P9-EEJ-304

# of Early Christianity

dary *REGIONS* Cities *Rivers* **SEAS**

Encyclopedia of Early Christianity

GARLAND REFERENCE LIBRARY OF THE HUMANITIES
(VOL. 846)

2nd ed. 1997 2 vols. Pf. xxvii + 1,213
rev.: JECS 6 (1998) 701-702 [Joseph F. Kelly].

This work commended by the American Society of Church History
in observation of its centennial year, 1988.

The North American Patristic Society commends the
Encyclopedia of Early Christianity as an important reference work
for students of early Christianity.

Encyclopedia of Early Christianity

EVERETT FERGUSON
Editor

MICHAEL P. McHUGH
FREDERICK W. NORRIS
Associate Editors

DAVID M. SCHOLER
Consulting Editor

GARLAND PUBLISHING, INC.
NEW YORK & LONDON   1990

© 1990 Everett Ferguson
All rights reserved

Library of Congress Cataloging-in-Publication Data

Encyclopedia of early christianity / Everett Ferguson,
    editor ... [et al.].
        p. cm. — (Garland reference library of the
    humanities ; vol. 846)
      Includes bibliographical references.
      ISBN 0-8240-5745-7
      1. Church history—Primitive and early church,
ca. 30–600—Dictionaries. I. Ferguson, Everett, 1933–
II. Series.
BR162.2.E53   1990
270.1'03—dc20   89-36997

Design and Electronic Page Layout: John M-Röblin

Printed on acid-free, 250-year-life paper

Manufactured in the United States of America

Contents

Preface

The *Encyclopedia of Early Christianity* addresses general readers, students, and professionals in other fields who want information about early Christianity. The articles, therefore, avoid technical language as much as possible, and where such is necessary provide definitions or explanations. Specialists in patristics and early Christian history will find the *Encyclopedia* useful for concise, accurate summaries, ready access to facts, and basic bibliographies.

One hundred and thirty-five writers have contributed the nine hundred and seventy-seven entries. Their varied academic and confessional backgrounds give a broadly international and ecumenical character to this volume.

The period chosen for coverage extends from the life of Jesus to approximately A.D. 600. The latter date, as any that might be chosen, is arbitrary, but conventional, and is not observed rigidly. A few modern scholars important in the study of early Christianity have been included, along with articles on conferences, institutes, journals, and learned societies, in order to give some sense of the history of scholarship.

Entries in the *Encyclopedia of Early Christianity* cover persons, places, doctrines, practices, art, liturgy, heresies, and schisms. Each entry begins with a brief definition, identification, or characterization. It proceeds with antecedents to the subject (if applicable) and then gives a chronological or topical development of the subject in early Christianity. The main patristic sources are listed at the close of the article.

Since there are excellent encyclopedias and dictionaries of the Bible available, the information on biblical persons and books concentrates on their significance and use in the postbiblical development.

Biographical articles cover the person's life, writings, teachings, importance, and influence—as applicable. Entries on saints note the feast day on which they are commemorated. Writers and writings are identified by their numbers in the *Clavis Patrum Latinorum* (CPL), *Clavis Patrum Graecorum* (CPG), and *Thesaurus Linguae Graecae* (TLG). Non-Christians important for the early history of Christianity, especially authors and rulers, have an appropriate place.

Doctrinal articles present the pertinent biblical data and trace the historical development through the term of the *Encyclopedia* or to whatever point provides a definitive or significant conclusion to the topic.

Regional surveys provide a sense of continuity in the early history while at the same time showing local variations in Christianity. The variety is further covered in the entries on heresies and schisms. Some synthetic articles treat issues of contemporary concern.

In order to avoid a one-sided reliance on written texts, entries are included on Christian art, archaeology, and architecture. Acknowledgments of the source accompany the illustrations. Photographs without a credit line were supplied by Everett Ferguson.

Greek and Latin sources referred to in the text of articles or in the bibliographies are cited by their English titles if an English translation exists, by their Latin titles if no English translation is available. References in parentheses are abbreviated: for Greek works the abbreviations are those in G.W.H. Lampe, *Patristic Greek Lexicon* (Oxford: Clarendon, 1961–1968); for Latin works, the abbreviations are those of A. Souter, *A Glossary of Later Latin* (Oxford: Clarendon, 1954).

The bibliographies that accompany most of the articles consist of patristic citations, editions of original works, translations, and studies, in that order, with the studies arranged chronologically.

The index is an essential part of the *Encyclopedia*, since it provides access to additional information on an item than is contained in the main entry and identifies many items for which there is not an entry.

There are specialized reference works in some of the areas covered by the *Encyclopedia of Early Christianity*: patrologies, dictionaries of Christian history and biography, substantive handbooks of church history. This *Encyclopedia* can only supplement and not supplant these works. The reader who needs more detailed or more technical information than is supplied here is referred to the publications listed in the general bibliography that follows.

THE EDITORS

General Bibliography

Altaner, B. *Patrology*, tr. H.C. Graef. Freiburg: Herder, 1960. 9th German ed. by A. Stuiber (Freiburg: Herder, 1980).

Baus, K. *From the Apostolic Community to Constantine*. Handbook of Church History, ed. H. Jedin. New York: Seabury, 1965.

Baus, K., et al. *The Imperial Church from Constantine to the Early Middle Ages*. Handbook of Church History, ed. H. Jedin. New York: Seabury, 1980.

Cabrol, F., ed. *Dictionnaire d'archéologie chrétienne et de liturgie*. 15 vols. Paris: Letouzey et Ané, 1907–1953.

Cross, F.L. and E.A. Livingstone, eds. *The Oxford Dictionary of the Christian Church*. 2nd ed. London: Oxford UP, 1974.

Di Berardino, A., ed. *Dizionario patristico e di antichità cristiane*. 3 vols. Casale Monferrato: Marietti, 1983–1988.

Frend, W.H.C. *The Rise of Christianity*. Philadelphia: Fortress, 1984.

Halton, T.P. *Early Christian Studies: A Bibliographical Guide*. Forthcoming.

Kelly, J.N.D. *Early Christian Doctrines*. 5th ed. New York: Harper and Row, 1978.

Kelly, J.N.D. *The Oxford Dictionary of Popes*. Oxford: Oxford UP, 1986.

Klauser, T., et al., eds. *Reallexikon für Antike und Christentum*. Stuttgart: Hiersemann, 1950–.

Krause, G., and G. Müller, eds. *Theologische Realenzyklopädie*. Berlin: de Gruyter, 1977–.

McDonald, W.J., et al., eds. *New Catholic Encyclopedia*. 15 vols. New York: McGraw-Hill, 1967, with supplementary vols. 16 (1974) and 17 (1979).

Pelikan, J. *The Christian Tradition*. Chicago: U of Chicago P, 1971, Vol. 1: *The Emergence of the Catholic Tradition (100–600)*.

Quasten, J., et al. *Patrology*. 4 vols. Westminster: Christian Classics, 1953–1986.

Smith, W., and H. Wace, eds. *A Dictionary of Christian Biography*. 4 vols. London: John Murray, 1877–1887.

Strayer, J.R., ed. *Dictionary of the Middle Ages*. 9 vols. New York: Scribner, 1982–.

Vacant, A., E. Mangenot, E. Amann, et al., eds. *Dictionnaire de théologie catholique*. 15 vols. Paris: Letouzey et Ané, 1903–1950.

Viller, M., et al., eds. *Dictionnaire de spiritualité, ascétique, et mystique*. Paris: Beauchesne, 1932–.

Abbreviations

CF *Classical Folia*

ChHist *Church History*

CHR *Catholic Historical Review*

CPG Clavis Patrum Graecorum, ed. M. Geerard. 5 vols. Turnhout: Brepols, 1974–1987.

CPh *Classical Philology*

CPL Clavis Patrum Latinorum, ed. E. Dekkers. 2nd ed. Steenbrugis: In Abbatia S. Petri, 1961.

CQ *Classical Quarterly*

CSCO Corpus scriptorum christianorum orientalium, ed. I.B. Chabot et al. Paris: Reipublicae; Leipzig: Harrassowitz, 1903–.

CSEL Corpus scriptorum ecclesiasticorum latinorum. Vienna: Geroldi, 1866–.

CW *The Classical World*

CWS Classics of Western Spirituality, ed. R.J. Payne et al. New York: Paulist, in progress.

DACL *Dictionnaire d'archéologie chrétienne et de liturgie,* ed. F. Cabrol. 15 vols. Paris: Letouzey et Ané, 1907–1953.

DCB *Dictionary of Christian Biography,* ed. W. Smith and H. Wace, 4 vols. London: John Murray, 1877–1887.

DOP *Dumbarton Oaks Papers*

DPAC *Dizionario patristico e di antichità cristiane,* ed. A. Di Berardino. 3 vols. Casale Monferrato: Marietti, 1983–1988.

DTC *Dictionnaire de théologie catholique,* ed. A. Vacant, E. Mangenot, E. Amann, et al. 15 vols. Paris: Letouzey et Ané, 1903–1950.

Duchesne Duchesne, L., ed. *Le Liber Pontificalis.* 2 vols. Paris: Thorin, 1886, 1892; repr. with 3rd vol. by C. Vogel, Paris: Boccard, 1955–1957.

ECR *Eastern Churches Review*

EMC *Echos du Monde Classique/ Classical Views*

EThL *Ephemerides Theologicae Lovanienses*

FMS *Frühmittelalterliche Studien*

FOTC The Fathers of the Church. Washington, D.C.: Catholic U of America P, 1947–.

Frend Frend, W.H.C. *The Rise of Christianity.* Philadelphia: Fortress, 1984.

FZPhTh *Freiburger Zeitschrift für Philosophie und Theologie*

GCS Die griechischen christlichen Schriftsteller. Berlin: Akademie, 1897–.

GOTR *Greek Orthodox Theological Review*

GR *Greece and Rome*

GRBS *Greek, Roman and Byzantine Studies*

HT *History Today*

HThR *Harvard Theological Review*

ICUR *Inscriptiones christianae urbis Romae,* ed. J.B. de Rossi. Rome: Libraria pontificia, 1857–1888; new series, ed. A. Silvagni, 1922–.

ILCV *Inscriptiones latinae christianae veteres,* ed. E. Diehl. 2nd ed. Berlin: Weidmann, 1961.

ITQ *Irish Theological Quarterly*

JAC *Jahrbuch für Antike und Christentum*

JBL *Journal of Biblical Literature*

JEH *Journal of Ecclesiastical History*

JMedHist   *Journal of Medieval History*

JRH   *Journal of Religious History*

JThS   *Journal of Theological Studies*

Kelly   Kelly, J.N.D. *Early Christian Doctrines.* 5th ed. New York: Harper and Row, 1978.

LCC   Library of Christian Classics, ed. J. Baillie et al. Philadelphia: Westminster, 1953–1966.

LCL   Loeb Classical Library. Cambridge: Harvard UP; London: Heinemann, 1912–.

Mansi   Mansi, G.D. *Sacrorum conciliorum nova et amplissima collectio.* Florence: Expensis Antonii Zatta, 1761–1762; repr. Graz, 1960–1961.

MEFR   *Mélanges d'archéologie et d'histoire de l'école française de Rome*

MGH   Monumenta Germaniae Historica. Berlin: Weidmann, 1877–, with several series, such as *Auctores Antiquissimi* and *Scriptores.*

MH   *Museum Helveticum*

MHA   *Memorias de historia antigua*

MSR   *Mélanges de science religieuse*

Musurillo   Musurillo, H., ed. and tr. *The Acts of the Christian Martyrs.* Oxford: Clarendon, 1972.

NCE   *New Catholic Encyclopedia,* ed. W.J. McDonald et al. 15 vols. New York: McGraw-Hill, 1967.

NHC   Nag Hammadi Codices, ed. with English tr., intro., and notes by the Institute for Antiquity and Christianity, *The Coptic Gnostic Library.* 15 vols. Leiden: Brill, 1975–.

NPNF   Nicene and Post-Nicene Fathers, ed. P. Schaff et al. 2 series of 14 vols. each. New York: Christian Literature, 1887–1894; repr. Grand Rapids: Eerdmans, 1952–1956.

NTA   *The New Testament Apocrypha,* ed. E. Hennecke and W. Schneemelcher; English tr. ed. R. McL. Wilson. 2 vols. Philadelphia: Westminster, 1963, 1966.

NTS   *New Testament Studies*

OC   *Oriens Christianus*

OECT   Oxford Early Christian Texts, ed. H. Chadwick. Oxford: Clarendon, 1970–.

ParOr   *Parole de l'Orient*

PEQ   *Palestine Exploration Quarterly*

PG   Patrologia Graeca, ed. J.-P. Migne. 162 vols. Paris, 1857–1886.

PL   Patrologia Latina, ed. J.-P. Migne. 217 vols. Paris, 1844–1864.

PO   Patrologia Orientalis, ed. R. Graffin and F. Nau. Paris: Firmin-Didot, 1907–1922.

PS   Patrologia Syriaca, rev. ed. I. Ortiz de Urbina. Rome: Pontifical Institute of Oriental Studies, 1965.

Quasten   Quasten, J. *Patrology.* 4 vols. Westminster: Christian Classics, 1953–1986.

RAC   *Rivista di archeologia cristiana*

RBén   *Revue Bénédictine*

REA   *Revue des études anciennes*

REAug   *Revue des études augustiniennes*

RecSR   *Recherches de science religieuse*

RecTh   *Recherches de théologie ancienne et médiévale*

REJ	*Revue des études juives*
RevThom	*Revue thomiste*
RH	*Revue historique*
RHE	*Revue d'histoire ecclésiastique*
RHPhR	*Revue d'histoire et de philosophie religieuse*
RHR	*Revue de l'histoire des religions*
RLAC	*Reallexikon für Antike und Christentum*, ed. T. Klauser et al. Stuttgart: Hiersemann, 1950–.
RomBarb	*Romanobarbarica*
RSLR	*Rivista di storia e letteratura religiosa*
RSR	*Revue de sciences religieuses*
SC	Sources chrétiennes, ed. H. deLubac, J. Daniélou, et al. Paris: Cerf, 1942–.
SCent	*The Second Century*
SEJG	*Sacris Erudiri: Jaarboek voor Godsdienstwetenschappen*
SP	*Studia patristica*
StudMed	*Studi medievali*
StudMon	*Studia monastica*

StudOv	*Studium Ovetense*
ThS	*Theological Studies*
ThZ	*Theologische Zeitschrift*
TLG	*Thesaurus linguae graecae: Canon of Greek Authors and Works*, ed. L. Berkowitz and K.A. Squitier. 2nd ed. Oxford: Oxford UP, 1986.
TLL	*Thesaurus linguae latinae.* Leipzig: Teubner, 1900–.
TRE	*Theologische Real-enzyklopädie*, ed. G. Krause and G. Müller. Berlin: de Gruyter, 1977–.
TS	*Texts and Studies.* Cambridge: Cambridge UP, 1891–.
TU	Texte und Untersuchungen. Berlin: Akademie, 1883–.
VChr	*Vigiliae Christianae*
WS	*Wiener Studien*
ZKG	*Zeitschrift für Kirchengeschichte*
ZNTW	*Zeitschrift für die neutestamentliche Wissenschaft*
ZRGG	*Zeitschrift für Religions–und Geistesgeschichte*
ZThK	*Zeitschrift für Theologie und Kirche*

Contributors

J.duQ.A. Jeremy duQ. Adams
Southern Methodist
University
Dallas, Texas

G.T.A. Gregory T. Armstrong
Sweet Briar College
Sweet Briar, Virginia

H.W.A. Harold W. Attridge
University of Notre Dame
Notre Dame, Indiana

D.E.A. David E. Aune
Saint Xavier College
Chicago, Illinois

W.S.B. William S. Babcock
Perkins School of Theology
Southern Methodist
University
Dallas, Texas

D.L.B. David L. Balás, O. Cist.
University of Dallas
Irving, Texas

B.B. Barry Baldwin
University of Calgary
Calgary, Alberta, Canada

P.M.B. Paul M. Bassett
Nazarene Theological
Seminary
Kansas City, Missouri

G.S.B. George S. Bebis
Holy Cross Greek Orthodox
School of Theology/
Hellenic College
Brookline, Massachusetts

R.M.B. Robert M. Berchman
Michigan State University
East Lansing, Michigan

G.C.B. George C. Berthold
Saint Anselm College
Manchester, New Hampshire

J.B. Jonathan Black
Hill Monastic Manuscript
Library
St. John's University
Collegeville, Minnesota

M.J.B. Monica J. Blanchard
Catholic University of
America
Washington, D.C.

P.M.Bl. Paul M. Blowers
Emmanuel School of
Religion
Johnson City, Tennessee

P.F.B. Paul F. Bradshaw
University of Notre Dame
Notre Dame, Indiana

P.B. Pamela Bright
Loyola University
Chicago, Illinois

J.A.B. James A. Brooks
Bethel Theological Seminary
St. Paul, Minnesota

J.J.B. Jorunn Jacobsen Buckley
Massachusetts Institute of
Technology
Cambridge, Massachusetts

D.B. David Bundy
Asbury Theological
Seminary
Wilmore, Kentucky

G.B. Gary Burke
Windsor Locks, Connecticut

J.P.B. J. Patout Burns
University of Florida
Gainesville, Florida

P.C.B. Paul C. Burns, C.S.B.
St. Mark's College
Vancouver, British
Columbia, Canada

J.H.C. James H. Charlesworth
Princeton Theological
Seminary
Princeton, New Jersey

E.A.C. Elizabeth A. Clark
Duke University
Durham, North Carolina

M.T.C. Mary T. Clark, R.S.C.J.
Manhattanville College
Purchase, New York

A.L.C. Allen L. Clayton
University of Texas at Dallas
Richardson, Texas

J.J.C. John J. Collins
University of Notre Dame
Notre Dame, Indiana

C.Co. Christopher Colvin
University of Dallas
Irving, Texas

J.H.Co. John H. Corbett
University of Toronto
Toronto, Ontario, Canada

C.C. Claude Cox
Grove Park Church of Christ
Barrie, Ontario, Canada

L.L.C. Lorin L. Cranford
Southwestern Baptist
Theological Seminary
Fort Worth, Texas

A.C. Agnes Cunningham,
S.S.C.M.
Mundelein Seminary
University of St. Mary of the
Lake
Mundelein, Illinois

B.E.D. Brian E. Daley
Weston School of Theology
Cambridge, Massachusetts

R.J.D. Robert J. Daly, S.J.
Boston College
Chestnut Hill, Massachusetts

G.D.D. George D. Dragas
University of Durham
Durham, England

R.B.E. Robert B. Eno, S.S.
Catholic University of
America
Washington, D.C.

G.H.E. Gerard H. Ettlinger
St. John's University
Jamaica, New York

D.F. Denis Farkasfalvy,
O. Cist.
Our Lady of Dallas
Cistercian Monastery
Irving, Texas

G.D.F. Gordon D. Fee
Regent College
Vancouver, British
Columbia, Canada

E.F. Everett Ferguson
Abilene Christian University
Abilene, Texas

T.M.F. Thomas M. Finn
College of William and Mary
Williamsburg, Virginia

P.C.F. Paul Corby Finney
University of Missouri–St.
Louis
St. Louis, Missouri

W.H.C.F. W.H.C. Frend
University of Glasgow
(emeritus)
Glasgow, Scotland

E.V.G. Eugene V. Gallagher
Connecticut College
New London, Connecticut

H.Y.G. Harry Y. Gamble
University of Virginia
Charlottesville, Virginia

J.L.G. James Leo Garrett
Southwestern Baptist
Theological Seminary
Fort Worth, Texas

J.E.G. James E. Goehring
Mary Washington College
Fredericksburg, Virginia

D.G. Deirdre Good
General Theological
Seminary
New York, New York

R.M.G. Robert M. Grant
University of Chicago
Chicago, Illinois

R.G. Rowan Greer
Yale University
New Haven, Connecticut

T.E.G. Timothy E. Gregory
Ohio State University
Columbus, Ohio

S.H.G. Sydney H. Griffith
Catholic University of
America
Washington, D.C.

D.E.G. Dennis E. Groh
Garrett-Evangelical
Theological Seminary
Evanston, Illinois

J.M.H. Joseph M. Hallman
College of St. Thomas
St. Paul, Minnesota

T.H. Thomas Halton
Catholic University of
America
Washington, D.C.

S.A.H. Susan Ashbrook Harvey
Brown University
Providence, Rhode Island

R.E.H. Ronald E. Heine
Institut zur Erforschung des
Urchristentums
Tübingen, West Germany

H.L.H. Holland L. Hendrix
Barnard College
New York, New York

A.H. Alisdair Heron
University of Erlangen
Erlangen, West Germany

E.G.H. E. Glenn Hinson
Southern Baptist
Theological Seminary
Louisville, Kentucky

W.D.H. William D. Howden
New Haven, Connecticut

R.J. Robert Jewett
Garrett-Evangelical
Theological Seminary
Evanston, Illinois

G.J.J. Gary J. Johnson
University of Richmond
Richmond, Virginia

F.S.J. F. Stanley Jones
California State
University–Long Beach
Long Beach, California

E.A.J. Edwin A. Judge
Macquarie University
Sydney, N.S.W., Australia

C.K. Charles Kannengiesser
University of Notre Dame
Notre Dame, Indiana

T.G.K. Terrence G. Kardong,
O.S.B.
Assumption Abbey
Richardton, North Dakota

J.F.K. Joseph F. Kelly
John Carroll University
Cleveland, Ohio

E.J.K. Edward J. Kilmartin, S.J.
Pontificio Istituto Orientale
Rome, Italy

K.L.K. Karen L. King
Occidental College
Los Angeles, California

W.E.K. W. Eugene Kleinbauer
Indiana University
Bloomington, Indiana

W.K. William Klingshirn
Catholic University of
America
Washington, D.C.

G.A.K. Glenn A. Koch
Eastern Baptist Theological
Seminary
Philadelphia, Pennsylvania

E.LaV. Eugene LaVerdiere, S.S.S.
Emmanuel Magazine
New York, New York

D.B.L. David B. Levenson
Florida State University
Tallahassee, Florida

J.P.L. Jack P. Lewis
Harding Graduate School of
Religion
Memphis, Tennessee

J.T.L.   Joseph T. Lienhard, S.J.
          Marquette University
          Milwaukee, Wisconsin

E.A.L.   Elizabeth A. Livingstone
          Oxford, England

R.L.   Rebecca Lyman
          Church Divinity School of
          the Pacific
          Berkeley, California

J.E.L.   John E. Lynch, C.S.P.
          Catholic University of
          America
          Washington, D.C.

L.S.B.MacC. Leslie S.B. MacCoull
          Society for Coptic
          Archaeology
          Washington, D.C.

C.T.McC. C. Thomas McCollough
          Center College
          Danville, Kentucky

L.M.McD. Lee M. McDonald
          Santa Clara First Baptist
          Church
          Santa Clara, California

M.P.McH. Michael P. McHugh
          University of Connecticut
          Storrs, Connecticut

J.McR.   John McRay
          Wheaton College
          Wheaton, Illinois

K.McV.   Kathleen McVey
          Princeton Theological
          Seminary
          Princeton, New Jersey

J.McW.   Joanne McWilliam
          University of Toronto
          Toronto, Ontario, Canada

R.W.M.   Ralph W. Mathisen
          University of South Carolina
          Columbia, South Carolina

B.M.M.   Bruce M. Metzger
          Princeton Theological
          Seminary
          Princeton, New Jersey

M.R.M.   Margaret R. Miles
          Harvard Divinity School
          Harvard University
          Cambridge, Massachusetts

P.C.M.   Patricia Cox Miller
          Syracuse University
          Syracuse, New York

F.X.M.   Francis X. Murphy,
          C.SS.R.
          St. Mary's Church
          Annapolis, Maryland

K.V.N.   Kenneth V. Neller
          Southside Church of Christ
          Lexington, Kentucky

F.W.N.   Frederick W. Norris
          Emmanuel School of
          Religion
          Johnson City, Tennessee

R.A.N.   Richard A. Norris
          Union Theological Seminary
          New York, New York

E.F.O.   Eric F. Osborn
          Queen's College
          University of Melbourne
          Parkville, Victoria, Australia

C.D.O.   Carroll D. Osburn
          Abilene Christian University
          Abilene, Texas

R.O.   Richard Oster
          Harding Graduate School of
          Religion
          Memphis, Tennessee

R.J.O.   Robert J. Owens
          Emmanuel School of
          Religion
          Johnson City, Tennessee

J.P.   John Painter
          LaTrobe University
          Bundoora, Victoria,
          Australia

L.G.P.   Lloyd G. Patterson
          Episcopal Divinity School
          Cambridge, Massachusetts

P.P.   Pheme Perkins
          Boston College
          Chestnut Hill, Massachusetts

W.H.P.   Walter H. Principe,
          C.S.B.
          Pontifical Institute of
          Mediaeval Studies
          Toronto, Ontario, Canada

R.R.   Robert Rea
          Lincoln Christian Seminary
          Lincoln, Illinois

H.E.R.   Harold E. Remus
          Wilfrid Laurier University
          Waterloo, Ontario, Canada

H.R.   Harry Rosenberg
          Colorado State University
          Fort Collins, Colorado

D.J.S. Daniel J. Sahas
University of Waterloo
Waterloo, Ontario, Canada

M.A.S. Margaret S. Schatkin
Boston College
Chestnut Hill, Massachusetts

D.M.S. David M. Scholer
North Park College and
Theological Seminary
Chicago, Illinois

L.P.S. Lawrence P. Schrenk
Catholic University of
America
Washington, D.C.

D.P.S. Donald P. Senior, C.P.
Catholic Theological Union
Chicago, Illinois

R.D.S. Robert D. Sider
Dickinson College
Carlisle, Pennsylvania

M.S. Michael Slusser
Duquesne University
Pittsburgh, Pennsylvania

C.C.S. Clyde Curry Smith
University of
Wisconsin–River Falls
River Falls, Wisconsin

G.F.S. Graydon F. Snyder
Chicago Theological
Seminary
Chicago, Illinois

H.F.S. Hendrik F. Stander
University of Pretoria
Pretoria, South Africa

T.S. Theodore Stylianopoulos
Holy Cross Greek Orthodox
School of Theology
Brookline, Massachusetts

W.M.S. Willard M. Swartley
Associated Mennonite
Biblical Seminaries
Elkhart, Indiana

L.J.S. Louis J. Swift
University of Kentucky
Lexington, Kentucky

K.J.T. Karen Jo Torjesen
Claremont Graduate School
Claremont, California

J.W.T. Joseph W. Trigg
St. Patrick's Church
Falls Church, Virginia

R.P.V. R.P. Vaggione, O.H.C.
Incarnation Priory
Berkeley, California

H.J.V. Hermann J. Vogt
University of Tübingen
Tübingen, West Germany

W.H.W. Walter H. Wagner
Muhlenberg College
Allentown, Pennsylvania

R.H.W. Rebecca H. Weaver
Union Theological Seminary
Richmond, Virginia

L.M.W. L. Michael White
Oberlin College
Oberlin, Ohio

L.R.W. Lionel R. Wickham
Cambridge University
Cambridge, England

R.Wi. Robert Wilken
University of Virginia
Charlottesville, Virginia

J.W. John Wilkinson
Washington, D.C.

R.L.W. Robert Lee Williams
Dallas, Texas

R.W. Rowan Williams
Oxford University
Oxford, England

D.F.W. Donald F. Winslow
Episcopal Divinity School
Cambridge, Massachusetts

D.F.Wr. David F. Wright
University of Edinburgh
Edinburgh, Scotland

F.Y. Frances Young
University of Birmingham
Birmingham, England

R.D.Y. Robin Darling Young
Catholic University of
America
Washington, D.C.

G.A.Z. Grover A. Zinn, Jr.
Oberlin College
Oberlin, Ohio

Chronology

Dates	Secular Rulers	Bishops of Rome	Church Leaders and Writers	Events
27 B.C.–A.D. 14	Augustus			
ca. 4 B.C.				Birth of Jesus
A.D. 14–37	Tiberius			
ca. 30				Death of Jesus
54–68	Nero			
ca. 62–68				Deaths of James, Peter, and Paul
70				Fall of Jerusalem
81–96	Domitian			
ca. 96			*1 Clement*	
98–117	Trajan			
ca. 115			Ignatius	
117–138	Hadrian			
135–165				Valentinus constructs Gnostic doctrine
144				Marcion disfellowshiped
ca. 150			Justin Martyr	
ca. 155				Death of Polycarp
161–180	Marcus Aurelius			
ca. 172				Montanist movement
ca. 180			Irenaeus	
189–199		Victor I		Paschal controversy
190–230				Monarchian controversies
193–211	Septimius Severus			
ca. 200			Tertullian	Beginnings of catacomb art
ca. 185–ca. 251			Origen	
217–222		Callistus I		Schism of Hippolytus
ca. 240				Christian church at Dura
248–258			Cyprian	
249–251	Decius			
251–253		Cornelius		Schism of Novatian
254–257		Stephen I		

Dates	Secular Rulers	Bishops of Rome	Church Leaders and Writers	Events
253–260	Valerian			
ca. 270				Anthony retires to the desert
284–305	Diocletian			Great Persecution
306–337	Constantine			
312				Donatist schism
313				Edict of Milan
ca. 315–339			Eusebius of Caesarea	
323				Pachomius's monastery
325				Council of Nicaea
328–373			Athanasius	
330				Founding of Constantinople
ca. 330–390			Three Cappadocians: Basil of Caesarea, Gregory of Nazianzus, Gregory of Nyssa	
337–361	Constantius II			
341				Ulfilas's mission to Goths
361–363	Julian			
363–373			Ephraem at Edessa	
366–384		Damasus I		
374–397			Ambrose	
379–395	Theodosius I			
381				Council of Constantinople
ca. 347–420			Jerome	
386–407			John Chrysostom	
ca. 400				Pilgrimage of Egeria
395–430			Augustine of Hippo	
408–450	Theodosius II			
410				Sack of Rome by Visigoths
411–430				Pelagian controversy
412–444			Cyril of Alexandria	
431				Council of Ephesus
ca. 432–ca. 461				Patrick to Ireland
440–461		Leo I		
450–457	Marcian and Pulcheria			
451				Council of Chalcedon
451				Defeat of Huns
474–491	Zeno			
476	Romulus Augustulus deposed			
481–511	Clovis			
484–519				Acacian schism
492–496		Gelasius I		
493–526	Theodoric			
527–565	Justinian			
529				Benedict founds Monte Cassino
537				Hagia Sophia
542–578			Jacob Baradaeus	
553				Council of Constantinople II
563				Columba to Iona
ca. 560–636			Isidore of Seville	
580–662			Maximus Confessor	
589				Council of Toledo
590–604		Gregory I		
597			Augustine of Canterbury	
ca. 650 or 675–ca. 749			John of Damascus	

The Encyclopedia

ABERCIUS (d. ca. 200). Bishop of Hierapolis in Phrygia, probably the Avircius Marcellus mentioned by Eusebius (*H.E.* 5.16.3). At age seventy-two, he composed and set up an epitaph for his own tomb. Two large fragments discovered by W.M. Ramsay are now in the Vatican Museum. The complete text has been restored from another inscription based on it and from the copy preserved in the fourth-century *S. Abercii vita*, which exists in three recensions. Abercius refers to his being a disciple of the "pure shepherd," his travels to Rome and Nisibis, Paul as his guide, the faith in Christ, the fish that the pure virgin caught, baptism ("seal"), and the eucharist. TLG 1353. *See also* Fish; Inscriptions; Pectorius; Shepherd.

[E.F.]

Bibliography

J.B. Lightfoot, *The Apostolic Fathers* (London: Macmillan, 1885), Vol. 2.1, pp. 476–485; T. Nissen, *S. Abercii vita* (Leipzig: Teubner, 1912); H. Leclercq, "Abercius," DACL (1924), Vol. 1, pp. 66–87; F. Dölger, *Ichthys: Das Fisch Symbol in frühchristlichen Zeit* (Münster: Aschendorff, 1928), Vol. 1, pp. 8ff., 87ff., 136ff.; Vol. 2, pp. 454–507; W.M. Calder, "The Epitaph of Avircius Marcellus," *JRS* 29 (1939):1–4; E. Ferguson, *Early Christians Speak* (Abilene: ACU, 1987), pp. 155f., 161f.; B. McNeil, "Avircius and the Song of Songs," *VChr* 31 (1977):23–34; W.K. Wischmeyer, "Die Aberkiosinschrift als Grabepigramm," *JAC* 23 (1980):22–47.

Restored Epitaph of Abercius (ca. 200) in Pio-Christian Museum, Vatican City, Italy.

3

ABGAR. Common name of the kings of Edessa. Probably after the conversion of Abgar (179–216), the legend developed of a correspondence between Abgar V (A.D. 9–46) and Jesus. Eusebius (*H.E.* 1.13) claims to translate from the archives of Edessa a letter sent by the sick king to Jesus requesting that he come to heal him and a reply from Jesus explaining that after his ascension he would send a disciple to cure him. According to Eusebius, Thomas sent Thaddaeus (Addai) to Edessa. *The Teaching of Addai* has Jesus send an oral reply, not a letter. The messenger from the king painted a portrait of Jesus that became a talisman protecting the city of Edessa from its enemies. *See also* Acts of Thaddaeus. [E.F.]

Bibliography
Eusebius, *Church History* 1.13; *Chronicle* ann. 218; Egeria, *Pilgrimage* 19; *The Teaching of Addai*; *Addai Thaddaei*.

S. Runciman, "Some Remarks on the Image of Edessa," *Cambridge Historical Journal* 3 (1929–1931):238–252; H.C. Youtie, "A Gothenburg Papyrus and the Letter of Abgar," *HThR* 23 (1930):299–302; idem, "Gothenburg Papyrus 21 and the Coptic Version of the Letter to Abgar," *HThR* 24 (1931):61–65; NTA (1963), Vol. 1, pp. 437–444; W. Bauer, *Orthodoxy and Heresy in Earliest Christianity* (Philadelphia: Fortress, 1971), pp. 2–12, 16–17, 35–39.

ABORTION. The voluntary expulsion of the human fetus was common in the ancient world. Plato (*Rep.* 5.9) and Aristotle (*Pol.* 7.14.10) suggested it as a way to limit the number of children. Wealthy and poor, wife and prostitute, practiced it. Yet the Hippocratic Oath specifically prohibited it, the Stoic Musonius Rufus (*Discourse* 15) argued against it, and Cicero (*In Defense of Cluentius* 32) demanded capital punishment for intentional abortions. Under Roman law, however, the fetus was not a person.

Jews found deliberate abortion unacceptable; they also rejected exposure of children. Yet their opinions differed widely as to the penalty for accidental or therapeutic abortions. Christians viewed the fetus as God's creation. They insisted that the destruction of the fetus was murder and that the perpetrators should be punished as murderers. *Didache* 2.2 and *Barnabas* 20.1–2 prohibited abortion as murder. The earliest information in the New Testament seems to occur in the vice lists, where *pharmakeia* may refer to the drug used in abortions. Clement of Alexandria (*Ecl.* 41; 48–49) quotes an earlier Christian writer who inferred from Luke 1:41 that life begins at conception. The apologists defended Christians against charges of immorality by noting the community's rejection of abortion.

Some Christians practiced abortion, however, as Hippolytus (*Haer.* 9.7) and Cyprian (*Ep.* 52.2) indicate. The Council of Elvira, ca. 305 (*can.* 63; 68), enacted punishments against infanticide, perhaps abortion. The Council of Ancyra, 314 (*can.* 21), prohibited abortion. Basil (*Ep.* 188.2), Ambrose (*Hex.* 5.18.58), and Jerome (*Ep.* 22.13) supported that stance. Augustine (*Quest. Exodus* 9.80 and *Quest. Hept.* 2) differed as to when life began, but he found intentional abortion of the formed fetus to be murder. John Chrysostom (*Hom.* 32 *in Rom.*) viewed deliberate abortion as murder. [F.W.N.]

Bibliography
M.J. Gorman, *Abortion and the Early Church: Christian, Jewish and Pagan Attitudes in the Greco-Roman World* (Downers Grove: InterVarsity, 1982).

ABRAHAM. The biblical patriarch (originally called Abram) who received God's call to leave his homeland and people and become the father of a new people (Gen. 11:26–25:11). Abraham's response in faith to God's call and to the promise of a land, a multitude of descendants, and a blessing to the nations, together with the fulfillment of that promise in the subsequent biblical narrative, made him the exemplar of faith and faithfulness in Jewish and Christian thought. The phrase "the God of Abraham, Isaac, and Jacob" (Exod. 3:6, 15; cf. Gen. 31:42; Mark 12:26) has become synonymous with "the God of the Bible." Jews, through Isaac, and Arabs, through Ishmael, consider Abraham their ancestor.

Abraham is prominent in rabbinical literature, in Jewish legend, and in the Hellenistic Jewish teacher Philo of Alexandria (*On Abraham* and other writings). Among the

Abraham's hospitality to the three heavenly visitors and his sacrifice of Isaac. Wall mosaic (sixth century) from the Church of S. Vitale, Ravenna, Italy. (Photograph Editore Dante, Ravenna)

Pseudepigrapha of the Old Testament are two writings of the late first or early second century A.D. associated with him, the *Apocalypse of Abraham* and the *Testament of Abraham*. Apart from scattered references in the Gospels, Romans 4 and Galatians 3 give major attention to Abraham. Hebrews 7 discusses the relationship between Melchizedek and Abraham (cf. Gen. 14) and understands Melchizedek as an anticipation of the priesthood of Christ.

Among the church fathers, Abraham himself was sometimes taken to be a type of Christ, but more often it was his son Isaac in the sacrifice on Mt. Moriah (Gen. 22). This scene was among the most frequent in early Christian art and persisted after most other Old Testament scenes had been dropped. In Christian biblical exegesis and in art, the hospitality of Abraham for the three heavenly visitors at Mamre (Gen. 18; Constantine built a martyrion here) is understood as a revelation of the Trinity. "The bosom of Abraham" is an expression for rest in God or paradise (Luke 16:22). Portions of the Abraham narrative found important places in the church's liturgy, including a reference to him in the canon of the Mass. *See also* Isaac.   [G.T.A.]

Bibliography

Origen, *Homilies on Genesis* 3–4; 6–11; Ambrose, *De Abrahamo.*

T. Klauser, "Abraham," and W. Staerk, "Abrahams Schoss," RLAC (1950), Vol. 1, cols. 18–28; D. Lerch, *Isaaks Opferung christlich gedeutet: Eine auslegungsgeschichtliche Untersuchung* (Tübingen: Mohr, 1950); K. Wessel, "Abraham," *Reallexikon zur byzantinischen Kunst,* ed. K. Wessel (Stuttgart: Hiersemann, 1966), Vol. 1, cols. 11–22; "Abraham," *Encyclopedia Judaica* (Jerusalem, 1971), Vol. 1, cols. 111–125; J. Van Seters, *Abraham in History and Tradition* (New Haven: Yale UP, 1975); F.L. Horton, *The Melchizedek Tradition: A Critical Examination of the Sources to the Fifth Century and in the Epistle to the Hebrews* (Cambridge: Cambridge UP, 1976); R. Martin-Achard et al., "Abraham," TRE (1977), Vol. 1, pp. 364–387.

ACACIUS OF CAESAREA (d. 365). Bishop of Caesarea in Palestine (341–365) and an Arian. Acacius succeeded Eusebius, but was deposed in 343 by the Council of Sardica. He became a Homoean, then accepted the Nicene Creed in 363, only to return to Arianism. He wrote comments on Romans and a treatise against Marcellus of Ancyra. A party bearing his name, "Acacians," gained influence in the late 350s. CPG II, 3510–3515. [F.W.N.]

Bibliography
Jerome, *Lives of Illustrious Men* 98; Socrates, *Church History* 2.4, 40, 44; 4.2; Sozomen, *Church History* 2.26; 3.2; 4.22, 26; Epiphanius, *Panarion* 72.6–10.
J.M. Leroux, "Acace, évêque de Césarée de Palestine (341–365)," *SP* 8 (=TU 93) (1966):82–85.

ACACIUS OF CONSTANTINOPLE (d. 489). Bishop (471–489). Acacius supported the compromise with the Monophysites expressed in the *Henoticon* issued by the emperor Zeno. His confirmation of Peter Mongus, a Monophysite, as patriarch of Alexandria led Felix II (III) of Rome to excommunicate him (484). Thus began the Acacian schism between Rome and Constantinople, which lasted to 518. CPG III, 5990–5991. *See also* Henoticon; Zeno. [E.F.]

Bibliography
Evagrius, *Church History* 3.4ff.; Simplicius, *Epistulae* 5–6; 14–15; 18–19; Felix, *Epistulae* 1–2; 9–12.
W.H.C. Frend, *The Rise of the Monophysite Movement* (Cambridge: Cambridge UP, 1972), pp. 143–254.

ACOLYTE. Highest of the minor orders in the Latin church, the others being lector, doorkeeper (also called porter), and exorcist (the latter two now abolished). The office of acolyte, derived from the ministry of the deacon, is first mentioned in letters of Cyprian (250). The duties of the acolyte included assistance to the celebrant at Mass, administration of the eucharist, and provision of relief to those in need. Acolytes often served as letter carriers. *See also* Deacon. [M.P.McH.]

Bibliography
Cyprian, *Letters* 7.1; 52.1; 59.1, 9; 77.3; 78.1; Eusebius, *Church History* 6.43.11.
J.G. Davies, "Deacons, Deaconesses and the Minor Orders in the Patristic Period," *JEH* 14 (1963):1–15.

ACTA SANCTORUM. See Bollandus, John, S.J.

ACTS OF ANDREW. A lost late-second-century apocryphal book closely associated with Tatian's Encratism rather than with Gnosticism. Cod. Vatic. Gr. 808 and Pap. Copt. Utrecht I contain fragments of the work; Gregory of Tours's *Liber de miraculis Beati Andreae Apostoli* includes a theologically transformed epitome of these acts. Eusebius (*H.E.* 3.35.6) mentions it; the fourth-century Manichaean *Psalm-book* knows its contents. The *Acts* described the apostle's miracles during a journey, his imprisonment at Patras in Achaia, his prosecution because of a life of ascetic practices, and his martyr's death. The *Martyrdom of Andrew*, a variant form of the *Acts*, contains the information that he was killed by crucifixion, but it does not mention the "St. Andrew's cross," which was associated with him no earlier than the fourteenth century. *See also* Andrew. [F.W.N.]

Bibliography
NTA, Vol. 2, pp. 390–424.
P.M. Peterson, *Andrew, Brother of Simon Peter: His History and Legends* (Leiden: Brill, 1958); J.M. Prieur, "La Figure de l'apôtre dans les Actes apocryphes d'André," *Les Actes apocryphes des Apôtres: Christianisme et monde païen* (Geneva: Labor et Fides, 1981), pp. 121–139.

ACTS OF APOLLONIUS. Apollonius, also called Sakkeas, was a Christian famous for his learning who was denounced by one of his slaves. His case was tried by Perennius, praetorian prefect of Rome (180–185) but described by the *Acts* (or *Martyrdom*) *of Apollonius* as proconsul of Asia. The *Acts*, which survive in an eleventh-century Greek manuscript and a fifth-century Armenian manuscript, include two speeches by Apollonius, which may preserve the apology of Apollonius that Eusebius says he delivered before the Roman senate. His martyrdom has been fixed on April 21, 183. TLG 0304. [E.F.]

Bibliography
Eusebius, *Church History* 5.21.2–5; Jerome, *Lives of Illustrious Men* 42.
F.C. Conybeare, *The Armenian Apology and Acts of Apollonius* (London: Sonnenschein, 1894); R. Freudenberger, "Die Überlieferung vom Martyrium des römischen Christen Apollonius," *ZNTW* 60

(1969):111–130; Musurillo, pp. xxiii–xxv, 90–105; H. Paulsen, "Erwägungen zu Acta Apollonii 14–22," *ZNTW* 66 (1975):117–126; V. Saxer, "L'Apologie au sénat du martyr romain Apollonius," *MEFR* 96 (1984):1017–1038.

ACTS OF CARPUS, PAPYLUS, AND AGATHONICE

ACTS OF CARPUS, PAPYLUS, AND AGATHONICE. Second–third-century account of martyrdom in Pergamum. Eusebius (*H.E.* 4.15.48) mentions the martyrs Carpus, Papylus, and Agathonice in the reign of Marcus Aurelius (161–180), but the Latin recension of their *Acts* places the martyrdom under Decius (250). Another possibility of date is under Septimius Severus (193–211). Carpus and Papylus, the latter a citizen of Thyatira, refused the imperial command to sacrifice to the gods and were burned at the stake by the proconsul. A woman standing by, Agathonice, felt herself called to martyrdom and threw herself upon the stake. Feast day April 13. TLG 0390.

[E.F.]

Bibliography
Musurillo, pp. xv–xvi, 22–37; J. den Boeft and J. Bremmer, "Notiunculae Martyrologicae II," *VChr* 36 (1982):384–385.

ACTS OF CYPRIAN

ACTS OF CYPRIAN. Account of the legal proceedings against Cyprian, bishop of Carthage, and his execution under Valerian and Gallienus (258). The *Acts of Cyprian* (CPL 53) consists of three parts: (1) Cyprian's hearing at Carthage and sentence of exile (August 30, 257); (2) his return to the city, arrest (September 13, 258), and trial (September 14, 258); (3) his execution by beheading (September 14, 258). The document is considered reliable.

There is also extant a *Life of Cyprian* (CPL 52), composed shortly after his death, according to Jerome (*Vir. ill.* 68), by his deacon Pontius. A panegyric, it won popularity but is not reliable. It was influenced by the account of the martyrdom of Perpetua and Felicitas (203). *See also* Cyprian. [M.P.McH.]

Bibliography
Acts of Cyprian: Musurillo, pp. xxx–xxxi, 168–175. *Life of Cyprian*: M.M. Müller and R.J. Deferrari, tr., "Life of St. Cyprian by Pontius," *Early Christian Biographies*, FOTC (1952), Vol. 15, pp. 1–24.

J. Aronen, "Indebtedness to *Passio Perpetuae* in Pontius' *Vita Cypriani*," *VChr* 38 (1984):67–76.

ACTS OF JOHN

ACTS OF JOHN. Gnostic legends (second or third century) about the apostle John. Some of the exoteric traditions in the *Acts of John* were known to Clement of Alexandria (*Adumb. in 1 Joh.* 1.1), but the references are too slight and varied to guarantee a second-century date for the *Acts*. It is part of the fourth-century *Manichaean Psalm-book*. Eusebius (*H.E.* 3.25.6) mentions it; Epiphanius (*Haer.* 47.1.5) says it was used by the Encratites. One textual puzzle of the Greek version suggests that it may have been written in Syriac or Aramaic. Although the work depicts John's activities in Asia Minor, it presents the wrong date for the destruction of Artemis's temple in Ephesus—it has John destroy it—and seems to have no local knowledge of the region.

The first sections of the *Acts of John* have been lost, but about seventy percent of the volume is extant, that is, if the *Stichometry* of Nicephorus, which contains descriptions of apostolic lives, is correct in saying that it was nearly as long as Matthew. It depicts John's miraculous adventures traveling from Miletus to Ephesus, his stay there, and trips to Smyrna, Laodicea, and back to Ephesus, where he met his death. A lost section probably included his conversion, an imprisonment, and the conversion of one Andronicus, as can be inferred from fragments and other references in the extant text. Perhaps the most interesting portion is the depiction of John preaching a gospel of Christ that has features reminiscent of those in Valentinian Gnosticism: dualism, a Christ figure who could change his physical characteristics, and the Ogdoad and Dodecad described in Valentinus's version of the aeons. It also contains Monarchian views of God.

Various theologically edited versions of the *Acts* exist that are interested primarily in the legends about the apostles. TLG 0317.

[F.W.N.]

Bibliography
E. Junod and J. D. Kaestli, eds., CC Ser. Apocryphorum (1983), Vols. 1–2; *Cahiers d'Orientalisme* (1983), Vol. 6.

NTA, Vol. 2, pp. 188–259.

E. Junod and J. D. Kaestli, *L'Histoire des Actes apocryphes des apôtres du IVe au IXe siècle: le cas des Actes de Jean* (Geneva: Revue de Théologie et de Philosophie, 1982); K. Schaeferdiek, "Herkunft und Interesse der alten Johannesakten," *ZNTW* 74 (1983):247–267; W.C. van Unnik, "A Note on the Dance of Jesus in the Acts of John," *Sparsa Collecta*, Part III (Leiden: Brill, 1983), Vol. 3, pp. 144–147.

ACTS OF PAUL. Christian apocryphal work (late second century). An unnamed presbyter in the province of Asia wrote the *Acts of Paul* "out of love for Paul" (Tertullian, *Bapt.* 17). Three major parts of the work circulated separately: (1) *Acts of Paul and Thecla*, in which Thecla, the principal character, after her conversion survives a fight with wild beasts and baptizes herself; (2) Correspondence of Paul and the Corinthians, in which the Corinthians respond to 2 Corinthians and Paul writes another letter to them (*3 Corinthians*, a work, strongly anti-Gnostic in content, that became for a time part of the Syriac and Armenian canons); (3) *Martyrdom of Paul*, in which Paul is beheaded and milk spurts from his neck on the clothes of the executioner. The author compiled oral traditions and legends combined with his own imagination to produce a narrative supplementing the canonical Acts of the Apostles in order to edify and entertain readers. The church rejected the work more for its fanciful content (Paul baptizing a lion and performing extraordinary miracles) than for heretical teaching, although it shares with other apocryphal acts an emphasis on fasting and continence. No single manuscript preserves the whole work, but substantial fragments are in Greek and Coptic. TLG 0388. *See also* Thecla. [E.F.]

Bibliography
Tertullian, *On Baptism* 17; Hippolytus, *Commentary on Daniel* 3.29; Origen, *On First Principles* 1.2.3; idem, *Commentary on John* 20.12; Eusebius, *Church History* 3.3.5; 3.25.4; Jerome, *Lives of Illustrious Men* 7.
NTA, Vol. 2, pp. 322–390.

ACTS OF PETER. Apocryphal work written in Greek in the east (late second century). The bulk of the *Acts of Peter* is extant in a seventh-century Latin manuscript from Vercelli, which contains an account of the apostle Peter's struggle with Simon Magus (cf. Acts 8:9–24) at Rome and Simon's death as the result of an attempt to fly to heaven from the Roman forum. A part of the text, known as the *Martyrdom of Peter*, survives in the original Greek as well. It reports (35) the *Quo vadis?* ("Whither goest thou?") incident, in which Christ meets Peter, who is fleeing from Rome along the Appian Way. Peter takes Christ's reply ("I go into Rome to be crucified") to his *Quo vadis?* question to apply to himself and returns to the city, where he undergoes crucifixion with head downward at his request (38). A Coptic fragment, which relates Peter's miraculous healing of his paralytic daughter, is also extant. The influence of pagan romance literature is evident in this as in other apocryphal acts and gospels. The work shows a tendency to Docetism, but probably not as the result of a formally adopted theological position; the writer was no theologian. It is not to be confused with the later (sixth-century?) Latin *Martyrium beati Petri Apostoli a Lino conscriptum* (*Martyrdom of Blessed Peter the Apostle Written by Linus*), which purports to furnish further details; the attribution to Linus, Peter's successor, is obviously fictitious. TLG 0389. *See also* Peter. [M.P.McH.]

Bibliography
Eusebius, *Church History* 3.3.2; Jerome, *Lives of Illustrious Men* 1.
M.R. James, tr., *The Apocryphal New Testament* (Oxford: Clarendon, 1924), pp. 300–336; NTA, Vol. 2, pp. 259–322.
J. D. Dubois, "The New *Series Apocryphorum* of the *Corpus Christianorum*," *SCent* 4 (1984):29–36.

ACTS OF PETER AND PAUL. Apocryphal writing (third century?). The *Acts of Peter and Paul* bears no relationship to either the *Acts of Paul* or the *Acts of Peter*. This text, extant only in Greek and Latin fragments, stresses the close relationship of Peter and Paul and their martyrdom in Rome. [D.M.S.]

ACTS OF PILATE. Apocryphal report of Pilate on Christ's trial, crucifixion, and resurrection, composed in Greek. Although there was a keen interest in Pilate in early Christianity and the existence of Acts of Pilate was known to second-century writers (Justin, *1 Apol.* 35.9; 48.3; cf. Tertullian, *Apol.* 21.24), the present *Acts of Pilate* dates from the fourth century or later; however, the use of earlier materials in its composition is likely. The *Acts of Pilate* proper may well have been intended as a response to forged Acts of Pilate spread by the Roman authorities in support of paganism under the emperor Maximinus Daia (311–312; cf. Eusebius, *H.E.* 1.9.3; 1.11.9; 9.5.1; 9.7.1). The work makes considerable use of the Gospel accounts and offers as well a report of debates in the Sanhedrin over the resurrection. Added to it in the early fifth century was a description of the harrowing of hell supposedly composed by two sons of the aged Simeon (cf. Luke 2:25–35), who served as witnesses (the narrative is suggested by 1 Peter 3:19). The two works together have been known as the *Gospel of Nicodemus* since the thirteenth century.

The popularity of the *Acts of Pilate* is attested by Latin, Syriac, Armenian, Coptic, and Arabic translations, alongside the original Greek. Pilate received veneration as a saint and martyr in Syria and Egypt and among the Copts. In the Middle Ages, the *Gospel of Nicodemus* was influential in the development of the legends of Joseph of Arimathea and of the Holy Grail besides being reflected in drama in the theme of the harrowing of hell.

[M.P.McH.]

Bibliography

H.C. Kim, ed., *The Gospel of Nicodemus: Gesta Salvatoris* (Toronto: Pontifical Institute of Mediaeval Studies, 1973).

M.R. James, tr., *The Apocryphal New Testament* (Oxford: Clarendon, 1924), pp. 94–147; NTA, Vol. 1, pp. 444–484.

D. Sheerin, "St. John the Baptist in the Lower World," *VChr* 30 (1976):1–22.

ACTS OF THADDAEUS. Apocryphal work composed in Syria (third century), now known from two sources. Eusebius quotes a purported correspondence between king Abgar V of Edessa (4 B.C.–A.D. 50) and Jesus. Subsequently, Thaddeus, identified as a disciple, was suppos-edly sent by the apostle Thomas to heal Abgar and to preach in Edessa (Eusebius, *H.E.* 1.13; for the identification of Thaddeus as an apostle, cf. 1.12.3; 2.1.6–7; the story is mentioned in *Pilgrimage of Egeria* 17; cf. 19). A later version, the *Doctrine of Addai* (ca. 400; Addai=Thaddeus), is substantially the same, except that the response to the king is spoken rather than written and the royal messenger conveys back to Abgar a portrait of Jesus. *See also* Abgar. [M.P.McH.]

Bibliography

The Teaching of Addai, tr. G. Howard (Chico: Scholars, 1981); NTA, Vol. 1, pp. 437–444.

ACTS OF THE APOSTLES. Fifth book of the New Testament, originally written as a companion volume to the Gospel of Luke (Luke 1:1–4; Acts 1:1). It is not possible to be precise regarding the date, origin, or even authorship of the Acts. The work could have been written as early as A.D. 65 (if written by Luke the companion of Paul—cf. Col. 4:14; 2 Tim. 4:11; Philem. 24) and possibly as late as 93–95; but if it was not composed by Luke, it could have been written well into the second century. Most scholars date the book ca. 80–85.

The traditional argument for Lucan authorship is based on the "we" passages of Acts 16:10–17; 20:5–15; 21:1–18; 27:1–28:16 and 11:28 in codex Bezae (cf. Irenaeus, *Haer.* 3.13.3; 3.14.1). In the list of Paul's missionary companions, only Luke and Jesus called Justus appear to be candidates for authorship; all early church tradition supports the former. Whoever wrote the book, the author intended the "we" passages to show that he was a participant in the journeys of Paul and was not simply using the conventional "we." Acts and other ancient historical writings made use of the first person plural in narrations of journeys to indicate participation (cf. esp. Polybius 36.12, but also 12.27.1–6; Lucian, *History* 47; Homer, *Odyssey* 12.402–425). Some scholars have questioned this conclusion, noting that were the author a companion of Paul, he would probably have shown awareness of Paul's epistles and major teachings and ascribed the title of apostle to Paul, who always so referred to himself. Also, the work's tendency to smooth out the differences in the early church, especially making Peter and Paul alike in regard to Gentile freedom and the Law (cf. Gal. 2:11–14), has caused some scholars to question its reliability.

Its full title, attached to Acts ca. 150, suggests that the book was about the apostles, but Luke shows little interest in the apostles as a group. Although not original to the document, the title is important evidence from the second century of the church's quest for faith to be rooted in apostolicity.

Acts concentrates its narrative around Peter (1–12) and Paul (13–28). The first half of the book tells the story of the early church in Jerusalem and Palestine/Syria from the resurrection of Christ to the departure of Peter from Jerusalem. Peter serves as the transition and authentication of the Gentile mission of the church, principally carried out by Paul. The career of the latter is structured in three missionary journeys from Antioch and Palestine/Syria to the west and a final journey as a prisoner to Rome. A feature of the contents is the frequent inclusion of speeches that summarize early Christian preaching and teaching (e.g., Acts 2; 3; 7; 13; 17; 20; 22; 26).

The author aimed at providing an "orderly account" of the birth and development of the Christian movement for his patron Theophilus (Luke 1:3–4), but he was also a zealous advocate for the Christian faith. He viewed the early Christians as models for conduct and wanted to show how the Christian movement, which began as a Jewish sect in Palestine, supplanted that group and grew to have universal appeal to both Jews and Gentiles. The author likewise stresses that the church and Rome were not in conflict.

Because of the length of Luke-Acts, the books were published in two separate volumes or scrolls of papyrus sheets, making it possible to circulate one without the other. Acts was separated from the Gospel of Luke at least by ca. 140, when an edited form of Luke became part of Marcion's "canon" along with ten of Paul's epistles. Acts was not used by Marcion probably because he was unaware of it.

Although some verbal parallels exist between Acts and 1 Clement, Barnabas, Polycarp, Didache, and Hermas, this may be evidence only of a common vocabulary in early Christianity. With Justin Martyr in the second century, however, there are apparent citations from Acts (compare Acts 1:8 with 1 Apol. 50.12 and Acts 17:23 with 2 Apol. 10.6). Irenaeus was the first writer to mention Acts by name and ascribe it to Luke. He also cited it in his attacks against Marcion (e.g., Haer. 3.1.1; 3.10.1; 3.12.1–5; 3.14.1–2). Acts is mentioned in the Anti-Marcionite Prologue of Luke (possibly as early as ca. 160–180 but probably later), which notes that Luke was a Syrian of Antioch, a disciple of the apostles who later followed Paul and who served the Lord as a single man until his death in Boeotia (Bithynia?) at the age of eighty-four. Clement of Alexandria frequently cited Acts in a scripturelike manner (e.g., Str. 3.6.49; 7.9.53). Origen made use of several texts in Acts, but was vague about its scriptural status (Or. 12.2; 13.6). Tertullian, like Irenaeus, appealed to Acts to refute Marcion (Marc. 5.1–2) and added that those who did not accept Acts as scripture were not of the Holy Spirit (Praescr. 22). In the third century, Hippolytus of Rome showed reliance on Acts for the story of Simon Magus of Samaria (Haer. 6.20.1–2); in the fourth, Eusebius used Acts as a model for his own history, claimed that Luke was its author (H.E. 3.4.4–11), and included it in his undisputed collection of New Testament scriptures (H.E. 3.25.1). Acts 7:6 was cited in the account of the Martyrs of Lyons (ca. 180–190—Eusebius, H.E. 5.2.5). After Eusebius Acts was acknowledged as scripture throughout the church both east and west, and by ca. 350 it appeared regularly in all church canons of scriptures, including the Muratorian Canon and Athanasius's Festal Letter for 367.

Five apocryphal acts—of Peter, Paul, John, Thomas, and Andrew—were anonymously written in the late second and early third centuries in Asia Minor and Syria. All were modeled after the New Testament Acts, but unlike Acts they are almost entirely fictional. In the third and fourth centuries, other apocryphal acts circulated in some churches but had no impact on the church's biblical canon.

Acts does not fit easily into any ancient pattern of historiography, although the author clearly had some acquaintance with the historian's craft and a working knowledge of Greek rhetoric. Acts itself is neither a biography nor a history after the usual ancient patterns, although the author uses both in his own way to underscore the validity of Christianity. There is no question that the author made use of sources for his work, but he has so completely rewritten them that they are hardly distinguishable. He shares in this practice with many ancient historians, such as Tacitus, Josephus, and even Dionysius of Halicarnassus (*Roman Antiquities* 5; 8) and Lucian (*History* 47), who claim to have neither added nor deleted anything but who also completely rewrote their sources. *See also* Luke. [L.M.McD.]

Bibliography

John Chrysostom, *Homilies on the Acts of the Apostles*, tr. J. Walker et al., NPNF, 1st ser. (1889), Vol. 11; Ephraem Syrus, *Commentary on Acts*, ed. F.C. Conybeare (F.J. Foakes Jackson and K. Lake, *The Beginnings of Christianity* [London: Macmillan, 1926], Vol. 3, pp. 373–453).

F.J. Foakes Jackson and K. Lake, *The Beginnings of Christianity. Part I: The Acts of the Apostles*, 5 vols. (London: Macmillan, 1920–1933); F.F. Bruce, *The Acts of the Apostles: The Greek Text with Introduction and Commentary* (Grand Rapids: Eerdmans, 1951); H.J. Cadbury, "'We' and 'I' Passages in Luke-Acts," *NTS* 3 (1956–1957):128–132; L.E. Keck and J.L. Martyn, eds., *Studies in Luke-Acts: Essays Presented in Honor of Paul Schubert* (Nashville: Abingdon, 1966); J.C. O'Neill, *The Theology of Acts in Its Historical Setting* (London: SPCK, 1970); E. Haenchen, *The Acts of the Apostles, A Commentary* (Philadelphia: Westminster, 1971); W.W. Gasque, *A History of the Criticism of the Acts of the Apostles* (Grand Rapids: Eerdmans, 1975); M. Hengel, *Acts and the History of Earliest Christianity* (Philadelphia: Fortress, 1980); H. Conzelmann, *Acts of the Apostles* (Philadelphia: Fortress, 1987); D.E. Aune, *The New Testament in Its Literary Environment* (Philadelphia: Westminster, 1987); C.J. Hemer, *The Book of Acts in the Setting of Hellenistic History* (Tübinger: Mohr, 1989).

ACTS OF THE MARTYRS OF EDESSA. Two Syriac cycles (fourth century?), one about Sarbel and Barsamja, the other about Gurja, Semma, and Habbib. The first is questionable as a historical source for persecution under Decius. The second, which is perhaps more reliable, contains stories of persecution in the reign of Diocletian. [F.W.N.]

Bibliography
PS 141.

ACTS OF THE PERSIAN MARTYRS. Diverse collection of narratives in Syriac—of uneven historical reliability—about Persian Christians who were put to death because of their faith by various Sassanian kings between 327 and 576. The largest group within the collection concerns the great persecutions during the reign of Sapor II (309–379). [R.J.O.]

Bibliography
PS 142.

ACTS OF THE SCILLITAN MARTYRS. Earliest account of martyrdom in Latin (second century). The *Acts of the Scillitan Martyrs* concerns twelve martyrs, seven men and five women, led by Speratus, from Scillium near Carthage, who were beheaded on July 17, 180. One of the earliest and most reliable martyr accounts, the work consists of the dialogue between the proconsul Saturninus (mentioned in Tertullian, *Scap.* 3.4) and the martyrs. This is the earliest dated document from the Latin church. In one of Speratus's responses, he refers to the "books [i.e., the Old Testament, the Gospels, or both] and letters of a just man named Paul," one of the earliest references to an authoritative collection of Paul's letters, important for New Testament canon history. This is also an early indication of a Latin translation of the Bible. [D.M.S.]

Bibliography
Musurillo, pp. xxii–xxiii; 86–89; B.M. Metzger, *The Canon of the New Testament* (Oxford: Clarendon, 1987), pp. 156–157.

ACTS OF THOMAS. Gnostic legendary account (third century?) of Thomas that conflates the apostle and a twin brother of Jesus and makes the character into a redeemer figure. Written in Syriac, the work was translated into a number of languages. The extant Greek text is closest to the original; the existing Syriac versions have been theologically adapted to orthodoxy.

The *Acts of Thomas* is the source of the connection between Thomas and India. Older traditions have Thomas die a natural death (Clement of Alexandria, *Str.* 4.71) or go to Parthia (Origen, *Hom. 3 in Gen.*). Coins found in Indian excavations speak of the kings mentioned in the legend but do not provide historicity for it.

The *Acts* originally used Tatian's *Diatessaron* as its source for Thomas's life with Jesus but was later adjusted to the four Gospels. It may have been known to Ephraem the Syrian and appears in the fourth-century *Manichaean Psalm-book*. Epiphanius (*Haer.* 47.1) is the first to speak of it by name; he sets it in Encratite circles. Augustine (*Faust.* 14; 22; passim) says that Manichaeans used it but that it was also popular in orthodox circles.

Somewhat influenced by Hellenistic-Oriental romances in its depiction of miracles, the work follows Thomas in his journey to India, describing his adventures and conversions, and ends with his martyrdom. A clearly developed Gnostic redeemer-myth marks the work. Accounts of conversion usually end in baptism, an anointing with oil, and a eucharistic celebration. The text contains both a "Wedding Hymn" and the beautiful "Hymn of the Pearl." The *Acts* has notable parallels with the *Acts of Paul*, but none with the *Acts of John*. Whether it depended upon the *Acts of Peter* is uncertain. TLG 2038. *See also* Thomas.

[F.W.N.]

Bibliography
PS 8; *Cahiers d'Orientalisme* (1983), Vol. 6.

A.F.J. Klijn, *The Acts of Thomas* (Leiden: Brill, 1962); NTA, Vol. 2, pp. 425–531.

P.H. Poirier, *L'Hymne de la perle des Actes de Thomas* (Louvain-la-Neuve: Université Catholique, 1981); M. Marcovich, "The Wedding Hymn of Acta Thomae," *Illinois Classical Studies* 6 (1981):367–385; G.L. Huxley, "Geography in the Acts of Thomas," *GRBS* 24 (1983):71–80.

ACTS OF XANTHIPPE AND POLYXENA.

According to the legendary account, Xanthippe, her husband, Probus, and her sister, Polyxena, were converted when Paul came to Spain. The *Acts of Paul* were a major source; the earliest possible date is the mid-third century. Feast day September 23. TLG 2248. [E.F.]

Bibliography
M.R. James, "Introduction to the Acts of Xanthippe and Polyxena" and "Acta Xanthippae et Polyxenae," *TS* 2.3 (1893):43–57, 58–85; W.A. Craigie, tr., ANF (1896), Vol. 10, pp. 203–217.

ADAM. First man in the accounts of creation in Genesis 1–2. *Adam* (Hebrew, "man") came to function as a proper name. Judaism considered Adam the founder of the human race and the ideal man. He became a central figure in later Christian, Gnostic, Manichaean, Mandaean, and Islamic thought. Patristic interpretations of Adam were conditioned by the Pauline (Rom. 5; 6; 15; 1 Cor. 15) and Lucan (Luke 3:38) usage. Paul understood Adam as a type of Christ, who, as the Second Adam, restored to humanity the state of grace to which Adam was party before the fall. Luke portrayed Adam as direct ancestor of Christ.

Patristic literature about Adam is extensive. He was important in the discussion of cosmology, creation, anthropology, spirituality, and Christology. Genesis, especially the narrative of the creation, became the focus of extensive exegetical effort. *See also* Christ, Christology; Eve; Genesis; Original Sin. [D.B.]

Bibliography
Basil of Seleucia, *Homiliae* 2 and 3 *in Adam* (PG 85.37–61).

T. Garcia de Orbiso, R. Aprile, and A. Rigoli, "Adamo," *Bibliotheca Sanctorum* (Rome: Istituto Giovanni XXIII, 1961), Vol. 1, pp. 201–226; P. Lengsfeld, *Adam und Christus* (Essen: Ludgerus, 1965); R. Scroggs, *The Last Adam: A Study in Pauline Anthropology* (Philadelphia: Fortress, 1966); H. Aurenhammer, "Adam," *Lexikon der christliche Ikonographie*, ed. E. Kirschbaum (Freiburg: Herder, 1968), Vol. 1, pp. 35–51; J.T. Nielsen, *Adam and Christ in the Theology of Irenaeus of Lyons* (Assen: Van Gorcum, 1968); O. Betz, P. Schafer, A. Hultgard, and F. Mildenberger, "Adam," TRE (1977), Vol. 10, pp. 414–437; F. Morard, "L'Apocalypse d'Adam de Nag Hammadi: une essai d'interprétation," *Gnosis and Gnosticism*, ed. M. Krause (Leiden: Brill, 1977), pp. 35–42; E. Pagels, *Adam, Eve, and the Serpent* (New York: Random House, 1988).

ADOPTIONISM. Term used by historians of doctrine, alongside "Dynamic Monarchianism" (with whose meaning it overlaps), to designate the idea that Jesus was a human being uniquely chosen to exercise the function or role of divine sovereignty and Sonship. Divine power (personal or impersonal) so resided in Jesus that he may be regarded as a uniquely inspired human person like, but far transcending, the Old Testament prophets; his anointing by the Spirit (whether at his baptism by John or at the moment of conception) created his Sonship, which thus falls in the same class with the Christian's adoptive sonship given at baptism.

This idea is a historian's abstraction, a line of thought never developed or presented complete by any one theologian. Probably no Christian theologian, not even those against whom the charge is leveled, taught its distinctive feature: that Christ is a "mere man" (*psilos anthropos*) by nature. Yet the abstraction points usefully to one of the two principles whose synthesis created ancient Catholic Christology: Christ's solidarity with us and his solidarity with the Father and Holy Spirit. Adoptionism achieves a type of expression in which the first principle predominates or appears to exclude the second; Docetism, in which the human Jesus is declared mere appearance, did the reverse. Although no full-fledged Adoptionist is to be found, certain themes and New Testament texts rang in the mind: the prominence given in the Gospels to Jesus' baptism and the descent of the Spirit (Mark 1:9ff. and parallels) and the liturgical recollection of this event not only at each Christian's baptism but at the feast of Epiphany (for many the most important Christian festival after Easter and Pentecost from the third century onward); and the texts that speak of Jesus as being "a man singled out by God" (Acts 2:22), as "advancing in wisdom and in favor with God and men" (Luke 2:52), and as having been "declared Son of God by a mighty act in that he rose from the dead" (Rom. 1:4). Perhaps, too, wherever a link with Judaism was cherished, the threat was felt of an Adoptionist reduction of Christ purely to the level of an adopted son of God, like one of the Old Testament saints (also called "sons of God"). Certainly, "Judaizing" usually meant something close to Adoptionism.

Although Adoptionism was never a possible choice for any theologian from subapos-

tolic times onward, all were forced by the Bible and by liturgy to attend to the Jesus who is like us and who, in his way, too, follows the Father's will. Two heretics, about whom we are badly informed, come closest to Adoptionism: Theodotus (cf. Hippolytus, *Haer.* 7.35), a late-second-century teacher from Byzantium who worked in Rome and allegedly taught that Jesus, born of a virgin and deeply devout, received the heavenly Christ in the form of a dove at his baptism; and Paul of Samosata, bishop of Antioch, who was condemned at a synod in Antioch in 268 for teaching that "Jesus Christ is from below" and "being unwilling to acknowledge . . . that the Son of God has come down from heaven" (Eusebius, *H.E.* 7.30). Later propagandists viewed Paul's teaching as heralding Nestorius's, but their reports of his words are unreliable. Otherwise, Adoptionism remained a Christology in search of a theologian until modern times. *See also* Christ, Christology; Monarchianism; Paul of Samosata; Theodotus the Leatherworker.   [L.R.W.]

Bibliography
A. Hilgenfeld, *Die Ketzergeschichte des Urchristentums, Urkundlich dargestellt* (Leipzig: Fues [R. Reisland], 1894), pp. 609–615; Kelly, pp. 115–119, 140.

AENEAS OF GAZA (d. 518). Christian Neoplatonic philosopher, friend of Procopius. In brilliant rhetorical style, Aeneas attacked the doctrine of preexistent souls and defended the immortal soul and the resurrected body. CPG III, 7450–7451.   [F.W.N.]

AETIUS (ca. 300–370). Leader of the Anomoean party within Arianism. Although reportedly a native of Cilicia, Aetius spent most of his career at Antioch. In spite of his humble origins, he aspired to become a sophist or rhetor and, while originally trained as a goldsmith, acquired considerable skill in logic and dialectic. Probably a convert to Christianity, Aetius received his training from some of Arius's earliest followers and himself became an ardent supporter. Ordained deacon by Leontius of Antioch in 344 or 345, he became one of the founding members of the Anomoean party, whose teachings were sometimes called Aetianism. As a friend of the Caesar Gallus, he was associated in his downfall and exiled (354), thus earning the gratitude of Gallus's brother, Julian the Apostate, who later rewarded him.

After a stormy career, he was condemned and exiled by councils at Ancyra (358) and Constantinople (360). Recalled by Julian, he was consecrated bishop, but without a specific see. Under Julian's successors, he lived in retirement and, although implicated in the revolt of Julian's cousin Procopius in 365, narrowly avoided condemnation. He died a few years later and was buried at Constantinople by his secretary, Eunomius. Apart from the fragments of some of his letters, his sole surviving work is that entitled *Syntagmation*. CPG II, 3445–3451. *See also* Anomoeans; Eunomius.

[R.P.V.]

Bibliography

G. Bardy, "L'Héritage littéraire d'Aétius," *RHE* 24 (1928):809–827; V. Grumel, "Les Textes monothélites d'Aétius," *Echos d'Orient* 28 (1929):156–166; L.R. Wickham, "The *Syntagmation* of Aetius the Anomoean," *JThS* 19 (1968):532–569.

AFRICA. Roman territory on the Mediterranean coast of northwest Africa. In the early Christian period, "Roman Africa" was sharply distinguished from Cyrenaica and Egypt to its east. In its broadest extent, it comprised a strip along the coast of modern Libya west from the Gulf of Sidra (Tripolitania) and much of the region north of the Sahara in present-day Tunisia and Algeria, with its influence extending into the territory of Morocco (Africa Proconsularis, Numidia, and the Mauretanias). Its population consisted originally of Libyans, or Berbers, who had immigrated from the area of the Levant several millennia before Christ.

Beginning in the ninth century B.C., Phoenicians from Tyre established maritime cities, of which Carthage became the most important. The Phoenicians appear to have been a courageous and passionate people, but also factious and cruel: in times of crisis they practiced child-sacrifice. When Carthage was destroyed by Rome in 146 B.C., its territory was organized into a Roman province; the Carthaginians moved to the hinterland, where they mingled with the Libyans. After its resettlement by Augustus, Carthage grew to become the largest city in North Africa. It had a cosmopolitan population with a large community of Jews and of Greeks.

As Carthage grew, Roman influence and administration extended throughout North Africa. The gradual Romanization of the territory brought urbanization, prosperity, Roman education, and an African Latin literature. Nevertheless, in many parts of North Africa, native identities were retained, and even in the time of Augustine there were native speakers who did not understand Latin.

Earliest Christianity in Africa. Our first witness to Christianity in North Africa comes in the form of an official record of the trial of the Scillitan martyrs in 180. They were evidently Latin-speakers (they carried a Latin Bible), but at least two of them bore names native to Africa. It is probable, however, that Christianity, perhaps conveyed by Greek merchants from the east, had originated somewhat earlier within the Greek-speaking community. The *Passion of Perpetua and Felicitas*, written just after 200, presupposes a strong Greek element in the community (*Pass. Perp.* 13.4), and Tertullian wrote in both Latin and Greek for the Christian community at Carthage. His writings indicate a community, at the beginning of the third century, already numerous and strong (*Scap.* 5.2); and Perpetua was from the upper classes (*Pass. Perp.* 2).

During the third century, Christianity continued to spread through the towns and countryside. Records attest that eighty-seven bishops attended the Council of Carthage in 256; they had come from Proconsular Africa, Numidia, Mauretania, and (at least one) from Tripolitania. The letters and treatises of Cyprian sharply illuminate the decade of the 250s. Many Christians lapsed during the persecution under Decius (249–250). Differing views on the appropriate treatment of the lapsed led to severe tensions in the Carthaginian church, and ultimately to the Novatian schism. In the same period, the African church asserted its independence from Rome over the question of the validity of baptism administered by heretics, when Cyprian refused (255–256) to accept the judgment of Stephen I, the bishop of Rome.

The African church again suffered severely during the persecution of Diocletian from 303 to 305 that led to the Donatist schism. Constantine's repeated decisions in favor of the Catholics at an early stage in the quarrel (312–317) put the Donatists in the position of the persecuted, and Donatism was able to take root as a movement not only of religious but also of social protest. Throughout the fourth century, the Donatists flourished under the leadership of such powerful bishops as Donatus, Parmenian, and Primian, and Catholics in Africa found themselves on the defensive. The imperial decision at the Council of Carthage in 411 in favor of the Catholics, however, entailed severe penalties for the Donatists, and their decline set in. The continuing growth of Christianity in North Africa is attested by the number of bishops present at this council—284 from the Donatists and 286 from the Catholics.

The Vandal Conquest. Almost immediately, the African church became embroiled in the Pelagian controversy, when Pelagius and Celestius arrived from Rome in 410. Several councils of Carthage from 411 to 418 condemned their views. Augustine continued to write against the Pelagian doctrines; at his death in 430, he left unfinished a work against Julian of Eclanum. By then, under their king Gaiseric, the Vandals had entered Africa. They captured Carthage in 439 and held power over much of Roman Africa for a century. The Vandals were Arian Christians; under their kings, Catholic Christianity lost the privileged position it had enjoyed under the Roman emperors. Catholic writers perhaps exaggerated the degree of persecution under the Vandals, but it is known that some Catholic bishops suffered exile, and some bishoprics were left vacant on the death of their incumbents.

After the defeat of the Vandals by the general Belisarius, sent by Justinian I to recapture Africa for the Roman empire (534–535), Catholic Christianity once more enjoyed a florescence. Relations with the eastern church can be documented. Already during the Vandal period, Vigilius of Thapsus, who wrote against the Monophysites and Arians, had fled to Constantinople. In the sixth century, Facundus, bishop of Hermione, went to Constantinople, where he completed an apology for those attacked in the Three Chapters.

Carthage fell to the Muslim armies in 698. Under the Arabs, Christianity in North Africa was slowly stifled, although there were still a few bishoprics in Africa in the eleventh century.

Intellectual Contributions. Several noteworthy features mark Christianity in North Africa. First, literary creativity was remarkably high, continuing under the Vandals (Victor of Vita, Vigilius of Thapsus, Fulgentius of Ruspe) into very late antiquity. The work of African Christians in apologetics is particularly distinguished, including such names as Tertullian in the late second century; Minucius Felix, Cyprian, and Arnobius in the third; Lactantius in the early fourth; and culminating in Augustine's *City of God* in the early fifth. Second, in spite of the many Christians who lapsed during the persecutions, African Christianity had a profound respect for the martyr, evident not only in the ecclesiastical conflicts that grew out of the persecutions but also in narratives commemorating martyrs (Perpetua, Cyprian, Maximilian) and in literature documenting attitudes (Tertullian, *Cor.* and *Fuga*; Augustine, *Conf.* 6.2). Third, African Christianity from its earliest days appears factious and schismatic. Before the great schisms of Novatian and Donatus, Montanism had won a place in Carthage, and such heretics as Hermogenes had found a home there. Finally, church councils played an important part in African Christianity. Of this, the Africans themselves were aware, and in 419 the African church collected the canons of its previous councils. These have come down as the code of canons of the African church, becoming a part of the canonical codes in both the eastern and western churches. *See also* Augustine; Carthage; Cyprian; Donatism; Pelagius, Pelagianism; Tertullian; Vandals. [R.D.S.]

Bibliography

P. Monceaux, *Histoire littéraire de l'Afrique chrétienne* (Paris: Leroux, 1901–1923); T.R.S. Broughton, *The Romanization of Africa Proconsu-*

Meal scene (late third century) from Catacomb of SS. Peter and Marcellinus, Rome, Italy. ("Irene, bring some hot." "Agape, mix it.") (Used by permission of Pontifical Commission of Sacred Archaeology.)

laris (Baltimore: Johns Hopkins P, 1929); W.H.C. Frend, *The Donatist Church: A Movement of Protest in Roman North Africa* (Oxford: Clarendon, 1952); B.H. Warmington, *The North African Provinces* (Cambridge: Cambridge UP, 1954); G.C. Picard, *La Civilization de l'Afrique romaine* (Paris: Plon, 1959); W.H.C. Frend, *Martyrdom and Persecution in the Early Church* (New York: New York UP, 1967 [1965]); P. Brown, *Augustine of Hippo* (Berkeley: U of California P, 1967); S. Raven, *Rome in Africa* (London: Evans, 1969); T.D. Barnes, *Tertullian: A Historical and Literary Study* (Oxford: Oxford UP, 1971); P. MacKendrick, *The North African Stones Speak* (Chapel Hill: U of North Carolina P, 1980); J. Cuoq, *L'Eglise d'Afrique du Nord des IIe au XIIe siècle* (Paris: Le Centurion, 1984).

AGAPE (LOVE FEAST). The Greek term *agapē* means "love." In early Christian theology, however, *agapē* refers to a distinctive kind of love, and in the early liturgy, to a special religious meal celebrated to alleviate the needs of the poor, the widows, and the orphans. Although the verb (*agapaō*) is common in classical Greek, the noun (*agapē*, Latin *caritas*) is seldom if ever found. Most scholars believe that the origin of the noun lies in Hellenistic Judaism, where it means sexual love (Septuagint), piety (*Aristeas* 229), the love of Wisdom personified (Wisd. Sol. 3:9; 6:18), love and fear (Philo, *Quod Deus immutabilis* 14.69), and the concrete love of neighbor expressed in philanthropy.

The New Testament gathers strands in Hellenistic Judaism to weave a distinctive theology of love: God, who is love, is embodied in Christ, who in turn is embodied in the community of believers (church), whose singular characteristic is that they love one another. Indeed, Paul (Gal. 5; Rom. 12; 1 Cor. 13), John (John 15; 1 John 3–5; 2 John), and James (James 2:1–6) maintain that Christian conduct is governed by this theology of agape. The giving of self is the connotation.

Among early Christians, both noun and verb remain the basic terms for God's attitude and action toward humans, for the reason why Christ came, and for Christian piety—agape in each case. Although patristic tradition reveals a variety of emphases, one finds the fundamental understanding of agape-theology already articulated in Clement of Rome at the end of the first century (*1 Clem.* 49–50): it is the binding power between God, Christ, and Christians, which in each case entails the giving of self for others.

In the history of early Christian practice, however, agape is also a liturgical term. Translated "love-feast" (Jude 12), it springs from the meal that the New Testament variously calls the "breaking of bread" (Acts 2:42–47; 20:7–12) and "eucharist" (1 Cor. 11:20–34). A core tradition in the early church, the meal explicitly recalls the meals Jesus celebrated with his disciples, especially the Last Supper (Mark 14; Matt. 26; Luke 22; John 13; 1 Cor. 11) and the postresurrection meals recounted in Luke 24 and John 20–21.

Although the evidence is scant and controversial, the breaking of bread/eucharist unquestionably was conditioned by religious meals in first-century Judaism, especially the fraternal meals that celebrated religious table-fellowship (*ḥaburah*) and in particular, the Passover meal. In time, the meal was also shaped by customs of the Greco-Roman world, especially the cult meals of the religious fraternities (*thiasoi, collegia*) and the funerary societies. When transported into a predominantly Hellenistic world, however, the meal was subject to serious abuses. Paul himself records heavy drinking, greed, disdain on the part of the well-off for the poor, and partisan strife (1 Cor. 11:17–22).

Eventually, abuses, coupled with imperial rescripts forbidding the meals of secret societies, brought about the separation of the fraternal meal (agape) and eucharist, but not everywhere and not at once. In Ignatius (ca. 110), for instance, the celebration of the agape is related to but distinct from the eucharist (*Smyrn.* 8.2); so also, the *Didache* 9; 10; 14. In Justin Martyr, the eucharist seems to have absorbed the fraternal functions characteristic of agape (*1 Apol.* 65; 67). Yet in the *Apostolic Tradition* of Hippolytus, there is a rubric (26) about the agape for widows, and Tertullian is quite clear about its social purpose: it is for the relief of the poor (*Apol.* 39). On the other hand, in Clement's Alexandria (ca. 200) agape and eucharist are joined, in spite of the signal abuses to which Clement gives witness (*Paed.* 2.5–10).

There is general agreement that from the mid-third century agape and eucharist go their separate ways, with the former becoming clearly a fraternal meal to relieve the distress of the needy. It remained such in North Africa, at least, into the fifth century, for Augustine (*Faust.* 20.20) distinguishes it sharply from the funerary meals (*refrigeria*), of which he disapproved. By the end of the patristic age, however, the agape had fallen into disuse. *See also* Almsgiving; Eucharist; Love. [T.M.F.]

Bibliography

Didache 9–10; Ignatius, *Smyrnaeans* 8; Clement of Alexandria, *Instructor* 2.1.4–9; Tertullian, *Apology* 39; Hippolytus, *Apostolic Tradition* 25–27; Augustine, *Against Faustus* 20. J. Keating, *The Agape and the Eucharist in the Early Church: Studies in the History of the Christian Love-Feasts* (London: Methuen, 1901); H. Leclercq, "Agape," DACL (1907), Vol. 1, pp. 775–848; W.O.E. Oesterley, *The Jewish Background of the Christian Liturgy* (Oxford: Clarendon, 1925); A. Nygren, *Agape and Eros* (Philadelphia: Westminster, 1953); H. Lietzmann, *Mass and Lord's Supper* (Leiden: Brill, 1953–1979); G.W.H. Lampe, *A Patristic Greek Lexicon* (Oxford: Clarendon, 1961); C. Spicq, *Agape in the New Testament*, 2 vols. (St. Louis: Herder, 1963–1965); E. Stauffer, "*Agapaō*," *Theological Dictionary of the New Testament*, ed. G. Kittel (Grand Rapids: Eerdmans, 1964), Vol. 1, pp. 21–55; J. Kilmartin, *The Eucharist in the Primitive Church* (Englewood Cliffs: Prentice-Hall, 1965); G.H. Outka, *Agape: An Ethical Analysis* (New Haven: Yale UP, 1972); E. Ferguson, *Early Christians Speak* (Abilene: ACU, 1987), pp. 129–136.

AGAPETUS I. Bishop of Rome (535–536). A firm defender of orthodoxy, Agapetus I excluded converts from Arianism from holding church office. He traveled to Constantinople at the request of the Gothic king Theodahad to dissuade Justinian I from his planned invasion of Italy but failed in this mission. He did, however, depose the Monophysite patriarch Anthimus, who enjoyed the empress Theodora's support, consecrated Menas in his place, and confirmed the orthodoxy of the Theopaschite formula. He died in Constantinople shortly thereafter. At Rome, he had established a library in his family home and had planned, along with Cassiodorus, a center of Christian education, a project that did not come to fruition.

He left six letters. Feast day April 22 (west), April 17 (east). CPL 1611, 1615, 1625, 1693.

[M.P.McH.]

Bibliography

Liber Pontificalis 59 (Duchesne 1.287–289).

H.I. Marrou, "Autour de la bibliothèque du Pape Agapit," *MEFR* 48 (1931):124–169; A. deVogüé, "Le Pape qui persécuta saint Equitius," *AB* 100 (1982):319–325.

AGRAPHA. Term (Greek, "unwritten things") used since the late eighteenth century to designate sayings of Jesus found outside the New Testament Gospels. Scholars of that period believed that the collection of these noncanonical sayings would help to "restore" the original Gospel. Such a view is no longer tenable, but the term has remained in scholarly vocabulary.

The transmission of sayings of Jesus closely parallels the history of the development of Gospel materials. From the period of Jesus' public ministry until the appearance of the first written Gospels, Jesus' story and words were transmitted orally. The production of written forms of the oral tradition (e.g., sayings of Jesus, miracle stories) carried into the second century. John's Gospel, last written of the canonical Gospels, ends with the admission that "there were many other things which Jesus did," which if all were written, the world could not contain (John 21:25). This would apply to Jesus' sayings as well.

Eusebius of Caesarea (*H.E.* 3.39.1) tells of the five-volume work by Papias (ca. 130), *Expositions of the Oracles of the Lord*, apparently an early collection of sayings of Jesus. The editors of Matthew and Luke may earlier have had at hand a document or oral tradition of sayings of Jesus (the so-called "Q" source), which they used to supplement the Marcan tradition. It was not until the late nineteenth and early twentieth centuries, however, that scholars began to collect Agrapha systematically.

The sources that produced Agrapha are: (1) New Testament writings other than Gospels; (2) manuscripts of the New Testament with different forms of sayings of Jesus; (3) church fathers, who often quote sections of apocryphal gospels; (4) the Talmud, the repository of Jewish traditions, which records sayings attributed to Jesus; (5) papyri discovered in Egypt written in Greek and Coptic; and (6) Islamic traditions dating from the eighth century and later. For historians, perhaps the most important is the Coptic *Gospel of Thomas*, discovered in 1946. It contains the largest single extant collection of sayings, 114 in all, many of which are variations on the canonical sayings of Jesus. The document is for the most part a list of sayings without a narrative context, which may have been used to support a Gnostic view of Jesus. Some of this document survives in Greek in the Oxyrhynchus papyri. The available forms of Agrapha give historians of religion an opportunity to trace the development of Gospel traditions. [G.A.K.]

Bibliography

J.H. Ropes, *Die Sprüche Jesu*, TU (1896), Vol. 14.2; idem, "Agrapha," *Hastings' Dictionary of the Bible*, Extra Vol. (New York: Scribner, 1904), pp. 343–352; A. Resch, *Agrapha: Aussercanonische Schriftfragmente*, 2nd ed., *TU* (1906), Vol. 15.3–4; J. Jeremias, *Unknown Sayings of Jesus* (London: SPCK, 1958; orig. German ed., 1951); A. Guillaumont et al., *The Gospel According to Thomas* (Leiden: Brill; New York: Harper, 1959); J. Finegan, *Hidden Records of the Life of Jesus* (Philadelphia: Pilgrim, 1969); F.F. Bruce, *Jesus and Christian Origins Outside the New Testament* (Grand Rapids: Eerdmans, 1974); H. Koester, "Apocryphal and Canonical Gospels," *HThR* 73 (1980):105–130; W. Stroker, *Extra Canonical Sayings of Jesus* (Atlanta: Scholars, 1989).

ALARIC (ca. 370–410). Ruler of the Visigoths (from ca. 395). An adherent of Arianism, Alaric led his people into Italy from Greece (401). Kept in check for a time by the Roman general Stilicho, he besieged Rome after Stilicho's death (408) and upon his third attempt entered and pillaged the city (410), from which he took as hostage Galla Placidia, sister of the emperor Honorius. He died of natural causes shortly thereafter, his plan to cross into Africa thwarted by the destruction of his ships in a storm. Augustine composed the *City of God* in response to the shock of the capture of Rome and the pagan arguments advanced to explain it. [M.P.McH.]

Bibliography

P. Courcelle, *Histoire littéraire des grandes invasions germaniques*, 3rd ed. (Paris: Etudes Augustiniennes, 1964), pp. 31–77; L. Musset, *The Germanic Invasions: The Making of Europe AD 400–600* (University Park: Pennsylvania State UP, 1975).

ALBAN (third–fourth century). By tradition Britain's first martyr, Alban may have been executed at Verulamium (St. Alban's) sometime between 209 and 305. Germanus of Auxerre visited his supposed tomb in 429; an important monastery was later founded on the site. The legend of his condemnation is preserved by Bede. Feast day June 20.

[M.P.McH.]

Bibliography

Constantius of Lyons, *Life of Germanus* 16; 18; Bede, *Ecclesiastical History* 1.7, 18.

ALBINUS (ca. 115–170). Important representative of second-century Middle Platonism. Nothing is known of his life, but Albinus's teachings are preserved in a handbook of Platonic doctrine, the *Didaskalikos*. This work contains teachings in dialectic, epistemology, and metaphysics.

Albinus's theology anticipates developments in later Hellenic and Christian Platonism (*Didas.* 10). He postulates three divine entities in a descending hierarchy of God, Mind, and Soul. God is an intellect above being; the Mind is the demiurge, who creates the universe; the Soul is an animate, partially rational and partially irrational being, who is the world-soul. *See also* Neoplatonism.

[R.M.B.]

Bibliography

C.F. Hermann, ed., *Platonis dialogi secundum Thrasylli tetralogias dispositi* (*Didaskalikos. Eisagōgē*) (Leipzig: Teubner, 1936), Vol. 6.

R.E. Witt, *Albinus and the History of Middle Platonism* (Cambridge: Cambridge UP, 1937); J.H. Leonen, "Albinus' Metaphysics: An Attempt at Rehabilitation," *Mnemosyne* 4.9 (1956):296–319; 4.10 (1957): 35–56; J. Dillon, *The Middle Platonists* (Cambridge: Duckworth, 1977), pp. 266–306; R.M. Berchman, *From Philo to Origen: Middle Platonism in Transition* (Chico: Scholars, 1984), pp. 83–104, 181–186.

"Alexamenos worships his God." Graffito now in the Palatine Antiquarium, Rome, Italy.

ALEXAMENOS. A graffito (second–third century?) found on the Palatine Hill in Rome shows a youth raising his hand in adoration toward a figure on a cross with the body of a man and the head of an ass. The inscription says in Greek, "Alexamenos worships his God." This caricature was prompted by the pagan notion that Jews and Christians worshiped a deity in the form of an ass (Tacitus, *Histories* 5.3f.; Minucius Felix, *Oct.* 9.3; cf. Epiphanius, *Haer.* 26.12).

[E.F.]

Bibliography

V. Väänänen, ed., *Graffiti del Palatino* (Helsinki: Akateeminen Kirjakauppa, 1966), Vol. 1: *Paedagogium*, ed. H. Solin and M. Iktonen-Kaila, pp. 209–212; G.M.A. Hanfmann, "The Crucified Donkey Man," *Studies in Classical Art and Archaeology: A Tribute to Peter Heinrich von Blanckenhagen*, ed. G. Kopcke and M.B. Moore (Locust Valley: Augustin, 1979), pp. 206–208.

ALEXANDER OF ALEXANDRIA (d. 328). Bishop (ca. 312–328). At the beginning of Alexander's episcopate, the church of Alexandria was preoccupied with the Melitian schism. Melitius, bishop of Lycopolis, took a rigorist position against the policies adopted by Peter, bishop of Alexandria, on the terms of readmitting to communion those who lapsed during the persecution under Diocletian. The problem was soon complicated and overshadowed by the teachings of Arius, a presbyter in Alexandria, who held that Christ was not eternal but created by God. Alexander moved cautiously but finally condemned Arius's views at a synod of about 100 bishops (ca. 319) and excommunicated him along with two bishops, five presbyters, and six deacons who held his views. Both Arius and Alexander wrote letters setting forth their positions; the controversy spread and came to the attention of the emperor Constantine. The Council of Nicaea (325) upheld Alexander's position on the co-eternity of Christ with God, anathematizing the views attributed to Arius, and adopted a policy on the treatment of Melitians, upholding the disciplinary and jurisdictional authority of the bishop of Alexandria in Egypt and adjacent territories. Alexander had the support throughout of his deacon Athanasius, who succeeded him as bishop. Feast day February 26 (west), May 29 (east), April 22 (Coptic). CPG II, 2000–2017. *See also* Arius; Athanasius; Melitius; Nicaea. [E.F.]

Bibliography
Athanasius, *Defense Against the Arians*; Socrates, *Church History* 1.5–6, 9; Sozomen, *Church History* 1.15; Theodoret, *Church History* 1.4; Epiphanius, *Panarion* 69.4.

H.G. Opitz, ed., *Athanasius Werke* (Berlin and Leipzig: de Gruyter, 1934–1935), pp. 6–11, 19–31; J.B. Hawkins, tr., ANF (1886), Vol. 6, pp. 289–304.

ALEXANDER SEVERUS (ca. 208–235).

Roman emperor (222–235). A cousin of the emperor Elagabalus, who designated him as Caesar, or co-ruler (221), Alexander became emperor upon Elagabalus's death. Throughout his rule, he was under the influence of his mother, Julia Mamaea. The jurist Ulpian also played a major role at first but was soon murdered (223) by mutinous praetorian troops. Justice was administered humanely and efforts were made to ensure civilian control, but military revolts persisted. A campaign to recover Mesopotamia from the Persians (232) met with some success. The emperor and his mother were killed by troops of the army on the Rhine.

Christians enjoyed toleration during the reign, and a number were members of the imperial court. Origen was active, and Julius Africanus dedicated his *Cesti* to the emperor. Alexander is reported to have had a statue of Christ placed in his private chapel among those of such other notables as Alexander the Great, Orpheus, and Abraham; they were enshrined as models of philosophic teaching rather than for purposes of religious devotion. At Rome, the schism that had arisen between the bishop Callistus and the antipope Hippolytus over Modalism and the reconciliation of Christians who had sinned after baptism apparently lingered under Urban I and Pontianus.

The reign was followed by that of Maximinus Thrax, who repudiated Alexander's policies and launched a period of persecution. A later tradition that Alexander was himself a persecutor, which doubtless arose over a confusion of dates, is to be rejected. [M.P.McH.]

Bibliography
Herodian, *Imperial History* 6; Dio Cassius, *Roman History* 79–80; Eusebius, *Church History* 6.21–28.

A. Jardé, *Etudes critiques sur la vie et le règne de Sévère Alexandre* (Paris: Boccard, 1925); R. Syme, *Emperors and Biography: Studies in the Historia Augusta* (Oxford: Clarendon, 1971), pp. 146–162; S. Settis, "Severo Alessandro e i suoi Lari (S.H.A., S.A., 29.2–3)," *Athenaeum* 50 (1972):237–251; R. Soraci, *L'opera legislativa e amministrativa dell' Imperatore Severo Alessandro* (Catania: Muglia, 1974); S.A. Stertz, "Christianity in the *Historia Augusta*," *Latomus* 36 (1977):694–715; N. Santos Yanguas, "La dinastia de los Severos y los christianos," *Euphrosyne* 11 (1981–1982):149–171.

ALEXANDRIA. Egyptian metropolis at the mouth of the Nile River. Alexander the Great laid out Alexandria sometime in 332–331 B.C. He chose a strip of land between Lake Mareotis and the Mediterranean Sea about one mile wide north and south and three miles long east and west, laid out the agora, the street grid, the city walls, and selected the temples (Strabo 17.791–795). Strategically, the city had connections to all points on the Mediterranean and through the Red Sea to the regions of southeast Asia. Alexandria had two harbors, east and west, that made it an excellent port.

The area within its walls was divided into five sections designated by Greek letters. One of these, known by the name Rakotis, was inhabited predominantly by native Egyptians; another was primarily Jewish. By the beginning of the Christian era, Jews were overflowing into a neighboring section. Their right to manage their own affairs almost as if they were a foreign government made relations with other Alexandrians difficult.

Alexandria was the home of many cults. The Rakotis section contained the famous Sarapeum. Sources make it clear that numerous Hellenistic gods were worshiped there, and various syncretistic religions also had their place.

Early Christian History. The emergence of Christianity in the city is difficult to date or describe. It probably began in connection with the Jewish community. There, it could have appealed to those like Philo, who allegorized the Old Testament, or it could have found a home with those linked to Jerusalem and perhaps more conservative in outlook. The western text of Acts 18:25 notes that Apollos was an Alexandrian who learned his Christianity in the city. Eusebius's legend concerning Mark's presence in the metropolis is late (*H.E.* 2.16), but the newly discovered letter by Clement of Alexandria shows the Marcan influence in the second century, both within more Gnostic and more orthodox communities. If the *Epistle of Barnabas, The Gospel of the Egyptians,* and *The Gospel to the Hebrews* come from Alexandria, the multiplex character of early Christianity there is clear. A letter attributed to Hadrian in the *Historia Augusta* (*Vita Saturnini* 8) comments on Alexandrian syncretism by noting that worshipers of Sarapis were Christians and Christians were Sarapis worshipers; it also notes that leaders in all religions, including Judaism, dabbled in astrology and the interpretation of animal sacrifices.

The dominant Christian figures known to us from the first half of the second century were Gnostic teachers: most notably Basilides, who apparently studied with Glaukios, a translator for Peter, and Valentinus, who almost became bishop of Rome. These men created Gnostic systems of intricacy and elegance. They may have been early directors of schools similar to that which emerged in the late second and early third centuries as the great catechetical school of Alexandria.

The first known orthodox teacher in Alexandria was Pantaenus, a shadowy figure who may have traveled to India and have been influenced by its philosophy and religion. His successor, Clement, wrote a number of works that give us a view of one who loved learning and found almost infinite ways to confront arguments against Christianity and to attack weaknesses in non-Christian religions. He emphasized the place of knowledge (*gnosis*) in faith but was not a Gnostic like Basilides or Valentinus.

The greatest figure in the catechetical school was Origen (ca. 185–ca. 251). Because of his love for the church, he had a concern for unlearned Christians, although his main interest was in the educated. Gregory Thaumaturgus's *Panegyric to Origen* describes how Origen taught his students to read biblical and non-Christian texts with care and insight by employing the interpretive tools of his day. He was the most creative theologian the eastern church ever produced, yet many of his ideas were condemned as heretical. Born in Alexandria, he spent only the first half of his life there, for he had conflict with his bishop and left for Caesarea of Palestine. After his departure, the school lacked forceful leadership. Interesting biblical criticism, however, was not lacking. Dionysius, bishop of Alexandria (d. 264), argued that the Greek of the Johannine corpus in the New Testament was so varied that no one author could have written the Gospel, the Epistles, and the Apocalypse.

Such literary criticism was common in Alexandrian intellectual life. A great library, started by Ptolemy Philadelphus, probably had burned during Caesar's attack on Antony in 48 B.C., but many books were still available in priestly libraries, particularly at the Sarapeum. The demands of the intellectual circles probably required the replacement of many volumes, a task made easier in Alexandria with its supply of papyrus. In Alexandria, philosophical figures held forth alongside historians and literary critics. Porphyry considered the Alexandrian Ammonius Saccas to be the best philosopher of the era (Eusebius, *H.E.* 6.19.6).

Doctrinal Controversies. One of the greatest crises within Christianity had its beginnings in Alexandria. Arius, a leading presbyter, attracted a large following. He could argue forcefully with the educated or write simple poetry for the masses. He returned to an older Christology that saw the Divine Son as a secondary figure, less than equal to the Father. Bishop Alexander found Arius's views heretical and excommunicated him. Arius had been educated in Antioch and had friends and supporters throughout the Mediterranean. At Nicaea in 325, Arius was condemned officially, but the next half-century saw considerable rancorous debate centered on both the issues and the personalities. Athanasius, eventually bishop of Alexandria and the noted defender of what came to be orthodoxy, fought Arianism most of his adult life. He was himself exiled a number of times. His ability to disappear into Egypt when sought by imperial authorities suggests that he had support in the Coptic-speaking Christian communities outside Alexandria.

Athanasius supported monasticism during his bishopric. He wrote a life of Anthony and was on good terms with the monks of the region, but monastic forces could be wielded for many purposes. Theophilus (bishop 385–412) used a monastic rabble to destroy the temple of Sarapis and its library in 391. His zeal in fighting false teaching involved him in hunting and destroying Origenist beliefs within monastic circles throughout Egypt.

His nephew Cyril (bishop 412–444) was a better man but also suffered from the climate of power. In 415, a mob attacked Hypatia, a gifted Neoplatonist philosopher, killed her, and dragged her body through the streets of the city. Her death went unpunished. Cyril turned his own attention to rooting out the unfaithful within. Like his uncle, who had worked for John Chrysostom's dismissal at Constantinople, Cyril set his hand against the Constantinopolitan bishop Nestorius. The main issues concerned political power and Christology. Nestorius developed an Antiochene position that emphasized the human and the divine in Christ at the expense of the unity of the one person. Cyril reacted strongly against Nestorius's teachings. His insistence on one divine nature involved a more simply understood view of

Christ's unified person. He reflected a deep Egyptian piety, based on the writings of Athanasius and Apollinarian treatises forged under Athanasius's name. He best represents the developed Alexandrian position, although occasionally his terminology is convoluted. At Ephesus in 431, Cyril achieved the condemnation of Nestorius but eventually created a peaceful understanding between himself and Antioch. The "one nature" emphasis, however, haunted Alexandrian circles. Dioscorus, Cyril's successor (444–451), took up Cyril's ambiguous terms and eventually was condemned and deposed at the Council of Chalcedon (451). He was an early representative of a Monophysite position (one nature) that almost denied a human nature in Christ. Timothy Aelurus (bishop 457–460 and again in 475–477) supported more moderate Monophysite views.

The sixth century saw orthodox and Monophysite struggles in the city and the development of various parties. Dioscorus II became bishop in 517 and continued the Monophysite views as the official Alexandrian position. He made alliances with Monophysites elsewhere in the east. Some in Alexandria wanted to avoid any sense of duality in Christ but insisted that the Son did assume a humanity like ours. Others, however, emphasized the "one nature" formula to the point that even Christ's human body was viewed as permanently incorruptible and immortal.

The emperor Justinian attempted to place a supporter of Chalcedon's Christology on the throne in Alexandria. Paul took charge of the official administration, but Monophysites only retreated to older churches or built new ones. Paul was deposed in 537. Although a Chalcedonian supporter became the official bishop in 570, the Monophysites were the clear majority.

Later Intellectual Life. These theological and political problems did not occupy all Christians of the era, however. John Philoponus, an Alexandrian Christian philosopher, argued against Proclus's and Plato's view of the eternity of the universe. His commentaries on Aristotelian treatises show an originality that may be his or reflect the views of his teacher, Ammonius. In any case, his cosmology is much more suited to twentieth-century physics than much ancient work. Elias and Stephen, other Christian philosophers, also wrote commentaries on various works of Aristotle.

Obviously, intellectual life in Alexandria was not limited to Christians. Ammonius, Philoponus's teacher, appears to have been a Platonist. Olympiodorus, a Neoplatonist, was able to continue his work without running into difficulty with Christianity. Both he and Ammonius produced commentaries on Aristotle and Plato. One of the interesting non-Christians of the sixth century was Eutocius of Ascalon, who at least visited Alexandria and perhaps taught there in the time of Philoponus. He studied mathematics and geometry and wrote commentaries on Apollonius and Archimedes. Alexandria fell to the Persians in 616 and the Muslims in 642. *See also* Egypt.   [F.W.N.]

Bibliography

H.I. Bell, "Alexandria," *Journal of Egyptian Archaeology* 13 (1927):171–189; E.R. Hardy, *Christian Egypt* (New York: Oxford UP, 1952); W. Bauer, *Orthodoxy and Heresy in Earliest Christianity*, 2nd rev. ed. G. Strecker (Philadelphia: Fortress, 1971), pp. 44–60; P.M. Fraser, *Ptolemaic Alexandria*, 3 vols. (Oxford: Clarendon, 1972); C.H. Roberts, *Manuscript, Society and Belief in Early Christian Egypt* (London: Oxford UP, 1979); N. Hinske, ed., *Alexandrien: Kulturbegegnungen dreier Jahrtausende im Schmelztiegel einer mediterranen Grosstadt* (Mainz am Rhein: Van Zabern, 1981); N.G. Wilson, *Scholars of Byzantium* (Baltimore: Johns Hopkins UP, 1983); B.A. Pearson and J. E. Goehring, eds., *The Roots of Egyptian Christianity* (Philadelphia: Fortress, 1986); R. Williams, *Arius: Heresy and Tradition* (London: Darton, Longman and Todd, 1987); *Alexandrina: Hellénisme, Judaisme, et Christianisme à Alexandrie. Mélanges . . . Mondésert* (Paris: Cerf, 1987).

ALLEGORY. Here figurative interpretation. "Allegory," from the Greek *alla*, "other," and *agoreuō*, "proclaim," referred originally to a figure of speech that Cicero defined as a "continuous stream of metaphors" (*Orator* 27.94). An early Christian example of allegory in that sense is the *Psychomachia* of Prudentius, an epic poem depicting the battle of personified virtues and vices in the soul. "Allegory" is here discussed in a derivative sense: interpretation of texts as if they were composed figuratively.

Hyponoia, "deeper meaning," was used by Plato and Xenophon to refer to the nonliteral interpretation. *Allēgoria*, a term coined by Hellenistic grammarians, gained currency in Christian circles through Paul's use of the verb *allēgoreō* (Gal. 4:24). Greek Christian writers also described allegory as *pneumatikē diēgēsis*, "spiritual interpretation"; *tropologia*, "figurative interpretation"; and *theōria*, "insight." In Latin, allegory is *allegoria* or *spiritalis interpretatio.*

Some scholars distinguish "allegory," defined as a method in which earthly realities are interpreted symbolically to refer to heavenly realities, from "typology," in which one historical reality is interpreted as foreshadowing another, especially the person and work of Christ. That modern distinction stems from Antiochene criticism of Alexandrian allegory, but it does not fully accommodate the wide variety of early Christian figurative interpretation.

Sources. Allegory originated in attempts by Greek thinkers to assimilate Homer and Hesiod to later scientific or religious outlooks. Thus, Theagenes of Rhegium (ca. 525 B.C.) defended Homer by interpreting the battles of the gods as a conflict between natural elements. Plato rejected morally offensive stories even if they should have a deeper meaning, but Stoicism perpetuated allegorical interpretation and passed it on to Hellenistic literary criticism. Stoic allegory survives in the work of Pseudo(?)-Heraclitus (first century A.D.), who claimed that everything in Homer is impious if nothing is allegorical (*Allegoriae Homericae* 1.1). Hellenistic authors also interpreted non-Greek myths allegorically; Plutarch (ca. A.D. 50–120) interpreted the Egyptian myth of Isis and Osiris so, and Numenius (second century A.D.) so interpreted the Old Testament.

Hellenistic Jewish authors, notably Philo, interpreted the Hebrew scriptures allegorically so as to find in them doctrines anticipating Greek philosophy. Such interpretation justified aspects of scripture that seemed barbarous in an alien cultural context. For example, in Philo's *On Mating with the Preliminary Stud-*

ies, Abraham's wife, Sarah, symbolizes philosophy; her handmaiden, Hagar, the general studies that prepare for philosophy; and Abraham, the soul that learns by instruction. Sarah gives Abraham Hagar because philosophy cannot bear fruit until the soul is prepared for it.

In Palestinian Jewish exegesis, allegory justified seeming anomalies in the Law and provided material for haggadah, the interpretation of the nonlegal passages of scripture. An example of the former is rabbi Jochanan ben Zakkai's (ca. A.D. 70) explanation that a robber receives a lighter punishment than a thief because the thief, acting secretly, has contempt for God's oversight. An example of the latter is the interpretation of unclean animals, such as the hare and the pig, to refer to Greece and Rome. Although Palestinian was generally more restrained than Hellenistic Jewish allegory and careful in particular to maintain legal validity, rabbi Akiba (ca. A.D. 50–132) could interpret the Song of Solomon allegorically to refer to the love between Israel and God.

The New Testament. The Gospels—unhistorically, in the view of most scholars—present Jesus using allegory as a rhetorical device in his own parables (cf. Matt. 13:18–35; Mark 4:12–20, 33–34; Luke 8:11–15) and interpreting allegorically the brazen serpent (Num. 21:9; John 3:14) and the two witnesses whose testimony is true (Deut. 19:15; John 8:17–18). Paul allegorized Abraham's wives, Hagar and Sarah, and the two mountains, Sinai and Zion, in Galatians 4. He also used allegory to apply cleaning out the old leaven at the Passover to maintaining the Christian community's purity (1 Cor. 5:6–8); to interpret the Deuteronomic command not to muzzle an ox treading grain in reference to the apostles' right to support (1 Cor. 9:8–14); and to make events in Exodus and Numbers prefigure Christian sacraments (1 Cor. 10:1–5). Hebrews 8–10 interprets the Levitical sanctuary and sacrificial system as a temporary earthly manifestation of a heavenly reality revealed in Christ.

The Second Century. Early Christian retention of the Old Testament as scripture made allegorical interpretation of the Old Testament attractive. The *Epistle of Barnabas* 9 contends that in the dietary laws Moses expounded moral principles in a spiritual manner, but the Jews, being carnal, misunderstood them to refer literally to foods. Moses forbade eating pork in order to discourage associating with swinish people, that is, people who remember the Lord only when they are in need, just as the pig pays no attention to its master while it is greedily feeding at the trough but squeals incessantly when it is hungry.

Marcion rejected allegory along with the Old Testament, but allegory played a role in much biblical interpretation in Gnosticism, which extended its use to the New Testament. Valentinus, for example, interpreted the woman in the parable of the leaven (Matt. 13:33–34; Luke 13:20–21) as the fallen aeon, Sophia; the three batches of meal as the three classes of human beings, material, psychic, and spiritual; and the leaven itself as the Savior (Irenaeus, *Haer.* 1.1.16). Valentinus's follower Heracleon interpreted the Gospel of John allegorically, presenting, for example, the "royal officer" of John 4:46–53 as the inferior Creator of the material world (Origen, *Jo.* 13.60.416).

Clement of Alexandria, who drew extensively on Philo, sought to obviate Gnostic interpretation of the Bible while providing a wide scope for allegory. Criticizing Gnostic allegory as arbitrary, he proposed that passages be interpreted (1) in a manner worthy of God, (2) consistently with the Bible as a whole, (3) in conformity to the church's traditional rule of faith (cf. *Str.* 7.16.96–104). He did not restrict allegory to the Old Testament, arguing, for example, that the wealth that Jesus advised the rich man who went away sorrowful to dispose of in order to be his disciple (Mark 10:17–22) was an overabundance of irrational emotions (*Q.d.s.*).

Origen. Origen provided a full theoretical justification for allegory in Book 4 of his treatise *On First Principles* and employed it continually in his extensive exegetical works. He presented the belief that the Bible is to be interpreted spiritually (i.e., allegorically), not simply literally, as a doctrine fundamental to the Christian faith (*Princ.*, prol. 8), providing a necessary defense against both Judaism and

Gnosticism. He complained that biblical literalists "believe such things about [God] as would not be believed of the most savage and unjust of men" (4.2.1) and drove intelligent Christians from the church. The Bible, Origen held, is so written that it meets the needs of Christians at every level of progress toward the knowledge of God. In this process, the letter (understood as the bare semantic information conveyed by the words on the page, not as the meaning intended by the author) is usually, although not always, as in the case of the Song of Solomon, edifying to simple believers. The biblical authors, he claimed, fully understood and intended to convey to spiritually advanced Christians worthy of them the mystical doctrines uncovered by the allegorical interpreter, inspired by God as they were. Such doctrines concern the soul and its relation to God, not historical events (*Jo.* 10.18.110).

For Origen, Greek philosophy was an essential preparation for the proper understanding of the Bible. He found in the Israelites' spoliation of the Egyptians at the time of the exodus an allegory of the Christian use of philosophy (*Ep.* 2). This image, mediated by Augustine (*Doctr. Christ.* 2.40.60), helped justify philosophical study in the Middle Ages. Origen also employed Hellenistic literary criticism to demonstrate the impossibility of the literal sense and hence the necessity of allegory. He held that the authors of scripture wove manifestly false information, including fictitious narrative, into their books in order to force the intelligent reader to seek a deeper meaning (*Princ.* 4.2.9). Origen's interpretation possessed a brilliance and consistency that gave it a compelling appeal but at the same time a boldness that made it increasingly controversial.

Eastern Patristic Tradition After Origen. Origen's allegorical interpretation was the basis of the Alexandrian school of biblical interpretation, which achieved its finest expression after him in Gregory of Nyssa and survives most extensively in the works of Cyril of Alexandria. By the fourth century, serious theological opposition to Origen had brought the word "allegory" into disrepute, and *theōria* replaced it. Basil the Great condemned allegorical interpretation of the creation narrative in Genesis,

contending that he interpreted "water" as water and "herb" as herb, not treating them as if they were dream fantasies (*Hex.* 9.1). Diodore of Tarsus and Theodore of Mopsuestia, interpreters of the Antiochene school, who were concerned to safeguard the historicity of the literal sense, articulated the case against Origen's allegory, which was, in their opinion, an arbitrary procedure that made the Bible incomprehensible and meaningless. Theodore's interpretation of Galatians 4:24 is a classic statement of their position (*Comm. Gal.*).

We find in the tradition exemplified by Ephraem the Syrian a use of allegory with affinities to Jewish and second-century Christian interpretation. Syriac authors made use of the concept of the *razā* (secret, mystery, or symbol), typified by Christological titles like "rock" or "vine," in the interpretation of scripture. Alexandrian allegory entered Syriac tradition in the writings of Philoxenus of Mabbug (d. 523) and others who knew Greek works in translation.

The West. Latin authors, beginning with Tertullian, used figurative interpretation when necessary in controversy but were suspicious of any speculative use of allegory. During the fourth century, however, Origen's works evoked considerable interest, and many are preserved in Latin translations. Augustine's ambivalent position best sums up the Latin tradition. He considered allegory essential to the defense of the Bible. He testifies that hearing Ambrose's allegorical interpretation of the Old Testament played a pivotal role in converting him from Manichaeism by demonstrating a deeper meaning beneath the crude and savage letter of the text (*Conf.* 5.14.24). He nevertheless became increasingly critical of allegory, insisting in his later works that a figurative interpretation did not preclude the literal, historical truth of the text. This is evident in his commentaries on the creation narrative in Genesis, which culminate in his significantly titled *Literal Commentary on Genesis.* Yet he did not give up allegory altogether, as demonstrated by his awkward insistence in that work that the "morning" and "evening" of Genesis 1 *literally* refer to the angels' awareness of creation (4.28.45).

Augustine's influential treatise *On Christian Teaching* provided a definitive defense of allegory while severely limiting its scope. On the one hand, he insisted that anything in the Bible performed by God or God's saints that seems shameful must be interpreted figuratively, the literal sense being removed as a husk from the edifying kernel (3.12.18). On the other hand, he warned against the abuse of allegory, claiming that heretics could always justify their errors by interpreting scriptural evidence against them figuratively (3.10.15). Augustine therefore denied the speculative use of allegory to search out mysteries nowhere apparent in the letter of scripture. He preferred to see allegory, in the Ciceronian sense, as entirely a matter of rhetoric, providing a pleasing intellectual stimulus. Thus, he wrote that the image of sheep in the Song of Solomon 4:2, which he interpreted to refer to the saints, made it possible for him to regard the saints more pleasantly, seeing them as the teeth of the church who cut men off from their errors and assimilate them into the body of the church after their hardness has been softened through chewing (2.6.7).

Conclusion. Gregory of Nyssa wrote that, much as wheat is turned into bread, allegory converts raw, unassimilable scripture into wholesome intellectual food (*Hom. in Cant.*, prol.). Allegorical interpretation was in no way hostile to a critical understanding of the letter and, indeed, encouraged it by freeing its conclusions from the need to harmonize with established doctrine or other scriptural passages. *See also* Interpretation of the Bible.   [J.W.T.]

Bibliography

W. den Boer, "Hermeneutic Problems in Early Christian Literature," *VChr* 1 (1947):150–167; R.M. Grant, *The Letter and the Spirit* (New York: Macmillan, 1957); R.P.C. Hanson, *Allegory and Event* (Richmond: John Knox, 1959); J. Daniélou, *From Shadows to Reality: Studies in the Biblical Typology of the Fathers* (Westminster: Newman, 1961); C.W. Macleod, "Allegory and Mysticism in Origen and Gregory of Nyssa," *JThS* n.s. 22 (1977):362–379; J. Pépin, *Mythe et allégorie: les origines grecques et les contestations judéo-chrétiennes*, 2nd ed. (Paris: Etudes Augustiniennes, 1979); S. Sandmel, *Philo of Alexandria: An Introduction* (New York and Oxford: Oxford UP, 1979); R. Heine, "Gregory of Nyssa's Apology for Allegory," *VChr* 38 (1984):360–370; K.

Froehlich, ed. and tr., *Biblical Interpretation in the Early Church* (Philadelphia: Fortress, 1984); S. Brock, *The Luminous Eye: The Spiritual World Vision of St. Ephrem* (Rome: CIIS, 1985); J.W. Trigg, ed. and tr., *Biblical Interpretation* (Wilmington: Glazier, 1987).

ALMSGIVING. Gifts of charity. Scriptural texts associating love for God with aid for the needy are common in both the Old Testament and the New (e.g., Isa. 58:6–12; Matt. 25:34–45; James 2:14–17), and examples of generosity are well attested in the primitive church (Acts 11:19–30; 2 Cor. 8:1–15). Following Jewish practice, the Christians tied almsgiving to prayer and fasting and viewed such activity both as a form of penance and as a means of gaining eternal reward. On the institutional level, the task of administering aid fell to deacons and widows and was under the direction of the local bishop. Prisoners, slaves, and travelers were common recipients of support. Except among the Gnostics, almsgiving was regarded as a serious obligation and a unifying force within Christian communities.

In post-Constantinian Christianity, the fortunes of aristocratic converts often provided support for the poor, but the needs were such that almsgiving became a common sermon topic, particularly in connection with ecclesiastical efforts to control material excesses among the rich. During this period, institutional resources (in the form of church wealth or public funds administered by ecclesiastics) played an increasing role, and church-sponsored activities, such as hospices and hospitals, grew continually in both the east and the west. Basil, John Chrysostom, and Ambrose were among the leaders in this development. From the fourth century onward, efforts to assist the poor were an organized part of monastic communities, and institutional services reached a peak in the early church under Gregory the Great. *See also* Offerings.   [L.J.S.]

Bibliography

G.L. Budde, "Christian Charity, Now and Always: The Fathers of the Church and Almsgiving," *American Ecclesiastical Review* 85 (1931):561–579; A. Hamman and F. Quéré-Jaulmes, *Riches et pauvres dans l'église ancienne* (Paris: Grasset, 1962); M. Hengel, *Property and Riches in the Early Church*

(Philadelphia: Fortress, 1974); R.M. Grant, *Early Christianity and Society: Seven Studies* (New York: Harper and Row, 1977), pp. 124–145; L. Countryman, *The Rich Christian in the Church of the Early Empire: Contradictions and Accommodations* (New York: Mellen, 1980); B. Ramsey, "Almsgiving in the Latin Church: The Late Fourth and Early Fifth Centuries," *ThS* 43 (1982):226–259; C. Osiek, *Rich and Poor in the Shepherd of Hermas* (Washington, D.C.: Catholic Biblical Association, 1983); E. Ferguson, *Early Christians Speak* (Abilene: ACU, 1987), pp. 207–218.

ALOGOI. Second-century Christian group in Asia Minor. The Alogoi apparently refused to acknowledge the divinity of Christ, the Word, perhaps in an attempt to protect the oneness of God. The name was given by their opponents to signify their opposition to the Word (*Logos*), but with the additional meaning of "those without reason." Little is known of the Alogoi, but their doctrines have interesting relations with early Christian literature. They did not find either the Gospel of John or the Book of Revelation to be authentic. John's Gospel contradicted the other Gospels particularly in chronology. It had no flight to Egypt and too many Passovers, and its numbers were incorrect. The Revelation was a vulgar treatise, fanciful and odd. One of their suggestions was that the Gnostic Cerinthus wrote both books. They opposed Montanist interest in those volumes. Epiphanius's account (*Haer.* 51), the main source of information, also indicates that they denied the divinity of the Spirit.

Irenaeus (*Haer.* 4.11.9) talks about those who rejected John, but he does not specify who they were. Hippolytus wrote against a Caius who rejected Revelation and attributed it to Cerinthus (Eusebius, *H.E.* 3.28), but we do not know if Caius refused the Gospel or if he was part of the Alogoi.

The relationship of the Alogoi to other groups is unclear. It is also uncertain whether their biblical criticism, their opposition to Montanists, or their rejection of the Son's and the Spirit's divinity is to be seen as fundamental to their beliefs. [F.W.N.]

Bibliography

A. Bludau, *Die ersten Gegner der Johannes-Schriften* (Freiburg: Herder, 1925).

ALTANER, BERTHOLD (1885–1964). Patristic scholar. After ordination as a priest (1910) and completion of advanced studies, Altaner taught patrology, church history, and Christian archaeology at the University of Breslau (1919–1933) but was deprived of his appointment by the Nazis. He then held a post at Breslau cathedral that enabled him to further his research until he was expelled by the Gestapo (1945). After the Second World War, he taught at Würzburg until his retirement (1950); he continued his scholarly activities thereafter. His earlier writings were on the history of the Dominican order, but he is best known for his *Patrologie: Leben, Schriften und Lehre der Kirchenväter* (Freiburg: Herder, 1938), which has passed through numerous editions and revisions. An English translation of the fifth German edition (1958) is available (Freiburg: Herder, 1960; tr. Hilda C. Graef); the most recent edition is the seventh, in German (rev. Alfred Stuiber, 1966, with a supplement, 1977). [M.P.McH.]

Bibliography

B. Altaner, *Verzeichnis meiner Veröffentlichungen 1907–1953* (Würzburg: Echter Verlag, 1953); "Bibliographie Berthold Altaner," *Historisches Jahrbuch* 77 (1958):576–600; J. Quasten, *CHR* 50 (1964):92–93.

ALTAR. Place where the eucharist is celebrated in a Christian church. In Judaism, the altar (Hebrew *mizbe'ah*) was the place where sacrificial slaughter and oblations of all kinds, including grain, wine, and incense, were offered. The temple had one central altar and an incense altar. Christianity replaced the Jewish altar with the eucharistic table. Of the two Greek words for altar, the church fathers preferred *thysiastērion* (Latin *altare*) to *bōmos* (Latin *ara*), which refers to pagan altars and sacrifices.

Since the eucharist is both a "bloodless sacrifice" in which Christ "the lamb of God is broken and distributed, broken but not divided, eaten yet never consumed" (liturgy of Saint John Chrysostom), as well as the reenactment of the Last Supper, the place of celebration is called both "altar," especially in the western

Altar over a box for relics in front of the bishop's chair and seats for the presbyters in the reconstructed early Christian church in the Byzantine Museum, Athens, Greece.

church (Tertullian, Cyprian, Ambrose, Augustine), and "table of the Lord" (1 Cor. 10:21) or holy table, especially in the eastern church. Ignatius (*Philad.* 4) refers to the eucharistic altar. Subsequent writers also speak of the table in the sense of altar (e.g., Eusebius, *H.E.* 7.9.4–5). Thus, "altar" and "table" have been used interchangeably.

An altar is made of wood or a slab of stone, for the eucharist was celebrated in early Christian antiquity either on a regular table (Latin *mensa*) in home churches, or on the tomb of a martyr, especially during the persecutions. Celebrating the eucharist on tombs of martyrs was an affirmation of faith in the communion of all saints, living and dead, as well as in the resurrection, because of the death and resurrection of Christ, "the first-born from the dead" (Col. 1:18); then arose the practice of a bishop consecrating a church by placing relics of saints or

martyrs in a crypt or in the four corners of the altar. In the eastern church, when the eucharist is celebrated on an unconsecrated altar, a piece of cloth with relics of martyrs sewn in its corners is placed on the altar for the celebration. This is called an "antimensis" (Greek *antimension*), "in the place of the table."

Around the altar and facing the congregation, there was the *synthronon*, a row of seats for the celebrant priests with the throne of the bishop, the chief celebrant, in the middle exactly behind the altar. Eventually, the western church moved the altar to the wall of the church building. The Second Vatican Council encouraged the removal of the altar from the outer wall toward the middle, so that the priest celebrates the eucharist facing the congregation.

The altar itself, standing on one or four legs, was surrounded in the eastern church by a canopy (*ciborium*), after the example of the imperial throne, so that it could be closed off with curtains at certain moments of the liturgy. The ciborium was later replaced by an *iconostasis*, or icon screen with doors, that divides the area of the altar from the nave. The ciborium itself became obsolete, and the whole area where the altar is located became known as the altar or holy place (*hieron*). The throne of the bishop was also moved into the nave at the head of the congregation; the ciborium became a smaller but elaborate container placed on the altar and containing the elements reserved from the liturgy on Good Thursday to be used for communion at times of urgent need. In the eastern church, only one eucharistic celebration may take place on a single altar on a given day. The need to celebrate several eucharistic services in the same church led to the establishment of two more altars in some churches, one on each niche on the right and left of the main altar in the *hieron*. In the western church, the desire of Christians to have private or family celebrations of the eucharist led to the designation and development of several chapels within the same church building, each one of them with its own altar.   [D.J.S.]

Bibliography
J. Mede, *The Name Altar, or Thysiasterion, Anciently Given to the Holy Table: A Common-place,*

or *Theologicall Discourse* (London: M. Felesher for J. Clark, 1637); H. Leclercq, "Autel," DACL (1924), Vol. 2, pp. 3155–3189; J.P. Kirsch and T. Klauser, "Altar," RLAC (1950), Vol. 1, pp. 334–354.

AMBO. Latin term for pulpit, derived from the Greek *ambon* ("crest of a hill"). The predecessor of the ambo was the *migdal* (Hebrew, "tower") of the synagogue. Surviving examples from early Christian church buildings are of marble but wood was also used. Most were elevated and reached by steps (sometimes two sets). They could be round, square, or polygonal in shape. Some had roofs or sounding boards above them. Their primary use was for the reading of the lessons out of the Bible, less commonly for sermons; John Chrysostom is a notable documented exception for preaching from the ambo. Some churches had two ambos, possibly for the reading of the Gospel and for the Epistle. In the Byzantine liturgy, the Gospel Book was carried from the altar to the ambo and back again. From the time of the Byzantine emperor Maurice at the end of the sixth century, the emperors were crowned in the ambo of the Church of Hagia Sophia in Constantinople.

The ambo was located in the nave of the typical early Christian basilica, sometimes in the center along the east-west axis of the building and sometimes slightly on one side, to the south or north. Often it was connected to the chancel (Latin *bema*) by a raised walkway (Latin *solea*). The chancel itself often projected into the nave from the apse. In taking communion, the Byzantine emperor came to the ambo and used the solea to go to the Holy Doors, where he entered the sanctuary. Not until the sixth century did the ambo become a standard part of church furnishings in Rome.

[G.T.A.]

Bibliography

A.M. Schneider, "Ambon," RLAC (1950), Vol. 1, cols. 363–365; T.F. Mathews, "An Early Roman

Reconstructed early Christian ambo from the Byzantine Museum, Athens, Greece.

Chancel Arrangement and Its Liturgical Functions," *RAC* 38 (1962):73–95; C. Delvoye, "Ambo," *Reallexikon zur byzantinischen Kunst*, ed. K. Wessel (Stuttgart: Hiersemann, 1966), Vol. 1, cols. 126–133; T.F. Mathews, *The Early Churches of Constantinople* (University Park: Pennsylvania State UP, 1971), esp. pp. 123, 124, 148–151, 172, 179; R. Krautheimer, *Early Christian and Byzantine Architecture*, 3rd ed. (Harmondsworth: Penguin, 1979), esp. pp. 107, 178.

AMBROSE (ca. 339–397). Bishop of Milan (374–397). One of the four doctors (with Augustine, Jerome, and Gregory the Great) of the western church, Ambrose came from a distinguished Christian background and was the son of the praetorian prefect of Gaul. After being educated at Rome, he began the practice of law ca. 365 at Sirmium and ca. 370 was appointed *consularis* (governor) of Aemilia and Liguria in northern Italy with headquarters in Milan. Four years later, when a riot threatened to break out among Catholics and Arians who were at odds over a successor to the deceased bishop Auxentius, Ambrose intervened to restore order and quickly found himself the unanimous choice for the episcopal see. Although only a catechumen at the time, he was baptized in short order and was consecrated bishop of Milan in early December 374.

In preparation for his episcopal duties, Ambrose threw himself into the study of theology and scripture under the direction of his former tutor, the learned and elderly Simplicianus, who later succeeded him in the bishopric of Milan. The new bishop's talent and inclinations were not in the field of speculative thought, but he quickly achieved a reputation as a pastor of souls, a firm defender of the orthodoxy of Nicaea and an effective preacher. His rhetorical style, characterized by long periodic sentences interspersed with direct and pithy statements, was rich in imagery derived from nature, scripture, and classical sources, such as Virgil and Cicero.

Writings. Ambrose's literary works, many of which were exegetical sermons hastily reworked for publication, reveal a heavy dependence on the Old Testament. Influenced by Philo and Origen, he accepted a threefold interpretation of the scriptural text (i.e., literal, moral, and allegorical/mystical), and he was fond of typology. It was the bishop's nonliteral approach that Augustine found so congenial to his own spiritual needs (*Conf.* 6.3–4), and in 387 he became Ambrose's most illustrious convert to Catholicism.

In contrast to many contemporary Christian bishops in the west, Ambrose knew Greek well, and his familiarity with such writers as Origen, Athanasius, Didymus the Blind, Cyril of Jerusalem, Basil, and Hippolytus, as well as the philosopher Plotinus, made him an important link between eastern Christianity and the western church. Although his theology was largely derivative, he expended considerable energy refuting Arian views on the Trinity and the incarnation (cf. *Fid.*; *Sp. Sanc.*; *Incarn. dom. sacram.*), and he is an important source of information on the ritual, symbols, and theology of the sacraments (cf. *Mys.*; *Sacram.*) in the fourth century.

The most notable of Ambrose's moral and ascetical writings is *On the Duties of the Clergy*, a compendium of Christian ethical teachings addressed to his own clergy but intended, probably, for the larger Christian community as well. The work is loosely modeled on Cicero's *On Duties*, but it draws a great deal from scripture and has a strong eschatological dimension. Ambrose frequently preached and wrote against the moral shortcomings of his time, particularly greed and luxury among the upper classes (cf. *Nabuth. hist.*; *Tobia*), and he was a zealous proponent of consecrated virginity (cf. *Virgin.*; *Virginit.*; *Instit. virg.*). In this context, he used Mary, the Blessed Virgin, as the model and patron of virgins and thereby became one of the earliest supporters of Marian devotion in the western church. The cult of the martyrs was also given prominence during his bishopric through the discovery in 386 of what were believed to be the remains of two Christian martyrs, Gervasius and Protasius, whose relics were deposited in the newly constructed Basilica Ambrosiana in Milan.

One of the pastoral achievements for which Ambrose is most famous is his work on Christian hymns. Although Hilary of Poitiers is credited with being the first to introduce liturgical hymns into the west, Ambrose's development of the genre into a simple, highly poetic, and very popular form justifies his title as "The Father of Liturgical Hymnody" in the western church. Countless hymns are attributed to him, but only the four attested by Augustine—*Aeterne rerum conditor, Deus creator omnium, Iam surgit hora tertia, Intende qui regis Israel*—are universally accepted by modern scholars.

The funeral orations that Ambrose delivered for his brother Satryus, for the emperor Valentinian II, and for Theodosius I, as well as the ninety-one extant letters, are valuable sources of information about the bishop's pastoral activities within the church and his prominent role in the political and religious affairs of the empire during the late fourth century.

Ecclesiastical Achievements. As a churchman, Ambrose was much committed to maintaining the ascendancy of Catholic orthodoxy in the face of both pagan and Arian opponents. With respect to the former, his most famous dispute had to do with the removal of the Altar of Victory from the Roman senate house in 382. The edict of Gratian (367–383) enjoining this action prompted a pagan embassy, led by Q. Aurelius Symmachus, to protest the emperor's decision, but at Ambrose's insistence the emperor refused the delegation an audience when it arrived at Milan. Two years later, Symmachus, who was now the Prefect of Rome, repeated his appeal in a famous *Relatio* addressed to Valentinian II (375–392). Ambrose again vehemently opposed any concession to pagan religion (*Ep.* 17; 18) and threatened to withdraw his support from Valentinian if the young emperor honored Symmachus's request. The appeal was denied, but for the next two years Ambrose's growing influence on Valentinian sparked a contest of wills between the bishop and the emperor's mother, Justina, who was a strong supporter of Arianism. Events centered on Arian rights to a basilica in Milan, and things came to a head in 386, when Ambrose literally stood his ground in the cathedral at Milan and forced the cancellation of an edict against the Catholics. It was on this occasion that he voiced the well-known words, "The emperor indeed is within the church, not above the church" (*Aux.* 36).

Ambrose exercised a similar orthodox influence over Valentinian's successor, Theodosius I (379–395). Their generally amicable relationship was severely strained on two occasions. In 388, when rioting Christians burned the synagogue at Callinicum, Theodosius ordered the local bishop to bear the cost of restoring the building, but Ambrose opposed this decision on grounds that such an action was tantamount to promoting the Jewish faith. Theodosius gave way to episcopal pressure, in which the bishop's zeal for orthodoxy obliterated his sense of justice. Two years later, in another riot, the people of Thessalonica murdered several imperial officials, and Theodosius exacted punishment by ordering the massacre of 7,000 citizens. When he learned of this action, Ambrose excommunicated the emperor and forced him to do public penance before readmitting him to communion with the church. The confrontation seems only to have sharpened Theodosius's concern for orthodoxy; not long afterward, he issued a decree outlawing the private and public practice of paganism throughout the realm.

Ambrose's championing of the church's interests as he saw them and his insistence that the emperors were subject to the moral law as interpreted and practiced by the church had a profound impact on the relations between church and state during the Middle Ages and in subsequent centuries. Feast day December 7. CPL 123–183. [L.J.S.]

Bibliography

Paulinus, *Life of Ambrose*, tr. J.A. Lacy, FOTC (1952), Vol. 15, pp. 27–66.

C. Schenkl et al., CSEL (1897–), Vols. 32, 62, 64, 73, 78, 79, 82; *De virginibus* and *De virginitate*, ed. E. Cazzaniga, *Corpus Scriptorum Latinorum Paravianum* (1948 and 1952); *Explanatio symboli ad initiandos*, ed. R.H. Connolly, TS 10(1952):1–39; *Expositio Evangelii secundum Lucam*, ed. G. Tissot, SC (1956–1958), Vols. 45 and 52; idem (with *Fragmenta in Esaiam*), ed. M. Adriaen, CCSL (1957), Vol. 14; *De sacramentis, De mysteriis, Explanatio symboli*, ed. B. Botte, SC (1961), Vol. 25 bis; *De Paenitentia*, ed. R. Gryson, SC (1971), Vol. 179; *De Nabuthae historia*, ed. M.G. Mara (L'Aquila: Japadre, 1975); *Apologia David*, ed. P. Hadot and M. Cordier, SC (1977), Vol. 239; *De officiis*, Book 1, ed. M. Testard (Paris: Les Belles Lettres, 1984).

H. de Romestin et al., tr., NPNF, 2nd ser. (1896), Vol. 10; M.M. Beyenka, J.J. Savage, R.J. Deferrari, M.P. McHugh, trs., FOTC (1947–), Vols. 22, 26, 42, 44, 65.

H. von Campenhausen, *Ambrosius von Mailand als Kirchenpolitiker* (Berlin: de Gruyter, 1929); J.R. Palanque, *Saint Ambrose et l'empire romain* (Paris: Boccard, 1933); F.H. Dudden, *The Life and Times of St. Ambrose*, 2 vols. (Oxford: Clarendon, 1935); *Sant' Ambrogio nel XVI centenario della nascita* (Milan: Vita e Pensiero, 1940); *Ambrosiana: Scritti di storia, archeologica et arte publicati nel XVI centenario della nascita di Sant' Ambrogio, CCCXL–MCMXL* (Milan: Biblioteca Ambrosiana, 1942); A. Paredi, *St. Ambrose*, tr. M.J. Costelloe (Notre Dame: U of Notre Dame P, 1964); E. Dassman, *Die Frömmigkeit des Kirchenvaters Ambrosius von Mailand* (Münster: Aschendorff, 1965); V. Hahn, *Das Wahre Gesetz: Eine Untersuchung der Auffassung des Ambrosius von Mailand vom Verhältnis der beiden Testamente* (Münster: Aschendorff, 1969); P. Courcelle, *Recherches sur saint Ambroise: "vies" anciennes, culture, iconographie* (Paris: Etudes Augustiniennes, 1973); *Ambroise de Milan, XVI Centenaire de son élection épiscopale* (Paris: Etudes Augustiniennes, 1974); G. Madec, *Saint Ambroise et la philosophie* (Paris: Etudes Augustiniennes, 1974); G. Lazzati, ed., *Ambrosius Episcopus: Atti del Congresso internazionale di studi ambrosiani nel XVI centenario della elevazione di sant' Ambrogio alla cattedra episcopale*, 2 vols. (Milan: Vita e Pensiero, 1976); H.J. auf der Maur, *Das Psalmenverständnis des Ambrosius von Mailand* (Leiden: Brill, 1977); H. Savon, *Saint Ambroise devant l'exégèse de Philon le Juif*, 2 vols. (Paris: Etudes Augustiniennes, 1977); L.F. Pizzolato, *La dottrina esegetica di sant' Ambrogio* (Milan: Vita e Pensiero, 1978); P.F. Beatrice et al., eds. *Cento anni bibliografia ambrosiana (1874–1974)* (Milan: Vita e Pensiero, 1981).

AMBROSIASTER (late fourth century). Name given by Erasmus to the anonymous author of a commentary—attributed to Ambrose throughout the Middle Ages—on the thirteen epistles of Paul. The commentary on Romans is extant in three versions, that on the two Corinthian letters in two, and each of the others in one; the commentary on Hebrews is of a later origin. Augustine (*C. Pelag.*4.4.7) assigned the work to a certain Hilary, but numerous attempts at identification of the author have failed to gain general acceptance.

The commentary was probably composed in Rome during the pontificate of Damasus I (366–384). The writer was well-read and knowledgeable about Jewish practices, perhaps a convert from Judaism or paganism. The exegesis is literal and historical; allegory is avoided. The work is polemical, in opposition to Arianism as well as to the teachings of Novatian and Photinus. With its abundant scriptural citations, it is a valuable witness to the Old Latin versions.

The British patristic scholar Alexander Souter established (1905) that the *Quaestiones Veteris et Novi Testamenti*, a collection of 150 questions in one version, or 127 in another (and 115 in a medieval version dating from between the eighth and twelfth centuries), long attributed to Augustine, is a work of Ambrosiaster. Like the commentary, it was probably written in Rome in the time of Damasus I. Most of the items in it are exegetical; some are of dogmatic or apologetic or historical interest. Fragments of other works and minor writings may also be assigned to the same author. CPL 184–188; see also 168, 189.

[M.P.McH.]

Bibliography
Quaestiones Veteris et Novi Testamenti, ed. A. Souter, CSEL (1908), Vol. 50; *Commentaria in XIII Epistulas Paulinas*, ed. H.J. Vogels, 3 vols., CSEL (1966–1969), Vol. 81.

A. Souter, *A Study of Ambrosiaster* (Cambridge: Cambridge UP, 1905); idem, *The Earliest Latin Commentaries on the Epistles of Saint Paul* (Oxford: Clarendon, 1927); H.J. Vogels, *Das Corpus Paulinum des Ambrosiaster* (Bonn: Hanstein, 1957); L.J. Speller, "New Light on the Photinians: The Evidence of Ambrosiaster," *JThS* n.s. 34 (1983):99–113.

AMEN. "'Amen' in Hebrew means 'may it be so'" (Justin, *1 Apol.* 65.4). The Hebrew root *amen* refers to what is dependable and so what is certain or true. "Amen" occurs in the Old Testament as a response to confirm an adjuration or curse (Num. 5:22; Deut. 27:15–26), to express agreement (1 Kings 1:36; Jer. 28:6), and to ratify doxologies (Neh. 8:6; 1 Chron. 16:36; Ps. 41:13). Greek versions either transliterated the word or translated it as "so be it" or "assuredly" (Eusebius, *Ps.* 71.18ff.). Saying

"Amen" made words one's own, and as a ratification "Amen" passed into the liturgy of the synagogue and the church.

Jesus emphasized the reliability and certainty of his words by prefacing them with "Amen" ("truly"; Matt. 5:18; Mark 8:12; John 1:51). He was himself called the "Amen" as the guarantee of God's promises (2 Cor. 1:20; Rev. 3:14). As Jews said "Amen" to any doxology, so words of praise in the New Testament are followed by "Amen" (Rom. 11:36; Gal. 1:5; Phil. 4:20). As a word of confirmation (Rev. 22:20), "Amen" occurs as the people's response to prayer, benediction, and doxology (1 Cor. 14:16; Gal. 6:18; Rev. 5:13; 7:12).

The biblical usage of "Amen" continued in the early church. Besides its occurrences in borrowed phrases and in exegetical passages, "Amen" is found predominantly in prayer. It was sung out as a unison congregational response to prayer (Tertullian, *Spec.* 25; Cyril of Jerusalem, *Catech.* 23.18; Theodoret, *Ps.* 105.48; Jerome, *Comm. Gal.* 1.2). It was also spoken by the believer at the reception of the eucharist (Hippolytus, *Trad. ap.* 23.6; *Const. app.* 8.13.15), and it occurs in hymns (*A. Jo.* 94) and at martyrdom (*Mart. Scill.* 17). *See also* Doxology; Prayer. [E.F.]

Bibliography
A. Stuiber, "Amen," *JAC* 1 (1958):153–159.

AMMIANUS MARCELLINUS (ca. 330–ca. 400). Roman historian. A Greek, born in Antioch, Ammianus served in the Roman army on the eastern frontier, in Gaul, and on Julian's ill-fated campaign in Persia (363). Having settled in Rome (after 378), he composed his *History* in Latin in thirty-one books as a continuation of the works of Tacitus. The period covered extended from the accession of Nerva (96) to the death of Valens (378). The first thirteen books are lost; the remaining eighteen span the years 353–378 and treat the reigns of Constantius II (in part), Julian, Jovian, Valentinian I, Valens, and Gratian (in part). The *History* is, on the whole, accurate, knowledgeable, and balanced. Little known in antiquity, it has been praised by Edward Gibbon among others in modern times.

Ammianus, himself a pagan, often mentions Christianity, which he terms a "plain and simple religion" (21.16.118). He reports Constantius's deposition of the Roman bishop Liberius for refusing to assent to the removal of Athanasius from the see of Alexandria (15.7.6–10); his is the earliest mention anywhere of the feast of the Epiphany in the west (21.2.5); he records the murderous riots that broke out between the followers of Damasus I and Ursinus over possession of the Roman see (27.3.12–15). Although twice protesting Julian's closing of the schools to Christian teachers (22.10.7; 25.4.20), he commends the same emperor for administering justice without religious bias (22.10.2). Likewise, he strongly approves of the tolerant religious policy of the Christian emperor Valentinian I (30.9.5). He is respectful of the martyrs (22.11.10) and praises the austere life of provincial bishops (27.3.15). His criticisms—directed against the savage hatred exhibited by Christians toward one another (22.5.4), for example, or against one particularly venomous bishop (22.11.3–8)—show no antipathy to Christian belief as such.

Ammianus's attitude toward Christianity has been a topic of scholarly discussion. It appears that he took it as a given in his society and was not unsympathetic to it. His view of religious matters reflects a certain detachment, although he does show disapproval of excessive imperial interference therein. [M.P.McH.]

Bibliography
Ammianus Marcellinus, tr. J.C. Rolfe, 3 vols., LCL (1935–1939); E.A. Thompson, *The Historical Work of Ammianus Marcellinus* (Cambridge: Cambridge UP, 1947).

R. Syme, *Ammianus Marcellinus and the Historia Augusta* (Oxford: Clarendon, 1968); R.C. Blockley, *Ammianus Marcellinus: A Study of His Historiography and Political Thought* (Brussels: Latomus, 1975); K. Rosen, *Ammianus Marcellinus* (Darmstadt: Wissenschaftliche Buchgesellschaft, 1982); B. Croke and A.M. Emmett, eds., *History and Historians in Late Antiquity* (Sydney: Pergamon, 1983), passim; V. Neri, *Ammiano e il cristianesimo: religione e politica nelle "Res gestae" di Ammiano Marcellino* (Bologna: CLUEB, 1985); E.D. Hunt, "Christians and Christianity in Ammianus Marcellinus," *CQ* 35 (1985):186–200; R.L. Rike, *Apex Omnium: Religion in the Res Gestae of Ammianus* (Berkeley: U of California P, 1987).

AMMONAS (fourth century). Desert father of Egypt. A disciple of Anthony, and his successor as head of the colony of hermits at Pispir (356), Ammonas was consecrated bishop by Athanasius. His letters—seven extant in a Greek version, fourteen in Syriac—are important evidence of early Christian mysticism. CPG II, 2380–2393. [M.P.McH.]

Bibliography

D.J. Chitty, *The Letters of Ammonas, Successor of St. Anthony* (Oxford: SLG, 1979).

AMMONIUS (fifth century). Monk of Nitria, one of the Tall Brothers. A learned man accused of Origenism by Theophilus of Alexandria and defended by John Chrysostom, Ammonius eventually submitted to Theophilus. *See also* Tall Brothers. [F.W.N.]

Bibliography

Sozomen, *Church History* 8.12–13, 15, 17; Palladius, *Lausiac History* 12.

AMMONIUS OF ALEXANDRIA (fifth or sixth century). Presbyter who wrote commentaries on Psalms, Daniel, John, Luke, Acts, 1 Corinthians, and 1 Peter, now extant only in fragments. The scholia on Matthew are not genuine. CPG III, 5500–5509. [F.W.N.]

Bibliography

PG 85.1361–1610; 1823–1826.

AMMONIUS SACCAS (ca. 175–244). Alexandrian philosopher. Ammonius Saccas was the primary teacher of Plotinus from 233 to 244. Although the "founder" of Neoplatonism, he wrote nothing and is known through Porphyry's *Life of Plotinus* 3 and 20 and Eusebius of Caesarea (*H.E.* 6.19.6–14). He may have been a Christian who converted to paganism and may have had Origen as one of his students.

[D.M.S.]

Bibliography

A.H. Armstrong, ed., *The Cambridge History of Later Greek and Early Medieval Philosophy* (Cambridge: Cambridge UP, 1967), pp. 196–200.

AMPHILOCHIUS (ca. 340–after 394). Bishop of Iconium in Asia Minor. Amphilochius studied rhetoric at Antioch and practiced law (364–370) in Constantinople. Several years after his retirement from public life, he became bishop of Iconium (373) at the instigation of Basil of Caesarea. Most of his writings are lost. Among his extant works are a synodal letter in defense of the divinity of the Holy Spirit issued after a council at Iconium (376); a treatise against the Messalians; homilies on liturgical feasts; the *Iambi ad Seleucum*; and numerous fragments. The iambic verses to Seleucus, preserved among the works of Amphilochius's cousin Gregory of Nazianzus, have some importance in the history of the canon of scripture, since they contain a list (verses 251–319) of the books known to Amphilochius to be genuine. He was held in esteem as a source of patristic teaching in the fifth century. Feast day November 23. CPG II, 3230–3254. TLG 2112. [M.P.McH.]

Bibliography

Amphilochii Iconiensis Iambi ad Seleucum, ed. E. Oberg (Berlin: de Gruyter, 1969); *Amphilochii Iconiensis opera: Orationes, pluraque alia quae supersunt, nonulla etiam spuria*, ed. C. Datema, CCSG (1978), Vol. 3; T.P. Halton and R.D. Sider, "A Decade of Patristic Scholarship 1970–1979," *CW* 76 (1982–1983):331–332 (bibliography).

ANACLETUS. Bishop of Rome (79–91?). According to the traditional order, Anacletus succeeded Linus and preceded Clement. An alternative report placed him after Clement and distinguished between a Cletus and an Anacletus. He is otherwise unknown. [E.F.]

Bibliography

Irenaeus, *Against Heresies* 3.3.3; Eusebius, *Church History* 3.13, 21; 5.6; *Liber Pontificalis* 3; 5 (Duchesne 1.125).

ANAPHORA. Prayer of consecration of the eucharist. "Anaphora" is the transliteration of a Greek term that has two general meanings and a variety of applications: (1) "lifting up," "carrying up," or "offering up," and (2) "relating to" or "referring to." Its specifically Christian usage is connected with the first meaning and refers to the sacrifice of Christ and its liturgical celebration in the liturgy of the eucharist. The biblical roots of this usage are to be traced to the Epistle to the Hebrews, where the cognate verb *anapherō* is used in a sacrificial sense to denote the unique sacrifice of Christ as the fulfillment and abolition of the Old Testament Levitical offerings (Heb. 7:27; 9:28; 13:15). It appears also in other New Testament writings (1 Peter 2:5, 24; James 2:21), but its older context is that of the Old Testament, especially the Septuagint, where this verb occurs in numerous places (Gen. 8:20; 22:2; 31:39; Exod. 18:19; 24:5; 29:18, 25; 30:9, 20). The term *anaphora*, meaning sacrifice, occurs in Psalm 51:19 (Greek 50:21).

In the liturgical context, "Anaphora" denotes the second part, the climax, of the eastern eucharistic liturgies—the first part being that of "Pro-Anaphora," or "Liturgy of the Catechumens." The Anaphora is known in the western eucharistic liturgies as the "Canon of the Mass" or "prayer of consecration." Since there are many eucharistic liturgies, there are also many Anaphoras. Broadly speaking, liturgists distinguish between eastern and western families, or types, of Anaphoras, subdividing them into Alexandrian (the Anaphora of St. Mark), East Syrian (the Anaphora of Addai and Mari, and of Theodore of Mopsuestia), West Syrian or Antiochene (the Anaphora of St. James), Byzantine (the Anaphoras of St. Basil and St. John Chrysostom), Roman, Gallican, Mozarabic, and others. The oldest surviving Anaphora is that in the *Apostolic Tradition* of Hippolytus (ca. 215); another ancient Anaphora is contained in the *Apostolic Constitutions* (8.12.4–51).

Several theories have been advocated by modern scholars about the interrelation of the various Anaphoras. The older view, which saw a basic common structure at the root of all the Anaphoras and relegated variations to secondary elements, is being convincingly reinstated today. This basic structure includes the following elements: (1) the introductory dialogue, (2) the eucharistic prayer, which is split into two parts by (3) the *Sanctus*, (4) the account of

the institution at the Last Supper, (5) the *anamnesis*, (6) the *epiclesis*, (7) the *diptychs*, and (8) the doxology. *See also* Epiclesis; Eucharist; Liturgy. [G.D.D.]

Bibliography

J. Quasten, *Florilegium Patristicum* 7, *Monumenta eucharistica et liturgica vetustissima* 1–7 (Bonn: Hanstein, 1935–1937); A. Hänggi and I. Pahl, *Prex eucharistica: Textus e variis liturgiis antiquioribus selecti* (Fribourg: Editions Universitaires, 1968).

W.H. Frere, *The Anaphora, or Great Eucharistic Prayer* (London: SPCK, 1938); G. Dix, *The Shape of the Liturgy* (London: Dacre, 1945); L. Bouyer, *Eucharist: Theology and Spirituality of the Eucharistic Prayer* (Notre Dame: U of Notre Dame P, 1968); W.J. Grisbrooke, "Anaphora," *A Dictionary of Liturgy and Worship*, ed. J.G. Davies (London: SCM, 1972); C. Jones, G. Wainwright, and E. Yarnold, eds., *The Study of the Liturgy* (London: SPCK, 1978), Ch. 3.

ANASTASIUS I. Bishop of Rome (399–401). Praised for his generosity and zeal by Jerome and Paulinus of Nola, Anastasius condemned the teachings of Origen at the instigation of Jerome's friends in Rome but received the defense of Rufinus of Aquileia against complicity in the heresy. Three of his letters on the Origenistic controversy are extant; he wrote as well to the Council of Carthage (401) against Donatism. CPL 1638–1640. [M.P.McH.]

Bibliography

Jerome, *Letters* 95 (by Anastasius); 127.10; 130.16; Paulinus of Nola, *Letter* 20.2; *Liber Pontificalis* 41 (Duchesne 1.218–219).

ANASTASIUS II. Bishop of Rome (496–498). Anastasius attempted to heal the schism that had begun with the excommunication of Acacius of Constantinople by Felix II (III) in the dispute over the *Henoticon* (484); for this he incurred the displeasure of some of the Roman clergy. Among his four extant letters are one upholding the validity of ordinations performed by Acacius and another, to the bishops of Gaul, in condemnation of traducianism. CPL 1677. [M.P.McH.]

Bibliography

Liber Pontificalis 52 (Duchesne 1.258–259).

ANASTASIUS I OF ANTIOCH (sixth century). Bishop (559–570, 593–598). Anastasius I opposed Justinian's support of the Aphthartodocetae, who claimed that Christ's body was always incorruptible. Justin II charged him with lavish expenditures and improper conduct and language. Gregory the Great defended him, as did the historian Evagrius. He left some letters and sermons. CPG III, 6944–6969. [F.W.N.]

ANASTASIUS II OF ANTIOCH (sixth–seventh century). Bishop (599–610). Anastasius II was supported by Gregory the Great and translated Gregory's *Pastoral Rule* into Greek. He died during a Jewish rebellion, his body mutilated and burned, perhaps in reaction to a Jewish persecution in 592–593.
[F.W.N.]

ANASTASIUS APOCRISARIUS (d. 666). Writer and theologian. *Apocrisarius* (representative) of the Roman church at Constantinople, Anastasius was exiled along with Maximus Confessor (655) for opposing the Monothelites, who maintained the existence of but a single will in Christ. Tried before a council at Constantinople, he and Maximus were tortured and banished to Colchis (662), where he died. He composed an account of the trial with other writings relating to the controversy. CPG III, 7733–7740. [M.P.McH.]

Bibliography
Repertorium Fontium Historiae Medii Aevi (Rome: Istituto Storico Italiano per il Medio Evo, 1967), Vol. 2, p. 220.

ANASTASIUS MONACHUS (d. 662). Disciple of Maximus Confessor. There survive from his pen a letter concerning the two wills of Christ (in Latin translation), a work on worship, and some new fragments on Luke. CPG III, 7725–7729. [F.W.N.]

ANASTASIUS SINAITA (d. ca. 700). Abbot of St. Catherine's monastery on Mt. Sinai. Anastasius apparently attacked Monophysitism

as early as 640. His *Viae dux* is primarily concerned with that understanding of Christ, but he attempted to uproot any heresy. The *Questiones et responsiones* include additions to his genuine comments. A number of homilies bear his name. CPG III, 7745–7758. [F.W.N.]

Bibliography
PG 44.1328–1345; 89.36–1288.
K.H. Uthemann, "Die dem Anastasios Sinaites zugeschriebene Synopsis des haeresibus et synodis: Einführung und Edition," *Annuarium historiae conciliorum* 14 (1982):58–94.

ANCHORITE. *See* Hermit.

ANCYRA (Angora, Ankara). Major city in the Roman province of Galatia. Ancyra became a significant center for Christianity in Asia Minor. Several synods of note were held there in the fourth century. The canons of the synod of 314 preserve one of the earliest orders of penance for those who apostatized (lapsed) during persecution. The first nine canons concern readmission to the church of both clergy and laity, prescribing penances according to clerical rank and circumstances of apostasy. The remaining fifteen canons address problems of ecclesiastical discipline and jurisdiction, such as the marriage of deacons, asceticism, and violence arising from clerical appointments (Mansi 2.513–540). In the midst of the Arian controversy, Basil, bishop of Ancyra, headed a synod in 358 that sought to reconcile the beleaguered eastern church by adopting a creed with the formula *homoiousian*, the Father and the Son defined as "of like substance." This creed proved to be unacceptable to the radical Arians, the Anomoeans, who denied any likeness of substance, and the Nicene supporters, who confessed "the same substance" in the Father and the Son (Mansi 3.265–290). A minor Arian synod held in Ancyra in 375 deposed a Nicene bishop, Hypsis of Parnassus, and attempted to depose Gregory of Nyssa (Basil, *Ep.* 237; 239). In addition to the synods, the monastic historian Palladius noted that the city was a center for ascetic life in the fourth century (*H. Laus.* 66–68). The temple of Augustus, which remains the most impressive of modern Ankara's ancient monuments, was converted into a Christian church in the fifth century. By the seventh century, Ancyra had become a metropolitan see of Constantinople and was fourth in rank after Caesarea, Ephesus, and Heracleia.   [R.L.]

Bibliography

Mansi, Vol. 2, cols. 513–540; Vol. 3, cols. 265–290.

C.J. Hefele, *The History of the Councils of the Church from the Original Documents* (Edinburgh: T. and T. Clark, 1888), Vol. 1, pp. 199–201; Vol. 2, pp. 228–231.

R.B. Rackham, "The Text of the Canons of Ancyra," *Studia Biblica et Ecclesiastica* 3 (1891):139–216; C.H. Turner, "Canon xiii of Ancyra," *The Church and the Ministry*, ed. C. Gore (London: SPCK, new ed. 1919), pp. 327–330; C. Karalevsky, "Ancyre," *Dictionnaire d'histoire et de géographie ecclésiastiques*, ed. A. Baudrillart (Paris: Letouzey et Ané, 1914), Vol. 2, cols. 1538–1543; P. Joannou, "Ancyra," NCE, Vol. 1, p. 488.

ANDREW. One of the twelve apostles of Jesus Christ, and brother of Simon Peter from Capernaum. Before joining Christ, Andrew was a disciple of John the Baptist (John 1:40–44). Apart from the few, although significant, references to him in the Gospels (Matt. 4:18; 10:2 and parallels; Mark 1:29; 13:3; John 6:8; 12:22), our knowledge of Andrew is derived from apocryphal sources and early church traditions.

The apocryphal sources include (1) the *Gospel of Andrew*, a lost work originally contained in the list of books condemned by the sixth-century *Decretum Gelasianum* 5; (2) the *Acts and Martyrdom of Andrew*, which mixes historical truth with legend; (3) the *Acts of Andrew and Matthias in the City of Cannibals* (i.e., in Sinope of Pontus), which became the basis for the tenth-century *Concerning the Life, Acts and End of St. Andrew the Protokletos* of Epiphanius the Monk (PG 120.216–260); (4) the *Acts and Journeys Joined with an Encomium*, which is similar in content to (3); (5) the *Acts of Peter and Andrew*; (6) the *Martyrdom of the Holy Apostle Andrew*; and (7) the *Acts of Andrew* (in Coptic and Ethiopic), which link Andrew's activity with that of Bartholomew and Paul.

Early church traditions about Andrew, which begin in the third century and reach their climax in eighth- and ninth-century Byzantium, associate Andrew's apostolic activity with Asia Minor, Thrace, and Greece and include his martyrdom in Patras in the northwest Peloponnesus. Origen, as Eusebius informs us (*H.E.* 3.1), supplies us with the most ancient reference to Andrew outside the New Testament. He tells us that he taught in Scythia (southern Russia). In the fourth century, Gregory of Nazianzus speaks of Andrew's missionary activity in Epirus and associates the mission in Achaia with Luke (*Or.* 33.11). Later authors, including Theodoret (*In Ps.* 116.1), Gaudentius of Brescia (*Serm.* 17), and Jerome (*Ep.* 59.5), knew of Andrew's activity in Achaia. Basil of Seleucia (d. 459) knew of Andrew's mission in Scythia, Thrace, and Achaia (*Enc. in And.* 6; PG 28.1108). We should also mention here two Latin texts: *Passio Sanct. Andreae Apostoli*, in the form of a letter from the priests and deacons of Achaia, describing Andrew's martyrdom, and Gregory of Tours's *Liber de miraculis beati Andreae Apostoli*. From the eighth and ninth centuries come the works of Epiphanius the Monk (PG 120.216–260), Pseudo-Dorotheus of Tyre (PG 92.1062–1072), the Synaxarium of the Church of Constantinople, and Nicephorus Kallistos (PG 145.860ff.).

According to these traditions, Andrew accompanied his brother Peter on an early mission in the Pontic region of Asia Minor and especially in the cities of Sinope, Amisus, and Trebizond, before turning to western Asia Minor (Phrygia, Mysia, and Bithynia). He returned to Pontus, where he was imprisoned and narrowly escaped death. He subsequently went to Scythia, Thrace (where he ordained Stachys as the first bishop of Byzantium), Thessaly, Greece, and Achaia. At Patras, he converted Maximilla, the wife of the Roman proconsul Aegeates, to Christ and as a result suffered martyrdom by crucifixion on a so-called St. Andrew's cross. His body was buried by bishop Stratocles of Patras; in 357, the relics were brought to Constantinople by Constantius II, but they were soon dispersed to various parts of

Christendom. Since the seventh century, Andrew has been regarded as the founder of the church of Constantinople. Churches in other regions, including those of Russia and Scotland, associated Andrew with their foundations. Feast day November 30. *See also* Acts of Andrew. [G.D.D.]

Bibliography

M.R. James, *The Apocryphal New Testament* (Oxford: Clarendon, 1924), pp. 337–363; NTA, Vol. 2, pp. 390–425.

F. Dvornik, *The Idea of Apostolicity in Byzantium and the Legend of the Apostle Andrew* (Cambridge: Harvard UP, 1958); P. Peterson, *Andrew, Brother of Simon Peter, His History and His Legends* (Leiden: Brill, 1958).

ANDREW OF CAESAREA (fifth century). Bishop of Caesarea in Cappadocia. Andrew apparently wrote the earliest Greek commentary on the Book of Revelation. Depending upon scattered comments on particular passages, he cautiously used a threefold interpretive method: historical, moral, and mystical. Because Revelation has fewer manuscripts than many other New Testament books, the text in Andrew's commentary is quite important. CPG III, 7478–7479. [F.W.N.]

Bibliography

J. Schmid, *Studien zur Geschichte des griechischen Apokalypse-Textes I. Der Apokalypse-kommentar des Andreas von Kaisareia* (Munich: Zink, 1955); A. Monaci Castagno, "Il problema della datazione dei commenti all'Apocalisse di Ecumenio e di Andrea di Caesarea," *Atti dell' Accademia delle Scienze di Torino: Classe di Scienze morali, storiche e filologiche* 114 (1980):223–246.

ANDREW OF CRETE (ca. 660–740). Born at Damascus, monk at Jerusalem, deacon at Constantinople, Andrew became archbishop of Gortyna, Crete. His sermons show oratorical excellence. He had a great interest in Mary. Among his hymns, the most famous is the "Great Canon," a penitential hymn in 250 strophes. Feast day July 4. CPG III, 8170–8219. [E.F.]

ANGELS. Spiritual beings, subordinate to God and superior to humans, who serve as God's agents in various ways and who together constitute the society of heaven united in unending worship and adoration of God. In contrast, the fallen angels, rebels against God and deprived of their heavenly status, represent a counterforce of evil (often indistinguishable from, although rarely identified with, the demons), which is doomed ultimately to defeat along with their head and leader, the devil.

The English "angel" (and its cognates in other modern languages) derives from the Greek *aggelos* through the Latin *angelus*. The classical Greek term means "messenger" and refers, first of all, to human messengers in human contexts (from Homer on); it was also applied, however, to those who bore messages from the gods (e.g., birds in Plutarch, *Oracles at Delphi* 22) and, in particular, to Hermes, the messenger of the gods (*Homeric Hymn to Demeter* 407). Only in the era of the Roman empire, and then chiefly in the Platonic philosophical tradition, did there emerge Greco-Roman references to angels as spiritual beings in something like the predominant Jewish or Christian sense (Porphyry in Augustine, *Civ. Dei* 10.9). Even later Christian usage, however, retained the notion that "angel" refers rather to an office than to the nature of the being who exercises the office (Hilary of Poitiers, *Trin.* 5.11; Augustine, *Serm.* 7.3).

Angels in Judaism. On the Jewish side, angels apparently go back to the earliest layers of Old Testament tradition. They function especially as messengers of God (Judg. 6:11–24 is perhaps a paradigm case); and collectively they are represented as the army (Gen. 32:1–2; cf. Josh. 5:13–14) or the heavenly court (1 Kings 22:19) of God, who, correspondingly, is designated the Lord or God of hosts (1 Sam. 1:3, 11; Ps. 24:10; Amos 3:13). The Old Testament cherubim (Gen 3:24; Exod. 25:18–22; Ps. 18:10; Ezek. 10:3–22) and seraphim (Isa. 6:2–7) were also reckoned among the angels by later Jewish (*1 Enoch* 61.10; 71.7) and Christian (Ps.-Dionysius, *C.H.* 7) traditions.

It was in postexilic Judaism, however, and especially in the apocalyptic tradition represented by Daniel, *1 Enoch*, and similar works, that angels came dramatically to the fore. The vast number of angels is emphasized (Dan. 7:10; *1 Enoch* 1.9; 14.22); they are arrayed in groups, hierarchically ordered, corresponding, for example, to the ascending sequence of the heavens as in *2 Enoch*, like an army (*2 Enoch* 1a.5–6) or a king's court surrounding the throne of God (Dan. 7:10; *1 Enoch* 60.2); they have leaders and commanders of whom the chief is most often the archangel Michael (*1 Enoch* 24.6; *Test. Abr.* 1.4). Thus, a complex heavenly society emerges that is at once magnified (reckoned on a supernatural scale) and humanized (given a recognizably human social structure) and finds its center in an unending worship of God (*2 Enoch* 19.3; 21.1; 22; Rev. 4; *Test. Adam* 4.8) that is obviously both a reflection of and a model for human worship on earth.

In this scheme, the angels retain the role of messenger (Tobit 12:6–22; *Test. Abr.* 1.4–7)

but now especially as bearers and interpreters of apocalyptic visions (Dan. 8; *1 Enoch* 1.2; *2 Enoch* 1), within which, too, they frequently serve as guides for journeys through the cosmos or as revealers of the secrets of the universe and its destiny (*1 Enoch*; *2 Enoch*). At the same time, angels acquire cosmic functions, such as directing the course of the stars (*2 Enoch* 4.1), and, on a more intimately human level, become linked to the religious and moral life, carrying prayers to God (Tobit 12:12; *Test. Abr.* 8.1; cf. *1 Enoch* 99.3), interceding before God on human behalf (*Test. Levi* 5.6; *Test. Dan.* 6.2), marking good and evil deeds (*2 Enoch* 19.5) and, above all, presiding over the judgment of souls (*Test. Abr.* 11–14), the vindication of the righteous (*1 Enoch* 100.5; *2 Enoch* 8–9), and the punishment of the evil (*2 Enoch* 10), both before and at the final judgment. In all this, angels are represented as figures of extraordinary power and command, striking in their beauty (Dan. 3:25; *1 Enoch*

Four angels alternating with the symbols of the four evangelists, vault mosaic (late fifth or early sixth century) of the Archbishop's Chapel, the Oratory of St. Andrew, in Ravenna, Italy. (The I and X are the first letters of Jesus Christ in Greek.) (Photograph Editore A. Longo, Ravenna)

106.5–6), fiery in aspect (*1 Enoch* 17.1; cf. Ps. 104:4), and awesome in their appearance to human beings (Dan. 8:17).

Postexilic Judaism also produced the mythic account of the fall of some angels through intercourse with the daughters of men (*1 Enoch* 6–10; cf. Gen. 6:1–4). These angels both violated their own spiritual status by intermingling with flesh and blood (*1 Enoch* 15.1–7) and became the teachers of secret and occult knowledge to humans (*1 Enoch* 10.7–8; 65.6–9), defiling themselves and corrupting the earth. As a result, they have been consigned to a place of punishment (*1 Enoch* 10) until the moment of their complete condemnation (*1 Enoch* 54). The evil angels, then, are the source of human knowledge of the arts of warfare, of cosmetics and sexual attraction, of metalwork and jewelry, of sorcery and incantation, even of writing with pen and ink (*1 Enoch* 8; 65; 69)—in short, of those cultural forms that were understood to deflect humans from God and to generate injustice among themselves. Thus, the angelic fall defines a cosmic setting for the human drama of good and evil, and invests it with more than human force (for later references, cf. *Jubilees* 4.22; 7.21–25; Philo, *Gig.*; Athenagoras, *Leg.* 24–25).

Angels in Christianity. Christianity inherited and developed the angelology of its Judaic environment, which is everywhere apparent at or just below the surface of the writings of the early period. Its angels bear the familiar names of their Jewish antecedents: Michael (Jude 9; Rev. 12:7; cf. *1 Enoch* 24.6); Gabriel (Luke 1:19, 26; Origen, *Princ.* 1.8.1; cf. Dan. 8:16); Raphael (Origen, *Princ.* 1.8.1; cf. Tobit 3:16); Uriel (*Apoc. Petr.* 4; 6; 12; cf. *1 Enoch* 9.1). They, too, are arranged in groups, at first rather unsystematically and without clear distinctions between them—as in the Pauline literature, which speaks of "powers" (Rom. 8:38; 1 Cor. 15:24), "authorities" (1 Cor. 15:24; Eph. 1:21; Col. 1:16), "principalities" (Rom. 8:38; 1 Cor. 15:24; Eph. 1:21), "dominions" (Eph. 1:21; Col. 1:16), and "thrones" (Col. 1:16), several of which are clearly hostile forces—and later in a systematically arrayed hierarchy of the nine orders of angels as in Pseudo-Dionysius (ca.

500), who lists, in descending order, seraphim, cherubim, thrones, dominions, powers, authorities, principalities, archangels, and finally angels (*C.H.* 6–9), each unambiguously good and wholly subordinated to God. They continue to serve as messengers (Matt. 2:13; Acts 8:26; 10:3–6; *Apoc. Paul.* 11). Similarly, they exercise various cosmic functions, appointed by God over the elements, the heavens, and the universe with all it contains (Athenagoras, *Leg.* 10; cf. *Diogn.* 7; Justin, *2 Apol.* 5; Origen, *Cels.* 8:31–36; Gregory of Nyssa, *Or. catech.* 6). At the same time, there are angels assigned to nations, to churches, and to individuals (Origen, *Princ.* 1.8.1; *Cels.* 8.34; Eusebius of Caesarea, *D.E.* 4.7–8); and the angels are intimately involved in the religious life, supervising repentance (Hermas, *passim*), praying with those in their charge (Origen, *Or.* 11.5; *Cels.* 8.34, 36), and carrying prayers to heaven (*Cels.* 5.4). According to some, each individual has been assigned a good angel and a bad angel and decides by free will which inclination to follow (Hermas, *Mand.* 5.1.1–4; Gregory of Nyssa, *V. Mos.* 2.45–47; cf. 1 QS 3–4). Above all, the angels are engaged in unending worship of God (Irenaeus, *Dem.* 9–10; Tertullian, *Or.* 3; Hilary of Poitiers, *Trin.* 3.7; *Apoc. Paul.* 7–8), circling in chorus around the divine being (Eusebius of Caesarea, *D.E.* 3.3; Gregory of Nazianzus, *Or.* 28.31) and providing a model for human imitation (Origen, *Cels.* 8.34).

If, in the Jewish traditions, angelic activity tended to focus on Israel, it was only natural that, in Christianity, the emphasis would shift to Christ and the church. Thus, the angels are represented in Christ's service (Matt. 4:6, 11), their roles concentrated around the events of his life and death (Luke 1; 2:8–14; Matt. 28), and they are associated with his return in judgment (Matt. 25:31); at the same time, Christ is portrayed as superior to and set above the angels (Eph. 1:20–21; Heb. 1:4–14). The angels minister to the church and preside over the processes by which it is built up (Hermas, *Vis.* 3.4; Origen, *Or.* 11.3); there are, for example, angels of baptism (Tertullian, *Bapt.* 4; 6) and of repentance (Hermas, *Vis.* 5.7 and *passim*; Clement of Alexandria, *Q.d.s.* 42), as well as an angel, Michael, charged with prayers and supplications (Origen, *Princ.* 1.8.1). In general, the aim of the angels, confirmed through the miracles performed by their agency, is to bring humans to blessedness through worship of God alone (Augustine, *Civ. Dei* 10.7–8, 12). At such points as these, early Christianity recast the heavenly society it had inherited from Judaism and gave it a peculiarly Christian stamp.

The development of early Christian theology, in relation both to Christian heresy and to non-Christian philosophy, forced further clarification of the place and role of the angels. Where it had been possible to rank Christ among the angels or even as an angel (Justin, *1 Apol.* 6; Origen, *Cels.* 5.58; Methodius, *Symp.* 3.4), in the Arian controversy it became important to specify that Christ is fully divine while the angels are created beings (Athanasius, *Ar.* 1.55, 62; 2.49). On another front, early Christianity was compelled to distinguish the angels from the gods and demons of Greco-Roman paganism, who, like the angels, were understood (in the philosophical traditions at least) as intermediary beings charged with the oversight of various regions of the cosmos and aspects of human affairs. Here, Christians insisted that the ministers of God are properly to be called angels, not gods (Lactantius, *Inst.* 1.67), and that, unlike the gods and demons, the angels claim no worship for themselves but rather direct humans entirely to God (Origen, *Cels.* 5.4–5; 8.31–36; Eusebius, *D.E.* 3.3; Augustine, *Civ. Dei* 10.7, 26). Finally, perhaps in relation to Gnosticism and its angelology, early Christianity shifted the fall of the evil angels back from Gen. 6:1–4 (still, e.g., in Justin, *2 Apol.* 5; Athenagoras, *Leg.* 24–25) to an earlier stage so that it anticipated and was correlated with the human fall from paradise (Irenaeus, *Dem.* 16 [but cf. 18]; Gregory of Nyssa, *Or. catech.* 6; Augustine, *Gen. ad litt.* 11), and the angelic sin came to be reckoned as envy or pride rather than lust (e.g., Gregory of Nyssa, *Or. catech.* 6; Augustine, *Gen. ad litt.* 11.14; *Civ. Dei* 11.13–15; 14.3). Particularly important in this regard is the fact that the angels were considered moral beings, pos-

sessed of reason and free will (Justin, *Dial.* 102; Irenaeus, *Haer.* 4.37.1, 6; Origen, *Princ.* 1.5.4–5; 1.8.1), so that evil was understood to have its root in the wrongful act of free agents, not in an evil nature inherently opposed to and incapable of the good (Augustine, *Gen. ad litt.* 11.20.27–21.28).

In contrast to the fallen angels, the good angels functioned in early Christianity to define the supramundane social context of Christian belief and life and to delineate the end and goal of human redemption. They were portrayed as an ordered society of created, rational beings united in the enjoyment of God, service to the divine will, and care for human well-being (Irenaeus, *Dem.* 9–10; Athanasius, *Ar.* 2.27; Gregory of Nazianzus, *Or.* 28.31; Ps.-Dionysius, *C.H.*; Augustine, *Civ. Dei* 22.29). True Christians, who became aliens and strangers in earthly society (1 Peter 2:19; Hermas, *Sim.* 1.1–7; *Diogn.* 5; Clement of Alexandria, *Str.* 7.12.78; Augustine, *Civ. Dei* 19.17), are reckoned kinsmen and friends by the angels (Origen, *Cels.* 8.34; cf. Augustine, *Civ. Dei* 19.9), and, with the angels, already belong to the eternal city of God (Augustine, *Civ. Dei* 12.1 and passim). The Christian life, insofar as it represents a turn away from the prevailing patterns of value and behavior in earthly society and toward love of God and one's fellow humans, becomes a kind of anticipation of the angelic life (Basil of Caesarea, *Hom.* 21.5; Gregory of Nyssa, *Virg.* 13; Theodoret, *H.E.* 4.21). Above all, the angels, in their ordered hierarchies, model that purified contemplation of God (esp. ps.-Dionysius, *C.H.*) and that love for and rejoicing in God that are the content of the eternal bliss and eternal peace of the redeemed following the final resurrection (Augustine, *Civ. Dei* 22.29–30; *Enchir.* 56–58). Thus, out of all proportion to its meager place in the New Testament (Luke 20:36; cf. Matt. 22:30; Mark 12:25), the notion of equality with the angels became central to the early Christian understanding of the postresurrection life of the redeemed (Clement of Alexandria, *Str.* 7.10.57; 7.12.78; Tertullian, *Res.* 36; Origen, *Cels.* 4.29; Gregory of Nyssa, *Virg.* 13; Augustine, *Civ. Dei* 9.23; 11.13), in which, according to Augustine, humans will be joined in one society with the angels who will be "our angels" (*Civ. Dei* 22.29; *Enchir.* 62–63). The principal role of the angels in early Christianity, then, was to delineate an alternative society, rightly directed to God and thus rightly ordered in itself, to which Christians could sense that they already belonged and with which they would be fully joined in the life to come. *See also* Demons; Satan. [W.S.B.]

Bibliography

1 Enoch; *2 Enoch*; *Testament of Abraham*; Hermas, *Shepherd*; Origen, *On First Principles* 1.5.1–5, 8.1–4; idem, *Against Celsus* 5.2–13, 52–58; 8.31–36; idem, *On Prayer* 11; Augustine, *City of God* 8–10; 11–14; 19–22; idem, *Enchiridion* 56–63; *Apocalypse of Paul*; Pseudo-Dionysius, *Celestial Hierarchy*.

J. Turmel, "Histoire de l'angélologie des temps apostoliques à la fin du Ve siècle," *Revue d'histoire et de littérature religieuses* 3 (1898):299–308, 407–434, 533–552; K. Pelz, *Die Engellehre des hl. Augustinus* (Münster: Aschendorff, 1912); C. Kaplan, "Angels in the Book of Enoch," *Anglican Theological Review* 12 (1930):423–437; E. Peterson, *Das Buch von den Engeln: Stellung und Bedeutung der hl. Engel im Kultus* (Leipzig: Hegner, 1935); E. Langton, *The Ministries of the Angelic Powers According to the Old Testament and Later Jewish Literature* (London: Clarke, 1936); N. Johannsson, *Parakletoi: Vorstellungen von Fürsprechern für den Menschen vor Gott in der alttestamentliche Religion, im Spätjudentum und Urchristentum* (Lund: Gleerup, 1940); J. Barbel, *Christos Angelos* (Bonn: Hanstein, 1941); H. Kühn, *Das Reich des lebendigen Lichtes: Die Engel in Lehre und Leben der Christenheit* (Berlin: Arnold, 1947); H. Kuhn, "The Angelology of the Non-Canonical Jewish Apocalypses," *JBL* 67 (1948):217–232; H. Bietenhard, *Die himmlische Welt im Urchristentum und Spätjudentum* (Tübingen: Mohr, 1951); B. Bamberger, *Fallen Angels* (Philadelphia: Jewish Publication Society of America, 1952); R. Roques, *L'Univers Dionysien* (Paris: Aubier, 1954); J.W. Moran, "St. Paul's Doctrine on Angels," *American Ecclesiastical Review* 132 (1955):378–384; J. Daniélou, *The Angels and Their Mission According to the Fathers of the Church*, tr. D. Heimann (Westminster: Newman, 1957); J. Michl and T. Klauser, "Engel," RLAC (1962), Vol. 5, pp. 54–322; W. Grundman, G. von Rad, and G. Kittel, "Aggelos," *Theological Dictionary of the New Testament*, ed. G. Kittel (Grand Rapids: Eerdmans, 1964), Vol. 1, pp. 74–87; G. Davidson, *A Dictionary of Angels* (New York: Free Press, 1967).

ANIANUS. Several persons of this name are known, among them a bishop of Alexandria (first century) and a bishop of Orleans (d. ca. 453) who helped organize the defense of that city against the Huns. The Alexandrian monk Anianus (fourth–fifth century), author of a chronicle known only in citations (CPG III, 5537), is perhaps to be identified with Anianus of Celeda. [M.P.McH.]

Bibliography

Anianus, bishop of Alexandria: Eusebius, *Church History* 2.24; 3.14, 21.

ANIANUS OF CELEDA (fifth century). A deacon with Pelagian leanings, Anianus caught Jerome's wrath. He translated some of John Chrysostom's homilies into Latin. CPL 771–772 (645 and 1147). [F.W.N.]

ANICETUS. Bishop of Rome (ca. 155–ca. 166). The episcopate of Anicetus is poorly known. Polycarp visited Rome and discussed with him the question of the proper date for the celebration of Easter, which in Asia Minor was kept on the fourteenth of the Jewish month Nisan. The Roman church before Soter (ca. 166–174) had no special Easter feast but observed the resurrection every Sunday. Although agreement could not be reached in this early stage of the Paschal controversy, the bishops parted amicably. The Gnostic Valentinus was in Rome until Anicetus's time. Hegesippus, author of a work against Gnosticism, and Justin Martyr were in the city during his episcopate. Anicetus probably built the shrine for Peter on the Vatican Hill that was excavated in modern times. Evidence for the tradition that he died a martyr is lacking. Feast day April 17.

[M.P.McH.]

Bibliography

Irenaeus, *Against Heresies* 3.3.3–4; 3.4.2; Eusebius, *Church History* 4.11.1–7; 4.14.1; 4.19; 4.22.3; 5.6.4–5; 5.24.14–17; *Liber Pontificalis* 12 (Duchesne 1.134).

M. Richard, "La Question pascale au IIe siècle," *L'Orient Syrien* 6 (1961):179–212.

ANOINTING. Religious application of olive oil. From cooking to cult, almost every aspect of life in the Greco-Roman world involved the use of oil. As a result, the practice of anointing was widespread. Although the customary Greek term, *chriein* (Latin *ung[u]ere*), literally means "to stroke" or "to rub," it came almost exclusively to denote the act of smearing with scented oil (Greek *chrisma, myron*; Latin *chrisma, unctio*; English "chrism"). Because of antiquity's pervasive ritual sense, anointing language is participatory, that is, it names an action through which a reality was seen to be conveyed. Thus, for instance, through the rite of anointing the king acquired power to rule both legitimately and effectively; the athlete, strength and stamina for the struggle; the sick, health-bearing force; the statue, divine power.

Biblical Anointing. The Bible reflects the range of Greco-Roman practice as well as its terminology and worldview, with this difference: biblical literature shows a marked tendency to emphasize sacred anointing. To be sure, there is a word for secular anointing, *sūk* (Septuagint *aleiphein*), but the far more frequent term is *māšaḥ* (Septuagint *chriein*), which denotes sacred anointing. The verbal adjective is *māšiaḥ* (Aramaic *mešiaḥ*; Septuagint *christos*; English "messiah"), "the anointed one," most often, "the anointed one of God." As for the sacred oil, it was compounded of myrrh, cinnamon, aromatic cane, and cassia (Exod. 30:22–25).

Like their neighbors, the Israelites anointed their sanctuaries and cult objects (Exod. 40:9–12). Easily the most common anointing in the Bible, however, is the anointing of the king, considered the heart of the rite of his enthronement. Thus, David and his descendants were called the "anointed of God" and seen to bear God's spirit (Isa. 11:2–9; Ps. 45; 89; 110). Also well attested is priestly anointing, particularly after the exile, when, in lieu of the monarchy, the temple priesthood moved center stage as God's anointed. Postexilic prophecy also shared the limelight. Deutero-Isaiah links anointing, prophetic office, and the gift of God's spirit (Isa. 42:1; 48:16; 61:1). In any case, the term "the anointed one" (mes-siah) in biblical tradition evoked the images of king, priest, and prophet, and could apply equally to Israel as a people as to individuals.

Against this background and the expectations to which it gave rise, the early Christians depicted Jesus as the anointed one—at once, king, priest, and prophet—sent to fulfill Israel's expectations for redemption and a new age. In the earliest layers of the traditions about Jesus, he is the *mešiaḥ/christos* anointed with the Holy Spirit and power by his Father (Acts 2:34; 4:18, 26–27; 10:38; Heb. 1:9; 2:1–18). Indeed, this early Christology of the "anointed one" permanently links the anointing of Jesus, his divine Sonship, and his constitution as Messiah.

Baptismal Anointing. Among the early Christians, the precise point at which Jesus became the Christ was a matter of dispute—his incarnation, baptism, and resurrection were the principal candidates. About the "christening" of the Christian, however, there was no dispute: baptism was the privileged moment. When Tertullian (ca. 200) wrote that Christians became christs through baptismal anointing (*Bapt.* 7), he was simply handing on a well-established tradition, which seems to have begun among Gnostic Christians in the early second century (Irenaeus, *Haer.* 1.21.3).

Although baptismal anointing differed from place to place, two dominant patterns developed early, the western and the Syrian. In the west, there were two separate anointings: one took place just before immersion in the baptismal water and the other, just after. Performed with olive oil (*elaion*)—generally exorcised (Hippolytus, *Trad. ap.* 21)—the first had in view healing, exorcism, and strengthening the candidate for combat with Satan; the second, performed with consecrated and scented olive oil (*chrisma, myron*), was associated with the gift of the Holy Spirit. Both the prebaptismal and the postbaptismal anointings covered the whole body, but the latter was done in two stages. In the *Apostolic Tradition* of Hippolytus (ca. 200), for instance, when the newly baptized emerged from the water, a presbyter anointed their bodies with chrism. After they had dried, dressed, and entered the church, however, the bishop imposed hands on them, poured chrism on their heads, and signed each on the forehead, presumably with the sign of the cross (*Trad. ap.* 22). The episcopal anointing with imposition and chrism generally bore the name "consignation (chrismation)." The two baptismal anointings are also discussed by Cyril of Jerusalem (ca. 350): The first conveys a participation in Christ, the olive tree, who drives out evil spirits and purges the traces of sin; the second conveys the descent of the Holy Spirit at the baptism of Christ and Christian alike (*Catech. mys.* 2.3; 3.1–6).

The second pattern of baptismal anointing is that of Syria. Until the fifth century, Syrian Christians knew only a prebaptismal anointing, the function of which was primarily exorcistic. In John Chrysostom's recently discovered baptismal instructions (ca. 385, Antioch), for instance, there is a two-part prebaptismal anointing but no postbaptismal rite (*Catech.* 2.21–27; cf. 11.27). On Good Friday, just after the candidates pledged allegiance to Christ, the bishop anointed the forehead of each with a cross. Then, during the Holy Saturday vigil and just before baptism, they were anointed from head to foot. The first anointing emphasized the presence of Christ and his protective power against Satan; the second, athletic preparation for baptismal combat with Satan. To be sure, three important Syrian works, the *Apostolic Constitutions* 7.22 (ca. 375), the *Baptismal Instructions* 5.27 of Theodore of Mopsuestia (ca. 420), and the *Testament of Our Lord* 2.8 (ca. 500) know of a postbaptismal anointing, which they associate with the descent of the Holy Spirit. In all three cases, however, the anointing appears to be a later addition, doubtless to bring the Syrian rites into line with general practice.

The importance of these originally divergent traditions is twofold: the Syrian emphasized the fact that baptism itself was the privileged moment of transformation through the descent of the Holy Spirit, whereas the western practice of postbaptismal anointing, especially consignation, focused attention on the ongoing work of the Holy Spirit in baptismal rebirth and postbaptismal life.

In the west, however, a wedge was gradually driven between the postbaptismal anointing of the body and consignation. By the fifth century, consignation was regularly separated from baptism and reserved to the bishop (Innocent I, *Ep.* 25.3.6). By the ninth century, the rite had become a separate sacrament (confirmation) at least for Rabanus Maurus (d. 856), who first provided its theology, namely, that the rite confers that distinctive gift of the Holy Spirit (already received in baptism) by which the Spirit strengthens one for life in Christ (*Inst. cler.* 1.28–30).

Anointing the Sick and the Dying. Anointing the sick was the earliest Christian rite of anointing (James 5:14–15). The rite seems originally to have been confined to Jewish Christianity. Origen (d. ca. 251), for instance, was the first actually to cite the text. In so doing, he interpolated a laying on of hands and connected the rite with the public reconciliation of sinners (*Hom. in Lev.* 2.4). Although others followed him (John Chrysostom, *Sac.* 3; Aphraates, *Dem.* 23.3), eastern documents dependent on the *Apostolic Tradition* link anointing and sickness, although without any reference to James 5:14–15. Serapion of Thmuis (ca. 350) goes further, recording a consecratory prayer over the oil that links anointing, sickness, sin, and forgiveness (*Euch.* 27), and Pseudo-Dionysius the Areopagite goes still further to describe a rite for anointing the dead (*E.H.* 7).

The links between sickness, sin, reconciliation, and death tended to be retained in several rites of anointing among Christians of the east, the most important of which is the solemn anointing of the sick involving seven priests and reminiscent of James 5:14–15. By the fifth century in the west, however, the links were preserved in a single rite, which Amalarius of Metz (d. ca. 850) would later identify as a sacrament and the liturgy of the Mozarabic rite would be the first to encode (*Liber ordinem*). By the twelfth century, it was clearly reserved for the gravely ill, those *in extremis*. Performed by a priest with oil consecrated by the bishop, usually on Holy Thursday, it was known as "Extreme Unction" and numbered among the seven sacraments (cf. Peter Lombard, *On the Sentences* 4, dist. 23). *See also* Baptism; Confirmation; Healing; Ordination; Sacraments.   [T.M.F.]

Bibliography

F.W. Puller, *The Anointing of the Sick in Scripture and Tradition with Some Consideration on the Numbering of the Sacraments* (London: Church Historical Society, 1904); P.F. Palmer, *Sacraments and Forgiveness* (Westminster: Newman, 1959), pp. 273–289; L.L. Mitchell, *Baptismal Anointing* (London: SPCK, 1966); T.M. Finn, *The Liturgy of Baptism in the Baptismal Instructions of St. John Chrysostom* (Washington, D.C.: Catholic U of America P, 1967); H.M. Riley, *Christian Initiation: A Comparative Study of the Baptismal Liturgy in the Mystagogical Writings of Cyril of Jerusalem, John Chrysostom, Theodore of Mopsuestia, and Ambrose of Milan* (Washington, D.C.: Catholic U of America P, 1974); N.D. Mitchell, "Dissolution of the Rite of Christian Initiation," *Made not Born* (Notre Dame: U Notre Dame P, 1976), pp. 50–82; *Temple of the Holy Spirit: Sickness and Death of the Christian in the Liturgy*, tr. M.J. O'Connell (New York: Pueblo, 1983) (tr. of the papers from the 21st Liturgical Study Week, St. Sergius, Paris, 1974).

ANOMOEANS. Those more radical followers of Arius (also known as Aetians, Eunomians, or Exoukontians) who, while accepting that the Father and Son are united in will, asserted that they are unlike or dissimilar (*anomoios*) in essence. The Anomoeans thus rejected both the *homoousios* of the Nicene party ("of one essence") and the *homoiousios* of the followers of Basil of Ancyra ("of similar essence") and clung to what appears to have been the original teaching of Arius in this respect. According to Athanasius and others, Arius had taught that the Son was *xenos* and *allotrios*, "extraneous" and "foreign," to the Father's essence and may also have used the word *anomoios* (Alexander of Alexandria, *Ep. encycl.* 13; Athanasius, *Decr.* 6.1; *Ar.* 1.6; 2.43). This aspect of his teaching, however, was comparatively neglected until, in reaction to various attempts at compromise, it was taken up with renewed vigor by Aetius and Eunomius in the 340s and 350s.

These men, whose names became virtually synonymous with "Anomoean," were not only followers but also critics of Arius. They were followers in that they viewed any admission of a similarity of essence between Father, Son, and Spirit as a Sabellian denial of their distinct identities and therefore asserted that such "Trinitarian" passages in the New Testament as Matthew 28:19 referred to three distinct and dissimilar beings: the Unbegotten God, creator of the Son and all that is; the Only-begotten God, God's instrument in creating all other things; and the Holy Spirit, the first and greatest creature of the Son, sent to sanctify the faithful. They were critics of Arius in that they specifically rejected two ideas espoused by earlier Arians: that the Son had been elevated to divine status through God's foreknowledge of his later moral advancement (*prokopē*); and that the Father's essence was unknown to the Son or to those to whom the Son chose to reveal him (cf. John 17:3). In their view, the latter teaching involved a blasphemous denial of the reality of revelation and made the knowledge of God impossible. They therefore asserted that the names of God revealed in or implied by scripture were directly revelatory of his essence, laying particular emphasis on the name *agennētos*, or "unbegotten."

Rejected by the "official" imperial Arian church, the Anomoeans developed an increasingly separate identity but remained a significant minority within the Arian movement until well after the triumph of Nicene orthodoxy in 381. Thereafter, while still maintaining a presence in Thrace, Cappadocia, and Syria, they were gradually driven underground. Later writers refer to them as "troglodytes" or "cave-dwellers," and although still mentioned as late as the sixth century, they disappear entirely thereafter. *See also* Aetius; Eunomius.

[R.P.V.]

Bibliography

Apart from the writings of Aetius and Eunomius, the principal surviving Anomoean works are as follows: Philostorgius, *Church History*, ed. J. Bidez, GCS (1913), Vol. 21; Pseudo-Chrysostom, *Deux homélies anoméennes pour l'octave de pâques*, ed. J. Liébert, SC (1969), Vol. 146; and *Der Hiobkommentar des arianers Julian*, ed. D. Hagedorn (Berlin: de Gruyter, 1973). There are also strong reasons for believing that the final editors of the *Apostolic Constitutions*, of the longer form of the *Letters* of St. Ignatius of Antioch, and of the Pseudo-Clementine *Recognitions* were Anomoeans.

M. Albertz, "Zur Geschichte der jung-arianischen Kirchengemeinschaft," *Theologische Studien und Kritiken* 82 (1909):205–278; J. de Ghellink, "Quelques appréciations de la dialectique d'Aristote durant les conflicts trinitaires du IVe siècle," *RHE* 26 (1930):5–42; T.A. Kopecek, *A History of Neo-Arianism*, 2 vols. (Cambridge: Philadelphia Patristic Foundation, 1979); idem, "Neo-Arian Religion: The Evidence of the Apostolic Constitutions," *Arianism: Historical and Theological Reassessments*, ed. R.C. Gregg (Cambridge: Philadelphia Patristic Foundation, 1985), pp. 153–179.

ANTHONY (ca. 251–356). Major figure in early Egyptian monasticism. According to Athanasius's *Life of Anthony* (ca. 357), the boy was raised in an economically comfortable Christian family and did not take to school. Anthony spoke Coptic and never learned Greek. In later years, he used translations or interpreters. By the age of twenty, he had lost both parents and was in charge of a young sister. After a series of experiences in communal worship during which the texts read seemed to give him personal instructions, he put his sister in a nunnery and took up the monastic life.

He is sometimes said to have been the first monk, but Athanasius's biography of him indicates that there were already monasteries near his village. Furthermore, some older men had moved to the edges of their towns and had entered a solitary life from their youth. If Anthony has a place as a pioneer, it is in his movement into the desert, or perhaps in the fame that came his way.

What we know of his life is complex. Anecdotes tell of his struggles with demons and thus his testing by the devil. Whatever the value of these stories, unusual events happened around him. Although he took little food or exercise when in seclusion, his spiritual and physical health seemed to be excellent. One unusual feature of Anthony's life as a hermit was his ability to move in and out of contact with people. In certain periods, he was willing to serve almost as a spiritual director among groups. But then he would move farther out into the desert to take up once again his solitary existence. He ended his life by going to Alexandria to be martyred.

His influence seems to have been strong not only in Egypt but elsewhere. Gregory of Nazianzus (*Or.* 21.5) in Cappadocia and Jerome (*Vir. ill.* 87–88) knew of his exploits. Augustine (*Conf.* 8.6) says that his deeds were known in Rome, Milan, and Trier. Doubtless, Athanasius's biography of him provided the source of some of that influence, but Anthony's significance was the reason that Athanasius wrote.

Athanasius tried to use the *Life* for his own purposes. It is difficult to accept that the intricacies of the Arian debate were of importance to this simple monk (*V. Anton.* 82). Jerome (*Vir. ill.* 88) knew of seven letters attributed to him, but those in a post-Renaissance edition are not genuine.

The number and kind of incidents attributed to him at times appear fanciful. But such heroic tales were a part both of the developing genre of hagiography and were in some ways necessary to accent his importance. The lives of saints remain a puzzle, because they often contain solid, historical materials alongside incredible stories. Feast day January 17. CPG II, 2330–2350.   [F.W.N.]

Bibliography
H. Dörries, *Die Vita Antonii als Geschichtsquelle* (Göttingen: Vandenhoeck & Ruprecht, 1949); L. Bouyer, *La Vie de S. Antoine*, 2nd ed. (Abbaye de Bellefontaine: Fontenelle, 1977); R.C. Gregg, tr., *Athanasius: The Life of Anthony and the Letter to Marcellinus* (New York: Paulist, 1980).

ANTHROPOLOGY. Examination of the capacities and destiny of human beings in virtue of their inherent relation to God. Although human nature was studied in terms of its differences from the divine nature, angelic nature, and irrational animal nature, particular attention was given to investigating those factors that were believed to underlie the peculiar character of the human condition itself: created good in paradise, humanity has suffered the debilitating consequences of sin but may be restored in Christ and perfected in eternity.

Attempts to describe the distinguishing features of human nature made use of images and teachings drawn from the Hebrew scriptures and Judaism, from an emerging canon of specifically Christian scriptures, and from contemporary Hellenistic religion and philosophy (e.g., Nemesius, *Nat. hom.*). Although this range of resources allowed some latitude of emphasis and interpretation, widely shared convictions regarding human capacities and destiny effectively regulated the pattern of components in any statement of Christian anthropology. Generally speaking, Christians described the human person as a rational being, a union of body and soul. Created in the image of God, individuals possess the capacity to live in subjection to the divine will as revealed in the Law and prophets of Israel and in the life and teachings of Christ. At the resurrection, all persons will be judged and either rewarded or punished on the basis of their free adherence to good or evil in their life on earth (cf. Athenagoras, *Res.*). The fall of Adam was believed to have diminished, to a greater or lesser extent, the human capacity for recognizing and choosing the good.

Determinism or Free Will in the Second Century. No one element consistently dominated this descriptive scheme, but in the debate against their pagan opponents Christians regularly stressed that the human will is free and thereby accountable. Although Platonism and some elements of Stoicism also taught free will, strong strains of fatalism had persisted in much of classical religion and philosophy from the writings of Homer through the first centuries of the church. The belief that human choice, action, and destiny are externally controlled, at least to some degree, by the gods or fate or the stars was widespread in the Greco-Roman world. The attraction of the Stoic doctrine of necessity and a pervasive interest in astrology and magic in the early centuries of the church attest to the increasing appeal of various forms of determinism or fatalism as explanations of the character of human life. Even in the most sophisticated philosophical discussions, the topic of fate had become a subject of serious inquiry (e.g., Cicero, *On Fate*; Ps.-Plutarch, *On Fate*; Alexander of Aphrodisias, *On Fate*). Belief in determinism came into conflict, however, with the convic-

tion of human responsibility and accountability that Christianity had inherited from Judaism, with its teaching of a revealed Law and divine retributive justice. The images of a final judgment derived from apocalyptic Judaism and contained in the sayings attributed to Christ strengthened the element of accountability in Christian teaching.

Some of the earliest and most forceful Christian resistance to a doctrine of determinism came from the apologists, writers of the second and early third century who sought to make a reasoned defense of Christian faith and practice to its pagan detractors. One of the apologists, Justin Martyr, argued that as humanity was created with reason, persons have the capacity to distinguish good from evil and the responsibility to pursue the good (*1 Apol.* 29). After death, all will receive eternal reward or punishment from a just God in accord with their freely chosen actions (*1 Apol.* 10;12). To suggest that persons are virtuous or evil as the result of an inevitable fate is to undermine human accountability and to rob the notions of vice and virtue of any content (*1 Apol.* 43). Justin tended to attribute the unreasonable and sinful character of human behavior to the work of demons who have kept the human mind in ignorance through distortion of the truth. Baptism, however, cleanses the penitent from sin and enables the penitent's will to operate in full freedom. As a result, Christians are the most reasonable of people in their free choice of the good.

Justin's concern to maintain the freedom of the will was shared by other apologists. Among them, Theophilus emphasized the function of the will in the first man. Influenced by Jewish teaching, Theophilus spoke of Adam as immature, an unfinished creature with the capacity either to choose obedience, which would lead to immortality, or to choose disobedience and become mortal (*Autol.* 2.24, 27). The effects of the punishment incurred by Adam's disobedience have continued in the subjection of his descendants to pain and death. Nevertheless, the intent of the hard life outside paradise was the education of the unfinished creature toward maturity and knowledge. Moreover, as death set a limit to sin, resurrection allowed restoration to new life (*Autol.* 2.26).

The portrayal of Adam as an immature creature in need of divine pedagogy would prove useful to Irenaeus of Lyons in the battle against Gnosticism. Although teachers of Gnosticism varied considerably in their estimate of the material world and the human condition, some general patterns of thought appear to have gained wide acceptance in Gnostic circles. Among these was a thoroughgoing dualism that not only set the cosmos and its creator, the demiurge, in opposition to the supreme God but also distinguished different natures among human beings. Those with a spiritual nature, as creations of the supreme God, were capable of redemption, whereas those with a material nature, as creations of the demiurge, were not. The result was an extreme form of determinism, which disallowed human responsibility for either good or ill.

Irenaeus rejected the Gnostic dualism of matter and spirit not only by arguing that all humanity shares one nature but also by insisting upon the identity of the supreme God with the creator God and affirming the goodness of the creation. Persons cannot be classified as having either a carnal or a spiritual nature, for each person is a combination of both the carnal and the spiritual. One can no more be a human being without flesh than without a soul (*Haer.* 5.6.1). Accordingly, there can be no distinction of origin nor determination of destiny based on nature. Instead, as creatures of a good and just God, all persons have a free will and will ultimately be rewarded or punished on the basis of the voluntary choices made during their lives (*Haer.* 4.15.2; 4.37.2–4).

These choices, Irenaeus insisted, were essential to the maturation of a person. Whereas the Gnostics attributed the imperfections of the human situation to the deficiencies of its creator, Irenaeus viewed these same imperfections as evidence of the accommodation of a gracious God to the unfinished condition of humankind (*Haer.* 4.14.2). In accord with the order of all creation, humanity had begun in an immature state and could receive the Spirit of God only in proportion to its developing

capacities (*Haer.* 4.38.1–4). Adam's sin resulted from his immaturity, but his freedom was essential for the possibility of growth. Experience of both the advantages of good and the disadvantages of evil is a necessary condition for a mature attachment to the good and for a true knowledge of self and God (*Haer.* 3.20.2; 4.37.6).

The Origenist Tradition of Reunion with God. In the second-century battle against various forms of determinism, the notions of free will and human accountability became well-established elements of Christian anthropology. Early in the third century, Origen was able to state that it was the universal teaching of the church received from the apostles that every rational soul has a free will, is subject to no necessity, and at the end of its life on earth will receive a just reward or punishment as its actions warrant (*Princ., praef.* 5; 3.1.1). This formulation suggests that by this time free will and divine justice had become coordinated notions. As Origen pointed out, however, scripture itself contained passages (e.g., Exod. 4:21; 7:3; Rom. 9:16, 18–19) that appeared to point to a divine determinism and thus contradict the church's teaching of human responsibility.

Origen dealt with the dilemma by enlarging the context of divine and human interaction. He speculated that the earth had been created as an arena of pedagogy for rational souls that had fallen from their original union with God. The harsh conditions of material existence provided a suitable context in which these fallen souls, now united with bodies, might learn the difficult lessons that would bring them once again to God (*Princ.* 1.8.1; 3.1.21–22). Instruction was not limited to earthly existence, however. Following the death of the body, medicinal punishment, as deserved, would assist the slow process of conversion and return of the soul to God.

Origen was convinced that every soul would ultimately be reunited with God but without any violation of the integrity of the human will. Divine actions noted in the scriptures that appear to harden the heart or to ensure conversion actually only illuminate and confirm the state of the soul as already hardened or healthy. The soul always responds to God freely according to its condition; yet with infinite patience God works with each soul to accomplish its ultimate restoration (*Princ.* 3.1.12–14).

One obvious aspect of Origen's treatment of the human condition is that the true self is the rational soul. The body functions as an instrument of divine instruction for the duration of the soul's life on this earth. Origen never made entirely clear whether the restoration of the soul to its true condition in union with God will be achieved in conjunction with the body.

More than a century later, Gregory of Nyssa, although greatly influenced by Origen, would insist that the body and the soul were united at creation and will be eternally joined at the resurrection. Both are essential components of human nature (*Hom. opif.* 8.4–5; 27.2). Thus, it was not material existence itself that resulted from the fall but the bodily processes, particularly sexuality, that humankind shares with the animals. As in the teaching of Origen, however, the alterations in life that resulted from the fall were intended for human benefit. The individual's absorption in carnality would eventually seem repugnant in contrast to the original human condition in which Adam had enjoyed a direct vision of God, free from passion. Accordingly, dissatisfaction with the present condition would initiate a renewal of the desire for God (*Virg.* 12). God's grace would thus have established the conditions leading to the return to God, but the decision would have been freely made out of the individual's own desire. Once undertaken, whether in this life or after death, the restoration to God would consist of an eternally deepening participation in God (*V. Mos.* 1.7–8), a process also known as deification (*theopoiēsis, theōsis*).

Although Gregory stressed the importance of the progressive purification of the self in the return to God, the most important figure in the actual systemization of the theory and practice of purification, that is, asceticism, was Evagrius Ponticus. Evagrius provided careful instruction for the identification and classification of thoughts, the eradication of evil ones and the attainment of virtuous ones. The objective of this process of ascesis was the achievement of a state of calm, *apatheia*, in which the passions or emotions would be rightly ordered, a precondition for contemplation and knowledge of God (*Cap. pract.* 81; 84).

Evagrius's pursuit of contemplation undistracted by passion was based on the conviction that the original condition and ultimate goal of the self is intellectual union with God. Soul and body are both the results of a primeval fall from a state of simple intelligence. Evagrius's scheme rested upon the twin assumptions that the will is free to choose between good and evil and that an individual has the capacity for self-purification. Nevertheless, the rigor of his system and the occasional references to the necessity of grace indicate the difficulty of attaining the goal.

All ascetics, of course, did not follow the scheme prescribed by Evagrius, although they did tend to share his confidence in the human capacity for self-generated movement toward the good. Generally, ascetics looked to the Law, the moral law of the Hebrew scriptures and the evangelical counsels (poverty, chastity, and obedience) as guides for the purification of the self. Obedience was the means of attaining perfection.

Pelagius and Augustine on Sin, Grace, and Predestination. One such ascetic who held a prominent, if negative, role in the development of Christian anthropology was Pelagius. Pelagius believed that persons are inherently capable of knowing and doing the good, although since Adam the habitual sin of both society and the individual has impaired these capacities (Pelagius, *Ep. Demetr.* 2; 3; 8). Through the operation of grace in the Law, the example and teaching of Christ, and the sacraments, however, the impediments to the exercise of the free will are removed. Lacking excuse, each person is accountable to God for success or failure in the achievement of perfection. This confidence in the Christian's power for self-determination elicited the sharp criticism of Augustine of Hippo.

Despite the fact that Augustine maintained the general descriptive scheme of human nature and destiny that had prevailed at least since Justin Martyr, he effected a transformation in the interpretation of key elements. In contrast to Pelagius, Augustine had no confidence in the human capacity to fulfill the Law apart from the work of the Spirit. Even before he encountered the work of Pelagius, Augustine had become convinced of the inability of the will to advance toward the good unless it also loves the good; yet love of the good is not a possibility inherent in the will. It is the gift of God (*Quaest. Simpl.* 1, qu. 2.21–22). In much the same way, Augustine argued against Pelagius that the will, even instructed by the Law, is incapable of obedience. The Holy Spirit must first transform the will so that it loves that which the Law commands and delights in doing it (*Spir. et litt.* 5). Delight, Augustine had come to believe, is not within the self's control but requires external intervention.

Augustine's argument reveals a distinctively different understanding of the capacities of the will from that held by Pelagius and perhaps even from that transmitted through the church's tradition. The freedom of the will was by now an integral component of the church's message, although, unlike Pelagius, most interpreters had tempered their assertions of human autonomy with acknowledgments of the complex and tenacious character of human sinfulness. Augustine agreed that the will is free in that it is subject to no external compulsion, but he was convinced that the will's neutral freedom for either good or evil was lost with Adam. As a result of Adam's choice of evil, the human will has become enslaved to sin and is no longer capable of loving the good and thus is no longer able to choose the good for its own sake (*Corrept.* 32). Volition remains but is governed by pride or by concupiscence, self-serving desire. Apart from the Spirit's gift of love, human choice can never be truly good.

Through grace, however, comes a restoration of the will's love for good and thus of its freedom to do the good. There is a corresponding loss of the will's attraction to and thus free choice of evil. Grace calls, prepares, converts, and upholds the will in the good in such a way

that perseverance is ensured (*Corrept.* 33–35). In this process, the will is never forced. Instead, grace transforms the desires of the will so that good finally becomes the object of unfailing delight. In contrast to Pelagius and ascetic theory generally, Augustine was insisting that progress toward eternal reward cannot be self-generated but is dependent upon the operation of grace.

Pelagianism was the subject of considerable controversy through most of the second decade of the fifth century, particularly in the west. The arguments of Augustine eventually prevailed. A series of North African councils condemned the perceived errors of Pelagian teaching, and in 418 Honorius, the western emperor, and Zosimus, the bishop of Rome, denounced both Pelagius and his follower Caelestius. It was not until 431 at the Council of Ephesus, thus after the death of Augustine, that Pelagian views received the condemnation of the entire church.

After 418, however, Augustine's case for the incapacity of the human will apart from the interior work of grace was recognized as authoritative in the west and no longer open to question. Nevertheless, the implications of his position for a doctrine of predestination remained the subject of heated debate for another century. Augustine's interpretation of the will's freedom for good as a consequence of the action of the Spirit seemed to require a predestined division of persons, some recipients of the work of the Spirit and others not. Augustine himself accepted predestination as an inscrutable mystery according to which God elects certain persons for salvation and allows the rest to continue in their enslavement to sin and its deserved punishment.

To many, a doctrine of predestination served only to introduce a new form of the very determinism against which the church had once so vigorously fought. An invincible judgment of God made in eternity on the basis of incomprehensible criteria would have the effect of setting an inevitable course for an individual's life and destiny. The determinations of the last judgment would merely be the outworking of an eternal, though hidden, divine judgment. Without human freedom, divine justice would be put in doubt. The now centuries-old characterization of the human being as capable of free choice and thus accountable at the last judgment had been retained but the meaning of its elements considerably altered.

The most serious opposition to a doctrine of predestination came from monks in southern Gaul who had been particularly influenced by the ascetic teaching of Origen and Evagrius. These opponents, the most prominent of whom was John Cassian, sought to maintain the possibility of limited autonomy in contrast to what appeared to be a fatalism that stripped moral effort of its significance and automatically excluded some from the possibility of salvation. Cassian agreed wholeheartedly with Augustine's teaching of the necessity of the interior operation of grace in the accomplishment of salvation, but he insisted on the capacity of the will to seek the good prior to the intervention of the Spirit (*Coll.* 13.11–12). The consequences of the fall and the effect of sin on human motivation were not as devastating in the eyes of Cassian as in those of Augustine.

A century later, a modified form of Augustinianism received official ecclesiastical endorsement, at least in the west. In the Synod of Orange (529), led by Caesarius of Arles, the devastating effects of the fall on body and soul of all Adam's descendants were affirmed. Specifically, the will has lost its capacity to turn to God apart from the operation of grace. Baptism does restore the freedom of the will; yet all good is still to be attributed primarily to God and only secondarily, if at all, to the individual. The synod explicitly rejected predestination to evil but was silent on the question of predestination to salvation.

The pronouncements of the synod vindicated Augustine's teaching on the debilitating effects of the fall and the consequent necessity of grace for the operation of a good will but carefully hedged its teaching against the charge of determinism. Although human nature and destiny were still to be characterized by responsibility and accountability, the capacity to exercise that responsibility in such a way as to give a good account at the last judgment was made absolutely dependent upon the work of grace. *See also* Body; Image of God; Immortality; Predestination; Soul; Spirit. [R.H.W.]

Bibliography

Cicero, *On Fate*, tr. H. Rackham, LCL (1960); Pseudo-Plutarch, *On Fate*, tr. P.H. DeLacy, LCL (1959); Alexander of Aphrodisias, *On Fate*, tr. R.W. Sharples (London: Duckworth, 1983).

Justin Martyr, *I Apology*, ANF (1885), Vol. 1; Athenagoras, *The Resurrection of the Dead*, tr. J.H. Crehan, ACW (1956), Vol. 23; Theophilus, *To Autolycus*, ANF (1885), Vol. 2; Irenaeus, *Against Heresies*, ANF (1885), Vol. 1; Origen, *On First Principles*, tr. G.W. Butterworth (London: SPCK, 1936); Gregory of Nyssa, *On Virginity; On the Making of Man; The Great Catechism*, tr. W. Moore and H.A. Wilson, NPNF, 2nd ser. (1893), Vol. 5; idem, *Life of Moses*, tr. A.J. Malherbe and E. Ferguson, CWS (1978); Evagrius Ponticus, *Praktikos* and *Chapters on Prayer*, tr. J.E. Bamberger (Kalamazoo: Cistercian, 1970); Nemesius of Emesa, *On the Nature of Man*, tr. W. Telfer, LCC (1955), Vol. 4; Pelagius, *Letter to Demetrias*, tr. J.P. Burns, *Theological Anthropology* (Philadelphia: Fortress, 1981); Augustine, *To Simplician on Various Questions*, tr. J.H.S. Burleigh, LCC (1953), Vol. 6; idem, *On the Spirit and the Letter; On Nature and Grace; On Rebuke and Grace; On the Predestination of the Saints; On the Gift of Perseverance*, tr. P. Holmes and R.E. Wallis, NPNF, 1st ser. (1887), Vol. 5; John Cassian, *Conference* 13, tr. E.C.S. Gibson, NPNF, 2nd ser. (1894), Vol. 11.

A. Vööbus, "Theological Reflections on Human Nature in Ancient Syrian Traditions," *The Scope of Grace*, ed. P. Hefner (Philadelphia: Fortress, 1964), pp. 101–119; E. Bréhier, *The Hellenistic and Roman Age* (Chicago: U of Chicago P, 1965); P. Brown, *Augustine of Hippo: A Biography* (Berkeley: U of California P, 1967); O. Chadwick, *John Cassian*, 2nd ed. (Cambridge: Cambridge UP, 1968); R.R. Evans, *Pelagius: Inquiries and Reappraisals* (New York: Seabury, 1968); E. TeSelle, *Augustine the Theologian* (London: Burns and Oates, 1970); J. Pelikan, *The Christian Tradition: A History of the Development of Doctrine* (Chicago: U of Chicago P, 1971), Vol. 1: *The Emergence of the Catholic Tradition (100–600)*; W.S. Babcock, "Grace, Freedom, and Justice: Augustine and the Christian Tradition," *Perkins Journal* 27 (1973):1–15; J. Daniélou, *A History of Early Christian Doctrine Before the Council of Nicaea* (London: Darton, Longman and Todd, 1973), Vol. 2: *Gospel Message and Hellenistic Culture*; H.W. Wolff, *Anthropology of the Old Testament* (London: SCM, 1974); J. Daniélou, Introduction to *From Glory to Glory: Texts from Gregory of Nyssa's Mystical Writings* (Crestwood: St. Vladimir's Seminary, 1979); J.P. Burns, *The Development of Augustine's Doctrine of Operative Grace* (Paris: Etudes Augustiniennes, 1980); J.P. Burns, tr. and ed., *Theo-*

logical Anthropology (Philadelphia: Fortress, 1981); N. El-Khoury, "Anthropological Concepts of the School of Antioch," *SP* 17.3 (1982):1359–1365; J.W. Trigg, *Origen: The Bible and Philosophy in the Third Century Church* (Atlanta: John Knox, 1983); P.C. Phan, *Grace and the Human Condition* (Wilmington: Glazier, 1989).

ANTI-MARCIONITE PROLOGUES. Prefaces to Mark, Luke, and John (the comparable prologue to Matthew is lost). Despite the modern designation, recent scholarship has judged that the Anti-Marcionite Prologues were not written against Marcion and did not have a common origin. The prologues, except for Luke, exist only in Latin. The only secure evidence of date is provided by the manuscripts in which they are found, but the prologue to Mark has contacts with second-century traditions. The prologue to Luke is later and provided the source for the longer Monarchian prologue. The prologue to John is late (at least fifth century) and unreliable. *See also* Marcion; Monarchian Prologues. [E.F.]

Bibliography

D. DeBruyne, "Les Plus Anciens Prologues latins des évangiles," *RBén* 40 (1928):193–214; B.W. Bacon, "The Anti-Marcionite Prologue to John," *JBL* 49 (1930):43–54; W.F. Howard, "The Anti-Marcionite Prologues to the Gospels," *Expository Times* 47 (1936):534–538; R.G. Heard, "The Old Gospel Prologues," *JThS* n.s. 6 (1955):1–16; J. Regul, *Die antimarcionistischen Evangelienprologe* (Freiburg: Herder, 1969).

ANTIOCH. City founded on the Orontes River in Syria by Seleucus I in 300 B.C. In the Christian era, Antioch became the third-ranking city of the Mediterranean world, behind only Rome and Alexandria until the rise of Constantinople. Antioch's fame rested partially upon its main street—two miles long with two-storied colonnades on each side, a large hippodrome,

Entrance to St. Peter's Church, a cave that tradition identifies as an early Christian meeting place in Antioch, Turkey.

at least two theaters, and a lovely imperial palace built by Diocletian. Numerous temples and a great octagonal church also served civic needs.

There was considerable strife, on both a cultural and a religious level, among Antioch, Alexandria, and Constantinople over which city was the queen of the east. During the fourth century, Antioch's eloquent preacher, John Chrysostom, was virtually kidnapped and taken to Constantinople, where he became the bishop. In the fifth century, Cyril of Alexandria worked diligently to secure the condemnation of Nestorius, the Antiochene theologian who became bishop of Constantinople.

According to the New Testament, early Palestinian Christians went to Antioch, where they preached to both Jews and Gentiles. Barnabas and Paul worked together there for about a year; the name "Christian" is said to have originated in the city (Acts 11:19–26). Paul's first missionary journey was begun from Antioch, where prophets and teachers in leadership agreed to support the undertaking (Acts 13:1–2). Galatians 1–2 indicates that Jewish and Gentile Christians there had difficulties; indeed, Peter himself disagreed with Paul's views.

Ignatius, bishop of Antioch (d. ca. 115), struggled with Judaizing Christians and Gnostics. Ignatius's epistles present a Christology that emphasizes both Christ's divinity and humanity and contain the strongest evidence for monepiscopacy to come from the subapostolic era.

Antioch attracted many Christian teachers, including Gnostics. Menander worked magic there perhaps in the last decade of the first century. During the second century, Saturninus (Satornilus), a native of Antioch, taught that Jesus only appeared to be human; in reality, he was the divine savior. Basilides, a famous Egyptian Gnostic, and Cerdo, a Syrian Gnostic, may have been in the city early in their careers, but Irenaeus's effort (*Haer.* 1.23–24) to trace these teachers back to Simon Magus is suspect.

The next important bishop was Theophilus. His *To Autolycus*, written ca. 180, relies primarily on Jewish apologetics; it has little specifically Christian content. Yet Theophilus introduced a Trinitarian concept and offered a view of the Christian scriptures as divinely inspired. Contemporary with Theophilus, Tatian, an Assyrian, taught in Antioch and had great success with his Encratite doctrines. Serapion, a bishop near the turn of the third century, thought that any gospel attributed to Peter must be genuine, but upon receiving a copy of the *Gospel of Peter* he banned it because of its Docetic teaching. He also battled against Montanism and Jewish proselytism.

In the third century, Origen visited Antioch at the request of Julia Mamaea, the mother of emperor Alexander Severus. He instructed her and others in the court on the nature of Christianity. No conversions are recorded, but that interest did provide tolerance for the faith. Under Decius, the situation deteriorated. Babylas, bishop of Antioch, died in prison there. In 256, Persians took the metropolis and carried a number of Christians into captivity, among them Demetrianus, the bishop. His successor, Paul of Samosata (260–268), was a high official in the Roman government, a *procurator ducenarius*. He taught that Jesus was a mere man and that the Son was not eternal. A council deposed him, but his political connections—and perhaps his support within the city—were so great that he held on to the church building for many months. Apollinarian forgeries from later centuries insisted that he had used the term *homoousios* ("of the same substance") in a heretical way and thus had tainted the term that was so important to Nicene Christology.

In the fourth century, Antioch became a center for theological controversy. Lucian, a scholar who had edited both the Septuagint and the New Testament text and was a respected martyr (312) in the persecution under Diocletian, was claimed as their founding teacher by Arius and his supporters. Eustathius, bishop of Antioch at the time of the Council of Nicaea in 325, attacked Arius and supported the position that the Son and the Father shared the same divine nature. A council in Antioch in 326, however, deposed Eustathius and brought great disorder to the city. In 350, Aetius, perhaps the most gifted logician of the Arian movement, was ordained a deacon in Antioch, but he was later dismissed from that post.

Paganism was not dead within the city, although it was weakened. In ca. 350, the relics of the martyr Babylas were moved to Daphne, a suburb of Antioch, next to the temple of Apollo and the spring of Castalia. In 362, emperor Julian had the relics removed, and the temple of Apollo was badly burned shortly afterward. Julian disliked Antioch, particularly because it rejected much of its ancient pagan heritage. He could not find many among the populace who would participate in the festivals, but he did have strong and influential pagan friends like the famous rhetorician Libanius. As late as 578, there were trials of practicing pagans in the metropolis.

The important Antiochene school of biblical exegesis and theology developed in the fourth century. It was marked by a more literal interpretation of scripture, probably influenced by Antiochene Judaism and the textual interpretation of Neoplatonists like Iamblichus, and a Christology that emphasized both Christ's humanity and divinity. Diodore of Tarsus (d. ca. 390) was one of its first representatives; Theodore of Mopsuestia (ca. 350–428) its best biblical commentator and theologian; Nestorius (d. ca. 451) its firebrand. John Chrysostom (ca. 347–407), its beloved preacher, represented Antiochene Christology in an orthodox manner. Because Nestorius was condemned in 431 and Theodore in 553, only modern scholarly interest has reclaimed the school's heritage. Yet the formula of union in 433 that presented a Christology agreeable to John of Antioch and to Cyril of Alexandria was fundamental for developing orthodoxy.

In the sixth century, a pillar saint, Symeon the Younger, located on a mountain not far from Antioch. He took his name Symeon from the more famous pillar saint of the previous century. Symeon the Younger's monastic complex was large and his influence was extensive. One of the great ironies of this century, however, was that Severus (ca. 465–538) became bishop of Antioch (512). The city that had seen the greatest theologians of the two-nature

doctrine of Christ was now dominated by the most important Monophysite ("one nature") theologian of the period. Yet perhaps because of his environment Severus often found ways to emphasize the humanity of Jesus.

The Persians sacked the city in 540, burned the suburbs in 573, and took the city again in 611. The Arabs took control in 637–638, but Christianity continued through the medieval period and still exists in modern Antakya.   [F.W.N.]

Bibliography
G. Elderkin, J. Lassus, R. Stillwell, D. Waagé, and F. Waagé, eds., *Antioch on the Orontes*, 5 vols. (Princeton: Princeton UP, 1934–1972); R. Devreesse, *Le Patriarcat d'Antioche, depuis la paix de l'église jusqu'à la conquête arabe* (Paris: Gabalda, 1945); A.J. Festugière, *Antioche païenne et chrétienne* (Paris: Boccard, 1959); G. Downey, *A History of Antioch in Syria from Seleucus to the Arab Conquest* (Princeton: Princeton UP, 1961); J.H.W.G. Liebeschuetz, *Antioch: City and Imperial Administration in the Later Roman Empire* (Oxford: Clarendon, 1972); W.A. Meeks and R.L. Wilken, *Jews and Christians in Antioch in the First Four Centuries of the Common Era* (Missoula: Scholars, 1978); D.S. Wallace-Hadrill, *Christian Antioch: A Study of Early Christian Thought in the East* (Cambridge: Cambridge UP, 1982); R. Brown and J.P. Meier, *Antioch and Rome: New Testament Cradles of Catholic Christianity* (New York: Paulist, 1983); S. Campbell, *The Mosaics of Antioch* (Leiden: Brill, 1988; F.W. Norris, "Antioch-on-the-Orontes as a Religious Center," *ANRW*, forthcoming.

ANTIOCHUS OF PTOLEMAIS (d. ca. 408).
Bishop of Acco in Phoenicia. Antiochus was one of the most bitter opponents of John Chrysostom. His writings are lost except for fragments. CPG II, 4296–4297.   [E.F.]

Bibliography
Socrates, *Church History* 6.11; Sozomen, *Church History* 8.10; Gennadius, *Lives of Illustrious Men* 20; Palladius, *Dialogue*; Theodoret, *Dialogues* 2.

ANTIOCHUS OF SABA (seventh century).
Monk. Antiochus, an eyewitness to the capture of Jerusalem by the forces of Persia (614) and to the sacking of his own nearby monastery of St. Saba, left an extensive collection of moralizing homilies in Greek based on scrip-

ture and the works of the fathers. CPG III, 7842–7844. [M.P.McH.]

Bibliography

Repertorium Fontium Historiae Medii Aevi (Rome: Istituto Storico Italiano per il Medio Evo, 1967), Vol. 2, p. 372.

ANTONINUS PIUS (86–161). Roman emperor (138–161). After rising through a series of public offices, Antoninus was adopted as successor by Hadrian (138); Antoninus in turn adopted Marcus Aurelius and Lucius Verus. As emperor, he showed respect to the position of the senate while extending the tenure of competent officeholders. Much of his effort was directed toward public-service projects in Rome and Italy.

The British frontier was extended, with a rampart, the Wall of Antoninus, constructed (142) to stabilize it. Despite occasional revolts and disturbances, the reign was marked by fiscal responsibility and a sense of well-being throughout the empire.

The era witnessed the development and strengthening of the monarchical episcopate in the church of Rome. It was under Antoninus that Justin Martyr arrived in Rome and founded his school there; his *Apology* is addressed to the emperor. The Gnostics Valentinus and Cerdo were active in the capital. Marcion was excommunicated by the Roman church (144) and went on to found his own religious community.

Antoninus's policy toward the Christians was generally tolerant, although a rescript issued by the emperor to the Council of Asia in their favor (Eusebius, *H.E.* 4.13) is considered a forgery by most scholars. Ptolemaeus and Lucius suffered martyrdom at Rome; it is uncertain whether Polycarp of Smyrna was put to death under Antoninus or subsequently. The temple of Antoninus and Faustina in the Forum was converted to use as a Christian church at a later period. [M.P.McH.]

Bibliography

Aelius Aristides, *To Rome;* Eusebius, *Church History* 4.10–14; 4.18.1–2.

M. Hammond, *The Antonine Monarchy* (Rome: American Academy in Rome, 1959); C. González

Román, "Problemas sociales y política religiosa: A propósito de los rescriptos de Trajano, Adriano y Antonino Pío sobre los cristianos," *MHA* 5 (1981):227–242; P. Keresztes, "Justin, Roman Law and the Logos," *Latomus* 45 (1986):339–346, esp. 344–345.

APELLES (second century). Disciple of Marcion in Rome. Apelles modified his master's dualism and Docetism but was still considered heretical by the church. Rhodo wrote against him. *See also* Marcion. [E.F.]

Bibliography

Eusebius, *Church History* 5.13; Tertullian, *Prescription of Heretics* 30; Pseudo-Tertullian, *Against All Heresies* 19; Hippolytus, *Refutation of All Heresies* 7.26; 10.16; Origen, *Homilies on Genesis* 2.2; idem, *Against Celsus* 5.54; Ambrose, *On Paradise* 5.28f.; 6.30–32; 7.35; 8.38–41; Epiphanius, *Panarion* 44.

A. von Harnack, *Marcion: Das Evangelium vom fremden Gott* (Leipzig: Hinrichs, 1924), pp. 177–196, 404–420; R.M. Grant, *Second Century Christianity: A Collection of Fragments* (London: SPCK, 1946), pp. 84–88.

APHRAATES (Syriac *Aphrahat*) (early fourth century). "The Persian Sage," a Syriac-speaking monk and cleric known for a set of twenty-three essays written between 337 and 345. In some ancient sources, the author of the essays is called Jacob, which may have been a second name taken at conversion or ordination.

The essays, or *Demonstrations,* mainly treat matters of Christian theology and spirituality: faith, love, fasting, prayer, war, monastic life, penitence, resurrection, humility, pastors, treatment of the poor, persecution, death, and the last times. One is a general letter to the bishops, presbyters, and laity of Seleucia-Ctesiphon, written on behalf of a church synod, which suggests that Aphrahat held high ecclesiastical office, perhaps bishop. *Demonstration* 23 is an elaborate chronological tabulation of biblical history.

Several of the *Demonstrations* debate with a real or hypothetical Jewish spokesman about circumcision, Passover, the sabbath, discrimination among foods, divine election of the Gentiles, the Messiah, virginity, and the Jews' expectation that they will be reunited. These reflect extensive contact with Jews and their interpretive traditions. It is noteworthy that Aphrahat displays none of the ill-feeling that marks many of his contemporaries.

Aphrahat, whom legend made head of the monastery of Mar Mattai near Mosul on the Tigris River, displays a purely Semitic form of Christian faith, rather ascetical, substantially orthodox, but untouched by the theological controversies of the Greek and Latin churches. His foundation is scripture, interpreted in a literal, historical manner. He cites the Bible over 1,000 times, usually from the Peshitta text. *See also* Persia; Syria, Syriac.   [R.J.O.]

Bibliography
W. Wright, ed., *The Homilies of Aphraates, the Persian Sage* (London: Williams and Norgate, 1869), Vol. 1: *The Syriac Text* (Vol. 2 was never published); I. Parisot, "Aphraatis sapientis persae, Demonstrationes," *Patrologia Syriaca*, ed. R. Graffin (Paris: Firmin-Didot, 1894–1907), Vols. 1, 2 (includes Latin translation).

J. Gwynn, "Selections Translated into English from the Hymns and Homilies of Ephraim the Syrian and from the Demonstrations of Aphrahat the Persian Sage," NPNF, 2nd ser. (1898), Vol. 13.2, pp. 115–433 (intro. and tr. of *Demonstrations* 1; 5; 6; 8; 10; 17; 21; 22); J. Neusner, *Aphrahat and Judaism* (Leiden: Brill, 1971) (tr. all or part of *Demonstrations* 11–13; 15–19; 21; 22). A complete English translation by R.J. Owens and R. Murray is in preparation.

APHTHARTODOCETAE. Sixth-century Monophysite sect. The leader of the Aphthartodocetae, Julian, bishop of Halicarnassus, taught that Christ's body was always incorruptible. The Monophysite leader Severus of Antioch, on the other hand, insisted that it was incorruptible only after the resurrection.

[F.W.N.]

APOCALYPSE OF PETER. Christian apocalypse from the mid-second century. The complete text of the *Apocalypse of Peter* is known from an Ethiopic translation; about one-half is known from Greek fragments. The work was accepted as canonical by Clement of Alexandria (in Eusebius, *H.E.* 6.14.1) and the Mura-

torian Canon but was thereafter rejected. In the work, Jesus describes to Peter and the disciples the gruesome punishments of the wicked in hell and, more briefly, the joys of the righteous in heaven. The motifs influenced later writings all the way to Dante. Two other compostions bear the same name: one in the Nag Hammadi Library (Codex VII, 3) and an Arabic text (ed. and tr. A. Mingana in *Woodbrooke Studies* 3.2 [Cambridge: Cambridge UP, 1931]). TLG 1159.   [E.F.]

Bibliography
Muratorian Canon 71–73; Clement of Alexandria, *Eclogues* 41; 48–49; Eusebius, *Church History* 3.3.2; 6.14.1; Methodius, *Symposium* 2.6; Sozomen, *Church History* 7.19; Macarius Magnes, *Apocritica* 4.6.16; 4.7.

M.R. James, *The Apocryphal New Testament* (Oxford: Clarendon, 1924), pp. 505–521; NTA, Vol. 2, pp. 663–683.

D.D. Buchholz, *Your Eyes Will Be Opened: A Study of the Greek (Ethiopic) Apocalypse of Peter* (Atlanta: Scholars, 1988).

APOCALYPSE OF STEPHEN. Otherwise-unknown work condemned in the *Decretum Gelasianum*, a sixth-century list of canonical and apocryphal books.   [D.M.S.]

APOCALYPSE OF THOMAS. Christian apocalyptic work (ca. 400). The *Apocalypse of Thomas* describes the events of the end times in a seven-day sequence. Since it reflects Manichaean and Priscillianist tendencies, it was condemned in the sixth-century *Decretum Gelasianum*. The work is known in a few Latin manuscripts and in an Old English sermon.

[D.M.S.]

Bibliography
M.R. James, *The Apocryphal New Testament* (Oxford: Clarendon, 1924), pp. 555–562; NTA, Vol. 2, pp. 798–803.

APOCALYPTIC LITERATURE. Apocalyptic literature takes its name from the Book of Revelation (or Apocalypse of John) in the New Testament. "Apocalypse" became a recognized genre in the Christian era, but several pre-Christian Jewish works are now recognized as pertaining to the same genre. An apocalypse may be defined as "a genre of revelatory literature with a narrative framework, in which a revelation is mediated by an otherworldly being to a human recipient, disclosing a transcendent reality that is both temporal, insofar as it envisages eschatological salvation, and spatial, insofar as it involves another supernatural world" (J.J. Collins, 1979). The adjective "apocalyptic" is often used loosely to refer to material that resembles the apocalypses in some significant respect.

The corpus of Jewish apocalypses is found primarily in the Pseudepigrapha: *1 Enoch, 2 Enoch, 2 Baruch, 3 Baruch, 4 Ezra, Apocalypse of Abraham* (*Jubilees* and *Testament of Abraham* are borderline cases). These books were composed between the late third century B.C. and the early second century A.D. They were not preserved in rabbinic Judaism but survived in various Christian churches in translations: Ethiopic (*1 Enoch*), Slavonic (*2 Enoch, Apocalypse of Abraham*), Syriac (*2 Baruch*), Greek (*3 Baruch, Testament of Abraham*), or Latin (*4 Ezra*). This was also true of related works like the *Testament of Moses* (Latin) and the *Testaments of the Twelve Patriarchs* (which may in part have been composed in Greek). The Aramaic original of parts of *1 Enoch* has recently been discovered among the Dead Sea Scrolls. The Qumran community that preserved the scrolls was heavily influenced by apocalyptic traditions, as can be seen from such compositions as *The Scroll of the War of the Sons of Light Against the Sons of Darkness*.

Only one full-fledged apocalypse, the Book of Daniel, was accepted into the Hebrew canon. Modern critical scholarship regards Daniel, like the other Jewish apocalypses, as a pseudepigraph, that is, a work attributed to a famous ancient person who was not its actual author. The visions in Daniel 7–12 are thought to have been written about the time of the Maccabean revolt (168–164 B.C.), but the tales in Daniel 1–6 are older, traditional narratives. Daniel, then, despite its canonical status, was not the first apocalypse, as several sections of *1 Enoch* are now known to be older.

Daniel 7–12 is a representative of one type of apocalypse, which may be called the "his-torical" type. Daniel receives his revelation in a dream-vision, in mysterious form: he sees beasts rising from the sea and a figure riding on clouds. This vision, explained to him by an angel, relates to the foreign overlords of the Jews and their impending judgment. The course of history is predetermined; there are four pagan kingdoms, and seventy weeks of years. At the end, the faithful Jews will triumph through the power of the archangel Michael. The final judgment will involve not only the restoration of Israel but also the resurrection of the individual dead for reward and punishment. A similar perspective on history is found in *4 Ezra, 2 Baruch*, and some sections of *1 Enoch*. Elements of this perspective are found already in some postexilic prophetic works in the Old Testament, notably Ezekiel 38–39 and the so-called "Apocalypse of Isaiah" (Isa. 24–27).

A different type of apocalypse is found in some of the Enoch literature, in which the visionary is taken up and guided through the heavenly world. Typically, he is shown the places of reward and punishment of the dead, the place of the coming judgment, the various ranks of angels, and ultimately the throne of God. This type of apocalypse is found in *1 Enoch* 1–36, *2 Enoch*, and *3 Baruch*. It represents an early stage of the Jewish mystical tradition.

The Book of Revelation in the New Testament is clearly in the tradition of Daniel, from which it derives much of its imagery. It is not, however, a pseudepigraph—John of Patmos was the actual author. Christ takes the place of Michael as the heavenly deliverer. This is the only full-fledged apocalypse in the New Testament. There are, however, other passages that have a strongly apocalyptic character, notably Mark 13 and parallels, which prophesy the coming of the Son of Man on the clouds (an allusion to Daniel 7, except that now the Son of Man should be identified as Christ rather than Michael).

The apocalyptic genre continued to flourish in Christianity after the New Testament period. The *Shepherd* of Hermas, like Revelation, is not a pseudepigraph, but the convention of pseudepigraphy reappears in the second century and later with apocalypses ascribed to

Peter, Paul, John, Mary, and others. Christians also adapted older Jewish apocalypses, such as *Ascension of Isaiah* and *2 Esdras.* The motif of the heavenly journey is especially prominent in the Christian apocalypses. The genre was also adapted in Gnosticism.

The function of apocalyptic literature is usually understood on the model of the Book of Daniel, which was written in a time of persecution, to give hope and comfort to the oppressed. The Book of Revelation, too, reflects a situation of oppression, although it now appears that it was not written during an intense persecution. Apocalypses are usually regarded as crisis literature. The crises, however, may have varied in kind and intensity. In some cases, the crisis may have been a general sense of alienation in a world dominated by pagan powers. In at least one case, *Testament of Abraham,* the crisis is the universal human crisis of death. What is common to the apocalypses is a search for salvation beyond this world, in a new creation or new Jerusalem and in a life free from death. This hope for transcendent salvation was crucial for the origin of Christianity, as it paved the way for the Christian belief in the resurrection of Jesus.   [J.J.C.]

Bibliography

J.H. Charlesworth, ed., *The Old Testament Pseudepigrapha* (Garden City: Doubleday, 1983), Vol. 1.

J.J. Collins, "Towards the Morphology of a Genre," and A.Y. Collins, "The Early Christian Apocalypses," *Semeia* 14 (1979), pp. 1–20, 61–121; C. Rowland, *The Open Heaven: A Study of Apocalyptic in Judaism and Christianity* (New York: Crossroad, 1982); J.J. Collins, *The Apocalyptic Imagination: An Introduction to the Jewish Matrix of Christianity* (New York: Crossroad, 1984); A.Y. Collins, ed., *Early Christian Apocalypticism: Genre and Social Setting, Semeia* 36 (Atlanta: Scholars, 1986); J.H. Charlesworth and J.R. Mueller, *The New Testament Apocrypha and Pseudepigrapha: A Guide to Publications, with Excursuses on Apocalypses* (Metuchen: Scarecrow, 1987).

APOCRYPHA, NEW TESTAMENT. *Apocrypha,* from earliest Greek, meant literally "hidden things." The term applies properly to the noncanonical books of the Old Testament. Already in antiquity, it could be extended equally to "unknown authorship" or "secretive usage." Measured against "recognized books," "apocrypha" took on successive implications of "dubious" or "illegitimate"; against "canonical," it took on the fully pejorative meaning "fabrications of heretics" (Eusebius, *H.E.* 3.25).

New Testament Apocrypha, in contrast to those of the Old Testament, is not a specific category. The problem has been what literature to include. Beginning with the *Muratorian Canon,* the most ancient lists of what constituted scripture as well as what lay outside have undergone variable development. With the *Decretum Gelasianum* (ca. 600), the list had begun to proscribe as "apocrypha" work of various patristic authors. It was not uncommon into the twentieth century to include the works of the apostolic fathers in printed translations of "New Testament Apocrypha." Yet for practical reasons, and under the impact of papyrological discoveries, such as the Nag Hammadi Library, whatever can better be treated elsewhere has to be excluded from this discussion of apocrypha. The larger interrelationships among the noncanonical works, however, ought not to be neglected.

Several difficulties make definition and classification problematic. The line between apocryphal New Testament and canonical New Testament was not at first clearly drawn. The increasing restrictions upon the former's being read "in church" precluded frequency of copy. Unavailability made some "apocryphal" books appear more esoteric than they actually are. Theological considerations of "normative orthodoxy" overwhelmed historical considerations of what may have been early. A distinction between "apocryphal" and "canonical" lies in a commitment to one variation within a larger variety of beliefs, or to a choice among historical possibilities. Yet the devotional and aesthetic capacities of "infancy accounts" and "martyrological narratives" continued to function dynamically within liturgy, church structure (both building and polity), and even creedal formulation at the same time that these literary materials were being suppressed. The suppression of what once had been, or even continued to be, influential upon some locations or aspects of variant Christian life, belief, or practice merely spawned newer examples in other places, east and west, and in different languages—Latin, Syriac, Coptic, Arabic, Ethiopic, Armenian.

Since other texts were not subject to the same stabilizing process at work in the canonical New Testament, the stream of any given "apocryphal tradition" could flow creatively: witness the "infancy accounts" associated with Thomas. What have been described as "modern forgeries" show that creative flow has not yet ceased, although such materials are not reckoned among the apocryphal New Testament.

The bias toward "canonical" goes so far that the total literature is fitted into the categories of "gospels," "acts," "epistles," or "apocalypses." Realistically, if these categories must be used, combinations would often better serve the specific example: the *Apocalypse of Peter* is a "teaching gospel" not unlike the "Little Apocalypse" of the Synoptics except now of the "Risen Christ."

Formally, only "epistle" is a real literary category, itself divisible into "model" and "actual" letters. Little remains of "apocryphal" correspondence: that of "the church at Corinth with Paul" (more frequently preserved with the *Acts of Paul*), that of "Abgar (of Edessa) with Jesus" (otherwise known within Eusebius, *H.E.* 1.13), that of "Paul and Seneca," and the *Epistle to Laodicea*. "Gospels" divide into stories, teachings, conversations, interrogations, and monologues, or some combination. They involve movements both "earthly" and "heavenly," before or after "the resurrection," in specific settings or of no apparent time and place. "Acts," or "histories," frequently fit into the Greco-Roman categories of "romances" or "lives," providing narrative or discourse set amidst quiescent or adventuresome contexts. Much is hagiographic, illustrating the history of Christian expansion less often than of ascetic or liturgical developments. "Apocalypses," implying "revelations," but cast commonly into the form of "itineraries," "heavenly" rather than geographic, blur formally with both "gospels" and "acts." The long-known "infancy gospel"

called since 1552 *Protevangelium of James* is entitled in the Bodmer papyrus codex "Genesis of Mary, Apocalypse to Jacob (James)."

Another category, not typically distinguished but very much in the scriptural tradition, is that of "hymns" (poems). Examples scattered through "apocryphal acts," or on papyri leaves as well as ostraca, some used like "creedal fragments" as amulets for the living or the dead, demonstrate their importance. A similar category is that of "prayer."

On another level of classification, the distinction could be "subject" rather than "form": Jesus, disciples and apostles, theological or ecclesiastical concerns. Those works related to Jesus show a further division, between "infancy" and "postresurrection" portraits; but no complete work illustrates the precrucifixion Teacher, at whom only the fragmentary Egerton "Unknown Gospel" temptingly hints. Oxyrhynchus fragments of "Sayings of Jesus" have proved to be a Greek version of the Coptic *Gospel of (Judas) Thomas* found at Nag Hammadi, wherein the discourse is with the "(ever-)living Jesus." The *Epistula Apostolorum* is a postresurrection "dialogue between Christ and his disciples" represented as a testamentary letter sent from "the Eleven" "to the Catholics of the four directions of the earth." "Subject" is as illusive as "form."

The view that the New Testament Apocrypha are illustrative of the "unlearned" or the "gnostic" mind only has been detrimental to its study. Linguistically, the apocryphal New Testament and the canonical New Testament belonged to the same larger world. Any "apocalypse" involving revelational "itineraries" cannot avoid comparison with episodes in Greek "magical" papyri: for example, *Apocalypse of Paul* with PGM I no. 4, lines 475–725, the "Mithras liturgy." This world ranges in intellectual capacities and achievements, as well as thought-processes, throughout the variety of participants and spectrum of human minds.

Were there exhaustive lexicons and concordances, grammars and syntaxes, for each separate entry that might be considered for inclusion within "Apocrypha, New Testament," they would help not merely to define form and intention of each work but also to reveal from the stockpile of particular vocabulary within each at what temporal boundaries the work is actually viable. This lack becomes even more acute in those instances for which versions in a wide variety of languages survived or have been recovered. The *Acts of Thomas* consists of examples in seven languages, of which Syriac is the probable original; but its "edition" is made even more complicated by translations back into Greek from languages translated from Greek. For many New Testament Apocrypha, the desideratum remains a critical edition.

"Apocryphal" materials are as well documented from the earliest known papyri as are "canonical." As papyri codices that include more than a single work are discovered, earliest collections show a randomness that cuts across the lines so conveniently erected between "apocryphal Old Testament," "pseudepigraphal Old Testament," "canonical New Testament," "apocryphal New Testament," "apostolic fathers," and even miscellaneous "classical" works. One codex in Greek of the third century (P. Bodmer V, VII–XIII, XX) contained in intentional numbered sequence the *Protevangelium*, the "correspondence of the Corinthian church with Paul," the eleventh *Ode of Solomon*, the Epistle of Jude, Melito's *Homily on the Passover*, a liturgical fragment, the *Apology* of Phileas, Psalms 33 and 34, and the epistles of Peter (constituting thereby the oldest known manuscript for three "Catholic" epistles). Other mixes become even more evident as time passes, with all kinds of preferences depending on whom or what is being "read." The Syriac *Acts of Philip* were included in a potpourri of eleven other kinds of treatises, including a *History of the Blessed Virgin*. Many motives may have been at work for what appear to be random collections.

Much of the remaining evidence is fragmentary. When we have only testimonia or incomplete texts, it is not really clear that we may rely on the accuracy of the former or the source of the latter. Papyrus evidence shows instead how "floating" some materials were. Considering the relative unreliability of the early patristic authors for the exact wording of "canonical" scripture, it is no wonder that so little correlation of testimonia, fragments, or titles with known texts can be ensured. The *Gospel of the Hebrews* or *Nazarenes* or *Ebionites* is a prime case in point. It remains equally difficult to identify the boundaries where "Agrapha" ceases and "Gospels," "apocryphal" or "canonical," begin.

These considerations point to the magnitude of the problems inherent in an amorphous, noncoherent corpus of "other early Christian literature," called collectively, for want of any other designation, "Apocrypha, New Testament." *See also* Acts of Paul; Acts of Peter; Acts of John; Agrapha; Apocalypse of Peter; Apocrypha, Old Testament; Canon; Epistle of Apostles; Gospel of Peter; Gospel of Thomas; Protevangelium of James.   [C.C.S.]

Bibliography

C. Tischendorf, *Evangelia Apocrypha*, 2nd ed. F. Wilbrandt (Leipzig: Mendelssohn, 1876); W. Wright, *Apocryphal Acts of the Apostles*, 2 vols. in 1 (1871; repr. Amsterdam: Philo, 1968); R.A. Lipsius and M. Bonnet, *Acta Apostolorum Apocrypha*, 2 vols. in 3 (Leipzig: Mendelssohn, 1891–1903); C. Tischendorf, *Apocalypses Apocryphae* (Leipzig: Mendelssohn, 1866); *Corpus Christianorum, Series Apocryphorum* (Turnhout: Brepols, 1983–).

M.R. James, *The Apocryphal New Testament* (Oxford: Clarendon, 1924); *NTA*, 2 vols.

A. Oepke and R. Meyer, "Kruptē," *Theological Dictionary of the New Testament* (Grand Rapids: Eerdmans, 1965 [orig. German ed., 1938]), Vol. 3, pp. 957–1000. S.E. Johnson, "Stray Pieces of Early Christian Writing," *Journal of Near Eastern Studies* 5 (1946):40–54; Quasten, Vol. 1, pp. 106–175; E.J. Goodspeed, *A History of Early Christian Literature*, rev. and enl. R.M. Grant (Chicago: U of Chicago P, 1966); J. Finegan, *Hidden Records of the Life of Jesus* (Philadelphia: Pilgrim, 1969); H. Koester, "Apocryphal and Canonical Gospels," *HThR* 73 (1980):105–130; idem, *Introduction to the New Testament* (Philadelphia: Fortress, 1982), Vol. 2: *History and Literature of Early Christianity*; J.D. Crossan, *Four Other Gospels: Shadows on the Contours of Canon* (Minneapolis: Winston, 1985); D. Wenham, ed., *Gospel Perspectives*, (Sheffield: JSOT, 1985), Vol. 5: *The Jesus Tradition Outside the Gospels*; J.H. Charlesworth and J.R. Mueller, *The New Testament Apocrypha and Pseudepigrapha: A Guide to Publications, with Excurses on Apocalypses* (Metuchen: Scarecrow, 1987).

APOCRYPHA, OLD TESTAMENT. *Apocrypha* (Greek, "hidden things") conventionally refers to those books that are included in the Old Testament of the Latin Vulgate but not in the Hebrew Bible: 1 and 2 Esdras, Tobit, Judith, Additions to Esther, Wisdom of Solomon, Ecclesiasticus (Ben Sira or Sirach), Baruch, Letter of Jeremiah, Prayers of Azariah and the Three Young Men, Susanna, Bel and the Dragon, Prayer of Manasseh, and 1 and 2 Maccabees. The latest edition of the Oxford Annotated Apocrypha includes also *3* and *4 Maccabees* and *Psalm 151*, which are found in some manuscripts of the Greek Bible.

2 Esdras (*4 Ezra*) 14:45–56 already distinguishes between twenty-four books that were to be made public and seventy that were to be restricted to the wise. Rabbinic literature distinguished three categories: books that defile the hands (canonical scriptures), books hidden away (*ganaz*) or withdrawn from circulation but that were still honored, and "outside books" (*separîm hîsônîm*) that were forbidden. When Origen refers to Jewish apocrypha, he presumably refers to the second category (*Ep.* 1.13). Sirach apparently fell in this category and may even have been regarded as canonical by some rabbis. It is not clear that there ever was an official Jewish collection of apocrypha.

The Greek-speaking Christian church accepted a larger collection of Jewish writings as authoritative than was included in the Hebrew canon. Alexandrian Judaism was formerly thought to have had a larger canon, but this idea has been discredited. It is disputed whether the canon of Alexandria extended beyond the Prophets or whether the list of Holy Writings was fixed in the first century. In any case, there was uncertainty in second-century Christianity as to which Old Testament books were canonical. The list of Melito of Sardis (Eusebius, *H.E.* 4.26.14) lacked the book of Esther. Tertullian argued for the inclusion of *1 Enoch* (*Cult. fem.* 1.3). The most widely accepted books were Wisdom of Solomon, Sirach, and Tobit; the additions to Daniel and Esther were accepted as part of those books, and Baruch was often cited as part of Jeremiah.

Jerome, in the Vulgate, distinguished those books that were not found in the Hebrew by comments in his prefaces but included the translations of some (see his comments in his *Preface to Samuel and Kings* and *Preface to Proverbs, Ecclesiastes,* and *Song of Solomon*). Gradually, the prefaces were ignored and all books of the Vulgate were recognized as scripture. This situation persisted until the Reformation. The Reformers acknowledged the utility of the Apocrypha but denied that they could be used to establish doctrine. The Council of Trent reacted by affirming the canonicity of the apocryphal books, with the exceptions of 1 and 2 Esdras and the Prayer of Manasseh, which were less firmly supported by tradition. Catholics often refer to the disputed books as "deuterocanonical," implying that they were written later than the protocanonical books. The Apocrypha were still included in the King James Version of 1611 but were often omitted in subsequent printings.

The Greek Orthodox Church accepts the full Catholic canon and in addition 1 Esdras, *Psalm 151*, Prayer of Manasseh, and *3 Maccabees*, with *4 Maccabees* in an appendix. The Russian Orthodox Church accepts 1 and 2 Esdras, *Psalm 151*, and *3 Maccabees*.

The books of the Apocrypha can be divided into two broad categories, narrative and discursive. The narrative books include works of historiography, historical fiction, and an apocalypse. 1 and 2 Maccabees may be classified as historiography. These books have their tendentious aspects and, in the case of 2 Maccabees, elements of fantasy, but they are constrained by the records and recollections of the early Maccabean period. Other historylike books observe no such constraints. Judith is set in the context of a fictional campaign in the reign of Nebuchadnezzar but mistakenly assumes that this was after the exile. Even the scene of the action, Bethulia, is fictional. The story of Darius's bodyguards in 1 Esdras 3:1–4:63 is a court tale of the same general type as the biblical stories of Joseph and Daniel. Bel and the Dragon is likewise set in a royal court but is dominated by polemic against idolatry, which was only a minor theme in Daniel 1–6. Susanna stands apart from the other Daniel stories and presents Daniel as a judge who exhibits Solomonic wisdom. His role as judge probably derives from a pun on the Hebrew meaning of *dan*. Tobit is a folktale, and it is significant that Tobit is said to be the uncle of Ahikar, hero of a widespread Near Eastern tale. *3 Maccabees* differs from most of these stories by the fact that it is set in Egypt. The story may be based on partial recollection of some historical episodes, but it is essentially a work of fantasy, reminiscent of Esther in its genre. Finally, there is the great apocalypse of *4 Ezra* (2 Esdras 3–14; 1–2 and 15–16 are made up of Christian oracles). Although the apocalypse climaxes in the eschatological visions, the work is held together by a narrative thread that relates the transformation of Ezra from skeptic to believer.

The discursive works include sapiential and hortatory writings and prayers. Sirach and Wisdom of Solomon were the most widely accepted of all the Apocrypha. Ben Sira (or Sirach) is on the whole a book of traditional proverbial literature, although it explicitly identifies wisdom with the Law (24.23). Wisdom of Solomon is quite different in character. It is noteworthy for its attempt to combine Greek philosophy with Jewish wisdom and its acceptance of the immortality of the soul. *4 Maccabees* is another Hellenistic work, which attempts to argue that obedience to the Law is in accordance with reason. It is a rhetorical piece rather than a coherent philosophical argument. Another hymn to wisdom is found in Baruch 3.9–4.4, which again identifies wisdom with the Law. A less sophisticated kind of argument is found in the Letter of Jeremiah, which is simply an attack on idolatry.

The additions to Esther and Daniel testify to the tendency of Hellenistic Jewish scribes to enhance the works they copied by inserting prayers. One of the Danielic insertions, the Prayer of Azariah, belongs to a widespread type of communal confession, based on Deuteronomic theology. Other examples are found in Nehemiah 9, Daniel 9, Baruch 1:15–3:8. A similar pattern is found in the independent Prayer of Manasseh, an individual prayer of repentance. Other apocryphal psalms are the exhortation to Zion in Baruch 4:5–5:9 and the reflection on David's career in *Psalm 151*. Other prayers are scattered throughout the books of the Apocrypha.

The Apocrypha represent only a selection of Jewish writings from the turn of the era. Remarkably few works of eschatological orientation are included: only one apocalypse (2 Esdras), no *Sibylline Oracles*, and testaments appearing only within larger narratives (in 1 Macc. 2 and Tobit 14). Yet the Apocrypha provide a salutary reminder that the canon was selected from a larger corpus of literature and that the line between canonical and noncanonical has often wavered. *See also* Apocrypha, New Testament. [J.J.C.]

Bibliography

B. Metzger, ed., *The Oxford Annotated Apocrypha*, expanded ed. (New York: Oxford UP, 1977).

G.W. Nickelsburg, *Jewish Literature Between the Bible and the Mishnah* (Philadelphia: Fortress, 1981); M.E. Stone, ed., *Jewish Writings of the Second Temple Period* (Philadelphia: Fortress, 1984).

APOKATASTASIS. Doctrine of universal salvation. The Greek word *apokatastasis* means primarily "restoration" or "reestablishment." In Hellenistic astronomy, the term referred to the return of the stars to the same place in the heavens and, especially according to the Stoics, to the periodic return of all constellations to their original place at the end of the cosmic cycle.

In the New Testament, the word is found only in Acts 3:21, where it refers to the fulfillment of God's promises in Jesus Christ. The verb *apokathistēmi* and the noun *apokatastasis* are often used in early Christian literature to express the restoration of the human condition to its divinely intended original state, and especially the glorious resurrection of the body.

In patristic thought, *apokatastasis* is often employed in a technical sense to refer to Origen's more or less firm hope of the restoration of all rational creatures to their original state of communion with God. The view that divine providence will eventually reduce all fallen minds, even those who became the devil and his angels, to their original union is clearly expressed in several texts of *On First Principles*. Since, according to Origen, God would bring this about without the violation of the freedom of his creatures, such a return may require indefinitely long periods of time. On the other hand, given Origen's conception of the original state, its restoration does not exclude a repeated falling away of rational creatures from God, which would imply the possibility of indefinite cycles of fall and return. Whereas these affirmations may appear as a definitive part of Origen's systematic thought, they do not belong to his rule of faith but rather are elements of his speculative synthesis. Furthermore, in a letter to his friends in Alexandria, he explicitly rejects the salvation of the devil. As H. Crouzel remarks, "The Origenian doctrine of *apokatastasis* is neither as simple nor as firm as that to which it was reduced by later Origenists and the controversies surrounding them."

In the fourth century, Gregory of Nyssa repeatedly expressed in his works the hope of a universal salvation of rational creatures, including even the devil and his angels. His notion of salvation, however, definitively excludes the possibility of a new fall. Traces of the same hope of universal salvation are found in several eastern fathers and also in some fathers of the west, such as Ambrose, who was heavily influenced by Origen and the Cappadocians. The doctrine of a necessary universal salvation was explicitly condemned in the course of the Origenistic controversies in the fifth and sixth centuries, especially at the Fifth Ecumenical Council in Constantinople (553). *See also* Eschatology; Hell. [D.L.B.]

Bibliography

Origen, *On First Principles* 1.6.3; 2.3; 3.5.6–6.6; Rufinus, *The Adulteration of the Works of Origen* 7; Jerome, *Apology Against Rufinus* 2.18 (for Origen's letter to his friends in Alexandria); Gregory of Nyssa, *On the Soul and the Resurrection* (PG 46.69C, 71A–72B); idem, *Catechetical Oration* 26; idem, *Life of Moses* 2.82; Ambrose, *On the Christian Faith* 5.150–179.

J. Daniélou, "L'Apocatastase chez saint Grégoire de Nysse," *RSR* 30 (1940):328–347; C. Lenz, "Apokatastasis," RLAC (1950), Vol. 1, pp. 510–516; J. Daniélou, *L'Être et le temps chez Grégoire de Nysse* (Leiden: Brill, 1970), Ch. 10; G. May, "Eschatologie V. Alte Kirche," TRE, Vol. 10, pp. 299–305; H. Crouzel, "L'Apocatastase chez Origène," *Origeniana Quarta: Die Referate des 4. Internationalen Origeneskongresses (Innsbruck, 2.–6. September 1985)*, ed. L. Lies (Innsbruck: Tyrolia, 1987), pp. 282–290.

APOLLINARIS OF HIERAPOLIS (second century).

Bishop of Hierapolis in Phrygia during the reign of Marcus Aurelius (161–180). Claudius Apollinari(u)s wrote various apologetical works, including one addressed to the emperor. He wrote also against the Montanists and on the Pasch. His involvement in the principal ecclesiastical problems of his day makes regrettable the loss of his writings. Feast day January 8. CPG I, 1103. TLG 1163. [E.F.]

Bibliography

Eusebius, *Church History* 4.21; 4.26.1; 4.27; 5.5.4; 5.16.1; 5.18.12–14; Jerome, *Letter 70 to Magnus* 4; Photius, *Library* 14.

APOLLINARIS OF LAODICEA (ca. 315–392).

Bishop and writer. Apollinaris's father (of the same name) was a native of Alexandria. As a priest and rhetor, Apollinaris the Elder taught grammar in Beirut before settling down in Laodicea. His son, born in Laodicea, became a lector in his local church. In 346, both of them welcomed in their home Athanasius, the bishop of Alexandria, on his return from an exile in the western part of the Roman empire. They were excommunicated by George, then bishop of Laodicea, who was committed to the Arian faith. When George lost his see at the Synod of Constantinople (360), his replacement was Pelagius, a member of the so-called Homoean party led by bishop Acacius of Caesarea. In their pro-Nicene opposition to Arianism, the two Apollinarises held strongly to their links with Athanasius. After the son replaced his father as the head of the Nicene community in Laodicea, he persistently claimed to be a true disciple of Athanasius. In the nearby Syrian metropolis of Antioch, Apollinaris sided with the conservative Nicene bishop Paulinus, himself in conflict with the moderate Nicaean Melitius. Along with delegates supporting both of them, Apollinaris sent his own monks to represent him at the pro-Nicene synod of union organized by Athanasius in Alexandria (362). The Christological divergences between the different delegations are witnessed by the synodal *Letter to the Antiochenes* 7, as transmitted under the name of

Athanasius, a document that for the first time briefly discusses the notion of God's incarnation later denominated as Apollinarianism.

The emperor Julian was at that time withdrawing Christians from the teaching of the classics. The two Apollinarises, in a final mutual undertaking, reacted with professional skill: the father composed poems inspired by the Old Testament in Homeric hexameters; the son wrote gospel dialogues in a style proper to contemporary rhetors.

In 363, Apollinaris, like the other pro-Nicene bishops in the area, delivered a personal statement about his form of orthodoxy to Julian's successor, the ephemeral Jovian. Whereas the elderly Athanasius added only a short comment to the Nicene formula of faith, the young Apollinaris wrote a genuine essay, containing already the main theses of his future heresy. The latter was censured for the first time as late as 377, in Rome, by the synod of the bishop Damasus I. A year earlier, Apollinaris had ordained his disciple Vitalis as a bishop in Antioch (in opposition to the moderate pro-Nicene administration of bishop Melitius). Damasus, counseled by Basil of Caesarea, had vainly attempted to reach an agreement that would have united Christian factions in the Syrian metropolis. The Roman censure was repeated by a synod in Antioch (379) and confirmed in the first canon of the imperial Synod of Constantinople (381). Apollinaris himself was not mentioned, but his disciples held their own synods and established a separate hierarchy in different churches. Gregory of Nyssa in Cappadocia first recognized the significance of the Apollinarian doctrine only in 382 on a trip to Jerusalem. He then wrote a refutation, the *Antirrheticus*, without ever having met Apollinaris. In 387, Gregory of Nazianzus asked the emperor Theodosius to protect him against the pressure of the Apollinarians as Theophilus of Alexandria had done in 385 or 386. The imperial administration issued anti-Apollinarian decrees from 388 on. Apollinaris died in 392; his followers in Antioch were reconciled with the Catholic church in 425. In other eastern churches, Apollinarianism kept a foot in the door for a few decades longer.

Many writings of the sect survived, through pseudonymity. They all focus on the theological formulation of the Christological dogma. Other apologetic works, like Apollinaris's lengthy treatise against Porphyry in thirty books and his pamphlet against Julian and Greek philosophers, seem to be lost. A numerous collection of quotations from Apollinarian exegesis are preserved, thanks to catenae. They still witness the scholarly gifts of Apollinaris as a commentator on scripture, in particular on Ecclesiastes, Isaiah, Hosea, Malachi, Psalms, Matthew, 1 Corinthians, Galatians, and Ephesians, according to references used by Jerome, who had been a student of Apollinaris. Other extracts are known and are partly available in critical editions, from commentaries on Proverbs, Song of Solomon, Isaiah, Ezekiel, Daniel, Luke, Romans, and James.

Apollinarianism is best summarized by the phrase "One nature of the Logos made flesh." Cyril of Alexandria took it as written by Athanasius, a blunder made possible by the fact that Athanasius also spoke of the "hypostasis," or the "person," of the divine Logos in terms of nature. In Apollinaris's view, the essential unity of the Logos with the Father served as a pattern for the Logos made flesh: his flesh could have no substantial reality outside his own divine nature, just as this nature could not make any sense out of the Father. Apollinaris concluded that there could be no human subject in Christ. After the imperial synods of Ephesus (431) and Chalcedon (451), his ideas survived only in the Monophysite churches. CPG II, 3645–3700. *See also* Christ, Christology.

[C.K.]

Bibliography

Pseudo-Athanasius, *De incarnatione contra Apollinarem*; Basil, *Letter* 263.4; Gregory of Nazianzus, *Letters* 101; 102; 202; Gregory of Nyssa, *Antirrheticus adversus Apollinarem*; Epiphanius, *Panarion* 77; Theodoret, *Fabulae haereticarum* 4.8; 5.9.

E. Raven, *Apollinarianism: An Essay on the Christology of the Early Church* (Cambridge: Cambridge UP, 1923); E. Muehlenberg, *Apollinaris von Laodicea* (Göttingen: Vandenhoeck & Ruprecht, 1969); E. Cattaneo, *Trois Homélies pseudo-Chrysostomiennes sur la Pâque comme oeuvre d'Apollinaire de Laodicée* (Paris: Beauchesne, 1980).

APOLOGETICS. Reasoned defense of belief or behavior. Apologetics was a persistent task of the ancient church, owing to the suspicion, criticism, and hostility encountered by Christianity. This effort spawned a distinctive type of literature, the "apology." In the Greek tradition, an apology (*apologia*, "defense") was, strictly speaking, a speech offered by the accused in a judicial proceeding, the most famous example being Socrates's answer in Plato's *Apology* to the charge of impiety. Christian apologies did not originate in legal proceedings, nor did they take the same literary form, but they all defended Christianity against criticism. Many and varied examples appear during the first five centuries, but second-century Christianity is sometimes called "the age of the apologists." Yet those apologists only strengthened a concern that had appeared here and there in the New Testament, and their work was continued by Christians of the third through fifth centuries who composed some of the most important apologies.

The apologists of the early church faced two distinct fronts, the Jewish and the Greco-Roman, and thus created two discrete bodies of apologetic literature.

Apologetics Toward Judaism. Since Christianity was a form of Judaism, the dialogue between Christianity and Judaism is virtually as old as Christianity itself. From the beginning, Christians used Jewish scriptures to argue their claim to the ancient revelation of Judaism, continuity with Jewish history, and the fulfillment of divine promises. The argument from scripture was developed largely, if not exclusively, against a Jewish denial of Christian claims and so had an apologetic motive. This exegetical effort began before the writing of the New Testament, but its traces are there: in quotations of Jewish scripture where the same text is given different applications (e.g., Isa. 6:9; John 12:39f.; Acts 28:25f.; Mark 4:11f.), in indications of stages of interpretation corresponding to changed situations, or in quotations of Jewish scripture where the text is actually modified to accommodate a specifically Christian sense. From an early time, the church had garnered from Jewish scripture a series of texts that were particularly useful in vindicating Christian claims against Jewish objections, and these texts were characteristically deployed in connection with key points of Christian preaching: the resurrection (Ps. 2:7–8; 16:9–10; 110:1; Dan. 7:13), passion (Isa. 52–53; Ps. 22; 34; 41; 69; 118:22; Zech. 9:9; 11:12f.; 12:10f.), and the origins of Jesus (Micah 5:1; Isa. 8:23–9:1), among others.

Beyond the routine use of such "testimonia," various writings of the New Testament are engaged in apologetics toward Judaism. The Gospel of Matthew, although written for Christians, consistently has an antagonistic Judaism in view. The author's use of quotations to support a prophecy-fulfillment scheme, his complaints against scribes and Pharisees (Matt. 23), and the legendary dimensions of his passion and resurrection stories (the suicide of Judas, the dream of Pilate's wife, the bribery of the guards at the tomb) all serve apologetic objectives. The Acts of the Apostles likewise embodies elements of apologetics toward Judaism, particularly in the speech of Stephen (Acts 7) and in the elaborate account of the initial reception of Gentiles (10–11). The apostle Paul writes to Gentile Christians, but elements of an apologetic toward Jews appear in his controversy with the Judaizing Christians of Galatia (esp. Gal. 3–4) and in his exposition of the gospel in Romans 2–4; 7; 9–11. The Epistle to the Hebrews, composed for Christians, is also an example of this genre, for it tries to justify the replacement of Judaism by Christianity, the suffering and death of Jesus, and Christianity's lack of a sacrificial cult.

In the second century, Christians wrote tracts whose sole purpose was to defend Christianity against Jewish objections and at the expense of Judaism. By then, the distinctions between Judaism and Christianity were clear both theologically and demographically, and mutual antagonism was commonplace. Among the earliest apologies was the *Epistle of Barnabas* (ca. 130). Not strictly directed toward Judaism, it nevertheless deals with the problem of how the Jewish scriptures were to be interpreted, a central issue in debate. The author argues in favor of an allegorical interpretation, dismissing the plain sense (and with it the ritual law) and discovering everywhere prophecies and prefigurations of the Christian religion. The *Dialogue Between Jason and Papiscus* (ca. 140), attributed to Aristo of Pella, is lost, but Celsus, Clement of Alexandria, Eusebius, and Jerome knew it and Origen preserves extracts in his *Against Celsus* (4.52). This work perhaps inaugurated the tendency in apologies *Adversus Judaeos* to employ the literary dialogue for juxtaposing Jewish and Christian positions and showing the superiority of the latter. The best-known and most valuable example of these is Justin Martyr's *Dialogue with Trypho* (ca. 155), which purports to be a record of an actual debate. Its length and detail suggest otherwise, although it probably draws on real discussions known to Justin.

Similar later works include the *Dialogue of Timothy and Aquila*, the *Dialogue Between Athanasius and Zacchaeus*, and the *Dialogue of Simon the Jew and Theophilus the Christian*. But Christian apologetics toward Judaism also took other forms: polemical tracts under the title *Adversus Judaeos*, as by Tertullian and Augustine, and collections of "testimonia," as by Cyprian or Gregory of Nyssa—scriptural texts gathered under argumentative headings, aiming to demonstrate the supersession of Judaism by Christianity and the fulfillment of messianic prophecies. Beyond these was homiletical literature, exemplified by Aphraates and John Chrysostom, insisting on the obsolescence of Judaism and the reallocation of the covenant to the (Gentile) church.

Despite the literary variety and chronological scope of these works, they possess a general consistency of argumentative methods and leading themes. Inevitably, the writings *Adversus Judaeos* focus on the scriptures of Judaism, a shared, authoritative divine revelation. The argument between Judaism and Christianity appears to be a clash between two distinct methods of scriptural interpretation: Jewish literalism and Christian typology, allegory, or prophecy-fulfillment. The methods did differ, but Judaism was not unaccustomed to allegorical interpretation nor were Christians indifferent to the literal sense of scripture. The

critical distinction rests in the Christian presupposition that Jewish scripture could be comprehended only on the basis of faith in Jesus as the Messiah and an exegetical method that was a consequence of this. Thus, Christians emphasized prophetic literature (including the Psalms) over narrative literature and prescinded from normal Jewish deference toward the Law. The Christians also depended upon the Greek version of Jewish scriptures, while Jews relied upon the original Hebrew text.

The agenda of the Christian apology toward Judaism was set partly by Jewish objections to Christianity and partly by the ambiguous relationship of the developing church to Judaism. The apologies could not refute Jewish objections and prove Christian claims by disavowing Judaism; the positive dependence of Christianity on Judaism required selective treatment. Hence, the argument with Judaism revolved around the principal issues that distinguished Christianity from Judaism: messianism, the role of the Law, and the place of Gentiles.

The assertion of Jesus' messiahship was largely inconsistent with common Jewish messianic ideas and therefore subject to various criticisms. The sufferings of Jesus and his death by crucifixion were especially alleged by Jews as disqualifications from messianic status. Christians countered with a proof from prophecy: suffering and even crucifixion had been predicted. Isaiah 53 and Psalms 22, neither messianically construed by Judaism, were frequent courts of Christian appeal for suffering; the crucifixion demanded ingenious typological prefigurations. Jesus' failure to fulfill traditional triumphant prerogatives was met by the distinction between two messianic advents, the first (and past) in humility and suffering, the second (and future) in power and glory. Against the Jewish insistence that the Messiah was human and that any other view compromised monotheism, Christian apologists mined Jewish scripture for indications of the preexistence and divinity of Christ, his activity in creation, and his participation in theophanies.

Torah, or the divine Law, was central to Jewish piety; it posed a basic problem for Christianity's claim to represent continuity with and fulfillment of scriptural revelation. The polemic against Judaism met this problem first by drawing a distinction, unknown in Judaism, between the moral and the ceremonial law, and then by maintaining that the moral law alone is permanent and universal, while the ceremonial was temporary and particular. The ceremonial law was no sign of elective favor, but a check against and even a punishment for Israel's stubborn disobedience. In proof of this claim, Christians pointed to the destruction of Jerusalem and the temple and the resulting impossibility of observing the cultic law. The moral law, however, was identified with the natural law attested by conscience and thus regarded as a matter of general rather than special revelation. Hence, apologists denied the validity of circumcision, sabbath observance, and dietary regulations, in addition to the laws governing the temple cult.

Along with this selective treatment of Torah, Christians asserted the rejection of the Jews as God's chosen people and their replacement by the Gentiles. Prophetic texts complaining of the infidelity of Israel and criticizing its cultic observance were cited against Judaism, while texts anticipating God's favor toward Gentiles were applied to the church. In addition, scriptural narratives about the primacy of younger sons over older brothers (Isaac and Ishmael, Jacob and Esau, Joseph and his brothers) were allegorically taken to portend the passing of covenant privilege from Israel to the Gentile church. Such arguments were buttressed by allusion to the empirical facts of the destruction of Jerusalem and the dispersion of Jews.

The thematic and argumentative similarities among these apologies pose the question whether and how far they betray a literary interdependence, a difficult puzzle indeed. Not unrelated is the further question whether the *Adversus Judaeos* literature was actually directed toward Jews or whether it was for Christian consumption only, or perhaps for potential Gentile converts to Christianity. Although the presentation of Judaism in this literature is often conventional and simplistic, and the character of the Jew somewhat stereotypical,

the ancient church was deeply engaged in debate with Judaism. It perceived in Judaism an important and persistent threat to Christian claims. Hence, even if the intended readers of apologies were not exclusively Jewish, the actual, longstanding problem of Jewish-Christian relationships was the chief motive in their production.

Apologetics Toward the Greco-Roman World. Through its missionary efforts among non-Jews and outside Palestine, Christianity came increasingly into contact with the Greco-Roman world, and progressively gained visibility in the larger society. Although many Gentiles were drawn to Christianity, many others perceived it as politically dangerous, socially offensive, or intellectually absurd.

Such negative perceptions are scarcely alluded to in the New Testament or the apostolic fathers. Those writings were directed to the Christian community and were not apologetic in the strict sense. Nevertheless, they occasionally reveal a sensitivity to the critical attitudes of outsiders and to problems of the relationship between Christians and the non-Christian environment. Thus, Paul had to take account of the interactions of Christians with the larger society (esp. 1 Cor. 1–2; 6; 8–10), and the author of 1 Peter knows the importance of not giving unnecessary offense and of making a defense (*apologia*) of one's convictions (3:13–17). The Acts of the Apostles shows a prominent apologetic interest, urging that Christianity, in spite of popular opposition, is politically innocuous, had been of positive interest to Gentiles, and had been tolerated by Roman officials. The Areopagus address attributed to Paul in Acts 17:22–31 adumbrates major themes of later apologetic literature.

Full apologies toward Greco-Roman society first appear during the second century. The earliest Greek ones were by Quadratus (between 117 and 138, lost) and Aristides (between 138 and 147). There followed the *Apology* of Justin Martyr (150), the *Address to the Greeks* of his pupil Tatian (170), the *Plea* of Athenagoras (ca. 177), the *To Autolycus* of Theophilus of Antioch (ca. 180), an apology by Melito of Sardis (ca. 175, lost) and another by Apollinaris of Hierapolis (ca. 175, lost), as well as the anonymous *Epistle to Diognetus*. The earliest Latin apologies include the *To the Heathen*, the *Apology*, and the *To Scapula* of Tertullian (ca. 200) and the *Octavius* of Minucius Felix.

With the exceptions of Melito and Tertullian, all of these writers are known principally as apologists. But in the following centuries many Christian writers not known chiefly as apologists composed some of the most impressive apologetic works, for example, Clement of Alexandria's *Protrepticus*, Origen's *Against Celsus*, Eusebius of Caesarea's *Preparation of the Gospel*, Theodoret's *Graecarum affectionum curatio*, and Augustine's *City of God*. This literature grew during a period when the church often attracted the attention and enmity of pagan society. Defense of the faith was needed not only to protect the church from popular violence and political repression but also to preserve the credibility of missionary appeals. These apologies respond to the criticisms—popular, political, and philosophical—directed against the church within Greco-Roman society.

Popular criticism appeared early and arose from perceptions of Christian behavior in ordinary social life. It was less concerned with matters of belief. The reticence of Christians toward routine social intercourse, civic responsibility, and public religious ceremony; their preference for private meetings, esoteric rituals, and close community; their predominantly proletarian constituency; and the peculiarity of their known beliefs all worked against them. Christians were viewed as misanthropists, who practiced atheism, ritual murder, cannibalism, incest, and magic. Such sensational suspicions were difficult to dislodge.

Political suspicion involved Christians' refusal to worship those gods honored as patrons and protectors of cities and of the empire. Christians seemed impious and antagonistic to public welfare. Their refusal to offer the token sacrifices to or on behalf of the emperor betrayed an ungovernable obstinacy or a revolutionary bent. That Christians venerated a figure executed under Roman law, that they

anticipated a different kind of kingdom, and that they gathered in associations (*collegia*) resembling those that nourished political opposition only fueled the supposition that they were dangerously disloyal. Popular criticism also supported this, since its allegations became "crimes associated with the name" (*flagitia cohaerentia nomini*), a principle on which Christians could be liable to prosecution because of their name alone.

Philosophical criticisms posed a still greater challenge. Lucian, Fronto, Galen, and Celsus in the second century, Porphyry in the third, and the emperor Julian in the fourth all attacked Christianity. The last three published influential works. Having acquainted themselves in detail with Christian history, literature, belief, and practice, they assessed Christianity against the sophisticated standard of the classical intellectual tradition. Their objections included social as well as intellectual matters, and they reveal something of the prejudice of an educated elite toward the largely lower-class constituency of the church. They saw the appeal of Christianity as limited to the uneducated and simple-minded. The narratives of scripture told foolish and often offensive stories and habitually represented God as subject to human emotions. Christian claims about Jesus were incredible: his virgin birth was devised to cover up his illegitimacy; his miracles were tricks of sorcery; his resurrection transpired in secret, witnessed only by women. Nobler figures were available in Greek stories. An incarnate God was inconceivable; an immutable and perfect being would not become a lesser, material being. Moreover, a God so recently and obscurely revealed in human history was unjust. Christian insistence that the world was theirs, that they were special objects of divine care, involved absurd self-importance and diminished divine providence, while ignoring the fact that Christians actually suffered more misfortune than most others. Christians required faith rather than reason and so recruited the thoughtless; they embraced immoral people as though virtue was irrelevant. They rejected the world and society, disparaging both in favor of a future that included the ludicrous expectation of a resurrection body rather than the immortality of the soul. Thus, philosophical critics judged Christian views as incoherent and incompatible with established principles. Christianity was an unsupportable novelty, disavowing even its own Jewish roots, yet remaining a barbarian superstition. Against such criticism Christian thinkers had either to argue on philosophical grounds or abandon any prospect of intellectual respectability.

The burgeoning number of apologies attests both the need and the effort of the church to respond. Apologists usually went beyond mere rebuttals of specific charges and pleas for toleration. They vigorously attacked popular religious ideas and practices and appealed to the thoughtful by representing Christianity as consistent with the best of classical philosophical reflection. They were defensive, polemical, and even evangelistic.

The apologists drew on various resources. One was the apologetic tradition of Hellenistic Judaism in its response to the ancient world. Since many of the criticisms leveled against Christianity had been lodged against Judaism, and since Christianity and Judaism had common theological ground, Jewish apologetics was helpful in the Christian cause. Another resource was the Greco-Roman philosophical tradition itself, both in its critical views of the mythological and cultic features of popular religion and in its constructive theological aspects, most especially in Middle Platonism. Then there were the Christian apologists themselves, many of whom had been well educated in pagan literature, philosophy, and rhetoric and were well equipped to articulate Christian positions in terms of the Greco-Roman world.

Because of the continuity of criticisms and the commonality of resources, these apologies comprise a coherent tradition. Although they took different literary forms, tones of argument, and special emphases, they shared a relatively stable set of themes and arguments. Against allegations of criminal behavior Christians issued denials, pointing both to an absence of evidence and to the contradictoriness of such acts to Christian morality. The charge of atheism could be admitted only so far as Christians

refused to worship popular gods, but this was justified, indeed required, by the Christians' worship of the one God, infinitely superior to idols. Moreover, cultic sacrifices were superfluous because God needed nothing. Prayer and virtuous living fulfilled his will. Some pagan philosophers had been "atheists" in that sense.

Against political suspicions it was argued that Christians were good citizens. Although they offered no sacrifices, they prayed for the welfare of the ruler and the state. They should not have been prosecuted for their name alone, something that the Roman legal system itself ordinarily stood against in cases where evidence of criminality was lacking.

The apologists used Jewish apologetics and Greek philosophical skepticism to denounce pagan popular religion. Relying on Jewish sources, they said that images were unworthy of reverence, being either lifeless and helpless or else the habitations of mere demons. Linking immorality and idolatry, they claimed that pagan cults were morally perverse. Employing Greek sources, they ridiculed anthropomorphism and immorality in classical mythology and adopted the theory of Euhemerus that the gods of popular worship were only historical heroes who had been overzealously deified.

The apologists' greatest energies, however, were devoted to philosophical criticisms. Christianity was not a novelty; it shared a continuity with ancient if "barbaric" Judaism. The argument from prophecy to fulfillment reinforced that claim and had some plausibility, given the pagan belief in prophets, oracles, and omens. Christian apologists followed Jewish apologists in their way of accounting for elements of Greek tradition that seemed amenable to Christian teaching: such ideas were plagiarized by Plato and other Greeks from the more ancient teachings of Moses but were not fully understood.

Apart from figures like Tatian and Tertullian, who were generally hostile to the classical philosophical tradition, most apologists valued it. The *logos* concept allowed them to accommodate that tradition to Christian teachings. From the Jewish background, the apologists correlated the biblical ideas of God's creation of the world by verbal command, the "word of the Lord" that revealed the divine will, and the personified "wisdom of God." Jesus was seen as the incarnation of the "word" (*logos*) of God. On the Greek side, Stoicism, followed by Middle Platonism, had formed a conception of *logos* as the fundamental principle of the cosmos, which shapes and orders the world but is also manifested in creatures, who possess its "seeds" (*logoi spermatikoi*). Beginning with Justin Martyr, the apologists conflated these biblical and Greek concepts, holding that there were valid revelations of *logos* among the Greeks. Although only partial, they were in continuity with Christianity, which proclaimed the ultimate *logos* in Christ and was itself the supremely true philosophy. Thus, Christianity was the consummation of the highest Greek aspirations. The *logos* concept also allowed Christians to preserve the transcendence and immutability of God—a presupposition shared with pagan intellectuals—while maintaining that God actively deals with the material world. Although this approach later required refinement in the Trinitarian controversy, it served apologetic needs well enough.

Yet many Christian beliefs lacked analogues in Greco-Roman thought and had to be argued against prevailing opinion. The creation of the world out of nothing (*ex nihilo*) opposed the Greek conception of the co-eternity of God and matter. In a similar way, a resurrection body was defended by appeal to divine omnipotence: if God created from nothing, he could surely reconstitute a body. The apologists also first argued a philosophy of historical process, a progressive movement toward a final consummation, over against common cyclic, fatalistic, or merely political conceptions of history. They gave up imminent expectations of the end of time but retained a teleological understanding of history.

These apologetic interests also influenced Christian exegesis. Typologies, developed against Jewish interpretations of scripture, became less useful in the Greco-Roman context, where allegories overcame patent anthropomorphism and other seeming barbarisms. Allegorical techniques were borrowed from Greek philosophy (although often by way of Hellenistic

Judaism), which had applied them to classical mythology. Yet appeals to scripture were less effective than appeals to reason, to conscience, and to principles current in Greco-Roman intellectual discourse.

The Christianity of the apologists, however, cannot be read off the apologies alone. Their projects were so focused on specific criticisms that they appear to support hardly more than monotheism, moral responsibility, and the expectation of resurrection and judgment and to be uninterested in Jesus as a human figure, in the corporate life of the Christian community, or in the deeper resources and expression of early Christian piety. The apologists were not disingenuous, but their task was of limited scope. Even so, apologetics was a task for Christian intellectuals, who by reason of their education and interests sometimes had almost as much in common with philosophically minded pagan critics as with the large numbers of uneducated fellow Christians.

Many critical issues of continuing importance were initially addressed in the debate between Christianity and the classical tradition. These included the relation of God and the world, the status of Jesus and his relation to God, the problem of faith and reason, the role of Christianity in society, the status of Christianity among other religions, including Judaism, the historical reliability of scripture, and the proper means of scripture interpretation. The intellectual challenge laid down by pagan critics compelled Christian thinkers to give more careful consideration to the elements of Christian belief, to specify their correlates and implications, and to set them forth in clear and systematic fashion. Thus, early Christian apologetics provided the context in which Christian thought moved beyond its early biblicism and took up the systematic and philosophical tasks of theology proper. *See also* Judaism and Christianity; Paganism and Christianity. [H.Y.G.]

Bibliography

Apologetics Toward Judaism: J.R. Harris, *Testimonies*, 2 vols. (Cambridge: Cambridge UP, 1916, 1920); A.L. Williams, *Adversus Judaeos: A Bird's Eye View of Christian Apologiae Until the Renaissance* (Cambridge: Cambridge UP, 1935); C.H. Dodd,

According to the Scriptures: The Sub-Structure of New Testament Theology (London: Nisbet, 1952); B. Lindars, *New Testament Apologetic* (London: SCM, 1961); M. Simon, *Verus Israel: A Study of the Relations Between Christians and Jews in the Roman Empire (135–425)* (New York: Oxford UP, 1986; orig. French ed. 1964); R.L. Wilken, *Judaism and the Early Christian Mind* (New Haven: Yale UP, 1971); D. Rokeah, *Jews, Pagans and Christians in Conflict* (Leiden: Brill, 1982); H. Schreckenberg, *Die christlichen Adversus-Judaeos-Texte und ihr literarisches und historisches Umfeld (1–11 Jh.)* (Berne: Lang, 1982).

Apologetics Toward the Greco-Roman World: M. Friedländer, *Geschichte der jüdischen Apologetik als Vorgeschichte des Christentums* (Zurich: Schmidt, 1903); J. Geffcken, *Zwei griechischen Apologeten* (Leipzig: Teubner, 1907); P. de Labriolle, *La Réaction païenne: étude sur la polémique antichrétienne du Ier au VIe siècle* (Paris: Artisan du Livre, 1934); G. Bardy, "Apologetik," RLAC (1950), Vol. 1, pp. 533–545; C. Andresen, "Justin und der mittlere Platonismus," *ZNTW* 44 (1952–1953):157–195; P. Dalbert, *Die Theologie der hellenistische-jüdischen Missions-Literatur unter Ausschluss von Philo und Josephus* (Hamburg: Reich, 1954); C. Andresen, *Logos und Nomos: Die Polemik des Kelsos wider das Christentum* (Berlin: de Gruyter, 1955); R. Holte, "*Logos Spermatikos*: Christianity and Ancient Philosophy According to St. Justin's Apologies," *Studia Theologica* 12 (1958):109–169; W. Jaeger, *Early Christianity and Greek Paideia* (Cambridge: Harvard UP, 1961); A.H. Armstrong and R.A. Markus, *Christian Faith and Greek Philosophy* (New York: Sheed and Ward, 1964); H. Chadwick, *Early Christian Thought and the Classical Tradition* (New York: Oxford UP, 1966); A. Dulles, *A History of Apologetics* (Philadelphia: Westminster, 1971); J. Daniélou, *Gospel Message and Hellenistic Culture* (Philadelphia: Westminster, 1973); R. Joly, *Christianisme et Philosophie* (Brussels: Université de Bruxelles, 1973); L.W. Barnard, "Apologetik (I)," TRE (1978), Vol. 3, pp. 371–411; S. Benko, "Pagan Criticism of Christianity During the First Two Centuries A.D.," ANRW (1980), Vol. 23.2, pp. 1055–1118; R.L. Wilken, *The Christians as the Romans Saw Them* (New Haven: Yale UP, 1984); R.M. Grant, *The Greek Apologists* (Philadelphia: Westminster, 1988).

APONIUS (beginning of fifth century). Writer at Rome. Aponius wrote an *Expositio in Canticum Canticorum*, which gives information about the Roman church and its Christology. CPL 194. [E.F.]

Bibliography
Apponni, *In Canticorum Expositio*, ed. B. de Vregille and L. Neyrand, CCSL (1987), Vol. 19.

A. Grillmeier, *Christ in Christian Tradition*, 2nd ed. (Atlanta: John Knox, 1975), Vol. 1, pp. 384–388; K.S. Frank, "Apponius, In Canticum Canticorum Explanatio," VChr 39 (1985):370–383.

APOPHTHEGMATA PATRUM. "Sayings of the Fathers," a collection of proverbs and anecdotes deriving from monks in the fourth and fifth centuries. Most of the sayings come from Egyptian monks, some from Syrians and Palestinians. The *Apophthegmata* were preserved orally in Coptic or Greek. The written collections are in three forms: the *Alphabetical Collection* (sixth century), the *Anonymous Collection*, and the *Systematic Collection* according to topics (transmitted principally in the west). The written collections exist in Greek, Coptic, Syriac, Armenian, and Latin. About one-seventh of the *Alphabetical Collection* is attributed to Poemen, and it may be that stories preserved by his disciples formed the nucleus of the whole collection. The collections underwent considerable development; wording was subordinated to the goal of edification.

The *Apophthegmata* come from anchoritic rather than cenobitic circles. Most of the hermits were unlearned, and their medium was not theological discourse but the pithy saying or anecdote expressing the practical wisdom born of experience. For this reason, the *Apophthegmata* are recognized as the best source for getting at the authentic spirit of the desert holy men. The sayings were addressed to specific situations, and the needs of the inquirer, not necessarily universal truth, made the teaching memorable. Among the recurring themes are humility, self-control, discretion, and vigilance. There frequently occurs the request, "Give me a word, father," and the Abba (or "father") spoke the life-giving response. CPG III, 5560–5615. *See also* Monasticism. [E.F.]

Bibliography
PG 65.71–440; F. Nau, *Revue de l'orient chrétien* 12–14 (1907–1909), 17–18 (1912–1913); PL 73.851–1052.

W. Budge, *The Wit and Wisdom of the Christian Fathers of Egypt* (Oxford: Oxford UP, 1934); B. Ward, *The Sayings of the Desert Fathers: The Alphabetical Collection* (Kalamazoo: Cistercian, 1975); idem, *The Wisdom of the Desert Fathers: Apophthegmata Patrum (The Anonymous Series)* (Oxford: SLG, 1975).

Twelve apostles flanking Christ, apse mosaic (fourth century) of the chapel of Sant'Aquilino in the Church of S. Lorenzo, Milan, Italy.

J.C. Guy, *Recherches sur la tradition Grecque des Apophthegmata Patrum* (Brussels: Société Bollandistes, 1962; 2nd ed. 1984); D. Chitty, *The Desert a City* (Oxford: Blackwell, 1966); A.C. Hamilton, "Spiritual Direction in the *Apophthegmata*," *Colloquium* 15 (1983):31–38.

APOSTLE. "Each person sent by someone is an apostle of the one sending" (Origen, *Jo.* 32.17). Since secular Greek use of *apostolos* hardly prepares for the Christian use, scholars have put forward three other proposals concerning the background of the New Testament concept of "apostle." (1) The rabbinic *shaliach* ("one sent") was a legal representative with power of attorney: "a man's *shaliach* is as himself" (*m. Ber* 5.5). The *shaliach*'s commission was for a specified function and was nontransferable. (2) Some Gnostic systems had an earthly redeemer-figure, a "sent man" who had a worldwide mission to communicate the saving knowledge he had received. (3) Since there is no documentary evidence for the existence of either the *shaliach* or the Gnostic redeemer prior to the New Testament, Jewish conventions of sending authorized representatives, especially the sending of prophets, perhaps provided precedent for the call and commission of the apostles. In this third view, the rabbinic *shaliach* and the Christian apostle were independent derivations from the same conceptions in earlier Jewish thought.

The New Testament uses the word "apostle" with reference to Jesus as God's messenger to the world (Heb. 3:1; cf. John 17:18), the "messengers of the churches" (2 Cor. 8:23; Phil. 2:25), and missionaries (Acts 14:4, 14; Rom. 16:7; 2 Cor. 11:13). The usage that came to prevail in Christianity, however, was the designation "apostle" for the twelve disciples specially chosen by Jesus as the nucleus of the new Israel (Luke 6:13–16; Matt. 10:1–4; names also in Mark 3:14–19; Acts 1:13f.) and for Paul (Gal. 1:1; Rom. 1:1; 1 Cor. 15:9). The names of the Twelve according to Matthew were Simon Peter, Andrew, James, John, Philip, Bartholomew, Thomas, Matthew, James the son of Alphaeus, Thaddaeus, Simon the Cananaean, and Judas Iscariot. These, who were personally chosen by Jesus and were witnesses of his resurrection—except Judas (Acts 1:21–26), by their testimony and work of planting churches formed the foundation of the church (Eph. 2:20; Rev. 21:14).

Later Christian literature occasionally uses "apostle" in the sense of missionary (*Did.* 11.3–6?; Ps.-Clement, *Hom.* 11.35; sarcastically in Cyprian, *Ep.* 55.24). Accordingly, the Seventy sent out by Jesus in Luke 10:1 are called apostles (Tertullian, *Marc.* 4.24). It is apparently in this missionary sense that Thecla is called an apostle (*Acts of Paul and Thecla*, title). Associates of the Twelve and Paul, as "apostolic men," are sometimes called apostles (Clement of Alexandria, *Str.* 4.17, of Clement of Rome; cf. *Martyrdom of Polycarp* 16.2). Otherwise, the overwhelming usage of "apostle" is as a technical term for the Twelve and Paul (Justin, *1 Apol.* 39; 49; *Dial.* 42; Irenaeus, *Haer.* 4.23f.). "The apostle" in the singular normally referred to Paul. In the lectionary, "the apostle" was the reading from the Epistles or Acts. The Gnostics emphasized the intimate secrets supposedly transmitted by the apostles, whereas the orthodox tradition made them missionaries to the Gentile world (*Asc. Isa.* 3.18f.; *Ep. apos.* 30; Eusebius, *H.E.* 3.1).

Since the apostles were the first bearers of the revelation of Christ, authenticated by their personal contact with him, there was a great concern on the part of the church in its controversies in the second century to establish the apostolic basis of Christianity. Hence, there was appeal to the collective witness of the apostles over against the appeals by Gnostics and others to traditions traced back to an individual disciple. The church claimed an apostolic faith, summarized in the Apostles' Creed, an apostolic scripture (an important but not decisive criterion for canonicity was authorship by an apostle or a close associate of an apostle), and an apostolic ministry, guaranteed by apostolic succession. The church orders, which described the organization and worship of the church, assigned apostolic institution to the practices of the church: the *Didache* ("The Teaching of the Lord Through the Twelve Apostles"), *Apostolic Tradition* (by Hippolytus), *Didascalia*, *Apostolic Church Order*, *Apostolic Constitutions*, and *Testament of Our Lord*. *See also* Apostles' Creed; Apostolic Succession; Evangelist; Ministry. [E.F.]

Bibliography

J.B. Lightfoot, "The Name and Office of Apostle," *St. Paul's Epistle to the Galatians*, 2nd ed. (London: Macmillan, 1866), pp. 92–101; A.F. Walls, "A Note on the Apostolic Claim in the Church Order Literature," *SP* 2 (1957):83–92; K.H. Rengstorf, "*Apostolos*," *Theological Dictionary of the New Testament*, ed. G. Kittel (Grand Rapids: Eerdmans, 1964), Vol. 1, pp. 407–447; W. Schmithals, *The Office of Apostle in the Early Church* (Nashville: Abingdon, 1969; orig. German ed. 1961); F.H. Agnew, "The Origin of the NT Apostle-Concept: A Review of Research," *JBL* 105 (1986):75–96.

APOSTLES' CREED. A baptismal confession of faith. Although the received text of the Apostles' Creed occurs first in the eighth century, the contents are essentially an expansion of the positive form (the Old Roman Symbol) of the questions asked candidates for baptism at Rome at the end of the second century. The baptizer asked the one to be baptized, "Do you believe in God the Father Almighty?" After the confession, "I believe," there was the first immersion. Then the baptizer asked, "Do you believe in Christ Jesus, the Son of God, who was born of the Holy Spirit and the Virgin Mary, who was crucified in the days of Pontius Pilate, and died, [and was buried,] and rose from the dead and ascended in the heavens and sat down at the right hand of the Father, and will come to judge the living and the dead?" The response, "I believe," was followed by the second immersion. The question, "Do you believe in the Holy Spirit in the holy church [and the resurrection of the flesh]?," and third confession led to the third immersion (Hippolytus, *Trad. ap.* 21.12–18). The interrogatory form of the baptismal confession is attested for this period in other sources (e.g., Cyprian, *Ep.* 69.7). It cannot be ascertained how old this practice was. A declaratory profession of faith in Christ is found in the western text (second century) of Acts 8:37.

The study of the early history of the Apostles' Creed has often confused it with the Rule of Faith (or Canon of Truth). Several second- and third-century authors refer to summaries of Christian teaching as the *regula fidei*. These varied widely in wording but had a similar content, based on the facts of the apostolic preaching. This content corresponds in many respects to the Apostles' Creed. There was obviously a close relationship between the faith that was taught and the faith that was confessed, but the *regula* and the *credo* had different functions: the former served as a summary of the preaching and the latter as an affirmation of faith. The confessions, probably because they had a regular liturgical function (as at baptism), acquired a fixity of wording that the Rule of Faith did not have.

The usual title in early sources for the Apostles' Creed was the Apostles' Symbol (*symbolon*). "Symbol" was used for a "standard" or a "formula," which could serve as a "badge" or a "sign" of one's identity. In reference to the baptismal confession, it represented a person's faith and the compact made with God.

The interrogatory creed of Hippolytus is found in declaratory form in two fourth-century sources, one Greek and one Latin but both associated with Rome. Marcellus of Ancyra sought to convince bishop Julius of Rome of his orthodoxy by stating his faith according to the Roman baptismal symbol (Epiphanius, *Haer.* 72.3). Rufinus of Aquileia wrote a *Commentary on the Apostles' Creed* (ca. 400) in which he compared the baptismal creed of his church with the wording used at Rome. The contents of the creed in Marcellus and Rufinus are virtually identical. The original language was apparently Greek, so this Old Roman Symbol (as it is usually called) presumably goes back at least to the third century. Plausible functions for the declaratory form were providing an outline for catechists in instructing candidates for baptism or serving as a text to be delivered to the candidate to learn in preparation for the baptism.

The name Apostles' Creed (Symbol) was first used a few years before Rufinus by Ambrose (*Ep.* 42.5), and Rufinus himself reports the tradition that the apostles after receiving the Holy Spirit and before dispersing to preach drew up this summary of the faith, each contributing a clause, in order to maintain unity of belief (cf. also *Const. app.* 6.14). By the sixth century, the contents of the Old Roman Symbol had been somewhat elaborated and the tradition of apostolic origin refined by identifying the clause contributed by each of the twelve apostles (Ps.-Augustine, *Serm. de symb.*). What had begun as a summary of the apostolic faith had come to be attributed to apostolic authorship.

The Roman church appears to have led the way in stabilizing the wording of the essentials of the apostolic faith. In doing so, it took phrases and ideas already in use and gave emphasis, formality, and fixity to the language. The Roman Symbol spread throughout the west, but it did not have any currency in the east, where different forms of baptismal creeds were in use. Usage produced some variation in the wording. A creed closely approximating the later received text of the Apostles' Creed is found in a sermon of Caesarius of Arles (*Sermo et sacramentum*), but the wording that became standard over western Europe from the reign of Charlemagne appears to have originated in southwestern France in the eighth century.

Confessions of faith were also used on occasions other than baptism: benedictions (2 Cor. 13:14; Polycarp, *Phil.* 12), hymns (Phil. 2:6–11; *Te Deum*), exorcism (Mark 3:11; 5:7; Justin, *Dial.* 30.3; 85.1f.; Origen, *Cels.* 1.6), combating heresy (1 John 4:2; Ignatius, *Magn.* 11; *Eph.* 18.2), persecution (1 Tim. 6:12–16; Tertullian, *Coron.* 11). These confessions might contain one member, confessing Christ (1 Cor. 15:1ff.; Ignatius, *Trall.* 9; Justin, *1 Apol.* 31.7), or less frequently God (Hermas, *Mand.* 1); two members—God and Christ (1 Cor. 8:6; Hippolytus, *Noet.* 1); or three members—God, Christ, and the Holy Spirit (2 Cor. 13:14; Irenaeus, *Dem.* 6). The single-member confessions about Christ were elaborated to cover the main facts of his life from birth, to death and resurrection, to second coming. It seems that the Apostles' Creed with its expanded statement about Christ resulted from combining a lengthy statement about Christ with a three-member confession. Other formulations were possible, for example, the *Epistle of the Apostles*

5 has a five-member confession, adding belief in the resurrection and the church to belief in the Father, the Savior, and the Holy Spirit. These items were normally incorporated into the third article (e.g., Hippolytus's baptismal confession) as expressions of the working of the Holy Spirit.

Much attention in the study of the creed has been given to its antiheretical thrust. The creed was not formulated specifically to counter heresy, for the content is found from the earliest periods of the church. The specific wording and some of the emphases may have been given in reaction to Marcion and the Gnostics. *See also* Confession of Faith; Creeds; Faith; Rule of Faith. [E.F.]

Bibliography
Rufinus, *Commentary on the Apostles' Creed*, tr. and notes J.N.D. Kelly, ACW (1955), Vol. 20; Ambrose, *Explanation of the Symbol*, R.H. Connolly, "The Explanatio Symboli ad Initiandos," *TS* 10 (1952):1–39.

A.C. McGiffert, *The Apostles' Creed* (New York: Scribner, 1902); H.B. Swete, *The Apostles' Creed: Its Relation to Primitive Christianity* (Cambridge: Cambridge UP, 1905); J. de Ghellinck, *Patristique et moyen-âge* (Gembloux: Duculot, 1949), Vol. 1: *Les Recherches sur les origines du symbole des apôtres*; J. Crehan, *Early Christian Baptism and the Creed* (London: Burns, Oates and Washbourne, 1950); J.N.D. Kelly, *Early Christian Creeds* (London: Longmans, 1960), pp. 1–181, 368–434; O.S. Barr, *From the Apostles' Faith to the Apostles' Creed* (New York: Oxford UP, 1964); D. Larrimore Holland, "The Earliest Text of the Old Roman Symbol: A Debate with Hans Lietzmann and J.N.D. Kelly," *CH* 34 (1965):262–281; E. Ferguson, *Early Christians Speak* (Abilene: ACU, 1987), pp. 23–32.

APOSTOLIC CHURCH ORDER (or *Ecclesiastical Canons of the Holy Apostles*). Compiled from earlier sources probably in Egypt ca. 300, the *Apostolic Church Order* gives ordinances ascribed individually to the twelve apostles (in a peculiar order), which they delivered in the presence of Martha and Mary. After an introduction (1–3), the first part (4–14) contains moral instructions similar to "the two ways" found in the *Didache* and other early Christian literature. The second part (15–30) legislates on church organization, providing for a bishop, presbyters, reader, deacons, and widows and excluding women from the ministry of sacrificing the body and blood. Originally in Greek, the work also survives in Latin, Syriac, Coptic, Arabic, and Ethiopic. CPG I, 1739. [E.F.]

Bibliography
A. Harnack, *Sources of the Apostolic Canons* (London: Black, 1895); J.P. Arendzen, "An Entire Syriac Text of the 'Apostolic Church Order'" (with Engl. tr.), *JThS* 3 (1901):59–80; G.W. Horner, *The Statutes of the Apostles or Canones ecclesiastici* (London: Williams and Norgate, 1904) (with Engl. tr.); T. Schermmann, *Die allgemeine Kirchenordnung, frühchristliche Liturgien und kirchliche Überlieferung* (Paderborn: Schöningh, 1914), Vol. 1, pp. 1–34; E. Hennecke, "Zur Apostolischen Kirchenordnung," *ZNTW* 20 (1921):241–248, cf. 254–256; J.V. Bartlett, *Church-Life and Church-Order During the First Four Centuries with Special Reference to the Early Eastern Church Orders* (Oxford: Blackwell, 1943), Ch. 5; A. Faivre, "Le Texte grec de la 'Constitution ecc. des apôtres' 16–20 et ses sources," *RSR* 5 (1981):31–42.

APOSTOLIC CONSTITUTIONS. Collection of materials on church order compiled sometime during the closing decades of the fourth century by a Semiarian or Apollinarian author, most probably the same one who interpolated and re-edited the letters of Ignatius of Antioch. The *Apostolic Constitutions* consists of eight books that deal with the following subjects: Christian behavior (1), ecclesiastical hierarchy (2), widows (3), orphans (4), martyrs (5), schisms (6), Christian morality and initiation (7), charismata, the eucharist, ordinations, and discipline (8). A great variety of other subjects emerge as important subthemes in these books, such as the forgiveness of penitents, almsgiving, the resurrection, the liturgical year, pastoral issues of all kinds, the organization and administration of the Christian communities, and all sorts of church discipline, whether moral, catechetical, or liturgical. As it stands, the *Apostolic Constitutions* does not represent a coherent whole, inasmuch as it repeats many of its subthemes in different places. It is in fact a compilation of already existing material.

Three major writings lie at the root of the *Apostolic Constitutions* (although other sources seem to have been adopted as well): the *Didas-*

calia Apostolorum (Const. app. 1–6), the Didache (Const. app. 7.1–32), and the Diataxeis of the Holy Apostles (Const. app. 8.3–45). The first source originated in Syria during the first decades of the third century, and its author must have been a clergyman, most probably a bishop. The second source also seems to have originated in Syria and belongs perhaps to the first century, but its authorship is unknown. The third document, which is in fact the Apostolic Tradition of Hippolytus (d. ca. 236), was probably made during the second decade of the third century; it itself is a compilation: 3–27 deal with ordination ceremonies and an elaborate version of the Antiochene, or Clementine, Liturgy, and 28–46 contain prescriptions for the life of the Christian community.

Among the other sources used in the Apostolic Constitutions are Jewish prayer formularies (7.33–38); rules pertaining to the training of catechumens and the administration of baptism (7.39–45); a list of the bishops consecrated by the apostles (7.46); Christian prayer formularies (7.47–49); a document on charismata (8.1–2); and the Apostolic Canons (8.47–85), which lists the acceptable books of the Bible, omitting the Revelation and adding the two letters of Clement of Rome and the Apostolic Constitutions itself.

The relation of the Apostolic Constitutions to other early church orders is not fully settled, since scholars disagree on their dependence or interdependence. These other writings include the Didascalia Arabica et Ethiopica (a recension of Const. app. 1–6), the Epitome of Hippolytus (Const. app. 8.1–2, 4–5, 16–18, 30–34, 42–46), the Egyptian Church Ordinance (Const. app. 8.47, can. 31–62), and the Testament of Our Lord and the Canons of Hippolytus (both connected with the previous text).   [G.D.D.]

Bibliography
M. Metzger, ed., SC (1985, 1986, 1987), Vols. 320, 329, 336.
ANF (1886), Vol. 7, pp. 385–505.

APOSTOLIC SUCCESSION. Doctrine that ministry in the church derives from the apostles in historical continuity. Succession lists of kings, periodically appointed magistrates, and heads of philosophical schools were kept in the Hellenistic world. The Jews had lists of prophets and rabbis, but most importantly of high priests. Although early Christians had an interest in the succession of their own prophets and teachers (particularly in the catechetical school in Alexandria), special attention attached to the succession of bishops, who by the end of the second century incorporated much of the authority and function of prophets and teachers into their office.

1 Clement 42–44 taught the apostolic institution of the offices of bishop and deacon in the church. After the appointment of the first bishops and deacons, the apostles provided for the continuation of these offices in the church. This was a different view from the later doctrine of apostolic succession, and it is to be noted that Clement included deacons as well as bishops in his statement. Ignatius, the first witness to only one bishop in a church, did not base his understanding of the ministry on succession. The one bishop was a representative of God the Father, and the presbyters had their model in the college of apostles (Trall. 3).

The first claim to a succession from the apostles in support of particular doctrines was made in the second century by the Gnostics. They claimed that the apostles had imparted certain secret teachings to some of their disciples and that these teachings had been passed down, thus having apostolic authority, even if different from what was proclaimed in the churches (Irenaeus, Haer. 3.2.1; cf. Ptolemy in Epiphanius, Haer. 33.7.9). Hegesippus, an opponent of Gnosticism, compiled a list of the bishops in Rome (Eusebius, H.E. 4.22.5f.).

Irenaeus of Lyons drew on the idea of the succession of bishops to formulate an orthodox response to the Gnostic claim of a secret tradition going back to the apostles. Irenaeus argued that if the apostles had any secrets to teach, they would have delivered them to those men to whom they committed the leadership of the churches. A person could go to the churches founded by apostles, Irenaeus contended, and determine what was taught in those churches by the succession of teachers since the days of the apostles. The constancy of this teaching was guaranteed by its public nature; any change could have been detected, since the teaching was open. The accuracy of the teaching in each church was confirmed by its agreement with what was taught in other churches. One and the same faith had been taught in all the churches since the time of the apostles.

Irenaeus's succession was collective rather than individual. He spoke of the succession of the presbyters (*Haer.* 3.2.2) or of the presbyters and bishops (4.26.2) as well as of the bishops (3.3.1). To be in the succession was not itself sufficient to guarantee correct doctrine. The succession functioned negatively to mark off the heretics who withdrew from the church. A holy life and sound teaching were also required of true leaders (4.26.5). The succession pertained to faith and life rather than to the transmission of special gifts. The "gift of truth" (*charisma veritatis*) received with the office of teaching (4.26.2) was not a gift guaranteeing that what was taught would be true, but was the truth itself as a gift. Each holder of the teaching chair in the church received the apostolic doctrine as a deposit to be faithfully transmitted to the church. Apostolic succession as formulated by Irenaeus was from one holder of the teaching chair in a church to the next and not from ordainer to ordained, as it became.

The church at Rome held a special place in Irenaeus's argument. It was the closest church to him founded by apostles, and it traced its teaching to the two leading apostles, Peter and Paul. Instead of listing the succession of bishops in all the churches, he gave the list of Rome alone as a demonstration of the continuity of apostolic teaching. Since the true apostolic doctrine was preserved there, every church must agree with what was taught at Rome (3.3.1–3).

Tertullian's *Prescription Against Heretics* 20–21; 32 made a similar argument. He included other churches besides Rome, making the point that it was unlikely for so many widely separated churches to have accidentally stumbled into the same doctrine. He referred only to bishops as belonging to the succession.

Churches were apostolic that agreed in the same faith, even if not founded by apostles.

Apostolic succession arose in a polemical situation as an effective argument for the truth of Catholic tradition against Gnostic teachings. As so often happens to successful arguments, it came to be regarded as an article of faith, not just a defense of the truth but a part of the truth itself.

Hippolytus is apparently the first for whom the bishops were not simply in the succession from the apostles but were themselves successors of the apostles (*Haer.*, praef.). When Eusebius of Caesarea used the lists of bishops as the framework for his *Church History*, he did not count the apostles in the episcopal lists. Cyprian, however, made an identification of the episcopate and the apostolate (*Ep.* 64.3; 66.4; cf. *Sent. epp.* 79 and Socrates, *H.E.* 6.8).

The view that bishops were truly successors of the apostles was accepted in Rome in the third century (Cyprian, *Ep.* 3.3; 66.4) and from the fourth century was the standard teaching of that church. This was applied to make the bishop of Rome the successor specifically to Peter and to hold a comparable place among the churches to the place of Peter in the apostolic church (Leo, *Serm.* 3.3–4; *Ep.* 45.2). This claim may be seen in the common designation of Rome as "the apostolic see."

Cyprian's view that sacraments administered outside the Catholic church were not valid (*Ep.* 73; cf. 75.7 for Firmilian) was slowly modified. Augustine extended the principle of the recognition of heretical or schismatic actions to a theory of the validity of ordination outside the Catholic church (*De bapt. c. Donat.* 1.1.2; *Ep.* 53.1–4, 6), but even for him such orders were probably not technically in the apostolic succession. The sacramental understanding of ordination that grew up in the fourth and fifth centuries shifted the emphasis to a succession from ordainer to ordained, but the earlier historical type of succession was preserved in the lists of local bishops. *See also* Bishop; Evangelist; Ordination; Sacraments.

[E.F.]

Bibliography
Irenaeus, *Against Heresies* 3.2.1–3.4.1; 4.26.2–5; 4.32.1–4.33.8; Tertullian, *Prescription Against Here-*

tics 20–21; 32; Hippolytus, *Refutation of All Heresies*, praef.; Cyprian, *Letters* 66.4; 75.16; *Judgment of 87 Bishops* 79; *Apostolic Constitutions* 8.46; Augustine, *On Baptism Against the Donatists* 1.1.2; idem, *Letter* 53.1–4, 6.

C.H. Turner, "Apostolic Succession," *Essays on the Early History of the Church and the Ministry*, ed. H.B. Swete (London: Macmillan, 1918), pp. 93–214; K.E. Kirk, ed., *The Apostolic Ministry* (New York: Morehouse-Gorham, 1947); T.W. Manson, *The Church's Ministry* (London: Hodder and Stoughton, 1948); E. Molland, "Irenaeus of Lugdunum and the Apostolic Succession," *JEH* 1 (1950):12–28; A. Ehrhardt, *The Apostolic Succession* (London: Lutterworth, 1953); E. Molland, "Le Développement de l'idée de succession apostolique," *RHPhR* 34 (1954):1–29; A.M. Javierre, "La Thème de la succession des apôtres dans la littérature chrétienne primitive," *L'Episcopat et l'église universelle*, ed. Y. Congar (Paris: Cerf, 1962); R.M. Grant, "Early Episcopal Succession," *SP* 11 (1972):179–184.

APRINGIUS OF BEJA (sixth century). Bishop and exegete. Apringius was the author of a Latin commentary, mostly derivative and of limited circulation, on the Book of Revelation, of which two large fragments survive. CPL 1093. [M.P.McH.]

Bibliography
Braulio of Saragossa, *Letter* 25.
Repertorium Fontium Historiae Medii Aevi (Rome: Istituto Storico Italiano per il Medio Evo, 1967), Vol. 2, p. 383.

APSE. Semicircular space at the end of the nave in the typical early Christian basilica. The term may also describe any similar space or opening whether or not the building is a church, and it is sometimes used for a freestanding structure. In most instances, the apse was roofed with a semidome or vault. The word comes from the Latin *apsis* (also spelled *absis* or *absida*) and the Greek *hapsis*, although the Greek word always means simply an arch. Latin synonyms include *concha*, *exedra*, and *tribunal*; the last two may also designate a lectern or pulpit (*ambo*), which in secular judicial basilicas was located in the apse. An apse was a common architectural feature in Roman imperial buildings. It often contained a throne or a statue of a deity or emperor.

In ecclesiastical usage, the apse was usually the location of clergy seats—sometimes arranged in tiers around the semicircle—and the bishop's throne, or *cathedra*, from which he preached and otherwise participated in the liturgy. In some church plans, a platform (*bema*) extended from the apse into the nave, and the entire area was known as the "sanctuary," where the eucharist was celebrated. It came to be marked off from the rest of the nave with railings. In many early Christian churches, the altar was not in the apse but in front of it in the nave.

In churches with two side-aisles, there might be apses at the end of each aisle—a triple-apse plan. With the establishment of the practice of orientation, the apse was regularly at the east end of the church. Basilicas in Algeria and Tunisia often had a second, counter-apse at the west end, which might house the relics of a saint or other special memorial. Churches of centralized plan also commonly had an apse opposite the entrance. There were usually three windows in the apse, and its exterior shape might be round or polygonal. In some plans, the apse was completely enclosed or inscribed within the flat east wall. The interior semidome was usually decorated, as in the churches of S. Vitale and of S. Apollinare in Classe at Ravenna. [G.T.A.]

Bibliography
A.M. Schneider, "Apsis," RLAC (1950), Vol. 1, cols. 571–573; C. Delvoye, "Etudes d'architecture paléochrétienne et byzantine," *Byzantion* 32 (1962):291–310, 489–547; idem, "Apsis," *Reallexikon zur byzantinischen Kunst*, ed. K. Wessel (Stuttgart: Hiersemann, 1966), Vol. 1, pp. 246–268 (with numerous plans); N. Duval, *Sbeitla et les églises africaines à deux absides*, 2 vols. (Paris: De Boccard, 1971, 1973); R. Krautheimer, *Early Christian and Byzantine Architecture*, 3rd ed. (Harmondsworth: Penguin, 1979), pp. 41–43 and passim (with illustrations, plans, and bibliography).

AQUILA (second century). Translator of the Old Testament into Greek. According to Epiphanius (*Mens.* 14), Aquila was a native of Sinope in Pontus. Having converted to Judaism, he came under the influence of the strictest Palestinian rabbinical exegesis. With the name of Aquila is connected a Greek translation of the Old Testament typified by extreme literalness. This translation, which Aquila worked upon ca. 130, replaced the Septuagint in Jewish circles and was used by Origen in the *Hexapla*. It is extant in fragments from Genesis, Kings, and Psalms; in marginal notes in Greek biblical manuscripts; and possibly as the translation of Ecclesiastes in Septuagint manuscripts. TLG 1768. *See also* Septuagint.

[C.C.]

Bibliography
J. Reider, *An Index to Aquila* (Leiden: Brill, 1966).

ARABIA. Peninsula between the Red Sea and Persian Gulf, and adjoining regions in southwest Asia. According to his own testimony, shortly after his conversion Paul set off to proclaim faith in Christ in Arabia (Gal. 1:15–17). Presumably, he preached among those people to the south and east of Damascus, whose civic center was the city of Bostra, the modern Buṣrâ in Syria, which became the capital of the Roman province of Arabia in A.D. 106. By the first half of the third century, Christianity was flourishing in this area, and the church of Bostra even boasted of having received Origen as a visitor on three different occasions. Moreover, the Roman emperor Philip "the Arab" (244–249), whom Eusebius and Jerome thought was a Christian, was born near Bostra. The people who lived in this border territory between Rome and the vast expanses of the Arabian desert were probably Arabic-speaking, although the widespread use of Greek and Syriac in the churches on the *limes arabicus* makes it uncertain whether Arabic was ever an ecclesiastical language there before the rise of Islam in the first half of the seventh century.

Nevertheless, it is clear that from the fifth century onward Christianity made steady progress among the Arabic-speaking tribes in Sinai and in Arabia proper. By the sixth century, central Arabia was virtually surrounded by Christian centers of influence. In the Holy Land, the monastery of St. Euthymius was the point of referral for an Arab tribe that had its own hereditary bishopric. In Judea, Gaza, the Negev, and the Sinai, communities of monks and hermits were familiar to the local Arabs, who often harassed them. On the borders with Syria, the Arabic-speaking tribes were regular visitors to the shrines of St. Sergius at Rusafa and of St. Symeon Stylites at Qalʿat Simʿân. By the late seventh century, ʿAqūla (Kūfa) was the seat of a bishop of the nomad Arabs.

Farther south, on the lower Euphrates, the town of Ḥīra was not only an important Arab tribal center, but it was ecclesiastically important among Syriac-speaking Christians as a center for missionary work among the Arabs of the peninsula. Arabia proper had a thriving Christian community in Najrān, which had active ties with Ḥīra. And to the south, the principalities of south Arabia had contacts with the Christian communities across the Red Sea in Ethiopia. So widespread did Christianity become among the trading communities in the tribal territories that even the later Islamic traditions recorded the presence of a cemetery for Christians in Mecca and reported that there was an icon of Mary the Mother of Jesus, and of her son, in the Kaaba in the prophet Muhammad's day. And numerous Islamic traditions report exchanges that Muhammad was supposed to have had with monks and other Christian Arabs.

The importance of recognizing the presence of Christianity in Arabia at least from the third century lies not least in the faith's strong showing among the people to whom Muhammad first preached Islam. In many ways, Islam was a direct challenge to the earlier spread of Christianity among the Arabs in the fifth and sixth centuries. [S.H.G.]

Bibliography
B.M. Metzger, *The Early Versions of the New Testament* (Oxford: Clarendon, 1977), pp. 257–268; J.S. Trimingham, *Christianity Among the Arabs in Pre-Islamic Times* (London and Beirut: Longman, 1979); G.W. Bowersock, *Roman Arabia* (Cambridge: Harvard UP, 1983); I. Shahid, *Rome and the Arabs: A Prolegomenon to the Study of Byzantium and the Arabs* (Washington, D.C.: Dumbarton Oaks, 1984); idem, *Byzantium and the Arabs in the Fourth Century* (Washington, D.C.: Dumbarton Oaks, 1984); idem, *Byzantium and the Arabs in the Fifth Century* (Washington, D.C.: Dumbarton Oaks, 1989).

ARATOR (d. ca. 550). Christian Latin poet. A protégé of Ennodius, Arator served in the court of the Ostrogothic kingdom and subsequently was ordained subdeacon. His epic poem *De actibus apostolorum*, dedicated to pope Vigilius (544), was based more or less on the Acts of the Apostles, but with considerable allegorical and mystical interpretation; it enjoyed widespread popularity in the Middle Ages. CPL 1504–1505.   [M.P.McH.]

Bibliography

Ennodius, *Epistulae* 8.4, 11, 33; 9.1; *Dictiones* 9; 11; 18; 22 *praef.*; *Carmina* 2.105, 114; Cassidorus, *Variae* 8.12.

Arator's De Actibus Apostolorum, ed. and tr. J.L. Roberts III, J.F. Makowski, and R.J. Schrader (Atlanta: Scholars, 1988).

F.J.E. Raby, *A History of Christian Latin Poetry*, 2nd ed. (Oxford: Clarendon, 1953), pp. 117–120; R.J. Schrader, "Arator: Revaluation," *CF* 31 (1977):64–77.

ARCHAEOLOGY. Study of the material remains of ancient cultures.

Historical Survey. Interest in early Christian remains began at the end of the fifteenth century with the study of the catacombs in Rome. The Renaissance opened up new fields of research for inquiring minds. Members of the newly founded Roman Academy explored the catacomb of Peter and Marcellinus, which originated at the end of the third century A.D.; they left their mark by carving on the walls their aim to be "researchers of antiquity."

During the century of the wars of religion (1530–1648), scholars continued to explore the catacombs. The most celebrated of these, Antonio Bosio (1576–1629), discovered the first Jewish catacomb, on the Via Nomentana, and so gave a tentative impulse to the comparative study of early Christian history; he preserved his work for posterity with fine representations of catacomb paintings. This period of research was succeeded by one in which scholarship gave way to the hunt for *objets d'art* to add to the splendor of the great houses of the wealthy. Only in the nineteenth century was scientific exploration of the catacombs resumed, with G. Marchi (1795–1860) and above all J.B. de Rossi

(1822–1894) laying the foundations for future scholarship.

Archaeological research in other areas rich in early Christian remains followed a similar pattern, made possible when the decline of the Turkish empire, from the end of the eighteenth century, opened the former Christian lands on the southern shores of the Mediterranean to Europeans. The discovery of the Rosetta Stone in Egypt in 1799 and its decipherment in the 1820s was followed by the excavations of Layard and Rawlinson in Mesopotamia. From the Babylonian library at Nineveh came tablets dating from ca. 1700 B.C. telling the story of the flood (Gen. 6) from the Babylonian point of view. With these discoveries, archaeology as applied to the Old and New Testaments began.

The next stage was a result of the French conquest of Algeria from 1830 to 1845. Early French settlers were amazed to find the ruins of Roman cities standing almost intact. Adrien Berbrugger's founding of the Société Historique Algérienne in 1856 opened the way for archaeological exploration there. It soon became clear that the remains of Roman villages and cities, such as Timgad and Cuicul, contained many Christian buildings unused since the sites were abandoned generally in the seventh and eighth centuries. In 1893, a survey by H. Graillot and S. Gsell of a large area north of the Aures Mountains revealed churches and chapels along with granaries and olive presses on village sites in what had once been the Roman province of Numidia and through inscriptions identified some of the buildings as belonging to the Donatist church. Archaeological discoveries confirmed the literary evidence provided by Optatus of Milevis and Augustine.

In Asia Minor, similar discoveries were being made by W.M. Ramsay, J.G.C. Anderson, and colleagues from Aberdeen University and by the Austrians J. Keil and G. von Premerstein. Keil and von Premerstein were tireless travelers and keen archaeologists and epigraphists. With W. Heberdey, they excavated the great theater at Ephesus on the hillside overlooking the harbor where Paul almost certainly faced his accusers in A.D. 53. Ramsay's discoveries confirmed the description in Acts 13–17 of the numerous Jewish communities in the cities of Asia Minor; with his younger colleagues, he found the first of the inscriptions containing the phrase "Christians for Christians" at sites of the imperial estates that covered part of the Tembris Valley in northern Phrygia. These inscriptions indicated that a strongly evangelical and confessional Christianity had taken root in that part of Asia Minor. Once again, archaeology had confirmed the literary accounts, in this case Eusebius of Caesarea's remarks on the strength of Montanism in Phrygia (*H.E.* 5.16–18). Both here and in Numidia, archaeology permitted a better understanding of the impact of nonorthodox Christianity on the rural populations of the Roman empire.

In 1900, scientific archaeology was still in its infancy, but the period after World War I witnessed dramatic changes. The extension of European influence throughout the Middle East opened up new, important sites for investigation. The single day's work by J.R. Breasted at Dura-Europos, the Roman frontier fortress on the Euphrates that was captured by the Persians in 256, fired the imagination of scholars and led to the successive seasons of work by Yale University in the 1920s and 1930s. At Dura, not only were the remains of a Jewish synagogue unearthed, with frescoes of Moses leading the people of Israel through the Red Sea, but also a Christian church, built ca. 240, with a baptistery and wall paintings of Old and New Testament scenes. The former scenes tended to foreshadow incidents in the latter, such as David's overthrow of Goliath, which prefigured Christ destroying Satan. Christians of the time were portraying their religion as one of liberation from traditional obeisance to idols and to the power of fate.

In Egypt, the study of papyri, extending back to the discovery in the 1890s of numerous fragments in the rubbish pits outside the town of Oxyrhynchus, was providing evidence of new, noncanonical gospels, such as the second-century fragments of an unknown gospel, published by H.I. Bell and T.C. Skeat, and the first fragment of what was identified later as the *Gospel of Thomas* (P. Oxy. i. 654, 655). In 1937, C.H. Roberts identified a small fragment of an early-second-century papyrus as John 18:31–33, 37–38 (Rylands Papyrus 457), thus effectively ending debate over a possible "late" date for the Fourth Gospel. The most sensational papyrological discovery of these years was that of a library of Manichaean tracts in Coptic, identified by K. Schmidt of the Pergamum Museum at Berlin. The manuscripts included Manichaean psalms and hymns as well as writings (lost during World War II) attributed to Mani himself.

In North Africa, the 1930s witnessed the continuation by scholars of the Ecole Française de Rome of the work in Numidia started by Gsell and Graillot, including the discovery of more Donatist sites, among them a large church dedicated to the memory of the Donatist martyr-bishop Marculus (d. ca. 348). Donatism was shown to be overwhelmingly the religion of the Numidian countryside.

Post–World War II research has been aided by the application of scientific dating techniques, such as carbon-14; by increased use of air photography; and by better methods of excavation, inspired largely by the work of R.E.M. Wheeler on Iron Age and Roman sites in Britain, and above all, new and effective means to preserve antiquities, especially frescoes.

A number of spectacular finds were made in the years 1945–1947. First, the Dead Sea Scrolls, the product of the Jewish sect of Covenanters, if not Essenes closely allied to them, shed light on the outlook of a pious Jewish community that flourished at the time of Jesus' ministry; the scrolls added to our knowledge of both the intellectual (strongly apocalyptic) background of Jesus' preaching and the text of the scriptures current in his day. Then, in Upper Egypt only a few miles from Pachomius's monastery at Chenoboskion (Nag Hammadi), a library of fifty-two separate Gnostic texts was found by Egyptian peasants, who handed them over to the local Coptic priest; from him they reached Cairo. After a history of academic bribery and intrigue, the whole library was translated into English and published by J.M. Robinson (*The Nag Hammadi Library in English*). This collection of religious texts, originally in Greek but found in Coptic translations, enabled the Gnostics of the second and third centuries to speak for themselves and not through the often distorting accounts of their Catholic opponents. They stand revealed as individuals who accepted that Christianity involved estrangement from the world, withdrawal from all that might contaminate the vision of reality they sought, and belief in a purely spiritual order and interpretation of scripture and the sacraments of the church. For them, the Christians' resurrection had already taken place. They had already died to the world and all that was material; they alone would receive the true revelation of Christ.

Regional Survey. Advances of historical scholarship all over the world have resulted in a great accumulation of archaeological material relating to early Christianity. Excavations in western Europe bear increasing witness to the religion's progress from the middle of the fourth century onward. The early Christian church had effectively replaced the pagan temples in many areas by the time of the barbarian onslaught in the first years of the fifth century. Especially in Britain, archaeological discoveries have supplemented the meager literary records. The treasure from Water Newton (near Peterborough) provided the earliest liturgical silver as yet found (mid-fourth century); the mosaic showing Christ as a beardless young man from the villa at Hinton St. Mary in Dorset, and the wall frescoes reconstructed from the villa at Lullingstone in Kent, reveal the new religion's success in penetrating the landowning class of society.

In Rome, the discovery of new catacombs, such as the Novaziono (in 1926), and Ponziano, and the Via Latina (1956), and new discoveries on older sites have proceeded year after year, until it has become possible to study the development of Christian art without a break from the late second to the fifth century. Of these new discoveries, originally undertaken to prepare a tomb for pope Pius X in 1939, the most important have been those beneath St. Peter's.

Excavations under the area of the high altar revealed well-preserved remains of a Roman cemetery dating to the second and third centuries A.D., which by the fourth century contained numerous Christian tombs. Much of this cemetery had been destroyed in 322 to make room for Constantine's basilica in honor of St. Peter. However, in one wall of a line of tombs, known as the Red Wall, had been built a small niched structure facing an open courtyard. This was in existence ca. 170 and is thought to mark the spot where Christians at that period believed Peter either to have died or to have been buried after his martyrdom at the hands of the emperor Nero in A.D. 64. In addition, it seems likely that this was the *tropaion,* or "trophy," seen on the Vatican Hill by the Roman presbyter Gaius ca. 200 and claimed by him to be a familiar object at the time to Roman Christians (Eusebius, *H.E.* 2.25.7). Unfortunately, the difficulties of excavation and, it must be admitted, the excavators' failure to observe stratigraphy, prevent a final verdict as to whether this indeed marked Peter's grave, or whether the cult-center on the Via Appia was the resting-place of the bones of Peter and Paul.

The 1960s saw a new, international approach to archaeological work. Even before Egypt gave notice in 1963 of the construction of the high dam at Aswan, which was designed to regulate the Nile's yearly flow but required the flooding of the country between Aswan and Wadi Halfa, survey work in the threatened Nubian sites had been under way. Mainly as a result of the efforts of H.S. Smith of the British Museum and W.Y. Adams of the University of Kentucky, sites were allotted to international teams with the objective of salvaging as much of the Nubian remains as was possible before the waters of the Nile rose to form Lake Nasser in 1965. Twenty-three nations from both eastern- and western-bloc countries cooperated. Two sites were the scene of particularly successful work. At Faras, across the Sudanese frontier, the Polish team, led by K. Michalowski, discovered the cathedral and governor's palace of the northern kingdom of Nobatia. The cathedral yielded a series of magnificent frescoes dating from between the eighth and twelfth centuries, including the famous St. Anne fresco of the eighth century, and a series of portraits of bishops mainly of the tenth and eleventh. In addition, a chronological list of bishops was found written in black ink on one wall, thus providing the history of Nobatia with a chronological framework. Q'asr Ibrim, an important fortified settlement about 100 miles to the north, was the site of a cathedral and at least two other churches, an official residence, and earlier temples and buildings extending back into pharaonic times. The settlement was situated on a cliff some 250 feet above the level of the Nile in 1963; work under the auspices of the Egypt Exploration society has gone on there continuously since then. Although no frescoes were found, the discovery at Q'asr Ibrim of what appears to have been the scattered remains of the cathedral library has clarified the liturgical significance of the frescoes at Faras. Fragments of Monophysite liturgies similar to the existing liturgies of St. Mark and St. James have been recovered, as well as a fragment of the *Acta* of the military martyrs Mercurius and George, who were represented at Faras. The cult of the military saints under the leadership of Michael and All Angels was shown to have been strong in Christian Nubia. The excavations also found title deeds of bishop Timotheus, buried with him and dated to 1374, which proved that organized Christianity had survived in Nobatia at least to that period. In further work, W.H.C. Frend found a group of nine leather scrolls concealed in a jar, the latest of which, dated precisely to 1464, recorded a "king Joel" and a "bishop Merkos." It is clear that Christianity in the Nile Valley did not fall before invading Muslim nomad tribes until the eve of European expansion in the last decade of the fifteenth century, which ended the advance of Islam.

Increased urbanization over the site of Carthage resulted in another international project of archaeological cooperation. Between 1976 and 1979, teams from fifteen countries worked on sites in the city area in close cooperation with Tunisian archaeologists. Notably successful on early Christian sites were teams representing English- and French-speaking Canada, led by E. Whitehead and J. Senay respectively, and from the University of Michigan, led by J. Humphrey. Discoveries included Byzantine churches and monuments, as well as evidence for the steady decline of living standards during the seventh century, the final period of Christian Carthage.

In recent years, Israeli archaeologists have added greatly to knowledge of Christian Palestine, and not the least to the identification of possible New Testament sites in Jerusalem, including perhaps Golgotha itself.

Contributions. The contributions of archaeology to the study of early Christianity can hardly be overestimated. Apart from the sheer bulk of new evidence, the archaeologist has cast a completely new light on the development of the early church. Nonorthodox traditions, such as the Gnostic, Manichaean, Donatist, Monophysite, and Montanist, can now speak for themselves from the indisputable evidence of discoveries from the ground. Christianity is revealed as never before as a religion of many traditions, in which various interpretations of the founder's life and work existed from earliest times. Something of the wholeness of the Christian faith has been revealed as well, and orthodoxy has become open to reinterpretation in the light of what is now known of other Christian traditions.

The organization of this new wealth of information has so far kept pace with the discoveries themselves. The quadrennial congresses devoted to Christian archaeology have enabled new discoveries to be announced and discussed. These conferences have been supplemented by national colloquia. Scholarly periodical literature is represented by the *Jahrbuch für Antike und Christentum*, published by the Franz Josef Dölger Institute at Bonn University, and by the *Rivista di archeologia cristiana*, published by the Pontifical Institute of Christian Archaeology at the Vatican. In Britain, the Society of Antiquaries of London yearly awards the Frend Medal for distinguished contributions to the archaeological study of early Christianity.

The prospects for continued archaeological work are good. Much depends, however, on political developments in the Mediterranean countries, and also on restraining growing populations from looting ancient sites for building stone. Against this, increased popular awareness of the importance of history in the cultural life of nations and the increasing search for self-identity expressed in the discovery of roots will help ensure the preservation of many antiquities of the Christian period. *See also* Art; Catacombs; Inscriptions; Papyri.

[W.H.C.F.]

Bibliography

L. Leschi, "Basilique et cimitère donatistes de Numidie (Ain Ghorab)," *Revue Africaine* 78 (1936):27–46; A. Berthier, *Les Vestiges du Christianisme antique dans la Numidie centrale* (Algiers: Imprimerie polyglotte africaine, Maison-Carrée, 1942); H.I. Bell, *Egypt from Alexander the Great to the Arab Conquests* (London: Oxford UP, 1948); E.A. Meates, *Lullingstone Roman Villa* (London: Heinemann, 1955); J.M.C. Toynbee and J. Ward Perkins, *The Shrine of St. Peter and the Vatican Excavations* (London: Longmans, Green, 1956); J.M.C. Toynbee, "A New Roman Mosaic Pavement Found in Dorset," *JRS* 54 (1964):7–14; D.J. Chitty, *The Desert a City* (Oxford: Blackwell, 1966); M. Gough, *The Early Christians* (London: Thames and Hudson, 1967); K. Michalowski, *Faras, die Kathedrale aus dem Wustensand* (Zurich: Benziger, 1967); C. Andresen, *Einführung in die Christliche Archäologie* (Göttingen: Vandenhoeck & Ruprecht, 1971); J. Jakobielski, *A History of the Bishopric of Pachoras on the Basis of Coptic Inscriptions* (Warsaw: Editions Scientifique de Pologne, 1972); M. Simon, *La Civilization de l'antiquité et Christianisme* (Paris: Arthaud, 1972); K.S. Painter, *The Water Newton Early Christian Treasure* (London: British Museum, 1977); J. Stevenson, *The Catacombs: Rediscovered Monuments of Early Christianity* (London: Thames and Hudson, 1978); A. Grabar, *L'Art paléochrétien et l'art byzantine* (London: Variorum, 1979); P. MacKendrick, *North African Stones Speak* (London: Croom Helm, 1980); C. Thomas, *Christianity in Roman Britain to A.D. 500* (London: Batsford, 1981); W.H.C. Frend, "Silent Witness: The Use and Limitation of Archaeological Research in the Problems of Early Christianity," *Römische Quartalschrift* 80 (1985):148–159; G. Snyder, *Ante Pacem: Archaeological Evidence of Church Life Before Constantine* (Macon: Mercer UP, 1985); W.H.C. Frend, *History and Archaeology in the Study of Early Christianity* (London: Variorum, 1988).

ARCHIMANDRITE. Head of a monastery or monasteries. The Greek term behind archimandrite ("ruler of the fold") has its roots in early eastern monasticism, appearing in the fourth century to denote a founder of one or more monasteries. It later came also to be synonymous with a "hegumen" or "abbot" and, later still, became a title of an office conferred on celibate priests by a bishop or patriarch (Mansi 7.61C–64C). Originally, however, this term was not necessarily tied to persons in holy orders.

According to Palladius, Pachomius (d. 346), the founder of the cenobitic system of monasticism, was called during his lifetime "an archimandrite of 3,000 monks" (*H. Laus.* 7). Another early reference occurs in a letter of Acacius and Paul ("Presbyters and Archimandrites, i.e., Fathers of Monasteries," from Coele-Syria) to Epiphanius of Salamis, which is reproduced at the beginning of the latter's *Panarion*. The same sense of the term is found in Cyril of Scythopolis, the sixth-century biographer of prominent Palestinian monks; in the acts of local councils (e.g., the Council of Constantinople [448], in which twenty-three archimandrites took part) and of ecumenical councils (Mansi 4.1101A; 5.1232A; 6.617D, 621C, 628CD, 629A, 677D, 793AB, 796C; Vol. 6 contains many references to Eutyches, the Monophysite archimandrite); and in state laws (Justinian, *Nov.* 5.7 for the year 535; 120.6 for the year 544; 123.34 for the year 546).

[G.D.D.]

ARIANISM. Patristic scholarship has for a long time been accustomed to using "Arianism" as a designation for all theologies at odds with the creed of Nicaea as promulgated in 325. This is in fact seriously misleading, insofar as it suggests that there was a single coherent "opposition party" deriving its ideas from the theology of Arius; recent research has more and more made plain the great diversity of anti-Nicene theology and the way in which Nicene polemic gives to the figure of Arius himself an importance not necessarily accorded him by opponents of the council of 325.

Doctrine of Arius. At the time of the initial outbreak of the doctrinal controversy (ca. 318 or 320/1), Arius was a senior presbyter in Alexandria, an influential teacher and ascetic, probably having links with the masters of the catechetical school. His bishop, Alexander, was struggling to secure the doctrinal and disciplinary cohesion of a church that had already been deeply scarred by dispute and schism, and he appears to have insisted upon his right to examine the exegesis of his clergy in their preaching. He also proposed in his own teaching a number of unfamiliar formulas, rooted in a tradition of Alexandrian theology but novel and problematic in expression. The doctrine that the Word is eternally generated from the Father, and that if God is rightly *called* Father he must always *be* the father of a son, goes back to Origen and is reflected in some of the surviving fragments of the teaching of Dionysius the Great (bishop of Alexandria from 259 to 268)—although other fragments put this in question. Alexander's version of this, expressed in slogans like "always God, always the Son," seemed to his critics to prejudice the integrity of monotheism, by suggesting either a second independent individual alongside God or else an eternal partition of God's substance (unthinkable in a nonmaterial reality). Or, if neither of these was acceptable as an interpretation, did not such language then suggest that the Word was really no more than an eternal nonindividuated "power" of God?

Arius attacked Alexander's theology on all these grounds and, according to the early chroniclers, was himself attacked by Alexander for his exegesis of certain biblical passages—almost certainly including Proverbs 8:22, "The Lord created me at the beginning of his ways." Arius's teaching represented a radicalized version of another strand in Alexandrian tradition, that which identified the Judeo-Christian God with the absolute primordial unity beyond all definition and categorization, and the Word, the Logos, with the foundational principle of the multiplicity of the world: the Father is purely one, *monas*, the Logos is many-in-one, the realm of ideas. If the *monas* is to be wholly itself, indivisible and self-sufficient, it must be capable of subsisting without the Logos: hence the slogan associated with Arius and his supporters, "there was when he [the Logos] was not"—although Arius himself was manifestly unhappy about the idea of a time interval preceding the generation of the Logos. His main point is that the Logos does not *have* to exist: God wills the Logos or Son to be, so that scripture can legitimately say (as in Proverbs 8:22) that Logos or Sophia is "created." But this is not to rank the Logos with other creatures, since all else depends on him; and although he is in principle capable of change and decline, he always freely adheres to the good and praises his Maker. Knowing this eternal fidelity, the Father gives him from the beginning all the divine glory a creature can possess, so that he becomes a mediator of the Father's glory, his life, his divine attributes, to the universe that comes to be through him.

This theology is a skillful and original blend of the biblical concern with a freely creating personal God and the philosophical concern with preservation of the pure singularity of the primal monad. This latter theme was becoming increasingly important in the philosophy of the day, as Neoplatonism gradually took shape, blending Platonic language and cosmology with Aristotelian logic and elements of Pythagorean numerology. We hear of Alexandrian Christians who had interests in all these areas; and it was known that Plotinus, father of Neoplatonism, had studied under the same teacher as the great Origen. It would be unsurprising for Arius to show signs of contact with this general philosophical current, and his language occasionally hints at it; but there is no absolutely clear evidence of specific indebtedness. Arius's early supporters showed few signs of metaphysical interest, although some were described as well-equipped dialecticians (as was Arius himself), and it is hard to see any signs of a definable group actually accepting Arius's theology and cosmology as a whole, let alone treating it as authoritative, outside his immediate circle in Alexandria.

Lucianists. After his predictable condemnation and deposition by Alexander and a large majority of the Alexandrian clergy, Arius swiftly became the figurehead of a campaign against Alexander's theology orchestrated by an influential group of clergy who had been students of the great exegete and martyr Lucian of Antioch (d. 311). Arius first gained some support in Palestine, not least from Eusebius of Caesarea, and then attracted the patronage of Eusebius of Nicomedia, the weightiest personality in the Lucianist circle. The subsequent history of "Arianism" is in large part the history of the Lucianists and those who traced their spiritual and intellectual descent from them. They regarded some features of Arius's theology with wariness, especially his stress on the absolute unknowability of God; Arius may well have composed his manifesto, the *Thalia* ("Banquet"), as it came to be called, in response to requests from the Lucianists for a clarification of his views. Lucianist theology, insofar as it can be clearly characterized, stressed the singleness of God the creator, his full revelation in the Son, his perfect and indefectible image, and the real and distinct subsistence (*hypostasis*) of each of the three divine subjects, united in a harmony of will and a hierarchical order. Like Arius, the supporters of this theology saw Alexander's views as menacing the unity and supremacy of the "true" God, the Father, and the reality of the Son as a hypostasis: Alexander's language could only mean either polytheism or Sabellianism. And the weakening of belief in the Son's hypostasis was also by now associated in the minds of many with Paul of Samosata's Christology: Jesus, a fully individuated human being, anointed and inspired by a Logos that remains in heaven. In contrast, Arius and the Lucianists almost certainly believed that the Logos acted as a soul in Jesus's body; being created and passible, it was able to undergo the experiences of Jesus' human nature. What was said in scripture about the weakness or suffering of Jesus was said directly of the Logos.

Nicaea. There was, then, enough common ground between Arius and the Lucianists to make a tactical alliance possible: there were clear common enemies. However, despite the skill and energy of the Eusebii and others in rallying support, the alliance disastrously failed to carry the day at Nicaea. The emperor Constantine's confidant Hosius of Cordova had been won over by Alexander, and imperial pressure was applied in favor of a settlement acceptable to Alexander (which meant a settlement unacceptable to Arius's supporters). The result was a creed asserting that the Son was generated "out of the Father's substance," "of the same substance [*homoousios*] with the Father"—both phrases known to be objectionable to Arius and the Lucianists. Arius's deposition was confirmed and he was exiled, as were two Libyan bishops who had taken his part; Eusebius of Nicomedia and two of his associates seem to have been given a "suspended sentence," but were exiled a few months later.

The creed was not a document commanding any significant degree of consensus, and subsequent events amply bear this out. Arius and Eusebius were both readmitted to communion, after declaring their assent to judiciously ambiguous formulas, by the end of 327; and although no new creed appeared, Nicaea seems to have become a dead letter by the 330s. Constantine was more concerned for unity than for absolute doctrinal probity and was prepared to tolerate some latitude over the details of Nicaea. Although he remained suspicious of and hostile to Arius, especially when the latter seemed to be threatening schism, he came increasingly to rely on Eusebius of Nicomedia, whose ascendancy survived the scandal of Arius's sudden death in 336 after a doubtfully candid recantation; it was Eusebius who finally baptized the emperor on his deathbed in 337.

Opposition to Nicaea. Part of the unease so widely felt about Nicaea arose from the fact that some of its defenders, notably Marcellus of Ancyra, gave it a practically Sabellian interpretation, vigorously repudiating a doctrine of three real divine subsistents (*hypostaseis*). Marcellus found a good deal of support in the west; but for most bishops in the eastern empire, the priority rapidly became and remained the reaffirmation of a three-hypostasis theology. In 341, the "Dedication" Council of Antioch, assembled for the consecration of a new basilica, produced a number of documents clearly expressing the consensus that had not prevailed at Nicaea. The bishops denied that they were followers of Arius, although they saw nothing objectionable in the theology he was assenting to at the end of his career. They put forward a short creed apparently ascribing eternal existence to the Son but noncommittal about the nature of the Son's unity with the Father. They also endorsed a creed said to derive from Lucian himself. This intriguing text emphasizes above all the Son's status as *perfect image* "of the substance and will and power and glory of the Father's divinity," and insists on the real distinction of Father, Son, and Spirit; to it are appended anathemas echoing those of Nicaea, directed against those who call the Son a creature or speak of a temporal interval before his begetting.

This creed was to be a point of reference over the next two decades for those who were unhappy with the *homoousios* but equally unhappy with Arius's stress on the contingency of the Son's generation—those who came to be known as "Homoiousians" for their belief that the Son was of "similar" substance to the Father, a group whose leader in this period was Basil of Ancyra. It is important to remember that this party accepted the anathemas against Arius's original views; they are not accurately called "Semiarians," as in some textbook accounts.

Neoarians. Within a decade of the Antiochene council, however, this party was already beginning to be outflanked by a far more radical transformation of "Lucianism," associated with the figure of Aetius. This remarkable man, of humble origin, had studied exegesis and dialectic with several prominent Lucianists of an older generation, although his personal relations with some of them were checkered. He clearly regarded many of the older Lucianists as too eager to compromise with Nicaea, and in the 350s and 360s, aided by his gifted pupil Eunomius, he helped to create a new power bloc in the eastern churches, hostile both to Nicaea and to the Homoiousians. In recent years, this party has come to be called Neoarian; this is a useful designation, but misleading to the extent that it suggests a conscious allegiance to Arius, whose memory was by no

means vivid among Nicaea's opponents. They have often been called "Anomoeans," from their arguing that Father and Son are "dissimilar," *anomoios*, but this title too has some drawbacks (it is not clear that *anomoios* was regularly used as a slogan by this party). Their insistence on denying the *homoiotēs* of Father and Son probably arose from the conviction that to call two subjects *homoios* was to include them both in a single genus (the logical terminology of the period would reinforce this): hence their opposition also to the mediating position of Acacius of Caesarea and his party in the 350s, that the Son was "like" the Father in will but not in substance. The Anomoeans, in other words, were not deliberately out to emphasize the gulf between Father and Son but to press home the logic of what they saw as implicit in the repudiation of Nicaea, the rejection of any formula that could suggest two coordinate independent deities.

The theoretical basis of this was stated in the *Syntagmation* of Aetius (359), written probably as a response to the Homoiousian Council of Seleucia in September 351, and to anti-Anomoean pressure from imperial authority (the emperor Constantius II was generally hostile to Nicaea but unsympathetic at this point to Aetius and his allies). Aetius's work consists of a brief preface and thirty-six articles syllogistically framed, setting out the implications of regarding *agennētos* ("unbegotten") as an exact designation of the divine nature and it alone. God remains unchanging in his uncaused nature and bestows immutability by his grace on the Son, who is caused and contingent in essence, existing "before the ages" but wholly dependent on God's will. The difference between this and Arius's theology lies chiefly in the stress on *agennētos* as a fully revelatory title—a point sharpened still further by Aetius's pupil Eunomius, later bishop of Cyzicus, who defended the idea of names as a kind of divinely ordered emanation from essences. Both Aetius and Eunomius attracted widespread mistrust and abuse because of their relentlessly dialectical methods; and Eunomius's claim that exactitude of theological language was vital to holiness, or even identical with holiness, drew forth some of the most effective polemic of the Cappadocian fathers in the 360s and 370s, based on an empiricist and functionalist view of language and a radical doctrine of divine incomprehensibility. This aspect of the controversy has tended to obscure the religious impulse of Neoarianism in defending the idea of a self-revealing *and* self-consistent God (clear in the remains we possess of Neoarian liturgy), and the concern of this group for fidelity to scripture.

New Consensus. However, the brief ascendancy of this party in 359–360, which saw the deposition of several prominent Homoiousians from their sees, succeeded in alienating the greater part of the eastern church; and Constantius's death and replacement by the pagan Julian in 361 meant that there was no longer an emperor whose shifting theological opinions could shift the balance of power in the church. In 360–361, the anti-Anomoean party consolidated itself in an alliance between Homoiousians and pro-Nicaeans. Athanasius, Alexander's successor at Alexandria, had for decades been attacking the enemies of Nicaea and creating the picture of an "Arian" party resisting the decrees of the council. The unhappy history of Marcellus, roundly condemned in the east, had produced in Athanasius a certain caution in stressing the *homoousios*; but toward the end of the 350s, he set out to show how no formula other than that of Nicaea would successfully rule out the Anomoean position that was so unpopular with most of the non-Nicaeans. His *On the Councils* (359) is one of the masterpieces of this skillful blend of polemic and conciliation, demonstrating that formulas dear to the Homoiousians were "Arian" by implication, open to the errors both of Arius and of Aetius, but also conceding an identity of *intention* between the Nicaeans and the Homoiousians of the 350s. The Council of Alexandria (362) confirmed the new alignment and spelled the beginning of the end for Neoarianism, which was increasingly pushed to the margins of the church in the empire. The work of the great Cappadocians gave a decisively Nicene stamp to the theological consensus in the east, and the Second Ecumenical Council at Constantinople (381) reaffirmed the faith of Nicaea in a slightly expanded creed—in substance, the Nicene Creed of today.

Arianism Outside the Empire. Thanks to the faithful labors of the Anomoean missionary Ulfilas, non-Nicene doctrine became the orthodoxy of the Goths who were converted to Christianity, and doctrinal dispute flared up here and there in the west, notably in Spain, after the Goths had overrun the western empire: the "Arian"-"Catholic" divide became a largely ethnic matter, although it continued to provoke terminological refinements in theology, in the form of the addition of the *Filioque* to the Niceno-Constantinopolitan Creed at successive Spanish and Frankish councils from the sixth century onward.

Significance. The doctrinal crisis of the fourth century decisively marked mainstream Christian doctrine in two crucial respects. As Athanasius insisted in his controversial writings, especially the *Discourses Against the Arians*, what was said about the generating of the Son had implications for our conception of the divine being as such: if the Son is an individual separate from the Father and existing by the Father's will, then it is hard to avoid the inference that "being Father," "being generative," is not essential to "being God." The generation of the son introduces an *arbitrary* extra qualification of the divine life, a sort of irrationality; there is no absolute continuity between what God is and what God does. Nicene Trinitarianism thus ruled out the idea of a progression in the divine life from a self-sufficient monad to a plurality: in other words, it separated the question of the "grammar" of talking about God from the question of cosmology or cosmogony. There is no "story" of the life of God or even of creation itself: there is the life of God, as eternal relatedness, Father, Word, Spirit, and there is the contingent order, defined simply by dependence on the life of God—on an act of generative will reflecting an unchanging generative nature. Nicaea thus intensified the distinction between creator and creature, and this had important consequences for anthropology and spirituality (what is the image of God in us?).

The controversy affected Christology. Arius, the Lucianists, and the Neoarians all seem to have agreed that the eternal Logos acted as a soul in the earthly Jesus. The doctrine of a human soul in Jesus was hopelessly tainted by association with Paul of Samosata, and the anti-Nicaeans vehemently rejected those who taught anything that smacked of this, notably the teachings of Photinus, the most radical of Marcellus's disciples. Although Arius and his first followers were charged with echoing Paul of Samosata, because they held to a doctrine of the Savior's mutability, the differences are massive; only a hint of Adoptionist language (divine glory in reward for virtue) appears in Arius, and it is rigorously excluded by later anti-Nicaeans. In principle mutable, the Son is *de facto* immutable in virtue. However, as a creature he can intelligibly be said to be subject to a variety of successive experiences and hence can be spoken of as subject of the human experience of Jesus (hunger, pain, and so on). On the other hand, if the Son is immutable in nature as in virtue—that is, of one nature with God—the idea of a human soul in Jesus has to be reviewed and rehabilitated, and a more "dualistic" Christology must be developed. In this sense, Nicaea led directly to Chalcedon; the "Arian" problematic was again directly formative of the prescriptions of orthodoxy.

Political Aspects. Although the Arian conflict must be viewed as a theological development, it had quite definite political features. When Constantine the Great called the Council at Nicaea, which met in 325, much if not all of his motivation was to keep the empire intact by having one solid religious pillar on which it could stand. He designated funds for travel and lodging, supplied the imperial palace at Nicaea as the meeting place, and himself participated in and oversaw the council. For him, the issue at stake was as much the unity of his empire as theology.

Arianism first represented a danger to political stability, but it soon penetrated the imperial circle and came to be viewed as basic to that stability. Constantine condemned Arius, but also exiled Athanasius, the defender of orthodoxy, for refusing politically helpful compromises. Constantius II supported an intermediate position and exiled both Athanasius and the Neoarian Aetius. The emperors who followed took up various positions; at one time, the "orthodox" would be turned out of office, at another their enemies. Athanasius was exiled or in flight in 336, 339, 356, 362, and 365. His career indicates how often and how easily things could be reversed. He, as much as his opponents, could be seen as a political menace: certain texts present him as one who tried to control the grain shipments north in an attempt to starve out his Arian enemies. Whether the documents are genuine, or perhaps forged as recent research suggests, they well indicate the economic and political struggles involved.

In the midst of these difficulties, the emperor Julian (361–363) attempted to bring all parties back into full battle so that his pagan revival would combat a weakened Christianity. His edicts of religious toleration were meant to produce that effect.

Rivalries between the great sees—Rome, Alexandria, Antioch, and the newly significant Constantinople—were also an important factor. Rome and Alexandria formed a tactical alliance that was to last for over a century and left its mark on the history of theological controversy. The incursions of the Arian Goths into the western empire in the fifth century provided another instance of external and internal political factors entering into the theological debates. *See also* Aetius; Anomoeans; Arius; Athanasius; Constantinople; Eunomius; Eusebius of Nicomedia; Homoeans; Lucian of Antioch; Nicaea. [R.W.]

Bibliography

M. Simonetti, *La crisi ariana nel IV secolo* (Rome: Institutum patristicum Augustinianum, 1975); T.A. Kopecek, *A History of Neo-Arianism*, 2 vols. (Cambridge: Philadelphia Patristic Foundation, 1979); R.C. Gregg and D.E. Groh, *Early Arianism: A View of Salvation* (Philadelphia: Fortress, 1981); R. Williams, "The Logic of Arianism," *JThS* n.s. 34 (1983):56–81; R.C. Gregg, ed., *Arianism: Historical and Theological Reassessments* (Cambridge: Philadelphia Patristic Foundation, 1985); R. Williams, *Arius: Heresy and Tradition* (London: Darton, Longman and Todd, 1987); R.P.C. Hanson, *The Search for the Christian Doctrine of God: The Arian Controversy 318–381* (Edinburgh: T. and T. Clark, 1988).

ARISTIDES (second century). Apologist. Aristides of Athens wrote the earliest preserved Christian apology. According to Eusebius (*H.E.* 4.3.3), Aristides presented his *Apology* to the emperor Hadrian ca. 125. The Syriac version, however, addresses the *Apology* to Antoninus Pius (138–161) early in his reign. Aristides divides humanity into four races: Barbarians, Greeks, Jews, and Christians. Chapters 1–14 describe the errors of Chaldeans, Greeks, Egyptians, and Jews. The Jews are better than the pagan nations because they worship the one God and have a superior morality, but they have rejected the Christ. Chapters 15–17 praise the manner of life of Christians as proof that Christianity is the worship of the one God. The text of Aristides's *Apology* has been reconstructed from the Syriac translation, some Armenian fragments, a revised Greek text in the *Life of Barlaam and Joasaph* 26–27 (eighth century), and Greek papyri fragments. The papryi show that the Syriac better represents the original than does the late Greek text. CPG I, 1062–1067. TLG 1184.   [E.F.]

Bibliography

J.A. Robinson and J.R. Harris, *The Apology of Aristides on Behalf of the Christians*, TS 1.1 (1891); J. Geffcken, *Zwei griechische Apologeten* (Leipzig: Teubner, 1907); B.P. Grenfell and A.S. Hunt, *The Oxyrhynchus Papyri* (London: Egypt Exploration Society, 1922), Vol. 15, no. 1778; H.J.M. Milne, "A New Fragment of the Apology of Aristides," *JThS* 25 (1923–1924):73–77.

D.M. Kay, tr., ANF (1896), Vol. 10, pp. 259–279.

R.L. Wolff, "The Apology of Aristides: A Reexamination," *HThR* 30 (1937):233–247; G.C. O'Ceallaigh, "Marcianus's Aristides on the Worship of God," *HThR* 51 (1958):227–254.

ARISTO OF PELLA (mid-second century). Apologist. According to a late (sixth-century) testimony, Aristo authored the first of the literary dialogues recording a debate between a Christian and a Jew, the lost *Dialogue Between Jason and Papiscus* (John of Scythopolis, *Comm. in Dion. Areop. De myst. theol.* 1). Origen summarizes the contents of this *Dialogue* as "a Christian [Jason, a Hebrew Christian] arguing with a Jew [Papiscus from Alexandria] from the Jewish scriptures, and show-ing that the prophecies concerning the Christ are applicable to Jesus" (*Cels.* 4.52). CPG I, 1101. TLG 1992.   [E.F.]

Bibliography

Origen, *Against Celsus* 4.52; Pseudo-Cyprian, *Ad Vigilium* 8 (preface to the Latin translation of the *Dialogue*); Eusebius, *Church History* 4.6.3; Jerome, *Commentarius in Galatas* 2.3; idem, *Quaestiones Hebraicae in Genesin* 1.1.

ARISTOTLE, ARISTOTELIANISM. Aristotle was born in Stagira in 384 B.C. He began his studies with Plato when he was seventeen and stayed in Athens until his teacher's death in 348/7. After he had spent five years in various Greek cities on the coast of Asia Minor, Philip of Macedon appointed him as tutor to his son Alexander at the Macedonian court at Pella. After the death of Philip in 335, Aristotle returned to Athens, where he established a school, the Lyceum. In 323, having been charged with impiety, he again left Athens for Chalcis, where he died the following year. This accusation probably resulted from the anti-Macedonian feelings following the death of Alexander the Great, his former student.

Aristotle's research and writings were encyclopedic in scope and volume. Although most of his works are now lost, his interests ranged from philosophical to scientific and political subjects; many of his most perceptive observations were in the field of biology. His earliest writings were popular dialogues highly regarded in antiquity for their literary style, but of these only fragments remain. Also lost are his large compendia of scientific and historical data, such as the collection of constitutions of the Greek states and lists of the Olympic victors. The extant treatises of the Aristotelian corpus are terse summaries (perhaps lecture notes), many of which have found their present form at the hands of later editors. The order of these writings is a matter of controversy; few regard his work as a "closed system" in which all the theories were held simultaneously, yet the problem of "development" in Aristotle remains vexing. In these writings, the philosopher develops a systematic yet commonsense philosophy that seeks to make intelligible the vast range of facts presented to the human mind.

Aristotle's Successors. At Aristotle's death, Theophrastus (ca. 370–288/5 B.C.) became head of the school, whose adherents are known as the Peripatetics. Although few of his writings have been preserved, many titles are known, and these suggest that his research developed in much the same way as his teacher's. Theophrastus's *Opinions of Natural Philosophers* was the first systematic history of philosophy and stands at the head of the long doxographical tradition; his *Laws* compared the laws and customs of the Greek states; his biological works classified and described plant life. Similar studies were undertaken by many of Aristotle's other students. Eudemus (second half of the fourth century B.C.) wrote histories of arithmetic, geometry, astronomy, and theology; Aristoxenus (b. 375/60 B.C.) produced works on music as well as studies in biography and history. As later heads of the school focused more on scientific topics—Straton of Lampsacus (d. 270/69), for instance, won fame for his physical theories—the school declined as a center of philosophical inquiry, and by the Hellenistic period the influence of Aristotelianism had waned. Although works of Aristotle were not unknown in this period, they appear to have had little influence on, for example, Stoic philosophy. Isolated Peripatetic philosophers are recorded, but little is known of their specific doctrines.

With the advent of the first century A.D., however, there was a renewed interest in Aristotelian philosophy. The writings of Aristotle had just been reedited by Andronicus of Rhodes (fl. 30 B.C.), and the eclectic Platonists of this period began to incorporate many Aristotelian features into their philosophies. Foremost among these was Albinus (fl. A.D. 50), whose philosophy included numerous Aristotelian elements in such areas as logic and epistemology. In the next two centuries, there developed a long tradition of producing commentaries on Aristotelian texts. While the earliest extant commentary (on the *Nicomachean Ethics*) was by Aspasius (first half of the second century A.D.), by far the most important and most able commentator of this period was Alexander of Aphrodisias (early third century).

He produced scholarly commentaries on a great range of Aristotelian texts as well as independent treatises, many of which survive; his renown earned him the title "The Commentator." Alexander's commentaries stand in contrast to later ones for their lack of Neoplatonic and mystical elements.

Influence on Neoplatonism. With Plotinus (205–269/70) began the Neoplatonic interpretation of Aristotle, which dominated Aristotelianism through the early-medieval world. Plotinus himself devoted several treatises to Aristotle, and his student Porphyry (232/3–ca. 305) commented extensively on him. His *Eisagoge*, an introduction to Aristotelian logic, became incorporated into the Aristotelian corpus and was itself the subject of further commentaries. For the Neoplatonists, Aristotle was the master of the physical world, while Plato's thought was supreme in metaphysics. This is reflected in the role of the Aristotelian treatises in education: the student would study the works of Aristotle, the "lesser mysteries," as preparation for the study of Plato, the "greater mysteries." Neoplatonists taught the essential harmony of Platonic and Aristotelian philosophy, and the theories of both philosophers now became synthesized into a new, unified Neoplatonic system; Neoplatonism is thus as much Neoaristotelian as Neoplatonic.

By the fifth and sixth centuries, Neoplatonic philosophy had become centered in Athens and Alexandria, and there was clearly interplay between philosophers in the two cities. Athenian Platonism is frequently characterized as speculative and Platonic, the Alexandrian as scholastic and Aristotelian, although these distinctions cannot be drawn too sharply. The commentary had now become an accepted genre for philosophical speculation; within these texts, philosophers frequently developed new theories and pursued lively philosophical debate. The bulk of the extant commentaries derive from this period, and the foremost commentators were the rivals Simplicius (sixth century) and John Philoponus (ca. 490–ca. 570).

Influence on Christianity. The antagonism between Christianity and paganism became a factor in philosophy. Porphyry had written *Against the Christians*, and Proclus had produced a treatise attacking the doctrine of the creation of the world. The challenge to Christianity was to present a plausible philosophical response. The Christian commentator Philoponus responded to Proclus's attack by arguing that creation was not only justified but required by Aristotle's own physical principles. In 529, the emperor Justinian forbade pagans to teach. While this order effectively ended the Athenian school, the Alexandrian tradition continued through such Christian commentators as David and Elias. The last Alexandrian commentator, Stephan (fl. 616), moved to Constantinople, and from him we can trace the development of Aristotelian philosophy in the Byzantine world. Here, the commentary tradition was continued by such men as Eustratius and Michael of Ephesus.

Aristotle's influence was not restricted to the pagan philosophers and their Christian successors. Although the response of some Greek fathers to Aristotle was hostile—he was condemned with many of the other "heretical" philosophers and associated with such Arian thinkers as Aetius and Eunomius—he did influence Clement, Basil, and Gregory of Nyssa, who used his scientific writings; and Aristotelian logic became an instrument in theological debates. Gregory of Nazianzus employed both Aristotelian logic and rhetoric in his battles with Neoarians.

Beginning in the mid-fifth century, many Aristotelian treatises and their accompanying commentaries were translated into Syriac and thus were available to Christian theologians using that language. In the Greek world, both Leontius of Byzantium and John of Damascus relied heavily upon Aristotelian categories for their theological endeavors. That is one reason both of them found Gregory of Nazianzus so helpful and that Thomas Aquinas used John of Damascus to such advantage. Aristotle became the propaedeutic for the study of theology. Particularly from the Syriac translations came the Islamic knowledge of Aristotle that eventually led to the reawakening in the Latin west of the full Aristotelian tradition. But it was also the appropriation of Aristotle by the church fathers that made the acceptance of Aristotle during the Middle Ages more palatable.

[L.P.S.]

Bibliography

H. Diels, ed., *Commentaria in Aristotelem Graeca*, 25 vols. (Berlin: Reimerus, 1881–1909); F. Wehrli, *Die Schule des Aristotles, Texte und Kommentar*, 10 vols. (Basel: Schwabe, 1944–1978); R. Sorabji, ed., *Ancient Commentators on Aristotle* (London: Duckworth, 1987–), Vols. 1–.

E. Renan, *De philosophia peripatetica apud Syros* (Paris: Durand, 1852); K. Praechter, "Die griechischen Aristoteleskommentare," *Byzantinische Zeitschrift* 18 (1909):516–538; J. de Ghellinck, "Quelques appréciations de la dialectique d'Aristote durant les conflits trinitaires du IV siècle," *RHE* 25 (1930):5–42; R.E. Witt, *Albinus and the History of Middle Platonism* (Cambridge: Cambridge UP, 1937); D. Ross, *Aristotle*, 5th ed. (Oxford: Oxford UP, 1949); B. Tatakis, *La Philosophie byzantine* (Paris: Presses Universitaires de France, 1949); H.D. Saffrey, "Le Chrétien Jean Philopon et la survivance de l'école d'Alexandrie au VIe siècle," *Revue des études grecques* 72 (1954):396–400; F.E. Peters, *Aristotle and the Arabs* (New York: New York UP, 1968); A.H. Armstrong, ed., *The Cambridge History of Later Greek and Early Medieval Philosophy* (Cambridge: Cambridge UP, 1970), pp. 39–52 and passim; J.P. Lynch, *Aristotle's School* (Berkeley: U of California P, 1972); J. Dillon, *The Middle Platonists: 80 B.C. to A.D. 220* (Ithaca: Cornell UP, 1977); H. Hunger, *Die hochsprachliche profane Literatur der Byzantiner* (Munich: Beck, 1978), Vol. 1 (Byzantinische Handbuch, Part 5, Vol. 1); P. Moraux, *Der Aristotelismus bei den Griechen*, 2 vols. (Berlin: de Gruyter, 1973–1984); R. Sorabji, ed., *Philoponus and the Rejection of Aristotelian Science* (London: Duckworth, 1987); D.T. Runia, "Festugière Revisited: Aristotle in the Greek Fathers," *VChr* 43 (1989):1–34.

ARIUS (ca. 260–336). Presbyter and theologian. Born in Libya or Alexandria, Arius is first mentioned during the time of Peter I, bishop of Alexandria, who died as a martyr in 311. He was then a temporary supporter of Peter's opponent, Melitius of Lycopolis. Under the successor of Peter, Achillas, in the spring of 312, Arius became a presbyter. Then Alexander, bishop from 312 to 328, put him in the top level of the local clergy and gave him the pastoral responsibility of Baucalis, a populated district near the harbor. Arius's fame as a preacher resulted from his interpretative techniques applied to scripture, by which he combined logical strength with a highly dogmatic speculation. As a leader in asceticism, Arius enjoyed notable popularity.

His clash with Alexander occurred ca. 318. Arius raised a loud protest in the midst of the congregation, while listening to one of the bishop's sermons, because the latter had stressed the equal eternity of the Father and the Son (Socrates, *H.E.* 1.5). The dramatic incident illustrates a long-lasting debate among Alexandrian theologians in the first two decades of the fourth century: how should one apply philosophical categories, mainly those taken over from Platonic cosmology, to express the Christian understanding of God as Creator and as Trinity? After several conciliatory conferences, a local synod of about 100 bishops and priests excluded Arius and his closest followers from communion, probably in 318 or 319. The synodal letter dictated by Alexander is preserved (Socrates, *H.E.* 1.6). It gives a clear idea of the Arian thesis as rejected by the local clergy: the Son is not eternal, nor equal to the Father; he is created as the principle of all things; his divine titles take their full value only after completion of the Father's salvific will on earth.

Before Arius left Alexandria, he wrote a pamphlet that came to be called the *Thalia* ("Banquet") in prose and verse, with which he hoped to reach a broader popular audience. He was supported by Eusebius, bishop of Nicomedia and close to the imperial court. Eusebius built up a coalition of eastern bishops opposed to Alexander. They asked for a readmission of Arius to the ranks of the Alexandrian clergy. Their letters led Alexander to publish a circular letter with a longer report on the dispute. We also possess this document, addressed to the bishop of Thessalonica (Theodoret, *H.E.* 1.4). The rule of the emperor Licinius in the east, who was unfriendly to the Christian churches, and his war against Constantine, coming from the west, delayed the solution of the Arian dispute until Constantine overcame his rival in the autumn of 324. Almost immediately, the new ruler of the whole Roman empire tried to secure peace among the Greek-speaking bishops. Finally, he convoked an imperial synod in the spring of 325, at Nicaea, not far from Nicomedia, in modern Turkey. Arius was then about sixty-five years old. The 250 bishops assembled in Nicaea confirmed his condemnation. In the creed, promulgated by this first "ecumenical council," they introduced anti-Arian phrases, like "true God from true God" and "one in substance [*homoousios*] with the Father," and they added to it a censure of the most striking Arian phrases: "There was once when he [the Son] was not," "he did not exist before he was born," "he came to be out of nothing."

Strikingly enough, the solemn act of Nicaea, far from settling the dispute, added new grist to the episcopal controversies. For the Nicene Creed was in important respects different from the creedal traditions established in the metropolitan churches of the east. In particular, the word *homoousios* was seen as a dubious innovation. As soon as 328, the bishops Eusebius of Nicomedia and Theognis of Nicaea, who had also been exiled like Arius in 325, regained their sees. Arius himself was rehabilitated by the eastern bishops at the imperial Synod of Tyre in 335. He was on the verge of being reintegrated into the Alexandrian clergy by the will of the versatile Constantine when he died on a Saturday in 336. His philosophical preconceptions, framing his notion of divine Trinity, died with him. His memory was soon repudiated by the bishops who had been his supporters. But the political and ideological controversy named after him was to last in the east and the west of the empire for at least four decades after his death. CPG II, 2025–2042. *See also* Arianism; Nicaea. [C.K.]

Bibliography

Athanasius, *Deposition of Arius*; idem, *Discourses Against the Arians* 1.1–3; 1.37; 2.17; idem, *On the Councils* 2.15–16; idem, *To the Bishops of Egypt* 2.12, 19; idem, *Defence of the Nicene Definition* 4.16; idem, *Letter* 54; Socrates, *Church History* 1.5–38; Sozomen, *Church History* 1.15–21; 2.27–30; Epiphanius, *Panarion* 68–69; Theodoret, *Church History* 1.1–6, 13.

T.E. Pollard, "The Exegesis of Scripture and the Arian Controversy," *BJRL* 41 (1959):414–429; L.W. Barnard, "The Antecedents of Arius," *VChr* 24 (1970):172–188; G.C. Stead, "The *Thalia* of Arius and the Testimony of Athanasius," *JThS* n.s. 29 (1978):20–52; T.A. Kopecek, *A History of Neo-Arianism*, 2 vols. (Cambridge: Philadelphia Patristic Foundation, 1979); R.C. Gregg and D.E. Groh, *Early Arianism: A View of Salvation* (Philadelphia: Fortress: 1981); C. Kannengiesser, *Holy Scripture and Hellenistic Hermeneutics in Alexandrian Christology: The Arian Crisis* (Berkeley: Center for Hermeneutical Studies, 1982); idem, "Arius and the Arians," *ThS* 44 (1983):456–475; R. Williams, *Arius: Heresy and Tradition* (London: Darton, Longman and Todd, 1987); R.P.C. Hanson, *The Search for the Christian Doctrine of God: The Arian Controversy 318–381* (Edinburgh: T. and T. Clark, 1988).

ARLES. Large and prosperous Roman city (Arelate) on the Rhône River north of the ancient Greek colony of Massilia (Marseilles). Its strategic location made Arles vital for commerce in Roman Gaul. Evidence of Christianity there prior to 250 is still unconfirmed, even though Christians were at other cities in the Rhône Valley, such as Lyons and Vienne, in the second century. Cyprian's reference to Arles as an episcopal city (*Ep.* 68.1) is the earliest documented reference to its ecclesiastical development. The Merovingian bishop-historian Gregory of Tours (*H.F.* 1.30) credits the possibly legendary bishop Trophimus as the evangelizer of the city. The see of Arles shared in the importance of secular, imperial Arles. The provincial capitals of Gaul from the late fourth century gave to their churches metropolitan status, a development true for Arles in the last decade of the century.

In the course of the controversy over Donatism, the bishop of Arles hosted a council of western bishops at Constantine's behest, the first of a succession of significant conciliar gatherings. This synod of 314 is noteworthy for the fact that participants included five churchmen from Britain, among whom were the bishops of London and York. The canons of the synod dealt with celibacy, the consecration of bishops, and rebaptism. Crucial dogmatic issues of the fourth and fifth centuries were reflected in the synods of 353 (Arianism) and 475 (predestination).

The jurisdiction of the church of Arles underwent significant and controversial changes during the patristic era. The Roman bishop Zosimus (417–418) designated the archbishop of Arles as papal vicar in Gaul with an extraordinary grant of responsibilities over the whole of the Gallic church and clergy, thus making Arles appear to be the supreme church in Gaul. Zosimus's unprecedented generosity irritated the Gallic church and was reversed in large part by his successor, Boniface I (418–422). But a legacy of intense rivalry remained, particularly between Arles and Vienne, whose archbishop, Avitus (494–518), vigorously pressed for his church's superiority. The rivalry was settled by the Roman bishop Symmachus in favor of Arles in 513.

Three bishops of Arles are important for the larger Christian community. Honoratus (426–429) was distinguished for his defense of Nicene orthodoxy and for his support of monasticism. Hilary from Lérins (428/9–449) during his twenty-year tenure was involved in major disputes as a spokesman for Semipelagianism and in a jurisdictional dispute of great consequence with pope Leo I. As a result, Arles lost its metropolitan status for a while. The confrontation enabled the papacy to obtain an imperial edict from emperor Valentinian III that declared all bishops of the western empire responsible to the bishop of Rome. Finally, Caesarius (502–542) elevated his church to a preeminent position again in Gaul as pope Symmachus made him the first western bishop to wear the pallium (symbol of special papal representative). Bishop Caesarius helped to shape early-medieval religious culture.

Arles was a center of the manufacture of Christian sarcophagi, and its museum of early Christian art has a collection second only to that in Rome. *See also* Caesarius of Arles; Gaul; Hilary of Arles.   [H.R.]

Bibliography
Gregory of Tours, *The History of the Franks*, tr. L. Thorpe (Harmondsworth: Penguin, 1974).

A. Malnory, *Saint Césaire, évêque d'Arles, 503–543* (Paris: Bouillon, 1894); L. Duchesne, *Fastes épiscopaux de l'ancienne Gaule*, 2nd rev. ed. (Paris: Fontemoing, 1907), Vol. 1; J. Hubert, "La Topographie religieuse d'Arles à l'époque paléochrétienne," *Cahiers Archéologiques* 2 (1947):17–27; H.G.J. Beck, *Pastoral Care of Souls in South-East France During the Sixth Century* (Rome: Gregorian University,1950); W.M. Daly, "Caesarius of Arles, a Precursor of Medieval Christendom," *Traditio* 26 (1970):1–28.

Cathedral of Etchmiadzin, Armenia (fourth–fifth century). (Photograph furnished by Claude Cox.)

ARMENIA. Nestled in the Caucasus, Armenia is today a Soviet Republic of some 18,750 square miles, an area that is a small fraction of its size at some points in its history. The terrain is one of mountains and gorges; the average altitude is almost 6,000 feet; the climate is warm in the summer (75–80 degrees F in July, in Yerevan) and mild in the winter (20–25 degrees F).

The Urartian kingdom came to an end in the sixth century B.C. and into its region in the Caucasus there moved a people from the west whom Hecataeus (fifth century B.C.) designates "Armenians" (*Armenioi*) and whose land Darius the Great (522–486) calls "Armenia" (*Armina*—in the Behistun Inscription). After domination by the Achaemenian Persians and then Syrians, and a period of independence, Armenia in the Christian era was fought over by the Romans and Persians and finally divided between them in 387.

These international connections much influenced the religion of Armenia. There is at Garni, seventeen miles from Yerevan, a delicate, reconstructed Greek temple dating from the first century. Iranian deities were revered; Zoroastrianism had widespread influence. Christian missionaries evangelized Armenia very early. This enterprise is associated especially with the name of Gregory the Illuminator (ca. 240–332), who converted king Tiridates ca. 301; Christianity became the national religion. Within a century, Mashtots and Sahak had invented an alphabet for Armenian, and the translation of the Bible initiated a period of vigorous scribal activity. Theological, homiletical, and other ecclesiastical documents generally were sought out and translated, an undertaking that has resulted in the preservation of important works not otherwise extant (e.g., by Philo, Irenaeus, Ephraem the Syrian). Significant Armenian writers, theologians, commentators, and historians emerged, including Koriun, Eznik of Kolb, and Lazar of Parp.

The Armenian church, while accepting the Councils of Nicaea, Constantinople, and

Ephesus, rejected the Council of Chalcedon (451) with its statement about "two natures" and thus went its own way as a "Monophysite" church, breaking with Constantinople. Today, the Catholicos of the Armenian Orthodox Church resides at Etchmiadzin in a complex next to the fifth-century cathedral at whose location St. Gregory had a vision of Jesus (*Etchmiadzin*, "the only-begotten descended") and which he was directed to build. The cathedral sits on a fire temple whose remains have been excavated beneath its altar. From an early period, the Armenian church functioned as a bastion of national self-identity against Persian, Greek, Arab, Turkish, and Russian influence and pressure. Wherever they went, Armenians built churches. Architectural treasures (churches and monasteries dating from the seventh and later centuries) dot the Armenian landscape and are scattered across eastern Turkey, in Georgia, and in Iran. Also, several thousand "stone crosses" (*khachkar*) have been preserved.

Armenians relatively early sought out Jerusalem, the Holy City, where the "Armenian Quarter" is home to a community with a patriarch, seminary, manuscript library, church, and printing press. Other manuscript libraries are found in Yerevan (the largest collection), Isfahan, Venice, and Vienna (the latter two run by the Mechitarist Fathers, a Catholic Armenian order).

Several journals are devoted to Armenian studies, including *Revue des études armeniennes*, *Annual of Armenian Linguistics*, and *Journal of the Society for Armenian Studies*. See also Eznik; Mashtots; Monophysites. [C.C.]

Bibliography

Moses Khorenats'i, History of the Armenians, tr. and comm. R.W. Thomson (Cambridge: Harvard UP, 1978).

S. Lyonnet, *Les Origines de la version arménienne et le Diatessaron* (Rome: Pontificio istituto biblico, 1950); K. Sarkissian, *The Council of Chalcedon and the Armenian Church* (London: SPCK, 1965); S. Der Nersessian, *The Armenians* (London: Thames and Hudson, 1969); K. Sarkissian, *A Brief Introduction to Armenian Christian Literature*, 2nd ed. (Bergenfield: Michael Barour, 1974); B.M. Metzger, *The Early Versions of the New Testament* (Oxford: Clarendon, 1977), pp. 153–181; B. Brentjes, S. Mnazakanjan, and N. Stepanjan, *Kunst des Mittelalters in Armenien* (Berlin: Union Verlag, 1981); C. Cox, "Biblical Studies and the Armenian Bible, 1955–1980," *Revue Biblique* 89 (1982): 99–113.

ARNOBIUS (d. ca. 327). Rhetorician and Christian apologist. A teacher of rhetoric at Sicca in North Africa under Diocletian (284–305)—Lactantius was his student while both were pagans—Arnobius became a Christian and, perhaps at the request of his bishop, composed *The Case Against the Pagans*. The work, in seven books, was probably written during the last of the persecutions (303–311). As much an invective against paganism as a defense of Christianity, it exhibits scant knowledge of the New Testament and virtually none of the Hebrew scriptures. Arnobius relied on Plato and other Greek philosophers; among the Latins, the influence of Varro is prominent, with echoes of Lucretius, Cicero, and even Ovid. Familiarity with Clement of Alexandria, Tertullian, and Minucius Felix is apparent. Similarities to Lactantius's *Divine Institutes* may be ascribed to use of a common source.

Arnobius seeks to rebut the charge that Christianity was responsible for recent disasters that had afflicted the empire. He stresses the transcendence of God at the expense of the immanence. He concludes that the human soul, because of its proclivity to sin and weakness, has its origin not from God directly but from some intermediate being (cf. Plato, *Timaeus*); thus it is not immortal in itself, although God may grant it immortality and will do so for the souls of those who have come to know him. Arnobius vigorously denounces paganism for its anthropomorphism, and the mystery cults come in for particular attack. He endorses the theory of Euhemerus of Messene (fl. 300 B.C.) that the gods were originally human beings who were deified upon death. He directs polemic against pagan temples, images, sacrifices, and the use of incense in pagan cults.

The work is valuable for the information it furnishes concerning contemporary paganism and accusations against Christianity.

Among the fourth-century fathers, it is apparently mentioned only by Jerome. Its influence on the Middle Ages was not significant, and it survives only in one ninth-century manuscript with a later (eleventh- or twelfth-century) transcription. CPL 93.   [M.P.McH.]

Bibliography

Jerome, *Chronicle* A.D. 253–327 ; idem, *Lives of Illustrious Men* 79; 80; idem, *Letters* 58.10; 70.5.

Arnobius of Sicca, The Case Against the Pagans, tr. G. McCracken, 2 vols., ACW (1949), Vols. 7, 8.

L.Berkowitz, *Index Arnobianus* (Hildesheim: Olms, 1967); J.D. Madden, "Jesus as Epicurus: Arnobius of Sicca's Borrowings from Lucretius," *CCC* 2 (1981):215–222; T.P. Halton and R.D. Sider, "A Decade of Patristic Scholarship 1970–1979," *CW* 76 (1982–1983):124–125 (bibliography); Y.-M. Duval, "Sur la biographie et les manuscrits d'Arnobe de Sicca: les informations de Jérome, leur sens et leurs sources possibles," *Latomus* 45 (1986):69–99; W.H.C. Frend, "Prelude to the Great Persecution: The Propaganda War," *JEH* 38 (1987):1–18, esp. 14–18.

ARNOBIUS THE YOUNGER (d. after 451). Christian writer. Little is known of Arnobius's life; he was a monk, quite possibly from Africa, who had lived for some time in Rome. His writings, in Latin, include the *Conflictus cum Serapione*, a dialogue between himself and the Egyptian Serapion, directed against the Monophysites; the *Expositiunculae in Evangelium*, notes on the Gospels of Matthew, Luke, and John; the *Liber ad Gregoriam*, a consolation to a Roman matron living in a difficult marriage; and the *Commentarii in Psalmos*, brief comments on the Psalms with an attack on Augustine's teaching on predestination. Another work, the *Praedestinatus*, has been ascribed to Arnobius, but it may derive from Julian of Eclanum or one of his adherents. In three books, it surveys some ninety heresies, almost all taken from Augustine's *De haeresibus*, and describes and refutes teachings on grace and predestination spread under Augustine's name. CPL 239–243.   [M.P.McH.]

Bibliography

Liber ad Gregoriam, ed. G. Morin, *Etudes, textes, découvertes* (Maredsous: Abbaye de Maredsous; Paris: Picard, 1913), pp. 383–439.

H. von Schubert, *Der sogennante Praedestinatus: Ein Beitrag zur Geschichte des Pelagianismus*, TU

(1903), Vol. 24.4: pp. 95–114; G. Morin, "Etude d'ensemble sur Arnobe le Jeune," *RBén* 28 (1911):154–190; H.A. Kayser, *Die Schriften des sogennanten Arnobius junior, dogmengeschichtlich und literarisch untersucht* (Gütersloh: Bertelsmann, 1912); H. Diepen, "La Pensée christologique d'Arnobe le Jeune: théologie de l'Assumptus Homo ou de l'Emmanuel?," *RevThom* 59 (1959):535–564; M. Simonetti, "Letteratura antimonofisita d'Occidente," *Augustinianum* 18 (1978):487–532.

ARNOLD, GOTTFRIED (1666–1714). German Protestant theologian. Arnold published *Die erste Liebe* in 1696, a study of earliest Christianity based on his patristic investigations and those of William Cave. Called to the chair of church history at Giessen in 1697, he became dissatisfied and returned to pastoral ministry. He published *Unparteiische Kirchen- und Ketzer-historie* in 1699–1700, a work noted for its insight into Protestant mysticism.

[F.W.N.]

Bibliography

F. Roberts, "Gottfried Arnold on Historical Understanding: An Early Pietist Approach," *Fides et Historia* 14 (1982):50–59.

ART. We can define early Christian art by the criteria of *iconography* (it comprises those images that illustrate Christian subjects, notably subjects drawn from the two Testaments and their respective Apocrypha and Pseudepigrapha); of *style* (it is the late-antique pictorial tradition that exhibits Christian styles of art); or of *patronage* (it comprises those late-antique works of art that Christian patrons commissioned in the third through the fifth centuries A.D.). None of these definitions is impeccable. For example, early Christian art embraces an iconographic repertory that includes many extrabiblical subjects, and thus to define it solely by its relation to the Old and New Testaments is reductionistic. As for the argument from style, it is problematic whether early Christians developed a distinctive style in art before 500 (Brandenburg, 1981). Patronage is still a good measure of late-antique art overall, but in practice it is often difficult or impossible to apply this criterion—most patrons, Christian or pagan, are simply unknown.

The chronological limits of early Christian art can be set at roughly 200 and 500. Before 200, we have no surviving images that can be linked unmistakably to Christian patronage. Christians probably bought art before the third century, but they must have made their purchases from the stock of images available at pagan markets. It is possible, if unprovable, that before 200 some men and women attached private, Christian meanings to selected images, such as the shepherd carrying a sheep (Good Shepherd), the personification of piety (the orant), or fishes, doves, anchors, loaves of bread, and so on.

The other end of the historical continuum must be defined more arbitrarily. In the east, a convenient *terminus ad quem* is 500, when we begin to encounter the early Byzantine style. Western art from the sixth through the eleventh centuries is best defined according to regional styles and traditions, but in broad terms it may be denominated "early-medieval" or "pre-Romanesque," not "early Christian."

Early Christian art reaches from the upper Tigris-Euphrates and eastern Syria to the northern Rhineland and Great Britain, from western Spain and Morocco to the Sinai, southern Jordan, and the first cataract of the Nile. The pattern of distribution follows the demography of the early church: most of it is urban, but there are numerous important rural enclaves, such as cemeteries, pilgrimage sites, and monasteries. The great workshops were located in cities, where rich patrons, most conspicuously emperors and bishops, could pay the price.

The range of monuments that constitute the evidence of early Christian art is broad. Architecture, painting, and sculpture are all represented, although not in all places or at all times. (Christian architecture, for example, is not found before the time of Constantine.) A fourth major art form, Christian mosaics, commences in the early Constantinian period, with Tomb M in the Vatican necropolis, the so-called Tomb of the Julii (ca. 300). The minor arts are also represented: we have ceramic, glass, and rock-crystal vessels; base- and precious-metal vessels; intaglios and perhaps a small number of cameos in semiprecious minerals; liturgical implements and jewelry; coins and medals; reliefs in ivory, bone, and wood. Textiles that are explicitly Christian (on the criterion of iconography) are wanting before 500.

The two traditional methods for the study of early Christian art are archaeology and art history. Archaeology, the older discipline, places objects within typologies according to a host of disparate attributes and without regard for the objects' quality. Chronology is paramount, and the best chronological indicators, such as inscriptions or coins, are external and documentary in character. Early Christian archaeology integrates the results of archaeological investigation with other areas of study, notably the history of Christian thought and practice, liturgy in particular. Art history groups objects, mostly figural in character, in chronological sequences that are inferred from typologies of style. The quality of the objects is a prime consideration. Art historians examine early Christian objects not so much in relation to other areas of historical research as in relation to other stylistic developments in the overall history of art. Intelligent study of early Christian art requires both archaeological and arthistorical methods. Furthermore, it is impossible to understand early Christian art without some knowledge of the literary and documentary sources produced by the early church.

Pre-Constantinian Period. Early Christian art falls into two periods: pre-Constantinian, and from Constantine to the end of the fifth century. The first is a period of beginnings and experimentation. The artistic record is fragmentary; in fact, the first two centuries of Christian history have left no material record in any form. There is no ideological reason to forbid the possibility that Christians patronized the pictorial arts, but we have no evidence that they did. First- and second-century Christians must have purchased objects necessary for everyday life, such as lamps, or signets emblazoned with images for use in attesting ownership of property, real or personal. Lamps and signets must have been purchased at pagan markets, and it is possible, on the evidence provided by Clement of Alexandria (*Paed.* 3.57.1–3.60.1), that Christians accepted some images and rejected others. This discrimination in turn must have provided the necessary precondition for the creation of the explicitly Christian forms of art that emerged gradually in the early third century, along with a new iconographic repertory that was rooted in the old types, now imbued with new meanings.

The study of Christian architecture in the pre-Constantinian period is beset with difficulties, not the least of them the lack of surviving material evidence. The only building that we have from this period is the Dura-Europos house church, which was in use as a Christian building for a mere decade (or slightly longer), perhaps 245–256. In its conception and original execution, this building was a secular domestic structure, a private house in a Syrian desert town, but toward the middle of the third century its first-floor interior was redesigned to accommodate the baptismal liturgy and possibly the eucharistic liturgy as well. Christian architecture understood as distinctively conceived and separately executed structures designed to house Christian cults did not commence until the last decade of the third century at the earliest; we have no surviving material evidence before 313. Architecture requires land, and before the fourth century most Christian communities did not have title to land on which they might build their churches. The Roman church probably did gain title to certain suburban funerary plots before the fourth century, and this in turn gave access to vast, uncharted subterranean zones—catacombs—where they could bury their dead.

The most extensive remains of pre-Constantinian Christian art consist in the many wall and ceiling paintings that survive in the oldest nuclei of the Roman catacombs. The oldest paintings overall come from two regions within the Callistus catacombs—Area I, including the so-called Crypt of the Popes, and about 500 feet to the northeast of Area I, the tomb of pope Cornelius (d. 253) and the so-called Crypt of Lucina (Reekmans's [1964] Hypogea α and β)—but there are fragments in Domitilla, and it is possible, although unlikely, that other early fragments survive in the Praetextatus and Priscilla catacombs as well. The paint-

ings in the Dura-Europos baptistery clearly belong to the period, and claims have been advanced for other places as well: a chamber underneath St. Felix at Cimitile near Nola, catacombs in Naples and Syracuse (Sicily), and Hadrumetum (Sousse in Tunisia), but the pre-Constantinian date of these monuments is far from clear. Near Porta Maggiore within the Aurelian wall on the Viale Manzoni in Rome, there are the remarkable paintings in the Hypogeum of the Aureli: they are clearly pre-Constantinian, but are they Christian?

In addition to the evidence of paintings, we have a small surviving corpus of pre-Constantinian Christian relief sculpture (on sarcophagi), and there is also the modest but important collection of freestanding statuettes in the Cleveland Art Museum (Kitzinger, 1978). Excepting the Cleveland marbles and a few masterpieces whose Christian attribution is disputed (e.g., the famous La Gayole sarcophagus in Brignoles [Var]), surviving pre-Constantinian Christian relief sculpture, on sarcophagi and on *loculus* plates in the catacombs, seems to have been manufactured primarily or perhaps exclusively in Roman workshops.

The iconography of pre-Constantinian Christian art falls into several categories: subjects drawn from the Bible; *interpretatio christiana* of pagan subjects, mythological and otherwise (e.g., Orpheus); and subjects that are decorative, some religiously neutral (e.g., candelabra), some perhaps religiously symbolic (e.g., grape vines). From the Old Testament, the most important subject is Jonah; from the New Testament, Jesus in the guise of a shepherd carrying a sheep. Both are soteriological images; they convey the idea of God's saving action, and they evidently carried special meaning in the context of death and dying, although they were not exclusively funereal iconographies, as the Dura-Europos shepherd clearly attests. Many of the same subjects that appear in a painted form also survive on pre-Constantinian Christian sarcophagi and *loculus* plates. The critical approach to this subject, however, requires that one distinguish between images that appear in the two settings. The catacomb paintings in Callistus, for example, are a communitarian and ecclesial art form: they were commissioned by a community of persons no doubt with the oversight of the clergy, and they must have been financed by a community purse. By contrast, the iconography on third-century Christian reliefs reflects choices made by the individuals (not groups) who commissioned and paid for sarcophagi. In both painting and sculpture, pagan workshops (*officinae*) played the major role in establishing the formal matrix and setting the formal limits of early Christian iconography throughout the third century.

Constantinian and Post-Constantinian Period. In art, as in other areas of life and thought, the Constantinian era was revolutionary. The single most important element in the Constantinian art revolution was the changed character of patronage. Before Constantine (primarily on the Roman evidence), Christian patrons came from the lower orders and their buying power was severely limited; in the early fourth century, thanks to the example set by the emperor, we encounter Christian patrons at the higher reaches of society. Whereas pre-Constantinian Christian art came mostly from mediocre Roman workshops, in the fourth century and later there were Christian buyers who could afford to patronize the best workshops and artists. These changed circumstances are reflected in all the arts, but the evidence of the minor arts is especially revealing. Luxury objects with Christian motifs and executed in costly materials, such as precious metals, fine glass, ivory, or semiprecious stones, begin to appear.

Constantine was the most important patron of the Christian arts in the fourth century. The emperor gave endowments of land to Christian communities and donated monies for the construction, furnishing, and maintenance of churches. Constantine's support meant that the church buildings he constructed belonged to the realm of public monumental architecture. The emperor's building program was an integral part of the new imperial policy whose goal was to give a prominent public place to the Christian church. Although the Con-

stantinian churches were under the jurisdiction of bishops, in fact they belonged to the public domain.

In addition to granting material support of land and monies, the emperor issued prescriptions about the shape of church buildings, but his words, partly preserved and partly invented by Eusebius, have a general character. More than once, Constantine suggests that church buildings should be lavishly appointed with architectural members and revetments in fine marbles, with gilded coffered ceilings, with altar vessels and candelabra in precious metals. The Constantinian donation lists incorporated in the *Liber Pontificalis* corroborate the impression, gained from the imperial rescripts and the Eusebian letters, that the Constantinian churches must have been richly fitted out on their interiors in a manner consistent with the emperor's intention to make these church buildings important and dignified symbols of religion in the public sphere. Details of design and construction were worked out on the local level, not personally directed by the emperor.

Insofar as they survive, the Constantinian architectural remains present a picture of extreme formal diversity. We have buildings that embody different functions, for example, martyr churches, palace churches, and covered-cemetery churches; buildings that were planned longitudinally, and others that have a centralized (e.g., cruciform) plan. Some Constantinian churches incorporate circular and octagonal halls; some have a single nave; others, a nave flanked by two or four aisles. Some terminate in an apse, others in a rectangular chancel bay or a transept. Some Constantinian churches have galleries, and some have windows lighting the nave. The fabric differs also from one building to the next: some are built of large ashlars, some of small ashlars, and some of concrete faced with brick. In short, variety of design and execution is the key, and this fact underscores the importance of decision making at the local level and of regional architectural and construction traditions in the implementation of the imperial architectural policy. At the same time, it is also possible (some would argue probable) that a certain uniformity of church design was envisaged and perhaps even promoted by Constantine—the model would have been the Lateran basilica (begun ca. 313), which was a longitudinal structure consisting of a nave with flanking parallel aisles and terminating in an apse.

During the fourth century, Christians continued to paint figural scenes on the walls and ceilings of their underground burial places. The most extensive Roman evidence comes from the catacomb of SS. Peter and Marcellinus (Deckers, 1988). Evidence of fourth-century Christian painting executed in contexts above ground is meager, although important fragments do survive, such as the late-fourth-century frescoes in the Memoria of the house beneath SS. Giovanni e Paolo (Rome) and the frescoes (ca. 350–400) in the so-called Christian Chapel of the Roman villa at Lullingstone in Kent, twenty miles east of London. With respect to subject matter, the most noteworthy fourth-century development is the expansion of the biblical repertory, to include especially New Testament scenes that relate to the politicization of the church, such as Pilate washing his hands and the seated or standing Christ-emperor, facing front and cast in the role of the lawgiver and/ or teacher.

Although not much fourth-century Christian painting survives above ground, there is a small extant corpus of Christian mosaics. To a considerable degree, developments in mosaic represent fourth-century pictorial traditions that must have been executed in painted form as well—the two media had so much in common that they may be called cognates. Painter and mosaicist employed different materials but had one goal—pictorial representation on a two-dimensional field—and they exploited the same iconographic repertory. Fourth-century Christian mosaics are found on floors, walls, and ceilings. We have examples in churches (Sta. Pudenziana in Rome, S. Aquilino in Milan, the Aquileia Cathedral), in baptisteries (the Lateran in Rome, S. Giovanni in Naples), and in mausolea above ground (Sta. Costanza in Rome, Centcelles near Tarragona). Triumphalism played an important iconographic role in several fourth-century mosaics, but nowhere was it more eloquently and poignantly rendered than in the famous apse mosaic (heavily restored) of Sta. Pudenziana, dated ca. 384–399. Here, a richly bearded and nimbed Christ-teacher-emperor sits facing front on a gem-encrusted throne amid apostles, evangelists (rendered symbolically), personifications of Jewish and Gentile societies, sacred buildings, and sacred places. Christ is seated here at the center of sacred history, indeed at the center of the cosmos itself, and his sacred presence is imaged in a manner reminiscent of secular society's highest authority, the emperor.

Sarcophagus fronts largely given over to S-shaped fluting (the so-called strigilate sarcophagi) continued to be popular in the fourth century, as they had been in the third. Fluted sarcophagi presented an attractive choice for the customer who wanted to economize; they required a minimum of figure-cutting, because the artists who specialized in the latter skill were the highest-paid members of Roman sculpture workshops. But for those willing to incur the expense, the more popular fourth-century Christian types were the continuous-frieze sarcophagi, in one or two registers, and the columnar sarcophagi. In the former, figures that belonged by virtue of their subject to narrative clusters were simply lined up along the front of the box without frame elements. In the columnar type, figures belonging to discrete narrative clusters were isolated and framed in niches consisting of columns surmounted by arches, pediments, or architraves. The so-called passion sarcophagi (see illustration under LABARUM) provide a good example of the columnar type in a fourth-century context.

In addition to architecture, painting, mosaic, and sculpture, the minor arts are a window onto the conditions of changed Christian patronage in the fourth century. Several late-fourth-century masterpieces fall into the category of luxury or sumptuary arts: the Brescia (Museo Cristiano) and Milan (Castello Sforzesco) ivory caskets; the silver caskets from Milan (S. Nazaro) and Thessalonica (excavations at Nea Herakleia); the glass cups encrusted with gold-glass medallions and the plates inlaid with gilded, polychromatic biblical scenes, both types produced in Rhenish workshops located somewhere near Cologne. There is a splendid fourth-century corpus of North African *terra sigillata* plates and bowls impressed with biblical scenes (many examples are in the Römisch-Germanisches Zentralmuseum, Mainz). Finally, there survives a substantial number of Christian intaglios and metal bezels on finger rings cut for fourth-century Christian patrons.

Under Theodosius I (379–395), scholars commonly see, especially in the pictorial arts, a kind of renaissance: their argument is based on style, specifically the presence of classicizing tendencies in relief and freestanding sculpture. Examples of this style are the bust of Arcadius in the Archaeological Museum (Istanbul) and the silver plate (*missorium*) of Theodosius in the Academia de la Historia (Madrid). The "Theodosian renaissance" appears to have been connected directly with the emperor as patron, and as such it is an eastern court style: its elements include symmetrical and abstract compositions together with supple, smooth renderings of human contours, especially physiognomies.

In the west, at the end of the fourth century, there was also a renaissance (or perhaps it is better thought of as a revival) of classical styles in the pictorial arts, but it was inspired by pagan, explicitly anti-Christian and anti-Theodosian, values. While the emperor was fostering the interests of the church, including Christian art, western men of rank like Nicomachus and Symmachus were attempting to resuscitate the forms and values of traditional Greco-Roman paganism. This effort left its mark in the pictorial arts at several levels, but the most striking evidence from the late fourth century onward appears on consular diptychs executed in ivory and exhibiting expressly pagan subjects. The great silver treasures of the late fourth century, those of Mildenhall, Esquiline, and Kaiseraugst (Kent and Painter, 1977), also attest the persistence of pagan iconography among the families of consular elites in the western half of the empire.

Fifth Century. The fifth century was a period of extraordinary creativity in the arts patronized by Christians. Surviving architectural monuments, including churches, baptisteries, mausolea, martyria, and monasteries, are impressive in numbers, in design and execution, and in geographical extent. From the Theodosian period onward, it became increasingly common for Christians to destroy non-Christian sanctuaries and then overbuild such places with churches. Longitudinally and centrally planned churches continued to be the two major types, although increasingly the properties of the two plans were merged.

Fifth-century fresco painting illustrating Christian subjects survives in small quantities, no doubt due mainly to accidents of preservation. The best-known frescoes of the period are in a funerary chapel at el-Bagawat, west of the Kharga Oasis, but there are fragments elsewhere (e.g., Antinoë, Deir Abu Hennis, Verona, Demetrias near Volos, Cimitile near Nola, and Iznik). The oldest surviving Christian paintings executed to accompany and illustrate a written text are thought to date approximately from the fifth century. These are the miniature illustrations that survive in fragmentary form from the *Quedlingburg Itala* (ca. 380–420; cf. Levin, 1985) and from the *Cotton Genesis* (possibly fifth century; cf. Weitzmann and Kessler, 1986).

To compensate for the sparse remains of fifth-century Christian wall painting, we have an abundance of figural wall, ceiling, and floor mosaics conceived and executed for Christian patrons. The major wall and ceiling monuments of the period are found in Ravenna (Mausoleum of Galla Placidia, Orthodox Baptistery), Rome (Sta. Pudenziana, Sta. Maria Maggiore, Sta. Sabina), Milan (S. Aquilino, S. Vittore in Ciel d'Oro), Naples (S. Giovanni in Fonte), and Thessalonica (St. George's Rotunda, St. David's). Important Christian floor mosaics of the period include examples at Misis/Mopsuestia near Adana (Budde, 1969) and at et Tâbgah-Heptapegon, south of Capernaum. Tunisia's national museum, the Bardo, contains several examples, although they are not dated securely.

Christian sculpture of the period is widely attested. The more than two dozen fifth-century Christian sarcophagi from Ravenna alone (Kollwitz and Herdejürgen, 1979) are executed according to eastern tradition, that is, all four sides of the chest are cut and displayed. In the west, the major fifth-century centers of sarcophagus manufacture were Ravenna and southern France. Freestanding statuary and portrait busts were manufactured in Constantinople, Attica, Rome, and western and southwestern Turkey. Constantinople was also an important center for the manufacture and distribution of architectural sculpture, such as column capitals, chancel screens, ambones. Sigma-shaped marble tabletops with a narrow frieze of reliefs along the borders were also produced in eastern workshops during the fifth century. The most important surviving fifth-century Christian wood sculptures are the reliefs on the doors of Sta. Sabina in Rome. Reliefs in ivory and in silver are also of great importance in defining the Christian art of the period.

In the category of minor art, we have fifth-century Christian figural pieces in virtually all media: glass (cut and gilded), rock crystal and other stones (intaglios, cameos, incised amulets), ivory (small rectangular, square, or circular boxes and the hinged rectangular tablets often called "diptychs"), base and precious metals (liturgical vessels, jewelry, revetments and inlays, lead ampullae), and terra-cotta (sigillata lamps, bowls, plates marked with raised images made from poinçon molds). Figural woven clavi and garment inserts are preserved to a considerable degree from fifth-century contexts, but Christian subjects are rare. *See also* Archaeology; Basilica; Catacombs; Dura-Europos; Shepherd, Good; Iconography; Mosaics; Orant; Ravenna; Rings; Sarcophagus.

[P.C.F.]

Bibliography

W.F. Volbach and M. Hirmer, *Early Christian Art* (New York: Abrams, 1962); L. Reekmans, *La Tombe du pape Corneille et sa region cémétériale* (Vatican City: Pontificio Istituto di Archeologia Cristiana, 1964); A. Grabar, *The Beginnings of Christian Art 200–395* (London: Thames and Hudson, 1967); F.W. Deichmann, G. Bovini, and H. Brandenburg, eds., *Repertorium der christlich-antiken Sarkophage* (Wiesbaden: Steiner, 1967); L. Budde, *Antike Mosaiken in Kilikien I: Frühchristliche Mosaiken in Misis-Mopsuhestia* (Recklingshausen: Bongers, 1969); R. Krautheimer, "Constantine's Church Foundations," *Congresso Internazionale di Archeologia Christiana VII. Atti* (Vatican City: Pontificio Istituto di Archeologia Cristiana, 1969), pp. 237–254; J. Beckwith, *Early Christian and Byzantine Art* (Harmondsworth: Penguin, 1970); P. du Bourguet, *Early Christian Art* (New York: Reynal, 1971); C. Davis-Weyer, *Early Medieval Art, 300–1150* (Englewood Cliffs: Prentice-Hall, 1971); C. Mango, *The Art of the Byzantine Empire, 312–1453* (Englewood Cliffs: Prentice-Hall, 1972); M. Gough, *The Origins of Christian Art* (London: Thames and Hudson, 1973); B. Brenk, *Spätantike und frühes Christentum* (Frankfurt, Berlin, and Vienna: Propyläen-Verlag, 1977); J.P.C. Kent and K.S. Painter, eds., *Wealth of the Roman World A.D. 300–700* (London: British Museum, 1977); E. Kitzinger, *Byzantine Art in the Making* (Cambridge: Harvard UP, 1977); idem, "The Cleveland Marbles," *Congresso Internazionale di Archeologia Christiana IX. Atti I* (Vatican City: Pontificio Istituto di Archeologia Cristiana, 1978), pp. 653–675; J. Kollwitz and H. Herdejürgen, *Die ravennatischen Sarkophage* (Berlin: Mann, 1979); R. Krautheimer, *Early Christian and Byzantine Architecture*, 3rd ed. (Harmondsworth: Penguin: 1979); H. Brandenburg, "Ars Humilis: Zur Frage eines christlichen Stils in der Kunst des 4. Jahrhunderts nach Christus," *JAC* 24 (1981):71–84; I. Levin, *The Quedlinburg Itala: The Oldest Illustrated Biblical Manuscript* (Leiden: Brill, 1985); K. Weitzmann and H.L. Kessler, *The Cotton Genesis: British Library Codex Cotton Otho B.VI* (Princeton: Princeton UP, 1986); J.G. Deckers, H.R. Seeliger, and G. Mietke, *Die Katakombe "Santi Marcellino e Pietro" Repertorium der Malereien* (Vatican City and Münster: Pontificio Istituto di Archeologia Cristiana/Aschendorff, 1988); R.L. Milburn, *Early Christian Art and Architecture* (Berkeley: U of California P, 1988).

ASCENSION OF ISAIAH. Christian expansion of a Jewish pseudepigraphical work. There are three main parts to the *Ascension of Isaiah*. The "Martyrdom of Isaiah" (1.1–3.12; 5.1–16) is a Jewish work relating the execution of the prophet Isaiah by king Manasseh. The "Testament of Hezekiah" (3.13–4.22) and "Vision of Isaiah" (6–11) are Christian compositions. The former contains a vision of Isaiah about the life and death of the Lord's Beloved, the corruption of the church, and the second coming. The latter relates Isaiah's journey through the seven heavens and the revelation to him of the miraculous birth, life, death, resurrection, and ascension of Christ. There are indications that the "Testament of Hezekiah" comes from the end of the first century, but the dates of the other parts and time of their combination are uncertain. The "Martyrdom" was composed in Hebrew and the other parts in Greek, but the work survives only in Ethiopic. TLG 1483. *See also* Isaiah. [E.F.]

Bibliography

NTA, Vol. 2, pp. 642–663; M.A. Knibb, "Martyrdom and Ascension of Isaiah," *The Old Testament Pseudepigrapha*, ed. J.H. Charlesworth (Garden City: Doubleday, 1985), Vol. 2, pp. 143–176.

ASCETICISM. Rigorous bodily self-denial. "Asceticism" is derived from the Greek noun *askēsis* meaning "exercise, practice, or training." The ascete (*askētēs*) is one who practices (*askeō*) a particular art, trade, or lifestyle. The term's origin lies in the athletic arena, where victory was won by those who had best trained their bodies in their respective sports. Its use broadened over time. Philosophical schools and religious sects made metaphorical use of the term as descriptive of the rigors of their chosen way of life. Within early Christian literature, it is but one of a number of metaphors borrowed from the world of athletic contests (e.g., 2 Tim. 4:7).

In religious parlance, asceticism denotes the voluntary exercise of self-denial designed to separate the individual from the human world and thereby facilitate access to the divine. The holiness and otherness of the divine lie at the heart of ascetic practice. By making oneself "other" from the world through such practices, one enhances one's access to the "otherness" of God. The motivation for using ascetic practices to facilitate the approach to the divine, however, varies. Fasting and sexual continence may result from demands of ritual purification, divinely imposed penance, or an anthropological view of humankind that emphasizes the distinction between the eternal soul and the temporal body. Food restrictions may depend upon forgotten ancient taboos (Lev. 11) or on theories of the transmigration of souls (Porphyry, *Abst.* 1.19). Regardless of the motivation, those who undertook the ascetic regimen understood it in terms of its positive dimension or goal. Separation from the lower, sensual, or physical realm enhanced one's rela-

tionship with the higher, noetic, or spiritual realm. The ascetic language of separation or withdrawal from the world must be read in terms of the purity, independence, or freedom it offered for the pursuit of a higher calling.

Antecedents. The ascetic impulse was widespread in the Greco-Roman world into which Christianity emerged. In Judaism, it was the holiness of God that called forth certain restrictions with respect to the world. Dietary prohibitions were imposed as part of a unique covenantal relationship with God and served to identify the Jews as his chosen people. Fasting served for penance, and sexual abstinence was observed only for brief periods to effect ritual purity (Exod. 19:15). The command to be fruitful and multiply (Gen. 1:28) was not abrogated. The outward practices that appear ascetic within Judaism depend on a dualism of pure and impure, clean and unclean, rather than on a dualism of body and soul. The latter dichotomy is not of Jewish origin. As a result, asceticism as a self-imposed discipline of the individual soul undertaken to raise one above the constraints imposed by the created world ran counter to general Jewish piety. Nonetheless, individual and communal lifestyles that imposed outward ascetic practices did occur in peripheral groups within later Judaism. The figures of John the Baptist and Josephus's teacher, Bannus (*Vit.* 2), call to mind the ascetic undertaking of the hermit. The Essene community at Qumran and the Therapeutae in Egypt (Philo, *Contemplative Life*) suggest the communal monastic lifestyle. The sharp dualism that lies behind the ascetic practices of John the Baptist and the Qumran community is not of body and soul but an eschatological dualism that separates the present age from the age to come. Such groups may have offered a pattern for the ascetic impulse of early Jewish Christianity, which was originally a peripheral group within Judaism. From there, it may well have influenced the rise of Encratism in Syria.

Plato supplied the philosophical basis of asceticism as it developed in the late-antique age and flourished in the emerging Christian church. He formulated a cosmological dualism between the home of the gods as a realm of ideas, being, and perfection and the human world of shadows, becoming, and imperfection. Human existence came to be seen as the temporary sojourn of the eternal soul, which comes from the realm of ideas, in a material body. The latter in fact imprisons the soul, which properly seeks its higher level. It is this dualism that leads the true philosopher to ascetic practices designed to free the inner self from the distractions of the body in order to effect a more focused contemplation of the superior world of ideas. Corporeal nature is transient and only interferes with the soul's quest to become like God. One must flee the world so that the soul, which comes from without, can move toward the divine (Plotinus, *Enn.* 2.3.4, 14f.). Spiritual withdrawal from the world into oneself was likewise a fundamental tenet of Stoicism. It offered a spiritual freedom from the bedlam of external society. Separation from the world supplied spiritual peace and tranquility (Seneca, *Ep. mor.* 56.6–7).

New Testament. Practices among the early Christians that appear ascetic, such as fasting and the renunciation of personal property, are dependent upon Jewish models. The Jesus of the Gospels was not ascetic (Matt. 11:19), although the blessing of the poor and the woes bestowed on the rich in the Synoptic Gospels suggest an association of spiritual wealth with earthly poverty. The calls to forsake one's parents and sell what one had, although they inspired many a later Christian to undertake the monastic life, were eschatologically motivated. Jesus spoke to those standing on the seam in time dividing this age from the age to come. Singular allegiance to God and his coming age was demanded. Parents and property were to be rejected as elements that bound one to the present age.

This view continued among the early Christians. The primitive communism of Acts (2:44–45; 4:35–5:2), which finds its closest parallel among the Essenes at Qumran, was motivated by an expectation of an imminent change in the world order, a change that would make private property meaningless. The Christian practice of fasting simply continued the Jewish precedent (Matt. 6:16–18; Acts 13:2;

14:23; 2 Cor. 11:27). In the *Didache* 8.1, Christians were advised to fast on Wednesdays and Fridays so as to distinguish themselves from the Jews, who fasted on Mondays and Thursdays. The Jewish origin of the practice is clear, and the motivation behind the shift in days seems obvious.

Paul likewise was not ascetic in the later sense of the word. There is no sharp dualism between body and soul in Paul. His stances toward the world that appear ascetic are motivated rather by his belief in the imminent return of Christ. It is because the time has grown short that he calls for those who have wives to live as though they had none (1 Cor. 7:29). Paul supports his position with language reminiscent of the Stoic vocabulary of independence and freedom from the anxieties of the world. It is better to refrain from marriage so as to be free from the worldly anxieties it produces. Such freedom enables one to be the more anxious about the affairs of the Lord (1 Cor. 7:32). Although Paul's call for continence is eschatologically motivated, it serves as the initial witness to the ideal of virginity as a higher calling within the church.

Early Christianity. As Christianity spread throughout the Greco-Roman world and assumed greater Hellenistic flavor, ascetic practices of varied form and degree became commonplace. The author of 1 John created a metaphysical dualism between flesh and spirit, light and darkness, truth and lie, that called forth ascetic stances to the world within the community (1 John 2:15–17). Virginity was extolled, continence in marriage advocated (Hermas, *Vis.* 2.2.3), and second marriages rejected (Athenagoras, *Leg.* 33). Ascetics were a recognized element within Christian communities, whose authority required control (Ignatius, *Polyc.* 5.2; cf. *1 Clem.* 38.2; Hermas, *Vis.* 1.2.3).

Ascetic practice knew no doctrinal bounds. Various Gnostic schools, Encratites, Montanists, Marcionites, and Manichaeans among others all advocated the ascetic life. Irenaeus (*Haer.* 1.24.2) asserted that the Gnostic Saturninus led many astray through a false continence, which included abstinence from meat and identification of marriage and procreation as works of Satan. Among the Montanists, strict ascetic practices ensured the gift of the Spirit within the community. The Syrian Encratites associated with Tatian rejected marriage as adultery and condemned the eating of meat and drinking of wine (Irenaeus, *Haer.* 1.28; Epiphanius, *Pan.* 46). For Marcion, opposition to the created world of the demiurge demanded an ascetic stance. Abstinence from meat and wine, extended fasts, and sexual continence evidenced the Marcionite's metaphysical alignment with the "good" God and against the God of creation. In such a view, marriage becomes "filthiness" and "obscene" (Tertullian, *Marc.* 1.19). Marcion represents an extreme view, but the praise of virginity and continence as higher forms of Christian life was seemingly universal. The *Acts of Thomas* 12–14 opposes intercourse and marriage as leading to destruction. In the *Acts of Paul and Thecla* 5–12, Paul blesses those who, although married, live a continent life. Jerome found the sole virtue in marriage in the fact that it bears virgin offspring (*Ep.* 22.20). The later Tertullian distinguished marriage and fornication only in the degree of their illegitimacy (*Castit.* 9). Conflicting pressures for virginity and marriage led to a common practice of spiritual marriage, in which a couple lived together in continence.

The ascetic ideal, to varying degrees, was part of most early Christian theology. It received especially strong support in the life and writings of Origen of Alexandria. Bodily asceticism was placed alongside of martyrdom as an expiation of sins and a means of focusing on the divine. Eusebius of Caesarea (*H.E.* 6) presents Origen as following a disciplined, philosophic way of life in which he trained himself by fasts, restricted hours of sleep (which were taken on the floor), continence, self-imposed poverty, and the avoidance of any material comforts. He encouraged others to follow his path to spiritual enlightenment. In the west, Tertullian, even before he embraced Montanism, favored a strict ascetic lifestyle. He reports large numbers of male and female ascetics in Carthage (*Cult. fem.* 2.9; *Ux.* 1.6; *Resurr.* 61) and presents them as the ideal core among the believers. In his later Montanist rigor, this core became a separate group distinguished from the lax majority.

With the rise of the monastic movement in the third and fourth centuries, the ascetic practice received an institutional framework. Withdrawal from the world took on a physical dimension as individuals departed for the desert, built walled communities separating themselves from society, or lived atop pillars or columns. The forms and rigors of the ascetic practice varied greatly. Excesses were commonplace. Monks extended their fasts to the entire week, mixed ashes with their food, slept standing up, burned fingers rather than give in to sexual desire, subjected their bodies to harsh physical discomfort and pain as acts of contrition. One hears of those who wore hair shirts or chains, who lived naked, who wandered, begged, and ate grass. The pagan Eunapius (346–414) describes Christian monks as men in appearance only who live the lives of swine (*V.S.* 472). But here again, one must view such practices against the positive goal of communion with the divine they were meant to facilitate. In general, monastic excesses are associated more with the anchorite or hermit, who sought to conquer the body in solitude. The cenobitic, or communal monastic, life found such ascetic striving divisive to the cohesion of the community. The monastic regulations of Pachomius in Egypt, Basil of Caesarea, and Benedict of Nursia all sought to curtail ascetic excess.

The ascetic impulse has been central to the Christian religion from its inception. Although the motivating force behind ascetic practices shifted, the dominance of asceticism as a Christian ideal only waxed stronger. The eschatological support for virginity in Paul became a statement of the ideal Christian life as being a bride of Christ. Although most could not accept a strict ascetic life, it was widely recognized as the path to follow to be numbered among the Christian elite. For many, including women, it offered an opportunity for advancement where none had been available to them before in society. Asceticism, like martyrdom, was open to all. *See also* Encratites; Hermit; Monasticism; Sexuality.   [J.E.G.]

Bibliography

A. von Harnack, *Monasticism: Its Ideals and History* (London: Williams and Norgate, 1901; orig. German ed., 1881); H.B. Workman, *The Evolution of the Monastic Ideal from the Earliest Time down to the Coming of the Friars* (London: Epworth, 1913); H. Strathmann, *Geschichte der frühchristlichen Askese bis zur Entstehung des Mönchtums im religiongeschichtlichen Zusammenhange* (Leipzig: Deichert, 1914); O. Hardman, *The Ideals of Asceticism: An Essay in the Comparative Study of Religion* (New York: Macmillan, 1924); H. von Campenhausen, "Early Christian Asceticism" and "The Ascetic Idea in Ancient and Early Medieval Monasticism," *Traditions and Life in the Church: Essays and Lectures in Church History* (Philadelphia: Fortress, 1968; orig. German ed., 1960); A. Vööbus, *History of Asceticism in the Syrian Orient*, 2 vols., CSCO (1958, 1960), Vols. 184, 197; G. Kretschmar, "Ein Beitrag zur Frage nach dem Ursprung frühchristlicher Askese," *ZThK* 61 (1964):27–67; P. Nagel, *Die Motivierung der Askese in der altern Kirche und der Ursprung des Mönchtums*, TU (1966), Vol. 95; P. Brown, *The Making of Late Antiquity* (Cambridge: Harvard UP, 1978); G. Winkler, "The Origins and Idiosyncrasies of the Earliest Form of Asceticism," *The Continuing Quest for God: Monastic Spirituality in Tradition and Transition*, ed. W. Skudlarek (Collegeville: Liturgical, 1982), pp. 9–43; V.L. Wimbush, "Renunciation Towards Social Engineering (An Apologia for the Study of Asceticism in Greco-Roman Antiquity)," *Occasional Papers of the Institute for Antiquity and Christianity* (Claremont: Institute for Antiquity and Christianity, 1986), No. 8; E.A. Clark, *Ascetic Piety and Women's Faith: Essays on Late Ancient Christianity* (Lewiston: Mellen, 1986); P. Brown, *The Body and Society: Men, Women, and Sexual Renunciation in Early Christianity* (New York: Columbia UP, 1988).

ASIA MINOR. Most of modern Turkey from the western coast east to the Taurus mountains, then north into the old Armenian plains. Early Christian texts referred to this unwieldy geographical region by the term "Asia," even though the Roman province of Asia was a much smaller area in southwestern Turkey.

When the Book of Acts details Paul's missionary journeys, it mentions cities and provinces in Asia Minor: Perga in Pamphylia, Pisidian Antioch, Iconium, Lystra, and Derbe; Phrygia, Galatia, Mysia, and Ephesus. Each of his overland trips went through Asia Minor. It is clear from those stories that both Jewish and pagan religions were entrenched in much of the region. Paul's Galatians, the epistle called Ephesians, and the correspondence with Timothy all have references to the area. The seven churches described in the Book of Revelation—Ephesus, Smyrna, Pergamum, Thyatira, Sardis, Philadelphia, and Laodicea—evidence Christianity in western Asia Minor. The total New Testament picture indicates that developing orthodoxy was present in the region but also that various understandings of the faith existed from an early period. For example, a small group of Christians in Ephesus (Acts 19) did not know of the Holy Spirit or Christian baptism. The writer of Revelation found some of the seven churches to be wanting.

In the second century, the Pliny-Trajan correspondence shows that the Roman government dealt with a Christianity spread through most social classes as a benign but stubborn superstition weak enough to be suppressed. Ignatius of Antioch traveled through the region on his way to martyrdom at Rome. To churches at Ephesus, Magnesia, Philadelphia, Tralles, and Smyrna, he wrote letters that demonstrate the presence both of developing orthodoxy and Judaizing as well as Gnostic elements in those Christian congregations. Melito of Sardis may have had a rancorous spirit, but his works and the later Sardis synagogue suggest that the struggles between Judaism and Christianity were continuing. Justin Martyr, while in Ephesus, may have begun his apologies for the Christian faith and perhaps even had some hand in the conversion of Tatian, another apologist who visited the city. Galen, a physician from Pergamum, considered Christianity an unreasonable superstition.

Irenaeus, the great bishop-missionary to France, was born in western Asia; knew Papias, who preferred oral tradition to written records of Jesus; and fought Gnostic influences in early Christianity. He had considerable influence in France and even in Rome, where he interceded for the practice in Asia Minor of dating Easter on the fourteenth day of Nisan (Quartodecimans), no matter what day, rather than on the following Sunday, arguing that the practice was an old one in western Asia Minor that went back to the time of the apostles.

Furthermore, he offered an interesting biblical theology organized around images and allegories, particularly certain parallels between Old and New Testament themes and the idea of restoration as central to the gospel. Friedrich Loofs, a learned historian of Christian doctrine, insisted that there was a settled Asia Minor theology to be found in Irenaeus and in Theophilus of Antioch. His theory is not currently accepted, but it does indicate the importance of figures from Asia Minor in early Christianity, both orthodox and otherwise.

Marcion from Sinope in Pontus, the wealthy son of a shipbuilder, jettisoned Jewish themes in the Christian faith, including the creator God, based his "scripture" on a shortened form of Luke and some of the Pauline epistles, and sounded much like some of the Gnostics of other regions. The Montanists, a Phrygian sect concerned with certain prophetic books and the Johannine literature, were noted for their charismatic aspects. Montanus claimed that the Holy Spirit spoke through him. Although the group started in Phrygia and thought that God's final kingdom on earth would be centered in the region, perhaps at Pepuza, it spread throughout the Mediterranean, partly because it called Christians back to earlier prophetic revival, Spirit-led experiences, and rigorous living. Tertullian, the famous North African, became a Montanist. Eusebius noticed that other Christians in Asia Minor saw the Montanists as wayward and threatening, held councils to discuss the problems, and ultimately condemned the sect.

In the third century, persecutions of Christians reached the area. Firmilian of Cappadocia describes such activity in the reign of Decius (ca. 250), after a series of earthquakes. The pagan aristocracy blamed Christians for the disasters, and the government responded with persecutions. Gregory Thaumaturgus ("The Wonder Worker"), a Cappadocian, learned much from his studies with Origen and became a powerful leader in his region. He seems to have been a theologian of some consequence, although an early creed attributed to him is Gregory of Nyssa's construction and his Trinitarian terminology is not precise. His

memory fills a number of hagiographies, which show his pastoral activity.

At the beginning of the fourth century, persecution of Christians intensified. Lactantius, a court rhetorician, describes the terror that plagued Nicomedia and the region of Bithynia during the most concerted effort to destroy Christianity yet mounted by the Roman government. But during the rest of the century after Constantine's victory, Asia Minor regained a dominant place in Christian theology. The Council of Nicaea, held in 325, attempted to settle the Arian controversy by condemning Arius's teachings and insisting that the Son and the Father were "of the same essence," *homoousios*. That council, called and funded by Constantine with clear political concerns for a unity of religion within the empire, in many ways failed. Arius was exiled in Asia Minor, but the emperor Constantius became a supporter of the Arian cause when he came under the influence of Eusebius of Nicomedia. Eusebius argued for the difference in nature between the Son and the Father, was able to get a number of Nicene defenders banned, and himself became bishop of Constantinople. Theognis of Nicaea and Asterius the Sophist supported the Arian cause, the one with political skill at the court, the other through writings; but Asterius seems to have been a bit less bold in his Arian views than Theognis. Basil of Ancyra appears to have accepted most of the content implied by the *homoousios* but was still troubled by the term. He well indicates the shades of opinion current at the time and is often referred to as a Semiarian, or a Homoiousian, one who could not bring himself to say that the Son was equal to the Father in nature but believed that he was of similar substance to the Father.

On the other side, Marcellus of Ancyra, Basil's predecessor, fought the Arians with every available means. His primary weapon was his pen. He wrote against Asterius with such force that he was accused of Sabellianism, of making no important distinctions between the Father and Son. Evidently, in his battle to defend the Son's divinity he more than once made statements that seemed to destroy differences between the two.

The Cappadocian fathers gave orthodoxy the defenders it so needed. Basil of Caesarea was one of the most astute theologian-bishops during the Arian crisis. He not only wrote important works against Eunomius and worked to place orthodox leaders in strategic positions but also was influential in monastic circles with his *Rule*. Gregory of Nyssa, his brother, was the most philosophically astute of the group and is well regarded among contemporary patrologists for his insightful theological treatises. Gregory of Nazianzus, a skilled rhetorician and logician, made his mark as a preacher. He is known as "the Theologian" in Eastern Orthodox circles to this day. Amphilochius of Iconium, perhaps a lesser light, also worked within this circle of remarkable talents.

These figures reflected Christian strength in the area and were influential within it. In the early 360s, the emperor Julian could still write to pagan leaders like Maximus of Ephesus, but his trip through Asia Minor on his way east led him to see how much the temples and their associated cultural events had been neglected. Paganism was weakened; Christianity had made an impact, but it was not yet an invincible victor. The letters of Nilus of Ancyra (d. 430), who began a monastery outside that city, indicate that paganism was still widespread and influential at least in the countryside during his lifetime.

During the fifth century, Asia Minor receded from its earlier importance. The Council of Chalcedon (451) was held in Asia Minor, as were both the Council of Ephesus (431) and the "Robber Council" of Ephesus (449). But the great parties in those debates were primarily Egyptian and Syrian in origin.

In the sixth century, Monophysite communities were more numerous than some now assume. Although Monophysite strength was concentrated in Syria, Palestine, and Egypt, a number of churches held such allegiances at least in Cilicia and Isauria. John of Hephaestus, in 540–541, made a missionary journey into Asia Minor and ordained clergy as he went. But Chalcedonian opinion also had its representatives. John the Grammarian of Cilicia was noted as one of the defenders of the council of 451.

Arab incursions into Asia Minor began in the second third of the seventh century. Christianity outlasted the forays but never again rose to its previous heights. *See also* Ancyra; Cappadocia; Ephesus; Galatia, Galatians; Nicaea.

[F.W.N.]

Bibliography
W.M. Ramsay, *The Cities and Bishoprics of Phrygia*, 2 vols. (Oxford: Clarendon, 1895–1897); W.M. Ramsay and G. Bell, *The Thousand and One Churches* (London: Hodder and Stoughton, 1909); F. Loofs, *Theophilus von Antiochen Adversus Marcionem und die anderen theologischen Quellen bei Irenaeus*, TU (1930), Vol. 46; D. Magie, *Roman Rule in Asia Minor to the End of the Third Century After Christ* (Princeton: Princeton UP, 1950); R.L. Wilken, *The Christians as the Romans Saw Them* (New Haven: Yale UP, 1984); T.A. Robinson, *The Bauer Thesis Examined: The Geography of Heresy in the Early Christian Church* (Lewiston: Mellen, 1988).

ASTERIUS (d. ca. 341). Supporter of Arius. Known as "the Sophist," Asterius was a pupil of Lucian of Antioch. As an articulate lay preacher and exegete, he was an important spokesman for Arian theology in his *Syntagmation*; only fragments of this Greek work are extant in the writings of his opponents, Athanasius and Marcellus of Ancyra. According to Jerome (*Vir. ill.* 94), Asterius also wrote commentaries on Romans and the Gospels, but only a few of his homilies on Easter and commentaries on the Psalms have been preserved. The Arian historian Philostorgius claimed that he later modified his Arian ideas; he was last noted as present at the Council of Antioch in 341. CPG II, 2815–2819. TLG 2061. [R.L.]

Bibliography
Fragments collected in G. Bardy, *Recherches sur St. Lucien d'Antioche et son école* (Paris: Beauchesne, 1936), pp. 341–354; M. Richard, *Asterii Sophistae Commentariorum in Psalmos* (Oslo: Brøgger, 1956).

H. Auf Der Maur, *Die Osterhomilien des Asterios Sophistes als Quelle für die Geschichte der Osterfeier* (Trier: Paulinus-Verlag, 1967); M.F. Wiles with R.C. Gregg, "Asterius: A New Chapter in the History of Arianism?," *Arianism: Historical and Theological Reassessments*, ed. R.C. Gregg (Cambridge: Philadelphia Patristic Foundation, 1985), pp. 111–151.

ATHANASIAN CREED. Western creed probably written in Latin during the late fifth or early sixth century in response to the Nestorian controversy (also known as the *Quicunque vult*, from its first two words). The appearance of the Athanasian Creed in a sermon by Caesarius of Arles and its similarity to the *Excerpta* of Vincent of Lérins suggests an origin in southern Gaul. The attribution to Athanasius is unsound, since the content and style, including certain technical terms, dictate that it cannot be a fourth-century document.

This creed deals, in two parts, with the doctrine of the Trinity and the incarnation. The first section operates primarily through thrice-repeated assertions of equal attributes—uncreated, unlimited, eternal, omnipotent—which are then said to make the Father, Son, and Holy Spirit not three but one. The second section enumerates events from the life of Jesus in a way similar to the Apostles' Creed, but unlike the Apostles' or the Niceno-Constantinopolitan creeds, it includes anathemas. At the beginning of each section and at the end of the whole, it declares belief in its statements necessary for salvation.

The Athanasian Creed forms an important part of Lutheran, Roman Catholic, and Anglican liturgies, but its inaccurate translations in some service books and a dislike of its condemnatory statements have led to its less-frequent use. It was never received as an Eastern Orthodox confession, although it has appeared—obviously without the *filioque* clause—in seventeenth-century Russian liturgical literature and in the Greek *Horologion* since the late eighteenth century. *See also* Creeds.

[F.W.N.]

Bibliography

A.E. Burn, *The Athanasian Creed and Its Early Commentaries* (Cambridge: Cambridge UP, 1896); idem, *The Athanasian Creed* (London: Rivington, 1930); H. Leith, *Creeds of the Church*, 3rd ed. (Atlanta: John Knox, 1982), pp. 704–706.

J.N.D. Kelly, *The Athanasian Creed* (London: Black, 1964); V.M. Lagorio, "The Text of the Quicunque vult in codex Ottob. Lat. 663," *JThS* 25 (1974):127–128; J.M. Perosanz, *El simbolo atanasiano* (Madrid: Ediciones Palabra, 1976).

ATHANASIUS (ca. 300–373). Bishop of Alexandria (328–373) and most dynamic leader of Egyptian Christianity in the fourth century.

Life. A chronicle of Athanasius's episcopal career, written soon after his death and put at the beginning of the collection of his Festal Letters, confesses that he was not yet the canonical age of thirty when elected a bishop of Alexandria in 328. A deacon under bishop Alexander (311–328), he acted as his secretary at the imperial Council of Nicaea (spring and summer 325), although his later autobiographical apologies never mention this trip. His predecessor had burdened him posthumously with the legacy of the Melitian schism and the Arian heresy, two causes of turmoil in the Alexandrian church for over three decades of his episcopacy.

The disciplinary decrees of Nicaea had fixed the rules for the readmission of the schismatic Melitians into the ranks of the Catholic clergy, but Alexander failed to apply those rules. A slight majority of clerics, including many bishops, along the Nile Valley and in Alexandria itself refused until his death to recognize his metropolitan authority. As his young successor showed himself to be more forceful, the leaders of the Melitian church sought external support among the episcopal coalition in the east hostile to the see of Alexandria. Athanasius, during his first five years in office, spent most of his energy in visiting the important monastic settlements in the desert areas of Egypt. He extended his authority as far as the border of modern Sudan and the western parts of Libya. By this historic initiative, Athanasius hoped to gain enough power to face the alliance of the Egyptian Melitians with the pro-Arian eastern bishops. His illusion was short-lived. In 335, he lost his see by the decision of an imperial synod held in Tyre, and on November 7 of that year he was exiled by Constantine to Trier, the northern capital of Gaul.

The core of the dispute was the case of Arius. Like his predecessor, Athanasius could not readmit the Alexandrian priest into communion, against both the canons of the local church and the solemn decision of Nicaea, which had confirmed the excommunication of

Arius as a heretic in 325. In his adversaries' view, statements issued by an imperial synod could always be revised by another synod of the same nature. They noted some affinities between their own theological traditions and Arius's doctrine concerning the Son of God. Their claim was that a doctrinal compromise should be reached, even after Nicaea. When Constantine died on May 22, 337 (Arius had passed away in the year before), Athanasius benefited from the support of Constantine II, Constantine's son, in Trier. He returned to Alexandria acclaimed as a hero by his people.

Only two years later, in 339, he was exiled again. In the east, the bishops opposing him, led by Eusebius of Nicomedia, did not see why they should tolerate his return to a position for which he had been invalidated by the synod of Tyre. They enjoyed the active support of another son of Constantine, Constantius II, who ruled over the eastern provinces of the empire. This time, Athanasius fled to Rome, where bishop Julius I welcomed him. He was recognized by Julius's local synod as the only legitimate bishop of Alexandria. In 343, a broader synod at Sardica convoked by yet another son of Constantine, Constans, ratified this recognition. In 346, thanks to the heavy political pressure of Constans upon Constantius II, his brother in the east, Athanasius returned to his see for ten years. Constans was murdered by a usurper in 350. Constantius, becoming sole ruler over the empire (Constantine II had been eliminated a few years earlier), decided to unify the religious policies in the line of the conservative majority of the eastern bishops, hostile to the creed of Nicaea. As Athanasius was the most steadfast and most famous supporter of Nicaea, the emperor's administration organized a vast campaign of synods and of individual signatures in east and west against him. Outlawed and sought by the secret police, which Constantius had recently reinforced, Athanasius vanished into the desert of Egypt from February 356 until November 361. Hidden by the monks, he continued to administer actively the vast territories under his jurisdiction, while his own intelligence service kept him informed about the ecclesiastical developments in Alexandria and abroad. When Constantius died in 361, Athanasius returned at once to Alexandria, even before ordered to return by the new emperor, Julian. In 362, he presided over a "synod of confessors" in his city, where the pro-Nicene factions achieved the basis for a firmer theological union. He was exiled again by Julian, because of his pastoral success, as a letter of the emperor to the Alexandrians pointed out. Athanasius withdrew for a short time from the city in 363. His last forced move occurred in the winter of 365/6, imposed on him by the Arian emperor Valens (364–378). But Valens needed popular support for his military campaign against the Goths, and called him back to his see on February 1, 366. Athanasius found himself reinstalled in Alexandria, where he died May 2, 373, at the age of seventy-four, after an unmatched forty-five years in office, including a total of fifteen years and ten months spent in exile.

Writings. At the time of his first exile (335–337), Athanasius completed the final draft of a double apology in Greek. The first part was a literary patchwork, *Against the Heathen*, collecting textbook notes from earlier years, framed by more personal remarks on the divine Logos. The second part, *On the Incarnation*, much more mature in its style and motives, witnesses the young bishop's theological intuitions concerning the basic teaching of the Christian doctrine. Both treatises offer close literary affinities with Athanasius's Festal Letters for Easter in the years 335, 336, and 337. Writing about the orientation to be taken in the catechesis of educated people in his local church, and aware of the emperor Constantine's rejection of any polemical mention of Arius, Athanasius omitted any open discussion of Arianism in this initial work. But soon after his return from Trier, he was requested, mainly by his monastic supporters, to give an account of his anti-Arian beliefs. The bulk of his *Orations Against the Arians* 1 and 2 was then distributed, in a confidential way, for a private reading among the monks at the start of his second exile, in 339. The text was quickly reworked and completed with documentary chapters, containing important extracts from Arius's *Thalia* and from a pamphlet of Asterius.

After his return from the second exile, Athanasius intended to secure once and for all the legitimacy of his title, still questioned by his episcopal adversaries at the imperial court. In the late 340s, he published a huge *Apology Against the Arians*, consisting mainly of synodal and epistolary documents. In the early 350s, a new generation of "Arian" opponents seemed to have introduced into the controversy revisionist ideas about the Alexandrian tradition. A *Letter on the Opinions of Dionysius*, bishop of Alexandria a century earlier, and a famous *Letter on the Decrees of Nicaea* reclaimed important aspects of earlier Alexandrian theology in favor, as Athanasius understood it, of the Nicene orthodoxy. These academic apologies were soon eclipsed by more militant writings, when he was thrown into the hazards of his third exile. A *Circular Letter to the Bishops of Egypt and Libya*, from 356, stresses the biblical arguments against Arius's *Thalia*, as already quoted in what now serves as a preface to the first of the *Orations Against the Arians*. The third exile brought Athanasius to the peak of his literary career: the *Apology to Constantius*, in which the passionate fighter gives up the hope of a reconciliation with the emperor; the *Letter About His Flight*; the *Letters to Serapion on the Divinity of the Holy Spirit*, laying down the foundations of the theological formula that would be canonized at Constantinople in 381; the *Life of Anthony*, using monastic records for writing what became a model of hagiography, filled with Greek and Alexandrian spirituality; and the ample apology *On the Synods of Rimini and Seleucia*, a documentary collection directed against the anti-Nicene party of Acacius of Caesarea and initiating a common front with the moderate Nicaeans gathered around Basil of Ancyra. These writings are only the best known from the years in the deserts (351–361). Of many private letters, only the letter to Rufinianus has come down to us. (The question has been raised if Athanasius wrote directly in Coptic. Many critics do consider as authentic some of the sermons transmitted under his name and known only in that language.)

Even in his later years, after his third exile, Athanasius continued to produce letters of a strong dogmatic content. The *Letter to the Antiochenes*, composed on behalf of the synod of 362, seems rather to be full of his spirit than to be written by himself. But the letters *To Adelphius* and *To Epictetus* are characteristic of his vocabulary and style of argument. From 329 through 372, we have partial records of almost all the homiletic Festal Letters sent out by Athanasius at the beginning of each year to prepare the communities for celebrating Easter at the correct date. They illustrate, like the other treatises and dogmatic letters, the bishop's theory of the salvific incarnation through which God acts in the church in its collective experience of faith and in its sacraments. Feast day May 2. CPG II, 2090–2309. TLG 2035.

[C.K.]

Bibliography
Athanasius necessarily bulks large in the histories of Socrates, Sozomen, and Theodoret and is frequently referred to in theologians of the fourth and subsequent centuries, e.g., Gregory of Nazianzus, *Orations* 21; Jerome, *Lives of Illustrious Men* 87.

St. Athanasius: Select Works and Letters, ed. A. Robertson, NPNF, 2nd ser. (1891), Vol. 4.

W. Bright, "St. Athanasius of Alexandria," DCB (1877), Vol. 1, pp. 179–203; E.P. Meijering, *Orthodoxy and Platonism in Athanasius: Synthesis or Antithesis?* (Leiden: Brill, 1974); C. Kannengiesser, ed., *Politique et théologie chez Athanase d'Alexandrie* (Paris: Beauchesne, 1974); A. Grillmeier, *Christ in Christian Tradition* (Atlanta: John Knox, 1975), Vol. 1, pp. 308–328; G.C. Stead, "Rhetorical Method in Athanasius," *VChr* 30 (1976):121–137; C. Kannengiesser, "Athanasius of Alexandria: Three Orations Against the Arians, a Reappraisal," *SP* 18 (1982):981–995; idem, *Athanase d'Alexandrie évêque et écrivain: une lecture des traités Contre les Ariens* (Paris: Beauchesne, 1983); idem, "The Athanasian Decade 1974–84: A Bibliographical Report," *ThS* 46 (1985):524–541; R.P.C. Hanson, *The Search for the Christian Doctrine of God: The Arian Controversy 318–381* (Edinburgh: T. and T. Clark, 1988).

ATHENAGORAS (latter half of second century). Christian apologist. Almost nothing is known about Athenagoras except what can be deduced from his two Greek works, namely his *Plea on Behalf of the Christians* and *On the Resurrection of the Dead*. In the Arethas Codex of the year 914, in which these two writings have been preserved, Athenagoras is described as a Christian philosopher of Athens. The information about Athenagoras's life given by Philip of Side, a historian of the fifth century, is suspect. The only other patristic writer to mention Athenagoras is Methodius (*Res.* 3.7).

Athenagoras's *Plea* was a defense of Christianity addressed to the emperors Marcus Aurelius and Commodus. It was probably written ca. 177. The main purpose of this work is to rebut accusations of atheism, cannibalism, and Oedipean incest. Athenagoras devotes the greater part of this work to the first charge. He argues that the pagan poets and philosophers themselves had largely abandoned their traditional polytheism, while the Christians had received their monotheistic belief from the prophets. The Christians also had reason on their side. In answer to the other two reproaches, Athenagoras cites the pure morality of the Christians. The accusations of the pagans can hardly be true in the light of the Christians' belief in a future judgment. In dealing with his subject matter, he displays a profound knowledge of Greek philosophy, literature, and mythology.

Athenagoras's authorship of the work *On the Resurrection* is disputed. This work has a philosophical character and sets out to prove the doctrine of the resurrection on rational premises. It consists of two main sections. In the first part, the author refutes the argument that the resurrection is impossible. He then emphasizes God's omnipotence. He argues that the dual nature of a person necessitates the perpetuity of existence. A person consists of body and soul, and this unity, which is destroyed by death, needs to be restored through the resurrection. Thus, the soul alone will not be rewarded or punished for deeds done in conjunction with the body.

A most significant aspect of the theology of Athenagoras is his well-developed teaching about the Trinity. In refuting the charge that Christians are atheists, Athenagoras calls attention to the distinctions within the Godhead while also demonstrating the unity of God. In line with his contemporaries, Athenagoras believed that the Holy Spirit was an effluence of God. He also strongly emphasized the existence of a large body of ministering angels.

It is sometimes asserted that Athenagoras was a Montanist because of his account of prophetic inspiration as well as his condemnation of second marriages. However, this could also be attributed to his Stoic and Platonist background and to the popularity of asceticism in the early church. Athenagoras was a philosophical theologian who exploited the best elements of Greek thought and culture in the service of Christian truth. He also believed that the prophets wrote their works under divine inspiration.   [H.F.S.]

Bibliography

Athenagoras: Legatio and De Resurrectione, ed. and tr. W.R. Schoedel, OECT (1972).

R.M. Grant, "Athenagoras or Pseudo-Athenagoras," *HThR* 47 (1954):121–129; L.W. Barnard, "The Embassy of Athenagoras—Two Notes," *VChr* 21 (1967):88–92; A.J. Malherbe, "The Holy Spirit in Athenagoras," *JThS* n.s. 20 (1969):538–542; idem, "The Structure of Athenagoras, Supplicatio pro Christianis," *VChr* 23 (1969):1–20; idem, "Athenagoras on Christian Ethics," *JEH* 20 (1969):1–5; idem, "Athenagoras and the Location of God," *ThZ* 26 (1970):46–52; idem, "Athenagoras on the Pagan Poets and Philosophers," *Kyriakon: Festschrift Johannes Quasten*, ed. P. Granfield and J.A. Jungman (Münster: Aschendorff, 1970), pp. 214–225; L.W. Barnard, *Athenagoras: A Study in Second Century Christian Apologetic* (Paris: Beauchesne, 1972).

ATHENS. Sometime political capital of Greece and the cultural capital of the ancient world. In spite of Athens's political depression following the classical period, it continued throughout antiquity as an educational center, especially for philosophy and rhetoric. In the republican period, Romans frequently visited the city to further their education. In 86 B.C., however, it was sacked by the Roman general Sulla. Status as an independent city was lost and with it political importance. Athens's prominence as an educational center also suffered. Philo of Larisa, the head of the Platonic Academy, and his student Antiochus of Ascalon fled to Rome. Although Antiochus did return to the city, the

Remains of basilica at Glyfada, Athens, viewed from west, showing narthex, nave, and at far end the apse; erected in the fourth century to mark traditional spot of Paul's landing on his arrival at Athens, Greece.

Platonic Academy had come to an end. During the Roman civil wars, inscriptions suggest a continued breakdown in civil order that harmed social institutions. There is evidence for some continued educational activity. In 44 B.C., for instance, Brutus attended the lectures of the Platonist Theomnestus. Yet in spite of the occasional patronage of such figures as Pompey and Julius Caesar, who began the construction of the "Roman" *agora* or marketplace in 47 B.C., the devastation of 86 B.C. led to an economic and probably cultural decline that did not subside until the reign of Augustus, who sponsored restoration and construction.

With the death of Augustus in A.D. 14, however, little imperial attention was directed toward Athens until the reign of Hadrian. Although sources are meager, there is evidence for some philosophical and educational activity during this time. Ammonius, the teacher of Plutarch of Chaeronea, taught an eclectic form of Platonism and had established a school there by A.D. 66-67, and the writings of Plutarch preserve descriptions of the informal "classes" or "lectures" held by Ammonius. The reigns of

Hadrian (117–138) and his successors mark a renaissance; Athens was to epitomize the best of Hellenic culture. The laws were reformed, new buildings constructed, and various other marks of patronage proliferated. Antoninus Pius (138–161), Hadrian's successor, appears to have established some type of institute of higher education. Aulus Gellius (*Attic Nights* 1.26; 17.20; 19.6) preserves reminiscences of his education under the Platonist Calvenus Taurus (ca. 145), and Apuleius speaks of studying poetry, geometry, music, and dialectic there ca. 150 (*Florida* 20.4). Marcus Aurelius (161–180) endowed four positions in philosophy, one for each of the major schools—Platonism, Aristotelianism, Stoicism, and Epicureanism—in 174 and added a position in rhetoric in 176. Lucian gives a humorous account of an election to one of these chairs in his *Eunuchus*.

The first report of a Christian community at Athens, aside from Acts 17:16–34, occurs in this period; Melito of Sardis (in Eusebius, *H.E.* 4.26.10) mentions that Antoninus Pius attempted to curtail the persecution of Christians there and elsewhere. The Athenian bishop

Publius was also martyred at this time. But beyond fragmentary references there is little evidence for Christian activity in the city prior to the Byzantine period, although several prominent Christians came from the city: Aristides, Athenagoras, and perhaps Clement of Alexandria. Athens's renewed prosperity continued into the third century, but in 267 the city was devastated by the invasion of the Heruli, a Germanic people. In spite of this attack, it remained a center of education, for in the next century we find three "official" sophists in addition to numerous private schools. Student riots were common, and rivalry was so strong that teachers might extract an oath of loyalty from students (Libanius 1.16, 20). Eunapius's *Lives of the Philosophers* describes Athenian life in this period, and Gregory of Nazianzus gives a portrait of students in Athens in the 350s, when he and Basil studied here (*Or.* 43.15–24). Yet the position of Athens was difficult; Synesius compared the city to a sacrificed animal (*Ep.* 136).

In 396, Alaric and his Goths approached the city but were apparently bought off. From the fifth century, we have two presentations of Athenian intellectual life, Marinus's *Life of Proclus* and Damascius's *Life of Isidore*. Educational studies in both philosophy and rhetoric focused on individual teachers and their often small number of students. Students studied at their teacher's home and may have lived there as well. In 426, Theodosius II converted pagan temples into Christian churches, and in 529 Justinian I forbade pagans to teach. Although this latter law probably had little effect on the teaching of rhetoric in Athens (by now most rhetoricians would have been Christian), it presumably closed the pagan philosophical schools. Seven Platonists departed for Persia and the court of king Chosroes. When this proved unsatisfactory, most seem to have returned to Greek territory, perhaps even Athens itself, and, although they could not teach, they did continue to produce philosophical treatises. The invasion of Greece by Slavs in 579 marks the end of Athens as a significant center of education, and the burden of providing education passed to Constantinople, Rome, and Alexandria.   [L.P.S.]

Bibliography

H.I. Marrou, *A History of Education in Antiquity* (New York: Sheed and Ward, 1956); H.A. Thompson, "Athenian Twilight: A.D. 267–600," *JRS* 49 (1959):61–72; A. Cameron, "The Last Days of the Academy at Athens," *Proceedings of the Cambridge Philological Society* 195 n.s. 15 (1969):7–29; J.P. Lynch, *Aristotle's School* (Berkeley: U of California P, 1972); S. Follet, *Athènes du IIe au IIIe siècle* (Paris: Les Belles Lettres, 1976); J. Dillon, *The Middle Platonists: 80 B.C. to A.D. 220* (Ithaca: Cornell UP, 1977); J. Oliver, "The *Diadochê* at Athens Under the Humanistic Emperors," *AJPh* 98 (1977):160–178; J. Glucker, *Antiochus and the Late Academy* (Göttingen: Vandenhoeck & Ruprecht, 1978); D.J. Geagan, "Roman Athens: Some Aspects of Life and Culture I. 86 B.C.–A.D. 267," *ANRW* (1979), Vol. 2.7.1, pp. 371–437; J. Oliver, "Roman Emperors and Athens," *Historia* 30 (1981):412–423; idem, "Marcus Aurelius and the Philosophical Schools at Athens," *AJPh* 102 (1981):213–225; G. Kennedy, *Greek Rhetoric Under Christian Emperors* (Princeton: Princeton UP, 1983).

ATONEMENT. Reconciliation through an act of reparation. Theologically, "atonement" is used for the work of Christ in reconciling God and humanity; theories of atonement speak of how that reconciliation was effected.

Concentrated theoretical discussion of atonement does not appear before the Middle Ages, but the doctrine is presupposed from the very beginning—indeed, many of the doctrinal controversies of the early centuries, particularly the Christological debates, were ultimately informed by presuppositions about salvation that created deep allegiances, although sometimes barely articulated. Study of the early period has often been distorted by the desire to find one or other of the later theories present in the New Testament or patristic material, whether the Anselmian (or penal substitution) view or the Abelardian (or moral influence) view. An attempt to break through this impasse was made by Gustaf Aulen, who in his book *Christus Victor* tried to rehabilitate what he called the "classic theory" of atonement. According to this exposition, the universal view of the early church was that Satan had usurped God's rule over the earth, and only triumph over his power could effect the salvation of humankind. This was what Christ had achieved. There is a great deal in Aulen's argument, but the wealth of imagery and ideas for expressing the work of Christ in both scripture and the patristic material cannot simply be forced into the "theory." More recent treatments of the material have tended to explore a variety of broad heads under which the ideas of the early church fall. This approach too has its problems, but it does provide a useful framework with which to start.

Educational View: Christ the Illuminator. In works like the *Didache* and the *Epistle of Barnabas*, which date from the early second century, we find mapped out a pattern of "two ways" of life; Christian teaching is presented as the true morality. Very quickly, apologists like Justin Martyr gave this a metaphysical basis: Christ was the embodiment of the Logos, the underlying rationality of the cosmos, the divine reason; he therefore confirmed and fulfilled the teaching of the great prophets and philosophers of all time and provided the final revelation of truth and goodness. In a culture that believed that sin was ignorance and virtue knowledge, a kind of skill that could be taught, it is not surprising that this could be regarded as the fundamental necessity for human beings, to be attracted away from wickedness and restored to communion with the divine. This was how humanity was rescued from idolatry and false religion and the true God was revealed. This was how his will was made known and the proper way of life made evident. Two centuries later, Eusebius of Caesarea still thought in these terms; Christianity was about monotheism and morality, revealed in Jesus Christ.

Two further factors contributed to the popularity of this kind of approach to atonement. On the one hand, the ever-present possibility of persecution and martyrdom in the early centuries encouraged emphasis on following the way revealed by Christ's example, not only by living a life of humility but also by being ready to die for one's faith—Ignatius wanted to "imitate the passion of my God" (*Rom.* 6.3). In the second place, the struggle with Gnosticism provoked a counteremphasis on the "illumination" brought by the "revealer," Jesus Christ. In the words of Irenaeus, "Not otherwise could we learn what God is if our Teacher the Word had not become Man. We could not otherwise learn unless we were to see our Teacher the Word and hear his voice with our ears, that we might become imitators of his actions and those who fulfill his words" (*Haer.* 5.1.1).

The educational view is associated particularly with the Alexandrian philosophers Clement and Origen. For Clement, Christ brought the true *gnosis*; for Origen, the plight of humanity dated from the tragic premundane fall of the eternal spirits created by God to enjoy contemplation of him, and the very creation of the world was an educational project to win back the redeemable—into this overall understanding of the purposes of God the work of Christ as revealer neatly fitted. The object of scriptural exegesis, of asceticism, of the eucharist, as of everything else was to enable souls to discern the spiritual realities and return to their lost home in heaven. Christ pioneered the way that all were to follow. He provided moral guidance in his teaching and an example in his life.

Emphasis on revelation and teaching is not confined to those for whom it was the overriding motif: it is found in the preaching and teaching of all the fathers. Reconciliation with God required repentance, a turning to the living God and abandonment of idolatry and immorality, which was brought about by Christ's revelation of the truth.

"Physical Theory": Christ the Restorer. For many of the early Christians, education alone was not sufficient for salvation. They recognized that the fundamental problem was that sin had mortal consequences: as the scripture said, "the wages of sin is death" (Rom. 6:23). So, from the earliest period, the Christian message included more than mere revelation. The *Didache* speaks of Christ as having revealed "immortality," as well as knowledge and faith; the eucharist was spiritual food and drink that effected eternal life. For Ignatius, the eucharist was the "medicine of immortality, an antidote to death" (*Eph.* 20.2). Irenaeus too can say, "So our bodies receiving the eucharist are no longer corruptible, having the hope of resurrection" (*Haer.* 4.31.4).

At first, the emphasis was eschatological: hope of a future life made Christian converts fearless in the face of death, not only prepared to face martyrdom but even, for example, to stay in plague-ridden cities to tend the sick when all others fled. The resurrection of Christ guaranteed their transcendence of death, and the eschatological future was made real in the sacraments. Christians already belonged to another world.

It was not long before the idea of the recreation of humanity through the incarnation began to predominate. Sin had mortal consequences: Adam's fall meant a loss that had to be restored. Irenaeus, writing against Gnostic dualism at the end of the second century, stresses the goodness of creation; salvation is not escape from an alien environment but rather the recreation of a world that has been corrupted. Adam was "a child, and it was necessary that he should grow and so come to his perfection" (*Dem.* 12), but he made the wrong choice and lost the "likeness" of God. He became mortal because of his fatal mistake. The new Adam, Christ, went over the ground again (recapitulated the story) and succeeded where Adam failed, so restoring the likeness of God and imparting immortality to humanity. "Out of his great love, he became what we are, that we might become what he is" (*Haer.* 5 praef.).

This last statement anticipates the theory of Athanasius: "He became human that we might become divine" (*Inc.* 54—*theopoiēsis*, or "divinization"). But Athanasius took a more serious view of the fall than had Irenaeus. Probably in a counterblast to Eusebius of Caesarea's "mere revelation" views, Athanasius wrote his *Contra gentes–De incarnatione*. Here, exploring the question why the incarnation had to happen, he spells out the dire consequences of Adam's sin. Adam was made in the image and likeness of God, that is, he was endowed with God's Logos, the principle of life and of reason, the true image and likeness of God— indeed, his Son. As a result of the fall, he lost the Logos. So he was progressively losing his reason and sinking into irrationality—hence, idolatry and sin: indeed, worse, he was returning to the "nothingness" out of which he had been created—hence, physical corruptibility and mortality. The only possible salvation was the restoration of the lost Logos to humanity—hence, the incarnation. Humanity is restored by the Logos himself taking human nature.

Athanasius understood human salvation to be realized by the participation of human beings in the archetypal Logos. He is truly Son of God; believers become sons of God by adoption into him. He is truly *homoousios tōi patri* ("one substance with the Father"), so participation in him effects *theopoiēsis*. The Arian suggestion that the Logos was a "derivative" being, creaturely like other creatures, threatened this perception of what constituted atonement, namely the restoration of the divine life to corrupted humanity. The later Alexandrian tradition struggled against Nestorianism precisely because it threatened this belief, that in Christ humanity was made divine, and by partaking of his flesh in the eucharist that divine life was received by the faithful. The sacramental dimension of this understanding was vital. Gregory of Nyssa spoke of Christ inserting himself as a kind of healing seed into the body of the believer as the eucharistic elements were received (*Or. catech.* 37). This idea of atonement was both "physical" and "mystical." In fact, it was deeply sacramental, as well as informed by the Platonic metaphysic.

Classic Theory: Christ the Victor. Even the "physical theory" of Athanasius, however, betrays a somewhat dualistic outlook: sin and death had to be "conquered." Human "irrationality" was compounded by the deceit of the demons who encouraged idolatry and false religion. According to the long recension of the *De incarnatione*, Christ had to die on a cross, because the demons inhabit the air and the air has to be purified so as to open up the way to heaven for us. An older but not unrelated assumption was that by his ascension Christ had broken through the ring of demons and the planetary spheres, breaking the astrological powers of fate and evil. The connection between these "victory" themes and the struggle with polytheism and idolatry, the "daemons" of the nations, should not be underestimated. But the ultimate background is the world of Jewish apocalyptic, which had such a formative influence on early Christian thinking. The work of Christ was the culminating act in the cosmic struggle between the hosts of God and the Satan and his angels: the victory theme was already present in the epistles of Paul and the Gospel of John—"Now is the Ruler of this world cast out" (John 12:31).

So Christ was proclaimed as the "slayer" of death and sin: "The word of God was made flesh in order that he might destroy death and bring us to life, for we were tied and bound in sin, we were born in sin and lived under the dominion of death," wrote Irenaeus (*Dem.* 37). As Origen put it, "Through his resurrection, he destroyed the kingdom of death, whence it is written that he freed captivity" (*Comm. in Rom.* 5.1). Later Christian art developed the icon of the Anastasis, in which Christ bursts the gates of Hades, tramples on Satan, and raises up Adam and Eve as he rises from the grave. The theme of victory pervades the homilies of the early church, and exorcism was an important feature of the baptismal rite: the convert put off the old allegiance to the world, the flesh, and the devil, and was sealed with the mark of the new allegiance to Christ (John Chrysostom strikingly exploits military metaphors in his catechetical lectures). The battle imagery could not fail to shape the assumptions of the Christian populace.

In this context, the blood of Christ was understood as the "ransom price" offered to the devil, and this led to some differences of opinion as to the status of the devil and God's dealings with him. For Irenaeus, the devil was simply a usurper, and in the earlier literature the ransom image comes from the battle imagery: it is the price for repurchasing captives. Tertullian and others, however, hazarded the view that the devil had rights over humanity—the rights of a slave owner, at least—and God had to deal with him on the basis of those rights. Origen and Gregory of Nyssa were prepared to speak of God deceiving the devil: as Gregory put it, "The Deity was hidden under the veil of our nature, that, as is done by greedy fish, the hook of the Deity might be gulped down along with the bait of the flesh and thus life be introduced into the house of death, and light shining in the darkness, that which is contrary to light and life might vanish away..." (*Or. catech.* 17–23). Gregory did not see anything

immoral about the deceiver being deceived, and like Origen he seems to have thought that it was permissible, since in the end it was for the devil's own good. Origen believed in the ultimate salvation of the devil and the restoration of all things to their pristine perfection. It is interesting how this highly mythological theme of conquest is particularly developed by sophisticated thinkers in the Platonic tradition like Origen and Gregory of Nyssa. Both stressed the love of God and the initiative of God in arranging for human salvation, while being somewhat embarrassed by the notion of God's wrath or the idea that God needed to change his mind. Seeing the work of Christ as God's way of dealing with an opposition absolved them from these difficulties.

But "who" achieved the victory? The recapitulation theory of Irenaeus integrated these victory themes with other motifs, and it is clear that in his view it was, and had to be, "humanity" that achieved the victory: "If man had not conquered the adversary of man, the enemy would not have been justly conquered" (*Haer.* 3.19.6). Yet in the same passage he adds, "If God had not given the salvation, we should not have securely obtained it, and if man had not been united to God, he could not have obtained incorruptibility." Christological ideas were never divorced from conceptions of salvation. For Irenaeus, it was essential that the victor be the "God-Man." But it took a long time for this to be effectively established in eastern theology. Athanasius, although so like Irenaeus in many of his views, clearly regarded the divinity of the Logos as the most important factor in achieving victory, and his grasp of the essential humanity of Christ is less than fully satisfactory. As the Christological debates developed in the late fourth and early fifth centuries, the Antiochenes put considerable emphasis upon the achievement of victory over sin and the devil by the "man assumed" by the Logos, thus ensuring that the balance was redressed in the eventual definition of the person of Christ at Chalcedon (451).

Gustav Aulen was certainly right in seeing that this "mythological" description of atonement had very deep roots in the patristic material and the life of the early church.

Sacrifice-Language: Christ as Victim. Gregory of Nazianzus was perplexed and offended by talk of God entering into deals or undertaking actions of dubious morality. He preferred to speak of "sacrifice" and the mystery of the "economy." He thus seems to imply that God, not the devil, needed atoning.

Ideas of sacrifice are deeply ingrained in the traditional language of the church. From the New Testament on, Christians had been affirming that they no longer offered "bloody sacrifices," since Christ had offered his sacrifice of obedience unto death and so fulfilled and annulled all sacrifice. Abraham's sacrifice of Isaac was seen as a "type" of the cross, and sacrifice language was also naturally used of Christian worship. Such sacrifices were offered to God. It was natural to assume that Christ as priest and victim offered a sacrifice to God for the sins of the whole world.

This notion is deeply pervasive in the homiletic literature. John Chrysostom took seriously the sacrificial language of the Epistle to the Hebrews and talked without embarrassment of the need for God's wrath to be propitiated by sacrifice. Here, he certainly operates with Greek pagan notions of how sacrifice worked—that sacrifice is usually a kind of bribe or bargain with the gods—rather than the more subtle biblical view; but one cannot help feeling that it was the natural reading of many biblical passages for pagan converts. His insistence on God's *philanthropia* may not seem entirely consistent with this, but there is in any case a paradox in Chrysostom, the stern prophet who was criticized for preaching free forgiveness to the repentant while threatening the rich and powerful with God's judgment. Unlike Origen, for whom the wrath of God was a kind of "pose" on God's part to discipline his recalcitrant children, Chrysostom sensed the need to do something about the offense to God caused by human sin. Humanity had to be reconciled with God. God was in some sense "enemy" as well as "friend."

Athanasius was the one eastern thinker to tackle this systematically. He outlines what has been described as the "divine dilemma": God had, so to speak, trapped himself by declaring that disobedience would lead to death.

He could not go back on his word, and yet he could not bear to see his most precious creature disappear into nothingness. So his saving action was necessary to his own integrity. God had, as it were, to "propitiate" himself.

It was in the west that this approach to atonement came to predominate. For Tertullian, Christ was sent to die: "For he had come for this purpose that he himself, free from sin and altogether holy, should die for sinners" (*Pud.* 22). Ambrose spoke of Christ taking our sins, and of God who spared not his own Son, acquitting us by making him to be sin for us. Augustine insists that if humanity had not sinned the Son of God would not have come; the sacrifice of Christ was promised in the sacrificial victims of old and is celebrated anew in the memorial sacrament. Various features of the western church encouraged this emphasis— the development of the penitential system, expressing the need to offer "satisfaction" for sin, the realistic representation of Christ's sacrifice in the form of the western eucharistic rites. Such features were already developing in the Latin Christianity of Tertullian and Cyprian in the third century. Here, no one was shy of speaking of God's wrath and judgment or of the need to pay the penalty. It was Christ who paid our debt, Augustine said: "Since death was our punishment for sin, his death was that of a sacrificial victim offered for sin" (*Trin.* 4.12.15).

Yet even in the west this understanding did not reach the status of a "theory," nor did it exclude other ways of understanding. "Our Lord Jesus Christ, the God-Man," wrote Augustine, "is both the evidence of the love of God toward us and an example of humility for men" (*Catech. rud.* 4.8); "the humility whereby God was born and led to death is the supreme medicine by which the swelling of our pride could be healed, and deep mystery by which our sin could be atoned" (*Trin.* 8.5.7).

Conclusion. It is in fact impossible to categorize neatly the thought of the major patristic writers on the subject of atonement. (Note how such figures as Irenaeus, Origen, and Athanasius appear in this article under several different headings.) A sentence in Irenaeus shows how the themes discussed above were woven together in patristic thought: "By his passion, the Lord destroyed death, dissipated error, rooted out corruption, destroyed ignorance, displayed life, showed truth, and deferred incorruptibility" (*Haer.* 2.20.2). Another problem is that the fundamental and pervasive tension between monism and dualism is left unresolved in the patristic literature. In preaching the need for salvation, Christians insisted on the devil's power over the world; but in opposing Manichaean dualism they insisted that this is God's world. As a result, attitudes to the things of this world—creation, sex, asceticism, beauty, enjoyment—were deeply ambivalent.

The four views of atonement presented here cannot do justice to the range of motifs and images that are found in describing the saving and atoning work of Christ. This article has dismembered several "systematic theologies" to illustrate common soteriological themes. These points need further exposition.

Patristic views of atonement can be appreciated only if one begins by recognizing the richness of typological and allegorical use of scripture, the multifaceted unity of imagery and allusion that pervades the literature. This can be seen most effectively in the catalogues of "names of Jesus," which are a feature of some of the homiletic literature—the sort of thing that Origen expounds in the first book of his *Commentary on John*. In such catalogues, we find Christ called Door, Way, Lamb, Shepherd, Stone, Pearl, Salt, Flower, Angel, Man, Light, Earth, Mustard-seed, Worm—each one backed up by a scriptural reference and each explained by some feature of his atoning work. In a sermonic address found in the *Martyrdom of St. Abo of Tiflis*, for example, Psalm 22 is quoted to justify the name "Worm," and then the fishhook image used by Gregory above is given as the explanation; "Mustard-seed" is accounted for as follows:"He made himself small and was made like us in our stature so that he might plant himself in the field of our soul and strike roots deep and might gather us upon the branches of his cross and be exalted and exalt us with him." This Georgian work of the eighth century certainly preserves ancient motifs and strikingly shows how the themes catalogued above appear in extraordinarily developed metaphors and parables based on scriptural material (cf. Birdsall below).

Although his list overlaps, Origen expounds many of the names differently, and unlike the popular homiletic tradition he presupposes a systematic theology. All these many titles are important because the one Christ is a "multitude of goods"; the Savior unites in himself the multiplicity of creation and the unity of God. Origen's fundamental idea of atonement, into which his use of the educational and victory themes is integrated, is the transcendent God and his marred creation remarried by means of their mutual consummation in this mediating "Second God," the One-Many of Middle Platonism.

Athanasius too lists the names of the Savior in the *Contra gentes*, not surprisingly including many of the same, since ultimately the lists were drawn from scripture. But despite some connections his fundamental system is very different from that of Origen. Where Origen could blur the distinction between God and the creation by conceiving of a hierarchy of being, a mediating link that he identified with the Logos, the Christ, the Savior, Athanasius certainly could not. For him, the Logos had to be the "absolute," absolute Wisdom, very Word, the Father's own power, absolute light, absolute holiness, quite different from creatures who merely "participate" in such absolutes. Athanasius's fundamental view of atonement is the taking up of the creation into God through participation—*theopoiēsis*, and this can be effected only through the Logos being fully divine, the true son into whose Sonship human beings are adopted. Into this systematic scheme, several of the themes treated above are integrated.

The successful doctrines of atonement found in the patristic writings are those that were able to integrate the range of imagery current in popular preaching. None achieved the status of an agreed creedal affirmation, and most belonged so intimately to a particular cultural setting that they did not succeed in transcending it. But there is more to patristic thought on the subject than is evident in studies that concentrate on simple transactional theories involving the appeasement of God or the devil, or focus exclusively on the subjective or objective aspects stressed in later formulations of the doctrine. Such approaches are destructive of the integrity of the patristic exegetical imagination and the systematic thought of the greatest among the fathers. *See also* Baptism; Christ, Christology; God; Salvation; Sin. [F.Y.]

Bibliography

J. Rivière, *The Doctrine of Atonement*, 2 vols. (St. Louis: Herder, 1909); R.S. Franks, *A History of the Doctrine of the Work of Christ* (New York: Hodder and Stoughton, 1918); H. Rashdall, *The Idea of Atonement in Christian Theology* (London: Macmillan, 1919); G. Aulen, *Christus Victor* (London: SPCK, 1931); H. Chadwick, "Eucharist and Christology in the Nestorian Controversy," *JThS* n.s. 2 (1951):145–164; H.E.W. Turner, *The Patristic Doctrine of Redemption* (London: Mowbray, 1952); F.W. Dillistone, *The Christian Understanding of Atonement* (London: Nisbet, 1968); F.M. Young, "Insight or Incoherence? The Greek Fathers on God and Evil," *JEH* 24 (1973): 113–126; J.N. Birdsall, "Diatessaric Readings in the 'Martyrdom of St. Abo of Tiflis'?," *New Testament Textual Criticism: Essays in Honour of Bruce M. Metzger*, ed. E.J. Epp and G.D. Fee (Oxford: Oxford UP, 1981), pp. 313–324; F.M. Young, "Allegory and Atonement," *Australian Biblical Review* 35 (1987): 107–114.

ATTILA

ATTILA (d. 453). Ruler of the Huns (434–453). Attila and his brother Bleda inherited the rule of the Huns from their uncles; he became sole ruler after killing Bleda (445). When the eastern emperor Marcian refused to pay further tribute, Attila invaded Gaul with Germanic allies; he withdrew after being checked in battle by a force of Visigoths and Franks under the Roman commander Aetius (451). He then entered Italy but departed after the plea of an embassy consisting of Leo I the Great and others (452), probably because of attrition of his forces and the pressure of an army at his rear sent by Marcian. His death, of natural causes, occurred shortly thereafter. Because of his reputation for cruelty, he became in Christian legend the "scourge of God," an instrument of divine retribution. [M.P.McH.]

Bibliography

E.A. Thompson, *A History of Attila and the Huns* (Oxford: Oxford UP, 1948); C.D. Gordon, *The Age of Attila: Fifth Century Byzantium and the Barbarians* (Ann Arbor: U of Michigan P, 1960).

AUGUSTINE (354–430). Bishop of Hippo in the Roman province of Numidia in North Africa. Augustine was born of a Christian mother, Monica, and a non-Christian father, Patricius. In his *Confessions*, written ca. 401, Augustine tells us more about his early life and struggles than does any other figure from late antiquity. His father was not a wealthy man, but Augustine received a classical education thanks to the generous support of a local dignitary, Romanianus. In 385, he became a professor of rhetoric in Milan. Although he achieved unusual success for a provincial, and was moving up in the volatile world of the late fourth century, he was, he tells us, desperately unhappy. At the age of nineteen, he was powerfully attracted to philosophy by reading the *Hortensius* of Cicero (*Conf.* 3.4). In spite of his mother's strong urgings that he convert to Christianity, Augustine followed worldly ambition until he was over thirty (*Conf.* 6.6), when he began to listen to the preaching of Ambrose, bishop of Milan, whose sermons he found remarkable for their philosophical acumen and religious insight. By this time, Augustine had become disillusioned with the Manichaean teachings he had eagerly followed for about nine years. Clearly, although Augustine himself presents his conversion to Christian faith as a dramatic release from his need for sex and worldly success, a long series of events had prepared him to turn to Christ, whom, he says, he had "drunk in with my mother's milk" (*Conf.* 3.4).

Augustine described sex as his particular compulsion; he had lived with one woman in faithfulness for thirteen years, and she had borne his son, Adeodatus. But when his engagement to an heiress came close to the time for marriage, his mother sent his companion back to North Africa. His marriage being delayed, Augustine soon found another concubine. Since sex was his addiction, it was sex from which he was "freed" at the time of his final conversion.

After retiring from professional life in order to live with his son and some friends with whom he could pursue study and conversation on philosophy and religion, Augustine spent some time at the country estate of Verecundus near

Milan, while preparing for baptism. His Cassiciacum dialogues, which date from this time, are more philosophical than Christian in content. He was baptized by Ambrose on Easter, 387. Augustine, along with his mother, son, and other close friends, prepared to return to North Africa to establish a monastic community. While the party waited in Ostia to sail, Monica died and was buried there. Returning to his birthplace, Thagaste, Augustine continued his philosophical inquiries. In the two years of his stay, both his dear friend Nebridius and his son, Adeodatus, died. As Augustine traveled through the town of Hippo Regius, looking for a place to found his monastery, he was made priest by popular acclaim; his life of philosophical leisure was over. The elderly bishop of Hippo, Valerius, soon gave Augustine preaching responsibilities, and within two years, in 393, he expounded the creed to bishops assembled in a general council of Africa.

After a brief period of retirement for the purpose of studying scripture, Augustine plunged into the life of a busy priest. In Hippo, Donatists outnumbered Catholics, and the Catholics' support was largely from distant Rome. In 395, on Valerius's retirement, Augustine was made bishop of Hippo, a post he held for the rest of his life.

During his ministry, doctrinal quarrels and schisms among Christians, as well as political and social calamity, upset the peace of North Africa and the Roman empire. In addition, Augustine spent several hours of every day adjudicating local lawsuits in the ecclesiastical court of Hippo, the alternative to the notoriously corrupt civil courts. In 410, Rome was conquered and sacked by the Goths under Alaric, a severe blow to the classical world. Refugees from Rome soon appeared in North Africa. At the end of Augustine's life, Hippo suffered a similar fate, as the Vandals besieged and, in the spring of 430, overran Numidia. Augustine died of a sudden fever in August 430, believing that the work of his entire life had come to nothing. Although Hippo was evacuated and burned a year after Augustine's death, his library was rescued. Augustine's writings began an immensely influential career.

Augustine and Manichaeism. Three great controversies shaped the teachings and writings of Augustine. Their chronological order indicates how the most characteristic Augustinian doctrines came to be formulated. These three controversies, prompted by Manichaeism, Donatism, and Pelagianism, can all be understood as conflicts over "anthropologies." The struggle with Manichaeism began with Augustine's attraction to Mani's intellectually satisfying identification of the origin and perpetuation of evil. Mani, a third-century Babylonian, taught that human beings are, in essence, rational and spiritual beings created by a supreme God, but this essential nature is unhappily bonded to a material body created by an evil demiurge. When, after nine years as a "hearer," or follower, of Manichaeism, Augustine came to find this doctrine unsatisfying, he was left with the need for a different comprehensive theory of the human situation. He articulated the doctrine of original sin to explain the irruption of evil in the midst of a good creation. Although earlier Latin authors had referred to original sin, they had given the doctrine no centrality or systematic development; neither baptismal creeds nor the Nicene Creed mentioned it. Augustine was the first to include a theory of the fall and original sin in the essentials of Christian faith and to articulate its intimate meaning for all human beings individually and for the human race collectively.

Although Augustine often spoke as if evil were a lack of knowledge, the development of his theology increasingly came to locate sin and evil in the human will, the energy of the whole human being, partly informed by intellect and partly by experience, feeling, and desire. The original created condition of human beings was to be oriented by delight to the intrinsically valuable object of this delight—God. From this orientation would flow a spontaneous ordering of objects of desire in which the goal would not be repression of attraction or rejection of "inferior" objects but the inclusion of all objects of delight in their order of value. In the first human beings, before the fall, the will was integrated, able to gather and focus the whole desire of human beings. The "first evil act" was a defection or falling away of the intentional will from God to the self. It was not a substantive evil; this act was, in the strictest sense, unnatural, a defect occurring in a good nature. Augustine's axiom "Whatever is, is good" (*Conf.* 7.12) insists that evil comes from the will that has lost its attraction to God and now seeks its own happiness in fragmentation in a world of diverse and competing objects of delight and desire. In the *Confessions*, Augustine describes his own experience of a divided will, dispersed and miserable in its search for happiness until God's grace intervened and Augustine, in his own phrase, "relaxed a little" (*cessavi de me paululum*) from himself (*Conf.* 7.14).

In the *City of God*, Augustine sets these same scenarios—on the one hand, fruitless and frustrating effort, and on the other, trusting acceptance of the grace of God—in an epic context of space and time. The city of humanity contrasts with the city of God; the struggles of secular human beings for sex, power, and possessions are juxtaposed with the condition of Christians who have surrendered their own desires and now regard themselves as journeying on a lifelong pilgrimage to the city of God. The distinction is not between church and secular culture; even the visible church is a *corpus permixtum*, a mixture of those predestined to eternal joy and those who share the fate of the *massa damnata*, eternal punishment. The ultimate fulfillment of human beings as individuals and as a race is the eschatological event of the resurrection of the body when body and soul are reunited to enjoy, or suffer, their eternal fate.

Augustine's construction of the saga of humanity postpones human perfection and completion until a time and space beyond present experience. This goes a long way toward explaining his sense of the problems that accompany life in the present; understanding his vision of the ultimate possibility of an integrated humanity in which a body no longer vulnerable to pain, disease, and death serves the soul as its intimate "spouse" allows us to sense his almost neurasthenic sympathy with, and distress over, suffering and the inability to achieve immediate happiness. His explanation of evil as temporary and originating in the human will was a pointed rebuttal of Mani's description of evil as necessary, permanent, and substantial.

The Donatist Controversy. The Donatist church in North Africa, a group larger than Catholic Christianity there, had split from the Catholic church over an issue of ecclesiastical purity long before Augustine became a priest. Donatists claimed that Catholic ordinations to the priesthood were traceable to bishops who had collaborated, by handing over holy books to the persecutors, in the Great Persecution of the church by Diocletian (303–305). In 311, a group of African bishops declared the bishop of Carthage, Caecilian, guilty of this offense and decreed his ordination invalid.

Although there were no major doctrinal differences between Catholics and Donatists, issues of ecclesiology were involved; different views of the church lay behind the political aspects of the schism. To the Donatists, the true church was a "pure" church, a church of the holy, separated from the surrounding secular society by participation in the sacraments dispensed by priests whose ordination was untainted by association with *traditores*, those who had betrayed the faith by cooperation with a persecuting state. Augustine began to debate with Donatists soon after his ordination to the priesthood, and the struggle was to continue until the suppression of Donatism after the edict against them resulting from the conference of 411. Augustine's idea of the church was strongly informed by his experience in Italy of a strong and self-confident body, able to assimilate and Christianize secular culture without fear of diluting acculturation. Contrasting metaphors permeated the conflict: for Donatists, the church was the "Bride of Christ, without spot or wrinkle"; for Augustine, the most adequate metaphor for the church was in the parable of the wheat and the tares, left together on the threshing floor until the day of judgment.

The sacraments were similarly understood in divergent ways by the two Christian groups. The Donatists held that the sacraments of baptism, eucharist, and ordination dispensed by clerics tainted by association with lapsed bishops in the distant past were not merely ineffectual but were actively contaminating. In his treatise *On Baptism, Against the Donatists,* Augustine worked out a theory of sacrament that did not rely on the purity of the priest but defined the sacraments as belonging to, and given by, Christ rather than the priest. Thus, the sacraments are efficacious even in the event of a priest's moral or spiritual failure. Against the Donatists' accurate invocation of the honored name of Cyprian, martyred bishop of Carthage (d. 258), who had favored the rebaptism of those converted to Catholic Christianity from schism, Augustine argued that Cyprian was more concerned with the unity of the church than with its purity.

The Donatist controversy prompted Augustine to construct a theology of the church as imperfect, struggling, a group of Christians engaged in the long "convalescence" that would terminate only in the perfected city of God in the day of resurrection. The political consequences of the debate were profound; the suppression of the Donatists became a model for future centuries of suppression of minority ideas and people by a powerful institutional church. Augustine came to the controversy believing that no persons should be compelled to embrace a faith that failed to attract and convince them. But his views changed as the result of his experience that people "compelled to enter" the Catholic body soon realized their former error. Augustine also found warrant in the forcible conversion of Paul on the road to Damascus for his advocacy of a political and legal resolution to a difference of religious perspectives (*Ep.* 185).

Pelagianism. The controversy over Pelagianism was the third lengthy intellectual and ecclesiastical battle in the context of which Augustine's theological ideas were formulated, especially those on predestination, original sin, and grace. When, in the second decade of the fifth century, Pelagius began to teach that it was possible—and therefore mandatory—that human beings strive toward and achieve perfection in the Christian life in the present, Augustine undertook to refute these teachings, arguing that perfection could not possibly be accomplished by human effort. Horrified by the pastoral implications of Augustine's statement

in the *Confessions,* "Command what you will: give what you command," Pelagius taught that the human being was responsible for the choice, self-definition, and conscious cultivation of perfection. He rejected a church characterized by a division between the professional full-time religious and the members who lived a secular life with a summary knowledge and practice of Christianity. Augustine saw the danger that laypeople would become discouraged by this teaching and despair of any Christian piety since they could not manage "perfect obedience." Pelagius's teaching had its foundation in an anthropology very different from Augustine's. Instead of Augustine's view of the disastrously undermining effect of original sin on the human race, Pelagius saw the slight undertow of bad habits as being socially conditioned and reversible with effort and conscious reconditioning. Pelagius assumed the freedom of the individual for self-definition. Although Augustine also wanted to maintain individual freedom enough to make the human will responsible for sin, he had a strong respect for the deadly inertia inherited from the parents of the human race in their act of disobedience. Also, although he did not draw the logical conclusion that whomever God did not, in his mercy, redeem from eternal damnation, he damned, Augustine insisted that God's foreknowledge predicted, but did not preordain, the eternal punishment of all people not selected for salvation.

Augustine's position reflected a perspective informed by three main components: his observation, his experience, and scriptural accounts of the human condition. Since Augustine's theology was strongly influenced by his own experience as well as by his observation of others, he began to puzzle over the fact that some people seem to learn increasingly to turn toward the light while others seem to dig themselves deeper and deeper into negative patterns of thought and destructive patterns of activity. How to explain this? Inadequate education? Poor parenting? Unfortunate circumstances? Yes, but more accurately these are the effects rather than the causes of sin. The *reason,* it seemed obvious to Augustine, was that some people have been given more grace than others, that increments of grace accompany and inform the daily decisions and acts of some, while others, of equal "merit" in the human view, do not receive enabling grace. Pelagius had argued that the grace of creation is enough to sustain and bring humans to perfection if they only use it and develop it.

Next to Pelagius, Augustine appeared to be morally tolerant. His interest, however, was not in promoting laziness in the Christian life but in giving full credit for human achievement to the grace of God and in emphasizing the imperfect pilgrim status of all Christians. The metaphors of the Christian life used by Pelagius and Augustine are significant: Pelagius exhorts Christians to grow to full adulthood, while Augustine emphasizes the dependency and helplessness of infants as the position of the Christian before God. Augustine's criterion of moral action carried out as the result of grace was spontaneity, effortlessness, not the teeth-gritting effort urged by Pelagius, an effort that was itself, for Augustine, the evidence of original sin.

As an old man, Augustine was still struggling against the Pelagianism of Julian of Eclanum, a wealthy and well-educated nobleman. Julian held a romantic notion of the origins of humankind in the Garden of Eden: Adam and Eve were simple, unsophisticated people, reveling in the beauty of nature and the goodness of God. It was human society in its gradual growth in numbers and interests that polluted the human race; individuals, however, could still choose to live in simplicity and trust. Baptism, he taught, returned the person to that original state, which could then be maintained throughout life. Accusing Augustine of a latent and endemic Manichaeism because of his teaching that the sexual act cannot, in the fallen state of the human race, be without sin, Julian wrote of the possibility of an integrated sexuality that Augustine had never imagined or achieved. In the course of these polemics with a brilliant younger man, Augustine insisted on the lifelong clash of reason and sexual desire, the permanent opposition of the will and sexuality. In *City of God* 14.16, his prime

example of the disjunction between the will and sexual desire was impotence; in his polemical works against Julian, Augustine identified the sexual act as the location of the transmission of original sin to the child propagated in this act (*Nupt. et concup.* 11.24.27).

Writings. The corpus of Augustine's writings is enormous. In the sixth century, Isidore of Seville wrote that anyone who claimed to have read all of Augustine's works could be immediately considered a liar. Augustine's writings fall into many literary categories and styles, from the lyrical *Soliloquies* of the Cassiciacum days to the acrimony of polemical treatises, from autobiography to homily and closely reasoned theological treatises. Numerous expositions of the creed, doctrinal teachings, and scriptural commentaries are also among Augustine's works. The three major volumes essential to understanding Augustine are the *Confessions*, the *City of God*, and *The Trinity*, but since Augustine was not a systematic writer, crucial pieces of his thought are dispersed throughout his corpus. In old age, Augustine attempted to review, evaluate, correct, and place his works in order of composition. The *Retractations* provide a guide not only to the chronological order of his works but also to the way his mind changed through his life. They remind students that in seeking to understand a fluent and lively mind like Augustine's it is never adequate to ascertain his view on an important issue at one time, as if it characterized his thinking throughout his life; rather, one must be careful to understand Augustine's development of thought, especially as pertaining to subtle features, like changes of underlying models—for example, his preference in maturity for temporal models of human life over the spatial models of his youth. Although *ascent* never disappears from Augustine's interpretive vocabulary, *pilgrimage* to the city of God comes to be his primary model.

Influence. The importance of Augustine has been profound to our own time. His powerful and rhetorically vivid description of the saga of humanity dominated the theological imagination of the Christian west from the medieval period forward. The institutions and attitudes of the west, both ecclesiastical and political, have formed around Augustine's interpretation of original sin, sacramental grace, the unruliness of sexuality, and the natural world as flawed along with human nature. In the reformations of the sixteenth century, both Protestant and Roman Catholic reformers appealed to different aspects of Augustine's teaching to support their claims. Roman Catholics cited his teachings on ecclesiology and his sacramental theology; Protestants invoked his teachings on the Christian's dependence on the grace of God for justification. Martin Luther quoted Augustine more than 100 times in his *Commentary on the Epistle to the Romans* alone. Augustine's ideas have provided arguments for political arrangements: his approval of the Donatists' suppression influenced theories of just war, and his social theory, described most concisely in *City of God* 19.13–15, urges the maintenance of hierarchical ordering in society. This order begins with the dominance of soul over body in the individual and moves to the familial dominance of husband over wife, children, and slaves, and on to society in the dominance of ruler over subjects. In the slippery world of the Roman empire, Augustine saw no alternative to this hierarchical ordering of human relations. Although the model of order he uses is that of body and soul, he does not envision, as his model might lead him to do, an alternative based on an articulated interdependence.

Many particular aspects of influence might be discussed regarding Augustine's importance in the Christian west, but it was primarily his grand, essentially biblical, scheme of creation, fall, redemption, and ultimate completion and perfection of humanity in the resurrection of the body that permeated the religious sensibilities of the west. His construction of human beings as essentially intentional—that is, not containing in themselves the possibility of integrated happiness but structured by the direction of their longings—simultaneously connects and explains the most intimate and personal of experiences with the cosmic and historical setting for the human pilgrimage. Feast day August 28. CPL 250–386. *See also* Anthropol-

ogy; Donatism; Mani, Manichaeism; Original Sin; Pelagius, Pelagianism; Predestination; Sacraments. [M.R.M.]

Bibliography

For editions and translations of Augustine's works, see A.DiBerardino, ed., *Patrology* (Westminster: Christian Classics, 1986), Vol. 4, pp. 342–462.

N.P. Williams, *The Ideas of the Fall and of Original Sin* (London: Longmans and Green, 1927); C.N. Cochrane, *Christianity and Classical Culture* (New York: Oxford UP, 1940); W.A. Schumacher, *Spiritus and Spiritualis: A Study in the Sermons of St. Augustine* (Mundelein: St. Mary of the Lake Seminary, 1957); E. Portalie, *A Guide to the Thought of St. Augustine* (London: Burns and Oates, 1960); G.I. Bonner, "Libido and Concupiscentia in St. Augustine," *SP* 6 (1962):303–314; P. Brown, *Augustine of Hippo* (Berkeley: U of California P, 1967); R.J. O'Connell, *St. Augustine's Early Theory of Man* (Cambridge: Harvard UP, 1968); R.A. Markus, *Saeculum: History and Society in the Theology of St. Augustine* (Cambridge: Cambridge UP, 1970); M.R. Miles, *Augustine on the Body* (Missoula: Scholars, 1979); idem, "Infancy, Parenting, and Nourishment in Augustine's Confessions," *Journal of the American Academy of Religion* 50 (1982):349–364; H. Chadwick, *Augustine* (New York: Oxford UP, 1986); A. Trapé, *St. Augustine: Man, Pastor, Mystic* (New York: Catholic Book, 1986); G. O'Daly, *Augustine's Philosophy of Mind* (Berkeley: U of California P, 1987); C. Mayer, ed., *Augustinus-Lexikon*, 5 vols. (Basel: Schwabe, 1986–).

AUGUSTINE OF CANTERBURY (d. before 610).

Missionary to England and first archbishop of Canterbury. Augustine, prior of a Roman monastery, was sent with some forty other monks by Gregory I the Great to evangelize the Anglo-Saxons (595 or 596). Nothing is known of his earlier career. His party fell into dissension while on the journey through Gaul. Augustine returned to Rome for further authorization and, having obtained it and been consecrated bishop in Gaul, proceeded to Great Britain (597). King Ethelbert of Kent, whose queen was Bertha, a Frankish Christian and great-granddaughter of Clovis, was converted with many of his subjects. Rome sent additional missionaries and granted Augustine metropolitan status. Gregory allowed him considerable freedom in the consecration of bishops and the adaptation of liturgical usages, while

St. Augustine's cross, erected in 1884 to mark site of his arrival in England, near Sandwich, Kent.

encouraging him to transform pagan temples and festivals for purposes of Christian worship.

Augustine established his see at Canterbury, where he built a cathedral and a nearby abbey; bishoprics were founded at London and Rochester. He held conferences on two occasions with the Celtic bishops of Wales and the western country in an attempt to bring about some uniformity of practice, particularly in regard to the date of the celebration of Easter, but without success.

The missionary effort made its immediate gains in Kent and adjacent regions, but it would eventually lead to the conversion of all England and, at the Synod of Whitby (663–664), the effective termination of the Paschal controversy in the west. Feast day May 26 (Episcopal), May 27 (Roman Catholic). CPL 1327, 1714.   [M.P.McH.]

Bibliography

Gregory the Great, *Letters* 6.51–59; 8.30; 9.11; 9.108; 9.109; 11.60; 11.61; 11.63; 11.64; 11.65; 11.66; 14.16; Bede, *Ecclesiastical History* 1.23–2.3.

H.F. Bing, "St. Augustine of Canterbury and the Saxon Church in Kent," *Archaeologia Cantiana* 62 (1949):108–129; M. Deanesly and P. Grosjean, "The Canterbury Edition of the Answers of Pope Gregory I to St. Augustine," *JEH* 10 (1959):1–49; P. Meyvaert, "Les 'Responsiones' de S. Grégoire le Grand à S. Augustin de Cantorbéry," *RHE* 54 (1959):879–894; J. Godfrey, *The Church in Anglo-Saxon England* (Cambridge: Cambridge UP, 1962); R.A. Markus, "The Chronology of the Gregorian Mission to England: Bede's Narrative and Gregory's Correspondence," *JEH* 14 (1963):16–30; M. Deanesly, *Augustine of Canterbury* (London: Nelson, 1964); P.H. Blair, *The World of Bede* (London: Secker and Warburg, 1970), pp. 41–88; J.W. Lamb, *The Archbishopric of Canterbury from Its Foundation to the Norman Conquest* (London: Faith, 1971); H. Mayr-Harting, *The Coming of Christianity to Anglo-Saxon England* (London: Batsford, 1972); C.E. Stancliffe, "Kings and Conversion: Some Comparisons Between the Roman Mission to England and Patrick's to Ireland," *Frühmittelalterliche Studien* 14 (1981):59–94.

AUGUSTUS (63 B.C.–A.D. 14). Roman emperor (27 B.C.–A.D. 14). Octavian was the grandnephew and adopted son of Julius Caesar. Although only eighteen at the latter's death, he gradually gained supremacy over Italy and, at the naval battle of Actium (31 B.C.), over the entire Roman world through his defeat of his rival Mark Antony and the Egyptian queen Cleopatra. His constitutional position was settled several years thereafter (27 B.C.), at which time he received the title Augustus. (The word *augustus* ["august, revered"] had an earlier precedent in Rome in a religious context [Ovid, *Fasti* 1.559–560] and would be held as a title by subsequent emperors.) His civil authority was based on his tribunician power (*tribunicia potestas*), his military status on a command superior to that of any other (*imperium maius*). Although theoretically sharing power in a dyarchy with the Roman senate, he was in fact supreme through his control of the army. He preferred to style himself *princeps* ("first citizen"), and the term "principate" has been used of his government.

Augustus effected a thorough reform and reorganization of the Roman state in almost every sphere, although retaining traditional practices insofar as possible. To defend the frontiers, he created a professional standing army, which looked for benefits to the emperor rather than to the commanders of its individual legions. The government made vigorous efforts to restore traditional Roman religion and morality; it encouraged the glorification of Rome and an Italian patriotic sentiment in art, sculpture, and literature. In this program, the emperor enjoyed considerable public support. He was above all hailed as the bestower of peace after a century of civil conflict.

Augustus oversaw a fundamental innovation, the promotion of the imperial cult, intended as a symbol of unity within the empire and a reinforcement of the loyalty of the army. The divine character of the imperial office would in time receive further emphasis, and the refusal to acknowledge the emperor's divine status would be construed as treason. In essence, political duty was cast in terms of religious obligation, a development that would occasion numerous persecutions of the early Christian church in one part of the empire or another.

It was in the reign of Augustus that Jesus Christ was born (Luke 2:1–7; cf. Eusebius, *H.E.* 1.5; the exact date of the census to which reference is made is disputed).　　[M.P.McH.]

Bibliography

Augustus, *The Acts of Augustus* (*Res gestae Divi Augusti*); Suetonius, *Life of Augustus*; Dio Cassius, *Roman History* 45–56; Valleius Paterculus, *History of Rome* 2.59–123.

L.R. Taylor, *The Divinity of the Roman Emperor* (Middletown: American Philological Association, 1931); S.A. Cook et al., *The Cambridge Ancient History* (Cambridge: Cambridge UP, 1934), Vol. 10, Chs. 1–18 and pp. 893–959 (bibliography); R. Syme, *The Roman Revolution* (Oxford: Clarendon, and New York: Oxford UP, 1939); V. Ehrenberg and A.H.M. Jones, *Documents Illustrating the Reigns of Augustus and Tiberius* (Oxford: Clarendon, 1955); M. Hammond, *The Augustan Principate in Theory and Practice During the Julio-Claudian Period* (New York: Russell and Russell, 1968); A.H.M. Jones, *Augustus* (New York: Norton, 1970); D. Kienast, *Augustus, Prinzeps und Monarch* (Darmstadt: Wissenschaftliche Buchgesellschaft, 1982); A. Kee, "The Imperial Cult: The Unmasking of an Ideology," *Scottish Journal of Religious Studies* 6 (1985):112–128.

AURELIAN (ca. 212–275). Roman emperor (270–275). A cavalry commander prior to his accession to the throne, and a strict disciplinarian, Aurelian sought to strengthen the frontiers of the empire and to restore internal unity. He defeated the Vandals in Pannonia, built the fortification wall that bears his name at Rome, and defeated and captured Zenobia, queen of Palmyra, who had attempted to establish her rule in Asia Minor, Syria, and Egypt. After putting a quick end to a rival Gallo-Roman empire in the west, he set out against Persia but was murdered in a military plot.

That Aurelian was largely successful in his aims was shown by his being hailed as *restitutor orbis* ("restorer of the world"). He reinstituted the Syrian cult of Sol Invictus, the unconquerable sun god, which had been discredited by the excesses of his predecessor Elagabalus, and evidently planned to make this worship the universal religion of the empire. Although intending to renew the persecution of Christians, he recognized the right of the church to own property in his decision awarding the episcopal residence at Antioch to Domnus, who was recognized by the bishop of Rome and the other Italian bishops, against the claims of Paul of Samosata.　　[M.P.McH.]

Bibliography

Eusebius, *Church History* 7.27–30.

AUSONIUS (ca. 310–ca. 395). Latin poet and rhetorician. Ausonius, a teacher of grammar and rhetoric at Bordeaux, was appointed tutor to the future emperor Gratian (ca. 365), by whom he was made consul (379). His numerous poems on secular subjects, including epigrams and versified epistles, are a valuable witness to Gallo-Roman civilization; the best known of them, the *Moselle*, describes the poet's journey on the river of that name. A few works of Christian tenor appear, among them a morning prayer contained in a poem describing the author's day and Paschal verses composed for the emperor Valentinian I. He addressed seven versified letters (*Ep.* 23–29 in Evelyn White's translation) to Paulinus of Nola. In the last three (*Ep.* 27–29), Ausonius attempted to dissuade Paulinus, a friend and former student, from entering the ascetic life, but Paulinus refused to heed his advice in two poems of reply (*Poems* 10; 11). CPL 1387–1422. [M.P.McH.]

Bibliography

Paulinus of Nola, *Poems* 10; 11 (=Ausonius, *Letters* 31 and 30 in Evelyn White's translation).

Ausonius, tr. H.G. Evelyn White, 2 vols., LCL (1919, 1921).

K. Chadwick, *Poetry and Letters in Early Christian Gaul* (London: Bowes and Bowes, 1955), pp. 47–62; C. Wittke, *Numen Litterarum: The Old and the New in Latin Poetry from Constantine to Gregory the Great* (Leiden: Brill, 1971), pp. 3–74; P.-M. Duval, *La Gaule jusqu'au milieu du Ve siècle* (Paris: Picard, 1971), Vol. 1.2, pp. 601–609, #256 (bibliography); H. Isbell, "Decimus Magnus Ausonius: The Poet and His World," *Latin Literature of the Fourth Century,* ed. J.W. Binns (London and Boston: Routledge and Kegan Paul, 1974); P.G. Walsh, tr., *The Poems of St. Paulinus of Nola,* ACW (1975), Vol. 4, pp. 20–24 (correspondence with Ausonius); T.P. Halton and R.D. Sider, "A Decade of Patristic Scholarship 1970–1979," *CW* 76 (1982–1983):357–358 (bibliography); A.D. Booth, "The Academic Career of Ausonius," *Phoenix* 36 (1982):329–343.

AUXENTIUS. There were two bishops of this name, both adherents of Arianism. Auxentius of Milan was appointed to that see in 355; despite his condemnation by several councils and by Hilary of Poitiers among others, he held office under the protection of the emperors Constantius II and Valentinian I until his death in 374. Ambrose was his successor. Auxentius of Durostorum in Lower Moesia (fourth century), who had been a student of Ulfilas, composed an important letter on the life of his former teacher. CPL 691. [M.P.McH.]

Bibliography

Auxentius of Milan: Hilary of Poitiers, *Contra Arianos vel Auxentium Mediolanensem.*

Auxentius of Durostorum: Repertorium Fontium Historiae Medii Aevi (Rome: Istituto Storico Italiano per il Medio Evo, 1967), Vol. 2, p. 426.

AVITUS (450–518). Bishop of Vienne (ca. 490–518). Influential in the church life of Burgundy, Avitus brought the Arian king Sigismund to Catholic belief. A strong supporter of the primacy of the papacy, he was the author of numerous letters, among them treatises against the teachings of Eutyches and Faustus of Riez. Besides homilies and a poem on virginity, he composed the *De spiritualis historiae gestis,* five Latin poems inspired by Genesis and Exodus, the first three of which are an early example of the theme of creation and fall (paradise lost). Feast day February 5. CPL 990–997. *See also* Burgundy. [M.P.McH.]

Bibliography

Gregory of Tours, *History of the Franks* 2.34; Sidonius Apollinaris, *Panegyric* 7 on *Avitus.*

Avitus: The Fall of Man: De spiritalis historiae gestis libri i–iii, ed. D.J. Nodes (Toronto: U of Toronto P, 1985).

Repertorium Fontium Historiae Medii Aevi (Rome: Istituto Storico Italiano per il Medio Evo, 1967), Vol. 2, pp. 427–430 (bibliography); M. Roberts, "The Prologue to Avitus' *De spiritalis historiae gestis*: Christian Poetry and Poetic License," *Traditio* 36 (1980):399–407; D.J. Nodes, *Avitus of Vienne's Spiritual History: Its Theme and Doctrinal Implications* (Ph.D. diss., University of Toronto, 1982); M. Roberts, "Rhetoric and Poetic Imitation in Avitus' Account of the Crossing of the Red Sea (*De spiritalis historiae gestis* 5.371–702)," *Traditio* 39 (1983):29–80; D.J. Nodes, "Avitus of Vienne's Spiritual History and the Semipelagian Controversy: The Doctrinal Implication of Books I–III," *VChr* 38 (1984):185–195; W. Ehlers, "Bibelszenen in epischer Gestalt: Ein Beitrag zu Alcimus Avitus," *VChr* 39 (1985):353–368.

B

BACHIARIUS (fourth–fifth century). Spanish monk and theologian. Suspected of involvement in the heresy of Priscillian, he departed his native land and composed, probably at Rome, a profession of faith, the *Libellus de fide* (ca. 383), notable for its orthodoxy. His other certainly genuine work, *De reparatione lapsi*, a plea to the abbot Januarius on behalf of a fallen monk, has importance for understanding the Spanish penitential system. CPL 568–570.

[M.P.McH.]

Bibliography

F.X. Murphy, "Bachiarius," *Leaders of Iberian Christianity*, ed. J. M.-F. Marique (Boston: St. Paul Editions, 1962), pp. 121–126.

BAPTISM. The rite of entrance into the church, normally administered by immersion to believers after a period of instruction.

Antecedents. Water was widely used in the ancient world as a means of purification. Washing was preliminary to initiation in some of the Hellenistic mystery religions.

The Law of Moses required a bath as a cleansing for certain impurities before participation in religious acts (Lev. 14–15; Num. 19). These baths were understood in New Testament times as requiring a pool large enough for an immersion. The cleansings were taken seriously by the Essenes, who practiced daily baths. Gentile converts to Judaism received circumcision, immersed themselves, and offered a sacrifice. Certain events in Old Testament history were treated in Christian literature as types of Christian baptism: notably the flood (Gen. 6–9; 1 Peter 3:20–21) and Israel's crossing of the Red Sea (Exod. 14; 1 Cor. 10:1–2).

The immediate antecedent to Christian baptism was the practice of John the Baptist. Like the Jewish washings, his baptism was an immersion, but unlike the other Jewish baths his was not self-administered, and the purification was given eschatological significance, so was not repeated (Mark 1:4–8). John's baptism, like Christian baptism, was related to repentance and the forgiveness of sins but differed from it in not having a specific connection with faith in Jesus ("in the name of Christ") and not promising the Holy Spirit (Acts 19:2–4). The foundations of Christian baptism were the baptism of Jesus by John the Baptist, at which time he was acknowledged as God's Son and received the Holy Spirit (Mark 1:9–11), and the command of the resurrected Jesus (Matt. 28:18–20).

Baptism of Christ performed by John the Baptist and witnessed by the personification of the Jordan River, mosaic (late fifth century) in the cupola of the Baptistery of the Arians, Ravenna, Italy. (Photograph Editore A. Longo, Ravenna)

Ceremony. The New Testament gives no description of ritual acts accompanying baptism. The practice seems to have been immediate baptism on acceptance of the gospel message (Acts 8:35–39; 16:30–33). Second-century sources indicate a period of moral instruction, prayer, and fasting prior to the baptism (*Did.* 7; Justin, *1 Apol.* 61). The *Apostolic Tradition* of Hippolytus, supplemented by references in Tertullian, provides an account of a developed ceremonial by A.D. 200. After a period of instruction that could last three years, the candidate was examined and prepared for the baptism to occur on the night before Easter Sunday. The Holy Spirit was petitioned to come upon the baptismal waters; the candidate disrobed, renounced Satan and all his works, and was anointed with the oil of exorcism to banish all evil spirits. Standing in the water, the candidate confessed faith in each person of the Trinity and was immersed three times, once after each confession. Then the candidate was anointed, reclothed, and anointed again with the laying on of hands (symbolizing the reception of the Holy Spirit). The congregation gave the kiss of peace and proceeded to the baptismal eucharist.

The basic outline of the ceremony continued to be observed, but in Syria the principal anointing came before and not after the baptism.

The catechetical lectures of church fathers in the fourth and fifth centuries are a rich source of information about baptismal doctrine and ritual. The creed was expounded in daily lectures during the weeks of Lent prior to Easter. During the week after baptism, lectures expounded the meaning of the event and its accompanying ceremonies.

Trine immersion may have been based on the command to baptize "in the name of the Father, the Son, and the Holy Spirit" (Matt. 28:19). That phrase is frequently attested in the second century as a formula accompanying baptism. Baptism "in the name of Jesus" appears to have been a description of the meaning of the act or a reference to the confession accompanying the baptism and not a formula pronounced at the baptism. Later, there was some discussion of triple versus single immersion. Gregory the Great (*Ep.* 43) approved a single ablution. The eastern churches have preserved the triple immersion; the western churches have various practices.

Action. The precedent of Jewish washings, the secular usage of *baptizein*, circumstantial accounts of baptism in early Christian literature, and the symbolism of baptism as burial and resurrection (Rom. 6:1–11; Col. 2:12) indicate that the normal practice in early Christian baptism was a dipping or plunging.

One of the earliest noncanonical documents, *Didache* 7, permits, in the absence of sufficient water for an immersion, pouring water three times on the head. Another occasion for an alternative to immersion was the baptism of a person confined to a sickbed. Cyprian defended this practice against reservations about its efficacy (*Ep.* 75).

The evidence of early baptisteries and Christian art has been open to varying interpretations. Some have contended that the candidate stood in a pool of water while water was poured over the head, a partial immersion. The literary accounts do not seem to bear this out (Cyril of Jerusalem, *Catech.* 17.14; Basil, *Spir.* 15.35; Ambrose, *Sacram.* 3.1.1f.; John Chrysostom, *Catech.* 2.26; *Hom. in Jo.* 25.2). The earliest baptismal font in the house church at Dura-Europos was sufficient for an immersion. Dimensions and shapes of other baptismal fonts from the fourth and following centuries vary, but most appear unnecessarily large for anything other than a complete washing.

A standard iconography of baptism soon established itself. The candidate was depicted nude, standing in water (varying from around the ankles to the waist), and smaller than the administrator, whose hand rested on the head of the candidate. The hand rested on the head at the moment of the confession of faith, according to Hippolytus, *Apostolic Tradition* 21. This gesture would also have been functional in guiding the head under the water, as in the literary sources. The nudity is a further indication of immersion. The water was alluded to by an economy of lines. The representations in art and the shape of the baptisteries may indicate that the administrator kept his hand on the head of the candidate, who kneeled in the water or bent the head forward (on the analogy of the self-washings in Judaism), rather than being laid back in a horizontal position.

Subjects. The accounts of conversion in the Acts of the Apostles follow the pattern of hearing the preaching, believing in Jesus and repenting of sins, and being baptized. The baptism of believers was normal in a missionary situation. It has been argued, however, that the references to the baptism of families (Acts 16:15, 33) and the analogy of proselyte baptism would have included children, even infants, or at least not have excluded them in principle.

The earliest explicit reference to infant baptism occurs ca. 200 in Tertullian, *On Baptism* 18, a passage that opposes what appears to be a relatively new practice. A few years later, Origen (*Comm. Rom.* 5.9) claimed infant baptism as a tradition from the apostles, and the ceremony of baptism in the *Apostolic Tradition* of Hippolytus makes provision for children (21.3–5). It and later baptismal liturgies, however, describe procedures that presuppose believers' baptism as the norm. Cyprian defended the validity of infant baptism (*Ep.* 58), but believers' baptism must have been frequent well into the fourth century, for the great church leaders, including those born to strong Christian parents (Basil, Gregory of Nyssa, Gregory of Nazianzus, John Chrysostom, Ephraem the Syrian, Jerome, Rufinus, Augustine), were not baptized until the end of their student days. The inscriptions that mention the baptism of children ordinarily place that baptism in close proximity to the death of the child, indicating that infant baptism was not routine but occurred as a precaution against death. The principal impetus for the rise and spread of infant baptism may have been the desire that the child not depart life without the safeguard of baptism. Infant baptism had become so common by the fifth century that Augustine used it as a decisive argument in support of original sin against Pelagius. Both men accepted the baptism of infants, and Augustine argued that, since baptism brought on the forgiveness of sins, the child must be born with sin (*Pecc. mer. et rem.* 1.23, 28, 39, 3.2.7; *C. Iul.* 3.5.11). Later, original sin was to be the principal theological basis for infant baptism, but the historical development followed the reverse sequence. The early Christian documents, in contrast, contain frequent reference to the sinlessness of children (Hermas, *Sim.* 9.29.1–3; *Barn.* 6; Aristides, *Apol.* 15.11; Athenagoras, *Res.* 14).

The emperor Justinian I made infant baptism compulsory in the sixth century. This broke down the practice of baptizing at special occasions and of having the bishops as the principal administrators.

Administrator. Tertullian stated the general patristic view that the usual minister of baptism was the bishop but, with his sanction, could be the presbyters or deacons; in case of need, any Christian man (but Tertullian drew the line against a woman baptizing) might baptize (*Bapt.* 17). In the Syrian *Didascalia*, deaconesses assisted in the baptism of women.

Controversy over the validity of baptism administered by "heretics" emerged in the third-century disagreement between Cyprian, who denied the validity of baptism administered by those outside the communion of the church, and Stephen I, who contended that water and the Trinitarian name made baptism valid regardless of the administrator. Cyprian reasoned that one who did not possess the Holy Spirit could not give the Spirit in baptism and that the person who did not have the church for mother could not have God for Father (*Ep.* 69–75). Stephen defended his practice as a tradition of the Roman church. Since the validity of one's baptism could not be left in the uncertainty of the standing of the administrator, opinion moved toward Stephen's opposition to rebaptism. The controversy flared up again in the fourth-century Donatist schism. With the Donatists, the problem had to do with the moral character, not doctrinal correctness, of the administrator. The Donatist position was rejected by the Council of Arles in 314 and was answered definitively by Augustine (*Ep.* 98). He established the objective holiness of the sacraments as determined by the appointment and action of God without dependence on the standing of the human administrator.

Doctrine. Baptism in the New Testament was an act of repentance (Acts 2:38; 3:19) and a confession of faith (Acts 18:8; Heb. 10:22f.; cf. Rom. 10:9f.). The connection of baptism with a confession of faith continued in the postapostolic period, as may be seen in the baptismal liturgies.

The New Testament further associates baptism with forgiveness of sins (Acts 2:38), gift of the Holy Spirit (idem), salvation (1 Peter 3:21), death and resurrection (Rom. 6:1–11), and incorporation into the church (1 Cor. 12:13). The postcanonical writings repeat these ideas (*Barn.* 11; Hermas, *Vis.* 3.3.1; *Mand.* 4.3.3; *Sim.* 9.13.3–6; Theophilus, *Autol.* 2.16; Irenaeus, *Dem.* 3; 42; Clement of Alexandria, *Paed.* 1.6.25–32). Baptism attained its importance because of its doctrinal association with the cross of Christ (Justin, *Dial.* 14; 86; 138). The strong emphasis on the necessity of baptism was reinforced by John 3:5, which was the favorite baptismal text of the early church. Only in some Gnostic circles was there a depreciation of the importance of baptism, a fact that called forth the earliest surviving treatise on baptism, written by Tertullian. That same author in another treatise summarized the benefits of baptism as forgiveness of sins, deliverance from death, regeneration, and the bestowal

of the Holy Spirit (*Marc.* 1.28). Such remained the view of the purpose of baptism throughout the patristic period.

An important exception to the normal necessity of receiving baptism was made in the case of martyrs. Martyrdom was viewed as bringing a forgiveness of sins (Cyprian, *Ep.* 73.22; Cyril of Jerusalem, *Catech.* 3.10). Hence, believers who had not yet been baptized were still assured that if they maintained their confession before the authorities they would enter heaven. *See also* Anointing; Baptistery; Catechesis; Confirmation; Epiclesis; Infant Baptism; Sacraments. [E.F.]

Bibliography

Tertullian, *On Baptism*; Hippolytus, *Apostolic Tradition* 16–23; Cyril of Jerusalem (?), *Catechetical Lectures* 19–21; John Chrysostom, *Baptismal Instructions*; Theodore of Mopsuestia, *Baptismal Homilies*; Ambrose, *On the Sacraments* and *On the Mysteries*; Chromatius of Aquileia, *Sermones* 14; 15; 19.

J. Corblet, *Histoire dogmatique, liturgique et archéologique du baptême*, 2 vols. (Paris: Palmé, 1881–1882); D. Stone, *Holy Baptism* (London: Longmans, 1917); J. Leipoldt, *Die urchristliche Taufe im Lichte der Religionsgeschichte* (Leipzig: Dörffling & Franke, 1928); P. Lundberg, *La Typologie baptismale dans l'ancienne église* (Uppsala and Leipzig: Lorentz, 1942); E.J. Duncan, *Baptism in the Demonstrations of Aphraates the Persian Sage* (Washington, D.C.: Catholic U of America P, 1945); J.H. Crehan, *Early Christian Baptism and the Creed* (London: Burns, Oates and Washbourne, 1950); G.W.H. Lampe, *The Seal of the Spirit* (London: Longmans, Green, 1951); A. Benoît, *Le Baptême chrétien au second siècle* (Paris: Presses Universitaires de France, 1953); G.R. Beasley-Murray, *Baptism in the New Testament* (New York: St. Martin, 1962); T. Maertens, *Histoire et pastorale du rituel du catéchuménat et du baptême* (Bruges: Biblica, 1962); L. DeBruyne, "L'Initiation chrétienne et ses reflets dans l'art paléochrétien," *RSR* 36 (1962):27–85; G. Kretschmar, *Die Geschichte des Taufgottesdienstes in der alter Kirche, Leiturgia* (1964–1966), Vol. 5; G. Wagner, *Pauline Baptism and the Pagan Mysteries* (Edinburgh: Oliver and Boyd, 1967); G. Ristow, *The Baptism of Christ* (Recklinghausen: Aurel Bongers, 1967); A. Hamman, *Baptism: Ancient Liturgies and Patristic Texts* (New York: Alba House, 1967); E.C. Whitaker, *Documents of the Baptismal Liturgy*, 2nd ed. (London: SPCK, 1970); K. Aland, *Taufe und Kindertaufe* (Gütersloh: Gütersloher Verlagshaus, 1971); H. Riley, *Christian Initiation* (Washington D.C.: Catholic U of America P, 1974); E. Ferguson, *Early Christians Speak* (Abilene: ACU, 1987), pp. 33–65.

BAPTISTERY. Building used for the performance of Christian baptism. Secular bathhouses sometimes became the site of Christian baptisteries and provided terminology for them. *Baptistērion* ("bathing or swimming pool") was the word for the building but could also be used of the font (*fons*), which was more commonly designated by the words *kolumbēthra* (Greek, "bathing pool") or *piscina* (Latin, "fish pond"). The Jews built synagogues near sources of water, which could be used for ritual purifications. In the period before A.D. 70, they had constructed immersion pools (*mikwaoth*) for performing ceremonial washings. These consisted of two pools connected by a channel to permit pure water to flow into the bathing pool. The addition of pure water purified the bathing pool. Rabbinic literature specified a minimum capacity (seventy-five gallons) and size that would permit covering the entire body.

The earliest Christian baptisms took place in natural sources of water (Mark 1:9f.; John 3:23; Acts 8:36; 16:13–15). The *Didache* 7 expressed a preference for baptism in running ("living") water, which would have accorded with the sentiments of Jews and others. Tertullian referred to baptism "in the sea or in a pool, in a river or a fountain, in a reservoir or a tub" (*Bapt.* 4). He insisted that it made no difference where the baptism was performed; for him, the effectiveness depended not on the kind of water but on the coming of the Holy Spirit on the water.

The earliest known baptistery is in the house church at Dura-Europos (ca. 240). One room was set aside as a baptistery and provided at one end with a baptismal pool, which measures five feet four inches in length by three feet to three feet four inches in width by three feet one inch in depth. Steps on the room side of the basin gave easier access. A ledge on the two short sides would permit a person seated to be immersed by bending over. The font was placed under a canopy on which was painted a blue sky and stars. On the wall behind the font (west end of the room) was a painting of the Good Shepherd and sheep, to which was added later a small Adam and Eve with the serpent in the garden. On the other walls were depicted the women approaching the tomb of

Baptistery of St. John (fifth century?), beside the present Church of Hagia Sophia, Thessalonica, Greece.

Jesus, Jesus and Peter walking on the water, Jesus healing a paralytic, the woman at the well in Samaria, and David and Goliath.

Over 400 baptisteries from the third to the seventh centuries have been catalogued. They exhibit a great architectural variety, and most are artistically unexceptional, being simple utilitarian structures adapted to the strict needs of the baptismal ceremony. Nonetheless, they testify to considerable unity in the Christian world and to the importance of baptism.

Some baptisteries were attached in one way or another to a church building, some were freestanding structures, and some formed a complex of more than one part. The independent structures were of various shapes—rectangular, square, but more often round, either a circle or an octagon. Tombs were often round in the Greco-Roman world, and this influenced the shape of martyria and baptisteries. The circular plan reinforced the imagery of baptism as a death and burial and the imagery of the baptismal font as a tomb. Baptism, moreover, was a resurrection, and this may have encouraged the use of an octagonal plan, for the number eight was a symbol for immortality, the world to come, and God's abode. Octagon-shaped baptisteries were especially popular in northern Italy and adjoining regions. The baptistery of St. John for the Church of St. Thecla in Milan, built by Ambrose, seemingly set the style. Its symbolism of new life was expressed by the inscription, probably by Ambrose: "Eight-niched soars this church destined for sacred rites, / eight corners has its font, which befits its gift. / Meet it was thus to build this fair baptismal hall / about this sacred eight: here is our race reborn." The baptismal waters were the womb of rebirth (Zeno of Verona, *Tract.* 1.49, 55) as well as a tomb of the old life. The fonts came in an even greater variety of shapes than the buildings or rooms that housed them: rectangle, square, circle, oval, hexagon, octagon, cross, clover-leaf. These shapes cannot be closely correlated with geographical regions or chronological periods. The shape of the basin often corresponded to the shape of the building. A ciborium sometimes enhanced the position of the font.

Corinth had at least three churches with baptisteries (Cenchreae Gate, Skutela, and Cemetery Church) in addition to the baptistery at the huge church at Lechaion (contrary to the rule of having a baptistery only at the bishop's church). One font is an octagon and another a Greek cross; the Lechaion font is something of a combination, for the octagonal pool has four arms (two of which are steps) giving the appearance of a cross. The baptismal font on the island of Delos is round. Its depth of thirty-eight inches corresponds to a common dimension of about one yard in smaller baptisteries. A simple rectangular pool may be seen at Augsburg. Timgad in ancient Numidia has a six-sided baptistery. Whereas eight was a symbol of resurrection, six was a symbol of death (Jesus was crucified on the sixth day and raised on the eighth). The large baptistery dedicated to John the Baptist at Thessalonica has six semicircular insets (for administrators?) in the pool, giving a floriated appearance. The largest existing baptismal pool is in the baptistery at St. John Lateran in Rome. The circular pool within the octagonal building is twenty-eight feet in diameter. Sixtus III supplied an inscription: "This is the fountain of life that purges the whole world."

An example of a baptistery with a complex of rooms is that of the urban basilica at Salona. There is a narthex, a room for catechumens, an auditorium, a dressing room, and the baptistery proper with a place for the baptismal anointing in the apse. The first font was a large hexagon in a square building. Next was a somewhat smaller hexagon; then a cruciform pool in an octagonal building. Such successive remodelings were not unusual, especially as modifications were required for the increasing frequency of infant baptism. However, all of the basins at Salona permitted immersion.

The most spectacularly decorated baptistery is the Baptistery of the Orthodox in Ravenna, furnished with mosaics by bishop Neon between 450 and 470. The octagonal building has a diameter of thirty-six feet; the octagonal font in the center has a diameter of eleven feet four inches and a depth of thirty-three inches. The four niches in the walls of the building have inscriptions quoting Matthew 14:29–32; Psalms 32:1; John 13:4–5; and Psalms 23:2. The inner slabs of the font have quotations from John 3:6; Galatians 3:27; and Acts 2:38. Three concentric circles of mosaics adorn the cupola. The outermost band is divided into eight sections by acanthus plants. Four thrones with a cushion on which stands a cross alternate with four altars bearing one of the four Gospels. The middle circle of mosaics is a procession of the twelve apostles in two groups led respectively by Peter and Paul. Each carries a crown in veiled hands. The central scene immediately above the font is the baptism of Jesus by John. The hand of God and the dove of the Holy Spirit gave a Trinitarian significance to the event. A personification of the river god in the waters of the Jordan represents Christ's victory over the forces of evil. A nineteenth-century restoration has incorrectly shown John pouring water on the head of Jesus, who stands naked and waist-deep in the water. The original would have had John's hand on Jesus' head, as in other representations of baptism and as in the nearly contemporary mosaic in the Baptistery of the Arians in Ravenna, which copied this baptistery. *See also* Baptism; Dura-Europos; Ravenna. [E.F.]

Bibliography

F.W. Deichmann, "Baptisterium," RLAC (1950), Vol. 1, cols. 1157–1167 (with listing and bibliography); W.M. Bedard, *The Symbolism of the Baptismal Font in Early Christian Thought* (Washington, D.C.: Catholic U of America P, 1951); *Acts du Ve Congrés international d'archéologie chrétienne*, Aix-en-Provence, September 1954 (Rome: Pontificio Istituto di Archeologia Cristiana, 1957); J.G. Davies, *The Architectural Setting of Baptism* (London: Barrie and Rockliff, 1962); A. Khatchatrian, *Les Baptistères paléochrétiens* (Paris: Imprimerie Nationale, 1962); S.K. Kostof, *The Orthodox Baptistery of Ravenna* (New Haven: Yale UP, 1965); C.H. Kraeling, *The Christian Building: The Excavations at Dura Europos*. Final Report VIII, II, ed. C.B. Welles (New Haven: Yale UP, 1967); P. van Dael, "Purpose and Function of Decoration-Schemes in Early Christian Baptisteries," *Fides Sacramenti. Sacramentum Fidei: Studies in Honor of P. Smulders*, ed. H.J. Auf der Maur, L. Bakker, et al. (Assen: Van Gorcum, 1981); A. Khatchatrian, *Origine et typologie des baptistères paléochrétiens* (Mulhouse: Centre de Culture Chrétienne, 1982).

BARDESANES (ca. 154–222). Syriac Christian poet whose name is also transcribed as Bardaisan (Bar Dayṣān). With his son, Harmonius, Bardesanes created a large body of Syriac hymns, no longer extant; he has been considered the father of Syriac hymnody.

The *Dialogue of Destiny*, or *The Book of the Laws of the Lands*, is extant in the original Syriac; fragments are preserved by Eusebius and other heresiologists. It refers to Bardesanes in the third person and evidently was written by his student Phillip, but it does contain the teachings of Bardesanes. There is a possibility that the *Acts of Thomas* came from his circle, but no evidence indicates that the *Acts* were written by him.

The teaching of Bardesanes has Gnostic elements, such as a dualism of darkness and light and the view that the material world was created by beings lesser than the one God. Yet he seems to be a convinced monotheist who avoids a physical dualism. Bardesanes evidently was much interested in astrology and the ways that custom and tradition influenced people's thoughts, but he had some sense of the importance of human freedom. Although good and evil beset men and women, each person who is in Christ can choose, because Christ countermands the force of the planets. Little is known, however, of Bardesanes's doctrines concerning the body and the soul, positions that would clearly specify how much he represented Gnostic views.

Ephraem the Syrian, who knew of a community that followed Bardesanes's teachings in the fourth century, says in his *Homily on the Life of the Pilgrim* that Bardesanes held a Docetic Christology, that he denied the resurrection body, and that he misunderstood the proper doctrine of creation. CPG I, 1152–1153. TLG 1214. [F.W.N.]

Bibliography

PS 10.

H.J.W. Drijvers, *The Book of the Laws of Countries: Dialogue on Faith of Bardaisan of Edessa* (Assen: Van Gorcum, 1965).

B. Ehlers, "Bardesanes von Edess—Ein syrischen Gnostiker," *ZKG* 81 (1970):334–351; E. Beck, "Bardaisan und seine Schule bei Ephram," *Le Muséon* 91 (1978):271–333; A. Dihle, "Zur Schicksalslehre des Bardesanes," *Kerygma und Logos: Festschrift für Carl Andresen* (Göttingen: Vandenhoeck & Ruprecht, 1979), pp. 123–135.

BARNABAS, EPISTLE OF. One of the apostolic fathers. Barnabas in the New Testament was a Hellenistic Jew from Cyprus, a Levite of some financial means (Acts 4:36f.). Enjoying the confidence of Christians in Jerusalem, he befriended Paul and became his companion in the Gentile mission (Acts 9:27; 11:22–26; 13:1f.). Although differing from Barnabas over personal (Acts 15:36–40) and policy matters (Gal. 2:13), Paul respected him (1 Cor. 9:6; Col. 4:10). Later tradition (Clement of Alexandria, *Str.* 2.20) counted Barnabas among the "Seventy" disciples sent out by Jesus (Luke 10:1), perhaps as explaining his designation as an "apostle" in Acts 14:4, 14. Tertullian considered Barnabas the author of the Epistle to the Hebrews (*Pud.* 20). The *Acta et passio Barnabae in Cypro* dates from the fifth century, and the *Evangelium Barnabae* mentioned in the *Decretum Gelasianum* is lost.

Modern scholarship has rejected the attribution of the *Epistle of Barnabas* to the Barnabas of the New Testament. The work itself does not name the author, who was evidently well known to the recipients, but the document was early attributed to him (Clement of Alexandria, *Str.* 2.6, 7), and "Epistle of Barnabas" is the title given in the manuscript tradition. The possibilities are as follows: (1) The document was pseudonymous; (2) it was written by another person named Barnabas who was then mistakenly identified with the better-known New Testament figure; or (3) an anonymous writing was mistakenly assigned to Barnabas. The author, by his disclaimers, was recognized as a teacher (*Barn.* 1.8; 4.9; but cf. 9.9), and his document is in form more of a treatise than an epistle.

The *Epistle of Barnabas* is usually dated 132–135, although an earlier date in the late 70s has had its champions, and 96–98 is a possibility. The internal evidence is inconclusive. The reference to ten kingdoms in 4.4f. is based on Daniel 7, and it is impossible to know which kings are included in the author's reckoning.

The language of rebuilding the temple in 16.3–5 refers to the spiritual temple of the heart of Gentile believers (any allusion to a physical temple in Jerusalem is doubtful).

The place of writing is usually taken to be Egypt, where the document was first attested (cf. references in Clement of Alexandria above), because of the Alexandrian type of nonliteral interpretation of the Bible. Recent scholars have also suggested Syria or Asia Minor.

The *Epistle of Barnabas* takes an original approach to the Christian debate with Jews over the question "To whom does the covenant belong?" The author argues in the first part of the work (2–17) that the Jewish people had rejected the Lord's covenant in the incident of the golden calf in Exodus 32 and that the covenant belongs to Christians, the new people (4.13–14). The Jews had understood the requirements of the Old Testament literally, but the Lord had intended them spiritually, and the Christians by keeping the ordinances of the Law of Moses spiritually were the people really living by its covenant. The sacrifices are fulfilled in the passion of Christ; circumcision is of the heart and hearing, not the flesh (9); the food laws mean that one should not associate with immoral persons (10); the washings do not bring forgiveness of sins, as baptism does (11); the sabbath has been surpassed by "the eighth day," Sunday (15); the true temple is God's dwelling in the heart (16). The second part (18–20) presents the "Two Ways" as the way of light and the way of darkness.

The *Epistle of Barnabas* was included in the biblical codex Sinaiticus after the Book of Revelation, and Origen seems to treat "the general epistle of Barnabas" as canonical (*Cels.* 1.63); but Eusebius listed it as rejected (*H.E.* 3.25.4). CPG I, 1050. TLG 1216.   [E.F.]

Bibliography

H. Windisch, *Der Barnabasbrief, Die Apostolischen Väter*, Vol. 3 of *Handbuch zum Neuen Testament* (Tübingen: Mohr, 1920); J.A. Kleist, *The Didache, The Epistle of Barnabas*, ACW (1948), Vol. 6; A. Hermans, "Le Pseudo-Barnabé est-il millénarist?," *Ephemerides theologicae Lovanienses* 35 (1959):849–876; S. Lowy, "The Confutation of Judaism in the Epistle of Barnabas," *Journal of Jew-*

ish *Studies* 11 (1960):1–33; R.A. Kraft, "Barnabas' Isaiah Text and the 'Testimony Book' Hypothesis," *JBL* 79 (1960):336–350 and 80 (1961):371–373; P. Prigent, *Les Testimonia dans la christianisme primitif: L'Epître de Barnabé I–XVI et ses sources* (Paris: Gabalda, 1961); R. Kraft, *Barnabas and the Didache*, Vol. 3 of *The Apostolic Fathers*, ed. R.M. Grant (New York: Nelson, 1965); L.W. Barnard, "Judaism in Egypt A.D. 70–135," "St. Stephen and Early Alexandrian Christianity," "Is the Epistle of Barnabas a Paschal Homily?," "The Dead Sea Scrolls, Barnabas, the *Didache* and the Later History of the 'Two Ways,'" "The Use of Testimonia in the Early Church and in the Epistle of Barnabas," *Studies in the Apostolic Fathers and Their Background* (New York: Schocken, 1966), pp. 41–55, 57–72, 73–85, 87–107, 109–135; K. Wengst, *Tradition und Theologie des Barnabasbrief* (Berlin: de Gruyter, 1965); R.A. Kraft, "An Unnoticed Papyrus Fragment of Barnabas," *VChr* 9 (1967):1–6; P. Prigent and R.A. Kraft, *Epître de Barnabé*, SC (1971), Vol. 172; P. Richardson and M.B. Shukster, "Barnabas, Nerva, and the Yavnean Rabbis," *JThS* n.s. 34 (1983):31–55.

BARSAUMA (ca. 415–ca. 495).

Nestorian bishop of Nisibis. Born in Persia and educated at Edessa under Ibas, Barsauma is considered, along with Narsai, the founder of the Persian Nestorian Church. [F.W.N.]

Bibliography
PS 48.
S. Gero, *Barsauma of Nisibis and Persian Christology in the Fifth Century* (Louvain: Peeters, 1981).

BASIL OF ANCYRA (d. after 363).

Bishop and leader of those who said that Christ was of similar substance (*homoiousia*) to God. A physician with good literary education, Basil was chosen bishop of Ancyra when Marcellus was deposed in 336. Although he enjoyed considerable influence with the emperor Constantius II, his radical Arian opponents secured his banishment from 343 (or 344) to 348 (or 353) and again from 360. He had a leading role at the councils of Sirmium (351, which condemned Photinus) and Ancyra (358). Epiphanius (*Haer.* 73.12–22) preserves a doctrinal statement that Basil composed in 359 along with George of Laodicea. The treatise *De virginitate*, attributed to Basil of Caesarea, is likely his. CPG II, 2825–2827. [E.F.]

Bibliography
Athanasius, *Defense Against the Arians* 3.49; idem, *To the Bishops of Egypt* 1.7; idem, *On the Councils* 41; Jerome, *Lives of Illustrious Men* 89; Socrates, *Church History* 1.36; 2.23, 26, 29, 30, 39, 42; 3.25; Sozomen, *Church History* 2.33; 3.12, 14; 4.2, 6, 13, 16, 24; 5.11; Epiphanius, *Panarion* 71.1–2; 73.1–28; Gregory of Nyssa, *Against Eunomius* 1.6; Philostorgius, *Church History* 3.16; 5.1; Theodoret, *Church History* 2.20.

BASIL OF CAESAREA (330–379).

Bishop, known as "the Great," one of the Cappadocian theologians.

Life. Basil was born into a Christian upper-class family. His father, also Basil, was a professor of rhetoric and had come from a well-off family in Pontus. His mother, Emmelia, however, provided the bulk of the wealth and status. There were nine children, five known by name: Macrina the Younger, Basil, Naucratius, Gregory of Nyssa, and Peter of Sebaste.

Basil's father died when he was a teenager. The home lessons in rhetoric were ended, and he went to school in Cappadocian Caesarea, where he met Gregory of Nazianzus. From there, he traveled to Constantinople, where he probably heard Libanius lecture. The finishing touches of his education were undertaken at Athens during a nearly six-year stay.

In 355, he returned home and taught rhetoric for a year. Then, much to his delight, he was able to make a tour with Eustathius the philosopher to visit monasteries in Syria, Mesopotamia, Palestine, and Egypt. These experiences were crucial for Basil and no doubt led to the writing of his monastic rule. He had felt the need for more exposure to the ascetic heroes and never forsook his concern for the monastic life even though he later became a bishop.

Upon his return from the tour, he was baptized and went to his father's estate at Annesi in Pontus. There, he was involved in a small ascetic community that included his sister, mother, and later Gregory of Nazianzus. In 358, he and Gregory evidently created the *Philocalia*, a selection of passages from Origen they found to be most significant.

Basil's entrance into public ministry was not forced or hurried. He was probably ordained a reader by Dianus, bishop of Caesarea in Cappadocia, in 360 and then ordained a presbyter by bishop Eusebius ca. 362. The emperor Julian, who had studied in Athens at the same time as Basil, evidently made an attempt to bring him to the court in Constantinople. But Basil still felt drawn to the ascetic life at Annesi. In 364, Eusebius, faced with the emperor Valens's Arianism, swallowed his pride and called Basil back to Caesarea to work with him as an auxiliary bishop, although that meant that he had to yield to Basil's superior talents.

During this period, Basil was occupied with both scholarly and benevolent work. He took seriously the threat of Neoarianism, as seen in the works of Aetius and Eunomius. But his pastoral heart and administrative skills came to the fore in 368, when famine overtook Cappadocia. By selling some of his own inheritance, dissuading many merchants who had sought to make a profit from the opportunity, and getting funds from the wealthy, he helped avert a serious disaster in Cappadocia.

Basil became bishop upon Eusebius's death in 370. For nearly nine years, he was active in doctrinal disputes and ecclesiastical politics. His opponents were many and powerful. The emperor Valens visited Caesarea in 372. A supporter of Arianism, he was yet impressed with Basil's wit and presence. When the provincial government was reorganized, the Arian bishop of Tyana demanded that a number of cities under Basil's authority should be under his jurisdiction. Each bishop rushed to put friends into the disputed towns. Basil angered his sensitive friend Gregory of Nazianzus by appointing him to the bishopric of a small town called Sasima.

In the same period, he entered the lists against the Arian Eustathius of Sebaste, a former mentor. Persuasion was to no avail. Eustathius remained an Arian and finally became the leader of the Pneumatomachians. Basil died in 379, in the midst of the Neoarian crisis.

Writings. Basil's writings are many and of uncommonly high quality. His style and arguments indicate his rhetorical training. His many letters are a goldmine of information about his life and also about the social, economic, political, and theological contexts of the period. They reveal him as both generous and cunning; they make clear that he would have been an unusual friend and a feared enemy.

One infamous piece, the *Address to Young Men*, reveals a side of Basil that is less than pleasing. He not only suggests what parts of pagan literature youth should be allowed to read, but also skews the pieces he chooses to interpret. Other theological writings, however, are of great merit. His *On the Holy Spirit* 1–3 (4–5 was probably written by Didymus of Alexandria) shows real penetration into Trinitarian issues and a certain biblical caution about what to claim for the Spirit. While never referring to the Spirit as God, Basil does argue for the Spirit's divinity. In his *Hexaemeron*, Basil interpreted the creation with an eye on both the text itself and the context of his day. Controlled allegorical and typological exegesis allowed him to make sense of the passages in light of contemporary science. His *Against Eunomius* shows rhetorical flourish and occasional sophistic cleverness while indicating a nuanced understanding of the problems. Basil saw that Eunomius shared neither his view that God's nature in itself is beyond human understanding nor his view that language never captured all truth. For him, the argument with the Arians was about theology and education.

Basil's contributions to theology are numerous. With the other Cappadocians, he worked out a sense of the Trinity that allowed for both unity and individuality. By employing various models, he helped form that doctrine in a way that is still basic to many eastern and western Christian communities. His sense of tradition is complex. He represents significant developments beyond what had gone before, but he was reluctant to see his work in those terms. He believed in the importance of unwritten traditions. (Erasmus, the sixteenth-century humanist and theologian, was shocked by Basil's position on such things.) By involving himself in public church life, he influenced the social concern of the church; by insisting on the ascetic life in his person and his *Rule*, he enabled others to see monasticism as both a spiritual and a social force. It is no wonder that Eastern Orthodoxy considers him as one of the three hierarchs, along with Gregory of Nazianzus and John Chrysostom. Feast day January 2 (west), January 1 (east). CPG II, 2835–3005. TLG 2040.   [F.W.N.]

Bibliography

Gregory of Nazianzus, *Oration* 20 "On St. Basil the Great"; Gregory of Nyssa, *Encomium on His Brother Basil*; Ephraem the Syrian, *Encomium in Magnum Basilium*; Socrates, *Church History* 4.26; Sozomen, *Church History* 6.15–17; Theodoret, *Church History* 4.16; Jerome, *Lives of Illustrious Men* 116; Photius, *Library* 141.

PG 29–32; *Sur le Saint-Esprit*, ed. B. Pruche, SC (1968), Vol. 17; *Homélies sur l'Hexaéméron*, ed. S. Giet, SC (1968), Vol. 26; *Sur l'origine de l'homme*, ed. A. Smets and M. Van Esbroeck, SC (1970), Vol. 160; *Contre Eunome*, ed. B. Sesboüé et al., SC (1982, 1983), Vols. 299, 305.

B. Jackson, tr., NPNF, 2nd ser. (1895), Vol. 8; *Saint Basil: Ascetical Works*, tr. M.M. Wagner, FOTC (1950), Vol. 9; *Saint Basil: Letters I, II* and *Exegetical Works*, tr. A.C. Way, FOTC (1951, 1955, 1963), Vols. 13, 28, 46.

M.M. Fox, *The Life and Times of St. Basil the Great as Revealed in his Works* (Washington, D.C.: Catholic UP, 1939); S. Giet, *Les Idées et l'action sociales de saint Basile le Grand* (Paris: Lecoffre, J. Gabalda, etc., 1941); H. Dörries, *De Spiritu Sancto. Der Beitrag des Basilius zum Abschluss des trinitarischen Dogmas* (Göttingen: Vandenhoeck & Ruprecht, 1956); Y. Courtonne, *Un Témoin du IVe siècle oriental, saint Basile et son temps d'après sa correspondance* (Paris: Les Belles Lettres, 1973); P.J. Fedwick, *St. Basil the Great and the Christian Ascetic Life* (Rome: Basilian, 1978); idem, *The Church and the Charisma of Leadership in Basil of Caesarea* (Toronto: Pontifical Institute of Mediaeval Studies, 1979); *Word and Spirit, A Monastic Review, I: In Honor of Saint Basil the Great* (Still River: St. Bede, 1979); P.J. Fedwick, *Basil of Caesarea: Christian, Humanist, Ascetic*, 2 vols. (Toronto: Pontifical Institute of Mediaeval Studies, 1981); *Atti del Congresso internazionale su Basilio di Cesarea, la sua eta e il Basilianesimo in Sicilia*, 2 vols. (Messina: Centro di Studi Umanistici, 1983); Metropolitan Georges, "Basil the Great, Bishop and Pastor," *St. Vladimir's Theological Quarterly* 29 (1985):5–27.

BASIL OF SELEUCIA (d. ca. 468). Bishop
(ca. 440–ca. 468). At the beginning of the controversy with the Monophysites, Basil condemned Eutyches (448) but soon reversed himself at the "Robber Council" of Ephesus (449), yet joined in the reversal of its decision at the Council of Chalcedon (451). Some forty homilies appear under his name; several of these influenced the hymnographer Romanos Melodos. A life of St. Thecla attributed to him is not his. CPG III, 6655–6675.   [M.P.McH.]

Bibliography

T.P. Halton and R.D. Sider, "A Decade of Patristic Scholarship 1970–1979," *CW* 76 (1982–1983):343–344 (bibliography).

BASILICA. Architecturally, a kind of building, and ecclesiastically, a category of church. The word basilica is Greek in origin (*basilikē*) and means "royal" or "pertaining to the king" (Greek *basileus*); it was used with the word *stoa* for the king's hall or throne room and in particular for the court of the *archon basileus* at Athens. It came to be applied to a variety of public and private buildings because they were royal in scale. Thus, in Roman architecture, any large, roofed hall might be called a basilica whether it functioned as a courtroom, market, or meeting place, and whether for secular or religious use. In a typical basilican plan, however, there was a wide but shallow entrance hall or narthex, a tall central hall or nave with windows (the clerestory) below the main roof but above the roofs over the parallel side-aisles, and a platform (tribunal) opposite the entrance for the presiding official, which was often set into a semicircular opening (apse) in the wall. In some cases, the apse was the setting for a statue of a deity or the reigning emperor. The side-aisles were set off by lines of columns or piers and were in many cases surmounted by galleries. Of special significance for the development of the basilica in early Christian architecture was the dominant longitudinal axis from entrance to apse.

In much later Roman Catholic usage, *basilica* became a title under church law for churches that enjoyed certain privileges. Major basilicas, for example, have the "holy door" and a papal altar, and minor basilicas take ecclesiastical precedence over other churches except for cathedrals.

Imperial Basilica (early fourth century) at Trier, West Germany. (Photograph furnished by G.T. Armstrong.)

The origins of the early Christian basilica have been the object of much study and debate. There can be no single answer because of the variety of antecedents in the architecture of the Roman empire and because of the variety of early Christian churches called basilicas. The term did not designate a single plan or design for those who were using it. The function of the building as a meeting place for Christians seems to have governed the usage as much as the form of the building. The origins of early Christian architecture are bound up with the debate over this term.

When the Christian church received official recognition from the emperor Constantine, it immediately needed suitable church buildings, buildings both larger and more monumental than any that Christians had previously been able or permitted to construct. Since the pattern of worship called for the gathering of the people together for the liturgy of the word and the eucharist, neither existing temple nor domestic architecture offered models for the rapidly growing church. The house churches

(*domus ecclesiae*) of the preceding period continued in use but were no longer adequate. A few churches were designated basilicas in texts of the early fourth century, but nothing is known of their architectural form. It is also unknown whether they survived the persecution of Diocletian. The pagan temples were shrines to house the cultic image of the deity, not places of communal worship. (In Christian usage, however, the church building could also be termed the palace of Christ or of God.) The form of building most suitable and adaptable for Christian worship was the Roman basilica. Moreover, the basilica was a conspicuous form of official or imperial architecture and thus a natural choice by imperial patrons of the church, such as Constantine and most of his successors. In the course of the fourth century, every major city of the empire, indeed every town with a bishop, received a church, to be called a cathedral because it sheltered the bishop's throne, or *cathedra*, and most of these churches were in the typical form of a basilica—a nave terminating in an apse, with two or four side-aisles. It was a hall for preaching and teaching, praying and singing, and it had its focus at the head of the nave, the longitudinal axis, in the chancel area in front of or within the apse, where the altar was located. The ambo, or pulpit, was in the nave, connected by a walkway to the chancel, or *bema*. There is no example of such a Christian building prior to Constantine because of the Diocletianic persecution, but the imperial basilicas of Leptis Magna (Tripolitana) and of Timgad and Tipasa (Algeria) in North Africa are examples of the form from the third century. The Basilica Ulpia in Trajan's Forum in Rome may be cited as an antecedent from the second century, and Greek examples would be even older. The imperial basilica in Trier from the early fourth century was also a forerunner, although it lacked side-aisles. All emphasized height and light, two important characteristics of the early Christian basilica.

The building program of Constantine opened the era of the Christian basilica with the Church of St. John Lateran in Rome, probably begun in 313, on imperial property. It could hold 3,000 worshipers and had double side-aisles, an apse, a clerestory, a timber roof, and an adjacent baptistery. The cathedral of the bishop of Rome, it was a monumental public building some 312 feet long, 180 feet wide, and 98 feet high, which made a statement about the emperor's feelings toward Christianity. It was an assembly hall like other, earlier imperial basilicas, and it was the audience hall of Christ, the heavenly king, richly decorated with multicolored marble columns, marble revetment, mosaics, and gold and silver furnishings. At this time, the bishops were granted a civil and judicial role by Constantine's religious legislation, so that the church building was also a court of law.

Double basilicas soon followed in Aquileia and Trier, important provincial cities. Other basilicas founded by the emperor are recorded by Eusebius, the church historian who was a contemporary of Constantine and wrote a biography of him (Eusebius, *V.C.* 3.25–43, 51–53). These include the Victoria basilica at the imperial residence of Nicomedia in Bithynia

(modern Izmit in Turkey); the Martyrion basilica, which was part of the complex constituting the Church of the Holy Sepulchre in Jerusalem; the Church of the Nativity in Bethlehem; and smaller basilicas at Mamre near Hebron and on the Mount of Olives in Jerusalem (the Eleona Church). From other sources, it is apparent that two important churches in Constantinople, the emperor's new capital, Hagia Irene, or Holy Peace, and Hagia Sophia, or Holy Wisdom, were associated with Constantine. Both seem to have been basilicas, and if Krautheimer is correct, the latter was similar to the basilica at the Church of the Holy Sepulchre with double side-aisles, galleries above them, a large atrium, and a propylaeum, or entrance gateway, on the street side of the atrium.

Still other Constantinian churches of the basilican plan were built in Rome adjacent to the tombs of the martyrs in the catacombs. These were marked by a single side-aisle that continued as an ambulatory around the circular west end. Inside each of them were the graves of Christians who wanted to be near the martyrs of the Roman church, and some noteworthy mausolea were built around them. By name, these basilicas were the Church of SS. Peter the Deacon and Marcellinus with the mausoleum of Helena, the emperor's mother; the Church of St. Agnes with the mausoleum of Constantina his daughter; the Church of the Apostles (later S. Sebastiano); and the Church of St. Lawrence. (The imperial basilicas of St. Lawrence and St. Agnes should not be confused with the later churches of the same name, S. Lorenzo f.l.M. and S. Agnese, which were built nearby directly over the catacombs.)

The most influential of Constantine's new buildings for subsequent church architecture in the west was that of St. Peter on the Vatican Hill, dating to the 320s (old St. Peter's in distinction from the Renaissance St. Peter's). It shared the established plan of nave and double side-aisles. The aisles were set off by a long colonnade supporting an architrave, above which rose the nave wall with its clerestory. The new and distinctive element was the large cross hall, or transept, at the west end of the nave opposite the entrance. This was the martyrion consecrated to the apostle Peter and erected over an ancient shrine to him. The building was larger than any other Constantinian church. A similar combination of basilican hall with a martyrion is found at the churches of the Holy Sepulchre and the Nativity built in the same decade. The Constantinian buildings were oriented along an east-west axis, with many having an eastern entrance, whereas by the fifth century the entrance of most churches was at the west. All of these buildings became centers of pilgrimage.

The subsequent development of the Christian basilica cannot be recounted here, but one must observe that it is related to the elaboration of the liturgy with processions and other priestly activities and with a need for special rooms, and to regional artistic traditions. The basilican plan as well as other plans developed by Constantine's architects functioned as models. It even appears that a number of synagogues of basilican plan from the next 250 years followed the same model, although none was of the size of the great Christian churches. Even a bare listing of examples will suggest the spread of the basilica to all corners of the empire.

Milan, a major administrative center and home of Ambrose, had a cathedral of basilican plan, Sta. Thecla (ca. 350), which was almost as large as the Lateran basilica, and like it with an adjacent baptistery. The cathedral at Trier was rebuilt in the 380s by the emperor Gratian, who with his co-emperors also built a new church similar to St. Peter's at the shrine of St. Paul outside Rome. The latter was distinguished by its tall transept and the use of an arcade above the nave columns. By the fifth century, the popes were important builders, as evidenced by the Church of Sta. Maria Maggiore in Rome, a major basilica of the 430s with elaborate mosaic decoration. For the same century, it is possible, as Krautheimer has done, to describe standard types of basilica for the three chief regions of the empire.

Notable monuments along the coastlands of the Aegean Sea include two basilicas at Thessalonica in northern Greece. The Church of the Acheiropoietos (ca. 450) has galleries and an inner as well as, originally, an outer narthex. The Church of Hagios Demetrios (St. Demetrius) is one of the most impressive cross-transept basilicas of the late fifth century, marked by double side-aisles, galleries, a rhythmic pattern of columns and piers supporting arcades at both floor and gallery levels, numerous round-headed windows of various sizes, and exposed timbered roofs. The extant building is a replica of the original, which burned down in 1917. In

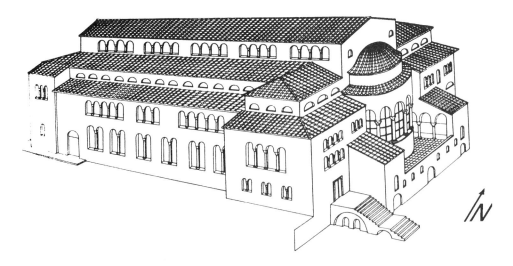

Reconstruction of Hagios Demetrios, Thessalonica, Greece, as in the late fifth century. (From R. Krautheimer, *Early Christian and Byzantine Architecture* [Harmondsworth: Penguin, 1986], fig. 79.)

Constantinople, the walls and one line of columns with the architrave from the monastery church of St. John Studios still stand. The plan of the Church of St. Mary in Ephesus (ca. 400), the site of the general council of 431, can still be seen in its ruins. It was a large basilica (279 feet long), with an equally large atrium and adjacent baptistery.

In the region of the Near East extending from Egypt to the highlands of Asia Minor and Armenia, Abu Mina in the desert west of Alexandria was the site of a basilica (ca. 113 by 98 feet) erected in 412 with imperial patronage at the burial place of St. Menas, which was remodeled and enlarged ca. 490 under the emperor Zeno. The new building had a transept almost as large as the basilica proper and an unusual narthex connecting the basilica to a tetraconch martyrion. Other Egyptian churches had a basilican plan with a triconch transept.

Perhaps the most remarkable use of the basilican plan is the martyrion of St. Symeon Stylites at Qal'at Si'man. Around a central shrine were four basilicas, each with a nave and side-aisles that formed a cross. Only that to the east had an apse, actually a central apse with smaller apses at the head of each side-aisle. This building also dates to the reign of Zeno. Gerasa (Jerash, Jordan) had seven basilicas; two of the largest, the cathedral (ca. 400) and the Church of St. Theodore (494–496), were aligned along a common east-west axis with an atrium between.

The churches of the Latin-speaking west preserved the simpler plans of the early Roman basilicas, and churches of the Romanesque and Gothic periods still followed a basilican plan. The Church of Sta. Sabina in Rome (422–432), for instance, has been compared with the imperial civil basilica in Trier in terms of its sense of space and light, although the church has an arcade of columns separating the nave from the side-aisles. Ravenna preserves three notable basilicas, each with arcades between the nave and single side-aisles: S. Giovanni Evangelista (424–434), S. Apollinare Nuovo (ca. 490), and S. Apollinare in Classe (532/6–549). Remains of basilicas in North Africa include some of great breadth, such as that in Tipasa (ca. 450)

with four aisles on each side of the nave, and some that hold the "Constantinian classicism" (Krautheimer), such as that in Tebessa (ca. 400) with galleries like the Church of the Holy Sepulchre and a trefoil martyrion on the south side.

The reign of the emperor Justinian (527–565) brought a flowering of churches with a central plan and vaulting, whose classical antecedents may be found in the Roman baths and the basilica of Maxentius in Rome and whose Christian antecedents are the martyria, the baptisteries, and a few palace churches. The new Church of Hagia Sophia (532–537) is the supreme achievement of this type and has been widely influential. Related to it is the domed basilica (a basilica with domes over the nave instead of timber roofing), of which the new Hagia Irene in Constantinople is a surviving example contemporary with Hagia Sophia—but here one leaves the early Christian period. *See also* Art; Hagia Sophia; Holy Sepulchre, Church of; Lateran; Martyrion; Nativity, Church of; Sabina; St. Paul's Outside the Walls; St. Peter, Church of; S. Apollinare in Classe; S. Apollinare Nuovo; Sta. Maria Maggiore. [G.T.A.]

Bibliography

R. Krautheimer, W. Frankl, S. Corbett, and A.K. Frazer, *Corpus Basilicarum Christianarum Romae: The Early Christian Basilicas of Rome (IV–X Cent.)*, 5 vols. (Vatican City: Pontificio Istituto di Archeologia Cristiana, and New York: Institute of Fine Arts, New York University, 1937–1977) (with plans and illustrations); E. Langlotz and F.W. Deichmann, "Basilika," RLAC (1950), Vol. 1, cols. 1225–1259 (with plans); G.T. Armstrong, "Imperial Church Building and Church-State Relations, A.D. 313–363," *ChHist* 36 (1967):3–17; idem, "Constantine's Churches," *Gesta* 6 (1967):1–9; R. Krautheimer, "The Constantinian Basilica," *DOP* 21 (1967):117–140 (with plans); C. Andresen, *Einführung in die christliche Archäologie* (Göttingen: Vandenhoeck & Ruprecht, 1971), Vol. 1B1 of *Die Kirche in ihrer Geschichte*, ed. K.D. Schmidt and E. Wolf, esp. for bibliography; T.F. Mathews, *The Early Churches of Constantinople: Architecture and Liturgy* (University Park: Pennsylvania State UP, 1971) (with plans); G.T. Armstrong, "Constantine's Churches: Symbol and Structure," *Journal of the Society of Architectural Historians* 33 (1974):5–16 (with plans and illustrations); B. Fletcher, *A History of Architecture*, 18th ed., rev. J.C. Palmes (New York: Scribner, 1975), pp. 256–402 (with plans and illustrations); B. Andreae, *The Art of Rome* (New York: Abrams, 1977), pp. 481–602 (with plans and illustrations); N. Duval, "Les Edifices de culte des origines à l'époque constantinienne," *Atti del IX Congresso Internazionale di Archeologia Cristiana, Roma 1975* (Vatican City: Pontificio Istituto di Archeologia Cristiana, 1978), Vol. 1: *Monumenti Cristiani Precostantiniani*, pp. 513–537; G. Stanzl, *Längsbau und Zentralbau als Grundthemen der frühchristlichen Architektur: Überlegungen zur Entstehung der Kuppelbasilika* (Vienna: Verlag der Österreichischen Akademie der Wissenschaften, 1979) (with plans); F. Sear, *Roman Architecture* (Ithaca: Cornell UP, 1982) (with plans and illustrations); F.W. Deichmann, *Einführung in die christliche Archäologie* (Darmstadt: Wissenschaftliche Buchgesellschaft, 1983), esp. ch. 6 (with bibliography); R. Krautheimer, *Three Christian Capitals: Topography and Politics* (Berkeley: U of California P, 1983) (with plans and illustrations); R. Krautheimer, *Early Christian and Byzantine Architecture*, 4th ed. (Harmondsworth: Penguin, 1986) (with plans, illustrations, and bibliography).

BASILIDES (second century). Teacher of Gnosticism. Probably born in Syria, Basilides taught in Alexandria during the second quarter of the second century. He apparently wrote a *Gospel*, an exegetical commentary on it in twenty-four books, and a collection of *Psalms* or *Odes*, but all those documents are lost.

The church fathers give varying reports concerning his teachings. Most scholars have suggested that the account of Irenaeus (*Haer.* 1.24) probably gives some sense of what his followers taught. In that view, a God beyond any description, "nonexistent," had *Nous, Logos, Phronesis, Sophia,* and *Dynamis* emanate from him. The last two created the first heaven, other powers made the second, and so forth until there were 365 heavens. Angels in the last heaven made the evil, material earth and separated its people into groups. The angels' leader is the God of the Jews, who taught those people to dominate others, but the others resisted. Prophecies and Law came from this evil leader and his angels.

Nous, who was Christ, opposed the powers of this world. He came to liberate souls from their oppression. He took the form of Simon of Cyrene and let that man be crucified, but he himself was unharmed. Only the foolish follow the crucified Simon through discipline and martyrdom. The wise follow *Nous* in a life of liberty, if not libertinism, and avoid martyrdom.

The other account of Basilides's teaching comes from Hippolytus (*Haer.* 7.20–27) and is supported by fragments in Clement, Origen, and Hegemonius. In this account, God is still inexpressible, but the world exists in his worldseed. There is no dualism of darkness and light, and no fall, only a type of monism. Three Sonships come from the seed: a light one, a heavier one, and one needing purification. The first ascends; the second needs the Holy Spirit to reach the upper world; the third is purified by carrying the souls of humans up with it. Two Archons and their sons also arise from the world-seed. The gospel, the light, appears, and the first son leads his father and the realm of eight (Ogdoad) to repentance. The second son learned from the first, and taught his father and the realm of seven (Hebdomad). The light that had descended through the eight and the seven descends on Jesus. Salvation is viewed as a kind of reincarnation that the world-seed controls. CPG I, 1127. *See also* Isidore.

[F.W.N.]

Bibliography

Irenaeus, *Against Heresies* 1.24; Hippolytus, *Refutation of All Heresies* 7.20–27; Epiphanius, *Panarion* 24; Theodoret, *Haereticarum fabularum compendium* 1.4; Philaster 32.

Fragments: Hegemonius, *Acta Archelai* 67; Clement of Alexandria, *Miscellanies* 1.21; 2.3, 6, 8, 20; 3.1; 4.12, 24, 26; 5.1; 6.6; 7.17; Origen, *In Romanos* 6.1.

W. Foerster, "Das System des Basilides," *NTS* 9 (1963):233–255; idem, *Gnosis: A Selection of Gnostic Texts* (Oxford: Clarendon, 1972), Vol. 1, pp. 59–83; W.P. Hauschild, "Christologie und Humanismus bei dem 'Gnostiker Basilides,'" *ZNTW* 68 (1977):67–92; R.M. Grant, "Place de Basilide dans la théologie chrétienne ancienne," *REA* 25 (1979):201–216; M. Jufresa, "Basilides: A Path to Plotinus," *VChr* 35 (1981):1–15.

BASILIUS CELIX (sixth century). Bishop of Irenopolis in Cilicia. Basilius Celix wrote an ecclesiastical history (450–527) filled with irrelevant episcopal letters (Photius, *Cod.* 42). He attacked John of Scythopolis and defended Diodore of Tarsus and Theodore of Mopsues-

Bibliography

P.T.R. Gray, *The Defense of Chalcedon in the East* (Leiden: Brill, 1979), pp. 111–113.

BAUR, FERDINAND CHRISTIAN

(1792–1860). Prominent German theologian and founder of the so-called Tübingen School in Germany, which emphasized a rationalistic historical approach to biblical literature and the study of early Christianity. Baur was one of the first to study the history of dogma and gave attention to determining the proper focus of church history.

Born in Schmiden, Germany, Baur was educated by his father, a Lutheran pastor in Blaubeuren, until he entered lower seminary at the age of thirteen; there, he was introduced to Greek, Latin, and Hebrew, as well as biblical exegesis, philosophy, and the classics. In 1809, he began his studies at Tübingen University, where he came under the influence of Ernst Gottlieb Bengel, who added to Baur's appreciation for historical theology. At Tübingen, his study of the German philosopher F.W.J. Schelling (1775–1854) had a major impact on his view of history as revelation and his attitude toward historical method. The genesis of Schelling's thought, as well as that of F.D.E. Schleiermacher (1768–1834), formed the backdrop for Baur's first book, *Symbolik und Mythologie, oder die Naturreligion des Alterthums* (1824–1825). Schleiermacher's *Glaubenslehre* (*On Christian Faith*) played a major role in Baur's formative theology, especially in his viewing Christianity from the perspective of the history of religions, but also from a critical historical stance.

Following two brief pastorates in Rosswaag and Mülhaufen, Baur joined the faculty at Blaubeuren in 1817. In 1826, he was appointed professor of theology at Tübingen and remained there until his death in 1860. He also accepted the invitation to be the university preacher during his tenure at Tübingen, insisting that Christian preaching and critical thought were compatible.

Baur is best known for his application of the Hegelian philosophy of history to early Christianity and his use of it in dating the New Testament writings. The extent to which Baur was dependent upon G.W.F. Hegel can be seen in his *Paulus, der Apostel Jesu Christi* (1845) and *Das Christenthum und die christliche Kirche der drei ersten Jahrhunderte* (1853), although that influence was perhaps not as strong as his most severe critics thought. He did not ignore history itself in favor of general theories about historical development, despite accusations to the contrary. Baur saw a conflict between the earliest strands of Jewish Christianity represented by James (thesis) and Gentile Christianity represented by Paul (antithesis), which was resolved in the second-century catholicizing tendencies of the church (synthesis) represented by Acts, which he believed was a second-century book, and also by Johannine Christianity. He believed that Matthew, the most Jewish Gospel, was the earliest of the four and that Paul wrote only 1 and 2 Corinthians, Romans, and Galatians. He dated all of the other Pauline literature in the second century. Although most of Baur's conclusions about the New Testament literature have proved false, his recognition of conflict in the early church and of the tendency of later generations to blur the conflict in favor of presenting a united church still has merit and is widely followed today.

Baur's most important works included *Geschichte der christlichen Kirche* (5 vols., 1853–1863), of which only Volume 1 was translated into English, as *The Church History of the First Three Centuries* (1878–1879); *Die Lehre von der Versöhnung* (1838); *Die christliche Lehre von der Dreieinigkeit* (1841–1843); *Kritische Untersuchungen über die kanonischen Evangelien* (1847); and *Vorlesungen über die christliche Dogmensgeschichte* (4 vols., edited by his son, F.F. Baur, 1865–1867).

[L.M.McD.]

Bibliography

P.C. Hodgson, *The Formation of Historical Theology: A Study of Ferdinand Christian Baur* (New York: Harper and Row, 1966); K. Löwith, *From Hegel to Nietzsche: The Revolution in Nineteenth-Century Thought* (Garden City: Doubleday, 1967); P.C. Hodgson, *Ferdinand Christian Baur on the Writing of Church History* (New York: Oxford UP, 1968); K. Barth, *Protestant Theology in the Nineteenth Century* (London: SCM, 1972).

BEDE (ca. 673–735). English monk and writer, known as "the Venerable." Educated by monks from the age of seven, Bede spent his life in the dual monastic foundations of Wearmouth and Jarrow, as monk, deacon (from age nineteen), and priest (from about age thirty). He never traveled beyond Northumbria (northeast England). A prolific writer, he composed scriptural exegeses, influenced by Augustine and Jerome; works, intended for the instruction of his students, on orthography, natural phenomena, and versification; chronologies; books of biography and hagiography; hymns and verse prayers; and several letters. His *Ecclesiastical History of the English Nation* (731), the principal source for the study of the early English church, is notable for its careful collection of data and sifting of fact from rumor. CPL 1343–1384; 1565–1567; 2318–2323.

[M.P.McH.]

Bibliography

Bede, *Ecclesiastical History* 5.24.

Critical editions of many of Bede's works are appearing in the series CCSL (1960–), to date in Vols. 118A–123C, 175; *Historia ecclesiastica gentis Anglorum*, ed. B. Colgrave and R.A.B. Mynors (Oxford: Clarendon, 1969).

A History of the English Church and People, tr. L. Sherley-Price (Harmondsworth: Penguin, 1955, rev. 1965); D. Hurst, tr., *Bede the Venerable: Commentary on the Seven Catholic Epistles* (Kalamazoo: Cistercian, 1985).

P.H. Blair, *The World of Bede* (London: Secker and Warburg, 1970); H. Ledoyen, "Bulletin d'histoire bénédictine, X," *RBén* 92 (1982):712*–718* (bibliography); T. Eckenrode, "The Venerable Bede: A Bibliographical Essay, 1970–1981," *American Benedictine Review* 36 (1985):172–194; *St. Bede: A Tribute (735–1985)* (Petersham: St. Bede's Publications, 1985); G.H. Brown, *Bede the Venerable* (Boston: Twayne, 1987); W. Goffart, *The Narrators of Barbarian History (A.D. 550–800)* (Princeton: Princeton UP, 1988); J.M. Wallace-Hadrill, *Bede's Ecclesiastical History of the English People: A Historical Commentary* (Oxford: Oxford UP, 1988).

BENEDICT OF NURSIA (ca. 480–540).

Monastic founder and author of the *Rule of Saint Benedict*, the most influential monastic rule in the Latin church. The only information we have for Benedict's life comes from the *Dialogues* of pope Gregory the Great (540–604), a highly stylized hagiographical account with heavy emphasis on miracles. Nevertheless, Gregory wrote only about fifty years after the death of the saint and he mentions places and persons well known to his readers, so we may take at least the broad outlines of his account as historically reliable. Benedict was born in the Apennine village of Nursia and was sent to Rome for a classical education. The decadence of the capital caused him to flee to a cave near Subiaco in the hills east of Rome for solitary contemplation. Although Benedict later insisted (*R.B.* 1) that a monk be trained as a cenobite (in community) before undertaking the anchorite (solitary) life, Gregory stresses that Benedict had to achieve personal integration through trials and sufferings before he could teach others the way to God (*Dial.* 2.2). (This same theme surfaces in many of Gregory's writings.) His spiritual renown soon attracted followers, whom he organized into small communities. He himself passed on to Monte Cassino, halfway between Rome and Naples, where he evangelized the population and founded a larger monastery. Monte Cassino served as a refuge from the Gothic wars that ravaged the Italian peninsula in the early sixth

St. Peter's Church, founded 674 (tower is later but before 686), Monkwearmouth, Tyne and Wear, England.

century. Gregory presents the last phase of Benedict's career as the full flowering of holiness. Not only was he able to thwart every attack of the devil; he was now able to see all passing worldly things in the light of the eternal vision of God (*Dial.* 2.35). As Gregory notes, Benedict was the author of a monastic rule noted for its "discernment" and "clarity of language."

The *Rule of Benedict* as we now have it, in seventy-three chapters, is roughly as long as one of the Gospels. Like the monastic rules of that time, it is a combination of spiritual doctrine and practical regulation, with emphasis mostly on the latter. A monastic rule for cenobites was seen as ascetical preparation for a life of contemplative prayer, but Benedict says little about this, except to refer his monks to such spiritual writers as John Cassian and Basil the Great (*R.B.* 73). After a prologue inviting the candidate to undertake monastic discipline so as to arrive at a condition of loving identification with Christ (*Prol.* 49–50), Benedict presents the abbot as the spiritual father and teacher of the monk (*R.B.* 2). The teaching of the abbot is crystallized into three basic monastic virtues: obedience, silence, and humility (*R.B.* 5–7), all of which center on the abandonment of self-will so as to learn the will of God through the monastic superior. The second half of the *Rule* applies these principles to practical aspects of the common life: Chapters 8–20 discuss the choral prayer or Divine Office; 23–30 and 43–46 present arrangements for the disciplining and rehabilitation of wayward monks; other chapters deal with sleep, diet, use of property, work, study, and training of novices. The last chapters (67–73) are concerned mostly with relations among the monks, culminating in a paean to mutual love (*R.B.* 72).

Because Benedict's rule became so dominant in subsequent centuries, it was once common to categorize him as a special genius who was able to avoid the excesses and narrowness of earlier writers. Today, however, most scholars see him as being in essential continuity with the general monastic tradition. It had always been evident that Benedict made use of earlier rules, such as those of Basil and Augustine, but it is now accepted that the principal prototype for Benedict's rule was the *Rule of the Master.* This long document from the early sixth century has some chapters that are almost identical with the *Rule of Benedict* and others that have obvious connections with it. Formerly, the *Rule of the Master* was considered an inferior later expansion of Benedict, but now Benedict is seen as a synthesizer of the earlier work and many other traditions. The true nature of Benedict's sources is now better known, and we can derive a clearer picture of the author through what he retains, what he modifies, and what he says when he is adding original material to the tradition. Compared with the Master, Benedict seems much more sensitive to human freedom and uniqueness. He leaves the abbot more leeway to adapt the regimen to local conditions, even inviting wholesale restructuring of something as sacred as the Divine Office (*R.B.* 18.22). Rather than stress external conformity, Benedict often manifests more concern for internal dispositions: everything must be done to preclude "sadness," "murmuring," and "contumacy." For all his humanity, however, Benedict shares with his predecessors an austere and even terrifying concept of God. Fear of the Lord is to pervade the atmosphere of the monastery and govern all its transactions (*R.B.* 7.10–13).

For all his later influence, Benedict was not famous in his lifetime, nor did he found an order of monks. The Lombards destroyed Monte Cassino ca. 570 and the monks fled to Rome, taking their rule with them. Popular legend assumed that Gregory the Great joined the community at that point and later, as pope, spread the rule throughout Europe. Modern scholarship has abandoned this view of the organic growth of Benedict's influence. In fact, we have no proof of any Italian monastery living according the *Rule of Benedict* before the tenth century. The rule begins to turn up in Gaul ca. 630 and in England ca. 660. At first, it was used in combination with other monastic rules, especially that of the Irishman Columbanus. Eventually, Charlemagne had Benedict's rule imposed on all the monasteries, in an attempt to standardize and Romanize his realm. After the collapse of the Carolingian empire in the ninth century, the monasteries retained the *Rule of Benedict* as their chief written guideline after the Bible: the document became indispensable to medieval monasticism. Feast day July 11 (west), March 14 (east). CPL 1852–1857, see also 1858. *See also* Monasticism; Monte Cassino.   [T.G.K.]

Bibliography
R. Hanslik, ed., *Benedicti Regula*, CSEL (1960, 1977), Vol. 75; J. Neufville and A. de Vogüe, *La Règle de saint Benoît* SC (1971–1972), Vols. 181–186; J.M. Clément, J. Neufville, and D. Demeslay, *La Règle du Maître*, SC (1964–1965), Vols. 105–107; A. de Vogüé and P. Antin, eds., *Grégoire le Grand, Dialogues*, SC (1978–1980), Vols. 251, 260, 265.

The Rule of St. Benedict in Latin and English with Notes, ed. T. Fry et al. (Collegeville: Liturgical, 1981); L. Eberle and C. Philippi, trs., *The Rule of the Master* (Kalamazoo: Cistercian, 1977); O. Zimmerman, *Dialogues*, FOTC (1959), Vol. 39.

J. Chapman, *Saint Benedict and the Sixth Century* (London: Sheed and Ward, 1929); L. von Matt and S. Hilpisch, *Saint Benedict* (Chicago: Regnery, 1961); D. Knowles, *Great Historical Enterprises* (London: Nelson, 1963), pp. 137–195; T. Kardong, *Together unto Life Everlasting: An Introduction to the Rule of Benedict*; idem, *Commmentaries on Benedict's Rule* (Richardton: Assumption Abbey, 1984, 1987).

BETHLEHEM. Traditional birthplace of King David and Jesus (1 Sam. 16:1, 4; Matt. 2:5; Luke 2:11; John 7:24), located five miles south of Jerusalem. Bethlehem attracted pilgrims at least from near the beginning of the second century (Justin, *Dial.* 78). Jerome (*Ep.* 58) states that the emperor Hadrian set up an Adonis shrine at the birthplace of Jesus, but Origen (*Cels.* 1.51) claimed that the cave and the manger were still in place. Constantine's mother, Helena, found a cave east of the city that she believed to be Jesus' birthplace. Constantine had the Church of the Nativity built at the site. There is a large grotto under its transept. The church suffered significant damage in a Samaritan revolt (521–528), but Justinian had it rebuilt in the basic form it has today.

Monasticism found a home in Bethlehem. John Cassian spent the years 380–386 with a friend, Germanus, in a cave there. Paula funded the construction of a monastery and a convent after 386. Jerome led the monastery; Paula and her daughter, Eustochium, led the convent. Paula, Eustochium, Jerome, and Eusebius of Cremona are buried in grottoes just outside the town near the Church of the Nativity.

Mosaics in the old St. Peter's, Sta. Constanza, Sta. Maria Maggiore, and SS. Cosma e Damiano in Rome depict two flocks of sheep, each turned toward the lamb of God in the center. A city on the left is named Jerusalem; a city on the right, Bethlehem. Some have interpreted "Jerusalem" as the Jewish Christian church and "Bethlehem" as the Gentile church. Others have suggested that the two cities depict the significance of Jesus for the church, his birth in Bethlehem, and his death and resurrection in Jerusalem. No texts speak to the issues. *See also* Church of the Nativity; Monasticism.   [F.W.N.]

Bibliography
A.M. Schneider, "Bethlehem," RLAC (1954), Vol. 2, pp. 224–228.

BIBLE. *See* Canon; Interpretation of the Bible; Manuscripts; Septuagint; Vulgate.

BISHOP. Overseer and pastor in the Christian church. The Greek *episkopos*, from which the English word "bishop" is derived, was a secular term. It referred to a diverse range of civil functionaries, such as an overseer of slaves, head of a mint, and construction foreman. Where it was used of officers in associations and cults, it had no priestly connotations, and, although financial affairs might be included in the oversight, this was not its technical meaning. A related word ("scout") was used of Cynic philosophers, and *episkopos* itself was used of the gods in their functions as guardians.

Functionaries more nearly comparable with the Christian bishop were found in Judaism, but they were not designated by this term. The ruler of the synagogue (*archisynagogos*) presided at its services, but we do not know that his activities went beyond this or that this function was confined to one person or always to the same person. The Essenes had an overseer (Hebrew *mebaqqer* or *paqid*; Greek *epimelētēs*) who was not a priest and whose tasks included receiving new members into the community, administering property, supervising labor (1QS vi. 11–23), and being a shepherd and teacher to the members (CD 13.7–15).

The New Testament uses "bishop" interchangeably with "pastor," "steward," and "presbyter" for the same community leaders (Acts 20:17, 28; 1 Peter 5:1–4; Titus 1:5–7). "Pastor" (shepherd) was common metaphorical language in the ancient world for those with the care and responsibility for people; "steward" (household manager) was a common secular term that could be applied to someone in a position of trust; "presbyter" (elder) seems to have come into Christian usage from the leaders of Jewish communities. The term "bishop" likely came from the Hellenistic vocabulary, but the function in the church developed from Christian requirements.

In the oldest sources, the word for bishop always occurs in the plural, with the exception of the Pastoral Epistles, where the singular is used in a generic sense (Titus 1:7; 1 Tim. 3:2). Since oversight is in its nature more commonly singular and the elders were always plural in Judaism, it was natural that "bishop" should have been chosen for the one head of a church and "presbyter" used for his council of advisers.

Clement of Rome in his discussion of the problems in the church at Corinth uses "bishops," as is typical in the New Testament, in the plural and as equivalent to "presbyters" as leaders of the church (*1 Clem.* 42; 44). He affirms that the apostles instituted the office, appointed the first bishops, and provided for the continuation of the office in the church. The appointment of bishops was with the consent of the whole congregation, but Clement does not judge it right to remove from the episcopate those who have blamelessly discharged their ministry.

Didache 15 instructs the church to elect (or appoint) "bishops and deacons." Their qualifications are similar, although more briefly stated, to those given in 1 Timothy 3:1ff. and

Titus 1:5ff. The bishops and deacons are stated to rank with the prophets and teachers as the honored men of the community, and the prophets and teachers are elsewhere stated to succeed to the financial support that Jewish communities gave to priests (*Did.* 13).

The first witness to monepiscopacy (only one bishop at the head of each local church) is found in the letters of Ignatius of Antioch. He gave theological justification to the one bishop, as the representative of the one God (e.g., *Magn.* 6.1). The episcopacy advocated by Ignatius is not described in priestly language (not even on the analogy of the Old Testament priesthood, as in Clement), is not based on apostolic succession, and is congregational (not diocesan). He normally mentions the bishop in conjunction with the presbyters and deacons, for the bishop functioned as the president of the presbytery, the "first among equals." The obedience that Ignatius enjoined on the churches included the presbyters and deacons as well as the bishop (*Polyc.* 6). The requirement to do nothing without the bishops—baptism, eucharist, agape (*Smyrn.* 8)—was a matter of good order, not of the validity of the acts, for the bishop could designate someone else to act for him. Ignatius's main concern was unity; and obedience to the clergy as the leaders of the community was essential to maintaining unity. Ignatius's reference to himself as "bishop of Syria" (*Rom.* 2.2) probably means "from Syria," or may be an indication that Antioch was the only church in Syria that had evolved a single bishop in his time. That monepiscopacy was a recent development is indicated by the tradition that he had only one predecessor at Antioch (Eusebius, *H.E.* 3.22). Furthermore, Ignatius may provide negative support for the evidence of Clement and Hermas (*Vis.* 2.4f.; 3.5.1) that monepiscopacy came somewhat later to Rome, for his letter to Rome makes no mention of church order, which is such a preoccupation of his other letters.

By the middle of the second century, the Ignatian type of church order, with a single bishop at the head of each Christian community, was generally observed. Justin Martyr's "president" or "ruler" of the assembly (*1 Apol.*

67) was presumably the bishop. Dionysius, bishop of Corinth, wrote letters to churches (ca. 170) in which he mentioned the bishop in each (Eusebius, *H.E.* 4.23), and Hegesippus about the same time drew up a list of bishops of Rome (Eusebius, *H.E.* 4.22).

The terminology of Irenaeus (*Haer.* 4.26.2; cf. 3.3.1f.) and Clement of Alexandria (*Str.* 7.1.3) preserved a certain interchangeability of the words "bishop" and "presbyter," because the bishop continued to be thought of as the head of the presbytery (but contrast *Haer.* 3.14.2, where Irenaeus fails to recognize the identity of bishops and presbyters in Acts 20:17, 28; and Clement of Alexandria, *Str.* 6.13.106; *Paed.* 3.12.97). The bishop could be called an elder, but an elder was not called a bishop.

Several factors were involved in the emergence of a single bishop: (1) There is a natural tendency in organizations toward a single head, and this was reinforced by the monarchical features of the Roman empire and the examples of religious and other associations in contemporary society. (2) Certain functions in the churches themselves were either necessarily or more expeditiously handled by one person—presiding at the assembly, handling finances, corresponding with other churches. (3) The need for authoritative teaching and a focus of unity brought forward one person with the gifts of teaching and administration who had connections with the previous traditions of the church.

The precedent of James and the elders of the church in Jerusalem (Acts 21:18) may have provided a model for the development of monepiscopacy. Although the title of bishop was applied to James only later, when monepiscopacy had become common in the church (apparently first by Clement of Alexandria, recorded by Eusebius, *H.E.* 1.1.3; cf. 7.19 and Ps.-Clement, *Ep. Petr.* and *Ep. Jac.*), the position of James has figured prominently in modern theories of the rise of monepiscopacy. Another theory sees the link between ministry in the apostolic age and the episcopal government of the church in the second century provided by such evangelists as Timothy and Titus, who were appointed by an apostle as his

delegates with the power of ordination (Theodore of Mopsuestia, *1 Tim.* 3.8; Theodoret, *1 Tim.* 3). This view too has been revived in modern times. Another effort to find apostolic institution of monepiscopacy looks to John at Ephesus, since this type of organization is attested first in Asia Minor and Antioch, and appeal can be made to Clement of Alexandria's report of John ordaining bishops (*Q.d.s.* 42), but Clement's passage uses "bishop" and "presbyter" interchangeably and does not specifically connect monepiscopacy with John. An alternative view, anticipated by Jerome (*Comm. Tit.* 1.7; cf. *Ep.* 146), sees the bishop as arising out of the council of presbyters and assuming some of the functions formerly performed by apostles, prophets, and evangelists, such as giving authoritative teaching and ordaining.

The functions of the bishop covered the principal activities of the church: presiding at church meetings (including eucharist, prayer, agape, and baptism—Ignatius, *Smyrn.* 8.2; *Magn.* 6–7), preaching and teaching (Ignatius, *Polyc.* 5; Eusebius, *H.E.* 4.22), administering benevolent funds (to assist orphans, widows, the sick, those in prison, and strangers—Hermas, *Sim.* 9.27.2; Eusebius, *H.E.* 4.23.10), and representing the church in correspondence and through messengers (Ignatius, *Polyc.* 7–8; Eusebius, *H.E.* 4.23). By the beginning of the third century, the bishops had assumed many of the preaching and teaching functions formerly associated with apostles, prophets, evangelists, and teachers. The distinguishing activity of the bishop, however, came to be regarded as ordination (John Chrysostom, *Hom.* 11 *in 1 Tim.* 3.8–10). Hippolytus, *Apostolic Tradition* 9, is our first source limiting the power of ordaining to a bishop. Normally, three bishops were required to ordain another bishop (Nicaea, can. 4).

Irenaeus's theory of apostolic succession (*Haer.* 3.3.1–3) did much to strengthen the episcopal organization of the church against heresy. Hippolytus's expectation that other bishops would be present to join with the ordaining bishop in the installation of a new bishop in a church furthered the idea that a bishop was not just the bishop of his own congregation but a bishop of the church. This view found full development in Cyprian, for whom the episcopate of the whole church was a single corporate possession, in which each individual bishop had a share (*Unit. eccl.* 5). In dealing with the problems posed by the persecution of Decius, Cyprian worked in concert with other North African bishops meeting in council. The model of the bishop had changed from the teacher on the teaching chair of the church (Irenaeus) to the magistrate making governmental and judicial decisions. Cyprian and his fellow bishops in synod corresponded to the governing councils of Roman colonies patterned on the senate in Rome. For Cyprian, "If any one is not with the bishop, he is not in the church" (*Ep.* 66.8).

In Cyprian, there is also a full development of the priestly terminology for the bishop, especially in reference to his celebrating the eucharist (*Ep.* 63.14; *Ep.* 3; *Unit. eccl.* 17). The analogy of the Old Testament priesthood was used in support of the demand for clerical, particularly episcopal, celibacy (Ambrose, *Off. minist.* 1.50.257–258, and Jerome, *Jov.* 1.34; the oldest requirement of celibacy is Elvira, *can.* 33). The specification of 1 Timothy 3:2 that a bishop be the "husband of one wife" was sometimes interpreted as "husband from one wife"— that is, a widower—so that the man did not have to be married but if he had been married (only once), his wife was now dead (*Const. app.* 2.2).

The growth of the church produced differentiation in rank among the bishops. The rule was one bishop to a city (Nicaea, *can.* 8), but not all cities were equal. As Christianity spread to rural districts, different procedures were adopted to provide spiritual leadership for the populace. One expedient was the chorepiscopus ("country bishop"). Chorepiscopi were especially numerous in Asia Minor, but their powers were limited: they could ordain only to the lower orders of the clergy, and they were subject to the nearest city bishop (Ancyra, *can.* 13; Antioch, *can.* 10). They were soon largely replaced by visiting presbyters (Sardica, *can.* 6; Laodicea, *can.* 57). On the other end of the scale, the bishop of the chief city of a province gained a precedence over other bishops in his province. The civil influence of provincial capitals encouraged this development, but it probably owed much to the mission strategy of the early church, whereby the gospel spread from major cities to neighboring cities and then to rural areas. New churches continued to look to the mother church from which they received the gospel. The term "metropolitan bishop" for the leading bishop of a province is first used in Canon 4 of the Council of Nicaea (325), but the influence was there from the third century. The metropolitan bishop presided at provincial synods and took the lead in the ordination of bishops in the province. The Council of Nicaea (*can.* 6) recognized some bishops as having wider than the usual metropolitan jurisdiction (Rome, Alexandria, Antioch, Caesarea). These protopatriarchs were reckoned at the Council of Chalcedon (451) as five (Rome, Constantinople, Alexandria, Antioch, and Jerusalem), and from the time of Justinian (sixth century) the title "patriarch" was in common use. The bishop of Rome, the only patriarch in the west and claiming a succession to Peter's place in the church, assumed monarchical (papal) authority.

Constantine incorporated the bishops into the governing structure of the empire by granting them judicial power. Litigants could choose to have their cases heard before a bishop, and his decisions had the validity of those made by civil magistrates and judges, thereby laying a basis for church courts.

Bishops of the fourth and fifth centuries continued to have the liturgical and preaching-teaching roles of their predecessors, but administrative duties increasingly infringed on pastoral work, although the great bishops remained closely involved with the lives of their people. As Augustine said, a bishop is "servant of the servants of God" (*Ep.* 217), a phrase that became a papal title with Gregory the Great (*Ep.* 1.1, 36; 6.51; 13.1).

The bishops gave an organizational strength and institutional stability to the church that made it a formidable power in the Roman empire. *See also* Apostolic Succession; Chorepiscopus; Councils; Election to Church

Office; Ministry; Ordination; Papacy; Patriarchs; Presbyter; Priesthood. [E.F.]

Bibliography

Ambrose, *On the Duties of the Clergy*; Gregory of Nazianzus, *Oration 2*; John Chrysostom, *On Priesthood*; Gregory I the Great, *Pastoral Rule*.

E. Hatch, *The Organization of the Early Christian Churches* (London: Rivingtons, 1888); C. Gore, *The Church and the Ministry*, rev. C.H. Turner (London: SPCK, 1936); G. Dix, "Ministry in the Early Church," *The Apostolic Ministry*, ed. K.E. Kirk (London: Hodder and Stoughton, 1946), pp. 185–303; J. Colson, *L'Evêque dans les communautés primitives* (Paris: Cerf, 1951); H.W. Beyer and H. Karpp, "Bischof," RLAC (1954), Vol. 2, pp. 394–407; W. Telfer, *The Office of a Bishop* (London: Darton, Longman and Todd, 1962); Y. Congar and B.-D. Dupuy, eds., *L'Episcopat et l'église universelle* (Paris: Cerf, 1962); J. Colson, *L'Episcopat catholique: collégialité et primauté dans les trois premiers siècles de l'église* (Paris: Cerf, 1963); E. Ferguson, "Church Order in the Sub-Apostolic Period: A Survey of Interpretations," *Restoration Quarterly* 11 (1968):225–248; R.E. Brown, *Priest and Bishop: Biblical Reflections* (Paramus: Paulist, 1970); W. Rordorf, "L'Ordination de l'évêque selon la Tradition Apostolique d'Hippolyte de Rome," *Questions liturgiques* 2–3 (1974):137–150; E. Dassman, "Zur Entstehung des Monepiskopats," *JAC* 17 (1974):74–90; E.G. Jay, "From Presbyter-Bishops to Bishops and Presbyters," *SCent* 1 (1981):125–162; A. Cunningham, *The Bishop in the Church: Patristic Texts on the Role of the Episkopos* (Wilmington: Glazier, 1985).

BLANDINA

BLANDINA (d. 177). Martyr of Lyons. Blandina, a female slave, was among the Christians whose martyrdom was narrated in the *Letter of the Churches of Lyons and Vienne* (Eusebius, *H.E.* 5.1.1–5.28). Although weak in body, she endured tortures that left her tormentors weary and encouraged other Christians to steadfastness. When she was hung on a post as bait for the wild animals, her fellow believers professed to see in her "him who was crucified for them." After being subjected to scourges, wild animals, and the hot griddle, she was tied in a net and killed by a bull. Feast day June 2 (west), July 25 (east). [E.F.]

Bibliography

Eusebius, *Church History* 5.1.17–19, 37, 41–42, 53–56.

BODY

BODY. The Greeks first used the term *sōma* ("body") to designate the dead body. The body in Greek thought was sharply distinguished from the life-giving breath or what the philosophers would later call "soul." The body for the Greeks was coextensive with physical existence, but the self was identified with the soul. Body also became a symbol of totality. The body as a totality of integrated and organized functions was governed and directed by the soul. This relation of body and soul provided a potent political symbol for the city-state, in which the rulers governed the body politic just as the soul governs the body.

As Plato elaborated these notions of body and soul, he evolved a dualism in which body was temporal, corporeal, and changeable and soul was eternal, incorporeal, and unchangeable. Thus, the soul had a kinship with the divine realm and the body was alien to it. Christian theology depended heavily on the categories of Greek philosophy and so had to struggle to articulate the importance of body in the doctrines of the incarnation and a bodily resurrection.

Jewish and Biblical Usage. In early Jewish thought, there was an organic unity of the self, and bodily life was coextensive with spiritual life. As intertestamental Judaism adopted the Greek language, the body-soul dichotomy was also adopted, but even then the idea of the original unity persisted, for body and soul together come to judgment and to resurrection. In Philo's thought, the body is strongly identified with the individual. The body represents the totality of the individual and is also characterized by its active participation and partnership with the soul. What renders suicide so reprehensible, according to Josephus, is that it severs that friendship between body and soul.

The Hebrew idea of the self as equated with bodily life shapes the New Testament teaching on resurrection. In Paul's thinking on the resurrected life, it is the body-self that is the subject, the "I." Resurrection life must be bodily life; the earthly body is transformed into a resurrected body. This contrasts with the Greek equation of the self with the soul as an incorporeal dimension of the self.

Paul, however, turns to a Greek motif in his use of the body as a metaphor for the Christian community. The church body represents the totality of functions over which Christ like the soul governs, directs, and rules. The body functions as a metaphor for community both because it is a metaphor for totality and because it can express that totality in terms of boundaries designating inside and outside. It is important to guard the integrity and the boundaries of the community by expelling the unworthy or the unclean. As the physical body is capable of pollution through sexual sin (i.e., incest and fornication), so the political body of the Christian community is capable of pollution. The pollution of the community can be neutralized by expelling the sinful member.

Second and Third Centuries. Although there is a diversity of views on the body among Gnostic writings, the body is always created by inferior deities, by either the archons, the angels, or the demiurge. The body functions as an instrument of the soul and mind, yet it is not itself the subject of salvation. Gnostic systems see salvation as deliverance from the body.

Irenaeus of Lyons, who took up the polemic against the Gnostic version of Christianity, affirms that the body was created by the one God the Father and that soul and body are together both in the image of God and both are the subject of salvation. The work of salvation, according to Irenaeus, requires that Christ the Logos take on full humanity, body and soul. The body was essential to salvation because it was the body that made it possible for Christ to undergo the suffering and the death inherent in human nature.

In the thought of Origen, the body was not a cause of sin; rather, it was created as a remedy for sin. Sin first occurred among incorporeal beings created before the existence of the material world. After their falling away, God created bodies and placed these souls into them to make them conscious of the distance of their fall from God.

In the ongoing controversy with the pagans, and specifically with pagan philosophers, Christian intellectuals like Origen found themselves having to defend the resurrection of the body. Christian theologians did find themselves in agreement with the philosophers on the notion that God had no body and that the divine was not embodied. (The Christian critique of polytheism found the philosophical notion of God very useful.) If God was without a body, however, then the Christian teachings on the resurrection of the body, implying that the self united with God was a bodily self, sounded absurd and ridiculous to the philosophers. Christian intellectuals like Origen affirmed the church's teaching on the resurrection of the body but attempted to describe the resurrected body as an immaterial one.

Athanasius, Ascetics, and Augustine. In Athanasius, the body of Christ is central to the two aspects of Christ's saving work. First, the body of Christ makes visible the invisible God and so makes God knowable. The visibility of the body of Christ restores the dim and darkened memory of the image of God through making the invisible God tangible, visible, and comprehensible. Second, since only the body can be subject to death, assuming a body is essential to the work of Christ. By joining himself to the body of death and surrendering himself to the death of the body, the immortality of the Logos conquers death in the body and restores the possibility of immortality and incorruptibility to humanity.

For the theologians of the ascetic movement, the incorporeal God was known through the contemplative activity of the mind. The body, because of its corporeality, could not be a vehicle for the knowledge of the incorporeal God and therefore acted as a weight on the mind as it sought to lose itself in the contemplation of God. The monastic disciplines of fasting, vigils, solitude, prayer, and exposure were designed to silence the clamor of the body so that the mind might ascend unimpeded to the contemplation of God. On the other hand, the body of the ascetic was an important symbol for the church of the presence of God. The bodily remains of martyrs and ascetics were reverently gathered and preserved; liturgical celebrations were held in the presence of their tombs on the anniversaries of their deaths; and eventually the bones of the martyrs and ascetics were placed under the altars of basilicas because of the sacred presence they bore.

Augustine rejected the idea that the opposition within the self came from a conflict between the desires of the body and the desires of the soul. Rather, he envisioned a unitary view of the human person in which all impulses originate in the soul or mind. The experience of internal conflict, according to Augustine, arises out of opposing tendencies in the mind rather than an opposition between mind and body. The original pre-fall unity of the self rested on the soul's total contemplation of the eternal truths. In Augustine's notion of the fall, the mind shifted from contemplation of the eternal truths to preoccupation with its own dominion and with the material world. The result of this shift is that the soul was no longer able to maintain the original harmony and unity of the body and soul operating together. Salvation in Christ restores this unity. See also Asceticism; Resurrection; Sexuality; Soul.   [K.J.T.]

Bibliography

Irenaeus, *Against Heresies*, tr. W.H. Rambaut, ANF (1885), Vol. 1; Tertullian, *On the Flesh of Christ*; idem, *The Resurrection of the Flesh*, tr. P. Holmes, ANF (1887), Vol. 3, pp. 163–214, 215–232; idem, *Exhortation to Chastity*, tr. S. Thelwall, ANF (1885), Vol. 4, pp. 1–20; Gregory of Nyssa, *On the Creation of Man*, tr. H.A. Wilson, NPNF, 2nd ser. (1893), Vol. 5, pp. 387–427; idem, *On Virginity*, tr. W. Moore, NPNF, 2nd ser. (1893), Vol. 5, pp. 343–371; Basil of Ancyra, *De virginitate*, PG 30.669–809; Ambrose, *De virginitate*, PL 16.279–316; Augustine, *On the Literal Meaning of Genesis*, tr. J.H. Taylor, ACW (1982), Vol. 41.

H. Chadwick, "Origen, Celsus and the Resurrection of the Body," *HThR* 41 (1948):83–102; E. Schweizer, "*Sōma*," *Theological Dictionary of the New Testament*, ed. G. Friedrich (Grand Rapids: Eerdmans, 1967), Vol. 7, pp. 1024–1094; R.H. Gundry, "*Sōma*" *in Biblical Theology* (Cambridge: Cambridge UP, 1976); M. Miles, *Augustine on the Body* (Missoula: Scholars, 1979); K.E. Børresen, "L'Anthropologie théologique d'Augustin et de Thomas d'Aquin: la typologie homme-femme dans la tradition et dans l'église d'aujourd'hui," *RecSR* 69 (1981):393–407; T.J. Dennis, "Gregory on the Resurrection of the Body," *The Easter Sermons of Gregory of Nyssa*, ed. A. Spira and C. Klock (Cambridge: Philadelphia Patristic Foundation, 1981), pp. 55–80; R. van den Broek, "The Creation of Adam's Psychic Body in the Apocryphon of John," *Studies in Gnosticism and Hellenistic Religion*, ed. R. van den Broek (Leiden: Brill, 1981), pp. 38–57; C. Blanc, "L'Attitude d'Origène à l'égard du corps et de la chair," *SP* 17.2 (1982):843–858; J. Gager, "Body-Symbols and Social Reality: Resurrection, Incarnation and Asceticism in Early Christianity," *Religion* 12 (1982):345–363; J.P. Burns, "Variations on a Dualist Theme: Augustine on the Body and Soul," *Interpreting Tradition*, ed. J. Kopas (Atlanta: Scholars, 1984), pp. 13–26; J. Fossum, "Genesis 1:26 and 2:7 in Judaism, Samaritanism and Gnosticism," *Journal for the Study of Judaism* 16 (1985):202–239; P. Brown, *The Body and Society: Men, Women, and Sexual Renunciation in Early Christianity* (New York: Columbia UP, 1988).

BOETHIUS (ca. 480–524/6). Statesman and philosopher. Anicius Manlius Severinus Boethius, born into a noble Roman family, was a cultured Christian well educated in and influenced by Neoplatonism, Aristotelianism, and Stoicism. His translation of Plato and Aristotle into Latin, intended to show the substantial identity of their thought, was left incomplete when he entered the service of the Ostrogothic rulers in Italy, becoming consul under Theodoric in 510 and master of the offices in 522. Accused of treasonable relations with Constantinople and unfairly condemned, he was imprisoned at Pavia (ancient Ticinum) and executed there between 524 and 526.

Boethius's writings—treatises on the *quadrivium*; grammatical, philosophical, and theological works; the *Consolation of Philosophy*—had an abiding influence. His translations of and commentaries on Porphyry's *Isagoge* and Aristotle's *Categories* and *On Interpretation*, along with his own logical treatises, formed the "old logic" (*logica vetus*) for generations of scholars. Boethius also raised for later thinkers the problem of universals, or the reality of general concepts. His methodological views provided for a certain autonomy of the sciences within sacred doctrine: for him, practical philosophy embraces ethics, politics, and economics, while speculative philosophy includes natural philosophy (the study of bodies in matter), mathematics (the study of forms abstracted from bodies and motion), and theology (the study of forms without matter and motion; e.g., God, angels, souls).

Although it had been doubted whether Boethius was a Christian, a text of Cassiodorus was found that affirmed his authorship of five theological opuscules (*opuscula sacra*), written between 512 and 520, which clearly show his Christian faith. *On the Catholic Faith*, whose authenticity, often questioned, is again being asserted, is likely the earliest of these. It is a simple presentation of what is to be believed on authority by contrast with what reason can grasp and elucidate. In the other four opuscules, Greek Neoplatonism and Aristotelianism serve Boethius's theology. Two opuscules on the Trinity use new vocabulary to restate the basically Augustinian doctrine of substance and relation. Boethius holds that every created subject (called *quod est*) is composed with various forms conferring being (*esse*) on it in various essentialist (not existential) ways. Individuals become such by their unique variety of collected accidents or properties. God, utterly simple, has no composition of subject and forms: the divine substance is pure form and absolutely one. Another opuscule, later called *De hebdomadibus*, concludes that the being of all existing things is good because God, who gave them being, is good. The fifth, *Against Eutyches and Nestorius*, transmits several definitions of "nature" and develops an influential definition of "person" ("individual substance of a rational nature") to show that Catholic doctrine on Christ is a mean between Monophysitism and Nestorianism.

In the *Consolation of Philosophy*, widely read in the Latin original and in later vernacular translations, Lady Philosophy comes to console Boethius in prison. Responding to his doubts about divine Providence, she shows the inconstancy of Fortune: no worldly desires can satisfy anyone. Although there is a natural desire for beatitude in all, true beatitude, which is "a state made perfect by the gathering together of all goods," can be found only in God. If evil seems to triumph, order will be restored in the next life according to personal deserts. God's knowledge of our future free acts (the source of merit) in no way impedes their freedom, since God is present to all our time by his eternity—eternity being "the total, perfect, and simultaneous possession of everlasting life." The *Consolation* contains no explicit mention of Christian mysteries and so has provoked various hypotheses about Boethius's Christianity and the nature of the work, but its doctrine is in fundamental accord with Christian faith and seems to imply it by its strong Augustinian background and by its subtle biblical and perhaps liturgical allusions.

Because Theodoric was an adherent of Arianism, Boethius's execution was later regarded as a martyrdom, and he has been venerated under the name "St. Severinus" in Pavia and elsewhere in northern Italy. CPL 878–894.

[W.H.P.]

Bibliography
The Theological Tractates, 2nd ed., E.K. Rand, tr. H.F. Stewart and E.K. Rand, LCL (1973); *Philosophiae Consolatio*, ed. L. Bieler, CCSL (1957), Vol. 94; for other editions, see CPL, to which add: *Boethius: De hypotheticis syllogismis*, ed. L. Obertello (Brescia: Paideia, 1969).

The Consolation of Philosophy, tr. W.V. Cooper (New York: Modern Library, 1943); tr. V.E. Watts (Harmondsworth: Penguin, 1969) tr. S.J. Tester, LCL (1973); *De topicis differentiis*, tr. E. Stump (Ithaca: Cornell UP, 1978).

L. Obertello, *Severino Boezio* (Genoa: Accademia Ligure di Scienze e Lettere, 1974), Vol. 1 (bibliography on Boethius); Vol. 2 (bibliography on his background and influence); J. Gruber, *Kommentar zu Boethius De consolatione Philosophiae* (Berlin: de Gruyter, 1978); H. Chadwick, *Boethius: The Consolations of Music, Logic, Theology, and Philosophy* (Oxford: Clarendon, 1981); M. Gibson, ed., *Boethius: His Life, Thought and Influence* (Oxford: Blackwell, 1981); L. Obertello, ed., *Atti del Congresso Internazionale di Studi Boeziani* (Rome: Herder, 1981); M. Fuhrmann and J. Gruber, eds., *Boethius* (Darmstadt: Wissenschaftliche Buchgesellschaft, 1984).

BOLLANDUS, JOHN, S.J. (1596–1665). Founder of the Bollandists and first editor of the *Acta Sanctorum*. A plan for the publication of critical editions of saints' lives available in the libraries of Belgium was conceived by Heribert Rosweyde (1569–1629), who, however, did not live to see its fulfillment. John Bollandus (Jean Bolland, John van Bolland), commissioned by his religious superiors to examine the material that Rosweyde had gathered, expanded the original design to include all saints known in the calendars, whether accounts of their lives were extant or not. A small group of Jesuits (never more than six, often fewer) was eventually organized to carry on the work. These Bollandists, as they are called, are chosen from a territory that corresponds approximately to modern Belgium and have their headquarters in Brussels.

The first two volumes of the projected series in hagiography, comprising the month of January, were published at Antwerp (1643) under the title *Acta Sanctorum*. Prominent among the early Bollandists were Godefroid (Gottfried) Henschenius (Henschens) (1601–1681), the first to be associated with Bollandus in the project, and Daniel Papebroch (van Papenbroek) (1628–1714), who was compelled to defend the Bollandists' work against the displeasure of the Carmelite order and attacks by the Spanish Inquisition. By the time of the suppression of the Jesuits (1773), fifty volumes of the *Acta Sanctorum* (through October 7) had appeared. Three additional volumes, prepared by former Jesuits and others, were issued shortly thereafter (1780, 1786, 1794). With the invasion of French revolutionary forces (1794), all work ceased and the library was dispersed with the loss of many manuscripts.

The modern history of the Bollandists begins with their reinstitution in 1837 and the resumption of the publication of the *Acta Sanctorum* in 1847. The *Acta* currently extends in sixty-seven volumes through November 10 (with an introductory volume to December), leaving fifty-one days to be covered, but in recent years the Bollandists have concentrated their efforts on other publications. The quarterly journal *Analecta Bollandiana* (*AB*: from 1882) publishes research articles, texts, commentaries, and manuscript catalogues, together with an up-to-date bibliography, *Bulletin de publications hagiographiques* (1891–). The series *Subsidia Hagiographica* (1886–) is designed for publication of catalogues of manuscripts, and of printed texts, commentaries, and studies, of a size and scope that exceeds the limits of the *Analecta Bollandiana*. The sources of saints' lives may be controlled through the

Bibliotheca Hagiographica Graeca (*BHG*), *Bibliotheca Hagiographica Latina* (*BHL*), and *Bibliographica Hagiographica Orientalis* (*BHO*), works of the late nineteenth or early twentieth centuries that are updated through supplements, new editions, and publications in the *Analecta Bollandiana*.   [M.P.McH.]

Bibliography
D. Knowles, "Great Historical Enterprises: The Bollandists," *Transactions of the Royal Historical Society* 8 (1958):147–166; repr. in *Great Historical Enterprises* (London: Nelson, 1963), pp. 3–32 (with bibliography); B. de Gaffier, "Les Bollandistes et les légendes hagiographiques," *Classica et Iberica: Festschrift Marique*, ed. P.T. Brannan (Worcester: Institute for Early Christian Iberian Studies, 1975), pp. 261–271; L.J. Swift, "The Bollandists," *Encyclopedia of Library and Information Science* (New York and Basel: Dekker, 1985), Vol. 38, supp. 3, pp. 37–53 (with bibliography).

BONIFACE I. Bishop of Rome (418–422). When his election to the Roman see was contested by the archdeacon Eulalius, Boniface received the support of the emperor Honorius. He upheld Augustine in the controversy with Pelagius, sustained the rights of the metropolitan bishops in Gaul, and defended the claim of Rome to immediate jurisdiction over Illyricum in opposition to Theodosius II. Several of his letters are extant. CPL 1648–1649.

[M.P.McH.]

Bibliography
Liber Pontificalis 44 (Duchesne 1.227–229).

BONIFACE II. Bishop of Rome (530–532). Boniface was designated by Felix III (IV) as his successor, but the Roman clergy elected Dioscorus, a deacon of Alexandria, who died shortly thereafter. Boniface in turn proposed that the pope have the right to choose his successor, and designated Vigilius, but subsequently rescinded the arrangement. He upheld the jurisdiction of Rome over Illyricum and, in his only extant work, a letter addressed to Caesarius of Arles, confirmed the acts of the second of the Councils of Orange against Pelagianism. CPL 1691.   [M.P.McH.]

Bibliography
Liber Pontificalis 57 (Duchesne 1.281–284).

BORDEAUX PILGRIM (333). Early Christian pilgrim from the west to Palestine. The Bordeaux Pilgrim, otherwise unidentified, traveled from Bordeaux to Jerusalem and, after a stay of several months in Palestine, returned by way of Milan, at which city his account concludes. His report, *Itinerarium Burdigalense*, lists the relay posts (*mutationes*) and hostels (*mansiones*) on the route and offers short descriptions of some monuments along with biblical reminiscences. It combines elements of the itineraries in use in the Roman army and postal service with those of an itinerary to the holy places having antecedents in earliest Christianity. CPL 2324. *See also* Pilgrimage.

[M.P.McH.]

Bibliography

P. Geyer and O. Cuntz, eds., *Itinerarium Burdigalense*, CCSL (1965), Vol. 175, pp. v–xiii, 1–26.

A. Stewart, tr., *Itinerary from Bordeaux to Jerusalem* (London: Palestine Pilgrims Text Society, 1887).

P.M. Duval, *La Gaule jusqu'au milieu du Ve siècle* (Paris: Picard, 1971), Vol. 1, pp. 558–560; C. Milani, "Strutture formulari nell' *Itinerarium Burdigalense* (a.333)," *Aevum* 57 (1983):99–108.

BREAD. The words for bread in Greek (*artos*) and Latin (*panis*) referred to the basic food of the ancient world. They naturally continued in Christian usage often to have simply the basic meaning of a loaf of bread. The petition of the Lord's prayer, "Give us this day our daily bread" (Matt. 6:11), perhaps originally associated with the messianic banquet (Matt. 8:11; Luke 13:29), was understood by some as literal food (Gregory of Nyssa, *Or. dom.* 4) but by others as spiritual nourishment (Origen, *Or.* 27). Bread often stood for all bodily nourishment (*1 Clem.* 34.1; Origen, *Or.* 27).

The distinctively Christian references to bread had to do with the eucharist. "Breaking bread" was among the earliest designations of the ceremony (Acts 2:42; *Did.* 14.1; Ignatius, *Eph.* 20.2). Ordinary bread was no longer considered ordinary (Justin, *1 Apol.* 66; Irenaeus, *Haer.* 4.18.5) after receiving the divine invocation. Fourth-century writers expressly stated that the bread was changed into the body of Jesus, either by calling on the Holy Spirit (Gregory of Nyssa, *Bapt. Chr.*; Theodore of Mopsuestia, *Cat.* 15.12) or by reciting the words of institution by Jesus (Ambrose, *Sacram.* 5.4.24). The eucharistic bread demonstrated the reality of the incarnation (Tertullian, *Marc.* 5.8.3) and passion of Christ (Ignatius, *Smyrn.* 7) and conferred immortality (Irenaeus, *Haer.* 4.18.5; Cyril of Alexandria, *Ador.* 3). The one bread was also expressive of the unity of the church (1 Cor. 10:17; *Did.* 9.4; Cyprian, *Ep.* 69.6).

Bread stamp (fourth century) with Chi-Rho monogram for the name of Christ in reverse (so as to print positive) from Eisenberg, now in Speyer Museum, West Germany.

Several Old Testament events were seen as prefiguring the eucharist. Encouraged by the comparison in John 6:30ff. of Jesus with the manna from heaven (Exod. 16:13ff.), many connected the manna with the eucharist (Cyprian, *Ep.* 69.14; Ambrose, *Mys.* 8.47–49). The manna was the "bread of angels" (Ps. 78:25; Justin, *Dial.* 57.2); it was not produced from the earth and so was a figure of the Logos, who like it could satisfy without surfeit (Gregory of Nyssa, *V. Mos.* 2.139–143). The twelve loaves of the "bread of the Presence" placed in the tabernacle (Exod. 25:30; Lev. 24:5–9) were similarly given a reference either to the eucharist (Hippolytus, *Trad. ap.* 36 [41]; Jerome, *Tit.* 1.8–9) or to Christ himself (Eusebius, *Ps.* 33.6–8; Cyril of Jerusalem, *Catech.* 22.5).

The believers brought an offering of bread and wine to be used at the eucharist; what was not used at the eucharist was blessed and given to the clergy and others (Athanasius, *Ep. encycl.* 4; Socrates, *H.E.* 7.12.9; Paulinus of Nola, *Ep.* 3.6; 4.5). Blessed bread (*eulogia*) as distinct from the eucharistic bread was eaten at the agape and could be given to catechumens or others excluded from communion (Hippolytus, *Trad. ap.* 25–27). It was also sent to the sick (Serapion, *Euch.* 17), eaten at funerary meals, and distributed on saints' days and at pilgrim shrines.

Bread was given various metaphorical meanings. The unleavened bread of the Passover was seen as signifying abstinence from evil deeds (Justin, *Dial.* 14). After the lead of John 6:35, "I am the bread of life," bread was often seen as signifying Christ (Tertullian, *Or.* 6.2; Gregory of Nazianzus, *Or.* 14.1). Bread was also identified among other things with scripture (Augustine, *Serm.* 95.1f.), wisdom (Gregory of Nyssa, *Hom.* 5 *in Eccl.*), love (Augustine, *Serm.* 105.6), martyrdom (Ignatius, *Rom.* 4.1), and Mary (Methodius, *Sym. et Ann.* 14).

Jesus' multiplication of loaves and fish (Mark 6:35–44; 8:1–8) was one of the most popular scenes in early Christian art, often in association with the turning of water into wine at Cana (John 2:1ff.). The baskets of bread gathered up after the feeding of the multitude influenced representations of other events as

well, for the bread is shown in baskets in the meal scenes in the catacombs and the "eucharistic Victory" in the floor mosaic at Aquileia is placed between a basket of bread and a chalice. Bread stamps, dated from the fourth century on, impressed distinctively Christian symbols on both the eucharistic and *eulogia* bread.

The different customs that figured in the medieval debates between the eastern and western churches about the bread in the eucharist (leavened in the Orthodox church and unleavened in the Roman Catholic church) appear not to have been a matter of discussion in ancient Christianity. *See also* Agape; Eucharist; Fish; Laying On of Hands; Paten; Wine. [E.F.]

Bibliography

G. Galavaris, *Bread and the Liturgy* (Madison: U of Wisconsin P, 1970).

BRITAIN. *See* Great Britain.

BURGUNDY. Region of central-eastern France deriving its name from the Germanic tribe of the Burgundians. The emperor Honorius established the Burgundians around Worms in the early fifth century, but following a brutal defeat by the Huns under Attila, they were relocated near Lake Geneva. As a result, there emerged a Burgundian kingdom under the able Gundobad (474–516) that included the early Catholic centers on the Rhône River, Lyons and Vienne. Catholic Christianity asserted itself through the leadership of bishop Avitus of Vienne (480–518). A member of a distinguished Gallo-Roman senatorial family, Avitus succeeded his father as bishop.

Gundobad, an adherent of Arianism, treated his Catholic bishop with great respect, giving him important governmental assignments and extraordinary leeway to propagate Catholicism even to the point of converting his son and heir, Sigismund. As a consequence, upon Sigismund's accession in 516, the Burgundian kingdom became the first Arian Germanic kingdom in the west to be converted to Catholic Christianity. A national Burgundian synod was convened by Avitus and his fellow metropolitan Viventiolus of Lyons at Epaon in

517; the Epaon canons reflect the growth of canon law in the Gallo-Roman church as it entered the Germanic era. The catholicizing of the Burgundians did not prevent the sons of the most notable royal Germanic convert to Catholic Christianity, Clovis, from completing the Frankish conquest of Roman Gaul by defeating Sigismund (534) and, in spite of an urgent plea from bishop Avitus, murdering the last Burgundian king. The memory of an independent Catholic kingdom of Burgundy remained a poignant legacy for France throughout the Middle Ages.   [H.R.]

Bibliography
Gregory of Tours, *The History of the Franks*, tr. L. Thorpe (Harmondsworth: Penguin, 1974).

T.S. Holmes, *The Origins and Development of the Christian Church in Gaul During the First Six Centuries of the Christian Era* (London: Macmillan, 1911); A. Coville, *Recherches sur l'histoire de Lyon au V aux IX siècle (450–800)* (Paris: Picard, 1928); O. Perrin, *Les Burgondes: leur histoire, des origines à la fin du premier royaume (534)* (Neuchâtel: Baconnière, 1968); H. Rosenberg, "Bishop Avitus of Vienne (c. 493–517) and the Burgundian Kingdom," *Journal of the Rocky Mountain Medieval-Renaissance Association* 3 (1982):1–12; E. James, *The Origins of France . . . 500–1000 A.D.* (New York: St. Martin, 1982).

BURIAL. From prehistoric times, disposition of the dead was a matter of duty, reflecting religious worldview and ideas about life, purity, and social obligation. There were basically two types of disposition in the environment of early Christianity: inhumation, or the interment of the intact corpse after mortuarial preparation, and cremation, or burning of the corpse to ashes, which may then be interred or dispersed. In both practices, elaborate ritual actions were observed.

Mortuarial Customs and Religious Outlook. In Jewish tradition, as in most of the ancient Near East, inhumation was the rule, except in extreme cases, such as plague (Amos 6:10). Burial was seen as a duty of the living, an act of piety toward the deceased (Tobit 1:16–20; 2:3–8).

Handling a corpse produced ritual impurity (Tobit 2:9). Hence, not only burial itself but correct procedures to ensure purity were necessary. Talmudic literature, especially the Tanaaitic tractate *Semahoth*, prescribed numerous procedures and provisions. Some of these likely go back to a considerably earlier period, such as closing the eyes of the deceased (Gen. 46:4), washing and anointing the body (John 12:7; Acts 9:37; *m. Shabbath* 23.5), and wrapping or binding to prevent undue distortion or swelling (John 11:44; 19:40; *Semahoth* 12.10). Embalming techniques, as in Egyptian mummification, were not widely used in Jewish custom, although they are known (Gen. 50:2–3, 26) and seem to have continued into the Roman period, especially among wealthy pagans and later among Coptic Christians.

Public displays of mourning were common to signal a death in a family, and funerary processions accompanied the burial proper. In all cases, burial in Judea-Palestine was prompt (*Semahoth* 11.1) and was an occasion for gathering of family and friends. The procession included arrangements for mourners and pipers (*Semahoth* 12.5; 14.7; Matt. 9:23; Josephus, *War* 3.437). There may have been other professionals who saw to preparation of the corpse.

In contrast to the Egyptian ideal of preserving the physical form of the body, Jewish

Arcosolium-type burial spot in vaulted chamber in the Domitilla Catacomb, Rome, Italy. (Used by permission of Pontifical Commission of Sacred Archaeology.)

custom (in keeping with its climate) expected decomposition. Initially, interment might include the primary mortuarial preparations with the body laid in a carved trough in the burial chamber until such time as decomposition was complete and final interment could occur. By the rabbinic period, second burials were common and entailed gathering up the bones of the deceased, which were then deposited in a small box or coffin, called an *ossuary* (*Semahoth* 12.9; *m. Sanhedrin* 6.6; *y. Sanhedrin* 6.23d). Reburial provided not only more space in the limited confines of family tombs but also an occasion for commemoration (*Semahoth* 12.4). Although not widespread before A.D. 70, the practice of transferring the bones to their final resting place (especially to *Eretz Israel*) became more common. Burial practice and piety reflect views of afterlife in the rabbinic notion of resurrection, which involved the physical body. At the same time, the expressions "sleeping with one's fathers" or being "gathered to one's people" preserve the intimate corporate quality of Jewish views of death. Excavated cemeteries at Beth Shearim and Jerusalem bear out these attitudes and show direct relationships to early Christian archaeological evidence. An artistic representation of such notions may be reflected in the Ezekiel panel from the third-century synagogue at Dura-Europos.

Both Cicero (*Laws* 2.22.56) and Pliny the Elder (*Natural History* 7.187) attest that cremation was the ancient ideal in Rome, although Greeks and Romans widely practiced inhumation from an early period. Cremation involved a different view of death, one that assumed continued existence of the soul alone. In Greek thought, this came to be connected with Orphic and later Platonic notions of the immortality of the soul; Roman tradition held a notion of the eternal "shade" (Latin, *manes*) of the deceased (Cicero, *Pis.* 7.16; Virgil, *Aeneid* 6.743). A common form of Roman funerary inscription began with *D.M.*, a salutation "To the divine shades" (*Dis manibus*). The tomb, then, was viewed as the place of final rest for the body, often pictured in eternal sleep. Elaborate provisions were common for disposition of the remains, whether cremated or inhumed.

Such gave rise to the production of *cineraria* ("ash chests") and sarcophagi (carved coffins) for burial, while the deceased was memorialized by inscriptions and effigies. Elaborate commemorative rites associated with the cult of the dead (funerary meals and libations poured over or into tombs) enhanced cemeterial complexes. Numerous epitaphs and a burgeoning consolation literature reflect Greek and Roman views of death.

Because a corpse was considered a defilement in both Greek and Roman tradition, laws regarding burial usually required disposition outside a city or beyond sacred limits. At Rome, all burials were outside the *pomerium* of the Servian wall, usually in a "burial city" (*necropolis*) above ground or in underground burial chambers. Roman law and custom set the *funus* (funeral), covering all responsibilities from the time of death to the postburial ceremonies, and carried status gradations for private and public (especially state or imperial) burials. Prior to the funeral rite, the deceased was washed and dressed to lie in state at home or (in state funerals) in a public building. A funeral procession led by torchbearers and mourners bore the burial couch to the site. The central rite of burial included throwing dirt on the corpse, even in cases of cremation. Following the disposition was a sacrifice. Upon returning from the funeral, those involved had to perform rites of purification and return to the grave for a meal. In state and imperial funerals, the processional became the occasion for great pomp and public feasts. Professional undertakers (*libitinarii*) handled such prescriptions for the wealthy. Guilds of "gravediggers" (*fossores*) also emerged, later prominent in Christian catacombs.

Cremation remained an expensive public ceremony available to few. By the early empire, inhumation had become the more common practice. An increasing foreign population in Roman cities encouraged burial societies (*collegia funeraticia*), most with some religious affiliation. Membership ensured that one would be buried properly. Such societies, using collective means, expanded communal burial sites, as in the catacombs at Rome. Significantly, Jewish burial societies are known, and the earliest Christian communities are often likened to burial societies.

Christian Burial, Catacombs, and Cult of Martyrs. Tombs observed in the Mediterranean world vary greatly owing to geological peculiarities. Cave tombs are common in Judea; catacombs occur primarily in the environs of Rome due to the peculiar geological composition of volcanic tufa. In the first two centuries, no distinctively Christian burial forms are known. The earliest Christians, it must be assumed, observed ancestral or local customs and conditions in burial.

The first evidence of uniquely Christian concerns in burial arises in the late second century. Tertullian (ca. 197) calls burial of the poor an act of piety and charity (*Apol.* 39.5f.). Acknowledgment of a venerated burial site and annual ceremonies for a Christian martyr commence with the *Martyrdom of Polycarp* 28.3 (bishop of Smyrna, d. ca. 156). The lengthy epitaph of Abercius from Hierapolis at the beginning of the third century shows the flowering of a Christian funerary tradition, although it draws heavily on pagan forms and content. From this same period comes the first datable Christian funerary art and symbolism, largely from sculpture on sarcophagi and the inscriptions and paintings of the catacombs.

The Roman catacombs were not exclusively Christian. Private family chambers and Jewish catacombs were numerous. The catacomb at S. Sebastiano became popular for Christian burial because of a tradition that associated it with the apostles Peter and Paul. Similarly, the tradition of Peter's tomb at the Vatican (originally a pagan necropolis, not a catacomb) seems to have made it a venerated site for pilgrimage and burial by Christians. In both cases, monumental church buildings were eventually erected over the early tombs to commemorate the funerary traditions.

Most of the Christian catacombs at Rome provide for modest burials in *loculi* dug into the walls of narrow tunnels in vertical rows. The wealthy were buried in large chambers (*cubicula*) with niches (*arcosolia*) hollowed out and decorated with the elaborate painted scenes that came to characterize the Christian burial tradition. In such areas, meals for the dead (*re-*

frigeria) were continued in the Christian tradition. Christian cemeteries from the third and fourth centuries are known from Carthage and Salona.

Some privately owned tombs, according to tradition, were donated to the church. Best known is the Domitilla catacomb in Rome, which traces its name to Flavia Domitilla, the wife of Flavius Clemens. The Callistus catacomb is thought to be on land owned by Zephyrinus, the bishop of Rome (199–217), who donated it for a Christian cemetery and put it under the deacon Callistus (who became the next bishop of Rome, 217–222). One of its chambers, called the "Crypt of the Popes," was especially venerated in epitaphs of bishop Damasus I (366–384) and in the later Roman papal tradition of the *Liber Pontificalis.* Pilgrimage, inscriptions, and art all attest to the vivid beliefs regarding death and burial as a central part of Christian faith and led to further developments toward exclusively Christian cemeteries and rituals. *See also* Art; Catacombs; Fossors; Martyrdom; Resurrection; Sarcophagi. [L.M.W.]

Bibliography

A.P. Bender, "Beliefs, Rites, and Customs of the Jews Connected with Death, Burial, and Mourning," *Jewish Quarterly Review* 6 (1893–1894):317–347, 664–671; 7 (1894–1895):101–118, 259–269; A.D. Nock, "Cremation and Burial in the Roman Empire," *HThR* 25 (1932):321–359; A. Grabar, *Martyrium: recherches sur le culte des reliques et l'art chrétien antique* (Paris: Boccard, 1946–1947); E.R. Goodenough, *Jewish Symbols in the Graeco-Roman Period* (New York: Bollingen, 1953), Vol. 1, pp. 61–177; O. Cullman, *Immortality of the Soul or Resurrection of the Dead* (London: SCM, 1958); H.J. Leon, *The Jews of Ancient Rome* (Philadelphia: Jewish Publications Society of America, 1960); R. Lattimore, *Themes in Greek and Latin Epitaphs* (Urbana: U of Illinois P, 1962); E.M. Meyers, "Second Burials in Palestine," *Biblical Archaeologist* 33 (1970):2–29; idem, *Jewish Ossuaries: Reburial and Rebirth* (Rome: Biblical Institute, 1971); J.M.C. Toynbee, *Death and Burial in the Roman World* (London: Thames and Hudson, 1971); E.M. Meyers and J.F. Strange, *Archaeology, the Rabbis, and Early Christianity* (Nashville: Abingdon, 1981), pp. 92–109; K. Hopkins, *Death and Revival* (Cambridge: Cambridge UP, 1983); G.F. Snyder, *ANTE PACEM: Archaeological Evidence of Church Life Before Constantine* (Macon: Mercer UP, 1985); S. Walker, *Memorials to the Roman Dead* (London: British Museum, 1985).

C

CAECILIAN (d. ca. 345). Archdeacon and later (311) bishop of Carthage. Caecilian acted in support of his bishop Mensurius to restrain excessive zeal for martyrdom during the persecution of Diocletian (303–305). Elected bishop of Carthage upon Mensurius's death, he found the validity of his ordination questioned, since one of his consecrators, Felix of Aptunga, was accused of being among the *traditores*, those who had surrendered sacred books to the persecutors. Under the influence of Donatus, Majorinus was elected as a rival bishop. The dispute was placed before synods at Rome (313), Arles (314), and Milan (316), all of which decided in Caecilian's favor. *See also* Donatism.   [M.P.McH.]

Bibliography

Optatus, *Against the Donatists* 1.16–27, Appendix; Eusebius, *Church History* 10.5–6; Augustine, *Letters* 43.2.3–5; 88.1–5; 173.7–9; 185.1.4–2.6.

CAESAREA. Major Roman city located on the eastern Mediterranean coast about halfway between modern Haifa and Tel Aviv in Israel. Herod the Great (37–4 B.C.) built Caesarea Maritima on a spot where no city had stood before, although a small settlement called Strato's Tower (Josephus, *War* 1.408) had arisen just to the north of the site in Hellenistic times. Immediately adjacent to the remains of the crusader fort presently marking the site, archaeologists have found the northern wall and gates of Herod's city. Two round towers are included in that wall, and a third, dating also to the time of Herod, was discovered in underwater excavation of the harbor.

Herod began construction of the city in 22 B.C.; it was finished in 10 B.C. and named Caesarea in honor of Augustus Caesar. The harbor was named Sebastos (Greek for Augustus). Many Jews lived there in addition to the Greeks and Romans, and it was they who initiated the hostilities that led to the first Jewish revolt (A.D. 66–70), which ended in the destruction of the temple of Jerusalem (Josephus, *Ant.* 20.173–178; *War* 2.266–270; 284–292). Some 20,000 Caesarean Jews were slaughtered during the riots that occurred at the outbreak of the revolt (*War* 2.457). A synagogue has been found along with numerous Jewish tombstones in the city's excavation. Excavations at Caesarea have revealed occupation from Hellenistic times, ca. 300 B.C., through the Roman, Byzantine, Arabic, and Crusader periods, ending in its final destruction in the thirteenth century. The city reached its zenith under the Byzantines.

Herod built Caesarea primarily as a commercial harbor that would enable him to conduct a lucrative trade between east and west. Josephus describes his harbor as being the size of Piraeus, the seaport for Athens (*Ant.* 15.332) or even larger (*War* 1.410). Underwater excavations have recently confirmed this estimate and revealed the nature of the harbor. It had a huge semicircular breakwater, extending as much as 1,500 feet from the shore, with a sixty-foot-wide entrance on the northwest, because of prevailing southerly currents. The northern breakwater was 150 feet wide and the southern one was 200 feet wide. Limestone blocks measuring fifty feet long, ten feet wide, and nine feet high (*War* 1.411) have been found here. An extension of the harbor was unearthed about 100 yards inland from the seashore of the present harbor. Enormous vaulted warehouses were discovered along the coast southward from the harbor to the theater and have been partially excavated. Each vault measures about ninety feet in length.

Aqueducts brought water to the city. A rock-hewn tunnel two and one-half feet wide by three feet high channeled water to Mt. Carmel from a point about six miles east; from there, the water was carried about eight miles to Caesarea through clay pipes on top of the prominent arched aqueduct that is one of the city's most visible monuments. To increase the water supply, a second aqueduct was built adjacent to this one, on the seaward side. Subsequently, a low-level aqueduct was built to bring water for irrigation from the Crocodile River about six miles north of Caesarea.

In the southern part of the city, Herod built a theater that has been partially restored by the Italian expedition that excavated it. The theater, whose floor was rebuilt at least fourteen times, testifying to its considerable use, would seat about 4,500. It is the only public building in Caesarea mentioned by Josephus that has been completely excavated. Between the theater and the sea are remains of ancient construction that may have been Herod's palace. A podium that supported the temple of Augustus has been found near the seacoast, built on top of the vaulted warehouses.

A prominent feature of the site today is the hippodrome, second in size only to the Circus Maximus in Rome. Recent excavation has determined that it was built no earlier than the third century A.D. The enormous size of the structure, about 1,400 feet long and almost 300 feet wide, indicates a sizable population in the region of Caesarea during the early Byzantine period. It would seat about 30,000.

Caesarea functioned as the Roman capital of Judea for about 600 years. Roman procurators like Felix and Festus (Acts 24:2, 27) had their residences here. American excavations over the past twenty years may have found one of these, dating to the third century. Roman legions were stationed here as well, and the excavation of the theater revealed an inscription containing the name of Pontius Pilate. An inscription on the seaward side of the high-level aqueduct mentions the Tenth Fretensis Legion. A Roman centurion named Cornelius was stationed here, who became the first non-Jewish convert to the Christian faith under the preaching of Simon Peter (Acts 10:1–11:11).

Caesarea is first mentioned in the New Testament as the place where Philip the evangelist preached (Acts 8:40; 21:8). Paul visited the city (Acts 9:30; 18:22; 21:8) and eventually spent two years there in prison (Acts 23:23; 24:27), appearing before Felix (Acts 23:24), Festus (Acts 25:6), and Agrippa II (Acts 25:23). In the second century, bishop Theophilus of Caesarea presided over a council of bishops in Palestine concerning the Pasch (Eusebius, *H.E.* 5.24.3). In the third century (231), Origen settled in Caesarea after being befriended by its bishop Theoctistus (Eusebius, *H.E.* 6.19.17; 6.27; other bishops mentioned in 7.14). In the fourth century (316), Eusebius, the noted church historian, was made bishop of Caesarea. The Council of Nicaea (325) recognized Caesarea as the metropolitan see of Palestine (*can.* 7), but the Council of Chalcedon (451) subordinated it to Jerusalem (session 7). The great library of Caesarea probably functioned until the Arabs devastated the city in 640. This conquest was responsible for the destruction of a public building, perhaps a praetorium, whose floor contains two mosaic inscriptions of Ro-

mans 13:3, which were excavated in 1972. The inscriptions probably date to the third century.
[J.McR.]

Bibliography

A. Negev, *Caesarea* (Tel Aviv: Lewin-Epstein, 1967); L.I. Levine, *Caesarea Under Roman Rule* (Leiden: Brill, 1975); C. Fritch, ed., *The Joint Expedition to Caesarea Maritima* (Missoula: Scholars, 1975), Vol. 1; R.J. Bull, "Caesarea," *Interpreter's Dictionary of the Bible, Supplementary Volume* (Nashville: Abingdon, 1976), p. 120; R. Hohlfelder et al., "Sebastos, Herod's Harbor at Caesarea Maritima," *Biblical Archaeologist* 46 (1983):133–143; K. Holum et al., *King Herod's Dream: Caesarea on the Sea* (New York: Norton, 1988).

CAESARIUS OF ARLES (469/70–542).

Bishop, abbot, and writer. The facts of Caesarius's life are known principally from the *Vita* written shortly after his death by five churchmen of his acquaintance. Born into a wealthy Gallo-Roman family in Châlon-sur-Saône, he entered the local clergy in his eighteenth year. Two years later, he departed for Lérins, where he remained for several years as a monk until illness forced him to Arles to recover. There, he studied with the rhetorician Julianus Pomerius and was ordained first a deacon and then a priest by bishop Aeonius. In 499, Caesarius was named abbot of a monastery in the suburbs of Arles, where he remained until chosen bishop of Arles in 502.

Caesarius was one of the most important figures in the sixth-century Gallic church, less for his theological achievements than for his efforts as a pastor to promote a Christian system of values, practices, and beliefs among his people. He was particularly well known for the women's monastery that he founded in Arles and for the rule that he composed for it; for the several regional councils over which he presided, including those of Agde (506) and Orange (529); and most of all for the sermons that he regularly delivered, "suitable to different festivals and places but also against the evils of drunkenness and lust, discord and hatred, wrath and pride . . . and other vices" (*Vita* 1.55).

These *Sermons*—now numbering almost 250—are Caesarius's most important writings,

and include both original compositions and revisions of other patristic sermons, especially those of Augustine. Their clarity, simplicity, and vigor gave them a wide circulation in his own time and throughout the Middle Ages. Caesarius's other writings include the *Regula monachorum*, two *Epistulae*, the *Testamentum*, and the *Rule for Nuns*, which had a measurable influence on later Gallic rules. Four theological treatises have also been plausibly attributed to Caesarius by Dom Morin (*Opusculum de gratia, Libellus de mysterio sanctae Trinitatis, Breviarium adversus haereticos, Expositio in Apocalypsim*), but their authenticity has not been universally accepted. Feast day August 27. CPL 1008–1019a. *See also* Arles; Orange, Councils of. [W.K.]

Bibliography

G. Morin, ed., *Sancti Caesarii episcopi Arelatensis Opera omnia nunc primum in unum collecta*, 2 vols. (Maredsous, 1937–1942); Vol. 1 contains the sermons, which have been repr. in CCSL (1953), Vols. 103–104, and Vol. 2 contains Caesarius's other works, as well as the *Vita Caesarii*, which is also available (with helpful notes) in B. Krusch, ed., *Scriptores rerum Merovingicarum*, MGH (Hannover: Hahn, 1896), Vol. 3, pp. 433–501.

M.M. Mueller, *Caesarius of Arles: Sermons*, 3 vols., FOTC (1956–1973), Vols. 31, 47, and 66; M.C. McCarthy, *The Rule for Nuns of St. Caesarius of Arles* (Washington, D.C.: Catholic U of America P, 1960); extensive selections from Book 1 of the *Vita Caesarii* are translated in J.N. Hillgarth, *Christianity and Paganism, 350–750: The Conversion of Western Europe* (Philadelphia: U of Pennsylvania P, 1986).

A. Malnory, *Saint Césaire, évêque d'Arles* (Paris: Bouillon, 1894); A. d'Alès, "Les Sermones de saint Césaire d'Arles," *RSR* 28 (1938):315–384; G. Bardy, "La Prédication de saint Césaire d'Arles," *Revue d'histoire de l'église de France* 29 (1943):201–236; idem, "L'Attitude politique de saint Césaire d'Arles," *Revue d'histoire de l'église de France* 33 (1947):241–256; M. Dorenkemper, *The Trinitarian Doctrine and Sources of St. Caesarius of Arles* (Fribourg: Fribourg UP, 1953); G. Terraneo, "Saggio bibliografico su Cesario vescovo di Arles," *La scuola cattolica* 91 (1963), Suppl. bibliog.:272–294; G. Langgärtner, "Der Apokalypse-Kommentar des Caesarius von Arles," *Theologie und Glaube* 57 (1967):210–225; P. Christophe, *Cassien et Césaire prédicateurs de la morale monastique* (Gembloux: Duculot, 1969); W.M. Daly, "Caesarius of Arles: A Precursor of Medieval Christendom," *Traditio* 26 (1970):1–28; A. de Vogüé, "La Règle de Césaire d'Arles pour les moines: un résumé de sa Régle pour les moniales," *Revue d'histoire de la spiritualité* 47 (1971):369–406; J. Courreau, "L'Exégèse allegorique de saint Césaire d'Arles," *BLE* 78 (1977):181–206, 241–268; W. Klingshirn, "Charity and Power: Caesarius of Arles and the Ransoming of Captives in Sub-Roman Gaul," *JRS* 75 (1985):183–203.

CAINITES. Gnostic sect. According to Irenaeus (*Haer.* 1.31.1–2), the Cainites associated Cain (as well as such figures as Esau, the tribe of Korah, and the Sodomites) with "the superior power"; attributed to Judas "the mystery of the betrayal," since he alone of all the apostles knew the truth; created such writings as the *Gospel of Judas*; attributed creation to *Hystera* (Womb); and maintained a soteriology that necessitated what Irenaeus viewed as licentious conduct. Similar features appear in the account of Pseudo-Tertullian (*Adv. omn. haer.* 7), where Abel is regarded as produced by an inferior power. Some Cainites claimed Judas as a benefactor to whom thanks should be offered rather than to Christ; others argued that since the suffering of Christ brought about salvation for humankind and was opposed by the powers of this world, Judas facilitated Christ's passion. From Tertullian (*Bapt.* 1.17), we learn that at least one woman occupied a position of leadership in a Cainite group.

The most extensive account of the Cainites is provided by Epiphanius (*Haer.* 38). It is in basic agreement with the accounts of Irenaeus and Pseudo-Tertullian and is probably dependent on them. The maker of this world, called Womb, is regarded as inferior to a higher power, called Wisdom. In *Panarion* 38.2.4, Epiphanius asserts his knowledge of their books, among which is an *Ascension of Paul* (cf. 2 Cor. 12:2–4). The bulk of Epiphanius's account is given over to a scriptural refutation of the Cainites' veneration of Judas.

There are some similarities between the Cainites and other groups described in the patristic accounts. Both Pseudo-Tertullian and Epiphanius continue their refutation by describing the Sethians. Epiphanius asserts that, like the Cainites, the Sethians believed humanity to be descended from primordial men, Cain and Abel. The higher power, called Mother, discovering that Abel had been killed, put her power in Seth and his race. Christ is a type of Seth and venerated by Sethians. The remainder of Epiphanius's account of the Sethians is probably based on first-hand information.

The publication of original Gnostic documents from Nag Hammadi supplements and corrects patristic accounts. Adulation of the Sodomites is also found in the *Paraphrase of Shem* (29,12–29), as is the personification of Womb (*Para. Shem.* 4,10–24; *Apocryphon of John* 5, 5; *Prayer of Thanksgiving* 64, 25–30). Included in the Nag Hammadi corpus is an *Apocalypse of Paul* loosely based on 2 Cor. 12:2–4 but more firmly connected with the genre of ascension (cf. the *Ascension of Isaiah*). An account of Cain and Abel as children of opposing powers is also found in *Origin of the World* (116, 33–117, 18). None of these Gnostic documents associates these teachings with the Cainites. What is most problematic about Irenaeus, and the more detailed account of Epiphanius, is the intimation of Gnostic licentiousness. Although the church fathers may have feared the libertine implications of Gnosticism, the writings at Nag Hammadi suggest that libertine Gnostics were a minority. *See also* Gnosticism. [D.G.]

Bibliography

Irenaeus, *Against Heresies* 1.31.1–2; Pseudo-Tertullian, *Against All Heresies* 7; Tertullian, *On Baptism* 1; Epiphanius, *Panarion* 38.

K. Rudolph, *Gnosis* (San Francisco: Harper and Row, 1985), pp. 17, 256–257; G. MacRae, *Studies in the New Testament and Gnosticism* (Wilmington: Glazier, 1987).

CALLISTUS I. Bishop of Rome (ca. 217–ca. 222). According to Hippolytus's polemical account, Callistus was a slave of Carpophorus entrusted with management of money. Sent to the mines in Sardinia as punishment for his Christian beliefs, he was released by the intervention of Marcia, the companion of emperor Commodus. Bishop Victor I gave him a pension for his suffering. Under bishop Zephyrinus (ca. 202), he was put in charge of the cemetery on the Appian Way, the first public Christian burial place, since called the catacomb of "San Callisto."

Callistus succeeded Zephyrinus as bishop of Rome ca. 217 and was attacked by his defeated rival, Hippolytus, on theological and moral charges. In his effort to find a middle theological course in Rome between Sabellius's Modalism and Hippolytus's Logos theology, Callistus may have taught a form of Monarchianism. He defended the unity of the Trinity by referring to one spirit, although he condemned Sabellius after becoming bishop. His alleged laxity is also questionable. He did allow ordination of remarried persons, objected to the deposition of bishops who had committed serious sins, and allowed marriage between persons of unequal social rank. An edict on forgiveness has sometimes been attributed to him (Tertullian, *Pud.* 1.6), but this is contested by modern scholars. He died a violent death—perhaps in a riot—ca. 222 and was the only bishop, apart from Peter, in the *Depositio martyrum*, the early Roman martyrology. His tomb, decorated with paintings of his supposed martyrdom, was discovered in 1960 in the cemetery of Calepodius on the Aurelian Way.[R.L.]

Bibliography

Hippolytus, *Refutation of All Heresies* 9.12; *Liber Pontificalis* 17 (Duchesne 1.141–142).

G.L. Prestige, *Fathers and Heretics* (London: SPCK, 1940), pp. 49–87; C.B. Daly, "The 'Edict of Callistus,'" *SP* 3 (1961):176–182; H. Gülzow, "Kallist von Rom, ein Beitrag zur Soziologie der römischen Gemeinde," *ZNTW* 58 (1967):102–121.

CANON (of scripture). Books of the Bible. The term "canon" (Greek *kanōn*, Hebrew *kaneh*) referred originally to a rule or measuring rod but in time came to be used of standards, precedents, and guidelines, whether for building a house, writing music, prose, or poetry, or, in the case of the early church, setting forth the essentials of Christian preaching, as in the *Regula fidei*. From the fourth century, the term was also regularly used by the church when referring to its collection of sacred writings, or scriptures.

The Old Testament Canon. The scriptures of the earliest Christian community were the Old Testament canon, still in process of final definition. The imprecise boundaries of the Old Testament canon for the early church are illustrated by the frequent references or allusions in the New Testament to the apocryphal and pseudepigraphal literature; the best-known example is Jude's appeal to *1 Enoch* 1.9 in Jude 14. The Jewish tripartite canon—i.e., the Law (Hebrew *torah*), Prophets (Hebrew *nebi'im*), and Writings (Hebrew *ketubim*, Greek *hagiographa*)—is not regularly cited in the New Testament. For the most part, only the Law and the Prophets are referred to (e.g., Matt. 5:17; Luke 24:27; Acts 28:23), although Luke 24:44 does refer to the Psalms as the third part of the Jewish scriptures. When Christianity moved away from the significant influences of Judaism, the church continued to appeal to the religious literature that was popular in Palestine before A.D. 70.

Soon after the return of the Jews from Babylon (ca. 530 B.C.), Israel's religious life was dominated by the interpretation of the Law. By ca. 400 B.C., the Prophets (Former Prophets: Joshua through Kings; Latter Prophets: Isaiah, Jeremiah, Ezekiel, and the Book of the Twelve or the Minor Prophets) also functioned as scripture in Israel. The third part, the Writings (in the Hebrew canon and the Protestant Old Testament canon, this includes Ruth, Job, Psalms, Ecclesiastes, Song of Solomon, Lamentations, Daniel, and Ezra-Nehemiah), was settled largely in the later first century or early second century. Melito (ca. A.D. 180) reports a Jewish canon of twenty-two books, which (by combining books) is the equivalent of the present Jewish and Protestant canon except for Esther (Eusebius, *H.E.* 4.26.13).

In the fourth and fifth centuries, however, apocryphal and pseudepigraphal writings were still found in Christian lists of Old Testament canonical scriptures. Athanasius, for example, in 367 listed in his Old Testament canon both Baruch and the Epistle of Jeremiah but omitted Esther (*Ep. fest.* 39). Also, many of the lists include one or more of the apocryphal writings (e.g., Origen, Cyril of Jerusalem, Hilary, Epiphanius, and others), but codex Sinaiticus and Gregory of Nazianzus (*Carm.* 1.12.5) omit Esther. The noncanonical books commonly referred to in these lists include

Judith, Tobit, Sirach, Baruch, 2 Esdras, Wisdom of Solomon, and the Epistle of Jeremiah. Only Jerome (347–420) appears to have accepted the Jewish biblical canon equivalent to the thirty-nine books that the Protestants later adopted.

The New Testament Canon. With one exception (Rev. 22:18–19), the New Testament writings appear not to have been written as sacred literature, but by the end of the first century New Testament literature was frequently used to settle disputes and address the life and ministerial needs of the church. From the early second century, some New Testament writings were called "scripture" or used authoritatively alongside the Old Testament in supporting the faith and ministerial practices of the church (e.g., *1 Clem.* 13.1–4; *2 Clem.* 2.4; 14.2; *Barn.* 4.14; Polycarp, *Phil.* 2.2–3; 7.1–2; 12.1; Ptolemy, *Letter to Flora* 3.6; Justin, *Dial.* 100.1f.; 101.3). The *Didache*, *1* and *2 Clement*, Ignatius's letters, the *Shepherd* of Hermas, and the *Epistle of Barnabas* frequently quote or allude to the New Testament writings, especially the Gospels and Paul, although generally not referring to these books by name.

By the mid-second century, the Gospels were regularly used with the Old Testament scriptures in the worship and ministry of many churches (Justin, *1 Apol.* 67) and functioned as sacred scripture in many churches. The formal recognition of New Testament literature as scripture is first attested by Irenaeus of Lyons (ca. 180), who was also the first to use the terms "Old Testament" and "New Testament" (*Haer.* 4.28.1–2). After him, there was widespread acceptance of New Testament writings as scripture, especially by Clement, Tertullian, and Origen.

Even though the New Testament writings themselves were not generally called "scripture" before the time of Irenaeus, the often-quoted words, ministry, passion, and resurrection of Jesus functioned as such from the very beginning of the church (e.g., 1 Cor. 7:10, 17; 11:23; 1 Thess. 4:15; Matt. 28:18; but also *1 Clem.* 13.1–4; Ignatius, *Philad.* 8.2; Polycarp, *Phil.* 2.2, 3).

Marcion (ca. 140) may well have drawn up the first closed collection of New Testament scriptures. However, he recognized only ten of Paul's epistles (he does not refer to the Pastorals) and an edited Gospel of Luke. His primary aim was the separation of Christianity from Judaism, claiming that the God of the Old Testament was not the God of Jesus and the apostles. He rejected both Judaism and its scriptures and believed that Paul, who rejected the Law as a means of salvation, best proclaimed the true Christian message. Excommunicated from the church in Rome, Marcion continued to have an impact on the church for several generations, an impact that led to lengthy refutations from Irenaeus and Tertullian. Although establishing a closed canon of scriptures was not Marcion's primary aim, his canon did have the effect of spurring the church into considering which Christian writings best defined its faith and mission. Justin Martyr (ca. 160) accepted the Synoptic Gospels as scripture, but his awareness of John is questioned. Irenaeus accepted all four of the canonical Gospels and urged that only those four be accepted as authoritative in the church (*Haer.* 3.11.8–9). Tertullian also accepted all four, Matthew and John as coming from apostles and Mark and Luke as presenting the teaching of Peter and Paul (*Marc.* 4.2.5).

The next writer for whom there is a list of his canon is Origen, but this list may have been an invention of Eusebius of Caesarea, since it is first found in Eusebius's writings (*H.E.* 6.25.3–14) and only later in Rufinus (345–410).

Historically, the church first recognized the New Testament writings as scripture and then moved toward a closed biblical canon. In that move, several historical factors seem to have influenced the church's decisions regarding its New Testament canon. Besides the impact made by Marcion and Irenaeus, a third factor that may have stimulated the church to clarify which Christian books should be acknowledged as scripture was the rejection of "inspired" books produced by the Montanists in the last half of the second century. Although there is little evidence of this literature in antiquity, Tertullian (possibly) wrote a defense of this "new prophecy" (*Pass. Perp.* 1.1), and a possible condemnation of it by a certain Apollinaris is recorded in Eusebius (*H.E.* 5.16.3–4).

In 303, the emperor Diocletian launched the last great empire-wide persecution against the Christians. In the first of four edicts, he demanded that the churches be destroyed and their sacred scriptures be confiscated and burned. Many Christians were persecuted and put to death because of their refusal to hand over their sacred books, and one can assume that the churches had already identified which books were demanded. Although the churches were not in complete agreement on which books were sacred, it is likely that most of them had by then decided the broad parameters of their biblical canon.

Constantine's conversion brought many benefits to the church, not the least of which was the cessation of persecution and the restoration of Christian property that had been confiscated or destroyed. The reign of Constantine (306–337), like that of Diocletian, was characterized by the pursuit of social and religious conformity (Eusebius, *V.C.* 2.65, 68); during and following his reign, there was a move in the church toward unity in theology and the biblical canon. Constantine requested Eusebius to produce fifty copies of scriptures for use in the new capital city of Constantinople (Eusebius, *V.C.* 3.37). Which scriptures to include in those copies was probably decided by Eusebius, but his choice was accepted by the emperor, a fact that would likely influence other Christians' decision on the matter.

Lists of New Testament Scriptures. After Eusebius, several lists or collections of biblical books began to circulate in eastern and western churches. Although a number of these lists reportedly derived from the second and third centuries, it is difficult to find any such lists in writings from that period. Only those lists produced in the fourth century and later were circulated as collections of sacred writings. These lists indicate the tendency toward a closed biblical canon.

Eusebius (ca. 325) established three categories for Christian books: those that were "accepted" as scripture, those that were "questionable" or "disputed," and those that were "spurious." He included in the first group twenty of the current New Testament books (the four Gospels, Acts, thirteen epistles of Paul, 1 John,

and 1 Peter). The "questionable" group—James, 2 Peter, Jude, 2 and 3 John, and possibly Hebrews and Revelation—was probably not a part of Eusebius's own canon. The "spurious" group was rejected outright and included such works as the *Gospels of Peter, Thomas,* and *Matthias;* the *Acts of Andrew, Paul,* and *John;* the *Didache;* and the *Apocalypse of Peter.* In time, the middle group was accepted by most churches, but the latter failed to find acceptance. The smaller canon closely approximated that accepted in the Syriac-speaking church in the fourth and fifth centuries.

The *Muratorian Canon,* a seventh- or eighth-century Latin translation of a list of sacred scriptures, is most commonly believed to have originated in or near Rome ca. 180–200. The list closely approximates the current New Testament collection, with the exception that 1 and 2 Peter and Hebrews are omitted but the *Apocalypse of Peter* and the Wisdom of Solomon are included. The dating of this fragment is questionable, since it does not represent the views of the church in either the east or the west in the late second century and it played no discernible role in the thinking of the church. The closest parallels to this document were produced only in the middle to late fourth century, and it is therefore probably best to date the fragment ca. 350.

Athanasius of Alexandria (367) produced the first list of New Testament books that corresponds to the twenty-seven–book New Testament canon used in the Catholic and Protestant churches today (*Ep. fest.* 39).

The most disputed New Testament books in the fourth to the sixth centuries were Hebrews, 2 Peter, Jude, and Revelation. On the other hand, several Greek manuscripts dating from the fourth century and even up to the eleventh century contain several noncanonical books. For example, codex Claramontanus (D) (fifth–sixth century) includes the *Epistle of Barnabas,* the *Shepherd* of Hermas, *Acts of Paul,* and the *Apocalypse of Peter* but omits Hebrews; codex Alexandrinus (A) (fifth century) includes both *1* and *2 Clement;* codex Constantinopolitanus (C) (eleventh century) includes *1* and *2 Clement,* the *Epistle of Barnabas,* the *Didache,* and an interpolated text of the letters of Ignatius; and codex Sinaiticus (fourth century) includes *Barnabas*. Clement of Alexandria called *Hermas* and *1 Clement* scripture; Origen called *1 Clement* a "Catholic epistle": there appears to have been broad agreement on the limits of the New Testament canon, but not unanimity.

Criteria. It is surprising that the ancient church left no record of the processes used to select its biblical canon, but some of these criteria are clear. (1) *Apostolicity.* If a writing was believed to have been written by an apostle, then it was recognized as scripture (see, e.g., Tertullian, *Marc.* 4.2.5). Apostolic authorship was not easily established, however, and this criterion does not account for Mark, Luke-Acts, Hebrews, or 2 and 3 John. (2) *Orthodoxy.* If a writing in question did not cohere with the core of teaching that was believed to have been passed on to the churches by the apostles through their successors, the bishops, the writing was unacceptable. But this "orthodoxy" or collection of teachings, which the church believed came from the earliest Christian communities, is not always clear in the ancient church. The belief in such a stable tradition nevertheless played a major role in Irenaeus's refutation and rejection of the Gnostic literature (*Haer.* 2.35.4; 3.3.3). The spectrum of theological perspectives in the New Testament itself shows that the early Christian community was often broader in its outlook than were succeeding generations of the church. (3) *Antiquity.* The dating of a book was often used to separate it from consideration. The author of the *Muratorian Canon*, for example, refused to accept the *Shepherd* of Hermas because it was not written in the apostolic age. (4) *Usage.* How a book served the churches' worship and instructional needs no doubt played a major role in determining which scriptures were preserved and became a part of the biblical canon. It is likely that the books recognized by the larger churches—Rome, Alexandria, or Antioch—influenced the decisions of the smaller churches. (5) *Inspiration.* What does not appear to have been a criterion for any of the early churches so much as a basic assumption was the notion of inspiration. Quite apart from the difficulty of distinguishing what was and

what was not inspired, a study of the church writings through the fifth century shows that whatever was believed to be true and faithful was also believed to be inspired. In the first five centuries, only heretical teaching was ever called uninspired. Both Clement of Rome (*1 Clem.* 63.2) and Ignatius (*Philad.* 7.1–2) claimed that their own writings were inspired, and the *Shepherd* of Hermas states that the prophecy of Eldad and Modat (now lost) was inspired. The author of *2 Clement* claimed that *1 Clement* was inspired (11.2; cf. *1 Clem.* 23.3–4).

Conclusion. Three facts are clear. The earliest and primary canon of the early church was the life, death, resurrection, and teachings of Jesus. The theology of the earliest Christians was informed by an array of writings wider than that included in the present-day Protestant or Catholic Old Testament. The churches of the fourth to the sixth centuries were in wide but not complete agreement on either their Old Testament or New Testament canons. A final determination was made for the Catholics at the Council of Trent (1545–1563) and for the Protestants during the time of the Reformation. The eastern Orthodox have an even larger biblical canon than either the Catholics or the Protestants: the Greeks add to the Apocrypha or Deuterocanonical books *2 Esdras* (Septuagint *1 Esdras*) and *3 Maccabees*, with *4 Maccabees* in an appendix, and the Russians add *3 Esdras* (Vulgate *4 Esdras*) and omit *4 Maccabees*. The Ethiopian biblical canon, which claims traditional roots back to the fourth century, contains eighty-one books. *See also* Apocrypha, New Testament; Apocrypha, Old Testament; Muratorian Canon; Peshitta; Pseudepigrapha; Septuagint; Vulgate.

[L.M.McD.]

Bibliography

Old Testament: Melito in Eusebius, *Church History* 6.26.14; Origen in Eusebius, *Church History* 6.25.2ff.; Athanasius, *Festal Letter* 39; Cyril of Jerusalem, *Catechetical Lectures* 35; Epiphanius, *Panarion* 1.1.8; idem, *On Weights and Measures* 4; 23; Gregory of Nazianzus, *Carmina* 1.12.5; 2.2.8; Laodicea, *Canon* 60; Hilary of Poitiers, *Commentary on Psalms* prol. 15; Jerome, *Letters* 53.8; idem, *Preface to Books of Samuel*; Rufinus, *Commentary on the Apostles Creed* 36–37; Augustine, *On Christian*

Doctrine 2.13; Council of Hippo, *Canon* 36. *New Testament: Muratorian Canon*; Eusebius, *Church History* 3.25; Cyril of Jerusalem, *Catechetical Lectures* 4.36; Laodicea, *Canon* 60; Athanasius, *Festal Letter* 39.

C.H. Turner, "Latin Lists of the Canonical Books," *JThS* 1 (1900):554–560; A.C. Sundberg, *The Old Testament of the Early Church* (Cambridge: Harvard UP, 1964); R.M. Grant, *The Formation of the New Testament* (New York: Harper and Row, 1965); J.C. Turro and R.E. Brown, "Canonicity," *Jerome Biblical Commentary*, ed. R.E. Brown et al. (Englewood Cliffs: Prentice-Hall, 1968), pp. 515–534; G.W. Anderson, "Canonical and Non-Canonical," *The Cambridge History of the Bible*, ed. P.R. Ackroyd and C.F. Evans (Cambridge: Cambridge UP, 1970), Vol. 1, pp. 113–158; H. von Campenhausen, *The Formation of the Christian Bible* (Philadelphia: Fortress, 1972); G.F. Moore, "The Definition of the Jewish Canon and the Repudiation of Christian Scriptures," *The Canon and Masorah of the New Hebrew Bible*, ed. S.Z. Leiman (New York: KTAV, 1974); A.C. Sundberg, "Canon Muratori: A Fourth-Century List," *HThR* 66 (1973):1–41; J.N. Lighthouse, "The Formation of the Biblical Canon in Judaism of Late Antiquity: Prolegomenon to a General Reassessment," *Studies in Religion* 8 (1978):135–142; E. Ferguson, "Canon Muratori: Date and Provenance," *SP* 18 (1982):677–683; W.R. Farmer and D. Farkasfalvy, *The Formation of the New Testament Canon*, ed. H.W. Attridge (New York: Paulist, 1983); H.Y. Gamble, *The New Testament Canon: Its Making and Meaning* (Philadelphia: Fortress, 1985); R. Beckwith, *The Old Testament Canon of the New Testament Church* (Grand Rapids: Eerdmans, 1986); B.M. Metzger, *The Canon of the New Testament: Its Origin, Development, and Significance* (Oxford: Clarendon, 1987); L.M. McDonald, *The Formation of the Christian Biblical Canon* (Nashville: Abingdon, 1988); F.F. Bruce, *The Canon of Scripture* (Downers Grove: InterVarsity, 1988); E. E. Ellis, "The Old Testament Canon in the Early Church," *Mikra*, ed. M.J. Mulder (Philadelphia: Fortress, 1988), pp. 653-690.

CANONS, CANON LAW. Ecclesiastical law as distinguished from the civil or Roman law. In Christian terminology, the Greek *kanōn* (a "rule" used by masons or carpenters) designated a standard or an approved list, as in "the canon of truth," "the canon of the Bible," "the canon [invariable part] of the Mass," and "the canons [clergy] of a cathedral." Much later, the church would "canonize" saints.

Apart from the New Testament, which has few specific norms applicable to daily life (Luke 12:13–16; Rom. 14:14; 1 Cor. 7:10; Acts 15:28–29), the oldest regulations are to be found in the church orders, such as the *Didache*, the *Apostolic Tradition* of Hippolytus, and the *Apostolic Constitutions*. Church orders are handbooks, supposedly emanating from all the apostles, that lay down directives for discipline and liturgical practice. These manuals really embody the customary observances in the area of their provenance. They flourished in the third century but were obsolete by the end of the fourth.

In a more formal sense, canon law originated in the enactments of councils or synods of the fourth century. Although in earlier documents there are indications of rulings on questions about rebaptism and the reconciliation of apostates, the first series of canons that have come down to us are probably from the councils of Elvira in Spain (ca. 300) and Arles in Gaul (314). The main line of development, however, occurred in Asia Minor and Northern Syria. Canons from the councils of Ancyra (modern Ankara), Neocaesarea, Antioch, Gangra, and Laodicea formed the nucleus of almost all future collections of church law. Pride of place was soon given to the canons of Nicaea (325), the first of the ecumenical councils.

These councils legislated, among other matters, on the qualifications for church office, the jurisdiction of such officials as the rural bishops, and church structures (the province, the exarchate, and the beginnings of the patriarchate). Many canons dealt with clerical discipline: deacons and presbyters, for example, were forbidden to marry after ordination, a policy still observed in the eastern churches. The marriages of Christians, the readmission of those in schism, public penance, and the ceremonies of the liturgy were also treated. Canonical decisions on matters of discipline, organization, and liturgy were subject to change, whereas matters of faith affirmed in the creeds were considered unalterable.

The lack of any discernible order among the canons of the individual councils is reflected in the first collections, which simply added the enactments of one council to those of another chronologically in a continuous enumeration. A *corpus canonum* (a body of law from Nicaea and other councils) representing the discipline of the region of Antioch was gradually elaborated in the latter half of the fourth century. This collection of Greek canons was soon translated into Syriac and Latin, either at Rome or in North Africa, and was used even by the church of Persia. It was referred to at the Council of Chalcedon (451).

Canonical activity in the west was also significant. The church in North Africa contributed three blocks of legislation: the *Breviarium* of the Synod of Hippo (393), the register of the Council of Carthage (419), and the material compiled in the case of the presbyter Apiarius, who had appealed to the bishop of Rome after being condemned by his own bishop (418). In Gaul, a collection of canons from three councils held in the region of Arles as well as the canons of Nicaea was compiled between 412 and 506. About the same time appeared the *Statuta ecclesiae antiqua*, the most important theological, canonical, and liturgical document of the Gallo-Roman church. An introductory part prescribing the examination and profession of faith for a candidate to the episcopacy is followed by eighty-nine disciplinary statutes modeled on the *Apostolic Constitutions* and a brief ritual of ordinations and blessings for bishops, presbyters, deacons, subdeacons, acolytes, exorcists, lectors, porters, psalmists, virgins, widows, and spouses.

Quite early in its development, church law was taken to include more than conciliar enactments. Papal rulings on certain practices were soon recognized as having legal force. When a question that could not be resolved by local authorities was referred to the bishop of Rome, he would issue an authoritative decision, or decretal. The first known decretal is to be attributed either to Damasus I (366–384) or to Siricius (384–399). The decretal activity of Innocent I (401–417) is particularly noteworthy. His letter to Decentius, bishop of Gubbio in Umbria (PL 20.551–561), dealt with matters pertaining to the eucharist, confirmation, reconciliation, and the anointing of the sick. Although addressed to a particular bishop or locality, the papal decretals found a wider public when incorporated into canonical collections.

In the Byzantine church, the canonical letters of twelve of the Greek fathers were also accepted as a source of law. Like the papal decretals, they were authoritative responses communicated to individuals. The most important were the epistles of Basil the Great (329–379) comprising ninety-six "canons." Six of the twelve fathers were bishops of Alexandria. A letter of Cyprian, bishop of Carthage (249–258), dealing with the rebaptism of heretics was also honored.

Perhaps even more significant for eastern canon law was imperial legislation. From the time of Constantine, the Roman emperors had assumed the role of protector of the church. The Theodosian code (438) and the Code of Justinian (534) dealt extensively with religious affairs. Justinian, for example, regulated the procedure for electing bishops and permitted divorce with the right of remarriage (*Novella* 22). Much of this legislation found its way into canonical collections. The church in addition borrowed many concepts and terms from Roman law.

Once the basic sources of ecclesiastical law had been agreed upon, canonists of the sixth century were in a position to compile great collections, which were to have enduring value. At Rome, ca. 525, the monk Dionysius Exiguus, for his *Liber canonum*, freshly translated from the Greek fifty of the so-called apostolic canons and the canons of eight councils (Nicaea, Ancyra, Neocaesarea, Gangra, Antioch, Laodicea, Constantinople, and Chalcedon). To these, he added the canons of the councils of Sardica (343) and Carthage (419). Shortly afterward, he published the *Liber decretorum*, thirty-nine papal decretals from Siricius (384–399) to Anastasius II (496–498). The two works together, known as the *Dionysiana*, became the preferred law book of the Roman church and the substance of the *Hadriana* that pope Hadrian I gave to Charlemagne (774). The second-most-important collection in the west was the *Hispana*, or *Isidoriana*; it ultimately included the canons of eleven Greek councils, eight African, thirty Spanish (up to the seventeenth council of Toledo in 694), and seventeen Gallic councils. The *Hispana* contained in addition 103 decretals ending with the pontificate of Gregory the Great (604).

About 570, John the Scholastic, patriarch of Constantinople, composed his *Collectio L [50] titulorum*, which arranged the canons under titles or subjects rather than chronologically. Along with the usual Greek councils were the entire eighty-five apostolic canons and sixty-seven fragments from the epistles of Basil. He also produced the *Collectio LXXXVII capitulorum* from the *Novellae*, or "New Constitutions," of Justinian. Toward the end of the century, a collection similar to that of John the Scholastic was subdivided into fourteen titles with a parallel compendium of imperial law under the same headings. Collections of both civil and canon law dealing with ecclesiastical matters are called *nomocanons*. The *Nomocanon XIV titulorum* reedited in the reign of Heraclius (630) is still the fundamental collection of the Orthodox churches. In 692, the Council of Trullo definitively approved the eastern canon law while adding 102 canons of its own. [J.E.L.]

Bibliography

F. Lauchert, *Die Kanones der wichtigsten altkirchlichen Councilien* (Freiburg: Mohr, 1896); tr. H.R. Percival, NPNF, 2nd ser. (1899), Vol. 14.

R.C. Mortimer, *Western Canon Law* (London: Black, 1953); J. Meyendorff, *Byzantine Theology* (New York: Fordham UP, 1974); J. Gaudemet, *Les Sources du droit de l'église en occident du IIe au VIIe siècle* (Paris: Cerf, 1985).

CANONS OF HIPPOLYTUS

CANONS OF HIPPOLYTUS. Church order based on the *Apostolic Tradition* of Hippolytus and variously dated from the fourth to the sixth century. The *Canons of Hippolytus* is available in Arabic, a translation of a Coptic version of the lost Greek original. The thirty-eight canons legislate mainly on matters of church organization and worship. Despite the late date and tertiary translation, the work may preserve at some places either the true reading of the *Apostolic Tradition* or an even earlier situation. CPG I, 1742. [E.F.]

Bibliography

R.G. Coquin, *Les Canons d'Hippolyte: édition critique de la version arabe* (with French tr.), PO (1966), Vol. 31.2, pp. 273–444.

W. Riedel, *Die Kirchenrechtsquellen des Patriarchats Alexandrien* (Leipzig: Deichert, 1900), pp. 193–200; R.H. Connolly, "The So-called Egyptian Church Order and Derived Documents," *TS* 8.4 (1916):50–134.

K. Müller, "6. Hippolyts *Apostolikē Paradosis* und die Canones Hippolyts," *ZNTW* 23 (1924):226–231; H. Brakmann, "Alexandreia und die Kanones des Hippolyt," *JAC* 22 (1979):139–149.

CAPPADOCIA. Roman province (from A.D. 17) located in east-central Asia Minor. Cappadocia's mountains and plains were rich in minerals, grains, and grass. As early as the Assyrian period, the region was noted for its fine horses; in Roman times, its horses were preferred for racing. Horse-racing imagery in the writings of Gregory of Nyssa (*V. Mos.*, prol. 1) and Gregory of Nazianzus (*Or.* 43, PG 36.513D–516A) suggests that racehorses continued to be raised there in the late fourth century.

Cappadocia had traditionally been under a feudal-type social system. This had two curious effects on the people and the land. The people had a reputation for being dependent. Strabo (12.2.11) relates the story that when the Romans granted them the right to live under their own laws, the Cappadocians responded by requesting that the Romans appoint them a king. The other consequence of the feudal system was that there were few cities in Cappadocia, but numerous small villages. When Cappadocia became a Roman province, it had only four cities: Mazaca, Tyana, Garsaura (later called Archelais), and Ariarathea. Mazaca, renamed Caesarea by Claudius, was the only major city.

There is no information about the planting of Christianity in Cappadocia. It was not included in the Pauline mission. It is mentioned only twice in the New Testament: Christians in Cappadocia are among those addressed in the salutation of 1 Peter, and Acts 2:9 lists Cappadocian Jews as part of the audience present at Pentecost. Perhaps Cappadocian converts at Pentecost were the first evangelists in the province.

Christianity must have spread extensively in the province in the second century, although again specific evidence is scarce. Eusebius (*H.E.* 5.5) indicates that there were Christians in Melitene, on the border of Armenia Minor, in the reign of Marcus Aurelius (161–180). Euelpistus, who stood trial as a Christian with Justin in Rome (ca. 165), asserted that he was of Christian parents in Cappadocia (*M. Just.* 4.7). Tertullian, in 212, related that Claudius Lucius Herminianus had persecuted the Christians in Cappadocia because of his wife's conversion (*Scap.* 3). Evidence also connects Symmachus, the second-century Ebionite, with Cappadocia (Eusebius, *H.E.* 6.17.1; Palladius, *H. Laus.* 64).

Alexander, the friend of Origen, prior to becoming bishop of Jerusalem in 212 had been a bishop in Cappadocia (Eusebius, *H.E.* 6.11.12), the first whose name is known.

In the third century, under the leadership of Firmilian, bishop of Caesarea (230–268), Cappadocia blossomed as a theological center recognized throughout the world. Like Alexander before him, Firmilian was an avid devotee of Origen (Eusebius, *H.E.* 6.27.1). If the note preserved by Palladius (*H. Laus.* 64; cf. Eusebius, *H.E.* 6.17.1) can be trusted, Origen spent two years in Firmilian's diocese, probably during the reign of Maximinus Thrax, being hidden by a virgin named Juliana.

The Cappadocian church under Firmilian was involved in the major debates of Christianity. Firmilian attended the Synod of Iconium, which dealt with Montanism, and was involved in the Novatianist controversy at Antioch. He supported Cyprian of Carthage against Stephen I of Rome in the controversy about heretical baptism and was influential in the dispute with Paul of Samosata.

Firmilian (Cyprian, *Ep.* 75.10) relates that there was a persecution in Cappadocia in 234 as the result of a series of earthquakes that devastated large portions of Cappadocia and Pontus. Many Christians fled the province to escape the persecution. Origen (*Comm. in Mt., ser.* 39) appears to refer to the same incident when he mentions a persecution and the burning of churches as the result of earthquakes. In the midst of this upheaval, an unnamed Montanist-type prophetess arose in Caesarea and

won a considerable following. In the latter part of Firmilian's life (ca. 258), the Goths raided Asia Minor and carried off a number of Cappadocian Christians (Philostorgius, *H.E.* 2.5). Among those captured were the parents of Ulfilas, who in the next generation would be known as the apostle to the Goths.

Cappadocian Christianity bore its most abundant fruit in the fourth century. The strength of the church in the province at the beginning of the century can be seen in the fact that the bishops from seven cities in Cappadocia attended the Council of Nicaea (325): Caesarea, Tyana, Colonia, Cybistra, Comana, Spania, and Parnassus.

The glory of the Cappadocian church, however, lies in the work of the so-called Cappadocian fathers: Basil, Gregory of Nyssa, and Gregory of Nazianzus, who were active in the second half of the fourth century. Origen's influence on Cappadocian theology continued in the work of these fathers, mediated in part by Gregory Thaumaturgus, the third-century bishop of Pontus who spent five years studying under Origen in Palestine. Macrina, the influential grandmother of Basil and Gregory of Nyssa, had been instructed by Gregory Thaumaturgus. So great was their esteem for the latter that Gregory of Nyssa later composed his *Life*.

Basil became bishop of Caesarea in 370; his nine years as bishop were both productive and stormy. In 371, the Arian emperor Valens divided Cappadocia into Cappadocia Prima, with Caesarea as its capital, and Cappadocia Secunda, with Tyana as its capital. Whether this was done to weaken Basil's power or only to improve the emperor's administrative and fiscal control in the province (cf. van Dam), the result was that it greatly increased Basil's problems by introducing a division within the Catholic camp. Anthimus, bishop of Tyana, with the approval of a number of bishops in Cappadocia Secunda, considered himself to have charge over all the churches in Cappadocia Secunda. Basil fought to maintain his control over the whole of Cappadocia by filling sees with bishops loyal to himself. He ordained his brother Gregory as bishop of Nyssa in Cappadocia Secunda, thus securing the loyalty of this diocese. He attempted the same thing at Sasima with his friend Gregory of Nazianzus. The latter attempt failed, however, because of Anthimus's opposition and Gregory of Nazianzus's lack of desire to be bishop of Sasima. The dispute with Anthimus lasted through 372.

Eunomius, the Neoarian of Cappadocian birth, had considerable success in the province in the 370s. A major literary debate erupted between himself and Basil. Gregory of Nyssa took up the Catholic side after Basil's death in 379. Although Arianism was not overcome in Basil's lifetime, the eventual victory was built on his achievements.

About 536, Justinian divided Cappadocia Secunda again. He made Mokissos the capital of Cappadocia Tertia, and renamed it Justinianopolis. [R.E.H.]

Bibliography
Strabo, *Geography* 12.1–2.

W.M. Ramsay, *The Historical Geography of Asia Minor* (London: Murray, 1890); A. von Harnack, *The Expansion of Christianity in the First Three Centuries* (New York: Putnam, 1905), Vol. 2; Ruge, "Kappadokia," *Paulys Real-Encyclopädie der classischen Altertumswissenschaft* (Stuttgart: Druckenmüller, 1919), Vol. 10, cols. 1910–1918; W.E. Gwatkin, *Cappadocia as a Roman Procuratorial Province* (Columbia: U of Missouri P, 1930); R. van Dam, "Emperor, Bishops, and Friends in Late Antique Cappadocia," *JThS* n.s. 37 (1986):53–76.

CARACALLA (188–217). Roman emperor (211–217). Aurelius Antoninus, nicknamed Caracalla, became emperor jointly with his brother Geta, whose murder he soon arranged (212). His military campaigns against the Germanic tribes were successful, but his eastern expeditions disappointing. He was assassinated at Carrhae (biblical Haran) in Mesopotamia. His principal legacy was the *Constitutio Antoniana* (212), which extended the Roman citizenship to all free inhabitants of the empire. His policy toward Christians was generally lenient. [M.P.McH.]

Bibliography
Tertullian, *To Scapula* 4.

P. Keresztes, "The *Constitutio Antoniana* and the Persecutions Under Caracalla," *AJPh* 90 (1970):446–459.

CARPOCRATES (second century). Gnostic leader. Carpocrates of Alexandria and his disciples, the Carpocratians, who existed into the fourth century, taught licentious living, transmigration of souls, and the natural conception of Jesus, committing their special *gnosis* to several works. Carpocrates's son, Epiphanes, wrote *On Justice*, a philosophical defense of a community of goods, including women. [R.R.]

Bibliography
Irenaeus, *Against Heresies* 1.25; Clement of Alexandria, *Miscellanies* 3.2; Hippolytus, *Refutation of All Heresies* 7.20; W. Völker, *Quellen zur Geschichte der christlichen Gnosis* (Tübingen: Mohr, 1932), pp. 33–38.

CARTHAGE. Roman city in North Africa. The Carthage known to early Christianity originated as a Roman colony established on the ruins of the Punic city destroyed in 146 B.C. by Scipio Africanus. The colony was not successfully established until 29 B.C. under Augustus, who named it Colonia Julia Carthago. It was a carefully planned city, with dwellings set out on a grid system and streets remarkable in antiquity for their breadth. Throughout the first and second centuries A.D., the city grew steadily and eventually came to be recognized as the greatest city in the western part of the empire, after Rome. Roman Carthage was built as an open city, and it was not until ca. 425, during the reign of Theodosius II, that the Theodosian wall was built, roughly coterminous with the circumference of the city planned by Augustus.

Christian Buildings. Before the legalization of Christianity, Christians owned burial grounds (*areae*) outside the city. After the peace established by Constantine, Christians were able to build churches. As in Rome, so in Carthage the church came to be administered through *regiones* (districts)—six such have been attested—each having its own churches, including possibly a basilica. From archaeological and literary evidence, eleven basilicas have been identified outside the Theodosian walls; from literary evidence, we know of eleven basilicas within them. After the Catholic-Donatist division in the fourth century, the Catholic cathedral appears to have been the Church of Restitutus, which was located within the walls, as was the Donatist cathedral, the Church of the Theoprepeia. The largest church, however, was evidently that now represented by the impressive ruins of Damous el karita, just outside the walls. There is also evidence of three monasteries, although monasticism did not flourish in Carthage until after 400. The construction of churches flourished in the late fourth and early fifth centuries, but Catholics lost many of their churches during the Vandal period (439–533). After the Byzantine conquest in 534, a program of restoration and building was undertaken. The first half of the seventh century appears to have been a time of relative prosperity, but recent excavations suggest that in the decades immediately preceding the fall of Carthage to the Arabs in 698 the churches suffered severely. The rapid decline appears to have been related to changing economic conditions occasioned by the Arab conquests in the east and the large number of people seeking refuge in Carthage.

Early Bishops. Records have not preserved for us an unbroken list of the bishops of Carthage in antiquity. Agrippinus is the first bishop to be attested (Cyprian, *Ep.* 71.4). He summoned a council to Carthage ca. 220 to debate the issue of the rebaptism of heretics, on which he took a hard line. Indeed, Carthaginian Christianity was for centuries characterized by a conflict between rigid and pliant attitudes toward moral and doctrinal issues. It is evidently a bishop of Carthage whom Tertullian (ca. 200), addressing as the "bishop of bishops" (*Pud.* 1.6), found too lenient in granting the church's peace to adulterers. Elsewhere, the same author gives us some vivid vignettes of the life of the Carthaginian church in the early third century. It was already a flourishing church (*Scap.* 5.2), ethnically mixed, with a strong Greek element. It contained an apparently conspicuous order of virgins (*Virg.* 10.1) and was not unaccustomed to the drama of exorcism (*Spect.* 26.1–4) and ecstasy (*An.* 9.4).

Cyprian, bishop from 248 to 258, brings the Carthaginian church sharply into view through his considerable correspondence and

his treatises. By mid-century, the church was not only populous but also relatively wealthy, and during the persecution of Decius (250), which threatened loss of property, many Carthaginian Christians lapsed. The bishop at first took an uncompromising attitude, but eventually a conciliatory resolution emerged from a council of African bishops that he called in 251. Henceforth, for several years, annual councils were held in Carthage. In these councils, the see of Carthage assumed a position of primacy among African churches, and Cyprian appears as the metropolitan. Indeed, Cyprian exerted influence beyond Africa: Cornelius, bishop of Rome, sought his recognition (*Ep.* 45.2); bishops in Spain turned to Carthage to mediate a dispute (*Ep.* 67.1); and Faustinus of Lyons requested Cyprian's support in an appeal to Stephen of Rome concerning the bishopric of Arles (*Ep.* 68).

Between Cyprian and Mensurius, who appears on the episcopal throne after the persecution of Diocletian (303–305), little is known of the bishops of Carthage. Nor is much known of the Carthaginian church during the second half of the third century. The persecution of Diocletian once more offered an occasion for conflict between purists and laxists. On the issue of *traditio*—handing over the scriptures to inquisitors during the persecution—Mensurius, as well as his deacon Caecilian, took a laxist position. They discouraged confrontation with the authorities and the excessive veneration of martyrs. Hostility arose, and when, after Mensurius's death (311), Caecilian succeeded to the episcopate, opponents charged that he had been consecrated by a *traditor* and an opposing bishop, Majorinus, was set up. The Donatist schism had begun.

Donatist Controversy. In the century that followed, the Donatists of Carthage appear to have had rather stronger leadership than the Catholics, as we may now call them. Majorinus died ca. 315, and the Donatist church in Carthage was ruled for a century by three powerful bishops—Donatus (315–ca. 350), Parmenian (ca. 355–391), and Primian (391–?). Sometime after the death of Caecilian (ca. 345), Donatus sought imperial recognition as the sole bishop of Carthage. The Donatists recurrently felt, however, the force of the imperial arm. In 317 under Constantine, and again in 347 under Constans, Donatism was severely repressed and its churches confiscated. Donatus went into exile in 347, and Carthage produced the Donatist martyrs Maximian and Isaac. Under Julian, their confiscated churches were restored, but after 404 the Carthaginian Donatists felt once more the severe penalties imposed by the law, and Primian went into exile. We hear little of the Donatist church of Carthage after the imperial proscription of Donatism following the Council of Carthage in 411.

If the Catholic bishops of Carthage were not, during most of the fourth century, a match for their Donatist counterparts in their own see, the respect paid to the Carthaginian episcopate abroad is attested by the presence of its bishops at some of the major councils of the period. At home, councils summoned by Gratus (in 349) and Genethlius (in 390) addressed the problem of the considerable moral and ecclesiastical corruption in the Catholic church. Under Aurelius (ca. 391–429), who gained strength through Augustine's support, councils were held with regularity in Carthage. These included the council of 411 resulting in the proscription of Donatism and that of 419, which challenged the jurisdiction of Rome in Africa and codified the canons of earlier African councils.

Vandals. Quodvultdeus was bishop in Carthage when, in 439, the Vandals, adherents of Arianism, took the city. A new and bitter hostility arose that was to last for almost a century. We are better informed about Catholic Christianity in Carthage than Arian. It was in general a difficult time for Catholics, who experienced at the hands of Arian Christians the intolerance with which Catholics had treated Donatists. Upon occupying Carthage, Gaiseric, the Vandal king, seized for the Arians the Catholic churches within the Theodosian walls, although he left for the Catholics some of their churches outside the walls; Quodvultdeus and some of his clergy went into exile. In 454, however, at the solicitation of

the western emperor Valentinian III, Gaiseric consented to the appointment of a new bishop, Deogratias, who died in 456 or 457. Huneric, Gaiseric's successor, began his reign with some significant concessions to Catholics, but he appears soon to have become embittered, for he ordered a general confiscation of Catholic churches and published a decree demanding that Catholics convert to Arianism on pain of confiscation of goods and exile. Bishop Eugenius and some 500 Carthaginian clergy went into exile. Under Gunthamund, Eugenius and other exiles returned, and Catholics in Carthage regained possession of their churches. Gunthamund, in his turn, ordered the churches closed and forbade the consecration of bishops. Many bishops refused to comply; Eugenius was again forced into exile, where he died. It was not until Hilderic ascended the throne in 523 that Catholics were granted freedom of worship and the right once again to ordain bishops.

Byzantine Rule. With the victory of Justinian's general Belisarius in 534, Africa came under the administrative authority of Constantinople. At once, the Catholics in Africa regained a favored position in relation to the imperial power. Already in 534, a council summoned by bishop Reparatus anticipated an influx of Arian converts, and few traces remain of Arianism in Carthage during the Byzantine period. Under Justinian, the metropolitan dignity of the Carthaginian episcopate was reaffirmed, although the imperial court was willing to deal directly with the primates of the African provinces.

Byzantine influence upon the church of Carthage was to be felt in a variety of ways. A church built in honor of the *Theotokos* ("mother of God") reflects the eastern interest in the cult of Mary. The affair of the Three Chapters brings into light once more the courageous independence of the Carthaginian episcopate. Reparatus's deacon, Ferrandus, wrote in opposition to Justinian's condemnation of the Three Chapters, and Reparatus supported him. Under his presidency, an African council (550) refused to condemn the Three Chapters, and broke relations with the Roman bishop Vigilius, who had succumbed to imperial pressure. Summoned to Constantinople, Reparatus refused to submit and was sent into exile, although not all his clergy shared Reparatus's stout conviction.

The long line of the Carthaginian bishops becomes in our sources indistinct and broken in the last century before the fall of the city to the Arabs in 698. *See also* Africa; Cyprian; Donatism. [R.D.S.]

Bibliography
C. Diehl, *L'Afrique byzantine: histoire de la domination byzantine en Afrique: 533–709*, 2 vols. (Paris, 1896; repr. New York: Burt Franklin, 1959); A. Audollent, *Carthage romaine* (Paris: Bibliothèque des Ecoles Françaises, 1901); C. Saumagne, "Colonia Julia Karthago," *Bulletin archéologique du Comité des travaux historique* (1924):131–139; W.H.C. Frend, *The Donatist Church: A Movement of Protest in Roman North Africa* (Oxford: Clarendon, 1952); C. Courtois, *Les Vandales et l'Afrique* (Paris: Arts et Métiers Graphiques, 1955); T.D. Barnes, *Tertullian: A Historical and Literary Study* (Oxford: Clarendon, 1971); J.-L. Maier, *L'Episcopat de l'Afrique romaine, vandale et byzantine* (Geneva: Institut Suisse de Rome, 1973); M.M. Sage, *Cyprian* (Philadelphia: Philadelphia Patristic Foundation, 1975); W.H.C. Frend, "The Early Christian Church in Carthage," *Excavations at Carthage 1976 Conducted by the University of Michigan*, ed. J.H. Humphrey (Ann Arbor: U of Michigan P, 1978), Vol. 3, pp. 21–40; F.M. Clover, "Carthage in the Age of Augustine," *Excavations at Carthage 1976 Conducted by the University of Michigan*, ed. J.H. Humphrey (Ann Arbor: U of Michigan P, 1978), Vol. 4, pp. 1–14; J.H. Humphrey, "Vandal and Byzantine Carthage: Some New Archaeological Evidence" and E.M. Wightman, "The Plan of Roman Carthage: Practicalities and Politics," *New Light on Ancient Carthage*, ed. J.G. Pedley (Ann Arbor: U of Michigan P, 1980), pp. 29–46; M.G. Fulford, "The Long Distance Trade and Communications of Carthage c. A.D. 400 to c. A.D. 650," *Excavations at Carthage: The British Mission*, ed. M.G. Fulford and D.P.S. Peacock (Sheffield: British Academy, 1984), Vol. 2, pp. 255–262.

CASSIAN, JOHN (ca. 365–ca. 433).

Monk and spiritual writer. According to Gennadius (*Vir. ill.* 62), Cassian was born in Scythia, present-day Romania. With his friend Germanus, he spent ten years in a monastery in Bethlehem and made extensive visits to monasteries in Egypt. Cassian went to Constantinople, where he was influenced by John Chrysostom, and ca. 405 went to Rome, where he became a friend of Leo, the future pope. By 415, he had settled in Marseilles and founded a monastery for men and one for women. He remained there until his death.

In Gaul, Cassian produced *The Institutes* and *The Conferences*, both influential contributions to the principles of monasticism and, indeed, to basic Christian spirituality. A third book, *On the Incarnation*, is an awkward defense of the unity of Christ against Nestorius, written at the request of Leo.

Books 1–4 of *The Institutes* identify the principles and spirit of monasticism by citing Egyptian experiences in such matters as dress and the prayer of the hours. Books 5–12 deal with eight sins: gluttony, fornication (omitted in Gibson's translation), covetousness, anger, dejection, accidie (weariness of heart, "noonday devil"), vanity, and pride. Cassian combined admiration for Egyptian models, ethical insight, discretion, and adaptability to Gallic experience.

The Conferences are dialogues with Egyptian abbots reconstructed by Cassian. The themes go beyond the patterns of communal life in *The Institutes* to the encounter of the individual with God. The dialogues take up renunciation, mortification, vices, demons, friendship, and prayer. They present the Christian as a soldier or athlete and warn him about the need for a director and for discretion. *Conference 16* praises the role of friendship in the spiritual life. *Conference 13* is a statement of Semipelagianism that acknowledges some possible initiative in free will prior to grace. This statement is more influenced by Chrysostom than by Augustine. *Conference 9* deals with four kinds of prayer and offers some reflections on the Lord's prayer. *Conference 10* provides a moving description of repetitive prayer. Feast day February 29 (east), July 23 (Marseilles). CPL 512–514. [P.C.B.]

Bibliography
M. Petschenig, ed., *Conlationes*, CSEL (1886), Vol. 13; idem, *De Incarnatione Domini contra Nestorium*, CSEL (1888), Vol. 17, pp. 239–391; idem, *De institutis coenobiorum et de octo principalium vitiorum remediis*, CSEL (1888), Vol. 17, pp. 3–231.

E.C.S. Gibson, tr., "John Cassian," NPNF, 2nd ser. (1894), Vol. 11, pp. 161–621; selections from *Conferences* in O. Chadwick, *Western Asceticism*, LCC, Vol. 12, pp. 190–289; C. Luibheid, tr., *John Cassian: Conferences*, CWS (1985).

P. Munz, "John Cassian," *JEH* 9 (1960):1–22; J.C. Guy, *Jean Cassien, vie et doctrine spirituelle* (Paris: Lethielleux, 1961); O. Chadwick, *John Cassian: A Study in Primitive Monasticism*, 2nd ed. (London: Cambridge UP, 1968); P. Rousseau, "Cassian, Contemplation and the Cenobitic Life," *JEH* 26 (1975):113–126; P. Rousseau, *Ascetics, Authority and the Church in the Age of Jerome and Cassian* (Oxford and New York: Oxford UP, 1978), pp. 153–234; D.J. MacQueen, "John Cassian on Grace and Free Will with Particular Reference to *Institutio* XIII and *Collatio* XII," *RecTh* 44 (1977):5–28; J. Rippinger, "The Concept of Obedience in the Monastic Writings of Basil and Cassian," *StudMon* 19 (1977):7–18; C. Folsam, "Anger, Dejection and Acedia in the Writings of John Cassian," *American Benedictine Review* 35 (1984):219–248.

CASSIODORUS (ca. 485–ca. 580). Statesman and ecclesiastical writer. Flavius Magnus Aurelius Cassiodorus, Senator, was born of south Italian nobility. His long life was divided into two distinct periods, the political and the scholarly-monastic. He served the Ostrogothic kings in Italy in various roles, as had his father before him. Cassiodorus was quaestor in 507, ordinary consul in 514, master of offices 523–527, and praetorian prefect 533–537.

Cassiodorus's chief value to the Goths lay in his literary talent, which he often used to glorify the regime. In 519, he produced the *Chronica*, a list of the Roman antecedents to Theodoric (ruled Italy 493–526) and his family. As prefect, the highest official beneath the king, Cassiodorus compiled the *Variae*, a collection of his official documents, meant to serve as models for his successors. His literary style is elaborate and artificial, which suited the pretensions of his masters. Neither original nor candid, he sets forth the events of his time in the best possible light, including his own succession as master of offices in place of the executed Boethius.

When Justinian's Byzantine armies recaptured Ravenna, Cassiodorus made his way to Constantinople. This marked the end of his political career but the beginning of an even longer career as an ecclesiastical writer. In the capital, he wrote a monumental *Expositio Psalmorum*, a complete commentary on the Psalms. The work is distinguished by orderly exegesis and a didactic approach to literary technique, an ideal introduction for young monks who pray the Psalms daily. Sometime before this, Cassiodorus founded the monastery of Vivarium on his family estate at Squillace on the southernmost coast of Italy. In 554, at age seventy, he returned home for a secluded life of contemplation and study, although he probably never took vows as a monk. His monastic ideal, unlike that of his contemporary Benedict of Nursia (ca. 480–540), was not a balance of work, prayer, and study, but rather emphasized study above all else. In 562, Cassiodorus wrote the *Institutions*, a kind of manual for monastic scholars and copyists. A unique catalogue of an ancient monastic library, it served as a model for many medieval book collections.

Although he may himself be considered one of the last of the ancient rhetors, Cassiodorus was not a promoter of the pagan classics. At Vivarium, bilingual scholars were imported to render Christian works into Latin from Greek, which he never learned well. Cassiodorus himself corrected Pelagius's New Testament commentary in a work entitled *Complexions*; at age ninety, he wrote a spelling manual for monks called *De orthographia*. That he had to provide such rudimentary education shows that Vivarium never lived up to the scholarly ideals of its master. Nor did the monastery have any impact on contemporary monastic or educational life. Only long after the death of Cassiodorus in 580 did books from the library find their way throughout Europe. CPL 896–911.

[T.G.K.]

Bibliography

Omnia Opera, 2 vols., PL 69–70; *Chronica*, ed. T. Mommsen, MGH Auct. Ant. (1894), Vol. 11; *Variae*, ed. T. Mommsen and L. Traube, MGH Auct. Ant. (1894), Vol. 12; A.J. Fridh, CCSL (1973), Vol. 96; *De anima*, ed. J.W. Halporn, CCSL (1973), Vol. 96; *Expositio Psalmorum*, ed. M. Adriaen, CCSL (1958), Vols. 97, 98; *De orthographia*, ed. H. Keil, *Grammatici Latini* (Leipzig: Teubner, 1880), Vol. 7, pp. 143–210; *Institutiones*, ed. R.A.B. Mynors (Oxford: Clarendon, 1937).

L.W. Jones, tr., *An Introduction to Divine and Human Readings by Cassiodorus* (New York: Columbia UP, 1946).

M.L.W. Laistner, "The Value and Influence of Cassiodorus's Ecclesiastical History," *HThR* 41 (1948):51–67; A. Momigliano, "Cassiodorus and Italian Culture of His Time," *Proceedings of the British Academy* 41 (1955):207–245; J.J. O'Donnell, *Cassiodorus* (Berkeley: U of California P, 1979); *Flavio Magno Aurelio Cassidoro: Atti della settimana di studi Cosenza-Squillace 19–24 settembre 1983*, ed. S. Leanza (Soveria Manelli, 1986); L. Viscido, *Studi sulle "Variae" di Cassidoro* (Calabria: Calabria Letteraria, 1987).

CATACOMBS. Term derived from the toponym *ad catacumbas* ("near the hollow"), the ancient description of a place on the Via Appia Antica in Rome at the third milestone adjacent to the Circus Maximus (map, no. 41) and possibly connected with the pozzolana quarry beneath S. Sebastiano (map, no. 47). The toponym indicated the place where the land dipped down, where there was a cavity, a depression, a hollow. The term became generic in the third century and came to denote any subterranean cemetery occupied by Christians.

"Catacomb" should be distinguished from "hypogeum," a privately owned and generally small underground burial complex consisting of one or more rooms joined by short passageways, corridors, and staircases. In matters religious, "hypogeum" is a neutral term: many religions in antiquity constructed funerary hypogea. "Catacomb," by contrast, implies a large subterranean cemetery consisting of several galleries (*dromoi*), often on more than one level, and rooms (*cubicula*) that adjoin and are cut off on the side of the galleries. Typically, superimposed *loculus* burials (in which the cadaver is emplaced in a horizontal wall niche cut parallel to the wall) line the walls of the galleries, and in the cubicula there are often *arcosolium* burials (cf. Kollwitz) cut into the walls and *forma* burials occasionally cut into the floor. Italian catacombs were constructed in the tufa subsoils that lined lands adjacent to cities. Fossors had the responsibility of cutting and excavating the vertical shafts (stair and light and air wells) that led down to the galleries as well as cutting and clearing the galleries and the rooms. Often they had to situate cubicula close to subsurface streams and wells so as to facilitate the washing and preparation of foods for the funerary refrigerium. They had to be informed about soil conditions, and they needed a rudimentary knowledge of the static properties of tufa. In short, given the complexities of this cunicular architectonic tradition, the fossors played a dual role: part laborer and part engineer. When Roman Christians began to construct catacombs in the early third century, they found that abandoned pozzolana quarries, or *arenaria*, such as the one beneath S. Sebastiano, were ideal places to begin the task of excavation and construction. Although there are some surviving non-Christian (e.g., Jewish) catacombs, in general it is correct to identify catacombs as the unique creation of early Christianity.

Origins and Antecedents. The idea of interring the dead in underground cavities is an old one. In Italy, where the overwhelming majority of early Christian catacombs survive, the Etruscans practiced hypogeal interment in *tumuli* and subterranean rooms from the seventh to the first century B.C. In addition to Rome, peninsular Italy (Campania), and Sicily, early Christian catacombs survive in North Africa (Algeria, Tunisia, Libya), in Greece and the Aegean Islands (notably Melos), on Malta, and in Alexandria. There is no evidence in any of these places that Christians were inspired to build catacombs on the model of Jewish precedents. In fact, the Roman Jews who built their own modest catacombs near the Via Appia Antica (Randanini catacomb), and on the Via Nomentana (Torlonia catacomb) could just as well have taken their cues from Christians.

We do not know where or how Christians buried their dead during the first and second centuries. It seems reasonable to suppose that in their earliest history Christians did not control (i.e., own) burial properties in any great degree. If this is correct, then it follows that the places where Christians buried their dead would have lacked distinction as Christian places of interment—indeed such places would have been controlled and owned by pagans and

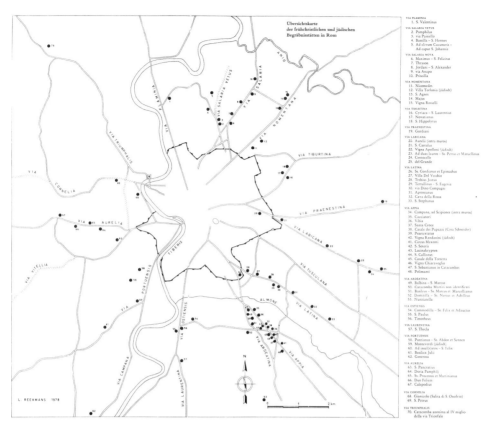

Übersichtskarte
der frühchristlichen und jüdischen
Begräbnisstätten in Rom

VIA FLAMINIA
1. S. Valentinus
VIA SALARIA VETUS
2. Pamphilus
3. via Paisiello
4. Bassilla – S. Hermes
5. Ad elivum Cucumeris –
   Ad caput S. Johannis
VIA SALARIA NOVA
6. Maximus – S. Felicitas
7. Thrason
8. Jordani – S. Alexander
9. via Anapo
10. Priscilla
VIA NOMENTANA
11. Nicomedes
12. Villa Torlonia (jüdisch)
13. S. Agnes
14. Maius
15. Vigna Rosuelli
VIA TIBURTINA
16. Cyriaca – S. Laurentius
17. Novatianus
18. S. Hippolytus
VIA PRAENESTINA
19. Gordiani
VIA LABICANA
20. Aurelii (intra muros)
21. S. Castulus
22. Vigna Apolloni (jüdisch)
23. Ad duos Justos – Ss. Petrus et Marcellinus
24. Centocelle
25. del Grande
VIA LATINA
26. Ss. Gordianus et Epimachus
27. Villa Del Vecchio
28. Trebius Justus
29. Tertullianus – S. Eugenia
30. via Dino Compagni
31. Aproniamus
32. Cava della Rossa
33. S. Stephanus
VIA APPIA
34. Campana, ad Scipiones (intra muros)
35. Cacciatori
36. Vibia
37. Santa Croce
38. Casale dei Pupazzi (Casa Schneider)
39. Praetextatus
40. Vigna Randanini (jüdisch)
41. Circus Maxenti
42. S. Soteris
43. Lucinakrypten
44. S. Callistus
45. Casale della Torretta
46. Vigna Chiaraviglio
47. S. Sebastianus in Catacumbas
48. Polimani
VIA ARDEATINA
49. Balbina – S. Marcus
50. Catacomba Mettis non identificati
51. Basileus – Ss. Marcus et Marcellianus
52. Domitilla – Ss. Nereus et Achilleus
53. Nunziatella
VIA OSTIENSIS
54. Commodilla – Ss. Felix et Adauctus
55. S. Paulus
56. Timotheus
VIA LAURENTINA
57. S. Thecla
VIA PORTUENSIS
58. Pontianus – Ss. Abdon et Sennen
59. Monteverdi (jüdisch)
60. Ad insalyxtos – S. Felix
61. Basilica Julii
62. Generosa
VIA AURELIA
63. S. Pancratius
64. Doria Pamphili
65. Ss. Processus et Martinianus
66. Duo Felices
67. Calepodius
VIA CORNELIA
68. Gianicolo (Salita di S. Onofrio)
69. S. Petrus
VIA TRIUMPHALIS
70. Catacomba anonima al IV miglio
    della via Trionfale

L. REEKMANS 1978

Sites of early Christian and Jewish catacombs, Rome, Italy. (From L. Reekmans, "Die Situation der Katakombenforschung in Rom," *Vorträge G. Rheinisch-westfälische Akademie der Wissenschaften: Geisteswissenschaften* 233 [Opladen: Westdeutscher Verlag, 1979].) (Used by permission.)

Jews. Second-century Roman Christians may have buried their dead in pagan plots that lay open to the sky (*sub divo*): the point has yet to be proved conclusively, but it is at least probable. Individual Christians may have wanted to segregate their dead during the earliest years of the movement (as might be argued from Tertullian, *Idol.* 14.5), but for the most part they lacked the control of property that would have made this possible.

History. The oldest surviving evidence of Christian catacomb interment is Roman (Callistus catacomb). According to Hippolytus, *Refutation of All Heresies* 9.12.14, bishop Zephyrinus (199–217) appointed the deacon Callistus to administer "the cemetery": this must correspond to the oldest centers of burial activity on Level 2 of the cemetery that came to be called by Callistus's name (even though his

body was buried in the Calepodius catacomb on the Via Aurelia, map, no. 67).

Within the vast Callistus complex, Area I on Level 2 is a region of about 100 by 230 feet and must correspond in contour and extent to a plot that the Christians from the late second century onward either owned or had access to. Area I also contained the "Crypt of the Popes," which housed the remains of several third-century Roman bishops. The second ancient nucleus in Callistus, roughly contemporary with Area I, and located 492 feet northeast of it, consisted of the tomb of pope Cornelius (d. 253) and a duplex or double cubiculum referred to popularly as the Crypt of Lucina. In Area I, as in this second nucleus, once the walls of individual cubicula had been filled with loculus burials, the ceiling and walls were then covered over with plaster, and the plaster was painted with pictorial subjects that contained Christian meanings relative to death and the afterlife.

The Callistus complex grew rapidly through the third, fourth, and early fifth centuries, as did a host of other Roman Christian catacombs. Burial activity to the southeast of the city was especially intense. The rate of growth is astonishing. Fossors must have worked day and night at breakneck speed to accommodate the burial needs of the burgeoning Roman Christian community.

As for material culture of artistic or aesthetic merit, the primary product of the catacombs was fresco painting. Although catacomb painting never rose to the level of great art, it constitutes an important last chapter in the history of painting in antiquity. Relief sculpture on sarcophagi was also preserved in the catacombs, together with a collection (of unknown size) of grave goods, including terracotta lamps and vessels, glass vessels (cups, beakers, and bowls decorated in the gold-glass technique), bone dolls, and perhaps an occasional early Christian intaglio or metal hoop worn as a finger ring.

The catacombs were church property, and what went on in them should be viewed as public and communitarian rather than private and individual. From the organizational and financial point of view, the Roman church's construction of vast suburban underground cemeteries was a brilliant solution to a potentially intractable problem: the availability of land for interment. Catacombs gave the church a cheap and hygienic means of disposing of its dead: once access (or title) to small subdial ("under the open sky") plots had been obtained, the only additional cost incurred by the construction and expansion of the catacombs was labor, and increasingly from the third through the fifth centuries the church coopted the fossors, which can only have had financial benefits to the institution.

The early Roman church, like others, also took seriously its commitment to eleemosynary works, of which the catacombs were a prime expression. The Roman church grew rapidly from 150 to 500, and many of the new converts were people of low social and financial status: the evidence of early Roman Christian epigraphy proves the point clearly. Many of these church members were people whose mortal remains, had it not been for catacombs, would have been tossed into common burial pits (*puticoli*), covered with lime, and forgotten. What the church guaranteed to such persons and their survivors was a dignified and orderly burial regardless of personal resources or station in life. *See also* Art; Burial; Fossors; Sarcophagi. [P.C.F.]

Bibliography

A. Bosio, *Roma sotteranea* (Rome: Facciottia, 1632); G.B. de Rossi, *La Roma sotteranea cristiana* (Rome: Cura della Commissione di Archeologia Sacra, 1864–1877), Vols. 1–3; H. Leclercq, "Catacombes," DACL (1910), Vol. 2.2, pp. 2376–2450; P. Styger, *Die römischen Katakomben* (Berlin: Verlag für Kunstwissenschaft, 1933); G. de Angelis D'Ossat, *La geologia delle catacombe romane* (Vatican City: Pontificio Istituto di Archeologia Cristiana, 1943); J. Kollwitz, "Arcosolium," RLAC (1950), Vol. 1, pp. 643–646; idem, "Arenarium," RLAC (1950), Vol. 1, pp. 646–647; F. Tolotti, *Memoria degli Apostoli in Catacumbas . . .* (Vatican City: Pontificio Istituto di Archeologia Cristiana, 1953); L. Hertling and E. Kirschbaum, *The Roman Catacombs* (London: Darton, Longman and Todd, 1960); H. Leon, *The Jews of Ancient Rome* (Philadelphia: Jewish Publication Society of America, 1960); L. Reekmans, *La Tombe du pape Corneille et sa région cémétériale* (Vatican City: Pontificio Istituto di Archeologia Cristiana, 1964); L. Reekmans, "Essais photogrammétriques dans les cryptes des martyrs romains," *Rendiconti della Pontificia Accademia Romana di Archeologia* 47 (1974–1975):129–138; F. Tolotti, "Ricerca dei luoghi venerati nella Spelunca Magna di Pretestato," *RAC* 53 (1977):7–102; J. Stevenson, *The Catacombs* (London: Thames and Hudson, 1978); U.M. Fasola and P. Testini, "I cimiteri cristiani," *Atti del IX.1 Congresso Internazionale di Archeologia Cristiana* (Vatican City: Pontificio Istituto di Archeologia Cristiana, 1978), pp. 103–139; L. Reekmans, "Die Situation der Katakombenforschung in Rom," *Vorträge G. Rheinisch-westfälische Akademie der Wissenschaften: Geisteswissenschaften* (Opladen: Westdeutscher Verlag, 1979), No. 233; F. Tolotti, "Le Cimitière de Priscille: synthèse d'une recherche," *RHE* 78 (1978):281–314; L. Reekmans, "Zur Problematik der römischen Katakombenforschung," *Boreas* 7 (1984):242–260.

CATECHESIS, CATECHUMENATE. Instruction of new converts to Christianity, from the Greek word *katecheō* ("teach"). Proselytes to Judaism were taught the commandments, and the meaning of conversion to Judaism, before and during the baptism of purification (*b. Yebam.* 47a–b). Although the Jewish instruction of proselytes is not specifically attested before New Testament times, it is assumed to have provided a pattern for Christian practice. The *Rule of the Community* from the Dead Sea Scrolls provides teaching for members of the community similar to that found in early Christian sources, such as the "Two Ways" in *Didache* and the *Epistle of Barnabas*.

Some parts of the epistles in the New Testament have been thought, if not to incorporate directly, at least to reflect blocks of catechetical material (1 Thess. 4:1–5:11; Col. 3:5–15; 1 Peter passim). Whether the instruction was before or after baptism in the earliest period of the church is not clear. The examples of immediate baptism (Acts 8:36–38; 16:33) would not have left time for any extensive prebaptismal teaching. The postcanonical sources, however, do indicate such instruction.

The earliest noncanonical sources also indicate a period of moral instruction prior to baptism. *Didache* 1–6 on the "way of life" and the "way of death" is presented as teaching to precede baptism (7.1). Justin Martyr also presupposes some doctrinal and moral instruction: "As many as are persuaded and believe that the things taught and said by us are true and promise to be able to live accordingly" are led to the water (*1 Apol.* 61).

The nature and purpose of Irenaeus's *Proof of the Apostolic Preaching* are in dispute. If, as seems likely, it was written as a guide for a catechist, it shows that the biblical history of God's dealings with human beings for salvation provided the framework of instruction for new converts at the end of the second century. The first half of the work tells the biblical story from creation to judgment, centering on Christ. The second half gives proof of the Christian message from the Old Testament prophets. The career of Christ is told from the prophets, whose material is organized according to his story, from preexistence to second coming (a similar arrangement of prophecy is found in Cyprian, *Quir.* 2, and Ps.-Epiphanius, *Testimony Book*).

The first evidence of an organized catechumenate is furnished by Hippolytus, *Apostolic Tradition* 16–20. It was clearly a well-developed institution at Rome in the early third century. Three years of instruction is called for before baptism, but it is explained that "it is not the time that is judged, but the conduct" (17). The treatise does not describe the content of instruction but implies a scriptural (17; 20; 35), doctrinal (21), and moral (42) teaching. About the same time, there is evidence of a catechetical school at Alexandria, whose most famous teacher was Origen (Eusebius, *H.E.* 6.3). The word "catechumen" emerged as a technical term also at this period (*Pass. Perp.* 2; Tertullian, *Praescr.* 41).

During the later third century, or certainly by the fourth century, there was observed a rule of secrecy (*disciplina arcani*), which not only excluded the unbaptized from the eucharistic assembly but also required avoidance of talk about Christian ceremonies in the presence of outsiders. Doctrinal instruction in this period took the form of delivering the creed to the new convert, who memorized it and repeated it before baptism.

The fourth and early fifth centuries, with the large influx of new converts into the church, constituted the great period of the catechumenate. Cyril of Jerusalem's *Catechetical Lectures*, delivered during the forty days preceding the Pasch (Easter), when baptism was administered, exemplify a predominantly doctrinal catechesis, expounding on each phrase of the Nicene Creed. Some moral content and biblical history were also included. The five *Mystagogical Catecheses* transmitted with the *Catechetical Lectures* may be by Cyril's successor, John. They were delivered during the week after Paschal Sunday and gave a liturgical catechesis on the meaning of baptism, chrism, and eucharist.

The catechetical sermons of several prominent fourth- and fifth-century bishops survive— those of Theodore of Mopsuestia, John Chrysostom, Ambrose, and Augustine. Some bishops also prepared guides for catechists. Gregory of Nyssa's *Catechetical Oration* is primarily doctrinal in content, offering an explanation of the Trinity and atonement. Augustine's *On Catechizing the Uninstructed* presents the outline of biblical history, leaving to the instructor to elaborate on points according to the hearer's needs. This history-of-salvation approach is represented in other sources (*Const. app.* 7.39; *Itin. Ether.* 46).

Modern scholars have shown most interest in the moral and doctrinal content of the catechesis. However, the biblical or historical (telling the story of Bible history) was another recognized pattern of catechesis and provided a framework holding together moral, doctrinal, and liturgical instruction.

During the fourth century, four distinct stages of catechetical instruction can be distinguished: (1) There was teaching for inquirers, for whom Augustine's *On Catechizing the Uninstructed* gives two sample discourses. (2) There was the catechumenate proper, for which there were rites of admission that varied from one locality to another. The delay of baptism by many in the fourth century meant that people might stay in the category of a catechumen for most of their lives. (3) The immediate preparation for baptism occurred in the forty days before the Pasch. The person submitted his or her name as desiring baptism and attended the preparatory lectures. The time was spent in fasting, penitence, confession, and listening to instruction. The exorcisms to deliver the person from the power of the devil became the scrutinies of the western rite. (4) Following the baptism, the new Christian wore a white garment and attended the postbaptism teaching on the meaning of the sacraments.

The spread of infant baptism in the fifth and sixth centuries brought about a decline in the catechumenate, which was designed for adult converts. This prepared the way for catechism to become in later times the instruction of children who had been baptized in infancy. *See also* Apostles' Creed; Baptism; Creeds; Rule of Faith. [E.F.]

Bibliography

Irenaeus, *Proof of the Apostolic Preaching*; Hippolytus, *Apostolic Tradition* 16–20; Cyril of Jerusalem, *Catechetical Lectures*; Theodore of Mopsuestia, *Catechetical Homilies*; John Chrysostom, *Baptismal Catecheses*; Ambrose, *On the Mysteries*; idem, *On the Sacraments*; idem, *Explanation of the Symbol*; Gregory of Nyssa, *Catechetical Oration*; Augustine, *On Catechizing the Uninstructed*; idem, *Sermons* 56–59; 212–216; Narsai, *Liturgical Homilies*.

P. Carrington, *The Primitive Christian Catechism* (Cambridge: Cambridge UP, 1940); W. Robinson, "Historical Survey of the Church's Treatment of New Converts with Reference to Pre- and Post-Baptismal Instruction," *JThS* 42 (1940):42–53; L.D. Folkemer, "A Study of the Catechumenate," *ChHist* 15 (1946):286–307; A. Turck, *Evangélisation et catéchèse aux deux premiers siècles* (Paris: Cerf, 1962); T. Maertens, *Histoire et pastorale du rituel du catéchuménat et du baptême* (Bruges: Biblica, 1962); J. Daniélou and R. du Charlat, *La Catéchèse aux premiers siècles* (Paris: Fayard-Mame, 1968); R.M. Grant, "Development of the Christian Catechumenate," *Made, Not Born: New Perspectives on Christian Initiation and the Catechumenate* (Notre Dame: U of Notre Dame P, 1976), pp. 32–49; M. Dujarier, *A History of the Catechumenate: The First Six Centuries* (New York: Sadlier, 1979); E. Ferguson, "Irenaeus' *Proof of the Apostolic Preaching* and Early Catechetical Instruction," *SP*, forthcoming.

CATENA. Linkage of excerpts from scriptural commentaries intended to give a fuller explanation of biblical passages (from Latin *catena*, "chain"). The excerpts, often taken from commentaries representing both the Antiochene and the Alexandrian schools of exegesis, were presented without comment by the compiler. The catena is therefore a special form of florilegium, that is, an anthology of quotations pertaining to a given subject; when the subject is scripture, the florilegium is called a "catena." The form has preserved much patristic exegesis (as well as heretical writings) that would otherwise have remained unknown.

Greek, Latin, and eastern catenae have come down to us. The scriptural text is often presented first, with the commentary written in parallel columns. Greek catenae date from the late fifth century, beginning with that of Procopius of Gaza, who drew his commentary on some Old Testament books from the works of Cyril of Alexandria, Basil the Great, and Gregory of Nyssa, followed by the catenae of Olympiodorus of Alexandria (sixth century),

John Drungarios (seventh century), Andreas the Presbyter (seventh century), and Nicetas of Heraclea (eleventh century). Latin catenists included Bede (seventh century), Alcuin (eighth century), Claudius of Turin (ninth century), Rabanus Maurus (ninth century), and Walafrid Strabo (ninth century). Later compilers were incompetent and careless, bringing disrepute to the form until the appearance of Thomas Aquinas's *Catena aurea*, a continuous exposition of excerpts from over eighty commentaries on the four Gospels. Syriac catenae were constructed by an anonymous writer of a *Garden of Delights* (seventh century), by Severus of Antioch (ninth century), by bishop Dionysius bar Salibi (twelfth century), and by Bar-Hebraeus, who wrote *Storehouse of Mysteries*, a commentary on the Old and New Testaments. CPG IV. *See also* Florilegium.

[M.T.C.]

Bibliography

J.A. Cramer, *Catenae Graecorum Patrum in Novum Testamentum*, 8 vols. (Oxford: E typographeo academico, 1838–1844).

CATHOLIC CHURCH. The first use of the term "catholic" (Greek *katholikos*, an adjective from the adverbial *kath' holou*, "in general, universal") to describe the church is in Ignatius of Antioch, ca. 110 (*Smyrn.* 8): "Let no one do anything with reference to the church without the bishop. Only that eucharist may be regarded as legitimate which is celebrated with the bishop or his delegate presiding. Where the bishop is, there let the community be, just as where Jesus Christ is, there is the catholic church." Here, "catholic" means less the universal church opposed to heresy than the "whole" church resistant by its very nature to division. With Clement of Alexandria, however, "catholic" is clearly defined (*Str.* 7.17.107): "It is evident that these later heresies and those that are still more recent are spurious innovations on the oldest and truest church. . . . We say that the ancient and catholic church stands alone in essence and idea and principle and preeminence." Cyprian's *The Unity of the Church* bases the need for unity in the local church on the unity required

in the universal, or catholic, church as Christ had founded it. For him (*Ep.* 66.8), the church that is not torn by schism or heresy is catholic. Eusebius of Caesarea quotes a letter in which Cornelius of Rome (251) sarcastically inquires whether Novatian did not know that there should be only one bishop in a catholic church. Finally, Cyril of Jerusalem (*Catech.* 18.22) summarizes all the meanings: "The church is called catholic because it is spread throughout the world, from end to end of the earth; also, because it teaches universally and completely all the doctrines that man should know concerning things visible and invisible, heavenly and earthly; and because it subjects to right worship all mankind, rulers and ruled, lettered and unlettered; further, because it treats and heals universally all kinds of sins committed by soul and body, and it possesses in itself every conceivable virtue, whether in deeds, in words, or in spiritual gifts of every kind."

Vincent, a monk on the island of Lérins, near Cannes, gave the classic definition of "catholic" (*Commonit.* 2.3): "Within the catholic church itself, great care must be taken that we hold on to that which has been believed everywhere at all times by all the faithful. This is what is truly and properly 'catholic' as the very force and meaning of the name indicates, that is, it includes everything universally. This will be the case if we follow universality, antiquity, consent. We shall follow universality in this way if we confess that to be the one true faith that is confessed by the whole church throughout the world; antiquity, if we never depart from the meaning that our forefathers declared sacrosanct; finally, consent, if in its very age we hold to the decisions and convictions of all, or almost all, the bishops and teachers." At the Council of Constantinople (381), the four notes of the church—one, holy, catholic, and apostolic—became official church teaching. Thus, "Catholic Church" became a regular name and the catholicity of the church an object of confession (Apostles' Creed). *See also* Church; Orthodox Church. [T.H.]

Bibliography

A. Garciadiego, *Katholiké Ekklesia* (Mexico City: Editorial Jus, 1953); J.N.D. Kelly, "'Catholique' et 'Apostolique' aux premiers siècles," *Istina* 14

(1969):33–45, esp. 34–39; R.P. Moroziut, "Meaning of Καθολικός in the Greek Fathers and Its Implications for Ecclesiology and Ecumenism," *Patristic and Byzantine Review* 4 (1985):90–104; idem, "Some Thoughts on the Meaning of ΚΑΘΟΛΙΚΗ in the Eighteenth Catechetical Lecture of Cyril of Jerusalem," *SP* 18.1 (1985):169–178.

CAVE, WILLIAM (1637–1713). Patristic scholar. Cave's *Apostolici* (1677), which provided a history of prominent figures in the first three centuries of the church, was followed by a second volume, *Ecclesiastici* (1683), which did the same for the fourth century. A defender of the Anglican church, he also wrote *Primitive Christianity: or The Religion of the Ancient Christians in the First Ages of the Gospel* (2 vols., 1673), which was frequently reprinted. [F.W.N.]

CELESTINE I. Bishop of Rome (422–432). Celestine acted vigorously against the followers of Novatian in Rome by confiscating their churches. He restored the basilica of Sta. Maria in Trastevere, damaged in Alaric's sack of the city (410), and the new basilica of Sta. Sabina was constructed during his episcopate. He worked to promote unity and discipline among the churches in Illyria, Italy, and Gaul; the bishops of Africa protested what they considered to be his unwarranted intervention in their affairs. He brought about the condemnation of Nestorius in a Roman synod (430) and delegated Cyril of Alexandria to carry out the sentence. He was a strong proponent of Rome's claim to primacy, most notably in his letter to the Council of Ephesus (431) and in his legate's statement there, but in his other correspondence as well. According to the report of Prosper of Aquitaine, he sent Germanus of Auxerre to combat Pelagianism in Britain (429) and made Palladius the first bishop of Ireland (431). CPL 1650–1654. [M.P.McH.]

Bibliography
Liber Pontificalis 45 (Duchesne 1.230–231); Prosper of Aquitaine, *Chronicum integrum* 744 (PL 51.594–595).

CELESTIUS (fifth century). Associate of Pelagius. A native of Great Britain, Celestius met Pelagius in Rome and became a principal supporter of his views. Although the two differed in approach, both denied the necessity of grace for the initial steps toward salvation. Celestius's teachings, condemned by several church councils from Carthage (411) to Ephesus (431), are known chiefly as reported by his opponent Augustine. CPL 767–770. [M.P.McH.]

Bibliography
Jerome, *Letter* 133.5; Augustine, *Letters* 157.22; 175; 176; 181 (=pope Innocent); 182 (=pope Innocent); idem, *On Man's Perfection in Righteousness*; idem, *On the Proceedings of Pelagius* (passim); idem, *On the Grace of Christ and on Original Sin* 1.30.32; 1.33.36; 2.2.2–2.7.8; 2.12.13; 2.22.25–2.23.26; idem, *Against Two Letters of the Pelagians* 3.5–4.8.

CELIBACY. *See* Asceticism; Clergy; Virgins.

CELSUS (late second century). Middle Platonist and author of the most comprehensive polemic against Christianity extant from the second century. Efforts to identify Celsus with any historical figure have failed, and nothing is known of him except what can be inferred from his writings. Celsus's sole work, *True Doctrine*, has survived only in quotations and paraphrases of it found in Origen's *Against Celsus*, which faithfully reproduces about ninety percent of the *True Doctrine*, most of it in direct quotations. Celsus's work can be dated no more precisely than the last third of the second century and is the earliest extended, systematic treatment of Christianity by an outsider.

Celsus was well informed, having obtained his information both from contact with Christians and from studying their writings. At the very least, he had read widely in Genesis, Matthew, and Luke, and to some extent in 1 Corinthians. Although direct dependence on any surviving apologetic writing has yet to be demonstrated, he was well acquainted with the religion of the Christian apologists, which he vigorously attacked. Celsus had considerable knowledge of several Gnostic and Marcionite sects and is the only source for the existence of some of them.

Encylopedic in his polemic, Celsus attacked the Christians' Jewish heritage, their founder and early leaders, and their theology and practice. He explained Jesus's miracles as worked by magical arts that Jesus learned in Egypt, and he claimed that Christians' appeal to faith instead of rational demonstration converted only women, children, and slaves. The bulk of his censure was directed toward the version of Christianity that came to be known as orthodox, adhered to, he says, by "the multitude." Celsus's historical importance is seen in the degree to which he accurately reflected the beliefs and practices of competing Christian groups, despite his polemical intent and tone. He provides historians with an excellent independent witness to the diverse forms of late-second-century Christianity.   [G.T.B.]

Bibliography

M. Borret, *Origène: Contre Celse*, SC (1967–1969, 1976), Vols. 132, 136, 147, 150, 227.

H. Chadwick, *Origen: Contra Celsum* (Cambridge: Cambridge UP, 1980); R.J. Hoffman, tr., *Celsus: On The True Doctrine: A Discourse Against the Christians* (New York: Oxford UP, 1986).

W. Völker, *Das Bild vom nichtgnostischen Christentum bei Celsus* (Halle: Buchhandlung des Waisenhauses, 1928); C. Andresen, *Logos und Nomos* (Berlin: de Gruyter, 1955); K. Pichler, *Streit um das Christentum* (Frankfurt and Berne: Lang, 1980); G. Burke, "Celsus and Late Second-Century Christianity" (Diss., University of Iowa, 1981); idem, "Walter Bauer and Celsus: The Shape of Late Second-Century Christianity," *SCent* 4 (1984):1–7; R.L. Wilken, *The Christians as the Romans Saw Them* (New Haven and London: Yale UP, 1984), pp. 94–125.

CELTIC CHRISTIANITY. Celtic Christianity is an inexact term, usually applied to the early Christianity (fifth to ninth centuries) of the Celtic peoples living in Ireland, western Britain, and Brittany but not, for example, to the Celts in Galatia or those Celts to whom Irenaeus said he preached in their own Gallic dialect. This Christianity has been of special interest to those who have interpreted it as a form of nonecclesiastical or at least noninstitutional religion. Earlier partisans saw the Celts as proto-Protestants, rejecting the works and pomp of Rome, but modern devotees concentrate more on a supposed Celtic individualism,

harmony with the natural world, and a constant awareness of the supernatural and mysterious.

Not surprisingly, these traits have appealed more to artists and poets than to historians, although a balance is now being reached. No one is sure when Christianity reached the western Celts. The evidence points to a standard western ecclesiastical influence, that is, governance by bishops, writing in Latin, participation in the affairs of the larger western Church. The originality of this Celtic fringe, on the surface so different from institutional religion, derived from three factors. First, Ireland had never been part of the Roman empire; Romanized Christianity had to mix with a completely Celtic culture. Second, the withdrawal of the Romans from Britain at the beginning of the fifth century encouraged a Celtic revival in the western part of the island, fortified by a sense of Roman desertion and the resistance to the ongoing Saxon invasion. Third, monasticism, the governing passion of Christian spiritual life at the end of the patristic period, reached the western Celts at a formative stage of their Christianity.

Most of the fifth- and sixth-century sources portray a typical western province. Evidence for a Celtic individualism dates from the seventh century or later, which makes it difficult to assess what is "native" Celtic and what is influenced by monasticism, especially Egyptian asceticism. Most scholars believe that Celtic Christianity is a combination of the two. When missionaries from Rome began to arrive in the British Isles at the end of the sixth century, adherents of old British Christianity clashed with advocates of Catholic Christianity over such customs as the date of Easter and the proper tonsure of monks. Roman customs prevailed after the Council of Whitby (664). The differences were more matters of national and ecclesiastical identity than doctrinal.

The demanding monasticism of the desert appealed to the heroic character of tribal Celtic society. Both emphasized individualism. The Egyptians went to desert retreats, the Celts to offshore islands; the Egyptians wandered in the unknown wilderness, the Irish ventured out on the uncharted North Atlantic. Both movements were products of a rural society. (The Irish cities, such as Dublin and Wexford, were founded by the Vikings in the ninth century.) The Egyptian portrayal of the desert as the symbolic Eden is reflected in the Celtic fondness for the natural world, so prevalent in vernacular poetry. In both regions, the saints did indeed live with animals, and their hagiography—especially the Celtic—includes tales of saints and animals. The desert fondness for tales of angelic visitors or demonic tempters mirrors pagan Celtic accounts of an ever-present otherworld. It seems most likely that many traits present in Celtic paganism were strengthened by the Egyptian influence.

It would, however, be misleading to present this as the Christianity of the Celts. Remarkable as the Celtic saints were, the theological literature, the penitential literature, and the canons of early councils make it clear that the vast majority of western Celtic Christians shared the rites and beliefs of their continental co-religionists. *See also* Gildas; Great Britain; Ireland; Patrick.   [J.F.K.]

Bibliography
N.K. Chadwick, *Studies in the Early British Church* (Cambridge: Cambridge UP, 1958); M. Deanesley, *The Pre-Conquest Church in England* (London: Black, 1961); J.T. McNeil, *The Celtic Churches: A History A.D. 200 to 1200* (Chicago: U of Chicago P, 1974); F.E. Warren, *The Liturgy and Ritual of the Celtic Church*, 2nd ed. J. Stevenson (Wolfeboro: Boydell, 1987).

CERINTHUS (first half of the second century). Jewish Christian Gnostic teacher. Branded a Judaizing "pseudo-Apostle" (*Ep. Apost.* 1.12; Epiphanius, *Haer.* 28.4.1ff.), Cerinthus flourished in Asia Minor. Patristic heresiologists attributed the following doctrines to Cerinthus: (1) a dualistic cosmology, which suggested that some debased demiurgic power created the world (Irenaeus, *Haer.* 1.26.1; Hippolytus, *Haer.* 7.33.1); (2) a Docetic Christology, wherein the Holy Spirit was believed to have descended on Jesus at his baptism and abandoned him at his death (Epiphanius, *Haer.* 28.1.5–7); and (3) a millenarian eschatology, in which it was claimed that, after the general resurrection, Christ would appear to establish an earthly kingdom (Eusebius, *H.E.* 3.28.2–4; 7.25.2–3). Polycarp reported an encounter of the apostle John with Cerinthus (Irenaeus, *Haer.* 3.3.4).

[P.M.Bl.]

Bibliography
G. Bardy, "Cerinthe," *Revue biblique* 30 (1921):344–373; J. Daniélou, *The Theology of Jewish Christianity* (London: Darton, Longman and Todd, 1964), pp. 68–69; A.F.J. Klijn and G.J. Reinink, *Patristic Evidence for Jewish-Christian Sects* (Leiden: Brill, 1973), pp. 3–19.

CHALCEDON, CHALCEDONIAN CREED. City in Asia Minor, location of the Fourth Ecumenical Council (451), important for its Definition of Faith on Christology. Chalcedon was situated not far from Constantinople. Although the decisions of the council that met there in 451 were hotly disputed, particularly in the east among supporters of a Monophysite Christology, it was becoming generally known by the seventh century as the Fourth Ecumenical Council, after Nicaea (325), Constantinople (381), and Ephesus (431).

Called by the emperor Marcian in order to bring religious unity to the empire so that political unity would emerge to help combat the military threat from the east, the council was led by an imperial commission of at least eighteen people headed by one Anatolius. It seemed needed because of the perceived debacle at Ephesus in 449, the *Latrocinium*, or "Robber Council," in which Dioscorus of Alexandria had played the dominant role. Dioscorus had seen to it that Eutyches, the archimandrite of Constantinople who refused all talk of two natures in Christ after the union of the divine and the human, was declared orthodox and that Flavian, bishop of Constantinople, was declared a heretic. In fact, Dioscorus had wielded such power of intimidation, backed by his own monks and imperial troops, that he had forced a number of reluctant bishops to sign the decisions and had been a party to the ultimately fatal beating of Flavian. The Robber Council had condemned Theodoret of Cyrus and Ibas of Edessa, proponents of an Antiochene Christology of two natures after the union. Both the west, particularly the papacy, and the Antiochene supporters of a two-nature Christology were incensed by that synod.

The complexity of the situation, however, was evident. Many eastern bishops insisted that Athanasius, Gregory of Nazianzus, and Cyril of Alexandria had taught a Christology in which the divine dominated the human to the point that it was proper to speak about one nature of the incarnate Logos. Although Athanasius's view did exclude the human will from any important attitudes or deeds, neither Gregory nor Cyril supported a view that excluded the humanity of Jesus as a subject. So many easterners were insistent upon the dominance of the divine in the person of Christ that any agreement at Chalcedon about Dioscorus's error at first could be reached only concerning his abuse of power. Many tended to agree that Eutyches should be condemned, but they found all two-nature language to be a Nestorian danger.

Dioscorus sat through the first session of the council (October 8). The imperial commissioners at the end of that session insisted that he and the leaders of the Robber Council be deposed, but some among the 500 bishops present still supported him. Their sentiment was clear when an uproar greeted the seating of Theodoret of Cyrus, a friend of Nestorius and an Antiochene theologian.

The commissioners demanded that the council draw up a statement of faith and turned its attention to that task in the second session (October 10). A number of the participants indicated that they preferred the statements of Nicaea and the writings of the fathers as sufficient. The creeds of Nicaea and Constantinople were read, as well as some of Cyril of Alexandria's letters against Nestorius and John of Antioch's treatise on the formula of reunion. Then pope Leo's *Tome* was read and hailed by the majority as true, but some bishops from Illyricum and Palestine heard overtones of Nestorius in it and pleaded for a reconsideration of the actions against the leaders of the Robber Council, a plan that went unheeded.

By the fourth session (October 17), the papal legates, the only western representatives at the council, had made a concerted attempt to put their stamp on the proceedings. In their view, the line of orthodoxy extended from Nicaea (325) through Constantinople (381) and Ephesus (431) to Leo's *Tome*. Eutyches and Nestorius represented the arch-Christological heretics, the first defending only one nature in Christ, the other defending two persons in Christ.

A first draft of the Chalcedonian creed—now lost—was presented to the fifth session (October 22). In its final form, it attempted to avoid the Eutychian error by incorporating the phrase "in two natures" and rejecting the phrase "out of two natures." The first phrase, and others in the creed, denoted that Jesus Christ was both fully human and fully divine and that the natures were not to be confused. With that kind of formulation, both the west, represented by Leo's legates, and the Antiochenes were assured that their insistence upon the manhood of Christ remained. Nestorius, still alive but in exile when the council met, approved of the creed, as his *Bazaar of Heracleides* shows. Theodoret was reinstated only after he anathematized Nestorius, and Ibas of Edessa was declared orthodox.

The eastern supporters of Cyril did not come away empty-handed. The Virgin Mary was called the *Theotokos* (literally, "god-bearer"), a term Nestorius had rejected and Cyril defended. The natures were viewed as neither divided nor separated, so that two persons or two Sons would be excluded. Recent research has indicated that this eastern group had a much more important role in the proceedings than has been assumed.

A number of eastern bishops, however, found Chalcedon improper, indeed heretical. Some of the Egyptian bishops declared that by custom they would have to await the appointment of a new bishop—Dioscorus having been deposed—until they could accept the decision. Yet many of them had not found the decision orthodox. The one-nature formula, thought to be from Athanasius but actually contained in Apollinarian forgeries, was dear to their sense of the faith. Some of these so-called Monophysites had an important place for the humanity of Christ, yet insisted on the predominance of the divinity on traditional and soteriological grounds. For such Christians all over the east, Dioscorus was a martyr.

The thirty canons of the council are of great interest to both the theological and social historian. The most important, Canon 28, gave Constantinople a place of honor second only to Rome. It was supposed to curtail the constant meddling of Alexandria in Constantinopolitan affairs and reflect the actual position of power. Rome accepted the council but not that canon. Other canons dealt with common problems: misuse of money, ordination, transfer of bishops to other sees, and attempts to undermine a bishop's authority.

After the seventh century, outside Monophysite circles, Chalcedon was viewed as an authoritative statement of Christology. Most Protestant, Roman Catholic, and Eastern Orthodox believers have found its positions fundamental. *See also* Christ, Christology; Ecumenical Councils; Eutyches; Leo the Great; Monophysites. [F.W.N.]

Bibliography

Mansi, Vol. 6, cols. 529–1230, and Vol. 7, cols. 1–872; ACO, Vol. 2; T.H. Bindley and F.W. Green, *The Oecumenical Documents of the Faith* (London: Methuen, 1950), pp. 85–235; A.J. Festugière, *Ephèse et Chalcédoine: actes des conciles* (Paris: Beauchesne, 1982).

A. Grillmeier and H. Bacht, *Das Konzil von Chalkedon: Geschichte und Gegenwart*, 3 vols., 4th ed. (Würzburg: Echter-Verlag, 1951–1954, 1973); R.V. Sellers, *The Council of Chalcedon: A Historical and Doctrinal Survey* (London: SPCK, 1953); P.T. Camelot, *Ephèse et Chalcédoine* (Paris: Orante, 1962); K. Sarkissian, *The Council of Chalcedon and the Armenian Church* (London: SPCK, 1965); A. Grillmeier, *Christ in Christian Tradition*, 2nd ed. (Atlanta: John Knox, 1975), pp. 520–557; P.T.R. Gray, *The Defence of Chalcedon in the East (451–553)* (Leiden: Brill, 1979); P. Stockmeier, "Das Konzil von Chalkedon: Probleme der Forschung," *Freiburger Zeitschrift für Philosophie und Theologie* 29 (1982):140–156; A. de Halleux, "La Reception du symbole oecuménique de Nicée à Chalcédoine," *Ephemerides theologicae lovanienses* 61 (1985):5–47; P.R. Fries and R. Nersoyan, eds., *Christ in East and West* (Macon: Mercer UP, 1987).

CHALICE. Community cup for eucharistic wine. Chalices are widely attested in early Christianity, from several kinds of sources, including literary-theological references, a few surviving early Christian examples, and numerous pictorial representations in painting, relief sculpture, mosaics, graffiti, ivories, and inta-

Cut-glass conical beaker (fourth century) with biblical scenes (Adam and Eve shown) of Rhenish provenance, now in the British Museum, London, England. (By courtesy of the Trustees of the British Museum.)

glios. Early on in the history of the church, chalice and paten became the quintessential sacred vessels.

On the literary side, the importance of the chalice derives from the Vulgate use of *calix* in reference to the cup of the Last Supper (Mark 14:23 and parallels; 1 Cor. 11:23–25). A long list of early Christian testimonies understand the chalice as eucharistic cup (cf. Klauser). On the basis of Tertullian's *On Modesty* 7.1 and 10.12, it seems highly probable that his Carthaginian Catholic opponents were using breakable (terra-cotta or, more likely, glass) eucharistic chalices at least by 210, if not earlier. The *Liber Pontificalis* 16 (Duchesne 1.139) says that Zephyrinus distributed glass patens to Roman clergy (as companion pieces glass chalices are probably implied), and idem 34 (Duchesne 1.170) says that chalices in precious metals were used under Sylvester I (314–335). Unfortunately, both these Roman testimonies are historically problematic. There are no surviving glass or metal chalices (understood as eucharistic cups) from either the third or fourth centuries.

Among surviving early Christian cups, the most famous is the Antioch chalice (ca. 500–550), but there is no certainty that it was originally conceived and executed with liturgical purposes in mind (cf. Weitzmann). Several surviving fourth- and fifth-century glass vessels are incised with Christian iconography; cups of this sort could have been put to use in eucharistic contexts, although it is impossible to prove the point (cf. Fremersdorf; also cf. the illustration of the British Museum's conical beaker incised with biblical scenes, Rhenish provenience). Eucharistic cups in the early Christian period were probably vessels with a large open mouth, handles at the shoulders, and a foot (cf. Klauser, 55–57).

Representations of drinking cups are ubiquitous in early Christian art: many examples appear in funerary contexts where it is correct to identify the vessels in question as cups for the refrigerium meal, not for the eucharist. Clement, *Instructor* 3.60.1, forbade Christians to emblazon cups on their finger rings; we have many third- and fourth-century Roman intaglios showing drinking cups, but much of this gemstone evidence cannot be linked to Christianity. *See also* Eucharist; Paten; Wine. [P.C.F.]

Bibliography
H. Leclercq, "Calice," DACL (1910), Vol. 2.2, cols. 1595–1645; J. Braun, *Das Christliche Altargerät in seinem Sein und in seiner Entwicklung* (Munich: Hueber, 1932), pp. 19–38; F.J. Dölger, "Der Kelch der Dämonen," *Antike und Christentum* 4 (1934):266–270; T. Klauser and S. Grün, "Becher," RLAC (1954), Vol. 2, cols. 37–62; P. Bruun, "Symboles, signes et monogrammes," *Acta Instituti Romani Finlandiae* (Helsinki, 1963), Vol. 1.2, pp. 84–85 ("Calix"); V. Elbern, *Der eucharistische Kelch im frühen Mittelalter* (Berlin: Deutscher Verein für Kunstwissenschaft, 1964); F. Fremersdorf, *Die römischen Gläser mit Schliff, Bemalung und Goldauflagen aus Köln* (Cologne: Verlag der Löwe, 1967); E. Dodd, *Byzantine Silver Treasures* (Berne: Abegg-Stiftung, 1973), figs. 5–10, 46; plates vii–x; K. Weitzmann, ed., *Age of Spirituality: Late Antique and Early Christian Art, Third to Seventh Century* (New York: Metropolitan Museum of Art, 1979), no. 542: Antioch Chalice; also nos. 531–532, 543–545.

CHARITY. *See* Agape; Almsgiving; Love.

CHILIASM. The hope, common to many religions, for a long period of God-given prosperity and peace on this earth, to be enjoyed by believers before the final consummation of history; also known as millennialism or millenarianism. The terms "chiliasm" and "millennialism" are derived from classical expressions for "thousand" (Greek *chilias*; Latin *mille*), since religious literature often speaks of such a "Golden Age" as lasting, like all idealized ages, for a thousand years.

In early Christian literature, chiliastic expectations form a recurrent if often controversial part of the church's future hope, appearing characteristically in works written during periods of persecution or by members of a small, sectarian community. Although the promise of a coming age of reward appears in a number of Jewish apocalyptic works, the normative scriptural text for Christian chiliasm is Revelation 20:1–7. There, the seer promises that after a first defeat of the forces presently oppressing the community, an angel of God will bind Satan in "the pit" for a thousand years; at the same time, Christian martyrs will rise from the dead in a "first resurrection" and reign for those thousand years with Christ. At the end of this age of peace and triumph, Satan will be loosed, to begin the great battle that will end in his final defeat (Rev. 20:10), the resurrection and judgment of all the dead (Rev. 20:12f.), and the creation of a "new heaven and a new earth" (Rev. 21:1ff.).

Second Century. Although the earliest extant noncanonical Christian document to speak of such a period of "rest" at the end of history is the *Epistle of Barnabas* (probably Alexandrian, ca. 130), the Christian chiliastic tradition seems to have been rooted in Phrygia, the region of western Asia Minor near the home of the Book of Revelation. Eusebius of Caesarea, writing in the early fourth century, cites earlier sources in describing the millenarian hopes of Cerinthus, a Judeo-Christian leader of apparently Gnostic tendency, who seems to have been active there ca. A.D. 100 (*H.E.* 3.28). According to another work cited by Eusebius (*H.E.* 7.25), some early Alexandrians rejected the canonicity of Revelation on the grounds that it was written by Cerinthus and that it presented an earthly, sensual picture of the coming kingdom of Christ.

Irenaeus (*Haer.* 5.33.3f.) attributes a similarly lavish description of the "kingdom of the righteous" to the now-lost writings of Papias, bishop of Hierapolis in Phrygia, whom he identifies as a disciple of the apostle John. This hope, which Irenaeus attributes to a whole group of "elders" belonging to the Johannine tradition, portrayed the millennium as a time of cosmic renewal, centered on the risen saints and characterized by fabulous fruitfulness, peace, and order.

Although his origin was in Palestine rather than Asia Minor, the apologist Justin Martyr asserts a millenarian hope, based on Old Testament prophecies as well as on Revelation 20. In his *Dialogue with Trypho* (written 155–165), an apologetic work cast as a conversation with a Jewish rabbi, Justin concedes that although all Christians hope for the resurrection of the

dead, some do not await a kingdom of earthly reward for the just. Following prophecy, however, he himself does look forward to a period of peace and plenty in a restored Jerusalem, before the general resurrection and judgment (*Dial.* 80f.; cf. 113; 139).

In adopting this hope as his own, Irenaeus (ca. 185) insists that one may not regard the biblical promises of earthly restoration for Israel simply as allegory (*Haer.* 5.35). He argues that it is fitting the just should be rewarded with happiness on this earth before the general resurrection and judgment, both because they have labored here for the love of God and because such a "righteous kingdom" will be a restoration of creation to its original state (*Haer.* 5.32.1). The purpose of this period of earthly beatitude is to allow the just to prepare gradually for the still greater fulfillment that is to follow, the opportunity to "grasp God" and participate in the divine nature (ibid.; cf. 5.praef.).

Although there is no direct evidence that the members of the Montanist sect, which originated in Phrygia ca. 170, were chiliasts, the extant fragments of prophecy attributed to their founders show a vivid expectation of the second coming of Christ and the conviction that the new Jerusalem, promised in Revelation 21, would descend from heaven on Pepuza, a village in their neighborhood. Tertullian of Carthage, who became a Montanist ca. 207, defends the chiliastic tradition in a work written shortly after his entry into the sect and argues that the material rewards promised the faithful in the millennial kingdom will be simply "a recompense for those things that, in the world, we have despised or lost" (*Marc.* 3.24). He suggests in this passage that the just will rise at various times during these thousand years of reward, according to their deserts. In later works from his Montanist period, however (e.g., *Resurr.* 26), Tertullian rejects any materialistic interpretation of the rewards promised the just and offers allegorical explanations of the biblical prophecies.

Third Century. In his *Commentary on Daniel,* the oldest extant scriptural commentary (ca. 204), Hippolytus foresees the end of the world as coming about 500 years after the birth of Christ, at the conclusion of the sixth millennium of created history. After this, Hippolytus awaits a thousand-year "sabbath" on earth for the saints, as described in Revelation, before the creation of a new cosmic order (4.23; cf. 4.10).

Origen, like all Greek commentators until the sixth century, was generally reticent about the Book of Revelation and allegorical in his interpretation of it; he considered any materialistic understanding of the biblical promises of reward a Judaizing aberration (*Princ.* 2.11.2; *Comm. in Mt.* 17.35). His pupil, bishop Dionysius of Alexandria, is reported by Eusebius (*H.E.* 7.24f.) to have written two pamphlets "On the Promises," directed against a chiliastic tract by Nepos, another Egyptian bishop and an opponent of Origen's allegorical method. Eusebius reports that Nepos's followers, led by a certain Korakion, formed a small schismatic church after Nepos's death, allegedly characterized by a historicizing, solely human understanding of Jesus and of the Christian hope (ibid.). The Palestinian chronographer Sextus Julius Africanus, also a friend of Origen, adopted the notion of a cosmic "week" of 7,000 years, familiar from apocalyptic and pagan speculation, as the underlying scheme of his own history; it is not clear, however, whether he imagined the coming final millennium or "sabbath" in the usual chiliastic terms.

Fourth Century. At the beginning of the fourth century, during the persecution of Diocletian, both Greek and Latin theologians showed a renewed interest in the millenarian tradition. Methodius of Olympus in southern Asia Minor, a disillusioned Origenist who became especially critical of Origen's spiritual notion of the resurrection body, insisted that the paradise in which the saints will rest is "a chosen spot on this earth" (*Res.* 1.55.1), and promised a "millennium of rest" with the risen Christ, to those who have "borne fruit" in this life by asceticism and consecrated chastity, before their final transformation and union with God (*Symp.* 9.5).

His contemporary Victorinus of Pettau, also a native Greek speaker (cf. Jerome, *Vir.*

ill. 74), wrote in Latin the first known commentary on the Book of Revelation, in which he offers a subdued but literal interpretation of that work's chiliastic vision. A brief Latin commentary on Matthew 24, published by G. Mercati in 1903 and C.H. Turner in 1904, which may also be by Victorinus, presents the chiliastic tradition in equally sober terms, insisting that the millennium will be a time of rest for the just but not of gross material pleasure; the author is also willing to accept the argument of antimillenarians that the "first resurrection" of Revelation 20:1–7 refers to baptism but argues that such a typological interpretation does not exclude a hope in its literal fulfillment.

Writing likewise in the first decade of the fourth century, the converted rhetorician Lactantius presents a dramatic apocalyptic scenario for the coming end of history in Book 7 of his *Divine Institutes*; there, he describes the thousand-year reign of the just, after Christ's triumphant return, as a time of marvelous prosperity, human fertility, and peace (*Inst.* 7.21–26)—a picture that owes as much of its detail to Virgil's fourth *Eclogue* and to the Christian *Sibylline Oracles* as to the Book of Revelation.

Both eastern and western Christian writers showed much less receptivity to chiliastic hopes in the century that followed Constantine's edict of toleration (313). Eusebius of Caesarea, Constantine's adviser and unabashed admirer, speaks of earlier millenarian hope as indicating the Judaizing sympathies and the small intelligence of its proponents (*H.E.* 3.39.13; 7.24.1). Apollinaris of Laodicea, condemned for his denial of a human soul in Christ, was also accused by Basil of Caesarea, Gregory of Nazianzus, and Jerome of reintroducing a "second Judaism" by espousing a chiliastic hope, although their contemporary the heresiologist Epiphanius of Salamis denies that he held such views (*Pan.* 77.36.5). Theodoret of Cyrus, writing his own heresiological work in the mid-fifth century, also rejects any terrestrial interpretation of the kingdom of God (*Haer.* 5.21).

Among Latin theologians of the late fourth century, Ambrose took the vision of a "first resurrection" in Revelation 20 to refer to the immediate admission of the just to beatitude after death and to their freedom from the purgative suffering that sinners must undergo before the "second" or universal bodily resurrection (*In Ps.* 1.47–54). Jerome rejected the chiliastic hope as a "fable" (*In Dan.* 2.7.17f.; *In Is.* 16.59.14), and in his *Commentary on Ezekiel* (after 411) takes Revelation 20 as referring allegorically to the time of the church; in this last passage, however, he is careful to recognize Christian chiliasm as a venerable tradition.

The African Donatist exegete Tyconius, in his commentary on Revelation, also interprets the thousand-year kingdom of Revelation 20 as referring to the present time of the church, in which the saints, "risen" from the death of sin in baptism, already reign with the risen Christ and enjoy his promises in a spiritual way. Augustine, who espoused an austere version of the millennial hope in his earlier works (e.g., *Serm.* [ed. Mai] 94.4f. [393–395]; *C. Adim.* 2.2 [394]; *Serm.* 259.2), later abandoned any literal interpretation of Revelation 20 in favor of Tyconius's ecclesiological reading (*Civ. Dei* 20.7ff.).

Fifth Century. The beginning of the fifth century, however, also witnessed another revival of millenarian expectations. The *Vision of Paul*, an apocalypse probably written in Greek ca. 400, presents a glimpse of a transformed world now standing ready in heaven, in which the Lord will reign for a thousand years; it is destined principally for those who have lived chastely in marriage, since virgins will receive rewards "seven times greater" (21f.). Bishop Gaudentius of Brescia also paints, in one of his sermons (*Tract.* 10.15–22), a portrait of a final age in which the saints will live free from fleshly drives and will have no other concern but to join the angels in praising God; it is not clear whether this is meant to refer to a penultimate, earthly stage of reward or whether it is simply a figure of eternal beatitude. In 397, the African bishop Quintus Julius Hilarianus, a neighbor of Augustine's, also wrote a millenarian tract on the coming end of history, based on the Book of Revelation.

Although there is wide disagreement about his date and place of origin, the Latin poet Commodian seems to fit most clearly into the brooding pessimism of the second half of the fifth century, a time of social and political decay. Commodian's poems speak of the age of the "first resurrection" as a time when God's poor will rise and live in peace and plenty in the heavenly Jerusalem, descended from heaven; there, they will marry and beget children, and have as their servants the rich who oppress them in the present age (*Instr.* 1.44.1–15; 2.35.12–16; *Carm.* 947–988).

The eastern church, however, seems to have shown little sympathy for the chiliastic tradition after the start of the fifth century. The Syrian bishop Philoxenus of Mabbug reports in his *Letter to Abraham and Orestes* that his anti-Chalcedonian colleague Stephen bar-Sudaili held a version of the millenarian hope in which the six ages of the present world will be followed by a "sabbath of rest" for the saints, before a final, universal transformation unites all creatures substantially with God. Philoxenus himself rejects this doctrine, as did, apparently, his anti-Chalcedonian contemporary the Pseudo-Dionysius (*E.H.* 7.1.2; cf. scholion of Ps.-Maximus Confessor *ad loc.*).

Sixth Century. The two sixth-century Greek commentators on the Book of Revelation, Oecumenius and Andrew of Caesarea, abandon all literal interpretation of Revelation 20, Oecumenius taking the passage as a typological reference to the time of Jesus' earthly life and Andrew concurring with Tyconius and Augustine in applying it to the present age of the church. The two Latin commentators on Revelation from the sixth century, Primasius of Hadrumetum and Apringius of Beja, likewise (and predictably) follow Augustine. Interest in the apocalyptic promises remained strong, and the sense that the world was near its end gained ground toward the end of the century, but it was now a foreboding that looked beyond the limits of the present world for its relief. *See also* Eschatology; Revelation, Book of.

[B.E.D.]

Bibliography

L. Gry, *Le Millénarisme dans ses origines et son développement* (Paris: Picard, 1904); G. Bardy, "Millénarisme," DTC, Vol. 10, pp. 1760–1763; A. Wikenhauser, "Weltwoche und tausendjähriges Reich," *Theologische Quartalschrift* 127

(1947):399–417; W. Bauer, "Chiliasmus," RLAC, Vol. 2, pp. 1073–1078; W. Nigg, *Das ewige Reich* (Munich and Hamburg: Siebenstern, 1967); H. Bietenhard, *Das tausendjährige Reich* (Zürich: Zwingli, 1955); A. Luneau, *L'Histoire du salut chez les pères de l'église: la doctrine des âges du monde* (Paris: Beauchesne, 1964); P. Bissels, "Die frühchristliche Lehre vom Gottesreich auf Erden," *Trierer theologische Zeitschrift* 84 (1975):44–47; B.E. Daley, *The Hope of the Early Church: Eschatology in the Patristic Age* (Cambridge: Cambridge UP, forthcoming).

CHOIR. Group of singers in church; then the place reserved for them. Special choruses sang at pagan festivals, and trained singers were among the musicians at the Jewish temple in Jerusalem. The sources are silent, however, about separate choirs in the church during the first two centuries. Ignatius of Antioch compared the congregation itself to a choir (*Eph.* 4). One of the charges against Paul of Samosata, the mid-third-century bishop of Antioch, was that he instituted a chorus of women singers (Eusebius, *H.E.* 7.30.10). More successful was the choir of virgins that Ephraem Syrus trained to sing hymns at the liturgy in order to combat the use of women choruses by heretics; but with some, any singing by women in church met with disapproval (e.g., Cyril of Jerusalem, *Procatech.* 14). Boys' choirs received more acceptance. From the fourth century, we hear of schools to train boys as lectors and cantors. The most famous of these was the *schola cantorum* traced to Gregory the Great.

As an architectural term, "choir" refers to the area where the seats of the clergy were located between the nave and altar, as part of what is also called the "chancel." The position of the clergy varied from church to church. In early basilicas, their seats were in a semicircle around the apse behind the altar, but in medieval cathedrals the stalls of the clergy were located west of the altar, in the "choir." The architectural use of the term was perhaps derived from the comparison of the clergy or singers to a crown surrounding the altar, but the medieval development was also influenced by the position where the monks gathered in monastic churches to say the Divine Office.

[E.F.]

Bibliography
J. Quasten, *Music and Worship in Pagan and Christian Antiquity* (Washington, D.C.: National Association of Pastoral Musicians, 1983; orig. German ed., 1973), pp. 75–92.

CHOREPISCOPUS. Bishop responsible for the care of people living in rural districts. The office is frequently mentioned in the fourth century in the east. There was a steady tendency to make the smaller bishoprics more dependent upon metropolitan sees; the country bishop was restricted in the use of the power of ordination and could ordain priests and deacons only with the consent of his metropolitan. The office gradually fell out of use in the Orthodox Church, but it continues in several eastern Catholic rites. In the west, it appeared in the eighth century, especially in the mission to Germany, but had disappeared everywhere by the twelfth. *See also* Bishop.   [M.P.McH.]

CHRIST, CHRISTOLOGY. "Christ" is an English transliteration of the Greek word for the Hebrew term *Messiah*, "the anointed one." Christology is the study of who Jesus Christ was and is. Within early Christianity, only Jesus of Nazareth was designated as the Christ (Matt. 16:16). For Christians, that title marked him as the savior of the world, including both Jews and Gentiles.

The life of Jesus is difficult to construct because the four Gospels are not biographies but rather documents of faith. Non-Christian sources know little of him. The Jewish historian Josephus (*Ant.* 20.9.1) describes the death of James, "the brother of Jesus who was called the Christ," but the longer description (*Ant.* 18.63–64) is a later Christian interpolation. Two Roman historians tell us a bit more. Suetonius (*Life of Claudius* 25.4) mentions public disturbances instigated by a Chrestus, perhaps a reference to Christ and thus to Jewish Christians. Tacitus (*Annals* 15.44.4) reports that Christus, the one from whom Christians take their name, suffered death at the hands of Pontius Pilate during the reign of Tiberius. Since the Enlightenment, a few scholars have

Youthful Christ, apse mosaic (fifth century) from the Church of Hosios David, Thessalonica, Greece.

gone so far as to question if Jesus existed or to restrict knowledge about him to the facts of his existence and his death. The basic assumption of these students has been that all data about him in the Gospels are postresurrection, colored by the commitments of the early Christian community—thus, not qualified to be viewed as "history"—and unbiased historians provide almost no information.

Others, while acknowledging that the entire New Testament is a document of faith, have sought ways to find traces of the historical Jesus. At the very least, he appears to have been a Jew born in Palestine during the time when Quirinius was governor of Syria, who became a traveling prophet, teacher, and miracle worker and was crucified in Jerusalem. He evidently made certain predictions about the coming Kingdom and the coming Son of Man. Sections of the New Testament identify those features with Jesus and his death and resurrection. Jesus taught in parables, pithy sayings, and perhaps in extended monologues and was opposed by important figures within established Palestinian Judaism.

Scholars who think that the Gospels provide this much about Jesus' life find those writings to be interested enough in reporting what unbelievers said that they have some claim to fairness and authenticity. Although all the records come through the life of the church, the early church itself was interested in getting the best possible evidence about this man Jesus. No consistent chronology of his life is possible, for even important events, such as his cleansing of the temple and the Last Supper, are not clearly dated within the four Gospels. Yet the church seems not only to have formed nuggets of memory to suit its continuing needs, but also to have patterned its own practice on the basis of memories about its Christ.

Literary, form, and redaction criticism—the study of the form of the stories and sayings, and the interests of each Gospel writer—have not necessarily led to the conclusion that little or nothing is known of Jesus' life. Even the death and resurrection of Jesus are treated by the Gospels in the form of realistic narratives, told as one would retell any occurrence. Although numerous post-Enlightenment scholars have rejected those claims, the intent of the New Testament is to give witness to things that its writers believed had happened.

Christology concerns questions about the nature of Christ's divinity, the nature of his humanity, and the oneness or wholeness of his person. Other theological themes are also involved. If Christ is divine, his relationship to God the Father requires an explanation. With the rise of questions concerning the Holy Spirit, particularly in the fourth century, the issue became a Trinitarian one. Because the coming of Christ for Christians is always a matter of salvation, no Christological concerns are ever completely separated from those of soteriology, the doctrine of salvation. If Christ must be fully divine to save, then his divinity cannot be sacrificed in any attempt to explain his person. If, however, he must be human to identify fully with the humanity he must save, then again his humanity cannot be sacrificed in order to describe his person. And if both divinity and humanity are necessary for reasons of salvation, then some explanation of his wholeness and oneness as a person is required.

The definition of Christology in the ancient church involved clashes of personality and politics. Doctrine was a part of life's full cloth, not merely an exercise for scholars.

New Testament. Earliest Christianity saw Jesus Christ as its center, but it struggled to explain his person. This was due not so much to philosophical systems adopted by the antagonists in the Christological debates as it was to the varied strains within the Christian tradition itself. Philosophical disagreements were at first latent; later arguments often focused on which models of explanation might be used to solve the puzzles, but the puzzles were there within the traditions. Obviously, the scriptures of Judaism set the tone, although no closed Jewish canon was available when Christianity emerged. The Gospels rework a number of Old Testament passages as keys to an understanding of who Jesus is. Isaiah 53 and 7:14 provide strong visions of his person, but they were interpreted in new ways. Proverbs 8:22 and Psalm 82:6 became important, but so at a later date, particularly in the fourth-century debates, did Baruch 3:33–35. The Gospel of Mark depicts a strong Son of God, while Matthew views Jesus as the promised Messiah. Luke sets him in a wider Gentile context; John sees him as a teacher of wisdom. Mark and John have no birth narrative, although John has his cosmic introduction. Yet the Gospels have a number of features in common. Each is basically a passion narrative with prologue. Each uses its introduction about Jesus' life to set the stage for his death and resurrection. Each sees Jesus as a miracle worker, one with great wisdom, yet filled with human emotions and compassion.

Internally, the Gospels can be intriguing if not confusing. John says that the Logos was God (1:1), has Jesus say that he and the Father are one (5:18), and speaks of the Christ as equal to the Father (10:30), but that same Gospel writer (14:28) also notes that Jesus said that the Father is greater than he. Matthew (1:18–2:12) provides narratives that tell of Jesus' virgin birth. Luke 2:52 provides the advancement (*prokopē*) theme, which notes that he grew in wisdom and stature. Each of the Gospels sets Jesus Christ's unusual strength of character, his sense of purpose, and his divine wisdom and works alongside his obvious human weaknesses.

These contrasts appear in other portions of the New Testament. Although a twenty-seven–book canon did not appear until the fourth century, the church struggled with the various images of Christ as it made decisions about the authority of the different books. Peter in Acts 2:36 speaks of Jesus being "made" both Lord and Christ. Colossians 1:15 calls him the "firstborn of all creation." Revelation 1:8 gives him the title of *pantocrator*, the Almighty, Ruler over all. 1 Timothy 2:5 refers to him as the "mediator"; Hebrews 4:15 finds him "tempted in all ways yet without sin"; 1 John 4:2–3 warns against any teaching that claims Christ only appeared to be in the flesh. Christology is thus a traditional, theological problem, not merely one that appears when the inquirer possesses a philosophical turn of mind. In the end, the most persuasive Christologies will be the ones that can make the most sense out of the most aspects of the Christian traditions.

Rejected Extremes. The crucible of Judaism in which Christianity emerged was itself formed by a strong sense of God's oneness: there are no other gods. It is thus understandable that few New Testament texts specifically call Jesus or the Christ God—although some texts can be read that way (John 1:1; Rom. 9:5)—and that there is evidence in Judeo-Christian communities of various Christologies that emphasize the manhood of the Messiah rather than his divinity. The indwelling of an angel in the man Jesus was one way to depict his superhuman power and yet avoid conflict with monotheism. This view illustrated part of a general pattern. The subordination of Christ's divinity, the description of it as something less than God himself, recurs throughout the history of Christology. It may or may not directly reflect Jewish influence, but it at least rests securely on a sense of God's oneness and his jealousy about polytheism. Even in the second or third century, an otherwise unknown Artemon, and Paul of Samosata, who followed him or taught views similar to his (Eusebius, *H.E.*

199

7.30.11), claimed that Jesus was a mere man composed of body and soul like any other human, one who did not preexist and did not come down from heaven. Others with understandings much like these were willing to speak of a divinity but saw it as a power that adopted the man Jesus, perhaps at infancy, but usually at the baptism or at the resurrection. According to this teaching, the one God in some way descended upon the person of Jesus and made him both Son and Christ, so that he could have divine power to fulfill the mission of salvation, but not be in conflict with the ultimate God. Such doctrines tended to balance the questions of soteriology, of how humans could be saved, by asserting the growth of virtue in the man Jesus, sometimes to the extent that he merited adoption as God's son, while understanding that in some way divine participation was important for salvation.

At the other extreme stood particular Gnostic teachers who found the created world so unworthy of the high God that a Docetic savior, a figure who only appeared to be human, was necessary. In these views, the divine but subordinate savior descended with the keys to unlock the earthly prison. In the last stages of his descent, he had to appear human in order to make his appeal to humankind; the pattern of salvific power, however, was not linked directly to human virtue but to divine knowledge. No one could be saved without divine intervention. Any involvement by ultimate divinity in this world as a full human being would represent a traitorous submission to the enemy who created the prison. Irenaeus, in *Against Heresy*, attempted to counter such views.

Although these extremes of subordination and docetism were often avoided, they continued to exert a powerful attraction. Views can be found that emphasize either the humanity or the divinity. Yet regional forms of Christianity, with their different languages and cultures, tended to develop along divergent lines that often crossed one another at important points, but still took varied approaches to and created different models of Jesus Christ.

Most of the developments in Christology took place in the eastern, Greek-speaking part of the empire, where the bulk of the Christian population lived and where the milieu encouraged creative discussions of Jesus' person. Origen, the east's counterpart of the west's Augustine, created a synthesis that only he could hold together. He was often subordinationist in his teaching about Christ's divinity, himself vigilant for Christian monotheism. He even had difficulty offering prayer in the name of Jesus (*Or.* 15–16). At the same time, he insisted on the importance of divine action for salvation and could speak of Christ's equality with God, particularly in his commentary on John's Gospel. He also drew a complicated picture by demanding that for the sake of salvation Jesus must have been fully human, containing body, mind, and soul (*Dial.* 7).

Arian Controversy. The great debates of the fourth and fifth centuries at first turned on the definition of the Logos, the divine Word. The inconsistent, wavering view of Origen offered support to both sides. Biblical interpreters trained in the school of Lucian of Antioch, himself a text critic and martyr, evidently noticed the fact that scripture did not often speak of Christ as God. They picked up on the Old Testament insistence on monotheism and suggested that the divine Christ must be subordinated to God the Father. They did not see themselves as innovators or philosophers but primarily as teachers of scripture and tradition. Arius, a presbyter of Alexandria, became their spokesman. A powerful teacher and popularizer with both rhetorical and poetic or hymnic skills, he was quite persuasive. Recent research has suggested that his views were almost totally influenced by soteriological concerns. Although that claim seems too broad, no one should deny that factors concerning salvation were quite significant in the debate. The view of a human Jesus who could grow in wisdom and virtue is specifically attacked by Cyril of Jerusalem (*Catech.* 10–11) as a tenet of early Arianism. That understanding could be a powerful motive for worshipers in their life of emulation. By emphasizing the progress of man, the average person would be encouraged to be like the Christ.

Athanasius, bishop of Alexandria, took the other side of the argument in his *Orations Against the Arians*. For him, the biblical passages that either express or imply the divinity of Christ are the central ones. Whatever monotheism is, it must include a plurality so that the full likeness of the Father and the Son may be proclaimed. Picking up a theme that had emerged as early as Irenaeus, Athanasius insisted soteriologically that unless Christ was divine he could not make us divine, he could not save us (*Decr.* 14). The entire reality of salvation hinged on the full divinity of the Son. Father and Son must be of the same essence or all hope of human restoration to God would be lost.

Athanasius saw himself as a biblical expositor, one who made the truth of scripture plain to the average Christian as well as the learned theologian. He saw the Arian subordination of the Son as wrongheaded from beginning to end. Were only questions of the Son's status raised, then the Arians would be wrong, for Christian tradition would not allow him to be less than the Father.

Athanasius was so vigilant and forceful in his views that his life is as interesting as his theological positions. He was exiled in the west or forced from his see at least three times and on other occasions had to blend into the Egyptian population to avoid arrest. His periods of exile allowed him to be a western influence for "orthodoxy" because he often was in Rome on the way to Trier and had correspondence with western bishops, particularly the bishop at Rome. He found ways to continue his influence in Egypt during his absence and ultimately triumphed in a most effective way; he outlived his opponents.

The Council of Nicaea (325) was called to settle the question of Christ's divinity. The emperor Constantine had learned the political importance of religious unity and put his power and influence behind the council. He summoned bishops and made available funds for travel and for the conference itself. Pressure to conform was evident, a weight that grew heavy for many of the participants. The council decided upon the term *homoousios*, pronouncing

that the Father and the Son were "of the same substance" or "essence." But the debate raged more strongly after the council than before. Within a year, Athanasius was both condemned and confirmed by a Jerusalem council. Emperors in Constantinople supported first Athanasian then Arian views. Not until the end of the fourth century did the scales tip toward an "orthodox" victory. Even then, Christianity among the Goths, propagated by Ulfilas, continued to have a solid Arian presence.

Within the wider debate, *homoiousians* (from *homoiousios*, "of like substance") insisted that there was more than an "iota" of difference between them and the *homoousians*. They were willing to see a strong similarity or likeness between Son and Father, but they were not willing to confess that the natures of the two were the same. Most members of this group eventually joined the *homoousians*, and their position concerning the divinity of Christ merged with that of the Nicaeans. Their intention was to emphasize the difference between Christ and creatures so that some sense of divinity was present. They were also most often convinced that only the divine could save, and they thus could be persuaded that the Son's divinity must be powerful enough to accomplish that task.

Apollinarianism. As is so often the case within theological controversies, no one schematic for the important questions about Christ's person was universally accepted. As the debates progressed, cracks in the various alliances continued to appear. Apollinaris of Laodicea was considered by Athanasius and the Cappadocian fathers to be a trusted supporter of an anti-Arian view. That he was. He insisted that the Son and the Father were of the same essence. But being a penetrating theologian, he moved on to other questions and thus worked out a particular sense of the wholeness or oneness of Christ's person. For him, the divine Logos took the place of the human mind and will in Jesus so that the divine would be predominant, sin avoided, and salvation ensured. No conflict of intellect or will could occur because Jesus had no human intellect or will. The oneness of Christ's person was clear, since only the unity of divine mind and soul with a human body could have provided all the parts of a human being necessary for existence. No closer union could be imagined.

It took Athanasius and the Cappadocians a number of years to recognize the danger of Apollinaris's position. He denied the soteriological tenet of Origen, that anything not assumed could not be saved. If humans were to be rescued, Christ would have to be fully human. Athanasius eventually looked at the issues from a different enough vantage point to see the problem with Apollinaris's Christology. But he was never able to express in his own doctrine of Christ any significant attitudes or actions that could be attributed to a human subject. For him, the unity of the person of Christ was basically due to a *Logos/sarx*, "Word/flesh," union. He insisted against Apollinaris that human intellect and will must be present in Jesus, but he could not bring himself to attribute actions or attitudes to Jesus' humanity.

The Cappadocians worked through the problems at a deeper level than did Athanasius, although like him they still found, both from Trinitarian and soteriological perspectives, that the predominance of the full divinity was the basic structure of Christology. The nature of the Father and the Son had to be the same in order to achieve the salvation of humanity. When pressed by later Arians, however, the Cappadocians developed a triple attribution. They viewed certain aspects of Jesus' story in scripture as acted out by the Logos before the incarnation, others by the Logos after the incarnation, and others by the humanity. In that way, they could avoid the Arian charges that the Logos had to be less than the Father because, for example, he felt pain, he cried, he hungered, he did not know: all biblical claims. They were not, however, willing to make triple predication a rule with no overlapping applications. They were wise enough to see that weakness or ignorance could be attributed to the Logos incarnate as a condition of his taking on human life for humanity's salvation or to the humanity in its ordinary circumstances.

The Cappadocians were also forced increasingly to argue philosophically with their Neoarian opponents, specifically Aetius and Eunomius, who had developed not only biblical positions but philosophical grounds for their views. More and more, the debates turned on the nature of the arguments presented for any position and along with that the nature of language. The Neoarians claimed that the Son was begotten and the Father unbegotten. Because the name of the Son's essence was "begotten," and names defined essence, the Son could not be equal to the Father, the name of whose essence was "unbegotten." The Cappadocians replied that God's nature was incomprehensible and that names do not signify essence. They also insisted that their view of Christ's full and equal divinity and his full humanity in one, whole person could make the best sense of the biblical and traditional sources.

Antiochenes and Alexandrians. Other approaches had been developed in different regions. In the debate with the early Arians, the Antiochene school had approached the issues from another vantage point. They agreed with Athanasius that the Son was of the same nature as the Father, but they also quickly recognized the problems that Apollinaris presented, difficulties that Athanasius and the Cappadocians did not see clearly for some time. Diodore of Tarsus and Theodore of Mopsuestia defended the divinity of the Logos by insisting upon a *Logos/anthropos*, "Word/man," union, one in which a full humanity of body, mind, and soul was present in Jesus. For them, the humanity of Jesus, not the Logos or the Son, was the subject of the weaknesses portrayed in scripture. They worked diligently to create an integral sense of the oneness or wholeness of Jesus—a prosopic union, as they called it, a unity of the person. The strength of their view was that they protected the full divinity of the Son and insisted that when the full humanity was assumed, humanity was saved in all its aspects. Yet their sense of the unity of the person was found to be weak by various "orthodox" opponents, not just Arian antagonists.

The beginning of the fifth century saw near warfare between Antiochene and Alexandrian views of Word/man and Word/flesh Christologies. Again, the political problems were major drawbacks to mutual comprehension. Alexandrian bishops felt themselves demeaned by the growing power of Constantinople and only partially satisfied with Rome's increasing centrality. They worked diligently to consolidate their influence, particularly in relation to Antioch, which was yet another strong see within the region. Thus, when an Antiochene presbyter, Nestorius, was named bishop of Constantinople, Alexandrian ears were alert to heretical sounds. Insensitive Nestorius obliged. He defended a Word/man Christology with a vengeance. If the Word joined the man in the incarnation, then it would be better to call the Virgin Mary the mother of Christ rather than the mother of God. For the Word was preexistent. Mary was the mother of the Word/man, the Christ, not God. The position made perfect sense within his understanding of Christology and indeed protected the place of the Word.

Popular piety was incensed, both in Alexandria and in some circles in Constantinople. The Virgin had been demeaned. Further investigations by Cyril, bishop of Alexandria, uncovered what he considered to be a two-son Christology, one divine and one human, taught by Nestorius. That resulted in a divided person, not a whole person. Cyril discovered a treatise attributed to Athanasius that insisted on the phrase "the one incarnate nature of the Son." Unfortunately, it was a forgery written by Apollinarians, but Cyril defended the "Athanasian" phrase against the "heretic" Nestorius. His influence was strong and Nestorius was hardly politic. In 431, the Council of Ephesus met, again under imperial leadership, and condemned Nestorius for dividing the person of Christ and degrading the Virgin. He was exiled.

Eventually Cyril and John of Antioch were able to sign a reunion document that attempted to heal the breach. Alexandrian and Antiochene theologians could find common ground, but one more outburst of bile was yet to come. At the Council of Ephesus in 449, eventually known as the "Robber Council," Dioscorus, bishop of Alexandria, used imperial troops to enforce the acceptance of "one nature after the union," a type of Apollinarian doctrine taught by Eutyches, an archimandrite of a monastery in Constantinople. According to Dioscorus and his cohorts, that teaching was from the fathers, particularly Athanasius and Cyril. Eutyches was declared orthodox; Flavian of Constantinople, who had reprimanded him, was declared heretical and beaten so badly that he soon died.

Chalcedon and Its Reception. In 451, the Council of Chalcedon met to talk once again about Christological issues. Although it was called by the emperor Marcian primarily to heal the political breach between east and west, it reflected the problem, particularly in its confession. Pope Leo's Tome represented the western contribution to the debate. His work did not contain the careful definitions so prevalent in the east, but it did present an outline that demanded full divinity and full humanity in one whole person. The two legates from Rome were able to get recognition from the council of pope Leo's contribution. Some easterners were satisfied with the confession because it stated their sentiments. Its fashioning was interesting. A number of negative adverbs were demanded by those who revered Cyril of Alexandria. The hope was that such descriptions as "undivided" would void the Antiochene influences, particularly what they viewed as the two-son doctrine of Nestorius. They wanted to make certain that the Antiochene error would not rise from its ashes. Recent research has indicated that that group extracted its price with more effectiveness than has previously been seen.

Others who had supported Dioscorus and found themselves unable to accept that both a full divinity and a full humanity were together in the person of Christ—that there were "two natures after the union" rather than the "one nature of the incarnate Logos"—were aggrieved by the compromise. Egyptian monks and prelates postponed signing the agreements because according to canon law they could not sign anything that the bishop of Alexandria had not signed. Because Dioscorus was deposed and no one occupied the Alexandrian see, they were correct in their position. In many instances, however, Egyptians refused to sign because they did not accept the Chalcedonian decision. As the so-called Monophysite, "one-nature," communities of the east heard about Chalcedon, many viewed it as a rebuke of both Athanasius and Cyril. Chalcedon became an anathema.

From his exile, Nestorius wrote the *Bazaar of Heracleides* in which he indicated his own acceptance of Chalcedon, indeed what he considered to be his own vindication in its insistence upon a full manhood. Thus, a number of those who supported a Word/man Christology found a benchmark at Chalcedon, even though some of their specific views were not confirmed. Groups of them, referred to by outsiders as the Nestorians, were eventually forced out of the empire by imperial law and persecution. They left their school at Edessa and moved to Nisibis, finally to Persia. They kept the Antiochene Christologies alive by translating many of the school's writings into Syriac, but they began to develop further definitions of prosopic union in order to satisfy their own sense of things and answer the charges that such views divided the Christ into two separate Sons. Babai the Great (seventh century) was one of the most successful in that effort.

The emperor Marcian had hoped that Chalcedon would provide a settlement so that the eastern and western portions of his empire would be religiously united, but his hope was not realized. Many Christian communities in what is now Egypt, Israel, and Turkey were incensed by the decisions. They went their own way in spite of imperial attempts to enforce the agreement. Although they put Cyril in their hall of saints, it was often Eutyches and Dioscorus who were seen as heroes. They had been deposed for keeping the faith. In spite of that lineage, however, a title like "Monophysite" was often a misnomer. More often than the simple definitions suggest, these churches and their leaders were concerned with questions of divine predominance in Jesus' person and a salvation described as divine intervention in order that humans might become divine (*theōsis*). Their soteriological interest, which went back to something like Origen's demand that a full manhood be assumed, led to occasional predication of acts and attitudes to the human subject. Even a "Monophysite"

stalwart like Severus of Antioch spoke of the human Jesus thinking, feeling, and doing certain things. It was the "Dyophysite" emphasis of Chalcedon, the hint of separation of the person or the equality of the two natures, that so troubled them. They continued to flourish, according to some estimates reaching their heights in the mid-sixth century.

Later Imperial Interventions. The tenacity of opponents of Chalcedon, the necessity of political support for imperial policies within the east, and the personal theological interests of two emperors led to two interesting attempts at union. Zeno's *Henoticon* (482) attempted to heal the breach between Constantinople and Alexandria that had marked the "Robber Council" and Chalcedon. Its language sought to allay the offense of Chalcedon by confirming the faith of the Councils of Nicaea (325), Constantinople (381), and Ephesus (431). It insisted that the Christ "is one, not two," condemning Nestorius and Eutyches and proclaiming Cyril's anathemas against Nestorius as one of the most important expositions of the faith. The attempt was to concede nearly every point at Chalcedon to the Monophysites without actually rejecting that council. It failed to receive support among the Monophysites and angered the Roman papacy, for "two-nature" formulas were important to the west.

The emperor Justinian tried another tack. He issued the *Three Chapters*, which condemned Theodore of Mopsuestia, Theodoret of Cyrus, and Ibas of Edessa, stalwarts of the Antiochene Word/man, two-nature Christologies. He also wrote a confession that viewed the divine nature in Christ as capable of suffering and the human nature as capable of existing only in the *hypostasis*, the person of Christ. The confession insisted that the humanity by itself never had any separate existence, a position proposed by Leontius. The Council of Constantinople (553)—noted for its condemnation of Origen and indeed confirming the right of later generations to declare the dead heretical—followed Justinian's lead, but it was too late. His efforts alienated the west. The Monophysites were not interested and the Nestorians were already more prominent in Persia than in the empire.

A final imperial effort by Heraclius resulted in the *Ekthesis*, a document written in 638 and meant once more to appeal to Monophysites in the midst of Persian and finally Muslim incursion in the east. A meeting in 624 between imperial advisers and leading Monophysites led to a definition of two natures in Christ, but only one mode of operation (*mia energeia*). Sergius, bishop of Constantinople, accepted the agreement and wrote to Honorius I, bishop of Rome, who himself offered the terminology of "one will." But later bishops in Rome and Constantinople rejected that formula. A Roman synod in 679 and a council in Constantinople in 680 rejected Monothelitism, the teaching of "one will" in Jesus Christ.

Western Christology. In the west, where Latin became the language of theology, the great Tertullian and most probably the early Latin translations of scripture formed the basis of attempts to explain Christ's person. In the late second–early third century, Tertullian was able to suggest ways in which both a divinity of full status and a complete humanity could exist in one person. Through his powerful rhetorical skill, he created formulas that were pithy, memorable, and inclusive. The old saw that the Romans were practical rather than speculative is in this instance true. The early creation of language that gave the appearance of solutions created a climate in which further speculation did not flourish as it did in the east. In fact, Gregory of Nazianzus (*Or.* 21.35) was so frustrated in his fourth-century contacts with Latin-speaking theologians that he claimed Latin itself did not have the power to support proper theology.

Yet Marius Victorinus was a sturdy defender of a Nicene Christology, in whose writings both philosophical sophistication and biblical learning are evident. Ambrose's allegorical interpretations of scripture allowed the Old Testament to be reclaimed for many purposes, including Christology. Certainly, there is no theological genius greater than that of Augustine. His writings indicate a deep speculative concern both with the unity within the Trinity and that between the divinity and humanity of Christ. He was able to improve some of the Latin formulas concerning the Christ by emphasizing the unitive aspects. He found a way to involve the human soul so that the problems of an Apollinaris or an Athanasius could be avoided, but he did not offer any significant assistance to the developments of eastern Christology in his time.

Conclusion. Ancient Christologies were always susceptible to different forms. Biblical and traditional sources demanded that. A philosophical, logical turn of mind often led to the insistence on a coherence and unity of view that excluded aspects of the Christian heritage. Four church councils—Nicaea (325), Constantinople (381), Ephesus (431), and Chalcedon (451)—have most often formed the consensus among Christians and have proved to be more confessional than reductionistically logical. They insisted that the Son is of the same nature as the Father, that both the human and the divine natures in Christ are full, and that together the two natures form only one, whole person. That consensus has been important into modern times, but the efforts of these four so-called ecumenical councils were not accepted by large groups of Christians who continued to take Jesus Christ as Lord and attempted to live out his will. In most ways, the confessions of those councils continue to offer a statement of the problems rather than a full solution. Yet they continue to be valuable as setting the boundaries if not providing a solution to speculations about Christology. *See also* Adoptionism; Arianism; Chalcedon; Docetism; Incarnation; Logos; Monarchianism; Monophysitism; Nicaea; Nestorianism; Trinity.

[F.W.N.]

Bibliography

Irenaeus, *Against Heresy*; Tertullian, *Against Praxeas*; Origen, *Dialogue with Heracleides*; Nicene Creed; Athanasius, *Orations Against the Arians*; Apollinaris of Laodicea, *On the Union in Christ of the Body with the Godhead*; Eunomius, *Apology*; Basil of Caesarea, *Against Eunomius*; Gregory of Nazianzus, *Theological Orations*; Niceno-Constantinopolitan Creed; Cyril of Alexandria, *Second and Third Letters to Nestorius*; idem, *Anathemas Against Nestorius*; Leo I the Great, *Tome*; Chalcedonian Creed; Nestorius, *Bazaar of Heracleides*; Zeno, *Henoticon*; Justinian I, *Three Chapters*; *Ekthesis*.

E. Weigl, *Christologie: Vom Tode des Athanasius bis zum Ausbruch des nestorianischen Streites (373–429)* (Munich: Kosel & Pustet, 1925); A. Gilg, *Weg und Bedeutung der altkirchlichen Christologie* (Munich: Kaiser, 1955); R. Bultmann, *Jesus and the Word* (New York: Scribner, 1958); A. Grillmeier, *Christ in Christian Tradition*, Vol. 1, 2nd ed., and Vol. 2 (Atlanta: John Knox, 1975, 1987); J. Jeremias, *The Problem of the Historical Jesus* (Philadelphia: Fortress, 1972); J. Meyendorff, *Christ in Eastern Christian Thought*, rev. ed. (Crestwood: St. Vladimir's Seminary, 1975); P.T.R. Gray, *The Defense of Chalcedon in the East (451–553)* (Leiden: Brill, 1979); R.A. Norris, tr. and ed., *The Christological Controversy* (Philadelphia: Fortress, 1980); B. Studer, *Gott and unsere Erlösung im Glauben der Alten Kirche* (Düsseldorf: Patmos, 1985); G.H. Ettlinger, *Jesus, Christ and Savior* (Wilmington: Glazier, 1987); P.R. Fries and T. Nersoyan, eds., *Christ in East and West* (Macon: Mercer UP, 1987); L.J. White, *Jesus the Christ: A Bibliography* (Wilmington: Glazier, 1988).

CHRISTMAS. From Old English "Mass of Christ," festival on December 25, celebrating the birth of Christ. This festival was not generally established before the end of the fourth century. The early Christians were far more concerned with the death and resurrection of Jesus, celebrated during Easter, than with his birth. Moreover, Origen said that Christians should not celebrate birthdays because it was a pagan custom, adhered to by unrighteous people, such as Pharaoh and Herod (*Comm. in Mt.* 10.22).

The exact date of Christ's birth is not known. There were individual efforts by some early Christians to determine the date of the nativity by indulging in fanciful arithmetic calculations. The *De Pascha computus*, composed in 243, is one such example. The author assigns the first day of creation to March 25, the vernal equinox. Thus, God made the sun on March 28, four days later. It follows that Christ, the "sun of righteousness" (Mal. 4:2), must have been born on March 28. Other authors favored other dates in spring, such as April 2, April 19, or May 20. Julius Africanus, however, argues in his *Chronicle* (A.D. 221) for a date in the winter, December 25. None of these dates enjoyed any preference or official recognition.

The true roots of what we know as Christmas lie in a feast celebrating the baptism of Christ on January 6. The heretical Basilideans taught that the divine Christ first *appeared* on earth at the baptism of Jesus and was then temporarily united with the human Jesus. The festival on January 6 was accordingly called Epiphany ("Appearance"). The orthodox church regarded Christ's birth as the real appearing of Christ upon the earth, and thus January 6 came to mark both the baptism and the nativity of Christ.

The Council of Nicaea (325) condemned the doctrine that God himself did not become incarnate in Jesus at birth. This Christological dogma probably caused the festival of Christ's birth to be separated from the heretical custom of commemorating Christ's "appearance" at baptism. The festival of the birth of Christ, who was hailed as "the light to lighten the Gentiles" (Luke 2:32; cf. Mal. 4:2), was then transferred to December 25, to counter a pagan festival held that day in honor of *Sol Invictus* ("The Invincible Sun").

The nativity festival was probably separated from Epiphany in Rome between 325 and 354. The first evidence of the celebration of Christ's birth on December 25 comes from Rome in the year 336, although the older Epiphany festival continued to exist for some time in its original form. Rome endeavored for many decades to establish the observance of December 25 in other regions as well. In 379, Gregory of Nazianzus introduced into Constantinople the celebration of Christ's birth on December 25.

In Antioch in 386, John Chrysostom delivered his well-known sermon *In diem natalem*, summoning the members of his church to observe the festival of December 25. It was only in 431 that Egypt decided to accept this festival. The strongest opposition, however, came from the Christians in Jerusalem, and it was not until the middle of the sixth century that Palestinian Christians accepted the festival of December 25. The Armenian church continues even today to commemorate Christ's birth on January 6. *See also* Epiphany.

[H.F.S.]

Bibliography

Clement of Alexandria, *Miscellanies* 1.21; Gregory of Nyssa, *In natalem Christi* (PG 46.1128–1149); Pseudo-Ambrose, *Sermo 6* (*De natali Domini* 4; PL 17.635ff.); John Chrysostom, *In diem natalem* (PG 49.351ff.); Augustine, *Sermons for Christmas and Epiphany*, tr. T.C. Lawler, ACW (1952), Vol. 15.

H. Usener, *Das Weihnachtsfest* (Bonn: Cohen, 1889); O. Cullmann, "The Origin of Christmas," *The Early Church* (Philadelphia: Westminster, 1956), pp. 17–36; A.T. Kraabel, "The Roots of Christmas," *Dialog* 21 (1982):274–280.

CHRYSIPPUS OF CAPPADOCIA (d. ca. 478). Monk. Coming from Cappadocia, Chrysippus entered the laura of St. Euthymius in Palestine and then became a presbyter at the Church of the Holy Sepulchre in Jerusalem. Four of his panegyrics survive. CPG III, 6705–6708. [E.F.]

Bibliography

Cyril of Scythopolis, *Vita S. Euthymii.*

CHURCH. The English word "church" derives from the Greek adjective *kuriakos*, "belonging to the Lord." It translates the Greek word *ekklēsia*, which in its beginnings in Christian usage referred to local assemblies of Christians (Gal. 1:22) meeting for worship, rather than to the locale of their assembly, since "church" as a distinctive building was a late development. At the outset, house churches were widely in use (Rom. 16:5). The rapid growth and prominence of such communities, first among Jews and then among Gentiles (Rom. 1:16), is attested for Rome as early as A.D. 58 and in A.D. 64 by the persecution under Nero of a huge crowd (*multitudo ingens*, Tacitus, *Annals* 15.44). The Gospel of Matthew, composed in Antioch ca. 80–90, formulated an end to Israel's tenure of the Old Testament title "people of God" and its inheritance by the church. The Greek word *ekklēsia* was already prominent in the Septuagint as a translation of the Hebrew *qahal*, "a convened assembly"; it appears frequently in the New Testament in this sense (1 Cor. 11:18; 14:19, 35). A virtual definition of "church" in the second century is found in the preamble of the *Martyrdom of Polycarp* (156), addressed from

"the church of God dwelling as a pilgrim at Smyrna to the church of God dwelling as a pilgrim at Philomelium and to all the congregations of the holy and catholic church in every place" (*M. Polyc.* prol.).

The history of the various local churches begins with the first Pentecost after the resurrection of Jesus, when Peter, the leader of the disciples, preached Jesus crucified and risen to the Jews in Jerusalem (Acts 2). The apostles, empowered by the Spirit, became "witnesses [to Christ] in Jerusalem, and in all Judea and Samaria and even to the uttermost ends of the earth" (Acts 1:8).

Apostolic Fathers. Among the writings of the apostolic fathers, Clement of Rome's epistle to the Corinthians, *1 Clement*, provides an instructive diptych of two churches, Rome and Corinth, at the end of the first century. From its opening line, it is clear that both are pilgrim churches, exiled from their heavenly home. The purpose of the letter is to rebuke the Corinthians for allowing their stable, ancient church to revolt against the presbyters. Sedition, quarrels, and schisms, they are told, should have no place in their community (*1 Clem.* 1). Some scholars anachronistically saw in the epistle an assertion of Roman primacy, but nowadays a hermeneutic of collegiality is more widely accepted. "Church" is identified as the assembly of the elect, sanctified by the will of God through the instrumentality of Jesus Christ (*1 Clem.* 42). Present are the elements of a hierarchical society: the equivalents of high priest, priests, levites, laity (40). Bishops and deacons were appointed after testing by the Spirit and had received the gospel from the apostles (42); bishops, when they died, had successors appointed in their place to preserve the permanence of the office (44). Such is the church in outline at the end of the first century.

The so-called *2 Clement* says: "But I do not think that you are unaware that the church is the body of Christ. For the scripture says: 'God made them male and female'; the male is Christ, the female is the church. And besides, the sacred books and the apostles say that the church is not of the present but existed from the very beginning" (*2 Clem.* 14).

The letters of Ignatius of Antioch (ca. 115) give valuable insights into the churches of Asia Minor and of Rome. There is much emphasis on the dangers of heresy and the need to obey bishops: "I exhort you to leave alone the foreign fodder of heresy and keep entirely to Christian food" (*Trall.* 6). "You must continue, then, to do nothing apart from the bishop. Be obedient, too, to the presbyters as to the apostles of Christ. . . . the deacons should please all in every way they can; for they are not merely ministers of food and drink but the servants of the church of God" (*Trall.* 2). These epistles have been called the epiphany of the monarchical episcopate or monepiscopate, and there have been renewed, although largely unsuccessful, attempts to prove that passages testifying to this phenomenon, uncomfortably early for some, have been interpolated. The important things stressed throughout are unity and charity, nurtured by the eucharist: "Come together in common, one and all without exception in charity, in one faith and in one Jesus Christ . . . so that with undivided mind you may obey the bishop and the presbyters, and break one bread that is the medicine of immortality and the antidote against death" (*Eph.* 20). The *Shepherd* of Hermas, written in Rome in the early second century, tells us that the church is an elderly lady, elderly "because she was created first of all, and for her the world was made" (*Vis.* 11.4).

Apologists. Among the second-century Greek apologists, Theophilus of Antioch (ca. 180) tells us: "For us the world is in the likeness of the sea. . . . And as in the sea there are some islands that . . . have anchorages and havens so that those who are tossed by storms can take refuge in them, so God gave the world, which is agitated and tossed by sins, certain assemblies called holy churches, in which as in havens with good mooring-places, are the teachings of truth. In these will take refuge those who wish to be saved . . ." (*Autol.* 2.14). He sustains the metaphor to describe erroneous heresies: "And as, again, there are other islands that are rocky and waterless and barren, full of wild beasts and uninhabitable, harmful to those who sail and are tossed by storms, islands on which ships are impaled and those who land perish, so also teach-

ings of error—I mean of the heresies—which destroy those who approach them." By Justin Martyr's time (d. ca. 165), a reasonably fixed liturgical service was in place. The "president" was responsible for leading the prayers, giving the instruction, and conducting the Lord's supper; but there was room left for improvisation (*1 Apol.* 65–67).

Early Theologians. Around 200, Irenaeus, as bishop of Lyons in France, gives us some idea of the rapid spread of the church: "Neither do the churches in Germany believe any differently, nor those in Spain, nor among the Celts, nor in the east, nor in Egypt, nor in Libya, nor in Jerusalem. But just as the sun is one and the same all over the world, so also the light, the proclamation of truth, shines forth everywhere" (*Haer.* 1.10).

At about the same time, Clement of Alexandria says: "The Father is one, the Word who belongs to all is one, the Holy Spirit is one. And one alone, too, is the virgin mother. I like to call her the church" (*Paed.* 1.6.42). Clement also stresses the need for unity: "It is evident that these later heresies and those that are still more recent are spurious innovations of the oldest and truest church. From what has been said, I think it has been made plain that unity is a characteristic of the true, the really ancient church" (*Str.* 7.17.107).

Origen's well-known words: "I want to be a man of the church; I do not want to be called by the name of some founder of a heresy" (*Hom.* 16 *in Lc.*) show his strong ecclesial awareness. For him, the church is the bride of Christ, who has existed since the creation of the world (*Cant.* 11.8).

The church, albeit built on a rock (Matt. 16:18), did not long remain monolithic. It underwent considerable fragmentation from within from the divisive forces of Marcionism, Gnosticism, and Montanism. Marcion was called "the first-born of Satan" by Polycarp of Smyrna (Irenaeus, *Haer.* 3.3.4) and was probably excommunicated by the church of Rome (ca. 144), only to set up his own, with a considerably abridged Bible and diluted Christology. Montanism emerged in the third quarter of the second century in Phrygia as a rigorous sect, first remaining within the church but later becoming schismatic and excommunicated. It emphasized strict asceticism, fasting, and encouraged ecstatic and prophetic utterance. Tertullian became its most illustrious adherent and articulate proponent in a series of treatises, including *On Modesty, On Monogamy,* and *Exhortation to Chastity.* He could speak of "the church of the spirit, not the church that consists of a number of bishops" (*Pud.* 21.17) and write: "But where no college of ministers has been appointed you the laity must celebrate the eucharist and baptize; . . . for where two or three are gathered together there is the church, even if these are lay people" (*Exh. cast.* 7). Earlier, he had been an ardent advocate of the hierarchical church that stemmed from the apostles and rejected as false whatever was unsupported in apostolic tradition.

When Cornelius became bishop of Rome in 251, a Roman priest named Novatian had himself consecrated bishop in opposition because of Cornelius's alleged laxity in readmitting to the church those who had lapsed during the Decian persecution (249–250). This was the start of Novatianism, which spread through Spain, Africa, and Phrygia and persisted down to the seventh century. Cyprian of Carthage elaborated a theology of the church in the wake of this Decian persecution. Unlike the unbending Novatians, he allowed the *lapsi,* if they had done penance for a long time and were in dangerous ill-health, to receive peace and reconciliation before death (*Ep.* 57.1). And again, against those who too readily readmitted apostates to communion, he said: "They who themselves have neither peace nor the church are now offering peace; they who have withdrawn from the church are permitting the bringing back and recalling of the lapsed. God is one and Christ one, and the church one, and the chair established upon Peter by the voice of the Lord one" (*Ep.* 43.5).

Writing to Stephen, bishop of Rome (254–257), Cyprian solicits his advice (*Ep.* 72.1) on the question of whether those who have been baptized outside the church, among heretics and schismatics, should be rebaptized "when they come to us and to the church that is one." He is unremittingly hard on Novatian: "Since the church alone has the life-giving water and the power of cleansing men, he who says with Novatian that anyone can be baptized and sanctified must first show that Novatian is in the church or presides over the church. For the church is one and what is one cannot be both within and without. For if it is with Novatian it was not with Cornelius. . . . Novatian is not in the church; nor can he be counted as a bishop, who, succeeding to no one and despising evangelical and apostolic tradition, has sprung from himself. For he who was not ordained in the church can neither have nor keep the church in any way." Cyprian's *On the Unity of the Church* 6 stresses the importance of membership in the one true church: "He cannot have God for his Father who has not the church for his mother."

Stephen insisted, against Cyprian, that those baptized in Novatian churches need not be rebaptized when they became Catholics. Other bishops rallied to Cyprian's side, notably Firmilian of Caesarea, who, in a letter to Cyprian, says: "And here I am justly outraged at such clear and open stupidity on the part of Stephen. Does he, who is so proud of the rank of his episcopal see and who claims for himself the honor of being the successor of Peter, on whom the foundations of the church were established, not see that he is bringing into existence other rocks and many new churches, since he, by his authority, defends the reality of their baptism?" (*Ep.* 75.17).

At the end of the third century, Methodius of Olympus, in his *Symposium,* gives a vivid description of the church as body of Christ: "The church could not conceive and bring forth anew the faithful by the laver of generation unless Christ emptied himself for them too for their conception of him . . . in the recapitulation of his passion, and came down from heaven to die again, and clung to his spouse, the church, allowing to be removed from his side a power by which all might grow strong who are built upon him, who have been born of the laver and receive of his flesh and bone, that which is holiness and glory" (*Symp.* 3.8).

Fourth and Fifth Centuries. Eusebius of Caesarea recorded the history of the church down to 303 in the first seven books of his *Church History;* he added Books 8–10 to cover the transition from the persecution of Diocletian to the reign of Constantine the Great. His euphoria is moving as he describes "the spectacle prayed and longed for by us all—dedication festivals in the cities and consecration of the newly built places of worship, convocations of bishops, gatherings of representatives from far-distant lands, friendly intercourse between congregation and congregation, unification of the members of Christ's body conjoint in one harmony" (*H.E.* 10.3).

Augustine, in his extended polemic against Manichaeans and Donatists, considerably deepened the theology of the church and of the sacraments. Against the former, he wrote, for instance, *The Catholic and Manichaean Ways of Life*. The Donatist church, from Donatus, schismatic bishop of Carthage (315–355), came into existence after the persecution of Diocletian, when rigorists claimed that Christians who had acquiesced in the persecutors' request to hand over the scriptures for burning had relinquished church membership. The Donatist church held supremacy within most of North Africa throughout the fourth century until Augustine, with help from the secular government, prevailed against them. Augustine wrote as many as thirteen works against the Donatists, and his ultimate triumph is documented in *Breviculus collationis cum Donatistis libri tres* and *Post collationem contra Donatistas liber 1*, associated with the Conference of Carthage, which he was instrumental in convening in 411. In Augustine's *Enchiridion* (421), we read: "The just order of the creed demanded that the church should follow after the Trinity as a house after its dweller, a temple after the god, a city after its founder. The whole church is to be understood here, not only that part which is on pilgrimage on the earth . . . but also that part which is always in heaven" (15.56).

By the mid-fifth century, it is clear from the letters of Leo I the Great, bishop of Rome, that he himself at least sees Rome as the center of the Christian church. Writing to the bishop of Antioch in 453, he says: "And so, dearest brother, it is fitting that you be mindful of that doctrine which the chief of the apostles . . . established by his uniform teaching throughout the world. . . . In that way, you will realize that

Peter, being preeminent in that place of residence where he was glorified, insists upon the institutions that he handed down, exactly as he received them from that very truth which he professed" (*Ep.* 119). *See also* Basilica; Catholic Church; Church and State; House Church; Orthodox Church. [T.H.]

Bibliography
1 Clement; Ignatius, *Ephesians* 1.3; 2.2; 4.1; idem, *Magnesians* 3.1; 6.1; idem, *Philadelphians* 2.2; 7.2; idem, *Smyrnaeans* 5.1; 8.1; Cyprian, *On the Unity of the Church*; Augustine, *Letter* 119; idem, *De unitate ecclesiae liber 1*.

W.H.C. Frend, *The Donatist Church: A Movement of Protest in Roman North Africa.* (Oxford: Clarendon, 1952); W. Simonis, *Ecclesia visibilis et invisibilis* (Frankfurt: Knecht, 1970); R.E. Brown and J.P. Meier, *Antioch and Rome: New Testament Cradles of Catholic Christianity* (New York: Paulist, 1983); R.B. Eno, *Teaching Authority in the Early Church* (Wilmington: Glazier, 1984); T. Halton, *The Church* (Wilmington: Glazier, 1985); A. Dulles and P. Granfield, *The Church: A Bibliography* (Wilmington: Glazier, 1985); E. Hinson, *Understandings of the Church* (Philadelphia: Fortress, 1986).

CHURCH AND STATE. The word "church" refers to that society of human beings which can be identified as the entire body of Christian believers. Here, we are concerned with the church as a Christian, ecclesiastical society that is to be distinguished from the state by its organization, its activities, and the realm in which its power is exercised. The church exists for the spiritual welfare of its members. It provides the possibility of achieving this end through the sacraments and other means of grace entrusted to it by the Lord. As a society that is also the body of Christ, the church is committed to continuing the salvific mission of Jesus Christ in the world through the ministerial and apostolic services exercised by its members.

As a society, the state is a body of human beings organized for effective governance through the exercise of civil authority and administration of political affairs. The power of the state applies to those areas of human life in which the well-being and welfare of citizens can and are to be ensured. Prior to the rise of Christianity, an essential element in the structure and activity of the state was an officially recognized religion.

This was particularly so in the ancient Near East and in the Mediterranean world, where religious and civil functions were understood to be inseparable.

Church-State Relationships. Many authors hold that church-state relationships, although varied, must always be dialectical, if not adversarial or conflictual. This view stems from an understanding of claims made on the loyalty of citizens to societies whose goals and purposes differ in kind.

Following the teaching of the New Testament (Mark 12:13–17; Rom. 13:1ff.; 1 Peter 2:13; 1 Tim. 2:2; Titus 3:1), early Christians understood that they were to obey and pray for the state (cf. *1 Clem.* 60.4–61.3). Because they lived in the Roman empire, taxes, military service, and political and social functions were important to Christians. When denied participation in any activities on the grounds of religious affiliation, Christians appealed to arguments of human rights, founded on Rome's reputation for justice (cf. Justin, *1 Apol.*).

Despite the good intent of Christians to live as citizens of two apparently incompatible societies, refusal to worship the state gods and goddesses along with rejection of the emperor as a god was considered by the authorities an act of treason. Reaction of the state toward this new religion was severe. Recognition of Christianity was withheld by the imperial government. Christianity was condemned as a religion and the church forbidden the right to assemble or to pursue in any way the activities of a legitimate society. Direct, overt, violent persecution of Christians was launched throughout the empire, with confiscation of property, imprisonment, torture, and death.

The persecutions of Decius (249–251), Diocletian (303–305), and Galerius (305–311) contributed to a new development in church-state relations. With the second-century apologists, Christians attempted to establish a dialogue with the state through a defense and explanation of their religious beliefs and practices. Christians also came to understand the value of a radical witness of fidelity to ethical norms and gospel values, affirmed in an irreproachable lifestyle and in the acceptance of death with courage

and hope. Martyrdom must be seen, from one perspective, as a unique phenomenon in the history of church-state relations. In 313, Constantine by the so-called Edict of Milan extended freedom of worship to Christians. The emperor Theodosius I (379–395) proclaimed Christianity the official religion of the empire, considered heresies legal offenses, proscribed sacrifices, and, for all practical purposes, suppressed paganism.

The term "Constantinian church" might lead to the impression that the Christian church and the Roman state achieved unity or even identity under Constantine. In fact, the distinction between the two societies became more clearly defined during this period. The emperor claimed the duty, if not the right, to interfere in the affairs of the church. He summoned the First Ecumenical Council (325) at Nicaea and acted to apply its decrees, by force if necessary. When the emperor's favor turned to the adherents of Arianism, he did not hesitate to exile Athanasius, defender of the Nicene faith.

Such measures contributed to a growing awareness by the church of its divine origin and mission. Although many of the organizational and administrative characteristics of Roman governance were adopted during the age of Constantine, a recognition of the rights and privileges proper to an ecclesiastical society also developed. The church willingly acknowledged the supremacy of the state in civil and political matters, while defending its own autonomy in the realm of the theological and the spiritual.

The greatest contribution to an understanding of church-state relations in the patristic age was made by Ambrose, bishop of Milan (ca. 374–397). As the son of a government official and as one who had himself followed a political career, Ambrose came to the episcopacy with a rich knowledge of the state. He defended the right of the church to autonomy and liberty in matters pertaining to faith and ecclesiastical jurisdiction. He did not hesitate to confront imperial rulers and call them to submission when occasion warranted it. According to Ambrose, the emperor's most honorable claim was that he was a "son of the Church." In some instances—for example, those regarding the restoration of the Altar of Victory and the burning of the synagogue at Callinicum—Ambrose seems to have acted from motives of prejudice. They were the result of his radical dedication to the liberty and autonomy of the church.

A new stage in church-state relations followed on the foundation of Constantinople, celebrated by Constantine as the "New Rome" (330), and the sack of "old" Rome by Alaric (410). These two events each contributed to a significant shift of power in the empire.

In the first place, frequent prolonged absences of the emperor from the capital forced the popes to assume authority for decisions that were civil as often as they were ecclesiastical. As Roman civil authority waned, the role of the popes became increasingly important. At the same time, the emperor's favor and support procured for the bishops of Constantinople growing influence and prestige. Affirmation of the primacy of the Roman see by Leo I the Great following the Council of Chalcedon (451) was a landmark in the growing tension between the east and the west.

In a similar manner, the barbarian invasions of Spain, Gaul, Africa, and the east marked, with the fall of Rome, the beginning of the end of Roman civil authority. Roman rule in the west came to a formal end when Romulus Augustulus was deposed in favor of the barbarian king Odoacer in 476.

Despite the blurring of distinctions that emerged as popes continued to exercise an influence in civil or political matters, the affirmation of two distinct, autonomous societies prevailed in the west. This "theory of the two powers," as it came to be called, was given definitive expression by Gelasius I, bishop of Rome (492–496), in a letter to the emperor Anastasius.

In the east, the vision of a single, unified society with the emperor as head was the goal. The Byzantine emperors held a theory of church-state relations in which they had a supervisory role over religious affairs (as earlier pagan emperors had) and a responsibility for the spiritual welfare of their subjects (as Jewish kings in the Old Testament had).

Theological Issues. Several theological issues can be identified in the changing pattern of church-state relations throughout the patristic

age. They point to a developing ecclesiology, or theology of church, one that was to serve as the foundation for ecclesiastical life, organization, and teaching in later centuries. This topic can be considered under three titles: the *mission*, the *nature*, and the *constitution* of the church.

The earliest Christian awareness of the church as a society with a mission came about through a gradual perception on the part of the followers of Jesus that they were a body distinct from the Jewish people. With the spread of Christianity throughout the Roman empire, Christians came to realize that they existed over against the state. Martyrdom, involving imprisonment, torture, and death, taught the Christians that they were to be in the world for the sake of others, as much as they were in the world for their own good. The sense of a mission confided to the church is reflected in documents from the beginning of the second century. This mission was to be realized by fidelity to a lifestyle that incarnated gospel values and the teachings of Jesus, transmitted through the apostles and the chosen leaders, the bishops. The Christian's mission in and to the world was to be found also in the witness of those who suffered martyrdom for their adherence to principles and values that often stood in contradiction to the mores of civil society. Finally, apologetics added a new dimension to the church's understanding of its mission. Defense of Christianity was carried out through an exposition of the truths professed by the believing community and by the stark contrast pointed out between the truth of the gospel and the limitations of Judaic or pagan philosophic teachings.

The writings of the apologists in the second century indicate an emerging discussion on the nature of the church. Although the classical vocabulary developed in medieval theology does not appear in the literature of this period, the divine origin and purpose of the church are nevertheless affirmed. It is the church that is to fulfill both the prophecies of the Old Testament and the aspirations of Greek philosophy. Pleas for the rights of Christians as loyal citizens of the empire are based on Rome's reputation for a justice that has its roots, according to Christian belief, in a theology of creation. The Christian God is the Creator who has willed that all good things be available to all human beings. The freedom of the church to dispense justice in its own right and to promote the works of charity toward the poor and needy is another result of this theology of creation, extended to embrace the notion of the church as the "new creation" in which God's promises are to be realized. The social thought of the church, found especially in the writings of Ambrose, underlines this dimension of its nature.

Finally, as the discussion of church-state relations clarified questions about the freedom and autonomy of an ecclesiastical society, the foundations for later teaching on the constitution of the church were laid. At this stage, development of church order, governance, and authority progressed and took the forms that would perdure in subsequent centuries. It is possible to trace the efforts of popes in the west to maintain the integrity of the church as a society apart from yet related to the state. Historical, cultural, and political influences have contributed to the strengths and limitations of each type of church-state relationship, not only in the patristic age but into the present. *See also* Martyr, Martyrdom; Persecution; Roman Empire.   [A.C.]

Bibliography
A.K. Ziegler, "Pope Gelasius I and His Teaching on the Relation of Church and State," *CHR* 27 (1942):3–28; S.Z. Ehler, ed. and tr., *Church and State Through the Centuries* (Westminster: Newman, 1954); K.F. Morrison, *Rome and the City of God* (Philadelphia: American Philosophical Society, 1964); R. Mikat, "Church and State," *Sacramentum Mundi: An Encyclopedia of Theology*, ed. K. Rahner (London: Burns and Oates, 1968), Vol. 1, pp. 337–346; C. Morino, *Church and State in the Teaching of St. Ambrose* (Washington, D.C.: Catholic U of America P, 1969); W.H.C. Frend, "Open Questions Concerning the Christians and the Roman Empire in the Age of the Severi," *JThS* 25 (1974):331–351; R.A. Sarno, *The Cruel Caesars: Their Impact on the Early Church* (New York: Alba House, 1976); A. Cunningham, ed., *The Early Church and the State* (Philadelphia: Fortress, 1982).

CIRCUMCELLIONS.
Members of a fourth-century protest movement in North Africa. The Circumcellions, often peasants, were fanatical Christians noted for martyrdom and for violence to others. Especially active in Numidia and Mauretania, they arose from extreme social conditions in which small farmers and slaves deeply felt their oppression. The Circumcellions attacked landowners and masters; they intimidated courts and debt collectors. Their social grievances were real. Yet they also saw themselves as soldiers of Christ (*agonistes*). Their name probably came either from the way they encircled estates for attack or the way they formed about small shrines where they could receive free food.

With clubs called "Israels," they might attack anyone at any place. But they could also show their religious fervor by offering their victims the chance of suicide, by throwing themselves onto altars of sacrifice at pagan festivals, or by committing mass ritual suicide. Arriving with their Israels, they might offer Christian relics for sale rather than engage in violence.

As terror squads among the Donatists, they brought little repute to that movement. Their lack of education, their real grievances, and their own mistreatment offer some explanation for their behavior. *See also* Donatism.   [F.W.N.]

Bibliography
Optatus, *Against the Donatists* 3.4; Augustine, *Contra Gaudentium* 1.28.32; idem, *Expositions in Psalms* 132.3, 6; idem, *De unitate ecclesiae* 19.50.

W.H.C. Frend, *The Donatist Church: A Movement of Protest in Roman North Africa.* (Oxford: Clarendon, 1952), pp. 172–178; idem, "Circumcellions and Monks," *JThS* n.s. 20 (1969):542–549.

CLAUDIANUS MAMERTUS (ca. 425–474).
Philosopher, monk, and priest of Vienne. Claudianus's work *De statu animae*, in defense of the teaching of Neoplatonism and of Augustine on the immortality of the soul against Faustus of Riez, was influential in early scholasticism. Letters to his close friend Sidonius Apollinaris and to the rhetorician Sapaudus are extant; the latter especially gives evidence of the cultural milieu of fifth-century Gaul. CPL 983–984. [M.P.McH.]

Bibliography
Sidonius Apollinaris, *Epistulae* 4.2, 3, 11; 5.2; Gennadius, *Lives of Illustrious Men* 83.

N.K. Chadwick, *Poetry and Letters in Early Christian Gaul* (London: Bowes and Bowes, 1955), pp. 207–210; *Repertorium Fontium Historiae Medii Aevi* (Rome: Istituto Storico Italiano per il Medio Evo, 1970), Vol. 3, pp. 490–491.

CLAUDIUS (10 B.C.–A.D. 54). Roman emperor (A.D. 41–54). While generally conciliatory toward the Jews, Claudius exiled some of them from Rome (ca. 49) because of disturbances over the name of "Chrestus" (Suetonius, *Life of Claudius* 25.4), who may well have been Christ. The edict of expulsion led the Jewish Christians Aquila and Priscilla to move to Corinth shortly before Paul's arrival there (Acts 18:2, 18–19; Rom. 16:3; 1 Cor. 16:19). It was under Claudius that a widespread famine afflicted the eastern provinces, especially Palestine (ca. 46–48; cf. Acts 11:28), possibly leading to the visit of Paul and Barnabas to Jerusalem (Acts 11:29–30; 12:25). His reign witnessed the first substantial missionary thrust of Christianity, with the journeys of Paul and others.   [M.P.McH.]

Bibliography

Tacitus, *Annals* 11–12; Dio Cassius, *Roman History* 60; Suetonius, *Life of Claudius*; Eusebius, *Church History* 2.8.

H.I. Bell, *Jews and Christians in Egypt* (Oxford: Oxford UP, 1926), pp. 1–37; A. Momigliano, *Claudius: The Emperor and His Achievement* (Oxford: Clarendon, 1934; repr. Cambridge: Heffer, 1961, and New York: Barnes and Noble, 1962, with new bibliography 1942–1959); V.M. Scramuzza, *The Emperor Claudius* (Cambridge: Harvard UP, 1940); F.F. Bruce, "Christianity Under Claudius," *BJRL* 44 (1961–1962):309–326; S. Benko, "The Edict of Claudius of A.D. 49 and the Instigator Chrestos," *ThZ* 25 (1969):406–418; R.E. Brown and J.P. Meier, *Antioch and Rome: New Testament Cradles of Catholic Christianity* (New York: Paulist, 1983), pp. 92–104.

CLAUDIUS CLAUDIANUS (d. ca. 404). Last significant Latin poet in the classical tradition. An Alexandrian, Claudian became court poet to the emperor Honorius and composed, in Greek and Latin, political panegyrics and invectives, mythological poems, epigrams, and miscellaneous short verse. He was at most a nominal Christian and was considered a pagan by Augustine and Orosius. Two short poems of Christian tenor, *De Salvatore* (or *Carmen paschale*) and *In Iacobum*, may well be his; if so, they are evidence of the religious syncretism possible in an age of transition. CPL 1461–1462.   [M.P.McH.]

Bibliography

Augustine, *City of God* 5.26; Orosius, *Against the Pagans* 7.35.

J.B. Hall, ed., *Claudii Claudiani carmina* (Leipzig: Teubner, 1985).

Claudian, tr. M. Platnauer, LCL (1922).

A. Cameron, *Claudian: Poetry and Propaganda at the Court of Honorius* (Oxford: Clarendon, 1970).

CLEMENT OF ALEXANDRIA (ca. 160–215). Christian writer (Titus Flavius Clemens Alexandrinus) who sought connections between Christianity and Greek culture. Except for one autobiographical reference and veiled comments about his teachers, nothing definite is known of Clement's life. He described himself as a Christian questing for understanding about God, traveling the Mediterranean to study under teachers from Italy to Palestine, and settling finally with an unnamed master in Egypt (*Str.* 1.1.11). His teachers, he claimed, gained their interpretations of the scriptures and discourses from Jesus' apostles. Their instruction included secret as well as public doctrines. The esoteric traditions were about heavenly beings and relationships as well as the eternal life prepared for all God's children.

Eusebius of Caesarea's biographical sketch may have some historical validity but is best used cautiously (*H.E.* 6.6; 6.11.6; 6.13–14). Other writers, both ancient and modern, extended that version, and it appears in numerous works about Clement. Eusebius posits that Clement headed an official catechetical school of the Alexandrian church and that he became Origen's teacher, thereby linking Origen and schools at which he taught to the apostles. There is, however, no non-Eusebian indication that a catechetical school existed in Alexandria prior to Origen or that Clement was his teacher.

From his writings and precedents, such as Justin, it appears that Clement headed an independent school that presented Christianity as the true philosophy, welcoming students from the level of prebaptismal inquirers to highly advanced scholars. He seems not to have been a presbyter and may have understood himself to be a Christian version of Sirach or Philo, Jewish sages whose works he used extensively. He knew wealthy Christians and advised them about the uses of their time and possessions. Above all, he was a learner and teacher of God's knowledge through Logos to salvation.

Clement's extant works include a trilogy—*Exhortation to the Greeks*, or *Protreptikos*; *Instructor*, or *Paidagogos*; and *Miscellanies*, or *Stromateis*; two sermonic essays—*Who Is the Rich Man Being Saved?* and *On Patience, to the Newly Baptized*; notes on a work by a heretical Gnostic—*Excerpts from Theodotos*; fragmentary outlines from biblical commentaries—*Hypotyposes*; and occasional lines attributed to him by later authors. Eusebius cited writings now lost, such as *On Passover, Fasting,* and *Judaizers*. There has recently been published a letter of Clement to a certain Theodore in which he quotes some passages from a secret version of the Gospel of Mark.

Several theories have been advanced about the trilogy. *Protreptikos* means exhortation toward actions, the philosopher's speech to attract students, and the exhorter-philosopher. The title applies to the introductory stage of philosophy and to unbaptized beginners interested in Christianity. *Paidagogos* concerns mostly the specific duties of ethics, the entry point of the next stage in philosophy, with some pointers toward the general principles undergirding ethics. This stage is appropriate for baptized students whose appetites and wills need further discipline. In an ultimate sense, Logos (Reason, both preincarnate and in Jesus) is humanity's Exhorter and Instructor. *Stromateis*, a multicolored patchwork cloth or bag, is an artful construction of clues, rooted in advanced ethics, directing disciplined and initiated Christian Gnostics toward the third stage of philosophy, esoteric knowledge (*gnosis*).

Clement held that God is the human-loving Creator who acts through Logos to educate women and men to their fulfillment as the highest angels (gods), bringing them to live in their proper heavenly mansions. Logos is the image and likeness of the Father; humans are in the image of Logos and grow, through disciplined education (*paideia*), into Logos's likeness. The Father became female to bear the Logos and Logos is the Father's breasts, nourishing humans. As Logos's *paideia* improves their souls, humans learn more of God's will, and they worship through praising God and educating others. True Gnostics are highly improved persons initiated

by other true Gnostics into the esoteric teachings given by Logos-Christ to the apostles. Clement's affirmations of creation and the incarnation distinguish him from heretical Gnostics, although his Christology has Docetic tendencies. Clement avoids apocalyptic language, substituting the ongoing progress of the soul through heavenly educational spheres for the resurrection of the dead and cosmic judgment.

Logos shaped and harmonized the cosmos, so wherever truth and reason are, there Logos has been. Philosophy is Logos's covenant with Gentiles, and Israel's scriptures are Logos's covenant with the Jews before the incarnation. Philosophy now is a means to understand truth in light of the incarnate Logos, and scripture is to be interpreted allegorically. Clement readily syncretized pagan and Jewish thought through the Logos.

Clement is regarded as the first self-conscious theologian and ethicist, a pioneer in Christian mysticism, and a contributor to the development of the concept of purgatory. His attitudes toward philosophy and pagan culture have been praised as being enlightened and criticized as diluting the gospel. Clement provides insights into the Alexandrian Christian, Jewish, and pagan milieu by reflecting on its intellectual and theological trends, biblical interpretations, and cultural concerns. His views on the true Gnostic and esoteric traditions have been used to promote elitist claims by theologians and clergy over other Christians. On balance, he attempted to present a comprehensive and coherent Logos-centered anthropology and theology.

Clement's theological style and Logos Christology, together with his educational and ethical emphases, have had lasting influence. His purported connection with Origen obscured Clement's unique contributions. He may have influenced Pseudo-Dionysius the Areopagite, and, through Dionysius, medieval mystics including Meister Eckhart. Fifteenth-century Florentines recovered his works for western Christianity. Servetus knew his writings and interpreted Clement as considering Logos to be the supreme angel. In the eighteenth century, John Wesley drew on Clement's depiction of the true Gnostic for his description of Christian perfection. Some nineteenth-century Anglicans took him as an example of Christian liberalism; others accused him of corrupting the gospel with Greek philosophy; and both used him to argue for a non–papally-centered church as well as for Victorian morality. Recently, scholars have gained from him understandings about the varieties of second-century Gnosticism, biblical texts and hermeneutics, and church life. CPG I, 1375–1399. TLG 0555. [W.H.W.]

Bibliography

O. Stählin, ed., GCS (1905–1980), Vols. 12, 15, 17, 52; C. Mondésert, F. Sagnard, H.I. Marrou, M. Harl, P.T. Camelot, A. LeBoulluec, eds., SC (1949–1981), Vols. 2, 23, 30, 38, 70, 108, 158, 278, 279.

W. Wilson, tr., ANF (1887), Vol. 2; R. Casey, ed., *Exerpta ex Theodoto of Clement of Alexandria* (London: Christophers, 1934); H. Chadwick, tr., *Alexandrian Christianity*, LCC (1954), Vol. 2; G.W. Butterworth, tr., *Clement of Alexandria*, LCL (1953); S. Wood, tr., *Clement of Alexandria: Christ the Educator*, FOTC (1954), Vol. 23; M. Smith, ed., *Clement of Alexandria and a Secret Gospel of Mark* (Cambridge: Harvard UP, 1973).

C. Bigg, *The Christian Platonists of Alexandria* (Oxford: Clarendon, 1913); R.B. Tollinton, *Clement of Alexandria: A Study in Christian Liberalism*, 2 vols. (London: Williams and Norgate, 1914); R. Casey, "Clement of Alexandria and the Beginnings of Christian Platonism," *HThR* 20 (1925):39–101; A. Outler, "The 'Platonism' of Clement of Alexandria," *Journal of Religion* 20 (1940):217–240; W. Voelker, *Der wahre Gnostiker nach Clemens Alexandrinus* (Leipzig: Akademie Verlag, 1952); E. Osborn, *The Philosophy of Clement of Alexandria* (Cambridge: Cambridge UP, 1957); H. von Campenhausen, *Fathers of the Greek Church* (London: Black, 1962), pp. 29–39; H. Chadwick, *Early Christian Thought and the Classical Tradition* (Oxford: Clarendon, 1966), pp. 31–65; W.H. Wagner, "Another Look at the Literary Problem in Clement of Alexandria's Major Writings," *ChHist* 37 (1968):251–260; S.A.C. Lilla, *Clement of Alexandria: A Study in Christian Platonism and Gnosticism* (Oxford: Oxford UP, 1971); J. Ferguson, *Clement of Alexandria* (New York: Twayne, 1974); E.A. Clark, *Clement's Use of Aristotle: The Aristotelian Contribution to Clement of Alexandria's Refutation of Gnosticism* (New York: Mellen, 1977).

CLEMENT OF ROME. Bishop of Rome (ca. A.D. 88–ca. 97) and traditional author of two works included in the writings of the apostolic fathers. Clement was reputed to be the bishop of Rome following Linus and Anacletus (Irenaeus, *Haer.* 3.3.1; Eusebius, *H.E.* 3.15.34). According to a rival tradition, Peter ordained Clement (Tertullian, *Praescr.* 32; cf. Epiphanius, *Haer.* 27.6). It was believed that Clement's home in Rome eventually became the titled (*titulus*) church called S. Clemente.

The letter called *1 Clement* was sent "by the church of God dwelling as a pilgrim in Rome to the church of God dwelling as a pilgrim in Corinth" (pref.). It was carried by three older messengers (63.3) who would report the effect of the letter upon their return to Rome (65.1). The letter addressed factionalism in the church at Corinth. Some younger members had managed to depose some of the older leaders (44). The author of *1 Clement* argues that the church has no right to terminate the ministry of elders, or their successors, appointed by the apostles.

The letter is of considerable value for understanding early Christianity. The author knows the Septuagint well. To support his argument, he uses the Jewish scriptures extensively. In the New Testament, he alludes to 1 Corinthians most often but knows also the Synoptic Gospels (and perhaps John), Acts, Romans, Galatians, Ephesians, Philippians, 1 Timothy, Titus, Hebrews, and 1 Peter. In three instances, the author quotes from "scriptures" that cannot be identified (17.6; 23.3; 46.2).

The tone of the letter is polite and conciliatory. It calls for a strong moral life and a secure church organization. Christian virtues include faith, hospitality, self-control, and humility. These virtues were ordered by the Creator God. Church order came from Jesus the Christ and the apostles (40–44). In one unique passage, the author proclaims the resurrection by means of an analogy to the phoenix rising from its own dead flesh (25). There is no hint of Roman ecclesiastical authority, yet the author does not clarify his right to "interfere" in the internal affairs of the church at Corinth.

The author does not identify himself (but see Hermas, *Vis.* 2.4.3). If the incidents mentioned in 1.1 refer to a persecution, then the most likely date for composition would be at Rome during the time of Domitian and the leadership of Clement (ca. 96). The letter might have been known to Ignatius of Antioch (ca. 117) and almost surely known to Polycarp, who wrote shortly after the death of Ignatius. *1 Clement* is included in the biblical codex Alexandrinus (fifth century) and was sometimes quoted as authoritative (e.g., Clement of Alexandria, *Str.* 4.17).

2 Clement is not a letter but a homily or appeal (17.3; 19.1) based on Isaiah 54:1 (cf. 2.1; 17.3; 19.1). As such, it is the oldest complete Christian sermon known. The preacher (different from the author of *1 Clement*) interprets the text in terms of the Gentile church called into being by Jesus Christ (1–2). Christians are to respond to this deed with virtuous living and mercy to others (3–4). But earthly life is a warfare that calls for repentance while there is yet time.

The homily was associated with *1 Clement* by the fourth century. Nothing is known of its provenance, date, or author. It is a rather ordinary composition that likely reflects the second century. Because of its association with *1 Clement*, one perhaps should assume a Roman origin for the sermon. *See also* Pseudo-Clementines. Feast day November 23 (west), November 24 or 25 (east). CPG I, 1001–1022. TLG 1271.

[G.F.S.]

Bibliography

J.B. Lightfoot, *Apostolic Fathers* (London: Macmillan, 1890), Part 1; R.M. Grant and H.H. Graham, *First and Second Clement* (New York: Nelson, 1965).

D.A. Hagner, *The Use of the Old and New Testaments in Clement of Rome* (Leiden: Brill, 1973); B. Bowe, *A Church in Crisis: Ecclesiology and Paraenesis in Clement of Rome* (Philadelphia: Fortress, 1988).

K.P. Donfried, *The Setting of Second Clement in Early Christianity* (Leiden: Brill, 1974).

CLERGY. Those Christians, as distinguished from "laity," who, by ordination, hold an office and exercise a permanent ministry in the church. In secular Greek, *klēros* meant "lot," either a token used in a lottery or an allotment or parcel of land. The Septuagint retained both meanings: victors cast lots when they divided spoils, and lots were cast as a sign of God's rule, as in the dividing of Canaan or the assigning of duties in the temple. The New Testament used the word of lots that are drawn, but more often of the portion allotted to someone. In the apostolic

fathers, the word usually meant the blessed lot that God would give Christians in the end-time (Ignatius, *Eph.* 11.2; *Trall.* 12.3; *Rom.* 1.2; *Philad.* 5.1; Polycarp, *Ep.* 12.2).

In Christian usage, *klēros* also came to mean "clergy." How the word acquired this meaning is unclear. Later fathers sought a biblical warrant for it. Jerome compared the Christian clergy to the Levites of the Old Testament, who received no land because the Lord was their lot (*Ep.* 52.5); Augustine wrote that the term recalls Matthias's election to the college of the apostles by lot in Acts 1:17, 26 (*In Psalm.* 67.19).

Clement of Alexandria was the first to use *klēros* to mean "clergy" (*Q.d.s.* 42); Clement of Rome had used the term "laic" earlier (*1 Clem.* 40). The meaning "clergy" for *klēros* soon became common; Tertullian, Hippolytus, Origen, and Cyprian all use it.

The distinction between clergy and laity is older than the terms. Presbyter-bishops were always distinct from deacons. By the mid-second century, most churches had one bishop at their head; a council of presbyters or elders who advised the bishop and could substitute for him; and deacons who assisted the bishop, especially in works of charity. ("Priest" was applied both to bishops and presbyters.) Tertullian distinguished clergy from laity (*Exh. cast.* 7); bishops and clergy from laics (*Monog.* 12); and bishops, presbyters, and deacons from laics (*Bapt.* 17).

The ranks of the clergy came to be called "orders" and induction into their ranks "ordination." The term "order" (Latin *ordo*) is borrowed from Roman society, where it meant the status of some persons, who, by office or privilege, had exceptional rights and duties. The Christian clergy formed a "clerical order." Tertullian uses the terms "ordination" (*Idol.* 7; *Exh. cast.* 7; *Praescr.* 41), "ecclesiastical orders" (*Monog.* 12), and "priestly order" (*Exh. cast.* 7).

In the late second and early third centuries, new ministries or orders, later called "lower clergy," emerged. Tertullian mentions lectors or readers (*Praescr.* 41). Hippolytus of Rome knows the offices of reader and subdeacon (*Trad. ap.* 11; 13). Cyprian is among the first to mention acolytes (*Ep.* 7) and exorcists (*Ep.* 69.15; cf. *Ep.* 75.10 by Firmilian of Caesarea). Cornelius of Rome, in a letter written ca. 250, gives a census of the clergy at Rome: one bishop, forty-six presbyters, seven deacons, seven subdeacons, forty-two acolytes, and fifty-two exorcists, readers, and doorkeepers (Eusebius, *H.E.* 6.43.11). The orders of subdeacon, acolyte, and doorkeeper (or porter) arose from divisions of the deacon's tasks. The office of reader originated independently and was later absorbed by the diaconate. Exorcists were originally charismatics rather than an order. Isidore of Seville lists the following clerical offices: doorkeeper, psalmist, reader, exorcist, acolyte, subdeacon, deacon, presbyter, bishop (*Etymol.* 7.12.3). Some churches counted gravediggers, singers, keepers of martyr's graves, hospital attendants, and others among the "lower clergy."

In the east, the order of deaconess emerged in the first half of the third century. Deaconesses were probably drawn from among those widows who exercised an active ministry; they had some of the functions of male deacons.

Clergy were elected or appointed. In the early centuries, the people chose the bishop and neighboring bishops ordained him. Later, the privilege of electing the bishop was restricted to certain classes, or to the clergy; the people sometimes retained the right of approving the candidate. Bishops were often chosen from among the presbyters or—as often at Rome—from among the deacons. Other clergy were either elected by the people, chosen by the bishop with the consent of the college of presbyters, or simply designated by the bishop.

Councils and synods, in their canons, legislated for the clergy. One of the earliest regulations forbade the ordination of a man who had married twice (cf. 1 Tim. 3:2, 12; Titus 1:6). Slaves and serfs were excluded from orders. The Council of Nicaea (325) forbade the ordination of voluntary eunuchs and neophytes (*can.* 1; 2). The eastern church eventually forbade deacons and priests to contract marriage but allowed married men to be ordained. Under Justinian, celibacy began to be required of bishops; if necessary, men elected bishops were to put their wives into distant convents. The western church more often expected men, after ordination to the diaconate, to live continently with their wives. The Council of Nicaea restricted the women who might live in a cleric's household to rela-

tives (*can.* 3). The same council forbade bishops, priests, and deacons to move from one diocese to another, or a bishop to receive another bishop's clerics (*can.* 15; 16). The Council of Chalcedon (451) allowed only those men to be ordained who were willing to exercise an office in their diocese. It also listed professions and activities forbidden to clerics, such as money-lending, holding public office, or administering property (*can.* 5). By the late fourth century, minimum ages for ordination were established, often thirty or thirty-five for the presbyterate.

From Constantine's time on, imperial legislation also dealt with clerics. Constantine exempted the clergy from certain taxes and services to the state and granted them privileges in the judicial forum. Later legislation forbade wealthy citizens or those who were essential to the functioning of the state to seek ordination. *See also* Ministry; Ordination; Priesthood.　　[J.T.L.]

Bibliography

H.J. Schroeder, *Disciplinary Decrees of the General Councils: Text, Translation, and Commentary* (St. Louis and London: Herder, 1937); Y.M.J. Congar, *Lay People in the Church: A Study for a Theology of the Laity* (Westminster: Newman, 1957), Ch. 1; G. Dix, "The Ministry of the Early Church," *The Apostolic Ministry*, ed. K.E. Kirk, 2nd ed. (London: Hodder and Stoughton, 1957), pp. 183–303; W.M. Plöchl, *Geschichte des Kirchenrechts*, 2nd ed. (Vienna and Munich: Verlag Herold, 1960), Vol. 1; P.M. Gy, "Notes on the Early Terminology of Christian Priesthood," *The Sacrament of Holy Orders* (London and Collegeville: Liturgical, 1962), pp. 98–115; P.R. Coleman-Norton, *Roman State and Christian Church: A Collection of Legal Documents to A.D. 535*, 3 vols. (London: SPCK, 1966); H. von Campenhausen, *Ecclesiastical Authority and Spiritual Power in the Church of the First Three Centuries*, tr. J.A. Baker (Stanford: Stanford UP, 1969); H.E. Feine, *Kirchliche Rechtsgeschichte. Die katholische Kirche*, 5th ed. (Cologne and Vienna: Bohlen Verlag, 1972); A.H.M. Jones, *The Later Roman Empire* (Oxford: Blackwell, 1973), Vol. 2, ch. 22; J.T. Lienhard, *Ministry* (Wilmington: Glazier, 1984).

CLOTILDA (ca. 470–545). Queen of the Franks (ca. 492–511). Clotilda, a princess of Burgundy, was married to Clovis, king of the Franks, for dynastic reasons. She brought about the conversion of her pagan husband to Catholic faith (496) and after his death (511) retired to an abbey, where she devoted herself to prayer and good works. Her later life was saddened by unremitting family conflicts. *See also* Clovis.

[M.P.McH.]

CLOVIS (ca. 466–511). Effective founder of the Frankish kingdom in Roman Gaul, the first continental Germanic state committed to Catholic Christianity by its ruler. Because of Clovis's conversion (496), the Franks had a special role in the emergence of early-medieval Europe and western Christendom. The major source for Clovis's career is a history of Merovingian (as Clovis's dynasty was known) Gaul by Gregory, bishop of Tours, the *History of the Franks* (entitled *Ten Books of History* by the author, who wrote it between 573 and 591). Gregory provides (2.27–43) a vivid account of Clovis's rise to power and his determined and mostly successful effort to bring Roman Gaul under his control. Initially, Clovis violated Christian churches, but at the end of his first decade of rule, his marriage to Clotilda, a Catholic princess and niece of the Arian Burgundian ruler, Gundobad, brought about a dramatic change. He became the object of an intensive proselytizing effort by his consort. The tense relations between the pagan husband and the Christian wife when their first infant son died after baptism led to an exchange of sharp words over the powers of their respective deities. Clovis's eventual conversion (2.30), with its far-reaching political consequences, was one of the most significant after that of Constantine the Great.

When faced with a losing battle against the Alamanni, Clovis invoked his wife's deity and then was able to tell Clotilda that he had gained a great victory by calling on the name of Christ. This led to consultation, at Clotilda's behest, between Clovis and Remigius, bishop of Rheims. There followed the king's baptism on Christmas Day, 496, according to the traditional date, and "three thousand of his army . . . at the same time." For the Catholic hierarchy of Gaul, a "new Constantine" had arrived, and the era of transition from Roman to Germanic Gaul was well underway, along with the Germanization of the Gallo-Roman church, by the seventh century. Although modern historians are skeptical as to the historical reliability of a Catholic bishop's

heroizing of a recent convert from paganism, who was fighting Arian Visigoths and Burgundians, there is nothing inherently improbable about Gregory's account, in which he does, occasionally if obliquely, criticize the "new Constantine." Furthermore, Gregory remains almost the sole extant source on Clovis's personal and political career. In the apt phrase of Wallace-Hadrill, "Clovis is Gregory's Clovis. . . ."

Clovis's military career and political successes led to the removal of any challenger among the Franks (Gregory's *History* is an awesome litany of political violence). He was recognized by the eastern emperor at Constantinople as the imperial consul in Gaul, he promulgated a law code (the *Lex Salica* in the Roman manner), and he made Paris his capital. Clovis is rightly recognized as the founder of medieval France. *See also* Clotilda; Franks.

[H.R.]

Bibliography

Gregory of Tours, *History of the Franks* 2.27–43.

S. Dill, *Roman Society in Gaul in the Merovingian Age* (1926; repr. New York: Barnes and Noble, 1966); F. Lot, *The End of the Ancient World and the Beginnings of the Middle Ages* (1931; repr. New York: Harper and Row, 1966); J.M. Wallace-Hadrill, *The Long Haired Kings and Other Studies in Frankish History* (New York: Barnes and Noble, 1962), pp. 49–70, 163–185; E. Ewig in K. Baus et al., eds., *The Imperial Church from Constantine to the Early Middle Ages* (New York: Seabury, 1980), ch. 34; E. James, *The Origins of France: From Clovis to the Capetians, 500–1000* (New York: St. Martin, 1982), esp. pp. 26ff. for most recent discussion of issues and evidence, especially archaeological; J.M. Wallace-Hadrill, *The Frankish Church* (Oxford: Clarendon, 1983).

CODEX. Book made by binding sheets together at the back or spine, in contrast to the scroll, which attaches sheets in a continuous roll. The Latin word *caudex* (referring to the trunk of a tree or a block of wood) was used for multileaved wooden tablets, which were bound together with rings or leather cords. They could be written on directly with ink, or more commonly were hollowed out in the central area, covered with wax, and written on with a stylus. Such wooden tablets were used as notebooks for business records, household accounts, school exercises, and first drafts of literary works. The word "codex" passed from tablets of wood to tablets of other materials bound in the same way. Notebooks of parchment are known from the first century and are referred to in 2 Timothy 4:13 (*membrana*, a Latin word borrowed in Greek).

At the beginning of the Christian era, the common form of a literary work was the papyrus roll; by the fourth century, it was the parchment codex. The change from papyrus to parchment in book production appears to have had no correlation with the change from the roll to the codex. The first undoubted reference to literary works in the codex form is in Martial's *Epigrams* 1.2 and 14 (*Apophoreta*) (ca. A.D. 85). He seems to refer to an innovation in the book trade, and the indications are that it was not successful. Surviving manuscripts indicate that the codex scarcely counted in the production of non-Christian Greek literary texts before A.D. 200 and achieved parity with the roll only ca. 300. By way of contrast, all surviving second-century Greek New Testament texts were written on papyrus codices, and the majority of Christian nonbiblical texts in the same period were in codex form.

Although it seems certain that the Christians were the first to make extensive use of the codex for books, explanations of the place, circumstances, and reason for the adoption of the codex remain speculative. Considerations of economy, compactness, convenience of use, and ease of reference may have somewhat influenced the spread of the codex, but these factors can be easily exaggerated and are not sufficient to account for such a major change in book-making. So widespread was the Christian use of the codex in the second century that its introduction must antedate 100. A date in the first century suggests that one of the Gospels may have been written on a papyrus codex and through circulation in the same form have set the pattern for later Christian usage. The collection of the letters of Paul may also have encouraged the adoption of the codex by Christians.

A codex was made by folding a sheet vertically in the middle to give two leaves (four pages), and each set of folded sheets was gathered and stitched. The standard form became a gathering of four sheets (eight leaves, sixteen pages), called in Latin *quaternion* ("set of four"), which gave to English the word "quire." The gatherings were made so that in a papyrus codex the horizontal fibers (*recto*) are at the same opening and

the vertical fibers (*verso*) at the next opening; similarly, in parchment codices two flesh sides and two hair sides were on facing pages. The size of pages could range from a height of just over ten inches to one inch and from a breadth of just over nine inches to one-half an inch (the smaller sizes in amulets). A great variety in numbers of pages is known. A few codices running to several hundred pages survive, but even large codices were normally less than 200 pages.

The codex distinguished Christian writings from the Jewish scrolls of scripture and pagan books (rolls). The earliest Christian manuscripts contain only one or two works in a codex, but by the third century the letters of Paul or the Gospels were being copied in single codices. Once adopted, the codex lent itself well to a canon of scripture, as in the great biblical codices of the fourth and fifth centuries, such as Vaticanus, Sinaiticus, and Alexandrinus. More than this cannot be said of a connection between the codex and the canon of the New Testament.

The earliest appearance in art of the codex for a book (and not for accounts) is a painting in the Catacomb of SS. Peter and Marcellinus (third century). Four codices represented the four Gospels, as in the mosaics of the Baptistery of the Orthodox at Ravenna. *See also* Manuscripts; Papyri; Parchment.   [E.F.]

Bibliography
F.G. Kenyon, *Books and Readers in Ancient Greece and Rome*, 2nd ed. (Oxford: Clarendon, 1951); E.G. Turner, *The Typology of the Early Codex* (Philadelphia: U of Pennsylvania P, 1977); C.H. Roberts and T.C. Skeat, *The Birth of the Codex* (London: Oxford UP for the British Academy, 1983).

COLOSSAE, COLOSSIANS. City in the eastern portion of the Lycus Valley in central Turkey, located on the southern bank of the Lycus River, about 100 miles east of Ephesus, to whose Christians was sent the New Testament book of Colossians. Today, there are few ruins marking the site of Colossae, which has never been excavated. Only a desolate mound now stands where this city once vibrated with life. Herodotus, in the fifth century B.C., called it "the large city of Colossae" (*History* 7.30), and Xenophon, about a century later, described it as large and prosperous (*Anabasis* 1.2.6). In the first centuries B.C.

and A.D., however, it was listed by Strabo among the smaller cities of the region (*Geography* 12.8.13) and was surpassed in size by its sister cities, Hierapolis and Laodicea, which were only about ten miles away. Yet, in this small three-city area, Cicero indicates that there may have been as many as 10,000 Jewish males (*Pro Flacco* 68). A significant Jewish presence at Colossae is indicated in the references in Paul's letter to circumcision (2:11ff.), sabbath (2:16), and the distinction between Jews and Gentiles (1:27; 3:11). The church in Colossae was probably founded not by Paul but by a convert of his named Epaphras (1:7), who was from Colossae (4:12) and who also evangelized Laodicea and Hierapolis (4:13). Since Onesimus was from Colossae (Col. 4:9), Philemon probably was also (Philem. 10–12). After the first century, Colossae disappeared from historical records.

The contents of the letter to the Colossians are closely related to the letter entitled Ephesians, except that the theme of Ephesians is "the church, the body of Christ" (Eph. 1:22–23), whereas the theme of Colossians is "Christ the head of the body, the church" (Col. 1:18). The letter opposes a false teaching that involved the worship of angels, ritualism, and asceticism (Col. 2:16–23). Against such practices Colossians emphasizes the unique person of Christ (Col. 2:9), the all-sufficiency of his atonement (Col. 2:13–15), and the conduct consequent to these doctrines (Col. 3:1–4:6).   [J.McR.]

Bibliography

John Chrysostom, *Homilies on Colossians*, tr. J. Ashworth, NPNF, 1st ser. (1889), Vol. 13; Theodoret, *Interpretatio epistulae ad Colossenses* (PG 82. 592–628); Pelagius, *Expositio in Colossenses*, ed. A. Souter, *TS* 9.2 (1926):451–473.

J.B. Lightfoot, *Saint Paul's Epistles to the Colossians and to Philemon* (London: Macmillan, 1879); E. Lohse, *Colossians and Philemon*, Hermeneia (Philadelphia: Fortress, 1971); E. Yamauchi, *The Archaeology of New Testament Cities in Western Asia Minor* (Grand Rapids: Baker Book House, 1980); P. O'Brien, *Colossians, Philemon*, Word Biblical Commentary 44 (Waco: Word, 1982).

COLUMBA (ca. 521–ca. 597). Monastic founder and missionary. Little is known with certainty of Columba's early life and education in Ireland. He is reported to have founded monasteries there and in Scotland. The most important, on the island of Iona off the Scottish coast, became a center for the evangelization of Scotland and later extended its influence to the north of England. He is claimed to be the author of a number of poems in Latin and in Gaelic, but only one of the Latin poems is probably his. His biography by Adamnan of Iona (composed ca. 690) must be used with care, but it has some historical value. Feast day June 9. CPL 1131–1135, 2012. *See also* Iona.   [M.P.McH.]

Bibliography

Adamnan of Iona, *Life of Columba* (*Adamnan's Life of Columba*, ed. A.O. and M.O. Anderson [Edinburgh: Nelson, 1961]); Bede, *Ecclesiastical History* 3.4, 25; 5.9, 24.

J.F. Kenney, *The Sources for the Early History of Ireland: An Introduction and Guide* (New York: Columbia UP, 1929), Vol. 1: *Ecclesiastical*, pp. 263–265, 422–442.

W.D. Simpson, *The Historical Saint Columba*, 3rd ed. (Edinburgh: Oliver and Boyd, 1963); D.A. Bullough, "Columba, Adamnan and the Achievement of Iona," *Scottish Historical Review* 43 (1964):111–130 and 44 (1965):17–33; M. Herbert, *Iona, Kells, and Derry: The History and Hagiography of the Monastic Familia of Columba* (New York: Oxford UP, 1988).

COLUMBANUS (d. 615). Missionary, abbot, and writer. Educated at the monastic school of Bangor in Ireland, Columbanus went (ca. 590) as a missionary to the Continent. In Burgundy, he founded Luxeuil and two other monasteries, from which numerous other foundations were established. His monastic rule, based on Irish practice, was rigorous. He fell into difficulty with the local bishops (603) over the date of Easter (the Paschal controversy), the refusal of the Irish abbots to accept episcopal authority, and the laxity of the Gallic church, but appealed for support to Gregory the Great. Generally unpopular with the royal court and the local clergy, he was expelled from Burgundy (610) and settled finally (ca. 612–615) at Bobbio in Italy. Letters, homilies, the monastic rule, and a penitential are attributed to him with reasonable certainty; the letters are important sources for matters in dispute between the Roman and Irish churches. The authenticity of the poetry under his name is in controversy; it shows a considerable knowledge of classical literature and mythology. Feast day November 23. CPL 1107–1119, see also

777, 978, 1862, 2278, 2317, and Addenda.

[M.P.McH.]

Bibliography

Jonas of Bobbio, *Life of Saint Columban*, tr. D.C. Munro (Philadelphia: U of Pennsylvania P, 1895).

Sancti Columbani Opera, ed. G.S.M. Walker (Dublin: Institute for Advanced Studies, 1957); J.F. Kenney, *The Sources for the Early History of Ireland: An Introduction and Guide* (New York: Columbia UP, 1929), Vol. 1: *Ecclesiastical*, pp. 186–205.

F. MacManus, *Saint Columban* (Dublin: Clonmore and Reynolds, and New York: Sheed and Ward, 1962); *Repertorium Fontium Historiae Medii Aevi* (Rome: Istituto Storico Italiano per il Medio Evo, 1970), Vol. 3, pp. 512–516; H.B. Clarke and M. Brennan, eds., *Columbanus and Merovingian Monasticism* (Oxford: British Archaeological Reports, 1981); M. Herren, "A Ninth-Century Poem for St. Gall's Feast Day and the *Ad Sethum* of Columbanus," *Studi Medievali* 24 (1983):487–520.

COMMODIAN (third, fourth, or fifth century). Christian Latin poet. The dates of Commodian's life, country of origin, and place of residence all remain in question. Most scholars would place him in the third century, quite possibly in Africa, although others would put him later, perhaps in fifth-century Gaul. Two poems are his, the *Instructions* and the *Carmen apologeticum*. The *Instructions*, eighty pieces of various lengths, mostly in acrostics, are apologetic and eschatological in tenor and contain an outline of the duties of Christians of every class. The *Carmen apologeticum* (*Carmen de duobus populis*), in paired hexameters, offers an explanation of Christianity with didactic intent. Both works show a good knowledge of scripture but little acquaintance with classical literature. They are based on accentual rhythm without attention to metrical quantities; their author composes in a popular language, ungrammatical and without stylistic pretensions. CPL 1470–1471.

[M.P.McH.]

Bibliography

Gennadius, *Lives of Illustrious Men* 15.

Commodianus, *Instructiones, Carmen de duobus populis*, ed. J. Martin, CCSL (1960), Vol. 128.

Commodianus, *Instructions*, tr. R.E. Wallis, ANF (1887), Vol. 4, pp. 201–219.

P.M. Duval, *La Gaule jusqu'au milieu du Ve siècle* (Paris: Picard, 1971), Vol. 1.2, pp. 763–764, #330 (bibliography); J. Fontaine, *Naissance de la poésie dans l'occident chrétien: esquisse d'une histoire de la poésie latine chrétienne du IIIe au VIe siècle* (Paris: Etudes Augustiniennes, 1981), pp. 39–52.

CONFERENCES. Gatherings of scholars to facilitate exchange of research results and cooperative work. The major international conference for early Christian studies, the Oxford International Conference on Patristic Studies, founded by F.M. Cross and continued by E.A. Livingstone, has met every four years since 1951. Papers (since 1955) are published in *Studia Patristica*.

Annual patristics conferences have been organized by the North American Patristic Society (since 1971) and the Canadian Society of Patristic Studies (since 1978). Patristic scholars may present their research at the annual and regional meetings of the American Academy of Religion, the Society of Biblical Literature, and the American Society of Church History. In Europe, the Istituto Patristico Augustinianum sponsors an annual patristics conference and frequent conferences on Augustine and Augustinian studies.

More specialized forums, such as the Congrés international d'archéologie chrétienne, have been developed as well. The Symposium Syriacum, Congress on Christian Arabic Studies, International Association of Armenian Studies, Society of Armenian Studies, and the International Association of Coptic Studies organize conferences that bring together specialists on Christianity outside or in the outlying provinces of the Roman empire. The Colloquium Origenianum, the International Colloquium on Gregory of Nyssa, and the Villanova Patristic, Medieval, and Renaissance Conference focus on Origen, Gregory of Nyssa, and Augustine-Augustinian studies respectively. *See also* Institutes; Societies.

[D.B.]

CONFESSION OF FAITH. The New Testament contains many statements of belief, but there was no effort to reduce these to a confession with a fixed wording. Seemingly, the earliest confessions affirmed that Jesus is the Christ (Messiah—Mark 8:29) or that Jesus is Lord (Rom. 10:9). Such a confession was made at baptism and may be the meaning of the phrase "baptized in the name of Jesus Christ" (Acts 2:38; 10:48; 19:5; cf. 22:16). Whether Matthew 28:19 refers to an expanded confession of "Father, Son, and Holy Spirit" or (as it has more commonly been understood) is a formula used by the administrator of baptism is in dispute. (No formula spoken by the administrator of baptism—other than the baptismal interrogation—is found in Hippolytus, *Apostolic Tradition* 21.) Hymnic material about Christ emphasized his descent and ascent (Phil. 2:5–11) or made a contrast between "according to the flesh" and "according to the spirit" (1 Tim. 3:16; 1 Peter 3:18, 22; Ignatius, *Eph.* 7.2), but other confessional summaries emphasized the facts of his life (1 Cor. 15:3ff.; cf. Ignatius, *Trall.* 9; *Smyrn.* 1). The name of Jesus was invoked in healings (Acts 3:6; 4:10f.) and exorcism (Acts 16:18; cf. 19:13). Some statements that seem confessional in their balanced phraseology connect Jesus with God (1 Cor. 8:6). A Trinitarian structure is seen in the benediction in 2 Corinthians 13:14. Some concise formularies present doctrinal content (Eph. 4:4–6).

This situation—a fairly fixed content of faith but varied wording, apart from a few fixed phrases—continued in second-century literature. Baptism was connected with faith in Father, Son, and Holy Spirit (*Didache* 7.1; Justin, *1 Apol.* 61; Irenaeus, *Dem.* 3). Prayers, doxologies, and hymns associated God and Christ (*1 Clem.* 61; *2 Clem.* 20.5) or included the entire Trinity (*M. Polyc.* 14; *Gloria; Phos Hilaron*). Summaries of belief addressed to pagans and summaries of preaching increasingly took a Trinitarian form (Justin, *1 Apol.* 6; Athenagoras, *Leg.* 10). Summations of the apostolic preaching occur particularly in the contexts of debate with heresies. The formulas of exorcism often contain some of the facts about Jesus Christ (Justin, *Dial.* 30; 76; 85; *2 Apol.* 6; 8). Times of persecution called for confession (Matt. 10:32f.), often in the form "I am a Christian" (*M. Just.* 3).

The proclamation of Christ was the starting point of every Christian confession. God was the Father of Jesus Christ who raised him from the dead (e.g., Polycarp, *Phil.* 2; 12), and the Spirit prophesied his coming (Justin, *1 Apol.* 31) and was his gift to believers (Tertullian, *Prax.* 2). Even the Trinitarian confessions were focused in Christ and gave more attention to him than to

the Father and the Spirit. And of Christ, it was his resurrection that formed the center of primitive Christian faith. It was in consequence of Jesus' death and resurrection that his divine Sonship and elevation to Lordship were declared.

Baptism continued in later centuries to be the principal occasion for the confession of faith (Tertullian, *Spec.* 4; Cyril of Jerusalem, *Cat. mys.* 2.4). So central was the confession that when infant baptism was practiced, provision was made for the parents or someone from their family to speak on behalf of the child (Hippolytus, *Trad. ap.* 21). From the third century, the baptismal confession in most places was standardized, a creed (as in the Apostles' Creed and Nicene Creed). *See also* Apostles' Creed; Creeds; Faith; Nicaea; Rule of Faith. [E.F.]

Bibliography

O. Cullmann, *The Earliest Christian Confessions* (London: Lutterworth, 1949); V. H. Neufeld, *The Earliest Christian Confessions* (Grand Rapids: Eerdmans, 1963); E. Ferguson, *Early Christians Speak* (Abilene: ACU, 1987), pp. 23–32.

CONFESSION OF SIN. Important element in the process of conversion and reconciliation in the early church. Practices varied greatly, but in general the development was from public confession of sinfulness to private confession of specific sins.

In the Gospels, confession refers to the sinner and the general condition of sinfulness rather than to sins—so Simon Peter, who confessed that he was a sinner (Luke 5:8). The same emphasis is found in Jesus' parables (Luke 15:18, 21; 18:13). Simon Peter's confession was related to his call to follow Jesus. In the Acts of the Apostles, we find confession associated with the moment of conversion (Acts 19:18). The parable of the lost son (Luke 15:11–32) shows how confession was related to the whole process of conversion, which included repentance, confession, forgiveness, reconciliation, and celebration. The confession of specific sins among Christians is presupposed in 1 John 1:9, which refers to the acknowledgment of sins as a condition of forgiveness, and in James 5:16, which urges its readers to confess their sins to one another.

At the end of the second century, Tertullian described a process of reconciliation in which Christians confessed or acknowledged their sinfulness, their need for the help of the church, and their confidence in the mercy of God: "This confession [*exomologesis*] is a disciplinary act of great humiliation . . . it teaches the penitent to cast himself at the feet of the presbyters, and to fall on his knees before the beloved of God, and to beg of all the brethren to intercede on his behalf" (*Paenit.* 9).

This penitential practice of confession was in place at the time of the persecution under Decius in the middle of the third century, when it became necessary to deal with the many who had apostatized—the *lapsi*—but who then wished to be reconciled. In this context, Cyprian described a process of reconciliation that included confession (*exomologesis*), and the laying on of hands, a gesture indicating readmission to full participation in the eucharist.

By the fifth century, the practice of public confession had been replaced by private confession, a change described by the Greek historian Sozomen: "Now in seeking pardon it is necessary to confess the sin, and since from the beginning the bishops decided, as is only right, that it was too much of a burden to announce one's sins as in a theater with the congregation of the church as witness, they appointed for this purpose a presbyter, a man of the best refinement, a man silent and prudent. To him sinners came and confessed their deeds . . ." (*H.E.* 7.16). *See also* Discipline; Penance; Repentance. [E.LaV.]

Bibliography

O.D. Watkins, *A History of Penance*, 2 vols. (London: Longmans, Green, 1920); P.F. Palmer, *Sacraments and Forgiveness* (Westminster: Newman, 1959); E. Ferguson, *Early Christians Speak* (Abilene: ACU, 1987), pp. 181–191.

CONFIRMATION. Medieval rite associated with baptism. *Confirmatio* was an early medieval Latin designation for the episcopal rite of laying hands on, and anointing with chrism, the heads of persons baptized on an earlier occasion by a priest alone. Where used in this sense, the term suggests both the ratification of the earlier rite and the strengthening of its effects. Although forms of the word occur in prayers ac- companying the hand-laying and chrismation from an early time, the term does not come to predominate over simple references to the action itself in the patristic period; it is occasionally used as well of the separate rite of episcopal hand-laying for restoring schismatics to the communion of the church (cf. Gennadius, *Eccl. dog.* 52).

The development of a separate rite, however designated, is part of the history of Christian initiation in the western churches between the recognition of the church by Constantine in the fourth century and the reign of Charlemagne in the ninth. Prior to that time, bishops had come to preside, in association with other ministers, over a single rite of baptism, which included, among other things and in various sequences, exorcisms and renunciations, a confession of Trinitarian faith closely connected with actual baptismal washing, and various anointings. The rite culminated in an episcopal hand-laying and chrismation later called the spiritual "seal" (*sphragis*), suggesting the stamping of the candidates with the identity of Christ in the way that coins were stamped with the image of Caesar. This single rite, normally celebrated at Easter but also at Pentecost and other occasions when necessary, led at once to admission to the eucharistic assembly.

The evidence of Hippolytus (early third century) shows that at Rome a final anointing was given by the bishop even though a priest had already performed an anointing with "oil of thanksgiving" as the candidates emerged from the water (*Trad. ap.* 21); this practice, although by no means exclusively Roman, continued in the Roman church through and beyond the fourth century. Elsewhere in the west, particularly where the newly rural society and a tendency toward routine baptism of infants without reference to the Paschal feast made it difficult for the bishop to preside, it became customary to regard washing and anointing by a priest as the basic initiatory rite. Evidence is insufficient to say whether the presbyteral anointing with oil blessed by the bishop was generally regarded as the equivalent of the seal, as was the case in the east.

Efforts of the Roman church to ensure that the practice of episcopal hand-laying with chrismation was continued or installed in the western churches are seen in letters of Innocent I (*Ep.* 25.3) and Gregory the Great (e.g., *Ep.* 13.2; cf. 4.26). But it was in the course of the effort to introduce Roman liturgical practices into the Frankish empire of Charlemagne that it was installed by synodical authority. In practice, the result was the introduction of what now appeared to be a rite separate from, however obviously associated with, baptism; in these circumstances, references in traditional prayer texts to a confirming of the Spirit through hand-laying and chrismation came to mind as a designation of what now appeared to be a "confirmation" of baptism.

It was left for later centuries to debate whether the Holy Spirit was conferred at baptism or confirmation, and whether those baptized should receive the eucharist before being confirmed—questions that could arise only with the establishment of the rite of confirmation as a separate sacrament. *See also* Anointing; Baptism; Laying On of Hands; Sacraments.

[L.G.P.]

Bibliography

G.W.H. Lampe, *The Seal of the Spirit* (London: Longmans, 1951); J.D.C. Fisher, *Christian Initiation: Baptism in the Medieval West* (London: SPCK, 1965); L.L. Mitchell, *Baptismal Anointing* (London: SPCK, 1966); B. Botte, *La Tradition apostolique de saint Hippolyte*, SC (1968), Vol. 11; E.C. Whitaker, *Documents of the Baptismal Liturgy*, 2nd ed. (London: SPCK, 1970); L. Ligier, *La Confirmation* (Paris: Beauchesne, 1973); N.D. Mitchell, "Dissolution of the Rite of Christian Initiation," *Made Not Born*, ed. A. Kavanaugh et al. (Notre Dame: U of Notre Dame P, 1976), pp. 50–82; A. Kavanaugh, *The Shape of Baptism* (New York: Pueblo, 1978); idem, *Confirmation: Origins and Reform* (New York: Pueblo, 1988).

CONON (d. ca. 250). Martyr in Pamphylia under Decius. Conon was a gardener from Nazareth. Nails were driven into his ankles, and he was forced to run. Later embellishments note his power over demons. Feast day January 26.

[F.W.N.]

Bibliography

Musurillo, pp. xxxii–xxxiii, 186–193.

CONSTANS (ca. 323–350). Youngest son of Constantine the Great and in 337 heir to Italy, Africa, and Illyricum. Constans defended Italy from his brother Constantine II and became emperor of the entire west in 340. Soon baptized, Constans provided gifts for the churches and the clergy. He was opposed to both pagans and Jews and favored the theological politics of Athanasius against the Arians. His goal was the unity of the church, and he therefore took steps against the Donatists in Africa in 347, although he proved unable to suppress them. The rebel Magnentius killed him near the Pyrenees in 350. *See also* Constantine; Constantius II. [R.M.G.]

CONSTANTINE THE GREAT (ca. 285–337). Roman emperor (306–337). Constantine was the son and heir of the Roman co-emperor Constantius I Chlorus and Helena, a woman of low rank who strongly influenced her son and was later named Augusta by him.

Constantine worked his way to supreme power through a series of alliances and military

Constantine the Great, Roman emperor (306–337), outside the Church of St. John Lateran, Rome, Italy.

campaigns. Apparently, he reached Britain in time for his dying father to appoint him his heir in 306, and his marriage to Fausta, daughter of the pagan emperor Maximian, helped confirm his position. He probably killed Maximian in 310 but executed Fausta and their son Crispus only in 326. He took Rome from his brother-in-law Maxentius in 312, using, at the battle of the Milvian Bridge just outside the city, booby-trapped pontoons but also relying on divine aid. A dozen years later, he attacked his sometime ally Licinius in order to establish sole rule for himself.

Constantine's reign was extremely important for the Christian church. In power in the west after 306, he tolerated Christians and, after the Milvian Bridge, in 313 at Milan agreed with Licinius that the church should recover confiscated property and obtain freedom of worship. At Rome, he continued Maxentius's policy of participation in church affairs, summoning a small synod in the palace of Fausta to consider the Donatist problem. Another synod had to be held at Arles in 314, and two years later, after a Donatist appeal, Constantine decided to hear the case himself. The Donatists rejected the adverse decision and for five years were repressed by force until Constantine abandoned his effort.

After defeating Licinius in 324, Constantine began rebuilding Byzantium as his new capital, to be named Constantinople. His mother visited the Holy Land, and often in her behalf he built and endowed many churches in Palestine and at Antioch and Rome, notably the basilica of St. Peter on the Vatican Hill. The later *Liber Pontificalis* preserves information about his gifts to the principal churches of Rome.

Within Licinius's realm, there had been fierce conflict among the bishops over the doctrines of Arius and his supporters. Constantine immediately told Arius and his accuser Alexander of Alexandria that the Arian question should never have been discussed at all, certainly not in public. He could see, however, that important questions of discipline as well as doctrine needed airing. His adviser Hosius of Cordova held a synod at Antioch around the end of 324, and its members denounced Arian supporters, who were given the right of appeal to a more representative

but still eastern council, held at Nicaea in the early summer of 325. The emperor attended but allowed eastern bishops to preside. The basic decision, reflected in the original creed of Nicaea, went against Arius, although for many years the question was not really settled. Politically, it was enforced by the emperor. Yet his policy was not fixed, and he may not have understood the theological issues. In 327, he pardoned Eusebius of Nicomedia and Arius, the next year banishing Marcellus of Ancyra and Eustathius of Antioch. In 336, he exiled Athanasius of Alexandria, the chief proponent of Nicene orthodoxy.

Although he was not baptized until his last year by the Arian bishop Eusebius of Nicomedia, Constantine had already spoken of himself as a Christian and provided Christianizing legislation on such matters as the observance of Sunday, the confiscation of temple treasures, and the exemption of the clergy from some taxes. He seems to have thought of himself as "the bishop of those outside," although this notion did not keep him from sending a representative of the Eleusinian mysteries on pilgrimage to Egypt the year after Nicaea. Obviously, he took seriously his responsibilities to Christians and pagans alike.

Most Christian leaders greatly admired him. Eusebius of Caesarea wrote a panegyric *Life of Constantine* in his honor (Nicaea had rescued the bishop from excommunication); the apologist Lactantius praised him. Both described his vision of a cross in the sky as the sign under which he would conquer at the battle of the Milvian Bridge, although in different ways. Hosius, bishop of Cordova in Spain, served as his troubleshooter in church affairs. Compared with his sons, the emperor worked wonders for the church.

Constantine was buried in the Church of the Twelve Apostles at Constantinople, almost certainly in the midst of the Twelve. In the eastern church, he has therefore been called the Thirteenth Apostle and as a saint has a feast day (May 21) with his mother, Helena. In the west, a Frankish document of the ninth century, the *Donation of Constantine*, showed him bestowing primacy and even the crown upon the bishop of Rome. It was recognized as a forgery six centuries later. During the Middle Ages, a famous bronze statue of Marcus Aurelius was preserved because it was supposed to represent Constantine. Opinions of Constantine have varied. Jacob Burkhardt wrote a fairly convincing diatribe against him, but modern scholars are generally more sympathetic to his goals and achievements in very difficult circumstances. The question as to whether he was a "genuine" Christian or not depends on somewhat subjective definitions. *See also* Labarum.   [R.M.G.]

Bibliography

Lactantius, *The Deaths of the Persecutors* 24–48; Eusebius, *Church History* 9–10; idem, *The Life of Constantine*; idem, *In Praise of Constantine*; [Ps?] Constantine, *To the Assembly of the Saints*; Socrates, *Church History* 1; Sozomen, *Church History* 1–2.

N.H. Baynes, *Constantine the Great and the Christian Church* (London: British Academy, 1932); A. Alföldi, *The Conversion of Constantine and Pagan Rome* (Oxford: Clarendon, 1948); J. Burckhardt, *The Age of Constantine the Great* (New York: Pantheon, 1949); E.B. Harrison, "The Constantinian Portrait," *DOP* 21 (1967):79–96 and plates; R. MacMullen, *Constantine* (New York: Dial, 1969); R.M. Grant, *Augustus to Constantine* (New York: Harper and Row, 1971), pp. 253–279; T.D. Barnes, *Constantine and Eusebius* (Cambridge: Harvard UP, 1981).

CONSTANTINOPLE. City on the Bosporus, on the site of ancient Greek Byzantium and modern Istanbul, Turkey. Founded by the emperor Constantine on November 8, 324, Constantinople was intended from its beginning to be the New Rome. Byzantium had occupied the tip of the promontory since 658 B.C. and had been enlarged by Septimius Severus in A.D. 196. The place was relatively easy to defend, being walled and surrounded on three sides by water. Its harbors were good and could be improved. Fine road systems led west and on the other side of the Bosporus to the east.

Fourth Century. Constantine increased the size of the site, traced out new western walls, and constructed buildings within old Byzantium. By 326, he had begun a cathedral and had a mint making coins; by 328, the walls enclosed about three square miles. Enough progress had been made by 330 that he consecrated the city at a ceremony in the Hippodrome. To spur the growth of population, Constantine repaired an aqueduct built by Hadrian and perhaps built another. The Marmara harbor was deepened to allow Alexandrian grain ships to dock. Senatorial

Church of Hagia Irene, Constantinople (Istanbul), site of the Second Ecumenical Council in 381.

families were offered land in nearby Asia Minor; middle-class folk were given free bread. Not surprisingly, the city grew.

Constantine's commitment to Christianity was on his own terms, but still a strong priority. He did not raze the pagan temples in Byzantium, but he did underwrite the building of Christian churches. The Church of the Twelve Apostles was completed not far from the new western wall and became his burial site. His Hagia Sophia was not completed until 360, well after his death.

A council in the metropolis, held during 360, affirmed the Semiarian decisions of Rimini and Seleucia: the Son was like (*homoios*) the Father in all things, not of the same nature (*homoousios*) as Nicaea had declared. Constantius II, the emperor, preferred this solution. He banned Aetius, a Neoarian theologian who opposed that formula, and exiled Athanasius, a supporter of Nicaea.

When Theodosius I took power, he returned to a more orthodox view. He brought Gregory of Nazianzus, a supporter of Nicaea, to the capital. There, Gregory rallied a small orthodox community and presided over some sessions of the ecumenical council of 381. The Neoarian community controlled most of the churches in the city, but Gregory had an impact. Yet he also had orthodox enemies. The bishop of Alexandria tried to assert his power in the city by supporting a usurper, Maximus. Alexandria and Constantinople were often rivals in various arenas, including ecclesiastical politics.

Approximately 150 Nicene and thirty-six Neoarian and Pneumatomachian bishops attended the council of 381, but no representatives of the west, either bishops or Roman legates, were present. The council basically ratified the decisions of Nicaea that the Son was of the same nature (*homoousios*) with the Father. It reaffirmed the Nicene Creed, created the Niceno-Constantinopolitan Creed that bears its name, and also extended the understanding of Christ by condemning Apollinaris's view that the human nature in Jesus was incomplete, lacking a human intelligent soul.

When Gregory became so disgusted with the wranglings that he resigned, Nectarius was named the new orthodox bishop of Constantinople. The attempt to settle a schism in Antioch went awry. Melitius, one bishop there, was invited to preside at the council but died during its proceedings. The selection of Flavian to succeed him ignored the claims of the esteemed older rival bishop Paulinus. The council gave a place of honor to the bishop of Constantinople above all except the bishop of Rome. The decision worsened antagonisms, which issued in repeated incursions into Constantinopolitan church affairs by Alexandrian bishops, particularly Theophilus and Cyril. Yet the confirmation at Chalcedon in 451 of Constantinople's position as the principal church in the east prepared for the recognition of its bishop as the leading patriarch in the Orthodox family of churches.

After a stunning career as a preacher in Antioch, John Chrysostom ("the golden-tongued") was kidnapped and made bishop of Constantinople in 398, but his career there was short and difficult. He was a strict moralist, a former monk who was offended by the materialism of the capital. He compared the empress Eudoxia to Jezebel or Salome, and thus quickly lost favor in the court. When some Origenist monks from Egypt, the Tall Brothers, appealed to Chrysostom to defend them against Theophilus, bishop of Alexandria, Theophilus sent messengers to Eudoxia and managed to get emperor Arcadius's agreement to hold a synod at which Chrysostom was condemned in 403. A near riot and an earthquake led Arcadius to recall Chrysostom, but in 404 the bishop was deposed and banned.

Fifth Century. When Theodosius II came to power in 408, the city had grown far beyond the walls built by Constantine. He began the great wall that defended the city for a thousand years. He started a "university" in 425 and recodified the laws by 438. During his reign, two Christian lawyers became church historians by updating the first ecclesiastical history of Eusebius. Socrates, a native of Constantinople, covered the period from 305 to 439. He used a number of good sources, which he cited, and offered a balanced, relatively objective viewpoint. Sozomen, born in Palestine but a resident of Constantinople when he wrote, is often disparaged. He did not cite his sources, yet he developed more fully some of the topics he treated and was much more of a literary stylist than Socrates.

Two important theological figures lived in Constantinople during Theodosius's reign. Nestorius, born in Syria, had been a monk in Antioch, where he gained a great reputation as a preacher. In 428, when the see of Constantinople was vacant, Theodosius invited him to the capital. Nestorius was not a moralist like Chrysostom, but he was still unsuited for the metropolis. He took it upon himself to attack heretics and schismatics. Full in the face of popular piety, he claimed that the Virgin Mary was not the mother of God (*Theotokos*) but rather the bearer of Christ (*Christotokos*). He emphasized the complete humanity of Christ as well as his divinity and downplayed the unity of the two aspects.

His positions created a furor in the metropolis and attracted the attention of the powerful and keen Cyril, bishop of Alexandria. The brash Nestorius did not explain his sense of the unity of Christ's person in terms acceptable to his opponents. Cyril, unwittingly quoting Apollinarian forgeries, insisted on a formula of one nature, a model that saw Christ's divinity completely dominate the humanity. Politics, personal temperaments, and different traditional views complicated matters. Nestorius was condemned at the Council of Ephesus in 431 and exiled. Cyril was later able to agree with John of Antioch on a compromise solution. When the Council of Chalcedon met in 451, Nestorius was still in disfavor, a position in which he died. But his *Bazaar of Heracleides*, extant only in Syriac, indicates that he thought Chalcedon vindicated his position.

Nestorius had powerful enemies in Constantinople also. Eutyches, the head of a monastery in the metropolis, opposed him. Monastic communities had become a substantial force in ecclesiastical politics. (The monastery of Isaac at Psmathia just outside the city, begun in 383, was one of the first monastic communities in Constantinople. A monastery of St. Andrew and another of Carpus and Papylus may have existed in the southern part of the city, where another church and a monastery, that of St. John Studios, begun during 463, can still be seen today. A monastery referred to as Hodigitria may have been built in the fifth century just east of Hagia Irene and Hagia Sophia. In Justin's reign [518–527] there were eighty-five monasteries in the metropolis.) Eutyches insisted that there were two natures, divine and human, in Christ before the union, but when they were united only one nature, the divine, remained. Christ's human nature was not the same as ours; it was much less. Flavian, bishop of Constantinople, called a council in 448 and excommunicated Eutyches. At the "Robber Council" of 449 in Ephesus, a high point of political power struggles among ecclesiastical leaders in Alexandria, Antioch, and Constantinople, Eutyches was acquitted, but at Chalcedon in 451 he was deposed and exiled. His views, however, were quite similar to those held by later Monophysites in Syria and Egypt.

In 482, the emperor Zeno, who needed the Monophysites' support for political reasons, tried to unite the Christian parties on a formula, the *Henoticon*, that condemned both Nestorius and Eutyches, affirmed the Niceno-Constantinopolitan Creed, and accepted Cyril of Alexandria's writings. Acacius, bishop of Constantinople, together with Peter Mongus, bishop of Alexandria, helped write the formula. Although accepted in the east, it failed in the west, partially because it did not discuss the problem of "natures" in specific language, and partially because it was an imposed political settlement.

Sixth Century. During the fifth century, at least one new church was built in the Blachernae region of the city near the northern end of Theodosius's wall. But the sixth century saw the greatest activity. From 527 to 565, Constantinople was dominated by the emperor Justinian. He reclaimed territory from the Vandals and Goths, recodified the laws—reenforcing the persecution of pagans through them—and showed himself to be a great builder and Christian apologist. From 527 to 536 he built the Church of St. Sergius and St. Bacchus. In the same period, he refurbished the Church of the Twelve Apostles. All did not go well, however. The Nika riot in 532 nearly destroyed the old center of the city and Justinian's reign. The emperor held out and used the destruction to his advantage. He rebuilt much of the city, including Hagia Irene and Hagia Sophia. The latter replaced the Constantinian structure with the present building. Begun five weeks after the fires set during the riot and completed in less than six years, Hagia Sophia became the most imposing structure in church architecture. The three-aisled building, with a round yet almost flat dome, was a marvel of engineering and art. Although the dome collapsed and had to be replaced, the basic structure and some of its later mosaics can be viewed today. The liturgy of Hagia Sophia became a standard for Eastern Orthodoxy.

When in 540 the plague killed thousands in Constantinople, Justinian enlarged the welfare system of the city, but the metropolis did not recover in population until the ninth century. The Sion silver hoard, displayed at Dumbarton Oaks in Washington, D.C., indicates the great skill of Constantinopolitan ateliers during this period. Procopius's description of Hagia Sophia makes it clear that there were many skilled craftsmen in the metropolis.

Still suffering politically from the religious divisions between Chalcedonians and Monophysites, Justinian decreed the *Three Chapters*, which condemned apparent supporters of Nestorius. Although dead, Theodore of Mopsuestia was to be excommunicated and his writings destroyed, and selected works of Theodoret of Cyrus and Ibas of Edessa would be banned. In 553, Justinian called a council in the city to decide such matters. Some 165 bishops, mostly from the east, attended. Fourteen anathemas were pronounced, twelve concerned with Theodore of Mopsuestia, one with Theodoret's writings, and one with Ibas's letter. Origen was also condemned as a heretic in the eleventh anathema. Vigilius of Rome did not attend and argued that Theodore had not been declared heretical by Ephesus or Chalcedon. He also noted that previous councils had not desecrated the dead. But he was exiled for a time, then brought back when he accepted the *Three Chapters*. Thus, this Fifth Ecumenical Council relegated two great eastern theologians, Origen and Theodore, to the ranks of the heretics. Only in modern times have their reputations been reestablished in some circles. When the Monophysites claimed that pope Julius and Athanasius supported their positions, Justinian countered that the citations were probably forgeries since they agreed with Apollinaris. Someone in the court was a worthy literary sleuth.

Theophylact Simocatta in his description of the Persian Wars under Maurice (582–602) implies that the bishop of Constantinople created a teaching post, perhaps a school, in relation to the patriarchate. There is some evidence for an ecclesiastical library as well.

Nicephorus, *Chronographia brevis* 8 (PG 100.1041ff.) provides the traditional list of the bishops of Constantinople. *See also* Hagia Sophia.
[F.W.N.]

Bibliography

J. Ebersolt, *Constantinople: recueil d'études, d'archéolgie et d'histoire* (Paris: Adrien-Maisonneuve, 1951); R. Janin, *Les Eglises et les monastères de Constantinople* (Paris: Centre National de la Recherche Scientifique, 1953), Vol. 3: La Géographie ecclésiastique de l'empire Byzantine: Première Partie, le siège de Constantinople et le patriarcat oecuménique; G. Downey, *Constantinople in the Age of Justinian* (Norman: U of Oklahoma P, 1960); J. Beckwith, *The Art of Constantinople* (Greenwich: New York Graphic Society, 1961); G. Every, *The Byzantine Patriarchate (451–1204)*, 2nd rev. ed. (London: SPCK, 1962); P. Sherrard, *Constantinople: Iconography of a Sacred City* (Oxford: Oxford UP, 1965); D.T. Rice, *Constantinople: From Byzantium to Istanbul* (New York: Stein and Day, 1965); T.F. Mathews, *The Early Churches of Constantinople: Architecture and Liturgy* (University Park: Pennsylvania State UP, 1971); *GOTR* 27.4 (1982):359–453, devoted to the Council of Constantinople, 381; N.G. Wilson, *Scholars of Byzantium* (Baltimore: Johns Hopkins UP, 1983); R. Krautheimer, *Three Christian Capitals* (Berkeley: U of California P, 1983).

ORTHODOX PATRIARCHS OF CONSTANTINOPLE, 315–606

Metrophanes	315–327?
Alexander	327?–340
Paul I	340–341
Eusebius	341–342
Paul I (again)	342–344
Macedonius I	342–348
Paul I (again)	348–350
Macedonius I (again)	350–360
Eudoxius	360–369
Demophilus	369–379
Evagrius	369–370
Gregory of Nazianzus	379–381
Maximus	381
Nectarius	381–397
John I Chrysostom	398–404
Arsacius	404–405
Atticus	405(406?)–425

Adapted from *History of the Byzantine State* by George Ostrogorsky. Copyright © 1969 by Rutgers, The State University. Printed with permission of Rutgers University Press.

Constantius I Chlorus (ca. 250–306), western emperor under Diocletian, in porphyry, now in the British Museum, London, England. (By courtesy of the Trustees of the British Museum.)

CONSTANTIUS I CHLORUS (ca. 250–306). Roman emperor in the west (305–306) and father of Constantine the Great. Constantius I Chlorus was an Illyrian army officer whose son Constantine was born to his concubine Helena ca. 285. Eight years later, after he had put away the concubine and married Theodora, stepdaughter of Maximian, the emperor in the west, the senior emperor Diocletian chose him to assist Maximian. He was expected to recover rebellious Britain and pacify Gaul; he succeeded in both tasks. When Diocletian abdicated in 305, Constantius became senior Augustus in the west. His son, kept as a hostage near the emperor Galerius in the east, escaped in 306 and joined his father in Britain for a successful campaign against the Picts. On his deathbed at York, Constantius seems to have designated Constantine as his heir. Diocletian had planned an imperial meritocracy, as in the second century, but Constantius disrupted the arrangement, first by marrying Theodora and then by selecting Constantine.

From 303 onward, Diocletian persecuted the Christian church, and in the east there were many martyrs. In the west, under Constantius, there were few if any, although occasional buildings were destroyed. Eusebius praises Constantius effusively, while Lactantius admits the destruction of buildings (*Mort. persec.* 15.7).

Constantius may have been a monotheist, but he was no Christian and took no interest in church problems. Constantine found him too plebeian and invented the legend of his descent from the emperor Claudius Gothicus. "Chlorus" is a medieval nickname perhaps meaning "pale." *See also* Constantine. [R.M.G.]

Bibliography

Lactantius, *Deaths of the Persecutors* 15; Eusebius, *Life of Constantine* 1.13–21; [Ammianus Marcellinus] *Excerpts of Valesius* 1–2.

CONSTANTIUS II (317–361). Roman emperor in the east (337–361). Constantius was the second son of Constantine and Fausta. At his father's death, the army killed many of his relatives, perhaps at his instigation, and the survivors—Constantine II, Constantius II, and Constans—divided the empire. Constantius took the eastern "dioceses" of Thrace, Macedonia, Greece, Asia, and Egypt, all with large Christian populations. To the east, the frontier was under attack by the Persians, but he was able to hold Nisibis from 338 to 350. In 340, Constantine II, ruler of Britain, Gaul, and Spain, was killed in Italy while attempting to overthrow Constans, himself killed a decade later. In 350, Constantius became ruler of the whole Roman empire, making his cousin Gallus the Caesar at Antioch in 351 but having him killed three years later. In 355, he made Gallus's half-brother, Julian, the Caesar in Gaul.

Constantius seems to have enjoyed theological debate, although he did not fully understand the issues. According to the pagan historian Ammianus Marcellinus, "He confused the plain and simple Christian religion with old women's superstitions, and in investigating it he aroused many controversies by complex discussions rather than serious attempts to settle matters. As they spread, he fed them by wordy contentions. As crowds of bishops went to and fro to the 'synods' as they call them, and he sought to make the whole religion conform to his will, he cut the sinews of the courier service" (21.16.18). Other passages explain some of the difficulties: "He made great pretensions to learning, but after failing in rhetoric because of dullness of mind, he turned to making verses but accomplished nothing worthwhile" (4). "Sometimes when dictating, he signed himself 'My Eternity' and in his own hand called himself 'Lord of the whole world'" (15.1.3).

In church affairs, Constantius usually supported the Arian party and opposed Athanasius, although his wavering policy involved not only exiling the bishop but also recalling him. (Both Constantine the Great and Julian also exiled Athanasius.) He held repeated councils in order to unify the church, beginning at Antioch in 341, with nearly 100 eastern bishops in attendance; continuing at Sardica in 343, where east separated from west; and reaching a climax in the west at Milan in 355 and at Sirmium in 357. At Milan, according to Athanasius (H. Ar. 33.7), the emperor insisted that his will was the rule for the church and that critics would be exiled. Before Sirmium, the aged Hosius of Cordova, who had served the emperor's father in religious

matters and had been active at Sardica, wrote him on the separation of church and state: "God has put in your hands the kingdom; to us he has entrusted the affairs of the church; and just as one who would steal the empire from you would resist God's ordinances, so you should fear that by taking the government of the church on yourself you would become guilty of a greater offense" (H. Ar. 44). Indeed, Hosius asked him to suspend the Council of Sirmium and stop meddling in church affairs, but he did not do so.

No one seems to have criticized his generous donations of tax exemption to the clergy. In 346, they were exempted from all supplementary taxes and levies, and further benefits extending to their wives, children, and slaves soon followed. At the Synod of Rimini, the clergy asked for total exemption from the land tax for themselves and for church property. Constantius permitted this exemption only for the church, but Julian evidently revoked it and it was not restored after his time.

Constantius was deeply impressed by his first visit to Rome in 357. Entering with his military escort and hailed as Augustus, he made an effort to look impassive, although he was "dazzled by the array of wonderful sights." He decided like the first Augustus to bring an obelisk from Egypt to adorn it (Ammianus 16.10). He removed the statue and altar of Victory from the Senate, but like his father he respected the privileges of the vestal virgins, distributed priestly offices among the nobles, and gave money for pagan rites (Symmachus, Ep. 10.61). His supposed attempts to suppress paganism had little result. In 341, he ordered sacrifices abolished (Cod. Thds. 16.10.2) but the next year required the temples in Rome to be left untouched (16.10.3). About 348, the Christian author Firmicus Maternus denounced pagan religions and urged Constantius to exercise greater harshness; five years later, he began attacks on paganism, in part because of his victory over the usurper Magnentius (Cod. Thds. 16.10.5). The visit to Rome and perhaps the tacit influence of Julian impelled him to modify this policy. In 357–358, he attacked barbarians on the Danube and then moved east to oppose renewed Persian attacks.

Athanasius had come to detest Constantius and in 358 denounced him as the forerunner of the Antichrist (*H. Ar.* 77). His pagan successor, Julian, also hated him and after tactfully praising him in three early panegyrics he denounced him as a murderer in orations and letters, as well as in a satire on the Caesars.

Racked by illness after the revolt of Julian, he was about to take an army westward through Asia to attack him when, overcome by illness, he was baptized by the Arian bishop of Antioch and died near Tarsus on November 3, 361. At his death, the Christian church was effectively Arian, but the pendulum was about to swing. *See also* Constans; Constantine.   [R.M.G.]

Bibliography

Ammianus Marcellinus, tr. by J.C. Rolfe, LCL (1935, 1937), Vols. 1 and 2; *The Works of the Emperor Julian*, tr. by W.C. Wright, LCL (1913), Vols. 1 and 2; J. Stevenson, ed., *Creeds, Councils, and Controversies* (New York: Seabury, 1966), pp. 1–50.

J. Vogt, "Pagans and Christians in the Family of Constantine the Great," *The Conflict Between Paganism and Christianity in the Fourth Century*, ed. A. Momigliano (Oxford: Clarendon, 1963), pp. 38–55; A.H.M. Jones, *The Later Roman Empire, A Social, Economic, and Administrative Survey*, 2 vols. (Norman: U of Oklahoma P, 1964), Vol. 1, pp. 112–120 and passim.

COPTS. Autochthonous Christians of Egypt. The name "Copts" is derived from the Greek *Aigyptioi* ("Egyptians") via the Arabic *Qibt*, meaning simply the indigenous population, descendants of those of pharaonic times and Christianized since the fourth century. After the Council of Chalcedon (451) resulted in the deposition of bishop Dioscorus I of Alexandria, the Egyptian Christians remained loyal to his ecclesiology and to Cyril's theology, refusing to accept the definition of Chalcedon and adhering to a church organization of their own, which came to be termed "Coptic Orthodox." "Copts" thus became a designation synonymous with "non-Chalcedonian Egyptian Christians," who used the Coptic language along with Greek in their liturgy and as a major carrier of their culture, thought, and theology. The label "Copt" does not, however, automatically connote a monoglot country dweller of the peasant class: Cyril of Alexandria was as much a Copt as Shenoute of Atripe.

The doctrinal position taken and defended by the Copts was essentially that of the Christology of Cyril, "one incarnate nature of God the Word," based on a semantics derived from Coptic and Syriac that understood *physis* and *hypostasis* as synonyms. Characteristic of the Coptic stance at the deepest level was a total rejection of the *Tome* of Leo and all it conveyed of accommodation to the Chalcedonian definition. By the end of the reign of Justinian (565), a separate non-Chalcedonian clerical structure, with bishoprics and buildings, dominated Egypt. Coptic spirituality and piety were intensely biblical and monastic, centered on local holy men.

The Coptic language, the latest stage of Egyptian but written in the Greek alphabet, grew to literary status through versions of the Bible and original writings of the Egyptian fathers, especially Shenoute: it was used for sermons, lives of the saints, and every kind of document of daily life from leases to lawsuits. Many thousands of papyri in Coptic survive, providing evidence for the life of the Copts from the fifth to the ninth century. The Copts were a culturally vigorous and creative ethnic group. They produced original works of theology based on strong biblical foundations and an abundant visual art in media from sculpture to textiles, one that blended classical and Egyptian elements to synthesize a new and striking transformation of Byzantine forms. The Coptic aristocrat land-

Coptic tapestry (ca. 500) depicting a cross, now in the British Museum, London, England. (By courtesy of the Trustees of the British Museum.)

owners of the sixth and early seventh centuries, classically educated and deeply religious, were the patrons of a flourishing cultural life in late-antique Christian Egypt.

The Arab conquest of 641 at first took over the local financial system of the Egyptian districts and continued to staff it with able Copts. But by Abbasid times (after 750), the Coptic language and culture began to give way to the Arabic of the Muslim overlords. The Copts became a "protected people" (*ahl al-dhimmi*), defined by their church adherence and subjected to social restrictions and a poll tax. Some eight to ten million Copts survive today, although persecuted, in Egypt, and another million in a diaspora in North America, western Europe, and Australia. *See also* Egypt; Monophysitism.

[L.S.B.MacC.]

Bibliography

B.M. Metzger, *The Early Versions of the New Testament* (Oxford: Clarendon, 1977), pp. 99–152; L.-A. Hunt, "Coptic Art," *Dictionary of the Middle Ages*, ed. J.R. Strayer (New York: Scribners, 1983), Vol. 3, pp. 585–593; B. Pearson and J. Goehring, eds., *The Roots of Egyptian Christianity* (Philadelphia: Fortress, 1986); J. Kamil, *Coptic Egypt: A History and Guide* (Cairo: American U of Cairo P, 1987); F. Friedman, ed., *Beyond the Pharaohs: Egypt and the Copts in the 2nd to 7th Centuries A.D.* (Providence: Museum of Art, Rhode Island School of Design, 1989); A.S. Atiya et al., eds., *The Coptic Encyclopedia* (Salt Lake City: Macmillan, forthcoming).

CORINTH, CORINTHIAN CORRESPONDENCE.

Roman colony, capital of Achaia, to whose church Paul wrote 1 and 2 Corinthians. Corinth was one of the largest cities in the Roman empire, reestablished in 46–43 B.C. after destruction a century earlier. Situated on the isthmus that joins northern Greece with the Peloponnesian peninsula, it developed rapidly with a mixed population of Roman freedmen, Greeks, and immigrants from other areas, including a substantial number of Jews. The economy was based on the transit of goods from the two harbors, Cenchreae to the east and Lechaion to the north and west, rendering unnecessary the dangerous sea passage to the south. Manufacturing, administration, and the Isthmian Games combined with an intensive road network to provide Corinth with a booming economy that reached its apex in the second century A.D. Corinth was also infamous for the sexual vices characteristic of a seaport, although Strabo's reference (8.6.20) to prostitutes in the temple of Aphrodite describes earlier conditions. The official language of Corinth was Latin, although church affairs were apparently conducted in Greek.

Paul's mission in Corinth probably began in the spring of A.D. 50, a date derived from the Gallio inscription, which establishes a tenure of July 1, 51, to July 1, 52, for the imperial proconsul before whom Paul appeared (Acts 18:12–17). This correlates with the encounter with Priscilla and Aquila, immigrants from Rome in 49, with whom Paul developed a tent-making business (Acts 18:1–3). Several house churches were established in Corinth and its two harbor towns, whose patrons sponsored various traveling evangelists and came to favor competing outlooks. The bulk of the converts were slaves and humble handworkers, led by such patrons as Gaius, Titius Justus, Chloe, Phoebe, Stephanus, Erastus, Priscilla, and Aquila. In the period between Paul's departure in 51 and his first return visit in 55, serious conflicts arose in the house churches, eliciting Paul's letters. Apollos, who evangelized in Corinth during this period, also played a prominent role in the development of the controversies. After the conflicts were resolved, Paul spent the winter of 56–57 in Corinth and Cenchreae before starting on his final trip to Jerusalem. Here, he found sufficient support to draft and refine his most elaborate letter, to the Romans.

Paul's correspondence with the Corinthian churches provides far more information than we have about any other area. It is appropriate to speak of the "Corinthian Correspondence" rather than simply 1 and 2 Corinthians, because there are direct references to two letters beyond the canonical epistles (1 Cor. 5:9; 2 Cor. 2:4). When one takes into account the changed attitude toward the Corinthian situation visible in 1 Corinthians 11:18–19 as compared with 1 Corinthians 1:10–14 and the abrupt shifts in subject matter and tone, it is likely that as many as seven letters were combined to create the canonical 1 and 2 Corinthians. There is more scholarly support for the redaction of 2 Corinthians than for 1 Corinthians, although some commentators still maintain the integrity of both. The discussion which follows treats the Corinthian correspondence in a possible chronological sequence.

In 1 Corinthians 11:2–34, Paul responds to hearsay information (11:18–19) about agitation concerning male and female hairstyles and disruptions of the Lord's supper. He urges the maintenance of traditional styles while arguing for interdependence between the sexes (11:11–12) and for respect for the body of Christ received in the Lord's supper. The letter suggesting avoidance of "immoral persons" (1 Cor. 5:9) probably originally began with 2 Corinthians 6:14–7:1, which demands recognition of the mutually exclusive spheres of Christ and pagan deities. This was followed by 1 Corinthians 6:12–20, which argues against pagan prostitution in response to proto-Gnostics who suggested that in Christ "everything is lawful." In 1 Corinthians 9:24–10:22, Paul goes on to support bodily discipline and a recognition that Christians cannot participate in pagan worship. In 1 Corinthians 15:1–58, Paul responds to contempt for the bodily component in the doctrine of resurrection.

The "answer letter" material in 1 Corinthians replies to a precise report from Chloe's people (1 Cor. 1:10–14) about intensified conflicts between Corinthian factions. In 1 Corinthians 1:1–6:11, Paul mounts an attack on the worldly wisdom causing factionalism, arguing that the "foolishness of God is wiser than men" and that the "weakness of the cross" alone is redemptive. He demands discipline for a church member demonstrating his spiritual prowess by violating the incest taboo (1 Cor. 5:1–13) and argues against worldly Christians settling their disputes in the courts (1 Cor. 6:1–11). In 1 Corinthians 7:1–9:23, Paul rejects Platonic marriage and develops a concept of complete sexual mutuality between married partners; he argues against violating the conscience of the weak by eating food offered to idols; and he defends his right to apostolic remuneration despite his having chosen not to use such privileges. In 1 Corinthians 12–14, he argues against the overvaluation of glossolalia and for a mutually edifying worship life based on the priority of love.

Most of 2 Corinthians deals with the challenge posed by invading missionaries with a "divine-man" orientation who criticized Paul's lack of speaking ability and personal charisma, his troubled relationship with various authorities, and his reluctance to tout his visionary experiences. These missionaries arrived in the midst of the ongoing conflicts, alienating the congregation. In 2 Corinthians 2:14–6:13 and 7:2–4, Paul responds to the missionaries' use of letters of recommendation showing their "sufficiency" in miracle working and allegorical interpretation. The Corinthians themselves are Paul's rightful letter of recommendation, he contends, while admitting that "we have this treasure in earthen vessels," susceptible to troubles and persecution on every hand.

After writing this letter, Paul apparently made a brief visit to Corinth, in which he was repudiated by the congregation swayed by the competing "superapostles" (2 Cor. 2:1; 13:2–6). He then wrote the harsh "letter of tears" (2 Cor. 2:4), developing a brilliant "fool's discourse" to reverse the claims of his pretentious opponents (2 Cor. 10:1–13:13). Forced into boasting to compete with the false apostles, he lists only the evidence of his vulnerability in the conviction that under the cross of Christ, divine power is "made perfect in weakness." The final components in the Corinthian correspondence indicate that the reading of the harsh letter produced reconciliation. A letter of reconciliation (2 Cor. 1:1–2:13; 7:5–8:24) recapitulates the conflict and its resolution. This is followed by instructions to reinstate efforts to collect the Jerusalem offering, disrupted by the conflict. In a separate administrative letter to the house churches of Achaia (2 Cor. 9:1–15), Paul describes the crucial role they should play in handling the offering.

The later history of the Corinthian church can be pieced together from details in *1 Clement* at the end of the first century, from a reference to Apollonius as a prominent defender of orthodoxy in the middle of the second century, and from letters exchanged with leaders in Rome and elsewhere. A prominent martyr by the name of Leonidas is described in the Martyrology of St. Jerome. Leaders of the Corinthian church attended the councils of Ephesus, Chalcedon, and Constantinople. There is evidence that the churches built after 325 in Corinth and in neighboring Lechaion developed into an important pilgrimage center. The basilica in Lechaion, for instance, rivaled in size that of St. Peter's in Rome. But the later church never played as prominent a role in the development of Christianity as the original congregation, as reflected in Paul's letters.   [R.J.]

Bibliography

John Chrysostom, *Homilies on the Two Epistles to the Corinthians*, tr. H.K. Cornish, J. Medley, and J. Ashworth, NPNF, 1st ser. (1889), Vol. 12; Theodoret, *Interpretatio Epistolae ad Corinthios* (PG 82.225–460); Cyril of Alexandria, *Explanatio in Epistolam I et II ad Corinthios* (PG 74.856–952); Pelagius, *Expositio in I et II Corinthios*, ed. A. Souter, *TS* 9.2 (1926):127–305.

On Corinth: R.L. Scranton, *Monuments in the Lower Agora and North of the Archaic Temple. Corinth: Results* (Princeton: Princeton UP, 1951); R.L. Scranton et al., *Kenchreai: Eastern Port of Corinth, I. Topography and Architecture* (Leiden: Brill, 1978); J. Wiseman, "Corinth and Rome, I: 228 B.C.–A.D. 267," *ANRW* II 7.1 (1979), pp. 438–548; N. Papahatzis, *Ancient Corinth* (Athens: Ekdotikē Athenōn, 1981); G. Theissen, *The Social Setting of Pauline Christianity: Essays on Corinth* (Philadelphia: Fortress, 1982); J. Murphy-O'Connor, *St. Paul's Corinth: Texts and Archeology* (Wilmington: Glazier, 1983).

On 1 Corinthians: H. Conzelmann, *1 Corinthians* (Philadelphia: Fortress, 1975); R. Jewett, "The Redaction of I Corinthians and the Trajectory of the Pauline School," *Journal of the American Academy of Religion, Supplement* 46 (1978): 389–444; J. Murphy-O'Connor, *1 Corinthians* (Wilmington: Glazier, 1979); J.C. Hurd, Jr., *The Origin of 1 Corinthians* (Macon: Mercer UP, 1983); R.P. Martin, *The Spirit and the Congregation: Studies in 1 Corinthians 12–15* (Grand Rapids: Eerdmans, 1984); W.L. Willis, *Idol Meat in Corinth: The Pauline Argument in 1 Corinthians 8 and 10* (Chico: Scholars, 1985); G.D. Fee, *The First Epistle to the Corinthians* (Grand Rapids: Eerdmans, 1987); R.A. Harrisville, *1 Corinthians* (Minneapolis: Augsburg, 1987).

On 2 Corinthians: F.T. Fallon, *2 Corinthians* (Wilmington: Glazier, 1980); V.P. Furnish, *II Corinthians* (Garden City: Doubleday, 1984); H.D. Betz, *Second Corinthians 8 and 9: A Commentary on Two Administrative Letters of the Apostle Paul* (Philadelphia: Fortress, 1985); D. Georgi, *The Opponents of Paul in Second Corinthians* (Philadelphia: Fortress, 1986); S.J. Hafemann, *Suffering and the Spirit: An Exegetical Study of II Cor. 2:14–3:3 within the Context of the Corinthian Correspondence* (Tübingen: Mohr-Siebeck, 1986); R.P. Martin, *2 Corinthians* (Waco: Word, 1986).

CORNELIUS. Bishop of Rome (251–253). Cornelius was elected to govern the Roman church after the see had been vacant for fourteen months following the death of the previous incumbent, Fabian, in the persecution under Decius. From the beginning, he met with strong opposition on the part of the Roman presbyter Novatian, who had himself consecrated bishop and went into schism over the issue of the treatment to be accorded to the *lapsi*, those who had lapsed in the persecutions. Novatian favored their complete and permanent exclusion from the church, whereas Cornelius would admit them again after a suitable period of penance, a position that also gained the adherence of Cyprian of Carthage and Dionysius of Alexandria. Novatian was excommunicated (251) at a large Roman synod attended by some sixty bishops. With the renewal of persecution under the emperor Gallus, Cornelius was banished (252) to Centumcellae (the modern Civitavecchia), where he died the following year. A fifth-century account of his martyrdom (CPL 2180) is without value, but the fact that he died in exile for the faith might well have given rise to the tradition that he died as a martyr.

Two letters of Cornelius concerning the schism of Novatian directed to Cyprian of Carthage appear in the correspondence of the latter (Cyprian, *Ep.* 49; 50). Eusebius of Caesarea quotes extensively (*H.E.* 6.43.5–22) from a letter directed to Fabius, bishop of Antioch, and indicates as well (6.43.3–4) the existence of other letters that were subsequently lost. The extant citations comprise a forceful if one-sided account of Novatian's activities; an incidental passage (6.43.11) furnishes valuable information on the organization of the Roman church and its provision for widows and other distressed persons. Feast day September 16. CPG I, 1850–1854; CPL 50. TLG 1842. [M.P.McH.]

Bibliography

O. Marucchi, *Christian Epigraphy* (Cambridge: Cambridge UP, 1912), no. 193, pp. 195–196; Cyprian, *Letters* 44–45; 47–48; 51–52; 59; 60; Eusebius, *Church History* 6.39–7.2; Jerome, *Lives of Illustrious Men* 66; *Liber Pontificalis* 22 (Duchesne 1.150–152).

P.F. de' Cavaliere, "La persecuzione di Gallo in Roma," *Studi e Testi* 33 (1920):181–210; M. Bévenot, "Cyprian and His Recognition of Cornelius," *JThS* 28

(1977):346–359; F. Jacques, "Le Schismatique, tyran furieux: le discours polémique de Cyprian de Carthage," *MEFR* 94 (1982):921–949.

COSMAS AND DAMIAN.

COSMAS AND DAMIAN. Twin brothers who were physicians. Cosmas and Damian offered their services without pay, and according to later legend they were martyrs. The Basilica of SS. Cosma e Damiano in Rome (built under Felix IV, 526–530) contains a splendid apse mosaic of the two martyrs introduced by Peter and Paul to Christ standing on the clouds of glory. Feast day September 26 (west), July 1 (east). [E.F.]

Bibliography

R. Krautheimer, *Corpus Basilicarum Christianarum Romae* (Vatican City: Pontificio Istituto di Archeologia Cristiana, 1946), Vol. 1.3, pp. 137–143; P. Chioccioni, *Illustrated Guide of the Basilica of Sts. Cosmas and Damian* (Rome, n.d.).

COSMAS INDICOPLEUSTES

COSMAS INDICOPLEUSTES (sixth century). "The Indian Navigator." Born in Egypt, Cosmas traveled as a merchant in the east, then retired to a monastery and wrote on cosmography and scriptural interpretation. The geographical descriptions in his *Christian Topography* are often correct, yet he based his defense of the earth as a flat plain on biblical texts, the fathers, and reason, and fought those who taught that it was a globe. CPG III, 7468. TLG 4061. [F.W.N.]

Bibliography

W. Wolska-Conus, ed., SC (1968, 1970, 1973), Vols. 141, 159, 197.

M.V. Anastos, "The Alexandrian Origin of the *Christian Topography* of Cosmas Indicopleustes," *DOP* 3 (1946):73–80.

COSMAS MELODOS

COSMAS MELODOS (d. ca. 760). Greek liturgical hymnographer. Said to have been an adoptive brother of John of Damascus, Cosmas Melodos entered the laura of St. Saba near Jerusalem (ca. 732) and later became bishop of Maïuma in Palestine (743). He is best known for his fourteen *canones*, hymns for major feasts, such as Easter and Nativity, which were incorporated into the eastern liturgy. He also composed *idiomela*, short religious poems, and is the probable author of a commentary on the poems of Gregory of Na-

zianzus. Since he was educated by a monk also named Cosmas, who was himself an author of religious poetry, there is some confusion about attribution of certain compositions to the one or the other. Feast day October 14 (east).

[M.P.McH.]

Bibliography

T.E. Detorakes, *Kosmas ho Melodos, Bios kai Ergo* [*Cosmas Melodos, Life and Work*]: *Analekta Blatadōn* 28 (Thessalonica: Institut Patriarcal des Etudes Patristiques, 1979); idem, "Vie inédite de Cosmas le Mélode," *AB* (1981):101–116.

COSMAS VESTITOR

COSMAS VESTITOR (seventh, eighth, or ninth century). Byzantine writer. Cosmas was an admirer of John Chrysostom, and his sermons on the death and assumption of Mary show the influence of Germanus of Constantinople. CPG III, 8142–8163. [E.F.]

COUNCILS.

COUNCILS. Gatherings of clergy (principally bishops) to decide questions of doctrine and discipline in the church; synods.

The biblical precedent for church councils was the meeting in Acts 15, when Paul and Barnabas, sent by the church at Antioch, met with the apostles, elders, and church in Jerusalem to discuss whether circumcision should be required of Gentile converts; but it was not until the fifth century that this "apostolic council" was taken as a model. A Greco-Roman precedent was the council (Greek *koinon*, Latin *concilium*) of leading men who represented provincial interests to the Roman authorities and demonstrated the province's loyalty to Rome through leadership in the imperial cult. The procedures of the Roman senate and colonial councils were followed in the church synods.

The first church councils were held in Asia Minor in the latter half of the second century to consider what to do about Montanism (Eusebius, *H.E.* 5.16.10; cf. Tertullian, *Jej.* 13, for councils in Greece). The prophetic power of speaking by the Holy Spirit claimed by Montanus came to be attributed to the bishops, especially when they were in council. Several councils of bishops were held a few years later in response to Victor of Rome's appeal to determine the practice of the churches in regard to the celebration of the Pasch (Eusebius, *H.E.* 5.23.2–4). Bishops of a province met annually under the presidency of the bishop of the chief city with some regularity in the mid-third century, particularly in North Africa, as is known from Cyprian of Carthage (*Ep.* 55; 67.1); we have the *Judgment of 87 Bishops* from one of these councils.

The first council of bishops from a significantly wider geographical area occurred at Arles in 314. It was called by Constantine to deal with questions posed by the Donatist schism in North Africa. Most of the western part of the empire, the territory then ruled by Constantine, was represented. This gathering provided precedent for the First Ecumenical Council, held at Nicaea in 325 to discuss the teachings of Arius. Although mostly eastern bishops were present at Nicaea, there were a few western representatives, giving the council a sense of truly representing the whole church. The organization of the early church had provided no machinery for settling disputes broader than those within a local church; councils became *the* way of dealing with larger issues. By the fourth century, it was common to speak of the council as convened in the Holy Spirit. Although other clergy or even laymen could participate in various ways, decisions were made by the bishops.

There were five types of councils: (1) *Ecumenical.* The Council of Chalcedon (451) defined the three authoritative councils in doctrinal matters up to its time. There had been a large number of councils, mostly concerned with Trinitarian and Christological doctrines, in the fourth and fifth centuries, and the defenders of the Nicene faith had contended that there could be only one council to define the one faith, so there had been no consensus on the number of authoritative councils. All the ecumenical meetings in the patristic period were convened by the emperor. (2) *Patriarchal.* Synods of Rome, Carthage, Alexandria, and Antioch already in the third century gathered bishops from outside their immediate province, anticipating the patriarchal organization of later times. (3) *Provincial.* The Council of Nicaea (*can.* 5) required the bishops of a province to come together twice a year. These provincial councils did not always

strictly follow political territorial lines, because missionary expansion or other factors often established relationships or dependency apart from shifting political authority. (4) *Diocesan.* The bishop of a city was expected to call together his clergy several times a year. This was made necessary by the fourth-century growth of the church; earlier, a bishop and his presbyters would have been together often. (5) *Endemic.* A peculiar type of council was the permanent or resident holy synod in Constantinople. After the transfer of the imperial government to Constantinople in the fourth century, there would be bishops from many places in the capital at any given time. The emperor would call in whatever clerics were in Constantinople at the time to meet with the local clergy on any matter of moment.

The acts (*acta*) of some of the councils have been preserved. Decisions on matters of faith are called "symbols" (creeds or definitions of faith). Decisions on disciplinary, liturgical, or organizational matters were framed in "canons." Athanasius saw it as significant that the bishops at Nicaea when they approved a statement of faith said, "This believes the Catholic church," for they could not define the faith but only confess that which had been delivered to them, but in their other decisions wrote, "It seemed good" (*Syn.* 1.5).

Theological reflection on the meaning and nature of councils began in the fourth century. Athanasius criticized the Arian councils as lacking the relative universality, freedom of action, and legitimacy of the participants at Nicaea (*Apol. sec.* 7; *Ep. Aeg. Lib.* 5–7). Augustine's conciliar theory emphasized the difference between scripture and the decrees of councils, for all councils are capable of being amended, yet he upheld the authority of a universal council as the voice of the Catholic church (*Bapt.* 2.3–4). Leo the Great provided a formal grounding for the authority of councils: the inspiration of the Holy Spirit, conformity with scripture, agreement with the universal and historical faith of the church, papal approval, and unity of councils (*Ep.* 13; 14; 106; 119; 129; 145–147; 162; 164; 166). New definitions of the faith were defended as required by new heresies. The most important criterion from the practical standpoint for recognizing the authority of a council was its reception by the faithful. Those councils "won" in the theological debates that were received by the greatest number as expressing their faith. *See also* Bishop; Church; Ecumenical Councils; Ministry. [E.F.]

Bibliography

C.J. Hefele and H. Leclercq, *Histoire des conciles*, 11 vols. (Paris: Letouzey et Ané, 1907–1952); ACO; J. Alberigo et al., *Conciliorum oecumenicorum decreta* (Freiburg: Herder, 1962).

H.J. Schroeder, *Disciplinary Decrees of the General Councils: Text, Translation, and Commentary* (St. Louis: Herder, 1937); *The Seven Ecumenical Councils*, ed. H.R. Percival, NPNF, 2nd ser. (1899), Vol. 14.

G. Kretschmar, "The Councils of the Ancient Church," *The Councils of the Church, History and Analysis*, ed. H.H. Margull (Philadelphia: Fortress, 1966); G.V. Florovsky, "The Authority of the Ancient Councils and the Tradition of the Fathers," *Glaube, Geist, Geschichte*, ed. G. Müller and W. Zeller (Leiden: Brill, 1967); R. Metz, *Histoire des conciles* (Paris: Presses Universitaires de France, 1968); H.J. Sieben, *Die Konzilsidee der alten Kirche* (Munich: Schöningh, 1979); P.R. Amidon, "The Procedure of St. Cyprian's Synods," *VChr* 37 (1983):328–339.

COVENANT. The exact etymology of the Hebrew word *berith* (translated "covenant") is disputed; consequently, its linguistic development is unclear. In usage, *berith* was associated, on the one hand, with imposition, law, commandment, or promise (Ps. 105:7–11). On the other hand, it was also associated with treaty, agreement, and so with people (Exod. 19:4–6) and relationships (e.g., marriage–Mal. 2:14). The translation of *berith* into Greek as *diathēkē* preserved the idea of disposition but introduced the legal concept of will or testament (Gal. 3:15; Heb. 9:16). The New Testament interpreted the blood of Jesus as a covenant sacrifice and the Lord's supper as a covenant meal (Matt. 26:28; 1 Cor. 11:25). Christian preachers saw in Christ the fulfillment of the covenant of God with David (Acts 13:34) and in Christians the fulfillment of the covenant with Abraham (Gal. 3:16–18), but they made a contrast between the Christian covenant and the Mosaic covenant (2 Cor. 3:7–18). Jeremiah's prophecy (31:31–34) of a new covenant was enormously influential on Christian thinking (Heb. 8:6–13).

As Christians sought to interpret their relationship to their Jewish heritage, various attitudes were taken toward the covenant. The *Epistle of Barnabas* understood Israel, when at Sinai it worshiped the golden calf and Moses broke the tablets of stone (Exod. 32), as having rejected the covenant offered by God, so that Christians now were the people who possessed the covenant, understanding the laws not literally but in their allegorical or spiritual sense (*Barn.* 4.13–14). In contrast, Marcion repudiated the Israelite covenant, declaring that it was given by the Creator God to the Jews, whereas the Father of Jesus Christ was a different God.

Justin Martyr (*Dial.* 10–11; 122–123) and Irenaeus (*Haer.* 4.32–34) took the intermediate position that God had made two successive covenants. The Mosaic covenant to Israel was historically valid and given by the same God who had now made a new and eternal covenant suited to all nations through Jesus Christ. The former covenant by its types and prophecies prepared for the covenant in Christ. In this way, the Jewish claims were relativized but the Jewish Bible was preserved for the church in response to Gnostic and Marcionite repudiation of the Jewish heritage. Although this historical periodization of the covenants as stages in God's revelation became characteristic of Christian thinking, there were different ways in which the significance of the Mosaic covenant was appropriated for Christian use. Broadly speaking, western authors frequently saw legal enactments in the Old Testament as furnishing justification for the binding nature of Christian counterparts. For instance, Cyprian argued that the clergy should not engage in secular work because the Levites were supported by tithes from the other tribes (*Ep.* 1.1). The translation of *diathēkē* into Latin as *testamentum* (Tertullian, *Marc.* 4.1; 5.4; *Prax.* 15) gave a decided legal cast to the understanding of "covenant" in western Christian thought. Other exegetes, more under the influence of Origen's allegories, saw the Old Testament as teaching spiritual lessons about the soul and the Christian life. For instance, Origen applied the instructions about building the tabernacle to mean "Each may construct in his own soul a tabernacle to God" (*Hom.* 9.4 *in Ex.*).

The old covenant was associated with Law and the new covenant with Gospel (Irenaeus, *Haer.* 4.9.1; Tertullian, *Marc.* 3.14), and Law and Gospel were both designations of the basic documents of Judaism and Christianity. Perhaps through this association, "old covenant" (testament) and "new covenant" (testament) became the designations for the bodies of literature that recorded the relationships of God with his people (Clement of Alexandria, *Str.* 5.6.38; 5.13.85). This terminology for the two parts of the Bible was well established from the third century (Origen, *Princ.* 4.1.1). *See also* Interpretation of Bible. [E.F.]

Bibliography

J. Behm, "Diathēkē," *Theological Dictionary of the New Testament*, ed. G. Kittel (Grand Rapids: Eerdmans, 1964), Vol. 2, pp. 106–134; K. Balzar, *Das Bundesformular* (Neukirchen: Kries Moers, 1964); D. Hillers, *Covenant: The History of a Biblical Idea* (Baltimore: Johns Hopkins UP, 1969); M. Weinfeld, "Berith," *Theological Dictionary of the Old Testament*, ed. G.J. Botterweck and H. Ringgren (Grand Rapids: Eerdmans, 1975), Vol. 2, pp. 253–279; E. Ferguson, "The Covenant Idea in the Second Century," *Texts and Testaments: Critical Essays on the Bible and Early Church Fathers*, ed. W.E. March (San Antonio: Trinity UP, 1980), pp. 135–162.

CREATION. Doctrine that God made the universe. Patristic speculation on the creation of the world answered the need both for a theologically acceptable interpretation of Genesis and for a continuing response to the perceived aberrations of Platonism, Gnosticism, and Origenism. Over against the Platonic cosmogony, which viewed matter as eternal and the created world as a quasi-necessary corollary of God's own being, second- and third-century Christian apologists expounded on the biblical account of the personal Creator creating solely by his sovereign will. The scriptural evidence was open to interpretation. The depiction of God fashioning the world from primeval chaos (Gen. 1:1ff.; cf. Wisd. Sol. 11:17) appeared superficially compatible with Plato's vision of the demiurge bringing order to eternal, formless matter (*Tim.* 30A; 48E–51B). Arguing that the biblical account was more ancient, and thus more veracious, Justin Martyr (*1 Apol.* 59) and ostensibly also

Clement of Alexandria (*Str.* 5.89.5–6) were content to affirm that God created the world by an ordering of preexistent matter. Other apologists, absolutizing the freedom of the Creator and the contingency of the world, espoused a creation *ex nihilo*, "out of nothing" (Tatian, *Or.* 5.1–3; Theophilus, *Autol.* 2.4; Tertullian, *Herm.* 21.2–3). Here too one could find corroborative biblical evidence (e.g., 2 Macc. 7:8; Rom. 4:17; Heb. 11:3).

Gnosticism posed the greatest threat to the formative Christian cosmology, attributing the material world to a process of devolution or degeneration from the divine pleroma, instigated by a subversive intermediary demiurge in some cases (as in Marcionism) identified with the Old Testament Creator. Irenaeus of Lyons took this radical Gnostic dualism to task in the first two books of his *Against Heresies*, insisting that the one high God was alone Creator, calling the world into existence *ex nihilo* and by the agency solely of his own Logos (*Haer.* 2.2.4–5; 2.9.1–2.10.4). In arguing for creation through the preexistent divine Logos, Irenaeus enjoyed the backing both of tradition (Justin, *2 Apol.* 6; *Dial.* 61–62; Tatian, *Or.* 5; Athenagoras, *Leg.* 10) and of abundant scriptural proof-texts (Gen. 1:26; Ps. 33:6; Prov. 8:22ff.; John 1:1–3; Col. 1:15–16; Heb. 1:2).

The involvement of patristic cosmology in Greek philosophy came to a head in the work of Origen of Alexandria. His treatise *On First Principles* (ca. 230), itself strongly anti-Gnostic, fused the salvation-historical perspective of scripture with the hierarchical worldview characteristic of Platonism. For Origen, there were in effect two creations. The Logos, eternally begotten from the Father, engendered a spiritual creation, a realm of noetic beings (*Princ.* 1.8.1; 2.8.3), which, in Origen's view, had to be co-eternal with God insofar as his abilities as Creator could never have been inoperative (*Princ.* 1.4.3–5; 2.1.1–5; 3.5.3). In turn, however, it was only in consequence of the fall of spiritual creatures that the material world as we know it, the realm of bodies, was created *ex nihilo* by God (*Princ.* 1.7.1–2.2.2). Although not evil in itself, the corporeal creation was for Origen a provisional and remedial state through which fallen souls would pass en route to being resolved again into their original spiritual condition (*Princ.* 2.3.1–7; 2.9.1–2.11.7; 3.5.1–3.6.9).

Despite Origen's insistence on the ontological subordination of this original spiritual creation to the Creator (*Princ.* 1.4.5), his hypotheses were hard to distinguish clearly from Platonic theories of generation or emanation. Fourth- and fifth-century authors responded by vigorously reasserting the doctrine of creation by divine volition alone. As Athanasius explained, God the Father "generated" his Son of his own essence, and, through his Son, he "created" the world entirely outside his proper being (*Ar.* 2.2). Generation was an act of nature, creation an act of will (*Ar.* 3.60–62; cf. Cyril of Alexandria, *Thes.* 15). As an external entity set apart from God by an insuperable hiatus of *diastema* (cf. Gregory of Nyssa, *Eun.* 2.69f.), the created world, in its spiritual and material dimensions, was the product of God's gratuitous love, called into being for a distinct providential purpose.

The patristic exegesis of Genesis reflected this urge not only to explain the modality of creation but also to affirm the purposefulness of the material cosmos within the divine economy. Apart from the more devotional Hexaemeral literature extolling the natural wonders of creation, such as Basil of Caesarea's *Homilies on the Hexaemeron* and Ambrose's *Hexaemeron*, a strongly philosophical exegetical tradition also took shape. Gregory of Nyssa argued that God's "six-day" work in Genesis 1 constituted not a preexistent spiritual creation, as Origen had envisioned, but an ideal, simultaneous creation, the providential pattern on which all creatures would unfold in orderly fashion in time (*Hex.*, PG 44.72B). Augustine reached a more elaborate view in the name of a "literal" interpretation of Genesis, distinguishing the pretemporal causation, or *conditio*, of creation from its *administratio* in space and time. God simultaneously conceived the seminal principles (*rationes seminales*) of his creatures in his Word, implanted those principles in his creatures when he made them, and then presided over their actual emergence according to this infused pattern (*Gen. ad litt.* 2.8.16–19; 4.33.51–4.35.56).

While continuing to depend on Platonic thought-forms in their cosmological specula-

tions, the later Greek church fathers remained faithful to the doctrine of the contingency of creation on the gratuitous will of God. For Pseudo-Dionysius the Areopagite, the created world comprised a graduated hierarchy (angelic, human) of participation in God's being (*C.H.* 3ff.)—not in God's internal nature, that is, but in his extraverted life and effective attributes (*D.N.* 11.6), his "energies," to use the earlier Cappadocian term. God's providential principles (*logoi*), implanted in the world and ordering created existent beings, were more than static metaphysical mechanisms; they were the very "intentions" (*thelēmata*) of God (*D.N.* 5.8), which communicated his glorious goal for created beings. Similarly, for Maximus Confessor (seventh century), these *logoi* conveyed the purposeful diversity in creation. They contained the pattern and goal (*telos*) of creaturely movement, which was not, as in Origenism, the recovery of a primitive spiritual condition but the attainment of a higher, ultimately supernatural mode of existence (*Thal.* 2.13; *Amb.* 7).   [P.M.Bl.]

Bibliography

Tatian, *Address to the Greeks* 5, tr. J.E. Ryland, ANF (1885), Vol. 2, pp. 59–83; Theophilus of Antioch, *To Autolycus* 10–18, tr. M. Dods, ANF (1885), Vol. 2, pp. 85–121; Tertullian, *Against Hermogenes*, tr. P. Holmes, ANF (1887), Vol. 3, pp. 477–502; Irenaeus, *Against Heresies*, 1–2, ANF (1885), Vol. 1, pp. 315–413; Origen, *On First Principles* 3.5, tr. G.W. Butterworth (London: SPCK, 1936); Basil of Caesarea, *Homilies on the Hexaemeron* tr. A.C. Way, FOTC (1963), Vol. 46, pp. 1–150; Ambrose, *Hexaemeron*, tr. J.J. Savage, FOTC (1961), Vol. 42, pp. 1–283; Augustine, *The Literal Meaning of Genesis*, tr. J.H. Taylor, ACW (1982), Vols. 41–42; Pseudo-Dionysius the Areopagite, *The Divine Names*, tr. C. Luibheid, CWS (1987), pp. 47–131; *The Celestial Hierarchy*, ibid., pp. 143–191.

F.E. Robbins, *The Hexameral Literature* (Chicago: U of Chicago P, 1912); W.A. Christian, "The Creation of the World," *A Companion to the Study of St. Augustine*, ed. R.W. Battenhouse (New York: Oxford UP, 1955), pp. 315–342; J.F. Callahan, "Greek Philosophy and the Cappadocian Cosmology," *DOP* 12 (1958):29–57; H. Cornélis, "Les Fondements cosmologiques de l'eschatologie d'Origène," *Revue des sciences philosophiques et théologiques* 43 (1959):32–80, 201–247; J. Pépin, *Théologie cosmique et théologie chrétienne* (Paris: Presses Universitaires de France, 1964); R.A. Norris, *God and World in Early Christian Theology* (New York: Seabury, 1965); H.A. Wolfson, "Patristic Arguments Against the Eternity of the

World," *HThR* 59 (1966):351–367; A. Ehrhardt, *The Beginning: A Study in the Greek Philosophical Approach to the Concept of Creation from Anaximander to St. John* (Manchester: Manchester UP, 1968); L. Scheffczyk, *Creation and Providence* (New York: Herder and Herder, 1970); G. Florovsky, "Creation and Creaturehood," *Creation and Redemption*, The Collected Works of George Florovsky (Belmont: Nordland, 1976), Vol. 3, pp. 43–78; G. May, *Schöpfung aus dem Nichts: Die Entstehung der Lehre von der Creatio ex Nihilo* (Berlin and New York: de Gruyter, 1978); H. Kaiser-Minn, *Die Erschaffung des Menschen auf den spätantiken Monumenten des 3. und 4. Jahrhunderts*, JAC, Ergänzungsband 6 (1981); R. Sorabji, *Time, Creation and the Continuum: Theories in Antiquity and the Early Middle Ages* (Ithaca: Cornell UP, 1983).

CREEDS. Official confessions of faith. The word "creed" is derived from the Latin *credo* ("I believe"). It is used now for formal, usually short, authorized statements of the main points of Christian belief.

Confessions of faith for the first 150 years of the church were not formalized with a fixed wording. There were many occasions for confessions of belief, and an ample supply of confessional material survives that forms the prehistory of formal creeds. Jesus Christ was the center of Christian faith, and most of the confessional statements center on his person and work. Under the influence of the baptismal confession (or was it already a formula?) of "Father, Son, and Holy Spirit" (Matt. 28:19), a Trinitarian pattern was soon impressed on affirmations of faith. Although the Trinitarian statements were initially short and balanced, they were soon expanded by the addition of longer Christological affirmations. This might be done by adding the historical facts about Jesus to the third article as predictions of the Holy Spirit through the prophets (Irenaeus, *Haer.* 1.10.1), but more commonly the facts about Jesus were incorporated in the second part, and other doctrinal items that seemed important to include were loosely attached at the end after mention of the Holy Spirit.

The first evidence for the employment of the formulas that became fixed in the Apostles' Creed is the set of questions asked of the candidate for baptism at Rome at the beginning of the third century (Hippolytus, *Trad. ap.* 21). This Old Roman (baptismal) Symbol, when put in declaratory form, is the earliest creed in the sense of a confession of faith given standardized wording and ecclesiastical authority. Slightly expanded and with its origin attributed to the apostles, it became the universal baptismal creed of the western churches, the Apostles' Creed. The emphasis was on the confession about Christ—born of the Holy Spirit and the Virgin Mary, crucified under Pontius Pilate, raised on the third day, ascended to heaven, and coming again as judge. This content remained characteristic of western baptismal creeds, which featured the primitive proclamation about Christ; the eastern creeds gave more attention to the cosmic setting of the drama of salvation.

The baptismal creed of the eastern churches after the fourth century was the Nicene Creed. It was apparently modified from one of the baptismal creeds in use in Palestine. Adopted at the Council of Nicaea in 325, it has an importance in the history of creeds beyond its eventual authoritative recognition (in expanded form) as the baptismal symbol in eastern churches and as the creed recited in the eucharistic liturgy of east and west. The council not only made additions to an existing symbol of faith but also, in order definitely to exclude what was considered erroneous in the teaching of Arius, attached anathemas to the end. The anathemas had the effect of turning the creed from a positive confession of faith into a negative test of fellowship. At Nicaea, it was not catechumens who needed a creed but bishops. The many creeds adopted at councils in the next half-century showed that it was not obvious to all that the Nicene Creed was the one universal creed of Christendom.

In fact, the creed recited in many churches today as the "Nicene Creed" is not the one approved at Nicaea but an enlargement of it associated with the Second Ecumenical Council at Constantinople in 381. This creed has also been given the clumsy but more precise name "Niceno-Constantinopolitan Creed." It differs from the creed approved in 325 in some points in the second article about Christ but principally in its greatly enlarged third article about the deity and work of the Holy Spirit, including reference to the church, baptism, resurrection, and eternal life. The Council of Chalcedon (451) identified this creed as approved at Constantinople in 381, but there are doubts, since the council in 381 affirmed that its faith was the same as Nicaea's. Moreover, the expanded creed is found in Epiphanius, *Ancoratus* 118, dated 374. It may be, however, that a scribe substituted for the original Nicene Creed in the text the later form of the creed with which he was more familiar. The exact origin of the "Constantinopolitan" version of the Nicene Creed remains obscure.

The Definition of Faith adopted at Chalcedon in 451 sought to accomplish for Christology what Nicaea and Constantinople had done for the Godhead. Its decision on the one person in two natures was widely (but not universally) accepted as setting the boundaries of orthodox Christological speculation; nevertheless, it did not achieve the liturgical use of the other creeds included in this survey.

A further extension of creeds into developed theology occurred with the so-called "Athanasian Creed" (also known from its opening words as *Quicunque vult*), a Latin creed which originated probably in southern Gaul. It appears in a sermon of Caesarius of Arles (sixth century), and from the seventh century it was attributed to Athanasius. Consisting of forty rhythmical sentences, the Athanasian Creed gives an exposition of the Trinity, the two natures of Christ, and the events of Christ's career similar to the Apostles' Creed.

The Third Council of Toledo (589), in signaling the conversion of the Visigothic kingdom from Arianism to the Catholic faith, added to the Niceno-Constantinopolitan Creed after "the Holy Spirit . . . proceeds from the Father" the phrase "and from the Son" (*Filioque* in Latin). This statement of the double procession of the Spirit was based on the theological expositions of the Trinity by Augustine and served to ensure the full deity of the Son. This addition to the Nicene Creed spread throughout the west and became an important point of theological difference between the western and eastern churches. The latter rejected the addition on the

grounds that no change could be made in the wording of the Creed and the addition introduced a second source besides the Father into the Godhead. *See also* Apostles' Creed; Athanasian Creed; Chalcedon; Confession of Faith; Faith; Filioque; Nicaea; Rule of Faith. [E.F.]

Bibliography
P. Schaff, *The Creeds of Christendom*, 3 vols. (New York: Harper, 1877); A.E. Burn, *An Introduction to the Creeds* (London: Methuen, 1899); F.J. Badcock, *The History of the Creeds* (New York: Macmillan, 1938); J.N.D. Kelly, *Early Christian Creeds* (London: Longmans, 1960).

CRISPINA (d. 304). Martyr in North Africa. Crispina was beheaded in Numidia under Diocletian for refusing to sacrifice to the Roman gods. The written record of her martyrdom appears authentic; her cult quickly became popular in North Africa. Augustine praised her sanctity and supplied further details concerning her family and social status. [M.P.McH.]

Bibliography
Augustine, *Sermons* 286.2; 354.5; idem, *Expositions on the Book of Psalms* 121(120).8; 138(137).2; idem, *Of Holy Virginity* 45.
Musurillo, pp. xliv, 302–309.

CROSS, FRANK LESLIE (1900–1968). Patristic scholar. Cross was priest-librarian of Pusey House (1927–1944), then Lady Margaret Professor of Divinity in the University of Oxford and Canon of Christ Church (1944–1968). He wrote seminal papers on the African canons and on western liturgical manuscripts; he edited, and largely wrote, the *Oxford Dictionary of the Christian Church* (London: Oxford UP, 1957; 2nd ed. 1974, with E.A. Livingstone). At four-year intervals, he organized International Conferences on Patristic Studies (from 1951) and on New Testament Studies (from 1957). Beginning at a time when ecumenical relations were strained, these gatherings enabled scholars from different countries and different churches to meet on common ground. [E.A.L.]

Bibliography
"Frank Leslie Cross, 1900–1968," *Oxford Dictionary of the Christian Church*, 2nd ed. (London: Oxford UP), pp. xxvii–xxxi.

Constanza gem, a carnelian intaglio, one of the earliest known representations of the crucifixion (fourth century?), now in the British Museum, London, England. (By courtesy of the Trustees of the British Museum.)

CROSS. According to the New Testament (Mark 15:22–26), the Romans executed Jesus of Nazareth by hanging his body on a cross. The form of the cross is not known. It could have consisted of a vertical shaft joined at its upper end to a horizontal cross beam so as to create a T. This is the form of the cross inferred, for example, from the remains of a crucified victim buried at Givat ha-Mivtar (cf. Strange; also *Israel Exploration Quarterly* 35.1 [1935]:22–27).

A well-attested tradition from the fourth or fifth century concerns the discovery of the cross on which Jesus was executed. Cyril of Jerusalem and Ambrose knew a version of the tale, as did Egeria, Melania the Elder, Paulinus of Nola, and the ecclesiastical historians Sozomen, Rufinus, and Socrates. A version of the story is transmitted in the *Teaching of Addai*, and the *Toledot Yeshu* contains yet another version hostile to Jesus and Christianity (cf. Leclercq).

Early Christian writers looked for prefigurations of the cross in a variety of places: they considered such anticipations as proofs of the truth of Christianity. In the literary realm, the process of ferreting out cruciform symbols began early in the second century. Christian writers mined both the Old Testament and pagan tradition. The Tree of Life in Paradise and Moses' staff, for example, were seen as prefigurations, as was Odysseus tied to the mast. They found cruciform symbols elsewhere as well, man-made objects, for example, such as the mast and yard of a ship or the warp and weft of a loom. In nature itself, the primary cruciform symbol seen by early Christians was that of a person standing erect with the arms extended outward from the trunk of the body: this, the so-called *orant* posture, was simultaneously a traditional prayer position and a reminder to early Christians of the cross.

As for surviving archaeological and art-historical evidences of cruciform symbolism, scholars have expended a great deal of energy in recent years sifting the sources in an effort to get at the facts. For the early or pre-Constantinian period, there is still some controversy on what constitutes admissible evidence. The cross marks on first- and second-century Palestinian ossuaries should not be interpreted in a Christian sense (cf. Smith), nor is there convincing evidence of Christian cruciform symbolism either at Pompeii or Herculaneum (cf. Dinkler, 1951). Certainly, one of the oldest surviving positive evidences of cruciform symbolism among early Christians is Constantine's use of the labarum. It is sometimes argued that the earliest appearance of Christian cruciform symbolism in intaglio form is pre-Constantinian, but the best-attested pieces, such as the British Museum's carnelian showing the crucifixion (pg. 244), are on iconographic grounds certainly fourth century or later. It was understandable, given the ubiquity of cruciform symbolism first in literature and subsequently in visual arts, that outsiders accused early Christians of worshiping the cross (Minucius Felix, *Oct.* 9.4; 29.6–8; Tertullian, *Nat.* 1.12.1; *Apol.* 16.6ff.), a charge that several early Christian authors vigorously denied.

The surviving visual record shows six principal types of early Christian crosses:

(1) ✝ the equilateral cross, in which the arms intersect at right angles, called *crux quadrata* or Greek cross;

(2) ✕ same as (1) but with arms displayed obliquely rather than vertically-horizontally, similar to the Greek *chi* and Latin X (the numerical equivalent of ten), called *crux decussata* or St. Andrew's cross;

(3) ⊤ like the Greek *tau* and Latin T, called *crux commissa*;

(4) ✝ same as (1) but with the horizontal bar intersecting the vertical about one-third of the distance from the top, called *crux immissa* or Latin cross;

(5) 卐 the equilateral cross that consists of four intersecting Greek capital *gammas*, joined at 90° angles, with the *gammas* turned to the right (as illustrated here) or to the left (less common), called *gammadion* or *crux gammata*, *swastika* (Sanskrit), *Hakenkreuz* (German);

(6) ☥ consists of a *tau* cross (3) surmounted by an oval, called *crux ansata*, handled cross, or *ankh* cross—this is essentially identical to the Egyptian *ankh* character, which meant "life" in hieroglyphs.

In addition, there are four cruciform ligatures or monograms attested in early Christian contexts, such as in painting, sculpture, mosaics, inscriptions; on various small finds; and in papyri;

(1) ⊞ *iota* plus *eta* could be interpreted to signify the first two letters of the name "Jesus" in Greek;

(2) ⊗ *iota* plus *chi* could be interpreted as the first two letters of "Jesus Christ" in Greek;

(3) ☧ *chi* plus *rho*, the Constantinian monogram (the labarum), joining the first two letters of "Christ" in Greek;

(4) ⳨ *tau* plus *rho*, which appears on the Beratius Nikatoras *forma* burial slab that dates before 275; this monogram also appears in certain Bodmer papyri (P^{66}, P^{75}) that predate Constantine and that contain sections of the canonical Gospels. Dinkler (1962) coined the term "staurogram" for this abbreviation. *See also* Labarum; Orant; Rings.   [P.C.F.]

Bibliography

Justin Martyr, *1 Apology* 55; *Dialogue* 86; 90; 97.

H. Leclercq, "Croix, crucifix," DACL (1914), Vol. 3.2, cols. 3045–3131; idem, "Croix (Invention et exaltation de la Vraie)," ibid., cols. 3131–3139; E. Dinkler, "Zur Geschichte des Kreuzsymbols," ZThK 48 (1951):148–172; repr. in *Signum Crucis* (Tübingen: Mohr, 1967), pp. 1–25; F.J. Dölger, "Beiträge zur Geschichte des Kreuzzeichens I–V," *JAC* 1–5 (1958–1962); E. Dinkler, "Kreuzzeichen und Kreuz–Tau, Chi und Stauros," *JAC* 5 (1962):93–112; repr. in *Signum Crucis* (Tübingen: Mohr, 1967), pp. 26–54; J.F. Strange, "Crucifixion, Method of," *Interpreter's Dictionary of the Bible. Supplementary Volume*, ed. K. Crim (Nashville: Abingdon: 1976), pp. 199–200; H. Rahner, *Greek Myths and Christian Mystery* (London and New York: Burns and Oates, 1963), pp. 46ff.; G.Q. Reijners, *The Terminology of the Holy Cross in Early Christian Literature* (Nijmegen: Dekker and Van de Vogt, 1965); J. Finegan, *The Archaeology of the New Testament* (Princeton: Princeton UP, 1969), pp. 220–260; G.Q. Reijners, "Cross

Symbolism in Hippolytus," *Mélanges Christine Mohrmann* (Utrecht and Anvers: Spectrum, 1973), pp. 13–24; R.H. Smith, "The Cross Marks on Jewish Ossuaries," *Palestine Exploration Quarterly* 106 (1974):53–66; P. Maser, "Die Kreuzigungsdarstellung auf einem Siegelstein," *RAC* 52 (1976):257–275; M. Hengel, *Crucifixion* (Philadelphia: Fortress, 1977); H.A. Drake, "Eusebius on the True Cross," *JEH* 36 (1985):1–22.

CYNICISM. Hellenistic philosophy. Rooted in the intellectual ferment of fifth- and fourth-century B.C. Athens, and inspired by the moral earnestness of the Socratic movement, Cynicism began as a radical critique of accepted cultural norms. Early Cynics, such as Antisthenes (ca. 446–ca. 366 B.C.), Diogenes (ca. 400–ca. 325) and Crates (ca. 365–285), advocated a life of virtuous simplicity and rejected ordinary conventions of speech and behavior as contrived pretense. This cultural critique was not merely theoretical but issued in a distinctive ascetical lifestyle. The ideal Cynic, exemplified by Diogenes, reduced wants to a minimum, wore only a cloak, bore only a staff and pouch, left hair and beard untrimmed, and exercised a bold "freedom of speech" to denounce stupidity and immorality. The very name, meaning "doglike," suggests characteristics of the Cynics, whose outrageous and deliberately provocative behavior often earned them opprobrium.

The influence of the early Cynics was felt throughout the Hellenistic period. Their orientation to ethics and their moral earnestness were appropriated by the Stoics, who also advocated life "in accordance with nature." Stoics, however, generally did not flout conventions in the radical Cynic fashion, and they developed a more comprehensive academic philosophical tradition.

With their practical, critical orientation, the Cynics produced no general ethical or metaphysical system. Some were, however, interested in fundamental philosophical questions and applied their standards of simplicity and naturalness in various ways. In theology, for example, some viewed the gods as mere human contrivances, advocated atheism, and rejected cultic practice as superstition. Others distinguished between the false gods of convention and the true god of nature.

In the early Christian period, the Cynic lifestyle of the wandering preacher continued to attract followers, and early Cynic rigorism remained popular. The sharp rhetoric of the preachers' harangues contributed to the more scholastic form of the "diatribe," which in turn influenced Christian hortatory style. Other Cynics of the period adopted a more moderate approach to the life of moral struggle. A related phenomenon was the idealization of the Cynic as the true philosopher by various moralists, such as the first-century Stoic Epictetus (*Diss.* 3.22). A similar idealization figures prominently in later Christian and pagan polemical writings, particularly in the emperor Julian's *Oration* 6.

The image of the Cynics that had become traditional by the period of the early church is accessible in the early-third-century work of Diogenes Laertius, *Lives of the Philosophers* 6, a collection of anecdotes about early Cynic heroes. The range of Cynic concerns, exemplifying their typical rhetoric, is attested in the Cynic epistles. These pseudepigraphical works, written in the Hellenistic and early Roman periods, were attributed to early Cynics and related philosophers. The Cynics' attire and renunciation of ordinary human life were part of the background of the Christian monk.   [H.W.A.]

Bibliography

D. Dudley, *A History of Cynicism* (London: Methuen, 1937); H.W. Attridge, *First-Century Cynicism in the Epistles of Heraclitus* (Missoula: Scholars, 1976); A.J. Malherbe, *The Cynic Epistles* (Missoula: Scholars, 1977); S.K. Stowers, *The Diatribe and Paul's Letter to the Romans* (Chico: Scholars, 1981); A.J. Malherbe, "Self-Definition Among Epicureans and Cynics," *Jewish and Christian Self-Definition*, ed. B.F. Meyer and E.P. Sanders (Philadelphia: Fortress, 1982), Vol. 3: *Self-Definition in the Greco-Roman World*, pp. 46–59.

CYPRIAN (ca. 200–258). Bishop of Carthage (ca. 248–258). Although his *Epistles* allow a rare insight into the career of Cyprian during most of his episcopacy, they have little to say about the course of his life prior to the persecution of Decius. Pontius, who may have been his deacon, wrote the narrative of his martyrdom with a short Life preceding it but provided few data from which to sketch an outline of his early life. A short account of his martyrdom is found in the brief *Acta proconsularia Cypriani*.

It is probable that Cyprian was born in Carthage into a family of some social standing and wealth. He became a distinguished rhetorician, widely known in the city, and acquired friends of political power. He was converted (ca. 245–246) under the influence of the aging Carthaginian presbyter Caecilius. With his conversion, he resolved on a life of celibacy, and, selling his considerable estate, he gave the proceeds (or most of the proceeds) to the needy. He was soon made a presbyter, and probably within a year—sometime between May 248 and May 249—was elected bishop of Carthage, with the strong approbation of the Christian people but with opposition from at least five presbyters who apparently envied his rapid rise to ecclesiastical power.

Episcopate. In January 250, shortly after the edict of Decius demanding the universal acknowledgment of the gods through sacrifice, Cyprian went into hiding in an unspecified place near Carthage, believing that as a man of distinction he would, if he remained in the city, provide a focus for pagan hostility to the Christians. He endeavored to rule his church from his hiding place by letters sent through faithful emissaries. In these letters, we witness the persecution waxing and waning over a few months. Within weeks, apparently vast numbers of Christians had lapsed and soon began to seek reconciliation. At first, Cyprian resolved that peace should not be extended to the lapsed until an appropriate response had been determined by the church in council. His position, however, was undermined by laxist presbyters who began to offer peace to those with certificates from confessors and martyrs, and further undermined by a letter from the Roman clergy to the church of Carthage highly critical of Cyprian as a "hireling" who had abandoned the flock. As Cyprian maneuvered for control, he gradually modified his position on the lapsed. Probably by early June, he had agreed that those who became severely ill and had done penance, could, provided they secured certificates from the confessors and martyrs, receive reconciliation from presbyters and even deacons (*Ep.* 18), and by midsummer he had accepted the

Roman position that all who had done penance could in the face of sickness be reconciled (*Ep.* 20). By late summer, he had received a letter of support from the Roman clergy (*Ep.* 30) and began making supportive clerical appointments at Carthage.

During the fall and winter, however, positions hardened; excommunication of the lapsed followed, and feelings ran so high that Cyprian was unable to return to Carthage until after Easter, 251. Shortly thereafter, the council of 251 adopted the position that peace should be granted only in severe illness to those who had actually sacrificed, while those who had by some means acquired certificates from the pagan authorities attesting that they had sacrificed, although in fact they had not, might be admitted to communion at once (*Ep.* 55.17). Eventually, under the threat of a new persecution by Trebonianus Gallus (emperor 251–253), Cyprian was prepared to grant reconciliation to all who sought it. Unfortunately, his efforts to make accommodation and at the same time maintain integrity resulted in the disruption of the unity of the Catholic church. By 252, two splinter groups each had its own bishop in Carthage, the rigorists, who took the position of Novatian, the schismatic bishop of Rome, and the laxists, who chose the presbyter Fortunatus as bishop.

The persecution had tested Cyprian's relations with Rome. If in 250 the Roman clergy had been slow to support him, in 251 he was cautious in recognizing Cornelius as the legitimate bishop of Rome, and only after careful investigation did he support Cornelius in opposition to the claims of Novatian. Cyprian's relations with Stephen I, elected bishop of Rome in 254, became strained. In that same year, Spanish bishops appealed to Cyprian from a decision of Stephen I, and a Gallic bishop sought his help to secure from Stephen a judgment against Marcian, who as bishop had declared himself a Novatianist. From 255, over the course of two years, Cyprian engaged in a bitter quarrel with Stephen concerning the rebaptism of heretics and schismatics; Stephen accepted the baptism of heretics and schismatics as valid, Cyprian denied it any efficacy whatever. But the end was near. Caught by the edict of Valerian requiring pagan sacrifice

(257), Cyprian was exiled to Curubis; the next year, unable to escape a new and more severe edict, he was returned to Carthage for trial before the proconsul, Galerius Maximus. Having confessed, he was immediately beheaded.

Writings. Among the writings of Cyprian, the corpus of his letters must be ranked of first importance as source for the history of a decade otherwise poorly documented. The majority of these letters find their occasion in persecution and its aftermath, above all the persecutions of Decius (250) and Valerian (257–258), and in an anticipated persecution by Trebonianus Gallus (252 or 253) (*Ep.* 57; 58; 60; 61). Nine letters (*Ep.* 67–75) document the rebaptism controversy, and a handful offer a glimpse into other aspects of life in the mid-third century, such as scandals among virgins (*Ep.* 4) and the devastation caused by barbarian raids (*Ep.* 62).

A dozen treatises from Cyprian's pen have come down to us; their subjects appear to be listed by Pontius (*Vita* 7) in an order that may reflect the sequence of their composition. Of two apologetic works, one, an appeal *To Donatus*, is clearly early—before 250; a second, *To Quirinus*, a compendium of scripture texts useful as testimonies, should also be dated before 250. The scandal among virgins apparently elicited the treatise *On the Dress of Virgins* (before 250). Out of the problems arising from the Decian persecution, Cyprian in the course of 251 wrote the treatises *On the Lapsed, On the Unity of the Church,* and probably also *On the Lord's Prayer,* which stresses the importance of unity. A severe plague in Carthage in 252 required a further apology from Cyprian, *To Demetrian,* showing that Christians are not the cause of national disasters, and evoked two pastoral treatises to Christians urging them not to forsake their responsibilities to the dead and the devastated (*On the Mortality, On Works and Alms*). Although the treatises *On the Good of Patience* and *On Jealousy and Envy* were evidently motivated by the baptismal controversy, they may also reflect Cyprian's patient endurance of opposition to his episcopacy. Finally, the treatise *To Fortunatus* is an exhortation to martyrdom in the face of the persecution of Valerian and can thus be dated to 257.

It is above all a theology of the church that emerges from these writings: by its possession of the Holy Spirit, the church of apostolic bishops is definitively demarcated from the so-called churches of those in schism and heresy. Cyprian did, however, obfuscate the relation of bishops to the papacy by publishing a second edition of *On the Unity of the Church,* in which changes to the text of the fourth and fifth chapters appear to qualify the Petrine supremacy.

Influence. Cyprian lived on in memory for centuries as a figure of vital importance, especially to Christianity in Africa. Lactantius regarded him as a distinguished, if not always satisfactory, apologist (*Div. inst.*); both Donatists and Catholics appealed to his authority in the fourth century; and at least three churches were built to his memory at Carthage. Under Damasus I (366–384), Rome acknowledged his greatness by including him in its festal calendar. The large number of extant manuscripts attest his popularity in medieval Europe. Feast day September 16 (Roman Catholic), September 26 (Episcopal). CPL 38–67. *See also* Acts of Cyprian. [R.D.S.]

Bibliography

W. Hartel, *Opera Omnia,* 3 parts, CSEL (1868–1871), Vol. 3; R. Weber and M. Bévenot, eds., CCSL (1972), Vol. 3; M. Simonetti and C. Moreschini, eds., [*Treatises*], CCSL (1976), Vol. 3A; *De Lapsis* and *De Ecclesiae Catholicae Unitate,* ed. M. Bévenot, OECT (1971).

R.E. Wallis, tr., ANF (1886), Vol. 5; M. Bévenot, *The Lapsed; The Unity of the Catholic Church,* ACW (1957), Vol. 25; R.J. Deferrari et al., *Treatises,* FOTC (1958), Vol. 36; R.B. Donna, *Letters,* FOTC (1964), Vol. 51; G.W. Clarke, *The Letters of St. Cyprian of Carthage,* 4 vols., ACW (1984, 1986, 1988), Vols. 43, 44, 46, 48.

P. Monceaux, *Histoire littéraire de l'Afrique chrétienne depuis les origines jusqu'à l'invasion arabe* (Paris: Leroux, 1902), Vol. 2; M.F. Wiles, "The Theological Legacy of St. Cyprian," *JEH* 14 (1963):139–149; G.S.M. Walker, *The Churchmanship of St. Cyprian* (London: Lutterworth, 1968); M.A. Fahey, *Cyprian and the Bible: A Study in Third Century Exegesis* (Tübingen: Mohr, 1971); P. Hinchcliff, *Cyprian of Carthage and the Unity of the Christian Church* (London: Chapman, 1974); M.M. Sage, *Cyprian* (Cambridge: Philadelphia Patristic Foundation, 1975); C. Saumagne, *Saint Cyprian, évêque de Carthage et "pape" d'Afrique* (Paris: CNRS, 1975).

CYPRIAN OF GAUL (fifth century). Christian Latin poet. Cyprian is the probable author of the *Heptateuchos*, a poetic paraphrase of the first seven books of the Old Testament, which evidences knowledge of the Latin poets both Christian and classical, Virgil especially. Other works attributed to him are dubious or spurious. Nothing is certain about his life, even the identification with Gaul being questioned.   CPL 1423–1430.   [M.P.McH.]

Bibliography

P.-M. Duval, *La Gaule jusqu'au milieu du Ve siècle* (Paris: Picard, 1971), Vol. 1.2, p. 805, #103A.

CYRIL OF ALEXANDRIA (ca. 375–444). The main architect of patristic Christology and bishop (412–444). Cyril was born in the small town of Theodosiou, about seventy miles east of Alexandria, of orthodox Christian parents. Little is known of his upbringing except that his writings show a solid foundation in biblical studies and standard theologians, particularly Athanasius. His mother's brother was Theophilus, bishop of Alexandria, trenchant critic of Origen, vigorous opponent of paganism, and tireless champion of his church's rights. Probably, Theophilus prepared Cyril for a church career, perhaps as his successor. He certainly took Cyril to attend him at the Synod of the Oak (403), where he secured the condemnation of John Chrysostom, bishop of Constantinople. Cyril succeeded Theophilus as bishop of Alexandria in 412 after a bloody and contested election. Violence marred the first years of his episcopate in a city prone to riots and lynchings. Quarrels among pagans, Jews, and Christians, and between Cyril and the governor, Orestes, culminated in the horrifying murder by a Christian mob of the distinguished pagan philosopher Hypatia (415), which "brought disgrace not only on Cyril but on the whole Alexandrian church" (Socrates, *H.E.* 7.15; cf. 7.13f., 16). That Cyril was responsible for the violence is a myth enshrined in Charles Kingsley's novel *Hypatia* and since perpetuated; that he was not, for some years, master of his own house is a fair deduction; and the government at the time did not condemn him personally.

Cyril's career as a theologian of international standing began with the ordination of Nestorius as bishop of Constantinople in 428. A controversy between the two, starting from a conflict of interests, broadened into a deep doctrinal division with consequences enduring to the present. Nestorius entertained complainants from Alexandria appealing to him for help; he preached with rigor the picture of Christ he had learned from his teacher at Antioch, Theodore of Mopsuestia: the true union by association of two personal subjects (*hypostases* or *prosopa*), God the Son and the Man, in Jesus Christ; the Blessed Virgin Mary could be called "mother of God" (*Theotokos*) only in a nuanced sense. Letters of increasing sharpness were exchanged; Cyril gained the vital support of the Roman bishop, Celestine; and a general council of bishops was convoked by the emperor, Theodosius II, to meet at Ephesus at Whitsuntide, 431. Cyril emerged as only imperfectly victorious. Nestorius resigned, but Cyril's sharp critique of his Christology, expressed in the twelve propositions annexed to his *Third Letter to Nestorius*, rankled in the minds of churchmen loyal, like Nestorius, to the memory of Theodore. A schism resulted between Cyril's party, principally Rome and Alexandria, and eastern churchmen, effectively Syria and Mesopotamia. It was healed only in 433, after lengthy and expensive negotiations, by a formula of reunion (*Ep.* 39.5) originating from the easterners led by John of Antioch, but accepted by Cyril and justified by a series of letters to friends and supporters. Cyril's standing was enhanced during his last ten years, as he rose to be a confidant of the imperial household. Although always suspected by eastern churchmen of bullying and intrigue, to the rest he appeared a pillar of orthodoxy upholding the faith at a moment when it was imperiled.

Writings. Among Cyril's surviving exegetical works are complete commentaries on the Pentateuch, the minor prophets, and John's Gospel, with fragments from commentaries on Romans, Hebrews (ca. 430), and other New Testament books, mostly antedating the Nestorian controversy. He was the author of a long apology against the apostate emperor Julian (written over many years), containing extensive quotations from Julian besides extracts from pagan philosophers; it survives incomplete. His dogmatic writings include the *Thesaurus de Trinitate*, an early work based largely on Athanasius's *Orations Against the Arians* but drawing on other sources; it is a collection of deductive and exegetical arguments designed to expound the Nicene faith. The later (prior to 429) dialogues *De Trinitate* set out in more elegant form the same general themes. Among Cyril's occasional writings are many letters (especially the important Second and Third to Nestorius, and that to John, bishop of Antioch, *Epistle 39*—see above) relating to all aspects of the Christological dispute; shorter works on Christology; and responses to doctrinal questions. His twenty-nine Festal Letters (annual letters to his diocese indicating the date of Easter and commenting on points of pastoral concern) are complete for the years 414–442.

Teaching and Spiritual Legacy. Cyril's reputation rests upon his teaching about the person and saving work of Christ. Strong in proclamation of biblical truth (as he saw it), it is weaker in explanation, and in some respects inconsistent. Christ is, for him, the eternal Son and Word of God, who has undertaken, without loss of his identity, for our salvation to live the human life, making all our natural limitations, sin excepted, his own. He is God and man at once, united as body and soul are united without coalescence. He is one nature or subject (*hypostasis*) having his source in two natures (he is "out of two natures") whose distinctions in him can be perceived only at the level of pure thought. Mary is mother of God-made-man; God died humanly on the cross; and the eucharist is the life-giving body of Life Divine itself made human. Cyril's technical terminology is casual (one nature/two natures, "out of," "hypostatic union"), but his religious message is clear. Its formal expression and interpretation were left to successive general councils. The Council of Chalcedon (451) made the *Second Letter to Nestorius* a norm of doctrine and drew largely, in its formula of faith, on the formula of reunion (433). Constantinople II (553) condemned opponents of the twelve propositions and thus canonized the whole of Cyril even at his sharpest and with his inconsistencies. Constantinople III (681) interpreted the spirit, at least, of Cyril, in assert-

ing a human will in Christ. But there remained and remains a substantial body of Christians, such as Copts, Jacobites (i.e., Syrian Christians, dating their break from Catholics to Jacob Baradaeus, in the sixth century), Armenians, and Ethiopians, for whom these councils represent a betrayal of Cyril's message. The present politics of the Middle East bear the marks of these old disagreements. Feast day February 9. CPG III, 5200–5438. [L.R.W.]

Bibliography

G.M. de Durand, *Cyrille d'Alexandrie: deux dialogues Christologiques*, SC (1964), Vol. 97; idem, *Cyrille d'Alexandrie: dialogues sur la Trinité*, SC (1976, 1977, 1978), Vols. 231, 237, 246.

Commentary on the Gospel of St. Luke by St. Cyril, Patriarch of Alexandria, 2 vols., tr. R. Payne Smith (Oxford: Oxford UP, 1859); *Cyril of Alexandria: Select Letters*, tr. and ed. L.R. Wickham (Oxford: Clarendon, 1983); *St. Cyril of Alexandria: Letters*, tr. J.I. McEnerny, FOTC (1987), Vols. 76, 77.

J. Liebaert, *La Doctrine christologique de s. Cyrille d'Alexandrie avant la querelle nestorienne* (Lille: Facultés Catholique, 1951); A. Kerrigan, *St. Cyril of Alexandria: Interpreter of the Old Testament* (Rome: Pontificio Istituto Biblico, 1952); W.J. Burghart, *The Image of God in Man According to Cyril of Alexandria* (Washington, D.C.: Catholic U of America P, 1957); R. Wilken, *Judaism and the Early Christian Mind: A Study of Cyril of Alexandria, Exegesis and Theology* (New Haven: Yale UP, 1971); W.J. Malley, *Hellenism and Christianity: The Conflict Between Hellenic and Christian Wisdom in the Contra Galilaeos of Julian the Apostate and the Contra Julianum of St. Cyril of Alexandria* (Rome: Università Gregoriana, 1978); P. Imhof and B. Lorenz, *Maria Theotokos bei Cyrill von Alexandrien: Zur Theotokos-Tradition und ihre Relevanz; eine dogmengeschichtliche Untersuchung zur Verwendung des Wortes Theotokos bei Cyrill von Alexandrien vor dem Konzil von Ephesus unter Berücksichtigung von Handschriften der direkten Überlieferung* (Munich: Kaffke, 1981); M. Simonetti, "Alcune osservazioni sul monofisimo di Cirillo d'Alessandria," *Augustinianum* 22 (1982):493–511; L.R. Wickham, "Symbols of the Incarnation in Cyril of Alexandria," *Typus, Symbol, Allegorie bei den östlichen Vätern und ihren Parallelen im Mittelalter: internationales Kolloquium, Eichstätt 1981*, ed. M. Schmidt with C.F. Geyer (Regensburg: Pustet, 1982), pp. 41–53.

CYRIL OF JERUSALEM (d. 387). Bishop (ca. 349, despite three banishments, until his death). Cyril was deeply involved in the Arian struggles and is noted for his catechetical lectures. His parents were both Christians. The family may have lived in Caesarea of Palestine, where his sister had residence. He rose through the ranks of clergy, probably as a deacon after 326 and a presbyter by 343.

A Jerusalem synod in 335 decided that Arius had been wrongly dismissed, but another in 346 received Athanasius back into communion (Athanasius, Apol. sec. 85; 57). Acacius of Caesarea, both an Arian and metropolitan of Palestine, disliked Cyril and his views. Cyril had not accepted the *homoousios* ("of the same nature") formula for the Son, but he did not support Arius either. Acacius was piqued by the seventh canon of Nicaea, which gave a place of honor to Jerusalem.

In 354–355, Cyril sold some expensive imperial artifacts given to the Jerusalem church. Sozomen (*H.E.* 4.25) says that the money helped the poor during a famine, but other sources are unclear. Acacius insisted Cyril report his sale to a synod. Cyril refused and the synod deposed him in 357. He went to Tarsus and endeared himself to the church there. By 359, imperial authority had put him back on the throne in Jerusalem and banished Acacius. But Acacius went to Constantinople, explained Cyril's sale to emperor Constantius, and got the decisions reversed in 360. Julian, however, returned Cyril to Jerusalem in 361, probably to ensure disruption among Christians.

In 366, Cyril appointed his nephew Gelasius bishop of Caesarea, perhaps the second time he had put a friend in that see (Epiphanius, *Haer.* 73). The emperor Valens reacted strongly to Cyril's meddling by exiling him to eastern Asia Minor.

When Valens died in 378, Cyril returned to Jerusalem. The nearly twelve years of banishment had seen Cyril move from his *Homoiousian* position to support of the Nicene party. Gregory of Nyssa traveled to Jerusalem in 379 to question Cyril on behalf of a council in Antioch that year. Gregory disliked the Jerusalem churches and despised the pilgrimage trade, but he found Cyril's

faith sound. In 381, at Constantinople, the council counted Cyril as a Nicene.

Cyril's views are known to us from his *Catechetical Lectures*, probably delivered ca. 350. They explain the faith to catechumens during the Lenten season. Although they were apparently taken down once by a scribe, the manuscripts and versions contain interesting variations. The lectures on the sacraments, often bound with the *Catechetical Lectures*, are also probably his work. Feast day March 18. CPG II, 3585–3618. TLG 2110. [F.W.N.]

Bibliography
Catéchèses Mystagogiques, ed. and tr. A. Piédagnel and P. Paris, SC (1966), Vol. 126; F.L. Cross, ed., *St. Cyril of Jerusalem's Lectures on the Christian Sacraments* (London: SPCK, 1951).

E.H. Gifford, tr., NPNF, 2nd ser. (1894), Vol. 7.

J. Lebon, "La Position de saint Cyrille de Jerusalem dans les luttes provoquees par l'arianisme," *RHE* 20 (1924):181–210, 357–386; A. Paulin, *Saint Cyrille de Jerusalem: catéchète* (Paris: Cerf, 1959); E. Yarnold, "The Authorship of the Mystagogic Catechesis Attributed to Cyril of Jerusalem," *Heythrop Journal* 19 (1978):143–161.

CYRIL OF SCYTHOPOLIS (sixth century) Monk. Born into a Palestinian family that provided a hospice for traveling monks, Cyril was tonsured in 543 and decided to live alone beside the Jordan. Later, he joined the lauras of St. Euthymius and St. Saba. He wrote the hagiographic lives of several Palestinian abbots. CPG III, 7535–7543. [F.W.N.]

Bibliography
Cyril of Scythopolis: The Lives of the Monks of Palestine, tr. R.M. Price (Kalamazoo: Cistercian, 1989).

CYRILLONAS (fourth century). Syriac poet. Cyrillonas wrote six hymns that concern the sacrificial character of the eucharist, Mariology, the adoration of the saints, and prayers for relief from disasters. [F.W.N.]

Bibliography
PS 27.

D

DAMASUS I. Bishop of Rome (366–384). Damasus's father, Antonius, perhaps of Spanish origin, followed an ecclesiastical career at Rome. Damasus himself served as a deacon under his predecessor, Liberius (352–366), and for a period supported the antipope Felix, although he was reconciled with Liberius shortly before the latter's death. His election to the Roman see was contested, since a minority faction had chosen the deacon Ursinus. Riots broke out in Rome in which more than 100 persons were killed. Ursinus was exiled by the imperial authorities but allowed to return to the city in the following year (367), at which time the violence was renewed. Banished from Rome a second time, he and his followers were permitted to settle in northern Italy. They instigated charges of adultery against Damasus (ca. 371), of which he was exonerated, although their strong opposition to him continued for some ten years thereafter.

The exact number, dates, and activities of the early synods held under Damasus are in controversy. He was a forceful opponent of Arianism and other forms of heresy; in this, he enjoyed the support of Peter of Alexandria. (In 380, the emperor Theodosius I declared Christianity in the form professed by Damasus and

Peter the state religion.) He deposed two Arian bishops in Illyricum (369), but his efforts against Auxentius of Milan apparently failed until the latter died and was replaced by Ambrose (374). He brought about the condemnation of the adherents of the rigorist Lucifer of Cagliari and opposed those who denied the divinity of the Holy Spirit. In eastern affairs, his relations with Basil the Great were difficult because of mutual misunderstandings over terminology used to discuss the Trinity as well as from Damasus's support of the claims of Paulinus of Antioch against Melitius, the bishop favored by Basil. After the deaths of Basil (379) and Melitius (381), he continued to recognize Paulinus against Melitius's successor, Flavian.

Damasus successfully worked to strengthen the position of the papacy. He was the first to apply consistently to Rome the term "Apostolic See." He set the administration of the papal archives and chancery on a firm basis. Latin was made the liturgical language of the Roman church. His interest in scripture was shown in his commission to his secretary, Jerome, to revise existing Old Latin versions of the Bible in light of the Greek text, an assignment that would eventually result in the Vulgate, along with his promulgation of a canon of scripture at a Roman council (382). He built several churches and a baptistery at the Church of St. Peter. His reopening and restoration of the catacombs advanced the cult of the martyrs and encouraged pilgrimage to Rome.

An integral part of the program of restoration of the martyrs' burial places was the provision of appropriate inscriptions, the *Epigrams*, composed by Damasus himself and engraved on marble slabs by the exceptionally talented artist Filocalus. Approximately sixty are extant together with additional fragments, most in honor of martyrs and others recently deceased, some in commemoration of various undertakings; they have importance for archaeology. A number of Damasus's letters survive, although the authenticity of some is doubtful. The fourth letter, the *Tome of Damasus*, is a summary of errors pertaining to the Trinity and to Christology in a profession of faith drawn up by a Roman council (382) and sent to Paulinus of Antioch. The genuineness of three letters in Damasus's name contained in the correspondence of Jerome has come into question. A decretal addressed to the bishops of Gaul on disciplinary matters is probably authentic. Damasus may have composed the first three parts of the *Decretum Gelasianum*, those on the Holy Spirit, the canon of scripture, and the Roman see as the source of authority, in connection with a Roman council (382), but the work as a whole is probably a product of southern Gaul in the later fifth or early sixth century. Jerome (*Ep.* 22.22) attributes to him works on virginity in both prose and verse, but these are now lost. In the Middle Ages, he was erroneously thought to have been the author of the *Liber Pontificalis*.

The pontificate of Damasus, despite its inauspicious beginnings, must be counted as among the most important in the early history of the papacy. Feast day December 4. CPL 1632–1636.   [M.P.McH.]

Bibliography

Ammianus Marcellinus, *History* 27.3.12–15; Ambrose, *Letter* 11; Jerome, *Lives of Illustrious Men* 103; idem, *Letters* 15–16; 22.22; 35–36; 45.3; 123.100; idem, *Preface to 4 Gospels*; *Liber Pontificalis* 39 (Duchesne 1.212–215).

M.A. Norton, "Prosopography of Pope Damasus," *Folia* 4 (1950):13–31; 5 (1951):30–55; 6 (1952): 16–39; repr. in *Leaders of Iberian Christianity*, ed. J.M.-F. Marique (Boston: Saint Paul, 1962), pp. 13–80; A. Lippold, "Ursinus und Damasus," *Historia* 14 (1965):105–128; T.C. Lawler, "Jerome's First Letter to Damasus," *Kyriakon: Festschrift Johannes Quasten*, ed. P. Granfield and J.A. Jungmann (Münster: Aschendorff, 1970), Vol. 2, pp. 548–552; M.H. Shepherd, "The Liturgical Reform of Damasus I," ibid., Vol. 2, pp. 847–863; C. Pietri, *Roma Christiana: recherches sur l'église de Rome (311–440)* (Rome: Ecole Française de Rome, 1976), Vol. 1, Chs. 6–10; J. Fontaine, *Naissance de la poésie dans l'occident chrétien* (Paris: Etudes Augustiniennes, 1981), pp. 115–125; P. Nautin, "Le Premier echange épistolaire entre Jérôme et Damase," *FZPhTh* 30 (1983):331–334.

DANIEL. Biblical book. The Book of Daniel (named for its main character) is found in the Christian Old Testament among the major prophets; in the Hebrew Bible, it is placed among the Writings. The textual history of Daniel is complicated. Until the mid-second century A.D., there were two and possibly three Greek versions used by Christian authors. The text known as Theodotion-Daniel became the one in common use in the east by the end of the second century A.D. and by the middle of the third century A.D. in the west also (Jerome, *Comm. in Dan.* 4.6). All of the Greek versions as well as the Vulgate included the material lacking in the Hebrew—the *Prayer of Azariah*, the *Song of the Three Young Men* (Dan. 3:24–90), *Susanna*, and *Bel and the Dragon* (Dan. 13–14).

The Book of Daniel figured prominently in early Christian literature. Significant uses of the book are found in *Epistle of Barnabas* 4; 6; 16; *1 Clement* 34; 50; Justin (*1 Apol.* 26; 51.9; *Dial.* 31–32; 110.1–3; 120.4–6), Clement of Alexandria (*Str.* 1.21; 6.15); Origen (*Princ.* 4.5; *Cels.* 2.49; 6.45; *Ep.* 1); Tertullian (*Marc.* 3; 4; *Jud.* 8.14; *Jej.*); Irenaeus (*Haer.* 3.21.7; 5.25–26; 34.2), Cyprian (*Quir.* 2.16–18; *Fort.* 11; *Op.* 5); Julius Africanus (*Chron.*); Hippolytus (*Antichr.* 21–26); Lactantius (*Div. inst.* 4.12, 21); Victorinus of Pettau (*Apoc.*); Eusebius of Caesarea (*D.E.* 8.2; *P.E.* 6.11); and Aphraates (*Demon.* 5).

Beginning with Hippolytus's *Commentary on Daniel* in 211 (the first full Greek commentary on a biblical book), commentaries were composed by a number of Christian interpreters in Greek, Latin, and Syriac. The Christian interpretation developed along three main lines: an apocalyptic and eschatological reading that focused on the dreams and visions of Chapters 2, 7, and 11, treating the imagery as prophecy of the end of the world order; a messianic reading that focused on Chapter 9 and interpreted the vision as a prophecy of the advent of Jesus as Messiah; a reading that used the first six chapters of the book for moral exhortation.

In terms of the apocalyptic-eschatological interpretation, there was widespread agreement that the statue made from the four elements in Daniel 2 and the four beasts of Daniel 7 represented the rise and fall of the Babylonian, Persian (or Medo-Persian), Greek, and Roman empires. The schemes into which the eschatological events and figures were placed varied. The earliest interpretive tradition, found in Irenaeus, Tertullian, and Hippolytus, tended to read Daniel as a prophecy of the end of the Roman empire and the coming of the thousand-year earthly reign of the saints. A later tradition, found in Eusebius, Jerome, and Theodoret, spurned this approach in favor of an eschatological interpretation that foresaw only a heavenly reign of the saints and portrayed the Roman empire as the predicted scene of the conflict between the Antichrist and the faithful. In the Syriac writers Ephraem the Syrian (or pseudo-Ephraem) and Aphraates and in the Greek commentary of Polychronius, bishop of Apamea, we find yet another exegetical tradition, which varied not only in its eschatological scheme but also in its interpretation of the imagery. These interpreters argued that Daniel's prophetic vision had as its ultimate point of reference the Seleucid empire governed by Antiochus Epiphanes (175–163 B.C.). All three interpreters go on to argue that the text points forward in an indirect or secondary sense to the events related to the advent of Jesus. This historicizing trend in the interpretation of Daniel probably arose as a consequence of the close proximity of the Syrian Christian community (and Apamea) to the large community of Jews living in the area of Edessa.

The Book of Daniel was frequently read and interpreted by Christians as prophetic testimony to the messianic status of Jesus (Jerome, *Comm. in Dan.* pref.). They interpreted the "anointed one" (Dan. 9:25–26) as a reference to Jesus.

Christian interpreters used the behavior of Daniel and his companions in the courts of the Babylonians (Dan. 1–6) for a variety of types of moral exhortation: against idolatry (Cyprian, *Fort.* 11); for fasting (Origen, *Cels.* 7.7; Tertullian, *Jej.* 9); against Jewish ritual (Theodoret, *Dan.* 10.4).

Daniel in the lions' den (Dan. 6) was one of the most popular scenes in early Christian art. *See also* Apocalyptic Literature.

[C.T.McC.]

Bibliography

Hippolytus, *Commentarius in Danielum*, ed. G.N. Bonwetsch, GCS (1897) 1.1, pp. 1–340; ed. M. Lefèvre, SC (1947), Vol. 14; Ephraem the Syrian, *Commentarii in Danielum*, ed. J.S. Assemanus, P. Benedictus, S.E. Assemanus, *Sanctus Ephraem Opera Omnia Quae Exstant* (1740), Vol. 2; Jerome, *Commentary on Daniel*, ed. F. Glorie, CCSL (1964), Vol. 75A; tr. G.L. Archer, *Jerome's Commentary on Daniel* (Grand Rapids: Baker, 1958); Polychronius, *Commentarius in Danielem*, ed. A. Mai, *Scriptorum Veterum Nova Collectio* (1825 and 1831), Vol. 1, pp. 1–27; Theodoret, *Interpretatio in Danielem*, ed. J. Schulze, PG (1864), Vol. 81, pp. 1255–1546.

H.H. Rowley, *Darius the Mede and the Four World Empires in the Book of Daniel* (Cardiff: U of Wales P, 1964); P.M. Casey, "Porphyry and the Origin of the Book of Daniel," *JThS* n.s. 27 (1976):15–33; J. Braverman, *Jerome's Commentary on Daniel: A Study of Comparative Jewish and Christian Interpretation of the Hebrew Bible* (Washington, D.C.: CBQ Monograph Series, 1978); M. Casey, *Son of Man: The Interpretation and Influence of Daniel 7* (London: SPCK, 1979); G.K. Beale, *The Use of Daniel in Jewish Apocalyptic Literature and in the Revelation of St. John* (New York: University Press of America, 1984); J. Gammie, "A Journey Through Danielic Spaces," *Interpretation* 39 (1985):117–130; R. Bodenmann, *Naissance d'une exégèse: Daniel dans l'église ancienne des trois premiers siècles* (Tübingen: Mohr, 1986).

DANIÉLOU, JEAN (1905–1974). Patristic scholar. Jean Daniélou was educated in France and received his doctorate from the Sorbonne in 1927. He became a Jesuit in 1929 and was ordained a priest in 1938. In 1969, he was appointed archbishop of Taormina and named a cardinal. He served as the professor of primitive Christianity at the Institut Catholique de Paris from 1943 to 1974.

Daniélou was most noted by the general public for his extensive writings on the relationship among modern culture, Christianity, and other religions. As a highly regarded historian of early Christianity, he made major contributions to the field, particularly in the interpretation of symbols, typology, and Jewish Christianity. His three-volume *History of Early Christian Doctrine Before the Council of Nicaea* (Philadelphia: Westminster, 1964–1977) is a classic example of his efforts. With Henri Marrou, he wrote the first volume of *The Christian Centuries: A New History of the Catholic Church, Vol. 1: The First Six Hundred Years* (New York: McGraw-Hill, 1964). Among others, Gregory of Nyssa (*Platonisme et théologie mystique*, 1944) and Origen (English tr. 1955) attracted his special attention.

In 1942, with Henri de Lubac, he founded the "Sources chrétiennes," the most productive series of ancient Christian texts and modern-language translations (in this case French) produced in the twentieth century. The series continues with over 300 volumes published.

[F.W.N.]

Bibliography
J. Fontaine and C. Kannengiesser, eds., *Epektasis: Mélanges patristiques offerts au cardinal Jean Daniélou* (Paris: Beauchesne, 1972).

DASIUS. Four martyrs of this name are known, but of only one is much known. The soldier Dasius was a martyr (303–304) under Diocletian; the *Martyrdom of Dasius* recounts the Roman army's celebration of the feast of Saturnalia. [E.F.]

Bibliography
Musurillo, pp. xl–xli, 272–279.

DAVID (late eleventh–early tenth century B.C.). King of Israel (1 Sam. 16–1 Kings 2, and, from another perspective, 1 Chron. 3; 10–29), traditionally considered the author of Psalms. David's descendants were to rule Israel in perpetuity (2 Sam. 7:12–16). Thus, in prophetic literature he became a model of the deliverer-restorer of the kingdom (Amos 9:11; Isa. 9:6; 11:1–10; Jer. 33:15–22). The Gospel writers assume the Davidic descent of Christ (Matt. 1:1; Luke 1:27), as do Paul (Rom. 1:3) and others (2 Tim. 2:8; Rev. 5:5; 22:16).

Patristic writers developed this tradition. Clement of Rome used David as an example (*1 Clem.* 4; 18) and like later writers saw Christ as speaking in the Psalms (16). Hippolytus, Ambrose, and John Chrysostom devoted major treatises to the significance of David for Christian theology. During the patristic period, David is considered, first, as the king of Israel who announces the Universal King; second, as a prophet; and third, as an exemplar of the Christian virtues required of a pastor. These images were represented in Christian art. [D.B.]

Bibliography
Hippolytus, *De David et Goliath* (CPG I, 1876); Ambrose, *The Prayer of Job and David* (CPL 135), tr. M.P. McHugh in FOTC (1972), Vol. 65; idem, *De apologia prophetae David* (CPL 135); John Chrysostom, *Homiliae 3 de Davide et Saule* (CPG II, 4412).

E. Lohse, "*Uios Dauid,*" *Theological Dictionary of the New Testament*, ed. G. Kittel (Grand Rapids: Eerdmans, 1972), Vol. 8, pp. 478–488; E.A. Gosselin, *The King's Progress to Jerusalem: Some Interpretations of David During the Reformation Period and Their Patristic and Medieval Background* (Malibu: Undena, 1976); L.A. Sinclair and C. Thoma, "David," TRE (1981), Vol. 8, pp. 378–388.

DAVID OF WALES (sixth century). Patron saint of Wales. David was active in the establishment of monastic foundations of great asceticism and probably attended synods called to combat Pelagianism. Many legends have accumulated around his life. The biography by Rhygyfarch (1056–1099), written to affirm the independence of the see of St. David's from Canterbury, is not reliable. Feast day March 1. [M.P.McH.]

Bibliography
Rhygyfarch, *Life of St. David*, ed. and tr. J.W. James (Cardiff: U of Wales P, 1967).

N.K. Chadwick et al., *Studies in the Early British Church* (Cambridge: Cambridge UP, 1958).

St. David's Cathedral, Wales (twelfth–fourteenth centuries), Britain's smallest cathedral.

DEACON. Servant or minister, a subordinate church official. Although nearly all religious and social groups have subordinate officials to assist the leaders, the principal non-Christian functionary who has been considered comparable with the Christian deacon is the *chazan* in the Jewish synagogue. The servant of the synagogue at different times and places was assigned a variety of tasks: assisting in the worship, caring for the building, executing punishment on offenders, and teaching children. Whatever his background, the deacon had a distinctive development in Christianity.

Diakonos ("deacon") is used in the New Testament in a nontechnical sense for a great variety of persons: waiters (John 2:5), government officials (Rom. 13:4), servants of Satan (2 Cor. 11:15), a disciple (Matt. 23:11), a messenger (Col. 4:7; 1 Thess. 3:2), evangelists and missionaries (1 Tim. 4:6; 2 Cor. 11:23), apostles (Matt 20:26; 2 Cor. 3:6), Christ (Rom. 15:8). "Deacon" as a technical term for a recognized ministry in the church with set qualifications is also attested in the New Testament (Phil. 1:1; 1 Tim. 3:8–13). The association of the deacons with bishops in these passages continued to be normal in Christian usage (*Did.* 15; *1 Clem.* 42), but there are also passages where deacons are paired with presbyters (elders—Polycarp, *Ep.* 5.2; Clement of Alexandria, *Str.* 3.12.90; 7.1.3). The deacons were the assistants of the spiritual leaders in the church, performing various services on behalf of the people. The deacons could, therefore, be seen as in a special way representing the serving attitude and work of Jesus (Ignatius, *Magn.* 6.1; *Trall.* 3.1; cf. Luke 22:27).

Deacons in the early centuries filled many functions. They distributed the eucharist in the Sunday assembly (Justin, *1 Apol.* 67); assisted at other liturgical functions, such as baptism and the agape (Hippolytus, *Trad. ap.* 21; 26); acted as ushers and kept order (*Didas.* 12); administered the benevolent relief of the church to widows and orphans (Hermas, *Sim.* 9.26.2); ministered to martyrs in prison (*Pass. Perp.* 3); served as messengers for churches (Ignatius, *Philad.* 10; *Smyrn.* 12); and administered church property (Cyprian, *Ep.* 52.1). Deacons had responsibility for burying the dead (Eusebius, *H.E.* 7.11.24), and in Rome a deacon was placed over the cemetery (Hippolytus, *Haer.* 9.7). The deacon was in especially close relations with the bishop, serving him, carrying out his instructions, and reporting to him (Hippolytus, *Trad. ap.* 9.2; 30). The deacons were the "eyes" (Ps.-Clement, *Ep. ad Jac.* 12) and "ears" (*Didas.* 11) of the bishop, constantly in contact with people, warning and exhorting, searching out the needy, and admonishing the wealthy (*Ap. Ch. Order* 20; 22). One deacon might become the right-hand man of the bishop, and bishops were more often chosen from the ranks of the diaconate than from the presbyterate. Deacons sometimes served rural parishes, but church councils disapproved (Elvira, *can.* 77; Arles, *can.* 16). The importance of the deacons became so great that at Rome they considered themselves superior to the presbyters, and their pretensions were opposed by those who emphasized the equivalence of presbyters and bishops (Jerome, *Ep.* 146; Ambrosiaster, *Quaes. V. et N. Test.* 127.101). Jerome first used the term "archdeacon" (*Ep.* 125.15; 146), a position that expanded considerably in the medieval west.

Some churches regarded the precedent of Acts 6:1–6 as limiting the number of deacons in a church to seven (Eusebius, *H.E.* 6.43.11; Neocaesarea, *can.* 15), but the *Apostolic Church Order* 20 provided for three, and the *Didascalia* 9 for as many as required (Sozomen, *H.E.* 7.19, said the number is irrelevant). *See also* Acolyte; Bishop; Deaconess; Ministry; Presbyter; Subdeacon.   [E.F.]

Bibliography

Special issue on "Deacons," *Theology* 58 (1955):403–429; J. Colson, *La Fonction diaconale aux origines de l'église* (Paris: Desclée de Brouwer, 1960); J.G. Davies, "Deacons, Deaconesses and the Minor Orders in the Patristic Period," *JEH* 14 (1963):1–15; *The Ministry of Deacons* (Geneva: World Council of Churches, 1965); G.W.H. Lampe, "Diakonia in the Early Church," *Service in Christ*, ed. J.I. McCord and J.H.L. Parker (Grand Rapids: Eerdmans, 1966), pp. 49–64; E.R. Hardy, "Deacons in History and Practice," *The Diaconate Now*, ed. R.T. Nolan (Washington, D.C.: Corpus, 1968); E.P. Echlin, *The Deacon in the Church* (New York: Alba House, 1971); J.M. Barnett, *The Diaconate: A Full and Equal Order* (New York: Seabury, 1981); L.R. Hennessey, "*Diakonia* and *Diakonoi* in the Pre-Nicene Church," *Diakonia: Studies in Honor of Robert T. Meyer*, ed. T. Halton and J.P. Williams (Washington, D.C.: Catholic U of America P, 1986), pp. 60–86.

DEACONESS. Female deacon. Discussion of the presence of deaconesses in the New Testament period has revolved around two texts. Romans 16:1 describes Phoebe as a "deacon" (*diakonos* as a feminine noun) of the church at Cenchreae. Does the word have its general sense of a servant or the technical meaning of

an official of the church? Perhaps more significant for the status of Phoebe is the description of her as a "helper," literally a patroness of the church, indicating wealth and the influence its use on behalf of the church would have given her. In 1 Timothy 3:11, "women" is ambiguous: "wives" (of deacons, and bishops?) or women deacons (so John Chrysostom, *Hom. 11 in 1 Tim.* 3.11)? The parallel construction with 3:1 and 8 would argue for a separate order of ministers, whereas the interruption in the description of deacons might favor the meaning "wives." Another possibility would be for these women to be female assistants to the deacons. Some independent confirmation for deaconesses from this early period is provided by Pliny the Younger (*Ep.* 96.8), who refers to his examination of "two female slaves, who were called deaconesses" (*ministrae*), but again, is this a technical use for an order?

The first extensive information on the deaconess comes from the third century in the *Didascalia* 16. The deaconesses did not perform baptism (cf. Tertullian, *Bapt.* 17) but assisted at the baptism of women. This was made necessary by the fact that baptism was normally received nude and was accompanied by an anointing. Women normally did not teach, but the deaconesses did give postbaptismal instruction on Christian living to other women. The deaconesses also ministered to women who were sick (cf. Epiphanius, *Haer.* 3.2.79).

The *Apostolic Constitutions* added to these duties arranging the place for women in the church building (8.28) and serving as a messenger for the church (3.19). This document required that she be a virgin or a once-married widow (6.17) and provided for an ordination by laying on of hands of the bishop and prayer (8.19f.). For the deaconess, it used the word *diakonissa*, which is first attested in the fourth century (Nicaea, *can.* 19). Clement of Alexandria earlier spoke of "women deacons" (*Str.* 3.6.53). The *Theodosian Code* (16.2.27) applied the requirement that enrolled widows be sixty years old (1 Tim. 5:9) to deaconesses, but the Council of Chalcedon (*can.* 15) set their minimum age at forty and forbade marriage to them after appointment.

Various serving ministries were also performed by virgins and widows.

With the decline of adult baptism, one of the important functions of deaconesses became unnecessary. The order of deaconesses appears to have been primarily an eastern creation and to have lasted longer there. Councils at Epaon (517) and Orleans (533) in France abolished the office, but there were survivals even in the west. *See also* Deacon; Virgins; Widows.

[E.F.]

Bibliography

C. Robinson, *The Ministry of Deaconesses* (London: Methuen, 1898); C.H. Turner, "Ministries of Women in the Primitive Church: Widow, Deaconess and Virgin in the First Four Christian Centuries," *Catholic and Apostolic*, ed. H.N. Bate (London: Mowbray, 1931), pp. 316–351; J. Mayer, *Monumenta de viduis, diaconissis, virginibusque tractantia* (Bonn: Hanstein, 1938); J.G. Davies, "Deacons, Deaconesses and the Minor Orders in the Patristic Period," *JEH* 14 (1963):1–15; *The Deaconess* (Geneva: World Council of Churches, 1966); J. Daniélou, *The Ministry of Women in the Ancient Church* (Westminster: Faith, 1974); R. Gryson, *The Ministry of Women in the Early Church* (Collegeville: Liturgical, 1976); A.G. Martimort, *Deaconesses: An Historical Study* (San Francisco: Ignatius, 1986).

DECIUS (201–251). Roman emperor (249–251). Gaius Messius Quintus Decius was a native of the middle-Danube region (Illyricum or Pannonia). He may have been prefect of the city of Rome ca. 248, when he was appointed by the emperor Philip the Arab (244–249) to restore order along the lower Danube. Roman troops were in revolt, and the area was under attack by the Goths. Decius's initial success was climaxed by his own (perhaps hesitant) acceptance of the imperial title, which was urged on him by the army. He marched on Italy, where he defeated Philip near Verona in 249.

Decius ruled with an unrelenting conservatism aimed at restoring the lost stability of an idealized Roman past, as exemplified by his adoption of the name "Trajan Decius" after his second-century predecessor. One manifestation of this conservatism was an order issued in 250 requiring all citizens of the empire to demonstrate their loyalty to the state gods by performing public sacrifice. The order seems not to have been directed expressly at Christians, but in practical fact it caused considerable problems for the church. Rigorous enforcement yielded a number of martyrs and a far greater number of apostates. But the immediate crisis was short-lived.

Campaigning against the Goths late in 250, Decius suffered a major defeat at Beroea. In midsummer of 251, he was defeated again and killed at Abrittus in the Dobrudja, the first Roman emperor to die in battle against foreign invaders. To the church, Decius's sudden demise seemed to represent the judgment of God. *See also* Persecution. [G.J.J.]

Bibliography

H.A. Pohlsander, "The Religious Policy of Decius," ANRW (1986), Vol. 2.16.3, pp. 1826–1842.

DEMONS. Beings intermediate between divine and human beings. The Greek word *daimon* (diminutive, *daimonion*) referred to a divine or superhuman power or activity. From the time of Homer and later, "demon" could be used for the gods in general, especially where the identity of the deity was unknown or the emphasis was on a power rather than on a specific being. This impersonal application of the word led to its usage for something heaven-sent, such as luck or chance. "Demon" was also the word for the soul of the deceased, a ghost. Another important usage was in reference to an individual guardian spirit accompanying each person, a meaning picked up especially by the Stoics. Important for the later development was the thought of Plato's student Xenocrates, who systematized views about demons as intermediary beings with divine power and human emotions. The reluctance to assign bad events to the gods meant that anything unpleasant was more often attributed to the demons, but in Greek thought demons remained capable of being either good or bad, unlike Jewish and Christian belief, which regularly considered them to be bad.

Although Jewish writers in Greek, such as Philo and Josephus, used "demon" with the same range of meaning that the word had in classical Greek, other Jewish writers preferred to speak of "evil spirits." Their origin was traced to the spirits of the giants that resulted from the intercourse of angels with women (*1 Enoch* 6; 15–16), to a pretemporal fall of some angels (*2 Enoch* 29.4f.), to a rebellion by angels prompted by jealousy over man's place in creation (*Life of Adam* 12–17), to punishment of the souls involved in building Babel (*b. Sanh.* 109a), or to a special creation by God (*Aboth* 5.6; *Midrash Rabbah, Genesis* 7.5, 5d). An important Jewish contribution to Christian thought was the identification of demons with the gods of pagan idolatry (Ps. 96:5 in the Septuagint was often cited).

Both Greeks and Jews considered it possible for demons to possess a person and resorted to magic or exorcism in order to expel such demons. Instances of demon possession stand out in the Gospels (Matt. 8:28–34; Luke 11:14–22). Indeed, demons appear in the New Testament mainly in the ministry of Jesus. They caused various kinds of illness (Luke 9:37–43; 13:10–16). Their appearance in the Gospel accounts mainly highlighted their supernatural witness to the divinity of Jesus (Mark 1:21–28; 3:11); their subjection to his authority enhanced his power (Luke 4:36; 10:17–20). The Pauline letters rarely use the terms "demons" (1 Cor. 10:19–21) or "evil spirits" but do use "principalities" and "powers" for intermediary beings (Rom. 8:38; Eph. 6:12).

Early Christian thought continued some of the variety in Jewish views about the origin of demons. The interpretation of Genesis 6:1–4 that demons resulted from the intercourse of "sons of God" (angels) with "daughters of men" was continued by some (Athenagoras, *Leg.* 24–25) but denied by others (Origen, *Cels.* 5.54f.). Some attributed the fall of angels to envy for men (Irenaeus, *Dem.* 16). The interpretation of Isaiah 14:12–15 and Ezekiel 28:1–19 as describing the fall of Satan because of pride is found fairly early (Tertullian, *Marc.* 2.10; Origen, *Princ.* 1.5.4–5). Christians did agree in considering the demons as creatures of God who sinned by their own free will (Origen, *Cels.* 4.65; 7.69; Tertullian, *Apol.* 22).

Demons assumed an important role in early Christian apologetics, especially in the work of Justin Martyr. Some Greek philosophers had already criticized certain features of pagan religion, such as magic and animal sacrifice, as involving the intermediary demons and not the highest gods. Because of the identification of pagan gods with demons, the apologists attributed all of pagan religion to the worship of demons (Minucius Felix, *Oct.* 26–27). The demons were considered responsible for the working of miracles (ibid., but cf. Tatian, *Or.* 18), the giving of prophecies at the oracles (Origen, *Cels.* 4.93), and the practice of astrology (Lactantius, *Div. inst.* 2.17). They were nourished by animal sacrifices (Athenagoras, *Leg.* 26–27; Origen, *Mart.* 45).

The demons were viewed as the cause of evils in the world. These included physical evils in the natural order (Origen, *Cels.* 1.31; 8.31). During the age of persecution, the Christian apologists said that the demons had incited the authorities to attack Christians (Justin, *1 Apol.* 5; 10; 57). Another demonic attack on Christianity was causing heresy (Hippolytus, *Haer.* 6.2). The moral evils of humanity, which were attributed to the demons' enticements to sin, were especially their work (Origen, *Princ.* 3.2.1; Tertullian, *Apol.* 22). The deception practiced by the devil and demons was a frequent theme (Justin, *1 Apol.* 5; Tatian, *Or.* 14). However, the demons could not compel human beings to sin (Irenaeus, *Haer.* 5.24.3). Sin came through free choice in response to temptations (Origen, *Princ.* 3.2.1–4). The close association of sins with demons and their working led to a personifying of sins. The *Testaments of the Twelve Patriarchs* show that in some Jewish circles sins were identified with the spirit that caused them (*Test. Reuben* 2). Similarly, the early Christian writer Hermas called certain sins demons (*Mand.* 2.3; *Sim.* 9.23.3). This tendency to internalize and psychologize the working of demons was carried farther by Origen (*Princ.* 3.3.4; *Hom. 12 in Jos.* 3; *Hom. 15 in Jos.* 5). In monastic literature, the demons appear mainly as allurements to sin (e.g., Athanasius, *V. Anton.* 5).

In the face of these powerful demonic influences, Christians remained confident that Christ had won a decisive victory over them and their ultimate defeat was ensured. The birth of Christ initiated the overthrow of demons (Justin, *Dial.* 45; 78). His ministry demonstrated his power over them (Origen, *Cels.* 8.64). The crucifixion was the climactic moment when the power of Satan and sin was broken (Justin, *Dial.* 49; 131). Only with the second coming of Christ, however, would the devil and demons be finally destroyed (Justin, *1 Apol.* 45; 52). In the meantime, the preaching of the gospel of Christ was the means of pushing back the realm of evil (Justin, *Dial.* 83; Origen, *Princ.* 3.5.7–8), and the demons were left inoperative when Christians resisted their temptations (Origen, *Hom. 15 in Jos.* 5). Christians at baptism shared in Christ's victory over the demonic forces (Origen, *Hom. 5 in Ex.* 1–2; Cyprian, *Ep.* 69.15). Martyrdom was a further means of sharing in the victory over demons (Origen, *Cels.* 8.44). An important demonstration of the truth and power of Christianity was the ability of Christians to drive demons out of those afflicted by them and to do this not by magical incantations but by the name of Jesus and simple words of prayer (Justin, *Dial.* 76; Origen, *Cels.* 1.6). It was confidently affirmed that the demons had no power or influence over Christians unless they chose to let them (Origen, *Cels.* 8.34, 36).

Papyri, inscriptions, and archaeological finds indicate that the line separating Christian practice from magic was not as clear as some of the literary sources would claim. Many Christians used the sign of the cross and amulets to ward off evil spirits.

In a world that was very conscious of supernatural power influencing human life, the Christian claim to offer deliverance from evil spirits was a powerful factor in the growth of the church. *See also* Angels; Exorcism; Magic; Satan.   [E.F.]

Bibliography

Plutarch, *Obsolescence of Oracles* 10–15 (*Moralia* 415A–418D); Justin Martyr, *1 Apology* 5; idem, *2 Apology* 5; Tertullian, *Apology* 22–23; Minucius Felix, *Octavius* 26–27; Pseudo-Clement, *Recognitions* 4.15–26; idem, *Homilies* 8.12–20; 9.9–23; Lactantius, *Divine Institutes* 2.15–18; Eusebius, *Preparation for the Gospel* 4.5, 15, 22–23; 5.1–17; 7.16.

A. von Harnack, *The Mission and Expansion of Christianity,* 2nd ed. (New York: Putnam, 1908), pp. 125-146. G.B. Caird, *Principalities and Powers: A Study in Pauline Theology* (Oxford: Clarendon, 1956); H. Wey, *Die Funktionen der bösen Geister bei den griechischen Apologeten des zweiten Jahrhunderts nach Christus* (Winterthur: Keller, 1957); F.X. Gokey, *The Terminology for the Devil and Evil Spirits in the Apostolic Fathers* (Washington, D.C.: Catholic U of America P, 1961); S. Eitrem, *Some Notes on the Demonology of the New Testament,* 2nd ed. (Oslo: Universitetsforlaget, 1966); C. Colpe et al., "Geister (Dämonen)," RLAC (1976), Vol. 9, pp. 546–797; F. Brenk, *In Mist Apparelled: Religious Themes in Plutarch's Moralia and Lives* (Leiden: Brill, 1977); M.P. McHugh, "The Demonology of Saint Ambrose in Light of the Tradition," WS 12[91] (1978):205–231; E. Ferguson, *Demonology of the Early Christian World* (New York: Mellen, 1984); F. Brenk, "In Light of the Moon: Demonology in the Early Imperial Period," ANRW (1986), Vol. 1.16.3, pp. 2068–2145.

DER BALIZEH PAPYRI. Sixth–seventh-century papyri preserved in the Bodleian Library, Oxford. The Christian texts include martyr accounts, hagiographical documents, prayers, a eucharistic liturgy close to the *Liturgy of St. Mark,* and a confession of faith similar to the baptismal confession in Hippolytus, *Apostolic Tradition.* The liturgical material reflects Egyptian usage in the fourth or even third century.
                    [E.F.]

Bibliography

C.H. Roberts and D.B. Capelle, *An Early Euchologium: The Dêr Balizeh Papyrus Enlarged and Reedited* (Louvain: Bibliothèque Muséon, 1949); P.E. Kahle, *Bala'izah: Coptic Texts from Deir El-Bala'izeh in Upper Egypt,* 2 vols. (London: Oxford UP, 1954); P.F. Palmer, *Sources of Christian Theology* (Westminster: Newman, 1955), Vol. 1: *Sacraments and Worship,* pp. 44–46.

DESERT FATHERS. *See* Monasticism.

DEVIL. *See* Satan.

DIADOCUS OF PHOTICE (fifth century). Bishop of Photice in Palestine (after 451). Diadocus wrote the *Capita centum,* describing how to reach spiritual perfection. Maximus Confessor, the *Doctrina Patrum,* and Photius evidence its popularity. CPG III, 6106–6111.
                    [F.W.N.]

Bibliography

PG 65.1141–1212; E. des Places, ed., SC (2nd ed., 1955), Vol. 5.

DIDACHE. "The Teaching of the Lord Through the Twelve Apostles to the Nations," a manual of church life included among the works of the apostolic fathers. It was characteristic of the church orders, of which the Didache is the first, to present their teachings as coming from the apostles. It was also characteristic for the contents to be revised and brought up to date as the practices of the church changed. The primitive prescriptions of the Didache soon no longer met the needs of later times. Only one manuscript, written in 1056, survives. There are, however, other witnesses to the text. The Didache influenced later documents; for instance, it was rewritten as Book 7 of the Apostolic Constitutions. There are papyrus fragments of the Greek, and parts are extant in Latin, Coptic, and Ethiopic.

The question of date is difficult to answer. Besides reckoning with possible later modifications in transmission, one must consider the evidences of compilation in the Didache. What is the date of the components? When were these compiled into a document? What is the date of later revisions or insertions? Dates from before A.D. 70 to a century later or some time between the late first or early second century have been proposed for the compilation. The place of origin is also disputed. Syria best fits the contents, but some aspects of the transmission and usage of the Didache support Egypt.

Chapters 1–6 present the "Two Ways" of life and death. This manner of setting forth moral instruction is based on Jewish patterns of teaching (as seen in Rule of the Community among the Dead Sea Scrolls), if not on a Jewish document. The parallels in the Epistle of Barnabas and Hermas may be due to independent appropriation of a common source rather than to a literary relation between these three documents. The specifically Christian part, a collection of sayings similar to Matthew and Luke's account of Jesus' teachings on the commandment to love one's neighbor (1.3–2.1), is missing from the Latin Doctrina Apostolorum (which otherwise substantially reproduces the "Two Ways" with a Christian doxology) and may be an interpolation to Christianize the Jewish teaching. This moral instruction was placed in the Didache as catechetical instruction preparatory to baptism.

Chapters 7–10 give liturgical instructions on baptism, fasting, prayer, and the eucharist. Immersion is preferred for baptism, but in the lack of sufficient water a triple affusion is permitted (a later modification?). Christian fast days are Wednesday and Friday, and the Lord's prayer (with doxology) is to be recited daily. The prayers in Chapters 9 and 10 have been much discussed. They are based on Jewish table prayers. It is not clear whether the thanksgivings are for the eucharist, an agape, or a eucharist followed by an agape.

Chapters 11–15 give instructions concerning the ministry: how to treat traveling apostles, prophets, and teachers (11–13); the need for reconciliation among members before coming together for the eucharist on the Lord's day (14); the election of bishops and deacons (15). Chapter 16 is an eschatological conclusion.

The Didache presents a church still in close proximity to Judaism and still developing its distinctive institutions. The document was highly valued in the early church. Eusebius placed it among the writings that were orthodox but rejected from the canon (H.E. 3.25.4), and Athanasius listed it as a book useful for catechumens (Ep. fest. 39). CPG I, 1735. TLG 1311.   [E.F.]

Bibliography

A. von Harnack, Die Lehre der zwölf Apostel, TU (1884), Vol. 2.1–2; W. Rordorf and A. Tuilier, La Doctrine des douze apôtres (Didachè), SC (1978), Vol. 248.

E.J. Goodspeed, The Apostolic Fathers: An American Translation (New York: Harper, 1950), pp. 1–18, 285–310; J.P. Audet, La Didachè, instructions des apôtres (Paris: Gabalda, 1958); R.A. Kraft, Barnabas and the Didache (New York: Nelson, 1965).

A. Vööbus, Liturgical Traditions in the Didache (Stockholm: Estonian Theological Society in Exile, 1968); B. Layton, "The Sources, Date, and Transmission of Didache 1.3b–2.1," HThR 61 (1968): 343–383; S. Giet, L'Enigma de la Didachè, (Paris: Ophrys, 1970); K. Niederwimmer, Die Didache (Göttingen: Vandenhoeck and Ruprecht, 1988).

DIDASCALIA. Combination church order and pastoral admonition entitled in Syriac "Catholic Teaching of the Twelve Apostles and Holy Disciples of our Savior." The *Didascalia* was composed in Greek in Syria in the first half of the third century. It survives entire in Syriac, but there is a Latin translation of about forty percent, and it is the basis of the first six books of the Greek *Apostolic Constitutions* and the Ethiopic and Arabic *Didascalia.* The fictitious setting is the gathering of the apostles in Acts 15, at which time they drew up this *Didascalia* for the ordering of the churches (24).

The community addressed was troubled by Jewish customs, and the author argues that only the moral law is binding and the ceremonial law ("the second legislation") has been abrogated (2; 26). Attention is given to proper conduct (1; 21), husbands and wives (2–3), and the upbringing of children (22). The bishop was the center of the community, and most of the directions are given to him, including information on the other ministers, among whom deaconesses and widows are prominent (4–9; 14–16). The baptismal ceremony follows the Syriac custom of anointing before the immersion with the Trinitarian formula (16). There is a description of how the clergy and people are to be seated in the church in order to preserve good conduct (12) and an encouragement to the people to be regular in assembling at church (13). The author advocates forgiveness for all sins—including adultery, idolatry, and apostasy—except the sin against the Holy Spirit, for those who repent and submit to discipline (6; 25). A strong stand is taken against heresy and schism (23), and the faithful are encouraged to martyrdom with the promise of the resurrection (19–20). CPG I, 1738. [E.F.]

Bibliography

R.H. Connolly, *Didascalia Apostolorum: The Syriac Version Translated and Accompanied by the Verona Latin Fragments* (Oxford: Clarendon, 1929); A. Vööbus, *The Didascalia Apostolorum in Syriac* I–II, CSCO (1978), Vols. 401, 407 (text) and 402, 408 (tr.); J.M. Hardin, *The Ethiopic Didascalia* (London: SPCK, 1920).

J.V. Bartlet, *Church-Life and Church-Order During the First Four Centuries with Special Reference to the Early Eastern Church-Orders* (Oxford: Blackwell, 1943).

DIDYMUS THE BLIND (313–398). Prominent representative of Alexandrian theology, orthodox in his stand on the Arian controversy but markedly Origenist in his biblical exegesis. Athanasius appointed Didymus to lead the catechetical school in Alexandria; that apart, we possess relatively little information on the course of his life, which seems to have been devoted largely to meditation, study, lecturing, and writing. Although blind from early childhood, he wrote prolifically on both dogmatic and exegetical subjects. His *De Spiritu Sancto,* preserved only in Jerome's Latin translation, is the one extant dogmatic work that can with certainty be ascribed to him; it shows him as a vigorous advocate of Nicene theology and of the divinity of the Holy Spirit. Many resemblances between this and a much longer study discovered in the eighteenth century (missing the title page and opening chapters) led to the identification of the latter with Didymus's lost *De Trinitate,* but his authorship remains uncertain, as does the more recent ascription to him of the fourth and fifth books appended to Basil of Caesarea, *Adversus Eunomium.* Today, more secure appears his authorship of a series of biblical commentaries discovered at Toura in Egypt in 1941, containing much allegory of an Origenist type. In the course of the Origenist controversies of the fifth and sixth centuries, Didymus's name fell into disrepute. This led to his posthumous condemnation along with Origen and Evagrius Ponticus around the time of the Fifth Ecumenical Council at Constantinople (553). CPG II, 2544–2572. TLG 2102.

[A.H.]

Bibliography

B. Krämer, "Didymos von Alexandrien," TRE (1981), Vol. 8, pp. 741–746 (bibliography).

DIOCLETIAN (ca. 240–316). Roman emperor (284–305). Gaius Aurelius Valerius Diocletianus laid the groundwork for the second phase of Roman imperial history, the "Dominate," or "Later Roman Empire"; the end of his reign saw the beginning of the most organized and extensive persecution of Christians, the so-called Great Persecution (303–311).

Marble fragment of a togate statue of the emperor Diocletian, ca. 295–300, in Asia Minor (height 14 inches). (The J. Paul Getty Museum, Malibu, California)

Originally named Diocles, Diocletian was a native of Dalmatia on the Adriatic coast of Yugoslavia, and like many humbly born Romans from backward provinces he pursued a career in the Roman army. By 284, he had risen to the rank of commander of the bodyguard of the emperor Numerian (282–284). On Numerian's assassination near Nicomedia in November 284, the army hailed Diocletian as emperor. Early the next year, he defeated Numerian's brother Carinus, becoming sole ruler.

The new emperor faced a host of problems. Since 235, civil wars and barbarian invasions had beset the empire, to the ruin of its economy. Diocletian, more administrator than general, took stern measures. To provide an imperial presence throughout the empire, he introduced the Tetrarchy, or Rule by Four. In 285, he named Maximian, his lieutenant, as Caesar (or junior emperor), assigning him the western half of the empire; a year later, he raised him to the rank of Augustus. In 293, he appointed two new Caesars, Constantius I Chlorus (the father of Constantine), who was given Gaul and Britain in the west, and Galerius, who was assigned the Balkans in the east. Each Augustus was to be succeeded by his respective Caesar. Diocletian thus hoped to solve the longstanding problem of imperial succession. (Diocletian and Maximian technically were of equal rank, but it always was clear that Diocletian was the real master.)

In the early years of his reign, Diocletian was able to restore and strengthen the borders of the empire. He brought the army (which had become accustomed to making and unmaking emperors) back under control by initiating several changes. He subdivided the roughly fifty existing provinces into approximately 100, putting less authority into the hands of each governor. The provinces were grouped into twelve dioceses, each under a vicar, and later into four prefectures, each under a praetorian prefect. One result was that the imperial bureaucracy became increasingly bloated. Diocletian began the policy of separating civil and military careers, so that provincial governors could not also be the commanders of armies. He began to divide the army itself into so-called border troops, actually an ineffective citizen militia, and palace troops, the real field army. To ensure the performance of necessary functions, he made certain occupations, such as those of soldier or tenant farmer (*colonus*), into compulsory services, which became hereditary duties.

Following the precedent of Aurelian (270–275), Diocletian transformed the emperorship into an oriental monarchy. The emperor now became a truly august, god-like figure, wearing gold and purple robes and a pearl diadem. Access to him became restricted, and he was addressed not as *princeps* ("first citizen") or with the soldierly title *imperator* ("general") but as *dominus noster* ("our lord"). Those in audience were required to prostrate themselves on the ground before him. Both Diocletian and Maximian adopted divine attributes, the former identified with Jupiter and the latter with Hercules.

Like Augustus and Decius, Diocletian attempted to use the state religion as a unifying element in society. Encouraged by the Caesar Galerius, he issued in 303 a series of four increasingly harsh decrees designed to compel Christians to take part in the imperial cult, the traditional means by which allegiance was pledged to the empire: (1) Church buildings were leveled, copies of the scriptures were burned, and Christians were removed from high offices; (2) bishops were imprisoned, but (3) released if they sacrificed; and (4) everyone was required to offer sacrifice. This began the Great Persecution.

Wearied by his twenty years in office, and determined to implement his method for the imperial succession, Diocletian abdicated on May 1, 305, and compelled his co-regent, Maximian, to do the same. Constantius I Chlorus and Galerius then became the new Augusti, and two new Caesars were selected, Maximinus Daia (305–313) in the east and Severus II (305–307) in the west. The bypassing of the sons of Maximian and Constantius eventually led to another round of civil wars, from which Constantine emerged the victor. Meanwhile, Diocletian retired to his palace at Split on the Yugoslavian coast. In 308, he declined an offer to reassume the purple. He died in 316. His reforms laid the foundation for the Byzantine empire. *See also* Persecution.

[R.W.M.]

Bibliography

Epitome de caesaribus; Eusebius, *Church History* 8–9; Eutropius, *Breviarium*; Lactantius, *The Deaths of the Persecutors; Panegyrici latini*; Sextus Aurelius Victor, *Liber de caesaribus.*

A.H.M. Jones, *The Later Roman Empire: A Social, Economic, and Administrative Survey* (Norman: U of Oklahoma P, 1964),Vol. 1, pp. 37ff.; T.D. Barnes, *The New Empire of Diocletian and Constantine* (Cambridge: Harvard UP, 1982); S. Williams, *Diocletian and the Roman Recovery* (New York: Methuen, 1985).

DIODORE OF TARSUS (d. ca. 390).

Bishop and theologian. Diodore was said by the emperor Julian (*Ep.* 55) to have studied in Athens. He wrote on philosophical topics, attacked the pagan opponents of Christianity, and was one of the chief foes of Julian's attempt to restore paganism (361–363). About this time, he became a strong supporter of Melitius, who became bishop of Antioch in 360 and who fought for the establishment of Nicene orthodoxy until his death in 381. Diodore founded a monastery and school near Antioch and was the teacher of Theodore of Mopsuestia and John Chrysostom. He was banished to Armenia in 372 but returned and became bishop of Tarsus in 378. He was one of the leading figures at the Council of Constantinople (381). Diodore was an opponent not only of the Arians but also of Apollinaris of Laodicea whose views may in part have been elaborated to reject Diodore's. Despite the fragmentary character of the evidence, we can conclude that Cyril of Alexandria was right in supposing that Diodore's Antiochene Christology, like Theodore's, was capable of being understood as an anticipation of Nestorianism. Diodore's interpretation of scripture was a second legacy to the Antiochenes. Fragments remain of his commentaries on Paul's epistles, and modern scholars have largely reconstructed his commentary on Psalms. His works display the characteristic features of Antiochene exegesis: Diodore opposed allegorism, insisted on the narrative meaning of scripture, and saw the relationship between the Old and New Testaments less as prophecy and more as typological fulfillment. CPG II, 3815–3822.

[R.G.]

Bibliography

Socrates, *Church History* 5.8; 6.3; Sozomen, *Church History* 5.7–11; 8.2; Theodoret, *Church History* 2.19, 23; 4.22, 24; 5.23; John Chrysostom, *Laus Diodori*; Jerome, *Lives of Illustrious Men* 119; 129.

PG 33.1561–1628; J. Deconinck, *Essai sur la chaîne de l'Octateuque avec une édition des Commentaires de Diodore de Tarse* (Paris: Champion, 1912); K. Staab, *Pauluskommentare aus der griechischen Kirche* (Münster: Aschendorff, 1933), pp. 83–112.

E. Schweizer, "Diodor von Tarsus als Exeget," *ZNTW* 40 (1941–1942):33–75; R. Abramowski, "Der theologische Nachlass des Diodor von Tarsus," *ZNTW* 42 (1949):19–69; L. Abramowski, "Streit um Diodor zwischen den bieden ephesianischen Konzilien," *ZKG* (1955):252–287; F.A. Sullivan, *The Christology of Theodore of Mopsuestia* (Rome: Universitas Gregoriana, 1956), pp. 181–196; C. Schaublin, "Zu Diodors von Tarsos Schrift gegen die

Astrologie (Phot. Bibl. Cod. 223)," *Rheinisches Museum für Philologie* 123 (1980):51–67.

DIOGNETUS, EPISTLE TO. Anonymous Christian apology in Greek (second century?). After its discovery in modern times, the work was incorrectly called an epistle because of its address to a certain Diognetus. Possible identifications for the addressee are a tutor of the emperor Marcus Aurelius (161–180) or a magistrate in Alexandria known from papyri dated between 197 and 203. On the basis of the contents, however, some think an earlier date more suitable. The author sets forth the superiority of the Christian religion over the idolatry of paganism and the ritualistic worship of the Jews (2–4). The most famous part of the work is the beautiful description of the Christian life (5–6). Chapters 7–8 affirm the divine origin of Christianity, which appeared late in human history because God allowed time to show the human need for salvation (9). Chapter 10 exhorts Diognetus to accept the Christian faith. Chapters 11–12 appear to be from a different work, in style a homily that speaks of the coming of the Logos to the world and the gathering of the church as paradise. The work is known from a single manuscript, marred by lacunae in Chapter 7 and after Chapter 10, that perished subsequent to its transcription. CPG I, 1112. TLG 1350. [E.F.]

Bibliography
H.G. Meecham, *The Epistle to Diognetus* (Manchester: Manchester UP, 1949); H.I. Marrou, ed., SC (1951, 1965), Vol. 33.
J.A. Kleist, tr., ACW (1948), Vol. 6, pp. 125–147.
R.H. Connolly, 'The Date and Authorship of the Epistle to Diognetus," *JThS* 36 (1935):347–353; idem, "Ad Diognetum XI–XII," *JThS* 37 (1936):2–15; P. Andriessen, "The Authorship of the Epistula ad Diognetum," *VChr* 1 (1947):129–136; L.W. Barnard, "The Epistle ad Diognetum: Two Units from One Author?," *ZNTW* 56 (1965):130–137; J.T. Lienhard, "The Christology of the Epistle to Diognetus," *VChr* 24 (1970):280–289; A.L. Townsley, "Notes for an Interpretation of the Epistle to Diognetus," *Rivista di studi classici* 24 (1976):5–20.

DIONYSIUS EXIGUUS (early sixth century). Monk from the Roman province of Scythia Minor who lived in Rome in the first half of the sixth century. Despite his self-designation as "the little" or "the less," as an expression of humility, Dionysius made important contributions to calendrical calculations and canonical collections. His calculations established the method of dating from the incarnation (*anno domini*, "in the year of the Lord"), but he miscalculated the date of Jesus' birth. His collection and translation of the canons of councils and decretals from the popes laid the basis for the canon law of the medieval church. CPL 653–654, 2284–2286. *See also* Canons, Canon Law. [E.F.]

Bibliography
Cassiodorus, *Introduction to Divine and Human Readings* 1.23.2–4.

DIONYSIUS OF ALEXANDRIA (d. 264/5). Bishop (247/8–264/5). Dionysius "the Great" was a pupil of Origen and successor of Heraclas first as head of the catechetical school (ca. 233–248) and then as bishop of Alexandria. He guided the Alexandrian church with moderation and broadmindedness during a time of famine and plague, civil war, and persecution. He fled the city during the Decian persecution and was banished to Libya during the Valerian persecution. His extensive correspondence and other writings are known only by mostly fragmentary quotations from later writers. Dionysius opposed Novatian and supported Cornelius and his policy of forgiveness for those who lapsed in persecution. He likewise sided with Stephen against Cyprian in rejecting the necessity of rebaptizing heretics and schismatics, but he would not break communion with those who did rebaptize. His opposition to Sabellianism produced statements suspected of tritheism, and for these he was taken to task by his namesake, Dionysius of Rome; but his more careful statement of his Trinitarian belief evidently was satisfactory. He was prevented by infirmity from participating in a synod at Antioch in 265 against Paul of Samosata. Dionysius won over chiliasts who, following the teachings of Nepos, bishop of Arsinoe, gave a literal interpretation to the Book of Revelation. In later expounding his position, Dionysius pointed to the stylistic differences between the Gospel of John and the Book of Revelation to argue that the John who wrote Revelation, although a "holy and inspired person," was not the apostle John. Feast day November 7 (west), October 3 (east). CPG I, 1550–1612. TLG 2952.   [E.F.]

Bibliography

Eusebius, *Church History* 3.28; 6.29, 35, 40–42, 44–46; 7.1–13, 20–29; idem, *Preparation for the Gospel* 7.19; 14.23–27; Athanasius, *Defense of Dionysius*; idem, *On the Councils* 44; idem, *Defense of the Nicene Definition* 25; Basil, *On the Holy Spirit* 29.72.

C.L. Feltoe, *Dionusiou Leipsana: The Letters and Other Remains of Dionysius of Alexandria* (Cambridge: Cambridge UP, 1904).

C.L. Feltoe, *St. Dionysius of Alexandria, Letters and Treatises* (London: SPCK, 1918).

F.C. Conybeare, "Newly Discovered Letters of Dionysius of Alexandria to the Popes Stephen and Xystus," *English Historical Review* 25 (1910):111–114; F.H. Colson, "Two Examples of Literary and Rhetorical Criticism in the Fathers," *JThS* 25 (1924):364–377; P. Nautin, *Lettres et écrivains chrétiens des IIe et IIIe siècles* (Paris: Cerf, 1961), pp. 143–165.

DIONYSIUS OF CORINTH (ca. 170). Bishop and letter writer. Dionysius composed eight letters, which were described by Eusebius of Caesarea (*H.E.* 4.23) but are no longer extant. Seven were directed to various churches, the eighth to a Christian woman, Chrysophora. Their authority was highly esteemed, to the point that attempts were made to misrepresent them; Eusebius had access to them in collected form.

In the letter to the Roman church and its bishop Soter (ca. 170), Dionysius praised the Romans' almsgiving, while also referring to a letter of Clement of Rome to the church at Corinth, *1 Clement* (ca. 96), that was customarily read at worship there, thus verifying its authorship by Clement. His letter to the Nicomedians was directed against the teachings of Marcion. That to the Athenians identified Dionysius the Areopagite (first century) as the first bishop of the church at Athens. Other letters were concerned with heresy, interpretation of scripture, and marriage and chastity.

In the Middle Ages, the bishop of Corinth was confused with both the Areopagite and Dionysius (Denis) of Paris (ca. 250), a patron saint of France. Feast day April 8 (west), November 29 (east). CPG I, 1336. TLG 1329.   [M.P.McH.]

Bibliography

Eusebius, *Church History* 2.25.8; 3.4.10, 4.21, 23; Jerome, *Lives of Illustrious Men* 27.

P. Nautin, *Lettres et écrivains chrétiens des IIe et IIIe siècles* (Paris: Cerf, 1961), pp. 13–32.

DIONYSIUS OF ROME. Bishop of Rome (ca. 260–ca. 268). A Roman presbyter, Dionysius succeeded Sixtus II after the see had been vacant some two years. As bishop, he reorganized the Roman church, which had suffered much from the persecution of Valerian. Prior to his accession, he had engaged in a correspondence with Dionysius of Alexandria concerning the validity of baptism administered by heretics. Athanasius cites two letters he wrote as bishop, one to the church of Alexandria concerning the teachings of Sabellius, the other to Dionysius of Alexandria against the latter's alleged acceptance of subordinationism, the position that the Son was subordinate to the Father in the Trinity. The Alexandrian bishop answered with a *Refutation and Apology*, which appears to have given sufficient proof of orthodoxy.

Basil the Great mentions Dionysius's charity to the church in Cappadocia when it was under barbarian attack. However, the genuineness of the quotations from his letters found in Athanasius and in Basil has been questioned. Along with Maximus of Alexandria, he was an addressee of a letter from a council at Antioch announcing the deposition of Paul of Samosata (ca. 268); it is uncertain whether he lived long enough to have received it. Feast day December 26. CPG I, 1860. TLG 2953.   [M.P.McH.]

Bibliography

Eusebius, *Church History* 7.5.6; 7.7.6; 7.9.6; 7.26.1; 7.27–30; Athanasius, *Defense of the Nicene Definition* 25–26; idem, *Defense of Dionysius*; Basil, *Letter* 70; *Liber Pontificalis* 26 (Duchesne 1.157).

J.F. Bethune-Baker, *An Introduction to the Early History of Christian Doctrine*, 7th ed. (London: Methuen, 1942), pp. 113–118; L. Abramowski, "Dionys von Rom (d 268) und Dionys von Alexandrien (d 264/5) in den arianischen Streitigkeiten des 4. Jahrhunderts," *ZKG* 93 (1982):240–272.

DIONYSIUS THE AREOPAGITE, PSEUDO-

(fl. 500). Writer in Syria who attempted to synthesize Christian theology and Neoplatonist philosophy and greatly influenced medieval Christian mysticism and theology. Acts 17:34 indicates that a member of the Court of Areopagus in Athens named Dionysius was converted by Paul. Eusebius (*H.E.* 4.23) cites Dionysius of Corinth as saying that this Dionysius became the bishop of Athens. Still later, he was confused with Dionysius of Paris (St. Denis).

A fifth- or sixth-century writer in Greek deliberately attributed his writings to the Areopagite in order to secure for them ancient and apostolic authority. In this, he was enormously successful, influencing such theologians, mystics, and poets in both east and west as Maximus Confessor, Gregory the Great, Andrew of Crete, John Scotus Erigena, Hugh of St.-Victor, Bonaventure, Albert the Great, the author of the *Cloud of Unknowing*, Dante, Meister Eckhart, John Tauler, and John Milton. Not until the sixteenth century was the authenticity of the writings seriously questioned by both Protestant and Catholic scholars, and not until the nineteenth century was the issue finally settled.

The main elements in Pseudo-Dionysius's theology can be seen in a brief summary of his writings. The *Divine Names* is concerned with the nature and attributes of God. He is the first principle who cannot be known directly but is suprapersonal and relates to humans only by his emanations. The *Celestial Hierarchy* describes how nine emanations of angels mediate between God and humans. God created the world through the emanations, but the world and the evil in it are unreal. Evil is merely the absence of good. Thus, God is absolved from involvement in evil. The *Ecclesiastical Hierarchy* shows how the heavenly emanations are continued in earthly ones: the three priestly orders (bishops, priests, and deacons), who employ three sacraments (baptism, the eucharist, and confirmation) to complete the mediation of the divine to monks, lay persons, and catechumens. The result of this elaborate scheme of mediation is purgation of sins, illu-

mination of the soul, and the mystic union with God. *Mystical Theology* describes the ascent of the soul to a state of passivity (the abandonment of sense perception and reason) and union with God or deification. Contemplation and prayer are major elements in this. They carry one outside of oneself to an ecstatic vision of God. There are also ten letters by Pseudo-Dionysius that elaborate on various aspects of this teaching.

All of these writings are heavily influenced by the teaching of Plotinus (d. 270) and Proclus (d. 447). The first to refer to the writings of Pseudo-Dionysius was Severus, the patriarch of Antioch (ca. 513). During the following years, various Monophysites appealed to them to support their position. CPG III, 6600–6635. *See also* Neoplatonism.   [J.A.B.]

Bibliography

J. Parker, ed., *Works of Dionysius the Areopagite*, 2 vols. (London: Parker, 1897–1899; repr. Merrick: Richwood, 1976), C.E. Rolt, tr., *Dionysius, the Areopagite, On the Divine Names and the Mystical Theology* (London: SPCK, 1920); J.D. Jones, tr., *Pseudo-Dionysius Areopagite: The Divine Names and Mystical Theology* (Milwaukee: Marquette UP, n.d.); *Dionysius the Areopagite, Mystical Theology and the Celestial Hierarchies*, tr. by the editors of The Shrine of Wisdom (North Godalming: Fintry Brook, 1949); C. Luibheid, ed., *Pseudo-Dionysius: The Complete Works*, CWS (1987), Vol. 54.

J. Vanneste, "La Théologie mystique de pseudo-Denys l'Aréopagite," *SP* 5 (=TU, Vol. 80) (1962):401–415; A.H. Armstrong, ed., *Cambridge History of Later Greek and Early Medieval Philosophy* (Cambridge: Cambridge UP, 1967), pp. 457–472; P. Rorem, *Biblical and Liturgical Symbols Within the Pseudo-Dionysian Synthesis* (Toronto: Pontifical Institute of Mediaeval Studies, 1984).

DIOSCORUS

(d. 454). Bishop of Alexandria (444–451). Dioscorus had served as an archdeacon under Cyril. Theodoret (*Ep.* 60), no doting friend, observes that he was virtuous and admired early in his reign, but the acts of the Council of Chalcedon (451) contain charges that he led an infamous life of extortion and terror (Mansi 6.1008f.). In both ecclesiastical politics and doctrine, Dioscorus followed Eutyches, the archimandrite of an important monastery in Constantinople, considered by many to be the father of Monophysitism. Eutyches had attacked all supporters of Nestorius and had insisted on the phrase "one incarnate nature of God the Word." Because that phrase was foundational to Cyril's anathemas against Nestorius, Dioscorus went to Eutyches's aid. In 449, he traveled to Ephesus in order to preside at a synod called by emperor Theodosius II, which probably included about 150 bishops. The synod's intent was to underwrite the Eutychian position. Dioscorus evidently made no attempt to be an impartial president. He bullied bishops to reject any "two-nature" language and worked toward the deposition of Flavian, bishop of Constantinople, and the restoration of Eutyches. Armed soldiers beat those who would not sign; Flavian died from his wounds. The synod became known as the *Latrocinium*, the "Robber Council."

At the third session of the Council of Chalcedon (451), Eutyches was condemned and Dioscorus was deposed, excommunicated, and exiled to Gangra in Paphlagonia. He was, however, viewed as a martyr by Monophysite churches.   [F.W.N.]

Bibliography

Theodoret, *Letters* 60; 83; 86; Evagrius, *Church History* 1.10; 2.2; 4–5; 18; Theopistus, *Historia Dioscuri*, ed. and tr. F. Nau, *Journal Asiatique, Series 10.1* (1903):5–108, 241–310; *ACO* 2; Mansi 6.

D.W. Johnson, ed. *Panegyric on Macarius, Bishop of Tkow, Attributed to Dioscorus of Alexandria*, CSCO (1980), Vol. 415.

R.V. Sellers, *The Council of Chalcedon* (London: SPCK, 1953), pp. 30–129; W.H.C. Frend, *The Rise of the Monophysite Movement* (Cambridge: Cambridge UP, 1972), pp. 25–54; B. Baldwin, "A Bishop and His Lady, AP 16.19," *VChr* 35 (1981):377–378.

DISCIPLINA ARCANI. "Rule of secrecy," the practice of not admitting the unbaptized to the eucharist and not talking about the sacraments in their presence. The early Christian apologists spoke openly about the activities in the Christian assemblies (Justin, *1 Apol.* 67), but, perhaps under the influence of the mystery religions and their secret rites of initiation, Christians began to restrict knowledge of their ceremonies to those who had received baptism. The problem posed by persecution and certain natural feelings of reverence for sacred rites may also have been factors in reserving explanation of the sacraments to full converts. The rule of secrecy was observed principally in the fourth and early fifth century (Cyril of Jerusalem, *Procatech.* 12). The great influx of new converts into the church included many who only registered as catechumens without going through the full initiation of baptism. This was sufficient for them to identify with the church without having to accept the full responsibilities of membership. The *disciplina arcani* functioned to make full membership more significant and attractive as preserving privileges that the nominal adherents did not have. It reinforced the importance of the catechumenate, which gave the instruction preparatory to full initiation. *See also* Catechesis, Catechumenate; Eucharist; Liturgy; Sacraments.   [E.F.]

DISCIPLINE, ECCLESIASTICAL. The notion of ecclesiastical discipline is concerned both with the doctrinal developments of repentance or penance and with the practical implementation of rules and sanctions within the religious community. In the latter vein, it is closely associated with recourse to exclusion from membership or fellowship, known variously as "excommunication," the "ban," or "shunning." Although reflections of community discipline in Judaism are seen in postexilic priestly reforms, more stringent ideals of purity are reflected in emerging apocalyptic and Hasidic piety from the Hellenistic period onward. Such may be seen especially in the sharp boundary definitions of the Qumran community, which made provision for rigorous scrutiny of the candidate for membership as well as censures for transgressions (*Rule* 5.1–9.26). The codified system included degrees of transgression and periods of discipline or exclusion until adequate expiation had been made (cf. *Rule* 6.24–7.12). Similarly, the emergent synagogue in the rabbinic period developed a system of disciplinary procedures (*Shammata*) that provided for temporary periods of censure (*nidduy, nezifa*) as well as total "ban" (*herem*; cf. *m.*

Yebamoth 47a, *m. Sanhedrin* 10.5; *t. Sanhedrin* 12.5; John 9:22, 34). The *ḥerem* came to be associated with imprecations against the offender, as in the addition of the "anathema" against the "heretics" (*Birkat ha-minim*) into Benediction 12 of the *Shemoneh esreh.*

In the New Testament period, the community practice of disciplinary exclusion, especially for moral offenses, can be seen in 1 Corinthians 5:1–5 and in Matthew 18:15–20. The former case seems to be closer to synagogue judicial practice, with the ultimate sanction being exclusion from the communion of the Lord's table. The latter has steps similar to those at Qumran, which resulted in the offender being considered outside the sectarian bounds of the elect community. In later documents of the period, disciplinary exclusion also dealt with matters of doctrine, as in the strictures against false teachers in 1 John 4:1 and 2 John 10 (cf. Jude 4; 2 Peter 2:1; Titus 3:9–10). Concern over gradation of sins calling for discipline, especially apostasy (cf. 1 John 5:16), gave rise to other regulations over readmission of offenders who showed due repentance. At least in some cases, however, it was assumed that no such repentance and readmission was possible (Heb. 6:4–6; 10:26; cf. Hermas, *Mand.* 4.3).

Along with the notions of excommunication and limited pardon for sins committed after baptism, there eventually came a gradation of sins, by which discipline was assigned. Ecclesiastical discipline as chastisement or "purging" of sins committed after baptism was offered in lieu of permanent excommunication (cf. Clement of Alexandria, *Str.* 2.13.56–58; 4.24.154; Eusebius, *H.E.* 5.28.12). Throughout the early centuries, the common practice involved actual or nominal exclusion followed by public confession before the congregation. Acts of self-abasement were enjoined to demonstrate the degree of one's sincerity in repentance. This public discipline came to be known in the west by the Greek word *exomologesis* ("confession"), designating a technical procedure of disciplinary exclusion, repentance, and readmission by the bishop (cf. Tertullian, *Paenit.* 9–10). In the Latin church, the domi-

nant term for this process was *paenitentiam agere*, which carried both the sense "to repent" and the more literal "to do (acts of) penance."

From the third century, however, this practice was modified, especially in the west, by the controversy over Christians who lapsed in time of persecution. More rigorous positions were adopted by Tertullian (in his Montanist period) and others, such as Hippolytus and Novatian, to suggest that there could be no repentance and no readmission (cf. Tertullian, *Pud.* 6; 13). The weight of experience and opinion would eventually side with Cyprian, who argued for a more lenient view of readmission, one that developed a refined procedure for returning penitents (cf. *De lapsis*). Thereupon arose the formal structures of public penance as normal grades of church discipline, including the status of the catechumen (cf. Gregory Thaumaturgus, *Ep. Can.* 11). Gradation of disciplinary actions correlated with gradation of sins (mortal and venial) would eventually come to be associated in the development of auricular or private penance through the assignment of acts of satisfaction in order to gain absolution and readmission to eucharistic fellowship. Hence, to "do penance" (*paenitentiam agere*) came to mean "acts of satisfaction" (*satisfactio operis*) by the time of Gregory the Great (*Moralia* 4). A parallel sense of disciplinary acts can be seen in the developing rigor of monastic piety from the fifth to seventh centuries (cf. Caesarius of Arles, Isidore of Seville). Especially in the west, then, "discipline," meaning both the attitude and the actions, came to be closely connected with medieval ideals of piety and can be traced in monastic and mystical traditions. The development of private penance (also called auricular confession) probably owes much to the stimulus of monastic piety, commencing especially with the Celtic tradition but evolving into the mainstream of western practice by the beginning of the Scholastic period. As a result, public church discipline and excommunication came to be restricted to the most serious of mortal sins or public transgressions, such as murder, heresy, or witchcraft. For the vast majority of personal sins, private confession before the priest alone was the rule, and the disciplinary sanctions evolved into a more refined system of penitential acts (*satisfactio operis*) assigned to be performed after absolution was granted. *See also* Confession of Sin; Excommunication; Penance; Repentance. [L.M.W.]

Bibliography

H. Koch, *Kallist und Tertullian* (Heidelberg: Winter, 1920); O.D. Watkins, *A History of Penance* (London: Longmans, Green, 1920); R.S.T. Haslehurst, *Penitential Discipline of the Early Church* (London: SPCK, 1921); P. Galtier, *L'Eglise et la rémission des péchés aux premiers siècles* (Paris: Beauchesne, 1932); J.T. McNeill, *Medieval Handbooks of Penance* (New York: Columbia UP, 1938); R.C. Mortimer, *The Origins of Private Penance in the Western Church* (Oxford: Clarendon, 1939); R.G. Smith, "Tertullian and Montanism," *Theology* 46 (1943):127–139; B. Poschmann, *Penance and the Anointing of the Sick* (London: Burns and Oates, 1964); E. Ferguson, *Early Christians Speak* (Abilene: ACU, 1987), pp. 181–191.

DIVORCE. Dissolution of marriage. The attitude of ecclesiastical authors of the first Christian centuries toward divorce is of great importance, for they were the closest heirs of the thought of the apostles and they lived in a period like our own, when the civil law accepted divorce and divorce was commonplace among the upper classes. Tertullian, at the end of the second century, contrasts the first 600 years of Roman history, when there was not a single divorce, with the morals of his own time, when women "long for divorce as though it were the natural consequence of marriage" (*Apol.* 6).

For the Jews as for the pagans of antiquity, every dissolution of marriage (either divorce by mutual consent or unilateral rejection) made possible a new marriage. Roman civil law, as promulgated by pagan and Christian emperors, viewed marriage as a contract between two persons, which could be dissolved by both parties mutually or, under certain conditions, by one person unilaterally. Many of the church fathers, both eastern and western, contrasted the law of God with the civil law, often denominated the "law of the pagans," even though during the fourth and fifth centuries the imperial power was officially Christian

(e.g., John Chrysostom, *Lib. rep.* 2.1). The fathers rejected the idea that marriage is an ordinary contract that can be set aside by any human institution (cf. Matt. 19:6). They termed unjust the pagan or Roman law that punished the adultery of the woman but did not consider the man guilty of adultery if his paramour was unmarried. It is therefore most unlikely that the sense and purport of Roman law constitutes a presumption in favor of the acceptability of remarriage among Christians. "The laws of Caesar are one thing, the law of Christ another; Papinian prescribes one thing, Paul something else," says Jerome in connection with Fabiola, who, after the death of her second husband, did penance for having remarried in violation of the laws of the church (*Ep.* 77). Augustine's treatise *On Faith and Works* reveals that the church in theory did not agree to receive remarried divorced people to baptism and the eucharist. It must be admitted, however, that the church's interdiction was not always the universal canonical practice.

Only one orthodox early Christian author, the obscure exegete known as Ambrosiaster, explicitly permits remarriage by reason of two limited circumstances: (1) a separation based upon fornication (Matt. 5:32), in which case a second marriage is permitted to the man alone; or (2) unbelief by the spouse (1 Cor. 7:15), in which case authorization is given to either sex. Otherwise, there is practical unanimity among the following authors and councils, who do not countenance remarriage after separation in general, or more particularly separation after adultery involving one or the other or both marriage partners: Hermas, Justin, Athenagoras, Theophilus of Antioch, Irenaeus, Clement of Alexandria, Origen, Tertullian, Council of Elvira, Council of Arles, Basil of Ancyra, Basil the Great, Gregory of Nazianzus, Apollinaris of Laodicea, Theodore of Mopsuestia, John Chrysostom, Theodoret of Cyrus, Epiphanius, Ambrose, Innocent I, Pelagius, Jerome, Leo the Great, and Augustine.

The American canonist Victor Pospishil contends that certain fathers permit remarriage *implicitly.* Henri Crouzel, however, believes that Pospishil, relying on the unspoken argument, distorts the meaning of the passages in question. The extreme rarity of explicit affirmations calls into question the accuracy of these "implicit allusions."

The majority of fathers teach that the innocent spouse is obligated to dismiss the adulterous spouse or risk endangering the holiness and integrity of the conjugal union. Basil the Great is an exception: he thinks that the woman should receive the man back from his errancy, whereas the man is obligated to send away an adulterous wife(*Ep.* 198.9). The fathers are divided on the related question of whether it is necessary to be reconciled with the guilty spouse who has repented. Augustine counsels reconciliation; John Chrysostom considers it problematic; Cyril of Alexandria advises against it; and Jerome, on the basis of the Old Testament, forbids it. The *Opus imperfectum in Matthaeum* states that Moses permitted a second marriage because of "hardness of heart" (Matt. 19:7–8), but the apostles made only a single concession in the controversy: second marriage after widowhood. One sees clearly that in most patristic writings the expressions "rupture" or "dissolution" of marriage by adultery do not have a juridical sense, that is, they do not signify that new marriages are permitted and refer only to the cessation of common life, without affecting the state of marriage. *See also* Marriage. [M.A.S.]

Bibliography

Gregory of Nazianzus, *Oration* 37 (NPNF, 2nd ser. [1894], Vol. 7); John Chrysostom, *De libello repudii* 2 (PG 51.217–226).

V.J. Pospishil, *Divorce and Remarriage: Toward a New Catholic Teaching* (New York: Herder and Herder, 1967); H. Crouzel, *L'Eglise primitive face au divorce, du premier au cinquième siècle* (Paris: Beauchesne, 1971).

DOCETISM. View that Christ's humanity was only an appearance (from Greek *dokēsis*) or disguise worn by the heavenly Redeemer. The spiritual Christ was frequently said to have entered the human Jesus at his baptism and to have departed prior to the crucifixion. Paul's description of the risen Christ as possessing a "spiritual body" (1 Cor. 15:42–50) was invoked to support the view that Christ was a spiritual and not a fleshly being.

The noun *dokētai*, "Docetists," is used by Serapion of Antioch (fl. A.D. 200; Eusebius, *H.E.* 6.12.6). Our earliest evidence for a group of Christians holding Docetic views of Christ concerns the opponents attacked in Ignatius of Antioch's letters (ca. A.D. 114) to the *Smyrneans* (2.1–8.2) and the *Trallians* (10). Against the Docetists, Ignatius insists upon the physical realities of Christ's birth, "bearing the flesh," suffering and death on the cross, and resurrection. One can speak of the crucified one as "God" suffering (cf. Ignatius, *Eph.* 1.1; *Rom.* 6.6). Without the resurrection of the "fleshly" Christ, human nature would not have been transformed (*Trall.* 9.2; *Smyrn.* 7.1). A variant of Luke 24:39 is cited to prove the fleshly reality of the risen Christ (*Smyrn.* 3.1). As a counter to the eucharists celebrated by the Docetists, Ignatius insists upon a realistic identification of the bread with the "flesh" of Jesus (*Smyrn.* 7.1).

Several of Ignatius's polemical arguments reappear in later patristic opposition to the Docetic Christologies advocated by Gnostic sects. Docetists are accused of making a mockery of the heroic suffering of martyrs (*Trall.* 10; *Smyrn.* 4.2; Irenaeus, *Haer.* 3.18.5; Clement of Alexandria, *Str.* 4.4.16.3; 4.9.73.1; Eusebius, *H.E.* 4.7.7). They have the same "unreality" as they ascribe to Christ (*Trall.* 10; Irenaeus, *Haer.* 4.33.5; Tertullian, *Val.* 27.3). A tendency toward Docetism grounded in the Fourth Gospel's portrayal of Christ as the descending and ascending revealer may have been manifested by the dissidents attacked for "denying that Jesus Christ has come in the flesh" (1 John 4:2; 2 John 7). Polycarp also attacks a group holding such a view (*Phil.* 7.1).

Gnostic sects frequently maintained a Docetic view of Christ, who is identified with a being from the heavenly realm of light. Salvation requires that the light trapped in the material world be freed by the Savior, who is not entangled in the darkness, passions, and forgetfulness of material reality. The demonic powers who opposed the revealer were deceived by the physical form that they crucified (sometimes "Jesus"; sometimes a substitute in Simon of Cyrene) into thinking that they had power over the Savior. In addition to patristic reports of such Docetic views (e.g., Irenaeus, *Haer.* 1.7.2; 1.26.1–7; 3.16.1–5; 3.18.6; 4.33.5; Hippolytus, *Haer.* 8.1–4; Tertullian, *Carn. Chr.* 3–5; *Marc.* 1.19), the Gnostic writings in the Nag Hammadi collection provide firsthand evidence for Docetic teaching among Gnostics (e.g., *First Apocalypse of James* V, 31, 15–26; *Second Logos of the Great Seth* VII 55, 9–56, 19; *Letter of Peter to Philip VIII* 139, 15–29). The Docetic Christology of the *First and Second Apocalypse of James* shows that Docetism could coexist with admiration for the heroic suffering of the martyr. The *Apocalypse of Peter* (cf. VII 81, 3–82, 14) has Jesus provide a vision of the crucifixion to Peter that shows his Spiritual Being untouched, watching the folly of the demons. This writing mocks those orthodox Christians who think they can attain salvation by worshiping a "dead man." A Docetic view of the crucifixion also appears in the *Acts of John* 97–104. *See also* Christology. [P.P.]

Bibliography

A. Grillmeier, *Christ in Christian Tradition* (Atlanta: John Knox, 1975), Vol. 1, pp. 78–79 and passim; Kelly, pp. 141-142; K. Rudolph, *Gnosis* (San Francisco: Harper and Row, 1983); W.R. Schoedel, *Ignatius of Antioch* (Philadelphia: Fortress, 1985), pp. 12, 20, 90–91, 124–125, 152–158, 220–246.

DOMITIAN (A.D. 51–96). Roman emperor (81–96). Domitian, son of the emperor Vespasian, succeeded his elder brother, Titus, to the throne; he had held no real power under either his father or his brother. His foreign policy was aimed at strengthening the frontiers of the Roman empire, while at home he had the reputation of an efficient and firm administrator. He commenced a building program and, despite his private vices, attempted to raise the standard of public morality. After crushing a revolt (88 or 89), he acted ruthlessly, instituting a reign of terror against opposition real or suspected. He revived the law against treason, encouraged the use of informers, and exiled philosophers and many others, perhaps the poet Juvenal among them. Unpopular for his tyranny and disregard of the senate as well as for his vices and arrogance, he was killed through a conspiracy of high-ranking officials in which his wife Domitia was involved.

Under Domitian, persecutions of Christians occurred at Rome and particularly in Asia, but there is not sufficient evidence to show that a decision was made to attack them throughout the empire as a matter of policy. The emperor's increasing suspicion and intolerance certainly played a role, and his assumption of the title "Lord and God" with the accompanying demand for divine homage was bound to bring him into conflict with the new religion (cf. Rev. 13:4; 14:9–11; 16:2). According to tradition, (Irenaeus, *Haer. 5.30.3*) it was in Domitian's reign that John, the writer of the Book of Revelation, was exiled to Patmos, where he received his apocalyptic visions; in the same book, mention is made of a martyrdom in Pergamum (2:13).

It is unlikely that Domitilla, Domitian's niece and the granddaughter of Vespasian, who was herself sent into exile (ca. 95), was a Christian. It is possible that she and her husband, the consul Flavius Clemens, who was executed at the same time, were "God-fearers," that is, Gentiles who shared in Jewish worship; or perhaps members of their household practiced Judaism or Christianity. Clement of Rome, the author of *1 Clement*, may possibly have served in the same family. The cemetery of Domitilla later became a Christian burial site. *See also* Persecution. [M.P.McH.]

Bibliography

Suetonius, *Life of Domitian*; Dio Cassius, *Roman History* 67; Eusebius, *Church History* 3.13–20.

E.M. Smallwood, "Domitian's Attitude Toward the Jews and Judaism," *CPh* 51 (1956):1–13; M. McCrum and A.G. Woodhead, *Select Documents of the Principates of the Flavian Emperors* (Cambridge: Cambridge UP, 1961); L.W. Barnard, "Clement of Rome and the Persecution of Domitian," *NTS* 10 (1963):251–260; P. Keresztes, "The Jews, the Christians and the Emperor Domitian," *VChr* 27 (1973):1–28; N. Santos Yanguas, "El emperador Domiciano y los christianos," *StudOv* 6–7 (1978–1979):165–185; A.Y. Collins, "Dating the Apocalypse of John," *Biblical Research* 26 (1981):33–45; R. Syme, "Domitian: The Last Years," *Chiron* (1983):121–146.

DONATISM. Schism that broke out in the church in North Africa after the Great Persecution in 303–305 and divided it throughout the fourth and early fifth centuries. Donatism declined after 411, when the imperial government declared its rival, led by Augustine, to be the true Catholic church in North Africa, but its continued existence can be traced until the Muslim invasion of the seventh century. It was in his campaign against the Donatists between 399 and 415 that Augustine formulated his characteristic doctrines concerning the nature of the church and its sacraments, but also his justification of repression by the state against individuals and organizations deemed to be heretical or in schism by the Catholic church.

Origins and History. The immediate cause of the schism was the situation in North Africa resulting from the Great Persecution under Diocletian. Many clergy had lapsed and handed over the scriptures to be burned at the demand of the authorities. These clergy were dubbed *traditores* ("betrayers") by those Christians who stood firm. Notable among the latter were a group of confessors from Abitina in western Tunisia who, while in prison, solemnly denounced *traditores* and declared that only those who followed their own steadfast example would share with them the joys of paradise (*Acta Saturnini* 18, PL 8.701). Their unbending attitude, however, displeased the Christian clergy at Carthage, notably the archdeacon Caecilian, who was later accused of preventing food from being brought into the prison by well-wishers.

Trouble came to a head in 311, when the bishop of Carthage, Mensurius, died and Caecilian was consecrated in his stead. Opposition developed immediately, Caecilian's enemies in Carthage being reinforced by the arrival of bishops from Numidia, whose primate had gained, in the previous forty years, the right to consecrate the bishop of Carthage but now found himself anticipated. Opposition was orchestrated by Donatus, a young bishop of the Numidian town of Casae Nigrae, who had already caused a schism by rebaptizing clergy who had lapsed in the recent persecution (Optatus, *Against the Donatists* 1.24; Augustine, *Brev. Coll. c. Don.* 3.12.24).

In 312, the Numidian primate, Secundus of Tigisis, held a council of seventy bishops in Carthage that deposed Caecilian on the grounds of uncanonical election, indiscipline, and cruelty toward confessors during the persecution (Augustine, *Brev. Coll.* 3.14.26; Anon., *Liber contra Fulgentium Donatistam* [fifth-century Catholic tract] 26, PL 43.774). In his place, the bishops consecrated the deacon Majorinus, who was chaplain to a rich Spanish woman, Lucilla. Lucilla had fallen foul of Caecilian before the persecution and had contributed largely toward the opposition (Augustine, *Unit. eccl.* 25.73, PL 43.443; Optatus, *Against the Donatists* 1.16, 19: Optatus reduces Majorinus to the grade of "lector" [reader]). Thus, in Optatus's picturesque phrase, "altar was set up against altar" (1.15, 19).

This was the situation in North Africa that confronted Constantine on the morrow of his victory over Maxentius on October 28, 312. The North African provinces surrendered to him without a blow, and the emperor hastened during the winter of 312–313 to extinguish all trace of the persecution. In so doing, he accepted Caecilian as rightful bishop of Carthage, provided him with a subsidy of 3,000 *folles* from the revenues of the imperial estates, and threatened criminal proceedings against his adversaries (Eusebius, *H.E.* 10.5.15–17; 10.6). When Constantine went further and ordered that clergy in communion with Caecilian should be exempted from municipal taxes (Eusebius, *H.E.* 10.7), his opponents appealed directly to him (Augustine, *Ep.* 88.2). For them, the excommunicated Caecilian was not even a cleric, and in appealing for judges from Gaul as being impartial, they also enclosed a list of Caecilian's alleged crimes. These documents were handed to the proconsul of Africa, Anulinus, who forwarded them to the emperor (Augustine, *Ep.* 88.2).

Constantine delegated the case to Miltiades, bishop of Rome, who was himself an African, and the hearing took place between October 2 and 5, 313. Majorinus had meanwhile passed from the scene and was replaced by Donatus. Miltiades decided against him (Optatus, *Against the Donatists* 1.24; Augustine, *Ep.* 43.5, 14–15).

The Donatists (as they were now known) appealed to Constantine again, charging that one of Caecilian's consecrators, Felix, bishop of Aptunga had been a *traditor* and hence that Caecilian's consecration was invalid. Constantine responded by summoning a new and larger council, representative of the area over which he ruled (the Prefecture of the Gauls and Italy) and by setting up a commission of inquiry in Carthage into the case of Felix (Optatus 1.25; Eusebius, *H.E.* 10.5.21–24).

The council met at Arles on August 1, 314, and the case again went against Donatus and his colleagues. In February 315, the proconsul, Aelianus, also pronounced in favor of Felix. Although Donatus was able to prolong the proceedings for another year and a half, Constantine finally decided in favor of Caecilian, and on November 10, 316, communicated his decision to the *vicarius* of Africa (Augustine, *C. Cresc.* 3.71.82; *Ad Don. post Coll.* 33.56).

This should have been the end of the matter, especially when in December 320 a spectacular trial was held before the *consularis* (governor) of Numidia, Zenophilus, at which it became clear that the chief opponents of Caecilian in that province had been themselves *traditores* (*Gesta Apud Zenophilum* = Appendix i, in CSEL ed. of Optatus, *De schismate*, Vol. 26, pp. 185–197).

The Donatists, however, went from strength to strength. That the schism did not end indicates that there were causes other than ecclesiastical behind the movement. Donatus was able to defy the emperor and his officials (Optatus 3.3) and ca. 336 held a council at which 270 bishops were present (Augustine, *Ep.* 93.43). The provinces of Numidia and Mauretania Sitifensis were overwhelmingly Donatist. Socially and economically, they differed to a profound degree from the more Romanized areas of proconsular Africa (Tunisia). Donatus's movement, however, was almost wholly confined to Africa, although he established a rival bishop in Rome (Optatus 2.4) in order to maintain communion with that see. This isolation proved a fatal weakness, for with the exception of the eastern churches at the time of the Council of Sardica in 342 or 343,

the rest of Christendom regarded Caecilian as bishop of Carthage. Donatus's efforts to reverse this position through the emperor Constans in 346 or 347 failed, and he ended his days (ca. 355) as an exile in Gaul (Optatus 3.1, 3).

The commission that Constans dispatched to Africa under two imperial notaries, Paul and Macarius, reestablished church unity in North Africa in 348 under the leadership of Caecilian's successor, Gratus. Their methods, however, were high-handed. They aroused popular resistance (Optatus 3.4) and caused alienation from the Caecilianist (now the "Catholic") cause. When in 362 the emperor Julian allowed the Donatist leaders to return (Augustine, *C. Litt. Petil.* 3.97.224), they reestablished the position of their church rapidly (Optatus 2.16–18). Only a few towns (among them Augustine's birthplace, Thagaste) failed to revert to Donatism.

Under a new Donatist bishop of Carthage, Parmenian, who was a Gaul or Spaniard by birth (Optatus 2.7), the Donatist position was consolidated. He ruled his church for thirty years, 362–392, during which time Donatism was indisputably the majority religion in North Africa (Jerome, *Vir. ill.* 93, written in 392) and produced, in the persons of Parmenian himself and the layman Tyconius (fl. ca. 380), an intellectual leadership that North African Christianity had lacked since the time of Cyprian.

The death of Parmenian was followed by a conflict in the Donatist church between his successor, Primian (392–412), and a more moderate party led by Maximian, a relative of Donatus. Schism broke out in June 393; Primian, charged with oppression, was condemned by a council of 100 bishops held at Cebarsussa in proconsular Africa on June 24, 393 (Augustine, *Ep.* 43.9.26). The Numidians, however, rallied to Primian and crushed his opponents at a council held at Bagai, a fortress town north of the Aures Mountains, on April 24, 394, at which 310 bishops were present. The damage was contained. Many of the Maximianist bishops returned to Donatist allegiance, and a series of lawsuits held before the imperial authorities in 395–398 against the remaining schismatics seemed to establish the Donatist church as the "Catholic" church in North Africa (Augustine, *C. Cresc.* 3.56.62; 4.3.3; 4.48.58). These years saw Donatism at the height of its influence and prosperity.

The support given by some Donatists, such as Optatus, bishop of Thamugadi (Timgad) in Numidia, to the rebellion of count Gildo against the imperial authorities in 397–398 gave the Catholics a real chance to turn the tables on their adversaries. In Augustine, bishop of Hippo, and his friend Aurelius, bishop of Carthage, they possessed intellectual and organizational leadership that enabled them to take full advantage of the rebellion's failure. Between 399 and 415, Augustine wrote a series of tracts attacking the Donatists as schismatics for being out of communion with the churches in the rest of the empire and heretics for insisting on repeating baptism for any convert. On historical grounds, also, their original break with Caecilian had been unjustified.

By the summer of 403, the Catholics felt strong enough to challenge their opponents to a conference whose aim would be to decide which party had the better claim to be the "Catholic" church in North Africa (text in PL 11.1200–1201; discussion in P. Monceaux, Vol. 4, pp. 128–131). Primian refused, but eighteen months later the Catholics succeeded in having the emperor Honorius promulgate specific edicts equating the Donatists with heretics, banning their church, and confiscating its property (*Cod. Thds.* 16.5.37, 38; and 6.4, 5, of February 12 and March 5, 405). The Donatists began to lose ground, as some of their more influential members succumbed to the pressure of the imperial laws. In May 411, the Catholics were at last able to force their opponents into a conference held on Catholic terms. It was convened at Carthage under the presidency of the imperial tribune and notary, Marcellinus. The Donatists and Catholics each mustered exactly 284 bishops. After three sessions, May 31–June 8, Marcellinus gave his decision against the Donatists (cf. S. Lancel, vol. 1), and they were banned by a severe and comprehensive edict on January 30, 412 *Cod. Thds.* (16.5.52).

This time, the emperor's measures were more effective; Donatism declined dramatically in the next seventeen years. Resistance tended to be isolated (cf. Augustine, *C. Gaud.*; *Ep.* 28, Divjak). In the Vandal period, the Donatists were quiescent and revived as a movement of any significance only in the later stages of the Byzantine occupation. Letters of Gregory I to his agents in North Africa and to imperial officials indicate the reemergence of Donatism in its former homeland of southern Numidia (*Ep.* 1.33; 3.32; 4.35; 6.34). The movement seems to have lived on until destroyed with the remainder of the Christian heritage in North Africa by the Arab invasions and the success of Islam (647–750).

Ideas and Doctrine. The Donatists believed themselves to be the true continuators of the church in North Africa as it had been before the Great Persecution, and in particular in the time of Cyprian. They emphasized the values of purity, holiness, and integrity against the Catholic stress on universality as the hallmark of a Christian community. This led them to an exclusive view of the church, following Tertullian (*Apol.* 39; *Spec.* 1) and Cyprian (*Ep.* 69.2; 74.11), comparing the church to a "sealed fountain" or "closed garden." As a result, they did not regard as valid any sacrament administered by a cleric in a state of sin (Caecilian, through his ordination by a *traditor*, was sinful by association), and hence baptism administered by any such must be renewed (it was not rebaptism).

Donatists regarded themselves as the suffering people of God, destined to undergo persecution and martyrdom for the sake of maintaining the integrity of the Christian community. The point is made by one of their leading bishops, Petilian of Constantine, ca. 400: "Therefore I say that he [Christ] ordained that we should undergo death for the faith, which each man should do for the communion of the church. For Christianity makes progress by the deaths of its followers" (quoted by Augustine, *C. Litt. Petil.* 2.89.196). This statement, written nearly a century after the emperor Constantine's conversion, illustrates the Donatist attitude toward the state. The Roman empire represented the world in an apocalyptic sense, ever hostile to the "saints" (i.e., the

Donatist Christians). With claims to sanctity went a proclamation of the ideal of apostolic poverty. The Donatists were the one Christian movement that attempted to change the social conditions of the empire. Although not in itself a political movement, its more extreme adherents in Numidia and Mauretania took the law into their own hands and from ca. 340 onward carried out attacks on landowners, forcing them to cancel debts and change places with their slaves (Optatus 3.4) or to perform slave labor (Augustine, *Ep.* 185.4.15). The terrorism extended to attacks on Catholic clergy (Augustine, *C. Cresc.* 3.43.47; *Ep.* 108; 111). These Circumcellions, as they were known, although armed with heavy clubs ("Israels"), regarded themselves primarily as men and women dedicated to holiness, and ultimately to martyrdom, and their war cry was *Deo Laudes* ("Praise to God") (Augustine, *Ep.* 108.5.14; *In Ps.* 132.6).

Not surprisingly, Donatist liturgy found scope for enthusiastic and ecstatic songs of praise as well as the celebration of the eucharist. "Praise ye the Lord and rejoice," an inscription over the entrance of a Donatist church at Thamalulla in Mauretania, sums up this outlook.

At the same time, Donatism produced able defenders and theologians, of whom Tyconius was outstanding. His teaching relating to the division of the saved and damned, who were the inhabitants of the city of God and the city of the devil, respectively, greatly influenced the theology of Augustine on the nature of the two cities representing the saved and the damned at final judgment. Donatism was a significant movement in the history of western Christianity. It preserved many of the church's values from the era before Constantine. Integrity, holiness, and readiness for self-sacrifice by the individual and the community have found their place among the values of many Protestant denominations. Similarly, the ideal of poverty, which also demanded active involvement to change society, has formed the background to many Christian movements of social reform. *See also* Augustine; Carthage; Circumcellions; Donatus the Great.   [W.H.C.F.]

Bibliography

Optatus, *Against the Donatists*, ed. C. Ziwsa, CSEL (1895), Vol. 26; tr. O.R. Vassall-Phillips, *The Work of St. Optatus Against the Donatists* (London: Longmans, Green, 1917); Augustine, Anti-Donatist works, PL 43 and CSEL, Vols. 51–53; tr. Marcus Dods, *The Anti-Donatist Works of St. Augustine*, NPNF 1st ser. (1872), Vol. 4; a number of letters concerned with the Donatist controversy are to be found in J.G. Cunningham's *Letters of St. Augustine*, 2 vols. (Edinburgh: T. and T. Clark, 1872); *Actes de la conférence de Carthage en 411*, ed. S. Lancel, SC (1972, 1975), Vols. 194, 195, 224; C. Lepelley, ed., *Les Lettres de saint Augustine découverts par Johannes Divjak* (Paris: Etudes Augustiniennes, 1983); A. Berthier et al., *Les Vestiges du Christianisme antique dans la Numidie centrale* (Algiers: Maison-Carrée, 1943), essential for the numerous archaeological remains of Donatism in eastern Algeria; J.L. Maier, *Le Dossier du Donatisme*, 2 vols., TU (1987–1988).

P. Monceaux, *Histoire littéraire de l'Afrique chrétienne* (Paris: Leroux, 1901–1923), Vols. 4–7; G.G. Willis, *St. Augustine and the Donatist Controversy* (London: SPCK, 1952); W.H.C. Frend, *The Donatist Church: A Movement of Protest in Roman North Africa* (Oxford: Clarendon, 1952); B.H. Warmington, *The North African Provinces from Diocletian to the Vandal Conquest* (Cambridge: Cambridge UP, 1954); J.B. Brisson, *Autonomisme et Christianisme dans l'Afrique romaine de Septime Sévère à l'invasion vandale* (Paris: Boccard, 1958); H.J. Diesner, *Kirche und Staat in spätrömischen Reich* (Berlin: Evangelische Verlagsanstalt, 1963); E. Tengström, *Donatisten und Katholiken: soziale, wirtsschaftliche und politische Aspekte eine Nordafrikanischen Kirchenspaltung* (Göteborg: Elanders, 1964); P. Brown, *Augustine of Hippo: A Biography* (London: Faber and Faber, and Berkeley: U of California P, 1967); R.A. Markus, *Saeculum: History and Society in the Theology of St. Augustine* (Cambridge: Cambridge UP, 1970); B. Kriegbaum, *Kirche der Traditoren oder Kirche der Martyrer? Die Vorgeschichte des Donatismus* (Innsbruck: Tyrolia, 1986).

DONATUS THE GREAT (d. 355). Bishop who gave his name to Donatist movement. Donatus, a Numidian, first appears as an opponent of those clergy who surrendered the scriptures to the authorities during the Great Persecution (303–305). Evidently already a bishop (Optatus, *Against the Donatists* 1.26) and a Carthaginian schismatic before Caecilian's election (Augustine, *Brev. Coll.* 3.12.24), he was consecrated a rival bishop of Carthage in 313.

He pled his case in Italy during the next few years (Optatus 1.26) but was condemned by Constantine in 316 (Augustine, *C. Cresc.* 3.71.82).

In 321, however, Constantine decreed that Donatist exiles could return. For the most part (Optatus 3.3), Donatus was left in peace until 346. According to Jerome (*Vir. ill.* 93), Donatus succeeded "in deceiving nearly all Africa." The 270 bishops who obeyed him and were summoned to a council ca. 336 formed the largest assembly of bishops anywhere in the empire to that date.

He failed finally because he overreached himself. In 346, an imperial commission sent to North Africa to look into his case was attacked by rural Donatist insurgents, the Circumcellions; Donatus and his chief supporters were then exiled (Optatus 3.4). He died in Gaul during 355.

None of his writings survived, but we know that theologically he was a disciple of Cyprian, although on the issue of rebaptism he was prepared to make concessions (Augustine, *Ep.* 93.63). He believed in the recompense of just and unjust, and that his church consisted only of the former, a gathered community outside of which no salvation was possible. In the same way, he accepted no interference from the state. "What has the emperor to do with the church?" (Optatus 3.3) was one of his most celebrated statements. A century after Donatus became bishop of Carthage, the grammarian Cresconius (Augustine, *C. Cresc.* 3.56.62) called him a religious reformer, who "purged the church of Carthage of error." Unfortunately for him and his followers, after the conversion of Constantine the ideal of the gathered church, dedicated to holiness and maintaining the commands of Christ in scripture in their complete integrity, gave way to the concept of the universal church in which sinners as well as saints had a place. *See also* Donatism. [W.H.C.F.]

Bibliography
P. Monceaux, *Histoire littéraire de l'Afrique chrétienne* (Paris: Leroux, 1901–1923), Vols. 4–7; W.H.C. Frend, *The Donatist Church: A Movement of Protest in Roman North Africa* (Oxford: Clarendon, 1952).

DOROTHEUS OF ANTIOCH (third century). Presbyter. A well-educated eunuch who knew Hebrew and the classics and a procurator of the dye works at Tyre, Dorotheus was a forerunner of Antiochene exegesis. [F.W.N.]

DOROTHEUS OF GAZA (sixth century). Founder of a monastery near Gaza (ca. 540). Dorotheus wrote a work against the errors of Origen and Evagrius, as well as instructions on the monastic life. The latter includes advice from earlier ascetics. CPG III, 7352–7360. [F.W.N.]

Bibliography
Dorotheos of Gaza: Discourses and Sayings, tr. E. Wheeler (Kalamazoo: Cistercian, 1977).

DOSITHEUS (second century). Founder of a heresy in Palestine. There is considerable confusion concerning the identity of Dositheus and the sect he founded. There may have been more than one person, and more than one religious group, of the same name, extending from the third century B.C. to the second century A.D. Dositheus was supposed to have been associated as both teacher and disciple with Simon Magus (Acts 8:9–24), himself alleged to have been the founder of Gnosticism. Dositheans practiced asceticism and stressed strict observance of the Sabbath and ritual purity. A short work, presented as a revelation of Dositheus, the *Three Steles of Seth,* was discovered at Nag Hammadi (NHC VII, 5); to whom it is to be attributed is uncertain. [M.P.McH.]

Bibliography
Hegesippus in Eusebius, *Church History* 4.22; Pseudo-Tertullian, *Against All Heresies* 1; Origen, *Against Celsus* 6.11; idem, *On First Principles* 4.3.2; Pseudo-Clement, *Recognitions* 1.54; 2.8; idem, *Homilies* 2.24.

S. Krauss, "Dosithée et les Dosithéens," *REJ* 42 (1901):27–42; K. Kohler, "Dositheus, the Samaritan Heresiarch, and his Relations to Jewish and Christian Doctrines and Sects," *American Journal of Theology* 15 (1911):404–435; R.McL. Wilson, "Simon, Dositheus, and the Dead Sea Scrolls," *ZRGG* 9 (1957):21–30; J. Fossum, "The Origen of the Gnostic Concept of the Demiurge," *EThL* 61 (1985):142–152.

DOVE. Most early Christian writers used the Greek word *peristera*—*Columba livia domestica* (house pigeon or dove)—instead of *peleia*—*Columbia livia* (wild pigeon). Early Christian nomenclature was shaped by Genesis 8:8–12 (Septuagint). A white dove was sacred to the Near Eastern goddess Astarte, and in the Hellenistic and Greco-Roman periods it became an attribute of Aphrodite-Venus. Doves were proverbially clean animals (e.g., Martial 1.109.2). Early Christians gave *peristera* (*columba*) a host of symbolic associations, but clearly the primary influence, fed by both Semitic and Greek tradition, is of the dove as a symbol or attribute of the Spirit that descended at Jesus' baptism (Mark 1:10 and parallels). The dove descending or hovering over the head of the baptizand (presumed, probably correctly, to be Jesus) is a popular subject in the earliest extant Christian iconography (e.g., Callistus, Area I.A3, west wall [PIAC, *Catalogo delle fotografie* (Città del Vaticano, 1973ff.) Cal E31, E32, E33]). The association of the dove with the Holy Spirit continued in the second century (Justin, *Dial.* 88.3–8; Clement of Alexandria, *Theod.* 16). In later tradition, such as the fifth-century wall mosaics of Sta. Maria Maggiore, the dove is associated with Noah, with Mary (as a sign of her purity), with Pentecost, with the church, with the individual soul, with humility and purity, and with numerous other types and virtues. In recommending to Christian addressees the use of the dove image to be emblazoned on finger rings (and worn as signets), Clement of Alexandria, *Instructor* 3.59.2, uses *peleia*, departing from the common Christian usage.   [P.C.F.]

Bibliography

O. Wasser, "Psyche (a) Der Seelenvogel," *Ausführliches Lexikon der griechischen und römischen Mythologie*, ed. W.H. Roscher (Leipzig: Akademie, 1902–1909), Vol. 3.2, pp. 3213–3222; J.P. Kirsch, "Colombe," DACL (1914), Vol. 3.2, cols. 2198–2231; H. Gressman, "Die Sage von der Taufe Jesu und die vorderorientalische Taubengöttin," *Archiv für Religionswissenschaft* 20 (1920–1921):1–40, 323–359; F. Sühling, *Die Taube als religiöses Symbol im christlichen Altertum* (Freiburg: Bolzano, 1930); idem, "Taube und Orante: Ein Beitrag zum Orantenproblem," *Römische Quartalschrift* 39 (1931):333–354; E.R. Goodenough, *Jewish Symbols in the Greco Roman Period* (New York: Pantheon, 1958), Vol. 8, pp. 27–46; L. Ginzburg and B. Cohen, "Dove," *The Legends of the Jews VII: Index* (Philadelphia: Jewish Publication Society of America, 1967), p. 117.

DOXOLOGY. From two Greek words, *doxa* and *logos*, basically meaning "words of praise" or "ascription of glory." In both Judaism and Christianity, doxologies praise or ascribe glory to God.

The Old Testament teems with doxologies, even in the oldest strata of text (e.g., Gen. 24:27). Their abundance in the Psalms (e.g., 8:1; 66:1–2; 96:6) connects them with Israel's worship, at least as early as the time of Solomon, and thence they came into synagogue rituals in the period just before the rise of Christianity. Only a small proportion of the biblical doxologies actually came into use in public worship.

Christian doxologies may be found in almost every book of the New Testament (e.g., Rom. 11:36; Gal. 1:5; Jude 25; Rev. 5:13). But again, only a few of these found use in public worship. In fact, earliest Christianity both used Old Testament doxologies in worship and developed its own as well. By the early second century, the uniquely Christian Trinitarian form was common, and at least in some cases it was intended by liturgical position and use to express both continuity and discontinuity with the Jewish tradition.

The earliest Christian doxologies are addressed to God the Father alone or the Father through the Son, in or with the Holy Spirit. By the fourth century, however, the Arians, and others unwilling to ascribe full divinity to Christ or full divine personality to the Spirit, used the traditional doxological expressions to support this subordinationism. This gave rise, in that century, to the orthodox form, which simply paralleled the ancient baptismal formula: "Glory [be] to the Father, and to the Son, and to the Holy Spirit."

In the fourth century, three principal forms of liturgical doxology became distinguishable. Probably the oldest is the Sanctus or Tersanctus, our first notice of which comes from the end of the first century. Its original form was probably "Holy, Holy, Holy, Lord of Hosts, all creation is full of thy glory" (*1 Clem.* 34). By the third century, it was incorporated into the prayer consecrating the eucharistic elements and had reached its full form (with some slight variations): "Holy, Holy, Holy, Lord God Almighty, heaven and earth are full of thy glory; Glory be to Thee, O Lord."

The *Gloria in excelsis*, a hymn based on Luke 2:14 that may date to the second century and that in the third century was used in the eastern liturgies as a "hymn at dawn," came to be sung in the fourth century in eastern liturgies at the close of the recitation of the Psalms, certainly in the morning and probably in the evening service. In Rome, by ca. 500, it came to be sung even before the scripture readings; there, it was often called the "Angel's Hymn." In both east and west, it was called the Greater Doxology. Pope Symmachus (498–514) ordered it to be sung on "every Sunday and martyr's feast."

What is now called the Gloria Patri was called the Lesser Doxology. It is a Christianizing and amplification of the Jewish tradition of "magnifying the Name." By the end of the third century, it was commonly recited at the close of the eucharistic prayer. In the fourth century, in noneucharistic services, it was sung as the close of each Psalm, except where several Psalms might be recited together, as a means of making them Christian. Much later, its use was more limited, but it retained its place and function. Its original form was simply "Glory [be] to God, Amen" or "Glory [be] to the Father, Amen," but already in the writings of Paul (Rom. 11:36) we see the additional phrase "forever," which was soon expanded to "is now and ever and in ages of ages" (i.e., the modern "is now and ever shall be, world without end"). By the fourth century, it had taken the Trinitarian form noted above. Sometime in the late fifth century, western Christians, reacting to Arianism, added "as it was in the beginning," but the eastern liturgies have never included the phrase.

In the eastern liturgies, after the mid-fifth century, the term "Angel's Hymn" often referred to quite another doxology, the Trisagion:

"Holy God, Holy and Mighty, Holy and Immortal, have mercy upon us." It played much the same role in eastern liturgies that the *Gloria in excelsis* played in the west, after ca. 450. It entered western liturgies only in the mid-sixth century or later, in the wake of Justinian I's attempts to restore the old empire. Its name reflects belief that it was revealed as a song sung by angels themselves. *See also* Gloria in excelsis; Trisagion.   [P.M.B.]

Bibliography
F.E. Warren, *The Liturgy and Ritual of the Ante-Nicene Church* , 2nd rev. ed. (London: SPCK, 1912); G. Dix, *The Shape of the Liturgy* (Westminster: Dacre, 1945); J.H. Srawley, *The Early History of the Liturgy* (Cambridge: Cambridge UP, 1947); J.A. Jungmann, *The Early Liturgy* (Notre Dame: U of Notre Dame P, 1959); G. Wainwright, *Doxology* (Oxford: Oxford UP, 1980).

DRACONTIUS (ca. 450–after 496). Latin poet and advocate. Trained in classical rhetoric at Carthage, Dracontius was imprisoned after the invasion of the Vandals for a poem he had composed in honor of the Roman emperor. Besides numerous secular poems, epithalamia, and epyllia on mythological figures, he is the author of the *Satisfactio*, a confession of guilt and request for pardon addressed to the Vandal king, and of the *De laudibus Dei*, verse in praise of God's goodness, the first book of which circulated separately in the Middle Ages as a *Hexaemeron*, or account of creation. CPL 1509–1514.   [M.P.McH.]

Bibliography
Dracontii Satisfactio, tr. M. St. Margaret (Ph.D. diss., University of Pennsylvania, 1935); *Liber I, Dracontii de Laudibus Dei*, tr. J.F. Irwin (Ph.D. diss., University of Pennsylvania, 1942); *Liber II, Dracontii de Laudibus Dei*, tr. J.E. Bresnahan (Ph.D. diss., University of Pennsylvania, 1949; Ann Arbor: University Microfilms, 1949).

F.J.E. Raby, *A History of Secular Latin Poetry*, 2 vols., 2nd ed. (Oxford: Clarendon, 1957), Vol. 1, pp. 105–112; Vol. 2, p. 367 (bibliography); D.F. Bright, *The Miniature Epic in Vandal Africa* (Norman: U of Oklahoma P, 1987).

DREAMS. In antiquity, communications from the spirit realm received in sleep. Although early Christianity rejected the profession of divination by dreams as magical meddling in the spirit world (Hippolytus, *Trad. ap.* 16), the signifying potential of dreams was affirmed, both in scriptural text (e.g., Acts 16:9; 18:9) and in personal experience. Early Christians shared in a widespread cultural attitude toward dreams, an attitude rooted in classical antiquity (Homer, the tragedians, Plato) that remained virtually unchanged for hundreds of years. Despite the few who scoffed at the attribution of meaning to dreams or saw demonic agitation at work in them, the majority of writers in late antiquity agreed with Tertullian's famous dictum in *On the Soul* 47.2 that dreams were a major source of insight about the divine world.

Citing the dream as a locus of interaction between human beings and gods, late-antique dream theory belonged to the branch of theology that explicated issues concerning the soul in both its imaginative and cognitive aspects. Like many others, Athanasius offered dream experience as proof that the soul was rational and immortal (*Gent.* 2.31; cf. Tertullian, *Anim.* 43; 45; Augustine, *Gen. ad litt.* 12; Clement of Alexandria, *Paed.* 2.9; Synesius of Cyrene, *Insomn.* 3–5). Early Christian authors adhered to the cultural convention that viewed dreams as witnesses to the intrusion of the future into the present rather than as explanations of the past. As phenomena of prophecy, dreams were prominent in two areas of early Christianity: in the interpretation of scripture, where the most popular dreamers were from the Hebrew tradition (Jacob, Daniel, Joseph); and in personal experience, in moments of intense social crisis or emotional upheaval. In scriptural interpretation, dreams were often part of the allegorical appropriation of the Hebrew tradition for Christology; hence, for example, Jacob's ladder became a sign of the cross. In personal experience, dreams figured prominently in the lives of martyrs (*M. Polyc.* 5.2; *Pass. Perp.* 4–10) and in conversion and the deepening of religious commitment (Gregory of Nazianzus, *Carm.* 2.1.45; Hermas, *Vis.* 1–5).

In general, late-antique thinkers viewed the dream as a phenomenon of the "middle realm" of the soul, situated between the human and the divine, the sensible and the intel-ligible, the earthly and heavenly, and activated by a conjunction of imagination and memory when these two are released into play as body and mind slumber. Dreams and the soul's reason formed a pair, and the conviction that dreams spoke with hermeneutical and spiritual authority was one that early Christianity embraced as part of its cultural milieu. *See also* Mysticism. [P.C.M.]

Bibliography

E.R. Dodds, *Pagan and Christian in an Age of Anxiety* (Cambridge: Cambridge UP, 1965), pp. 37–68; C.A. Behr, *Aelius Aristides and the Sacred Tales* (Amsterdam: Hakkert, 1968); M. Dulaey, *Le Rêve dans la vie et la pensée de saint Augustin* (Paris: Etudes Augustiniennes, 1973); P.C. Miller, "'A Dubious Twilight': Reflections on Dreams in Patristic Literature," *ChHist* 55 (1986):153–164.

DUALISM. Any belief that explains the world in terms of a pair (or pairs) of opposing principles. The most archaic forms of dualism are found in mythologies that pit good and evil or earthly and heavenly gods against one another. Order, creation, and civilization become possible only when the "sky gods" are able to subdue the dragonlike monster associated with the watery chaos out of which earth emerged. Genesis 1 rejects this ancient Near Eastern mythic pattern by insisting that God's creative power operates through the divine word, not a cosmic battle. The mythic imagery stayed alive in poetic texts, however, such as the description of Yahweh's battle with the sea in Isaiah 51:9. The theme is recaptured in the defeat of the dragon that opposes God's people in Revelation 12–13.

The primitive dualism of mythology was transformed into a dualism of opposing principles by peoples who saw in the myths the conflict of forces of light and darkness, good and evil. The myths of the Persian Zoroastrian religion described the world as locked in conflict between forces of good (light) and evil. Those who followed the teachings of the prophet Zoroaster would assist the process of separating truth from falsehood that was required for the final victory of the good. Thus, the dualism is mythic, cosmological, and ethical, since the ethical life of individuals is shaped by the necessity to assist the victory of light.

Iranian dualism is thought to have influenced the emergence of dualism in Jewish apocalyptic writings, which place much more emphasis upon the struggle with demonic powers than one finds in canonical texts. In some writings, like Daniel, the enemies of Israel's righteous are identified with the dragon figure. The righteous await a final heavenly battle between angelic forces led by Michael, in which Satan will be defeated forever. The writings of the Essene sect exhibit both cosmic-eschatological dualism and ethical dualism. The *War Scroll* describes the final battles in which the forces of Michael and Satan struggle with each other until the final victory. The *Community Rule* likens the dualism of two angels, of light and darkness, to the ethical life of the righteous. The good are led by the angel of light; the wicked by the angel of darkness. Until the end of time, however, human beings also experience the conflict of the two powers within their hearts. This view influenced early Christian ethics through descriptions of the "Two Ways" of life and death, such as one finds in the *Epistle of Barnabas.* Paul also uses dualistic language about the opposition of "Spirit" and "flesh" (e.g., Gal. 5:16–26; Rom. 7:13–8:13).

Another development in dualistic speculation was the contrasting of two ages, the present evil age with the future age of righteousness that follows upon God's victory over the Satanic forces of evil. Paul thinks of Christian life in the Spirit as a manifestation of that new age while Christians are still living in the "evil age." They must be warned not to share the values of the present age (Rom. 12:2). Paul can also speak in mythic language of the powers or gods of this age (1 Cor. 2:6–8; 2 Cor. 4:4).

The sharp division between those who are righteous and the majority of humanity who are "the wicked" often suggests an anthropological dualism. Some persons are "good" either by nature or by divine destiny, which has singled them out and endowed them with the revelation or divine spirit necessary to attain salvation. The rest are doomed to remain cap-

tive to sin and death. The Fourth Gospel exhibits this kind of dualism when it speaks of believers as those whom the Father has "given" to the Son (e.g., John 3:18–21, 31–36; 5:19–24; 10:22–30).

Religious dualism of this sort is always linked with a strong sense of revelation. This world is too corrupt for humans to find the truth about God on their own. Jewish and Christian apocalypses convey revelation through heavenly visions and journeys. The Fourth Gospel pictures Jesus as the only revealer to have come from heaven. Consequently, the saving knowledge of God is available only to persons who believe in Jesus (e.g., John 1:1–18). Because of their belief, Christians may claim a heavenly destiny. They may even insist that they are "not of this world" in the way that other persons are (e.g., John 17:14–16).

Another type of dualism developed in the Greek philosophical tradition. Empedocles described the cycles of the world as the interacting principles of love and hate. Pythagorean traditions elaborated a series of opposed principles, some derived from mathematical speculation about the causes of the universe, such as limited/unlimited, odd/even, unity/multiplicity. Parmenides spoke of a way of truth leading to knowledge that was opposed to the illusion of those trapped in the senses. Elements of all these emerge in the philosophical traditions inaugurated by Plato. Platonism insists upon the sharp difference between the world of sensible, changing reality and the world of truth, which can be reached only through reason. The body belongs to the former; the soul to the latter. The world of the divine contains the true forms, Ideas, for all that exists. The philosopher who is able to contemplate that world becomes as much like the gods as is possible for any human being. Its ability to enter that world shows that the soul is not a material entity but is immortal and divine.

Platonism had a long history in Christian thought, since it seemed to provide the best philosophical basis for Christian beliefs about God and the soul. The contrast between the realities of the heavenly sanctuary and its earthly images that dominates the Epistle to the Hebrews has its origin in the Jewish philosopher Philo's application of Platonic philosophy to biblical interpretation. God created the visible world according to the heavenly ideas.

The radical dualism of Gnostic speculation challenged both Christianity and Platonism. Gnostics insisted that the material world was not merely an imperfect reflection of the divine but was created by an ignorant demon to keep the divine light that had become trapped there from recognizing its true divine home. Gnostics employed all forms of dualism—mythic, religious, ethical, cosmic, and philosophical—in expounding their system. Only those who hear the call of the heavenly revealer, who reject this world and its passions and authorities and prepare their soul for its reunification with its heavenly origin are saved. Some Gnostic writings expounded this system using Jewish and Christian mythic themes. Others took over the philosophic ascent of the soul from Platonism. Some required a severely ascetic renunciation of the body. Others appear to have sought "reunification" through cultic practices. Gnostic dualism lived on in Manichaeism and related religious movements, such as those of the medieval Bogomils and Cathars.

Both Christian opponents like Irenaeus and Origen and philosophic opponents like Plotinus rejected the radical dualism and world-denying character of Gnostic dualism. They insisted that divine power and goodness are reflected even in the material world. Irenaeus emphasized the image of God in humanity as restored through the incarnation to prove that the radical separation of God and the world presupposed in the Gnostic systems is wrong (e.g., *Haer.* 5.6). Plotinus castigated his Gnostic opponents for destroying all the beauty and order in the cosmos (*Enneads* 2.9). Dualism within Christian theology must always be constrained by the conviction that the world is the creation of a good God and that salvation is mediated through, not in opposition to, incarnate reality. *See also* Apocalyptic Literature; Gnosticism; Mani, Manichaeism.   [P.P.]

Bibliography

J. Daniélou, *Gospel Message and Hellenistic Culture* (Philadelphia: Westminster, 1973); J. Gammie, "Spatial and Ethical Dualism in Jewish Wisdom and Apocalyptic Literature," *JBL* 93 (1974):356–385; A. Wedberg, *A History of Philosophy* (Oxford: Clarendon, 1982), Vol. 1; K. Rudolph, *Gnosis* (San Francisco: Harper and Row, 1983); J.J. Collins, *The Apocalyptic Imagination* (New York: Crossroads, 1984).

DURA-EUROPOS. City on the middle Euphrates River in Roman Syria (at Es-Salihiyeh in modern Iraq), discovered by British soldiers in 1920 and given its double name from the ancient geographer Isidore of Charax. Excavations were begun in 1922 by the French Academy of Inscriptions and Letters and then jointly with Yale University until 1939. Findings proved important for two reasons. First, the city was strategically located on the eastern frontier of the Roman empire. It was a crossroads of trade and cultures, having been founded, after Alexander's conquests, by the Seleucids, ceded to the Parthians, and then taken over and expanded by the Romans during the second century A.D. Second, the city was completely destroyed, and partially buried in the process, in 256 during Sassanian incursions. The remains were consequently preserved in a state of "suspended animation."

Among the discoveries were the central market and the military garrison (with records and documents). Abundant art, including painting and sculpture, reflects both eastern and western styles and has been termed "proto-Byzantine." Especially noteworthy is the religious architecture, thirteen temples of Greek, Roman, Parthian, and Palmyrene deities. This syncretistic environment produced a uniquely Durene temple style, which has Hellenistic as well as Near Eastern influences. Also discovered were three minor religious sanctuaries that had been renovated from private homes near the city's West Wall. They include a Mithraeum, a Jewish synagogue, and the earliest known Christian church building.

In the synagogue (two adjacent houses), the assembly hall was decorated with spectacular narrative scenes illustrating biblical themes,

Baptistery of the Christian church at Dura-Europos, Syria (240s), as formerly reconstructed at the Yale University Art Gallery, New Haven, Connecticut. (Dura-Europos Collection, Yale University Art Gallery)

such as the crossing of the Red Sea, the anointing of David, the Purim triumph, and the temple, all grouped around one of the earliest known Torah shrines. Prior to this discovery, such use of pictorial art was thought impossible in early synagogues. The narrative scenes show extensive use of midrashic traditions and programmatic composition to enhance the worship space. The artistic program is datable to 244–245.

The Christian building proved an equally spectacular find, although inferior in size and aesthetic quality to the synagogue. On the exterior, the house remained unchanged; only on the interior were renovations undertaken to transform it from domestic to church use. Two rooms were combined to form a rectangular assembly hall. Another small room was transformed into a baptistery, with a canopied font set into the floor at one end. This room was also decorated with narrative scenes from the Gospels, including the women at the tomb, Jesus' miracles, and a Good Shepherd. This remains the earliest known church building and baptistery, the earliest (and most clearly datable) Christian art outside the catacombs, and the earliest datable pictorial representation of Jesus. *See also* Art; Baptistery; House Church.

[L.M.W.]

Bibliography

J.H. Breasted, *Oriental Forerunners of Byzantine Painting* (Chicago: U of Chicago, 1924); M. Rostovtzeff, *Dura-Europos and Its Art* (Oxford: Clarendon, 1938); C.H. Kraeling, *The Synagogue, Final Reports* VIII:1 (New Haven: Yale UP, 1956); E.R. Goodenough, *Jewish Symbols in the Graeco-Roman Period* (New York: Pantheon, 1964–1968), Vols. 9–11; C.H. Kraeling, *The Christian Building, Final Reports* VIII:2 (New Haven: Yale UP, 1967); J. Gutmann, ed., *The Dura-Europos Synagogue: A Reevaluation (1932–1972)* (Missoula: Scholars, 1973); A. Perkins, *The Art of Dura-Europos* (Oxford: Clarendon, 1973); C. Hopkins, *The Discovery of Dura-Europos* (New Haven: Yale UP, 1979); L.M. White, *Building God's House in the Roman World: Architectural Adaptation Among Pagans, Jews, and Christians* (Baltimore: Johns Hopkins UP, 1989).

DYOPHYSITISM. Belief that Christ had two natures, from the Greek *duo* ("two") and *phuseis* ("natures"). Dyophysites were those who accepted the definition worked out by the Council of Chalcedon (451), which stated that the Christ consisted of two distinct natures, one divine and one human, in one person. The term was applied to those who accepted the "two-natures" theology by their opponents, the Monophysites, who believed that the incarnate Christ consisted of only one nature.

This controversy over the relationship between the divine and human natures in Christ was rooted in the differing views of the schools of Alexandria and Antioch. The theologians of Antioch, the most notable of whom in this controversy was Nestorius, but whose views had their antecedents in Diodore of Tarsus and Theodore of Mopsuestia, taught that there were two natures in Christ without confusion and without division. The Godhead in Christ, they argued, maintains its immutability and impassibility, and the manhood maintains all the characteristics of perfect humanity. The Alexandrians, on the contrary, represented in the pre-Chalcedonian period of the debate preeminently by Cyril of Alexandria, took over the formula of Apollinaris that Christ possessed one nature. Modern scholarship has argued that the two sides, with the exception of a few extremists, were not as far apart as they thought. Nevertheless, Cyril managed to get Nestorius removed from the see of Constantinople as a heretic.

The Council of Chalcedon was convoked in 451 to settle the issue of the natures of Christ and thus restore peace to the church. Its definition is a compromise between the two positions. It keeps the two natures distinct, as in the Antiochene position, but proclaims the oneness of Christ, as in the Alexandrian, in his person and *hypostasis*. The Christ has two natures, the definition asserts, both perfect God and perfect man, but is not two persons. The unity in person, on the other hand, does not confuse the distinction in the natures.

Although Chalcedon provided the formula that was to prevail as orthodox Christology, it did not bring an immediate peace to the church. The Monophysites rejected the definition, and the Monophysite-Dyophysite controversy raged on for more than a century after the so-called Christological settlement at Chalcedon. *See also* Chalcedon; Christ, Christology; Cyril of Alexandria; Monophysites; Nestorianism; Nestorius. [R.E.H.]

Bibliography

P. Schaff, *The Creeds of Christendom* (1877; repr. Grand Rapids: Baker, 1977), Vol. 2, pp. 62–65.

R.V. Sellers, *The Council of Chalcedon* (London: SPCK, 1953); idem, *Two Ancient Christologies* (London: SPCK, 1954); A. Grillmeier, *Christ in Christian Tradition*, 2nd ed. (Atlanta: John Knox, 1975); F. Young, *From Nicaea to Chalcedon* (Philadelphia: Fortress, 1983).

E

EASTER. *See* Pasch, Paschal Controversy.

EBIONITES. One of the names applied to Jewish Christians by the church fathers. "Ebionites" in Greek is a transliteration of the Hebrew (more accurately, an Aramaic variation on the Hebrew), which means "poor." The precise origins of this name are not known. Paul was ordered to organize a collection for the "poor" in Jerusalem (Gal. 2:10), and this has sometimes been taken as evidence that the early Jerusalem congregation called itself "the poor," a term similarly used in the Qumran writings for the people with whom they were sympathetic (e.g., *Commentary on Psalm 37* 2.9; 3.10; *Commentary on Habakkuk* 12.3). Yet Paul's further statement in Romans 15:26 that the offering was for "the poor *among* the saints in Jerusalem" indicates not a messianic designation of the entire Jerusalem community but a descriptive term for the economically deprived.

The use of the term at Qumran, in the Old Testament, and in the New Testament does, however, shed light on what must have eventually become an honorific self-designation of at least some Jewish Christians. Irenaeus knows of a group of Christians called the Ebionites (*Haer.* 1.26.2—the first witness to this usage), and Origen is aware of the Hebrew meaning of the name (*Cels.* 2.1; *Princ.* 4.3.8).

Irenaeus ascribes the following doctrines and practices to the Ebionites: rejection of Paul as an apostate from the Law; use of only Matthew's Gospel; veneration of Jerusalem; observance of circumcision, the Law, and a Jewish way of life; rejection of the virgin birth; unusual exposition of the prophets; and possibly the use of water in the eucharist. Origen confirms several of these traits, insinuates that the Ebionites observed the Passover, and states that one group of the Ebionites actually accepted the virgin birth.

A number of other church fathers mention these and other features. For example, the notion that the Ebionites were founded by the heretical leader Ebion, which is first witnessed by Tertullian and Hippolytus and brings the Ebionites into line with other sects, was rapidly adopted in antiheretical literature. Epiphanius of Salamis, in particular, adds much more information about the Ebionites and their writings. He provides, for example, the only excerpts we have from a Jewish Christian gospel identified by modern scholars as the *Gospel of* the Ebionites. He also supplies the only information we have on the scurrilous anti-Pauline *Anabathmoi Jakobou* (*Haer*. 30.16.7–9).

Although some investigators, ancient and modern, have attempted to isolate the Ebionites as a distinct body within the larger class of Jewish Christians (the Ebionites are often seen as the stricter, more radical group), the notices of the church fathers are more amenable to the view that "Ebionites" was just one appellation (among others, particularly "Nazoraeans") of Jewish Christians and, moreover, that the Jewish Christians included a variety of groups and communities. *See also* Jewish Christianity; Pseudo-Clementines. [F.S.J.]

Bibliography

Irenaeus, *Against Heresies* 1.26.2, 3.21.1, 5.1.3; Hippolytus, *Refutation of All Heresies* 7.22; Tertullian, *Prescription Against Heretics* 33; Origen, *Against Celsus* 2.1; idem, *On First Principles* 4.3.8; Pseudo-Tertullian, *Against All Heresies* 11; Eusebius, *Church History* 3.27; Epiphanius, *Panarion* 29–30.

F.J.A. Hort, *Judaistic Christianity* (Cambridge and London: Macmillan, 1894); L.E. Keck, "The Poor Among the Saints in the New Testament," *ZNTW* 56 (1965):100–129; idem, "The Poor Among the Saints in Jewish Christianity and Qumran," *ZNTW* 57 (1966):54–78; G. Strecker, "On the Problem of Jewish Christianity," in W. Bauer, *Orthodoxy and Heresy in Early Christianity*, ed. R.A. Kraft and G. Krodel (Philadelphia: Fortress, 1971; orig. German ed., 1964), pp. 241–285; A.F.J. Klijn and G.J. Reinink, *Patristic Evidence for Jewish-Christian Sects* (Leiden: Brill, 1973).

ECCLESIOLOGY. *See* Church.

ECSTASY. Concept signifying a wide variety of practices and attitudes that are functions of the desire to see, experience, and be moved by the divine. The word "ecstasy" (from Greek) literally means "to stand outside oneself." It is an experience known in shamanism, Hinduism, Buddhism, Greco-Roman religion, Judaism, Islam, and Christianity.

The biblical texts of both Testaments reflect a positive view of ecstatic rhetoric and experiences. The patristic writers, influenced by contemporary Greco-Roman culture, especially Middle Platonic and Neoplatonic philosophy, developed the concept. Montanism caused a reaction against linking too closely the human and the divine. However, the concern to experience the divine remained central to spirituality. Clement of Alexandria articulated an understanding of perfection and orthodox *gnosis*. Origen translated this into levels of spiritual development, which were refined by the Cappadocians, Evagrius of Pontus, Pseudo-Dionysius the Areopagite, and Maximus Confessor. Within the eastern monastic tradition, ecstasy was joined to asceticism, as can be seen in the numerous saints' lives and the theoretical literature produced by such authors as John the Solitary, Isaac of Ninevah, and Macarius. In the west, an ecstatic tradition, influenced by the east but distinct, can be traced through Augustine, John Cassian, and Gregory the Great. *See also* Mysticism. [D.B.]

Bibliography

H. Weinel, *Die Wirkung des Geistes und der Geister im nachapostolischen Zeitalter bis auf Irenaeus* (Freiburg: Herder, 1899); H.K. La Rondelle, *Perfection and Perfectionism* (Kampen: Kok, 1971); C.G. Williams, *Tongue of the Spirit: A Study of Pentecostal Glossolalia and Related Phenomena* (Cardiff: U of Wales P, 1981).

ECUMENICAL COUNCILS. Synods representing the universal church. The institution of ecumenical councils, or synods, is related to Christianity's rise as the state religion of the Roman empire. The first ecumenical council was summoned by the emperor Constantine the Great in 325, and the succeeding ones were summoned by his successors.

The emergence of an ecumenical council presupposes two conditions: (1) the understanding of the Roman state as the *oikumenē*, a Greek term denoting an inhabited or civilized region, particular or universal, and the understanding of the church's historical boundaries as coextensive with those of the "Roman" world-empire (Matt. 24:14; Acts 17:6, 31; Rom. 10:18; Rev. 3:10); and (2) the development of the "conciliar procedure" of the church, which had its precedent in the so-called apostolic council of Jerusalem described in Acts 15 and proceeded with the development of episcopal church structures along the lines of the political structures of the Roman state. Provincial and regional church councils competent to deal with matters of faith and order were established before the First Ecumenical Council of Nicaea in 325.

Nicaea was the first instance of the highest development of the church's conciliar structure and procedure since apostolic times. It marked the first occasion when representatives of the entire church met in council to deal with a theological problem—Arianism, the denial of the true Godhead of Christ—fundamental to its common faith and with matters of order affecting the entire church, such as the date of Easter. Although the Council of Nicaea styled itself "Great and Holy" (cf. its *Epistle to the Church of Alexandria* in Socrates, *H.E.* 1.9), Eusebius calls it "ecumenical" (*V.C.* 3.6); and so does Athanasius (*Ep. Afr.* 1), who provides in his defenses of the Nicene faith the first statements of the criteria for an ecumenical council: the Council of Nicaea was ecumenical because it was representative of the entire church through its bishops (*Apol. sec.* 23; *Ep. Aeg. Lib.* 5; 13), because it had an "obvious and just cause" (*Syn.* 5f.), and because it issued a free and unanimous decision (*Ep. Aeg. Lib* 13) that was identical with the traditional and apostolic faith of the church (*Ep. Aeg. Lib.* 8; *Ep. Jov.* 1f.; *Ep. Afr.* 1). Although an extraordinary council, as compared with many earlier ones, the Council of Nicaea gained universal authority for its creed (matters of faith) and its canons (matters of church order).

The Second Ecumenical Council, summoned at Constantinople in 381 by Theodosius I to deal with Pneumatomachians and other heretics, was initially a council of the eastern Roman empire (Theodoret, *H.E.* 5.7, 8; Socrates, *H.E.* 5.7) but was later recognized as ecumenical on account of its faith and the great sanctity of its members. Its creed, which represented an expansion of the creed of Nicaea, became the universal creed of Christendom. The Third Ecumenical Council of Ephesus (431), which condemned the heresy of Nestorius and dealt with several other matters, was summoned as "ecumenical" (Evagrius, *H.E.* 1.8) and called itself such (cf. *can.* 1; ACO 1.3, p.

47). The same applies to the Fourth Ecumenical Council of Chalcedon (451), which condemned Eutychianism (ACO 1.3, pp. 99, 116, 122), and to the subsequent Ecumenical Councils—the Fifth, of Constantinople (553), which dealt with the controversy of the Three Chapters and possibly Origenism; the Sixth, of Constantinople (680–681), which dealt with Monenergism and Monotheletism; the completion of the Fifth and Sixth, of Trullo in Constantinople (691–692), which was legislative; and the Seventh, of Nicaea (787), which dealt with the use of icons in the church.

Other church councils had been summoned as ecumenical but were not recognized as such. These include the councils of Sardica (343) and Ariminum (359), according to the historian Socrates (*H.E.* 2.20, 37); the "Robber Council" of Ephesus (449), under the presidency of Dioscorus of Alexandria, who was condemned at Chalcedon; and the Iconoclastic Council of Hieria (754), summoned by the emperor Constantine V. The church did not approve these councils because they did not meet the criteria that Athanasius and later church fathers outlined. The so-called Eighth Ecumenical Council of Constantinople (880), which reinstated Photius of Constantinople, was originally accepted by both the eastern and the western churches, but the Latin church, after it broke relations with the east, replaced it in its list of ecumenical councils with an earlier Council of Constantinople (870) that had condemned Photius. The schism of 1054, which divided the western from the eastern church, marked a new era in ecumenical councils. Apart from the uniate councils of Lyons (1274) and of Ferrara-Florence (1439), which attempted to heal the schism between the western and eastern churches and which were styled as "ecumenical," there were other ecumenical councils in both east and west whose status is accepted only by the respective church. *See also* Chalcedon; Constantinople; Councils; Ephesus; Nicaea. [G.D.D.]

Bibliography

Mansi; ACO.

H.R. Percival, ed., *The Seven Ecumenical Councils*, NPNF, 2nd ser. (1899), Vol. 14; C.J. Hefele, *A History of the Councils of the Church from the Origi-*

nal *Documents* (Edinburgh: Clark, 1896; repr. New York: AMS, 1972), Vols. 1–5.

G. Dumeige, ed., *Histoire des conciles oecuméniques* (Paris: Orante, 1962–1978), Vols. 1–4; H.J. Margull, ed., *The Councils of the Church: History and Analysis* (Philadelphia: Fortress, 1966); World Council of Churches, *Councils and the Ecumenical Movement* (Geneva: WCC, 1968); L.D. Davis, *The First Seven Ecumenical Councils (325–787): Their History and Theology* (Wilmington: Glazier, 1987).

EDESSA. Northern Mesopotamian center of Syriac Christianity, modern Urfa. Founded by Seleucus I Nicator in 303/2 B.C., Edessa had a strategic location that made it important to both Roman and Byzantine governments as an outpost against eastern enemies. Native kings ruled from ca. 130 B.C. to A.D. 243.

Legend relates that its king Abgar wrote to Christ and received a letter from him by the hand of Addai (Eusebius, *H.E.* 1.13). Christianity in the city was perhaps Gnostic and Marcionite first, then more orthodox. The *Acts of Thomas* may have been written there. Bardesanes (154–222), a noted poet, wrote against Marcionites but was opposed for his Gnostic speculations. His followers existed in Edessa until the eighth century. He attempted to combine Chaldean astrology and philosophical speculation with his religion.

Ephraem, born in Nisibis in 306, died in Edessa in 373 after ten years in the city. An ascetic, he composed hymns, homilies, commentaries, expository sermons, and polemical treatises. Often called "The Harp of the Holy Spirit," he was a master of Syriac style. Since he attacked Marcion, Bardesanes, Arius, and Mani, it is possible that he met followers of each in Edessa.

Rabbula, bishop of Edessa (412–435), had difficulty with Bardesanes's followers and suppressed Tatian's *Diatessaron*. He baptized some Arians and Marcionites. Although he fought Nestorians bitterly, Ibas, his successor, supported them. In 471, bishop Cyrus had the theological school of Edessa disbanded for its Nestorian leanings.

The city fell to the Persians in 609 and the Muslims in 639.   [F.W.N.]

Bibliography
J.B. Segal, *Edessa "The Blessed City"* (Oxford: Oxford UP, 1970); H.J.W. Drijvers, *Cults and Beliefs at Edessa* (Leiden: Brill, 1980).

EGERIA, PILGRIMAGE OF. Early-fifth-century diary concerning the travels of Egeria to Sinai and Palestine, rediscovered in one incomplete copy in 1884. The *Pilgrimage of Egeria* has been known under various names, including Eutheria, Aetheria, and Silvia, primarily because of different spellings within the traditions or conjectures about her identity; but references in library catalogues indicate that her name was Egeria. A nun from northwestern Spain, the region of Galicia, she wrote the account for her religious community there.

The extant text begins with Egeria's arrival at Mt. Sinai and stops in the midst of her description of the Feast of Dedications at Jerusalem. Some chapters have lacunae. An account of her journey in a letter of the seventh-century Spanish monk Valerius indicates that she had visited many sites for pilgrims in Egypt, Judea, and Galilee, including quite isolated monasteries. The first preserved sections of her diary detail visits to places mentioned in the Old Testament. She was often shown them by ascetics living in the regions, who kept some traditions of their locations alive. She tried to follow the route of the Exodus and visited Mt. Nebo and the tomb of Job at Carneas in Hauran, the tomb of St. Thomas the Apostle in Edessa, and the house of Abraham in Carrhae. In Constantinople, on the return trip, she spent time at the tomb of St. Thecla near Seleucia in Isauria and the Basilica of St. Euphemia in Chalcedon.

The last half of the volume describes the celebration of the liturgy in Jerusalem, both daily and within the yearly cycle. This liturgical information is invaluable in the history of liturgy. The diary also mentions six churches—the Holy Sepulchre, the Church of Sion, the Imbomon and the Eleona on the Mount of Olives, the Basilica of the Nativity in Bethlehem, and the Church of Lazarus in Bethany—and thus is helpful in the study of early church architecture. CPL 2325. *See also* Pilgrimage.
               [F.W.N.]

Bibliography

A. Franceschini and R. Weber, eds., CCSL (1958), Vol. 175, pp. 29–103.

G. Gingras, *Egeria: Diary of a Pilgrimage*, ACW (1970), Vol. 38; J. Wilkinson, tr. and ed., *Egeria's Travels to the Holy Land*, rev. ed. (Warminster: Aris and Phillips, 1981).

M. Starowieski, "Itinerarium Egeriae (Quaestiones criticae)," *Menander* 33 (1978):93–108, 133–145; idem, "Bibliografia Egeriana," *Augustinianum* 19 (1979): 297–318; P. Devos, "Egeriania," *AB* 105 (1987): 159–166, 415–424; V.Väänänen, *Le Journal-Epître d'Egérie* (Itinerarum Egerie): *Etude linguistique* (Helsinki: Suomalainen Tiedeakatemia, 1987); H. Sivan, "Who Was Egeria? Piety and Pilgrimage in the Age of Gratian," *HThR* 81 (1988):59–72.

EGYPT. Although the origins of Christianity in Egypt lie shrouded in uncertainty, the significance of Egypt in the development of Christian thought and practice in the early centuries of the common era can hardly be overestimated. The rich intellectual environment of Alexandria provided strong impetus to Christian theological speculation. A center of Greek philosophy and learning, it became a center of Christian theology as well, as the two confronted and influenced each other, and among the results were the cosmopolitan teaching of Clement of Alexandria, the allegorical exegesis and speculative theology of Origen, and a variety of Gnostic teachers. It was in Egypt that Arius first propounded his theory of the Son of God as a creature, and it was Egypt that supplied the most effective rebuttal to Arius in the person of Athanasius. Among the less speculative native Egyptian population, one finds influential innovation in Christian practice. Although the monastic lifestyle was not solely the product of Egypt, its Egyptian forms and heroes were renowned throughout the empire. Both the life of the hermit (anchoritic) monk and the communal (cenobitic) monastic life gained classic expression in Egypt, influencing the development of monasticism throughout Christian history.

Culture. The Egypt to which Christianity came in the middle of the first century offered a diversity of cultural elements. The native Egyptian population, the source of the wonders of the pharaonic past, had long been subjugated to foreign rule. Three centuries of Greek domination, from Egypt's conquest by Alexander in 332 B.C. to its acquisition as a Roman province under Octavian in 30 B.C., left a significant stamp on its government, culture, and identity. Greek became the dominant language of business and government and continued as such through the era of Roman rule. Alexandria, founded by Alexander, had become a major center of learning. The second city of the empire after Rome, it was renowned for its beauty, its library, and its scholarly activity. It also was home to one of the major populations of Jews outside of Palestine, a population that produced the Greek translation of the Hebrew Bible, the Septuagint, and the wedding of Jewish and Greek thought represented in the interpretative philosophy of Philo of Alexandria (ca. 20 B.C.–A.D. 50), both of which strongly influenced early Christian development.

The cultural matrix of Greeks, Jews, native Egyptians, and Romans aided the interaction of ideas, but it also proved divisive, as the various populations sought to improve their respective positions. Alexandria, a city created by the Greeks on the Mediterranean coast, was viewed with suspicion, at best, by the native population. One spoke of Alexandria *and* Egypt rather than of Alexandria *in* Egypt. As the native Egyptians despised Greek domination, so later many Greeks despised Roman rule. Jews held positions of authority within the government, but antagonism toward the Jewish population was common. Riots, oppression, and persecution among the ethnic populations were all too frequent.

Introduction of Christianity. It is an enigma of Christian history that mention of the earliest mission to a province and city of such significance is absent from the surviving sources. Paul shows no interest in Egypt, and the Book of Acts, which traces the spread of Christianity around the northern side of the Mediterranean Sea, says nothing of its arrival there (except the allusion in the western text of Acts 18:25). Church tradition recognizes the evangelist Mark as the founder of Christianity in Egypt (Eusebius, *H.E.* 2.16; Clement of Alexandria, fragmentary letter to Theodore containing the *Secret Gospel of Mark*), but the evidence is late and thus of questionable historical reliability. Christianity surely arrived in Egypt within the first generation after the death of Jesus, most likely from Palestine through the large Jewish population, probably in Alexandria.

Although the earliest Christian mission to Egypt thus appears to bear a strong Jewish stamp, when it emerges into the light of day in surviving second-century sources, it is decidedly Greek in flavor. A strong Gnostic presence, witnessed in such renowned teachers as Basilides, Valentinus, and the Marcionite Apelles, led Walter Bauer to argue in 1934 that the earliest form of Christianity in Egypt was Gnostic. He accounted for the silence concerning Christianity's early years in Egypt by arguing that the "orthodox" victors had simply excised the earlier history as a Gnostic history. While a strong Gnostic presence in Egypt is clear, recent scholarship has rejected Bauer's thesis as an oversimplification. The silence is more likely the result of the decidedly Jewish flavor of earliest Egyptian Christianity. When Egyptian Jewry was virtually annihilated during the reign of Trajan (A.D. 98–117), the Jewish Christian mission, little differentiated from Judaism in general by outsiders, disappeared along with it. Subsequent Christian development in Egypt occurred first in the Gentile or Greek population and only later began to affect native Egyptians.

The philosophical schools of Alexandria formed a speculative milieu in which Christian theological inquiry first spread its wings. Although major Gnostic thinkers flourished in second-century Alexandria, they were not alone in their quest for Christian understanding. A certain Stoic convert named Pantaenus (d. A.D. 190) produced a non-Gnostic scholarly tradition strongly influenced by Platonic thought and the methods of allegorical exegesis. His approach is best represented in the writings of Clement of Alexandria (150–215) and Origen (185–254).

Third Century. By the end of the second century, the bishop of Alexandria was clearly emerging as a major ecclesiastical power. Although Eusebius of Caesarea traces the Alexandrian episcopacy back to Mark (*H.E.* 2.16),

it is only with the episcopate of Demetrius (190–232) that there emerges any significant information beyond mere names. Thereafter, the authority and influence of the office continued to increase. In the episcopate of Dionysius (247–264), while the church suffered under the Decian persecution, the authority of the office was brought to bear both over the broader Egyptian church beyond Alexandria and outside of Egypt in Catholic theological issues. Dionysius corrected the erring Egyptian bishop Nepos of the Arsinoite nome and communicated frequently by letter with bishops of cities outside of Egypt. He was himself accused of tritheism by the bishop of Rome for his perhaps overvigorous attack on the Sabellian heresy.

It is in this era between Demetrius and Dionysius that one begins to witness the rapid growth of Christianity among the native population. The rise of the Coptic language (from the Arabic *Kibt*, which in turn derives from the Greek word for Egyptian) appears closely linked to this missionary effort. One should distinguish in general between the more highly theological, Alexandria-centered Christianity of the Greek-speaking Egyptians and the simpler, more practical Christianity of the native Egyptians or Copts.

Egyptian Christians of both varieties periodically suffered persecution. The extent of the martyr literature and the number of martyrs commemorated in the *Synaxarium* attest to the impact of these persecutions on the Coptic church. The Great Persecution under the emperor Diocletian was particularly severe in Egypt. In later years, the Coptic church marked the year of Diocletian's accession (284) as the Era of the Martyrs and used the date as the beginning of the Coptic era. The Era of the Martyrs ended with the execution in 311 of Peter, the bishop of Alexandria, who henceforth was known as the last, or "seal," of the martyrs. Different opinions on the treatment of Christians who compromised their faith produced a schism led by the rigorist Melitius of Lycopolis.

The last half of the third century also marked the rise of the monastic enterprise in Egypt. Anthony (251–356) took up the ascetic life ca. 269. Others soon followed. Theirs was the life of an anchorite or hermit, although they often gathered their cells in relative proximity to one another. The desert soon blossomed with such settlements, which became pilgrimage goals for visitors from the city and other lands. Even the Alexandrian archbishop was known to visit the ascetic holy men. In Upper Egypt, Pachomius (292–346) first developed cenobitic monasticism, in which the monks shared a lifestyle within a walled community under a monastic rule. Pachomius's rule served as a model for later monastic development. The writings of the monk Shenoute.(d. 452), superior of the White Monastery near Sohag in Upper Egypt, are considered the highwater mark of Coptic literature. In 431, he attended the Council of Ephesus, where, with Cyril of Alexandria, he opposed Nestorius.

Fourth and Fifth Centuries. The fourth and fifth centuries found Egyptian Christianity embroiled in the major theological issues of the day. The Alexandrian priest Arius (ca. 260–336) raised the question of the relationship between God the Father and the Son. He asserted that the Son, as the first born of creation, was subordinate to the Father. The Council of Nicaea (325) rejected Arius, but his teachings continued to cause controversy and conflict until 381. Central in the orthodox struggle against Arius was the Alexandrian bishop Athanasius (ca. 300–373), whose voluminous writings are our major source on the Arian debate. His significance for all Christendom was quickly recognized. Within ten years of his death, Gregory of Nazianzus eulogized Athanasius from the pulpit in Constantinople as the pillar of the church of his time (*Or.* 21.1).

The ecclesiastical and political power of the patriarch of Alexandria both within Egypt and beyond was established. Those who occupied the see through the middle of the fifth century continued active involvement in international ecclesiastical politics. Theophilus, bishop of Alexandria (385–412), whose methods were unscrupulous, actively suppressed the remnants of pagan religion in the city, destroying the famous temple of Sarapis in 391. He also waged a vicious campaign against Origen-

ism. In this campaign, through political maneuvering at the Synod of the Oak (403), he effected the condemnation of the Constantinopolitan bishop John Chrysostom. Theophilus's successor, Cyril (412–444), carried on a similarly unyielding attack against Nestorius, who was condemned at the Council of Ephesus (431), which was under Cyril's control.

The major fifth-century struggle centered on the relationship between the human and divine nature in Christ. The letter of pope Leo I of Rome, issued in 449, maintained that the two natures remained unconfused and unmixed in their union in the person of Christ (Dyophysitism). The more Monophysite Copts of Egypt rejected the letter, which came to bear the label of "the hated tome" in subsequent Coptic literature. With the decision of the Council of Chalcedon (451) to support the Dyophysite position and its condemnation of the Alexandrian patriarch Dioscorus, the Coptic church became increasingly isolated. Efforts by Constantinople to force compliance with the rulings of Chalcedon only hardened Egyptian opposition. The subsequent century witnessed rival Chalcedonian and non–Chalcedonian patriarchs and periods of persecution of the non–Chalcedonian Copts.

The Greek rulers, whose allegiance lay with Constantinople, thus had little Coptic support. When the Arab armies arrived in Alexandria to complete their conquest of Egypt in 642, one suspects that the Monophysite Copts felt little loss at the defeat and final departure of their Greek Dyophysite oppressors.

Egypt has proven to be a valuable source of primary data for the study of early Christianity. Its dry sands and its monasteries have preserved countless documents that would otherwise have been lost. Papyrus finds have supplied the earliest surviving evidence of many biblical texts. Noncanonical, heterodox material, such as the predominantly Gnostic collection of texts found at Nag Hammadi, have offered a unique window into the diversity of earliest Christianity. Finally, a wealth of private, business, and legal documents have begun to shed significant light on the social world of the early Christians. *See also* Alexandria;

Anthony; Arius; Athanasius; Clement of Alexandria; Copts; Cyril of Alexandria; Dyophisitism; Gnosticism; Monasticism; Monophysitism; Pachomius; Shenoute; Theophilus of Alexandria. [J.E.G.]

Bibliography

E.L. Butcher, *The Story of the Church of Egypt: Being an Outline of the History of the Egyptians Under Their Successive Masters from the Roman Conquest Until Now* (London: Smith, Elder, 1897); J.G. Milne, *A History of Egypt Under Roman Rule*, 3rd ed. (London: Methuen, 1924); W. Bauer, *Orthodoxy and Heresy in Early Christianity*, ed. R.A. Kraft and G. Krodel (Philadelphia: Fortress, 1971; orig. German ed.,1964); H.I. Bell, *Egypt from Alexander the Great to the Arab Conquest: A Study in the Diffusion and Decay of Hellenism* (Oxford: Clarendon, 1948); E.R. Hardy, *Christian Egypt: Church and People: Christianity and Nationalism in the Patriarchate of Alexandria* (New York: Oxford UP, 1952); M. Roncaglia, *Histoire de l'église copte* (Beirut: Dar al-Kalima, 1966–1973); C.H. Roberts, *Manuscript, Society and Belief in Early Christian Egypt* (London: Oxford UP, 1979); C.W. Griggs, "The History of Christianity in Egypt to 451 A.D." (Ph.D. diss., University of California, Berkeley, 1979); N. Lewis, *Life in Egypt Under Roman Rule* (Oxford: Clarendon, 1983); B.A. Pearson and J.E. Goehring, eds., *The Roots of Egyptian Christianity* (Philadelphia: Fortress, 1986); A.K. Bowman, *Egypt after the Pharaohs: 332 B.C.–A.D.642: From Alexander to the Arab Conquest* (Berkeley: U of California Press, 1986).

ELECTION TO CHURCH OFFICE. Magistrates in Greece were elected by the citizens. The vote was taken by a show of hands, which was the original meaning of *cheirotonia*, the word for ordination in later Christian usage. Republican Rome and the Romanized towns under the early empire chose their magistrates by election, the outcome of which was determined by the majority in the various voting divisions. The imperial system reduced the role of popular elections in Rome, but elsewhere political offices on the local level continued to be filled by this method. Both Greek and Roman private associations chose their officers by election, and some civic priesthoods in Greece were filled in this manner.

The evidence for election among the Jews is not so extensive, but there are indications that Hellenistic Jews followed Greek precedents in electing their community officers. At least some leaders of the Essenes were chosen by the congregation (1QSA 1.13–17; CD 10.4–6).

The Book of Acts gives considerable emphasis to community choice among the early Christians: the choice of two candidates to succeed Judas as an apostle (Acts 1:23), the selection of seven ministers of benevolence in Jerusalem (6:3–5), the approval of the Holy Spirit's call of Paul and Barnabas to mission work (13:2f.), the deliberations over circumcision and choice of delegates by the Jerusalem church (15:22; cf. 2 Cor. 8:19).

The *Didache* 15 enjoined Christians to "elect for yourselves bishops and deacons," and *1 Clement* 44 referred to bishops "appointed by the apostles and afterward by other eminent men with the consent of the whole church." Ignatius expected a congregational election of a church's delegates (*Philad.* 10.1; *Smyrn.* 11.2; *Polyc.* 7.2). Election by the people was one of the methods of appointment known to Origen (*Hom.* 13 *in Num.* 4). Cyprian described a procedure of selection involving clerical nomination, popular election, and episcopal ordination (*Ep.* 55.8f.; cf. 67.3f.) that became widespread in the western half of the church (cf. Hippolytus, *Trad. ap.* 2.1–5). The will of the populace could prevail over clerical opposition (Sulpicius Severus, *V. Mart.* 9).

In the Greek east, episcopal elections seem to have followed closely what is known of procedures in Greek civil elections. There were "those presiding at the vote"; nomination was important (related in the Christian context to the expectation of divine guidance); the votes (taken down by the deacons) often resulted in a division in which there was no clear majority; but the desire was to secure as unanimous a decision as possible (*V. Polyc.* 22; Gregory of Nyssa, *V. Gr. Thaum.* [PG 46.933ff.]). Unanimity was taken as an indication of God's choice (Ambrose, *Ep.* 63.2; Gregory of Nyssa, *Ep.* 17). Omens or signs sometimes swayed the people's choice, as a dove settling on the head of Fabian (Eusebius, *H.E.* 6.29) or the child's exclamation "Ambrose bishop!" (Paulinus, *V.S. Amb.* 3.6).

Episcopal elections could generate all the fervor of modern political campaigns: "The populace was divided into several parties, each with its own candidate, as is usual in such cases . . .; but at last the whole people came to an agreement, and with the aid of a band of soldiers . . . brought him against his will to the sanctuary, and setting him before the bishops, begged with entreaties mingled with violence that he might be consecrated" (Gregory of Nazianzus, *Or.* 18.33). Such displays prompted the clergy to keep a tight hold on the process of election (Laodicea, *can.* 13). Even in circumstances where the choice of bishops was made by the clergy, the people gave their approbation through the acclamation that the candidate was "worthy" (Athanasius, *Apol. sec.* 6; Theodoret, *H.E.* 4.20; Theophilus of Alexandria, *can.* 6). *See also* Ordination.

[E.F.]

Bibliography

E. Staveley, *Greek and Roman Voting and Elections* (Ithaca: Cornell UP, 1972); E. Ferguson, "Qumran and Codex D," *Revue de Qumran* 8 (1972):75–80; idem, "Origen and the Election of Bishops," *ChHist* 43 (1974):26–33.

ELECTION TO SALVATION. Act of the divine will referring to God's choice of persons to salvation. The term "election" is often used in close connection with "predestination." The latter term suggests that God's sovereign choice was exercised from eternity prior to a person's existence (cf. Eph. 1:4). However, "election" and "predestination" are frequently used interchangeably.

God's election of people is wholly an act of grace and is in no way dependent upon human achievement (Rom. 11:6). Nevertheless, Christians are exhorted to make their gratuitous election sure by living in obedience to the call of the sovereign God (2 Peter 1:10). The objects of the divine choice are both individual and corporate. In the Pauline writings, the election of ethnic Israel is extended to the election of a spiritual community of believers in Christ consisting of Jews and Gentiles, identified as a "new Israel" (Rom. 9–11). In subsequent centuries, the patristic theologians reiterated the idea that the election of the Christian church replaced the election of Israel. It

has been argued that the popularity of this theme in patristic writings can be ascribed to the early Christians' polemic against Judaism.

In the first four centuries, the doctrine of election was not formally treated, and all the patristic references to this teaching are incidental. The views of the early theologians cover the whole spectrum, from a fatalistic concept of God's election on the one hand to a strong emphasis on the free will of a person to choose good or bad on the other. Thus, Clement of Rome (*1 Clem.* 2.4) equates those who are saved with those who are elected by God, while Clement of Alexandria (*Str.* 5; 6.6) says that one should blame oneself if one is not elected and choose rather to leap out of the ship into the sea. It seems as if the church fathers believed that God especially elected the martyrs from among the believers and that they formed an elite group within the elect (*M. Polyc.* 20.1).

The idea of election was prominent in sects associated with Gnosticism. The Manichaeans, for instance, distinguished between an elite circle of elect and a mass of laymen known as hearers. The elect, who were always few in number, were ascetics and vegetarians and were distinguished by white robes.

Around 400, the issue of election, as well as the agelong controversy over determinism and indeterminism (debated also by pagan philosophers), was brought to a head by Pelagius. He taught that everyone had free will to resist God's call. One can choose either to do evil or to keep the commandments of God, if one really desires to do so. Augustine opposed Pelagius and taught that all people were sinners. From these sinners, a strictly limited number were elected to receive God's unmerited grace in order to replace the fallen angels (*Enchir.* 61–62; but cf. *Civ. Dei* 22.1). This operation of God's grace in the hearts of the elect was irresistible. At the Council of Carthage (418), Pelagianism was condemned. In 529, the Council of Orange upheld the Augustinian position on the necessity and priority of grace for salvation. *See also* Grace; Predestination.

[H.F.S.]

Bibliography

Clement of Alexandria, *Miscellanies* 5.13; Pelagius, *De natura*; idem, *De libero arbitrio*; idem,

De induratione cordis Pharaonis; Augustine, *On Nature and Grace*; idem, *Letter* 140; idem, *On the Grace of Christ*; idem, *On the Proceedings of Pelagius*; idem, *On the Predestination of Saints.*

G.S. Faber, *The Primitive Doctrine of Election*, 2nd ed. (London: Blenkarn, 1842); E. Jauncey, *The Doctrine of Grace up to the End of the Pelagian Controversy* (New York: Macmillan, 1925); H.H. Rowley, *The Biblical Doctrine of Election* (London: Lutterworth, 1950); G.C. Berkouwer, *Divine Election* (Grand Rapids: Eerdmans, 1960).

ELEUTHERUS. Bishop of Rome (ca. 171–189). Eusebius (*H.E.* 5.3.4) says that letters concerning Montanus from martyrs in Lyons and Vienne were addressed to him. Tertullian (*Prax.* 1) mentions a Roman bishop who supported Montanus, then changed his mind, but he does not name him. Bede (*H.E.* 4) connects Eleutherus with the origin of British Christianity, but his evidence is late and confused. Feast day May 26. [F.W.N.]

Bibliography
Eusebius, *Church History* 4.22.3; 5. pref.; 5.4–6; *Liber Pontificalis* 14 (Duchesne 1.136).

ELISHE VARDAPET (d. ca. 480). Bishop in Armenia. A student of Mashtots, Elishe (Elisaeus) was among the founders of Armenian literature. His authorship of the most famous work attributed to him, a history of the Vardanian War (449–451), in which the Armenians fought for independence from Persia, is questioned. [E.F.]

Bibliography
R.W. Thompson, tr., *History of Vardan and the Armenian War* (Cambridge: Harvard UP, 1982).

ELKESAITES. Jewish-Christian Gnostic sect. The Elkesaites are mentioned in Origen's "public address on the 82nd Psalm," which is included only as a fragment cited by Eusebius (*H.E.* 6.38); the first extensive treatment of the Elkesaites occurs in Hippolytus (*Haer.* 9.8–12; 10.25). These two third-century descriptions were elaborated during the fourth and fifth centuries in the heresiological writings of both Epiphanius of Salamis (*Haer.* 19; 30.17; 53) and Theodoret of Cyrus (*Haer.* 2.7), who seems not to know Epiphanius's reference.

According to Hippolytus, the Elkesaites arrived in Rome in the second century in the person of Alcibiades from Apameia of Syria, castigated as a despicable character. He brought a book of revelatory instructions, assumed to have been obtained by one Elkesai. Origen, followed by Theodoret, merely relates that the book was said "to have fallen out of the heavens." Hippolytus, however, details the time, the location, and the process: he refers twice, within what appear to be direct quotations, to "the third year of Trajan's reign" (100/1), a date that had eschatological significance for the group's originating prophecy. The book had appeared in Parthia, at a place called Sera, or among a group named Sēres (cf. Ps.-Clementines, *Recog.* 8.48; 9.19). It was brought by angels, each ninety-six Roman miles tall, one male (the Son of God), the other female (the Holy Spirit—a gender designation appropriate only in a Semitic environment), who, through Elkesai, delivered the book's contents to one Sobiai.

Hippolytus claims to have resisted the movement's arrival in Rome; according to Eusebius, it had no sooner begun than it was quenched. But Epiphanius still knew of members who survived into his time, including two women, Marthus and Marthana. (The old suggestion that these are instead two "bishops" each with the Syriac honorific title *Mar* could indicate a more thriving group.) These two were claimed to be descendants of Ieksai (Aramaic, "hidden lord"), brother of Elkesai ("hidden power"). If Sobiai is any clue, there may well be a tie to the familiar Quranic correlation of the three groups that lie behind Islam—Jews, Christians, and Sabaeans—a suggestion made by the tenth-century Islamic encyclopedist Ishāq an-Nadīm in his list of authors, *Kitab al-Fihrist*: there was a sect of Sabaeans of the marshlands who practiced frequent religious washings and who identified al-Hasīh as their founder (9.1, Dodge ed. II, 811).

Although the Elkesaites had Jewish origins with respect to the doctrine of creation and the validity of the Law for circumcision and life, a peculiar Christological motif entered with a suggestion of "transmigration" into different bodies at different times, of which the "transmigration" into Jesus is but one in the series, followed by one into the Spirit, and so on. The church fathers admit the Elkesaites' use of scripture, noting only their complete rejection of the apostle Paul. It is impossible to ascertain if "transmigration" was in the Elkesaite sources or represents part of the heresiological denigration. Yet the Elkesaites do appear to "gather myths from different systems," including those of astrologers, mathematicians, and magicians.

The Elkesaites were rebaptizers, even for severe breaches of sexual conduct. Epiphanius accused them of holding the belief that idolatry could be acceptable when one is under severe persecution. At their baptisms, there were "seven witnesses adjured by incantation" (or "elements confessed by chants" in Theodoret): the heavens, the water, the holy spirits, the angels of prayer, the oil, the salt, and the earth. Hippolytus gives but a few examples of their formulary but implies similar resorts for medicinal and exorcistic purposes and for the regulation of the influence of astral phenomena. Epiphanius notes the rejection of sacrifices and priestly rites, since fire rather than water is alien to God. Prayer was to be oriented toward Jerusalem alone. Epiphanius preserves one example of words not to be interpreted but to be included in one's prayer, which appear to be Aramaic preserved in Greek letters, with reversed spelling, and repeated twice from middle out to both ends: "I am a witness over you on the day of the great judgment." Hippolytus's final citation indicates the book is not to be read at all, although the precepts are to be carefully guarded, "because not all men are faithful, nor all women upright."

Efforts to tie the Elkesaites to the same source that lies beneath the Pseudo-Clementine *Recognitions* and *Homilies* remain unresolved—awaiting, like the group itself, original documentation. Similarly, the "guilt by association" tendencies of Epiphanius, who brought Essenes or Ebionites into the discussion, seem unwarranted. The Elkesaites have assumed new importance in religious history with the recent discovery that Mani grew up in an Elkesaite community. The Elkesaites remain essentially unknown, save as the first of those Christian-izing splinters upon whom a revelatory book fell directly out of the heavens. *See also* Mani, Manichaeism. [C.C.S.]

Bibliography
Hippolytus, *Refutation of All Heresies* 9.8–12; 10.25; Eusebius, *Church History* 6.38; Epiphanius, *Panarion* 19; 20; 30; 53; Theodoret, *Haereticarum fabularum compendium* 2.7.

The Fihrist of al-Nadīm, ed. and tr. B. Dodge, Vol. 2 (New York: Columbia UP, 1970), pp. 745–825; *Der Kölner Mani-Kodex,* ed. L. Koenen and C. Römer (Bonn: Habelt, 1985).

W. Brandt, *Elchasai: Ein Religionsstifter und sein Werk* (Leipzig: Hinrichs, 1912); H. Waitz, "Das Buch des Elchasai," *Harnack-ehrung* (Leipzig: Hinrichs, 1921), pp. 87–104; J. Irmscher, "The Book of Elchasai," NTA, Vol. 2, pp. 745–750; The Cologne Mani Codex (P. Colon. inv. nr. 4780), *Concerning the Origin of His Body,* tr. R. Cameron and A.J. Dewey (Missoula: Scholars, 1979), pp. 74–79; G.P. Luttikhuizen, *The Revelation of Elchasai: Investigations into the Evidence for a Mesopotamian Jewish Apocalypse of the Second Century and Its Reception by Judeo-Christian Propagandists* (Tübingen: Mohr, 1985).

ELVIRA. City (Roman Illiberis) in southern Spain (near Granada) where the earliest church council known to have been held in Spain met during the first decade of the fourth century. Nineteen bishops, among them Hosius of Cordova, and more than twenty priests were in attendance; the churches represented were located mostly in southern Spain. The council at Elvira dealt primarily with moral issues and the question of pagan influences on church life in what were evidently mixed communities of pagans and Christians. It also considered the situation of the *lapsi,* Christians who had renounced their faith under persecutions. The eighty-one canons adopted, most of them disciplinary in nature, were remarkably severe. Certain of them decreed excommunication without any possibility of reconciliation even at the point of death. Elvira was the first council to impose penalties upon consecrated women who proved unfaithful to their pledge of virginity; they were to be excommunicated and allowed communion only at the end of their lives (*can.* 13). Bishops, priests, deacons, and other ministers were forbidden to live with their wives and to father children under penalty of removal from the clerical state (*can.* 33), the oldest legislation ordering clerical continence. Religious images were prohibited on the walls of Christian churches (*can.* 36), probably to avoid confusion with pagan practice. Two canons, 63 and 68, were directed against either abortion or infanticide; the Council of Ancyra (314) would condemn both practices, although changing the lifelong excommunication imposed by Elvira to ten years' duration. One effect of the Elvira council was to strengthen the authority of the bishops. Attempts to question the authenticity of its canons by ascribing them to a later compilation have not met with general acceptance. [M.P.McH.]

Bibliography

A.C. Vega, ed., *De la Santa Iglesia Apostólica de Eliberri (Granada)*, 4 vols. (Madrid: Maestre, 1957, 1961); J. Vives et al., *Concilios visigóticos e hispano-romanos* (Madrid: Instituto Enrique Flores, 1963), pp. 1–15.

S. Laeuchli, *Power and Sexuality: The Emergence of Canon Law at the Synod of Elvira* (Philadelphia: Temple UP, 1972); rev. in *VChr* 29 (1975):75f.; M. Meigne, "Concile ou collection d'Elvire?," *RHE* 70 (1975):361–387; R. Grigg, "Aniconic Worship and the Apologetic Tradition: A Note on Canon 36 of the Council of Elvira," *ChHist* 45 (1976):428–433; R. García Villoslada, *Historia de la Iglesia en España I* (Madrid: Edica, 1979), pp. 81–119; J. Orlandis and D. Ramos Lisson, *Die Synoden auf der Iberischen Halbinsel bis zum Einbruch des Islam (711)* (Paderborn: Schöningh, 1981), pp. 3–30.

ENCRATITES. Christian sect characterized by strict regulations and ascetic tendencies. The name Encratites ("Abstinents") is derived from a Greek word (*enkrateia*) denoting "continence" or "self-control." The sect of the Encratites originated in the second century, but the name was also indiscriminately applied to many different groups with rigorous teachings.

Irenaeus relates that the Encratites proceeded from Saturninus and Marcion (*Haer.* 1.28); however, both Eusebius (*H.E.* 4.29.6) and Jerome (*Jov.* 1.3) describe Tatian, a Syrian by birth, as the founder of the sect of the Encratites. Tatian became a Christian in Rome, but he gradually adopted an ascetic form of Christian life. He broke away from the church, and ca. 172 he returned to his native Mesopotamia, which was more favorable to his ascetic views. Encratite tendencies had probably already appeared in Syria and Mesopotamia before Tatian's return and had come down from the Jewish Christian origins of the church. Nevertheless, Tatian became an important exponent of the teachings of the Encratites.

According to Irenaeus, Tatian condemned matrimony and regarded all sexual relations as impure. Jerome states that Tatian's Encratite view of marriage was based on the text "For he who sows to his own flesh will from the flesh reap corruption" (Gal. 6:8). Tatian explained this verse as meaning that he who has intercourse with his wife will reap perdition. Tatian even compared marriage with fornication and the corruption of boys (*Orat.* 8).

The Encratites condemned the use of wine and even substituted water for wine in the eucharist. Thus, they and other groups adhering to this practice, such as the Ebionites, acquired the titles *Hydroparastatae* ("water supporters") and *Aquarii* ("water-carriers"). The Encratites also refrained from the use of animal food. In the name of Christian perfection, they denounced all worldly goods and practiced an ascetic form of life.

According to Hippolytus (*Haer.* 8.13), the doctrine of some Encratites concerning God and Christ resembled that of the orthodox church. He says that the Encratites differed from their orthodox brothers only in the radicalism of their mode of life. Many of the Encratites, however, were dualists. They regarded flesh as evil and spirit as good. This also explains their emphasis on abstinence.

Eusebius (*H.E.* 4.29) writes that some of them rejected the epistles of Paul and the Acts of the Apostles. Tatian gave this sect a more complete canon, including Paul's epistles, and he also compiled the *Diatessaron*, a harmony of the four Gospels. Many Encratite ideas are embodied in the Apocryphal Acts. Epiphanius writes that the Encratites also used the "so-called *Acts of Andrew, of Thomas,* and *of John.*"

Other prominent figures in the Encratite movement were Julius Cassianus (Clement of Alexandria, *Str.* 1.21) and Severus (Eusebius,

H.E. 4.29). Sozomen also writes about Busiris, a member of the Encratites, who was imprisoned during the time of Julian for ridiculing the pagans (*H.E.* 5.11). The adherents of the Encratite sect were gradually absorbed by other ascetic movements. [H.F.S.]

Bibliography

Irenaeus, *Against Heresies* 1.28; Clement of Alexandria, *Miscellanies* 7.17.108.2; Hippolytus, *Refutation of All Heresies* 8; 13; Eusebius, *Church History* 4.29; Epiphanius, *Panarion* 46–47; Jerome, *Against Jovinian* 1.3; idem, *Commentarii in epistulam ad Galatas* 6; Sozomen, *Church History* 5.11.

G. Blond, "L'Hérésie encratite vers la fin du quatrième siècle," *RecSR* 31 (1944):159–210; R.M. Grant, "The Heresy of Tatian," *JThS* n.s. 5 (1954):62–68; L.W. Barnard, "The Heresy of Tatian—Once Again," *JEH* 19 (1968):1–10.

ENGLAND. *See* Great Britain.

ENNODIUS (ca. 473–521). Bishop, rhetorician, and writer. Probably a native of Arles, Ennodius entered the clerical state (ca. 494) in Pavia, where he had been brought up. He spent many years in Milan, writing and teaching rhetoric, until his consecration as bishop of Pavia (ca. 511). Pope Hormisdas twice sent him (515, 517) to bring about a reconciliation of the schism resulting from the excommunication of Acacius of Constantinople. A prolific writer, Ennodius is the author of some 300 letters, which are important source material for the early sixth century; he also wrote discourses (*Dictiones*) on diverse topics sacred and secular; poetry, including hymns modeled on those of Ambrose, and epigrams; a panegyric on the Arian king Theodoric; biographies of his predecessor, Epiphanius of Pavia (d. 496), and of the monk Anthony of Lérins; the *Eucharisticon*, a religious autobiography modeled on the *Confessions* of Augustine; and other works. A defender of pope Symmachus in the latter's dispute with Laurentius over the papal succession, Ennodius upheld the exemption of the papacy from interference by secular authority. CPL 1487–1503. [M.P.McH.]

Bibliography

Life of St. Epiphanius, tr. G.M. Cook, *Early Christian Biographies,* FOTC (1952), Vol. 15, pp. 301–351;

Repertorium Fontium Historiae Medii Aevi (Rome: Istituto Storico Italiano per il Medio Evo, 1976), Vol. 4, pp. 328–330 (bibliography).

ENOCH. Antediluvian patriarch (Gen. 5:24). Jews developed many legends about Enoch, and Hebrews 11:5 includes him in its roll call of faith. The longest and for religious ideas the most significant book in the Old Testament Pseudepigrapha is *1 Enoch,* whose language and ideas have many points of contact with the New Testament (quoted in Jude 14–15). *1 Enoch* is a composite of at least five writings from the second century B.C. to the first century A.D. It survives entire only in Ethiopic, but there are important Aramaic fragments from the Dead Sea Scrolls. The contents include information on the origin of evil and demons, the expectation of a "Son of Man," astrology, the punishment of sinners, and the blessedness of the righteous. *1 Enoch* was occasionally treated as inspired scripture in the early church (*Barn.* 16.4; Tertullian, *Cult. fem.* 1.3.1), but generally it was rejected (Origen, *Cels.* 5.54; cf. *Princ.* 4.4.8). *2 Enoch* survives only in Slavonic and comes from the early centuries of the Christian era. It recounts how Enoch was taken through the seven heavens and was shown the future. [E.F.]

Bibliography

M.A. Knibb and E. Ullendorff, *The Ethiopic Book of Enoch: A New Edition in the Light of the Aramaic Dead Sea Fragments,* 2 vols. (Oxford: Clarendon, 1978).

E. Isaac, "1 (Ethiopic Apocalypse of) Enoch," and F.I. Anderson, "2 (Slavonic Apocalypse of) Enoch," *The Old Testament Pseudepigrapha,* ed. J.H. Charlesworth (Garden City: Doubleday, 1983), Vol. 1, pp. 5–221; M. Black, *The Book of Enoch or 1 Enoch: A New English Edition with Commentary and Textual Notes* (Leiden: Brill, 1985).

EPARCHY. Province, from the Greek word equivalent to the Latin *provincia.* In early Christian times, an eparchy was a fundamental administrative unit in the political structure of the Roman empire; it had Greek antecedents. It was always a region with several small towns or cities located around a mother town or city, the "metropolis." Several eparchies formed a diocese (*dioicesis* or *administratio*); and several of these formed the hyparchy or prefecture. From the second century onward, the church, as a result of its steady growth within the Roman empire, adopted this political-administrative structure, a structure that came to include groups of bishops belonging to the same province and forming a provincial synod, which was centered on or chaired by a metropolitan bishop. The grouping in turn of metropolitans around the bishop of a city of higher political rank led to the institution of the patriarchate.

Under Constantine, the Roman state was divided into four great hyparchies (*praefecturae*): the East, Illyricum, Italy, and Gaul. The hyparchy of the East was subdivided into five dioceses—the diocese of the East, comprising fifteen eparchies and centered on the metropolis of Antioch; Egypt, comprising six eparchies and centered on the metropolis of Alexandria; Asia, comprising ten eparchies and centered on the metropolis of Ephesus; Pontus, comprising eleven eparchies and centered on the metropolis of Caesarea of Cappadocia; and Thrace, comprising six eparchies and centered on the metropolis of Constantinople. The hyparchy of Illyricum was subdivided into two dioceses—Macedonia, with seven eparchies and Thessalonica as the metropolis, and Dacia, with five eparchies. The hyparchy of Italy had four dioceses—Rome, with ten eparchies; Italy with six eparchies and Milan as the metropolis; West Africa, with six eparchies and Carthage as the metropolis; and West Illyria, with six eparchies and Sirmium as the metropolis. The hyparchy of Gaul comprised three dioceses—Gaul, with fourteen eparchies; Spain, with seven; and Britain, with five.

The structure of the church exactly reflected this division of the Roman empire, and later modifications did not alter its fundamental shape. The canons of many early councils, local or universal, dealt with matters relating to ecclesiastical eparchies, to metropolitans, and to exarchs or patriarchs (e.g., Nicaea, *can.* 4–7; Constantinople, *can.* 2–3; 6; Ephesus, *can.* 1–2; 8; Chalcedon, *can.* 12; 17; 19; 28). The Council of Chalcedon (451) was decisive for establishing the so-called pentarchy of patriarchs (Rome, Constantinople, Alexandria, Antioch, and Jerusalem), under which the various ecclesiastical eparchies in east and west were grouped and which survived until the division of the eastern and western churches.   [G.D.D.]

Bibliography

W.H. Bright, *The Definitions of the Catholic Faith and the Canons of Discipline of the First Four General Councils of the Universal Church* [in Greek and English] (Oxford: James Parker, 1874); G.B. Howard, *The Canons of the Primitive Church* (Oxford: James Parker, 1896).

W.H. Bright, *Notes on the Canons of the First Four General Councils* (Oxford: Clarendon, 1882); E.W. Kemp, "Councils and Provinces in the Early Church," *Council and Consent* (London: SPCK, 1961); W. De Vries, *Orient et Occident* (Paris: Cerf, 1974); Maximus, Metropolitan of Sardes, *The Ecumenical Patriarchate in the Orthodox Church* (Thessalonica: Patriarchal Institute of Patristic Studies, 1976); V. Phidas, *The Institution of the Pentarchy of the Patriarchs* [in Greek], 2 vols. (Athens, 1977).

EPHESUS, EPHESIANS. Principal city of Roman province of Asia and New Testament epistle. Scholars have vigorously debated the destination and authorship of the epistle to the Ephesians for decades. Resolution of the issue of authorship depends on the flexibility and variety one allows in Paul's correspondence. The omission at Ephesians 1:1 of the phrase *en Epheso* in the Chester Beatty Papyri and several important witnesses has led some scholars to regard the document as originally a circular letter wherein the names of various destinations could be added when appropriate. Although initially attractive, this theory is improbable, since undisputed circular letters preserved in the New Testament (Rev.; 1 Peter; Gal.) never reflect this procedure. The ostensible lack of specificity in the epistle has also been used to advance the idea that Ephesians was an encyclical letter. However, only when it is judged by criteria of other Pauline letters and not on its own terms is one led to conclude that Ephesians was not occasional like the other Pauline letters.

Studies in ancient Greek letter writing have demonstrated that authors often use *parakalo* ("urge, beseech, implore") to highlight the intent of their letters. Therefore, the use of *parakalo* in Ephesians 4:1 should mark it not

Ruins of the Church of St. Mary (from the well in the courtyard toward the nave),
where the Third Ecumenical Council, 431, met in Ephesus, Turkey.

only as the thematic verse, but also as the hinge that joins the indicative (doctrinal) and imperative (practical) components that are so typical of Pauline letters. The use of the *mēketi* ("no longer—Eph. 4:14, 17, 28) and the present active imperative (Eph. 4:26, 29, 30; 5:7, 11, 15, 17, 18; 6:4) reveals specific behavioral problems in the Ephesian community that served as the occasion of writing. One may paraphrase 4:1 as "walk and live in a way that is commensurate with the divine election that you received." Accordingly, chapters 1–3 are a presentation of this election and calling of the saints; chapters 4–6 depict the ethical lifestyle and moral imperatives that form the appropriate response to God's merciful election and grace.

The concentration of Old Testament and Jewish themes and terms in Chapters 1–3 can best be explained by positing a situation wherein a predominantly Gentile church (e.g., Eph. 2:11; 3:1; 4:17) had forsaken its Old Testament heritage and identity, perhaps in response to pervasive Greco-Roman anti-Semi-

tism, and thereby assumed an ethical posture not substantially different from its pagan environment. This would explain the strong Jewish vocabulary used in Ephesians 2:11–22 to interpret a Gentile church's self-identity.

Ephesus. Ephesus was a major urban port in antiquity located on the western coast of Turkey. It is mentioned in Hittite texts, and the earliest artifacts there date from the late Bronze Age. Its propitious site at the nexus of travel and commerce between Greece and the east ensured it a place in the mainstream of Hellenistic, Roman, and Byzantine culture and history.

Contrary to common conjecture, the harbor at Ephesus was still functional in the later Roman era. Fifth-century ecclesiastical officials chose Ephesus as the site for the councils of 431 and 449, in part, because of the city's accessibility to those arriving by land or by sea (ACO 1.1.3.31). The problem of alluvium in the harbor did not arrest the city's prosperity and growth (est. pop. 250,000) during the Roman and early Byzantine periods. Earthquakes and invasions were of more significance than the silting harbor. These finally led to a severe diminution of the city's size in the Byzantine period, followed by the relocation (made possible by the construction of an aqueduct) of the city's center to Ayasolouk Hill.

According to Acts 19, Paul was significant in introducing the gospel to Ephesus. It became the matrix of early Pauline and Johannine Christianity as well as a literary center of primitive Christianity. Paul's longest recorded missionary effort was at Ephesus (Acts 19:10; 20:31). 1 and 2 Corinthians and Romans were written during or shortly after Paul's stay there. 1 and 2 Timothy were written to Timothy at Ephesus, and an Ephesian incarceration may have provided the context for certain Pauline "Prison Epistles." Timothy reportedly became bishop of Ephesus and was martyred there (Eusebius, H.E. 3.4.5). His relics were later (356) transported to Constantinople.

The New Testament never places the apostle John's residence in Ephesus, though this belief appears early in Christian tradition (Irenaeus, Haer. 2.22.5; 3.3.4; Clement of Alexandria, Q.d.s. 42). The issue of John's presence in Ephesus is connected with literary questions regarding the Epistles of John, the Gospel of John, and the Revelation of John. For a variety of reasons, some have postulated the existence of two different writers of this name, one an important Christian leader in the Asian church and the other the apostle of Jesus (cf. Dionysius of Alexandria in Eusebius, H.E. 3.39.5–7; 7.24.7). The prevailing, although not unanimous, verdict of the ancient church (Justin, Dial. 81.4, for Revelation; Eusebius, H.E. 3.1.1; 3.23.4–5; 3.24–25) was that the apostle authored the Epistles, the Gospel, and the Revelation and was subsequently buried at Ephesus.

By the second century (M. Polyc. 17–18), some Christians were interpreting the graves and remains of the martyrs and spiritual leaders in ways adapted from pagan hero cults. Such was the attitude toward John's grave even in the pre-Constantinian period. This led later to the construction of a chapel over the side of his interment. Byzantine pilgrims visited the grave for cures, and a cathedral was built over the purported grave by the emperor Justinian.

At the outset of Ephesian Christianity, issues of orthodoxy and heterodoxy were recurrent. The presence of heresy can be inferred from Acts 20:29–30; 1 Timothy 1:3, 18–20; 4:1–5 (cf. 1 Cor. 15:32; 16:9b) and the patent theological focus of the Johannine Epistles and Gospel. The Epistles, as well as later tradition (Irenaeus, Haer. 3.3.4), are clear about John's opposition to inchoate Gnosticism at Ephesus. By the early second century, however, primitive orthodoxy was secured. There is no reason to doubt contemporary authors who express confidence that the Ephesian church neither brooked false apostles (Rev. 2:2) nor allowed evil doctrine to be sown in the hearing of Christians (Ignatius, Eph. 9). Nevertheless, the city was no stranger to controversy. The Ephesian bishop Polycrates opposed Victor of Rome in the Quartodeciman issue at the end of the second century, and later many of its bishops were Arians. Ephesus eventually lost its position as the ecclesiastical metropolis of Asia Minor to Constantinople, although not without a fight.

Later Ephesian ecclesiastical history is associated with Mary, the mother of Jesus. Roman Catholic interpreters usually point to Revelation 12:1–6 and Ignatius of Antioch's Ephesians 18–19 to support early veneration of the Blessed Virgin Mary, particularly in Roman Asia. The later touchstone for the veneration of Mary was the term Theotokos ("God-bearer"). A Byzantine inscriptional intercessory prayer addressed to Mary as Theotokos was discovered at Ephesus. The Greek epithet Aeiparthenos ("perpetual virgin"), employed earlier in Ephesian epigraphy for the goddess Hestia, was also a favorite term among the Monophysites.

In the fifth century, Nestorius and other anti-Monophysites disavowed Theotokos because of its dangerous theological implications regarding the nature of Christ; Cyril of Alexandria and others, including the Roman bishop Celestine I, supported it. The Council of Ephesus in 431 sided with Cyril in legitimating Theotokos. Although ordered to attend the council meetings, Nestorius chose to remain under the protection of armed guards at his place of lodging. Many of his supporters avoided the meeting, while others had not yet arrived. With no opposition present, the proceedings of the council were conducted quickly. Cyril had Nestorius's views recapitulated and condemned. Memnon, bishop of Ephesus, aligned himself with Cyril. He may have been partially motivated by the desire to forge an alliance with Cyril of Alexandria against Nestorius of Constantinople, since the see of Constantinople was encroaching upon Ephesus's ecclesiastical hegemony.

The "Robber Council" of Ephesus (*Latrocinium*) in 449 centered on Monophysite personalities and issues. Eutyches of Constantinople had been convicted of Christological heresy in 448, accused by bishop Eusebius of Doryleum, who had also accused Nestorius two decades earlier in 431. Through Eutyches's nepotistic influence with the court of Theodosius II, a council was convened to exonerate him. The council was labeled "robber" by pope Leo (451) because of its violent character and theological error. The reprieve for Eutyches and Monophysitism was temporary, as both were condemned at the Council of Chalcedon (451).

An abundance of Christian material culture and ruins has been excavated at Ephesus during the past century. This includes over a dozen church buildings and shrines, especially the Church of St. John, the Church of St. Mary, and the Cave of the Seven Sleepers; scores of inscriptions and graffiti written by indigenous and pilgrim Christians; three baptisteries (the Church of St. Mary, the Church of St. John, the Temple of Sarapis); and numerous Christian symbols and artworks. A lintel inscription containing apocryphal correspondence between Jesus and Abgar (cf. Eusebius, *H.E.* 1.13.5) was erected in the fifth–sixth century to protect the city of Ephesus by means of its supposed apotropaic qualities. Epigraphical documents from a sixth-century bishop of Ephesus, Hypatius, have been discovered. During his tenure as bishop, Hypatius's well-known defense of icons came to concrete expression in the construction of the Church of St. John, which abounded in images and biblical scenes.

The monasteries and numerous pilgrimage sites in Ephesus—such as relics of Timothy, relics and the church of St. John, the tomb of Mary Magdalene, the tomb of the virgin daughters of Philip, the Cave of the Seven Sleepers—further attest to the city's significance in Byzantine Christianity.

Acts 19, the apocryphal *Acts of John*, and the works of later fathers testify to various stages of conflict between Christianity and the religion of the Ephesian Artemis. Although Paul was first mentioned in this connection (Acts 19), the apostle John is usually the Christian protagonist in later literature. In one Syriac account, he converted 40,000 Ephesians. With the damage (whose extent is debated) brought by Gothic armies of the third century and the subsequent conversion of Constantine, the official influence of the cult of Artemis waned. Her unofficial influence, some have suggested, continued through the rise of the cult of the Blessed Virgin Mary. The vast amount of marble from the temple of Artemis was eventually taken and used in ecclesiastical and secular buildings of the Byzantine period. The fragmentary remains of her temple foundation were discovered only in the nineteenth century. *See also* Christ, Christology; Cyril of Alexandria; Nestorius. [R.O.]

Bibliography

John Chrysostom, *Homilies on Ephesians*, tr. W.J. Copeland, NPNF, 1st ser. (1889), Vol. 13; Marius Victorinus, *Commentarii in Epistulam ad Ephesios*, PL 8.1255–1294; Ambrosiaster, *Commentarius in Epistolam ad Ephesios*, ed. H.J. Vogels, CSEL (1966–1969), Vol. 81; Pelagius, *Expositio in Ephesios*, ed. A. Souter, TS 9.2 (1926):344–386; Jerome, *Commentarii in Epistulam ad Ephesios*, PL 26.467–590; Theodoret, *Interpretatio Epistolae ad Ephesios*, PG 82.505–557.

B.F. Westcott, *Saint Paul's Epistle to the Ephesians* (London: Macmillan, 1906); M. Barth, *Ephesians*, 2 vols. (Garden City: Doubleday, 1974); F.F. Bruce, *The Epistles to the Colossians, to Philemon, and to the Ephesians* (Grand Rapids: Eerdmans, 1984).

ACO; A. d'Alès, *Le Dogme d'Ephèse*, 2nd ed. (Paris: Beauchesne, 1931); P.-T. Camelot, *Ephèse et Chalcédoine* (Paris: Orante, 1962); A.J. Festugière, *Ephèse et Chalcédoine: Actes des conciles* (Paris: Beauchesne, 1982); M. O'Carroll, *Theotokos: A Theological Encyclopedia of the Blessed Virgin Mary* (Wilmington: Glazier, 1983).

D. Knibbe, "Ephesos: A. Historisch-epigraphischer Teil," W. Alzinger, "Ephesos: B. Archäeologischer Teil," and S. Karwiese, "Ephesos: C. Numismatischer Teil," in *Paulys Realencyclopädie der classischen Altertumswissenschaft*, Supplementband 12, ed. K. Ziegler (Stuttgart: Druckenmuller, 1970), pp. 248–297, 1588–1704, 297–364; R. Oster, "The Ephesian Artemis as an Opponent of Early Christianity," *JAC* 19 (1976):24–44; B. Kötting, *Peregrinatio Religiosa: Wallfahrten in der Antike und das Pilgerwesen in der alten Kirche*, 2nd ed. (Münster: Antiquariat Stenderhoff, 1980); C. Foss, *Ephesus After Antiquity: A Late Antique, Byzantine, and Turkish City* (Cambridge: Cambridge UP, 1979); T. Klauser, "Gottesgebärerin," RLAC (1981), Vol. 11, pp. 1071–1103; W. Elliger, *Ephesos: Geschichte einer antiken Weltstadt* (Stuttgart: Kohlhammer, 1985); R. Oster, *A Bibliography of Ancient Ephesus* (Metuchen: Scarecrow, 1987).

EPHRAEM THE SYRIAN (ca. 306–373). Syrian hymnist (known as "Harp of the Spirit"), exegete, teacher, deacon, of Nisibis and Edessa. Born to Christian parents (*C.H.* 26.10), in or near Nisibis (Sozomen, *H.E.* 3.16), but baptized as a youth (*C.H.* 3.13; *Virg.* 37.10.1–4), Ephraem composed hymns, homilies, and commentaries and taught under the auspices of the orthodox bishops Jacob, Babu, Vologeses, and Abraham (*C. Nis.* 13–21). When Rome ceded Nisibis to Persia in 363, Ephraem went to Edessa, where he established a school of biblical and theological studies (PO [1907], Vol. 4, p. 377) and women's choirs to sing his hymns (AMS, Vol. 3, pp. 665–678). Ordained to the diaconate, he died ministering to victims of the plague on June 9, 373 (*C.H.* 56.10).

As early as the fifth century, Ephraem's hymns (Syriac *madrāshē*) were gathered according to melody or theme for liturgical use into the following collections: Hymns on Faith (*H.F.*), Hymns Against Heresies (*C.H.*), Hymns on Paradise (*Parad.*), Hymns Against Julian (*C.J.*), Hymns on the Nativity (*Nat.*), Hymns on the Epiphany (*Epiph.*), Hymns on the Church (*Eccl.*), Hymns on Nisibis (*C. Nis.*), Hymns on Virginity (*Virg.*), Hymns on Fasting (*Ieiun.*), Hymns on Unleavened Bread (*Azym.*), Hymns on the Crucifixion (*Cruc.*), Hymns on the Resurrection (*Res.*), Hymns on Abraham Quidunaya (*Abr.*), and Hymns on Juliana Saba (*Jul. Sab.*). He also composed metrical homi-

lies (*mēmrē*) and prose sermons, of which the best known are the anti-Arian *mēmrē* on Faith (*S.F.*) and the Sermon on Our Lord. Other extant prose works are the Letter to Publius, Refutations of Mani, Marcion, Bardesanes, and the astrologers (*Pr. Ref.*), and commentaries on Genesis and Exodus (*Comm. Gen. Ex.*) and on the *Diatessaron* (*Comm. Diat.*), the latter fully extant only in Armenian. Commentaries on other Old Testament books survive in catenae.

Beginning characteristically with the unique Syriac type of ante-Nicene Christianity—with its Encratism, Gnosticism, and special relationship with Judaism—Ephraem introduced these features into an orthodox Christian framework, based upon a vision of the world as a vast system of symbols or mysteries. History and nature constitute the warp and woof of reality. At the center of all is Jesus Christ, the incarnate "Word of the Most High," who plays on "three harps," the Old and New Testaments and Nature (*Virg.* 28–30, esp. 29.1). Because biblical typology plays the central role among the historical symbols, his works provide many examples of typological exegesis. All historical events have religious significance, however, and Ephraem, like the Jewish prophets, contemplates contemporary political and military events in the light of ethics and theology, seeking evidence of divine activity and edifying moral lessons (*C.J.* and *C. Nis.*). Nature, too, is replete with intimations of the presence of God. In creating the world, God deliberately presented humanity not only with examples of beauty and order but also with symbols that allude more richly to the identity of their Creator (*Virg.* 20.12).

A central theological theme is the incarnation as the miraculous and paradoxical self-abasement of God out of love for humankind and the consequent intimacy between the Creator and human beings both collectively and individually (*Nat.* 1.99; 8.2; 21.12.5–6; *Virg.* 1.1–8; 2.15; 23–25). Although it is clear that human beings enjoy a unique position in the world, certain material things, such as oil or ointment, also have a privileged place rooted in nature, in their physical properties, and in their names (*Virg.* 4–7). This concept characterizes but is not limited to Ephraem's sacramental theology; the hymns are rich in imagery drawn from nature or from the world of the artist and artisan. Mariology is closely related to the understanding of the incarnation and the sacraments, and Mary's significance is interpreted through an array of Old Testament types: Eve, Sarah, Rachel, Anna, Tamar, Ruth, and Rahab, and even the table of the Law and the ark of the covenant (*Nat.* 8.13; 13.2–5; 9.7–16; 15.8; 16.12, 16–17).

Although he freely adopted imagery from the noncanonical and possibly heterodox literature of the early Syriac tradition, such as Tatian's *Diatessaron*, the *Odes of Solomon*, and the *Acts of Thomas*, Ephraem's work is consciously orthodox and often polemical in tone. He attacks Mani, Marcion, and Bardesanes (*C.H.*; *Pr. Ref.*), the astrologers (*C.H.*; *Pr. Ref.*; *C.J.*), the Arians (*S.F.*; *H.F.*; *C. Nis.*), the emperor Julian and paganism (*C.J.*), and aspects of Judaism (*Ieiun.*; *Azym.*; *Cruc.*; *Res.*; *Nat.*; *C.J.*). With respect to Judaism, he is unusually well informed despite his frequently bitter polemic; the Hymns on Paradise and Commentaries on Genesis and Exodus are permeated with noncanonical Jewish traditions.

Ephraem's hymns became central to both east and west Syrian liturgical traditions, and his works have influenced all aspects of Syrian ecclesiastical life. His reputation as a hymnodist and ascetic spread to all branches of the church. Greek, Latin, Armenian, Georgian, Slavonic, Coptic, Arabic, and Syro-Palestinian translations of his hymns abound; many, however, are spurious.   [K.McV.]

Bibliography

Syriac hymns and homilies, ed. E. Beck, CSCO 154–413 passim; *Comm. Diat.*, ed. L. Leloir (Dublin: Hodges Figgis, 1963); French tr. L. Leloir, SC (1966), Vol. 121; *Pr. Ref.*, ed. and Engl. tr. C.W. Mitchell, E.A. Bevan, and F.C. Burkitt (London: Williams and Norgate, 1912, 1921); *Comm. Gen. Ex.*, ed. R.-M. Tonneau, CSCO (1955), Vols. 152–153; S. Brock, *The Harp of the Spirit*, 2nd ed. (London: Fellowship of St. Alban and St. Sergius, 1983); K. McVey, *Ephrem the Syrian* (New York: Paulist, 1989). Information on other eds. and trs. in R. Murray, "Ephraem Syrus," TRE (1982), Vol. 9.5, pp. 755–762; S. Brock, "Syriac Studies 1971–1980, a Classified Bibliography," *ParOr* 10 (1981–1982):320–327; J. Melki, "Saint Ephrem: bilan de l'édition critique," *ParOr* 11 (1983):3–88.

E. Beck, et al., "Ephrem le Syrien," *Dictionnaire de Spiritualité*, ed. M. Viller (Paris: Beauchesne, 1960), Vol. 4, cols. 788–822; B. Outtier, "Saint Ephrem d'après ses biographes et ses oeuvres," *ParOr* 4 (1973):11–33; R. Murray, *Symbols of Church and Kingdom: A Study in Early Syriac Tradition* (Cambridge: Cambridge UP, 1975); S. Brock, *The Luminous Eye: The Spiritual World Vision of St. Ephrem* (Rome: Centre for Indian and Inter-Religious Studies, 1985); W.L. Petersen, *The Diatessaron and Ephrem Syrus as Sources of Romanos the Melodist*, CSCO (1986), Vol. 466; S. Griffith, "Ephraem, the Deacon of Edessa, and the Church of the Empire," *Diakonia: Studies in Honor of Robert T. Meyer*, ed. T. Halton and J.P. Williams (Washington, D.C.: Catholic U of America P, 1986), pp. 22–52; P. Tanios Bou Mansour, *La Pensée symbolique de Saint Ephrem le Syrien* (Kaslik: Liban, 1988).

EPICLESIS. Calling-upon or invocation (Greek *epiklēsis*; Latin *invocatio*); technical term for the liturgical invocation of the Holy Spirit, or more properly the invocation of God to send the Holy Spirit. "Epiclesis" is used particularly of the characteristic element of the eucharistic prayers (*anaphorae*) of the eastern churches from the fourth century onward in which God is called upon or invoked to send the Spirit on the offerings of bread and wine in order that they may be or become the body and blood of Christ.

Invocation is, however, a much more general feature of early Christian prayer than this technical use of the term might suggest. The pattern of early Christian prayer, inherited from Jewish prayer, is one in which God is thanked or blessed for the redemptive acts recalled by the people, and implicitly or explicitly called upon to continue those acts on behalf of those who address him. Invocation is thus an implication of all prayers rather than a special feature of some of them; the significance of particular invocations, whatever their precise form, needs to be considered in this wider context. The later western tendency to concentrate on the eucharistic epiclesis, and to regard it as the specific point at which a transformation of the bread and wine is effected, has allowed medieval and Reformation disputes about a "moment of consecration" to obscure this fact.

Specific liturgical invocation of the Spirit upon the water of baptism is probably assumed in Tertullian (*Bapt.* 4) and appears in the prayer text of Serapion (*Euch.* 7). But such an invocation of the Spirit, or of all the persons of the Trinity, is frequently mentioned (Irenaeus, *Frg.* 33; Origen, *Frg.* 36 *in Jo.*; Cyril of Jerusalem, *Catech.* 3.3; Gregory of Nyssa, *Or. catech.* 33), and later appears in the Gelasian and Ambrosian rites in the west. The precise form of the invocation is perhaps less important, especially in view of the oral-formal character of early Christian liturgical prayer, than the underlying conviction that God, through the Spirit, will make the water the effective means of rebirth in Christ.

The earliest explicit reference to invocation in the eucharist is Irenaeus's assertion (*Haer.* 4.31.4) that it is by "the invocation of God" that the eucharistic bread and wine cease to be ordinary bread and wine and become the body and blood of Christ; the first specific invocation of the Spirit appears in Hippolytus (*Trad. ap.* 4), where, after the memorial of the bread and wine, God is asked to send the Spirit "on the offering of your holy church" in order to effect its eschatological unity. Hippolytus's language appears, in retrospect, to lack clarity. But there is good reason to think that it is the basis on which the invocations of Cyril of Jerusalem (*Catech. myst.* 5.7), the *Apostolic Constitutions* 8, Theodore of Mopsuestia (*Serm. catech.* 6), and the liturgies of St. Basil and St. John Chrysostom took shape. Thus, the dual stress on the action of the Spirit upon the bread and wine and upon the community was made more explicit. A different pattern of eucharistic invocation is found in Serapion (*Euch.* 13), where God is asked to send the Spirit upon the church prior to the memorial and to send the Word upon the bread and wine at a later point. Traces of this pattern remain in eastern prayers, and it may have had some influence on the order of petitions in the Roman Canon. But the increasing eastern stress on the Spirit as making the bread and wine to be the body and blood of Christ, in parallel with reference to God's effecting the incarnation of the Word, represents a development of the main pattern

in the circumstances of the Trinitarian controversy, as a way of emphasizing the equal significance of Spirit and Word. Here again, however, the underlying theme is that of God's providing the means of renewing the church through the work of the Spirit in making the bread and wine the body and blood of Christ.

In current ecumenical discussion, the eastern churches vigorously deny the western assumption that the invocation of the Spirit constitutes a "moment of consecration" different from the recitation of the "words of institution." At the same time, both eastern and western churches are studying the more general place of invocation in the pattern of early Christian prayer. *See also* Baptism; Eucharist; Prayer. [L.G.P.]

Bibliography

A.G. Hebert, "The Meaning of the Epiclesis," *Theology* 27 (1933):198–210, and "Theology" Reprints, No. 14 (London: SPCK, n.d.); F.S.B. Gavin, *The Jewish Antecedents of the Christian Sacraments* (London: SPCK, 1928); A.Z. Idelsohn, *The Jewish Liturgy and Its Development* (New York: Holt, 1932); E.G.C.F. Atchley, *On the Epiclesis of the Eucharistic Liturgy and in the Consecration of the Font* (Oxford: Oxford UP, 1935); H. Lietzmann, *Mass and Lord's Supper* (Leiden: Brill, 1953); J. Jungmann, *The Mass of the Roman Rite* (New York: Benziger, 1959); L. Bouyer, *Eucharist* (Notre Dame: Notre Dame UP, 1968); V. Lossky, *Orthodox Theology* (Crestwood: St. Vladimir's Seminary, 1978); idem, "The Invocation of the Spirit in the Eucharist," *Anglican-Orthodox Dialogue*, Moscow Statement 1976, Section 7; repr. in H. Meyer and L. Vischer, eds., *Growth in Agreement* (New York: Paulist, 1984).

EPICUREANISM. Philosophy whose goal was the eradication of fear through a scientific or natural understanding of the world. This understanding is based on hedonism (the goal of life is pleasure) and atomism (the world is composed of atoms and space); the elimination of fear leads to a life of tranquility. Pleasure is the absence of pain, and the greatest pleasures are those of the soul. Science, by denying the immortality of the soul and the gods' involvement in human affairs, frees us from fear of death and the supernatural. The doctrines of Epicurus (341–270 B.C.) are most fully and systematically expounded in the *De rerum natura* of Lucretius (ca. 94–55 B.C.), as well as in the writings of Philodemus of Gadara (ca. 110–ca. 40 B.C.) and those of Epicurus himself. Further, several dialogues by Cicero (106–43 B.C.), such as *De natura deorum*, have Epicurean interlocutors.

The spread of Epicureanism was often greeted with hostility; such pagans as Cicero and Plutarch (ca. A.D. 50–ca. 120) and numerous Christian fathers opposed it. By the time of its founder's death, Epicurean communities had been established in several Greek cities; others soon followed in Antioch and Alexandria and later throughout Gaul and Italy. By the second century B.C., the philosophy had supporters in Rome; Gaius Amafinius was the first to present a Latin version of Epicureanism (*Tusc.* 4.3.6). Its popularity reached its height during the late republican period, when it counted among its followers such men as Calpurnius Piso, Cassius, and perhaps Julius Caesar. The school continued to flourish in the first century A.D., when Paul met both Epicurean and Stoic philosophers in Athens (Acts 17:18). In the next century, the emperor Marcus Aurelius established at least one teaching position for an Epicurean philosopher. At the same time, in the obscure town of Oenoanda, Turkey, Diogenes, a devout follower and a local aristocrat, had a large wall inscribed with Epicurean maxims.

The denial of a benevolent and concerned divinity established Epicurus as an enemy of Christianity, and many patristic authors, while showing a familiarity with this philosophy, vigorously attacked it: Hippolytus (*Haer.* 1.19), Origen (in Gregory Thaumaturgus, *Panegyr.* 13), Arnobius (*Adv. nat.* 2.9, 30), Dionysius of Alexandria (in Eusebius, *P.E.* 14.23–27), Tertullian (*Praescr.* 7.4), Lactantius (*Div. inst.* 1.11; 3.17; 7.3; *Ira* 4.8; *Op. Dei* 6). By the fourth century, as both Julian the Apostate (*Letter to a Priest* 301c) and Augustine (*Ep.* 118.2.12, 21) attest, Epicureanism had come to an end. [L.P.S.]

Bibliography

N.W. de Witt, "Notes on the History of Epicureanism," *Transactions of the American Philological Association* 63 (1932):166–176; P. Giuffrida,

L'epicureismo nella letteratura latina del I secolo a.C., 2 vols. (Turin: Paravia, 1940–1948); A.D. Simpson, "Epicureans, Christians, Atheists in the Second Century," *Transactions of the American Philological Association* 72 (1941):372–381; P.H. de Lacy, "Lucretius and the History of Epicureanism," *Transactions of the American Philological Association* 79 (1948):12–23; N.W. de Witt, *St. Paul and Epicurus* (Minneapolis: U of Minnesota P, 1956); W. Schmid, "Epikur," RLAC (1961), Vol. 5, pp. 681–819; R. Jungkuntz, "Christian Approval of Epicureanism," *ChHist* 31 (1962):279–293; idem, "Fathers, Heretics, and Epicureans," *JEH* 17 (1966):3–10; M. Gigante, *Richerche Filodemee* (Naples: Macchiarol, 1969); E. Paratore, "La problematica sull'epicureismo a Roma," ANRW (1973), Vol. 1.4, pp. 116–204; P.H. and E. de Lacy, *Philodemus, On Methods of Inference*, 2nd ed. (Naples: Bibliopolis, 1978).

EPIGONUS (ca. 200). Monarchian teacher at Rome. Epigonus was a disciple of Noetus and the teacher of Cleomenes. [E.F.]

Bibliography
Hippolytus, *Refutation of All Heresies* 9.2.

EPIGRAPHY. *See* Inscriptions.

EPIPHANES (second century). Carpocratian Gnostic writer. Epiphanes, son of the Gnostic leader Carpocrates, died at age 17. He composed *On Justice*, which reflects Platonic influence and advocates radical community of all things, including the sharing of women. CPG I, 1123. TLG 1348. [R.R.]

Bibliography
Clement of Alexandria, *Miscellanies* 3.2.
W. Völker, *Quellen zur Geschichte der christlichen Gnosis* (Tübingen: Mohr, 1932), pp. 33–36.

EPIPHANIUS OF SALAMIS (ca. 315–403). Native of Palestine and bishop of Salamis in Cyprus. Epiphanius was a heresy hunter who insisted on Nicene orthodoxy. He founded a monastery at Eleutheropolis in Judea (ca. 335). The bishops of Cyprus made him their metropolitan in 367, because of his sincere concern for the faith and his organizational abilities.

Epiphanius's reputation rests primarily on his attempts to refute heresy and uphold Nicene

Orthodoxy. He wrote the *Panarion*, often referred to as *Haereses*, in which he attacked every heretical opinion and group known to him from the beginning of the church through his own era. Although the work is poorly organized, too trusting of friends, and too scathing toward opponents, it does contain information unavailable elsewhere.

Epiphanius labored to eradicate Apollinarian and Melitian sympathizers. After meeting Jerome in Rome during 392, he joined forces with him in attempting to root out Origenistic influence, particularly within monastic communities. He attacked John, bishop of Jerusalem, as an Origenist while a guest preaching in John's pulpit. In 400, he made his way to Constantinople to assist Theophilus of Alexandria's apparent efforts against Origenism. But when he discovered that Theophilus's real intent was to unseat John Chrysostom, he left Constantinople and died on the journey back to Cyprus. His *Ancoratus*, a doctrinal treatise, does not contain the Niceno-Constantinopolitan Creed, which some scribe added to the manuscript. He wrote two other extant treatises, *On Measures and Weights* and *On Gems*, as well as a number of letters and some scriptural scholia. Feast day May 12. CPG II, 3744–3807. TLG 2021.   [F.W.N.]

Bibliography

PG 41–43; I. Hilberg, ed., *Epistulae* 51 and 91, CSEL (1910–1918), Vol. 54, pp. 395–412, and Vol. 55, pp. 145–146; J. Lebon, ed., *Epistulae* [fragments in Severus of Antioch], CSCO (1933), Vol. 102, pp. 235ff.; K. Holl, ed., GCS (1915, 1922, 1933), Vols. 25, 31, 37.

P.R. Blake and H. deVis, *Epiphanius: De Gemmis* (London: Christophers, 1934); J.E. Dean, *Epiphanius' Treatise on Weights and Measures: The Syriac Version* (Chicago: U of Chicago P, 1935); F. Williams, *Panarion, Book I (1–46)* (Leiden: Brill, 1987).

F. Young, "Did Epiphanius Know What He Meant by 'Heresy'?" *SP* 17.1 (1982):199–205; J. Dechow, *Dogma and Mysticism in Early Christianity: Epiphanius of Cyprus and the Legacy of Origen* (Macon: Mercer UP, 1988).

EPIPHANY. Christian feast, from the Greek word for "manifestation" or "appearance." The earliest known Christian use of "Epiphany" to designate a feast day is from the late second century: the Basilidians, a heretical sect in Egypt, celebrated the baptism of Jesus on January 6 (Clement of Alexandria, *Str.* 1.21). The earliest known account of orthodox Christians celebrating Epiphany comes from a report of a visit of the emperor Julian to a church in Vienne in Gaul, in early 361, while he was still only Caesar in the west, "on the feast day in January celebrated by the Christians as Epiphany" (Ammianus Marcellinus, *History* 21.2).

Some Christians from Greece and Egypt eastward may have used the term as the name for their annual celebration of the nativity of Jesus Christ (in most places, January 6) as early as the second century. Certainly by the third century, most eastern Christians were doing so, and it is quite probable that the church in Vienne, which had close ties with the east, was following eastern practice. But the actual date of Christ's birth was not certain, so while by the last quarter of the fourth century Christians almost everywhere had come to celebrate January 6 as Epiphany, the Day of Manifestation, at least four other significant manifestations of Christ's glory beside the nativity were commemorated on this date at different places: the visit of the Magi to the infant Jesus (Matt. 2), Jesus' baptism (Matt. 3), the wedding at Cana (John 2:1–11), and the feeding of the five thousand (Matt. 14:13–21).

No later than the mid-fourth century, the church in Rome made the commemoration of the visit of the Magi the principal theme of its celebration of Epiphany and thereby set the pattern for much of the west. This practice seems to be related to the fact that sometime before 354 the Roman Christians had begun to celebrate December 25 as the feast of the nativity. It seems likely that Rome celebrated Epiphany before it began to celebrate December 25, but the available data mention no such feast. So one may only speculate that the celebration of the nativity on December 25 was an addition to a calendar that already included Epiphany on January 6, and that the addition simply separated the nativity theme from the other Epiphany themes. Why the manifestation to the Magi would then become the principal theme of Epiphany remains uncertain.

On the other hand, December 25 was not celebrated in the east until ca. 385, when it was commemorated in both Antioch and Constantinople. Not until sometime after 430 was it celebrated in the sees of Alexandria and Jerusalem. And even with this acceptance of a western practice, the east tended to retain the note of nativity in the January 6 celebration and give Epiphany much more prominence than it gave December 25.

The dates for both Christmas and Epiphany, as authentic anniversaries, lack any grounding in history. Most likely, both dates were originally connected with one or another pagan deity and were adopted and adapted by the church. *See also* Christmas.   [P.M.B.]

Bibliography
B. Botte, *Les Origines de la Noël et de l'Epiphanie* (Louvain: Abbaye du Mont César, 1932); A.A. McArthur, *The Evolution of the Christian Year* (London: SCM, 1953); P.G. Cobb, "The History of the Christian Year," *The Study of Liturgy,* ed. C. Jones, G. Wainwright, and E. Yarnold (London: SPCK; New York: Oxford UP, 1978), pp. 414–415.

EPISTLE. Reading in the liturgy taken from the epistles of the New Testament and from the Acts of the Apostles. The Epistle was originally called, as it still is in the eastern churches, the "Apostle," as distinct from the "Prophecy" and the "Gospel." In the east, the Epistle followed the reading of the lections from the Old Testament (the "Prophecy"), wherever and whenever these were included, and preceded the reading from the Gospel. In the west, it often included Old Testament readings. In both east and west, the term came to denote the book that contained the readings. The Apostle of the eastern churches begins with the Acts of the Apostles, which is read between Easter and Pentecost, and then goes through the Pauline and the Catholic Epistles. This arrangement seems to go back at least to John Chrysostom's time. The contents of the Apostle in the western churches have varied considerably, especially from the seventh century onward, because they seem to have evolved around different principles; but it is not clear how far back this divergence goes. *See also* Gospel; Lectionary.   [G.D.D.]

Bibliography
G. Dix, *The Shape of the Liturgy* (London: Dacre, 1945), esp. pp. 360ff. and 470ff.; C. Jones, G. Wainwright, and E. Yarnold, eds., *The Study of the Liturgy* (London: SPCK, 1978).

EPISTLE OF THE APOSTLES. Apocryphal work, ca. 150. The *Epistle of the Apostles* relates a dialogue of Jesus with the eleven disciples (incorrectly named) placed in the period between his resurrection and ascension. Although beginning as a letter, the work's literary form is that of a postresurrection revelation, a genre well represented among the documents from Nag Hammadi. The author, it seems, used a favorite Gnostic literary form to oppose Gnostic ideas, for he emphasizes the full humanity of Christ, the resurrection of the flesh, and the necessity of water baptism for salvation and warns against Simon Magus and Cerinthus. Although written in Greek, the *Epistle of the Apostles* survives only in Ethiopic and less completely in Coptic.   [E.F.]

Bibliography
NTA, Vol. 1, pp. 189–227.
J. Hills, *Tradition and Composition in the* Epistula Apostolorum (Philadelphia: Fortress, 1989).

EPISTLE OF TITUS. Latin pseudepigraphal writing from the fourth or fifth century. The *Epistle of Titus, the Disciple of Paul, on the Estate of Chastity* is actually a treatise on celibacy addressed to ascetics of both sexes. The author commends virginity and warns against the abuse of "spiritual marriage," in which a man and woman dedicated to chastity lived in the same house. The Priscillianist movement in Spain appears to be the environment in which the work was produced. *See also* Titus.   [E.F.]

Bibliography
NTA, Vol. 2, pp. 141–166.
A. von Harnack, "Der apokryphe *Brief des Paulusschulers Titus,*" *Sitzungsberichte der Berliner Akademie* 17 (1925):180–213.

ESCHATOLOGY. Doctrine of last things. Eschatology, in Christian terms, is theological reflection on the hope of believers: hope in God's final resolution of the ambiguities of history and in the final salvation of both individual and community from death and sin, rooted in the conviction that this final resolution and salvation have already begun in the resurrection of the crucified Jesus.

The apocalyptic tradition of late Judaism looked for God to intervene soon in human affairs, bringing a dramatic end to the present social and natural order and creating a new world, in which the dead would rise, the just would be rewarded forever, and their oppressors would be forever punished. Reflected in Jesus' own preaching, this scheme of expectation was readily adopted by Paul (e.g., 1 Thess. 4:13–5:11; 2 Thess. 2:1–12; 1 Cor. 15) and other New Testament writings (e.g., 1 Peter 4:7–19; 2 Peter 2–3; Jude; Rev.); quite naturally, it provided the main images and conceptual structure for the hope of the early Christian communities.

Second Century. Second-century Christians of Jewish background produced several works that depicted, in vivid apocalyptic colors, the coming end of the world and the advent of Christ as glorious judge of history: chief among them are the *Apocalypse of Peter* (mid-second century), the *Ascension of Isaiah* (second century?), the *Epistle of the Apostles* (ca. 150), and Books 7 and 8 of the *Sibylline Oracles* (150–200). Other writings of the same period and cultural milieu, those of the apostolic fathers, reflect varying senses of the nearness of these final events. Although the *Didache*, the *Epistle of Barnabas*, and the homily known as *2 Clement* speak of history's final crisis as imminent (*Barn.* 4; *Did.* 16; *2 Clem.* 5.5; 7.1; 8.1–3) and express a longing for Jesus' coming (*Did.* 10.6; cf. *Barn.* 21.1), other works, such as *1 Clement* and the *Shepherd* of Hermas, refer to these things in the context of the continuing process of history and emphasize that sinners still have time to repent (*1 Clem.* 23.3–4; 28; Hermas, *Vis.* 3.8.9). Still other works of the first half of the second century reflect a strongly "realized" eschatology: the sense that final salvation is already real and available for the Christian. So the letters of

Ignatius of Antioch and the Syriac *Odes of Solomon* speak of eternal life and incorruptibility as present gifts in the community of faith (Ignatius, *Philad.* 9.2; *Odes* 15.8; 17.1–4; 25.8) and see in the death of the martyr a direct means of access to union with the risen Lord (Ignatius, *Rom.* 6.1f.; cf. Polycarp, *Ep.* 9.2; *M. Polyc.* 17.1).

The Greek apologists of the mid-second century, in their dialogue with Christianity's Hellenistic critics, present the Christian expectation of a bodily resurrection and judgment for all people as the basis of ethical behavior, something required by belief in a just and provident God (Justin, *1 Apol.* 14; *2 Apol.* 1). These writers considered the human soul not to be naturally immortal but saw eternal life as participation, by divine gift, in the life of God (Tatian, *Orat.* 13; Athenagoras, *Leg.* 4; 31). Two treatises on the resurrection from the apologetic milieu, one attributed to Justin and the other, with more likelihood of authenticity, to Athenagoras, attempt to refute philosophical criticisms of the Christian hope in bodily resurrection by appealing to the creative power of God and to the requirements of justice. In Roman Africa during the same decades, Minucius Felix and Tertullian echoed this apologetic and its frankly materialistic conception of the risen state.

Gnostic Christians of the late second century generally took a less literal approach to the resurrection hope, corresponding to their view of the material world as the creation of lesser forces than the redeeming God. Although the charge of orthodox critics, such as Irenaeus and Tertullian, that the Gnostics denied any share in future salvation to the body or the material world, is an oversimplification, most Gnostic groups saw the Christian hope primarily as promising a fulfillment of the spiritual enlightenment presently available to their own initiates; so the Valentinian *Treatise on the Resurrection* conceives this as the restoration (*apokatastasis*) of luminous heavenly reality, now weighed down by flesh, to its original state. In response to Gnostic interpretations, Irenaeus of Lyons strongly stressed the unity of the world and its history as the creation of a single God and saw the resurrection of the body and the transformation of the material world as the culmination of a consistent plan of salvation centered on Christ.

Third Century. Third-century western writers, faced with persecution and mounting social disintegration, reflected the popular view that the world was "growing old" and nearing a fiery end. Tertullian, who joined the Montanist sect ca. 207, reflected that group's millenarian hope (*Marc.* 3.24) and concern for the life of the individual after death; he conceived this as a period of detention in huge "reception rooms" under the earth, where souls anticipate imaginatively the reward or punishment they will receive after the bodily resurrection (*Anim.* 55–58). The *Passion of Perpetua and Felicitas*, narrating the execution of several (Montanist?) Christians in Carthage in 203 and sometimes said to have been edited by Tertullian, presents several visions of the reward promised martyrs after death and of the effects of their prayers in easing the suffering of those who died outside the faith.

The eschatology of Alexandrian theologians at the beginning of the third century shows a more optimistic and intellectual character. Although his popular writings reflect traditional apocalyptic views of the afterlife and the end of history, Clement of Alexandria suggests, in works for his advanced readers, that the beatitude for which Christians hope is really a full realization of the loving, contemplative union with God that the disciplined and intelligent disciple can experience in this life (*Str.* 7.11.63.1f). Clement suggests cautiously that all intellectual creatures will eventually be saved (*Str.* 7.2.12.2ff.) and interprets the biblical picture of the fire of Gehenna as a purifying suffering imposed after death to bring sinners to repentance (*Str.* 7.6.34.4; 7.12.78.3).

A generation younger than Clement, Origen wrote in the same rich cultural and religious milieu and shared many of Clement's ideas; nevertheless, his eschatological doctrine is fuller and more complex, due to his concern to be a pastoral interpreter of scripture and church tradition and a spiritual guide as well as a systematic thinker. So Origen takes the apoca-

lyptic passages of the New Testament to have both a literal sense, as predictions of the future, and a metaphorical reference to the present spiritual lives of believers (*Comm. ser.* 32–60 *in Mt.*). In general, Origen sees the eschatological goal of human life as the union of all created intellects with God and each other in a loving relationship that is forged on earth but will never cease to grow (*Princ.* 3.6.6; *Jo.* 1.16.92; *Hom.* 17 *in Num.*). This doctrine, shared with Clement and many later writers, became controversial even during Origen's lifetime because of his stress on the universality of salvation, possibly even including the evil spirits, and because of his conception of this as the restoration (*apokatastasis*) of souls to an "original" state of bliss that preceded the existence of the material world (*Princ.* 1.6.2f.; *Jo.* 1.16.91; *Comm. in Rom.* 5.10; 9.41). Like Clement, he regarded the punishment of sinners to be intelligible only as a kind of self-generated internal suffering, allowed by God as part of an educative and purgative process (*Princ.* 2.10.4; *Or.* 29.15).

Origen's conception of the resurrection proved to be equally controversial. Although he affirmed the church's conviction that our present bodies will rise "in some form" (*Princ.* 2.10.1f.), he emphasized, following 1 Corinthians 15, their future spiritual character and was critical of the materialistic notions of popular Christian hope (*Cels.* 5.18–23). As the principle of continuity in a constantly changing corporeal existence, the soul will form the matter it needs to support itself into a condition appropriate to life in union with God (Frg. of *Comm. in Ps.* 1.5 in Methodius, *Res.* 1.20–24). It is unclear, however, whether Origen speculated that all bodily existence would eventually pass away; in *On First Principles* 2.3.7, he seems content to leave the question open.

Fourth Century. The turn of the fourth century witnessed the revival of more literal interpretations of the eschatological tradition. Both Peter of Alexandria and Methodius of Olympus, in the first years of the century, criticized Origen sharply for failing to take the material character of the risen body seriously.

The Latin writers Victorinus of Pettau and Lactantius, at about the same time, revived interest in biblical apocalyptic: the former by composing the first extant commentary on Revelation, the latter by expanding and systematizing the scenario of that book into a dramatic description of the climax of history, which Lactantius expected about the year 500 (*Div. inst.* 7).

The fourth-century Syriac writers Aphraates and Ephraem the Syrian also echoed earlier expectations of a coming judgment and a material resurrection; in addition, they spoke of death as a personal force, eager to subdue or devour the human race (Aphraates, *Dem.* 22; Ephraem the Syrian, *C. Nis.* 52–68). For both of them, the period between the individual's death and the resurrection is a dreamless sleep in a dark and airless underworld (Ephraem the Syrian, *C. Nis.* 36f.). Ephraem's *Hymns on Paradise* provide a lyrical and imaginative description of the promised life of the blessed in a rich garden, whose center is the glorified Christ. Fourth- and fifth-century ascetical writings from Egypt, including Athanasius's influential *Life of Anthony*, the *Sayings of the Desert Fathers*, and the Pachomian corpus, also stress traditional expectations of the judgment and the eternal punishment of sinners as important themes for the meditation of monks (*Apophth. Patr.*; Evagrius 1; Theophilus 4f.); they speak in graphic terms of the struggle between angel guardians and demonic "customs officials" over the souls of the dying (*V. Anton.* 65).

In the mainstream of Greek theology after Nicaea, Eusebius of Caesarea showed a suspicious attitude toward the apocalyptic tradition and open contempt for millenarianism (*H.E.* 3.39.13; 7.24.1); in the historical reign and patronage of Constantine, he saw the first signs of the coming of Christ's eternal kingdom (*V.C.* 1.33). His opponent on Trinitarian issues, Marcellus of Ancyra, conceived of the goal of the divine plan of salvation as the unity of all creation, including the risen Christ, in the radical unity of God. To avoid the accusation of thereby denying the eternal validity of Christ's rule, Marcellus subsequently argued that

the goal of the divine plan is simply an end to the separateness of humanity from God (Ps.-Athanasius, *Inc. et ctr. Ar.* 20f.).

Later in the fourth century, the three great Cappadocian fathers reflected a modified revival of Origen's eschatology. Basil of Caesarea, although holding the eternity of both beatitude and damnation, stressed the centrality of the direct and transforming knowledge of God in human fulfillment. His friend Gregory of Nazianzus also interpreted traditional expectations in a spiritual sense, cautiously adopting Origen's "medicinal" explanation of divine punishment and his hope for universal salvation (*Or.* 30.6; 40.36). Basil's brother, Gregory of Nyssa, refined the Origenist hope still further, insisting that sin and its punishment cannot be eternal because evil, as a mere privation or disfigurement of the good created by God, must eventually come to an end (*Hom. opif.* 21.1). At the resurrection, human nature will be restored to its original state of material and spiritual integrity, realizing the fullness of what God has eternally intended it to be (*Hom. opif.* 16). The agent of this reintegration will be the indestructible soul, which remains related to the particles that it once formed into a body, even in their state of dissolution (*Anim. et res.* [PG 46.128]). Gregory also emphasized that the human spirit can never be satiated in its desire for God; thus, beatitude will be an endless growth both in that desire and its fulfillment (*V. Mos.* 2.239).

Contemporary with the Cappadocians were two Origenists writing in Egypt, Didymus the Blind and Evagrius of Pontus, whose radical eschatological doctrines were condemned both in their own time and in the sixth century. Both conceived of human fulfillment as the restoration of an "original" bodiless existence of souls, a state of substantial, totally immaterial union with God that will eradicate all individuality. On the other hand, John Chrysostom, who as bishop of Constantinople gave shelter to some fifty of Evagrius's disciples who had been driven from Egypt in 401, preached a more traditional doctrine of bodily resurrection and eternal punishment for sin and considered the prospect of divine sanctions after death a sign of the nobility of the human person (*Hom.* 3 *in Philm.* 2).

John's Antiochene friend Theodore of Mopsuestia emphasized the radical distinction between our present "state" (*katastasis*), as the time in which salvation is promised to the believer and signified typologically in scripture and the church's sacraments, and our longed-for final state of incorruptible existence as friends of God (*Jo.* 14.6; 17.11). Theodore's disciple Theodoret of Cyrus maintained the same tension between present and future but spoke also of eschatological salvation as a real union, by grace or "good pleasure," between God and creatures (*In Eph.* 1.23; *In 1 Cor.* 15.28).

In the Latin west, the issues raised by the Origenist revival also influenced the eschatological thought of late-fourth-century writers. Ambrose of Milan adhered, in some passages, to the traditional doctrine of eternal punishment for sinners (*Fid.* 2.119), while in others he saw punishment as medicinal (*In Ps.* 1.47) and hoped that all people, or at least all Christians, would be saved (*Exc. Sat.* 116; *In Ps.* 39.17). Jerome, too, despite his violent repudiation of Origen's teaching from 393 on, continued to maintain the hope that all believers in Christ will be saved (*Ep.* 119.7). Along with Hilary of Poitiers, both these writers emphasized the ecclesial character of final beatitude and suggested that Christ's judgment would concern only believers whose virtues and vices were not already apparent.

Fifth and Sixth Centuries. It was Augustine's synthesis of biblical and traditional hope, however, that proved most influential on later Latin eschatology. Despite the heightened sense of many of his contemporaries that the end of the world was near, the mature Augustine remained agnostic about its coming (*Ep.* 199) and cautiously literal in his interpretation of the biblical scenario of judgment and retribution (*Civ. Dei* 20–22). The key element in his own speculations is his distinction between time, as the measure of the changing consciousness of finite spirits embodied in a world of growth and corruption, and the simple, self-contained stability of God's eternal exis-

tence. Without destroying the reality of the flesh or its cosmic environment, resurrection will be, in Augustine's view, a transformation of human existence from this temporal mode to a participation in God's timeless being (*In Ps.* 101.10; *In Evang. Ioh.* 31.5), the repose of God's "eternal sabbath" (*Conf.* 13.37). Following the Donatist Tyconius, Augustine interpreted the "millennium" of Revelation 20:3 as referring to the present age of the church; so those who have died in grace still belong to time and to the church and share its life of prayer (*Civ. Dei* 20.9). Although the dead already anticipate in their consciousness the destinies that will be theirs, the full reality of both reward and punishment must await the end of time, when the damned will be consigned to eternal torture and the blessed will join in the "society of angels" as a community eternally contemplating God (*Civ. Dei* 19.13, 17).

Spiritual writers in the fifth and sixth centuries, such as the author(s) of the Pseudo-Macarian homilies and Diadochus of Photice in the east and Julian Pomerius in the west, emphasized the continuity between the contemplative union with God that is possible in the present life and its transformation in eternal beatitude. A revival of Origenist eschatology in its extreme Evagrian form around the turn of the sixth century, notably in the Syriac writings of Philoxenus of Mabbug and Stephen bar-Sudaili, met strong opposition both within their own anti-Chalcedonian camp and among the Chalcedonian establishment and led to the condemnation of Origenist theses by the emperor Justinian in 543 and by the Second Council of Constantinople (553). Greek philosophical doctrines of the preexistence and reincarnation of souls and the eternity of the material world were directly attacked from the point of view of traditional Christian eschatology by the controversialist Aeneas of Gaza early in the sixth century and by Zachary of Mytilene a generation later. John Philoponus, the anti-Chalcedonian Christian philosopher of Alexandria who wrote major commentaries on Aristotle, also rejected the eternity of matter and interpreted the resurrection of the body as the complete recreation of the human person, body and soul—a view later attacked by orthodox theologians.

The sixth century witnessed another revival of interest in the apocalyptic genre in both east and west: this time, however, without the sense of impending doom that had previously been associated with it. Besides the anonymous "Oracle of Baalbek" and other pseudo-Sibylline works from the first decade of the century, this is exemplified in Oecumenius's commentary on the Book of Revelation, a sober and learned work with an Origenist tinge composed ca. 510, the first such commentary in Greek. This was followed later in the century by Andrew of Caesarea's more explicitly orthodox Greek exposition of the same book, as well as by two careful and balanced Latin commentaries, works of the African Primasius of Hadrumetum and the Spaniard Apringius of Beja.

At the end of the sixth century, pope Gregory the Great again reflected the anxieties of the Latin west in the face of barbarian invasion and general social decline by his vivid foreboding that the world was approaching its end. Yet his confidence in the health of the expanding church gave him hope and turned his interest more directly toward preparing his contemporaries for their own death. His picture of the judgment, purgative suffering, and reward or punishment that awaits each individual at death, especially as he describes them in Book 4 of his *Dialogues*, provided both a focus of interest and a rich supply of images for medieval Latin eschatology.

In the first half of the seventh century, Maximus Confessor's remarkable synthesis of earlier Greek theology included an emphasis on the divinization of the human person by grace as the goal of God's eternal plan of creation (*Amb. Joan.* 7). Echoing this hope half a century later, John of Damascus (*Imag.* 1) summarized and systematized the traditional arguments for the bodily resurrection and the traditional expectation of Christ's coming and judgment with a comprehensiveness and clarity that was to become the basis for classical Byzantine eschatology (*F.O.* 99f.). In the east as in the west, early Christian hope for final salvation had itself reached its final form. *See also* Apokatastasis; Chiliasm; Heaven; Hell; Judgment; Purgatory.　　　　[B.E.D.]

Bibliography

L. Atzberger, *Geschichte der christlichen Eschatologie innerhalb der vornicänischen Zeit* (Freiburg: Herder, 1896); R. Frick, *Die Geschichte des Reich-Gottes-Gedankens in der alten Kirche bis zu Origenes und Augustin* (Giessen: Töpelmann, 1928); J. Gross, *La Divinisation du chrétien d'après les pères grecs* (Paris: Gabalda, 1938); J. Daniélou, "La Doctrine de la mort chez les pères de l'église," *Mystère de la mort et sa célébration* (Paris: Cerf, 1951), pp. 134–156; E. Staehelin, *Die Verkündigung des Reiches Gottes in der Kirche Jesu Christi*, 2 vols. (Basel: Reinhardt, 1951–1953); G.W.H. Lampe, "Early Patristic Eschatology," *Eschatology*, ed. W. Manson et al. (Edinburgh and London: Oliver and Boyd, 1953), pp. 17–35; G. Florovsky, "Eschatology in the Patristic Age," *GOTR* 2 (1956): 27–40; H.A. Wolfson, "Immortality of the Soul and Resurrection in the Philosophy of the Church Fathers," *Harvard Divinity School Bulletin* 22 (1956–1957): 5–40; J. Pelikan, *The Shape of Death: Life, Death and Immortality in the Early Fathers* (Nashville: Abingdon, 1961); H. Rondet, *Fins de l'homme et fin du monde* (Paris: Fayard, 1966); S. Prete, *La escatologia e parenesi negli scrittori cristiani latini* (Bologna: Zanichelli, 1966); L.G. Patterson, *God and History in Early Christian Thought* (London: Black, 1967); B. McGinn, *Visions of the End* (New York: Columbia UP, 1979); J. LeGoff, *The Birth of Purgatory* (London: Scolar, 1984); B.E. Daley, *The Hope of the Early Church: Eschatology in the Patristic Age* (Cambridge: Cambridge UP, forthcoming).

ESTHER. Queen of Persia, book of Bible. The Book of Esther occurs in various positions as one of the five scrolls in the division of the Hebrew Bible named the Writings (Hagiographa). No fragments of the book were found in the Qumran literature; it is not mentioned in the New Testament; and it does not appear in the canonical list of Melito of Sardis (Eusebius, *H.E.* 4.26.13f.). Esther occupies various positions in Greek manuscripts and canonical lists of the church fathers but is last in the lists of Origen (Eusebius, *H.E.* 6.25.2) and Athanasius (*Ep. fest.* 39). Athanasius recommended it only for the reading of catechumens. The Council of Carthage (397) recognized the Book of Esther, including the sections drawn from the Septuagint, as having a place in the Christian scriptures.

The Septuagint has 107 verses not in the Hebrew text. Jerome translated Esther into Latin at Bethlehem in 405, and the added verses were excerpted and included as an appendix to the book. These additions are commonly printed in collections of Apocrypha.

Esther (or Hadassah), Jewish queen of Persia in the reign of Xerxes I (Ahasuerus, 485–465 B.C.), kinswoman of the Jew Mordecai, delivered her people from the plot of Haman. The event is commemorated in the feast of Purim. Purim itself is first mentioned in 2 Maccabees 15:36. The story is then surveyed by Josephus (*Ant.* 11.6.1–13 [159–296]) and is the subject of the Mishnah tractate *Megilla.*

Esther's deliverance is included in the survey of noble women in *1 Clement* 55.6, and she is mentioned by Clement of Alexandria and Origen.   [J.P.L.]

Bibliography

J. Allenbach et al., *Biblia Patristica*, 4 vols. and Supplement (Paris: Editions du Centre National de la Recherche Scientifique, 1975–1987); C.A. Moore, *Esther* (Garden City: Doubleday, 1977).

ETHELBERT (d. 616). King of Kent. Ethelbert married the Christian princess Bertha, daughter of Charibert, king of the Franks. This connection led to the mission of Augustine of Canterbury, sent by Gregory the Great for the evangelization of England. Ethelbert was himself converted, becoming the first Christian Anglo-Saxon king. He founded churches at Canterbury and Rochester, and St. Paul's in London, while ensuring that the primatial see would remain in Canterbury. Through his influence, the kings of Essex and East Anglia became Christians. A code of laws (604), in which punishments were decreed for robbers of church property, is attributed to him. He is depicted in art holding a sword and a church.
CPL 1827.   [M.P.McH.]

Bibliography

Bede, *Ecclesiastical History* 1.25–26, 32–33; 2.2–5; 5.24.

F.L. Attenborough, *The Laws of the Earliest English Kings* (Cambridge: Cambridge UP, 1922), pp. 4–17.

ETHERIA. *See Egeria, Pilgrimage of.*

ETHICS. Human conduct; principles or rules for regulating attitudes and actions. Ethics may also include arguments meant to adjudicate differences in various ethical systems. Early Christian ethics participates in that discussion, but it is most often centered on individual and communal identity as determining conduct. To put the point in terms of modern ethics, early Christian ethics was basically neither deontological, consequential, nor utilitarian.

Were one to focus only on virtues and vices or rules and regulations, the New Testament would at many points show the same lists of virtues as those of various Jewish and Stoic codes. Yet Jesus is credited with contrasting his views with those of the old Law and Pharisaical or Sadducean interpretations (Matt. 5:17–48). Much of what he taught can be found in the Talmud or the Mishnah. Paul's codes of morals (Rom. 12:9–21; Gal. 5:19–23) are often duplicated in Stoic fragments. Neither leader had difficulty acknowledging the force of earlier tradition. Jesus summed up the Law and the prophets as loving God and your neighbor as yourself (Matt. 22:34–41). Paul noted that a number of the virtues he espoused had no laws written against them (Gal. 5:23). Each virtue, however, had a quality indicating that Christian ethics was something different.

Distinctiveness. The distinctiveness of early Christian ethics is its central concern for Christian identity. The call is to be a child of God, to become who the believer is. Christians are to be members of God's kingdom (Mark 1:14–20); they should imitate Paul as he imitates Christ (1 Cor. 11:1). Yet as members of the body of Christ, as participants in one another, their identity is not only individual but communal (1 Cor. 12).

That type of concern is continued in early Christian literature outside the New Testament. *1 Clement* 30–33 bases its exhortations on the identity of Christians: they are a part of what is holy, called by the will of God in Christ, sanctified through grace. Because that is who they are, they should shun unrighteous deeds and thoughts and do the tasks of a good worker or soldier. Ignatius gives various churches ethical advice (*Eph.* 1.3–8, 10; *Magn.* 6–7) that he grounds in their faith and identity. They are to imitate God and Christ, to follow the Lord's example, to love others in harmony with the mind of God, to confirm God's ways. From that sense of who they are, they can discover which specific acts and attitudes to choose. The *Epistle to Diognetus* 5 views Christians as the soul of the world. Justin Martyr (*1 Apol.* 1.16) warns them not to imitate the evildoers. Tatian (*Orat.* 15) emphasizes that humans are in the image and likeness of God and thus should surpass animals and even apparently normal human activity in striving to be like God. For Irenaeus (*Haer.* 4.39–40; *Dem.* 96), Adam and Eve were children whom God intended to grow toward maturity, but they showed their immaturity in rebellion. Therefore, Christ came in human flesh to save both body and soul, to restore the identity of humanity. When restored, humans will not need the Law as a teacher but will be able to live the life of faith by not even thinking about the temptations that beset the immature.

Free Will and Grace. Both Clement of Alexandria (*Str.* 1.11.52) and Origen (*Princ.* 3.6.1) emphasize the image of God and insist that even after the rebellion of Adam and Eve, free will is still present in humankind. In fact, there is a strong sense of human freedom to choose the good or the evil at the same time that there is a deep sense of difficulty in doing the good. Athanasius (*Gent.* 34.3; *Inc.* 4.4) notes that humans were made in the image of God. They chose, because of outside distractions, to turn away from their own being and reject their nature. The Word came to teach them, to repaint the image. Their present condition is controlled by temptation and is indeed ruled by death, but through Christ they can return to their intended place. Even in their present state, they can repent and turn again to God. For Gregory of Nazianzus (*Carm.* 1.1.8; *Or.* 37.13) and Basil of Caesarea (*Hom. in Ps.* 1.3), sin has defaced the image of God, but it is still intact at least to the point that sinful humans can choose to do what God

commands. They cannot be saved by their own actions, but they do have the ability to respond to the gospel of Christ. The human soul always hates its slavery to sin but is still enslaved. It must be a both/and situation, not an either/or. If human wills were not free in some effective manner even after Adam's deed, then God would in some horrid way be responsible for evil itself, and human responsibility would be vitiated. Although no one would deny that salvation comes from God's grace in Christ, neither would one accept a bold predestinarian view in which the soul's destiny had been totally predetermined without reference to the person's decision.

This balanced concern for a modicum of free choice and the necessity of grace is not a position taken only in the east. Tertullian (*Paenit.* 3.5) emphasizes the freedom of human will, although he often uses it as an explanation of why people cannot blame external circumstances for their own evil deeds. The assumption, however, is that humans are responsible for their attitudes and actions because they could have chosen otherwise. Cyprian (*Ad Donat.* 1) also wrestles with these questions. He finds that in his own sinfulness he could still consider what was promised to him by divine grace. He is aware that he could not extricate himself from his former ways, but he could decide to be baptized. In that washing, he began to feel his reconstruction as a new man, as one indwelt by the Spirit. Hilary of Poitiers (*In Psalm.* 14) found the kingly stature of humans in Adam's gift of free will. Even after their sin, humans are saved by God's grace, taught the knowledge of God that they can receive.

These examples are not meant to suggest that Augustine and Gregory the Great are alone in their insistence upon an original sin that deprives humans of making their own choices. Augustine eventually came to support single predestination (God's decree to save the elect) and imply a double predestination (election of the saved and reprobation of the lost) in which the majesty of God was fully displayed. He found humans to be conceived in sin and thus personally incapable of receiving or accepting their own salvation. The deep love of God is thus demonstrated in his salvation of some humans, for all were destined for damnation (*Grat.*; *Corrept.*; *Retract.* 1.8, 76, 98f.). Yet even Augustine, before the conflict with Pelagius, in his writings against the Manichaeans, had noticed that the will must be operative if people are to be responsible and punishment is to be just (*Lib. arb.* 1.1; 3.1, 17). Gregory the Great (*Moral.* 24.10.24; 27.25.28) insisted that conscience and reason held each human accountable for his or her evil deeds. All know what they are doing and know that it is wrong, but the freedom to choose good deeds is provided by grace. In spite of these strong western positions on the bondage of the will, it is not clear from early Christian tradition that Christian ethics always involved the claim that the human will is completely enslaved as the result of original sin.

Vices and Virtues. Once the issues of identity, grace, predestination, and free will have been explored, it is important to turn toward some of the descriptions of vice and virtue that one finds in this early literature. Jesus is recorded as having taught the "two ways," one leading to destruction and the other to life, a popular device in the writings outside the New Testament (Matt. 7:13–14). A large section of the *Didache* (1–6) is devoted to that topic. Irenaeus (*Dem.* 1–2; *Haer.* 4.40) describes the contest between virtue and vice in a manner that appears to be related to the two-ways metaphor when he mentions the straight path. Origen (*Princ.* 3.2.4) explicitly employs the terminology of two ways.

Other early Christian writers followed the lead of Paul, who mentioned lists of vices and virtues that closely parallel those found in Stoic writings. Ignatius (*Polyc.* 1–5) praises justice, humility, and continence. Justin Martyr (*1 Apol.* 1.16) speaks against troublemakers and urges Christians to be patient, meek, and constant in their lives while avoiding indecency, cupidity, violence, swearing, and tyrannical behavior. Irenaeus (*Dem.* 1–2) exhorts his hearers or readers to courage, determination, and perseverance. Clement of Alexandria relies on C. Musonius Rufus and Epictetus at

particular points. He advises temperance, modesty, obedience, and charity, indeed full self-mastery, and rejects pride, softness, gluttony, and sexual immorality (*Paed.* 4.10.1). Origen (*Cels.* 3) warns against pride, avarice, a wicked tongue, and falsehoods, in the midst of praising virginity. John Chrysostom (*Hom.* 13 in *Mt.*) picks up the Beatitudes from Jesus' Sermon on the Mount, but he lists them in much the way that a Stoic would and even drops the praise of peacemakers.

The western leaders of Christianity hold similar views. Tertullian (*Pat.*) rails against various vices and praises virtues that a Stoic would applaud. He became disenchanted with the Catholic church primarily because of what he saw as its infidelity to Christian ethics and joined the stricter Montanists. Hilary of Poitiers (*In Psalm.* 14) exhorts Christians to justice, innocence, self-control, and perfection and insists that pride and tyranny be avoided. Brothers and sisters in Christ should correct one another with gentleness. Ambrose (*Off. minis.* 24; 28; 124) finds Panaetius and Cicero to be good teachers about duty; indeed, he orders his discussion around the four classic Stoic virtues of prudence, justice, strength, and temperance. Jerome (*In Matt.* 2.13) offers Plato as a guide to the three major passions of the human soul: reason, wrath, and desire. Yet in many cases, some biblical personage or admonition is given as the basis for the selection of these particular virtues and vices.

Specifics of Conduct. Various positive commands and admonitions mark early Christian literature. The *Epistle to Diognetus* rejects abortion, a note sounded throughout the early heritage. Ignatius offers advice on how to treat widows and slaves and the relationship between husbands and wives. Cyprian (*Quir.*) built a work on 120 commands found in the Gospels. A number of the leaders, such as Athanasius (*V. Anton.*), Basil (*Moral.*), and Gregory of Nyssa (*Instit.*) insist that the ascetic life is the proper one. Although they do not belittle marriage, they do sound the note raised in Paul's first Corinthian letter (1 Cor. 7): the single life is more suited to one serving God because it offers fewer distractions. Fornication and adultery are eschewed by all at the level of teaching, although the repeated emphasis makes it clear that the demands were not always obeyed.

Remarriage was often denied, unless the spouse was dead, as Ambrose (*Vid.* 11.68–69) indicates. Pope Leo I (*Ep.* 15) specified that no one could become a bishop if he had married a second time or was married to a widow.

Some Christians found full involvement in the larger arena of life within the city or the empire to be difficult. Tertullian (*Spec.; Idol.*) offered long lists of occupations that Christians should not pursue, expanding the hints found in the Pauline epistles. Discipleship meant the denial of the trappings demanded by power. Paul of Samosata, doubtless called to account for his Christological teaching, was rejected as the bishop of Antioch because he used his position as a procurator in the Roman government as the model for a Christian bishop. However, by the time that Rufinus translated those sections from Eusebius's *Church History* that dealt with Paul (7.30.6–16), he misunderstood the decision of the synod at Antioch (268) that deposed Paul. Rufinus thought that it was the abuse of such aspects as the high throne, the private audience chamber, and church funds that was at issue. In his era, bishops took their cues from Roman officials, while emperors had a loud voice and a strong arm in church councils.

Most Christians viewed the use of force as illicit in spite of centurions who believed without giving up their positions (Matt. 8:5–13; Acts 10:17–48). Some believers served both in the police force and in standing legions, such as the one Eusebius (*H.E.* 5.1–8) describes. Augustine even went so far as to develop a theory of the just war (*Civ. Dei* 19; *C. Faust.* 22).

Summary. Establishment of Christianity as a licit religion in the Roman empire gave much of Christian ethics a more accommodating stance in relationship to contemporary culture. Yet the root of Christian identity in its own community, formed by the person, life, and teaching of Christ and by the primitive congregations, meant that a reforming impetus was always available. Asceticism and monasticism offered a demanding model, even though they could be deformed in their own special ways. Ethics was always an important arena for Christians. Origen (*Cels.*) argued the superiority of Christian conduct when compared with that of classical Rome or Greece. John Chrysostom's *Homilies on Romans* interpreted that highly theological epistle in basically a moral tone. Theodoret's (*Haer.* 5) unique systematic theological treatment of the Christian faith deals with a number of pressing ethical issues. The mixed witness of these early figures still provides a unifying picture of identity, character, virtue, and active concern for all aspects of life. *See also* Love; Sin. [F.W.N.]

Bibliography

Epistle to Diognetus; Clement of Alexandria, *Miscellanies*; Tertullian, *On Idolatry*; Cyprian, *Testimonies*; Origen, *Against Celsus*; Athanasius, *Life of Anthony*; Basil of Caesarea, *Moralia*; John Chrysostom, *Homilies on Romans*; Augustine, *City of God*; Theodoret, *Haereticarum fabularum compendium* 5.

H.H. Scullard, *Early Christian Ethics in the West from Clement to Ambrose* (London: Williams and Norgate, 1907); F.J. Cadoux, *The Early Church and the World* (Edinburgh: T. and T. Clark, 1925); K.E. Kirk, *The Vision of God* (London: Longmans, Green, 1931); J. Leipoldt, *Der soziale Gedanke in den Alten Kirche* (Leipzig: Koehler and Amelung, 1952); A. Dihle, "Ethik," RLAC (1966), Vol. 6, pp. 646–796; M. Spanneut, *Tertullien et les premiers moralistes africains* (Gembloux: Duculot, 1969); E. Arnold, *The Early Christians After the Death of the Apostles* (Rifton: Plough, 1970); E. Osborn, *Ethical Patterns in Early Christian Thought* (Cambridge: Cambridge UP, 1976); G. Forell, *History of Christian Ethics* (Minneapolis: Augsburg, 1979), Vol. 1; R. Greer, *Broken Lights and Mended Lives: Theology and Common Life in the Early Church* (University Park: Pennsylvania State UP, 1986); A. Malherbe, ed., *Moral Exhortation: A Greco-Roman Sourcebook* (Philadelphia: Westminster, 1986); W. Meeks, *The Moral World of the First Christians* (Philadelphia: Westminster, 1986); F.X. Murphy, *The Christian Way of Life* (Wilmington: Glazier, 1986); J.L. Womer, *Morality and Ethics in Early Christianity* (Philadelphia: Fortress, 1987).

ETHIOPIA. Ancient writers called various geographical areas south of Egypt and as far away as India by the name "Ethiopia." In the Septuagint, Ethiopia usually identifies ancient

Cush or Meroe, which later became Christian Nubia. Queen Candace of Ethiopia and her treasurer, the eunuch baptized by the evangelist Philip (Acts 8:27), were Nubian, not Ethiopian—Candace is a Meroitic title for "queen mother." The Ethiopian kingdom of Axum, named for its capital, was southeast of Nubia. Located in the northern Ethiopian plateau, and including the coastal lowlands, Axum controlled the Red Sea trade from its major seaport at Adulis.

The introduction of Christianity to Ethiopia in the early fourth century is described in Rufinus's *Ecclesiastical History* 1.9–10 (ca. 401). Frumentius and Aedesius, brothers from Tyre, are said to have been shipwrecked off the Ethiopian coast; they were rescued and became distinguished officials of the royal court at Axum. Frumentius is said to have visited Athanasius in Alexandria to request a bishop for Ethiopia. Athanasius consecrated him, and he returned to Axum as the first of a long line of bishops, or *abunas* as they are called locally, who came to Ethiopia by way of Egypt. The chronology is anchored by the letter of the emperor Constantius II to the rulers of Axum, written ca. 356 in an unsuccessful attempt to replace Frumentius with an Arian bishop. The text is preserved in Athanasius's *Apology to the Emperor Constantius* 31 (ca. 356/7). Numismatic and epigraphical materials from Axum confirm the Christian conversion of the Ethiopian royal family in the fourth century, but the new religion spread slowly throughout the country.

After the Council of Chalcedon (451), the church in Ethiopia became identified with Monophysitism. In the second half of the fifth century, Ethiopia was the fertile ground for the missionary activities of Syrian and Egyptian ascetics, some of whom probably were Monophysite refugees. The best known of these visitors are the "Nine Saints," Syrian monks who traversed the country building churches and monasteries. In all likelihood, the Bible was translated into Ge'ez (classical Ethiopic) in the fifth century. The Old Testament text is based largely on the Septuagint. The New Testament text shows Syriac as well as Greek influences.

There are also versions of important apocrypha, such as *Enoch* (complete only in Ethiopic), *Jubilees*, and the *Ascension of Isaiah*. Early translations of patristic texts include the *Shepherd* of Hermas, the *Rule* of Pachomius, the *Physiologus*, and the *Qerillos*, a collection mainly of Christological texts.

By the early sixth century, Cosmas Indicopleustes in his *Christian Topography* could describe Ethiopia as a thoroughly Christian land. During the reign of the Axumite emperor Kālēb (514–542), an Ethiopian expedition (523–525) was sent to South Arabia, at the request of the Chalcedonian emperor Justin I, to rescue the Christians of Najrān from the persecution of a local king, Dhū Nuwās, who was a Jewish convert and Persian ally. Accounts of this successful expedition survive in the Greek and oriental versions of the *Martyrdom of St. Arethas* (ca. 535–545), the Syriac *Book of the Himyarites* (ca. 526–635), two Syriac letters (518/9) of Symeon of Bēth-Arshām (d. ca. 540), and the Syriac *Letter to the People of Najrān* by Jacob of Sarug (d. 521). In the seventh century, the advance of Islam effectively isolated Ethiopia from the rest of the Christian world. *See also* Nubia.   [M.J.B.]

Bibliography

E. Ullendorff, *Ethiopia and the Bible* (London: Oxford UP, 1968); F. Altheim and R. Stiehl, *Christentum am Roten Meer* (Berlin and New York: de Gruyter, 1971), Vol. 1; I. Shahid, *The Martyrs of Najrân: New Documents* (Brussels: Société des Bollandistes, 1971); Y.M. Kobishchanov, *Axum* (University Park: Pennsylvania State UP, 1979); J.S. Trimingham, *Christianity Among the Arabs in Pre-Islamic Times* (London and Beirut: Longman and Librairie du Liban, 1979); F. Thelamon, *Païens et chrétiens au IVe siècle: l'apport de l'"Histoire ecclésiastique" de Rufin d'Aquilée* (Paris: Etudes Augustiniennes, 1981); H.W. Lockot, *Bibliographia Aethiopica: Die äthiopienkundliche Literatur des deutschsprachigen Raums* (Wiesbaden: Steiner, 1982); J. Bonk, *An Annotated and Classified Bibliography of English Literature Pertaining to the Ethiopian Orthodox Church* (Metuchen: Scarecrow, 1984); B.W.W. Dombrowski and F.A. Dombrowski, "Frumentius/Abbā Salāmā: Zu den Nachrichten über die Anfänge des Christentums in Äthiopien," *OC* 68 (1984):114–169; A. Taklahāymānot, "The Egyptian Metropolitan of the Ethiopian Church," *Orientalia Christiana Periodica* 54 (1988):175–222.

EUCHARIST. The consecration and communion of bread and wine as a memorial of Christ's death and resurrection in the Christian liturgy.

Terminology. From the second century on, *eucharistia* (Greek, "thanksgiving") was the most common term for the central act of the Christian assembly (Ignatius, *Philad.* 4). The verb form, "to give thanks," was used in the accounts of Jesus' Last Supper with his disciples (Matt. 26:27). The word could be applied to the prayer of thanksgiving (*Did.* 9), to the elements for which thanks were said (Justin, *1 Apol.* 66), and to the whole action (Ignatius, *Eph.* 13.1). The earliest name for the observance was "the breaking of bread," which could refer to the opening act of an ordinary meal (Acts 27:35) as well as to a religious ceremony (Acts 2:42; Serapion, *Euch.* 2 tit.). The Pauline term "Lord's supper" (1 Cor. 11:20) did not prevail in Christian terminology (but cf. Basil, *Reg. br.* 310), perhaps as a result of the separation of the memorial of Christ from the evening meal (Tertullian, *Cor.* 3). The word *agapē* ("love feast") was occasionally used to include the eucharist (*Ep. apos.* 15). *Anamnēsis* ("memorial" or "remembrance"—1 Cor. 11:24f.; Justin, *Dial.* 70.4) and *koinōnia* ("communion"—1 Cor. 10:16; Serapion, *Euch.* 2) were

Christ administering communion to the apostles on a paten (565–578) found at Riha, Syria. (Courtesy of The Byzantine Collection, neg. 54.89.21, © 1989 Dumbarton Oaks, Trustees of Harvard University, Washington, D.C. 20007.)

also used. The common terms in later patristic times became in Greek *mystērion* ("mystery"— Eusebius, *D.E.* 1.10) and in Latin *sacramentum* (Cyprian, *Ep.* 63.16).

Antecedents. Religious meals of various types were known in Greek and Roman religion. They have been classified as (1) eating together in a cult society, to express fellowship or commemorate a founder or benefactor; (2) eating together when a deity was considered to preside; and (3) ecstatic rending of animals and eating their raw flesh. None offers an exact parallel to the Christian commemoration of Christ's death.

Judaism provided the immediate background to the Christian practice and concepts. Eating together served to confirm and remember covenants (Exod. 24:3–11; cf. the Passover—Deut. 16:1–8; *b. Pes.* 10.5). Jesus' Last Supper occurred at Passover. Although there are difficulties of chronology, the meal, if not actually the Passover, was at Passover season and was permeated with Passover motifs (Matt. 26:17–30 and parallels). The Jews had other religious meals, such as the meal on Sabbath eve, which concluded with the *Kiddush*, a blessing of a cup of wine and water for the sanctification of the Sabbath and whose wording influenced Christian prayers (*Prayer Book*, p. 122). Jewish meals included a blessing over bread and wine, and this assumed special importance in the eschatological meal described in the Dead Sea Scrolls (1QSa 18–22). Although Judaism provided several features to the Christian eucharist, the specific connection with Christ was a new development.

New Testament Origins. Despite differences in details between Mark 14:22–25 and 1 Corinthians 11:20–30, there is no reason to question the origin of the Christian eucharist in the Last Supper of Jesus with his disciples before the crucifixion. Also important were the meals of Jesus with his disciples after the resurrection (Luke 24:13–43; John 21:4–14). These would account for the Sunday observance and the frequency of fish symbolism in connection with the eucharist. Very early, a pattern of weekly meeting to break bread was established (Acts 20:7; cf. *Did.* 14). If Acts 2:46 referred

to a daily eucharist (other interpretations are possible), it was exceptional in the early centuries. The accounts of the institution of the Lord's supper in the Gospels already show the bringing together of the blessings of the bread and wine, which at the Last Supper came at the beginning and end of the meal respectively, and thus the separation of the memorial of Christ from the meal context.

Ceremony. The connection of the Lord's supper with the resurrection faith early established the morning, the time of the resurrection, as the appropriate time for taking the bread and wine (Tertullian, *Coron.* 3; cf. the explanation of the Passover meal as in the evening because of the Exodus at night—Deut. 16:6). The meal context for the eucharist was still preserved in the instructions in *Didache* 9–10, but there are uncertainties about the relation of the prayers preserved there to the eucharist, reinforced by the anomaly of the reverse order of the cup before the bread. Eating of the eucharist was limited to the baptized (9) and was to be preceded by reconciliation of any quarrels (14). Ignatius insisted on a single eucharist by the whole congregation under the presidency of the bishop or someone chosen by him (*Smyrn.* 8).

The earliest full accounts of the eucharist, both at baptism and the regular Sunday assemblies (Justin, *1 Apol.* 65; 67), include the presenting of bread and wine mixed with water to the president (offertory), the thanksgiving prayer for the gifts of creation and redemption (cf. Justin, *Dial.* 41) ratified by the congregational "Amen," and the communion, with the consecrated elements administered by the deacons and taken by them to those who had to be absent from the assembly.

The main features of the later eucharistic liturgies are found in the *Apostolic Tradition* (4) of Hippolytus. The deacons brought the elements to the bishop, and there was an introductory dialogue between the bishop and the people (*Sursum corda*). With his hands on the elements, the bishop said the prayer, which developed the history of salvation in a manner parallel to the baptismal catechesis. The prayer included the repetition of Jesus' words of institution, along with a statement of the remembrance of his death and resurrection (*anamnesis*) and of the offering of the bread and cup (oblation), and concluded with a petition for the coming of the Holy Spirit (*epiclesis*) "upon the offering of your holy church, that [God] would grant to all who partake of the holy [mysteries] to be united that they may be filled with the Holy Spirit." The congregation received the elements from the presbyters and deacons and said "Amen." At the baptismal eucharist, the new Christian was given a cup of milk with honey and a cup of water in addition (23).

The change of the bread and wine into the body and blood of Jesus came to be identified in later western thought with the repetition of the words of institution (Ambrose, *Sacram.* 4.4.14–4.5.23) and in later eastern thought with the invocation of the Holy Spirit (*Const. app.* 8.2.12). Both the *anamnesis* and the *epiclesis* would have been aspects of the early eucharistic celebration, but the earliest attitudes would probably have followed Jewish thought that the prayer of thanksgiving itself dedicated something to the purpose for which it was intended (cf. 1 Tim. 4:4f. and Justin, *1 Apol.* 66). Hippolytus wrote a model prayer to be followed by the bishop but specified that each one might pray according to his own ability, provided that the prayer be correct and orthodox (10.4). He stood midway between free prayer (Justin, *1 Apol.* 67) and the prescribed prayers of the liturgies.

Catechetical Lecture 23, ascribed to Cyril of Jerusalem, and *Apostolic Constitutions* 8.6–15 provide evidence of more developed eucharistic liturgies in the fourth century, just before the formation of the main eastern liturgies. The service may be outlined as follows: (1) the *lavabo*, a ceremonial washing of their hands by the presbyters; (2) kiss of peace as a sign of brotherly love and reconciliation by the congregation; (3) preface, including *Sursum corda*; (4) thanksgiving, followed by the singing of the *sanctus* (from Isa. 6:2, 3); (5) *epiclesis* for the change of the elements; (6) great intercession on behalf of the living and the dead; (7) Lord's prayer; (8) invitation to communion ("holy things for the holy," to which the people responded, "One is Holy, One is Lord, Jesus Christ," and the chanter sang Psalms 33:9); (9) reception of communion with a voiced "Amen"; (10) benediction.

Doctrine. The terminology employed indicates the important doctrinal ideas associated with the eucharist. The very name points to this act as the church's great moment of thanksgiving. The prayer was primarily a prayer of thanksgiving, and the whole service commemorated God's actions for human salvation, especially in the death and resurrection of Christ.

The prayer of thanksgiving was the basis for the extensive employment of sacrificial language in reference to the eucharist, for it was viewed as a thank offering (Justin, *Dial.* 41; Irenaeus, *Haer.* 4.17.5; 4.18.4). Malachi 1:11f., with its reference to the Lord's table and a pure offering, and the greatness of the Lord's name among the nations, made it the favorite text of the second-century church. The Lord's death was itself viewed as a sacrifice, and Cyprian combined the ideas of prayer as the pure sacrifice, the offering of bread and wine, and the association of the elements with the body and blood of Christ into the interpretation that "the Lord's passion is the sacrifice that we offer" (*Ep.* 63.17). The idea that the eucharist participated in and in some way perpetuated the sacrifice of Christ on the cross was to dominate later western thinking, giving the eucharist the character of a redemptive sacrifice (cf. Cyril of Jerusalem, *Catech.* 23.8–10) as well as a thank offering.

Jesus had identified the bread and the fruit of the vine with his body and blood (Mark 14:22), and this identification continued in Christian thought (Justin, *1 Apol.* 66), especially in arguments against Docetists and Gnostics who denied the reality of Jesus' human nature (Ignatius, *Smyrn.* 7; Irenaeus, *Haer.* 4.18.4f.; 5.2f.). Although some authors preferred to speak of the elements as a figure (*figura*— Tertullian, *Marc.* 4.40) or symbol (*symbolon*— Clement of Alexandria, *Paed.* 2.2.19f.; Origen, *Comm. in Mt.* 11.14), ancient thought gave a close correspondence between the symbol and that which was symbolized. Two strands of thought about the real presence were transmitted in the later tradition of the church. One line of interpretation maintained the symbolism of the visible signs and the reality of the supernatural and invisible gift of grace and divine life imparted through the symbols (dynamic symbolism—maintained in the Middle Ages especially through the influence of Augustine; cf. *In evang. Ioh.* 26.11[13]). Another strand of thought emphasized a change by which the sign and the reality became virtually identical (Ambrose, *Sacram.* 4.4.14–5.23).

By the sacrificial aspect of the eucharist, human beings were brought to God through the offering of the memorial of Christ's sacrifice, and by the real presence, God was brought to human beings in the spiritual food of the communion.

The memorial of Christ's death and resurrection held the historical aspect of Christian faith before the believers (John Chrysostom, *Hom.* 25.3 *in Mt.*). The liturgies either referred to the institution of the eucharist or substantially repeated it. The eschatological anticipation of the Lord's return so prominent at the beginning (1 Cor. 11:26; *Did.* 9–10) continued to be expressed in the expectation of the heavenly banquet and left a residue in the liturgy, such as the custom of facing east in prayer, for this was the direction of paradise from which Christ would return. The communion aspect, emphasizing the unity of the church (*Did.* 9), continued to be affirmed (Augustine, *Serm.* 272).

Art. The catacomb paintings include a large number of meal scenes. The interpretations of these have suggested many alternatives: the Last Supper, a eucharist, an agape, one of the meals from the Gospels (the multiplication of bread and fish or the postresurrection meal in John 21), a funerary meal, or the heavenly banquet. Different scenes may represent any one of these, and in some cases motifs from more than one model may have been combined. A few scenes seem to make direct allusion to the eucharist. A painting in St. Callistus (Foto Cal C 33) depicts an *orant* (praying figure) and another person with hands placed on a large fish on a tripod (for the fish symbolism in the eucharist, see the epitaph of Abercius), and a painting in SS. Peter and Marcellinus (Wilpert 159, 2) shows a seated figure blessing a loaf on a table. The most common way of referring to the bread and wine, in other media (notably on sarcophagi) as well as catacomb paintings, was by juxtaposing the miracles of the multiplication of the loaves and the turning of the water to wine at Cana (cf. Irenaeus, *Haer.* 3.11.5, for the association of these with the eucharist). The eucharist was also alluded to by representation of the Old Testament types. The bringing of bread and wine to Abraham by Melchizedek (Gen. 14:18) was an obvious type (already in Clement of Alexandria, *Str.* 4.25.161; Cyprian, *Ep.* 63.8; and cf. the location nearest the altar in the nave mosaics at Sta. Maria Maggiore). Abraham's sacrifice of Isaac (Gen. 22:1–18) was a popular type of the sacrifice of Christ and so was brought into association with the eucharist (note its combination in St. Callistus with a meal scene and the eucharistic fish mentioned above). The mosaics flanking the altar at S. Vitale show the sacrifice of Isaac, Melchizedek bringing bread and wine to Abraham, the sacrifice of Abel (Gen. 4:4), and the hospitality of Abraham to the heavenly visitors (Gen. 18:1–8). The combination of these scenes suggests the sacrificial and communion aspects of the eucharist.

In the oldest representations of the Last Supper—an ivory diptych in the cathedral treasury in Milan (fifth century) and the narrative cycle of mosaics in the nave of S. Apollinare Nuovo in Ravenna—perhaps under the influence of the early symbolic representations (and if so, confirming their eucharistic allusion), a fish is on the table. The moment most often chosen for representations of the Last Supper was the prediction of the betrayal, as in the sixth-century miniature in the Rossano Gospels. The table was normally a *sigma*-shape (semicircular) with Christ seated at the left (but he is at the center in an illuminated manuscript [No. 286, fol. 125] at Corpus Christi College, Cambridge—sixth century?—one of the rare early representations of the institution itself). From the sixth century, it became popular in the east to depict the Last Supper according to current liturgical practice as the "Apostles' First Communion." Communion in both kinds is emphasized by a double scene in which Christ presides at the altar and the apostles approach from each side to receive the bread and wine respectively (Rabbula Gospels and silver patens in Istanbul and Dumbarton Oaks).

Art, literature, and liturgy attest to the fundamental place of the eucharist as proclaiming the central aspects of Christian faith—the death and resurrection of Christ. *See also* Abercius; Agape; Anaphora; Bread; Epiclesis; Excommunication; Liturgy; Mass; Offerings; Real Presence; Sacraments; Sacrifice; S. Apollinare Nuovo; S. Vitale; Sunday; Wine.   [E.F.]

Bibliography

Didache 9–10, 14; Justin, *1 Apology* 65; 67; Hippolytus, *Apostolic Tradition* 4; Cyprian, *Letter* 63; Serapion, *Prayerbook* 1–2; Cyril of Jerusalem, *Catechetical Lectures* 23; *Apostolic Constitutions* 8.12–15; Ambrose, *On the Sacraments* 4.3–5.3; 6.1; *On the Mysteries* 8.43–9.59; Augustine, *Homilies on the Gospel of John* 26.10–20; 27.11.

H.B. Swete, "Eucharistic Belief in the Second and Third Centuries," *JThS* 3 (1902):161–177; Y. Brilioth, *Eucharistic Faith and Practice Evangelical and Catholic* (London: SPCK, 1930); E.G.C.F. Atchley, *On the Epiclesis of the Eucharistic Liturgy and the Consecration of the Font* (London: Oxford UP, 1935); J. Quasten, *Monumenta eucharistica et liturgica vetustissima* (Bonn: Hanstein, 1935–1937); F.L. Cirlot, *The Early Eucharist* (London: SPCK, 1939); G. Dix, *The Shape of the Liturgy* (Westminster: Dacre, 1945); M. Vloberg, *L'Eucharistie dans l'art* (Grenoble and Paris: Arthaud, 1946); E. Dekkers, "L'Eglise ancienne a-t-elle connu la messe du soir?," *Miscellanea Liturgica in Honorem L. Cuniberti Mohlberg* (Rome, 1948), Vol. 1, pp. 231–257; J. Solano, ed., *Textos eucaristicos primitivos*, 2 vols. (Madrid: La Editorial Catolica, 1952); G. Mathew, "The Origins of Eucharistic Symbolism," *Dominican Studies* 5 (1953):1–11; H. Lietzmann, *Mass and Lord's Supper* (Leiden: Brill, 1953–1979); R.L.P. Milburn, "Symbolism and Realism in Post-Nicene Representations of the Eucharist," *JEH* 8 (1957):1–16; J. Baum, "Symbolic Representations of the Eucharist," *Pagan and Christian Mysteries* (New York: Harper, 1963), pp. 70–82; A.D. Nock, "Hellenistic Mysteries and Christian Sacraments," *Early Gentile Christianity and Its Hellenistic Background* (New York: Harper Torchbooks, 1964), pp. 109–145; K. Wessel, *The Last Supper* (Recklinghausen: Aurel Bongers, 1967); W. Rordorf et al., *The Eucharist of the Early Christians* (New York: Pueblo, 1978); E. Lodi, *Enchiridion euchologicum fontium liturgicorum* (Rome: C.L.V.-Edizioni liturgiche, 1979); G. Wainwright, *Eucharist and Eschatology* (New York: Oxford UP, 1981); A. Bouley, *From Freedom to Formula: The Evolution of the Eucharistic Prayer from Oral Improvisation to Written Text* (Washington, D.C.: Catholic U of America P, 1981); D.J. Sheerin, *The Eucharist* (Wilmington: Glazier, 1986); E. Ferguson, *Early Christians Speak* (Abilene: ACU, 1987), pp. 93–105.

EUCHERIUS OF LYONS (d. ca. 449). Bishop and writer. Eucherius, a member of an aristocratic Gallo-Roman family, entered the monastic life after having held high imperial office; he was elected to the see of Lyons in 434. An esteemed preacher and correspondent with such prominent figures as Paulinus of Nola and Sidonius Apollinaris, he was the author of exegetical treatises important for the history of the biblical text as well as of exhortations to the ascetic life. A hagiographical work on the Theban legion, soldiers from the Thebaid martyred according to tradition under emperor Maximian (285–293), is also his. CPL 488–498.   [M.P.McH.]

Bibliography

Paulinus of Nola, *Letter* 51; Sidonius, *Letter* 4.3.7; *Poem* 16.115; Cassiodorus, *Divine and Human Readings* 1.10.1.

N.K. Chadwick, *Poetry and Letters in Early Christian Gaul* (London: Bowes and Bowes, 1955), pp. 151–160; P.-M. Duval, *La Gaule jusqu'au milieu du Ve siècle* (Paris: Picard, 1971), Vol. 1.2, pp. 728–732 (bibliography).

EUGIPPIUS (d. ca. 535). Abbot and writer. A disciple of Severinus of Noricum, Eugippius migrated to Italy sometime after Severinus's death in 482 and eventually became abbot of the monastery of Lucullanum near Naples. A friend of Cassiodorus, he presided over a flourishing monastic scriptorium, the manuscripts of which were diffused throughout Italy and North Africa. He composed the *Life of Saint Severin*, an important source for the history of the area about the Danube, and compiled a selection of extracts from the works of Augustine that was popular in the Middle Ages. Toward the end of his life, he wrote a rule for his monks, derived in great part from Augustine and the anonymous *Regula Magistri*, or *Rule of the Master.* CPL 676–679. [M.P.McH.]

Bibliography

Eugipii Regula, ed. F. Villegas and A. de Vogüé, CSEL (1976), Vol. 87.

The Life of Saint Severin, tr. L. Bieler with L. Krestan, FOTC (1965), Vol. 55.

Repertorium Fontium Historiae Medii Aevi (Rome: Istituto Storico Italiano per il Medio Evo, 1976), Vol. 4, pp. 389–390; R. Noll, "Literatur zur Vita Sancti Severini aus den Jahren 1975–1980," *AAWW* 118 (1981):196–221.

EULOGIUS OF ALEXANDRIA (d. 608).

Patriarch of Alexandria (580–608). Eulogius combatted Monophysites and other heretics. A letter from his friend Gregory the Great (*Ep.* 8.30) suggests that he supported the mission to Britain. [F.W.N.]

Bibliography

Gregory the Great, *Letters* 1.25; 5.43; 6.60; 7.34, 40; 8.29–30; 9.78; 10.35, 39; 12.50; 13.41–42.

EUNOMIUS OF CYZICUS (ca. 325–ca. 395).

One of the principal leaders of the Anomoean party within Arianism. Born to comparatively humble parents in rural Cappadocia and originally trained as a shorthand writer, Eunomius went on to become a rhetor, studying first at Constantinople and later at Antioch. He continued his studies at Alexandria, becoming both the disciple and the secretary of the Anomoean leader Aetius, who was then resident there. Returning to Antioch with his master, he became prominent in the Anomoean party and indeed later so eclipsed his teacher that the movement is often called "Eunomianism" after him. Although he shared Aetius's exile after the Council of Ancyra (358), he was vindicated at the Council of Constantinople (360) and made bishop of Cyzicus by Eudoxius, bishop of Constantinople. Deposed not long after and then exiled under the emperor Valens (369/70), he became the leader of the Anomoean party after Aetius's death. He was released from exile after the battle of Adrianople (379) and took up residence at Constantinople but was again exiled under Theodosius I. He died at Dakora near Caesarea in Cappadocia.

Eunomius's teaching was a formidable expression of the Anomoean position and provoked extensive refutations from his theological contemporaries, notably Basil the Great and Gregory of Nyssa. He is one of the few Arian authors whose dogmatic writings have survived. These include his *Apology* (preserved entire), his *Apology for the Apology* (preserved in extensive quotations by Gregory of Nyssa), and his *Confession of Faith* (also preserved entire). Fragments of other works also survive. His lost works include a commentary on Romans and some forty letters. CPG II, 3455–3460. *See also* Aetius; Anomoeans. [R.P.V.]

Bibliography

Basil of Caesarea, *Adversus Eunomium*; Gregory of Nyssa, *Against Eunomius*; Socrates, *Church History* 4.7; 5.24; Sozomen, *Church History* 6.8, 26–27; 7.17; Photius, *Library* 138.

Eunomius, *The Extant Works*, ed. and tr. R.P. Vaggione, OECT (1987).

E. Vandenbussche, "La Part de la dialectique dans la théologie d'Eunomius 'le technologue,'" *RHE* 40 (1944–1945): 47–72; J. Daniélou, "Eunome l'Arian et l'exégèse platonicienne du Cratyle," *Revue des études grecques* 69 (1956):412–432; L.R. Wickham, "The Date of Eunomius' *Apology*: A Reconsideration," *JThS* 20 (1969):231–240; E. Cavalcanti, *Studi Eunomiani* (Rome: Pontificium Institutum Orientalium Studiorum, 1976).

EUSEBIUS OF CAESAREA (ca. 260–ca. 339).

Bishop of Caesarea and the first major historian of the church. Eusebius was also a biblical exegete, an apologist for Christianity against paganism, an activist in the Arian controversy, and an early interpreter of the duties of a Christian emperor. Although not an eloquent writer or original thinker, he preserved precious documents and valuable reflections on Christian life and thought in a transitional period.

In Caesarea, the young Eusebius studied with Pamphilus, a noted Christian teacher with a remarkable theological library and an admiration for Origen. Eusebius devoted himself to scholarship and to Pamphilus, even taking the name of his teacher, Eusebius Pamphili ("the son of Pamphilus"); together they wrote *A Defense of Origen*. Among his early works were *Against Hierocles*, a short apology defending the miracles of Jesus; the *Onomasticon*, a study of biblical place-names and geography; and the *Chronicle*, a chronology of biblical and historical events. These writings reflect Eusebius's lifelong interest in proving the truth of Christianity by showing the fulfillment of prophecy and scripture in historical events. He later commented that "works are plainer than words" (*P.E.* 1.3), and his many writings reveal his attention to the literal or historical interpretation of scripture rather than to allegorical exegesis or theological reflection, in spite of his admiration for Origen.

Building on these early writings, Eusebius began his most famous work, the *Church History*. Its purpose was to show in fullest detail the dispensation and divinity of Christ through the story of Christians, who had cast out error, endured persecution, fulfilled Hebrew prophecy, and seen their enemies punished by divine providence. Although these themes had been part of earlier apologies and were used by Eusebius to present a highly sympathetic view of the Christian past, his breadth of vision and extensive quotation of original sources make his history essential to any study of early eastern Christianity. The first draft was perhaps written before 300, but Eusebius continued to revise it in light of new events during the next twenty years, including the Diocletian persecution (303) and the tolerance of Christianity granted under Constantine (313).

During the Diocletian persecution, Pamphilus was imprisoned and eventually martyred. After his teacher's death in 310, Eusebius traveled through Palestine and Egypt. The result of his experiences was a remarkable work, *The Martyrs of Palestine* (later incorporated into the *History*), an eyewitness account of the torture and heroism of Christian martyrs. He himself was imprisoned in Egypt. Shortly afterward (ca. 313), he became bishop of Caesarea and continued his historical and apologetic writings. In reply to the devastating polemic against Christian interpretation of scripture by the philosopher Porphyry, Eusebius wrote two massive apologetic works that drew on his knowledge of scripture and Greek literature. In *The Preparation for the Gospel*, he compared scripture with Greek literature to show the superiority of Jewish and Christian teaching to Hellenic mythology and philosophy. In the companion work, *The Proof of the Gospel*, Eusebius continued his apology by showing in detail how Christ's life fulfilled Hebrew prophecy and made Christians the true heirs to the Jewish covenant. Both works tend to rest on sheer volume of quotation rather than cogent argument. A later work by Eusebius, the *Theophany*, drew on both these works to defend the incarnation.

Theologically, Eusebius played an active role in the Arian controversy. As a scholar and student of Origen's thought, he initially defended Arius's theology as giving proper ontological and scriptural prominence to the Father. After his condemnation at the Council of Antioch in 324, he sought to make peace with the larger church at Nicaea in 325. He accepted the creed of Nicaea and *homoousios* with certain elucidations to protect the superiority of the Father (Athanasius, *Decr.* 3; Sozomen, *H.E.* 1.21). Wary of possible Sabellian interpretations of the creed, Eusebius joined with those who attacked and ousted Eustathius of Antioch (Theodoret, *H.E.* 1.20; Sozomen, *H.E.* 2.18–19). In 335, he participated in the exiling of Athanasius (Athanasius, *Apol. sec.* 87.1). He also wrote against Marcellus of Ancyra, whom he suspected with some justification of Sabellianism. In *Contra Marcellum* and *De ecclesiastica theologia*, Eusebius presented the traditional faith of the church as teaching three preexistent and separate *hypostases*; the Son was begotten by the Father but was clearly secondary. Although Eusebius may have been defending a traditional subordinationism common in the eastern church, his theological reputation was tarnished for later generations.

The favors granted Christianity under Constantine confirmed Eusebius's vision of the historical triumph of the church, and his reflections on Constantine's rule celebrated the new union of spiritual and temporal power. His orations to the emperor, *In Praise of Constantine* and *On Christ's Sepulchre*, on the occasion of Constantine's thirtieth anniversary as emperor (335), preserve his high hopes for Christian imperial power. Combining Greek rhetorical forms with Christian theology, Eusebius compared Constantine to Christ as the ruler of his people; as the Word brought peace and order, so should the emperor as the image of the Word. A similar theology was expressed in the unfinished *Life of Constantine*. These optimistic reflections laid the foundation for later political theory in the Byzantine empire. In his later life, Eusebius also finished two commentaries on biblical books he had used extensively throughout his life: Psalms and Isaiah. Both works reflected his textual and historical interests. He died ca. 339, a respected scholar and bishop. CPG II, 3465–3507. TLG 2018. *See also* Martyrs of Palestine.   [R.L.]

Bibliography

Editions of Greek texts in PG 19–24; *Eusebius Werke*, GCS (1902–1983), Vols. 7, 9, 11, 14, 20, 23, 43, 47; Greek and French texts in *Histoire ecclésiastique*, ed. G. Bardy, SC (1952–1958), Vols. 31, 41, 55, 73; *La Préparation évangélique*, ed. E. des Places, J. Sirinelli, and O. Zink, SC (1974–), Vols. 206, 215, 228, 262, 266, 292, 307.

Against Hierocles in Flavius Philostratus, *The Life of Apollonius of Tyana, the Epistles of Apollonius, and the Treatise of Eusebius*, tr. F.C. Conybeare, LCL (1912); *Church History, Life of Constantine the Great*, and *Oration in Praise of Constantine*, tr. A.C. McGiffert and E.C. Richardson, NPNF, 2nd ser. (1890; repr. 1978), Vol. 1; *The Ecclesiastical History*, tr. K. Lake and J.E.L. Oulton, 2 vols., LCL (1926–1932); *The Ecclesiastical History* and *The Martyrs of Palestine*, tr. H.J. Lawlor and J.E.L. Oulton (London: SPCK, 1928); *In Praise of Constantine, A Historical Study and New Translation of Eusebius's Tricennial Orations*, tr. H.A. Drake (Berkeley: U of California P, 1976); *The Preparation of the Gospel*, tr. E.H. Gifford, 2 vols. (Oxford: Clarendon, 1903); *The Proof of the Gospel*, tr. W.J. Ferrar, 2 vols. (London: SPCK, 1920); *The Theophania*, tr. S.E. Lee (Cambridge: Cambridge UP, 1893).

J.B. Lightfoot, "Eusebius of Caesarea," DCB (1880), Vol. 2, pp. 308–348; H.J. Lawlor, *Eusebiana: Essays on the Ecclesiastical History of Eusebius* (Oxford: Clarendon, 1912); J. Stevenson, *Studies in Eusebius* (Cambridge: Cambridge UP, 1929); N.H. Baynes, "Eusebius and the Christian Empire," *Mélanges Bidez* (Brussels: Secrétariat de l'Institut, 1934), pp. 13–18; H. Berkhof, *Die Theologie des Eusebius von Caesarea* (Amsterdam: Uitgeversmaatschappij Holland, 1939); D.S. Wallace-Hadrill, *Eusebius of Caesarea* (London: Mowbray, 1960); C.U. Wolf, "Eusebius of Caesarea and the *Onomasticon*," *Biblical Archaeologist* 27 (1964):66–96; A. Weber, *APXH: Ein Beitrag zur Christologie des Eusebius von Caesarea* (Rome: Pontificia Universitas Gregoriana, 1965); C. Sant, *The Old Testament Interpretation of Eusebius of Caesarea* (Malta: Royal University of Malta, 1967); F. Ricken, "Die Logoslehre des Eusebius von Caesarea und der Mittelplatonismus," *Theologie und Philosophie* 42 (1967):341–358; G.C. Stead, "Eusebius and the Council of Nicaea," *JThS* n.s. 24 (1973):85–100; J.E. Bruns, "The 'Agreement of Moses and Jesus' in the *Demonstratio Evangelica* of Eusebius," *VChr* 31 (1977):117–125; C. Luibheid, *Eusebius of Caesarea and the Arian Crisis* (Dublin: Irish Academic Press, 1978); A.A. Mosshammer, *The Chronicle of Eusebius and Greek Chronographic Tradition* (Lewisburg: Bucknell UP, 1979); R.M. Grant, *Eusebius as Church Historian* (Oxford: Clarendon, 1980); T.D. Barnes, *Constantine and Eusebius* (Cambridge: Harvard UP, 1981); S. Gero, "The True Image of Christ: Eusebius's Letter to Constantine Reconsidered," *JThS* n.s. 32 (1981):460–470; E. des Places, *Eusèbe de Césarée Commentateur: Platonisme et écriture sainte* (Paris: Beauchesne, 1982).

EUSEBIUS OF NICOMEDIA (d. 342). Bishop (317–342). Eusebius acquired the see of Nicomedia during the reign of the eastern Roman emperor Licinius (308–324), perhaps ca. 317, when Licinius himself took up residence in Nicomedia. Connections at the imperial court in fact may have facilitated Eusebius's rise to prominence, for he had been previously bishop of Berytus, and his critics criticized the move to Nicomedia as uncanonical. As bishop of the emperor's city, he apparently enjoyed a considerable prestige among his colleagues. This prestige, perhaps more than Eusebius's known theological predilections, may have prompted the recently excommunicated Arius to appeal his case to Eusebius shortly before 324. Eusebius's favorable endorsement of Arius's petition put him at the center of the Arian controversy, which dominated the remainder of his professional life.

Eusebius accepted the anti-Arian creed formulated by the Council of Nicaea (325) but refused to recognize the council's confirmation of Arius's excommunication. For this refusal, presumably, the emperor Constantine deposed and banished him in 325. He was reinstated at Nicomedia, however, scarcely two years later; became thereafter Constantine's primary ecclesiastical adviser; and himself administered Constantine's deathbed baptism—all the while continuing to fight for the reinstatement of Arius.

That the death of Constantine did not reduce Eusebius's prominence is shown by the pro-Arian attitude of Constantine's heir in the east, Constantius II. Just prior to his own death in 342, Eusebius became bishop of the new capital, Constantinople. CPG II, 2045–2056.

[G.J.J.]

Bibliography
Socrates, Church History 1–2; Sozomen, Church History 1–2; Theodoret, Church History 1.
T.D. Barnes, Constantine and Eusebius [of Caesarea] (Cambridge: Harvard UP, 1981).

EUSEBIUS OF VERCELLI (d. 370/1). Native of Sardinia, cleric at Rome, after 344 first bishop of Vercelli, opponent of Arianism. At pope Liberius's request, Eusebius was (with Lucifer of Cagliari) a leader of the western supporters of Nicaea after the Arianizing Synod of Arles in 353. At the Synod of Milan in 355, he resisted the condemnation of Athanasius and asked the bishops to sign the creed of Nicaea. He was exiled to the east from 355 to 361. In 362, he signed Athanasius's Tome to the Antiochenes and carried it to Antioch. Three of his letters are extant. A work on the Trinity is inauthentic. Eusebius introduced monastic life for diocesan clergy. CPL 105–111e. [J.T.L.]

Bibliography
Hilary of Poitiers, Fragmenta historica 11.5; Lucifer of Cagliari, Epistula 1; Liberius, Epistulae iv ad Eusebium; Ambrose, Letter 63; Jerome, Lives of Illustrious Men 96.
J.T. Lienhard, "Patristic Sermons on Eusebius of Vercelli and Their Relation to Monasticism," RBén 87 (1977):164–172.

EUSTATHIUS OF ANTIOCH (fl. 325). Bishop of Berea, then bishop of Antioch toward the end of 324. Eustathius was one of the leaders of the anti-Arians at Nicaea in 325 and a staunch defender of the council, attacking Eusebius of Caesarea as an Arian and attacked by Eusebius as a Sabellian. By the end of 326, the Arians succeeded in deposing him. Fragments of his dogmatic writings show that his theology foreshadows the Antiochene Christology. His homily on the witch of Endor (1 Sam. 28) rejects Origen's interpretation of the

story as too literal but also attacks Origen's allegorical exegesis. CPG II, 3350–3398.

[R.A.G.]

Bibliography
M. Spanneut, Recherches sur les écrits d'Eustathe d'Antioche avec une édition nouvelle des fragments dogmatiques et exégétiques (Lille: Facultés catholiques de Lille, 1948).

EUTHERIUS OF TYANA (fifth century). Bishop of Tyana. Eutherius supported Nestorius and attacked Cyril of Alexandria as an Apollinarian. He attended the Council of Ephesus (431), where he voted to wait until the Antiochenes could arrive. When his party lost the vote, he was deposed. CPG III, 6147–6153.

[F.W.N.]

Bibliography
PG 28.1337–1394; 84.681–685, 726–731, 815–826.

EUTROPIUS (fourth–fifth centuries). Chief adviser of the emperor Arcadius (383–408). Eutropius arranged the marriage of Arcadius with Eudoxia in 395 and supported the election of John Chrysostom as bishop of Constantinople in 397. He was at the height of his influence as consul when he fell from favor in 399. He was noted for pride and avarice. [E.F.]

Bibliography
John Chrysostom, Two Homilies on Eutropius, tr. W.R.W. Stephens, NPNF, 1st ser. (1889), Vol. 9, pp. 245–265; Claudian, In Eutropium 1–2; Sozomen, Church History 8.7; Zosimus, New History 5.3, 8–14, 17–18.

EUTROPIUS (fl. 415). Presbyter. Active in Aquitaine or northern Spain, Eutropius wrote four short treatises displaying a high degree of classical education and representing the tradition of spiritual exegesis employed in support of the ascetic life. CPL 565–567. [E.F.]

Bibliography
Gennadius, Lives of Illustrious Men 49.
F. Cavallera, "L'Héritage littéraire et spirituel du prêtre Eutrope," Revue d'ascétique et de mystique 24 (1948):60–71; P. Courcelle, "Un Nouveau Traité d'Eutrope, prêtre aquitain, vers l'an 400," REA 61

(1954):377–390; H. Savon, "Le Prêtre Eutrope et la 'vraie circoncision,'" *RHR* 199 (1982):273–302, 381–404.

EUTYCHES (fl. 450).

Archimandrite of a monastery in Constantinople. Eutyches was the godfather of Chrysaphius, the emperor Theodosius II's grand chamberlain, and had the support not only of the imperial court but also of Dioscorus, the powerful patriarch of Alexandria. By 447, his theological views were causing controversy in Constantinople; his insistence on the one nature of the incarnate Word, together with his view that even Christ's sufferings were the Word's, appeared to deny the full humanity of Christ. In November 448, Flavian, the patriarch of Constantinople, summoned a council that condemned Eutyches, who immediately appealed the decision. The result was a council (the *Latrocinium*, or "Robber Council") held in Ephesus in 449 at which Dioscorus, supported by the imperial court, vindicated Eutyches. The *Tome* of Leo, bishop of Rome, was not read, even though it was a response to Flavian regarding the controversy. In the summer of 450, the tide turned when Theodosius II died and Chrysaphius was deposed. A new council met at Chalcedon in 451. Eutyches was condemned, and Dioscorus was deposed. The Chalcedonian Definition of Faith insisted upon the phrase "*in* two natures," and by rejecting the phrase "*out of* two natures" excluded any use of the one-nature (Monophysite) formula. It is difficult to be sure exactly what Eutyches taught, largely because he seems to have shifted his views under pressure. He was prepared to recognize two natures of Christ before the incarnation but remained insistent that the incarnate Lord was one nature fashioned out of the two. He seems to have died not long after Chalcedon. CPG III, 5945–5954.   [R.A.G.]

Bibliography

Leo the Great, *Letters* 20–26; 28; 31; 34; 35; 38; 85; 87; 98; 124; 134; 164; tr. C.L. Feltoe, NPNF, 2nd ser. (1895), Vol. 12; Peter Chrysologus, *Letter to Eutyches*, tr. G.E. Ganss, FOTC (1953), Vol. 17, pp. 285–287.

E. Schwarz, "Der Prozess des Eutyches," *Sitzungsberichte der bayerischen Akademie der Wissenschaften* (Munich: Bayerischen Akademie der Wissenschaften, 1929); R. Draguet, "La Christologie d'Eutyches d'après les Actes du Synode de Flavien (448)," *Byzantion* 6 (1931):441–457; T. Camelot, "De Nestorius à Eutyches: l'opposition de deux christologies," *Das Konzil von Chalkedon*, ed. A. Grillmeier and H. Bacht (Wurzburg: Echter-Verlag, 1951), Vol. 1, pp. 213–242; A. Grillmeier, *Christ in Christian Tradition*, 2nd ed. (Atlanta: John Knox, 1975), Vol. 1, pp. 523–534, 537–538.

EVAGRIUS OF PONTUS (345–399).

Monk who developed Gnostic, Origenist spirituality. Born into a Christian family, Evagrius was a student of Gregory of Nazianzus, who ordained him a deacon in 379. Later, he traveled to Jerusalem, where he entered a monastery on the Mount of Olives along with Melania the Elder and Rufinus. By 383, he was in Egypt at Nitria, where he met Palladius, Macarius, and other monastic leaders.

Evagrius spent his life mostly in monastic seclusion and the study of Origen. His works portray a type of Origenistic spirituality that sees intelligent souls as once part of a great divine unity. Each soul fell and was joined to a body but through practical asceticism and Gnostic contemplation could eventually return to that unity with God. Although his Christology was at first much like that of Gregory of Nazianzus, eventually he reduced the incarnation to a vision of a great intellect that gave souls knowledge in order to return to God.

Evagrius's influence was wide, as much for his practical advice in ascetic practices as for his doctrines. In the fifth and sixth centuries, his works were often at the center of the Origenist controversy, but they had an effect on John Cassian, Maximus Confessor, John Climacus, and various Monophysite and Nestorian leaders. His writings in Greek—works on spirituality, as well as extensive biblical commentaries—are extant only in Syriac and Armenian. Some pieces attributed to Nilus of Ancyra may be the work of Evagrius. CPG II, 2430–2482. TLG 4110.   [F.W.N.]

Bibliography

Socrates, *Church History* 4.23; Sozomen, *Church History* 6.30; Gennadius, *Lives of Illustrious Men* 11; Palladius, *Lausiac History* 38.

Evagrius Ponticus: Praktikos and Chapters on Prayer (Kalamazoo: Cistercian, 1989).

A. Guillaumont, *Les "Kephalaia Gnostica" d'Evagre le Pontique et l'histoire de l'origénisme chez les Grecs et chez les Syriens* (Paris: Seuil, 1962); K. Beyschlag, "Was heisst mystische Erfahrung?," *Evangelium als Schicksal: 5 Studien zur Geschichte der alten Kirche* (Munich: Claudius, 1979), pp. 113–134; P. Gehin, "Un Nouvel Inédit d'Evagre le Pontique: son commentaire de l'Ecclésiaste," *Byzantion* 49 (1979):188–198; J. Paramelle, "Les Chapitres des Disciples d'Evagre," *Annuaire de l'Ecole pratique des Hautes Etudes, Ve section, Sciences religieuses* 88 (1979–1980):348–385; A. Guillaumont, "Le Corpus des 62 lettres d'Evagre le pontique," *Annuaire de l'Ecole pratique des Hautes Etudes, Ve section, Sciences religieuses* 89 (1980–1981):471–472.

EVAGRIUS SCHOLASTICUS (ca. 535–600).

Church historian. Born in Coele Syria and a lawyer in Antioch, Evagrius treated the church histories of Eusebius, Socrates, Sozomen, and Theodoret as classics. He wrote his own history ca. 593, beginning with events in 428. His viewpoint was influenced by his position of power; he was well established at Antioch and even knew the family of the emperor Maurice.

Unlike Eusebius, Evagrius found the tides of fortune in human affairs overwhelming. Although he largely Christianized the theme of fortune, he found many events to be beyond the control of those involved in them. He encouraged virtue but saw much of life through the eyes of a Greek tragedian.

Although not gifted theologically and credulous about saints' legends, Evagrius did carry on an interesting polemic against other historians. He insists that Zacharias Rhetor, a Monophysite historian, skewed his facts and that Zosimus, a vigorous anti-Christian, could not support his case that Christians were the cause of the empire's decline. Like Eusebius, he sees God's hand in the developments of the empire.

Evagrius used a number of fine sources (Eustathius the Syrian, Procopius of Caesarea, Agathus, and others), which he tends to quote rather than merely mention. They greatly enhance the value of his history. CPG III, 7500.

[F.W.N.]

Bibliography
Evagrius, Ecclesiastical History, tr. E. Walford (London: Bagster, 1846).

P. Allen, *Evagrius Scholasticus, the Church Historian* (Leuven: Peeters, 1981); G. Chesnut, *The First Christian Histories: Eusebius, Socrates, Sozomen, Theodoret, and Evagrius*, 2nd ed. (Macon: Mercer UP, 1986).

EVANGELIST.

Preacher of the gospel. The New Testament uses the word "evangelist" three times. Ephesians 4:11 lists evangelists among the ministers who are Christ's gifts to the church. Acts 21:8 calls Philip (cf. Acts 6:8) an evangelist. 2 Timothy 4:5 exhorts Timothy to "do the work of an evangelist." This "work," according to the letters to Timothy and Titus, included "reading [the scriptures], teaching, and exhorting" (1 Tim. 4:13) in the assembly; preaching the word, which involved "convincing, rebuking, and exhorting" (2 Tim. 4:2); preserving sound doctrine (1 Tim. 1:3ff.; 6:20); training others to continue the ministry (2 Tim. 2:2); and giving organizational structure to local churches (Titus 1:5). The function of preaching the gospel is much more frequent than the title of evangelist (e.g., Acts 8:4; 11:20; Rom. 10:15; 1 Peter 1:12).

This title is rare in early Christian literature, but it seems that much of the function was continued by those known as "teachers" (Hermas, *Sim.* 9.15.4?), such as Justin Martyr (Eusebius, *H.E.* 4.11.8) and Pantaenus (idem, *H.E.* 5.10.2). Where the word "evangelist" occurs, it is often in reference to missionary preaching; Eusebius used it for those who along with the apostles and then in succession to them preached the gospel and established churches throughout the world (*H.E.* 2.3.1f.; 3.37). Origen described the activity without use of the word "evangelist" (*Cels.* 3.9). Theodoret explained evangelists as "those who going about preached" (*Eph.* 4.11). Since the apostles were known as "those who preach the gospel" (Gal. 1:8; *1 Clem.* 42.1; Polycarp, *Ep.* 6.3; *Barn.* 8.3), the evangelists were closely associated with them. Thus, Tertullian asked, "Who are the false apostles but the preachers of a spurious gospel?" (*Praescr.* 4; cf. *Coron.* 9). Hippolytus called Luke an "apostle and evangelist" (*Antichr.* 56; cf. Origen, *Jo.* 2.4). It was later said that "all apostles are evangelists, but not all evangelists are apostles" (Ps.-Jerome, *In Eph.* 4.11; cf. John Chrysostom, *Hom.* 11.2 *in Eph.* 4.11).

The association of evangelists with apostles led to the theory that they were the link in the apostolic succession from apostles to bishops (Theodore of Mopsuestia, *1 Tim.* 3.8; Theodoret, *1 Tim.* 3.1). Origen says that it sometimes happened that a Christian arrived in a town, taught, converted some, and finally became the bishop (*Hom.* 11 *in Num.* 4). This was a natural enough process but was distinct from the dogmatic theory that made such men as Timothy and Titus the bearers of apostolic authority transmitted to bishops.

The reader of the scriptures in the assembly was said to assume "the position of an evangelist" (*Ap. Ch. Order* 19). Eusebius chose to restrict his account of "shepherds and evangelists" to those "who transmitted the apostolic doctrine to us in writings still extant" (*H.E.* 3.37). This transfer from the preacher to the writer became characteristic of Christian usage, and the name "evangelist" came to refer to the writers of the four Gospels (Origen, *Jo.* 10.31; John Chrysostom, *Hom.* 1.2 *in Mt.*). The term "evangelist" first referred to a proclaimer of the gospel, then a reader of the gospel, and finally a writer of the gospel. *See also* Apostolic Succession; Bishop; Ministry; Reader.

[E.F.]

Bibliography

E. Ferguson, "The Ministry of the Word in the First Two Centuries," *Restoration Quarterly* 1 (1957):21–31.

EVE. First woman (Gen. 2:20–23; 3:20). The initial references to Eve in the Christian tradition link her with sinfulness (2 Cor. 11:3; 1 Tim. 2:11–15). According to the author of 1 Timothy, Eve had a secondary status for two reasons: she was created second (Gen. 2:21–22) and she, not Adam, was first deceived (Gen. 3:1–6). Because of her sin, women of the author's time were not to teach or to have authority over men.

Eve, Adam, and tree of the knowledge of good and evil (third century), from chamber 14 of the Catacomb of SS. Peter and Marcellinus, Rome, Italy. (Used by permission of Pontifical Commission of Sacred Archaeology.)

Christian writers from the second century onward adapted Paul's theme of the parallel between Adam and Christ (Rom. 5; 1 Cor. 15) to parallel Eve with Mary: both were virgins, but one brought forth disobedience while the other obediently gave herself to become the mother of the Savior (Justin, *Dial.* 100; Irenaeus, *Haer.* 3.22.4). In addition, patristic authors frequently commented on the sentence passed on Eve in Genesis 3:16, believing that the verse gave biblical justification for the male domination of women. Thus, Tertullian (*Cult. fem.* 1.1.1) reminds a female audience that as Eve's descendants, they are "the devil's gateway" and are responsible for the Son of God having had to die. Although a few authors attempted to mitigate Eve's role in the sin (e.g., Ambrose, *Parad.* 12.56), the tendency was to blame her more heavily.

Another area of speculation surrounding the figure of Eve was whether she had received the "image of God" as completely as Adam had: 1 Corinthians 11:7 could be taken to imply that she had not. If the woman was inferior even at creation, women of the present could be reminded of their "natural" inferiority (e.g., Augustine, *Gen. ad litt.* 11.42; John Chrysostom, *Hom.* 26 *in 1 Cor.* 5; *Serm.* 2 *in Gen.* 2; *Hom.* 8 *in Gen.* 4).

Gnostic and Manichaean literature commented on Eve as well. Although Manichaean mythology interpreted Eve negatively (since the scheme of reproduction that further disperses the particles of light in dark materiality begins with her), Gnostic texts could offer a more positive interpretation, since eating of the tree in the Garden of Eden was the introduction to "knowledge." Eve even functions as a spiritual principle who awakens Adam and is his teacher (e.g., *On the Origin of the World* 115–116; *Apocalypse of Adam* 64). *See also* Women.

[E.A.C.]

Bibliography

J.A. Phillips, *Eve: The History of an Idea* (San Francisco: Harper and Row, 1984); K. King, ed., *Gnosticism and Images of the Feminine* (Philadelphia: Fortress, 1988); E. Pagels, *Adam, Eve, and the Serpent* (New York: Random House, 1988).

EXCOMMUNICATION. Exclusion from the communion of the church for disciplinary purposes. Rabbinic literature distinguished levels of discipline in Judaism. The most severe was the *ḥerem*, which excluded a person from public worship and social intercourse except with wife and children and denied to him anything other than the bare necessities of life from other Jews. The *nidduy* was inflicted for less severe offenses and lasted for thirty days, during which time the person dressed as a mourner. This punishment was removed after due signs of repentance. The Dead Sea Scrolls show comparable disciplinary procedures in sectarian Judaism contemporary with the New Testament. Various offenses brought exclusion for one or two years, but apostasy by a member of more than ten years brought lifetime exclusion (1QS vi.24–vii.25). The Gospel of Matthew records Jesus' instructions that a person who rejected admonition was to be excluded from the community (Matt. 18:15–17), and Paul taught that the church was not to eat with a person guilty of immorality (1 Cor. 5:1–13).

Only the baptized could share in the eucharist (Justin, *1 Apol.* 66), and the *Didache* 9 understood Jesus' words, "Give not that which is holy to the dogs" (Matt. 7:6), as applying to the eucharist. This principle had as its corollary that a Christian who did not live as required by the gospel was excluded from the communion. The *Didache* 14 required reconciliation of those who quarreled before the church assembled. The eucharist was defined in terms of communion: "*Koinōnia* [communion] is the name for the reception of the divine mysteries, for thereby we receive the gift of being made one with Christ and partakers of his kingdom" (Isidore of Pelusium, *Ep.* 1.228). The phrase *communio sanctorum* in the Apostles' Creed, usually translated "communion of the saints," probably meant originally "the communion of holy things" (the sacrament). The celebration of the eucharist was the basic expression of fellowship within and between congregations.

The breaking of fellowship involved separation from communion. Tertullian speaks of "one who has sinned so grievously as to be excluded from the fellowship of prayer, assembly, and all observance of holy things" (*Apol.* 39.4). Faithful Christians were not to pray with a person placed under discipline (*Didas.* 6.14; *Can. app.* 11). However, discipline especially involved exclusion from the eucharist (Elvira, *can.* 34; Arles, *can.* 4–5). Reconciliation to the church was readmission to communion (Elvira, *can.* 9; 46; 69; 78). The canonical legislation of the church established varying periods of discipline for different offenses and different stages in reconciliation to the church (Gregory Thaumaturgus, *Ep. can.* 11; Basil, *Can.* 4; 56; 82f.). The reconciliation to the church of those dying involved giving the eucharist to the person (Eusebius, *H.E.* 6.44.2–6; Nicaea, *can.* 13). The western church tended to see excommunication more in terms of punishment; the eastern preferred to speak of discipline as therapeutic (Gregory of Nyssa, *Ep. can.* 1).

Excommunication was imposed for moral failures and for doctrinal errors that denied the confession of the church (*Didas.* 12; *Const. app.* 8.12.1–2). Letters informed other churches about those in fellowship and those excluded. *See also* Discipline; Eucharist; Penance; Repentance. [E.F.]

Bibliography

W. Doskocil, *Der Bann in der Urkirche* (Munich: Zink, 1958); W. Elert, *Eucharist and Church Fellowship in the First Four Centuries* (St. Louis: Concordia, 1966).

EXODUS. Second book of the Pentateuch, named for the Exodus from Egypt, which gave Israel its independence. The word "exodus" occurs in the Greek Bible at Exodus 19:1. In its forty chapters, Exodus covers history from the death of Joseph to the setting up of the tabernacle at Mt. Sinai in the second year of the Exodus. The larger part of the book deals with God's giving of the Law to Israel on Mt. Sinai and details the building and furnishing of the tabernacle.

In the Old Testament, the Exodus is alluded to in Psalm 78:43–53 and Micah 6:4–5. The prophets develop the idea of the second Exodus, the return from captivity (Isa. 43:16–20; 48:21–22; Jer. 16:14f.; 23:7f.; Hosea 11:11). Scholars have seen an "Exodus" pattern in the Gospels of Matthew, Luke (cf. use of *exodos* in 9:31), and John. The narratives of the Egyptian bondage or the crossing of the sea are included in New Testament summaries of biblical history (Acts 7:14ff.; 13:17; Heb. 11:23ff.).

Philo of Alexandria allegorized the account of the Exodus as stages in the soul's return to God. Paul's use of the typology of baptism in the cloud and sea (1 Cor. 10:2) and reference to the manna and water from the rock (1 Cor. 10:3–4) set the Exodus typology for the church.

In Melito's *Homily on the Passover*, the Exodus and its commemoration as Passover prefigure the passion of Christ and the deliverance it brings. Origen combined Philo's and Paul's approaches, seeing in the journey from Egypt to the promised land a route to be followed in the spiritual life.

In Christian typology, the crossing of the sea is baptism and the manna is the eucharist (Tertullian, *Bapt.* 8; 9; Didymus the Blind, *Trin.*

2.14; Ambrose, *Mys.* 3:14; Basil, *Spir.* 14). Theodoret (*Qu. 27 in Ex.*, PG 80.257) and Ambrose (*Sacr.* 5.1) make the connection between water and manna and the eucharist. Augustine (*Faust.* 12.29–30) brings together all the types of the Exodus. *See also* Moses.

[J.P.L.]

Bibliography

Origen, *Homilies on Exodus*, tr. R.E. Heine, FOTC (1982) Vol. 71; Gregory of Nyssa, *Life of Moses*, tr. A.J. Malherbe and E. Ferguson, CWS (1978); Cyril of Alexandria, *Glaphyra in Pentateuchum*, PG 69; Zeno of Verona, *Sermones*, CCSL (1971), Vol. 22; Gaudentius of Brescia, *Tractatus*, CSEL (1936), Vol. 68.

P. Lundberg, *La Typologie baptismale dans l'ancienne église* (Leipzig: Lorentz, 1942); R. Devreesse, *Les Anciens Commentateurs grecs de l'Octateuque et des Rois* (Vatican City: Biblioteca Apostolica Vaticana, 1959); J. Daniélou, *From Shadows to Reality* (London: Burns and Oates, 1960), pp. 153–228; R.E. Nixon, *The Exodus in the New Testament* (London: Tyndale, 1963); D. Daube, *The Exodus Pattern in the Bible* (London: Faber and Faber, 1963); B. Childs, *The Book of Exodus: A Critical, Theological Commentary* (Philadelphia: Westminster, 1974); J.P. Hyatt, *Exodus* (Grand Rapids: Eerdmans, 1980).

EXORCISM. Expulsion of evil spirits. The Greek *exorkizō* and *orkizō* meant to place under oath (Matt. 26:63), to adjure, and so to give a solemn command or to compel a spirit to obey. These words are not used of Christian activity in the New Testament (Mark 5:7; Acts 19:11–16). Jesus' authority was shown in that he "cast out" (*ekballō*) demons (Mark 1:34, 39). Later Christian writers did use the words in reference to Christians expelling evil spirits (Justin, *Dial.* 76.6; 85.2).

Healers and magicians in the Greco-Roman world claimed to be able to cure those possessed by reciting formulas and performing magical actions (Plutarch, *Mor.* 706E; cf. Xenophon of Ephesus, *An Ephesian Tale* 1.5). Accounts of pagan exorcists near New Testament times are found in Philostratus, *Life of Apollonius* (2.4; 3.38; 4.4, 20, 25, 44), and Lucian of Samosata, *Lover of Lies* 16. The magical papyri provide numerous examples of the procedures and formulas in use. The typical procedure was to identify the demonic power being invoked with a considerable elaboration of names, to address him with the words, "I adjure you," and to give specific commands. The practice involved purifications, sacrifices, and the preparation of various material elements. Jews were quite prominent among the practitioners of magic and exorcism (Acts 13:6; 19:14), and Josephus records an exorcism by a Jew that is similar to stories found in Greco-Roman authors (*Ant.* 8.46–49).

Jesus' mastery over demons is prominent in the Gospels (Luke 4:31–37; 8:26–39). His expulsion of demons was a sign of the coming of the kingdom of God (Luke 11:14–22). Although Jesus occasionally used techniques parallel to those of the time (Mark 7:33f.), observers were impressed that "he cast out the spirits with a word" (Matt. 8:16) and showed his authority by direct imperative and not by elaborate invocations and rituals. His disciples shared his power by the use of his name (Luke 9:49f.; 10:17; Acts 16:18).

Some accounts of exorcism in early Christian literature are similar to Greco-Roman accounts (e.g., *A. Petr.* 11). Pagan critics of Christianity, such as Celsus, charged that Christian exorcisms were done by magical means (Origen, *Cels.* 1.6). Christians claimed, however, that they banished demons by the power of the name of Jesus, employing only prayer, the words of the scriptures, and simple gestures (Justin, *Dial.* 76; Tertullian, *Apol.* 23; Origen, *Cels.* 7.4; 7.57; *Comm. in Mt.* 13.7). One of the fullest passages on proper conduct in casting out demons is found in Pseudo-Clement, *On Virginity* 1.12. Christian practice had formal similarities with the pagan, in the invocation of a deity, recitation of formulas, and use of physical actions, such as laying on of hands and anointing; but the content was different: prayer instead of adjuration, use of the name of Jesus and the historical facts about him instead of extended names of deities, and an attitude of faith and humility instead of compulsion. Christians emphasized the moral effects of their teaching in contrast to self-interest (Origen, *Cels.* 1.68).

Distinct from the exorcism of the possessed and ill (mentally or physically) was the routine exorcism of candidates for baptism in order to remove them from the moral influence of evil spirits (first attested in Hippolytus, *Trad. ap.* 20–21). The baptismal exorcisms might involve oil, water, laying on of hands, the sign of the cross, breathing (*exsufflatio*), and prayers. Cornelius of Rome mentions exorcists among the clergy in the mid-third century (Eusebius, *H.E.* 6.43.11). *See also* Demons. [E.F.]

Bibliography

F.J. Dölger, *Der Exorzismus im altchristlichen Taufritual* (Paderborn: Schöningh, 1909); C. Bonner, "Traces of Thaumaturgic Technique in the Miracles," *HThR* 20 (1927):171–181; W.L. Knox, "Jewish Liturgical Exorcism," *HThR* 31 (1938):191–203; C. Bonner, "The Technique of Exorcism," *HThR* 36 (1943):39–49; S. Eitrem, *Some Notes on the Demonology of the New Testament* (Oslo: Universitetsforlaget, 1966); K. Thraede, "Exorzismus," *RLAC* (1969), Vol. 7, pp. 44–117; E. Ferguson, *Demonology of the Early Christian World* (New York: Mellen, 1984); D.C. Duling, "The Eleazar Miracle and Solomon's Magical Wisdom in Flavius Josephus's *Ant. Jud.* 8.42–49," *HThR* 78 (1985):1–25; H.A. Kelly, *The Devil at Baptism: Ritual, Theology, and Drama* (Ithaca: Cornell UP, 1985); H.D. Betz, *The Greek Magical Papyri in Translation* (Chicago: U of Chicago P, 1986).

EZEKIEL (seventh century B.C.). Hebrew prophet and book in the major prophets of the Old Testament. The Book of Ezekiel is named after the prophet, who used oracles and visions to accuse the community, call it to repentance, and reveal the fortunes of the people who would return to Jerusalem and reestablish the cult and the temple. Christians commonly used the Septuagint version, although translations by Aquila and Symmachus were also known. Jerome translated the Hebrew text into Latin in 392–393. Prior to Origen, no Christian exegete undertook the difficult task of composing a full commentary on this complex prophetic book. Origen wrote his commentary on the book in Caesarea and followed it with a series of homilies on key passages. Origen's commentary is essentially lost, but Jerome translated large portions of the homilies in the early fifth century and incorporated them into his own *Commentarii in Ezechielem*. In the east, the only full commentary on Ezekiel to have survived is that of Theodoret of Cyrus (436), who refs to commentaries written by Apollinaris of Laodicea, Theodore of Mopsuestia, and Polychronius of Apamea; apart from a few fragments in catenae, all of these have been lost. This sparsity reflects Ezekiel's size and complexity more than its perceived importance and relevance. The book is quoted frequently and in a wide spectrum of early Christian texts from the end of the New Testament period, and the suviving commentaries display the importance of the prophecy for various apologetic and theological claims.

The Christian interpretation of Ezekiel developed around three main themes: the nature of God and Christ as revealed through the throne-vision of Chapters 1 and 10; the promises of redemption and restoration, especially in Chapters 36 and 37, and the related theme of the events at the end of the age (i.e., references to Gog and Magog in Chapter 38); and the judgment on Jewish life and ritual.

From an early time, the throne-vision was the source for the description of theophanies in Jewish and Christian literature. Interpreters were led to questions about the nature of God and the relationship between God and Christ. Irenaeus, for example, cites the text against those who claim to know the true nature of God, saying that Ezekiel was given a vision "only of the likeness of God" (*Haer.* 4.15). Tertullian cites Ezekiel 1:26 in *Against Praxeas* as a way to argue that the Son, "who is the visible manifestation of the invisible God," is distinct from and has his being derived from God. Likewise, Theodoret and Jerome argue that the throne-vision (esp. 1:27) refers to the visible and thus "human attributes" of Christ.

The references to God's judgment of individuals (e.g., 14:14) and his desiring repentance and restoration (e.g., 36–37) rather than punishment (e.g., 18:23) led to extended discussions of the individual nature of salvation and the coming of Christ as manifesting the mercy of God. Frequently, Ezekiel 36:25–26 was incorporated in discussions of the "new covenant" and the promise of new life brought through the advent of Christ. Cyprian, for example, uses the text in a discussion of baptism, claiming that the new heart and new spirit promised by

the prophecy are a result of "the application of the cleansing water" (*Ep.* 69.12). Likewise, Augustine contrasts the judgment rendered in Ezekiel 36:17–18 with the promise of "new heart and a new spirit" in Ezekiel 36:23–29, arguing that the former applies to "the carnal people of Israel" while the latter is a promise to "spiritual Israel which is one people by the newness of grace" (*Doctr. Christ.* 3.48).

The references to Gog and Magog in Ezekiel 38, another favorite point of entry for Christian interpreters, were a cause of diversity and dissension. Although some linked the figures to such threats as the Goths (Ambrose, *Fid.* 2.16), others (Augustine, *Civ. Dei* 20.11; Theodoret, *Ezech.* 39.29) rejected this sort of millenarian interpretation. Theodoret, for example, says, "I am amazed not only at the folly of the Jews but of others who have the name of Christian, who hold fast to Jewish myths and say that the invasion of Gog and Magog has not taken place . . ." (*Ezech.* 39.29). It is likely that the concern over this millennial interpretation was linked to a related concern over a rising tide of Jewish messianic expectation, which used this text in conjunction with the reference to a new Jerusalem in Ezekiel 48 to argue for the renewal of the Jewish cult and the revitalization of Jerusalem as the center of the cult.

Several portions of Ezekiel factor heavily into the Christian attack on the legitimacy of Jewish worship and life. In fact, Ezekiel can be seen as providing the interpretive key for Christians in their response to the issue of the ongoing efficacy of Jewish ritual and worship. Both Justin Martyr (*Dial.* 19.6) and Tertullian (*Jud.* 4.11) use Ezekiel to argue that the dispersion of the Jews is God's punishment and that such rituals as Sabbath were instituted as a temporary means to discipline an unruly people.

[C.T.McC.]

Bibliography

Origen, *Homiliae in Ezechielem*, ed. W.A. Baehrens, GCS (1925), Vol. 33, pp. 319–354; Jerome, *Commentarii in Ezechielem*, ed. M. Adriaen and F. Glorie, CCSL (1964), Vol. 75; Theodoret, *Interpretatio in Ezechielem*, ed. J. Schulze, PG 81.801–1256.

H.L. Ellison, *Ezekiel, the Man and His Message* (Grand Rapids: Eerdmans, 1956); W. Eichrodt, *Ezek-*

iel: A Commentary (Philadelphia: Westminster, 1970); W. Zimmerli, *Ezekiel*, 2 vols. (Philadelphia: Fortress, 1979, 1983); W. Brownlee, *Ezekiel* (Waco: Word, 1986).

J. Daniélou, *Etudes d'exégèse judéo-chrétienne* (Paris: Beauchesne, 1966); G. Otranto, "Ezechiele 37, 1–14 nell' esegesi patristica del secondo secolo," *Vetera Christianorum* 9 (1972):55–76; G.W. Ashby, *Theodoret of Cyrus as Exegete of the Old Testament* (Grahamstown: Rhodes UP, 1972); C. Rowland, "The Influence of the First Chapter of Ezekiel on Jewish and Early Christian Literature" (Ph.D. diss., Cambridge University, 1974); G. Quispel, "Ezekiel 1.26 in Jewish Mysticism and Gnosis," *VChr* 34 (1980):1–13; D. Halperin, "Origen, Ezekiel's Merkabah, and the Ascension of Moses," *ChHist* 50 (1981):261–275; E. Dassman, "Trinitarische und christologische Auslegung der Thronvision Ezechiels in der patristischen Theologie," *Im Gesprach mit dem dreieinen Gott, Festschrift W. Breuning* (Dusseldorf: Patmos, 1985), pp. 159–174.

EZNIK (fourth–fifth centuries). Bishop of Bagrevand in Armenia. Eznik of Kolb, a village in the Ayrarat region of Armenia, was a student of Mashtots, inventor of the Armenian alphabet, and of his colleague the catholicos Sahak. He traveled with other students to Edessa and Constantinople to translate church literature and, shortly after the Council of Ephesus (431), helped Sahak check the existing Armenian Bible translation on the basis of Greek manuscripts acquired in Constantinople. Eznik is known especially for his treatise *Against the Sects*, written in the 440s. He describes, using quotations, and then refutes, by practical argument and scriptural exegesis: (1) pagan heresies, (2) Zoroastrianism, (3) Greek schools of thought (Pythagoreans, Platonists, Stoics, Epicureans), and (4) Marcionism. This treatise is an invaluable patristic source for (2) and (4) in particular; at the same time, it illuminates the philosophical and theological situation in Armenia in the fifth century. *See also* Armenia; Marcion; Mashtots. [C.C.]

Bibliography
L. Mariès and C. Mercier, eds., *Eznik de Kolb: De Deo*, PO (1959), Vol. 28.3–4.

EZRA (ESDRAS) (fourth or fifth century B.C.). Leader of the Jews who returned to Jerusalem after the exile in Babylonia; book in the Bible. Ezra was a priest and teacher of the Law. The Book of Ezra tells of the restoration of the Law under the leadership of Ezra in the postexilic Jewish community. Later Jewish tradition regarded Ezra as collecting and transmitting the Hebrew scriptures and apocryphal works (4 Ezra 14). The Hebrew Bible treats Ezra and its companion book, Nehemiah, which tells of the rebuilding of the walls of Jerusalem under the governor Nehemiah, as one book (1 and 2 Esdras in the Vulgate).

The Greek and Latin form of Ezra's name, Esdras, is employed in the title of 1 Esdras (3 Esdras in the Vulgate), a Greek version of Ezra-Nehemiah based on a text different from that in the Hebrew Bible. Apocalyptic works were later attributed to Ezra. 2 Esdras of the Apocrypha (*4 Esdras* or *4 Ezra* of the Latin), written toward the end of the first century, wrestles with the problem of the destruction of Jerusalem in A.D. 70. This work was preserved by Christians in Latin with the addition of two chapters at the beginning (*5 Ezra*) and two at the end (*6 Ezra*). Other apocalypses ascribed to Ezra are the *Greek Apocalypse of Ezra, Vision of Ezra, Questions of Ezra,* and *Revelation of Ezra.* [E.F.]

Bibliography
J.M. Myers, *Ezra–Nehemiah* (Garden City: Doubleday, 1965).

B.M. Metzger, "The Fourth Book of Ezra," M.E. Stone, "Greek Apocalypse of Ezra," J.A. Mueller and G.A. Robbins, "Vision of Ezra," M.E. Stone, "Questions of Ezra," and D.A. Fiensy, "Revelation of Ezra," *The Old Testament Pseudepigrapha*, ed. J.H. Charlesworth (Garden City: Doubleday, 1983), Vol. 1, pp. 517–604.

F

FABIAN. Bishop of Rome (236–250). The story was told that Fabian was chosen bishop when a dove alighting on his head was taken as a sign of divine election. A later report made Fabian responsible for assigning the seven deacons and seven subdeacons to the fourteen regions of Rome. He became one of the first martyrs of the persecution under Decius. Feast day January 20.   [E.F.]

Bibliography
O. Marucchi, *Christian Epigraphy* (Cambridge: Cambridge UP, 1912), no. 192, p. 195; Cyprian, *Letters* 9; 30; Eusebius, *Church History* 6.29; 6.36.4; 6.39.1; *Liber Pontificalis* 21 (Duchesne 1.148–149).

FACUNDUS OF HERMIANE (sixth century). Bishop and theologian in North Africa. A defender of the independence of the church from civil authority, Facundus was active in the disputes of his time over Christology in opposition to the position taken by the emperor Justinian and pope Vigilius on the *Three Chapters*. His writings supply important documentation for the events surrounding the Second Council of Constantinople (553). CPL 866–868.   [M.P.McH.]

Bibliography
Facundus Hermianensis, Opera Omnia, ed. J.-M. Clement and R. Vander Plaetse, CCSL (1974), Vol. 90A; *Repertorium Fontium Historiae Medii Aevi* (Rome: Istituto Storico Italiano per il Medio Evo, 1976), Vol. 4, pp. 418–419; R.B. Eno, "Doctrinal Authority in the African Ecclesiology of the Sixth Century: Ferrandus and Facundus," *REAug* 22 (1976):95–113.

FAITH. Act or state of believing and that which is believed. The word "faith" is a noun that correlates with the verb "to believe" and carries most of the substantival meanings implied by the verb. In English Bibles, "faith" usually translates the Hebrew noun '*emunah* and the Greek noun *pistis* and their cognates. Historically, it has borne both objective and subjective connotations. Objectively, it denotes that which is believed or that to which assent and affirmation are given. Subjectively, it refers to the disposition to believe, assent, or affirm, or to the act of believing, assenting, or affirming.

In the Old Testament, the word "faith" usually refers to God's faithfulness, but in a few passages (e.g., Hab. 2:4) it refers to human faithfulness to God. In the New Testament, as a nearly technical term, it is used in four basic ways: to denote truth believed or to be believed (Eph. 4:5); to describe a sure confidence that issues in activity (Acts 6:8; Heb. 11:4, 5,

7); to denote implicit trust (Matt. 6:30; 8:26); and to denote intellectual assent (James 2:26). However, the writers insist that faith that is mere intellectual assent is spiritually deficient.

All New Testament uses of the term "faith" finally have to do with Jesus of Nazareth. Each reflects or implies belief in one or more of the following: Jesus' unique kinship to God the Father (Matt. 16:13–20); his person and work as the fulfillment of the scriptural promises of a Messiah and a messianic kingdom (Matt. 11:2–6), the full realization of which is yet to come (Rev. 21:1–8); his power over nature and over evil (Luke 8:26–39); his moral and spiritual lordship over humankind by way of his teachings, his person, and his atoning work (Matt. 28:16–20); the reality of redemption from sin and victory over death in and through him (1 Cor. 15:12–28).

In its proclamation of these beliefs, the primitive church did not aim primarily at careful intellectual articulation. It usually understood specific declarations of belief to refer to some aspect of personal or communal relationship to Christ and, through him, with others.

The most comprehensive expression and definition of faith was not a dogmatic or creedal statement but a cultic act, the celebration of the eucharist, or Lord's supper, in which only the baptized could participate. Christians believed that their faith entailed a radical change in relationship with God and with others, sufficiently radical to be described by such terms as "the new birth" and "regeneration." Baptism, as a part of this change, was itself a confession of faith. Christians also believed that the practical, daily ethic of the believer and the Christian community should and would arise out of reflection on these two acts of faith and on biblical teaching.

The early Christians, then, would have defined faith in terms of two elements: trust in the redeeming work of Christ and belief that such trust begets specific ethical commitments. However, they debated the specific means of ethical expression.

Gnosticism and the Rule of Faith. In the second century, Gnosticism pushed Christians into refining their understanding of faith. Gnostics insisted that faith, as Christians usu-

ally defined it, was at best an inferior foundation for salvation and at worst a damning false piety, trapped in the matter of the earth. They believed that salvation came through "the knowledge," a divinely revealed system of intellectually articulated information about the spiritual structure of the universe and how that structure relates to salvation. Details of the system varied among them, but all insisted that without "the knowledge" there was no true salvation. Most Gnostics seem to have believed that this knowledge required the use of special language, myths, and esoteric rites known and open only to the properly initiated.

Three aspects of Gnostic belief in particular were at issue: the denial of legitimacy to nonintellectual aspects of believing, the denial of value to the material creation, and the denial of a genuine incarnation of God in Christ and therefore the rejection of God's own fundamental self-revelation, which for Christians is the very means of salvation. Christians began to argue the certainty of their faith as they had historically held it. Essentially, it consisted not in dogmatic affirmation but in the relationship of Christians to Christ, and to each other through him. This certainty, they said, came to them in the proclamation of the church in word and sacrament, both of which were based on the person and work of Christ. But for all that they resisted definitive rational confessions, by the mid-second century they were developing the idea of the "rule of faith" (or the "canon of truth").

Although the "rule of faith" was not an intellectually articulated doctrinal statement with a universally accepted or exact form, it did bespeak a tendency in that direction. Originally, it seems to have consisted of a few somewhat formal assertions, which varied according to time and place, although they were based upon what was thought to be apostolic testimony. Increasingly, however, it took on an identity of its own and began to serve as a norm for theological reflection.

Early Fathers. Clement of Alexandria (d. ca. 215), confronting Gnosticism directly, saw the rule of faith as the essential antonymn to Gnostic speculation and to non-Christian philosophy in general. And, less tentative than his theological predecessors about the place of intellectual assent in the process of believing, he argued that intellect is a divine gift and therefore an asset to faith, not a liability. For Clement, the faith is a certain truth revealed by divine power; it is "a grace [*charis*] of God" (*Str.* 1.7.38.4). The faithful are those "taught by God, through the instruction of the Son, in writings that are indeed sacred" (*Str.* 1.20.98.4). So faith is that which is taught by God, through Christ, in a written revelation, and it is belief in that which is taught. Faith is also that which can be concluded by syllogistic reasoning from the revealed texts and teachings, and, further, it is belief in those conclusions (*Str.* 2.2.8.4; 8.3.7.6). For Clement, then, theological conclusions, if they begin from revealed premises and are logically appropriate, are to be accepted on faith as articles of faith. With Clement, we take long steps toward the understanding that faith is intellectual assent to theological propositions.

Although Clement sought to show that the Christian is the true Gnostic, his contemporary Tertullian sought to contradict the Gnostics directly. To do this, he appealed to the "rule of faith" over against Gnostic "knowledge" and in contrast to Greek philosophy in general: "To know nothing against the rule of faith is to know everything" (*Praescr.* 7). As Tertullian saw it, the content of the truth that Christians believe is revealed and may not be obtained in any way but by revelation. It is beyond the reach of intellect. And the very act of believing is grace-enabled. Faith is precisely that act. Tertullian does occasionally refer to that which is believed as the faith, but even his appeal to the rule of faith is an appeal to a process of affirming as much as it is to a list of affirmations.

Origen, a younger contemporary of both Clement and Tertullian, modified Clement's understanding of faith by way of his concern with human free will. Origen understood faith to be both a human act, arising out of the human's own capacities, and an effect of divine grace (*Cels.* 8.43), and he accepted the Gnostic criticism of the faith held by most Christians as an unreflective acceptance or affirmation of gradually learned beliefs as they

are imposed by authority. He then set out to define faith in such a way as to counteract the criticism and at the same time to encourage Christians to deeper and broader piety and understanding. That is to say, he wished to reassert the primacy of faith as the basis of the believers' relationships to God and others and faith as the expression of those relationships.

In line with the tradition to his time, Origen believed that forgiveness of sins and eternal salvation depend upon faith. But "bare faith," as he called it, is insufficient, for it is often no more than simple confidence in authority, or even belief motivated by fear. Such faith must be matured into "reason and wisdom" on the way to authentic *gnosis*, or knowledge and understanding. The highest grade of faith is true *gnosis* (*Cels.* 1.11, 13). But authentic *gnosis*, according to Origen, is still essentially soteriological. It is the knowledge or understanding that has to do with salvation, not knowledge and understanding in general or esoteric insight into the mysteries of the universe or the divine nature. It is finally a matter of knowing Christ (*Princ.* 1. pref. 1–4; 1.2.1–13). Authentic *gnosis* is still tied to the rule of faith, to the doctrines taught by the church. These *dogmata*, as Origen called them, are the objects of all the grades of faith, from "bare faith" to "true *gnosis*" (*Jo.* 32.9).

As Origen understood it, the notion of "faith" carries both an ethical and an intellectual meaning. Faith is the basis of true piety, of right and of rightly motivated behavior (*Cels.* 3.69). It must express itself in repentance and good works (*Cels.* 3.71, 57; 8.10). To live righteously, one must exercise faith (i.e., the knowledge and understanding of salvation that one has); if one does not live righteously, one's faith cannot develop. Faith (again, true knowledge and understanding) and morality are thus absolutely interdependent (*Jo.* 19.6). To believe truly is to know and to understand truly; and to know and to understand truly is to believe truly.

Cyprian, a Latin-speaking contemporary of Origen, understood faith to be intellectual and practical acceptance and affirmation of God's law and God's promises, especially the law of love and the promises of redemption and eternal life as they are revealed by and in Christ (*Mort.* 6.22, 24; *Ad Demet.* 20). But Cyprian was more concerned than earlier or contemporary writers to articulate the role of the church in inciting, defining, and directing that acceptance and affirmation. He emphasized the eucharist as the principal expression of the person and work of Christ, whom he understood to be the focus and source of faith. But the eucharist could be offered only in the church and only by a duly ordained priest. The existence and definition of the church thus depended upon its celebration and, by extension, upon the ministrations of duly ordained clergy. Cyprian moved theology quite far toward insisting that "faith" means acceptance and affirmation of the teachings and the teaching authority of the church and of its sacramental ministry, a direction long since taken in common practice.

The early church kept the ancient idea that faith is essentially a living, personal, and communal relationship to God and to others in and through Christ. Nonetheless, as it articulated this relationship with increasing theological precision, especially in the third, fourth, and fifth centuries, in the face of heresy and of its own ever more complex and demanding place in society at large, the ideas of intellectual assent and affirmation, even of submission to the church, came to dominate the definition and understanding of the term. Articulation and affirmation became more and more technical, philosophically complex, and ideologically weighted, and therefore beyond the intellectual reach of most believers. Still, although the majority of Christians may not have been able to fathom much of what they were implying in their liturgical confessions of faith, these could not be suspended, for they were elements in the unity, catholicity, and apostolicity of the church. Encouraging the faithful to trust and believe the church (i.e., the theological experts and caretakers of the tradition), and defining that trust and belief as faith, came to be almost standard pastoral practice.

Creeds. Of special importance to the development of the idea of "faith" in the fourth and fifth centuries are the creeds that the church, in the persons of its bishops, produced, accepted, or mandated to be used liturgically.

The so-called Apostles' Creed seems to have been in common use in something like its present form by the fourth century, although its roots reach back to the second century. Its importance to the development of the idea of faith lies in the fact that it is self-consciously a confession of faith, used liturgically, not an academically formal declaration of essentially intellectual commitments. It begins "I believe in . . . ," not "I believe that . . . ." In fact, the Synod of Milan (390) called it the Apostles' Symbol, emphasizing its confessional, as over against any essentially intellectual, character.

However, by the late fourth century, if not earlier, this creed, in various but related forms, had become both the principal confession of the faith of the church in the west and an outline for catechetical instruction. Other modes and forms of confession of faith remained and were exercised, but this one statement was taken generally throughout the western church as the declaration that made one Christian (at baptism) and as the declaration by means of which one remained Christian. To recite it was to exercise faith as well as to confess faith. And its use as an instrument of catechesis gave it importance exactly as a declaration of essentially intellectual commitments. Christians understood it to be the faith, rationally summarized.

But the Apostles' Creed, under whatever name, had no universally official standing. The first official creed for the entire church was that created by the Council of Nicaea (325), to contradict the rationalistic, "scientific" Christology of Arius of Alexandria and his followers. In its principal affirmation—that only God, truly God incarnate but still God in substance, could redeem fallen humanity and reconcile it to God—it was quite wittingly "unscientific." It deliberately set faith and philosophy (as then usually defined) at odds.

What we now call the Nicene Creed (the Niceno-Constantinopolitan Creed) is, as it were, a gradually edited version of that creed of 325. It strengthens the "unscientific," anti-rationalistic character of the creed of 325 by dropping the anathemas against the Arians and by adding confessions concerning the Holy Spirit and the unity of the true church. And yet the very editing, and the uses to which the Nicene Creed soon came to be put, speak of an intellectualizing process that worked at cross-purposes with the original intention of the council.

The church created this creed for liturgical recital, but it came to serve as an outline in catechesis and in more advanced theological study. Further, the bishops more or less mandated its use, in one form or another, for the entire church. So to recite the Nicene Creed was to confess the faith, that is, to say something of one's living relationship to God and to others as these were determined by the person and work of Christ. But to recite the creed was also to express certain intellectual commitments regarding the way in which the faith was to be confessed and to declare fidelity and submission to the church as a hierarchical institution. Intellectual commitment with specific philosophical and theological content and allegiance to the church as institution now became integral aspects of the confession of faith and of faith itself. Subsequent creeds from the same centuries, such as that which is now called the Athanasian Creed or the *Quicunque vult*, clearly illustrate the point.

Augustine. A half-century after the Nicene Creed came to have much the same form that it now has, Augustine, bishop of Hippo, gave the idea of faith the form that it was to carry in the west for at least a millennium. His most characteristic and broadly applicable definition comes from his controversy with the Pelagians: faith is "the disposition and will of the person who believes" (*Grat.* 28). True faith pertains to believers only, and only divine, sovereign grace makes one a believer.

And what does a believer believe? Augustine understood that, ultimately, one is a believer because, enabled by grace, one places trust and confidence in the atoning work of God in Christ. But Augustine was convinced that the believer comes to that place of trust and confidence by submitting to the church, for it is the church alone that inerrantly ex-

presses and applies the benefits of that work to humankind. This it does through the proclamation of the word and the celebration of the sacraments. Augustine said: "For my part, I should not believe the gospel except as moved by the authority of the Catholic church" (*C. epist. fund.* 6).

Augustine emphasized trust or assent in his understanding of faith. And although that trust or assent is intelligent and finally rests on the revelation, that is, on Christ and the biblical word, one submits to the church as the custodian, proclaimer, and dispenser of the benefits of Christ and that word. Faith is essentially spiritual propensity or bent of heart and intellect and will. The source of that propensity is the predestining grace of God, and the object also of that propensity or bent is the grace of God in Christ, as proclaimed, taught, and celebrated by the church.

The teaching of the church is not the faith. It is true knowledge, and is the object of faith. Augustine does not seem to have given much attention to the idea of faith as the content of belief, to the idea that faith is what the church believes. "Faith" describes believers in the act of believing; it does not usually refer to what they believe.

With this understanding, Augustine altered the traditional Christian comprehension of the relationship between the faith and knowledge. Earlier Christianity had tended to think of faith as both revealed content and grace-impelled affirmation of that content. Knowledge came through rational reflection on the revealed content. Opinion varied as to the soteriological significance of such knowledge. Augustine retained the idea that faith is grace-impelled affirmation, but he tended to think of the revealed content as true knowledge, not as faith, and of the knowledge gained by rational reflection upon the revealed content as having little or no necessary soteriological value.

An ambiguity in Augustine's thought that affected Christian theology for centuries appears in his understanding of the nature and role of the creed. For Augustine, recital of the creed was itself an act of faith, but he also understood the creed to be the faith taught by the church, to which one submits in the very act of recitation. So Augustine held that faith is (1) the very act of reciting the creed, (2) the affirmation of the creed's propositions as such, (3) submission to the church, which is implicit in the act of reciting, and (4) the propositions of the creed in themselves.

By the mid-fifth century, Augustine's view prevailed in the west, but in a truncated form. The ancient understanding of faith as living relationship to God and thereby to others, in and through Christ, did not disappear. In many persons and places it lived in full vigor, especially in nascent cenobitic monasticism and along the ancient frontiers of the old empire. But apparently among very large numbers, especially around the Mediterranean coast, it withdrew into the shadows. "Faith" had come most commonly to mean assent to and affirmation of the teaching of the church. "The Faith" was the creed itself—the Apostles' Creed or any of the conciliar professions—understood to be an intellectual summary of the church's teaching and proclamation. *See also* Apostles' Creed; Athanasian Creed; Confession of Faith; Creeds; Rule of Faith.   [P.M.B.]

Bibliography
Clement of Alexandria, *Miscellanies* 2.1–6, 11–12; 5.1; Ambrose, *On the Faith*; Augustine, *On the Value of Believing*; idem, *On Faith in Things Not Seen*.

H.A. Wolfson, *Philosophy of the Church Fathers* (Cambridge: Harvard UP, 1956), pp. 102–140; K. Haacker, "Glaube II/III," TRE (1984), Vol. 13, pp. 277–304; S.G. Hall, "Glaube IV," TRE, Vol. 13, pp. 304–308; C. Becker, "Fides," RLAC (1969), Vol. 7, pp. 801–839; D. Lührman, "Glaube," RLAC (1981), Vol. 11, pp. 48–122.

FALL. First sin by human beings. The narrative of Adam and Eve's primitive transgression and expulsion from paradise (Gen. 3:1–24) was the consistent starting-point for patristic inquiry into the origin of evil and sin in the world. The church fathers closely followed Paul in linking universal sinfulness to the one man Adam (Rom. 5:12ff.), having as its corollary the universality of salvation in the one man Christ (5:15). Yet this invited deeper speculation on the interconnected themes of Adam's paradisiac condition, the actual cause and con-sequences of the lapse, and the logical difficulty that the fall posed with regard to divine providence.

The earlier Greek fathers in general pinned responsibility for the fall on an abuse of free will, in which all humanity had participated by emulating Adam's disobedience. Although seduced by the devil (serpent) or assisted by fallen angels, it was humanity by its own moral failure that produced evil (cf. Justin, *2 Apol.* 5; *Dial.* 88; Tatian, *Orat.* 7–9; 11; Theophilus, *Autol.* 2.27; Origen, *Princ.* 3.2.2; *Cels.* 4.65–66). The punitive consequences of Adam's fall, mortality and subjection to the passions (Tatian, *Orat.* 11; Theophilus, *Autol.* 2.26; Clement of Alexandria, *Str.* 3.12.88ff.; 3.17.103; Methodius, *Res.* 1.38f.; 2.1–4), were traditionally juxtaposed with the conditions of his original, unfallen state. Adam was variously portrayed in paradise as having been suspended between potential mortality or immortality (Theophilus, *Autol.* 2.24) or as having enjoyed an immortality of childlike innocence and purity (Clement of Alexandria, *Prot.* 11.111; Methodius, *Res.* 1.88; 2.2–4).

Such depictions were common in later Greek writers as well. Athanasius theorized that humanity in paradise was subject to physical corruption like other creatures but, having been endowed with the grace of the image of God, could also remain perfect through uninterrupted contemplation of the Word (*Inc.* 3–4). Basil of Caesarea (*Hom.* 9.6), Gregory of Nyssa (*Hom. opif.* 17.2–5), and John Chrysostom (*Stat.* 11; 12; *Hom.* 16 *in Gen.* 5) all envisioned Adam as having enjoyed a quasiangelic life in paradise. In the west too, Ambrose graphically described Adam's lofty state before his lapse as equivalent to being in the "third heaven" in 2 Corinthians 12:4–5 (*Parad.* 42; 53). Ambrosiaster, anticipating Augustine, suggested by contrast that Adam had been mortal by nature but remained incorruptible by partaking of the Tree of Life (*Quaest.* 19).

A principal theological difficulty, however, lay in explaining how Adam, having once tasted God's goodness, could have chosen to transgress God's law. Granted he abused his freedom, a defective choice would seem to presuppose a defective nature or, as was suggested in certain early rabbinic explanations, an innate inclination toward evil. As early as Justin Martyr (*2 Apol.* 14.1), attempts were made to characterize the primal sin as an intellectual failure, an ignorance of the good (Athanasius, *Gent.* 7; Gregory of Nyssa, *Mort.*, PG 46.497B–C). In a more dramatic hypothesis, Origen, who interpreted Genesis 3 purely allegorically, had postulated that all souls, having once enjoyed a preexistent life of union with God, became surfeited with his goodness and lapsed through sheer negligence, for which embodiment itself was punishment (*Princ.* 1.4.1ff.; 2.9.1–8). Methodius (*Res.,* passim) and the Cappadocian fathers rejected this theory. Gregory of Nyssa in particular speculated as to whether sin originated more specifically from the human creature's natural passibility. But if, as Gregory affirmed, subjection to passions was itself part of the punishment for Adam's sin (*Anim. et res.,* PG 46.148Cff.; *Or. catech.* 8), how could passions at once be considered the prior cause of that sin? Gregory's tentative answer was that God had superadded the passions to human nature in prevision of the fall. They were part of God's "ideal" creation, becoming dysfunctional only after Adam fell prey to sensual pleasure (*Hom. opif.* 18; *Virg.* 13). The focus of Gregory's ascetic doctrine of the fall was not, then, the paradisiac Adam, who fades into the background, but Adam the "image of God," the pleroma of humanity, struggling to overcome carnality and become like God. The tendency in certain schools of Greek patristic anthropology was to view Adam's "natural," unfallen state more theoretically than historically. Thus, Maximus Confessor, in the seventh century, held that Adam's original perfection had been potential and without duration, and that he actually fell "at the very instant of his creation" by squandering his capacity for spiritual pleasure on sensible objects (*Thal.* 61).

In the west, Augustine settled on a literal interpretation of Genesis 3. Adam and Eve each had a natural body (*corpus animale*) in paradise (*Gen. ad litt.* 9.10.16–18) and were able to hold off lustful desire and bodily decay by feeding on the Tree of Life, a primordial *sacramentum* (8.4.8–8.5.11; 11.18.23–24). Their liberty was utterly relative, a freedom to persevere in the good, a *posse non peccare,* or "ability not to sin" (*Corrept.* 12.33), which presupposed still a certain creaturely liability to defect from the good (*Civ. Dei* 14.11ff.). The primal sin was a spiritual one, a deliberate disobedience of God's law, an act of pride and cognate vices (*Enchir.* 45; *Civ. Dei* 14.13; *Gen. ad litt.* 11.41.56ff.), punished with unbridled concupiscence and death (*Gen. ad litt.* 11.31.40ff.; *Nupt. et concup.* 1.23.25ff.) and, most tragically, with the hereditary transmission of Adam's guilt to his human posterity (*Nupt. et concup.* 2.8.20; 2.34.58, etc.).

For all its disastrous results, the fathers still generally concluded that the fall, viewed *ex post facto,* did not ultimately frustrate God's original plan for humanity. Irenaeus, in the second century, having portrayed Adam in paradise as a spiritual infant summoned to mature through assimilation to God (*Dem.* 12; *Haer.* 4.38.1–4), highlighted the pedagogical value of the experience of evil in pressing humanity toward the good (*Haer.* 3.20.1–2). Origen, too, took heart in the realization that the punitive result of the fall, the experience of corporeality, would quicken souls toward spiritual truth (*Cels.* 6.44, 54–56). The experience of moral evil and carnal torments had a certain provisional, pedagogical value for Gregory of Nyssa as well (*Hom. opif.* 21; *Or. catech.* 8). The doctrine of divine providence and defense of human freedom against Gnostic determinism (cf. Tertullian, *Marc.* 2.5ff.) seemed to demand such convictions, although the fathers consistently stopped short of affirming that the fall had been a "necessary" prerequisite for the incarnation and for salvation in Christ.
See also Adam; Anthropology; Creation; Eve; Original Sin; Sin.   [P.M.Bl.]

Bibliography

Irenaeus, *Against Heresies* 3–5, ANF (1885), Vol. 1, pp. 414–567; Origen, *On First Principles,* tr. G.W. Butterworth (London: SPCK, 1936); Methodius, *On the Resurrection,* tr. W.R. Clark, ANF (1888), Vol. 6, pp. 364–377; Gregory of Nyssa, *On the Making of Man,* tr. H.A. Wilson, NPNF, 2nd ser. (1893), Vol. 5, pp. 387–427; idem, *The Great Catechism,* tr. W.

Moore, ibid., pp. 473–509; Ambrose, *On Paradise*, tr. J.J. Savage, FOTC (1961), Vol. 42, pp. 287–356; Augustine, *The Literal Meaning of Genesis*, tr. J.H. Taylor, ACW (1982), Vols. 41–42; idem, *On Rebuke and Grace*, tr. P. Holmes and R.E. Wallis, NPNF, 1st ser. (1887), Vol. 5, pp. 471–491.

F.R. Tennant, *The Sources of the Doctrines of the Fall and Original Sin* (Cambridge: Cambridge UP, 1903); N.P. Williams, *The Ideas of the Fall and of Original Sin* (London: Longmans, Green, 1927); E.V. McClear, "The Fall of Man and Original Sin in the Theology of Gregory of Nyssa," *ThS* 9 (1948):175–212; B. Otis, "Cappadocian Thought as a Coherent System," *DOP* 12 (1958): 95–124; R. Niebuhr, *The Nature and Destiny of Man* (New York: Scribner, 1964), Vol. 1; M. Harl, "Recherches sur l'origénisme d'Origène: la 'satiété' (*koros*) de la contemplation comme motif de la chute des âmes," *SP* 8 (1966):373–405; Kelly, Chs. 7 and 13; J. Barr, "The Authority of Scripture: The Book of Genesis and the Origin of Evil in Jewish and Christian Tradition," *Christian Authority: Essays in Honour of Henry Chadwick*, ed. G.R. Evans (Oxford: Oxford UP, 1988), pp. 59–75.

FASTIDIUS (fifth century). British church historian. Fastidius probably wrote the *Corpus Pelagianum* and the *De vita christiana*, often attributed to Pelagius or Pseudo-Augustine. He criticized some Pelagian-sounding doctrines but apparently followed Pelagius's advice on prayer. CPL 763 (736). [F.W.N.]

FASTING. Abstinence from, diminution of, or delay of food usually for a stated period of time. Early Christians practiced various kinds of fasts. Some of these they inherited from Judaism; others they developed anew. Customs varied from place to place. By at least A.D. 100, Christians in some areas fasted twice a week, on Wednesdays and Fridays. According to the *Didache* 8, they chose these days to distinguish themselves from Jews, who fasted on Mondays and Thursdays. Weekly fasts did not become universal, however, until the later fourth century (Epiphanius, *Haer.* 65.6; *Exp. fid.* 22).

The *Didache* 6.4 prescribed one or two days of fasting before baptism for the baptizand, baptizer, and others. Mentioned also by Justin (*1 Apol.* 61) and Tertullian (*Bapt.* 20),

fasting on Friday and Saturday before baptism on Easter Sunday as a spiritual preparation had become customary for candidates by the fourth century.

Probably an elaboration of the baptismal fast, fasting during the time of the Pasch was first noted by Irenaeus in his letter to Victor during the Easter controversy, ca. 195 (Eusebius, *H.E.* 5.24). At this time, customs varied. Some fasted one day, others two or more, and some for still longer periods. Shortly afterward, Tertullian referred to a general custom of fasting on the "day of the Passion," that is, Good Friday (*Or.* 18). Not until the fourth century did a forty-day fast become widespread (Nicaea, can. 5; *Itin. Aeth.* 27–28), and even then the manner of observing it varied, some churches emphasizing prayer rather than fasting. Holy Week, added to the church calendar during the fourth century, became the preeminent time for fasting. Customs continued to vary considerably even after the fourth century. Fasting was forbidden between Easter and Pentecost.

Fasting as preparation for ordination or other special occasions was common. Several church orders urged widows to observe voluntary fasts (e.g., *Test. Dom.* 1.42). Fasting before communion did not become common until the fourth century. Fasting was required of persons doing penance. Monks made fasting a regular feature of their *askēsis* ("training").

The Montanist sect increased the number and severity of the church's fasts in accordance with their conviction that the dawning of the era of the Paraclete with Montanus enabled Christians to pursue more rigorous discipline. Montanists kept two weeks of partial fasts (xerophagies), exempting Saturdays and Sundays (Tertullian, *Ieiun.* 15). They also extended biweekly fasts to a later hour and restricted food intake more strictly than Catholics, who permitted considerable latitude.

Early Christian fasting served several purposes: a demonstration of ethical sincerity (e.g., saving food to give as an offering for the needy—Hermas, *Sim.* 5.3.7); a sign of authentic repentance both before and during penance; preparation for significant religious moments, such as baptism, eucharist, or ordination; a means of intensifying prayer; and a symbol of identification with the passion of Christ. *See also* Asceticism; Lent. [E.G.H.]

Bibliography

Tertullian, *On Fasting; Didascalia* 21; *Apostolic Constitutions* 5.3; Basil of Caesarea, *Homilia* 1–2 (PG 31.163–198).

L. Duchesne, *Christian Worship: Its Origin and Evolution*, 5th ed. (London: SPCK, 1927), Ch. 8; A.J. Mclean, "Fasting (Christian)," *Encyclopedia of Religion and Ethics*, ed. J. Hastings (Edinburgh: T. and T. Clark, 1937), Vol. 5, pp. 765–771; W.L. Johnson, Jr., "Motivations for Fasting in Early Christianity to A.D. 270" (Th.M. thesis, Southern Baptist Theological Seminary, 1978).

FATHERS OF THE CHURCH. Term used broadly to designate the theological writers of the first six centuries, to Gregory the Great (d. 604) in the west and to John of Damascus (d. 749) in the east, specifically those who came to be regarded as orthodox.

In its origin, "fathers" in a religious sense refers to persons to whom is owed spiritual generation and formation in teaching and style of life (cf. 1 Kings 20:35, but also 1 Cor. 4:15; 1 Peter 5:12; and later *M. Polyc.* 12.2; Irenaeus, *Haer.* 4.41.2; Clement of Alexandria, *Str.* 1.1.2–2.1; Origen in Eusebius, *H.E.* 6.14.9). The apostles or patriarchs are designated "fathers" in *1 Clement* 62.2. Since bishops came to be regarded as "fathers" of Christians in this sense, they were so addressed from the second century onward (cf. *Letter of the Churches of Lyons and Vienne* in Eusebius, *H.E.* 5.4.2; Cyprian, *Ep.* 30; 31; 36).

It was in the midst of the controversies of the fourth and following centuries that the term came to be used in particular of those bishops who were remembered as exponents of orthodox teaching (Basil, *Ep.* 140.2; Gregory of Nazianzus, *Or.* 33.5; Cyril of Alexandria, *Ep.* 39); it is used in this sense preeminently of the bishops of the Council of Nicaea (Basil, *Ep.* 52.1; Gregory of Nyssa, *Ep. can.*; Ephesus [431], *can.* 7), and of the bishops of the councils of Nicaea and Constantinople (Chalcedon, *Def.* 2; 4). These were the "fathers" to whom regard was due for having affirmed the Catholic faith in a special sense.

It is but a step from here to the point where the term begins to be used more generally of those whose teaching can be appealed to for the establishment of orthodox doctrine. Thus, Jerome, in recording the works of early writers, finds it convenient to distinguish the fathers from other "ecclesiastical writers" (*Vir. ill.*, prol.; *Ep.* 113.3). Augustine is prepared to include Jerome himself, although not a bishop, among the fathers on account of his teaching (*C. Jul.* 1.7.34). And Vincent of Lérins, disputing the value of Augustine's teaching against the Pelagians in his *Commonitory* (434), does not find it supported by the "fathers," who "each in his own time and place, remaining in the unity of communion and faith, were accepted as approved masters" (41). In the same vein, the sixth-century *Decretum Gelasianum* provides a list of fathers of the church that singles out those who laid the basis of the faith of the Roman church.

A closely related development is the designation of certain of the fathers as doctors (teachers) of the church in a special sense. Although eastern liturgical books single out Basil the Great, Gregory of Nazianzus, and John Chrysostom as "great ecumenical teachers," the west by the time of Charlemagne came to set Ambrose, Augustine, Jerome, and Gregory the Great in this category, and to add Athanasius, with his western connections, to the eastern triad. The western list of doctors has subsequently been filled out with theologians whose views are counted worthy of note without reference to their patristic character.

The advent of modern critical scholarship, as well as the disputes of the Reformation period regarding the sources of doctrine, gave rise to differing estimates of the place of the fathers in the establishment of orthodox teaching, without in any way calling into question their significance in the formation of Christian theology. [L.G.P.]

Bibliography

G.L. Prestige, *Fathers and Heretics* (London: SPCK, 1940); H.E.W. Turner, *The Pattern of Christian Truth* (London: Macmillan, 1954); Quasten, Vol. 1, pp. 1–22; Altaner, pp. 1–44; F.L. Cross, *Early Christian Fathers* (London: Duckworth, 1960); J. Pelikan, *The Emergence of the Catholic Tradition*

(Chicago: U of Chicago P, 1971); H. von Campenhausen, *Ecclesiastical Authority and Spiritual Power in the Church of the First Three Centuries* (London: Stanford, 1972).

FAUSTINUS (fourth century). Latin theological writer and adherent of Lucifer of Cagliari. A priest at Rome, Faustinus composed (ca. 380–385) a treatise on the Trinity, written at the request of Flacilla, wife of the emperor Theodosius I, and directed against Arianism; appended to it is a short creed addressed to the emperor. Along with another Luciferian priest, Marcellinus, Faustinus sent to Theodosius a petition for the protection of the adherents of Lucifer against persecution (384); the work is important in understanding the nature of the schism (CPL 119, 120, 1571).

Among numerous others named Faustinus are a supposed martyr, along with his brother Jovita, at Brescia (second century), and a bishop of Lyons (mid-third century) who, in a (lost) letter to the Roman bishop Stephen I, denounced Marcian of Arles as an adherent of the schism of Novatian.   [M.P.McH.]

Bibliography
Faustinus, Latin theological writer: Gennadius, *Lives of Illustrious Men* 16.

M. Simonetti, ed., *Faustinus Luciferianus, Opera*, CCSL (1969), Vol. 69, pp. 287–392, 410–437.

M. Simonetti, "Note su Faustino," *SEJG* 14 (1963):50–98.

Faustinus, bishop of Lyons: Cyprian, *Letter* 68.

FAUSTUS OF BYZANTIUM (ca. 400). The foundation of our knowledge of Christian Armenia is a history of the country covering the years 317 to 387, written by Faustus in Greek but surviving in Armenian.   [E.F.]

FAUSTUS OF RIEZ (d. ca. 490). Abbot, bishop, and writer. Faustus became bishop of Lérins (ca. 433) and later bishop of Riez in Provence (ca. 458). For a number of years (ca. 478–485), he suffered exile under Euric, Arian king of the Goths, but returned on the latter's death. His writings include *De gratia Dei*, a work on grace and free choice, and *De Spiritu*

Sancto, on the divinity of the Holy Spirit, as well as letters and homilies. The *De gratia Dei* has caused him to be considered, along with John Cassian, as one of the principal proponents of Semipelagianism, although he rejected Pelagianism itself. In the early sixth century, John Maxentius denounced the work as heretical; through the agency of Fulgentius of Ruspe and Caesarius of Arles, Semipelagian teachings were condemned at the second of the councils of Orange (529). Faustus also accepted traducianism, the materiality in some sense of the human soul, in which he was opposed by Claudianus Mamertus.   CPL 961–977.

[M.P.McH.]

Bibliography
Gennadius, *Lives of Illustrious Men* 85.

G. Weigel, *Faustus of Riez: An Historical Introduction* (Philadelphia: Dolphin, 1938); P.-M. Duval, *La Gaule jusqu'au milieu du Ve siècle* (Paris: Picard, 1971), Vol. 1.2, pp. 745–748, #322 (bibliography); *Repertorium Fontium Historiae Medii Aevi* (Rome: Istituto Storico Italiano per il Medio Evo, 1976), Vol. 4, pp. 435–436 (bibliography).

FELICITAS. *See* Perpetua.

FELIX I. Bishop of Rome (269–274). Little is known of Felix's life. He probably replied to a report sent to his predecessor Dionysius on the deposition of Paul of Samosata, but the letter is not extant.   [M.P.McH.]

Bibliography
Eusebius, *Church History* 7.30, 32; *Liber Pontificalis* 27 (Duchesne 1.158).

FELIX II (III). Bishop of Rome (483–492). (The variation in number results from the removal of a fourth-century claimant to the episcopal see from the list of popes.) Felix rejected the *Henoticon*, a theological formula promoted by the emperor Zeno to effect reunion with the Monophysites and, in 484, excommunicated the patriarch Acacius of Constantinople. His eighteen extant letters are concerned mostly with eastern affairs.   CPL 1665–1666.   [M.P.McH.]

Bibliography

Liber Pontificalis 50 (Duchesne 1.252–254).

P. Nautin, "La Lettre de Félix III à André de Thessalonique et sa doctrine sur l'église et l'empire," *RHE* 77 (1982):5–34.

FELIX III (IV). Bishop of Rome (526–530). Made pope through the influence of the Gothic king Theodoric, Felix transmitted to the second of the councils of Orange (529) propositions on grace, drawn in large measure from Augustine, which effectively put an end to Pelagianism. He began the practice of adapting buildings in the Roman forum to the needs of Christian worship. CPL 1625; 1686–1690. *See also* Felix II (III). [M.P.McH.]

Bibliography

Liber Pontificalis 56 (Duchesne 1.279–280); Cassiodorus, *Variae* 8.15.

FELIX OF NOLA (third century). Priest of the church of Nola in southern Italy and martyr. Felix gained renown for courage and zeal during the persecution of the church, perhaps under Decius (250–251) or Valerian (258), or both. His cult, already popular locally, was spread by Paulinus of Nola through a series of some fifteen *carmina natalicia*, or birthday poems (395–ca. 409), intended to be recited each year on the day of the saint's death, or birth into eternal life, January 14. [M.P.McH.]

Bibliography

Paulinus of Nola, *Poems* 12–16; 18–21; 23; 26–28; 29.

P.G. Walsh, tr., *The Poems of St. Paulinus of Nola*, ACW (1975), Vol. 40, pp. 6–13.

FILASTRIUS OF BRESCIA (d. ca. 397). Bishop and writer. Filastrius, a vigorous opponent of Arianism, preached at Milan against the Arian bishop Auxentius. His *Diversarum haereseon liber*, a catalogue of 156 heresies, is based largely upon Epiphanius of Salamis, as well as Irenaeus. The work is confusing, since its definition of heresy is unclear, but Augustine used it in his *De haeresibus.* CPL 121, 121a.
[M.P.McH.]

Bibliography

Gaudentius of Brescia, *Sermon* 21.

FILIOQUE. Latin phrase meaning "and from the Son," added in the west to the statement "The Holy Spirit proceeds from the Father" in the so-called Niceno-Constantinopolitan Creed associated with the First Council of Constantinople (381).

The original creedal statement reflects the tradition of the east, which, while maintaining that the Holy Spirit proceeds from the Father in a way differing from the Son's generation, hesitated to say more about the Holy Spirit's origin than the text of John 15:26: "The Spirit of truth, who proceeds from the Father." The Greek fathers stressed the monarchy of the Father, that is, his unity and his role as the sole cause (*aitia*) or principle (*archē*) of the Son and the Holy Spirit, which for them guarantees the divinity and unity of the Son and Spirit. When they link the Spirit with the Son, they refer not to the inner life of the Trinity but rather to the economy of salvation, where the Spirit's role follows that of the Son. This seems to be the case with their statements, based on scripture, that the Holy Spirit is "the Spirit of the Son" as well as of the Father (Athanasius, *Ep. Serap.* 3.1; Gregory of Nyssa, *Eun.* 1.378), "the Image and Spirit of the Son" (Athanasius, *Ep. Serap.* 1.24), "the Spirit of Christ" (Gregory of Nyssa, *Diff. ess.* 4 [in Basil, *Ep.* 38]), and "the Spirit of the Power [i.e., the Son]" (Gregory of Nyssa, *Maced.* 13). Gregory of Nyssa speaks of the Son's mediation or middle position (*mesiteia*) with respect to the Spirit, which, however, "does not exclude the Spirit's natural relation (*physikē . . . schesis*) with the Father" (*Tres Dii.*).

This theme was developed later by John of Damascus, who, calling the Holy Spirit the "Spirit of the Son" but denying that the Son is "cause" (*aitios*) or that the Holy Spirit is "from the Son" (*ek tou Uiou*) (*F.O.* 1.8), says that "the Spirit of the Son proceeds, not as from him (*ex autou*), but as through him (*di'autou*) from the Father" (*F.O.* 1.12). The phrase "through the Son" was added to the Niceno-Constantinopolitan Creed in the solemn profession of faith sent in 784 by Tarasius, patriarch of Constantinople, to the eastern patriarchs. His profession, with the addition, was examined without rejection at the Second

Council of Nicaea (787). In Greek patristic thought, however, the phrase "proceeds through the Son" occurs less often than is usually said, and, when used, it frequently applies only to the central role of the Son in the economy of salvation and not to the immanent procession of the Spirit.

A somewhat different tradition developed in the west. Tertullian says that he preserves the monarchy of the Father when he holds that "the Spirit comes from no other source than from the Father through the Son" (*Prax.* 4.1). Hilary of Poitiers says that the Holy Spirit expresses the unity of the Trinity because the Spirit "receives from both" the Father and the Son (*Op. hist. frg.* 2.31). Marius Victorinus writes that the Father is principally (*principaliter*) the source of the Holy Spirit (*Adv. Arium* 3.8) and that "the Spirit receives from Christ, Christ having received from the Father, so that the Spirit also receives from the Father" (*Adv. Arium* 1.13); this statement seems to imply a certain mediatory position or influence of the Son. Ambrose holds that the Holy Spirit is not separated from the Father and the Son "when he proceeds from the Father and the Son" (*Sp. Sanct.* 1.11.120). Although in these texts Hilary, Victorinus, and Ambrose speak directly of the saving missions of the Spirit, they tend to move from these temporal missions or processions toward the eternal procession.

Against this traditional background, Augustine developed a clearer, more explicit doctrine about the immanent procession of the Holy Spirit. "The Son," he says, "is born of the Father, and the Holy Spirit proceeds from the Father principally and (by [the Father's] gift and with no lapse of time) commonly from both" (*Trin.* 15.26.47); he adds that the Son "has it from the Father that the Holy Spirit should also proceed from him" (ibid.). This carefully phrased Augustinian doctrine was already simplified in the western creed known as *Quicunque vult*, reverenced as bearing the authority of its supposed author, Athanasius; it said that "the Holy Spirit is from the Father and the Son, not made or created or begotten, but proceeding." This creed, together with Augustine's theology, influenced the Third

Council of Toledo (589) to teach, with less care than had Augustine, that the Holy Spirit *proceeds* from the Father *and the Son* (*ex Patre ET FILIO procedere*) and to anathematize "those who do not believe . . . that the Holy Spirit proceeds from the Father and the Son" (ed. Vives, pp. 109, 118); however, the text of the Niceno-Constantinopolitan Creed, including the phrase "proceeding from the Father and the Son," was added to the manuscripts of this council only at a later date. The Niceno-Constantinopolitan Creed had been sung for some time in the eucharist in Spain; it was perhaps in 675, at the Third (provincial) Council of Braga, that the phrase "and from the Son" was added to "proceeds from the Father" so that the creed used in the eucharist now read that the Holy Spirit "proceeds from the Father *and the Son*." Some scholars hold that the phrase was added in order to emphasize, against Arianism, the Son's equality and consubstantiality with the Father; others maintain it was simply a normal development growing out of western theology.

In a synodal letter to Constantinople in 649, pope Martin I caused irritation by including the phrase "and from the Son." But it was Charlemagne's introduction of the singing of the creed (including the *Filioque*) into the imperial liturgy that led to difficulties. In 807, some Latin monks, after visiting Aachen, began singing the creed, with the *Filioque*, in the liturgy of their Jerusalem monastery. This action drew bitter protests from Greek monks in the Holy City: their patriarch protested to pope Leo III, and the Latin monks appealed to the pope for a decision.

Two issues were involved. The first was the addition to the Niceno-Constantinopolitan Creed, because the councils of Ephesus (431) and Chalcedon (451) had forbidden any faith diverse from that of Nicaea. For the Greeks, this meant prohibition of verbal additions, whereas the Latins held that a change of faith, not of words, was proscribed. In fact, Ephesus had spoken of the creed of Nicaea without the additions of Constantinople (although Chalcedon referred to the entire creed) and the Second Council of Nicaea (787) heard, without dissent, the creed of Tarasius with the addition of "through the Son," a phrase that brought objections from the *Libri Carolini* written at Charlemagne's court in opposition to this council, including its acceptance of Tarasius' altered creed.

The second issue was that of doctrine. The phrase *Filioque* seemed to the Greeks to make the Son unoriginate and, with respect to the Holy Spirit's origin, totally equal. The Greek verb *ekporeuesthai*, which corresponds to the Latin *procedere*, implies that the subject of the verb, designated as the source of the procession, is without origin; hence, for the Greeks the subject of *ekporeuesthai* could be only the unoriginate Father. The Greeks were concerned to maintain the equality and consubstantiality of the Holy Spirit with the Father against the *Pneumatomachi* ("Spirit-Fighters"), who, they feared, might argue that the Spirit's procession from the Son would imply that the Spirit originates from the Father only mediately and is therefore inferior in being to the Father. They also thought that the *Filioque* would make the Father's originating role imperfect and partial.

Charlemagne's theologians, informed by pope Leo III, produced several works defending the doctrine of the procession of the Holy Spirit from the Son as well as from the Father; they accused the Greeks of heresy in their doctrine of the procession. Although declaring the western view orthodox, pope Leo III refused to allow the insertion of the creed, with the *Filioque*, into the Roman liturgy and counseled the Spanish and Frankish churches to remove the creed gradually from their liturgies. He also had placed before the tomb of St. Peter two plates containing the creed, written in Latin and Greek and without the *Filioque* or its Greek equivalent. The Frankish court of Charlemagne nevertheless continued to use it, in part to assert itself politically against the eastern empire. Use of the creed with the *Filioque* gradually spread in the west and at a later date (perhaps ca. 1013) entered the liturgy of Rome itself.

In 867, Photius, patriarch of Constantinople, protested against the presence of Latin missionaries in Bulgaria, insisting that this area depended on him as patriarch; in the same letter, he accused them of heresy because they recited the creed with the added *Filioque*. Photius insisted that the Holy Spirit proceeds "from the Father only." Ratramnus of Corbie wrote his *Contra Graecorum opposita* to answer Greek attacks on the west. Concerning the Holy Spirit he argued, among other things, from scriptural use of "Spirit of the Son" or "Spirit of Christ," from Christ's promising to send the Spirit from the Father (John 15:26), and from Christ's saying that the Holy Spirit would "receive" from Christ (John 16:14). In 879–880, Photius led a council in the presence of legates of pope John VIII that condemned the addition of the *Filioque*, and wrote a letter (PG 102.793B–821B) and a treatise, the *Mystagogia* (PG 102.280A–400A), to answer the arguments of the Latins.

Although the west seems to have recognized the "Photian" council for some time, in the eleventh century cardinal Humbert, on a mission to Constantinople, actually accused the Greeks of omitting the phrase from where it should be in the creed. Michael Caerularius, patriarch of Constantinople, discovering only later that it was a Latin addition, used this fact in his disputes with Rome.

Two later attempts at reconciliation between the eastern and western churches, the Second Council of Lyons (1274) and the Council of Florence (1439), reached agreement on accepting the *Filioque* but the Greek clergy and people rejected the concessions made by their delegates. Today, more objective discussions of the issue have led to better mutual understanding and some conciliatory gestures.

[W.H.P.]

Bibliography

J. Vives et al., eds., *Concilios Visigóticos e Hispano-Romanos* (Barcelona and Madrid: Consejo Superior de Investigaciones Científicas, Instituto Enrique Flóres, 1963).

M. Jugie, *De Processione Spiritus Sancti ex fontibus Revelationis et secundum Orientales dissidentes* (Rome: Facultas Theologica Pontificii Athenaei Seminarii Romani, 1936); J. Meyendorff, "La Procession du Saint-Esprit chez les Pères orientaux," *Russie et Chrétienté*, 4ème série-2ème année, nos. 3–4 (1950):158–178; T. Camelot, "La Tradition latine sur la procession du Saint-Esprit 'a Filio' ou 'ab utroque,'" ibid., pp. 179–192 ("échange de vues" on Meyendorff and Camelot ibid., pp. 193–196); M.-J. Le Guillou, "Filioque," Catholicisme (Paris: Letouzey et Ané, 1956), Vol. 4, cols. 1279–1286; J.N.D. Kelly, Early Christian Creeds, 3rd ed. (London: Longmans, 1972), pp. 358–367; R. Haugh, Photius and the Carolingians: The Trinitarian Controversy (Belmont: Nordland, 1975).

FINNIAN. Finnian of Clonard (d. ca. 549), abbot, founded the monastery of Clonard, County Meath, Ireland. He supposedly had connections with the Welsh church, especially with St. David, and was also a famous teacher whose leading disciples were known as the Twelve Apostles of Ireland. He is the likely author of the earliest Irish penitential book.

Finnian of Moville (d. ca. 579), another sixth-century abbot, is credited with introducing the Vulgate into Ireland. He was supposedly a student of the British saint Nennius, but accounts of Finnian's life are late and are of dubious value. [J.F.K.]

FIRMICUS MATERNUS (d. after 350). Rhetorician and Christian apologist. Born into a senatorial family in Sicily, Firmicus Maternus received the customary education in rhetoric and philosophy; his writings abound in reminiscences of classical literature. As a pagan, he wrote (ca. 335) the Mathesis in eight books, an extensive manual of, and an apology for, astrology; the work shows influence of Neoplatonism. After his conversion, Firmicus attacked the pagan mystery cults and in The Error of the Pagan Religions (ca. 347) urged the emperors Constantius and Constans to destroy them; he appeals to the authority of scripture, mostly to the Testimonia of Cyprian, but his theological knowledge is scant. The Consultationes Zacchei et Apollonii, a report of a discussion extending over three days that leads to Zaccheus's conversion of Apollonius to Christianity, has been attributed to Firmicus, but it is probably not his. CPL 101–103. [M.P.McH.]

Bibliography
Firmicus Maternus, The Error of the Pagan Religions, tr. C.A. Forbes, ACW (1970), Vol. 37; Ancient Astrology, Theory and Practice: Matheseos Libri VIII, tr. J.R. Bram (Park Ridge: Noyes, 1975).

R.P.C. Hanson, "The Christian Attitude to Pagan Religions," ANRW (1980), Vol. 2.23.2, pp. 910–973; repr. in R.P.C. Hanson, Studies in Christian Antiquity (Edinburgh: T. and T. Clark, 1985), pp. 144–229.

FIRMILIAN (d. 268). Bishop of Caesarea in Cappadocia (ca. 230–268). Firmilian was an admirer of Origen, and he corresponded with Dionysius of Alexandria concerning Novatianism. His only extant writing is a letter to Cyprian, supporting him against Stephen I of Rome on the necessity of rebaptizing those baptized by heretics and schismatics (Cyprian, Ep. 75). Firmilian presided at the first council in Antioch (264) to consider the orthodoxy of Paul of Samosata. Feast day October 28. CPG I, 1760. [E.F.]

Bibliography
Eusebius, Church History 6.27; 6.46.3; 7.5, 14, 28, 30.4f.; Basil, On the Holy Spirit 29.74; idem, Letter 188.1.

G.A. Mitchell, "Firmilian and Eucharistic Consecration," JThS n.s. 5 (1954):215–220.

FISH. Frequent early Christian symbol. Fish occur in the Gospels in the miracles of multiplication, when Jesus fed the 5,000 with five loaves and two fish (Mark 6:35–44) and the 4,000 with seven loaves and a few fish (Mark 8:1–8), and in the postresurrection meals, when Jesus appeared to the disciples in Jerusalem on the evening of the resurrection (Luke 24:41–43) and later to seven disciples beside the Sea of Galilee (John 21:1–14). The multiplication of the bread and fish became a favorite scene in early Christian art, both in catacomb paintings and on sarcophagi. The eucharistic interpretation of the multiplication of the bread and fish (Irenaeus, Haer. 3.11.5) and the presence of fish in meal scenes perhaps influenced artists to show fish on the table in depictions of the Last Supper (as at S. Apollinare Nuovo in Ravenna).

Fish also occur in nautical scenes, sometimes in association with a fisherman (as in the baptismal representation in the Catacomb of St. Callistus—Foto Cal E 32) and some-

Fish and anchor inscribed on grave slab in Catacomb of Domitilla. (Used by permission of Pontifical Commission of Sacred Archaeology.)

times with an anchor. Tertullian gave a baptismal interpretation to the fish symbol: "We as little fishes, in accordance with our *ichthys* [Greek, "fish"] Jesus Christ, are born in water" (*Bapt.* 1). *Piscina* ("fish pond") became one of the terms for a baptistery.

There is no need to distinguish rigidly the nautical (baptismal) and meal (eucharistic) usages of the fish. They are combined in the epitaph of Abercius: "Everywhere faith led the way and set before me food, everywhere the fish from the spring, mighty and pure, whom the pure virgin caught and gave this to the friends to eat always, having sweet wine, giving mixed wine with bread." Paulinus of Nola (ca. 396) also associated the images: "I see the congregated people so arranged in order on the couches and all so filled with abundant food that before my eyes arise the richness of the evangelical benediction and the image of the people whom Christ fed with five loaves and

two fishes, himself the true bread and fish of the living water" (*Ep.* 13.11).

The words of Abercius may have pictorial illustration in the painting in the Catacomb of St. Callistus called the "eucharistic fish" (Foto Cal E 25), which shows a large fish on a small table with one person laying hands on it in blessing and another lifting hands in prayer. The words of Paulinus may have a bearing on a grave inscription now in the Vatican Museum, "Fish of the Living," accompanying two fish with an anchor between them. Is it "fish of the living waters," or is "fish" the acrostic "Jesus Christ, God's Son, Savior" of the living ones?

The various uses of the fish symbolism are united by the identification of the fish with Christ (cf. Origen, *Comm. in Mt.* 13.10). This identification is expressed most clearly in the acrostic on the word "fish." The letters of the Greek word for fish (*ichthys*) formed the first letters of the words in the phrase "Jesus Christ, God's Son, Savior." This acrostic is presumably behind Tertullian's allusion to the Greek word in his Latin treatise *On Baptism* cited above. The whole phrase is spelled out in the acrostic poem found in the *Sibylline Oracles* 8.217–250. It is not clear whether the confessional formula gave rise to the fish symbolism or some use of the symbol (whether borrowed from the environment or originating within Christianity) prompted the acrostic.

Besides the many appearances of fish on funerary inscriptions, the fish was one of the emblems considered suitable on seals for Christians (Clement of Alexandria, *Paed.* 3.11). *See also* Abercius; Baptism; Bread; Eucharist; Iconography; Inscriptions; Laying On of Hands; Wine. [E.F.]

Bibliography

C.R. Morey, "The Origin of the Fish Symbol," *Princeton Theological Review* 8 (1910):93–106, 231–246, 401–432; 9 (1911):268–289; 10 (1912):278–298; F. Dölger, *Ichthys: Das Fisch Symbol in frühchristlichen Zeit* (Münster: Aschendorff, 1928); G.F. Snyder, *Ante Pacem: Archaeological Evidence of Church Life Before Constantine* (Macon: Mercer UP, 1985), pp. 24–26.

FISHER, GEORGE PARK (1827–1909). Historian and theologian. Fisher was Professor of Ecclesiastical History at Yale Divinity School from 1861 to 1901. He wrote *The Beginnings of Christianity* (New York: Scribner, 1877) and a *History of Christian Doctrine* (New York: Scribner, 1896). Fisher was quite interested in Christian life and worship as well as doctrine. As a theologian, he was a moderate conservative interested in Christian evidences based primarily on moral teachings but also on miracles. He resisted both a more radical biblical criticism and archconservative insistence on biblical authority as the foundation of faith. [F.W.N.]

FLAVIAN (d. 449). Bishop of Constantinople (446–449). In his battle against Monophysite influence, Flavian excommunicated Eutyches, an archimandrite in Constantinople, at a synod there in 448. Emperor Theodosius II sought to reverse that verdict by calling a general council at Ephesus in 449. There, Dioscorus, bishop of Alexandria, terrorized those present into supporting Eutyches and denouncing Flavian. A number of bishops were beaten by soldiers armed with clubs, but Flavian evidently took such abuse that he died a few days later. For its action, this synod became known as the *Latrocinium*, the "Robber Council." CPG III, 5930–5938. [F.W.N.]

Bibliography

Leo the Great, *Letters* 22–23; 26–28; 36; 38–39; 49; Theodoret, *Letters* 11, 86, 104.

W.H.C. Frend, *The Rise of Christianity* (Philadelphia: Fortress, 1984), pp. 763–770.

FLORILEGIUM. A set of selections from earlier authors arranged topically. From two Latin words, *flores* and *legere*, "to gather flowers," "florilegium" is the equivalent of the Greek derivative, "anthology," and means a collection of flowers, that is, excerpts worthy of being preserved. These excerpts represent the quintessence of prior writings and offer themselves as an aid to memory. They are aptly called "borrowed" literature. The genre appears in the first Christian generations with the collections of the *logia*, or the sayings of Jesus or of the apostles, and with lists of "authorities" and "testimonies," which represent the earliest effort to compose a catechism or to present liturgical formularies or Christian moral teachings. Later came the anthologies of sentences or propositions, of which Isidore of Seville was the first great compiler and which continued on into the age of Scholasticism.

Florilegia can be classified according to their sources or their objectives. Their sources are either profane or Christian, or a mixture of these two. The Christian florilegia can be subdivided into biblical, patristic, biblical-patristic, and sacred-profane anthologies. Their objectives are either scriptural (and then they are called *catenae*) or dogmatic-apologetic, liturgical, homiletic, moral, or canonical. The dogmatic florilegia were often drawn up to establish the orthodoxy or the heterodoxy of individual theologians, and many of them became incorporated in the *Acta* of church councils.

Gregory of Nazianzus and Basil the Great collected extracts from the writings of Origen; the anthology is known as *Philocalia* (ca. 362). There are also many spiritual florilegia oriented toward meditation and prayer.

In an age when books were not readily available, the florilegium provided citations from many sources on a given topic. The genre is pervasive in Latin literary history; most of this literature is as yet unedited. The florilegia have preserved excerpts from many works no longer in existence, sometimes allowing reconstruction of the original work. Florilegia also indicate what texts have been most influential in a given period and provide insights into its culture. On the other hand, because the excerpt has been separated from the context, it can also give a misleading picture of an author's opinion. *See also* Catena.   [M.T.C.]

Bibliography

H.M. Rochais et al., "Florilèges spirituels," *Dictionnaire de spiritualité ascétique et mystique* (Paris: Beauchesne, 1964), Vol. 5, pp. 435–512.

FLORINUS (second century). Roman presbyter and follower of the Gnostic Valentinus. Florinus was the addressee of a letter of Irenaeus of Lyons directed against his teachings; they had known one another when both were associated with Polycarp in Asia Minor. Irenaeus also wrote against him a lost treatise, *On the Ogdoad*, and a letter to the Roman bishop Victor I (189–198), extant only in a Syriac fragment.   [M.P.McH.]

Bibliography

Eusebius, *Church History* 5.15, 20.

FONT. *See* Baptistery

FOSSORS. In strict sense, laborers who dig soil (*TLL* 6.1 [Leipzig, 1912–1926], col. 1214); but for early Christianity, gravediggers. The term fossor is certainly attested epigraphically in the pre-Constantinian period (e.g., *ICUR* n.s. 4.12228: from the Catacomb of Callistus).

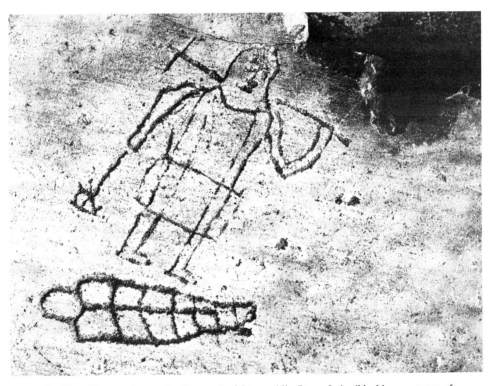

Graffito of fossor and corpse in Catacomb of Commodilla, Rome, Italy. (Used by permission of Pontifical Commission of Sacred Archaeology, catalogue number Com Ts 1.)

Also possibly from the third century is ICUR n.s. 2.6446, which shows, in graffito form, a fossor dressed in a short, sleeveless, and belted tunic with a pickaxe (*dolabra*; cf. Gaitzsch) mounted on a long staff slung over his shoulder, a lamp hanging from the right hand, and in front, supine, a cadaver wrapped in linens (see illustration). Fossors dug the catacomb galleries, *cubicula* ("burial rooms"), *loculi* (horizontal burial niches in walls), *formae* (burial cists in floors), and *arcosolia* (vaults above interments); hence, they were vital personnel in the funerary bureaucracy of early Christian Rome. Fossors may also have functioned in the capacity of plasterers and painters in the catacombs, but this is speculation.

Based on the labors they performed, fossors probably came from the lower classes. It appears that some succeeded in improving their condition: during the fourth and fifth centuries, fossors were admitted to a minor order within the clerical hierarchy, and it is conceivable that in this same period a few industrious and enterprising fossors accumulated some capital through the sale of their products, *loculi, arcosolia, formae,* and *cubicula.* But the amounts of money attested epigraphically for the sale of such products are not great. In addition to digging subterranean burial places in Rome, fossors performed other functions, such as guarding catacomb entrances and maintaining catacombs and lands (including gardens) above ground. The amount of subterranean labor (digging and clearing and carrying soil) performed by fossors in the years 200–500 was immense. *See also* Burial; Catacombs.

[P.C.F.]

Bibliography

H. Leclercq, "Fossoyeurs," DACL (1923), Vol. 5.2, cols. 2065–2092; J. Guyon, "La Vente des tombes à travers l'épigraphie de la Rome chrétienne (IIIe–VIIe siècles): le rôle des *fossores, mansionarii praepositi* et prêtres," *MEFR* 86.1 (1974):549–596; E. Condi Guerri, *Los "fossores" de Roma paleocristiana* (Vatican City: Pontificio Istituto di Archeologia Cristiana, 1979); W. Gaitzsch, "Werkzeuge und Geräte in der römischen Kaiserzeit: Eine Übersicht," ANRW (1985), Vol. 2.12, pp. 170–204.

FRANKS. Coalition of Germanic peoples who appeared between the Weser and Rhine rivers during the troubled times of the third century A.D. The most influential group among the Franks, or "Free Men," apparently was that of the Sicambrians, or Salians, mentioned in the first century by Pliny the Elder. By the third century, the name "Francia" was applied to the right bank of the lower and middle Rhine. Between 253 and 276, the Franks raided Gaul and even Spain. In the 350s, a horde of Franks and Alamanni invaded Gaul, but were defeated by the emperor Julian. He confirmed the Salians in their possession of Toxandria (northern Belgium).

Thereafter, many Franks, such as Richomer, Arbogast, Merobaudes, and Bauto, the father-in-law of the emperor Arcadius (395–408), entered the service of the Romans and reached high office. During the massive barbarian invasions of 406, the Franks remained remarkably loyal to Rome, although they did sack Trier four times.

In legend, the ruling Merovingian family was founded by a certain Pharamund, but the first known Salian king was Chlogio, who after ca. 420 expanded the kingdom to the Somme River. It may have been at this time that the *Lex Salica* of the Franks was first drawn up. At the same time, the Ripuarian Franks crossed the middle Rhine, near Trier and Cologne; other Franks remained east of the river. Chlogio's successor, Merovechus, led the Salians in 451 when they joined with the Roman general Aetius and the Visigoths to defeat Attila and the Huns. By the reign of Childeric (ca. 456–ca. 481), the Franks had occupied Cambrai, where Childeric's grave was discovered in 1653. A reliable tradition suggests that the Roman general Aegidius replaced him as king for a few years.

At this time, the Salian Franks were few in number, perhaps only 6,000 warriors, and were fragmented into several groups. The real expansion and unification of the kingdom did not occur until the reign of Childeric's son Clovis (ca. 480–511). In 486, he overcame the Roman "king" Syagrius of Soissons, and occupied the Roman province of Belgica Secunda. In the 490s, he defeated the Alamanni, and in 500 he also defeated the Burgundians. In 507, he inflicted a disastrous defeat upon the Visigoths of Alaric II (485–507) at Vouillé near Poitiers. Clovis then overthrew the other Frankish kings, such as Chlodericus, king of the Ripuarians, and Ragnacharius, king of Cambrai, and brought all the Franks under his own rule.

Clovis's baptism as an orthodox Christian by bishop Remigius of Rheims in the late 490s did much to conciliate the Gallo-Roman aristocracy and in particular the powerful Gallo-Roman bishops. Later Frankish kings, however, interfered regularly in ecclesiastical affairs, bestowing sees on their favorites and often appropriating church property. The Franks also absorbed elements of classical culture, including the Latin language itself, which eventually evolved into modern-day French.

By the time of Clovis's death in 511, the Franks controlled most of central and northern Gaul. His kingdom then was partitioned among his four sons. This Merovingian practice was to be the bane of the dynasty, preventing the unification of the kingdom and encouraging the intrigues and quarreling for which the Merovingian kings became so well known.

Frankish rule in Gaul was never very secure. As a barbarian drop in a Roman sea, Frankish rulers always had to be wary of antagonizing the powerful old Gallo-Roman landed aristocracy. Nor was their control over their own nobility any more firm. The central administration consisted primarily of the king's household. A "referendary," later a "chancellor," oversaw court business. The administration was decentralized, with most real authority in the hands of local potentates, whether officials like dukes (military governors) and counts (city administrators), bishops, or landed magnates.

In the seventh century, the "mayors of the palace" appropriated increasing authority, and in the middle of the eighth century they appropriated the kingship as well, establishing the Carolingian dynasty. *See also* Clovis; Gaul; Gregory of Tours. [R.W.M.]

Bibliography

Chronicle of Fredegarius (CPL 1314), ed. B. Krusch, MGH, *Scriptores Rerum Merovingicarum* (1888), Vol. 2, pp. 1–193; *Lex Salica*, ed. J.H. Hessels and H. Kern (London: Murray, 1880), and ed. H.

Geffcken (Leipzig: Veit, 1898); *Vita Remigii*, ed. B. Krusch, MGH *Scriptores Rerum Merovingicarum* (1896), Vol. 3, pp. 239–336; *Vita Genovefae* (CPL 2104): Text A, ed. B. Krusch, MGH, *Merovingicarum* (1896), Vol. 3, pp. 204–238; Text B, ed. C. Kohler, *Etude critique sur le texte de la vie de sainte Geneviève* (Paris: Vieweg, 1881), pp. 5–47; Text C, ed. C. Künstle, *Vita S. Genovefae* (Leipzig: Teubner, 1910).

Gregory of Tours, *History of the Franks,* tr. L. Thorpe (Harmondsworth: Penguin, 1974); *Liber historiae Francorum,* tr. B.S. Bachrach (Lawrence: Coronado, 1973); J.M. Wallace-Hadrill, *The Fourth Book of the Chronicle of Fredegarius with Its Continuations* (London and New York: Nelson, 1960).

S. Dill, *Roman Society in Gaul in the Merovingian Age* (London: Macmillan, 1926); J.M. Wallace-Hadrill, *The Long-Haired Kings and Other Studies in Frankish History* (London: Methuen, 1962); E. Zöllner, *Geschichte der Franken bis zur Mitte des sechsten Jahrhunderts* (Munich: Beck, 1970); B.S. Bachrach, *Merovingian Military Organization 481–751* (Minneapolis: U of Minnesota P, 1972); J.M. Wallace-Hadrill, *The Frankish Church* (Oxford: Clarendon, 1983).

FULGENTIUS OF RUSPE (ca. 467–533).

Bishop and writer. According to his biographer, Ferrandus (PL 65.117–150), Fulgentius was born at Telepta in the central-western section of the North African province of Byzcena. His family, the Gordiani, belonged to the senatorial class at Carthage and had suffered under the ruling Vandals, adherents of Arianism. His mother was active in his education. After a period as procurator of his hometown, Fulgentius resigned in order to become a monk. In 507, he was elected bishop of Ruspe on the east coast of Byzcena. The Vandal king Thrasamund, an Arian, soon banished him to Sardinia with sixty other bishops. Recalled from 515 to 517 to negotiate with the Arians, Fulgentius remained an exile until the death of Thrasamund in 523. He returned to Ruspe to serve as bishop until his own death ten years later.

Fulgentius's extant corpus of letters, treatises, sermons, and an acrostic hymn all deal with Christian issues (not mythology). He discussed ascetical life in letters to Galla (*Ep.* 2), Proba (*Ep.* 3; 4), and Eugippus (*Ep.* 5). Against the Arian Vandals of North Africa, he defended orthodox Trinitarian belief. Not very original,

Fulgentius used Ambrose, Hilary (*Ep.* 14), and especially Augustine to present the full divinity of the Son (and sometimes of the Holy Spirit). He defended the full and unconfused divinity and humanity in Jesus Christ, referring to the virginity of Mary (*Ver. praed.* 1.100–101) and borrowing the language of Leo (*Ep.* 14). Against the Semipelagians of southern Gaul, Fulgentius employed Augustine's positions on predestination, the necessity of prevenient (or prior) grace, and infant baptism (*Ep.* 17). One work, popular in the Middle Ages, is a basic outline of the faith with forty rules for a simple pilgrim named Peter (*De fide ad Petrum*). Feast day January 1. CPL 814–846. [P.C.B.]

Bibliography

J. Fraipont, ed., *Sancti Fulgentii Episcopi Ruspensis Opera*, CCSL (1968), Vols. 91, 91A.

G.G. Lapeyre, *S. Fulgence de Ruspe: un évêque africain sous la domination vandale: essai historique* (Paris: Lethielleux, 1929); J.J. Gavigan, "Fulgentius of Ruspe on Baptism," *Traditio* 5 (1947):313–322; M.L.W. Laistner, "Fulgentius in the Carolingian Age," *The Intellectual Heritage of the Early Middle Ages*, ed. C.G. Starr (Ithaca: Cornell UP, 1957), pp. 202–215; J.J. Gavigan, "Vita monastica in Africa desiitne cum invasione Wandalorum?," *Augustinianum* 1 (1961):7–49; W.G. Rusch, *The Later Latin Fathers* (London: Duckworth, 1977), pp. 192–197; S.T. Stevens, "The Circle of Bishop Fulgentius," *Traditio* 38 (1982):327–341.

G

GAISERIC (d. 477). King of the Vandals (428–477). Gaiseric brought the Vandals from Spain to North Africa (429) and captured much of the territory within a few years. Augustine died at Hippo while the city was under Vandal siege (430). With the fall of Carthage (439), Gaiseric gained a capital for his kingdom. He subsequently won control of the western Mediterranean, through his fleet, and sacked Rome (455). An astute ruler, he was an adherent of Arianism; under him, the Catholic church suffered the exile of some of its bishops and confiscation of properties. *See also* Vandals.

[M.P.McH.]

GAIUS (late second–early third century). Roman presbyter and writer. Gaius is the author of a dialogue against Proclus, an adherent of Montanism, fragments of which are preserved by Eusebius of Caesarea. His reference to the memorials of Peter and Paul (Eusebius, *H.E.* 2.25.7) appears to be confirmed by the excavations under the church of St. Peter. In regard to the canon of scripture, Gaius accepted the epistles of Paul (not the Epistle to the Hebrews), but apparently rejected John's Gospel and the Book of Revelation as the work of Cerinthus. In this, he was opposed by Hippolytus; several works of the latter have been erroneously attributed to Gaius.   [M.P.McH.]

Bibliography

Eusebius, *Church History* 2.25.5–7; 3.28.1–2; 3.31.4; 6.20.3; Jerome, *Lives of Illustrious Men* 59.

GAIUS. Bishop of Rome (283–296). Nothing is known for certain of Gaius's activities; the account in the *Liber Pontificalis* is not reliable. During his episcopate, the Roman church enjoyed a period of relative tranquility prior to the persecution under Diocletian; he probably did not die a martyr. He is the last Roman bishop for whom an epitaph in Greek is preserved. Feast day April 22.   [M.P.McH.]

Bibliography

O. Marucchi, *Christian Epigraphy* (Cambridge UP, 1912), no. 196, pp. 196–197; Eusebius, *Church History* 7.32.1; *Liber Pontificalis* 29 (Duchesne 1.161).

GALATIA, GALATIANS. Both a small region north of the center of Asia Minor that had been settled in the third century B.C. by marauding Gauls called Galatians and a larger Roman province encompassing much of central Asia Minor. Galatians is one of the most important letters of Paul.

The authenticity of Galatians is universally accepted. The main problems are destination and date. In favor of a north Galatian destination are the references to Galatia in Acts 16:6 and 18:23 (because Luke usually uses geographical rather than political terminology) and the reference to the Galatians in Galatians 3:1 (because it is doubtful that the term would have been applied to any except the descendants of the Gauls). In favor of a south Galatian destination are the reference to Galatia in Galatians 1:3 (because Paul usually uses political terminology), the references to Barnabas in Galatians 2:1, 9, 13 (because he was with Paul only when Paul founded the churches in south Galatia according to Acts 13–14), the improbability that Paul would have gone to north Galatia to recover from the illness mentioned in Galatians 4:13, and the certainty that Paul evangelized south Galatia. Most American and British scholars favor the southern theory, most Germans the northern.

If Galatians 4:13 indicates that Paul had visited Galatia at least twice at the time of writing, then on the basis of the north Galatian theory the letter could not have been written before Paul came to Ephesus ca. 53 on what Acts describes as his third missionary journey, because the only passages that could refer to north Galatia are 16:6 (set at the beginning of the second journey) and 18:23 (beginning of third). On the basis of the southern theory, it could have been written anytime after the end of the first journey, because according to Acts 14:21–25 Paul revisited the south Galatian churches while still on that journey. Some who hold the southern theory date the letter in 48 or 49 before the Jerusalem Council of Acts 15—thus making it the earliest of Paul's letters. Others adopt the same late date that is necessary on the basis of the northern theory. Much depends on how one relates Paul's visits to Jerusalem as described in Galatians to those described in Acts—a problem on which no consensus has been reached. Another consideration is the extent of the historical and chronological accuracy of Acts. Most American scholars adopt the late date, most British the early date.

The Galatian churches were troubled by a Judaizing teaching that required Gentile converts to keep parts of the Law of Moses, especially circumcision (Gal. 6:12–13), in order to be a part of God's people. Paul responds with a personal defense of his apostleship (Gal. 1–2), a doctrinal argument affirming that the true heirs of Abraham are such by faith in Christ and not by works of Law (Gal. 3–4), and a practical conclusion on the morality according to the Spirit that is free from legalistic requirements (Gal. 5–6). Paul's argument established a Gentile Christianity that maintained its continuity with the Old Testament but its freedom from circumcision and other ceremonial aspects of the Mosaic law. A minor problem is whether Paul wrote against only the Judaizers or whether he also opposed some libertines. Most take the former position.

Galatians headed the list of Paul's epistles in Marcion's Bible.   [J.A.B.]

Bibliography

John Chrysostom, *Commentary on Galatians*, NPNF, 2nd ser. (1890), Vol. 13, pp. 1–45; Theodoret, *Interpretatio Epistolae ad Galatas*, PG 82.460–504; Marius Victorinus, *Commentarii in Epistulam ad Galatas* (PL 8.1145–1198); Jerome, *Commentarii in epistulam ad Galatas*, PL 26.331–468; Pelagius, *Expositio in Galatas*, TS 9.2 (1926):306–343.

W.M. Ramsay, *St. Paul the Traveller and Roman Citizen* (London: Hodder and Stoughton, 1895); idem, *The Cities of St. Paul* (London: Hodder and Stoughton, 1907); R.K. Sherk, "Roman Galatia: The Governors from 25 B.C. to A.D. 114," and S. Mitchell, "Population and Land in Roman Galatia," ANRW (1980), Vol.7.2.2, pp. 954–1052, 1053–1081.

J.B. Lightfoot, *The Epistle of St. Paul to the Galatians* (London: Macmillan, 1866); E.D. Burton, *The Epistle to the Galatians* (Edinburgh: T. and T. Clark, 1921); H.D. Betz, *Galatians* (Philadelphia: Fortress, 1979); F.F. Bruce, *Commentary on Galatians* (Grand Rapids: Eerdmans, 1982).

GALERIUS (ca. 250–311). Roman emperor (305–311). An Illyrian of humble birth, Galerius rose through the military ranks to be appointed Caesar of the east by Diocletian upon the latter's reorganization of the imperial system (293); at that time, he married Diocletian's daughter Valeria. (In the new arrangement, government was to be in the hands of a tetrarchy consisting of two emperors, or Augusti, for west and east, each seconded by a Caesar). As Caesar, he won victories over the Germans in defense of the frontiers along the Danube (293–295) and, after an initial setback, against Narses I of Persia (298). It is likely that he was influential in persuading Diocletian to initiate the Great Persecution against Christians (303–311), although other factors were doubtless involved.

Upon the abdication of Diocletian (305), Galerius became Augustus for the east; he appointed his nephew, Maximinus Daia, as his Caesar. After the death of the western Augustus, Constantius I Chlorus (306), Galerius conferred the title on the western Caesar, Severus, and sent him to Rome against Maxentius, who claimed the imperial office for himself. Severus met with defeat and, after the failure of an attempted invasion of Italy, Galerius himself was forced to withdraw. In an effort to save the tetrarchy, Licinius was appointed Augustus of the west and Maxentius declared a public enemy (308).

Persecutions continued and indeed intensified in the east, although they had virtually ceased in the west. One of Galerius's final acts, however, was the issuance of an edict of toleration (311) permitting Christians to rebuild their places of worship. He died shortly thereafter, with the tetrarchic system on the point of breakup. A final outburst of persecution occurred in the territories subject to Maximinus Daia for a short time afterward (311–312). The motives for Galerius's termination of the persecution, like those for his initiation of it, are not certain. Political intrigue and the effects of his terminal disease may have played a role at the end; it is certain that he recognized the failure of his policy at a time of imperial crisis. *See also* Diocletian; Persecutions.

[M.P.McH.]

Bibliography

Lactantius, *The Deaths of the Persecutors* 9–14; 18–35; Eusebius, *Church History* 8.16–17; idem, *Martyrs of Palestine* 1;4; [Ammianus Marcellinus], *Excerpts of Valesius* 1.1–4.11.

P. Keresztes, "From the Great Persecution to the Peace of Galerius," *VChr* 37 (1983):379–399; O. Nicholson, "The Wild Man of the Tetrarchy: A

Divine Companion for the Emperor Galerius," *Byzantion* 54 (1984):253–275.

GALLA PLACIDIA (ca. 392–450). Roman empress. The daughter of the emperor Theodosius I, Galla Placidia was taken as a hostage by the Visigothic ruler Alaric upon his sack of Rome (410). She married Alaric's brother-in-law and successor, Ataulf (414), and after his murder was returned to the western emperor Honorius, her stepbrother. She was then married to Constantius (417), who died shortly afterward (421). Bitter quarrels with Honorius drove her and her children to take refuge in Constantinople with the eastern emperor Theodosius II. After her stepbrother's death (423), the rule was secured (425) for Valentinian III, her young son by Constantius. She acted as effective ruler for many years, although her power was eventually rivaled by that of the general Aetius.

Galla Placidia influenced Honorius in favor of Boniface I when Eulalius contested his election to the Roman see (418–419). She is reported to have esteemed Germanus of Auxerre and to have arranged the return of his body to Gaul upon his death at Ravenna (ca. 437–446). An uncompromising adherent of Catholic orthodoxy, she was vigorous in opposition to the supporters of Pelagianism and Manichaeism. She upheld the position of Leo the Great in his condemnation of Eutyches (449). Two of her letters concerning this matter, addressed respectively to Theodosius II and his sister Pulcheria, are extant in the correspondence of Leo (*Ep.* 56; 58).

Although Galla Placidia died in Rome, it is possible she was buried in the mausoleum she had constructed in Ravenna; the structure, dedicated to St. Lawrence, is renowned for its mosaics, especially that of Christ as the Good Shepherd. *See also* Ravenna. [M.P.McH.]

Bibliography

V.A. Sirago, *Galla Placidia e la trasformazione politica dell' Occidente* (Louvain: Bibliothèque de l'Université, 1961); S.I. Oost, *Galla Placidia Augusta: A Biographical Essay* (Chicago and London: U of Chicago P, 1968); L. Storoni-Mazzolani, *Vita di Galla Placidia* (Milan: Rizzoli, 1975); P. Caffin, *Galla Placidia: la dernière impératrice de Rome* (Paris: Perrin,

1977); S. Rebenich, "Gratian, A Son of Theodosius, and the Birth of Galla Placidia," *Historia* 34 (1985):372–385.

GALLICAN RITE. Form of the liturgy used in Gaul until the second half of the eighth century. The Gallican rite was one of several ancient versions that existed in the regions of the west before the Roman rite became universal. As a distinct form, it had its own Mass, Divine Office, liturgy of baptism, and other ceremonies, which differed from those of the Roman rite in their components, texts, and style of chant. But even within Gaul, liturgical usages differed from one diocese to the next, and the Gallican rite encompasses all of these.

The date at which the rite was established in Gaul has been placed as early as the second century or as late as the fifth, and there are various opinions concerning its ultimate origin. It contains many eastern elements and some that had been used in the early stages of the Roman liturgy. It flourished in the fifth and sixth centuries, when it influenced other major rites of the west. By the seventh century, Roman liturgical books that were brought to Gaul resulted in a hybrid liturgy, and in the second half of the eighth century, under the legislation of Pippin and Charlemagne, the Roman rite supplanted the Gallican.

The structure of the Gallican Mass is known to us through the *Expositio* of Pseudo-Germanus. In this commentary, the seventh- or eighth-century author describes most of the components of the Mass and provides a context in which we can place additional components (mostly orations—i.e., prayers—called *collectiones*) known from extant liturgical books. The Mass consists of the following elements: (1) a chant *ad praelegendum*, corresponding to the Roman Introit; (2) the *Silentium* (calling for silence) and the formula "Dominus sit semper vobiscum" ("May the Lord be with you always"); (3) the *Aius* (a threefold *Sanctus* in Greek and Latin) and a threefold *Kyrie Eleison*; (4) the *Prophetia* (Zachariah's canticle from Luke 1) and a *collectio post prophetiam*; (5) two readings, usually from the Old Testament and the Epistles; (6) the *Benedictio*

(canticle from Daniel 3); (7) an *Aius*, a Gospel reading, a *Sanctus*, and a homily; (8) *preces pro populo* (litany verses), *collectio post precem*, and dismissal of nonbaptized; (9) the *Sonum* (an Offertory chant), *laudes* (Allelulia), *praefatio*, and *collectio*, the last corresponding to the Roman Secret; (10) a recital of names of the dead (*Nomina*) and *collectio post nomina*; (11) the Kiss of Peace (not at its place in the Roman Mass just before the communion) and a *collectio ad pacem*; (12) dialogue (as in the Roman Mass), a *contestatio* (Proper Preface), *Sanctus,* and *collectio post sanctus*; (13) the Canon (less extensive than the Roman Canon) and a *collectio post secreta*; (14) an antiphon at the Fraction, Lord's prayer, and benediction; (15) the *Trecanum* (communion chant) and Postcommunion oration; (16) dismissal and *eulogia* (giving bread to those not receiving communion). Even when the actual orations in Gallican books are Roman, they may bear the characteristically Gallican labels.

According to the sixth-century monastic rules of Caesarius and Aurelianus of Arles, monks and nuns observed a daily Office consisting of a full set of canonical hours. The extensive recitation of Psalms, and the use of chants, hymns, and lessons, may be distinguished from the corresponding features of the Office in other rites. Attempts were made to institute many of these daily hours in the cathedrals, but the clergy was normally obliged to attend only Lauds and Vespers.   [J.B.]

Bibliography

E.C. Ratcliff, ed., *Expositio Antiquae Liturgiae Gallicanae* (London: Henry Bradshaw Society, 1971); L.C. Mohlberg, ed., *Missale Gallicanum Vetus* (Rome: Herder, 1958); idem, ed., *Missale Gothicum* (Rome: Herder, 1961); E.A. Lowe, *The Bobbio Missal: A Gallican Mass-Book* (London: Henry Bradshaw Society, 1920); P. Salmon, ed., *Le Lectionnaire de Luxeuil* (Rome: Abbaye Saint-Jerome, 1944).

J. Quasten, "Oriental Influence in the Gallican Liturgy," *Traditio* 1 (1943):55–78; H.G.J. Beck, *The Pastoral Care of Souls in South-East France During the Sixth Century* (Rome: Gregorian University, 1950); W.S. Porter, *The Gallican Rite* (London: Mowbray, 1958); A.A. King, "Gallican Rite," *Liturgies of the Past* (London: Longmans, 1959), pp. 77–185; K. Gamber, *Codices Liturgici Latini Antiquiores* (Freiburg: Universitätsverlag, 1968), Vol. 1, pp. 56–66, 153–193.

GALLIENUS (ca. 218–268). Roman emperor (253–268). Gallienus was associated with his father, Valerian, in the rule of the empire upon the latter's accession to the throne (253). Assigned to defend the west, he thwarted the attempt of the Germanic tribes to invade Gaul and repulsed the Alamanni from Italy. After his father's capture by the forces of Persia (260), he confronted repeated internal crises and invasions in both east and west. He was killed by his officers at Milan. In reversal of his father's policy, he issued an edict (260) that ended coercion against Christians; further, he restored to the bishops the care of churches and cemeteries. These decisions were made pragmatically, because of the failure of the former course of action; occasional local incidents of persecution continued to occur.   [M.P.McH.]

Bibliography
Eusebius, *Church History* 7.10.1, 7.13.1; 7.22.12–23.4; 7.28.3–4.

M.M. Sage, "The Persecution of Valerian and the Peace of Gallienus," *WS* 17 (1983):137–159.

GANGRA. City in Paphlagonia (today Turkish Çankiri). Gangra was part of the Roman province of Galatia from the year 6/5 B.C. Although the date of the introduction of Christianity is not known, the names of martyrs have survived. Novatianism was strong in the region. A council at Gangra in the 340s adopted twenty canons against the extreme asceticism of Eustathius of Sebaste. An epilogue ("Canon 21") explains true asceticism. In the mid-fifth century, its church was under the patriarchate of Constantinople. CPG IV, 8553.   [E.F.]

Bibliography
Socrates, *Church History* 2.38; 2.43; Sozomen, *Church History* 3.14; 4.24.

F. Lauchert, *Die Kanones der wichtigsten altkirchlichen Concilien* (Frankfurt: Minerva, 1961), pp. 79–83; J. Hefele and H. Leclercq, *Histoire des conciles* (Paris: Letouzey et Ané, 1907), Vol. 1.2, pp. 1029–1045.

H.R. Percival, tr., NPNF, 2nd ser. (1899), Vol. 14, pp. 91–101.

H.M. Gwatkin, *Studies of Arianism* (1882; repr. New York: AMS, 1978), pp. 185–188; A.H.M. Jones, *Cities of the Eastern Roman Provinces*, 2nd ed. (Oxford: Clarendon, 1971), pp. 166f., 559.

GAUDENTIUS OF BRESCIA (late fourth–early fifth century). Bishop and preacher. Chosen bishop of Brescia while on a journey to the east (ca. 397), Gaudentius accepted the office through the persuasion of Ambrose and other bishops. At the request of emperor Honorius and pope Innocent I, he went to Constantinople to plead for the return of John Chrysostom from exile, but without success. His twenty-one extant sermons show a good grasp of theology and a solid classical training; the last of these, *Sermon* 21, is a panegyric on his predecessor, Filastrius of Brescia. CPL 215–216.   [M.P.McH.]

Bibliography
John Chrysostom, *Letter* 184.

Gaudentius of Brescia, Sermons and Letters, tr. S.L. Boehrer (S.T.D. thesis, The Catholic University of America, 1965).

C. Truzzi, *Zeno, Gaudenzio e Cromazio, Testi e contenuti della predicazione cristiana per le chiese di Verona, Brescia e Aquileia (360–410 ca)* (Brescia: Paideia, 1985); P. Meyvaert, "Excerpts from an Unknown Treatise of Jerome to Gaudentius of Brescia," *RBén* 96 (1986): 203–218; Y.-M. Duval, "Le *Liber Hieronymi ad Gaudentium*. Rufin d'Aquilée, Gaudence de Brescia et Eusèbe de Crémone," *RBén* 97 (1987): 163–186.

GAUL. According to the geographers of antiquity, the lands bounded by the Alps, the Mediterranean, the Pyrenees, the Atlantic, and the Rhine (Strabo 2.5.28). The population was mainly Celtic (the Gauls) with some Germanic elements in the north and Greek colonies in the south. Largely under Roman control by Julius Caesar's death in 44 B.C., Gaul was divided by Augustus in 27 B.C. into the four provinces of Aquitania, Gallia Narbonensis, Lugdunensis, and Belgica, each of which was then subdivided into a number of smaller regions (*civitates*), usually on the basis of existing tribal boundaries. Within each *civitas*, one town was designated as the *civitas* capital, which served as the center for the *civitas* government and, in Christian times, as the residence of the local bishop.

Christianity, in the words of Sulpicius Severus (ca. 360–ca. 420), "was received across the Alps rather late" (*Chron.* 2.32.1). When it did arrive in Gaul, the new religion made its first attested appearance in the mid-second century in the *civitas*-capitals of Vienne (Narbonensis) and Lyons (Lugdunensis), river ports along the principal trade route between the Mediterranean Sea and the Rhine frontier. A letter written by the Christians of those towns, and preserved in Eusebius (*H.E.* 5.1–4), conveys to their "brethren in the provinces of Asia and Phrygia" news of the martyrdom in 177 of about fifty of their number at Lyons. Until put to death in 177, Pothinus served as bishop of Lyons and also appears to have been responsible in some way for the community at Vienne. He was in fact probably the only bishop in Gaul at the time, as was his successor, the celebrated Irenaeus of Lyons (d. ca. 200).

The growth of Christianity in Gaul during the third century can to some extent be measured by the increase in the number of bishoprics for which evidence is available, especially in the more heavily urbanized regions of Narbonensis and Lugdenensis. By the mid-third century, bishops are well attested for Lyons, Arles, Vienne, Toulouse, Rheims, Paris, and Trier, and half a century later, at the Council of Arles (314), sixteen Gallic bishoprics were represented, perhaps half of those in existence at the time. That Christians in late-third-century Gaul probably constituted a small proportion of the population, however, is suggested by the relatively limited number of Gallic martyrs known to have perished in the persecutions of Decius (250–251), Valerian (257–260), and Diocletian (303–305), despite the best efforts of later hagiographers to publicize the heroic feats of their Christian ancestors.

Although they were already numerous by the early fourth century, the bishops of Gaul were slow to become involved in the Arian controversy. Only one Gallic bishop was present at the Council of Nicaea in 325, and only two appeared at the Council of Sardica in 343. Gallic bishops were, in fact, not drawn into the controversy until Constantius II convened a council at Arles in 353, forced the assembled bishops to sign a condemnation of Athanasius, and exiled the only bishop who refused. A similar pattern of events unfolded at the councils of Béziers (356) and Rimini (359), at which several Gallic bishops were deposed, including Hilary of Poitiers, who spent the period between 356 and 360 in Phrygia composing treatises against Arianism. The Arian controversy in Gaul came to an end when Julian was proclaimed emperor in Paris in 360. Constantius lost control of the region, the exiles were recalled, and the Gallic bishops, under the leadership of Hilary, proclaimed their allegiance to the Council of Nicaea.

Just before he went into exile, Hilary came into contact with a recently discharged Pannonian soldier named Martin, who was destined by the efforts of Sulpicius Severus, Paulinus of Périgueux, Gregory of Tours, and others to become the most famous religious figure in late Roman Gaul, first as a monk in Ligugé, near Poitiers (360–ca. 371), and then as the third bishop of Tours (ca. 371–397). As bishop, Martin was known chiefly for his foundation of a monastery nearby at Marmoutier, and for his efforts to convert the still overwhelmingly pagan peasantry to Christianity, a process not completed until several centuries later.

Yet, as an unkempt ascetic, the son of a soldier, and an ex-soldier himself, Martin was hardly a typical Gallic bishop of the late fourth century (Sulpicius Severus, *Mart.* 9.3). In fact, the majority of his episcopal colleagues appear to have been members of those aristocratic families that had traditionally exercised local authority in Roman Gaul. Traditional patterns were also followed in the organization of the church in Gaul, as they were elsewhere. By the late fourth century, in most cases, the boundaries of the Christian dioceses in Gaul coincided with those of the *civitates*; the ecclesiastical provinces into which these dioceses were distributed largely corresponded to the seventeen civil provinces created by the third-century reorganization of Diocletian; and, in accordance with the Council of Nicaea, bishops of metropolitan *civitates* gradually came to be considered superior in prestige to their comprovincial bishops, although not without some bitter disagreements within provinces about the right to metropolitan status. The best known of these rivalries arose in the late fourth century between the bishops of Arles and Vienne.

With the barbarian invasions of 406–407 and later, and the settlement of Franks, Visigoths, and Burgundians on Gallic soil, imperial control over Gaul began to slip away. By ca. 476, nearly the whole of Gaul had fallen into barbarian hands. In the insecurity of these times—clearly reflected in the writings of Paulinus of Pella and Salvian of Marseilles, among others—the local strength of the Gallo-Roman church and its leaders became evident, as such bishops as Germanus of Auxerre, Sidonius Apollinaris, and Caesarius of Arles organized defenses against the barbarians, negotiated tax remissions for lands devastated by warfare, supplied food in times of famine, and ransomed prisoners of war from captivity.

The fifth century saw not only warfare but also the strengthening of ecclesiastical institutions in Gaul. The monastic movement, which had effectively begun with Martin's foundations at Ligugé and Marmoutier, continued to grow in popularity with the establishment of monasteries by John Cassian at Marseilles (ca. 415), Romanus at Condat in the Jura Mountains (ca. 440), and Honoratus at Lérins (ca. 400). The last of these became well known as a training ground for distinguished bishops and a center of Semipelagianism. This period also saw the construction of many baptisteries, shrines, and basilicas (e.g., Gregory of Tours, *H.F.* 2.14–17) and the establishment of parish churches in numerous villages and villas (e.g., *H.F.* 10.31).

Political stability returned to Gaul in the sixth century as the Franks, having gradually converted to Catholic Christianity after Clovis's baptism, progressively won control over Visigothic Aquitaine (507), Burgundy (534), and Ostrogothic Provence (536). By the end of the sixth century, the slow transformation of Gaul from a Roman province to a Frankish kingdom was well under way, a process most vividly illustrated in the historical and hagiographical writings of Gregory of Tours. *See also* Arles; Clovis; Franks; Gregory of Tours; Irenaeus; Martin of Tours.   [W.E.K.]

Bibliography

D. de Sainte-Marthe et al., *Gallia christiana*, 16 vols. (Paris, 1715–1865); J.-H. Albanès and U. Chevalier, *Gallia christiana novissima*, 7 vols. (Montbéliard and Valence, 1895–1920); C. Munier, *Concilia Galliae, 314–506*, CCSL (1963), Vol. 148; C. de Clercq, *Concilia Galliae, 511–695*, CCSL (1963), Vol. 148A; E. Le Blant, ed, *Inscriptions chrétiennes de la Gaule antérieures au VIIIe siècle*, 2 vols. (Paris: L'Imprimerie Impériale, 1856–1865); E. Le Blant, ed., *Noveau recueil des inscriptions chrétiennes de la Gaule antérieures au VIIIe siècle* (Paris: L'Imprimerie Nationale, 1892); N. Gauthier, *Première Belgique, Recueil des inscriptions chrétiennes de la Gaule antérieures à la renaissance carolingienne*, 19 vols. when completed, ed. H.-I. Marrou (Paris: CNRS, 1975), Vol. 1.

L. Duchesne, *Fastes épiscopaux de l'ancienne Gaule*, 2nd ed., 3 vols. (Paris: Fontemoing, 1907–1915); T.S. Holmes, *The Origin and Development of the Christian Church in Gaul During the First Six Centuries of the Christian Era* (London: Macmillan, 1911); S. Dill, *Roman Society in Gaul in the Merovingian Age* (London: Macmillan, 1926); A. Grenier, *Manuel d'archéologie gallo-romaine*, 4 vols. (Paris: Picard, 1931–1960); H.G.J. Beck, *The Pastoral Care of Souls in South-East France During the Sixth Century* (Rome: Gregorian University, 1950); E. Mâle, *La Fin du paganisme en Gaule* (Paris: Flammarion, 1950); F. Benoit, *Sarcophages paléochrétiens d'Arles et de Marseille, Gallia*, Suppl. 5 (1954); N.K. Chadwick, *Poetry and Letters in Early Christian Gaul* (London: Bowes and Bowes, 1955); J.M. Wallace-Hadrill, *The Long-Haired Kings and Other Studies in Frankish History* (London: Methuen, 1962); E. Griffe, *La Gaule chrétienne à l'époque romaine*, 2nd ed., 3 vols. (Paris: Letouzey et Ané, 1964–1966); P.-M. Duval, *La Gaule jusqu'au milieu du Ve siècle*, 2 vols. (Paris: Picard, 1971), annually updated in the "Chronique gallo-romaine" in *REA*; J.F. Drinkwater, *Roman Gaul* (Ithaca: Cornell UP, 1983); J.M. Wallace-Hadrill, *The Frankish Church* (Oxford: Clarendon, 1983); R. Van Dam, *Leadership and Community in Late Antique Gaul* (Berkeley: U of California P, 1985); R.W. Mathisen, *Ecclesiastical Factionalism and Religious Controversy in Fifth-Century Gaul* (Washington, D.C.: Catholic U of America P, 1988); idem, "The Theme of Literary Decline in Late Roman Gaul," *CP* 83 (1988): 45–52.

GELASIUS I. Bishop of Rome (492–496). Gelasius served as an influential adviser to his immediate predecessor, Felix II (III), and drafted many of Felix's letters. On his own accession, he continued to uphold the primacy of the papacy in the course of the Acacian schism, which had arisen (482) over the *Henoticon* issued by the emperor Zeno and the subsequent excommunication of the patriarch of Constantinople, Acacius. In answer to the overtures of Acacius's successor, Euphemius, Gelasius replied that reconciliation was possible only if the names of Acacius and others who had supported the *Henoticon* were removed from the diptychs, or lists of those to be included in public prayer. This was in effect a demand that the excommunication be acknowledged.

In a letter (*Ep.* 12) to the emperor Anastasius I, Gelasius advanced the theory of the two powers ("two swords"), that is, that the world was governed by the spiritual authority of the Roman see, directed toward eternal life, and the temporal power of the emperor over earthly affairs, both being subject to the lordship of Christ. (This position had earlier been set forth by Felix II [III] in a letter to Andrew of Thessalonica.) The theory was to undergo subsequent development and serve as the basis for much teaching and speculation concerning the relationship of church and state in the Middle Ages. Gelasius further claimed as a papal prerogative the right to ratify the decrees of councils and, at a Roman synod in 495, was the first Roman bishop to receive the title "Vicar of Christ." In his formulation of the role of the papacy, he owed much to the thought of Ambrose and of Leo the Great. His pontificate may be viewed as the culmination of developments initiated more than a century before under Damasus I (366–384).

Against Manichaeism, Gelasius insisted on the reception of the eucharist in both forms, bread and wine. He warned against a resurgence of the remnants of Pelagianism in letters to the bishops in Picenum and Dalmatia, apparently the last papal directives issued on the subject. He opposed a revival of the pagan festival of Lupercalia (February 15) at Rome. He sought to improve the training of the clergy and showed a pastoral concern for the poor.

Approximately 100 letters of Gelasius survive, whole or in fragments, as well as six theological treatises, including one on the two natures in Christ directed against Eutyches and Nestorius. An extant litany is his, as well as eighteen Mass formulas incorporated into the *Leonine (Verona) Sacramentary* (early seventh century). The so-called *Gelasian Sacramentary*

(mid-eighth century) is not his, nor is the *Decretum Gelasianum* (sixth century), the first three parts of which may have been the work of Damasus I; its fourth part deals with the orthodox fathers and councils of the church; the fifth part, with books to be received (works of the fathers) and those to be rejected (apocryphal writings, biblical and patristic, and patristic writings of dubious orthodoxy). Feast day November 21. CPL 1667–1676.

[M.P.McH.]

Bibliography

Gennadius, *Lives of Illustrious Men* 94 (96) (added to the original by a later hand); *Liber Pontificalis* 51 (Duchesne 1.255–257).

A.K. Ziegler, "Pope Gelasius I and His Teaching on the Relation of Church and State," *CHR* 27 (1942):3–28; A.W.J. Hollemann, *Pope Gelasius I and the Lupercalia* (Amsterdam: Hakkert, 1974); J. Taylor, "The Early Papacy at Work: Gelasius I (492–496)," *JRH* 8 (1974–1975):317–332; W. Ullmann, *Gelasius I (492–496): Das Papsttum an der Wende der Spätantike zum Mittelalter* (Stuttgart: Hiersemann, 1981); R.L. Benson, "The Gelasian Doctrine: Uses and Transformations," *La Notion d'autorité au Moyen Age: Islam, Byzance, Occident,* ed. G. Makdisi et al. (Paris: Presses Universitaires de France, 1982), pp. 13–44; P. Nautin, "La Lettre de Félix III à André de Thessalonique et sa doctrine sur l'église et l'empire," *RHE* 77 (1982):5–34.

GELASIUS OF CAESAREA (d. 395). Bishop of Palestinian Caesarea (367–395). A nephew of Cyril of Jerusalem, Gelasius participated in the Council of Constantinople in 381. He wrote a continuation of Eusebius's church history and a treatise against Eunomians. CPG II, 3520s.

[F.W.N.]

GELASIUS OF CYZICUS (late fifth century). Church historian. Gelasius wrote a *Historia ecclesiastica* (or *Acta*) about the events at the Council of Nicaea in 325. The work, although based on good sources, is neither independent of other documents nor proof that Nicaea published official *Acta.* CPG III, 6034. [F.W.N.]

Bibliography

PG 85.1191–1360; G. Loeschcke and M. Heinemann, eds., GCS (1918), Vol. 28.

GENESIS. First book of Moses or of the Pentateuch, named in Hebrew from its opening word, *Bereshith*, and in Greek, Latin, and English named "Genesis" from a word that occurs at Genesis 2:4. In fifty chapters, the book covers salvation history from creation to the death of Joseph. It is punctuated by ten occurrences of the phrase "These are the generations of. . . ."

Chapters 1–11 deal with creation, the flood, and the story of humankind in general. Chapters 12–50 tell the story of Abraham and his descendants. The call of Abraham and the promises made to him (12:1–3), including the land (12:7) and the covenant sealed by circumcision (17), are essential for understanding the remainder of the Bible.

The Christian church accepted Genesis as a part of the canon from its earliest days, and it is one of the most frequently cited (and echoed) Old Testament books. Creation, the account of Adam and Eve, the flood, the promise to Abraham, Melchizedek, and Joseph's experiences are all essential to New Testament thought in explaining the background and significance of the coming of Jesus. In the Pauline epistles, the promise to Abraham that in his descendants all nations would be blessed is accomplished in the evangelization of the Gentiles (Rom. 4; Gal. 3). These trends were continued in the postapostolic church.

Whereas Marcion rejected the entire Old Testament, insisting that the characters of Genesis had served the demiurge rather than the true God, the Gnostics allegorized Genesis as a support of their system. The orthodox claimed the patriarchs as their spiritual ancestors, denying that contemporary Jews were the faithful descendants of Abraham.

Genesis heads the earliest canonical list, that of Melito of Sardis (Eusebius, *H.E.* 4.26.13f.), and this practice is constant across the first six Christian centuries. Genesis also heads the lists of biblical books in the Greek codices.

In the Berlin Genesis, a Greek papyrus thought to be of the third century, the preserved text begins at Genesis 1:16 and continues to 35:8 with numerous breaks. Portions of Genesis are missing in codices Alexandrinus, Sinaiticus, and Vaticanus. Genesis was illustrated with miniatures in two important early Christian manuscripts, the Vienna Genesis and the Cotton Genesis, and was popular among Christian commentators. The account of creation called forth a large body of literature on the six days of creation (*hexaemeron*). [J.P.L.]

Vienna Genesis, illuminated manuscript (sixth century), covenant of God with Noah and his sons under the rainbow. (H. Gerstinger, Die Wiener Genesis [Vienna: 1931], pl. 5.)

Bibliography

Hippolytus, *Fragmenta in Genesim*, GCS 1.2; Origen, *Homilies on Genesis*, tr. R.E. Heine, FOTC (1982), Vol. 71; Ephraem the Syrian, *Commentarii in Genesim*, CSCO, Scrip. Syr. (1955), Vol. 71; John Chrysostom, *Homiliae in Genesim*, PG 53–54; Theodoret, *Quaestiones in Genesim*, PG 80.77–225; Jerome, *Quaestiones Hebraicae in Genesim*, PL 23; Augustine, *The Literal Meaning of Genesis*, tr. J.H. Taylor, ACW (1982), Vols. 41–42; Claudius Marius Victorius, *Alethia*, PL 61, CCSL 128.111–198, CSEL 16.1; Cyril of Alexandria, *Glaphyra*, PG 69.13–386.

F.E. Robbins, *The Hexaemeral Literature* (Chicago: U of Chicago P, 1912); A. Levene, *The Early Syrian Fathers on Genesis* (London: Taylor's Foreign Press, 1951); G.T. Armstrong, *Die Genesis in der alten Kirche* (Tübingen: Mohr, 1962); D. Kidner, *Genesis: An Introduction and Commentary* (Chicago: InterVarsity, 1967); J. Allenbach et al., *Biblia Patristica* (Paris: Centre National de la Recherche

Scientifique, 1975–1987); G.A. Robbins, ed., *Genesis 1–3 in the History of Exegesis: Intrigue in the Garden* (Lewiston: Mellen, 1988).

GENNADIUS (d. near the end of the fifth century). Presbyter at Marseilles. Gennadius is remembered chiefly for his continuation of Jerome's *Lives of Illustrious Men,* in which he discussed in 100 chapters the Christian authors of the fifth century. The accounts are brief, but the information is valuable. His other works are lost, except for the *Liber ecclesiasticorum dogmatum,* wrongly attributed to Augustine. He was probably of Semipelagian persuasion. CPL 957–959.   [E.F.]

Bibliography
Cassiodorus, *Introduction to Divine and Human Readings* 1.17.2.
Gennadius, *Lives of Illustrious Men,* tr. E.C. Richardson, NPNF (1892), Vol. 3, pp. 385–402.

GENNADIUS I OF CONSTANTINOPLE (d. 471). Bishop (458–471), exegete, and theologian. Prior to his election, Gennadius had vigorously attacked the Christological teaching of Cyril of Alexandria. An able administrator, he convoked a synod to deal with the problem of clerical simony (ca. 459). He was a strong opponent of the Monophysites and received a letter from Leo the Great directed against the activities of Timothy Aelurus, the Monophysite patriarch of Alexandria. His many homiletic writings are lost. Fragments of the attack on Cyril are preserved by Facundus of Hermiane. Fragments of his scriptural commentaries survive mainly in catenae; those on Genesis and the Epistle to the Romans are important for exegesis and spiritual life. A synodal letter on simony is his only work to come down in its entirety. CPG III, 5970–5986. TLG 2762.   [M.P.McH.]

Bibliography
Leo the Great, *Letter* 170; Gennadius, *Lives of Illustrious Men* 89 (90).

GEORGE, ST. Popular Christian saint, whose fame is widespread but whose real story is obscure, not least because of the legends that were attached to his name. George, from a Cappadocian family resident in Armenia, was a soldier in the Roman army. Because of his confession of Christ, he suffered martyrdom during the persecution under Diocletian (284–305) at Lydda (Diospolis) of Palestine, where his tomb and shrine have been shown from early times. The *Acts of St. George,* derived from Pasicrates, survive in Greek, Syriac, Coptic, Armenian, and Latin but seem to have suffered interpolations. Feast day April 23.   [G.D.D.]

Bibliography
Acta Sanctorum (Paris: Palmé, 1865), Vol. 10, April 3: 101–165; H. Delehaye, *Les Légendes grecques de saints militaires* (Paris: Picard, 1909), pp. 145–176.

GEORGE OF LAODICEA (fourth century). Bishop of Laodicea in Syria (335–347), native of Alexandria. An early supporter of Arius, George switched his allegiance first to the Semiarians (or Homoeans) and then to the Neoarians (Anomoeans). CPG II, 3555–3558.
[F.W.N.]

GEORGE OF PISIDIA (seventh century). Constantinopolitan deacon and poet. Responsible for the archives or sacred vessels at Hagia Sophia, George wrote contemporary political history and religious poetry. CPG III, 7827–7839.   [F.W.N.]

Bibliography
J.D. Frendo, "Classical and Christian Influences in the *Heracliad* of George of Pisidia," *Classical Bulletin* 62 (1986):53–61.

GEORGIA. Area of over 47,000 square miles at the eastern end of the Black Sea. More than half the country is mountainous, with the remainder hills and plateaus or plains and valleys. Citrus fruits, tea, and vineyards thrive in a temperate climate. The Georgians, who call themselves "Kartvelians," get their English name from the names given by modern Arabs and Persians: "Kurj" or "Gurj." From pre-Christian times, there have been, aside from Georgian proper, two other linguistic groups, Svan and Mingrelo-Laz, comprising the Caucasian family of languages. Georgia has been inhabited since the Stone Age and, in the historical period, Assyrians, Urartians, Scythians, Cimmerians, Persians, Greeks, Romans, and Arabs all left their imprint.

The conversion of Georgia to Christianity is ascribed to Nino (ca. 330). Previous to this, Georgia had a mixture of religions, including Zoroastrianism, devotion to Greek deities, lunar worship, and folk religion of various kinds. Before Nino, Greek missionaries had already worked in the cities along the Black Sea coast in western Georgia.

The Georgian church was initially under the aegis of Antioch. Along with Copts, Syrians, and Armenians, the Georgians opposed the creedal statement of the Council of Chalcedon (451), and at the Synod of Dvin (506) a majority of Georgian bishops condemned it. From the time of king Vaghtan Gorgaslan (ca. 446–510), the Georgian church has been an independent national church. It elects its own Catholicos-Patriarch, who resides in Tbilisi and conducts worship at the Sioni Cathedral (built in the sixth–seventh centuries).

At an early date, the Georgian church developed an active monastic tradition. Peter the Iberian built a monastery near Bethlehem and other monks lived at Mt. Athos, at St. Catherine's monastery in the Sinai, as well as in Georgia.

Following the Islamic conquest in the seventh century, an Arab viceroy lived in Tbilisi; however, the city prospered because of its location along busy trade routes. *See also* Nino. [C.C.]

Bibliography

R.P. Blake, "Georgian Theological Literature," *JThS* 26 (1924):50–64; P. Peeters, "Le Début du Christianisme en Georgie d'après les sources hagiographiques," *AB* 50 (1932):5–58; M. Tarchnisvili, *Geschichte der kirchlichen georgischen Literatur* (Vatican City: Biblioteca Apostolica Vaticana, 1955); D.M. Lang, *Lives and Legends of the Georgian Saints* (New York: Macmillan, 1956); D.M. Lang, *The Georgians* (London: Thames and Hudson, 1966); M. van Esbroeck, *Les Plus Anciens Homeliaires géorgians: étude descriptive et historique* (Louvain: Université Catholique, 1975); R. Mepisashvili and V. Tsintsadze, *The Arts of Ancient Georgia* (London: Thames and Hudson, 1979); J.N. Birdsall, "Georgian Studies and the New Testament," *NTS* 29 (1983):306–320.

GERMANUS OF AUXERRE (ca. 375–ca. 437/446).

Bishop of Auxerre (from 418). A member of the Gallo-Roman aristocracy, Germanus was educated in Gaul and at Rome, where he studied rhetoric and law. He entered on a career in the civil service and married. During his tenure as military governor in Armorica (later Brittany), he was elected bishop of Auxerre. He traveled to Britain (429) to combat Pelagianism there; in the course of this visit, he saw the supposed tomb of the British martyr Alban and perhaps promoted the saint's cult as a bond of orthodoxy. Later (ca. 436/444), he revisited the island, again in order to oppose Pelagianism. He died at Ravenna, where he had gone to intercede with the emperor Valentinian III and his mother, Galla Placidia, on behalf of Armorican rebels. His biography, written (ca. 480) by Constantius of Lyons, has value as a source for the period; Bede derived most of his account of Germanus's activities in Britain from it. [M.P.McH.]

Bibliography

Constantius of Lyons, *Life of Saint Germanus of Auxerre*, tr. in F.R. Hoare, *The Western Fathers* (New York: Sheed and Ward, 1954); Bede, *Ecclesiastical History* 1.17–21.

R.W. Mathisen, "The Last Year of Saint Germanus of Auxerre," *AB* 99 (1981):151–159; E.A. Thompson, *Saint Germanus of Auxerre and the End of Roman Britain* (Woodbridge: Boydell, 1984); R.A. Markus, "Pelagianism: Britain and the Continent," *JEH* 37 (1986):191–204.

GERMANUS OF CONSTANTINOPLE (ca. 634–ca. 733).

Patriarch of Constantinople (715–730), stalwart fighter against Iconoclasm. Although many of Germanus's writings were destroyed, the historical work *De haeresibus et synodis*, some letters on the iconoclastic controversy, homilies on the Blessed Virgin Mary, and the *Historia mystica ecclesiae catholicae* (a commentary on Byzantine liturgy), demonstrate his importance. Feast day May 12. CPG III, 8001–8033. [F.W.N.]

Bibliography
PG 98.9–453.
R. Taft, "Liturgy of the Great Church: An Initial Synthesis of Structure and Interpretation on the Eve of Iconoclasm," *DOP* 34–35 (1980–1981):45–75.

GERMANY. To the Romans, the area (*Germania*) north and east of the Rhine River. The name "German" was applied to any invader from across the Rhine. The Rhine also marked the northern boundary of the Roman empire, and Germany was to serve as a staging ground for raids that would culminate in the "barbarian invasions" of the fifth century.

The best ancient account of the Germans is that of the Roman historian Tacitus. In his *Germania* (A.D. 98), he described them as meat-eating, beer- and milk-drinking pastoralists who dressed in skins and refused to acquire property. He said of them, "They transact no business, public or private, without being armed . . ." (13). "It is well known that the peoples of Germany never live in cities . . ." (16). Of their women, he noted, "Armies already wavering and on the point of collapse have been rallied by the women. . . . They believe that there reside in women an element of holiness and a gift of prophecy; and so they do not scorn to ask their advice. . ." (8).

The extent to which the western Germans were different from the Celts remains unclear. Recent opinion favors the view that cultural differences between them were not as great as once thought. Many place-names between the Rhine and Elbe, for example, tend to be Celtic rather than Germanic, and in antiquity it was assumed that *Germania* was merely the part of *Celtica* (central and northern Gaul) on the other side of the Rhine. It may be that the name "Germans" originated as the name of Celts east and north of the Rhine. No ancient "Germans" ever called themselves that.

Farther to the east, however, there did live true "Teutonic" Germans, such as the Goths, Vandals, Burgundians, and Lombards. These Germans, who were only distantly related to the west Germans of the Rhine and upper Danube, apparently had their origin on the Baltic coast and in Scandinavia.

Several groups of Germans made their way into Gaul. In the second century B.C., the warlike Belgae occupied the lower Rhine; the middle Rhine was taken by the Treveri. The first Germans to attract the notice of the Romans were the Cimbri and Teutones, who invaded southern Europe ca. 110 B.C. Early in the first century B.C., some of the large group called the Suevi began to cross the Rhine but were defeated and forced to retire by Julius Caesar in 58 B.C.

The emperor Augustus (27 B.C.–A.D. 14) initially intended to occupy Germania between the Rhine and Elbe rivers. His stepsons Drusus and Tiberius had some initial successes in this project. A premature attempt to introduce Roman laws and customs into the province, however, resulted in a revolt led by the chieftain of the Cherusci, Arminius. In A.D. 9, Augustus's legate Varus and three legions were lured into an ambush in the Teutoburg Forest and virtually annihilated. After this disaster, the frontier was moved permanently back to the Rhine. To conceal the disgrace of the defeat, areas of Gaul on the left bank of the Rhine were later renamed "Upper" and "Lower Germany."

The Roman emperors were continuously concerned with protecting the northern frontier. Domitian (A.D. 81–96) annexed the exposed area between the Rhine and Danube, the *Agri Decumates*, and protected it with a line of fortifications (the *limes*) consisting of wooden palisades and towers. Hadrian (117–138) rebuilt these defenses in stone. Marcus Aurelius (161–180) campaigned extensively against the Marcomanni and Quadi on the upper Danube. During the troubled times of the third century, a coalition of Germans known as the Franks crossed the middle and lower Rhine. Another such coalition, the Alamanni, broke through the *limes* ca. 260 and raided as far as Italy. More and more Germans were recruited into the Roman army, some reaching high rank. During the fifth century, several east Germanic peoples, as well as the Franks, occupied most of the western half of the empire.

Tacitus claimed that "the Germans do not think it in keeping with the divine majesty to confine gods within walls or to portray them in the likeness of any human countenance. Their holy places are woods and groves . . ." (*Germania* 9). Their main deities were Tiu, a war god; Wodan, a god of the dead; and the thunder god Donar (or Thor). The Romans equated these three with Mars, Mercury, and Jupiter (or Hercules). Their names eventually were given to the days of the week also assigned to their Roman counterparts (Tuesday, Wednesday, and Thursday). Wodan's wife, Frija, likewise gave her name to the Roman day of Venus (Friday). Whereas many of the east Germans had adhered to Arianism by the time they arrived in the empire, most of the west Germans remained pagans and therefore were more easily converted to Catholicism.

Literary and archaeological remains give evidence for the existence of Christianity in Germany by the late second or early third century. By the middle of the third century, there was a bishop, Eucharius, in Trier, the imperial capital, and shortly thereafter one in Cologne; there were almost certainly bishops in Augsburg and Mainz as well. A bishop of Cologne, Maternus, attended councils in Rome (313) and Arles (314). Around that time, there were virgin martyrs of uncertain name, number, and origin in Cologne; by the ninth century, they were referred to as Ursula and her companions. The martyrdom of Afra (ca. 304) reveals the presence of Christians in Augsburg before the accession of Constantine; by the sixth century, the tomb and chapel of the martyr would become a place of pilgrimage. The presence of a Christian community in Mainz is attested ca. 200. In the fifth century, Severinus worked in Raetia, where the existence of bishoprics and monasteries is presupposed. A number of Christian communities survived the migrations of peoples in the fifth century with varying fortunes. *See also* Franks; Goths; Vandals.

[R.W.M.]

Bibliography

Tacitus, *Germania*, tr. H. Mattingly (Harmondsworth: Penguin, 1970).

L. Schmidt, *Geschichte der deutschen Stämme bis zum Ausgang der Völkerwanderung*, 2nd ed., 2 vols. (Munich: Beck, 1934–1941); A.C. Levy, *Barbarians on Roman Imperial Coins and Sculpture* (New York: American Numismatic Society, 1952); M. Wheeler, *Rome Beyond the Imperial Frontiers* (Harmondsworth: Penguin, 1955); P. Courcelle, *Histoire littéraire des grandes invasions germaniques*, 3rd ed. (Paris: Etudes Augustiniennes, 1964); E.A. Thompson, *The Early Germans* (Oxford: Oxford UP, 1965); P.L. MacKendrick, *Romans on the Rhine: Archaeology in Germany* (New York: Funk and Wagnalls, 1970); K. Schäferdiek, "Germanenmission," and H. von Petrikovits, "Germania," RLAC (1978), Vol. 10, pp. 492–654.

GIBBON, EDWARD (1737–1794). English historian, whose monumental *Decline and Fall of the Roman Empire* (6 vols., 1776–1788) ushered in a new era for the historical study of Christianity. Gibbon accomplished this in a dramatic manner with Chapters 15 and 16 of Volume 1. Although anticipated by others, it was Gibbon's analysis of the "human causes of the progress and establishment" of Christianity in the early Roman empire that captivated, challenged, and provoked his contemporaries. His brilliant style, with its vivid rhetorical flourishes and keen sense of irony, yielded a narrative that was an immediate sensation. Gibbon's emphasis upon natural and secular factors aroused much criticism; his ironic comments on the miraculous element in Christianity as well as his disparagement of ecclesiastical events and personalities angered many. His criticisms of ecclesiastical personalities and secular imperial figures, who yielded to the burgeoning power of the church from the time of Constantine the Great, demonstrate that for Gibbon history was "essentially personal and dramatic" (Low). Gibbon saw in Christianity's ascetic and world-denying tendencies, as well as in its drawing some of the most able men away from the service of the state, causes for the fall of the empire.

Although reared a Protestant, Gibbon underwent a brief conversion to Roman Catholicism, following a short and unhappy sojourn at Oxford. He returned to his original religious persuasion after his father sent him to Lausanne, Switzerland, for tutoring by a Calvinist minister. This Lausanne interlude of five years was vital to Gibbon's intellectual formation. Here he completed his thorough grounding in Greek and especially Latin classics and in French literary culture. The classics opened the Roman world to him, and French introduced him to the best scholarship available on antiquity, a subject that the French dominated during the seventeenth and eighteenth centuries. Gibbon's *Decline and Fall* is unique for its extensive and often generous citation of earlier writers—especially the Catholic historians Baronius and Tillemont and the Protestant Milman—but many forerunners were savaged by Gibbon's wit.

To many of his contemporaries, Gibbon was an "infidel." After preparing a "Vindication" in 1779 as a response to his religious critics, Gibbon states in his *Memoirs/Autobiography* that he dealt with further criticism "by pure and placid indifference." For all of his disparagement of the church and its institutional practices, Gibbon in fact was deeply attracted to church history. The interaction between the most powerful empire and the radical religious sect resulted in more than the "triumph of barbarism and religion." Out of this complex historical confrontation, there emerged European civilization and the *Christianized* Roman empire, which gave substance and form to this grand historico-cultural entity. Its first modern and greatest secular historian was Edward Gibbon.   [H.R.]

Bibliography

Definitive edition of the *Decline and Fall* is that by J.B. Bury, beginning in 1899 and reaching a ninth edition in seven volumes (London: Methuen, 1925); a convenient edition of Gibbon's complicated memoirs and autobiography is available in M.M. Reese, ed., *Gibbon's Autobiography* (London: Routledge and Kegan Paul, 1970); P.B. Craddock, ed., "A Vindication of Some Passages in the Fifteenth and Sixteenth Chapters of the . . . *Decline and Fall*. . . .1779," *The English Essays of Edward Gibbon* (Oxford: Clarendon, 1972), pp. 231–313 and editor's "Notes," pp. 570ff.

S.T. McCloy, *Gibbon's Antagonism to Christianity* (1933; repr. New York: Burt Franklin, 1966); D.M. Low, *Edward Gibbon, 1737–1794* (New York: Random House, 1937); J.W. Swain, *Edward Gibbon the Historian* (London: Macmillan, 1966); L. White, ed., *The Transformation of the Roman World: Gibbon's Problem After Two Centuries* (Berkeley: U of California P, 1966), esp. G.B. Ladner, "The Impact of Christianity," pp. 59–91; D.P. Jordan, *Gibbon and His Roman Empire* (Urbana: U of Illinois P, 1971); G.W. Bowersock, J. Clive, and S.R. Graubard, *Edward Gibbon and the Decline and Fall of the Roman Empire* (Cambridge: Harvard UP, 1977), esp. O. Chadwick, "Gibbon and the Church Historians," pp. 219–231; J.W. Burrow, *Gibbon* (New York: Oxford UP, 1985); P.B. Craddock, *Edward Gibbon, a Reference Guide* (Boston: G.K. Hall, 1987); idem, *Edward Gibbon, Luminous Historian, 1772-1794* (Baltimore: Johns Hopkins UP, 1988); D. Womersley, *The Transformation of "The Decline and Fall of the Roman Empire"* (Cambridge: Cambridge UP, 1988).

GILDAS (fifth–sixth century). British monk. Gildas was a reformer, indeed a Jeremiah, and his only large work, the *Destruction of Britain*, deals largely with the sins, both great and small, of Romano-British clergy and aristocracy. Written in Latin, it tells of the pagan Anglo-Saxon invasion of Romanized Britain; it includes the stories of the Roman desertion of Britain, the feats of Ambrosius Aurelianus, and the battle of Badon Hill (although he does not mention Arthur). A fragmentary letter and a probably inauthentic penitential are also attributed to him. Feast day January 29. CPL 1319–1324. *See also* Great Britain.   [J.F.K.]

Bibliography

M. Winterbottom, ed., *Gildas: The Ruin of Britain and Other Works* (Chichester: Phillimore, 1978).

T.D. O'Sullivan, *The De Excidio of Gildas: Its Authenticity and Date* (Leiden: Brill, 1978); M. Lapidge and D. Dumville, *Gildas: New Approaches* (Woodbridge: Boydell, 1984).

GLORIA IN EXCELSIS. "Glory to God in the highest" (Latin), a doxology, or hymn of praise. The opening words are those of the song of the angels at Christ's birth (Luke 2:14). Among the oldest of extant Christian hymns, the *Gloria* was composed on the model of the Psalms. It appears in both Greek and Syriac versions, but its date and authorship are unknown. Use of the *Gloria* in the Divine Office in both east and west preceded its use in the Roman Mass, a practice that did not become general before the eleventh century, and then only for Sundays and certain other major feasts. *See also* Doxology; Hymn.   [M.P.McH.]

Bibliography

Pseudo–Athanasius, *De virginitate* 20.

B. Capelle, "Le Texte du 'Gloria in excelsis,'" *RHE* 44 (1949):439–457; J.A. Jungmann, *The Mass of the Roman Rite: Its Origins and Development (Missarum Sollemnia)* (New York: Benziger, 1951), Vol. 1, pp. 346–359.

GNOSTICISM. Derived from the Greek for "knowledge," *gnōsis*, the term "Gnosticism" covers a number of religious and quasiphilosophical movements that developed in the religious pluralism of the Hellenistic world and flourished from the second to the fifth centuries A.D.

Gnōsis does not refer to understanding of truths about the human and natural world that can be reached through reason. It refers to a "revealed knowledge" available only to those who have received the secret teachings of a heavenly revealer. All other humans are trapped in ignorance of the true divine world and the destiny of the Gnostic soul to return to its home there. For some Gnostic groups, the return of the soul to the divine was pictured as a reunion with a heavenly counterpart. Ritual enactment of the "marriage" between the soul and her consort seems to have been typical of groups that traced their teaching to Valentinus, a Gnostic teacher active among Christians in Rome in the middle of the second century A.D. Other groups placed more emphasis on freeing the soul from all its attachments to the material world by an ascetic overcoming of the passions. For them, sexuality and femininity were evils that had to be rejected at every turn. The Gnostic Thomas traditions that may have originated in Syria represent this approach. Those influenced by the mystical side of Platonism seem to have practiced rituals in which the soul ascended to contemplation of the divine. The philosopher Plotinus opposed the claims of such persons among his disciples.

Worldview. One of the most striking features of Gnostic teaching is the elaborate mythology that explains how this world of darkness, dominated by a demonic god and his powers, came into being. Most of these myths begin with a harmonious unfolding of the heavenly world from an indescribable divinity. The divinity may be represented as a "one" beyond all beings or may be given the epithet "mother-father." Since matter, passions, darkness, and discord have nothing in common with the divine, the myths eventually tell the story of a "fall" or a "flaw" in the heavenly realm. Often, this flaw is the restless desire of the youngest of the divine beings, Wisdom (Greek *Sophia*). She may be seeking the divine Father above. Or she may try to give birth without her heavenly consort, as the Mother-Father does.

The result of Sophia's passion is often described as a dark creature with animal-like features. He is cast out of the divine world, often by his mother, who wants to hide the result of her passion. She too is separated from the divine, frequently in a realm between that of her offspring and the heavens that Gnostics refer to as the "All" or the "Fullness" (Greek *Plērōma*). Sophia's offspring creates his own world of powers in imitation of the heavenly structure, although they contain the seeds of discord and destruction.

Jewish Sources. Many of these Gnostic accounts parody themes from the Old Testament and from other Jewish exegetical traditions. The creator of this world boasts in the words of Yahweh that he alone is God. Such blasphemy is met by a voice from his mother or by a revelation of the true heavenly Adam figure, or both. The creator and his minions try to copy that figure when they create Adam-Eve. But unknown to them, the power that the creator breathes into Adam-Eve to get the being to stand is the portion of the divine light-world that had fallen with the creator. Adam-Eve does not belong to the creator god but to the heavenly world. Other elements in the Genesis stories, such as the fall of Eve and the flood, are rendered as attempts by the demonic powers to keep Adam-Eve from recognizing his/her heavenly origin.

Sometimes, Gnosticism presents various "Eves." The heavenly Eve, a spiritual representation of Sophia, awakens Adam to the truth. In other versions of the story, angelic beings come to rescue the ancestress of the Gnostics from attacks by the demonic powers. A number of Gnostic groups identified themselves with

Seth (and his sister Norea). They embody the spiritual seed of Adam, which has been preserved throughout history. Revelations by the heavenly Seth have made it possible for the Sethians to know their true identity. They will return to their heavenly home.

The basic outlines of such Gnostic readings of Genesis were already known to scholars from the accounts given by the church fathers. Irenaeus's *Against Heresies* preserves fragments of this mythology and spends much of its second book refuting the Gnostic understanding of God and creation. Neither orthodox Jews nor orthodox Christians could accept a rendering of Genesis that turned its God and creation against humanity in the name of some other divine world. Another example of Gnostic cosmology incorporating the images of Genesis into its speculation was known from the first tractate of the *Corpus Hermeticum*, called *Poimandres* ("shepherd of men"). A pagan collection of mysticism and magical writings from Greek-speaking Alexandria, the *Corpus Hermeticum* claimed to be the revelation of the "Thrice Great Hermes," the Egyptian god of wisdom, Thot. Hermetic wisdom does not appear as dualistic as cosmologies that are more clearly identified with Gnostic sects, since the god and administrators of the lower world are not evil. Nor is a descent of the heavenly revealer necessary to enlighten humanity. The myth does, however, emphasize the divided origins of humanity. The enlightened soul will ascend beyond what is bodily and mortal and break the bond of eros. Echoes of the Greek Old Testament are found in its story of the material creation.

Poimandres shows that Jewish creation stories could be incorporated into speculative mythology of a Gnostic sort quite apart from any direct engagement of the adherents with either Judaism or Christianity. But the preoccupation with Jewish traditions as structural elements in so many variants of Gnostic myth has often led scholars to surmise that the roots of Gnostic speculation lay in sectarian Judaism. Discovery of the Nag Hammadi Library, a collection of Coptic codices containing some fifty texts, most of them Gnostic tracts, has

added considerable evidence to the case for Jewish origins. Discovered in 1946, the manuscripts had a checkered history on the antiquities market. A few writings that provided striking examples of the teaching of Gnostic Christians were published within a decade and became well known: *Gospel of Truth* (a meditation on the Gnostic "gospel" of salvation); *Treatise on Resurrection* (also called the *Letter to Rheginus*); *Gospel of Thomas* (a collection of sayings and parables of the risen Jesus that contains parallels to material in the Synoptic Gospels); *Gospel of Philip* (an exposition of Gnostic sacraments); and the *Apocryphon* ("Secret Book") *of John* (a Gnostic cosmology framed as a revelation of the risen Jesus to John; Irenaeus apparently used a variant of its myth in his account of the Barbelo Gnostics). But much of the rest of the collection was either published in European books and journals that were difficult to obtain or not published at all. Only in 1977 did a provisional English translation of the entire find appear, edited by J.M. Robinson.

These writings have yielded extensive evidence for Jewish traditions in the formation of Gnostic speculation. Semitic etymologies for names of Eve and angelic beings are evident. References to Enoch and traditions from the Enoch apocrypha are evident in stories of the fallen angels. Legends about David, Solomon, and demons are referred to. The angelic Melchizedek figure appears in Gnostic Christian dress. The Sophia figure of Gnostic myth appears to be indebted to Jewish wisdom traditions.

The general reader can gain a feel for the "Jewishness" of much Gnostic speculation by reading three works from the Nag Hammadi collection: *Apocalypse of Adam* (NHLE 256–264; Foerster, 2.13–23), *Hypostasis of the Archons* (NHLE 152–160; Foerster, 2.40–52), and *Apocryphon of John* (NHLE 98–116, the long version; Foerster, 1.105–120, the short version). The *Apocalypse of Adam* reflects Jewish speculation about Adam-Eve and even uses a common literary type in Jewish apocrypha, revelation by a dying patriarch to his son (here, Seth). Yet this revelation shows "god" to be a malicious fraud who seeks only to enslave humanity. *Hypostasis of the Archons* contains two sections, both of which have literary parallels in Jewish apocrypha: the first provides an exegesis of Genesis 1–6, the second a revelation to Norea, ancestress of the Gnostics, by the angel Eleleth. The exegesis of Genesis follows the text so closely that it may even be described as "midrash" (a Jewish style of commentary that interprets texts by weaving them together in new combinations). Eleleth's revelation contains an interesting middle section in which one of the sons of the creator god, called by the divine epithet *Sabaoth*, repents and is given a kingdom above that of his father. Although he remains outside the divine Pleroma, the Sabaoth figure appears to partially rehabilitate the Jewish god.

The Genesis myth of *Apocryphon of John* has many similarities to the type of Sethian interpretation evident in the previous two tracts. The author of the work has, however, placed this material in a Christianizing framework. Revelation to Seth or Norea does not take place in primordial time. It is a revelation of the risen Jesus to the apostle John that the author claims to preserve. Glosses, which differ in the long and short versions, identify Christ with various heavenly figures. In the short version, "Thought" (derived from Sophia) teaches Adam-Eve from the tree; in the long version, Christ does so. But much of the work remains untouched by Christianity, and parallels to Jewish speculation are numerous.

Although the new evidence has helped make a strong case for the origins of much Gnostic speculation and mythology in heterodox Jewish circles, scholars have so far found it difficult to say just who belonged to those circles. The biography of Mani, the third-century A.D. founder of Manichaeism, speaks of the prophet's father as a member of a Gnosticizing baptismal sect. Some scholars think the sect may have been the Jewish Christian Elkesaites, founded in Syria ca. A.D. 100. Sethian traditions like *Apocalypse of Adam* contain allusions to baptismal rites. Many Gnostic Christian teachers had ties to Alexandria, which had an extensive, educated, and

pluralistic Jewish community. Papyri evidence also shows strong links between Judaism and Christianity in Alexandria and Palestine. In addition, perhaps as a result of the grain trade between Egypt and Rome, one finds teachers with Alexandrian roots, like the Platonist Plotinus and the Gnostic Valentinus, in Rome.

Gnostic Teachers. Whatever the origins of Gnosticism, the expansion of Gnostic sects and speculation in the second century is directly linked to teachers who claimed to preserve the true revelation of Christ. Basilides, a teacher active in Alexandria (ca. 117–160), is said to have composed a gospel, odes, and twenty-four books of exegesis. He claimed to have had access to secret apostolic tradition passed down through a disciple of Peter and Matthias. His teaching was continued by a disciple, or "true son," Isidore. Clement of Alexandria says that the Basilidians celebrated Jesus' baptism (January 6 or 10) as the day on which he received heavenly enlightenment.

The most prolific "school" of Gnostic teachers derived from the Alexandrian Valentinus, who had moved to Rome ca. 140. Tertullian even claims that Valentinus was almost elected bishop but was then expelled as a heretic, although he continued teaching for another twenty years. Other Valentinian teachers included Ptolemy, whose letter to a female patron, Flora, was preserved by Epiphanius (Foerster, 1.154–161); Theodotus, some of whose sayings were preserved by Clement of Alexandria (Foerster, 1.222–238); and Heracleon, fragments of whose commentary on John were included in Origen's commentary (Foerster, 1.162–283). Valentinian teachers wrote treatises in the Nag Hammadi collection: *Gospel of Truth; Treatise on Resurrection; Tripartite Tractate; Gospel of Philip; Valentinian Exposition with On the Anointing, On Baptism, and On the Eucharist.* Another Valentinian teacher, Marcus, had followers who reached the Rhône Valley and may have been sources for much of Irenaeus's information about Gnostic sects.

Relations with Christianity. Their orthodox Christian opponents complained about the multiplicity of Gnostic sects and the ease with which Gnostics might appear to be Christians. Indeed, many Gnostic teachers spoke of Christians in general as "psychics" (from Greek for "soul") who lacked the Gnostic enlightenment that would make them "pneumatics" (Greek for "spirit") or Gnostics. Although they would not be part of the gathering of the Gnostic church in the Pleroma, they might come to a lower heavenly realm. Christian sacraments were seen as poor images of the true sacraments celebrated by Gnostics.

From the Gnostic point of view, most Christians were captive to a materialist blindness that kept them from seeing the truth. Orthodox Christians believed in resurrection of a material body, when they should have recognized that resurrection refers to the union of the soul with the Savior. They believed that the physical death of Jesus and material washings take away sin, when they should have recognized the absurdity of thinking that the heavenly revealer actually died on the cross. All that was hung on the cross was the material body that had served the revealer as a vehicle during this life. (Some Gnostic writings even speak of the Savior looking on with laughter as the evil powers thought they were killing him.) Most Christians read the scriptures literally, while Jesus taught that they held hidden meanings. They focused attention on the earthly life of Jesus and were ignorant of the revelations that the risen Lord gave to his disciples. They had a literalist interpretation of judgment at the end of the world, but judgment takes place as the individual soul leaves the body at death. The "end of the world" images refer to the collapse of this world of darkness that will result when all of the light returns to the heavenly world.

As Christians sought to answer the challenge posed by the Gnostics, they insisted on those points that their Gnostic adversaries had put in question. The "Father" referred to in Jesus' teaching is not some god superior to the Creator of the Old Testament. Christians worship the God of Judaism and retain its scriptures as their own. Christians must reject the Docetic understanding of Jesus as the material form for a heavenly revealer. The reality of Jesus' humanity and suffering death is fundamental Christian teaching. The resurrection does not refer to the soul but to God's creative power in transforming the body at the judgment. Against Gnostic charges of literalism, Irenaeus insists upon the narrative unity of the New Testament. He maintains that Gnostic interpretation chops up and fragments texts. Further, the witness of the apostles as a whole stands with one unified voice. Gnostics carve up apostolic tradition into a number of different traditions, none of which is universally recognized in the churches.

Gnostic devaluation of the material world implied that nothing from the material world could play a role in salvation. Therefore, Gnostic groups were divided in their understanding of ritual. Some argued that only liberation of the soul from the material world through asceticism and knowledge could bring salvation. They interpreted the baptism of Jesus as the moment in which saving knowledge destroys the hold of evil powers over the world. This type of argument is advanced in a Nag Hammadi treatise, *Testimony of Truth.* The author goes on to attack Basilides, Isidore, and Valentinus for not being sufficiently ascetic, and to warn that people who think that martyrdom and the hope of bodily resurrection will save them are lost in error.

The writings in the Nag Hammadi collection generally represent an ascetic position with regard to the material world and its passions. The *Gospel of Thomas* in its rendering of familiar parables also includes attacks on those who are merchants. Those who fail to accept the invitation to the banquet include one who is buying a house and another who is collecting rent on a farm he has just purchased. This version concludes with the pronouncement: "Businessmen and merchants will not enter the places of my Father" (*Gos. Thom.* 64; NHLE 125). The man who finds treasure in a field uses his windfall to lend money at interest (*Gos. Thom.* 109; NHLE 129). But the church fathers frequently accused Gnostics of immorality. Irenaeus claimed that Marcus deceived women followers by first allowing them to be prophetesses in the eucharistic cult and then taking advantage of them sexually (Foerster, 1.200–202). He insisted that such libertine behavior resulted from the Gnostic claim to be superior to the powers that rule this world. Epiphanius claimed that he was seduced by members of a Gnostic sect he had joined as a young man, whom he accuses of sexual excesses in ritualized contexts (Foerster, 1.313–325). Although such extravagant descriptions suggest polemic rather than fact, some Gnostic sects may have enacted their rejection of human sexuality and procreative conventions in libertine behavior.

The antiheretical writers of the church used arguments from reason and from the interpretation of scripture in order to refute Gnostic teachings. They emphasized the doctrines of creation, redemption, and resurrection, which they saw particularly threatened by Gnostic interpretations. On the institutional level, the church strengthened the position of the bishops through the doctrine of apostolic succession. Its teachers emphasized the rule of faith (the summary of the apostolic teaching) as a guide to interpreting scripture and sharpened the confessions to bring out their antiheretical content. The leaders of the church moved to define more carefully the canon of scripture where the authentic apostolic tradition was to be found. The great church survived, in part, because its strong organizational ties gave it a stability missing in the loosely organized and diverse Gnostic groups.

Women. References to women in Marcosian cult feed speculation about the place of women in Gnostic groups. Mary Magdalene plays an important role in some Gnostic works as the one whom Jesus loved and who received special revelations from him (as in *Gospel of Mary*; NHLE 471–474). Women figure as part of the chain of secret tradition in *First Apocalypse of James* (NHLE 248). Gnostic speculation included feminine attributes of the deity, androgynous pairs of heavenly "aeons" and similar pairs in the restoration of the soul, a revaluation of the "Tree of Knowledge" and the "fall of Eve," and a goddess figure in the story of Sophia and her offspring. On the other hand, ascetic writings like *Thomas the Con-*

tender are hostile to sexuality and urge the Gnostic to avoid the "works of femaleness." Although her passion may be the archetype of the Gnostic soul, the fall is still the result of Sophia's weakness, and she must be set right by a male consort. Peter's hostility toward Mary at the conclusion of *Gospel of Thomas* is answered by the affirmation that the savior will "make her male."

Although some have been quick to herald the Gnostics as exponents of women's liberation in a church that was becoming dominated by the patriarchy of episcopal hierarchy, the evidence is far from conclusive. Anthropologists have shown that the presence of female divinities and imagery does not of itself advance the position of women in a society. Religious historians have demonstrated that men and women often appropriate the same symbols in different ways. Such studies are warning against overdramatization of the novelty of Gnosticism for the "liberation" of women.

Both women and men may have been attracted by the promise of "knowledge," salvation, and insight not shared by the larger community. Or, in some cases, they may have found the teaching of someone like Valentinus more persuasive than that in the larger community. Responding to Gnostic teachings, the Alexandrians, Clement and Origen, were particularly sensitive to the intellectual and theological challenge they posed. Augustine later claimed that the system of the Manichaeans held his allegiance until he had been schooled out of materialism by Platonism and out of literalist reading of the Bible by Ambrose. Only after some time was he able to appreciate the significance of Christian teaching about incarnation in contrast to the crude materialism of the Manichaean teachers.

Relation to Monasticism. The bindings of the Nag Hammadi codices contained papyri from the Pachomian monasteries of the region in the mid-fourth century. The area in which the documents are alleged to have been found shows a Pachomian monastic settlement. Some of the tractates are not Gnostic but are general pieces of ascetic wisdom (cf. *Teachings of Silvanus*, which contains a section from a sermon attributed to Anthony, and *Sentences of Sextus*, as well as three Hermetic tracts). These facts have led to some speculation about the collection itself. Were the codices copied and used by Egyptian monks for their ascetic and mystical value? Or were they collected for purposes of combating Gnostic tendencies? Were they hidden away by the monks when the bishop of Alexandria came to exercise more direct control over the orthodoxy of the monastic settlements in the desert some 400 miles away? We may never know. Similarly, we know that Gnostic groups continued into the fourth century. But by the end of fifth century, Gnosticism and its most successful incarnation as a "world religion," Manichaeism, had faded from the scene. Ecclesiastical censure and opposition are only part of the explanation. Changes within Christian communities and the larger world of which people were a part must also be assigned a role. But Gnostic speculation in the broad sense remained part of the human symbolic world to reemerge in the future. *See also* Mani, Manichaeism; Nag Hammadi. [P.P.]

Bibliography

W. Foerster and R.McL. Wilson, eds., *Gnosis: A Selection of Gnostic Texts* (Oxford: Clarendon, 1972–1974), Vol. 1: *Patristic Evidence;* Vol. 2: *Coptic and Mandaic Sources;* Institute for Antiquity and Christianity, *The Coptic Gnostic Library,* 15 vols. (Leiden: Brill, 1975–); B. Layton, *The Gnostic Scriptures* (Garden City: Doubleday, 1987); J.M. Robinson, ed., *The Nag Hammadi Library in English,* rev. ed. (San Francisco: Harper and Row, 1988).

H. Jonas, *The Gnostic Religion* (Boston: Beacon, 1963); D.M. Scholer, *Nag Hammadi Bibliography 1948–1969* (Leiden: Brill, 1971) continued in *Novum Testamentum* annually from 13 (1971); P. Perkins, *The Gnostic Dialogue: The Early Church and the Crisis of Gnosticism* (New York: Paulist, 1980); K. Rudolph, *Gnosis: The Nature and History of Gnosticism* (San Francisco: Harper and Row, 1983); H.A. Green, *The Economic and Social Origins of Gnosticism* (Atlanta: Scholars, 1985); C.W. Hedrick and R. Hodgson, eds., *Nag Hammadi, Gnosticism and Early Christianity* (Peabody: Hendrickson, 1986).

GOD. Greco-Roman paganism exhibited a variety of beliefs about the divine. Alongside the traditional deities (both the anthropomorphic deities of Greek mythology and the spe-cialized supernatural powers in nature worshiped by the Romans), there were tendencies, especially in philosophical circles, toward monotheism. Philosophers, however, usually thought more in terms of an intellectual principle—incapable of feelings and manifested in the traditional deities, who were subordinated to it—than in terms of a personal God. Among the Jews, the uncompromising monotheism of the prophets was modified in some circles by speculation about the divine attributes and about beings who could mediate the presence of God.

Early Christians were firmly committed to belief in one God and to worship of him. Their faith originated in Judaism, was founded on the Old Testament, and was reinforced by their understanding of the life and teaching of Jesus and their belief in and experience of the work of the Holy Spirit. The essential feature of Christian belief was thus a latent Trinitarianism, which, expressed in worship, was gradually and not always successfully worked out by major theologians both before and after the Council of Nicaea.

Early Christians. Early writers referred to the reality of the Father, the Son, and the Holy Spirit, but without specifying the precise function of each "person" or their interrelations; the references were controversial. Jewish Christians who used the apocryphal *Gospel of the Hebrews* held the unusual view that Christ spoke of the Holy Spirit as his mother. Gnostics offered various substitutes for the more conventional Christian doctrines (in the *Apocryphon of John* we find Father-Mother-Son); but although followers of Montanus's apocalyptic schism located the Holy Spirit within Montanus, they continued to use the terms Father, Son, and Holy Spirit.

Paul, with Old Testament authors, insisted that God is the creator, sustainer, providential ruler, and future judge of the universe. The Gnostics denied this belief, whether they viewed the creator god as defective, merely just rather than good (cf. Marcion), or definitively evil. They separated redemption from creation and dualistically assigned different sources to each. Although their views of God were not uniform, they usually asked how a perfect God or "fullness" (*Plērōma*) of divine beings could have produced or generated a defective world like the one in which we human beings live. The classical Gnostic explanation was that spiritual beings emanated from "the top down," but then an unruly female being spontaneously produced a defective son—who joined his own defective products in making our world and the first human being. Human beings owe any excellence they may have to a divine spark slipped into them from the world above: almost all of them, however, forget it. The prophets were therefore sent from above to recall the spark or spirit to itself, and finally the savior came to bring it back above. Since Gnostics often called the defective son either "the Creator" or "the God of the Jews," they evidently strayed far from Judeo-Christian monotheism.

In Christianity, the nature and functions of the Son inevitably influenced the picture of the Father, and questions naturally arose about the Son's divinity because of his ungodlike suffering and death. In the common pagan philosophical theology of the day, God was infinite, intangible, uncontained, immortal—all the "negative attributes" developed in Middle Platonism and set forth, for example, by the Jewish writer Philo of Alexandria. If the Son suffered, some supposed, he could not be divine. The apostle Paul, on the other hand, insisted that the Son of God "loved me and gave himself for me" (Gal. 2:20). Although he originally possessed equality with God or could acquire it, he "emptied himself" of the divine attributes (Phil. 2:6–7).

Johannine Theology. The Johannine writings spoke of God as eternally invisible but emphasized the person and functions of the Logos, or Word of God, especially as incarnate (John 1:14). The Father is greater than the Son, but the Son is "in the bosom of the Father" (1:14, 18) and is one with him (10:30); the Father is in the Son and the Son in the Father. For this reason, he who has seen the Son has seen the Father (14:9–10). A disciple addresses the risen Jesus as "my Lord and my God" (20:28). On the other hand, the incarnate Lord is human; he is tired and thirsty (4:6–7; cf. 19:28), loves (11:5), weeps (11:35), and is wounded (20:25–27).

"Preaching of Peter" and Ignatius. An important step toward a more philosophical (Platonic) theology is reflected in the apocryphal *Preaching of Peter*, of uncertain date, which describes God as "the invisible who sees all, uncontained who contains all, without needs whom all need and because of whom they exist, incomprehensible, eternal, imperishable, unmade who made all things by the word of his might" (in Clement of Alexandria, *Str.* 6.39.3). This doctrine underlies what Ignatius of Antioch, as well as his Docetic opponents, had to say about the divine Christ. Ignatius describes Christ as "the one who is above seasons, timeless, invisible who for us became visible, intangible, impassible who for us became passible, who in every way endured for us" (*Polyc.* 3.2). The Docetists apply the "negative attributes" to Christ. Ignatius agrees but insists on the paradox of the incarnation, using the term "for us," which comes from Paul. Ignatius recognizes the paradox, unlike his opponents.

Aristides. Aristides's apology (early second century) begins with a Stoic-Platonic picture of God as the incomprehensible mover of the universe, unoriginate, uncreated, comprehended by none but comprehending all, without beginning or end, immutable, immortal, perfect, without name, form, or members, thus recalling the *Preaching of Peter.* Aristides uses this definition to attack the pagan gods, identified with the mutable elements or the vulnerable and sinful deities of mythology. Christians, as the *Preaching of Peter* had said, alone rightly worship the true God.

Justin. The apologetic work of Justin, who wrote at Rome in the middle of the second century, is more original. Justin held that God is eternally immutable and the source of all existence. He has no name, for a name is given by someone older than the one named. Terms used about him come from his relations with man and the universe. Justin rejects any literal interpretation of biblical metaphors. God does not have hands, feet, fingers, or soul, for his is not a composite being. Although he can be called "in the heavens" or "above heaven" or "above the universe," he is not in space at all.

Like Philo and later Christian apologists, Justin understands God's work in the world in relation to the figure of Sophia, or Wisdom, in Proverbs 8:22ff., identifying it with the Logos, or Word of God.

Athenagoras. The theology of Athenagoras (ca. 177, Athens) was deeply influenced by the popular Platonism that he knew well. Like the Platonist Albinus, he summarizes: God is "uncreated, eternal, invisible, impassible, incomprehensible, and infinite." He "can be apprehended by mind and reason alone." He is "encompassed by light, beauty, spirit, and indescribable power" (*Leg.* 10.1). He created and adorned the universe and now rules it. Athenagoras was the first apologist to identify God as Mind (10.3). Philo occasionally referred to God in this way, treating him as "the active cause, the most pure and unsullied Mind of the universe" (*On the Creation of the World* 8), but such a doctrine was only one of his interpretations. Athenagoras himself also used the term "Mind" in regard to the Son.

Athenagoras was the first Christian to provide logical proof for the existence of only one God (*Leg.* 8). This he called "the reasoning that supports our faith." The argument seems to run as follows: Two gods (or more) have to be in (1) the same category or (2) different categories (1.1). As gods, uncreated, they could not belong to the same category. If they were created, they would belong to the same category because made after the same model, but uncreated things are dissimilar (1.2). God is not composite and divisible into complementary parts (i.e., gods). Against Stoic doctrine, he is "uncreated, impassible, and indivisible." As gods, they could not be independent (2.1). The Maker of the world is above and around the spherical creation and governs it, and therefore there is no place for other god(s) (2.1.1). Such a god could not be in the world since it belongs to God (2.1.2). Such a god could not be around the world since God is above it (2.2). Such a god could not be above the world and God in another world and around it (2.2.1). For if he is in or around another world, he is not around us, since the Maker rules our world, and (2.2.2) his power is not great since he is in a limited place (so he is not God) (2.3). And if he is not in or around another world, he does not exist, since there is no place for him or anything for him to do. Therefore, there is one God, the Creator of the World.

An eclectic philosophical treatise ascribed to Aristotle (*De Melisso Xenophane Gorgia*), but really from the Roman period, contains similar arguments, beginning with the assertion that "what comes into existence must come either from like or from unlike" and concluding that God is eternal. Then, "if he is most powerful of all, he must be one. For if there were two or more, he would not be most powerful and best of all." The argument goes on to consider motion and shape in regard to God, although not place, on which Athenagoras lays emphasis.

Both Athenagoras and Theophilus are willing to call the Son or Logos the Mind of the Father (Clement calls the Logos the Son of the Father-Mind). He is the "first being begotten by the Father" (Athenagoras, *Leg.* 10), as he is for Justin. In Athenagoras's background, there thus seems to be a doctrine of a primal Logos-Sophia. In his view, it is based on what "the prophetic Spirit" said in the name of the Son: "The Lord made me the beginning of his ways for his works" (Prov. 8:22). The Son as Logos of the Father "came forth to serve as Ideal Form and Energizing Power" for the creation (*Leg.* 10.2–3). Here, the terms used recall the Platonic *idea* ("idea" or "form") and the Aristotelian *energeia* ("energizing force"). He also calls the Son the Mind, Logos, and Sophia of the Father, thus pointing to his being "united in power yet distinguished in rank." There is a divine Spirit that moved the Old Testament prophets "in the ecstasy of their thoughts" and blew through them like musical instruments." This same Holy Spirit, which is active in those who speak prophetically, we regard as an emanation of God like a ray of the sun or like fire from fire" (*Leg.* 10.4; 24.2). Here, "emanation" echoes what Wisdom of Solomon 7:25 says about Sophia, but Athenagoras adds the thought that the Spirit "flows forth" from God and "returns like a ray of the sun" (*Leg.* 10).

Elsewhere, he notes, in language used of *pneuma* by Philo, that "the Spirit is an emanation like fire from fire" (*Leg.* 24.2), and the comparison to both fire and light occurs in Justin, although applied to the Logos.

Beyond that, the Spirit is also the source of the unity between Father and Son. "The Son is in the Father and the Father in the Son by a powerful unity [or, by the unity and power] of spirit [or, of the Spirit]" (10.2). The language is unquestionably Johannine (John 10:38), and Athenagoras may also be thinking of the Paraclete sayings where the Father will send the Holy Spirit in Jesus' name (John 14:26) or Jesus himself will send him from the Father (15:26). One might also compare 2 Corinthians 13:13: "the grace of the Lord Jesus Christ and the love of God and the fellowship [*koinonia*] of the Holy Spirit."

The explicit doctrine of the Trinity in Athenagoras is the oldest that we know. He speaks of "God the Father, God the Son, and the Holy Spirit" and intimates that Christians "proclaim both their power in their unity and their diversity in rank" (10.5; repeated in 24.2). There is a unity between Son and Father and a communion between Father and Son, and there is a unity of Spirit, Son, and Father as well as a distinction among them. The Spirit is obviously the source of prophetic inspiration; greater than that, but not called God.

Although Theophilus, a contemporary of Athenagoras, speaks of God and his Word and his Wisdom as a "triad" (*Autol.* 2.15), he says that if man is added to the triad it becomes a tetrad: evidently, he was not thinking in Trinitarian terms.

Tatian. Tatian's ideas about the nature of God resemble those of his teacher, Justin, but his language is sometimes closer to Gnostic authors. In the *Oration* (ca. 178) he uses Gnostic terms in speaking of "the perfect God" (*Orat.* 4) and calling the Logos "the God who suffered" (13). The contemporary Gnostic Ptolemy differentiated the perfect God from the creator and spoke of Sophia as "the Aeon who suffered." Tatian, however, did not at first have a perfect God above the Creator or any doctrine of Sophia. Later, he moved into Gnosticism.

In the *Oration*, the doctrine of God is straightforward Middle Platonism, with occasional echoes of isolated New Testament passages. "God has no constitution in time but is alone without beginning: he is the beginning of everything" (*Orat.* 4). Thus, philosophy explains the terms of John 4:24, "God is spirit." In addition, God is invisible and intangible. "We know him through his creation and we recognize his invisible power in his works"—an echo of Romans 1:20.

Justin had developed a semiphilosophical doctrine of the Logos but always gave it content out of biblical passages, especially from the Old Testament. Tatian, on the other hand, does away with much of the biblical content, perhaps because he is addressing outsiders, and what he retains seems not far from Christian apologetic theology at Antioch or Gnostic theology. God exercises his creative power through his Logos. He was originally alone, but the whole power or potentiality of things visible and invisible is with him through his logical power. (Conceivably, these expressions are built on Hebrews 1:3.) In response to God's pure will, the Logos "leapt forth" (an echo of Justin) as his "firstborn work" (cf. Col. 1:15). It originated by division, not abscission, or, as Whittaker translates, "by partition, not by section." In other words, it remains essentially united with its source. To explain this notion, Tatian relies on two analogies. First, many fires come from one torch (an image taken from Justin and indirectly from Philo). Second, a speaker is not "empty" of thought when he expresses what is in his mind. The second metaphor comes from what may be called linguistic psychology.

Theophilus of Antioch. Like Philo, Theophilus (ca. 180) sets forth a doctrine of God essentially Jewish in nature even though expressed in the language of Middle Platonism. He says that "we acknowledge (1) a God; (2) but only one, (3) the Founder and Maker and Demiurge (4) of this whole cosmos, (5) and we know that everything is governed by providence, by him alone" (*Autol.* 3.9). These five points are exactly the same as those listed by Philo in a "creed" toward the end of *On the*

Creation of the World. Theophilus, an heir of Hellenistic Judaism, must reflect some of its major developments in the second century. He uses biblical texts for making philosophical statements about God. After the *Preaching of Peter,* he employs the traditional "negative attributes." Indeed, he claims that one can speak only of functions or aspects of God, never of God in himself. Justin had already presented the idea in abbreviated form. Because of Theophilus's concern for scripture, one might expect a more detailed picture of how God works, but he does not provide one. Instead, he treats God's Logos as equivalent to his Mind, Spirit, Wisdom, and Forethought. Like Irenaeus, he refuses to differentiate mental activities within God, so as not to feed Gnostic theories about sequential emanations.

Theophilus insists on the transcendence of God and points out that all God's "appellations" refer to his characteristics, attributes, or activities, not to his nature in itself. Biblical names, such as Light, Logos, Mind, Spirit, Wisdom, Strength, Power, Providence, Kingdom, Lord, Judge, Father, and Fire, refer to attributes or aspects. The terms are symbolic because they refer to the ineffable transcendent God. Yet Theophilus, like Justin, is not an orthodox Platonist philosopher. His list of names and attributes has biblical and Christian antecedents and ends on a biblical note. "If I call him Fire I speak of his wrath" (*Autol.* 1.3). His correspondent asks, "Will you tell me that God is angry?" Theophilus replies, "Certainly; he is angry with those who commit evil deeds but good and merciful toward those who love and fear him [Exod. 20:5–6; 34:6–7; Deut. 5:9–10; 7:9–10]. For he is the instructor of the pious and father of the just, but judge and punisher of the impious" (*Autol.* 1.3). Here, he is on firm ground both biblical and Stoic; Plutarch notes that in the Stoic view God punishes evil and does much to punish wicked men. But Theophilus explicitly opposes the great majority of Greek philosophers, as well as the Marcionites, who taught that "the Good does not condemn those who have disobeyed him." For Theophilus, the God of Christians is both good and just.

Theophilus then returns to philosophy and continues with school definitions and etymologies (from Herodotus and Plato), following with a collection of Old Testament verses to illustrate God's creative power. He uses Pauline epistles and the Gospel of John but also makes use of both Platonic and Stoic categories. He lists "negative attributes" of God in Platonic fashion but treats the Logos or Son of God in a Stoic manner, differentiating the *logos endiathetos* within God from the *logos prophorikos* that he expressed. Theophilus's language is fluid. Sometimes he treats Logos as different from Wisdom; sometimes he identifies them. Like Philo, he calls Logos and Sophia "God's hands" and identifies God's Sophia with his Logos.

At times, he assigns creative activity to Sophia. "God by Sophia founded the earth" (Prov. 3:19). God generated his Logos together with his own Sophia, the latter as his helper in creation (Prov. 8:27–29), who named the stars, created fish and birds, and inspired the prophets. Theophilus also calls Sophia God's "offspring," pointing toward Proverbs 8:25, in Christian exegesis already referred to the Logos.

"God made everything through his Logos and Sophia," says Theophilus, citing biblical texts that mention Logos and Spirit or Sophia, Intelligence, and Perception. Later on, he turns to the Gospel of John to indicate that "through him he made everything" or that "by his Logos God made heaven and earth and what is in them" (*Autol.* 2.10). In the beginning, the Spirit was "above the water" and nourished it, giving life to the creation. But Logos is the same as Spirit and Sophia, and "Light is the beginning of the creation." The Logos (Word) was made manifest when God said, "Let there be light," for "the Command of God (by which is meant his Logos) shone like a lamp in a closed room and illuminated the region under the heaven" (*Autol.* 2.13).

After creation, the Logos appeared in Eden (cf. Philo and Justin), for Adam stated that he heard the voice of God, who was walking in paradise (Gen. 3:10). Since God cannot be present in a particular place, Adam must have heard his creative Logos, called Voice and identified as his Power and Sophia (cf. 1 Cor. 1:24). The Logos was "assuming the role" (literally "face") of God—since according to Genesis 3:8 Adam and Eve hid from the "face" of God.

Theophilus's Logos is essentially an emissary of the Father. He probably knows Justin's idea that the prophets, inspired by the divine Logos, spoke "as in the role of God the Father and Master of all" or in the role of Christ or of "the people replying to him or to his Father" (Justin, *1 Apol.* 36). For Theophilus as for his predecessors, the Logos (or Sophia, or Spirit) inspired the prophets. God sent them "from among their brothers" (Deut. 18:15) to "teach and remind" the people of the content of the Mosaic law. According to John 14:26, the Paraclete, the Holy Spirit, will "teach and remind" believers of everything Jesus said to his disciples. Combined, these allusions show that Jesus must have reiterated the law of Moses— the law of God. Theophilus seems to regard the Logos on earth as more like a prophet than anything else. Clement of Alexandria sets forth the role of the Logos more carefully (*Prot.* 110.1–2): "The divine Logos, the most manifest real God [cf. John 17:3], the one made equal [Phil. 2:6] to the Master of all—for he was his Son and 'the Logos was in God' [John 1:2]—. . .assuming the role of a man and fashioned in flesh, played the saving drama of humanity."

Irenaeus. In the second century, Irenaeus, the bishop of Lyons, echoes a discussion of God by the pre-Socratic philosopher Xenophanes (Frg. 24 Diels-Kranz) no fewer than five times in his *Against Heresy*, the most important citations are 2.13.3, where Irenaeus says that God is entirely mind, spirit, thinking, notion, reason, hearing, eye, light, source of all good things—"as it is suitable for religious and pious people to say of God"; and 2.28.4, a slightly more biblical list, with the comment that thus "it is useful for us to know about God and we learn from the scriptures." Presumably, Irenaeus's "religious and pious people" were Platonists, whose basic idea of God was shared with Christians who read the Bible. They used Plato's expression "source of all good things."

This reflection of Xenophanes is important; although Christians had enunciated the basic thought even before Irenaeus's time, his influence meant that philosophical theology could be used, with some restrictions, not just among apologists or at Alexandria but among theologians generally.

Irenaeus's theology is by no means exclusively philosophical. He read his Bible, especially the Old Testament, with care, and his ideas are closer to "ordinary" or "simple" Christianity than those of most apologists. His God actively intervenes in human affairs. He loves humanity and wants to educate and save it. He has acted notably in the incarnation of his Son ("the Son of God became Son of Man so that the sons of men might become sons of God"— *Haer.* 3.10.2), and he will establish his reign on earth, not somewhere in the heavens.

Alexandrian Theology. The apologists anticipated much of the Alexandrian theology, but Clement and Origen expressed it with greater precision. The idea of impassibility was especially important at Alexandria, where Christians were so much under the spell of philosophy (as mediated, for example, by Philo) that they treated biblical language about divine emotions as allegorical. Philo had insisted that "God is not like a man" (Num. 12:19), favoring this text over the many anthropomorphic pictures in the Old Testament. And in his *Commentary on John*, Origen extended the notion of divine immutability by arguing that the divine Christ really did not cleanse the temple, for as God he could not be in a particular place or time or do anything in particular.

Clement of Alexandria in the late second century recognized that the doctrine of God as Mind is Platonic, but his slightly later contemporary Origen, in his early treatise *On First Principles*, called God "the Mind that is the source of every intellectual nature or mind" (1.1.6). On the other hand, in later writings he calls him "Mind or beyond Mind," reiterating a hypothesis of Aristotle: "God is either Mind or something beyond Mind" (Frg. 49, *On Prayer*). A similar oscillation occurs in Philo, Clement, Platonism, and Gnosticism (cf. H.

Crouzel, *Origène: Traité des Principes* II [Paris: Cerf, 1978], p. 25). There are pagan and Christian analogies, for example, *Corpus Hermeticum* 2.14, "God is not Mind but cause of the existence of mind," and Theophilus, "If I call him Mind, I speak [only] of his intelligence" (*Autol.* 1.3).

Not all Jews or Christians shared these philosophical interpretations, although most of the nontheological literature has perished and we know the "literalists" largely through attacks by the Alexandrians. Philo attacks Jewish literalists for supposing that God could repent or experience wrath. Origen claims that simple believers make God worse than the most savage and unjust man. Ultimately, however, Origen's own ideas underwent change. In his later years, he read the emotional letters of the martyr Ignatius and began thinking about the Father and his suffering on our behalf (*Hom. in Ezech.* 6.6). Such ideas obviously contradict his earlier insistence on impassibility; he did not integrate his new picture, closer to that of the Bible, into his theology as a whole. Patristic and medieval theologians often drew away from "biblical realism" in favor of rational constructions. *See also* Christ; Holy Spirit; Trinity.   [R.M.G.]

Bibliography
G.L. Prestige, *God in Patristic Thought*, 2nd ed. (London: SPCK, 1952); G. Kretschmar, *Studien zur frühchristlichen Trinitätstheologie* (Tübingen: Mohr-Siebeck, 1956); R.M. Grant, *The Early Christian Doctrine of God* (Charlottesville: U of Virginia P, 1966); G. af Haellstroem, Fides Simpliciorum *According to Origen of Alexandria* (Helsinki: Societas Scientiarum Fennica, 1984); R.M. Grant, *Gods and the One God* (Philadelphia: Westminster, 1986).

GOSPEL. Readings from the New Testament Gospels recited over the course of the liturgical year, or the liturgical book from which these readings are taken. In the liturgies of the east and west, the Gospel was the final scriptural reading of the Mass, and it was normally recited by the deacon. Before the reading, the Gospel book was brought from the altar to an ambo or lectern from which the Gospel would be recited.

In the early liturgy, the Gospel reading for each Mass may have been selected by the celebrant, and in some liturgies of the east readings were simply presented in their scriptural order. After the fourth century, as the liturgical year developed, cycles of predetermined readings for the entire year were established in the various regional liturgies. The readings in these fixed cycles evoked themes that were appropriate for the feast or liturgical season.

At first, the readings were taken from a book containing the four Gospels, sometimes with marginal cues indicating the readings for the individual Masses. After the sixth century, the readings for all the Masses in the year were either listed in a short *capitulare* after the four Gospels or presented in full within a different type of liturgical book, an *evangelistarium* or lectionary. In sixth- and seventh-century books, such as the purple Rossano Gospels (Greek; Rossano, Cathedral), Rabbula Gospels (Syriac; Florence, Bibl. Laurentiana, cod. Plut. I, 56), and Gospels of St. Augustine (Latin; Cambridge, Corpus Christi College 286), the Gospel texts are preceded by illustrations of Gospel scenes in addition to the customary canon tables and portraits of the evangelists and their symbols. *See also* Epistle; Lectionary.   [J.B.]

Bibliography
T. Klauser, *Das römische Capitulare Evangeliorum* (Münster: Aschendorf, 1935); J.A. Jungmann, *The Mass of the Roman Rite* (New York: Benziger, 1951), Vol. 1, pp. 391–461; C. Vogel, *Medieval Liturgy: An Introduction to the Sources* (Washington, D.C.: Pastoral, 1986), pp. 292–355.

GOSPEL ACCORDING TO THE HEBREWS. Noncanonical gospel. Originating probably in early-second-century Egypt, and in use predominantly among Jewish Christians, the *Gospel According to the Hebrews* came to be quoted in a number of patristic authorities interested in its apocryphal traditions of sayings of Jesus (Clement of Alexandria, *Str.* 2.45; 5.96; Origen, *Jo.* 2.12; Eusebius, *H.E.* 4.22.7; Jerome, *Vir. illus.* 2).   TLG 1374.   [P.M.Bl.]

Bibliography
NTA, Vol. 1, pp. 158–165.

GOSPEL OF ANDREW. Apocryphal writing. It is not certain whether the *Gospel of Andrew* actually existed. This title appears in the sixth-century *Decretum Gelasianum* but may represent a confusion with the *Acts of Andrew*. It could refer to a Gnostic text to which Augustine may make reference (*Adv. leg. et proph.* 1.20). [D.M.S.]

GOSPEL OF BARNABAS. Italian Renaissance forgery that presents Jesus from an Islamic point of view. It is possible that the *Gospel of Barnabas* contains some ancient Jewish Christian traditions. It is not the work of the same title, now lost, condemned in the *Decretum Gelasianum* (early sixth century). [D.M.S.]

Bibliography
P. Beskow, *Strange Tales About Jesus: A Survey of Unfamiliar Gospels* (Philadelphia: Fortress, 1983), pp. 11–15.

GOSPEL OF MATTHIAS. Gnostic gospel (early second century?). The *Gospel of Matthias* is mentioned by Origen and Eusebius and is believed by many to be identical with the *Traditions of Matthew* mentioned by Clement of Alexandria. It called for a strict ascetic life and was especially popular among the Basilidians (possibly used by Basilides and his son Isidore). Now lost, it likely was written in Egypt, perhaps at Alexandria. [R.R.]

Bibliography
Origen, *Homilia 1 in Lucam.*; Eusebius, *Church History* 3.25.6–7; Clement of Alexandria, *Miscellanies* 2.9; 7.13, 17.
NTA, Vol. 1, pp. 308–313.

GOSPEL OF PETER. Apocryphal New Testament writing (second century). Scholarly opinion on the date of composition of the *Gospel of Peter* is divided. It was discovered in 1886–1887 by Urbain Bouriant in an eighth-century manuscript from a tomb at Akhmîm in Upper Egypt but originated in Syria. Serapion, bishop of Antioch, in a letter to the church of Rhossus in Cilicia (ca. 190) reproduced by Eusebius of Caesarea (*H.E.* 6.12.2–6), testified to its use while finding in it elements of Docetism. Yet whether it contains formal heresy is doubtful; it may well be merely a work of popular Christianity. Origen in the third century knew of it.

The *Gospel of Peter* gives an account of the passion, death, burial, and resurrection of Christ; the resurrection narrative is expanded with accounts of miracles. Responsibility for Christ's death is laid upon the Jews; Herod, not Pontius Pilate, orders the crucifixion. The possibility has been advanced that papyrus fragments of an *Unknown Gospel* probably from Oxyrhynchus in Egypt may belong to the *Gospel of Peter.* TLG 1371. [M.P.McH.]

Bibliography
Origen, *Commentary on Matthew* 10.17; Eusebius, *Church History* 3.3.2; 6.12.2–6.
M.G. Mara, ed., *Evangile de Pierre*, SC (1973), Vol. 201.
NTA, Vol. 1, pp. 179–187.
J.W. McCant, "The Gospel of Peter: Docetism Reconsidered," *NTS* 30 (1984):258–273; R. Brown, "The *Gospel of Peter* and Canonical Gospel Priority," *NTS* 33 (1987):321–343; J.B. Green, "The Gospel of Peter: Source for a Pre-Canonical Passion Narrative?," *ZNTW* 78 (1987):293–301; D.F. Wright, "Papyrus Egerton 2 (the *Unknown Gospel*)—Part of the *Gospel of Peter?*," *SCent* 5 (1985–1986=1988): 129–150.

GOSPEL OF PHILIP. One of the Coptic texts of the Nag Hammadi collection, the *Gospel of Philip* (NHC II, 3) is a Christian Gnostic work (third century?) with affinities to the Valentinian school. Despite its title, it is neither a narrative of the life of Jesus, like the canonical Gospels, nor a collection of sayings, like the *Gospel of Thomas,* nor a meditative homily on the gospel, like the *Gospel of Truth.* It is rather a collection of discrete comments on various theological matters, the random character of which suggests that they are excerpts from other works. The text survives in Coptic but was probably originally compiled in Greek, although some sections display familiarity with Syriac. A precise date for the work cannot be determined. Since it presupposes substantial development in the Valentinian tradition, it was probably written after 200 but before 350, the approximate date of the Coptic manuscript.

The comments are diverse, yet certain concerns pervade the work. A dichotomy between the spiritual world of truth and light and the corrupt world of matter is fundamental. Salvation involves restoration of the soul to the supernal world from which it came. This was made possible by the coming of Jesus Christ, who ransomed souls held captive by hostile cosmic forces. The process of restoration is mediated through an elaborate sacramental system involving baptism, anointing, eucharist, ransom, and the bridal chamber. The status of the last two "sacraments" has been much debated, and it is unclear whether they involve distinct rituals or are merely interpretations of the spiritual effects of common rites. The prominent "bridal chamber," in any case, refers not to earthly matrimony but to a spiritual union, apparently of the soul with its heavenly counterpart. [H.W.A.]

Bibliography

B. Layton, "The Gospel of Philip," in *Nag Hammadi Codex II, 2-7, Together with XIII, 2, Brit. Lib. Or. 4926(1) and P. Oxy. 1, 654, 655* (Leiden: Brill, 1989).

R.M. Wilson, *The Gospel of Philip, Translated from the Coptic Text, with an Introduction and Commentary* (London: Mowbray, 1962); B. Layton, *The Gnostic Scriptures* (Garden City: Doubleday, 1987), pp. 329–353.

E. Segelberg, "The Coptic Gnostic Gospel According to Philip and Its Sacramental System," *Numen* 7 (1960):189–200; R.M. Grant, "The Mystery of Marriage in the Gospel of Philip," *V Chr* 15 (1961): 129–140; J.-E. Ménard, *L'Evangile selon Philippe* (Montreal: Université de Montreal, 1964); J.J. Buckley, "A Cult Mystery in the Gospel of Philip," *JBL* 99 (1980):569–581; D.H. Tripp, "The Sacramental System of the Gospel of Philip," *SP* 17.1 (1982):251–260.

GOSPEL OF THE EGYPTIANS. Apocryphal gospel (second century). The *Gospel of the Egyptians* is a highly ascetic work written in Egypt. Although only a few quotations survive, it was apparently quite popular and circulated widely. Called heretical by the church fathers, it was used by Encratites (Julius Cassianus, to abolish marriage), Naassenes (to prove theories of the soul), and Sabellians (to prove Trinitarian Modalism). [R.R.]

Bibliography

Clement of Alexandria, *Miscellanies* 3.9, 13; Hippolytus, *Refutation of All Heresies* 5.2; Epiphanius, *Panarion* 62.2.

NTA, Vol. 1, pp. 166–178.

GOSPEL OF THOMAS (Infancy). Apocryphal gospel. Although part of the material (6) is attested at the end of the second century (Irenaeus, *Haer.* 1.20.1), the *Gospel of Thomas* in its present form is considerably later, perhaps from the sixth century. The work describes miracles performed by the child Jesus between five and twelve years of age. These deeds are prodigies that—were the name of Jesus not attached to them—one would not suspect of pertaining to the Jesus of the Gospels, such as giving life to toy clay birds and striking dead a playmate who had bumped into him. The work survives in Greek, Latin, Syriac, Armenian, and Georgian versions, with considerable variation among them. Patristic references to a *Gospel of Thomas* are likely to the Gnostic sayings gospel of the same name (Hippolytus, *Haer.* 5.2—a quotation found in neither but with a motif similar to the Coptic gospel; Origen, *Hom.* 1 *in Lc.* 2; Cyril of Jerusalem, *Catech.* 4.36; 6.31). [E.F.]

Bibliography

NTA, Vol. 1, pp. 388–401.

GOSPEL OF THOMAS (Sayings). Collection of 114 sayings, or *logia*, purportedly uttered by Jesus during his earthly ministry. The *Gospel of Thomas* is part of the Gnostic library discovered at Nag Hammadi, Egypt, in 1945. Unlike the canonical Gospels, it is almost devoid of both narration and any readily discernible outline.

The *Gospel of Thomas* was probably written ca. 140. Although some scholars think the collection originated in Greek, its roots could well go back to a Semitic language, either Aramaic or Syriac. The copy discovered at Nag Hammadi was written in Coptic around the late fourth or early fifth century. The only other surviving witnesses are three Greek fragments in a slightly different version, discovered at

Oxyrhynchus and dating from as early as the first part of the third century. The collection may have originated with some Gnostic group, but it has also been suggested that it was used first by Jewish Christians, perhaps with ascetic tendencies (Encratites).

Some sayings in the *Gospel of Thomas* are almost identical to those found in the canonical Gospels (cf. Matt. 15:14 with logion 34: "Jesus said: If a blind man leads a blind man, they will both fall into a pit"); others only loosely resemble canonical material (cf. logion 75, "Jesus said: There are many standing at the door, but it is the solitary who will enter the bridal chamber," with Matt. 7:13–14; 22:14; 25:1–3). A few sayings are recorded in no other writing yet because of their authentic "ring" could conceivably go back to Jesus. One of these sayings is logion 82: "Jesus said: He who is near me is near to the fire, and he who is far from me is far from the kingdom." On the other hand, many sayings are so foreign to Jesus' teaching that they were obviously composed by those who had a theological bias. A good example is logion 114: "Simon Peter said to them: Let Mary leave us, for women are not worthy of life. Jesus said: I myself shall lead her, in order to make her male, so that she too may become a living spirit resembling you males. For every woman who will make herself male will enter the kingdom of heaven."

Although the origins of the *Gospel of Thomas* are not known, one may postulate that a collection of sayings was assembled, perhaps in Syria, under the pseudonym of Didymus Judas Thomas sometime in the mid-second century. Some material in the collection could have been as old as or older than the canonical Gospels. Other sayings could have been gleaned from the traditions of that time. The sayings collection would then have made its way to Egypt, being translated first into Greek, then into Coptic, all the while being revised to suit the theology of its various users through the modification and the addition of sayings. Possibly, the original collection was theologically neutral but went through an evolutionary process until it came to be the *Gospel of Thomas* acceptable to Gnostics that we possess today.

See also Gnosticism; Nag Hammadi. [K.V.N.]

Bibliography
The Facsimile Edition of the Nag Hammadi Codices. Codex II (Leiden: Brill, 1974); B. Layton, ed., *Nag Hammadi Codex II, 2–7, The Coptic Gnostic Library* (Leiden: Brill, 1989).

H. Koester and T.O. Lambdin, "The Gospel of Thomas," *The Nag Hammadi Library in English*, ed. J.M. Robinson, rev. ed. (San Francisco: Harper and Row, 1988), pp. 124–138.

R.McL. Wilson, *Studies in the Gospel of Thomas* (London: Mowbray, 1960); B. Gärtner, *The Theology of the Gospel of Thomas* (London: Collins, 1961); J.E. Ménard, *L'Evangile selon Thomas* (Leiden: Brill, 1975); B. Lincoln, "Thomas-Gospel and Thomas-Community: A New Approach to a Familiar Text," *Novum Testamentum* 19 (1977):65–76; S.L. Davies, *The Gospel of Thomas and Christian Wisdom* (New York: Seabury, 1983); C. Tuckett, "Thomas and the Synoptics," *Novum Testamentum* 30 (1988): 132–157.

GOSPELS. *See* John, Luke, Mark, Matthew.

GOTHS. People who seem to have originated in the area of the Baltic Sea. By the first century A.D., the Goths were on the lower Vistula River. In A.D. 98, Tacitus writes of "the Gothones, who are governed by kings. Their rule is somewhat more autocratic than in the other German states, but not so much that freedom is destroyed" (*Germania* 44). In the latter half of the second century, they appeared in what is now Poland and by the early third century they had moved to the northern coast of the Black Sea, where they became divided into the Ostrogoths ("East Goths") and Visigoths ("West Goths").

During the troubled third century, the Goths made many serious attacks upon the Roman provinces in the Balkans and even crossed the Black Sea to raid Anatolia. They killed the emperor Decius in battle in the Dobruja (251) and sacked the old Greek cities of Corinth, Argos, Sparta, and Athens (267). The Goths were eventually driven back by the emperors Gallienus (260–268) and Claudius II (268–270), who then took the surname Gothicus. Nevertheless, the emperor Aurelian (270–275) subsequently abandoned the trans-

Danubian province of Dacia, which the Visigoths then occupied. The Ostrogoths, meanwhile, under the royal family of the Amals, established an empire in the Ukraine.

Throughout the succeeding years, the Goths maintained close contact with the empire, often serving in the Roman army. In the mid-fourth century, the Goth Ulfilas, an Arian Christian, served as a missionary to his countrymen and translated the Bible into Gothic. Many Goths were converted. Similarly, other Germanic peoples—Vandals, Burgundians, Suevi, Lombards—also adopted the Arian faith. This Germanic Arianism later was to cause problems with the Catholic population after the Germans entered the empire.

In 375, the eastern emperor Valens (364–378) allowed the Visigoths, terrified by the approach of the Huns, to settle on deserted land in Thrace. But the Visigoths then took to raiding, and on August 9, 378, under their chief Fritigern, they inflicted a disastrous defeat on the Romans at Adrianople, just northwest of Constantinople. The emperor Theodosius I (379–395) could do no better than to recognize them as Roman "allies" and confirm them in possession of the Danubian province of Lower Moesia. Under their leader Alaric (ca. 391–410), they again took to ravaging the Balkans and Greece, and in 401 they invaded Italy. In 410, they seized Rome, although the three-day "sack" actually did little damage. After an abortive invasion of Africa, the Visigoths then moved to Gaul.

In 416, the Roman general Constantius compelled the Visigoths to attack the Vandals and Alans in Spain; they were rewarded in 418 by being allowed to settle in Aquitania Secunda (southwestern Gaul), where they had their capital at Toulouse. During the fifth century, they gradually increased their hold on southwestern Gaul. In 451, under their king Theodoric I (not to be confused with the Ostrogothic king Theodoric the Great), they joined with Aetius and the Franks to defeat Attila and the Huns. Under Theodoric II (453–466), the Visigoths occupied most of Roman Spain.

The able Visigothic king Euric (466–484) conquered the remainder of southwestern Gaul, including Provence and the Auvergne. Unlike his Arian predecessors, he was increasingly harsh in his treatment of the Catholic hierarchy. Some bishops were exiled, and cities that had lost their bishops were forbidden to ordain successors. His son Alaric II (484–507) attempted to reach a rapprochement with the Gallo-Romans. He sponsored a church council at Agatha in 506 and issued a new law code that protected the rights of the Roman population. In 507, however, he was killed at the battle of Vouillé against the Franks. As a result, the Visigoths lost all their Gallic possessions except for a Mediterranean strip and subsequently were limited to Spain. Later kings were tolerant of the Catholic religion. In the early 550s, the Byzantine emperor Justinian (527–565) reconquered the southern part of Spain, but it was gradually lost. In 589, under Reccared, the Visigoths formally converted to Catholicism. The kingdom persisted until the Islamic conquest of 711.

The Ostrogoths under Hermanaric, meanwhile, had been overcome by the Huns in the 370s and remained subjected to them until 454, when the Huns were overthrown in a rebellion of subject peoples at the Battle of the Nedao River. Under Valamer (ca. 447–ca. 465), the Ostrogoths then settled within the Roman empire in Pannonia (Hungary). In the early 470s, a portion of them joined the Visigoths in Gaul.

The remainder, under Theodoric (471–526), invaded Italy in 489 at the behest of the emperor Zeno (474–491) and overthrew the barbarian king Odoacer. Theodoric then established the Ostrogothic kingdom of Italy, which also included Provence and the Dalmatian coast. He was tolerant of the Catholic religion, retained the Roman administrative system, and worked closely with the old Roman senatorial aristocracy. His capital was at Ravenna, where he built a great Arian basilica to Christ the savior. He maintained good relations with the Byzantine empire.

In the last few years of his reign, however, Theodoric unwisely antagonized the Roman population. The influential senators Boethius and Symmachus were executed, and pope John I (523–526) was ill-treated. Theodoric also ordered the appropriation of all the Catholic churches but died in 526 before the order could take effect. The murder in 533 of the pro-Roman regent Amalasuntha gave the Byzantine emperor Justinian the pretext to invade Italy. During the ensuing warfare, lasting from 536 to 552, the Ostrogoths were destroyed by the Byzantine generals Belisarius and Narses, and much of Italy was left devastated. *See also* Alaric; Theodoric; Ulfilas. [R.W.M.]

Bibliography

Jordanes, *De origine actibusque Getarum*, tr. C.C. Mierow, *The Gothic History of Jordanes in English Version* (Princeton: Princeton UP, 1915); Ammianus Marcellinus, *Res gestae* (the period 353–378); Claudian, *De bello gothico* (402); Zosimus, *Historia nova* (fourth and fifth centuries); and Procopius, *De bello gothico* (sixth century).

H. Bradley, *The Goths: From the Earliest Times to the End of the Gothic Dominion in Spain* (London: Unwin, 1887); A.A. Vasiliev, *The Goths in the Crimea* (Cambridge: Medieval Academy of America, 1936); E.A. Thompson, "The Visigoths from Fritigern to Euric," *Historia* 12 (1963):105–126; idem, *The Visigoths in the Time of Ulfila* (Oxford: Oxford UP, 1966); idem, *The Goths in Spain* (Oxford: Oxford UP, 1969); B.M. Metzger, *The Early Versions of the New Testament* (Oxford: Clarendon, 1977), pp. 375–393; W. Goffart, *Barbarians and Romans, A.D. 418–584: The Techniques of Accommodation* (Princeton: Princeton UP, 1980); E.A. Thompson, *Romans and Barbarians: The Decline of the Western Empire* (Madison: U of Wisconsin P, 1982); T. Burns, *A History of the Ostrogoths* (Bloomington, Indiana UP, 1984); P. Heather, "The Crossing of the Danube and the Gothic Conversion," *GRBS* 27 (1986): 289–318; H. Sivan, "On Foederati, Hospitalitas,* and the Settlement of the Goths in A.D. 418," *AJPh* 108 (1987): 759–772; H. Wolfram, *History of the Goths* (Berkeley: U of California P, 1988).

GRACE. The Greek term for grace, *charis*, appears in a variety of contexts associated with graciousness and benevolence before the early Christian appropriation of the term as a theological concept for the divine favor. In the Old Testament literature, three words carry the meanings clustered around *charis*: *hen* was used for a master's favorable disposition toward his slave; *hesed* was used for steadfast mercy in the context of covenant relationships; *rahamin* (womb love or compassion) was used of God's

acts that spring from the pangs of mother love. In Jewish wisdom literature, the graciousness of God was seen in God's mercy toward the sinner.

In New Testament writings, *charis* appears frequently in liturgical passages, but it is Paul who appropriates the term as a theological concept—the grace of God as expressed in the death and resurrection of the Son. In Paul's elaboration of the concept of grace, he coins a new word, *charisma*, to designate the powers of God within the individual, such as love, trust, hope, and comfort, and the ministries of the empowered individual to the community. Paul proposed a dialectical tension between Law (Torah) and grace; God's activity operated through both. As the message of Christianity was carried to the pagan world, the dialectic between grace and Torah was no longer relevant. The accent fell on the grace of God, mediated through baptism, which brought forgiveness, a new life, and a new morality.

Gnostics and their Opponents. Marcion built his interpretation of Christian theology around Paul's doctrine of grace and radicalized the Pauline tension between Law and grace. The Law was created and mediated by an inferior creator god who was responsible for this world. Grace was mediated through Jesus Christ, who was sent as a redeemer by an unknown God of love and benevolence. In the Gnostic systems, saving grace took the form of knowledge of the Father (who was differentiated from the creator god) and knowledge of the true identity of the soul (that it came from the realm of the Father). The basis for this salvation lay exclusively in the goodness and benevolence of the Father.

Although the Gnostics rejected the role of the creator god and the Jewish people in the process of salvation, Irenaeus affirmed both. The grace of God in salvation, according to Irenaeus, begins with the creation of human beings in the image and likeness of God and continues into Jewish history as a first stage in the process of Christian salvation history. For Clement of Alexandria also, God's gracious activity in salvation goes back to the original creation of humanity in the image of God. The grace of salvation works through an educational process that transforms the person so that he or she is eventually capable of perfect fellowship with God. *Charis* designates the gracious, gentle, and forgiving work of God with a person; *nomos* designates the corrective and disciplinary activity of God.

Origen elaborates Clement's doctrine of salvation while at the same time strenuously resisting the Gnostic idea that the basis for salvation was the possession of a nature alien to this world that belonged to the spiritual world of the Father. Instead, Origen insists on the free will of all rational souls; God's gracious activity in salvation takes place under the conditions of human free will. This leads Origen to postulate two creation events: first, the creation of the rational souls with free will, who lived in fellowship with God before the fall, and then the creation of bodies after the fall and incorporation of these rational souls into bodies to enable them to experience their fall away from God. Through their bodily existence, a process of education and transformation would restore them to the original fellowship with God. In Origen's system, then, the entire cosmos and human history become one vast educational process issuing from God's gracious intention to save all the souls that he created. In this context, Origen uses *charis* and *charisma* most frequently to designate the knowledge that is mediated to the soul by the Logos in the process of salvation.

Salvation and the process of the divinization of the human person created in the image of God set the framework for the fourth-century controversy over the person of Christ. Athanasius, in response to the Arian position, which made the Logos the Son of God by the grace of adoption, distinguished between Sonship according to nature and Sonship according to grace. Christ is a Son according to nature, being generated from the essence of the Father rather than created. Believers are sons and daughters of God by grace rather than by nature.

Asceticism. The ascetic life created a new context for reflection upon the nature of grace. In Athanasius's *Life of Anthony*, the *charis* of

God is recognized in the *charisma* manifest in the ascetics. Among the manifestations of grace in the ascetics were the discernment of demons, the power to cast out demons, and the gifts of long-suffering, humility, and compassion.

In Christian theology, God's gracious activity had long been identified with the presence of the Holy Spirit. Basil of Caesarea offered as proof that the Holy Spirit is divine the activity of the Holy Spirit in effecting all of the operations of salvation. The Holy Spirit is identified not only with the grace that is operative within the individual but also with the grace that is operative within the community and above all in the monastic community, where the grace of God and the presence of the Holy Spirit are experienced in the diversity of gifts and ministries operating within the community.

The soul in its virginal state before the fall possessed grace, beauty, and charm, because of its creation in the image of God. The ascetic life, and specifically virginity, represented a return to this paradisiacal state and to the original grace and beauty of the soul. Gregory of Nyssa was the first to articulate the long-standing experience of the ascetics that no act of virtue could be achieved without the help of grace and that the efforts and exertions of the ascetic were met by God's responsive grace. Gregory articulated this as *synergia*, a working together of human effort and God's grace.

Pelagius, Augustine, and Cassian. Pelagius stands in line with the traditional understanding that grace is operative in the new covenant, that the whole operation of salvation history is an expression of God's grace, and that the grace of forgiveness in baptism is not merited. According to Pelagius, grace was mediated through the example of Christ and through his teachings. The grace with which human nature was endowed includes free will, the gift of conscience, the power of reason to distinguish, and the gift of the freedom and power to choose. He resisted the idea of grace operating directly on the will in such a way that the will is overcome and is no longer free.

Augustine's innovative doctrine of grace, which was determinative for both medieval and

Reformation understandings, was formulated during the controversy with Pelagius. He traced his own innovative doctrine to an exegetical insight during his studies of Paul's letters, although it was not developed until this controversy. Fundamental to this doctrine were views on anthropology developing in the Latin church. The starting point of Latin anthropology was the damage done to human nature as a result of the fall, in contrast to the Greek emphasis on the grace inherent in the image of God in the original creation of human persons. Against the Manichaeans, Augustine argued that the origin of evil lay not in a spiritual principle but in the will, which can dispose itself toward good or evil.

Augustine's description of his conversion in the *Confessions* provides a useful paradigm for his notion of grace. After pages of agonizing description of an interior conflict where Augustine wished to renounce sexual passions in favor of Christian celibacy but could not will it, he was encountered in a dramatic moment by an interior grace that enabled him to will and choose what he wished. Accordingly, in Augustine's doctrine of grace, grace operates within; it is infused, hidden, and operates in increments on the will. Grace achieves a genuine freedom of will, because through the operations of grace the will is at last free and empowered to choose what it wishes.

For Augustine, the damage done in the fall was done to the will, rendering it impotent and therefore not free. This original insight implied that if the will cannot act apart from God's grace, then the initiative of God's grace is required for the initial act of believing and so for conversion. Since the experience of history demonstrates that many are not converted, their fate lies in the predestination of God, who failed to provide the necessary grace. Monastic thinkers in southern Gaul strenuously resisted the predestinarian consequences of Augustine's doctrine of grace.

John Cassian, carefully distancing himself from both Pelagius and from Augustine, affirmed that God's will to save included all persons. His compromise formulation affirmed that sometimes God appeals to free will (as in the case of Zacchaeus) or that sometimes he inter-

venes with an overriding grace (as in the case of Paul). The disputants took their issues to the bishops. In 411, a synod was convened at Carthage, where a disciple of Pelagius, Celestius, was accused of heresy. In 418, a synod convened again and repudiated the idea that grace operates primarily through teaching and knowledge and affirmed that grace operates directly on the will. The Council of Ephesus (431), alongside the Christological issue, took the time to condemn Pelagianism. Finally, in 529, the Council of Orange made the Augustinian doctrine of grace, without its predestinarian aspects, authoritative for the early-medieval church. *See also* Augustine; Caesarius of Arles; Cassian, John; Election to Salvation; Orange, Councils of; Pelagius; Predestination; Semipelagianism.   [K.J.T.]

Bibliography

Irenaeus, *Against Heresies*, tr. W.H. Rambaut, ANF (1885), Vol. 1; Athanasius, *On the Incarnation*, tr. A. Robertson, NPNF, 2nd ser. (1892), Vol. 4, pp. 1–30; Basil of Caesarea, *On the Holy Spirit*, tr. B. Jackson, NPNF, 2nd ser. (1895), Vol. 8, pp. 2–80; Pelagius, *Letter to Demetrias on True Humility* ed. and tr. K.C. Krabbe (Washington, D.C.: Catholic U of America P, 1965); Augustine, *On the Grace of Christ and Original Sin*; idem, *On Nature and Grace*, tr. R. Holmes and R.E. Wallis, NPNF, 1st ser. (1887), Vol. 5, pp. 121–151, 217–236.

E. Jauncey, *The Doctrine of Grace up to the End of the Pelagian Controversy* (New York: Macmillan, 1925); T. Torrance, *The Doctrine of Grace in the Apostolic Fathers* (Edinburgh: Oliver and Boyd, 1950); M.F. Wiles, *The Divine Apostle: The Interpretation of St. Paul's Epistles in the Early Church* (Cambridge: Cambridge UP, 1967); H. Conzelmann, "Charis," *Theological Dictionary of the New Testament*, ed. G. Friedrich (Grand Rapids: Eerdmans, 1974), Vol. 9, pp. 359–418; D.I. Macqueen, "John Cassian on Grace and Free Will," *RecTh* 44 (1977):5–28; E. Mühlenberg, "Synergism in Gregory of Nyssa," *ZNTW* 68 (1977):93–122; P.J. Fedwick, *The Church and the Charisma of Leadership in Basil of Caesarea* (Toronto: Pontifical Institute of Medieval Studies, 1979); A. Schindler, "Gnade," *RLAC* (1981), Vol. 11, pp. 314–446; A. Dihle, *The Theory of the Will in Classical Antiquity* (Berkeley: U of California P, 1982); J. Koenig, "Occasions of Grace in Paul, Luke and First Century Judaism," *Anglican Theological Review* 64 (1982):562–576; J.P. Burns, "Grace: The Augustinian Foundation," *Christian Spirituality*, ed. B. McGinn and J. Meyendorff (New York: Crossroad, 1985), pp. 331–349; P.C. Phan, *Grace and the Human Condition* (Wilmington: Glazier, 1989).

GRATIAN (359–383). Roman emperor (375–383). The son of Valentinian I, Gratian became western emperor upon his father's sudden death, although his half-brother Valentinian II, only four years of age at the time, had a nominal share in the rule; their uncle Valens governed the east. The rhetorician and poet Ausonius, who had been appointed Gratian's tutor (ca. 365), was influential in the reign. After removing unpopular ministers, Gratian issued a series of laws to remedy abuses and mitigate his father's harsh actions against opponents. He devoted much attention to the defense of Gaul and won an important victory over the Alamanni, a Germanic people (377). He made Theodosius I emperor in the east (379) after Valens's death in battle against the Visigoths at Adrianople (378).

In his religious policy, Gratian was influenced by Theodosius I, by the Roman bishop Damasus I, but above all by Ambrose, who composed the first two books of *The Faith* in response to his request for instruction on Arianism (378). Three additional books of the same title (380) and *The Holy Spirit* in three books (381) followed in answer to the emperor's further request. Ambrose's *De Noe* (ca. 378–384) likened Gratian to the patriarch Noah. A defender of Nicene orthodoxy, like Theodosius I in the east, Gratian issued a series of enactments against heresy and returned to Ambrose (380) a basilica that had passed into Arian control. Arianism would be driven from the empire through councils held in his and Theodosius's reigns at Aquileia in the west and Constantinople in the east (381).

The Spanish bishops Idatius and Ithacius obtained from him a decree against Manichaeism, which was construed broadly enough to include Priscillian and his followers, but it was annulled on the intervention of court officials (ca. 382). Gratian was adamant in his opposition to paganism. The first emperor to refuse the title *pontifex maximus,* he abolished support of the pagan priesthoods at public expense and over the protests of Symmachus removed the altar and statue of the goddess Victory from the senate house at Rome (382).

Gratian was killed at Lyons after the desertion of most of his troops in the revolt of Maximus "the Usurper," an imperial claimant from Great Britain (383). Ambrose asked for the body from the victor; it was eventually buried in Milan. Besides the usual imperial rescripts, the short letter of invitation and request for further information addressed to Ambrose that led to the composition of *The Holy Spirit* is extant (PL 16.875–876). CPL 160, 160a, 1574–1575. *See also* Ambrose.

[M.P.McH.]

Bibliography

Ammianus Marcellinus, *History* 27–31; Ausonius 1 (*Prefatory Pieces*) 1.23–38, 18 (*Epistles*) 22.80–93, 19 (*Epigrams*) 26–27; idem, *Thanksgiving for His Consulship*; Symmachus, *Epistulae* 1.13; 10.2; idem, *Oratio* 2; Ambrose, *De Noe*; idem, *Enarratio in Psalmum LXI* passim; idem, *The Faith* passim; idem, *The Holy Spirit* 1.1.19–21; idem, *The Sacrament of the Incarnation of Our Lord* 8.79–10.116; idem, *On the Death of Valentinian (II)* 71–81; idem, *On the Death of Theodosius* 39–40; 52; idem, *Letters* 1; 10; 11; 12; 24.9–11; Sozomen, *Church History* 7.1–4; Zosimus, *New History* 4.12, 19, 24, 32–37; Bede, *Ecclesiastical History* 1.9.

M. Fortina, *L'imperatore Graziano* (Turin: Società Editrice Internazionale, 1953); H. Glaesener, "L'Empereur Gratien et S. Ambroise," *RHE* 52 (1957):466–488; J. Cameron, "Gratian's Repudiation of the Pontifical Robe," *JRS* 58 (1968):96–102; G. Gottlieb, "Gratianus," RLAC (1983), Vol. 12, pp. 718–732.

GREAT BRITAIN. Legend attributed the founding of Christianity in Britain to Joseph of Arimathea (commemorated in a medieval monastery at Glastonbury), a charming but unprovable possibility. Most likely, Christian missionaries arrived in the second or even late first century, when the Romans had pacified the southern two-thirds of the island. Written evidence for the development of British Christianity is sparse; literally no extant documents survive from Britain itself until the sixth century. There are references to British Christianity in a number of continental and Mediterranean writers—Origen (*Hom.* 4 *in Ezech.*), Tertullian (*Adv. Iud.* 7), Athanasius (*Ep.* 56 *to Jovian*), Jerome (*Ep.* 46.10)—and there survive writings from Britons who left their homelands, for example, Pelagius in Italy and Patrick in Ireland, as well as some anonymous pieces. Scholars have relied heavily on these references, and on references in such later writers as Gildas and Bede, and on archaeological evidence.

The earliest mentions of Christianity in Great Britain appear ca. 200 in Origen and Tertullian, but they say nothing about the British church, only that Christianity was so widespread in the Roman world that it had reached even that distant island. Writing ca. 480, the Gallic monk Constantius of Lyons (*V. Germ.* 18) speaks of a martyr named Alban, who most likely died in the Decian persecution (250). Gildas speaks of two other martyrs, Aaron and Julius, contemporaries of Alban.

In 314, five Britons attended the Council of Arles; Athanasius says that the British bishops accepted the decrees of Nicaea (325) and supported him at the Council of Sardica (343); the western Nicaean Hilary of Poitiers claimed British support in his struggle with the Arians. None of this is surprising; most westerners supported Nicaea, and the British were geographically so far removed from the sites of the controversy that they would have followed the lead of the larger continental churches. The attendance of the British bishops at the Council of Arles (314) suggests that ecclesiastically Britain was allied with the Prefecture of the Gauls, though the exact nature of the relationship is impossible to gauge.

Archaeological evidence points to a church that was initially urban, largely episcopal, and materially well off. In the fourth century, Christianity spread to the great rural estates, whose owners practiced a mild syncretism, although the extent to which the countryside was evangelized remains uncertain. The large and impressive floor mosaic from a villa at Hinton St. Mary in Dorset shows a mixture of pagan and Christian motifs. The famous Mildenhall (Suffolk) silver treasure of the fourth century contains both large dishes with pagan motifs and spoons that apparently had Christian liturgical functions.

There are, however, some finds that are predominantly, if not unquestionably, Christian, again from the fourth century. The Water Newton treasure hoard includes liturgical silver with Christian designs, such as the chi-rho or the alpha and omega or a combination of these. From the villa at Lullingstone in Kent come wall plasters with Christian designs, including orant figures and two large chi-rhos with alpha and omega set in the wedges made by the arms of the rho. Clearly, Christianity could claim the allegiance of wealthy and powerful people. Furthermore, the artistic designs of these surviving pieces indicate a ready acquaintance with movements on the Continent. Archaeologists can certify only two buildings as churches; these are at Silchester (Hampshire) and Richborough (Kent).

The flourishing condition of the British church may also be seen in its effort to evangelize its pagan neighbors. Ninian worked among the southern Picts, according to Bede (*H.E.* 3.4.1), while Patrick, who came from a minor landowning family in western Britain, was sent to Ireland.

The relation of Pelagius to Britain remains a mystery. He was clearly British, and his teachings were popular enough on the island to warrant a corrective visit there by Germanus of Auxerre in 429. None of his writings, however, originated in his homeland, and there is no reason to consider his views to be those of British ecclesiastics in general. His career raises two other questions. First, where did he receive his education? He arrived in Italy as a spiritual adviser to wealthy Christians, so he apparently got his education in Britain, but under what circumstances we do not know. Second, he is referred to by his opponents as a monk, but there is, in fact, no evidence for monasticism in Britain before the fifth century.

In the mid-fifth century, Roman Britain—separated from the empire since 406—was invaded by pagans from Germany. The Anglo-Saxons occupied the eastern half of the island and continued to push the British to the west, leaving them only Wales and Cornwall. Clearly, the British were not exterminated in the eastern parts of the island, but when Roman missionaries to the Anglo-Saxons led by Augustine arrived at Canterbury in 598, they found only a ruined church dedicated to St. Martin of Tours. Monks like Gildas, David (Dewi), and

Samson now led the British church, which retained a measure of independence until the Norman Conquest, when at long last it too became part of the continental system. *See also* Augustine of Canterbury; Celtic Christianity; Ireland. [J.F.K.]

Bibliography

J.M.C. Toynbee, "Christianity in Roman Britain," *Journal of the British Archaeological Association* 16 (1953):1–24; M.W. Barley and R.P.C. Hanson, eds., *Christianity in Britain, 300–700* (Leicester: Leicester UP, 1968); R. Grant, "Christianity in Roman Britain," *Anglican Theological Review* 51 (1969):78–96; C. Thomas, *Christianity in Roman Britain to A.D. 500* (Berkeley: U of California P, 1981); E. Harbert, "Gran Bretagna," and K. Painter, "Gran Bretagna e Irlanda," DPAC (1984), Vol. 2, pp. 1654–1677; K. Painter, "Recent Discoveries in Britain," *Actes XIe Congrès d'archéologie chrétienne,* Lyons, 21–28 Septembre 1986, forthcoming.

GREECE, GREEK. In early Christian times, the name Greece (Hellas) refers in a narrow sense to the Roman province of Achaia (founded 29 B.C.), located in the southern part of the Greek peninsula with the Peloponnesus as its heartland and Corinth as its first capital. In a broader sense, it refers to the whole Greek peninsula, which came to form the Roman diocese of East Illyricum, whose capital was first Sirmium and subsequently Thessalonica; this regional usage, which came in at the time of Diocletian (284–305), comprises also Macedonia, Epirus, and the islands on both sides of the peninsula, including Crete. Strabo mentions both senses (*Geography* 8.1.1–3; 17.3.25). The reference to Greece in Acts 20:2 is in line with the narrower sense. Eusebius of Caesarea knows both senses of the name (*H.E.* 5.22; *V.C.* 3.19). The provincial usage is found in the minutes of various councils: Sardica (342–343) (Mansi 3.38ff.), the Third Ecumenical Council at Ephesus (431), the Fourth at Chalcedon (451), the Fifth at Constantinople (533), and the Sixth at Constantinople (680–681) (Mansi 6.608; 7.4, 101–102; 11.613, 625, 628, 641, 644, 669, and 672). When in 733 an edict of Leo the Isaurian placed the eastern provinces of East Illyricum and of South Italy under the jurisdiction of the patriarch of Constantinople, the province of Greece

(Achaia) was divided into two: the province of Peloponnesus with Corinth as the metropolis and the province of Greece with Athens as the metropolis. The autocephalous archdiocese of Patras was also given the name of Greece (*Codex Parisinus graecus* 1555A).

Christianity arrived in Greece (in the regional sense) with the missionary work of Paul, after his vision at Troas (Acts 16:9ff.) ca. A.D. 50. The Acts of the Apostles provides the first records of the ecclesiastical history of this region. In Paul's time, many churches were founded, including Thessalonica and Philippi in Macedonia, Corinth in Achaia, Nicopolis in Epirus, and Gortyna in Crete. Although not a great episcopal center, Athens became important theologically, mainly by providing such important second-century apologists as Aristides, Athenagoras, and Clement of Alexandria. During the first three centuries, these churches and many others enlarged their membership and organized themselves with bishops and metropolitans. The early history of this region can be divided into five periods: from apostolic times to the Council of Nicaea (50–325); from Nicaea to the foundation of the archdiocese of Justiniana Prima (325–535); from the foundation of Justiniana to the transference of East Illyricum to the jurisdiction of Constantinople (535–732/3); from the Iconoclastic controversy to the sacking of Constantinople by the Crusaders (733–1204); and from the sacking of Constantinople to its capture by the Turks (1204–1453).

Greek culture influenced almost the whole Roman empire but especially its eastern regions, including Asia Minor, Syria, Palestine, and Egypt. These regions had been Hellenized since Alexander the Great and his successors. The Roman empire entered into this political-cultural heritage to such an extent that it may be characterized as Greco-Roman. References to "Greeks" in this wider cultural sense abound in the New Testament (John 7:35; 12:20; Acts 11:20; 14:1; 19:10, 17; Rom. 1:14, 16; Gal. 3:28; Col. 3:11), but this usage became a characteristic feature of the early church as it moved out of its first home in Palestine into the wider Hellenistic world.

The adoption of the Greek language by the church and the Christianization of the Hellenized provinces of the Roman empire "turned the world into a sort of Athens and Greece through the word of the Teacher of the Christians," as Clement of Alexandria put it (*Prot.* 6.18.167). Origen speaks of "Greece in the whole ecumene" and of "the Greeks" in contrast to "the land of the barbarians" and "the barbarians" (*Princ.* 4.1.1; *Cels.* 1.27). The term "Greek" long remained synonymous with the ancient traditions of Greece, including its paganism and philosophy, but the Christian Hellenism that replaced them constituted the heart of the Catholic church in the Roman empire. Even in Rome, the church used the Greek language, as attested by the letter of Clement of Rome (*1 Clem.*) and its earliest great theologian, Hippolytus (ca. 170–235), who wrote in Greek. The same must have been the case in Gaul, where Irenaeus (ca. 115–ca. 202), a Greek from Smyrna, wrote his famous anti-Gnostic work *Against Heresies* in Greek, as well as the *Demonstration of the Apostolic Preaching.* Throughout the first centuries, the theologians of the western Roman provinces—Tertullian, Hilary of Poitiers, Ambrose, Jerome, Rufinus (but not Augustine)—knew Greek, and many of them translated or paraphrased Greek theological works into Latin.

In the east, Greek language and education were the chief characteristics of the church. The liturgies, the theological and ecclesiastical literature, the structures, and the ethos of the church were Greek. Its many great theologians, such as the early Alexandrians Clement and Origen, or the later fathers, such as Athanasius, Basil the Great, Gregory of Nazianzus, Gregory of Nyssa, John Chrysostom, Cyril of Jerusalem, Cyril of Alexandria, and Theodoret of Cyrus, have left monuments of a Christianized Hellenism that became fundamental for later Christianity. All the eastern patriarchates were Greek in this wider Christian sense, and all the ecumenical councils took place in Greek-speaking lands and published their deliberations in Greek. Although both Latin and Greek were the official languages of the Roman empire, the dominance of Greek through-out the early centuries, especially in the east, is indisputable. Even in the west, this Greek image of early Christianity was altered only as it gradually came under the influence of new invaders and was politically cut off from the east Roman empire. The distinction between the Latin west and the Greek east is from a much later date: it came in with the political changes in western Europe that broke up the ancient image of the Roman empire and restricted it to the eastern Roman state, which came to be called the Greek Kingdom of Byzantium. *See also* Athens; Corinth; Philippi; Thessalonica. [G.D.D.]

Bibliography
A. von Harnack, *The Expansion of Christianity in the First Three Centuries*, 2 vols. (New York: Putnam, 1904–1905); K.S. Latourette, *A History of the Expansion of Christianity* (New York: Harper, 1937–1938), Vols. 1–2; "Hellas," *Thrēskeutikē kai Ethikē Egkuklopaideia* (Athens, 1964), Vol. 5, pp. 593–649; K. Baus, *From the Apostolic Community to Constantine* (New York: Herder, 1965); V. Phidas, "Schediasma Ekklēsiastikēs Historias tēs Hellados," *Nea Ziōn* (Jerusalem, 1981); W.H.C. Frend, *The Rise of Christianity* (Philadelphia: Fortress, 1984).

GREGORY I THE GREAT (ca. 540–604). Bishop of Rome (590–604), civil official, monk, and writer. Little is known about the life of Gregory; almost all the information we have comes from the letter prefaced to his *Magna moralia in Job* and from remarks scattered in other letters and works. No contemporary Lives exist, and authors of medieval Lives (with the exception of the anonymous monk of Whitby, who may have known oral traditions going back to persons who had known Gregory) depended upon the same sources available to modern historians.

Early Life. Gregory was born to an aristocratic Roman family that had been Christian for several generations: Gregory's great-great-grandfather was pope Felix II (III) (483–492), and pope Agapetus I (535–536) was another paternal ancestor. Gregory's father, Gordianus, was a senator and probably held a minor ecclesiastical office (*regionarius* or *defensor*). Gregory mentions his mother once, but her name,

Sylvia, is first found in the *Life* of Gregory by the anonymous monk of Whitby. Gregory had a brother and three sisters. The sisters embraced the life of Christian virgins. Tarsilla and Aemiliana were known for their asceticism and prayer; Gordiana eventually abandoned the dedicated life and married the steward of her estates. In 573, Gregory was prefect, highest civil administrator in Rome. Shortly after this date, he abandoned public life to become a Christian monk. He gave away his inherited family wealth (his father had died and his mother had taken up the life of an ascetic widow), founded the monastery of St. Andrew in the family mansion on the Caelian Hill overlooking the Colosseum, and used family lands in Sicily to establish and endow six monasteries there.

A quiet life of self-denial and prayer in the company of other monks at St. Andrew's was not Gregory's destiny. Summoned back to service in the church of Rome by Pelagius II, Gregory was ordained deacon and sent to Constantinople as episcopal representative (*apocrisarius*). He resided there from 579 until 586, when he was recalled to Rome. Monks from St. Andrew's accompanied him to Constantinople, and he began the famous *Magna moralia in Job* as a commentary on the Book of Job delivered orally to them. While in Constantinople, Gregory seems to have associated mostly with western clerics, notably Leander, another aristocrat-turned-monk, who later became bishop of Seville. Gregory engaged in an acrimonious theological debate with the patriarch Eutyches. His knowledge of Greek is currently under renewed discussion; it would seem that he did not know the language but depended on translations, written or oral. His knowledge of eastern theology, monastic practices, and ascetic traditions can be explained by a shared background for later Greek and Latin traditions just as easily as by recourse to materials now extant only in Greek.

Upon his return to Rome, Gregory lived again in the monastery of St. Andrew as a simple monk (not as abbot, as some scholars have suggested) and assisted Pelagius II with papal business. When Pelagius died in 590 during a time of plague, Gregory was the unanimous choice of the people for bishop. Gregory resisted, even writing the emperor Maurice to ask that he not approve the election. Gregory finally acquiesced and even before the emperor's confirmation reached Rome was rallying the population through his preaching. To seek divine mercy and a cessation of the plague, he organized a set of penitential processions that set out from various city churches and converged on the basilica of Sta. Maria Maggiore. Later tradition spoke of the appearance over Hadrian's mausoleum (now the Castel San Angelo) of an angel sheathing a sword to signify the end of the plague.

Episcopate. Gregory's episcopate was significant for the Roman church. He was the first monk chosen bishop, and he sought to fill positions in his household with monks as well, thus apparently provoking a reaction among the clerics in his time and in the decades following. He put the administration of the bishopric's lands, which were scattered throughout Italy, Gaul, North Africa, and elsewhere, on a much firmer footing, showing the administrative skills that earlier had propelled him to the office of prefect. His letters to civil officials in east and west, to bishops, priests, and other ecclesiastical leaders, and to laypersons, reveal the mind of a leader who could be demanding or conciliatory, blunt or restrained, as the situation demanded. He was mindful equally of the supreme authority claimed by the Roman bishopric and of the need to keep that claim in proper perspective. He rejected the title of "ecumenical" patriarch when applied to him or to other bishops. Supreme authority, as he understood it, meant the power to intervene to regulate disorders, not the right to dominate in all matters.

Gregory was much affected by the destruction and suffering caused by both the Gothic Wars waged by Justinian I to reestablish imperial control over the Italian countryside and by the invasion of Italy by the Lombards, who, from 586, laid siege to cities, devastated the countryside, and struck fear in the hearts of all. With an energy typical of the best Roman administrators, Gregory resolutely faced the diminishment of resources, dislocation of population, shortages of food, and flood of refugees entering Rome. He provided for the needs of people, but more importantly he negotiated with the Lombards and brought peace to Italy, although such an independent settlement provoked the ire of the emperor resident in Constantinople.

Writings. During, and indeed before, his episcopacy, Gregory gave himself to the task of interpreting scripture. After he became bishop, scripture interpretation bore fruit in sermons delivered to the people of Rome on Sundays and feast days. Of his sermons, there survive several series: on the liturgical cycle of Gospel lessons, on the opening and closing chapters of the Book of Ezekiel, and two on the Song of Solomon. The surviving commentaries on scripture cover the books of Job and 1 Kings. Now lost are commentaries on Proverbs, the Song of Solomon, the books of the prophets, all of Kings, and Genesis through Judges. As later rearrangements and digests of the *Magna moralia in Job* were to prove, Gregory's lengthy commentary on that biblical book could be viewed as a commentary on all of scripture, since he wove into his exegesis comments on numerous passages from other books of the Bible. In the letter prefaced to the commentary on Job, Gregory likened biblical interpretation to building a house: the literal-historical sense lays the foundation, the allegorical sense erects the walls in a structure of doctrine, and the moral interpretation spreads the beauty of color over the structure. He gave attention to all three senses and thus set an important pattern for medieval exegetes.

In addition to writings on scripture, two other works deserve special mention, the *Dialogues* and the *Pastoral Rule (Regula pastoralis).* The *Dialogues,* in four books, recounts the lives and miracles of holy men and women in Italy. This influential work is often cited as evidence for the decline of religious sensibilities and the rise of superstition in sixth-century Italy, but recent studies have established a more balanced interpretation. Considered in light of similar narratives of lives of eastern ascetics and the rise of the cult of the saints in

the west, this work is evidence not so much for superstition as for an increased awareness of divine power and presence mediated in the lives of holy persons, and for the existence of a worldview that allowed for miracles and "paranormal" phenomena, such as visions or clairvoyance. The second book of the *Dialogues* recounts the life and miracles of Benedict of Nursia, founder of the Abbey of Monte Cassino and author of the Benedictine *Rule.* The earliest account of Benedict's life, it draws on materials that Gregory gathered from persons who had known the great abbot. Although Gregory knew of Benedict's *Rule* (he mentions it in the *Dialogues*), it is unlikely that the monastery of St. Andrew founded by Gregory followed the *Rule,* whose dominance in European monasticism was a development of the Carolingian period.

The *Pastoral Rule* takes up the question of the effective ministry of bishops in their dioceses, and especially the matter of preaching. Although lamenting the loss of peace and quiet when he was called out of his monastic life to serve as emissary of the Roman church in Constantinople and later as bishop, Gregory nonetheless threw himself unreservedly into the demanding work of service. In the *Pastoral Rule,* written shortly after he became bishop, Gregory sought to sketch the duties of the ideal shepherd (pastor) of souls. He gives attention to matters of behavior, spiritual advice, administration, and organization. His overarching concern is with the bishop as speaker for the divine Word, a spiritual model who preaches to the Christians in his care by word and by example. The impact of this view on the medieval church was far-reaching.

Although Gregory's name is attached to a sacramentary and to a form of liturgical chanting, it is now generally recognized that his connection with either of them is slight. His presence in the liturgy comes through prayers that he wrote and through sermons and extracts from commentaries that were incorporated into service books.

Spiritual Teachings. Gregory was not an innovative theologian, but he did form a vocabulary and emphasize themes that shaped the life and thought of subsequent generations of Christians. He was an important transmitter of patristic thought, especially that of Augustine, from whom he took many of his theological clues: the fallen state of human beings (with the pervasive effects of original sin), the primacy of grace in salvation, the doctrine of predestination, the mediating role of the sacraments, the significance of history, and the spiritual quest for the immediate awareness of God in mystical experience. On one topic, the understanding of heaven and the distinction between the saved and the damned, Gregory made a significant contribution; his consideration of the punishment of the unjust and of the possibility of an after-death purgation of sins contributed to the gradual elaboration of a doctrine of purgatory.

Although Gregory was a monk, his spiritual teaching did not assume a commitment to the monastic life conceived in an institutional sense. Discipline of mind and body and dedication to prayer were possible for the married and the celibate, the monk and the layperson, male and female. The monastic life, however, offered the best possibility of sustained discipline and prayer, without the distractions of family, public service, and other forms of attachment and duty incumbent on those who lived in the world. Gregory himself was concerned with the balance between the active life of service to others and to the church in the world and the contemplative life of discipline and prayer. His contributions to the delineation of this dialectic and the description of the life of asceticism and prayer are central for the development of the western mystical tradition in the medieval period. In his *Magna moralia in Job*, Gregory wrote perceptively and movingly about the discipline of life leading to mystical, or contemplative, experiences. He drew on his predecessors in the west and the Christian east to form a distinctive presentation of the path to contemplation. One of the enduring marks of his thought is the use of polar opposites to convey the need to strike a balance in life, such as the need to join humility to severity in the effective exercise of authority. The potential ambiguity of set patterns,

such as solitude for prayer, is also very much in evidence, for he points out that for some people solitude produces temptation and sloth rather than the peace and inwardness that lead to the heights of prayer. The situation of the individual is of paramount importance; some require the active life, others the contemplative, and to force a person to follow the wrong way is a serious mistake.

Gregory's contributions to the Roman church amply justify the designation of "the Great." His unending labors on behalf of the citizens of the city, his numerous sermons (many delivered when he was severely ill) that eloquently address the spiritual and material concerns of the Christians of Rome, his skilled administration of the temporal possessions of the church, and his clear communication of an ideal of asceticism, prayer, and contemplation all were combined in a life that could be presented as a model of the ideal pastor, which for Gregory was the true calling of the bishop. Feast day September 3 (formerly March 12). CPL 1708–1723. *See also* Papacy. [G.A.Z.]

Bibliography

Liber Pontificalis 66 (Duchesne 1.312–314); *The Earliest Life of Gregory the Great,* by an Anonymous Monk of Whitby, tr. B. Colgrave (Cambridge: Cambridge UP, 1986).

Opera, ed. D. de Sainte-Marthe, PL 75–79; *Registrum epistularum,* ed. D. Norberg, CCSL (1982), Vols. 140, 140A; *Homiliae in Hiezechielem,* ed. M. Adriaen, CCSL (1971), Vol. 142; *Moralia in Iob,* ed. M. Adriaen, CCSL (1979–1985), Vols. 143, 143A, 143B; *In canticum canticorum, in librum primum regum,* ed. P. Verbraken, CCSL (1963), Vol. 144; *Dialogues,* ed. A. de Vogüé, SC (1978, 1979, 1980), Vols. 251, 260, 265.

Book of Pastoral Rule and Selected Epistles, tr. J. Barmby, NPNF, 2nd ser. (1895, 1898), Vols. 12–13; *Pastoral Rule,* tr. H. Davis, ACW (1950), Vol. 11; *Dialogues,* tr. O.J. Zimmermann, FOTC (1959), Vol. 39; *Dialogues, Book II,* tr. M. Uhlfelder (Indianapolis and New York: Bobbs-Merrill, 1967).

F.H. Dudden, *Gregory the Great,* 2 vols. (London: Longmans, 1905); E.C. Butler, *Western Mysticism,* 2nd ed. (New York: Harper and Row, 1966); C. Dagens, *Saint Grégoire le Grand: culture et expérience chrétiennes* (Paris: Etudes Augustiniennes, 1977); P. Meyvaert, *Benedict, Gregory, Bede, and Others* (London: Variorum Reprints, 1977); J. Richards, *Consul of God: The Life and Times of Gregory the Great* (London and Boston: Routledge and Kegan Paul, 1980); R.A. Markus, *From Augustine* to *Gregory the Great* (London: Variorum Reprints, 1983); G.R. Evans, *The Thought of Gregory the Great* (Cambridge: Cambridge UP, 1986); J. Fontaine et al., eds., *Grégoire le Grand* (Paris: CNRS, 1986); M. Baasten, *Pride According to Gregory the Great: A Study of the Moralia* (Lewiston: Mellen, 1986); C. Straw, *Gregory the Great: Perfection in Imperfection* (Berkeley: U of California P, 1988); W.D. McCready, *Signs of Sanctity: Miracles in the Thought of Gregory the Great* (Toronto: Pontifical Institute of Mediaeval Studies, 1988).

GREGORY OF AGRIGENTUM (late sixth century). Bishop of Agrigentum in Sicily. To Gregory is attributed a commentary on Ecclesiastes in ten books. Feast day November 23. CPG III, 7950.   [E.F.]

Bibliography

Gregory the Great, *Letters* 1.72; 2.33; 3.12; 5.12; 8.23; Leontius, *Vita Gregorii* (PG 98.525–740).

G.H. Ettlinger, "The Form and Method of the Commentary on Ecclesiastes by Gregory of Agrigentum," *SP* 18.1 (1985):317–320.

GREGORY OF ELVIRA (ca. 320–after 392). Bishop, exegete, and homilist. Gregory was a strong opponent of Arianism and an adherent of the creed of Nicaea, both in his resistance to Hosius of Cordova and the other bishops who yielded at the Council of Rimini (359) and throughout his career. He supported the position of Lucifer of Cagliari against allowing repentant Arians to continue in ecclesiastical office. Gregory's writings have often been attributed to others. He is the author of a defense of Nicene orthodoxy, as well as of scriptural exegeses that make much use of allegory; his homilies on the Song of Solomon are notable for their application of bridal imagery to Christ and the church. CCSL 546–557.

[M.P.McH.]

Bibliography

Eusebius of Vercelli, *Epistula* 3; Faustinus and Marcellinus, *De confessione verae fidei* (=*Libellus precum*) 9.33–11.41; Jerome, *Lives of Illustrious Men* 105.

Gregorius Iliberritanus et ps.-Gregorius Iliberritanus, Opera quae supersunt, ed. V. Bulhart and J. Fraipont, CCSL (1967), Vol. 69.

T.P. Halton and R.D. Sider, "A Decade of Patristic Scholarship 1970–1979," *CW* 76 (1982–1983):379 (bibliography).

GREGORY OF NAZIANZUS (ca. 329–390). Bishop of Constantinople (379–381). Gregory's title, "The Theologian," which appears as early as the Council of Chalcedon (451), is shared only with the apostle John. Along with John Chrysostom and Basil of Caesarea, he is considered by the eastern Orthodox as one of the hierarchs of the faith. Although he wrote in Greek and did not become as famous as John Chrysostom in the west, 1,200–1,500 manuscripts of his works survive.

Life. Gregory was born into an upper-class, landholding family in Cappadocia. His father, also a Gregory, was able to pay most of the cost of a new church building in Nazianzus. He had not always held Christianity in such high regard; his family had belonged to the Hypsistarii, a Hellenized Jewish sect that worshiped one God, observed the Sabbath, and kept the food laws but rejected circumcision. When the elder Gregory became a Christian, his paternal grandmother disowned him for a time. But during the younger Gregory's early adult years, Gregory the elder was bishop of Nazianzus. He appears to have been a good pastor and administrator but not an able theologian. On one occasion, he signed an Arian creed, only later recognizing what it meant and rejecting its tenets. Gregory's mother, Nonna, evidently was the Christian center of the family. She had come from a Christian background, influenced her husband to become a believer, and provided the sense of faith that nurtured the children. A younger brother, Caesarius, chose medicine as a career and was a physician in the court of Constantinople; he later served as treasurer in Bithynia, but he died in mid-life. Gorgonia, a sister, also preceded Gregory in death.

Gregory received the benefits of an excellent education. His family had the financial resources and the sense of what such an education could provide. He studied at Nazianzus, Caesarea in Cappadocia (where he first met Basil of Caesarea), Caesarea in Palestine, Alexandria, and finally Athens. At Caesarea in Palestine, his love of Origen was probably strengthened if not begun; he was also able to learn from Thespesius, a noted rhetorician there. In Alexandria, he must have heard about Athanasius and may have studied with Didymus the Blind. In Athens, he studied under Himerius, who understood the use of Aristotelian enthymemes—a two-part "if–then" type of argument used for probability questions or informal presentation of syllogistically demonstrable issues. He also learned from Prohaeresius, a fellow Cappadocian Christian, who was noted for his memory and rhetorical power. Although we have none of his works, Prohaeresius may well have been one of the most significant figures in helping Gregory see the relationship between education and theology. At least, he was an impressive teacher of rhetoric; the emperor Julian allowed him to teach when he had banned all other Christians from teaching in the normal schools.

During the stay in Athens, Gregory became reacquainted with Basil. They grew to be fast friends even though their temperaments were quite different. They planned a life of monastic contemplation together, but Basil left Athens early to travel to monasteries in Palestine and Egypt. Gregory turned down the students' call for him to teach rhetoric in Athens, eventually making his way back home, and then to Pontus, where he joined Basil in a small ascetic retreat. Although the enterprise was a failure, they probably did assemble the *Philocalia* there, a digest of Origen's works. Despite differences, the friendship of the two struck deep roots and grew to something they would come both to cherish and regret.

Gregory returned in 358–359 to his home, taught rhetoric, and made occasional visits back to Pontus. Yet the tension between ascetic withdrawal and public performance plagued him all his life. He had the theological and preaching gifts to be a bishop, but the details of public administration found no resonance in his person. He more than once fled into monastic retreat after periods of difficult community demands.

In 361, his father forced ordination on him. Again, he left for Pontus, but by Easter of 362 he was back and ready to assist his father with the church duties. In 370, Basil tricked Gregory into coming to Caesarea to help him

secure the bishopric after Eusebius's death. Gregory was deeply hurt. The problems grew in 371, when Basil, now bishop, tried to appoint Gregory bishop of Sasima, a tiny town of no significance, as part of his effort to mute Arian influence in the region. Gregory was again piqued. In his funeral oration for Basil, he was to mention this betrayal of their friendship.

In 374, both of Gregory's parents passed away. He was now freed from familial demands for a life of public service, but the bishops of the region and the people of Nazianzus wanted him to follow his father. He fled to the convent of St. Thecla in Seleucia and stayed there for four years. Although we have no information that can be securely dated to that period, interesting changes occur after it. The threat of Apollinarianism (which compromised the full humanity of Christ), for example, had not been clear to Gregory when he entered this stage of study and contemplation, but he was able to combat it effectively not long after this stay (*Ep.* 101). Perhaps more information about its character had come to him in Seleucia. At any rate, he was prepared to recognize its dangers when he reached Constantinople.

Finally, a call came that caught his attention: to become the preacher for the small orthodox congregation in Constantinople. Gregory had been in a period of seclusion and probably was not averse to life in the metropolis, at least to its cultural aspects. In the period 379–381, most of his orations were given and his career enhanced. He was the defender of orthodoxy when Theodosius I ascended the throne. But his previous life plagued him. Alexandrian opponents at the Council of Constantinople (381) insisted that since Gregory had been a bishop elsewhere he had broken canon law in accepting the position in the capital. Even though he had not served at Sasima and had been only an auxiliary at Nazianzus, he did not find the dispute worth the effort. Complaining of ill health, he resigned from his positions as bishop and president of the council and left for Nazianzus. There, after a year's wrangling with those who wanted him to assume the bishopric, he took up the post.

In 384, once more citing ill health, he retired to the family estate at Arianzus to devote himself to writing. Having written most things during his lifetime with a view to a larger public, he was now able to collect his letters and to edit and publish various other works. He died in 390.

Works. In his writings, Gregory turned Hellenic and Hellenistic tradition to Christian use. He wrote more than 17,000 verses. Unlike the two Apollinarii of Laodicea, he did not think of versifying the Bible but of making Greek poetry carry Christian content. Although his lines are not always markedly creative, he did write good elegies. His theological poetry, if often bland, fits the classical forms well. He used classical vocabulary and meter in works featuring Christian concepts and heroes. His greatest achievement in verse, however, is his autobiographical poetry, which marks a new level of autobiography, both in poetic form and in personal reflection. Only Augustine's *Confessions*, many times longer and in prose, is more revealing.

Gregory appears to be the first Christian to make a collection of his own letters. This sense of his own talent and mission is striking. At times, the early epistles show an immaturity of interest and character, but some of them are priceless. Three letters (*Ep.* 101–102; 202) are of such theological importance for Apollinarianism that they belong to a separate manuscript tradition. One letter to Nicobulus (*Ep.* 51) about writing letters had pointed advice for any author. Gregory pleads for conciseness yet comprehensiveness, grace and style, and understandability.

Gregory's most important works are the *Orations.* Forty-four genuine discourses have come down to us. The bulk of them were preached at church services and festivals. They reveal Gregory at his best, both as orator and as Christian believer. His funeral oration for Basil is often considered the best since Demosthenes. Byzantine commentators on rhetorical works frequently replaced examples taken from Demosthenes with ones from Gregory.

His most complex discourses are the five *Theological Orations.* Forced by the later Ari-

ans to defend his positions publicly, Gregory left his usual homiletical practice and argued at length for a particular method in theology. He insisted that God's nature was incomprehensible but that God had made his existence and his character known. At last, Gregory put his education in philosophical rhetoric to good use in his attack on the Eunomians, who tried to make theology into a logical science by seeing language as a God-given system, names as indicative of essence, and theological knowledge as propositional, capable of syllogistic demonstration.

Gregory contended that theology was more a discipline of probabilities, even poetic in nature. He showed that Aristotle had dealt with probability questions, not merely demonstrable ones. Gregory knew a tradition of Aristotelian scholarship that viewed the *Rhetoric* as part of the logical treatises, not a separate work that treated the art of persuasion as if it were only salesmanship. That tradition, often referred to as philosophical rhetoric, as opposed to sophistic rhetoric, knew both the limits of syllogistic reasoning and the danger of arguing a case through any appropriate means for an end. As a philosophical rhetorician, Gregory kept his confessional stance intact, refusing to see theology as a systematic, syllogistic science, but he did not withdraw into irrationality.

Doctrinally, he and the other Cappadocians fashioned a Trinitarian view that emphasized both the one nature of God and the three persons of Father, Son, and Holy Spirit. Gregory insisted that the Holy Spirit was God, a position Basil implied but would not take publicly. In Christology, Gregory defended both the full humanity and the divinity of the Son in one complete person. He could speak of the Son before the incarnation, the Son incarnate, or the man Jesus as the subject of various biblical passages. For him, the Son was one; the impassible could suffer the passion. His views were more inclusive than many later positions. In soteriology, he became the champion of the *theōsis* concept, the view that incarnation and salvation were balanced. The Son became human so that humans could become divine. These positions stood firmly against what he saw as the dangers of Neoarians, Apollinarians, and Pneumatomachians. Feast day January 2 (west, with Basil of Caesarea), January 25 and 30 (east). CPG II, 3010–3125. TLG 2022. [F.W.N.]

Bibliography

PG 35–38; A. Tulier, P. Gallay, J. Bernardi, J. Mossay, eds., SC (1969–1985), Vols. 149, 208, 247, 250, 270, 284, 309, 318.

C.G. Browne and J.E. Swallow, eds., NPNF, 2nd ser. (1894), Vol. 7, pp. 185–498; L.P. McCauley et al., tr., *Funeral Orations by Saint Gregory Nazianzen and Saint Ambrose,* FOTC (1953), Vol. 22; E.R. Hardy, ed., *Christology of the Later Fathers,* LCC (1954), Vol. 3, pp. 113–232; J. McGuckin, tr., *Gregory Nazianzen: Selected Poems* (Oxford: SLB, 1986); D. Meehan, tr., *Saint Gregory of Nazianzus: Three Poems,* FOTC (1987), Vol. 75.

R.R. Ruether, *Gregory of Nazianzus: Rhetor and Philosopher* (Oxford: Clarendon, 1969); F. Trisoglio, *San Gregorio di Nazianzo in un quarantennio di studi (1925–1965)* (Turin: Collegio San Giuseppe, 1974); D.F. Winslow, *The Dynamics of Salvation: A Study in Gregory of Nazianzus* (Cambridge: Philadelphia Patristic Foundation, 1979); A.-S. Ellverson, *The Dual Nature of Man: A Study in the Theological Anthropology of Gregory of Nazianzus* (Uppsala: Almqvist & Wiksel, 1981); J. Mossay, *Repertorium Nazianzenum, Orationes, Textus Graecus, I: Codices Galliae* (Paderborn: Schöningh, 1981); R.E. Snee, "Gregory Nazianzen's Constantinopolitan Career, A.D. 379–381" (Diss., University of Washington, 1981); G.A. Kennedy, *Greek Rhetoric Under Christian Emperors* (Princeton: Princeton UP, 1983), pp. 215–239; B. Wyss, "Gregor II (Gregor von Nazianz)," RLAC (1983), Vol. 12, pp. 793–863; J. Mossay, *2. Symposium Nazianzenum, Louvain-la Neuve 25–28 août, 1981. Actes du colloque international organisé avec le soutien du Fonds National Belge de la Recherche Scientifique et de la Görres-Gesellschaft zur Pflege der Wissenschaft* (Paderborn: Schöningh, 1983); F.W. Norris, "Of Thorns and Roses: The Logic of Belief in Gregory Nazianzen," *ChHist* 53 (1984):455–464; idem, *Faith Gives Fullness to Reasoning: The Five Theological Orations of Gregory Nazianzen* (Leiden: Brill, forthcoming).

GREGORY OF NYSSA (331/40–ca. 395).

Bishop, the youngest of the "three great Cappadocians." Gregory was born into an influential and deeply Christian family. His year of birth is uncertain, but he was at least a few years younger than his brother Basil, the later bishop of Caesarea. His education seems to have been influenced especially by his oldest sibling, Macrina ("the younger"), and later in both rhetoric and theology by Basil. Unlike Basil and Gregory of Nazianzus, he did not study at the great centers of higher learning, but on his own he absorbed, remarkably well, the rhetorical and philosophical culture of his time, including much of what we would call "natural sciences." Starting early in ecclesiastical service, he gave up his lectorate in the church to become a rhetor (Gregory of Nazianzus, *Ep.* 11). He was certainly married, and did not join Basil and Gregory of Nazianzus in their monastic retirement. He did return, however, into the full service of the church and was ordained by Basil in 372 to the modest bishopric of Nyssa in Cappadocia. As an administrator, he was a disappointment to Basil (*Ep.* 58; 60; 100); because of accusations of mismanagement raised by the Arians, he was deposed in 376 but returned to his bishopric only two years later.

After Basil's death on January 1, 379, Gregory became his recognized heir (Gregory of Nazianzus, *Ep.* 76) in the struggle against extreme Arianism, as represented by Eunomius, and began the most fruitful period of his life. In 379, he took part in the synod of the Nicene party held in Antioch; returning from there, he visited his dying sister Macrina, superior of a monastery of women in Annesi (*Ep.* 19; *V. Macr.*). Soon afterward, he traveled to Ibora and Sebaste in order to supervise the election of new bishops (*Ep.* 15; 18; 19; 22); in Sebaste, Gregory himself was elected bishop, but he extricated himself, and, a short time afterward, his youngest brother, Peter, became bishop there.

From May to July 381, Gregory played an important role at the Council of Constantinople convoked by Theodosius I, later recognized as the Second Ecumenical Council. Theodosius then designated him one of those bishops communion with whom was a necessary condition for being recognized as orthodox (*Cod. Thds.* 16.1.3). On a mandate of the council, Gregory traveled in the same year to the Roman province of Arabia to intervene in a conflict concerning the bishopric of its capital, Bostra. On this trip, he also visited Jerusalem to mediate in ecclesiastical controversies (*Ep.* 2.11–12) and in the process was constrained to defend the orthodoxy of his own Christology (*Ep.* 3). Although himself highly moved by his visit to the holy places in Jerusalem (*Ep.* 3.1–4), Gregory, because of the moral dangers involved, advised women committed to the monastic life against such pilgrimages (*Ep.* 2).

Gregory's presence at the Constantinopolitan synod of 383 is attested by a sermon (*Deit.*). He delivered sermons in the capital on the occasions of the death of the young princess Pulcheria and the empress Flacilla. After 385, the sources are silent, although Gregory's literary activity continued, especially in the area of the theology of Christian perfection. We know that he was present at the synod of Constantinople in 394; he died probably soon afterward.

Writings. We possess a substantial body of writings from Gregory (only his epistles seem to have been preserved incompletely). The following selection will treat some of the more important works in probable chronological order.

On Virginity is Gregory's first published writing, although its date can be set only approximately, between 370 and 379 (probably in the earlier years of this period). Several other works may be assigned to the same period, such as the homilies on the Lord's prayer, the Beatitudes, and the Psalms, as well as *In Ecclesiasten.*

Many of Gregory's important writings can be dated with relative accuracy to the period following the death of Basil (379). *On the Making of Man* and *Hexaemeron* explicitly complete and correct Basil's homilies on creation and stem probably from 379–389. Close to them is *On the Soul and the Resurrection,* presented as a dialogue with the dying Macrina (who functions as the teacher of Gregory), and the *Life of Macrina.*

The most important dogmatic works of Gregory, the books *Against Eunomius,* can, thanks to the research of Diekamp and Jaeger, be dated rather closely: Books 1 and 2 (in older editions and translations 1 and 12B) were written, hastily, in 380–381 (certainly before the Council of Constantinople); 3 (in older editions 3–12), in 381–383; the *Refutatio confes-*

sionis Eunomii (in older editions 2), shortly after 383. The so-called shorter Trinitarian writings can also be assigned, on the basis of internal indications, to this period, as can the brief treatise *Ad Petrum fratrem de differentia essentiae et hypostaseos* (transmitted also as *Ep.* 38 of Basil, but today generally attributed to Gregory), *On the Holy Spirit,* and *In illud: Tunc et ipse filius.* The treatise *Adversus Arium et Sabellium* is not universally accepted as Gregory's.

The *Great Catechism,* a summary but relatively comprehensive theological synthesis for catechists, seems to have followed the Trinitarian writings. From the subsequent years date Gregory's refutations of the Christology of Apollinaris: the short treatise *Ad Theophilum, Adversus Apollinaristas,* written in 385 or later, and the substantial *Antirrheticus adversus Apollinarem.*

One of Gregory's most extensive and mature works, the *In Canticum canticorum,* and the *Life of Moses,* both treating especially the nature of Christian perfection as continuous progress, stem probably from Gregory's last years (391–395).

Difficult to locate chronologically is the treatise *On the Christian Mode of Life,* a reworking of the so-called "Great Letter" of Pseudo-Macarius. Its attribution to Gregory is generally but not universally accepted.

Theology. Earlier scholars generally underestimated Gregory in relation to the other great Cappadocians, Basil of Caesarea and Gregory of Nazianzus, but recent patristic research has resulted in a positive reevaluation, both of his role in church history and of the quality of his rhetoric. It is, however, primarily as a Christian thinker and spiritual guide that Gregory has won widespread recognition.

Gifted with an outstanding ability for speculative thought, Gregory was better acquainted with the Greek philosophy of the day, especially Middle and Neoplatonism, than were most of his Christian contemporaries, and he put it to use in the service of a genuinely Christian theology and spirituality. Radically transforming the Platonic-Neoplatonic notion of participation, he elaborated the fundamental

Christian distinction between God and creatures, excluding within the divinity any subordinationism (against the Neoarians and Pneumatomachians). He affirmed unequivocally both the full divinity (against Eunomius) and the full humanity (against Apollinaris) of Christ, by whose incarnation, death, and resurrection the human race has been restored to communion with God. In his anthropology, he refuted the preexistence of souls, which had been affirmed by both Origen and the Neoplatonists, and considered humanity as that part of the rational or intellectual creation through which the material universe also was destined to partake of God. Conceiving the vocation of man as a neverending growth in sharing God's life, he preserved the primacy of God as the infinite source of all good, while maintaining human responsibility in freely responding to God's call by a continuous process of conversion.

Gregory's influence on writers of both the east—Pseudo-Dionysius, Maximus Confessor, John of Damascus, Gregory Palamas—and the west—John Scotus Eriugena, the theological anthropology of the twelfth century—is in the process of being better investigated. Feast day March 9. CPG II, 3135–3226. TLG 2017. *See also* Participation. [D.L.B.]

Bibliography

PG 44–46; W. Jaeger et al., *Gregorii Nysseni Opera* (Leiden: Brill, 1952–); R. Staats, ed., *Makarios-Symeon Epistola Magna: Eine messalianische Mönchsregel und ihre Umschrift in Gregors von Nyssa "De instituto christiano"* (Göttingen: Vandenhoeck & Ruprecht, 1984).

W. Moore and H.A. Wilson, eds., NPNF, 2nd ser. (1893), Vol. 5; H.C.Graef, tr., *St. Gregory of Nyssa, The Lord's Prayer, The Beatitudes*, ACW (1954), Vol. 18; E.R. Hardy and C.C. Richardson, eds., *Christology of the Later Fathers*, LCC (1954), Vol. 3; H. Musurillo, ed., *From Glory to Glory: Texts from Gregory of Nyssa's Mystical Writings* (New York: Scribner, 1961); V.W. Callahan, tr., *Saint Gregory of Nyssa, Ascetical Works*, FOTC (1967), Vol. 58; A.J. Malherbe and E. Ferguson, tr., *Gregory of Nyssa: The Life of Moses*, CWS (1978); A. Spira and C. Klock, eds., *The Easter Sermons of Gregory of Nyssa: Translation and Commentary* (Cambridge: Philadelphia Patristic Foundation, 1981); C. McCambley, tr., *Saint Gregory of Nyssa: Commentary on the Song of Songs* (Brookline: Hellenic College, 1988).

J. Daniélou, *Platonisme et théologie mystique: doctrine spirituelle de saint Grégoire de Nysse* (Paris: Aubier, 1944; rev. ed. 1954); idem, "La Chronologie des sermons de Grégoire de Nysse," *RSR* 29 (1955):346–372; W. Völker, *Gregor von Nyssa als Mystiker* (Wiesbaden: Steiner, 1955); D.L. Balas, *"Metousia Theou": Man's Participation in God's Perfections According to St. Gregory of Nyssa* (Rome: Herder, 1966); E. Mühlenberg, *Die Unendlichkeit Gottes bei Gregor von Nyssa: Gregors Kritik am Gottesbegriff der klassischen Metaphysik* (Göttingen: Vandenhoeck & Ruprecht, 1966); J. Daniélou, *L'Etre et le temps chez Grégoire de Nysse* (Leiden: Brill, 1970); M. Harl, ed., *Ecriture et culture philosophique dans la pensée de Grégoire de Nysse: Acts du colloque de Chevetogne (22–26 Septembre, 1969)* (Leiden: Brill, 1971); R.M. Hübner, *Die Einheit des Leibes Christi bei Gregor von Nyssa: Untersuchungen zum Ursprung der "physischen" Erlösungslehre* (Leiden: Brill, 1974); H. Dörrie, M. Altenburger, U. Schramm, eds., *Gregor von Nyssa und die Philosophie*, Zweites Internationales Kolloquium über Gregor von Nyssa, Freckenhorst bei Münster 18.–23. September, 1972 (Leiden: Brill, 1976); M. Canévet, *Grégoire de Nysse et l'hermeneutique biblique: étude des rapports entre le langage et la connaissance de Dieu* (Paris: Etudes Augustiniennes, 1983); H.B. Wicher, *Gregorius Nyssenus: Catalogus translationum et commentariorum: Mediaeval and Renaissance Latin Translations and Commentaries: Annotated Lists and Guides* (Washington, D.C.: Catholic U of America P, 1984), Vol. 5; A. Spira, ed., *The Biographical Works of Gregory of Nyssa*, Proceedings of the Fifth International Colloquium on Gregory of Nyssa, Mainz, 6–10 September, 1982 (Cambridge: Philadelphia Patristic Foundation, 1984); L.F. Mateo-Seco and J.L. Bastero, eds., *El "Contra Eunomium I" en la Produccion Literaria de Gregorio de Nisa*, VI Coloquio Internacional sobre Gregorio de Nisa (Pamplona: Ediciones Universidad de Navarra, 1988); M. Altenburger and F. Mann, eds., *Bibliographie zu Gregor von Nyssa: Editionen-Übersetzungen-Literatur* (Leiden: Brill, 1988); H.R. Drobner, *Bibelindex zu den Werken Gregors von Nyssa* (Paderborn: Selbstverlag, 1988).

GREGORY OF TOURS (538–593/4). Bishop and writer. Born November 538, in Auvergne in Gaul, he took the name Gregorius after an ancestor who was bishop of Langres. He came from a Gallo-Roman senatorial family with a long record of service in the church. Gregory received a normal education, although he was sensitive about its limitations. He is apologetic about his rustic Latin (*H.F.* 5.6; 10.31) but can refer to Virgil's *Aeneid* (*H.F.* 2.29; 4.30, 46;

8.22; 9.6). He has some awareness of the liberal arts in the writings of Martianus Capella (*H.F.* 4.8; 5.49; 7.1; 10.31). In 573, Gregory became the nineteenth bishop of Tours, the thirteenth member of his family to hold this office (*H.F.* 5.49). He remained bishop until his death.

Gregory wrote a number of works: *De cursu stellarum ratio; Vitae patrum; In Psalterium; De miraculis beati Andreae; Passio sanctorum Martyrum Septem Dormientium;* and the famous *History of the Franks* in ten books. Some of these works are brief translations or survive only in fragments. *De cursu stellarum ratio* attempts to fix the hours for the nocturnal recitation of the Divine Office. Gregory demonstrates a rudimentary knowledge of astronomy and of curiosities, listing, for example, the wonders of the world. His works on the miracles associated with martyrs and confessors are an important contribution to hagiography and reflect his deep interest in Martin of Tours (*De virtutibus beati Martini*).

The History of the Franks, or *Ten Books of History* (written between 573 and 591), opens with a sweeping review of history from Adam and Eve down to the death of Martin. Then Gregory moves slowly through the careers of Clovis and his sons. The core of the work, Books 5–10, deals with contemporary events, 573–591. Book 10 concludes with a list of the bishops of Tours and a list of Gregory's writings.

Although Gregory is gullible, he does acknowledge a range of sources: the Bible, Eusebius (in translation), Orosius, Gallic authors, and seven documents (in Books 9 and 10). Gregory's viewpoint is that of a bishop who regards the church as the source of goodness and value in a barbarian age. He possesses a lively narrative style and portrays his characters in an effective dramatic fashion. Sigibert is a good soldier, diplomat, and husband; Chilperic is vicious, vindictive, and lusty. Their respective queens, Brunhild and Fredegund, are also presented in sharply contrasting moral categories. It is noteworthy, however, that Gregory's portrait of the beautiful and generous Brunhild is not corroborated by the contemporary account by "Fredegarius." Feast day November 14. CPL 1023–1032. *See also* Clovis; Franks. [P.C.B.]

Bibliography
W. Arendt, B. Krutsch, M. Bonnet, eds., *MGH, Scriptores Rerum Merovingicarum,* Vol. 1 (Hanover: Hahn, 1884–1885); Vol. 7 (1919–1920), pp. 757–769.

O.M. Dalton, tr., *The History of The Franks by Gregory of Tours: Introduction, Translation and Notes,* 2 vols. (Oxford: Clarendon, 1927); *Gregory of Tours: The History of the Franks,* tr. L. Thorpe (Harmondsworth: Penguin, 1974); W.C. McDermott, tr., "Selections," *Monks, Bishops and Pagans: Christian Culture in Gaul and Italy 500–700,* ed. E. Peters (Philadelphia: U of Pennsylvania P, 1975); E. James, tr., *Gregory of Tours: Life of the Fathers* (Liverpool: Liverpool UP, 1985); R. Van Dam, tr., *Gregory of Tours: Glory of the Confessors* (Liverpool: Liverpool UP, 1985); idem, *Gregory of Tours: Glory of the Martyrs* (Liverpool: Liverpool UP, 1988).

S. Dill, *Roman Society in Gaul in the Merovingian Age* (London: Macmillan, 1926); O. Chadwick, "Gregory of Tours and Gregory the Great," *JThS* 50 (1949):38–49; J.M. Wallace-Hadrill, "The Work of Gregory of Tours in Light of Modern Research," *Transactions of the RHS* (1951):25–45; repr. in *The Long Haired Kings*. . . (see below), pp. 49–70; M.L.W. Laistner, *Thought and Letters in Western Europe A.D. 500–900,* 2nd ed. (Ithaca: Cornell UP, 1957), pp. 129–135; J.M. Wallace-Hadrill, *The Long-Haired Kings and Other Studies in Frankish History* (London: Methuen, 1962); A. Erikson, "The Problem of Authorship in the Chronicle of Fredegar," *Eranos* 63 (1965):47–76; B. Vettere, *Struttiere e modelli culturali nella Società merovingia: Gregorio di Tours* (Galatina: Congedo, 1979), pp. 9–34; F.R. Newbold, "Patterns of Communication and Movement in Ammianus and Gregory of Tours," *History and Historians in Late Antiquity,* ed. B. Croke and A. Emmett (Elmsford: Pergamon, 1983); W. Goffart, *The Narrators of Barbarian History (A.D. 550–800)* (Princeton: Princeton UP, 1988).

GREGORY THAUMATURGUS (ca. 210–260).

Bishop of Neocaesarea. Gregory Thaumaturgus ("The Wonder Worker") was born into a pagan family in Cappadocian Pontus. After the death of his parents, he studied rhetoric, then law. Intending to go to Beirut to further his legal education in 233, he instead went with his brother to study with Origen at Caesarea in Palestine. By 238, he had returned to Pontus and sometime in the 240s became bishop of Neocaesarea. He fled the Decian persecution, lived through gruesome attacks by Goths in the 250s and took part in the synod that excommunicated Paul of Samosata in the 260s.

Perhaps his most noted work is a eulogy for Origen, which describes in detail how the great theologian taught, leading students through the classics and helping them see their values and dangers. A communal letter that deals with pastoral problems during the Gothic invasion is extant, as is a treatise for preachers on how to interpret the Septuagint. A piece dedicated to Philogrius, which deals with the doctrine of the Trinity and exists only in Syriac, is probably authentic. The confession of faith attributed to him by Gregory of Nyssa is the latter's own composition. Some Apollinarian forgeries were transmitted under his name.

Gregory's influence depended much upon the widely circulating tales of his miracles. Lives written by Gregory of Nyssa and others ap-pearing independently in Latin, Syriac, and Armenian show the extent of his fame. Feast day November 17. CPG I, 1763–1794. TLG 2063. [F.W.N.]

Bibliography

Gregory of Nyssa, *Vita Gregorii Thaumaturgi.*
W. Telfer, "The Cultus of St. Gregory Thaumaturgus," *HThR* 29 (1936):225–234; L. Abramowski, "Das Bekenntnis des Gregor Thaumaturgus bei Gregor von Nyssa und Das Problem seiner Echtheit," *ZKG* 87 (1976):145–166; idem, "Die Schrift Gregors des Lehrers Ad Theopompum und Philoxenus von Mabbug," *ZKG* 89 (1978):273–290; H. Crouzel, "Faut-il voir trois personnages en Grégoire le Thaumaturge? A propos du 'Remercîment à Origène' et de la 'Lettre à Grégoire,'" *Gregorianum* 60 (1979):287–320; H. Crouzel, "La christologia in Gregorio Taumaturgo," *Gregorianum* 61 (1980):745–755; R. Riedinger, "Das Bekenntnis des Gregor Thaumaturgus bei Sophronius von Jerusalem und Macarius von Antiochia," *ZKG* 92 (1981):311–314; S. Brock, "Clavis Patrum Graecorum III, 7717," *JThS* n.s. 32 (1981):176–178.

H

HADES. Abode or state of the dead prior to their eternal disposition at the last judgment. Although Hades is translated as "hell" in some English versions of the Bible, "hell" more properly translates *gehenna*, the true hell of everlasting punishment. Hades was originally the name of the Greek god of the underworld. Hellenistic Judaism, however, appropriated the term as the equivalent of the Hebrew *sheol*, the realm of the dead. *Sheol*-Hades was believed to be located in the heart of the earth (Ps. 26:5; Matt. 11:23; Luke 10:15). In the New Testament, Hades is the interim place of the dead between death and resurrection (Luke 16:23; Rev. 6:8; 1 Cor. 15:55; Rev. 20:14). At the last judgment, it is cast into *gehenna* (Rev. 20:14f.).

By Jesus' time, two main conceptions about Hades had arisen among the Jews and had passed into the New Testament literature. One school of thought held that all souls, both just and unjust, went to Hades but were separated into different locations in the underworld. The righteous went to a place of consolation; the unrighteous were tormented elsewhere. Such is the notion behind the parable of the rich man and Lazarus (Luke 16:19–31): Lazarus is carried by angels to "Abraham's bosom" while Dives suffers in fiery torment. A second view held that only the souls of the ungodly went to Hades; the righteous went to "paradise" (Luke 23:43) or to be "with the Lord" (2 Cor. 5:8).

According to Irenaeus (ca. 115–ca. 202), the Gnostics substituted a belief that righteous souls bypassed Hades and went straight to heaven in place of a belief in the resurrection from the dead (Haer. 5.31.1–2)—a teaching that was known also to Justin Martyr (*Dial.* 80). Irenaeus combated the Gnostics by looking to the experience of Christ. Upon his death, Jesus "dwelt in the place of the dead for three days." He was next resurrected and then ascended into heaven. Likewise, the souls of his disciples will first "sojourn to the invisible place allotted to them by God" and remain there until the resurrection. Only when they again "receive their bodies" and are resurrected will they enter into God's presence.

Hippolytus (ca. 170–ca. 236) wrote the first Christian descriptive geography of the underworld. In *On the Universe, Against the Greeks and Plato* 1, Hippolytus locates Hades beneath the earth, far removed from the light of the sun. Souls arriving at its one gate are separated by angels according to their righteousness. Just souls are conducted to the "right" and brought to a place of light called "Abraham's bosom." There, they glimpse their future heavenly reward and await their reception of it. They are not tormented but are at rest. The unrighteous, on the other hand, are dragged away to the left of the gate by angels. They are taken lower and lower into the depths until they are able to feel the "hot smoke" and see the flames of the lake of fire (*gehenna*), which is in the vicinity of Hades but is as yet uninhabited. The unrighteous "shudder" in terror at the expectation of their future judgment, while the remorse is enhanced by their ability to see the saints at rest in Abraham's bosom across the unbridgeable chasm that divides Hades.

Tertullian (ca. 160–ca. 225) also believed righteous and unrighteous souls would descend into Hades to await the resurrection. Some had argued that Christ's descent into Hades had freed the saints from the obligation of sojourning there when they died; rather, they could enter immediately into paradise. Tertullian denied that the just go to paradise immediately, with the exception of the martyrs, who did indeed bypass Hades. One's own lifeblood, Tertullian asserted, was "the only key to unlock paradise" (*Anim.* 55). Moreover, he believed that the time spent in Hades by the just was remedial in character. Souls underwent "some compensatory discipline" there while awaiting the resurrection and final judgment (*Anim.* 58; *Marc.* 4.34), and the intercession of the living could bring relief to the soul of the righteous departed (*Monog.* 10). Tertullian's opinion that the souls of some saints could escape Hades by their deeds in this life, that is, by martyrdom, while others had need of penitential cleansing in the afterlife before receiving their final reward, anticipated the doctrine of purgatory that would arise later in the west.

Origen (ca. 185–ca. 251) defined Hades as a dark underground place—the lowest of three levels of the world (heaven, earth, Hades)—which was the abode of demonic powers. His reading of 1 Corinthians 3:12–15, however, prevented him from accepting the traditional view that both saints and sinners

went to Hades. In his homily on 1 Samuel 28:3–25, Origen insisted that Christ's descent into Hades and subsequent resurrection were not a pattern to be followed by all believers (as Irenaeus had insisted) but represented the liberation of the righteous from incarceration in Hades. Henceforth, all righteous souls went immediately to paradise.

After Origen, speculation about Hades tended to wane in favor of a debate over the question of the nature of the punishment of the wicked. Gregory of Nyssa (ca. 330–395), perhaps expanding on Origen's spiritualized depiction of hell as a place filled with remorse and separated from God (*Princ.* 2.10.4), asserted that Hades was not a locality but a spiritual state, since souls were not corporeal and hence could not be confined in a place (*Anim. et res.* 37–40). Gregory the Great (ca. 540–604) agreed with the Alexandrians that the harrowing of Hades removed the need for the righteous to go there (*Moral.* 12.13). Finally, John of Damascus (ca. 675–749), reflecting the exalted status of the Virgin Mary in popular piety, denied that her soul was in Hades (*Carm. dorm. BVM* 1.12).

The question of Hades remained ambiguous in Christian thought. By the end of the fourth century, it was popularly believed that the punishment of the damned began immediately upon death and did not await the final judgment (Hilary of Poitiers, *In Psalm.* 51.22f.; 57.5; Jerome, *In Joel* 2.1; Augustine, *Praed. sanct.* 24). Speculation about an intermediate state between death and resurrection focused solely on the state of the redeemed. In the west, the doctrine of purgatory eventually evolved. The east, on the other hand, came to see sin not so much in terms of wrongful acts that required a period of penance in either this or the next life but as a moral and spiritual disease healable by divine grace. Thus, although not necessarily disagreeing with the Latins about the existence of an intermediate state between death and resurrection where the purgation of the soul took place, the east tended to be ambiguous about the particulars of the place or state. The west moved toward ever-greater precision in its understanding of the time after death and before the resurrection. *See also* Harrowing of Hell; Heaven; Hell; Purgatory. [A.L.C.]

Bibliography
R.H. Charles, A *Critical History of the Doctrine of a Future Life in Israel, in Judaism, and in Christianity,* 2nd ed. (London: Black, 1913); L. Prestige, "Hades in the Greek Fathers," *JThS* 24 (1922):476–485; M. Richard, "Enfer," *DTC* (1924), Vol. 5, pp. 27–119; A. Adam, "Hölle," *Lexikon für Theologie und Kirche* (Freiburg: Herder, 1960), Vol. 5, pp. 446–450; J. Jeremias, *"Hades,"* *Theological Dictionary of the New Testament,* ed. G. Kittel (Grand Rapids: Eerdmans, 1964), Vol. 1, pp. 146–149; H. Bietenhard, "Hell," *The New International Dictionary of New Testament Theology,* ed. C. Brown (Grand Rapids: Zondervan, 1976), Vol. 2, pp. 205–210; H. Crouzel, "Hades et la gehenne selon Origène," *Gregorianum* 50 (1978):291–331; G.A. Lee, "Hades," *International Standard Bible Encyclopedia,* ed. G.W. Bromiley (Grand Rapids: Eerdmans, 1982), Vol. 2, pp. 591–592; J. Le Goff, *The Birth of Purgatory* (Chicago: U of Chicago P, 1983).

HADRIAN (76–138).

Roman emperor (117–138). Upon his father's death (85), Hadrian became the ward of Trajan, the future emperor, whom he eventually succeeded. His policy was directed toward securing the frontiers of the empire; he spent much of his time in travel to that purpose. He abandoned his predecessor's conquests beyond the natural eastern boundary, the Euphrates, and built Hadrian's Wall in Britain (122–126). The failure of the revolt of Bar Kochba in Judea (131–135) brought to an end Jewish hopes for the restoration of Israel until modern times. In an imperial rescript to Minucius Fundanus, the proconsul of Asia, Hadrian attempted to ensure due process for Christians in court and to check the activities of informers. Despite the general tolerance of his reign, a number of Christians suffered martyrdom, probably including the Roman bishop Telesphorus (ca. 136), unless, as stated by Eusebius (*H.E.* 4.10), he died under Antoninus Pius. [M.P.McH.]

Bibliography
Eusebius, *Church History* 4.3–6, 8–10.

B.W. Henderson, *The Life and Principate of the Emperor Hadrian* (London: Methuen, 1923); S. Perowne, *Hadrian* (London: Hodder and Stoughton, 1960); C. Gonzalez Roman, "Problemas sociales y política religiosa: A propósitio ·de los rescriptos de Trajano, Adriano y Antonino Pio sobre los cristianos," *MHA* 5 (1981):227–242; S. Applebaum, The Second Jewish Revolt (AD 131–135)," *PEQ* 116 (1984):35–41; M.T. Boatwright, *Hadrian and the City of Rome* (Princeton: Princeton UP, 1987).

HAGIA SOPHIA.

Justinian I's church in Constantinople, still extant. The most famous church building of antiquity, Hagia Sophia is a domed basilica constructed between 532 and 537. The impact on the visitor comes from the spaciousness of the building. In its present form—the dome has fallen more than once, minarets were added by Turkish conquerors and the forecourt removed—the church is a 220-by-250-foot structure whose dome rises 180 feet from the floor. The inner chamber rests on 104 monolithic columns, which tilt inward, giving more emphasis to the building's height.

An earlier structure, started by Constantine, had stood on the spot. Completed in 360 and also called Hagia Sophia at a later date, it was burned during the Nika revolt in 532. Anthemius of Tralles and Isidore of Miletus planned the new building and are responsible for the concept of so large a domed basilica. One hundred foremen oversaw the work of artisans assembled from all over the empire. Some 40,000 pounds of silver were fashioned into its furnishings, a golden altar held the central place, and marble floors reflected the building's beauty. Both Paul the Silentiary and Procopius provide rich descriptions of its appearance. The earliest mosaics contained patterns and at least one cross. The lovely ones now partially restored date from the ninth century, after the Iconoclastic controversy was resolved. [F.W.N.]

Bibliography
Paul the Silentiary, *Descriptio S. Sophiae;* idem, *Descriptio ambonis* 50ff.; Procopius, *Buildings* 1.1.22ff.; Evagrius, *Church History* 4.31; Agathias, *Historiarum* 5.9.2–5.

R.L. Van Nice, *Saint Sophia in Istanbul: An Architectural Survey, Installments I and II* (Washington, D.C.: Dumbarton Oaks, 1966 and 1986); T. Klauser, "Hagia Sophia," *JAC* 13 (1970):107–118; T. Mathews, *The Early Churches of Constantinople: Architecture and Liturgy* (University Park: Pennsylvania State UP, 1971); C. Mango, *The Art of the*

Church of Hagia Sophia in Istanbul, Turkey, from the south, now a museum. Built 532–537 under the emperor Justinian and dedicated to Christ as the "Holy Wisdom."

Byzantine Empire 312–1453 (New York: Prentice-Hall, 1972); idem, Byzantine Architecture (New York: Rizzoli International, 1985); R. Mainstone, Hagia Sophia: Architecture, Structure and Liturgy of Justinian's Great Church (London: Thames and Hudson, 1988).

HAGIOGRAPHY. Greek term for writing (graphē) about saints (hagioi), to inspire remembrance and imitation of their lives and deeds. The honoring of saints has played a central role in Christian practice and spirituality. Christianity considers all persons baptized in the Trinity as saints. Paul called all Christians saints, and he addressed his letters "to the saints of such and such city. . . ." Holiness in the Christian tradition is not an abstract notion and goal but an incarnate reality, manifested and witnessed to in the life of Christians. A Christian is an imitator of a life of witness, holiness, and even sacrifice, in the example of Christ. Ignatius, bishop of Antioch (d. ca. 110), died as a martyr "so as not only to be called, but to be found to be a Christian as well" (Ignatius, Rom. 2.1; 3.2). To the earliest Christians, martyrdom was another form of baptism, a baptism of blood, through which one rises into the life of eternity and incor-

ruptibility. Thus, martyrs and those who die in Christ do not perish but live with him forever. The church then is a communion of saints, living and "fallen asleep" alike.

The drive to remember, honor, and imitate the lives of martyrs led to the designation of the anniversary of their death as a special day, which was actually called "birthday" (Greek genēthlios hēmera, Latin natale). Such a commemoration was marked by liturgical celebrations on the tombs of martyrs and accompanied by a reading of narratives of their life and death. The need for and attraction of such material is manifested by the proliferation of legendary Acts of Christ and of apostles produced in the apocryphal literature, although the canonical Acts of the Apostles can be considered as the first hagiography. The accounts of Christian martyrdoms may be divided into three groups, Acta or Gesta (accounts of trials and condemnations written for the purpose of spiritual reading and edification), Passiones or Martyria (descriptions of the martyr's life and death by eyewitnesses or trustworthy contemporaries), and Martyr's Legends (legendary stories and narratives of later times). It was the Acta that were mainly read on the anniversary celebrations at the tombs of martyrs. Written in the hundreds during the fourth and fifth centuries, they contain a historical core, although such *Acta* must be studied critically when used as historical documents.

Having survived the persecutions and emerged victorious, the church in the fourth century started taking stock of its heroes and martyrs; the result was the compilation of abridged lives and lessons of saints in order of their appearance in the calendar for liturgical purposes throughout the ecclesiastical year. These collections are known by such names as *depositiones* and *martyrologia* in the Latin church, or *synaxaria* ("gatherings") and *menaea* ("monthly liturgical books") in the Greek.

Because physical martyrdom as an ultimate act of imitation of Christ was not always possible, monasticism—dying to the world, and living for Christ—became an alternative to martyrdom and another kind of baptism—the baptism of tears (of repentance). Martyrs became the prototypes for ascetics, contemplatives, and defenders of the orthodox faith. To them, the lives of martyrs and saints were records of paramount importance. No wonder, therefore, that monastic communities became centers for hagiography. Asceticism and monasticism constitute an imitation of the life of martyrs and a continuation of their tradition—thus, the acknowledgment as saints of saintly men and women from the monastic community. In the fourth century, there were even some zealots, like the Eustathians, who went so far as to maintain that the true saints were the ascetics and monks who suffered not for a moment as did the martyrs, but for life. Monasteries became places where the lives of martyrs, spiritual masters, fathers of the church, and other confessors of faith, both men and women, were intensely remembered and celebrated.

Lives of saints constituted the main reading material in refectories of monasteries during meals, on festive occasions, and especially on the name day of a saint. The *Life of Anthony* by Athanasius (ca. 300–373) became a blueprint for such hagiographies. The *Lausiac History* of Palladius (d. ca. 430) is a hagiography of saintly monks. Sozomen (early fifth century) and Theodoret of Cyrus (ca. 393–ca. 466) compiled legends of monks and the miracles they performed. The east produced far more lives of saints than did the west. Saints' lives took the form of narratives, homilies, and sermons, as well as hymns for easier memorization by the populace and for use in liturgical services. Hagiography is intrinsically related to hymnology.

It was also related to iconography. Depiction of the martyrdoms and the lives of saints in painted icons is another early Christian tradition. Icons retell a sacred story through colors. (The word *graphē* in fact means both writing and painting, and the word *historeō*, composing a story, refers to both written and painted narratives.) It was no surprise, therefore, that eighth-century iconoclasm turned with vehemence against both the making of icons and the honoring of saints, the monasteries becoming the key target of the iconoclasts. In the Eastern Orthodox world, "hagiography" means narration of something sacred by means of either writing or painting. As the *synodikon* of the Council of Constantinople (843) states, ". . .we confess Christ our true God and his holy saints: to honor them by means of words, of writings, of gestures, of sacrifices, of churches, of icons." The honoring of saints and the retelling of their lives form a comprehensive expression of the church that is not limited to writing.

The study of saints' lives has been enhanced by the specialist work of the Bollandists. *See also* Bollandus, John; Martyrs; Monasticism; Saints.   [D.J.S.]

Bibliography
W.H.C. Frend, *Martyrdom and Persecution in the Early Church* (Garden City: Doubleday, 1967); H. Delehaye, *The Legends of the Saints: An Introduction to Hagiography* (Norwood: Norwood, 1974); P. Brown, *The Cult of the Saints: Its Rise and Function in Latin Christianity* (Chicago: U of Chicago P, 1981); S. Wilson, ed., *Saints and Their Cults: Studies in Religious Sociology, Folklore, and History* (New York: Cambridge UP, 1984); D.J. Sahas, *Icon and Logos: Sources in Eighth-Century Iconoclasm* (Toronto: U of Toronto P, 1986); A.G. Elliott, *Roads to Paradise: Reading the Lives of the Early Saints* (Hanover: UP of New England, 1987).

HALO. Luminous disc or circle surrounding the head or body of a divinity or semidivine figure in iconography and art. The halo, perhaps originally a protective device for statues, became symbolic of divinity during the Hellenistic period. It is found in Greco-Roman mosaics depicting Jupiter, Apollo, Venus, and other gods or demigods.

The earliest extant examples of the halo in Christian usage are in the Roman catacombs, where it indicates symbols of Christ, such as a ship's pilot, Jonah, a shepherd, and eventually is applied to depictions of Christ himself. It appears in later iconography on the apostles, saints, and the Virgin Mary. Christ's halo came to be differentiated by the addition of the Greek letters *alpha* and *omega*, one on each side of his head. The halo became a standard feature of Christian art and iconography. It generally disappeared from western art during the Renaissance but remains in Orthodox iconography.

[D.B.]

Bibliography

A. Krucke, *Der Nimbus und verwandte Attribute in der frühchristlichen Kunst* (Strassburg: Heitz, 1905); J. Wilpert, *Die römischen Mosaiken und*

Bust of bearded Christ with halo (nimbus) and Greek letters alpha and omega. Catacomb of Commodilla, Rome, mid-fourth century.
(Used by permission of Pontifical Commission of Sacred Archaeology.)

Malereien der kirchlichen Bauten vom 4. bis 13. Jahrhundert (Freiburg: Herder, 1917); M. C. Guerin, *Histoire du nimbe des origines aux temps modernes* (Paris: Latines, 1961).

HARNACK, ADOLF VON (1851–1930). German Protestant church historian and theologian. Harnack's historical studies often brought him into disagreement with the German Lutheran Church, although he himself saw no conflict between his work and belief. His undergraduate years were spent at Dorpat and Leipzig. The latter university offered him a professorship after the completion of his doctorate and Habilitationsschrift. In his five years there (1874–1879), he published over ninety articles and books. During his professorship at Giessen (1879–1886) and then at Marburg (1886–1888), he wrote his *History of Dogma* (3 vols.; Freiburg: Mohr, 1885–1889; Engl. tr. London: Williams and Norgate, 1896–1899). That work, heavily influenced by Albrecht Ritschl's interpretation of the gospel as one of virtue and morality, is a classic and by 1909 had appeared in its fourth edition. Yet its publication created problems for Harnack. When the University of Berlin offered him a chair in 1888, it did so over the objections of the Lutheran Church Senate. In 1900, he wrote the influential *What Is Christianity?* (Leipzig: Hinrichs, 1901; Engl. tr. London: Williams and Norgate, 1901), a classic of liberal Protestantism, as well as the history of the Prussian Academy of Science, of which he was a member, on the occasion of its 200th anniversary. He was more than once snubbed by the church but was frequently honored by the academy. One branch of the church, however, did recognize his importance; he served as president of the Lutheran Social Congress, 1903–1911.

In many ways, Harnack embodied the modern beginnings of patristic studies. His *Patrum Apostolicorum Opera* (3 vols.; 1875–1877), written with O. von Gebhardt and Theodore Zahn, laid the foundations for such investigations. His *Geschichte der altchristlichen Literatur bis Eusebius* (2 vols.; Leipzig: Hinrichs, 1893 and 1903; 2nd ed. 1958) has proved to be a standard for questions of chronology and background. With Theodor

Mommsen, he helped found a commission on the church fathers that published editions of the Greek fathers from the first three centuries. Often referred to as the Berlin Corpus, *Die griechischen christlichen Schriftsteller* has only recently fallen on hard times, as East Germany has not viewed it as a priority; counting the editions replaced with reprints or updated works, it has produced over sixty volumes. Equally important was the foundation with O. von Gebhardt of the series *Texte und Untersuchungen zur Geschichte der altchristlichen Literatur*, which continues to publish and has now issued over 130 volumes. *Theologische Literaturzeitung*, started with E. Schürer, still publishes articles and reviews and in 1989 was in its 114th year.

Certain of Harnack's own studies have become standards. His *Mission and Expansion of Christianity in the First Three Centuries* (Leipzig: Hinrichs, 1902 and 1924; Engl. tr. London: Williams and Norgate, 1908) assembled so many data and offered so many solid interpretations that it is still the beginning point for church and social historians, although it must be supplemented. His *Marcion* (Leipzig: Hinrichs, 1924) is only now being superseded by modern scholarship, but it still possesses worth as the major work on its subject.

[F.W.N.]

Bibliography

G.W. Glick, *The Reality of Christianity* (New York: Harper and Row, 1967); W. Pauck, *Harnack and Troeltsch: Two Historical Theologians* (New York: Oxford UP, 1968); E.P. Meijering, *Theologische Urteile über die Dogmengeschichte: Ritschl's Einfluss auf von Harnack* (Leiden: Brill, 1978); W. Dobertin, *Adolf von Harnack: Theologe, Pädagoge, Wissenschaftspolitiker* (Frankfurt: Lang, 1985).

HARROWING OF HELL. Medieval English term for Christ's descent into Hades understood as the moment of his victory over Satan and conquest of the powers of death and evil (the episode is included, for example, in several English mystery-play cycles). In early Christianity, Christ's descent was widely, perhaps universally, affirmed as a point of belief. Its meaning, however, was interpreted in a variety of ways; and no one view appears to have become dominant or to have excluded the others.

Christ's descent, in the three-day interval (the *triduum*) between his death and resurrection, seems to be stated or implied in several New Testament texts (e.g., Matt. 12:40; Acts 2:24, 27, 31; Rom. 10:7; Eph. 4:9; Col. 1:18 [the well-known 1 Peter 3:18 and 4:6 are more ambiguous cases; cf. Augustine, *Ep.* 164]); and it appears to have echoes in certain writings of the apostolic fathers (Ignatius, *Magn.* 9.2 [and *Philad.* 9.1?]; Polycarp, *Ep.* 1.2; and perhaps Hermas, *Sim.* 9.16). By the end of the second century, it was apparently known to at least some pagans as a Christian belief (Origen, *Cels.* 2.43). In the fourth century, it began to acquire creedal status, first perhaps in Syriac Christianity, although no known examples survive (but cf. Eusebius, *H.E.* 1.13.20), and then, in the Greek arena, in the fourth formula of Sirmium (the "Dated Creed" of 359) and the conciliar creed produced at Constantinople in 360 (these had an Arian tinge, however, and none passed into general use). In the Latin west, the descent appeared first in the baptismal creed of the Italian see of Aquileia (Rufinus, *Symb.* 18; 28) and then in the widely circulated Apostles' and Athanasian Creeds. For Augustine, despite his own uncertainties about its meaning, it was a traditional and undeniable article of belief (*Ep.* 164.3, 14).

Interpretations of the descent varied widely. It could mean simply that Christ died (Rufinus, *Symb.* 18), following the universal rule of human death (Irenaeus, *Haer.* 5.31.1–2; Tertullian, *Anim.* 55), and that God released him from death's hold (Acts 2:24, 27, 31). In the second century, correlated with a spurious verse from Jeremiah, it was included in the pattern of Old Testament prophecy and New Testament fulfillment that was taken to show that Christ was no mere man, but the very Word of God and the realization of God's ancient purposes (Justin, *Dial.* 72; Irenaeus, *Haer.* 3.20.4; 4.33.1; *Dem.* 78). An earlier and more enduring version of the pattern correlated the descent with various texts from the Psalms (Acts 2:24–31; Irenaeus, *Haer.* 5.31.1; Rufinus, *Symb.* 28; Augustine, *Ep.* 164.3).

In one prominent interpretation (perhaps sparked by a phrase in the pseudo-Jeremiah text: "he descended to preach the gospel"), Christ descended to proclaim salvation to those who had lived justly before his coming, both Jew and Greek, but had died without faith (Irenaeus, *Haer.* 4.22.1–2; Clement of Alexandria, *Str.* 6.6.44–51; cf. Origen, *Cels.* 2.43), thus providing an opportunity for repentance to those who had preceded as well as to those who succeeded him in time (but note Augustine's objections to this view, *Ep.* 164.12). The descent was also understood to have brought release from the pangs of hell to prominent Old Testament figures who in one way or another had anticipated Christ, especially Adam, the patriarchs, and the prophets, including John the Baptist (Ignatius, *Philad.* 9.1?; Origen, *Hom.* 15 *in Gen.* 5; Cyril of Jerusalem, *Catech.* 4.11; 14.19; Augustine, *Ep.* 164.6 [but also the questions he poses in sections 7–9]). Finally, the descent was construed to represent Christ's victory over death and over Satan as holding the power of death (Origen, *Hom.* 17 *in Gen.* 5; Cyril of Jerusalem, *Catech.* 14.17–19), after which, as "first-born of the dead" (Col. 1:18), he led forth his saints as a mighty band (also Irenaeus, *Dem.* 39; Clement of Alexandria, *Str.* 6.6.47; and cf. Eusebius, *H.E.* 1.13.20)—although Tertullian insisted that heaven would not be opened until the end-time (*Anim.* 55). The *Gospel of Nicodemus*, possibly dating from the fourth century, combined the last two of these interpretations in what was certainly the most dramatic early Christian presentation of Christ's descent and also the most immediate early Christian ancestor of the medieval versions of the harrowing of hell.

Stories of descent into the underworld were also told, of course, of Greek and Roman heroes and gods, such as Odysseus, Hercules, Persephone, and Aeneas. But the accounts of Christ's descent bear faint, if any, relation to these; they show no interest, for example, in either his journey to or his journey from hell. It is probably best to say that they represent a specifically Christian theme, widely adopted but never fully or consistently elaborated in the early period.   [W.S.B.]

Bibliography

Irenaeus, *Against Heresies* 3.20.4; 4.22.1–2; 4.33.1; 5.31.1–2; Tertullian, *On the Soul* 7; 55; Clement of Alexandria, *Miscellanies* 6.6.44–51; Cyril of Jerusalem, *Catechetical Lectures* 4.11; 14.17–20; Augustine, *Letter* 164; *Gospel of Nicodemus*.

R.H. Connolly, "The Early Syriac Creed," *ZNTW* 7 (1906):202–223; F. Loofs, "Descent to Hades (Christ's)," *Encyclopedia of Religion and Ethics*, ed. J. Hastings (New York: Scribner, 1912), Vol. 4, pp. 654–663; J.A. MacCulloch, *The Harrowing of Hell: A Comparative Study of an Early Christian Doctrine* (Edinburgh: T. and T. Clark, 1930); J. Kroll, *Gott und Hölle: Der Mythos vom Descensuskampfe* (Leipzig and Berlin: Teubner, 1932); H. Quilliet, "Descente de Jésus aux enfers," *DTC* (1939), Vol. 4, pp. 565–619; B. Reicke, *The Disobedient Spirits and Christian Baptism: A Study of 1 Pet. III.19 and Its Context* (Copenhagen: Munksgaard, 1946); W. Bieder, *Die Vorstellung von der Höllenfahrt Jesu Christi* (Zurich: Zwingli Verlag, 1949); A. Grillmeier, "Der Gottessohn im Totenreich," *Zeitschrift für katholische Theologie* 71 (1949):1–53, 184–203; A. Cabaniss, "The Harrowing of Hell, Psalm 24, and Pliny the Younger," *VChr* 7 (1953):65–74; J.N.D. Kelly, *Early Christian Creeds*, 3rd ed. (New York: McKay, 1972); P. Happé, ed., *English Mystery Plays* (Harmondsworth: Penguin, 1975); D. Sheerin, "St. John the Baptist in the Lower World," *VChr* 30 (1976):1–22.

HEALING, RELIGIOUS. Overcoming bodily weakness or disease by divine power. Religious healing was as persistent a feature of early Christianity as of the pagan religious cults of the Greco-Roman world. Not surprisingly, the terms used for healing through the power of Christ were the same as those appearing in other religions of the time, as well as in contemporary medical practice. The Greek word *iaomai* broadly referred to the occurrence of healing or curing (Matt. 8:5–10; Mark 5:29; Luke 5:17; cf. Justin, *2 Apol.* 6.6; Origen, *Cels.* 5.58; Athanasius, *Inc.* 18.4), and *therapeuō* to the provision of healing or curing (Matt. 4:23–24; Mark 1:13–14; 4:23; cf. Justin, *1 Apol.* 18; Tatian, *Orat.* 16; Origen, *Cels.* 2.45; Athanasius, *Inc.* 49.1); these terms, however, were in practice used interchangeably, as were other terms that had broader meanings: *hygiainō* was used of having or receiving good health (Matt. 12:13; Mark 3:5; Luke 5:31), and *sōzō* of saving in the sense of preserving or rescuing from serious illness or death (Matt.

9:21–22; Mark 5:23; Luke 7:3). The latter terms tended later to be taken up into more spiritualized conceptions of health and salvation (but cf. *1 Clem.* 59.4; Justin, *Dial.* 91.4; 112.1; Basil, *Hom. in Ps.* 7). Such modern derivatives as "therapy," "hygiene," and even "saving" retain the same range of meanings when used of the curing and prevention of disease.

Accounts of healings, from an early time (John 20:30f.), were designed to elicit faith or were said to have done so (1 Cor. 2:4; 2 Cor. 12:12; Acts 2:43; 3:6–10; 5:12–16; 9:32–35; 14:3; *A. Paul.* 50–55; *A. Jo.* 38–45). Healings by those awaiting martyrdom (e.g., Eusebius, *Mart. Pal.* 1.1; *Pass. Perp.* 9.1; 16.4) and by ascetics (e.g., Athanasius, *V. Ant.* 80; Gregory of Nyssa, *V. Gr. Thaum.* PG 46.916A; Jerome, *V. Hilar.* 8.8) were frequent. Bishop Novatian of Rome was said to have been converted through being healed (Eusebius, *H.E.* 6.43.14). The phenomenon of healing was an important factor in the growth of the church.

At the same time, evidence of difficulty with those who used the name of Christ simply as a technique for healing was already seen in the account of the seven sons of Sceva (Acts 19:13–17; cf. 8:9–13). Celsus summarizes the intellectual pagan view of Jesus as a trickster whose disciples led astray the uninformed (Origen, *Cels.* 3.52), and Origen's careful treatment of healings is written with this charge in mind (*Cels.*, 1.46; 3.71ff.). The early designation of the elders of the church as the appropriate healers (James 5:14–16) may be read in this context. Moreover, although Hippolytus (*Trad. ap.* 1.5) says that those with power to heal are to be acknowledged but not ordained, mention of the gift of healing is made in later ordination prayers (*Const. app.* 8.16, 26); baptismal exorcisms and the eucharistic communion are also noticed as occasions of healing (Tertullian, *Bapt.* 5; Cyprian, *Ep.* 75.15; Irenaeus, *Haer.* 4.18.2; 5.2.2). Some concern to contain or regularize indiscriminate healing stands alongside general acceptance of the phenomenon.

Christian interpretation of healings proceeds on the common assumption that illness results from possession by demons or acquies-

cence in the powers of evil. Healings done by Jesus or in his name are marks of the inbreaking of the power of the kingdom of God or of release from the bondage of sin (Matt. 12:27–28; Mark 3:22–27; Luke 4:31–37; cf. Matt. 10:7–16; Mark 6:8–11; Luke 10:3–12). For Paul, those who have the power to heal are taken together with those who can preach, prophesy, speak with tongues, and the like, as possessing *charismata* or gifts of the Holy Spirit poured out in the last days for the recreation of humanity through Christ (1 Cor. 12:9). Elaboration of these themes throughout the period stresses healings as evidence of the continuation of the saving work of Christ (Justin, *2 Apol.* 13; *Dial.* 17; 30; Irenaeus, *Haer.* 3.18.4; 4.20.2; 5.3.1ff.; Origen, *Cels.* 7.32; Cyprian, *Ep.* 74.2; 76.2), of the goodness of the body (Justin, *1 Apol.* 18ff.; Tatian, *Orat.* 6; 16; 20; Theophilus, *Autol.* 1.7; 2.26; Irenaeus, *Haer.* 5.12.6; Origen, *Cels.* 5.19), and of the possibility of its resurrection (Tertullian, *Resurr.* 12; Gregory of Nyssa, *Hom. opif.* 25.6ff.; Augustine, *Civ. Dei* 22.5, 8ff.). Healings thus witness to God's purpose to free the whole creation for eternal life with him.

In general, early Christian writers assumed that healings were manifestations of the redemptive power of God; they were more concerned to keep them in this perspective than, as in our time, either to promote healings as central to Christian experience or to deny their occurrence. *See also* Anointing.   [L.G.P.]

Bibliography

A. von Harnack, *The Mission and Expansion of Christianity in the First Three Centuries* (London: Williams and Norgate, 1908), pp. 101–124; C.H. Harris, "Visitation of the Sick," *Liturgy and Worship*, ed. W.K. Lowther Clarke (London: SPCK, 1932), pp. 472–540; S.V. McCasland, *By the Finger of God* (New York: Macmillan, 1951); R.M. Grant, *Miracle and Natural Law in Graeco-Roman and Early Christian Thought* (Amsterdam: North-Holland, 1952); J. Kallas, The *Significance of the Gospel Miracles* (New York: Seabury, 1961); B. Poschmann, *Penance and the Anointing of the Sick* (New York: Herder and Herder, 1964); R. MacMullen, *Christianizing the Roman Empire (A.D. 100–400)* (New Haven: Yale UP, 1984); H.C. Kee, *Medicine, Miracle, and Magic in Early Christian Times* (Cambridge: Cambridge UP, 1986).

HEAVEN. Dwelling-place of God and the angels and the ultimate place or state of eternal reward for the redeemed. In scripture, heaven is principally God's sphere, so much so that postexilic Judaism began the practice—frequent also in the New Testament—of using "heaven" as an alternative for "God" (Dan. 4:23; Luke 15:21; Matt. 21:25; 23:22; John 3:27). Hellenistic influences in the apostolic church's concept of heaven are evidenced in Paul's notion of a series of heavens (Eph. 4:10; 2 Cor. 12:2–4) and in the idea that heaven is a place of great conflict between the demonic powers that populate some of its regions and the saints and angelic host (Eph. 6:12; Rom. 8:38; Rev. 12:7–9). Ultimately, the New Testament looks forward to the creation of a new heaven and a new earth. Then will the New Jerusalem descend to earth from heaven and inalienably establish God's presence and glory upon earth (Rev. 21:1–14).

As the goal of the Christian's salvation, the fulfillment of all spiritual desire and yearning, heaven was of widespread interest in ancient Christianity. Early on, it was conceived of as a place where the believer enjoyed an ultraterrestrial life full of joy that was human in character. Scenes from the catacombs in Rome depict heavenly life as a banquet or as a landscape filled with playing children; and funerary inscriptions refer to the deceased as "gone to God," "living with Christ," or as "refreshed and joyful among the stars."

By the end of the fourth century, the indescribable joy of heaven was defined less in terms of sensual delights and more in terms of the beatifying (in the west) or deifying (in the east) vision of God. As early as the second century, Clement of Alexandria had spoken of heaven as the place where the elect receive from Christ the vision of God (*Str.* 5.1; *Prot.* 1.97). For Gregory of Nazianzus (ca. 329–390), heaven represents the end of a journey and the beginning of a new life. There, the Christian pilgrim finds complete release from life's vicissitudes (*Or.* 16.9; 40.5), and tastes in full what only could be sampled in this life: the knowledge of God, nearness to the divine presence, and joyful life in Christ (*Or.* 7.17; 8.23). It is

in this future heavenly life that believers fully become what they were meant to be when they were created in the divine image (*Or.* 2.22; 28.17; 38.11–12).

A prominent issue in the development of a doctrine of heaven in the early church was whether the tension between the current manifestation of the kingdom of God in the world and the future revelation of that kingdom carried over into the realm of the departed souls. God's kingdom, as taught by Jesus and transmitted through the apostolic teaching, was both already present and not yet revealed. Between these two poles oscillates the Christian life. Did death stop the oscillation or was it continued into the afterlife? Christians were convinced from the beginning that death ushered them into the presence of God and Christ, but at that moment did they find in that presence the final consummation of their hope or were they still awaiting the complete revelation of the kingdom?

Critically important to the church's answer was its understandings of the last judgment and the resurrection from the dead. By the second century, Christ was being referred to in formulas as the coming "judge of the living and the dead" (Acts 10:42; 1 Peter 4:5; 2 Tim. 4:1; Polycarp, *Ep.* 2.1; *Barn.* 7.2; *2 Clem.* 1.1). But when did the judgment of the dead take place? The Book of Revelation said it was at the end of time, when death and Hades would give up the dead and the eternal disposition of every soul would be determined on the basis of inclusion in the book of life (Rev. 20:11–15). However, the parable of the rich man and Lazarus (Luke 16:19–31) implied that some sort of judgment took place at death that resulted in rest for the righteous and punishment for the wicked. Tertullian (ca. 160–ca. 225) knew of eucharistic commemorations for the dead wherein prayers were offered for their repose, refreshment, and/or peace (*Anim.* 51; *Monog.* 10; *Coron.* 3). Moreover, there are hints of an idea of an individual judgment immediately after death in writings from the early second century (*1 Clem.* 5.4–7; 6.1–2; 50.3–4; *M. Polyc.* 17.1), although the church in the main taught that judgment lay in the future. But by the beginning of the fifth century, the idea of an individual judgment seemed to be the majority position. For Augustine (354–430), a judgment took place at the moment of death that anticipated the verdict of the final judgment (*Enchir.* 109–110; *In evang. Ioh.* 49.10; *Gen. ad litt.* 12.32).

Did the particular judgment at death usher the soul of the believer into complete heavenly bliss? Since the apostolic age, the church consistently had maintained that full and complete salvation included the resurrection from the dead. Life in heaven, in some way, was to be a life lived in a body (*Barn.* 5.7; 21.1; Irenaeus, *Haer.* 1.10.1; 3.9.1; 5.13.2–3; 5.20.1; *1 Clem.* 49.6; *2 Clem.* 9.1–5; Justin, *Dial.* 80; Tertullian, *Resurr.*). This notion was established firmly in the east with the settling of a dispute over the nature of the resurrected body. Origen (ca. 185–ca. 251) had taught that the resurrected body, although identical in "form" with the material body, is actually of a wholly different quality. All that unites the two bodies is a "seed," present in the material body, from which the resurrected, spiritual body is germinated (*Princ.* 2.10.3). Origen's ideas were soundly rejected by Peter of Alexandria (d. 311) and Methodius of Olympus (d. ca. 311). Thereafter, it was impossible to maintain anything less than the complete identity of the material body with the resurrected one. Consequently, in the east complete salvation had to await the day of resurrection. Basil of Caesarea (ca. 330–379), for instance, asserted that it was only after the saints had become the "sons of the resurrection" that they could obtain the "face to face" knowledge of God presently enjoyed by the angels (*Hom. in Ps.* 33.11).

In the west, on the other hand, the relation of the general resurrection to the attainment of salvation was less clear. Augustine taught that although resurrection from the dead would enhance the joys of salvation already available to the departed soul, it was not a precondition for completely realizing the heavenly reward; the departed soul could enjoy the beatifying presence of the Godhead without being reunited to the body in resurrection (*Ep.*

164; 187.3, 6–7; *Retract.* 1.14(13).2; *In evang. Ioh.* 49.10; cf. *Ps.* 36.10).

Left unanswered was the question of the relationship of a developing doctrine of purgatory to the notion that the saints were granted the complete vision of God upon death. Augustine divided humanity into three types: the good, the evil, and those in between (*Enchir.* 110). He believed the souls of the latter could benefit from the celebration of the eucharist or from the giving of alms in their remembrance (*Enchir.* 110; *Anim.* 15; *Civ. Dei* 21.24). It is unclear, however, where those souls are. Augustine admitted in one place that Abraham's bosom and paradise (the traditional abode of such souls) might be different names for heaven itself (*Gen. ad litt.* 1.12) and argued in another that Christ's soul had no need to descend into Abraham's bosom after the crucifixion since the souls there were already enjoying the beatifying presence of the Godhead (*Ep.* 164.3, 8). Not until 1336 would the matter be cleared up in the west, when pope Benedict XII in the bull *Benedictus Deus* asserted that the individual judgment at death admitted the soul immediately either to the beatific vision in heaven, to purgatory, or to hell. *See also* Hades; Hell; Judgment; Martyrdom; Purgatory; Resurrection; Salvation.   [A.L.C.]

Bibliography

U. Simon, *Heaven in the Christian Tradition* (New York: Harper, 1958); H. Traub, *"Ouranos," Theological Dictionary of the New Testament,* ed. G. Friedrich (Grand Rapids: Eerdmans, 1967), Vol. 5, pp. 497–543; J. A. Mourant, *Augustine on Immortality* (Philadelphia: Villanova UP, 1969); R.H. Mounce, *The Book of Revelation* (Grand Rapids: Eerdmans, 1977); Kelly, pp. 459–489; D.F. Winslow, *The Dynamics of Salvation: A Study in Gregory of Nazianzus* (Cambridge: Philadelphia Patristic Foundation, 1979); D.W. Lotz, "Heaven and Hell in the Christian Tradition," *Religion in Life* 48 (1979):77–92; R. Attwell, "Aspects in St. Augustine of Hippo's Thought and Spirituality Concerning the State of the Faithful Departed, 354–430," *The End of Strife,* ed. D. Loades (Edinburgh: T. and T. Clark, 1984), pp. 3–13; A. Clayton, "The Orthodox Recovery of a Heretical Proof-Text: Athanasius of Alexandria's Interpretation of Proverbs 8:22–30 in Conflict with the Arians" (Ph.D. diss., Southern Methodist University, 1988), pp. 85–95.

HEBREWS, EPISTLE TO THE. New Testament book. The document known as the Epistle of Paul to the Hebrews is neither an epistle, nor is it by Paul, nor is it necessarily to "Hebrews." It is rather a homily, with a short epistolary conclusion. Although speculation has continued since the early church, there is no solid evidence about the author, who remains anonymous. Its addressees are equally obscure. The work's closest affiliations are to documents emanating from Rome, and it is likely that the work was addressed to Roman Christians sometime in the last third of the first century. Attempts to be more precise about the date, particularly on the basis of its cultic arguments, are unpersuasive.

This homily aims to revitalize the faith of a congregation some of whose members have become disaffected (10:25). This situation probably had complex causes, including persecution (10:32–34; 12:3; 13:3), doubt occasioned by delay of the coming "day" (10:25), and Judaizing pressure (13:9). Hebrews responds by exhorting its audience to hold fast (3:14) with faithful endurance (10:36–12:13) and issues stern warnings against apostasy (2:1–4; 6:4–8; 10:26–31; 12:14–17).

Hebrews' rhetorical strategy involves not only exhortation but also reflection on Christ and his salvific work. It develops traditions known to the addressees and labeled their "confession" (3:1; 4:14). These included affirmations about Christ as the eternal Son (1:3), become incarnate to lead his brethren to heavenly glory (2:5–10), and, as Psalm 110 suggests, exalted after death to God's right hand (1:5–14), where he functions as priestly intercessor (2:17–18).

These affirmations are creatively interpreted in Hebrews' central exposition. The heavenly character of the priestly Son is affirmed in Chapter 7 through exegesis of Psalm 110:4. The verse, otherwise ignored in early Christianity, speaks of a priest "after the order of Melchizedek." Inspired by speculation on the mysterious biblical figure, Hebrews takes the remark to refer to the eternal realm. An elaborate exposition in Chapters 8–10 begins with Christ as priest in a heavenly temple (8:1–6) but ultimately interprets his "heavenly" offering as conformity to God's will in a bodily self-sacrifice (10:1–10). His death established a sanctifying covenant in which sins are truly forgiven, access to God provided (10:11–20), and the meaning of faithful endurance exemplified (12:1–13).

The first use of Hebrews, in *1 Clement*, develops the priestly imagery, but with an interest in church office. Tertullian, in his Montanist phase, found the rigorism of Hebrews appealing, although he maintained that Barnabas was the author (*Pud.* 20). Similar skepticism about the apostolicity of Hebrews characterized the west down to the fourth century. The Alexandrians, Clement and Origen, appreciated Hebrews for its handling of scripture and its image of Christ as the first martyr. They preserve the tradition of Pauline authorship with theories of an assistant or translator (Eusebius, *H.E.* 3.38.1; 6.25.14). The high Christology of Hebrews contributed to the controversies of the fourth century. This most elaborate homily inspired further homiletic reflection, particularly by John Chrysostom (PG 63). [H.W.A.]

Bibliography

John Chrysostom, *Homilies on Hebrews*, tr. T. Keble, NPNF, 2nd ser. (1889), Vol. 14; Cyril of Alexandria, *In Epistolam ad Hebraeos* (PG 74.953–1006); Theodoret, *Interpretatio Epistolae ad Hebraeos* (PG 82.673–786).

B.F. Westcott, *The Epistle to the Hebrews*, 3rd. ed. (London: Macmillan, 1903); F.F. Bruce, *The Epistle to the Hebrews* (Grand Rapids: Eerdmans, 1964); R.A. Greer, *The Captain of Our Salvation: A Study in the Patristic Exegesis of Hebrews* (Tübingen: Mohr-Siebeck, 1973); P.E. Hughes, *A Commentary on the Epistle to the Hebrews* (Grand Rapids: Eerdmans, 1977); H.W. Attridge, *Hebrews* (Philadelphia: Fortress, 1989).

HEGEMONIUS (fourth century?). Author or scribe who wrote the *Acta Archelai*. The work dealt with heretics: Manichaeans, Photinians, Apollinarians, and Donatists. It was probably written in Rome. CPG II, 3570s; CPL 122.

[F.W.N.]

HEGESIPPUS (ca. 110–180). Christian Greek author of *Hypomnemata,* or *Memoirs,* in five books, fragments of which are preserved in Eusebius, *Church History.* Perhaps of Jewish origin, Hegesippus made a voyage by sea via Corinth to Rome during which he made contact with many bishops and found the same doctrine among them all. On arrival at Rome, he made a succession list (*diadochē*) down to Anicetus (d. ca. 168), who was succeeded by Soter and by Eleutherus. He was also interested in the succession in the see of Jerusalem, the origin of heresies, and apostolic succession in important episcopacies as a guarantee of orthodoxy. CPG I, 1302. [T.H.]

Bibliography
Eusebius, *Church History* 2.23; 3.11–12, 16, 19–20, 32; 4.7–8, 11, 21–22.

HELENA (ca. 250–ca. 330). Mother of Constantine the Great. Helena shared a modest social background with Constantine's father, Constantius I, whose legal wife she became ca. 270. In 293, Constantius had to divorce Helena in order to consolidate a dynastic marriage alliance with the senior emperor in the west, the Augustus Maximian, by marrying his step-daughter Theodora. Helena continued to be associated with her son, but sources for the next thirty years are scant.

Helena comes to prominence again at a critical juncture in Constantine's reign: his victory over Licinius in 324, which made him sole ruler of the Roman empire, and the tragic conflict within the imperial family that led to the execution of his second wife, Fausta, and his son Crispus. (Helena was involved in her daughter-in-law's downfall on the erroneous charge of adultery, which may have caused a sense of guilt and desire to do penance expressed by her precedent-setting journey to Jerusalem in 326.) At this time, Helena, as an empress mother and Augusta, wielded considerable power. Her role in church history was due to her partnership in Constantine's program of church building at Bethlehem and Jerusalem and to her discovery of what she believed to be the true cross, both of which led to the revival of Jerusalem and the encouragement of pilgrimage to the Holy Land.

Helena provided a prototype for the Christian Augustae who would help to govern the Christianized Roman empire. Feast day May 21 (east). [H.R.]

Bibliography
Eusebius, *Life of Constantine* 3.
A.H.M. Jones et al., eds., *The Prosopography of the Later Roman Empire* (Cambridge: Cambridge UP, 1971), Vol. 1: *A.D. 260–395,* pp. 410–411 [most complete listing of ancient sources]; J.H. Smith, *Constantine the Great* (New York: Scribner, 1971); D. Bowder, *The Age of Constantine and Julian* (London: Elek, 1978); T.D. Barnes, *Constantine and Eusebius* (Cambridge: Harvard UP, 1981); idem, *The New Empire of Diocletian and Constantine* (Cambridge: Harvard UP, 1982); K.G. Holum, *Theodosian Empresses: Women and Imperial Dominion in Late Antiquity* (Berkeley: U of California P, 1986); R. Klein, "Helena II (Kaiserin)," RLAC (1987), Vol. 14, cols. 355–375.

HELL. Place or state of final punishment for the damned. Although some biblical translations employ the term "hell" for both *hades* and *gehenna,* the latter properly denotes "hell"; the former, the intermediate place or state between death and the last judgment. Literally speaking, *gehenna* refers to the Valley of Hinnom (Josh. 15:8), a place infamous for pagan rites, including child sacrifice (2 Kings 16:3; 23:10). Jeremiah prophesied that God's judgment would fall on it (Jer. 19:6f.). By New Testament times, Jeremiah's prophecy had been intermingled with speculation about the end of time. Thus, *gehenna* had come to be considered as the place of final judgment or hell itself, the fiery abyss (Matt. 13:42, 50; Rev. 20:10). New Testament writers also distinguished it sharply from Hades. In their view, Hades is an intermediate place or state of the soul between death and final judgment, but *gehenna* is an everlasting fire into which both the souls and the bodies of the wicked are cast, together with Satan and the demons (Mark 9:43, 45, 47f.; Matt. 8:29; 10:28; 25:41; cf. the lake of fire in Rev. 19:20; 20:10, 14f.). Although there was some question about the reality of the fires of hell, early Christians generally accepted the existence of a place of final punishment.

What the church struggled with in regard to hell was the question of the duration of its punishment. Some scholars have argued that a notion of the annihilation of the wicked, and not eternal punishment, is present in the writings of such thinkers as Justin Martyr, Irenaeus, and Arnobius. The textual evidence, however, does not seem to bear the weight of this conclusion.

The overwhelming majority of Christian writers held that the wicked were to be eternally punished. This group includes Ignatius of Antioch, Justin Martyr, Minucius Felix, Tertullian, Cyprian of Carthage, Basil of Caesarea, John Chrysostom, and Augustine. Tertullian, for example, held that one of the joys of heaven would be the ability of the saints to watch the damned tormented forever in hell (*Spect.* 30). The ablest exponent of eternal damnation was Augustine. In his *City of God,* the bishop of Hippo challenged the idea that the length or the quality of the punishments of those who had rejected God's offer of redemption would be less than eternal or severe (*Civ. Dei* 21.9–18).

Augustine was attempting to refute a notion about punishment that is evidenced as early as the second century in the writings of Clement of Alexandria. At about the same time that Tertullian was rejoicing in the eternal doom of the wicked, Clement expressed reservations about an everlasting chastisement. In the *Miscellanies,* he argued that God does not punish, he corrects; the punishing actions of God are remedial in nature (*Str.* 7.16). Thus, the wicked do not suffer forever but are eventually brought to repentance (*Str.* 7.12). Unfortunately, Clement was not altogether clear on the idea of remedial punishment. In several other places, he writes of hell as a place of everlasting punishment of the wicked (e.g., *Str.* 1.7; 7.10; *Prot.* 9; *Q.d.s.* 1; 26; 33).

No such equivocation is found in the writings of Origen. Origen agreed with Clement that God did not chasten vindictively, but remedially. More important, however, was the fact that everlasting punishment meant that someone was capable of thwarting the will of

God forever, since it was the divine will that all be saved and come to the knowledge of the truth (1 Tim. 2:4; *Princ.* 3.6.5). As long as hell remained, all were not redeemed and God's will was frustrated. For Origen, there was no soul so wicked that it could not be cleansed eventually from its evil (*Cels.* 6.25–26). Indeed, every soul was in need of purification because every soul had been tainted by its union with the flesh (*Hom. 8 in Lev.*). All souls must therefore endure the trial by fire mentioned in 1 Corinthians 3:10–15, which "awaits us all at the end of life" (*Hom. 24 in Lc.*). The length of purgation depended on the soiled condition of the soul. Those souls that were merely tainted by the flesh could be purified in an instant, whereas those that had been truly contaminated by sin would require a longer period of cleansing

In Origen's view, hell would eventually be emptied of the wicked because the punishment of fire would eventually burn off the dross of the soul and enable it to turn once again to God. Indeed, even Satan himself would one day return to God as an obedient servant (*Princ.* 3.6.5–6; cf. Jerome, *Epist. Pachom.* 7). Origen was the first Christian theologian to assert that there was a possibility of purification after death. In this sense, he was a contributor to the development of the doctrine of purgatory. His notion of a finite length of punishment for the wicked also found favor among several eastern Christian thinkers: Ephraem the Syrian, Didymus the Blind, Gregory of Nyssa, Gregory of Nazianzus, Diodore of Tarsus, and Theodore of Mopsuestia. The idea, like its author, however, was always controversial. Basil of Caesarea, for example, asserted that the repentance of the wicked in hell was impossible, for in hell the sinful soul was cut off from the Holy Spirit and therefore could not repent (*Spir.* 40). Notions of remedial punishment were also found in the west, and, as we have seen, evoked a lengthy response from Augustine (*Civ. Dei* 21). In 543, the doctrine of universal salvation was condemned in the ninth anathema of Justinian's edict against Origen. Ten years later, the Fifth General Council, meeting at Constantinople, sustained this denunciation. *See also* Apokatastasis; Hades; Harrowing of Hell; Heaven; Purgatory; Satan.   [A.L.C.]

Bibliography

R.H. Charles, *A Critical History of the Doctrine of a Future Life in Israel, in Judaism, and in Christianity*, 2nd ed. (London: Black, 1913); M. Richard, "Enfer," DTC (1924), Vol. 5, pp. 27–119; A. Adam, "Hölle," *Die Religion in Geschichte und Gegenwart*, 3rd ed. (Tübingen: Mohr, 1959), Vol. 3, pp. 399–407; K. Beitl, "Hölle," *Lexikon für Theologie und Kirche* (Freiburg: Herder, 1960), Vol. 5, pp. 446–450; D.P. Walker, *The Decline of Hell* (Chicago: U of Chicago P, 1964); J. Jeremias, "Gehenna," *Theological Dictionary of the New Testament*, ed. G. Kittel (Grand Rapids: Eerdmans, 1964), Vol. 1, pp. 657–658; H. Bietenhard, "Hell," *The New International Dictionary of New Testament Theology*, ed. C. Brown (Grand Rapids: Zondervan, 1976), Vol. 2, pp. 205–210; H. Crouzel, "Hades et la gehenne selon Origène," *Gregorianum* 50 (1978):291–331; Kelly, pp. 473, 483f.; J. Meyendorff, *Byzantine Theology: Historical Trends and Doctrinal Themes*, 2nd ed. (New York: Fordham UP, 1979), pp. 218–222; J.B. Russell, *Satan: The Early Christian Tradition* (Ithaca: Cornell UP, 1981); G.W. Bromiley, "Hell, History of the Doctrine of," *International Standard Bible Encyclopedia*, ed. G.W. Bromiley (Grand Rapids: Eerdmans, 1982), Vol. 2, pp. 677–679; J. Le Goff, *The Birth of Purgatory* (Chicago: U of Chicago P, 1983).

HELVIDIUS (fl. 380s). Latin theologian. When Jerome was aggressively asserting the spiritual virtues of virginity at Rome, Helvidius objected with a treatise that rejected Jerome's arguments, which focused particularly on the perpetual virginity of Mary. Jerome's refutation of Helvidius, *Against Helvidius,* and his polemics against Jovinian and Vigilantius were critical in the establishment of the ascetic values that were to be so influential in shaping European religious and social experience.

Helvidius was representative of those in the fourth-century Italian church who, like Jovinian, objected to the elevation of celibacy over marriage as a qualification for spiritual excellence, but it was Jerome's view that prevailed. Helvidius disappeared after his brief public confrontation with his acerbic and prolific scholarly opponent. *See also* Jerome.

[H.R.]

Bibliography

Jerome, *Against Helvidius*, tr. J.N. Hritzu, FOTC (1965), Vol. 53, pp. 3–34.

J.N.D. Kelly, *Jerome: His Life, Writings and Controversies* (New York: Harper and Row, 1975), pp. 104–110.

HENOTICON. Formula of union for Monophysites and the orthodox, written in 482. Emperor Zeno, needing political assistance from the regions of the eastern empire in which the Monophysites were strong, asked Acacius, bishop of Constantinople, to assist him. Acacius sensed that his Chalcedonian position and that of the anti-Chalcedonian or Monophysite Christians had points of contact and even similarity. He entered conversations with Peter Mongus, bishop of Alexandria, to see what agreement could be reached. The resultant document condemns both Nestorius, as the representative of a divisive, two-nature Christology that endangered the unity of the person of Christ, and Eutyches, as the representative of a restrictive, one-nature Christology that threatened the humanity of Jesus.

The formula, however, never discusses in explicit terms the problems involved in the language of "nature," one or two. Because both Acacius and Zeno wanted to end the separation between Constantinople and Alexandria that had arisen when Dioscorus, the Alexandrian bishop, had been deposed at Chalcedon, they sought to concede nearly any point but the acceptance of Chalcedon's decrees. They proposed union on the basis of the Niceno-Constantinopolitan Creed and the Twelve Anathemas of Cyril against Nestorius.

Many of the Monophysites accepted the *Henoticon*, but lack of mention of Leo's *Tome* made Rome suspicious. Felix II (III) even excommunicated Acacius, causing a schism that lasted thirty-five years. The effort at union thus proved to be a failure. *See also* Acacius of Constantinople; Felix II (III); Monophysites; Zeno.

[F.W.N.]

Bibliography

Evagrius, *Church History* 3.14.

J.C. Ayer, *A Source Book for Ancient Church History* (New York: Scribner, 1941), pp. 526–529; W.H.C. Frend, *The Rise of Christianity* (Philadelphia: Fortress, 1984), pp. 809–811, 846, 850–851; A. Grillmeier, *Christ in Christian Tradition* (Atlanta: John Knox, 1987), Vol. 2, pp. 247–317.

HERACLEON (second century). Gnostic teacher. Together with Ptolemy, Heracleon was a leading representative of the Italian school of Valentinian Gnosticism centered at Rome in the third quarter of the second century (Hippolytus, *Haer.* 6.35.5–7). Fragments of his exegetical scholia on the Gospels have been preserved in Clement of Alexandria (*Ecl.* 25.1; *Str.* 4.71–72) and, more extensively, in Origen's *Commentary on John* (esp. Book 13). In his exegesis of John, Heracleon allegorizes events in the ministry of Jesus in terms of the Redeemer's condescension into material reality, the realm of the demiurge, to bestow saving gnosis on the pneumatic elect. CPG I, 1137. TLG 1403.   [P.M.Bl.]

Bibliography

A.E. Brooke, ed. *The Fragments of Heracleon*, TS 1.4 (1891).

W. Foerster and R.McL. Wilson, eds. *Gnosis: A Selection of Gnostic Texts* (Oxford: Clarendon, 1972), Vol. 1, pp. 162–183; E.H. Pagels, *The Johanine Gospel in Gnostic Exegesis* (New York: Abingdon, 1973).

HERDER, JOHANN GOTTFRIED (1744 –1803). German critic and philosopher. Noted for his part in Romanticism, his literary criticism within the *Sturm und Drang* movement, and his philosophy of history, Herder wrote the *Christliche Schriften,* in which he voiced his sense of Jesus as the noblest figure in human history. Herder downplayed miracles, refused the description of early Christians as enthusiasts, rejected the influence of Greek and oriental myths on the gospel, and developed the use of historical critical methods on the Gospels.   [F.W.N.]

Bibliography

F. McEachran, *Life and Philosophy of Johann Gottfried Herder* (Oxford: Clarendon, 1939); W. Koepke, *Johann Gottfried Herder* (Boston: Twayne, 1987).

HERESY. Term deriving from the Greek word *hairesis,* which originally meant "choice" but by the beginning of the Christian era had come also to be applied to a religious or philosophical sect. In a Christian context, "heresy" normally refers to a false religious sect or to erroneous teaching and is consequently the opposite of "orthodoxy." Understood this way, the chief issue becomes what criteria distinguish true from false doctrine. Irenaeus (fl. 180–200), although he depends upon earlier writers, notably Justin Martyr, gives us our first evidence for how the developing Great Church (or "early Catholicism") attempted to define heresy. Any opinions that contradicted or subverted the apostolic faith were heretical. What Irenaeus means by the apostolic faith is scripture and the rule of faith. By scripture, he understands the Septuagint translation of the Old Testament together with a closed collection of apostolic writings nearly identical with what we call the New Testament. By rule of faith, he understands a flexible, creedlike summary of the meaning of scripture. These two elements of the apostolic faith coinhere and are guarded by the bishops who succeeded the apostles. It is on this basis that Irenaeus rejected the Gnostics and the Marcionites as heretics. They misused scripture, and their views contradicted the rule of faith.

In practice, however, Irenaeus's definition of heresy proved insufficient. Bishops could disagree as to what followed the apostolic faith, and what was orthodox in one church could be regarded as heretical in another. As a result, the church began to call councils to adjudicate charges of heresy. To some degree, conciliar activity may be found in the church before the Constantinian revolution. In the first half of the third century, Origen acted as a theological expert in what amounted to ecclesiastical courts summoned to hear heresy charges. In 268, a council in Antioch condemned as heretical Paul of Samosata's views of Christ. Nevertheless, ecumenical councils were held only after imperial patronage had come into play. The councils of Nicaea (325) and Constantinople (381) formulated the dogma of the Trinity and defined Arianism and Apollinarianism as heresies. The councils of Ephesus (431) and Chalcedon (451) defined the dogma of Christ's person, rejecting Nestorius and Eutyches as heretics. Later ecumenical councils continued to deal with the problem of Christ's person. It must be added that the authority of the so-called ecumenical councils derived not only from imperial authority but also from general acceptance by the church.

Heresy therefore remains in theory a denial of orthodox doctrine, which is itself based upon scripture and the rule of faith (or the creeds); but in practice, attempts to purge the church of heresy involved questions of ecclesiastical authority and of the relation of the church to the Roman empire. A list of heresies in the early church would include the various forms of Gnosticism, Marcionitism, Montanism, Monarchianism, Arianism, Apollinarianism, Nestorianism, Monophysitism, Manichaeism, Pelagianism, and Priscillianism. *See also* Rule of Faith; Schism.   [R.A.G.]

Bibliography

H.E.W. Turner, *The Pattern of Christian Truth* (London: Mowbray, 1954); W. Bauer, *Orthodoxy and Heresy in Earliest Christianity* (Philadelphia: Fortress, 1971; orig. German ed., 1934); E.P. Sanders, et al., eds. *Jewish and Christian Self-Definition,* 3 vols, (Philadelphia: Fortress, 1980–1982); H.O.J. Brown, *Heresies: The Image of Christ in the Mirror of Heresy and Orthodoxy from the Apostles to the Present* (Garden City: Doubleday, 1984); A. Le Boulluec, *La Notion d'hérésie dans la littérature grecque IIe–IIIe siècles,* 2 vols. (Paris: Etudes Augustiniennes, 1985).

HERMAS. One of the apostolic fathers. The *Shepherd* of Hermas is a complex Christian apocalypse written in Greek in stages from ca. A.D. 90 to 150. The author repeatedly calls himself Hermas. He was probably a freedman formerly owned by a woman named Rhoda who lived in Rome (*Vis.* 1.1). He was married and had children but was later persuaded to practice sexual continence (*Vis.* 2.3). He was a contemporary of Clement (*Vis.* 2.4.3), possibly identical with the author of *1 Clement,* who died ca. 101 (Eusebius, *H.E.* 3.34). The Muratorian Canon (ca. 170), however, identifies Hermas as the brother of Pius, bishop of Rome (d. ca. 154). This disparity in dating reflects the composite literary character of the *Shepherd.* In its present form, the text is made up of a series of visions purportedly experienced by Hermas arranged in three sections, consisting of five *Visions,* twelve *Mandates,* and ten *Similitudes.* The earliest stratum of the work, *Visions* 1–4, constituted an independent apoca-

lypse written during the last decade of the first century. In this part of the work, the otherworldly revealer is an old woman who later appears younger. The first four *Visions* also have an eschatological emphasis lacking in the rest of the work. The imminence of the great tribulation is mentioned several times (*Vis.* 2.3.4; 4.1, 5). From *Vision* 5 through *Similitude* 10, the angel of repentance, in the guise of a shepherd, becomes Hermas's supernatural guide, providing the name for the entire work.

In spite of its complicated compositional history, the central theme of the *Shepherd* is the possibility of a second and final repentance. Repentance had come to be understood as a once-for-all act associated with baptism, which cleansed the recipient from sin (*Mand.* 4.3.1). Postbaptismal sins were problematic, causing Christians to postpone baptism as long as possible. The possibility of a *second* (and final) repentance proposed by Hermas (*Vis.* 2.2.4–5; *Mand.* 4.4.4) and legitimated by special revelations granted to him was an attempt to solve a critical religious and theological problem. The author functioned as a prophet, even though he does not claim prophetic status.

Hermas wrote down his visionary revelations for both oral presentation to leaders and members of local churches in and around Rome (*Vis.* 2.2.6; 3.8.10; 3.9.7) and written distribution (*Vis.* 2.4.3). The ethical rigorism of the *Shepherd* together with its implicit claim to divine inspiration made it popular during the second and third centuries, when the New Testament canon was in formation. Irenaeus (*Haer.* 4.20), the early Tertullian (*Or.* 16; cf. *Pud.* 10), Clement of Alexandria (*Str.* 1.29; 2.1), and Origen (*Comm. in Rom.* 16.14) all treated it with respect. Eusebius of Caesarea categorized the *Shepherd* as a writing received by some but not all (*H.E.* 3.4.6; 3.25.4). It was part of the great fourth-century biblical codex Sinaiticus. CPG I, 1052. TLG 1419.

[D.E.A.]

Bibliography

M. Whitaker, *Die apostolischen Väter I: Der Hirt des Hermas,* GCS (1967), Vol. 48, pp. 1–98.

G. Snyder, *The Shepherd of Hermas* (Camden: Nelson, 1968); L.W. Barnard, "The Shepherd of Hermas in Recent Study," *Heythrop Journal* 9

(1968):29–36; J. Reiling, *Hermas and Christian Prophecy: A Study of the Eleventh Mandate* (Leiden: Brill, 1973); R.J. Bauckham, "The Great Tribulation in the Shepherd of Hermas," *JThS* n.s. 25 (1974):27–40; C. Osiek, *Rich and Poor in the Shepherd of Hermas: An Exegetical-Social Investigation* (Washington, D.C.: Catholic Biblical Association, 1983); D.E. Aune, *Prophecy in Early Christianity and the Ancient Mediterranean World* (Grand Rapids: Eerdmans, 1983), pp. 299–310.

HERMIT. Solitary ascetic, anchorite. The term "hermit" derives from the Greek *erēmitēs* (Latin *eremita* m., *eremitis* f.), "one who resides in the desert" (*erēmos*). Its use in the early church is associated with the rise of the monastic movement in the third and fourth centuries, and it identifies those individuals who practiced the ascetic life in solitude by separating themselves from the world to live alone. The separation, particularly in Egypt, was most often accomplished by withdrawal (Greek *anachōrēsis*) to the desert; hence, the use of "anchorite" as a meaningful equivalent of hermit. Both terms are used to distinguish the monk who lived alone from the one who shared with others a common life in an ascetic community. These latter were called cenobites, a term derived from this common (Greek *koinos*) or shared lifestyle.

The use and meaning of these terms shifted over time and space. One must be careful to test the meaning of the term through the life and actions of the individual it describes rather than use a given meaning uncritically to define the individual. Thus, it was the solitary lifestyle rather than the linguistic (and perhaps original) linkage of the term "hermit" with the desert that became the definitive element for its use in the early church. The centrality of the desert in the monastic tradition of Egypt did not translate well to many other locations. Likewise, the demand of physical remoteness was a major variable in the definition of *anachōrēsis*, or withdrawal. Often, hermits lived in close proximity to one another, with frequent communication and sharing of tasks. Individuals living the life of a hermit could be found outside of the desert, even in villages and towns.

In early Christian literature, Anthony of Egypt is represented as the preeminent hermit or anchorite. The story of his life by Athanasius, *Life of Anthony*, recounts his increasing physical withdrawal from the world: from his home, to the outskirts of his village, to a nearby tomb, to the distant desert. This preeminence is, however, largely literary. The solitary life of the hermit both preceded Anthony in Egypt (*V. Anton.* 3) and developed independently in other parts of the ancient world.

A peculiar development in Syria was the "pillar saints," who took up residence on the top of columns and had food hoisted up to them. Symeon Stylites is the best known of these practitioners of extreme anchorite spirituality.

The hermit was rarely successful in the quest for solitude. Success inevitably brought fame, which in turn led others to seek out the hermit for advice, patronage, and prayers. Prospective monks often sought out famous hermits as spiritual guides. The hermit had a limited need of the world as a source of food and other physical necessities: Anthony, for example, wove baskets that he exchanged with visitors for articles he needed (*V. Anton.* 53). The sources of early monastic history are replete with references to such contact between the hermit and the world. *See also* Monasticism.　　　　　　　　　　　　[J.E.G.]

Bibliography

D.J. Chitty, *The Desert a City: An Introduction to the Study of Egyptian and Palestinian Monasticism Under the Christian Empire* (Oxford: Blackwell, 1966); P. Brown, "The Rise and Function of the Holy Man in Late Antiquity," *JRS* 61 (1971):80–101; E.A. Judge, "The Earliest Use of Monachos for 'Monk' (P. Coll. Youtie 77) and the Origins of Monasticism," *JAC* 20 (1977):72–89; P. Brown, *The Making of Late Antiquity* (Cambridge: Harvard UP, 1978), esp. Ch. 4; J.E. Goehring, "The World Engaged: The Social and Economic Context of Early Egyptian Monasticism," *Essays on Antiquity and Christianity in Honor of James M. Robinson*, Vol. 2, *Gnosticism and the Early Christian World*, ed. J. Sanders, J.E. Goehring and C. Hedrick (Sonoma: Polebridge, forthcoming).

HESYCHIUS OF EGYPT (ca. 300). Jerome speaks of the text of the Septuagint used in

Egypt as the work of Hesychius. An important revision of the text of the Bible was made in Egypt about the beginning of the fourth century, but Jerome's disparaging comments about interpolations made by Hesychius raise a question about whether they are the same. The *Decretum Gelasianum* calls his work on the Gospels "apocryphal." There is doubt whether he is to be identified with the bishop martyred under Diocletian (Eusebius, *H.E.* 8.13.7) or one of the four Egyptian bishops who wrote a letter rebuking Melitius. Hesychius the lexicographer, who lived later, was probably a pagan. [E.F.]

Bibliography

Eusebius, *Church History* 8.13.7; Jerome, *Praefatio in Paralipomena;* idem, *Apology Against Rufinus* 2.27; idem, *In Isaiam* 58.11; idem, *Preface to the Four Gospels; Decretum Gelasianum.*

F.G. Kenyon, "Hesychius and the Text of the New Testament," *Mémorial Lagrange* (Paris: Gabalda, 1940), pp. 245–250.

HESYCHIUS OF JERUSALEM (d. after 451).

Exegete and homilist. Little is known of Hesychius's life. He was a monk and probably a priest of the church in Jerusalem; his contemporaries regarded him highly as a theologian and preacher. His death occurred after the Council of Chalcedon (451). His extensive surviving works include commentaries on Leviticus, Job, and Psalms and scholia on Isaiah and the minor prophets; he is said to have commented on all of scripture. His exegetical principles were derived from Origen. He is the author of numerous homilies; a church history (ca. 428), now lost, in which he opposed Nestorianism; and an extant treatise on apparent discrepancies in the Gospels. He figures in discussions on Christology—his own treatment of the subject being based on Cyril of Alexandria—and on original sin. An opponent of Arianism, he is considered to have affinities with the Monophysites. CPG III, 6550–6596.
[M.P.McH.]

Bibliography

Les Homélies festales d'Hésychius de Jérusalem, ed. M. Aubineau, 2 vols. (Brussels: Société des Bollandistes, 1978, 1980); "Une Homélie perdue d'Hésychius de Jérusalem, sur saint Jean-Baptiste, retrouvée en version arménienne," ed. C. Renoux and M. Aubineau, *AB* 99 (1981):45–63; *Hésychius de Jérusalem, Homélies sur Job: Version arménienne,* ed. C. Renoux and C. Mercier, 2 vols., PO (1983), Vol. 42.1, 2; H. Savon, "Les Homélies festales d'Hésychius de Jérusalem," *RHR* 197 (1980):429–450; T.P. Halton and R.D. Sider, "A Decade of Patristic Scholarship 1970–1979," *CW* 76 (1982–1983):342 (bibliography).

HEXAPLA. Work of Old Testament textual criticism by Origen. The Bible of the earliest church was for the most part the Old Testament in the Greek translation known as the Septuagint or "LXX." When the church and the synagogue parted ways, the church took the LXX with it as the inspired word of God. For its part, the synagogue then returned to the Hebrew and disparaged the traditional Greek version. Among the Jews, other more "faithful" versions replaced the LXX, such as the translations of Aquila and Theodotion. The debate between Jews and Christians over who possessed the inspired text did not subside.

Origen (ca. 185–ca. 251) was a brilliant and prodigious biblical scholar and commentator who attempted to resolve this issue by carefully comparing the LXX with the traditional Hebrew text of his day. He did this in an immense book, now lost, that ran to an estimated 6,000 pages. In six columns (hence *hexapla*), word by word or phrase by phrase down the page, he set forth (1) the Hebrew, (2) a transliteration of the Hebrew into Greek, the independent translations of (3) Aquila and (4) Symmachus, (5) the LXX, and (6) the translation by Theodotion.

Where the LXX was longer than the Hebrew text, Origen marked those words with an obelus (÷) in front and a metobelus (:) following. Where the LXX was shorter than the Hebrew, Origen added (usually from Theodotion) the word or words necessary to make its length correspond to the Hebrew, marking what he had added with an asterisk (※) before and a metobelus following. Origen's great work of scholarship was never recopied in its entirety and presumably was destroyed at Caesarea in the seventh century during the Muslim conquest of Palestine. However, the fifth column, the result of Origen's editorial work, was very popular and circulated widely, eventually corrupting most of the textual tradition of the Old Testament in Greek. Today, the preservation of the signs in Greek, Syriac, and Armenian witnesses allows textual critics to reckon precisely the state of the LXX in the third century. TLG 2042,083. *See also* Aquila; Origen; Septuagint; Symmachus; Theodotion. [C.C.]

Bibliography

F. Field, *Origenis Hexaplorum* (Oxford: Clarendon, 1875).

H.B. Swete, *An Introduction to the Old Testament in Greek,* rev. R.R. Ottley (Cambridge: Cambridge UP, 1902); S. Jellicoe, *The Septuagint and Modern Study* (Oxford: Clarendon, 1968); C. Cox, *Hexaplaric Materials Preserved in the Armenian Version* (Atlanta: Scholars, 1986).

HIEROCLES (third–fourth century). Governor of Bithynia (303) with interest in Neoplatonic philosophy, who led persecutions against Christians. Hierocles wrote two (now lost) tracts against Christianity entitled *Philaletheis* ("Friend of Truth") that were cleverly worded as if expressing a sympathetic understanding of its faults. Working from a detailed knowledge, he pointed out internal contradictions in scripture and charged the disciples with proclaiming falsehoods and being crude and uneducated. Lactantius (*Div. inst. 5.2–4; Mort. pers.* 16) thought that Hierocles might have been a Christian previously. Hierocles employed arguments similar to those of Celsus and claimed that Apollonius of Tyana had done equal or greater works than had Jesus, who was a magician and a robber (Eusebius, *Hierocl.*). [F.W.N.]

Bibliography

M. Forrat and E. des Places, eds., *Eusèbe de Cesarée: Contre Hiéroclès,* SC (1986), Vol. 333.

F.C. Conybeare, tr., "The Treatise of Eusebius . . . Against . . . Hierocles," *Philostratus,* Vol. 2, LCL (1912).

M. Kertsch, "Traditionelle Rhetorik und Philosophie in Eusebius' Antirrhetikos gegen Hierokles," *VChr* 34 (1980):145–171.

HILARY. Bishop of Rome (461–468). A native of Sardinia, Hilary served as legate of Leo the Great to the "Robber Council" of Ephesus (449); but he withdrew in fear of his life because of his support of Flavian, patriarch of Constantinople, against Dioscorus, patriarch of Alexandria. His own pontificate, however, was concerned mostly with affairs in the west. His efforts to reestablish the jurisdiction of Arles in Gaul were thwarted, but a synod convoked by him in the church of Sta. Maria Maggiore in Rome (465) settled disputes among the Spanish bishops. In thanksgiving for his deliverance at Ephesus, he built chapels adjoining the baptistery of the Lateran. His letters are concerned mostly with events in Gaul and Spain. CPL 1662–1663. [M.P.McH.]

Bibliography

Leo the Great, *Letter* 44; *Liber Pontificalis* 48 (Duchesne 1.242–248).

HILARY OF ARLES (401–449). Bishop and theologian. Hilary's career reflects some of the significant developments in the western church during the first half of the fifth century, developments that profoundly affected western Christendom. He was born in northern Gaul, to the Gallo-Roman aristocracy. His few extant authentic writings—a sermon, a letter, and some verses—indicate that he was given the classical literary education, with an emphasis on rhetoric and philosophy, that was readily available in the Gallic schools of the fifth century. After an early career in public service, Hilary responded to his cousin Honoratus's call to ascetical life on the island of Lerinum (Lérins). Here, Honoratus had founded a monastic community ca. 410. In 426, Hilary reluctantly followed Honoratus to Arles; like many other fifth-century Gallic cities, this major urban center in southern Gaul drew upon the monastic community of Lérins for episcopal leadership. Before his death ca. 430, Honoratus designated his young disciple as his successor. Although he could not return to his monastic retreat, Hilary's devotion to the monastic ideal and to Lérins's emphasis in theology characterized his episcopal career until his death.

As bishop, Hilary gained fame as a fearless preacher. He also shared in the raging theological discussion in the Gallic church over Augustinianism, and, although he was in general devoted to the teaching of the bishop of

Hippo, he did have reservations about Augustine's doctrine of irresistible grace. As bishop of Arles, Hilary had metropolitan jurisdiction, and his application of this authority led him to a dispute with pope Leo I. Hilary's deposition of a bishop outside of his metropolitan jurisdiction and Celidon of Besançon's appeal to Rome for restoration resulted in a definitive assertion of papal primacy, with resolute imperial support, over the western church. Leo the Great rejected Hilary's in-person appeal and restored Celidon; in addition, he obtained in 445 at Rome an imperial decree issued by Valentinian III in the names of Valentinian and the eastern emperor Theodosius II. This document harshly criticized Hilary as "contumacious" and vigorously supported the jurisdiction of the papacy over "Gallican bishops as well as those of other provinces."

Although a reconciliation with Leo was not achieved before Hilary's death in 449, the papal comment that Hilary was one of "holy memory" is an appropriate epitaph. Feast day May 5. CPL 500–509.   [H.R.]

Bibliography

Gennadius, *Lives of Illustrious Men* 70; Leo the Great, *Letters* 10; 40; 66; 165.

S.J. Cavellin, ed., *Vitae sanctorum Honorati et Hilarii, episcoporum Arelatensium* (Lund: Gleerup, 1952).

A.C. Cooper-Marsdin, *The History of the Islands of the Lerins* (Cambridge: Cambridge UP, 1913), pp. 185–191; T.G. Jalland, *The Life and Times of St. Leo the Great* (London: SPCK, 1941); P.R. Coleman-Norton, *Roman State and Christian Church* (London: SPCK, 1966), Vol. 3, pp. 732–736 (tr. of the imperial rescript with notes); K.F. Stroheker, *Der senatorische Adel im spätantiken Gallien* (Darmstadt: Wissenschaftliche Buchgesellschaft, 1970), pp. 182–183; P. Riché, *Education and Culture in the Barbarian West: Sixth Through Eighth Centuries*, tr. J.J. Contreni (Columbia: U of South Carolina P, 1976).

HILARY OF POITIERS (ca. 315–ca. 367). Bishop and church father. Hilary was born and died in Poitiers, France. His distinguished pagan family gave him an education in philosophy and classics. As a young man, he was converted to Christianity by reading the Bible. He married and had one daughter, Abra. Elected bishop of Poitiers by popular acclaim (353), he began to defend the doctrine of the Trinity declared at Nicaea in 325 against the Arians. In his day, the emperor Constantius II favored the Arians and was opposed by Athanasius. At the Council of Béziers (356), he refused to condemn Athanasius and was exiled to Phrygia by the emperor. There, he learned Greek and studied the works of the Greek fathers. In 359, he attended the Council of Seleucia, where he upheld the orthodox doctrine of the Trinity, and the Council of Rimini, where the emperor Constantius forced the orthodox bishops to subscribe to an Arian creed. Considered a troublemaker, Hilary was sent back to Gaul without having his banishment annulled. He then worked vigorously on behalf of the unity of the Trinity, first in Gaul, then in Italy, from which he was finally ordered back to Gaul.

Hilary's writings were important in the development of Latin theology. *On the Trinity* has twelve books, the first three written before 356, the last nine during the exile in Phrygia. It is the first extended study of this doctrine in Latin. *On the Councils*, written in Phrygia, explains why the eastern clergy were dissatisfied with the expression *homoousios* ("of one substance") in the Nicene Creed and provides citations and explanations of the eastern professions of faith. *Fragmenta ex opere historico* contains documents pertaining to Arianism. *Tractatus super Matthaeum* was written before the exile, and *Tractatus super Psalmos*, inspired by Origen, after the exile. *Contra Constantium* was directed against Constantius II, whose religious policy was causing disunity in the church. Three incomplete hymns make Hilary the first known hymnodist in the western church.

Hilary taught that the existence of God could be known by reason but that the nature of God is incomprehensible. Knowledge of the Trinity comes from the Son's revelation, from the Son who said: "I in Thee and Thou in me" (John 14:4). From this, we know of the *circumincessio/perichoresis*, that is, the coinherence of the Father and Son, and of the Spirit who unites Father and Son as substantial love. Hilary ascribed the same attributes to the Holy

Spirit as to the Father and Son and taught that in Christ there is one divine person in two natures, human and divine.

Called "The Athanasius of the West," Hilary preached, wrote, and suffered exile in defense of the divinity of Christ. Through this exile, he was able to acquaint the Latin west with the theological riches of the Greek fathers. In 1851, Pius IX declared him doctor of the universal church. His name is given to the spring term at the English law courts and at Oxford and Durham universities. Feast day January 14. CPL 427–472.   [M.T.C.]

Bibliography

Jerome, *Lives of Illustrious Men* 100.

Tractatus super Psalmos, ed. A. Zingerle, CSEL (1891), Vol. 22; *De trinitate,* ed. P. Smulders, CCSL (1979, 1980), Vols. 62, 62A; *Tractatus mysteriorum* and *Hymni,* ed. A. Feder, CSEL (1916), Vol. 65; *Tractatus mysteriorum,* ed. J.-P. Brisson, SC (1947), Vol. 19; *Commentarius in Euangelium Matthaei,* ed. J. Doignon, SC (1979), Vols. 254, 258.

On the Councils, tr. W. Sanday, NPNF, 2nd ser. (1898), Vol. 9; "The Hymns of Saint Hilary of Poitiers," tr. W.N. Myers (Thesis, University of Pennsylvania, 1928); *The Trinity,* tr. S. McKenna, FOTC (1954), Vol. 25.

P.T. Wild, *The Divinization of Man According to St. Hilary of Poitiers* (Mundelein: St. Mary of the Lake Seminary, 1950); P. Galtier, *Saint Hilaire de Poitiers: le premier docteur de l'église latine* (Paris: Beauchesne, 1960); C.F.A. Borchardt, *Hilary of Poitiers' Role in the Arian Struggle* (The Hague: Martinus Nijhoff, 1966); E.P. Meijering, *Hilary of Poitiers on the Trinity* (Leiden: Brill, 1982).

HIPPOLYTUS (ca. 170–ca. 236). Presbyter, rival bishop at Rome, and martyr. Ancient sources show confusion about Hippolytus's identity and modern scholars disagree on key points; the following account will take a conventional approach.

A learned and cultivated person whose heritage derived from the Greek-speaking east, Hippolytus became a leading theologian in the church at Rome. He found himself in sharp disagreement with the bishops Zephyrinus and Callistus, and the most likely explanation for his designation in mainly eastern sources as a bishop (e.g., Eusebius, *H.E.* 6.20) is that he became the bishop of a schismatic community in Rome. In 235, the emperor Maximinus

Statue of Hippolytus at the entrance to the Apostolic Library, Vatican City, Italy.

Thrax exiled both Hippolytus and bishop Pontianus to Sardinia. Before their martyrdom, they were apparently reconciled, for bishop Fabian brought the two bodies back to Rome to be buried on the same day, August 13 (Hippolytus in the cemetery on the Via Tiburtina and Pontianus in the cemetery of St. Callistus—*Liber Pontificalis* 19), and bishop Damasus I later honored Hippolytus (incorrectly identified as a follower of Novatian, whose views on the nature of the church he anticipated) with an inscription identifying him as a martyr.

Since he was a schismatic and the last prominent writer of the Roman church to use Greek, his works suffered much in transmission, often preserved only in translations. Excavations at the Via Tiburtina and Via Nomentana in 1551 uncovered a statue of a person seated on a chair that has inscribed on one side a table for calculating the date of Easter coinciding with Eusebius's description of Hippolytus's Paschal cycle and on the other side a list of writings with similarities to the writings by Hippolytus known to Eusebius (*H.E.*

6.22) and Jerome (*Vir. ill.* 61). The statue was apparently a second-century work reused and provided with a new head by Hippolytus's followers and inscribed during his lifetime.

The most important work ascribed to Hippolytus is the *Refutation of All Heresies,* which finds the origin of Christian heresies in the philosophical schools of the Greeks. However, not all scholars accept the attribution. The recovery of Hippolytus's *Apostolic Tradition* from the later church-order literature that incorporated it has given valuable information on ordination, ministries in the church, the catechumenate, baptism, eucharist, the agape, and other church practices. The *Commentary on Daniel,* preserved in its entirety in Slavonic, is the earliest orthodox commentary to survive. Among other notable works by Hippolytus are a treatise *On Christ and Antichrist,* a *Homily on the Heresy of Noetus, Benedictiones Isaac et Iacob,* and *Benedictiones Moysis.*

Hippolytus resembled Irenaeus in theology, Origen in scholarship, and Tertullian in attitudes but was inferior to all three in originality and achievement. His debt to Irenaeus's theology is seen especially in his doctrine of salvation. Christ took on flesh and reversed the experience of Adam in order to confer immortality on the human race. Hippolytus clashed with Callistus on Christology and on the nature of the church and forgiveness. He followed the apologists in distinguishing three stages in the divine Word: as the immanent reason within the mind of God, as the spoken word of creation, and as the incarnate word in Jesus Christ. The Word (Christ) was distinguished from the Father in such a way that Callistus accused him of believing in two gods. Hippolytus wanted a church of the pure and took a rigorist position against forgiving those guilty of serious sins after receiving baptism. Feast day August 13 (west), January 30 (east). CPG I, 1870–1925. TLG 2115. *See also* Callistus; Christ; Penance.   [E.F.]

Bibliography

N. Bonwetsch et al., eds. *Hippolytus Werke* GCS (1897–), Vols. 1, 26, 36; M. Marcovich, ed. *Hippolytus: Refutatio Omnium Haeresium* (Berlin: de Gruyter, 1986).

B. Botte, *La Tradition apostolique de s. Hippolyte* (Munster: Aschendorff, 1963); G. Dix, tr, *The Treatise on the Apostolic Tradition of St. Hippolytus of Rome* (London: SPCK, 1968); R. Butterworth, tr, *Hippolytus of Rome, Contra Noetum* (London: U of London P, 1977).

J.J.I. von Döllinger, *Hippolytus and Callistus* (Edinburgh: T. and T. Clark, 1876); C. Wordsworth, *Hippolytus and the Church of Rome* (London: Rivingtons, 1880); A. d'Alès, *La Théologie de saint Hippolyte* (Paris: Beauchesne, 1906); R.H. Connolly, *The So-Called Egyptian Church Order and Derived Documents* (Cambridge: Cambridge UP, 1916); P. Nautin, *Hippolyte et Josipe* (Paris: Cerf, 1947); idem, *Le Dossier d'Hippolyte et de Meliton* (Paris: Cerf, 1953); J.M. Hanssens, *La Liturgie d'Hippolyte* (Rome: Gregoriana, 1970); D.L. Powell, "The Schism of Hippolytus," *SP* 12 (TU 115) (1975):449–456; A. Zani, *La cristologia di Ippolito* (Brescia: Morcelliana, 1983); D.G. Dunbar, "The Delay of the Parousia in Hippolytus," *VChr* 37 (1983):313–327; C. Osborne, *Rethinking Early Greek Philosophy: Hippolytus of Rome and the Presocratics* (Ithaca: Cornell UP, 1987).

HISTORY OF JOSEPH THE CARPENTER.

Apocryphal life of Joseph, composed in Egypt, during the fourth–fifth century, supposedly told by Jesus to his disciples on the Mount of Olives. Containing material inspired by the *Protevangelium of James* and the *Infancy Gospel of Thomas,* the *History of Joseph the Carpenter* is extant in a Coptic version and an Arabic translation with later additions. The work furnishes early evidence for the veneration of Joseph. Popular in the east, it was brought into Latin in the fourteenth century.   [M.P.McH.]

Bibliography

S. Morenz, ed., *Die Geschichte von Joseph dem Zimmermann* (Berlin: Akademie, 1951).

M.R. James, tr., *The Apocryphal New Testament* (Oxford: Clarendon, 1924), pp. 84–86.

HOLY SEPULCHRE, CHURCH OF THE.

The existing church of this name in Jerusalem consists of a rebuilding of the original rotunda in the eleventh century, after it had been destroyed in 1009, and a new church joined to it by the crusaders in the twelfth century. Recent archaeological excavations have established that the extant structures incorporate substantial elements of the buildings of the fourth

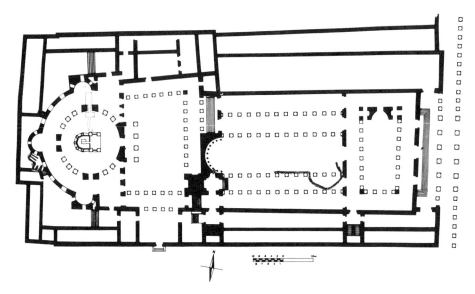

Church of the Holy Sepulchre (fourth-century plan), Jerusalem, Israel. (Plan furnished by G.T. Armstrong.)

century, most notably the walls of the rotunda to a height of 36 feet.

The original Church of the Holy Sepulchre was built between 326 and 335 at the direction of the emperor Constantine, who wrote the bishop of Jerusalem to express his desire "that it should surpass all the churches of the world in the beauty of its walls, columns, and marbles" (Eusebius, *V.C.* 3.31). This church included two major buildings, a semicircular rotunda with an inner circle of columns and piers around the empty tomb of Christ and to the east of it a large basilica. The rotunda was often called the Anastasis (Greek, "resurrection") and may not have been completed within the lifetime of Constantine; the basilica was often called the Martyrion (Greek, "witness"). In Cyril of Jerusalem's *Catechetical Lectures,* the whole complex is called Martyrion on the basis of the Septuagint version (followed also by the R.S.V.) of Zephaniah 3:8. Only the foundations of the basilica survive beneath the extant building, but the placement of its apse, double side-aisles, and exterior walls has been established. Eusebius in his *Life of Constantine* describes galleries, a gilded, coffered ceiling, and marble sheathing on the walls. Between these two principal buildings was a courtyard with porticoes. In its southeastern corner adjacent to the basilica stood the rock of Golgotha or Calvary, the place of the crucifixion.

The main entrance to the basilica was from an atrium at its east end, which in turn had a monumental gateway along the principal north-south street (the Roman *cardo*) of the city. The complex had a clear east-west axis, although the rotunda and basilica were not perfectly aligned along it. Its total length was 384 feet, almost as great as that of the Church of St. Peter in Rome without its atrium. Like the Church of the Nativity in Bethlehem, there was a basilica for congregational worship and a centralized martyrion at the holy place proper, the tomb of Christ.

Although the authenticity of the site has been much debated in the modern period, a good case can be made for it, and it is certainly the site revered by Jerusalem Christians at the time of Constantine as containing the empty tomb. To reveal the tomb and construct the church here, a Roman temple to Aphrodite had to be removed and the site cleared. The location was on the north side of the forum of Roman Jerusalem, which the emperor Hadrian had rebuilt after the Second Jewish Revolt in 132. Hadrianic foundations have been found beneath the church as well as ancient cisterns and a quarry. Some rock tombs have also been found.

The Church of the Holy Sepulchre has always been the preeminent center of pilgrimage in Christendom, and control of the buildings today is shared by the representatives of seven different churches. The design of the building had a wide influence on later church architecture. [G.T.A.]

Bibliography

Eusebius, *Life of Constantine* 3.25–40.

C. Coüasnon, *The Church of the Holy Sepulchre in Jerusalem* (London: Oxford UP for the British Academy, 1974); R. Krautheimer, *Early Christian and Byzantine Architecture*, 3rd ed. (Harmondsworth: Penguin, 1979), pp. 62–70, 77–78, and passim; V.C. Corbo, *Il Santo Sepolcro di Gerusalemme: aspetti archeologici dalle origini al periodo crociato*, 3 vols. (Jerusalem: Franciscan Printing Press, 1981, 1982), with Engl. summary in Vol. 1, pp. 219–235, and captions to the plates in Italian and English; D. Bahat, "Does the Holy Sepulchre Church Mark the Burial of Jesus?," *Biblical Archaeology Review* 12.3 (May-June 1986):26–45.

HOLY SPIRIT. "Spirit" *(rûah)*—literally "wind," "breath," or "soul"—is commonly used in the Old Testament to describe God's active presence in the world. It is associated especially with the creation and support of life, with artistic or ecstatic prophetic gifts, and with the hope for the future Davidic king and the restoration of Israel. The term "Holy Spirit" appears only in the late passages Isaiah 63 and Psalm 51, and the great classic prophets do not appear to have claimed to be inspired by God's "Spirit," although it came to be a tenet of later Judaism that the prophets were indeed so inspired and that the age of such inspiration had passed.

Intertestamental Judaism brought an intensified interest in the workings of the divine Spirit, both in apocalyptic writing, which was eschatologically and messianically oriented, and in the more cosmologically interested and Hellenistically colored Wisdom literature. But it is in the New Testament that the Holy Spirit becomes a central theological theme in the light of the message that Jesus Christ was in a special way both the recipient and the mediator of the Spirit. The Synoptic writers, Paul, and the Fourth Gospel unfold distinct perspectives, shaped respectively by the history of salvation culminating in Jesus Christ, the antithesis of "spirit" and "flesh," and the awareness of the "Spirit who proceeds from the Father" as "the other Paraclete" continuing in the church the work of Jesus Christ and his victorious conflict with "the world." Already in the New Testament period, tension can be seen between a "charismatic" emphasis on particular "gifts of the Spirit" (such as "speaking in tongues") and the insistence of Paul on the *kerygma* "received from the Lord" and the criterion of upbuilding the community of faith (cf. 1 Cor. 12–14).

Second Century. The conflict between more "institutional" and more "charismatic" pneumatologies—a conflict that has marked the life of the church ever since the New Testament—was particularly acute in the second century. The Gnostic systems of belief, teaching, and piety that flourished then, and briefly constituted a serious challenge to Catholic Christianity, developed their own notion of "redemption," by pushing the contrast between "spirit" and "flesh" to the point of an extreme dualism in which the material creation, the incarnation, and the institutional church were practically denied all saving significance. This was reflected, in another form, in Marcion's disjunction between the "just" God of the Old Testament, the creator of the material world, and the "alien God of love" proclaimed in the New Testament. Different again was the Montanist movement in the last third of the second century, a "prophetic" and "revivalist" cult, nourished by apocalyptic utterances, that awaited the descent of the New Jerusalem upon a village in Asia Minor. The leader of the movement, Montanus, is said to have claimed to be "the Father and the Son and the Paraclete," or at least to have spoken in their names.

Against these movements, the apologists in the mid-second century insisted that Jesus Christ was the bringer of the true knowledge of God adumbrated both in the Old Testament and in the pagan *praeparatio Evangelii*. Like the apostolic fathers before them, they emphasized the continuity between the Old and New Testaments, the saving significance of the incarnation, and the connection between the Holy Spirit and the history of salvation culminating in Jesus Christ. Similarly, in the next generation, Irenaeus of Lyons described the Holy Spirit and the Word incarnate in Jesus Christ as "the two hands of God," by whom God worked both creation and redemption, and insisted upon the relation between the Holy Spirit and the church: "Where the church is, there is the Spirit of God; and where the Spirit is, there is the church and every kind of grace." Irenaeus's reaffirmation of the theological tradition he had learned in his home in Asia Minor laid the foundation for the dogmatic pneumatology articulated in the fourth century.

Third Century. The third century gave a new, intensified, but also more narrowly specified twist to the arguments over who belonged to the church in the proper sense. Gnosticism and Montanism were no longer the issue, although both movements still survived. Christian faith spread ever more widely, became more and more "respectable"; the attempts of pagan emperors to suppress it grew more despairing but also more violent. Persecutions and betrayals led to a demand for a new and more rigorous "perfection," for the exclusion of those who had not stood fast in the face of political pressure and the threat of torture, for the refusal of recognition to "heretical" or "schismatic" baptism and the like. Some of the "confessors" (*confessores*) stood over against those who had fallen and demanded their exclusion from the body of the church. Specifically pneumatological arguments played little role in the resulting debates, but the dispute can properly be seen as carrying forward the argument over the criteria for church membership, which in earlier generations had a more markedly pneumatological character and direction. It is of abiding significance that the Catholic church of the period, rejecting the rigorism of Tertullian, Novatian, and the Donatists, insisted that the church is not a body of those who are already perfect but the community of those whose sins are being forgiven. The "spiritual" church is not a community of perfect spiritual holiness

but a community being made spiritually holy by the ongoing work of the Holy Spirit.

The development of the doctrine of the Holy Spirit advanced toward more precise formulation in the third century in the context of the doctrine of the Trinity. Tertullian's *Adversus Praxean* (before ca. 220) introduced such technical terms as *trinitas, substantia,* and *persona* and offered illustrations—e.g., root, branch, and shoot, or source, ray, and illumination—to suggest how the divine triunity could be conceived as a "monarchy" unfolding in an "economy" or "dispensation." Toward the middle of the century, Origen provided the first extended systematic treatment of the person and work of the Holy Spirit in relation to and in distinction from those of the Father and the Son: created beings "derive existence from God the Father, rationality from the Word, sanctity from the Holy Spirit" (*Princ.* 1.3.8). The tendency of both Tertullian's and Origen's thought remained, however, markedly subordinationist, assigning the Son (or Word) a lower dignity and status than the Father, and the Holy Spirit a lesser still. The Arian controversy of the fourth century forced further reflection, leading to the rejection of such subordinationism in all but the most refined sense.

Fourth Century. In the initial stages of the Arian controversy, up to about the middle of the fourth century, the status of the Holy Spirit was not a central issue; the creed approved by the Council of Nicaea in 325 powerfully emphasized the consubstantiality of the Son with the Father but concluded with the simple, traditional affirmation, "And [we believe] in the Holy Spirit." By the time that the Council of Constantinople terminated the controversy in 381 and promulgated what is today known as the Nicene Creed, the third article had been considerably expanded to read, *inter alia,* "And in the Holy Spirit, the Lord, the Life Giver, who proceeds from the Father, who with the Father and the Son is worshiped and glorified, who spoke by the prophets." These formulations, although not explicitly calling the Spirit "God" or "consubstantial" with the Father and the Son, are nevertheless clear enough in their intention. The Spirit is

"Lord" (a divine title) and "Life Giver" (i.e., creator), comes forth "from the Father" (as does the Son), is worshiped "with the Father and the Son," and is the same Spirit in the Old Testament ("who spoke by the prophets") as in the New.

Behind these deliberate formulations lay a series of debates and controversies that erupted in the third quarter of the fourth century. The divinity of the Holy Spirit was doubted on the one hand by conservative Egyptian Christians, who rejected Arianism in Christology but regarded the Spirit as a "creature" and an "angel"; on the other by radical Arians, the "Anomoeans," who insisted on the "unlikeness" of the Son to the Father and, by the same token, on the inferiority of the Spirit; and from yet a third side by the Pneumatomachians, representatives of the "Homoean" party who in the 360s and 370s parted company with the great Cappadocian theologians Basil of Caesarea, Gregory of Nyssa, and Gregory of Nazianzus, who were reaching a rapprochement with Athanasius and the Nicene party, and denied the propriety of worshiping the Spirit. Several orthodox writings between the middle of the century and the Council of Constantinople clarified the issues. The results are largely collated and summarized in the *Pseudo-Athanasian Dialogues* and in the *De Trinitate* ascribed to Didymus, both dating from the last decades of the fourth century.

Fifth Century. As in the earlier stages of the Arian controversy, the debate of the fourth century concerning the status, dignity, and working of the Holy Spirit was carried on for the most part in the eastern church, although echoed in the west by such writers as Hilary of Poitiers and Ambrose of Milan. When a major new western initiative emerged in the form of Augustine's *On the Trinity* (completed ca. 420), it was to prove controversial and ultimately divisive between east and west. Augustine put western Trinitarian reflection on a new tack; he did not carry on the debate with Arianism but assumed its rejection, setting out instead to pursue the question of how God could be thought of as triune, "one substance in three persons." In the later books of *On the Trinity,* he developed the conception of the structure of the human self as a *vestigium trinitatis:* mind, knowledge, and love, or memory, intelligence, and will, offered themselves as the best available analogies to the divine triunity. The Holy Spirit, as corresponding to the third term in these analogies, was to be conceived as the mutual love of the Father for the Son and the Son for the Father, and by extension as their common gift to humankind. From this, it followed that the Holy Spirit may properly be said to proceed "from the Father *and the Son*" (*Filioque*), and this view became standard in western pneumatology, eventually leading to the incorporation of the *Filioque* clause in the Nicene Creed—an insertion that remains a point of controversy between the eastern and western churches, although recent ecumenical conversations hold out hope that the controversy may yet be laid to rest. *See also* Filioque; God; Pneumatomachians; Spirit; Trinity. [A.H.]

Bibliography

Tertullian, *Against Praxeas* 25; Origen, *On First Principles* 1.3; Novatian, *On the Trinity* 29; Athanasius, *Letters to Serapion* (C.R.B. Shapland, *The Letters of St. Athanasius Concerning the Holy Spirit* [New York: Philosophical Library, 1951]); Hilary, *On the Trinity* 2.29–35; Cyril of Jerusalem, *Catechetical Lectures* 16; Basil of Caesarea, *On the Holy Spirit*; Didymus the Blind, *De Spiritu Sancto*; Ambrose, *On the Holy Spirit*; Gregory of Nazianzus, *Theological Orations* 5 [=Or. 31]; Augustine, *On the Trinity* 2.5–7; 4.21; 5.11–15; 7.3; 15.17–19, 26–27; John of Damascus, *Orthodox Faith* 1.7–8.

H.B. Swete, *The Holy Spirit in the Ancient Church* (London: Macmillan, 1912); L. Vischer, ed., *Spirit of God, Spirit of Christ: Ecumenical Reflections on the Filioque Controversy* (London: SPCK, and Geneva: WCC, 1981); A.I.C. Heron, *The Holy Spirit* (Edinburgh: Handsel, and Philadelphia: Westminster, 1983), pp. 63–98; W.-D. Hauschild, "Geist/Heiliger Geist/Geistesgaben IV: Dogmengeschichtlich," *TRE* 12 (1984):196–217 (bibliography); S.M. Burgess, *The Spirit and the Church: Antiquity* (Peabody: Hendrickson, 1984); J.P. Burns and G.M. Fagin, *The Holy Spirit* (Wilmington: Glazier, 1984).

HOMILY. In Christian usage, a discourse given on a biblical text for a congregation as part of a service of worship. The Greek word *homilia* meant "company" or "converse" but also "instruction" or "lecture"; it could designate the instruction that a philosopher gave his pupils in familiar conversation. Unlike the more formal *logos,* or "sermon," the homily was originally simple, unadorned, and conversational. Among Christian writers, Ignatius of Antioch was the first to use *homilia* in this sense (*Polyc.* 5.1). It was a technical term for the president's discourse at the liturgy by the early fourth century (Ancyra, *can.* 1). Latin writers began to use it as a loan-word at the end of the fourth century; Augustine had to explain it (*In Psalm.* 118 [119], pref.; *Ep.* 224).

The homily is distinct from two other kinds of discourse in early Christianity: the missionary sermon and catechesis. The homily had three characteristics: as liturgical, it belonged to the order of Christian worship; as exegetical, it explained a text from the Bible, God's living word to his people; as prophetic, it demonstrated the significance of the text for the hearers.

The Jewish sermon developed in the postexilic synagogue. Jesus preached in the synagogue at Nazareth on a passage from Isaiah (Luke 4:16–21). The New Testament probably contains fragments of homilies, such as the allegorical explanation of Jesus' parable of the sower (Mark 4:14–20).

The oldest Christian homily—*2 Clement,* included among the apostolic fathers—is a straightforward exhortation to repentance, wholehearted service of God, and hope in the resurrection. The second-oldest is Melito of Sardis's Paschal homily (late second century): a complex, florid, poetic sermon on Exodus 12 delivered at the liturgical service that commemorated Jesus' death and resurrection. As Justin Martyr described the second-century eucharistic liturgy, the homily followed a reading from the Old Testament or apostolic writings (*1 Apol.* 67); later, three readings were customary.

The oldest extant corpus of Christian homilies comes from Origen. Most are on the Old Testament, but thirty-nine are on Luke. They are a running exposition of the text (a biblical book was read serially) and usually end with a doxology. Origen often strained to extract a doctrinal or ethical teaching for his hearers even from obscure passages.

During the fourth century, changes in the church led to far-reaching changes in preaching. Preaching the homily was generally reserved to the bishop. He preached usually from the throne, seated, but sometimes from the ambo. Once men educated in rhetoric became bishops, they cultivated style and form, and the Christian homily or sermon (the distinction was blurred) became the last great flowering of ancient rhetoric. Basil the Great and John Chrysostom used the plain and terse but sometimes pedantic Attic style; Gregory of Nazianzus was a master of the florid and heavy Asiatic style. Awkward biblical prose, both Greek and Latin, influenced the preachers' idiom. As the Christian calendar of feast days and fasts developed, the serial reading of the Bible gave way to topical readings (at least on Sundays and feasts) and eventually to a lectionary, and the subjects of homilies changed accordingly. Celebration of the eucharist on weekdays gave rise to series of homilies. Better-educated congregations expected more artful, and longer, homilies. Finally, theological conflict became an important occasion for preaching.

After Origen, the three Cappadocian fathers are the next important Greek homilists. Among Basil the Great's works are nine homilies on the Hexaemeron (the six days of creation) and fourteen on the Psalms, and twenty-four occasional sermons. Forty-four of Gregory of Nazianzus's orations are extant, including homilies for liturgical feasts, encomia of the saints, and funeral orations. Gregory of Nyssa has eight homilies on Ecclesiastes, fifteen on the *Song of Solomon,* five on the Lord's Prayer, and eight on the Beatitudes, as well as many occasional sermons

The master of the Greek homily was John Chrysostom, 140 of whose homilies on the Old Testament are extant, mostly on Genesis and the Psalms, as well as about ninety each on Matthew and John, fifty-five on the Acts of the Apostles, and over 200 on fourteen Pauline letters. Chrysostom's exposition of the scriptures is straightforward and historical, in the exegetical tradition of Antioch that he learned from Diodore of Tarsus. He often preached daily, sometimes twice. On a feast day, he might preach for two hours. His homilies suggest his lively contact as preacher with his congregation and include frequent digressions. Chrysostom's *On the Priesthood* contains a chapter on the office of preaching.

Homilies survive from "Macarius the Great" (probably Symeon of Mesopotamia), Amphilochius of Iconium, Severian of Gabala, Asterius of Amasea, Cyril of Alexandria, Theodoret of Cyrus, and others, but they never equaled Chrysostom. Among preachers in Syriac, Ephraem the Syrian was outstanding. The monastic homily, an exhortation to monks, emerged as a distinct form.

Few Latin homilies from before the late fourth century are extant, although some works by Cyprian and Hilary of Poitiers probably originated as homilies. The oldest corpus of Latin homilies is from Zeno of Verona. Ambrose's preaching impressed Augustine (*Conf.* 6.2–3); his works on Psalm 118 (119) and Luke began as homilies. Chromatius of Aquileia and Maximus of Turin also left collections of homilies.

The greatest Latin preacher was Augustine. More than 500 occasional homilies and sermons are extant, and his works on the Psalms, John, and 1 John were originally homilies. He was keenly aware of his congregation and made determined efforts to hold their attention; his sermons are filled with plays on sounds and words, stylistic flourishes, and aphorisms. He often alludes to the liturgical setting. His weekday homilies were sometimes no more than ten minutes long. The fourth book of his *On Christian Doctrine* is the first Christian treatise on homiletics.

After Augustine, the Latin homily became more stylized. Important collections survive from Peter Chrysologus of Ravenna, Leo the Great, Faustus of Riez, Caesarius of Arles, and Gregory the Great. Some authors began reworking the homilies of Augustine and others and eventually produced homiliaries, books of homilies that priests were to read to their congregations on Sundays and feast days. *See also* Preaching.   [J.T.L.]

Bibliography
F. van der Meer, *Augustine the Bishop: The Life and Work of a Father of the Church* (London and New York: Sheed and Ward, 1961), Part 3: "Preaching"; Y. Brilioth, *A Brief History of Preaching* (Philadelphia: Fortress, 1965); J. Bernardi, *La Prédication des pères cappadociens* (Paris: Presses Universitaires de France, 1968); J.B. Schneyer, *Geschichte der katholischen Predigt* (Freiburg: Seelsorge Verlag, 1969); T.K. Carroll, *Preaching the Word* (Wilmington: Glazier, 1984).

HOMOEANS. Theological and ecclesiastical party formed in 359 during the Arian controversy under the leadership of Acacius, who had succeeded Eusebius as bishop of Caesarea in 340. The Homoeans sought to establish a compromise formula defining Christ as like or similar (*homoios*) to God, omitting any reference to essence (*ousia*). The compromise failed to gain the acceptance of moderate opinion in the east because it was increasingly seen as a mask for Arianism.

The background for the Homoeans may be sought in the reaction of the church to the Council of Nicaea (325). The Nicene watchword *homoousios* ("of one substance") was suspect to most Christians in the east both because the word was not in scripture and because it had been condemned as Sabellian by the council in Antioch that deposed Paul of Samosata in 268. The defenders of Nicaea, including Athanasius, were widely regarded as neo-Sabellians; and the situation after Nicaea was complicated by the fact that the Arians gained the confidence of moderate eastern opinion by espousing formulations that were scriptural and traditional and that clearly insisted in opposition to Sabellianism upon the distinct character of the Son of God. The real difficulty was to formulate an anti-Sabellian understanding of the Son that would not be Arian.

By the late 350s, three significant parties had arisen, all of which opposed Nicaea and the Homoousians. The Danubian bishops Valens of Mursia and Ursacius of Singidunum held a western synod at Sirmium in the summer of 357 that condemned the use of *homoousios* and *homoiousios* ("of similar substance") and insisted upon restricting theology to scriptural terms. Hilary of Poitiers called the decree of the synod "the blasphemy of Sirmium." Partly in reaction to the Danubians, Basil of Ancyra held a synod in 358 that organized a party under the watchword *homoiousios*. This party has sometimes been called "Semiarian." During the same period, the Neoarians (Anomoeans), led by Aetius and his follower Eunomius, formed a party by winning to their cause George of Cappadocia, who had replaced Athanasius in Alexandria, and Eudoxius of Antioch. Attempts to effect a compromise that would satisfy all three groups led to the double synod of Rimini (west) and Seleucia (east) in 359. Acacius of Caesarea joined an alliance of the Danubians and the Neoarians and sought to impose on the Synod of Seleucia a compromise formula that included the words "we distinctly acknowledge the likeness [*homoios*] of the Son to the Father."

Although Acacius and the Danubian bishops failed to convince the majority of the bishops at Rimini and Seleucia, the emperor Constantius II accepted the Homoean compromise in December 359 on the condition that Acacius repudiate the Neoarians. In January 360, at a synod in Constantinople, Acacius ratified this decision, condemning the Neoarians and deposing the Homoiousians on nontheological charges. Acacius apparently believed that the compromise could succeed only by eliminating what he regarded as the extremist parties. The triumph of the Homoeans was short-lived and did not survive the death of Constantius in 361 and the pagan reaction under his successor, Julian. Acacius himself was deposed by the Homoiousians in 365, the year before his death. *See also* Acacius; Anomoeans; Homoousios. [R.A.G.]

Bibliography

Frend, pp. 617–623; T.A. Kopecek, *A History of Neo-Arianism* (Cambridge: Philadelphia Patristic Foundation, 1979); R.P.C. Hanson, *The Search for the Christian Doctrine of God: The Arian Controversy 318–381 A.D.* (Edinburgh: T. and T. Clark, 1988).

HOMOOUSIOS. Key word in the Nicene Creed that describes the Father and the Son as of the same nature or substance. *Homoousios*

first appeared among Christians in Gnostic circles, where it was used to compare humans with godlike figures, good and evil (Origen, *Jo.* 13.25; 20.20, 24 about Heracleon), or divine beings of the same spirit (Irenaeus, *Haer.* 1.5.1; Clement of Alexandria, *Exc. Thdot.* 50; Tertullian, *Hermog.* 44 [Latin *consubstantialis*]).

Origen (*Ps.* 54.4; *Fr. in Heb.* [PG 14.1308]; *Princ.* 4.4.1) evidently used the term to mean that the Son is what the Father is, but kept intact a subordination of the Son to the Father. *Homoousios* may have been debated at the Council of Antioch (268), which deposed Paul of Samosata (Athanasius, *Syn.* 45; Hilary, *Syn.* 81; Basil, *Ep.* 52.1), but it is difficult to say what it meant if it was in fact used. Dionysius of Alexandria rejected the term because it was not biblical. When questioned by Dionysius of Rome about possible subordinationist leanings, he said that he believed about the Son what the term *homoousios* was intended to safeguard about the Son's nature (Athanasius, *Dion.* 18).

At the Council of Nicaea (325), emperor Constantine was behind the introduction of *homoousios*. His western adviser, Hosius of Cordova, probably saw the term as asserting the numerical identity of nature shared by Father and Son—Tertullian (*Prax.* 2 [Latin *consubstantialis*]) had already expounded that view. The majority of the council, however, were conservatives who found *homoousios* to be unbiblical and supported a significant priority of the Father. Thus, at Nicaea the term had only a generic meaning, one affirming the full deity of the Son, not a numerical identity of essence. Yet it did expose Arius and his circle's subordination of the Son. They had thought the term described a material unity (Arius, *Ep. Alex.*) and had rejected it.

Councils at Antioch (341 and 344) and Philippopolis (342) disagreed with Arian teaching but refused to employ *homoousios*. Councils at Sardica (343), Sirmium (357), Nike in Thrace (359), and Constantinople (360)—influenced by emperor Constantius II—rejected the Nicene position in favor of Arianism. Athanasius only late used *homoousios* as the keystone of his teaching (*Syn.* 53). He insisted that although it was not in scripture its meaning was scriptural (*Decr.* 21). The majority of Christian leaders in the 360s and 370s preferred a lack of definition. Cyril of Jerusalem (*Catech.* 4.7; 6.6; 11.16) taught that the Son was "like" (*homoiousios*) the Father in all things. Athanasius (*Syn.* 41) and Hilary (*Syn.* 67–71) courted these circles because they were anti-Arian. The *homoiousian* party eventually became a part of the *homoousian* party. This is the source of the English phrase "not an iota of difference."

In the 360s, the *homoousios* was applied to the Spirit (Athanasius, *Ep. Serap.* 1.2, 20–21; 3.7). Gregory of Nazianzus (*Or.* 31.5) noted in 380 that various views existed. Basil never used the term of the Spirit. Pneumatomachians claimed that the Spirit was not of the same nature as the Father, but the Council of Constantinople (381) extended that sameness to the Spirit.

During the fifth and sixth centuries, a numerical unity of Father, Son, and Holy Spirit was understood as the meaning of *homoousios*. Leontius of Byzantium (*Nest. et Eut.*, PG 86.1289A) also taught the unity of the Son's human nature with that of all humanity, as did John the Grammarian (PG 86.2945B) and Ephraem of Amid (Photius, *Cod.* 229).

This latter view emphasizes that the use of *homoousios* involved more than a restricted, metaphysical debate. At least during the conflict between Arius and Alexander, it entailed a different understanding of soteriology, the teaching about how God could save humanity. At the end of the patristic period, nearly all Christian teachers thought that Jesus Christ must be of the same nature as the Father and the Spirit to effect salvation; many also thought he must be of the same nature as humankind to reach that goal. *See also* Arianism; Athanasius; Nicaea, Council of. [F.W.N.]

Bibliography

J.F. Bethune-Baker, *The Meaning of Homoousios in the Constantinopolitan Creed* (Cambridge: Cambridge UP, 1901); G.L. Prestige, *God in Patristic Thought*, 2nd ed. (London: SPCK, 1952); I. Ortiz de Urbina, "L'Homoousios' preniceno," *Orientalia Christiana Periodica* (1942):194–209; P.T.R. Gray, *The Defense of Chalcedon in the East (451–553)* (Leiden: Brill, 1979); R.C. Gregg and D.E. Groh, *Early Arianism—A View of Salvation* (Philadelphia: Fortress, 1981); Archbishop Methodius, "The Homoousion," and A.I.C. Heron, "Homoousios with the Father," *The Incarnation: Ecumenical Studies in the Nicene-Constantinopolitan Creed, A.D. 381*, ed. T.F. Torrance (Edinburgh: Handsel, 1981), pp. 1–15, 58–87; Kelly, pp. 233–255.

HOMOSEXUALITY. Sexual activity between persons of the same sex. Homosexual behavior was widespread in Greek society from at least the sixth century B.C., nearly always between males and chiefly in relationships between (active) young adults and (passive) teenagers. Although it enjoyed general acceptance, a current of critical disapproval is evident from the fifth century onward. Moreover, "Greek love" rarely found more than marginal favor in the Roman world.

Homosexuality was largely unknown in Judaism, but Christianity inherited unqualified condemnations of male homosexual practices in Leviticus 18:22 and 20:13. (The import of these verses cannot be limited to behavior associated with pagan cults, any more than the prohibition of child sacrifice in 18:21 or bestiality in 20:15.) Postbiblical Judaism stressed the homosexual element in the Sodomites' attempted rape of Lot's male guests (Gen. 19:4–5; cf. Judg. 19:22), and Hellenistic Jewish writers denounced homosexuality as frequently as any sin.

Paul declared both male and female homosexual activity (i.e., not merely pederasty) to be contrary to nature and symptomatic of the depravity of fallen humanity (Rom. 1:26–27). He also included male homosexuality in catalogues of vices, along lines familiar from Hellenistic Jewish literature. The Greek word *arsenokoitai* in 1 Corinthians 6:9 and 1 Timothy 1:10, denoting literally (males) "who lie [sleep] with males," was almost certainly formed under the influence of the Septuagint text of Leviticus 18:22 and 20:13. Although first attested in Paul, the term also occurs in Hellenistic Jewish texts (*Sibyll. Or.* 2.73, influenced by Pseudo-Phocylides's *Sentences*).

The church fathers universally condemned male homosexual behavior. In a standard triad of sexual sins that includes adultery and fornication, *arsenokoitia* (same root as Paul's term) appears interchangeably with *paidophthoria* ("perversion of boys"; e.g., *Did.* 2.2; Theophilus, *Autol.* 1.2, 14; Origen, *Comm. in Mt.* 14.10). Although the Levitical prohibition was not frequently cited (but cf. Tertullian, *Marc.* 1.29.4; Origen, *Comm. in Rom.* 4.4; Eusebius, *D.E.* 1.6.67; 4.10.6; *P.E.* 13.20.7; *Const. app.* 6.28; 7.2), no evidence suggests that it was felt to be no longer binding or to condemn only ceremonial uncleanness. Many fathers emphasized the homosexual lust of the Sodomites (e.g., Methodius, *Symp.* 5.5; John Chrysostom, *Hom. in Gen.* 43.4; Macarius, *Hom.* 4.22; Augustine, *Conf.* 3.8.15; Gregory the Great, *Moral.* 14.19). Some criticized other aspects of their depravity, but no patristic source excludes a homosexual interpretation of their conduct.

Stoic influence reinforced Paul's portrayal of homosexuality as unnatural, and early Christian writers regularly characterized it in these terms (Tertullian, *Coron.* 6; Clement of Alexandria, *Paed.* 2.83ff.; Lactantius, *Div. inst.* 6.23; Ambrose, *De Abrahamo* 1.6.52; Cyril of Alexandria, *Ador.* 1). They clearly regarded it as contrary to the created constitution and function of men and women, and not merely to the dispositions of particular individuals. Their occasional objections to the passivity or effeminacy involved in such acts simply illustrate their view of them as against nature. Although antiquity was scarcely aware of homosexuality as a sexual orientation, the prominence of the argument from nature suggests that patristic judgment would have deemed it an index of the moral disorder of humanity.

The frequency with which John Chrysostom, for example, attacked homosexual behavior shows that some in the church, including monks, indulged in it. Attempts to characterize particular relationships as homosexual, such as those between Perpetua and Felicitas or Ausonius and Paulinus, even without physical acts, are unconvincing.

All the evidence indicates that the teaching mind of the early church unreservedly condemned homosexual activity. Yet, although clearly viewed as contrary to God's will in scrip-ture and nature, it was not singled out for special execration. Its practitioners were debarred from the catechumenate by the church orders and condemned by councils from the early fourth century (e.g., Elvira, *can.* 71; Ancyra, *can.* 17), but conciliar reprobation was not frequent. The legislation of Christian emperors, picking up earlier Roman enactments (*Lex Scantinia, Lex Julia*), is of uncertain import until Justinian's time, when homosexual conduct was made a capital offense like adultery under the *Lex Julia* (*Inst.* 4.18.4). Yet Justinian's new laws against it were more hortatory than harshly condemnatory (*Nov.* 77; 141). *See also* Sexuality. [D.F.Wr.]

Bibliography
D.S. Bailey, *Homosexuality and the Western Christian Tradition* (London: Longmans, Green, 1955); K.J. Dover, *Greek Homosexuality* (London: Duckworth, 1978); V.P. Furnish, *The Moral Teaching of Paul* (Nashville: Abingdon, 1979), pp. 52–82; L.P. Wilkinson, *Classical Attitudes to Modern Issues* (London: Kimber, 1979); J. Boswell, *Christianity, Social Tolerance and Homosexuality* (Chicago: U of Chicago P, 1980) (influential but highly misleading on the early church); R. MacMullen, "Roman Attitudes to Greek Love," *Historia* 27 (1982):484–502; J.J. Collins, *Between Athens and Jerusalem: Jewish Identity in the Hellenistic Diaspora* (New York: Crossroad, 1983), pp. 141–153; S. Lilja, *Homosexuality in Republican and Augustan Rome* (Helsinki: Societas Scientiarum Fennica, 1983); D.F. Wright, "Homosexuals or Prostitutes? The Meaning of *arsenokoitai* (1 Cor. 6:9; 1 Tim. 1:10)," *VChr* 38 (1984):125–153; idem, "Early Christian Attitudes to Homosexuality," *SP* (forthcoming).

HONORATUS OF LERINS (ca. 350–ca. 430). Notable figure in the emergence of western monasticism because of the monastery he founded ca. 410 on the island of Lérins (off modern Cannes). Honoratus soon attracted many disciples, for whom he developed a rule. His monastery produced generations of churchmen who gave spiritual and intellectual leadership to the western church during the fifth and sixth centuries. His great reputation for sanctity caused him to be called from Lérins in 428 to serve briefly as bishop of Arles before his death ca. 430. *See also* Hilary of Arles.

[H.R.]

Bibliography

Hilary of Arles, *Life of St. Honoratus,* tr. F.R. Hoare in *The Western Fathers* (New York: Sheed and Ward, 1954), pp. 247–280.

HONORIUS (384–423). Western emperor (395–423). Honorius became emperor in the west upon the death of his father, Theodosius I. (Theodosius's elder son, Arcadius, became ruler in the east.) He ruled, under the protection of the general Stilicho, first from Milan and later (402) from Ravenna. Throughout his reign, the empire was troubled both by usurpers and by external attacks. Stilicho, who had handled the crises of the regime with some success, was executed (408), and Alaric besieged Rome (408–410). Constantius, Stilicho's successor, eventually became co-ruler (421) but died shortly thereafter. Honorius soon followed him in death and was buried at Ravenna.

The policies of the reign were in large part those of the emperor's advisers. Laws against pagans and heretics were reaffirmed (395), and stern decrees were issued against Donatism (405 and subsequently) and Pelagianism (418). A delegation sent to Constantinople on behalf of the deposed John Chrysostom was forcibly rebuffed. Honorius recognized the election of Boniface I to the Roman see against the claims of Eulalius (419). CPL 262, 1577, 1580, 1582, 1585, 1587, 1589, 1591, 1592, 1623, 1641, 1644, 1648.   [M.P.McH.]

HOPE. Christian virtue of confidence in God, especially concerning the future. Soon after the crucifixion of Jesus, two disciples remarked: "But we had hoped that he was the one to redeem Israel" (Luke 24:21). They referred to what is commonly called the "messianic hope," the age-long expectation that God would send his Messiah or "anointed one" to restore the Davidic monarchy, drive out the foreign occupying armies, and reestablish the glory of Israel. When Jesus' followers identified him as the Messiah or Christ (e.g., Mark 8:29), it appears that this identification did not include the eventuality of Jesus' suffering and death. The subsequent experience of his resurrection radically changed these early expectations: the anticipation of a political Messiah was replaced by the conviction that Jesus Christ was indeed God's agent—even God's only Son—sent to offer salvation from sin and death. "Redemption" took on a specifically soteriological meaning. The saving acts of God in Christ now offered hope for "eternal life" (Titus 3:7), for "salvation" (1 Thess. 5:8), and for "glory" (Col. 1:27).

The Pauline writings express this hope both in personal and in cosmic terms. For the individual, there is the hope that one shares (or will share) in Christ's resurrection (e.g., Rom. 6:5; 1 Cor. 15). The whole of creation itself participates in this hope as well, for it will be set free from bondage to decay (Rom. 8:21) and become, as God intends, a "new creation" (Gal. 6:15). God, for Paul, is indeed the "God of hope" (Rom. 15:13). The Christian's hope, then, exists as a present possession: through Christ, there is access to God's grace, so that the believer can now "rejoice in hope of sharing the glory of God," and this hope "does not disappoint" (Rom. 5:2, 5). Hope is also a future expectation: as the author of the Epistle to the Hebrews puts it, faith is the "assurance of things hoped for, the conviction of things not seen" (Heb. 11:1).

In the New Testament as well as in the subapostolic period, this tension between the present and the future was sharpened when articulated against the backdrop of eschatological expectations. Salvation, eternal life, and participation in Christ's victory were available, but the end (parousia) was not yet (Augustine, *Civ. Dei* 19.4). Stated often in apocalyptic dress, there was the conviction that Jesus was to return so as to establish the godly commonwealth and to judge the living and the dead; then would be the time when all things would be subjected to God and God would be "all in all" (1 Cor. 15:28). It was initially believed that this cosmic event would take place while the majority of first-generation Christians were still alive. It was the delay of the longed-for second coming, however, that altered the nature of the Christian hope as radically as the death of Jesus had altered the disciples' understanding of Jesus' messiahship. The tension between the "now" and the "then" was bound to increase. In the Johannine literature, for instance, there exist side by side the assertion that eternal life is a present possession (John 17:3) and several references to Jesus' return (14:3), to the resurrection at the last day (6:39), and to the future day of judgment (1 John 4:17).

In subsequent generations, as the hope for an imminent end receded, there still survived the hope that in the death and resurrection of Jesus God had acted decisively for the whole of humankind, at least potentially. There were some, like the adherents of Montanism, who continued to believe that the cataclysmic end of time was soon to come, but they were in the minority. During the age of persecutions, many believed that the martyrs would upon death go directly to heaven, win the crown of immortality, and even sit with Christ in judgment upon their tormentors (e.g., Origen, *Mart.* 28). With the end of persecution, in Constantine's reign, two new kinds of hope emerged. There was the hope, now that the empire was nominally Christian, that soon all persons would be brought into the Christian fold. In opposition to all this, however, were the growing number of monastics (cenobites as well as anchorites) who thought the church had become too worldly; they sought a life of asceticism, which they hoped was as near to the heavenly state as possible in this life.

Another factor affecting the nature of the early Christian hope was a difference of opinion as to how many people would ultimately be saved. For Origen, there was the hope that eventually all people, even the whole of creation, would be restored to their original intimacy and union with God; in this, he was followed by Gregory of Nyssa and to some extent by Gregory of Nazianzus. A dissenting voice to this universalism was Augustine; for all his many observations on the nature of hope, as in his *Enchiridion,* he claimed that only those souls who had been predestined to glory would be saved; all others were lost.

In the early church, the delay of the parousia had one palpable effect. It gave rise to chiliasm, or millenarianism, the belief that

Christ would return for a thousand-year reign on earth (Justin, *Dial.* 81; Irenaeus, *Haer.* 5.26–36). Although initially popular, chiliasm was later rejected.

Whatever shape the Christian hope took, common to its varying and often contradictory expressions was the sustained conviction that the ground of hope lies ultimately in God. Athanasius, for instance, could advise his correspondent Marcellus to read the Psalms, for there, he said, one can find that our souls may be "cheered by the hope we place in God" (*Ep. Marcell.* 19). And John Chrysostom, nicely assuaging the tension between the "now" and the "then," asks, What is the hope that is set before us? His reply is noteworthy. Even though we still live in this world, we live surrounded by God's promises, since "through hope we are already in heaven" (*Hom. in Heb.* 11.3).

[D.F.W.]

Bibliography
P.G. Walsh, "Spes romana, spes christiana," *Prudentia* 6 (1974):33–42; B. Hebblethwaite, *The Christian Hope* (Grand Rapids: Eerdmans, 1984).

HORMISDAS. Bishop of Rome (514–523). Hormisdas was a native of Frusino in Campania. Because of Vitalian's revolt, emperor Anastasius sought to heal the Acacian schism between Rome and Constantinople that had arisen in 484 over the Eutychian heresy. The effort failed, but Hormisdas later arranged an agreement on Chalcedonian orthodoxy with eastern bishops, which the emperor Justinian enforced. Feast day August 6. CPL 1683s.

[F.W.N.]

Bibliography
W.H.C. Frend, *The Rise of the Monophysite Movement* (Cambridge: Cambridge UP, 1972), pp. 229–247.

HOSIUS OF CORDOVA (ca. 257–ca. 357). Bishop and theologian. Bishop of Cordova in Spain (from ca. 295), Hosius suffered persecution under Maximian (303–305) and took part in the Council of Elvira (ca. 306). An opponent of Donatism and Arianism, he served as adviser to the emperor Constantine on ecclesiastical affairs (312–326). He had an important role at the Council of Nicaea (325) and presided at that of Sardica (343). Because of his resistance to the efforts of the emperor Constantius II to gain the condemnation of Athanasius, he was detained at Sirmium. There, under duress, he signed (357) a creed put forward by the Anomoeans, which involved concessions to the Arians. Allowed to return to his diocese, he repudiated his signature shortly before his death. He published no major works. CPL 537–539; see also 449, 578. *See also* Sardica. [M.P.McH.]

Bibliography
Isidore of Seville, *De viris illustribus* 5.6–7.
V.C. DeClercq, *Ossius of Cordova: A Contribution to the History of the Constantinian Period* (Washington, D.C.: Catholic U of America P, 1954); idem, "Ossius (Hosius) of Cordova," *Leaders of Iberian Christianity*, ed. J.M.-F. Marique (Boston: St. Paul, 1962), pp. 127–140.

HOUSE CHURCH. As a movement within Second Temple Judaism, Christianity began with no distinct institutions and no church buildings. The earliest description shows followers of Jesus continuing in Jewish temple piety and table fellowship "from house to house" (Acts 2:46; 5:42). This picture is enhanced by references to household conversions (Acts 16:15, 34; 18:8; 1 Cor. 1:16; 16:15). Paul sends salutations to "the church in the house of so-and-so" (1 Cor. 16:19; Rom. 16:5; Philem. 2; Col. 4:15), which is distinguished from more general references to "church" (Greek *ekklēsia*). The phrase suggests that existing households served as the nucleus of Christian organization with cellular communities formed around them. The extended household included not only the immediate family members but also other relatives and domestic slaves plus a coterie of freedmen, hired workers, and business associates and clients. There were several such house-church cells in larger cities, such as Corinth and Rome, and diversity was likely in both worship and group organization.

Places of meeting in the New Testament period included domestic "upper rooms" (Acts 20:7f.) as well as "halls" (*scholē*—Acts 19:9) and "warehouses" (*horreum*—*Passio Pauli* 1), but the most common reference is to private houses. It is also noteworthy that other religious groups and associations were accustomed to adapt houses and private buildings for assembly. Most of the Jewish synagogues from the Roman period were renovated private houses (e.g., at Dura-Europos). None of the earliest house-church meetingplaces can be positively identified archaeologically, as the house-church organization implies that no specific changes were made in the building itself.

The earliest evidence of a house converted architecturally into a place of Christian worship is from Dura-Europos, dated ca. 241–256. It is a typical house with rooms grouped around a central court. It is significant, however, that at this conversion all domestic functions ceased, and the building was given over completely to religious use; it was a "church building." Other sites that may provide valuable data for buildings of the third century and earlier are the excavated remains at Rome of a large apartment building that was taken over in the construction of the Church of SS. Giovanni e Paolo and a public building below the lower basilica of S. Clemente.

Christian writers of the third century also seem to reflect a transformation to known church buildings. Such edifices were at times called *oikos ekklēsias* (Latin *domus ecclesiae*) or *oikos kyriakou* (cf. Eusebius, *H.E.* 7.30.19; 8.1.5). Although the terminology has been inconsistent, for reasons of clarity it is preferable to distinguish between the unrenovated "house church" of the New Testament period and the renovated *domus ecclesiae*, beginning especially in the third century. At the same time, a distinction is made between these simpler church edifices (which may have evolved from a variety of existing buildings) and the beginnings of a formal church architecture with the introduction of the Christian basilica under the emperor Constantine in the early fourth century. *See also* Basilica; Church; Dura-Europos. [L.M.W.]

Bibliography
F.V. Filson, "The Significance of Early Christian House Churches," *JBL* 58 (1939):105–112; E.A.

439

Judge, *The Social Organization of Christian Groups in the First Century* (London: Tyndale, 1960); C.H. Kraeling, *The Christian Building* (New Haven: Yale UP, 1967); J.M. Petersen, "House Churches in Rome," *VChr* 23 (1969):264–272; R. Krautheimer, *Early Christian and Byzantine Architecture,* 3rd ed. (Harmondsworth: Penguin, 1979); R. Banks, *Paul's Idea of Community: The Early House Churches in Their Historical Setting* (Grand Rapids: Eerdmans, 1980); E.M. Meyers and J.F. Strange, *Archaeology, the Rabbis, and Early Christianity* (Nashville: Abingdon, 1981); W.A. Meeks, *The First Urban Christians* (New Haven: Yale UP, 1982); A.J. Malherbe, *Social Aspects of Early Christianity,* 2nd ed. (Philadelphia: Fortress, 1983); H.-J. Klauck, *Hausgemeinde und Hauskirche im frühen Christentum* (Stuttgart: Katholische Bibelwerk, 1983); S. Barton, "Paul's Sense of Place: An Anthropological Approach," *NTS* 32 (1986):225–246; P.C. Finney, "Early Christian Architecture: The Beginnings (A Review Article)," HTR 81 (1988):319–339; L.M. White, *Building God's House in the Roman World: Architectural Adaptation among Pagans, Jews, and Christians* (ASOR; Baltimore: Johns Hopkins UP, 1989).

HUMILITY. Christian virtue of lowering oneself. The New Testament twice quotes a well-known passage from Proverbs 3:34: "God opposes the haughty, but to the humble he gives grace" (James 4:6; 1 Peter 5:5). Indeed, throughout the New Testament are countless allusions to humility as the appropriate ethical posture for the Christian. Colossians 3:12, for instance, enjoins the Christian to put on "mercy, kindness, humility, gentleness, and patience," characteristics said to be the components of genuine love (Col. 3:14; cf. 1 Cor. 13:4–5). This emphasis on humility is even more often articulated in the Gospel accounts of Jesus' teaching, but with what might strike the reader as an ironic twist: that humility is the pathway to greatness. Those who humble themselves and become like children are the "greatest" in God's kingdom (Matt. 18:4); similarly, those who exalt themselves will be humbled and those who humble themselves will be exalted (Luke 14:11; cf. Matt. 23:12 and Luke 18:14). This persistent theme may best be expressed by the saying attributed to Jesus: "Many that are first will be last, and the last first" (Mark 10:31; cf. Matt. 19:30; 20:16; Luke 13:30).

Given this scriptural stress on the virtue of humility, it is not surprising that the subapos-

tolic writings continue the theme. Ignatius of Antioch, for instance, quotes Proverbs 3:34 as he urges respect for one's bishop, a respect, he says, that is analogous to one's humility before God (*Eph.* 5.3). Clement of Rome also refers to the passage from Proverbs in his admonition that we clothe ourselves in humility, the one sure antidote to "loathsome pride" (*1 Clem.* 30.1–3). Arrogance and boldness, he continues, are the attributes of those accursed by God, while the gentle and the humble are blessed by God (30.8).

As frequent as such passages are, more important are the references not to the humility of the Christian but to the humility of Christ. Clement, who was certainly more of a moralist than a theologian, claimed that Christ, who is the "scepter of God's majesty," came to us not with pomp and pride but in all humility (*1 Clem.* 16.1). Successive generations of Christian writers reiterate this and similar statements with increasing frequency, so much so that humility soon becomes a specifically Christological concept. With Philippians 2:5–11 as the scriptural warrant, the incarnation is conceived as a "coming down," a "condescension," or a "self-emptying," and the crucifixion as the truest mark of humble obedience. Ethically, then, those who humble themselves will be exalted; Christologically, Christ humbled himself that we might be exalted. He it is who "lowered himself" to our human nature that we might be "raised" to his divine nature. Athanasius described this mutual exchange in his assertion that Christ "became human that we might become divine" (*Inc.* 54). He goes on to say, however, that Christ's "humility and simplicity" belong only to the first coming; the second coming will be "glorious" (56).

As the Trinitarian controversies reached a tentative resolution at the councils of Nicaea (325) and Constantinople (381), where the preexistent Son was declared to be "of the same substance with the Father," humility began to take on specifically theological connotations. The humility of Christ, that is, came to be perceived as the humility of God. In spite of valiant efforts to preserve the Hellenic doctrine of God's impassibility, the majority of

Christian writers saw in Christ God's own self-emptying. As early as the second century, Ignatius of Antioch could speak of the "passion of my God" (*Rom.* 6.3) and Melito of Sardis could claim that "God has been murdered" (*Pass.* 96). In the fourth century, Gregory of Nazianzus spoke of Christ as "God made to suffer for our sake" (*Or.* 30.1) and boldly preached a "crucified God" (*Or.* 45.28).

It was divine humility, then, that was embodied and articulated by Jesus Christ. Centuries before Christ, the prophet Micah could ask (Micah 6:8): "What does the Lord require of you but to do justice, to love kindness, and to walk humbly with your God?" And centuries after the death of Christ, Augustine (for whom pride was at the root of all sin) could claim (*Enchir.* 108) that human pride could best be exposed and cured by the "humility of God" (*per humilitatem Dei*)—or again, that God was made humble (*Deus factus est humilis*) so that the pride of the human race might not prevent people from following in God's own footsteps (*In Psalm.* 33; *Enarr.* 1.4).   [D.F.W.]

Bibliography

John Chrysostom, *Concerning Lowliness of Mind*, tr. R. Blackburn, NPNF, 1st ser. (1889), Vol. 9.

J. Macquarrie, *The Humility of God* (Philadelphia: Westminster, 1978).

HYMNS. A hymn, according to Augustine, "is a song with praise of God. If you praise God and do not sing, you do not utter a hymn; if you sing and do not praise God, you do not utter a hymn" (*In Psalm.* 148.11).

Hymnos (Greek) and *carmen* (Latin) commonly had a religious connotation. Since there was often little difference between formal prayer and song, hymn could be used for any vocal expression of praise, but it referred especially to sung praise. In ecclesiastical Latin, *hymnus* came to refer to a religious song composed according to rules of measure and rhythm.

Hymns were used in the worship of the Greek and Roman gods, as shown by sources as diverse as the *Homeric Hymns*, Horace's *Carmen saeculare*, inscriptions, and a painting from Herculaneum depicting a choir in front of a temple to Isis, "for," as Plutarch writes, "it is an act of piety to sing hymns to the gods" (*On Music* 2 [1131D]).

The Psalms of the Old Testament were sometimes called hymns by Jewish and Christian authors. They have always held a prominent place in Christian devotional and liturgical practice. Other praise songs continued to be produced by Jews, as witnessed by the pseudepigraphal *Psalms of Solomon*, the Thanksgiving (*Hodayot*) Hymns from Qumran, and Philo's description of the sect of Therapeutae (*Contemplative Life* 80). The later Hebrew *piyytim* sometimes were constructed according to an equal number of stressed syllables in each unit, as in the Hebrew Psalms, but more commonly have an equal number of syllables in each unit.

Christians adopted for singing other poetic pieces from the Bible besides the Psalms. The codex Alexandrinus of the Bible (Greek) groups fourteen such pieces. Nine became "canonical" in the Greek church as Biblical Odes (or Canticles): Exodus 15:1–18; Deuteronomy 32:1–43; 1 Samuel 2:1–10; Habakkuk 3:2–19; Isaiah 26:9–21; Jonah 2:2–9; Daniel 3:26–45, 52–56, 57–90; and Luke 1:46–56, 68–79. There does not appear to have been any clear distinction in practice in the first century between "psalms, hymns, and spiritual songs [odes]" (Eph. 5:19; Col. 3:16).

In addition to the fixed passages from the Bible, the early Christians had their own new compositions. Fragments of Christian hymns have been identified in the New Testament—Philippians 2:6–11; 1 Timothy 3:16; Ephesians 5:14; Colossians 1:15–20—and in other early Christian literature, such as Ignatius, *Romans* 7.2. The Book of Revelation contains many hymnic passages (4:11; 5:9f.; 7:15–17f.; 11:17f.; 15:3f.), some of which may reflect liturgical usage.

The presence of song in Christian assemblies is indicated by 1 Corinthians 14:15, 26, and Hebrews 2:12 (cf. Matt. 26:30). The earliest official notice of Christian meetings by a Roman governor reported that the Christians met "on a certain fixed day before it was light, when they sang in alternate verses a hymn to Christ as to a god" (Pliny the Younger, *Ep.*

10.96). The Christ-centered content is a principal feature of Christian hymns (cf. Eusebius, *H.E.* 5.28.6). There are many patristic references to hymns and songs in the liturgy (Clement of Alexandria, *Paed.* 3.11.80.4; Tertullian, *Or.* 28; Hippolytus, *Dan.* [PG 10.693D]; Origen, *Hom.* 6.1 and 3 *in Jud.*; Eusebius, *Ps.* 65.10–15).

The earliest Christian hymns were not constructed according to the metrical rhythm of classical poetry but did borrow some rhetorical features from Hellenistic prose hymns. Of greater influence on Christian hymns was the accentual rhythm of Semitic poetry (an equal number of accented syllables in each verse). Rhyme was incidental before the fifth century.

Some early hymns continue in use in Christian liturgies. *Phos Hilaron* ("Joyous Light") from the second or third century became the Evening Hymn of the Greek church. The Morning Hymn in its Latin version (*Gloria*) has been popular in western Christianity.

A few Gnostic hymns have been preserved: the hymn of Christ in *Acts of John* 94–96; a hymn by Valentinus (Hippolytus, *Haer.* 6.37); a Naassene hymn (ibid. 5.5), which is in classical meter; and the "Hymn of the Pearl" (or "Hymn of the Soul") in *Acts of Thomas* 108–113. The production of heretical hymns, as by the Arians in the fourth century, led to occasional unsuccessful efforts to limit songs in church to biblical material (Laodicea, *can.* 59).

The earliest collection of Christian hymns, the *Odes of Solomon* (second or third century), survives in Syriac, which may be the original language of composition. The Syriac-speaking church was fertile in the production of hymns, but the hymns of its first poet known by name, Bardesanes, were not preserved because of doubts about their orthodoxy. The classic Syriac poet is Ephraem the Syrian, "The Harp of the Holy Spirit." His hymns make use of acrostics and a strophic (stanzaic) structure, as does other Semitic poetry. He employs an equal number of syllables for each verse, however, which is not done in the Hebrew Psalms.

The use of acrostics, the isosyllabic structure of verses, and refrains were important Semitic influences on Byzantine hymns. The greatest early Byzantine hymn writer is Roma-

nos Melodos, who developed the *kontakion*.

Clement of Alexandria at the end of the second century wrote the first known orthodox hymn using the quantitative metrical form of the Greeks (*Paed.* 3.12 end). The earliest Christian hymn known to be sung according to the Greek tonal system is the fragment in Oxyrhynchus Papyri XV.1786, the earliest (third-century) Christian hymn with musical notations. It is composed in rhythmic prose and contains directions for singing like the cantillation employed in Jewish and early Christian liturgy. The words praise the Trinity (cf. Origen, *Cels.* 8.67).

The standard form of Latin Christian hymnody began with Ambrose. The exact number of the hymns attributed to him that are genuine is disputed. The Ambrosian hymns have eight strophes of four lines each. A later Latin hymn writer of note is Venantius Fortunatus.

Hymns were employed at weddings and funerals. The church fathers recommended also that religious songs replace instruments and secular songs in the home (Clement of Alexandria, *Paed.* 2.4.43–44; John Chrysostom, *Exp. in Ps.* 41.2f.; *Hom.* 1 *in Col.* 1.5). CPG I, 1355–1359. *See also* Gloria in Excelsis; Music; Phos Hilaron; Poetry; Prayer; Psalms; Romanos Melodos; Te Deum.   [E.F.]

Bibliography

J. Mearns, *The Canticles of the Christian Church* (Cambridge: Cambridge UP, 1914); J. Kroll, *Die christliche Hymnodik bis zu Klemens von Alexandreia* (Königsberg: Hartung, 1921); A.S. Walpole, *Early Latin Hymns* (Cambridge: Cambridge UP, 1922); E. Wellesz, "The Earliest Example of Christian Hymnody," *CQ* 39 (1945):34–45; idem, *A History of Byzantine Music and Hymnography* (Oxford: Clarendon, 1961); L. Deiss, *Hymnes et prières des premiers siècles* (Paris: Fleurus, 1963); G. Schille, *Frühchristliche Hymnen* (Berlin: Evangelische Verlagsanstalt, 1965); R.P. Martin, "The Bithynian Christians' *Carmen Christo*," *SP* 8 (TU 93) (1966):259–265; R. Deichgräber, *Gotteshymnus und Christushymnus in der frühen Christenheit* (Göttingen: Vandenhoeck & Ruprecht, 1967); H. Darre, "De l'usage des hymnes dans l'église des origines à s. Grégoire le Grand," *Etudes gregoriennes* 9 (1968):25–36; K. Mitsakis, "The Hymnography of the Greek Church in the Early Christian Centuries," *Jahrbuch der Österreichischen Byzantinischen Gesellschaft* 20 (1970):31–49; A.W.J. Holleman,

"The Oxyrhynchus Papyrus 1786 and the Relationship Between Ancient Greek and Early Christian Music," *VChr* 26 (1972):1–17; J.H. Charlesworth, *Odes of Solomon* (Missoula: Scholars, 1977); J. Szövérffy, *A Guide to Byzantine Hymnography* (Leiden: Brill, 1978); idem, *A Concise History of Medieval Latin Hymnody* (Leiden: Brill, 1985); E. Ferguson, *Early Christians Speak* (Abilene: ACU, 1987), pp. 149–165; F.F. Church and T.J. Mulry, *The Macmillan Book of Earliest Christian Hymns* (New York: Macmillan, 1988).

HYPATIA (d. 415). Pagan philosopher of Alexandria. An adherent of Neoplatonism, Hypatia was the daughter of the philosopher-mathematician Theon. One of her students was Synesius of Cyrene, who corresponded with her and sent her his work *On Dreams* (ca. 403–404). She composed lost works on philosophy and mathematics.

Hypatia was killed by a Christian mob in Alexandria. The involvement of Cyril of Alexandria in her murder is debated; he certainly maintained an intolerant climate of opinion in the city that made it possible.   [M.P.McH.]

Bibliography
Synesius of Cyrene, *Letters* 10; 15; 16; 33; 80; 124; 153; Socrates, *Church History* 7.15.

J.M. Rist, "Hypatia," *Phoenix* 19 (1965):214–225; V. Lambropoulou, "Hypatia, the Alexandrian Philosopher," *Hypatia, Feminist Studies I* (Athens, 1984):3–11; R.J. Penella, "When Was Hypatia Born?," *Historia* 33 (1984):126–128; K. Wider, "Women Philosophers in the Ancient Greek World: Donning the Mantle," *Hypatia: A Journal of Feminist Philosophy* 1 (1986):21–62, esp. 52–62; M.E. Waithe, ed., *A History of Women Philosophers,* (Dordrecht, Boston, and Lancaster: Martinus Nijhoff, 1987), Vol. 1: *Ancient Women Philosophers 600 B.C.–A.D. 500.*

HYPATIUS (d. after 537). Bishop of Ephesus (531–after 537). Hypatius was adviser to the emperor Justinian and spokesman for the orthodox in negotiations with the Monophysites. He secured papal recognition of the Theopaschite formula, and he approved the use of images. CPG III, 6805–6807. *See also* Ephesus.

[E.F.]

Bibliography
P.J. Alexander, "Hypatius of Ephesus, A Note on Image Worship in the Sixth Century," *HThR* 45 (1952):177–184.

HYPOSTASIS. Greek word variously rendered in English as "person," "substance," "subject," or "subsistence." A noun formed from the verb *hyphistēmi* (stand under, support, stand off or down from), *hypostasis* first achieved wide currency as a medical term meaning a deposit, sediment, or precipitate. It joined the language of philosophy, under Stoic auspices, as signifying real, concretely existent being, that is, the actual "deposit" or "precipitate" in reality of unactualized possibility. In this sense, hypostasis was also contrasted with insubstantial appearance or merely notional existence. Thus, it came to mean the actuality or reality of something (whether in the sense of its nature, its existence, or its source), or simply as an actuality, a real thing (*pragma*): connotations that, it is important to note, could also attach to the term "substance" (*ousia*). "Hypostasis" often bore the sense of that which lies behind and beneath an appearance (its reality) or an activity (its plan or purpose); but just as frequently it was used to emphasize the fact of concrete existence.

"Hypostasis" figured in the theological language of the patristic era in two primary ways: in the development of the doctrine of the Trinity and in the formulation of the doctrine of the incarnation.

Trinity. The custom of referring to the triad of the baptismal confession—God, God's Son, and God's Spirit—as hypostases (plural) goes back at least to the age of Origen and Hippolytus. There can be little doubt that the primary intent of this usage was to mark them out as three distinct and objective realities: the same intent, indeed, that lies behind Tertullian's application to them of the term *persona.* Since, however, "hypostasis" was not a technical term with an exact, delimited connotation, and since its meaning overlapped that of "substance," it was natural to interpret the formula "three hypostases" as meaning not merely three distinct realities, but three realities hierarchically graded according to nature, or status, or both; and other considerations—e.g., the desire to preserve monotheism—made such an understanding of it seem necessary. This so-called "subordinationist" tendency was present in Origen himself and had its most extreme representative in Arius. Hence, by the time of the Council of Nicaea (325), a traditionalist teacher like Eusebius of Caesarea could believe firmly that the Nicene Creed's affirmation of the homoousios ("of one substance") with regard to Father and Son contradicted the doctrine that they were distinct in hypostasis. Not unnaturally, then, the formula "three hypostases" was taken, in the early phases of the Arian controversy, as a rallying cry for the opponents of Nicaea, of whatever sort or degree; and this situation was only exacerbated by the fact that the Latin tongue had in practice only one word—*substantia*—for the two Greek terms *hypostasis* and *ousia*.

The settlement of the Trinitarian controversy therefore entailed, among other things, a more exact definition of "hypostasis": one that would differentiate it from "substance." This was supplied by the Cappadocian fathers, who identified hypostasis with *to idion* as opposed to *to koinon*: the particular individual (defined by a set of differentiating characteristics) as distinct from specific or generic nature. Thus, just as they interpreted "substance" to mean "nature," they interpreted "hypostasis" as connoting an individual reality, a notion for which *prosōpon,* the Greek equivalent of the Latin "person," could also be used. The hypostases of the Trinity, then, were objective realities that completely shared the same nature or substance, but were differentiated from one another, and so individualized, by the relations of origination and derivation in which they stood to one another.

Christology. The same period in which this Trinitarian settlement was being worked out saw "hypostasis" introduced into the language of Christology. The first author known to have employed it in this way was Apollinaris of Laodicea (fl. 375). He interpreted the union of Word and flesh in Christ (cf. John 1:14) to mean that the Word of God took the place of the "spirit" or "intellect" in a human organism, so becoming its governing, life-giving principle. The result of this union he described as a single nature (*physis*), a single substance (*ousia*), and a single hypostasis.

In Apollinaris's formula, then, the terms "nature," "substance," and "hypostasis" are used

as rough equivalents in the sense that each refers to a concrete individual: to the Son of God as owning a human organism. In the reaction to this picture of Christ, two issues were prominent: whether it was right to conceive the creaturely component in Christ as incomplete (that is, as lacking its own intellect); and whether it was right to make the Son of God the subject of human passions and limitations. Answering both of these questions in the negative, the Antiochene theologian Theodore of Mopsuestia (d. 428) set out a Christology that insisted that the humanity of Christ is a nature and a hypostasis in its own right, and hence that in Christ there are two hypostases and two natures, which are unified because the divine Son identifies himself with "the Man" by indwelling. In Theodore's usage, "hypostasis" and "nature" were still equivalents. Both denote a real, concrete individual considered both as an independent subject of action and attribution and as having a distinctive constitution or character. In the Nestorian controversy (428–431), Cyril of Alexandria, although firmly repudiating Apollinaris's denial of a rational human soul in Christ, insisted nonetheless that there is only one subject of attribution in Christ: the Son of God, who has "emptied himself" by taking the human way of being as his own. Hence, Cyril continued, against Theodore and Nestorius, to speak of Christ as one hypostasis and one nature. In his case, as in Theodore's, "hypostasis" means an individual reality—that of the Son of God; but for him this hypostasis is the sole "subject" in Christ, and specifically the subject of a genuinely human existence. But in following Theodore by continuing to use "nature" as an equivalent for "hypostasis," and so speaking of "one nature," Cyril gave the impression of failing to see a distinction in Christ between being divine and being human.

It was at the Council of Chalcedon (451) that the Christological use of "hypostasis" was finally clarified and brought into line with its Trinitarian use. Chalcedon insisted with Cyril that there is in Christ one sole hypostasis— that of the divine Son, considered as a real individual who is the ontological subject of an incarnate life. It refused, however, to allow the confusion of hypostasis with nature, which it seems to have taken, in line with the established terminology of the doctrine of the Trinity, to mean a generic (and not an individualized) nature. Thus, it could speak of the Christ as one divine hypostasis (or *prosōpon:* "person") having two unconfused but inseparable "natures," divine and human, that is, as the rightful individual subject of two distinct systems of predication. *See also* Arianism; Homoousios; Incarnation; Nicaea, Council of; Substance; Trinity.   [R.A.N.]

Bibliography

R.E. Witt, "Hypostasis," *Amicitiae Corolla: Essays Presented to J. Rendel Harris,* ed. H.G. Wood (London: U of London, 1933); M. Richard, "L'Introduction du mot 'hypostase' dans la théologie de l'incarnation," *MSR* 2 (1945):5–32, 243–270; G.L. Prestige, *God in Patristic Thought,* 2nd ed. (London: SPCK, 1952), pp. 162–190; H. Dörrie, "Hypostasis: Wort- und Bedeutungsgeschichte," *Nachrichten von der Akademie der Wissenschaften in Göttingen, phil.-hist. Kl.* (1955); A. Grillmeier, *Christ in Christian Tradition,* 2nd ed. (Atlanta: John Knox, 1975).

1

IAMBLICHUS (ca. 245–330). Preeminent Neoplatonist of his age. Born in Chalcis, Syria, Iamblichus was a defender of traditional Roman culture and philosophy against Christianity. A prolific writer, he broadened Neoplatonism to include religious themes. This is most evident in his elevation of the *Chaldean Oracles* (second-century Greek religious verses) to the status of divine revelation and of theurgy (summoning divine power by magic) as the principal means for the soul's salvation.

Iamblichus's Neoplatonism represents a continuation and expansion of the teachings of Plotinus and Porphyry. His influence on later Neoplatonism was deep and long-lasting. *See also* Neoplatonism.   [R.M.B.]

Bibliography
Critical editions in the Teubner texts; in E. des Places, ed. and tr., *Les Mystères d' Egypte* (Paris: Budé, 1966); and in J. Dillon, ed. and tr., *Iamblichi Chalcidensis* (*In Platonis Dialogos Commentariorum Fragmenta*) (Leiden: Brill, 1973).

H. Lewy, *Chaldaean Oracles and Theurgy* (Cairo: Institut Français d'Archéologie Orientale, 1956); C. Steel, *The Changing Self: A Study on the Soul in Later Neoplatonism: Iamblichus, Damascius, and Priscianus* (Brussels: Koninklijke Academie voor Wetenschappen, Letteren en Schone Kunsten van België, 1978); S. Gersch, *From Iamblichus to Eriugena. An Investigation of the Prehistory of the Evolution of the Pseudo-Dionysian Tradition* (Leiden: Brill, 1978); J. Finamore, *Iamblichus and the Theory of the Vehicle of the Soul* (Chico: Scholars, 1985).

IBAS (d. 457). Bishop of Edessa (435–449, 451–457) and a leader in the theological school there. Ibas translated into Syriac some of the works of Theodore of Mopsuestia, Theodoret of Cyrus, and Diodore of Tarsus. Following his famous letter to Mari, a bishop in Persia, he was vigorously attacked for Nestorianism. He was deposed in 449 by the "Robber Council" at Ephesus, exonerated by the Council of Chalcedon (451) and restored to office, but condemned by the Council of Constantinople (553). His Christological position seems to have been a mediating one between Nestorianism and Chalcedonian orthodoxy. None of the hymns, homilies, or commentaries reputedly authored by him has survived. CPG III, 6500–6501. *See also* Three Chapters. [R.J.O.]

Bibliography
ACO, Vol. 2, i/3, pp. 32–34; iii/3, pp. 39–43; and Vol. 4, i, pp. 138–140.

ICON. Religious painting or holy image (Greek *eikōn*) to which special veneration is given. In Christianity, icons can represent Christ, the Virgin, saints, angels either individually or in groups, as well as scenes from the lives of these personages, or even theological concepts. Early icons either were portable (and hence privately owned, unless they were intended to be placed upon an icon stand, *proskynētarion*, in a church) or were permanently affixed to the walls or columns of a church or to its chancel screen. Portable icons assume various shapes: usually rectangular, but also square or circular. They normally comprise single panels but were also produced as folding pairs (diptychs) or as a central panel to which a pair of wings was attached (triptychs). Single panels sometimes featured a raised frame into which a sliding lid could be inserted so that they could be carried about. The frames customarily held dedicatory inscriptions. Most commonly, early icons were of wood, such as cypress or sycamore, which was covered usually on one side in one of two techniques: tempera (pigment mixed with egg yolk) or encaustic (colored, molten wax in which the wax is fused with the gessoed surface by the application of hot irons). The wood could be covered with canvas upon which the gesso was applied and then the encaustic or tempera. Materials other than wood were also employed, including ivory, textiles, and, on the wall of a chapel or church, fresco. In contrast to the post-Iconoclastic period (after the eighth century), early Christian icons survive in small numbers. Nearly all of the preserved early examples are sheltered in the monastery of St. Catherine at Mt. Sinai or were formerly housed there.

Painted Christian icons descend from Greek Hellenistic and Roman portraits of gods, emperors, state officials, writers, philosophers, or, in private homes, ancestors. Surviving examples of painted portraits of gods and emperors (the latter known as *laurata*) provide direct sources not only of single or grouped Christian figures but also of rectangular and circular formats, of diptychs and triptychs, and of the encaustic and tempera techniques.

Although the evidence is scattered and spotty, the veneration of icons seems to have evolved from pre-Christian practices that survived into Christian times. Tapers and incense burners were placed in front of or beside icons, curtains adorned them, they were decorated with flowers, and prayers were said before them. This relates to the cult of the portrait of rulers, which was complete with propitiatory sacrifices, the burning of candles and incense, and prayers and apotropaic supplications. By ca. A.D. 400, Christians held a belief in the magical efficacy of their images. Icons were placed as apotropaia at the entrances of churches, public places, public gateways, and workshops, indicating the prophylactic capacity of saints' portraits. By the sixth century, genuflection and bowing (*proskynēsis*) were commonly practiced before images in churches, and these icons were also kissed. Icons were carried in solemn processions, as was traditional in the cult of the imperial image, and they were used as palladia in battle. Hence, they were sometimes carried at the rebuilding of a church and were displayed to help protect a city in time of defense. Moreover, a cult of images, arising in part from the cult of relics, intensified in the sixth and seventh centuries, when it was officially promoted.

Early icons were made by artists (whose names are almost never recorded) or were *acheiropoietai*, images not made by human hands. *Acheiropoietai* were of two kinds. Either they were images believed to have been made by hands other than those of ordinary mortals, or else they were said to be mechanical, although miraculous, impressions of the original. The most renowned example is the Christ image of Edessa, which had been created when Christ pressed a piece of cloth against his face and which he allegedly sent to king Abgar of Edessa. This *acheiropoietos* is claimed to have been exhibited during the Persian siege of Edessa in 544.

Although authors in the early Christian period mention icons (e.g., Basil, *Spir.* 18.45; Gregory of Nyssa, *Hom. opif.* 16.13), no truly systematic attempt was made to establish a Christian theory of images prior to the sixth century. Some Christian writers were opposed to the use of icons and considered them a form of idolatry. Early Christianity, however, saw an increasing preoccupation in theological writings with the relationship of the image to its prototype rather than to the worshiper, as well as an increasing belief in the potentialities of the image as an instrument of divine power. Nevertheless, there is no proof that the painters and the artists of religious images in other media were familiar with this body of literature. See also Art; Images.   [W.E.K.]

Bibliography

A. Grabar, *Martyrium*, 2 vols. (Paris: Collège de France, 1943–1946); E. Kitzinger, "The Cult of Images in the Age Before Iconoclasm," *DOP* 8 (1954):83–150; repr. in *The Art of Byzantium and the Medieval West: Selected Studies by Ernst Kitzinger*, ed. W.E. Kleinbauer (Bloomington: Indiana UP, 1976), pp. 90–156, with author's "Postscript" on pp. 390–391; N.H. Baynes, "The Icons Before Iconoclasm," *Byzantine Studies and Other Essays* (London: Althone, 1955), pp. 226–239; D. Shepherd, "An Icon of the Virgin: A Sixth-Century Tapestry Panel from Egypt," *Bulletin of the Cleveland Museum of Art* 56 (1969):90–120; K. Weitzmann, *The Monastery of Saint Catherine at Mount Sinai: The Icons* (Princeton: Princeton UP, 1976), Vol. 1: *From the Sixth to the Tenth Century*; idem, *The Icon: Holy Images—Sixth to Fourteenth Century* (New York: Braziller, 1978); V. Lossky and L. Ouspensky, *The Meaning of Icons* (Crestwood: St. Vladimir's Seminary 1980).

ICONOGRAPHY. The reasoning behind Christian art. Christian iconography owed a great deal to Jews and to their cultural context in the Mediterranean. Admittedly, the second of the Ten Commandments might be understood as prohibiting any "likeness" of living beings, but in the reign of Herod the Great some secular Jewish buildings in Jerusalem had wall paintings representing birds. A stricter interpretation was required for religious buildings, and the few notices of the Jewish temple indicate its sculptures consisted of geometrical designs, formalized plants, and stars or flowers. Although their style is certainly borrowed from the Greek world, the subjects were taken from the biblical descriptions of the temple and had their own history among the Jews. For example, in Solomon's time the cherubim had been sphinxes, yet Josephus, when he described the cherubim that decorated the temple veil (cf. 2 Chron. 3:14), said that the forms of living creatures were avoided, and the cherubim were represented by stars or flowers (*War* 5.214; *Ant.* 3.126). Josephus thus interprets the second commandment strictly, but two centuries later this particular kind of strictness had been relaxed in the decoration of synagogues, for instance, in Hammath Tiberias.

Sources. There are several categories of early Christian art: sculptures, mosaics or wall frescoes in churches or tombs, and small pictures, manuscripts, ivories, jewelry, or metalwork. Any upper-class Roman villa would have contained exemplars of most of these forms, and at the outset the style of Christian art depended on the fashion in secular art. Techniques for the decoration of buildings had been established for centuries, and only in the reign of Augustus, at a much later stage, did an architect explain how to make the floor on which the mosaic cubes were laid, and criticized wall paintings (Vitruvius, *Arch.* 7.1, 5). Artists took great care over the design of mosaics, and in some cases carefully worked it out on the plaster underneath the cubes. Identical designs found in sites that are geographically far apart indicate the use of pattern books. Irregular execution was often caused by the fact that a team of craftsmen laid the cubes. Designs of wall paintings had to be carefully worked out beforehand, since the final painting was rapid and had to be done while the plaster was still wet. Early Christians bought objects from secular shops; Clement of Alexandria (ca. 200) recommended what signets to buy: "Let the signets be for us a dove, or a fish, or a ship in full sail, or a harmonious lyre, like the one that was used by Polycrates" (*Paed.* 3.11.59.1). Although jewelers made the typical "lyre of Polycrates" signet for any customer who would buy it, its meaning for Christians was the harmony of worship. Purchase from secular factories seems to have continued: a sixth-century factory has been found in Palestine that produced glass flasks for both Jews and Christians. Christians often made use of Greco-Roman models. Thus, Christ was represented by the long-familiar Roman motif of the Good Shepherd. A Jewish version of the Roman design of "Orpheus and the Animals" in Gaza has the label "David" over the central figure, and the same design is used in a church at Huarté in Syria with the label "Adam." Even specifically Jewish or Christian designs are seen through the dominant Roman style. Christ is often represented as an emperor, and even the archangels Michael and Gabriel in S. Apollinare in Classe, Ravenna, are dressed like Roman officers.

Interpretation. Churches and works of art that people saw on pilgrimages contributed to the development of Christian art. Monza and Bobbio have collections of flasks from Jerusalem that were embossed with pictures to commemorate the pilgrimage. In any case, Christians traveled a great deal, so it is not surprising that their art forms all over the empire have much in common. The interpretation of Christian art was based on interpretation of the Bible, with a sense that might be literal but was also in many cases allegorical. The latter reflected Greco-Roman thought. The *Picture of Cebes* (ca. A.D. 50) describes a picture in a Greek temple and argues that its meaning appeared only when the priest had interpreted it allegorically. In a similar way, Clement of Alexandria claims that Egyptian hieroglyphs, or the Hebrew tabernacle, are not to be understood literally but have an allegorical meaning that concerns divine things; and this interpretation is known only to the initiated members of the group (*Str.* 5.4.20f., 41). In the *Liber formularum spiritalis intelligentiae* (PL 50.727–772), Eucherius of Lyons interprets the meaning of biblical allegories; he also deals with some difficulties of interpretation, as when, for example, in different contexts allegories mean contradictory things. In Christian art, a literal interpretation perhaps suffices for the New Testament scenes that line the nave of S. Apollinare Nuovo, Ravenna. These are simply reminders of the literal text of the Gospels. But another scene, which must be allegorical, is the picture of emperor Justinian and empress Theodora with their suites in S. Vitale, Ravenna. Doubtless, these particular rulers gave the church offerings at its dedication, but they had never been in Ravenna, and this representation of them, surrounded as they are by the clergy of the city, is true only in the sense that they were benefactors. Old Testament scenes in early Christian art are likely to be given a double meaning, as they were in the commen-

taries. Another mosaic in S. Vitale literally represents Abraham entertaining the three men (Gen. 18) and depends on its Christian identification as the occasion when Abraham saw Christ (John 8:56). The source of the pictures has also to be taken into account. Some motifs and pictures were derived from the Jews. An excellent example is the stars on Christian liturgical fans, which clearly represent cherubim, just as they did in the Jewish temple according to Josephus. A different problem arises when Christians borrowed directly from pagan sources. Thus, in two fourth-century Christian sites in England are mosaics of Bellerophon slaying the chimaera. They cannot be interpreted literally and must be allegories of Michael slaying "a great red dragon, with seven heads and ten horns" (Rev. 12:3, 8). Living in a culture where Greco-Roman designs were still dominant, early Christians constantly borrowed Greek or Roman pagan motifs, but they admitted these motifs only on their own terms. They did so often enough that such borrowings cannot be held to be unorthodox.

One of the main questions for the art historian is what, at their stage of the Greco-Roman culture, Christians would have found understandable. If they turned to the Book of Ezekiel, they saw that angels could be symbolized by eagles. But they did not therefore think that because eagles were a possible symbol, angels had feathers (Ps.-Dionysius, *C.H.* 2). Greco-Roman symbols of heavenly beings who carried men's souls from earth to heaven included griffins. And even though Christians could find no supporting passage in the Bible, they accepted griffins as symbols for angels simply because the symbol was familiar. An excellent instance of Christians taking over pagan art occurs in a story about Alexandria, when the temple to Sarapis was destroyed (Socrates, *H.E.* 5.7). The Christians found stones inscribed with hieroglyphics shaped like a cross with a loop replacing its upper member—in other words, the *ankh*. Some Christians claimed that this letter belonged to them, since it contained the cross, but others, who were recent converts from the worship of Sarapis, explained that it really meant "the future life." The Christians accepted this new interpretation; and it seems from about this time the *ankh* appears in Egypt with a Christian meaning. *See also* Art; Dove; Fish; Mosaics; Phoenix.   [J.W.]

Bibliography

E.E. Urbach, "The Rabbinic Laws of Idolatry," *Israel Exploration Journal* 3–4 (1959–1960):149ff., 229ff; J.M.C. Toynbee, "A New Roman Mosaic Pavement Found in Dorset," *JRS* 54 (1964):7–14; J. Daniélou, *Primitive Christian Symbols* (Baltimore: Helicon, 1964); A. Grabar, *Christian Iconography* (Princeton: Princeton UP, 1968); E. Kirschbaum, *Lexikon der christlichen Ikonographie*, 8 vols. (Freiburg: Herder, 1968–1976); D. Barag, "Glass Pilgrim Vessels from Jerusalem," *Journal of Glass Studies* 12–13 (1970–1971):35ff., 45ff.; G. Schiller, *Iconography of Christian Art* (Greenwich: New York Graphic Society, 1971); M.-T. and P. Canivet, "La Mosaique d'Adam," *Cahiers archéologiques* 24 (1975):46–49; J. Beckwith, *Early Christian and Byzantine Art* (Harmondsworth: Penguin, 1979).

IGNATIUS OF ANTIOCH (beginning of second century). Bishop and one of the apostolic fathers. Nothing is known of Ignatius prior to his assuming the office of bishop, nor is anything known of the office itself prior to Ignatius. Toward the end of the reign of Trajan (98–117), Ignatius was arrested and, like Paul (Acts 25:11), taken to Rome for judgment. Ignatius expected to be killed in the arena by wild beasts. En route to Rome, Ignatius wrote seven letters. From Smyrna, he wrote letters to the churches at Ephesus, Magnesia, Tralles, and Rome. Later, at Troas, he wrote to the churches at Philadelphia and Smyrna, with an additional personal letter to Polycarp, bishop of Smyrna.

The letters witness to a unique understanding of the office of bishop. The bishop relates to the church as did Jesus Christ (*Eph.* 6) or even God (*Magn.* 6; *Smyrn.* 9). The church cannot function without a bishop present (*Smyrn.* 8; *Trall.* 2.2; 7; *Magn.* 7; *Polyc.* 4). Indeed, the church cannot worship, baptize, celebrate the eucharist, or solemnize a marriage without the bishop (*Smyrn.* 8; *Polyc.* 5). At all times, the congregation must be subject to the bishop (*Eph.* 2.2; 4.1; 5.1; *Magn.* 2.13; *Philad.* 7). The bishop has been appointed by Christ, not the church (*Eph.* 3), although in the bishop one can see the whole church (*Eph.*

1.3). It is not clear whether this exalted understanding of his office (later called a monarchical bishop) simply continues the organization found in the New Testament (Acts 21:18), first advocates the ultimate authority of a bishop, or just represents a unique personal position not shared by the nascent church.

Ignatius did not want the church at Rome to interfere with his impending martyrdom. He understood that his life and his office compelled him to act in consonance with his calling (*Rom.* 7.2). By giving his life for God's sake, he could become a true disciple (*Eph.* 3.1–2; *Rom.* 4.2). At martyrdom, he would cease being a voice or sound and would become a "word of God" (*logos theou*) congruent with his faith (*Rom.* 2.1). Ignatius was conscious of his role and accepted it. He spoke of himself as the presence of God (note the name he gave himself, Theophoros—*Eph.* inscrip.).

Ignatius was profoundly aware of spiritual oneness with God (*Trall.* 11.2; *Philad.* 8.1; 9.1; *Polyc.* 8.3). He sought the same spiritual unity for the church (*Eph.* inscrip.; 4.2; 5.1; *Magn.* 6.2; 14.1; *Philad.* 2.2; 3.2; 7.2; 8.1; *Polyc.* 1.2). Such oneness was for Ignatius a wholeness of life. He wished for Christians to be one in flesh and spirit (*Rom.* inscrip.; *Magn.* 13.2), one in faith and love (*Eph.* 14.1), as are Jesus and the Father (*Eph.* 5.1; *Magn.* 7.1; *Smyrn.* 3.3). He understands these three pairs to be parallel elements of the Christian unity (*Magn.* 1.2). Such unity comes when flesh suffers spiritually as Jesus Christ suffered (*Eph.* 8.2). Indeed, the celebration of the passion of Jesus, the eucharist, or the breaking of one bread together, also serves as a medicine for creating unity (*Eph.* 20). If the church is not united in this way, then Ignatius's death will have no meaning (*Eph.* 3; 11.2; *Magn.* 1.1; 14.1; *Philad.* 10.1; *Smyrn.* 11). In fact, he cannot easily distinguish his death from the death of Jesus and the eucharist (*Rom.* 2). As he is "ground by the teeth of the wild beasts," he prays he will be "found the pure bread of Christ" (*Rom.* 4.1).

The letters of Ignatius to the churches and Polycarp were collected by Polycarp, whose own epistle was a cover letter for the collection (13.2). During succeeding centuries, many additions were made to the collection. Only in the latter part of the nineteenth century did scholars reconstruct the original seven.

[G.F.S.]

Bibliography

Eusebius, *Church History* 3.22; 3.36; *Apostolic Constitutions* 7.46; John Chrysostom, *In S. Ignatium Martyrem* (PG 50.587–596).

J.B. Lightfoot, *The Apostolic Fathers* (London: Macmillan, 1889), Part 2, Vols. 1–3.

R.M. Grant, *Ignatius of Antioch* (Camden: Nelson, 1966); W. Schoedel, *Ignatius of Antioch* (Philadelphia: Fortress, 1985); H. Paulsen, *Die Brief des Ignatius von Antiochia und der Brief des Polykarp von Smyrna* (Tübingen: Mohr, 1985).

ILDEFONSUS OF TOLEDO (ca. 610–667). Archbishop and writer. Abbot of a community of monks near Toledo, Ildefonsus was chosen archbishop of the city, where he served for nearly a decade (657–667). He was active in the development of the Mozarabic rite. His work on the perpetual virginity of Mary, *De virginitate perpetua beatae Mariae*, besides showing his own strong devotion, played a part in the growth of Marian piety in Spain; the legend that Mary presented him with a chasuble in gratitude appeared in medieval collections and was popular with Spanish artists. The *De cognitione baptismi*, on baptism and the preparation of catechumens, is useful for the information it furnishes on the administration of the sacrament. A sequel, the *De itinere deserti*, compares the journey of the soul after baptism to the wanderings of the Israelites in the desert. The *De viris illustribus*, in the tradition of similar works by Jerome, Gennadius of Marseilles, and Isidore of Seville, comprises fourteen biographies; it is a source for Spanish church history. Feast day January 23. CPL 1247–1257.

[M.P.McH.]

Bibliography

Julian of Toledo, *Elogium S. Ildefonsi* (see CPL 1252).

A. Braegelmann, *Life and Writings of St. Ildefonsus of Toledo* (Washington, D.C.: Catholic U of America P, 1942).

IMAGE OF GOD. Only in Genesis 1:26–27 and 5:1 does the Old Testament teach that human beings were created in the image (*tselem*) and after the likeness (*demuth*) of God. Such image is associated with maleness and femaleness (1:27) and with human dominion over the rest of creation (1:26). Its endurance after the advent of sin can be seen in that the image was the basis for a law against murder (9:6) (cf. Wisd. Sol. 2:23; Sirach 17:3). Only in the Pauline epistles, with one exception (James 3:9—*homoiōsis*), does the New Testament specifically teach the doctrine of the image (*eikōn*). Since something major has happened to this image, through Jesus Christ it must be renewed (Col. 3:10) and humans must be changed (2 Cor. 3:18) and conformed to the image of Christ (Rom. 8:29).

Among the advocates of the view that image (*tselem*) and likeness (*demuth*) are quite distinct were the Valentinian Gnostics, Irenaeus (*Haer.* 5.16.2), Clement of Alexandria (*Prot.* 12), Origen (*Princ.* 3.6.1; *Cels.* 4.30), Cyril of Jerusalem (*Catech.* 14.10), and others. For Irenaeus, *tselem* meant natural gifts that cannot be lost and *demuth* the supernatural lost in Adam and restored through Christ. For Clement and Origen, the image was given at creation but the likeness is attainable only through perfection. Holding, on the contrary, to the view that *tselem* and *demuth* are synonyms were Athanasius (*Gent.* 34; *Inc.* 13), Didymus the Blind (*Trin.* 2.12), Cyril of Alexandria (*Dogm.* 3), and others. The view of Gregory of Nyssa, more complex and subtle, reckoned *tselem* as the more static and *demuth* the more dynamic aspects of the same reality.

The church fathers were nearly unanimous in concluding, as Philo had done, that the image was locatable in man's soul (or mind or spirit), not in his body: Clement of Alexandria (*Str.* 2.19), Tatian (*Orat.* 12; 15), Athanasius (*Gent.* 34), Cyril of Jerusalem (*Catech.* 4.18), John Chrysostom (*Hom. in Gen.* 8.3–4), Ambrose (*Hexameron* 6.7.40, 43; 6.8.44–46), Cyril of Alexandria (*Mt.* 6.23; *Hom. in Lc.* 96), and Augustine of Hippo (*Trin.* 14.4; *Civ. Dei* 12.23; *Gen. ad litt.* 10.2; *Ep.* 166.12).

Also widely held among the fathers was the idea that the image is to be identified with reason (*logos*) or mind (*nous*): Clement of Alexandria (*Str.* 5.14), Origen (*Cels.* 4.85),

Methodius (*Symp.* 6.1), Eusebius of Caesarea (*H.E.* 10.4.56), Gregory of Nazianzus (*Or.* 38.11), Gregory of Nyssa (*Hom. opif.* 5), and Augustine of Hippo (*Gen. ad litt.* 3.20; 6.12; *In evang. Ioh.* 3.4; *In Psalm.* 49.9). But especially for Athanasius (*Inc.* 3; 11) and Cyril of Alexandria (*Jo.* 3.4; 6) this image involves human participation in the Logos.

Common to the fathers also was the identification of the image with free will as to good and evil: Irenaeus (*Haer.* 4.4.3; 4.38.4), Tertullian (*Marc.* 2.6), Basil the Great (*Quod Deus non est auctor malorum* 6), Gregory of Nyssa (*Virg.* 12; *Or. catech.* 5), and Cyril of Alexandria (*Jo.* 1.7–8; 9.1).

Some fathers reckoned man's dominion over irrational creatures as an aspect or a corollary of the image: Eusebius of Caesarea (*D.E.* 4.6), Gregory of Nyssa (*Hom. opif.* 4), Severian of Gabala (*Creat.* 5.4), Diodore of Tarsus (*Gen. on* 1.26), John Chrysostom (*Stat.* 7.3), Cyril of Alexandria (*Glaph. Gen.* 1; *Ep. Calos.*), and Theodoret of Cyrus (*Qu. in Gen.* 20). For Ambrosiaster (*Quaest. vet. et novi test.* 127; 45), dominion was Adam's headship over Eve; for Gregory of Nyssa (*Hom. opif.* 16.7–9), maleness and femaleness occurred after an androgynous beginning; and for Isidore of Pelusium (*Ep.* 3.95), Eve shared in the dominion only until the fall.

Likewise, some fathers taught that the image/likeness must and can be restored through Jesus Christ with resultant adoptive sonship, holiness, and victory over death: Irenaeus (*Haer.* 3.18.1; 4.38.4; 5.16.2), Origen (*Cant.* 3.8; *Hom. in Gen.* 1.13), Hilary of Poitiers (*Trin.* 11.49), Basil of Caesarea (*Bapt.* 2; *Ascet. disc.* 1), Didymus the Blind (*Trin.* 2.12), Gregory of Nyssa (*Or. catech.* 5; *Or. dom.* 1; 2), Cyril of Alexandria (*Jo.* 1.9; 9.1; 11.11; 12.1; *Resp.* 10; *Nest.* 3.2; *Trin.* 6), Leo the Great (*Serm.* 12.1), and Diadochus of Photice (*Cent. chap.* 89). But Epiphanius of Salamis (Jerome, *Ep.* 51.6–7) argued against the Origenists that Adam had never lost the image, and the later Augustine sought a *via media* between an unharmed image and a totally lost image (*Trin.* 14.4; *Retract.* 1.25). Building upon but modifying the emanationism of Plotinus, Augustine concluded that there are various vestiges of the

Trinity in the minds of human beings (*Trin.* 8–10; 14). *See also* Images.   [J.L.G.]

Bibliography

A. Struker, *Die Gottebenbildlichkeit des Menschen in der christlichen Literatur der ersten zwei Jahrhunderte* (Münster: Aschendorff, 1913); A. Mayer, *Das Gottesbild im Menschen nach Clemens von Alexandrien* (Rome: Pontificium Istitutum S. Anselmi, 1942); J.T. Muckle, "The Doctrine of St. Gregory of Nyssa on Man as the Image of God," *Mediaeval Studies* 7 (1945):55–84; R. Leys, *L'Image de Dieu chez saint Grégoire de Nysse* (Brussels: L'Edition Universelle; Paris: Desclée de Brouwer, 1951); R. Bernard, *L'Image de Dieu d'après saint Athanase* (Paris: Aubier, 1952); D. Cairns, *The Image of God in Man* (London: SCM, 1953), Chs. 1–8; H. Crouzel, *Théologie de l'image de Dieu chez Origène* (Paris: Aubier, 1956); W.J. Burghardt, "The Image of God in Man According to Cyril of Alexandria" (S.T.D. diss., Catholic University of America, 1957); J.E. Sullivan, *The Image of God: The Doctrine of St. Augustine and Its Influence* (Dubuque: Priory, 1963).

IMAGES. The word "image" (representation) is used variously in the scriptures, and this variety is reflected in the writings of early church authors. Broadly speaking, there are two kinds of images: essential and imitative, that is, images that are the visible aspect of an invisible reality, and images that symbolically represent realities that lie beyond them.

In the Old Testament, there are several imitative images that were used in the context of Israel's worship, some of them with religious significations, for example, the cherubim above the ark of the covenant in the temple (Exod. 25:18–22; 37:7–9; 1 Kings 6:23–28), and others purely decorative, such as the decorations of the walls of the temple (1 Kings 6:29–35; Ezek. 41:18–20). No image of God, however, was allowed (Exod. 20:4, 5), and God was regarded as invisible and undepictable. All representations of God were regarded as idols. Although upholding the invisibility of God, the Old Testament does say that human beings were made "after the image and likeness of God" (Gen. 1:26f.; cf. 5:1 and 9:6). Judaism remained opposed to any representation of God. For Philo, the great Hellenized spokesman of Judaism, God was as far beyond representation as he was anonymous (*Decalogue* 66–76).

In the New Testament, the apostle Paul identifies God's image with Jesus Christ, God's Son (Col. 1:15; 2 Cor. 4:4), thereby suggesting that the invisible God has become visible in Christ and therefore that Genesis 1:26f. must be understood in terms of Christ. He teaches that the human being is *an* image of God (1 Cor. 11:7), as distinct from *the* image that is Christ, and that it is by being in Christ that this condition is restored to humanity. In fact, in Christ human beings are putting on the image of a second type of humanity, that of the heavenly man who is the Lord Jesus Christ, as distinct from the first type of the earthly man, Adam (1 Cor. 15:49; Col. 3:10; Rom. 8:29; 2 Cor. 3:18). Important also is the contrast made in the Epistle to the Hebrews between the Old Testament Law and Christ, or, more specifically, between the sacrifices of the Law and the sacrifice of Christ, presented in terms of "shadow" and "image" (Heb. 10:1).

The Pauline teaching on God's image revealed in Christ and restored to humanity is fundamental to the teaching of early church theologians, who treat it frequently in their writings, giving it a variable but rich content. The image of God in humanity is located primarily in the soul, and from this basis the theologians spun out many profound elaborations, which may be classified as either external or internal. The external understanding of the image of God in humanity refers to the human lordship and dominion over the rest of creation. Internally examined, it refers to the rational, noetic, and self-determining capacities of the soul that enable humanity to participate in God's nature or energies. These two aspects are so interconnected that the one explains the other. The dominion of humanity over the rest of creation is realized in terms of the external understanding, explaining and determining the life movement of the internal. Humanity is engaged in the life of creation in such a way that it participates in and cooperates with God. All this is curtailed, obscured, even lost to humanity because of the fall into sin, but it is restored in and through Christ, the image of God, who has become human without ceasing to be divine.

As the doctrine of the person of Christ was formulated against various heresies, the precise way in which image language must be understood in relation to God, Christ, and humanity is more clearly explained and elaborated. Inasmuch as Christ is both God and man, he is the living image of God in a divine and in a human way. In other words, in Christ we have both God's very image and its reflection in humanity. During the fourth century, the divine image in Christ received increasing stress in the context of the Arian controversy, while the human reflection of this image in Christ was stressed against Apollinarianism. The fifth-century Nestorian controversy introduced yet another nuance concerning the application of image language to Christ, namely its relation to Christ's one divine human person, or hypostasis. Image language and Christology reappear in the post-Chalcedonian Christological discussions, reaching their climax in the Fifth (533) and Sixth (680–681) Ecumenical Councils, which respectively stressed the unity of person and the duality of natures in Christ. It is, however, in the eighth century that image language in relation to Christology and anthropology was more thoroughly discussed as a result of the Iconoclastic controversy.

An icon (Greek *eikōn,* "image") is a flat image, usually painted, of Christ or of the events and persons associated with him in sacred history. Icons in the broad sense were introduced very early, as we see in the Christian catacombs and sarcophagi. It seems clear that icons differed from other images, especially from those associated with pagan idols, which were for Christians the object of frequent attack, as they had been for Jews and Neoplatonic philosophers. Yet liturgical practice gave rise to a fierce dispute concerning the theological legitimacy of the use of icons, a dispute that shook the Roman world and the church for over a century (726–843). The use of icons was eventually upheld, as explained by the Seventh Ecumenical Council (787). Iconophile theologians, such as John of Damascus, Theodore the Studite, the patriarchs of Constantinople Nicephorus and Methodius, and the 350 fathers of the Seventh Ecumenical Council, explained the manifold meanings of the word "image" and how images were employed in the liturgical practice of the church. John of Damascus, for example, speaks of five or six senses of the term "image" (*Imag.* 1.9; 3.18–23).

In the last analysis, this explanation was Christological. Icons did not depict the invisible Godhead, but the form that the Son of God irrevocably assumed at his incarnation. Icons of saints depicted the transformation of human beings after Christ's image. Consequently, to use human images/icons of Christ, and of the persons and events connected with his saving person and work, is legitimate, inasmuch as it constitutes a confession of God's incarnate and saving economy. If the One Christ is truly both God and man, then he must be both undepictable in his Godhead and depictable in his manhood. To refuse to depict his humanity means either to sever it from his divine person and suggest the error of Nestorianism, or to confuse it with his Godhead and suggest the error of Eutychianism. Thus, the same truths that are expressed through sacred words in the patristic dogmas are expressed through sacred images. The icon is not a mere symbol but has a dogmatic and mystagogical character. It leads from the copy to the prototype, from the human to the divine, from the created to the uncreated, provided that it is approached with faith and is understood to be a channel of the sanctifying grace of the Savior. *See also* Icon; Image of God.   [G.D.D.]

Bibliography

John of Damascus, *On the Divine Images,* tr. D. Anderson (Crestwood: St. Vladimir's Seminary, 1980); Theodore the Studite, *On the Holy Icons,* tr. C.P. Roth (Crestwood: St. Vladimir's Seminary, 1981); D.J. Sahas, *Icon and Logos: Sources in Eighth Century Iconoclasm* (Toronto: U of Toronto P, 1986).

G.B. Ladner, "The Concept of the Image in the Greek Fathers and the Byzantine Iconoclastic Controversy," *DOP* 8 (1953): 3–34; L. Ouspensky and V. Lossky, *The Meaning of Icons* (Boston: Boston Book and Art Shop, 1969); G.V. Florovsky, "The Iconoclastic Controversy," *Christianity and Culture* (Belmont: Norland, 1974), Vol. 2, pp. 101–119; C. Von Schoenborn, *L'Icône du Christ* (Fribourg: Editions Universitaires, 1976); *Iconoclasm,* Papers Given at the Ninth Spring Symposium of Byzantine Studies, University of Birmingham, March 1975 (Birmingham: Center of Byzantine Studies, University of Birmingham, 1977); L. Ouspensky, *Theology of the Icon* (Crestwood: St. Vladimir's Seminary, 1978); A.G. Hamman, *L'Homme image de Dieu* (Paris: Desclée, 1987).

IMMORTALITY. The self's or soul's survival of bodily death. Neither the early Jewish scriptures nor the early literature of the Greeks considered such a notion. For the Greeks, on the contrary, immortality (*athanasia*) was an exclusive property of the gods and connoted both everlastingness and blessedness, even as, among the Hebrews, it was the Lord alone who is "everlasting" (Ps. 90:2), while "all flesh is grass" (Isa. 40:6). The persistence of a "shade," or *eidolon,* in the underworld of Hades or Sheol was acknowledged in both cultures; in both, however, this underworld was the realm of death, not of life. To go there was simply to depart from substantive reality and enter a shadow-realm.

In both cultures, these early conceptions underwent revision and, at least initially, for the same fundamental reason: that the moral sense of the individual human life seemed unfulfilled apart from the assumption of an afterlife. At stake was the possibility either of human blessedness, which would entail some sort of share in the life of the divine realm, or of an ultimate punishment for those who had violated the moral order of things.

Greek Philosophy. Among the Greeks, it appears to have been in Orphic and Pythagorean circles that the soul, by now understood as the essential human "self," was first conceived to survive death, that is, the dissolution of body and soul; and this doctrine was closely joined to a belief that souls are rewarded or punished in the afterlife for their virtue or lack of it. Socrates, in Plato's *Phaedo* 107D–114, tells a "story" about the soul's fate after death that echoes these Orphic and Pythagorean ideas. The story's plausibility, however, is made to depend upon an earlier "physical" argument for the soul's immortality and incorruptibility (*aphtharsia*). This argument turns on the proposition that soul, as the principle of life and of motion in bodies, is by definition incapable of death and thus everlasting, without beginning or end. Plato's thinking on this subject, in which the *Phaedo* marks only a first stage, is thus conditioned not only by an interest in the destiny of the human person considered as a moral agent but also by the fact that in his picture of the cosmos soul—or at any rate rational soul in its various grades and manifestations, from the Soul of the world down to that of an individual human being—is the self-moving source of ordered motion in the realm of "becoming" and thus a necessary and eternal principle of the natural order, something intrinsically divine. In the case of human souls, however, immortality in the sense of everlastingness does not strictly entail immortality in the sense of blessedness; the latter depends on the acquisition of moral excellence.

Neither Aristotle nor the Epicureans followed Plato in these teachings, and indeed they denied even the idea that the individual human soul survives death, although Aristotle ascribes immortality to "active intellect," which he does not conceive to be individuated but describes as "immortal and eternal," that is, divine (*On the Soul* 430a17, 24). The Stoics, who envisaged the soul as a spark or offshoot of the divine "Spirit" that informs and governs the cosmos, sometimes contemplated a survival of the soul up until the periodic resolution of the cosmos into fire; but they were clear, as against Plato, that the human soul "is subject to generation and destruction." Hopes of immortality, in this case, of a blessed life with the gods, were encouraged by the Hellenistic mystery cults; however, these hopes did not presuppose a natural immortality that belongs to the individual soul automatically.

Jewish Thought. It was at a relatively late date that a notion of the individual's survival of death appeared in the traditions that produced the Hebrew scriptures. The classical Hebraic view was that the individual is strictly and justly rewarded or punished by God in the present life. Skepticism about this teaching (as expressed, for example, in Ecclesiastes and Job) did not, nevertheless, lead directly to belief in an afterlife. Such a belief first appears in clear form in Daniel 12:1–2, written during the crisis of faith occasioned by the oppressive policies of Antiochus IV. It takes the form of an assertion that "many of those who sleep in the dust of the earth shall awake," that is, it posits a final resurrection of the dead and associates this with a divine judgment that will vindicate the righteous and punish the wicked. In later apocalyptic literature, although all the dead are judged, the general tendency is to affirm full resurrection only in the case of the righteous, who are raised to "eternal life" or to "the world to come." This resurrection of course affects the person as such, and since Hebraic tradition did not identify the soul as the essential "self," it is generally taken to be corporeal. Nevertheless, *1 Enoch* 92–93 appears to contemplate a spiritual resurrection that pertains to the soul, and Josephus attributes to the Essenes the view that, although bodies are perishable, souls perdure and are punished by torment or rewarded with bliss (cf. *Wisd. Sol.* 3:1). The Sadducees in the time of Jesus and Paul were notorious for their rejection of the doctrine that God will quicken the dead and bring the righteous to a blessed immortality; but the Pharisaic party accepted it, and later Judaism affirmed the soul's immortality, that is, its survival, as well as the resurrection of the dead. In Jewish tradition, however, the possibility of an ultimate human blessedness and of the survival that it presupposes are made to depend upon God's will and not, as for Plato, on the soul's intrinsic divinity or everlastingness.

New Testament. It is against this background, in which a variety of conceptions deriving from different traditions were being employed to affirm both an afterlife for the individual and a share in God's blessed eternity for the righteous, that the teaching of the New Testament and other primitive Christian literature must be read. These writings contain no affirmation that the "soul" naturally survives death and certainly no allegation of its intrinsic divinity; but they evince a clear faith that God has already raised Jesus from the dead and will in the end raise believers to share his risen life. The term "immortality" itself appears only three times in the New Testament. 1 Timothy 6:16 sees immortality as the exclusive possession of God, a view that agrees with Paul's blunt description of human beings considered as "flesh" or "body" as "mortal" (e.g., Rom. 6:12;

2 Cor. 4:11). Nevertheless, Paul himself employs the Greek words for "immortality" and "incorruptibility" to define the state of the person who shall have been raised to the new life in Christ (1 Cor. 15:53f.). In other words, Paul uses "immortality" to denote not an inborn capacity to survive death but one aspect of the state of salvation, a gift of God. For him, it means roughly the same thing as "eternal life." The same appears to be true of other early Christian writers, such as Ignatius of Antioch, for whom immortality is equivalent to life "in Jesus Christ" (*Eph.* 20.2), and *1 Clement* (35.4), which characterizes "life in immortality" as one of the gifts of God that Christians wait for.

Justin, Irenaeus, and Origen. With Justin Martyr in the middle of the second century, however, there appears explicitly in Christian tradition the idea that the soul survives its separation from the body in death. Justin is careful to deny that the soul is immortal in the Platonist sense of ungenerate and eternal (*Dial.* 5.2, 4) or that it is incapable of ceasing to exist (6.1f.), and he repudiates those who think that because the soul is immortal it "needs nothing from God" (1.5), a view that he probably associated more with Christian Gnostics than with Plato.

He nevertheless affirms that souls survive death and continue to exist "as long as God wills them to exist" (5.3). The word "immortal," however, he reserves, when speaking for himself, to describe the gift of Christ at his second coming, when believers will become "impassible and immortal as God is" (124.4). Much the same set of ideas appears in Irenaeus. Like Justin, he sees the human person as a composite of soul and body and agrees that the soul, the seat of intelligence and freedom, survives its separation from the body for "a long series of ages" (*Haer.* 2.34.2). He can even describe such survival as "immortality" (5.4.1). Normally, however, Irenaeus too prefers to use "immortality," closely associated in his mind with "incorruptibility," to describe "the glory of the uncreated One," which human beings can hope to share only as, through the gift of the Spirit and the whole-hearted obedience to

God that it enables (4.5.1; 4.38.3), they enter into *koinōnia* with God (5.1.1). This eschatological immortality, moreover, must embrace body as well as soul, since Irenaeus identifies the human person not with the soul as such but with the union of soul and body.

Even Origen, who plainly teaches that the human soul is "incorruptible and immortal," qualifies the assertion in three ways. First, he sees this as testifying not to the necessary blessedness of the soul but merely to the fact that even as a creature it has a certain affinity for the divine and is "capable of receiving God" (*Princ.* 4.4.9). Second, he explains the phrase "Who alone has immortality" (1 Tim. 6:16) as meaning that blessedness belongs only to God by nature (*Jo.* 2.12). Finally, unlike Plato, he envisages the soul as "generate" and hence as dependent on God for its "natural" capacity to survive bodily death as well as for its capacity to enjoy the blessedness of eternal life.

Later Usage. In this way, then, the word "immortality" in patristic usage became ambiguous. On the one hand, it came to denote merely the soul's capacity to survive separation from the body in death, its persistence in being; on the other, it continued to refer to the eschatological reality of the resurrection, "eternal life." A resolution of the ambiguity came about only gradually, a resolution that turned on the fact that death was regularly conceived as a separation of soul and body in which, while the whole person is said to die, it is the body alone that is actually dissolved. Given this understanding of death, it was possible to describe humanity's ultimate blessedness differently for soul on the one hand and for body on the other. Thus, Athanasius uses "incorruption" or "immortality" to denote the fruit of Christ's overcoming of death as it touches the body, while blessedness for the soul, which is already immortal in the minimal sense that it persists in being, is characterized as its restoration to the image of God through knowledge of God (e.g., *Inc.* 20). In still later writers, the word "immortality" is less and less used even with regard to the body (or, for that matter, the whole person) in its redeemed state, and the term is thus voided on the whole of any eschatological connotation.

Instead, the words "resurrection" or "incorruption" are preferred to describe the body's state in the age of the new creation or "eternal life." Augustine, for example, when discussing the destiny of the human body, sometimes employs "immortal" or "immortality" (*Civ. Dei* 20.20), but he prefers to speak in other terms, as "the resurrection of incorruptible bodies" (13.19). By the end of the patristic period, "immortality" was on its way to losing its connotation of ultimate blessedness, and its primary sense had become that of the soul's survival of death. *See also* Resurrection; Soul.   [R.A.N.]

Bibliography

E. Rohde, *Psyche* (New York: Harcourt, Brace, 1925); A.-J. Festugière, *La Révélation d'Hermès Trismégiste* (Paris: Lecoffre, 1953), Vol. 3: *Les Doctrines de l'âme*; O. Cullmann, *Immortality of the Soul or Resurrection of the Dead?* (London: Macmillan, 1958); F. Refoulé, "Immortalité de l'âme et résurrection de la chair," *RHR* 163 (1963):11–52; H.A. Wolfson, "Immortality and Resurrection in the Philosophy of the Church Fathers," *Immortality and Resurrection*, ed. K. Stendahl (New York: Macmillan, 1965), pp. 54–96; R. Norris, "Immortality," *The Interpreter's Dictionary of the Bible*, ed. K. Crim (Nashville: Abingdon, 1976), Supplementary Volume, pp. 426–428; H. Sonnemans, *Seele: Unsterblichkeit–Auferstehung* (Freiburg-im-Br.: Herder, 1984); A.H. Armstrong, *Expectations of Immortality in Late Antiquity* (Milwaukee: Marquette UP, 1987).

IMPASSIBILITY. Doctrine that God is incapable of suffering. The English word "impassibility" translates the Greek noun *apatheia* (adjective, *apathēs*), which has two meanings: the incapacity for suffering or the inability to have feeling. Several Greek philosophers and Christian thinkers following them associated suffering and emotion with imperfection. A being that suffers is imperfect because it is under the control of another. Emotion seems to imply lack of rational self-control. Hence, *apatheia* is attributed to the divine, and is thought of, especially by the Stoics, as an ethical ideal.

There are several good examples of this characterization of the divine in the pre-Socratics: Anaxagoras (Diels A56–II.20.34; 100–II.29.31), Democritus (A132–II.114.13), Xenophanes (A35–I.124, 7–8; A31–I.121.32),

and Antiphones the Sophist (B5–II.339.15). For Plato, God does not grieve or laugh (*Rep.* 3.388; *Phil.* 33 B, C). Aristotle states that the divine substance is impassible and immutable (*apathēs kai analloioton*—*Met.* 12, 7.13–1073 A.11; cf. *On the Heavens* I.III–270 b.2f; *Topica* 148 a.20; *On the Soul* 408 b.25–29; 430 a.18; 405 b.20; cf. Plotinus, *Enn.* 1.2.3; 4.3.32; 1.2.5; 5.5.11).

Several modern writers have noted that the Bible knows neither an unemotional nonsuffering God nor unfeeling human persons. The God of Israel regularly becomes angry or is jealous; he feels compassion, pity, mercy. Also important is the insistence in some parts of the New Testament that God was literally present in the life, preaching, and death of the man Jesus of Nazareth, which might suggest divine passibility (John 1:14). This is precisely the criticism of Christianity given by the Middle Platonist Celsus (Origen, *Cels.* 4.14–16; 7.13–17). In spite of this, Christian writers, following the lead of Philo of Alexandria, developed a portrait of God that included impassibility in both senses. Some also, influenced especially by the Stoics, saw human impassibility as a Christian virtue.

For the apologists Justin (*1 Apol.* 25.2), Aristides (*Apol.* 1.5), Athenagoras (*Leg.* 21; 22; 29), Theophilus (*Autol.* 2.4), and Irenaeus (*Haer.* 2.21.4–2.23), God is impassible. Clement of Alexandria is the best example of complete absorption of this idea into Christian theology. Not only is God impassible, but also Jesus' human soul. The Christian Gnostic strives to attain the condition of *apatheia* in imitation of God and of Jesus, and this is the essence of true piety. Although Origen did not follow Clement's Christology, the idea of impassible deity is the same except for a few texts, principally *Homilia in Ezechiel* 6.6, where he attributes suffering to God. The most important document questioning divine impassibility in the east is a post-Origenistic work ascribed to Gregory Thaumaturgus, *Ad Theopompum*. Latin writers holding the concept of God's impassibility include Tertullian, Arnobius, Novatian, Lactantius, Hilary, and especially Augustine. Both Tertullian (*Marc.* 2.16) and Lactantius (*Ira Dei*), however, deny it at times.

The question of the impassibility of the Logos became crucial during the Arian debate. If the Logos is passible, he is not divine. Nevertheless, for Athanasius in some paradoxical way the Word that became flesh truly suffered while remaining impassible (*Ep. Epict.* 6). Eventually, the two-nature doctrine propounded at Chalcedon (451) tried to preserve both passible humanity and impassible deity in Jesus. In spite of Chalcedon's doctrine of two unmixed natures, Monophysites continued to hold to a more dynamic Christology associated with the Athanasian paradox. The view that one of the Trinity suffered was affirmed in the Theopaschite formula. *Apatheia* became important in spiritual teaching especially in the east toward the end of the patristic era. *See also* Modalism; Theopaschite Formula. [J.M.H.]

Bibliography

H.F.A. von Arnim, *Stoicorum veterum fragmenta*, 4 vols. (Leipzig: Teubner, 1903–1924); H. Diels, *Doxographi graeci* (Berlin: de Gruyter, 1929).

J.K. Mozeley, *The Impassibility of God: A Survey of Christian Thought* (Cambridge: Cambridge UP, 1926); W. Elert, *Der Ausgang der altkirchlichen Christologie* (Berlin: Lutherisches Verlagshaus, 1957); W. Maas, *Unveränderlichkeit Gottes* (Munich: Schoningh, 1974); J.C. McLelland, *God the Anonymous: A Study in Alexandrian Philosophical Theology* (Cambridge: Philadelphia Patristic Foundation, 1976); J.M. Hallman, "The Mutability of God: Tertullian to Lactantius," *ThS* (1981):373–393.

INCARNATION. Existence in flesh. As the expression of a Christian doctrine, incarnation refers to the belief that the eternal Word of God existed in the flesh as a human being after being born, through the power of the Holy Spirit, from the Virgin Mary. Jesus of Nazareth, as the incarnate Word of God, was therefore believed to be both God and a human being. No member of the early Christian church would have denied the basic doctrine of the incarnation, but explanations of its meaning varied, so that mainstream Christianity displayed a pluralism that disappeared only as time passed. What Christians did reject was any view that denied either the divinity or the humanity of the incarnate Word, for linked always to the doctrine of the incarnation was the belief

that, to be the Savior of humanity, the incarnate Word must be both divine and human. (In this context, it is necessary to note that, although the Word became incarnate in human history as a male, what is important is not his maleness but his humanity.)

In a general way, the entire New Testament was a relevant source for this doctrine, insofar as it presented Jesus as Son of God and son of Mary; the same is true for the Old Testament passages that promised a savior. Although the word "incarnation" does not occur, some texts were especially crucial for the idea; in Luke 1:26–35, the angel told Mary about the child she was to bear; Luke 2 spoke of the birth, infancy, and childhood of Jesus; John 1:14 was the source of much discussion—"the Word became flesh"; Philippians 2:6–7 introduced "form of God" and "form of a servant."

The earliest postscriptural writers, the apostolic fathers, did not attempt to explain the meaning of the incarnation: for them, it was simply a datum of revelation, a central doctrine of faith, without which there was no salvation. Ignatius of Antioch spoke often and vividly of the Savior who was truly God and truly human; the letter of Clement of Rome to the Corinthians promised salvation through the Savior's blood; the *Shepherd* of Hermas, on the other hand, seemed to confuse the Son with one or another angel. In the second half of the second century, such apologists as Justin and Athenagoras attempted to prove that their new faith was rational because it was God's Word (*Logos*, which also means "reason") that became flesh in order to save human beings, who possess the power of reason. Irenaeus of Lyons, their contemporary, was less philosophically inclined and presented the incarnate Word as the one who recapitulated, or summed up in himself, all of humanity; the Savior was therefore the second Adam who freed humanity from the condemnation owing to the sin of the first Adam. At Alexandria in the early third century, Clement and Origen tended to emphasize the divine character of the incarnate Word, although both of them realized that the Savior also had to be human, if humanity was to achieve knowledge of, and union with, God through him.

Although the fourth-century Arian controversy was technically a Trinitarian problem, it also touched the doctrine of the incarnation. The Arians were perceived as teaching that God's Word was a creature and therefore not divine; if this is true, the incarnation loses its significance, for the incarnate Word can no longer save humanity from sin and death. Athanasius of Alexandria employed an argument based on the incarnation and salvation to refute Arianism. In the last quarter of the fourth century, Apollinaris of Laodicea offered an apparently brilliant resolution of the Arian problems concerning the unity of the divine and human; but his teaching was rejected, since he seemed to deny that the Savior had a rational soul and thus seriously compromised the humanity of the incarnate Word.

Theological controversy now focused primarily on the incarnation, and two diverse approaches appeared. These have traditionally, if not always accurately, been associated with the cities of Alexandria and Antioch. The Alexandrian tradition stressed the divinity of the incarnate Word, as Apollinaris did, and concentrated on the Savior as one person, the divine Word united to flesh. The Antiochene tradition, represented in the late fourth century by Theodore of Mopsuestia, emphasized the humanity of the incarnate Word and thus spoke more often of the Savior's two natures. Theodore said that the human Jesus progressed through his life, death, and resurrection to a share in the glorification of the Word, with whom he was united; this explanation resembled the thought of Gregory of Nyssa, but even though Theodore was considered an outstanding teacher during his lifetime he was condemned years after his death as a forerunner of Nestorianism.

Nestorius, who became bishop of Constantinople in 428, objected to the practice, in prayer, of calling Mary "the mother of God" (*Theotokos*). His attempts to explain her motherhood led his opponents, headed by Cyril of Alexandria, to conclude that he was actually preaching two sons, one divine and one human, who were joined into a kind of third reality, the Christ, who was certainly human, but

not clearly divine; if that were true, then the Word of God did not truly become flesh. After an exchange of letters marked by misunderstanding and hostility, the teachings of Cyril and Nestorius were examined at a meeting of bishops in Ephesus in 431; this gathering, later recognized as a general council, vindicated Cyril and condemned Nestorius. Although Cyril and John, bishop of Antioch, reached an agreement in 433, some felt that Cyril had denied the Savior's humanity, and others thought that two natures implied two sons. The ideas of a monk named Eutyches brought the controversy to a climax; he was accused of a Monophysite view of the incarnation for teaching that the Savior was truly one divine person in flesh, while actually suppressing his humanity.

In 449, a meeting at Ephesus, which came to be known as the "Robber Council," declared Eutyches orthodox and condemned his opponents. This action was overthrown in 451 at Chalcedon by a general council that issued a declaration of faith based on the writings of Cyril, on those of certain of his opponents, and on those of Leo I, the bishop of Rome; it rejected the teaching of both Eutyches and Nestorius and declared that Jesus Christ was one person, the divine Word, who, to save the human race, existed in two complete natures, the human and the divine.

The Council of Chalcedon closed an era in the history of early Christian thought on the incarnation, but it did not definitively solve all problems, for it was rejected by those who felt that it was not faithful to the teaching of Cyril. Most of the theological struggles of the next 150 years reflected this tension. Anti-Chalcedonians (who were usually thought to be Monophysites) tended to view the council's supporters as Nestorians because they insisted on the Savior's two natures. *See also* Christ, Christology; Logos.   [G.H.E.]

Bibliography.

Representative patristic texts are collected in E.R. Hardy, *Christology of the Later Fathers*, LCC (1954), Vol. 3; R.A. Norris, *The Christological Controversy* (Philadelphia: Fortress, 1980); G.H. Ettlinger, *Jesus, Christ and Savior* (Wilmington: Glazier, 1987).

R.V. Sellers, *Two Ancient Christologies* (London: SPCK, 1954); O. Cullmann, *The Christology of the*

New Testament, rev. ed. (Philadelphia: Westminster, 1959); R.H. Fuller, *The Foundations of New Testament Christology* (New York: Scribner, 1965); E. Schendel, *Herrschaft und Unterwerfung Christi* (Tübingen: Mohr-Siebeck, 1971); A. Grillmeier, *Christ in Christian Tradition*, 2 vols. (Atlanta: John Knox, 1975 and 1987); H. Küng, *On Being a Christian* (Garden City: Doubleday, 1976); C.F.D. Moule, *The Origin of Christology* (Cambridge: Cambridge UP, 1978); E. Schillebeeckx, *Jesus: An Experiment in Christology* (New York: Seabury, 1979); idem, *Christ: The Experience of Jesus as Lord* (New York: Seabury, 1980); G.H. Tavard, *Images of the Christ: An Enquiry into Christology* (Lanham: UP of America, 1982); R.H. Fuller and P. Perkins, *Who Is This Christ?* (Philadelphia: Fortress, 1983); F.M. Young, *From Nicaea to Chalcedon* (Philadelphia: Fortress, 1983).

INFANT BAPTISM. Christian custom of baptizing infants or very young children, ordinarily by immersion in water. Whether infant baptism was practiced in the earliest period of Christian history has been debated since the sixteenth century.

The first explicit evidence for baptism of very young children appears in Tertullian's *On Baptism*, composed before his conversion to Montanism ca. 206. In this instruction, Tertullian objected to the practice, asking why "the innocent period of life" should cause haste to obtain "remission of sins." Building a case, he warned that it could put the sponsors in danger should they fail to fulfill their promises by dying themselves in persecution or by the infants' failure to hold to their baptismal vow. Hence, he urged, "Let them 'come,' while they are growing up; let them 'come' while they are learning, while they are learning where to come; let them become Christians when they have become able to know Christ" (*Bapt.* 18).

By the mid-third century, baptism of infants was being viewed as a well-established tradition dating from the earliest period of Christian history. Although Origen left no comment on the matter that can be attributed to his Alexandrian period (202–232), in Caesarea (232–254/5) he remarked in a *Commentary on Romans* (5.9) that "the church has received a tradition from the apostles to give baptism even to little children." In sermons, he cited this tradition to prove that infants inherited sin and guilt. Commenting on Leviticus 12:2 (*Hom. in Lev.* 8.3), he demanded to know why infants should be baptized "according to church custom," since, "if there were nothing in infants that required forgiveness and pardon, the grace of baptism would seem superfluous" (cf. *Hom. in Lc.* 14). At about the same time, Cyprian, bishop of Carthage, reported the consensus of an African council of bishops that swept aside arguments of bishop Fidus for delay of baptism until the eighth day with the contention that, although infants have not committed willful acts of sin, as descendants of Adam they have "contracted the contagion of the ancient death" at the instant of birth and thus must receive forgiveness not of their own but of Adam's sin (*Ep.* 58.5).

From the mid-third century on, baptism of infants was standard practice in both east and west. Deferral of baptisms in the fourth century has sometimes been cited as evidence that the custom developed late and with opposition, but these cases may have been mentioned because they were exceptional. Other motives, often not worthy ones, were frequently at work. The strongest of these was probably the reluctance pagans felt about surrendering to the demands made by the Christian faith, particularly under some duress. "If baptism washed away all past sins," many reasoned, "why not delay it until the end and thus ensure direct entrance into heaven?"

Whether Christians baptized infants prior to the third century depends on indirect evidence. The scholar Joachim Jeremias has set forth the following arguments: (1) References in early Christian writings to baptism of "households" (1 Cor. 1:16; Acts 11:14; 16:15, 33; 18:8) would probably include children, for family solidarity was strong in the ancient world. (2) Christian baptism paralleled proselyte baptism and circumcision (Col. 2:11), in which it was taken for granted that even the smallest children would enter the covenant along with their parents. (3) Acts 2:38f. extends the invitation for baptism directly to the hearers and their children. (4) Several passages in the New Testament imply that children born to Christian parents received baptism. Since baptism replaced circumcision, it is probable that prohibition of circumcision of children by parents of Jewish descent, according to Acts 21:21, necessitated baptism of the children. In the early Christian churches, moreover, the story about Jesus' rebuking of the disciples for "hindering" the little children from coming to him (Mark 10:13–16) may allude to the baptism of children, for the word "hinder" belonged to a baptismal formula. (5) A few references in the second-century church fathers allow one to infer the practice. Justin alluded to "many men and women of the age of sixty and seventy years who have been disciples of Christ from childhood" (*1 Apol.* 15.6). Polycarp of Smyrna claimed to have served Christ "eighty-six years," surely meaning from infancy (*M. Polyc.* 18.3). Clement of Alexandria, soon after 195, spoke in an allegorical figure of "children being drawn up out of the water" (*Str.* 3.59.2).

Jeremias supplemented these data with several arguments from silence: (1) If infants had not been baptized, there would be evidence of two kinds of Christians—baptized and unbaptized—but there is none. (2) There is "no information about the introduction of a practice deviating from previous custom." (3) No special rite was introduced for the baptism of children. (4) The custom nowhere appears "as the special doctrine of a party or sect." (5) Both east and west agreed in tracing the custom back to apostolic times.

Kurt Aland, although accepting infant baptism on theological grounds, contested Jeremias's argument on all other points, forcing him to admit the uncertainty of the crucial prop—the baptism of "households." The New Testament evidence neither confirms nor denies whether "households" necessarily included children.

In the absence of conclusive evidence for infant baptism prior to the early third century, other scholars have based their case for the practice on theological reasons. According to Oscar Cullmann, for instance, Christ procured "a general baptism" for all persons in his death and resurrection. By grace, God enables all to partake of that once-for-all saving event

through baptism. The decisive thing is faith "as response to this grace." By its very nature, baptism completes proselyte baptism and circumcision.

Roman Catholics have stressed the need to accept developments in the life of the church beyond the apostolic era. Although most Protestants have done the same in fact, they have hesitated to acknowledge this in theory, since it weakens the means by which they propose to maintain a continuous reform of the church, that is, testing by scriptures. If infant baptism was a later development, one can only speculate as to the reasons for it. These may have included pressure from parents anxious about their children's salvation, the intensity of Christian efforts to win adherents, a shift in theological perceptions from childhood innocence to inheritance of sin and guilt, and the influence of Judaism or other competitors. *See also* Baptism; Sacraments.   [E.G.H.]

Bibliography.

Tertullian, *On Baptism* 18; Origen, *Homiliae in Leviticum* 8.3; idem, *Homiliae in Lucam* 14; idem, *Commentarii in Epistulam ad Romanos* 5.9; Cyprian, *Letter* 58; Gregory of Nazianzus, *Oration on Baptism* 28; John Chrysostom, *Homily 25 on John*.

O. Cullmann, *Baptism in the New Testament* (Chicago: Regnery, 1950); A.W. Argyle, "Baptism in the Early Christian Centuries," *Christian Baptism*, ed. A. Gilmore (Philadelphia: Judson, 1959), pp. 187–222; J. Jeremias, *Infant Baptism in the First Four Centuries* (Philadelphia: Westminster, 1960); K. Aland, *Did the Early Church Baptize Infants?* (Philadelphia: Westminster, 1963); J. Jeremias, *The Origins of Infant Baptism* (London: SCM, 1963); K. Aland, *Die Stellung der Kinder in den frühen christlichen Gemeinden—und ihre Taufe* (Munich: Kaiser, 1967); E. Ferguson, "Inscriptions and the Origin of Infant Baptism," *JThS* n.s. 30 (1979):37–46; D.F. Wright, "The Origins of Infant Baptism—Child Believers' Baptism?," *Scottish Journal of Theology* 40 (1987):1–23.

INNOCENT I. Bishop of Rome (402–417). Innocent was bishop of the Roman church during the siege of Rome by Alaric (408–410) but was not present at the taking of the city, as he had gone to Ravenna in a vain effort to arrange a truce with the western emperor Honorius. He returned to his see only several years later (412).

Innocent's letter to Decentius, bishop of Gubbio in Umbria (416; *Ep.* 25), figures in the development of the canon of the Roman liturgy; the same letter witnesses to the anointing of the sick and distinguishes the rite of confirmation from that of baptism. Other letters to western bishops are concerned with upholding the prerogatives of the papacy—as all western churches owed their beginnings to Peter and his successors, Roman liturgical customs were to be kept and major disputes were to be referred to Rome. Likewise, Roman prerogatives were upheld over eastern Illyricum, which fell under the civil jurisdiction of the eastern empire.

Innocent affirmed the position of the bishops of Africa in their condemnation of Pelagius, Celestius, and their adherents. In his correspondence on this matter (*Ep.* 29–31), he interpreted the Africans' request as an appeal to the judgment of his see, whereas they had asked only that he add the authority of the apostolic see to their own. In the east, he maintained communion with John Chrysostom of Constantinople after John was deposed and exiled (404), and he broke off relations with the sees of Alexandria and Antioch over the dispute. He gave staunch support to Jerome and the latter's companions Eustochium and her niece Paula the younger when their monasteries were attacked and was critical of John, bishop of Jerusalem, for his failure to check the assaults. Thirty-six of Innocent's letters are extant; they constitute the principal source for his activities. Feast day July 28. CPL 1641–1643. [M.P.McH.]

Bibliography

Gennadius, *Lives of Illustrious Men* 43; *Liber Pontificalis* 42 (Duchesne 1.220–224).

G. Ellard, "How Fifth-Century Rome Administered Sacraments: St. Innocent I Advises an Umbrian Bishop," *ThS* 9 (1948):3–19; B. Capelle, "Innocent Ier et le Canon de la Messe," *RecTh* 19 (1952):5–16; E. Demougeot, "A propos des interventions du Pape Innocent Ier dans la politique séculière," *RH* 78 (1954):23–38; M.R. Green, "Pope Innocent I" (Ph.D. diss., Oxford University, 1973); O. Wermelinger, *Rom und Pelagius: Die theologische Position der römischen Bischöfe im pelagianischen Streit in den Jahren 411–432* (Stuttgart: Hiersemann, 1975); E. Lanne, "Les Sacrements de l'initiation chrétienne et la confirmation dans l'Eglise d'Occident, pt. 2," *Irénikon* 57 (1984):323–346.

INSCRIPTIONS. Writings on durable materials, most often stone or metal. Inscriptions are identifiable as Christian by their content, their use of specifically Christian formulas or names (often pejorative and adopted or given out of a sense of humility), and the presence of distinctively Christian symbols. These latter include the cross, the Greek letters alpha and omega (cf. Rev. 1:8; 21:6; 22:13), the fish (Greek *ichthys*, derived from the first letters of the words for "Jesus Christ, Son of God, Savior"), palm branches (cf. John 12:12–13), the victor's crown, the anchor of hope, and the dove and olive branches of peace. Funeral texts, inscribed or scratched (graffiti), comprise by far the largest class. Professions of faith appear, along with scriptural quotations, prayers, and, later, the graffiti of pilgrims, dedications of churches, and literary texts in honor of martyrs and other saints.

The number of discovered inscriptions dating from before the third century is small. There are more from that century, and they are quite common from the fourth century on. Their exact total will never be known, since it is sometimes difficult to distinguish between genuine and spurious inscriptions, some once discovered have been destroyed or exist only in manuscript form, and new ones are found every year. Most of the texts are in Greek or in Latin, and of these the Latin far outnumber the Greek.

Greek inscriptions have been found in the largest quantity in Asia Minor and other regions of the east; in the west, they appear chiefly in Rome and Sicily. As an international center, Rome had many Greek-speaking residents, and the language of the liturgy was Greek into the fourth century. The Greek inscriptions found in the city approximately equal the Latin in number in the third century, but their numbers show a rapid decline thereafter. Among Greek inscriptions important for their doctrinal or historical content are that of Abercius (late second century) from Phrygia, the epitaph of Pectorius (fourth century, but perhaps employing older material) from Autun, and one in honor of a missionary from Laodicea in Syria who worked among the Celts (late second century), discovered at Lyons.

Latin inscriptions come in greatest quantity from Rome and its neighborhood. They are frequent in Africa, Gaul, Italy, and Spain but less so in more northern regions, such as Germany or Great Britain, or in the east. Since most of them, along with the majority of similar pagan inscriptions, are composed in vulgar Latin, that is, the spoken Latin of the time, they offer important evidence for the process of transition from Latin to the early Romance languages.

The graffiti found in or near the catacombs of Rome, under the Church of St. Peter and elsewhere, have special significance. Scratched in Greek or in Latin by mourners or pilgrims, and extending from the third to as late as the eighth century, they give evidence of religious and cultural development and continuity over a considerable period. They testify as well to the substantial role of the cult of the martyrs in the city.

Devotion of the martyrs culminated under Damasus I (366–384) in the Latin *Epigrams* that he composed in the course of his restoration of their burial places and had inscribed by the noted engraver Filocalus (CPL 1635, 1636). These epitaphs, which furnish evidence of Damasus's zeal in discovering and preserving the tombs, supply information about his life and family as well. Although their importance to hagiography is clear, they are not considered to be of high literary merit. Some can be read on their original marble slabs, but most are extant only in medieval manuscripts.

Leo I the Great (440–461) composed an inscription placed in the baptistery of the Lateran basilica (CPL 1657b). Other inscriptions assigned to him are probably not his.

The earliest Christian epitaphs, in Greek or in Latin, often reveal the humble origin of the deceased and are without indication of date, which must be deduced when possible from archaeology and often scant internal evidence. Indications of date become more frequent from the mid-fourth century on. In the west, dating

is most often by reference to the Roman consuls, who continued to be appointed even after the collapse of the western empire, although Spain and Africa have systems of their own. In the east, dating follows a wide variety of local or regional systems. But inscriptions were not dated from the supposed year of Christ's birth prior to the early Middle Ages.

Although the earlier epitaphs generally omit the mention of profession or trade or social standing, such references increase from the mid-fourth century. Thenceforth, Christians appear in virtually all the occupations known to antiquity and in every social class, from noble to slave. Like their pagan counterparts, these Christian inscriptions offer an invaluable look into the activities of everyday life. Yet, except for Filocalus, the identities of their engravers are unknown.

Christian funeral inscriptions are often like pagan ones in their style and in the expression of a natural grief before the fact of death, but they differ above all in exhibiting a confident and clear hope of resurrection. They tend consequently to sound a more cheerful and even triumphant note. The Christian's true birthday (*dies natalis*) is considered to be the day of his death, reckoned as birth into the fullness of eternal life. The familiar alpha-omega symbol sometimes appears in reverse order (omega preceding alpha, the final letter of the alphabet before the first) in order to indicate this concept of the ending of life as leading to the beginning of a new life.

Inscriptions testify to the belief of ordinary Christians in such basic teachings as the Trinity and the divinity of Christ, although hardly with the degree of exactness to be expected of doctrinal writings in manuscript form. They reflect Christian practice in regard to baptism and the eucharist and reveal a strong belief in the efficacy of prayer. (Often, the prayer texts themselves reflect formulas of the primitive liturgy.) They give witness to the organization of the church and the clergy, the division into various orders major and minor, and the terminology of monasticism. They record the foundation and dedication of churches and the celebration of Easter and other feasts.

Some have value for the investigation of schismatic movements, such as Montanism and Donatism.

Epigraphy, or the study of inscriptions, is an indispensable component of the study of early Christianity. In medieval and later times, although still valuable, it plays a less important role as manuscript evidence is more abundant. *See also* Abercius; Archaeology; Damasus I; Numismatics; Pectorius, Epitaph of.

[M.P.McH.]

Bibliography

Corpus Inscriptionum Graecarum, ed. A. Boeckh et al. (Berlin: Reimer, 1828–1877), esp. Vol. 4, part 40, "Inscriptiones Christianae" (1877); the *CIG* is continued by *Inscriptiones Graecae* (Berlin: Reimer, 1873–1932, and, from 1932, de Gruyter); *Corpus Inscriptionum Latinarum* (Berlin: Reimer, 1862–1932, and de Gruyter, 1933–); E. LeBlant, *L'Epigraphie chrétienne en Gaule et dans l'Afrique Romaine* (Paris: Leroux, 1890); G. Lefebvre, *Recueil des inscriptions grecques-chrétiennes d'Egypte* (Cairo: Institut Français, 1907); A. Silvagni and A. Ferrua, eds., *Inscriptiones Christianae Urbis Romae*, nova series (Vol. 1, Rome: Befani; Vol. 2, Rome; Vols. 3–, Vatican City: Pontificium Institutum Archaeologiae Christianae, 1922–); E. Diehl, ed., *Inscriptiones Latinae Christianae Veteres*, 3 vols. (Berlin: Weidmann, 1924–1931; 2nd ed. 1961, ed. J. Moreau), Vol. 4 *Supplementum* , ed. J. Moreau and H.I. Marrou (Dublin and Zurich, 1967); H. Lietzmann, N.A. Bees, and G. Sotiriu, eds., *Corpus der Griechisch-Christlichen Inschriften von Hellas*. 1. *Die Griechisch-Christlichen Inschriften des Peloponnes* (Athens: Christlich-Archäologische Gesellschaft, 1941); A.C. Bandy, *The Greek Christian Inscriptions of Crete* (Athens: Christian Archaeological Society, 1970); D. Feissel, *Recueil des inscriptions chrétiennes de Macédoine du IIIe au VIe siècle*, Bulletin de correspondance hellénique, suppl. 8 (Paris: Boccard, 1983).

O. Marucchi, *Christian Epigraphy* (Cambridge: Cambridge UP, 1912); R. Cagnat, *Cours d'épigraphie latine*, 4th ed. (Paris: Fontemoing, 1914); A. Ferrua, *Epigrammata Damasiana* (Rome: Pontificio Istituto di Archeologia Cristiana, 1942); R. Lattimore, *Themes in Greek and Latin Epitaphs* (Urbana: U of Illinois P, 1942), pp. 301–340); M. Guarducci, *Epigrafia Greca*, 4 vols. (Rome: Istituto Poligrafico dello Stato, 1967–1978), esp. Vol. 4: *Epigrafi sacre pagane e cristiane* (1978); G. Susini, *The Roman Stonecutter: An Introduction to Latin Epigraphy* (Totowa: Rowman and Littlefield, 1973); G.H.R. Horsley, *New Documents Illustrating Early Christianity: A Review of the Greek Inscriptions and Papyri Published in 1976–* (North Ryde: Ancient History Documentary Research Centre, Macquarrie University, 1981–1983, and Sydney: Macquarrie University, 1987–); A.G. Woodhead, *The Study of Greek Inscriptions*, 2nd ed.(Cambridge: Cambridge UP, 1981); A.E. Gordon, *Illustrated Introduction to Latin Epigraphy* (Berkeley: U of California P, 1983).

INSTITUTES. Research centers organized to expedite the study of early Christianity in its larger context. The longest sustained research effort has been that of the Bollandists (Jesuits) in Brussels, who have specialized in the study of hagiography since 1615. Modern institutes have been influenced by Adolf von Harnack, who organized the Kirchenväter Kommission in Berlin, which undertook publication of Die Griechischen Christlichen Schriftsteller. This has been supplemented by, among others, the work of the Corpus Christianorum Center at the Katholieke Universiteit te Leuven, and the Institut des Sources Chrétiennes in Lyons.

Other institutes complement the research with traditional academic organization and goals. The Pontificio Istituto Orientale was organized in Rome in 1917 to examine the development of Christianity in the Near East. The Istituto Patristico Augustinianum in Rome initially focused on Augustine but has expanded to include research on all aspects of early Christianity. It has produced the *Dizionario patristico e di antichità cristiane* (1983–1988) and has brought to completion the *Patrology* of Johannes Quasten (1978, Engl. tr. 1986). As an example of a specialized institute, the Forschungsstelle Gregor von Nyssa an der Westfälischen Wilhelms-Universität in Münster is bringing to completion the critical edition of Gregory of Nyssa's works with complete lexicon and classified bibliography.

In North America, Harvard's Dumbarton Oaks in Washington, D.C., has focused on the Byzantine period. More recently, the Institute for Antiquity and Christianity in Claremont, California, has coordinated research on the Christianity of the Copts, asceticism, and Christian origins. Other institutes functioning as units of a regular university program are found at the Catholic University of America and the universities of Montreal, Princeton, Toronto, and Villanova.

[D.B]

INTERPRETATION OF THE BIBLE. Born with a set of sacred writings, the Christian church has always linked its self-understanding to the interpretation of its scriptures inherited from Judaism. The Synoptic Gospels portray Jesus as the founder of Christian exegesis: he explains the scriptures in the synagogues (cf. Luke 4:16–23), quotes them in disputes (Matt. 22:29, 37, 41–45 and parallels), and proposes his own teaching in reference to them (Matt. 5:17–48; 10:10; Mark 4:11–12; 13:14–15; Luke 7:27). His death and resurrection are described as their fulfillment and also as the key to their ultimate, divinely willed meaning (Matt. 21:4–5, 13, 16, 42; 26:24; Mark 12:10; 14:21; 15:28; Luke 22:37; 24:27). In Luke's account of the final appearance, the risen Christ opens the disciples' minds to understand the scriptures (Luke 24:44–45, where "law, prophets, and psalms" means the whole Jewish Bible).

The letters of Paul express a conscious claim that the Christian church is the rightful owner of the Jewish scriptural heritage: "whatever was written in former days was written for our instruction" (Rom. 15:4; cf. 1 Cor. 10:11). Paul makes a similar generalization about "the law and the prophets" (cf. Rom. 3:21), and he gives numerous examples of Christological exegesis (cf. Rom. 4:23; 8:36; 10:18–21; 11:2–6; 1 Cor. 9:9–10; 10:1–5; Gal. 3:6–14; 4:21–31). The Johannine writings state the same principle: "If you believed Moses, you would believe me, for he wrote of me" (John 5:46). But although the scriptures lead to belief in Jesus, Jesus is said to transcend Moses: "grace and truth" transcend the law (John 1:17), and true worship "in spirit and truth" makes the cult of the temple obsolete (John 4:24). We see here two complementary features: (1) all Jewish writings are considered prophetic in reference to the deeds, the teaching, and the person of Jesus; and (2) their fulfillment leads to a "fullness" substantially superior to what had been possessed by the first recipients of the biblical texts.

The Epistle to the Hebrews is an important milestone in the formation of early Christian exegesis. It provides the framework of a comprehensive Christological exegesis for the most important personalities (Abraham, Moses, Aaron, Joshua, and David) and the basic institutions (the kingdom, the land, the temple) of the Jewish past. Christ is presented as the Messiah (king and Son of God), leading the people to the final destination of the Jewish exodus, and as the high priest who offered a conclusive, comprehensive, and everlasting sacrifice. His death and resurrection constitute a new covenant that both fulfills and supersedes (makes "old") the previous one (Heb. 8:13).

Jewish Interpretation. The Christological interpretation of the Old Testament as practiced by the first Christians stands in direct dependence upon the views and practices found in first-century Judaism. The connections are most evident with regard to biblical inspiration and the authority of the sacred texts, but at numerous instances also the methods and procedures of rabbinic exegesis have been borrowed or imitated. When using scriptural texts, the authors of the New Testament use the same freedom and inventiveness found in the *midrashim* of the rabbis. The Hebrew midrash (from *darash*, "to search") is a theological study of the biblical text, freely expanding the subject matter beyond the literal meaning. Whether providing interpretation of a legal text (*halakah*) or of a religious narrative (*haggadah*), the midrash is determined equally by objective and subjective factors: it seeks to find a meaning relevant to the religious and practical needs of the reader. The program of the Christian midrash as both dependent upon and theologically conflicting with rabbinic exegesis is succinctly expressed by the Johannine Christ addressing a Jewish audience: "You search the scriptures because you think that in them you have eternal life; and it is they that bear witness to me" (John 5:39).

Presuppositions of Christian Interpretation. At an early stage, this exegesis practiced by the church brings to focus the idea that the Old Testament receives its full meaning from the proclamation of Christ, that is, "the gospel" (cf. Gal. 1:16–17), standing for both the teaching *of* Jesus and the teaching *about* Jesus, both transmitted by authoritative witnesses, who were chosen and empowered by Jesus himself: "the apostles." The church's teaching has therefore a double foundation: the prophetic word of the Old Testament and the divinely authorized preaching of the first Christian missionaries, an idea expressed by the formula "prophets and apostles." Although "the prophets" meant more exactly "the Law and the prophets" (a Jewish expression for the totality of the scriptures), what is meant by "the apostles" also allows further division: Christ's own words (the gospel in a restricted sense) and the apostolic teaching that witnesses to Jesus and interprets his words and deeds. Such an understanding by the church of its own preaching created the Christian canon of scriptures: besides the books of the Old Testament, a second set of holy and normative writings contains the gospel of Jesus according to four renditions, Matthew, Mark, Luke, and John; an ancient summary of the church's formative history (Acts); and a collection of apostolic letters. Only one "prophetic book" is appended to this "New Testament," the Book of Revelation, which, despite its purported authorship by the apostle John, the epistolary form of its first chapters, and the repeated references to its inspired origin and unchangeably sacred text (22:7, 9, 18–19), received canonicity in the whole church only after centuries of controversy.

This process by which the Christian Bible came about determined the essential features of patristic exegesis. A theory of interpretation emerged at the same time as the canon was formed. By the end of the second century, we find it in all provinces where Christianity had spread. A forerunner of this interpretation is Justin Martyr, who, by presenting Christ as the eternal Logos of God, identifies the principle of all divine revelation with the preexistent Christ through whom God has spoken to the patriarchs, to Moses, and to all prophets. Following in his footsteps, Irenaeus, bishop of Lyons in Gaul, Tertullian of Carthage in North Africa, bishop Theophilus of Antioch in Syria, the Alexandrian Clement in Egypt, and Hippolytus in Rome use essentially the same method of interpretation based on the unity of the "two Testaments." They believe that the

two are intimately connected and theologically harmonized, affirming at the same time the New Testament's guiding role and supremacy, and, within the New Testament, the supremacy of the Gospels. Faced with divisive heresies (chiefly Gnosticism and Marcionism), these theologians, who were also churchmen, defended the unity of the scriptures on the basis of a unified and unique salvation history. They speak of the one and same God, the Creator and Father, of the one and only Son, through whom the world was created and redeemed, as well as of the one and same sanctifying Spirit, who moved the prophets and the apostles to preaching and writing. The church gathered by God the Father and participating in the filiation of the Son is the social setting in which the correct understanding of the scriptures takes place through the power of the same Spirit who originated them.

Origen. Early Christian biblical interpretation gained its next major impetus from the work of one of the greatest of all exegetes, Origen of Alexandria, in the third century. His influence has been lasting in two major areas. First, he made the church aware that the transmission and translation of its sacred texts needs to be watched and controlled. His *Hexapla*, a sixfold presentation of various textual traditions of the Old Testament, survived only in fragments, but the lesson was not lost. Christians became aware of both the weaknesses and variations of the Septuagint and realized the problems of textual transmission also for the New Testament. Second, Origen was the first Christian exegete to show the need for a method and even epistemological and anthropological foundations to Christian exegesis. His solution was expressed in the following scheme. He speaks of the three "meanings" or "senses" of scripture, signifying three consecutive steps in the exegetical process. The first is the "literal" or "historical" meaning that results from the application of linguistic, grammatical, and literary tools. In narrative texts, this leads to the understanding of empirical facts; in other texts, such as the Psalms or the prophetic works, it provides access to a set of images or mental representations that, however, reflect the material world and are known to man through bodily senses. The second meaning of the text can be reached only by transcending the "literal" or "historical" meaning and gaining insight into its revelatory significance. This meaning is referred to as "allegorical" (at other times as "figurative," "symbolic," or "spiritual"), a meaning hidden "under the letter." Here, Origen's thought and language owe much to a Platonic conception of the world and were influenced by the Alexandrian intellectual climate, not only through the biblical commentaries of the Jewish philosopher Philo but also through the allegorical interpretation of the Homeric poems fashionable in Alexandrian literary circles. Yet what Origen calls "allegorical meaning" provides Christian substance: it is usually based on the Christological relevance of a text and as such is dependent on specifically Christian teaching. He constantly refers to Pauline and Johannine texts (some of them quoted above), since he wants to promote the exegesis exemplified in their writings. The allegorical meaning is either of doctrinal or of moral character or quite often of both: instruction of Christian faith turns into conclusions about Christian conduct. Furthermore, within this "allegorical" or "spiritual" phase of interpretation, Origen also explores the eschatological implications of what was said about Christian faith and life.

These different meanings ("letter" and "spirit") of the same text are presented in a threefold (letter, allegory, morality) or fourfold (in which the eschatological meaning or *anagoge* appears under a separate heading) scheme. But sometimes, especially in his homilies, Origen prefers to distinguish only between two meanings, the literal and the "spiritual," the latter standing for whatever allegorical, moral, or eschatological meaning the text conveys. Although his schematization may vary, most important is the parallel that he draws between the (three) meanings of scripture and the composite structure of human nature. Just as man consists of "body, soul, and spirit" (a Platonic trichotomy supported by 1 Thess. 5:23), so does the biblical text reveal three layers of meaning (literal, moral, and allegorical/

eschatological). By this, he proposes an anthropological model for biblical interpretation that has startling consequences. It logically implies that man's penetration of the sacred text must be regarded as coextensive with his own self-discovery. We understand the Bible's spiritual message to the extent we can face and actualize our own nature as spiritual beings, created to God's image and likeness. By means of this anthropological model, Origen easily fuses his "spiritual" or "allegorical" interpretation with a set of Neoplatonic and dualistic presuppositions, running the risk that biblical ideas and philosophical premises may coalesce with unresolved ambiguity.

Origen's influence can hardly be exaggerated. In the east, the Cappadocian fathers, Basil, Gregory of Nyssa, and Gregory of Nazianzus, and in the west, the four most influential patristic figures, Jerome, Ambrose, Augustine, and Gregory the Great, were greatly indebted to him. After the Council of Nicaea, however, with Christianity entering the Constantinian period, the task of the church and its exegesis changed considerably. On the one hand, the need arose to provide solid biblical basis for specific answers to the Trinitarian and Christological problems, which had been formulated mostly in nonbiblical terms. On the other hand, the church needed to take a stand on practically all issues of social and public life and thus provide support and guidance toward building a Christian empire. Cautions, restrictions, and reservations necessarily arose with respect to Origen's allegory. An exegetical tradition established itself in Antioch, which, following the lead of bishop Theodore of Mopsuestia, refused to accept allegorization and claimed to base all scriptural arguments on historical interpretation. This "historical exegesis" did not practice historical inquiry in the modern sense of the term. It was opposed, however, to the Alexandrian tradition insofar as it sought, while abstaining from the use of symbolism, to establish the Christological relevance of each text by placing it into the whole of salvation history, that is, assigning its place within a divinely willed historical scheme with Christ as its center and peak. The influence of the Antiochenes helped preserve the balance between history and allegory; the Trinitarian controversies helped clarify the limits imposed by faith on the use of ancient philosophical terms and theories.

The commentaries written in the "golden age of patristics" both filtered and transmitted the influence of Origen. They became models of exegesis for at least a millennium. Their use of historical and linguistic tools, employed to decipher the literal meaning, ensured the survival of rudimentary textual and critical concerns. Their theological and pastoral orientation influenced the church in subsequent centuries to use the biblical texts in service of orthodox doctrine, moral instruction, theological discovery, and spiritual guidance. *See also* Allegory; Canon.   [D.F.]

Bibliography

Origen, *On First Principles* 4; Ambrose, *Expositio Psalmi 118;* Gregory of Nyssa, *Commentary on the Song of Songs;* Jerome, *Commentarius in Matthaeum* (SC [1977], Vol. 242); Augustine, *On Christian Doctrine;* idem, *The Literal Meaning of Genesis;* Gregory the Great, *Moralia in Job.*

G. Bardy, "L'Interprétation chez les pères," *Supplément du Dictionnaire de la Bible* (Paris: Letouzey et Ané, 1949), Vol. 4, pp. 569–571; H. de Lubac, *Histoire et esprit: l'intelligence de l'Ecriture d'après Origène* (Paris: Aubier, 1950); A. Penna, *Principi e carattere dell'esegesi di San Gerolamo* (Rome: Pontificio Istituto Biblico, 1950); A. Kerrigan, *St. Cyril of Alexandria: Interpreter of the Old Testament* (Rome: Pontificio Istituto Biblico, 1952); R.M. Grant, *The Letter and the Spirit* (London: SPCK, 1957); R.P.C. Hanson, *Allegory and Event* (Richmond: John Knox, 1959); H. de Lubac, *Exégèse médievale: les quatre sens de l'Ecriture* (Paris: Aubier, 1961), Vol. 1; P.R. Ackroyd and C.F. Evans, eds., *The Cambridge History of the Bible* (Cambridge: Cambridge UP, 1970), Vol. 1; M. Simonetti, *Profilo storico dell' esegesi patristica* (Rome: Augustinianum, 1981); B. de Margerie, *Introduction à l'histoire de l'exégèse* (Paris: Cerf, 1982, 1983), Vols. 1–2; W.R. Farmer and D. Farkasfalvy, *The Formation of the New Testament Canon* (New York: Paulist, 1983); R.M. Grant and D. Tracy, *A Short History of the Interpretation of the Bible* (Philadelphia: Fortress, 1984); C. Mondésert, ed., *Le Monde grec ancien et la Bible* (Paris: Beauchesne, 1984); K. Froelich, *Biblical Interpretation in the Early Church* (Philadelphia: Fortress, 1984); K.J. Torjesen, *Hermeneutical Procedure and Theological Method in Origen's Exegesis* (Berlin: de Gruyter, 1986); J.L. Kugel and R.A. Greer, *Early Christian Interpretation* (Philadelphia: Westminster, 1986); W. Trigg, *Biblical Interpretation* (Wilmington: Glazier, 1988).

IONA. Small island of the Scottish Hebrides just west of the isle of Mull; center of Irish Celtic monasticism. Adamnan's *Life of Columba* describes events on Iona in the sixth and seventh centuries (although it must be used with care). Columba evidently began the monastery. Monks from Iona went as missionaries into Northumbria and among the Pictish churches of eastern Scotland. Modern excavations around the medieval abbey on Iona uncovered remains of buildings that apparently

Iona Abbey, restored in the early twentieth century, on or near the site of Columba's settlement (sixth century) on the island of Iona, Scotland.

go back to the early period. Various carved stones, including the famous Celtic crosses, also may date from as early as the eighth century. The Irish kings Niall Frossach and Artgall became monks there in that same century.

Presently, the island is dominated by the restored medieval abbey, a good museum, and the St. Martin Cross. (Pieces of the St. John Cross now rest in Edinburgh.)   [F.W.N.]

Bibliography.

Argyll: An Inventory of Monuments (Edinburgh: Royal Commission on the Ancient and Historical Monuments of Scotland, 1982), Vol. 4: *Iona.*

IRELAND. The origins of Christianity in Ireland are obscure. Medieval legends tell of saints who lived in southern Ireland before St. Patrick, and archaeologists have discovered some Christian artifacts from the fourth century, but these could have come from trade or plunder. The first reliable information is given by the Gallic chronicler Prosper of Aquitaine (*Chronicle* ann. 431), who says that in 431 a Roman deacon named Palladius was sent by pope Celestine I "to the Irish believing in Christ." Who they were is unknown; scholars assume Christianity came to Ireland via contacts with Christians in Britain. (Since these contacts were often with southern Ireland, it is likely that the medieval legends of pre-Patrician saints in the south have some historical basis.) Who Palladius was is also unknown; scholars assume that the pope was concerned that Pelagianism, a serious problem in Britain, would spread to the nascent Irish church, and so he sent someone he could trust to the scene. What Palladius did in Ireland is also unknown. Later accounts, usually lives of Patrick, say that Palladius died a martyr or that he went back to

High cross (eighth–ninth century) at Moone, Ireland, seen through the gateway of the monastery building.

Britain. Since these remarks are intended to glorify Patrick by playing down Palladius, they should not be taken seriously. A bishop sent to strengthen the faith of an existing Christian community would not have led the life from which legends grow; we may assume that Palladius had a quiet and probably effective episcopate.

Shortly after Palladius arrived, a British missionary bishop named Patrick came to work among the pagans in the north. As a teenager, Patrick had been kidnapped to Ireland and sold into slavery as a shepherd. He escaped to Britain, entered clerical life, and now returned as a bishop, apparently sent by the British church. He spoke the Irish language, knew some of the countryside, and was a man of great faith and courage. He labored among the pagans for almost thirty years. His success was phenomenal; where he planted Christianity, it flourished, and there were no retrograde pagan revivals. He died ca. 461. His two brief writings (*Confessions* and *Letter to Coroticus*) are the earliest documents known to be composed in Ireland.

Patrick came as a missionary bishop, and we may assume that he brought the organization he knew in Britain and Gaul with him to Ireland. Later legends that picture him going about the country alone (and in full episcopal regalia!) cannot be taken seriously. He certainly would have had assistants—at the very least he would have needed people to carry the liturgical vessels, books, and the like necessary for founding a church—and he trained a native clergy. But Ireland was not to be a reproduction of the British model.

After Patrick's death, a veil descends upon Irish history, and it does not lift until the late sixth century. When it does, paganism was still a force in Ireland but one clearly in retreat. Monasteries had considerable importance, and all the great names of history and legend from this period are monks and nuns: Columba, Brigid, Brendan, the Finnians, Columbanus. The monastery was a rural institution that fit well into the cityless Irish landscape, and even bishops were associated with monasteries. Not until Viking invaders established such trading centers as Dublin and Wexford in the ninth century did Ireland get the urban episcopacy so common in Romanized territories.

Irish Christianity had its idiosyncrasies, such as the "wandering for Christ" in which a person would go into voluntary exile as an act of asceticism, a variation on the eastern monks' flight to the desert and a contradiction to the increasing *stabilitas* of the western monks. On the other hand, the Irish stood clearly in the Latin Christian tradition. Their famous and not so famous authors wrote in Latin, and they used existing Latin forms, such as biblical commentaries and saints' lives. Some charming Christian nature poetry, extolling the goodness of creation, survives in the vernacular.

Because Ireland was spared the barbarian invasions that ended the Roman empire, its Christian learned tradition was strong when much of continental Europe's was weak. Consequently, in the sixth and seventh centuries, Irish saints and scholars helped to evangelize northern England and to re-evangelize much of France. Furthermore, Irish manuscripts are among the earliest witnesses to the works of Latin writers, such as Gregory the Great and Pelagius, the biblical Apocrypha, and the Latin versions of the Bible. This last portion of western Europe to be converted during the Roman period played a significant role in adapting Christianity to the post-Roman world. *See also* Celtic Christianity; Great Britain; Patrick.

[J.F.K.]

Bibliography

N.K. Chadwick, *The Age of the Saints in the Early Celtic Church* (London: Oxford UP, 1961); L. Bieler, *Ireland: Harbinger of the Middle Ages* (London: Oxford UP, 1963); K. Hughes, *The Church in Early Irish Society* (Ithaca: Cornell UP, 1966); idem, *Early Christian Ireland: Introduction to the Sources* (Ithaca: Cornell UP, 1972); J.T. McNeill, *The Celtic Churches: A History, A.D. 200 to 1200* (Chicago: U of Chicago P, 1974); K. Hughes and A. Hamlin, *The Modern Traveller to the Early Irish Church* (London: SPCK, 1977).

IRENAEUS (ca. 115– ca. 202). Bishop of Lyons and church father. Irenaeus was born in Smyrna, Asia Minor, where he knew bishop Polycarp and from him learned of the Johannine tradition. He studied and taught at Rome before going to Lyons. As a presbyter, he went on a mission to bishop Eleutherus of Rome to urge toleration with regard to adherents of Montanism in Asia Minor.

Among Irenaeus's writings is the *Demonstration*, or *Epideixis*, a work on the apostolic preaching; recovered in 1904 in an Armenian translation, it explains Christian doctrine and then proves it from Old Testament prophecies. *Against Heresies*, or *Adversus haereses*, is available in a Latin translation. Book 1 refutes Gnostic arguments by reason; Book 2 sets forth the traits of false Gnosis and the history of Gnosticism; Book 3 refutes Gnosticism from the teaching and tradition of the apostles; Book 4 refutes it from the sayings of Jesus; Book 5 treats of the things to come, with remarks on millenarianism.

Fragments of the original Greek of the *Adversus haereses* are found in the writings of Hippolytus of Rome, Eusebius of Caesarea, Epiphanius of Salamis, and Theodoret of Cyrus, as well as in catenae and papyri. There are twenty-three fragments extant in Syriac; Books 4 and 5 are available in an Armenian translation.

In opposition to Gnostic dualism, Irenaeus teaches that there is but one God who is the Creator of the world and the Father of Jesus Christ, that there is one divine economy of salvation and one revelation. The visible creation is good, not evil, and the body will rise again.

Irenaeus was a pastoral bishop concerned with protecting Christians against Gnosticism. He was interested in philosophy only insofar as it could help one to penetrate more deeply into what one believed. He taught that human thinking is powerless to know God and his dispensation for the salvation of all people. Although the Gnostics thought that they could arrive at saving knowledge through human effort, true salvation is attained only through faith in what God has revealed and in what he has done. One must give complete acceptance to revelation, which defines the content of the Christian's faith upon which life is to be based. In opposition to the "private revelations" put forth by the Gnostics, Irenaeus states that

Christians have been given the same four Gospels so that they may know the same tradition as handed down by the apostles and bishops who succeeded them.

Irenaeus's solution to the problem of faith and reason is fundamentally the one that the church has accepted: human reason and divine revelation are different dimensions of reality. Man's intellectual quest can never become God's self-communication in revelation nor can it substitute for it. In working out the solution to this problem, he found himself teaching the nature of theology, which begins with scriptural statements and the positions of the teaching authority of the church and then uses all the resources of human intelligence to understand these truths. This is the activity of the intelligent Christian who deems faith to be an important and interesting object of study. In the ancient world, philosophy was concerned with the quest for happiness but sought it through the use of the autonomous reason. Christians had the need to relate that reason to the guidance of faith. Revelation, according to Irenaeus, is public and common to all Christians. No secret tradition supersedes the church tradition. The apostles established the organs by which their teaching was to be transmitted, and the bishops have the responsibility of guarding the conformity of church teaching with revelation. The unity of doctrine is found in the Rule of Faith.

The center of Irenaeus's theology is Paul's doctrine of the "recapitulation of all things in Christ." Human nature in its entirety is assumed by the Word of God. Christ as the new Adam renews all creation and leads it back to its author through the incarnation and redemption. Mary is the new Eve, the mother of all the living. Human existence finds its exemplar in the humanity of the incarnate Christ in whom the human race is unified. Irenaeus employed the learning of his day but subordinated it to the purpose of the "restoration of all things in Christ." Through communion with Christ in the Holy Spirit, human beings are made incorruptible and through redemption are made like God. In union with Christ, the world and humanity fulfill their divine destiny.

Irenaeus upheld the teaching of the bishops, the heirs of the apostles' authority, as preferable to that of the heads of schools of theology. He developed a theology of ecclesiastical institution by establishing the apostolic origin of episcopal succession: John by way of Polycarp in the case of Smyrna, Paul in the case of Ephesus, and Peter and Paul in the case of Rome. His treatment of the relation of faith and reason was to influence Augustine's position: one believes in order to understand. In his thought and action, he was an important link between east and west. Among the sources for his teaching are Justin Martyr, Theophilus of Antioch, and Ignatius of Antioch.

Irenaeus was the first great Catholic theologian, one who emphasized the role of the church, the canon of scripture, and the religious and theological tradition. In the sixth century, Gregory of Tours refers to Irenaeus as a martyr. Feast day June 28. CPG I, 1306–1321. TLG 1447. *See also* Apostolic Succession.

[M.T.C.]

Bibliography

Irénée de Lyon: Contre les Heresies, ed. A. Rousseau, L. Doutreleau, and C. Mercier, SC (1965–1982), Vols. 100, 152, 153, 210, 211, 263, 264, 293, 294.

St. Irenaeus, Proof of the Apostolic Preaching, tr. J.P. Smith, ACW (1952), Vol. 16; *Irenaeus, Writings*, tr. A. Roberts and W.H. Rambaut, ANF (1884), Vol. 1.

J. Lawson, *The Biblical Theology of St. Irenaeus* (London: Epworth, 1948); A. Houssiau, *La Christologie de saint Irénée* (Gembloux: Duculot, 1955); G. Wingren, *Man and Incarnation: A Study in the Biblical Theology of Irenaeus* (Philadelphia: Muhlenberg, 1959); J. Ochagavía, *Visibile Patris Filius: A Study of Irenaeus' Teaching on Revelation and Tradition* (Rome: Pontificium Institutum Orientalium Studiorum, 1964); J.T. Nielsen, *Adam and Christ in the Theology of Irenaeus of Lyons* (Assen: Van Gorcum, 1968); A. Orbe, *Antropología de san Ireneo* (Madrid: La Editorial Catolica, 1961); H.B. Timothy, *The Early Christian Apologists and Greek Philosophy* (Assen: Van Gorcum, 1973); G. Vallée, *A Study in Anti-Gnostic Polemics: Irenaeus, Hippolytus, and Epiphanius* (Waterloo: Wilfrid Laurier UP, 1981); R. Kereszty, "The Unity of the Church in the Theology of Irenaeus," *SCent* 4 (1984):202–218; M.A. Donovan, "Irenaeus in Recent Scholarship," *SCent* 4 (1984):219–241; R.M. Grant, "Carpocratians and Curriculum: Irenaeus' Reply," *HThR* 79 (1986):

127–136; Y. de Andia, *Homo Vivens: Incorruptibilité et divinisation de l'homme selon Irénée de Lyon* (Paris: Etudes Augustiniennes, 1986).

ISAAC. Son of Abraham and father of Jacob and Esau. The life of Isaac is recounted in Genesis 21–28. The only son of Abraham and Sarah, Isaac was given his name, meaning "he laughs," because of the response of his aged mother to the divine promise of a son (Gen. 18:10–15). He is contrasted with his half-brother, Ishmael, in the Genesis narrative. The biblical portrayal of the choice of Isaac over Ishmael as heir to the patriarchal tradition became significant in early Christian exegesis because of Paul's analysis (Rom. 9:7; Gal. 4:21–31).

Abraham's sacrifice of Isaac, during which the boy consented to death but was delivered by God (Gen. 22:1–19), became a type of Christ's sacrifice and resurrection, implied already in Hebrews 11:17–19. Patristic writers developed this type in detail, and it became a recurring feature of exegesis and theological analysis. Thus, Golgotha was considered the site of the event, Isaac carrying the wood was a type of Christ bearing the cross, and the substitutionary ram provided by God in the Old Testament narrative offered another type of Christ. Iconographical representations of Isaac and the interpretation of his story as a type of Christ are present in Christian art from the earliest period. [D.B.]

Bibliography

Melito, *On Pascha* 59; 69; Ambrose, *Isaac or the Soul*, tr. M.P. McHugh, FOTC (1972), Vol. 85.

J. Daniélou, "La Typologie d'Isaac dans le christianisme primitif," *Biblica* 28 (1947):363–393; I.S. van Woerden, "The Iconography of the Sacrifice of Abraham," *VChr* 15 (1961):214–255 (includes a complete list of representations); R.L. Wilken, "Melito, the Jewish Community at Sardis, and the Sacrifice of Isaac," *ThS* 37 (1976):53–69.

ISAAC OF ANTIOCH (d. ca. 460). Orthodox priest and abbot of a convent near Antioch. Among Syriac churchmen, Isaac was second only to Ephraem in the quantity and variety of his writings. In the manuscripts, his works are mingled with those of three other Isaacs of the fifth and sixth centuries, as well as with some by Ephraem the Syrian. [R.J.O.]

Bibliography

Gennadius, *Lives of Illustrious Men* 67.

Isaac's works are not all published; the major editions are G. Bickell, *Isaac Antiocheni, opera omnia*, 2 vols. (Giessen: Richeri, 1873–1877), and P. Bedjan, *Homiliae S. Isaaci syri Antiocheni* (Paris and Leipzig: Harrassowitz, 1903).

ISAAC OF NINEVEH (d. ca. 700). Syriac-speaking monk. Except for five months as bishop of Nineveh, Isaac lived in solitude and wrote extensively about ascetic spirituality. Sebastian Brock's recent discovery of a Syriac manuscript at the Bodleian Library in Oxford has doubled the extant works of Isaac. His writings are not all published and have been confused somewhat with those of Isaac of Antioch. [R.J.O.]

Bibliography

The Ascetical Homilies of St. Isaac the Syrian (Boston: Holy Transfiguration Monastery, 1984).

ISAIAH (eighth century B.C.). Hebrew prophet and longest of the prophetic books in the Bible. Isaiah was son of Amoz, about whom no more is known. (The Septuagint and Vulgate spelled this name and that of Amos the prophet alike, and some Christian writers confused the two [Clement of Alexandria, *Str.* 1.20; Greek translator of *Ascension of Isaiah*; and Augustine, *Civ. Dei* 18.27].) Isaiah was a Judean prophet in Jerusalem, whose book of sixty-six chapters is regularly placed first in Jewish canonical lists of the latter prophets as well as in Christian lists, where prophetic books seem to be arranged by length. A major prophet by Augustine's evaluation, Isaiah precedes Jeremiah.

The first half of Isaiah (1–39) has its setting in the Assyrian crisis of the late eighth century B.C. that brought about the downfall of the northern kingdom of Israel (721 B.C.) and threatened the existence of Judah. Isaiah rebuked the people and rulers for their sins and called on them to trust God rather than Egypt. The second half of the book (40–66) has as its setting the Babylonian exile and restoration of the Jews to Jerusalem by the Persians in the sixth century B.C.; hence, most scholars think another prophet ("Second Isaiah") or prophets wrote this part. The message of hope in this part of Isaiah sets forth the universalism of the one God and his call to his people to be a blessing to all nations.

Isaiah is said to have written "the rest of the acts of Uzziah" (2 Chron. 26:22); 2 Chronicles 32:32 alludes to a text called the "vision of Isaiah the prophet, the son of Amoz, in the book of the kings of Judah and Israel." Isaiah is honored in Sirach's list of worthies (Sir. 48:22–25). The Qumran community valued his book, as is shown by manuscript fragments, a commentary, and citations. His career is surveyed by Josephus (*Ant.* 9.13.3 [276]; 10.2.1–2 [27–35]; 10.3.1 [37]).

The *Lives of the Prophets* of Pseudo-Epiphanius has Isaiah killed by Manasseh, king of Judah, and buried at the oak of Rogel near Siloam. The name Siloam is interpreted as "sent" (cf. John 9:7), from the fact that the spring gave water for Jews but withheld it from besieging foreigners. The pool miraculously sent Isaiah water in answer to his prayers before he died. The intermittent flow of the water is explained as coming through Isaiah, who was buried here to ensure the continued flow. The tomb is said to be near the tomb of the kings but east of the tomb of the priests. The site described is not now locatable.

The *Ascension of Isaiah* was probably composed by a Jew in Hebrew or Aramaic, ca. A.D. 150–200; a Christian writer later inserted an apocalypse (3.13–4.22). In this treatise, a false prophet, Belchira, accuses Isaiah of prophesying falsely against Israel and Judah and of saying, "I have seen God and behold I live." Beliar, angered by Isaiah's vision, instigates Manasseh to seize Isaiah and saw him asunder while Belchira stands laughing. Isaiah had a vision in which an angel carried him through seven heavens, showing him the world hidden to the flesh. He saw the descent of the Christ, the incarnation, the passion, ascension, and commissioning of the disciples. He described the reign of Beliar and the Lord's second coming to punish Beliar and his host.

Christian writers considered Isaiah as a martyr (allusions to the wooden saw are found in Justin [*Dial.* 120.5], Tertullian [*Pat.* 14; *Scorp.* 8], and others). Writers interpreted Hebrews 11:37 ("sawn asunder") in this light (Origen, *Ep.* 1.9; *Mt.* 10.18).

The Book of Isaiah is the most frequently cited prophetic book in the New Testament. Receiving most attention are the voice in the desert (Isa. 40:3; cf. Matt. 3:1–3), the Immanuel prophecy (7:14; cf. Matt. 2:20–23), the unbelief of Israel and the idea of the remnant (1:9; 59:7–8; cf. Rom. 3:15; 9:29), the prince of peace (9:2–7; cf. Matt. 4:14–16), and the suffering Servant (Isa. 53:1ff.; cf. Acts 8:27–35). Writers of the second and later centuries used these quotations and referred to others. Isaiah's prediction of the virgin birth became a motif of early Christian art, identified in frescoes in the Catacombs of Priscilla and Domitilla. Vatican Greek MS 699 of the sixth century has a miniature of the world with Isaiah announcing the child to Mary. Artists were deterred from depicting Jesus by the interpretation of Isaiah 53:2 that "he had no form or comeliness" (Clement of Alexandria, *Paed.* 3.1; Tertullian, *Carn. Chr.* 9; Origen, *Cels.* 6.75). On the other hand, the catacomb shepherd image may have been influenced by Isaiah 40:11 as well as by Ezekiel 34. *See also* Ascension of Isaiah.

[J.P.L.]

Bibliography
Eusebius of Caesarea, *Commentarii in Isaiam* (PG 24.89–526); Pseudo-Basil, *Enarratio in prophetam Isaiam* (PG 30.117–668); Zeno of Verona, *Sermones* (PL 11.462–473); Cyril of Alexandria, *Commentarius in Isaiam* (PG 70.9–1449); Jerome, *Commentarii in Isaiam* (PL 24.17–678); Theodoret of Cyrus, *Interpretatio in Isaiam* (PG 81.216–493); Hesychius of Jerusalem, *Interpretatio Isaiae* (PG 93.1369–1385); Procopius of Gaza, *Catena in Isaiam* (PG 87, 2.1817–2717).

G.A. Smith, *The Book of Isaiah*, 2 vols. (New York: Armstrong, 1908); C.R. North, *The Second Isaiah* (Oxford: Clarendon, 1964); B.S. Childs, *Isaiah and the Assyrian Crisis* (London: SCM, 1967); J.L. McKenzie, *Second Isaiah* (Garden City: Doubleday, 1968); C. Westermann, *Isaiah 40–66* (Philadelphia: Westminster, 1969); E.J. Young, *The Book of Isaiah*, 3 vols. (Grand Rapids: Eerdmans, 1970–1972); O. Kaiser, *Isaiah 1–12* and *13–39*, 2 vols. (Philadelphia: Westminster, 1972, 1974); A.S. Herbert, *The Book of the Prophet Isaiah 1–39* and *40–66* (Cambridge: Cambridge UP, 1973, 1975).

ISIDORE (second century). Disciple, perhaps son, of the Gnostic Basilides. Clement of Alexandria (*Str.* 2.20; 6.6) says Isidore authored a commentary on a prophet named Parchor and a treatise on ethics. In the commentary, Isidore claimed that Aristotle and other Greek philosophers borrowed teachings from that prophet. In the treatise on ethics, he distinguished between passions that can upset the soul and an inner soul or self that must resist them.

[F.W.N.]

Bibliography
Clement of Alexandria, *Miscellanies* 2.20; 3.1.3; 6.6; Hippolytus, *Refutation of All Heresies* 7.8.

ISIDORE OF PELUSIUM (ca. 360–ca. 435). Presbyter at Pelusium, Egypt. Isidore was known for his ascetic piety and his biblical and secular learning. Monks honored him as a teacher of the spiritual life. His letters (about 2,000 are extant) show him a master of style. Born in Alexandria, Isidore upheld the orthodox Christology of Alexandria but practiced the literal and historical hermeneutics of Antioch. CPG III, 5557–5558.

[E.F.]

Bibliography
Apophthegmata Patrum, "Isidore"; Nicephorus Callistus, *Historia ecclesiastica* 14.53; Photius, *Epistulae* 2.44.

PG 78.

C.H. Turner, "The Letters of Isidore of Pelusium," *JThS* 6 (1905):70–86; K. Lake, "Further Notes on the MSS of Isidore of Pelusium," *JThS* 6 (1905):270–282; M. Smith, "The Manuscript Tradition of Isidore of Pelusium," *HThR* 47 (1954):205–210.

ISIDORE OF SEVILLE (ca. 560–636). Archbishop and writer. The last of the fathers of the church in the west, Isidore was probably born in Cartagena, then under Byzantine rule. The family moved to Seville, where he was taught by his elder brother Leander, whom he succeeded as metropolitan (ca. 600). As archbishop, he worked vigorously to promote Catholicism. He had a major role at the fourth of the councils of Toledo (633), which dealt with the education of the clergy and sought to secure uniformity of liturgical practice within the Mozarabic rite. The same council promoted a close tie between church and state by its decision in favor of the claim of Sisenand to the throne of the Goths against the reigning king Suinthila. Isidore's aim of a renewed church in a united Visigothic kingdom was thus realized.

A prolific writer, Isidore is best known for his *Etymologiae*, or *Origines*, an encyclopedia of the knowledge of his time, undertaken (ca. 620) at the request of king Sisebut; left incomplete at Isidore's death, it was ordered and edited by Braulio of Saragossa. Intended as a work of reference for scholarly consultation, it relied mostly on later sources, such as Martianus Capella, Cassiodorus, and diverse manuals and school textbooks. The *De natura rerum* (612–613), also dedicated to Sisebut, was a scientific work meant to supply rational explanations for natural phenomena. Isidore's historical writings consist of the *Chronica maiora*, a history extending from creation to 615; *The History of the Goths, Vandals, and Suevi*, a source for the advance of the Goths in Spain; and *De viris illustribus*, a series of short biographies modeled on those of Jerome and Gennadius of Marseilles.

The dogmatic works include *Sententiarum libri tres*, a manual directed toward clerical formation, and *De fide catholica*, a presentation of Christology intended for Jews and based on prophecies from the Hebrew scriptures. *Synonymorum libri duo* is a work of spirituality cast in the form of a dialogue between man and reason. *De ecclesiasticis officiis* deals with liturgy, including the Divine Office, and the various ranks of clergy and faithful. A number of exegetical works are extant, in which the stress is laid on allegory and the interpretation of scripture in a moral sense, as well as letters, several minor pieces, and compositions of doubtful authenticity.

Isidore holds a position as a vital link between the learning of antiquity and that of the Middle Ages. His writings were used by countless medieval authors, and he exercised a pervasive influence on medieval thought. Feast day April 4. CPL 1186–1229, 1868.

[M.P.McH.]

Bibliography

Braulio of Saragossa, *List of the Books of Isidore*; Ildefonsus of Toledo, *De viris illustribus* 9 (8).

E. Bréhaut, *An Encyclopaedist of the Dark Ages, Isidore of Seville* (New York: Columbia UP, 1912); J. Fontaine, *Isidore de Séville et la culture classique dans l'Espagne wisigothique* (Paris: Etudes Augustiniennes, 1959), reissued with addition of a third vol., *Notes complémentaires et supplément bibliographique* (Paris: Etudes Augustiniennes, 1983); J.N. Hillgarth, "The Position of Isidorian Studies: A Critical Review of the Literature 1936–1975," *StudMed* 24 (1983): 817–905; J. Fontaine, *Tradition et actualité chez Isidore de Seville* (London: Variorum Reprints, 1988).

ISIS. Egyptian goddess who became in the Hellenistic and Roman periods the focus of a Mediterranean-wide cult. Isis was an ideal of motherhood and marriage who bore Isiris a son, Horus, and gathered the pieces of Osiris's body after he had been slain by Seth. Her tears formed much of the Nile, and thus she was worshiped during the annual floods. At some point, she was joined with Anubis, a dog-headed god. In all these myths, she was seen as powerful, the giver of life and immortality. In Hellenistic times, when linked with her consort Sarapis, she was worshiped throughout the Mediterranean region. As one of the great female deities to emerge in the ancient world, she drew to her identity a number of other goddesses from other areas. Herodotus (2.59) saw her as Demeter. Apuleius's *Golden Ass* records her claim that she was worshiped throughout the world under different names. Lists of her shrines support that claim, as do excavated temple sites, artifacts, and inscriptions.

Isis was not always well regarded. In ca. 54 B.C., her temples in Italy were destroyed by the authorities and her followers hounded, although by 43 B.C. she had a temple in Rome. Yet Augustus and Tiberius persecuted her worshipers. Isis was often paired with Sarapis, and when the Sarapeum in Alexandria was burned in A.D. 391, the center of the cult was gone.

Worship of Isis included a secret initiation preceded by washings, purifications, and abstinence from meat and wine for certain periods. The actual ceremonies of the mystery initiation are not known, but Isis was regarded as a savior goddess. The figure of Isis nursing Horus is thought by some to have had a deep influence on Christian iconography of Mary and the child Jesus. [F.W.N.]

Bibliography

V. Tran Tinh, *Isis Lactans* (Leiden: Brill, 1973); F. Le Corsa, *Isis, mythe et mystères* (Paris: Les Belles Lettres, 1977); F. Solmsen, *Isis Among the Greeks and Romans* (Cambridge: Harvard UP, 1979); R.A. Wild, *Water in the Cultic Worship of Isis and Sarapis* (Leiden: Brill, 1981); F.W. Norris, "Isis, Sarapis, and Demeter in Antioch of Syria," *HThR* (1982):189–207.

ITALY. Home of the greatest empire of antiquity and among the most significant areas in the development of early Christianity. The concluding chapter of Paul's letter to the Romans, with its numerous references to individuals and families in the imperial capital, attests to the arrival of the gospel well before he wrote (ca. 55). Suetonius refers to the presence of Christians at Rome as early as 49 or 50, when he describes the emperor Claudius's edict expelling the Jews from Rome because of disturbance among them "at the instigation of Chrestus" (*V. Claud.* 25.4). The number of Christians at Rome was considerable by the time of the persecution under Nero in 64 as reported by Suetonius (*V. Nero.* 16.2) and Tacitus (*Annals* 15.44). They do not identify any individual; however, Clement, the late-first-century bishop of Rome, confirms the deaths of Paul and Peter on the occasion of the first imperial persecution, which was restricted apparently to the capital city (*1 Clem.* 5). Their martyrdom guaranteed the city and its church a degree of sanctity second only to that of Jerusalem and the holy places of Judea. Second-century sources attest as well to the growth of the Christian community in central and southern Italy.

A distinctive feature of the earliest Christian community of Rome was its Greek social and linguistic texture. Only at the end of the second century did the church there begin to reflect its Latin environment, with the election of Victor I as bishop. The role of the Roman church in the second and third centuries corresponded to the status of the city as the imperial capital. From Christian sources, we learn of a parade of Christian writers, orthodox and heterodox, who gravitated to Rome, contributing to its importance in the larger Christian community. By the late second century, according to Irenaeus of Lyons, the city had gained a reputation as a defender of orthodoxy; in addition, a Roman sense of order and history is shown in the first recorded roster of bishops for an urban church, preserved in Irenaeus and quoted by Eusebius of Caesarea in his *Church History* 5.6.

Continued growth at Rome necessitated a more elaborate pastoral organization by the middle of the third century. Eusebius (*H.E.* 6.43) preserves precious information that demonstrates concretely the growth of the Roman church; Christians in Rome may have numbered anywhere from 10,000 to 40,000, out of a total population of about 750,000. Complementing the capital city's growth (although we lack detailed contemporary documentation) was the missionary outreach of the Roman church into central and southern Italy, whose success is confirmed by the synod of sixty Italian bishops convened at Rome by bishop Cornelius in 251. But northwestern and northern Italy remained largely untouched by Christianity until the fourth century.

On the Adriatic side of the peninsula, communities of Christians appear in the third century at Ravenna and Rimini; a martyrdom at Piacenza hints at the existence of a church there. Aquileia is credited with a bishop early and in turn sponsored bishoprics at Verona and Brescia in the fourth century. The great city of the late-fourth-century empire, Milan, with a trio of third-century martyrs, may have episcopal beginnings that reach back to the early fourth century. Sicily and Sardinia had Christian origins at least in the third century (and perhaps earlier in the case of Sardinia, due to the sentencing of Roman Christians to the mines there).

Constantine the Great's victory over Maximian (312) and then over Licinius (324) united the empire under a single ruler and inaugurated dramatic changes in the status and role of Christianity in Italy and the empire at large. The church of Rome benefited from the emperor's largesse and the entire Christian church from his pro-Christian legislation. In addition, Constantine's church-building program in Rome ushered in a new era for Christian congregations there and elsewhere, as the Roman basilica was adapted to accommodate the needs of a religion now far beyond the era of the house church.

Constantine's impact on the church led it into its imperial era; his fourth-century successors, except for the neopagan Julian, increasingly involved themselves in its internal affairs, including such major dogmatic disputes as that over Arianism. Imperial attitudes dictated events within the church. Theological leadership in Italy in the contest with Arianism came from Milan, where the extraordinary churchman Ambrose was bishop. By the 370s, Milan had replaced Rome as the imperial residence in the west. Although Milan, Aquileia, and Ravenna could maintain their independence from the Roman church, the bishops of Rome during the fourth century began to assert themselves in ways that pointed toward the appearance of the medieval papacy. The emperor Gratian issued a rescript during the pontificate of Damasus I (366–384) that recognized the bishop's appellate jurisdiction over the bishops of Italy and the west. Damasus also took the lead in advancing the triumph of Latin culture in the Roman church by commissioning Jerome's new Latin version of the scriptures; the Vulgate would profoundly shape the literary culture and religious experience of western Christendom. Along with the Vulgate, Damasus's innovations in Latinizing the Roman liturgy provided the essential ingredients for the unity of Christianity in Italy and eventually the west.

Damasus's vital pontificate, however, witnessed storm warnings for Italy and Rome. Within a generation, the Eternal City would be confronted for the first time in eight centuries by barbarian occupiers, who were also heretics. In 378, the Arian Visigoths, following their startling triumph over the emperor Valens and his legions at Adrianople, began their wanderings within the empire that led them to Italy and the sack of Rome in 410. Arian Germanic peoples now became a factor in the life of Italian Christianity. After Alaric and the Visigoths, Rome had to deal with the Vandals led by Gaiseric from their African base; pope Leo I the Great in 451 turned from heretical barbarians to simple pagan ones when he negotiated with Attila and spared Italy and Rome from a Hunnic invasion. With Theodoric and his Ostrogoths, a permanent Arian kingdom appeared in Italy. Theodoric (ruler in Italy, 493–526) followed a policy of toleration toward the Catholic church, seeking to bring about the assimilation of Germans and Italians. But his suspicions as to the loyalty of Catholic Roman senators in his service, notably Boethius, led to bitter antagonism at the end of his reign.

The gloomy atmosphere of Theodoric's final years was an ominous preview of sixth-century Italy. Justinian, the orthodox emperor at Constantinople and vice-regent of Christ, now had the opportunity to fulfill his political ambition: to restore the empire by reconquering the west. For Italy, this meant the Gothic wars, which dragged on for a quarter of a century with devastating consequences for its population and economy. The gravity of the situation was compounded by a series of famines and plagues. A Byzantine administration established by Justinian at Ravenna, the Exarchate, was unable to deal with the arrival of the last major Germanic tribe to settle within the boundaries of the old Roman empire. In 568, the Arian Lombards swept into the Po Valley. A Lombard kingdom with Pavia as its capital, as well as Lombard duchies in central Italy, posed a grave threat to the integrity of the papal position in Rome, since the popes were by now *de facto* rulers of the city and its environs.

In this extremely difficult situation, there appeared a truly brilliant churchman, pope Gregory the Great (590–604). He provided inspiring leadership in confronting the welter of religious, socioeconomic, and political problems that enmeshed sixth-century Italy. He was closely associated with one of the most influential personalities in the development of monasticism, Benedict of Nursia (488–525), whose *Rule,* along with the Vulgate and a succession of remarkable Roman bishops, were among the Italian church's lasting contributions to the development of western Christendom. *See also* Ambrose; Damasus; Goths; Milan; Ravenna; Rome; Theodoric; Victor.   [H.R.]

Bibliography

J. Daniélou and H. Marrou, *The First Six Hundred Years* (New York: McGraw-Hill, 1964); K. Baus, *From the Apostolic Community to Constantine* (New York: Herder and Herder, 1965); H. Chadwick, *The Early Church* (Harmondsworth: Penguin, 1967); P. Brown, *The World of Late Antiquity* (New York: Harcourt Brace Jovanovich, 1971); J.G. Davies, *The Early Christian Church: A History of Its First Five Centuries* (London: Weidenfeld and Nicolson, 1965); K. Baus, *The Imperial Church from Constantine to the Early Middle Ages* (New York: Herder and Herder, 1980); W.H.C. Frend, *The Rise of Christianity* (Philadelphia: Fortress, 1984).

J

JACOB BARADAEUS (ca. 500–578). Missionary bishop and organizer of Monophysite churches. The name of Jacob Baradaeus ("the ragged") was applied in the eighth century to the non-Chalcedonian, "Monophysite," churches in Asia Minor, Syria, Lebanon, and Palestine—the "Jacobites." The son of a priest of Tella, Syria, Jacob became a monk at the monastery of Pesilto in the region of Nisibis. With Sargis, another monk of his house, he went in 527 to Constantinople as an ambassador for the interests of the non-Chalcedonians in Syria. The empress Theodora was noted for her sympathy to the non-Chalcedonian party. After fifteen years at a monastery in the capital, Jacob was made bishop of Edessa. At the same time, a fellow Monophysite, Theodosius, became bishop of Bostra in response to a request from Harith ibn-Gabala, sheikh of the Ghassanid Arab tribes at the eastern Roman border, for an "orthodox," that is, Monophysite, leader. Making the most of his appointment, Jacob began to fill numerous bishoprics in Asia Minor and Syria with non-Chalcedonians, often monks from prominent Syrian monasteries. He thus reestablished a Monophysite hierarchy disrupted after the ouster in 518 of Severus, patriarch of Antioch. His appointment of Sargis as patriarch of Antioch completed the task.

Jacob's sobriquet in Syriac, Burdᶜono (Greek Baradaios), signifies the ragged cloak of felt that he wore to disguise himself as a beggar and elude imperial agents during his journeys throughout the territory. Building a heroic reputation, he reconstituted a hierarchy said to number twenty-seven bishops and 100,000 clergy, according to his biographer, Pseudo-John of Ephesus. At the time of his death, on July 30, 578, the Monophysite churches were in schism over a contested election to the key patriarchate of Antioch.

[R.D.Y.]

Bibliography
Pseudo-John of Ephesus, *Vita Baradaei*, ed. E.W. Brooks, PO (1926), Vol. 19, pp. 228–268.

A. Baumstark, *Geschichte der syrischen Literatur* (Bonn: Marcus & Weber, 1922); E. Honigmann, *Evêques et évêchés monophysites d'Asie antérieure au VIe siècle* (Louvain: Durbecq, 1951).

JACOB OF SARUG (ca. 451–521). Syriac-speaking priest whose learning and piety, expressed in numerous writings, earned him esteem as "flute of the Holy Spirit and harp of the orthodox church." Born at Kurtam in

Osrhoene (Mesopotamia), Jacob was educated at Edessa prior to ordination. He was appointed *periōdeutes* (itinerant priest over villages of the region) at Haura in 503 and in 519 became bishop of Batnan, chief city of Sarug. Although some prose compositions, especially letters, survive, he is most famous for about 760 homiletical poems (*memre*), about half of which are extant. He generally avoided theological controversy, and scholars have debated his doctrinal position. Most today judge him to have been a Monophysite.   [R.J.O.]

Bibliography

Metrical homilies ed. A. Vööbus, *Handschriftliche Überlieferung der Meemre-Dichtung des Jaʿqob von Sereug*, CSCO (1973, 1980), Vols. 344–345, 421–422; other eds. listed in *PS*, pp. 104–109, and A. Baumstark, *Geschichte der syrischen Literatur* (Bonn: Marcus & Weber, 1922).

JAMES. Book in New Testament; brother of Jesus. The Epistle of James, counted as one of the "General Epistles" because it was addressed to "the twelve tribes in the Dispersion" rather than to a specific congregation, has been traditionally ascribed to "James, the brother of the Lord." The author simply styles himself as "James, a servant of God and of the Lord Jesus Christ" (James 1:1). Of the five persons called by this name in the New Testament, only the brother of Jesus, who was martyred ca. A.D. 62 (Josephus, *Ant.* 20.9.1), seems a reasonable choice, although it is questioned why he did not refer to himself as the "brother of Jesus" directly. No early sources associated the work with Jesus' brother, and the very lack of information regarding its author hindered its early acceptance in the canon of the New Testament. A common modern view is that the work is pseudonymous. A reasonable estimate of its date of composition is the second half of the first century.

Epistle of James. Although cast in the form of a letter, James is really a sermon dealing with ethical admonition. The salutation alone corresponds to epistolary form; there are no personal greetings, which one would expect if it were truly a letter. The sermon gives the impression of comprising pieces of ethical admonition loosely joined together. Its charac-

ter is Jewish, since the admonition takes as examples Old Testament worthies (prophets, Job, Elijah) rather than Jesus. The ideas and use of imperatives link it closely to the sayings of Jesus represented in the Sermon on the Mount/Plain (Matt. 5–7 and parallels in Luke). James undoubtedly represents the same ethical and wisdom traditions as those sections of the Gospel tradition.

The language of the author is that of an educated Greek who uses rhetorical devices, alliteration, word play, and elevated vocabulary. His considerable skill places him among the most literate of New Testament authors.

A theme throughout James is that of the poor and the rich (1:9–11; 2:1–7; 5:1–6). To be poor is to be pious, a view found in both Old and New Testaments (e.g., Ps. 86:1f.; Luke 6:20). Another important theme is that of faith and works (2:14–26). Works are a proof of the vitality of faith; "faith without works is dead." This argument has been viewed as a corrective to the Pauline position that faith is the essential ingredient for salvation. It is not clear that James is trying to correct Paul, but the book does show that the relation of faith and works was a matter of discussion in some early Christian communities. Other themes found in James are those of temptation (1:12–15), the use and abuse of the tongue (1:26; 3:1–12), and patience (5:7–11).

Person of James. Mark 6:3 and Matthew 13:55 establish the tradition that Jesus had a relative by the name of James. The relationship has been interpreted as half brother, stepbrother, or cousin. Paul likely referred to this person when he recited the list of resurrection appearances of Christ (1 Cor. 15:7), and he certainly identifies him as the "brother of the Lord" in an autobiographical section dealing with events after his own conversion (Gal. 1:19; 2:9, 12). James's prominence in Galatians seems to indicate that he held some position of authority in the Jerusalem church, appearing to be even more prominent than Peter (Cephas).

This picture is elaborated in the Acts of the Apostles, where again James seems to be a leading figure in the Jerusalem church (Acts 12:17; 21:18). He played a significant role in the so-called Jerusalem Council by mediating the dispute between Paul and the Jerusalem church (Acts 15:13f.).

Other information about James comes from later sources. Eusebius of Caesarea, quoting Clement of Alexandria, claims that James the "just" was chosen as "bishop" of Jerusalem after Jesus' ascension (*H.E.* 2.1.3; 7.19; also Ps.-Clement, *Rec.* 1.43; *Const. app.* 8.35; John Chrysostom, *Hom.* 38 *in 1 Cor.*). Eusebius goes on to quote Hegesippus, claiming that James was holy from his mother's womb, did not drink wine or strong drink, did not cut his hair, ate no meat, and neither anointed himself with oil nor bathed. He was constantly in prayer on his knees, so that they became hard like those of a camel (*H.E.* 2.23.5f.). Such ascetic tendencies, whether James engaged in them or not, were attributed to James by groups who practiced them. The Coptic *Gospel of Thomas* 12 makes the high claim that heaven and earth came into being for the sake of James, which demonstrates the power of James's reputation in some early groups.

It is doubtful that James was bishop of the Jerusalem church, since the monarchical episcopate does not seem to have been established until the second century. More likely is that James held leadership with Peter and John, but what the exact relationship was among the three cannot be determined.

James seems to be described as a high priest in Hegesippus's traditions recorded by Eusebius (*H.E.* 2.23.6) and Epiphanius (*Haer.* 78.14), but it is also possible to understand Eusebius's text in such as way as not to postulate high-priesthood. The Pseudo-Clementine literature attests the way in which Jewish Christianity looked back to James as its hero and leader. *See also* Jewish Christianity.   [G.A.K.]

Bibliography

A. Meyer and W. Bauer, "The Relatives of Jesus," NTA, Vol. 1, pp. 418–432; B. Reicke, *The Epistles of James, Peter, and Jude* (Garden City: Doubleday, 1964); P. Feine and J. Behm, *Introduction to the New Testament*, ed. W.G. Kümmel, 14th rev. ed. (New York and Nashville: Abingdon, 1966), pp. 284–292; M. Dibelius, *James: A Commentary on the Epistle of James* (Philadelphia: Fortress, 1976); W. Pratscher, *Der Herrenbruder Jakobus und die Jakobustradition* (Göttingen: Vandenhoeck & Ruprecht, 1987).

JEREMIAH. Hebrew prophet and book in Bible. Jeremiah was a Judean prophet of the late Babylonian period, from the thirteenth year of king Josiah of Judah (621 B.C.) to the fall of Jerusalem to the Babylonians (587 B.C.), when he was carried off by his compatriots to Egypt. He is mentioned in Daniel 9:2 and 1 Esdras 1:32 and is praised in Sirach 49:6 (8); Josephus surveys his career (*War* 5.391–392; *Ant.* 10.78–179; 11.1). In Jewish tradition, Jeremiah wrote the Book of Kings, Lamentations, and his own book (*b. Baba Bathra* 14b); in Christian legend, he fought in Egypt against idols (*Apocrypha Anecdota*, TS 5.1 [1897]:164). The tradition that he was stoned by the Jews is found in the "Rest of the Words of Baruch" (*2* and *4 Baruch*) and in the *Lives of the Prophets*. His martyrdom is mentioned in *Apocalypse of Paul* 49 and in Hippolytus, *Susanna* 1.1. He is counted among martyrs by Victorinus of Pettau, *Apocalypse of John* 11.5, and Pseudo-Tertullian, *Five Books in Reply to Marcion* 3.230–245.

In the New Testament, some supposed that Jesus was Jeremiah come to life again (Matt. 16:14). Prophecies from the Book of Jeremiah are cited by name in Matthew 2:17 (Jer. 31:15) and 27:9; however, the second of these seems connected with Zechariah 11:12–13 (cf. Jer. 18:2–3; 32:6–15). It was Jeremiah's prophecy of a new covenant (Jer. 31:31–34) that was most influential in Christian thought (Matt. 26:28; Mark 14:24; Heb. 8:8–12; 10:16, 17). Without identification of the source, Jeremiah's temple sermon (Jer. 7:11) is cited in Matthew 21:13 (Mark 11:17; Luke 19:46) and his statement about the wise man not glorying in his wisdom (Jer. 9:23) in 1 Corinthians 1:31 and 2 Corinthians 10:17.

The Greek text of Jeremiah is one-third shorter than the Hebrew Masoretic text. Jeremiah 33:14–26 is missing, and the oracles on foreign nations (Jer. 46–51) follow Jeremiah 25. Within the section, the nations are dealt with in a different order. The arrangement problem is noticed in Origen, *Epistle to Africanus* 4, and in Jerome, *Preface to Jeremiah*.

Jeremiah was quite popular in writers of the second century. In Christian canonical lists beginning with Melito of Sardis, Jeremiah occupies second place in the prophets, following Isaiah.

The Lamentations of Jeremiah is one of the five scrolls in the division of the Writings (Hagiographa), which in the Septuagint and Vulgate follows Jeremiah. The book comprises five elegiac poems lamenting the destruction of Jerusalem. In the Christian church, Lamentations has commonly been interpreted in reference to Christ's passion.

A pseudepigraphical Epistle of Jeremiah, which is an attack on idolatry based on the Aramaic verse in Jeremiah 10:11, is included in the Apocrypha, as is also the book of Baruch, who was Jeremiah's secretary.   [J.P.L.]

Bibliography

Origen, *Homiliae in Ieremiam*, ed. P. Nautin and P. Husson, SC (1976), Vol. 232 and (1977), Vol. 238; Ephraem the Syrian (*Opera Syrica* 98–102); Pseudo-Chrysostom, *Fragmenta in Ieremiam*, PG 64.740–1037; Theodoret of Cyrus, *Interpretatio in Ieremiam*, PG 81.496–805; Jerome, *In Hieremiam*, ed. S. Reiter, CCSL (1960), Vol. 74; Olympiodorus, *Commentarii in Ieremiam*, PG 93.628–725.

C. Wolff, *Jeremia in Frühjudentum und Urchristentum*, TU (1976), Vol. 118.

E.A. Leslie, *Jeremiah* (Nashville: Abingdon, 1954); J. Bright, *Jeremiah* (Garden City: Doubleday, 1965); E.W. Nicholson, *Jeremiah 1–25* and *26–52*, 2 vols. (Cambridge: Cambridge UP, 1973, 1975); J.A. Thompson, *The Book of Jeremiah* (Grand Rapids: Eerdmans, 1980).

Modern statue of Jerome (ca. 347–420) in Bethlehem.

JEROME (ca. 347–419/20). Scripture scholar, translator, polemicist, and ascetic. Jerome (Eusebius Hieronymus) was born in the remote town of Stridon somewhere on the border of Dalmatia. His younger brother, Paulinian, together with a younger sister, would follow his example in taking up the ascetic life. From ca. 360 to 366, he studied at Rome, where one of his teachers was Aelius Donatus, a renowned grammarian and commentator on Terence and Virgil. It was at Rome, in 366, that he received baptism. After a stay in Trier, he spent some time in Aquileia; there, with several friends, among them Rufinus of Aquileia, he devoted himself to asceticism.

Setting out for the east ca. 372, he stayed first at Antioch, where he continued his study of Greek. He lived for several years (ca. 375–377) as a hermit in the desert region of Chalcis in Syria, where he began his study of Hebrew. Again at Antioch, he was ordained a priest by Paulinus, one of the contenders for the bishopric of that city during the schism that arose over the theology of Melitius of Antioch. Jerome is not, however, known to have functioned as a priest. While in the city, he attended the lectures of Apollinaris of Laodicea.

Jerome accompanied his bishop to the Second Ecumenical Council of Constantinople (381), where he made the acquaintance of

Gregory of Nazianzus and Gregory of Nyssa. He went on to Rome with Paulinus to gain the support of Damasus I in the controversy with Melitius. While in Rome (382–385), he served as Damasus's secretary and became the spiritual counselor of a group of noble Roman women, among them Paula and her daughter Eustochium. After Damasus's death and the election of Siricius to the see in 384, he departed, under some compulsion, for the east. He had made enemies by his rigorous ascetical teachings and stringent censures of Roman laxity and did not enjoy Siricius's support.

After a period of travel about the east, he founded, along with Paula, a double monastery of men and women at Bethlehem in 386. There, he would devote his life to his scriptural studies and voluminous writings. He was at first favorable to the works of Origen and enjoyed cordial relations with his old friends Rufinus and Melania the Younger, who themselves had founded a double monastery in Jerusalem on the Mount of Olives. The subsequent bitter dispute between Jerome and Rufinus would continue, despite a brief period of reconciliation (397), until Rufinus's death. When Jerome's monastery was attacked by a marauding gang in 416, the Roman bishop Innocent I criticized John of Jerusalem for his failure to prevent the assault (Innocent, *Ep.* 35 = Jerome, *Ep.* 137). Jerome died a few years thereafter.

Writings. Jerome is known first and foremost for his translations and revisions of the biblical books—the Vulgate—which became the accepted text in the Latin West. He translated at Constantinople (380) the *Chronicle* of Eusebius of Caesarea and carried it forward from its original ending in 325 to the death of Valens in 378. In 390, he translated and revised Eusebius's *Onomasticon*, a gazetteer of biblical places, and issued a second *Onomasticon*, a book of biblical personal names that shows heavy dependence on Philo and Origen. His work *On the Lives of Illustrious Men*, modeled on Suetonius, depends for the first seventy-eight of its 135 lives on Eusebius's *Chronicle* and *Church History*. Extending from Peter (1) to Jerome himself (135), it includes the Jewish authors Philo (11) and Josephus (13)

and the pagan Seneca the Younger (12) as well as a number of heretical writers. A source for the history of ancient Christian literature, it was continued by Gennadius, Isidore of Seville, and Ildefonsus of Toledo.

The translations (from 381 on) of numerous homilies of Origen on the prophets and the Song of Solomon were followed (ca. 392) by a rendering of that author's thirty-nine homilies on the Gospel of Luke, a version directed against the supposed deficiencies of a similar commentary by Ambrose. In the course of the controversy with Rufinus, Jerome issued (399) his own translation of Origen's *On First Principles* to counter that of his former friend. His translation of the work of Didymus the Blind on the Holy Spirit (387–390), the only extant version, was again directed against a treatise of Ambrose.

Scattered throughout Jerome's correspondence are translations of writings of Epiphanius of Salamis and Theophilus of Alexandria among others. His Latin version of the *Rule* of Pachomius, made from a Greek rendering of the Coptic original, preserved that work and allowed for its influence on western monasticism.

Among Jerome's biblical commentaries are four written in haste in 386 on the Pauline epistles (Philemon, Galatians, Ephesians, Titus), a commentary on Ecclesiastes (ca. 389), notes on the Psalms (ca. 390), a technical work on Genesis (ca. 392), a brief commentary on the Gospel of Matthew done upon request (398), and a revision of Victorinus of Pettau's Latin treatise on the Book of Revelation (date uncertain; early). But his most extensive works in this area are his series of commentaries on all of the minor (393–406) and major (407 on) prophets. The latter work was ended by his death, so that the final commentary, on Jeremiah, is incomplete. Although showing considerable dependence on earlier exegetes, the commentaries manifest Jerome's own considerable erudition.

A series of homilies given in Bethlehem ca. 400 is based mainly on the Psalms and Gospels, especially Mark; many are related to the cycle of the liturgical year. Three lives of ascetics contain much legendary material in furtherance of the monastic ideal—one (ca. 375–379) of Paul of Thebes, an obscure figure of the Egyptian desert, another (ca. 386–390) of Hilarion of Gaza, spiritual father of Epiphanius of Salamis, and the third (ca. 390) of Malchus, whom Jerome had met during his stay in the desert of Chalcis.

Jerome's polemical works are directed against the adherents of Lucifer of Cagliari (ca. 379); against Helvidius (ca. 383), who asserted that Mary had other children after Jesus' birth; against Jovinian (393), who taught that the reward of heaven would be equal for all and that virginity was not superior to marriage; against John of Jerusalem (397), a refutation of the teachings of Origen and defense of Epiphanius; against Rufinus in three books composed (401–402) in the course of the Origenist controversy; against Vigilantius (406), a defense of the veneration of martyrs, monasticism, and clerical celibacy; and against the adherents of Pelagius, a dialogue in three books (415). Most of these writings are abusive, teeming with bitter invective, although those against the Luciferians and the Pelagians are civil in tone.

The correspondence of Jerome includes the prefaces to his translations, letters relating to scriptural interpretation, the monastic life, the clergy, virgins, widows, and a defense (*Ep.* 57) of his own translation practices, as well as a number of funeral eulogies. This material has considerable historical importance in addition to its innate interest.

Among the numerous spurious works under his name is the *Martyrologium Hieronymianum*, a martyrology compiled in the north of Italy (fifth century) and revised in Gaul (ca. 600).

Significance. Jerome is a major bridge figure in the transition to the Middle Ages in the west. Although his reputation grew above all from his work on the Vulgate, his scriptural commentaries and his translation and expansion of Eusebius's *Chronicle* would also prove to have a substantial influence. His views on monasticism, celibacy, the virginity of Mary, and the cult of saints prevailed in medieval Catholic piety.

In medieval art, he is often portrayed with a lion and a cardinal's hat, the former because of a ninth-century legend that he tamed a lion by removing a thorn from its paw, the latter on the anachronistic (twelfth-century) assumption that Damasus I had made him a cardinal. The report (ca. 1290) of the removal of his remains to the Church of Sta. Maria Maggiore in Rome is unfounded.

The cult of Jerome as scholar gained popularity among the Renaissance humanists. Erasmus published (1516) the first successful critical biography to accompany his edition of Jerome's works. CPL 580–642. Feast day September 30. *See also* Jerusalem; Rufinus; Vulgate. [M.P.McH.]

Bibliography

Jerome, *Lives of Illustrious Men* 135.

PL 22–30; *De viris illustribus*, ed. E.C. Richardson, TU (1896), Vol. 14.1a; *Epistulae*, ed. I. Hilberg, CSEL (1910), Vol. 54; (1912), Vol. 55; (1918), Vol. 56; various biblical commentaries and polemical works appear in CCSL (1958–), Vols. 72–80.

Lives of Illustrious Men, tr. E.C. Richardson, NPNF, 2nd ser. (1892), Vol. 3, pp. 359–384; *Letters and Select Works*, tr. W.H. Fremantle et al., NPNF, 2nd ser. (1893), Vol. 6; *Life of Paul, Life of Hilarion, Life of Malchus*, tr. M.L. Ewald, *Early Christian Biographies*, ed. R.J. Deferrari, FOTC (1952), Vol. 15, pp. 217–297; *Letters*, Vol. 1 [Letters 1–22], tr. C.C. Mierow, ACW (1963), Vol. 33; *Homilies*, tr. M.L. Ewald, FOTC (1964, 1966), Vols. 48, 57; *Dogmatic and Polemical Works*, tr. J.N. Hritzu, FOTC (1965), Vol. 53.

F. Cavallera, *Saint Jérôme, sa vie et son oeuvre* (Louvain: Spicilegium Sacrum Lovaniense, and Paris: Champion, 1922); P. Antin, *Essai sur s. Jérôme* (Paris: Letouzey et Ané, 1951); F.X. Murphy, ed., *A Monument to Saint Jerome: Essays on Some Aspects of His Life, Works and Influence* (New York: Sheed and Ward, 1952); H. Hagendahl, *Latin Fathers and the Classics: A Study on the Apologists, Jerome and Other Christian Writers* (Göteborg: Almqvist & Wiksell, 1958), pp. 91–328 (updated in idem, "Jerome and the Latin Classics," *VChr* 28 [1974]:216–227); D.S. Wiesen, *St. Jerome as a Satirist: A Study in Christian Latin Thought and Letters* (Ithaca: Cornell UP, 1964); P. Antin, *Recueil sur saint Jérôme* (Brussels: Latomus, 1968); P. Courcelle, *Late Latin Writers and Their Greek Sources* (Cambridge: Harvard UP, 1969), pp. 48–127; H.F.D. Sparks, "Jerome as Biblical Scholar," *The Cambridge History of the Bible*, ed. P.R. Ackroyd and C.F. Evans, (Cambridge: Cambridge UP, 1970), Vol. 1, pp. 510–541; J.N.D. Kelly, *Jerome: His Life, Writings, and Controversies* (London: Duckworth, and New York: Harper and Row, 1975); R.J. O'Connell, "When Saintly Fathers Feuded: The Correspondence Between Augustine and Jerome," *Thought* 54 (1979):344–364; A.D. Booth, "The Chronology of Jerome's Early Years," *Phoenix* 25 (1981):237–259; T.P. Halton and R.D. Sider, "A Decade of Patristic Scholarship 1970–1979," *CW* 76 (1982–1983): 353–356 (bibliography); W.C. McDermott, "Saint Jerome and Pagan Greek Literature," *VChr* 36 (1982):372–382; E.F. Rice, Jr., *Saint Jerome in the Renaissance* (Baltimore: Johns Hopkins UP, 1985); P. Jay, *L'Exégèse de saint Jérôme d'après son Commentaire sur Isaïe* (Paris: Etudes Augustiennes, 1985); E.A. Clark, "The Place of Jerome's Commentary on Ephesians in the Origenist Controversy: The Apokatastasis and Ascetic Ideals," *VChr* 41 (1987):154–171; Y.M. Duval, *Jérôme entre l'Occident et l'Orient, 16e centenaire du départ de Jérôme de Rome et son installation à Bethléem: Actes du Colloque de Chantilly (septembre 1986)* (Turnhout: Brepols, 1988).

JERUSALEM. King David's capital city and important early Christian center. Jesus had part of his ministry in Jerusalem, died there, and was raised there. All the apostles were at one time or another in the city, including Paul. The first conference, if not council, to decide a disputed issue in the church was held in Jerusalem (Acts 15).

Yet Jerusalem's environs were not always inviting to Christians. Stephen was stoned there, and others were scattered in the midst of persecution. During the First Jewish Revolt (A.D. 66–70), the temple was destroyed, deeply affecting both Jews and Christians. Some Christians fled to Pella, a naturally fortified city in central Palestine, perhaps to return when fighting stopped (Epiphanius, *Haer.* 29; *Mens.* 15). They may have been the Christian community that created the *nomina sacra*, the abbreviations of sacred names in biblical manuscripts that mark Christian copyists. The Bar Kochba revolt of A.D. 132, which resisted Hadrian's attempt to turn the ruins of the temple into a shrine for Jupiter Capitolinus, led to another Roman show of force. Hadrian may have found Christian churches within Jerusalem at the restoration in A.D. 135; Eusebius of Caesarea (*D.E.* 3.5.108) speaks of one large building built by Jews, perhaps Jewish Christians.

Although early bishops' lists that Eusebius supplies (*H.E.* 4.5; 5.12; 7.32) seem forced, some bishops of the third century are plausible. Narcissus (*H.E.* 5.23) dealt with the Quartodeciman problem (whether Easter should be observed on the fourteenth day of Nisan or on the Sunday near that date). During his episcopate, Origen taught at Caesarea in Palestine and made visits to Jerusalem. Alexander, a bishop in Cappadocia, came to Jerusalem to visit the historical sites; he is one of the first recorded pilgrims. Made bishop of Jerusalem, he died in the Decian persecution (*H.E.* 6.11, 39).

In the fourth century, a new era dawned. Helena, Constantine's mother, probably had a hand in the emperor's building projects in Jerusalem. Eusebius describes a number of churches, the most important being the Church of the Holy Sepulchre (*V.C.* 3.25–40; 4.40), which Constantine himself dedicated in 335. It was built on Golgotha, where Hadrian had constructed a temple apparently dedicated to Venus or Aphrodite (Eusebius, *H.E.* 3.26; Jerome, *Ep.* 58.3). Evidently, when the razing of these structures took place, a cave was discovered that was thought to be the tomb of Jesus. About A.D. 380, a church was built in Gethsemane.

The pilgrim of Bordeaux visited the city at about this time. Egeria's early-fifth-century travel accounts, discovered only in the nineteenth century, indicate that she too was in Jerusalem and knew of the Sion church as well as the Eleona and Imbomon churches on the Mount of Olives. Although her work is fragmentary, one section describes in detail the Christian liturgy of Jerusalem. Her diary and the lectures of Cyril, bishop of Jerusalem, supply a wealth of information about Christian worship.

Two synods in Jerusalem—one in 335, which restored Arius's memory to a favored position, and another in 346, which readmitted Athanasius to communion—indicate how turbulent the Arian conflict was within the city. Cyril of Jerusalem offers evidence of early Arian themes, particularly the importance of growth in Jesus for the process of salvation.

His rejection of such positions in his catechetical orations offers a broader view of Arianism.

In 361, emperor Julian tried to rebuild the Jewish temple; he hoped thereby to honor a group that still offered sacrifices and to weaken Christian claims of being God's Israel. Pockets of gas that had accumulated in the ruined foundations thwarted his efforts. The site caught fire, and the project was abandoned.

Jerusalem continued to attract prominent Christians. Palladius, the historian of early monasticism, evidently lived there from 386 to 388. Jerome, perhaps the finest scholar the western church produced in the patristic period, moved to Bethlehem in 386 and resided there until his death in 419/20. At first, he and bishop John of Jerusalem were close friends. Some of Jerome's sermons that describe scenes in the city suggest that they were preached there. In 395, however, he and John had a violent quarrel. John went so far as to ban Jerome and his Bethlehem monastery. Jerome had grown distrustful of John's orthodoxy, believing that John had some Arian leanings and lived in too grand a style. Those events reflect Jerome's conflict with the monastery on the Mount of Olives, which had a more relaxed attitude toward life and was itself noted for important inhabitants. Rufinus, a boyhood friend of Jerome, had lived in that monastery for some time, as had Melania the Elder. Both had supported John. Such issues as the orthodoxy of Origen, the proper translation of the Old Testament, and the reading of pagan literature began to separate the former friends. Epiphanius of Salamis had no small part in the affair; at one point, as an invited guest, he attacked John from John's own pulpit. He urged Jerome on and worsened the situation.

New building projects and ecclesiastical politics dominated the beginning of the fifth century. Within the city, the churches of St. Stephen in Eudocia and St. John were built. The Origenist struggle continued. Furthermore, Juvenal, bishop of Jerusalem, supported Cyril of Alexandria in his battle with Nestorius, for reasons of both faith and political favor. Like Cyril, he wished to weaken Constantinople's place as second to Rome and sought to further Jerusalem's claim to a patriarchate. Although

Juvenal failed in 431 at Ephesus, he achieved his goal in 451 at Chalcedon.

The sixth century saw Jerusalem profit from Justinian's building programs. He refurbished the Anastasis (the Chapel of the Resurrection) and completed the new Church of St. Mary, dedicated in 543. The Madeba mosaic gives an interesting view of the city in this century. The churches of St. Sophia, St. Peter in Gallicanta, and Probatica Piscina probably date from this period.

The patriarchate remained basically orthodox in the early part of the century, when Saba (439–532) was so influential. Although his monastery lay between Jerusalem and the Dead Sea, in Wadi en-Nar, his presence was felt in the city. The patriarch had made him the superior of all monk-hermits throughout Palestine in 493. Saba continued the struggle with Origenist monks in the region.

Persians sacked the city in 614, killing thousands and burning most of the churches and monasteries. Jerusalem did not fully recover before the Muslim invasions. *See also* Holy Sepulchre, Church of the. [F.W.N.]

Bibliography

F.M. Abel, "Jerusalem," DACL (1926), Vol. 7.2, pp. 2304–2374; M. Join-Lambert, *Jerusalem* (New York: Ungar, 1958); J.D. Wilkinson, *Jerusalem Pilgrims Before the Crusades* (Warminster: Aris and Phillips, 1981); idem, *Egeria's Travels in the Holy Land*, rev. ed. (Warminster: Aris and Phillips, 1981); F.E. Peters, *Jerusalem: The Holy City in the Eyes of Chroniclers, Visitors, Pilgrims, and Prophets from the Days of Abraham to the Beginnings of Modern Times* (Princeton: Princeton UP, 1985); J.D. Purvis, *Jerusalem, The Holy City: A Bibliography* (Metuchen: Scarecrow, 1988).

JESUS. *See* Christ, Christology.

JEWISH CHRISTIANITY. The phenomenon known as Jewish Christianity is complex. One should not think of it as a unity but as a variety of religious developments. A review of the scholarly literature reveals four working definitions:

(1) "Jewish Christianity" refers to the earliest level of the Christian church, where Christians were those who had been born Jews but

had come to accept Jesus as the Messiah/Christ. Modern authors at times describe this type as Palestinian, New Testament, or Judaizing Christianity—terms that are not necessarily synonymous but are generally used to characterize nascent Christianity.

(2) The term is used for a kind of Jewish legalism in which the injunctions of the Torah are binding but in which belief in Jesus has been incorporated. This Jewish Christianity has as its main characteristic opposition to Gentile Christianity, as represented by Paul and his mission, which had freed itself from the demands of Torah. In the view of F.C. Baur, these two opposing forces in the early church found a synthesis in the development of Catholicism. In this definition, Jewish Christianity is sometimes referred to as "original" or "legalistic," and Gentile Christianity as "Hellenistic" or "Pauline."

(3) The term is used in a general fashion to include Jewish apocalyptic thought in Christian contexts. It is assumed that Jewish Christian groups promulgated this type of literature and had a distinct "theology." J. Daniélou postulates three distinct expressions of early Christian theology: Jewish, Hellenistic, and Latin. The method used to determine such a Jewish Christianity is eclectic and probably does not fully represent any specific group.

(4) The term is used to represent groups that both the Catholic church of the second century and the synagogue viewed as being outside their mainstream—thus, a kind of "middle ground." Sometimes, such scholars as H.-J. Schoeps wholly identify this Jewish Christianity with the Ebionites, but this is too narrow a definition. Groups within this category have been described as "heretical," "vegetarian," "Gnostic," "syncretistic," and simply as "later." Not all of these adjectives, of course, apply to every group: besides Ebionites, there were Cerinthians, Symmachians, Elkesaites, and Nazoraeans, whom the church fathers identified as bearers of heresy and who belong in this category of Jewish Christianity, as well as groups named more generally, such as Hemerobaptists and other baptizing sects inhabiting the Jordan and Transjordan areas. Certain of these groups existed until the fourth and fifth centuries but

disappeared in the Transjordan thereafter. Their views probably influenced Nestorian Christianity and may have found representation in the Christianity known to Muhammad.

Sources. Early Christian sources have been used in a variety of ways to derive these definitions, sometimes to support contradictory positions. The following sources, however, are pivotal.

In the New Testament, the Acts of the Apostles 1–12 represents Palestinian sources and shows the early Jewish Christian communities struggling with relationships with Hellenistic-oriented communities. Some of the struggle reflects that within Judaism between Judean and diaspora communities. Some Jewish Christians strongly opposed Paul's gospel that freed Gentile converts from observance of the Law (Acts 15; 21:17–40). The Epistle of James is widely recognized as offering an early Jewish Christian perspective, and the Johannine corpus reflects perspectives of a Christianity heavily indebted to Judaism.

In the apostolic fathers, the *Epistle of Barnabas*, the *Didache*, and the *Shepherd* of Hermas show authors influenced by Jewish concepts and texts who are in the process of incorporating and processing these materials for their respective Christian communities.

Among the church fathers, the heresiologists have passed down the names of Jewish Christian groups and the ideas with which they were associated, but little of their primary source material has been preserved. The exception is Jewish Christian gospels, which have been transmitted in fragmentary form (cf. NTA, Vol. 1, pp. 117–165). The writings of Irenaeus (*Haer.*), Pseudo-Clement (*Hom.*; *Recogn.*), Eusebius of Caesarea (*H.E.*), Jerome (*Ep.*; *Prol. Gal.*, *Vir. ill.*), and Epiphanius (*Haer.*) have been of significant value in presenting Jewish Christian thought. However, the fathers' references to these groups must be assessed in light of their hostility to Jewish Christianity.

The Pseudo-Clementine *Homilies* and *Recognitions* contain the remnants of earlier Jewish Christian materials. Two major sources embedded in the Pseudo-Clementines are the *Preachings of Peter* and the *Acts of Peter*. These are of uncertain Jewish Christian provenance.

Jewish Christian gospel materials have traditionally been assigned the names of *Gospel of the Nazaraeans*, *Gospel of the Ebionites*, and *Gospel according to the Hebrews*. Although it is not entirely clear that the extant fragments can be assigned with precision to one or the other of these "gospels," it is certain that the gospels were a source of contention among Jewish Christian groups. The *Gospel of the Nazaraeans* is thought to be an Aramaic version or targum of the Gospel of Matthew. Fragments assigned to this gospel do not reveal any heretical tendencies. The *Gospel of the Ebionites* is known by fragments preserved only in Epiphanius. They are described as being from an abridged or falsified Matthew from which references to Jesus' miraculous birth had been excised, as well as other traditions that seemed to indicate that Jesus was divine. The fragments appear to have been written in Greek; they show knowledge of the Synoptic Gospels and probably cannot be dated any earlier than the second half of the second century. The *Gospel according to the Hebrews*, according to Jerome (*Tract. in Esai.* 11.2), was written in Hebrew and used by the Nazoraeans. This is the Jewish Christian gospel most often mentioned by title. Its "Hebrew" original has not survived but is known through Greek, Latin, and Coptic fragments. Apparently, this gospel was almost as long as our canonical Matthew and probably contained accounts of Jesus' preexistence or birth, baptism and some of his teachings, and his passion and resurrection. In this gospel, James, the Lord's brother, was present at the Last Supper and was a witness of the resurrection, which made James the highest authority among the disciples.

History. The Christian movement began in Galilee with Jesus and his disciples. Early Christians were converts from Judaism. These disciples made missionary forays into the Decapolis, the territories and cities north and east of Galilee. Consequently, it is in Galilee that the center of early Jewish Christianity must be found. After A.D. 70, Jewish Christianity would be located in many of the Galilean and Transjordanian villages and cities. In Galilee, the villages of Kokaba and Nazara are named

as Jewish Christian centers; in the Transjordan, Pella, Beroea, Basanitis, Nabatea, Paneas, Moabitis, and Adraoi are given as specific locations. In the fourth century, a group is also found on the island of Cyprus.

At the beginnings of the Jewish war against Rome in A.D. 66, Jewish Christians in Jerusalem and perhaps also in Galilee escaped to Pella in Perea (Eusebius, *H.E.* 3.5.3), impelled "by a revelation." This pivotal event, denied as historical by some scholars, situated the Jewish Christians for the most part in the Transjordan for the remainder of their history.

Certain of the Jewish Christian communities revered Peter, who is described in the Pseudo-Clementine literature as one who kept the ritual laws of Judaism. Other communities revered James, the brother of Jesus, martyred in A.D. 62. Evidently, his family relationship to Jesus, as well as his devotion to Torah, were the principal reasons for his veneration. Other members of Jesus' family succeeded James in the leadership of the Jerusalem Christian community—Simon bar Clopus, a cousin (Eusebius, *H.E.* 3.11.1) or uncle (*H.E.* 3.32.6), and Justus, who may have been a relative, who succeeded Simon.

After the fall of Jerusalem in 70, Christians were excluded from participation in synagogues, and sometime later the curse against heretics used in synagogue worship was formulated. This was directed principally toward Jewish Christians. The Gospel of John 12:42 and 16:2, written in the 90s, makes reference to the excommunication of Christians from synagogues. Jewish Christianity in this situation probably began to use and adapt the traditions of the Gospel of Matthew, which had come into written form in the 80s, for worship and catechetical purposes. The patristic accounts, however, seem to indicate that the Matthew used by Jewish Christianity was in the "Hebrew" language. This may have been a retroversion of canonical Matthew, which almost certainly was originally written in Greek. Apparently, Matthew was used instead of other Gospels that may have been available due to its Jewish perspective. With the beginning of the second century, the heretical and schismatic era of Jewish Christianity began. In the tenth year of Trajan's reign (107), Simon bar Clopus, perhaps the final relative of Jesus, was martyred, reputedly at the age of 120 (Eusebius, *H.E.* 3.32.3). No longer would there be eyewitnesses who could correct the traditions circulated about Jesus. In 135, the Bar Kochba rebellion was quelled by the Romans, which marked the end of Jewish Christianity in Jerusalem. For the next 300 years, according to patristic records, Jewish Christianity would exist in the Transjordanian territories and then fade out of historical record. Whether there were viable Jewish Christian communities in the fifth century or only literary traditions perpetuated by the church fathers is not entirely clear. That their memory was kept alive is certain.

Some of the heretical Jewish Christian groups became syncretistic in their beliefs, combining traditional Jewish customs and practices with Gnostic beliefs and exotic religious notions. The Elkesaites were one such group; they blended elements of Judaism, Gnosticism, magic, and astrology (Hippolytus, *Haer.* 9.8–12; 10.25). That these groups should disappear is not surprising, since they did not fit either into posttemple Judaism nor into the emerging Catholic church with its concerns for orthodoxy. *See also* Ebionites; Elkesaites; James; Judaism and Christianity; Pseudo-Clementines. [G.A.K.]

Bibliography

G. Hoennicke, *Das Judenchristentum in ersten und zweiten Jahrhunderte* (Berlin: Trowitzsch, 1908); J. Thomas, *Le Mouvement baptiste en Palestine et Syrie (150 av. J.-C.–300 ap. J.-C.)* (Gembloux: Duculot, 1935); H.J. Schonfield, *The History of Jewish Christianity: From the First to the Twentieth Century* (London: Duckworth, 1936); H.-J. Schoeps, *Theologie und Geschichte des Judenchristentums* (Tübingen: Mohr, 1949); J.A. Fitzmyer, "The Qumran Scrolls, the Ebionites and Their Literature," *ThS* 16 (1955):335–372; J. Munck, "Jewish Christianity in Post-Apostolic Times," *NTS* 6 (1959–1960):103–116; M. Simon, *Recherches d'histoire Judéo-Chrétienne* (Paris: Mouton, 1962); P. Vielhauer, "Jewish Christian Gospels," NTA, Vol. 1, pp. 117–165; J. Daniélou, *The Theology of Jewish Christianity* (London: Darton, Longman and Todd, 1964); H.D. Betz, "Orthodoxy and Heresy in Primitive Christianity," *Interpretation* 19 (1965):299–311; M. Simon, "Problèmes du Judéo-Christianisme," *Aspects du Judéo-Christianisme: Colloque de Strasbourg 23–25 Avril 1964* (Paris: Presses Universitaires de France, 1965), pp. 1–17; S. Pines, *The Jewish Christians of the Early Centuries of Christianity According to a New Source* (Jerusalem: Central Press, 1966); G. Quispel, "The Discussion of Judaic Christianity," *VChr* 22 (1968):81–93; H.-J. Schoeps, *Jewish Christianity* (Philadelphia: Fortress, 1969); I. Mancini, *Archaeological Discoveries Relative to the Judaeo-Christians* (Jerusalem: Franciscan Printing Press, 1970); G. Strecker, "On the Problem of Jewish Christianity," *Orthodoxy and Heresy in Earliest Christianity*, ed. R.A. Kraft and G. Krodel (Philadelphia: Fortress, 1971), pp. 241–285; R.A. Kraft, "In Search of 'Jewish Christianity' and Its Theology': Problems of Definition and Methodology," *RecSR* 60 (1972):81–92; A.F.J. Klijn and G.F. Reinink, *Patristic Evidence for Jewish-Christian Sects* (Leiden: Brill, 1973); A.F.J. Klijn, "The Study of Jewish Christianity," *NTS* 20 (1973):419–431; R. Murray, "Defining Judaeo-Christianity," *Heythrop Journal* 15 (1974):303–310; R.A. Kraft, "The Multiform Jewish Heritage of Early Christianity," *Christianity, Judaism and Other Greco-Roman Cults*, ed. J. Neusner (Leiden: Brill, 1975), pp. 174–199; F. Manns, "Bibliographie de Judéo-Christianisme," *Studium Biblicum Franciscanum* (Jerusalem: Franciscan Printing Press, 1979); R.A. Pritz, *Nazarene Jewish Christianity* (Leiden: Brill, 1988).

JOB. Named for its major character, the Book of Job is classified in the division of the Writings in the Hebrew Bible; in the Greek, Latin, and English Bibles, Job is the first of the poetic books. Job has a prose prologue and epilogue but otherwise is in verse. Commonly classified as Wisdom literature, the book discusses how the suffering of the righteous is to be harmonized with the ways of a God who is righteous and all-powerful. The wealthy and righteous Job loses his possessions, family, and health. In three cycles, Job's three friends speak, accusing him of sin because he was suffering, and are answered by Job. Elihu speaks, and God speaks out of the whirlwind. Job is in the end restored to prosperity. There is also in Greek a Jewish apocryphal *Testament of Job*, in which Job recounts his life and sufferings in order to encourage patience and endurance.

In the Old Testament, Job is an example of the eminently righteous man (Ezek. 14:14, 20), and in the New Testament he is praised for his steadfastness (James 5:11). The church fathers often referred to Job, but few complete commentaries have come down to us: fragments of commentaries are found from Clement of Alexandria (PG 9), Origen (PG 12; 17), Athanasius (PG 27), and John Chrysostom (PG 64). There are works by Ambrose (PL 14), Augustine (PL 34), and Gregory the Great (PL 75).

The resurrection affirmation in the Septuagint wording of Job 19:26 led Christians (cf. *1 Clem.* 26) to see in Job a notable symbol of the resurrection. Job was an example of steadfastness and as a sufferer who was eventually vindicated could be regarded as a type of Christ himself.

Job is occasionally a subject in early Christian art. He is usually a solitary seated figure, but sometimes his wife is shown offering him food on a rod or stick, but not touching him because of his sores.   [J.P.L.]

Bibliography
Didymus der Blinde, Kommentar zur Hiob, ed. A. Henrichs, L. Koene, U. and D. Hagedorn (Bonn: Habelt, 1968–); D. Hagedorn, ed., *Der Hiobkommentar des Arianers Julian* (Berlin: de Gruyter, 1973); Olympiodorus of Alexandria, *Kommentar zu Hiob*, ed. U. and D. Hagedorn (Berlin: de Gruyter, 1984).

L. Leclercq, "Job," DACL (1926), Vol. 7.2, pp. 2554–2570; H.H. Rowley, *Job* (Grand Rapids: Eerdmans, 1970).

JOHN, JOHANNINE LITERATURE. Apostle and supposed author of the Gospel and Epistles now bearing his name and of the Revelation of John. The Gospel and three Epistles are strictly anonymous, although the author of second and third Epistles designates himself the Elder (*presbyteros*). Only in the Book of Revelation does the author refer to himself as John, "your brother," naming Patmos as the location of the visions recorded in this book of prophecy (Rev. 1:3, 9). Yet tradition, which can be traced back to Irenaeus of Lyons (*Haer.* 2.22.5; 3.3.4; 3.16.5; 4.20.11), ascribed all five books to John the son of Zebedee and identified him with the Beloved Disciple of the Fourth Gospel.

The reasons for attributing the Johannine corpus to John the son of Zebedee, from the inner circle of Jesus' twelve disciples (Mark 9:2; 14:33), and naming him the Beloved Disciple, are far from clear. In what appears to be an appendix (21:24–25), authorship of the Gospel is attributed to the Beloved Disciple mentioned in 13:23; 19.26; 20:2; 21:7, 20; and perhaps also in 1:35; 18:15–16; 19:35. Nevertheless, his identity remains hidden: either John the son of Zebedee or an otherwise unnamed disciple may have been intended. Whoever is intended, the Beloved Disciple serves as an ideal figure, appearing in tandem with Peter. All of these references may be later additions belonging to a time when the Johannine Christians were attempting to come to terms with Petrine Christianity, here represented by Peter.

The Gospel of John takes a different approach to telling the story of Jesus from that of the Synoptic Gospels (Matthew, Mark, Luke). Where the same event is related (as the cleansing of the temple), it is put in a different chronological setting: the beginning of Jesus' ministry (John 2:13–25) instead of the end (Mark 11:15–18). The Fourth Gospel includes many long discourses by Jesus, such as the "Farewell Discourse" (John 14–17). These often relate to one of the seven "signs" (mighty works) done by Jesus: changing the water into wine (2:1–11), healing the nobleman's son (4:46–54), healing the lame man (5:2–18) followed by discourse on authority (5:19–47), feeding the multitude (6:4–13) with discourse on "bread of life" (6:25–71), walking on the water (6:16–21), healing the man born blind (9:1–41, including discussion of spiritual sight) and raising Lazarus (11:1–44, including discussion of resurrection). The epistles of John show a more obviously polemical situation. They oppose a schismatic movement that minimized the real humanity of Jesus (1 John 2:22; 4:2; 2 John 7), claimed a moral superiority over sin (1 John 1:8, 10), and neglected the expressions of Christian fellowship (1 John 2:9–11; 3:15–18; 4:20f.).

Evidence for the Gospel is found in a fragment of John 18:31–33, 37, 38 (Rylands Papyrus 457), which must be dated between A.D. 120 and 150 (cf. Egerton Papyrus 2). Had the Gospel been written by John the apostle, we would expect evidence of widespread use reflecting its authority. Apparent echoes of the Gospel in Ignatius of Antioch and Justin Mar-

Church of St. John, Ephesus, Turkey, built under the emperor Justinian (527–565). View from the altar area and traditional site of the grave of the apostle John (bottom right) through the nave to the entrance.

tyr (mid-second century) could be derived from a wider tradition rather than from the Gospel itself. Justin certainly knew Revelation and attributed it to John the apostle (*Dial.* 81). Justin's pupil Tatian made use of the Gospel in his *Diatessaron*, thus indicating that he regarded it as an equal authority with the Synoptics. Melito of Sardis (ca. 165) also used it, and Polycrates of Ephesus (ca. 190) asserts that John, who leaned on the Lord's breast, sleeps at Ephesus (Eusebius, *H.E.* 3.31.2–4). More importantly, Irenaeus appeals to the witness of Polycarp and Papias of Hierapolis, claiming that they knew John the apostle. This is called into question by Eusebius of Caesarea (324), who asserts that Papias knew John the elder, not the apostle, quoting from the lost works of Papias to make his point (*H.E.* 3.29.1–7). This quotation is not quite straightforward but probably does imply two different Johns. Eusebius attributed the Gospel to the apostle and the Book of Revelation to the elder.

This reading of the evidence by Eusebius implies an early death of the apostle, a view supported by Philip of Side (ca. 430) and George Hamartolos (ninth century). Both appeal to the second book of Papias in a way that suggests George might be dependent on Philip. The early-fifth-century martyrology drawn up in Edessa and the early-sixth-century Calendar of Carthage both assert that John met an early death as a martyr. These works are too late to be reliable and may be dependent on Mark 10:39, although it can be argued that, had the sons of Zebedee not both been dead, this text would not have been recorded. This tradition might have been supressed in the interest of the position supported by Irenaeus.

The adherents of Montanism (mid-second century) made use of the Gospel's teaching about the Spirit/Paraclete (John 14–16), and the vision of the descent of the heavenly Jerusalem (Rev. 21). The first known commentary on a book in the New Testament is that of the Valentinian Gnostic Heracleon on the Fourth Gospel, which is preserved only in the commentary of Origen (early third century). The commentary of the Gnostic Ptolemy on the prologue of the Gospel is preserved by Irenaeus (*Haer.* 1.8.5). According to Hippolytus (*Haer.* 5.2–4, 11–12), the Naassenes and Peratae had also made wide use of John, virtually ignoring the Synoptics. The prevalence of the Gospel in Gnosticism might have given the impression that it was a Gnostic book. Indeed, according to Epiphanius of Salamis (*Haer.* 51.2–3), the Alogoi, who opposed the doctrine of the Logos, attributed both the Gospel and Revelation to the archheretic Cerinthus. Irenaeus saw the Valentinian position to be so dependent on John that the only way to refute it was to set out a valid interpretation of the Gospel (*Haer.* 3.11.7). He also recounts a tradition of the opposition of John to Cerinthus (*Haer.* 3.3.4).

What attracted the Gnostics to the Gospel was the cosmological framework of the prologue and the symbolism of the Gospel as a whole, which led Clement of Alexandria to refer to it as "the spiritual Gospel." In all probability, the *Gospel of Truth* (part of the Nag Hammadi Library) is a Valentinian meditation on the Gospel of John, which was also a fertile source for the development of the theology of the great church, although presuppositions derived from Platonism and Stoicism often influenced interpretation.

The Logos doctrine of John 1:1–18 continued to be significant in the development of Christology up to the Council of Chalcedon (451). The teaching about the Paraclete/Spirit of Truth (14:15–17, 25–26; 15:26–27; 16:7–15) also contributed strongly to the ultimate recognition of the Holy Spirit as a third divine person in relation to the Father and the Son. Indeed, it was the Gospel that provided the resources from which the church constructed its doctrine of the Trinity in terms of Father, Son, and Holy Spirit, although the doctrine was embryonic in certain formulas known to Paul and Matthew (2 Cor. 13:13; Matt. 28:19).

The Fourth Gospel emerges from the mists only in the middle of the second century, but by the end of the patristic period it held central stage and influenced the development of doctrine perhaps more than any other single work. The other representatives of the Johan-

nine literature did not prove to be so influential. Revelation declined in influence, probably because of the Montanist heresy and growing skepticism concerning millenarianism, and the Epistles paled to insignificance alongside the more vital and impressive Gospel. Feast day December 27 (west), September 26 (east). *See also* Revelation, Book of. [J.P.]

Bibliography

Origen, *Commentary on John*, tr. A. Menzies, ANF (1896), Vol. 10; John Chrysostom, *Homilies on St. John*, tr. C. Marriott, NPNF, 1st ser. (1889), Vol. 14; Theodore of Mopsuestia, *Commentarius in evangelium Johannis*, CSCO (1940), Vols. 115–116; Cyril of Alexandria, *Commentary on the Gospel According to John*, 2 vols., Library of the Fathers of the Church (Oxford: UP, 1832, 1835); Augustine, *Tractates on the Gospel According to St. John* and *Homilies on the Epistle of John*, tr. J. Gibb, J. Innes, and H. Browne, NPNF, 1st ser. (1888), Vol. 7.

K. Aland, ed., *Synopsis Quattuor Evangeliorum* (Stuttgart: Wurtembergische Bibelanstalt, 1964), pp. 531–548.

B.F. Westcott, *The Gospel According to St. John* (London: Murray, 1908); R.E. Brown, *The Gospel According to John*, 2 vols. (Garden City: Doubleday, 1966, 1970); L. Morris, *The Gospel According to John* (Grand Rapids: Eerdmans, 1971); C.K. Barrett, *The Gospel According to St. John* (London: SPCK, 1978).

R.E. Brown, *The Epistles of John* (Garden City: Doubleday, 1982); J.M. Lieu, *The Second and Third Epistles of John* (Edinburgh: T. and T. Clark, 1986).

V.H. Stanton, *The Gospels as Historical Documents* (Cambridge: Cambridge UP, 1903); J.N. Sanders, *The Fourth Gospel in the Early Church: Its Origin and Influence on Christian Theology up to Irenaeus* (Cambridge: Cambridge UP, 1943); C.H. Dodd, *The Interpretation of the Fourth Gospel* (Cambridge: Cambridge UP, 1953); M.F. Wiles, *The Spiritual Gospel: The Interpretation of the Fourth Gospel in the Early Church* (Cambridge: Cambridge UP, 1960); T.E. Pollard, *Johannine Christology and the Early Church* (Cambridge: Cambridge UP, 1970); E.H. Pagels, *The Johannine Gospel in Gnostic Exegesis* (New York: Abingdon, 1973); D.M. Smith, *Johannine Christianity: Essays on its Setting, Sources and Theology* (Edinburgh: T.and T. Clark, 1987); R.E. Heine, "The Role of the Gospel of John in the Montanist Controversy," *SCent* 6 (1987/1988): 1–19.

JOHN II. Bishop of Rome (532–535). Originally named Mercurius, John was the first pope to change his name upon election. He accepted the Theopaschite formula that the emperor

Justinian I had inserted in a dogmatic decree defining the faith of Chalcedon against the *acoemetae*, or "sleepless monks," of Constantinople, who denied to Mary the title *Theotokos*, or "mother of God." In correspondence with Caesarius of Arles, he ordered an errant bishop to be deposed and confined to a monastery. Five of his letters are extant. CPL 1613, 1625, 1692.   [M.P.McH.]

Bibliography

Liber Pontificalis 58 (Duchesne 1.285–286).

JOHN CHRYSOSTOM (ca. 347–407). Bishop of Constantinople (from 398) and the greatest preacher in the early church, hence the name *Chrysostomos* ("golden-mouthed"). John lived during the golden age of early Christian literature; like others who were part of the blossoming of Christian cultural and spiritual life in this period—Basil of Caesarea, Gregory of Nyssa, and Gregory of Nazianzus—he was thoroughly educated in the rhetorical and literary traditions of Greek culture, while surpassing all his contemporaries in the purity and elegance of his style. Widely admired by modern classical scholars, his prose has been described as "the harmonious expression of an Attic soul." John put his literary and rhetorical gifts at the service of Christ, and most of his writings are sermons based on the books of the Bible, homilies on festivals and saints' days, and treatises on the Christian life. He also wrote the first Christian treatise on the office of the ministry, *On the Priesthood*. In the Middle Ages, he was the most beloved among all the early Christian writers from the east, as hundreds of manuscripts of his writings testify. Less than a decade after his death, the first biography appeared, written by Palladius, bishop of Helenopolis; and several generations later, the epithet Chrysostom had begun to replace his given name.

John was born in Antioch in Syria into a good, if undistinguished, family of the educated upper class. Until he was made bishop of Constantinople in 398, he lived in Antioch and its environs. His father, a civil servant, died while John was a child, and he was raised by his mother, Anthusa. As a young man, he studied with Libanius, the outstanding rhetorician of the day. Because of his exceptional gifts, it was assumed he would pursue a career in law or the civil service. During his teens, however, John cast his lot with the church and made the first steps leading to the Christian ministry, a profession in which his rhetorical education would serve him well. Baptized in 368, he began the study of the scriptures under the bishop of Antioch, Melitius. After three years, he was ordained lector (reader), one of the minor offices; but before pursuing a clerical career, John went to live in the countryside, under the tutelage of an aged monk, in order to practice the disciplines of mortification of the body and solitude of the soul. Although his ascetic ideals were later tempered by his pastoral experience, throughout his life he continued to hold up the solitary life as the highest form of Christian devotion.

In 381, John was ordained deacon, and five years later, presbyter (priest). The next decade was the most productive in his life. He preached regularly at the several churches in the city of Antioch and took an active interest in civic affairs. From this period come his sermons on Genesis, Matthew, John, Romans, Galatians, 1 and 2 Corinthians, Ephesians, Timothy, and Titus. They are marked by a warm devotion to Christ and a lively interest in applying the biblical text to the spiritual and moral lives of the faithful. They are also a rich source of evidence for life in Antioch in late antiquity and for differences within the Christian community at that time. From this period also comes a series of sermons, *Homilies on the Statues*, occasioned by civic violence against statues of the emperor and his family in Antioch. While the bishop was in Constantinople pleading for clemency, John preached twenty-one sermons, at once castigating the people for their wrongdoings and consoling them in the face of the emperor's wrath. During these years, he preached a series of sermons against a group of radical Arian Christians in the city, *On the Incomprehensibility of God*, as well as eight sermons, *Against Judaizing Christians*, warning the faithful against the dangers of participating in Jewish festivals, such

John Chrysostom. Mosaic (tenth century) from the nave of Hagia Sophia, Istanbul, Turkey.

as Rosh Hashanah and Yom Kippur, and observing the Sabbath. The Jews were a lively presence in the city, and some Christians found their rites irresistible. In the sermons, John is on the defensive and his language is often harsh and bellicose. When these sermons were copied or translated in medieval Europe, a society in which Christianity was the dominant religion, their defamatory and abusive language helped foster anti-Jewish attitudes among Christians.

In 398, John was forced to accept appointment as bishop of Constantinople. From this point on, he became enmeshed in imperial and ecclesiastical politics, fields in which he was much less adept than in preaching and pastoral work. Even before becoming bishop, he had acquired enemies. The man who had consecrated him, Theophilus, bishop of Alexandria, a rival episcopal see, had lent his support to another candidate and was displeased with John's election. But the first two years in office were relatively untroubled, and John devoted

himself to preaching in the capital and overseeing the churches in the city. He supported mission efforts among the Gothic tribes in the Balkans and encouraged preaching in their language and translations of the Bible into Gothic. At first, he was on good terms with the empress Eudoxia, but his uncompromising zeal for reform, his disdain for the opulent life and manners of the court, his reclusiveness, and his "liberty of speech" (tactlessness) created new enemies. The trouble began when he overstepped his episcopal authority by deposing several bishops in Ephesus, a city not under his jurisdiction, for selling church offices and appropriating church money for personal use. During the three months he spent in Ephesus adjudicating this matter, his enemies plotted against him.

On his return, an injudicious reference in a sermon to the empress as "Jezebel" mobilized his foes. The key figure was Theophilus, who had been waiting for the first misstep by the new bishop. By humiliating the bishop of Constantinople, Theophilus hoped to aggrandize his own see, Alexandria. A group of monks from Egypt, the "Tall Brothers," had been charged with "Origenism." Their case was brought to Constantinople, but John refused to condemn them without a hearing. As a result, Theophilus used the trial of the Tall Brothers as a ruse to attack John. A synod was held across the Bosporus from Constantinople in a suburb of Chalcedon, at a place called the "Oak," in 403. Theophilus packed it with Egyptian bishops, who became John's judges and accusers. Instead of hearing the case of the monks, they condemned John on a series of concocted charges, among which was uttering defamatory and treasonable words against the empress. Declared guilty and deposed from his office, John left Constantinople by night for a town on the Black Sea, but he was immediately recalled and reinstated.

New friction, however, developed with the empress, and he was charged with assuming the duties of his office without being properly reinstated. Again, he was deposed and exiled near Antioch and then banished to an isolated village on the Black Sea. Although he received support from all over the Christian world, including from the bishop of Rome, he lived out his final days in exile. During this period, he wrote many letters that are still extant. One group, to an old friend and confidant, Olympias, a religious woman, is a touching testimony to the deep respect and admiration that on occasion existed between Christian clergy and women in the early church. He died on September 14, 407, and his body was removed to Constantinople thirty years later. Feast day January 27. CPG II, 4305–5197.   [R.Wi.]

Bibliography
Palladius, *Dialogue Concerning the Life of Chrysostom*; Socrates, *Church History* 6.2–23; 7.25–45; Sozomen, *Church History* 8.2–8; Theodoret, *Church History* 5.27–36; Isidore of Pelusium, *Epistulae* 2.42.
PG 47–62; SC (1968–1983), Vols. 13, 28, 50, 79, 103, 117, 125, 138, 188, 272, 277, 300, 304.
NPNF, 1st ser. (1888–1893), Vols. 9–14; FOTC (1957–1986), Vols. 33, 41, 68, 72, 73, 74; ACW (1963, 1985), Vols. 31, 45.
A.J. Festugière, *Antioche païenne et chrétienne* (Paris: Boccard, 1959); C. Baur, *John Chrysostom and His Time*, 2 vols. (London: Sands, 1960); R. Carter, "The Chronology of St. John Chrysostom's Early Life," *Traditio* 18 (1962):357–364; E.A. Clark, *Jerome, Chrysostom, and Friends: Essays and Translations* (New York: Mellen, 1979); R.L. Wilken, *John Chrysostom and the Jews: Rhetoric and Reality in the Late Fourth Century* (Berkeley: U of California P, 1983).

JOHN CLIMACUS (ca. 579–649). Abbot at Sinai. John wrote *The Ladder of Divine Ascent (or of Paradise)*, an influential ascetic work of the eastern church. Feast day March 30. CPG III, 7850–7853.   [F.W.N.]

Bibliography
C. Luibheid and N. Russells, trs., *John Climacus: The Ladder of Divine Ascent* (New York: Paulist, 1982).

JOHN MALALAS (sixth century). Historian. John's *Chronographia* gives a history from creation to his time, nine books up to the incarnation, nine afterward. He includes references to historians otherwise unknown. Much of his grasp of Roman history is shaky, but he has important details for the history of Antioch in Syria. CPG III, 7511.   [F.W.N.]

Bibliography
E. Jeffreys, M. Jeffreys, R. Scott, et al., trs., *The Chronicle of John Malalas: A Translation* (Melbourne: Australian Association of Byzantine Studies, 1986).

JOHN MAXENTIUS (sixth century). Priest and monk. A leader of monks from Scythia who was active 519–533 in support of the Theopaschite formula of faith, John Maxentius may well be the person of the same name who is the author of a profession of faith, attacks on Nestorianism and Pelagianism, and a sharp criticism of pope Hormisdas. His identification with John, bishop of Tomis, is uncertain. CPL 656–665.   [M.P.McH.]

Bibliography
Maxentius aliique Scythae monachi necnon Iohannes Tomitanus, Opuscula, ed. F. Glorie, CCSL (1978), Vol. 85A.

JOHN MOSCHUS (ca. 550–619). Author of the *Pratum spirituale* (or "The Spiritual Meadow"), a piece that contains many monastic anecdotes. John Moschus spent most of his adult years at the monastery of St. Theodosius outside Jerusalem but traveled to various important monastic centers, such as Alexandria, Antioch, Rome, and Samos, where he gained firsthand experience with spiritual leaders. The *Pratum spirituale* exists in many recensions because it was both popular for its insights and often added to. CPG III, 7376–7377.[F.W.N.]

Bibliography
H. Chadwick, "John Moschus and His Friend Sophronius the Sophist," *JThS* n.s. 25 (1974):41–74.

JOHN OF ANTIOCH (d. 441). Bishop (428–441), moderate supporter of Nestorius in his battle with Cyril of Alexandria. John led an Antiochene contingent to the Council of Ephesus (431). His party was delayed by weather and reached the city only after Cyril and his group had condemned Nestorius. When John's party arrived, they held their own council, condemned Cyril, and backed Nestorius.

In 433, John and Cyril were able to agree on a formula that pushed Cyril to confess publicly the full humanity of Christ and demanded that John concede the dangers of a divisive Christology in two natures. Cyril gained support, but John lost influence due to the compromise. CPG III, 6301–6360.   [F.W.N.]

Bibliography
Cyril of Alexandria, *Letters* [to John and from John] 13; 22; 35; 38–39; 47; 52; 61–63; 66–67; 89–91; 102–104.
R.V. Sellers, *The Council of Chalcedon: A Historical and Doctrinal Survey* (London: SPCK, 1953), pp. 6–34.

JOHN OF CAESAREA (sixth century). Grammarian and bishop. An early representative of Neochalcedonian Christology, John wrote (ca. 515) an apology for the faith of Chalcedon, known from its refutation by Severus of Antioch. CPG III, 6855–6862.   [E.F.]

Bibliography
Severus, *Liber contra impium Grammaticum.*

JOHN OF CARPATHUS (fifth, sixth, or seventh century). Perhaps bishop of the island of Carpathus in the Aegean, John is the author of didactic and hortatory works directed to monks. CPG III, 7855–7859.   [M.P.McH.]

Bibliography
"St. John of Karpathos," *The Philokalia, the Complete Text Compiled by St. Nikodimos of the Holy Mountain and St. Makarios of Corinth,* tr. G.E.H. Palmer, P. Sherrard, and K. Ware (London: Faber and Faber, 1979), Vol. 1, pp. 297–326.

JOHN OF DAMASCUS (ca. 650 [or 675?]–ca. 749). Byzantine monk and theologian. Born in Damascus of the prosperous Mansur family, John was well educated in both Greek and Arabic. Following his grandfather and father in ministerial posts, Yanah ibn Mansur ibn Sargun, as he was called, resigned his position at the caliph's court to enter the monastery of Mar Saba (St. Saba) near Jerusalem and was ordained a priest.

Little is known of his life, as the traditional biography dates only from the eleventh century. In 726, the emperor Leo the Isaurian issued his first edict against images. Theophanes the Chronicler relates that John was a forceful resister of this policy. In his *Apostolic Discourses,* John produced a theologically reasoned defense of the veneration of holy images that earned him the bitter enmity of the emperors and the anathema of the iconoclast council of 753. Out of the reach of the emperors in Muslim territory, John could continue to write and preach at his monastery and also in the churches of Jerusalem. Of the thirteen homilies attributed to him only nine are certainly genuine, but they are an eloquent testimony to his abilities as preacher and theologian. The four homilies on the Virgin Mary offer devout evidence of a developed Mariology. Surnamed Chrysorrhoas ("Golden-flowing"), John was also adept at Greek liturgical poetry and shared in the composition of the Byzantine liturgical office. His *Sacra parallela* is a vast compilation of scriptural and patristic material on the moral and ascetical life, although the exact extent of his contribution is uncertain. Most of his works were written for a monastic audience.

He wrote defenses of orthodox Christianity against the Nestorians, Paulicians, Monophysites, Monothelites, and also against Muslim fatalism. But the greatest of his works by far is his *Fount of Knowledge*, which he intended to be a compendium of Christian truth gathered from previous authors. The first part of the work is a philosophical introduction (*Philosophical Chapters* or *Dialectica*); the second part is a historical introduction in which he summarizes eighty chapters of Epiphanius's *Panarion* while adding twenty others from various sources (*On Heresies in Epitome*); the main body of the work is entitled *An Exact Exposition of the Orthodox Faith*. This last, the best-known part, consists of 100 dogmatic chapters (a "century") usually divided into four books. It is a systematic treatment of all theological questions from the triune God to the resurrection of the dead based on the teachings of the Nicene and post-Nicene Greek fathers (and Leo the Great), especially Gregory of Nazianzus. An admirable synthesis of Greek theology, it is a practical *summa* that has had great influence in the east and (from the twelfth century onward) in the west. In general, John is a coherent transmitter and exponent of the Greek Christian tradition who uses the fathers as authoritative interpreters of scripture and of orthodox theology. Feast day March 27 (west), December 4 (east). CPG III, 8040–8127.

[G.C.B.]

Bibliography
Works in PG 94–96; a critical ed. of the entire corpus has been begun under the auspices of the Abbey of Scheyern in Bavaria: *Die Schriften des Johannes von Damaskus I* (Berlin: de Gruyter, 1969-).
Exposition of the Orthodox Faith, tr. S.D.F. Salmond, NPNF, 2nd ser. (1899), Vol. 9; *Fount of Knowledge*, tr. F.H. Chase, FOTC (1958), Vol. 37; *On the Divine Images*, tr. D. Anderson (Crestwood: St. Vladimir's Seminary, 1980); the homilies on the dormition and the nativity, ed. and tr. (into French) P. Voulet, SC (1961), Vol. 80.
V.A. Mitchel, *The Mariology of Saint John Damascene* (Kirkwood: Maryhurst Normal, 1930); J. Nasrallah, *Saint Jean de Damas: son époque, sa vie, son oeuvre* (Harissa: St. Paul, 1950); K. Rosemond, *La Christologie de saint Jean Damascene* (Ettal: Buch Kunstverlag, 1959); L. Sweeney, "John Damascene and the Divine Infinity," *New Scholasticism* 35 (1961):76–106; idem, "John Damascene's 'Infinite Sea of Essence,'" TU (1962), Vol. 81, pp. 248–263; M. O'Rourke Boyle, "Christ the Eikon in the Apologies for Holy Images of John of Damascus," *GOTR* 15 (1970):175–186; D.J. Sahas, *John of Damascus on Islam: The "Heresy of the Ishmaelites"* (Leiden: Brill, 1972).

JOHN OF EPHESUS (or John of Asia, ca. 507–589). Monophysite monk, missionary, bishop, and historian from north Mesopotamia. John spent much of his career in exile during anti-Monophysite persecutions, traveling throughout the eastern empire or living with refugees in Constantinople. Enigmatically, the emperor Justinian chose John to lead a missionary campaign in Asia Minor. John claimed to have converted 80,000 pagans and schismatics (notably Montanists). He endured lengthy imprisonments because of his Monophysite beliefs.

Two important Syriac works by John survive: the *Lives of the Eastern Saints*, fifty-eight short biographies of holy men and women he knew; and his *Ecclesiastical History*. Both provide invaluable material on sixth-century life in the Byzantine east.　　　　　　[S.A.H.]

Bibliography
Lives of the Eastern Saints, ed. and tr. E.W. Brooks, PO (1923–1925), Vols. 17–19. John's *Ecclesiastical History* was written in three parts; only a few fragments of Part 1 survive. Part 2 survives in the Chronicle of Pseudo-Dionysus of Tell-Mahre; for the passages by John (with French tr.), see F. Nau, "Analyse de la seconde partie inédite de l'Histoire Ecclésiastique de Jean d'Asie," *Revue de l'orient chrétien* 2 (1897):455–493, and for the text, *Incerti Auctoris Chronicon Pseudo-Dionysianum Vulgo Dictum* II, ed. I.B. Chabot, Vol. 2, and *Accedunt Ioannis Ephesini Fragmenta*, ed. E. W. Brooks, CSCO (1952), Vol. 104,153. Part 3 survives intact: *Ioannis Ephesini Historiae Ecclesiasticae Pars Tertia*, ed. and tr. E.W. Brooks, CSCO (1935), Vols. 105, 154 and 106, 155.
P. Brown, "Eastern and Western Christendom in Late Antiquity: A Parting of the Ways," *The Orthodox Churches and the West*, ed. D. Baker (Oxford: Blackwell, 1976), pp. 1–24; S.A. Harvey, "Physicians and Ascetics in John of Ephesus: An Expedient Alliance," *DOP* 38 (1984):87–93; S.A. Harvey, *Asceticism and Society in Crisis: John of Ephesus and the "Lives of the Eastern Saints"* (Berkeley: U of California P, forthcoming).

JOHN OF EUBOEA (eighth century). Monk and presbyter perhaps from Euroia near Damascus rather than from Euboea in Greece. A younger contemporary of John of Damascus and a skilled preacher who often raved against Jews, he wrote panegyrics for saints Paraskeue and Anastasia. CPG III, 8134–8138.   [F.W.N.]

JOHN OF GAZA (sixth century). Poet. Around 530, John of Gaza wrote *An Explanation of the Map of the World* in trimetrical poetic form. His effort became a model for poetic literature in the Byzantine period.
                                              [F.W.N.]

JOHN OF SCYTHOPOLIS (early sixth century). Bishop of Scythopolis in Palestine. An influential early Neochalcedonian theologian, John wrote a commentary on the Pseudo-Dionysius. Only fragments of his literary output survive. CPG III, 6850–6852.   [E.F.]

JOHN PHILOPONUS (ca. 490–570s). Christian Aristotelian philosopher who lived and studied at Alexandria. The writings of John Philoponus include commentaries on Aristotle, other philosophical treatises, and theological works. He led the overthrow of Aristotelian science by espousing the creation of the world. For philosophical reasons, he rejected Chalcedonian Christology and later held tritheistic views. Near the end of his life, he argued that those resurrected will have a different substance and nature. Although his theological views had little impact (some were condemned in 680), his philosophical and scientific theories exerted an influence in the Renaissance.   [L.P.S.]

Bibliography
Against Aristotle, on the Eternity of the World, tr. C. Wildberg (Ithaca: Cornell UP, 1987).
R. Sorabji, ed., *Philoponus and the Rejection of Aristotelian Science* (London: Duckworth, 1987).

JOHN THE BAPTIST. Ascetic preacher of baptism and repentance. Early Christianity viewed John the Baptist preeminently as the "forerunner" of Christ, following the tradition of Mark 1:2, where the "messenger" of Malachi 3:1 is seen as coming before the Christ rather than simply before "the Lord." John's preaching is thus an integral part of the course of events marking the incarnation, and his baptism of Jesus is taken, following the tradition of Matthew 3:13–17 (cf. 28:19), as anticipating the baptism of Christians. Origen speculates that John was an embodied angelic spirit ("messenger"—*Jo.* 2.25), and others, even those more wary, at least follow him in taking the Lucan account of John's "leaping in his mother's womb" at Mary's visit to Elizabeth (Luke 1:41) as anticipating John's later recognition of Jesus as "Lamb of God" (John 1:29).

Modern critical questions as to whether John regarded himself, or was regarded, as a messianic figure in the form of "Elijah to come," and as to whether Baptist messianic materials underlie the Lucan account of John's birth, were not generally considered in the patristic period. However, Justin Martyr knew that some regarded John as Messiah (*Dial.* 88).

John figures in early Christian iconography in scenes of Jesus' baptism and is portrayed as a desert prophet seeing a vision of the coming Christ and as a figure pointing to a representation of the "Lamb of God." John's death was celebrated on August 29, and reference is made to his tomb at Sebaste, destroyed by Julian the Apostate (ca. 360). In the fourth- and fifth-century elaboration of festivals based on the birth narratives, the nativity of John came to be celebrated on June 24–25.   [L.G.P.]

Bibliography
Pseudo-Chrysostom, *In Praecursorem* (PG 59.489–492); idem, *In laudem conceptionis S. Joannis Baptistae* (PG 50.787–792); idem, *In Natale S. Joannis Baptistae* (PG 61.757–762); idem, *In decollationem Praecursoris* (PG 59.485–490).
J. Daniélou, *Jean-Baptiste, témoin de l'Agneau* (Paris: Seuil, 1964); C.H.H. Scobie, *John the Baptist* (Philadelphia: Fortress, 1964); W. Wink, *John the Baptist in the Gospel Tradition* (London: Cambridge UP, 1968); A. Kavanagh, *The Shape of Baptism: The Rite of Christian Initiation* (New York: Pueblo, 1978); L.F. Badia, *The Qumran Baptism and John the Baptist* (Lanham: UP of America, 1980).

JONAH. One of the twelve "minor prophets." The Book of Jonah tells the story of the prophet (2 Kings 14:25) sent by God to preach to Nineveh, capital of Assyria, the enemy of Israel. Instead of obeying, Jonah took a ship in the opposite direction, but he was swallowed by a great fish. The fish deposited Jonah on land, and he went to Nineveh, whose inhabitants repented at his preaching. The book is an important testimony in the Old Testament to God's concern for nations other than Israel. In the New Testament, Jonah was cited as a sign of the ministry of Jesus and of his resurrection (Luke 11:29f.; Matt. 12:39–41; 16:4).

Jonah was the minor prophet most often referred to in the early church. The Christological interpretation with reference to the passion and resurrection of Christ was the most common use of Jonah (beginning with Justin, *Dial.* 107–108). The experience of Jonah also became a testimony to the resurrection of individual believers (Irenaeus, *Haer.* 5.5.2; Tertullian, *Res.* 58). Other lessons drawn from Jonah included repentance (*1 Clem.* 7.7), God's mercy (Tertullian, *Marc.* 2.24), the conversion of pagans (Clement of Alexandria, *Prot.* 10.99.4), and obedience (John Chrysostom, *Stat.* 5.15–17; cf. 20.21f.).

The story of Jonah was far and away the Old Testament scene occurring most frequently in early Christian art. Although there are variations, the most common representation is a three-part cycle showing Jonah swallowed by a sea monster, spewed out of its mouth, and at rest in the pose of Endymion under a gourd vine. Various interpretations have been offered, but a plausible meaning for the sequence is death, resurrection, and eternal bliss. If so, the art represents a change in the message away from Jonah's preaching, repentance, and God's rebuke of the prophet to a symbol of deliverance. This would fit the funerary setting of the catacombs and sarcophagi, but the Jonah cycle was popular in all forms of art, for instance the marble statuettes in the Cleveland Museum, among the rare examples of three-dimensional sculpture in early Christian art. *See also* Minor Prophets.   [E.F.]

Bibliography

Jerome, *In Jonam*, SC (1985), Vol. 323; Theodore of Mopsuestia, *In Jonam*, PG 66.317–346; Cyril of Alexandria, *In Jonam* , PG 71.597–638; Theodoret, *In Jonam*, PG 81.1719–1740.

E. Stommel, "Zum Problem der frühchristlichen Jonasdarstellungen," *JAC* 1 (1958):112–115; M. Lawrence, "Three Pagan Themes in Christian Art," *De Artibus Opuscula XL: Essays in Honor of Erwin Panofsky*, ed. M. Meiss (New York: New York UP, 1961), pp. 323–334; M. Lawrence, "Ships, Monsters, and Jonah," *American Journal of Archaeology* 66 (1962):289–296; W.D. Wixom, "Early Christian Sculptures at Cleveland," *Cleveland Museum of Art Bulletin* 54 (1967): 67–89; J. Allenbach, "La Figure de Jonas dans les textes preconstantiniens ou l'histoire de l'exégèse au secours de l'iconographie," *La Bible et les Pères*, ed. A. Benoit et al. (Paris: Presses Universitaires de France, 1971); Y.-M. Duval, *Le Livre de Jonas dans la littérature chrétienne grecque et latine: sources et influence du Commentaire sur Jonas de saint Jérôme* (Paris: Etudes Augustiniennes, 1973).

JOSEPHUS (ca. A.D. 35–100). Jewish priest, military leader, and historian. Josephus ben Matthias, or, as later known, Flavius Josephus, wrote works that are essential sources for first-century history. A Jerusalem aristocrat, he participated in the revolt against Rome (A.D. 66–70) as a leader of Galilean forces. After surrender to Roman troops, he prophesied that their general, Vespasian, would become emperor. With the prediction fulfilled, he was released from bonds and served Titus, Vespasian's son, as a translator during the siege of Jerusalem. After the war, under imperial patronage, he resided in Rome and composed four works. *The Jewish War* is a seven-book account of the revolt, prefaced by a review of Jewish history during the Hellenistic period. Although eliciting sympathy for the nation as a whole, it castigates the Jewish revolutionaries. *The Antiquities of the Jews* recounts in twenty books the course of Jewish history from Adam to the mid-first century. The first half paraphrases scripture; the second provides important information about Herod and Hellenistic Jewish history. The apologetic tract *Against Apion* refutes anti-Jewish slanders and emphasizes Israel's antiquity and the Torah's ideals. The *Life* appended to the *Antiquities* briefly recounts Josephus's conduct during the revolt.

Josephus found no Jewish imitators but proved invaluable for Christian historians from Eusebius onward for information about the environment of early Christianity, as a model of theological historiography, and as an apologetic tool in Christian-Jewish controversy. The reference to Jesus as the Christ in *Antiquities* 18.3.3 [63–54] (cf. 20.9.1[200]) is in its present form a Christian interpolation but may have contributed to the legend that Josephus became a Christian and a bishop. TLG 0526. [H.W.A.]

Bibliography

H. St. J. Thackeray, ed. and tr., *Josephus*, 9 vols., LCL (1956–1965); K.H. Rengstorf, *A Complete Concordance to Flavius Josephus*, 4 vols. (Leiden: Brill, 1973–1983).

H. Schreckenberg, *Bibliographie zu Flavius Josephus* (Leiden: Brill, 1968); idem, *Die Flauius-Josephus-Tradition in Antike und Mittelalter* (Leiden: Brill, 1972); H.W. Attridge, *The Interpretation of Biblical History in the Antiquitates Judaicae of Flavius Josephus* (Missoula: Scholars, 1976); H. Schreckenberg, *Rezeptionsgeschichtliche und Textkritische Untersuchungen zu Flavius Josephus* (Leiden: Brill, 1977); S.J.D. Cohen, *Josephus in Galilee and Rome: His Vita and Development as a Historian* (Leiden: Brill, 1979); L.H. Feldman, *Josephus: A Supplementary Bibliography* (New York: Garland, 1986); G.F. Chestnut, *The First Christian Histories: Eusebius, Socrates, Sozomen, Theodoret and Evagrius*, 2nd ed. (Macon: Mercer UP, 1986); L.H. Feldman and G. Hata, eds., *Josephus, Judaism, and Christianity* (Detroit: Wayne State UP, 1987).

JOSHUA. Sixth book of the Old Testament, named after its major character, who succeeded Moses. In twenty-four chapters, the Book of Joshua covers the story of the conquest of Palestine and the allotment of the land among the various tribes. The conquest is alluded to in other Old Testament summaries, and Joshua is mentioned in Sirach 46:1, 4, and in 4 Ezra 7:107.

The New Testament alludes to the conquest of the land by Joshua and the burial of Joseph's bones (Acts 7:16, 45; 13:19) and the conquest and the act of Rahab (Heb. 11:30, 31; cf. James 2:25; Matt. 1:5); the name of Joshua appears in the allegorical argument of Hebrews 4:8.

In contrast to the Jewish interpretation of Joshua as a disciple of Moses, Christian typo-logy exalted Joshua at the expense of Moses. Moses could not lead the people into rest, but Joshua did. The point of reference is that the names of Joshua and Jesus are identical in Greek. Jesus gives rest (cf. Ps. 95:11; Heb. 3:11, 18; 4:8, 9). Another element in the typology is Joshua's victory over Amalek (Exod. 17:12–13), representing the powers of evil (*Barn.* 12.7–10; 17.14, Justin, *Dial.* 75; 89; 90; 99; Origen, *Hom. in Jos.* 1.1; 2.1; Gregory of Nyssa, *V. Moys.* 2.148; Cyprian, *Test.* 2.21; Tertullian, *Marc.* 3.18; Prudentius, *Cath.* 12.169). Justin made Moses with his outstretched arms a symbol of the first advent and the cross and Joshua a type of the second advent. He also made a connection between Jesus the stone and the stone knives used in circumcision (*Dial.* 113).

For Irenaeus, Moses was a type of the Law and Joshua of the New Testament. Origen declared that the whole book of Joshua is a *sacramentum* ("sign" or type) of Christ. The succession of Joshua to Moses indicated that the Gospel replaces the Law. Eusebius gave attention to this typology (*H.E.* 1.3.4), as did Lactantius (*Div. inst.* 4.17). Zeno of Verona (1.13) and Jerome (*Ep.* 53) made Joshua the type of Christ both in his name and his work. Augustine took up the typological significance of the name and of Joshua's leading the people into the promised land (*C. Faust.* 12.322). In other Joshua typology, the crossing of the Jordan became a type of baptism, Rahab of the church, and the fall of Jericho of the end of the world.

Joshua is a theme in Christian art. In the nave of Sta. Maria Maggiore in Rome, for example, is a series of mosaics from the Book of Joshua. [J.P.L.]

Bibliography

Origen, *Homiliae in Jesu Nave*, ed. A. Jaubert, SC (1960), Vol. 71; Augustine, *Locutiones Heptateuchum* and *Quaestiones in Heptateuchum*, ed. J. Fraipont, CCSL (1958), Vol. 33; Theodoret, *Quaestiones in Josuam*, PG 80.457–485; Procopius of Gaza, *Catena in Octateuchum*, PG 87.

J. Daniélou, *From Shadows to Reality* (London: Burns and Oates, 1960), pp. 229–286; J. Soggin, *Joshua: A Commentary* (Philadelphia: Westminster, 1972); J. Allenbach et al., *Biblia Patristica* (Paris: Centre National de Recherche Scientifique, 1975–1982), lists citations in the first three centuries.

JOURNALS. Patristic scholarship appears in over 200 journals published around the world, and a number of specialized periodicals are essential to its development. In the United States, *The Second Century* (1981–), *Patristic and Byzantine Review* (1982–), and *Augustinian Studies* (1970–) are significant. *Patristics* (1972–) publishes book reviews. *Harvard Theological Review* (1908–), *Anglican Theological Review* (1918–), *Church History* (1932–), and *Greek Orthodox Theological Review* (1954–) have published important research. Major British journals in this field include the *Journal of Theological Studies* (1899–) and the *Journal of Ecclesiastical History* (1950–), although many other journals publish an occasional article on patristics.

The important continental journals are *Vigiliae Christianae* (1948–), *Bulletin de littérature ecclésiastique* (1877–), *Revue d'histoire ecclésiastique* (1900–), *Ephemerides Theologicae Lovanienses* (1924–), *Revue théologique de Louvain* (1970–), *Byzantion* (1924–), *Analecta Bollandiana* (1882– , devoted to hagiography), *Augustinianum* (1961–), *Vetera Christianorum* (1964–), *Byzantinisches Zeitschrift* (1892–), *Zeitschrift für Kirchengeschichte* (1877–), and *Zeitschrift für die neutestamentliche Wissenschaft und die Kunde der älteren Kirche* (1900–).

Research on oriental patristics is published in *Le Muséon* (1882–), *Oriens Christianus* (1901–), *Orientalia Christiania Periodica* (1935–), *Orientalia Lovaniensia Periodica* (1970–), *Revue des études arméniennes* (1920–1930; 1964–), *Handes Amsorya* (1887–), *Parole de l'Orient* (1970–), *MIDEO, Mélanges de l'institut dominicain d'études orientales du Caire* (1954–).

Essential indexes include *Religion Index I and II*, *Bibliographia Patristica*, *Revue d'histoire ecclésiastique*, *Byzantinisches Zeitschrift*, *Ephemerides Theologicae Lovaniensia*, and *L'Année philologique*.   [D.B.]

JOVIAN (ca. 331–364). Roman emperor (363–364). Jovian took office in the Persian campaign when Julian was killed. He made a humiliating agreement, ceding five Mesopotamian provinces and much of Armenia to the Persians. Although he restored Christian privileges, he perhaps tolerated some pagan practices. He died in an accident in the year following his accession.   [F.W.N.]

Bibliography
Socrates, *Church History* 3.22, 24–26; Sozomen, *Church History* 6.3–6; Ammianus Marcellinus, *History* 25–26, passim.

JOVINIAN (d. ca. 406). Monk from Milan. Jovinian's career highlights an era crucial in the social development of the western church. During the late fourth century, the spiritual excellence of a life committed to asceticism and virginity or celibacy was increasingly accepted. Jovinian, like his contemporary Helvidius, argued for spiritual equality regardless of one's sexual status. He wrote a book, now lost, strongly supportive of marriage and opposed the concept of the perpetual virginity of Mary.

Vigorous responses came from an array of powerful, articulate opponents: Ambrose of Milan, Siricius of Rome, Augustine of Hippo, Pelagius, and the champion of asceticism, virginity, and Mary's unique sexual status, Jerome (*Against Jovinian*). The preeminent polemicist and satirist among the western fathers, Jerome appears to have been guilty of overkill in his polemic, for a close friend tried to recall all copies of the treatise. Although Jerome was disappointed by the reception given his treatise in Rome, his views were to prevail in western Christianity, and Jovinian was exiled by imperial decree. *See also* Jerome.   [H.R.]

Bibliography
Jerome, *Against Jovinian*, tr. W.H. Fremantle, NPNF, 2nd ser. (1894), Vol. 6, pp. 340–416; Augustine, *On the Good of Marriage* and *Of Holy Virginity*, tr. C.L. Cornish, NPNF, 1st ser. (1887), Vol. 3, pp. 397–438.
J.N.D. Kelly, *Jerome: His Life, Writings, and Controversies* (London: Duckworth, and New York: Harper and Row, 1975), pp. 180–189.

JUDAISM AND CHRISTIANITY. From the first century, relations between Jews and Christians were marked by hostility—the opposition between an established religion and an offshoot claiming to have supplanted it. Leaders of each religion criticized the other faith. In particular, Christian ecclesiastical authorities and writers developed a set of themes designed to demonstrate to Christians and potential converts the inauthenticity of Judaism; they often preserve the counterarguments of their real or fictional opponents. Among Jews, a slanderous biography of Jesus circulated (the principal elements of which are preserved in the medieval *Sepher Toledoth Jeshu*). From the fourth century, local and ecumenical Christian councils enacted legislation designed to separate the two religious groups. Imperial legislation, such as the *Code of Justinian*, made these strictures public, along with certain other disabilities. Nevertheless, close connections between Judaism and Christianity persisted in popular practice and among scholars and leaders. Furthermore, groups of Jewish Christians continued late into the fifth century to combine a belief in the messianic status of Jesus with a mixture of Jewish and Christian practices, forming a *tertium quid* condemned by both sides.

The traditional attraction of Jewish scriptures, practice, and thought for some Christians, and the continued flourishing of Jewish communities in the Christian empire along with the occasional case of political subversion or proselytization by Jews or, in one case, Jewish persecution of Christians outside the empire, provoked Christian authors to develop the *Adversus Judaeos* ("Against the Jews") tradition; these works continued into the medieval and Byzantine period as evidence of mutual attraction and repulsion.

First Century. Recent scholarship has demonstrated both the Jewishness of Jesus and the complexity of Palestinian Judaism in the first century. Jesus' criticism of current Jewish leaders and practice, as well as his positive statements of theological truth and religious obligation, are part of the intra-Jewish debate exemplified also by the Qumran documents and preserved in later rabbinic writings. All four Gospels give early Christian views of Jesus' growing conflict with Jewish authorities, but Mat-

thew establishes the theme of the transfer of the promises of Israel to the church, and John portrays Jesus' career as one of opposition to the Jews. These documents reflect the late-first-century separation of early Christianity from Judaism. The authentic Pauline epistles, written earlier, are complex: they reject the universal applicability of Torah and regard it, and Judaism, as of real though limited validity (e.g., Rom. 2–4; 9–11). Later New Testament writings demonstrated the continuity of the old covenant with the church, entirely abrogating Judaism; Acts demonstrates early Jewish hostility to Christian preaching. The destruction of Jerusalem and the temple in A.D. 70 forced all Jewish groups to reorganize and added impetus to the diaspora of early Christianity into the rest of the Mediterranean and Near Eastern world. Other early writings, such as the *Didache* and Ignatius, warn against Judaizing and manifest the growing separation of the two religions.

Nevertheless, the preservation in Christianity of Jewish practice and literature ensured a sense of both continuity and relationship between the two and may have aroused the curiosity of some Christian believers. The weekly gathering of Christians for prayer, regular fast days, reading of scriptures, including the Old Testament, with an interpretive homily, the centrality of the Psalms, and the importance of liturgical rites like baptism and eucharist, with their roots in observable Jewish ritual—all these suggested a certain similarity to Judaism. Use of Jewish literature, such as the Old Testament Apocrypha, rhetorical devices, and literary genres, such as biblical exegesis, apology, prayers, and litanies, expressed the link between the two religions despite the changes shaping and separating each community.

Second to Fourth Centuries. By the second century, the Christian apologists and homilists had amassed a collection of themes to defend themselves against pagan charges of novelty and to provide answers to continued Jewish opposition. The *Adversus Judaeos* tradition, a broad literary stream within early Christianity, depends upon two elements: a collection of proof-texts (*testimonia*) from the Old Testament to demonstrate the basis of Christian claims to the divinity of Christ and the extension of the Mosaic covenant to the Gentiles, and a group of ideas based on earliest Christian literature that became common from this period onward. These ideas are that the church is the true Israel; that Christ perfected and abrogated all Law secondary to the Ten Commandments; and that Judaism, always rebellious and inclined toward idolatry, as evidenced by its refusal to obey the prophetic injunctions, was now completely exhausted and continued to exist primarily as an example of degradation. The destruction of Jerusalem, and chiefly of the temple and its cult, was the historical confirmation of God's reprobation of the Jews. These themes were gathered first by Justin Martyr in the *Dialogue with Trypho* (ca. 155) but were used by Christian apologists in their defenses of Christianity to pagan imperial officials. Homilists, such as Melito of Sardis in *On the Passover* (ca. 190), used the *Adversus Judaeos* genre to convince Christian congregations of their superior standing in a city where Jews were actually more secure, more numerous, and more prosperous. In fact, the relatively high standing of Jews in Greco-Roman society seems to have made Christian authors even more concerned to refute their religious views.

During this period, when opposition to Judaism was becoming better articulated among Christians, the Jews in general enjoyed a period of security within both the Roman and Persian empires. Despite the rebellions by Jews in the first and second centuries, their communities were strong in Syria, Palestine, and Egypt; Christian theologians sometimes turned to the scholars of these communities for aid in interpreting the scriptures. Origen in Palestinian Caesarea consulted Jewish teachers of the rabbinical school there and used contemporary Jewish tradition in interpreting scripture, along with the allegorical-philosophical method of Philo, the Alexandrian Jewish author. Origen's *Hexapla*, begun in Alexandria and completed in Palestine in 245, demonstrates his preference for beginning with the Hebrew tradition in matters of text and interpretation. Origen

put the church's arguments against Jews on a firm foundation and provided Christians with protection against Jewish arguments. Likewise, in the fourth century, Jerome learned Hebrew from a Jew, obtained from Jewish communities copies of the Hebrew Bible to aid in the production of the Vulgate, and consulted a Jewish scholar on points of translation. Similar scholarly discussions went on in Antioch and elsewhere in Syriac-speaking communities. In early-fourth-century Persia, the *Demonstrations* of Aphraates (ca. 337–345) show firsthand contact with Jewish knowledge, as does other early Syriac literature. The presence of flourishing Jewish communities in Persian Mesopotamia, with a well-known rabbinic academy in Nisibis, accounts for this knowledge, reflected also in the Targum-traditions present in a fourth-century author like Ephraem the Syrian.

Although Jews had resorted to apologies in their own defense (e.g., Josephus, *Against Apion*) and had suffered military defeats in Palestine (A.D. 66–73 and 132–135) and anti-Jewish riots in Alexandria (A.D. 38–41; 115–117), they were sometimes accorded a high status in the pagan but religiously tolerant culture of the second- and third-century empire. Official Roman policy from the second century B.C. to the early fifth century A.D. allowed Jews to live according to their customs, to collect money for the temple among the diaspora communities (until 70), to rule their own internal affairs, and to preserve the Sabbath rest. On the popular level, Jews seemed to have enjoyed a reputation for magic and astrology, as reflected in the beliefs that Moses and Solomon were practitioners of magical arts; this attitude persisted in Christian communities, and the accompanying admiration of Jewish rabbis irritated later Christian authors.

Jewish Response to Christianity. Judaism of the first century A.D. was surrounded by imitators who, although they did not actually become converts, were attracted to Jewish moral standards, ritual, or dietary practice. They received the approval of the Jewish community despite their non-Jewish status. Christians and Jewish Christians, however, came to be condemned because they rejected the essential requirements of Judaism as defined by the Tan-naitic rabbis: acceptance of the entire written and oral Torah, circumcision, purification immersions, and sacrifice (until 70). It is likely that the *birkat ha-minim* (benediction against the heretics) was composed before the mid-second century to exclude Jewish Christians from leading or participating in synagogue services (cf. Justin, *Dial.* 16.4, "You . . . curse the Christians in your synagogues . . ."). Origen (*Hom.* 2.8 *in Ps.* 37), Epiphanius (*Haer.* 29.2), and Jerome (*Isa.* 5.18–19; *Amos* 1.11–12) all attest to the thrice-daily curse of Christians in synagogue prayers. By the mid-fourth century, a curse against *noserim*, or (Gentile) Christians (*nazaraioi*), was added to that against the *minim.* In addition, the Tannaim (rabbis of the second–third centuries) rejected Christian scriptures (the Septuagint) and seem to have rejected Philo because of his wide use by Christians.

Nevertheless, Christians continued to attend synagogue into the late fourth century, as the writings of Origen, Jerome, John Chrysostom, and others show. Some Christians seem to have maintained Jewish practices, including the reckoning of the date of Easter by 14 Nisan, the date of the Jewish Passover, which led to the Paschal controversy in the church.

Christian-Jewish Relations from the Fourth Century. From the early fourth century, a series of church councils enacted canons seeking to restrict Christian participation in Jewish ceremonies along with other Christian-Jewish contact, including mixed marriages. Legislation from the synods of Elvira (306), Antioch (341), Nicaea (325), and Laodicea (365?) is evidence that Christians, including clergy, were enjoying Jewish hospitality, participating in Jewish festivals, seeking blessings from Jewish rabbis, and participating in the Passover. These canons could not, however, seek to regulate internal Jewish life, which continued to be protected under the *lex Judaeorum* through the fifth century. The *Theodosian Code*, for instance, employs the terminology of abuse against Judaism but affirms certain traditional rights of the Jewish community, which by the end of the fourth century included members of no little

wealth and was governed by a powerful patriarch resident in Palestine. Jews continued to receive imperial privileges and exemptions even though there is some evidence of active Jewish proselytization during the period (despite legal punishments designed to halt this). The code also extended protection to Jews and their synagogues and allowed reconstruction of those razed by fire; this, despite the famous episode of Ambrose's opposition to the rebuilding the synagogue at Callinicum destroyed by a Christian mob.

The *Code of Justinian* in 534 withdrew some traditional Jewish privileges and imposed new disabilities, such as the exclusion of non-orthodox (including Jews) from the imperial legions, disqualification of Jews and heretics as witnesses against the orthodox, and prohibitions against Jewish ownership of Christian slaves and the building of new synagogues. Most interesting is *Novella* 146, which intervenes in an internal Jewish conflict over using languages other than Hebrew in the synagogue. The law mandates that congregations can choose their language and that readings from the Greek Old Testament must come from the Septuagint or the version of Aquila; prohibits the Mishna and the holding of "Sadducean" opinions on resurrection, last judgment, and angels; and imposes various punishments for violation of these laws.

From the fourth century, especially in the east, where Jewish communities were strongest, Christian leaders employed the *Adversus Judaeos* genre in sermons or treatises to dissuade Christians from an apparently customary association with Jews, including participation in Jewish festivals, consultation of rabbis, and reverence for Jewish scriptures. Most notable are John Chrysostom's sermons on Judaizers, given 386–387 in Antioch; but the accounts of Jerome, Rufinus, and Theodoret of Cyrus all indicate that Christians "Judaized," as do sources for the Syriac-speaking territory: the *Didascalia Apostolorum* (third century), Aphraates and Ephraem the Syrian (fourth century), Isaac of Antioch (fifth century), and Jacob of Sarug (sixth century) with his seven sermons *Contra Judaeos.*

Church leaders particularly abhorred the attempt of the emperor Julian (361–363) to rebuild the temple. This return to the pre-Constantinian *status quo ante* would have destroyed one critical argument *Adversus Judaeos*, and it seemed to give Jewish communities some hope of lasting imperial favor. The program's termination in 363 by a natural disaster may not have quelled Jewish expectations for a restoration of the building and of Jerusalem as a Jewish city, expectations that frightened Christian authors and heightened their use of the anti-Jewish arguments.

Outside the Roman empire, Christian-Jewish relations differed significantly. In the Sassanid realm of Persia and its client states, Jews generally had a higher status than that of Christians and may have encouraged the occasional persecutions of Christians that occurred there. A Jewish king of Himyar in south Arabia subjected Christian communities to persecution and martyrdom at an uncertain date between 518 and 523; the martyrs were promptly included in the hagiographical traditions of the eastern churches.

Up to and beyond the end of the early Christian period, ecclesiastical writers continued to use the *Adversus Judaeos* genre to distinguish Christianity from Judaism, to prevent conversions, and to discourage participation in Jewish religious life. Meanwhile, Jewish communities developed a *modus vivendi* in which religious and communal life survived and attracted both the interest of lay Christians and the conditional toleration of such authors as Augustine and Gregory the Great. *See also* Apologetics; Jewish Christianity; Josephus; Philo.   [R.D.Y.]

Bibliography

S. Krauss, "The Jews in the Works of the Church Fathers," *Jewish Quarterly Review* 5 (1893):122–157; 6 (1894):82–99; J. Juster, *Les Juifs dans l'Empire Romain: leur condition juridique, économique et sociale*, 2 vols. (Paris: Geuther, 1914); A.L. Williams, *Adversus Judaeos: A Bird's-eye View of Christian Apologiae Until the Renaissance* (Cambridge: Cambridge UP, 1935); W. Cramer, *Kirche und Synagoge: Handbuch zur Geschichte von Christen und Juden: Darstellung mit Quellen* (Stuttgart: Klett, 1967–1970); J. Neusner, *Aphrahat and Judaism: The Christian Jewish Argument in Fourth-Century Iran* (Leiden: Brill, 1971); I. Shahid, *The Martyrs of Najran* (Brussels: Subsidia Hagiographica, 1971); J. Parkes, *The Conflict of the Church and the Synagogue: A Study in the Origins of Antisemitism* (New York: Atheneum, 1974); M. Stern, *Greek and Latin Authors on Judaism*, 2 vols. (Jerusalem, 1974, 1980); N. De Lange, *Origen and the Jews: Studies in Jewish-Christian Relations in Third-Century Palestine* (Cambridge: Cambridge UP, 1976); A.F. Segal, *Two Powers in Heaven: Early Rabbinic Reports About Christianity and Gnosticism* (Leiden: Brill, 1977); D. Levenson, "A Source and Tradition Critical Study of the Stories of Julian's Attempt to Rebuild the Jerusalem Temple " (Ph.D. diss., Harvard University, 1979); L.H. Schiffmann, "At the Crossroads: Tannaitic Perspectives on the Jewish-Christian Schism," and R. Kimelman, "Birkat Ha-Minim and the Lack of Evidence for an Anti-Christian Jewish Prayer in Late Antiquity," *Jewish and Christian Self-Definition*, ed. E.P. Sanders with A.I. Baumgarten and A. Mendelson (Philadelphia: Fortress, 1981), Vol. 2: *Aspects of Judaism in the Greco-Roman Period*, pp. 115–156, 226–244; H. Schreckenberg, *Die christlichen Adversus-Judaeos-Texte und ihr literarisches und historisches Umfeld (1.–11. Jh)* (Frankfurt and Berne: Lang, 1982); J.G. Gager, *The Origins of Anti-Semitism: Attitudes Toward Judaism in Pagan and Christian Antiquity* (New York: Oxford UP, 1983); R.L. Wilken, *John Chrysostom and the Jews: Rhetoric and Reality in the Late Fourth Century* (Berkeley: U of California P, 1983); J. Neusner and E. Frerichs, eds., *"To See Ourselves As Others See Us": Christians, Jews, "Others" in Late Antiquity* (Chico: Scholars, 1985); M. Simon, *Verus Israel: A Study of the Relations Between Christians and Jews in the Roman Empire (135–425)* (Oxford: Oxford UP, 1986; orig. French ed., 1948); S. Wilson, ed., *Anti-Judaism in Early Christianity 2: Separation and Polemic* (Waterloo: Wilfrid Laurier UP, 1986); A. Linder, *The Jews in Roman Imperial Legislation* (Detroit: Wayne State UP, 1987); J. Neusner, *Judaism and Christianity in the Age of Constantine* (Chicago: U of Chicago P, 1987).

JUDAS ISCARIOT. Name given in lists of the original twelve disciples as that of the one who would betray Jesus (Mark 3:19; 14:10; Matt. 10:4; 14:10, 43ff.; Luke 6:16; 22:3f., 47f.; Acts 1:16–20, 25). In John 6:71; 13:21, he is called "Judas son of Simon Iscariot." Textual variants preserve early difficulties in understanding the name; for example, codex Sinaiticus (at John 6:17) reads it as a Semitism meaning "man of Kerioth"; codex Bezae (John 6:71; Matt. 10:4; Luke 6:12) reads a form of *Skariotēs* or *Skarioth*, possibly taken to reflect the Latin *sicarii*, a common designation for the "knife-wielding" Zealots (cf. Josephus, *War* 2.254). Judas appears to be the lone Judean among the twelve, and he is sometimes associated directly with Jewish revolutionaries. The Gospels offer various reflections on his role; for instance, only John 12:6; 13:39 designates him as treasurer; the accounts of his remorse and death after the crucifixion in Matthew 27:3–10 and Acts 1:16–20 differ in details that possibly reflect earlier Jewish traditions of divine retribution (e.g., 2 Macc. 9:5–13). The enigma has led to complex attempts to understand both Judas's background and the motivation and nature of his betrayal of Jesus, but none has found universal acceptance. Later Christian tradition continued to develop the characterization of Judas, as seen in the fragments of Papias (cf. Irenaeus, *Haer.* 5.33.4), and his name was associated with a Gnostic sect, the "Cainites," in an otherwise lost document called the *Gospel of Judas* (cf. Irenaeus, *Haer.* 1.28.9; Epiphanius, *Haer.* 38.1.5). [L.M.W.]

Bibliography
P.F. Baum, "The Medieval Legend of Judas Iscariot," *Proceedings of the Modern Language Association* n.s. 24 (1916):481–632; K. Lake, "The Death of Judas," *The Beginnings of Christianity*, ed. F.J. Foakes Jackson and K. Lake (London: Macmillan, 1933), Vol. 5, pp. 22–30; C.C. Torrey, "The Name 'Iscariot,'" *HThR* 36 (1943):51–62; R.B. Halas, *Judas Iscariot* (Washington, D.C.: Catholic U of America P, 1946); H. Ingholt, "The Surname of Judas Iscariot," *Studia orientalia Ioanni Pedersen* (Copenhagen: Munksgaard, 1953); R.McL. Wilson, "Gospel of Judas," NTA, Vol. 1, pp. 313f.; M. Smith, "Zealots and Sicarii: Their Origins and Relations," *HThR* 64 (1971):1–19; A. Ehrman, "Judas Iscariot and Abba Saqqara," *JBL* 97 (1978):572–573; Y. Arbeitman, "The Suffix of Iscariot," *JBL* 99 (1980):122–124; J. Fitzmyer, *Gospel According to Luke* (Garden City: Doubleday, 1981), Vol. 1, p. 620.

JUDE (first century). Name of an apostle and of a brother of James and Jesus; book in the New Testament. Jude (or Judas, not Iscariot) the apostle, sometimes called Thaddeus (Luke 6:16; Acts 1:13; Matt. 10:3; Mark 3:18), is probably to be distinguished from the Jude of the New Testament epistle, the brother of a James (Jude 1:1), perhaps the brother of Jesus. Jude 1:17 speaks of the apostles in the third person and past tense. Some commentators, however, see the letter as pseudonymous.

The Epistle of Jude has a learned Greek style and quotes the apocryphal books of the *Assumption of Moses* 9 and *1 Enoch* 14–15. 2 Peter edits but copies sections of Jude. The opponents mentioned in Jude appear to be antinomian Christian pre-Gnostics. The epistle confronts them by mentioning the Father, Son, and Holy Spirit, the deposit of faith, a sense of angels—both good and bad—and eternal life. Feast day (apostle Jude) October 28 (west), June 19 (east). [F.W.N.]

Bibliography
Muratorian Canon 68; Clement of Alexandria, *Comments on Epistle of Jude* 2; Tertullian, *On Apparel of Women* 1.3; Eusebius, *Church History* 2.23.25; Didymus the Blind, *In epistulas catholicas*, PG 39.1811–1818.
K. Staab, "Die griechischen Katenenkommentare zu den katholischen Briefen," *Biblica* 5 (1924):296–353; E.M. Sidebottom, *James, Jude and 2 Peter* (New York: Nelson, 1967); J. Gunther, "The Alexandrian Epistle of Jude," *NTS* 30 (1984):549–562; C. Osburn, "I Enoch 80:2–8 (67:5–7) and Jude 12–13," *CBQ* 47 (1985):296–303; G. Sellin, "Die Häretiker des Judasbriefes," *ZNTW* 77 (1986):206–225; M. Green, *2 Peter and Jude* (Grand Rapids: Eerdmans, 1987); R. Bauckham, "The Letter of Jude: An Account of Research," *ANRW* (1989), Vol. 2.25.5.

JUDGMENT. God's punishment of the wicked and reward of the righteous. The Old Testament portrays God as the judge of all the earth. Generally, his judgment is expected within the course of history and takes the form of the vindication of the righteous and the punishment of the wicked. The notion of judgment at the end-time grew out of the awareness that justice was not done in the events of this world, a development that appears to have been furthered by the destruction of Jerusalem and the captivity in Babylon. The Jews reworked ancient Babylonian myths in such a way that what was originally cosmological in orientation took on an eschatological meaning. Daniel 12:2 speaks of the resurrection of the righteous and the wicked in a way that foreshadows later

Christian depictions of the last judgment. That text might not assert universal resurrection; although the word "many" in biblical language can mean "all," it need not. Postexilic descriptions of God's judgment adopted apocalyptic features that emphasized the punishment of God's enemies. The resurrection of the wicked for punishment could be called the resurrection of judgment (John 5:29).

According to the Synoptic Gospels, Jesus often spoke of the coming judgment. Of special importance is his depiction of the gathering of the nations and their judgment before the throne of the Son of man (Matt. 25:31–46). The tradition that God himself will be the judge continued (Rev. 14:7), but through apocalyptic influence there emerged the theme that the judgment will be carried out by the vice-regent of God, the Son of man. Alongside the emphasis on imminent future judgment is the assertion that judgment has begun with the appearance of Jesus (John 3:19–21; 9:39; 12:31). In John 5:24–29, the two themes appear side by side, a feature that may be comparable with Jesus' proclamation of the kingdom of God as already present and as imminently coming. Other important New Testament texts dealing with judgment are Paul's letters to the Thessalonians (1 Thess. 1:10; 2:19; 4:13–18; 5:1–11; 2 Thess. 1:3–2:12; cf. 1 Cor. 15:50–58) and the Book of Revelation (esp. 20:1–22:5). Here, it becomes clear that there are four closely related themes: the return of Christ (the *parousia*); the general resurrection; the judgment; and the end of the world. Indeed, in Revelation 20:4–5, 11–15, there appear to be two resurrections, the first of the martyrs, and then that of the rest. The latter is universal in scope and is the precursor of the universal judgment in which those whose names are not written in the book of life are cast into the lake of fire. In the interpretation of the subsequent centuries, it is not always clear in what order these events will occur.

The themes of the New Testament are repeated in the apostolic fathers (*1 Clem.* 16; 28; Ignatius, *Eph.* 16.2; *Polyc.* 2; Polycarp, *Ep.* 2; 7; *Didache* 16; Hermas, *Vis.* 3.8.9; 4.3; *Sim.* 9.18.2; 9.27.3) in more or less the same unre-

flective form. Jesus, who had come to save, would come again to judge the world. The dead would be raised in the flesh after the pattern of Jesus' own resurrection. The time of the coming is uncertain but imminent. The hiatus between the righteous dead going immediately to paradise and the general resurrection on the last day as the precursor of the judgment of living and dead remains. The messianic reign of Christ on earth for a thousand years (Rev. 20:2–5) prior to the coming of the final reign of God, was taken up by the apologists (Justin, *Dial.* 80–81) and then by the great theologians (Irenaeus, *Haer.* 5.35; Tertullian, *Marc.* 3.24; Hippolytus, *Antichr.*), who attempted to uphold traditional eschatology against Gnosticism. They defended their interpretation of the physical resurrection at the last judgment against the Gnostic view that the soul passed immediately to heaven at death. Opposition to the millenarian doctrine, however, was growing, fueled in part by the opposition to Montanism, which on the basis of Revelation 21 had asserted that the new Jerusalem would come down from heaven in Phrygia, an interpretation discredited by its nonfulfillment.

In the third century, Origen taught the resurrection of a spiritual body and affirmed that there was an intermediate state (*Princ.* 2.9.8–103; 3.1.1; 3.6.6). The judgment would separate good and bad according to their works. Punishment would take place in the consciousness of the wicked; it would be temporary and remedial. In the end, the goodness of God and the freedom of all creatures would lead to the salvation of all. In the fourth and fifth centuries, concentration on parousia and judgment continued, although Origen's critique was so effective that millenarianism went on the wane in the west as well as the east, as is evidenced by Augustine. But Origen's own interpretation of the judgment was rejected. The punishment of the wicked was generally held to be eternal with no hope of salvation, although doubts along the lines of Origen's teaching continue to appear until the end of the fifth century. Augustine represents the majority view in seeing that justice is done if wickedness is balanced by punishment (*Civ. Dei* 20.1–3). By this time, the distinction between the eternal punishment of the wicked and the temporary, purging punishment of Christian sinners had become important. *See also* Eschatology. [J.P.]

Bibliography

J.A. Baird, *The Justice of God in the Teaching of Jesus* (London: SCM, 1963); J. Daniélou, *The Theology of Jewish Christianity* (London: Darton, Longman and Todd, 1964), pp. 192–204, 377–396; idem, *The Gospel Message and Hellenistic Culture* (London: Darton, Longman and Todd, 1973), pp. 20–22, 124, 206–207; Kelly, pp. 461–485; J.M. Court, *Myth and History in the Book of Revelation* (London: SPCK, 1979).

JULIAN (331 or 332–363). Roman emperor (361–363). Son of Julius Constantius, Constantine's half-brother, and Basilina, Flavius Claudius Julianus lost his mother while he was an infant. His father and an older brother were murdered at the accession of Constantius II (September 337). Julian was entrusted to Eusebius of Nicomedia and educated in the Greek classics by Mardonius. He and his half-brother, Gallus, were sequestered at Macellum in Cappadocia for six years (342–348), supervised by George of Cappadocia, the future Arian bishop of Alexandria (who was to be lynched at the beginning of Julian's reign). Julian continued his education in rhetoric and philosophy with some of his era's most prominent teachers, predominantly pagan, in Constantinople, Nicomedia, Pergamum, Ephesus, and Athens, where he came to know Basil of Caesarea and Gregory of Nazianzus.

After the execution of Gallus (354), whom Constantius had appointed Caesar in 351, Julian's interests were protected by the emperor's wife, Eusebia. On November 6, 355, Julian was made Caesar, married to Constantius's sister Helena, and sent to Gaul, where he proved to be a successful governor and general. When Constantius summoned the heart of Julian's troops to the Persian front, they rebelled and proclaimed Julian Augustus (February 360). Civil war was averted only by Constantius's death on November 3, 361.

On December 11, 361, Julian entered Constantinople as Augustus and initiated a series of political, economic, and religious measures aimed at eliminating corruption, reducing taxes, and promoting religious toleration and the revival of paganism. In May 362, Julian left the capital for Antioch to prepare for a military campaign against Persia. His ascetic paganism and attempted economic reforms proved immensely unpopular in Antioch, inspiring him to write the *Misopogon* ("The Beard Hater"), a bitter satire on his relations with the Antiochenes. Julian set out for Persia on March 5, 363. Although enjoying initial success, he could not take Ctesiphon and died on June 26 after being struck by a spear in a battle near that city.

Although raised a Christian, by 351 Julian had privately rejected Christianity and become a passionate adherent of Greek and Roman paganism. Influenced deeply by the theurgist Maximus of Ephesus, he adopted the Neoplatonism of the school of Iamblichus, which taught that union with the divine was to be achieved by ritual, especially animal sacrifice. He was particularly devoted to the solar deity Helios, whom he saw as the mediator between the visible and higher realms (cf. *Hymn to King Helios*). In the Neoplatonic tradition, he understood myths allegorically, especially those connected with the mysteries (cf. *Hymn to the Mother of the Gods*), into several of which—Eleusis, probably Mithras, and Cybele-Attis—he was initiated.

With Constantius's death, Julian openly declared his paganism. As emperor, he saw himself as restorer of the temples and ancient traditions and attempted to reform and reorganize paganism with himself as *pontifex maximus* and various regional high priests under him. Although a staunch opponent of the Christians, whom he styled "Galileans," Julian attempted to create an impression of fairness. He recalled the orthodox bishops, including Athanasius, exiled under the Arian Constantius (February 9, 362) and tried to maintain cordial relations with Christian intellectuals like Basil, Aetius, and Prohaeresius. Nevertheless, he clearly favored pagans in his appointments, swiftly punished antipagan actions, revoked the privileges of the clergy, exiled church leaders, such as Athanasius, who opposed his program, and forbade Christians to teach the Greek classics (June 17, 362; *Cod. Thds.* 13.3.5; *Ep.* 61). While in Antioch, he ordered the removal of the remains of St. Babylas from the environs of the temple of Apollo in Daphne. When, soon after, fire destroyed the temple, he closed the great church at Antioch.

Armed with a much more sophisticated knowledge of Christianity than previous anti-Christian polemicists, Julian composed a treatise *Against the Galileans* (winter 362/3), of which substantial fragments are preserved in Cyril of Alexandria's *Against Julian*, written ca. 440. The refutation of Julian's work by Philip of Side (early fifth century) is lost. Although he regarded the biblical account of creation as inferior to the Platonic and the prophets as inferior to the oracles, he respected the Jews as adherents of a traditional religion based on sacrifice. For that reason, and to refute Christian claims of the obsolescence of Judaism, he issued orders in early 363 to rebuild the Jerusalem temple (*Ep.* 204), a project that was aborted by fires on the site.

Although he reigned less than two years, Julian became an important symbol in the ideological and political battle between pagans and Christians that continued through the beginning of the fifth century. Up to the modern period, the failure of the "apostate" has served the church—western, Byzantine, and oriental—as a powerful proof of the working of divine providence. A rich hagiographical tradition developed around martyrs under Julian. The emperor's death, with the famous cry, "You have conquered, O Galilean"—found first in Theodoret, *Church History* 3.20—and the account of the martyrs who were revivified to slay him, has been a particularly fertile area for legendary elaboration.   [D.B.L.]

Bibliography

Pagan sources: Julian, *Works*, ed. and tr. W.C. Wright, LCL, 3 vols. (1913–1923); *Iuliani imperatoris epistulae leges poemata fragmenta varia*, ed. J. Bidez and F. Cumont (Paris: Les Belles Lettres, 1922 [standard enumeration of letters]); *Iuliani imperatoris librorum contra Christianos quae supersunt*, ed. C.J. Neumann (Leipzig: Teubner, 1880); Ammianus Marcellinus, *History*, Books 14–25 ed. E. Galletier, J. Fontaine and G. Sabbah, 4 vols. (Paris: Les Belles Lettres, 1968–1977); tr. J.C. Rolfe, LCL, 3 vols. (1935–1939); Libanius, *Julianic Orations*, ed. and tr. A.F. Norman, LCL (1969); Zosimus, *New History*, Books 1–5 ed. F. Paschoud, 3 vols. (Paris: Les Belles Lettres 1971–86); tr. R.T. Ridley (Sydney: Australian Association for Byzantine Studies, 1982); Eunapius, *Lives of the Sophists*, ed. and tr. W.C. Wright, LCL (1921); *History*, ed. and tr. R.C. Blockley, *The Fragmentary Classicising Historians of the Later Roman Empire*, 2 vols. (Wolfeboro: Longwood, 1981–1983).

Christian sources: Gregory of Nazianzus, *Invectives Against Julian* (Or. 4–5), ed. J. Bernardi, SC (1983), Vol. 309; tr. in C.W. King, *Julian the Emperor* (London: Bell, 1888); Ephraem the Syrian, *Hymns Against Julian*, ed. E. Beck, CSCO (1957), Vols. 174–175; tr. K. McVey, CWS (forthcoming); John Chrysostom, *On St. Babylas Against Julian and the Greeks*, ed. M. Schatkin, SC (forthcoming); tr. M. Schatkin, *St. John Chrysostom Apologist*, FOTC (1985), Vol. 73; Cyril of Alexandria, *Contra Julianum* (PG 76.489–1058), Books 1–2 ed. P. Burguiere and P. Evieux, SC (1985), Vol. 322; Church Histories of Rufinus, Philostorgius, Socrates, Sozomen, and Theodoret (see relevant entries for texts and translations); Zonaras, *Epitome Historiarum*, ed. Dindorf, Vol. 3 (Leipzig: Teubner, 1870); M. DiMaio, "Zonaras' Account of the Neo-Flavian Emperors" (Ph.D. diss., University of Missouri, 1977); *Syriac Julian Romance*, tr. H. Gollancz, *Julian the Apostate* (London: Milford, Oxford UP, 1928). S.N.C. Lieu, ed., *The Emperor Julian: Panegyric and Polemic* (Liverpool: Liverpool UP, 1986 [translations of Mamertinus, John Chrysostom, and Ephraem]).

J. Bidez: *La Vie de l'empereur Julien* (Paris, 1930); J. Vogt, *Kaiser Julian und das Judentum* (Leipzig: Hinrichs, 1939); R. Browning, *The Emperor Julian* (Berkeley: U of California P, 1975); S.P. Brock "A Letter Attributed to Cyril of Jerusalem on the Rebuilding of the Temple," *Bulletin of the School of Oriental and African Studies* 40 (1977):267–286; G. Bowersock, *Julian the Apostate* (Cambridge: Harvard UP, 1978); W.J. Malley, *Hellenism and Christianity* (Rome: Universitas Gregoriana, 1978); R. Klein, ed., *Julian Apostata* (Darmstadt: Wissenschaftliche Buchgesselschaft, 1978); R. Braun and J. Richer, eds., *L'empereur Julien. De l'historie à la legende (331–1715)* (Paris: Les Belles Lettres, 1978); J. Richer, *L'empereur Julien. De la legende au mythe* (Paris: Les Belles Lettres, 1981); F. Blanchetière, "Julien, philhellène, philosémite, antichrétien," *Journal of Jewish Studies* 31 (1980):61–81. D.B. Levenson, "A Source and Tradition Critical Study of the Emperor Julian's Attempt to Rebuild the Jerusalem Temple" (Ph.D. diss., Harvard University, 1980); P. Athanassiadi-Fowden, *Julian and Hellenism* (Oxford: Clarendon, 1981); R. Wilken, *The Christians as the Romans Saw Them* (New Haven: Yale UP, 1984), pp. 164–196; S.H. Griffith, "Ephrem the Syrian's

Hymns 'Against Julian,'" *VChr* 41 (1987):238–266; D.B. Levenson, *Julian and the Jerusalem Temple* (forthcoming).

JULIAN OF ECLANUM (ca. 380–455).

Bishop and adherent of Pelagianism. Julian was born in the district of Apulia in south-central Italy. His father, Memorius, was a bishop enjoying friendly relations with Paulinus of Nola and Augustine of Hippo. Julian married the daughter of Aemilius, bishop of Beneventum. After Julian became a deacon in 408, Augustine invited him for a visit (*Ep.* 101.4). Around 416, Julian became bishop of Eclanum in Apulia. In 418, he resisted pope Zosimus's initiatives against the Pelagians and was exiled with eighteen other bishops. Around 429, he appealed, in vain, to bishop Nestorius and emperor Theodosius II. Condemned at Ephesus in 431, Julian settled in Sicily, where he taught rhetoric. In 439, he made an unsuccessful attempt at reconciliation with the church. Julian was an accomplished exegete. Extant works attributed to him include treatments of Job, the Minor Prophets, and the Song of Solomon and a Latin translation of Theodore of Mopsuestia's *Commentary on the Psalms.*

Julian's vigorous defense of Pelagianism is extant chiefly in citations in the writings of his principal adversary, Augustine. After Julian's letters to Zosimus and Valerius, Augustine wrote the first book of his *On Marriage and Concupiscence.* This sparked a polemical exchange that included Julian's four books *Ad Turbantium* and eight books *Ad Florum.* Accusing Augustine of residual Manichaeism or puritanism, Julian attacked his notion of original sin, its consequences, and its transmission through procreation. Julian argued that marriage, conjugal union, and offspring are good. For Julian, concupiscence is evil only in excess and infant baptism is superfluous. CPL 773–777. [P.C.B.]

Bibliography

A. Bruckner, *Die vier Bücher von Julianus von Eclanum an Turbantius* (Berlin: Trowitzsch, 1910); L. de Coninck, ed., *Iuliani Aeclanensis, Expositio Libri Iob, Tractatus Prophetarum Osee, Iohel et Amos . . . accedunt operum deperditorum fragmenta . . . collecta, aucta, ordinata,* CCSL 88 (1977), Vol. 88; idem, *Theodori Mopsuesteni Expositionis in Psalmos Iuliano Aeclanensi interprete in Latinam versae quae supersunt,* CCSL (1977), Vol. 88A.

A. Bruckner, *Julian von Eclanum: Sein Leben und seine Lehre: Ein Beitrag zur Geschichte des Pelagianismus,* TU (1897), Vol. 15.3; M. Meslin, "Sainteté et mariage au cours de la seconde querelle pélagienne: saint Augustin et Julien d'Eclane," *Etudes Carmélitianes* 31 (1952):293–307; G. Bouwman, *Des Julian von Aeclanum, Kommentar zu den Propheten Osee, Joel, und Amos. Ein Beitrag zur Geschichte der Exegese,* in *Analecta Biblica* 9 (Rome: Pontificium Institutum Biblicum, 1958); F. Refoulé, "Julien d'Eclane: théologien et philosophie," *RSR* 52 (1964):42–84, 233–247; G.R. Evans, "Neither a Pelagian nor a Manichee," *VChr* 35 (1981):232–244; P. Brown, "Sexuality and Society in the Fifth Century A.D.: Augustine and Julian of Eclanum," *Tria Corda, Scritti in onore di A. Momigliano,* ed. E. Gabba (Athenaeum I Como: New Press, 1983), pp. 49–70; A.E. McGrath, "Divine Justice and Divine Equity in the Controversy Between Augustine and Julian of Eclanum," *Downside Review* 101 (1983):312–319.

JULIAN OF HALICARNASSUS (d. after

527). Bishop and theological writer. A Monophysite, Julian was expelled from his see of Halicarnassus by the emperor Justin I and took refuge in Alexandria (518). There, he became leader of the Aphthartodocetae, who taught the incorruptibility of the body of Christ. He wrote four treatises against Severus of Antioch in the course of the controversy over this teaching; substantial fragments are extant. Some letters also survive. A commentary on Job once attributed to him is not his. CPG III, 7125–7127. [M.P.McH.]

Bibliography

R. Draguet, *Julien d'Halicarnasse et sa controverse avec Sévère d'Antioche sur l'incorruptibilité du corps du Christ* (Louvain: Imprimerie P. Smeesters, 1924); A. Sanda, ed., *Severi Antiiulianistica* (Beirut: Typographia Catholica, 1931).

JULIAN POMERIUS (late fifth–early sixth

century). Ascetical writer. A native of Mauretania, Julian lived in Gaul, where he taught Caesarius of Arles and was ordained a priest. His Latin work *The Contemplative Life* describes the ideals of both the contemplative and the active life; its first two books were intended as a pastoral manual for clerics; the third was directed to all Christians. Formerly attributed incorrectly to Prosper of Aquitaine, it was popular throughout the Middle Ages. Another work, on the nature of the soul, is known only in summary and fragments; other ascetical writings are lost. CPL 998, 998a.

[M.P.McH.]

Bibliography

Ennodius, *Epistula* 2.6; Gennadius, *Lives of Illustrious Men* 95 (98); Isidore of Seville, *De viris illustribus* 12 (25).

Julianus Pomerius, The Contemplative Life, tr. M.J. Suelzer, ACW (1947), Vol. 4.

JULIUS I. Bishop of Rome (337–352). The support that Julius gave to Athanasius was an important contribution to the eventual triumph of Nicene orthodoxy in the Arian controversy. He convened a council of more than fifty bishops in Rome (341) that acquitted Athanasius of the charges against him and also declared Marcellus of Ancyra orthodox. The Council of Sardica in 343 approved in its Canon 3 (Greek) the right of bishops condemned by a synod to appeal their case to Julius. Feast day April 12. CPL 1627.   [E.F.]

Bibliography

Athanasius, *Apology Against the Arians* 20–35; 41–53; 58; idem, *History of the Arians* 2.9, 11; Hilary of Poitiers, *Fragmenta Historica* B, 2.2–4 (letter of the council of Sardica to Julius—tr. in J.T. Shotwell and L.R. Loomis, *The See of Peter* [New York: Columbia UP, 1927], pp. 527–529); Socrates, *Church History* 2.8, 15, 17, 20, 23, 34; Sozomen, *Church History* 3.8, 10–11; 4.8; *Liber Pontificalis* 36 (Duchesne 1.205–206).

E.G. Weltin, *The Ancient Popes* (Westminster: Newman, 1964), pp. 177–190.

JULIUS AFRICANUS, SEXTUS (ca. 160–ca. 240). Christian writer. Probably born in Jerusalem, Sextus Julius Africanus served under the emperor Septimius Severus and was closely connected with the royal house of Edessa in Syria. Sent to Rome by a colony in Palestine to plead its case, he remained there to organize the public library in the Pantheon under Alexander Severus. His *Chronicles*, extant only in fragments, contained regnal, archon, and consul lists, along with genealogies, from the creation to A.D. 220. The work has affinities to chiliasm, since Julius maintained that Christ was born in the year 5500 from the creation and would return in the year 6000. It served as a source for Eusebius of Caesarea, but the invention of the Christian world chronicle is to be ascribed to the latter. Julius's *Cesti*, parts of which survive, is a work in twenty-four books on a miscellany of subjects. Dedicated to Alexander Severus, it shows a mixture of superstition and Christianity. Two letters are also extant. In one, to Origen, the authenticity of the story of Susanna (Dan. 13:1–64) is denied; the other, to Aristides, contains discussion of the genealogies of Christ as reported in Matthew and Luke. CPG I, 1690–1695. TLG 2956.

[M.P.McH.]

Bibliography

Eusebius, *Church History* 1.6.2; 6.31.1–3; 7.1–16; Jerome, *Lives of Illustrious Men* 63.

Les "Cestes" de Julius Africanus: étude sur l'ensemble des fragments, ed. J.R. Viellefond (Florence: Sansoni Antiquariato, and Paris: Didier, 1970).

Chronicles and *Letter to Aristides*, tr. S.D.F. Salmond, and *Letter to Origen*, tr. F. Crombie, ANF (1886), Vol. 6, pp. 130–138 (*Chronicles*) and 125–127 (*Letter to Aristides*), and Vol. 4, p. 385 (*Letter to Origen*).

F. Granger, "Julius Africanus and the Library of the Pantheon," *JThS* 34 (1933):157–161; E.H. Blakeney, "Julius Africanus: A Letter to Origen," *Theology* 29 (1934):361–368; B. Croke, "The Originality of Eusebius' *Chronicle*," *AJPh* 103 (1982):195–200; F.C.R. Thee, *Julius Africanus and the Early Christian View of Magic* (Tübingen: Mohr, 1984).

JULIUS THE VETERAN (third–fourth century). Martyr. The tradition that Julius, a Roman legionary, was martyred in Lower Moesia (modern Bulgaria) probably deserves acceptance; the date of his martyrdom is uncertain, being perhaps as early as 200 or as late as 305.

[M.P.McH.]

Bibliography

Musurillo, pp. xxxix, 260–265.

J. den Boeft and J. Bremmer, "Notiunculae Martyrologicae II," *VChr* 36 (1982):383–402, esp. pp. 395–397 (discussion of date).

JUSTIN, GNOSTIC (second century). Early Gnostic teacher. Justin is known only from an abstract of his *Book of Baruch* preserved by Hippolytus (*Haer.* 5.18–23; 10.11). The book offers a Gnostic interpretation of the origin and history of the universe based on Genesis but drawing also on Greek mythology. Justin has three supreme principles: the Good Being; Elohim, the male creator; and Eden, the female principle and mate of Elohim. Elohim and Eden produced twenty-four angels, twelve for each. The third of the paternal and the third of the maternal angels, Baruch and Naas, possessed special properties. Baruch was the revealer angel of the Good Being and Naas (Hebrew, "serpent"; cf. the Naassenes) was the teacher of transgression. TLG 1454.   [E.F.]

Bibliography

R. Haardt, *Die Gnosis, Wesen und Zeugnisse* (Salzburg: Müller, 1967), pp. 98–105; W. Foerster and R.McL. Wilson, eds. *Gnosis: A Selection of Texts* (Oxford: Clarendon, 1972), Vol. 1, pp. 48–58.

JUSTIN MARTYR (d. ca. 165). Apologist and martyr. As an exegete, teacher, and prolific author writing in Greek, Justin Martyr is one of the most important witnesses of the life, faith, and worship of second-century Christianity. He contended with great zeal on various fronts, against the Roman state, pagan philosophy, Judaism, and heretical Christianity. He proved to be one of the preeminent interpreters of the Christian faith between the apostle Paul and Origen, integrating the insights of his Christian predecessors and laying new foundations for future thinkers, such as Irenaeus, Tertullian, and the Alexandrians. The magnitude of Justin's originality and achievement has not always sufficiently been recognized by scholars, but in recent years students of Justin have come to see him as "one of the most original thinkers Christianity produced" (Osborn, p. 201).

Life. Although the details are hazy, an outline of Justin's life may be drawn from his own writings. He identifies himself as "Justin, son of Priscus and grandson of Baccius, of Flavia Neapolis in Syrian Palestine" (*1 Apol.* 1.1), a city established by Vespasian as a Roman colony in the region of Samaria, near the ruins of ancient Shechem, and now called Nablus. Nothing is known of his early youth. At the time of his debate with the Jew Trypho, dated by Trypho's mention of the Bar Kochba War in *Dialogue* 1.3 and 9.3 (132–135), Justin had reached manhood, had studied philosophy, and was now doing evangelistic work, probably all in Ephesus. He was thus born in either the late first century or the early second, perhaps of Roman descent, as his name and that of his father indicate. Although he once refers to himself as a Samaritan (*Dial.* 120.6), he clearly viewed himself as a Gentile, uncircumcised and ignorant of Moses and the prophets until his conversion to Christianity as an adult in passionate search for truth. The story of his intellectual odyssey and his dramatic conversion to Christianity, no doubt to some degree idealized, is told in *Dialogue* 2–8. Left dissatisfied by successive encounters with philosophical schools—Stoics, Peripatetics, Pythagoreans, as well as Platonists, whom he greatly favored for a time—Justin was led by a wise old man to the revealed truth spoken by the Old Testament prophets and fulfilled by Christ. "Immediately a fire was kindled in my soul," writes Justin, who then embraced Christianity as "the only safe and beneficial philosophy" (*Dial.* 8.1). The courage of Christians in the face of death, which had previously impressed him (*2 Apol.* 12.1), may also have played a role in his conversion.

Like other itinerant pagan and Christian teachers, Justin found his way to Rome, where he carried on a long teaching ministry during the reign of Antoninus Pius (138–161), to whom he addressed his *First Apology*. One of his pupils was Tatian, the apologist. There in the marketplace of philosophies and religions, and continuing to wear the cloak of a philosopher (*pallium*), Justin conducted vigorous debates with proponents of various ideologies, including Crescens, a Cynic philosopher and vehement opponent of Justin (*2 Apol.* 3.1), as well as heretical Christian groups, such as the Valentinians and Marcionites, against whom he wrote a lost treatise (*1 Apol.* 26.8). He no doubt also disputed with Jews, and it was probably in Rome that he put into writing his *Dia-*

logue with Trypho the Jew, a full apology of Christian claims over against Judaism. The fateful part of his work, and that for which Christian tradition honors him, however, was his bold engagement of the Roman judicial system for its totally unjustified mortal persecution of Christians because of the "name" only. As the foreboding Second Apology addressed to the Roman senate anticipates, this courageous witness brought him into collision with the Roman state in the person of the prefect Junius Rusticus (162–168) early in Marcus Aurelius's reign. Upon confession of faith and refusal to sacrifice to the gods, Justin and six other Christians were, according to a later but reliable account of Justin's martyrdom (Acts of Justin), condemned by Rusticus, scourged, and beheaded.

Writings. Although Eusebius mentions numerous works by Justin, only three survive, in a single fourteenth-century manuscript (Paris, No. 450). The First Apology is an earnest appeal for justice and liberty on behalf of Christians, who are to be judged not on the basis of irrational hatred and slanders about atheism, immorality, and disloyalty but on the basis of their moral life and the truth they hold. They are monotheists but also believe in Christ the only Son of God and preexistent Logos (Word), who inspired both Old Testament figures and Greek philosophers and who is fully vindicated by the incontrovertible fulfillment of prophecy and his supreme teachings—unless one is blinded by demons. Justin also offers valuable accounts of the celebration of early Christian baptism and the eucharist, concluding with Hadrian's letter to Minucius Fundanus directing that Christians should be fairly tried on the basis of criminal evidence only. Intended probably as a supplement, the brief Second Apology expresses Justin's indignation at a recent beheading of three Christians at the instigation of a dissolute pagan whose Christian wife had censured him for his immoral life. This writing answers slanders and concentrates on the meaning of suffering, the courage of Christians, and the superiority of Christianity as the whole revelation of God's truth. Nearly as lengthy as the four Gospels combined, the Dia-

logue opens with an extensive philosophical prologue in which Justin concedes nothing to philosophy but rests the burden of truth on the divine scriptures and the words of the Savior. The bulk of this work is a massive collection of elaborate interpretations based on the Old Testament regarding the role of the Mosaic law, the person of Christ as Son and Logos of God, and the church as the true Israel. Convinced that he has the gift of understanding and interpreting scripture (Dial. 58.1), Justin makes his appeal to many readers but especially to an eschatological remnant of Jews who are still open to the gospel (Dial. 55.3; 64.2–3). Of his lost writings, the Syntagma Against All Heresies (1 Apol. 26.8) and the Syntagma Against Marcion (perhaps the same work) used by Irenaeus (Haer. 4.6.2) indicate his antiheretical interest and the reason he impressed his successors as a "heresiologist."

Thought. Too much is sometimes made of Justin's philosophical background because of his teaching about the seminal Logos and his discussion of philosophical schools in the Dialogue. Although Platonist influence on his concepts of God's transcendence and of a universal moral law is unmistakable, the controlling center of Justin's thought is orthodox Christianity and its teachings about creation, incarnation, atonement, resurrection, church, sacraments, and moral life. Far from being an academic or eclectic philosopher, Justin sits in judgment on philosophy and is uncompromising about biblical truth. His focus is Christ, the consummate truth of all, and his criterion is scripture, the word of God that discloses supernatural, not human, wisdom. He is ready to proclaim the truth of the gospel to all alike, pagans, Jews, and heretical Christians, facing real issues of life and risking daily threat of death. Justin is "philosophical" in that he seeks in a truly pioneering achievement to provide an intelligent argument in defense of the gospel on the basis of prophecy, miracles, the quality of Christian life, and the principles of justice and reasonable discourse. Yet his deepest conviction is that God's truth itself, which one must proclaim or face God's judgment (Dial. 82.3), wins the day by its own supernatural power. A great Christian apologist, Justin is in the end an earnest evangelist of Christ speaking on behalf of Christians who, although cursed and persecuted, say lovingly to all: "You are our brothers, come to know the truth of God" (*Dial.* 96.2). Feast day June 1. CPG I, 1073–1089. TLG 0645.   [T.S.]

Bibliography

E.J. Goodspeed, *Die ältesten Apologeten* (Göttingen: Vandenhoeck & Ruprecht, 1914).

A. Roberts and J. Donaldson, eds., "Justin Martyr," ANF (1885), Vol. 1; A.L. Williams, *The Dialogue with Trypho* (London: SPCK, 1930).

E.R. Goodenough, *The Theology of Justin Martyr* (Jena: Frommann, 1923); R. Holte, "Logos Spermatikos: Christianity and Ancient Philosophy According to St. Justin's Apologies," *Studia Theologica* 12 (1958):109–168; J.S. Sibinga, *The Old Testament Text of Justin Martyr* (Leiden: Brill, 1963); P. Prigent, *Justin et l'Ancien Testament* (Paris: Lecoffre, 1964); W.A. Shotwell, *The Biblical Exegesis of Justin Martyr* (London: SPCK, 1965); H. Chadwick, *Early Christian Thought and the Classical Tradition* (Oxford: Clarendon, 1966), pp. 1–30; L.W. Barnard, *Justin Martyr: His Life and Thought* (Cambridge: Cambridge UP, 1967); A.J. Bellinzoni, *The Sayings of Jesus in the Writings of Justin Martyr* (Leiden: Brill, 1967); J.C.M. van Winden, *An Early Christian Philosopher: Justin Martyr's Dialogue with Trypho Chapters One to Nine* (Leiden: Brill, 1971); E.F. Osborn, *Justin Martyr* (Tübingen: Mohr, 1973); T. Stylianopoulos, *Justin Martyr and the Mosaic Law* (Missoula: Scholars, 1975); D. Trakatellis, *The Pre-Existence of Christ in Justin Martyr* (Missoula: Scholars, 1976); O. Skarsaune, "The Conversion of Justin Martyr," *Studia Theologica* 30 (1976):53–73; J. Nilson, "To Whom Is Justin's *Dialogue with Trypho* Addressed?," *ThS* 38 (1977):538–546; O. Skarsaune, *The Proof from Prophecy: A Study in Justin Martyr's Proof-Text Tradition* (Leiden: Brill, 1987).

JUSTINIAN I (482–565). Roman emperor (527–565). Born in Tauresium in the region of Scopia into a Greek-Illyrian family, Flavius Petrus Justinianus succeeded his uncle Justin (518–527) as emperor in Constantinople. He had come to the capital through his uncle's initiative and studied law and theology before serving as prefect. His rise to the throne was resisted by the relatives of emperor Anastasius, Justin's predecessor, who instigated an insurrection against him that resulted in the Nika riots (532–537), which were finally and deci-

sively suppressed through the daring interference of the empress Theodora and the sheer strength and ability of Justinian's general Belisarius. Having firmly established his authority, Justinian emerged as one of the greatest emperors, placing the stamp of his extraordinary personality on almost every aspect of Roman-Byzantine history and affairs, especially in the political, legislative, and religious spheres.

Justinian was a man of ascetical disposition who generally assumed an austere manner of life—sometimes not eating for two whole days—and delighting in working for most of his time in the library. He was popular and easily approachable, as the historian Procopius tells us, and was magnanimous toward his enemies. Able to recognize the abilities of others, he attracted such noteworthy collaborators as the generals Belisarius, Narses, Germanus, and Sittis; the Greek lawyer Tribonianus; the economist John the Cappadocian, who became Prefect of the Royal City; the architects Anthimus of Tralles and Isidore of Miletus, the designers of Hagia Sophia; and the empress Theodora. His wife, originally from either Cyprus or Monophysite Egypt, proved a faithful and honorable companion to Justinian, although she had many enemies and was often unjustly accused. It was through her influence that her husband became involved in pro-Monophysite policies.

Justinian sought to serve the unity and growth of both the empire "of the blessed race of the Romans" (*Cod.* 2nd prol.) and of the church (*Nov.* 6). He regained lost territories in Africa, Italy, and Spain, defeating respectively the Vandals (534), the Ostrogoths (540), and the Visigoths (555), who had inflicted blows against orthodoxy through their Arian sympathies. That success, however, left other borders, especially those in the southeast and the northeast, open to other enemies—Persians, Arabs, Avars, and Slavs.

Justinian's first and perhaps most brilliant legacy was the reform of the law, which he brought about by personal involvement and by employing distinguished lawyers under the leadership of Tribonianus. This achievement includes the *Codex Justinianus* (529 and 534), which governed the empire until its fall and through it passed to the Slavs and to western Europe; the *Digests* or *Pandects* (533); the *Institutiones* (533), which formed the *Juris civilis* (Civil Code); and the *Novellae* or *Nearai* (new laws).

Justinian commissioned extensive public building throughout the empire, most notably Hagia Sophia in Constantinople, which survives to this day, and such great monastic fortresses as those of St. Catherine's in Sinai and St. Saba in Palestine.

Justinian was the first emperor to take a personal interest in theology. Unlike his predecessors, he understood his role to be not that of an external arbiter or reconciler but that of an internal regulator, who actively participated in theological discussions and often resolved or settled them of his own will without recourse to ecclesiastical channels. He established the archdiocese of Justiniana in his own birthplace; ninety of his *Novellae* dealt with ecclesiastical matters. Justinian had prompted his uncle to

revoke Zeno's *Henoticon* (481), which had lasted thirty years in the east, and to replace it with pope Hormisdas's *Libellus*, thus mending relations between the east Romans and west Romans, which had been broken since 484. As emperor, he attempted to suppress the remnants of paganism, putting an end to the Academy in Athens (529), and of the heresies—Manichaeism, Montanism, Arianism, Pneumatomachianism—by excluding their followers from high office.

Justinian held a different attitude to the Monophysites, choosing to argue with them by means of extensive writing. In this, he may have been influenced by his wife (who was of Monophysite persuasion), by political considerations (the bulk of his subjects, especially in Egypt and Syria, were Monophysites), and by his own Neochalcedonian theological position (which combined acceptance of the Chalcedonian formula and of Cyril of Alexandria's entire doctrine, including his "one-nature" Christological formula).

Emperor Justinian (527–565) carrying a gold paten and preceded by a subdeacon swinging a censer, a deacon carrying the gospels, and bishop Maximian of Ravenna (546–556). Mosaic in church of S. Vitale, Ravenna, Italy.

In 533, Justinian called a theological consultation in Constantinople in which twelve bishops (six orthodox and six Severian Monophysites), other clergy, and himself participated. (The minutes of this meeting are lost, but for accounts cf. ACO 4.2, pp. 169–1840; Mansi, 8.81–834.) From this meeting, Justinian learned that the principal Monophysite objections to Chalcedon were that it implied separation of the two natures and that it reinstated previously deposed Nestorianizing bishops. He tried to answer these objections by two edicts (*diatagmata*). The first of these approved of the second Theopaschite Formula, "one of the Trinity has suffered in the flesh," which denoted the communication of the idioms of the two natures in the one person and thus averted the "division" of Dyophysitism so strongly objected to by Monophysites. This position is perfectly exemplified in Justinian's famous hymn that was incorporated into the Greek Orthodox liturgy and is sung to this day, "The Only-begotten Son and Logos of God. . . ." Particularly important here are the phrases "who was crucified, Christ the God . . . being one of the Trinity." In 543 (or 545 or 546), Justinian issued another edict, which condemned the *Three Chapters* (the person and writings of Theodore of Mopsuestia, the writings of Theodoret of Cyrus against Cyril of Alexandria, and the Epistle of Ibas of Edessa to Maris). Only extracts from this edict have survived, but there are extant a new edict (or confession of faith) issued in 551 and dealing with the same subject and a reply to a memorandum of the bishops of Illyricum, written in 550 in favor of the *Three Chapters*.

In the meantime, Theodora had followed her own independent church policy. Since 531, she had converted Hormisdas's palace in Constantinople into a monastery for 500 Monophysites from the east. In 535, she managed to raise to the episcopal throne of Constantinople a certain Anthimus of Trebizond, a Monophysite. In the following year, Anthimus was deposed by a synod summoned under a new bishop, Menas of Constantinople; the synod condemned Severus of Antioch, against Theodora's wishes. Her revenge was to raise

Vigilius, who had been Rome's *apocrisiarius* (or representative) in Constantinople, to the see of Old Rome. Vigilius's attitude to the dogmatic disputes proved inconsistent, inasmuch as he attempted to strike a balance between the Chalcedonian formula and Neochalcedonianism. Theodora was also able to reorganize the Monophysites of Syria, establishing Jacob Baradaeus as their first bishop (he was made bishop of Edessa) and allowing them to organize themselves into a separate church. In 542, Justinian's edict on Monophysitism, occasioned by the return to orthodoxy of Monophysite monks through the efforts of Zoilus of Alexandria, did not result in any major conversion of the Monophysites, who continued to regard him as an oppressor and heretic.

A new edict in 543 condemned Origenism, which had been the subject of a great dispute in Palestine. Justinian based this edict on the teachings of the fathers and sent it to bishop Menas with the demand that it should be ratified by a council. In 553, Justinian summoned the Fifth Ecumenical Council, which ratified the condemnation of the *Three Chapters* and perhaps Origenism. Vigilius accepted these decisions with great hesitation, but died on his way to Rome after a long compulsory stay in the eastern capital.

In spite of all his efforts and the Fifth Ecumenical Council, Justinian did not achieve the reconciliation of the Monophysites, many of whom had adopted extreme points of view and did not desire union with the orthodox church. It seems, however, that he never gave up on his vision. At the end of his life, according to the reports of the historians, he seems to have adopted the point of view of the Aphthartodocetae, the group of the Monophysites under Julian of Halicarnassus who, explaining Eutyches's position, believed that Christ's body was free from the corruption incurred by a natural conception and that his sufferings took place as a result of a special miraculous operation. Justinian, persuaded by the bishop of Ioppa that this teaching could be understood in an orthodox way, attempted to impose it on the church with an edict. Eutychius of Constantinople refused to accept it and was dethroned, and the same would have happened to the other patriarchs had Justinian not met with his death. The edict has not survived (Evagrius, *H.E.* 4.39 ff.) and perhaps was never published. The question remains why Justinian in the end preferred Aphthartodocetism to the moderate Monophysitism of Severus. There is no easy answer to this: not only is primary historical evidence lacking, but Justinian's alleged Aphthartodocetism can in fact be seriously disputed—especially in view of his acceptance of the elevation of the Neochalcedonian John Scholasticus to the throne of Constantinople. It is a paradox that the emperor who more than any other established orthodoxy in the Old and New Romes should have left the impression that he was a Monophysite Aphthartodocetist. *See also* Hagia Sophia; Procopius of Caesarea; Theodora; Theopaschite Formula; Three Chapters. CPG III, 6865-6893.

[G.D.D.]

Bibliography

Procopius, *History of the Wars, Buildings,* and *Secret History,* tr. H.B. Dewing, LCL, 7 vols. (1914–1940).

PL 63.430–510; 66.14–43; 69.30–37, 119–120, 177–327; 72.976–984; PG 86.945–1150.

J.V. Bryce, "The Life of Justinian by Theophilus," *English Historical Review* 2 (1887):657–686; M. Hasset, "The Reign of Justinian," *American Catholic Quarterly Review* 37 (1912):266–285; G.P. Baker, *Justinian* (New York: Dodd, Mead, 1931); M.V. Anastos, "The Immutability of Christ and Justinian's Condemnation of Theodore of Mopsuestia," *DOP* 6 (1951):123–160; P.N. Ure, *Justinian and His Age* (Harmondsworth: Penguin, 1951); G. Downey, *Constantinople in the Age of Justinian* (Norman: U of Oklahoma P, 1961); D.J. Constantellos, "Justinian and the Three Chapters Controversy," *GOTR* 8 (1962–1963):71–94; A.H.M. Jones, *The Later Roman Empire, 284–602,* 2 vols. (Norman: U of Oklahoma P, 1964); J.W. Barker, *Justinian and the Later Roman Empire* (Madison: U of Wisconsin P, 1966); J. Meyendorff, "Justinian, the Empire and the Church," *DOP* 22 (1968):45–60; E. Chrysos, *The Ecclesiastical Policy of Justinian in the Controversy of the Three Chapters and the Fifth Ecumenical Council* [in Greek] (Thessalonica, 1969); R.

Browning, *Justinian and Theodora* (New York: Praeger, 1971); W.H.C. Frend, *The Rise of the Monophysite Movement* (Cambridge: Cambridge UP, 1972); V. Phidas, *The Institution of the Pentarchy of the Patriarchs* [in Greek], 2 vols. (Athens, 1977); S.P. Brock, "The Conversations with the Syrian Orthodox Under Justinian (532)," *Orientalia Christiana Periodica* 47 (1981):87–121; A. Gerostergios, *Justinian the Great, the Emperor and Saint* (Belmont: Institute for Byzantine and Modern Greek Studies, 1982); A. Cameron, *Procopius and the Sixth Century* (Berkeley: U of California P, 1985).

JUSTUS OF URGEL (d. after 546). Bishop and exegete. A participant in the second of the councils of Toledo (527) and in that of Lerida (546), Justus wrote a brief explanation of the Song of Solomon employing allegory, in which allusion is made to the persecution of the church in Spain by the Goths—adherents of Arianism—as well as a sermon on the feast of Vincent of Saragossa. CPL 1091–1092.

[M.P.McH.]

Bibliography

Isidore of Seville, *De viris illustribus* 33–34.

JUVENCUS (early fourth century). Christian Latin poet. Juvencus, a Spanish priest, wrote the *Evangeliorum libri IV,* a poetic paraphrase in Latin of the life of Christ based on the Gospel narratives, Matthew especially, but also much influenced in its form by Virgil and other classical poets. The first Christian epic, the work was popular throughout the Middle Ages. Other works, not extant, dealt with the sacraments; the *Heptateuchos,* once ascribed to Juvencus, is probably by Cyprian of Gaul. CPL 1385.

[M.P.McH.]

Bibliography

Jerome, *Lives of Illustrious Men* 84; idem, *Letter* 70.5.

M.A. Norton, "Prosopography of Juvencus," *Folia* 4 (1950):38–42; repr. in *Leaders of Iberian Christianity,* ed. J.M.-F. Marique (Boston: St. Paul, 1962), pp. 114–120.

K

KINGS. Book(s) of Bible. The books of Kings were considered one unified book in Hebrew manuscripts (*b. Baba Bathra* 14b) but were divided first by the Septuagint and later in the Vulgate and English Bibles. The division was introduced into Hebrew Bibles in the Bomberg edition of 1518.

Classified by the rabbis among the former prophets, the book of Kings, a continuation of the books of Samuel and designated 3–4 *Basileion* (Reigns or Kingdoms) by the Greeks and *Regum Tertius et Quartus* by the Latins, are classified by Christians as historical books covering the period from the old age of David (ca. 971 B.C.) and the rise of Solomon through the fall of Jerusalem in 587 B.C. and the exaltation of king Jehoiachin by the Babylonian ruler Evil-Merodach during the exile (561 B.C.). Since Martin Noth, the books of Kings are often spoken of as "Deuteronomic History" (applying the teachings of the Book of Deuteronomy to the interpretation of Israel's history).

A part of scripture taken over by the church from the Jewish community, the books of Kings are frequently cited or echoed in the New Testament and appear in Christian canonical lists from the time of Melito of Sardis.

[J.P.L.]

Bibliography

Theodoret of Cyrus, *Quaestiones in libros Regnorum* PG 80.667–800; Procopius of Gaza, *Catena in Octateuchum* PG 87.1147–1200.

J.A. Montgomery, *A Critical and Exegetical Commentary on the Books of Kings* (New York: Scribner, 1951); M. Noth, *The History of Israel* (London: Black, 1958), pp. 42, 203–249, 288–289; E.R. Thiele, *The Mysterious Numbers of the Hebrew Kings,* rev. ed. (Grand Rapids: Eerdmans, 1965); J. Gray, *I & II Kings,* 2nd ed. (Philadelphia: Westminster, 1970); J.H. Hayes and P.K. Hooker, *A New Chronology of the Kings of Israel and Judah* (Philadelphia: John Knox, 1988).

KISS OF PEACE. Originally an expression of Christian love and fellowship, later an act of liturgical worship. The term "kiss of peace" itself does not appear in the New Testament, but the origin of the rite is the "holy kiss" of Romans 16:16; 1 Corinthians 16:20; 2 Corinthians 13:12; and 1 Thessalonians 5:26 and the "kiss of love" of 1 Peter 5:14. The earliest reference to the kiss in formal worship is in Justin (*1 Apol.* 65.2): "After the prayers have been completed, we greet each other with a kiss." The rite was easily abused, however. Clement of Alexandria (*Paed.* 3.11.81) complains about shameless and resounding kissing in churches, and Hippolytus (*Trad. ap.* 2.18) directs that men shall kiss men only and women likewise (he further indicates that catechumens shall not participate). Tertullian (*Or.* 18), who calls the rite simply "the Peace," also connects it with prayers in worship and with reconciliation and urges those who are fasting not to refuse it. In the eastern liturgy, it has retained its position after the prayers, but in the western church it was moved during the fifth or sixth century to the celebration of the eucharist. Other occasions for the practice in the early church were baptism, ordination, marriage, the veneration of martyrs, and burial. The practice tended to die out in the late Middle Ages and to be replaced by kissing altars, icons, the cup, and the Bible. There has been a revival in recent times. [J.A.B.]

Bibliography

F. Cabrol, "Baiser," DACL (1925), Vol. 2.1, cols. 117–130; K. Thraede, "Ursprung und Formen des 'hl. Kuss' in frühen Christentum," *JAC* 11/12 (1968–1969):124–180; idem., "Friedenskuss," RLAC (1972), Vol. 8, pp. 505–519. G. Stählin, "Phileō," *Theological Dictionary of the New Testament,* ed. G. Friedrich (Grand Rapids: Eerdmans, 1974), Vol. 9, pp. 118–127, 138–146; E. Kreider, "Let the Faithful Greet Each Other: The Kiss of Peace," *Conrad Grebel Review* (1987):29–49.

KYRIE ELEISON. "Lord, have mercy." This Greek prayer of supplication first appeared, in the mid-fourth century, in the liturgy in the east, where it was recited or sung as part of a litany in response to the deacon or other leader. Pope Gelasius I (492–496) inserted it into the Roman Mass as a response. Gregory the Great (590–604) dropped the invocations for many masses—soon they would disappear entirely—but retained the *Kyrie* and authorized the addition of the phrase *Christe eleison,* "Christ, have mercy." In the present Roman Mass, the *Kyrie* appears immediately before the *Gloria in excelsis* when that prayer is recited; each of the petitions—"Lord, have mercy; Christ, have mercy; Lord, have mercy"—is said or sung by the celebrant and repeated by the congregation as a response, normally in the vernacular. *See also* Litany.   [M.P.McH.]

Bibliography

B. Capelle, "Le Kyrie de la messe et le pape Gélase," *RBén* 46 (1934):126–144; repr. in *Travaux liturgiques de doctrine et d'histoire II. Histoire: La Messe* (Louvain: Centre Liturgique, Abbaye du Mont César, 1962), pp. 116–134; C. Callewaert, "Les Etapes de l'histoire du Kyrie: S. Gélase, S. Benoît, S. Grégoire," *RHE* 38 (1942):20–45; J.A. Jungmann, *The Mass of the Roman Rite: Its Origins and Development (Missarum Sollemnia)* (New York: Benziger, 1951), Vol. 1, pp. 333–346.

L

LABARUM. Imperial standard adopted by Constantine. Lactantius, a contemporary, in *The Deaths of the Persecutors* 44.5f., says that on the night before the Battle of the Milvian Bridge (October 28, 312) Constantine received a command from God to mark his men's shields with an $\times$ bisected by a I ($\maltese$) with a circumflex at its upper end. Evidently, what Lactantius meant was an $\times$ bisected by a P, or $\maltese$. According to Eusebius (*V.C.* 1.26–31), before the battle Constantine adapted the Roman cavalry standard (*vexillum*). It consisted of a gilded vertical shaft with a transverse bar forming a cross surmounted by a wreath of gold and precious stones enclosing the chi-rho ligature (or monogram): $\maltese$ A purple banner hung from the transverse bar, and on it was inscribed in Greek "by this conquer." There were also medallions of Constantine and his sons above the banner. The *labarum* can be reconstructed on the evidence of these literary sources—Lactantius, who has the chi-rho monogram alone, and Eusebius, who has the monogram circumscribed within a wreath surmounted on a cruciform *vexillum*.

Eusebius does not use the term *labarum*; it is not attested literarily until the middle of the fourth century, when it was used for the first

171

Sarcophagus (fourth century) depicting the soldiers who guarded the tomb of Jesus asleep under the *labarum* of Constantine. (Formerly Lateran inv. no. 171; now in Pio Christian Museum, Vatican City, Italy.) (Courtesy Monumenti Musei e Gallerie Pontificie.)

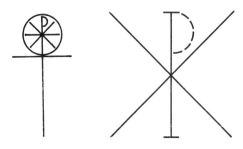

EUSEBIUS   LACTANTIUS

Schematic drawings of the *labarum* based on the
accounts of Eusebius (*V.C.* 1.26–31) and Lactantius
(*Mort. per.* 44.52). (Furnished by P.C. Finney.)

time by the unknown compiler of the chapter
indices to the *Life of Constantine* at 1.31. Its
derivation is obscure, although a Celtic root is
probable (cf. Egger). Key military personnel at
the Battle of the Milvian Bridge were the Celts
and Germans, and they would have understood
the term. Greeks in the east clearly did not.

For a time, the *labarum* was the Constantinian insignia par excellence. It appeared
in a wide variety of material contexts, for example, emblazoned on Constantine's helmet
represented on a silver medallion struck at
Ticinum in 315 (cf. Bruun). Several Constantinian coin issues bore the *labarum.* It is
shown in the accompanying illustration as the
central symbol on the front of a Roman Christian sarcophagus that dates to the first half of
the fourth century. *See also* Cross.   [P.C.F.]

Bibliography
H. von Campenhausen, "Die Passionssarkophage:
Zur Geschichte eines altchristlichen Bildkreises,"
Marburger Jahrbuch für Kunstwissenschaft 5
(1929):39–86; R. Egger, "Das Labarum, die Kaiser-
standarte der Spätantike," *Sitzungsberichte der Öster-
reichischen Akademie der Wissenschaft in Wien:
Philosophisch-historische Klasse* 234.1 (1960):3–26;
P. Bruun, "The Christian Signs on the Coins of
Constantine," *Arctos* n.s. 3 (1962):5–35; E. Dinkler,
"Das Kreuz als Siegeszeichen," *ZThK* 62 (1965):1–20;
repr. in *Signum Crucis* (Tübingen: Mohr, 1967), pp.
55–76.

LACTANTIUS (ca. 250–ca. 325). Christian
Latin apologist. Born in North Africa, Lactantius was a student of Arnobius the Elder there
when both were still pagans. Appointed by
Diocletian as teacher of Latin rhetoric in Nicomedia, he lost his post in the persecution of
Christians under that emperor (303); the exact date of his conversion is uncertain. He left
Nicomedia (ca. 305–306) and eventually was
made tutor to Crispus, eldest son of Constantine, at the imperial court at Trier in Gaul
(ca. 317).

Of his writings, *The Workmanship of God*
(303–304) presents an argument for divine
providence based on the workings of the human body. *The Divine Institutes* (ca. 308–309)
offers a philosophy of religion, refuting attacks
on Christianity and setting forth its doctrine
and worship with extensive consideration of
eschatology. It exhibits many classical quotations, from Cicero and Virgil especially, and
relies on the *Sibylline Oracles* among other
sources. It was eventually supplemented (ca.
317) by an *Epitome,* an abridged and edited
version.

The Wrath of God (313–314) offers a
demonstration, against Epicureanism, that such
emotions as anger and kindness are not inconsistent with the nature of God, and, against
Stoicism, that God's anger is as necessary as
his kindness. *The Deaths of the Persecutors*
(ca. 314–315) is intended to demonstrate that
all persecutors must meet with a bad end; the
focus is on such contemporaries as Diocletian,
Galerius, and Maximinus Daia. The work is a
significant historical source for its period. *The
Phoenix,* a poem based on the myth of that
bird, is so constructed that much of the work
can be read in either a pagan or a Christian
sense. Certain references, however, strongly
suggest that it is Christian in its intent. (The
poem appears in an expanded and allegorized
form in the Old English Exeter Book.) Several
other works of Lactantius are lost.

A rhetorician and not a theologian, Lactantius emphasizes the providence of God,
martyrdom, love of God and neighbor, and such
virtues as humility and chastity. He apparently
does not teach a Holy Spirit distinct from Father and Son. He upholds a dualism of soul
and body, good and evil. His eschatology has

an element of chiliasm. Lactantius enjoyed a special favor with the humanists of the Renaissance, who called him "the Christian Cicero." CPL 85–92. *See also* Phoenix.   [M.P.McH.]

Bibliography

Jerome, *Lives of Illustrious Men* 80.

Lactantius: Institutions divines II, ed. P. Monat, SC (1987), Vol. 337; *Epitomé des institutions divines,* ed. M. Perrin, SC (1987), Vol. 335.

Lactantius: De Mortibus Persecutorum, ed. and tr. J.L. Creed (Oxford: Clarendon, 1984); *Lactantius: The Divine Institutes Books 1–7* and *Lactantius: The Minor Works,* tr. M.F. McDonald, FOTC (1964, 1965), Vols. 49, 54.

J. Stevenson, "The Life and Literary Activity of Lactantius," *SP* 1 (1957):661–677; idem, "Aspects of the Relations Between Lactantius and the Classics," *SP* 4 (1961):497–503; R.M. Ogilvie, *The Library of Lactantius* (Oxford: Clarendon, 1978); J. Fontaine and M. Perrin, eds., *Lactance et son temps* (Paris: Beauchesne, 1978); A. Søby-Christensen, *Lactantius the Historian: An Analysis of the De Mortibus Persecutorum* (Copenhagen: Museum Tusculanum, 1980); T.P. Halton and R.D. Sider, "A Decade of Patristic Scholarship 1970–1979," *CW* 76 (1982–1983): 125–127 (bibliography); P. Monat, *Lactance et la Bible: une propédeutique latine à la lecture de la Bible dans l'Occident constantinien,* 2 vols. (Paris: Etudes Augustiniennes, 1982); P. McGuckin, "The Christology of Lactantius," *SP* 17.2 (1982):813–820; M.L. Colish, *The Stoic Tradition from Antiquity to the Middle Ages* (Leiden: Brill, 1985), Vol. 2, pp. 37–47; O.P. Nicholson, "The Source of the Dates in Lactantius' *Divine Institutes,*" *JThS* 36 (1985):291–310; C. Ocker, "Unius Arbitrio Mundum Regi Necesse Est: Lactantius' Concern for the Preservation of Roman Society," *VChr* 40 (1986):348–364; P.A. Roots, "The *De Opificio Dei:* The Workmanship of God and Lactantius," *CQ* 37 (1987): 466–486; E. Heck, "Lactanz und die Klassiker: Zu Theorie und Praxis der Verwendung heidnischer Literatur in christlicher Apologetik bei Lactanz," *Philologus* 132 (1988): 160–179.

LAITY. "People" (from Greek *laos*), the ordinary believers in contrast to the clergy, those who hold office in the church. A layperson may also be defined as one living in the world in distinction to a monk (e.g., Palladius, *V. Chrys.* 19). The body of the laity consists of two classes: the baptized members and the catechumens, who are preparing for baptism.

In the Old Testament, the Israelites were distinguished from Gentiles as "God's people" (Exod. 6:7; Deut. 14:2) and were identified as "the people" in contrast to their own rulers and priests (Exod. 19:24; Lev. 4:3; Deut. 18:3). The Old Testament antithesis of priest and people being foreign to the New Testament, the apostle Peter calls the whole church "a royal priesthood" and "the people of God" (1 Peter 2:9–10). The church is the "new people" (*Barn.* 5.7; 7.5; 13.6; Aristides, *Apol.* 16; Constantine, *Or.s.c.* 19), and "the people of the Lord, and the people that consists of those who bear a new name" (Hippolytus, *Dan. 4.9*). Clement of Rome (A.D. 96) introduced the term "layman" into Christian literature, by analogy from Judaism, to describe one who does not hold any office in the Christian community (*1 Clem.* 40).

Despite the growing distinction between clergy and laity, the concept of universal priesthood was not lost sight of. Irenaeus of Lyons, for example, states that all who are justified have the "sacerdotal order" (*Haer.* 4.8.3; cf. 4.17; 5.34). Tertullian as a Montanist writes: "Are we laypeople not priests also? It is written, 'He hath made us kings and priests' [Rev. 1:6]. It is the authority of the church alone that has made a distinction between clergy and laity" (*Exh. cast.* 7). Origen addresses his congregation as follows: "Do you not recognize that the priesthood has been given to you also, that is to the whole church of God and the nation of believers?. . . You have therefore a priesthood, being 'a priestly nation'" (*Hom.* 10.1 *in Lev.*). To John Chrysostom, the entire people gathered in prayer constitutes the "fullness of priesthood" (*Hom.* 3.4 *in Phil.*).

Functions of the Laity. During the pontificate of Damasus I (366–384), the pseudonymous writer known as Ambrosiaster described the gradual restriction of lay participation in church functions as follows: "At first, all taught and baptized on whatever days and seasons occasion required. . . . That the people might grow and multiply, it was at the beginning permitted to all to preach the gospel, and to baptize, and to explain the scriptures in church, but when the church embraced all places, houses of assembly were constituted, and rulers and the other offices in the church were instituted" (*Comm. in Eph.* 4.11, 12). Despite the obvious clericalization of the church, other activities outside church governance remained open to laypeople, such as evangelism, teaching, and studying scripture.

Early Christians, living in a world of pagans and unbelievers, were expected to preach the gospel as opportunity presented itself. The mission of Christianity in antiquity was carried out largely by informal missionaries (Origen, *Cels.* 3.55). Lay missionaries include Pantaenus, who is said to have traveled to India (Eusebius, *H.E.* 5.10), and a female prisoner, later called Nino, who began the conversion of Georgia by evangelizing its king (Socrates, *H.E.* 1.20). Each Christian was expected to bring his neighbor from error to truth.

Following Jewish custom, laymen were permitted to preach in church up to the time of Origen (ca. 230). The bishops of Jerusalem and Caesarea invited the lay teacher Origen to expound the scriptures to their congregations. This was made the basis of an accusation against him by Demetrius, bishop of Alexandria, that Origen had preached "in the presence of bishops" (Eusebius, *H.E.* 6.19). Origen states: "In many so-called churches, especially those in large cities, one can see rulers of the people of God who do not allow anyone, sometimes not even the noblest of Jesus' disciples, to speak with them on equal terms" (*Comm. in Mt.* 16.8). Lay teachers were still approved by the *Apostolic Constitutions*: "Although a man be a layman, if experienced in the delivery of instruction, and reverent in habit, he may teach; for the scripture says: 'They shall be all taught of God'" (8.31). The Fourth General Council at Carthage (398) prohibited laymen from teaching in the presence of clergymen and without their consent (*can.* 98); Canon 99 forbids women, no matter how "learned or holy," to "presume to teach men in a meeting." We do not find in the east, however, the schism that will establish itself in the west between clergy and laity in the realm of theological interest and competence.

Laypeople, not just priests and monks, had the obligation to read and study the scriptures. Origen thinks that from one to two hours of prayer and Bible reading is barely an adequate minimum for the individual Christian (*Hom. 2 in Num.*). According to Jerome, Pamphilus at Caesarea readily provided Bibles to men and women who liked to read (*Adv. Rufin.* 1.9). Those who could not read or were too poor to purchase the books were to nourish themselves from the official explication of the Bible in church (John Chrysostom, *Hom.* 72.4 *in Mt.*). Parents were obliged to instruct their children at home, since the secular schools were largely pagan (John Chrysostom, *Inan. gl.* 19).

Laity in the World. As the word "vocation" implies, the laity were "called" to practice Christianity in the world. Even the inferior members of the church were morally superior to the pagans living around them (Origen, *Cels.* 3.29). Ignatius of Antioch always made mention of his title of "Christian" or "disciple" when he wished to make known his innermost identity. He desired that he and all Christians might *be* what their name meant (*Rom.* 3.2; *Magn.* 4). The baptismal catecheses never ceased to insist on the moral exigencies of the name Christian. The duty of laypeople was to oppose the then prevalent sins of abortion and homosexuality and to combat greed and dishonesty in business life (Tertullian, *Idol.* 11f.).

Every Christian, owing to his or her baptismal profession, was at risk for martyrdom, which was considered the summit of perfection in the early church. In fact, the laity constituted the majority of martyrs, since all of the female martyrs were lay, one of the most renowned being the Gallic woman Blandina (Eusebius, *H.E.* 5.1.17).

Every Christian was called to become perfect (Matt. 5:48) and to obey all the precepts of the Sermon on the Mount. Far from encouraging the laity to resign themselves to an inferior status, as being the normal condition of one not a monk, the Greek fathers endeavored to broaden the dimensions of the generosity of the faithful to include the example of the monks. John Chrysostom states paradoxically: "The holy scriptures want all to lead the life of monks, even if they are married" (*Oppugn.* 3.15). This definition of the layperson as a "monk in the world" is based upon the Christian virtues that the laity were obliged to practice. For example, the laywoman Martha (d. 551), mother of Symeon Stylites the Younger, carried out extensive charitable work in her native city of Edessa in Syria.

The church fathers in their preaching make frequent pronouncements about the role of the laity, to the effect that the clergy alone cannot carry the burden, and that many apostolic works cannot be carried on without the laity's help. *See also* Clergy; Priesthood.

[M.A.S.]

Bibliography

P. Dabin, *La Sacerdoce royale des fidèles* (Brussels: L'Edition Universelle, 1950); Y. Congar, *Lay People in the Church* (Westminster: Newman, 1957); G.H. Williams, "The Role of the Layman in the Ancient Church," *Greek and Byzantine Studies* 1 (1958):9–42; L. Ryan, "Patristic Teaching on the Priesthood of the Faithful," *ITQ* 29 (1962):25–51; W.H.C. Frend, "The Church of the Roman Empire 313–600," *The Layman in Christian History*, ed. S.C. Neill and H.-R. Weber (Philadelphia: Westminster, 1963), pp. 57–87; J.L. Garrett, Jr., "The Pre-Cyprianic Doctrine of the Priesthood of All Christians," *Continuity and Discontinuity in Church History*, ed. F.F. Church and T. George (Leiden: Brill, 1979), pp. 45–61; A. Faivre, "The Laity in the First Centuries: Issues Revealed by Historical Research," *Lumen Vitae* 42 (1987):129–139; L. Doohan, *The Laity: A Bibliography* (Wilmington: Glazier, 1987); J.L. Garrett, "The Priesthood of All Christians: From Cyprian to John Chrysostom," *Southwestern Journal of Theology* 30 (1988):22–33.

LAODICEA. Along with Hierapolis and Colossae, one of the triple cities of the Lycus Valley in the Roman province of Asia in the first century (Col. 4:13; Rev. 3:14–22), in the province of Phrygia Pacatiana in the fourth century. The letter referred to in Colossians 4:15–16 may have been Ephesians, which epistle was known by Marcionites as Laodiceans (Tertullian, *Marc.* 5.17; cf. *Can. Mur.* 64). A Latin apocryphal *Epistle to the Laodiceans* of uncertain date survives. Sixty canons associated with a council of Laodicea of uncertain date in the late fourth century became a part of the early collections of canon law. They cover a wide variety of subjects—various heresies, liturgy, marriage, and church order. The sixtieth canon, which may be later than the others, lists the books of the Old Testament (without the Apocrypha except for Baruch and the Epistle of Jeremiah) and New Testament (omitting Revelation).

[E.F.]

Bibliography

C.J. Hemer, *The Letters to the Seven Churches of Asia in Their Local Setting* (Sheffield: JSOT, 1986), pp. 178–209.

B.F. Westcott, *A General Survey of the History of the Canon of the New Testament* (London: Macmillan, 1875), pp. 427–435; J.B. Lightfoot, *St. Paul's Epistles to the Colossians and to Philemon* (London: Macmillan, 1879), pp. 1–72, 274–300; NTA, Vol. 2, pp. 128–132.

C.J. Hefele and H. Leclercq, *Histoire des conciles* (Paris: Letouzey et Ané, 1907), Vol. 1, pp. 989–1028; H.R. Percival, tr., NPNF, 2nd ser. (1899), Vol. 14, pp. 123–160.

LATERAN. Constantinian church in Rome, on the site of the palace of the Laterani family, which was the episcopal seat and residence of the popes from the fourth to the fourteenth centuries. The only early Christian buildings in the Lateran complex (which consists of several medieval and later structures) are the rectangular basilica (246 feet long, 180 feet wide) and the octagonal baptistery, both situated on the eastern rise of the Caelian Hill in the southeast part of ancient Rome. The nucleus of the whole complex, the basilica, was built on land given to the church by Constantine. The exact date on which construction was begun is not known, but on the evidence of the Constantinian foundation walls, some of which are still in place, 313 is a reasonable *terminus a quo*. The construction of the building may have

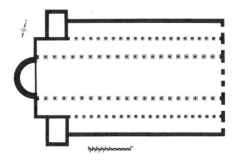

Lateran basilica, Rome, Italy.
(Plan by G. T. Armstrong.)

extended over a period of from one to five centuries.

The nave of the church ran east and west and was flanked by two aisles on either side. Four rows of twenty columns each supported the superstructure. A large apse terminated the nave to the west, and the so-called fastigium (fastidium) of *Liber Pontificalis* 34 (Duchesne 1.172, Sylvester, 314–325) is said to have extended across the apse opening. The exterior of the building was plain, but its interior, decorated with colored marbles and precious metals, must have been jewellike. The baptistery, also begun by Constantine, lies adjacent to the basilica on its southwest. *See also* Basilica.

[P.C.F.]

Bibliography

M. Teasdale Smith, "The Lateran Fastigium, a Gift of Constantine the Great," *RAC* 46 (1970):149–175; R. Krautheimer, S. Corbett, and A.K. Frazer, *Corpus Basilicarum Christianarum Romae* (Vatican City: Pontificio Istituto di Archeologia Cristiana, 1977), Vol. 5, pp. 1–92; R. Krautheimer, *Early Christian and Byzantine Architecture*, 3rd ed. (Harmondsworth: Penguin, 1981), pp. 46ff., 94 (baptistery).

LATOURETTE, KENNETH SCOTT

(1884–1968). Historian of Christian missions. Latourette received a B.S. degree in chemistry from Linfield College in 1904, and the B.A., M.A., and Ph.D. degrees in history from Yale. After holding teaching positions in the Yale in China program at Changsha, China, and at Reed College, and a chaplaincy at Denison University, he was named the D. Willis James Professor of Missions at Yale in 1921. He was appointed professor of missions and oriental history in 1925 and a Sterling Professor in 1949. Latourette retired from Yale in 1951 and taught at Union Theological Seminary in New York from 1955 to 1964.

Although the majority of his books deal with the Far East, many of them with Christian missions there, his classic work is *A History of the Expansion of Christianity* (7 vols.; New York: Harper, 1937–1945). The first volume, *The First Five Centuries* (1937), although dated, remains a helpful guide, being well written and relying heavily on ancient sources. The second volume, *The Thousand Years of Uncertainty* (1938), indicates its Protestant viewpoint. The first six chapters are concerned with the spread of Christianity up to the rise of Islam. Latourette's interest in the global expansion of Christianity led him to deal with the mission history of eastern churches as well as those in the west, an all too rare accomplishment in his time. The remaining volumes continue the history of missions to the modern era.

[F.W.N.]

Bibliography

K.S. Latourette, "The Christian Understanding of History," *American Historical Review* 54 (1949):259–276; W.C. Harr, ed., *Frontiers of the Christian World Mission Since 1938: Essays in Honor of Kenneth Scott Latourette* (New York: Harper, 1962); K.S. Latourette, *Beyond the Ranges: An Autobiography* (Grand Rapids: Eerdmans, 1967).

LAURA (LAVRA). Individual monastic cells grouped around a central opening (Greek, "lane" or "alley"). In this arrangement, monks could live together either as hermits or as a community, hold common services, and allow novices to enter training. Hermits could be in solitude without cooked meals or contact with others for five days and then receive warm meals and fellowship for two days.

The first laura apparently was started in 328–335 by Chariton; it was located at Fara, about four miles northwest of Jerusalem. He founded another later at Douka in present-day Jordan. During the next two centuries, lauras were formed in Palestine by Euthymius the Great (d. 473), Gerasimus (d. 475), and Saba (d. 532). By the end of the seventh century, approximately twenty of the 130 monasteries in Palestine were lauras.

John Moschus in his *Pratum Spirituale* records a number of anecdotes about life in the lauras of the early seventh century. The system spread to Arabia, Egypt, Syria, and elsewhere. The Great Laura at Mt. Athos in Greece once was operated in this fashion, although it now functions as a communal monastery with no facilities for hermits. Saba's Laura still exists at Mar Saba in Israel. *See also* Monasticism.

[F.W.N.]

St. Lawrence, mosaic from the Mausoleum of Galla Placidia (fifth century), Ravenna, Italy.
(Photograph Editore Dante, Ravenna.)

Bibliography

D.J. Chitty, *The Desert a City: An Introduction to the Study of Egyptian and Palestinian Monasticism Under the Christian Empire* (Oxford: Blackwell, 1966).

LAVABO. Washing of the celebrant's fingers after the presentation of the offertory gifts of bread and wine in the liturgy (from the Latin, "I will wash"). This action, which at first had the practical purpose of cleansing the hands of the celebrant after he had received diverse gifts from the congregation, was originally performed in silence. Later, Psalm 26:6–12 was appointed for recitation; *Lavabo,* the initial word of the selection from the Psalm in the Latin Vulgate, was thus employed to designate the action. In the revised Roman liturgy (1969), the prayer was replaced by Psalm 51:4.   [M.P.McH.]

Bibliography

J.A. Jungmann, *The Mass of the Roman Rite: Its Origins and Development (Missarum Sollemnia)* (New York: Benziger, 1955), Vol. 2, pp. 76–82.

LAWRENCE (d. 258). Roman deacon and martyr. Lawrence suffered martyrdom, probably by beheading, under the emperor Valerian (253–260) several days after the Roman bishop Sixtus II (257–258). Little is known of his life; as a deacon, he would have been associated with Sixtus in almsgiving. The well-known legend that he was roasted to death on a gridiron because, upon being requested to surrender the wealth of the church, he presented a crowd of the poor and disabled, is without merit. Devotion to him spread throughout the west from the fourth century, his name being included in the canon of the Roman Mass. It was promoted by Ambrose and Prudentius among others, and he was portrayed on the mosaics of the mausoleum of Galla Placidia in Ravenna. Churches were dedicated to him in Rome. The church built (ca. 330) above his tomb in a catacomb was an object of pilgrimage; under Pelagius II (579–590), it was expanded into the basilica of St. Lawrence-Outside-the-Walls (S. Lorenzo fuori le Mura). Bede (*H.E.* 3.29) reports that pope Vitalian (657–672) sent relics of Lawrence and other saints to Oswy, the

Saxon king of Northumbria. In art, Lawrence is depicted with the gridiron and sometimes with the purse of almsgiving. Feast day August 10. [M.P.McH.]

Bibliography

Ambrose, *On the Duties of the Clergy* 1.41.204–206; 2.28.140–141; idem, *Letter* 37.36–37; Prudentius, *Crowns of Martyrdom* 2.

L. Huetter, *S. Lorenzo in Lucina* (Rome: Danesi, 1931); H. Delehaye, "Recherches sur le légendier romain," *AB* 51 (1933):34–98; V.L. Kennedy, *The Saints of the Canon of the Mass* (Vatican City: Pontificio Istituto di Archeologia Cristiana, 1938), pp. 124–128; W. Frankl et al., "Le esplorazioni nella basilica di S. Lorenzo nell' Agro Verano," *RAC* 26 (1950):9–48; R. Krautheimer et al., *Corpus Basilicarum Christianarum Romae* (Vatican City: Pontificio Istituto di Archeologia Cristiana, 1962), Vol. 2, pp. 1–146; W. McCarthy, "Prudentius, Peristephanon 2: Vapor and the Martyrdom of Lawrence," *VChr* 36 (1982):282–286; M.T. Tavormina, "A Liturgical Allusion in the *Scottish Legendary*: The Largesse of Saint Lawrence," *Notes and Queries* n.s. 33 (1986):154–157.

LAYING ON OF HANDS. Placing the hand or hands on another's head in blessing. Although the gesture of laying on of hands was known in the Greco-Roman world, the Jewish usage provided the background for the Christian act. The Hebrew word *samakh* ("to lean upon") is used in the Old Testament for a worshiper on an animal brought for sacrifice (Leviticus), for witnesses on the blasphemer who is to be stoned (Lev. 24:14), for the people in consecrating the Levites (Num. 8:10), and for Moses on Joshua in appointing him his successor (Num. 27:15ff.; Deut. 34:9). This gesture signified a transfer from one to another or the creating of a substitute. Other words, *shith* and *sim* ("to put or place" [the hands]), are used in the bestowal of the patriarchal blessings (Gen. 48:14ff.). In postbiblical Judaism, "laying on of hands" could be used for blessing (*Jubilees* 25) and for healing (*samakh—Genesis Apocryphon* 20.22, 29). From *samakh* derived the noun *semikah*, which became the technical term for the ordination of rabbis. Rabbis in the period after A.D. 70 ordained their students by an imposition of hands as successors in the role of religious judges.

In the New Testament, the gesture of laying on of hands occurs in a simple benediction (Mark 10:13–16), in healings (Mark 5:23; 6:5; Acts 28:8), in appointments to church office (Acts 6:6; 13:3), and in conferring the Holy Spirit (Acts 8:14–24). Early church literature provides further testimony to the use of laying on of hands: in benedictions (*A. Jo.* 46; Clement of Alexandria, *Paed.* 3.11), in healings (*A. Petr.* 20; Ps.-Clement, *Hom.* 8.24; 9.23), in the reconciliation of penitents (Cyprian, *Ep.* 19.2; 74.1), in ordination (*A. Petr.* 10; *Trad. ap.* 2.3, 5; 8.1; 9.1), and at various points in the baptismal ceremony—in the prebaptismal exorcism, at the baptismal confession of faith, in the actual immersing, and at the postbaptismal blessing and anointing (*Trad. ap.* 20.8; 21.12, 14; 22.1, 2). The postbaptismal imposition of hands was identified by Tertullian with the gift of the Holy Spirit to the baptized (*Bapt.* 8; *Res.* 9). This was the starting point for the separation of confirmation from baptism as a distinct sacrament in the western church. References to the imposition of hands in the reconciliation of heretics are disputed as to whether the meaning was penance or confirmation.

The idea that unites all these occasions for the laying on of hands is the bestowal of a blessing, whether of a general prayer of benediction, the special blessing of health, the forgiveness and readmission to the fellowship of the church, the divine favor and human recognition manifest in accession to ministry, or the specific blessing of the bestowal of the Holy Spirit. Several considerations show that the underlying idea was the petition for divine blessing. Laying on of hands in Christian usage was normally associated with prayer. The accompanying prayer is expressly mentioned in several of the above references; in addition, the laying on of hands is interpreted in terms of prayer in the reconciliation of penitents (*Didas.* 10; Augustine, *Bapt.* 3.16.21), in confirmation (Ps.-Cyprian, *Rebap.* 3–4; Tertullian, *Bapt.* 9), in ordination (Theodoret, *H.E.* 4.23), in healing (Origen, *Lev.* 2.4, cites James 5:14 as "laying on of hands" instead of "pray" as in the text), and in connection with baptism (*Didas.* 9). The prayer explained the kind of blessing intended, even as the laying on of hands made specific the person for whom the divine favor was asked.

Syriac, which was Christian Aramaic, a language closely related to Hebrew, provides a significant argument for the linguistic background of Christian usage. The Syriac translation of the New Testament regularly uses the equivalent of the Hebrew *sim* for the laying on of hands and so points to the blessing background for the Christian understanding of the act.

Early Christian art provides a further argument for the Christian understanding of the laying on of hands. Biblical texts that use the verb "bless" are depicted with a laying on of hands, even where this gesture is not mentioned in the Bible. For example, Isaac's blessing of Jacob (Gen. 27:26–30) is portrayed in the mosaics of Sta. Maria Maggiore in Rome with Isaac's right hand on Jacob's head. Jesus' multiplying of the loaves and fish (Matt. 14:29 and parallels) was regularly shown on Christian sarcophagi with Jesus placing one hand on the bread and the other on the fish. The multiplication of bread and fish is the only scene in early Christian art in which the laying on of hands is applied to inanimate objects. Hands were placed on the bread during the eucharistic prayer (Hippolytus, *Trad. ap.* 4; cf. the scene in the Catacomb of St. Callistus of a person with hand extended to a fish on a tripod while another figure stands by with hands uplifted in prayer).

The association of the laying on of hands with the Holy Spirit, as in the postbaptismal rite and in the petition for the Holy Spirit in ordination, led to viewing this gift as the primary meaning of the laying on of hands. Accordingly, Gregory of Nazianzus spoke of the dying Basil, who "by ordaining the most excellent of his attendants, bestowed upon them both his hand and the Spirit" (*Or.* 43.78). This appears to have been a secondary development by which one specific application of the gesture overshadowed the underlying significance. *See also* Anointing; Baptism; Confirmation; Eucharist; Healing; Holy Spirit; Ordination; Penance; Prayer.   [E.F.]

Bibliography

J. Behm, *Die Handauflegung im Urchristentum nach Verwendung, Herkunft, und Bedeutung* (Leipzig: Deichert, 1911); J. Coppens, *L'Imposition des mains et les rites connexes dans le Nouveau Testament et dans l'église ancienne* (Paris: Gabalda, 1925); L. de Bruyne, "L'Imposition des mains dans l'art chrétien ancien," *RAC* 20 (1943):113–278; D. Daube, *The New Testament and Rabbinic Judaism* (London: Athlone, 1956), pp. 244–246; J. MacDonald, "Imposition of Hands in the Letters of Innocent I," *SP* 2 (1957):49–53; J.K. Parratt, "The Laying On of Hands in the New Testament: A Re-examination in the Light of the Hebrew Terminology," *Expository Times* 80 (1969):210–214; E. Ferguson, "Laying On of Hands: Its Significance in Ordination," *JThS* n.s. 26 (1975):1–12.

LEANDER OF SEVILLE (ca. 540–ca. 600).

Archbishop and writer. The elder brother of Isidore of Seville, Leander traveled to Constantinople (ca. 582) either on church business or as an exile. There, he knew Gregory the Great, who later (595) dedicated to him the *Moralia,* or *Commentary on Job* (CPL 1708). As archbishop of Seville in Spain (from ca. 584), he effected the conversion from Arianism of Recared, king of the Visigoths (587), and shortly thereafter, at the third of the councils of Toledo (589), brought about the organization of the church in the Visigothic kingdom. At his death, he was succeeded in his see by Isidore. His extant writings are *On the Training of Nuns,* a work of asceticism dedicated to his sister, and *The Triumph of the Church,* a sermon delivered at the council in Toledo in which he expresses his joy at the end of religious disunity in Spain.   CPL 1183–1185.   [M.P.McH.]

Bibliography

Isidore of Seville, *De viris illustribus* 41.57–59; Gregory the Great, *Epistles* 1.43; 5.49; 9.121; idem, *Dialogues* 3.31.

Iberian Fathers, Vol. 1: *Writings of Martin of Braga, Paschasius of Dumium, Leander of Seville,* tr. C.W. Barlow, FOTC (1969), Vol. 62.

LECLERCQ, HENRI (1869–1945). Historian

of the early church. A monk of Solesmes, France, from 1895, Henri Leclercq was sent in 1896 to Farnborough Priory in England, where he began research projects in early Christian liturgy and archaeology with his superior, Dom Fernand Cabrol. Since his work required that he spend each day in the British Museum, Leclercq lived in London from 1908 on and was canonically released from his monastic vows in 1924. He was a self-taught polymath who collected sources and wrote on many historical subjects. Leclercq's main achievement was the *Dictionnaire d'archéologie chrétienne et de liturgie* (1903–1953), which he composed virtually singlehanded. His works are marred by prejudice and inaccuracy but remain valuable sources of information. [B.E.D.]

Bibliography

T. Klauser, *Henri Leclercq (1869–1945): Vom Autodidakten zum Kompilator grossen Stils* (Münster: Aschendorff, 1977).

LECTIONARY. Liturgical book that provides the scriptural readings necessary for the Mass or Divine Office. In the strict sense of the term, the lectionary is a volume containing *pericopes*, or lessons written out in full for the individual Masses or Offices in the liturgical year. However, other classes of books were also used for the readings in the Mass, and the historical development of the lectionary emerges through the study of all these books.

The lectionary was not required in the first four centuries of Christianity: the liturgical year had not yet been extensively developed, and the Bible alone was sufficient. Scriptures could be read continuously from one Mass to the next, or appropriate lessons could be selected for certain feasts through a process of improvisation.

By the fifth century, specific readings had been assigned to the feasts in the year, and there are references to Gallican lectionaries compiled by Musaeus of Marseilles and Claudianus Mamertus of Vienne in the middle of that century. Some scholars identify Musaeus's compilation with the earliest extant lectionary, a palimpsest from the beginning of the sixth century (Wolfenbüttel, Herzog August Bibliothek, codex Weissenburgensis 76). This document presents three lessons for each Mass: an Old Testament reading, an Epistle, and a Gospel. Three readings were used at Mass not only in the Gallican rite but also in other ancient rites and apparently even in Rome until the first reading was dropped in the sixth century. Lectionaries comparable with the Wolfenbüttel palimpsest, with *pericopes* for all the readings in each Mass, were not regularly used in the Roman rite until a few centuries later.

The more common books from the early period fall into several classes: one consists of Bibles having marginal notes indicating the liturgical application of the individual passages, and a second consists of *capitularia*, which provide the opening and concluding phrases of the *pericopes* for each Mass in the liturgical year (normally starting with Christmas). A *capitulare* may list the Epistle readings alone (including Old Testament lessons), the Gospel readings alone, or both readings for each Mass. The Gospel *capitularia* are often found in lavish evangeliaries, together with the four Gospels and Eusebian canon tables, which indicate parallel passages among the Gospels. A third class consists of books containing the actual *pericopes* for each Mass. A book may contain *pericopes* for the Epistle alone (*liber comitis*) or for the Gospel alone (*evangelistarium*). The full lectionary, mentioned above, completes the list of possible books for the Mass readings.

The different types of Gospel *capitularia* of the Roman rite reflect the development of the liturgical year after 600. The Epistle *capitularia* also reflect this development, but the Epistle and Gospel *capitularia* developed somewhat independently. Although the earliest known form of each is found in a manuscript (Würzburg, Universitätsbibliothek, M. p. th. f. 62) from the early eighth century, the Epistle *capitulare* in this manuscript is less developed than the accompanying Gospel *capitulare*.

Lessons for the Office on certain feasts are found in some non-Roman Mass lectionaries. Lectionaries specifically for the Office are not extant before the ninth century. The Bible could be read in its entirety over the course of the year in the lessons at Matins, and it was necessary only to list the order in which the books of scripture were to be read.

Greek lectionary manuscripts provide an important witness to the text of the Bible. *See also* Epistle; Gospel. [J.B.]

Bibliography

W.H. Frere, *Studies in Early Roman Liturgy* (Oxford: Oxford UP, 1934, 1935), Vols. 2–3; T. Klauser, *Das römische Capitulare Evangeliorum* (Münster: Aschendorff, 1935).

E.C. Colwell and D.W. Riddle, *Prolegomena to the Study of the Lectionary Text of the Gospels* (Chicago: U of Chicago P, 1933); K. Gamber, *Codices Liturgici Latini Antiquiores* (Freiburg: Universitätsverlag, 1968), Vol. 1, pp. 170–180; Vol. 2, pp. 429–439, 446–491; C. Vogel, *Introduction aux sources de l'histoire du culte chrétien au moyen âge* (Spoleto: Centro Italiano di Studi sull' Alto Medioevo, 1975), pp. 239–328.

LECTOR. *See* Reader.

LENT. Forty-day fast period before Easter, "the feast of the feasts" of Christianity. Resurrection is the cornerstone and the very ethos of Christianity. In the words of Paul, "If Christ has not been risen then our preaching is in vain and your faith is in vain" (1 Cor. 15:14). Lent is not an end in itself. It was instituted as a means of penitential preparation as well as a period of preparation for baptism, which in the early church customarily took place on Easter Sunday. The word "Lent" comes from the Anglo-Saxon *lencten,* meaning "spring," and is associated with the season of Easter.

The tradition of the fast is an early one, but originally neither the duration nor the strictness of the fasting was definite. It seems that earliest Christians kept complete fasting, that is, complete abstention from food, for two days or forty hours, the time from the crucifixion to the resurrection, during which Christ was under the power of death (Irenaeus in Eusebius, *H.E.* 5.24.12). Voluntary fasting beyond this limit was called *superpositio.* The Easter fast was extended to one week sometime in the early third century (Dionysius of Alexandria, *Ep. Bas.,* PG 10.1278). It was further extended to forty days (Greek *tessarakastē,* Latin *quadragesima*) sometime between 300 and 325, as the fifth canon of the First Ecumenical Council of Nicaea (325) refers to it as an es-

tablished practice. Augustine (*Ep.* 55.28) and Jerome (*In Isa.* 58), both of the early fifth century, claim that the extension to forty days was introduced for the first time in the church during the persecutions of Galerius, Maximinus Daia, and Licinius (306–323) in accordance with the example of Moses (Exod. 34:28), Elijah (1 Kings 19:18), and Christ (Matt. 4:2). The Council of Laodicea, Canon 50 (ca. 365), expressly commanded its observance. The extension of fasting for forty days possibly had its origin in monastic communities. During the second part of the third century, there were ascetics who kept the forty-day fast before Easter. In the east, fasting was observed for seven weeks excluding Saturdays and Sundays; in the west, it was observed for six weeks excluding only Sundays, or actually for thirty-six days. To compensate for the four missing days, the western church in the seventh century moved the beginning of the fast to Ash Wednesday.

Observance of fasting, although not always uniform, meant abstention from flesh, fish, eggs, and dairy products. Epiphanius of Salamis (d. 403) and the *Apostolic Constitutions* 5.18 mandate the eating of bread, salt, water, and boiled vegetables only. Some Christians had only one light meal toward the end of the day. Fasting rules relaxed after the ninth century. The eastern church retains both the duration and the strictness of fasting of the early centuries. The fast was a period of penitence and spiritual preparation for the baptized Christians and a period of instruction for the catechumens, as the *Catecheses* of Cyril of Jerusalem (d. 386) indicate. Baptism of the catechumens took place on Easter Sunday followed by their first communion, thus exemplifying Paul's words "all of us who have been baptized into Christ Jesus were baptized into his death. We were buried therefore with him by baptism into death, so that as Christ was raised from the dead. . . we too might walk in newness of life" (Rom. 6:3–4). The feast of Easter celebrated, precisely, this newness of life. *See also* Fasting; Pasch. [D.J.S.]

Bibliography

H. Franke, *Lent and Easter: The Church's Spring* (Westminster: Newman, 1955); A. Schmemann,

Great Lent (Crestwood: St. Vladimir's Seminary, 1974).

LEO I (ca. 400–474). Eastern Roman emperor (457–474). Born in Thrace, Leo served as a military tribune prior to his accession. The first emperor to be crowned rather than simply acclaimed, he was placed on the throne through the efforts of Aspar, the commander of his guard of Goths. He eventually dismissed Aspar from military command (467), and later had him executed for conspiracy (471). He proceeded to rule in his own name with the help of the Isaurians, a people of Anatolia; his elder daughter, Ariadne, had been given in marriage (466) to an Isaurian chief who would succeed him as the emperor Zeno. His plan for a large naval expedition, under the command of his brother-in-law, Basiliscus, to dislodge Gaiseric and the Vandals from North Africa met with disaster (468). By refusing (468–469) to open market towns to the Huns, he effectively contributed to the dispersal of that people.

Almost immediately after his accession, Leo was called upon to decide the case of Timothy Aelurus, an adherent of the Monophysites, who became patriarch of Alexandria after his predecessor had been lynched by a mob. The response to the emperor's circular letter to metropolitan bishops and certain hermits was virtually unanimous in favor of upholding the decisions of the Council of Chalcedon (451) and refusing recognition to Timothy. Accordingly, the latter was banished from his see (460) despite the influence exerted in his behalf by Aspar. The responses of the bishops have been gathered in the codex Encyclius (458; CPG IV, 9089). A number of letters of pope Leo the Great to the emperor regarding the controversy are extant (CPG IV, 9078, 9081, 9089 [7], 9094, 9096, 9097, 9100), as well as one from Timothy (CPG IV, 9098; III, 5485). Later, the Monophysite sympathizer Peter the Fuller, who had usurped the see of Antioch, would be removed from it by imperial authority.

The emperor Leo supported the claims of Acacius, patriarch of Constantinople (472–489), to a status for his see equivalent to that of Rome, basing his position on a disciplinary decision of the Council of Chalcedon (CPG IV, 9015, 9018), against the position taken by the Roman bishop Simplicius. He was personally devoted to the pillar saints, such as Symeon Stylites and Daniel Stylites, and quite active in ecclesiastical legislation, issuing decrees against simony in episcopal elections and in favor of a strict Sunday observance among others. He also promoted the development of hospitals.   [M.P.McH.]

Bibliography

Evagrius, *Church History* 2; Procopius, *History of the Wars* 3.5.7–3.7.2; Anonymous, *Vita S. Danielis Stylitae*, ed. H. Delehaye, *AB* 32 (1913):121–229.

E.A. Thompson, *Romans and Barbarians: The Decline of the Western Empire* (Madison: U of Wisconsin P, 1982), pp. 223–226; G. Dagron, "Le Fils de Léon Ier (463): Témoignages concordants de l'hagiographie et de l'astrologie," *AB* 100 (1982):271–275.

LEO I, THE GREAT. Bishop of Rome (440–461). Little is known of Leo's life before his election to the bishopric of Rome. He was quite possibly of Tuscan origin. As an influential deacon of the Roman church, he assisted both of his predecessors in their administration of the Roman church and was in Gaul on a diplomatic mission for the imperial court when elected bishop.

Leo lived during times that were difficult politically, socially, and theologically. He vigorously advocated the primacy of the Roman bishop, opposed heresy in the west and east, sought to protect Rome from military invasion, and preached eloquently to the populace. When the Huns under Attila invaded Italy, Leo met Attila near Mantua and persuaded him to withdraw. In 455, Leo confronted the Vandal leader Gaiseric outside the city of Rome and managed to lessen the level of violence against the city and the people. Leo foreshadowed the increased role that later bishops would play in the life of Rome.

Leo was instrumental in pressing the claims of the bishop of Rome to primacy within the church. He asserted that as successors to the apostle Peter the bishops of Rome were given authority over all other bishops and that the voice of the Roman bishop was in effect the voice of Peter. Leo asserted his authority not only over bishops in Italy, but also those in Gaul, North Africa, Spain, and elsewhere in the west. Although he confirmed the doctrinal decisions of the Council of Chalcedon (451), he totally rejected Canon 28 of that council, which declared that the see of Constantinople should be recognized as having dignity equal to that of Rome.

Leo was a staunch opponent of heresy, denouncing in sermons and letters Manichaeans, Nestorians, Pelagians, Priscillianists, and the Monophysite Christology of Eutyches. It was in connection with the controversy over Eutyches's teaching that Leo achieved one of his most significant triumphs. In 449, Leo sent a letter, now known as the *Tome,* to Flavian, bishop of Constantinople, in opposition to Eutyches's declaration that the person of the incarnate Christ was composed of only one nature, the divine (hence, "Monophysitism"). Leo held, in concert with the traditional teaching of the western church, that Christ's one person had two natures, one divine and one human, so related that they were neither confused and mixed together nor absolutely separated from each other. That year, Leo's legates presented the *Tome* at a synod convened at Ephesus, but the assembled bishops rejected Leo's point of view and affirmed that of Eutyches. Leo denounced the synod as a *latrocinium* (a violent robbery) and pressed for a new council. In 451, the emperor convened the Fourth Ecumenical Council at Chalcedon. Leo did not attend, but his legates again presented the *Tome.* This time, the Council not only heard the letter read but acclaimed Leo's doctrine as the orthodox position. Leo's letter was a fundamental influence on the language of that section of the creed of Chalcedon dealing with the relationship of the human and divine natures within the one person of the incarnate Christ. For the western church, the Council of Chalcedon and the *Tome* essentially mark the end of Christological debate, with the exception of Spanish Adoptionism and some twelfth- and thirteenth-century controversies. For the eastern church, however, debate, dissension, and division on Christological topics continued for several centuries.

Leo's sermons and letters open a window on the lives of Christians in fifth-century Rome and elsewhere. Ninety-six sermons and 123 letters are accepted as genuine. The sermons, which span the entire cycle of the liturgical year, display a polished Latin style and address directly and eloquently the spiritual needs of the populace. In them, one can see Leo resolutely opposing astrology and customs derived from traditional Roman religious practices, as well as the dominant heresies of the day. The sermons delivered during Lent give insight into penitential practice and Leo's conception of the role of bishops in this. Leo was also concerned with liturgical matters, especially liturgical conformity among dioceses, but scholars debate his connection with the Leonine Sacramentary, a connection that is slight at best.

Leo's episcopate left a distinctive mark on the Roman church, which was strengthened by his administrative capabilities. His vigorous assertion of Petrine primacy over the universal church laid the foundation for later claims of papal supremacy, and his active opposition to heresy and equally active promotion of what he held to be orthodox doctrine, as witnessed especially in the *Tome,* provided an important theological legacy. His sermons reveal a bishop's deep concern for the needs of those Christians committed to his care, while his letters show his vigorous assertion of papal prerogatives. Leo stands as one of the most outstanding early bishops of Rome. Feast day November 10 (formerly April 11) (west), February 18 (east). CPL 1656–1661. *See also* Papacy.   [G.A.Z.]

Bibliography

Liber Pontificalis 47 (Duchesne 1.238–241).

Opera, ed. P. and H. Ballerini, PL 54–56; *Tractatus (=Sermones),* ed. A. Chavasse, CCSL (1973), Vols. 138–138A.

Select Letters and Sermons, tr. C.L. Feltoe, NPNF, 2nd ser. (1895), Vol. 12; *Letters,* tr. E. Hunt, FOTC (1957), Vol. 34.

T.G. Jalland, *The Life and Times of St. Leo the Great* (London: SPCK, and New York: Macmillan, 1941); W. Ullman, "Leo I and the Theory of Papal Primacy," *JThS* n.s. 11 (1960):25–51; A.S. McGrade, "Two Fifth-Century Conceptions of Papal Primacy," *Studies in Medieval and Renaissance History* (Lincoln: U of Nebraska P, 1970), Vol. 7, pp. 1–45; S.O. Horn, *Petrou Kathedra: Der Bischof von Rome und die Synoden von Ephesus (449) und Chalcedon* (Paderborn: Bonifatius, 1982).

LEONTIUS OF BYZANTIUM (d. ca. 543). Monk who defended Chalcedonian Christology. Although he clearly attacked Monophysite and Nestorian Christologies, Leontius remains a puzzle. Little is known of his early life, except that he had viewed Chalcedon through the interpretation of Diodore of Tarsus and Theodore of Mopsuestia but then changed his mind. Despite his claim not to have received much formal education, his work shows both dialectical and rhetorical skill.

Leontius apparently went to Palestine between 510 and 520 to live the monastic life. By 531, he was in Constantinople on a mission from a prominent monastery in Palestine. Evidently, he stayed there, living as a hermit and representing Palestinian, Chalcedonian causes at synods in 532 and 536. Soon after that, he returned to Palestine, but by 540 he was back in Constantinople.

The great question is Leontius's own theological stance. Some think that two works attributed to him, *Contra Monophysitas* and *Adversus Nestorianus*, were written by Leontius of Jerusalem. He defended Origenists but probably not the doctrines later condemned at the council in 553. What he encouraged was the value of speculation and the dangers of both absolutely divisive or unitive Christologies. He was a Dyophysite himself, at least one who insisted on the full manhood of Christ.

His work against Nestorians may contain the only Greek fragments of sixth-century Nestorians known to us. Thus, his efforts not only show his own prowess but also contain precious evidence of his opponents. He apparently wrote six treatises in Greek that have recently received a new edition. CPG III, 6813–6820.   [F.W.N.]

Bibliography
B.E. Daley, "Leontius of Byzantium: A Critical Edition of His Works, with Prolegomena" (Ph.D. diss., Oxford University, 1978); *Leontii Presbyteri Constantinopolitani Homiliae*, ed. C. Datema and P. Allen, CCSG (1987), Vol. 17.

M. Richard, "Léonce de Byzance était-il origéniste?," *Revue des études byzantines* 5 (1947):31–66; D.B. Evans, *Leontius of Byzantium: An Origenist Christology* (Washington, D.C.: Dumbarton Oaks, 1970); B.E. Daley, "The Origenism of Leontius of Byzantium," *JThS* n.s. 27 (1976):333–369;

L. Perrone, "Il 'Dialog contro gli aftartodoceti' di Leonzio di Bisanzio e Severo di Antiochia," *Cristianesimo nella Storia* 1 (1980):411–442; L. Abramowski, "Ein nestorianischen Traktat bei Leontius von Jerusalem," *Orientalia Christiana Analecta* 221 (1983):57–63; M. van Esbroeck, "La date et l'auteur du *De Sectis* attribué à Léonce de Byzance," *After Chalcedon: Studies in Theology and Church History Offered to Professor Albert van Roey for His Seventieth Birthday* (Leuven: Peeters, 1985), pp. 415–424.

LETTER OF THE CHURCHES OF LYONS AND VIENNE. Account of the persecution in Lyons in 177, written shortly after the event. The churches in Gaul wrote to their brothers in Asia and Phrygia, whence many of their members came, a letter preserved in Eusebius's *Church History* (5.1.3–5.3.3). Animosity against Christians among the populace provoked the authorities to take action. Pagan slaves, under threat of torture, accused their Christian owners of heinous crimes. Christians experienced cruel punishments in the amphitheater as part of the gladiatorial and wild beast contests. The letter provides a vivid account of the persecution and Christian reactions to it (from apostasy to heroic resistance) and includes material for a theology of martyrdom, according to which the glory of Christ is seen in the martyrs. *See also* Blandina.   [E.F.]

Bibliography
H. Musurillo, pp. xx–xxii, 62–85.

W.H.C. Frend, *Martyrdom and Persecution in the Early Church* (Oxford: Blackwell, 1965); T.D. Barnes, "Pre-Decian *Acta Martyrum*," *JThS* n.s. 19 (1968):517–519.

LIBER PONTIFICALIS. "Book of the Popes," a collection of the lives of the Roman bishops from Peter to Pius II (d. 1464). There were two editions of the original compilation, made in the sixth or seventh century. The work was begun perhaps under Hormisdas (514–523) or Boniface II (530–532). The first compiler may have belonged to the Roman clergy; the work was continued by various hands. Sources for the *Liber* include the *Liberian Catalogue,* itself a list of the Roman bishops down to Liberius (352–366) contained within a larger compila-

Amphitheater at Lyons, France, where Christians were martyred in A.D. 177.

tion made in the fourth century by the so-called Chronographer of 354, as well as Jerome's *Lives of Illustrious Men*. The accounts tend to be composed in stereotyped formulas; those in the earlier part of the work are mostly short. The earlier lives are the less reliable, intermingling the authentic with the spurious, but beginning with Anastasius II (496–498), they become more trustworthy. Used in the education of aspiring clergy in the church at Rome and as an administrative abstract and archival inventory of that church, the *Liber* became influential in the formation of medieval concepts of the papacy.   [M.P.McH.]

Bibliography

Le Liber Pontificalis, ed. L. Duchesne, 2 vols. (Paris: Thorin, 1886, 1892); repr. with third vol. of additions and corrections by C. Vogel (Paris: Boccard, 1955–1957).

The Book of the Popes, tr. L.R. Loomis (New York: Columbia UP, 1916); *Liber Pontificalis to 715 A.D.,* tr. R. Van Dam (Liverpool: Liverpool UP, 1989).

T.F.X. Noble, "A New Look at the *Liber Pontificalis,*" *Archivum Historiae Pontificiae* 23 (1985):347–358.

LIBERATUS (sixth century). Deacon at Carthage. About 560, Liberatus wrote *Breviarium causae Nestorianorum et Eutychianorum,* a history of the Christological controversies up to 553. He was a champion of the Three Chapters. CPL 865.   [E.F.]

LIBERIUS. Bishop of Rome (352–366). For refusing to accept the condemnation of Athanasius, the champion of the orthodox creed of Nicaea, Liberius was deposed (355) by the emperor Constantius, an adherent of Arianism. But after being brought to Milan and then banished to Thrace and later to Sirmium, he changed his position (357) and was allowed to reoccupy his see (358). His submission has been attributed to various factors, among them ill health and the rigors of exile. After the emperor's death (361), Liberius offered pardon (362) to a group of bishops who had participated in the Arian synod of Rimini (359) on condition that they adhere to the faith of Nicaea. He likewise required the eastern bishops who later sought his support to adhere to the

Nicene Creed (366). He built a basilica in Rome that would become Sta. Maria Maggiore, and consecrated Marcellina, sister of Ambrose, to a life of virginity.

Fragments of thirteen letters under his name are extant, including three addressed to Eusebius of Vercelli and four, cited by Hilary of Poitiers, to various eastern bishops. The latter group of letters figures in the debate over the precise nature of the formula to which he subscribed in exile, although their authenticity has been questioned. CPL 1628–1631.

[M.P.McH.]

Bibliography
Ammianus Marcellinus, *History* 15.7.6–10; Sozomen, *Church History* 4.11, 15; 6.10, 11; *Liber Pontificalis* 37 (Duchesne 1.207–210).

LIBYA. Modern Libya includes Roman Cyrenaica and Tripolitana. Cyrene was the capital of the province of Cyrenaica, which included the Pentapolis and Crete.

The Jews of Cyrene, who had earlier enjoyed the favor of both the Ptolemies and Romans, instigated an unsuccessful insurrection that spilled over into other Jewish communities of the east from 115 to 117 (Dio Cassius 68.32; Eusebius, *H.E.* 4.2).

New Testament writers reflect the activities of several Cyrenians in Palestine and Syria. Simon of Cyrene carried Jesus' cross (Mark 15:21 and parallels). On Pentecost, Jews from "the parts of Libya toward Cyrene" heard Peter's sermon (Acts 2:10). The dispute that led to Stephen's death began in a Cyrenian synagogue in Jerusalem (Acts 6:9). Christians from Cyrene were among the group who first evangelized the Greeks in Antioch (Acts 11:20), and Lucius of Cyrene was one of the prophets and teachers of the same church (Acts 13:1).

Few details of Christianity in Cyrenaica during the patristic period have survived. Certain fourth- and fifth-century fathers connected Sabellius originally with Libya, but this may simply be based on the prevalence of his teaching in Cyrenaica in the third century. Dionysius, bishop of Alexandria (247–264), is known to have concerned himself with Cyrenian Sabellianism. Canon 6 of the Coun-

cil of Nicaea affirmed an "ancient" custom that placed Libya and Pentapolis under the ecclesiastical jurisdiction of Alexandria. The Libyan bishops Secundus and Theonas were the first bishops to take up Arius's cause, and they never deserted him.

Synesius (ca. 370–ca. 414), the Neoplatonic philosopher who studied under Hypatia in Alexandria, so endeared himself to the Pentapolis for defending Cyrene from marauding tribes in 405–406 that he was elevated to bishop of Ptolemais in 410. In the Chalcedonian-Monophysite controversy of the sixth century, the Chalcedonian party held the upper hand in Cyrenaica. Although impressive archaeological remains testify to Christian vitality, especially in the sixth century, the expansion of Christianity was arrested when the Muslims gained control of Cyrenaica in 642.   [G.T.B.]

Bibliography
J.B. Ward-Perkins, "Christian Antiquities of the Cyrenaican Pentapolis," *Bulletin de la Société d'Archéologie Copte* 9 (1943):123–139; A. Rowe, *A History of Ancient Cyrenaica* (Cairo: Institut Français d'Archéologie Orientale, 1948); J.M. Reynolds and J.B. Ward-Perkins, eds., *Inscriptions of Roman Tripolitania* (Rome: British School, 1952); J.B. Ward-Perkins and R.G. Goodchild, "The Christian Antiquities of Tripolitania," *Archaeologia* 95 (1953):1–82; A.H.M. Jones, *Cities of the Eastern Roman Provinces*, 2nd ed. (Oxford: Clarendon, 1971), pp. 349–362; J.D. Fage, ed., *The Cambridge History of Africa* (Cambridge: Cambridge UP, 1978), Vol. 2, pp. 107–116, 140–147, 164–167, 197–209; E.A. Rosenbaum and J.B. Ward-Perkins, *Justinianic Mosaic Pavements in Cyrenaican Churches* (Rome: British School, 1980).

LICINIAN (sixth century). Bishop of Cartagena in Spain. Licinian wrote on various topics: baptism and chrism for infants, the incorporeality of human souls, and angels. Isidore of Seville knew Licinian's works. CPL 1097.

[F.W.N.]

LICINIUS (ca. 250–324). Eastern Roman emperor (308–324). A Dacian peasant who soldiered with the eastern emperor Galerius, Licinius had been named emperor of the west by Galerius at an imperial conference in 308.

But since Maxentius held Rome, Italy, and Africa, while Constantine acquired Gaul, Licinius was left with nothing but the eastern coast of the Adriatic. After Galerius's death in 311, Licinius married Constantine's sister Constantia at Milan before defending himself against Maximinus Daia, Galerius's nephew and successor, and seizing his territory. At Milan, Constantine and Licinius joined in publishing official letters to extend toleration to the Christian churches. (These are given in Greek by Eusebius, in Latin by Lactantius.) After tension and occasional military conflict arose between the two emperors, Licinius withdrew his concessions to the Christians and renewed the persecution (ca. 320). Eusebius lists the measures he took (*V.C.* 1.51–54). He forbade synods to meet, banished Christians of high rank from the imperial palaces, deprived them of rank and honor, imposed fines, and threatened death, while soldiers (as usual) had to sacrifice to the gods. In addition, he forbade church meetings except in the countryside and regulated worship and instruction by separating the sexes; he executed several bishops.

By 324, Constantine invaded his lands, and after serious defeats by land and sea Licinius surrendered. Eusebius of Nicomedia won from the victor a promise to spare his life, but Licinius was put to death a few months later. Constantine's council at Nicaea in 325 was meant partly to produce the unity not achieved during Licinius's persecution. On arriving, many bishops denounced one another for having collaborated with him; presumably, a main target was Eusebius of Nicomedia, who supported Arius as well.

Lactantius and Eusebius regarded him as a convert to Christianity. This seems unlikely, although his prohibition of councils may mean only that, like Constantine, he had little use for theological debates. He lacked Constantine's expert advisers and his talent for dealing with church affairs. [R.M.G.]

Bibliography

Lactantius, *Deaths of the Persecutors* 25; 32; 35–52; Eusebius, *Church History* 8.13.15; 8.15.17; 9.9–10; 10.5, 8–9.

LIGHTFOOT, JOSEPH BARBER (1828–1889). Anglican biblical scholar, patrologist, and bishop. Lightfoot studied and worked with B.F. Westcott and F.J.A. Hort at Cambridge and spent much of his life in that university. In 1879, he became bishop of Durham. Lightfoot's commentaries on the epistles of Paul are marked by historical insight and a thorough sense of classical context and patristic interpretation. His work *The Apostolic Fathers* (London: Macmillan, 1885–1890) was without peer in English-language scholarship and still contains much helpful information. [F.W.N.]

Bibliography

G.R. Eden and F.C. MacDonald, eds., *Lightfoot of Durham: Memories and Appreciations* (Cambridge: Cambridge UP, 1932).

LINUS. Bishop of Rome (d. ca. 80). According to tradition, Linus was the immediate successor of Peter in the Roman church. He was identified with the Linus of 2 Timothy 4:21, a disciple of Paul at Rome. Nothing is known of his life or career; an account of Peter's martyrdom ascribed to him is a sixth-century legend. [M.P.McH.]

Bibliography

Irenaeus, *Against Heresies* 3.3.3; Eusebius, *Church History* 3.2.1; 3.4.8; 3.13.1; 3.21.1; 5.6.1; *Liber Pontificalis* 2 (Duchesne 1.121).

LITANY. Religious procession and type of congregational prayer; from a Greek word meaning a public procession or act accompanied by supplication or prayer to God for a particular cause. It appears that litany was adopted as a form of religious ceremonial by Christians from Greek and Jewish antecedents, although its Christian content was quite different. The most famous Greek litanies were those of the Panathenaean and Eleusinian mysteries. The most characteristic Jewish litany is the procession of the priests with the ark of the covenant around Jericho (cf. Josh. 6; 2 Macc. 3:15–20; 10:16).

Christian liturgical processions emerged in the ante-Nicene era, but they became prominent only after Nicaea, when they were connected with the cross, the Gospel, the relics of saints, and, later, the holy icons. Practiced especially on occasions of natural disasters and wars, they were also incorporated into feasts in honor of the Lord, the Virgin Mary, and the saints. Evagrius records such a litany with the relic of the holy cross in Apamea in response to a fire that was miraculously stopped (*H.E.* 4.26). A similar litany on account of an earthquake during the reign of Theodosius II (408–450) led to the establishment of an annual litany in Byzantium on October 26. Mamertus of Vienne composed a litany in 467 as a consequence of another earthquake. One famous example is the "Sevenfold Litany" of Gregory the Great, written on the occasion of a pestilence in Rome; this came to be known as the Great Litany of St. Mark (Mansi 12.400).

The word "litany" also denotes a prayer of supplication incorporated into the celebration of the eucharist or any other sacrament, or indeed, into the office of daily prayer. Such a prayer takes the form of fixed petitions and short responses (e.g., *Kyrie eleison*) by the clergy and the people. These litanies, known in the eastern churches as "Petitions," "Additional Supplications," or "Fervent Supplications," originated in Antioch in the fourth century and were transmitted to the east and west after their adoption by the church of Constantinople. Modern liturgists have argued that the earliest litany of this kind in the west is the fifth-century "Supplication of Pope Gelasius" (492–496). Other examples are found in the Ambrosian and Mozarabic liturgical rites. *See also* Kyrie Eleison; Liturgy. [G.D.D.]

Bibliography

W.J. Grisbrooke, "Litany," *A Dictionary of Liturgy and Worship*, ed. J.G. Davies (London: SCM, 1972), pp. 215–216; C. Jones, G. Wainwright, and E. Yarnold, eds., *The Study of Liturgy* (London: SPCK, 1978).

LITURGY. Formal or public worship. "Liturgy" (Greek *leitourgia*) embraces service, freely given or obligatory, on behalf of the state, private sector, or a divinity. New Testament texts employ the word for the service of Christ (Heb.

8:6), and of Christians for others (Phil. 2:30). The field of meaning was extended to include the worship prescribed by the Mosaic Law in the Greek Old Testament and to Christian worship in Clement of Rome's comparison between cultic institutions of the old and new covenant (*1 Clem.* 40–41; 44). It is uncertain whether the application to the ministry of Christian leaders in the Acts of the Apostles 13:2 and *Didache* 15.1 includes cultic functions. Hippolytus uses it in this latter sense: a cleric (*kleros*) is qualified through ordination (*cheirotonia*) for the service of worship (*Trad. ap.* 10). In the church of the empire, liturgy was the eastern technical term for public worship; the western equivalent was *ministerium, officium,* or *munus.*

The earliest Christian community of Jerusalem participated in Jewish worship and followed the custom of other sectarian groups of holding private meetings. Under the conviction that God's promise had been realized in Jesus' glorification, Christian communal worship was charged with the expectation of the imminent coming of the kingdom. The definitive break with official Judaism, within three decades, and the establishment of the Christian churches in new cultural contexts, occasioned significant changes in the shape of the Christian worship. But the structure of synagogue services was observed: reading and exposition of scripture within the context of prayer and confession. Jewish psalms, hymns, songs, and prayers were adapted. Also the Jewish practice of morning and evening prayer was retained (Mark 1:35; 6:46; Luke 10:17), a custom that was highly esteemed in later generations. (Partial descriptions of communal worship are found in 1 Cor. 11:17ff.; Acts 2:42, 46; 5:42; 20:7ff.) Doxologies and closing formulas of letters are often precipitates of liturgical prayer. The link made on Christological grounds between the earthly and heavenly liturgy in the Epistle to the Hebrews and the Book of Revelation became a central theme in later liturgical prayer and the theology of worship.

The history of the origin, universal usage, and ritual of baptism in the earliest period remains obscure. New Testament evidence indicates the tendency toward the development of a uniform rite, probably determined by Jewish practices, such as proselyte baptism. New Testament sources do not provide sufficient data for a detailed description of the typical place, time, frequency, and procedure for the Christian communal meal. The general structure of a Jewish festive meal was retained, and the observance was grounded on a command of Jesus (Luke 22:19). A specific type of Jewish meal may have contributed significantly to the beginnings of a normative order. The Jewish thank-offering meal (*tōdah*) is suggested because it offers a striking analogy to the external shape of the second-century eucharist. The extent to which Christians borrowed from meals of other religious groups remains an open question.

Celebrated as a memorial of the Christ-event, this meal was animated by the experience of the risen Lord and the hope of his second coming. Initially, the accent may have been placed on Christ's resurrection; later, the death of the Lord (1 Cor. 11:26) became a prominent aspect of the celebration. Following the example of Jesus at the Last Supper, a solemn prayer was spoken over the bread and cup, shared as a way of realizing unity of the participants with Christ and one another (1 Cor. 10:16–17). Models of eucharistic prayer are not found in the New Testament. But internal evidence, confirmed by later use in the formulation of eucharistic prayers, indicates that Colossians 1:12–20 may be an adaptation of this liturgical source.

Unresolved problems exist regarding the process of reconciliation of sinners, as well as the procedure for installation of local leaders. References to a rite of laying on of hands and prayer (Acts 6:1–6; 13:1–3; 20:28; 1 Tim. 4:14; 5:22; 2 Tim. 1:6) suggest that a normative form of ordination existed at an early date. Attempts to relate this to a contemporary Jewish practice have been inconclusive.

The custom of assembling on the first day of the week for the celebration of the eucharist was widespread by the end of the first century, but not universal. Acts 20:7–11 may be the earliest witness to this practice, also recorded in an old pericope of the *Didache* (14.1). The annual Paschal feast has roots in New Testament communities, but the data are lacking for an accurate description of the meaning, time, and ordering of the celebration.

Second and Third Centuries. Forms of worship were developed by church leaders under the inspiration of the moment, and guided by the Gospels and apostolic letters. They were marked by simplicity and intelligibility and oriented to the second coming of Christ. The roles of liturgical ministers reflected the social structure of the community. These liturgies, despite minor differences, are remarkably similar, due in great part to the communication among local churches. Justin Martyr gives the first description of a Sunday service (*1 Apol.* 67). Saturday was generally considered a day of preparation for Sunday, as was to be the case later on in the east.

The annual Paschal feast was observed very early in Asia Minor and was probably introduced elsewhere after 135. The *Epistle of the Apostles* (130–140) supplies the first textual witness, and attributes the feast to a command of the Lord (15). The implication of the second-century Paschal controversy remain obscure. As observed by the Quartodecimans at the Jewish Passover, 14/15 Nisan, the feast was the memorial of Jesus' death; the Palestinian-Roman tradition celebrated Easter as the feast of Jesus' resurrection on Sunday. An important development took place in the third century. Under the influence of Origen, who was inspired by the baptismal theology of Paul (Rom. 6:1ff.), the Alexandrian tradition interpreted Easter as the feast of passage of the faithful from death to life. The order of the Paschal feast included a night vigil, with readings from scripture and a homily. The celebration of the eucharist toward morning signaled the transition to the joyful fifty days following.

Early descriptions of the rite of baptism are found in *Didache* 7.1–2 and Justin Martyr's *1 Apology* 61; the full western rite is in Hippolytus's *Apostolic Tradition* 15–21. The kernel of this latter liturgy includes the bath and interrogation of the faith, laying on of hands and prayer, anointing and the sign of the cross. The Syrian practice placed the anointing and laying on of hands before the bath (*Didas.* 3.2[6]; orthodox interpolations in the *A. Thom.* 25–27). Baptism was not administered only at a particular time. However, under the influence of Origen's interpretation of the Paschal feast, the Easter vigil became recognized as the proper occasion for Christian initiation.

In Greek-speaking communities of the second century, *eucharistia* was a technical term for the Lord's supper. It is employed in the letters of Ignatius of Antioch; Justin Martyr uses it for the eucharistic prayer as well as the elements of bread and wine (*Dial.* 41.1). At an unknown date, and for unknown reasons, the meal was dropped. However, the later Egyptian custom of linking a meal with the eucharist suggests that the more original practice of the first century was retained in some second-century churches.

Justin (*1 Apol.* 65; 67) gives the first detailed description of the assembly. Reading from the prophets and the Gospels and apostolic letters was followed by prayer over bread and wine and the ceremonial taking of the food and drink. The same procedure is found in the rite of *Apostolic Tradition* 4. Examples of eucharistic prayers of the ante-Nicene period are *Didache* 9–10, the older parts of the *Anaphora of Addai and Mari,* and the *Anaphora of St. Mark* (Strasbourg, gr. 254). The oldest available full text of a eucharistic prayer seems to be that of *Apostolic Tradition* 4. It constitutes a single act over the bread and wine. Attempts to trace the origin and development of these prayers back to specific Jewish types have not been completely successful.

The typical eucharistic prayer began with thankful praise for God's work in Christ, including the institution of the eucharist. This was linked often to an invocation (*epiklēsis*) for the coming of the Spirit (identified with the Logos), and occasionally the Logos is explicitly named. From this advent, the faithful expect to be made worthy to participate in Christ's body and blood. The earliest forms do not include an explicit petition for the sancti-

fication of the elements. These prayers concluded with various petitions: for the sanctification of the faithful, the eschatological gathering of the church, or the coming of the kingdom.

By this time, a rite of reconciliation of sinners with the church, applicable once, had been established. A laying on of hands with prayer by the leader(s) of the community was preceded by a period of public penance and followed by readmission to full participation in the eucharist.

The threefold hierarchical structure of bishop, presbyter, and deacon, attested in the letters of Ignatius of Antioch, existed everywhere at the end of the second century. The rites of ordination to these offices are given in *Apostolic Tradition* 2–3; 7–8. The only other third-century detailed account of ordination procedures is found in the Pseudo-Clementines, where the custom observed in Transjordan (ca. 220) is recorded (*Clem. Ep.*; *Hom.* 3.60–72).

The *Apostolic Tradition* describes a ritual of evening worship (25), and the custom of prayer in the morning (32), at the third, sixth, and ninth hours; before retiring; and at midnight (41). Tertullian also provides information about such practices, the forerunners of the later liturgy of the hours.

Fourth to Seventh Century. As local churches moved toward institutionalized centers, pluriformity of liturgies yielded to distinct types in the east. These were associated with Alexandria (Coptic), Jerusalem-Antioch (East and West Syrian), Cappadocia (Armenian), and Constantinople (Byzantine). The last represents a synthesis of the total spiritual heritage of the eastern churches. Although the western liturgical families are not so particularized as those of the east, a distinction can be made between local liturgical traditions: Roman, Milanese, Spanish, Gallican, North African, and Celtic. Three of the practices of the church of Jerusalem, a center of pilgrimage, became models for the worship of the church of the empire: the structure and organization of daily hours of prayer, the celebrations of feasts of the year, and Christian initiation.

In the east, the freedom to improvise was abandoned very early in favor of transmitted texts. But the inherited texts were soon expanded by the insertion of quotations from scripture, current theological insights, and additional prayers. Central rites were enriched by accidental accretions. As a result, the original simplicity and directness was lost. Corresponding western developments occurred at a slower pace. Restrictive legislation concerning the freedom to formulate liturgical prayers was enacted in North Africa at the end of the fourth and beginning of the fifth century (Council of Hippo, 393: confirmed by the *Breuiarium, can.* 21, of the Council of Carthage, 397; Council of Carthage, 407). Similar legislation, also aimed at securing purity of doctrinal expression, is found in Spanish councils of the next two centuries (councils of Gerunda, 517, and Toledo, 633).

The liturgy of daily prayer at fixed hours first begins to appear in this period. Here, the most significant contribution of monasticism to the liturgy was made. In the west, a gradual clericalization of daily communal prayer led to loss of its popularity with the common people, but analogous development in the east did not weaken lay participation in morning and evening prayer.

Sunday had become the official day of rest in the empire (321), intended for assembly in the church. At the same time, the number of annual feasts increased. The interpretation of Easter underwent some development. The Alexandrians, associating the feast with the passage of the faithful from death to life, linked it to the passage of Israel through the sea (Exod. 13–14) and played down the relation to the Jewish Passover. The typical Greek approach, while maintaining the interpretation of Origen, brought in the older tradition so that the connection with Exodus 12, the theology of the Passover lamb, was recovered. The Syrian churches, more conservative, followed the synoptic tradition. Here, Thursday and Friday of Holy Week were joined together. Friday was the Paschal feast, the memorial of the death of the Lord, the new Passover lamb. In the west, under the influence of Augustine, the concept of passage through passion came to the foreground. Thus, the passion of Jesus and that of Christians were held together as a single event.

Lent, the forty days before Easter, was given a structure that would long endure. Feasts of the Ascension (fortieth day after Easter) and Pentecost (fifty days after Easter) were established, along with Christmas (December 25) and Epiphany (January 6). The last, of eastern origin, was related initially to both the baptism and the birth of Jesus. Preceded by Advent, Christmas and Epiphany began to develop as the second great cycle of the church year. Annual memorial days of apostles, martyrs, and confessors, and of the *Theotokos*, were also introduced.

The baptismal catecheses of Cyril of Jerusalem, Theodore of Mopsuestia, and Ambrose, and the sermons of such bishops as John Chrysostom and Augustine, indicate that developments had taken place in the rite of Christian initiation. The ritual battle against Satan was especially amplified. In the environs of Antioch, in the sixth century, the indicative passive formula ("May the servant be baptized. . .") was substituted for the interrogation of the faith. The indicative active formula ("I baptize you. . .") was definitively established in the west in the eighth century.

In the east, the liturgy of the eucharist was expanded through the introduction of more elaborate rituals, such as the Great Entrance, and accretions to the communion rite. The eucharistic prayer now included an invocation for the sending of the Holy Spirit to sanctify the gifts of bread and wine, a consequence of the development of the theology of the divinity and personal mission of the Holy Spirit. The narrative of the institution of the eucharist was dealt with in a free way, various actions of the Lord being added as the basis for a ritual performance of the presiding minister. The accent shifted to some extent from the more original proclamation of the death of the Lord to a dramatic representation of this mystery. Examples of these prayers are the Byzantine anaphora of Basil the Great and the anaphoras of John Chrysostom and the Twelve Apostles, both of which derive from a fourth-century Greek source.

Western liturgies are more sober, with only minor additions made to earlier forms. The old Roman canon does not emphasize praise of God, and there is no epiclesis for the coming of the Holy Spirit. Attention is focused on the activity of the congregation and the gifts offered. The prayer conceives the celebration as involving a twofold movement: the presentation of the gifts, and their return. There is a solemn petition that the hallowing of the gifts of the community by God may cause them to become the sacrament of Christ's sacrifice.

There was little change in the rites of reconciliation of sinners and ordination. The first signs of a liturgical celebration of marriage are found at this time. The crowning (east), the veiling of the bride (*velatio*) at Rome, and the joining of hands are not specifically Christian. But there was added prayer by the church leader. Burial customs were an important element of the daily life of non-Christians and Christians. The latter borrowed local practices and to some extent Christianized them. The meal for the dead, despite the opposition of church leaders, continued in many places. Eventually, the eucharist was made to serve as a substitute.

Developments that took place in the church of the empire determined later practice. Traditional structures remained, although sometimes obscured by embellishments. As the church became reconciled to time, liturgy was no longer animated by the expectation of the imminent coming of the kingdom. Rather, the Christian experience became one of the power of the liturgy to communicate the grace of salvation here and now. *See also* Eucharist; Mass; Office, Divine.   [E.J.K.]

Bibliography

Didache 7; 9–10; 14; Justin Martyr, *I Apology* 61; 65; 67; Tertullian, *On Baptism*; Hippolytus, *Apostolic Tradition* 4; 15–21; Syriac *Didascalia; Leonine Sacramentary* (Rome); *Pilgrimage of Egeria*, and *Armenian* and *Georgian Lectionaries* (Jerusalem); *Apostolic Constitutions* (Antioch); *The Testament of Our Lord* (Syria).

J.S. Srawley, *The Early History of the Liturgy*, 2nd ed. (Cambridge: Cambridge UP, 1947); J. Daniélou, *The Bible and the Liturgy* (Notre Dame: Notre Dame UP, 1956); A. Baumstark, *Comparative Liturgy* (London: Mowbray, 1958); J.A. Jungmann, *The Early Liturgy to the Time of Gregory the Great* (Notre Dame: Notre Dame UP, 1959); L. Deiss, *Early Sources of the Liturgy* (London: Chapman, 1967); F. Hahn, *The Worship of the Early Church* (Philadelphia: Fortress, 1973); C. Vogel, *Introduction aux sources de l'histoire du culte chrétien au moyen âge*, ed. B. Botte (Spoleto: Centro Italiano di Studi sull' Alto Medioevo, 1975); C. Jones, G. Wainwright, and E. Yarnold, eds., *The Study of Liturgy* (New York: Oxford UP, 1978); T. Klausner, *A Short History of the Western Liturgy*, 2nd ed. (Oxford: Oxford UP, 1979); H. Wegman, *Christian Worship in East and West* (New York: Pueblo, 1985); H.-J. Schultz, *The Byzantine Liturgy* (New York: Pueblo, 1986); T.K. Carroll and T. Halton, *Liturgical Practice in the Fathers* (Wilmington: Glazier, 1988).

LOGOS. The Greek term *logos* is patient of many meanings and, depending on the context, can be translated in a seemingly infinite variety of ways: "speech," "discourse," "proclamation," "story," "reason," "rational principle," "logic," "commandment." For the theology of the early church, however, its most significant, and at the same time most problematic, rendering is as "word" or "Word," and it is as a pivotal term in the Prologue (Fore-"word") to the Fourth Gospel that *logos* was to become highly determinative for the development of Christian doctrine.

Gospel of John. Theologians of varying, and often competing, persuasions appealed to John 1:1–14 as the scriptural warrant for their views. Yet the precise meaning of *logos* in this text has been open to a wide spectrum of interpretations.

"In the beginning was the Word" clearly points to some kind of cosmic preexistence; "the Word was with God" suggests a divine relationship; "and the Word was God" (or, as the NEB translates, "what God was, the Word was") connotes divine status; "all things were made through him [the Word]" implies a specific function in the economy of creation; "the Word became flesh and dwelt among us" intimates a special relationship between Christ and humankind. Most of these assertions as to the status, function, and relationship of the Logos are sustained, nuanced, and further explicated in the subsequent chapters of John's Gospel (e.g., 1:15; 5:17–18; 8:58; 12:45; 14:7–11; 17:5); but never again after the Prologue, in the whole of the Johannine corpus, does the term "Logos" appear as a synonym for Christ (unless the "word of life" in 1 John 1:1 can be so construed; cf. Rev. 19:13). Rather, John's characteristic designation for Christ is "Son," and thus for God is "Father." The palpable difference between God/Word and Father/Son terminology posed difficulties for future theologians.

Jewish Background. It is impossible to determine with any accuracy the extent to which John's use of "Logos" was a conscious inheritance from Hebrew scriptures or a conscious (or unconscious) derivation from Hellenic philosophy. The first phrase of John's Gospel (*en arche*) certainly brings to mind the opening words of Genesis: "In the beginning. . . ." In this creation narrative, it is quite natural to think of God's "word" as the agent of creation: God "spoke" and the successive elements of the created order came into being (cf. Ps. 33:6–9). Important also, in the prophetic literature, is the relationship between God's word and the prophetic word. It is in fact God's word that is spoken *to* the prophet ("The word of the Lord came unto me. . .") as well as spoken *by* the prophet ("Thus says the Lord. . ."). Yet this is more than verbal communication among God, God's prophet, and God's people; God's word has a dynamic and substantive existence of its own: "[S]o shall my word be that goes forth from my mouth; it shall not return to me empty, but it shall accomplish that which I purpose, and prosper in the thing for which I sent it" (Isa. 55:11). God's word, then, as in the Fourth Gospel, preexists creation and, in bringing order out of chaos, is the agent of creation; it is a word operative in the human sphere, a word of revelation to be spoken and to be responded to; and it is a word that itself brings about the purpose for which it was originally articulated. No wonder that the early Christians would think of scripture itself as the "word of God"; and no wonder they would think of Christ, "the Word," as the divinely planned fulfillment of God's creative and redemptive plan, to which the whole of Hebrew scriptures, they believed, bore ample testimony.

It is within the Wisdom literature of the Old Testament, however, that even more striking parallels to the Prologue of John are to be found, especially in respect to preexistence and to creativity. But here, rather than *logos,* the term *sophia* ("wisdom") is used, and it is Proverbs 8:22, a text with a prolific exegetical history, that is most often cited: "The Lord created me [Sophia] at the beginning of his work, the first of his acts of old." Implicit in this sentence is the assertion that Sophia existed prior to the creation of the world (as the later Athanasians would argue), but it also implies that the Son (=Sophia) was a "creature" (as the Arians would argue). A few verses later (8:30), there is a description of a "delightful" relationship between God and Sophia that existed before the formation of the earth and the heavens. In the apocryphal Wisdom of Solomon, we find Logos and Sophia joined together as the agents of creation: "O God of my fathers and Lord of mercy, who has made all things by thy Logos and by thy Sophia has formed man. . . ." (9:1–2). The Jewish philosopher Philo of Alexandria used the concept of *logos* extensively in his interpretation of Judaism in terms of Greek philosophy. It is important to note, however, in spite of the many possible parallels, that in neither the Hebrew perception of the "word of God" nor in the understanding of Sophia in the world of Hellenized Judaism is there any indication of "incarnation." The key phrase, "and the Word became flesh," is a uniquely Christian concept (even though, interestingly, the word "incarnation" nowhere appears in the New Testament).

Greek Background. In pre-Christian Greek philosophy, especially among the Stoics, *logos* was a significant concept, the more so because of its later appropriation by Christian theologians. In this philosophical context, *logos* is perhaps better translated as "reason" than as "word," or, perhaps, as "rational principle." For most of these writers, the universe, both in its initial formation as well as in its subsequent evolution, was subject, as if to "natural law," to a rational (or logical) principle of governance, a predominant "power" upon which all things depend for their very existence. This rational principle, or *logos,* was accordingly perceived to have divine or semidivine attributes and on occasion was even denominated "God" (*theos*). Central to this subtle and often wondrously complex doctrine were three technical terms that were to become part of Christian theological discourse. (1) Human beings, like all of creation, are indwelt by the *logos* (or at least a portion of the *logos*), by token of which the *logos* was perceived to function in a seminal or germinal capacity. This was called the *logos spermatikos*. (2) As a dynamic rational principle, the *logos* had its distinct existence as an unspoken word or thought, existing in the mind of God but not yet uttered, a thought having as it were the potential for articulation. This was called the *logos endiathetos*. (3) Once the silent thought was expressed, however, it went out from the mind of God as a verbal emanation. This was called the *logos prophorikos*. (One cannot help but wonder if Ignatius of Antioch—no philosopher he!—had this latter in mind when he spoke of God revealing [expressing?] himself in "Jesus Christ, his Son, who is the *logos* proceeding from silence" [*Magn.* 8.1].)

The Apologists. These technical terms, and the concepts relating to them, were to find further elucidation at the hands of the major second-century Christian apologists, Theophilus of Antioch, Athenagoras, and especially Justin Martyr. The philosophical background just sketched, along with Hebrew and Christian scriptures, provided these apologists with a conceptual vocabulary by which they sought to identify Jesus Christ as *the* Logos. As such, their writings were to have a direct bearing upon the subsequent development of Trinitarian and Christological doctrine.

Theophilus describes the preexistence of the Logos in this way: "When God wished to make what he planned to make, he generated [*egennesen*] this Logos as the firstborn of all creation. He. . .generated the Logos and constantly converses with him. . . . [John's Gospel] shows that originally God was alone and the Logos was in him" (*Autol.* 2.22). The Logos's role in creation is also described, and with striking imagery drawn from Hebrew scriptures: "God, having his own Logos innate in his bowels, generated him together with his own

Sophia, vomiting him forth before everything else. He used the Logos as his servant in the things created by him, and through him he made all things" (2.10). For all the apparent dependence on John 1:1–3, it is strange (but hardly unique in this literature) that Sophia and Logos are said to have been generated as two separate beings; it is even more strange that, throughout the whole of Theophilus's treatise, John 1:14 is not once mentioned.

The *Legatio* of Athenagoras expresses similar as well as divergent views. In line with the traditional tenets of Hellenistic theology, Athenagoras defines God as "uncreated, eternal, invisible, impassible, incomprehensible, and infinite," yet he can be apprehended by mind (*nous*) and reason (*logos*) (*Leg.* 10.2). And it is through the Logos, which issues from God, that the universe is ruled. This Logos, Athenagoras goes on to say (combining some interesting philosophical categories), is the "Logos of the Father in ideal form and energizing power," through whom all things came into existence (10.2). United by the power of the Spirit, the Father and the Son dwell in each other mutually (cf. John 17:21). Here, we see intimations of Trinitarian thought, but as yet conceptually inchoate. Athenagoras does indeed speak of "God the Father, God the Son, and God the Holy Spirit," but for him, although these three are "one," they are at the same time diverse in rank (*taxis*) (10.5).

This implicit subordination of the Logos, and the Spirit, to God appears even more deliberately stated in the writings of Justin Martyr. For Justin, as for the other apologists, the Logos was certainly preexistent and was also God's agent of creation: "And [God's] Son, who alone is properly called Son, the Logos, who was also with him and was begotten before the works [of creation], when at first he created and arranged all things by him [the Logos], is called Christ" (*2 Apol.* 6). More than this, all human beings, whether Jew or Gentile, could and did participate in the Logos, since the Logos was from the beginning present in the whole of creation, and the extent to which these people lived in accordance with the Logos is the extent to which they could not inappropriately be called "Christians," even though by some they have been regarded as "atheists" (*1 Apol.* 46). (One is reminded of Gregory of Nazianzus's assertion in respect to the pre-Christian piety of the Maccabean martyrs: "The Word. . . did appear later at specific time, but it had been known earlier by those who were pure in heart" [*Or.* 15].) For this reason, then, Justin, as Clement of Alexandria was later to suggest, believed that the mythology and philosophy of the Greeks, as well as the writings of Moses and the prophets, pointed equally to the fulfillment of the gospel in Jesus Christ (*1 Apol.* 20–21). There is a difference, however; these "pre-Christian Christians" participated only partially in the Logos and, however well-spoken, only in proportion to the share they had in the *logos spermatikos* (*2 Apol.* 13), whereas it is only in Christ that the Logos in its fullness dwelt. Yet Justin was hardly precise in his explanation of the Logos, often to the point, one must admit, of being confusing. This remarkable sentence is but one of many such instances: "God begat before all creatures a Beginning, a certain rational power [proceeding] from himself, who by the Holy Spirit is called, now the 'Glory of the Lord,' now the 'Son,' again 'Sophia,' again an 'Angel,' then 'God,' and then 'Lord' and 'Logos'" (*Dial.* 61). Further, in spite of references to the Logos as deserving to be worshiped "as God and as Christ" (*Dial.* 63), the Logos for Justin was radically subordinated to God (the Father), "numerically distinct" (*Dial.* 62), and the one whom we worship "in second place" to God himself (*1 Apol.* 13).

Later Developments. The "Logos theology" of the apologists, then, was more speculative than consistently grounded in scripture, clearly eclectic in the resources upon which it drew, and not without its conceptual difficulties. For all these writers' insistence upon the preexistent Logos, its role in the "work" of creation, and its sure identity with Jesus Christ, the Logos apparently was for them an "intermediary" between God and the created order and therefore necessarily subordinate to the God from whom it "issued forth." The Logos theology prevailed over competing Monarchian

views in the third century; nevertheless, with its difficulties it was not sufficient to resolve the Trinitarian debates of the third and fourth centuries. In these debates, two pivotal questions were being asked: (1) To what extent, in spite of the occasional vocabulary of the apologists, can one equate the Logos with God (cf. John 1:1–"and the Word was God"), or at least assign to the Logos fully divine status or attributes? And (2) to what extent, given the scriptural and philosophical background, is the Logos the more appropriate term by which to designate Jesus Christ? Origen's masterly and sophisticated theology was quite specific in respect to both these questions: (1) The Logos is a "second God" (*Cels.* 5.39; cf. 6.61). And (2) although "Son" and "Logos" are equivalent terms, the Son is also the "very wisdom [Sophia] and Word [Logos] and Life of God" (*Princ.* 1.2.3–4). In its opposition to the apologists as well as to Origen (although its primary target was the radical subordination of Arius and his followers), the Council of Nicaea spoke definitively to this twofold set of issues. By declaring the Son to be "of one essence with the Father," the council posited the fully divine status of Jesus Christ, an assertion, it must be admitted, that was made more to exclude Arian views than to articulate a well-thought-out theological position on its own behalf. And, although the "Creed" that Eusebius of Caesarea presented initially to the Council spoke of Jesus both as "Word of God" and "only-begotten Son," the final form of the Symbol of Nicaea was content to speak of Jesus Christ simply as the "Son of God," as did the "Creed of the 150" at Constantinople in 381 and the Definition of Chalcedon in 451.

It is clear, then, that the theology of the apologists was ultimately to be found wanting. They, in their wisdom, had subordinated the Logos to God so as to preserve God's oneness, to distinguish God, that is, from all that was not God, including God's innate and articulated Logos. They could speak of the Logos's preexistence; they could refer to the Logos's role in creation; they could speak of the Logos's intimacy with God and indwelling of the created order; and they could identify the Logos with Jesus Christ. But they could not and did not refer unequivocally to the Logos as "God" or as "God incarnate" ("the Word made flesh"). The Nicaeans, on the other hand, largely for soteriological reasons, insisted on the full divinity of the Word that both "was with God" and "was God." In so doing, they created a "Trinity" of co-equal persons, each subsisting eternally in the one divine *ousia* ("substance"). This was clearly a radical shift of paradigm, one in which the "Father" was no longer exclusively "God" but one person in the divine Triad. If the God/Logos model was not without difficulties, the Father/Son model was now to encounter difficulties as well. If the apologists saw in the Logos the "articulation" of God, the framers of the Nicene Symbol saw the Word as the "embodiment" of God. There is a considerable difference, both philosophically and theologically. Some would see the difference as one between a "rational and impersonal" philosophy and a "metaphysical but personal" theology.

Accordingly, in the post-Nicene era, "Logos" was no longer used exclusively, or even predominantly, of Jesus; rather, it become one of many synonyms for Jesus, including such terms as Sophia or Power (*dynamis*). As the Trinitarian debates waned after Nicaea, "Logos" became an important but relatively short-lived Christological term, creating what some historians have referred to as the controversy between the *Logos/sarx* (Word/flesh) model of the Alexandrian school and the *Logos/anthropos* (Word/man) model of the Antiochenes. One example of the former will have to suffice. Apollinaris supported the Nicene assertion as to the Son's consubstantiality with the Father, but he was at the same time concerned to preserve the unity of Christ, the unity, that is, of the divine and human in the incarnate Logos (the second person of the Trinity). He suggested, therefore, that at the incarnation the human "mind" or "spirit" of Jesus was replaced by the Logos, the result being that the incarnate Lord (Son) was indeed one person but with a humanity limited to flesh (body) and soul, whereas his rational and therefore governing principle was the Logos. Not surprisingly, Gregory of Nazianzus, among others, pil-

loried Apollinaris's view as a "mindless" Christology, insisting that it is the *whole* of human nature that was assumed by the Word, including the mind ("where sin first entered in"), since only "that which is assumed can be saved" (*Ep.* 101; 202).

In subsequent generations, the Prologue to the Gospel of John remained the key text for most theologians, although they tended to interpret it, and the Gospel as a whole, through Nicene glasses. (Cyril of Alexandria's *Commentary on John* is perhaps the most glaring example of this.) Yet those who, by the middle of the fifth century, were to be called orthodox were firmly convinced that human beings could be saved neither by a "spoken word" nor by a "rational principle": rather, they proclaimed that salvation could be achieved only by a God (Father) who sent his only Son, that "whoever believes in him should not perish but have eternal life" (John 3:16). *See also* Christ, Christology; God; Incarnation; Monarchianism; Philo; Trinity.   [D.F.W.]

Bibliography

G.L. Prestige, *God in Patristic Thought* (London: SPCK, 1936); W. Kelber, *Die Logoslehre von Heraklit bis Origenes* (Stuttgart: Urachhaus, 1958, 1976); H.A. Wolfson, *The Philosophy of the Church Fathers*, 2nd ed. (Cambridge: Harvard UP, 1964); J. Daniélou, *Gospel Message and Hellenistic Culture* (Philadelphia: Westminster, 1973); A. Heron, "Logos, Image, Son: Some Models and Paradigms in Early Christology," *Creation, Christ, and Culture*, ed. R.W.A. McKinney (Edinburgh: T. and T. Clark, 1976), pp. 43–62; D.C. Trakatellis, *The Pre-existence of Christ in Justin Martyr* (Missoula: Scholars, 1976).

LONGINUS. Name given to the soldier who thrust his spear into the side of Jesus (John 19:34). Through confusion with the centurion who confessed Christ as Son of God (Mark 15:39), Longinus was made a Christian and then a martyr. Feast day March 15 (west), October 16 (east).   [E.F.]

Bibliography

Acts of Pilate 16.7.

R.J. Peebles, *The Legend of Longinus in Ecclesiastical Tradition and in English Literature and Its Connection with the Grail* (Bryn Mawr: Bryn Mawr College Monographs, 1911).

LORD'S PRAYER. Model prayer taught by Jesus to his disciples (Matt. 6:9–13; Luke 11:2–4). In Matthew, the Lord's prayer is included in the Sermon on the Mount; in Luke, it is given in answer to a request from the disciples and shows signs of modification for a later Gentile community. Despite similarity between the prayer and Jewish liturgical formulas, there is not sufficient evidence to argue against its Christian origin and character. The concluding doxology is reminiscent of acclamations in use at the time of Christ, although it is probably an interpolation added to Matthew's text in early times by Greek scribes.

At an early period, the Lord's prayer was translated into Greek from the original Aramaic. This facilitated its use for the rites of Christian initiation. A short time before their baptism, fourth-century catechumens received instructions on the Lord's prayer, the Creed, the Trinity, and the incarnation. Only baptized Christians were allowed to use the formula as a prayer. The *oratio fidelium* ("believer's prayer"), as Augustine called it, was also to be the *oratio quotidiana*, the prayer recited three times daily.

Although the practice is known to have begun earlier, the first witness to incorporation of the Lord's prayer into the eucharist is Cyril of Jerusalem in the fourth century (*Catech.* 23.11). It held a privileged place also in the liturgy of John Chrysostom. Augustine knew that it followed the breaking of the bread, immediately before the kiss of peace and communion, as in the Ambrosian liturgy and Mozarabic rite. Pope Gregory the Great (d. 604) directed that the Lord's prayer be recited immediately after the canon and before the *fractio* (breaking of the bread). In the celebration of Mass in the Roman Catholic church today, the prayer follows the eucharistic prayer and precedes the sign of peace. In other Christian celebrations of the Lord's supper or in communion services, the Lord's prayer is always granted a place of honor, according to the custom or form of the ritual.

With the development of western monasticism and the introduction of Latin into the liturgy, the Lord's prayer became known in that language. Lay brothers were allowed to substitute for the Divine Office the multiple recitation of the *Pater noster* ("Our Father"). This practice continued into the Middle Ages, when the prayer was universally said in Latin.

From earliest times, Christians have looked on this prayer as a model, taught by Jesus as a form or pattern of how his disciples were to pray and what requests they were to address to the heavenly Father. The importance accorded it is reflected in the commentaries on the text written by both Greek and Latin fathers of the church.

The earliest commentary on the prayer was that of Tertullian (ca. 198), who called it an "epitome of the whole gospel." Following Tertullian (his "master"), Cyprian (ca. 251) also wrote a treatise, in which he emphasized the "public and common" character of the prayer. Origen (ca. 233) applied allegory to each of the petitions of the prayer. In the fourth and fifth centuries, Jerome changed *quotidianum* ("daily") in Matthew to *supersubstantialem* ("supersubstantial," that is, supernatural), following Origen's interpretation.

Cyril of Jerusalem presented a brief commentary on the prayer in his catechetical lectures; Gregory of Nyssa devoted five sermons to it. Augustine, for whom it was the source of all other prayers, appealed to its teaching on more than one occasion but developed a major explanation of it in his commentary on the Sermon on the Mount (2.15–39). In the seventh century, Maximus Confessor added an important contribution to patristic literature on the prayer. Throughout the period of early Christianity, only the followers of Pelagius expressed dislike of this prayer, because its teaching stood in contradiction to theirs. Since they were perfect, they could pray only that *others* be forgiven.

From the fathers of the church, more than from any other source, a rich spiritual and theological doctrine has been developed out of the prayer. This doctrine can be summarized under three headings: simplicity, community, and mission. *See also* Prayer.   [A.C.]

Bibliography
Tertullian, *On Prayer*, tr. E.J. Daly, FOTC (1959), Vol. 40, pp. 157–188; Origen, *On Prayer*, tr. and ann. J.J. O'Meara, ACW (1954), Vol. 19, pp. 3–140;

Cyprian of Carthage, *On the Lord's Prayer*, tr. R.J. Deferrari, FOTC (1958), Vol. 36, pp. 127–159; Cyril of Jerusalem, *Catechetical Lectures* 7, tr. L.P. Mc-Cauley, FOTC (1963), Vol. 61, pp. 170–179; Gregory of Nyssa, *The Lord's Prayer*, tr. and ann. H.C. Graef, ACW (1954), Vol. 18, pp. 21–84; Augustine, *The Lord's Sermon on the Mount*, tr. J.J. Jepson, ACW (1948), Vol. 5, pp. 4–11, 103–127; Maximus Confessor, *Commentary on the Our Father*, tr. G.C. Berthold, CWS (1985), pp. 101–125.

F.H. Chase, *The Lord's Prayer in the Early Church* (Cambridge: Cambridge UP, 1891); J. Lowe, *The Interpretation of the Lord's Prayer* (Evanston: Seabury–Western Theological Seminary, 1955; exp. and rev. C.S.C. Williams, Oxford: Clarendon, 1962); R.E. Brown, "The Pater Noster as an Eschatological Prayer," *ThS* 22 (1961):175–208; H. vanden Bussche, *Understanding the Lord's Prayer* (New York: Sheed and Ward, 1963); R.L. Simpson, *The Interpretation of Prayer in the Early Church* (Philadelphia: Westminster, 1965); J. Jeremias, *The Prayers of Jesus* (Naperville: Allenson, 1967); T. Corbishley, *The Prayer of Jesus* (New York: Doubleday, 1977); J.J. Petuchowski and M. Brocke, eds., *The Lord's Prayer and the Jewish Liturgy* (New York: Seabury, 1978); L. Boff, *The Lord's Prayer* (Maryknoll: Orbis, 1983); M.-B. von Stritzky, *Studien zur Überlieferung und Interpretation des Vaterunsers in der frühchristlichen Literatur* (Münster: Aschendorff, 1989).

LORD'S SUPPER. *See* Eucharist.

LOVE. Supreme Christian virtue of willing and acting for the best of others in unity with God. Although it is wrong to reduce all Christian ethics, either in the New Testament or among the fathers, to the love command, there is no doubt that love is the supreme virtue, which unifies righteousness, obedience, faith, humility, and other values. The development of early Christian ethics shows different ways in which love was seen to unite all virtues and to join the believer to God. These may be summarized as the philosophy, community, preaching, and order of love.

New Testament. Love, as defined by the life, death, and teaching of Jesus of Nazareth, dominates the writings of the New Testament. The command to love God is joined by the command to love both neighbors and enemies. The four evangelists make different points. Mark contrasts the morality of love with exter-

nal acts of worship (12:28–34), Matthew takes love as the heart of the Law (22:34–40), Luke's good Samaritan underlines the need for practical expression (10:25–37), John finds in love a divine source of unity and the distinctive mark of the Christian disciple (13:34–35; 14:20–24).

For Paul, the supreme value is love; nothing has any value without it. His description of love recalls the life of Jesus. Love belongs to the new age and defines the realm of grace. Love is the power of the new creation by which the world is reconciled to God (2 Cor. 5:17). All is transitory, except for faith, hope, and love; of these, the greatest is love (1 Cor. 13). Love comes from God, who has wrought our whole salvation in a single act of love upon the cross. Paul lives by the faith of the Son of God, who, on the cross, loved him and gave himself for him. Believers are joined in the body of Christ by their varying gifts. None of these gifts can function and the body cannot exist without love. The Law is summed up in the command to love (Rom. 13:9). Yet Paul also sums up the Law as "thou shalt not covet" (Rom. 7:7), so there is a place in the ethics of the New Testament for more than one precept. Further, the love command is not an alternative to rules; rather, it goes beyond the rules without going against them.

John describes Jesus loving his own in the world and loving them to the end (John 13:1). He washes their feet and gives them a new Law that links their love to his: "Love as I have loved you." He is the pattern and cause of love, among those who love because he has first loved them. The prayer of Jesus, that all might be one, points to love as the substance of the divine unity. Jesus prays to the Father "that the love with which you have loved me may be in them and I in them" (John 17:26).

Early Writers. The themes of the New Testament are taken up and developed in the early period of Christian thought. In the apostolic fathers and the apologists, the love command is directed to the will rather than to the emotions, and the unique love of the only God points the way to perfection; love creates the Christian community and sin's failure to fulfill the command is overcome by the grace of divine love. Clement of Rome shows how the love command moves from indicative to imperative, "Let him that has love in Christ fulfill the commands of Christ" (*1 Clem.* 49), how it "joins us to God in its perfection, for it is great and wonderful and perfect beyond telling" (*1 Clem.* 50), and calls for love to heal the divided community and to cover a multitude of sins.

In the *Didache,* the "way of life" begins with the command to love (*Did.* 1). Justin Martyr (*Dial.* 93) claims the love command as the universal rational rule that shows the maturity of the Christian position. All righteousness and piety is brought together in one perfect command (*Dial.* 93). Love of neighbor includes every human being, every rational animal with similar feelings.

Irenaeus of Lyons proves the unity of God's saving history from the identity of the commands to love in Moses and Jesus, for Jesus did not take away from the Law but renewed it. The one God, who gave the one Law of love to Moses, gave it to the disciples of Jesus, who perfected it. "He who loves God is perfect both in this age and in that to come. . . . For we never cease from loving God but the more we shall gaze upon him, the more we shall love him" (*Haer.* 4.12.2).

Tertullian points to the unity, universality, and eternity of the command to love God (*Jud.* 2). God, who made the universe and rules the world, could not have given his Law to one race; it was given at the beginning to Adam and Eve and contained all the precepts of later laws: that we should love God and neighbor. Our first parents disobeyed this Law; all who receive the new Law become part of God's new people (*Jud.* 3). Tertullian also uses the love command to point to the one God of both testaments (*Marc.* 5.8).

Philosophy of Love: Clement of Alexandria. For Paul, the cross became the power and wisdom of God; by divine love, the new creation grows and all things work together for good. Clement of Alexandria developed the rationality of love as the principle that guides the good life and that leads to unity with God. Just as the Platonist strove toward the good by

which all else is known, so Clement unites the believer with God in love. For Clement as for Plato, likeness to God is the one end of moral activity and stretches from simple human acts to divine encounter. Clement stresses the contingency and perfection of love. In the *Instructor,* he gives a detailed account of right Christian behavior. Love is the heavenly food on which reason feeds. It bears all things and never fails; it is the staple diet of the kingdom of God (*Paed.* 2.1.5.3). It rejects the artificial and superfluous and brings true beauty in the place of pretense (3.1.3.1–2). The story of the good Samaritan shows how "love bursts out in good works" (*Q.d.s.* 28). Love of Christ, who is our nearest neighbor, leads to love of Christ's brethren and service to the needy; but rich people need our love too, for they need to be shown how their salvation is possible (*Q.d.s.* 3).

According to Clement, the perfection of love is evident from the way it brings all virtues together (*Str.* 2.9.45). Beyond this, it is the means of entering into God, "for the more a man loves God, the more closely he enters into God" (*Q.d.s.* 27), where he grows toward the divine perfection (*Q.d.s.* 38). Such love is free from passion and desire, for all has been fulfilled. The perfect Christian and true Gnostic (to be distinguished always, in Clement, from the heretical Gnostic) has anticipated hope by knowledge and "remains in the one unchanging disposition, knowing and loving; he will not try to be like beautiful things for he possesses beauty itself through love" (*Str.* 6.9.73.3). As Plato insists, like is known by like, so only those who love can see and know the God of love (7.11.67f.). Love is the one thing necessary for the philosopher who seeks after truth.

Clement's account of Christian perfection in *Miscellanies* 7 was without antecedent and influenced nearly all subsequent thinking about humankind and God. The true Gnostic is a person in love with God (7.11.67f.). Such a one anticipates the life of heaven so as to "feast on that clearest and purest insatiable vision which is granted to greatly loving souls." The person's whole life is a festival of praise, spent in declaring love for God in every activity and praying continuously with inner, unspoken attention (7.7.43.5).

Martyrdom is the supreme act of love and faithfulness. "Without hesitation, we call martyrdom perfection, not because someone has reached, as all must, the end of his life but because he has demonstrated the perfect work of love" (*Str.* 4.4.14.3). The martyr gladly and lovingly gives up human life, when the God whom the martyr loves asks for it (4.9.75.4). In death as in life, the perfect Christian is made one with God by love, being so assimilated to God as to become a third divine likeness.

Community of Love: Basil the Great. The same call to constant prayer and union with God in love is found in Basil the Great, but it is now the basis of life within a religious community rather than a private philosophic quest. The monk is a Christian soldier who takes the kingdom by storm, the athlete who strains every sinew, and the simple child who trusts. He knows that God has made us, like different parts of a body, so that we need the help of one another (*Reg. fus.* 7). The soul cannot leave unsatisfied its longing for God, for it is wounded with love (*Reg. fus.* 2.1). Every Christian, especially the monk, aims to be joined to God by love. This love is implanted in every soul at its creation, and, despite the damage of sin, grace leads the soul to perfect fellowship with God. Basil gives greater emphasis than earlier writers to the community of love. Whatever is done for the least of the brethren is done for their Lord (*Reg. fus.* 3). Love is the sure sign of the disciple of Christ who is a person of peace. Yet there can be times when one may grieve another for the other's good (*Moral.* 5). The monk loves the Lord with all his heart, mind, and strength (*Ep.* 23). When others hate him, he returns love for their hate (*Ep.* 43). Love never fails, and when it is subject to others, it can never suffer humiliation (*Ep.* 65).

The community that Basil defines is built on love and thus is natural for human beings: "Who does not know that man is a tame and sociable animal, and not a solitary and fierce one? For there is nothing so characteristic of our nature as to associate with one another, to need one another, and to love our kind" (*Reg.*

fus. 3). The unity of believers in the body of Christ is a unity of love. There will, however, be disputes, and there must be a way to settle them (*Reg. fus.* 49). Basil is less than confident that Christians will find the way of love and peace. He longs to restore the peace and love of the fathers (*Ep.* 70). In the beginning, the churches flourished because they were joined in faith and love into one body. Now, peace and unity are gone. Christians have become worse than animals, who at least know how to herd together. "But our most savage warfare is with our own people" (*Hom.* 30.78). Only a renewal of the Holy Spirit, who distributes gifts to the many members of the body, can restore the love that unites.

Preaching of Love: John Chrysostom. It was left to a great preacher to delineate most powerfully the supremacy of love. Unlike Clement and Basil, John Chrysostom was not concerned with a spiritual elite. He places the perfection of love within the reach of all Christians. He attributes the vitality and force of Paul, who is his chief source, to the supremacy that Paul gave to love (*Incomprehens.* 1). Every virtue springs from love (*Hom. in 1 Cor.* 33.9). "Virtue is born from love and love from virtue. They produce one another" (*Hom. in Eph.* 9.3). Miracles have brought many converts; but miracles were effective only because love broke open the way for them (*Hom. in Jo.* 72.4). The power of love transforms us into the likeness of God, whose love is seen in creation and redemption and in the providence that watches over us "with an infinite love, a love sincere, indestructible, unquenchable" (*Non desp.* 6). The sublimity of love is seen in Paul, who so loved that he "burnt brighter than any flame, for as iron when thrown into the fire becomes fire itself, so Paul animated by the fire of love became love itself" (*Laud. Paul.* 3). The power of love means that nothing can threaten those whom Christ loves. Their love is their constant theme and they pass on the flame (*Compunct.* 1.1.8). Love looks for no reward but to please God and by its works to proclaim the good news of his love.

According to Chrysostom, community is natural to human beings because a good Creator has made them that way. The order of the world requires that we live in communities and families, for the advantage of our neighbor coincides with our own. God has made chains of love to bind us together in many ways through mutual need and friendship (*Hom. in 1 Cor.* 34.4). Love is the life of the church. The preacher cares only for the holiness of his congregation, with whom he is bound by mutual love. As soon as he begins to preach, all weariness leaves him, for "neither sickness nor a thousand other obstacles would be able to separate me from your surrounding love" (*Terr. mot.*). John deplores disputes in the church and insists that unity is more important than liturgical details.

One dramatic episode provides Chrysostom with an opportunity to demonstrate the love of the church. Eutropius, who had been no friend of the church, fell from imperial favor and influence; in fear for his life, he took refuge in the sanctuary, where he clung to the column of the altar, while John preached on the text "Vanity of vanities, all is vanity." John defended the sanctuary of the church against those who thought that Eutropius should not benefit from the institution that he had, when in power, attacked. Now the opportunity had come to show both the power and the love of the church. The power was evident because her enemy had been brought low. Love was proved "in that she whom he attacked now holds her shield before him and takes him under her protecting wings. She makes him quite safe, forgets all resentment for past wrongs and lovingly receives him in her embrace" (*Eutrop.* 1.3).

John's enthusiasm shows in his call to perfection, which extends to every Christian and which rejects all mediocrity. "It is not enough that love should be sincere. It should be violent, hot, and boiling" (*Hom. in Rom.* 21.10). "The measure of love is that it never stops" (*Hom. in Phil.* 2.1). Love is never canceled by strenuous works of charity; these serve only to intensify the love from which they spring.

John had unbounded confidence in the power of love to transform moral failures, such as those who are fearful, violent, rude, wanton, or lustful. Love receives all such into her school and changes them by her power. "Love is the great teacher. She has the power to free men from error, to form their minds, to take them by the hand and lead them on to wisdom" (*Hom. in 1 Cor.* 33.8).

Order of Love: Augustine of Hippo. As in so many areas, Augustine's account of love, both more extensive and more rational than that given by other writers, draws together and provides a structure for earlier tendencies. Order is what brings us to God. Measure, form, and order are universal values. Righteousness in God does not vary, but in humans it varies and grows as they attain the order of right reason. Love is rational: "The lover. . .will find justice through this rule of life, that he shall with perfect readiness serve the God whom he loves, the highest good, wisdom and peace" (*Mor. eccl.* 24.44).

Augustine continues to move the readers of his *Confessions* by his sense of the immediacy of God. This intimacy permeates his other writings: "Following after God is the desire of happiness; reaching God is happiness itself. We follow after God by loving him" (*Mor. eccl.* 1.1). The love of God and neighbor includes all goodness (*Serm.* 350.2f.). The grace of God restores freedom to the captive will, and "the law of liberty is the law of charity" (*Ep.* 167.19). Christian life is built on the foundation of humility and the service of love.

Love is the universal and sufficient Christian virtue, "so that temperance is love keeping itself entire and incorrupt for the beloved, courage is love bearing everything gladly for the sake of the beloved, righteousness is love serving the beloved only, and prudence is love wisely discriminating between what helps and what hinders it" (*Mor. eccl.* 33.73). Love of human beings leads to love of God, which is a holy longing or desire. The world is a wilderness. "If you do not want to die in that desert from thirst, drink love" (*In epist. Ioh.* 7.1). Love is the weight that draws us to various levels of good. It is a necessity for life but can go wrong: "Are you told not to love anything? Not at all. If you are to love nothing you will be sluggish, dead, detestable, wretched. Love, but be careful what you love" (*In psalm.* 31.5). The order of love begins with love of the world, which is good, proceeds to love of self, then love of neighbor, and finally to love of God. Love of God is love of being and life, of truth and knowledge, and finally of love, for God "is that very love which links in the bond of holiness all the good angels and all the servants of God and joins us and them to one another in obedience to himself" (*Trin.* 8.12).

The church is the one Christ loving himself (*In epist. Ioh.* 10.3). Love is a uniting force that flows from Christ to his members. "The effect of his love is so to bind us to one another in mutual love that we become the body of which he is the head" (*In evang. Ioh.* 65.2). This love is most evident in monasticism. At the commencement of Augustine's monastic rule, the commands to love God and neighbor stand supreme. The command "Love and do what you will" has been misapplied in modern times. Augustine used it as an explanation of the severity of love and the exercise of contradictory attitudes. "Once for all, then, a short precept is given you: love and do what you will; if you are silent, be silent from love; if you cry out, cry out from love; if you correct, correct from love; if you spare, spare through love; let the root of love be within, nothing but good can come from this root" (*In epist. Ioh.* 7.8).

Love dominates early Christian ethics and permeates Christian philosophy, community, preaching, and law. All this rests on the scriptural basis that is found in Paul and John and the Sermon on the Mount. *See also* Agape; Ethics.   [E.O.]

Bibliography

A.D. Lindsay, *The Moral Teaching of Jesus* (London: Hodder and Stoughton, 1937); J. Burnaby, *Amor Dei: A Study of St. Augustine's Teaching on the Love of God as the Motive of Christian Life* (London: Hodder and Stoughton, 1938); M. Spanneut, *Tertullien et les premiers moralistes africains* (Gembloux: Duculot, 1969); V.P. Furnish, *The Love Command in the New Testament* (New York: Abingdon, 1972); E.F. Osborn, *Ethical Patterns in Early Christian Thought* (Cambridge: Cambridge UP, 1976); G. Strecker, "Strukturen einer neutestamentlichen Ethik," *ZThK* 75 (1978):117–146; W. Schrage, *Ethik des neuen Testaments* (Göttingen: Vanden-

hoeck & Ruprecht, 1982); idem, "Ethik IV, Neves Testament, " *TRE* (1982), Vol. 10, pp. 435–462; E.F. Osborn, "Ethik V, Alte Kirche," TRE (1982), Vol. 10, pp. 463–473; G. Strecker, *Die Bergpredigt* (Göttingen: Vandenhoeck & Ruprecht, 1984).

LUCIAN OF ANTIOCH (d. 312). Presbyter at Antioch, scholar, and martyr. Lucian edited a revised text of both the Septuagint and the Gospels. His Septuagint revision soon became the standard Old Testament text in Syria, Asia Minor, and Constantinople. His New Testament text is basic to what is known as the Textus Receptus, the text found in the bulk of Greek manuscripts.

Some early Arians, including Arius himself and Eusebius of Nicomedia, claimed that Lucian's teaching was fundamental to their doctrine. He thus is credited with subordinationist views of Christ.

Lucian, after much torture, was martyred in Nicomedia. Feast day January 7 (west), October 15 (east).   [F.W.N.]

Bibliography

Eusebius, *Church History* 8.13.2; 9.6.3; Jerome, *Lives of Illustrious Men* 77.

G. Bardy, *Recherches sur Lucien d'Antioche et son école* (Paris: Beauchesne, 1936).

LUCIAN OF SAMOSATA (ca. 115–200). Pagan Greek satirist. In *The Passing of Peregrinus,* Lucian describes the life of the title character, evidently a historical person who forsook paganism to become a Christian. Peregrinus went to prison for his faith and was well treated by his fellow believers, but later he became a Cynic. Banned from Rome, he traveled to Athens and had himself burned to death there. In this tale, Lucian depicts Christians as ethical but ignorant, duped by a charlatan. In *Alexander the False Prophet,* Lucian ridicules Alexander of Abonuteichus, another religious huckster, who created a huge puppet of a snake that awed those who visited his shrine.

[F.W.N.]

Bibliography

B. Baldwin, *Studies in Lucian* (Toronto: Hakkert, 1973); J. Hall, *Lucian's Satire* (New York: Arno, 1981).

LUCIFER OF CAGLIARI (d. ca. 370). Bishop of Cagliari in Sardinia and fierce opponent of Arianism. With Eusebius of Vercelli, Lucifer was exiled by the emperor Constantius II for his vigorous defense of Athanasius. Released on the accession of Julian (362), he became entangled in the controversy between the followers of Melitius and Eustathius at Antioch. By consecrating an adherent of Eustathius as bishop there, he gave rise to the Melitian schism. It is uncertain whether he himself died a schismatic, although that is suggested by references in Ambrose (*Exces. frat.* 1.47) and Augustine (*Ep.* 185.47). He is the author of five vitriolic polemics, addressed to Constantius, which rely heavily on scripture copiously cited from the Old Latin versions. His followers endorsed his rigorist views. Attacked by Jerome in the *Dialogue Against the Luciferians,* they disappeared early in the fifth century. CPL 112–118. [M.P.McH.]

Bibliography

Jerome, *Lives of Illustrious Men* 95.

Opera quae supersunt, ed. G.F. Diercks, CCSL (1978), Vol. 8; "El tratado *De regibus apostolicis* de Lucifer de Cagliari (estudio crítico y edición)," ed. J. Avilés, *Analecta Sacra Tarraconensia* 49–50 (1976–1977 [1979]):345–437; "El tratado *Moriundum esse pro Dei filio* de Lucifer de Cagliari (comentarios y edición crítica)," ed. L. Ferreres, *Analecta Sacra Tarraconensia* 53–54 (1980–1981 [1984]):1–99.

T.P. Halton and R.D. Sider, "A Decade of Patristic Scholarship 1970–1979," *CW* 76 (1982–1983):380 (bibliography).

LUCILLA (fourth century). Wealthy woman from Spain who lived in Carthage and evidently supported the Donatists. Lucilla probably bought the condemnation by the Numidian bishops of Caecilian, bishop of Carthage, that precipitated the Donatist schism. He had opposed her extreme veneration of a martyr's bone and had demanded the return of church plate after the cessation of persecution. *See also* Donatism. [F.W.N.]

Bibliography

Optatus, *Against the Donatists* 1.16, 18–19; Augustine, *Letter* 43.17; idem, *Contra epistolam Parmeniani* 1.3.5; idem, *Contra Cresconium* 3.29.33; idem, *De unitate ecclesiae* 3.6; 18.46; 25.73.

LUCIUS I. Bishop of Rome (253–254). Banished from Rome under the emperor Gallus (251–253), Lucius I was allowed to return shortly thereafter under Valerian (253–260). Little is known of his episcopate. In opposition to the adherents of Novatian, he continued the liberal policy of his predecessor Cornelius in receiving back into communion the *lapsi,* those who had yielded under persecution. He presumably died a natural death; the story of his martyrdom is apocryphal. Feast day March 4. CPL 62. [M.P.McH.]

Bibliography

Cyprian, *Letters* 61; 68.5; Eusebius, *Church History* 7.2; *Liber Pontificalis* 23 (Duchesne 1.153).

LUKE. Traditional author of the Gospel bearing his name and also of the Book of Acts. Both books are strictly anonymous, although their prefaces, the common addressee (Theophilus), and the similarities of style and outlook have convinced most scholars of their common authorship. The "we" sections of Acts (16:10–17; 20:5–15; 21:1–18; 27:1–28:16; and 11:28 in codex Bezae) imply that the author was a companion of Paul on his second and third missionary journeys as well as the journey to Rome. This companion was soon identified with the Luke of Colossians 4:14, Philemon 24, and 2 Timothy 4:11. From these texts, it appears that Luke was a physician, a Gentile by birth, and a worker with Paul. It may be that the same Luke is in view in Acts 13:1 (11:28) and Romans 16:21. If this is the case, Luke could have been a native of Syrian Antioch, as is suggested by the *Anti-Marcionite Prologue,* Eusebius (*H.E.* 3.4.6), and Jerome (*Vir. ill.* 7), or a native of Philippi, as may be suggested by the commencement of the "we" sections.

In addition to the basic outline of the ministry of Jesus reflected in Mark's Gospel, Luke has a large block of mostly distinctive material (Luke 9:51–18:14) placed in the context of the last journey to Jerusalem. Luke contains also an extensive infancy narrative (Luke 1–2) and is the only record of some of the best-known parables of Jesus—the good Samaritan (10:25–37), the prodigal son (15:11–32), the Pharisee and the publican (18:9–14). Luke is distinctive for his emphasis on thanksgiving and praise (2:20; 5:25; 7:16; 13:13; 17:15; 18:43; 23:47), prayer (3:21f.; 5:16; 6:12; 9:29; 11:5–13; 18:1–8; 23:34; 23:46), and the Holy Spirit (4:1, 14, 18; 11:23; 24:49), and his interest in those usually despised in his day—the poor (2:7f., 24; 6:20; 9:58; 14:21), women (7:11, 37; 8:2f.; 9:38; 18:15), Samaritans (10:25–37; 17:16), and Gentiles (4:24f.; 23:28f.).

Evidence of the use of Luke's Gospel in the early church prior to Tatian is ambiguous. Although there may be echoes of Luke in the *Didache,* in the letters of Clement of Rome and Ignatius, and in Justin, it is also possible that they made use of gospel tradition, not Luke, because they do not actually quote him. Both Tatian, in his *Diatessaron,* and Celsus, in his attack on Christianity in his *True Word,* give evidence of their knowledge of the Gospel, but without actually ascribing it to Luke. The Gospel was known to the Gnostic teachers Basilides and Valentinus and was commented on by Heracleon. Marcion's scriptures consisted of his own edited version of Luke as representing Paul's gospel and his own edition of the Pauline letters, purged of what he perceived as Judaizing tendencies (Tertullian, *Marc.* 4.2, 5).

From the time of Origen (*Hom. 1 in Lc.*), it was common to refer 2 Corinthians 8:18 to Luke and identify his Gospel as that of Paul. The *Anti-Marcionite Prologue* says that Luke did not marry, and died, full of the Holy Spirit, in Bithynia (or Boeotia) aged seventy-four. Ire-

naeus (180) and the *Muratorian Canon* connect the New Testament references to Luke the companion of Paul with the author of the Gospel and Acts (Irenaeus, *Haer.* 3.1.1; 3.10.1; 3.12.12; 3.14.1–4; 3.22.4). The Gospel is ascribed to Luke and quoted by Clement of Alexandria (*Hyp.* on 1 Peter 5:13) and Tertullian (*Marc.* 4.2). Thenceforth, the common assumption was that Luke was the author of the Gospel and Acts. In the symbolism of the Gospels, Luke was represented by a bull. Feast day October 18. *See also* Acts of the Apostles; Mark; Matthew.   [J.P.]

Bibliography
Origen, *Homiliae in Lucam,* SC (1962), Vol. 87; Eusebius of Caesarea, *Commentaria in Lucam,* PG 24.529–606; Titus of Bostra, *Commentaria in Lucam,* TU (1901), Vol. 21; Ambrose, *Expositio Evangelii secundum Lucam,* CCSL (1957), Vol. 14; Cyril of Alexandria, *Commentary on the Gospel According to Saint Luke,* tr. R.P. Smith (Oxford: Oxford UP, 1859; repr. Studion, 1953); J. Reuss, *Lukas Kommentare aus der griechischen Kirche,* TU (1984), Vol. 130.

A. Plummer, *A Critical and Exegetical Commentary on the Gospel According to St. Luke* (Edinburgh: T. & T. Clark, 1896), esp. pp. xi–xxii, lxxiii–lxxxii; V.H. Stanton, *The Gospels as Historical Documents* (Cambridge: Cambridge UP, 1903), Part 1: *The Early Use of the Gospels;* K. Aland, ed., *Synopsis Quattuor Evangeliorum* (Stuttgart: Württembergische Bibelanstalt, 1964), pp. 531–548; E.E. Ellis, *The Gospel of Luke* (London: Oliphants, 1974); I.H. Marshall, *The Gospel of Luke* (Grand Rapids: Eerdmans, 1978); J.A. Fitzmyer, *The Gospel According to Luke* (New York: Doubleday, 1981); International New Testament Greek Project, *The New Testament in Greek* (Oxford: Clarendon, 1984), Vol. 3: *The Gospel According to St. Luke.*

ᑕᑐ

MACARIUS MAGNES (early fifth century?). Apologist. Probably a bishop of Magnesia, Macarius is the author of the *Apocriticus,* a fictional dialogue between a pagan and a Christian that may contain material from a lost work of Porphyry, the champion of Neoplatonism. Passages from the dialogue were invoked in the ninth-century iconoclastic dispute and by the Jesuit Francesco Torres (Turrianus) in the Reformation controversy over the eucharist. CPG III, 6115–6118.   [M.P.McH.]

Bibliography
The Apocriticus of Macarius Magnes, tr. T.W. Crafer (London: SPCK, and New York: Macmillan, 1919).

T.P. Halton and R.D. Sider, "A Decade of Patristic Scholarship 1970–1979," *CW* 76 (1982–1983):341 (bibliography).

MACARIUS THE GREAT (ca. 300–ca. 390). Egyptian monk. Macarius founded the monastery in the Desert of Scete that became a significant center of asceticism. What little we know of him comes from the *Apophthegmata patrum,* Palladius's *Lausiac History,* and the *Historia monachorum.* According to these sources, he began the monastery at age thirty and was ordained a priest by age forty.

The works attributed to him are not certainly his. Some have been viewed as written by Gregory of Nyssa, others as coming from Gnostic or Messalian communities. It is even probable that the bulk of them come from Syria rather than Egypt. CPG II, 2400–2427. TLG 2109. *See also* Monasticism.   [F.W.N.]

MACRINA THE YOUNGER (ca. 327–379/ 80). Oldest child of Basil the Elder and Emmelia and sister of Basil of Caesarea and Gregory of Nyssa; called "the younger" to distinguish her from her grandmother Macrina, a disciple of Gregory Thaumaturgus, bishop of Neocaesarea, and the mother of Basil the Elder. Macrina's life is known to us through the hagiographical biography written by Gregory of Nyssa as well as from his *Letter* 19. She is also introduced, in an obviously fictitious manner, although perhaps not without some historical foundation, in his dialogue *On the Soul and the Resurrection* as teaching him, from her deathbed, on the nature and destiny of the human soul. Gregory of Nazianzus's *Letter* 163 contains only a brief praise of her; Basil of Caesarea never mentions his sister in his writings.

From Gregory of Nyssa's writings, we gain the image of a well-educated woman who had a major part in the education and spiritual development of her brothers. After the death of her fiancé, Macrina, about twelve years old at the time, decided to remain a virgin and stay with her mother. Eventually, they transformed their household at Annesi in Pontus, Asia Minor, into a monastery of which Macrina became the superior. Gregory gives us a vivid description of his visit to his dying sister. Her death has usually been dated to December 379, but recent study has reaffirmed July 19, 380, the date given by the earlier hagiographical traditions. Feast day July 19.   [D.L.B.]

Bibliography

Gregory of Nyssa, *Life of Macrina,* ed. P. Maraval, SC (1971), Vol. 178; tr. V. Woods Callahan, FOTC (1967), Vol. 58, pp. 161–191; idem, *On the Soul and the Resurrection,* tr. V. Woods Callahan, FOTC (1967), Vol. 58, pp. 195–272; idem, *Letter* 19.

P. Wilson-Kastner, "Macrina: Virgin and Teacher," *Andrews University Seminary Studies* 17 (1979):105–117; J. LaPorte, *The Role of Women in Early Christianity* (New York and Toronto: Mellen, 1982), pp. 80–88, 103–105; A. Meredith, "A Comparison Between the *Vita Sanctae Macrinae* of Gregory of Nyssa, the *Vita Plotini* of Porphyry and the *De Vita Pythagorica* of Iamblichus," *The Biographical Works of Gregory of Nyssa,* ed. A. Spira (Cambridge: Philadelphia Patristic Foundation, 1984), pp. 181–195; R. Albrecht, *Das Leben der heiligen Makrina auf dem Hintergrund der Thekla-Traditionen: Studien zu den Ursprungen des weiblichen Mönchtums im 4. Jahrhundert in Kleinasien* (Göttingen: Vandenhoeck & Ruprecht, 1986).

MADEBA MAP. Oldest extant cartographical representation of Israel, Jordan, and adjacent areas, dating to the reign of the emperor Justinian, probably between 560 and 565. The map is a partially damaged mosaic floor, originally about eighty feet by four feet, discovered in 1896 when the Greek Orthodox church in Madeba, Jordan, was constructing a new building over the old one. The mosaic contained 2,300,000 cubes and would have required a full year's work for three persons. It was thus an expensive undertaking during the Byzantine era, when Christians in the east were building important monuments throughout the Holy Land. The surviving portion of the map depicts an area extending on the north from Aenon near Salim (south of the Sea of Galilee) to a considerable distance south of the Dead Sea, and

Floor mosaic (sixth century) from Madeba, Jordan, centering on the city of Jerusalem.

on the west from the Mediterranean Sea to about five miles east of the Dead Sea. The original map would have included an area considerably larger, extending from Byblos and Damascus on the north to Mt. Sinai and Thebes in Egypt on the south, and from the Mediterranean on the west to Amman on the east. The Nile River is represented as branching into seven arms to produce the famous seven mouths of the Nile (Herodotus 2.17). Like most ancient maps, this one is not made to scale. Its major source is the fourth-century *Onomasticon* of Eusebius of Caesarea. Jerusalem is detailed in the center with many buildings, including the Church of the Holy Sepulchre and the recently excavated New Church of Justinian. [J.McR.]

Bibliography

M. Avi Yonah, *The Madeba Mosaic Map* (Jerusalem: Israel Exploration Society, 1954); V.R. Gold, "The Mosaic Map of Madeba," *Biblical Archaeologist* 21 (1958):50–71.

MAGIC. Use of ceremonies and formulas to influence a supernatural power to produce or prevent a given result. Many people practiced magic in late antiquity; few admitted it. Attempts to capture the heart of a potential lover, ensure the success of a favorite horse, punish an enemy, or achieve intimacy with the divine through ritual actions and recitations might appear to constitute magic or one of the closely related occult arts like divination, astrology, or alchemy. They were, however, not always viewed as such. One person's magic, spell, or demonic ritual was another person's miracle, prayer, or sacrament. Such differences depend on an observer's fundamental perception that magic was something done by *someone else.* That perception was reinforced by the fact that the practice of magic in its various forms was generally illegal.

Anyone who had a stake in the social, political, or religious status quo was justifiably wary of attempts to change it through invisible means. Roman emperors, for example, were notably sensitive to attempts to establish the time of their death by divination, for fear that their opponents might want to ensure the ac-

curacy of the divination through assassination. Magic was perceived as a disruptive force. Consequently, to describe a belief or practice as magical was to stigmatize it as threatening, antisocial, immoral, and criminal. Practitioners, such as those represented in the magical papyri of the second century B.C. through the fifth century A.D., preferred to present their activities as a "mystery" and to concentrate on the technology for acquiring divine revelations (cf. *PGM* 1.54ff.; 4.475; 5.110; 13.1ff.). Apuleius, when accused of magically luring an attractive older widow into marriage, responded that the actions in question might resemble those of philosophers, natural scientists like Aristotle, or even the sacred practices of the Persian Magi but were certainly not magic (*Apology* 3.5; 25.5–10; 26.1–5). Thus, despite attempts to distinguish magic from religion, science, medicine, and philosophy, the boundaries remained fluid and the distinctions were largely polemical.

Charges of magic attended the birth and growth of the Christian movement. The Synoptic Gospels report that Jesus' enemies attributed his miracles to magic (Mark 3:19–30; Matt. 12:22–37; Luke 11:14–23) but that Jesus himself attributed them to divine power. The Acts of the Apostles depicts the apostles as triumphing over the opposition of magicians and persuading many to give up the practice of magic (Acts 13:4–12; 19:13–20). In the second century, Celsus made the accusation that Jesus practiced magic the centerpiece of his broadside against the new movement (Origen, *Cels.* 1.6, 38). Later critics, like Hierocles in the third century, took up the same cry (Eusebius, *Hierocl.* 2). They aimed to discredit both the movement and its founder by exposing their deceptive missionary practices. Since magic was patently deceitful, any intelligent, upright citizen would of course be immune to its attractions. For Celsus, it follows that Jesus "won over only ten sailors and tax collectors of the most abominable character" (Origen, *Cels.* 2.46), and that later Christian missionaries found their converts among "wool workers, cobblers, laundry workers, and the most illiterate and bucolic yokels" (*Cels.* 3.55).

Christians were quick to draw different boundaries. Both the Gospels and later texts sharply distinguished Jesus' miracles from the actions of magicians on account of their truly divine power and moral effects. In an elaborate set-piece, the apocryphal *Acts of Peter* dramatizes the impotence of Simon Magus's magic in the face of Peter's Christian miracles (23–27). Converts left behind a world of magic and demons. As Justin Martyr notes in a series of contrasts between behavior before and after conversion: "Those who [once] made use of magic arts have dedicated themselves to the good and unbegotten God" (*1 Apol.* 14). For Justin, Hippolytus, Tertullian, and many other Christians, the ritual of baptism marked the threshold between the demonic world of magic, immorality, and ignorance and the blessed haven of the Christian life. Exorcism at baptism ensured that the new convert was purified. The community of the faithful was conceived as an enclave tentatively secured against onslaughts of the demons.

Despite efforts to exclude magic from Christian practice, it exerted a powerful attraction. Ignatius of Antioch describes the eucharist as the "medicine of immortality" (*Eph.* 20.2), a phrase reminiscent of the magical papyri. The canons of the Synod of Elvira (ca. 306) reveal a disquieting tendency of the faithful to dabble in magic. John Chrysostom inveighs against Antiochene Christians who sought healing from Jewish "charms, incantations, and amulets" (*Jud.* 8.5–7). It seems clear that, like those addressed at Elvira, at least some Jews and Christians in Chrysostom's Antioch incorporated magic into their traditional religious practices. The complicated religious situations of fourth-century Spain and Antioch show that distinctions that seem clear in theory and polemic may not hold fast in practice. Augustine outlines a similar situation in fifth-century North Africa (*Serm.* 9.3; 56.12; 88.25).

The attraction of magic was in the promises it made. Magic offered power. To turn indifference into passion, enmity into injury, isolation into intimacy with the divine—such were the desires of the magician (and the client). But for everyone who found these turns of events attractive, another person might be threatened. The spouse of the object of a love charm, a public official, the priest of a local temple—all could perceive magic as a threat. In a climate charged with uncertainty, unanticipated and unwelcome change aroused suspicions of magic.

It is not surprising that the success of the Christian movement attracted accusations that magic was at its root. Nor is it surprising that the enterprising magicians tried to use the powerful name of Jesus (Origen, *Cels.* 1.6; *PGM* 123.50; 128.1). For magic always represents an alternative. As a new religion, Christianity was suspect and hence open to charges of magic; as it demonstrated its hold on people, magicians tried to borrow its power; when it became an established faith, some Christians sought additional power outside of its boundaries. *See also* Demons; Miracle; Testament of Solomon.

[E.V.G.]

Bibliography

K. Preisendanz, ed. *Papryi graecae magicae: Die griechischen Zauberpapryi*, 2nd ed. (Stuttgart: Teubner, 1973–1974).

H.D. Betz, ed., *The Greek Magical Papyri in Translation* (Chicago: U of Chicago P, 1986); *The Testament of Solomon*, tr. D.C. Duling in J.H. Charlesworth, ed., *The Old Testament Pseudepigrapha* (Garden City: Doubleday, 1983), Vol. 1, pp. 935–987; G. Luck, *Arcana Mundi: Magic and the Occult in the Greek and Roman Worlds* (Baltimore: Johns Hopkins UP, 1985).

R. MacMullen, *Enemies of the Roman Order* (Cambridge: Harvard UP, 1966); J.M. Hull, *Hellenistic Magic and the Synoptic Tradition* (Naperville: Allenson, 1974); M. Smith, *Jesus the Magician* (New York: Harper and Row, 1978); D.E. Aune, "Magic in Early Christianity," ANRW (1980), Vol. 23.2, pp. 1507–1557; E.V. Gallagher, *Divine Man or Magician? Celsus and Origen on Jesus* (Chico: Scholars, 1982); H.C. Kee, *Miracle in the Early Christian World* (New Haven: Yale UP, 1983); H. Remus, *Pagan-Christian Conflict over Miracle in the Second Century* (Cambridge: Philadelphia Patristic Foundation, 1983); H.C. Kee, *Medicine, Miracle, and Magic in New Testament Times* (Cambridge: Cambridge UP, 1986).

MAJORINUS (d. ca. 313/314). Claimant of the episcopal see of Carthage. After the death of Mensurius, bishop of Carthage, in 311, a council of bishops of Numidia met and chose Majorinus for the see (312) in opposition to

Caecilian, previously elected successor; this marked an early stage in the schism that would become known as Donatism. The election of Majorinus, a lector under Mensurius, was promoted by Lucilla, a wealthy woman who had been criticized by Caecilian for excessive zeal. Majorinus lived only a short time thereafter, being succeeded in his claim by Donatus. *See also* Donatism. [M.P.McH.]

MALCHION (third century). Presbyter at Antioch in Syria. The head of a rhetorical school, Malchion interrogated Paul of Samosata and drafted the conciliar letter denouncing him as a doctrinal heretic and an unworthy disciple. [F.W.N.]

Bibliography
Eusebius, *Church History* 7.29–30; Jerome, *Lives of Illustrious Men* 71.

MANDAEISM. Religion of the Ṣubbi (Mandaic, "baptizers") along the rivers and canals of southern Iraq and southwest Iran. Reaching back at least into the third century A.D., this Gnostic religion shows affinities with both Judaism and Christianity. Since the seventh century, Mandaeism has survived, at times tenuously, under Islamic rule. Sometime during the first three Christian centuries, the Mandaeans emigrated from the Jordan Valley eastward to their present habitat. The Mandaic language belongs among the East Aramaic dialects, and it contains West Syrian elements that are particularly evident in central religious terms (e.g., *yardna*, Jordan, "running water," and *manda*, "knowledge").

Mandaeans possess a voluminous, complex literature, the chief texts being the *Ginza* ("Treasure"), divided into *Right* and *Left Ginza* (the latter contains mainly hymnic material); a collection of hymns and prayers dating at least in part to the third century; and the *Book of John*, like the *Ginza* a collection of myths, exhortations, and revelations. Other texts, some as yet unpublished, contain ritual instructions and commentaries as well as other forms of priestly instructions. There are also inscribed Mandaean clay bowls and lead strips.

In the first part of the twentieth century, the study of Mandaeism enjoyed great popularity among European scholars, due chiefly to Lidzbarski's fine translation of the Mandaean sources. Drower's fieldwork and editions of Mandaean texts, from the 1930s to the 1960s, brought new insights and a widened scope to scholarship on the Mandaeans. In recent decades, language studies by Macuch and Rudolph's monographs on Mandaean religion mark further advances.

The Mandaean mythology is characterized by a tempered dualism in which forces of light and dark continually strive against one another but also mingle and cooperate. A preexistent Lightworld harbors a number of beings, *'utria*, some of whom are responsible for the creation of the material world, the soul's fall into the material body, and the soul's eventual return to its heavenly home. Of these *'utria*, Manda d-Hiia ("Knowledge-of-life") is a revealer and a savior, Ptahil is one of the world creators, and his father, Abatur, personifies the scales of judgment. John the Baptist is the traditional Mandaean prophet, but this idea marks a late mythological development without historical foundation.

In the *Book of John*, however, he is the baptizer *par excellence*, for repeated baptism, *maṣbuta*, is the most conspicuous among Mandaean rituals. Mandaeans also celebrate various ritual meals for their dead, among them the complex death-mass, *masiqta* ("raising up"). The secret initiations of priests secure the continuation of the two priestly classes, *tarmidas* and *ganzibras*. Laypeople and priests are divided in terms of access to religious texts and knowledge, but the two groups support one another. Mandaeans today number perhaps 14,000, but exact figures, especially after the close of the Iran-Iraq war (1980–1988), are unavailable. Long before and during the war, a considerable number of Mandaeans emigrated to other countries, where many of them try to maintain their traditions and religious identity. [J.J.B.]

Bibliography
M. Lidzbarski, ed., *Ginza: Der Schatz oder das grosse Buch der Mandäer* (Göttingen: Vandenhoeck & Ruprecht, 1925); idem, *Das Johannesbuch* (Giessen: Töpelmann, 1915).

E.S. Drower, *The Canonical Prayerbook of the Mandaeans* (Leiden: Brill, 1959); W. Foerster and R.McL. Wilson, eds., *Gnosis: A Selection of Gnostic Texts* (Oxford: Clarendon, 1974), Vol. 2: *Coptic and Mandaean Sources,* pp. 123–317.

E.S. Drower, *The Mandaeans of Iraq and Iran* (Oxford: Clarendon, 1937); K. Rudolph, *Theogonie, Kosmogonie und Anthropogonie in den mandäischen Schriften* (Göttingen: Vandenhoeck & Ruprecht, 1965); R. Macuch, ed., *Zur Sprache und Literatur de Mandäer: Studia Mandaica* (Berlin: de Gruyter, 1976), Vol. 1; K. Rudolph, *Gnosis* (San Francisco: Harper and Row, 1983), pp. 343–366.

MANI, MANICHAEISM. Founder of the last great religious movement to make its way from the eastern frontiers into Roman society (third century). Mani sought a religious movement that would unite both east and west. Patterning his missionary zeal on Paul's call, Mani claimed to be an apostle. His religious vision incorporated influences from the heterodox Jewish Christian baptismal sect in which he had been brought up, as well as from Zoroastrianism and Buddhism.

Life and Early History. Mani was born in southern Mesopotamia on April 14, 216. His mother was said to have been of noble Persian lineage. His father had joined the Jewish Christian baptismal sect of the Elkesaites. Biographical material about the prophet's life and revelations collected by early followers survives in a small Greek codex of some 200 pages entitled *Concerning the Origin of His Body.* ("Body" refers to the founding of the Manichaean church by the prophet.) Mani claimed to have had revelations from his "heavenly twin" from the age of twelve. As visions of the Paraclete (Spirit) led him to question the practices of the baptismal sect to which he belonged, Mani engaged in disputes with its elders. At age twenty-four, on April 19, 240, Mani received his heavenly call to become the "apostle of light." Expelled from the sect with his father and two disciples, Mani began to send out emissaries. Upon his return from a journey to India in 242, Mani was able to convert members of the Persian royal court and had apparently gained a hearing from its new ruler, Sapor I (242–273). With the ascension of Bahram I (274–277), a reforming Zoroastrian priest, Kar-

tir, instigated persecution of Mani and his followers. Mani was imprisoned and died a martyr in the spring of 276.

Although the dissension and schism that resulted from the persecution led to the near eradication of Manichaeism in Persia itself, the movement flourished both in the west, where it entered the Roman empire, and in the east, where it reached central Asia. Manichaeism responded to persecution by "Christianizing" its organizational structure, with intensive preaching by wandering missionaries, and relying upon the support of "hearers"—merchants and other patrons whose sins were forgiven by the "elect" but who did not take on the elect's ascetic lifestyle.

As it came to be considered a Christian heresy, Manichaeism found itself the object of persecution by Christian bishops backed by the authority of the state in the Roman west. But its eventual decline in the sixth century may have been due as much to loss of its base of "hearers" as to measures against the sect. Manichaeism was liberated from persecution in the east by the rise of Islam. In central Asia, it flourished along with Buddhism and Nestorian Christianity until the Mongol attacks of the thirteenth century. During medieval times, it reemerged in the west in the sectarian forms of the Paulicians, Bogomils, and Catharists. Portuguese traders reported the existence of Manichaeans in southern China in the seventeenth century.

Doctrines. Although only fragments of his own writings remain, Mani himself claimed distinction from earlier religious founders by composing his own doctrinal, liturgical, and homiletic works. He devised a characteristic script and even composed one volume that contained illustrations of his doctrine. The Manichaeans were known for the beauty of their manuscripts, especially in their attention to the decoration. Manichaean material, much of it unedited, survives in Greek, Coptic, Syriac, Turkish, and Chinese, a diversity that reflects the global mission undertaken by Manichaean preachers.

Mani's religious system is grounded on a radical dualism of light and darkness. His dualism has affinities with Gnosticizing trends in Christianity, which he had probably encountered in their Syriac versions. An elaborate procedure of redemption is required for the particles of light that are trapped in this world to be liberated and returned to the heavenly world. Manichaeans saw the Milky Way as the great cosmic ladder by which such particles made their return and pointed to the waxing and waning of the moon as evidence for the collection and departure of light particles in the heavenly realm. The adepts of the sect, the elect, devoted their lives to freeing particles of light entrapped in matter. Mani's biography includes scenes in which he hears the anguished cries of plants and vegetables being cut. Meat-eating was forbidden; the elect took a daily common meal of fruits like melons, bread, and water. They also abstained from creating new prisons for light through sex and sought to avoid harm to living beings by any act of violence, including most forms of work. Consequently, their needs had to be supplied by the "hearers" of the movement. The elect devoted themselves to preaching, study, and copying manuscripts. They were required to fast 100 days a year, including a thirty-day fast before the annual festival of Mani's death.

Mythic stories tell of the mixing of the realms of light and dark, as well as the great "evocation" of God necessary to draw light out of darkness. The demonic powers of the lower world had created the human body in the form of the heavenly prototype of humanity, an androgynous Adam/Eve. As a result of the heavenly origins of their spirits, humans could become vehicles for the liberation of light. Only those who belonged to the elect would leave this world at death to return to the light realm. Women might also be among the elect, although they could not hold offices within the sect. The elect forgave the sins of the hearers who provided their support. In return for such a life, the hearer might expect to be reincarnated as one of the elect or one of the light-bearing plants and so achieve salvation.

Adaptation of Christian themes led to the depiction of Jesus as a variety of figures; for example, in North Africa the suffering Jesus represented the suffering particles of light. Augustine is perhaps the most famous Manichaean "hearer" in western Christian tradition. He owed his appointment to the chair of rhetoric in Milan to Manichaean supporters. But the teachings of Ambrose gave him a deeper understanding of Christianity, as Neoplatonism deepened his understanding of the nature of the soul and its relationship to the divine. He came to see Manichaeism as a crude mythologizing and found that its preachers were unable to answer the intellectual questions put to them. The life of Christian monks provided a better expression of asceticism, he thought, than did that of the vagrant and unkempt Manichaean preachers. [P.P.]

Bibliography
R. Cameron and A. Dewey, eds. and trs., *The Cologne Mani Codex: "Concerning the Origin of His Body"* (Missoula: Scholars, 1979).

P. Brown, "The Diffusion of Manichaeism in the Roman Empire," *Religion and Society in the Age of St. Augustine* (London: Faber and Faber, 1972), pp. 94–118; K. Rudolph, *Gnosis* (San Francisco: Harper and Row, 1983), pp. 326–342; S.N.C. Lieu, *Manichaeism in the Later Roman Empire and Medieval China: A Historical Survey* (Manchester: Manchester UP, 1985); S. Stroumsa and C.G. Stroumsa, "Aspects of Anti-Manichaean Polemics in Late Antiquity and under Early Islam," *HThR* 81 (1988):37–58.

MANUSCRIPTS. From the Latin *manu scriptus*, "written by the hand." Until the advent of printing with movable type in the fifteenth century, ancient texts could be transmitted only by being copied laboriously letter by letter. Principal writing materials were papyrus and parchment, with paper becoming popular in the late Middle Ages. A sharpened reed with a slit commonly served as a pen; from the seventh century, the quill became popular for writing on parchment. Black ink was made from various materials, such as charcoal or lampblack mixed with gum and water; ink made from nutgalls produced a rusty-brown color. Other colors, such as red, purple, gold, and silver, occasionally occur (cf. Jerome, *Ep.* 22.32).

Down to the second century A.D., literary works were customarily published in scroll form, separate sheets being attached side by side and rolled around a stick. Writing on the scroll ran at right angles to the stick and was arranged in a series of columns, each usually about two or three inches wide. Although such scrolls rarely exceeded thirty-five feet in length, the roll was relatively inconvenient to use. Early in the second century, the codex, or leaf-form of book, became popular among Christians; Jewish manuscripts continued to be written primarily in scroll form. Although the first mention of literary works being published in parchment codices is found in Martial 1.2.7–8 (late first century), the codex did not predominate in pagan literature until the third or fourth century. The codex form, created by folding one or more sheets in the middle and sewing them together, had a number of advantages: it was handier than the bulky roll; with writing possible on both sides of the page, it could contain more text and reduce costs; and it made texts easier to consult. The codex became the principal format for the transmission of the New Testament (cf. 2 Tim. 4:13) and patristic literature.

Scribal Activity. The earlier practice in the church, of individuals making copies of biblical documents, gave way in the fourth century, when Christianity received official sanction from the government, to the production of books in scriptoria. Several scribes sitting in a scriptorium could write copies as a lector slowly read aloud the text of the exemplar. To catch errors, manuscripts produced in scriptoria were commonly checked by a corrector, whose alterations are usually detectable by differences in handwriting and shades of ink. Scribes working in scriptoria usually were paid according to the number of lines copied, a normal line (or stichos) having fifteen or sixteen syllables. In 301, a price-fixing edict of Diocletian, *De pretiis rerum venalium* 7.39, set a standard rate.

Texts were written without word division, that is, in continuous script (*scriptio continua*), and frequently without sentence division. Prior to the eighth century, punctuation rarely occurs. Sections or chapters were sometimes marked, the earliest being in the margins of the fourth-century codex Vaticanus. Chapter

titles begin to appear with the fifth-century codex Alexandrinus.

Later, in the Byzantine period, books were usually produced by monks in monasteries, often working by themselves in their cells and copying by looking to the side at an exemplar. This procedure also resulted in copying mistakes. About 800, Theodore the Studite, abbot of the monastery of the Studium at Constantinople, established severe rules for monks not careful in copying manuscripts (PG 99.1739).

Corrected manuscripts were often sent to miniators, who added ornamental letters and artistic designs. Excellent examples of early Christian manuscript illumination are codex Amiatinus in the Laurentian Library at Florence, the Lindisfarne Gospels in the British Museum, and the Book of Kells at Trinity College, Dublin. Jerome (*Ep.* 22.32; 107.12) cautioned against gilding, arabesque patterns, and bindings decked with jewels at the expense of textual exactitude.

Earlier Greek manuscripts were written in uncials, or capital letters, but from the ninth century a smaller script in a running hand, called minuscule, became popular. This more compact script had the advantages of speed in writing and utilizing less parchment, thus reducing costs.

Collections of Manuscripts. The multiplication and circulation of copies (cf. Plato, *Apology* 26; Ps.-Plutarch, *Lives of the Ten Orators* 841F) resulted in collections of manuscripts. Strabo 13.1.54 states that Aristotle built up a large collection that served as a model for the establishment of the famous library at Alexandria, which contained more than 200,000 volumes (*Ep. Aristeas* 10). Earlier, Callimachus had compiled the *Pinakes,* a 120-book guide to the manuscripts in the library. As manuscripts of a given work did not always contain identical texts, one particularly important aspect of work at the library in Alexandria was sorting through the various manuscripts of the work and arriving at a standard text. The great library at Pergamum, established in the second century B.C. by king Eumenes II, then came to rival the Alexandrian library and was noted for its bibliographical work but not for any significant editorial activity.

By the middle of the second century B.C., Rome possessed a considerable body of literature of her own, but nothing is said of a book trade at Rome prior to Cicero. Augustus founded two public libraries, after which libraries became common both in Rome and in the provinces, and by the fourth century, Rome could boast twenty-eight public libraries. Significant private collections were not uncommon (cf. Jerome, *Ep.* 22.30). By the sixth century, however, monasteries had become the principal centers for manuscript collection and production. For example, the monastery of Vivarium, which Cassiodorus founded in southern Italy sometime after 540, owed much of its interest in education and copying manuscripts, both religious and secular, to the impending devastation of war and conquest that threatened to destroy manuscripts, and thus learning and literacy (cf. Cassiodorus, *Inst.*). The founding of Monte Cassino by Benedict of Nursia (ca. 529) effectively laid the foundation upon which monastic life in the west was based for centuries, and although the copying of manuscripts was not explicitly said to be part of the monastic ideal, reading was required and thus manuscripts were essential. The great monastery of Bobbio, founded in northern Italy in 614, was the scene of much scribal activity as the early Middle Ages grew near. The sixth century witnessed the collapse of what remained of the Roman empire in the west, and the ravages of conquest and barbarism dealt serious blows to both classical and religious manuscripts. Missionary expansion of the church in northern Europe, however, continued to necessitate the production of manuscripts in Britain and on the Continent.

Pagan Manuscripts and the Early Church. The fourth-century clash between Christianity and paganism, from which the church emerged victorious, did not result in the elimination of pagan manuscripts. Although such texts did contain much that was inimical to the Christian faith, patristic writers discovered that they could still benefit from them. When Gregory Thaumaturgus attended Origen's school at Caesarea (ca. 233–238), he found Origen encouraging pupils to read classical literature (PG 10.1088A, 1093A). Origen also had adapted the system of marginal signs used by the Alexandrian critics in his textual criticism. Basil wrote a short treatise (*Hom.* 22) on the best method of profiting from Greek literature, and Gregory of Nazianzus criticized the complete rejection of pagan works (PG 36.508B). Ambrose was able to produce his *On the Duties of the Clergy*, an influential manual of Christian ethics, by reworking the essentially Stoic content of Cicero's *On Duties.* Likewise, Augustine adapted classical Roman rhetoric from Cicero's *Orator* in his *On Christian Teaching* to meet the needs of Christian preachers. Jerome (*Ep.* 70.2) concluded that, on the analogy of Deuteronomy 21:10–13, just as a captive woman may be taken as wife when her head has been shaved and her nails pared, so pagan literature could be utilized with profit.

It is sometimes said that the church burned pagan manuscripts as a matter of policy, but the burning of the library at Antioch by Jovian in 363 was an isolated incident, and the statement of Petrus Alcyonius (1486–1527) that the church burned pagan manuscripts is unsupported by other evidence. Although the Byzantine church burned the works of heretics, no evidence exists to indicate that the church took such measures against classical texts.

Manuscripts of the New Testament. Colossians 4:16, "When this letter has been read among you, have it read also in the church of the Laodiceans; and see that you read also the letter from Laodicea," reflects in all probability the practice of the early church. Small collections of manuscripts in local churches grew by a process of exchange until the late second century, when Irenaeus of Lyons mentions a collection of four Gospels regarded as equally authoritative accounts and the *Muratorian Canon* gives a canonical list of New Testament documents. The earliest manuscript of the Pauline letters, *p46*, evidences a standard collection by ca. 200. However, variant readings in the Greek manuscript tradition of the New Testament multiplied. Since the autographs are no longer extant, the science of textual criticism addresses the varied problems in the transmission, corruption, and restoration of the New Testament text.

From 200, regional languages became a popular medium for Christian missions. Augustine (*Doctr. christ.* 2.11), however, complained that translation of the early versions was often by individuals unskilled in Greek. This, coupled with the significant differences between Greek and other ancient languages, resulted in divergences of readings. Consequently, the manuscripts of the ancient versions, such as Latin, Coptic, Syriac, Ethiopic, Georgian, and Armenian, present a variety of text-critical problems not unlike those of the Greek manuscripts.

Patristic citations, of great value for locating given readings geographically and chronologically, also present a variety of readings. Of particular value are those places where writers comment upon variant readings known to them. However, as the manuscripts of the fathers have been modified in the course of copying and are often separated from their autographs by several centuries, one must first ascertain the true text of the father. Then, one must decide whether the citation is genuine or merely an adaptation or allusion. Obviously, longer and verbally exact citations are of greater value than shorter, inexact citations in determining the biblical text of a patristic writer. Patristic writers sometimes altered biblical texts consciously, often for theological reasons, as is observed in the fragment of an anonymous treatise preserved in Eusebius (*H.E.* 5.28.1–6). Dating from the early third century, this document specifically charges certain Monarchians with altering biblical manuscripts to prove their own doctrine: "For this purpose they fearlessly lay their hands upon the holy scriptures, saying that they have corrected them. . . . Copies of many you may find in abundance, altered, by the eagerness of their disciples to insert each one his own corrections, as they call them, i.e., their corruptions." *See also* Codex; Papyri; Parchment; Text Criticism.   [C.D.O.]

Bibliography
E.M. Thompson, *Greek and Latin Palaeography* (Oxford: Clarendon, 1912); K. Weitzmann, *Illustration in Roll and Codex: A Study of the Origin and Method of Text Illustration* (Princeton: Princeton UP, 1947); K. Aland, *Kurzgefasste Liste der griechischen Handschriften des Neuen Testaments* (Berlin: de Gruyter, 1963); B.M. Metzger, *The Text of the New Testament: Its Transmission, Corruption, and Restoration*, 2nd ed. (New York: Oxford UP, 1968); idem, "Patristic Evidence and the Textual Criticism of the New Testament," *NTS* 18 (1972):379–400; L.D. Reynolds and N.G. Wilson, *Scribes and Scholars: A Guide to the Transmission of Greek and Latin Literature*, 2nd ed. (Oxford: Clarendon, 1974); B.M. Metzger, *The Early Versions of the New Testament* (Oxford: Clarendon, 1977); J.K. Elliott, *A Bibliography of Greek New Testament Manuscripts* (Cambridge: Cambridge UP, 1988).

MARCELLINUS. Bishop of Rome (296–304). It is likely that Marcellinus somehow compromised his faith in the persecution under Diocletian. Augustine rejected a report, circulated by the adherents of Donatism, that Marcellinus sacrificed to the gods and surrendered the sacred books to the authorities. The legend that Marcellinus judged himself for his actions before a synod of bishops, because the primatial see could be judged by no one else, was circulated to support the position of Symmachus against the schism of Laurentius (cf. CPL 1679). An inscription referring to Marcellinus gives the first usage of "pope" for the bishop of Rome (DACL, Vol. 3, cols. 3169–3170). Feast day June 2.   [M.P.McH.]

Bibliography
Eusebius, *Church History* 7.32.1; Augustine, *Answer to the Letters of Petilian* 2.93.202; idem, *De unico baptismo* 16.27, 30; *Liber Pontificalis* 30 (Duchesne 1.162–163).

MARCELLUS (d. 298). Martyr. Marcellus, a centurion in Tingis, Mauretania, threw down his soldier's belt, was tried for treason, and was executed by the sword. The *Acts of Marcellus* exist in two recensions.   [E.F.]

Bibliography
Musurillo, pp. xxxvii–xxxix, 250–259.
J. den Boeft and J. Bremmer, "Notiunculae Martyrologicae," *VChr* 35 (1981):52.

MARCELLUS OF ANCYRA (ca. 280–374). Bishop of Ancyra and an unyielding but controversial opponent of Arianism and defender of the Nicene Creed. Marcellus was listed as present at the Synod of Ancyra in 314. He attended the Council of Nicaea in 325, but his support of the *homoousian* ("same substance") formula led to "impiety diametrically opposed to Arius" (Basil, *Ep.* 69). On the basis of a work written against Asterius, Marcellus was suspected of Modalism by eastern bishops, such as Eusebius of Caesarea. According to his critics, and confirmed by the few extant fragments of this work, Marcellus held an extreme monotheism that defined God and the Word as identical (one *hypostasis* or *ousia*); the distinction of this monad into Son and Spirit occurred only for the purpose of the incarnation and salvation. On the basis of 1 Corinthians 15:24–28, Marcellus argued that at the end the Son would deliver all to the Father and "God will be all in all." Deposed by eastern bishops at a synod in 336 at Constantinople, he was repeatedly condemned by them—at councils held at Antioch (341), at Sardica (343), and again at Antioch (345). In Rome, however, Marcellus's statement of faith (Epiphanius, *Haer.* 72.2, 3) was accepted, and he together with Athanasius was acquitted of heresy in 340 and again by the western bishops at Sardica in 343. Athanasius later withdrew his support, and Marcellus was increasingly associated with the teachings of his pupil, Photinus. Marcellus was condemned with Photinus at the Council of Constantinople in 381; the line "whose kingdom will have no end" was inserted in the creed to refute his interpretation of 1 Corinthians 15:24–28. Due to the fragmentary condition of his work, reconstruction of his teachings and attribution of his writings remain controversial. CPG II, 2800–2806.

[R.L.]

Bibliography
Fragments in *Eusebius Werke*, ed. E. Klostermann, GCS (1906), Vol. 4, pp. 183–215.
M.-D. Chenu, "Marcel d'Ancyre," DTC (1927), Vol. 9.2, cols. 1993–1998; G.W.H. Lampe, "Some Notes on the Significance of BASILEIA TOU THEOU, BASILEIA CHRISTOU in the Greek Fathers," *JThS* 49 (1948):58–73; idem, "Exegesis of Some Biblical Texts by Marcellus of Ancyra and Pseudo-Chrysostom's Homily on Psalm 96," *JThS* 49 (1948):169–175; M. Richard, "Un Opuscule méconnu de Marcel évêque d'Ancyre," *MSR* 6 (1949):5–28; T.E. Pollard, "Marcellus of Ancyra: A Neglected Father," *Epektasis*, ed. J. Fontaine and C. Kannengiesser (Paris: Beauchesne, 1972), pp. 187–196; J.T. Lienhard, "Marcellus of Ancyra in Modern Research," *ThS* 43 (1982):486–503; idem, "The Exegesis of 1 Cor. 15, 24–28 from Marcellus of Ancyra to Theodoret of Cyrus," *VChr* 37 (1983):340–359; idem, "Basil of Caesarea, Marcellus of Ancyra, and 'Sabellius,'" *ChHist* 58 (1989): 157–167.

MARCIA (d. 193). Formerly the concubine of Quadratus, the nephew of Marcus Aurelius, Marcia became part of the emperor Commodus's household in 183, when he had Quadratus killed. Given honors as an empress, she used her influence in behalf of Christians. She was raised by a Christian presbyter but may not have been a Christian herself. Didius Julianus put her to death in 193 for her part in Commodus's murder.   [F.W.N.]

Bibliography
Hippolytus, *Refutation of All Heresies* 9.7; Dio Cassius 73.4, 22; 74.16.

MARCIAN (ca. 392–457). Eastern Roman emperor (450–457). Marcian was born and bred to a modest military career that included service in Lydia and Africa and concluded at Constantinople as an assistant to Aspar, the imperial chief of staff and power behind the throne. At the initiative of Aspar and Pulcheria, sister of the deceased emperor Theodosius II, Marcian entered imperial and church history in 450, when he married Pulcheria, with an arrangement that allowed her to continue the vow of perpetual virginity she took at age fifteen.

Pulcheria's influence was apparent immediately in Marcian's ecclesiastical policies. The convoluted controversies involving Monophysitism, the "Robber Council" of Ephesus (449), and pope Leo I's *Tome,* as well as Marcian's desire to have his election recognized by the western emperor Valentinian III and the pope, led Marcian to convene the Fourth Ecumenical Council at Chalcedon in 451. At Chalcedon, the imperial couple oversaw the declaration of Christological orthodoxy, and also, in spite of concern for pope Leo's goodwill, the emergence of Constantinople's episcopal parity with Rome (*can.* 28), the completion of a process that began at the Second Ecumenical Council at Constantinople in 381 (*can.* 3).

Marcian's religious policy sorely offended the eastern provinces of Syria and Egypt, which had Monophysite sympathies, but justified his recognition as the defender of Christological orthodoxy in the Greek core of the eastern empire and the Catholic west. *See also* Chalcedon; Pulcheria.   [H.R.]

Bibliography

A.H.M. Jones, *The Later Roman Empire, 264–602: A Social, Economic and Administrative History,* 2 vols. (Norman: U of Oklahoma P, 1964); K. Baus et al., *The Imperial Church From Constantine to the Early Middle Ages* (New York: Seabury, 1980), pp. 115–118, 268; J.R. Martindale, *The Prosopography of the Later Roman Empire* (Cambridge: Cambridge UP, 1980), Vol. 2, A.D. 395–527, pp. 714–715; K.G. Holum, *Theodosian Empresses: Women and Imperial Domination in Late Antiquity* (Berkeley: U of California P, 1982).

MARCIANUS (late fourth century). Syrian monk. To Marcianus have been assigned treatises, mainly on ascetic subjects, that survive largely in Syriac. An alternative attribution is to a fifth-century monk of Bethlehem. CPG II, 3885–3900.   [E.F.]

Bibliography

Theodoret, *History of the Monks* 3(25); idem, *Church History* 4.25; Cyril of Scythopolis, *Vita Euthymii* 123 (PG 114.701); Zachariah, *Historia ecclesiastica* 3.3 (PG 85.1152).

MARCION (d. ca. 154). One of the most influential heretics of the second century. Marcion was born in Sinope, a port on the Black Sea in the province of Pontus. Marcion was the son of a bishop and a prosperous ship owner. The tradition that he was expelled from the local church by his father because of the seduction of a virgin is questioned by modern scholars. Marcion went to Rome ca. 140; there, he was for some time a member of the Roman church, to which he gave a large sum of money, and came under the influence of Cerdo, a Gnostic teacher, whose ideas he developed.

Marcion openly expounded his beliefs to the leaders of the church in Rome, whereupon he was excommunicated in July 144. His money was also returned to him.

Thereafter, Marcion founded his own church with an organization and a ritual similar to that of the Roman church, so similar, in fact, that Cyril of Jerusalem found it necessary to warn Christians not to enter a Marcionite church by mistake (*Catech.* 4.4). Marcion was clearly a successful heretic, and according to Justin Martyr his ideas were widely disseminated all over the Roman empire by the year 150.

Marcion's church posed a real threat, and almost all the prominent patristic writers felt constrained to denounce him. His movement spread rapidly through the Roman empire and flourished for nearly a century, with small numbers of adherents lingering on to a much later date. Many Marcionites were swallowed up by Manichaeism. Irenaeus of Lyons reckoned Marcion among the Gnostics. But although Marcionism did have much in common with Gnosticism, it differed in several important respects, for instance, in its lack of speculation about a series of aeons emanating from an original divine being.

According to Marcion, there was a radical dichotomy between the Old and the New Testament, between the Law and the Gospel. He also sharply distinguished between an inferior creator God, or Demiurge, of the Old Testament and the Supreme God of the New Testament. The creator God's incompetence, ignorance, and wickedness were revealed throughout the Old Testament: as the creator of Adam, he was responsible for the entrance of evil into the world; he was ignorant and could not find Adam, and thus he had to ask Adam where he was. The imperfection of the world is a reflection of the imperfection of the Demiurge, who was also characterized by contradictory actions. After forbidding the making of images, he ordered Moses to set up a brazen serpent. The vengeful Jewish God also taught "an eye for an eye and a tooth for a tooth." Christ, however, commanded love even toward one's enemies. The God of the New Testament alone was worthy to be called God.

Likewise, Marcion believed that the Christ of the prophets was not to be identified with the Christ of the new dispensation. The Jewish Messiah would bring back the Jews from their dispersion, and this event had still to happen. Marcion's Messiah was a universal savior. Another important aspect of his Christology is its Docetism. He denied that Christ was born of a woman and that his body was material. This view was derived from Marcion's belief that matter is evil. Thus, an earthly body cannot serve as a dwelling place for the divine.

Although Marcion rejected the religion of the Old Testament as irrelevant to Christianity, he did not deny that the Old Testament had some value. He regarded it as an accurate historical document of the past and of the Jewish race in particular. Marcion interpreted each verse literally, rejecting the allegorical method of exegesis; he even disregarded figurative meanings. The church fathers ridiculed Marcion because he repudiated all attempts to see the suffering Messiah as the fulfillment of Old Testament prophecy. He did have some appreciation for the Old Testament as an ethical code, but he believed it had validity only until the beginning of the Christian era.

Concerning the New Testament, Marcion believed that only Paul correctly understood Jesus' teaching and rejected the twelve apostles as Judaizers who taught a modified Judaism repugnant to God. Much in Paul's epistles was arbitrarily used by Marcion in support of his own doctrines, for example, that the old dispensation of the Law and the prophets had passed away. Passages in the Pauline epistles that could be interpreted as assigning validity to the Old Testament Marcion rejected as interpolations and simply removed.

Marcion deduced from Galatians 1:8–9 that there was only one Gospel, which he identified with Luke, who was a friend and companion of Paul; the other Gospels were contaminated by Jewish influences. Although Luke was the closest to the original Gospel, it too was nevertheless perverted by Judaizers and contained elements that had to be discarded, such as the Jewish genealogy and the infancy narrative.

Marcion was the first person to compile a collection of canonical New Testament scriptures. This consisted of one Gospel (an abridgment of the Gospel of Luke) and ten expurgated Pauline epistles (known as the *Apostolicon*). The Pastoral Epistles and the Epistle to the Hebrews were excluded as being non-Pauline. (Marcion also changed the title of the Epistle to the Ephesians to the *Epistle to the Laodiceans*.) In his *Antitheses*, Marcion justified his criticism of the scriptures and his formation of a canon. This work had a creedlike status in the Marcionite church, but only quotations from it have been preserved. Marcion's activities impelled Christians to study the relationship between the Old and New Testament and gave an important impetus to the formation of the canon.   [H.F.S.]

Bibliography

Irenaeus, *Against Heresies* 1.27; 4.8, 34; Tertullian, *Prescription Against Heretics* 30–44; Clement of Alexandria, *Miscellanies* 3.3–4; Origen, *Against Celsus* 6.53, 74; Eusebius, *Church History* 4.11, 29; Epiphanius, *Panarion* 42.

Tertullianus: Adversus Marcionem, ed. and tr. E. Evans, OECT, 2 vols. (1972).

R.S. Wilson, *Marcion: A Study of a Second-Century Heretic* (London: Clarke, 1933); J. Knox, *Marcion and the New Testament* (Chicago: U of Chicago P, 1942); E.C. Blackman, *Marcion and His Influence* (London: SPCK, 1948); D. Balas, "Marcion Revisited: A 'Post-Harnack' Perspective," *Texts and Testament: Critical Essays on the Bible and Early Church Fathers*, ed. W.E. March (San Antonio: Trinity UP, 1980), pp. 95–108; R.J. Hoffman, *Marcion: On the Restitution of Christianity: An Essay on the Development of Radical Paulinist Theology in the Second Century* (Chico: Scholars, 1984); G. May, "Marcion in Contemporary Views: Results and Open Questions," H.J.W. Drijvers, "Marcionism in Syria: Principles, Problems, and Polemics," and R.J. Hoffmann, "How Then Know This Troublous Teacher? Further Reflections on Marcion and his Church," special issue of *SCent* 6 (1987/1988): 129–191; A. von Harnack, *Marcion: The Gospel of the Alien God* (Durham: Labyrinth, 1989; orig. German ed. 1921).

MARCIONITE PROLOGUES. Most manuscripts of the Latin Vulgate contain brief prologues to the letters of Paul identifying the recipients and giving the letters' place of composition and purpose. They seem to have originated in Greek in the late second century and to presuppose the order of Paul's letters as given in Marcion's edition. The prefaces to 2 Corinthians, 2 Thessalonians, and letters to individuals appear to be later additions. It is still debated whether these prologues derived from Marcionite circles or are evidence of Marcion using an already existing order of Paul's letters. Their content does not reflect distinctive Marcionite teaching. *See also* Marcion; Vulgate. [E.F.]

Bibliography

J. Wordsworth and H. White, eds., *Novum Testamentum Domini Nostri Jesu Christi Latine* (Oxford: Clarendon, 1913–1941), Vol. 2.

D.J. Theron, *Evidence of Tradition* (Grand Rapids: Baker Book House, 1958), pp. 78–83.

N. Dahl, "The Origin of the Earliest Prologues to the Pauline Letters," *Semeia* 12 (1978):233–277.

MARCUS

MARCUS (second century). Gnostic leader; adherent of Valentinus in Asia Minor. Marcus is depicted in negative terms by the only extant primary source, Irenaeus of Lyons, who reported that he employed magic in the celebration of a kind of eucharist and seduced women with potions and love charms. He and his followers, the Marcosians, who had spread to the region of the Rhône in Gaul, were said to have engaged in extensive alphabetic and numerical speculations. Their scriptures included the *Acts of Thomas* and other apocrypha. *See also* Gnosticism. [M.P.McH.]

Bibliography

Irenaeus, *Against Heresies* 1.7–14.

F. Sagnard, *La Gnose valentinienne et le témoignage de st. Irénée* (Paris: Vrin, 1947), pp. 358–386; M. Simonetti, *Testi gnostici cristiani* (Bari: Laterza, 1970), pp. 219–224; R.J. Hoffman, "The 'Eucharist' of Marcus Magus: A Test-Case in Gnostic Social Theory," *Patristic and Byzantine Review* 3 (1984):82–88; D.J. Good, "Sophia in Valentinianism," *SCent* 4 (1984):193–201.

MARCUS AURELIUS

MARCUS AURELIUS (121–180). Roman emperor (161–180) and philosopher. Adopted by his predecessor, Antoninus Pius, Marcus Aurelius was married (145) to Antoninus's daughter, Faustina the Younger (d. 175). He abandoned rhetorical studies to devote himself to Stoicism (146–147). Upon his accession to the throne, he shared authority with a co-emperor, Lucius Verus, after whose death (169) he ruled alone. The reign was troubled by wars, including a Parthian invasion (163–166), nominally handled by Verus, although others were in fact responsible for the Roman victory; a plague (166–167) that brought about a substantial loss in population; a revolt in Syria and Egypt (175); and repeated fighting against Germanic tribes on the northern frontiers (166–168, 170–175, 178–180).

The last of the five "good emperors," Marcus showed a profound concern for the spiritual and material welfare of the Roman empire. The judiciary was reformed and the civil service improved and enlarged to meet the increasing complexity of administration, but the depletion of funds from the long series of wars would prove irreparable. The emperor sought to gain public recognition for philosophy by establishing chairs at Athens (176) for the four main schools: Platonism, Aristotelianism, Stoicism, and Epicureanism. His writings consist of letters, mostly in Latin, to his onetime tutor in Latin rhetoric, Fronto, and the Greek *Meditations*, a series of philosophic reflections in no particular order, intended for his personal use and probably transcribed from his notebooks after his death. Consistent themes in his philosophy are the tension between the desire for reflection and repose and the obligations of social duty, and the inevitability of death and need for resignation to it. His Stoicism, while not original, was deeply felt.

As an upholder of the traditional religion, he considered Christianity a danger to the state and judged that the Christians' refusal to sacrifice to the gods was obstinate and theatrical (*Meditations* 11.3). Although no general persecution is attributable to him, he allowed the local persecutions that arose to some extent from the superstitious fears of a population suffering from the misfortunes of the time. In reply to a question from the governor at Lyons, he held that Christians, even those who were Roman citizens, were to be executed unless they recanted (177). Among those who suffered death under his rule were Justin Martyr along with six companions at Rome (ca. 165) and a group of some forty-eight at Lyons, including Pothinus, the aged bishop of the city, and Blandina, a young slave girl (177). Certain other martyrdoms assigned to the reign may not in fact have taken place during it. A number of Christian apologists directed their protests to the emperor. Those of Athenagoras and Theophilus of Antioch are extant; the addresses of Miltiades, Apollinaris of Hierapolis, and Melito of Sardis are lost.   [M.P.McH.]

Bibliography

Dio Cassius, *Roman History* 71–72; *Historia Augusta, Life of Marcus Aurelius*; Eusebius, *Church History* 4.14.10–5.9.1.

Marcus Aurelius, *Meditations,* tr. M. Staniforth (Harmondsworth: Penguin, 1964); Marcus Aurelius, *Meditations,* tr. G.M.A. Grube (Indianapolis: Bobbs-Merrill, 1963).

H. Sedgwick, *Marcus Aurelius: A Biography* (New Haven: Yale UP, 1921); P.A. Brunt, "Marcus Aurelius and the Christians," *Studies in Latin Literature and Roman History*, ed. C. Deroux (Brussels: Latomus, 1979), Vol. 1, pp. 483–520; J.H. Oliver, "Marcus Aurelius and the Philosophical Schools at Athens," *AJPh* 102 (1981):213–225; P. Hadot, "Les Pensées de Marc Aurèle," *BAGB* (1981):183–191; A. Birley, *Marcus Aurelius: A Biography*, 2nd ed. (New Haven: Yale UP, 1987); R.M. Grant, "Five Apologists and Marcus Aurelius," *VChr* 42 (1988):1–17.

MARINUS. Several persons of this name appear in the sources. The best known are a Roman legionary martyred at Caesarea in Palestine (ca. 260) and the patron saint of the Republic of San Marino (fourth century?). The latter was, according to legend, a deacon and a hermit, but nothing is known of his life with certainty.   [M.P.McH.]

Bibliography

[Marinus, martyr of Caesarea]: Eusebius, *Church History* 7.15–16; Musurillo, pp. xxxvi, 240–243.

MARIUS MERCATOR (fifth century). North African who combated Pelagianism, particularly that of Celestius and Julian. Marius also attacked Theodore of Mopsuestia as the source of Pelagian and Nestorian error. He was bilingual, equally competent in Greek and Latin. CPL 780–781 (200, 754, 775).   [F.W.N.]

MARK. Member of the primitive Jerusalem church and missionary companion of Paul, Barnabas, and probably Peter; traditional author of Second Gospel. The name "Mark" (a common Latin name in antiquity) occurs eight times in the New Testament, presumably all of them referring to the same person. Five of these occurrences are in Acts, where John Mark is introduced as the son of a Mary in whose Jerusalem home Peter took refuge after being miraculously freed from Herod's prison (Acts 12:12). This same John Mark is mentioned as accompanying Barnabas and Saul from Antioch when they brought relief to the Jerusalem church (Acts 12:25; cf. 11:27–30). The last set of references in Acts is found in 15:37–39; because John Mark had apparently withdrawn from a previous missionary trip in Pamphylia (13:13), Paul did not want his company on another trip. This led to a rift with Barnabas, who took Mark with him to Cyprus, while Paul chose Silas as his associate.

If the "Mark" referred to in the Pauline correspondence is the same John Mark, then the rift must have eventually healed. He is mentioned in Colossians 4:10 as "Mark the cousin of Barnabas" and in Philemon 24 as "fellow worker" of Paul. In the probably Deutero-Pauline 2 Timothy, the author describes Mark as "very useful in serving me" (4:11).

The final New Testament reference to Mark is found in 1 Peter 5:13, where the author calls Mark "my son" and depicts him as joining Peter in sending greetings from Rome to the churches of northern Asia Minor.

Although there is little doubt that John Mark was a significant missionary figure in the earliest church, there is some debate about his possible connection with Peter in the composition of the Gospel attributed to his name. The earliest attestation of Mark as the evangelist is found in Eusebius (*H.E.* 3.39.15), who cites Papias (ca. 125–130), who in turn refers to the testimony of John the elder. Papias's claim is that Mark was the "interpreter" of Peter during his stay in Rome and wrote from memory the materials Peter had used in his preaching, thus materials already adapted to an audience. Later variations on this tradition (e.g., Origen in Eusebius, *H.E.* 6.25.5) give Peter a more direct role, along with Mark, in the composition of the Gospel. Available sources do not permit certitude, but there seems to be no good reason to doubt that Mark was associated with Peter (as already indicated in Acts 12:12 and 1 Peter 5:13), was the author of the Gospel attributed to him, and may have been part of Peter's missionary group located in Rome.

The outline of Jesus' ministry in the Gospel of Mark provides the basic structure of the Synoptic Gospels: (1) Preliminaries of the ministry of John the Baptist leading to the baptism and temptation of Jesus (1:1–13). (2) Opening of the Galilean ministry, leading to the appointment of the Twelve (1:14–3:19). (3) Height of the Galilean ministry, climaxing in the rejection at Nazareth and mission charge to the Twelve (3:20–6:13). (4) Ministry outside Galilee, climaxing in the confession of Jesus' messiahship (6:14–8:30). (5) Journey to Jerusalem, during which the meaning of messiahship was clarified (8:31–10:52). (6) Ministry in Jerusalem, closing with the apocalyptic discourse (11:1–13:37). (7) Passion and resurrection (14:1 to the ending, on which the manuscripts differ). The Gospel of Mark is a fast-moving narrative with vivid details in which the emphasis is on the mighty deeds of Jesus more than on the content of his teaching. Greatest attention centers on the passion of Jesus and its meaning.

Mark was neglected by patristic commentators. Later writers identify Mark as the founder of the church of Alexandria. Although there is little historical grounding for this, it is an important part of Coptic church tradition. Mark was represented in Christian art by a lion (although Irenaeus ascribed to him the eagle—*Haer.* 3.11.8). Feast day April 25.   [D.P.S.]

Bibliography

V. Taylor, *The Gospel According to St. Mark* (London: Macmillan, 1959); R.P. Martin, *Mark: Evangelist and Theologian* (Grand Rapids: Zondervan, 1973); M. Smith, *Clement of Alexandria and a Secret Gospel of Mark* (Cambridge: Harvard UP, 1973); W.L. Lane, *The Gospel According to Mark* (Grand Rapids: Eerdmans, 1974); S. Kealy, *Mark's Gospel: A History of Its Interpretation* (New York: Paulist, 1982); R. Brown and J. Meier, *Antioch and Rome* (New York: Paulist, 1983), pp. 191–201; H.-M. Schenke, "The Mystery of the Gospel of Mark," *SCent* 4 (1984): 65–82; M. Hengel, *Studies in the Gospel of Mark* (Philadelphia: Fortress, 1985), pp. 1–58; B. Orchard, "The Historical Tradition," *The Order of the Synoptics: Why Three Synoptic Gospels?* ed. B. Orchard and H. Riley (Macon: Mercer UP, 1987), pp. 111–226.

MARRIAGE. According to Christian teaching, the union of one man and one woman for life for procreation and companionship. The church fathers repeated what Jesus and the apostles taught about the indissolubility of marriage and the mutual obligations of the husband and wife (Matt. 19:1–12; 1 Cor. 7; Eph. 5:22 ff.). There are three areas, however, in which they advanced the New Testament teaching: the comparison of marriage with virginity, the sacramental doctrine of marriage, and the role of the church in matrimonial affairs.

Heretical and Orthodox Views of Marriage. The true thought of the fathers on marriage is found less in their ascetical writings, in which they compare it unfavorably with virginity, than in their apologetic works, where they defend marriage against heretical excesses of the day, two of them in particular. The first was Encratism, which held that the marriage act was sinful and had to be renounced, a teaching associated with Tatian (Jerome, *Comm. Gal.*). Tertullian attributed the similar teaching against marriage cited in 1 Timothy 4:3 ("forbidding marriage") to Marcion and Apelles (*Praesc.* 33). The other heresy was that promoting communal sex, which condemned marriage but permitted sexual intercourse. This seems to have been the teaching of the Nicolaitans (Eusebius, *H.E.* 3.29). Carpocrates and Epiphanes also taught that wives were to be held in common (Clement of Alexandria, *Str.* 3.2).

The orthodox Christian writers, rejecting both the rigorism and the promiscuity of the heretics, asserted the legitimacy and sanctity of marriage. Clement of Alexandria refuted those who deprecated marriage by listing the apostles known to have been married and by telling a story about Peter's devotion to his wife (Eusebius, *H.E.* 3.30). Clement denied that procreation was a sin or that parenthood was a distraction from holy living. He condemned wantonness and excess, however; the marital act must be chaste. He upheld monogamy strictly as the only legitimate form of marriage, against those adherents of Gnosticism, the Carpocratians, who held their women in common and against pagan immorality in general (Tertullian, *Apol.* 39.11–13). According to Augustine, marriage is the foundation of all social relationships (*Fid. invis.* 4).

Of all the Greek fathers, it was John Chrysostom, in *On Marriage and Family Life*, who treated the moral aspects of marriage most extensively. His main ideas were three. First, marriage is not an obstacle to salvation; otherwise, God would not have instituted it. A married person, if the will is present, can fulfill his or her religious duties. Second, God established marriage for the procreation of children; sin, however, has destroyed the original divine intent, so much so that contemporary humanity has substituted the indulgence and satisfaction of the sexual instinct as the primary purpose of marriage (cf. 1 Cor. 7:9). Marriage is thus a harbor in which tempted or weak souls take refuge, whereas strong and noble souls have the capacity for virginity. Third, marriage is nevertheless a praiseworthy state and not a sinful one, although its origin is tainted with corruption. Marriage, with its capacity to repress evil desires and promiscuity, simultaneously promotes the spiritual and like virginity can be a means to procure salvation. Chrysostom also discusses the desirability of family life and the role of the Christian wife (*Hom.* 4.2f. in Is. 6:1).

Tertullian wrote one of the most impressive eulogies of Christian marriage, *To His Wife,* showing the esteem in which the church held marriage. The work depicts divine benediction, human happiness, and the harmonious life of the pair under the protection of God and in union with Christ (*Ux.* 2). Ambrose taught that the virtue of chastity embraces marriage along with widowhood and virginity; heaven would be monotonous if only the continent were admitted there (*Vid.* 4). He also praised pregnancy and maternity, using the Virgin Mary as an example (*Expos. Luc.* 2.2). Jerome, on the contrary, favored virginity to such an extent that he had to defend himself against the charge of being an enemy of marriage (*Ep.* 48).

Augustine provided the definitive exposition of the patristic doctrine of the virtue of marriage in *On the Good of Marriage* and *On Marriage and Concupiscence.* Marriage is not blameworthy; it was instituted and blessed by God at creation and then elevated by Jesus to the status of a symbol of his union with the church. Marriage is good because it offers three good things: *proles,* the procreation of infants by the conjugal act; *fides,* the chastity of the spouses in reciprocal fidelity; and *sacramentum,* the indissoluble union of the spouses. Augustine's positive estimate of the conjugal act was an advance on the thought of his predecessors; he believed concupiscence to be an evil, but not the act of marriage itself; when spouses have the procreation of infants as their goal, the conjugal act is sinless and legitimate.

Influence of Christianity upon Marriage. Christianity made marriage a matter of free choice. Although recommending celibacy, the fathers respected the liberty of the individual and let the person decide whether to marry. The second-century pagan apologist Celsus, while noting the aversion Christians had for holding public office, says nothing about any repugnance on their part to marriage. Only in the second half of the fourth century, when monasticism was reaching its apogee, was the church accused of destroying the family and depopulating the empire.

Christianity gave marriage its due honor, treating it as a divine institution rather than as a civic duty; its model was the relationship between Christ and his church. The foundation of marriage thus became conjugal love, which mitigated the harshness of the husband's role as master. Even more significant was the change in the wife's position. Pagan antiquity generally did not concede to women the full status of a human being; in relation to her husband, she was deprived of basic rights to the point of enslavement. Christianity made the wife equal to the husband, sharing the same perfection, in relation to Christ and the kingdom of God. The subordination of the wife was now voluntary, not natural, and her role was valued positively.

Matrimony was contracted within the Christian community. The first witness of the intervention of the church in marriage is Ignatius of Antioch (ca. 110), who wrote: "It is right for men and women who marry to be united with the consent of the bishop, that the marriage be according to the Lord and not according to lust" (*Polyc.* 5.2). The fourth-century church fathers frowned upon marriages between Christians and pagans or Jews, although the contemporary councils did not regard such marriages as invalid but merely inflicted penance on the couple or their parents (Elvira, *can.* 15–17; Chalcedon, *can.* 14). The civil law was stricter, sometimes punishing marriages between Christians and Jews with the death penalty (*Cod. Thds.* 16.8.6 [339]; 3.7.2 [388]).

The pagan customs surrounding weddings were modified to conform to Christian sensitivity. John Chrysostom opposed the pagan practice of dancing at weddings, saying: "Is the wedding then a theater? It is a sacrament, a mystery, and a model of the Church of Christ, and still you invite dissolute women to it! . . . But why is there any need of dancing at all? They dance at pagan ceremonies; but at ours, silence and decorum should prevail, respect and modesty. Here, a great mystery is accomplished; away with the dissolute women, away with the profane!" (*Hom.* 12.4 *in Col*; cf. *Inan. gl. 88*).

Among the essentials of Christian marriage were mutual consent and the blessing of prayer, often including the eucharist. Secular customs of joining right hands, giving a ring, taking a veil, and (in the east) crowning were continued in the wedding ceremony (Stevenson, Ch. 1). The equating of the marriage rite with other sacraments belongs to a later period. Christian iconography continued the Roman custom of depicting a marriage by showing the couple joining right hands, but Christ replaced Juno as the deity uniting the couple.

[M.A.S.]

Bibliography

Clement of Alexandria, *Miscellanies* 3, tr. H. Chadwick, LCC (1954), Vol. 2; Tertullian, *To His Wife* and *Monogamy*, tr. W.P. LeSaint, ACW (1951), Vol. 13; John Chrysostom, *On Marriage and Family Life*, tr. C.P. Roth and D. Anderson (Crestwood: St. Vladimir's Seminary, 1986); Augustine, *On the Good of Marriage*, tr. T. Wilcox, FOTC (1955), Vol. 27; idem, *On Marriage and Concupiscence*, tr. R. Holmes and R.E. Wallis, NPNF, 1st ser. (1887), Vol. 5.

A. Moulard, *Saint Jean Chrysostome, le défenseur du mariage et l'apôtre de la virginité* (Paris: Gabalda, 1923); G.H. Joyce, *Christian Marriage: An Historical and Doctrinal Study*, 2nd ed. (London: Sheed and Ward, 1948); J. Noonan, *Contraception: A History of Its Treatment by the Catholic Theologians and Canonists*, 2nd ed. (Cambridge: Belknap, 1966); J.J. Hugo, *St. Augustine on Nature, Sex, and Marriage* (Chicago: Scepter, 1969); K. Stevenson, *Nuptial Blessing: A Study of Christian Marriage Rites* (New York: Oxford UP, 1983); O.L. Yarbrough, *Not Like the Gentiles: Marriage Rules in the Letters of Paul* (Atlanta: Scholars, 1985); C. Munier, *Ehe und Ehelosigkeit in der Alten Kirche* (Bern: Lang, 1987).

MARTIN OF BRAGA (ca. 520–ca. 580). Archbishop, missionary, and writer. Born in Pannonia, Martin, who had become a monk in Palestine, entered Gallaecia (modern Galicia in Spain and northern Portugal) ca. 550; there, he became abbot then bishop of Dumio, and archbishop of Braga. He was active in the conversion of the Sueves from Arianism to orthodox belief. His many writings reflect both theological and pastoral interests, as well as a sound classical knowledge. *Sayings from the Egyptian Fathers* is a translation from the Greek for his monks. The three short essays *Driving Away Vanity, Pride,* and *Exhortation to Humility* show the influence of John Cassian. A collection of canons from eastern, African, and Spanish synods has come down under his name; some elements of it are his. The moral treatise *Anger* is based on Seneca; very popular in the Middle Ages, and likewise based on Seneca (the lost *De officiis*), was the treatise *Rules for an Honest Life,* which deals with the four cardinal virtues. The sermon *Reforming the Rustics* shows the persistence of pagan beliefs among the rural population of the region. *Triple Immersion* is directed against the practice of using a single immersion at baptism. Feast day

March 20. CPL 1079c–1090; see 1787–1790a.

[M.P.McH.]

Bibliography

Gregory of Tours, *De virtutibus Sancti Martini Turonensis* 1.11; idem, *History of the Franks* 5.37; Venantius Fortunatus, *Carmina* 5.1, 2; Isidore of Seville, *De viris illustribus* 22 (35).

Writings of Martin of Braga, tr. C.W. Barlow, in *Iberian Fathers*, Vol. 1, FOTC (1969), Vol. 62, pp. 3–109.

C.W. Barlow, "Martin of Braga," *Leaders of Iberian Christianity*, ed. J.M.-F. Marique (Boston: St. Paul, 1962), pp. 103–113 (valuable collection of the evidence); A. Ferreiro, "The Missionary Labors of St. Martin of Braga in 6th Century Galicia," *StudMon* 23 (1981):11–26; idem, "St. Martin of Braga's Policy Toward Heretics and Pagan Practices," *American Benedictine Review* 34 (1983):372–395.

MARTIN OF TOURS (ca. 316–397).

Monk and bishop. A convert from paganism, Martin, after service in the Roman army, eventually took up the monastic life, first at Milan and later (ca. 360) in Gaul. As bishop of Tours (from ca. 372), he continued to encourage monasticism. He devoted much effort to the evangelization of the pagan countryside, introducing the beginnings of a parochial system. His intercession against the execution of Priscillian by the emperor Maximus was in vain. Upon his death, his cult spread widely; many churches and monasteries were dedicated to him throughout the Middle Ages. Gregory of Tours devoted four of his *Miraculorum Libri viii* to miracles worked by his relics. The story that Martin, as a solider, once shared his cloak with a beggar, is apocryphal. A confession of faith, once attributed to him, is not his. Feast day November 11 (west), November 12 (east). CPL 1748a. *See also* Sulpicius Severus.

[M.P.McH.]

Bibliography

Sulpicius Severus, *Life of St. Martin, Letters, Dialogues*, tr. B.M. Peebles, FOTC (1949), Vol. 7; Paulinus of Périgueux, *Vita S. Martini*; Gregory of Tours, *De virtutibus Sancti Martini Turonensis*; idem, *History of the Franks* passim, tr. O.M. Dalton (Oxford: Clarendon, 1927); Venantius Fortunatus, *Vita S. Martini*.

N.K. Chadwick, *Poetry and Letters in Early Christian Gaul* (London: Bowes and Bowes, 1955), pp. 89–121; C. Stancliffe, *St. Martin and His Hagiographer: History and Miracle in Sulpicius Severus* (Oxford: Clarendon, 1983); on the development of the cult, see J.H. Corbett, "The Saint as Patron in the Work of Gregory of Tours," *JMedHist* 7 (1981):1–13; L. Pietri, *La Ville de Tours du IVe au VIe siècle: naissance d'une cité chrétienne* (Rome: Ecole Française de Rome, 1983); B.W. Reynolds, "Familia Sancti Martini: Domus Ecclesiae on Earth As It Is in Heaven," *JMedHist* 11 (1985):137–143.

MARTYR, MARTYRDOM.

Giving one's life because of one's faith. The Greek word *martus* ("martyr") meant "witness" and the verb form, *martureo*, meant "to testify." In the New Testament, the writings of Luke use the noun for one who had seen the resurrected Christ, an "eyewitness," and so one who could literally bear witness to him or attest his resurrection (Luke 24:48; Acts 1:22). The Johannine writings use the verb in the sense of testimony for Christ as Son of God, to confess him (John 1:15; 5:36f.; Rev. 1:2). Revelation 2:13 uses "martyr" of a "blood witness," one who was killed for his confession of faith, and before the end of the second century the word had become technical in this sense (*M. Polyc.* 2; Irenaeus, *Haer.* 5.9.2; Clement of Alexandria, *Str.* 4.4–5, 21). The idea of "eyewitness" was not lost, for the martyrs were accorded a vision of Christ (Acts 7:56; 22:20?; *M. Carp.* 39; 42). A distinction was made between those who confessed before the authorities and survived ("confessors") and those who died, to whom alone the name "martyrs" was given (cf. Eusebius, *H.E.* 5.2.2–4).

Background and History. There survive some records of proceedings against dissidents to Roman rule known as *The Acts of the Pagan Martyrs* (ed. H. Musurillo [Oxford: Clarendon, 1954]), but the title reflects the application of Christian terminology to those whose protest was political. Accounts of the deaths of illustrious men, particularly philosophers and preeminently Socrates, were appropriated to describe Christian martyrs as seekers of truth who despised death. Among the Jews, there were accounts of the sufferings of the prophets (*Lives of the Prophets*) and accounts of rabbis who died for the Law and sanctification of the name of God, but there is missing the idea of witness or testimony, which is emphasized in the Christian terminology. The "Maccabean

Front of the procession of twenty-six martyrs led by St. Martin from the mosaic decoration (557–572) of the south wall of S. Apollinare Nuovo, Ravenna, Italy. (Photograph Editore Dante, Ravenna.)

Martyrs" (the aged Eleazar and a mother with her seven sons) are the only martyrs commemorated by both Jews and Christians, and their story in 2 Maccabees 6:18–7:41 and *4 Maccabees* was influential in the Christian literature and theology of martyrdom.

Although persecution was not a constant experience for early Christians, it was a possibility with which all had to reckon. In this atmosphere, religious confession took on its special meaning of "blood witness." A few Christians were deliberately provocative to the authorities, but they and those who came forward asking for martyrdom did not represent the thinking of the church at large, which took the position that one should be faithful if brought to trial but should not seek out martyrdom. Tertullian, as a Montanist, voiced enthusiasm for martyrdom (*Fug.* 9), but such an attitude was found in the Catholic church also (*Scap.* 5). The steadfastness of Christians under persecution led some observers to conversion (Justin, *2 Apol.* 12; Tertullian, *Apol.* 50),

but other pagans treated the enthusiasm for martyrdom with scorn (Marcus Aurelius, *Meditations* 11.3; Epictetus, *Discourses* 4.7.6). The Gnostics in general avoided martyrdom. The Christians who were steadfast in the face of persecution were fewer than those who fell away or went into hiding. The martyrs, therefore, were the heroes of the church, and a high regard for them is already evident in the first document devoted to martyrdom, the *Martyrdom of Polycarp* (ca. 155/6 or 167). A theology of martyrdom was early elaborated. A beginning is present in the letter of Ignatius to the *Romans*, and it was fully developed in the literature of martyrdom in the second and third centuries.

The greatest number of martyrs was made during the persecutions of Decius and Diocletian in the mid-third and early fourth centuries. In the third century, the cultic veneration of martyrs spread throughout the church. With the coming of peace to the church in the fourth and fifth centuries, the expressions of honor for the martyrs knew no bounds, and the cult of the martyrs was fully accomplished. Likewise, since martyrs were no longer being made by pagan Rome, cultic veneration began to be freed from its original limitation to martyrs and extended to monks and bishops as spiritual martyrs. A basis for this development had been laid in the theology of Origen, who, denied the martyrdom he desired, had fashioned under the influence of the ascetic piety of late antiquity the ideal of interior martyrdom, which became the spiritual basis of Christian monasticism. Literal martyrdom continued to be experienced by Christians in Persia during the fourth and fifth centuries, and within the Roman empire heretics experienced persecution from the Christian rulers.

Literature. The authentic accounts of martyrdom come in two literary forms: the *passiones* or *martyria* and the *acta* or *gesta.* The passions are accounts of the last days and of the death of the martyr. The two earliest are letters from the home churches of the martyrs, setting forth their conduct and death as models for others: The *Martyrdom of Polycarp,* depicting a "martyrdom according to the gospel," that is, according to the will of God; and the *Letter of the Churches of Lyons and Vienne* (ca. 177—Eusebius, *H.E.* 5.1.3-63), presenting Christ as suffering in the martyrs. The Latin passions emphasized the visions received by the martyrs and presented the martyrs as possessors of the prophetic gift and so as successors of the prophets. Quite notable is the *Passion of Perpetua and Felicitas,* because it incorporates the diary of Perpetua and the account of the vision of Saturus written by himself. In the later Donatist passions, polemics against the Catholic church take precedence over history.

The acts of the martyrs recount their trials before the authorities. They are not transcripts of the court proceedings, and even where they may be based on such official documents they have undergone Christian editing and adaptation. The earliest, the *Acts of Justin,* exists in three recensions that show the progressive editing that was done to these works. Others, such as the *Acts of SS. Carpus, Papylus, and*

Agathonice, show later reworking. One of the earliest documents of Christian Latin is the *Acts of the Scillitan Martyrs* from North Africa. A characteristic of the Latin acts was the formula by the martyr, *Deo gratias* ("thanks to God").

The reality of martyrdom and the difficulty of facing it led to the writing of exhortations to martyrdom: Tertullian, *To the Martyrs;* Origen, *Exhortation to Martyrdom;* Cyprian, *To Fortunatus;* Pseudo-Cyprian, *Glory of Martyrdom.* These were written to encourage Christians facing persecution.

The annual commemoration of the death of a martyr included from the fourth century the preaching of a panegyric on his or her life. The eulogies delivered by the great bishops and preachers of the fourth and fifth centuries established a new branch of classical epideictic literature. Basil, Gregory of Nazianzus, Gregory of Nyssa, Ephraem the Syrian, John Chrysostom, and Asterius of Amasea were among the great panegyrists. Drawing on the fragments of tradition available, they used hyperbole to enhance the virtues of the martyrs. Since the goal was edification, they exhorted the hearers to the imitation of the martyrs.

History became even more subordinate to "edification" in the legends and lives of the saints that came to be written. Jerome's *Life of Paul* the hermit, for example, may not have had much more than the name of the hero as its historical core. The panegyrists had extended the honors originally reserved for martyrs to bishops, ascetics, and virgins, and this was continued in the hagiographical texts.

Theology. The significance of martyrdom in the early church is shown by the important theological premises that were used to interpret the event. Martyrdom was a grace not given by God to everyone. Since martyrdom was a bit capricious as to whom it came, there was a strong sense that one was chosen by God for this experience (*A. Cyp.* 2.1; Ps.-Cyprian, *Laud. mart.* 23; Hippolytus, *Dan.* 3.26). To be a martyr was to be counted worthy by God (*M. Polyc.* 14; 20; *M. Iren.* 5.2). For this reason, Christians were not to rush into martyrdom (*M. Polyc.* 4).

Martyrdom was an imitation and participation in the sufferings of Christ (*M. Polyc.* 1; 6ff.; Origen, *Mart.* 42), who was present with the martyr, strengthening him or her (*M. Polyc.* 2; Eusebius, *H.E.* 5.1.22). The Holy Spirit filled the martyrs (*M. Agap.* 1) and inspired them with eloquence (Hippolytus, *Dan.* 2.21). Martyrdom was a fight with the devil and his demons (*Pass. Perp.* 10.14), in which victory was won by the martyr (Eusebius, *H.E.* 5.1.23, 27; Origen, *Mart.* 42). Athletic imagery was common. The martyr was assured of an eternal reward, whereas denial brought eternal punishment (*M. Polyc.* 2; 11; Tertullian, *Mart.* 2; *M. Pion.* 20.5). Martyrdom was described in eucharistic (*M. Polyc.* 14) and baptismal (*Pass. Marian. et Jac.* 11.10) language. As a baptism of blood, it brought forgiveness of sins (Tertullian, *Bapt.* 16; Origen, *Mart.* 30). Martyrdom was a witness to the state of its subordination to the God of heaven (*Pass. Jul.* 2.5f.; 3.3; *A. Max.* 2.1) and to unbelievers of the truth of the gospel (*Pass. Perp.* 1; *Pass. Fruct.* 6.3).

Because those who confessed Christ before the authorities were viewed as possessing the Holy Spirit (on the basis of Luke 12:11f.), the martyrs-to-be and confessors were believed to have the power to forgive sins and reconcile penitents to the church (Tertullian, *Mart.* 1; *Pud.* 22; Cyprian, *Ep.* 26; Eusebius, *H.E.* 5.2.5). This created problems in discipline and organization, so that Cyprian and other bishops had to insist on the prerogatives of the bishop in determining reconciliation with the church. The confessor was considered to belong to the rank of the presbyters without benefit of ordination (Hippolytus, *Trad. ap.* 10).

Cult. The marks of respect and veneration (*M. Polyc.*) were not manifestations of cult. The special privileges granted to them were the basis for the cult of the martyrs. The great promises of the gospel were granted to them in a special way: forgiveness of sins, the gift of the Holy Spirit, and eternal life. Martyrs as the perfect disciples immediately realized the blessings promised to all Christians and entered directly on death into the presence of God and Christ in heaven and did not have to await the general resurrection in an intermediate

abode of the dead, as did others (Tertullian, *Anim.* 55; *Res.* 43). Martyrs had won freedom of speech with God and so could serve as intercessors. Invocation of the martyrs to pray for the believer on earth (Cyprian, *Fort.* 11; Ps.-Cyprian, *Laud. mart.* 30) was based on their privileged condition and the practice of intercession for one another. This invocation of the martyrs still stood in relation to the Lord, since they were his servants, and did not become an independent cult separate from Christ (Augustine, *Civ. Dei* 8.27). Given the exceptional place of the martyrs in the church and ancient ideas of the rapport of the dead with the living, the practice of invocation of the saints was not strange to the people of classical antiquity.

Greeks and Romans held funerary meals in honor of a deceased family member annually on the person's birthday. This practice was continued in the church, but with important modifications. The meal was held on the anniversary of the death instead of the birth, for the martyr's death was a birthday to eternity. The family of the deceased was now the Christian community, which formed his or her spiritual family, and this ensured perpetuity of commemoration of those noted for their faith. The commemoration was local at first, and the lists of anniversaries to celebrate in each church constituted the first martyrologies. In time, churches borrowed one another's saints to commemorate. The commemorative meals of paganism became an agape and eucharist in Christianity (Cyprian, *Ep.* 12.2; 39.3).

The cult of the martyrs became public after the recognition of the church. Great numbers of the faithful participated, and there was much show. Memorial buildings (*martyria*) were built. The burial places had earlier been places of prayer, and the place of the tomb governed the location of the edifice. The funeral banquets took on the character of a popular feast more than of religious solemnity, and abuses connected with them led to efforts by church leaders to suppress them (Augustine, *Conf.* 6.2). The commemorative banquet was accompanied by a vigil of prayer, scripture readings, songs, and preaching (a panegyric on the martyr). The relics of the saints were regarded as having power over demons and power to effect healings. Christian preferred to be buried in the vicinity of the martyrs' tombs so as to share in their power at the resurrection. Pilgrims to the sites of martyrs' burials left inscriptions asking them to pray for them. The names of the martyrs were given to the children of the faithful. The cult of the martyrs was particularly prominent in North Africa. Pilgrimage to the grave of a martyr and belief in intercession by a saint had Jewish analogues.

A characteristic phenomenon was the finding of the remains of martyrs hitherto forgotten or unknown. Usually, a dream or a vision revealed the location. The first recorded example of the translation of the bones of a martyr (which would have been quite sacrilegious to pagan Greeks and Romans, but this time was commanded by the emperor Julian) concerned the remains of Babylas of Antioch (Sozomen, *H.E.* 5.19). A famous example was Ambrose's vision revealing the location of the burial of Protasius and Gervasius and his removal of their bones to the Ambrosian basilica in Milan (*Ep.* 22.2).

John of Damascus gave the classic clarification of the distinction according to which veneration belongs to the relic of the saints but true worship is given to God alone (*F.O.* 4.15).

The cult of the martyrs had a Christian origin and development, but pagan and Jewish ideas influenced it, increasingly so with time. The way in which Christian beliefs were expressed stemmed largely from traditional practices. *See also* Hagiography; Martyrion; Paganism and Christianity; Persecution; Relics; Saints.   [E.F.]

Bibliography

Martyrdom of Polycarp; Eusebius, *Church History* 5.1–3; *Passion of Perpetua and Felicitas*; Tertullian, *To the Martyrs*; Origen, *Exhortation to Martyrdom*; Cyprian, *To Fortunatus*; Pseudo-Cyprian, *Glory of Martyrdom*.

H. Musurillo, *The Acts of the Christian Martyrs* (Oxford: Clarendon, 1972).

H. Delehaye, *Les Passions des martyrs et les genres littéraires* (Brussels: Bollandists, 1921); idem, *Sanctus: essai sur le cult des saints dans l'antiquité* (Brussels: Bollandists, 1927); D.W. Riddle, *The Martyrs: A Study in Social Control* (Chicago: U of Chicago P, 1931); H. Delehaye, *Les Origines du culte des martyrs* (Brussels: Bollandists, 1933); M. Lods, *Confesseurs et martyrs: successeurs des prophètes dans l'église des trois premiers siècles* (Neuchâtel: Delachaux & Niestlé, 1958); T. Klauser, *Christlicher Märtyrerkult, heidnischer Heroenkult und spätjüdische Heiligverehrung: Neue Einsichten und neue Probleme* (Cologne: Westdeutscher, 1960); N. Brox, *Zeuge und Märtyrer: Untersuchungen zur frühchristlichen Zeugnis-Terminologie* (Munich: Kösel, 1961); H. von Campenhausen, *Die Idee des Martyriums in der alten Kirche* (Göttingen: Vandenhoeck & Ruprecht, 1964); W.H.C. Frend, *Martyrdom and Persecution in the Early Church* (Oxford: Blackwell, 1965); T. Baumeister, *Die Anfänge der Theologie des Martyriums* (Münster: Aschendorff, 1980); V. Saxer, *Morts, martyrs, reliques en Afrique chrétienne aux premiers siècles* (Paris: Beauchesne, 1980); W.C. Weinrich, *Spirit and Martyrdom: A Study of the Work of the Holy Spirit in Contexts of Persecution and Martyrdom in the New Testament and Early Christian Literature* (Washington, D.C.: UP of America, 1981); B. Dehandschutter, "Le Martyre de Polycarpe et le développement de la conception du martyre au deuxième siècle," *SP* 17.2 (1982):659–668; W. Tabbernee, "Early Montanism and Voluntary Martyrdom," *Colloquium* 17 (1985):33–44; G.A. Bisbee, *Pre-Decian Acts of Martyrs and Commentarii* (Philadelphia: Fortress, 1988); A. Droge and J. Tabor, *A Noble Death: Suicide and Martyrdom Among Ancient Jews, Christians, Greeks, and Romans* (San Francisco: Harper and Row, 1989).

MARTYRDOM OF AGAPE, IRENE, CHIONE, AND COMPANIONS.

Account of the arrest and trials of seven women in Thessalonica in 304. Agape, Irene, and Chione were executed. Its Thessalonian setting is also reflected in its citations of Paul's 1 Thessalonians.   [D.M.S.]

Bibliography

Musurillo, pp. xlii–xliii, 280–293.

MARTYRDOM OF FRUCTUOSUS AND COMPANIONS.

Account of the martyrdom of bishop Fructuosus of Tarragona, Spain, and his two deacons in 259. It is quoted by Augustine (*Serm.* 273) and paraphrased by Prudentius (*Peristeph.* 6). CPL 2056.   [D.M.S.]

Bibliography

Musurillo, pp. xxxii, 176–185.

MARTYRDOM OF MARIAN AND JAMES.

Latin account of martyrdom (third century). The *Martyrdom of Marian and James* was known to Augustine. It tells of the prophetic visions and death of James, a deacon, and Marian, a reader, on May 6, 259, near Cirta in Numidia, during the Valerian persecution. CPL 2050. [D.M.S.]

Bibliography
Augustine, *Sermon* 284.
Musurillo, pp. xxxiii–xxxiv, 194–213.

MARTYRDOM OF MONTANUS AND LUCIUS.

Latin account of martyrdom (third century). The *Martyrdom of Montanus and Lucius* was modeled on the *Martyrdom of Perpetua and Felicitas* to such a degree that its complete historicity is questionable. In the form of a letter to the church in Carthage, it tells of the visions and death of these two clergymen in Carthage on May 23, 259, during the Valerian persecution. CPL 2051. [D.M.S.]

Bibliography
Musurillo, pp. xxxiv–xxxvi, 214–239.

MARTYRDOM OF POLYCARP (ca. 155/6?).

Oldest account of a Christian martyrdom. The *Martyrdom of Polycarp* is a letter from the church at Smyrna to the church at Philomelium in Phrygia recounting the death of the bishop Polycarp, written shortly after the event, to which short appendices were later added. The date of Polycarp's martyrdom is much controverted: between 155 and 159, in 166/7, or in 177. The letter is famous for perhaps the first documentation of the use of "martyr" (Greek *martus*, "witness") in a technical sense (clearly so in 1.1; 2.2; and 19.1); for the courageous declaration of Polycarp before the governor, "For eighty-six years I have served Christ and he has done me no wrong; how can I blaspheme against my king and savior?" (9.3); and for the prayer of the martyr at the stake (14). The document is important also because the parallels to the death of Jesus and the biblical language and imagery (e.g., the "cup of Christ" for death—14) influenced the theology of martyrdom. Polycarp's death was set forth as an example of a "martyrdom according to the gospel" (1.1): he did not volunteer for martyrdom (in contrast to the person who gave himself up to the authorities but then failed to maintain his confession—4) but rather retired in order to save his life; when arrested, he faced his accusers and death with dignity and firmness. CPG I, 1045. TLG 1484. *See also* Martyr, Martyrdom; Polycarp. [E.F.]

Bibliography
Eusebius, *Church History* 4.15.
B. Dehandschutter, *Martyrium Polycarpi: Een Literaair-Kritische Studie* (Louvain: Universitaire Pers, 1979).
Musurillo, pp. xiii–xv, 2–21.
T.D. Barnes, "A Note on Polycarp," *JThS* n.s. 18 (1967):433–437; idem, "Pre-Decian *Acta Martyrum*," *JThS* n.s. 19 (1968):510–514; T. Baumeister, *Die Anfänge der Theologie des Martyriums* (Münster: Aschendorff, 1980), pp. 289–306.

MARTYRDOM OF POTAMIANA AND BASILIDES.

Account of martyrdom (ca. 205–210). Eusebius reports the martyrdom of Potamiana in Egypt, the first recorded to have been inflicted by the pouring of boiling pitch, followed by the martyrdom of Basilides, the soldier who had led her to her death. A vision of Potamiana led him to become a Christian three days later, and he was put to death the next day. He is the first recorded soldier to convert to Christianity as a direct result of a martyr's witness. [D.M.S.]

Bibliography
Eusebius, *Church History* 6.5; Palladius, *Lausiac History* 3.
Musurillo, pp. xxvii–xxviii, 132–135.

MARTYRION.

Greek word (plural *martyria*) designating a place of witness (from *martyrein*, "to witness") and more particularly a church or shrine built to commemorate a place associated with Jesus Christ, with an appearance of God in the biblical narrative, or with the Virgin Mary or other saint of the Christian church, or to house the relics of any of them. In the history of early Christian art and architecture, the term "martyrion" (or *martyrium* following the Latin spelling, although the equivalent Latin term is *memoria*; *martyry* in British usage) has come to refer to a major category of church buildings in distinction from such other categories as the basilica for congregational worship and the baptistery. André Grabar, who published the pioneering work on this category of church in 1946, believed that the martyrion derived from the funerary architecture of the later Roman empire and developed with the Christian cult of the dead, especially the cult of the relics of Christ and the saints.

Today, it is clear that this category of buildings emerged from many sources within Roman imperial architecture. Due recognition must also be given to the creativity of the architects of Constantine, the first Christian ruler of the Roman empire, in designing martyria. The direct connection, which Grabar stressed, between the martyrion and the pagan *heroön*, a building or monument in honor of a hero or

city founder, has been largely rejected because the *heroön* was based on a practice of the earlier Hellenistic era; still, the *heroön* survived in relation to the emperors themselves and could have been adapted to Christ as the founder of the New Jerusalem in the planning of the Church of the Holy Sepulchre in Jerusalem. Cyril of Jerusalem (*Catech.* 14.6) cites Zephaniah 3:8, which in the Septuagint and Revised Standard Version connects resurrection and witness, as the reason for calling this particular church the Martyrion.

The martyrion was typically a centralized structure, as opposed to a hall with a definite axis, such as the basilica; it was focused on a sacred object or place—the remains of a martyr saint, for example, or the burning bush at Mt. Sinai, where the sixth-century emperor Justinian built the monastery of St. Catherine.

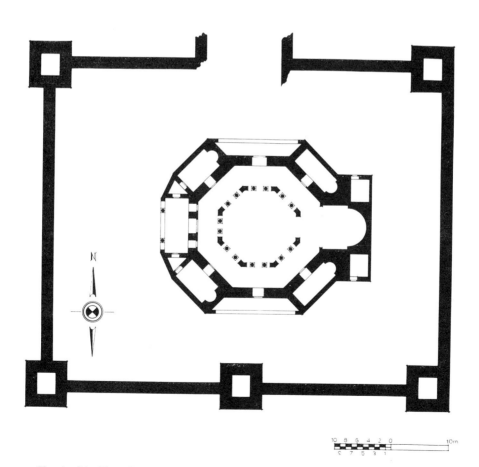

Church of the Theotokos (ca. 484), Mt. Gerizim, Israel. (Plan furnished by G.T. Armstrong.)

When, however, the practice of placing a relic of a saint in or beneath every altar developed in the later fourth century, and became normative for the western church somewhat later, the distinction between the martyrion and the congregational basilica was blurred, although a separate architectural setting for relics, such as an adjacent chapel or a special apse or niche, was often provided.

Grabar described seven kinds of martyria in terms of their plan or shape: (1) those of the square plan, most of which have been incorporated into larger and more complex buildings; (2) those of rectangular plan; (3) those consisting of an isolated apse or exedra (such as were found in pagan cemeteries), which were not of great importance by themselves but became common elements in more elaborate buildings with the same function; (4) those in the form of a triconch, or three apses opening out from a central square; (5) those marked by a transverse or transeptal hall or enclosure; (6) circular or polygonal martyria; and (7) martyria in the shape of a cross, whether in a freestanding cruciform plan that was visible externally or as an arrangement within a larger building, the so-called inscribed cross. The last of course had a particular symbolic significance for Christians, as did the octagonal martyrion (the number eight symbolized the resurrection). The provision of an ambulatory around the simple circular or polygonal structure seems to have been a new design created by Constantine's architects for the Church of the Holy Sepulchre and was often copied thereafter.

Martyria have been found in all parts of the ancient Christian world, from Egypt and Syria to the Balkans, Gaul, and North Africa. The first and most important for the cult of relics and the practice of pilgrimage were those built under the patronage of Constantine, who made the veneration of the martyrs a state cult (cf. Eusebius, *V.C.* 4.23). These include the Church of the Holy Sepulchre and the Eleona Church on the Mount of Olives in Jerusalem, the Church of the Nativity in Bethlehem, and the church at Mamre south of Bethlehem, which commemorated God's appearance to Abraham in the form of three heavenly visitors (Gen. 18). Constantine also founded the Church of St. Peter on the Vatican Hill in Rome, which became especially influential for medieval church architecture, and the first Church of St. Paul Outside the Walls, and he or his family were associated with the building of four cemeterial basilicas adjacent to important catacombs in Rome, which shared many of the characteristics of the martyrion in their function if not in their form. Finally, two martyria dedicated to local saints and the Church of the Twelve Apostles, the burial place of Constantine, are attributed to him in his new capital, Constantinople. The Church of the Twelve Apostles exercised a far-reaching influence on the architecture of the eastern church. This building, which reached its final form in 370, had a cruciform plan. The relics of SS. Andrew, Timothy, and Luke were placed here in 356 or 357. Its site is now occupied by the Fatih Mosque in modern Istanbul.

Other notable martyria are the second Church of St. Paul's Outside the Walls, in Rome, built under imperial patronage in 385 as a copy of St. Peter's, and the well-preserved Church of S. Stefano (468–483); the Church of St. John in Ephesus (ca. 450 and rebuilt on an even larger scale in the next century), sections of which have been reconstructed in recent years; the Church of St. Menas (ca. 412) at Abu Mîna west of Alexandria in Egypt; the church (ca. 480–490) enclosing the pillar of Symeon Stylites at Qal'at Si'man, from whose central octagon four basilicas extended to give it the form of a cross; and the Church of the Theotokos (484) on Mt. Gerizim in Palestine. The last two were built under the patronage of the emperor Zeno, and the Church of St. Menas was remodeled by him. Such imperial patronage continued under Justinian in the sixth century, and centrally planned buildings became the norm for ecclesiastical architecture whatever the function and continued to be the norm throughout the Byzantine empire and its dependencies. *See also* Baptistery; Basilica; Holy Sepulchre, Church of; Martyr, Martyrdom; Nativity, Church of; Pilgrimage; Relics; St. Paul's Outside the Walls, Church of; St. Peter, Church of. [G.T.A.]

Bibliography

A. Grabar, *Martryium: recherches sur le culte des reliques et l'art chrétien antique*, 2 vols. (Paris: Collège de France, 1946, plates, 1943); idem, "From the Martyrium to the Church: Christian Architecture, East and West," *Archaeology* 2 (1949):95–104; J.P. Kirsch and T. Klauser, "Altar III (christlich)," RLAC (1950), Vol. 1, cols. 334–354; J.B. Ward-Perkins, "Memoria, Martyr's Tomb and Martyr's Church," *JThS* n.s. 17 (1966):20–38, and *Akten des VII. Internationalen Kongresses für christliche Archäologie, Trier 1965* (Vatican City and Berlin, 1969), pp. 3–27 (related studies appear in the same Congress volume); G.T. Armstrong, "Fifth and Sixth Century Church Buildings in the Holy Land," *GOTR* 14 (1969):17–30; C. Andresen, *Einführung in die christliche Archäologie*, Vol. I.B.1 of *Die Kirche in ihrer Geschichte*, ed. K.D. Schmidt and E. Wolf (Göttingen: Vandenhoeck & Ruprecht, 1971) (esp. for bibliography); G.T. Armstrong, "Constantine's Churches: Symbol and Structure," *Journal of the Society of Architectural Historians* 33 (1974):5–16; R. Krautheimer, *Early Christian and Byzantine Architecture*, 3rd ed. (Harmondsworth: Penguin, 1979) (with additional bibliography); F.W. Deichmann, *Einführung in die christliche Archäologie* (Darmstadt: Wissenschaftliche Buchgesellschaft, 1983), esp. Ch. 5 (bibliography); K. Stähler, "Grabbau," RLAC (1983), Vol. 12, cols. 397–429. (Grabar, Armstrong, and Krautheimer provide plans and illustrations of martyria.)

MARTYRS OF PALESTINE. Record of martyrdoms in Palestine from 303 to 311 written by Eusebius of Caesarea. The *Martyrs of Palestine* is extant in a Greek recension preserved as part of the eighth book of Eusebius's *Church History* and in a Syriac one, which is independent and much longer. The account, which Eusebius says comes from personal acquaintance (*H.E.* 8.13.7), mentions eighty-three martyrs and refers to countless others who were maimed or sent to copper mines (*H.E.* 8.12.10) and others who apostatized. The work indicates that persecution of those who refused to sacrifice to the emperor and eat sacrificial meat was worse under Maximinus Daia than under Diocletian. CPG II, 3490. *See also* Eusebius of Caesarea.

[F.W.N.]

Bibliography

E. Schwartz, ed., GCS (1908), Vol. 9.2, pp. 907–950; W. Cureton, *History of the Martyrs of Palestine* (London: Williams and Norgate, 1861). H.J. Lawlor and J.E.L. Oulton, trs., *Eusebius, The Ecclesiastical History and Martyrs of Palestine* (London: SPCK, 1928), Vol. 2.

T. Christensen, "The So-Called Appendix to Eusebius' Historia Ecclesiastica VIII," *Classica et mediaevalia* 34 (1983):177–209.

MARY. Mother of Jesus. Mary is mentioned several times in the New Testament, and she has a particularly important role in the beginning of Luke's Gospel and in the Gospel according to John. She also played a significant role in the development of early Christian theology beyond the New Testament era. From the second century to the middle of the fifth, the focus of theological reflection on Mary was primarily Christological. Already from the third century, however, and up to the end of the sixth, it gradually shifted toward ecclesiological concerns.

The mother of Jesus is one of several women named Mary in the New Testament. Her name renders the Greek *Maria* (also *Mariam*), which is from the Hebrew name *Miriam.* The most prominent person in the Old Testament to bear that name was the sister of Moses (Exod. 15:20; Num. 26:59). A third Greek form of the name, *Mariamme*, also was in use in the first century A.D. (Josephus, *Ant.* 3.2.4.54).

New Testament. The first reference in Mark to Mary's name is in 6:3 (cf. Matt. 13:55); earlier in the Gospel, Mark had referred to "the mother of Jesus" (3:31–35; cf. Matt. 12:46–50; Luke 8:19–21), without mentioning her name. At that point, however, the Gospel's concern was not with the person of Mary but with her relationship to Jesus and with the nature of a true relationship with him. The account draws attention away from a merely biological relationship to a Christological one. It does the same for the brothers and sisters of Jesus (cf. 1 Cor. 9:5; Gal. 1:19; Acts 1:14; John 2:12). Years earlier, Paul had done the opposite in emphasizing the biological relationship in order to bring out the humanity of God's Son: "God sent his Son, born of a woman" (Gal. 4:4).

In the introduction of Matthew's Gospel, Mary, the betrothed and later the wife of Joseph (1:18, 24), is presented as the virginal mother (1:18, 25) of Jesus the Christ (1:16). Throughout the introduction, Matthew's emphasis is not on Mary but on her husband, Joseph, who must come to terms with Jesus' conception by the Holy Spirit. For Matthew, the virginal conception has significant bearing on Jesus' identity as Emmanuel (cf. Isa. 7:14), "God with us" (Matt. 1:23).

Luke, the evangelist most sensitive to the role of women in the story of Jesus, is also the New Testament writer who developed Mary's role most extensively. Unlike Matthew, his introduction, which tells of the ultimate origins (1:5–2:40) and destiny (2:41–52) of Jesus, emphasizes the role of Mary and not that of Joseph. Several stories in the first two chapters have Mary at their center: the announcement of the conception of Jesus (1:26–38), Mary's visit to Elizabeth (1:39–56), the birth of Jesus (2:1–7), and the finding of Jesus in the temple (2:41–52). These stories include many of the most prominent themes later developed in the Gospel and in Luke's second volume, the Acts of the Apostles. Their focus on the identity of

Mary's Son as the Son of the Most High (1:32) and as the Lord (1:43) who must be with his Father (2:49), highlights their Christological nature. Mary's own role in these stories as the servant of the Lord (1:38), who sings the praises of the Lord (1:46–55) and brings him into the world (2:6–7) but must accept his return to the Father (2:49), shows her as a type of the church and underlines their ecclesiological nature. Later, in Acts 1:13–14, Mary the mother of Jesus is presented as a disciple at prayer with the apostles, some women, and the brothers of Jesus.

John's Gospel introduces Mary at the beginning in the story of the marriage feast at Cana (2:1–12) and again at the end in the story of Jesus' exaltation on the cross (19:25–27). At Cana, Mary draws Jesus' attention to the fact that there was no more wine, a situation that allows Jesus to point to the future, to "his hour" and the eschatological wedding banquet. At the cross, when all that Jesus had been sent to do was finished, his hour had arrived. Jesus' mother is to be mother of the

Virgin Mary with Christ Child flanked by four archangels, early-sixth-century wall mosaic in S. Apollinare Nuovo, Ravenna, Italy. (Photograph Editore Dante, Ravenna.)

beloved disciple as well, and he himself is to recognize her as his mother. Both at Cana and at the cross, Jesus addresses Mary as "woman." In all of Greek literature, including the Septuagint, there is absolutely no precedent for a son addressing his mother by the title "woman." In doing so, the Jesus of John's Gospel focuses on Mary, the mother, precisely as the woman. In all likelihood, the Gospel intends to evoke the figure of Eve, the woman who was the mother of all.

Second Century. The patristic era drew heavily on all of these New Testament themes and developed them much further. Throughout the second century, interest in Mary was almost exclusively Christological. In Ignatius of Antioch, the primary emphasis was on the reality of the incarnation and Mary's motherhood. In Justin Martyr and Irenaeus of Lyons, it shifted to the work of redemption and the contrasting roles of Mary and Eve.

The earliest patristic references to Mary are in the letters of Ignatius (ca. 110), who strongly affirmed the reality of the incarnation in response to Docetic tendencies. In doing this, he insisted on the genuineness of Mary's childbirth: "Our God, Jesus Christ, was borne in the womb of Mary according to the divine economy" (*Eph.* 18.2). As the son of Mary and of God, he was truly born (*Eph.* 7.2; *Trall.* 9.1; cf. *Eph.* 19.1; *Smyrn.* 1.1).

Like Ignatius, Justin Martyr, the foremost Greek apologist of the second century, referred to Mary's role in the incarnation but placed greater emphasis on her role in the work of redemption. His *Dialogue with Trypho* provides our oldest witness to the parallel roles of Mary and Eve, an extension of the Pauline antithesis between Christ and Adam. Reflecting on Luke 1:26–38, Justin wrote: "Christ became man by the virgin in order that the disobedience that proceeded from the serpent might receive its destruction in the same manner in which it derived its origin" (*Dial.* 100.4–6). He was also the first after Luke (cf. Luke 1:27) to call Mary "the virgin" (*hē parthenos—Dial.* 87.2; passim).

Irenaeus, the most important theologian of the second century, developed the Mary-Eve antithesis in the context of his theology of recapitulation. For Irenaeus, all of humankind is taken up in Christ, so that what was lost in Adam is regained in Christ. In this plan of salvation, Mary's role parallels that of Eve. Eve, while yet a virgin, disobeyed and became the cause of death for herself and the whole human race. Mary, as a virgin, obeyed and became a cause of salvation for herself and the whole human race (*Haer.* 3.22.4). By restoring the image and likeness of God that had been lost in Adam, Christ offered salvation to Adam (*Haer.* 3.18.1). As the human race fell into the bondage of death by means of a virgin, so was it rescued by a virgin (*Haer.* 5.19.1).

In her role, Mary was both the virginal mother of Christ and an intercessor: "Adam had necessarily to be restored in Christ, that mortality be absorbed in immortality, and Eve in Mary, that a virgin advocate of a virgin should undo and destroy virginal disobedience by virginal obedience" (*Dem.* 33). Mary's advocacy in behalf of Eve was not of the same order as the redemption effected in and through Christ, whose birth was that of "the pure one purely opening the pure womb that regenerates the human race unto God" (*Haer.* 4.33.11).

Christological Controversies. Early in the third century, Tertullian pursued the Mary-Eve antithesis: the virgin Eve listened to the word of the serpent and engendered death. The virgin Mary listened to the word of Gabriel, and God sent his Word into her womb. Tertullian also brought an original element to his presentation: just as the first Adam was formed from virginal soil, in which no seed had as yet been planted, so the new Adam was formed from the virginal ground of Mary (*Carn. Chr.* 17).

From the third to the fifth centuries, the major Christological controversies focused on Christ's incarnate person as both human and divine. These discussions led to refinements in the understanding of Mary's role as mother.

Beginning with the Latin translation of Hippolytus, Mary is referred to as *Deipara*, that is, "Bringer-forth of God." This may represent an attempt to render the Greek title *Theotokos*, "God-bearer." Hippolytus would then provide the oldest attestation of this title. But the title's popularity is due especially to Cyril of Alexandria (d. 444), who advanced it in the disputes with Nestorius (d. 451); the latter accepted the title *Christotokos*, "Christ-bearer," but not *Theotokos*.

Theotokos was proclaimed as a proper title of Mary at the Council of Ephesus (431) and was accepted by orthodox Christians of both east and west. Its intent was to affirm that the person Mary bore was truly God as well as truly man. A few years later, when the Monophysites used the title *Theotokos* in a heretical sense denying the humanity of Jesus, orthodox Christians reaffirmed its rightness but also turned to the title *Mother of God*, which had the advantage of including Mary's spiritual as well as physical motherhood.

Ecclesiological Use. Beginning with Irenaeus in the late second century, many of the fathers also presented Mary in an ecclesiological context. For Irenaeus, "Mary cried out prophetically in the name of the church" when she responded to Elizabeth's greeting with the *Magnificat* (*Haer.* 3.10.2).

Origen saw Mary as a model of Christian living, especially in her virginity. He also had a distinctive ecclesiological interpretation of Jesus' words to Mary in John 19:25–27: it can be said of all who are perfect that it is no longer they who live but Christ who lives in them; Jesus' message to Mary concerning the beloved disciple consequently must be understood as, "Behold your son, Christ" (*Jo.* 1.4, PG 14.32). For Origen, the beloved disciple was not an additional son, but one in whom her only son abided. This position was consistent with his emphasis on Mary's perpetual virginity, a theme dear to the Alexandrians. Athanasius even referred to her with the title *aeiparthenos*, "ever virgin" (*Ar.* 270).

The view of Mary's virginity as a model for the Christian life, held by both the Alexandrians and the Cappadocians, was even more highly developed in the writings of Ambrose and Augustine, who presented Mary's virginity, sinlessness, and Christian perfection as a type of the church. For Ambrose, "The role of the church, like that of Mary, is to conceive by the Spirit and to bring new children into the world" (*Expos. in Lc.* 2.7). For all her gran-

deur, however, Mary was not to be adored. "Mary was the temple of god, not the God of the temple" (*Sp. Sanct.* 3.80).

The various themes found in Ambrose received a more ample expression and development in the writings of Augustine, but he too brought some unique perspectives. Augustine placed great emphasis on Mary's faith: "Mary believed, and what she believed was done in her; let us too believe that what was done in her might benefit us" (*Serm.* 215.4, PL 38.1319). For Augustine, it was greater for Mary to be a disciple and a person of faith than to be the mother of Christ: "Mary is more blessed for grasping faith in Christ than for conceiving his flesh; the maternal relationship would not have profited Mary had she not borne Christ in her heart more happily than in her womb" (*Sanct. Virg.* 3.3, PL 40.398).

Assumption. The absence of biographical information about Mary in the New Testament led early to the production of apocryphal accounts. The second-century *Protevangelium of James* used the birth narratives of Jesus as a model for that of Mary. An additional theme that appears from the late fourth century onward is that of Mary's assumption into heaven, initially only of her soul (*Falling Asleep of Mary; Passing of Mary*). This development, which viewed Mary, the one who had such an important role in Jesus' entry into the world, as being associated in his return to the Father, found its earliest expression in apocryphal documents. It is only from the time of Gregory of Tours (d. 593), however, whose formulation of the belief was inspired by the apocrypha, that it became widely accepted. Mary's body was "borne on a cloud into paradise, where it was reunited with her soul and now rejoices with the elect" (*Glor. beat. mart.* 4, PL 71.70). *See also* Protevangelium of James; Theotokos.

[E.LaV.]

Bibliography

P.F. Palmer, *Mary in the Documents of the Church* (Westminster: Newman, 1952); G. Miegge, *The Virgin Mary* (Philadelphia: Westminster, 1955); W.J. Burghardt, "The Testimony of the Patristic Age Concerning Mary's Death," *Marian Studies* 8 (1957):58–99; H. Graef, *Mary: A History of Doctrine and Devotion,* 2 vols. (New York: Sheed and

Ward, 1963); R.E. Brown, K.P. Donfried, J.A. Fitzmyer, and J. Reumann, *Mary in the New Testament: A Collaborative Assessment by Protestant and Roman Catholic Scholars* (Philadelphia: Fortress, and New York, Ramsey, and Toronto: Paulist, 1978); P. Grelot, "Marie (vierge)," *Dictionnaire de spiritualité* (Paris: Beauchesne, 1980), Vol. 10, cols. 409–440; M. O'Carroll, *Theotokos: A Theological Encyclopedia of the Blessed Virgin Mary* (Wilmington: Glazier, 1983).

MASHTOTS (361/2–440). Armenian bishop and scholar. The basic source for our knowledge of Mashtots, later also called Mesrop or Mesrob, is Koriun's *Life of Mashtots*. Koriun relates how Mashtots was born in the Armenian village of Hatsek, in the region of Tarawn. He grew up and became a civil servant and a soldier and then, through his study of the Bible, renounced the world for the life of a hermit. Mashtots is important because he created the Armenian alphabet, the incentive for which was the desire to translate the Bible. Koriun also credits Mashtots with the creation of alphabets for Georgia and Caucasian Albania. His invention of the Armenian alphabet in Samosata was undertaken with the cooperation of the Catholicos Sahak (350–439), who thereafter was much involved with him in translating the Bible. (Mashtots succeeded Sahak as patriarch in 440, shortly before his own death.) The invention of the alphabet and the translation of the Bible into Armenian were of inestimable significance for the development of the Armenian church (which hitherto had relied on Greek and Syriac versions of the scriptures), Armenian literature, and Armenian self-identity.

Mashtots preached widely in Armenia and Georgia and, with Sahak, sent out students to Edessa and Constantinople to translate and acquire ecclesiastical writings. Throughout all this, he carried on his monastic endeavors. Together with Sahak, Koriun says, Mashtots opposed the teachings of Theodore of Mopsuestia. Students of Mashtots and Sahak became the preachers, translators, writers, and church leaders of the "Golden Period" of Armenian literature, the fifth century. Feast day February 19 (Armenia), November 25 (west). [C.C.]

Bibliography
The critical ed. of Koriun's *Life of Mashtots* is *Vark' Mashtots'*, ed. M. Abeghyan (Yerevan: Haypethrat, 1941; repr. with Engl. tr. Delmar: Caravan, 1985).
C. Cox, "The Purpose of Koriun's Life of Mashtots," *Christian Teaching, Studies in Honor of LeMoine G. Lewis*, ed. E. Ferguson (Abilene: ACU, 1981), pp. 303–311.

MASS. Liturgical rite in the Catholic Church. The Latin word *missa* is found in a number of different senses in early western liturgical usage. First, it can mean the dismissal of groups of people from a liturgical rite. Thus, Augustine uses the phrase *missa catechumenis* to refer to the dismissal of the unbaptized after the homily and before the eucharist (*Serm.* 49.8), and John Cassian speaks of a monk who wished to function as a deacon and perform the *missam catechumenis* (*Inst.* 11.16). Although the word is not frequently found in the west in the fourth and fifth centuries, it does occur seventy-two times in the *Pilgrimage of Egeria*, an account of a visit to Jerusalem with a description of its liturgy written apparently toward the end of the fourth century by a nun of Gallic or Spanish origin. It is employed in more than one sense here, but "dismissal" is still the most common meaning. The author uses it, however, not simply to refer to the departure of a specific group of individuals from an act of worship but to designate the dismissal of the whole congregation at the end of the rite itself. A similar usage can be seen in the prescriptions for the daily services in the sixth-century *Rule* of Benedict of Nursia (17; cf. 60, where it is probably to be interpreted in the same sense).

Second, in the monastic traditions of Gaul and Spain, *missa* denotes a standard liturgical unit that was repeated a number of times within a rite. The monastic rules of Caesarius of Arles and his successor, Aurelian, make reference to a variable number of *missae* to be used in the course of the night, each made up of three readings, three prayers, and three Psalms; in Spain, Isidore of Seville speaks of a monastic night office that includes several *missae*, here composed of three Psalms or canticles and prayers (*Eccl. off.* 6.4).

Third, *missa* can describe a complete liturgical rite. This usage can already be seen in Egeria (42; 43.3) and in Cassian (*Inst.* 3.6, 8), as well as in other later western writings (e.g., Council of Agde, *can.* 30).

Fourth, *missa* can be a technical term for the eucharistic rite. Although some claim that Ambrose used the word this way in a letter to his sister written in 385 (*Ep.* 20.5), this is most probably only a further instance of the more general sense of "liturgical rite." It is not until the beginning of the sixth century that unambiguous examples of its use with this more restricted meaning are encountered—Cassiodorus (*Exp. Ps.* 25; 33) appears to be the earliest—but thereafter this meaning becomes very common.

Various theories have been offered concerning the origin of the term in Christian liturgical usage. The most probable explanation is that the word is derived from *dismissio* ("dismissal"). *Missa* rarely occurs outside a liturgical context, but when it is found in secular Latin it always has that sense, and its earliest appearances in Christian literature are with the same meaning. But why should a word that originally designated the end of a rite also be extended to describe liturgical units within a service, and even the whole act of worship itself?

It is evident from early liturgical sources that the conclusion of an act of worship did not generally consist merely of a brief sentence of dismissal but was an elaborate and important element that occupied a substantial amount of time within the totality of the rite. Egeria tells, for example, how at the end of each of the various services held in the course of an ordinary weekday at Jerusalem, even when another act of worship was about to follow immediately afterward, the deacon would call upon the catechumens to stand and bow their heads while the bishop said a prayer over them; the procedure would then be repeated for the faithful; and finally each person would come up to the bishop and receive an individual laying on of hands from him (24.2–7).

In later liturgical practice, this ritual tended to be drastically curtailed, no doubt because of its time-consuming nature. Nevertheless, once the extent of its original form is appreciated, it becomes much easier to understand a terminological evolution that otherwise seems somewhat strange, in which the word that had originally described the last major section of a rite might also be used to designate other liturgical units, and ultimately the whole rite itself. *See also* Eucharist; Liturgy.

[P.F.B.]

Bibliography

J. Pinell, "Las missas, grupos de cantos y oraciones en el officio de la antigua liturgia hispana," *Archivos Leonenses* 8 (1954):145–185; C. Mohrmann, "Missa," *VChr* 12 (1958):67–92; J.A. Jungmann, *The Mass of the Roman Rite,* new ed. (New York: Benziger, 1959); K. Gamber, *Missa romensis* (Regensburg: Pustet, 1970), pp. 170–186; A. Kavanagh, *Confirmation: Origins and Reform* (New York: Pueblo, 1988), pp. 3–38.

MATTHEW. One of the twelve apostles and the name given in later tradition to the writer of the first Gospel. The name Matthew is found in all of the New Testament lists of the twelve (Matt. 10:3; Mark 3:18; Luke 6:15; Acts 1:13). The name also occurs in Matthew 9:9 in the story of Jesus' call of the tax collector. Matthew is depicted as sitting at a tax or toll booth near Capernaum. He immediately followed Jesus' invitation; the subsequent story presents Jesus as eating with "many tax collectors and sinners," something that provoked a strong reaction from the Pharisees (Matt. 9:10–13). The evangelist follows through on this by identifying Matthew as "the tax collector" in the list of the twelve (Matt. 10:3). The source for this identification is not clear. In Mark's account, the tax collector called by Jesus is named "Levi the son of Alphaeus" (Mark 2:14). If, as most New Testament scholars now believe, Mark was written prior to Matthew, then Matthew may have changed "Levi" to "Matthew" in the call story to bring it into accord with "Matthew the tax collector" in his list of the twelve. Others have attempted to harmonize the two accounts by suggesting that "Matthew" and "Levi" were two names for the "son of Alphaeus," just as Peter was also called Simon.

A tradition dating back to Papias (writing ca. 125–130), cited by Eusebius (*H.E.* 3.39.16), attributed the authorship of the Gospel to Matthew the apostle, who is supposed to have written the discourses (*ta logia*) of Jesus in the "Hebrew dialect"; these were then translated by others as they were able. Much confusion surrounds this assertion. No Hebrew or Aramaic version of the Gospel from early times exists, and there is little evidence that the present Greek version was translated from a Semitic source. Its content and style suggest a Greek-speaking, Jewish Christian author writing in the last quarter of the first century, probably at Antioch. Therefore, most contemporary scholars consider it improbable that the Galilean tax collector Matthew was in fact the author of the Gospel. One cannot rule out the possibility that the apostle may have been connected with the church from which the Gospel ultimately emerged and that this became a basis for attributing the Gospel to his authorship. From the time of Irenaeus (*Haer.* 3.1.1), the first Gospel was uniformly attributed to the apostle Matthew.

Matthew's Gospel is "the teaching Gospel." Not only does it give prominence to Jesus' ministry as a teacher (Matt. 4:23; 9:35), but it also has proved to be so admirably arranged for teaching purposes that it has remained the most widely used of the four Gospels. In addition to the basic outline of the ministry of Jesus reflected in Mark, Matthew, like Luke, contains a genealogy and account of Jesus' birth and infancy (Matt. 1–2) and blocks of its own distinctive material. The most characteristic contents of Matthew are found in five discourses by Jesus: (1) on discipleship (the "Sermon on the Mount"—Matt. 5–7); (2) on apostleship, or missionaries (Matt. 10); (3) the parables of the kingdom (Matt. 13); (4) church discipline (Matt. 18); and (5) on present and future judgment (Matt. 23–25).

Matthew was not only first in the canonical lists but was also regarded by the ancient church as the first written (e.g., Augustine, *Consen. ev.* 1.4). It was the most frequently quoted Gospel in the early church. Matthew's

symbol in art was a man. Feast day September 21 (west), November 16 (east). *See also* Luke; Mark.						[D.P.S.]

Bibliography

Origen, *Commentary on Matthew*, ANF (1896), Vol. 9; repr. Vol. 10 (1951); John Chrysostom, *Homilies on St. Matthew*, NPNF, 1st ser. (1888), Vol. 10; Pseudo-Chrysostom, *Opus imperfectum in Matthaeum*, CPG II, 4569/CPL 707; Hilary of Poitiers, *Commentarius in Euangelium Matthaei*, SC, (1978–1979), Vols. 254, 258; Chromatius of Aquileia, *Tractatus in Matthaeum*, CCSL (1974–1977), Vol. 9A and Suppl.; Jerome, *Commentarii in Euangelium Matthaei*, CCSL (1969), Vol. 7; Augustine, *Our Lord's Sermon on the Mount*, NPNF, 1st ser. (1888), Vol. 6.

C.H. Turner, "Early Greek Commentators on the Gospel According to St. Matthew," *JThS* 12 (1911):99–112; D. Hill, *The Gospel of Matthew*, (London: Oliphants, 1972), pp. 22–38; W. Kümmel, *Introduction to the New Testament* (Nashville: Abingdon, rev. Engl. ed., 1975), pp. 120–121; D. Senior, *What Are They Saying About Matthew?* (New York: Paulist, 1983); E. Massaux, *Influence de l'Evangile de saint Matthieu sur la littérature chrétienne avant saint Irénée* (Louvain: Peeters, 1986); B. Orchard, "The Historical Tradition," *The Order of the Synoptics: Why Three Synoptic Gospels?*, ed. B. Orchard and H. Riley (Macon: Mercer UP, 1987), pp. 111–226.

MAURISTS. French Benedictine congregation, founded in 1621 and destroyed during the French Revolution (1790). The congregation, under the patronage of St. Maurus (sixth century), a disciple of Benedict of Nursia, had its headquarters at Saint-Germain-des-Prés in Paris; most French Benedictine monasteries were members. Maurists were educators and preachers, but they are best known for their scholarship, characterized by its thoroughness and objectivity. Their development and employment of the sciences auxiliary to history, such as paleography, chronology, and numismatics, are noteworthy. Their interests ranged over a wide variety of historical and literary works; Maurist editions of many of the writings of the church fathers were incorporated into the *Patrologia Graeca* and *Patrologia Latina* of Jacques Paul Migne. A number of their other publications were continued in the nineteenth century through the efforts of learned societies and individuals.					[M.P.McH.]

Bibliography
D. Knowles, *Great Historical Enterprises* (London: Nelson, 1963), pp. 33–62.

MAXENTIUS (ca. 279–312). Claimant to the imperial throne. Son of the emperor Maximian, Maxentius was not chosen in his father's place when Maximian, along with Diocletian, resigned the rule of the empire (305). He was soon (306) proclaimed emperor at Rome, initially with his father's support. He maintained his position for several years in Italy, held Spain for a time (ca. 308–310), but faced resistance in Africa that led to the loss of the grain supply. He was defeated and killed in battle against Constantine. His policy of toleration made possible the elevation of Marcellus to the Roman see (306 or 308) after a vacancy of several years, but the latter's imposition of strict penance on those who had lapsed during persecutions resulted in dissension and public disorder. Maxentius exiled him from Rome, and he died shortly thereafter.   [M.P.McH.]

Bibliography
Lactantius, *Deaths of the Persecutors* 18; 26; 28; 43–44; Eusebius, *Church History* 8.14.1–6, 16–18; 9.9.1–11; *Excerpts of Valesius* 3.6–4.12.

MAXIMIANUS (d. 434). Bishop of Constantinople (431–434). Maximianus was elected to replace Nestorius, deposed at the Council of Ephesus (431); much of his administration was devoted to dealing with Nestorianism. Although he deposed four Nestorian bishops who refused to enter into communion with him, his policy of seeking reconciliation met with some success, and peace was made between Cyril of Alexandria and John of Antioch. One letter, to Cyril, is extant. CPG III, 5770–5773.

[M.P.McH.]

Bibliography
Celestine I, *Epistulae* 24; 25.19; Sixtus III, *Epistula* 3 (= John of Antioch).

MAXIMILIAN (d. 295). Martyr at Tebessa in Numidia. When Maximilian at age twenty-one was called to military service, he refused on the grounds that as a Christian he could not serve. He was executed by the sword, and a pious woman took his body to Carthage for burial next to the body of Cyprian. Feast day March 12. CPL 2052.   [E.F.]

Bibliography
Musurillo, pp. xxxvii, 244–249.

MAXIMINUS (early fifth century). Arian author and bishop. Maximinus is the best Arian writer in Latin. In 427 or 428, he had a public debate with Augustine at Hippo, preserved in Augustine's *Collatio Augustini cum Maximino*. Maximinus's *Dissertatio Maximini contra Ambrosium* includes important information on other figures. Other polemical works and homilies are attributed to him. CPL 692–702.[E.F.]

MAXIMINUS DAIA (d. 313). Claimant to the imperial throne. Adopted by his uncle Galerius upon the latter's accession to the throne (305), Maximinus was made Caesar and given rule of Syria, Egypt, and part of Asia Minor. He assumed the title of emperor (310) just as the imperial system of two emperors, *Augusti*, each assisted by a Caesar, was breaking down. Shortly after Constantine defeated Maxentius in the west (312), Licinius defeated Maximinus, who died as a fugitive. A persecutor of Christians, he made a final attempt to destroy the church in Syria and Egypt (311–312). He sought to revive paganism and to reorganize its priesthood. His campaign of defamation against the Christians led to the composition, in reply, of the apocryphal *Gospel of Nicodemus* (fifth century). [M.P.McH.]

Bibliography
Lactantius, *Deaths of the Persecutors* 18–19; 36–49; Eusebius, *Church History* 8.14.7–16.2; 9.1.1–9.9.1; 9.12–11.8; idem, *Martyrs of Palestine*.
P. Keresztes, "From the Great Persecution to the Peace of Galerius," *VChr* 37 (1983):379–399.

MAXIMUS CONFESSOR (580–662). Byzantine theologian and ascetical writer. Born either in Constantinople (as the traditional biography has it) or in Palestine, according to the near-contemporary and unfriendly Maronite biography (*AB* 91 [1973]:299–346), Maximus led a long and eventful life as a monk (not a priest) and theologian in both the east and the west. Driven westward by the Persian advance, he spent about a dozen years at a Byzantine monastery at Carthage after stays in Crete and perhaps also Cyprus. It was at this monastery that Maximus produced the works for which he is best known: *Questions to Thalassius*, a long exegetical discussion of scriptural texts; *Ambigua*, explications of troublesome passages in Gregory of Nazianzus and Pseudo-Dionysius mostly of a Christological nature; *Mystagogy*, a treatise of spiritual advancement in the form of a commentary on the eucharistic liturgy; *Centuries on Love* and *Centuries on Theology and the Economy* (*Gnostic Centuries*), maxims on the Christian life arranged in groups of 100; and *Commentary on the Our Father*. These works are characterized by a creative rehandling of traditional ideas from Origen, Evagrius, Pseudo-Dionysius, and others as corrected and balanced in the light of Gregory of Nyssa and Gregory of Nazianzus, to whom Maximus was much indebted.

While Maximus was at Carthage, the Monothelite controversy broke out as a result of a compromise aimed at appeasing the Monophysites. Sophronius, his first superior there, later patriarch of Jerusalem, helped him to see the dogmatic issue involved, and Maximus resolutely took a position against the heresy in a series of *opuscula*. When Pyrrhus, the deposed Monothelite patriarch of Constantinople, came to Carthage, a celebrated debate was held between the two protagonists before many North African bishops, which resulted in the capitulation of Pyrrhus (645). Both he and Maximus sailed for Rome, where the deposed patriarch delivered his personal submission to the pope. When political circumstances changed, however, Pyrrhus retracted the submission and fled to Constantinople, where he was reinstated as patriarch. The Lateran Synod was held under the presidency of pope Martin I (649) and Monothelitism was condemned as a deviation from Christian truth. It is possible that Maximus is the author of the *acta* of the synod, which would have been subscribed to by the pope and bishops present. The synod's action

was in violation of the emperor's decree enjoining silence in the matter of Christ's wills. In consequence, Martin and Maximus were arrested in Rome (653), to be carried off to Constantinople; the pope died en route. In the capital, Maximus was put on trial and exiled to Thrace. Brought back to Constantinople (658), he refused to compromise the Dyothelite position and was returned to exile. In 662, he was sentenced anew to exile, and after torture and mutilation of his tongue and right hand he was deported to Lazica in Russian Georgia, where he died.

A champion of the integrity, freedom, and functioning of the human and divine wills in Christ, Maximus saw his teaching as faithful to the full consequences of the Christology of Chalcedon (and was so vindicated at the Sixth Ecumenical Council in 680). His spiritual doctrine, or theory of divinization, was firmly anchored in the incarnation of the eternal Logos in Christ and as confessed and experienced in the church's life and worship. The incarnation of the Logos leads to the divinization of man through a love made possible by grace. Maximus had an enormous influence over subsequent Byzantine theology and monastic practice. Feast day August 13 (west), January 21 (east). CPG III, 7688–7721.   [G.C.B.]

Bibliography

PG 90–91; *Centuries on Love*, ed. A. Ceresa-Gastaldo (Rome: Studium, 1963); *Quaestiones ad Thalassium I–LV*, ed. C. Laga and C. Steel, CCSG (1980), Vol. 7; *Quaestiones et Dubia*, ed. J. Declerck, CCSG (1982), Vol. 10; *Ambigua ad Iohannem*, ed. E. Jeauneau, CCSG (1988), Vol. 18; further vols. in progress in CCSG.

The Ascetic Life and *Four Centuries on Charity*, tr. P. Sherwood, ACW (1955), Vol. 21; *Chapters on Love, Our Father, Chapters on Knowledge, Mystagogy*, and trial proceedings, tr. G. Berthold, CWS (1985).

P. Sherwood, *An Annotated Date-List of the Works of Maximus the Confessor* (Rome: Herder, 1952); idem, *The Earlier Ambigua of Saint Maximus the Confessor and His Refutation of Origenism* (Rome: Herder, 1952); H.U. von Balthasar, *Kosmische Liturgie*, 2nd ed. (Einsiedeln: Johannes-Verlag, 1961); L. Thunberg, *Microcosm and Mediator* (Lund: Gleerup, 1965); W. Völker, *Maximus Confessor als Meister des geistlichen Lebens* (Wiesbaden: Fisteiner, 1965); A. Riou, *Le Monde et l'église selon Maxime le Confesseur* (Paris: Beauchesne, 1973); J.-M.

Garrigues, *Maxime le Confesseur: la charité avenir divin de l'homme* (Paris: Beauchesne, 1976); F. Heinzer and C. von Schönborn, *Maximus Confessor* (Fribourg: Herder, 1982).

MAXIMUS OF TURIN (d. between 408 and 423). Bishop and homilist. Although little is known of his life, Maximus's Latin homilies, of which over 100 survive, show him to have been a zealous pastor and a skillful preacher who made much use of allegory. They furnish considerable information about liturgy and church practice and provide good evidence for the nature and survival of pagan beliefs in north Italy. Several were circulated in medieval collections. CPL 220–226b.   [M.P.McH.]

Bibliography
Gennadius, *Lives of Illustrious Men* 40.
The Sermons of St. Maximus of Turin, tr. B. Ramsey, ACW (1989), Vol. 50.
M.C. Conroy, *Imagery in the Sermones of Maximus of Turin* (Washington, D.C.: Catholic U of America P, 1965); D. Devoti, "Massimo di Torino e il suo pubblico," *Augustinianum* 21 (1981):153–167; M. Pellegrino, "Martiri e martirio in S. Massimo di Torino," *RSLR* 17 (1981): 169–192.

MELANIA THE ELDER (ca. 342–ca. 410). Ascetic. A Roman woman of considerable wealth, Melania adopted a life of asceticism upon the early death of her husband (ca. 365). She left Rome for Egypt (ca. 372) and eventually Palestine, where with Rufinus of Aquileia she established a double monastery for men and women on the Mount of Olives (ca. 379). Upon her return to Italy (400), she visited Paulinus of Nola; several years later, she went back to Jerusalem and died at her monastery there. Although praised by Jerome, she incurred his enmity for her support of Rufinus in his defense of the orthodoxy of Origen. [M.P.McH.]

Bibliography
Palladius, *Lausiac History* 46; 54; 55; Jerome, *Letters* 3.3; 4.2; 39.5; 45.4; 133.3; Paulinus of Nola, *Letters* 28.5; 29.5–14; 31.1; 32.11; 45.2–3.
F.X. Murphy, "Melania the Elder: A Biographical Note," *Traditio* 5 (1947):59–77.

MELANIA THE YOUNGER (ca. 383–439). Ascetic. The granddaughter of Melania the Elder, Melania entered on a life of asceticism together with her husband, Pinian. Having fled from Italy before the invasion of the Goths, they settled (410) at Thagaste in North Africa, where they met Augustine. In 417, they went to Jerusalem, where, after Pinian's death (431 or 432), Melania founded religious establishments on the Mount of Olives. She is known to have visited Constantinople (436), where she met with the empress Eudoxia. Her life was written (ca. 440) by Gerontius, a priest and monk who succeeded her in the direction of the monasteries (CPL 2211). Feast day December 31.   [M.P.McH.]

Bibliography
Jerome, *Letter* 143.2; Augustine, *Letters* 124–126; idem, *On the Grace of Christ* 1.1.
E.A. Clark, *The Life of Melania the Younger: Introduction, Translation, and Commentary* (New York: Mellen, 1984); idem, "Claims on the Bones of Saint Stephen: The Partisans of Melania and Eudocia," *ChHist* 51 (1982):141–156.

MELCHIZEDEKIANS. Two early Christian sects that were known under the name of the Old Testament priest Melchizedek (Gen. 14:18–20; cf. Heb. 5:1–10). Epiphanius (*Haer.* 55) calls those who followed Theodotus the Banker Melchizedekians, because Theodotus taught that Melchizedek was a deity above Christ, was a priest without a father, was incomprehensible in his nature, and was a priest for angels and powers.

Timothy the Presbyter (*Cotel. mon. ecc. gr.* 3.392) mentions a different group called Melchizedekians who lived in Phrygia, observed the Sabbath but rejected circumcision, and would not allow themselves to be touched by anyone outside their sect. They accepted objects from others only if those objects were first placed on the ground.   [F.W.N.]

MELITIUS OF ANTIOCH (d. 381). Bishop (360–381). Appointed to the see of Antioch after having been bishop of Sebaste, Melitius was exiled almost at once by the emperor Constantius II, an adherent of Arianism, when his orthodoxy became apparent in his inaugural sermon. He was restored to the see (362) after

Julian became emperor but was banished twice more (365–366; 371–378) under the Arian emperor Valens. Restored a final time (378), he presided at the Council of Constantinople (381), during which he died. A synodal letter to the emperor Jovian is reported under his name in Socrates Scholasticus and a homily in Epiphanius of Salamis; most of the writings attributed to him are dubious.

The Melitian schism in Antioch (not to be confused with the schism in Alexandria revolving around Melitius of Lycopolis) was a dispute between two orthodox factions, which arose when Lucifer of Cagliari consecrated Paulinus to the see of Antioch (362); Paulinus, a follower of Eustathius (bishop ca. 324–330), was put forward by a party that questioned the theology of Melitius and his followers. Melitius refused communion with Athanasius, who then supported Paulinus; Basil the Great upheld Melitius's cause throughout. For a number of years, bishops continued in both lines, the schism at last ending with the recognition of Melitius's successor by the Eustathian party. Feast day February 2. CPG II, 3415–3425.

[M.P.McH.]

Bibliography

Epiphanius, *Panarion* 3.1.73.29–33; Socrates, *Church History* 2.44; 3.9, 25; 4.2, 26; 5.5, 9; Sozomen, *Church History* 4.25, 28; 5.13; 6.4, 7; 7.3, 7, 10.

F. Cavallera, *Le Schisme d'Antioche (IVe–Ve siècle)* (Paris: Picard, 1905); W.A. Jurgens, "A Letter of Meletius of Antioch," *HThR* 53 (1960):251–260.

MELITIUS OF LYCOPOLIS (early fourth century).

Schismatic bishop. Little is known of Melitius's life. He entered into schism against Peter, bishop of Alexandria (300–311), over the latter's lenient policy toward those who had lapsed under persecution and was deposed from office by an Egyptian synod (ca. 306). (It is debated whether one of his supporters, Arius, is to be identified with the founder of Arianism.) The schism, restricted mostly to the Alexandrian church and its suffragan jurisdictions, persisted under Peter's successors, Achillas and Alexander. The Council of Nicaea (325) determined that the clergy ordained by Melitius could continue in a position subordinate to those ordained by Alexander, except for Melitius himself, who was deprived of episcopal authority. He complied for a time and submitted to Alexander a list of some twenty-eight bishops whom he had ordained. Upon the election of Athanasius to the see of Alexandria (328), the dispute was renewed with the encouragement of Eusebius of Nicomedia, an adherent of Arianism. Melitian theology came increasingly under Arian influence as a result of the alliance of the two parties. The schism evidently continued for several centuries; it is not to be confused with the schism of the same name centered on Melitius, bishop of Antioch. TLG 2955. *See also* Peter of Alexandria.

[M.P.McH.]

Bibliography

Peter of Alexandria, *The Letter to the Alexandrians on Meletius*; Athanasius, *Apology Against the Arians*; idem, *Circular to the Bishops of Egypt* 21–23; idem, *History of the Arians* 78–80; idem, *First Oration Against the Arians* 3; Socrates, *Church History* 1.6.9; Sozomen, *Church History* 1.15, 24; 2.18, 21–23, 25; *Codex Veronensis LX (58)* (see W. Telfer, "The Codex Verona LX [58]," *HThR* 36 [1943]:169–246).

H.I. Bell, *Jews and Christians in Egypt* (London: British Museum, and Oxford: Oxford UP, 1924), pp. 38–99; W. Telfer, "St. Peter of Alexandria and Arius," *AB* 67 (1949):117–130; idem, "Meletius of Lycopolis and Episcopal Succession in Egypt," *HThR* 48 (1955):227–237; R. Williams, "Arius and the Melitian Schism," *JThS* n.s. 37 (1986):35–52.

MELITO (last third of second century).

Bishop of Sardis in Asia Minor. The main sources are Eusebius's discussion *(H.E.* 4.26.1–14) and Melito's surviving Passover/Easter sermon, *On the Pasch,* a Greek text of which was discovered in 1932 and identified in 1936.

According to Eusebius, Melito was a Quartodeciman (one who observed the Pasch on the exact day of the Jewish Passover) and the author of at least seventeen works, which he lists (*H.E.* 4.26.2; cf. Jerome, *Vir. ill.* 24). These works include treatises on baptism and on the book of Revelation and an apology addressed to the emperor Marcus Aurelius. Brief fragments of some of these works survive.

Melito traveled to Palestine (Eusebius, *H.E.* 4.26.12–14), the first recorded Christian pilgrim to the Holy Land, in order to visit the place "where it was proclaimed and done" and to get exact information on the canon of the Old Covenant. Melito's use of this term is the first known designation of the Hebrew Bible as the Old Testament. His list, the first Christian list of the Old Testament canon, is the same as the Jewish Hebrew Bible canon at this time, except for his omission of Esther.

Melito's *On the Pasch,* known also in part in Latin, Syriac, Coptic, and Georgian translations, is a powerful typological sermon in the current Greek rhetorical style on the Passover as finding its fulfillment in Christ. The sermon is characterized further by its vivid descriptions, high Christology, and strong anti-Judaism. Feast day April 1. CPG I, 1092–1098. TLG 1495. [D.M.S.]

Bibliography

Eusebius, *Church History* 4.26.1–14; 5.24.5; 5.28.5; 6.13.9; Jerome, *Lives of Illustrious Men* 24.

O. Perler, *Méliton de Sardes, Sur la pâque et fragments,* SC (1966), Vol. 123; S.G. Hall, *Melito of Sardis, On Pascha and Fragments* (Oxford: Clarendon, 1979).

E. Werner, "Melito of Sardes, the First Poet of Deicide," *Hebrew Union College Annual* 37 (1966):191–210; A.T. Kraabel, "Melito the Bishop and the Synagogue at Sardis: Text and Context," *Studies Presented to George M.A. Hanfmann,* ed. D.G. Mitten et al. (Mainz: Verlag Philipp von Zabern, 1971), pp. 77–85; G.F. Hawthorne, "Christian Baptism and the Contribution of Melito of Sardis," *Studies in New Testament and Early Christian Literature: Essays in Honor of Allen P. Wikgren,* ed. D.E. Aune (Leiden: Brill, 1972), pp. 241–251; R.L. Wilken, "Melito, the Jewish Community at Sardis, and the Sacrifice of Isaac," *ThS* 37 (1976):53–69; T.P. Halton and R.D. Sider, "A Decade of Patristic Scholarship 1970–1979," *CW* 76 (1982–1983): 91–92 (bibliography); F.W. Norris, "Melito's Motivation," *Anglican Theological Review* 68 (1986):16–24.

MENANDER (second century). Samaritan Gnostic, born in Capparatea. Menander may have been a disciple of Simon Magus. In Antioch of Syria, he had considerable teaching success (Justin, *1 Apol.* 26; 56). According to Irenaeus (*Haer.* 1.23), he taught that the world was created by angels, not God himself, and that he himself had been sent as a savior to help humans overcome the power of those

angels. Menander promised his followers that they would neither age nor die. Serious belief in his doctrines soon required allegorical interpretation. Since antiheretical writers delighted in providing a lineage from Simon Magus, neither that affiliation for Menander nor the claim of a Samaritan pedigree for other Gnostics may be taken at face value. [F.W.N.]

MENAS (third or fourth century). Egyptian martyr. Menas may have been born and martyred in Egypt, but the story of his life has been conflated with that of another person who was killed in Phrygia during the Diocletianic persecution (303–311). Whether that person was St. Gordian or someone named Menas is unknown.

A shrine was erected in his honor southwest of Lake Mareotis not far from Alexandria. Thought to be his birthplace, it became a center for pilgrims who sought water cures for their maladies. The site was excavated in 1905–1908; a church and ampullae (flasks) depicting Menas between two camels were found. His cult, viewing him particularly as a helper of merchants, has been encountered in Gaul, Germany, Greece, and Italy. [F.W.N.]

Bibliography

"Acta S. Menae," *AB* 3 (1884):258–270; C.M. Kaufmann, *Die Menasstadt und das Nationalheiligtum der altchristlichen Agypter in der Westalexandrinischen Wüste* (Leipzig: Hiersemann, 1910).

MENAS OF CONSTANTINOPLE (d. 552). Alexandrian-born bishop of Constantinople (536–552, including two periods of excommunication). Menas was set in office by pope Agapetus after Anthimus, the Monophysite bishop, had been deposed. Menas presided at an anti-Monophysite synod in 543 and with some reservations supported Justinian's edict against the Three Chapters in that same year. When those under his jurisdiction appealed to pope Vigilius, Menas was twice excommunicated, in 547 and 551. The emperor, however, put pressure on Vigilius and in each case Menas was restored. His tenure of office saw what was probably the most intricate struggle between the imperial and papal thrones over the see of Constantinople. Feast day August 25. CPG III, 6923–6932. [F.W.N.]

Bibliography

W.H.C. Frend, *The Rise of the Monophysite Movement* (Cambridge: Cambridge UP, 1972), pp. 272–273, 281.

MESROB. *See* Mashtots.

MESSALIANS. Ascetic sect. Also known as Euchites (Greek for "praying ones"), the Messalians (their Syriac name) originated shortly after the mid-fourth century. They held that only intense and ceaseless prayer could eliminate the passion and desire by which demons held power over a person; consequently, they refused work and lived on alms. They were attacked by Ephraem the Syrian, Flavian of Antioch, Amphilochius of Iconium, and Epiphanius and were condemned at Antioch (ca. 385), Side (383), Constantinople (426), and Ephesus (431). Possible connections with Eustathius of Sebaste, Diadochus, Gregory of Nyssa, and Pseudo-Macarius have been debated. They are last heard of in the seventh century. [E.F.]

Bibliography

Ephraem the Syrian, *Homilia* 22; Epiphanius, *Panarion* 80; Theodoret, *Church History* 4.10; idem, *Haereticarum fabularum compendium* 4.11; Photius, *Library* 52; John of Damascus, *Liber de haeresibus* 80 (PG 94.728ff.); M. Kmosko, App. I, "Antiquorum testimonia de historia et doctrina Messalianorum sectae," *Patrologia syriaca*, ed. R. Graffin (Paris: Firmin-Didot, 1926), Vol. 3, cols. clxxi–ccxciii.

G.L. Marriott, "The Messalians; and the Discovery of Their Ascetic Book," *HThR* 19 (1926):191–198; E. des Places, ed., *Diadoque de Photicé, Oeuvres spirituelles*, SC (1955), Vol. 5, pp. 12–22; R. Staats, *Gregor von Nyssa und die Messalianer* (Berlin: de Gruyter, 1968); J. Gribomont, "Le Dossier des origines du messalianisme," *Epektasis: Mélanges J. Daniélou* (Paris: Beauchesne, 1972), pp. 611–625; A. Louth, "Messalianism and Pelagianism," *SP* 17.1 (1982):127–135.

METHODIUS (d. ca. 311). Bishop of Olympus in Lycia and opponent of Origen. The works of Methodius are mostly lost or available only in fragments. That is tragic because they con-

tained a response to Porphyry's *Against Christianity*; commentaries on Genesis, the Song of Solomon, and Job; a treatise on martyrs; and an unusual work entitled *Against Origen Concerning the Female Python.* This last piece and another on *Creation* probably dealt with Origen's teaching about creation and the eternity of the world.

Six treatises exist primarily in Old Church Slavonic translations that are occasionally fragmentary or abridged. Three of them indicate how Methodius interpreted scripture: *The Leech and the Verse*, on Proverbs 30:10ff. and Psalm 18; *To Sistelius on Leprosy*, on Leviticus 13; and *The Jewish Foods and the Red Heifer*, on food laws and Numbers 19. In each case, Methodius develops an allegorical interpretation of the passage. Of the other three treatises, one, *Life and Rational Activity*, is a fragment on hope in God, and two are polemical: *Free Will* attacks a Gnostic or a Neoplatonist explanation of the origin of evil or perhaps Origen himself; the *Treatise on the Resurrection of the Body* insists that the earthly body is identified with the resurrection body (an attack on Origen's conception of a spiritual body in the resurrection).

The one work extant in Greek, *The Banquet*, is a manual of Christian doctrine focused on the ascetic life that includes many theological topics discussed in dialogue form. Feast day September 18 (west), June 20 (east). CPG I, 1810–1830. TLG 2959. [F.W.N.]

Bibliography

W.R. Clarke, tr., ANF (1888), Vol. 6, pp. 305–402; *Methodius of Olympus: The Symposium, a Treatise on Chastity*, tr. H. Musurillo, ACW (1958), Vol. 27.

L.G. Patterson, "De libero arbitrio and Methodius' Attack on Origen," *SP* 14 (1971):160–166; T.D. Barnes, "Methodius, Maximian, and Valentinus," *JThS* n.s. 30 (1979):47–55; A. Vitores, *Identidad entre el cuerpo meurto y resucitado en Orígenes según el "De Resurrectione" de Metodia de Olimpo* (Jerusalem: Franciscan Printing Press, 1981); L.G. Patterson, "Methodius, Origen and the Arian Dispute," *SP* 17.2 (1982):912–923.

MIGNE, JACQUES PAUL (1800–1875). Ecclesiastical editor and publisher. Migne served for some time (1824–1833) as a parish priest in

Orléans, near his birthplace of Saint-Flour. He was permitted to leave for Paris because of difficulties with his bishop over a pamphlet he had published on the Revolution of 1830. He engaged in ecclesiastical journalism in the French capital for a few years but then determined (1836) to publish a universal library for the clergy. From the publishing house that he established in Paris, he issued courses of theology and scripture and collections of apologetics, French sermons, church history, and writings on Mary.

His best-known publications are the series on the Greek and Latin ecclesiastical writers. The *Patrologia Graeca* (*PG*) in 167 volumes (1857–1866) extends through the Council of Florence (1439); the *Patrologia Latina* (*PL*) in 221 volumes (1844–1855) ends with Innocent III (1216). (There is a five-volume supplement to the *Patrologia Latina* [1958–1974] by A. Hamman.) Migne incorporated into these collections many of the texts of the Maurists along with their notes and prefatory material. Although he urged his collaborators to correct or reedit texts, his aim throughout was to provide the best versions available under the constraint of time. Migne's editions are being replaced, slowly yet steadily, most notably by volumes in the series *Corpus Scriptorum Ecclesiasticorum Latinorum* (*CSEL*), *Griechischen Christlichen Schriftsteller* (*GCS*), *Corpus Christianorum* (*CC*), and *Sources chrétiennes* (*SC*), but also by volumes in other series and through the publication of individual works. However, they remain standard for many authors.

After losing his printing house to fire (1868), Migne was able to rebuild but incurred the displeasure of the archbishop of Paris over his attempts to finance the new establishment. He died virtually blind.   [M.P.McH.]

Bibliography

A.C. Cotter, "Abbé Migne and the Catholic Tradition," *ThS* 7 (1946):46–71; P. Glorieux, "Pour revaloriser Migne: tables rectificatives," *MSR* 9 supplement (1952):1–82; L.C. Sheppard, "The Abbé Jacques Paul Migne," *American Benedictine Review* 7 (1956–1957):112–128; A. Hamman, *Jacques Paul Migne: le retour aux Pères de l'église* (Paris: Beauchesne, 1975); A. Mandouze and J. Fouilheron, eds., *Migne et le renouveau des études patristiques: actes du colloque de Saint-Flour, 7–8 juillet 1975* (Paris: Beauchesne, 1985).

MILAN. City at the heart of continental Italy in the valley of the Po River. Christianity was associated with Milan almost from the beginning of its emergence as an imperial colony in the second century A.D. Its strategic location made it a provincial capital and ensured its political and administrative ascendancy. As a result of the far-reaching constitutional and administrative reorganization of the empire by Diocletian (285–305), Milan became one of the four capital cities in the tetrarchy. By this time, its episcopal organization was in place; its growth and importance are attested by the fact that its sixth bishop, Merocles, attended the synods devoted to the Donatist controversy at Rome and Arles in 313 and 314. Milan loomed large during the fourth century, when the church's status was rapidly changing; with the "Edict of Milan" (313), by which Constantine and Licinius granted toleration to Christianity, the church entered an era of increasing imperial favor and support. Milan's period of glory came in the post-Constantinian era, when the empire was effectively divided into eastern and western halves with the dual capitals of Constantinople and Milan; the latter enjoyed this status from 354 to 404. The city's political eminence was complemented by its ecclesiastical importance, which was due to the extraordinary career of its bishop Ambrose (374–397), whose statesmanship and aggressive leadership enabled him to prevail over Arian rulers and bishops. Exerting an influence greater than that of the bishop of Rome, he had a major role in putting down paganism, preserving the church's independence from the emperor, and developing such aspects of church life as the cult of the martyrs, worship, and asceticism.

Milan's imperial ascendancy witnessed a time of extensive church building (S. Tecla, S. Ambrogio, S. Lorenzo Maggiore). During this era, the church of Milan enjoyed administrative jurisdiction over northern Italy and beyond the Alps in a territory equivalent to modern Switzerland, a jurisdiction that was, however, steadily reduced as new metropolitan jurisdictions emerged at Aquileia and Ravenna.

The fourth-century bishops were responsible for an aggressive missionary thrust in northern Italy, especially during Ambrose's time. Milan hosted significant synods in the fourth and fifth centuries; that of 355 is particularly noteworthy because of the Arian emperor Constantius II's efforts to have Athanasius condemned. Associated with the liturgy of the Milanese church is the so-called Ambrosian rite, one of the few western liturgies besides that of Rome to survive in the Roman Catholic Church.

The continuous invasions of Italy battered Milan in the fifth and sixth centuries. The Huns sacked the city in 452; the Byzantine-Gothic war caused great destruction, including an appalling massacre by the Goths. With the arrival of the Arian Lombards in 568, the last major Germanic people to settle in the western half of the Roman empire, Milan lost its political and religious dominance to Pavia. The successors to Ambrose took refuge in Genoa for nearly three quarters of a century. But the memory of Milan's imperial grandeur would assert itself during the later medieval era when Milan once more became the leading city of northern Italy. *See also* Ambrose. [H.R.]

Bibliography
H. Leclercq, "Milan," DACL (1933), Vol. 11, cols. 983–1102; J.-R. Palanque, *Saint Ambroise et l'empire romain* (Paris: Boccard, 1933); F.H. Dudden, *The Life and Times of St. Ambrose* (Oxford: Clarendon, 1935); S. Bottari, ed., *Tesori d'arte cristiana* (Milan: Libreria Commissionaria Italiana, 1966), Vol. 1.8: *Milano, Basilica di S. Ambrogio*; C. Wickham, *Early Medieval Italy: Central Power and Local Society, 400–1000* (Totowa: Barnes and Noble, 1981); R. Krautheimer, *Three Christian Capitals: Topography and Politics: Rome, Constantinople, Milan* (Berkeley: U of California P, 1983), pp. 69–92.

MILLENNIALISM. *See* Chiliasm.

MILTIADES (second century). Greek apologist from Asia Minor. Miltiades wrote (ca. 179–190) the *Apology for Christian Philosophy, Against the Greeks, Against the Jews, That a Prophet Should Not Speak in Ecstasy* (an anti-Montanist work), and a treatise against Valentinian Gnostics. His works are lost but are described, with some citations, by later writers. [D.M.S.]

Bibliography
Tertullian, *Against Valentinus* 5; Eusebius, *Church History* 5.16.3; 5.17.1, 5; 5.28.4; Jerome, *Lives of Illustrious Men* 39.

MINISTRY. The ancient world, as a broad generalization, knew three types of leadership structure: leaders chosen to make the decisions and exercise authority (this was characteristic of the Romans); leaders chosen to carry out the will of the people (characteristic of the Greeks); and a society of unequal members in which leaders make decisions in conjunction with the other members (characteristic of the Jews). This last type of community structure has received a fairly detailed illustration in the Qumran sect (1QS v.11f.; vi.16; viii.1), which had elements of monarchy (the overseer), oligarchy (the council of 12 [15]), and democracy (the session of the "many"). The early church has been compared with the Qumran community as having a similar concept of unequal members functioning as a unit. An important difference was that the church did not have a distinct priestly class exercising the influence of priests at Qumran.

The community organization of the Jews provided the immediate background for leadership structures in the early church. Jewish communities in Palestine were overseen by a plurality of elders (*zekenim*, "presbyters"). Diaspora communities had a multiplicity of functionaries, but they also were overseen by a council of older men, designated by varying terminology. The synagogue gatherings were presided over by a "ruler of the synagogue," who selected those who took a public part (cf. Acts 13:15 for "rulers"). A synagogue had a servant (*chazan*), who might be called on to perform several subordinate functions.

Ministry in the church was seen as deriving from Jesus. The various ministries in the church were his gifts (Eph. 4:11; cf. John 20:21; Gal. 1:1), and Jesus was the model for the different ministries in the church—apostle (Heb. 3:1), prophet (Acts 3:22ff.), preacher and teacher (Matt. 4:23), shepherd and bishop (1 Peter 2:25), deacon (Rom. 15:8). The Holy Spirit inspired a great variety of ministries in the apostolic age (1 Cor. 12:4–11, 28–30; Rom. 12:6–8). These varied ministries could be summarized as speaking ministries and serving ministries (1 Peter 4:10f.; cf. Acts 6:2–4 for the ministry of the word and the ministry of mercy). Overlapping with the inspired ministries were local leaders, chosen under the direction of apostles and missionary evangelists (Acts 6:1–6; 14:23; Titus 1:5), who provided continuity after the death of the apostles and the decline of prophets (Did. 11; 13; 15).

The latest books of the New Testament and the earliest writings outside it provide evidence for a twofold ministry of presbyter-bishops assisted by deacons in the churches over a wide geographical area in the latter part of the first century and beginning of the second: Jerusalem and Judea (Acts 11:30; 15:6; James 5:14), Syria (Did. 15.1), Galatia (Acts 14:23), Asia Minor (1 Peter 5:1–4), Ephesus (Acts 20:17, 28; 1 Tim. 3), Philippi (Phil. 1:1; Polycarp, Ep. 6); Corinth (1 Clem. 42.4), Crete (Titus 1:5–7), and Rome (1 Clem. 42; 44; Hermas, Vis. 2.4.2f.; 3.5.1). Later testimony would presumably add Alexandria to the list (Jerome, Ep. 146; Severus, ed. Brooks, II, 213).

Ignatius of Antioch early in the second century provides the first testimony to a threefold ministry of bishop, presbyters, and deacons, in which the bishop is clearly distinguished from (although closely associated with) the presbytery of which he was the chairman (Eph. 4.1; Philad. 7.1). Ignatius wanted to bring all church activities under the supervision of the bishop in order to maintain unity (Smyrn. 8). The Ignatian pattern of ministry was generally observed by the middle of the second century and was universal by its end. The bishop took on the roles of prophet, evangelist, and teacher as well as presided over the presbyters. Ignatius's description of the bishop as representing God, the presbyters the apostles, and the deacons Christ was adopted by the Didascalia 9, adding that deaconesses represented the Holy Spirit.

The view that the apostles had established ministry in the church and that there had been a continuous succession of bishops and presbyters in the churches (apostolic succession) became a powerful weapon against heresy and strengthened the authority of the ministry.

The growth of the churches occasioned the institution of additional orders of ministry. Cornelius in the mid-third century reports that the church at Rome included one bishop; forty-six presbyters; seven deacons; seven subdeacons; forty-two acolytes; fifty-two exorcists, readers, and doorkeepers; and about 1,500 widows (Eusebius, H.E. 6.43.11). A fifth-century document lists the seven orders of the clergy in ascending order as gravedigger, doorkeeper, reader, subdeacon, deacon, presbyter, and bishop (Ps.-Jerome [Faustus?], De septem ordinibus ecclesiae). Under Justinian (535), the church at Constantinople had sixty presbyters, 100 deacons, forty deaconesses, ninety subdeacons, 110 lectors, twenty-five cantors, and 100 doorkeepers (Nov. 3.1). As newer ministries were instituted in the churches, these orders too were traced back to apostolic institution (Const. app. 8.19–26, 28, 46). The orders of ministry in the church were increasingly thought of on the analogy of officers in the civil government, with the result that a person was expected to pass through the lower grades of the clergy in advancement to the higher offices. Proclus is only one of many whose career proceeded from reader, to deacon, to presbyter, to bishop (Socrates, H.E. 7.40–41). Ambrose was one of the exceptions who went immediately from baptism to bishop (Paulinus, V. Amb. 3.9).

The ordination prayers in the church orders give the conception of ministry for each rank. Common to these prayers is the invocation of the Holy Spirit on the ordained. Special treatises were written, however, only about bishops, for they were considered the supreme embodiment of ministry.

Many images were held up as models for the exercise of ministry: shepherd, preacher, judge, teacher. Especially notable was the adoption of the priestly image, comparing bishops, presbyters, and deacons to the priests and Levites of the Old Testament (*Const. app.* 8.46.1–6). *1 Clement* 40 used the Old Testament orders of ministers as an illustration of good order in the church. Origen in his commentaries on the Old Testament adapted the instructions to priests to the Christian ministry, calling the ministers in the church "priests" but explaining this usage by typology (*Jo.* 1.3; *Hom.* 5 *in Lev.* 4; *Hom.* 12 *in Jer.* 3). Cyprian freely used "priest" for the "bishop" (*Ep.* 63). Although monasticism began as a lay movement, its ideals influenced the conception of the ministry, giving impetus to the ideal of celibacy and encouraging a distinctive dress and hair style. Pseudo-Dionysius the Areopagite (*E.H.* 1.2–3; 5.1ff.) saw the ministry as an earthly counterpart to the angelic hierarchy and had a great influence on later conceptions of the ministry in the eastern churches. *See also* Apostolic Succession; Bishop; Church; Clergy; Deacon; Deaconess; Evangelist; Ordination; Presbyter; Priesthood; Teacher.   [E.F.]

Bibliography

T.M. Lindsay, *The Church and the Ministry in the Early Centuries* (London: Hodder and Stoughton, 1902); A. von Harnack, *The Constitution and Law of the Church in the First Two Centuries* (London: Norgate and Williams, 1910); J.B. Lightfoot, "The Christian Ministry," *Saint Paul's Epistle to the Philippians* (Grand Rapids: Zondervan, 1953 repr.), pp. 181–269; G.H. Williams, "The Ministry of the Ante-Nicene Church" and "The Ministry in the Later Patristic Period," *The Ministry in Historical Perspectives*, ed. H.R. Niebuhr and D.D. Williams (New York: Harper, 1956), pp. 27–81; B. Reicke, "The Constitution of the Primitive Church in the Light of Jewish Documents," *The Scrolls and the New Testament*, ed. K. Stendahl (New York: Harper, 1957), pp. 143–156; C. Vogel, "Unité de l'église et pluralité des formes historiques d'organisation ecclésiastique de IIIe au Ve siècle," *Unam Sanctam* 39 (1962):591–636; W. Rordorf, "La Théologie du ministère dans l'église ancienne," *Ministères et laïcat* (Taizé: Presses de Taizé, 1964), pp. 84–104; S.L. Greenslade, "The Unit of Pastoral Care in the Early Church," *Studies in Church History*, ed. G.J. Cuming (London: Nelson, 1965), Vol. 2, pp. 102–118; H. von Campenhausen, *Ecclesiastical Authority and Spiritual Power in the Church of the First Three Centuries* (London: Black, 1969); J.T. Lienhard, *Ministry* (Wilmington: Glazier, 1984); E. Ferguson, *Early Christians Speak* (Abilene: ACU, 1987), pp. 167–179.

MINOR PROPHETS. The twelve shorter prophetic books in the Hebrew Bible: Hosea, Joel, Amos, Obadiah, Jonah, Micah, Nahum, Habakkuk, Zephaniah, Haggai, Zechariah, and Malachi. They first appear as a literary unit ca. 180 B.C. in Sirach 49:10. Eight incomplete manuscript copies of these prophets have been identified in the Qumran Caves, plus fragments of commentaries on Hosea, Micah, Nahum, Habakkuk, and Zephaniah. There is a second-century A.D. manuscript from Wadi Murabba'at, as well as a Greek text from the Nahal Hever. A third-century Greek manuscript is in the Freer collection, and these prophets are included in codices Vaticanus and Alexandrinus but are incomplete in Sinaiticus (lacking Hosea, Amos, and Micah).

Early Christianity followed the Hebrew tradition that spoke of "twelve prophets." Although quotations from most of these prophets appear in the New Testament, and they are quoted in other early Christian writings, it is not until Melito of Sardis that reference is made again to the twelve as a unit. He speaks of the "twelve in a single book" (Eusebius, *H.E.* 4.26.13f.).

These prophets are often quoted by name in Christian writings, but the canonical lists of both the eastern and western churches, rather than giving their individual names, customarily designated the group as "the twelve" (cf. Sundberg). Gregory of Nazianzus broke the pattern in the eastern church and Augustine in the western by listing individual books.

It is to Augustine (*Civ. Dei* 18.29) that the designation "minor prophets" is owed. Augustine distinguished between those "who are called minor because of the brevity of their writings, as compared with those who are called the greater prophets because they published larger volumes." These prophets are not minor in importance. *See also* Jonah; Prophets.

[J.P.L.]

Bibliography

Jerome, *Commentarii in prophetas minores*, ed. M. Adriaen, CCSL (1969, 1970), Vols. 76, 76A; Theodore of Mopsuestia, *Commentarius in xii prophetas minores*, PG 66.124–652; Cyril of Alexandria, *Commentarius in xii prophetas minores*, ed. P.E.

Pusey (Oxford: Clarendon, 1868); Theodoret, *Interpretatio in xii prophetas minores*, PG 81.1545–1988.

G.L. Robinson, *The Twelve Minor Prophets* (New York: Harper, 1926); G.A. Smith, *The Book of the Twelve Prophets* (New York: Harper, 1929); A.C. Sundberg, Jr., *The Old Testament of the Early Church* (Cambridge: Harvard UP, 1964), pp. 58–59; D.A. Schneider, "The Unity of the Book of the Twelve" (Ph.D. diss., Yale University, 1979).

MINUCIUS FELIX (late second or early third century). Christian Latin apologist. A Roman advocate, probably from Africa, Minucius Felix wrote the *Octavius*, a dialogue between the Christian Octavius, an advocate from overseas who had died prior to the composition of the work, and the pagan Caecilius from Cirta in Numidia, who is depicted as having been persuaded by the force of the arguments to become a believer. Directed primarily to pagan readers, the *Octavius* relies extensively on Stoicism; Cicero and Seneca the Younger are major sources. Since Christianity is treated from the standpoint of philosophy, scripture is not cited nor are major biblical teachings much discussed. The emphasis is on monotheism, divine providence, a belief in immortality, and ethical standards; pagan mythology is attacked vigorously. Often edited and translated, the work is useful for its portrayal of the contemporary religious and social situation as well as for its indications of the relations between Roman Christianity and that of Africa. There is a long history of scholarly dispute over the relationship of the *Octavius* and the *Apology* of Tertullian (197). It is certain only that one of these writings must have depended on the other. A work, *De fato*, promised in the *Octavius* (36.2), either is lost or was never written. CPL 37, 37a.   [M.P.McH.]

Bibliography

Lactantius, *Divine Institutes* 1.11.55 (=*Octavius* 21.5–7); 5.1.22; Jerome, *Lives of Illustrious Men* 58; idem, *Letters* 49.13; 60.10; 70.5.

Octavius, ed. M. Pellegrino (Turin: Paravia, 1963); ed. J. Beaujeu (Paris: Les Belles Lettres, 1964); ed. B. Kytzler (Leipzig: Teubner, 1982).

Octavius, tr. G.H. Rendall, LCL (1931); tr. R. Arbesmann et al., FOTC (1950), Vol. 10; tr. G.W. Clarke, ACW (1974), Vol. 39.

H.J. Baylis, *Minucius Felix and His Place Among the Early Fathers of the Latin Church* (London: SPCK, and New York and Toronto: Macmillan, 1928); G.W. Clarke, "The Literary Setting of the *Octavius* of Minucius Felix," *JRH* 3 (1965):195–211; idem, "The Historical Setting of the *Octavius* of Minucius Felix," *JRH* 4 (1967):267–286; T.P. Halton and R.D. Sider, "A Decade of Patristic Scholarship 1970–1979," *CW* 76 (1982–1983):112 (bibliography); A.J. Cappelletti, "Minucio Félix y su filosofía de la religión," *Revista Venezolana de Filosofía* 19 (1985):7–62; M.L. Colish, *The Stoic Tradition from Antiquity to the Early Middle Ages* (Leiden: Brill, 1985), Vol. 2, pp. 29–33.

MIRACLE. Wondrous deed attributed to divine power. The variety of Greek and Latin terms both for the phenomena called "miracles" and for the people who perform wondrous feats attests the fact that thaumaturgy (miracle working) and thaumaturges (miracle workers) were common in the Greco-Roman world in which Christianity came into being.

Extraordinary happenings, or accounts of such, are subject to dispute and can lead to conflict. They may, for example, be deemed improbable (John 9:32). In the *Acts of Thomas*, a pagan husband tells his Christian wife that "never was it heard in this world that anyone raised a dead person" (*A. Thom*: 96; cf. Origen, *Cels.* 2.55). That some things were considered impossible—e.g., rivers running backward, the sun standing still (Apuleius, *Metam.* 1.3)—was a commonplace, one used in fact as a literary device. A supposedly extraordinary phenomenon might also be questioned on epistemological grounds. At Jesus' baptism, who besides Jesus heard the wondrous voice from heaven or saw the bird?, asks the pagan Celsus (*Cels.* 1.41). Who saw Jesus risen from the dead and how often did he appear? Only once, and stealthily (7.35), to a frenzied woman whose mental state disposed her to dreaming (2.55).

Even if a phenomenon was accepted as extraordinary, the agency or means by which it occurred might be questioned. Jesus was accused of casting out demons by aid of Beelzebul, the prince of demons (Mark 3:22; Matt. 12:24; Luke 11:15), and his enemies feared that his disciples would steal his body and say he had risen (Matt. 27:63–64). A common means of discrediting a "miracle" was to attribute it to sleight of hand (Origen, *Cels.* 1.68) or to magical tricks (Irenaeus, *Haer.* 1.13.1; Hippolytus, *Haer.* 4.28) or to magic worked with the aid of demonic forces (Justin, *1 Apol.* 14.1; 26.2; *2 Apol.* 5.4; Irenaeus, *Haer.* 1.13; 2.31.2–3; 2.32).

A number of factors underlay such disputes. One was level of education. Rank-and-file Roman soldiers might interpret a lunar eclipse as a dire omen, a wondrous sign from the gods, while their officers might understand it as an unusual but natural event caused by the earth's shadow (Livy, *History* 44.37). The "ignorant multitude" at the time of Romulus did not understand the reason for a solar eclipse, says Augustine (*Civ. Dei* 3.15), who was himself freed from belief in astrology through reading books by astronomers that explained the causes of eclipses (*Conf.* 5.4.6). Another factor was group loyalty: the miracle claims of a group of which one is suspicious or to which one is hostile were apt to be discounted, as is evident in some of the examples cited above. In early Christianity, one finds these same factors operative as Christians disputed with Jews, pagans, and other Christians over miracle claims.

Early Christian sources depict Christians performing miracles (2 Cor. 12:12; Rom. 15:19; Acts 3:1–11). Although Christians took pains to distinguish their efforts from those of pagans (e.g., Irenaeus, *Haer.* 3.32.5; Origen, *Cels.* 7.4), their techniques were similar. Christian sources mention material means (handkerchiefs or aprons, Acts 19:12; a shadow, Acts 5:15; oil, James 5:14), laying on of hands (Acts 28:18), "adjurations" (Origen, *Cels.* 7.4), the invoking of a powerful name (i.e., Jesus: Acts 3:6; 4:10, 30; Justin, *2 Apol.* 6.6; *Dial.* 30.3; 76.7; 85.2–3; Irenaeus, *Haer.* 2.32.4; Origen, *Cels.* 1.6), the recital of "formulas from the holy scriptures" (ibid 7.67). The "formulas" Origen refers to may be the Christian credos, summarizing the Jesus story or his miracles, that early sources say were employed in Christian thaumaturgy (Justin, *2 Apol.* 6.6; *Dial.* 30.3; 76.7; 85.2–3; Iren., *Haer.* 2.32.4; Origen, *Cels.* 1.6; *M. Petr. et Paul.* 56; *A. Petr. et Paul.* 77; *A. Jo.* 70; *A. Thom.* 47–48).

Appealing to the power of Jesus, by invoking his name or reciting credos about him, involved Christians in a paradox basic to the early Christian message: where was the power in a person who, in contrast to accepted ideas of deity, was himself so helpless that ordinary mortals put him to death (Origen, *Cels.* 2.9, 55; 6.10), and indeed a death reserved for the worst offenders and the lowest strata of society? Thus, Paul can point to "signs and wonders and mighty works" that he wrought as authentication of his apostleship (2 Cor. 12:12; cf. Rom. 15:19), yet he regards such recitals as foolishness to those outside the Christian fold (1 Cor. 1:18–25) and says he will boast, instead, of his weakness, persecutions, and the like, on behalf of Christ, "for when I am weak, then I am strong" (2 Cor. 12:9–11). The many miracles wrought by Jesus in the Gospel of Mark are put in perspective by the evangelist's portrait of Jesus as one who must suffer and die and whose miraculous powers must therefore be kept secret (1:34, 43; 3:12; 5:43; 7:36) until it is clear that he accomplishes God's purposes through dying (8:31–33; 14:61–62).

The New Testament writings are nonetheless post-Easter documents, and the Christ they depict is both the serving, suffering, dying Jesus and the risen, exalted Lord of the church, who, as he once worked miracles, can now do so again for or through his followers. Healings and mighty works were present gifts of the Spirit to Jesus' followers, reports Paul (1 Cor. 12:9–10). In the Gospel of John, Jesus tells his hearers that even if they do not believe him, they should believe his mighty works (10:27); but these works are signs that, for those whose eyes are opened (9), point beyond themselves to the one who while multiplying earthly loaves is himself the life-giving bread from heaven (6) and who, in the cross and its aftermath, reascends to the Father. The tension inherent in these accounts between a miracle-working and a suffering, dying Jesus—a figure of the past as well as a presence in Christian communities—lessened as Christians increased in numbers and made their presence felt in the empire. Christian apologists cited the miracles wrought by Jesus or his followers as proof of his power and of his superiority to pagan and Jewish thaumaturges; they sought to defend the miracles of Jesus and his followers against charges that they were wrought by sleight of hand or by magic with the assertion that his followers have left magic and magical arts behind. The cross became "the mightiest symbol of [God's] strength and dominion" (Justin, *1 Apol.* 55.2; examples in 55.3–8); moreover, Jesus' suffering and death were not shameful—sons of Zeus, too, suffered and died (Justin, *1 Apol.* 22.3–4).

Resurrection. What is perhaps the key Christian miracle, the resurrection of Jesus and of believers, is sometimes portrayed in stark physical terms (John 11:1–44; Luke 24:36–43; John 20:24–27; cf. Origen, *Cels.* 5.14). Such interpretations raised the problem of how a body consumed by an animal, which is in turn consumed by another animal or a human, could be raised (Athenagoras, *Res.* 4; Methodius, *Res.* 1.20.4; Porphyry, Frg. 94, Harnack; Augustine, *Civ. Dei* 22.20). "With God all things are possible" was a common reply (*Apoc. Petr.* 4; Athenagoras, *Res.* 5.1; Porphyry, Frg. 94, Harnack), as it was to objections to Christian resurrection claims generally (*1 Clem.* 27.2; Justin, *1 Apol.* 18.6; 19.6; *Dial.* 69; Tertullian, *Res.* 57; Origen, *Cels.* 5.14). Philosophically schooled Christians were apt to reject literalist views of resurrection and, in the case of Origen, to posit an interpretation that drew on Paul's comparison of resurrection to the growth of a grain of wheat (1 Cor. 15:35ff.) but was informed by Stoicism and Platonism. Gnostic Christians, although sometimes ostensibly affirming resurrection in the flesh (*Gosp. Philip.* 23; *Ep. Rheg.* 47.2ff.), more typically interpreted resurrection, whether of Jesus or of Christians, nonliterally or "spiritually" (Hippolytus, *Haer.* 7.27.10; Clement of Alexandria, *Exc. Thdot.* 61.7; Irenaeus, *Haer.* 1.30.13; 2.31.2; *Gosp. Philip* 21–23; 90; *Ep. Rheg.* 45.30ff.; 49.15; cf. 2 Tim. 2:18).

Interpretation. The contrast between literal and nonliteral interpretation of miracles evident in these examples is found in early Christian interpretation of miracles generally. Marcion, operating on the principle that texts should be read literally unless they themselves indicate otherwise, contrasted the injurious nature of the miracles of the just God of the old covenant and their use of material means with the beneficent wonders worked with a mere word by the Christ of the good God of the new covenant (Tertullian, *Marc.* 4.9.7). Having rejected typological interpretations of the Jewish scriptures and proofs from Jewish prophecy to establish Christ's divinity, Marcion counted on Christ's miracles to accomplish this purpose (Tertullian, *Marc.* 3.3.1). Apelles, one of Marcion's followers, turned the incredibility of the creator God's miracles against him, asking, for example, how a small ark could hold so many animals and their food for a whole year, and concluding that such tales were false (Origen, *Hom. in Gen.* 2.2).

More common, however, was nonliteral interpretation of miracle accounts, those in the Jewish scriptures (especially those accounts considered offensive) as well as those in Christian writings. Such interpretation, which did not necessarily preclude literal acceptance, came to predominate in mainstream Christianity but was found also in Gnosticism. Heracleon, for example, gives allegorical interpretations of the healing of the official's son (John 4:46–53) that accord with Gnostic thought (Origen, *Jo.* 13.60; cf. 13.11). Typical examples of mainstream Christian interpretation are Tertullian, who, against Marcion's literal reading of Christ's healing of a blind man, sees the blind as a symbol of the Jewish people (*Marc.* 4.36.13); or Clement of Alexandria, who regards the five barley loaves in the story of Christ's feeding of the multitude (Mark 6:30–44; Matt. 14:13–21; Luke 9:10–17) as the preparation of Greeks and Jews for "the divine wheat," that is, the food cultivated by the Law, because barley ripens before wheat, while the two fish signify Greek philosophy, generated and borne on the Gentile wave (*Str.* 6.11.24); or Origen, who sees the waterpots in the water-into-wine story (John 2:1–11) as the scriptures that cleanse and the two or three measures they contain as three senses of scripture (*Princ.* 4.2.5); or Augustine, who says that Aaron's rod, changed into a serpent, is Christ put to death, and the serpent changed back into a rod is Christ resurrected, along with his body the church, while the serpents that the Egyptian magicians produced from their rods and that were swallowed up by Aaron's serpent (Exod. 7:10–12) are like persons dead in the world who will not rise with Christ unless, by believing in him, they are swallowed up as it were and enter into his body, the church (*Trin.* 3.20).

Such interpretations did not preclude literal acceptance and interpretations of miracle accounts. Origen could take miracle stories literally (e.g., *Cels.* 2.33.34; *Cat. Matt.* 8.5–9, 28–30, 32–33 [frgs. 154, 164, 168 in Klostermann and Benz, 1941]); but in accord with the principle that all of scripture has a spiritual meaning (*Princ.* 4.3.5), he might, alongside, also give a nonliteral interpretation or application (*Cat. Matt.* 8.32 [frg. 189 in Klostermann and Benz, 1941]).

In several passages, Augustine reflects on the nature of miracles. Miracles are not against nature but against nature as humans know it (*Gen. ad litt.* 6.13.24). Angels, good or evil, know more of nature than do humans and can therefore work what appears miraculous to humans (*Trin.* 3.8.13; 10.20). But had the Creator not implanted causal principles in the visible world, the angels or their human agents, such as magicians, could accomplish nothing—they are not creators (*Trin.* 3.8.13). These principles or seeds can operate over a period of time, as in normal human or animal development or the making of wine, or instantaneously, as in the creation of Adam (Gen. 1:27) or the turning of a rod into a snake (Exod. 4:3; 7:10–12) or water into wine (John 2:1–11) (*Gen. ad litt.* 6.13.24; 14.25; *Trin.* 3.5.11), for the Lord is the author of time (*Gen. ad litt.* 6.13.24). Both what is perceived as miraculous and what as ordinary are caused by God's power and in accord with his will (*Trin.* 3.2.7; 5.11; 10.19), but it is only the unusual thing that is considered miraculous (3.5.11; 6.11). Miracles may be wrought directly by God or through angels or the spirits of martyrs (*Civ. Dei* 22.9). These distinctions, and Augustine's reflections on miracles generally, were developed further by medieval scholastics.

As a young Platonist, Augustine had distanced himself from miracles, saying their novelty was necessary in Jesus' day to persuade the multitude, which relies on the senses, while their beneficence moved it to love the Lord (*Util. cred.* 16.34). Miracles did not continue, however, so that the soul would not seek visible things and because their very continuance would make them customary and therefore no longer wondrous (*Vera relig.* 25.47). In his old age, Augustine stated that he meant, not that no miracles occurred at present, but rather that none such or so many as occurred in Jesus' day; indeed, he himself knew of some miracles (*Retract.* 1.12.7; 1.13.5; cf. *Civ. Dei* 22.8). In the exercise of his bishop's office, confronting sickness, heresy, and pagan dismissal of Christian miracle claims, he saw miracles as a comfort to believers and a defense against their enemies, including magicians and theurgists who invoked demons to work their wonders (*Civ. Dei* 10.9–10).

Saints, Relics, Symbols, Sacraments. Christian miracle piety came to be focused on martyrs, whose faithfulness was rewarded by the Lord, who performed miracles at their tombs or through their remains; on practitioners of asceticism, through whom the savior worked miracles; and on Christian symbols and sacraments.

In the Greco-Roman world, persons renowned for various reasons—"heroes"—were believed to exert power from their graves, with the result that their remains were carefully preserved. Christians, too, carefully preserved the precious remains of their heroes, the martyrs (e.g., *M. Polyc.* 18; Paulinus, *V. Amb.* 32–33). Pagans might protest that Christian martyrs were in fact convicted criminals (Eunapius, *V. Soph.* 472) and that to fill every place with tombs and monuments and then grovel among them was to go against Jesus' characterization (Matt. 23:27) of tombs as unclean (Julian, *Galil.* 335B-D). For Christians, however, the martyrs were powerfully present in their tombs and in their enshrined remains, indeed in anything that even touched the remains (*A. Thom.* 170), and the proof was the many healings, exorcisms, and other miracles wrought by the sainted martyrs. Incubation—the practice of sleeping at a temple of the pagan hero-deity Asclepius in the hope of miraculous healings— also came to be practiced at martyrs' shrines (e.g., Gregory the Great, *Dial.* 2.38).

In the ascetics, whose rigorous life became the new form of martyrdom, Christians found another locus of power, as is evident in the many accounts of their lives. An early Life, that of Pachomius, attributes exorcisms, healings, and clairvoyance to this Egyptian ascetic (*V. Pach.* 41; 43–45; 112) but also reports instances where his prayers for healing were not answered (45), or where he expounded on the resurrection but did not raise the dead (62). Miracles are more frequent in Athanasius's *Life of Anthony* (14; 48; 50; 54; 57; 58; 60; 61; 63; 71; 86) and other such Lives of the fourth and fifth centuries; by the time of the *Dialogues* ascribed to Gregory the Great, miracles are as frequent as they are astounding (*Dial.* 1.1–5, etc.).

The Lives of saints are careful to provide biblical precedents for such miracles and to portray them as less than Christ's and worked by divine power through the ascetics (e.g., Athanasius, *V. Anton.* 56; 59; Gregory the Great, *Dial.* 2.8) or through the faith of the supplicants after instruction by an ascetic (e.g., Athanasius, *V. Anton.* 48), though sometimes the ascetic is himself said to possess miraculous power (Gregory the Great, *Dial.* 2.30). As with the martyrs, posthumous miracles came to be attributed to them (Jerome, *V. Paul.* 16; *V. Hilar.* 47; Paulinus, *V. Amb.* 52; 54).

Although the authors of the Lives stressed that virtue and the ascetic life ranked above miraculous power (Athanasius, *V. Anton.* 38; Jerome, *V. Hilar.* 38; Gregory the Great, *Dial.* 1.12) and indeed accounted for that power (Athanasius, *V. Anton.* 34; 65; Jerome, *V. Hilar.* 18), for supplicants what mattered most was that the power was there, whether in a past or present saint—both of whom were still powerfully present—or in holy water (Jerome, *V. Hilar.* 20; Gregory the Great, *Dial.* 1.10; cf. *A. Thom.* 52; Augustine, *Civ. Dei* 22.8) or the holy eucharist (Gregory the Great, *Dial.* 2.24; cf. *A. Thom.* 51) or the sign of the once shame-

ful but now potent cross (Athanasius, *V. Anton.* 23; 80; Jerome, *V. Hilar.* 6; 40; Gregory the Great, *Dial.* 1.10; 2.3). Miracles were both a deliverance from present evils and a foretaste of the ultimate victory.

However one characterizes or explains the phenomena that early Christians called "miracles," without them early Christianity would be inconceivable and the medieval landscape unrecognizable. *See also* Magic.   [H.E.R.]

Bibliography

M. Hamilton, *Incubation or The Cure of Disease in Pagan Temples and Christian Churches* (St. Andrews: Henderson, and London: Simpkin, Marshall, Hamilton, Kent, 1906); H. Chadwick, "Origen, Celsus, and the Resurrection of the Body," *HThR* 41 (1948):83–102; E.R. Dodds, *The Greeks and the Irrational* (Berkeley: U of California P, 1951); R.M. Grant, *Miracle and Natural Law in Graeco-Roman and Early Christian Thought* (Amsterdam: North-Holland, 1952); J.A. Hardon, "The Concept of Miracle from St. Augustine to Modern Apologetics," *ThS* 15 (1954):229–257; G. Bornkamm, "The Stilling of the Storm in Matthew," and H.J. Held, "Matthew as Interpreter of the Miracle Stories," *Tradition and Interpretation in Matthew*, ed. G. Bornkamm, G. Barth, and H.J. Held (Philadelphia: Westminster, 1963), pp. 52–57, 165–299; J. Becker, "Wunder und Christologie: Zum literarkritischen und christologischen Problem der Wunder im Johannesevangelium," *NTS* 16 (1969–1970):130–148; P. Boglioni, "Miracle et nature chez Grégoire le Grand," *Cahier d'études médiévales* (Montreal: Bellarmin, and Paris: Vrin, 1974), Vol. 1: *Epopées, légendes et miracles*, pp. 11–102; J.M. McColloh, "The Cult of Relics in the Letters and 'Dialogs' of Pope Gregory the Great," *Traditio* 32 (1976):145–184; P. Brown, *The Cult of the Saints: Its Rise and Function in Latin Christianity* (Chicago: U of Chicago P, 1981); H. Remus, "Does Terminology Distinguish Early Christian from Pagan Miracles?," *JBL* 101 (1982):531–551; idem, "'Magic or Miracle'? Some Second-Century Instances," *SCent* 2 (1982):127–156; B. Ward, *Miracles and the Medieval Mind: Theory, Record and Event 1000–1215* (Philadelphia: U of Pennsylvania P, 1982); J. Helgeland, "The Transformation of Christianity into Roman Religion," *Traditions in Contact and Change: Selected Proceedings of the XIVth Congress of the International Association for the History of Religions*, ed. P. Slater and D. Wiebe (Waterloo: Wilfrid Laurier UP, 1983); H. Remus, *Pagan-Christian Conflict over Miracle in the Second Century* (Cambridge: Philadelphia Patristic Foundation, 1983); H.C. Kee, *Miracle in the Early Christian World* (New Haven: Yale UP, 1983); J.M. Peterson, *The Dialogues of Gregory the Great in*

Their Late Antique Cultural Background (Toronto: Pontifical Institute of Mediaeval Studies, 1984); H.C. Kee, *Medicine, Miracle, and Magic in New Testament Times* (Cambridge: Cambridge UP, 1986); R.A. Greer, *The Fear of Freedom: A Study of Miracles in the Roman Imperial Church* (State College: Pennsylvania State UP, 1989).

MISSIONS (SPREAD OF CHRISTIANITY).

Efforts to win adherents. Missionaries relied largely on the planting of churches in urban centers from which the process could move outward. The conversion of Constantine (ca. 312) resulted in state support of evangelistic efforts within the Roman empire and ensured Christianity's triumph over its competitors—the old state cults, the oriental mysteries, as well as its parent religion, Judaism. Although Christian missionaries registered their most noteworthy successes within the empire, they extended their efforts well beyond it throughout the ancient world. Armenia, in fact, was the first nation to convert officially to the Christian faith (ca. 301). Before the end of the seventh century, missionaries had penetrated as far east as India and China, as far south as Abyssinia, as far west as the British Isles, and as far north as Germany.

Geographical Spread. Christianity began as a sect of Judaism, the first (Jewish) converts not distinguishing themselves from other Jews save in their conviction that Jesus had fulfilled long-awaited Jewish expectations of a Messiah through his death and resurrection and would soon return to consummate God's purpose for the people of the covenant. Debate within the Jewish communities over these claims, however, soon resulted in persecution led by the rabbi Saul of Tarsus that scattered believers from Jerusalem to other parts of Palestine and beyond. Wherever Christians went, they carried with them a vital missionary impulse (Acts 8:4), but the conversion of their one-time persecutor supplied the mission effort with a fervent leadership (Acts 9; Gal. 1:13ff.). Saul, renamed Paul, formulated a strategy for the evangelization of the Roman empire that continued to serve the mission effort throughout subsequent centuries despite heated debate over

accepting Gentiles without requiring them first to become Jews (Acts 11; 15).

Even before the Jewish revolts (A.D. 66–70, 132–135) closed Jerusalem to Christians, many of whom fled to Transjordan, the focus of mission activities shifted to Antioch in Syria, whence Paul and Barnabas launched the first of their missionary journeys to Cyprus and Cilicia in Asia Minor (Acts 13–14). Fired by expectation of the imminent return of Christ, they went first to Jewish communities to win converts. When opposition forced them out of the synagogues, they started churches separated from them, Paul focusing his efforts on winning Gentiles, even thinking of himself as "apostle to the Gentiles" (Gal. 2:8). Separating from Barnabas after one foray (Acts 15:36–41), Paul formulated a strategy for planting the seed of the gospel in major hubs of commerce and culture, moving gradually westward as far as Spain. Before his last trip to Jerusalem (A.D. 58), which resulted in imprisonment at Caesarea (58–60) and later at Rome (60–62), he managed to start churches in numerous cities in Asia Minor and the Greek peninsula.

Taking advantage of fields tilled by Jews, and free of some of the demands made by the Jewish faith, Christianity soon outstripped its parent. Whereas Judaism accounted for an estimated seven percent of the population of the Roman empire during the first century, by the time of Constantine Christianity could claim an estimated five to fifteen percent, with its best showing in cities where Judaism had been strong. According to the painstaking study of A. von Harnack, by the Council of Nicaea (325) Christianity represented nearly half of the population in Asia Minor, Thrace opposite Bithynia, Cyprus, and Edessa, as well as Armenia. Christians constituted an important segment of the population in Antioch and Coele-Syria; Alexandria together with Egypt and the Thebaid; Rome, lower Italy, and certain parts of middle Italy; proconsular Africa and Numidia; Spain; and parts of Achaia, Thessaly, Macedonia, the islands, and southern Gaul. They were thinly scattered in Palestine, Phoenicia, Arabia, the Greek peninsula, the northern region of middle Italy and eastern region of upper Italy, and Mauretania and Tripolitana. There is evidence for a Christian presence in the towns of ancient Philistia, the north and northwestern coasts of the Black Sea, western upper Italy, middle and upper Gaul, Belgica, Germany, and Raetia, although Christianity was obviously a negligible factor in such places. The evangelization of the countryside did not proceed with any speed until after Constantine's conversion.

Constantine gave Christianity an immense boost. Although forced initially to treat the religions of the empire impartially, the emperor immediately bestowed favors on the churches, the clergy, and individual believers. Following his defeat of Licinius (324), he increasingly applied his powers to secure the triumph of Christianity and the eradication of its competitors, envisioning himself as a thirteenth apostle and a bishop to those outside the church. He and his mother, Helena, set an example for the Roman upper classes in erecting grand basilicas. Disappointment that he could not win over the city of Rome to his faith contributed to Constantine's decision to move his capital to Byzantium (330). Thereafter, he threw himself energetically into the task of Christianizing not only the new capital but the entire empire. In a hierarchical society, imperial assistance obviously aided the churches immensely in their evangelistic efforts, although there is ample evidence of resistance to the increasing pressures to abandon the ancestral faith. The emperor Julian (361–363) slowed Christianity's advance somewhat, but his brief reign did not allow him to move far in his effort to restore the ancient cultus. In 391, the emperor Theodosius declared open war on paganism, although he failed to extirpate it. In 529, Justinian ordered all non-Christians to come to the church, receive instruction, and be baptized under penalty of confiscation and exile. A series of laws subsequently inflicted increasing penalties upon pagans, Jews, Samaritans, and heretics.

Immediately after Constantine's conversion, the churches expanded their network of bishoprics throughout the empire so as to leave no nook or cranny without a witness. The number of bishops multiplied especially in Italy, Gaul, other parts of the west, and in Egypt, where they had been few. The early councils of the Constantinian and post-Constantinian era brought the churches' jurisdictional areas into approximate line with the dioceses and provinces of the empire. A system of parishes may also have emerged during the fourth century. Two letters of pope Zosimus (417 and 418) offer convincing proof for parochial organization along the coast of Gaul. The evangelization of rural areas proceeded less regularly than that of cities. In the east, *chorepiscopi*, or rural bishops, were evidently appointed in order to supply the small villages and country places without increasing the number of bishops unduly.

In the meantime, however, the collapse of the western portion of the Roman empire created a new missionary challenge. From the third century, the barbarian tribes in Europe had been breaching the empire's defenses and steadily pressing southward. Missionaries, most of them monks, worked among the various tribes, establishing monasteries and building churches. In Gaul, Martin, bishop of Tours (ca. 371–397), carried out remarkably effective work in the countryside around Tours, introducing a rudimentary parochial system. Arian missionaries evangelized the Visigoths and Burgundians before the fifth century. The Franks accepted Catholic Christianity after the conversion of their king, Clovis, baptized on Christmas Day, 496, by Remigius, bishop of Rheims. In this, Clovis yielded to the pleas of his wife, the Burgundian princess Clotilda, after winning a victory over the Alamanni. The Goths were early evangelized by Catholic missionaries and by Audians, but the Arian Ulfilas (ca. 311–383), a Cappadocian born among the Goths, proved more effective. Shortly after his consecration as a bishop by Eusebius of Nicomedia, he returned to Gothic territory, where he was the first to translate the Bible (omitting the books of Kings as too warlike) into their language.

Christianity evidently came to the British Isles as early as the first century by way of Roman soldiers and then (ca. 300) from Gaul, but the Angles and Saxons almost wiped out all traces in the late-fifth-century invasions. Patrick (ca. 390–460), reared as a Christian in Britain, was captured by pirates and spent six years in Ireland before escaping. After some training in Britain or Gaul, he returned to Ireland as a kind of itinerant bishop and spent the rest of his life evangelizing local chieftains, educating their children, ordaining clergy, and establishing monasteries for both men and women. Patrick's contemporary Ninian (ca. 360–ca. 432), son of a converted chieftain of the Cumbrian Britons, received instruction in the faith at Rome and, after consecration as a bishop (394), did mission work in Scotland and Wales. Candida Casa (Whithorn) became a center from which Ninian and his monks went out to convert Britons and Picts and served as a seat of learning for Welsh and Irish missionaries.

In the east, Constantine's zealous activities on behalf of Christianity proved disastrous for Christians in Armenia, Georgia, and Persia, for Persian invaders suspected Christians of being agents of the Romans. Armenia, evangelized by Gregory the Illuminator (ca. 300), suffered persecution when Sapor II seized the Christian king Tigranes and occupied his kingdom. The Bible was translated into Armenian ca. 400. Georgia, evangelized, according to tradition, through a miraculous healing of the king, Mirian, by a captive Christian woman named Nino or Nina, also suffered in the Persian invasion after establishing ties with Constantinople. In the second half of the fifth century, however, Vakhtang I (446–499) freed the nation from Zoroastrianism and reinstituted the Georgian church. Even before Constantine, Christianity had made strong inroads into the east, becoming well established in Edessa and Adiabene, and reaching the Hephthalite Huns and Turks. Severe persecution broke out after Constantine sought to intercede with Sapor II on behalf of Christians in Persia, whose fortunes fluctuated with Roman policy. In the fifth century, the Persian church sided with Nestorius.

Although most scholars remain skeptical of legends about mission work in India and Ceylon by the apostle Thomas, more definite evidence exists for the late fourth and fifth centuries. By 500, Christianity was well represented in Arabia, and its influence increased rapidly during the next century.

Abyssinia became a Christian state under 'Ezana, a king probably won to Christianity by Frumentius (fourth century). Frumentius was a captive who, with another youth, rose to high posts in service of his captors. Caring for merchants from the Roman empire who came to Axum, he went to Alexandria and asked Athanasius for a bishop for the Christians of his adopted country. Athanasius proceeded to appoint and ordain Frumentius himself. In the second half of the fifth and in the sixth century, a large number of monks made their way to Abyssinia; some of them translated the Bible into Ethiopic.

Methods. The influence of money and power doubtless figured prominently in the success of Christianity after the conversion of Constantine, for it grew from a sizable minority faith to become the established religion of the empire. Help of emperors, however, cannot explain the significant impact that Christianity had already made in some parts of the empire and stood ready to make elsewhere.

Foremost in the process of evangelization was the establishment of organized communities that could carry on a quiet witness in time of persecution. By ca. 200, the churches had gradually fashioned a five-stage process for the enlistment and incorporation of new members. In a culture saturated with religious anxiety and searching for security, Christians had a ready-made supply of inquirers who might have heard about their cult through casual contact with Christians, through experience of Christian charity, through witnessing martyrdom, through Christian writings, or, in times when popular hostility abated, through more direct efforts to win converts. As Hippolytus, schismatic bishop of Rome (217–235), outlined the procedure, inquirers first heard a brief summary of the Christian message. If they wished to proceed, those persons in occupations deemed unsuitable for Christians, because immoral or too closely connected with the pagan cultus, had to relinquish them or be rejected. Magicians were ineligible, presumably because they were agents of the devil. Standards of admission, however, probably varied considerably from area to area, and it must be remembered that Hippolytus himself was a rigorist. Approved candidates then entered a formation process lasting, according to Hippolytus, up to three years. Instruction in this period consisted chiefly of attendance during the service for catechumens to hear the sermon. Added to it, however, were regular exorcisms to expel the malevolent demons that the ancients believed to control their lives. In effect, catechumens were undergoing a "psyching" process that could equip them to rise above the popular level of morality and even, if necessary, give their lives for their faith. As floods of converts entered during the fourth century, the catechumenate was abbreviated, sometimes to as little as ten days before baptism.

Preparation of converts to register a firm commitment reached a peak immediately prior to and in the baptismal service itself. Unlike its chief competitors, the oriental mystery religions, Christianity demanded absolute loyalty to the point of intolerance. What was initially a two-day period of fasting and final instruction before baptism was elongated, at least by the fourth century, into the forty days of Lent, during which the bishop exorcized the baptizands. Baptism itself, normally administered at dawn on Easter Sunday (although, according to Tertullian, it could take place also on Pentecost Sunday), brought the preparatory process to its climax. Here, baptizands symbolically severed all ties with their old lives and bonded themselves to the One God—Father, Son, and Holy Spirit—with an oath (*sacramentum*). They were baptized nude to symbolize their complete break with the old life and anointed with an oil of exorcism. Facing westward while standing in water over which the Holy Spirit had been invoked, they renounced Satan. Turning toward the east, they received baptism after responding to each of the three articles of an interrogatory baptismal confession of faith. In some churches, after reclothing, they took milk and honey before communion with the assembled congregation, which awaited their return from the baptistery. The week following baptism, possibly as early as the third but definitely by the fourth century, the newly baptized received instruction in the "mysteries," that is, baptism, Lord's supper or eucharist, and, in some places, the creed.

During the first century and a half, Christianity presented itself largely as a competitor of the oriental cults that appealed so strongly to people throughout the ancient world, and thereafter as a philosophy as well. It offered salvation from sin, forgiveness, regeneration, and participation in Christ's victory over the demonic through sacraments. It extended love, fellowship, and charity without regard for social standing, culture, or education, astounding the ancient world by the extent of its care for widows and orphans, the indigent, prisoners, the sick and disabled, and persons overwhelmed by calamities of one kind or another. It presented itself as a religion of spirit and power through miracles of healing and prophecy. The miraculous proved convincing in a world where people constantly sought ways to deal with demons, departed spirits, and evil powers. Pagan polemicists came up with an answer to Jesus in the guise of Apollonius of Tyana, a Neopythagorean philosopher who died ca. A.D. 98.

The liabilities inherent in argument from miracles caused some shift in Christian self-depiction after ca. 150. Either in connection with catechetical instruction or, more likely, on personal initiative, Christian philosopher-evangelists founded schools designed to win the growing number of cultured Romans who manifested interest in Christianity. Several Gnostic teachers, such as Valentinus, gathered disciples and developed systems of thought characterized especially by a syncretism that would appeal to a variety of people. In Rome, Justin, a native of Samaria, established a school in which he trained several significant figures in early Christian missionary history, including Tatian. Martyred under Marcus Aurelius (ca. 165), Justin argued that Christianity is the "true philosophy." The universal Logos ("Reason") has taught truth in piecemeal fashion through Greek philosophers and Hebrew prophets, but in Jesus of Nazareth he became incarnate so that humankind can know how to live as they should to attain immortality. In Alexandria, Pantaenus, about whom little else is known, started an apologetic tradition continued by Clement and Origen, both of whom carried the argument for Christianity to new heights. Clement had a special interest in making the faith intelligible and attractive to a wealthy and educated elite who sought admission to the church from ca. 175.

As Christianity moved up the social ladder, devotees of traditional Roman religions and philosophies—such as Celsus (who composed his *True Discourses* ca. 175), the Stoic emperor Marcus Aurelius, the physician Galen, and later the Neoplatonist Porphyry—took note of the new religion, necessitating greater care in Christian self-presentation. By the middle of the third century, however, Christianity had become sufficiently well established everywhere to incite systematic efforts on an empirewide basis to repress it—under Decius (251–253), Valerian (257–260), and Diocletian (303–311). Decius feared that he was confronted with "an empire within the empire." In choosing Christianity over the solar monotheism of Mithras, Constantine wanted to take advantage of the feature Decius dreaded most: Christianity's well-organized network throughout the empire.

[E.G.H.]

Bibliography

A. von Harnack, *The Mission and Expansion of Christianity in the First Three Centuries*, 2nd ed. (New York: Putnam, 1908); A.D. Nock, *Conversion* (London: Oxford UP, 1933); K.S. Latourette, *A History of the Expansion of Christianity*, 7 vols. (New York: Harper, 1937–1945); M. Green, *Evangelism in the Early Church* (London: Hodder and Stoughton, 1970); E.G. Hinson, *The Evangelization of the Roman Empire* (Macon: Mercer UP, 1981); Frend, passim; R. MacMullen, *Christianizing the Roman Empire (A.D. 100–400)* (New Haven: Yale UP, 1984); J.N. Hillgarth, ed., *Christianity and Paganism, 350–750: The Conversion of Western Europe* (Philadelphia: U of Pennsylvania P, 1986).

MITHRAISM. Religion of the Persian god Mithras, which entered the Greco-Roman world in the first century B.C. An enigmatic mythic figure, Mithras seems to have originated in Hittite Anatolia, but he became prominent in the early Iranian pantheon. He was associated closely with Ahura-Mazda and was translated to India, surviving as Mitra or Mithra in the *Vedas* and the Persian *Avesta*. In Persian Zoroastrianism, Mithras's role diminished, and much early material is lost. Mithras appears in nature, as hunter and keeper of the fertile plains. In the *Vedas*, he is attendant to Varuna, the Lord of Heaven, and is closely connected with the power of sun and light and with the bull, symbol of life and fecundity.

Prior to its emergence under Rome, a distinct cult of Mithras is not known. Its new form borrowed elements from astrology and the mysteries. The central mythic cycle focused on the birth of Mithras (December 25) and his victory over the bull, commonly depicted in the *tauroctone*, a highly stylized scene of Mithras slaying the bull. The cycle carried a number of overt symbols, including those of astrology, which would have been immediately apprehensible to an initiate. The most common epithet for the god in later Roman times, after equation with the sun god had become complete, was *Sol Invictus Mithras* ("Mithras, the Invincible Sun"). Mithras's victory in returning life to the earth was somehow understood as an offer of personal "salvation." The initiation ritual is shrouded in mystery but seems to have included moments of suffering or struggle, mock or real. There were multiple grades of initiation, sometimes associated with the seven planetary spheres or ranks known from Mithraic art: Raven, Bride, Soldier, Lion, Persian, Heliodromos, Father. Passing through these grades, the worshiper advanced in the cult and in closeness to Mithras.

Mithraic practices and membership are known from numerous archaeological remains, including cult buildings, art, and inscriptions. The cult building, or *Mithraeum*, was usually a narrow rectangular hall, intentionally made to resemble a cave. On one end stood the central objects of interest: an altar and a painting or sculpture of the *tauroctone*. Flanking the walls were benches on which the worshipers sat or reclined. There they also held a communal meal, which early Christians considered dangerously similar to the eucharist (cf. Justin, *1 Apol.* 66; Tertullian, *Praescr.* 40).

The cult of Mithras was indeed one of Christianity's chief competitors. Its small cells excluded women and had neither professional clergy nor public festivals; therefore, participation was exclusive to initiates. In the provinces, from Parthia to Britain, Mithraism was especially popular among the military, but it also attracted a large following at Rome, where it was favored by several of the emperors, such as Commodus. [L.M.W.]

Bibliography

F. Cumont, *The Mysteries of Mithra* (Brussels: Lamertin, 1913 [in French]; Engl. tr. New York: Dover, 1956); A.D. Nock, "The Genius of Mithraism," *JRS* 27 (1937):109ff.; M.J. Vermaseren, *Corpus inscriptionum et monumentorum religionis Mithraicae*, 2 vols. (The Hague: Van Gorcum, 1956, 1960); idem, *Mithras, the Secret God* (London: Chatto and Windus, 1963); S. Laeuchli, *Mithraism in Ostia* (Evanston: Northwestern UP, 1967); idem, "Urban Mithraism," *Biblical Archaeologist* 31 (1968):73–99; H.D. Betz, "The Mithraic Inscriptions of Santa Prisca and the New Testament," *Novum Testamentum* 10 (1968):62–80; L. Campbell, *Mithraic Iconography and Ideology* (Leiden: Brill, 1968); R.L. Gordon, "Mithraism and Roman Society: Social Factors in the Explanation of Religious Change in the Roman Empire," *Religion* 2 (1972):92–121; J.R. Hinnells, ed., *Mithraic Studies*, 2 vols. (Manchester: Manchester UP, 1975); U. Bianchi, *Mysteria Mithrae* (Leiden: Brill, 1979); M.P. Speidel, *Mithras-Orion: Greek Hero and Roman Army God* (Leiden: Brill, 1980); R. MacMullen, *Paganism in the Roman Empire* (New Haven: Yale UP, 1981); R. Merkelbach, *Mithras* (Königstein: Hain, 1984); L.M. White, *Building God's House in the Roman World: Architectural Adaptation Among Pagans, Jews, and Christians* (Baltimore: Johns Hopkins UP, 1989).

MODALISM. Doctrine that denied any permanent distinctions within the Godhead and emphasized divine unity by describing "Father," "Son," and "Holy Spirit" as temporary modes for the purpose of creation or redemption. The name "Modalism" was suggested by the nineteenth-century historian Adolf von Harnack, but in ancient literature this theology was called Monarchianism, or "Patripassianism" in the west and "Sabellianism" in the east. *See also* Monarchianism. [R.L.]

MÖHLER, JOHANN ADAM (1796–1838). German church historian and theologian. Möhler taught church history in the Catholic Faculty at Tübingen from 1819 to 1835, then at Munich until his death. He opened fruitful contacts with the Protestant theologians of his day, including Friedrich Schleiermacher. Traveling throughout Germany, he found much in the Protestant faculties with which he agreed. Möhler is most noted for his book *Die Einheit der Kirche* (1825), which took a sympathetic and creative view of Catholic-Protestant relations. On the subject of early Christianity, he wrote a *Patrologie*, a work on Athanasius, and numerous articles on Jerome, Augustine, and other fathers. [F.W.N.]

Bibliography

P.-W. Scheele, *Johann Adam Möhler* (Graz: Styria, 1969).

MONARCHIAN PROLOGUES. Many Latin manuscripts of the Gospels contain prologues composed by Priscillian or one of his followers (late fourth or early fifth century). These prologues were composed in Latin and followed the Old Latin order of the Gospels—Matthew, John, Luke, and Mark. They teach that the Father is identical with the Son (the Father became the Son by the incarnation) and that in the incarnation God assumed a human body (the divine nature constituted Christ's soul). The historical notices rest on no sound tradition, and the style is (perhaps intentionally) obscure. [E.F.]

Bibliography

J. Wordsworth and H.J. White, *Novum Testamentum Domini Nostri Jesu Christi, Latine* (Oxford: Clarendon, 1889–1898), Vol. 1, pp. 15–17, 171–173, 269–271, 485–487; J. Chapman, *Notes on the Early History of the Vulgate Gospels* (Oxford: Clarendon, 1908), pp. 217–288; D.J. Theron, *Evidence of Tradition* (Grand Rapids: Baker Book House, 1958), pp. 56–65; K. Aland, ed., *Synopsis Quattuor Evangeliorum* (Stuttgart: Württembergische Bibelanstalt, 1964), pp. 538–539; J. Regul, *Die antimarcionitischen Evangelienprologe* (Freiburg: Herder, 1969), pp. 40–50, 207–262; H. Chadwick, *Priscillian of Avila* (Oxford: Clarendon, 1976), pp. 102–109.

MONARCHIANISM. Doctrine, most prominent in the second and third centuries, that emphasized the unity of divine being (*monarchia*, "one rule or power") at the expense of separate and permanent identities of Father, Son, and Holy Spirit in the Godhead. The nineteenth-century scholar Adolf von Harnack distinguished two types of Monarchianism: "Modalist Monarchianism" and "Dynamic Monarchianism." Historically, however, Monarchianism referred to a theological movement in Rome based on the teachings of Noetus, Praxeas, and Sabellius (Harnack's Modalist Monarchians), which prompted controversy with Tertullian and Hippolytus. Tertullian first called them "Monarchian" (*Prax.* 10.1), and his writings together with those of Hippolytus remain the major sources for Monarchian theology.

Like the Jews, the early Christians were identified in ancient society by their uncompromising monotheism. Martyrs confessed their confidence in "one God who made heaven and earth" (Acts 4:24). Apologists, such as Justin Martyr and Theophilus of Antioch, argued that Christian monotheism was more rational than polytheism, for the same god who exercised rule (*monarchia*) was bringing the world to salvation (Justin, *Dial.* 1; Theophilus, *Autol.* 2.8). One of the earliest theological problems in Christianity, therefore, was the relation of this one God to Jesus the Christ. Some Christians, such as Ignatius of Antioch and Melito of Sardis, called Jesus "God" unreservedly; others, like Justin and Hippolytus, used Wisdom literature and Logos theology to argue that the Son was divine, but a distinct being from the Father. Those who have been called Monarchians sought to reconcile the tension between scriptural monotheism and the divinity of Jesus in two ways.

The Modalist Monarchians taught that one divine being had revealed itself as "Father," "Son," and "Holy Spirit" but that these names referred only to temporary modes of activity and were not eternal characters within the Godhead. According to Hippolytus, Noetus of Smyrna (ca. 190) first taught a form of this doctrine, which was later brought to Rome (*Haer.* 9.1, 5). Appealing to biblical passages, such as Isaiah 45:14 and John 10:30, Noetus and his pupil Epigonus seemed to be defending both devotion to Christ and traditional monotheism. When he was criticized and condemned

by the church, Noetus replied, "But what harm do I do in glorifying Christ?" (Hippolytus, *Noet.* 1.2). Cleomenes, a pupil of Epigonus, was reported to have taught that Christ "confessed himself to be the Son to those who saw him, while to those who could receive it, he did not hide the fact that he was the Father" (Hippolytus, *Haer.* 9.5). Tertullian described the teaching of Praxeas in a similar way; to protect the unity of divine being, the "Father" and "Son" were defined as one entity (*Prax.* 10). According to Epiphanius, writing against this doctrine a century later, another teacher, Sabellius, also taught and was condemned in Rome ca. 220 (*Haer.* 62; Hippolytus, *Haer.* 9.6). Sabellius, who may have had some connection with the Roman bishop Callistus, allegedly taught that God was a monad with three energies that appeared in history for the purpose of creation and salvation as "Father," "Son," and "Holy Spirit."

In spite of its devotional appeal in proclaiming the divinity of Christ, the church rejected Monarchianism, or Sabellianism as it was called in the east, for several reasons. Using the prologue of John, Hippolytus and Tertullian argued that scripture did indeed reveal two eternal facets of one God in the Father and the Son. Equally important, the simple identification of Jesus with the Father resulted in a confusion of the works of salvation (Hippolytus, *Haer.* 9.6). According to Tertullian, Praxeas taught that the Father was born, suffered, and died (*Prax.* 27–29). This not only contradicted scripture but also violated the contemporary definition of the impassibility of God. In the west, therefore, the Monarchians were derided as "Patripassians," or those who claimed that the Father suffered. Although the language of God suffering in Jesus was acceptable devotionally, it could not be a theological definition of the Father without distortion of scripture.

Dynamic Monarchianism also defended monotheism but had a different Christology. Jesus was not some form of God incarnate but rather a man who received divine power (*dynamis*) from the one God. It was thus a form of Adoptionism. Early opponents of the Monarchians, such as Origen and Hippolytus, grouped the Modalists and the Adoptionists together because their defense of divine unity focused in the Father could result in denying divinity to Jesus, who became only the human locus for divine activity. However, the origins and teachings of the figures traditionally grouped under the category "Dynamic Monarchianism" were historically and probably theologically diverse. Theodotus was mentioned by Hippolytus as coming from Byzantium and teaching in Rome in 190; using Luke 1:35, Theodotus described Jesus as a man who received divine power at baptism (*Haer.* 7.23). He was condemned by the Roman bishop Victor, but his theology may have been continued in some way by Theodotus the Banker, who portrayed Jesus as the new Melchizedek, mediator between God and humanity, probably on the basis of the Epistle to the Hebrews (Hippolytus, *Haer.* 7.24). Another teacher, Artemon, argued in the middle of the third century that Adoptionism was the true apostolic tradition, which the church had abandoned for Logos theology (Eusebius, *H.E.* 5.28.3). Paul of Samosata, bishop of Antioch, is traditionally linked to these Adoptionists, but his theological and ecclesiastical motivations remain obscure. Condemned by a council in 268, Paul objected to the worship of Christ and taught that Jesus was an inspired man rather than the incarnate, preexistent Word of God (Eusebius, *H.E.* 7.27–30). Adoptionism in many forms was repeatedly condemned and often called "Psilanthropism" (*psilos anthropos*, "mere man").

The results of the Monarchian movement were the first reflections on the doctrine of the Trinity. Labeled "ditheists" by the Monarchians, Tertullian, Hippolytus, and Origen attempted to create a vocabulary to express the distinctions within the one God. Sabellianism and Psilanthropism became the borders of the developing theological inquiry and were used as categories to condemn individuals in succeeding centuries. Thus, Dionysius, bishop of Alexandria, wrote against Sabellianism in Libya in the third century, but his refutation was criticized by Dionysius, bishop of Rome, for its sharp distinctions between the Father and the Son (Athanasius, *Dion.* 5ff.). Arius cited Sabellianism as a position he wished to avoid (Alexander, *Ep. Alex.*). Marcellus of Ancyra,

a critic of Arius, was condemned in the east in 336 for holding a form of Sabellianism but was acquitted in the west; he taught that God was a monad who became a triad only for the purpose of salvation. He and his pupil Photinus were condemned at the Council of Constantinople (381). Forms of Modalist Monarchianism therefore proved attractive to Christians as a defense of traditional monotheism and a confession of the divinity of Christ. Monarchianism, however, was consistently rejected as the primary definition of divine being because it tended to blur the identities and roles of the Father and Son or lead to Adoptionism. *See also* Adoptionism; Christ, Christology; Modalism. [R.L.]

Bibliography

Hippolytus: Refutatio Omnium Haeresium, ed. M. Marcovich (Berlin: de Gruyter, 1986); idem, *Contra Noetum*, PG 10.803–830; *Hippolyte contre les heresies fragment*, ed. P. Nautin (Paris: Cerf, 1949); *Tertullian's Treatise Against Praxeas*, ed. and tr. E. Evans (London: SPCK, 1948).

Hippolytus, *Contra Noetum*, tr. R. Butterworth (London: Heythrop College, 1977); idem, *Philosophumena*, or *The Refutation of All Heresies*, tr. F. Legge (New York: Macmillan, 1921); Origen, "Dialogue with Heraclides," *Alexandrian Christianity*, ed. H. Chadwick, LCC (1954), Vol. 2, pp. 430–455; C.L. Feltoe, *The Letters of Dionysius of Alexandria* (Cambridge: Cambridge UP, 1904).

C.H. Turner, "The 'Blessed Presbyters' Who Condemned Noetus," *JThS* 23 (1921–1922):28–35; G. La Piana, "The Roman Church at the End of the Second Century," *HThR* 18 (1925):201–277; G. Bardy, "Monarchianisme," DTC (1927), Vol. 10.2, cols. 2193–2209; G.L. Prestige, *God in Patristic Thought* (London: SPCK, 1952); H. de Riedmatten, *Les Actes du procès de Paul de Samosate* (Fribourg en Suisse: St–Paul, 1952); H.J. Carpenter, "Popular Christianity and the Theologians in the Early Centuries," *JThS* 14 (1963):294–310; E. Klinger, "Modalism," *Sacramentum Mundi* (New York: Herder and Herder, 1969), Vol. 4, pp. 88–90; Kelly, pp. 115–126; R. Sample, "The Christology of the Council of Antioch (268 C.E.) Reconsidered," *ChHist* 48 (1979):18–26.

MONASTICISM. Life of separation from the world and commitment to the spiritual struggle toward perfection. Asceticism, contemplation, and service to God and humanity, all in markedly varied forms and degrees, are part of the monastic life. The term "monasticism" derives

Fortified monastery (sixth to fifteenth centuries) on the coast of the island of St. Honorat, Lérins, France.

from the Greek *monastērion*, which was used in antiquity for both the individual hermit's cell and the more familiar communal cloister. The Greek *monos* means "alone," and a *monachos* is a "solitary one." The earliest attested use of *monachos* for a Christian monk occurs on an Egyptian papyrus document (*P. Coll. Youtie* 77) dated to 324. It refers to an individual named Isaac, who, together with a deacon, interceded in a village dispute.

Origins. The rise and development of Christian monasticism are best examined within the early Christian movement as a whole. Although the communal life of the Essenes at Qumran and of the Jewish Therapeutae in Egypt (Philo, *Contemplative Life*) resembles that of the Christian monks, no direct historical link has been established. Likewise, early attempts to find a Greco-Roman precedent in the religious recluses of the temples of Sarapis have proved ill-founded. Influences from Judaism, Greco-Roman philosophy, and oriental religions are certainly present in Christian monastic development, but the widespread ascetic impulse in this era led to parallel practices and lifestyles that were fairly common.

The origin of the Christian monastic life is instead found in the transformation of the eschatological communion of saints brought on by the delay of the second coming of Christ and the increasing success of Christianity. In the second and third centuries, before the conversion of the emperor Constantine, martyrdom was the ultimate expression of Christian commitment. The martyr chose death rather than conformity to the Roman way of life. With the peace that ensued in the fourth century and the concomitant influx of new members, Christians began to conform to the ways of the world. In this new environment, the monastic life developed in part as a statement against this growing conformity. The monk replaced the martyr as Christian hero, as the one who chose to die to a secular lifestyle. These men and women, who were in the world but not of the world, became the earthly embodiment of the heavenly communion of saints. Their authority as holy men and women of God made them popular sources of divine power and wisdom among the people—and a concern to the ecclesiastical authorities, who sought to bring them under their own control.

Forms of Monasticism. The ascetic impulse found early expression in the Christian movement as men and women equated abstinence from things of this world with devotion to the world to come. A devout religious life of prayer, spiritual exercise, and charity often brought with it abstinence from meat, strong drink, adorning dress and cosmetics, sexuality, and marriage. Initially, those men and women who practiced the more austere way of life did so within their homes or on the outskirts of their village. Theodore, a fourth-century Pachomian abbot of Upper Egypt, began his life of abstinence within an isolated room in his parent's home (Bohairic *Life of Pachomius* 31). The *Life of Anthony* 3 (ca. 357) reports that those who wished to concern themselves with their own destiny practiced asceticism by themselves not far from their villages. Houses of virgins seem also to have existed from a relatively early date. The *Life of Anthony*, attributed to Athanasius, relates that Anthony, who is presented as the founder of the monastic life, placed his younger sister with "known and trusted virgins" before embarking on his own religious quest.

In the late third and fourth centuries, the classic forms of the monastic life arose. These included at the one extreme the solitary life of the hermit (anchoritic monasticism), who sought to maximize his or her separation from the world, and at the other extreme the fully communal life (cenobitic monasticism), in which the monks lived together in a community under a common monastic rule. Between the two, other patterns existed, the most familiar being the semieremitic life, in which groups of monks constructed their solitary cells in relatively close proximity to one another.

The surviving sources that narrate this development must be treated with care. In many ways, they represent the propaganda of "orthodoxy," and their modern readers likewise often fall victim to their own cultural biases when interpreting them. Thus, the notion of the Egyptian origin of monasticism, still frequently asserted, is a result of western scholarship's predominant reliance on Greek and Latin sources. The early and independent rise of monasticism in Syria and the east can

no longer be disputed. Likewise, the presentation of particular forms of the monastic enterprise as the creation of certain individuals has as much to do with the nature of the sources as with reality. Without denying Anthony's significance in monastic history, his unique place in that history is in large part a result of the *Life of Anthony*, a work more of propaganda than of history. The *Life* itself acknowledges that when Anthony first took up the monastic life there was an old man in the neighboring village who had lived the ascetic life in solitude from his youth. Similarly, Pachomius, who is often credited with founding the first communal monastery, is reported to have received preexisting communities of monks into his monastic system. Theodore, one of Pachomius's successors, came to Pachomius's monastery from a non-Pachomian monastery in the southern diocese of Sne (Bohairic *Life of Pachomius* 29–32). Recent scholarship has suggested that the influence of early Manichaean monastic settlements in Egypt may have been seminal to the Pachomian innovation.

Ideology. The various early ascetic practices, as well as the later forms of monasticism, were clearly not the product of any one theological point of view. The impulse to asceticism was widespread in late antiquity, and it flourished in Christian circles of diverse theological perspective. Although the major surviving sources seek to align the monastic movement with the "orthodox" church, clearly such an alignment is a product of time and the eventual "orthodox" control of history. The ascetic life was central to many Gnostic Christians, and heterodox Melitian monasteries of the fourth century are recorded in papyrus documents from Egypt. Early types of wandering monks were rebuked in later monastic sources and church canons. The Boskoi, or Grazing Ascetes, around Nisibis lived on grass as a result of their interpretation of Psalm 49:20 (Septuagint), which led them to believe that they might recover the lost likeness of God by living like cattle (Sozomen, *H.E.* 6.33). Monks holding to the Origenist persuasion were forced out of Egypt at the end of the fourth century by bishop Theophilus, who in turn was influenced against them by anthropomorphist monks, who held, against the Origenists, that God possessed a human form.

In a similar fashion, although the sources emphasize the role of men in the monastic undertaking, recent scholarship has recognized that the ascetic life allowed women many opportunities that were closed to them in the larger society. If there is neither male nor female in the perfect existence of the kingdom of God (Gal. 3:28), monasticism offered some women the closest proximity to that state here on earth. Stories from the desert tell of monks who were not discovered to be female until their death. Among the noble women of Rome, ascetic renunciation became an avenue for their own advancement.

Early Leaders in Egypt. In early-third-century Egypt, the Greek Platonic theology of Origen gave a strong impetus to the ascetic movement. When the monastic life began to emerge as a distinct institution later in the century, however, its leading practitioners came from among the native Egyptian, or Coptic, population. Jerome, in what appears to be a legendary account of a hermit named Paul, the *Vita Pauli*, linked the origins of monasticism with Christian withdrawal (*anachorēsis*) to the desert during the Decian persecution. Such early hermits may indeed have existed, but tradition has identified the Coptic peasant Anthony as the father of anchoritic monasticism. He is, however, more properly understood as its model than as its founder.

Anthony (ca. 251–356), whose parents died when he was twenty years old, embarked on the monastic life when he heard in church the scripture reading, "If you would be perfect, go, sell what you possess and give to the poor; and come, follow me, and you will have treasure in heaven" (Matt. 19:21). He sold his inheritance and gave the proceeds to the poor, entrusted his younger sister to local virgins, and devoted himself to a life of self-denial and asceticism near his own home. He soon moved from the edge of the village to more distant tombs and then across the Nile to a deserted fort, seeking to avoid human contact. He continued in seclusion for twenty years, during

which time he was victorious against the powerful onslaught of demons. When he eventually was forced out of his shrine by those who wished to imitate him, he emerged "as one initiated into the sacred mysteries and filled with the spirit of God" (Athanasius, *V. Anton.* 14). His fame spread, and pilgrims came to set up their own monastic cells in his vicinity, turning to him as their spiritual guide. When he withdrew deeper into the wilderness near the Red Sea (the site of the present Monastery of St. Anthony), his admirers followed, and he eventually accepted his calling as the spiritual father of a loose community of independent anchorites. The *Life of Anthony* emphasizes the monk's austerity and his zeal for orthodoxy during the Arian struggles of the fourth century. One must use such evidence with caution, however, since the surviving letters and sayings attributed to Anthony do not reveal these same concerns. The effort of the author of the *Life of Anthony* must be viewed as church propaganda, designed to co-opt the growing power and authority of the nascent monastic movement for the "orthodox" church. Through his efforts, Anthony became the preeminent model of the monastic life in service of the church.

Ammun (d. ca. 350), a contemporary of Anthony, founded a semieremitic monastic settlement in the desert at the Mount of Nitria in the southwestern portion of the Nile Delta. An orphan, compelled by his uncle to marry at age twenty-two, he lived a celibate life together with his wife for eighteen years, after which (ca. 315) he retired to the desert at the Mount of Nitria (Palladius, *H. Laus.* 8). Others soon imitated his way of life, and an important community of hermits arose. They eventually established a second community of cells, Cellia, some twelve miles farther into the desert. Macarius the Great (ca. 300–ca. 390), who as a village anchorite was falsely accused by a village maiden of begetting her child and then vindicated, retired for solitude (ca. 330) to the desert of the Wâdi n' Natrûn, some forty miles farther south. Again, as his fame spread, disciples arrived to join him. The result was the eremitic settlement of Scete in the Wâdi n'

Natrûn, a site that still preserves several functioning Coptic monasteries. These three settlements in Lower Egypt are the major source of the sayings or apophthegms of the desert fathers that are preserved in early collections (*Apophthegmata Patrum*). Although their interpretation is fraught with difficulty, the sayings offer a unique window into the lives of these early ascetics, who appear therein in less redacted form than in such secondary accounts as the *Life of Anthony*.

Pachomius (292–346), an Upper Egyptian pagan by birth, is credited with the innovation of a communal monastic life of shared work and worship under a common monastic rule. This form of the monastic life, termed "cenobitic" from the Greek word for "common," was destined to become the predominant form in Christendom. A recipient of Christian charity, Pachomius was baptized and after three years took up the monastic life of a hermit under the direction of the anchorite Palamon (316). While collecting wood at the nearby deserted village of Tabennesi, he received a vision that instructed him to remain at that site and build a monastery (323). He complied, and after initial difficulties brethren began to join in increasing numbers. Within six years, a second monastery was founded at nearby Pbow to accommodate them. At the time of Pachomius's death, some 3,000 monks were under his control. They resided in nine separate monasteries and two affiliated nunneries along the Nile in Upper Egypt. Pachomius's monasteries were walled communities situated within the greenbelt of the Nile Valley. The members shared a life of meals, work, worship, and adherence to the rule begun by Pachomius. The community of monasteries was well organized, with the individual abbots under the leadership of the abbot of the central monastery at Pbow. Although the sources portray a close link between the Pachomian movement and the ecclesiastical authorities, friction did exist, as witnessed by the questioning of Pachomius's clairvoyant powers at the Synod of Latopolis.

Shenoute (334–450) was abbot of the famous White Monastery at Sohag in Upper Egypt. He governed his cenobitic monastery with somewhat harsher rules than those of Pachomius. He was heavily involved in the wider community of Upper Egypt and struck out violently against the remnants of pagan culture. His participation at the Council of Ephesus (431) underscores the growing monastic influence in the church at large. As an author, Shenoute marks the highest development of Coptic literature. But because he wrote at a time when Coptic Christianity was becoming increasingly isolated from most of Christendom, his works were never translated into Greek, and as a result his history and significance were forgotten outside of Egypt. Today, he is recognized as one of the preeminent figures in Coptic Christianity.

The sources are replete with evidence for the widespread existence of monks and monasteries up and down the Nile Valley. A party of travelers who visited the monasteries of Egypt in 394 reported in their *Historia monachorum* the seemingly endless number of monastic establishments of varied type between Lycopolis (Assuit) and Alexandria. In the town of Oxyrhynchus, they noted that "the city is so full of monasteries that the very walls resound with the voices of monks. Other monasteries encircle it outside, so that the outer city forms another town alongside the inner. The temples and capitals of the city were bursting with monks; every quarter of the city was inhabited by them" (Russell, p. 67). The account may be exaggerated, but it portrays well the influence of the monastic enterprise in Egypt. The renown of the Egyptian monks made them the goal of visitors from within and without the country. The Alexandrian bishop Theophilus visited Abba Pambo in Scete, and foreign visitors frequented the monastic enclaves. The important narratives recorded in the anonymous *Historia monachorum* (ca. 400), the *Lausiac History* of the Galatian bishop Palladius (ca. 419), and the *Institutes* and *Conferences* of John Cassian (ca. 420) are all products of such pilgrimages.

Eastern Monasticism Outside Egypt. The ascetic impulse was also leading to monastic undertakings in Syria and Palestine, sometimes with Egyptian influences. Strong Encratite leanings, represented by Tatian, expressed themselves in the severity of Syriac asceticism.

Among certain Syriac Christians, baptism involved a commitment to continence. A spiritual elite, called the Sons of the Covenant, formed in some communities. Although they are not to be equated with the monastic movement *per se*, they did represent a claim of a higher or more perfect Christian way of life.

The most famous innovation in Syriac monasticism was that of the stylite monk, who withdrew from the world atop a pillar or column. Its first and most famous representative was Symeon the Elder or Stylites (388–459). A native of Cilicia, he began his career within a community of monks. Driven to live a life that would shine forth as a symbol of faith, he withdrew as a hermit, first shutting himself within a cell for three years and eventually establishing his abode on the top of a pedestal or column, near Antioch. He progressed through four columns, each higher than the last; the final thirty years of his life were spent on top of a column more than fifty feet high. Symeon's fame spread, and crowds gathered to admire his piety. They came seeking advice, miracles, intercession, and even approval of the decrees of ecclesiastical councils. After his death, his column was enclosed by a huge martyrion, the impressive remains of which are still visible. Symeon's stylite innovation led to imitators, the most famous of whom are Daniel Stylites, who resided on his columns at Anaplous on the Bosphorus in the latter half of the fifth century, and Symeon the Younger of Antioch, who ascended his pillar at age seven.

In Palestine, the beginning of the anchoritic life is traced to a certain Hilarion (293–371). Although Jerome's account of his life is full of legendary accretions, it is most probable that Hilarion was a historical figure. He was first attracted to the monastic life in Egypt upon hearing of the exploits of Anthony. He returned to his native Gaza and took up the solitary life. He spent twenty-two years in solitude, after which others began to join him in the desert. Monasteries soon followed, one of the first being the establishment (ca. 335) of his disciple Epiphanius, the later bishop of Salamis, near Eleutheropolis between Gaza and Jerusalem. In the Judean wilderness east of Jerusalem, a location that brings to mind the

desert life of Elijah, Elisha, John the Baptist, and the Qumran Essenes, monastic communities were in existence at least as early as the beginning of the fourth century. Late sources report the activity of Chariton, a confessor under Aurelian, who established three monasteries in the Judean wilderness in the last quarter of the third century, the first at Fara. His assemblages were termed "lauras," a development that appears to be of Palestinian origin. The laura, a colony of anchorite monks who resided in separate cells but owed allegiance to a central abbot, contained shared central buildings, including a church at which the monks gathered on Saturdays and Sundays. The rest of the week was spent in their individual cells. Among the most famous later lauras was that founded at Khan el Ahmar by Euthymius (377–473), who learned the monastic life at the laura of Fara. His disciple Saba (439–532) in turn founded a large laura in 478, which survives today as the functioning monastery of Mar Saba. Many other lauras sprang up as well in the Judean wilderness.

Eustathius (ca. 300–ca. 377), bishop of Sebaste, pioneered the ascetic movement in eastern Asia Minor. His ascetic ideals drew to him the Cappadocians Basil of Caesarea and Gregory of Nazianzus. Basil (330–379), who lived as a monk in Syria and Egypt before settling in the vicinity of Neocaesarea, established the organizational basis of Greek monasticism. His monastic rule, composed 358–364, accented the superior nature of the cenobitic way of life in opposition to the solitary undertaking of the anchorite. He rejected excessive ascetic practices in favor of a view of asceticism as service to God expressed through obedience to one's superiors within the community, liturgical and private prayer, charity to the poor, and manual labor. The Basilian form of monasticism has continued to define the Greek and Slavonic monastic enterprise.

Western Monasticism. The monastic life reached the west through Athanasius as a result of his exile in Trier and Rome. In the west, the movement had its initial success in the higher classes of society. Jerome (342–420), after a period of training in the desert near Antioch, returned to Rome, where, under

Damasus I, he became a major spokesperson for the monastic ideal. His ascetic propaganda proved especially successful among widows and virgins of the senatorial aristocracy, who became his disciples. He left Rome in 385, followed by several of these ascetic women. After completing the usual pilgrimages to Syria and Egypt, he settled near Bethlehem in a monastery founded by Paula, one of his Roman disciples. Her daughter, Eustochium, eventually succeeded her. Another Roman matron, Melania the Elder, founded a convent of cloistered nuns near Jerusalem.

It was also in the west that the monastic ideal was closely linked to the clerical life. Eusebius of Vercelli (d. 371) organized a community of clergy dedicated to an ascetic life. His ideas are paralleled in the efforts of Ambrose of Milan and Augustine of Hippo in North Africa. The merging of the clerical and monastic life in the later canons regular in the west represents an outgrowth of this tradition.

The spread of monasticism to Gaul is attributed by the sources to the efforts of Martin of Tours (ca. 316–397). After receiving his initial training in northern Italy, he founded the first monastery in Gaul at Ligugé near Poitiers (ca. 360). His election as bishop of Tours in 372 did not dissuade him from his monastic life. It led rather to his founding of the famous monastery at Marmoutier near Tours, which enabled him to continue to live as a monk while serving in the ecclesiastical office.

John Cassian founded two monasteries in Marseilles (ca. 415), for which his famous *Institutes* and *Conferences* were written. These writings depend heavily upon Cassian's early sojourn among the monks of Egypt and betray the strong influence of eastern traditions in Gaul. From Gaul, the monastic movement spread to the Celtic regions of the British Isles. It expanded rapidly in the sixth century and became, notably in Ireland, the defining force not only of the church but also of the society at large. The Rule of Columbanus (543–615), the Irish-born missionary to Gaul, was the only serious rival to the Rule of Benedict in the west.

Benedict of Nursia (480–540) wrote an organizational rule that eventually supplanted the earlier profusion of rules in the west and became the guiding principle of western monasticism through the Middle Ages. He initially withdrew from the world as a hermit in a cave at Subiaco (ca. 500). His fame soon brought disciples, who established small monasteries around him. He departed to found the monastery of Monte Cassino (ca. 529), where he remained until his death. The rule that Benedict devised drew on the earlier work of Basil and others. It organized the community under an elected abbot, who was himself subject to the rule. The monastic life was a training ground in the service of God, the central act of which was the common, public celebration of the Divine Office. Private prayer and labor filled the remainder of the day. Continuity in the monastic life was encouraged through the binding of the monk and the community together for life. The earlier practice of wandering between monasteries was thus precluded. Benedict's legacy is witnessed in the widespread propagation of Benedictine monasticism in the medieval west.

Influence. As a way of life, monasticism was not limited to any one theological persuasion, and throughout its history movements ultimately labeled heretical by the church often flourished within monastic circles. The Messalians in the east and the Priscillianist movement in Spain are notable examples. But it was never the monastic life itself that came into question.

In the age of Constantine and beyond, the monks had become the new martyrs. Their life represented a total commitment to God, an undertaking that made them strangers on earth. It offered in the eyes of many the best path toward the perfection that represented the new ultimate, although perhaps unattainable, goal of all Christians. As the new holy men of the Christian age, they became recognized sources of divine power and authority. They were instrumental in the spread of Christianity, particularly in the countryside. And they served others as a prescience of their own future life in the heavenly communion of saints.

See also Anthony; Archimandrite; Asceticism; Basil of Casearea; Benedict of Nursia; Cassian,

John; Hermit; Laura; Pachomius; Shenoute; Symeon Stylites. [J.E.G.]

Bibliography

J. Fontaine, *Vie de saint Martin*, SC (1967–1969), Vols. 133–135; A. de Vogüé and J. Neufville, *La Règle de S. Benoit*, SC (1971–1972), Vols. 181–186; P. Canivet and A. Leroy-Molinghen, *Histoire des moines de Syrie: histoire Philothée: Théodoret de Cyr*, SC (1977), Vol. 234.

W.K.L. Clarke, *The Ascetic Works of Saint Basil* (New York: Macmillan, 1925); H. Waddell, *The Desert Fathers* (London: Constable, 1931); R.T. Meyer, *St. Athanasius: The Life of Saint Antony*, ACW (1950), Vol. 10; O. Chadwick, *Western Asceticism*, LCC (1958), Vol. 12; A.-J. Festugière, *Les Moines d'orient* (Paris: Cerf, 1961–1965); R.T. Meyer, *Palladius: The Lausiac History*, ACW (1964), Vol. 34; B. Ward, *The Sayings of the Desert Fathers: The Alphabetical Collection* (London: Mowbray, 1975); L. Eberle, *The Rule of the Master* (Kalamazoo: Cistercian Publications, 1977); R.C. Gregg, *Athanasius: The Life of Antony and the Letter to Marcellinus*, CWS (1980); N. Russell, *The Lives of the Desert Fathers: The Historia Monachorum in Aegypto* (London: Mowbray, 1981); A. Veilleux, *Pachomian Koinonia* (Kalamazoo: Cistercian Publications, 1980–1982), Vols. 1–3; D.N. Bell, *Besa: The Life of Shenoute* (Kalamazoo: Cistercian Publications, 1983); E.A. Clark, *The Life of Melania the Younger: Introduction, Translation, and Commentary* (New York: Mellen, 1984).

C. Butler, *The Lausiac History of Palladius: A Critical Discussion Together with Notes on Early Egyptian Monasticism* (Cambridge: Cambridge UP, 1898); S. Schiwietz, *Das morgenländische Mönchtum* (Mainz: Kirchheim, 1904–1938), Vols. 1–3; W.K.L. Clarke, *St. Basil the Great: A Study in Monasticism* (Cambridge: Cambridge UP, 1913); H. Delehaye, *Les Saints stylites* (Brussels: Société des Bollandistes, 1923); C. Butler, *Benedictine Monasticism: Studies in the Benedictine Life and Rule*, 2nd ed. (London: Longmans, 1924); M.G. Murphy, *St. Basil and Monasticism* (Washington, D.C.: Catholic U of America P, 1930); H.G. Evelyn White, *The Monasteries of the Wâdi n' Natrûn* (New York: Metropolitan Museum of Art, 1932), Vol. 2: *The History of the Monasteries of Nitria and Scetis*; K. Heussi, *Der Ursprung des Mönchtums* (Tübingen: Mohr, 1936); D. Amand, *L'Ascèse monastique de saint Basile de Césarée* (Liège: Maredsous, 1949); E.E. Malone, *The Monk and the Martyr: The Monk as the Successor of the Martyr* (Washington, D.C.: Catholic U of America P, 1950); A. Vööbus, *History of Asceticism in the Syrian Orient: A Contribution to the History of Culture in the Near East*, Vols. 1–2, CSCO (1958–1960), Vols. 184, 197; J. Gribomont, "Le Monachisme au sein de l'église en Syrie et en Cappadoce," *StudMon* 7 (1965):7–24; D.J. Chitty, *The Desert a City: An Introduction to the Study of Egyptian and Palestinian Monasticism Under the Christian Empire* (Oxford: Blackwell, 1966); G. Nedungatt, "The Covenanters of the Early Syriac-speaking Church," *Orientalia Christiana Periodica* 39 (1973):191–215, 419–444; P. Brown, *The Making of Late Antiquity* (Cambridge: Harvard UP, 1978); P. Rousseau, *Ascetics, Authority, and the Church in the Age of Jerome and Cassian* (Oxford: Oxford UP, 1978); A. Guillaumont, *Aux Origines du monachisme chrétien: pour une phénoménologie du monachisme* (Bégrolles: Maine et Loire, 1979); E.A. Clark, "Ascetic Renunciation and Feminine Advancement: A Paradox of Late Ancient Christianity," *Anglican Theological Review* 63 (1981):240–257; P. Rousseau, *Pachomius: The Making of a Community in Fourth-Century Egypt* (Berkeley: U of California P, 1985); A. de Vogüé, *Les Règles monastiques anciennes (400–700)* (Turnhout: Brepols, 1985) (typology); J.E. Goehring, *The Letter of Ammon and Pachomian Monasticism* (Berlin and New York: de Gruyter, 1986); P. Brown, *The Body and Society: Men, Women, and Sexual Renunciation in Early Christianity* (New York: Columbia UP, 1988).

MONICA (ca. 331–387). Mother of Augustine. A Berber North African woman, Monica is known to us only in the writings of her eldest son, Augustine. A son's description of his mother is likely to be highly subjective, but there is no other evidence that would enable us to understand Monica's experience from her own perspective. Married to Patricius, who was a pagan until near the end of his life, she was also the mother of two other children. According to Augustine's account in the *Confessions*, his conversion to Christianity was the insistent, if not dominating, focus of Monica's prayers and efforts. Monica was respected by the Christian community into which she was born and in which she was raised and was powerful in her sphere of family and friends, both in avoiding her husband's abuse and in her instrumentality in Augustine's conversion. Augustine wrote, "I thought that you [God] were silent and that it was my mother who was speaking; but you were not silent; you spoke to me through her" (*Conf.* 2.3). Monica followed Augustine to Milan, where, presaged by a dream she had, his conversion occurred and he was baptized by Ambrose.

Augustine also described Monica's participation in the small community of lovers of wisdom who retired from business occupations to study and converse about religious and philosophical matters at Cassiciacum after his conversion. Although lacking a formal education, he wrote, she demonstrated the profound wisdom that is the result of living as a devoted Christian. At the end of her life, Monica shared with Augustine the mystical experience recorded in *Confessions* 9.10. She died at Ostia, no longer insisting on burial with her husband, and confident of resurrection. For more than 1,000 years after her death, her devotion to Augustine's conversion was repeatedly cited as a model for other mothers. Feast day August 27. *See also* Augustine.   [M.R.M.]

Bibliography

Augustine, *Confessions* 9 and passim.

R.J. O'Connell, *St. Augustine's Early Theory of Man* (Cambridge: Harvard UP, 1968), pp. 227–231; P. Brown, *Augustine of Hippo* (Berkeley: U of California P, 1969), pp. 28–34; C.W. Atkinson, "'Your Servant, My Mother': The Figure of St. Monica in the Ideology of Christian Motherhood," *Immaculate and Powerful: The Female in Sacred Image and Secular Culture*, ed. C. Atkinson, C. Buchanan, and M. Miles (Boston: Beacon, 1985), pp. 139–172.

MONOPHYSITISM. Movement that emphasized the divine nature of Christ in the Christological disputes of the fifth century, from a Greek term meaning "one nature." Monophysitism designates a specific theological tradition associated initially with the city of Alexandria, but the name in time came to be used more generally to identify those Christian communions of the east that do not accept the decrees of the Council of Chalcedon (451): the Copts in Egypt, the Jacobites in Syria, and the Armenian Orthodox Church. Modern scholars regard Monophysitism as less a doctrinal deviation than a schism. In most respects, the Monophysite churches do not differ from other eastern Christian churches in doctrine, polity, or liturgy. But to understand their origins one must examine the theological disputes that engendered the schism.

At the time of the Council of Chalcedon, most Christians accepted the Nicene Creed, which affirmed that Christ was fully God, "of one substance with the Father," and that the Son, eternally begotten of God the Father, had "become incarnate," that is, entered fully into human nature. In the decades before the council, however, disputes had arisen about how best to express the relation between the divine and human in Christ. One school, that of Alexandria, taught that the eternal Word of God had *become* the person of Jesus of Nazareth; another school, that of Antioch, believed that the eternal Word had entered into the man Jesus of Nazareth as the Spirit had descended on the prophets but more fully and intimately, "as in a son." To explain their respective beliefs, each tradition used the term "nature" (*physis*) in a different sense. Cyril, bishop of Alexandria (412–444) and a disciple of the great Christian leader of the fourth century Athanasius of Alexandria, understood the term "nature" to refer to the second person of the Trinity, the divine and eternal Word of God (as in John 1:1). In his view, and the tradition he represented, there was one "nature," the divine Word, and this Word had become incarnate in Jesus Christ. For him, then, the term "nature" referred to a concrete and complete entity, the Word begotten of the Father, what we would call a "person." The other group of Christian thinkers, located primarily in the vicinity of Antioch in Syria, represented by Theodore of Mopsuestia, Theodoret of Cyrus, and Nestorius of Constantinople, used the term "nature" in a different sense. "Nature" for them designated a quality or a character, like "brownness" or "density," not a concrete entity. Just as "brownness" designated the quality of being brown, so human nature referred to the quality of being human. Peter was human, Paul was human, and Jesus was human, but each was a distinct individual person.

The question, then, arose as to whether it was proper to say that Christ had two natures, divine and human. For Antiochene theologians, the answer was "yes." Christ possessed the quality of humanity and the quality of divinity. For Cyril of Alexandria and his followers, talk of "two natures" was confusing because it implied there were two Christs (i.e., two distinct and separate entities), two persons, one who was the eternal Word of God and the other the human being Jesus of Nazareth. Hence, they preferred to speak of "one nature" in Christ.

The possibility for conflict and misunderstanding is apparent.

As is often the case in theological disputes among Christians, each appealed to different passages from the scriptures. The Alexandrian theologians cited such passages as "The Word was made flesh and dwelt among us" (John 1:14), and the Antiochene theologians pointed, for example, to the descent of the Holy Spirit on Christ in baptism (Matt. 3:16).

At the Council of Chalcedon, leaders of the churches from throughout the Christian world tried to reconcile these two traditions with the formulation "one person in two natures" (divine and human). Although there was precedent for this wording, political divisions among the churches made the compromise formula suspect. The council deposed and excommunicated the bishop of Alexandria, Dioscorus, angering the faithful in Egypt. One document adopted at the council, the *Tome* (*Ep.* 28) of Leo I, bishop of Rome, seemed, in the view of the Alexandrians, to divide Christ's work into separate human and divine activities. The council also repudiated Eutyches, archimandrite of a monastery in Constantinople. Eutyches had defended a formulation used earlier in Alexandria, "two natures before but only one after the union," which was discarded at the council. As a consequence, bishops of Egypt felt that the tradition of their church was being abandoned. When the Egyptian bishops realized that the council would adopt the formula "two natures," they were reported to have said: "We shall be killed if we subscribe to the *Tome* of Leo. We would prefer to die at the hands of the emperor and the council than at home" (Mansi, 7.58–60). After the council, feeling ran so high in Alexandria that the pro-Chalcedonian bishop, Proterius, appointed after Dioscorus's deposition, was lynched by a mob.

In the decades after Chalcedon, efforts were made to reconcile the conflicting views and heal the impending schism, all without success. In 482, emperor Zeno proposed a compromise document, the *Henoticon*, which omitted the offensive language of "two natures." Although it gained support in the east, it displeased the bishop of Rome (because of its studied ambiguity and slight of the role of Leo I at

Chalcedon). As a result, Rome severed relations with Constantinople. By the early part of the sixth century, with no resolution in sight, the non-Chalcedonian churches (Monophysites) in Syria began to ordain priests and deacons to serve their members, and from this time we can date the formal and institutional beginning of Monophysitism as a separate ecclesiastical communion. The Armenians were not represented at the Council of Chalcedon and were not involved in the disputes after the council, but early in the sixth century they rejected Chalcedon and for that reason are considered Monophysites.

Monophysitism was as much a political and ecclesiastical movement as it was a theological doctrine. Its institutional origins lie in the period after Chalcedon, when the council's decrees were repudiated by the faithful in Egypt, Palestine, Syria, and other parts of the Christian east. Hence, the term "non-Chalcedonian" is a more accurate way to refer to the "Monophysite" churches. In some regions, notably Upper Egypt (where Coptic was spoken) and Syria, the Monophysites were the only Christians. In these areas, Monophysitism was the continuation of the same form of Christianity that had existed there for centuries. Like other Christians, the Monophysites accepted the decrees of Nicaea (325), revered the early Christian writers and teachers, celebrated the traditional liturgy, and in other ways practiced the "Catholic faith." They differed from others in believing that no further definition of the faith beyond Nicaea (namely Chalcedon) was necessary. Jacob Baradaeus (ca. 500–578), a monk from east Syria, was responsible for spreading Monophysitism and establishing new churches all over the Christian east as far as the Euphrates River. For this reason, the Monophysite Christians of Syria are sometimes called the Jacobites.

The Monophysites produced a number of outstanding Christian teachers and spiritual writers, among them Severus of Antioch, Jacob of Sarug, Philoxenus of Mabbug, John of Tella, and Theodore of Arabia. Deviant forms of Monophysitism also developed, as for example the teaching of Julian, bishop of Halicarnassus, who taught that Christ's body was incorruptible (that is, not fully human). His teaching, however, was repudiated by Severus of Antioch. *See also* Aphthartodocetae; Chalcedon; Christ, Christology; Cyril of Alexandria; Nestorianism.

[R.Wi.]

Bibliography

J. Lebon, *Le Monophysisme sévérien* (Louvain: van Linthout, 1909); W.A. Wigram, *The Separation of the Monophysites* (London: Faith, 1923); E. Honigman, *Evêques et evêchés monophysites d'Asie antérieure au VIe siècle* (Louvain: Durbecq, 1951); A. Grillmeier and H. Bacht, *Das Konzil von Chalkedon: Geschichte und Gegenwart*, 3 vols. (Würzburg: Echter, 1953–1962); A.D. Halleux, *Philoxène de Mabbog, sa vie, ses écrites et sa théologie* (Louvain: Imprimerie Orientaliste, 1963); K. Sarkissian, *The Council of Chalcedon and the Armenian Church* (London: SPCK, 1965); W.H.C. Frend, *The Rise of the Monophysite Movement* (Cambridge: Cambridge UP, 1972); A. Grillmeier, *Christ in Christian Tradition*, 2 vols. (Atlanta: John Knox, 1975, 1987).

MONTANISM. Ecstatic prophetic movement in the Christianity of Asia Minor, dating primarily to the late second and early third centuries. Known as "the Phrygian heresy" in early Christian sources until the fourth century (after its place of origin and greatest support), Montanism was subsequently named after its founder and first prophet, Montanus (ca. 170). Montanist prophets claimed direct ecstatic revelations from God to support their teachings on disciplinary questions, especially extended hours of fasting and asceticism, and on eschatology. Montanists differed from Catholics in their insistence that a true prophet spoke in unconscious ecstasy and in their emphasis upon greater disciplinary rigor. Charges that they were doctrinal heretics are unfounded.

Sources on the date of the outbreak of the Montanist controversy are confused, but a date ca. 170 is to be preferred. A "newly baptized" Christian named Montanus began ecstatic prophesying in the Spirit (Eusebius, *H.E.* 5.16.7) in the village of Ardabav in southern Phrygia. He was joined shortly thereafter by two prophetesses, Maximilla (5.16.13) and Priscilla. Christianity in Asia Minor had long treasured the Gospel of John, with its promise of the Paraclete, and was the setting of the eschatological prophecy of the Book of Reve-

lation. The daughters of Philip had resided in Asia Minor and were held to be prophetesses (Eusebius, *H.E.* 5.17.3). Such circles seem the best explanation for the backgrounds of the movement, rather than pagan ecstatic religion or Judaism.

Both the anonymous source quoted by Eusebius (*H.E.* 5.17.1–14) and a Catholic redaction of an early Montanist source preserved by Epiphanius (*Haer.* 48) make it clear that the theological aspect of the controversy turned on the point of whether a true prophet spoke in ecstasy without the cooperation, and hence potential corruption, of the prophet's rational mind (the Montanist position) or whether the true prophet spoke in possession of his or her sense, that is, nonecstatically (the Catholic position).

The source preserved by Epiphanius shows some of the scriptural examples put forward by the Montanists to prove their point. Among other texts, the Montanists used Genesis 2:21 (Adam's ecstatic sleep) to show a scriptural prophecy (cf. Eph. 5:31–32) delivered in ecstasy (*Haer.* 48.5–6). The Montanist prophets also seem to have practiced "charismatic exegesis," in which the text of scripture was actually cited in their oracles in such a way as to include their eschatological key to the scriptures within the text. For example, an oracle of "self-commendation" (Aune's term) of Montanus quotes the Septuagint text of Isaiah 63:9: "Neither a messenger nor an ambassador [*presbys*] but I the Lord God Father came." The Montanist oracles that have been preserved are excerpted from their original literary settings and so are difficult to interpret correctly. A handful of authentic Montanist inscriptions have been identified. One authentic late Montanist inscription substantiates Epiphanius's charge (*Haer.* 49) that the Montanists allowed female clergy.

The literary warfare that followed the outbreak of the controversy culminated in a series of synods of churches in Asia Minor, the first such regional synods in Christian history, in which the Montanists were excommunicated (Eusebius, *H.E.* 5.16.10). The controversy spread by 177 to Rome, where the Montanists were excommunicated by bishop Eleutherus.

Just after 208, Montanism gained its most famous convert, Tertullian of Carthage. His later treatises, beginning with Book 4 of *Against Marcion*, include Montanist passages and show that Tertullian had access to the same early Montanist source preserved in Epiphanius. North African Montanism in Tertullian's day continued to emphasize long fasts, prohibited second marriages and flight to avoid martyrdom (Tertullian, *Fug.*), and specified the exact length of veils to be worn by women. The Montanist prophets also announced an eschatological vision of the heavenly Jerusalem, seen suspended over geographical Jerusalem (Tertullian, *Marc.* 3.24.4). Spiritual psalms, visions, and prayers (*Marc.* 5.8.12) also played a part in community life.

Almost nothing is known about post-third-century Montanism. A Montanist martyr appears in Eusebius of Caesarea's *Martyrs of Palestine* 3.1 in the persecutions of 303–311. Montanism continued to be mentioned in writers through the seventh century and later, but these references tend to be secondary notices about the origins of the movement. *See also* Chiliasm; Schism; Tertullian.   [D.E.G.]

Bibliography
Eusebius, *Church History* 5.3.4; 5.14–18; Epiphanius, *Panarion* 48.

P. de Labriolle, *Les Sources de l'histoire du Montanisme: textes grecs, latins, syriaques* (Fribourg and Paris: L'Université de Fribourg [Suisse], 1913); E. Gibson, *The "Christians for Christians" Inscriptions of Phrygia* (Missoula: Scholars, 1978); R.E. Heine, *The Montanist Oracles and Testimonia* (Macon: Mercer UP, 1989).

W. Schepelern, *Der Montanismus und die phrygischen Kulte* (Tübingen: Mohr, 1929); J.M. Ford, "Was Montanism a Jewish-Christian Heresy?," *JEH* 17 (1966):145–158; T.D. Barnes, "The Chronology of Montanism," *JThS* n.s. 21 (1970):403–408; J.A. Fischer, "Die antimontanistischen Synoden des 2./3. Jahrhunderts," *Annuarium Historiae Conciliorum* 6 (1974):241–273; F.C. Klawiter, "The New Prophecy in Early Christianity: The Origin, Nature and Development of Montanism, A.D. 165–220" (Ph.D. diss., University of Chicago, 1975); D.E. Aune, *Prophecy in Early Christianity and the Ancient Mediterranean World* (Grand Rapids: Eerdmans, 1983); T.D. Barnes, *Tertullian: A Historical and Literary Study* (Oxford: Oxford UP, 1985); D.E. Groh, "Utterance and Exegesis: Biblical Interpretation in the Montanist Crisis," *The Living Text: Essays in Honor of Ernest W. Saunders*, ed. D.E. Groh and R. Jewett (Lanham: UP of America, 1985), pp. 73–95; R.E. Heine, "The Role of the Gospel of John in the Montanist Controversy," *SCent* 6 (1987–1988):1–21.

MONTE CASSINO. Benedictine monastery, located between Rome and Naples, founded by Benedict of Nursia (ca. 529). After leaving Subiaco, Benedict constructed two chapels at Monte Cassino, where a temple of Apollo once stood. Upon the destruction of the monastery by the Lombards (ca. 580), the community took refuge in the Lateran basilica in Rome; the site was not reoccupied for almost a century and a half (ca. 720). Subsequently, the abbey suffered from the Saracens (883), as well as from earthquake (1349) and aerial attack (1944). The principal Benedictine house, Monte Cassino had a considerable influence on the development of western monasticism; Benedict is thought to have composed his rule there. *See also* Benedict of Nursia; Monasticism.

[M.P.McH.]

Bibliography
H. Bloch, "Monte Cassino, Byzantium, and the West in the Earlier Middle Ages," *DOP* 3 (1946):163–224; idem, *Monte Cassino in the Middle Ages* (Cambridge: Harvard UP, 1983).

MOSAICS. Technique used to decorate pavements, walls, and vaults of buildings. Mosaics were adopted by Christians in the fourth to sixth centuries as one of their principal means of artistic expression. Some of the greatest glories of early Christian and early Byzantine art were in this medium. Mosaics served didactic as well as decorative purposes.

The edict of Diocletian on prices in 301 (7.8, 9) mentions two categories of mosaicist, *musearius* and *tessellarius*, indicating that two separate crafts likely had been distinguished by the late empire. In all probability, the former was a wall mosaicist, while the latter laid floor mosaics (cf. *Cod. Thds.* 13.4.2).

Mosaicists were specialists, and a number of them were required to produce a wall mosaic. Wall mosaics were done *in situ* rather than in the workshop. Whether the painting of the setting bed and the actual placement of the tesserae there (see below) were normally entrusted to a single master or to diverse specialists is unknown. If a team of craftsmen was involved in a large commission, the master or masters presumably were responsible for the faces and possibly the rest of the human figures, and assistants for decorative motifs, especially recurrent ones. For a small commission, one mosaicist might undertake all the tasks. In the vast majority of cases, early Christian mosaicists remain anonymous.

Techniques, Materials, Placement. In the absence of surviving manuals or treatises, our knowledge of the workshop practices of early Christian mosaicists must derive from close study of surviving examples. Three layers of plaster were generally applied to the walls or vaults, with the tesserae inserted into the third layer, called the setting bed. The first two layers comprised a simple mixture of lime, marble, or brick dust and chopped straw and measured about seven-tenths and six-tenths of an inch, respectively, in depth. Composed of lime and marble dust, the setting bed was of a finer consistency and averaged about one-half inch. Each of the layers was executed in turn. The size of the work area for the first layer is unknown, but the second coat was applied in patches that the mosaicist thought he could complete in a day, before the plaster of this application as well as the setting bed, which was to be quickly laid over it, could begin to solidify. The second layer retarded the drying of the setting bed. In extant mosaics, the breaks between the different stages of mosaic work are hard to detect.

The three layers were made to adhere by keying the surfaces and in some instances by hammering iron nails into the joints of the masonry before the plastering began. The setting bed covered these nail heads. Casual, isolated markings, rough preparatory drawings, or even compositional tryouts might be made on the bare masonry of the first or second layer, but these drawings were not necessarily to be reproduced on the setting bed. Such drawings are recorded in Sta. Maria Maggiore at Rome, the Rotunda at Thessalonica, and at Zsromi in Russian Georgia. Far more commonly, it seems, the setting bed was completely painted in various colors and some degree of shading. These sketches served as guides for the laying of the tesserae but were not necessarily closely followed. No evidence of underdrawings or fully sketched compositions (*sinopia*) intended for the guidance of the painter of the setting bed has so far been discovered from this period. The role of model books and sketches on parchment remains in doubt. Programs of decoration and recurrent motifs may have been inspired by model books or sketches, perhaps composed of outline drawings with or without colors; none survives, however, and the relative scarcity of parchment makes their existence questionable. Designs drawn or painted on wood or papyrus, on the other hand, seem more likely (cf. Paulinus of Nola, *Ep.* 32.9, 10, 17).

The materials used in wall and vault mosaics were cut and uncut stone (marble, limestone, black basalt), red terra-cotta, glass (including gold and silver), glazed pottery, infrequently mother of pearl, and, in the provinces, shell. These materials were cut in rectangular, trapezoidal, and triangular shapes or were splintered. The pieces are called "tesserae" (Latin *tessellae, tesserae,* "cubes" or "dice"). The size of these cubes varied considerably. The largest usually appear in backgrounds (measuring about one-third by two-fifths of an inch), and the smallest in the faces of human figures (often as small as one-fifth inch square). The tesserae were never completely inserted in the setting bed; one-fourth to one-third of their thickness normally projects from the surface. As many as fifty or more hues have been identified in a single monument, for instance, in the Rotunda at Thessalonica. Usually, all the glass tesserae (except those capped with gold or silver) are opaque rather than translucent. Marble and stone could be employed in their natural hues; marble tesserae are found pigmented with earth colors that had been applied before insertion in the setting bed.

Stone and glass tesserae covered with gold had been used by the Romans in both floors and on vaults. But the early Christians employed gold and silver tesserae in ways far more diverse and spectacular. Made with an application of a metal foil applied or encased in transparent glass, gold and silver tesserae gave mirrorlike reflections of high intensity. The early

Christians used gold for garments, haloes, jewelry, accessories like swords, and especially for backgrounds, whether plain or architectural. It also was employed for depicting light emanating from the Lord as early as the late-third-century mausoleum of the Julii beneath St. Peter's at Rome. The earliest gold ground in a monumental apse background occurs in S. Aquilino at Milan (ca. 350–375?), where it signifies divine light. When used for large expanses of background, the gold tesserae were sometimes set in reverse, in order to avoid an uneven gleam. The first known gold ground in a dome mosaic is probably that in the (imperial?) mausoleum at Centcelles (now Constanti) in Tarragona in Spain (mid-fourth century). Thenceforth, throughout the Mediterranean world gold was used in the grounds for appearances of God or theophanies. Silver, too, was used to depict divine light emanating from Christ. Christ and archangels sometimes wear silver haloes. In the Rotunda at Thessalonica, the fifth-century background of the medallion in the summit of the dome that contained the standing figure of Christ was rendered in silver, as were the haloes of the angels supporting the medallion. In addition, silver was used for accessories like swords, and it could highlight garments.

Tesserae were spaced and angled according to the intended overall effect. Sixth-century mosaicists set gold and silver cubes at extremely sharp angles to enhance reflection. Maximum light effects resulted when the mirror ends were angled downward toward the beholder. A prime example is the original sixth-century mosaic decoration in Hagia Sophia at Constantinople, where even in one dark corner of the edifice the tesserae are not only tilted downward but are also turned slightly sideways to catch the light from a nearby window. In other sixth- and seventh-century mosaics in the eastern Mediterranean, the tesserae in haloes were commonly tilted.

Early Christian mosaics adorned churches, baptisteries and baptismal tanks, mausolea and tombs, catacombs, palaces, villas, houses, bath buildings, and other civic edifices. The technique occasionally was applied to exterior walls and curved surfaces (e.g., tombs in Asia Minor and churches at Thessalonica, Rome, Poreč, and probably Bethlehem). In the interiors of churches, mosaics decorated domes, half-domes, the semidomes of apses, vertical walls, pavements, and liturgical furnishings (e.g., a pulpit [ambo] at Nicopolis in Epirus). Not uncommonly, the technique appeared in combination with other decorative devices, such as marble revetment, stuccoes, painted carved capitals, and even frescoes.

The most prevalent type of church building in the early Christian period was the wooden-roofed, aisled basilica. In such basilicas, mosaics could adorn the semidome of the apse (or apses) in the sanctuary and the triumphal arch wall in front of the apse, as in the early-sixth-century Church of SS. Cosma e Damiano at Rome. Here were positioned the mosaics that were the most important in content. In addition, the wall surfaces above the nave colonnades and those of the entrance wall were also sometimes carpeted with mosaics, and these surfaces could be adorned with extensive cycles of scenes from the Old Testament, the New Testament, or both. The pavements of basilicas were also sometimes made of mosaic, at least in the eastern Mediterranean until the reign of the Justinian. Such mosaics adhere to a late-antique tradition of placing religious pictures in pavements.

Because mosaics were expensive, the medium has important implications for patronage. A donor or group of donors might provide the funds for just one panel of mosaic, an entire mosaic cycle, or the entire building including its decoration.

Iconographic Programs. Early Christian mosaic programs described in literary sources as well as extant cycles demonstrate that no single canon was followed in the positioning of the scenes on the walls or in their scale relationships. The most important figures or scenes were not necessarily larger than less important ones. More or less unified iconographic programs existed for some monuments, such as the mausoleum of Galla Placidia and the Church of S. Vitale, both at Ravenna, but no two sets of mosaics known to us exemplify exactly the same program. The sixth-century apse mosaics of S. Apollinare in Classe and the monastery church of St. Catherine on Mt. Sinai both depict the transfiguration of Christ but treat the theme in radically different ways, the first symbolically and the second literally. Individual programs were fluid, often revealing two or more levels of meaning, as in the apse and triumphal-arch wall mosaics in the church on Mt. Sinai. Many preserved programs are difficult to decode in detail; others, like the mosaics in the Rotunda at Thessalonica and in Sta. Maria Maggiore at Rome, remain enigmatic in salient respects. Local determinants, such as patronage, the liturgy, and iconographic traditions, explain this striking diversity and difficulty of interpretation. By contrast, Byzantine cycles of mosaic decoration in the post-Iconoclastic period follow a generally well defined *system* of decoration, as at Hosios Loukas and Daphne in Greece.

Pre-Christian cult buildings featured mosaics that conveyed religious ideas. A *Mithraeum* at Ostia, for example, housed a niche decorated with a mosaic, possibly of the third or early fourth century A.D., which represented the god Silvanus. In the fourth century, the Christians depended to a large extent upon iconography derived from the pagans, and a mixture of pagan and Christian themes occurs in some Christian monuments of that century, such as the mausoleum at Centcelles and the early-fourth-century hypogeum under the Via Livenza at Rome. By the fifth century, a thoroughly Christian iconography had been worked out at most sites, but its formal motifs were generally based on pre-Christian sources, pagan as well as secular and even some times Jewish.

One early Christian iconographic innovation was the role of the single figure or a few figures within a church, as in the destroyed mosaics in the Church of St. Demetrius at Thessalonica. Isolated, frontally disposed figures of saints, sometimes repeated in a single building, began to appear in the fifth and sixth centuries, probably in response to the growing cult of relics (e.g., the late-fifth-century mosaic in the dome of the chapel of S. Vittore in Ciel d'Oro attached to S. Ambrogio at Milan).

A combination of Old and New Testament figures and scenes characterizes many early Christian mosaics, such as those in the third-century mausoleum of the Julii beneath St. Peter's at Rome and the mausoleum at Centcelles. The oldest surviving Old Testament cycle occurs on the nave walls of Sta. Maria Maggiore at Rome (432–440), where twenty-seven of the original forty-two panels are preserved (although restored); the earliest extant New Testament cycle runs down the upper nave walls of S. Apollinare Nuovo at Ravenna (ca. 493–526). Compositions of purely theological content occur as well, such as the so-called liturgical *maiestas* in the apse mosaic of Hosios David at Thessalonica (ca. 500). Images of donors in the presence of divinity are also widespread, an example being the apse mosaic of SS. Cosma e Damiano at Rome. *See also* Art; Iconography; Ravenna. [W.E.K.]

Bibliography

M. van Berchem and E. Clouzot, *Mosaiques chrétiennes du IVe au Xe siècle* (Geneva: Les Presses de l'Imprimerie du "Journal de Genève," 1924); D. Levi, *Antioch Mosaic Pavements*, 2 vols. (Princeton: Princeton UP, 1947); F.W. Deichmann, *Frühchristliche Bauten und Mosaiken von Ravenna* (Baden-Baden: Grimm, 1958); H. Stern, "Les Mosaïques de l'église de Sainte-Constance à Rome," *DOP* 12 (1958):157–218; C. Ihm, *Die Programme der christlichen Apsismalerei vom vierten Jahrhundert bis zur Mitte des achten Jahrhunderts* (Wiesbaden: Steiner, 1960); E. Kitzinger, *Israeli Mosaics of the Byzantine Period* (Geneva: UNESCO, 1960); H. Torp, *Mosaikkene i St. Georg-Rotunden i Thessaloniki* (Oslo: Gyldendal Norsk Forlag, 1963); H.P. L'Orange and P.J. Nordhagen, *Mosaics* (London: Methuen, 1966); W. Oakeshott, *The Mosaics of Rome, from the Third to the Fourteenth Centuries* (Greenwich: New York Graphic Society, 1967); L. Budde, *Antike Mosaiken in Kilikien*, 2 vols. (Recklinghausen: Bongers, 1969–1972); R.S. Cormack, "The Mosaic Decoration of S. Demetrios, Thessaloniki," *Annual of the British School at Athens* 64 (1969):17–52; W. Deichmann, *Ravenna: Hauptstadt des spätantiken Abendlandes*, 2 vols. in 4 (Wiesbaden: Steiner 1969–1974); B. Brenk, "Early Gold Mosaics in Christian Art," *Palette*, no. 38 (Basel: Sandoz, 1971), pp. 16–25; W.E. Kleinbauer, "The Iconography and the Date of the Mosaics of the Rotunda of Hagios Georgios, Thessaloniki," *Viator* 3 (1972):27–107; G.H. Forsyth and K. Weitzmann, *The Monastery of Saint Catherine at Mt. Sinai: The Church and Fortress of Justinian* (Ann Arbor: U of Michigan P, 1973); B. Brenk, *Die frühchristlichen Mosaiken in S. Maria Maggiore zu Rom* (Wiesbaden: Steiner, 1975); N. Duval, *La Mosaïque funéraire dans l'art paléochrétien* (Ravenna:

Longo, 1976); J. Wilpert and W.N. Schumacher, *Die römischen Mosaiken der kirchlichen Bauten vom IV.–XIII. Jahrhundert* (Freiburg, Basel, and Vienna: Herder, 1976); E. Kitzinger, *Byzantine Art in the Making: Main Lines of Stylistic Development in Mediterranean Art, 3rd–7th Century* (London: Faber and Faber, 1977; rev. ed.: *Byzantinische Kunst im Werden: Stilentwicklungen in der Mittelmeerkunst vom 3. bis zum 7. Jahrhundert* (Cologne: DuMont Buchverlag, 1984); A.H.S. Megaw and E.J.W. Hawkins, *The Church of the Panagia Kanakariá at Lythrankomi in Cyprus: Its Mosaics and Frescoes* (Washington, D.C.: Dumbarton Oaks, 1977); F.B. Sear, *Roman Wall and Vault Mosaics* (Heidelberg: Kerle, 1977); M. Spiro, *Critical Corpus of the Mosaic Pavements on the Greek Mainland, Fourth/Sixth Centuries, with Architectural Survey,* 2 vols. (New York: Garland, 1978); M. Picirillo, *Chiese e mosaici della Giordania settentrionale* (Jerusalem: Studium Biblicum Franciscanum, 1981); S. Campbell, *The Mosaics of Antioch* (Toronto: Pontifical Institute of Medieval Studies, 1988).

MOSES. The key events in the formation of Israel as the covenant people of God—the deliverance from bondage in Egypt and the giving of the Law on Mt. Sinai—were associated with Moses. In Jewish and Christian tradition, Moses was the author of the first five books of the Bible. Postbiblical Jewish writings exalted the figure of Moses and added legendary features to his life, particularly in regard to his birth and early life and to his death. Philo, the apologist of Hellenistic Judaism, presented him as a king, lawgiver, priest, and prophet. Moses was known by pagans as the lawgiver of the Jews, as leader of the exodus, and as a magician.

Moses is referred to in the New Testament as lawgiver (John 1:17; 2 Cor. 3:7ff.) and as associated with prophets (Acts 26:22). Christ is presented as the prophet like Moses (Acts 3:22ff.; 7:37 citing Deut. 18:15–19). The superiority of Christ over Moses is affirmed (Heb. 3:3–5; 12:18–24). The basis was thereby laid for the dual evaluation of Moses in Christian thought: positive as the prophet and type of Christ and negative as the representative of the Jewish Law.

Jewish influence was strong on the Syriac church, which cited Moses as the model of all virtues. The Latin church fathers, concerned with moral and practical matters, appealed to

Moses as the leader of the people, the messenger of God, and the forerunner of Christ. Moses was viewed as a mediator in bringing liberation to the people, in interceding when they sinned, and in legislating conduct. Gregory of Nyssa was representative of the Greek fathers in employing typological and allegorical interpretations of Moses in relation to Christ and the church. He made a distinctive contribution in using Moses as a model of the spiritual life understood as perpetual progress toward perfection.

Moses appears frequently in Christian art, most often in the crossing of the Red Sea, receiving the Law from the hand of God, and (assimilated to Peter) in bringing water from the rock. *See also* Exodus.   [E.F.]

Bibliography
Philo, *Life of Moses*; Gregory of Nyssa, *Life of Moses* (tr., intro., and notes A.J. Malherbe and E. Ferguson, CWS [1978]).

H. Cazelles et al., *Moïse l'homme de l'alliance* (Paris: Desclée, 1955); J.G. Gager, *Moses in Greco-Roman Paganism* (Nashville: Abingdon, 1972).

MOSHEIM, JOHANN LORENZ VON (1694–1755). German Protestant church historian. Mosheim is most noted for his influence at Göttingen as both professor and chancellor from 1747 to his death. He insisted that the church was a human organization, not the kingdom of God, and that its history should be treated under secular canons. He thus attacked the conception of ecclesiastical history as primarily theological and polemical. His *Institutes of Christian History* (1755) has often been revised and used as a textbook, but its interpretations are sparse and its treatment basically a rehearsal of facts.   [F.W.N.]

Bibliography
K. Heussi, *Johann Lorenz Mosheim: Ein Beitrag zur Kirchengeschichte der achtzehnten Jahrhunderte* (Tübingen: Mohr, 1906).

MOZARABIC RITE. The Mozarabic liturgy originated quite early in the Iberian peninsula, perhaps with the first Christian missionaries; it attained a high degree of development in the era of the Visigoths, especially in the seventh century. The rite is a western liturgy, with Roman and Gothic antecedents; eastern and African elements also appear. Attempts were made to ensure uniformity of practice, most notably at the fourth of the councils of Toledo (633). A number of bishops introduced new liturgical texts, among them the archbishops of Toledo Ildefonsus (657–667) and Julianus (680–690). Upon the Arab invasion of Spain (711), Christians living under Islamic rule continued to practice the rite—indeed, these Christians, known as Mozarabs, gave their name to it. At the time of the reconquest, it was ordered replaced by the Roman rite (1080). But its decline was gradual; it continues in limited use in Toledo, and there is some interest in its revival. [M.P.McH.]

Bibliography

W.C. Bishop, *The Mozarabic and Ambrosian Rites: Four Essays in Comparative Liturgiology* (London: Mowbray, and Milwaukee: Morehouse, 1924), pp. 1–97; J. Pinell, "Boletín de liturgia hispano-visigótica," *Hispania Sacra* 9 (1956):405–428; J.F. Rivera Recio, ed., *Estudios sobre la liturgia mozárabe* (Toledo: Diputacion Provincial, 1965), with lists of primary sources (pp. 109–164) and bibliography (pp. 165–187); J. María de Mora Ontalva, "Nuevo boletín de liturgia hispánica antigua," *Hispania Sacra* 26 (1973):209–236.

MURATORIAN CANON. Account in Latin of the books in the New Testament. L.A. Muratori discovered in the Ambrosian Library in Milan (Cod. 101, fol. 10–11) a fragment of eighty-five lines discussing the canonical books of the New Testament and published it in 1740. The Latin codex from which the document came was written in the seventh or eighth century and had belonged to Columbanus's monastery at Bobbio. Some pieces of the same work were found in four eleventh-to-twelfth-century manuscripts of Paul's epistles at Monte Cassino. Most scholars have taken the reference to the *Shepherd* of Hermas ("written recently in our own time while his brother Pius" was bishop of Rome) as indicating the latter half of the second century as the date and Italy (perhaps Rome) as the place for the original composition. Although it has been argued that the original derived from fourth-century Palestine or Syria, the contents of the document support the traditional date and locale. The original language presumably was Greek. The Latin is clumsy, and the text has suffered in transmission by a poorly educated scribe. If the traditional date is maintained, the *Muratorian Canon* is the earliest surviving list of New Testament books and so of great interest for the history of the canon.

Although there are unique features to the Muratorian list, its description of the canon parallels what is found in the usage of writers ca. 200. The author knew a two-part Bible of "prophets and apostles" (lines 79–80). Mutilated at the beginning, the text begins with words that can be matched elsewhere as describing Mark. The first complete sentence names Luke as the third Gospel. The New Testament has the form of the present canon: four Gospels, Acts, Letters of Paul to churches and then to individuals, other Letters, and Apocalypses. The author had a special concern to affirm the authority of the Gospel of John as written at the request of all the apostles (lines 9ff.), perhaps responding to questions about the Fourth Gospel and expressing the interest in united apostolic authority against the Gnostic preference for individual disciples. He saw a significance in Paul writing to seven churches (nine letters) as indicating that his letters were intended for the whole church, even as the Revelation of John was written to seven churches (lines 49f.). The *Muratorian Canon* differs from the present canon in the absence of Hebrews, James, 1 and 2 Peter, and 3 John(?). The fragmentary nature of the work allows for the possibility that some of these books were mentioned in what is now lost. It accepted two books that are not in the present canon—*Apocalypse of Peter* (noted by the author as not received by all) and *Wisdom of Solomon* (there is a possibility that the translator or a transcriber has made a mistake here)—and rejected heretical books by Marcionites, Gnostics, and Montanists. The *Shepherd* of Hermas was acknowledged as orthodox but was written too late to be included in the canon.

The author did not set forth a theory of canonicity, but his statements show an interest in inspiration, as a precondition of canonicity (lines 19f.); apostolicity (or antiquity), as giving authenticity; usefulness to and acceptance by all the churches (catholicity), as determinative of authority; and reading in the assembly, as a result of canonicity (line 78). CPG I, 1862. *See also* Canon (of scripture).   [E.F.]

Bibliography

S.P. Tregelles, *Canon Muratorianus* (Oxford: Clarendon, 1867); T. Zahn, *Geschichte des neutestamentlichen Kanons* (Erlangen: Deichert, 1890), Vol. 2.1; J.B. Lightfoot, *The Apostolic Fathers* (London: Macmillan, 1890), Vol. 1.2, pp. 405–413; G. Kuhn, *Das muratorische Fragment über die Bücher des Neuen Testaments* (Zurich: Höhr, 1892); B.F. Westcott, *A General Survey of the History of the Canon of the New Testament* (London: Macmillan, 1896), pp. 214–224, 530–547.

J. Stevenson, *A New Eusebius* (London: SPCK, 1957), pp. 144–147; D.J. Theron, *The Evidence of Tradition* (Grand Rapids: Baker Book House, 1958), pp. 106–113.

N. Dahl, "Welche Ordnung der Paulusbriefe wird vom Muratorischen Kanon vorausgesetzt," *ZNTW* 52 (1961):39–53; H. von Campenhausen, *The Formation of the Christian Bible* (Philadelphia: Fortress, 1972), pp. 243–263; J. Beumer, "Das Fragmentum Muratori und seine Rätsel," *Theologie und Philosophie* 48 (1973):534–550; A.C. Sundberg, Jr., "Canon Muratori: A Fourth-Century List," *HThR* 66 (1973):1–41; E. Ferguson, "Canon Muratori: Date and Provenance," *SP* 18 (1982):677–683; G. Hahneman, "The Muratorian Fragment and the Development of the Canon" (Ph.D. diss., Oxford University, 1988).

MUSIC. The functions of music in Greco-Roman society are summarized in the response to the question, "What is the business of a pipe player?" "Why, what else, except that the mourner may have his sorrow lulled to sleep by the pipe, and that they who rejoice may have their cheerfulness enhanced, and the lover may wax warmer in his passion, and that the lover of sacrifice may become more inspired and full of sacred song?" (Philostratus, *Life of Apollonius* 5.21). Music had a prominent place in military life, at the theater, at games in the arena, in entertainment and dance, and at banquets in the home.

The Greeks gave music an important place in education as an influence in shaping attitudes and character (e.g., Plutarch, *On Music* 26–27; 33; 41). Music exemplified the harmony

that was the goal of moral education (Strabo 10.3.9f.).

Music was especially prominent in religious activities. Ancient authors claimed that music was pleasing to the gods (Horace, *Odes* 1.36.1ff.) and could be used to invoke their presence (Plutarch, *Table Talk* 4.6.2). Instrumental music, particularly that of the pipe, nearly always accompanied the offering of the sacrifice (Plutarch, *On Music* 14; *How to Study Poetry* 16; Lucian, *Dance* 16), and sometimes writers offered the utilitarian function of covering up the noise of the animals as the explanation for its presence (Plutarch, *Superstition* 13.171). Modern authors have emphasized rather the magical function of music in warding off evil spirits, and this has support in the ancient sources (Plutarch, *Isis and Osiris* 63; Pliny the Elder, *Natural History* 28.3.11). Certain cults used music to induce ecstasy (Strabo 10.3.7; Lucian, *Harmonides* 1; Aristotle, *Politics* 8.7.1342b).

The principal wind instruments were the Greek *aulos* (pipe, or "flute"), often a double pipe, and the Latin *tibia* (pipe); the principal stringed instruments were the lyre and *kithara* ("zither"). The trumpet was used mainly in the military. Certain instruments had a particular association with certain cults: the syrinx (the small shepherd's pipes) with Pan and later Attis, the tympanum ("cymbals") with Cybele, the sistrum (a type of rattle) with Isis.

Philosophers valued the lyre (as producing a soothing sound) over the pipe (a shrill sound producing excitement), vocal music over instrumental, and silent meditation over song (Plato, *Republic* 399E; *Laws* 669E; Philo, *Noah as Planter* 2.126; Porphyry, *De abstinentia* 2.34). In contrast to Plato and others who attributed great power to music, Philodemus denied to music other effects than pleasure.

Jewish Background. Although the Bible assigned instrumental music, among other aspects of civilization, to the lineage of Cain (Gen. 4:21), the Jews and their neighbors in the ancient Near East employed many instruments, even in their worship (Ps. 150). The Law of Moses authorized blowing trumpets at appointed festivals and sacrifice (Num. 10:10). The organization of cultic music was attributed to David, even as most of the Psalms were attributed to him (1 Chron. 15:16–28; 16:4–6; 23:5; 25:1, 6f.). Music in the temple service at the beginning of the Christian era is described in Sirach 50:11–20 and Mishna *Tamid* and *Sukka* 5.

The synagogue, on the other hand, developed an exclusively vocal type of music. After the destruction of the temple in A.D. 70, the prohibition of instruments was explained as due to mourning for its loss, and there were some efforts to extend the prohibition to daily life as well (*b. Gittin* 7a; *b. Sotah* 48a). This appears to have been an explanation after the fact, for instruments were seemingly absent from the synagogues before A.D. 70. From the chanting of prayers and the cantillation of scripture readings, there developed a psalmody for which instrumental accompaniment was irrelevant.

From Philo and the Talmud, there is information about the manner of performing religious songs among the Jews. Philo's description of the Therapeutae mentions solos in various "measures and melodies," responses in unison by men and women in the congregation, antiphonal singing by the group divided into two choruses that kept time with hands and feet, and singing together as one choir (*Contemplative Life* 80; 83–87). A later text mentions similar methods: a leader reciting the text with the congregation responding after each line with a leading word or by repeating the words of the leader, or the congregation all together joining with the leader after he has begun (*b. Sotah* 30b).

New Testament References. The New Testament refers to the ordinary instruments of the time in illustrations (1 Cor. 13:7; cf. Rev. 18:22) and the use of instruments at weddings (Matt. 11:17) and funerals (Matt. 9:23) and in warfare (1 Cor. 13:8). A trumpet will announce the end of the age (Matt. 24:31), and stringed instruments, based on the imagery of the Jewish temple, are present in the heavenly worship (Rev. 5:8; cf. 15:2 and 14:2f.). The principal form of music in early Christianity was singing "psalms, hymns, and spiritual songs" (Eph. 5:19; Col. 3:16; cf. Matt. 26:30), and this was in close association with prayer (1 Cor. 14:15; Acts 16:25; James 5:13).

Christian Singing. Christian music was vocal and monodic. References to Christians singing abound in patristic literature: as an illustration (Ignatius, *Rom.* 2.2), in general statements (Clement of Alexandria, *Str.* 6.14.113), as a spiritual sacrifice in place of pagan sacrifice (Justin, *1 Apol.* 13; *Orac. Sib.* 8.482–499), at the agape (Tertullian, *Apol.* 39.18), at martyrdom (Eusebius, *H.E.* 8.9.5), and especially at the regular assemblies of the church (see references below).

Jewish psalmody presumably provided the model for Christian song, but if so, Greek melodies soon had their influence. More is known about the manner of performance than about the melody or chant employed. Solo rendition, in which one person sang and others listened, is known among monks (John Cassian, *Inst.* 2.5, 12). Basil of Caesarea describes three types of congregational participation in the rendering of the Psalms: responsorial singing, in which the precentor or reader (cf. Jewish cantor) sang the body of the text and the people responded with a refrain; antiphonal singing, in which the congregation was divided into two groups and alternated singing; and unison or corporate singing, in which all united (*Ep.* 207). Each is confirmed by other texts. The most common and presumably the earliest form of singing in church was responsorial (Tertullian, *Or.* 27; John Chrysostom, *Hom.* 36 *in 1 Cor.* 14:33; *Const. app.* 2.57.6; *Test. Dom.* 2.11, 22; Pliny the Younger, *Ep.* 10.96, may be responsorial rather than antiphonal). The congregational response was a word, such as "Hallelujah" or "Amen," or a verse, such as "His mercy endures forever."

Responsorial singing gave rise to antiphons. These originated in the repetition of one psalm verse as a refrain sung by the congregation alternating with another verse by the precentor. The antiphons were separated from the Psalms and elaborated. In the west, they were mainly scripture verses, but in the east they were new metrical creations.

One report attributed the introduction of antiphonal singing to Ignatius of Antioch (Socrates, *H.E.* 6.8), but other testimony placed its introduction in Antioch at the middle of the fourth century (Theodoret, *H.E.* 2.19). It was practiced earlier in the Syriac church. Since antiphonal singing allowed a greater congregational participation than responsorial singing, it spread rapidly in the east (cf. *Itin. Aeth.* 27 for Jerusalem). This was the type of "congregational singing" that Ambrose introduced at Milan (Augustine, *Conf.* 9.7; cf. Paulinus, *V. Amb.* 4.13). It was introduced into the liturgy at Rome in the fifth century by Celestine (*Lib. Pontif.* 45), although it had been used earlier at vigils.

Some passages stress that the whole congregation participated in the singing (John Chrysostom, *Exp. Ps.* 150; Basil, *Hom. in Ps.* 1.2). This emphasis occurred especially in connection with the phrase "one voice" (Ignatius, *Eph.* 4; Eusebius, *Ps.* 91.2f.). Some descriptions of unison singing make explicit that voices of young and old, men and women, were included (John Chrysostom, *Hom. in Ps.* 145.2; Ambrose, *Ps.* 1, *Exp.* 9). Since voices differ according to age and sex, the emphasis must have been on total participation and the unity and harmony of the church more than on maintaining the same tone.

There was opposition to women singing in church (Cyril of Jerusalem, *Procatech.* 14; Isidore of Pelusium, *Ep.* 1.90). Their silence in the synagogue, the immoral connotations of female singers, and the use of choruses of women by heretics were factors in this opposition. Paul of Samosata, while bishop of Antioch in the mid-third century, is the first known to have introduced the practice of a women's chorus (Eusebius, *H.E.* 7.30.10). Among the orthodox, choirs of virgins are known from Ephraem the Syrian. The opposition to women's choruses was extended to all participation in the liturgy, in spite of the defense by Ambrose cited above.

Many church writers made the point that the music must be not only with the voice but also from the heart (*2 Clem.* 9.10; Basil, *Hom. in Ps.* 29.3; John Chrysostom, *Hom.* 19 *in Eph.* 5:19).

Opposition to Instruments. The earliest references to Christian services mention singing but are silent about instruments. In the fourth century, some writers took note of the difference between the non-use of instruments among Christians and their prominence in pagan sacrifices and in the Jewish temple. Theodoret (*Quaes. et resp. ad Orth.* 107) and Niceta (*Util. hymn.* 9) explained that instrumental music belonged to the childhood state of God's people and was among those practices of the Old Testament, such as sacrifice, circumcision, sabbath, that had been abrogated in the New Testament, whereas singing without accompaniment was useful for quieting the passions and lifting the thoughts to God. Explanations of the absence of instruments in Christian worship were commonly occasioned by comments on the passages in Psalms that mention instruments. Two types of approach were adopted. One was the historical, covenantal distinction represented by Theodoret and Niceta. God allowed instrumental music to prevent the Jews being led by attraction to it into idolatry (Theodoret, *Affect.* 7.16; *Ps.* 150:4; John Chrysostom, *Exp. Ps.* 149:2). Another approach was to give an allegorical or spiritual interpretation of the instruments named in the Old Testament. The instruments were not to be taken literally but as descriptions of the parts of the human body, the true instrument for praising God (Clement of Alexandria, *Paed.* 2.4.41–42; John Chrysostom, *Exp. Ps.* 150; *Hom. in Ps.* 145:2, 3; Athanasius, *Ep. Marcell.* 29; Jerome, *Hom.* 21 *in Ps.* 91; Augustine, *In Ps.* 43.5; 92.5).

The opposition to instruments was extended by some to their use in private life. The antagonism to idolatry and immorality associated with banquets, the theater, and other entertainments caused instruments to be included in these strictures (Ps.-Clement, *Recogn.* 4.13; Tertullian, *Marc.* 5.18; Epiphanius, *Haer.* 25.4; John Chrysostom, *Hom.* 1 *in Col.* 1:5; Gregory of Nazianzus, *Or.* 5.25). One of the few favorable references to instrumental music in patristic literature comes from Clement of Alexandria: "Even if you wish to sing and make melody to the accompaniment of the kithara or lyre, there is no blame" (*Paed.* 2.4.43). Clement here agrees with the philosophical approval of stringed instruments in contrast to wind instruments. In spite of efforts to apply the passage to the agape, or even the liturgy, Clement's context is proper conduct at an ordinary home banquet.

Later Developments. The Christian heritage of vocal music was transmitted to the Middle Ages in the west by the Gregorian chant, or plainsong. The connection of Gregory the Great with this style of singing is disputed. The Gregorian chant incorporated elements from Jewish and Roman song as developed in the early church. It preserved early Christian characteristics, such as the absence of instrumental accompaniment, of polyphony, and of strict time values. Byzantine music preserved a greater variety of melodies.

The organ appears to have moved from the court ceremony of the emperor to the church, but only in the west, and it is debated whether this occurred in the seventh century or the tenth.

When Christians came to write on musical theory, they largely transmitted the thoughts of their Greek predecessors. Theoretical treatises dealing with the abstract characteristics of music had little or nothing to do with ecclesiastical music. The word *musica* rarely was used with reference to Christian song, indicating the recognition that classical music was something different.

Purpose of Music. When Christians did reflect on the nature of their own music, they called attention to its moral purpose. There is a rapport between the movements of the soul and music, so music by combining pleasure with profit is a means of giving beauty to the moral character (Athanasius, *Ep. Marcell.*; Basil, *Hom. in Ps.* 1.2; Clement of Alexandria, *Str.* 6.11; John Chrysostom, *Exp. Ps.* 134.1; Augustine, *Conf.* 9.6.14; 10.33.50). Christians applied the philosophical commonplace about the cosmic harmony of the spheres to the singing of Psalms as being consonant with human nature and as an imitation of the God who created harmony (Gregory of Nyssa, *Pss. Titt.* 1.3). Christian music was intended to glorify God, to edify the faithful by lifting thoughts above and reaffirming the faith, to improve conduct, and to proclaim the truth. *See also* Hymns; Psalms. [E.F.]

Bibliography

Clement of Alexandria, *Instructor* 2.4.41–44; Niceta, *On the Utility of Hymn Singing*; Augustine, *De musica*; Boethius, *De institutione musica*; Martianus Capella, *Marriage of Philology and Mercury* 9.

T. Gérold, *Les Pères de l'église et la musique* (Paris: Alcan, 1931); E. Wellesz, "Early Christian Music," *New Oxford History of Music*, ed. A. Hughes (London: Oxford UP, 1954), Vol. 2: *Early Medieval Music up to 1300*; C.H. Kraeling, "Music in the Bible," and E. Werner, "The Music of Post-Biblical Judaism," *New Oxford History of Music*, ed. E. Wellesz (London: Oxford UP, 1957), Vol. 1: *Ancient and Oriental Music*; E. Werner, *The Sacred Bridge*, Vol. 1 (New York: Columbia UP, 1959); Vol. 2 (New York: KTAV, 1984); E. Wellesz, *A History of Byzantine Music and Hymnography* (Oxford: Clarendon, 1961); W.S. Smith, *Musical Aspects of the New Testament* (Amsterdam: ten Have, 1962); J. Mountford, "Music and the Romans," *BJRL* 47 (1964):198–211; J.W. McKinnon, "The Meaning of the Patristic Polemic Against Musical Instruments," *Current Musicology* (Spring 1965):69–82; W.D. Anderson, *Ethos and Education in Greek Music* (Cambridge: Harvard UP, 1966); J.A. Haldane, "Musical Instruments in Greek Worship," *Greece and Rome* 13 (1966):98–107; O. Söhngen, *Theologie der Musik* (Kassel: Stauda, 1967); G. Wille, *Musica Romana* (Amsterdam: Schippers, 1967); A.W.J. Holleman, "Early Christian Liturgical Music," *Studia Liturgica* 8 (1971–1972):185–192; E. Ferguson, *A Cappella Music in the Public Worship of the Church* (Abilene: ACU, 1972); H.I. Marrou, "Une Théologie de la musique chez Gregoire de Nysse?," *Epektasis*, ed. J. Fontaine and C. Kannengiesser (Paris: Beauchesne, 1972), pp. 501–508; R.A. Skeris, Chroma Theou: *On the Origins and Theological Interpretation of the Musical Imagery Used by the Ecclesiastical Writers of the First Three Centuries with Special Reference to the Image of Orpheus* (Altötting: Coppenrath, 1976); R.F. Hayburn, *Papal Legislation on Sacred Music 95 A.D. to 1977 A.D.* (Collegeville: Liturgical, 1979); J. Quasten, *Music and Worship in Pagan and Christian Antiquity* (Washington, D.C.: National Association of Pastoral Musicians, 1983; orig. German ed., 1973); J.A. Smith, "The Ancient Synagogue, the Early Church, and Singing," *Music and Letters* 65 (1984): 1–16; G. Cattin, *Music of the Middle Ages* (Cambridge: Cambridge UP, 1985), Vol. 1; R.R. La Croix, ed., *Augustine on Music: An Interdisciplinary Collection of Essays* (Lewiston: Mellen, 1987); J.W. McKinnon, ed., *Music in Early Christian Literature* (New York: Cambridge UP, 1987).

MYSTICISM. Spiritual union with the divine; from the Greek verbs *múein* ("to abandon corporeal sensations and replace them by suprasensible illumination") and *mueîn,* ("to introduce into, or to lead to, something that is a secret, a mystery"). The word "mysticism" does not appear in the scriptures or in patristic Christian literature. Christian authors, however, do use related forms—"mystery," "mystic(al)," "mystagogy," "mystagogue"—in connection with initiation, including instruction about the divine revelation and especially participation in the "mysteries" (sacraments) of Christianity.

Christian mysticism is distinguished to a greater or lesser degree from other forms of mysticism, such as the mystery religions, the Platonic and Neoplatonic philosophies, the nonorthodox movements Gnosticism and Montanism, and the Jewish mystical theology of Philo. Centered upon Christ's divine-human person his teaching and his example, it transforms and confirms human beings in their particularity and freedom. Christian mysticism can thus be defined as the free union and communion of the human being with the divine, without confusion, in Jesus Christ and in the church, although this broad understanding may receive different emphases and contexts in different authors: liturgical, ascetical, theoretical, and practical.

The roots of Christian mysticism appear in the New Testament, particularly in the teachings of Paul and John concerning union with Christ and the experience of God's presence and love. These teachings were taken up and expounded by subsequent authors. The elementary spiritual teaching of the apostolic fathers and the apologists became more elaborate in the writings of Irenaeus, the Alexandrians Clement and Origen, and especially in the liturgical, ascetical, and spiritual writings of fourth- and fifth-century authors. Modern scholars have focused on the mystical aspects of Origen, Macarius, Gregory of Nazianzus, Gregory of Nyssa, Cyril of Alexandria, and Augustine and have variously assessed their connection with the mysticism of Neoplatonism.

At the end of the fifth century, the first systematic exposition of a Christian mysticism appears in the work of the unknown Syrian Christian author who wrote under the pseudonym Dionysius the Areopagite. Pseudo-Dionysius distinguishes between two theological procedures, the *kataphatic* (affirmative) and the *apophatic* (negative), and connects the latter with what he calls "mystical theology." Here, he claims that God is "above every being and knowlege" (*D.N.* 1.4) and "dwells in divine darkness, that is, in unapproachable light" (*Myst.* 1). As such, he is "above every affirmation and negation" (*Myst.* 5), and therefore it is only through the "pure and spotless spirit and prayer" (*D.N.* 3.1) that human beings can approach God. God cannot be known "out of his being but in the negation of all things as in the thought of transcendence and in the thought of the cause of all things" (*Myst.* 5). This knowledge, which rests upon a mystic union between the human spirit and God, is the ultimate goal of Christian initiation. Patristic scholars have pointed out the parallels and the differences between the mysticism of Pseudo-Dionysius and of Greek Neoplatonic philosophers—Proclus, Damascius, and others. John of Scythopolis and Maximus Confessor were the patristic authors who "domesticated" Pseudo-Dionysius's theology for the Christian church.

In the sixth century, John Climacus developed a practical Christian mysticism for his monks through his monastic manual *The Ladder of Divine Ascent.* In the seventh century, Maximus Confessor wrote several works directly related to a Christian mysticism that is more than intellectual and is explained in a variety of ways, especially in terms of "being," "knowledge," and "love." In the tenth century, Symeon the New Theologian attempted to synthesize the spiritual and theoretical mysticism of Maximus with the practical and ascetical mysticism of John Climacus, taking up the work of other ascetical mystical theologians like Theodore the Studite and his successors and the great spiritual masters of the monastery of St. Mamas in Constantinople. His contribution marked a return to the central datum of Christian mysticism, the divine-human mystery of Christ and the union of human beings in it. *See also* Dionysius the Areopagite, Pseudo-; Ecstasy; Maximus Confessor.   [G.D.D.]

Bibliography

Pseudo-Dionysius: The Complete Works, tr. C. Luibhéid, CWS (1987); *Maximus Confessor: Selected Writings,* tr. G. Berthold, CWS (1985); *John Climacus, The Ladder of Divine Ascent,* tr. C. Luibhéid, CWS (1982).

E.C. Butler, *Western Mysticism* (London: Constable, 1922; 2nd ed. 1927; 3rd ed. 1967); M. Smith, *Studies in Early Mysticism in the Near and Middle East* (London: Sheldon, 1931); V. Lossky, *The Mystical Theology of the Eastern Church* (London: James Clark, 1957); L. Bouyer, *A History of Christian Spirituality* (London: Burns and Oates, 1963), Vol. 1: *The Spirituality of the New Testament and the Fathers;* A. Louth, *The Origins of the Christian Mystical Tradition (From Plato to Denys)* (Oxford: Clarendon, 1981); C. Jones et al., eds., *The Study of Spirituality* (London: SPCK, 1986); T. Špidlík, *The Spirituality of the Christian East* (Kalamazoo: Cistercian, 1986).

N

NAASSENES, OPHITES. Gnostic sect(s). The only account of the Naassenes is found in Hippolytus (*Haer.* 5.6.3–11.1 and summarized at 10.9.1–3). The Naassenes adhered to a Gnostic system that described the generation of the world through three principles, a teaching also found in the *Megale Apophasis* and in descriptions of the Peratae, the Sethians/Archontics, and the Docetists.

According to Hippolytus, the Naassenes derive their name from the Hebrew word for serpent, *naḥash*, rendered in Greek as *naas*. It is a term for the middle principle, the self-originate, personified as the bisexual Adam, who is compared to the seed, the water, the serpent, and the soul. Every nature seeks after this element, without which nothing, whether inanimate or animate, can exist. It is also compared to the great ocean that flows downward (meaning that humanity is born) and upward (meaning the "gods" come into being and the divine element in humanity returns to its true home). The other two primary elements are the preexistent and the outpoured chaos. The human soul is seen as universally desirable, and although sexual activity describes human interaction on earth, it is regarded as a necessary evil. In the highest realm, asexuality seems to be preferred. In the realms below, humanity is kept enslaved by the creator Esaldaeus. From this condition of slavery, humans must awaken the Christ in themselves and be "born again." Jesus is the redeemer who releases humanity from its captivity, and by "entering through the third door" (probably a reference to a Gnostic sacrament) salvation is attained. The account ends with the famous Naassene hymn in which Christ is described as Redeemer.

The Ophites, like the Naassenes, posited three divine principles and venerated the serpent (Greek *ophis*) as a medium of divine revelation. These principles are described by Irenaeus (*Haer.* 1.30.1–5) as First Anthropos (Man), Second Anthropos, and Holy Spirit/Woman. Christ is the product of all three figures. Material creation results from the "overflowing" of the Mother and is called Sophia (Wisdom) and Man-Woman. Being weighed down by a material body, she nevertheless gathered power to leap upward and become the visible heaven. Her son, Ialdabaoth, begot seven sons, and claimed his uniqueness in language from the Old Testament: "I am Father and God and above me there is none." This was refuted by a cry from his Mother, and so a rivalry between mother and son was established in which humans struggle to regain awareness of their higher origins, aided by Sophia, while her son, the creator God of the Old Testament, strives to keep them ensnared. One form of Sophia's aid is Christ, who descended into Jesus but departed before the crucifixion. Some Ophites claimed that Sophia became the serpent in Genesis 3:1, since the serpent opposes the Hebrew God. More information about the Ophites comes from Epiphanius (*Haer.* 37.5–8), who describes the involvement of a snake in Ophite sacramental rites.

For the second-century pagan Celsus, Christians were indistinguishable from Gnostic sects, and thanks to Origen, who preserves Celsus's writings for the purpose of refuting them, we possess a diagram from the Ophites (*Cels.* 6.24–28). Although difficult to reconstruct, the diagram shows seven concentric spheres through which the soul passes by addressing the guardians of each in specific formulas. In obscure sacraments and ritual descriptions, these accounts show the Gnostic concern for salvation. *See also* Gnosticism.[D.G.]

Bibliography

Irenaeus, *Against Heresies* 1.30.1–15; Hippolytus, *Refutation of All Heresies* 5.6.3–11.1; 10.9.1–3; Pseudo-Tertullian, *Against All Heresies* 6; Origen, *Against Celsus* 6.24–38; 3.13; Epiphanius, *Panarion* 37.

H. Schlier, "Der Mensch im Gnostizismus," *Studies in the History of Religions*, ed. C.J. Bleeker (Leiden: Brill, 1955), pp. 60–76; H.-C. Puech, "Archontiker," RLAC (1950), Vol. 1, pp. 634–643; A.J. Welburn, "Reconstructing the Ophite Diagram," *Novum Testamentum* 23 (1981):261–287; J. Frickel, *Hellenistische Erlösung in christlicher Deutung: Die gnostischer Naassenerschrift* (Leiden: Brill, 1984).

NAG HAMMADI. Village in Upper Egypt near the place in which a jar containing the remains of thirteen codices from the fourth century A.D. was discovered. The codices contain Coptic versions of some fifty-one writings, most of them representing Gnostic speculation. The jar was uncovered by a camel driver digging for fertilizer in 1945. One of the codices appears to have been mutilated after its discovery. The find made its way into the hands of various antiquities dealers and was only slowly acquired by the Coptic Museum in Cairo, where the volumes are now housed. Codex I reached Belgium and was eventually acquired by the Bollingen Foundation for Carl Jung. Hence, it is sometimes referred to as the "Jung codex." It too has been returned to Cairo. Numerous delays hampered the scholarly publication of the find. Thanks to UNESCO, a complete photographic edition has been published and a team from the Institute for Antiquity and Christianity at Claremont, California, was able to publish a provisional English translation of the whole collection in 1977. Scholarly editions of the texts with translations are also being prepared by the Claremont group as well as groups at the University of Laval (French) and Berlin (German).

Analysis of the materials used in the bindings of the codices shows that they were produced in the area in which they were found. Dates on letters and grain receipts indicate a date in the mid-fourth century A.D. Place references as well as a reference to "Father Pachom" suggest that the volumes may have been the possession of Pachomian monks known to have inhabited the area. Archaeological surveys have uncovered the remains of a Pachomian basilica. However, there are no remains to indicate exactly where the codices were stored or produced. Some scholars think that the monks may have collected these writings either to refute heresies or because of their world-renouncing ascetic tone and then hidden them away when Athanasius in 367 sent out a letter condemning apocryphal books.

The writings in the collection were translated into Coptic from Greek. One of the most famous, the *Gospel of Thomas* (NHC II, *2*), contains a collection of sayings attributed to Jesus. Greek variants of some of the sayings were found among the Oxyrhynchus Papyri. Other sayings in the *Gospel of Thomas* are variants of those known to us from the Synoptic Gospels, such as the parables of the sower, the mustard seed, and the great banquet. Another writing, the *Wisdom of Jesus Christ* (NHC III, *4*), survives in an additional Coptic version in the Berlin codex, which also contains a short version of another work, the *Apoc-*

ryphon of John, which is found in both longer and shorter versions at Nag Hammadi (NHC II, *1,* and IV, *1* [long]; NHC III, *1* [short]). A Greek fragment of the *Wisdom of Jesus Christ* survives. What appears to be a variant of the cosmological speculation of the *Apocryphon of John* is quoted by Irenaeus of Lyons (*Haer.* 1.29).

The *Wisdom of Jesus Christ* and the *Apocryphon of John* are examples of a common type of Gnostic writing, a dialogue between the risen Jesus and one or more disciples in which Jesus reveals Gnostic teaching. Although the framework makes Jesus the revealer, the content of the dialogue contains philosophical speculation about the transcendence of God and a radical revision of Genesis speculation designed to show the hostility of the creator God to Gnostics. In some versions, the female principle derived from the Godhead, a Wisdom figure, appears to be the original revealer. Such evidence suggests that Christian Gnostics appropriated their myths, speculation, and exegesis from traditions that were not originally Christian. They "Christianized" such material by identifying Jesus, or the risen Christ, with a heavenly figure. This impression is strengthened by the fact that in the Nag Hammadi collection the treatise just before the *Wisdom of Jesus Christ,* the *Letter of Eugnostos, the Blessed,* contains the content of the former's revelation about the origins of the heavens without its dialogue or other evidently Christian features. On the other hand, many of the treatises suggest that Gnostic mythology could not have developed without elaborating on and radically reversing Jewish traditions, especially those connected to Genesis. *The Nature of the Archons* (NHC II, *4*) and the *Apocalypse of Adam* (NHC V, *5*) provide examples of such interpretation.

It has proven difficult to match treatises from Nag Hammadi with the various "schools" of heretics reported by the church fathers. Similarities between their mythological structure and that of the "Sethian Ophites" in Irenaeus (*Haer.* 1.30) have led some scholars to propose that writings like the *Apocryphon of John,* the *Apocalypse of Adam,* the *Wisdom of Jesus Christ,* and the *Gospel of the Egyptians* belong to a broad type of Gnosticism called "Sethian." Some of the writings in Codex VI are clearly of the hermetic type. Others appear to stem from the Valentinian schools of Christian Gnosticism. The most famous are the *Treatise on the Resurrection* (NHC I, *4*), the *Gospel of Truth* (NHC I, *3*), and the *Gospel of Philip* (NHC II, *3*).

Other writings in the collection represent an interpretation of Gnostic enlightenment that has been shaped to fit Platonic speculation about the ascent of the soul to a vision of the divine. Two of them, *Zostrianos* (NHC VIII, *1*) and *Allogenes* (NHC XI, *3*), are reported to have been read by members of Plotinus's circle.

In addition to Gnostic and hermetic writings, the Nag Hammadi collection contains some writings that appear to have been preserved as general wisdom or ascetic teaching. They are not explicitly Gnostic in their speculation. Such writings include a collection of pagan proverbs, the *Sentences of Sextus* (NHC XII, *1*); a wisdom homily, the *Teaching of Silvanus,* which incorporates part of a sermon of Anthony (NHC VII, *4*); a translation of a section of Plato's *Republic;* and a general apocryphal story about Peter and the apostles, the *Acts of Peter and the Twelve Apostles* (NHC VI, *1*).

The Nag Hammadi library provides a wide variety of Gnostic and even some non-Gnostic writings from the second and third centuries. It gives further evidence for the development of Gnosticism as a Christian heresy through the transformation of myths and speculative materials from a heterodox Jewish or even pagan and philosophical background. It suggests that quite a diversity of material was available to the ascetic communities of the Egyptian desert. Consequently, the Nag Hammadi find will continue to enrich scholarly understanding of the diversity in the thought-world of second- and third-century Christianity. *See also* Egypt; Gnosticism. [P.P.]

Bibliography

J.M. Robinson, *The Nag Hammadi Library in English* (San Francisco: Harper and Row, 1978, rev. ed. 1988); J.M. Robinson and B. Van Elderen, "The Nag

Hammadi Excavations," *The Institute for Antiquity and Christianity Report 1972–1980*, ed. M.W. Meyer (Claremont: Institute for Antiquity and Christianity, 1981), pp. 37–44; K. Rudolph, *Gnosis* (San Francisco: Harper and Row, 1983); J.M. Robinson, *The Facsimile Edition of the Nag Hammadi Codices: Introduction* (Leiden: Brill, 1984).

NARSAI (ca. 399–ca. 503). Nestorian teacher (also Narses). Left an orphan at an early age, Narsai was reared in a monastery where his uncle was abbot. He studied in the school of Edessa, becoming its director in 451. Narsai followed the theology of Theodore of Mopsuestia and was a friend of Ibas, bishop of Edessa. When the latter died and a strong opponent of Nestorianism became bishop, Narsai was forced to flee. The bishop of Nisibis, Barsauma (Barsumas), persuaded him to settle at Nisibis, where he taught for the rest of his life. (He was later to come into conflict with Barsauma.) Although not an especially original theologian, Narsai became the most influential exponent of Nestorian doctrine. Over eighty metrical homilies by him survive. These Syriac homilies treat liturgical, theological, exegetical, and moral subjects. Exegetical works mentioned by later authors appear not to have survived, and there is doubt about the authenticity of liturgical poems ascribed to him. *See also* Barsauma; Nestorianism; Nisibis; Theodore of Mopsuestia.   [E.F.]

Bibliography
F. Martin, "Homélie de Narsès sur les trois docteurs nestoriens," *Journal Asiatique* 14 (1899):446–492 and 15 (1900):469–525; A. Mingana, *Narsai Doctoris Syri Homiliae et Carmina*, 2 vols. (Mossul: Fratrum Praedicatorum, 1905); R.H. Connolly, *The Liturgical Homilies of Narsai* (Cambridge: Cambridge UP, 1909); P. Gignoux, *Homélies de Narsai sur la création*, PO (1968), Vol. 34, pp. 415–716; F.G. McLeod, *Narsai's Metrical Homilies on the Nativity, Epiphany, Passion, Resurrection, and Ascension*, PO (1979), Vol. 40, pp. 1–193.

A. Vööbus, *History of the School of Nisibis*, CSCO (1965), Vol. 266, Subs. 26, pp. 57–65; F.G. McLeod, "Man as the Image of God: Its Meaning and Theological Significance in Narsai," *ThS* 42 (1981):458–467.

NARTHEX. Greek word for the porch outside or the vestibule inside the entrance of a church.

It extended across the width of the building and was set off by columns or an arcade. If there was an atrium in front of the church, the narthex formed the side of it adjacent to the façade of the church. With the adoption of orientation for churches, this meant that it was on the east side of the atrium and at the west end of the church. In some cases, such as Hagia Sophia, there were two narthexes, outside and inside the building, known, respectively, as the exonarthex and esonarthex. From the narthex, one could look into the church either through doors or through a colonnade.

The common opinion that the narthex was the only part of the church to which catechumens and penitents were admitted has been challenged by Thomas Mathews. In the early Byzantine liturgy, the First Entrance was made from the narthex through the central or Royal Door into the nave. When the emperor took part in the liturgy, he met the patriarch in the narthex. The clergy and the people entered at the same time. Catechumens seem to have been sent to the galleries or excluded from the church altogether during the eucharist.

In the late-fifth-century Church of St. Demetrius in Thessalonica, Greece, and elsewhere, the nave arcades turned in at the west end of the nave to enclose the esonarthex, forming what Greeks in later times called the *tribelon* ("place of three curtains"). Semicircular openings or apsidoles sometimes terminated each end of the narthex. Double-storied narthexes were found in the Byzantine east, and in some buildings steps led from the narthex directly to galleries above the side-aisles. The narthex is characteristic of the early Christian basilica, as well as most Byzantine and some Romanesque churches, but it is seldom found in the Gothic period. *See also* Basilica.   [G.T.A.]

Bibliography
T.F. Mathews, *The Early Churches of Constantinople: Architecture and Liturgy* (University Park: Pennsylvania State UP, 1971), pp. 125–130, 139–149; B. Fletcher, *A History of Architecture*, 18th ed., rev. J.C. Palmes (New York: Scribner, 1975), pp. 347–386; R. Krautheimer, *Early Christian and Byzantine Architecture*, 3rd ed. (Harmondsworth: Penguin, 1979), esp. pp. 98–99, 105–108, 129–131, 180–181 (with

illustrations, plans, and additional bibliography on individual churches).

NATIVITY, CHURCH OF THE.

Church in Bethlehem, one of three founded by the emperor Constantine about the time of the Council of Nicaea (325) in commemoration of the major events of the life of Christ. The Church of the Nativity combined an octagonal structure at its eastern end, around and over the cave in which it was believed Jesus was born, with a basilica consisting of a colonnaded nave and double side-aisles. The octagon was the martyrion proper and was as wide as the nave and inner side-aisles (about fifty-nine feet). It probably had a wooden pyramidal roof with an opening in the center corresponding to an opening over the cave itself. The basilica was nearly square (ninety-four by ninety-five feet), with a clerestory. On the western end, there was a colonnaded atrium at least as long as the basilica and a forecourt in front of it. The mosaic pavements of this church probably date to the end of the century.

Between 560 and 604 (earlier according to some scholars), the octagon was replaced by a greatly enlarged choir area with a trefoil transept wider than the basilica, a large chancel, and an eastern apse with clergy seats. A narthex was added and the west wall extended by another set of columns to give an overall length of 210 feet, imposing but still only a little more than half the length of the Church of St. Peter in Rome and two-thirds of Justinian's Church of Hagia Sophia in Constantinople. Except for the atrium, this rebuilding has survived to the present despite damage from earthquake and fire. *See also* Basilica.   [G.T.A.]

Bibliography

R.W. Hamilton, *The Church of the Nativity, Bethlehem* (Jerusalem: Department of Antiquities, 1947); G.T. Armstrong, "Imperial Church Building in the Holy Land in the Fourth Century," *Biblical Archaeologist* 30 (1967):90–102; idem, "Fifth and Sixth Century Church Buildings in the Holy Land," *GOTR* 14 (1969):23–25; R. Krautheimer, *Early Christian and Byzantine Architecture*, 3rd ed. (Harmondsworth: Penguin, 1979), pp. 91–93.

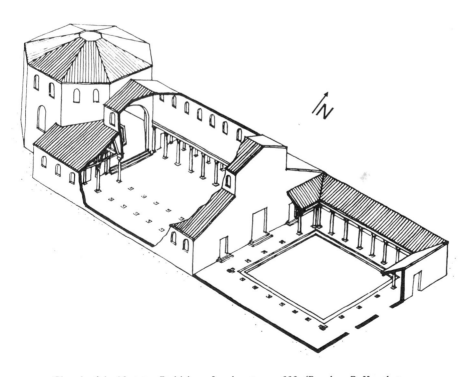

Church of the Nativity, Bethlehem, Israel, as in A.D. 333. (Based on R. Krautheimer, *Early Christian and Byzantine Architecture* [Harmondsworth: Penguin, 1986], fig. 26.)

NEANDER, AUGUST (1789–1850). German Protestant church historian. Born into a Jewish family, Neander became a Christian in 1806. After completing his formal education, he took a professorship at Heidelberg in 1812, but from 1813 until his death he taught in Berlin.

For Neander, church history was a dialectical process worked out between the Spirit of Christ and the spirit of the world; it was in a certain sense a history of piety. He carried out his historical research and teaching under the influence of Schleiermacher. His books indicate a good knowledge of the sources and are marked by interesting portrayals of individuals, but they suffer from a lack of clarified conceptions and systematic overview.

Neander's six-volume *General History of the Christian Religion and Church* (1825–1852, tr. 1847–1852) covered the beginnings to 1431. He was the author of *Julian the Apostate* (1812, tr. 1850), *Gnosis* (1818), *John Chrysostom* (1822, tr. 1838), *Tertullian, The Age of the Apostles* (1832), and the *Life of Jesus* (1837, tr. 1841).

Both A. von Harnack and Phillip Schaff gave important speeches in appreciation of his work in 1889 on the 100th anniversary of his birth. [F.W.N.]

Bibliography
P. Schaff, *Saint Augustine, Melanchthon, Neander: Three Biographies* (New York: Funk and Wagnalls, 1886).

NECTARIUS (fourth century). Bishop of Constantinople (381–397). Nectarius was born at Tarsus in Cilicia and climbed the political ladder in Constantinople to the rank of *praetor*. He succeeded Gregory of Nazianzus when Gregory resigned the see in 381. Nectarius presided over the rest of the Ecumenical Council of 381. His baptism had come just before his elevation to bishop. Although he occupied the bishopric nearly two decades, very little is known about him or his work. Feast day October 11. CPG II, 4300–4301. [F.W.N.]

Bibliography
Socrates, *Church History* 5.8, 10, 19; Sozomen, *Church History* 6.27; 7.8; Theodoret, *Church History* 5.8–9.

NEMESIUS (fl. ca. 390). Bishop of Emesa in Syria. Nemesius wrote *On the Nature of Man*, a Christian anthropology setting forth the intimate union of soul and body. He was knowledgeable in philosophy and medicine and was interested in ethics and defending providence against fatalism. CPG II, 3550. TLG 0743. [E.F.]

Bibliography
Maximus Confessor, *Opuscula theologica et polemica*, PG 91.277; Anastasius Sinaita, *Quaestiones* 18, PG 99.505; John of Damascus, *Orthodox Faith* 2.12–29.
Nemesius, *On the Nature of Man*, tr. W. Telfer, LCC (1955), Vol. 4, pp. 203–455.

NEOCAESAREA. Three bishoprics of this name are known. (1) Neocaesarea of Bithynia. Two of its bishops were present at councils in Constantinople—Olympias in 381 and Cyriacus in 518. (2) Neocaesarea in Syria. Paul, its bishop, who had lost the use of his hands under torture for the faith during the reign of Licinius, attended the Council of Nicaea (325). (3) Neocaesarea in Pontus. Gregory Thaumaturgus was born there (ca. 213) and was its bishop (ca. 240–ca. 270). Basil the Great took up the cenobitic life there (ca. 358–ca. 364) and renewed his friendship with Gregory of Nazianzus during his stay. A council held there passed fifteen canons dealing with matrimonial and disciplinary issues, including regulation of the catechumenate. These canons, together with legislation issued at Ancyra and Gangra, formed the early Greek canonical corpus. Extant in many eastern versions, it was translated into Latin (before 451) and came to form part of canon law in the west as well as the east. [M.P.McH.]

Bibliography
For the canons of Neocaesarea (3), see CPG IV, 8504–8505. Engl. tr. in NPNF, 2nd. ser. (1899), Vol. 14, pp. 79–86.

NEOPLATONISM. A variety of Platonisms from the third to the sixth century A.D. The founder of Neoplatonism was Plotinus (205–270). His influence extended into the Hellenic Neoplatonisms of Porphyry, Iamblichus, Syrianus, Proclus, and Damascius, and into the Christian Neoplatonisms of Basil of Caesarea, Gregory of Nyssa, Gregory of Nazianzus, Synesius of Cyrene, and Pseudo-Dionysius among Greek-speaking Christians, and Marius Victorinus, Ambrose, Augustine, and Boethius in the Latin west.

Neoplatonism's sources are the dialogues of Plato, the writings of Aristotle, and (depending on the kind of Neoplatonism) various religious texts. These last include the *Chaldean Oracles,* the Hermetic writings, and the Old and New Testaments. From these sources, Neoplatonism proposes a metaphysical system that appeals to a hierarchy of beings, the reality of first principles, a tripartite theory of the soul, and a tripartite doctrine of knowledge. After Plotinus, there is a shared Neoplatonic assumption that revelation is the source of all logical knowledge. From this flows the attempt to systematize and attain a rational grasp of the revelation of the gods for a true understanding of the nature of reality.

Neoplatonic doctrines are based on theories proposed in earlier Platonism, Aristotelianism, and Stoicism. Neoplatonism differs from Platonism in its novel combinations of previously disparate theories and in its profoundly religious orientation. Its hypostatic doctrines, its views of the relation between the spheres of being, its conceptions of the nature and function of knowledge, and its understanding of the nature and destiny of the human soul flow from philosophical exegesis and from revelatory wisdom. Neoplatonism quarried ancient philosophical and religious sources; however, its arrangement and interpretation of Platonic doctrine were fresh and novel.

At the center of Neoplatonic metaphysics is a hypostatic theology. In general, Neoplatonists postulated three or four hypostases, called One, Mind, Soul, and Nature. The One is God, who is above all being and intellect but is the principle of being and intellect. The One is the source and end of all things. From the One emanates Mind. This absolutely unwavering intellect thinks itself and the ideas (the ideal forms of reality). Mind produces the Soul of the All. The Soul is a cosmic intellect that contains all the general and specific ideas that become explicit in the universe. The universe is called Nature, and it is the realm of all physical things, the natural order whose causes and effects are logical. It has the character of natural necessity for Hellenic Neoplatonists and of the divinely established laws of nature for Christian Neoplatonists.

Each hypostasis refers to a distinct level of reality. Everything is in all; each level of being contains the whole of possible reality, but under a different aspect, and in its own way. The human soul is a microcosm of reality partaking of all its realms. By way of recollection and conversion to the divine reason in the soul, an individual soul ascends from its manifold sensible knowledge to a unitive intellectual knowledge, and finally to a supranoetic, mystical union with God.

Neoplatonism focuses upon issues of the human soul's fall into matter and its redemption. Neoplatonists teach that once the human soul descends into matter it is separated from God. To overcome this separation, the soul must shed its passionate and appetitive impulses and cultivate its rational and divine potentials.

"Conversion" and "procession" are the key terms of Neoplatonic soteriological doctrine. Through its conversion to reason, the soul proceeds upward to God. This process is conceived as an ascent from the material world to the intelligible world and finally to the divine world. To attain salvation, Neoplatonists invoked not only the teachings of Greco-Roman philosophy, but primarily the revelations of God. Divine revelation took manifold forms. Hellenic Neoplatonists relied on the sacred scriptures of the Hellenistic and Roman religions. Christian Neoplatonists turned to the Bible. From this confluence of philosophy and religion, a set of norms was postulated that, if followed, led to the soul's salvation and union with God.

After Plotinus, Neoplatonists synthesized and expanded his interpretation of Plato. Foremost among these interpreters was Plotinus's student Porphyry, who bequeathed Plotinian Platonism to both pagans and Christians.

Porphyry commented upon the *Chaldean Oracles,* a second-century collection of gnomic sayings, expounding divine revelation that disclosed the full truth of Platonism. These writings provided a knowledge of theurgy (rites to induce the presence of deity) that permitted many souls to attain salvation without knowing philosophy. The *Chaldean Oracles* were to become the Bible of Hellenic Neoplatonists from Iamblichus to Proclus.

The later Hellenic Neoplatonists synthesized the teachings of Plotinus, Porphyry, and the *Chaldean Oracles.* Chief among them was Iamblichus, who expanded the intermediate hypostases between the One and the levels of reality. Believing the soul to be fully fallen and separated from God, Iamblichus multiplied the sources of divine revelation to encompass most of the religious writings of Greco-Roman antiquity; he placed theurgy at the center of Neoplatonic speculation about attaining salvation. Syrianus and Proclus continued this tendency, constructing a complex synthesis of Neoplatonism, Chaldeanism, and Orphism. On the basis of the principles of analogy and mediation, they postulated that each level of reality imitates a higher level, and each is analogous to the highest level of all. In imitating transcendent unity, each level of reality is endowed with a ternary structure that departs from unity, unfolds itself in multiplicity, and then by its spiritual conversion returns to unity.

Hellenic Neoplatonism was anti-Christian. Porphyry wrote works against the faith, and Iamblichus was the spiritual mentor of the pagan emperor Julian the Apostate. After the triumph of Christianity in the fourth century, Hellenic Neoplatonists muted their criticisms. Neoplatonic academies existed in Athens and Alexandria into the sixth century.

Christian Neoplatonism, whose leading exponents were Gregory of Nyssa and Augustine, flourished from the fourth century onward. Its origins can be traced back to the second and third centuries A.D. Clement and Origen of Alexandria understood Christian revelation in Platonic terms. Combining the teachings of Origen and Plotinus, Christian Neoplatonists fashioned a distinct Neoplatonism. Culling from philosophy and from the Bible and church doctrine, they erected a Platonic interpretation that lasted through the Christian Middle Ages. Specifically, based on a close reading of the Bible and Plato, their contributions to Neoplatonism's legacy were theological. The Trinitarian doctrines of Marius Victorinus and Augustine are based on Porphyry's interpretation of the unity of substance between the three divine hypostases. Gregory of Nyssa and Synesius of Cyrene employed Plotinian theological language and theory to conceptualize understandings of the nature of God. Trinitarian and mystical theologies of Neoplatonic cast were carried by Boethius and Pseudo-Dionysius into the medieval period. Neoplatonism provided interpretations of God, cosmos, soul, and knowledge that largely framed later Christian self-definitions. *See also* Iamblichus; Philosophy; Plato; Plotinus; Porphyry.   [R.M.B.]

Bibliography

E. Zeller, *Die Philosophie der Griechen* (Leipzig, 1868; repr. Darmstadt: Wissenschaftliche Buchgesellschaft, 1963), Vols. 4–6; C. Bigg, *The Christian Platonists of Alexandria* (Oxford: Oxford UP, 1913); T. Whittaker, *The Neo-Platonists* (Cambridge: Cambridge UP, 1928); E.R. Dodds, "The Parmenides of Plato and the Origin of the Neo-Platonic One," *CQ* 22 (1928):129–142; W. Theiler, *Die Vorbereitung des Neuplatonismus* (Berlin: Weidmann, 1930); A.H. Armstrong, *The Architecture of the Intelligible Universe in the Philosophy of Plotinus* (Cambridge: Cambridge UP, 1940); C.J. DeVogel, "On the Neoplatonic Character of Platonism and the Platonic Character of Neoplatonism," *Mind* 62 (1953):43–64; W.K.C. Guthrie, *A History of Greek Philosophy* (Cambridge: Cambridge UP, 1962–1965), Vols. 1–2; H. Chadwick, *Early Christian Thought and the Classical Tradition* (Oxford: Oxford UP, 1967); A.H. Armstrong, ed., *The Cambridge History of Later Greek and Early Medieval Philosophy* (Cambridge: Cambridge UP, 1967); P. Merlan, *From Platonism to Neoplatonism,* 3rd ed. (The Hague: Nijhoff, 1968); H.J. Krämer, *Der Ursprung der Geistmetaphysik* (Amsterdam: Grüner, 1969); R.T. Wallis, *The Neoplatonists* (London: Duckworth, 1972); E.P. Meijering, *God Being History: Studies in Patristic Philosophy* (Amsterdam, Oxford, and New York: North Holland, 1975); H. Dörrie, M. Altenburger, and U. Schramm, eds., *Gregor von Nyssa und die Philosophie* (Leiden: Brill, 1976); C. Steel, *The Changing Self: A Study on the Soul in Later Neoplatonism: Iamblichus, Damascius and Priscianus* (Brussels: Koninklijke Academie voor Wetenschappen, Letteren en Schone Kunsten van België, 1978); J. Geffcken, *The Last Days of Greco-Roman Paganism* (Amsterdam, New York, and Oxford: North Holland, 1978; orig. German ed., 1920); D.J. O'Meara, ed., *Neoplatonism and Christian Thought* (Albany: SUNY Press, 1982); R.B. Harris, ed., *The Structure of Being: A Neoplatonic Approach* (Albany: SUNY Press, 1982); S. Gersh, *Middle Platonism and Neoplatonism: The Latin Tradition*, 2 vols. (Notre Dame: U of Notre Dame P, 1986).

NEOPYTHAGOREANISM. Revived Pythagorean school of the first century B.C. In 530 B.C., Pythagoras of Samos immigrated to Italy and settled in Croton, where he founded a society that was both a scientific school and a religious community. A conspiracy against this society caused Pythagoras to flee to Metapontum, where he died. Pythagoras discovered the mathematical basis of the basic intervals of Greek music. He and his followers laid the foundations of Greek mathematics and hoped to find in it the key to the understanding of the universe. They regarded the whole universe as a harmonious world-order dependent on arithmetical relations. Pythagoras, influenced by the Orphic cult, taught the doctrine of transmigration. He also took over from the Orphics certain ascetic practices and stressed the need for the soul to be purified from bodily influences. The members of the Pythagorean sect regulated their lives by religious and ethical principles. The Pythagorean philosophy as such apparently disappeared in the course of the fifth century B.C.

In the first century B.C., there occurred a revival of Pythagorean ideas. Some scholars assert that Neopythagoreanism originated in Rome with Publius Nigidius Figulus (d. 45 B.C.), a friend of Cicero; others argue that it originated in Alexandria with Eudorus and Arius Didymus. Another leading exponent of Neopythagoreanism was Moderatus of Gades, who lived in the second half of the first century A.D. and whose writings were very influential. We also have a substantial part of the writings of Nicomachus of Gerasa (fl. ca. A.D. 100).

The most significant Neopythagorean was Apollonius of Tyana (d. ca. A.D. 98). Apollonius was an itinerant teacher, sage, and ascetic, and he had the reputation of a magician. He traversed the Roman empire and even went as far as India. Our main source for his life and teachings is the *Life of Apollonius* written by Flavius Philostratus (ca. 170–249). Later in the third century, the pagan Hierocles, governor of Bithynia, used the life of Apollonius to argue against the originality and divine nature of Christ; his work is known from the refutation written by Eusebius of Caesarea. Numenius of Apamea, who lived in the late second century, was the last major Neopythagorean philosopher, and he has been called a Platonist as well as a Neopythagorean.

The Neopythagoreans borrowed elements from Platonic, Peripatetic (Aristotelian), and Stoic schools and gave the credit for this refurbished philosophy to Pythagoras. Two tendencies can be distinguished within the Neopythagorean system, one toward Stoic monism and the other toward Platonic dualism. A distinctive feature of Neopythagoreanism was its theological speculation. The Neopythagoreans had a refined idea of God and placed him so far above the finite that he could never come into contact with anything corporeal. They also demanded a spiritual worship of God and insisted on purity of life. This could be achieved through abstinence from meat and sex. They also believed in demons and displayed an interest in astral theology and number-mysticism. One should nevertheless remember that within these common beliefs there were many variations. The Neopythagorean disparagement of the material world could have been a source of Gnostic dualism of spirit and matter.

Neopythagoreanism was intellectual and scientific in form and appealed only to an elite group with sound philosophical education. In the third century A.D., Neopythagoreanism merged into Neoplatonism. *See also* Philosophy.   [H.F.S.]

Bibliography

Pseudo-Justin, *Hortatory Address to the Greeks* 4; 19; Irenaeus, *Against Heresy* 2.14; Hippolytus, *Refutation of All Heresies* 1.2; 6.16–24; Tertullian, *On the Soul* 28–35; Origen, *Against Celsus* 1.15; Lactantius, *Divine Institutes* 1.5; 3.18; idem, *Epitome* 36; Eusebius, *Against Hierocles*.

J.E. Raven, *Pythagoreans and Eleatics* (Cambridge: Cambridge UP, 1948); H. Thesleff, *An Introduction to the Pythagorean Writings of the Hellenistic Period* (Abo: Abo Akademi, 1961); C.J. De Vogel, *Pythagoras and Early Pythagoreanism* (Assen: Van Gorcum, 1966); J.A. Philip, *Pythagoras and Early Pythagoreanism* (Toronto: U of Toronto P, 1966); P. Gorman, *Pythagoras: A Life* (London: Routledge and Kegan Paul, 1979).

NEREUS AND ACHILLEUS. Roman martyrs. The Roman soldiers Nereus and Achilleus were beheaded for their faith and buried in the Catacomb of Domitilla. Although dates as early as the first century have been proposed for them, the earliest evidence of their martyrdom is from the fourth century: an inscription authorized by Damasus I and a carving on a column in the cemetery basilica dedicated to them. The later *Passio SS. Nerei, Achillei et sociorum* is legendary. Feast day May 12. CPL 2214.   [E.F.]

Bibliography
H. Achelis, *Acta SS. Nerei et Achillei,* TU (1893), Vol. 11.2.

NERO (A.D. 37–68). Roman emperor (54–68). The last emperor descended from Augustus, Nero was adopted in A.D. 50 by the emperor Claudius at the behest of his mother, Agrippina the Younger, who was both Claudius's wife and niece. He married Octavia, daughter of Claudius, in 53 and came to the throne at the age of sixteen, when his predecessor was poisoned at the order of Agrippina. He conducted the earlier years of his reign under the guidance of the philosopher Seneca, his tutor, and Burrus, the commander of his guard. Administration was efficient and enlightened, and Roman authority was advanced in Armenia and Britain. Yet, in this period, the emperor had Claudius's son Britannicus poisoned (55)—Agrippina was intending to support his claim to rule—and, weary of his mother's intrigues, had her murdered too (59). He divorced Octavia and married a mistress, Poppaea (62); in the same year, Burrus died and Seneca retired.

Nero's last years, under the influence of new advisers, degenerated into a reign of terror and a time of unrestrained self-indulgence. A conspiracy against him failed through hesitation (65) but led to a further round of repression, which brought about the deaths of Seneca and many others. Finally, the armies of Gaul and Spain revolted, his guard deserted, and he committed suicide.

It was to Nero that Paul appealed, exercising his right as a Roman citizen when accused before the governor at Caesarea (Acts 25:1–12), although it is not likely that the emperor tried the case in person. In order to direct blame for the great fire at Rome (64) from himself, Nero fixed upon the Christians as scapegoats and had many executed in cruel and ingenious ways (Tacitus, *Annals* 15.44). This first of the Roman persecutions seems to have taken place mainly in the city itself. There is evidence for the martyrdom of Peter and Paul at Rome around this time (ca. 64–67) in *1 Clement* 5–6, which gives the earliest witness to the persecution. The *Ascension of Isaiah* 4.2–3 depicts Peter as being delivered into the hands of a king (Nero) who had killed his own mother.

A popular belief that Nero would return may be reflected in the person of the second beast in Revelation 13:11–18, where the beast's number is given as 666. Each letter of the Greek and Hebrew alphabets has a numerical value; Nero's name in Hebrew would give the required total.   [M.P.McH.]

Bibliography
Tacitus, *Annals* 13–16; Suetonius, *Life of Nero;* Dio Cassius, *Roman History* 61–63; Eusebius, *Church History* 2.20–3.4.
J. Beaujeu, "L'Incendie de Rome en 64 et les Chrétiens," *Latomus* 19 (1960):65–80, 291–311; J.H. Bishop, *Nero: The Man and the Legend* (London: Robert Hale, 1964); B.H. Warmington, *Nero: Reality and Legend* (New York: Norton, 1970); M. Grant, *Nero: Emperor in Revolt* (New York: American Heritage, 1970); W. Rordorf, "Die neronische Christenverfolgung in Spiegel der apokryphen Paulusakten," *NTS* 27–28 (1982):365–374; M. Griffin, *Nero: The End of a Dynasty* (London: Batsford, 1984, and New Haven: Yale UP, 1985).

NESTORIANISM. Popular but inaccurate name for the Dyophysite church that emerged from the Christological controversies of the fifth century. It subsequently developed as the "Church of the East" (the members' preferred name), centered in Persia and having the eastern dialect of Syriac as its primary language.

The Nestorians take their name from Nestorius, bishop of Constantinople (428–431), who was deposed and exiled for propagating Dyophysite theology to its heretical extreme: teaching that the second person of the Trinity was two persons, the man Jesus who was born, suffered, and died, and the divine Logos, eternal and unbegotten. Nestorius was in fact unjustly accused in this matter. Moreover, the movement that bears his name did not involve him and does not itself deserve the heretical label, although it does represent a Christology that emphasizes the distinction between (as opposed to the unity of) Christ's human and divine natures ("Dyophysites" from the Greek *dyo physeis*, "two natures").

Early Teachers. Nestorianism grew out of the Christology developed at the school of Antioch by Diodore of Tarsus (d. before 394), Theodore of Mopsuestia (ca. 350–428), and Nestorius (ca. 381–451). Later Nestorians referred to these as the "Three Great Lights" of the church. All three followed the Antiochene tradition of historical exegesis rather than the allegorical tradition of the school of Alexandria. Diodore presented Christ in two natures, human and divine. In the womb of Mary, the Logos had fashioned a temple for himself, in which he dwelt. This temple, the man Jesus, was the subject of Christ's human experiences of suffering. The full divinity of the Logos was thus protected from any hint of diminishment. Diodore prepared the way for the work of his student Theodore, who taught two clearly defined natures of Christ: the assumed Man, perfect and complete in his humanity, and the Logos, the Son, true God of true God and consubstantial with the Father, complete and perfect in his divinity. These two natures (*physeis*) were united by God in grace in one person (*prosōpon*). The unity did not produce a "mixture" of the two natures but an equality in which each was left whole and intact. Theodore also stressed the theological significance of history as a progressive enactment of God's purpose and thereby justified theologically the Antiochene exegetical methods.

Diodore and Theodore were considered "orthodox" during their own lifetimes but came under suspicion during the Christological controversies of the fifth century as the two teachers who had sown the seeds for Nestorius's "heresy." Later, the writings of both were condemned, by virtue of their association with the deposed patriarch. The irony of the creed adopted at the Council of Chalcedon (451) was its strongly Dyophysite base, defining Christ as one person "*in* two natures" (rather than the Monophysite "*out of* two natures"). The formula was carried through in the name of Cyril of Alexandria, and the "Nestorian" heresy was condemned, despite Nestorius's propagation of this very position.

Edessa. Another theological center cultivating a Dyophysite Christology was the school of Edessa, which during the fifth century undertook to translate the works of Diodore and Theodore into Syriac. It is largely these translations from the Greek that have survived, because of their significance for the Nestorian church. Theodore, revered as the "Interpreter," exerted the greatest influence on Nestorian doctrine. Nestorius himself was held in high honor—his *Bazaar of Heracleides* was translated into Syriac in the 530s—but the actual impact of his work was less significant.

The school of Edessa had been the major training center of clergy for the whole of the Syrian Orient, including Persia, and had disseminated widely an appreciation for Dyophysite Christology. Following the condemnation of Nestorius at the Council of Ephesus (431), the Antiochenes were increasingly pressured to modify their views, and some began to migrate east to the more sympathetic atmosphere of Edessa. But Edessa itself became entangled in the heightening controversy; many Dyophysites moved on into Persia, and in 489 the school of Edessa was officially expelled by order of the emperor Zeno. It was soon reestablished in Nisibis, where a small school already existed, and soon regained its eminent reputation.

Persia. Many of the exiled Dyophysites were received by the Persian Christians into important ecclesiastical positions. Between the Dyophysite sympathies of its church structure and the impact of the school of Nisibis, the Persian church was by the sixth century largely "Nestorianized." Several factors encouraged this process. Because of its geographical and political isolation, the church in Persia had for the most part developed independently of that in the Greco-Latin realm and had of necessity been largely self-governing. Again, the severing of ties with the west due to persecution in Persia took place just at the inception of the Christological controversies after the Council of Nicaea (325). The Persian church thus had little contact with this dispute and remained uninterested due to the urgent nature of its own problems. When the Nestorians began to move into Persia, they did not carry the stigma of heresy in the eyes of the Persian Christians.

The arrival of the Dyophysites did raise the issue of political loyalties. To receive the Nestorians with honor was to further the identification of the eastern church as nonwestern or non-Roman. For the Persian state, this may have alleviated some of the concern about Christian allegiance to Constantinople; it may also have encouraged the eastern church to develop itself accordingly.

The Dyophysites arrived to find the eastern church already very different from that of the west. We are fortunate in possessing a large collection in Syriac of synodical texts, the *Synodicon Orientale,* first assembled in its present form in the eleventh century and including documents dating back to the earliest development of the Church of the East. From these, we learn, for example, that the Persian Christians conducted their first major synod in 410 at Seleucia. This council was in fact summoned at the behest of the western church by the bishop Marutha of Maipherqat (Martyropolis). It was a time of relative peace between Byzantium and Persia, which allowed the eastern church to collect itself after a long and harsh period of persecution. Fittingly, the synod was concerned with organizational issues. In what was essentially the consecration of an autocephalous ecclesiastical structure, the synod established the bishop of Seleucia-Ctesiphon as "Catholicos and Archbishop of all the Orient," independent of the see of Antioch, and henceforth of equal primacy with the western patriarchates in the eyes of the eastern church. Just as important was the synod's action of offi-

cially recognizing the creed and canons of the Council of Nicaea (325). This was not the first attempt of the church in Persia to define its creed but was rather an action in which an older Persian creed was redefined in light of Nicaea, affirming Nicaea's creed as the measure of orthodoxy for the entire church.

In these circumstances, the Dyophysite movement from the west came to be grafted onto the eastern church in the course of the fifth century, producing the "Nestorian" Church of the East. At the synod of 486, the Church of the East chose to adopt an Antiochene Christology—its first creedal statement after the Council of Chalcedon and one that subsequent synods strengthened. Much later, at the Synod of 585, the Dyophysite position was joined with the canonization of the writings of Theodore of Mopsuestia (defended as early as the irregular Synod of 484) and by the specific anathematization of the "heresy of Eutyches" (i.e., true Monophysitism). Although the Church of the East continued to redefine its Christology, it has never taught a heretical Dyophysitism: two Sons, or two Christs, or two persons (*prosōpa*).

The synod of 486 marked another significant departure for the eastern Syrian church, in the validation of married clergy even at the episcopal rank and even in the instance of widowhood. This stance may have reflected the specific cultural setting of the Persian empire, as celibacy was a practice particularly loathsome to Zoroastrianism. As a minority religion, Christianity remained in an insecure position, dependent always upon the (unreliable) favor of the government. To be less at odds with Zoroastrian society was to keep a lower profile. The synodical documents repeatedly stress their debt to the good will of the Shah-in-Shah.

The ecclesiastical consolidation of the Nestorian church was accompanied by an intellectual flowering, especially through the school of Nisibis. The great hymn writer Narsai took over the leadership of the school in 451, while it was still in Edessa. He preceded the school's official exile, arriving in Nisibis perhaps as early as 471, and did much to prepare for the impending institutional transplant. He remained a leader of the school until his death (ca. 503). Narsai's writings offered a creative response, especially to those of the Monophysites Severus of Antioch and Jacob of Sarug.

Eventually, Narsai came into conflict with Barsauma, the bishop of Nisibis. Barsauma had been a student at the school of Edessa contemporaneously with the future Monophysite leader Philoxenus of Mabbug, and perhaps also with Jacob of Sarug. He was consecrated to the see of Nisibis ca. 435. A passionate leader, Barsauma evoked controversy throughout his episcopal career. He introduced legislation on clerical marriage—he himself married a former nun—and led an internal revolt against the Catholicos Babowai during the 480s. Barsauma seems to have conducted a disciplinary campaign on behalf of the Dyophysite stance, which later Monophysite sources have portrayed as a persecution. Although that exaggerates the severity of the action, there was a growing anti-Dyophysite presence in the Persian church. Those places that resisted Barsauma's authority later emerged as centers for the eastern Monophysite church.

There was thus by the end of the fifth century a nascent community that opposed the sharpening Dyophysite identity of the Church of the East. It formed a receptive base for the Monophysites who began to cross into Persia when the Byzantine persecutions against them commenced in 519. These persecutions were directed against the monasteries and clergy, and it was hence the monasteries in Persia that were quickly turned to Monophysite support. The sixth century witnessed a volatile situation for the Christians in Persia, with Dyophysites and Monophysites in open conflict and considerable movement across factional lines. The Monophysite historian John of Ephesus (*Lives* 10) portrays at least some of this rivalry being played out in the Sassanian court, where both sides vied for respectability. The *Synodicon Orientale* shows the Dyophysite synods of 554, 585, 596, and 605 all recording theological statements against Monophysite positions and showing much alarm. By the turn of the seventh century, there were two churches in the Persian domain, each with its own ecclesiastical structure.

Characteristics. The Church of the East began as a Christian community separate from the Christian empire; it became "Nestorian" in circumstances that added theological weight to a political situation. At no time in its history has the Church of the East been able to identify itself with a political authority. Not only has it always been a minority religion, but it has been so in a context containing "other" Christian churches. Consequently, it has had to define itself from within its own body rather than through geographical or political boundaries. It may be this lack of political identification that enabled the Church of the East to undertake an early missionary effort unparalleled for centuries thereafter. We find its traces in India, Soghdiana, Turkestan, Turfan, Manchuria, Siberia, and above all, between the sixth and ninth centuries, in a particular flowering in China. But in the Middle East, India, and North America, the Church of the East continues, a living tradition still. *See also* Christ, Christology; Edessa; Monophysitism; Narsai; Nestorius; Nisibis; Persia.   [S.A.H.]

Bibliography

Synodicon Orientale ou Recueil de Synodes Nestoriens, ed. and tr. J.-B. Chabot (Paris: Imprimerie Nationale, Librairie C. Klincksieck, 1902); L. Abramowski and A.E. Goodman, *A Nestorian Collection of Christological Texts* (Cambridge: Cambridge UP, 1972).

W.A. Wigram, *An Introduction to the History of the Assyrian Church: or the Church of the Sassanid Persian Empire 100–640 AD* (London: SPCK, 1910); R. Abramowski, "Der theologische Nachlass des Diodor von Tarsus," *ZNTW* 30 (1931):234–262; R.A. Norris, *Manhood and Christ: A Study in the Christology of Theodore of Mopsuestia* (Oxford: Clarendon, 1963); A. Vööbus, *History of the School of Nisibis,* CSCO (1965), Vol. 266, Subs. 26; R.A. Greer, "The Antiochene Christology of Diodore of Tarsus," *JThS* n.s.17 (1966):327–341; J.M. Fiey, *Jalons pour une histoire de l'église en Iraq,* CSCO (1970), Vol. 310, Subs. 36; S. Gero, *Barsauma of Nisibis and Persian Christianity in the Fifth Century,* CSCO (1981), Vol. 426, Subs. 63; S.P. Brock, "The Christology of the Church of the East in the Synods of the Fifth to Early Seventh Centuries: Preliminary Considerations and Materials," *Aksum-Thyateira: A Festschrift for Archbishop Methodius of Thyateira and Great Britain* (Athens, 1985), pp. 125–142.

NESTORIUS (ca. 381–451). Theologian and preacher. Nestorius trained at the school of Antioch and was consecrated bishop of Constantinople in 428. He perpetrated harsh persecutions against heretics and within a year of gaining office had provoked a major controversy, in part for his theology and in part for arousing jealousy among his colleagues.

Nestorius's greatest adversary was Cyril, bishop of Alexandria (412–444). Himself a profound theologian, Cyril was a product of the Alexandrian school. To some extent, the rivalry between these men played out the tensions between the two schools: the Antiochene with its emphasis on historical exegesis, and the Alexandrian with its allegorical tradition. But Cyril was also driven by his own ambitions—the desire to assert Alexandria's primacy over the other eastern sees and the submission of Constantinople to his authority.

Nestorius was accused of teaching that the historical Jesus had been a "mere man." He took offense at the title *Theotokos*—literally "God-bearer" or "mother of God"—used in reference to the Virgin Mary and especially championed by Cyril. For Nestorius, this was an impious title. He saw the title *Anthropotokos,* "Man-bearer," as more accurate but promulgated *Christotokos,* "Christ-bearer," as the most appropriate. The *Theotokos* controversy became a violent issue for the church at every level, popular, hierarchical, papal, and imperial. As the historian Socrates admitted (*H.E.* 7), the conflict was unjustly exaggerated: Nestorius overreacted to the title's implications, and Cyril misrepresented Nestorius's position.

Nestorius was deposed by the Council of Ephesus (431); in 435, Theodosius II ordered his writings burned. The Council of Chalcedon convened (451) to settle the Christological question. Ironically, the council's final definition of Christ as "one person in two natures" was seen by Nestorius as vindicating his own teachings, an interpretation shared by his Monophysite opponents. In fact, Nestorius condemned the heresy falsely attributed to him—the extreme view that the human Jesus and divine Christ were two different persons—and the separation of the Dyophysite Christians into their own church (the "Nestorian" Church of the East) did not involve him. For Nestorius himself, salvation required that both the human and divine natures of Christ be complete, to guarantee the integrity of the incarnation and to protect the divine Logos from the blasphemous assertion that God could suffer pain or weakness. Instead, Nestorius asserted that Jesus Christ was one Lord, indivisible in his person (*prosōpon*), but containing two natures (*ousiai*), the divine and the human. Thus, the union and the separation exist in two distinct spheres of existence, just as in the Trinity there is one nature (*ousia*) in three persons (*prosōpa*).

Nestorius lived the last twenty years of his life in exile, enduring much suffering. During this time, he wrote the book preserved in Syriac under the (mistranslated) title *Bazaar of Heracleides*, his own version of his life. He did not understate the personal animosity between himself and Cyril or the bitterness of his trials. But in the *Bazaar*, Nestorius ultimately presents himself as a man of true humility, seeking that God's truth should prevail whatever his own fate. CPG III, 5665–5766. *See also* Christ, Christology; Cyril of Alexandria; Nestorianism; Theotokos.   [S.A.H.]

Bibliography

Socrates, *Church History* 7.

Nestoriana: Die Fragmente des Nestorius, ed. and tr. F. Loofs (Halle: Niemeyer, 1905); *Le Livre d'Héraclide de Damas,* ed. and tr. F. Nau (Paris: Letouzey et Ané, 1910); *Nestorius: The Bazaar of Heracleides,* ed. and tr. G.R. Driver and L. Hodgson (Oxford: Oxford UP, 1925).

J.F. Bethune-Baker, *Nestorius and His Teaching* (Cambridge: Cambridge UP, 1908); F. Loofs, *Nestorius and His Place in the History of Christian Doctrine* (Cambridge: Cambridge UP, 1914); M.V. Anastos, "Nestorius Was Orthodox," *DOP* 16 (1962):119–140; R.A. Greer, "The Image of God and the Prosopic Union in Nestorius' *Bazaar of Heracleides,*" *Lux in Lumine: Essays in Honor of W.N. Pittenger,* ed. R.A. Norris (New York: Seabury, 1966), pp. 46–61; H.E.W. Turner, "Nestorius Reconsidered," *SP* 13 (1975):306–321; R.C. Chesnut, "The Two Prosopa in Nestorius' *Bazaar of Heraclides,*" *JThS* n.s. 29 (1978):392–409.

NICAEA, COUNCIL OF; NICENE CREED.
First Ecumenical Council and its confession of faith (325).

Seats for the presbyters in the apse of the Church of Hagia Sophia (Holy Wisdom) in Nicaea (Iznik, Turkey), established in the fourth century and site of the Seventh Ecumenical Council in 787.

Occasion. Immediately after his victory in 324 over Licinius, the emperor of the east, Constantine the Great discovered the Christological disputes that had broken out well before 318 in Alexandria and had spread throughout the whole east. Some found the oneness of God threatened by a fully divine Son; others did not. Some suggested a kind of salvation in which the Son's moral progress provided the example; others emphasized the Son's full divinity as necessary for salvation.

Constantine sent his theological adviser, bishop Hosius of Cordova, to Alexandria to restore peace among the parties. Hosius must have recognized that his mission was unsuccessful. On his return trip, he presided over a council in Antioch, which, although convened originally to elect a bishop, provisionally condemned three other bishops, among them Eusebius of Caesarea, the church historian, because of their false teachings. The final judgment would be left to a great synod, one planned for the winter of 324/5 in Ancyra. (The report about the council of Antioch and the

invitation to Ancyra, extant only in Syriac, appears to be genuine.) Constantine, however, changed his mind and invited the bishops to Nicaea, a city near the imperial residence at Nicomedia that possessed a royal palace with a sufficiently large assembly hall. He made this decision despite his previous failure to settle the Donatist dispute through conciliar politics (primarily the Council of Arles in 314).

Proceedings. At Nicaea, philosophers and theologians, not only those of episcopal rank, apparently discussed the essence of Christ and his relationship to the Father. A welcoming speech by the emperor opened the gathering. The friends of Arius (who taught that the Son's divinity was not equal to that of the Father), above all Eusebius of Nicomedia, laid before the assembly a confession of faith in which the Son of God was completely subordinated to the Father and was designated as of a different nature. When the majority angrily rejected this text, Eusebius of Caesarea—as he himself says in a letter to his home church—offered the baptismal confession of that congregation, to which he appears to have added an emphasis on the individual personality of the Father, Son, and Spirit. But the majority accused him of false teaching, and Eusebius attempted to justify himself. His defense received the full approval of the emperor, who was not yet baptized and held beliefs quite similar to those of Eusebius.

The council was called on to accept this confession of faith, although, according to Eusebius, Constantine did desire the insertion of the word *homoousios* ("of the same nature" or "same essence"). He must have known that this word was controversial. He gave it, as Eusebius reports, a philosophical explanation: no one should use it to attach corporeality to divine essence. In constructing its creed, however, the council evidently neither inserted *homoousios* into the creed from Caesarea nor formulated a completely new confession of faith. Instead, it adopted a text related to the confession of Jerusalem—as later attested in Cyril of Jerusalem's *Catechetical Orations*—to which it then added condemnations of the Arian teaching. Only two bishops refused to sign the council's documents; they were removed and sent into exile by the emperor. Eusebius of Nicomedia withdrew his signature and met the same fate. Eusebius of Caesarea, with many others, gave the confession a false interpretation, as if it only referred to Christ's existing in some manner before his earthly life. They did not at any time disavow Arius.

The council then took up the calculation of Easter (to fall on the first Sunday after the first full spring moon), the Melitian schism in Egypt (*Letter to the Church in Alexandria*), and a list of questions concerning ecclesiastical law (twenty canons). The sixth canon, which referred to the geographically uncircumscribed preeminence of the bishop of Rome, guaranteed the jurisdiction of the bishop of Alexandria over Egypt, Libya, and the Pentapolis. In the same way, the traditional preeminence of Antioch and that of bishops in other provinces was recognized as valid. Canon 7 ensured an honored place to the bishop of Aelia (Jerusalem), although he still remained under the metropolitan of Caesarea in Palestine. All these decisions deeply affected ecclesiastical politics.

A Roman-Alexandrian axis was developing that would feel threatened by Antioch and Constantinople.

Meaning of the Creed. A full understanding of this council's confession of faith, the Nicene Creed, depends not only on the parts that derive from traditional confessions—like that of Jerusalem or Caesarea—but also on those parts that are not found in the text that was finally adopted. Even if the Caesarean Creed was not the foundational document, and thus expressions were not struck out of its text to form the Nicene Creed, some of its contents still would have appeared to be inappropriate to the participants. Its reference to Christ as the "firstborn of all creation" (Col. 1:15), which stands in the first part of its second article, concerns his preexistence, his relationship to the Father. It must have shocked the bishops, because it already placed the preexistent one within the creation, an act that appears to jeopardize his infinity. Similarly important was its designation of the procreation of the Son as "before all ages," a phrase absent in the Nicene Creed that reappears in the Niceno-Constantinopolitan Creed. It is also significant that in the Nicene Creed, as in the Caesarean Creed, Christ was not called first of all "the Logos of God" but rather "Son of God." Such phrases would not have aided the framers of the Nicene Creed in their battle with Arianism.

The text of the Nicene Creed betrays not only a certain editorial clumsiness—the expression "true God from true God" doubling the preceding "God from God"—but also a polemical purpose. It does not follow strictly in the line of positively formulated baptismal confessions. It inserts both the negative statement "not created" and also the explanation "that is, out of the essence of the Father," thus excluding the thought that the Son originated, like all other things, by the will of the Father—that he was created. The most important addition, however, is naturally "of one nature with the Father." Yet behind that terminology lies neither a speculation about the "essence" or "nature" (*ousia*) of the triune God nor careless words about the special relationship between the Father and Son in the Godhead. The expression probably was chosen because it had the same meaning for the Latins—not only for Hosius but also for Constantine himself—as the "one substance" in the language of Tertullian. The immediate reason, however, was Arius's refusal of the word. Thus, its meaning is in the first instance negative; within the body of the confession, it excludes Arianism, as later the anathemas more clearly and fully do. Arius refused inner-divine procreation as incompatible with the pure spiritual nature of God and had already rejected the word *homoousios*. He wanted to recognize the Father's place as Creator as the only correct mode of relationship of the Father-God to others, including the Son. Therefore in this context—and on the basis of Constantine's explanation—the phrase "of one nature with the Father" certainly means nothing other than this: a genuine Father-Son relationship, a real procreation in God, and God's pure spiritual nature must be held firm. The additional condemnations concern three statements of Arius: (1) "There was when he [the Son of God] was not"; (2) "Before he was made, he was not"; and (3) "He originated out of nothing." Those who wanted to trace the Son of God back to a different *hypostasis* or *ousia* were condemned. Whether talk of direct closeness or of the "nothingness" formed the context, any expressions were refused that grounded the existence of the Son in some previously existing matter. The background is thus more truly that of a cosmogony than that of another matter. Characterizing the Son as not "made or changeable or variable" excludes not only the Arian statement about his origin, but also the divine Son's morally exemplary and servantlike progress toward "divine" being. These anathemas became superfluous not only because the Arian danger abated, but also because the meaning of the term *homoousios* was developed (and expanded to the Spirit) through the teaching by the Cappadocians of the "Three Hypostases," that is, a doctrine of God that emphasizes one nature and three persons within the Trinity. *See also* Arianism; Creeds; Homoousios. [H.J.V.]

Bibliography

Mansi 2. 635–1082; I. Ortiz de Urbina, *Nicée et Constantinople* (Paris: Editions de l'Orante, 1963); G.L Dossetti, *Il simbolo di Nicea e di Costantinopli, ed. critica* (Rome: Herder, 1967).

D.L. Holland, "Die Synode von Antiochien (324/325) und ihre Bedeutung für Eusebius von Casarea und das Konzil von Nizäa," *ZKG* 81 (1970):163–181; J.N.D. Kelly, *Early Christian Creeds*, 3rd ed. (London: Longmans, 1972), pp. 205–262; M. Simonetti, *La crisi ariana nel IV secolo* (Rome: Institutum Patristicum Augustinianum, 1975); H.-J. Sieben, *Die Konzilsidee der Alten Kirche* (Paderborn: Ferdinand Schoningh, 1979); J. St. O'Leary, "Has the Nicene Creed Become Inaccessible?," *ITQ* 48 (1981):240–255; J.N.D. Kelly, "The Nicene Creed: A Turning Point," *Scottish Journal of Theology* 36 (1983):23–39; A. de Halleux, "La Réception du Symbole Oecuménique, de Nicée à Chalcédoine," *Ephemerides Theologicae Lovanienses* 61 (1985):1–47.

NICETA OF REMESIANA (d. ca. 414).

Bishop (370–ca.414). Remesiana, the present Bela Palanka in Yugoslavia, stood on the border between east and west, with contacts in both directions. Although Niceta's works were transmitted under the names of other men, he has in this century been credited with the *Explanation of the Creed*. An excellent source for the history of the Apostles' Creed, it uses significant technical phrases, such as *communio sanctorum* ("community of the holy"). He wrote treatises against Arians and Pneumatomachians, as well as pieces that deal with liturgical issues. He may have been the author of the *Te Deum Laudamus*. Feast day June 22. CPL 646–652. [F.W.N.]

Bibliography

Paulinus of Nola, *Poems* 17; 27; idem, *Letter* 29.16; Gennadius, *Lives of Illustrious Men* 22.

A.E. Burn, *Nicetas of Remesiana: His Life and Work* (Cambridge: Cambridge UP, 1905); C. Turner, "Niceta of Remesiana II. Introduction and Text of *De psalmodiae bono*," *JThS* 24 (1922–1923): 225–250.

"Writings of Niceta of Remesiana," tr. G.G. Walsh, FOTC (1949), Vol. 7, pp. 1–76.

NICHOLAS, ST. (fourth century). Bishop of

Myra in Lycia. Although Nicholas was one of the most popular saints in both east and west, there exists no historically trustworthy evidence concerning his life. According to tradition, he was imprisoned for his faith in the persecution under Diocletian (303–311). He is also reputed to have attended the Council of Nicaea (325), where he condemned Arianism, but the authenticity of this account is doubted. On May 9, 1087, the inhabitants of Bari, Italy, obtained possession of his relics. Legends associated with Nicholas caused him to be venerated as the patron saint of various groups, especially of sailors and children. His gifts to the latter were the basis of his later association (as Santa Claus) with Christmas. Feast day December 6.

[H.F.S.]

Bibliography

E. Crozier, *The Life and Legends of Saint Nicholas, the Patron Saint of Children* (London: Duckworth, 1949); A.D. De Groot, *Saint Nicholas: A Psychoanalytic Study of His History and Myth* (New York: Basic Books, 1965); C.W. Jones, *Saint Nicholas of Myra, Bari and Manhattan* (Chicago: U of Chicago P, 1978).

NICOLAITANS.

Early Christian sect. Revelation 2:6 and 15 mention the Nicolaitans; Acts 6:5 speaks of a deacon in Jerusalem, Nicolaus of Antioch. Various early Christian writers describe the sect as marked by eating meat offered to idols and practicing sexual immorality, particularly fornication and adultery.

Irenaeus (*Haer.* 1.26; 3.11), Hippolytus (*Haer.* 7.36), and Epiphanius (*Haer.* 25) make the Nicolaus of Acts responsible for the original errors. Clement of Alexandria (*Str.* 2.20; 3.24), Eusebius (*H.E.* 3.29), and Theodoret (*Haer. fab.* 3.1), however, describe Nicolaus as an ascetic who gave his wife to another in marriage and had no sexual relations with any others. They depict his daughters as virgins and his son as uncorrupted. [F.W.N.]

NILUS OF ANCYRA

(d. ca. 430). Disciple of John Chrysostom and founder of monastery near Ancyra. Nilus wrote ascetic and moral tracts and some biblical comments. His letters provide information concerning the survival of paganism. CPG III, 6043–6084. [F.W.N.]

Bibliography
PG 79.

NINIAN

(ca. 360–ca. 432). Evangelist to Scotland. Ninian (or Nynia) is known only from a reference in Bede's *Ecclesiastical History of the English People* 3.4.1, written in 731. Bede says that Ninian was a British bishop who evangelized among the southern Picts, a people that occupied what is now Scotland. He built a stone church in Whithorn, called Candida Casa ("white house") because of its color, and he dedicated it to Martin of Tours. An earlier generation of scholars saw in Ninian the "apostle of the Picts," indeed the apostle to most of Scotland, but scholars today see him working in a more limited geographical area of southwestern Scotland. An anonymous eighth-century poem about him provides no biographical evidence. Feast day September 16. [J.F.K.]

Bibliography

N. Chadwick, "St. Ninian: A Preliminary Study of Sources," *Transactions of the Dumfriesshire and Galloway Natural History and Antiquarian Society* 27 (1950):9–53.

NINO

(fl. ca. 330). Missionary to Georgia. Information about Nino, the "apostle of Georgia," is preserved by Rufinus in his *Historia ecclesiastica*, where he claims the story was related to him in Jerusalem by a Georgian priest named Bakur. Rufinus's account, set down ca. 395, was heavily embellished in later centuries.

It was through Nino that Georgia was converted to Christianity. In Rufinus's account, she was a Cappadocian slave, whose miraculous healing abilities came to the attention of the queen (Nana) of Georgia, who was gravely ill. Nino healed her by placing a hair cloak on her and calling on Christ's name. In addition, by calling on Christ, the king (Mirian) was delivered from engulfment in pitch-black darkness (an eclipse?) while hunting. Following his conversion, the king, at Nino's admonition, built a church at Mtskheta, a few miles from modern-day Tbilisi, an event itself attended by a great miracle. An embassy was sent to Constantine the Great soliciting priests to come to Georgia to teach.

Like Gregory the Illuminator in Armenia three decades earlier, Nino oriented Georgia away from Zoroastrian Iran (and later Islam) and toward orthodox Christianity. Georgian historical writing is connected with the recording of the lives of early saints; the earliest chronicle, the *Conversion of Iberia,* composed in the seventh century, centers on Nino.

Nino died a natural death and was buried at Bodbe in Kakheti province. Feast day January 14. *See also* Georgia.   [C.C.]

Bibliography
Rufinus, *Historia ecclesiastica* 10.11.
D.M. Lang, *Lives and Legends of the Georgian Saints* (New York: Macmillan, 1956).

NISIBIS. Commercial city in northeastern Mesopotamia (modern Nusaybin). Long home to a significant Jewish population, after ca. 300 Nisibis also became an important Christian center. Its famous Nestorian theological school, devoted especially to the works of Theodore of Mopsuestia, dominated the Persian church in the fifth and sixth centuries. *See also* Barsauma; Narsai; Nestorianism; Persia.   [R.J.O.]

NOAH. In the Old Testament, builder of the ark, survivor of the flood, and ancestor of the whole human race. Genesis describes Noah as a man "righteous in his generation" (Gen. 5:29–9:28). He was remembered as an eminently righteous man (Ezek. 14:14, 20; cf. Sirach 44:17; and Wisd. Sol. 10:4).

The Gospel of Luke includes Noah in the genealogy of Jesus (Luke 3:36); his days illustrated the carelessness of the human race (Matt. 24:38; Luke 17:26). To the writer of the Epistle to the Hebrews, Noah was a man of faith (Heb. 11:7); in the Epistles of Peter, Noah was a preacher of righteousness, and the flood was a type of baptism (1 Peter 3:20f.; 2 Peter 2:5).

Second-century writers developed these motifs. Noah became an example of obedience who preached repentance to his generation (*1 Clem.* 9.1, 4; cf. Theophilus, *Autol.* 3.19). Marcion, on the other hand, denied that Noah and the other patriarchs were righteous (Irenaeus, *Haer.* 1.27.3). In spite of major differences in the two stories, the Christian apologists claimed that Noah was the same as the

Greek flood hero Deucalion (Justin, *2 Apol.* 7.2; cf. Theophilus, *Autol.* 3.19). Irenaeus gives a survey of the flood episode (*Dem.* 19–22).

In the church, Noah became a type of Christ (Justin, *Dial.* 138). This typology developed out of the Greek words describing Noah, translated "end," "beginning," "righteous," and "rest." (He was the end of one race and the beginning of another.) Noah's drunkenness became a classic example of the evils of inebriation, but by the time of Cyprian (*Ep.* 63.6) his nakedness became a type of the passion of Jesus.

Noah and his ark, which was depicted as a box, became a favorite motif in catacomb paintings and on sarcophagi as an example of deliverance. Third-century coins from Apamea in Phrygia also show Noah and the ark. [J.P.L.]

Bibliography
J. Hooyman, "Die Noe–Darstellung in der frühchristlichen Kunst," *VChr* 12 (1958):113–136; J.P. Lewis, *A Study of the Interpretation of Noah and the Flood in Jewish and Christian Literature* (Leiden: Brill, 1968); J.A. Maritz "Noah's Ark and the Animals of Early Christian Art," *Akroterion* 28 (1983):102–108; J.P. Lewis, "Noah and the Flood in Jewish, Christian and Muslim Tradition," *Biblical Archaeology* 47 (1984):175–176.

NOETUS (fl. ca. 200). Adherent of Modalism. A native of Asia Minor, probably of Smyrna, Noetus taught Modalism—a form of Monarchianism—and its corollary, Patripassianism, that is, the belief that God the Father was born in the incarnation, and suffered and died. Interpreting the prologue of the Gospel of John (1:1–18) as allegory, Noetus rejected the orthodox doctrine of the Logos. He was excommunicated by a synod of presbyters (ca. 200).

[M.P.McH.]

Bibliography
Hippolytus, *Refutation of All Heresies* 9.2.7–10; 10.27; idem, *Homily on the Heresy of Noetus;* Epiphanius, *Panarion* 57; Theodoret, *Haereticarum fabularum compendium* 3.3.

NONNUS OF PANOPOLIS (b. ca. 400). Poet. Nonnus was born in Upper Egypt. Two poems under his name are known. The *Dionysiaca* recounts in forty-eight books the legend of

Dionysus and is wholly pagan in content. The *Paraphrasis in Iohannem* paraphrases John's Gospel in hexameters. CPG III, 5641–5642.

[E.F.]

Bibliography
Dionysiaca, tr. W.H.D. Rouse, 3 vols., LCL (1940).

NOVATIAN (mid-third century). Presbyter and then counter-bishop in Rome. Novatian was ordained to the office of presbyter by bishop Fabian (ca. 249) without having had to rise through the clerical ranks. He appears to have been baptized in the midst of a difficult illness (Eusebius, *H.E.* 4.43.13). His reputation was ensured by his *On the Trinity*, a piece unequaled theologically in the west before 350; his letters in the Cyprian corpus, nos. 30 and 36, also surpass the rest of Roman correspondence and not merely stylistically. His opponents Cornelius, bishop of Rome, and Cyprian, bishop of Carthage (*Ep.* 55.24), and the unknown author of *Against Novatian* hold him in high esteem. During the vacancy of the Roman see following the martyrdom of Fabian in the spring of 250, Novatian quickly took over the leadership of the clergy and intensified the penitential discipline (Cyprian, *Ep.* 8; 30.8).

Because the moderate Cornelius eventually was elected bishop of Rome, Novatian believed the holiness of the church was in danger through permitting apostates to return to communion and allowed himself to be ordained by three Italian bishops. He attracted a few bishops to his side, and installed rival bishops in some sees.

Novatian's *On the Trinity* never uses the word *trinitas* and never names the Holy Spirit "God" or "person." Only the baptismal formula and rational inferences required that one speak of the Spirit. Novatian's composition is mainly a discussion of Christ's divinity and the unity (not identity) of the Father and the Son (*Trin.* 9–28); salvation is not understood as atonement for sins. Because the Son of God has become man, he can lead humankind to eternal salvation. Here, faith and ethics appear to be intertwined. Novatian's *On Jewish Meats*, written before the Decian persecution, depicts the unclean foods of the Old Testament allegorically as vices. *On Public Shows* opposes Christians who would attempt to make the Christian and Roman cultures compatible. *On the Advantages of Chastity*, written after Novatian's consecration as bishop, calls the members of the "virgin church" to remain pure as the dwelling place of the Holy Spirit. CPL 68–76.

[H.J.V.]

Bibliography
H. Weyer, *Novatianus. De Trinitate. Über den dreieinigen Gott. Text, Übersetzung, Einleitung, Kommentar* (Darmstadt: Wissenschaftliche Buchgesellschaft, 1962); *Novatianus, Opera quae supersunt*, ed. G.F. Diercks, CCSL (1972), Vol. 4.

R.J. De Simone, *The Treatise of Novatian the Roman Presbyter on the Trinity* (Rome: Institutum Patristicum Augustinianum, 1970); *The Trinity, The Spectacle, Jewish Foods, In Praise of Purity, Letters*, tr. R.J. DeSimone, FOTC (1974), Vol. 67.

H.J. Vogt, *Coetus Sanctorum: Der Kirchenbegriff des Novatian und die Geschichte seiner Sonderkirche* (Bonn: Hanstein, 1968); H. Gülzow, *Cyprian und Novatian: Der Briefwechsel zwischen den Gemeinden Rom und Kartago zur Zeit der Verfolgung des Kaisers Decius* (Tübingen: Mohr, 1975); R. Kydd, "Novatian's De Trinitate 29: Evidence of the Charismatic?," *Scottish Journal of Theology* 30 (1977):313–318; G. Pelland, "Un Passage difficile de Novatien sur I Cor. 15:17–28," *Gregorianum* 66 (1985):25–52.

NUBIA. Territory occupied for some 900 years (550–1450) by the three Christian kingdoms of Nobatia, Makurrah, and Alwah, extending down the Nile Valley from Aswan to beyond Soba toward the Ethiopian frontier.

Literary sources, particularly the Monophysite writer John of Ephesus (ca. 507–589), have left vivid descriptions of the successful mission to the Nobatian court in 542, under the patronage of the empress Theodora, that resulted in the conversion of the most important of the three kingdoms to Monophysite Christianity. The writer of the *History of the Patriarchs*, Severus el-Ashmunein, included brief accounts of the unification of the three kingdoms under king Mercurius of Nobatia (ca. 710) and also of Nubia's relations with the Muslim caliphate at Baghdad and emirate at Cairo, as well as with the Coptic patriarchate.

It was not, however, until the early twentieth century that archaeology disclosed the full extent and variety of the Nubian Christian heritage. Cut off from the rest of the Byzantine world by Islamic kingdoms, Christian Nubia survived for some 900 years, during which time, especially in the ninth and tenth centuries, it achieved remarkable wealth and splendor.

The years leading into the building of the high dam at Aswan in 1965 witnessed further surveys and excavations, particularly at Faras, noted for its frescoes, and at Q'asr Ibrim, renowned for its new documentary finds, all undertaken on an international scale. Polish and West German teams continue to work on sites below the second cataract, and British teams at Q'asr Ibrim. *See also* Ethiopia.

[W.H.C.F.]

Bibliography

Severus el-Ashmunein, *History of the Patriarchate of Alexandria*, ed. and tr. B.T.A. Evetts, PO (1907; 1910), Vols. 1 and 5; John of Ephesus, *Historiae ecclesiasticae*, ed. with a Latin tr. E.W. Brooks, CSCO, Scriptores Syrii (1935–1936), Vol. 3.3; *Oriental Sources Concerning Nubia*, ed. G. Vantini (Heidelberg: Heidelberger Akademie der Wissenschaften, and Warsaw: Polish Academy of Sciences, 1975).

K. Michalowski, *Faras, die Kathedrale aus dem Wüstensand* (Zurich: Benzinger, 1967); E.R. Dinkler, ed. *Kunst und Geschichte Nubiens in Christlicher Zeit* (Recklinghausen: Bongers, 1970); J. Jakobielski, *A History of the Bishopric of Pachoras on the Basis of Coptic Inscriptions* (Warsaw: Editions Scientifique de Pologne, 1972); W.Y. Adams, *Nubia, A Corridor to Africa* (London: Allen Lane, 1977); P.L. Shinnie, "Christian Nubia," *Cambridge History of Africa*, ed. J.D. Fage (Cambridge: Cambridge UP, 1978), Vol. 2, Chap. 9; W.H.C. Frend, "The Exploration of Christian Nubia: Retrospect and Prospect," *Proceedings of the Patristic, Medieval, and Renaissance Conference* (Villanova: Augustinian Historical Institute, Villanova U, 1985), Vol. 6, pp. 51–74.

NUMENIUS (late second century). Neopythagorean philosopher from Apamea in Syria. Numenius may be described as a "Platonizing Pythagorean." He anticipated Plotinus's three ultimate principles or three gods. For Numenius, they were the Absolute Good (the Pythagorean Monad), the Demiurge (or Intelligence), and the Sensible Universe (or World Soul). He knew the works of Moses and described Plato as "Moses speaking Attic Greek" (Clement of Alexandria, *Str.* 1.22). He influenced, besides Plotinus and Porphyry, the Christians Origen, Eusebius of Caesarea, and Nemesius of Emesa. TLG 1542. *See also* Neopythagoreanism.

[E.F.]

Bibliography

Eusebius, *Preparation for the Gospel* 9.7–8; idem, *Church History* 6.19.8; Nemesius, *On the Nature of Man* 2.

E. Des Places, *Numénius Fragments* (Paris: Les Belles Lettres, 1973).

P. Merlan in *Cambridge History of Later Greek and Early Medieval Philosophy*, ed. A.H. Armstrong (Cambridge: Cambridge UP, 1967), pp. 96–106.

NUMISMATICS. The study of coins. Ancient coins provide a wealth of information about the civilizations that minted them, although this wealth is often untapped by modern historians of early Christianity. Greek, Roman, Jewish, and Christian coins illumine such areas as international, national, regional, and urban political history, ancient chronology, religion and mythology, civic and cultic monuments, fiscal reforms and policies, military history, and iconography.

Several characteristics make ancient coinage important. Coins usually provide more contemporary evidence than does literature. Since their legends and imagery were usually altered to respond to current events, government programs, and other immediate concerns, coins functioned much like commemorative stamps. Like modern urban billboards, they reflected the contemporary ethos. The smaller denominations were more widely disseminated among the common people in diverse regions than either literature or large monuments could be. Coinage was a preeminently versatile medium for political and religious propaganda, especially among the Romans.

The corpus of ancient Jewish coinage is relatively small and aesthetically inferior to contemporary Greek and Roman mintage. It is quite valuable, nonetheless, for interpreting Jewish political history as well as possible Jewish assimilation of pagan symbols.

Cities and federations of the Greek east were usually allowed to continue minting coins under Roman supervision. These imperial Greek coins are extremely helpful in understanding both the urban context of Christian history in the east and local circumstances.

Official Roman coins from the late republic and empire are replete with references to historical events and with visual imagery relevant to the study of early Christianity—for example, the destruction of Jerusalem; the veneration and cult of the emperor; belief in nativity stars and astrology; gestures, rites, and myths of numerous religions that competed with Christianity; and iconography portraying Roman aspirations.

Starting with Constantine, both pagan and Christian emblems and terminology began to appear on the official coinage of the Christian empire, typically continuing the propagandistic use of coins that was so successful in earlier periods. *See also* Iconography.   [R.O.]

Bibliography
J. Maurice, *Numismatique constantinienne*, 3 vols. (Paris: Leroux, 1908–1912); C.H.V. Sutherland et al., *Roman Imperial Coinage* (London: Spink, 1967–1981), Vols. 6–9.

O

OAK, SYNOD OF THE. Church council held in 403 near Chalcedon. Theophilus, bishop of Alexandria, had accused John Chrysostom, bishop of Constantinople, of misconduct regarding the Tall Brothers. The synod, composed of thirty-six to forty-five bishops mostly from Egypt, deposed Chrysostom on false charges. The emperor, Arcadius, sent him into exile in Bithynia, but popular outcry and an earthquake led to his reinstatement in a matter of days. *See also* John Chrysostom; Tall Brothers.

[F.W.N.]

ODES OF SOLOMON. Earliest Christian hymnbook (late first–early third century). The *Odes of Solomon* consists of forty-two odes preserved in Syriac (the second ode is missing). The ascription to Solomon is unexplained, for nothing in the contents, overt or implicit, makes one think of Solomon. Although a Greek original has been advocated (*Ode* 11 exists in Greek in Papyrus Bodmer XI, third century), the majority of scholars hold to a Syriac original. Some of the ambiguity perhaps arises from the author having been bilingual. Dates from the late first to the early third century have been proposed, but most place the work at the earlier end of the time span. Syria or Palestine seems to be the country of origin. Although Jewish or Gnostic derivation for the songs have been argued, the case for a Christian origin is strong. The frequent baptismal imagery has suggested a baptismal setting, but this claims too much. In spite of the individualized piety, the hymns seem designed for church use. The Semitic imagery is often strange to modern western readers, but many passages of pure spirituality still resonate with all believers. Stylistic features include introductions by the odist, frequent use of comparisons, Christ speaking in the first person, and Hallelujah at the close. TLG 1243.

[E.F.]

Bibliography

Lactantius, *Divine Institutes* 4.12; *Pistis Sophia* 58–59; 65; 69; 71 (quotes in Coptic *Odes* 1; 5–6; 22; 25); Pseudo-Athanasius, *Synopsis scripturae sacrae* 74 (PG 28.432); Nicephorus, *Chronographia brevis*.

J.R. Harris and A. Mingana, eds. and trs., *The Odes and Psalms of Solomon*, 2 vols. (Manchester: Manchester UP, 1916, 1920); J.H. Charlesworth, ed. and tr., *The Odes of Solomon* (Missoula: Scholars, 1977); M. Lattke, *Die Oden Salomos in ihrer Bedeutung für Neues Testament und Gnosis*, 4 vols. (Göttingen: Vandenhoeck & Ruprecht, 1979–).

J.H. Bernard, *The Odes of Solomon*, TS 8.3 (1912); J.H. Charlesworth, "Odes of Solomon," *The Old Testament Pseudepigrapha*, ed. J.H. Charlesworth (Garden City: Doubleday, 1985), Vol. 2, pp. 725–771.

ODOACER (ca. 434–493). Barbarian (Germanic) ruler of Italy. After service under Roman command in a mercenary capacity, Odoacer rebelled and established his rule over Italy (476) with the deposition of Romulus Augustulus, often called the last Roman emperor in the west. At first, Odoacer recognized the eastern emperor Zeno as nominal overlord. Later, after several years of fighting (489–493), he was defeated and killed through treachery at Ravenna by Theodoric, ruler of the Goths, who had been delegated by Zeno to occupy Italy. An adherent of Arianism, Odoacer interfered little in church affairs; he favored Severinus of Noricum and played a role in the election of Felix II (III) to the Roman see (483).

[M.P.McH.]

Bibliography

Excerpts of Valesius 8.37–38; 10.45–11.56; Eugippius, *Life of Saint Severin* 7.1; 32.1–2; 44.4–5.

J.M. Wallace–Hadrill, *The Barbarian West 400–1000* (London and New York: Hutchinson's University Library, 1952); A.H.M. Jones, "The Constitutional Position of Odoacer and Theoderic," *JRS* 52 (1962):126–130; L. Musset, *The Germanic Invasions: The Making of Europe A.D. 400–600* (University Park: Pennsylvania State UP, 1975); E.A. Thompson, *Romans and Barbarians: The Decline of the Western Empire* (Madison: U of Wisconsin P, 1982); B. Macbain, "Odovacer the Hun?," *CPh* 78 (1983):323–327.

OECUMENIUS (sixth century). Named the Rhetor or the Philosopher. Oecumenius wrote the earliest extant Greek commentary on Revelation, treating it as a canonical book and a guide to the past, present, and future. He mentions no earlier commentaries but cites Athanasius, Basil, Gregory of Nazianzus, and Evagrius. Fragments of his comments on Paul's epistles and scholia on John Chrysostom are also extant. CPG III, 7470–7475.   [F.W.N.]

Bibliography

H.C. Hoskier, ed., *The Complete Commentary of Oecumenius on the Apocalypse* (Ann Arbor: U of Michigan P, 1928).

A. Monaci Castagno, "Il problema della datazione dei commenti all'Apocalisse di Ecumenio e di Andrea di Caesarea," *Atti della Accademia delle Scienze di Torino. Classe di Scienze morali, storiche e filologiche* 114 (1980):223–246.

OFFERINGS. Gifts to God and the church, especially as made in the context of the liturgy. The New Testament employs cultic terminology (e.g., *prosphorein*, *prosphora*) to express the idea of consecration of created beings for the service of God. Self-offering is the primary category: the surrender of the whole of human existence to the will of God in order to receive from him the meaning of one's life. The paradigm is the self-emptying of Jesus (Heb. 9:14), concretely realized by the ordering of all his activity to express his love for his Father, and to reveal the love of the Father for all humanity so that they too might come to love him. The self-offering of Christians committed to the way of Jesus embraces the whole range of human activity (Rom. 12:1–2; 15:16), including the priestly ministry of preaching the word (Rom. 15:15), praise of God, and generosity toward others (Heb. 13:15–16).

The Old and New Testaments place great value on almsgiving, as do later Christians. Collections for the needy were made at the Sunday gatherings in the Pauline churches (1 Cor. 16:1–2) and presumably elsewhere. This practice became normative in the second century. Justin Martyr does not call the weekly collections "offerings" (*1 Apol.* 67.1); but the contemporary *Shepherd* of Hermas describes almsgiving as an acceptable sacrifice (*Sim.* 5.3). Polycarp of Smyrna likens widows to an altar on which offerings of the faithful are made to God (*Phil.* 2.4.3). In the second century, no direct connection is made between the offering of the eucharistic sacrifice and contribution of bread and wine, or gifts for the needy, made in the weekly assembly.

Originally, in accord with contemporary meal customs, the faithful supplied bread and wine for the eucharist without ceremony. After the meal was dropped, a ritual presentation to the leader of the eucharist was made (Justin, *1 Apol.* 65; 67). This practice later took on symbolic overtones. However, second-century reflection on the link between the eucharistic prayer of thanksgiving and the bread and wine led to the notion of the offering of bread and wine as the community's expression of gratitude for creation and redemption (Justin, *Dial.* 41.1; Irenaeus, *Haer.* 4.17–18).

Table for offerings or an agape table,
Corinth Museum, Greece.

In third-century North Africa, the presentation of bread and wine at the eucharist was understood to express the co-offering of the faithful with the bishop. On the other hand, the north Syrian *Didascalia* teaches that the bishop alone offers the gifts brought by the faithful, along with the eucharistic sacrifice itself (2.26.2f.). Here, the Old Testament sacrificial system grounds the view that other sacrifices can be made alongside the eucharistic oblation. These two modes of presentation of gifts at the eucharist coexist from the fourth century onward. In the east, the gifts of the faithful were brought to the sacristy and were considered to be almsgiving. In Egypt, North Africa, and Rome, great significance was awarded to the offertory procession, a liturgical expression of the co-offering of the laity. The floor mosaic of the double church at Aquileia depicts an offertory procession of the people. Elsewhere in the west, the Gallican church was guided by the Old Testament sacrificial system and the mode of offering in the east. This practice influenced the Visigothic liturgy, which it handed on to the Celtic church. Subsequently, the Celtic church adopted the Roman custom of presentation of gifts at the altar, but not the sacrificial concept underlying the offertory procession.

In the church of the empire, for a number of reasons, the practice of making offerings at the eucharist became more related to the personal salvation of the donor, which had first become a growing concern in Gaul and Great Britain, or to the donor's petition for other individuals, living or dead. This contrasts with ante-Nicene thought, in which the accent was on offering for God and the gifts had their purpose in the service of God's poor. Now, the offerings were associated more with the spiritual welfare of individuals. Recompense for a gift, however, was not strictly claimed. In Roman law, the concept of free donation without recompense excluded this. In the early Middle Ages, the position of German law—that it belongs to the essence of a gift to be sealed by recompense—took hold in the west and led to a new understanding of the relation of a gift to the salvation of the donor. *See also* Almsgiving; Eucharist.   [E.J.K.]

Bibliography

G. Dix, *The Shape of the Liturgy* (Westminster: Dacre, 1945), pp. 110–123; J.A. Jungmann, *Missarum Sollemnia*, 2nd ed. (Vienna: Herder, 1952); idem, *The Mass of the Roman Rite* (New York: Benziger, 1959), pp. 314–344; A. Mayer, *Triebkräfte und Grundlinien der Entstehen des Messstipendiums* (St. Ottilien: EOS, 1976), pp. 1–133.

OFFICE, DIVINE. Liturgical fulfillment of scriptural precepts for praying continuously or at regular intervals. Unlike other parts of the liturgy, in which chants and prayers center on a sacramental rite, the Divine Office has as its essence the recitation of chants, readings, and prayers at determined hours of the day. The number of hours observed daily could vary from one tradition to the next in the early liturgy, but eight was to become the standard number: Matins (midnight), Lauds (before sunrise), Prime (6 A.M.), Terce (9 A.M.), Sext (noon), None (3 P.M.), Vespers (before sunset), and Compline (before bed).

The individual hours consist of the following elements: the recitation of entire Psalms and biblical canticles, with an antiphon chanted after each Psalm or group of Psalms (originally after each Psalm verse); the reading of scriptural lessons at night, or a short *capitulum* at the other hours, with a responsory chanted after each lesson; a hymn; at some hours, litanies and Psalm verses known as *preces* and versicles; a collect or oration (petition or prayer). The hours differ in the arrangement of these elements and in the number of Psalms and antiphons. Terce, Sext, and None, however, have a common structure.

Some of the Psalms, chants, and orations that appear in the Office are repeated each day, particularly those that have references to the appropriate time of day. Others vary from day to day. The variable pieces in the Office are arranged in such a way that the entire Psalter is recited in the course of the week or even in a shorter period, the entire Bible is read in the course of the year, and the individual feasts of the liturgical year have their own proper chants, readings, and orations.

In the first three centuries of Christianity, the Office consisted merely of public gatherings in the morning and evening, gatherings that had Jewish precedents. The daily vigils (Matins) appeared only with the formation of monastic communities in Egypt and Asia Minor during the fourth century. The practice of reciting the entire Psalter over a certain number of days has its origins in the monastic Office, and there are references to the private observance of the other hours in these monastic circles. In fourth-century Jerusalem, the monks observed a night Office together with some of the laity, and by daybreak the clergy arrived in order to attend Lauds.

The same situation is evident in the basilicas of fifth-century Rome. The monks observed a full set of daily hours with a weekly recitation of the Psalter, but the clergy was obliged to attend only Lauds, Vespers, and, by the sixth century, Matins. The other ancient rites of the west (Gallican, Old Spanish, Celtic, and Ambrosian) had Office traditions of their own, and, as in Rome, the clergy observed only two or three hours while the monks observed a full set with more extensive Psalm singing.

Another sixth-century development was the formation of the Benedictine Office. This Office had as its model the monastic Office of Rome, but Benedict redistributed the Psalms and modified the structure of the individual hours. The Roman monastic Office of this time and the Benedictine Office have coexisted down to the present, with one important change: by the end of the eighth century, the Benedictine Office began to be observed universally by monks, while the clergy throughout the Frankish realm observed the full set of hours in the formerly monastic Roman Office, now known as the secular Office. *See also* Liturgy.

[J.B.]

Bibliography

R.-J. Hesbert, *Corpus Antiphonalium Officii*, Vols. 1–4, Rerum Ecclesiasticarum Documenta, Series Maior, Fontes 7–10 (Rome: Herder, 1963–1970).

C. Callewaert, *Sacris Erudiri* (Steenbrugge: Abbatia S. Petri, 1940), pp. 53–168; J.M. Hanssens, *Nature et genèse de l'Office des Matines* (Rome: Universitas Gregoriana, 1952); O. Heiming, "Zum monastischen Offizium von Kassianus bis Kolumbanus," *Archiv für Liturgiewissenschaft* 7 (1961):89–156; J.A. Jungmann, *Pastoral Liturgy* (London: Challoner, 1962), pp. 105–200; P. Salmon, *The Breviary Through the Centuries* (Collegeville: Liturgical, 1962); C.W. Dugmore, *The Influence of the Synagogue upon the Divine Office* (Westminster: Faith, 1966); P.F. Bradshaw, *Daily Prayer in the Early Church* (New York: Oxford UP, 1982); R. Taft, *The Liturgy of the Hours in East and West: The Liturgy of the Divine Office and Its Meaning for Today* (Collegeville: Liturgical, 1986).

OILS, HOLY. *See* Anointing.

OLD LATIN VERSIONS. Translations of the Bible into Latin that existed prior to the revision that Jerome began ca. 384 (the Vulgate). As Augustine (*Doct. Chris.* 2.16) and Jerome (*Preface* to his revision of the Gospels) expressly state and as a study of the manuscripts preserving the Old Latin versions shows, there were several varieties of the pre-Jerome Latin Bible. Their origin is obscure. Because the language of the church at Rome was Greek till the mid-third century, the Old Latin versions could not have originated there, but rather within those early Christian communities, as in North Africa and Italy, that used Latin. At various places and times, translators rendered this or that book of the scriptures. The manuscripts preserving these early efforts bear texts that fall into African and European types; the latter can be subdivided into Gallic and Italian types. Old Testament books seem to have been translated from an early Christian pre-*Hexapla* form of the

Greek Septuagint; New Testament books rest upon a fluid Greek text, commonly known as the "Western" text.

The pre-Jerome translations in general lack polish, are painfully literal, and are occasionally of dubious Latinity. Here and there, one finds noteworthy additions; for example, when Jesus "was baptized, a tremendous light flashed forth from the water, so that all who were present feared" (Matt. 3:15 ms. *a*); the Synoptic Gospels give various names to the two thieves who were crucified with Jesus; and Mark's account of Jesus' resurrection is expanded (Mark 16:3 ms. *k*). The Gospels in the early versions are in the order Matthew, John, Luke, Mark (mss. *a, b, d, e, ff*, *q, r*).

No complete Bible of any of the Old Latin versions has been preserved in a single volume, and some of the manuscripts show a "mixed" form of the text. It is remarkable that long after Jerome's Vulgate was published, people continued to make copies of Old Latin texts. The principal manuscripts of the Old Testament are codex Wirceburgensis (sixth century; Pentateuch and the Prophets) and codex Lugdunensis (sixth century; Heptateuch). For the Gospels, the African text is best represented in codices Bobbiensis and Patatinus (both fifth century) and less strongly in Colbertinus (twelfth century).

The standard edition of the whole Old Latin version is still that of Pièrre Sabatier, whose posthumously published *Bibliorum sacrorum Latinae versiones antiquae . . .*, 3 vols. (Rheims: R. Florentain, 1743–1749), remains indispensable, for it includes evidence of manuscripts that subsequently were lost. The Old Latin text of the Gospels was edited by Giuseppe Bianchini (Rome: A. de Rubeis, 1749; repr. in Migne, PL 12.141–946) and by Adolf Jülicher, Walter Matzkow, and Kurt Aland (Berlin: de Gruyter, 1938–). A monumental project was planned by Teófilo Ayuso Marazuela, *La Vetus Latina Hispana*, of which only Volume 1, *Prolegómenos* (Madrid: Consejo Superior de Investigaciones científicas, 1953), and several volumes of the Old Testament have appeared (Vol. 2: *El Octateuco; introducción general y edición crítica*, 1967;

and Vol. 5: *El Salterio*, 3 vols., 1962). After collecting material for many years, scholars at the Monastery of Beuron in Germany have begun to publish editions of books of the Bible based on extensive collections of patristic quotations of the Old Latin; the project is entitled *Vetus Latina; Die Reste der altlateinischen Bibel nach Petrus Sabatier neu gesammelt . . .* (Freiburg: Herder, 1949–). [B.M.M.]

Bibliography
B.M. Metzger, *The Early Versions of the New Testament, Their Origin, Transmission, and Limitations* (Oxford: Clarendon, 1977), pp. 285–330.

OLYMPIAS (ca. 365–ca. 410). Deaconess in Constantinople. A woman of great wealth and high standing, Olympias was briefly married to Nebridius (appointed prefect of the city in 386). Upon his death in 386 or 387, she refused remarriage, despite pressure from the emperor Theodosius I, and adopted an ascetic mode of life. She founded and headed a community of women immediately adjoining the cathedral, dispensing much charity and hospitality. She became a powerful friend and supporter of bishop Nectarius, who ordained her deaconess even though she was far below the canonical sixty years of age, and of his successor, John Chrysostom, seventeen of whose letters to her survive. In 404, she was embroiled in the bitter struggles that led to Chrysostom's exile and was herself tried, fined, and exiled. Her death date—after 407, before 419—remains uncertain. Feast day December 17 (west), July 25 (east).

[W.S.B.]

Bibliography
John Chrysostom, *Epistulae* 1–17, SC (1964), Vol. 103; idem, *Life of Olympias*, tr. E.A. Clark, *Jerome, Chrysostom, and Friends* (New York: Mellen, 1979); Palladius, *Dialogue* 10.16; idem, *Lausiac History* 56.1; 61.3; Sozomen, *Church History* 8.9, 24, 27.

OLYMPIODORUS (early sixth century). Exegete and deacon of Alexandria. Olympiodorus is known for his commentaries, preserved in part, mostly in catenae, on Job, Ecclesiastes, Jeremiah, Lamentations, and Baruch. A commentary on the Psalms exists in fragmentary form, and only a single short fragment of his work against the Monophysite Severus of Antioch survives, published with the writings of Anastasius Sinaita. CPG III, 7453–7464.

[M.P.McH.]

Bibliography

Olympiodorus of Alexandria, *Kommentar zu Hiob*, ed. U. and D. Hagedorn (Berlin: de Gruyter, 1984).

OPHITES. *See* Naassenes.

OPTATUS OF MILEVIS (fourth century). Bishop in North Africa. Optatus wrote a treatise in six books (ca. 367), *Against the Donatists*, directed against Parmenian, their bishop of Carthage. (A seventh was added ca. 385.) The work contains many of the positions later taken by Augustine in his battles with Donatists. Optatus sketched the history of the Donatists and argued against both their catholicity and their holiness. He dealt with the problems of church and state, discussed the nature of baptism, and indicated how Donatists could return to the church. A collection of documents at the end of his work pertaining to the Donatist controversy is a historical gold mine. Feast day June 4. CPL 244–249 (368, serm. 131). [F.W.N.]

Bibliography

Jerome, *Lives of Illustrious Men* 110; Augustine, *De unitate ecclesiae* 19.50; idem, *Against the Letter of Paymonides* 1.3.5.

R. Vassal-Phillips, *The Work of St. Optatus Against the Donatists* (London: Longmans, Green, 1917).

N.H. Baynes, "Optatus," *JThS* 26 (1925): 37–44; C.H. Turner, "Adversaria Critica: Notes on the Anti-Donatist Dossier and on Optatus, Books I, II," *JThS* 27 (1926): 283–296.

ORANGE, COUNCILS OF. Orange, the ancient Roman city of Arausio in Gaul, located on the lower Rhône River, hosted councils in 441 and in 529 with the metropolitan bishops of Arles presiding. In 441, Hilary of Arles convened sixteen bishops from cities of southern Gaul. The council's thirty canons (decrees) dealt with disciplinary and administrative matters: a bishop's jurisdiction over churches located on the estates of great landowners (anticipating the thorny problem of the medieval "proprietary" churches), the manumission of slaves by and in the church, and, with Canon 21, the acceptance by the Gallic church of papal guidelines for clerical marriage, which declared that married men joining the clergy had to take the vow of continence along with their wives.

It is the second council, held at Orange in 529, however, that has loomed large in the history of councils and theological definition. Convened by Caesarius of Arles, one of the extraordinary bishops of the age and a determined advocate of Augustinianism, this synod brought the half-century-long debate in the church of southern Gaul to a conclusion with its rejection of Semipelagianism. Backed by a strongly supportive letter from pope Felix III (IV), Caesarius presented twenty-five canons that dealt with original sin, with the need for grace, and with predestination to evil (which he rejected). The triumph of Augustine's views on sin and grace at Orange represented the culmination of decades of effort by popes and by Prosper of Aquitaine to remove any vestige of Pelagianism in the Gallic church. With the adoption of Caesarius's proposals, the church of Gaul found itself in harmony with the Roman view of Augustine. Two years later, pope Felix's successor, Boniface II, gave his approval to the decrees of Orange II. [H.R.]

Bibliography

C. Munier, ed., *Concilia Galliae A. 314–A. 506*, CCSL (1963), Vol. 148; C. DeClercq, ed., *Concilia Gailiae A. 511–A. 695*, CCSL (1963), Vol. 148A.

K.J. Hefele, *A History of Christian Councils*, tr. from German by H. Plumptre, Vol. 3 (Edinburgh: T. and T. Clark, 1883) and by W.R. Clark, Vol. 4 (Edinburgh: T. and T. Clark, 1895); K.J. Hefele and H. Leclercq, *Histoire des conciles d'après les documents originaux* (Paris: Letouzey et Ané, 1908), Vol. 2.1–2 (with extensive bibliography).

J. Pelikan, *The Christian Tradition*. (Chicago: U of Chicago P, 1971), Vol. 1: *The Emergence of the Catholic Tradition (100–600)*, pp. 327–331.

ORANT. The posture symbolizing prayer, from Latin *orans* ("one who prays"). Typically, in early Christian art, the orant is represented by a standing female facing front, arms raised and extended outward from the body. The central

Orant on front of the Via Lungara sarcophagus (late third century), Museo Nazionale delle Terme, Rome, Italy. (Used by permission of Pontifical Commission of Sacred Archaeology, catalogue number Na A 11.)

figure on the Christian third-century sarcophagus in Rome's Museo delle Terme, (see illustration) represents the type. The posture is the one observed for prayer in several ancient cultures. On Roman coin reverses, for example (cf. Klauser), the same prayer figure appears as a personification of *Pietas*, the virtue of care, especially womanly care, in relation to one's family and by extension to the larger family of the state. The posture was common in Jewish (1 Kings 8:22; 2 Macc. 3:20; *Berakoth* 3.5; 5.1) and Christian prayer (1 Tim. 2:8; Tertullian, *Apol.* 30.4; Origen, *On Prayer* 31). The figure is widely attested in the very earliest Christian art (in painted form within the oldest nucleii of the Callistus catacomb, for example), but there has been a long history of controversy surrounding its interpretation (cf. Wessel). Because this image is often attested in funerary contexts, many interpreters have sought an eschatological-symbolic explanation: the orant is a symbol of the soul in paradise, or of the church (feminine) at prayer anticipating the next life.

Theodor Klauser revolutionized the study of this subject by arguing (1) that the orant is widely attested in pre-Christian and non-Christian contexts (an indisputable fact and indeed something of a commonplace recognized long before Klauser's work); (2) that in the Roman numismatic context the figure personifies *Pietas*; (3) that in many iconographic contexts

(such as the sarcophagi of La Gayole, Sta. Maria Antiqua, and the Via Salaria) the orant represents not a generalized concept but instead a quite specific person—i.e., the deceased—in portrait; and (4) that the facts indicate that the image scarcely ever conveys an explicitly Christian (i.e., biblical) meaning but instead carries the meanings given it in pre-Christian or non-Christian contexts.

If Klauser is right, the orant cannot be considered one of the traditionally early Christian images, since in his view wherever and whenever the image appears it conveys non-Christian meanings, primarily of pagan piety associated especially with the lives of persons (mainly women) commemorated on sarcophagi. Klauser's orderly and exhaustive presentation of the evidence is a significant contribution to the study of early Christian art, but whether his conclusions will stand the test of time remains to be seen. The frequency of the orant in a Christian context shows at the very least that early Christians found in the image powerful symbolic associations. *See also* Art; Prayer.   [P.C.F.]

Bibliography

A. Bosio, *Roma sotterranea* (Rome: Facciotti, 1632), pp. 631–632; W. Neuss, "Die Oranten in der altchristlicher Kunst," *Festschrift Paul Clemens* (Bonn: Schwann, 1926), pp. 130–149; H. Leclercq, "Orant, orante," DACL (1936), Vol. 12.2, cols. 2291–2322; K. Wessel, "Ecclesia orans," *Archäologischer Anzeiger* 70 (1955):315–334; A. Stuiber,

Refrigerium interim (Bonn: Hanstein, 1957), pp. 130–149; T. Klauser, "Studien zur Entstehungsgeschichte der christlichen Kunst II.6–10," *JAC* 2 (1959):115–131; idem, "III.11," *JAC* 3 (1960):112–133; idem, "VII.16," *JAC* 7 (1964):67–76; F. Matz, "Das Problem der Orans und ein Sarkophag in Cordoba," *Madrider Mitteilungen* 9 (1968):300–310.

ORDERS, ORGANIZATION OF THE CHURCH. *See* Ministry.

ORDINATION. Appointment to church office. The words *cheirotonia* (Greek) and *ordinatio* (Latin) at different times in their historical development referred to the selection of a person for a function, the installation of a person into an office, or both together. They eventually became the technical terms in Christianity for the formal bestowal of holy orders, later counted as one of the seven sacraments of the Roman Catholic and Eastern Orthodox churches.

Greco-Roman society knew several methods for selecting political and religious functionaries: cooptation by those already performing the task, designation by a person in authority, popular election, taking lots to determine the divine will, and inheritance. Each of these methods was known in Judaism at one time or another.

The methods for installing a person into an office in the ancient world were equally varied and carried no necessary correlation with the methods of selection. Divine invocation was common, the form varying with the culture, but oath-taking and some form of prayer were especially frequent. The first performance of the duties of an office was a widespread method of demonstrating accession to the office. Formal seating in a chair, the bestowal of the emblems of the office, investiture with the clothing pertaining to a function, and giving the name or title of the function were natural and obvious ways of marking entrance into the exercise of an office.

Rabbinic ordination has often been interpreted as the antecedent to Christian ordination; however, since rabbinic ordination began after A.D. 70, a preferable view is to see both as independent developments out of a common Jewish background. Christian ordination gave a central importance to prayer, which is not accorded a constitutive place in rabbinic ordination. The Christian technical terminology for ordination in Syriac (a cognate language to Hebrew) was derived from a root different from that employed for rabbinic ordination.

The New Testament provides examples of persons being chosen by Christ (Luke 6:13; Acts 1:23–26; Gal. 1:1), by the Holy Spirit through prophetic revelation (Acts 13:1–3; 1 Tim. 1:18; 4:14; Acts 20:28), by apostles and evangelists (Acts 14:23?), and by election by the whole church (Acts 6:5; 2 Cor. 8:19). Wherever the initiative in the selection lay, these sources indicate that the process was a corporate one in which the other parties concerned gave their assent.

Variety in methods of selecting bishops is attested in the succeeding centuries. Sometimes, a bishop designated his successor (Theodoret, *H.E.* 4.20; 5.23), a practice forbidden by canon law (Antioch, *can.* 23). The bishop normally did have the right to appoint the lesser clergy, even presbyters (*Didas.* 9), although this customarily required the approval of the people (Cyprian, *Ep.* 38.1f.). The presbyters in their turn had an important role in the selection of bishops by giving their testimony to a candidate's worthiness or putting forward a candidate for consideration (Cyprian, *Ep.* 55.8; Hippolytus, *Trad. ap.* 2.2). According to later testimonies, the practice at Alexandria up to the third century was for the twelve presbyters who led the church to elect the bishop out of their own number, ordain him, and select his successor as a presbyter (Jerome, *Ep.* 146; Eutychius, *Annals*, PG 111.982). The most common method of selecting a bishop in the early centuries was congregational election (*1 Clem.* 44; Cyprian, *Ep.* 59.5f.; 67.3; Gregory of Nyssa, *V. Gr. Thaum.*, PG 46.933ff.). Whether the initiative for selection rested with neighboring bishops, the local clergy, or the people, the sources are agreed in considering the concurrence of all as necessary and as an indication of the divine choice (Cyprian, *Ep.* 55.8f.; 68.2).

Although various ways of showing entrance into office found a place in the ceremony of ordination, the passages that give details show a remarkable similarity in including prayer and the laying on of hands. This was true already in New Testament accounts of appointment: of evangelists (1 Tim. 4:14), missionaries (Acts 13:1–3), presbyters (1 Tim. 5:22; Acts 14:23?), and the seven, who were prototypes of deacons (Acts 6:6). The laying on of hands was done by evangelists (1 Tim. 5:22; Titus 1:5), the presbytery (1 Tim. 4:14), or apostles and prophets acting for the church (Acts 6:6; 13:3). This action in Christian usage signified the bestowal of a blessing. The significance of ordination in the New Testament is brought out by Acts 14:26, which refers to 13:3 in this way: "They had been commended to the grace of God for the work which they had fulfilled." The gesture of laying on hands was an accompaniment to prayer, reinforcing it and marking out the person for whom the divine approval and favor were sought. The fourth-century *Life of Polycarp* 11 describes an ordination as "to cover such a head with his hand and to bless so noble a soul with his voice." Several references to ordination put the emphasis on the prayer as the central element in an appointment. Thus, Jerome defines the Greek word *cheirotonia* as "the ordination of the clergy that is accomplished not only at the verbal prayer but at the imposition of the hand (lest indeed in mockery someone be ordained ignorantly to the clergy by a secret prayer)" (*In Isa.* 16.58). The prayer is constitutive for Jerome, and the imposition of hands had a purely functional role. John Chrysostom in commenting on Acts 6:6 speaks similarly, for he wants to stress God's appointment: "For Luke says not how, but simply that they were ordained by prayer: for this is the ordination. The hand of man is laid on, but God performs everything, and it is his hand that touches the head of the one being ordained, if he is truly ordained" (*Hom.* 14 *in Acts*).

A minimum of three bishops were expected to be present for the ordination of another bishop (Arles, *can.* 20; Nicaea, *can.* 4). From the time of the *Apostolic Tradition* of Hippolytus, the power of ordination was confined to the bishop. The ordination prayers preserved in this document and later sources reflect common ideas about ordination. The prayers acknowledge God as the one who appoints ministers for his church. They contain praise of God, who has provided leaders for his people, and petition for divine favor upon the person in the performance of his task. In the *Apostolic Tradition*, the other presbyters gave their personal benediction by jointly laying on hands at the ordination of a presbyter and praying silently at the ordination of a bishop while one bishop ordained (8.1; 9.6; 2.3f.). It was common in the ordination prayers for presbyters to recall the precedent of the seventy elders chosen to assist Moses in overseeing Israel (Num. 11:16–25) and in the ordination prayers for deacons to recall Stephen and the seven servants in Acts 6 as models. The heart of the ordination prayers was a petition for the Holy Spirit to enable the person to fulfill the ministry for which he was chosen.

The special gift of the Holy Spirit on the ordinand led to ideas of a sacramental change. Gregory of Nyssa gives one of the first such expressions, comparing ordination to baptism and the eucharist: "Although before the benediction [these objects] are of little value, after the sanctification bestowed by the Spirit each has its several operations. The same power of the word also makes the priest venerable, honorable, and separated by the benediction bestowed on him from the common mass. . . . While continuing to be in all appearance the man he was before, by some unseen power and grace the unseen soul is transformed for the better" (*Bapt. Chr.*). Augustine gave classic expression to this understanding of ordination with his idea of an indelible character impressed on the soul (*De bapt. c. Donat.* 1.1.2; cf. Gregory the Great, *Ep.* 2.46). The sacramental idea of ordination encouraged the development that saw it not just as appointment to serve a particular church (Nicaea, *can.* 8; 16; *Can. ap.* 68; Theodoret, *H.E.* 1.9.7ff.) but as an individual prerogative apart from a local community. The Syriac church saw ordination by the laying on of hands as transmitting the priesthood from the Old Testament (*Edessene Canons*, Cureton, p. 24; Ephraem, *Hymn c. Haer.* 22.18ff.). Ordination was normally required for the exercise of the eucharistic ministry, but a few texts seem to indicate this was not always the case (Tertullian, *Exh. cast.* 7; Hippolytus, *Trad. ap.* 10). *See also* Anointing; Clergy; Election to Church Office; Laying On of Hands; Ministry; Sacraments. [E.F.]

Bibliography

Hippolytus, *Apostolic Tradition* 2–3; 8–15; Serapion, *Prayerbook* 12–14; *Apostolic Constitutions* 3.20; 8.3–5, 16–28; *Testament of Our Lord* 1.21, 30, 38; Augustine, *On Baptism Against the Donatists* 1.1.2; idem, *On the Good of Marriage* 24 (32); idem, *Against the Letter of Parmenides* 2.13.28ff.; *Statuta ecclesiae antiqua* 90–92.

W.H. Frere, "Early Forms of Ordination," *Essays on the Early History of the Church and the Ministry*, ed. H.B. Swete (London: Macmillan, 1918), pp. 263–312; M.A. Siotis, "Die klassische und die christliche Cheirotonie," *Theologia* [Greek] 20–22 (1949–1950); J. Newman, *Semikhah* (Manchester: Manchester UP, 1950); E. Lohse, *Die Ordination im Spätjudentum und im Neuen Testament* (Göttingen: Vandenhoeck & Ruprecht, 1951); A. Ehrhardt, "Jewish and Christian Ordination," *JEH* 5 (1954):125–138; E. Ferguson, "Ordination in the Ancient Church, 1–4," *Restoration Quarterly* 4 (1960):117–138 and 5 (1961):17–32, 67–82, 130–146; idem, "Eusebius and Ordination," *JEH* 13 (1962):139–144; idem, "Jewish and Christian Ordination," *HThR* 56 (1963):13–19; H.B. Porter, Jr., *The Ordination Prayers of the Ancient Western Churches* (London: SPCK, 1967); O. Bârlea, *Die Weihe der Bischöfe, Presbyter, und Diakone in vornicänischer Zeit* (Munich: Societas Academica Dacoromana, 1969); E. Ferguson, "Attitudes to Schism at the Council of Nicaea," *Schism, Heresy, and Religious Protest* (Cambridge: Cambridge UP, 1972), pp. 57–63; idem, "Selection and Installation to Office in Roman, Greek, Jewish and Christian Antiquity," *ThZ* 30 (1974):273–284; P. van Beneden, *Aux Origines d'une terminologie sacramentelle: Ordo, ordinare, ordinatio dans la littérature chrétienne avant 313* (Louvain: Spicilegium sacrum Lovaniense, 1974); P.-M. Gy, "Ancient Ordination Prayers," *Studia Liturgica* 13 (1979):70–93; J. Lécuyer, *Le Sacrement de l'ordination: recherche historique et théologique* (Paris: Beauchesne, 1983).

ORIENTATION. The practice of building churches along an east-west axis. Some of the earliest churches, such as several of those built under the patronage of the emperor Con-stantine in the first half of the fourth century, had the entrance at the east end and the apse and altar at the west; others had apse and altar to the east; and still others were not aligned to an east-west axis at all, due perhaps to local custom or to topographical conditions of the site. By the fifth century, despite occasional exceptions, particularly in Africa, the prevailing custom throughout the Christian world was to place the entrance to the west and the apse to the east: worshipers thus faced the east and the rising sun, the direction of prayer for many Christians from at least the second century. This was also the standard plan for churches throughout the Middle Ages.

Orientation may have had a precedent in the cosmic orientation of the entrances of many temples toward the east in the Greek and Roman world as well as in Mesopotamia and Egypt. Jewish synagogues, on the other hand, were commonly aligned toward Jerusalem, as mosques in the Muslim world would be aligned toward Mecca, but many synagogues had an east-west axis with an eastern entrance like the Jerusalem temple. The cathedral of Tyre and the Church of the Holy Sepulchre in Jerusalem, both of which Eusebius describes in detail, follow this latter plan; Constantine's church on the Mount of Olives and the Church of the Nativity at Bethlehem have the entrance to the west.

Christians associated Christ and his second coming in glory with the east on the basis of Matthew 24:27 and his ascension from the Mount of Olives in Jerusalem, which is east of the city proper. The *Shepherd* of Hermas has been cited as the earliest Christian writing to make an allusion to prayer directed toward the east, but the apocryphal *Acts of Paul* (11.5) from the late second century gives the first certain evidence. Tertullian mentions the practice in his *Apology* 16 and *To the Nations* 1.13; Clement of Alexandria (*Str.* 7.43.6f.) and Origen (*Jo.* 1.24; *Or.* 32) endorse it—the latter citing Jesus' teachings about light, from the Gospel of John. Christian theologians came to equate the risen Christ of Easter morning with the rising sun. The Syrian *Didascalia* 3 repeats the ideas of Origen and adds the expectation of paradise out of the east. Basil of Caesarea speaks of prayer directed toward the east as showing the desire for paradise (*Spir.* 27.66). In many early Christian and Byzantine churches, these ideas received architectural expression in the mosaic decoration of the semidome of the apse with a large cross or an image of Christ. [G.T.A.]

Bibliography

C. Vogel, "Orientation of Churches," NCE (1967), Vol. 10, p. 767; E. von Severus, "Gebet I," *RLAC* (1972), Vol. 8, cols. 1225–1226; R. Krautheimer, *Early Christian and Byzantine Architecture*, 3rd ed. (Harmondsworth: Penguin, 1979), p. 99; F.W. Deichmann, *Einführung in die christliche Archäologie* (Darmstadt: Wissenschaftliche Buchgesellschaft, 1983), pp. 90, 103; S.C. Herbert, "The Orientation of Greek Temples," *PEQ* (1984):31–34; J. Wilkinson, "Orientation, Jewish and Christian," *PEQ* (1984):16–30.

ORIGEN (ca. 185–ca. 251). One of the most learned teachers and prolific authors of the early church. After the hagiographical elements are weeded out from Eusebius's *Church History* 6, a reasonably reliable biographical sketch of Origen emerges. He was born in Alexandria of devout Christian parents. His father, Leonides, was martyred ca. 201. Precocious in virtue and learning, he was from his early twenties entrusted with the catechetical instruction of converts while also dedicating himself to the study of philosophy under Ammonius Saccas and the other, mostly eclectic Neoplatonist, thinkers of Alexandria. He was also acquainted by travel with churches across the empire: Rome (where he apparently came into contact with Hippolytus), Athens, Caesarea, parts of Asia Minor, and "Arabia." To non-Christians, he was known as a great Christian savant. Among Christians, his reception was mixed: assailed by some—especially his own bishop in Alexandria, who eventually forced his departure from that city—for his spiritualizing biblical interpretation, and hailed by others—especially the bishops of Jerusalem and Caesarea, where he spent his last eighteen and most productive years—as a great Christian teacher and arbiter of orthodoxy. He died sometime after June 251 after suffering imprisonment and torture in the Decian persecution.

Origen was perhaps the most prolific writer in antiquity, producing by dictation some 2,000 works: commentaries on almost every book of the Bible, foremost among them the *Commentary on John* and several commentaries on the Psalms; hundreds of homilies; numerous scholia on particular passages; and the prodigious *Hexapla*, whose philological sophistication was not approached again until the sixteenth century. There are also two major "uncharacteristic" works: the apologetic *Against Celsus* and the speculative *On First Principles*. Among his treatises are two works often included in anthologies (because of their convenient brevity): *On Prayer* and *On Martyrdom*. Only a small, but still impressive, part of this massive edifice remains: fragments of the *Hexapla*; nine of thirty-two books of the *Commentary on John*; the latter half of the *Commentary on Matthew* (some of this only in an anonymous fifth-century Latin translation); a somewhat abbreviated Latin translation by Rufinus of the *Commentary on Romans*; Rufinus's Latin version of the prologue and Books 1–3 (out of ten) of the *Commentary on the Song of Solomon;* 279 mostly Old Testament homilies (only twenty-one of them in Greek, the rest in the Latin of Rufinus and Jerome); Rufinus's translation of *On First Principles*; the treatises on prayer, martyrdom, and the Passover; the *Dialogue with Heraclides*; the eight books *Against Celsus*; the *Philocalia* (an anthology compiled by the great Cappadocians who deeply revered him, Basil of Caesarea and Gregory of Nazianzus); and assorted fragments from the rest.

All these works come from Origen's mature, final twenty years and reveal no substantial internal development, although the late, Matthaean commentary is more pastoral and less speculative than the earlier one on John. The Latin translations of Rufinus, formerly suspect, have been proven, by comparison with genuine Greek fragments, to be substantially accurate.

There are many Origens: philosopher and scholar, mystic, systematician, proponent of an esoteric system, exegete and/or allegorist, saint (even martyr), true gnostic (in the sense of Clement of Alexandria), one for whom mystical knowledge is the way to salvation, Hellenist, Platonist, moralist, ascetic, eunuch, syncretist, and man of the church. Which was the true Origen? His own response is consistent with the witness of his life: "I want to be a man of the church . . . to be called by the name . . . of Christ, and to bear that name which is blessed on the earth" (*Hom.* 16 *in Lc.*).

Origen was above all a biblical theologian—there was at that time no other kind—committed to handing on the church's rule of faith by expounding the many ways in which the eternal Word is *now* incarnate—i.e., present and speaking to us—in the word of scripture. Thus, every word of scripture is sacred because, beyond the literal or historical meaning, which is not always present in every passage, stands always a *spiritual meaning*, which is Christ or points to Christ, if not literally then at least metaphorically, typologically, or allegorically. This is not precisely the historical Jesus but the personally identical glorified eternal Logos, who, having returned to the Father, is now present to Christians spiritually and in mystery.

This is the heart and soul of Origen's thought. Even *On First Principles*, his most systematic or speculative work, supports this. Apart from external evidence suggesting that Origen's purpose was to defend his spiritualizing method of exegesis, the internal evidence is strong. The prologue gives a detailed outline of the church's rule of faith, which is then expounded, after the manner of contemporary philosophical treatises on first principles, in a sometimes highly speculative but always carefully qualified way. In this, he uses scripture both as exposition and as proof in precisely the same way he does in the commentaries. The final section, Book 4, describes his exegetical method.

Later theology judges Origen to have put insufficient emphasis on the historical incarnation of Christ and the literal meaning of scripture. His obvious subordinationist tendencies, however, are something he shares with most Christian thinkers a century before Nicaea. He rejected reincarnation but speculated about preexistence of souls. He also speculated

that the love of God, after untold eons of purification, would eventually accomplish universal salvation. Such speculations, which Origen himself always carefully qualified, were subsequently turned into dogmas by overenthusiastic followers, the Origenists. This Origenism so clouded Origen's fame that he was anathematized by the emperor Justinian I in the Second Council of Constantinople (553), quite unjustly it seems, since the fifteen anathemas laid at his door were actually based on statements by one of these Origenists, Evagrius of Pontus.

Thus, for many, Origen has been a sign of contradiction. Yet not only because he was so admired by the great Cappadocians, but also because even "enemies" like Jerome copied extensively from his works into their own, he has exerted an influence on Christian thought, exceeded perhaps by no one except the apostle Paul himself. CPG I, 1410–1525. TLG 2042. *See also* Allegory; Hexapla; Interpretation of the Bible.   [R.J.D.]

Bibliography

PG 11–14; 17; P. Koetschau, E. Klostermann, E. Preuschen, W.A. Baehrens, and M. Rauer, eds., GCS (1899–1959), Vols. 2, 3, 6, 10, 22, 29, 30, 35, 49; L. Doutreleau, P. Fortier, A. Méhat, O. Rousseau, J. Scherer, A. Jaubert, C. Blanc, M. Borret, H. Crouzel, R. Girod, P. Nautin, et al., eds., SC (1942–), Vols. 7 (bis), 16 (bis), 29 (bis), 37 (bis), 67, 71, 87, 120, 132, 136, 147, 148, 150, 157, 162, 189, 190, 222, 226, 227, 232, 238, 252, 253, 268, 269, 286, 287, 290, 302, 312.

F. Crombie, A. Menzies, and J. Patrick, ANF (1885), Vols. 4, 10; *Philocalia*, tr. G. Lewis (Edinburgh: T. and T. Clark, 1911); *On First Principles*, tr. G.W. Butterworth (London: SPCK, 1936); *Against Celsus*, tr. H. Chadwick (London: Cambridge UP, 1953); *On Prayer and Exhortation to Martyrdom*, tr. J.J. O'Meara, ACW (1954), Vol. 19; *Commentary on the Song of Songs and Homilies on the Song of Songs*, tr. R.P. Lawson, ACW (1957), Vol. 26; *Homilies on Genesis and Exodus*, tr. R. Heine, FOTC (1982), Vol. 71; H.U. von Balthasar, *Origen, Spirit and Fire: A Thematic Anthology of His Writings* (Washington, D.C.: Catholic U of America P, 1984).

H. Crouzel, *Bibliographie critique d'Origène; Bibliographie critique d'Origène: Supplément 1* (The Hague: Nijhoff, 1971, 1982); idem, "Chronique origénienne," *Bulletin de littérature ecclésiastique* (an annual bibliographic review of the most important studies published in the previous year).

An extensive and representative selection of articles on Origen can be found in *SP* 1–18 (1957–), and in the proceedings of the International Origen Congresses held at four-year intervals since 1973: *Origeniana*, ed. H. Crouzel, G. Lomiento, and J. Rius-Camps (Bari: Istituto di Letteratura Cristiana Antica, 1975); *Origeniana Secunda*, ed. H. Crouzel and A. Quacquarelli (Rome: Edizioni dell'Ateneo, 1980); *Origeniana Tertia*, ed. R. Hanson and H. Crouzel (Rome: Edizioni dell'Ateneo, 1985); *Origeniana Quarta*, ed. L. Lies (Innsbruck and Vienna: Tyrolia, 1987).

J. Daniélou, *Origen* (New York: Sheed and Ward, 1955); J.W. Trigg, *Origen: The Bible and Philosophy in the Third-Century Church* (Atlanta: John Knox, 1983); C. Kannengiesser and W.L. Petersen, eds., *Origen of Alexandria: His World and His Legacy* (Notre Dame: Notre Dame UP, 1988); H. Crouzel, *Origen* (San Francisco: Harper and Row, 1989).

ORIGINAL SIN. Doctrine that the primitive transgression and curse of Adam (Gen. 3:1–24) somehow implicated his entire human posterity. The rich diversity of early Christian expositions of this concept is explained in part by the lack of a systematic doctrine of sin in scripture itself. Texts traditionally adduced as evidence for original sin (e.g., Job 15:14–15; Ps. 51:5; Eccles. 7:20), including the *locus classicus*, Romans 5:12–21, drew divergent interpretations among early Christian writers. Granted that all humanity participated in Adam's fall (Rom. 5:12), the church fathers sought to spell out the nature of that solidarity theologically, defining whether human beings shared Adam's actual guilt or only the repercussions of his primal sin.

There is little evidence among the Greek fathers for a notion of inherited guilt or physically transmitted sinfulness. With the apologists, culpability was principally a matter of the individual's exercise of free will, of personal sins for which Adam's disobedience was only a prototype (Tatian, *Or.* 11; Justin, *2 Apol.* 7; *Dial.* 88). Greek writers consistently espoused the sinlessness of infants (*Barn.* 6; Aristides, *Apol.* 15; Clement of Alexandria, *Str.* 4.25.160; Gregory of Nyssa, *Infant.* passim; John Chrysostom, *Hom.* 28 *in Mt.* 3), thereby precluding original guilt as a basis for infant baptism (Gregory of Nazianzus, *Or.* 40.17, 28; Theodoret, *Haer.* 5.18). Irenaeus indicated explicitly that humanity shared in Adam's actual disobedience, but the upshot was more a

mystical solidarity with Adam than a genetic fault that might impair individual freedom (*Haer.* 3.18.7). Origen too stressed that individual souls were punished precisely according to their respective sins (*Princ.* 2.9.6). This characteristic emphasis on personal responsibility (Cyril of Jerusalem, *Catech.* 4.18–21; John Chrysostom, *Hom.* 10 *in Rom.*), coupled with the belief that moral evil had no "natural" status in creation but resulted only from human volition (Athanasius, *Gent.* 6–7; Gregory of Nyssa, *Or. catech.* 7), continued to militate against a doctrine of genetically transmitted sin in the Christian east.

A graver picture of human solidarity with Adam emerged among the earlier Latin fathers. Tertullian, although defending individual responsibility (*Marc.* 2.5–7, 9), nevertheless postulated a real infection of human nature through Adam, an irrational predisposition to sin inseminated in each new soul through its parent (*Anim.* 16, 39–41; *Test. anim.* 3). Cyprian was the first to postulate the physical inheritance of the "contagion of death" from Adam as grounds for baptizing infants (*Ep.* 64.5). Both Ambrosiaster (*Rom.* 5.12ff.) and Ambrose (*Enar. in Ps.* 38.29) emphasized the corporate participation in Adam's sin, Ambrose even alluding to an inheritance of his guilt (*Exc. Sat.* 2.6); but both authors concluded that individuals were ultimately accountable only for their own sins (Ambrosiaster, *Quaest.* 21f.; Ambrose, *Enar. in Ps.* 48.9).

A crucial scriptural text in debates over original sin was Romans 5:12: "Sin came into the world through one man and death through sin, and so death spread to all men *because* (eph hō) all men sinned...." The Greek fathers generally deduced from Paul's statement that humanity inherited not Adam's actual sin, but his punishment of "death," be it mortality (John Chrysostom, *Hom.* 10 *in Rom.*; Theodore of Mopsuestia, *Rom.* 5.13-14), bodily corruption (Athanasius, *Inc.* 4-5; Cyril of Alexandria, *Rom.*, PG 74.789B), or subjugation to lustful passions (Methodius, *Res.* 2.1-4; Gregory of Nyssa, *Anim. et res.*, PG 46.148Cff; Maximus, *Thal.* prol.). This "death" did not vitiate human nature and volition, but did leave persons frail, and was conducive to the further proliferation of sin (cf. Cyril of Alexandria, *Rom.*, PG 74.788D-789B; Theodore of Mopsuestia, *Rom.* 5.21; Theodoret, *Rom.* 5.21). Human beings grew up with sin such that it became second nature for them (Gregory of Nyssa, *Beat.* 6). "Original sin" was thus a sort of chain reaction precipitated by Adam, a continuing—but not predetermined—cycle of disobedience and death.

In the west, the Old Latin text of Romans 5.12 rendered the Greek phrase *eph hō* with *in quo*, suggesting that "death spread to all men *in whom* [i.e., Adam] all men sinned." Humanity sinned with Adam "as in a lump" (Ambrosiaster, *Rom.* 5.12; cf. Augustine, *Pecc. mer.* 1.10.11; *C. Pelag.* 4.4.7). Augustine took this to mean that humanity hereditarily bore Adam's guilt (*Nupt. et concup.* 2.5.15). His arch-opponent Pelagius, teaching at Rome in the early fifth century, had flatly denied this interpretation of Romans 5:12 (*Rom.* 5.12–19). For Pelagius, guilt was incurred only through individual sins, committed "by the example of Adam's disobedience" (*exemplo inobedientiae Adae*). Evil or guilt could never be said to dwell naturally in human beings, compelling them to sin; sin was principally a matter of personal actions (Augustine, *Nat. et grat.* 19.21; *Pecc. orig.* 13.14). Logically, infants were to be baptized not for inborn guilt but for sanctification (Augustine, *Pecc. orig.* 18.20ff.; *C. Iul. op. imperf.* 1.53). Pelagius did affirm, to be sure, a certain social or environmental legacy of sin, the learned wickedness that fostered habitual sin in human beings; but always there remained in them the power to shun vice and embrace virtue (*Ep. ad Dem.* 8; 17).

Challenged by more aggressive Pelagians like Celestius and Julian of Eclanum, Augustine formulated his mature doctrine of original sin in what was really a debate over the efficacy of divine grace in human salvation. If humanity was saved absolutely in the one man Christ, it was utterly guilt-ridden through the one man Adam, and was perpetuating that guilt by natural descent (*Pecc. mer.* 1.12.15–1.16.21; *Nupt. et. concup.* 2.34.57–58). Rampant concupiscence had accompanied Adam's transgression,

and thus his sin was transmitted by sexual procreation, through the medium of lust (ibid. 1.6.7; 1.24.27; passim). Like Jerome (*Dial. adv. Pelag.* 17–19), Augustine concluded that even infants were not exempt from guilt and thus required baptism (*Pecc. mer.* 1.9.24ff.). Accused of Manichaeism for attaching original sin to human nature itself (*Nupt. et concup.* 2.29.49), Augustine conceded that a certain creaturely dignity remained in that nature but that it had been persuaded into evil by the devil and was diseased (ibid. 2.34.57; cf. *Nat. et grat.* 3.3). Therein, humanity had lost the freedom of paradise, the ability not to sin, and was captive to a certain necessity of sinning (cf. *C. Pelag.* 1.2.5; *Perf. iust.* 1–3). Only Christ's grace could redeem the deviant will from original sin, enabling it to do good and be saved (*Grat.* 4.7ff.). Augustine's theory of original sin won the favor of African bishops in councils at Carthage in 416 and 418 and was pivotal for the later development of the doctrine of sin in the Christian west. *See also* Anthropology; Fall; Sin.

[P.M.Bl.]

Bibliography

J.P. Burns, ed. and tr., *Theological Anthropology* (Philadelphia: Fortress, 1981); Tertullian, *On the Soul*, tr. P. Holmes, ANF (1887), Vol. 3, pp. 181–235; Cyprian, *Letter* 64, tr. G.W. Clarke, ACW (1986), Vol. 46, pp. 109–112; Gregory of Nyssa, *On the Making of Man*, tr. H.A. Wilson, NPNF, 2nd ser. (1893), Vol. 5, pp. 387–427; idem, *The Great Catechism*, tr. W. Moore, ibid., pp. 473–509; idem, *On Infants' Early Deaths*, tr. W. Moore, ibid., pp. 372–381; John Chrysostom, *Homily 10 in Romans*, tr. J.B. Morris et al., NPNF, 1st ser. (1888), Vol. 11, pp. 401–408; Augustine, *On the Merits and Forgiveness of Sins, and on the Baptism of Infants*, tr. P. Holmes and R.E. Wallis, NPNF, 1st ser. (1887), Vol. 5, pp. 15–78; idem, *On Nature and Grace*, ibid., pp. 121–151; idem, *On Man's Perfection in Righteousness*, ibid., pp. 159–176; idem, *On the Grace of Christ, and on Original Sin*, ibid., pp. 217–255; idem, *On Marriage and Concupiscence*, ibid., pp. 263–308.

F.R. Tennant, *The Sources of the Doctrines of the Fall and Original Sin* (Cambridge: Cambridge UP, 1903); N.P. Williams, *The Ideas of the Fall and of Original Sin* (London: Longmans, Green, 1927); A Gaudel, "Péché originel" (Parts 1–4), DTC (1933), Vol. 12.1, pp. 275–432; J. Ferguson, *Pelagius: A Historical and Theological Study* (Cambridge: Heffer, 1956); J. Gross, *Geschichte des Erbsündendogmas* (Munich and Basel: Reinhardt, 1960), Vol. 1: *Entstehungsgeschichte des Erbsündendogmas von der*

Bibel bis Augustinus; A. Sage, "Le Péché originel dans le pensée de saint Augustin, de 412 à 430," *REAug* 15 (1969):75–112; H. Rondet, *Original Sin: The Patristic and Theological Background* (Shannon: Ecclesia, 1972); Kelly, Chs. 7 and 13; D. Weaver, "From Paul to Augustine: Romans 5:12 in Early Christian Exegesis," *St. Vladimir's Theological Quarterly* 27 (1983):187–206; idem, Pts. 2–3, "The Exegesis of Romans 5:12 Among the Greek Fathers and Its Implications for the Doctrine of Original Sin: The 5th–12th Centuries," *St. Vladimir's Theological Quarterly* 29 (1985):133–159, 231–257.

OROSIUS (early fifth century). Presbyter and Christian historian from Spain. Orosius wrote a treatise against the Priscillianists. When in 414 he visited North Africa, he came under the influence of Augustine, who sent him to Palestine to support Jerome in his fight against Pelagius. The Council of Diospolis in Palestine, however, sided with the latter. That led Orosius to write a piece in defense of his own views. By 417, he had returned to the west. His Latin *History Against the Pagans*, unlike the work of the Greek ecclesiastical historians of the period, viewed history through the perspective of Augustine's *City of God* and attacked the pagans on Augustine's grounds. Although the work begins with the foundation of Rome, its greatest value is its treatment of the years 378–417. CPL 571–574.   [F.W.N.]

Bibliography

Gennadius, *Lives of Illustrious Men* 40.

R.J. Deferarri, *Paulus Orosius: The Seven Books of History Against the Pagans*, FOTC (1964), Vol. 50.

B. Lacroix, *Orose et ses idées* (Montréal: Institut d'Études Médiévales, 1965); Y. Janvier, *La Géographie d'Orose* (Paris: Les Belles Lettres, 1982).

ORTHODOX CHURCH. The terms "orthodox" and "orthodoxy" (from the Greek *orthos*, "right," and *doxa*, "opinion" or "doctrine"), appeared in the fifth century A.D., but they acquired their technical meaning by the ninth century, when they were used to refer to "true doctrine" and "true practice." The term Orthodox Church now refers to those churches also known as the Eastern Orthodox Church, the Orthodox Catholic Church, or the Greek Orthodox Church, which derive from the four ancient patriarchates—Constantinople, Alexandria, Jerusalem, and Antioch—as well as other national, autocephalous churches and their daughter churches in communion with them. "Orthodox" in this modern sense contrasts with Roman Catholic, Protestant, Nestorian, and Coptic churches of the east. The Niceno-Constantinopolitan Creed (381) defined the church as "one, holy, catholic, and apostolic" without use of the term "orthodox," because it and other creeds were themselves a definition of what right doctrine was.

The terminology of the orthodox church arose (e.g., Justinian, *Cod.* 1.5.21) in contrast to positions defined by the ancient church as heretical. The basic doctrinal affirmations of orthodoxy involved God, Christ, the church, eschatology, the sacraments, and spiritual life. The ultimate source of divine revelation was held to be the Trinity, one in essence and three in persons, both unity and multiplicity, with the understanding that the Father is the First Cause in relation to the Son and the Holy Spirit. Although the divine essence of the Trinity is incomprehensible, a partial knowledge of the divine energies and attributes of God is attainable. The second person of the Holy Trinity, Jesus Christ, was affirmed to be the Son of God who in due time became man for human salvation. He is perfect God and perfect man, and the two natures in him are united, according to the definition of the Fourth Ecumenical Council (Chalcedon, 451), "without confusion, without change, without division, without separation," but in a perfect hypostatic union. Although Christ, or the Logos, was born of the Father before all ages, he was born as a human being of the Virgin Mary, was baptized by John the Baptist, preached his gospel, was arrested and crucified under Pontius Pilate, arose in three days, ascended to the heavens, and on the day of Pentecost sent the Holy Spirit on his twelve apostles and founded his church.

According to orthodox doctrine, the church is the body of Christ, both in her universal and local aspects, and the unity and catholicity of the church is lived and practiced in the sacraments, especially in the eucharist. Christology and ecclesiology are combined in the eucharistic community, in which redemption in Christ becomes a present reality and an eschatological anticipation. Although the faithful anticipate and pretaste the fruits of the life after death in the life of the church, the second coming of the Lord and the general and final judgment are integral parts of the teaching. The unrighteous are believed to receive eternal punishment, whereas the righteous will be transformed and transfigured with and into the eternal glory of God, a process called "divinization" (theōsis).

This ultimate goal was presented as the result of constant and unending effort of spiritual life on this earth. The fathers of the church described the spiritual life as a continuous and strenuous ascent (Gregory of Nyssa) or a continuous exertion and exhausting climbing on the ladder of spiritual perfection (John of Sinai). In this effort, the imagination of the faithful has to be cleansed of all shameful thought. The eastern fathers saw repentance, silence, tears, fasting, humility, contrition, and purity as bringing about the illuminating and sanctifying power of the Holy Spirit. This ultimate communion of man and God is strengthened, also, through an active and continuous participation of the faithful in the liturgical and sacramental life of the church. Thus the faithful were to live out in the liturgical, mystical, and spiritual life of the church the totality of the great mystery of salvation in Jesus Christ as Lord and Savior. *See also* Catholic Church; Church; Heresy; Holy Spirit; Trinity. [G.S.B.]

Bibliography

S. Bulgakov, *The Orthodox Church* (London: Centenary, 1935); H.E.W. Turner, *The Pattern of Christian Truth* (London: Mowbray, 1954); V. Lossky, *The Mystical Theology of the Eastern Church* (London: Clarke, 1957); J. Meyendorff, *The Orthodox Church* (New York: Pantheon, 1962); T.K. Ware, *The Orthodox Church* (Baltimore: Penguin, 1963); G. Florovsky, *Bible, Church, Tradition: An Eastern Orthodox View* (Belmont: Nordland, 1972); J. Karmiris, *A Synopsis of the Dogmatic Theology of the Orthodox Catholic Church* (Scranton: Christian Orthodox Edition, 1973); A. Schmemann, *The Historical Road of Eastern Orthodoxy* (Crestwood: St. Vladimir's Seminary, 1977); T.K. Ware, *The Orthodox Way* (Crestwood: St. Vladimir's Seminary, 1979); D.J. Constantelos, *Understanding the Greek Orthodox Church: Its Faith, History, and Practice* (New York: Seabury, 1982); H.O.J. Brown, *Heresies: The Image of Christ in the Mirror of Heresy and Orthodoxy from the Apostles to the Present* (Garden City: Doubleday, 1984); C. Cavarnos, *Byzantine Sacred Art*, 2nd ed. (Belmont: Institute for Byzantine and Modern Greek Studies, 1985); J.M. Hussey, *The Orthodox Church in the Byzantine Empire* (Oxford: Clarendon, 1986); P. Nellas, *Deification in Christ* (Crestwood: St. Vladimir's Seminary, 1987).

P

PACHOMIUS (ca. 292–346). Credited by church tradition with the establishment of cenobitic monasticism, in which monks live together in a single monastic complex under a common rule. Prior to this innovation, the monastic enterprise was dominated by the hermit monk, best represented by the Egyptian Anthony, who withdrew from the world in solitude (anchoritic monasticism). Pachomius is also credited with devising the first monastic rule for governing monks in the common economic and spiritual life of shared meals, work, and prayer within a walled complex. Recent scholarship has suggested that early Manichaean communities in Egypt may have influenced Pachomius's efforts.

A native Egyptian, Pachomius converted to Christianity at age twenty, when as a conscript in the army he experienced the kindness of Christian charity. Upon his release at war's end, he returned to the Upper Egyptian village of Chenoboskion to be baptized. A few years later, he took up the monastic life, living as a hermit and practicing harsh forms of ascesis under his spiritual father, Apa Palamon.

In 323, while collecting firewood at the deserted village of Tabennesi, the young monk received a vision in which a voice instructed him to "dwell in this place and build a monastery; for many will come to you to become monks, and they will profit their souls" (Bohairic, *Life of Pachomius* 17, tr. A. Veilleux, 1.39). The resulting community is presented as the beginning of cenobitic monasticism. After initial difficulties, Pachomius's new experiment grew rapidly. Within six years, the number of monks had grown so large as to require the establishment of a second monastery nearby at Pbow, which was destined to become the central monastery, and the largest, of the Pachomian system. As Pachomius's fame spread, other existing groups of monks petitioned to join the movement, and more distant monasteries were established along the Nile in Upper Egypt. When Pachomius died in the plague that ravaged his communities in 346, a total of nine monasteries and two affiliated nunneries were under his control. According to Palladius, writing ca. 420, some 3,000 monks belonged to the movement in Pachomius's day (*H. Laus.* 26.18–20).

The community continued to grow after Pachomius's death, first under the leadership of Theodore and then under Horsiesi. A major five-aisle basilica, the largest in Egypt (240 by 118 feet), was constructed at Pbow in the fifth century and dedicated by the archbishop of Alexandria. The Pachomian movement disappeared as an Egyptian institution in the latter part of the fifth century, a casualty of the Christological controversies brought on by the Council of Chalcedon (451). By this time, however, its fame and its rule had reached beyond Egypt and continued to influence Christian monastic development.

Pachomian sources include a complex tradition of the *Life of Pachomius*, chronicles, rules, instructions, letters, and other writings. *See also* Monasticism. [J.E.G.]

Bibliography

L.T. Lefort, *S. Pachomii vitae bohairice scriptae*, CSCO (1925), Vol. 89; idem, *S. Pachomii vitae sahidice scriptae*, CSCO (1933–1934), Vols. 99–100; F. Halkin, *Sancti Pachomii vitae graecae* (Brussels: Société des Bollandistes, 1932); L.T. Lefort, *Les Vies coptes de saint Pachome et de ses premiers successeurs* (Louvain: Bureaux du Muséon, 1943); idem, *Ouevres de s. Pachome et de ses disciples*, CSCO (1956), Vols. 159–169.

A.N. Athanassakis, tr. *The Life of Pachomius* (Missoula: Scholars, 1975); A. Veilleux, *Pachomian Koinonia* (Kalamazoo: Cistercian Publications, 1980–1982), Vols. 1–3; J.E. Goehring, *The Letter of Ammon and Pachomian Monasticism* (Berlin: de Gruyter, 1986).

D.J. Chitty, *The Desert a City: An Introduction to the Study of Egyptian and Palestinian Monasticism Under the Christian Empire* (Oxford: Blackwell, 1966); A. Veilleux, *La Liturgie dans le cénobitisme pachomien au quatrième siècle* (Rome: Herder, 1968); P. Rousseau, *Pachomius: The Making of a Community in Fourth-Century Egypt* (Berkeley: U of California P, 1985); J.E. Goehring, "New Frontiers in Pachomian Studies," *The Roots of Egyptian Christianity*, ed. A. Pearson and J.E. Goehring (Philadelphia: Fortress, 1986), pp. 236–257.

PACIAN OF BARCELONA (ca. 310–d. before 392). Bishop and writer. Little is known of Pacian's life; Jerome dedicated *On the Lives of Illustrious Men* to Pacian's son, the praetorian prefect Flavius Dexter. Pacian's works include a homily to catechumens on baptism and the effects of original sin; three letters to one Sympronian in defense of the right of the church to absolve sins committed after baptism, against the position taken by the followers of Novatian; and an exhortation to pen-

ance, which furnishes source material for the study of the penitential system in Spain. Feast day March 9. CPL 561–563. [M.P.McH.]

Bibliography

Jerome, *Lives of Illustrious Men* 106 (cf. 132).

PAGANISM AND CHRISTIANITY. It was in Antioch that the disciples first received the name of Christians (Acts 11:26); the context suggests that the name was originally applied to followers of Christ by outsiders, as elsewhere by king Agrippa (Acts 26:28) or by persecutors (1 Peter 4:16). The Roman sources make it evident that the designation was both official and popular at Rome from an early date; the form of the word itself indicates its origin in Latin and attests that Christians were believed to form a sociopolitical grouping organized around a leader whose personal name was Christus. This was an accurate, if hostile, designation that Christian believers were pleased to take up (Ignatius, *Rom.* 3.2).

Social Basis of Persecution. Among the Roman sources, the casual allusions of Suetonius may be taken as accurately reflecting attitudes current in their context: disturbances instigated by one "Chrestus" offered a pretext for expelling the Jews from Rome (*Claudius* 25.4); by Nero's time (A.D. 54–68), the Christians were seen as a distinct class of people given to a new and wicked superstition (*Nero* 16.2). Tacitus's more detailed description of the persecution under Nero should be read as reflecting the animus arising among Romans from the Jewish War (*Histories* 5), although the details are accurate enough (*Annals* 15.44): the mob that gave the Christians their name hated them for their crimes; their leader had been put to death under Pontius Pilate, but the "deadly superstition" spread throughout Judea and even to Rome. Some confessed their faith and were arrested; on their testimony, a multitude were convicted of arson, but also of hatred of the human race.

A generation later (ca. 112), Pliny the Younger encountered much the same situation in a remote corner of Pontus (*Letters* 10.96–97): there had been trials of Christians, but they were uncommon, for Pliny had doubts about details. Was the profession alone (*nomen*) to be punished, or only the crimes associated with it? Interrogation and confession were followed by threat of punishment and the opportunity to recant: characteristic was the inflexible obstinacy of the believers. They were widely hated and subject to anonymous denunciation, perhaps in part because the temples and festivals had been abandoned and the demand for sacrificial animals had fallen off. We see here the social basis of popular resentment that will be common in the acts of the martyrs. Christians already formed a private, if not secret, society (*hetaeria*) of the sort so feared by the Roman state (Pliny the Younger, *Letters,* 10.34); they might protest that they met only for hymns and solemn oaths of philanthropy, followed by an innocent meal. They were suspect, nonetheless, even if the torture of female slaves confirmed only that their superstition, not their conduct, was depraved. To be noted here also is the ritual imposed on those who denied the name of Christian: they were to call on the gods and make an offering to the emperor's image; then they were to curse Christ.

All these details, and their hostile tone, are confirmed by the martyr literature. Already, Polycarp (ca. 156/7) was pressed to say "Caesar is Lord," to swear by the genius of the emperor, to say, "Away with the atheists!," and to curse Christ (*M. Polyc.* 8–9). He responded by professing, "I am a Christian" (10). Widespread popular resentment also figured here (12) and the clear sense that the eternal reign of Christ was opposed to the power of the Roman state. The martyrs earned their status as friends of God, their identification with Christ, by bearing witness in death; around them they assembled "families" of followers, their "children in the Lord" (*M. Carp.,* Latin recension 3); here, even the hostile crowds recognized the image as alluding to the Christian community. Likewise, the agents of the Roman state are identified as the "devil's henchmen" (4). Examples could be multiplied; all the Roman sources and the martyr acts agree in their descriptions of the Christian movement and of the punishment awaiting those who professed

the Christian name. There remains the question of the crimes. Apart from atheism and antisocial behavior, the Roman sources are silent. The fair-minded Pliny found none. But even here there are hints of popular slanders soon to become specific. Pliny's Christians as early as 112 felt compelled to assert the innocence of their meals. By 177, servants were being terrified into denouncing "Oedipean marriages and dinners in the manner of Thyestes" (Eusebius, *H.E.* 5.1.14), while Blandina protested under torture that "we do nothing to be ashamed of" (5.1.19). The charge of obscene rites suggests the traditional Roman horror of conspiratorial movements, of which they were prepared to believe anything.

Strangely enough, the Christian apologists consistently report the details of these same slanderous accusations. Already by ca. 155, Justin Martyr alluded to allegations that Christians met in secret to eat human flesh and, once the lamps had been upset, to participate in promiscuous, perhaps incestuous, intercourse (*1 Apol.* 26.7); Athenagoras echoes the charges repudiated by the contemporary martyrs at Lyons (*Leg.* 3.1; 31–32). Tertullian (ca. 199) developed the theme with savage irony (*Apol.* 7–8); and somewhat later it appears fully formed in the *Octavius* 9 of Minucius Felix: Christians form a secret society of people "who fall in love almost before they are acquainted"; the names of brother and sister hallow fornication as incest. Their foolish superstition makes a boast of crime; a condemned criminal and his cross are fitting objects of their veneration. Finally, there is infant murder (here a part of initiation), cannibalism, and the banquet with promiscuous incestuous intercourse. It should be noted that Christians made similar charges against the Gnostics in the second century (Clement of Alexandria, *Str.* 3.2.10); a sharp-eyed Greek critic, no lover of the Christians, recognized in them no crime except "atheism," but rather the practice of brotherly love (Lucian, *Passing of Peregrinus* 11–13; 16).

One modern scholar is willing to believe that there is some basis to these charges (Wilken, p. 19f.); and Epiphanius, a later heresiologist, reports a sect in which ritual intercourse was reported under the name of the agape (*Haer.* 26.4–5). The indignation of Jerome (*Ep.* 22) and the embarrassment of Augustine that his mother engaged in festive banqueting by night at martyrs' shrines, when such practices had just been forbidden by Ambrose (*Conf.* 6.2), should remind us that such charges were not altogether fanciful. Certainly, few will believe the idealized picture of the Christian movement presented by the second-century apologists. Arguing against the Jews, they would have it that the church was the true Israel (Justin, *Dial.*). Addressing Greco-Roman philosophers, they presented the Christian faith as true philosophy (Justin, *Apol.*; Minucius Felix, *Octavius*), a view consistent with that held by the outsider Galen (Wilken, Ch. 2). Celsus was not convinced: with all their merits and pretensions, the Christians were an illegal movement that was undermining the state (Origen, *Cels.*), a judgment that recalls the charges made by the Roman authorities, the popular slanders, and the dramatic confrontations reported in the martyr acts.

Religion and the State. Christian "atheism" was, after all, treason against the Roman state; and it was the Roman state, not the imaginary entity known to moderns as "paganism," that orchestrated the opposition to the Christian movement. The civic fathers of the Greco-Roman world might respond to the Christian counterculture with distaste and small-scale violence, but it was the willingness of the Roman state and its rulers to support the civic religion that made Christian conduct subversive. The political disorders of the mid-third century were no doubt the proximate cause for the disappearance of many traditional cults: the hieroglyphic script became extinct in Egypt after Decius (249–251); at Rome, the Arval Brothers ceased to keep records from 241; and the last cultic inscriptions at Olympia date from the 260s (Geffcken, pp. 26–30). The persecutions of the Christians under Decius (250) and Diocletian (303) in particular increasingly took on the character of a holy war. Not only intending to break the church, they aimed to revive traditional cults, building and restoring temples and patronizing the priesthoods

(Eusebius, *H.E.* 8.14.9; 9.4.2). Emperors made a point of consulting oracles publicly; they sought out new cults (the cult of Mithras became the imperial faith); Diocletian and Maximian took the titles Jovius and Herculius; philosophers were encouraged to attack the new faith (Geffcken, pp. 31–33). The reign of Constantine was simply the turning point in the long struggle for legitimacy. In that struggle, the martyrs in the arena, even if few in number, were the banner carriers for the church. Symbolically, the arena was the scene of confrontation: attended by the masses, patronized by the imperial family, publicly legitimized by its parodic appropriation of traditional cult, and always a center for the cult of the ruler himself, the arena was well suited to this role.

The Public Games. Tertullian's denunciation of the games, *The Shows*, is harsh but coherent. God created everything; but rival powers perverted his plan by abusing creation; such abuse is idolatry (2). For a baptized Christian to attend the games is to participate in idolatry, in the work of the demons that he had renounced. The demonic nature of the games can be demonstrated from their origin, their names, their conduct, and the superstition they serve (4). From the beginning, games were either sacred or funereal—but they were associated with a wide range of social events, from royal birthdays and major victories to small-town celebrations (6). All the games required religious rites in which guilds, priesthoods, and magistrates took part—a demonic conclave (7). The circus was marred only by the cult of the gods; as the shrine of Venus, the theater was more alarming (8–10). But the gladiatorial games attract the harshest condemnation (12ff.): originating in human sacrifice to the dead, these developed as a refined form of sadism. Their demonic origin was patent: the crowd was maddened and merciless, obsessed with filth and violence, the sexual perversity of the plays, the savagery of the gladiators and beast shows (13–23). The gladiator personified the perversity of this culture: officially he was despised and excluded, but all sought him out, to sell their souls or bodies (22). Participation in the games often led to demonic possession (26); the games should be left to the devil's followers (28). Now they rejoiced; soon enough they would mourn (29–30). Featured in the final cataclysm will be "the magistrates who persecuted the name of Jesus" (30). It is easy to dismiss Tertullian's fervor; the games were a familiar feature of Roman life. Their pervasive influence has been underestimated by students of antiquity. Decorative art in the later empire attests their popularity—with all their lust and violence (cf. Martial, *On the Spectacles* 5). All this was familiar to Tertullian and essential to understanding the confrontation between church and society.

Ruler Cult. As the martyr literature makes clear, the imperial cult was central to this public ritual. Not that anyone viewed the emperor, alive or dead, as a god in the normal sense: he was *divus* not *deus*; he did not supplant the traditional deities but appropriated them to legitimize his rule (Bowersock, p. 172). As universal benefactor, the emperor personified the state; hence, he was everywhere. The second and third centuries saw the construction of new temples for the ruler cult become the most conspicuous form of building activity in the Roman world (Bowersock, p. 173). But it was the games, honoring the imperial house as universal benefactor, with which the imperial cult was most closely associated, whether in small-town festivals or at Rome itself: here was paraded the bust or statue that alone made the ruler familiar to the ruled (Bowersock, p. 173).

Omnipresent, the ruler cult was taken for granted except when resisted by Jews or opposed by Christians. But they opposed it only when it served the demons; it is now clear that the ruler cult persisted, indeed, that it was appropriated by the church under Constantine; so long as sacrifice was forbidden, temples could remain and games could continue, except for the gladiatorial shows. The apotheosis of Constantine in imperial iconography served only as the basis for his cult as a saint, well established by the fifth century. It was only after the Christians had shown the way that Julian was addressed in prayer, on the model of Christian prayer to the saints, something unheard of in the imperial cult before Constantine. Only

Ambrose and a few other church fathers perceived the danger of a religious authority vested in the emperor (Bowersock, p. 182).

The Heart of the Conflict. From the beginning, Christians had been recognized as a conspiratorial group, a social and political organization that did not acknowledge the legitimacy of the Roman state. This was no mere philosophical school, whatever the apologists might argue. The popular slanders were closer to the mark when they described the Christians as a secret society of initiates whose oaths of fraternal love were legitimized by ritual acts. Celsus too recognized that Jesus was no mere philosopher (Wilken, Ch. 5); more likely, he was a magician; how else could he perform miracles? Christian doctrine, in Celsus's view, was shameful, with its talk of god made man and of bodily resurrection; Christian history was founded on apostasy from Judaism; the Christian movement was revolutionary; it would lead to the overthrow of the empire. It is no surprise that such views prompted persecution.

Coexistence was never a possibility, and the victory of the church thus led to that takeover of the Roman state evident in Constantine's preferential legislation and his measures against Jews and heretics. Or perhaps it was rather that the Roman state had appropriated the church as a new source of legitimacy. The pagan emperor Julian understood this very well. Persecution would be counterproductive; it was more effective to encourage the Christian propensity for active dissent. However, the educational and philanthropic accomplishments of the church as a human organization could not be overlooked; they were to be imitated by a revived "paganism," itself now organized into something resembling a "church." The effort proved too late; but, perhaps paradoxically, Julian's realism decisively reshaped the struggle between Christians and followers of the traditional cults.

Pagan philosophers and statesmen alike were convinced of the necessity for social unity and systematic polemic; this very recognition acknowledged that their efforts were futile. The Greco-Roman cities, with their institutions and culture, had all but passed away; and with them faded their traditional cult. A certain legacy remained in philosophy and scholarship—and in the Christian obsession with demons. *See also* Apologetics; Church and State; Isis; Mithraism; Persecution; Philosophy; Roman Empire. [J.H.Co.]

Bibliography

Martial, *On the Spectacles*; Pliny the Younger, *Letters* 10.96, 97; Suetonius, *Claudius* 25.4; idem, *Nero* 16.2; Tacitus, *Annals* 15.44; idem, *Histories* 5; Lucian, *Passing of Peregrinus* 11–13; 16.

Ignatius, *Romans* 3.2; Justin Martyr, *1 Apology* 26.7; idem, *Dialogue with Trypho*; *Martyrdom of Polycarp* 8–12; *Acts of Carpus, Papylus, and Agathonice* (Latin) 3–4; Athenagoras, *Plea* 3.1; 31–32; Clement of Alexandria, *Miscellanies* 3.2.10; Tertullian, *Apology* 7–8; idem, *On the Shows*; Minucius Felix, *Octavius*; Origen, *Against Celsus*; Eusebius, *Church History* 5.1.14–19; 8.14.9; 9.4.2; Epiphanius, *Panarion* 26.4–5; Jerome, *Letter* 22; Augustine, *Confessions* 6.2.

P. de Labriolle, *La Réaction païenne: étude sur le polémique antichrétienne du Ier au VIe siècle* (Paris: L'Artisan du Livre, 1934); R. Walzer, *Galen on Jews and Christians* (London: Oxford UP, 1949); C. Andresen, *Logos und Nomos: Die Polemik des Kelsos wider des Christentums* (Berlin: de Gruyter, 1955); A.D. Nock, *Conversion: The Old and the New in Religion from Alexander the Great to Augustine of Hippo* (London: Oxford UP, 1961); J. Geffcken, *The Last Days of Greco-Roman Paganism* (Amsterdam: North-Holland, 1978); R.P.C. Hanson, "The Christian Attitude to Pagan Religions up to the Time of Constantine the Great," ANRW (1980), Vol. 23.2, pp. 910–973; R. MacMullen, *Paganism in the Roman Empire* (New Haven: Yale UP, 1981); G.W. Bowersock, "The Imperial Cult: Perceptions and Persistence," *Jewish and Christian Self-Definition II: Self-Definition in the Greco-Roman World*, ed. B.F. Meyer and E.P. Sanders (Philadelphia: Fortress, 1982), pp. 171–182; E.V. Gallagher, *Divine Man or Magician? Celsus and Origen on Jesus* (Chico: Scholars, 1982); R.L. Wilken, *The Christians as the Romans Saw Them* (New Haven: Yale UP, 1984); R.L. Fox, *Pagans and Christians* (New York: Knopf, 1987).

PALESTINE. Region of Jesus' ministry. Herod the Great (37–4 B.C.) had renewed the country through his great wealth. He added significant buildings to Jerusalem, the capital, and built his remarkable seaport, Caesarea Maritima, which brought lucrative trade to the land.

The First Jewish War (A.D. 66–70) seriously weakened the country. Much of Jerusalem was destroyed, including Herod's temple. The emperor Julian (361–363) attempted to rebuild the Jerusalem temple under his policy of religious toleration, but evidently hidden pockets of gas caused explosions and fires that stopped the project. Palestinian Judaism, however, remade itself without its cultic center. Johanan Ben Zakkai began an academy in Jamnia ca. A.D. 70. Although Jerusalem was renamed Aelia Capitolina by Hadrian after the Bar Kochba revolt in 135 and pagan temples were built on sacred sites, the Jewish community recovered. It worked through the process of closing its own canon of scriptures and developed the strong rabbinic tradition found in the Mishnah. The Palestinian Talmud was produced in academies at Tiberias, Caesarea, and Sepphoris (Diocaesarea) during the third through the fifith centuries. Indeed, Origen (*Sel. in Ps.*) and Jerome (*Praef. in Job* 1) learned Hebrew, Jewish tradition, and scriptural interpretation from Palestinian rabbis.

Both Paul's epistles and the Book of Acts refer to Christianity in Palestine. During the First Jewish War, some Jewish Christians left Jerusalem for Pella, the naturally fortified city in central Palestine, perhaps to return later. Jewish Christians, both more orthodox and more Gnostic groups, persisted. Origen (*Cel.* 2.1), Epiphanius (*Haer.* 29; 36), and Jerome (*Ep. ad Aug.* 89.13; *In Isa.* 5.18ff.), all with experience in Palestine, knew the differences between the groups, which the heresiologists misunderstood. Eusebius's unhistorical list of Jerusalem bishops (*H.E.* 3.35; 4.5–6) unfortunately does not give us good information about second-century Palestinian Christians.

The major figure in the third century was Origen. Born in Alexandria and a teacher there for years, Origen (ca. 185–251), while on a trip to Palestine, was ordained a presbyter in 230 by Theoctistus and Alexander, the bishops of Caesarea and Jerusalem respectively (Eusebius, *H.E.* 6.19). That so angered Demetrius, Origen's bishop in Alexandria, that he dismissed Origen from his teaching position and forced him to leave Egypt. Origen took up residence in Caesarea of Palestine, where he continued his biblical commentaries and other writings. He died as a result of injuries received during the Decian persecution (Eusebius, *H.E.* 6.32, 39), but his influence in the region was strong well into the sixth century. Pamphilus, the teacher of Eusebius, carefully watched over the library that Origen had assembled at Caesarea (*H.E.* 6.32). Later, Euzoius (Jerome, *Vir. ill.* 113) had the deteriorating papyrus volumes recopied on parchment.

In the Valerian persecution (257–259), a number of Christians were martyred, both orthodox and Marcionite (Eusebius, *H.E.* 7.12, 15). Under Diocletian (284–305), martyrdom in Palestine was evidently widespread and intense. Eusebius devoted a treatise to *The Martyrs of Palestine*, perhaps because of his closeness to the sources. Procopius, a lector who translated Greek into Aramaic, had lived in Scythopolis. He and a number of leaders from smaller churches in the region around Caesarea were tortured. Other Christians were put to the test in Gaza, Tyre, and Ascalon. People traveling in other areas were taken prisoner; at least one Palestinian died in Antioch. People from Gadera, Diospolis (a village near Eleutheropolis), Jamnia, and Maganaea (perhaps Batanea in northeastern Palestine) were affected. Judaism was not involved, because it was a recognized religion of the empire.

Pilgrims came to Palestine well before the fourth century. Although not a pilgrim in the usual sense, Melito of Sardis visited the area in the middle of the second century to find out exactly which books the Jews accepted in their canon (Eusebius, *H.E.* 4.26.14). Alexander, a bishop in Cappadocia, may be the first recorded visitor to have sought out the holy places. The first known personal record of such travels is that of the anonymous pilgrim from Bordeaux. Another famous traveler, Egeria, wrote about her travels from Spain to Palestine and Sinai, probably in the early fifth century. Earlier figures like the elder and younger Melanias, Paula, and Eustochium, as well as Basil of Caesarea and Jerome, came partially as pilgrims. When Julian became emperor (361), pagan riots throughout Palestine destroyed sites marked for pilgrims. Eusebius (*H.E.* 6.18) had seen a statue in Caesarea Philippi said to be of Jesus and the woman with the issue of blood, but it was destroyed by pagans in Julian's reign (Philostorgius, *H.E.* 7.3).

Some Christians disliked the trappings of pilgrimages. Gregory of Nyssa, sent to Palestine by a council in Antioch to investigate Jerusalem's orthodoxy, was shocked by the immorality they had spawned (*Ep.* 2, *On Pilgrimages*; but cf. *Ep.* 3, *To Eustathia et al.*). Jerome, however (*Ep.* 46; 58), defended the practice. Christian iconography was permanently affected by pilgrimage sites in Palestine; various artifacts found elsewhere in the Christian world depict not only the treasures within pilgrimage shrines but the shrines themselves. This is especially true of, but not limited to, depictions of Jerusalem.

Conflict with Judaism continued during the third and fourth centuries. Lydda (Diospolis), Tiberias, and Caesarea all had strong Jewish and Christian communities. One note in the Talmud speaks of a rabbi in Caesarea who could argue about Christian doctrine in ways that a visiting rabbi from Babylon did not know or understand (*b. Ab. Zara* 4a). Proselytism probably was practiced by both sides.

Palestine was also notable as a center of developing Christian monasticism. In the early fourth century, Chariton, a pilgrim from Iconium, was attacked by robbers and held in a cave near Fara. When his captors died (apparently from poisoned wine), he felt miraculously saved and stayed in the cave as a hermit. By 330, he had agreed to allow others to join him and is credited with creating the first laura, eventually called the Old Laura, a communal organization of hermits' cells. Hilarion (ca. 291–371), perhaps the first anchorite in Palestine, is said to have visited Anthony in Egypt while studying in Alexandria. He returned to his village near Gaza and went into the desert a few miles away from the sea (Sozomen, *H.E.* 3.14). Sozomen tells of a number of people who set up monasteries in the region of Gaza and Jerusalem (*H.E.* 6.32).

In the early fifth century, Euthymius, an Armenian pilgrim, went to the Old Laura. By 420, he and a friend had built their own laura, in which Euthymius was active until his death in 473. Saba, a Cappadocian pilgrim, became an anchorite and began at least seven monasteries in the region of the Kidron Valley. By 494, he was made archimandrite of all the hermits in Palestine, a position he held until his death in 531. Cyril of Scythopolis, who lived in the monasteries of St. Euthymius and St. Saba, wrote hagiographic lives of each of them.

Three important theological issues touched Palestine in the fifth and sixth centuries. In the first, Pelagius, a British defender of free will and ethical responsibility who was eventually condemned in the west, went to Palestine and was declared orthodox by a synod at Lydda (Diospolis) in 415. Neither Jerome in Palestine nor Augustine in North Africa could influence the decision otherwise. The second, Origenism, was enlivened by great personalities. Rufinus and Jerome, earlier friends and fellow students, had both learned much from Origen. Rufinus continued his support of the brilliant theologian, but Jerome was concerned about Origen's views on universal salvation, the humanity of Jesus, and the place of human souls. When Epiphanius, born in Palestine, then bishop of Salamis in Cyprus, sought to root out Origenism, Rufinus and John, bishop of Jerusalem, stood against him, but Jerome joined his cause. The monks of Palestine were divided. During the early sixth century, Saba fought Origenism, but other monks left Mar Saba and built their own laura. In 553, the Second Ecumenical Council of Constantinople condemned Origen. Eustochius of Alexandria, made bishop of Jerusalem, used imperial troops to clean out the "heretics" in the monasteries.

A third issue was Christology. Many in Palestine had developed a view of Jesus similar to that held by Cyril of Alexandria, which emphasized the divinity of Christ, even to the point of attributing one nature to the Son. Nestorius, a supporter of two natures, was seen as an enemy. When Juvenal, bishop of Jerusalem, returned in 451 from the Council of Chalcedon, which defined Jesus as one person in two natures, he was driven out of the city for signing its statement of faith, as were other Palestinian bishops who supported that council. Euthymius, however, stayed loyal to the imperial settlement. The empress Eudoxia controlled troops in Jerusalem, and Juvenal was able to return, forcing some of his opponents to flee to Egypt. In 482, when Zeno tried to reinterpret Chalcedon in his *Henoticon*, many Palestinian monasteries and some bishops accepted his compromise, which did not challenge Monophysite (one-nature) views. Saba, however, the founder of a large monastery outside Jerusalem, supported Chalcedon. But Peter the Iberian, leader of a monastery in Maiuma, continued his Monophysite teaching. Sophronius says that by the time of the Arab conquest in the seventh century there were 137 anti-Chalcedonian monasteries in Palestine. *See also* Caesarea; Jerusalem; Monasticism; Pilgrimage. [F.W.N.]

Bibliography

F. Abel, *Histoire de la Palestine depuis la conquête d'Alexandre jusqu'à l'invasion arabe* (Paris: Gabalda, 1952); A. Ovadiah, *Corpus of the Byzantine Churches in the Holy Land* (Bonn: Hanstein, 1970); P.B. Bagatti, *The Church from the Circumcision and the Church from the Gentiles in Palestine* (Jerusalem: Franciscan, 1971); K. Weitzmann, "*Loca Sancta* and the Representational Arts of Palestine," *DOP* 28 (1974):31–55; L. Perrone, *La chiesa di Palestina e le controversie Cristologiche* (Brescia: Paideia, 1980); F. Heyer, *Kirchengeschichte des Heiligen Landes* (Stuttgart: Kohlhammer, 1984); M. Simon, *Verus Israel: A Study of the Relation Between Christians and Jews in the Roman Empire (135–425)* (Engl. trans. of 1964 French with postscript) (Oxford: Oxford UP, 1986); G. Viken, *Pilgrimage Art* (Washington, D.C.: Dumbarton Oaks, 1986).

PALLADIUS (ca. 365–425). Historian of monasticism. Born in Galatia, Palladius studied classical literature and theology, particularly with Evagrius of Pontus. His brothers and sisters had entered monasteries; he began that life in a community at the Mount of Olives. He later lived with ascetics in Alexandria, Nitria, and Cellia, but his health broke and he returned to Palestine. From there he went to Helenopolis in Bithynia, where he became bishop, eventually holding the same post at Aspuna. He is best known for his *Lausiac History* (419–420), which contains many anecdotes about famous ascetic figures of the period. CPG III, 6036–6038. TLG 2111.

[F.W.N.]

Bibliography

R. T. Meyer, tr., *Palladius: The Lausiac History*, ACW (1965), Vol. 34; idem, *Palladius: Dialogue on the Life of St. John Chrysostom*, ACW (1985), Vol. 45.

E.D. Hunt, "Palladius of Helenopolis: A Party and Its Supporters in the Church of the Late Fourth Century," *JThS* 24 (1973):456–480.

PAMPHILUS (ca. 240–309). Presbyter at Caesarea in Palestine and scholar. After studying at Alexandria, Pamphilus established a school at Caesarea. An ardent admirer of Origen, he wrote an *Apologia* for Origen, only partially preserved in a Latin translation. Pamphilus assembled a large library, used by his student Eusebius, who took his name (Eusebius Pamphilus) and wrote his *Life*, now lost. A two-year imprisonment in the persecution under Maximinus Daia ended in his martyrdom. Feast day June 1 (west), February 16 (east). CPG I, 1715–1716. TLG 2961. [E.F.]

Bibliography

Eusebius, *Church History* 6.32.3; 6.33.4; 7.32.25; 8.13.6; Jerome, *Lives of Illustrious Men* 75; idem, *Preface to Chronicles*; idem, *Against Rufinus* 1.2, 9; 2.6, 27; idem, *Letter* 84.10; Photius, *Library* 118.

PANTAENUS (late second century). Teacher at Alexandria. Pantaenus is apparently referred to as "the Sicilian bee" by his student Clement of Alexandria (*Str.* 1.1). Eusebius reports his mission work in India (H.E. 5.10). He was interested in reconciling Greek learning and Christianity and pioneered in the spiritual interpretation of the scriptures. Feast day July 7 (Coptic, June 22). [E.F.]

Bibliography

Clement of Alexandria, *Miscellanies* 1.1; *Selections from Prophetic Scriptures* 56.2; Eusebius, *Church History* 5.10–11; 6.6; 6.13.2; 6.14.9; 6.19.13; Maximus Confessor, *De variis difficilibus locis Dionysii et Gregorii* , PG 91.1085A–B; Photius, *Library* 118.

PAPACY. Institution of the bishop of Rome as holding primacy within the universal church. Attention came to focus on the leader of the Roman church as representing the primacy of Rome, although the monepiscopate may not have been clearly established there until the mid-second century. Later theologians cited certain New Testament passages as basic to Roman claims, for example, Matthew 16:16–18; Luke 22:31f.; and John 21:15–18, Jesus' commission to Peter as leader of the twelve. But use of these passages did not figure prominently in earlier decades.

Against the adherents of Gnosticism in particular, the church fathers stressed the idea of an apostolic succession found in the churches but centered especially in the bishops as leaders of the communities. Among all the sees in the world, certain ones stood out because of their historical links to the first generation of founding apostles. Hegesippus, a Jewish Christian of the mid-second century, traveled the Mediterranean to verify the uniformity of teaching within the church. He made a list of Roman bishops, but unfortunately the citation in Eusebius of Caesarea does not give the list itself (*H.E.* 4.22). The first such list comes a little later in Irenaeus of Lyons (*Haer.* 3.3.3). Such lists do not prove the existence of the monepiscopate in the first century. Linus, Cletus, and others counted as early bishops may have been outstanding members of the collective leadership of Roman Christians.

Why did the church of Rome rise to such a position of leadership? Most emphasize the role of Peter and Paul. After centuries of debate, their presence in Rome is generally conceded. In the narrow, literal sense, they were not the founders of the Christian community there, but most would see them as founders in a moral sense. Moreover, they died as martyrs and their remains were a proud possession of the Roman church, a fact that would be of increasing significance in time to come. They were the reason for Rome's special position (Irenaeus, *Haer.* 3.3.2).

Although there were many sees of apostolic foundation in the east, the west had only one (Carthage never made such a claim). Because of Peter and Paul, Rome was the outstanding apostolic see in the church as a whole. Did such moral authority translate into power of command? Roman authority was clearest in practice in Italy, although this was modified somewhat with the emergence of Milan as the metropolitan see of northern Italy in the late fourth century. It was also acknowledged in Gaul and Spain. Latin North Africa sometimes contested Roman intervention but at other times sought Roman action. The problematic area lay in relations with the east.

In the early centuries, the Greek east was the center of almost all theological activity and consequently of doctrinal controversy. Rival sees sought Roman support for themselves and their views. In hindsight, the Roman record for supporting orthodoxy was outstanding, whereas the record of the principal eastern sees was much more checkered. Rome reacted much more than it acted. Its function might best be characterized as one of vigilance, on guard against error, and of confirming or rejecting the positions of others. But from the point of view of theological creativity, Rome was a negligible quantity. In the area of discipline, the Roman ideal was that others should conform to Roman ways (e.g., the letter of Innocent I to bishop Decentius of Gubbio, 416), but in practice the see had much less success in this endeavor. Thus, the question of who held the ultimate decision-making power in the church remained unsettled. By the fifth century, if not before, the Roman view was that it had that power whereas others, especially in the east, looked to the ecumenical council as the supreme authority.

Historical Developments. Looking first at the period before Nicaea, one must keep in mind the fragmentary state of the evidence. Among documents emanating from Rome is the letter of Clement, *1 Clement* (ca. 96), from the Roman Christians to the community of Corinth. Longstanding discussions range around the issue of whether this document should be regarded as an instance of authoritative Roman intervention in the affairs of a distant (and apostolic) church or as an exercise in fraternal correction.

A clearer instance of the exercise of Roman authority in the church at large came at the end of the second century in the course of the Paschal controversy, concerning the method for determining the date of Easter.

Although it probably started as a dispute between the bishop of Rome and an eastern community settled in Rome itself, it soon escalated into a conflict of traditions between Rome and Christians of the province of Asia. Victor I of Rome (189–198) threatened to cut off the dissenters. The practice of the rest of the church agreed with that of Rome, but many bishops, including Irenaeus (Eusebius, *H.E.* 5.24.11), thought the Roman threat excessive. The issue does not seem to have been resolved at this time.

Among non-Roman witnesses is the work of Irenaeus of Lyons (d. ca. 202), *Against Heresies.* Irenaeus developed the classic argument that the teaching of Christ is to be found in the doctrine preached publicly in the churches. In their historical link to the receding past, the apostolic sees play an indispensable role in preserving this rule of faith, and the church of Rome is the outstanding apostolic see, "one with which all must be in agreement" (3.3.2).

A few decades later, Cyprian, bishop of Carthage (d. 258), used a much-controverted expression: the "chair of Peter." In his letters and his treatise *On the Unity of the Church,* Cyprian is concerned primarily with the unity of the local church. Each legitimate bishop in his own see holds the "chair of Peter" against usurpers. He honored the see of Rome but also in later years came into serious conflict with Stephen I of Rome over the rebaptism of heretics. Although we do not have Stephen's own words, a letter of bishop Firmilian of Caesarea in Cappadocia (hostile to Stephen) indicates that Stephen based his claims on his holding the historical "chair of Peter" in Rome.

The first half of the fourth century saw little activity by the Roman bishops. Medieval legends about Constantine and Sylvester I (314–335) seem to have arisen from the later presumption that the church of Rome must have played a more prominent role than it actually did. Both the Lateran basilica and the Church of St. Peter derive from Constantine's beneficence. At the beginning of the controversy over Donatism, he asked the Roman bishop Miltiades to hear the appeals, but the decision of a Roman council was put aside and the case judged afresh by the Council of Arles (314). Rome played little part in the Council of Nicaea (325) called by the emperor.

The western role began to emerge more sharply in the long aftermath of Nicaea, when Rome became the champion of the fugitive Athanasius (d. 373). The rejection (340) by Julius I of the condemnation of Athanasius raised the issue of how such east-west confrontations could be settled. The eastern enemies of the Alexandrian bishop claimed that their decisions were not subject to further appeal. The Council of Sardica (343) was intended to reconcile east and west. Although it failed in this, the western bishops with Athanasius and his fellow exiles promulgated canons that specified that for the "honor of the memory of Peter" the bishop of Rome should henceforward be a court of appeal. These canons seem to have had few echoes in other churches in the ancient period. When Constantius II became sole emperor in 351, he enforced his will on the western church. Bishop Liberius of Rome was exiled (355–358) and ultimately capitulated, although the prestige of his see does not appear to have suffered.

As Constantinople's ecclesiastical importance increased, its episcopal leadership was formalized in the third canon of the council of 381. Later to be considered the Second Ecumenical Council, this was, even more than Nicaea, an eastern council. The third canon recognized Constantinople as the "New Rome," second in primacy of honor after "Old Rome." Its view that the importance of a see was intimately connected with its civil rank clashed with the increasingly clear Roman insistence that Rome was the primatial see by divine right; political and historical significance was irrelevant.

Indeed, it is in the mid-fourth century, as Rome's civil importance rapidly began to decline, that there is extant an abundance of documentary material from a succession of strong bishops, asserting their authority in no uncertain terms. From the time of Damasus I (366–384), Roman letters refer to the local church as *the* apostolic see. Zosimus (417–418) and Boniface I (418–422) stressed that Roman

decisions can be neither appealed nor reversed. The letters of Innocent I (401–417) use language that fast became commonplace, for example, that major cases are to be brought to Rome's attention "as the synod decided" (Letter to Victricius of Rouen, 416). The apostle Peter continues to act in each succeeding Roman bishop (ibid.—an idea that goes back at least to Siricius [384–399]). Decrees from the western emperors Gratian (ca. 378) and Valentinian III (445) supported Rome's position.

The ambivalence of the African church is seen in its eager soliciting of Innocent's approval of its condemnation of Pelagius (416–417) and its angry reaction, on the other hand, to Roman intervention in the case of Apiarius (418–424). The recent publication of hitherto unknown letters of Augustine shows that the traditional view of African reluctance to consult with Rome has been exaggerated. Roman bishops at this time also sought to reinforce their influence beyond Italy by the establishment of vicariates in places like Thessalonica (Damasus) and Arles (Zosimus). From Siricius (385) come the first known papal decretals, that is, canonical decisions issued simply by the bishop of Rome without a council. The Roman church, he insisted, is the head of the body. Perhaps in answer to the third canon of the council of 381, a Roman council in 382 elaborated the view that the eastern sees of Alexandria and Antioch were of significance only because they had once been associated with Peter (or Mark, in the case of Alexandria). Constantinople, with no Petrine connection, was eliminated from consideration. The rise of Roman prestige and power also had its dark side in the menace of corruption through wealth and arrogance, as sketched in Ammianus Marcellinus (*History* 27.3.12–15) and exemplified in the violence that sometimes accompanied papal elections.

The Christological developments of the fifth century derive from the theological movements in the east. The authority of Celestine I (d. 432) was associated with the triumph of Cyril of Alexandria over Nestorius of Constantinople at the Council of Ephesus (431).

The high point of the ancient papacy is usually seen in the time of Leo I the Great (440–461), the first Roman bishop from whom we have homilies as well as letters. His *Tome* expressing the western view of the relation between the divine and the human in Christ was at first suppressed at Ephesus (449) but, with the help of a new ruler, triumphed at Chalcedon two years later. Leo's victory was, however, lessened by the even stronger assertion of Constantinople's standing as the New Rome in Canon 28, which he vehemently rejected.

The brief reign of Gelasius I (492–496) presages the medieval papacy. Gelasius asserted Rome's authority in clear and often harsh terms, showed only contempt for Constantinople's claims, and declared the power of priests superior to that of kings. The rise of the Monophysites after Chalcedon led the eastern emperors to seek theological accommodation with them for the sake of political unity. One such attempt by the emperor Zeno (482) led to the Acacian schism between Rome and Constantinople, ending only with the accession of the emperor Justin I (518), who insisted on its termination. The formula of union of Hormisdas was more or less imposed on the eastern churchmen. Among its phrases was: ". . . in the apostolic see, the Catholic religion has always been preserved immaculate . . . ."

This seemingly irresistible rise of the Roman see suffered a serious setback in the sixth century during the reign of the emperor Justinian I (527–565). Justinian also sought to appease the Monophysites by condemning long-dead theologians and their works. This controversy, known as the Three Chapters, was perceived in the west as an attack on the now untouchable Council of Chalcedon. Vigilius (537–555) was long imprisoned and mistreated in Constantinople. His frequent vacillations and ultimate approval of the Second Council of Constantinople (553) stirred widespread anger in the west. His successors in the sixth century were faced with a stubborn schism in northern Italy. Gregory the Great (590–604) helped to heal that wound and restore much of the damaged prestige of the Roman see. *See also* Election to Church Office; Peter; Rome.

[R.B.E.]

Bibliography

C. Mirbt and K. Aland, *Quellen zur Geschichte des Papsttums und des römischen Katholizismus*, Bd. 1, *Von den Anfängen bis zum Tridentinum*, 6. Auflage (Tübingen: Mohr–Siebeck, 1967).

L. R. Loomis, *The Book of the Popes to the Pontificate of Gregory I* (New York: Columbia UP, 1916; repr. New York: Octagon, 1965); J.T. Shotwell and L.R. Loomis, *The See of Peter* (New York: Columbia UP, 1927; repr. New York: Octagon, 1965); E. Giles, *Documents Illustrating Papal Authority A. D. 96–454* (London: SPCK, 1952); H. Burn-Murdoch, *The Development of the Papacy* (London: Faber and Faber, 1954); R. Davis, *The Book of Pontiffs* (Liverpool: Liverpool UP, 1989).

E. Caspar, *Geschichte des Papsttums von den Anfängen bis zur Höhe der Weltherrschaft. 2 bde.* (Tübingen: Mohr-Siebeck, 1930–1933); E. G. Weltin, *The Ancient Popes* (Westminster: Newman, 1964); R. Brown et al., *Peter in the New Testament* (Minneapolis: Augsburg, and New York: Paulist, 1973); A. C. Piepkorn and J. McCue, "The Roman Primacy in The Patristic Era," *Papal Primacy and the Universal Church*, ed. P. Empie and A. Murphy (Minneapolis: Augsburg, 1974), pp. 43–97; W. De Vries, *Orient et Occident: les structures ecclésiales vues dans l'histoire des sept premiers conciles oecuméniques* (Paris: Cerf, 1974); C. Pietri, *Roma Christiana: recherches sur l'église de Rome, son organisation, sa politique, son idéologie de Miltiade à Sixte III (311–440)*, 2 vols. (Rome: Ecole Française, 1976); J. Richards, *The Popes and the Papacy in the Early Middle Ages 476–752* (Boston: Routledge and Kegan Paul, 1979); M. Woytowytsch, *Papsttum und Konzile von den Anfängen bis zu Leo I (440–461)* (Stuttgart: Hiersemann, 1981); J.N.D. Kelly, *The Oxford Dictionary of Popes* (New York: Oxford UP, 1986); P. Lampe, *Die stadtrömischen Christen in den ersten beiden Jahrhunderten* (Tübingen: Mohr-Siebeck, 1987).

POPES

Information includes the name of the pope, in many cases his name before becoming pope, his birthplace or country of origin, the date of accession to the papacy, and the date of the end of reign, which, in all but a few cases, was the date of death. Double dates indicate times of election and coronation. Source: *1987 Catholic Almanac*, ed. F.A. Foy (Huntington: *Our Sunday Visitor*, 1987), p. 123, based on *Annuario Pontificio*.

St. Peter (Simon Bar-Jona): Bethsaida in Galilee; d. ca. 64 or 67.

St. Linus: Tuscany; 67–76.

St. Anacletus (Cletus): Rome; 76–88.

St. Clement: Rome; 88–97.

St. Evaristus: Greece; 97–105.

St. Alexander I: Rome; 105–115.

St. Sixtus I: Rome; 115–125.

St. Telesphorus: Greece; 125–136.

St. Hyginus: Greece; 136–140.

St. Pius I: Aquileia; 140–155.

St. Anicetus: Syria; 155–166.

St. Soter: Campania; 166–175.

St. Eleutherius: Nicopolis in Epirus; 175–189.

Up to the time of St. Eleutherius, the years indicated for the beginning and end of pontificates are not absolutely certain. Also, up to the middle of the eleventh century, there are some doubts about the exact days and months given in chronological tables.

St. Victor I: Africa; 189–199.

St. Zephyrinus: Rome; 199–217.

St. Callistus I: Rome; 217–222.

St. Urban I: Rome; 222–230.

St. Pontian: Rome; July 21, 230, to Sept. 28, 235.

St. Anterus: Greece; Nov. 21, 235, to Jan. 3, 236.

St. Fabian: Rome; Jan. 10, 236, to Jan. 20, 250.

St. Cornelius: Rome; Mar. 251 to June 253.

St. Lucius I: Rome; June 25, 253, to Mar. 5, 254.

St. Stephen I: Rome; May 12, 254, to Aug. 2, 257.

St. Sixtus II: Greece; Aug. 30, 257, to Aug. 6, 258.

St. Dionysius: July 22, 259, to Dec. 26, 268.

St. Felix I: Rome; Jan. 5, 269, to Dec. 30, 274.

St. Eutychian: Luni; Jan. 4, 275, to Dec. 7, 283.

St. Caius: Dalmatia; Dec. 17, 283, to Apr. 22, 296.

St. Marcellinus: Rome; June 30, 296, to Oct. 25, 304.

St. Marcellus I: Rome; May 27, 308, or June 26, 308, to Jan. 16, 309.

St. Eusebius: Greece; Apr. 18, 309 or 310, to Aug. 17, 309 or 310.

St. Melchiades (Miltiades): Africa; July 2, 311, to Jan. 11, 314.

St. Sylvester I: Rome; Jan. 31, 314, to Dec. 31, 335.

(Most of the popes before St. Sylvester I were martyrs.)

St. Marcus: Rome; Jan. 18, 336, to Oct. 7, 336.

St. Julius I: Rome; Feb. 6, 337, to Apr. 12, 352.

Liberius: Rome; May 17, 352, to Sept. 24, 366.

St. Damasus I: Spain; Oct. 1, 366, to Dec. 11, 384.

St. Siricius: Rome; Dec. 15, or 22 or 29, 384, to Nov. 26, 399.

St. Anastasius I: Rome; Nov. 27, 399, to Dec. 19, 401.

St. Innocent I: Albano; Dec. 22, 401, to Mar. 12, 417.

St. Zosimus: Greece; Mar. 18, 417, to Dec. 26, 418.

St. Boniface I: Rome; Dec. 28 or 29, 418, to Sept. 4, 422.

St. Celestine I: Campania; Sept. 10, 422, to July 27, 432.

St. Sixtus III: Rome; July 31, 432, to Aug. 19, 440.

St. Leo I (the Great): Tuscany; Sept. 29, 440, to Nov. 10, 461.

St. Hilary: Sardinia; Nov. 19, 461, to Feb. 29, 468.

St. Simplicius: Tivoli; Mar. 3, 468, to Mar. 10, 483.

St. Felix III (II): Rome; Mar. 13, 483, to Mar. 1, 492.

He should be called Felix II, and his successors of the same name should be numbered accordingly. The discrepancy in the numerical designation of popes named Felix was caused by the erroneous insertion in some lists of the name of St. Felix of Rome, a martyr.

St. Gelasius I: Africa; Mar. 1, 492, to Nov. 21, 496.

Anastasius II: Rome; Nov. 24, 496, to Nov. 19, 498.

St. Symmachus: Sardinia; Nov. 22, 498, to July 19, 514.

St. Hormisdas: Frosinone; July 20, 514, to Aug. 6, 523.

St. John I, Martyr: Tuscany; Aug. 13, 523, to May 18, 526.

St. Felix IV (III): Samnium; July 12, 526, to Sept. 22, 530.

Boniface II: Rome; Sept. 22, 530, to Oct. 17, 532.

John II: Rome; Jan. 2, 533, to May 8, 535.

John II was the first pope to change his name. His given name was Mercurius.

St. Agapetus I: Rome; May 13, 535, to Apr. 22, 536.

St. Silverius, Martyr: Campania; June 1 or 8, 536, to Nov. 11, 537 (d. Dec. 2, 537).

St. Silverius was violently deposed in March 537, and abdicated Nov. 11, 537. His successor, Vigilius, was not recognized as pope by all the Roman clergy until his abdication.

Vigilius: Rome; Mar. 29, 537, to June 7, 555.

Pelagius I: Rome; Apr. 16, 556, to Mar. 4, 561.

John III: Rome; July 17, 561, to July 13, 574.

Benedict I: Rome; June 2, 575, to July 30, 579.

Pelagius II: Rome; Nov. 26, 579, to Feb. 7, 590.

St. Gregory I (the Great): Rome; Sept. 3, 590, to Mar. 12, 604.

PAPIAS (early second century). Bishop of Hierapolis in Phrygia and apostolic father. Papias wrote *Expositions of the Oracles of the Lord* (ca. 130) in five books, known only from fragmentary quotations in later writers. Especially notable is his testimony concerning the writing of Matthew (originally, he says, in Hebrew) and Mark (faithfully recording the preaching of Peter but not set out in good order). Papias, in commenting on the oracles of the Lord, declared a preference for what he heard from the "living voice" of the elders who heard the teachings of the disciples of the Lord over what was written in books. His materialistic view of the millennium later brought him into disfavor. CPG I, 1047. TLG 1558. [E.F.]

Bibliography

Irenaeus, *Against Heresies* 5.33.4; Eusebius, *Church History* 2.15.2; 3.36.2; 3.39; Jerome, *Lives of Illustrious Men* 18.

J.B. Lightfoot, *Apostolic Fathers* (London: Macmillan, 1907), pp. 514–535.

U.H.J. Körtner, *Papias von Hierapolis: Ein Beitrag zur Geschichte des frühen Christentums* (Göttingen: Vandenhoeck & Ruprecht, 1983); J. Kürzinger, *Papias von Hierapolis und die Evangelien des Neuen Testaments* (Regensburg: Pustet, 1983).

PAPYRI. Common writing material in antiquity. The papyrus reed grew abundantly in Egypt. The stems were sliced into strips laid across each other, and beaten into paperlike sheets (Pliny the Elder, *Natural History* 13.68–83), then often made up into rolls or codices (books of the modern type).

As a category of modern study, papyrology includes texts on other materials used in antiquity to carry writing—parchment, wooden tablets, ostraca (pottery shards)—but recovered in Egypt or occasionally elsewhere in modern times. Being ancient copies directly retrieved, papyri are distinguished from "manuscripts" preserved in libraries as the result of repeated copying during late antiquity and the Middle Ages. In the history of a literary text, the "papyri" generally represent an older and less standardized stage of the "manuscript" tradition. With the Greek Bible, for example, the modern text rests upon the great library codices of the fourth century, but some 150 fragments found in Egypt in the twentieth century have taken us back to an earlier date. Many ancient works not surviving through library transmission have been partially retrieved from papyri.

Over 3,000 Greek or Latin literary papyri have been found, and a further 600 biblical and patristic texts. There are scores of thousands of documentary papyri, such as government or business records and private letters. Many include dates or are dated on other internal evidence quite closely, so that the changing styles of writing in Egypt during Ptolemaic, Roman, and Byzantine times are well defined, often allowing paleographers to assign undated Greek documents to the nearest century. With the far fewer Latin papyri, and the more stereotyped Coptic ones, dating is more problematic.

Early Christianity is documented by more than 300 papyri prior to its establishment under Constantine. Half of these are biblical texts and a quarter belong to other literary or sublit-erary types (liturgical, magical), while the re-mainder include some thirty letters and thirty other documents. Christians presumably wrote or are referred to in other extant documents without our being able to identify them. After the time of Constantine, signs of Christian belief become common in texts of all kinds. It can be argued on this basis and that of name usage in the papyri that a quarter of the people of Egypt were Christian by ca. 325 and a half by 400.

Official Traces of Christians. Official re-action to the church is first marked in the pa-pyri by the affirmations of sacrifice submitted in 250 under the edict of the emperor Decius (*New Documents 1977*, no. 105). These pa-pyri, and a half-dozen others documenting the measures of Valerian, Diocletian, and Galerius, with Maximinus Daia's edict of 312 preserved in Eusebius and its two epigraphic fragments, are the only direct sources from the third or fourth centuries that convey the government's policy against the Christians. Decius was ap-parently the first to enforce a standard prac-tice. To the ageold Roman custom of national sacrifice (*supplicatio*) in an emergency, he added a striking novelty: all were to lodge an officially attested declaration (*libellus*) that they had always persisted in sacrificing and on this occasion had personally tasted the offering. The uniformity of the *libelli* (forty-four survive, from seven different places) at these two key points proves that the form of words, as well as the procedure, was prescribed. The file-number preserved in one case and the duplicate in another (also the pattern of folding) show that individuals had to be able to produce their signed claim for verification against the cen-tral record. Whether any extant copy was lodged by a Christian cannot be proved, but the earliest attestation of the name Thecla (*P. Oxy.* 1464), and her being covered by a vicari-ous offering, suggests it. From the renewal of the test under Diocletian in 304, we have the letter of Copres (*P. Oxy.* 2601), a Christian who arranged a substitute to sacrifice for him.

The earliest references to "Christians" in the papyri come under Valerian, in an order for arrest dated to 256 (*P. Oxy.* 3035) and in a property(?) assessment of 259/60(?) (*P. Oxy.* 3119). From February 5, 304, under Diocletian, comes the affirmation of a "reader" that his former "church"—the earliest certainly Chris-tian instances of these two terms in the pa-pyri—had been in possession of no property apart from what had already been confiscated: bronze "goods" (not a "gate," as first read in *P. Oxy.* 2673, and thus not the earliest reference to a church building; "church" was still nor-mally used for an association). The interroga-tions of Dioscorus (*P. Oxy.* 3529) and Phileas (*P. Chester Beatty* XV, ed. Pietersma) by Cul-cianus in 307 take us close to the court tran-scripts lying behind the martyr acts (*New Documents 1977*, no. 106). Constantine's let-ter to the provincials of Palestine, of which Eusebius (*V.C.* 2.24–42) claimed to have a personally signed copy, is attested by a frag-ment preserved on the back of a document apparently dated 319/20 (*P. Lond.* 878, with *JEH* 5 [1954]: 196–200).

Such terms as *ekklēsia* ("church," "assembly"), *presbyteros* ("presbyter," "elder"), *diakonos* ("deacon," "servant"), and *anagnōstēs* ("reader") occur in documents of the third and early fourth centuries but may refer to either ecclesiastical or civil institutions. A *monachos* ("monk") and a *diakon* ("deacon"), together in a petition of June 6, 324 (*New Documents 1976*, no. 81), seem to imply the official ac-ceptance of ecclesiastical titles, and that just prior to Constantine's taking Egypt from Lic-inius. If so, this is the earliest attestation of the term "monk" from any source. From October 2, 325, we have the first reference in a civil document to "the Lord's day" (*P. Oxy.* 3759), Sunday having been made the legal holiday in 321 in place of Thursday. From then on, overt reference to Christian institutions becomes common in the papyri.

Christian Papyri. Monotheistic expres-sions, and other attitudes suggestive of Chris-tian belief, begin to appear in documents of the third century, but in no case do these prove Christian origin. With letters, however, there are several indicators taken as decisive, such as the abbreviated *nomina sacra* ("sacred names," and the phrase "in the Lord." By such criteria, the earliest extant Christian letters could be from the Great Oasis, on the affairs of a family of the governing class (Naldini 4), and a family letter (from Oxyrhynchus?) mentioning "the Paschal festival" (Naldini 5), both of which have been dated to early in the third century. From later in that century come a letter between minor tax officials (Naldini 13, Oxyrhynchus) and a business letter from Rome referring to the *papas* Maximus, presumably the bishop of Alexandria, 264–282 (Naldini 6, Fayum). This had been folded with Hebrews 1:1 written above the text, and on the back both the Septuagint and Aquila versions of Genesis 1:1–5, perhaps converting it into an amulet. Several private letters even of the second century have been claimed as Christian but lack the decisive signs of belief (*New Documents 1977*, no. 22; *1978*, no. 2; *1979*, no. 16).

Letters of recommendation for travelers follow a set pattern in nine letters of the late third or fourth century (e.g., Naldini 19, 20, 28, 29, 50, 94) from one community to another. Presbyters, deacons, and, in three cases, a *papas*, Sotas, are mentioned. The travelers are sometimes catechumens, "at the beginning of the gospel" in one case, "up to Genesis" in another. Other travelers are to be received "in peace." One name was apparently entered later in the blank space left for the purpose. Since it is not possible to tie these letters to monasticism, they may be taken as evidence of the network of hospitality set up between churches. Other ecclesiastical correspondence of the early period may be seen in Naldini 21 and 23 (on travel in difficult times) and 30 (on property transfer); Naldini 37 and 38 document a circle of Christian women (not monastics) actively engaged in trade. The archive of Apa Paieous (*P. Lond.* 1913–1922) documents a monastic community of Melitians and its struggle against the followers of Athanasius at Alexandria. The archive of Apa Paphnutius (*P. Lond.* 1923–1929; *New Documents 1979*, no. 123) consists of the pleas for intercession sent to the anchorite by his cultivated correspondents. The archive of Abinnaeus, a military commander of the Fayum in the mid-fourth century, shows the influential position held by Apa Mios in a community by now extensively Christianized.

Magical Papyri. The magical papyri, mainly from the first four centuries, contain a few allusions to Jewish or Christian beliefs. But the appeal to "Jesus, God of the Hebrews" (PGM IV, 3019–3020), shows that the users were neither Jews nor Christians. Practitioners of magic aimed to tap any source of power, and the church fathers tried to keep them at arm's length. Prior to Naldini 6 (above), only one Christian text (Haelst 275), citing powerful words from Job 33 and 34, seems to have a magical intention. The practice of excerpting from scripture becomes established only in the fourth century; prior to that, the surviving fragments normally come from whole books. By the sixth century, a quarter of all Christian literary papyri can be assigned a magical use. One might string together creedal phrases or Gospel incipits with the opening of Psalm 91 (LXX 90), allusions to the healing miracles, and a prayer for healing (*New Documents 1978*, no. 93). The tight folding and the use of the magical color red (e.g., for the string that fastened the little package) may indicate that such texts were made to be worn as charms rather than to be displayed for reading. By contrast, *Oxyrhynchus Papyrus* 407 (late third century or fourth) bears a carefully formulated first-person-singular prayer to God the Creator for help, mercy, and deliverance from sin, offered through Christ, with doxology. On the back of the sheet is written the word *proseuchē*, "a prayer." There seems no reason to link a prayer like this with magic at all. Tables of set questions and answers for telling one's fortune, called *sortes Astrampsychi* (*New Documents 1977*, no. 8), were devised in Egypt in the third century and Christianized by the sixth.

Liturgical Texts. Liturgical prayers and hymns are preserved by nearly 200 papyri, not counting the many ostraca and graffiti from monastic sites. A third-century hymn to the Trinity (*P. Oxy.* 1786), equipped with an alphabetic indication of the musical notes, is the earliest example of church music. Also possibly liturgical is a single line provided with four or more settings (*P. Oxy.* 3705). A later Epiphany hymn is written out with doubled vowels to help the singer observe the long notes (*New Documents 1977*, no. 100 [2]). A codex in Barcelona combines classical and Christian texts in both Greek and Latin. Among the latter is a rhythmic and rhyming hymn beginning with a refrain in honor of Christ the Liberator, followed by a stanza for each letter of the alphabet. The graphic narrative takes the congregation through the episodes of Christ's origin, birth, and life. It is close in content to the *Protevangelium of James*. Because the papyrus breaks off at the wedding at Cana, it was taken at first as a hymn to Mary (*New Documents 1977*, no. 92). But this is unlikely, given the fourth-century date of the codex. The earliest prayer to the Virgin, a precursor of the one used in the west, the *Sub tuum praesidium*, is written in the chancery style common in the third century but with the brown ink that becomes common in the fourth (Haelst 983). It contains the term "Mother of God" (*Theotokos*), which also came into currency in the fourth century. The Lord's prayer is found from the third century (*New Documents 1978*, no. 88), and there is a sixth-century accentual hymn to the Trinity related to the *Te Deum* (*P. Lond.* 1029). Creedal papyri are also found (*New Documents 1976*, no. 66; *1977*, no. 110; *1978*, no. 93).

Christian Literary Works. Unidentified literary works, often assumed to be homilies, survive in 100 fragments, twenty dated prior to Constantine. With known authors, the proportions are much the same. Hermas is the early favorite, reflecting his close association with the canonical books: there are two fragments dated second–third century, ten in all by the early fourth, and another eight later (*New Documents 1977*, no. 98, with *P. Oxy.* 3527). Pre-Constantinian authors attested by papyri of their own epoch are Philo (two third-century papyrus codices confirm the Christian associations of this book form by their use of the abbreviated "sacred names" and by the New Testament fragments in the binding of one), *Barnabas*, Aristides, Tatian, Irenaeus, Origen, Julius Africanus, and Eusebius. From the later epoch, there are further papyri of some of these authors, as also of Ignatius, Melito, Hippolytus, Athanasius, Basil, the Gregories of Nazianzus and of Nyssa, Didymus the Blind, John Chrysostom, and Cyril. Didymus the Blind (*New Documents 1979*, no. 107), whose works are otherwise mostly lost, is now extensively restored by five of the papyrus codices of the sixth–seventh century found at Tura, a 2,000-page find including also works of Origen.

Apocryphal and Gnostic Writings. Apocryphal and Gnostic writings survive in sixty fragments, twenty prior to Constantine. These are sometimes the only Greek remains of works preserved by later versions in other languages. They include the *Sibylline Oracles*; the *Apocryphon of Moses*; the *Penitence of Jannes and Jambres* (twice); the *Odes of Solomon*; *Sophia of Jesus Christ*; the *Protevangelium of James*; the gospels of *Peter*, *Thomas* (three times), *Mary*, and two otherwise unknown gospels; the *Acts of Paul* and the *Acts of Peter*; the Pseudo-Clementine *Recognitions*; and the *Apocalypse of Peter*. Of later material, easily the most important is the fifth-century miniature biography of Mani (*New Documents 1979*, no. 132), now fully published.

Biblical Material. Biblical papyri outnumber all other Christian literary and subliterary papyrus texts together over the four centuries, third to sixth, of well-documented Greek-Christian culture in Egypt, and in the pre-Constantinian period they are twice as common. This preference and its great variety of expressions attest the centrality of biblical texts in church life. Above all, the relatively unprofessional copying and the popular use of the books demonstrate the highly unclassical phenomenon of a general movement of thought and practice across the community, inspired by books.

The reading of the Bible is illustrated by codex sheets from two bilingual lectionaries of the fourth century, the one a set of Greek extracts from Matthew on parchment, with Coptic translations (Haelst 351), the other Ephesians on papyrus, written out in sense lines with Latin translation (Haelst 523). A fourth-century Psalm text written from memory on the back of a papyrus roll bearing a speech of Isocrates is apparently marked up for reading aloud, with double-consonants separated and points inserted to mark syllables (Haelst 109), and a third-century papyrus roll has excerpts from Exodus, in a library hand, similarly marked (*P. Harr.* II, 166). A pair of excerpts from Acts on a folded papyrus double-sheet reproduces parts of the episodes of the Ethiopian and of Cornelius in a painstaking, unprofessional hand, much corrected by the writer and marked up for reading (Haelst 482)—a preacher's copy perhaps?

Bible study frequently leaves its mark. Almost all the following texts are from the third or early fourth centuries. An ostracon (Haelst 1101) bears three columns of words and names from both Old and New Testaments, in alphabetical order. A papyrus roll (Haelst 286) bears Greek verses from Hosea and Amos translated into Coptic; it is perhaps a teaching aid. Another (Haelst 1158) lists Hebrew proper names, in Greek letters, with interpretations of their meaning. A similar list appears on a single papyrus sheet (Haelst 1136). An unpublished Chester Beatty codex (*New Documents 1979*, p. 192) contains a Greco-Latin lexicon of the Pauline letters along with conjugation tables for Greek verbs. An unusually early example of Origen's "Hexaplaric" recension of Wisdom of Solomon has been found (*P. Köln* IV, 167); the textual criticism of the Septuagint independent of Origen and with reference to the Hebrew is seen in the Minor Prophets codex (Halest 284), which carries glosses in Greek and Coptic. School copies are found of Psalm 1 from a papyrus roll (*P. Laur.* IV, 140) and of Psalm 92 (Haelst 205), Psalm 146 (Haelst 239), and Psalm 46 (Coptic, *ZPE* 6 [1970]:133–149), all on wooden tablets, the last two combined with secular school texts. A library catalogue on papyrus lists Exodus, Leviticus, Job, and Acts, along with Origen on John, the *Shepherd* of Hermas, and other works (Haelst 1192).

Combinations of biblical books in one codex occur early for the Pentateuch, Wisdom literature, the Minor Propets, the Gospels (sometimes with Acts), and the Pauline epistles. Prior to the great fourth-century parchment codices Sinaiticus and Vaticanus, which first present the whole Bible as one book, there is only one papyrus, a roll, that seems to link Old and New Testaments, the fragment having Exodus (Haelst 44) on the recto and Revelation (Haelst 559) on the verso. Combinations with nonbiblical books occur quite often. Besides those mentioned above, early examples are the Song of Solomon (Haelst 269) with Aristides (Haelst 624); the Minor Prophets (Haelst 284) with Clement of Alexandria (?, Haelst 636) in different hands; Bel and the Dragon (Haelst 323) with a homily (Haelst 1083) and a Latin text; Ecclesiastes (Haelst 263) in both Greek and Coptic with the *Acts of Paul* (Haelst 605) and Coptic translations of the Song of Solomon and Lamentations; Hebrews (Haelst 537) on the verso of a roll bearing an *Epitome* of Livy. Excerpts from scripture are often found on the back of documents, confirming that people were free to copy it at will without enshrining the text in a sanctified format.

All the books of the New Testament are attested in Greek papyrus fragments or excerpts, and all of the Old except Ruth, 2 Kings, 1 Chronicles, and Lamentations. In order of frequency come Psalms, Matthew, John, Genesis, Luke, Acts, Isaiah, Exodus, Mark, and Romans. The Old Testament is somewhat more frequently found than the New. Of the pre-Constantinian copies, a dozen are on rolls, the standard book form in classical antiquity and Judaism (the Dead Sea Scrolls are mostly of parchment or leather); some ninety have the codex form, as in a modern book, which became normative in Christian use. Eighty of these are of papyrus; a dozen use the parchment that was soon to become standard for the codex.

The Berlin Acts (Haelst 479) is one of the earliest parchment codices known, coming from the second or third centuries. The Yale Genesis (Haelst 12), a papyrus codex strongly claimed for the late first century, has also been assigned to the second or third. Seven Christian copies of Old Testament texts have been attributed to the second century, and four copies of New Testament texts. Depending as they do upon paleographic comparison with other papyri, the datings must remain vague. But given that a half-dozen other biblical texts are assigned to the second or third century, and dozens more to the third, the general conclusion is clear. The presence of an active Christian community in Egypt is well established by a strong wave of biblical fragments that precede the emergence of other forms of papyrus documentation of early Christianity in the mid-to late third century. *See also* Codex; Manuscripts; Parchment. [E.A.J.]

Bibliography

Greek Papyri in the British Museum (London: British Museum, 1893–); *The Oxyrhynchus Papyri* (London: Egypt Exploration Society, 1898–); *The Abinnaeus Archive: Papers of a Roman Officer in the Reign of Constantius II* (Oxford: Clarendon, 1962); M. Naldini, *Il cristianesimo in Egitto: lettere private nei papiri dei secoli II–IV* (Florence: Le Monnier, 1968); *Kölner Papyri* (Opladen: Westdeutscher Verlag, 1976–); *Dai papiri della Biblioteca Medicea Laurenziana* (Florence: Gonelli, 1976–); G.H.R. Horsely, ed., *New Documents Illustrating Early Christianity: A Review of the Greek Inscriptions and Papyri Published in 1976* (Sydney: Macquarie U, 1981); *1977* (1982); *1978* (1983); *1979* (1987); A. Pietersma, ed., *The Acts of Phileas, Bishop of Thmuis, P. Chester Beatty XV* (Geneva: Cramer, 1984); *The Rendel Harris Papyri* (Zutphen: Terra, 1985), Vol. 2.

H.D. Betz, ed., *The Greek Magical Papyri* (Chicago: U of Chicago P, 1986).

J. van Haelst, *Catalogue des papyrus littéraires juifs et chrétiens* (Paris: Publications de la Sorbonne, 1976); E.A. Judge and S.R. Pickering, "Papyrus Documentation of Church and Community in Egypt to the Mid-Fourth Century," *JAC* 20 (1977):47–71; idem, "Biblical Papyri Prior to Constantine: Some Cultural Implications of Their Physical Form," *Prudentia* 10 (1978):1–13; C.H. Roberts, *Manuscript, Society and Belief in Early Christian Egypt* (London: Oxford UP, 1979); E.G. Turner, *Greek Papyri: An Introduction*, 2nd ed. (Oxford: Oxford UP, 1981); E.A. Judge, "The Magical Use of Scripture in the Papyri," *Perspectives on Language and Text*, ed. E.W. Conrad and E.G. Newing (Winona Lake: Eisenbrauns, 1987), pp. 339–349.

PARCHMENT. Writing material made from the skins of cattle, goats, sheep, and donkeys, as well as from wild animals, such as antelope and wolves. After the grease had been removed by soaking the skins in lime solution, the hair was removed by scraping. The skins were then washed, stretched out on frames, dried, and rubbed smooth with pumice stone before finally being rubbed with fine chalk. "Vellum" commonly refers to a finer type of parchment, usually made from the skins of calves and lambs. Isidore of Seville (*Etym.* 6.11.1–5) mentions three sorts of parchment, white, yellow, and purple, noting that as early as Pliny parchment was of the dirty yellow type with some already being tinted purple to heighten the gold and silver lettering of luxurious manuscripts (cf. Jerome, *Ep.* 22.32; 107.12). The process for whitening parchment was discovered somewhat later.

According to Pliny the Elder (*Natural History* 13.21), Eumenes II, king of Pergamum in Asia Minor 197–159 B.C., planned to found a library that would rival the great library at Alexandria. The resultant displeasure of Ptolemy of Egypt led to an embargo being placed upon the export of Egyptian papyrus. Since papyrus was the principal writing medium of the period, Eumenes was forced to develop the production of an alternative, which from its place of origin was called in Greek *pergamēnē*, from which the English term "parchment" is derived. However, as this writing material had been used among the Greeks and Persians before the time of Eumenes, it is more likely that due to this embargo Pergamum was the site of the development of a high quality of parchment and that the city was noted for its manufacture and export.

Papyrus was gradually supplanted by parchment. The *membranae* to which Catullus and other writers of the first century B.C. and the first century A.D. refer were likely parchment documents. Suetonius (*Lives of the Caesars* 1.56.6) says that Caesar sent reports to the senate on parchment, and it is probable that his diaries of the Gallic war were also written on this material. Cicero is reported by Pliny to have seen the entire *Iliad* written on parchment. Earlier, the Jews had sent to Ptolemy a copy of the Old Testament written on parchment.

The first recorded use of the material among Christians is 2 Timothy 4:13, although the precise content of those documents remains uncertain. About A.D. 84, Martial (1.2.7–8) referred to the extensive use of parchment for literary works. From the fifth to the fifteenth century, practically all manuscripts were written on parchment. During this period, production grew into an industry, and workers were called *pergaminarii*. For economy, unimportant or antiquated documents were reused after the writing had been washed out of the parchment and the underlying text of these palimpsests can now be read with the use of chemical reagents or with ultraviolet light. After the advent of paper from China in the late Middle Ages and the development of the printing press, calligraphy declined and with it the use of parchment. *See also* Codex; Manuscripts; Papyri.   [C.D.O.]

PARTICIPATION. "Participation," derived from the Latin *participatio* (from *pars* and *capere*), means literally the receiving of a part, and thus partaking of or sharing in something, and, in a wider sense, fellowship or communion with someone.

Philosophical and Biblical Background. The idea of participation has always been a fundamental category of religious and metaphysical reflection. The first systematic elaboration is found in the dialogues of Plato, where the idea of participation (the Greek expressions being the verb *metechein* and the nouns *methexis* and *metochē,* less frequently the verb *koinōnein* and the noun *koinōnia*) serves primarily to express the relationship between the many sensible instances and the one form, and so generally the relationship between the sensible universe and the intelligible world (in some texts we find a kind of participation also between the forms themselves). Middle Platonism and Neoplatonism revived the idea of participation, which for the most part expressed the relationship between the sensible and the intelligible but came increasingly also to express the relationship between the levels of the intelligible world itself, as, for example, in Plotinus, between the Soul and the Intellect and the Intellect and the One. In the later Neoplatonists, such as Proclus, it served in a more elaborate form, to structure the whole system of emanations.

In the Old Testament, especially in the Septuagint, the idea of participation occurs in a religious context. Much more significant for patristic literature, however, is its use in the New Testament. Although there is no evidence that the technical-philosophical understanding of the term influenced the New Testament writers, they did use "participation" to express, on the one hand, human sharing in the Holy Spirit and the communion with Christ and through him God the Father, and, on the other hand, the communion between the individual Christians and Christian churches within the total Christian community.

Second and Third Centuries. The earliest Christian literature of course continues the New Testament usage, but a more technical understanding of the term occurs sporadically, notably in Justin Martyr, who expresses the partaking in the Logos of even pre-Christian Greek philosophers, such as Socrates, with a Middle Platonic terminology of participation. A similar use of the idea of participation was its application to the relationship of the individual Christian to Christ and to that of divinized humans to God.

Irenaeus repeatedly uses the terminology of participation to express the initial vocation of humanity created in the image and likeness of God and the progressive restoration of this likeness, lost by the sin of Adam. Whereas human beings are in the *image* of God by virtue of their nature, including a body and a rational soul possessing understanding and freedom, the *likeness* consists in a participation of the Holy Spirit. In the Spirit, Christians have access to the Son, who, by his very incarnation as man, restored the lost communion between human beings and God. Finally, the soul's true life is participation in God the Father, fulfilled in eternal vision of him.

There are several instances of participation in Clement of Alexandria, who, as Irenaeus did before, expressed "divinization" as participation in God. A much more extensive and systematic use of the category of participation is found in Origen, who expressed the dynamism of the participation of rational creatures in the Trinitarian life of God. On the level of "nature," every being partakes in God the Father, whereas only rational creatures partake of the Logos. On the level of "grace," this natural participation in the Logos is the presupposition of the capacity to partake of God in a higher manner. The first stage of this higher participation consists in partaking of the Holy Spirit, who renders the rational creatures holy and in turn makes them participants of the Son insofar as he is Wisdom and Justice. Finally, eternal happiness is that "true existence" which consists in a higher participation in God the Father.

A special feature of Origen's theology is the expression of the relationship between the divine persons themselves in terms of participation. The Holy Spirit receives all that he is by participating in the Son, whereas the Son, who is Logos and Wisdom "by itself," is in turn truly "good" and especially "God" only by participating in the Father, who is "goodness itself" and "divinity itself" (autoagathos, autotheos). The value of his synthesis is its unified vision of the dynamics of participation on all its levels. But Origen's use of the same terms to express, on the one hand, the relationship between rational creatures and the divine persons, and, on the other hand, the relationship between the divine persons themselves, introduced a subordinationist tendency into his Trinitarian theology, a tendency that, in an exaggerated form, was misused by the Arians.

Gregory of Nyssa. The great post-Nicene theologians assimilated and transformed Origen's system. Gregory of Nyssa, who has probably the fullest theology of participation among the Greek fathers, used the concept as frequently and as systematically as Origen but in full harmony with Nicene orthodoxy. Much more clearly than Origen, he transformed the Platonic hierarchy of beings, dominated by the distinction between the intelligible and the sensible world, into one dominated by the distinction between the Uncreated and the created. Creatures in turn are divided into intellectual and sensible, with humanity the link between the two, not as a result of a fall, as in the case of Origen, but as part of God's original plan, as in Irenaeus. "Participation" ex-

presses the relationship between the intellectual creatures, especially human beings, and God. Whereas God possesses all pure perfections (divinity, goodness, holiness) essentially, by nature, human beings receive them only by participation. The very nature of human beings as image and likeness of God is constituted by an initial participation in some of the divine attributes, primarily reason and freedom; but this initial participation is only the foundation for a call to the continuous dynamic participation in God's goodness that constitutes the life of the created spirit. Gregory developed the idea that human perfection not only is capable of growth but consists of a never ending, progressive participation in the infinite goodness of God. Origen's ambiguous use of the terminology of participation within the Trinity was corrected by Gregory's consistent distinction between this "vertical" participation of creatures in God and a "horizontal" participation of individuals in a common specific nature. This concept of horizontal participation was extended to the three divine persons (hypostaseis), who share in the one divine nature. They are distinguished in Gregory by their "mode of existence," the Father being unoriginated, the Son being generated by the Father, and the Spirit proceeding from the Father (through the Son), but they are not subordinated to each other since they share equally in the one infinitely perfect divine essence. Of course, Gregory maintained, with Origen and the whole previous Christian tradition, that all divine benefits come to human beings from the Father through the incarnate Son in the Spirit, although, sharing the anti-Arian preoccupation of almost all post-Nicene fathers, he tended to minimize the differences among human relationships to the three divine persons. That human beings are sanctified especially by participation in the Holy Spirit and are children of God especially by sharing in the Sonship of Christ was affirmed by Gregory too. But the emphasis was more on the participation in the divine perfections common to the whole Trinity.

Other Greek Theologians. The main elements of Gregory of Nyssa's theology of participation occur in practically all subsequent Greek fathers, although there are considerable differences among authors. For example, Theodore of Mopsuestia, following Gregory of Nyssa, used the terminology of deification (*theopoiesis*) and divinization (*theosis*) sparingly, while his great contemporary Gregory of Nazianzus used it without inhibition. With Arianism fading, the Greek fathers were more emphatic in making divinization central to their theology of grace, retaining, however, the fundamental teaching of the earlier fathers that we are "divine" only by participation and thus radically distinguished from the essential divinity of the divine persons.

At the end of the patristic period, a new factor in the development of the idea of participation was introduced by the writings of Pseudo-Dionysius the Areopagite, who adapted the triadic hierarchies of Proclus to express the hierarchical structure of the angelic world and the church. Although influential primarily in the Latin Middle Ages, his thought, transformed by Maximus Confessor and others, did exert an influence on Byzantine theology as well.

Latin Theologians. The idea of the divinization of human beings, not by nature but by grace, is found in early Latin writers, such as Tertullian, but the terminology of participation seems to appear extensively only in the fourth century. One of the important mediators between Greek and Latin patristic theology is Ambrose, many of whose works are paraphrases of the writings of the eastern fathers. Augustine assimilated yet also critically confronted the Platonic tradition, especially in its Neoplatonic form, as in Plotinus and Porphyry, and developed an original version of the theology of participation. More than the Greek fathers, he included in his synthesis a Christian version of the Platonic "ideas" located in the eternal Logos. The participation of creatures and, especially, rational creatures in the divine perfections is thus mediated from the beginning through the Logos. After the fall, of which Augustine had a more pessimistic view than did the Greek tradition, it is the incarnate Logos, more precisely "the man Jesus Christ,"

who is the mediator of the restoration of participation in the divine life. Particularly rich is his theology of the ecclesial dimension of participation within the one body of Christ. Through Augustine, all the essential lines of the patristic theology of participation, including an insistence on a true but participated divinization by grace, have been transmitted to the subsequent western tradition, but enriched and modified by specifically Augustinian emphases—original sin, the powerlessness of the will without grace—that account for many of the differences between medieval Latin and contemporary Byzantine theology. [D.L.B.]

Bibliography

Justin Martyr, *1 Apology* 46.2; idem, *2 Apology* 13; idem, *Dialogue with Trypho* 6; 63.5; 124; Irenaeus, *Against Heresies* 2.34; 3.18.7; 4.praef. 4; 4.1.1–2; 4.20.5; 4.38.4; 5.3.2–3; 5.8.1; 5.12.2–3; 5.27.2; Clement of Alexandria, *Exhortation* 1.8.4; idem, *Instructor* 1.6.26.1–2; idem, *Miscellanies* 2.22.131.6; Origen, *On First Principles* 1.1.3; 1.3.3–8; 1.6.2; 2.6.3; 4.4.5, 9; idem, *Commentary on John* 2.11–33; 2.75–77; idem, *Against Celsus* 6.64; Gregory of Nyssa, *On the Soul and the Resurrection*, PG 46.105; idem, *Against Eunomius* 1.270–293; 2.69–70; 3.6.66–80; idem, *Homilies in Canticles* 6; 8; 9; idem, *On the Making of Man* 12; 16; idem, *On Infants Who Die Prematurely*, GNO 3.2, pp. 78–81; idem, *Catechetical Oration* 1.6; 5.3–7; idem, *On the Lord's Prayer* 5; idem, *On Not Three Gods* GNO 3.1, pp. 40–41; idem, *Life of Moses* 1.7–8; 2.22–25; idem, *On Virginity* 1; Pseudo-Dionysius, *On Divine Names* 1.2.10; 2.4.47; 2.5.49–2.6.52; 4.1.96–107; 4.7.132–141; 4.20.196–204; 5.1.257–5.5.67; Ambrose, *Hexaemeron* 6.7–8; idem, *Flight from the World* 4.17; 6.36; idem, *On the Holy Spirit* 6.80; Augustine, *Answers to Eighty-three Different Questions* 23; 46; idem, *Confessions* 7.9; 13.1–5; idem, *On the Trinity* 14.(8)11; (12)15; (17)23–(19)25; idem, *Commentary on Psalms* 118.16; idem, *City of God* 8.1; 9.15, 23; 10.2; 11.10–12; 20.16; 22.29–30.

W.J. Burghardt, *The Image of God in Man According to Cyril of Alexandria* (Woodstock: Woodstock College, 1957); L. Abramowski, "Zur Theologie Theodors von Mopsuestia," *ZKG* 72 (1961):263–293; D.L. Balás, "Christian Transformation of Greek Philosophy Illustrated by Gregory of Nyssa's Use of the Notion of Participation," *Proceedings of the American Catholic Philosophical Association* (Washington, D.C.: Catholic U of America P, 1966), pp. 152–157; idem, *METOUSIA THEOU: Man's Participation in God's Perfections According to Saint Gregory of Nyssa* (Rome: Herder, 1966); idem, "Participation in the Specific Nature According to Gregory of Nyssa: Aristotelian Logic or Platonic Ontology?," *Arts libéraux et philosophie au moyen âge: actes du quatrième congrès international de philosophie mediévale* (Montreal: Institut d'Etudes Mediévales, Paris: Vrin, 1969), pp. 1079–1085; idem, "The Idea of Participation in the Structure of Origen's Thought: Christian Transposition of a Theme of the Platonic Tradition," *Origeniana* (Bari: Istituto di Letteratura Cristiana Antica—Università di Bari, 1975), pp. 257–275; P. Wilson-Kastner, "Grace as Participation in the Divine Life in the Theology of Augustine of Hippo," *AugStud* 7 (1976):135–152; F. Normann, *Teilhabe—Ein Schlüsselwort der Vätertheologie* (Münster: Aschendorff, 1978); W.J. Caroll, "Participation in Selected Texts of Pseudo-Dionysius the Areopagite's *The Divine Names*" (Diss., Catholic University of America, 1981).

PASCH, PASCHAL CONTROVERSY. Early Christian term for the Jewish Passover; Easter. *Pascha,* the Greek form of the Hebrew *pasaḥ* and Aramaic *pasḥa,* has no true English equivalent—thus, the transliterations "Pasch" and "Paschal." For the early Christians, the term evoked the complex themes of Israel's Exodus tradition (Exod. 12–15). It was used in four related ways to refer to (1) the Jewish Passover festival; (2) the Passover meal, or seder; (3) the Paschal lamb; and (4) the Christian festival later called Holy Week and Easter. In addition, the term was used to describe controversies that surrounded computation of the day and date for celebrating the passion and resurrection of Jesus.

The Christian Pasch. The New Testament is replete with references to the Jewish Passover festival as *pascha.* Sometimes, the term simply expresses a temporal reference point in Christ's life; more often, it provides the context and interpretation of his life and death as a new Passover/Exodus, a theme central to the patristic period.

A closely related early Christian use of *pascha* was to denote the Last Supper, about which there are two early traditions. The Synoptic Gospels identify it as the Passover meal, or seder (Mark 14:12–16; Matt. 26:1–35; Luke 22:1–19). Yet in John the Supper is not a seder, and the entire account implies a chronology of Holy Week different from the Synoptic tradition (John 13:1; 19:31). In spite of this

dissonance of traditions, the Last Supper was clearly regarded as Paschal by the mid-second century, thus imbuing the Paschal eucharist and the weekly Lord's day eucharist with the Passover-seder motif—the meal was seen to recapitulate, fulfill, and replace the Passover and its seder, heralding the new Exodus.

The earliest Christian use of *pascha,* however, is also its most striking: to Christ as the Passover lamb. The identification is first made by Paul (1 Cor. 5:6–8) and then is richly developed in subsequent literature. In the Johannine tradition, for instance, Jesus is designated lamb of God (John 1:20) at the outset of his public life; the Passover occupies a central interpretive place in the narrative sections (John 2:23; 6:5; 11:55; 12:1, 20; 13:1; 18:39; 19:31); and the Holy Week chronology discloses that Jesus dies as the Paschal lambs are sacrificed in the temple. In the Book of Revelation, the lamb is a primary symbol for Christ (Rev. 5:6–10; 6:1–4; 7:14; 8:1; 14:1, 11; 19:7, 9; 21:14, 22–27; 22:1–5). By the middle of the second century, Melito of Sardis preached a now-famous homily, *On the Pasch,* which celebrated the theme of Christ as the Passover lamb and his death as the new Passover/Exodus.

These closely related uses of *pascha* signal the fact that Jewish Christianity had early adapted the Jewish Passover festival for Christian use. Melito's Paschal homily reveals the earliest structure of the Christian Pasch: it was celebrated during Passover (sunset to midnight) on 14 Nisan (15 in Jewish reckoning) and consisted of fasting, scripture reading (especially Exod. 12), chanting, and the eucharist, at which a homily on the Pasch was delivered. Whether the rite already included baptism is not certain. By the end of the second century, however, Tertullian's *On Baptism* testifies to baptism at this time, followed by a week of special liturgical instruction and celebration. At the beginning of the third century, essentials of what would become Holy Week, Easter, and Easter Week were in place. By the end of the fourth century, the "Forty Days," or Lent, had developed as a period of intense catechetical and ritual preparation for baptism, which together with the eucharist and chrismation comprised the solemn Paschal liturgy of Christian tradition for centuries to come.

Paschal Controversies. There were two issues. The first had to do with the proper day for observance of the Christian *pascha*: should the festival coincide with the Jewish Passover or be celebrated on the Sunday following? Melito represents the primitive tradition already widespread in Asia Minor and Syria, namely, that they should coincide. This usage was called "Quartodeciman," because the official Jewish calendar set Passover to begin at the close of the fourteenth day (*die quarto decima*) after the full moon that fell on or following the spring equinox (14/15 Nisan). As the church spread among Gentiles, however, the "Sunday following" tradition developed, largely because Christian Gentiles measured the seasons by the solar Julian calendar rather than the lunar Jewish calendar. The traditions came into sharp conflict during the second century, pitting the churches of Asia Minor against those that looked to Rome and leading the Roman bishop Victor I to excommunicate the Quartodecimans. Eusebius of Caesarea has left a detailed account in his *Church History* 5.23–25. The conflict was acute because of the centrality of the resurrection of Jesus to Christian faith, and different customs in its observance threatened that faith.

The controversy was compounded by the related problem of establishing the proper date. As noted, the Julian calendar, which the empire followed, was solar and thus incommensurate with the lunar calendar. Further, neither calendar is precisely divisible by the length of a day, resulting in complex intercalations. Finally, there were two standards of reckoning for the Julian calendar; at Rome the spring equinox was March 25, and at Alexandria March 21.

The Council of Nicaea (325) addressed the problems of both day and date, decreeing (1) that the Christian *pascha* be celebrated on the Sunday immediately following the full moon that fell on or after the spring equinox and (2) that the equinox be reckoned as March 21 (Eusebius, *V.C.* 3.18). Since no British bishops were present at Nicaea, the Celtic church

observed a different method of calculating Easter, and this became a point of conflict when Roman Christianity was introduced into the British Isles at the end of the sixth century. The controversies resonated in the west until the close of the eighth century, largely because of the computational difficulties in establishing a uniform cycle of dates ("Paschal tables"). Later calendar changes in the west would result in different calculations of the date of Easter by the eastern and western churches. *See also* Lent. [T.M.F.]

Bibliography

P.T. Weller, *Selected Easter Sermons of St. Augustine* (St. Louis: Herder, 1959); A. Hamman, *The Paschal Mystery* (New York: Alba House, 1969); E. Yarnold, *The Awe-Inspiring Rites of Initiation: Baptismal Homilies of the Fourth Century* (Slough: St. Paul, 1972); R. Cantalamessa, *Ostern in der Alten Kirche* (Berne: Peter Lang, 1981); A. Strobel, *Texte zur Geschichte des frühchristlichen Osterkalenders* (Münster: Aschendorff, 1984); D.J. Sheerin, *The Eucharist* (Wilmington: Glazier, 1986); T.M. Finn, *Early Christian Baptism and the Catechumenate* (Wilmington: Glazier, 1989).

C.J. Hefele, *A History of the Councils of the Church* (Edinburgh: T. and T. Clark, 1894), Vol. 1, pp. 298–324; J. Daniélou, *The Bible and the Liturgy* (Notre Dame: U of Notre Dame P, 1956); N.M. Denis-Boulet, *The Christian Calendar* (New York: Hawthorn, 1960); A. Jaubert, *The Date of the Last Supper* (New York: Alba House, 1965); T.M. Finn, *The Liturgy of Baptism in the Baptismal Instructions of St. John Chrysostom* (Washington, D.C.: Catholic U of America P, 1967); W. Huber, *Passa und Ostern: Untersuchungen zur Osterfeier der alten Kirche* (Berlin: Topelman, 1969); A. Strobel, *Ursprung und Geschichte des frühchristlichen Osterkalendars* (Berlin: Akademie-Verlag, 1977); S.G. Hall, "The Origins of Easter," *SP* 15 (1984):554–567; "Pâques (histoire et liturgie)," *Catholicisme Hier, Aujourd'hui, Demain* (Paris: Letouzey et Ané, 1985), Vol. 9, pp. 572–592; T. Talley, *The Origins of the Liturgical Year* (New York: Pueblo, 1986).

PATEN. In early Christian usage, a shallow (slightly concave) rounded dish of glass, metal, wood, or even terra cotta for the eucharistic bread. Because of their association with the sacramental elements, the wine and bread, the chalice (cup) and paten came to be viewed as sacred vessels. It became common to execute the paten in precious metals; the oldest surviv-

Line drawing of a glass plate (fourth century) from Ursulagartenstrasse, Cologne, West Germany, now in the British Museum, London, England. (By courtesy of the Trustees of the British Museum.)

ing examples, in silver, belong to the sixth century. The large fourth-century silver dish from the Water Newton treasury is marked with a chi-rho and an alpha and omega in the central roundel. It could have been used as a eucharistic paten, although this cannot be proved. The *Liber Pontificalis* 18 (Duchesne 1.143) mentions silver patens under bishop Urban I (222–230), and 34 (Duchesne 1.176ff.) reports gold and silver chalices and patens in the Roman churches under Sylvester I (314–335), but we have no metal vessels that clearly served as patens and that predate the early Byzantine period.

The *Liber Pontificalis* 16 (Duchesne 1.139) says that under Zephyrinus (199–217) glass patens were distributed to urban churches. Again, we have no surviving glass vessels to prove the point; however, there survive cer-

tain fourth-century Rhenish glass plates marked with Christian iconography that could have been used as patens. The Ursulagartenstrasse plate (see illustration), discovered in 1866 in Cologne, is probably the supreme example, but the function of that vessel is also a matter for speculation. *See also* Bread; Chalice; Eucharist. [P.C.F.]

Bibliography

O.M. Dalton, *Catalogue of Early Christian Antiquities and Objects from the Christian East. . .in the British Museum* (London: British Museum, 1901), no. 628 (Ursulagartenstrasse plate); J. Braun, *Das christliche Altargerät in seinem Sein und in seiner Entwicklung* (Munich: Hueber, 1932), pp. 197–246; E.C. Dodd, *Byzantine Silver Treasures* (Berne: Abegg-Stiftung, 1973), figs. 19–25, 35–38; K.S. Painter, *The Water Newton Early Christian Silver* (London: British Museum, 1977); J.L. Schrader, "Antique and Early Christian Sources for the Riha and Stuma Patens,"

Gesta 18 (1979):147–156; K. Weitzmann, ed., *Age of Spirituality: Late Antique and Early Christian Art, Third to Seventh Century* (New York: Metropolitan Museum of Art, 1979), nos. 482, 533, 546–548; A.V. Bank, *Byzantine Art in the Collections of Soviet Museums* (Leningrad: Aurora, and Chicago: Imported Publications, 1985), plates 66–68, 78.

PATRIARCH. Father, ruler, or leader of a family or tribe. In both the Old and the New Testaments, "patriarch" refers to the forefathers of the human race and more specifically and more frequently to Abraham, Isaac, Jacob, and Jacob's twelve sons (Gen. 12–50; Acts 7:8ff.; Heb. 7:4; in Acts 2:29, the term applies to David). In the fourth century, the term was used, as, for instance, by Gregory of Nazianzus (*Or.* 42.23), as a title of honor for older bishops. Gradually, by the fifth century, the term became more specific; emperor Theodosius II called the bishops of Rome and of Constantinople patriarchs. The word acquired its technical meaning with the 123rd novella of emperor Justinian I, which in the third chapter speaks about the "most blessed archbishops and patriarchs of the old Rome and Constantinople and Alexandria and Antioch and Jerusalem." The 123rd novella confirmed the existing ecclesiastical reality, by which the bishops of these great apostolic sees had become exarchs, or superintendents of large territories over which they exercised canonical jurisdiction. Thus, the bishop of Rome exercised his authority over Italy; the bishop of Constantinople over Thrace, Asia, Pontus, and Greece; the bishop of Alexandria over Egypt and Libya; the bishop of Antioch over part of Asia Minor and Syria; and the bishop of Jerusalem over Palestine. The patriarchs had the right to ordain metropolitans, that is, the bishops of the capitals or principal sees of their provinces. They acquired the authority to hear appeals and to become the judges over canonical and moral issues of their bishops. Finally, the title entered the synodical language of the church with the second and seventh canons of the Council of Trullo in 692 (Quinisext).

Gradually, out of this ecclesiastical accommodation, the doctrine of "Pentarchy" was developed. According to this view, the five apostolic sees were more or less equal, and the church was to be governed through cooperation, mutual respect, and mutual recognition. Commenting on Matthew 16:18–19, Theodore the Studite, a monk of the ninth century of Constantinople and founder of the Studion Monastery, wrote: "Who are the men to whom this order is given? The apostles and their successors. And who are their successors? He who occupies the throne of Rome, which is the first; he who occupies the throne of Constantinople, which is the second; and after them those who occupy the thrones of Alexandria, Antioch, and Jerusalem. This is pentarchic [*pentēkoryphos*] authority in the church, and these [patriarchs] have jurisdiction over divine dogmas" (*Ep.* 124; PG 99.1417). Emperor Basil the Macedonian proclaimed that "God established his church on the foundation of the five patriarchs, and he has defined in his holy Gospels that they would never fail altogether, because they are the heads of the church" (Acts of the Council of Constantinople [869], Ch. 8; Mansi 16.140).

During the reign of Justinian I, the patriarch of Constantinople acquired the title "Ecumenical"—applied for the first time to patriarch John II, the Cappadocian (518–520), in the sense that he presided over the Byzantine empire. The title of patriarch was later granted to the bishops of the capital sees of national churches, such as Moscow. The election of the patriarchs takes place in accordance with the canonical rules of each patriarchate, but the election is carried out mainly by the Home or Resident Synods of the patriarchates. The Ecumenical Patriarchate of Constantinople is considered first among equals (*primus inter pares*) in the Orthodox family of churches.

The title patriarch is used by some bishops of the west, like that of Venice, and by some eastern bishops in communion with Rome, such as the Melchites and Maronites. It is used also by some Monophysite and Nestorian bishops in Egypt and India.   [G.S.B.]

Bibliography

Agapius and Nicodemus of the Holy Mountain, *The Rudder [Pedalion] of the Orthodox Christians, or All the Sacred and Divine Canons* (Chicago: Orthodox Christian Educational Society, 1957); Maximos of Sardes, *The Oecumenical Patriarchate* in the Orthodox Church (Thessalonica: Patriarchal Institute for Patristic Studies, 1976); J. Pelikan, *The Christian Tradition: A History of the Development of Doctrine* (Chicago: U of Chicago P, 1977), Vol. 2: *The Spirit of Eastern Christendom (600–1700)*, pp. 164–166; N.D. Patrinacos, *A Dictionary of Greek Orthodoxy* (New York: Greek Orthodox Archdiocese of North and South America, 1984), s.v.

PATRICK (d. ca. 460). Missionary to Ireland. Patrick was born in western Roman Britain toward the end of the fourth century. Kidnapped at the age of fifteen by Irish pirates, he spent six years in slavery as a shepherd in western Ireland before running away and escaping on, most likely, a pirate ship. He eventually returned home to Britain and entered the clerical life. In 431, a Roman deacon named Palladius was sent as bishop to the small Irish Christian community. Shortly thereafter, possibly as early as 432, Patrick, now a bishop, went to Ireland, but unlike his predecessor, he labored among the pagans. He definitely worked in the northeast and probably in the northwest as well but apparently not in the south.

He left behind two writings. One is a brief but moving *Letter to the Soldiers of Coroticus,* deploring the kidnapping of some of his converts by a Christian British prince and demanding their return. It is not known if the letter achieved its goal. His other writing is a *Confession,* which defends his mission against critics in the British church. He speaks of suffering, hardship, danger, and imprisonment but always of how his faith sustained him. The miracle-working Patrick of the snakes and shamrocks is a creation of medieval legend; the historical Patrick was a great missionary who worked for thirty years, earning the title "apostle of Ireland." Feast day March 17. CPL 1099–1106. *See also* Great Britain; Ireland.

[J.F.K.]

Bibliography

L. Bieler, tr., *The Works of St. Patrick,* ACW (1953), Vol. 17.

L. Bieler, *The Life and Legend of St. Patrick* (Dublin: Clonmore and Reynolds, 1949); R.P.C. Hanson, *Saint Patrick: His Origins and Career* (New York: Oxford UP, 1968); idem, *Life and Writings of the Historical St. Patrick* (San Francisco: Harper and Row, 1983); J.F. Kelly, "The Escape of Saint Patrick from Ireland," *SP* 18 (1985):41–45.

PATRISTICS. *See* Fathers of the Church.

PATROLOGIA GRAECA, PATROLOGIA LATINA. See Migne, Jacques Paul.

PAUL (d. ca. 65). Apostle to the Gentiles (Gal. 2:7–9). The apostle Paul was the most effective early Christian missionary, and his letters became part of the New Testament canon. He now appears as a thoroughly apocalyptic thinker whose religious orientation was marked by spiritual enthusiasm and radical criticism of the contemporary world order. He advocated a revolutionary form of congregational life, marked by equality and guided by Spirit-inspired leadership committed to a crucified Lord. The volatile life of these churches, shaped by external pressures and internal conflicts, evoked the letters that offer unparalleled insights into the life of the primitive church.

Life. Paul's career needs to be reconstructed mainly on the basis of his authentic

Paul with container for scrolls, fresco (fourth century) from Catacomb of Domitilla, Rome, Italy. (Used by permission of Pontifical Commission of Sacred Archaeology.)

letters, with evidence from the book of Acts when it does not conflict with this primary evidence. He was born around the beginning of the first century in a Hellenistic Jewish family from Tarsus in Asia Minor and named Saul. His persecution of early Christians as heretics indicates that he belonged to a radical strain of the Pharisee movement (Phil. 3:3–4; Gal. 1:13–24). Since Paul held Roman citizenship, practiced a trade as a tentmaker, and had received a sophisticated education in Greek rhetoric, it is clear that his family had some prominence. Paul's vision of the resurrected Jesus (ca. A.D. 34) altered his legalism and zealotry into its opposite, an advocacy of including Gentiles in the church on the basis of grace alone. In place of the Pharisaic commitment to legal obedience, there emerged an identification with Jesus, whose lordship offered a new basis of world transformation and unification (Phil. 3:7–11; 2 Cor. 5:16–21).

Paul's early missionary activities in Arabia, Syria, and his native Cilicia (Gal. 1:17–21) were conducted in part in cooperation with the church at Antioch of Syria (Acts 13–14). In the early part of this period (A.D. 37), he experienced the first troubles with political authorities (2 Cor. 11:32–33). In travels touching north Galatia, Macedonia, and Greece (Acts 15:36–18:21), Paul and his colleagues founded the churches reflected in the letters. His early preaching centered on the dawn of a new age with Jesus as an end-time savior (1 Thess. 1:9–10; 2:9–13).

By A.D. 48, Paul reached Philippi to establish a Gentile congregation that provided financial support for later missionary activities (2 Cor. 11:9; Phil. 4:10–20). This church had some divisive qualities (Phil. 4:2–3) and a tendency toward spiritual arrogance (Phil. 2:1–16), which probably contributed to the mob violence and judicial punishment that ended Paul's mission there (1 Thess. 2:2; Acts 16:19–40). Paul's apocalyptic gospel probably also contributed to civil disturbances that led to the premature closure of his Thessalonian ministry in the summer of 49. His proclamation provoked some radical responses within the Thessalonian congregation, including misunderstanding about the new age as if it were fully present. This resulted in a series of difficulties, including shocked disappointment at the death of congregational members and the renewal of persecution (1 Thess. 3:1–5; 4:13–18). 1 Thessalonians was directed to this situation in A.D. 50, clarifying the nature of the new age as an era of faith, love, and hope for a future parousia of Christ. This effort to explain an eschatology combining the "already" with the "not yet" was apparently misunderstood. 2 Thessalonians summarizes the message of the first letter and emphatically denies that Paul taught that the "Day of the Lord has already come" (2 Thess. 2:2).

After a brief mission in Beroea that also ended in civil disturbances (Acts 17:10–14) and an attempt to found a congregation in Athens (Acts 17:33–34), Paul arrived in Corinth in the winter of 49/50. He began an eighteen-month ministry with a congregation that proved formative for his theology and ethic. This period ended with a hearing before Gallio, the proconsul of Achaia, in response to disorders and charges from a local synagogue (Acts 18:12–17). In response to conflicts between house churches sponsored by competing patrons in Corinth, Paul wrote a series of letters that were later woven into canonical 1 and 2 Corinthians. Dealing with troubles provoked by indigenous proto-Gnostics, Paul developed distinctive ideas about the church as the "body of Christ" (1 Cor. 12:27), marriage as mutual submission in the body (1 Cor. 7:1–40), respect for conscience even when it is misguided (1 Cor. 8; 10), a theology of the cross that transcends human wisdom (1 Cor. 1:18–31), Christian freedom that is capable of renouncing itself in service of others (1 Cor. 9), and an egalitarian theory of church leadership and worship (1 Cor. 12–14) marked by a doctrine of the superiority of love over faith and hope (1 Cor. 13). In response to criticism from missionaries arriving in Corinth with a triumphalist theology, Paul developed a theology of the cross that allows one to be honest about human weakness (2 Cor. 12:7–10) and to respect barriers against human pride (2 Cor. 10:7–18). He worked out a distinctive theology of Christ's reconciling atonement (2 Cor. 5:16–21) and suggested guidelines for a nonauthoritarian interpretation of scripture (2 Cor. 3:1–18).

In A.D. 51, Paul participated in the Jerusalem conference called in response to the demand of Judaizers that Gentile Christians be circumcised (Gal. 2:1–10; Acts 15:1–35). Paul's account of this meeting between advocates of the Gentile mission—Barnabas, Titus, and himself—and the leaders of Jewish Christianity—James, Peter, and John—stresses the significance of preserving the "freedom" of Gentile Christians from the burdens of the Jewish Law (Gal. 2:4). His description of the motivation of the Judaizers in Galatians 6:12–13 indicates that they wished to avoid persecution by compelling Gentile Christians to be circumcised. The likely background for this campaign was Zealot pressure in the late 40s and early 50s on Judean Christians to avoid relations with the uncircumcised (2 Thess. 1:14–16). Paul resisted this campaign because it would undermine the prospects of the Gentile mission and destroy the equality between Jews and Gentiles. His distinctive doctrine of justification by faith rather than by works of the Law emerged from this conflict (Gal. 2:11–21). The conference resulted in acknowledgment of the Gentile mission free from the obligation of the Jewish Law, but the question of how Jews and Gentiles would coexist in local churches was left unresolved. Several months after the council, this issue emerged in Antioch when a delegation from the party of James compelled Peter to refrain from eating with Gentile Christians (Gal. 2:11–14). Paul opposed this violation of the principle of justification by faith alone with its corollary of fellowship between those who conformed to the Law and those who did not. Several years later, the Jerusalem authorities attempted to provide a new basis for fellowship in a letter imposing the obligation on Gentiles to conform to a minimum level of Law (Acts 21:25), but there is no evidence that Paul ever accepted such a ruling (Gal. 2:6). His advocacy of freedom from the Law resulted in conflicts that continued even after his death.

Paul's letter to the Galatian churches reflects the ongoing conflict over the Law. A group of Judaizers arrived in Galatia shortly after Paul had revisited his churches on the way from Antioch to Ephesus. They advocated circumcision and adherence to Jewish festivals as a means of achieving perfection. Paul argued that for Gentiles to accept the Law was to repudiate the Spirit (Gal. 3:2–5) and to revert to a position of slaves (Gal. 4:1–11). Even the Hebrew scriptures, which the Judaizers touted, spoke in Paul's view in support of the premise that Gentiles become sons of Abraham through faith alone (Gal. 3:6–29). In an allegorical treatment of the two sons of Abraham (Gal. 4:21–31), Paul developed antitheses between flesh and spirit, slavery and freedom, Law and promise, and the contemporary Jerusalem whence the Judaizers came and the "Jerusalem above" that was the true home of Christians. This argument, set forth with the eloquent resources of Greek rhetoric and Hebrew exegesis, proved to be immensely influential. But Paul's mission continued to be plagued by conflicts with Judaizers, reflected in Paul's next letter to the Philippians (ca. 54–55) and in his last letter to the Romans (ca. 56–57).

Paul's Asian ministry, centering in Ephesus, commenced in A.D. 52 and lasted around three years. With a large number of missionary colleagues, satellite churches were established in such cities as Laodicea, Hierapolis, and Colossae. Public disorders and the imprisonment reflected in the Philippian letter probably ended the Ephesian ministry, which was followed by travels to Macedonia, Asia, and Illyricum until Paul arrived in Corinth for his final visit in the winter of 56/7. At least one additional imprisonment may have occurred during this time, as reflected in the writing of Philemon and probably also Colossians (A.D. 55–56). Paul's efforts to raise funds for the offering that had been agreed at the Jerusalem conference were delayed by imprisonments and church conflicts (2 Cor. 8–9).

Paul's most important letter, to the Romans, was written in the winter of 56/7 to prepare for an intended mission to Spain. Working under the patronage of Phoebe, the leader of a church near Corinth (Rom. 16:1–2), Paul hoped to use the resources of the splintered

Roman house churches to penetrate Spain. The letter to the Romans clarifies the gospel to be proclaimed in Spain, starting with the theme of the righteousness of God revealed in the Christ event that must be received by faith (Rom. 1:16–17). No culture has lived up to the demands of this impartial righteousness (Rom. 1:18–3:20), so salvation is a matter of everyone accepting grace and ceasing to boast (Rom. 3:21–31). The true children of Abraham live by faith (Rom. 4) and are set free from sin and the Law (Rom. 5–7) to be led by the Spirit (Rom. 8). Despite the temporary resistance of unbelieving Jews, the gospel will succeed in unifying the human race (Rom. 9–11). The new life of responsible love and equality (Rom. 12–13) should be particularly visible in the mutual welcome between competitive house churches in Rome (Rom. 14:1–15:13). If this gospel is embodied in the life of the Roman churches, their participation in the mission to the barbarians will follow (Rom. 15:14–16:23).

After completing Romans, Paul set off for Jerusalem with the offering, only to become involved in civil disturbances once again, resulting in a two-year imprisonment at Caesarea (Acts 24:24–26:32). After appealing his case to Rome, he was under house arrest in the imperial city from A.D. 60 to 62 and was executed then or at a later arrest.

Influence. Paul's influence was assured by the Book of Acts and the publication of his letters, which provided the basis for extensive conflicts between conservative and Gnostic Christians for the next several centuries. The use of his thought by heretical factions was countered by the composition of 1 and 2 Timothy and Titus by a Pauline school centered in Ephesus. (Other epistles, such as Jude, James, 2 Peter, and the letters in the Book of Revelation, were also written to refute libertinistic and Gnostic interpreters.)

The influence of Paul is visible in *1 Clement,* written to Corinth toward the end of the first century, which uses the career and martyrdom of the apostle to urge unity in the congregation. Ignatius (*Rom.* 4.3) and Polycarp (*Ep.* 9.1) honored and used Paul's letters; Marcion seized on the radical potential of Paul's thought, giving precedence to Galatians as the source of anti-Judaistic doctrine. Marcion developed Paul's distinction between God and the "god of this world" (2 Cor. 4:4) into a systematic ditheism to resolve the problem of evil and the fallen nature of humankind. He used the dualistic potential of Paul's anthropology to teach that the spirit originated with the true God while the body and soul were the creation of the Jewish God of this world. Both the high Christology and the Docetic potential (Phil. 2) of Pauline thought were used. Similarly, Valentinus revered Paul as the primary source of the Gnostic understanding of secret wisdom (1 Cor. 2:7) concerning freedom from the Law and from human authority along with salvation by grace. The Pauline categories of flesh, soul, and spirit were used to define the three classes of humans, of which the spiritual Gnostics alone are assured of salvation.

The church fathers of the second century, led by Irenaeus of Lyons, sought to reclaim Paul as the apostle of orthodoxy, reading the authentic Pauline letters through the lenses of the Pastoral Epistles and the book of Acts. Paul was claimed along with Peter as the co-founder of the orthodox church in Rome, and by the third century the expression "the apostle" refers to Paul alone. A central place for Paul is visible from Origen through John Chrysostom; his thought was absolutely formative for Augustine. Other strands of Christian tradition were also influenced by Paul. In the *Acts of Paul,* the authority of the apostle is used in support of an apocalyptic, countercultural, and ascetic orientation giving prominent place to female leadership. The Ebionites, on the other hand, expressed contempt for Paul and rejected his letters as the source of antinomian heresy. Similarly, the Pseudo-Clementine writings denigrate Paul in favor of Peter. Of the major streams in early Christianity, therefore, only the radical Jewish Christians repudiated Paul. All others, whether Gnostic or orthodox, relied on various aspects of the Pauline legacy. *See also* Acts of Paul; Vision of Paul.   [R.J.]

Bibliography

K. Staab, *Pauluskommentare aus der griechischen Kirche* (Münster: Aschendorff, 1933).

M.F. Wiles, *The Divine Apostle: The Interpretation of St. Paul's Epistles in the Early Church* (Cambridge: Cambridge UP, 1967); E.H. Pagels, *The Gnostic Paul: Gnostic Exegesis of the Pauline Letters* (Philadelphia: Fortress, 1975); K. Stendahl, *Paul Among Jews and Gentiles* (Philadelphia: Fortress, 1976); F.F. Bruce, *Paul: Apostle of the Heart Set Free* (Grand Rapids: Eerdmans, 1977); B. Holmberg, *Paul and Power* (Philadelphia: Fortress, 1978); E. Dassmann, *Der Stachelm im Fleisch: Paulus in der frühchristlichen Literatur bis Irenäus* (Münster: Aschendorff, 1979); R. Jewett, *A Chronology of Paul's Life* (Philadelphia: Fortress, 1979); A. Lindemann, *Paulus im ältesten Christentum* (Tübingen: Mohr-Siebeck, 1979); R.F. Hock, *The Social Context of Paul's Ministry: Tent-Making and Apostleship* (Philadelphia: Fortress, 1980); J. Murphy-O'Connor, *Becoming Human Together: The Pastoral Anthropology of St. Paul* (Wilmington: Glazier, 1982); C.J. Roetzel, *The Letters of Paul: Conversations in Context* (Atlanta: John Knox, 1982); W.A. Meeks, *The First Urban Christians: The Social World of the Apostle Paul* (New Haven: Yale UP, 198); E.P. Sanders, *Paul, the Law, and the Jewish People* (Philadelphia: Fortress, 1983); J. Zeisler, *Pauline Christianity* (Oxford: Oxford UP, 1983); D.R. MacDonald, *The Legend and the Apostle: The Battle for Paul in Story and Canon* (Philadelphia: Fortress, 1983); G. Luedemann, *Paul, Apostle to the Gentiles: Studies in Chronology* (Philadelphia: Fortress, 1984); J.C. Beker, *Paul the Apostle: The Triumph of God in Life and Thought* (Philadelphia: Fortress, 1984); L.E. Keck, *Paul and His Letters*, 2nd ed. (Philadelphia: Fortress, 1988).

PAUL OF SAMOSATA (third century).

Bishop of Antioch (ca. 260–268). A native of Samosata, Paul came either from a poor background or from a well-to-do family that had been economically ruined. Although often described as a procurator ducenarius under Zenobia, queen of Palmyra, he was most probably such a procurator in the Roman bureaucracy, for Palmyrene hegemony over Antioch did not begin until after he was deposed in 268. As a powerful Roman official, he fits the description found in Eusebius (*H.E.* 7.28–30) of one who had a personal bodyguard strong enough to keep control of the church building even after he was deposed, who had secretaries for writing letters, and who introduced into the church building a high throne, a tribunal (raised stage), and a *secretum*, a small chamber for private discussions. Paul offers significant evi-

dence that urban churches were seeking men of power and culture for their bishops.

Paul is usually noted for his place in Christological issues, but that position is clouded. He emphasized a Christology from below, rejecting the Son's preexistence and descent and stressing Jesus' ordinary manhood of body and soul. Synods in Antioch in 264 and 268 condemned these teachings. The later documents, which claim to give a transcript of his heresy trial, are most probably Apollinarian forgeries that sought to disparage the term *homoousios* and attack Antiochene Christology. [F.W.N.]

Bibliography
Eusebius, *Church History* 7. 28–30; Theodoret, *Haereticum fabularum compendium* 2.11; Epiphanius, *Panarion* 65.

H.J. Lawlor, "The Sayings of Paul of Samosata," *JThS* 19 (1917–1918):20–45, 115–120.

F.W. Norris, "Paul of Samosata: Procurator Ducenarius," *JThS* n.s. 35 (1984):50–70; H.C. Brennecke, "Zum Prozess gegen Paul von Samosata. Die Frage nach der Verurteilung des Homoousios," *ZNTW* 75 (1984):270–290; J.A. Fischer, "Die antiochenischen Synoden gegen Paul von Samosata," *Annuarium historiae conciliorum* 18 (1986):9–30.

PAULA (374–404).

Roman widow and disciple of Jerome. The mother of five children, Paula was one of a number of women for whom Jerome provided spiritual counsel. With her daughter Eustochium, she followed him to the east (385). After visits to the holy places there and to the desert hermits of Egypt, she founded several monastic establishments in Bethlehem. Paula's life was devoted to asceticism and good works. She was a knowledgeable student of scripture. Jerome wrote her eulogy; Eustochium assumed the direction of the monasteries upon her mother's death. A letter (*Ep.* 46) from Paula and Eustochium appears among the writings of Jerome. CPL 620. [M.P.McH.]

Bibliography
Jerome, *Letter* 108.

PAULINUS OF NOLA (355–431).

Bishop, monk, and Christian poet. A native of Aquitaine, Paulinus was educated at Bordeaux by Ausonius and was governor of Campania in

379. He met Martin of Tours and made friends with Sulpicius Severus. He married the Spaniard Therasia; their child died in infancy. Paulinus was baptized at Bordeaux (389) and ordained a priest in Barcelona (394). He and Therasia renounced their property, moved to Nola (near Naples) and founded a monastery at the tomb of St. Felix (395). Paulinus corresponded with Augustine and Jerome and knew Ambrose, both Melanias, Niceta of Remesiana, Victricius of Rouen, Julian of Eclanum, and others. In 417, Augustine warned him against Pelagianism (*Ep.* 186). About fifty letters and thirty poems are extant. CPL 202–207. *See also* Fish.   [J.T.L.]

Bibliography

Ausonius, *Carmina* 27.2; idem, *Epistulae* 19–25; Augustine, *Letters* 27; 31; 42; 45; 80; 95; 149; 196; Jerome, *Letters* 53; 58; 85; emperor Honorius, *Epistula* 25 in *Collectio Avellana* (CSEL, Vol. 35); Gennadius, *Lives of Illustrious Men* 49; Uranius, *Epistula de obitu Paulini ad Pacatum* (PL 53.859–866).

Letters, . . . Poems of St. Paulinus of Nola, tr. P.G. Walsh, ACW (1966, 1967, 1975), Vols. 35, 36, 40.

PECTORIUS, EPITAPH OF.

PECTORIUS, EPITAPH OF. Greek inscription, found near Autun, France, comprising three distichs (six lines) and five hexameters. Although inscribed in the fourth century, the Epitaph of Pectorius in its first part borrows language from the epitaph of Abercius or a poem of Abercius's time. The first five lines form an acrostic for the Greek word for "fish." Baptism is called "the immortal fountain of divine water," and the eucharist is alluded to in the phrase "holding the Fish in your hands." In the second part, Pectorius prays for his mother and asks her, his father, Aschandius, and his brothers to pray for him "in the peace of the Fish." *See also* Abercius; Fish; Inscriptions.   [E.F.]

Bibliography

K.M. Kaufmann, *Handbuch der altchristlichen Epigraphik* (Freiburg im Breslau: Herder, 1917), pp. 178–180; F.J. Dölger, *Ichthys: Das Fisch Symbol in frühchristlichen Zeit* (Münster: Aschendorff, 1928), Vol. 1, pp. 12–15, 177–183; Vol. 2, pp. 507–515; Quasten, Vol. 1, pp. 173–175; G. Grabka, "Eucharistic Belief Manifest in the Epitaphs of Abercius and Pectorius," *American Ecclesiastical Review* 131 (1954):254–255.

PELAGIUS, PELAGIANISM.

PELAGIUS, PELAGIANISM. Ascetic (ca. 350–ca. 425), founder of movement emphasizing free will and good works.

Life and Works. Pelagius is thought to have been British by birth and appears to have belonged to a family that could educate him well. By 390, he is known to have been in Rome, the leader of one of the many reform-minded, ascetical groups of the late fourth century. Celestius and Rufinus the Syrian were among his better-known followers, and it was this group's understanding of the freedom of human actions, for good or bad, in relation to the help given the human person by God, that led to the controversy with Augustine that left an enduring mark on western thought. The measure of Pelagius and Pelagianism has traditionally been Augustinianism. Yet Pelagius was nearing the end of his life when the quarrel with Augustine broke out, and his most important writing was done in other contexts. Moreover, the term "Pelagianism" gives the wrong impression. It was not a matter of a few disciples echoing their master's thought, but of a widespread, multifaceted movement with its own internal differences.

The *corpus* of Pelagius's own works is disputed. At the beginning of this century, all that was known of his extant writings were the letters to Demetrias and Celantia, a corrupt text of a commentary on the Pauline epistles and fragments quoted by Augustine. In 1934, this list was expanded dramatically to twenty-nine items. Although accepted by the editor of the Supplement to the *Patrologia Latina*, the expanded list has not gained widespread acceptance. De Plinval's (1934) methodology, based on parallelisms between texts and similarities of word usage and style, has met severe criticism. In one of the earliest and most serious challenges (Evans, 1962), the number of authentic works was cut to twelve—seven complete extant works, including five letters, the *Libellus fidei* sent to Innocent I, and the *Commentary on Thirteen Pauline Epistles*, and fragments surviving from five other works. This list has in turn been challenged, and the debate continues.

The *Commentary on Thirteen Pauline Epistles* (part of which has recently been translated into English for the first time; deBruyn, 1987) is important, not only for the opportunity it gives to assess Pelagius's thought outside the context of the quarrel with Augustine, but also for the light it sheds on the history of the Latin biblical text. If Pelagius's text is predominantly from the Vulgate, as some argue, and not the Old Latin versions, it is an early and valuable witness to the former.

Controversy with Augustine. Also in dispute are the circumstances surrounding the beginning of the Augustinian controversy with the Pelagians. Traditionally, it has been thought that Augustine's *On Merit and the Forgiveness of Sins* (412), a reply to Celestius's denial of the transmission of sin, was the first shot fired, and some still hold that view. But others see the beginning earlier in replies to Augustine's *Ad Simplicianum*, whether the *Liber de induratione cordis Pharaonis* written ca. 404 by an unknown author, or the *Liber de fide* of Rufinus the Syrian, written ca. 400, or Pelagius's objection to the sentence in the *Confessions*, "Command what you will, and give what you command" (reported by Augustine, *Praed. Sanct.* 2.53).

There is little dispute about the course of the controversy once begun. Celestius was the first to clash publicly with the North Africans. His application for ordination was refused and the six following propositions, taken from his works, were condemned by a synod at Carthage in 411: (1) Adam was created mortal and would have died even if he had not sinned. (2) Adam's sin affected only himself, not the whole human race. (3) Children are born into the same state as that of Adam before he sinned. (4) The human race does not die corporately with Adam or rise corporately with Christ. (5) The law as well as the gospel offers entrance to the kingdom of heaven. (6) Even before the coming of Christ, there were human persons without sin. Celestius appealed his condemnation to Rome, but left Africa and made his way to Ephesus, where he was ordained in 415.

Pelagius had fled Rome when it was invaded in 410 and visited Sicily and North Africa briefly before going on to Palestine. In 413, he was invited, as were Augustine and Jerome, to address a letter to Demetrias on the occasion of her formal adoption of the ascetic life. Apart from the *Commentary*, this letter is the writing of Pelagius that best reveals his understanding of human nature and the interaction of human effort and divine help. While in Palestine, Pelagius wrote, among other things, his treatise *De natura*, to which Augustine responded with *On Nature and Grace*. Pelagius had already earned the enmity of Jerome, and this increased when, in 415, Augustine informed Jerome of his differences with Pelagius. Jerome, in turn, wrote his *Dialogues* against the Pelagians, interpreting their teaching on the possibility of sinlessness as the *apatheia* of Stoicism.

The possibility of sinlessness was the focus of a synod held in 415 at Diospolis in Palestine to adjudicate charges against Pelagius and Celestius. Pelagius satisfied the synod of his orthodoxy, and both he and Celestius were declared in communion with the church. Augustine and the African bishops launched a successful counter-appeal to Rome, which resulted in Innocent I's excommunication of Pelagius and Celestius (January 417). Innocent, however, died in March 417, and the letters the two accused had written in their own defense were received by the new Roman bishop, Zosimus. Less sympathetic to the African cause, he reinstated Pelagius and Celestius and rebuked those who had brought the charges against them. But before his decision reached North Africa, pressure had been brought to bear on the imperial court at Ravenna, and the pendulum swung again. In April 418, the emperor, Honorius, issued a condemnatory rescript, to be followed two months later by the *Tractoria* of Zosimus, which not only condemned Pelagius and Celestius, but demanded that the Italian bishops endorse the decision. A second civil document banished both Pelagius and Celestius from the Italian peninsula. Pelagius escaped to a wandering life in the east. He is thought to have died in Egypt, but the date is unknown. Celestius became entangled in the controversy over Nestorianism and vanished from history ca. 431.

An aspect of the Pelagian controversy to which attention has only recently been paid is the intertwining of theological questions and ecclesiastical politics in the condemnations of 418. The condemnation of Pelagius should be seen in the context of the efforts of Rome to extend its hegemony, efforts reinforced by the appeals of the North African bishops, however selective. On the other hand, the decision of the Africans to deal directly with the court at Ravenna and the submission of Zosimus to Honorius's decree has been seen as an African triumph over Roman control.

The Pelagian cause was taken up by Julian of Eclanum, one of eighteen Italian bishops who had refused to sign the *Tractoria*. Julian, a man of intelligence and learning, saw Manichaeism in Augustine's teaching, and a relentless pamphlet war raged between them during the 420s. Julian has received attention from recent scholarship, especially for his keen philosophical mind and his scriptural commentaries in the tradition of Theodore of Mopsuestia.

Pelagianism should not be seen apart from the other controversies of the period. Jerome's attacks on Pelagius were due in part to the legacy of teachings passing under the name of Origen that he saw in his writings. Pelagius, who apparently occupied the middle ground between Jerome and Jovinian on the question of the relative value of married and celibate life, accused Augustine of Manichaeism, in which he was followed by Julian. The further charge, originating with Cyril of Alexandria and passed on by Marius Mercator, that Nestorianism and Pelagianism were allied, has no foundation. Nor should the Pelagian controversy be studied in isolation from its historical context. Its literature, it has been said, is "the best witness to various ways in which thinking men reacted to the fall of Rome" (Morris, 1965).

Doctrines. Was Pelagius "Pelagian"? This has been seen as a real question more in the past fifty years than in any period since the

fifth century. It is now recognized that the questions in dispute (the natural immortality of Adam, the inheritance of guilt, the vitiation of human nature) were open ones and that Pelagius's answers to them were at least as much in the Christian tradition, particularly that of the eastern church, as those of his attacker. Very few twentieth-century writers would echo the Augustinian charge that Pelagius denied the human need of divine grace. The Pelagian affirmation of the human ability to avoid sin was posited in opposition to theories of a determined future. The ability is not self-given, but a fruit of divine gifts to the human person. There is now a greater appreciation of Pelagius's thought as reacting against determinism of any kind, and the importance of love in his theological ethics is recognized.

The "creationist" nature of Pelagius's theology, which Augustine criticized, has been explicated and his anthropology (rightly seen by Augustine and many since him to be at the core of the dispute) has been systematically explored. The rationality and liberty given to the human person in creation (the defining *bonum naturae*) are, in Pelagius's eyes, divine gifts, not achievements, and those gifts properly used bring human persons into conformity with God. Pelagius's Christological and Trinitarian thought has never been seriously challenged, although some fault him for placing the solidarity of human persons more in their [re]conciliation with the Creator than in their incorporation in Christ.

Pelagianism. It is one thing to talk of the thought of Pelagius, another of that of the "Pelagians." Among the works accepted by de Plinval were the six ascetical and moral treatises edited by Caspari in 1890. While they are generally agreed to be the work of one author, it has been argued that these writings could not be attributed to Pelagius himself "because the ascetical teaching on marriage and continence . . . is not of a piece with the teaching on this subject to be found in the assured writings of Pelagius" (Evans, 1968, p. 38). In 1962, a hypothesis was put forward that has found a certain acceptance among English-speaking scholars. The six treatises, it argued, were written by a Briton living in Sicily whose "singular argument on poverty and riches . . . [was] unique in his own time" (Morris, p. 44). The greater rigor on sexual and social questions revealed in these six treatises (whoever their author) is one index of the diversity of outlook among Pelagians. Even between the two best known of the Pelagians—Pelagius himself and Celestius—there were differences, and the thought of Julian of Eclanum, a generation later, can be distinguished from that of either. The six "Caspari" treatises are but part of a body of pseudonymous literature commonly termed "Pelagian," but which, while it has a certain shared idiom, is far from monolithic in teaching and attitude.

The existence of this body of writing and the continued mining of Pelagius's *Commentary* through the late patristic period and Middle Ages are witnesses to the persistence of the "Pelagian" cast of mind. It has recently been plausibly conjectured that the traditional picture of Pelagianism in Great Britain as "a fairly new heresy . . . faced with an established Catholic orthodoxy" is false, that there existed instead "a range of views," some of which became "heresy" only in relation to the theology of continental churches, and that even the label "heresy" disappeared within a century. "[I]f heresy and orthodoxy were never separated in Britain, . . . how effective and how long-lasting was their separation elsewhere in Western Europe?" (Markus, 1986).

If an anonymous Pelagianism did, in fact, occupy one pole of the ongoing Christian tradition, it was always balanced by the other pole of Augustinianism. The Pelagian controversy involved "two elements . . . that must always be held in tension. . . . The Pelagians did not deny grace, they affirmed it. But grace was first of all man's own freedom, his God-given ability to decide between good and evil." Efforts to occupy a middle ground, affirming a cooperation of divine grace and human free will, associated with John Cassian and other teachers in southern Gaul, have been labeled Semipelagianism. The view that came to prevail, emphasizing the priority of grace in salvation (prevenient grace) but not accepting all of Augustine's views on predestination, has in turn been termed Semiaugustinianism. While Pelagius's idea of grace may have been too facile, Augustine was equally unappreciative of the ideal of human freedom. Recognition of the value and need of the two approaches to grace and freedom is a mark of most late twentieth-century scholarship on the subject. CPL 728–779. *See also* Augustine; Grace; Julian of Eclanum.   [J.McW.]

Bibliography

For the text of Pelagius see *PL Supplementum* 1.1110–1570 (to be used with care); A. Souter, *TS* 9.1–3 (1922–1931). For Rufinus of Syria, see M.W. Miller, *Rufini presbyteri Liber de Fide: A Critical Text and Translation, with Introduction and Commentary* (Washington, D.C.: Catholic U of America P, 1964).

R. Evans, *Four Letters of Pelagius* (London: Black, 1968); T. deBruyn, *A Translation, with Introduction and Notes, of Pelagius's "Commentary on Romans"* Unpublished (Ph.D. diss, University of St. Michael's College, Toronto, 1987).

G. de Plinval, "Recherches sur l'oeuvre littéraire de Pélage," *Revue de philologie, de littérature et d'histoire anciennes* 60 (1934):1–42; idem, *Pélage: ses écrits, sa vie et sa reforme. Etude d'histoire littéraire et religieuse* (Lausanne: Payot, 1943); J. Rivière, "Héterodoxie des pélagiens en fait de rédemption?," *RHE* 41 (1946):5–43; T. Bohlin, *Die Theologie des Pelagius und ihre Genesis* (Lundequist and Wiesbaden: Harrassowitz, 1957); J.N.L. Myres, "Pelagius and the End of Roman Rule in Britain," *JRS* 50 (1960):21–36; R. Evans, "Pelagius: Fastidius and the Pseudo-Augustinian *De vita Christiana*," *JThS* n.s. 13 (1962):72–98; J. Morris, "Pelagian Literature," *JThS* n.s. 16 (1965):26–60; P. Brown, "Pelagius and His Supporters: Aims and Environment," *JThS* n.s. 19 (1968):83–114; R. Evans, *Pelagius: Inquiries and Reappraisals* (New York: Seabury, 1968); P. Brown, "The Patrons of Pelagius: The Roman Aristocracy Between East and West," *JThS* n.s. 21 (1970):56–72; G. Bonner, *Augustine and Modern Research on Pelagianism* (Villanova: Villanova UP, 1972); G. Greshake, *Gnade als konkrete Freiheit: Eine Untersuchung zur Gnadenlehre des Pelagius* (Mainz: Matthias-Grunewald Verlag, 1972); E. TeSelle, "Rufinus the Syrian, Caelestius, Pelagius: Explorations in the Prehistory of the Pelagian Controversy," *AugStud* 3 (1972):61–95; R. Haight, "Notes on the Pelagian Controversy," *Philippian Studies* 22 (1974):26–48; O. Wermelinger, *Rom und Pelagius: Die theologische Position der römischen Bischofe im pelagianischen Streit in den Jahren 411–432* (Stuttgart: Hiersemann, 1975); C. Pietri, *Roma Christiana. Recherches sur l'église de*

Rome, son organisation, sa politique, son idéologie de Miltiade à Sixte III (311–440), 2 vols. (Rome: Ecole Française de Rome, 1976); J.P. Burns, "Augustine's Role in the Imperial Action against Pelagius," *JThS* n.s. 30 (1979):67–83; J.B. Valero, *Las bases antopologicas de Pelagio en su tratado de las "Expositiones"* (Madrid: Publicaciones de la Universidad Pontificia Commillas, 1980); R.A. Markus, "Pelagianism: Britain and the Continent," *JEH* 37 (1986):191–204; A. Solignac, "Pélage et Pélagianisme," *Dictionnaire de Spiritualité* 12 (Paris: Beauchesne, 1986), cols. 2889–2942; B.R. Rees, *Pelagius: A Reluctant Heretic* (Wolfeboro: Boydell, 1988).

PELAGIUS I. Bishop of Rome (556–561). A Roman deacon and, for a time, representative (*apocrisarius*) of the Roman church at Constantinople, Pelagius wrote in defense of the Three Chapters, subjects condemned by the emperor Justinian in an attempt to reconcile the Monophysites. In this work, which opposed the position then taken by pope Vigilius, he made extensive use of the writings of Facundus of Hermiane. When elected pope (at the insistence of Justinian), Pelagius accepted the decrees of the Second Council of Constantinople (553) and tried in many of his letters to overcome strong western opposition to the condemnation of the Three Chapters. Much of his pontificate was spent in rebuilding Rome and aiding the poor. CPL 1698–1703. [M.P.McH.]

Bibliography
Liber Pontificalis 62 (Duchesne 1.303–304).

PELAGIUS II. Bishop of Rome (579–590). Elected when Rome was threatened by the Lombards, Pelagius sent the future Gregory the Great as his representative (*apocrisarius*) to Constantinople to seek help. When the Byzantine emperor Tiberius was unable to comply, the pope appealed to the Franks; a truce was finally arranged (585) by the Byzantine exarch of Ravenna. Pelagius attempted without success to heal a schism that arose in northern Italy because of the lingering dispute over the Three Chapters. He refused to recognize the title "ecumenical patriarch" used by the bishop of Constantinople. His building and renovation projects at the Church of St. Peter and other religious establishments were extensive. He died in a plague; six of his letters are extant. CPL 1705–1707.   [M.P.McH.]

Bibliography
Liber Pontificalis 65 (Duchesne 1.309–311).

PENANCE. Sacrament for forgiveness of postbaptismal sin. The Christian practice of penance is closely associated with the notion of repentance and conversion from sin, and also with practical matters of discipline or sanctions, both of which have roots in Jewish and Hellenistic thought.

Early Practices. According to the earliest traditions, conversion and repentance were stressed in the apocalyptic preaching of Jesus (Matt. 4:17; Mark 1:15). Almost from the beginning, questions arose concerning the treatment of Christians whose behavior did not conform. One who sinned after baptism was to be considered an "outcast" and was to be barred (or "excommunicated") from the communion of the saints, both for the good of the church and for the good of the sinner (1 Cor. 5:3–6; Matt. 18:15–20). The issue then came to be whether and how such a person might obtain forgiveness. Early on, there are indications that such secondary remission of sins was thought impossible since one no longer had recourse to baptism (Heb. 6:4–6), and this view was commonly held through the middle of the second century (Hermas, *Mand.* 4). In other documents from the same period, forgiveness and reconciliation among Christians are required (James 5:15–16; *Did.* 8.2; 14.2); regular confession of sins and weeping in prayer ensure one's purity before communion (*Did.* 14.1; *1 Clem.* 40). The earliest writing devoted to the issue of postbaptismal sins is the homily *2 Clement.* It includes acts of penitence that secure forgiveness, such as fasting, prayer, and especially almsgiving or acts of charity (*2 Clem.* 16.14; cf. *Did.* 4.6; *Barn.* 19.10). Thus, the view emerged that lesser (or venial) sins were covered by contrite confession and prayer, while more serious (or mortal) sins were still liable to excommunication and more stringent discipline. The excommunicated sinner was treated like the unbaptized in that the granting of reconciliation and forgiveness was signified in the readmission to eucharistic fellowship. In both Ignatius (*Philad.* 3.2; 8.1) and Polycarp (*Phil.* 6.1), reconciliation was to be administered by the bishop as a public act (cf. Hermas, *Vis.* 2.4).

Through the beginning of the third century, opinions as to the possibility of remission for postbaptismal sins varied, although ecclesiastical "confession" was widely practiced (Justin, *Dial.* 141; Dionysius of Corinth in Eusebius, *H.E.* 4.23; Irenaeus, *Haer.* 1.8; 3.4). One stimulus toward further systematization may have been the rigorism of the Montanist movement, which reasserted the position that there was no repentance after baptism. The majority of writers through the third century took a more lenient stand, although there are notable exceptions, such as Hippolytus at Rome (*Haer.* 9.7). Clement of Alexandria admitted one repentance after baptism (*Str.* 2.13; cf. *Q.d.s.* 42), and he was generally followed by Origen and the eastern fathers. Origen offered one of the first explanations of the mechanism of penitential remission; he suggested that penance itself is the counterpart of the blood of Christ that ransoms the sinner through baptism. For Origen, acts of penitence, like martyrdom, constitute a "second baptism" and thereby remission of sins (*Hom. in Lev.* 2; *Or.* 28; *Mart.* 30).

Third-Century Controversies. The first major controversies over penitential practice came in the third century in North Africa. Tertullian adopted Irenaeus's theory of recapitulation (*Haer.* 3.21; 4.27; 5.16, 19) to suggest that Christ's death attained remission of sins by means of compensation. Thus, Tertullian made the mechanism of repentance its compensatory effect, picking up on a Latin word play: God "offers release from penalty [*poena*] at the compensating exchange of penitence [*paenitentiam*]" (*Paenit.* 6). This legal metaphor of penitential compensation, which he also calls "satisfaction" (*Paenit.* 5), would provide the dominant model and vocabulary for the doctrine of penance in the west throughout the Middle Ages.

In the earlier phase of his Christian writings, Tertullian accepted the possibility of one repentance after baptism and so defined the conventional practice of public penance, or *exomologēsis*, the Greek term for "confession" (*Paenit.* 9). It included acts of self-humiliation before the entire congregation as appeasement to God through which satisfaction and absolution were obtained. In this period, public penance was clearly an ecclesiastical cycle administered by the bishop. Later, however, Tertullian converted to the stricter Montanist position, which had become popular in North Africa. In *De pudicitia*, he repudiated lenient postbaptismal reconciliation. Apparently taken in direct response to actions by the bishop of Carthage, Tertullian's stricter position did not affect treatment of venial sins but was directed at mortal sins, especially murder, idolatry, and adultery, which he said could never be forgiven on earth (*Pud.* 7; 9).

Tertullian's sobering attack probably exerted wide influence, if one may judge from the magnitude of the next crisis over penance that arose in North African Christianity. It concerned the treatment of Christians who, under the Decian persecution, "lapsed" into idolatry by offering sacrifice. When the persecution eased, readmission of the lapsed became an issue. Despite the rigorist tradition of Tertullian, some of the Carthaginian clergy (including martyrs in prison) were granting reconciliation to the lapsed. Others, such as the rigorist schismatic Novatian from Rome, denied any possibility of reconciliation, while demanding that the lapsed nonetheless be enrolled as penitents. The bishop of Carthage, Cyprian, sought to show mercy to the lapsed but also demanded that correct ecclesiastical procedures be observed. Cyprian called for a long and laborious process of examination for the penitent, which he set out in stages, beginning with acts of satisfaction to demonstrate contrition, followed by public *exomologēsis* before the church, and finally public reconciliation to the "peace of the church" at the hands of the priest (*Laps.* 16; cf. *Ep.* 4; 15–17; 31). Cyprian built upon Tertullian's legal metaphor of compensation toward a sacramental notion of penance by calling it an expiation for sin and the "medicine of atonement" through satisfaction (*Laps.* 15–16). An important distinction was also made in dissociating the reconciliation of penance (for postbaptismal sins) from the forgiveness obtained through baptism.

Fourth to Sixth Centuries. Cyprian's position, expressed through synodal decrees, established both the tone and the vocabulary for future doctrinal developments in the west. The right of the church to govern reconciliation was central in the North African Donatist controversy, most notably in the writings of Augustine. Also, the legal metaphor used by Tertullian and Cyprian for penitential reconciliation was more broadly applied by Augustine to questions of sin and grace in that he distinguishes prebaptismal "penance" not only from the continual penance offered for venial sins but also from penance in the technical sense for grave sins (*Symb.* 7–8; 15–16). Augustine thus upheld the ecclesiastical practice of public penance for mortal sins. From the time of Augustine, a more formalized liturgy of penance began to evolve. Beginning in the Roman rite of the fifth and sixth centuries, penance was enjoined on all (for the sake of secret sins) in Lent followed by a public rite of reconciliation on Maundy Thursday prior to Easter communion (Innocent I, *Ep.* 25.7). The practice became formalized by the time of the *Gelasian Sacramentary* (dating probably from the eighth century). During this period, penance was becoming especially popular for the sick and dying, and Lent was becoming more specifically a time for all to do penance.

By the time of Gregory the Great (d. 604), penance had received most of its formal elements. Drawing on Augustine, Gregory could say that baptism, now becoming restricted to infants, was exclusively for the remission of original sin, while all other sins had to find recourse in the baptism of tears in a contrite heart (*Moral.* 9.84; *Hom. in Evang.* 10.7; *Exp. in Sept. Psalm. poenit.* 2.1). Gregory further specified three aspects or steps of penance as "conversion in mind, confession with the mouth, and vindication from sin": *conversio mentis, confessio oris, vindicata peccati* (*Exp.*

in Prim. Reg. 6.2). Here, Gregory clearly sets the stage for the Scholastic definition of the stages of penance as contrition of heart (*contritio cordis*), confession of mouth (*confessio oris*), and works of satisfaction (*satisfactio operis*). Moreover, in extending the Latin legal metaphor in conjunction with the Augustinian distinction between forgiveness for original sin and forgiveness for sins committed after baptism, Gregory was the first to formalize a more complete doctrine of purgatory as the penance that continues after death (*Dial.* 4.25, 39, 48, 56; *Hom. in Evang.* 19.4).

For Gregory, penance was still a public ecclesiastical act. Only by the end of the sixth century would the new practice known as auricular or semiprivate confession emerge, especially through the Celtic rite. As it became prominent in medieval monastic practice, private penance to an individual priest-confessor became the norm by the twelfth century and was systematically ordered in Scholastic treatises. Since baptism had largely become a sacrament of infancy, penance stood alongside the Mass as the primary sacraments of western piety through the high Middle Ages. Its pervasive influence can be seen in Anselm's "satisfaction theory" of the atonement, which viewed Christ's death as a supreme act of penance for the sins of humanity. Numerous handbooks for confessors (called *summae confessorum*) further specified proper ways of interrogating penitents to determine grades of sin. Corresponding gradations of acts of satisfaction were defined to be assigned after absolution was granted. The Fourth Lateran Council (1215) decreed that all Christians must receive the eucharist at least once a year, and such observance mandated attendance at confessional before communion. *See also* Confession of Sin; Discipline; Repentance.   [L.M.W.]

Bibliography

O.D. Watkins, *A History of Penance* (London: Longmans, Green, 1920); R.S.T. Haslehurst, *Penitential Discipline in the Early Church* (London: SPCK, 1921); P. Galtier, *L'Eglise et la rémission des péches aux premiers siècles* (Paris: Beauchesne, 1932); J.T. McNeill, *Medieval Handbooks of Penance* (New York: Columbia UP, 1938); R.C. Mortimer, *The Origins of Private Penance in the Western Church*

(Oxford: Clarendon, 1939); B. Poschmann, *Paenitentia Secunda* (Bonn: Hanstein, 1940); P. Galtier, *Aux Origens du sacrement de pénitence* (Rome: Gregorianum, 1951); P. Anciaux, *La Théologie du sacrement de pénitence au XIIe siècle* (Louvain: Nauwelaerts, 1952); H.E.W. Turner, *Patristic Doctrine of Redemption* (London: Mowbray, 1952); M. Bévenot, "The Sacrament of Penance and St. Cyprian's *De Lapsis*," *ThS* 16 (1955):175–213; G.H. Williams, "The Sacramental Presuppositions of Anselm's *Cur Deus Homo*," *ChHist* 26 (1957):245–274; E. Langstadt, "Tertullian's Doctrine of Sin and the Power of Absolution in *De Pudicitia*," *SP* 2 (TU 64) (1957):251–257; P.F. Palmer, *Sacraments and Forgiveness* (Westminster: Newman, 1959); W. Telfer, *The Forgiveness of Sins* (London: SCM, 1960); P. Anciaux, *The Sacrament of Penance* (New York: Sheed and Ward, 1962); B. Poschmann, *Penance and the Anointing of the Sick* (London: Burns and Oates, 1964); A. Kavanaugh et al., "Penance: The Ministry of Reconciliation," *Resonance* 2 (1966):1–135; H. Karpp, *Die Busse: Quellen zur Entstehung des altkirchlichen Busswesens* (Berne: Peter Lang, 1969); T. Tentler, *Sin and Confession on the Eve of the Reformation* (Princeton: Princeton UP, 1977); L.M. White, "Transactionalism in the Penitential Thought of Gregory the Great," *Restoration Quarterly* 21 (1978):33–51; Groupe de la Bussiere, *Pratiques de la confession, des pères du désert à Vatican II* (Paris, 1983).

Pentecost, Mary with the twelve apostles, the Rabbula Gospels (sixth century), folio 14b (C. Cecchelli, *The Rabbula Gospels* [Olten and Lausanne: Urs Graf-Verlag, 1959]).

PENTECOST. Jewish and Christian feast; derived from the Greek word for "the fiftieth." In early Christian usage, Pentecost denoted the fiftieth day after the resurrection of Christ (Acts 2:1ff.), when the Holy Spirit descended on his disciples. The Christian calendar followed the Jewish (cf. Acts 20:16; 1 Cor. 16:8), the day corresponding to the Old Testament "feast of the weeks" or "harvest" (cf. Exod. 23:16; 34:22; Deut. 16:10, 16), later called Pentecost and associated with the reception of the Law by Moses from God (Exod. 19:1ff.). Augustine (*Ep.* 55) explains the difference between the Jewish and the Christian feasts of Pentecost in terms of the difference between the gift of the Law and the gift of the Holy Spirit.

Up to the middle of the fourth century, it appears that the feast of Pentecost commemorated the ascension of Christ into heaven as well as the descent of the Holy Spirit and also that it was not restricted to the fiftieth day after Christ's resurrection but included all the fifty days from the resurrection to the descent of the Spirit (Tertullian, *Idol.* 12; Origen, *Cels.* 8:22; Council of Antioch [341], *can.* 20; Basil, *Spir.* 27; Gregory of Nyssa, *Spir.*, PG 46.697). Other characteristic features of this feast and of the whole period from Easter to Pentecost were the administration of baptism and the prohibition of kneeling and fasting, as a sign of the exaltation of Christ and the coming general resurrection. The latter feature, already known to Tertullian (*Coron.* 3) at the beginning of the third century, was given canonical status by the Council of Nicaea (325), Canon 20. The many superb sermons on Pentecost by the early fathers indicate the early church's awareness of the significance of the person and work of the Holy Spirit. [G.D.D.]

Bibliography

Gregory of Nazianzus, *Oration* 41; Gregory of Nyssa, *In pentecosten*; John Chrysostom, *De Sancta Pentecoste, Homiliae* 1–2.

A.A. McArthur, *The Evolution of the Christian Year* (London: SCM, 1953); idem, *The Christian Year and Lectionary Reform* (London: SCM, 1958); F.X. Weiser, *Handbook of Christian Feasts and Customs* (New York: Harcourt, Brace, 1958); J. Gunstone, *The Feast of Pentecost: The Great Fifty Days in the Liturgy* (Westminster: Faith, 1967); C. Jones, G. Wainwright, and E. Yarnold, eds., *The Study of the Liturgy* (London: SPCK, 1978).

PERPETUA AND FELICITAS (d. 203). Martyrs, whose experience is preserved in the *Passion of Perpetua and Felicitas*. These two women, along with Saturninus, Secundulus, Revocatus, and Saturus, all catechumens, were martyred in Carthage, North Africa, in 203. Felicitas and Revocatus were slaves. The account of their martyrdom is especially important because it contains the prison diaries of Perpetua (3–10) and Saturus (11–13). An editor, often incorrectly identified as Tertullian, has provided a narrative framework (1–2; 14–21).

Perpetua's diary recounts the attempts of her pagan father to dissuade her from her Christian faith and her struggle over her infant son, whom she eventually gave up to her father. The diary also describes Perpetua's four visions. The second and third visions (7–8) are about her deceased brother, Dinocrates, and imply that her prayers were effective in delivering him from suffering in the afterlife. The first and fourth visions (4; 10) are about her martyrdom and include her statement that she "became a man" in the arena (10.7). Felicitas bore a daughter in prison who was raised by a Christian woman (15). Saturus's diary recounts a heavenly vision in which the martyr Perpetua settles a dispute between a bishop and a presbyter.

The editor, probably a Montanist, argues strongly that the visions of Perpetua and Saturus are the continuing work of the Holy Spirit and are as significant as the old visions recorded in the Bible. This martyr account probably reflects the contemporary conflicts over authority with respect both to martyrs and to followers of Montanism, the New Prophecy.

Augustine preached four sermons on Perpetua and Felicitas on their feast day. He discusses explicitly his admiration for Perpetua's faith and heroic strength in the context of his generally negative view of women and female sexuality. Feast day March 6. CPL 32.

[D.M.S.]

Bibliography

Tertullian, *On the Soul* 55.4; Augustine, *Sermons* 280–283; Quodvultdeus (?), *Sermo de SS. Perpetua et Felicitate*.

W.H. Shewring, *The Passion of SS. Perpetua and Felicity: New Edition and Translation of the Latin Text, Together with the Sermons of St. Augustine upon These Saints* (London: Sheed and Ward, 1931); Musurillo, pp. xxv–xxvii, 106–131.

M.R. Lefkowitz, "The Motivations for St. Perpetua's Martyrdom," *Journal of the American Academy of Religion* 44 (1976):417–421; W.H.C. Frend, "Blandina and Perpetua: Two Early Christian Martyrs," *Les Martyrs de Lyon (177)* (Paris: Centre National de la Recherche Scientifique, 1978), pp. 167–177; M.A. Rossi, "The Passion of Perpetua, Everywoman of Late Antiquity," *Pagan and Christian Anxiety: A Response to E.R. Dodds*, ed. R.C. Smith and J. Lounibos (Lanham: UP of America, 1984), pp. 53–86; E.A. Petroff, *Medieval Woman's Visionary Literature* (Oxford: Oxford UP, 1986), pp. 60–82; A. Pettersen, "Perpetua—Prisoner of Conscience," *VChr* 41 (1987):139–153.

PERSECUTION. Harassment or oppression of people for their religious faith, usually including infliction of death.

Background. The first Christians were conditioned to expect persecution even before they experienced it. Among the Jews, the prophets had proclaimed that the faithful would suffer at the hands of the unrighteous, even as an atonement for their sins (Isa. 53). In the Maccabean revolt of 167 B.C., events gave this perspective its paradigmatic formulation for the Jews. Suffering in persecution was the willing sacrifice made by the righteous for the sins of the unrighteous (2 Macc. 7:32–37). Such acceptance, and even expectation, of persecution had become entrenched in Jewish tradition by the time Jesus began his ministry.

Seeing himself as a servant reminiscent of the figure in Isaiah 53 (Matt. 20:26–28), Jesus warned his followers not to be surprised at persecution (Matt. 10:16–25). He then himself died a martyr's death at the instigation of the Jewish establishment, led by the high priest Caiaphas, with the cooperation of the Roman governor Pontius Pilate.

Persecution of Christians in the Roman empire can be divided into three periods.

Jewish Persecution of Christians from Jesus' Death to the Great Fire in Rome, A.D. 64. In the first period of persecution, Christianity appeared as a sect within Judaism, which was a legal religion in the Roman empire. Jewish religious authorities considered the new group to be their responsibility, and Roman authorities generally agreed. Christians lived with the ambiguity of toleration by Rome and persecution by Jewish authorities. The Jewish persecution consisted of considerable harassment (Acts 4–5) and a few deaths (Acts 6–8). About A.D. 44, Herod Agrippa I, Rome's "king" of the Jews, in the interests of the Jerusalem authorities, executed the apostle James, brother of John, and jailed the apostle Peter (Acts 12). Subsequently, ca. A.D. 62, the high priest Ananus executed James, the brother of Jesus (Josephus, *Antiquities* 20.200–201; Eusebius, *H.E.* 2.23).

Around the Mediterranean, Jews during this period, presumably synagogue leaders in many cases, took similar actions against the representatives of the new Jewish sect (Acts 13–14). Similar resistance by unconverted Jews may have been the underlying cause of Claudius's expulsion of Jews from Rome about the same time (Acts 18; Suetonius, *Claudius* 25; cf. Heb. 10:32–34). In the early 50s, the pattern reported in Acts 16–19 was one of local groups, usually unconverted Jews with Gentile assistance, either pressing the Roman authorities to incarcerate the missionaries or driving the missionaries out of town by unofficial citizen action. In the late 50s, Paul was attacked in Jerusalem by some Jews from the Ephesus area and was given protective custody there by Roman authorities (Acts 21–22). Upon discovery of a plot to kill him, the authorities transferred him to Caesarea, where he was held for two years, and later, on appeal, to Rome (Acts 23–25; 28).

Roman Persecution Instigated by Society, 64–250. As Christianity became distinguished from Judaism as a new religion, it suffered the disapproval of both the Jews and the larger Gentile public. Nero (A.D. 54–68) was the first Roman emperor to persecute Christians. Nero's action against them evidently should be associated not with the fire in Rome in the summer of 64, as commonly deduced from Tacitus (*Annals* 15.44), but with the "novel enactments" including "punishments . . . inflicted on the Christians" subsequently (64–68), according to Suetonius (*Nero* 16; cf. Tertullian's

institutum Neronianum in *Nat.* 1.7).The law probably made it a capital offense to be a Christian (cf. 1 Peter 4:12–17), regardless of any *flagitia* (abominable acts), and can plausibly be attributed to the influence of Nero's mistress and second wife Poppaea Sabina, known to intercede for Jewish causes (Josephus, *Antiquities* 20.195). *1 Clement* 5–6 relates the persecution to Jewish intrigue. Early tradition places Peter and Paul among the martyrs in Rome at this time (*1 Clem.* 5; 1 Peter 5:13, identifying "Babylon" with Rome).

About the year 95, Domitian (80–96), according to Eusebius (*H.E.* 3.18.4), banished "many" Christians from Rome, including Flavia Domitilla, niece of the prominent consul Flavius Clemens. *1 Clement* 1 and 7 suggest recent persecution in Rome, as does the apostle John's banishment to Patmos off the coast of Asia probably about the same time (Rev. 1:9). In Pliny's letter to the emperor Trajan (*Ep.* 10.96), the Christians who had given up their faith twenty years earlier may have been apostates under Domitian's rule. If there was a plot against Domitian in 95 (Suetonius, *Domitian* 15; Dio 77.14), the emperor's banishment of Christians from Rome may be connected with it in some way. Contemporaneous persecution in Asia Minor may have been mob action inspired by Christian refusal to take the emperor's loyalty oath. What truth there is in Hegesippus's account of Domitian's interrogation of two grandsons of Jude (Eusebius, *H.E.* 3.20.1–6) seems to be related to Domitian's concern about tax evasion by Jews (Suetonius, *Domitian* 12). The grandsons' release suggests a clear distinction between Jews living as Christians, in this case, and Jews living as Jews, still subject to Rome's tax on the Jews, the *fiscus Iudaicus.*

Under Trajan (98–117), it becomes clear that simply being a Christian was a capital offense (Pliny the Younger, *Ep.* 10.96). Pliny, Trajan's governor for Bithynia and Pontus probably from late 111 to early 113, indicates that he was involved in a large-scale matter: "A great many individuals of every age and class, both men and women, are being brought to trial, and this is likely to continue." Presumably, "many" were also "led away for execution," although he found that many others would recant their Christianity given the "opportunity." In his rescript, Trajan commends Pliny and adds, procedurally, that persons charged "must not be hunted down" nor should their names be taken from "pamphlets circulated anonymously" (Pliny the Younger, *Ep.* 10.97). Hegesippus a few decades later wrote similarly that Trajan's reign involved persecution initiated by the populace "sporadically, in some cities" (Eusebius, *H.E.* 3.32.1). Along with these nameless martyrs in Bithynia are two from other parts of the empire who do have names. Simon the son of Clopas, bishop of the Jerusalem church after James's death, was arrested after accusation from "heretics" within his Davidic clan, tortured, and crucified, presumably in Jerusalem, during Trajan's reign (Eusebius, *H.E.* 3.32). Ignatius, bishop of Antioch, was also arrested, perhaps from a similar "insider" accusation to a Roman authority in Antioch, and taken to Rome for execution under Trajan.

Hadrian (117–138) sent a rescript in 124–125 to Minucius Fundanus, governor of Asia (Justin, *2 Apol.* 68), with two procedural stipulations similar to Trajan's regarding accusation of Christians. Accusation must be made by an individual in court, not by "outcries" from a mob, and false accusations must receive "more severe punishment." Christianity remained illegal, but its adherents gained procedural protection from mob accusation. Antoninus Pius (138–161) in a rescript to the Council of Asia alluded to problems of mob violence against Christians in Greece and Asia (Eusebius, *H.E.* 4.26.10; Justin, *1 Apol.* 68), evidently in reaction to natural disasters. Specific instances of persecution are limited to the martyrdom of Telesphorus, bishop of Rome, in 138 (Eusebius, *H.E.* 5.6.4), and that of an unnamed woman, her teacher, Ptolemaus, and a bystander, Lucius (Justin, *2 Apol.* 2).

Under Marcus Aurelius (161–180), violence against Christians became more widespread. At some point between 161 and 168, eleven Christians of Philadelphia in Asia were arrested and taken to Smyrna to be killed in the provincial games (*M. Polyc.* 19). Shortly

thereafter, Polycarp, bishop of Smyrna, was arrested and executed. About the same time, two others in Smyrna, three in Pergamum, the church leader Publius in Athens, and the apologist Justin in Rome were martyred (Eusebius, *H.E.* 4.15.46–48; 16.1; 23.2). This rash of executions is probably to be dated close to 168. Anti-Christian feeling in society was no doubt intensified by a Parthian attack ca. 165, then a plague and a German invasion, and was probably mobilized by an imperial decree (*V. Aberc.* 1) requiring sacrifices to the gods across the empire. In 177, mass persecution took place in Vienne and Lyons in Gaul (Eusebius, *H.E.* 5.1–3). The record of the persecution names eight Christians who died and indicates that the total number was large. The extraordinary mob violence, followed by government brutality, was triggered by a senate decree in early 177, the so-called *senatus consultum de pretiis gladiatorum minuendis*, allowing provincial officials to purchase condemned criminals more cheaply and to employ them as gladiators in the public games. Eusebius considered it likely that similar atrocities occurred in other provinces (*H.E.* 5.2.1). His view is supported by the writing of an unusual number of apologetic works from Greece to Syria in the years 177–180. Melito of Sardis mentions "new decrees throughout Asia" resulting in "brigandage by mob" (Eusebius, *H.E.* 4.26.5–6), legislation likely inspired by the senate's new decree. Intense anti-Christian feelings in society emerged in print in the pagan writings of Lucian in 165 and Celsus ca. 178.

Commodus (180–192) was notable for the "milder treatment" afforded Christians under his reign (Eusebius, *H.E.* 5.21.1). In 180, a dozen Christians from Scilli in North Africa were executed by the Roman governor. A prominent Roman, Apollonius, was martyred in this period on accusation by a servant (Eusebius, *H.E.* 5.21.2–5). Tertullian indicates that a number of fanatical, possibly Montanist, Christians were executed in Asia ca. 184–185 (*Scap.* 5.1).

The "Caesar's decree" mentioned by Hippolytus (*Dan.* 1.20) has been identified with a prohibition of conversions to Christianity by

Septimus Severus ca. 201 or 202, but this is unsubstantiated. By contrast, the *Passion of Perpetua and Felicitas* confirms the martyrdom of five African Christians at Carthage in 202. Probably in the same year, Leonides, Origen's father, was executed in Alexandria (Eusebius, *H.E.* 6.2.12). Eusebius names eight of Origen's students who were executed in 206 (*H.E.* 6.4–5). He claims, questionably, that Severus stirred up persecution "in every place" (*H.E.* 6.1.1). Severus's role in the persecutions, in fact, remains obscure.

During the joint rule of Caracalla and Geta (211), a Christian soldier was executed for refusing to wear a laurel wreath along with his fellow soldiers (Tertullian, *Coron.* 1.1). A year later, Caracalla killed Geta, and in an ensuing purge of Geta's loyalists, Christians were persecuted at least in Africa. Some avoided the persecution at this time by taking flight or by buying immunity (Tertullian, *Fug.* 5.5; 12.1; 13.3).

Maximinus Thrax (235–238) executed some Christians in a purge of Alexander Severus's imperial court (Herodian, *Hist.* 7.1.2–4). Eusebius writes of a persecution against "only the leaders of the church" (*H.E.* 6.28). However, only in Rome and in Caesarea, with its imperial connection, were leaders persecuted: two rival Roman bishops, Pontianus and Hippolytus, were deported, and a wealthy deacon, Ambrose, and a presbyter were jailed in Caesarea. Severe persecution arose at this time in Pontus and Cappadocia. Earthquakes led to mob violence that was supported by the governor Serenianus's action against both Christians and their church buildings (Origen, *Comm. Ser. Mt.* 39; Cyprian, *Ep.* 75.10).

During the reign of Philip (244–249), himself friendly toward Christians, mob persecution broke out in Alexandria, probably in connection with celebration of Rome's thousand years of existence in 247–248 and with a renewed enthusiasm for older local religion. Dionysius, bishop of Alexandria, names four Christians and indicates many others who suffered "for a long time" (Cyprian, *Ep.* 37.2; 43.3; Eusebius, *H.E.* 6.41.1–9).

Roman Persecution Initiated by the Government, 250–313. Decius (249–251), in an effort to revitalize traditional paganism, issued an edict in late 249 or early 250 requiring sacrifice to the gods (Cyprian, *Ep.* 37.2; 43.3; Eusebius, *H.E.* 6.41.10). Like Maximinus Thrax, he focused attention on the clergy. In Rome, bishop Fabian was executed (*H.E.* 6.39.1); his successor, Cornelius, was exiled for a time in 253. In Egypt, Dionysius of Alexandria, himself jailed and later released, names twenty Christians tortured or killed, and notes that "many others throughout the cities and villages were torn in pieces" (*H.E.* 6.41.1–42.1). In Jerusalem and Antioch, the bishops Alexander and Babylas died in prison (*H.E.* 6.39.2–4). Origen was tortured in Caesarea (*H.E.* 6.39.5).

On the other hand, the elderly Chaeremon, bishop of Nilopolis, fled his city and "many of the more eminent persons" offered sacrifice (*H.E.* 6.42.3). At Carthage, bishop Cyprian disappeared and most of the church did similarly or offered sacrifice (Cyprian, *Ep.* 17.1); the Spanish bishops Martialis and Basilides circumvented sacrifice by purchasing *libelli*, certificates verifying sacrifice (Cyprian, *Ep.* 67.1). Bishop Euctemon in Smyrna apostatized (*M. Pion.* 18.13). Decius was able to weaken the churches by throwing them into internal chaos. An estimate of martyrdoms during the Decian persecution is placed in the hundreds; that of apostasies, considerably higher. The question of readmission of the "lapsed" loomed large.

When Valerian (253–260) came to power, persecution stopped because of Gothic invasions; it resumed in 257 during an improved military situation. A decree required church leaders to sacrifice and forbade Christian assemblies on church property. Cyprian and Dionysius were exiled at this point (Cyprian, *Ep.* 77–81; Eusebius, *H.E.* 7.11.8–10). The following year, a harsher order prescribed more severe punishment for Christians of higher church rank or social class, including some loss of property, and a broader requirement of sacrifice. The Roman bishop Sixtus II, seven deacons, and some women of the aristocracy were executed at this time (Cyprian, *Ep.* 80.1). In Africa, the same fate befell the bishop Cyprian and three other bishops, four other named leaders, and possibly many more unnamed. Fructuosus and two deacons were burned alive in Tarragona, Spain (*M. Fruct.* 2.4). Three Christians in Palestine were voluntary martyrs (Eusebius, *H.E.* 7.12).

Gallienus (260–268) ushered in a new if not permanent era of peace for the Christians. By decree, the new emperor immediately returned church property to the bishops' control and permitted them, officially for the first time, to resume their duties (Eusebius, *H.E.* 7.13). Persecution was limited to one Christian soldier at Caesarea who refused to sacrifice while being promoted (*H.E.* 7.15). Christianity came to enjoy a protected status it had not had since Nero first clearly differentiated it from Judaism nearly 200 years earlier.

With Diocletian (284–305) came the sequence of events ending the first peace of the church and beginning the "Great Persecution." Anti-Christian sentiment was ascendant, both in society, as seen in Porphyry's writings, and in government. In 297, Manichaeism was banned as doctrine hostile to Rome. Sometime between 297 and 301, Christians making the sign of the cross on a certain occasion were considered by Diocletian and Galerius to be the cause of bad omens. Diocletian ordered all palace and military personnel to sacrifice (Eusebius, *H.E.* 8.4.3; Lactantius, *Mort. pers.* 10). The economy of the empire was deteriorating, and Christianity was blamed for that as well (Arnobius, *Adv. nat.* 1.3, 13–14).

Following conferences in Nicomedia (302–303) among Diocletian, the Caesar Galerius, and their chief adviser, Hierocles, Diocletian decided to "terminate" Christianity (Lactantius, *Mort. pers.* 16.4). The result was four edicts of increasing severity issued in 303–304. On February 23, 303, officers looted and demolished the church near the palace in Nicomedia and burned its scriptures. The next day, an edict was published mandating destruction of all churches and sacred books and depriving Christians of all class privileges (*Mort. pers.* 11–13; Eusebius, *H.E.* 8.2.4). Palace fires and eastern provincial revolts followed. In response, Diocletian executed 268 Christians in Nicomedia (*P. Oxy.* 10.15; Eusebius, *H.E.* 8.6.6–7). A second edict was issued to imprison all higher clergy (Eusebius, *H.E.* 8.6.8–9). Prison overcrowding led to a third edict, in November, offering amnesty on the condition of sacrifice (*H.E.* 8.2.5; 8.6.9–10).

To this point, no death penalty had been stipulated. By the spring of 304, however, government demands escalated, and a fourth edict, promulgated by Galerius, required all people to sacrifice, on pain of death or forced labor (Eusebius, *M.P.* 3.1; *V.C.* 2.34). Enforcement was lighter in the west under Maximian than in the east under Diocletian. Gaul and Britain lost few churches and no Christians (Lactantius, *Mort. pers.* 15.6; Eusebius, *H.E.* 8.13.13). Only at Haidra in North Africa were martyrs reported (*Inscr. Lat. de la Tunis.* 470). In the west, Christian controversy swirled mainly around surrendering of the scriptures. In the east, persecution was intense, and later debate centered on sacrificing to the gods.

In 305, the emperors Diocletian and Maximian retired in favor of their Caesars, Galerius (305–311) in the east and Constantius (305–306) in the west. This brought a lull in the persecution. Two edicts followed. Galerius's own Caesar, Maximinus Daia, issued an edict in 306 requiring sacrifice, but problems of reorganization inhibited its enforcement. Eusebius knows of only three martyrs in Palestine from that renewed persecution (*M.P.* 4.6, 8–15). In 307–308, however, 227 Christians were arrested in Egypt and suffered savage mutilation before being released (Eusebius, *M.P.* 8.1, 5–13).

In 309, a second edict from Maximinus Daia specified rebuilding of pagan temples and public sacrifice (*M.P.* 9.2). Eusebius counts twenty-one Christian executions in Palestine from 309 to 311 (*M.P.* 9.2–11, 31); some Christians fled the empire (*M.P.* 11.8–12; *V.C.* 2.53).

On April 30, 311, the ailing Galerius issued his famous Edict of Toleration, admitting failure in the restoration of Roman religion and allowing Christians freedom "to live as Christians" (Lactantius, *Mort. pers.* 34; Eusebius, *H.E.* 8.17.3–11), and Maxentius followed suit in Italy (Augustine, *Coll. c. Don.* 34). Taking charge in the east after Galerius's death, Maximinus Daia (311–313) made attempts at counteracting Galerius's edict (Eusebius, *H.E.*

9.2, 7.3–14), largely ineffectual except for the extraordinary brutality in Egypt (*H.E.* 8.9.4–5). By 313, Maximinus gave up and issued notices declaring toleration of Christians (*H.E.* 9.9a.1–9; 9.10.7–11). The Great Persecution had come to an end.

Meanwhile, Constantine (312–337) had identified his cause with the Christian God and in 313, with his ally in the east, Licinius (308–324), drew up a notice of toleration similar to that of Galerius, the "Edict" of Milan, issued on June 13 (Lactantius, *Mort. pers.* 48.2–12; Eusebius, *H.E.* 10.5.2–14). It stipulated freedom of religious choice and return of all church property to Christians. Christianity became a religion supported by the imperial treasury and by a converted emperor, Constantine.

In an effort to overcome Constantine, Licinius futilely attempted a renewal of persecution in 322–323. It cost him his life in 324. With little more success, the emperor Julian the Apostate (360–363), a nephew of Constantine, attempted a revival of paganism by restitution of temple property in Christian hands, by depriving Christian clergy of imperial financial support, and by recalling from exile schismatic Christian bishops. His death in 363 cut short any possibility of breathing life into the old Roman religion. Persecution was now to become the prerogative of the victorious church against those deemed heretics or schismatics, although Christians outside the Roman empire, as in Persia, were still to experience persecution from a non-Christian government. *See also* Church and State; Martyr, Martyrdom; Paganism and Christianity; Roman Empire. [R.L.W.]

Bibliography

Suetonius, *Lives of the Caesars* (*Claudius* 25, *Nero* 16, *Domitian* 15); Tacitus, *Annals* 15.44; Pliny the Younger, *Letters* 10.96, 97; Josephus, *Jewish Antiquities* 20.195–203; Justin, *1 Apology* 68; idem, *2 Apology* 2; *Martyrdom of Polycarp; Acts of the Scillitan Martyrs; Letter of the Churches of Lyons and Vienne* in Eusebius, *Church History* 5.1–3; Tertullian, *To the Heathen* 1.6–7; idem, *Apology* 1–5; idem, *Crown* 1.1; Cyprian, *On the Lapsed* 8; 25; 27; idem, *Letters* 11.1; 24; 55.14; 67.1; 75.10; 77–80; Lactantius, *On the Deaths of the Persecutors* 6; 10–13; 15.6; 16.4; 48.2–12; Eusebius, *Church History* 2.10, 22–23, 25; 3.12, 17–19, 32–33, 36; 4.9, 12–17; 5.1–5, 21; 6.1–2, 4–5, 28, 39–42; 7.1–4, 10–13, 15, 30; 8.1.1–10.5.14; idem, *Martyrs of Palestine* 3.1; 4–6; 8.1.5–13; 9.2–11.31; idem, *Life of Constantine* 1.27–32; 2.34, 53.

C. Callewaert, "La Méthode dans la recherche de la base juridique des premiers persécutions," *RHE* 12 (1911):5–16, 633–657; A. Alföldi, "Die Hauptereignisse der Jahre 253–261 n. Chr. im Orient im Spiegel der Münzprägung," *Berytus* 4 (1937):41–68; H.M. Last, "The Study of the 'Persecutions'" *JRS* 27 (1937):80–92; N.H. Baynes, "The Great Persecution," *Cambridge Ancient History* (Cambridge: Cambridge UP, 1939), Vol. 12, pp. 646–677, 789–795; A.N. Sherwin-White, "The Early Persecutions and Roman Law Again," *JThS* n.s. 3 (1952):199–213; R.M. Grant, *The Sword and the Cross* (New York: Macmillan, 1955); E.M. Smallwood, "The Legislation of Hadrian and Antoninus Pius Against Circumcision," *Latomus* 18 (1959):334–347; G.E.M. de Ste. Croix, "Why Were the Early Christians Persecuted?," *Past and Present* 26 (1963):6–38; H. Grégoire, *Les Persécutions dans l'empire romain*, 2nd ed. (Brussels: Palisades Académies, 1964); W.H.C. Frend, *Martyrdom and Persecution in the Early Church* (Garden City: Doubleday, 1964); T.D. Barnes, "Legislation Against the Christians," *JRS* 58 (1968):32–50; J. Moreau, *Die Christenverfolgung im römischen Reich* (Berlin: de Gruyter, 1971); P. Keresztes, "The Imperial Roman Government and the Christian Church, I. From Nero to the Severi," and "II. From Gallienus to the Great Persecution," ANRW (1979), Vol. 2.23.1, pp. 247–315, 375–386.

PERSIA. Christianity in Persia was a minority religion among other strong religions—Judaism, Manichaeism, and especially the state religion, Zoroastrianism. Christianity may have started within the Jewish community at Adiabene, having followed the trade routes. Its language was Syriac, later primarily an ecclesiastical language. Christians also came with the deportation of war prisoners taken during conflicts with Rome in 256, 260, and 360. The deported Christians tended to retain their use of Greek and their own clerical structure.

Reliable evidence begins with Aphraates, the "Persian Sage," whose twenty-three *Demonstrations* date between 337 and 345. Aphraates presents a biblically centered Christianity, in dialogue with Judaism but otherwise ecclesiastically isolated. He mentions neither the Arian crisis nor the Council of Nicaea. Although not indicating an organized monastic movement, Aphraates does speak within a protomonastic community, practicing celibacy and other forms of self-discipline.

Apart from a brief and contained episode in the 270s under Vahran II, Persian Christianity first experienced widespread persecution under the Sassanid king Sapor II between 340 and 372. There is some evidence that Constantine had designs on Persia; however, officially he spoke out on behalf of the Christians in a letter to Sapor stressing the need for cordial relations. The question of loyalties to the now-Christian Roman empire became an ongoing concern for the Sassanids. Persecutions prevailed during periods of war, and toleration, sometimes with active support, during times of peace. Persecution generally focused on Christian leaders, converts from Zoroastrianism, and high-ranking officials in the Sassanian court.

In 410, the first general synod of the Persian church met, initiated by Marutha of Maipherqat on embassy from the west. Territorial administration was a major issue, as was the adoption of the Nicene Creed and canons. Subsequent synods repeatedly sought reconciliation with the western church on doctrinal matters, but eventually the Persian church declared its independence. Communications with the west were problematic, and the fluctuating political situation necessitated an autonomous structure.

In 489, the Byzantine emperor Zeno closed the school of Edessa because of its strongly Antiochene Christological stance. Many of its members fled to Persia. The school was refounded at Nisibis under the direction of Narsai. The Persian church took a decisive turn toward the Christology of Nestorius, sometimes violently so, under the influence of Narsai and the bishop Barsauma. The Sassanid court at least tacitly encouraged this move, thinking Nestorians might be more loyal to the Persian than to the Byzantine empire, which had exiled and anathematized their advocates. The Synod of 554 adopted Theodore of Mopsuestia's interpretation of the Nicene Creed (*can.* 40), and Theodore was continually cited in later synods.

The monastic movement and the sixth-century persecutions in Byzantine territory

brought a growing Monophysite presence in Persia. The efforts of John of Tella, Symeon of Beth Arsham, and Ahudemmeh resulted in a separate and substantial Monophysite community by the seventh century.

For the eastern church, faith had never coincided with political boundaries. This encouraged the vigorous tradition of missionary activity, especially for the Nestorians, that reached as far as China. For Christians in Persia, religion and not empire provided the source of self-identity. *See also* Nestorianism.

[S.A.H.]

Bibliography

J. Labourt, *Le Christianisme dans l'empire Perse sous le dynastie sassanide* (224–632), 2nd ed. (Paris: Lecoffre, 1904); W.A. Wigram, *An Introduction to the History of the Assyrian Church 100–640 AD* (London: SPCK, 1910); J.-M. Fiey, *Jalons pour une histoire de l'église en Iraq*, CSCO (1970), Vol. 310, Subs. 36; W.G. Young, *Patriarch, Shah, and Caliph* (Rawalpindi: Christian Study Centre, 1974); S.P. Brock, "A Martyr at the Sasanid Court under Vahran II: Candida," *AB* 96 (1978):167–181; idem, "Christians in the Sasanian Empire: A Case of Divided Loyalties," *Religion and National Identity*, ed. S. Mews (Oxford: Blackwell, 1982), pp. 1–19.

PESHITTA. Most important ancient Syriac translation of the Bible. Syriac was the Aramaic dialect of the city of Edessa that was widely used in Syria, Mesopotamia, and Persia from the first century A.D. until well into the Middle Ages and later. The precise significance of the name (Syriac *p^esitta* means "simple") is not certain, but it probably meant a straight translation without interpretative expansions or a translation easy to read because unencumbered with a critical apparatus (in contrast to the Harklean and Syro-*Hexapla* versions). No reliable account about the origin of the Peshitta survives. Certainly, it was not produced all at once; marked differences among the books and sections reflect a variety of translators and settings.

Most scholars today believe that the Peshitta Old Testament originated in Edessa, although some maintain the theory of Paul Kahle that it was begun in Adiabene in connection with the conversion of the royal house to Judaism. It is impossible to determine whether it was undertaken first by Jews or by Jewish Christians. The Pentateuch (along with Proverbs and Chronicles) contains a few readings that resemble Jewish Aramaic targums (interpretive translations of the Hebrew scriptures), and it has been proposed that it was actually made from such a targum, then later corrected to the Hebrew text. Recent studies, however, have demonstrated that the targumic elements are not as prominent as sometimes suggested and that the earliest stages of the Peshitta textual tradition show the least difference from the Hebrew text. Affinities with the Septuagint suggest that it too influenced some of the Syriac translators, but the picture is far from clear and such influence should not be overemphasized.

In general, the Peshitta Old Testament seems to have been based on a Hebrew text similar to the Hebrew Masoretic text. It probably originated in the late first or second century A.D., although manuscripts survive only from the fifth century and later. All the canonical books, as well as the Apocrypha, were included, the latter having been translated from the Greek (except for Sirach). Because of its antiquity and because the Syriac language is so closely related to Hebrew, the Peshitta Old Testament is an important resource for study of the history of the biblical text.

The Peshitta New Testament seems to have come into existence more gradually, through revision of earlier Syriac translations. Scholars have been unable to clarify the process absolutely, but a tentative outline is visible. Tatian produced a harmony of the four Gospels, the *Diatessaron*, ca. 170. Somewhat later—surely by the fourth century—another Syriac translation was made of the four separate Gospels, Acts, and the fourteen Pauline letters. This version, called today Vetus Syra (Old Syriac), appears to have been based at least partly on the Syriac text of the *Diatessaron* but also displays clear affinities with the major Greek manuscripts of the New Testament. Subsequently, a version of this Vetus Syra was itself revised further according to the Greek text, and this process of revision led to what is now known as the Peshitta New Testament.

This text as it had developed by the fifth century may have been sanctioned by Rabbula, bishop of Edessa, but was not created by him. The Peshitta New Testament includes only twenty-two books, omitting 2 Peter, 2 and 3 John, Jude, and Revelation.

Once formed, the Peshitta Old and New Testament text became quite stable; the surviving manuscripts do not differ dramatically from one another. Other Syriac Bible translations were also produced: the Syro-*Hexapla* (Old Testament), the one by Jacob of Edessa (Old Testament), the Philoxenian (New Testament), and the Harklean (New Testament). But it was the Peshitta that remained the esteemed Bible of both the eastern and western branches of the Syriac-speaking church.

[R.J.O.]

Bibliography

P.E. Pusey and G.H. Gwilliam, eds., *Tetraeuangelium sanctum juxta simplicem Syrorum versionem* (Oxford: Clarendon, 1901); idem, *The New Testament in Syriac* (London: British and Foreign Bible Society, 1920); a complete critical edition of the Old Testament and Apocrypha is in process by the Peshitta Institute at the University of Leiden, The Netherlands, and is scheduled to be finished by about 1990: *The Old Testament in Syriac According to the Peshitta Version* (Leiden: Brill).

A. Vööbus, "Syriac Versions," *Interpreter's Dictionary of the Bible, Supplementary Volume* (Nashville: Abingdon, 1976), pp. 848–854; B. Metzger, *The Early Versions of the New Testament* (Oxford: Clarendon, 1977), pp. 3–98; E. Würthwein, *The Text of the Old Testament* (Grand Rapids: Eerdmans, 1979), pp. 80–83; S. Brock and B. Aland, "Bibelübersetzungen I.4: Die Übersetzungen ins Syrische," TRE (1980), Vol. 6, pp. 181–196; P.A.H. de Boer, "Peshitta Institute Communication XVI: Towards an Edition of the Syriac Version of the Old Testament," *Vetus Testamentum* 31 (1981):346–357; A. Gelston, *The Peshitta of the Twelve Prophets* (Oxford: Clarendon, 1987).

PETER (d. ca. 64). One of the twelve apostles of Christ and a leading figure in the life and mission of the early church. There are abundant references to Peter in the Synoptic Gospels and the Acts of the Apostles, in John, and several references in the Pauline correspondence. Two New Testament letters also appear under his name.

Peter, fresco in Catacomb of Domitilla, Rome, Italy. (Used by permission of Pontifical Commission of Sacred Archaeology.)

Although influenced by later theological and ecclesial concerns, the Gospel portrayal of Peter does provide some basic biographical information. Peter belonged to the inner circle of Jesus' first followers. John's Gospel identifies him as a disciple of John the Baptist prior to meeting Jesus (John 1:40–42). The Synoptic Gospels describe him as a Galilean fisherman with family in Capernaum (Mark 1:16–18); his mother-in-law was cured by Jesus (Mark 1:29–31). In all four Gospels, he is among the first called by Jesus to be a disciple.

His original name was apparently Simon Bar-Jona, or son of John; Matthew's Gospel depicts Jesus as assigning him the name "Peter" or "rock" (*kepha* in Aramaic; cf. Matt. 16:18; John 1:42). Traces of this tradition may be found in the other Gospels, where the name "Simon" still lingers (Matt. 10:2; 17:25; Luke 6:14; 22:31; the composite "Simon Peter" is used repeatedly in John). Paul consistently uses "Peter" or "Cephas," a transliteration from the Aramaic form of the name (cf. 1 Cor. 15:5; Gal. 1:18).

There is little doubt that Peter played a prominent role in the circle of Jesus' disciples. With James and John, he was a privileged witness at the raising of Jairus's daughter (Mark 5:37), at the transfiguration (Mark 9:2), and in Gethsemane (Mark 14:33). At several points

in the Gospels, he is depicted as spokesperson for the group (e.g., Mark 10:28). In all three Synoptics, it is Peter who answers the key question about Jesus' identity (cf. Mark 8:29 and parallels); a corresponding type of confession is found in John 6:68. The tradition about Peter's betrayal is a negative confirmation of his prominence; unlike the other disciples whose flight is described en masse (at least in Matthew and Mark), Peter's failure is told in detail (Mark 14:66–72). In Matthew's Gospel, stories concerning Peter are more prominent: he miraculously walked on the water toward Jesus (Matt. 14:28–31), received a special blessing because of his confession of Jesus (16:17–19), was the intermediary for paying the temple tax (17:24–27), and questioned Jesus about the limits of forgiveness (18:21–22).

In John's Gospel, Peter shares prominence with the unnamed Beloved Disciple, whose closeness to Jesus and faith in him seem to outshine that of the apostle. Nevertheless, Peter is also quite visible; here, too, he was among the first called to be a disciple (John 1:40), expressed deep faith in Jesus (6:68), was addressed by Jesus at the washing of the feet (13:6–10), requested information about Jesus' betrayer (13:24), expressed his loyalty to Jesus (13:36–37), struck one of Jesus' captors with a sword (18:10–11), was present for the trial of Jesus (18:15–18), publicly denied his master (18:25–27), was a witness, along with the Beloved Disciple, to the empty tomb (20:1–10), and was a prominent character in the Galilean appearance stories of chapter 21.

Considerable attention is also given to Peter in the Acts of the Apostles, where is he is clearly designated as the most prominent leader of the Jerusalem church through the first fifteen chapters. Luke's schema has Peter dominating the early chapters of Acts, only to fade from the scene after Chapter 12, when Paul's missions become the focus (except for Acts 15, where Peter makes one last significant appearance at the Jerusalem council). But in the opening chapters, Peter is clearly to the fore. He guided the meeting of the eleven for the choice of Matthias (Acts 1:15) and was the one who delivered the first great missionary speech of Acts at Pentecost (2:14–42). He along with

John performed the first healing (3:1–10) and delivered the discourse that followed (3:11–26). Further cures at his hand are described in 5:12–16, 9:32–35, and 9:40–41. Peter is also among the apostles who were persecuted and repeatedly imprisoned for their bold preaching (Acts 4:3; 5:18; 12:3) but also received miraculous deliverance (5:19; 12:6–11). Ananias and Sapphira experienced judgment for their dishonesty in Peter's presence (5:1–11), as did Simon Magus (8:14–24). Luke highlights the role of Peter in the developing universal mission. He and John were sent to investigate the fact that Samaritans had responded to gospel preaching, and they received them into the community (8:14–17). Through a vision, Peter was guided to the Gentile Cornelius and baptized him and his household (10–11). At the Jerusalem council, the last of Peter's appearances in Acts, his intervention was decisive for accommodating the Gentile mission (15:7–11). Luke portrays these events as pivotal for the early community.

The general picture of Peter as a leading apostle is corroborated in the Pauline literature. The important text of 1 Corinthians 15:3 places "Cephas" as the first among the twelve to receive a resurrection appearance. In Galatians, Paul notes that he "went up to Jerusalem to visit Cephas" after his three-year stay in Arabia and Damascus (Gal. 1:18); although Paul does not expressly say so, this visit seems intended to validate his new-found Christian identity in view of his previous reputation as a persecutor of the church (cf. Gal. 1:22–24). The missionary role of Peter is difficult to pinpoint on the basis of Paul's writings. In Galatians, Paul emphasizes Peter's role as missionary to the Jews (the "circumcised"—cf. Gal. 1:7–8), a role the risen Christ had entrusted to Peter just as the Gentile mission had been entrusted to Paul (Gal. 1:8). Paul refers to Peter, James, and John as the reputed "pillars" (Gal. 1:9); while his characterization may have some degree of irony, he does not really dispute the important role of these leaders (cf. 1 Cor. 9:4).

Paul also provides evidence that Peter's role was more extensive than merely heading a mission to the circumcised. In Galatians 2:11–14, he excoriates Cephas for withdrawing from table fellowship with Gentiles in Antioch under pressure from Jewish Christians sent by James. The intensity of Paul's anger and the fact that he cites this incident to the Christians of Galatia imply that Peter had exercised some sort of public mediating role between Jews and Gentiles and, in this instance, was violating that trust. This may be the historical grounding for Luke's portrayal of Peter in Acts 10–11, where he is the apostle who first brings Gentiles into the community. The existence of more wide-ranging missionary activity on the part of Peter may also be reflected in the presence of Petrine factions in the church of Corinth (cf. 1 Cor. 1:12; 3:22). That the letters of Peter would later originate from the Roman church may also be evidence that the apostle had left his mark there.

The New Testament evidence suggests that Peter was a leading disciple of Jesus and continued to play a major role in the apostolic church. Although a member of the Jerusalem circle and involved in the Jewish Christian mission, there is evidence that he exercised some sort of bridging role to the Gentile churches as well, although the nature and extent of that activity are difficult to determine. As reflected in Matthew 16 and John 21, the later New Testament traditions (cf. 1 Peter 5:1 and 2 Peter) portray Peter in a more pastoral than missionary role. This is similar to the portrayal of Paul in the Pastoral Epistles, where he is depicted as an elder concerned for the good order of the churches and the solidity of their leadership.

Peter in Rome. Some recent scholarship, however, suggests that Peter's role in early Christianity was much greater than a surface reading of the New Testament reveals. Hengel, for example, believes that Mark's narrative theology (and therefore subsequent Synoptic tradition) actually represents the "Petrine kerygma," that is, reflects the style and emphasis of Peter's own missionary proclamation. Elliott and others have predicated a Petrine circle at Rome, where more synoptically oriented theology was melded with Pauline traditions that had been absorbed into the Roman community; from such a circle of later disciples of Peter and Paul would have developed the letter of 1 Peter.

The earliest literary evidence places Peter in Rome and refers to his martyrdom there (John 21:18–19; 1 Peter 5:13; Ignatius, *Rom.* 4.3; *1 Clem.* 4–6; Gaius of Rome in Eusebius, *H.E.* 2.25.6), although the New Testament provides nothing on his life beyond the period of Paul's activity. The first traditions outside the New Testament do not agree on the length of Peter's stay in Rome, the motive and nature of his martyrdom, or his involvement in the leadership structure of Roman Christianity.

Even if Peter was indeed martyred during the Neronian persecution, it is improbable that his body was claimed by Christians during such dangerous times and that the bones discovered during twentieth-century excavations at the Vatican are his. Yet it is quite possible that Christians remembered and marked in some approximate way the place of his death. The Aedicula on the Vatican is probably the trophaeum mentioned by Gaius ca. 200, but the Circus of Nero to the south of the Vatican Hill, where one finds the building of the Red Wall, may mark the first spot honored by Christian communities. The relationship of the Vatican sites and the shrine at the catacomb of S. Sebastiano is difficult to assess. Perhaps schismatics wishing to claim Peter's authority for their own are responsible for the catacomb cultic center; or the orthodox may have used it during the persecutions under Valerian, when it would have been dangerous to celebrate Peter's memory at the traditional places.

The lateness of the singular devotion to Peter by the Roman community is significant. Up until the third century, Peter *and* Paul usually form the pair who carry the most weight in early Christian circles, including Rome. The city of Antioch could also insist that both ministered within its walls, as could Jerusalem. Rome, however, did hold that both apostles had been martyred there. The growing attempts of the Roman bishops in the late second century to claim universal leadership of the Christian community perhaps led to the veneration of Peter over other apostles, on the basis of the interpretation of Matthew 16:16, the sense of Rome's centrist Christian tradition, and its political and economic position. This veneration formed the context for Peter's legendary twenty-five-year episcopacy at Rome as the city's first bishop. No early evidence exists to support that claim.

The Petrine Letters. It is unlikely that Peter wrote either of the letters attributed to him, although authorship is more probable in the case of 1 Peter than 2 Peter. The dating of the former letter is difficult; a period sometime in the decade of the 70s is mostly likely.

1 Peter was written from Rome ("Babylon," 5:13) to a number of churches in Asia Minor (1:1). It terms the recipients "exiles of the diaspora" (1:1) and "aliens" (2:11). Although traditional interpretation understood these terms as spiritual metaphors—that is, as referring to exile from heaven—recent exegesis has suggested that the recipients of the letter may in fact have been social and ethnic outcasts. Much of the letter is concerned with the relationship of the Christian communities to the surrounding, sometimes hostile, culture. The author urges a strong sense of Christian identity based on baptism, exhorting the most vulnerable members of the community—slaves and wives of non-Christian husbands—to maintain proper conduct so as to give witness to the non-Christian heads of their households. The letter also exhibits a rich and vibrant theology, emphasizing the redemptive and exemplary power of the sufferings of Jesus (2:19–25; 3:17–22), the foundation of hope based on the resurrection (e.g., 1:3–9), and the need for charity within the Christian community (e.g., 2:8; 4:8–11). The author also speaks of impending trial (4:12) that will usher in the final days.

The second letter of Peter differs in style and tone. It is presumably written from Rome (there is a reference to 1 Peter in 3:1) but the identity of the recipients is unknown. Even though Petrine authorship is much less likely for this letter, the effort at pseudonymity is much greater: the letter is presented as a kind of valedictory in view of approaching death (1:13–14); Peter's presence at the transfiguration is cited (1:17–18); Paul is referred to as his "brother" (3:15).

Whereas the threats to the communities addressed in 1 Peter were external, the problems in 2 Peter are mainly internal. False teachers are plaguing the community. They are arrogant and corrupt and lead astray especially those who are newly converted (2:18); to combat their influence, the author uses material similar to that found in Jude (cf. 2 Peter 2:1–18 with Jude 4–16). There are also those in the community whose faith in the parousia is waning (3:1–10), and a problem has arisen with regard to misinterpretation of Paul's writings (3:15–17). The letter combats these problems both by a scorching indictment of the false teachers and by emphasizing the soundness of the tradition handed on through the apostolic teaching; the latter is based on the prophetic authority of the apostles, whose experience of the Holy Spirit is manifestly genuine (1:19–21).

That the author cites Paul's writings as "scripture" (3:16), uses several strongly Hellenistic categories (e.g., "divine nature," 1:4), and deals with the problem of the delay of the parousia is taken as evidence that this is one of the latest New Testament books, perhaps written in the early part of the second century.

Outside the New Testament, the power of Peter's person to attract attention becomes evident. Pieces from the second century through the sixth, some in more than one version, carry his name: *Apocalypse of Peter, Doctrine of Peter, Gospel of Peter, Preaching of Peter, Acts of Peter, Acts of Peter and Paul, Passion of Peter and Paul, Martyrdom of Peter*. The recently discovered library at Nag Hammadi includes its own *Apocalypse of Peter* and *Acts of Peter*, as well as the *Letter of Peter to Philip*. In each of these writings, a Christian community, often with developed Gnostic doctrines, claimed Peter's authority for its views. Feast day (with Paul) June 29. *See also* Acts of Peter; Apocalypse of Peter; Gospel of Peter; Papacy. [D.P.S. and F.W.N.]

Bibliography

Eusebius, *Church History* 2.14.4–15.2; 2.25.5–8; 3.2.1–3.4.11; 3.25; 3.30.1; 6.14.5–7; 6.25.5; 7.25.14; Jerome, *Lives of Illustrious Men* 1; *Liber Pontificalis* 1 (Duchesne 1.118–120).

M. Guarducci, *The Tomb of St. Peter: The New Discoveries in the Sacred Grottoes of the Vatican* (New York: Hawthorn, 1960); O. Cullmann, *Peter, Disciple, Apostle, Martyr*, 2nd ed. (Philadelphia: Westminster, 1962); D.W. O'Connor, *Peter in Rome: The Literary, Liturgical, and Archaeological Evidence* (New York: Columbia UP, 1969); R. Brown, K. Donfried, and J. Reumann, *Peter in the New Testament* (Minneapolis: Augsburg, and New York: Paulist, 1973); J.D. Kingsbury, "The Figure of Peter in Matthew's Gospel as a Theological Problem," *JBL* 98 (1979):68–83; M. Hengel, *Studies in the Gospel of Mark* (Philadelphia: Fortress, 1985), esp. pp. 50–63; T.V. Smith, *Petrine Controversies in Early Christianity: Attitudes Toward Peter in Christian Writings of the First Two Centuries* (Tübingen: Mohr-Siebeck, 1985).

E.G. Selwyn, *The First Epistle of Saint Peter* (London: Macmillan, 1947); D. Senior, *1 & 2 Peter* (Wilmington: Glazier, 1980); J.H. Elliott, *A Home for the Homeless: A Sociological Exegesis of 1 Peter, Its Situation and Strategy* (Philadelphia: Fortress, 1981); R. Bauckham, *Jude, 2 Peter* (Waco: Word, 1983); D. Farkasfalvy, "The Ecclesial Setting of Pseudepigraphy in Second Peter," *SCent* 5 (1985–1986):3–29.

PETER CHRYSOLOGUS (ca. 400–454). First metropolitan bishop of Ravenna (433–454). Peter fought stubborn pagan practices and worked to undergird Christian doctrine and life. He replied to Eutyches and urged him to submit to Rome and its orthodoxy. Despite his epithet (Chrysologus), his sermons show no sign of the oratorical brilliance attributed to him and are simple expositions of scripture. Feast day July 30. CPL 227–237. [F.W.N.]

Bibliography

Agnellus, *Liber Pontificalis Ecclesiae Ravennatis. Saint Peter Chrysologus: Selected Sermons*, tr. G.E. Ganss, FOTC (1953), Vol. 17.

PETER OF ALEXANDRIA (third–fourth century). Bishop of Alexandria (ca. 300–ca. 311) and martyr. The persecution under Diocletian forced Peter into hiding from ca. 306 to 311. The efforts of Melitius of Lycopolis to take over Peter's duties, and Peter's policy of moderation in dealing with those who lapsed in persecution, provoked the Melitian schism. Peter returned after the Edict of Toleration by Galerius, but he was beheaded when Maximinus Daia resumed persecution. His writings survive only in fragments; most important are fourteen canons dealing with problems caused by the persecution and works opposing Origen's views on the soul and the resurrection body. Feast day November 26 (west), November 24 (east), November 25 (Ethiopia). CPG I, 1635–1662. TLG 2962. *See also* Melitius of Lycopolis.

[E.F.]

Bibliography

Eusebius, *Church History* 7.32.31; 8.13.7; 9.6.2; Socrates, *Church History* 1.5, 6; Sozomen, *Church History* 1.15, 24; Athanasius, *Defense Against the Arians* 59.

T. Vivian, *St. Peter of Alexandria: Bishop and Martyr* (Philadelphia: Fortress, 1988).

PETER THE FULLER (d. 488). Monophysite bishop of Antioch. Peter joined the monastic community of the Acoemetae at Constantinople in his early years and learned the trade of a fuller. Although banned because of his Monophysite views, he returned to the city and came to know the emperor Zeno. During bishop Martyrius's absence from Antioch, Zeno backed Peter's ascension to the episcopal throne there (470), but Gennadius, bishop of Constantinople, had Peter imprisoned in the Acoemetae monastery. Back in Antioch by 475, he was again deposed in 477. He signed Zeno's *Henoticon* in 482, and then occupied the see until his death in 488. He apparently added "who was crucified for us" to the Trisagion and made other liturgical changes. CPG III, 6522–6525.

[F.W.N.]

Bibliography

Evagrius, *Church History* 3.5, 8, 16; Theodore Lector, *Ecclesiasticae historiae* 1.20.

W.H.C. Frend, *The Rise of the Monophysite Movement* (Cambridge: Cambridge UP, 1972), pp. 167–170, 188–190.

PHILEAS (d. between 304 and 307). Bishop of Thmuis in the Nile Delta and martyr. Eusebius preserved Phileas's letter from prison to his church (*H.E.* 8.10). The *Acts of Phileas*, containing his apology on behalf of basic Christian teachings before the prefect Culcianus in Alexandria, is preserved among the Bodmer papyri, among the Chester Beatty papyri, and

in a Latin version. Feast day February 4. CPG I, 1671–1672. TLG 2013, 2014, 2966.   [E.F.]

Bibliography

Musurillo, pp. xlvi–xlviii, 320–353; A. Pietersma, *The Acts of Phileas Bishop of Thmuis* (Geneva: Cramer, 1984).

PHILIP OF SIDE (early fifth century). Church historian. A priest and friend of John Chrysostom, Philip was an unsuccessful candidate for the patriarchate of Constantinople three times (426, 428, 431). His Christian history (434–439), treating events from creation to his own time in thirty-six books, survives only in fragments, including an excerpt from Papias of Hierapolis (Papias, frg. 11), and a discussion of the catechetical school of Alexandria. Other works, including a refutation of Julian the Apostate's writings against the Christians, are lost. CPG III, 6026.   [M.P.McH.]

Bibliography

John Chrysostom, *Letter* 213; Socrates, *Church History* 7.26, 27, 29, 35; Photius, *Library* 35.

PHILIP THE ARABIAN (ca. 204–249). Roman emperor (244–249). Successor to Gordian III, Philip concluded a pact of peace with Persia, then proceeded to Rome, where he celebrated the 1,000th birthday of the city (248). The last years of his reign were troubled by an invasion of the Goths and usurpers within the empire. He died fighting near Verona against Decius, whom the army on the Danube had acclaimed emperor. Christian writers favored him in contrast to Decius, a notorious persecutor. He may well have been sympathetic to Christianity. That he and his wife were the recipients of a letter from Origen is at least possible, but it is improbable that he was himself a Christian.   [M.P.McH.]

Bibliography

Excerpts of Valesius 6.33; Eusebius, *Church History* 6.34.1–6.39.1; Zosimus, *Historia nova* 1.18–22.

D. MacDonald, "The Death of Gordian III—Another Tradition," *Historia* 30 (1981):502–508; H.A. Pohlsander, "Did Decius Kill the Philippi?," *Historia* 31 (1982):214–222; G.W. Bowersock, *Roman Arabia* (Cambridge: Harvard UP, 1983), pp. 121–127.

PHILIPPI, PHILIPPIANS. City of Macedonia to whose Christians Paul wrote a letter. Pausanius, who traveled in Greece during the reign of Hadrian (117–138), called Philippi "the youngest city in Macedonia . . . , which was named after its founder, Philip, son of Amyntas" (*Guide to Greece* 6.10; cf. Diodorus 16.3.7, 8.6). Philip II, father of Alexander the Great, took the city in 356 B.C., four years after colonists from Thasos built it. They had called it Krenides (although some identify it with Daton), but after Philip conquered and fortified it, he named it for himself. A number of ancient authors mention the city (Dio Cassius 47.35–49; Appian, *Civil Wars* 4.102–138; Plutarch, *Brutus* 38–53). The goldmines there provided Philip with needed revenue, as much as 1,000 talents a year (Diodorus 16.8.6; Strabo 7, frg. 34).

The city dramatically emerged from obscurity in 42 B.C., when the Caesarians, Octavian and Antony, defeated the Republicans, Cassius and Brutus, on the plains of Philippi. The city was immediately colonized with Roman veterans and made a Roman city—Colonia Augusta Julia Philippensis (Strabo 7, frg. 41; Pliny the Elder, *Natural History* 4.42; Diodorus 51.4.6).

The apostle Paul first visited the city in A.D. 49 (Acts 16:11–40), just before going to Corinth, where his arrival may be dated to the winter of 49. The Christians at Philippi sent contributions to Paul, and his letter to the Philippians thanked the church for their support (Phil. 4:15–18). The letter shows a close relationship between the Philippians and Paul. It is rich in information about Paul's circumstances and co-workers (Phil. 1:12–26; 2:19–30) and in various exhortations (1:27–2:18; 4:1–9). It warns against the errors of false teachers (3) and frequently hints at threats to the unity of the congregation (most explicitly in 4:1–3). The hymn to Christ in Philippians 2:5–11 commends the incarnation and crucifixion as examples of humility.

The church at Philippi received correspondence from Polycarp in the early second century. Subsequently, Philippi became an important Christian center containing a metropolitan bishop. The bishop Porphyry named in a

Looking toward the west entrance of Basilica B (sixth century) at Philippi, Greece.

mosaic inscription is presumably to be identified with the Porphyry present at the Council of Sardica (343).

French and Greek excavations have revealed four large basilicas and an octagonal church of the early Byzantine period. A cemetery of this period has recently been found east of the forum. Remains from the earlier Roman period include a large forum, about 330 feet by 165 feet, with buildings that can be dated by inscriptions to the reign of Marcus Aurelius. The forum was larger prior to this time. On the north side, in the center, are a rostrum for public speaking and two monuments, each of which is flanked by a fountain. On the west are a temple and government buildings; the east is encompassed by another temple, a monument, and a large library. The western, southern, and eastern sides of the forum were surrounded by a wide portico, some columns of which may still be seen.

Few remains date to Paul's time. The theater, which was built in the time of Philip II, enlarged and modified in the second century A.D. and destroyed at the beginning of the fifth century, was standing at the time of Paul's visit. Sections of the Egnatian Way, the major road running east and west along the north side of the forum, are well preserved. Houses of the Augustan period were replaced by buildings on the south side of the forum. Since the fifth century, a vault on the north side of the forum has been shown as Paul's prison.   [J.McR.]

Bibliography

John Chrysostom, *Homilies on Philippians*, NPNF, 1st ser. (1889), Vol. 13; Theodoret, *Interpretatio Epistolae ad Philippenses*, PG 82.557–589; Marius Victorinus, *Commentarii in Epistulam ad Philippenses*, PL 8 1197–1236; Ambrosiaster, *Commentarius in Epistolam ad Philippenses*, CSEL (1966–1969), Vol. 81; Pelagius, *Expositio in Philippenses*, ed. A. Souter, *TS* 9.2 (1926):387–416.

J.B. Lightfoot, *Saint Paul's Epistle to the Philippians* (London: Macmillan, 1913); F.W. Beare, *A Commentary on the Epistle to the Philippians* (New York: Harper, 1959); R.P. Martin, *Carmen Christi* (London: Cambridge UP, 1967); idem, *Philippians* (Grand Rapids: Eerdmans, 1980).

R.F. Hoddinot, *Early Byzantine Churches in Macedonia and Southern Serbia* (London: Macmillan, 1963), pp. 99–116, 169–173, 188–193; R. Stillwell et al., *Princeton Encyclopedia of Classical Sites* (Princeton: Princeton UP, 1976), pp. 704–705; *Journal of Hellenic Studies, Archaeological Reports*, nos. 27–32 (1981–1986).

PHILO OF ALEXANDRIA (ca. 20 B.C.–ca. A.D. 50).

Jewish writer and philosopher. Philo was a member of one of the richest and most prominent Jewish families of Alexandria. His brother Alexander was a high imperial tax official; his nephew Tiberius Julius Alexander was procurator of Judea in A.D. 46 and, under Nero, prefect of Egypt (Josephus, *Antiquities* 20.100). A leader of the Alexandrian Jewish community, Philo led an unsuccessful embassy to Caligula (ca. 39–40) to protest assaults on the Jewish community by the Alexandrians. He tells the story in his *Ad Gaium*, referring to himself as an old man. From this, we assume he was approaching sixty at this time.

Philo received a Hellenic education, although thoroughly trained in Judaism. Fully versed in literature, grammar, rhetoric, and philosophy, he represents a type of Judaism extant in Alexandria if not in the other great cities of the Roman empire. Working from the Septuagint, Philo set forth a Jewish version of the Platonisms current in his age.

Philo's prolific writings fall into four groups: historical and apologetical, expository on the books of Moses, allegorical on Genesis, and philosophical. These works became the basis of later Alexandrian Christian exposition, allegorization, and philosophical interpretation of scripture.

As a commentator on scripture, Philo limited himself to the books of Moses. His approach is allegorical. Applying the "physical" allegory that the Stoics employed on Homer to Jewish scripture, he interpreted the "philosophy" of Moses as symbolic of Middle Platonic "natural" philosophy. His vocabulary and theories exhibit a thorough knowledge of contemporary Alexandrian Platonism. His philosophical antecedents were likely Eudorus of Alexandria, Antiochus of Ascalon, and perhaps Posidonius of Apamea. He also displays a profound knowledge of the Pythagorica of the late first century B.C., offering a philosophical theology and physics fully at home in "contemporary" Platonic and Neopythagorean arithmological speculation.

Philo's metaphysic begins with a gradation of being, leading from the highest original intellect, God, through his Logos, who contains the divine ideas and who creates the physical universe. His God is beyond description and is called the One. His Logos is a demiurgic intellect who fashions the universe on the models of the divine ideas, as the extension of the divine mind above and within the world. His theory of knowledge complements his view of reality. The soul is capable of knowing the physical and the intellectual worlds. He assumes that revelation is the first principle of all discursive knowledge. From a knowledge of scripture flows a comprehension of the nature of reality and God's law (nomos). To know reality and the norms of ethical and pious behavior, one studies God's revelation allegorically. All wisdom and virtue are mediated through Mosaic prophecy. Following it, the soul becomes good and attains a "likeness to God," living in concordance with nature.

Philo's Judaism is optimistic and hopeful. The universe created by God's Logos is good, and humanity is capable of attaining goodness and unity with the divine. His view of reality, and the nature and destiny of humankind, became a pillar for the self-definition of later Christian Platonism. Alexandrian Christian thinkers, such as Clement, Origen, and Cyril, were well acquainted with Philo, but so too were Eusebius of Caesarea, Gregory of Nyssa, Jerome, and many others.   [R.M.B.]

Bibliography

Eusebius, *Church History* 2.16–18.

L. Cohn and P. Wendland, eds., *Philonis Alexandrini Opera quae supersunt*, 7 vols. (Berlin: Reiter, 1896–1930); F.H. Colson, G.H. Whittaker, and R. Marcus, *Philo*, 12 vols., LCL (1929–1963); E.M. Smallwood, *Philonis Alexandrini Legatio ad Gaium* (Leiden: Brill, 1961); G. Mayer, *Index Philoneus* (Berlin: de Gruyter, 1974).

E.R. Goodenough, *An Introduction to Philo Judaeus* (New Haven: Yale UP, 1940); H.A. Wolfson, *Philo*, 2 vols. (Cambridge: Harvard UP, 1947); idem, *Religious Philosophy: A Group of Essays* (Cambridge: Harvard UP, 1961); J. Whittaker, "God, Time and Being in Philo of Alexandria," *Symbolae Osloenses* 23 (1971):33–57; B.L. Mack, "Exegetical Traditions in Alexandrian Judaism: A Program for the Analysis of the Philonic Corpus," *Studia Philonica* 3 (1974–1975):71–112; J. Laporte, "Philo in the Tradition of Wisdom," *Aspects of Wisdom in Judaism and Early Christianity*, ed. R. Wilken (Notre Dame: Notre Dame UP, 1975); J. Dillon, "The Transcendence of God in Philo," *Colloquy* 16 (Berkeley: Center for Hermeneutical Studies, 1975); idem, *The Middle Platonists* (Cambridge: Duckworth, 1977); H.R. Moehring, "Arithmology as an Exegetical Tool in the Writings of Philo of Alexandria," *Society of Biblical Literature Seminar Papers* 1 (1978):191–228; S. Sandmel, *Philo of Alexandria: An Introduction* (New York: Oxford UP, 1979); D. Winston and J. Dillon, eds., *Two Treatises of Philo of Alexandria* (Chico: Scholars, 1983); R.M. Berchman, *From Philo to Origen: Middle Platonism in Transition* (Chico: Scholars, 1984); D. Winston, *Logos and Mystical Theology in Philo of Alexandria* (Cincinnati: Hebrew Union College of America, 1985); D.T. Runia, *Philo of Alexandria and the Timaeus of Plato* (Leiden: Brill, 1986); A. van den Hoek, *Clement of Alexandria and His Use of Philo in the* Stromateis (Leiden: Brill, 1988); R. Radice and D.T. Runia, *Philo of Alexandria: An Annotated Bibliography 1937–1986* (Leiden: Brill, 1988).

PHILOSOPHY. Inquiry into the ultimate nature and principles of reality as a whole. The original meaning of the Greek word *philosophia* was "love of wisdom." Today, in a more technical sense, "philosophy" refers to a critical and systematic inquiry into reality by reason alone, but it was used in a much wider sense in classical and Christian antiquity. The church fathers often called their faith-based quest for wisdom "philosophy." The present article, however, will focus on the encounter between early Christianity and philosophy in a stricter sense, one that originated primarily in Presocratic Greek thought, reached a fully developed form in Plato and Aristotle, and was continued in the various philosophical schools of Hellenism.

Historical Sketch. Although in the Old Testament God's self-revelation was received by thinking human beings who used the terms, images, and thought-forms of their culture for a deeper understanding of both what had been revealed and of reality in general in the light of that revelation, one cannot speak of a philosophy in any strict sense within the Old Testament. There was, however, an encounter with philosophy, in the form of late Stoicism and beginning Middle Platonism, in several later writings of the Old Testament period, notably in the Wisdom of Solomon (an apocryphon in the Protestant Bible but part of the Catholic canon). Outside of the scriptures, some Jewish writers, especially Philo of Alexandria, used Hellenistic philosophy, primarily the Platonic tradition, in the allegorical interpretation of the inspired books. The New Testament is obviously dominated by God's self-revelation in Christ witnessed to by the apostles and apostolic men whose understanding was shaped primarily by Jewish categories. Nevertheless, already in the New Testament writings, especially in the Pauline and Johannine corpus, several terms and ideas from popular Hellenistic philosophy were used for the understanding and presentation of the Christian message.

A similar situation holds for the apostolic fathers, even though the use of the terms and ideas of Hellenistic culture was increasing, as in, for example, Clement of Rome and Ignatius of Antioch. A more explicit and substantial encounter between early Christianity and Hellenistic philosophy took place in the second-century apologists, particularly Justin Martyr, who not only made wide use of the categories of Middle Platonism in his defense and exposition of Christianity but also developed a rationale for a positive appreciation of the best of Greek philosophers based on the theory that they participated in the same Logos who became incarnate in Jesus Christ. A seemingly contradictory attitude was taken by Tertullian, whose "What has Athens to do with Jerusalem?" (*Praescr.* 7) has often been quoted. It is true that Tertullian's explicit judgments on Greek philosophy were overwhelmingly negative; nevertheless, he too used Hellenistic philosophy, especially Stoicism, extensively. For Clement of Alexandria, "philosophy educated the Greek world as the Law did the Hebrews to bring them to Christ" (*Str.* 1.28.3). He made use of Hellenistic philosophy, especially Stoicism and Middle Platonism, in a critical manner, transforming it in a Christian sense.

Origen's view was less optimistic, even though in his theological synthesis, found most explicitly in the *First Principles* but underlying

also his other writings, he was deeply influenced by Middle and beginning Neoplatonism—to the extent that several of their features, such as the descending hierarchy within the divine and the preexistence of souls, in spite of his orthodox intentions, endangered essential elements of his Christian faith. A special place in the encounter between Hellenistic philosophy and Christianity is due Eusebius of Caesarea, whose *Preparation for the Gospel*, as the title indicates, intended to show how Greek thought had positively prepared for (although it did not attain to) the truth of Judeo-Christian revelation. In the process, he provided us with many fragments of Hellenistic philosophy not found elsewhere, notably of Neopythagorean and Middle Platonic authors.

The Arian crisis of the fourth century constituted also a crisis of the Middle and Neoplatonic interpretation of Christianity found in Origen, Eusebius, and others. The Councils of Nicaea (325) and Constantinople (381) clearly rejected any subordinationism within the Trinity, and the orthodox Greek theologians of the fourth century, more consciously than before, distinguished the Christian worldview from that of Hellenistic philosophy. Thus, for example, Gregory of Nyssa, while fully acquainted with the language, images, and thought-forms of Middle and beginning Neoplatonism and using them extensively in his theology, almost always purified them from all that contradicts Christian faith and inserted them in a radically transformed sense within a genuinely Christian synthesis. Although not always equally philosophically minded, the Greek fathers of the following centuries basically followed the same model. A renewed impact of Neoplatonism in its later, more scholastic form (as in Proclus) is found in the works of Pseudo-Dionysius the Areopagite, whose system, certainly Christian in its intention and substance, is nevertheless problematic in its rigidly triadic structure and some specific details. Most of these defects were corrected through its subsequent use by the great eastern theologians, such as Maximus Confessor.

In fourth-century Latin theology, Neoplatonism had a major impact on Marius Victorinus, whose Trinitarian doctrine, although explicitly anti-Arian, closely reflects some of the terms and ideas of Plotinus and especially Porphyry. In Milan, Neoplatonism was positively received as a possible resource for Christian theology by Simplicianus and Ambrose. In this context, Neoplatonism had an important role in the conversion of Augustine (*Conf.* 7). He read the Neoplatonists Plotinus and Porphyry, aware of their fundamental shortcomings in relation to Christianity, such as absence of the doctrine of incarnation and consequently of a universal mediator between God and humanity, and of divine grace. In his *City of God* in particular, Augustine confronts the Neoplatonic doctrine of salvation even more explicitly and subjects it to a thorough Christian criticism (6–10). His own theological synthesis, not less than that of Gregory of Nyssa, makes extensive use of Middle and Neoplatonic terms and ideas, but always corrected, transformed, and inserted into a Christian whole.

Christianity as Philosophy. Even though the fathers did not develop the idea of philosophy as a discipline independent from the understanding of Christian faith, that is, from theology in its contemporary sense, they were, with a few exceptions (e.g., Tatian and Tertullian—in profession but not in practice), certainly not hostile to human reason and to the use of its results in their Christian reflections. Hellenistic philosophy itself was generally not conceived as a rationalistic enterprise but was rather indebted to a quasireligious tradition, especially in the case of Middle and Neoplatonism, and presented itself not only as a theoretical view of reality but also as a way of life and even of salvation. It is thus understandable that Christian thought conceived itself implicitly or explicitly as the true philosophy. Furthermore, since many of the Platonists defended the pagan religions, and several of the later Neoplatonists combined the claim of special divine oracles and the use of magical practices with their philosophy, the claim of Christian thinkers of being true philosophers is, especially in the context of their own times, both intelligible and well founded.

The Christian authors were generally convinced that, since human reason is itself a gift of God, its use in the service of understanding faith is both legitimate and necessary. Quite logically, they extended this notion also to the use of those elements of pagan philosophy that, in the light of revelation and reason, they found true and valuable. That reason and philosophy were "used" does not depreciate their intrinsic value; rather, it emphasizes the primacy of divine revelation and faith in their thought.

Which Philosophies? Among the Hellenistic philosophies that influenced and were used by the church fathers, Stoicism was certainly important, but the prevailing Hellenistic philosophy already in the time of Philo (ca. 20 B.C.–ca. A.D. 50) was increasingly the Platonic tradition, which in the form of Middle Platonism assimilated also Aristotelian, Stoic, and Neopythagorean elements in an essentially Platonic framework. This Middle Platonism constituted the main philosophical background not only of the church fathers of the second and the early third century but persisted in its influence even after the rise of Neoplatonism. As for Neoplatonism, the works of Plotinus were read by several fathers, such as Gregory of Nyssa and Augustine, yet the more popular Porphyrian version had an even more widespread influence.

It would, however, be misleading to speak without strong qualifications of a patristic "Stoicism" or "Platonism" or "Neoplatonism." First of all, no one belonging to these philosophical schools would have recognized a Christian author as a fellow member. Despite the common (when considered in isolation) expressions, ideas, and doctrines in the writings of the church fathers and the pagan philosophers, the essential question is *how* these elements were used. In fact, they were radically transformed in the service of an essentially Christian worldview.

Hellenization of Christianity. This may be the proper place to assess the validity of Harnack's influential assertion of a "Hellenization of Christianity" in the patristic period. There can be no doubt that a certain Hellenization of Christianity occurred, but this should be taken first of all in a theologically neutral sense; it means that the presentation of the Christian message within a Hellenistic milieu took place quite naturally in the contemporary Greek language and with the use of images and thought-forms from contemporary Hellenistic culture. The beginnings of such a process are already found within Judaism, as witnessed by the Septuagint and other Greek translations of the Old Testament, as well as the Jewish intertestamental literature written in the Greek language. The New Testament itself is a prime example of this process, which is quite naturally continued by the early church. A certain Hellenization occurred also, although much less often than implied by Harnack, in a theologically pejorative sense, insofar as the use of Hellenistic language and thought-forms resulted in some instances in a distortion of more or less important elements of the Christian message, an example being Origen.

Nevertheless, the idea of a Hellenization of Christianity in the patristic period has to be complemented and corrected by two other formulas emphasized again and again in recent literature: the "de-Hellenization of Christianity" and the "Christianization of Hellenism." As several authors have pointed out, the development of early Christian dogma as formulated by the first four ecumenical councils, even though it could not have taken place without the use of Greek language and thought-forms, represented in opposition to preceding "Platonizing tendencies" of subordinationism more a de-Hellenization than a Hellenization of Christianity. The consubstantiality of the three divine persons instead of a descending hierarchy—affirmed by Nicaea (325) and Constantinople (381)—and the view of Christ as fully God and fully man in a concrete individual person instead of a cosmic intermediary who would be neither God nor man—affirmed by Ephesus (431) and especially Chalcedon (451)—show how radically early Christian doctrines contradicted the prevailing tendencies of Hellenistic philosophy.

As to the Christianization of Hellenism, the elements of Hellenistic philosophy found in the fathers in most cases not only were consciously purified of whatever was contradictory to Christian faith but, by being inserted in a different historical, metaphysical, and existential structure, came to be profoundly transformed in their meaning and significance. These elements, corrected and transformed, served the early Christian thinkers to elaborate a deeper understanding of their Christian faith and its philosophical presuppositions. Thus, for example, the fundamental distinction between God the Creator and the created world and the notion of God as the only necessary Being and yet personal in an infinitely perfect sense, and free Creator of every other being that came into existence out of nothing, are not found in any of the Greek philosophical systems. In a similar way, Christian anthropology presented a radically new and yet profoundly realistic vision of human existence. It did so by affirming both the spiritual and the bodily dimension of man as incarnate spirit and by emphasizing both the dignity of being created to the image of God (manifested especially in understanding and freedom) and the creaturely limitation of the human being in need of a continuous conversion to God sustained and perfected by God's prevenient grace. Although affirming God's timeless eternity, Christian thought was able to recognize the positive meaning of time and history in God's plan. Human beings can achieve their God-given vocation only within a temporal process. Moreover, their vocation to perfection is an essentially communitarian one, and the community of salvation is shaped and realized in a historical drama in which the divine persons are the primary actors while, at the same time, humanity is called to a conscious and free cooperation. The final consummation of salvation was not conceived simply as an intellectual union of the individual with the first principle but as an assumption of the human community into the very communion of God's Trinitarian life.

Patristic thought on these matters contributed to the elaboration and development of strictly philosophical ideas and doctrines that have profoundly influenced not only subsequent medieval thought but—and this is often overlooked—also modern and contemporary philosophy. *See also* Aristotle, Aristotelianism; Epicureanism; Neoplatonism; Neopythagoreanism; Participation; Plato, Platonism; Plotinus; Porphyry; Socrates; Stoicism. [D.L.B.]

Bibliography

A. von Harnack, *History of Dogma* (London: Constable, 1900), Vol. 2, pp. 169–229; H.A. Wolfson, *The Philosophy of the Church Fathers* (Cambridge: Harvard UP, 1956), Vol. 1: *Faith, Trinity, Incarnation*; J.H. Waszink, "Der Platonismus und die altchristliche Gedankenwelt," *Recherches sur la tradition platonicienne*, ed. P. Courcelle et al. (Geneva: Vandoeuvres, 1958), pp. 139–179; A.H. Armstrong and R.A. Markus, *Christian Faith and Greek Philosophy* (London: Darton, Longman and Todd, 1960); E. Gilson, *The Christian Philosophy of Saint Augustine* (New York: Random House, 1960); A.M. Malingrey, *"Philosophia": étude d'un groupe de mots dans la littérature grecque, des Présocratiques au IVe siècle après J.-C.* (Paris: Klincksieck, 1961); W. Jaeger, *Early Christianity and Greek Paideia* (Cambridge: Harvard UP, 1961); C. Tresmontant, *La Métaphysique du christianisme et la naissance de la philosophie chrétienne: problèmes de la création et de l'anthropologie des origines à saint Augustin* (Paris: Seuil, 1961); A. Momigliano, ed., *The Conflict Between Paganism and Christianity in the Fourth Century* (Oxford: Clarendon, 1963); C. Tresmontant, *The Origins of Christian Philosophy* (New York: Hawthorn, 1963); E. von Ivanka, *Plato Christianus: Übernahme und Umgestaltung des Platonismus durch die Väter* (Einsiedeln: Johannes Verlag, 1964); J.H. Waszink, "Bemerkungen zum Einfluss des Platonismus im frühen Christentum," *VChr* 19 (1965): 129–162; A.H. Armstrong, ed., *The Cambridge History of Later Greek and Early Medieval Philosophy* (Cambridge: Cambridge UP, 1967); idem, *St. Augustine and Christian Platonism* (Villanova: Villanova UP, 1967); D.L. Balás, "The Encounter Between Christianity and Contemporary Philosophy in the Second Century," *Anglican Theological Review* 50 (1968):3–15; M. Harl, ed., *Ecriture et culture philosophique dans la pensée de Grégoire de Nysse* (Leiden: Brill, 1971); W. Pannenberg, "The Appropriation of the Philosophical Concept of God as a Dogmatic Problem of Early Christian Theology," *Basic Questions in Theology* (Philadelphia: Fortress, 1971), Vol. 2, pp. 119–183; H. Dörrie, "Was ist 'Spätantiker Platonismus'? Überlegungen zur Grenzziehung zwischen Platonismus und Christentum," *Theologische Rundschau* 36 (1972):285–302; J. Daniélou, *Gospel Message and Hellenistic Culture* (London: Darton, Longman and Todd, 1973); A. Warkotsch, *Antike Philosophie im Urteil der Kirchenväter. Christlicher Glaube im Widerstreit der Philosophien. Texte in Übersetzungen* (Paderborn: Schöningh, 1973); E.P. Meijering, *Orthodoxy and Platonism in Athanasius: Synthesis or Antithesis?*, 2nd ed. (Leiden: Brill, 1974); idem, "Wie platonisierten Christen? Zur Grenzziehung zwischen Platonismus, kirchlichem Credo und patristischer Theologie," *God Being History: Studies in Patristic Philosophy* (Amsterdam: North-Holland, 1975), pp. 133–146; M. Altenburger, H. Dörrie, and V. Schramm, eds., *Gregor von Nyssa und die Philosophie* (Leiden: Brill, 1976); J. Dillon, *The Middle Platonists: 80 B.C. to A.D. 220* (Ithaca: Cornell UP, 1977); A.H. Armstrong, *Plotinian and Christian Studies* (London: Variorum Reprints, 1979); H. Dörrie, "Die Andere Theologie: Wie stellten die frühchristlichen Theologen des 2.–4. Jahrhunderts ihren Lesern die 'Griechische Weisheit' (= den Platonismus) dar?," *Theologie und Philosophie* 56 (1981):1–46; E. Osborn, *The Beginning of Christian Philosophy* (Cambridge: Cambridge UP, 1981); J.M. Rist, "Basil's 'Neoplatonism': Its Background and Nature," *Basil of Caesarea: Christian, Humanist, Ascetic: A Sixteen-Hundredth Anniversary Symposium: Part One* (Toronto: Pontifical Institute of Mediaeval Studies, 1981), pp. 137–220; D.J. O'Meara, ed., *Neoplatonism and Christian Thought* (Norfolk: International Society for Neoplatonic Studies, 1982); A.M. Ritter, "Platonismus und Christentum in der Spätantike," *Theologische Rundschau* 49 (1984):31–56; C. Gnilka, *CHRESIS: Die Methode der Kirchenväter im Umgang mit der antiken Kultur: I. Der Begriff des "rechten Gebrauchs"* (Basel: Schwabe, 1984); M.L. Colish, *The Stoic Tradition from Antiquity to the Early Middle Ages: II. Stoicism in Christian Latin Thought Through the Sixth Century* (Leiden: Brill, 1985); S. Gersh, *Middle Platonism and Neoplatonism: The Latin Tradition*, 2 vols. (Notre Dame: U of Notre Dame P, 1986).

PHILOSTORGIUS

PHILOSTORGIUS (ca. 368–ca. 439). Arian church historian. Philostorgius was born at Borissus in Cappadocia. The fragments of his history of the Arian controversy from ca. 300 to 430 are found in the *Passion of Artemius* (an Arian martyr) and in the epitome of Photius. Philostorgius is important for his Arian perspective, an inside view from the losing side; for his use of reliable sources, sources that were not always used by the more orthodox historians; for his detailed characterizations of Arian leaders; and for his geographical descriptions. CPG III, 6032. TLG 2058. [F.W.N.]

Bibliography

Photius, *Library* 40.

Philostorgius, *Kirchengeschichte*, ed. J. Bidez, 2. Auflage, F. Winkelmann, GCS (1972), Vol. 21.

E. Walford, *The Ecclesiastical History of Sozomen . . . also the Ecclesiastical History of Philostorgius as Epitomized by Photius* (London: Bohn, 1855).

PHILOXENUS OF MABBUG (ca. 440–523).

Bishop and theologian. Philoxenus (Akhsenaya in Syriac) was born in Persia and educated at the school of Edessa. Ardently Monophysite, he was consecrated bishop of Mabbug (Hierapolis) in Syria in 485, and emerged with Severus of Antioch as a powerful leader. His influence extended to the imperial throne under Anastasius I. In 519, on the accession of Justin I, he was captured and exiled. He died in 523, apparently by suffocation from smoke.

Philoxenus represented the finest synthesis of Greek and Syriac intellectual tradition. Devoted to Syriac culture, he wrote only in Syriac and initiated a new translation of the Bible. His works include commentaries on the Gospels, homilies, liturgical pieces, and letters.

[S.A.H.]

Bibliography

Philoxenus of Mabbug, Discourses, ed. and tr. E.A.W. Budge, 2 vols. (London: Asher, 1893–1894); *Three Letters of Philoxenus of Mabbogh*, ed. and tr. A. Vaschalde (Rome: Tipografia della R. Accademia dei Lincei, 1902); *Philoxène, Lettre aux moines de Senoun*, ed. and tr. A. de Halleux, CSCO (1963), Vols. 231–232, Scrip. Syr. 98–99; D.J. Fox, *The Matthew-Luke Commentary of Philoxenus* (Atlanta: Scholars, 1979).

A. de Halleux, *Philoxène de Mabbog: sa vie, ses écrits, sa théologie* (Louvain: Orientaliste, 1963); R.C. Chesnut, *Three Monophysite Christologies: Severus of Antioch, Philoxenus of Mabbog, and Jacob of Sarug* (Oxford: Oxford UP, 1972).

PHOENIX.

Legendary bird, symbol of immortality or resurrection. According to several ancient versions of the story, the Phoenix lived a fabulously long time, died at the end of its life cycle, then miraculously regenerated itself out of its own decomposing remains (Herodotus 2.73; Pliny the Elder, *Natural History* 10.2.3–5; Ovid, *Metamorphoses* 15.392–407; Aelian, *Nature of Animals* 6.58). The story probably originated in Asia, perhaps in India or Arabia, but in most of the later versions Syria and Egypt play a significant role in the legend, which was adopted by many cultures throughout the ancient world, from the Mediterranean to China. The Romans, under Hadrian and under Constantine and his sons, for example, used the

Inscribed image of a Phoenix from Catacomb of Callistus, Rome, Italy. (Used by permission of Pontifical Commission of Sacred Archaeology, catalogue number Cal Ts 3.)

symbol on their coin reverses to symbolize the eternity of the empire.

Early Christians saw in the phoenix a pagan anticipation of Christianity. The literary tradition began with *1 Clement* 25–26 in support of the resurrection, and was followed by a steady stream of patristic writers. In the seventh chapter of the *Physiologus*, the phoenix is made into a highly evocative symbol of Christ.

Representations of the phoenix in art are numerous (cf. Türk). In the world of early Christians, the image was common on Constantinian coins, on magical amulets, and occasionally on early Christian sarcophagi, mosaics, and paintings, as well as on funerary epitaphs: the incuse funerary image from the Callistus catacomb (see illustration) depicts the bird radiate and nimbed. *See also* Lactantius; Resurrection.

[P.C.F.]

Bibliography

1 Clement 25–26; Tertullian, *On the Resurrection of the Flesh* 13; Commodian, *Carmen apologeticum* 13.9; [Lactantius], *The Phoenix*; Eusebius, *Life of Constantine* 4.72; Cyril of Jerusalem, *Catechetical Lectures* 18.8; Ambrose, *On the Decease of His Brother Satyrus* 2.59.

G. Türk, "Phoinix," *Roschers Ausführliches Lexikon der griechischen und römischen Mythologie* (Leipzig: Teubner, 1884–1937), Vol. 3.2, cols. 3450–3472; J. Hubaux and M. Leroy, *Le Mythe du Phénix dans les littérature grecque et latine* (Liège: Droz, 1939); M.F. McDonald, "Phoenix redivivus,"

Phoenix 14 (1960):187–202; R. van den Broek, *The Myth of the Phoenix According to Classical and Early Christian Traditions* (Leiden: Brill, 1972).

PHOS HILARON. Hymn. "Hail Gladdening Light" (literally "Joyous Light") is still sung in the Eastern Orthodox evening service. It is also known as the "Lamplighting Hymn of Thanksgiving." According to the first explicit literary reference, in the fourth century, the hymn was already of great antiquity and so must go back to the second or third century. The custom of prayer and song at the time of lamplighting in the evening is attested early (Hippolytus, *Trad. ap.*, Ethiopic version; Cyprian, *Dom. or.* 35). Christians used the *Phos Hilaron* both publicly and privately on this occasion. It praises the Trinity but especially exalts Christ, the true light and giver of life. CPG I, 1355. *See also* Hymns. [E.F.]

Bibliography
Basil, *On the Holy Spirit* 29.73.
A. Tripolitis, "Phos Hilaron: Ancient Hymn and Modern Enigma," *VChr* 24 (1970):189–196; A. Hamman, "Comment analyser un texte patristique," *L'Enseignement de la patristique/The Teaching of Patristics*, ed. C. Beauvalet (Paris: Saint-Sulpice, 1987), pp. 76–80.

PHOTINUS (d. 376). Bishop of Sirmium (ca. 344–351). Photinus was deposed for his Christological views. Because none of his works is extant and his opponents give different descriptions of his teachings, his errors are obscure. He is often linked with Sabellius as one who rejected the preexistence of Christ. Well educated and rhetorically skilled, with knowledge of both Greek and Latin, he wrote against heretics and pagans. He had continuing influence after his exile, even after his death. Photinians were expressly condemned at the Council of Constantinople in 381 and again by Theodosius II in 428. [F.W.N.]

Bibliography
Socrates, *Church History* 2.18, 29, 30; Sozomen, *Church History* 4.6; Epiphanius, *Panarion* 71.

PHOTIUS (ca. 810–ca. 895). Patriarch of Constantinople (858–869, 877–886). The depo-

sition of patriarch Ignatius and appointment of Photius by emperor Michael III, not accepted by pope Nicholas I, provoked the Photian schism between Constantinople and Rome, one of a series of temporary breaks in communion between the two sees. The authority of the pope and jurisdiction over mission work in Bulgaria seem to have been the principal points in dispute, but Photius's criticisms of the *Filioque* gave the basis for dogmatic differences between the Catholic and Orthodox churches. Photius has a place in the study of early Christianity because he wrote a summary and evaluation of his reading, the *Library*, which preserves analyses and quotations of many patristic works now lost. Feast day February 6 (Greek). TLG 4040. [E.F.]

Bibliography
R. Henry, ed., *Photius. Bibliothèque.* 8 vols. (Paris: Les Belles Lettres, 1959–1977).
J.H. Freese, tr., *The Library of Photius* (1–165) (London: SPCK, 1920), Vol. 1.
E. Dvornik, *The Photian Schism* (Cambridge: Cambridge UP, 1948).

PHYSIOLOGUS. One who interpreted metaphysically the natural world. An anonymous Christian author took legends about nature, mostly animals, and gave moral and mystical interpretations to them. The Greek original of the *Physiologus* allegorized about fifty objects. Produced probably in Egypt and dated variously from the second to the late fourth century, the work became enormously popular, and translations appeared in nearly every European vernacular. Its allegories, such as those of the pelican and the phoenix, influenced much of the symbolism in Christian art. The work led to the development of the medieval bestiaries. CPG II, 3766. TLG 2654. [E.F.]

Bibliography
F. Sbordone, ed., *Physiologi Graeci* (Milan: Dante Alighieri, 1936); K. Kaimakis, *Der Physiologus nach der ersten Redaktion* (Meisenheim am Glan: Hain, 1974).
J. Carlill, "Physiologus," *The Epic of the Beast*, ed. W. Rose (New York: Dutton, 1924); F. Carmody, *Physiologus: The Very Ancient Book of Beasts, Plants, and Stones* (San Francisco: Book Club of California, 1953); M.J. Curley, tr., *Physiologus* (Austin: U of Texas P, 1979).

733

F. Lauchert, *Geschichte des Physiologus* (Strassburg: Trübner, 1889); F. Klingender, *Animals in Art and Thought to the End of the Middle Ages* (Cambridge: MIT, 1971); R. van den Broek, *The Myth of the Phoenix According to Classical and Early Christian Traditions* (Leiden: Brill, 1972); P. Cox, "The *Physiologus*: A *Poiēsis* of Nature," *ChHist* 52 (1983):433–443.

PIERIUS (third century). Presbyter at Alexandria. Pierius was head of the catechetical school in 265 and later lived in Rome. Jerome (*Vir. ill.* 76) knew a number of his treatises; Photius (*Cod.* 119) speaks of a homily on Hosea and twelve books on Luke. Epiphanius mentions a church dedicated to Pierius in Alexandria. Feast day November 4. CPG I, 1630. TLG 2963.   [F.W.N.]

Bibliography
Eusebius, *Church History* 7.32.
L.B. Radford, *Three Teachers of Alexandria: Theognostus, Pierius, Peter* (Cambridge: Cambridge UP, 1908), pp. 44–57.

PILGRIMAGE. Journey taken as an expression of religious devotion to a place believed to be especially sacred or holy. As early as the mid-second century, Christians were traveling to places intimately associated with Christ and the apostles, especially those in Palestine. The end of official opposition to the church by the Roman imperial government, in the 310s, allowed a great increase in such trips.

The earliest known Christian pilgrim is Melito of Sardis (d. ca. 190), who seems to have gone to Palestine and perhaps the Sinai peninsula largely to verify biblical data (Eusebius, *H.E.* 4.26.14). The next pilgrim of whom we know was Alexander (d. 251), a bishop from Cappadocia, who was made bishop of Jerusalem while on pilgrimage there (Eusebius, *H.E.* 6.11.2). Origen, a friend of Alexander, writing ca. 230, looked with the eyes of a pilgrim upon his own sojourn in Palestine, although he was actually in ecclesiastical exile (*Jo.* 4.24). His student Firmilian, bishop of Caesarea in Cappadocia, is reported by Jerome to have gone to Palestine "influenced by [*sub occasione(m)*] the holy places"

(Jerome, *Vir. ill.* 54). Pionius (d. 251), a presbyter whom we know through a heavily edited martyrdom, also is said to have traveled to Palestine on pilgrimage (Eusebius, *H.E.* 4.15.46–47).

Several fourth-century sources, the most important being Paula and Eustochium (Jerome, *Ep.* 46) and Eusebius (*V.C.* 3.26), assume that Christians had made pilgrimages to Palestine from the church's earliest days. Sozomen (d. ca. 439) did not see it that way but believed that the pagans had deliberately buried the sacred places in Palestine, so the Christians would not frequent them (*H.E.* 2.1).

The earliest extant account of a Christian pilgrimage is that of the anonymous Bordeaux Pilgrim, which recounts the stops along the way to Palestine ca. 333. More extensive, and more descriptive of the activities at the holy sites themselves, is the *Pilgrimage of Egeria*, recounting travels with a devotional purpose in the Sinai, Egypt, Palestine, Mesopotamia, and Asia Minor ca. 400. The author was a woman from either southern Gaul or northern Spain, perhaps but not certainly a monastic.

By the late fourth century, Rome too, especially the places associated with Peter and Paul, attracted large numbers of Christian pilgrims. But until the late seventh century, Palestine remained far and away the most important of the destinations of pilgrims.

The earliest known Christian pilgrims made their journeys both to enrich their understanding of the Bible and to pray at particularly holy places. By the late fourth century, many went to the holy places to fulfill vows— for example, to be baptized in the Jordan or to pray for some specific boon. The latter practice, especially, led to concern lest piety and superstition be confused, especially as the number of sites and objects believed to have been associated with Christ and the apostles grew. Gregory of Nyssa warned against the moral dangers of pilgrimage (*Ep.* 2) but also spoke of the spiritual thrill of seeing the holy places (*Ep.* 3). Pilgrimage was not imposed as a public penance until at least the sixth century, although it may have been undertaken as a means of voluntary penance by the late fifth century. *See also* Bordeaux Pilgrim; Egeria, Pilgrimage of. [P.M.B.]

Bibliography

P. Geyer, ed., *Itinera Hierosolymitana Saeculi iiii–viii*, CSEL (1898), Vol. 39; *Itineraria et Alia Geographica*, ed. P. Geyer et al., CCSL (1965), Vols. 175, 176.

J. Leclercq, "Pèlerinages," DACL (1939), Vol. 14, pp. 65–176; E.D. Hunt, *Holy Land Pilgrimages in the Later Roman Empire, A.D. 312–460* (Oxford: Clarendon, 1982); P. Maraval, *Lieux saints et pèlerinages d'Orient: histoire et géographie des origines à la conquête arabe* (Paris: Cerf, 1985).

PIONIUS (d. 250). Presbyter of Smyrna and martyr. Pionius was martyred at Smyrna in the persecution under Decius. He was reported to have been arrested while commemorating the anniversary of Polycarp's martyrdom (February 23). To judge by the account given in the *Martyrdom of Pionius*, he was a forceful speaker and had traveled extensively. The *Martyrdom* is useful both as a rare extant account of proceedings under the Decian persecution and for its depiction of life in Smyrna in the mid-third century. A *Life of Polycarp*, attributed to Pionius is spurious and was probably composed (ca. 400) as a supplement to the authentic account of that saint's death. Feast day February 1 (Roman martyrology), March 12 (east). TLG 2005. [M.P.McH.]

Bibliography

Eusebius, *Church History* 4.15.46–47.
Musurillo, pp. xxviii–xxx, 136–137.

V. Saxer, "Les Actes des 'martyrs anciens' chez Eusèbe de Césarée et dans les martyrologes Syriaque et Hiéronymien," *AB* 102 (1984):85–95; J. den Boeft and J. Bremmer, "Notiunculae Martyrologicae III: Some Observations on the Martyrologia of Polycarp and Pionius," *VChr* 39 (1985):110–130.

PIUS I. Bishop of Rome (mid-second century). Pius was perhaps a brother of the Hermas who composed the *Shepherd*. His pontificate witnessed the growth of Gnosticism as well as the advance of Rome as a major Christian center, visited by such figures as Hegesippus, Irenaeus of Lyons, Justin Martyr, and Polycarp. [M.P.McH.]

Bibliography

Eusebius, *Church History* 4.11; 5.6, 24; *Liber Pontificalis* 11 (Duchesne 1.132–133).

PLATO, PLATONISM. Founder of one of the major philosophies of the ancient world. Plato (428–346 B.C.), grew up as an aristocrat in the Athens of the Peloponnesian War. The subsequent trial and execution of his friend and mentor, Socrates, led Plato to turn from a career in politics to consideration of the larger political question of a just society. Sometime between 389 and 367 B.C., Plato organized a school and began teaching near the grove of Academus outside Athens. This was the founding of the Academy, which survived until closed by Justinian I in A.D. 529. The Academy attracted a number of outstanding minds, among them Aristotle.

Writings and Teaching. Thirty-five dialogues are attributed to Plato, twenty-five of which, including the best-known dialogues, are generally accepted as genuine. There are also thirteen letters, few of which are thought to be genuine; but the seventh, the most substantial and interesting for its details of Plato's life and philosophy, probably is at least a reasonably accurate portrayal.

The dialogues can be loosely grouped into three periods. The early, Socratic, dialogues, such as the *Euthyphro* or *Lysis*, have Socrates engaged in a lively conversation about some ethical matter. Socrates examines a respondent's claims to knowledge about piety, friendship, or whatever the topic. The dramatic result is bafflement (*aporia*) when no account of the matter proves coherent or adequate. In the middle dialogues, Socrates, still at center stage, suggests positive doctrine: about justice, for example, in the *Republic*, or love in the *Symposium*, or the soul in the *Phaedo*. In the late dialogues, Socrates is a secondary or even, as in the *Timaeus* or *Sophist*, a minor character. The dramatic element is less lively and the discussion more abstruse. In the last and longest dialogue, the *Laws*, a detailed discussion of legislation for a better state, Socrates is altogether absent.

A direct presentation of Plato's teaching is hampered by the indirect presentation of the dialogues. Then too there is a perennial debate whether Plato changed his philosophy or developed a single philosophy, the view followed here.

The early dialogues take over the Socratic themes and arguments. They are concerned with ethical knowledge, specifically knowledge of the virtues. The conversation takes the form of an inquiry into an ethical term seeking a general definition. The result is an impasse when no adequate definition is found. Nevertheless, a number of theses are affirmed, among them: that whatever is good is beneficial; that the virtues are unified; and that wrongdoing is ignorance and virtue is knowledge. The ethical agent, it is argued, must look to some ideal as a guide for action in ever-changing contexts. The condition for virtue, then, is to know this ideal.

The middle dialogues examine the nature of these ideals and present what is called the theory of Ideas. The ideals, such as beauty or justice, are taken to be real entities and not relative to different people or contexts but absolute standards, always the same. Further, these ideals, called Ideas or Forms, are in some manner the explanation of or cause of their individual examples. In turn, the examples are said to participate in the Ideas. Humans grasp such Ideas with the mind only, directly apprehending them in a previous disembodied existence and recollecting these Ideas in this life through reminders and imitations provided by sensible reality. The *Phaedo* is the most frequently cited source for both the theory of Ideas and its correlative, the doctrine of recollection. The *Symposium* takes up the relation between Ideas and their instances, and the *Republic* puts forward a program for a society based on the Ideas, unified by the Idea of the Good. With the theory of Ideas comes a sharp dichotomy between sensation and thought, between flux and stability. The physical world, grasped by the senses, is in incessant change; the world of Ideas and numbers, grasped by the mind, is not. The stability of knowledge reflects the reliability and stability of what is known and more real, the Ideas or Forms.

The dichotomy also separates body and soul. The body is part of the world of change and opinion, the soul is not. The accounts of the soul in the *Phaedo, Phaedrus, Republic*, and *Timaeus* do not offer a coherent theory, although they affirm that at least part of the soul is separable from the body and immortal. The myths in these dialogues and the *Gorgias* tell of a cycle of reincarnations through which one ascends by virtuous living and which one can ultimately escape to a blessed, everlasting existence. The *Republic* proposes a tripartite soul. The highest part is reason, which should rule the other parts. Its authority follows from its knowlege of reality. Then there is a "spirited" portion, which inclines to the noble and good. Lastly, there are the desires, which, having no sense of measure, require the guidance of reason and the discipline of the spirited part. The pursuit of philosophy is a right ordering of the soul and a purification, turning one from the physical world toward spiritual reality, the Ideas.

The later dialogues slight the theory of Ideas and look to principles of reality and reasoning in general. The *Timaeus* expounds a theory of the ultimate originating principles of the cosmos and explains in great detail elements, change, sensible phenomena, and the human body and soul. The theory is related in the form of a creation myth in which a divine demiurge fashions the visible and sensible cosmos after an eternal and changeless paradigm. The *Sophist* and *Statesman*, in seeking to define their respective topics, reflect on a method for defining kinds, the method of collection and division.

Aristotle and other later sources write of Plato's "unwritten doctrine," which seems to have been speculation on the ultimate principles of knowing and reality, taking mathematics as the paradigm. Traces of the unwritten doctrine are most evident in the *Parmenides* and the *Philebus*.

Later Developments. The unwritten doctrine, as well as the categorial schemes and the levels of reality, were the most influential portions of Plato in Neoplatonism. Immediately after Plato, the theory of Ideas and method of collection and division were neglected, the former falling to Aristotle's trenchant criticisms, the latter to his version of real definition by genus and species. A century after Plato's death, the Academy, taking up the aporetic style of the dialogues, turned to skepticism under Arcesilaus (315–241 B.C.) and remained the center for skepticism until Antiochus (d. 68 B.C.) adopted a more eclectic approach in 78 B.C.

Before Plotinus (ca. 205–270), the Academy made some syncretic accommodation with Stoicism and with Aristotle, especially with the *Categories* and Aristotelian logic and psychology. The degree of accommodation depended on the head of the Academy. Neopythagoreanism also influenced Academic teaching, although the exact nature of the influence is confused by the obvious reliance of Neopythagoreanism on Academic doctrines and the unwritten doctrine. Albinus (mid-second century A.D.) held that Ideas were thoughts in the mind of an Aristotelian God, a notion the Neoplatonists took up. Through the Neoplatonists, Plato influenced Christian thought, especially on such subjects as the nature of the deity, creation, and the soul. *See also* Creation; Dualism; Immortality; Neoplatonism; Philosophy; Socrates; Soul. [C.Co.]

Bibliography

Plato, *Opera*, ed. J. Burnet (Oxford: Clarendon, 1902–1906).

Plato, *Dialogues*, tr. B. Jowett, 4th ed. (Oxford: Oxford UP, 1953).

W.D. Ross, *Plato's Theory of Ideas* (Oxford: Clarendon, 1951); P. Courcelle et al., *Recherches sur la tradition platonicienne* (Geneva: Vandoeuvres, 1955); P. Merlan, *From Platonism to Neoplatonism*, 2nd ed. (The Hague: Nijhoff, 1960); E. von Ivanka, *Plato Christianus: Übernahme und Umgestaltung des Platonismus durch die Väter* (Einsiedeln: Johannes Verlag, 1964); R.E. Allen, ed., *Studies in Plato's Metaphysics* (London: Routledge and Kegan Paul, 1965); D.L. Balás, "Christian Transformation of Greek Philosophy Illustrated by Gregory of Nyssa's Use of the Notion of Participation," *Proceedings of the American Catholic Philosophical Association* (1966), Vol. 40, pp. 152–157; G. Vlastos, ed., *Plato*, 2 vols. (Garden City: Anchor, 1971), Vol. 1: *Metaphysics and Epistemology*; Vol. 2: *Ethics, Politics, and Philosophy of Art and Religion*; J. Daniélou, *Gospel Message and Hellenstic Culture* (Philadelphia: Westminster, 1973); J.N. Findlay, *Plato: The Written and Unwritten Doctrines* (London: Routledge and Kegan Paul, 1974); J. Dillon, *The Middle Platonists: 80 B.C. to A.D. 220* (Ithaca: Cornell UP,

1977); G. Vlastos, *Platonic Studies* (Princeton: Princeton UP, 1981); K.M. Sayre, *Plato's Late Ontology* (Princeton: Princeton UP, 1983); T. Szlezák, *Platon und die Schrift-lichkeit der Philosophie* (Berlin: de Gruyter, 1985); J.M. Rist, *Platonism and Its Christian Heritage* (London: Variorum, 1986); C. Fabricius, "Zu den Aussagen der griechischen Kirchenväter über Platon," *VChr* 42 (1988):179–187.

PLINY THE YOUNGER (ca. A.D. 61–ca. 113). Roman writer, orator, and public official. The extant writings of Pliny the Younger are a *Panegyric on the Emperor Trajan* (100) and ten books of letters, the first nine of which (published 100–109) are literary in nature and cover a wide variety of themes. The tenth book consists of administrative letters from Pliny to the emperor Trajan concerning affairs in the province of Bithynia, of which Pliny was governor, together with the emperor's replies. This correspondence is valuable as an account of Roman provincial administration. Two letters in particular (10.96 and 97; written in 112) are important for the light they shed on Roman policy toward Christians. Pliny in his letter (10.96) seeks guidance on procedure and inquires whether Christians are to be punished for their membership in a secret society; he describes early Christian assemblies with probable reference to an agape. It is quite possible that the charges brought before Pliny against Christians were motivated more or less by factional or personal animosities. Trajan's reply that Christians were guilty for membership in the group but were not to be sought out or accused anonymously guided imperial policy for the next century and a half. *See also* Persecution; Trajan. [M.P.McH.]

Bibliography

Tertullian, *Apology* 2.6–9; Eusebius, *Church History* 3.33.

Pliny the Younger, *Letters*, tr. W. Melmoth, 2 vols., LCL (1915); *The Letters of the Younger Pliny*, tr. B. Radice (Harmondsworth: Penguin, 1963).

R. Hanslik, "Der Forschungsbericht: Plinius der Jüngere, I Bericht," *AAHG* 8 (1955):1–18; "II Bericht," *AAHG* 17 (1964):1–16; F. Römer, "III Bericht," *AAHG* 28 (1975):153–200; "IV Bericht," *AAHG* 40 (1987):153–198; A.N. Sherwin-White, *The Letters of Pliny: A Historical and Social Commentary* (Oxford: Clarendon, 1966), esp. pp. 691–712; R.J.A. Talbert, "Pliny the Younger as Governor of Bithynia-Pontus," *Studies in Latin Literature and Roman History*, ed. C. Deroux, 2nd ed. (Brussels: Latomus, 1980), pp. 412–435; R.L. Wilken, *The Christians as the Romans Saw Them* (New Haven: Yale UP, 1984), pp. 1–30; G.J. Johnson, "*De conspiratione delatorum*: Pliny and the Christians Revisited," *Latomus* 47 (1988):417–422.

PLOTINUS (ca. 205–270). Founder of Neoplatonism. Details of his life and teachings are preserved in Porphyry's *Life of Plotinus* and in his own *Enneads* (edited by Porphyry). Plotinus combined Platonism, Aristotelianism, and Stoicism into a series of novel teachings in metaphysics, epistemology, psychology, and ethics. His influence was immense. Among those indebted to Plotinus were the Hellenic Neoplatonists Porphyry, Iamblichus, Syrianus, Proclus, and Damascius and the Christian Neoplatonists Gregory of Nyssa, Marius Victorinus, Augustine, Pseudo-Dionysius, and Boethius.

Plotinus provided the philosophical framework in which many Christian thinkers expressed their theology and psychology. He postulated three divine hypostases (entities)—God, Mind, and Soul. God is radically transcendent beyond being and intellect. Mind is a primary intellect who creates the universe. Soul is an animate intellect who is the extension of the divine in the physical universe. By a process of necessary emanation, God produces the Mind, who contains within himself the divine ideas and constitutes the intelligible universe. On the level of Mind, being, intellect, and life appear. From the Mind emanates the Soul, who is the principle of life and growth. Soul, or Nature, animates and contains within itself the whole of the physical universe.

Fundamental to Plotinus's metaphysics is the notion that each of the lower hypostases proceeds from the one above. Turning back in contemplation on its source, it gains full constitution through the ontological and logical laws of procession and return. On the basis of these laws, Plotinus affirms an essential connection between the hypostases, and between divinity and creation. *See also* Neoplatonism.

[R.M.B.]

Bibliography

E. Bréhier, ed., *Opera*, 7 vols. (Paris: Budé, 1924–1938); P. Henry and H.R. Schwyzer, *Opera*, 2 vols. (Paris and Brussels: Museum Lessianum, 1951–1959).

A.H. Armstrong, tr., *Plotinus*, 7 vols., LCL (1966–1988).

T. Whittaker, *The Neo-Platonists*, 2nd ed. (Cambridge: Cambridge UP, 1928); A.H. Armstrong, "Emanation in Plotinus," *Mind* 46 (1937):61–66; idem, *The Architecture of the Intelligible Universe in the Philosophy of Plotinus* (Cambridge: Cambridge UP, 1940); J.M. Rist, *Plotinus, The Road to Reality* (Cambridge: Cambridge UP, 1967); A.H. Armstrong, ed., *The Cambridge History of Later Greek and Early Medieval Philosophy* (Cambridge: Cambridge UP, 1967), pp. 195–268; H.J. Blumenthal, "Plotinus in the Light of Twenty Years' Scholarship, 1951–1971," ANRW (1988), Vol. 2.36.1, pp. 528–570; K. Corrigan and P. O'Cleirigh, "The Course of Plotinian Scholarship from 1971 to 1986," ANRW (1988), Vol. 2.36.1, pp. 571–623.

PNEUMATOMACHIANS. Fourth-century Christians who denied the divinity of the Holy Spirit. Fifth-century writers, such as Sozomen, Socrates, Jerome, and Rufinus, identify the Pneumatomachians as Macedonians, claiming that Macedonius, a Semiarian bishop of Constantinople (ca. 342–360), was the founder of the sect. It may be that his followers joined the Pneumatomachians after his deposition in 360. In the 360s, the sect held its own councils and occupied a position in Christology somewhere between the western position and the Neoarians (Sozomen, *H.E.* 5.14). In the next decade, the Pneumatomachians became fragmented. One group not only rejected the Holy Spirit's divinity but also that of the Son (Gregory of Nazianzus, *Or.* 31). Perhaps they had previously been Semiarians, supporters of the Council of Seleucia. Yet Sozomen (*H.E.* 4.27) notes that Macedonius rejected his former views and claimed that the Son (although not the Holy Spirit) was God, a position that would be consistent with the views of the other group in the sect (Gregory of Nazianzus, *Or.* 31).

During the 370s, Eustathius of Sebaste, who had supported the *homoousios* position concerning the Son—that the Son was "of the same essence" as the Father—denied the divinity of the Spirit and became the leader of the Pneumatomachians. Orthodox Christians had themselves not been united in their views of the Spirit. Basil of Caesarea, a former friend of Eustathius, defended the Spirit's divinity but would not say or write that he was God because he thought the time was not right to say this openly. On the other hand, Gregory of Nazianzus (*Or.* 31) boldly said that the Spirit was God.

Sozomen (*H.E.* 4.27) claims that the Pneumatomachians were numerous in Constantinople and in Bithynia, Thrace, the Hellespont, and other neighboring provinces. During Valens's reign (364–378), the group was persecuted by the government; they were probably a strong force, perhaps even a majority, in those provinces (Sozomen, *H.E.* 6.10). They attempted a reconciliation with Rome in the 370s, when Eustathius of Sebaste, Theophilus, bishop of Castabalis, and Silvanus, bishop of Tarsus, went there as an embassy (Sozomen, *H.E.* 6.9; Socrates, *H.E.* 4.12). Sabinus, a "Macedonian" and a bishop of Heracleon in Thrace, claimed in his collection of synodal decisions that his group had accepted the *homoousios*, at least for the Son (Socrates, *H.E.* 1.8; 4.12).

In 381, Pneumatomachians were invited to the Council of Constantinople. Led by Eleusius of Cyzicus and Marcion of Lampsacus, they were represented by thirty-six persons, probably bishops, who were mostly from the Hellespont. They refused to acknowledge the statement made by their leader to the Roman bishop, Liberius; rejected the *homoousios* as descriptive of the Son and the Spirit; and withdrew from the council (Socrates, *H.E.* 5.8; Sozomen, *H.E.* 7.7). Although Pneumatomachians were branded an illegal sect and were deprived of their churches by the *Theodosian Code* of 383, they seem to have lasted into the fifth century. They did not again have bishops until the reign of Arcadius (395–408—Sozomen, *H.E.* 8.1). [F.W.N.]

Bibliography

Socrates, *Church History* 2.45; Sozomen, *Church History* 4.27; Theodoret, *Church History* 2.5; 5.9.

P. Meinhold, "Pneumatomachoi," *Paulys Realencyclopädie* (Stuttgart: Druckenmüller, 1951), Vol. 41, cols. 1066–1101; W.-D. Hauschild, *Die Pneumatomachen* (Diss., University of Hamburg, 1967); S. Papadopoulos, *Gregorios ho Theologos kai hai prohypotheseis Pneumatologias autou* (Athens: n.p., 1975); R.P.C. Hanson, *The Search for the Christian Doctrine of God: The Arian Controversy 318–381* (Edinburgh: T. and T. Clark, 1988), pp. 760–772.

POETRY. For the early Christian era, any rhythmical or metrical composition, including the texts of hymns.

About a third of the Hebrew Bible is in verse. Most notable are the Psalms, which even in translation retain characteristics of Hebrew poetry. The Psalter was the church's first hymn book; but Christians also composed new works in the style of the Psalms. The New Testament includes some early Christian poetic compositions (e.g., Luke 1:46–55, 68–79; 2:29–32; 1 Tim. 3:16; 2 Tim. 2:11–13; Rev. 5:9–10; 15:3–4). In the second century, the Gnostics composed far more poetry than did orthodox Christians.

Secular Greek and Roman poetry began to influence Christian literature in the third century, when those educated in the schools of rhetoric (which taught the study and composition of poetry) began to convert. Augustine's *Confessions*, for example, show how deeply his schooling in Virgil's *Aeneid* affected him. Through the fifth or sixth century, Christian poets, although rejecting the values of pagan education, owed their training to the schools of rhetoric. Christian authors employed most of the literary forms of secular poetry, such as epic, epistle, lyric, epigram, and (rarely) drama.

Christian poetry falls into four principal classes: didactic, liturgical, literary, and monumental. Many poems instructed readers in the faith, warned them against error, or exhorted them to virtue. Other poems, especially hymns, were meant for liturgical use. Still others, like the retellings of biblical narratives or the metrical lives of saints, were literary exercises intended for pious entertainment or edification. Some poems were written to be inscribed on churches, pictures, tombs, and monuments.

All poetry is rhythmic or metrical. Hebrew poetry achieved its effect primarily by the parallelism of clauses but also by parallel stress, alliteration, assonance, paronomasia, and onomatopoeia. Some Psalms were divided into strophes; others were abecedarian or used refrains. Classical Greek poetry was quantitative: it achieved its rhythm by a fixed pattern of alternating long and short syllables, a fixed number of feet in a line, and (in lyric poetry) a fixed length for stanzas. Lines did not have a fixed number of syllables, rhyme was generally avoided, and the stress accent of words played no role. One common meter was dactylic hexameter, used especially in epic poetry; others were elegiac couplets, iambic dimeter, and trochaic tetrameter. Latin poetry simply took over the prosody and forms of Greek poetry.

Several Christian poets, through the sixth century and later, tried to write in classical, quantitative verse; some succeeded better than others. But others abandoned the classical meters, which in any case were no longer fully understood, and introduced new rhythmical or metrical principles, replacing the fixed number of feet in a line with a fixed number of syllables, and sometimes taking account of the stress accent of words and employing rhyme and assonance. Acrostic or abecedarian structure sometimes served as a further ornament: either the first letters of each line spelled a word or a phrase, or successive lines or verses began with successive letters of the alphabet (a technique already used in Hebrew poetry). But purely accentual verse and consistent rhyme are medieval.

Syriac Christian Poetry. Syriac writers were the first to develop an original Christian poetry. The *Odes of Solomon* are probably an early Syriac composition. Bardesanes of Edessa (154–222) and his son Harmonius composed 150 hymns. Ephraem the Syrian (ca. 306–373) wrote *memre*, or metrical sermons, in verses of (usually) seven syllables and stanzas of four lines, and *madrasha*, which were hymns or texts of songs composed in strophes with a refrain; he has hymns on the Nativity, Lent, Easter, and saints and martyrs. Later Syriac authors are Cyrillonas, Balai, Isaac of Antioch, Narsai (a Nestorian), and Jacob of Sarug (a Monophysite).

Greek Christian Poetry. Until the fifth century, relatively few Greek-speaking Chris-

tians wrote poetry; monastic biblicism and, perhaps, residual fear of Gnosticism hindered them. Still, Clement of Alexandria (d. before 215) has a beautiful hymn to Christ at the end of the *Instructor*. Methodius (late third century?) wrote a hymn to Christ, the bridegroom, and to the church, his bride, in his *Symposium*. The oldest known Christian example of hexametric poetry (ca. 300) has been published from the Bodmer papyri (no. 29). Arius (d. 336) wrote the *Thalia*, in prose and verse, to popularize his doctrines; in this case, poetry served theological propaganda. After Julian the Apostate forbade Christians to teach pagan literature, Apollinaris of Laodicea (ca. 315–392) tried to recast biblical material in epic, lyric, and dramatic form to serve as Christian textbooks, but only a version of the Psalms, in hexameters, remains. Gregory of Nazianzus (ca. 329–ca. 390) stands out as the most prolific Greek Christian poet of the first five centuries and is almost the only one who assiduously cultivated classical forms and meters. His dogmatic and moral poems are didactic and generally uninspired; his narrative poems are quite personal, often describing the state of his soul. They have authentic poetic feeling, as does his autobiography, in almost 2,000 iambic trimeters. Synesius of Cyrene (ca. 370–414) composed nine or ten hymns in Doric dialect and classical prosody that mix Neoplatonic and Christian thoughts with religious sentiment.

Greek Christian poetry began to flourish in the sixth century. Romanos Melodos (ca. 485–ca. 560) is the greatest of the early Byzantine poets. He wrote *kontakia*, or homilies in the form of songs, probably under Syrian influence. The poems treat Christ's life and work, biblical persons, Gospel parables, and saints. The famous *akathistos* hymn (so called because it is never sung sitting) is an anonymous abecedarian song of praise to Mary in twenty-four strophes. Sophronius of Jerusalem (d. 639) wrote anacreontic odes for liturgical feasts. Other early Byzantine hymnographers are George of Pisidia (d. mid-seventh century), Andrew of Crete (ca. 660–740), and Cosmas Melodos (d. mid-eighth century).

Latin Christian Poetry. Commodian (third, fourth, or fifth century) was possibly the first Christian Latin poet. He wrote the *Instructions* in two books of eighty poems in acrostic or abecedarian form. The poems are didactic, probably intended for catechumens. His *Carmen apologeticum*, in more than 1,000 hexameters, is an exposition of Christian doctrine. Much early Christian Latin verse is anonymous, such as the *Phoenix*, attributed to Lactantius; the *Laudes Domini*, a poem about a miracle; and poems on biblical material: *De Sodoma*, *De Iona*, and a poem on the Maccabees (ascribed to the philosopher Marius Victorinus).

Christian Latin poetry first flourished in the fourth century, beginning with Juvencus, a Spanish priest, who composed (ca. 330) a poetic paraphrase of the Gospels in more than 3,000 hexameters; it is the first attempt to write a Christian substitute for pagan literature and the first of many biblical epics. Proba, a Roman woman, wrote (ca. 360) a Virgilian *cento* (that is, a poem composed entirely of lines and half-lines from Virgil) that describes the early history from Genesis and the life of Christ; the effect is often bizarre. Another Spaniard, pope Damasus I (366–384), composed inscriptions for the tombs of saints and martyrs; about sixty are extant, two-thirds still on the original marble. Ausonius (ca. 310–ca. 395), a distinguished teacher and statesman in Gaul, composed verses at the end of his life that are more notable for technique than for inspiration. His exchanges of letters in verse with his pupil Paulinus of Nola, in which he tried to deter Paulinus from the monastic life, are noteworthy. (Paulinus's answers, also in verse, are extant.) Ambrose of Milan (ca. 339–397), "the father of Latin hymnody," not only wrote magnificent hymns himself (perhaps fourteen of his survive, many still used in the liturgy of the hours) but began the long tradition of Ambrosian hymnody. Ambrose abandoned classical forms and wrote in stanzas of four eight-syllable lines without rhyme. The anonymous *Carmen aduersus Marcionitas*, a tract in verse against the Marcionites once attributed to Tertullian, dates probably from the fourth century.

Prudentius (348–after 405) was undoubtedly the greatest Christian Latin poet of antiquity. Imaginative and sensitive, he commanded rich poetic language and imagery. He published his collected works in eight books at the end of his life. His topics are varied: poems for times of the day, defense of the doctrine of the Trinity, apologies against heathenism, praise of the martyrs. Augustine of Hippo (354–430) wrote the abecedarian *Psalmus contra partem Donati*, a refutation of Donatism written for Catholics in a meter that is easily memorized and sung, with a refrain. Paulinus of Nola (351–431), whom Ausonius had educated, versified some Psalms and wrote epigrams and epigraphs, but his largest work is a series of fourteen birthday odes (*carmina natalicia*) for Felix of Nola, his patron. Paulinus also wrote a Christian wedding-song (*epithalamium*) for Julian of Eclanum, a *propempticon* (farewell to a traveler) for Niceta of Remesiana, and the first Christian elegy.

In Gaul in the fifth century, Christian poetry flourished until the barbarians overran the land and the public schools closed. Cyprian (early fifth century) versified the first seven books of the Bible in hexameters, with a few lyric passages. Sedulius (from southern Gaul or Italy) wrote, sometime before 431, a *Paschale carmen* in five books, about biblical miracles. His language is lively and his technique almost classical. Orientius, also from Gaul, wrote (ca. 440) the *Commonitorium*, perhaps the best Christian didactic poem, in elegiac couplets. Claudius Marius Victorius of Marseilles (d. 425–450), in his *Alethia*, reworked the early chapters of Genesis into hexameters. Prosper of Aquitaine versified (ca. 450) sentences from Augustine. Ausonius's grandson Paulinus of Pella (376–after 459), toward the end of his life, wrote his autobiography, called *Eucharisticos*, in about 600 hexameters. Paulinus of Périgueux wrote (ca. 470) the life of Martin of Tours in some 3,500 hexameters. Sidonius Apollinaris (ca. 430–ca. 487), bishop of Clermont, wrote poems, epitaphs, and inscriptions, which are included in his letters. Rusticus Helpidius (d. 501/2), bishop of Lyons and a friend of Sidonius Apollinaris, wrote a poem on Christ and epigrams for pictures in churches. Avitus of Vienne (450–518) turned Genesis and Exodus into hexameters, a kind of "Paradise Lost."

Venantius Fortunatus (ca. 535–ca. 610), bishop of Poitiers, was the most impressive Christian Latin poet of the sixth century. Among his more than 300 poems in many genres are the hymns for Passiontide, *Vexilla regis* and *Pange lingua . . . proelium*, which are still used in the liturgy of the hours. He also wrote an extensive life of Martin of Tours in hexameters. His form is classical, but his sensibility is already medieval.

Dracontius (late fifth century), who lived in Carthage, was the most important African poet. His longest work is *De laudibus Dei,* a sort of theodicy, in three books. Arator (Rome, mid-sixth century) wrote a long epic based on the Acts of the Apostles. Other sixth-century Italian poets were Boethius and Ennodius. CPL 1385–1542. *See also* Hymns; Psalms. [J.T.L.]

Bibliography

W.v. Christ and M. Paranikas, eds., *Anthologia graeca carminum Christianorum* (Leipzig: Teubner, 1871); P. Maas, ed., *Frühbyzantinische Kirchenpoesie* I (Bonn: Marcus & Weber, 1910); M. Pellegrino, ed., *La poesia greca cristiana dei primi secoli,* 2 vols. (Turin: Gheroni, 1952, 1963); J.J. Thierry, *Christ in Early Christian Greek Poetry: An Anthology* (Leiden: Brill, 1972); A.H.M. Kessels and P.W. Van der Horst, "The Vision of Dorotheus (Pap. Bodmer 29)," *VChr* 41 (1987):313–359.

O.J. Kuhnmuench, *Early Christian Latin Poets: From the Fourth to the Sixth Century* (Chicago: Loyola, 1929); E. Wellesz, *A History of Byzantine Music and Hymnography* (Oxford: Clarendon, 1949); F.J.E. Raby, *A History of Christian-Latin Poetry from the Beginnings to the Close of the Middle Ages,* 2nd ed. (Oxford: Clarendon, 1953); N.K. Chadwick, *Poetry and Letters in Early Christian Gaul* (London: Bowes and Bowes, 1955); E. Werner, *The Sacred Bridge: The Interdependence of Liturgy and Music in Synagogue and Church During the First Millennium* (London: Dobson, and New York: Columbia UP, 1959); C. Witke, *Numen Litterarum: The Old and the New in Latin Poetry from Constantine to Gregory the Great* (Leiden: Brill, 1971); J.W. Binns, ed., *Latin Literature of the Fourth Century* (London and Boston: Routledge and Kegan Paul, 1974); J. Fontaine, *Naissance de la poésie dans l'occident chrétien* (Paris: Etudes Augustiniennes, 1981).

POLYCARP (d. ca. 156). Bishop of Smyrna and one of the apostolic fathers. Polycarp is known to us from his letter to the Philippians and the *Martyrdom of Polycarp.* Except for a brief encounter with Marcion (Eusebius, *H.E.* 4.14.7), nothing is known of his life. His death is described in the *Martyrdom,* written by his church within a year of the event (*M. Polyc.* 18.3). Polycarp links the apostolic era with the next generation, for Irenaeus (Eusebius, *H.E.* 5.20.6) claimed that Polycarp sat at the feet of the apostle John and that he was appointed to his office at Smyrna by the apostles themselves.

According to Irenaeus (Eusebius, *H.E.* 5.20.8), Polycarp wrote several letters to neighboring congregations, but only the letter to the Philippian Christians is extant. It was occasioned primarily by a request from the community at Philippi for copies of the letters by Ignatius (*Ep.* 13.2). Polycarp honored the request and added a cover letter for the collection. A secondary occasion for the letter was the apparent abuse of his office by a certain elder (11.1–2). The letter consists primarily of collected quotes, especially from apostolic writings. Although he writes just after the death of Ignatius (ca. 117?), Polycarp shows a significant knowledge of the New Testament. He knows a collection of the Pauline letters (3.2) but never mentions a collection of four Gospels. The Christianity reflected in the letter of Polycarp parallels that found in the Pastoral Epistles: strong morality, anti-Doceticism, respect for tradition, and a concern for the poor.

In the *Martyrdom,* the church at Smyrna describes the arrest of Polycarp (6.1–7.3), his short trial (9.1–11.2), and his immediate execution, first by an unsuccessful burning, then by the dagger of the executioner (16.1). Not only is the *Martyrdom of Polycarp* the first Christian account of martyrdom, but it is the earliest witness to the practices of Christians having a meal for the dead, especially the martyrs (17.1–18.3), and the formation of a martyrs' calendar (18.3). Feast Day February 23. CPG I, 1040–1042. TLG 1622. *See also* Martyrdom of Polycarp. [G.F.S.]

Bibliography

Irenaeus, *Against Heresies* 3.3.4; Tertullian, *Against Heretics* 32.2; Eusebius, *Church History* 3.36.1, 10; 4.14.1–9; 5.20.4–8.

J.B. Lightfoot, *Apostolic Fathers* (London: Macmillan, 1885), Part 2, Vol. 3, pp. 897–1086.

W.R. Schoedel, *Polycarp, Martyrdom of Polycarp, Fragments of Papias* (Camden: Nelson, 1967).

P.N. Harrison, *Polycarp's Two Epistles to the Philippians* (Cambridge: Cambridge UP, 1936); H. Koester, *Introduction to the New Testament* (Philadelphia: Fortress, 1982), Vol. 2, pp. 306–308.

POLYCRATES (late second century). Bishop of Ephesus. In the Paschal controversy, Polycrates was the spokesman for the Quartodecimans, who observed the annual celebration of the resurrection of Jesus on the fourteenth day of the Jewish month Nisan. Victor I, bishop of Rome, asked for meetings of bishops in different provinces to determine when they celebrated the Pasch. Other regions reported that they observed it only on Sunday, but Polycrates,writing for other bishops of the province of Asia, defended the Quartodeciman practice as the tradition of the apostles Philip and John and of the bishops Polycarp, Melito, and seven of his own kindred. CPG I, 1338. TLG 1626. *See also* Pasch; Victor I.   [E.F.]

Bibliography
Eusebius, *Church History* 3.31.3; 5.24.1–8.

PONTIANUS. Bishop of Rome (230–235). Pontianus agreed to the condemnation of Origen by Demetrius of Alexandria (Jerome, *Ep.* 33.4). He was banished by emperor Maximinus to Sardinia, where he died. His remains along with those of Hippolytus were returned to Rome in 237, and an inscription commemorated his burial. Feast day November 19.[E.F.]

Bibliography
O. Marucchi, *Christian Epigraphy* (Cambridge: Cambridge UP, 1912), no. 190, p. 194; Eusebius, *Church History* 6.23.3; 6.29.1; *Liber Pontificalis* 19 (Duchesne 1.145–146).

PORPHYRY (ca. 232–ca. 305). Pagan Neoplatonic philosopher, student of Plotinus. Born in Tyre, Porphyry went to Athens for further education and there studied under the Platonist Longinus. In 263, he left for Rome, where he studied with Plotinus for six years. After settling for a period in Sicily, he returned to Rome sometime after Plotinus's death.

Few of Porphyry's voluminous writings survive. The most significant are his *Life of Plotinus, Eisagogē* (an introduction to Aristotelian logic), *Sentences Leading to the Intelligible World* (a systematic work), and several letters. He also edited Plotinus's *Enneads*. His interests ranged from philosophy and religion to philology and allegorical interpretation. He focused on the moral and religious aspects of philosophy, but he was also a scholastic commentator on Plato, Aristotle, and Plotinus. His writings popularized the thought of Plotinus, especially in the Latin west.

In the lost *Against the Christians*, Porphyry attacked Christianity by applying historical criticism to biblical texts, such as the Book of Daniel. Eusebius of Caesarea, Apollinaris of Laodicea, Macarius Magnes, and Philostorgius all wrote refutations of Porphyry that are lost, but Eusebius's *Demonstration of the Gospel* and *Preparation of the Gospel* are both directed against this work.   [L.P.S.]

Bibliography
H. Dörrie et al., *Porphyre, Entretiens sur l'antiquité classique* (Geneva: Foundation Hardt, 1966), Vol. 12; M.V. Anastos, "Porphyry's Attack on the Bible," *The Classical Tradition . . . in Honor of H. Caplan*, ed. L. Wallach (Ithaca: Cornell UP, 1966); P. Hadot, *Porphyre et Victorinus*, 2 vols. (Paris: Etudes Augustiniennes, 1968); A.H. Armstrong, ed., *The Cambridge History of Later Greek and Early Medieval Philosophy* (Cambridge: Cambridge UP, 1970), pp. 272–297; T.D. Barnes, "Porphyry *Against the Christians*: Date and Attribution of Fragments," *JThS* n.s. 24 (1973):424–442; A. Smith, *Porphyry's Place in the Neoplatonic Tradition* (The Hague: Nijhoff, 1974); B. Croke, "Porphyry's Anti-Christian Chronology," *JThS* n.s. 34 (1983):168–185; R.L. Wilken, *The Christians as the Romans Saw Them* (New Haven: Yale UP, 1984), pp. 126–163; A. Smith, "Porphyrian Studies since 1913," ANRW (1988), Vol. 2.36.2, pp. 717–773.

POTAMIUS OF LISBON (d. after 359). Bishop and writer. The first known bishop of Lisbon, Potamius signed and circulated the "Blasphemy of Sirmium," a doctrinal formula that reflected the teachings of extreme Arianism. It is probable that he returned to orthodoxy together with many other bishops after the Synod of Rimini (359). Of his writings, two dogmatic letters (one of them addressed to

Athanasius) and two homilies (on Lazarus and on Isaiah) survive. CPL 541–544. [M.P.McH.]

Bibliography

Hilary of Poitiers, *On the Councils* 3; 10; 11; Phoebadius, *Contra Arianos* 5.

PRAXEAS (second–third century). Teacher of Modalist Monarchianism. Praxeas moved from Asia Minor to Rome ca. 200. The only source of information on him is Tertullian's *Against Praxeas*, in which he is described as an anti-Montanist and a Patripassian. [D.M.S.]

Bibliography

E. Evans, ed. and tr., *Q. S. Fl. Tertullianus, Treatise Against Praxeas* (London: SPCK, 1948).

PRAYER. "Prayer is conversation with God," according to John Chrysostom (*Hom. in Gen.* 30.5; cf. Clement of Alexandria, *Str.* 7.7; Gregory of Nyssa, *Or. Dom.* 1). Origen distinguished the words for prayer in 1 Timothy 2:1: supplication is a "petition offered with entreaty" by one who needs something; prayer "is offered in a dignified manner with praise concerning matters of importance"; intercession "is a request to God . . . made by one who possesses more than usual confidence"; and thanksgiving "is an acknowledgment that blessings have been obtained from God" (*Or.* 14.2).

Background. Greek and Roman religion was characterized by the attitude "I give in order that you may give to me" (Plato, *Euthyphro*). Prayer spelled out the benefits expected to be received in return for sacrifices. Philosophers and poets, however, advocated a more unselfish view of prayer and emphasized inner qualities (Plato, *Phaedrus* 279B–C). Greek prayers followed a standard pattern: invocation of the deity, identified by names and titles; praise of his or her deeds or attributes; petition to be present, to accept the offering, and to give favors to the worshiper(s).

Much of the language and practice of Christian prayer is derived from the Jewish Bible and Jewish prayer life at the beginning of the Christian era. Observant Jews recited the *Shema* (Deut. 6:4–9 expanded) twice daily and prayed three times a day (*Berakoth* 1.1–2; 4.1).

The classic prayer of Judaism, used both in the synagogue and in private devotion, is the *Shemoneh Esreh*, the "Eighteen Benedictions," the components of which are first century or earlier in date. Jewish prayers generally followed one of two structures: the *berakah* form ("Blessed be the Lord"), after naming the Lord, gave the ground of the blessing in the activity of God by recalling his deeds, made petition and intercession, and concluded with further words of benediction to God; the *hodayah* form ("I give thanks to you, O Lord") addressed God directly in the second person and after expressing the reason for the praise proceeded with the same elements as the blessing form. The rabbis established the *berakah* formula, found in the *Shemoneh Esreh*, as the standard form of prayer. Christians generally adopted the thanksgiving form, but the principal difference between Jewish and Christian prayer is the place given by Christians to the mediation of Christ.

New Testament. The example and teaching of Jesus provided the basis of Christian prayer. His prayer life is noted in all the Gospels but is given special prominence by Luke. Jesus' teaching about prayer, as on other subjects, emphasized simplicity, humility, and inner motives (Matt. 6:5–15; Luke 11:1–3; 18:1–14). The model prayer that Jesus taught his disciples, the "Lord's prayer" (Matt. 6:9-13; cf. Luke 11:1–4), took the place in Christian practice of the *Shemoneh Esreh* in Judaism. The most important contribution of Jesus to the Christian understanding of prayer was his intimate relationship with God as "Father" (Mark 14:36), which he taught his disciples to share.

Paul's letters contain many prayers, and the opening thanksgiving sets the theme of each letter. Much of his theology may be learned from his prayers. The distinctive note of Christian prayer as prayed "in the name of Jesus Christ" is expressed in John (14:13f.; 15:16; 16:24, 26). These words, which seldom occur in surviving prayers, mean that the prayer is offered because of him and in service to him. Since the language of worship tends to be conservative, it is not surprising that some Aramaic words from the early days of the church continued in the Greek-speaking church: "Abba" ("Father") in addressing God (Gal. 4:6), "Amen" ("May it be so") as a ratification of prayer (1 Cor. 14:16), and "Maranatha" ("Our Lord, come"—1 Cor. 16:22) as an expression of eschatological hope.

Literature. The practice of prayer, both personal and corporate, is often referred to in early Christian writings, and these also often contain prayers. The earliest treatises on prayer usually took the form of commentaries on the Lord's prayer. Collections of prayers began to be made in the fourth century, and the written liturgies contain prayers for corporate worship. The commentaries on the Psalms are often treatises on prayer. Augustine's *Confessions* is written as a long sustained prayer to God, an instance of prayer providing the form of a literary work. Many prayers were written on scraps of papyrus or on ostraca or were inscribed on tombstones, churches, houses, utensils, and jewelry, indicating their pervasiveness in the lives of the people.

Occasions. Prayer was a part of all religious activities, both public and private. It was prominent in the Sunday assembly of the church (1 Cor. 14:15; Tertullian, *Apol.* 39). The long prayer near the close of *1 Clement* (59–61) probably reflects the style and content of prayer that the author was accustomed to lead in the church at Rome. Origen regularly closed his homilies with prayer. The great prayer of the congregational assembly was the eucharistic prayer, led by the bishop and responded to by the people in unison with "Amen" (Justin, *1 Apol.* 65; 67). The early practice was free prayer, although with recurring themes and some relatively fixed formulas, but soon written guides standardized the eucharistic prayer (Hippolytus, *Trad. ap.* 10). Many cities had daily assemblies of the church for instruction and prayer (Hippolytus, *Trad. ap.* 35). Bishops' churches came to have regular morning and evening services (John Chrysostom, *Catech.* 8.17–18; *Const. app.* 2.59.2; 8.35–39). Prayer accompanied the agape of the church (Tertullian, *Apol.* 39.16–18; Hippolytus, *Trad. ap.* 25–27), as it did ordinary meals (1 Tim.

4:4f.; Aristides, *Apol.* 15). Martyrs faced death with prayer (*M. Polyc.* 7–8; 14). Prayer blessed Christian marriage (Gregory of Nazianzus, *Ep.* 231), comforted the bereaved at funerals (funeral orations regularly concluded with prayer— e.g., Gregory of Nazianzus, *Or.* 7.24), and indeed accompanied all of life (Gregory of Nyssa, *Or. Dom.* 1).

Times of Prayer. In addition to the public, corporate prayers, individuals observed private, daily times of prayer. The *Didache* 8.2, 3 enjoined the use of the Lord's prayer three times a day. Tertullian refers to prayer in the morning, 9 a.m., 12 noon, 3 p.m., in the evening, and in the night in addition to mealtimes (*Or.* 24–25). These times of prayer became institutionalized in monasticism as the offices of Lauds, Prime, Terce, Sext, None, Vespers, Compline, and Midnight (Benedict, *Rule* 16). Clement of Alexandria knew fixed times of prayer but like many others emphasized that the true Christian "prays throughout his whole life" (*Str.* 7.7.40, 49). Silent or mental prayer could be observed at any time (ibid.; John Chrysostom, *Hom. prec.* 1–2). Paul's admonition to "pray without ceasing" (1 Thess. 5:17) received various interpretations. Origen understood praying to include doing virtuous deeds and obeying God's commands; these complemented the minimum expression of formal prayer at morning, noon, evening, and midnight (*Or.* 12.2). Some monks, such as the Messalians, sought a more literal fulfillment in unceasing prayer. Certain spiritual writers commended constant meditation on the name of Jesus in whatever one was doing (Diadochus, *Cap.* 31f.; 61; 88; John Climacus, *Scal.* 28), which practice developed in the Orthodox Church into the "Jesus prayer" ("Lord Jesus Christ, Son of God, have mercy on me").

Posture. Both kneeling and standing had early precedent in Christian practice (Acts 20:36; Mark 11:25). Kneeling expressed humility and penitence and so was used on fast days; standing expressed joy and confidence and so was adopted on Sunday, the day of the resurrection (Tertullian, *Coron.* 3; *Or.* 23). In both cases, in keeping with a normal practice of the ancient world, the arms were outstretched to the side with the hands slightly elevated and the palms turned upward (1 Tim. 2:8; Origen, *Or.* 31.2f.). The outstretched arms were understood by Christians as representing the crucifixion of Christ (Tertullian, *Or.* 14; cf. 17; *Odes of Solomon* 42.1f.). The *orant* posture in early Christian art shows the ubiquity of this symbol of prayer. The *orantes* normally have their head covered, perhaps because they represent a deceased person or are stylized representations of the soul (and so female); Christian practice, however, was for men to pray with head uncovered (1 Cor. 11:4; Tertullian, *Apol.* 30.4). Prayer was normally made facing east, the direction of paradise and the direction from which Christ (the true Light) would come (Origen, *Or.* 32; Basil, *Spir.* 27.66).

Formal Aspects. Origen outlined prayer according to the following subjects: "At the beginning and preamble of the prayer, God is to be glorified. . . . And next in order after this, each one must offer general thanksgiving including blessings bestowed on many besides himself, together with those he has personally obtained from God. After thanksgiving . . . he ought to accuse himself bitterly before God for his own sins, and then ask God, first for healing that he may be delivered from the habit that causes him to sin, and secondly for forgiveness of the past. After confession, in the fourth place, he should add his request for great and heavenly things, his own and general, and also for his family and his dear ones. And finally, he should bring his prayer to a close glorifying God through Christ in the Holy Spirit" (*Or.* 33.1). Not all prayers followed this outline of praise, thanksgiving, confession, petition, and doxology, or contained all these elements; but this represents the classic structure of prayer.

Christian prayer is normally addressed to God as Father, although there are early examples of prayers addressed to Christ. With the rise of the cult of the saints, petitions were directed also to Mary and the saints as intercessors before God. Expressions of praise to God (doxologies) were taken over from Judaism, but the distinctively Christian doxologies included Christ and the Holy Spirit, either as joint re-

cipients of the praise with the Father or as the basis and means of the praise being offered. In corporate prayer, besides the "Amen" by which the congregation made the words spoken by the leader its own, other brief prayer acclamations were used in various contexts: "Hallelujah" ("Praise the Lord"), "Hosannah" ("Save now, we pray"), the Trisagion ("Holy, Holy, Holy"), "Kyrie eleison" ("Lord, have mercy"), "Dominus vobiscum" ("the Lord be with you"), "Pax vobiscum" ("Peace be with you"), "Gratias Deo" ("Thanks be to God").

Content. The words of praise and thanksgiving were often phrased with a view to the petitions and intercessions to be made. The central affirmation of Christian prayer, as of Christian faith, was what God had done in and through Jesus Christ. Many times, this was set in the context of a history of salvation, which recited God's acts prior to the coming of Christ and sometimes referred to important developments for his people after Christ's coming. The recitation of God's benefits included material as well as spiritual blessings (Justin, *1 Apol.* 13; *P. Oxy.* 18.430; 3.407). The wide range of petitions in early Christian prayer is illustrated by the prayer in *1 Clement* 59–61, in part: "Save those of us in affliction, have mercy on the humble, raise up the fallen, manifest yourself to those in need, heal the sick, bring back those of your people who are straying. Feed the hungry, ransom our prisoners, raise up the weak, comfort the fainthearted." Especially notable in the days of persecution were the prayers for rulers (1 Tim. 2:2; Polycarp, *Ep.* 12; Tertullian, *Apol.* 30; 39).

Theology. The nature of God and faith in him formed the basis of Christian prayer. Prayer was thus always also a confession of faith, a confession of who God is, of what he has done and can do, and of one's relation to him. Without neglecting God's other attributes, such as his role as Creator, the Christian approached him in prayer as Father on the ground that this relationship had been created by Jesus Christ. Although prayer to Christ was not frequent (Acts 7:39), the salvation accomplished by his death and resurrection was the basis of access to God, and he was the mediator of prayer. He imparted his Sonship to his people. Prayer, furthermore, was prompted by the Holy Spirit, who, having given new life and providing the link between the believer and God, inspired the address to God as Father. The possession of the Spirit united believers to one another and so gave a community expression to prayer. The Christian prays *"Our* Father," in consciousness of being one with all redeemed people, sharing a mutual salvation and mutual concerns. Prayer as the "spiritual oblation that has abolished the former sacrifices" (Tertullian, *Or.* 27–28; cf. Clement of Alexandria, *Str.* 7.7) made one a living sacrifice. Effective prayer had to be joined to a moral life and be prompted by sincere motives. The resulting service of God to which prayer was related was directed toward the future coming of Christ and eternal life with God. *See also* Amen; Doxology; Epiclesis; Eucharist; Hymns; Kyrie eleison; Litany; Liturgy; Lord's Prayer; Office, Divine; Orant; Ordination; Psalms; Sacramentary; Trisagion.   [E.F.]

Bibliography

Clement of Alexandria, *Miscellanies* 7.6–7; Tertullian, *On Prayer*; Origen, *On Prayer*, E.G. Jay, *Origen's Treatise on Prayer* (London: SPCK, 1954); Cyprian, *On the Lord's Prayer;* Serapion, *Prayerbook*, J. Wordsworth, *Bishop Serapion's Prayerbook* (London: SPCK, 1923); Cyril of Jerusalem, *Catechetical Lectures* 5; Gregory of Nyssa, *The Lord's Prayer*, tr. H. Graef, ACW (1954), Vol. 18; Aphraates, *Demonstration* 4; Evagrius Ponticus, *De oratione;* Theodore of Mopsuestia, *Catechetical Homily* 11; John Cassian, *Conferences* 9–10; Augustine, *Letter 130 to Proba*; C. del Grande, *Liturgiae Preces Hymni Christianorum* (Naples, 1934) (critical edition of prayers and hymns from papyri).

F. Cabrol, *Liturgical Prayer* (London: Burns, Oates and Washbourne, 1922); A. Hamman, *Early Christian Prayers* (Chicago: Regnery, 1961); idem, *La Prière* (Tournai: Desclée, 1963), Vol. 2: *Les Trois premiers siècles*; R.L. Simpson, *The Interpretation of Prayer in the Early Church* (Philadelphia: Westminster, 1965); P. Bradshaw, *Daily Prayer in the Early Church* (London: SPCK, 1981; and New York: Oxford UP, 1982); A. Cunningham, *Prayer: Personal and Liturgical* (Wilmington: Glazier, 1985); S. Brock, *The Syriac Fathers on Prayer and the Spiritual Life* (Kalamazoo: Cistercian Publications, 1987); E. Ferguson, *Early Christians Speak* (Abilene: ACU, 1987), pp. 137–147; F.F. Chruch and T.J. Mulry, *The Macmillan Book of Earliest Christian Prayers* (New York: Macmillan, 1988).

PREACHING. Oral proclamation and interpretation of the gospel tradition, usually authorized by the church and addressed to a group, that calls for some response by the hearers. In early Christianity, there was missionary preaching, preaching to catechumens (those being instructed in the faith), and preaching as part of the regular liturgy. Christian liturgical preaching was heavily influenced by the pattern of synagogue worship, in which a reading from scripture was followed by an explanation of the passage. Missionary preaching and, to a lesser degree, other types of preaching may also have been influenced by the practices of Hellenistic philosophical groups. The preaching to Jewish audiences reported in the New Testament shows the influence of Old Testament prophecy, reinterpreting the tradition of Israel in a new situation.

Although preaching played a prominent role in church life from the beginning, there are few extant sermons from earlier than the middle of the third century. Origen is the first preacher whose sermons have survived in any number. The legal recognition of Christianity in the early fourth century gave preaching a greater prominence in society, and preachers arose who deserved such prominence. The fourth and early fifth centuries are generally recognized as a "golden age" of preaching, in both the eastern and western church. Such preachers as John Chrysostom, Basil, Gregory of Nazianzus, Ambrose, and Augustine attracted large crowds. Their sermons were written down for posterity, and, along with those of Origen, provided influential models for later centuries. The quality of preaching tended to decline in the fifth and sixth centuries, although church leaders like Leo the Great, Caesarius of Arles, and Gregory the Great were also known for their preaching.

Preaching in the New Testament. Oral proclamation played a major role in the ministry of both John the Baptist and Jesus (Mark 1:4, 14 and parallels). The Gospels report that Jesus commissioned his disciples to preach, both during his ministry (Mark 6:7–12; Matt. 10:7 and parallels) and after his resurrection (Matt. 28:18–20; Luke 24:45–49). Acts and the

Pauline epistles indicate that preaching was a major tool in the early church's evangelism. Although the Gospels provide no clear example, liturgical preaching and catechetical instruction probably helped shape the oral tradition that stands behind them. Other writings, such as 1 Peter, may be based on sermons. Since many of the New Testament books were written to be read aloud in worship, they may reflect the nature of first-century liturgical preaching.

Missionary Preaching. The historical accuracy of the sermon reports in Acts is debated. At the very least, these reports indicate what a later generation of Christians thought early missionary preaching was like: The dawn of the messianic age was proclaimed, usually with reference to Old Testament prophecy; this age had been inaugurated through the life, death, resurrection, and exaltation of Jesus Christ; forgiveness of sins was offered to those who repented and believed.

Although much evangelism was carried out by ordinary Christians through their everyday contacts, there were itinerant missionaries in the second and third centuries. None of their sermons is extant. Missionary preaching to pagan audiences probably exhorted them to reject idols, turn to the one true God, and learn of Christ and his significance (cf. 1 Thess. 1:9–10). Miracles and the ethical behavior of Christians were cited as evidence of the superiority of the Christian faith.

After the time of Constantine, when most residents of the empire were at least nominally Christian, missionary preaching continued on the fringes of the empire. Ulfilas (ca. 311–383), missionary to the Goths in the region of the Danube, and Patrick (d. ca. 460), in Ireland, were two such missionaries, but there are no records of their preaching.

Liturgical Setting. Although preaching took place in other contexts, most extant sermons were a part of Christian assemblies. The sermon immediately followed the reading of lessons from the Old and New Testaments, even as early as the middle of the second century (Justin, *1 Apol.* 67). From the third century, only baptized Christians were allowed to be present at the eucharistic liturgy, but the liturgy of the word, including the sermon, remained open to catechumens and other interested hearers. After Christianity was recognized as a legitimate religion, preaching became popular: large crowds would occasionally interrupt the preacher with applause. The preacher normally spoke while seated; the congregation stood. Sermons seem to have varied greatly in length but occasionally lasted more than an hour. Sometimes, more than one preacher would preach during a single service. Preaching was not limited to Sunday. Several fourth-century preachers are known to have preached on weekdays, at least during festivals or seasons of fasting, as had Origen in the third century. Not all preachers were so diligent, however. Especially in the fifth and sixth centuries, one finds bishops exhorting the clergy to preach more frequently.

Use of Scripture. Early Christian preaching was biblical preaching. Numerous scripture passages—often dozens—were cited in a single sermon. From the time of Origen onward, the most common form of sermon was the exegetical homily, the phrase-by-phrase exposition of a particular passage, usually the text read for the day. Even in such homilies, many other scriptures were cited. Whether or not a sermon centered on a single text, scripture was almost always the authority given for the claims made in preaching. The goal of preaching, however, was never simply that the hearers understand scripture. The exposition of the text was accompanied by application (sometimes implicit, but usually explicit), calling the hearers to respond to the message of the gospel. The Old and New Testaments, especially the former, were often interpreted typologically or allegorically, so that the Christian gospel was found in all the scripture.

Catechetical Preaching. Catechumens heard many sermons. Especially important were those preached shortly before, or immediately after, their baptism. Usually preached on successive days, these didactic sermons explained the central mysteries of the faith to the new Christians. The homily form was normally maintained, but the text expounded was not from scripture but from the liturgy: the baptismal rite, the eucharist, the creed, the Lord's prayer. Although these sermons still came after the reading of the scripture text for the day, and many scriptures were cited during the sermon, it was the liturgy itself that was expounded step-by-step.

Panegyrical Preaching. Devotion to the saints and martyrs, and celebration of festival days in their honor, increased greatly in the fourth century. The sermons for these festival days took the form of praise of the life of the saint. Christian morality and sound doctrine were promoted by presenting the saint as a model to be emulated. Scripture was often cited as authority in these sermons, but it was usually the life of the saint, not a text, that formed the basis of the sermon.

The Preacher. In the first century, it seems that any member of a congregation or visiting Christian could be asked to speak. Soon, however, preaching became a task restricted to the clergy. By the middle of the second century, *2 Clement* 17.3–5 indicates that preaching was the normal task of presbyters; Justin (*1 Apol.* 67) describes the sermon as given by the "president" (*proestos*—the bishop?) of the congregation. Later, preaching became the clear responsibility of the bishop, although he often delegated this responsibility to presbyters. A storm of controversy broke out in the third century when Origen began preaching without ordination, even though he had been asked to preach by two bishops (Eusebius, *H.E.* 6.19.16–18). Bishops would sometimes prepare written sermons that were then read in the outlying churches of the diocese by presbyters or deacons. By the sixth century, written sermons from the church fathers were authorized to be read by deacons in village churches.

Rhetoric and Style. Among the characteristics of early Christian preaching, appeal to the authority of scripture and tradition is prominent: logical argument plays a secondary role. It was generally assumed that preaching was made effective through the work of the Holy Spirit. Structurally, a sermon passage expounding a biblical text is often followed by another applying the scripture to the lives of the hear-

ers. This pattern sometimes constitutes the two major parts of the sermon outline, or it may appear as a repeating cycle throughout the sermon. Paradox is frequently used (because it is appropriate to the nature of the gospel, and already appears in many scripture texts). Many sermons end with a doxology.

Despite these commonalities, there was also considerable diversity. The two extant sermons from the second century stand in sharp contrast. The style of *2 Clement* is mundane and plodding, but Melito of Sardis's *On the Passover* is polished and eloquent, using a wide variety of rhetorical devices. Some sermons were carefully written out before delivery; others were delivered extemporaneously. Both John Chrysostom and Augustine used the homily form, but Chrysostom was given to frequent digressions, while Augustine usually remained close to his text. There was simply no single way in which to preach a Christian sermon.

The tools of rhetoric became more prominent in Christian preaching after the third century. As the church was allowed to proclaim its message freely, in a society where rhetoric was the core of a good education, skillful rhetoric became important in attracting and convincing hearers. All of the greatest preachers of the fourth century had studied rhetoric, and several had taught rhetoric before their ordination.

Again, there was diversity in the degree to which rhetorical conventions were adopted, but usually Christian preachers exercised some restraint. Although Chrysostom was a master rhetorician, he wrote, "Let a [preacher's] diction be poor and his style simple and unornamented; but let him not be unskilled in the knowledge and accurate explanation of doctrine" (*Sac.* 4.6). Augustine's *On Christian Doctrine* was the earliest book on homiletics. He urged that preachers use rhetoric to promote truth, just as others used it to promote falsehood. He adapted the three goals of Ciceronian rhetoric—to teach, to please, and to move—for Christian preaching. The preacher was "not only to teach that he may instruct and to please that he may hold attention, but also to persuade that he may be victorious"

(4.13.29). Moving, or persuading, was to be the most important goal of preaching. Teaching was the secondary goal. Pleasing was never to be the goal of a sermon, only a means of achieving the goal.

The use of illustrations varied greatly. Some sermons used hardly any, except those drawn from scripture. This is especially true of earlier sermons but is also characteristic of the catechetical sermons of Cyril of Jerusalem (ca. 348). Other preachers, such as Chrysostom, depicted aspects of everyday life. Gregory of Nazianzus used illustrations drawn from pagan authors; Basil is noted for his illustrations drawn from nature. Anecdotes from the lives of the saints were also employed from the fourth century onward.

The Purpose of Preaching. As we have seen, preaching played many roles in the life of the early church. Preaching won converts, interpreted the faith of the church for its members, and gave Christians guidance for daily living. For Irenaeus (*Haer.* 1.10), preaching was the means by which the tradition of the faith was explained, clarified, and passed on to others. During periods of doctrinal controversy, sermons were often used to expose the errors of theological opponents and to defend the true gospel.

Exhortation to live a proper Christian life was common. At times, such exhortation degenerated into tedious moralizing or, in the fifth and sixth centuries, admonitions to perform one's churchly duties. At other times, for example in the sermons of Chrysostom, one finds powerful, theologically based critiques of sub-Christian practices, both in individual lives and in society.

Preaching sought to promote both the knowledge of Christian doctrine and the practice of Christian faith. In its sermons, the early church proclaimed Jesus Christ and interpreted what it meant to be his church. *See also* Homily; Rhetoric.   [W.D.H.]

Bibliography

M.F. Toal, ed., *The Sunday Sermons of the Great Fathers*, 4 vols. (Chicago: Regnery, 1958–1963); C.E. Fant, Jr., and W.M. Pinson, Jr., eds., *20 Centuries of Great Preaching* (Waco: Word, 1971), Vol. 1.

E.C. Dargan, *A History of Preaching* (New York: Armstrong, 1905); C.H. Dodd, *The Apostolic Preaching and Its Developments* (London: Hodder and Stoughton, 1936); H.T. Kerr, *Preaching in the Early Church* (New York: Revell, 1942); J. Foster, *After the Apostles* (London: SCM, 1951); A. Niebergall, "Die Geschichte der christlichen Predigt," *Leiturgia,* ed. K.F. Müller and W. Blankenburg (Kassel: Stauda, 1955), Vol. 2, pp. 181–352; Y. Brilioth, *A Brief History of Preaching* (Philadelphia: Fortress, 1965); W. Schütz, *Geschichte der christlichen Predigt* (Berlin: de Gruyter, 1972); D.T. Holland, *The Preaching Tradition* (Nashville: Abingdon, 1980); G.A. Kennedy, *Classic Rhetoric and Its Christian and Secular Tradition* (Chapel Hill: U of North Carolina P, 1980); idem, *Greek Rhetoric Under Christian Emperors* (Princeton: Princeton UP, 1983); R.D. Sider, *The Gospel and Its Proclamation* (Wilmington: Glazier, 1983); T.K. Carroll, *Preaching the Word* (Wilmington: Glazier, 1984); D.G. Hunter, *Preaching in the Patristic Age* (New York: Paulist, 1989)

PREDESTINATION. God's determination of the ultimate destiny of individual human beings and the operations through which he brings each person to the chosen end. During the patristic period, predestination refers only to those being brought to salvation, not to the damned. God's election is based upon no prior merits of those who are to be saved: it precedes and actually effects the good willing and performance that make one worthy of eternal life. In contrast, God knows (foreknowledge) but does not will or cause, either by acting or failing to act, the sins for which the condemned are judged. Moreover, the theory of predestination is applied only to those who have fallen in Adam and are saved in Christ: God knew but did not produce either the fidelity of the angels or the sin of Adam and the demons.

The biblical foundation of the doctrine of predestination is twofold. The scriptural narrative portrays God acting without regard for or even against human qualifications and achievements in assigning roles in the economy of salvation: the favoring of Jacob over Esau provides a signal but hardly isolated instance of this divine sovereignty. God's purposes, moreover, were accomplished even in the actions of those who appear to be acting against them: Pharaoh's resistance to Moses and Judas's betrayal of Jesus both advanced God's plan. Paul's assertion (Rom. 8–11) of the gratuity of salvation and the efficacy of God's treatment of Jacob and Esau, Israel and the nations, provided the foundation for the patristic doctrine of predestination. Additional evidence was found especially in Matthew 20:23; John 6:44–45, 66; and Ephesians 1:3–14.

Christian apologists in the second and third centuries ignored this biblical theme; in their struggle against Gnosticism and other forms of determinism, they insisted upon the role of individual free choice in both good and evil. They explained the sovereignty of divine governance over all creation through God's exhaustive knowledge of the intentions and actions of the creatures. Each individual's free choices are integrated into the divine plan for the whole. Although insisting upon individual responsibility, these and subsequent Christian writers also asserted the gratuity of the divine mercy and the divine initiative in the saving activity of Christ.

At the end of the fourth century, Augustine initiated a different interpretation of the text of Romans and a new understanding of divine sovereignty. In his *To Simplician on Various Questions*, he asserted that without regard for their prior or subsequent merits, God chooses certain individuals for conversion and actually effects their own saving faith in Christ. A later treatise, *On Correction and Grace*, applied the principles derived from Romans, and elaborated by reference to an array of scriptural texts, to perseverance in Christian faith and good works, which were judged necessary for salvation. God freely elects individuals, moves them to believe in Christ, grants them the power to fulfill his commandments, and ensures their performance of good works and repentance for failures. Thus does God bring the elect to glory, without regard for any independent or autonomous merits of their own.

The doctrine of God's predestination of the elect assigns to God all glory for salvation; the creature can claim no credit for initiative or even independent cooperation with the divine mercy. Failure and damnation, however, are assigned to the independent choice of the creature. Augustine explained that initially God

had endowed humanity with the capacity for meritorious action enjoyed by the angels; through this, humans might have earned eternal beatitude. In Adam, all human beings failed and merited damnation. Those whom God elects in Christ are saved not by their own power or even by their cooperation with divine assistance but through the efficacy of divine mercy. All others are condemned in God's justice for their participation in Adam's sin and for the sins that they have personally added.

The Augustinian theory of predestination met widespread resistance. Predestination of the elect seemed logically to entail a divine decision to withhold necessary assistance and thereby to condemn the nonelect. In addition, the theory postulated that God chooses some for Christian faith but not for eternal life. Through the Council of Orange (529), the western church accepted the doctrine that God elects individuals for Christian faith without regard to their merits and actually causes their own free conversion. The council ignored Augustine's assertion of divine predestination of individuals to salvation or glory that would be accomplished through the grace of perseverance and without regard to merits. In the ninth century, the church condemned the teaching of the monk Gottschalk that God predestines some to damnation. The eastern church did not share Augustine's doctrine of divine influence over human willing, through which the saving purpose is effected. *See also* Augustine; Election to Salvation; Original Sin; Pelagius, Pelagianism; Prevenient Grace.

[J.P.B.]

Bibliography

Augustine, *To Simplician on Various Questions*, ed. A. Mutzenbecher, CCSL, (1970), Vol. 44, tr. J. Burleigh, *Augustine: Earlier Writings* (Philadelphia: Westminster, 1952), pp. 372–406; idem, *On Rebuke and Grace*, PL 44.915–946, tr. P. Holmes and R.E. Wallis, NPNF, 1st ser. (1887), Vol. 5, pp. 468–491; idem, *On the Predestination of the Saints*, PL 44.959–992, tr. P. Holmes and R.E. Wallis, NPNF, 1st ser. (1887), Vol. 5, pp. 495–519; *Concilia Galliae (A.D. 511–695)*, ed. C. de Clercq, CCSL (1963), Vol. 148A.

R. Bernard, "La Prédestination du Christ total selon saint Augustin," *Recherches augustiniennes* 3 (1965):1–58; J.M. Rist, "Augustine on Free Will and

Predestination," *JThS* n.s. 20 (1969):420–447; J.P. Burns, *The Development of Augustine's Doctrine of Operative Grace* (Paris: Etudes Augustiniennes, 1980).

PRESBYTER. A rank of Christian minister: an elder, later a priest. *Presbuteros* in Greek designated an older man and was rarely used of an official. In Rome, the senators derived their name from the adjective *senex* ("old"). In Judaism, "elder" (*zaken*) was a technical term for a member of the council of community leaders. Each Jewish community had a group of older men responsible for interpreting the Law and deciding disputes within the community. The primarily judicial nature of this function is indicated already in the Old Testament (e.g., Deut. 21:18–21; 1 Kings 21:8ff.). The Jewish elders mentioned in the New Testament were primarily members of the Great Sanhedrin in Jerusalem (e.g., Mark 11:27; 14:53; local elders in Luke 7:3), whose number of seventy was based on the precedent of Numbers 11:16–24 (m. Sanh. 1.6). Rabbinic literature required the presence of three ordained men for the ordination of an elder (b. Sanh. 13b) and set forth qualifications for the office (*Deut. Rab.* 1; b. Sanh. 17a). Diaspora synagogues were governed by a council; its members, however, were not normally called "elders" but *archons* ("rulers") or collectively *gerousia* ("council of elders").

The presbyters in early Christian congregations (Acts 14:23; James 5:14) were apparently derived from the elders of Jewish communities; the literal translation of *zaken* into Greek gave *presbuteros* a technical sense. The early Christian elders had comparable functions in overseeing community affairs, deciding disputes, and preserving the teachings (Acts 11:30; 15:6, 22; 1 Tim. 5:17). The apostle Peter was ranked among the Christian elders (1 Peter 5:1). The author of 2 and 3 John identified himself as "the Elder," a rare use of the term as an individual title, since the office was normally plural (cf. 1 Tim. 4:14; 1 Tim. 5:19 is generic).

"Presbyter" occasionally had in early Christian usage a semitechnical reference to disciples of Jesus (Papias in Eusebius, *H.E.* 3.39.4) and then to their disciples, who could serve as guar-antors of the tradition from apostolic days (Irenaeus, *Haer.* 4.27.1; 5.33.3). Its predominant usage, however, was in the plural for members of the council who provided spiritual leadership for a local group.

Several early noncanonical documents reflect a situation where a plurality of presbyters was at the head of a congregation (Polycarp, *Ep.* 5–6, cf. 11; *2 Clem.* 17.3; *Asc. Isa.* 3.23f.; *Orac. Sib.* 2.264f.). Even where the single bishop was clearly distinct from the presbyters, as in Ignatius, the presbyters were in close association with the bishop and in their plurality represented the college of apostles (Ignatius, *Polyc.* 6; *Trall.* 3; *Smyrn.* 8). The church at Alexandria, according to later reports (Jerome, *Ep.* 146; Eutychius, *Annals*, PG 111.982), was led by twelve presbyters, who chose a president as bishop out of their own number.

Although by the end of the second century the term "bishop" was confined to the president of the council of presbyters, bishops could also be called "elders" (Irenaeus in Eusebius, *H.E.* 5.20.7; 5.24.14; Clement of Alexandria, *Str.* 3.12.90), and many fourth-century writers remembered that in the New Testament there was an identity of elders and bishops (Jerome, *Ep.* 146; *Ad Tit.* 1:5; Ambrosiaster, *In Eph.* 4.11; *In 1 Tim.* 3.10; Theodore of Mopsuestia, *1 Tim.* 3; John Chrysostom, *Hom.* 2 *on Phil.* 1.1). Gnostics were careless about distinctions in the ministry (Tertullian, *Praescr.* 41).

The presbyters formed a council of advisers and associates of the bishop (*Didas.* 26). The presbyters, like the Jewish elders, were especially involved in the exercise of discipline and giving judgment (Tertullian, *Apol.* 39; *Paenit.* 9; Ps.-Clement, *Ep. Jac.* 10; Hippolytus, *C. Noetum* 1; Epiphanius, *Haer.* 42). Teaching became mainly the task of the bishop, but in carrying out their disciplinary role the presbyters taught morals (Ps.-Clement, *Hom.* 3.65–68; *Ep. Jac.* 7). Cyprian found it necessary to bring even discipline more closely under the supervision of the bishop (*Ep.* 15.1; 16).

Origen (*Hom.* 4 *in Gen.* 4) explained that "presbyter" was ascribed to the holy persons of old "not by reason of longevity but of maturity." The Council of Neocaesarea (*can.* 11) set thirty years as the minimum age for ordination as a presbyter (*Const. app.* 2.1 recommended fifty for a bishop).

With the growth of churches in the large cities, it was necessary to have several different meeting places in addition to the bishop's church. As these different meeting places emerged as stable parishes, it became customary to designate a presbyter to preside over each. In this way, liturgical functions that had earlier been performed exclusively or primarily by the bishop devolved regularly on the presbyters. The presbyter became the celebrant of the eucharist at the parish churches. A presbyter might be designated by the bishop to preach (as Origen at Caesarea and John Chrysostom at Antioch). Similarly, the terminology of "priest" passed from the bishop to the presbyter, which word provides the etymological derivation of the English word "priest," so that in modern churches of the Catholic tradition the terminology is bishop, priests, and deacons.

The Eastern Orthodox churches extended the functions of the priesthood more fully to presbyters than did western Catholics, for Orthodox priests administered confirmation, a function long reserved normally to the bishop in the Catholic church. On the other hand, the requirement of celibacy did not apply to priests in the eastern churches. *See also* Bishop; Deacon; Ministry; Ordination; Priesthood.

[E.F.]

Bibliography

Jerome, *Letter* 52.

G. Bornkamm, "*Presbus, Presbuteros*," *Theological Dictionary of the New Testament*, ed. G. Friedrich (Grand Rapids: Eerdmans, 1968), Vol. 6, pp. 651–680; J.G. Sobosam, "The Role of the Presbyter: An Investigation into the *Adversus Haereses* of Saint Irenaeus," *Scottish Journal of Theology* 27 (1974):129–146; A.E. Harvey, "Elders," *JThS* n.s. 25 (1974):318–332; C.H. Roberts, "Elders: A Note," *JThS* n.s. 26 (1975):403–405; D. Powell, "Ordo Presbyterii," *JThS* n.s. 26 (1976):290–328.

PREVENIENT GRACE. Divine operation that precedes all human efforts and begins the process of conversion. The teaching of prevenient grace (grace that "goes before") asserts that as a consequence of the fall of humanity in Adam individuals will not or cannot take the initial step toward salvation or do anything that would make them worthy of forgiveness and assistance. By sheer gratuity, God moves a person to repent for sin and believe in Jesus Christ.

The scriptures and the fathers of the church both asserted that God has taken the initiative for the salvation of humanity as a whole. In Romans and Galatians, Paul insisted that, unlike the legal covenants that required action of both parties, the foundational covenant that began with Abraham and was fulfilled in Christ was established by God alone and need only be received in faith. In various ways, the apologists and the defenders of the Nicene definition of faith, as well as the parties to the fifth-century Christological debates, all argued that the salvation of humanity required a divine intervention that was gratuitous and efficacious.

The doctrine of prevenient grace arose rather in consideration of the application of the work of Christ to individuals. Christian theologians generally believed that salvation was attained only through faith in Christ and participation in the communion of the church. Thus, they recognized the priority of the preaching of the gospel to the individual's response of faith. During the first part of the fifth century, in a controversy with Augustine of Hippo, the British ascetic Pelagius asserted that the capacity to choose between good and evil is an inalienable endowment of rational nature, given by God in the creation itself. God requires that a person respond to the admonitions of the natural or Mosaic Law and to the preaching of the gospel, which offers forgiveness for past sins and promises an eternal reward for living according to God's commandments. God provides assistance to those who have already shown themselves worthy or those who God knows will prove worthy by their response.

Augustine, however, insisted that in the sin of Adam all humanity lost the freedom to do good and avoid sin. God's grace comes to an individual whose only merits are evil and who can respond to the admonition of the Law and the preaching of the gospel only through a prevenient grace that moves the person to repentance and to place faith and hope in Christ. God then rewards faith with charity, the indwelling of the Holy Spirit, whereby the convert loves God and gains the freedom to live according to the commandments. God's operation is a prevenient grace, preceding all human merits and producing its own free acceptance.

Unlike his teaching on the gift of perseverance, Augustine's theory of a prevenient divine operation or grace that initiates the process of individual salvation met with widespread acceptance. Through the Council of Orange (529), the western church affirmed its foundations and implications. It became an element in the medieval synthesis, and although it was questioned in the fourteenth and fifteenth centuries, the gratuity, priority, and efficacy of the divine grace in justification were recognized by Reformers and Catholics alike. *See also* Augustine; Election to Salvation; Grace; Pelagius, Pelagianism; Predestination.

[J.P.B.]

Bibliography

Augustine, *On Rebuke and Grace*, tr. P. Holmes and R.E. Wallis, NPNF, 1st ser. (1887), Vol. 5, pp. 468–491; *Concilia Galliae (A.D. 511–695)*, ed. C. de Clercq, CCSL, (1963), Vol. 148A.

A. Sage, "Praeparatur voluntas a Domino," *REAug* 10 (1964):1–20.

PRIESTHOOD. Term used in churches of the Catholic tradition for the ministry of bishops and presbyters. The terms *archiereus*, *hiereus*, and *hierōsunē* are applied to Christ in the New Testament. The Epistle to the Hebrews 10:10–12 describes Christ as exercising a high-priestly ministry that fulfills all human priesthood once for all. Priesthood (*hierateuma*), predicated of the chosen people (Exod. 19:6), describes the status of the new people of God (1 Peter 2:5, 9), and the individual Christian (*hiereis*—Rev. 1:6; 5:10; 20:6). On Christological grounds, Christians share in the holiness of Christ and make an acceptable offering of their lives through invoking his unique sacrifice.

The New Testament does not employ the title "priest" for those who exercise special ministries, but Paul does use priestly language to describe his apostolic work of preaching (Rom. 15:16). Since Christians took over the synagogue structure, with elders or overseers, an analogy with the Levitical priesthood is not to be expected. Clement of Rome, however, possibly drawing on a liturgical collection of Old Testament *testimonia* and the Epistle to the Hebrews, compares the Old Testament high priests, priests, and Levites to contemporary counterparts in the church (*1 Clem.* 40–41; elsewhere in the document, Christ is the high priest—36; 61; 64), and speaks of a liturgical offering of "gifts" proper to the episcopate (44.4).

Up to the end of the second century, the terms "priest" and "priesthood" were not used for ecclesiastical officers. Polycrates of Ephesus (ca. 195) calls the apostle John a teacher and priest (*hiereus*), who wears the "sacerdotal tiara" (Eusebius, *H.E.* 5.24.3). Tertullian refers to bishops as priests, and once as *summus sacerdos* (*Bapt.* 17.1–2). He also calls all Christians priests (*Monog.* 7.8). Presbyters are said to belong to the *ordo sacerdotalis* (*Exhort.* 7), but it is not certain that Tertullian names them priests (*Pudic.* 20; *Idol.* 7.6). Presumably under the influence of the terminology of *1 Clement*, the *Apostolic Tradition* of Hippolytus applies the notion of priesthood to both bishops and presbyters as a quality properly pertaining to them. The ordination prayer for the bishop refers to his exercise of sovereign priesthood (*archierateuein*—*Trad. ap.* 3), and once the title *archiereus* is used for the bishop (34). Deacons are distinguished from presbyters because they are not ordained to the priesthood (8). Cyprian, who frequently uses *sacerdos* for bishops (*Ep.* 63.14.4), associates presbyters with the bishop in the sacerdotal order (*sacerdotali honore coniuncti*—*Ep.* 61.3.1). With one possible exception (*Ep.* 40.1.2), the term "priest" is applied to presbyters by the bishop of Carthage insofar as they form a single body of *sacerdotes*. Origen attributes a priesthood to the whole church (*Hom. in Lev. 9.1*), and to individuals who fulfill the law of God (*Hom. in Jos. 9.5*). In the hierarchy of ministries, bishops are priests par excellence (*Hom. in Lev. 6.6*). At least sixteen times, presbyters, who pertain to the sacerdotal order (*Hom. in Num.* 2.1), are named priests. Origen's view that presbyters have an inferior priesthood (*Hom. in Ex.* 2.6), probably inspired by 2 Kings 23:4, is taken up by later writers. Among the first, Optatus of Milevis (ca. 370) ranks presbyters in the second order of *sacerdotium*, and deacons in the third order (*C. Parm. Donat.* 1.1.3).

In the second half of the fourth century and in the fifth, "priest" normally meant "bishop" in the east and west, although occasionally it was applied to presbyters. Augustine attributes *sacerdos* to bishops, presbyters, and ordinary Christians, as members of the High Priest, Christ (*Civ. Dei* 10.20). He uses the title, in the narrower sense, for bishops and presbyters less frequently than his contemporaries. His caution in this regard is at least partially due to the need to insist on the unique priesthood of Christ in the ongoing debate with the adherents of Donatism. Parmenian, who had succeeded Donatus as leader of the Donatist church, equated *sacerdotium* with holiness and taught that unworthy bishops and presbyters could not administer sacraments. According to Augustine, the minister is only the servant of Christ and does not lose the capability to exercise his offices because of sinfulness (*C. Parm.* 2.28). Augustine, as well as Pseudo-Dionysius the Areopagite, transfers the meaning of baptism as a seal of the Master to orders. The bishop of Hippo, who attributes the right to baptize to ministerial priests, says that this right can no more be lost than baptism itself. The implication that ordination confers a permanent sealing lies behind the later western theology of the priestly *character*.

Although the priestly terminology derives from the Old Testament, it must be understood in terms of the functions associated with it. The special priestly ministry of bishops included the offering of the eucharistic sacrifice, completing the Christian initiation, reconciling sinners, and ordaining other ministers. Fourth- and fifth-century patristic writers describe the office of priest as ordered to the ministry of teaching, baptizing, reconciliation of sinners, and eucharist. In virtue of the ministry of education, regeneration, and reconcili-

ation, the priest's role was conceived as that of spiritual fatherhood. However, a new understanding of the priest emerged as a consequence of sixth-century developments: doctrinal teaching became less common with the end of the great heresies; catechumenate instruction was greatly reduced as infant baptism became widespread; and opportunities for the ministry of pastoral correction decreased with the decline of the discipline of public penance. Attention increasingly focused on the ritual activity of priests. As a result, a theology of priesthood began to be formulated on the basis of Old Testament types.

In the west, the tension between the old and the new is exemplified by Isidore of Seville in the late sixth and early seventh centuries. His *Etymologiae* defines the priest as one who "consecrates and sanctifies" (7.12.17); *De ecclesiasticis officiis* relates the sacerdotal order of the New Law to the power of the keys and preaching, when referring to the bishop (2.5.5). In regard to the presbyter, Isidore mentions the priestly functions of presiding over the church, celebrating the eucharist, and preaching the word (27.1–2). *See also* Bishop; Clergy; Laity; Ministry; Presbyter.   [E.J.K.]

Bibliography

Gregory of Nazianzus, *Oration* 2, tr. C.G. Browne, NPNF, 2nd ser. (1894), Vol. 7; John Chrysostom, *On the Priesthood*, tr. W.R.W. Stephens, NPNF, 1st ser. (1889), Vol. 9; Gregory the Great, *Pastoral Rule*, tr. H. Davis, ACW (1950), Vol. 11.

P.M. Gy, "Notes on the Early Terminology of Christian Priesthood," *The Sacrament of Holy Orders* (Collegeville: Liturgical, 1962), pp. 98–115; L. Ryan, "Patristic Teaching on the Priesthood of the Faithful," *ITQ* 19 (1962):25–51; D. Power, *Ministers of Christ and His Church* (London: Chapman, 1969), pp. 1–88; L. Sabourin, *Priesthood: A Comparative Study* (Leiden: Brill, 1973); M. Bévenot, "Tertullian's Thoughts About the Christian 'Priesthood,'" *Corona Gratiarum . . . E. Dekkers* (Bruges: Sint Pietersabdij, 1975), Vol. 1, pp. 125–137; idem, "'Sacerdos' As Understood by Cyprian," *JThS* n.s. 30 (1979):421–423.

PRIMASIUS

PRIMASIUS (sixth century). Exegete and bishop of Hadrumetum in North Africa. An adherent of pope Vigilius in his condemnation of the Three Chapters, Primasius wrote a Latin commentary on the Book of Revelation. Valuable as a witness for the lost work of Tyconius, although derived from Augustine as well, this commentary furnishes important evidence for the history of the Old Latin version of the New Testament. CPL 873.   [M.P.McH.]

Bibliography

Primasius, Commentarius in Apocalypsin, ed. A.W. Adams, CCSL (1985), Vol. 92.

PRISCILLIAN (ca. 340–ca. 387). Bishop of Avila in Spain. Priscillian was born probably in the Roman province of Galicia in Spain. His family was wealthy, probably Roman, and perhaps senatorial. He seems to have studied the Bible extensively and given much thought to theological and spiritual issues, but he was probably not formally educated. Sometime before 370, perhaps in consequence of his studies, he was converted to Christianity and baptized. Soon he adopted a lifestyle characterized by asceticism. His sharp rejection of all secularism, which nevertheless did not require total withdrawal from the ordinary world, the persuasiveness of his call to an all-absorbing love of God, and his insistence on thorough Bible study, all of which implied the necessity for reform of the church, and all of which came at a time of high anticipation of the imminence of the second coming of Christ, created both disciples and enemies, principally in the south and west of the Iberian Peninsula, in the Balearics, and in southern Gaul.

Among the bitterest of his enemies were Ithacius, bishop of Ossonuba (Faro, Portugal), and his metropolitan, Hydatius or Idatius of Emerita Augusta (Mérida, Spain). Their distaste, and the report that at least two bishops in Hydatius's province, Instantius and Salvianus (sees unknown), had bound themselves to Priscillian by an oath, helped to precipitate the Council of Zaragoza in October 380, which ten of the twenty-six or more bishops in Spain and two bishops from southern Gaul attended. Debate at the council was apparently sharp, because Priscillian's teachings and practices could be given a generally orthodox, if clearly ascetic, reading. Equally sharp was subsequent debate over whether Priscillian personally, or any of his disciples, was explicitly condemned by the council.

The Priscillianists' liturgical use of texts already adjudged apocryphal by many, but in common use among the Manichaeans, and their appeal to them to advocate clerical and perhaps general celibacy, left Priscillian and his friends open to charges of Manichaean dualism. Their punctilious asceticism only made this charge more credible.

Early in 381, bishops Instantius and Salvianus, both put under a cloud by the council of 380 if not officially censured, secured the election of Priscillian (still a layman) as bishop of Avila. Hydatius, infuriated, enlisted the influence of Ambrose of Milan and obtained an imperial rescript ordering the deposition and banishment of any "pseudo-bishops and Manichaeans" in his province, naming no one in particular. Priscillian, the two bishops, and three female supporters gained on the journey through Aquitaine then went on to Rome to plead their cause, attest their theological orthodoxy, and call for an ecclesiastical, rather than a civil, inquiry and trial, although they did not insist on the last point. Pope Damasus I refused to see them. They then went to Milan, hoping to change Ambrose's mind and enlist his aid; he too refused them audience. They next turned to Macedonius, perhaps a pagan, the master of the offices, a man jealous of Ambrose. Through his influence, the emperor Gratian issued a rescript restoring Priscillian and Instantius to their sees (Salvianus had died in Rome). Back in Spain, they pressed charges against their enemy, Ithacius. Ithacius then fled to Trier and got Gratian to call for a hearing of the whole affair there. Macedonius intervened, but only to transfer it to Spain.

That hearing never took place. In August 383, Gratian was murdered, and Magnus Maximus was acclaimed Augustus, but not universally. Maximus made his orthodoxy a political tool, and the festering issue involving Priscillian became a principal occasion of its use. He called for an ecclesiastical synod at Bordeaux to hear and resolve the matter. There, Instantius was deposed, and Priscillian, apparently believing that there would be scant justice for him in that synod, got the hearing transferred to Maximus's imperial court at Trier. The trial gave Maximus a chance to show that, unlike Gratian, he would not tolerate either paganism or heresy. As bishops from Gaul and Spain came in, he entertained them lavishly, and they responded with sycophancy, some of it cynical. Only Martin of Tours, and perhaps one other, resisted the imperial blandishment.

Priscillian was charged with sorcery, a crime closely associated with suspicions of treason and therefore almost always accompanied by severe torture to extract confession. Priscillian confessed to having had an interest in magic, to having conducted nighttime meetings with women, and to having prayed naked, all of these actions being associated with sorcery. Further, sorcery and Manichaeism were popularly associated. But it was of sorcery that he was found guilty. He was imprisoned, and the matter of sentencing was left to the emperor. In the meantime, Ithacius withdrew from the prosecution, having encountered severe criticism for his participation in a trial on a capital charge of one believed by many to be a bishop. This necessitated a second trial, which had the same end. And this time, Maximus sentenced Priscillian, two other clergy, a wealthy female supporter, a well-known Christian poet, and perhaps one other person to be executed. The sentence was carried out sometime between 385 and 387 in Trier, to the satisfaction of Ithacius and Hydatius but to the dismay of such persons as Ambrose, who opposed Priscillian but believed capital punishment to be inappropriate at best and usually unequivocally evil, and to the profound disgust of Martin of Tours, who saw in the affair a deep perversion of both Christian faith and civil justice.   [P.M.B.]

Bibliography
G. Schepss, ed., CSEL (1889), Vol. 18; A. Hamman, ed., Patrologia Latina Supplementum (Paris, 1958ff.), Vol. 2, pp. 1391–1507.

B. Vollmann, "Priscillianus," Paulys Realenzyklopädie der klassischen Altertumswissenschaft, Supplement 14 (Munich: Druckenmüller, 1974), pp. 485–559; H. Chadwick, Priscillian of Avila (Oxford: Clarendon, 1976); R. Van Dam, Leadership and Community in Late Antique Gaul (Berkeley: U of California P, 1985).

PROBA (fourth century). Christian Latin poet. Proba, a woman of the Roman nobility, composed (ca. 360) a cento of 694 verses, drawn from Virgil and treating biblical events, particularly the creation story from Genesis and the life of Christ. Perhaps written in reaction to an edict of Julian the Apostate (ca. 362) that forbade Christians to teach classical texts, the work was for a long time used as a schoolbook. An earlier poem by Proba, an epic on the civil war between Constantius II and Magnentius, is lost. CPL 1480.   [M.P.McH.]

Bibliography
E.A. Clark and D.F. Hatch, The Golden Bough, The Oaken Cross: The Vergilian Cento of Faltonia Betitia Proba (Chico: Scholars, 1981); idem, "Jesus as Hero in the Vergilian Cento of Faltonia Betitia Proba," Vergilius 27 (1981):31–39.

PROCLUS OF CONSTANTINOPLE (d. 446). Bishop of Constantinople (434–446). As a priest at Constantinople, Proclus opposed Nestorius in 428 by preaching a sermon eventually placed in the acts of the Council of Ephesus (431). His Tome, a letter to eastern bishops (437), condemned Christological positions like those held by Theodore of Mopsuestia but did not condemn Theodore himself. Feast day October 24 (west), November 20 (east). CPG III, 5800–5915.   [F.W.N.]

Bibliography
Socrates, Church History 7.26, 28, 40–43, 48; Theodoret, Letter 47.

PROCOPIUS OF CAESAREA (ca. 500–ca. 565). Historian. Procopius is the principal source for the reign of Justinian (527–565). His History of the Wars recounts the campaigns of Belisarius, and his Buildings the constructions of Justinian. The Secret History (Anecdota), not published until after his death, has intrigued historians because its dark picture of Justinian and Theodora contrasts sharply with his other works. Similarly problematical is Procopius's religion: he accepted some Christian tenets but at other times expressed a non-Christian viewpoint.   [E.F.]

Bibliography

Procopius, *History of the Wars, Buildings, and Secret History*, 7 vols., tr. H.B. Dewing, LCL (1914–1940).

J.A.S. Evans, "Christianity and Paganism in Procopius of Caesarea," *GRBS* 12 (1971):81–100; A. Cameron, *Procopius and the Sixth Century* (Berkeley: U of California P, 1985).

PROCOPIUS OF GAZA (ca. 475–ca. 538).

Rhetorician and biblical interpreter. Probably the outstanding figure of the Christian rhetorical school at Gaza, Procopius wrote comments on the Octateuch (first eight books of the Old Testament) and other Old Testament books by quoting previous exegetes like Philo, Origen, Basil of Caesarea, Theodoret of Cyrus, and Cyril of Alexandria. His letters are highly stylized, helpful for descriptions of the period, but theologically of little interest. CPG III, 7430–7448. [F.W.N.]

Bibliography

PG 87.1–2838; S. Leanza, ed., CCSG (1978), Vol. 4 and Supplementum (1983); R. Hercher, *Epistolographi Graeci* (Paris: Firmin-Didot, 1873), pp. 533–598.

PROPHET, PROPHECY.

A prophet is a spokesperson for a deity; prophecy is the oral or written message delivered or produced by prophets and regarded as divine revelation by those who accept their credentials. These revelatory messages provide a divine perspective on human affairs and occasionally predict future events. Prophets typically communicate with the supernatural world by means of one of two types of altered states of consciousness. The "vision trance" involves visions, hallucinations, heavenly ascents, and out-of-body experiences. Jewish and Christian apocalypses, like Revelation, the *Shepherd* of Hermas, and the *Apocalypse of Peter*, are a type of revelatory literature consisting primarily of reports of such visionary experiences. The "possession trance" involves possession by a spirit who speaks and acts through the prophet. Israelite and early Christian prophets claimed such revelatory experiences, reflected through the use of such introductory formulas as "thus says the Lord" (characteristic of Old Testament prophets) or "thus says the Holy Spirit" (occasionally used by early Christian prophets). Although prophets and prophecy were a central feature of first-century Christianity, during the course of the second century they were marginalized and became largely associated with protest movements within Christianity, such as Montanism.

Earliest Christianity began as one among many sects and movements within early Judaism in which prophets and prophecy played a major role. John the Baptist was popularly regarded as a prophet (Matt. 14:5; Mark 11:32). Although John did not claim divine inspiration, he did preach the necessity of repentance in preparation for the impending judgment of God in a style reminiscent of Old Testament prophets (Matt. 3:7–10; Luke 3:7–9). Jesus too was thought to be a prophet (Matt. 21:46; Mark 6:15; 8:28; Luke 7:16; John 6:14) and probably regarded himself as one (Mark 6:4; Luke 13:31–33). Among the eschatological deliverers anticipated in early Judaism were the prophets Elijah and Moses, who were expected to return just before the end. Early Christianity identified John the Baptist with the eschatological Elijah, the forerunner of the Messiah (Matt. 11:12–14; Mark 1:2–4). Jesus, usually identified as the expected Messiah, was occasionally considered to be the eschatological Moses (Acts 3:22; 7:37).

Although early Judaism usually reserved the term "prophet" for Israelite prophets of the past or eschatological prophets of the future, early Christians frequently used the word for those of their number who were channels of divine communication. The widespread existence of prophetic phenomena, including glossolalia, in the early church was related to the general Christian conviction that the Spirit of God (expected by early Judaism to return in the eschaton) was now present and active in the midst of the people of God, that is, Christians (Rom. 8:9–11; 1 Cor. 6:19; 1 Thess. 4:8). The Spirit was active in a particular way in those who had the gift of prophecy (1 Cor. 12:4–11; 1 Thess. 5:29; Acts 4:8). The letters of Paul, the earliest sources for first-century Christianity (written between A.D. 49 and 64), reveal the central importance of prophecy in the Pauline churches. 1 Thessalonians and 1 Corinthians particularly (supplemented by Acts) indicate that those who prophesied did not, like bishops or elders, occupy a particular office in particular churches but rather filled a particular function (Eph. 2:20; 3:5; 4:11). Theoretically, all Christians could prophesy (1 Cor. 14:1-5, 39; Acts 2:17), but not all actually did (Rom. 12:6; 1 Cor. 12:28). Prophets were ordinarily members of local communities who prophesied primarily in the setting of Christian worship (1 Thess. 5:19; 1 Cor. 14:20-36). This suggests that prophets had a considerable degree of control in the exercise of their prophetic gifts (1 Cor. 14:29-33). Prophetic utterances were subject to evaluation by other prophets (1 Cor. 14:29) or other Christians (1 Thess. 5:21). According to Paul, prophetic speech ought to edify, encourage, and console those present (1 Cor. 14:3). Prophets reportedly had clairvoyant powers that enabled them to expose the inner secrets of others, resulting in their repentance (1 Cor. 14:24-25). According to Acts, prophecy also functioned to select particular people for special tasks (13:1-3), to provide guidance in making crucial decisions (16:6-10), to predict the future (11:27-28; 20:23; 21:10-11), and to resolve disputes (15:28, 32). John, the author of Revelation, regarded himself as a prophet (Rev. 10:11; 22:9, 16) and repeatedly calls the apocalypse he wrote a "prophetic book" (1:3; 22:7, 10, 18). John's familiarity with the situations of each of the seven churches addressed suggests that he was part of a prophetic circle that exercised an itinerant ministry in the Roman province of Asia (22:9; apostles also were itinerants, cf. 2:2). Revelation exhibits a clear instance of conflict between prophets. John opposes the prophetess "Jezebel," whom he charges with encouraging the Christians of Thyatira to eat meat sacrificed to idols (a Jewish taboo, cf. Acts 15:29) and to practice immorality, possibly with prophetic authority.

During the first half of the second century, the role of prophecy experienced a number of gradual changes. By the end of the century, the church's experience with Montanism,

and with Gnostic sects in which prophecy played a prominent role, had left both prophecy and prophets largely discredited. For Ignatius (ca. 115), prophecy was a gift that he exercised in a congregational setting and that exposed congregational secrets (*Philad.* 7:1-2). In the *Didache*, prophets as well as apostles are depicted as itinerants (11-13), although some settled permanently (12.3-4). Christian communities were widely scattered but maintained communication through traveling Christians, including apostles, prophets, and teachers (cf. 3 John 5-8), to whom they offered hospitality. Some of these travelers were charlatans intent on fleecing the flock (Hermas, *Mand.* 11.12; *Did.* 11.6) and on freeloading (*Did.* 11.9; 12.1-4). Tests for determining the genuineness of the prophet (or apostle, or teacher) were therefore devised (1 John 4:1-3; *Did.* 11-12; Hermas, *Mand.* 11). A few prophetic figures of the early second century, such as Ammia of Philadelphia (Eusebius, *H.E.* 5.17.3-4) and Quadratus (ibid., 3.37.1), were remembered as orthodox Christian prophets.

Montanism, also called the "New Prophecy," was a prophetic and apocalyptic movement originating in Asia Minor in 156 or 172. Montanus, the prophetic founder of the movement, was joined by two prophetesses, Priscilla and Maximilla (Eusebius, *H.E.* 5.16.6-9; 6.20.3; Hippolytus, *Haer.* 7.19.1). Montanism was particularly dependent on the Gospel and Revelation of John. The movement espoused a rigorous ethic, placed a high value on martyrdom, and expected the imminent arrival of the great persecution and the descent of the heavenly Jerusalem at Pepuza, seventy miles east of Philadelphia. Although Montanism was a popular movement (Tertullian was a convert), it was strongly opposed by Christian heresiologists. *See also* Ezekiel; Isaiah; Jeremiah; Minor Prophets; Montanism. [D.E.A.]

Bibliography

D. Hill, *New Testament Prophecy* (Atlanta: John Knox, 1970); J. Reiling, *Hermas and Christian Prophecy: A Study of the Eleventh Mandate* (Leiden: Brill, 1973); G. Dautzenberg, *Urchristliche Prophetie: Ihre Erforschung, ihre Voraussetzungen im Judentum und ihre Struktur im ersten Korintherbrief* (Stuttgart: Kohlhammer, 1975); U.B. Müller, *Prophetie und*

Predigt im Neuen Testament: Formgeschichtliche Untersuchungen zur urchristlichen Prophetie (Gütersloh: Verlagshaus Gerd Mohn, 1975); J. Panagopoulos, ed., *Prophetic Vocation in the New Testament and Today* (Leiden: Brill, 1977); M.E. Boring, *Sayings of the Risen Jesus: Christian Prophecy in the Synoptic Tradition* (Cambridge: Cambridge UP, 1982); D.E. Aune, *Prophecy in Early Christianity and the Ancient Mediterranean World* (Grand Rapids: Eerdmans, 1983); H.K. Stander, "Prophets in the Early Christian Church," *Ekklesiastikos Pharos* [Greek] 66–67 (1984–1985):113–122.

PROSPER OF AQUITAINE (ca. 390–after 455).

Theologian, poet, and chronicler. The life of Prosper of Aquitaine can be traced only in outline. His writings show that he received a solid education in the schools of Roman Gaul. He went from Aquitaine to Marseilles, where he enjoyed some kind of association with nearby monasteries. When controversy arose there (ca. 426) over the teachings of Augustine on grace, he defended them against the Semipelagianism advanced by the adherents of John Cassian. He went to Rome after Augustine's death to seek the support of the Roman bishop Celestine I (431). Celestine replied in a letter to the bishops of Gaul (*Ep.* 21), which, although urging great respect for the teachings of Augustine, did not uphold him specifically on every point of doctrine.

Prosper resumed the debate at Marseilles, where he issued his major theological writings over a short period of time (431–434). With the death of John Cassian (435), the controversy subsided. On the accession of Leo the Great (440), Prosper returned to Rome to offer Leo his services. The works of his later period (from ca. 435 on) are less polemical in tone. That he died after 455 is shown by the termination of his chronicle with that year.

Prosper's earlier writings include letters to a certain Rufinus and to Augustine himself, valuable for the evidence they give of the reaction in southern Gaul to Augustine's teaching on predestination; the *Poem on the Ungrateful* in refutation of Pelagian and Semipelagian teachings; and several short poems, one aimed at John Cassian and another directed against Nestorianism and Pelagianism, both of which had been condemned at the Council of Eph-

esus (431). There are also prose replies to objections raised to Augustinian theology by critics in Gaul, by Vincent of Lérins (probably), and by two priests of Genoa, as well as an attack on the views advanced by Cassian.

The later works include one on the last third of the Book of Psalms, which is itself a florilegium from Augustine, and the *Liber sententiarum*, a compilation of 392 extracts from works of Augustine taken out of context. The latter work was further condensed into the *Epigrammata*, 106 items in a mixture of prose and verse. Prosper's chronicle is based on Jerome and Eusebius of Caesarea for its account of the earlier period (to 378), then shows reliance on Sulpicius Severus and Orosius (to 417). Its narrative account of the later period (to 455), based on the author's personal knowledge, is especially valuable.

Several of the numerous other writings found under Prosper's name are probably his, including the so-called *Chapters of Celestine*, a survey of the teachings of the Roman see on the doctrine of grace found appended to the letter of Celestine I to the Gallic bishops; *The Call of All Nations*, in which God's universal will for the salvation of all is affirmed; and a *Letter to Demetrias Concerning True Humility*, directed to a consecrated virgin at Rome. Moreover, there is solid evidence to suggest attribution to Prosper of the *Poem on Divine Providence*, a consideration of providence set against the background of recent invasions of Gaul by Vandals and Goths, although the matter remains in controversy.

It was through Prosper that much of Augustine's thought was transmitted to the second of the councils of Orange (529) and eventually diffused throughout the Middle Ages. Feast day July 7. CPL 516–535, 2257.

[M.P.McH.]

Bibliography

Gennadius, *Lives of Illustrious Men* 84.

Prosper Aquitanus, Expositio Psalmorum C–CL, ed. P. Callens, and *Liber Sententiarum* ed. M. Gastaldo, CCSL (1972), Vol. 68A; *De providentia Dei*, ed. and tr. M. Marcovich (Leiden: Brill, 1989).

Prosper of Aquitaine: Grace and Free Will, tr. J.R. O'Donnell, FOTC (1949), Vol. 7; *St. Prosper of Aquitaine, The Call of All Nations*, tr. P. De Letter, ACW (1952), Vol. 14; *Carmen de Ingratis S. Pro-*

speri Aquitani, tr. C.T. Huegelmeyer (Washington, D.C.: Catholic U of America P, 1962) (*Poem on the Ungrateful*); *Prosper of Aquitaine, Defense of St. Augustine*, tr. P. De Letter, ACW (1963), Vol. 32; *The Carmen de Providentia Dei Attributed to Prosper of Aquitaine*, tr. M. McHugh (Washington, D.C.: Catholic U of America P, 1964) (*Poem on Divine Providence*); *Epistula ad Demetriadem de Vera Humilitate*, tr. M.K.C. Krabbe (Washington, D.C.: Catholic U of America P, 1965) (*Letter to Demetrias Concerning True Humility*); *A Poem on Divine Providence*, tr. J. Walsh and P.G. Walsh, *Divine Providence and Human Suffering* (Wilmington: Glazier, 1985), pp. 64–91.

L. Valentin, *Saint Prosper d'Aquitaine: étude sur la littérature latine ecclésiastique au 5e siècle en Gaule* (Toulouse: Privat, 1900); G. de Plinval, "Prosper d'Aquitaine interprète de saint Augustin," *REAug* 1 (1958):339–355; R. Lorenz, "Der Augustinismus Prospers von Aquitanien," *ZKG* 73 (1962):217–252; C. Bartnik, "L'Universalisme de l'histoire du salut dans le *De vocatione omnium gentium*," *RHE* 68 (1973):731–758.

PROTEVANGELIUM OF JAMES.

PROTEVANGELIUM OF JAMES. Apocryphal narrative of Jesus' infancy, known also as the *Gospel of James* or *Book of James;* the work received its present title from the Latin translation of G. Postel (Basel, 1552). The *Protevangelium of James* is found in a Greek text that dates from the fourth century. It enjoyed considerable popularity, appearing in more than thirty Greek manuscripts and in Syriac, Armenian, Coptic, and Old Slavonic translations. It was known probably to Justin Martyr (*Dial.* 78.5) and Clement of Alexandria (*Str.* 7.93.7) and certainly to Origen (*Comm. in Mt.* 10.17). The author of the *Protevangelium* in its original form (there were later additions) was probably a mid-second-century Jewish Christian living outside of Palestine, perhaps in Egypt. To lend authority to the work, he claimed identity with James, a relative of Christ, witness of the resurrection, and leader of the early Jerusalem Christian community.

The narrative supplies the names of Joachim and Anne as Mary's parents and claims that she was born to them in their old age. It goes on to describe Mary's presentation in the temple in her third year. There, she was educated until the age of twelve, when she was espoused to Joseph, an aged widower with children. Afterward, the priests assigned her the task of weaving part of a curtain for the temple. The annunciation, or declaration that she was to bear Jesus, took place as she was engaged in her weaving at home, after a preliminary annunciation heard while she was drawing water from a well. Mary's virginal birth of Jesus, which takes place in a cave, is established on the testimony of a midwife; throughout, the work is intended to uphold Mary's perpetual virginity before, in, and after the birth of Christ. The *Protevangelium* concludes with the slaughter of the Holy Innocents, the martyrdom of Zechariah, father of John the Baptist, and the death of Herod.

Although the work was rejected as uncanonical by the *Decretum Gelasianum* in the sixth century, the *Protevangelium* has had a considerable influence in liturgy and art. From it, there developed the Feast of the Presentation of Mary in the Temple (November 21, east and west) and the devotion to St. Anne. Legends surrounding the annunciation were popular in medieval art from the fifth century on. Mary is shown holding the wool from her weaving in the mosaics of the church of Sta. Maria Maggiore in Rome as well as in later depictions through the tenth century; the preliminary annunciation at the well is frequently represented in Byzantine art. TLG 1637.

[M.P.McH.]

Bibliography

E. de Strycker, ed. and tr., *La Forme la plus ancienne du Protévangile de Jacques* (Brussels: Société des Bollandistes, 1961).

NTA, Vol. 1, pp. 370–388.

E.A.W. Budge, *Legends of Our Lady the Perpetual Virgin and Her Mother Hanna* (London: Medici Society, 1922, and London: Oxford UP and H. Milford, 1933); G. Schiller, *Iconography of Christian Art* (Greenwich: New York Graphic Society, 1971), Vol. 1; idem, *Ikonographie der christlichen Kunst* (Gütersloh: Gütersloher Verlagshaus Gerd Mohn, 1980), Vol. 4.2; J. Vogt, *Ancient Slavery and the Ideal of Man* (Cambridge: Harvard UP, 1975), pp. 159–161.

PROVIDENCE.

PROVIDENCE. "The care that God takes over existing things," or "the will of God through which all existing things receive their final issue" (John of Damascus, *F.O.* 2.29). The concept of providence predates Christianity. Plato

(*Timaeus* 40–44) was the first philosopher to speak of an ordering principle in the universe; in contrast, the church fathers frequently criticized Aristotle for saying that providence extended only to the regions above the moon. The church fathers were concerned to show that God's overruling care for his creation and his people was different from fatalistic determinism (astrology and Stoic philosophy) and from capricious chance or fortune (deified as the goddess Tyche).

Among the apostolic fathers, *1 Clement* 20 is an extended panegyric on the harmony in the cosmos, in terms similar to the *Epistle to Diognetus* 7 (second century), and owing something to Stoicism. Among the Greek apologists, Justin Martyr (*Dial.* 1) complained that the majority of the philosophers neglected the question of a divine providence, as if this knowledge were unnecessary to human happiness. In his *1 Apology* 44, he wrote that God has foreknowledge of what all will do and has ordained that each will be rewarded for meritorious acts, since he cares and provides for the human race. Theophilus of Antioch (*Autol.* 2.8) quoted several Greek poets who championed providence and repudiated philosophers like Euhemerus, Epicurus, and Pythagoras for rejecting it. Athenagoras (*Leg.* 24.3) wrote that the angels were led into being by God, so that God would have universal providence over all things, whereas the angels would be over particular things. He quoted the Stoics (19.3) as saying that there are two causes, one active and efficacious insofar as it is providence, the other passive and immutable insofar as it is matter.

Irenaeus, in combating Gnosticism, insisted on one God who is both Father and providential ruler (*Haer.* 3.25) and on the unity of Jesus Christ (3.16), denying the Gnostic belief that the Suffering One somehow proceeded not from the Father but from a Demiurge. He stressed (*Haer.* 1.10, 22; 2.1–4) that there is but one God, maker of heaven, earth, and sea and everything in them. The Lord Jesus Christ, the only begotten Word, took up man into himself, recapitulates all things in himself, constitutes himself head of the church, and will draw all things to himself in due time (3.16.6).

The Alexandrians Clement and Origen developed the view of the action of providence as a pedagogical exercise, a graduated education leading the soul toward salvation. For Clement, even the rebellious are guided by a universal providence to a salutary end (*Str.* 1.17), and the greatest achievement of providence is in not allowing evil to remain unredeemed. Origen sees providence at work in everything; the peace brought about under Augustus in the Roman empire, for example, aided the growth of the nascent church (*Cels.* 2.30). Echoing Stoic doctrines, Origen believed that providence created all things for the sake of rational beings (*Cels.* 4.81). The Latin writer Lactantius reiterated that the marvelous harmony in creation is planned and effected by God's providence, acknowledging Cicero and the Stoics as his sources (*Div. inst.* 1.2); he claimed that human beings alone among creatures are made upright looking toward heaven because immortality has been provided as the reward of virtue (7.5). He was concerned particularly to refute Epicurus's rejection of providence and advocacy of the view that adversities will always befall the good, while the wicked enjoy wealth and honors (*Div. inst.* 3.17).

In the late fourth century, John Chrysostom was the great theologian of providence, to which he devoted a monograph and many homilies. Theodoret of Cyrus wrote a *De providentia*. The first half established the divine order and harmony in the universe and human control over the animal and vegetable worlds; the second half tried to come to grips with some of the anomalies pointed out by critics of providence, such as the gap between rich and poor and the danger of wicked masters corrupting virtuous slaves. Theodoret offers little besides a plea to accept the *status quo* in the hope that the final resurrection of the body, guaranteed by Christ's death and resurrection, will rectify present imbalances. Christ's incarnation is seen as the supreme manifestation of divine providence.

Augustine, in his *Confessions* 6.6, affirmed that none of the objections in the manifold writings of mutually opposed philosophers ever forced him to disbelieve in God's governance of human affairs. Yet in his *De ordine* and throughout his writings, he tried to reconcile God's concern with human affairs with the perversity that seems so pervasive that it could not derive from his governance or even from a hireling of his (*Ord.* 1). Augustine nonetheless stressed the gubernatorial and administrative role of providence as it pilots the church and the entire City of God (*Civ. Dei* 15.27).

[T.H.]

Bibliography

John Chrysostom, *No One Can Harm the Man Who Does Not Injure Himself,* tr. W.R. Stephens, NPNF, 1st ser. (1889), Vol. 9; Theodoret of Cyrus, *On Divine Providence,* tr. T. Halton, ACW (1988), Vol. 49; Augustine, *Divine Providence,* tr. R.P. Russell, FOTC (1948), Vol. 5; Salvian, *The Governance of God,* tr. J.F. O'Sullivan, FOTC (1947), Vol. 3.

J. and P.G. Walsh, *Divine Providence and Human Suffering* (Wilmington: Glazier, 1985).

PRUDENTIUS (ca. 348–after 405). Christian Latin poet. Knowledge of Prudentius's life is based mostly on his writings. Born in Spain, he practiced law and had a successful career as a civil administrator, finally holding a position at the imperial court. Thereafter, he resolved to devote himself to Christian poetry. He published most of his writings in a collection when he was fifty-seven (405) and probably did not live much longer.

His *Hymns for Every Day* comprises twelve poems, six for use at various hours of the day and six occasional pieces. *The Divinity of Christ* treats the nature of Christ and errors concerning it. *The Origin of Sin* is directed against the teachings of Marcion. *The Spiritual Combat* is a work of asceticism presented in the form of an allegory of combat between virtues and vices; its conclusion is based on the Book of Revelation.

Against Symmachus, in two books, is directed to the controversy that arose over the removal of the altar of Victory from the Roman senate house (382). Prudentius's arguments resemble those made by Ambrose. Notable is the vision of the empire as a single people; the work closes with an appeal to the emperor Honorius against gladiatorial combats. The

Martyrs' Crowns consists of fourteen hymns, each devoted to a martyr; most of those honored are Spanish or Italian. Half of the work was composed before a journey to Rome (ca. 401–403), the rest during the trip or upon the return. The *Twofold Nourishment,* or *Scenes from Sacred History,* is a series of short verses, each of four lines, on forty-nine scenes from scripture, evidently composed to accompany paintings; the pieces belong as much to the history of early Christian art as to poetry.

Prudentius's writings exhibit a good knowledge of such classical poets as Lucretius, Horace, and Juvenal, but above all of Virgil. Hymns from *The Martyrs' Crowns* and *Hymns for Every Day* were incorporated into the breviary of the Mozarabic rite. *The Spiritual Combat* developed a theme influential in medieval Latin poetry. Although Prudentius's reputation declined after the Renaissance, it has undergone a vigorous revival in the light of recent scholarship. CPL 1437–1446.   [M.P.McH.]

Bibliography

Aurelius Prudentius Clemens, Carmina, ed. M.P. Cunningham, CCSL (1966), Vol. 126.

Prudentius, tr. H.J. Thomson, 2 vols., LCL (Vol. 1—1949, 1961; Vol. 2—1953, 1961); *The Poems of Prudentius,* tr. M. Clement Eagen, 2 vols., FOTC (1962, 1965), Vols. 43, 52.

B.M. Peebles, *The Poet Prudentius* (New York: McMullen, 1951); R.E. Messenger, "Aurelius Prudentius Clemens: A Biographical Study," *Leaders of Iberian Christianity 50–650 A.D.,* ed. J.M.-F. Marique (Boston: St. Paul, 1962), pp. 81–102; J. Fontaine, *Naissance de la poésie dans l'occident chrétien: esquisse d'une histoire de la poésie latine chrétienne du IIIe au VIe siècle* (Paris: Etudes Augustiniennes, 1981); T.P. Halton and R.D. Sider, "A Decade of Patristic Scholarship 1970–1979," *CW* 76 (1982–1983):358–360 (bibliography); J. Harries, "Prudentius and Theodosius," *Latomus* 43 (1984): 69–84; A.-M. Palmer, *Prudentius on the Martyrs* (Oxford: Clarendon, 1989).

PSALMS. Biblical book. The Psalms are a collection of Hebrew religious poetry composed over several centuries, from the early monarchy (tenth century B.C.) to the postexilic period (fifth or fourth century B.C.). The largest number are attributed to David, but many are assigned to other authors, and many are anonymous. The canonical collection of 150

Psalms was compiled from earlier collections and was divided into five books: Psalms 1–41, 42–72, 73–89, 90–106, 107–150.

The numbering of the Psalms is different in the Hebrew (followed by the English) and the Greek (followed by the Latin and other ancient versions). Psalms 9 and 10 of the Hebrew are one Psalm in the Greek, so the Greek remains one number behind the Hebrew up to Psalm 114. Psalms 114 and 115 (Hebrew) are combined in the Greek, but Psalm 116 of the Hebrew is divided into two in the Greek, so the Greek is once more one number behind the Hebrew up to Psalm 147, which the Greek divides into two. The result is that only the first eight and the last three Psalms have the same number in the Hebrew and in the Greek.

The headings that accompany many of the Psalms do not appear in most cases to have been original, and their value varies. These headings offer some historical information, such as the names of authors or circumstances of writing, but especially musical directions, such as the type of Psalm, the occasion for use, and instructions about performance. Patristic commentators drew upon them for their interpretation of the Psalms (e.g., Gregory of Nyssa, *Inscrip. Psal.*).

Hebrew poetry achieved rhythm by stress on important words, not by the number of syllables. Its most distinguishing feature is the use of parallelism, a balancing of thought in consecutive lines. The principal types of parallelism are synonymous (the same thought repeated in similar words), antithetic (the thought in one line contrasted with the next), synthetic or climactic (a second or even third line built on and advancing the thought of the first), and chiastic (a parallelism of first and fourth lines and second and third lines).

The many types of Psalms—hymns of praise, songs of thanksgiving, laments both individual and communal, royal Psalms, wisdom Psalms—reflect a wide variety of emotions as well as occasions in personal and community life. It has been common since the patristic commentaries to see the Psalms as reflecting all human moods and containing words suitable for all religious needs.

The Jews continued to produce religious poetry of the same type. A 151st Psalm has long been known from the Septuagint. In more recent years, the Dead Sea Scrolls have yielded manuscripts of the Psalms containing other noncanonical Hebrew Psalms; the Qumran Psalter indicates either a stage in the transmission of the Psalms before the final determination of the canon or the continued writing of Psalm-type pieces (cf. the *Thanksgiving Hymns* also from Qumran). Although the word "Psalms" referred especially to the biblical collection, it could also be used for hymns of the same type, as in the pseudepigraphical *Psalms of Solomon* from the first century B.C.

Jewish usage as reflected in the headings of the Psalms in the Septuagint and in the *Psalms of Solomon* does not permit a clear differentiation among "psalms, hymns, and spiritual songs [odes]" (Eph. 5:19; Col. 3:16). The later church fathers gave etymological distinctions among these terms as a basis for allegorical interpretation. Since the Greek *psalmos* originally referred to the sound made by plucking on the strings of an instrument and so could be understood as referring to physical activity, the church fathers gave a higher evaluation to odes and hymns as representing an intellectual or spiritual activity (Didymus, *Exp. in Ps.* 4; Ps.-Hippolytus in PG 10.717B–C; John Chrysostom, *Hom.* 9 *in Col.* 3.13). This interpretation was only theoretical, in order to teach the need for both contemplation and good deeds, and there is no evidence that it corresponded to any actual depreciation of psalmody in the practice of the church.

The musical notations accompanying them have led to the description of the Psalms as the "hymn book" of the postexilic Jewish temple. From the temple, the Psalms passed into the Jewish synagogue, and from there into the early church.

Psalms is the most-quoted Old Testament book in the New Testament, and it has continued to be popular in Christian usage. The Psalms were interspersed with the scripture readings in the synaxis (or liturgy of the word) and were employed in connection with the eucharist. Patristic references to the singing of the Psalms in the Sunday assembly are numerous (Tertullian, *Anim.* 9; Eusebius, *H.E.* 10.3.3; Cyril of Jerusalem, *Catech.* 23.20; *Const. app.* 2.57.6; Ambrose, *Ps.* 1, *Exp.* 9; John Chrysostom, *Hom.* 36.9 *in 1 Cor.* 14.33; idem, *Hom. in Ps.* 145). There were efforts, finally unsuccessful, to limit what was sung in church to the biblical Psalms and odes (Laodicea, *can.* 59; *Can. Basil.* 97). The Psalms were also used in the daily office (*Itin. Ether.* 4; 21; 24; John Cassian, *Inst.* 2.4–5), at baptism (Cyril of Jerusalem, *Procatech.* 15), the agape (Tertullian, *Apol.* 39.18), at funerals (*Const. app.* 6.30; Gregory of Nyssa, *V. Macr.*), and on other occasions, as well as in private devotions. The Psalms had great use in monastic circles. Their popularity with ordinary Christians is shown by their use, especially Psalm 90, in phylacteries. Many of the church fathers wrote commentaries on the Psalms or preached homilies on them. Some of Origen's comments have been preserved, and he seems to have been particularly influential on later spiritual interpretations of the Psalms.

Christian interpretation related the Psalms to Christ, either as Christ speaking through the Psalms (already in the New Testament—Heb. 2:12) or Christ as the one spoken about (e.g., the frequent New Testament use of Psalm 22 in connection with the passion and Psalms 2 and 110 in connection with the Sonship and priesthood of Christ). Athanasius's *Epistle to Marcellinus, On the Interpretation of the Psalms* provides a good introduction to the Christian use of the Psalms—liturgical, devotional, Christological, and doctrinal. Athanasius justified the use of melody or chant in the recitation of the Psalms as symbolizing the harmony within the soul and as elevating one's soul above earthly distractions to higher things. *See also* Hymns; Music; Office, Divine; Vision of Paul. [E.F.]

Bibliography

Athanasius, Epistle to Marcellinus, tr. E. Ferguson, *Ekklesiastikos Pharos* 60 (1978):378–403, and R. Gregg, *Athanasius: The Life of Antony and the Letter to Marcellinus*, CWS (1980); Eusebius, *Commentarius in Psalmos*, PG 23; Asterius, *Homiliae in Psalmos*, ed., M. Richard, *Asterii Sophistae* (Oslo, 1956); Didymus the Blind, *Expositio in Psalmos*, ed., L.

Doutreleau, A. Gesché, and M. Gronewald, *Didymos der Blinde, Psalmenkommentar 1–4* (Bonn, 1968–1970); Theodore of Mopsuestia, *Commentarii in Psalmos*, ed., R. Devreesse, *Le Commentaire de Théodore de Mopsueste sur les Psaumes* (Vatican City, 1939); John Chrysostom, *Homilia in Psalmos*, PG 55; Hilary, *Commentary on the Psalms*, tr. W. Sanday, NPNF, 2nd ser. (1895), Vol. 9; Ambrose, *Enarrationes in XII Psalmos*, ed., M. Petschenig, CSEL (1919), Vol. 64; Augustine, *Expositions on the Psalms*, tr. S. Hebgin and F. Corrigan, ACW (1960), pp. 29–30; Jerome, *Homilies on the Psalms*, tr. M.L. Ewald, FOTC (1964, 1967), Vols. 48, 57; Cassiodorus, *Expositio Psalmorum*, ed. M. Adriaen, CCSL (1958), Vols. 97–98.

On the biblical book: S. Mowinckel, *The Psalms in Israel's Worship*, 2 vols. (Oxford: Blackwell, 1962); H. Guthrie, *Israel's Sacred Songs* (New York: Seabury, 1966); M. Dahood, *Psalms*, 3 vols. (Garden City: Doubleday, 1966); C.F. Barth, *Introduction to the Psalms* (New York: Scribner, 1966); J.A. Sanders, *The Dead Sea Psalms Scroll* (Ithaca: Cornell UP, 1967); E. Werner, *The Sacred Bridge* (New York: KTAV, 1984), Vol. 2, pp. 51–107.

On Christian usage: J.A. Lamb, *The Psalms in Christian Worship* (London: Faith, 1962); R. Devreesse, *Les Anciens commentateurs grecs des Psaumes* (Vatican City: Biblioteca Apostolica Vaticana, 1970); E. Mühlenberg, *Psalmenkommentare aus der Katenenüberlieferung I–III* (Berlin: de Gruyter, 1975–1978); M.-J. Rondeau, *Les Commentaires patristiques du Psautier*, 2 vols. (Rome: Pontificum Istitium Studiorum Orientalium, 1982, 1985); E. Ferguson, "The Active and Contemplative Lives: The Patristic Interpretation of Some Musical Terms," and idem, "Athanasius' 'Epistola ad Marcellinum in interpretationem Psalmorum,'" *SP* 16.2 (1985):15–23, 295–308.

PSEUDEPIGRAPHY. False attribution of a writing to another person. A falsely ascribed writing is called a "pseudepigraphon" (plural "pseudepigrapha"). Both terms derive from the Greek *pseudepigraphos* ("false superscription"). In reference to the New Testament and early Christian literature, "pseudepigrapha" indicates works ascribed to an author other than the real one. In reference to the Old Testament, pseudepigrapha denotes Jewish literature not in the Old Testament but often considered sacred in many early Jewish and Christian communities.

In the late second century A.D., Serapion of Antioch used *ta pseudepigrapha* (Eusebius, *H.E.* 6.12) to brand documents he considered falsely credited to a New Testament author. In antiquity, attempts were made to reject literary forgeries; Galen wrote *On His Own Books* to separate his genuine compositions from false attributions. Classical scholars today use the terms "pseudepigraphy" or "pseudepigrapha" to describe writings incorrectly attributed to thinkers like Anacharsis, Apollonius, Crates, Diogenes, Heraclitus, Plato, Pythagoras, Socrates, and Xenophon. Biblical scholars use "pseudepigrapha" to denote a large number of texts improperly attributed originally or subsequently to a person mentioned in the Christian Bible or to an author of one of the biblical books. Scholars judge only the attributions to be "false"; the writings themselves are invaluable for clarifying the complexities and diversities in both early Judaism—as with *1 Enoch*, a collection of books written from 250 B.C. to ca. A.D. 70 but ascribed to the antediluvian sage—and early Christianity—as with the *Odes of Solomon*, a collection of hymns composed probably by a convert from Judaism to Christianity, perhaps in the early second century.

"Pseudepigraphy" covers a wide range of writings, extending from what may be partly authentic to what is clearly spurious. Some biblical books, such as the Psalms of David and Proverbs of Solomon, or sections of them, such as Isaiah 24–27, 2 Corinthians 6:14–7:1, and the speeches by Peter, Stephen, and Paul in Acts, are pseudepigraphical, but scholars use other terms to describe them (one reason being that canonical, and most extracanonical, pseudepigrapha are categorically different from ancient forgeries). "Pseudepigraphy" in early Christianity can be studied in seven interrelated literary categories (the examples are selective according to widely held views of New Testament scholars): (1) works not by an author but probably containing some of his own thoughts (Ephesians and probably Colossians); (2) documents by someone who was influenced by another person to whom the work is ascribed (1 Peter and maybe James); (3) compositions influenced by earlier works of an author to whom they are assigned (1 Timothy, 2 Timothy, Titus); (4) Gospels (eventually) attributed to an apostle but deriving from later circles or

schools of learned individuals (Matthew and John); (5) Christian writings attributed by their authors to an Old Testament personality (*Testament of Adam, Odes of Solomon, Apocalypse of Elijah, Ascension of Isaiah*); (6) once-anonymous works now correctly (perhaps Mark, Luke, and Acts) or incorrectly credited to someone (some manuscripts attribute Hebrews to Paul); (7) compositions that intentionally try to deceive the reader into thinking the author is someone famous (2 Peter).

Pseudepigraphy must not be equated with literary forgery, since many pseudepigrapha were not intended to deceive the reader. Many early Christians considered it proper to attribute thoughts or documents to someone who had inspired them; they employed no footnotes to hide the fact that almost all thoughts are derivative. Iamblichus (ca. 245–ca. 330) even argued that honor often demanded attributing one's own work to Pythagoras.

By at least the year 120, pseudepigraphy was the norm for writing in many Christian groups. Some of the canonical works are authentic (Romans, 1 and 2 Corinthians, Galatians, Philippians, 1 Thessalonians, Philemon, Revelation). Others are anonymous (Mark, Luke, Acts, Hebrews). Most, according to current scholarship, are ultimately pseudonymous or incorrectly attributed to someone (Matthew, John, 1 and 2 Peter, James, Jude, 1, 2, and 3 John, 1 and 2 Timothy, Titus, Ephesians, and probably Colossians and 2 Thessalonians). Of the twenty-seven documents in the New Testament canon, fifteen are now judged by many to result from pseudepigraphy. These writings, however, enjoyed widespread acceptance in early Christian groups, among whom they were *not* in fact considered pseudepigraphical.

Paul was the author to whom most documents later considered canonical were falsely credited. Outside the canon, some other works were incorrectly attributed to Paul (written as if composed by him or claiming to contain authentic data about him): *3 Corinthians, Epistle to the Alexandrians, Epistle to the Laodiceans, Correspondence Between Seneca and Paul, Apocalypse of Paul, Vision of Paul, Martyrdom of Paul, Passions of Peter and Paul*, and the

Acts of Paul, whose author, when discovered, confessed that he had written only out of "love for" the apostle (cf. Tertullian, *Bapt.* 17). Numerous documents were also falsely attributed to Peter, namely the *Apocalypse of Peter*, *Gospel of Peter*, *Preaching of Peter*, *Acts of Peter*, *Acts of Andrew and Peter*, and *Martyrdom of Peter*. Beginning around the middle of the second century, the interest in Jesus' mother gave rise to many pseudepigrapha, notably *Birth of Mary*, *Gospel of the Birth of Mary*, *Passing of Mary*, *Questions of Mary*, *Apocalypse of the Virgin*, *Assumption of the Virgin*, and the Coptic *Lives of the Virgin*.

Early biblical exegesis in Christian circles frequently took the form of pseudepigraphy. Dogma, curiosity, apologetics, and especially the need to fill in gaps in the history of the drama of salvation gave rise to legends, storytelling, and pseudepigraphy. It is worthy of note that the *Apostolic Constitutions* warn against pseudepigraphical works; but this text itself must be categorized as pseudepigraphy.

To conclude that a work is "pseudepigraphical" depends on the perspective of the judge, in both antiquity and modernity. No clear distinction separates, for example, Paul's own writings from Pauline pseudepigrapha; scholars are divided regarding the Pauline authorship of 2 Thessalonians and Colossians. No formula can be used to prove an attribution. Each work must be carefully studied in terms of its own form, content, and function. Judgments will certainly vary and are often inchoate. Specialists take the following into consideration: (1) reflections of social and ecclesiastical conditions atypical of the alleged person's own time (Matthew, John, 1 and 2 Peter, 1, 2, and 3 John, Pastoral Epistles); (2) contradictions of a putative author's thought, especially in ecclesiology (Colossians), eschatology (2 Thessalonians, Titus), and the concept of faith (Pastoral Epistles); (3) a description that cannot be a self-portrait by the alleged author (2 Timothy, Colossians 1:24–25); (4) a perception or depiction of others, especially rivals, that is uncharacteristic of the alleged author (Jude, Pastoral Epistles); (5) appreciable differences between the alleged author's own intentions and the actual writer's purpose; (6) contrasting linguistic styles (Ephesians), absence of key terms or concerns (Colossians and Ephesians do not contain some of Paul's major theological ideas and omit customary attempts to finance his mission), and appearance of *hapax legomena*, or unique vocabulary (Ephesians, Hebrews, Pastoral Epistles); (7) the alteration of an alleged author's use of terms, like "hope" (Colossians); (8) a means of argumentation or rhetoric unlike that used by the alleged author (Pastoral Epistles); (9) literary dependence on a document that postdates a historical person (2 Peter is influenced by Jude and 1 Peter); and (10) general alignment with the development of thought subsequent to the time of the alleged author (1, 2, and 3 John, Pastoral Epistles).

Pseudonymity is not anonymity. A pseudepigraphon must be related in some way, perhaps through a "school," to a recognizable person. Pseudepigraphy must not be studied through the attempt to remove anonymity but through the links that connect the writing with the honored historical or legendary individual to whom it is attributed. One must always ask the question, "*Why* did the author write pseudepigraphically?" Some of the works were produced by learned and gifted scholars; many of them are essential reading for a balanced view of Christian origins. *See also* Apocrypha, New Testament; Apocrypha, Old Testament.

[J.H.C.]

Bibliography

E.J. Goodspeed, "Pseudonymity and Pseudepigraphy in Early Christian Literature," *New Chapters in New Testament Study* (New York: Macmillan, 1937), pp. 169–188; K. Aland, "The Problem of Anonymity and Pseudonymity in Christian Literature of the First Two Centuries," *The Authorship and Integrity of the New Testament* (London: SPCK, 1965), pp. 1–13; D. Guthrie, "Acts and Epistles in Aprocryphal Writings," *Apostolic History and the Gospel*, ed. W. Ward Gasque and R.P. Martin (Grand Rapids: Eerdmans, 1970), pp. 328–345; W. Speyer, *Die literarische Falschung im heidnischen und christlichen Altertum: Ein Versuch ihrer Deutung* (Munich: Beck, 1971); B.M. Metzger, "Literary Forgeries and Canonical Pseudepigrapha," *JBL* 91 (1972):3–24; M. Rist, "Pseudepigraphy and the Early Christians," *Studies in New Testament and Early Christian Literature: Essays in Honor of Allen P. Wikgren*, ed. D.E. Aune

(Leiden: Brill, 1972), pp. 75–91; N. Brox, *Falsche Verfasserangaben: Zur Erklärung der frühchristlichen Pseudepigraphie* (Stuttgart: KBW, 1975); J.H. Charlesworth, *The Old Testament Pseudepigrapha*, 2 vols. (Garden City: Doubleday, 1983, 1985); L.R. Donelson, *Pseudepigraphy and Ethical Argument in the Pastoral Epistles* (Tübingen: Mohr-Siebeck, 1986); M. Kiley, *Colossians as Pseudepigraphy* (Sheffield: JSOT, 1986); D.G. Meade, *Pseudonymity and Canon: An Investigation into the Relationship of Authority and Authority in Jewish and Earliest Christian Tradition* (Tübingen: Mohr-Siebeck, 1986; Grand Rapids: Eerdmans, 1987); J.H. Charlesworth and J.R. Mueller, *The New Testament Apocrypha and Pseudepigrapha: A Guide to Publications with Excursuses on Apocalypses* (Metuchen: Scarecrow, 1987).

PSEUDO-CLEMENTINES. Specific set of pseudonymous works bearing the name of Clement of Rome (late first century); the term only secondarily refers to other anonymous or pseudonymous writings associated with Clement. Running through the *Pseudo-Clementines* is an entertaining story of Clement's conversion to Christianity, travels with Peter, and recovery of his family, which had been scattered by a series of misfortunes.

The main constituents of the *Pseudo-Clementines* are the *Homilies* and the *Recognitions*, both of which originated in fourth-century Syria. A letter of Peter to James (*Epistula Petri*), an account of James's response (*Contestatio*), and a letter of Clement to James (*Epistula Clementis*) precede the *Homilies* in the extant copies. The other texts are mostly abridgments of these writings. Although two fairly late Greek manuscripts have preserved the *Homilies* in their original language, the *Recognitions* have survived, apart from small fragments, only in Latin and Syriac translations. Since the *Homilies* and the *Recognitions* share much material and often agree word for word with each other, especially in the details of Clement's life history, some sort of literary dependency is obviously involved. Nineteenth-century scholars disagreed over whether the *Homilies* were dependent on the *Recognitions* or vice versa; in the twentieth century, the prevailing view is that both derive from an earlier work, called the "basic writing," or

Grundschrift. It is disputed whether fragments of the basic writing may be salvaged from certain citations by early Christian writers.

The *Pseudo-Clementines* are significant as the first full-scale Christian adoption of the literary genre of the novel. The motif of "recognitions," in which individuals recognize members of their long-lost family, is used to illustrate how Christian faith leads to the resolution of difficulties in life. The *Pseudo-Clementines* are of even greater significance for yet another reason: the long discourses of Peter quoted in the works present a version of Christianity more Jewish than the form that gained dominance in the early church. Particularly because certain passages are also vehemently anti-Pauline (*Hom.* 17.13–19; *Recogn.* 1.70–71; *Ep. Petr.* 2), many scholars since F.C. Baur in the early nineteenth century have viewed the *Pseudo-Clementines* as one of the few surviving witnesses to a widespread early Jewish Christianity and not just as an expression of late Judaizing tendencies.

Because traces of the fourth-century Arian debate reveal the two existing renditions of the *Pseudo-Clementines* to be of much later date than Baur thought, scholars have postulated various sources to account for the Jewish Christian elements as well as other material. The Jewish Christian passages have often been assigned to a source called the *Kerygmata Petrou* (*Preachings of Peter*), but the existence of this writing is far from certain. A Hellenistic Jewish Christian source more likely stands behind large portions of *Recognitions* 1.27–71, which is an arresting survey of salvation history from creation to the seventh year after Jesus' crucifixion. Passages relating to Greek mythology and theology (partially Orphic) preserve details not found elsewhere, some of which seem to derive from handbooks. The suspicion that the novel of recognitions was adopted *en bloc* from an earlier work is unfounded; the author probably just pieced together various motifs into a new romance. To assume one particular source for the unusual sayings of Jesus is also unwarranted.

In their Latin version, the *Pseudo-Clementines* had a considerable impact on western literature. The figure of Faust, for example, is modeled on the Pseudo-Clementine Simon Magus. CPG I, 1015. TLG 1271.003–009, 011–012.   [F.S.J.]

Bibliography
B. Rehm, ed., *Die Pseudoklementinen I: Homilien*, prepared for the press by J. Irmscher, rev. by F. Paschke, GCS (1969), Vol. 42, 2nd ed., rev.; W. Frankenberg, ed., *Die syrischen Clementinen mit griechischem Paralleltext: Eine Vorarbeit zu dem literargeschichtlichen Problem der Sammlung*, TU (1937), Vol. 48.3; B. Rehm, ed., *Die Pseudoklementinen II: Rekognitionen in Rufins Übersetzung*, prepared for the press by F. Paschke, GCS (1965), Vol. 51; G. Strecker, *Die Pseudoklementinen III–IV: Konkordanz zu den Pseudoklementinen*, GCS (1986–1990).

T. Smith, tr., "Pseudo-Clementine Literature," ANF (1886), Vol. 8, pp. 67–346; G. Strecker, tr., "The Kerygmata Petrou," and J. Irmscher, tr., "The Pseudo-Clementines," NTA, Vol. 2, pp. 102–127, 532–570.

E.C. Richardson, "Faust and the Clementine Recognitions," *Papers of the American Society of the Church History* 6 (1894):133–145; F.J.A. Hort, *Notes Introductory to the Study of the Clementine Recognitions: A Course of Lectures* (London: Macmillan, 1901); H. Waitz, *Die Pseudoklementinen, Homilien und Rekognitionen: Eine quellenkritische Untersuchung*, TU, n.s., 10.4 (1904); B. Rehm, "Zur Entstehung der pseudoclementinischen Schriften," *ZNTW* 37 (1938):77–184; L.L. Kline, *The Sayings of Jesus in the Pseudo-Clementine Homilies* (Missoula: Scholars 1975); G. Strecker, *Das Judenchristentum in den Pseudoklementinen*, TU (1981), Vol. 70, 2nd ed., rev.; F.S. Jones, "The Pseudo-Clementines: A History of Research," *SCent* 2 (1982):1–33, 63–96.

PTOLEMY (second century). Gnostic teacher; prominent adherent of Valentinus in Italy. Ptolemy's *Letter to Flora*, preserved in the writings of Epiphanius of Salamis (*Haer.* 33.3–7), concerns the value of the Mosaic Law, the precepts of which are divided into three parts: the first coming from God, the second from Moses' own speculations, and the third from the Jewish elders. Yet since the Law is itself imperfect, it cannot have come from the perfect God, but must have been given by the demiurge, the creator of the present world, who occupies a middle position between the perfect God and the devil. The work is important as a representative of extant Gnostic literature and as an effort to place the interpretation of scripture on a scientific basis.

Little is known of Ptolemy's life. He may have been the Christian teacher who, according to Justin Martyr (*2 Apol.* 2.1–9), suffered as a martyr on the accusation of an aggrieved husband who was attempting to retain his wife's dowry. At least, the justification of divorce in the *Letter to Flora* appears appropriate to Justin's story. CPG I, 1135. TLG 1641. *See also* Gnosticism.   [M.P.McH.]

Bibliography
Justin Martyr, *2 Apology* 2.1–9 (= Eusebius, *Church History* 4.17); Irenaeus, *Against Heresies* 1.1.1–8.5; Epiphanius, *Panarion* 33.3–7.

G. Quispel, ed., *Ptolémée, Letter à Flora*, SC (1949, 1966), Vol. 24.

W. Foerster and R.McL. Wilson, *Gnosis: A Selection of Gnostic Texts* (Oxford: Clarendon, 1972), Vol. 1, pp. 121–161.

R.M. Grant, "A Woman of Rome: The Matron in Justin, 2 Apology 2.1–9," *ChHist* 54 (1985):461–472.

PULCHERIA (399–453). Daughter of the eastern Roman emperor Arcadius (395–408) and older sister of the emperor Theodosius II (408–450). Entrusted by the senate in Constantinople with the education and guardianship of her brother, Pulcheria was declared Augusta in 414 and virtually ran the affairs of the empire. Her influence was eclipsed by that of the eunuch Chrysaphius after 439, but on the death of Theodosius II in 450 she became empress and took as her consort the general Marcian. Learned and vigorous, she was known for her piety, asceticism, and orthodoxy. She arranged to have the bones of John Chrysostom returned to Constantinople, opposed Nestorianism, and arranged for the Council of Chalcedon in 451. Feast day September 10. *See also* Marcian.   [E.F.]

Bibliography
Sozomen, *Church History* 9.1–2; Leo the Great, *Letters* 31; 45; 58; 61; 70; 74; 77; 94; 95; Theodoret, *Letter* 43.

K.G. Holum, *Theodosian Empresses: Women and Imperial Domination in Late Antiquity* (Berkeley: U of California P, 1982).

PURGATORY. Place or state, intermediate between heaven and hell, where after death and prior to final judgment certain souls are purged of their remaining minor (venial) sins through penal suffering and so attain salvation. The Latin noun *purgatorium*, as distinct from the adjective *purgatorius*, does not occur before the twelfth century, nor does the idea itself in its full and characteristic form (and then only in Latin or western Christianity). Several of the elements that would contribute to the notion of purgatory did, however, begin to take shape in early Christianity.

The traditions of Jewish (e.g., *1 Enoch*; *4 Ezra*) and Christian (e.g., *Apoc. Petr.*, *Vis. Paul.*) apocalyptic gave birth to an imagined geography of the otherworld. Various groups of the righteous and especially of the unrighteous were assigned to different regions either of rest and refreshment or of pain and torment, thus producing a vivid topography of heaven and hell correlated with the moral goodness or evil shown by persons prior to death (cf., e.g., Gregory the Great, *Dial.* 4.36). Such descriptions delineated the setting in which purgatory would appear as a place of temporary punishment for souls immediately assigned neither to heaven nor to hell; they also supplied much of the imagery of torment that would characterize purgatorial suffering. Most important, they introduced a more highly differentiated classification of human beings by moral status than mere division into the saved and the damned.

Intermittently, too, early Christianity intimated that a person's fate may not be settled at death (only to be confirmed and enforced at the last judgment) and pictured divine punishment as a purifying fire (cf. Isa. 66:15–16; Mal. 3:2–3; 1 Cor. 3:11–15), purgative rather than punitive in force. Clement of Alexandria mentions instructive as well as punitive correction and speaks of a discerning fire that penetrates the soul (*Str.* 4.26; 6.6; 7.6); Origen sketches an entire theory of punishment as purification (e.g., *Princ.* 2.10.4–8). In particular, using imagery from 1 Corinthians 3:11–15 and Ezekiel 22:18, Origen distinguished the righteous (works in gold, silver, precious stones); those guilty only of lesser sins (wood, hay, stubble);

and the evil (iron, lead, bronze) (cf. *Princ.* 2.10.4; *Cels.* 4.13; 5.15; 6.70; *Hom.* 15 in *Lev.* 3). The first group passes unscathed through the purifying fire; the second is quickly purged; the third requires a lengthy and painful purgation and purification. Origen never clearly separated purgation from final judgment, however; and the early church finally rejected his claim that ultimately all (even the demons) would be purged and saved. It was Augustine (and the Latin tradition), not Origen, who shaped the view that would endure.

Augustine interpreted 1 Corinthians 3:11–15 in Origen's manner but construed the three groups quite differently. The first consists of the saved, the third of the damned; only the middle group—who have made Christ their foundation but remain attached to earthly things in lesser ways—may be purified in a process that, begun in this life, may also extend beyond death (*Enchir.* 67–69; *Civ. Dei* 21.26). Augustine explicitly opposes the idea that all or even many can be saved through postmortem purification (*Civ. Dei* 21.13–25); his view represents a distinct narrowing of the theory of purgative punishment. It does, however, establish three critical points: some people can be assigned at death neither directly to the saved nor directly to the damned (a threefold, not a twofold, moral classification); these people are guilty of lesser sins ("minor" rather than "capital" sins; cf. Caesarius of Arles, *Serm.* 179), which alone are subject to postmortem purification; and so, for these people at least, death does not settle ultimate destiny. It is in this context, then, that belief in a cleansing fire after death can be affirmed (Gregory the Great, *Dial.* 4.41).

Finally, early Christianity contributed to the later idea of purgatory the sense that the interventions of the living—in the eucharist, in prayer, in almsgiving—can relieve or reduce the sufferings of the dead. This sense lay behind the universal early Christian practice of prayer for the dead in the liturgy. But it also produced vivid stories in which the dead were actually "seen," through visions or appearances, to be helped (e.g., *Pass. Perp.* 7–8; Gregory the Great, *Dial.* 4.42); and it was formulated abstractly in the claim that the souls of the dead, if properly prepared in life, benefit from the aid offered by friends and relatives among the living (Augustine, *Cur. mort.* 18; *Enchir.* 110). If in some contexts Christianity tended to shatter the bonds of kinship and friendship (cf., e.g., Matt. 10:35–37; *Pass. Perp.* 3), here it cemented them and so prepared the way for the medieval pattern of interventions designed to alleviate the suffering of souls in purgatory. *See also* Hades; Heaven; Hell. [W.S.B.]

Bibliography

Passion of Perpetua and Felicitas; Vision of Paul; Origen, *On First Principles* 2.10.4–8; idem, *Against Celsus* 4.13; 5.15; 6.70; Augustine, *Enchiridion* 67–69, 110; idem, *City of God* 21.13–26; idem, *The Care to Be Taken for the Dead;* Caesarius of Arles, *Sermon* 179; Gregory the Great, *Dialogues* 4.

G. Anrich, "Clemens und Origines als Begründer der Lehre vom Fegfeuer," *Theologische Abhandlungen, Festgabe für H.J. Holtzmann,* ed. W. Nowack et al. (Tübingen: Mohr-Siebeck, 1902), pp. 95–120; A. Landgraf, "I Kor. 3, 10–17 bei den lateinischen Vätern und in der Frühscholastik," *Biblica* 5 (1924):140–172; T. Silverstein, *Visio Sancti Pauli: The History of the Apocalypse in Latin, Together with Nine Texts* (London: Christophers, 1935); A. Michel, "Purgatoire," DTC (1936), Vol. 13, cols. 1163–1326; C.M. Edsman, *Ignis Divinus: le feu comme moyen de rejeunissement et d'immortalité: contes, légendes, mythes et rites* (Lund: Gleerup, 1949); J. Gnilka, *Ist 1 Kor. 3, 10–15 ein Schriftzeugnis für das Fegfeuer? Eine exegetischhistorische Untersuchung* (Dusseldorf: Triltsch, 1955); P. Jay, "Le Purgatoire dans la prédication de saint Césaire d'Arles," *RecTh* 24 (1957):5–14; N. Konde, *L'Evolution de la doctrine du purgatoire chez saint Augustin* (Paris: Etudes Augustiniennes, 1966); C. Dagens, *St. Grégoire le Grand: culture et expérience chrétiennes* (Paris: Etudes Augustiniennes, 1977); J. Le Goff, *The Birth of Purgatory* (Chicago: U of Chicago P, 1984); R.R. Atwell, "From Augustine to Gregory the Great: An Evaluation of the Emergence of the Doctrine of Purgatory," *JEH* 38 (1987):173–186.

Q

QUADRATUS (second century). Probably the earliest Christian apologist. According to Eusebius, who preserves the only known fragment of this work, Quadratus wrote (ca. 120–130) in Asia Minor an apology to the Roman emperor Hadrian (117–138). The fragment comments on the continuing testimony of persons healed and raised from the dead by Jesus, some of whom Quadratus claimed to have known. This Quadratus is not the bishop of Athens (late second century) mentioned by Jerome. Feast day May 26. CPG I, 1060. TLG 1652.   [D.M.S.]

Bibliography
Eusebius, *Church History* 4.3.1–2; Jerome, *Lives of Illustrious Men* 19; idem, *Letter* 70.4.

QUASTEN, JOHANNES (1900–1987). German patristic scholar. Educated at the Gymnasium, Moers, and in the University of Münster, where he studied under F.J. Dölger, Quasten in 1930 published his dissertation, *Musik und Gesang in den Kulten der heidnischen Antike und christlichen Frühzeit* (English tr. Washington, D.C.: National Association of Pastoral Musicians, 1983). Quasten did extensive archaeological work in Rome, Sicily, Yugoslavia, and North Africa. After the Nazis revoked his *licentia docendi* at Münster in 1937, he became professor of patristics at the Catholic University of America in 1938. He founded the important series Ancient Christian Writers and Studies in Christian Antiquity. In 1950, he published the first volume of his *Patrology* (Utrecht: Spectrum; Westminster: Newman), followed in 1953 and 1960 by Volumes 2 and 3. Just before his death, a fourth volume appeared in English translation from the faculty of the Institutum Patristicum, Rome.   [T.H.]

Bibliography
P. Granfield and J.A. Jungmann, eds., *Kyriakon: Festschrift Johannes Quasten,* 2 vols. (Münster: Aschendorff, 1970), Vol. 2, pp. 924–938.

QUODVULTDEUS (d. ca. 453). Bishop and writer. As a deacon of the church of Carthage, Quodvultdeus sent two letters to Augustine (*Ep.* 221 and 223 among the works of the latter) requesting a compilation of heresies; Augustine responded with his work *De haeresibus* (428–429), left incomplete at his death. Quodvultdeus became bishop of Carthage ca. 437 but was expelled from the see upon the capture of the city by Gaiseric two years later;

he died in exile at Naples. Besides the letters to Augustine, the *De promissionibus et prae-dictionibus Dei,* long attributed to Prosper of Aquitaine, is the work of Quodvultdeus. A source for the African catechesis of baptism, it exhibits quotations from the classical poets, Virgil especially, taken in a Christian sense. Quodvultdeus is also the author of a number of homilies, some having to do with baptism and others concerning the spread of Arianism. CPL 262, 401–417, addenda 401–412, 413.

[M.P.McH.]

Bibliography

Opera Quodvultdeo Carthaginiensi Episcopo Trib-uta, ed. R. Braun, CCSL (1976), Vol. 60.

R

RABBULA (d. 435). Bishop of Edessa (411/2–435). Born in Chalcis of a pagan father and Christian mother, Rabbula converted to Christianity ca. 400 and soon turned to asceticism. He was influential in both Syrian Christianity and the larger eastern church. In Edessa, he led a campaign against pagans, heretics, and Jews, destroying four pagan temples and a synagogue. He championed the use of the separated Gospels and is said to have destroyed 400 copies of Tatian's *Diatessaron*. He may have sponsored the Peshitta Syriac translation of the Bible. A stern administrator, Rabbula used the church's resources for the care of the poor and the building of infirmaries for the sick and destitute. He is credited with a set of strict rules for clergy, monks, and nuns.

Edessa was linked by tradition to the teachings of Diodore of Tarsus and Theodore of Mopsuestia, and at the Council of Ephesus (431) Rabbula sided with Nestorius's supporters. Shortly thereafter, he was converted to Cyril of Alexandria's Christological position and worked vigorously on Cyril's behalf, although this meant opposing the views of some of his own clergy. He banned the writings of Theodore and Diodore and circulated Cyril's work in Syriac.

During his term as bishop, Edessa saw much cultural vitality; important hagiographical texts were produced for the cults of the Edessan martyrs and saints, as well as chronicles of the city's Christian history. On his death, he was succeeded by the "Nestorian" Ibas. CPG III, 6490–6497.   [S.A.H.]

Bibliography

P. Bedjan, ed., *Acta Martyrum et Sanctorum* IV (Paris: Harrassowitz, 1904), pp. 396–450; A. Vööbus, ed. and tr., *Syriac and Arabic Documents Regarding Legislation Relative to Syrian Asceticism* (Stockholm: Etse, 1960), pp. 24–33.

G.G. Blum, *Rabbula von Edessa*, CSCO (1969), Vol. 300, Sub. 34; P. Peeters, "La Vie de Rabbula, évêque d'Edesse," *Recherches d'histoire et de philologie orientales* (Brussels: Société des Bollandistes, 1951), pp. 139–170.

RAVENNA. City in northern Italy. Ravenna assumed importance in the Roman empire when Augustus established a port for the navy nearby at Classe and built a canal connecting the city with the Po River. The first archaeological remains of Christians in the region pertain to Classe at the end of the second and beginning of the third century. The first bishop was Apollinaris, known from *Sermon* 128 of Peter Chrysologus, the earliest ecclesiastical author of Ravenna. Apollinaris was a martyr (*Mart. hier.*, July 23) and was reported by a seventh-century legend to have been a disciple of Peter.

The greatest growth of Ravenna occurred after emperor Honorius, faced with the invasion of Alaric, decided in 402 to move the imperial residence there from Milan. In consequence, Ravenna's bishop acquired metropolitan standing; the city's first great monuments of Christian art were constructed in the mid-fifth century. These included the Church of Sta. Croce and adjoining it the so-called Mausoleum of Galla Placidia, adorned with magnificent mosaics striking for their rich blue color, which became an oratory. Hardly anything remains of the cathedral built by bishop Ursus, but the cathedral baptistery does survive. Its mosaics were commissioned by bishop Neon. Two other basilicas were built in this period: the Church of St. John the Evangelist (restored since World War II) and the Church of the Apostles, now dedicated to St. Francis.

The Ostrogothic king Theodoric captured Ravenna in 493, and his reign (to 526) marked the second, or Arian, phase of Christian building in the city. Theodoric built a palace, the appearance of which is known from a mosaic in the Church of S. Apollinare Nuovo; his mausoleum, which is still standing; a church on the site of Santo Spirito; its baptistery, the baptistery of the Arians, which imitated the form and in an inferior way the mosaic of the baptism of Christ in the Orthodox Baptistery; and the basilica dedicated to the Savior, now known as S. Apollinare Nuovo. To the reign of Theodoric belongs also the Archbishop's Chapel (Oratory of St. Andrew), with its splendid mosaic of Christ the Victor.

In 540, Justinian's general Belisarius captured Ravenna for the Byzantine empire, and in 554 it became the headquarters of the Exarch, who represented Byzantine authority in Italy. The Church of the Savior was rededicated to St. Martin and new mosaics were added. Newer constructions brought to completion the basilica of S. Apollinare in Classe and the crown of Ravenna's Christian architecture and mosaics—S. Vitale. Both were consecrated near mid-century by bishop Maximian, whose ivory episcopal throne with carvings of biblical scenes is one of the most beautiful works in ivory to come down from the ancient world.

Two significant councils met in Ravenna, in 419 and 499, to decide disputed papal elections. The Byzantine period at Ravenna ended in 751 with the Lombard conquest of the city.

The Christian mosaics of Ravenna are without rival in the study of early Christian and early Byzantine art. They belong chronologically, geographically, and artistically between two worlds: to the times of transition from Christian antiquity to the Middle Ages; to the meeting place of the Roman west and the Byzantine east; and to the transition from early Christian to Byzantine art. Ravenna well deserves its designation as "an art city." *See also* Baptistery; Galla Placidia; Justinian; Mosaics; Peter Chrysologus; S. Apollinare in Classe; S. Apollinare Nuovo; S. Vitale; Theodoric. [E.F.]

Bibliography

Andreas Agnellus, *Liber Pontificalis Ecclesiae Ravennatis.*

M. Lawrence, *The Sarcophagi of Ravenna* (New York: Archaeological Institute of America, 1945); G. Bovini, *Ravenna Mosaics* (Greenwich: New York Graphic Society, 1956); S.K. Kostof, *The Orthodox Baptistery of Ravenna* (New Haven: Yale UP, 1965); G. Bovini, *Ravenna: An Art City* (Ravenna: Longo, n.d.); *Ravenna Felix* (Ravenna: Longo, n.d.); F.W. Deichmann, *Ravenna: Hauptstadt des spätantiken Abendlandes*, 2 vols. (Wiesbaden: Steiner, 1969, 1974); O.G. von Simson, *Sacred Fortress: Byzantine Art and Statecraft in Ravenna* (Princeton: Princeton UP, 1987).

READER. The lector, a person who read the scriptures in the liturgy. The reading of the scriptures was one of the foci of the synagogue service (Luke 4:16f.; Acts 13:15) and continued to be characteristic of Christian assemblies (1 Tim. 4:13; Rev. 1:3). The earliest references to scripture reading give no indication of a special order assigned this task (Justin, *1 Apol.* 67; Tertullian, *Apol.* 39). Tertullian makes the first use of the noun "reader" (*Praescr.* 41). Hippolytus prescribed that "the reader is appointed by the bishop giving him the book, for he is not ordained" (*Trad. ap.* 12; cf. IV Carthage, *can.* 8), but the *Apostolic Constitutions* 8.22 provided for ordination by prayer and the laying on of hands. The fullest account of the reader as a distinct office in the church is found in the *Apostolic Church Order* 19: "For Reader, one should be appointed, after he has been carefully proved; . . .of a plain utterance, and capable of clearly interpreting, mindful that he assumes the position of an evangelist." Commodian says, "You [readers] are flowers in the congregation; you are Christ's lanterns" (*Instruct.* 2.26[67]). From the mid-third century, the readers were counted as a definite order in the clergy (Cyprian, *Ep.* 39.1, 4; Origen, *Hom.* 15 *in Num.* 1; *Didas.* 9; Laodicea, *can.* 24; *Const. app.* 6.17). The office of reader became the first step in the advancement in the clergy (Cyprian, *Ep.* 38.2).

In the basilicas of the fourth and fifth centuries, the reader read from the ambo (Sozomen, *H.E.* 9.2). By the fourth century, the reader, although reading lessons from other parts of scripture, no longer read the Gospel, an honor given to a deacon or higher clergy (*Const. app.* 2.57; Jerome, *Ep.* 147.6). The deacons gradually absorbed the functions of the reader. *See also* Deacon; Lectionary.   [E.F.]

Bibliography

A. von Harnack, *Sources of the Apostolic Canons with a Treatise on Origin of the Readership and the Lower Orders* (London: Norgate, 1895); J.G. Davies, "Deacons, Deaconnesses and the Minor Orders in the Patristic Period," *JEH* 14 (1963):10–14; R. Martineau, *Office and Work of a Reader* (Oxford: Mowbray, 1970).

REAL PRESENCE. Doctrine that the body and blood of Christ are in some sense truly present at the eucharist. Its biblical basis was Jesus' words at the Last Supper about the bread, "This is my body," and about the cup, "This is my blood" (Mark 14:22f.), and the teaching of John 6:48–65 that it is necessary to eat his flesh and drink his blood to receive eternal life. On the other hand, it has been argued that in a Jewish setting Jesus' words at the institution of the eucharist were not meant literally but constituted prophetic symbolism, meaning "This represents" my body and blood (cf. Exod. 12:11; Gal. 4:24). Similarly, John 6 has been interpreted as expressing symbolically the divine life that the Holy Spirit makes available by reason of the flesh and blood of Christ, likened to the manna of Exodus 16. As Christianity moved outside the Jewish context into the world of Greek thought, the language of Jesus took on a realistic meaning. This is illustrated by Justin's ambiguous (to modern readers) effort to explain Jewish ideas of a prayer of consecration, which changed something's purpose or function (1 Tim. 4:4f.), by using physical analogies (*1 Apol.* 66).

Realist language about the eucharist occurs in the second century mainly to counter Docetic and Gnostic ideas that denied to Christ a real physical body. Ignatius referred to those who avoided the eucharist because of its association with the flesh of Christ (*Smyrn.* 7). Irenaeus made the eucharist an important argument against the Gnostics. The invocation of God adds a heavenly reality to the material elements, and the one who eats the eucharist is nourished by the body and blood of Christ. How then can the Gnostics deny the incarnation of Christ or say that human flesh is incapable of receiving resurrection (*Haer.* 4.18.4f.; 5.2.2f.)? Tertullian wrote less realistically, preferring to speak of the "figure" of Christ's body (*Marc.* 4.40), but he also argued that there could not be a figure unless there was the real body of which it was a figure. In spite of their language of "figure," Tertullian (*Cor.* 3.4) and Cyprian (*Laps.* 25) show a considerable reverence for the consecrated elements. Nevertheless, the true literalists were some of the Gnostics themselves, and their language may have influenced the realist language of popular piety (Irenaeus, *Haer.* 1.13.2; Clement of Alexandria, *Exc. Thdot.* 82).

The Alexandrians expressed an understanding similar to what has been termed dynamic symbolism, according to which the Holy Spirit works through the consecrated elements to bring divine life and blessings to the recipient (Clement of Alexandria, *Paed.* 1.6.43; 2.2.19f.; Origen, *Comm. in Mt.* 11.14; *Cels.*

8.33; *Hom.* 8.5 *in Lev.*). This language of symbolism continued in Greek writers of the fourth century, but the most influential exponent of the view that the realism pertains to the divine gifts and not to the elements was Augustine. "The sacrament is one thing, the power of the sacrament another" (*In evang. Ioh.* 26.11[13]; cf. *Civ. Dei* 21.25; *Doctr. Christ.* 3.16.24 for the figurative interpretation of John 6:53). The consecrated elements for Augustine are holy symbols possessing the significance or value of the body and blood. One thing is seen (bread and wine), but by faith an unseen reality is understood (body and blood)—cf. the definition of a sign in *Christian Doctrine* 2.1.

A real presence and/or realistic understanding of the benefits of communion were not the same as a change in the elements. One of the first clear statements of a change in the elements themselves, and not simply in their use or effects, is found in Cyril of Jerusalem, who assigns the change to the invocation of the Holy Spirit (*Catech.* 19.7; 22.7). Gregory of Nyssa employed the term "transelements" (i.e., transforms) in describing the change by which Christ through the prayer of benediction imparts his immortal life to the bread and wine (*Or. catech.* 37). Ambrose introduced the idea of a sacramental change in the elements to the west, and he identified the change with reciting Jesus' words of institution (*Sacram.* 4.4.14–4.5.23).

Although Augustine's dynamic symbolism and Ambrose's realism were to coexist in western thought, the latter's views prevailed in the Middle Ages and the former's views were reappropriated at the Reformation. *See also* Bread; Eucharist; Sacrifice.   [E.F.]

Bibliography
Justin Martyr, *1 Apology* 66; Irenaeus, *Against Heresies* 4.18.4f.; 5.2.2f.; Cyprian, *Letter* 63.2; Cyril of Jerusalem, *Catechetical Lectures* 19.7; 22.3, 7; Gregory of Nyssa, *Catechetical Oration* 37; Ambrose, *On the Sacraments* 4.4.14–4.5.23; Augustine, *Sermons* 227; 272; idem, *Homilies on the Gospel of John* 26.13.11; 50.12.13; idem, *Letter* 98.9.

D. Stone, *The Holy Communion* (London: Longmans, Green, 1904), pp. 36–57; A.J. MacDonald, ed., *The Evangelical Doctrine of Holy Communion* (Cambridge: Heffer, 1930); C.W. Dugmore, "Sacrament and Sacrifice in the Early Fathers," *JEH* 2 (1951):24–37; G.W.H. Lampe, "The Eucharist in the Thought of the Early Church," *Eucharistic Theology Then and Now* (London: SPCK, 1968), pp. 34–58; E. Ferguson, *Early Christians Speak* (Abilene: ACU, 1987), pp. 107–118.

RELICS. Remains of martyrs and saints. The bones of condemned criminals, observes the hostile Eunapius (ca. 391), were essential to Christian cult, which recognized the dead as martyrs and ambassadors to God (*V. Sophis.* 472). The early acts of the martyrs also describe the martyrs as loyal disciples of the Lord (*M. Polyc.* 17–18; *Pass. Perp.* 21; *A. Cyp.* 5; *Pass. Fruct.* 6). Instead of "relics" (Latin *reliquiae,* "remains"), believers in late antiquity described the bodies of the special dead as their "memory," their "blessings," as "tokens" of a warm affection.

The powers of the friends of God were associated with their bones and their possessions in the Hebrew Bible (2 Kings 2:14; 13:21), as also in the Christian community (Matt. 9:20; Acts 5:15; 19:12). The power of the martyrs arose from their proximity to Christ as well as from the manner of their death (Acts 1:8, 22), a relationship consistently emphasized in the acts of the martyrs. Cyprian justifies veneration of the instruments of the martyr's suffering by insisting that the bodies of Christ's prisoners sanctified their chains (*Ep.* 76.2). After Constantine, objects associated with confessors, heroes of the early church, and even the prophets and patriarchs were now held to represent the power of the special friends of God (Eusebius, *H.E.* 6.9f.; 7.19). The Council of Gangra (ca. 340) decreed excommunication for those who despised relics. In the east the desert fathers and the stylites and in the west Martin of Tours were soon to prove rich sources of such tokens.

By the end of the fourth century, the role of relics in Christian cult had become clearly defined. The invention, or discovery and identification, of relics was an occasion of rejoicing when "deeds of power" (Latin *virtutes,* "miracles") were experienced. Prototypical for the west was the discovery in 386 of the remains of Gervasius and Protasius at Milan (Paulinus, *V.*

Amb. 14). The discovery was usually followed by a translation, or transfer of the relics, to a location more suited to popular devotion: in 351, Babylas was translated at Antioch (Sozomen, *H.E.* 5.19). Anthony feared something similar (Athanasius, *V. Anton.* 90). A century later, the people of Antioch refused to surrender the body of Symeon Stylites even to the emperor (Evagrius, *H.E.* 1.13). A natural extension was the sale and, still more so, the theft of relics. Such practices caused scandal (Augustine, *Op. monach.* 28.36); later, they were a major means of diffusion of relics.

Despite the reservations of Augustine about the efficacy of burial next to the saints (*Cura mort.*), relics were common and highly prized, in the east (Theodoret, *Ep.* 131; 145), as in the west (Paulinus of Nola, *Ep.* 32.17; Gaudentius of Brescia, *Tract.* 17). The early fathers consistently emphasized that relics attest to the special relationship of the saints to God (summarized by Isidore of Seville, *Eccl. off.* 1.25.1–6). This relationship was realized in the social sphere by the reverence of the faithful and confirmed in great liturgical dramas staged by the bishops. Competition for relics was keen, but the rewards of possessing them were great—no less than kinship with the special dead, the friends of God.

This social interpretation of the cult of relics is substantiated by a new understanding of ancient Jewish burial practices and beliefs. As with the patriarchs, so throughout antiquity Jews "gathered up" the bones of their kin for secondary burial in ossuaries. "The memory of the righteous is for a blessing" (Prov. 10:7); but this memory was a social fact, not a given. To gather up bones was to claim kinship with the righteous dead, patriarch or Maccabean hero, saint or martyr, and paradoxically by this act to establish the one so commemorated as a friend of God. These claims of kinship were reflected in the rich vocabulary that expresses the relationship between believer and saint, between saint and God. A relic was thus not so much a magical object in itself, at least in the early Christian centuries, as a token of memory and affection, the outward manifestation of a blessing and the realization of a rela-tionship with a special friend of God. *See also* Martyr, Martyrdom; Saints. [J.H.Co.]

Bibliography

Martyrdom of Polycarp 17–18; *Passion of Perpetua* 21; Cyprian, *Letter* 76.2; *Acts of Cyprian* 5; *Martyrdom of Fructuosus* 6; Eusebius, *Church History* 6.9–10; 7.19; Athanasius, *Life of Anthony* 90; Eunapius, *Lives of the Sophists* 472; Ambrose, *Letter* 61; Paulinus, *Life of Ambrose* 14; Augustine, *The Work of Monks* 28.36; idem, *The Care to Be Taken for the Dead*; idem, *Confessions* 9.7; idem, *City of God* 22.8; Sozomen, *Church History* 5.19; Theodoret, *Letters* 130; 144; Evagrius, *Church History* 1.13; Gaudentius of Brescia, *Tractatus* 17; Paulinus of Nola, *Letter* 32.17.

H. Leclercq, "Relics et reliquaires," DACL (1948), Vol. 14, cols. 2294–2359; F. Chiovaro, "Relics," NCE (1967), Vol. 12, pp. 234–240; E.M. Meyers, *Jewish Ossuaries: Reburial and Rebirth, Secondary Burials in their Ancient Near Eastern Setting* (Rome: Biblical Institute, 1971); P. Brown, "Relics and Social Status in the Age of Gregory of Tours," *Society and the Holy in Late Antiquity* (Berkeley: U of California P, 1982), pp. 222–250; P.J. Geary, *Furta Sacra: Theft of Relics in the Central Middle Ages* (Princeton: Princeton UP, 1978); L. Rothkrug, "The 'Odour of Sanctity' and the Hebrew Origins of Christian Relic Veneration," *Historical Reflexions, Reflexions Historiques* 8 (1981):95–142; P. Brown, *The Cult of the Saints: Its Rise and Function in Latin Christianity* (Chicago: U of Chicago P, 1987).

REPENTANCE. Change of heart expressed in change of life. The concept of repentance in early Christianity seems to stem from a combination of Jewish and Greek ideas current in the Hellenistic age. The Greek terms *metanoia, metanoein* (meaning a change or conversion of mind) are rare in classical usage but more common in *koinē*. The sense of "remorse" is given by the term *metamelesthai*; by the first century A.D., however, philosophical moralists could use the two terms synonymously as referring to the turning from vice to virtue (e.g., *Tabula of Cebes* 10.4f.; 35.4). In Jewish tradition, "turning" from sin (Hebrew *shub*) is especially connected with the prophetic call to repentance (cf. Amos 4:6; Hosea 5:4; Jer. 4:1; 26:3; 36:3). Yet the greater weight given to the concept as central to Jewish piety must be attributed to postexilic developments of apocalyptic and reflections on divine punishment for Israel's sin of idolatry and the necessity of conversion (Ezek. 14:6; 18:30). In the Septuagint, *metanoia* is used to translate both the sense of "remorse" (Hebrew *nacham*) and of "conversion" (*shub*), and thence it is found more regularly in Hellenistic Jewish literature (cf. Sirach 48:15; *Test. Zeb.* 9.7; Prayer of Manasseh 8; 13). Finally, in Philo (*Leg. spec.* 4.18; *Virt.* 152; 208; *V. Mos.* 1.167; *Leg. alleg.* 3.211) the term takes on elements of both Jewish piety (as turning from sin or idolatry to God) and Hellenistic ethics (as turning from vice to virtue).

In the New Testament, the sense of conversion is associated with the apocalyptic preaching of both John the Baptist and Jesus (Matt. 3:2; 4:17; Mark 1:4, 14). In Paul, both remorse and conversion are necessary for the proper walk of faith and salvation (cf. 2 Cor. 7:9f.; Rom. 2:4). Yet in Paul, *metanoia* is more commonly associated with turning to Christ rather than with a Christian's repentance for sins (cf. Matt. 18:15, 21; Luke 17:3f.). The question of a second *metanoia* for sins after baptism is first raised in Hebrews 6:4–6 (cf. 10:26f.). It is particularly this notion that comes to be associated with the development of ecclesiastical discipline and the doctrine of penance in the early church.

The dual sense of repentance, for the new convert as well as for the fallen Christian, can be seen in the apostolic fathers. In *Didache* 14 and *1 Clement* 57.1, repentance is expressed through confession of sins. The unrepentant sinner was normally excommunicated until such confession was made (cf. Ignatius, *Smyrn.* 4; *Eph.* 7; *Philad.* 3; 8). Yet repentance was seen as the indispensable conversion of mind to God (cf. *2 Clem.* 9), which calls forth "fruits befitting repentance" (*2 Clem.* 16). Explicit differentiation in the concept is made first by the Roman writer Hermas in his *Shepherd* (from the middle of the second century). He relaxes his stringent morality only to the extent of allowing one "repentance" after baptismal repentance (*Mand.* 4.3). The postbaptismal repentance is equated with humiliation, self-affliction, and "torment of the soul" (*Sim.* 7.4). This distinction would become especially important in the developing Latin theological idiom of

the west. Beginning with Tertullian, the Greek *metanoia* was translated by the Latin *paenitentia*, but the verbal form used was *paenitentiam agere* (Tertullian, *Paenit.* 6; 9). In Tertullian, this term clearly comes to signify the act of "penitence," although it contains both confession and remorse. Thus, in medieval Latin thought beginning with Gregory the Great, the threefold constitution of penance (*paenitentia*) included change of mind (*conversio mentis*), oral confession (*confessio oris*), and works of satisfaction (*satisfactio operis*) (*Mor.* 4; 16; *In prim. Reg.* 6.2). This analysis would carry through into the Scholastic development of the sacramental doctrine of penance. *See also* Confession of Sin; Discipline; Penance.

[L.M.W.]

Bibliography

Tertullian, *On Repentance;* ANF (1887) Vol. 1; Cyril of Jerusalem, *Catechetical Lectures* 2, tr. E.H. Gifford, NPNF, 2nd ser. (1893), Vol. 7; Ambrose, *Concerning Repentance*, SC (1971), Vol. 179, NPNF, 2nd ser. (1896), Vol. 10.

O.D. Watkins, *A History of Penance* (London: Longmans, Green, 1920); R.S.T. Haselhurst, *Penitential Discipline of the Early Church* (London: SPCK, 1921); A.D. Nock, *Conversion* (Oxford: Clarendon, 1933); P. Galtier, *Aux origines du sacrement de pénitence* (Rome: Gregoriana, 1951); W. Telfer, *The Forgiveness of Sins* (London: SCM, 1960); B. Poschmann, *Penance and the Anointing of the Sick* (London: Burns and Oates, 1964); S. Richter, *Metanoia* (New York: Sheed and Ward, 1966); J. Behm and E. Wurthwein, "*Metanoia, Metanoeō*," and O. Michel, "*Metamelomai*," *Theological Dictionary of the New Testament*, ed. G. Kittel (Grand Rapids: Eerdmans, 1967), Vol. 4, pp. 975–1008 and 626–629; E. Ferguson, *Early Christians Speak* (Abilene: ACU, 1987), pp. 181–191.

RESURRECTION. God's returning the righteous to life at the end-time; in Christian writings, the resurrection of Jesus after his crucifixion. Less frequently, the wicked are also spoken of as resurrected to suffer punishment (e.g., the "second death" in Rev. 20:11–15). Unlike immortality, an inherent property of the soul in contrast to the perishable body, resurrection is an act of divine power in calling persons to a new form of life eternally in God's presence.

Images of resurrection emerge in Judaism during the second century B.C. A restoration of life awaits those who suffered martyrdom for their religion (Dan. 12:1–2; 2 Macc. 7). In the first century A.D., resurrection was a "sectarian" belief, defended by the Pharisees and rejected by the Sadducees (Josephus, *War* 18.11–22). Jesus defended the belief against the paradoxes created by a materialistic reading on the part of Sadducee opponents in Mark 12:18–27. Other Jewish writings speak of immortality as belonging to the true image of God in Adam (Wisd. Sol. 2:23). Paul uses this imagery in speaking of the risen Christ as the spiritual Adam (1 Cor. 15:45–49).

Belief that God had raised Jesus after the crucifixion is central to Christianity. The parallel conviction that the crucified had been exalted to the right hand of God forged links with the figure of the exalted Son of Man in Daniel 7:14ff. (Mark 14:62; Rev. 1:7) and supported attribution of other divine titles like Lord to Jesus (Phil. 2:6–11). Our earliest witnesses to the emergence of this belief speak of appearances "from heaven" to various followers who were witnesses to the resurrection (Gal. 1:16; 1 Cor. 15:3–10). The temporal marker "on the third day" connects the resurrection with the crucifixion; the visionary experiences indicate that the risen Jesus was exalted with God in heaven, not merely a resuscitated corpse. Thus, resurrection/exaltation served as divine vindication of Jesus' ministry.

Although resurrection images spoke of persons becoming like stars or angels, they appear to presume that the bodies of the righteous would no longer be in the grave, as in the proleptic resurrection of the righteous at the hour of Jesus' crucifixion (Matt. 27:51–53). Tradition holds that Jesus' tomb was found to be empty but that the initial response to such a phenomenon was not the conclusion that "he is raised" (a message that Gospel reports link to angelic revelation at the tomb; e.g., Mark 16:6) but rather bewilderment (Luke 24:22–24) or the supposition of tomb robbery (John 20:2, 13, 15; Matt. 27:62–65). Thus, the empty tomb only confirms a faith in Jesus' resurrection that had its origins in independent acts of divine revelation.

Short narratives about Jesus' appearances served to show Christians the reestablishment of the community of disciples and their commissioning to spread the message about Jesus after the crucifixion. The earliest version of Mark contained only a reference to a Galilee vision of the Lord (Mark 16:7; Mark 16:9–20 is a later addition in some text traditions). Matthew 28:9–10 and John 20:11–18 knew a tradition of an appearance to women near the tomb. Matthew 28:16–20 crafts a commissioning vision out of a series of sayings of the Lord. Diverse traditions preserved in Luke and John speak of appearances to disciples, in meal settings, around Jerusalem (Luke 24:13–49; John 20:19–29). John 21:1–23 has crafted an elaborate commissioning of disciples and Peter from a tradition of appearances in Galilee. Luke 24:41–43 and John 20:25–27 emphasize the bodily continuity of the risen Jesus with the crucified. These passages would later play an important role in the argument against those who argued that the risen Lord was a purely divine, spiritual being and that resurrection of the faithful meant ascent of the soul to that heavenly status, not transformation of the embodied person. Such arguments were often advanced in Gnosticism, as in the treatise *On the Resurrection* from Nag Hammadi. In that context, "resurrection" could be predicated of the enlightened soul while it was still in this life. 2 Timothy 2:18 refers to some who claimed that resurrection had come already.

Apocryphal traditions from later centuries expanded the canonical narratives with details of Jesus' actual emergence from the tomb (*Ev. Petr.* 9–14; *Ascens. Is.* 3.16–18). Gnostic writings are particularly fond of picturing the risen Lord as a luminous, polymorphous, divine being (e.g., *A. Thom.* 27; *Ap. John* 2.1.32–2.9). This tendency toward spiritualizing the resurrection was countered by emphasis on the material reality of the risen Lord (e.g., *Ep. Apos.* 11; 24–26) and insistence that the New Testament taught that resurrection implied transformation of the body (Irenaeus, *Haer.* 5.7.1–2; 5.13.1, with reference to the raising of Lazarus).

Christian writers also had to defend belief in resurrection against philosophic paganism, which claimed immortality to be a natural property of the soul and perishability an unalterable fact of material reality. They answered that the soul, like the body, was God's creation and not naturally immortal (Tatian, *Or.* 13–16). The "image of God" in Genesis included the body, so God's creative power could transform it to receive immortality along with the soul (Irenaeus, *Haer.* 5.3.2–13; Justin, *1 Apol.* 18–19; Tatian, *Or.* 5.3–6.1; Theophilus, *Autol.* 1.7–8). Other arguments in favor of resurrection included references to cyclic phenomena in nature, to the legend of the Phoenix, and to various pagan myths of dying and rising gods (*1 Clem.* 24–26; Justin, *1 Apol.* 18–20; Tertullian, *Resurr.* 11–13). Origen tackled the "scientific" objections of the third century based on the nature of matter by arguing that the "eternal stars" were both material and eternal (*Cels.* 4.61) and that besides changeable matter there was a "matter" that served as the abiding substrate of identity (*Cels.* 4.55–56).

The traditional link between resurrection and judgment led to arguments that stress the appropriateness of the body, the medium through which persons have done good or evil, sharing in the reward that follows upon those acts (*2 Clem.* 8.4–6; Athenagoras, *Leg.* 36; Tertullian, *Resurr.* 14–17). Justin Martyr argued that the body was necessary for the personal identity of individuals in the judgment (*Dial.* 45). By the end of the second century, the bodily resurrection of Jesus and the bodily resurrection of the faithful at the second coming were established Christian doctrine. The creedal formula "I believe in the resurrection of the body and in life eternal" makes explicit the originating connection between resurrection and eternal life in the presence of God. *See also* Immortality. [P.P.]

Bibliography

Athenagoras, *On the Resurrection of the Dead,* ed. and tr. W.R. Schoedel, OECT (1972); Tertullian, *The Resurrection of the Flesh,* tr. P. Holmes, ANF (1887), Vol. 3; Origen, *On First Principles* 2.10–11, tr. G. W. Butterworth (London: SPCK, 1936); Methodius, *On the Resurrection,* tr. W.R. Clark, ANF (1886), Vol. 6; Gregory of Nyssa, *On the Soul and Resurrection,* tr. W. Moore, NPNF, 2nd ser. (1892), Vol. 5; Ambrose, *On Belief in the Resurrection,* tr. H. De Romestin, NPNF, 2nd ser. (1896), Vol. 10.

H.A. Wolfson, "Immortality and Resurrection in the Philosophy of the Church Fathers," *Immortality and Resurrection,* ed. K. Stendahl (New York: Macmillan, 1965); C.F. Evans, *Resurrection and the New Testament* (London: SCM, 1970); A.H.C. van Eijk, "'Only That Can Rise Which Has Previously Fallen': The History of a Formula," *JThS* n.s. 22 (1971):517–529; J.G. Davies, "Factors Leading to the Emergence of Belief in the Resurrection of the Flesh," *JThS* n.s. 23 (1972):448–455; G. Nickelsburg, *Resurrection, Immortality and Eternal Life in Intertestamental Judaism* (Cambridge: Harvard UP, 1972); A.H.C. van Eijk, "Resurrection-Language: Its Various Meanings in Early Christian Literature," *SP* 12 (1975):271–276; H. Hendrickx, *Resurrection Narratives of the Synoptic Gospels* (London: Chapman, 1984); P. Perkins, *Resurrection: New Testament Witness and Contemporary Reflection* (Garden City: Doubleday, 1984); J.E. McWilliam Dewart, *Death and Resurrection* (Wilmington: Glazier, 1986); G. O'Collins, *Interpreting the Resurrection: Examining the Major Problems in the Stories of Jesus' Resurrection* (New York: Paulist, 1988).

REVELATION, BOOK OF (the Apocalypse).

Last book and only apocalypse in the New Testament, and one of the most controversial canonical writings in the ancient church. The author of Revelation repeatedly mentions that his name is John (1:4, 9; 22:8) and implies that he is a prophet (1:3; 22:9) but otherwise provides no more specific clues to his identity. By the late second century, the author was widely identified with the apostle John, the son of Zebedee (Justin, *Dial.* 81.4; Irenaeus, *Haer.* 4.20.11), to whom the Gospel of John and the three Johannine letters were also ascribed.

For the ancient church, the most controversial part of Revelation, and the part that fueled doubts about its authorship, was 20:4–6, which was invoked to support the view that Christ would return to the earth and establish a temporary messianic kingdom for 1,000 years. The literal understanding of this intermediate kingdom, called "chiliasm" or "millenarianism," met with favor among Christians with a strong Jewish theological heritage, such as Papias, Justin, and Irenaeus. Those with a more Hellenistic orientation tended to reject it. Dionysius of Alexandria (d. 264/5) rejected millenarianism and argued on stylistic grounds that the Gospel and Revelation of John were not written by the same person. He proposed *two* Johns;

the author of the Gospel was John the apostle (Eusebius, *H.E.* 7.25). Eusebius of Caesarea agreed and proposed that Revelation was written by a shadowy figure called John the Presbyter (*H.E.* 7.25). Montanism, a Christian reform movement arising in Phrygia in the second half of the second century, found support for its distinctive beliefs in the Gospel and Revelation of John, including an imminent great tribulation and the descent of the heavenly Jerusalem at Pepuza, seventy miles east of Philadelphia (cf. Rev. 3:7–13). Such use of Revelation caused many to question its authority, but the Alogoi, a Christian sect contemporaneous with Montanism, were extreme in ascribing both the Gospel and Revelation of John to the Gnostic heretic Cerinthus (Epiphanius, *Haer.* 51).

The traditional date of composition is ca. A.D. 95, toward the end of the reign of the emperor Domitian (Irenaeus, *Haer.* 5.30.3), widely regarded as a persecutor of Christians (Eusebius, *H.E.* 3.17). There is little evidence of "official" Roman repression of Christianity between the persecutions of Nero (A.D. 64) and Decius (250), yet being a Christian was considered a capital offense (Pliny the Younger, *Ep.* 10.96.2–3). Actual punishment depended on public opinion, the zeal of informants, and the cooperation of provincial governors. Pressure to participate in the imperial cult in the province of Asia made it easy to identify Christians, some of whom had been executed (Rev. 2:13; 6:9–11). John himself had suffered exile (1:9).

The Book of Revelation was written to inspire hope in Christians facing persecution and martyrdom. It assured them that God is in control, that Christ is "Lord of lords and King of kings" (Rev. 17:14), and that any and all opposition powers will come to destruction (17:1–19:20) and the faithful will inherit the heavenly Jerusalem (21:1–22:5). The contents are built up from a series of symbols and visions grouped by sevens: letters to seven churches (2–3); a scroll sealed with seven seals (5:1–8:5); seven angels with seven trumpets (8:6–11:19); seven angels with seven bowls of wrath (15:1–16:21).

The central theme of Revelation, summarily expressed in the speech of God in Revelation 21:6–8, is justice: faithful Christians will be rewarded with eternal bliss; lapsed Christians and unbelievers will suffer eternal punishment. John, like the Old Testament prophets with whom he identified, predicts the coming of eschatological judgments to punish the wicked and unrepentant, and at the same time offers comfort and encouragement to Christians by preparing them for the coming trials and presenting them with a preview of the eternal state of blessedness awaiting the faithful, particularly the martyrs. *See also* Apocalyptic Literature.   [D.E.A.]

Bibliography
Victorinus of Pettau, *Commentary on the Apocalypse,* ANF (1886), Vol. 7, pp. 344–360; Tyconius, *Commentarius in Apocalypsin,* in F. LoBue and G.C. Willis, *The Turin Fragments of Tyconius' Commentary on Revelation* (Cambridge: Cambridge UP, 1963); Jerome, *Commentarii in Apocalypsim,* CSEL (1916), Vol. 49.

H.B. Swete, *The Apocalypse of St. John,* 3rd ed. (London: Macmillan, 1911); G.R. Beasley-Murray, *The Book of Revelation,* rev. ed. (Grand Rapids: Eerdmans, 1978); G.B. Caird, *A Commentary on the Revelation of St. John the Divine* (New York: Harper and Row, 1966); G. Maier, *Die Johannesoffenbarung und die Kirche* (Tübingen: Mohr–Siebeck, 1981); A.Y. Collins, *Crisis and Catharsis: The Power of the Apocalypse* (Philadelphia: Westminster, 1984).

REVELATION, DOCTRINE OF. The term "revelation" conveys the notion of uncovering something not previously known. In Christian history, it has been used primarily as a technical theological word to denote the self-manifestation of God and his will. Although a number of verbs and their derivatives can be translated as "reveal," the primary Old Testament verb (no noun exists) is *gālah.* The concept of revelation is implicit in many additional expressions having to do with God speaking and acting in a way that is audible, visible, or both. New Testament words that connote the idea of revelation include *apokaluptein, apokalupsis, phaneroun,* and *dēloun.*

The biblical terms, although not implying all that historical theology suggests, do imply the essential idea of divine self-disclosure. Of importance also is the initiative of God in this action of self-revealing; humanity discovers God only as he chooses to make himself known. More than just the providing of information about who God is and what he does, revelation is *encounter* with God and thus has a redemptive purpose.

Judaism. In the Old Testament era, the revelation of God occurred "in many and various ways" (Heb. 1:1; cf. Eichrodt 2.15–45). God is depicted as revealing himself through natural phenomena (Exod. 19:9ff.; Deut. 5:22ff.; Ps. 18:11; 104:3; Amos 1:2; Hab. 3:9f., 14; Isa. 30:27). Visions and dreams also served as vehicles of divine revelation (Exod. 33:22; Num. 24:4; Isa. 6:1ff.; Gen. 28:11ff.; 1 Sam. 28:6). Additionally, the theophany of Yahweh sometimes took on human form (Num. 12:8; Exod. 33:23; Deut. 34:10; Judg. 6:22). There is, however, a tendency to underscore the transcendence of God and thus to portray the revelation of Yahweh either through an angel of God (Gen. 16:7, 9–11; Judg. 6:20; 2 Sam. 17:17, 20) or through a manifestation of divine glory (Ps. 29; Exod. 24:15–17; Ezek. 43:1–4). Seeking the face of God is frequently a means of coming to know Yahweh and his will and blessing (Gen. 32:30; 2 Sam. 21:1; 2 Chron. 7:14; Job 33:25). Knowledge of the name of God means insight into the divine character and essence (Ps. 118:26; Jer. 7:12; 1 Kings 8:33).

Most importantly, the revelation of God takes place directly in the words of God spoken to individuals. The use of the verbs for "say" with God as their subject is exceedingly numerous throughout the Old Testament (Gen. 1:28; Exod. 7:13; 2 Kings 1:3; Ezek. 2:8); similar is the use of the phrase "word(s) of the Lord" (Gen. 15:1; Exod. 4:28; 1 Sam. 3:1; Ps. 119; Jer. 6:10; 8:9; Dan. 9:2; Amos 3:1; Micah 1:1). The prophetic "thus says the Lord" became a pivotal vehicle for revealing God's will to the people of Israel. The writing down of those words became important, from the recording of the ten words on the tables of stone at Sinai by the finger of God (Exod. 31:18) to the command to Jeremiah to "write in a book all the words that I have spoken to you" (Jer. 30:2). The actions of God in the history of

individuals (Ps. 3:1ff.; 118:13–14) and of Israel (Ps. 98:2–3; Jer. 33:16) stand as a major channel of divine revelation as well. The full revelation of God and the culmination of his will are seen in the eschatological "Day of the Lord" (Hosea 2:19ff.; Jer. 31:31ff.). Although scholars debate the key context for the divine self-manifestation—the acts of God in history (Wright); the covenant relation (Eichrodt); the cultic centers of worship (von Rad)—the clear emphasis of the Old Testament is that God has made known both himself (as Lord of history, as holy and gracious, and as the Creator and Sustainer of the world) and his will, especially to his people "in many and various ways" (Heb. 1:1).

In rabbinic Judaism, the revelation of God was focused in the Torah, the Law of Yahweh. The developing oral tradition was understood as a precise exposition of the will of God based upon the Torah. Messianic expectation largely anticipated a superb exposition of the Torah. In Jewish apocalypticism, however, the revelation of God to the great figures of the past, now sealed, was to be disclosed at the end of time when the messianic age would burst in upon this present evil age. A third approach to revelation in ancient Judaism is represented by Philo and the Jewish Wisdom literature: the one-sided apocalyptic emphasis upon the transcendence of God was replaced in Hellenistic Judaism by an emphasis upon the immanence of God as revealed in creation and in philosophy.

New Testament. The New Testament reaches behind early Judaism to the Old Testament understanding of divine revelation, especially to the prophets. Yet early Judaism does exert influence upon the New Testament view, especially at the point of an eschatological outlook.

In the Synoptic Gospels, Jesus is both the focus and the bearer of divine revelation. The content of this revelation is the manifestation of God in and through the coming of his kingdom (Mark 1:14–15 and parallels; Matt. 4:12–17; Luke 4:14–15). Simeon speaks of the infant Jesus as "a light for revelation [*apokalupsin*] to the Gentiles" (Luke 2:32; cf. Isa. 42:6;

49:6). In Jesus is the unique and exclusive revelation of the Father: "All things have been delivered to me by my Father; and no one knows the Son except the Father, and no one knows the Father except the Son and any one to whom the Son chooses to reveal him" (Matt. 11:27; cf. Luke 10:21–22). The words and the deeds (especially the miracles; cf. Matt. 9:32–33) of Jesus were the means of divine manifestation. Mere human comprehension is insufficient to receive this revelation (Matt. 11:6; Luke 7:23); this knowledge of salvation is denied to the wise but made available to those willing to receive it in faith and love (Matt. 11:25). The eschatological fullness of this revelation will be disclosed at the return of the Son of man (Luke 17:30).

The apostle Paul likewise understood revelation not merely as the imparting of divine knowledge but primarily as the coming of God, as the disclosure of the world to come, which took place in a historical development up to the death and resurrection of Jesus in the last time (1 Cor. 10:11; cf. Heb. 1:1–4) and which will culminate in the cosmic catastrophe at the end of history. *Apokalupsis* and its derivatives are significant in the Pauline letters. Although God has revealed himself in creation (Rom. 1:19) and in the human moral consciousness (Rom. 2:13–16), a greater saving revelation is needed. The gospel of Christ has been revealed to Paul (1 Cor. 2:10; Gal. 1:11–12, 16), and thus he claimed apostolic authority as a bearer of that revelation (Gal. 1:1, 13–17; cf. Rom 15:15–21; 2 Cor. 13:2–4). The focus of this revelation is Christ (Rom. 1:2–6); but included in it is the righteousness of God (Rom. 1:17), the wrath of God (Rom. 1:18), and the unity of humanity in redemption (Eph. 3:3–6). This revelation composes the Word of God (1 Thess. 2:13; Col. 1:25–29). *Apokalupsis* can also refer to specific manifestations of the will of God (Gal. 2:2; Phil. 3:15) as well as to ecstatic experiences (1 Cor. 14:6; 2 Cor. 12:1). The eschatological culmination will be in the revelation of Christ at the end of the ages (1 Cor. 1:7; Rom. 8:18; cf. 1 Peter 1:5; 5:1) together with judgment (1 Cor. 3:13) and the appearance of the Antichrist (2 Thess. 2:3, 6, 8).

The Johannine writings express the idea of revelation primarily through the *phaneroun* group. The incarnate Word has revealed the glory of the Father to believing eyes (John 1:9–18). Through his deeds and words, Jesus revealed himself and the Father's will (John 1:31; 2:11; 7:4; 9:3; 14:21; 17:6; 21:1, 14; 1 John 1:2; 3:5, 8; 4:9).

In summary, revelation in the New Testament denotes the unveiling of the salvation of God in the redemptive work of his Son. The gospel message came into being as the apostolic witness to this saving act of God in Christ. Yet the revelation of God will be unveiled in its completeness only with the return of the Son at the close of the age.

Apostolic Fathers. As with the biblical materials, no systematic presentation or treatise on the doctrine of revelation exists in any of the church fathers. Yet the concept of revelation is certainly present in their writings. In the apostolic fathers, the variation of vocabulary is similar to that of the New Testament in reference to the phenomena of divine revelation: most important are the terms *apokaluptein* ("reveal") and *phaneroun* ("make manifest"), along with their cognates. Also significant are *dēloun* ("show") and *gnōrizein* ("make known") as well as the noun *oikonomia* ("administration," plan of salvation). God has revealed himself in the Word: ". . .there is one God, who manifested himself through Jesus Christ his Son, who is his Word proceeding from silence, who in all respects was well pleasing to him that sent him" (Ignatius, *Magn.* 8.2). This revelation was for the salvation of sinful humanity (Ignatius, *Eph.* 19:2–3). Thus, the hearing and obeying of the word of the Lord, as a tradition passed down through the true descendants of the apostles, became pivotal (*Did.* 4.1; *Barn.* 9.9; *1 Clem.* 2.1; Ignatius, *Eph.* 15.2); the tradition found its scriptural basis in the Old Testament revelation (*1 Clem.* 13.1; *Barn.* 6). Also, this revelation of Christ could come directly through visions and dreams (Hermas, *Vis.* 3.1.2; *Sim.* 2.1; *M. Polyc.* 22.3). The question of an established written canon delimiting the parameters of revelation was not an issue with the apostolic fathers. The basic theme of revelation was the universal rule of God that became visible in the cosmos and in the Christ event.

Apologists. Justin Martyr and others sought in Hellenistic philosophy a means of showing the superiority of Christianity. They argued that Greek philosophy, based upon human reason, gives limited access to truth, whereas Christianity, based upon divine revelation, provides total access. The key is Christ as Logos, the divine Reason. God as pure Spirit (thus transcendent and inaccessible) made himself accessible through the Logos.

Justin Martyr produced the most extensive development of the Logos theme. He adapted the Stoic concept of the Logos as the Reason behind creation to the Logos motif in the New Testament. Through the Logos, God created all things (*2 Apol.* 6.3), and through him God continues to speak (*Dial.* 62.4). All truth has its origin in the Logos. There is a seed (*sperma tou Logou*) in every person providing a partial knowledge of truth (*2 Apol.* 8.1; 13.5); Greek philosophy thus reflects partial insight into divine truth (*1 Apol.* 46.2–3). The revelatory action of the Logos is seen better in the patriarchs and the prophets: "Jesus is the one who appeared and spoke to Moses, Abraham, and, in a word, to all the patriarchs" (*Dial.* 113.4; cf. 37.4; 58.3; 7.1–2). But in the incarnation of the Word, divine revelation reaches its highpoint (*Dial.* 127.4; *1 Apol.* 63). Thus, in Jesus there is exclusive knowledge of the Father (*1 Apol.* 13.3; 63.13; *Dial.* 121.4). This knowledge comprises the superior doctrine that is contained in the memoirs of the apostles, "which are called Gospels" (*1 Apol.* 66.3; *Dial.* 102.5; 103.6–8; 104.1).

Theophilus of Antioch held a similar view of the revelation of the transcendent God through the divine Logos (*Autol.* 2.22). Athenagoras (esp. *Leg.* 10) and the *Epistle to Diognetus* (7.1–9.6) shared in the Logos doctrine of Justin, although they did not develop it as extensively.

Antiheretical Writings. Parallel to the defense of Christianity against Jews and pagans without was the defense of orthodoxy against the substantial influence of Gnosticism within.

Drawing on aspects of Greek philosophy, Gnostic teachers, such as Basilides and Valentinus (Marcion can be included although not a Gnostic in the strictest sense), set forth Christ as the revealer of the unknown God; Yahweh is a mere demiurge, a secondary reflection of God. The Old Testament thus is either radically reinterpreted or else is rejected outright as having no revelatory value (Marcion). In the "Christianizing" of Greek mythology, Gnosticism found an immediate revelation through its possession of special *gnōsis* ("knowledge"). This in turn was supported, especially by Marcion, through the development of a written canon of New Testament scriptures as authoritative revelation.

In response, Irenaeus of Lyons (esp. *Haer.* 2) argued for the unity of the revelation of God in both Testaments, basing his argument on the doctrine of the Trinity. Christ as the Word (much as the Logos concept of Justin) is the unifying source who becomes the manifestation of God through special Old Testament theophanies, for example, to Abraham (*Haer.* 4.7.1–3), although these but foreshadow the supreme New Testament manifestation in the incarnation of the Word (*Haer.* 4.20.5). The terminus of this revelatory activity is the doctrine taught by Christ, preserved by his apostles and entrusted to his church to guard faithfully (*Haer.* 1.8.1; 1.10.2; 2.9.1). The whole issue of the New Testament canon thus emerged in response to Marcion's efforts.

Similarly, Tertullian deals with the understanding of revelation in connection with the question of the knowledge of God. He basically disallowed philosophy as a means of revelation (*Apol.* 47) in favor of the Old and New Testament scriptures (*Apol.* 18–23); the apostles had been entrusted with that complete revelation (*Praescr.* 20–21). Only the orthodox church possessing the rule of faith (*regula fidei*), the oral tradition established through proper succession of the bishops from the apostles, can correctly use and appeal to the scriptures (*Praescr.* 19). The tradition and the scriptures contain the identical content: the saving knowledge of God (*Praescr.* 38). Because the heretics use only a mutilated version of the scriptures, they possess no saving knowledge of God (*Praescr.* 35–39).

Eastern Fathers. Clement of Alexandria combined the philosophically oriented Logos doctrine of Justin with Irenaeus's Christian interpretation of the Old Testament (*Str.* 6.15). The Logos as divine light is the source of true revelation as found in philosophy (*Str.* 1.19–20), in the Law (*Paed.* 11), and supremely in the New Testament gospel (*Str.* 5.34; *Prot.* 10.1). The church stands as the recipient of that full illumination of the incarnate Logos (*Str.* 1.98.4; *Prot.* 112.2) received as the gift of faith (*Str.* 1.35.2–4). Once received, the true *gnōsis* blossoms through contemplation, obedience, and movement to perfection (*Str.* 2.46.1).

Origen also based his concept of revelation on the Logos doctrine (*Princ.* 1.1.1; *Jo.* 1.16–23). In reaction to the Marcionite rejection of the Old Testament, Origen stressed its revelatory character and unity with the New Testament (*Princ.* pref. 4). The scriptures must then be understood through the spirit of the Logos (*Princ.* 4.2.3), since he stands behind them. Through spiritual purification, the believer can move toward the perfect knowledge to be given in the eternal gospel unveiled at the second coming of Christ (*Comm. in Rom.* 1.4; *Comm. in Mt.* 17.19).

Later, Athanasius and Cyril of Alexandria largely repeated and extended the concepts set forth by Clement and Origen, while focusing on Christological insights in the context of opposition to Arianism and Nestorianism. Athanasius underscored three sources of revelatory knowledge of God: Christ as the illuminating Word (*Gent.* 42), creation illumined by the Word (*Gent.* 35), and the internal image of God (*Gent.* 34). The incarnation of the Word manifests Christ as a divine person (*Inc.* 14) and his doctrine of salvation (*Inc.* 3; *Ar.* 2.55). Cyril of Alexandria stressed Christ as revealing light (*Jo.* 5.2 [PG 73.777]; 6 [73.993]).

The Cappadocian fathers, Basil, Gregory of Nyssa, and Gregory of Nazianzus, were concerned to refute the teaching of Eunomius that the divine essence could be known by the human mind and therefore was not mysterious

to those who adhered to the true doctrine. Their response was to reemphasize the incomprehensible character of the very divine essence that remains a mystery even to the one enlightened by revelation (Basil, *Hom. Spir.* 16.38 [PG 32.136–140]; Gregory of Nyssa, *Beat.* 6 [44.1269]; Gregory of Nazianzus, *Or.* 31.26). In a similar vein, the Antiochene John Chrysostom stressed, against the Anomoeans, the incomprehensibleness of God from a pastoral stance. One must stand in awe before this hiddenness of God, which can be penetrated only by the Son and the Spirit (*Incomprehens.* 1–3 [PG 48.701–728]; *Hom.* 15 *in Jo.* 1 [59.98]). Only in Christ are believers given a glimpse into the mystery hidden from the nations and from the angels (*Hom.* 5 *in Col.* 1–2 [62.331–333]).

Western Fathers. The west saw less of a tendency toward speculative theology. Following in the train of Tertullian, Cyprian of Carthage stressed obedience to the "tradition of the Lord" as the focal point of divine revelation (*Ep.* 63.2–10): "Neither the apostle [Paul] himself nor an angel from heaven can preach or teach any otherwise than Christ has once taught and his apostles have announced" (*Ep.* 63.11). The source of that tradition is the gospel and the apostolic tradition as recorded in the scriptures.

In the fourth century, Hilary of Poitiers and Ambrose emphasized a more mystical tone via influence from the eastern tradition and thus prepared the way for Augustine. In Hilary's view, the mind has to advance "beyond the knowledge of natural reason" to a faith that "rejects the captious and useless questions of philosophy" and grasps the "deeds of God" in the incarnation of Christ (*Trin.* 1.13). The Holy Spirit's guidance in this quest for knowledge is crucial (*Trin.* 1.38).

Augustine made use of motifs from the Johannine writings in the New Testament in order to focus upon Christ as the Way and Mediator of the revelation of the Father. The Son uniquely makes the Father known to humanity (*Trin.* 8.3; *In epist. Ioh.* 47.3). He is the Prophet (*In epist. Ioh.* 24.7), the Master of both the Old and New Testaments (*In epist.*

Ioh. 45.9) who teaches the truths of salvation (*In epist. Ioh.* 17.15; 21.7). The apostles and prophets stand as witnesses to Christ the Light, and their testimony must be believed if the invisible realities are to be grasped (*Civ. Dei* 11.3). The apostles, the scriptures, and the church are the links to Christ and guarantee the authenticity of the faith (*In epist. Ioh.* 109.1; *Fid. et symb.* 1.1; *Enchir.* 1.4; *Util. cred.* 8.20). Revelation (*revelatio*) is closely identified with illumination (*illuminatio*): "Unless he who dwells within reveals, to what purpose do I speak?" (*In epist. Ioh.* 26.7). [L.L.C.]

Bibliography

G.E. Wright and R.H. Fuller, *The Book of the Acts of God* (Garden City: Doubleday, 1957); M. Harl, *Origène et la fonction révélatrice du Verbe incarné* (Paris: Seuil, 1958); C.-M. Edsman, W. Eichrodt, E.L. Dietrich, O.A. Piper, L. Richter, and G. Gloeger, "Offenbarung," *Die Religion in Geschichte und Gegenwart,* rev. 3rd ed., ed. K. Galling (Tübingen: Mohr–Siebeck, 1960); W. Eichrodt, *Theology of the Old Testament,* 2 vols. (Philadelphia: Westminster, 1961, 1967); C.F.D. Moule, "Revelation," *The Interpreter's Dictionary of the Bible,* ed. G.A. Buttrick (Nashville: Abingdon, 1962); G. von Rad, *Old Testament Theology,* 2 vols. (New York: Harper and Row, 1962, 1965); A. Oepke, *"Apokaluptō, apokalupsis," Theological Dictionary of the New Testament,* ed. G. Kittel and G. Friedrich (Grand Rapids: Eerdmans, 1964–1976); Y.M.-J. Congar, *Tradition and Traditions: An Historical and a Theological Essay* (New York: Macmillan, 1966); G. Moran, *Theology of Revelation* (New York: Herder and Herder, 1966); E. Schillebeeckx, *Revelation and Theology* (New York: Sheed and Ward, 1967); A. Dulles, *Revelation Theology: A History* (New York: Herder and Herder, 1969); H. von Campenhausen, *The Formation of the Christian Bible* (Philadelphia: Fortress, 1972); M. Schmaus, A. Grillmeier, and L. Scheffczyk, eds., *Handbuch der Dogmengeschichte,* Vol. 1.1A: M. Seybold et al., *Offenbarung: Von der Schrift bis zum Ausgang der Scholastik* (Freiburg: Herder, 1971); W. Mundle, B. Gärtner, and C. Brown, "Revelation," *The New International Dictionary of New Testament Theology,* ed. C. Brown (Grand Rapids: Zondervan, 1975–1978); J. Barr, "Revelation in History," *The Interpreter's Dictionary of the Bible: Supplementary Volume,* ed. K. Crim (Nashville: Abingdon, 1976); Kelly, pp. 29–79; W. Wieland, *Offenbarung bei Augustinus* (Mainz: Mattias-Brunewald-Verlag, 1978); D.A. Pailin, "Revelation," *The Westminster Dictionary of Christian Theology,* ed. A. Richardson and J. Bowden (Philadelphia: Westminster, 1983).

RHETORIC. Art of persuasion. Rhetoric recognizes the importance of how something is said or written as well as what is argued. Since the classical period, it has been closely allied with studies of grammar, literature, and logic.

Greek and Roman Rhetoric. The reputation of rhetoric became tarnished even among the ancient Greeks. Plato, in his *Gorgias,* attacked it as an art without a subject, a sham that encouraged its practitioners to sell their skills to the highest bidder with little or no concern for questions of truth. Usage of the term today, particularly in comments about political issues, commonly refers to talk without substance.

There is no doubt that various rhetoricians have concentrated on technical rhetoric rather than the deeper questions involved in the topics discussed. For much of its history in Greek and Roman culture, the discipline was dominated by handbooks that gave detailed analysis of the forms of persuasion. Among the most famous were those of the Greeks Hermagoras and Hermogenes and the Romans Cicero and Quintilian. These handbooks prepared students for the process of argument before various audiences—particularly political bodies—and thus continued to be useful guides for the study of law and the rudiments of psychology and political science. Throughout the early Christian and patristic period, promising children were trained in the study of rhetoric in order to prepare them for a life of public service.

Early Christian literature has sometimes been misinterpreted from the assumption that rhetoric is concerned entirely with form. Plato, in his *Phaedrus,* insisted that rhetoric and philosophy shared important interests. His view of "philosophical rhetoric" was further developed by his pupil, Aristotle, whose lectures on the topic have come down to us as his *Rhetoric.* Although that discipline, for Aristotle, concentrated on the character of the speaker and the audience, it was a part of dialectic. Closely related to philosophy and logic, rhetoric was especially adapted to the discussion of probability questions that could not be treated in a formal, syllogistic way.

Aristotle described an *enthymeme*, a two-proposition form of argument, that could be employed in two different ways. First, it could represent an argument that could also be given the threefold syllogistic form. Aristotle noted that audiences often would not follow a speech that made its case in terms of syllogisms, such as: All men are mortal, Socrates is a man, therefore Socrates is mortal. But an audience well might be intrigued by the statement: "Socrates is mortal, for Socrates is a man," or "if Socrates is a man, then Socrates is mortal." That form of presentation demanded that the audience provide the missing proposition of the syllogism. But the argument itself could be decided through the testing of syllogistic validity that is detailed in Aristotle's *Organon,* the so-called logical treatises.

The second use of the *enthymeme* concerned probability questions, problems that were not amenable to formal demonstration through syllogisms: "The sun has always come up, so it will come up tomorrow," "Athenians are reasonable people; they will support democracy." Such issues demanded attention and as much rigor as one could muster, but they defied syllogistic treatment.

Arabic and Syriac translators of Aristotle's works were so taken by this distinction between demonstrable and probability questions that they included Aristotle's *Rhetoric* and his *Poetics* within his logical treatises called the *Organon.* Later Byzantine manuscripts of Aristotle, however, separate them and thus lose the logical connections of philosophy and rhetoric that were also important to Stoic and Neoplatonic philosophers.

Primary evidence supports the view that during the Christian era, indeed at the beginning of the Roman imperial period, there was little conflict between rhetoric and philosophy as competing views of education. Unfortunately, much secondary literature has supposed the opposite, relying on Plato's *Gorgias.* Rhetorical schools studied philosophy at least at a handbook level and often beyond that, while philosophical schools paid attention to rhetorical handbooks. The conflict between Plato and Gorgias over the artlessness of rhetoric, its lack of integrity and solid argument, had basically been resolved along lines found in Plato's *Phaedrus* and Aristotle's larger canon of logical treatises that included at least the *Rhetoric.*

New Testament. This interaction of philosophy and rhetoric becomes extremely important as the context of early Christian literature. The central conception of faith within the New Testament is set on foundations from the Greek rhetorical tradition of persuasion. If "faith" (*pistis*) is a form of "persuade" (*pithanomai*), then it has connections with discussions of philosophical demonstration and rhetorical probability. The recovery of rhetoric as an interpretive tool has led to other interesting insights into the New Testament. A variety of rhetorical forms is to be found in both the Gospels and the Epistles: deliberative rhetoric seeks to move an audience toward an action in the future; epideictic rhetoric tries to influence an audience's views of a present issue by praising or denouncing it; judicial rhetoric attempts to convince an audience about the value of something from the past. The Sermon on the Mount is informed by deliberative rhetoric, John 13–17 by epideictic rhetoric, and 2 Corinthians by judicial rhetoric. All three forms are found in Paul's epistles.

Rhetorical criticism applied to scripture clarifies at least two major positions. First, sophistic, technical rhetoric is absent from the New Testament; indeed, Paul denies its validity (1 Thess. 2:4). No arguments within the New Testament are constructed without concern for their truth or with interest in bringing material gain to their writers. Second, the apparently illogical character of the arguments often dissolves when rhetorical canons are employed instead of syllogistic ones. For example, attempts to break the Corinthian epistles of Paul into more than two letters, attempts made with little or no manuscript evidence, show themselves to be based on a misunderstanding of the type of argument employed. Rhetoric encouraged asides that broke into linear presentation of the cases.

Second and Third Centuries. The study of rhetoric is necessary to the investigation of early Christian writers after the New Testament, casting light on types of appeals, figures, even the epistolary or homiletical forms. The concern for symmetry and the necessity of prolixity lie behind much of the literature. The writers' use of balanced phrases and clauses is attractive to modern readers, but not the incessant "mixed metaphors." They draw images from all areas of life. Word play, punning, oxymoron, and paradox are frequent, as are exaggeration and feigned ignorance or denial of interest in eloquence. (These denials are often the most eloquently written passages within the work.)

Many second-century Christian writers can be understood only when viewed through a deep appreciation of rhetoric. The letters written by Ignatius of Antioch and the homily on the Passover preached by Melito of Sardis represent an Asiatic style with the hymnic cadences and well-accepted forms of argument that make up that tradition. Tatian, in his *Discourse to the Greeks*, argues the bankruptcy of Greek learning and culture in a style that shows both his dependence upon rhetorical canons and a study of Greek philosophy that was both deeper and broader than that of Justin Martyr.

In the third century, the strength of Tertullian's Latin, the unusual balance of his arguments, matching the beginning with the ending, the second section with the penultimate section, and so on, comes from careful mastery of rhetorical canons. Origen's *Against Celsus* evidences his grasp of the relationship between logic and rhetoric. He shows a mastery of Stoic formal logic and the use of plausibility and probability arguments.

Fourth and Fifth Centuries. A number of preachers and theologians of the fourth century were rhetoricians of the finest art. Many taught the subject. John Chrysostom's homilies in Attic Greek, perhaps the best from early Christianity, are concerned most often with biblical exegesis, but both his interpretive tools and his forms of presentation fit the rhetorical canons of his day. His exegetical sermons are often helpful thanks to his interest in the grammatical, literary character of the texts. His concern for symmetry and paradox creates both phrases and paragraphs that are memorable.

Gregory of Nazianzus, perhaps the greatest Greek orator since Demosthenes, could move audiences by his mastery of the art of persuasion and an inventive choice of figures. He was one of the first Christian writers to collect his own letters; he wrote over 17,000 lines of verse, including an autobiography of unusual depth, surpassed only by Augustine's *Confessions*. During his bitter debates with the Neoarians, he attacked their grasp of logic and use of rhetoric, particularly their understanding of Aristotle. Gregory's famous *Theological Orations* cannot be understood outside the context of philosophical rhetoric. He used both forms of enthymematic arguments. His grasp of theology was dependent as much on his understanding of rhetoric as on his sense of Christian tradition. He recognized that theology was a probabilistic discipline whose coherence could be argued logically but whose basis would need to be presented persuasively on the grounds of faith, not reason. For him, faith gave fullness to reason. Gregory is the most-quoted Orthodox theologian; his works are commonly quoted in Byzantine rhetorical handbooks for examples of rhetorical figures, precisely at the spots where ancient rhetoricians like Demosthenes were cited in classical and Hellenistic Greek handbooks.

Augustine's handbook *On Christian Doctrine* is concerned primarily with the problems of biblical interpretation. He employed rhetorical canons, beginning with the reading of a work aloud so as to reveal any textual corruptions. His concerns with pronunciation and cadence, dependent as they are on oral communication, are sometimes difficult for us to grasp fully today. Augustine offered various examples of how texts could be interpreted and particularly studied a work on hermeneutics written by Tyconius, thus indicating how interpretation and hermeneutics formed part of a rhetorical study. The final section of this treatise is devoted to the specific study of rhetoric, particularly that of Cicero, teaching biblical students to present their views persuasively. No other work on the relationship of rhetoric and Christian faith had such widespread influence. Many positions concerning persuasion and rhetoric taken during the western Middle Ages

were dependent upon this treatise of Augustine.
See also Preaching. [F.W.N.]

Bibliography

G. Kennedy, *The Art of Persuasion in Greece* (Princeton: Princeton UP, 1963); R.D. Sider, *Ancient Rhetoric and the Art of Tertullian* (Oxford: Oxford UP, 1971); G. Kennedy, *The Art of Rhetoric in the Roman World* (Princeton: Princeton UP, 1972); H. Lansberg, *Handbuch der literarischen Rhetorik: eine Grundlegung der Literaturwissenschaft,* 2 vols., 2. Auflage (Munich: Max Hueber, 1973); G. Kennedy, *Greek Rhetoric Under Christian Emperors* (Princeton: Princeton UP, 1983); idem, *New Testament Interpretation Through Rhetorical Criticism* (Chapel Hill: U of North Carolina P, 1984); J.L. Kinneavy, *Greek Rhetorical Origins of Christian Faith: An Inquiry* (Oxford: Oxford UP, 1987); J.J. Murphy, *Medieval Rhetoric: A Select Bibliography,* 2nd ed. (Toronto: U of Toronto P, 1989); F.W. Norris, *Faith Gives Fullness to Reasoning: A Commentary on Gregory Nazianzen's Theological Orations* (Leiden: Brill, forthcoming).

RINGS. Clement's *Instructor* indicates that Alexandrian Christians in the late second and early third centuries wore finger rings (signets or intaglios) that they used, in the common secular manner, to mark personal property against theft and to attest documents. Clement specifies certain subjects, such as dove, fish, lyre, and anchor, that in his view Christian signet owners could emblazon on their rings in good conscience and forbids others, such as idol, sword, bow, cup, lovers, and *hetairai.* We have no way of knowing to what extent Christians of the period heeded Clement's prescriptions.

The earliest surviving rings (intaglios enclosed in bezels surmounted on hoops, hoops alone marked with incuse epigraphy and symbols, and metal bezels surmounted on hoops) that can be positively linked on iconographic or epigraphic grounds to Christian owners date to the Constantinian period. The objects and scenes depicted on these rings accord with what is known in other media, although glyptic iconography, which pursues magical purposes (cf. Smith), exhibits a wide range of variants from the norm as known, for example, in painting or in sculpture. The greatest collections of rings are in London (cf. Dalton), Paris (uncatalogued), and Rome (uncatalogued). *See also* Art; Iconography. [P.C.F.]

Bibliography

Clement of Alexandria, *Instructor* 3.57.1–60.1.

O.M. Dalton, *Catalogue of Early Christian Antiquities and Objects from the Christian East. . .in the British Museum* (London: British Museum, 1901); H. Leclercq, "Gemmes," DACL (1924), Vol. 6.1, cols. 794–864; P. Maser, "Die Kreuzigungsdarstellung auf einem Siegelstein," *RAC* 52 (1976):257–275; J. Engeman, "Glyptik," RLAC (1981), Vol. 11, cols. 270–313; M. Smith, "Old Testament Motifs in the Iconography of the British Museum's Magical Gems," *Coins, Culture and History in the Ancient World . . . in Honor of Bluma Trell,* ed. L. Casson (Detroit: Wayne State UP, 1981), pp. 187–194.

ROMAN EMPIRE. The reign of the first Roman emperor, Augustus (27 B.C.–A.D. 14), coincided with the birth of Christ, a synchrony often remarked upon by Christian chroniclers. By then, most of the Roman empire in Europe and the Greek east had been acquired by a mixture of force and diplomacy, and consolidation of the acquisitions was proceeding apace. One such area was Judea, conquered by Pompey in the 60s B.C. The Romans respected tough enemies, and none came tougher than the Jews. This, allied to their uncompromising religion, a source of puzzlement and resentment to the more theologically complacent Romans, had an important consequence: the Romans would have been much less worried by Christ and his message had he not been a Jew.

First Century. During the first century A.D., the empire periodically increased, despite the policy of nonexpansion recommended by Augustus to his successor, Tiberius (A.D. 14–37), in whose reign the crucifixion took place. Major developments included the gradual conquest of Britain, begun under Claudius (41–54), and of Dacia (roughly modern Romania) by Trajan (98–117). Wars against the independent empire of Parthia in the east were concluded to Roman advantage under Nero (54–68) and Trajan, while the Jewish rebellion was put down over some years (66–74), largely by the future emperors Vespasian (69–79) and Titus (79–81); the city and temple of Jerusalem were destroyed, resistance ended with the celebrated siege of Masada, and the Jewish diaspora was extended. A consequence of this last was the growth of a substantial Jewish ghetto in the city of Rome (there already was one at Alexandria in Egypt, the second-largest city of the empire); its existence is clear enough from the anti-Jewish sentiments of the satirist Juvenal (ca. A.D. 100) in his poem on the horrors of Rome (*Satire* 3.14; cf. 14.96–106), a pagan pendant to the contemporary diatribe of the Book of Revelation, although it is notable that his full racist venom is reserved for Greeks.

Christians are not directly mentioned by Juvenal (an oblique reference to their punishment under Nero occurs in his *Satire* 1.155–157), a reticence due perhaps to contempt and the fact that the word *Christiani* would not fit his meter, although there were ways around that, rather than ignorance. Suetonius, in his *Claudius* 25, claims that emperor expelled Jews from Rome because of their constant rioting "at the instigation of Chrestus." It remains unclear whether this alludes to Christ (Tertullian, *Apol.* 3, complains of this misspelling, but Suetonius can spell *Christiani* correctly at *Nero* 16) or to some local agitator (Chrestus is a name suiting a freedman or foreigner—a praetorian prefect bore it in the early third century). There is no need to accuse Suetonius of chronological error here, as some do. There is documentary evidence of Claudius having to deal with Jewish-Greek clashes at Alexandria; similar outbreaks at Rome and their suppression can readily be accepted.

Nero notoriously used the Christians as scapegoats for the fire that destroyed much of Rome in 64. He might well have exploited the (at this time) better-known Jews (the Romans had by now developed a repertoire of Jewish jokes, but no Christian counterparts), had not their powerful patronage by his wife, Poppaea, and a favored actor, Aliturus, deflected him. It is only Tacitus (*Annals* 15.43–44) who formally connects the fire with the persecution, remarking that these Christians deserved what they got but adding that public opinion was appalled by their cruel punishments. Suetonius places the persecution in his list of Nero's good deeds (*Nero* 16); neither the Christians nor any other scapegoats appear in his account of the fire, and the same is true in the Byzantine epitome of the other major source, the third-century historian Dio Cassius (62.16–18).

One modern theory is that some apocalyptically-minded Christians, taking the burning city to portend the return of Christ, sought to help God's work by spreading the flames; these would be the self-confessed arsonists mentioned by Tacitus. Although such admissions might be worthless, being extracted under torture, the notion remains reasonable.

Domitian (81–96) is alleged by some Christian sources, notably Eusebius of Caesarea (*H.E.* 3.17–20), who also says he canceled it, to have promoted the second persecution; his pagan critics Suetonius (*Domitian* 12, with circumstantial detail) and Dio Cassius saw him rather as an enemy of Jews, an attitude that would suit the younger son and brother of Vespasian and Titus; Eusebius affirms that Vespasian did not persecute Christians.

So far, the early attacks, genuine and alleged, were confined to emperors conventionally regarded as "bad." But this changed dramatically. It is also notable that they occurred when Rome was under stress of war or natural calamity. There are no precise links of cause and effect, but the times were right for fear of the unusual, especially a militant foreign cult, and attempts to extirpate it.

Second Century. During the reign of Trajan, the second of Edward Gibbon's "five good emperors" and one later sufficiently reverenced by European Christians to be included in Dante's *Paradiso*, the lawyer and *littérateur* Pliny the Younger, while governing the eastern province of Bithynia, wrote to his emperor for advice on a local problem—the Christians (*Ep.* 10.96). Pliny's ignorance of what to do (allowing for his usual hyperconscientiousness in clearing policy with Trajan first), along with Trajan's opening remark that "it is impossible to lay down a general rule with a fixed formula," suggests that there was no clearcut Roman law against Christianity. It is commonly and reasonably thought that Christians would come under the ban on assemblies (*collegia*) imposed by Julius Caesar. The attitude of Pliny is odd. He attended no formal trials of accused religionists (although he did torture two deaconesses), felt that most of what the Christians did was socially harmless, yet concluded that they were "only a degenerate and fanatical cult"—a curious combination of terms! But it is clear that neither Pliny nor Trajan wanted to unleash an empirewide persecution.

The second century, especially after Hadrian (117–138), in whose reign Christianity was not an issue (albeit some sources credit him with sympathetic protection), is poorly documented. An item in Dio Cassius (69.3) commends Antoninus Pius (138–161, a sobriquet *not* earned by this policy) for not persecuting. With tragic paradox, it was in the reign of the otherwise admirable Marcus Aurelius (161–180) that Christianity widely and enduringly came into prominence. His reign was an age of martyrdoms, although it may be fair to say that Marcus permitted rather than promoted anti-Christian outbursts. The times were again ripe for fears of this sect—plague, barbarian invasion of Italy, war with Parthia, and civil war conspired to take their toll of normal Roman common sense and toleration. Marcus seems also unduly bothered by occasional Christian refusals to serve in the army at a time when pacifism was singularly unwelcome at Rome. It is symptomatic that the otherwise decent and educated Fronto, the African-born intellectual and imperial tutor, could accuse the Christians of secret intoxication and sexual orgies. The same attitude is manifest in the apparent allusion in the fictional *Metamorphoses* (or *Golden Ass*) of the contemporary Apuleius, in which a disreputable woman "rejects all true religion for a fantastic and blasphemous only God, in whose honor she drank from morning and whored at all hours" (9.14). Christianity also attracted the attention of the satirist Lucian of Samosata; although speaking kindly (*Passing of Peregrinus* 13) of their charitable works and mutual support, he ridicules the Christians' belief in eternal life and speaks of Christ as a "crucified sophist." This latter term was less offensive than some suppose (Lucian was himself a sophist!), and his mild remarks hardly deserved the Byzantine label of "anti-Christ" or his inclusion in the old Catholic Index. Lucian also mentions Christians in his *Alexander,* a pamphlet addressed to Celsus, probably that Celsus who penned *The True Word,* the first serious pagan attempt to counter Christianity intellectually.

Third Century. The century after Marcus is again badly documented on the pagan side; the Christian view of things is increasingly heard, in Greek and Latin. There are tantalizing glimpses—for instance, Dio Cassius's mention (72.4.7) of the emperor Commodus's (180–192) mistress Marcia as a protector of Christians, also the claim in the unreliable pagan *Historia Augusta* that Alexander Severus (222–235) had a statue of Christ in his private chapel. Late tradition made Philip the Arabian (244–249) the first (albeit crypto) Christian emperor, a fancy no doubt tailored to fit the fact that Rome celebrated its millenary in his reign. During the half-century of anarchy (235–285), an age of constant civil war if little loss of imperial territory, some emperors earned notoriety as persecutors, notably Decius (249–251) and Valerian (253–260). The latter, the first Roman emperor ever to be taken and held prisoner of war, was captured by the Sassanian rulers of Persia, the new and militant replacement for the Parthians in the east, whose own ardent Zoroastrianism was a novel and complicating factor in Roman religious policy; Mani was executed by them at this time, and a desire to appease Persia may have contributed to Diocletian's persecution.

Fourth Century. Diocletian (285–305) himself had less stomach for this last and worst attack (303–311) than his colleagues Galerius and Maximian. He became emperor in what has been characterized as the "Age of Anxiety," inheriting every conceivable secular problem. His own aversion to Christianity seems due largely to personal faith in paganism and unwarranted fear of the pacifist strain in some Christian sects. Nor was it simple capitulation to an ignorant mob demanding "the Christians to the lions." Some Neoplatonist philosophers urged the persecution, and Porphyry's influential tract *Against the Christians* came out at this time.

Everything changed with Constantine, sole emperor after 324. His motives for favoring Christianity have been endlessly debated. Genuine faith and conversion or political expediency: every theory has its problems. After Constantine (306–337), every Roman and

Byzantine emperor was nominally Christian, with the notorious exception of Julian "the Apostate" (361–363). Julian pursued what Jerome neatly dubbed "the gentle persecution," fomenting splits between Christian leaders and followers that they might destroy each other, adding his own intellectual stimulus in many writings, notably *Against the Galileans* (incomplete, but showing impressive knowledge of the Old Testament). It seems unlikely that a longer reign would have turned back the religious clock. His successor, Jovian, was a Christian, and there were no more Julians; his own substitute faith was a mélange well beyond the comprehension of ordinary people, and as he himself admitted, the "Galileans" were outdoing his pagans in the vital area of charity.

The boot was now on the other foot. Paganism was persecuted with varying degrees of severity. But there was no sustained bloodbath; individual pagans were often tolerated and advanced, and paganism hung on for several centuries. Christian treatment of other Christians was frequently far sorrier, often being based on such concepts as "orthodoxy" and "heresy." As Ammianus Marcellinus, a contemporary historian and far from purblind admirer of Julian, remarked, "No wild beast is so savage toward mankind as are Christians to each other"; he overstated his case, but there was a case to be overstated.

The fourth century completed the secular as well as the religious transformation of antiquity. On May 11, 330, Constantine inaugurated his new city of Constantinople, destined to be the capital of the Byzantine empire until its fall in 1453. The always Christian Byzantines, although eastern and hellenophone, thought of themselves as new Romans, not new Athenians.

Christian Attitudes Toward the Empire. The Goths and Vandals likewise turned themselves into ersatz Romans; Orosius (7.43.6) among others approved this process. Why did Christians not start again with a completely new beginning? Largely because church tradition had not been against the Roman empire as such. It preferred a Christian Rome to a Romeless world. This attitude was consonant with Christ's "Render unto Caesar" injunction and with Paul's pride in his Roman citizenship (Acts 16:37–38; 22:27, 29). The apocalyptic anti-Romanism of Revelation, in which Rome is denounced not by name but through the figurative Babylon, is unusual, being closer in sentiment to its contemporary pagan counterpart, Juvenal's *Third Satire,* as well as the *Sibylline Oracles.* Christianity did not monopolize dire predictions. Scipio had foretold the end of Rome while watching Carthage burn in 146 B.C., and the emperors Tiberius and Nero liked to quote the Greek "When I am dead, let fire consume the earth" (Dio Cassius 58.23.4; Suetonius, *Nero* 38.1). Christian and pagan moralizing shared many assumptions. Early Greek fathers, such as Clement of Alexandria, Justin Martyr, and Tatian, fulminated against the immorality and absurdity of classical religion, but their terms of reference were identical with those of paganism's own critics, above all Lucian.

Antipathy to Rome was softened by contacts with the wider benefits of the *Pax Romana* and with contemporary Hellenism, a process exemplified by Philo, who combined Jewishness with admiration of Augustus (*Embassy to Gaius* 3–5; 144), and by Tertullian, who renounced classical culture ("What has Athens to do with Jerusalem?") but insisted that Christians prayed to their God for the empire's well-being (*Apol.* 30.1; 32.1). Harsher notes were sounded by Minucius Felix, who denounced Roman imperialism in Tacitean tones and prefigured the view that all empires must fall (*Oct.* 25.5, 13), and by Commodian, who warned against the treacherous seductions of peace (*Instr.* 2.21).

The grim view resulted from local sufferings; almost all the western martyrdoms up to 300 were in Africa. Likewise, the fifth-century gloom of Salvian of Marseilles ("Rome dies laughing"—a Juvenalian epigram) came from contemporary troubles and his own sour temperament. He was well out of the mainstream. With the advent of Constantine, Christians lost all reason to pray for the empire's end. Eusebius, notably in his *Theophany,* hastened to promote the requisite ideology: the empire had paved the way for the Word of God; henceforth, Christ would be its partner in success.

During Alaric's sieges of Rome (408–410), the Christian authorities were desperate enough to permit pagan rites in the city's defense; but no one could be found to perform them (Zosimus, *H.E.* 5.41). To Socrates Scholasticus in Constantinople, Rome's capture was an event hardly worth noticing, certainly no cause for threnody (*H.E.* 7.11). But to Jerome in Bethlehem, it was the end of the world (*Ep.* 128).

An anonymous late epigram in the *Greek Anthology* sums it up: "Rome [i.e., Constantinople], queen of the world, your fame will live for ever, for Victory is wingless and so cannot fly away" (9.647). The point is, this couplet could have been penned at any time, in old or new Rome, by a pagan or a Christian.

End of the Empire. In 395, the Roman empire was divided into two halves, east and west, with separate rulers, courts, and (increasingly) languages. Apart from the ephemeral efforts of Justinian I (527–565), best regarded as both the last Roman and first real Byzantine emperor, to regain the "lost territories," this division would be permanent, albeit soon made meaningless by the transformation of the west into separate kingdoms founded by the different Germanic peoples (Vandals, Goths, Franks) in the fifth century. In his attempts to establish religious orthodoxy by law and sword, Justinian also crystallized the old and the new.

The old empire was gone, and the Roman map of the world was redrawn with the genesis of some modern countries. Secular events prompted the now-venerable debate over the "decline and fall." Every theory has its problems; none, for instance, will work that does not account for the survival of the east along with the nonsurvival (in its old form) of the west. Those with a partiality for Occam's razor might see the relative internal stability and freedom from foreign invasions enjoyed by the east as a critical factor. Many pagans understandably blamed the Christians, a point of view countered by Augustine and Orosius, among others, in their piling-up of lists of similar disasters suffered before God had ousted Jupiter. Gibbon's formulation of the same explanation

is, much as one admires the incomparable elegance and wit of his narrative, conditioned by some obvious eighteenth-century prejudices (aversion to "superstition," the unfortunate return of the "noble savage" theory), and ultimately unhistorical. Christianity, along with Marxism and Islam, remains one of the three movements that shape nearly every country on the planet earth and can thereby be considered as the largest and most vital survival of the classical heritage. *See also* Church and State; Eparchy; Paganism and Christianity; Persecution; Rome. [B.B.]

Bibliography

E. Gibbon, *The Decline and Fall of the Roman Empire,* ed. J.B. Bury, 7 vols. (London: Dent, 1909–1914); A.H.M. Jones, *Constantine and the Conversion of Europe* (London: English Universities P, 1948); M. Chambers, ed., *The Fall of Rome: Can It Be Explained?* (New York: Holt, Rinehart and Winston, 1963); A.N. Sherwin-White, *Roman Society and Roman Law in the New Testament* (Oxford: Oxford UP, 1963); E.R. Dodds, *Pagan and Christian in an Age of Anxiety* (Cambridge: Cambridge UP, 1965); W. Kaegi, *Byzantium and the Decline of Rome* (Princeton: Princeton UP, 1968); R.P.C. Hanson, "The Reaction of the Church to the Collapse of the Western Roman Empire in the Fifth Century," *VChr* 26 (1972):272–287; A. Garzetti, *From Tiberius to the Antonines* (London: Methuen, 1974); P. Brown, *The Making of Late Antiquity* (Cambridge: Harvard UP, 1978); J.P.V.D. Balsdon, *Romans and Aliens* (London: Duckworth, 1979); C. Mango, *Byzantium: The Empire of New Rome* (London: Weidenfeld and Nicolson, 1980); T.D. Barnes, *Constantine and Eusebius* (Cambridge: Harvard UP, 1981); R.L. Wilken, *The Christians as the Romans Saw Them* (New Haven: Yale UP, 1984); C.M. Wells, *The Roman Empire* (London: Fontana, 1984); T.D. Barnes, *Early Christianity and the Roman Empire* (London: Variorum Reprints, 1985); R. MacMullen, *Christianizing the Roman Empire* (New Haven: Yale UP, 1985); B. Baldwin, *Studies on Greek and Roman History and Literature* (Amsterdam: Gieben, 1985); A. Ferrill, *The Fall of the Roman Empire: The Military Explanation* (London: Thames and Hudson, 1986); J. Herrin, *The Formation of Christendom* (Princeton UP, 1987).

ROMAN EMPERORS

Augustus	27 B.C.–A.D. 14
Tiberius	A.D. 14–37
Gaius (Caligula)	37–41
Claudius	41–54
Nero	54–68

ROMANOS MELODOS (ca. 485–ca. 560). Eastern religious poet and hymnographer. Born at Emesa in Syria, Romanos was for a time a deacon in Beirut but is known for his work at Constantinople. He is the most significant composer of *kontakia* (verse sermons chanted to music, based on a stress accent). About eighty pieces appear under his name, although not all are genuine. Some, such as those on the nativity and on the resurrection, are critically acclaimed. The extent of Romanos's indebtedness to Ephraem the Syrian and to the *Diatessaron* of Tatian is debated.   CPG III, 7570.   [M.P.McH.]

Bibliography

Sancti Romani Melodi Cantica, ed. P. Maas and C.A. Trypanis, Vol. 1: *Cantica Genuina* (Oxford: Clarendon, 1963); Vol. 2: *Cantica Dubia* (Berlin: de Gruyter, 1970); *Romanos le Mélode, Hymnes*, ed. J. Grosdidier de Matons, 5 vols., SC (1964–1981), Vols. 99, 110, 114, 128, 283; *Kontakia of Romanos, Byzantine Melodist*, tr. M. Carpenter, 2 vols. (Columbia: U of Missouri P, 1970, 1973).

J. Grosdidier de Matons, *Romanos le Mélode et les origines de la poésie religieuse à Byzance* (Paris: Beauchesne, 1977); E.C. Topping, "St. Romanos the Melodos: Prince of Byzantine Poets," *GOTR* 24 (1979):65–75; W.L. Petersen, "The Dependence of Romanos the Melodist upon the Syrian Ephrem: Its Importance for the Origin of the Kontakion," *VChr* 39 (1985):171–187.

ROMANS. Letter of Paul "to all God's beloved in Rome" (1:7). Addressed to the congregation or congregations of Christians in the imperial capital, which Paul was intent on visiting (1:10), Romans was generally accessible to early Christians as part of the collection of Pauline letters published early in the second century.

Romans itself is commonly regarded as among the earlier letters of Paul, although John Knox argues cogently that it may have been among the last. In either case, it is closely associated with the letter to the Galatians, asserting in much the same language but at greater length that in Christ all believers are presented righteous before God on the basis of faith rather than obedience to the Law (3:19–26). It is thus in part a defense of Paul's view that the law of circumcision has been abrogated, and that Jews and Gentiles alike are made Christians through confession of faith and baptism alone (6:1–12; 8:1–18). This new dispensation is seen as foreshadowed in God's acceptance of Abraham's faith before the giving of the Law and in connection with the promise that Abraham will be the "father of many nations" (4:1–4, 16–25).

Romans came to controversial prominence in connection with Marcion's interpretation of Paul as having distinguished an evil God of the Law, bent on subjecting the creation to condemnation for disobedience, from the true God and Father of our Lord Jesus Christ, who saves through faith. Although Marcion placed Galatians first in his list of Pauline letters, Romans also had a place in Marcion's new scriptures with which he sought to replace the Law and Prophets. The letter also played a part in Gnosticism, particularly in the efforts of the Valentinians to find support in Paul for their teaching about an imperfect creator different from the true God who gives "knowledge" to spiritual Christians through the Savior.

In reply to both Marcion and the Valentinians, Irenaeus of Lyons interpreted Paul in the light of the stress in Ephesians 1:10 on Christ as "recapitulating" or "heading-up-again" the human nature disfigured by Adam and subjected to sin and death. Irenaeus stresses the relation of the covenants of Law and grace against Marcion and begins the emphasis, pressed by Origen in his commentary on Romans, on Paul's teaching about the freedom of the will in contrast to Valentinian teaching about the salvation of a spiritual elect.

A quite different approach to Romans is taken by Augustine of Hippo, in early fragmentary comments in the *Letter to Simplician*, in the major writings, and in the dispute with Pelagius and his followers. Here, Paul is treated as an analyst of the way in which every person discovers guilt through the imposition of Law and is saved only by the grace that enables the will to overcome the bondage to sin that Law reveals. Augustine's approach is perhaps no less "psychological" than those of Origen and other Greek commentators, but it marks a new departure in the treatment of Romans, which made it a central document in the controversies of the Reformation.

The present problem is to discover the real Paul behind these patristic interpretations so as to let them stand out in their own right as reflecting the questions to which answers were sought from the readings of Paul's work.

[L.G.P.]

Bibliography

Origen, *In epistulam Pauli ad Romanos* (see CPG I, 1457); John Chrysostom, *Homilies on Romans*, tr. J.B. Morris, NPNF, 1st ser. (1889), Vol. 11, pp. 335–564; Theodore of Mopsuestia, *In epistulam ad Romanos*, PG 66.787–876; Cyril of Alexandria, *Explanatio in epistulam ad Romanos*, PG 74.773–856; Theodoret, *Interpretatio epistulae ad Romanos*, PG

82.36ff.; Ambrosiaster, *Commentarius in epistulam ad Romanos*, ed. H.J. Vogels, CSEL (1966), Vol. 81; Pelagius, *Expositiones epistularum Pauli*, ed. A. Souter, TS 9.2 (1926):6–126; Augustine, *Propositions from the Epistle to the Romans and Unfinished Commentary on the Epistle to the Romans*, ed. P.F. Landes (Chico: Scholars, 1982).

J. Murray, *The Epistle to the Romans* (Grand Rapids: Eerdmans, 1968); E. Käsemann, *Commentary on Romans* (Grand Rapids: Eerdmans, 1980).

J. Knox, *Marcion and the New Testament* (Chicago: U of Chicago P, 1942); idem, *Chapters in a Life of Paul* (New York: Abingdon-Cokesbury, 1950); A. Benoit, *Saint Irénée: introduction à l'étude de sa théologie* (Paris: Presses Universitaires de France, 1960); P. Brown, *Augustine of Hippo: A Biography* (Berkeley: U of California P, 1967); M.F. Wiles, *The Divine Apostle: The Interpretation of St. Paul's Epistles in the Early Church* (Cambridge: Cambridge UP, 1967); K. Stendahl, "The Apostle Paul and the Introspective Conscience of the West," *The Writings of St. Paul*, ed. W. Meeks (New York: Norton, 1972); E.H. Pagels, *The Gnostic Paul: Gnostic Exegesis of the Pauline Letters* (Philadelphia: Fortress, 1975); H. Gamble, *The Textual History of the Letter to the Romans* (Grand Rapids: Eerdmans, 1977); K.P. Donfried, ed., *The Romans Debate* (Minneapolis: Augsburg, 1977); P. Gorday, *Principles of Patristic Exegesis: Romans 9–11 in Origen, John Chrysostom, and Augustine* (New York: Mellen, 1983).

ROME. Capital of the Roman empire and largest city of the Mediterranean world. Legend had it that the city was founded on April 20, 753 B.C., by the twins Romulus and Remus on the Tiber River in central Italy. Settlement spread to the "seven hills," and the site has been continuously inhabited ever since.

Rome was one of the most important early Christian centers. According to tradition, it was the site of the martyrdoms of both Peter and Paul in the 60s A.D. Subsequently, the bishops of Rome gained an increasing role as church leaders; by the sixth century, they alone came to use the title "pope." By the eighth century, the popes increasingly were able to exercise their independence of the Byzantine emperors.

Early History. Archaeological investigations indicate that by the mid-eighth century B.C. the only habitation on the site of Rome consisted of huts on several of the hills. The lower, marshy area was used only as a burial ground. Rome did not become urbanized until it was annexed by the Etruscans in the late seventh century B.C.

The Roman tradition that the city was originally ruled by kings appears to be true, as does the belief that the last of the Etruscan kings, Tarquin the Proud, was expelled ca. 509 B.C. The period of the kings was followed by what the Romans called the *res publica.* The republic was actually an aristocracy, later an oligarchy, in which the real power lay in the hands of a narrow group of large landowners whose members made up the senate. The chief executive officers were two consuls, elected every year, whose primary responsibility was to lead the army.

Beginning in the mid-fourth century B.C., Rome began to extend its influence over Italy. To facilitate communications, the famous Roman road system was begun in 312 B.C. with the Via Appia to Campania. At the same time, the first aqueduct, the Aqua Appia, was built to bring water into the city. By 268 B.C., Rome had completed its conquest of the Italian peoples, and between 264 and 201 the Romans fought their most difficult wars, with the city of Carthage in North Africa (modern Tunisia).

The second century B.C. saw the defeat of the other Mediterranean powers, including Antigonid Macedonia and Seleucid Syria. Although the Romans initially had been reluctant to acquire overseas provinces, for which they did not have an effective administrative machinery, by 130 B.C. Roman territory included lands from Spain to Anatolia.

Native Roman religion was essentially contractual in nature and was concerned with propitiating vague, ill-defined forces called *numina.* This concept of the *quid pro quo* ("this for that") had an important influence upon the later development of Roman law. The Roman presence in the eastern Mediterranean saw the rise of philhellenism; the Romans gradually adopted much of Greek culture, including literature, mythology, and religion.

The increasing wealth and power of Rome were reflected in the growing magnificence of the city. In the second century B.C., the Basilica Aemilia, a law court, was built in the Forum, and two new aqueducts were also constructed. In 78 B.C., the Tabularium, or state records office, was built on the slopes of the Capitoline Hill. Subsequently, powerful, ambitious senators endowed the city with additional buildings. In 55 B.C., Pompey built the city's first permanent stone theater. In the early 40s, Julius Caesar began the practice of building new fora; his own was focused on a temple of Venus the Ancestress.

The Early Empire. The establishment of the Roman empire by Octavian (Augustus, 27 B.C.–A.D. 14) saw an explosion of building activity in Rome as successive emperors attempted not only to outdo their predecessors but also to impress people of the city with their devotion. Augustus is known as the emperor who changed Rome "from a city of brick into a city of marble," and he was in fact responsible for much renovation and new construction (*Res gestae* 19–21).

Building activities continued under the subsequent Julio-Claudian emperors.

During the reign of Claudius, probably in 51 or 52, the Christians made their first attested appearance in Rome. Suetonius notes that at this time "[Claudius] expelled from Rome the Jews, who were assiduously creating disturbances at the instigation of Chrestus" (*Claudius* 25). Other Roman sources refer to the early Christians as *Chrestiani.* This same expulsion of the Jews is mentioned in Acts 18:2. These Roman disturbances probably are similar to other ones caused by Christian preaching in the Jewish communities in other parts of the empire. At this time, of course, the Roman authorities could not distinguish between Jews and Christians. By the time Paul wrote his letter to the Romans (ca. 58), the church of Rome seems to have been firmly established: at the end of the letter, he mentions twenty-four Roman Christians by name.

In the year A.D. 64, during the reign of Nero (54–68), a great fire destroyed much of central Rome, as reported by the historian Tacitus: "Disaster followed, in the form of the most terrible and destructive fire Rome has ever known. Whether this fire was accidental, or elaborately contrived by the emperor, is uncer-

tain. . . . It began in the part of the Circus Maximus [the chariot racecourse] that is close to the Palatine and Caelian Hills, and among shops whose wares included inflammable goods. The fire took hold at once, and the wind very quickly spread it the length of the Circus. . . . First it swept through all the level ground, then climbed the hills, then returned again to destroy the lower districts. The speed with which it spread, and the all-too-combustible nature of the old city, with its narrow winding streets and irregular buildings, nullified all attempts to contain it. . . . The fire was brought to a halt on the sixth day. . . " (*Annals* 15.38–41). Suetonius (*Nero* 38) gives a similar account and notes that "Nero's men destroyed. . .every ancient monument of historical interest that had hitherto survived."

In order to escape accusations that he had been behind this disaster, Nero affixed the blame for the fire upon the small Christian community of Rome (Tacitus, *Annals* 15.44). He thus brought about the first persecution of the Christians, during which both Peter and Paul were said to have been martyred. After this extensive destruction, the city was rebuilt in a more organized fashion. This new Neronian city was to last in substantially the same form until the end of the imperial period.

Nero was the last of the relatives of Augustus to hold the throne. After a short period of civil war (68–69), the general Vespasian (69–79) founded the second imperial dynasty, that of the Flavians (69–96). Under them, much new building occurred, including the Flavian amphitheater, otherwise known as the Colosseum. Vespasian's elder son, Titus (79–81), built a Temple of the Deified Vespasian; his younger son, Domitian (81–96), erected a triumphal arch in the Republican Forum in honor of his brother Titus's victory over the Jews and the sack of Jerusalem (A.D. 70).

At this time, a number of high-ranking members of Roman society began to adopt the Christian religion. Manlius Acilius Glabrio, consul in 91, and Flavius Clemens, the cousin of the emperor Domitian and consul in 95, for example, both may have been Christians. The latter's wife, Flavia Domitilla (Domitian's niece), owned the land that in the early third century became a Christian burial place, the cemetery of Domitilla. The two were charged with "atheism" and the adoption of Jewish ways; Clemens was executed and Domitilla was exiled.

Five Good Emperors. After the murder of Domitian in 96, Rome was ruled by the Antonine emperors, the first five of whom were also known as the "five good emperors" (96–180), who were chosen on the basis of their ability, not because of their blood relationship to the previous emperor. The first of them, the elderly senator Nerva (96–98), completed the forum begun by Domitian. It probably was during the reign of Nerva that Clement, one of the first bishops of Rome (ca. 88–97), wrote his letter to the church of Corinth. Clement, the son of the Roman Faustinus and of Jewish descent, was said to have been a convert and follower of Paul and to have been named bishop of Rome by Peter, although he is in fact listed as the third Roman bishop after Peter. His house was used as a church during the early centuries of the Christian era; in the third century, part of it served as a shrine of the Persian god Mithras. In the early fourth century, a much larger basilica was built atop the house and in 1108 another basilica (S. Clemente) was built on top of this one. The lower basilica was not rediscovered until 1857, and beneath it lies the small stuccoed chamber identified as part of Clement's house.

Nerva's successor, the popular army commander Trajan (98–117), embarked on some ambitious building projects in Rome, including a triumphal arch, a new bath complex, and the last, and most ambitious, of the imperial fora, Trajan's Forum.

The emperor Hadrian (117–138) was responsible for the construction of many new monuments and even designed some of them. In the Forum across from the Colosseum, he built an elaborate architectural pun, the Temple of Venus and Rome. This temple was actually two temples, back-to-back and mirror images of each other, one in honor of Venus (*Amor*, or love) and the other in honor of Rome

(*Roma*). He also renovated or rebuilt many of the buildings in Rome, leaving on them the names of their original builders. The most noteworthy of these was the round Pantheon, a temple of all the gods, the largest surviving roofed building in Rome. (Until 1892, it was thought to have been built by Agrippa, whose name is the only one to appear on it.)

Antoninus Pius (138–161) constructed a well-preserved temple in the Forum for his deified wife, Faustina; after his death, it became his own temple as well. The last of the "five good emperors," Marcus Aurelius (161–180), raised his own column, which depicts scenes from his wars against the Germans, as well as a column of Antoninus Pius, which now exists only in fragments.

According to tradition, another early Christian church, that of St. Praxedis, dates to the Antonine period. Praxedis and Pudentiana were said to have been the daughters of the senator Pudens, whom they persuaded to give refuge to Peter in his house on the Viminal Hill. In the 140s, the house was said to have been consecrated as a church. The existing Church of St. Praxedis dates to 822. Also ca. 140, the Roman Christian Hermas, probably a freedman and the brother of the Roman bishop Pius I (ca. 140–155), completed his famous work the *Shepherd*. At the end of the second century, Victor I (ca. 189–199) became the first Roman bishop to attempt to regulate the practices of all the churches, by his involvement in the Paschal controversy.

From Severus to Constantine. The Severan dynasty (193–235) saw some of the last new extensive imperial construction in Rome. Septimius Severus (193–211) built a new imperial palace on the Palatine Hill, the arch of Severus in the Forum, the arch in the Forum Boarium, and the Septizonium, a gateway that survived until 1588.

Severus's son Caracalla (211–217) was responsible for a new aqueduct and the well-preserved Baths of Caracalla. Not many years after his assassination, however, Rome entered the trying period of the imperial crisis, or military anarchy (235–284), and the empire was racked by civil wars and foreign invasions.

Under the emperor Decius (249–251), there occurred the first empirewide persecution of the Christians. Many of the martyrs of this and other persecutions were buried in the underground cemeteries of Rome located outside the walls. Important catacombs include those of Callistus, Cecilia, Domitilla, and Sebastian. Catacombs, as places of burial, were the sites of commemorations of the martyrs, but they do not seem to have been used as places of refuge, for their existence was well known. In the persecution of Valerian, in 258, for example, they were the first places to be searched.

In the 250s, the church of Rome became embroiled in the Novatianist controversy, when the rivals Cornelius, who eventually prevailed, and Novatian contended for the see. At the same time, the Roman bishops began to build on the tradition that they were the successors to Peter, as they emphasized later in the African Donatist controversy of the fourth century.

Little building was done until the reign of Aurelian (270–275), when a new wall was hurriedly constructed around the city. Aurelian also built a temple of the sun. Under Diocletian (284–305), a good deal of restoration work was undertaken in the Forum. The Curia was rebuilt in its present form, and the partially extant Baths of Diocletian also were erected. Maxentius (306–312) began work on a new basilica, the last major building in the Republican Forum, completed under Constantine (306–337). The Arch of Constantine next to the Colosseum, commemorating Constantine's victory over Maxentius at the battle of the Milvian Bridge (312), was decorated primarily with artwork cannibalized from monuments of earlier emperors. At the same time, however, the lessened importance of Rome as an imperial city was marked by the founding of Constantinople as a second capital in the east (330).

Christian Rome. The first great age of church construction in Rome began with Constantine, who demonstrated his support of the Christian faith by building no fewer than ten churches in and around Rome, including the basilica of St. John in the Lateran (the "Constantinian basilica," which collapsed in 877) to serve as the seat of the bishop of Rome. Also constructed, primarily in the episcopate of Sylvester I (314–335), were the churches of the Apostles (Peter and Paul), of SS. Marcellinus and Peter, of the Holy Cross in Jerusalem, of St. Agnes, of St. Laurence, of St. Paul, the *titulus Equitii* (Church of St. Martin), the *titulus Marci* (Church of St. Mark), and the basilica of St. Peter in the modern Vatican (demolished in the Renaissance to make way for the present basilica). The dedicatory inscription of the last of these reads "because under Your leadership the world has risen triumphant to the stars, Constantine the Victor has founded this church for You" (Diehl, *I.L.C.V.*, Vol. 1, no. 1752).

The new alliance of state and church meant that the position of Rome as imperial capital gave added luster to the prestige of the bishop of Rome. Later centuries even gave rise to the legend that there had been a "Donation of Constantine," which granted to Sylvester I and his successors dominion over the entire western empire. As papal authority grew, conflicts over the episcopal office became even more heated, notably in 366–367, when blood ran in the streets during the conflict between Damasus I (366–384) and Ursinus (366–367). The pagan senator Praetextatus cynically commented that if he could be pope, he too would become a Christian (Jerome, *C. Ioh. Hieros.* 8).

Also in the fourth century were built the basilica of Julius, later Sta. Maria in Trastevere, under Julius I (337–352), and the basilica of Liberius, later Sta. Maria Maggiore, under Liberius (352–366), and Sta. Lorenzo in Damaso under Damasus I. Damasus also was largely responsible for the repair and restoration of the catacombs: he cleaned them out, added skylights, identified many of the burials, and discouraged new graves.

By this time, however, numerous splinter sects had established themselves at Rome. The Novatianists continued to choose their own bishops, as did the Luciferians and the African Donatists. Also present were the Marcionites, Montanists, Sabellians, and Valentinians.

During the fifth century, the bishops of Rome, with the support of the imperial government, began to assert increasing authority. Innocent I (402–417) solidified a papal vicariate in Illyricum, and Celestine I (422–432) closed the last Novatianist churches in Rome. Several imperial decrees were issued against the "Manichaeans" (a catchall epithet for heretics) who supposedly infested Rome. Leo I the Great (440–461) extended his jurisdiction into Spain and succeeded in gaining from the emperor Valentinian III (425–455) a rescript granting him authority over the entire western church.

The increasing status of the church of Rome was reflected in another round of church building. The *titulus Vestinae* (a church of SS. Gervasius and Protasius, now St. Vitale) was built under Innocent I (402–417), and the basilicas of Sta. Sabina and of St. Lawrence outside the walls under Sixtus III (432–440), the latter with the help of the emperor Valentinian III. Simplicius (468–483) was responsible for the basilica of St. Stephen ("S. Stefano Rotundo").

Decline of Rome. Meanwhile, the secular authority of the western Roman empire had been undergoing a rapid decline. In 402, the Visigoths invaded Italy, and in 410, under their leader Alaric, they occupied Rome, but the three-day sack did more psychological than architectural damage. In 455, a seventeen-day sack by the Vandals, who had occupied North Africa, was more ruinous. On this occasion, the treasures Titus had brought back from the Jewish temple of Jerusalem were carried off, although they subsequently were lost at sea. The declining architectural condition of Rome in the mid-fifth century is aptly described by a law of the emperor Majorian (457–461): "We are anxious to correct the obnoxious practices that have long been allowed to deface the appearance of the Venerable City. For it is obvious that public buildings . . . are on all sides being destroyed by the most deplorable connivance of the city administration. While the requisite materials for public buildings are being collected, the noble constructions of antiquity are torn down, and a great desecration is committed to allow a trivial repair. . . . We therefore proclaim by a general law that all public

buildings . . . may not be destroyed by anyone . . ." (*Nov. Maj.* 4: A.D. 458). The very need to issue such a law indicates the prevalence of such practices and suggests that by the fifth century many of the monuments of classical Rome were rapidly approaching a state of decrepitude if not ruin. By this time, the western empire had been reduced to Italy and southern Gaul. Milan and then Ravenna had long since replaced Rome as the *de facto* capital of the western empire.

The year 404 saw the last gladiatorial combats in the Colosseum and 523 the last wild animal hunts. The last new monument in the old Republican Forum was a column of the Byzantine usurper Phocas (602–610), erected by Gregory the Great (590–604). Church building did continue, even if at a reduced pace. For instance, Felix III (IV) (526–530) converted an old Roman archive building into the surviving basilica of SS. Cosma e Damiano.

In 536, the Byzantine general Belisarius invaded Italy to reclaim it from the Ostrogoths. The subsequent twenty-six years of warfare completed the ruin of classical Rome. During several sieges of the city, the aqueducts were cut, the walls broken, and the city often virtually deserted. The emperor Justinian I's attempts to restore the condition of Italy were forestalled by the invasion of the Lombards in 568. For the rest of the century, little new building activity took place; Pelagius II (579–590) rebuilt the basilica of St. Lawrence essentially in its present form.

As the Byzantine control of Rome weakened in the seventh century, the bishops of Rome became ever more independent. Throughout the Middle Ages, Rome became increasingly important as a western Christian center. But of the ancient secular monuments, only those that had been converted into churches, such as the archives, Curia, and Pantheon, were to survive intact. *See also* Catacombs; Italy; Papacy; Roman Empire.

[R.W.M.]

Bibliography

D.R. Dudley, *Urbs Roma: A Source Book of the Classical Texts on the City and Its Monuments* (Aberdeen: Phaidon, 1967); F. Gregorovius, *Rome and Medieval Culture: Selections from the History* of the City of Rome in the Middle Ages (Chicago: U of Chicago P, 1971); A.G. McKay, Roma Antiqua: Latium and Etruria, A Sourcebook of Classical Texts (Lanham: UP of America, 1986).

S.B. Platner and T. Ashby, A Topographical Dictionary of Ancient Rome (London: Oxford UP, H. Milford, 1929); J. Carcopino, Daily Life in Ancient Rome (New Haven: Yale UP, 1940); D.M. Robathan, The Monuments of Ancient Rome (Rome: Bretschneider, 1950); P.L. MacKendrick, The Mute Stones Speak: The Story of Archaeology in Italy (New York: St. Martin, 1960); E. Nash, A Pictorial Dictionary of Ancient Rome (London: Swemmer, and New York: Praeger, 1961); H.T. Rowell, Rome in the Augustan Age (Norman: U of Oklahoma P, 1962); D. Thompson, The Idea of Rome from Antiquity to the Renaissance (Albuquerque: U of New Mexico P, 1971); E. Crucitti-Raber, Rome: Pagan and Christian (Rome: Fratelli Palombi, 1975); R. Lanciani, The Ruins and Excavations of Ancient Rome (New York: Bell, 1979); R.E. Brown and J.P. Meier, Antioch and Rome: New Testament Cradles of Catholic Christianity (New York: Paulist, 1983).

ROTAS SATOR (first century). Latin word square that spells the same words in every direction:

```
R   O   T   A   S
O   P   E   R   A
T   E   N   E   T
A   R   E   P   O
S   A   T   O   R
```

Excavations have revealed examples from Britain, Pompeii, and Dura-Europos. The association with Christianity depends on the arrangement of the letters to spell Pater Noster ("Our Father") in Latin with the letters A and O (alpha and omega) left over:

```
              P
              A
          A   T   O
              E
              R
P A T E R N O S T E R
              O
              S
          A   T   O
              E
              R
```

Although the result is striking, the interpretation rests on unlikely assumptions, and a non-Christian meaning is more probable.   [E.F.]

Bibliography

D. Fishwick, "On the Origin of the Rotas-Sator Square," HThR 57 (1964):39–53; E. Dinkler, Signum Crucis (Tübingen: Mohr, 1967), pp. 160–173; W.O. Moeller, The Mithraic Origin and Meanings of the Rotas-Sator Square (Leiden: Brill, 1973); W. Baines, "The Rotas-Sator Square: A New Investigation," NTS 33 (1987): 469–476.

RUFINUS OF AQUILEIA (ca. 345–410). Monk and translator. Born near Aquileia, Rufinus studied at Rome, where he first met Jerome. Returning home, he lived for a time (368–373) in a community devoted to practices of asceticism. He spent the years 373–380 in Egypt, where he visited the desert fathers and became a student of Didymus the Blind, who was influenced by the teachings of Origen. He then joined with Melania the Elder in founding a double monastery for men and women in Jerusalem on the Mount of Olives (381). Jerome, who settled in Bethlehem (386), supported Epiphanius of Salamis in challenging the orthodoxy of the teachings of Origen against the position taken by Rufinus and bishop John of Jerusalem. The conflict was resolved for the moment through the efforts of Theophilus of Alexandria. Rufinus returned to Italy in 397 and to Aquileia two years later.

Thenceforward, Rufinus's literary production was impressive, although prior to that time he had published nothing. Most of his work consisted of translations into Latin of Greek church fathers, Origen especially, at a period when knowledge of Greek was in decline in the west. He deeply offended Jerome by his translation of Origen's On First Principles (398), in which he represented Jerome as having once been an admirer of Origen. Stung by the bitter attacks that issued from Bethlehem, he defended his position in a profession of faith to the Roman bishop Anastasius I (400). He died in Sicily as mainland Italy was overrun by Alaric and the Goths.

Defending his work on Origen, Rufinus began by translating the first book of Pamphilus's apology on Origen's behalf along with a treatise on interpolation in Origen's works. He maintained that unorthodox doctrinal passages in Origen's writings were later insertions; he thus felt free to delete them in his versions. The translations followed rapidly, starting with *On First Principles,* a systematic manual of Christian theology, and continuing with homilies on Joshua, Judges, several Psalms, Genesis, Exodus, Leviticus, and Numbers, and commentaries on Romans and the Song of Solomon. Much of Origen's work survives only in Rufinus's translations.

He also translated the shorter *Asceticon* of Basil the Great, a series of questions and replies on the monastic life; through this Latin version, the work exercised some influence on western monasticism. To his translation of Eusebius of Caesarea's *Church History,* he added two books reaching to the death of Theodosius I (395). Other writings that came into Latin under his hand include the *Sentences* of Evagrius Ponticus and the *Sentences* of one Sextus, a Pythagorean philosopher whom he erroneously identified with Sixtus II of Rome; an anonymous history of the Egyptian monks, replete with fables; homilies of Basil and of Gregory of Nazianzus; and the *Recognitions,* falsely attributed to Clement of Rome.

Rufinus's original works include two apologies on the Origenist controversy, one of shorter length to Anastasius I (see above) and the other in two books to Jerome, in answer to the latter's accusations. (This last piece was itself answered by a further attack from Jerome.) There are also a commentary on the Apostles' Creed, which shows dependence on Cyril of Jerusalem, and a short treatise on Jacob's blessings of the twelve patriarchs (Gen. 49). His letters are lost. CPL 195–201; see also, for Jerome, CPL 613–614. [M.P.McH.]

Bibliography

Jerome, *Apology Against Rufinus;* idem, *Letters* 3–5; 51; 57; 80–84; 97; 125; 133; Paulinus, *Letters* 28.5; 40.6; 46; 47; Augustine, *Letters* 63; 156; Palladius, *Lausiac History* 46.5; Sidonius Apollinaris, *Letter* 4.3; Gennadius, *Lives of Illustrious Men* 17.

Tyrannius Rufinus, Opera, ed. M. Simonetti, CCSL (1961), Vol. 20.

Rufinus: A Commentary on the Apostles' Creed, tr. J.N.D. Kelly, ACW (1955), Vol. 20.

F.X. Murphy, *Rufinus of Aquileia, 345–411* (Washington, D.C.: Catholic U of America P, 1945); C.P. Hammond, "The Last Ten Years of Rufinus' Life and the Date of His Move South from Aquileia," *JThS* n.s. 28 (1977):372–429 (includes table of dates for his literary work); H. Ledoyen, "Saint Basile dans la tradition monastique occidentale," *Irénikon* 53 (1980):30–45; T.P. Halton and R.D. Sider, "A Decade of Patristic Scholarship 1970–1979," *CW* 76 (1982–1983):356–357 (bibliography); F. Thélamon, *Paiens et chrétiens au IVe siècle: l'apport de l'histoire ecclésiastique de Rufin d'Aquilée* (Paris: Etudes Augustiniennes, 1981).

RULE OF FAITH. Summary of the main points of Christian teaching. Church writers from the end of the second century used in Latin *regula fidei* or in Greek *kanōn* ("canon of truth") or similar terms when referring to the apostolic preaching that served as the norm of Christian faith. The terminology may have been suggested by Paul's language in Galatians 2:14 and 6:16.

The Book of Acts includes sermons preached to Jews (Acts 2; 3; 10; 13) that are constructed on a similar plan and make the following points: Jesus Christ was killed, raised, and exalted; these things happened in fulfillment of the Old Testament prophecies and were attested by the witness of the apostles; God now offered salvation to those who believed, repented, and were baptized. Sermons to pagans were constructed differently and had first to present the creator God of the Bible but also came around to the resurrection of Jesus and judgment (Acts 17:30f.; cf. 1 Thess. 1:9f.). Paul outlined the gospel in terms of Jesus' death, burial, and resurrection, all in accordance with the scriptures, and affirmed that he and the twelve preached the same gospel (1 Cor. 15:1–11).

Postcanonical documents continued to present the heart of the Christian message as the events connected with Christ and these as the activity of God (Ignatius, *Eph.* 18.2) and the fulfillment of what was said by the prophets inspired by the Spirit (Justin, *1 Apol.* 31.7). Increasingly, a Trinitarian structure was given to these summaries of apostolic teaching, perhaps under the influence of the baptismal confession (Matt. 28:19). God was presented as one, the Creator, and the Father of Jesus Christ.

Faith in Christ was related to his virgin birth, ministry, death, resurrection, ascension, and coming again in judgment. The Holy Spirit too was described in terms of his activity—inspiring the prophets, renewing humanity to God, and guiding believers (Irenaeus, *Dem.* 6; *Haer.* 1.10.1; Tertullian, *Praesc.* 13).

The Rule of Faith has often been studied as an antecedent to the Apostles' Creed. The content of the preaching was obviously related to the faith that was confessed, but its function was different from the creed's. The Rule was a summary of the teaching presented, perhaps especially to new converts in preparation for baptism. This aspect accounts for the lack of conformity in wording or even in the order of the main points, a feature that was bothersome to those who related the Rule to the development of creeds. The essential message was fixed by the facts of the gospel and the structure of Christian belief in one God, reception of salvation in Christ, and experience of the Holy Spirit; but each teacher had his own way of stating or elaborating these points. The Rule of Faith never attained the standardization of wording that its counterpart, the baptismal confession of faith (Apostles' Creed), did.

The Rule of Faith assumed an important place in the controversies with heretics in the second century (Clement of Alexandria, *Str.* 7.15–16), and it is to this polemical situation that we owe most of the statements of the content of the Rule. Some authors, in fact, specifically elaborate portions of the Rule with a polemical intention in mind or stress the uniform nature of the contents wherever the church existed (Irenaeus, *Haer.* 1.10.1). The challenge of Marcion and the Gnostics perhaps encouraged efforts to instruct new converts more carefully in the facts of the gospel and the basic Christian worldview. The catechesis in preparation for baptism gave a common basis from which to argue against variant forms of the Christian message. The "canon of truth," as preserving the essential content of scripture, could be seen as explaining the meaning of scripture (Clement of Alexandria, *Str.* 6.15). Somewhat later, Origen could take the Rule of Faith as the groundwork from which to launch his theological speculations into areas where the faith of the church was not already settled (*Princ.* pref.). *See also* Apostles' Creed; Confession of Faith; Creeds; Faith. [E.F.]

Bibliography

Irenaeus, *Proof of the Apostolic Preaching* 6; idem, *Against Heresies* 1.10.1; 3.4.2; Tertullian, *Prescription of Heretics* 13; idem, *Veiling of Virgins* 1.3; idem, *Against Praxeas* 2.1–2; Origen, *On First Principles* pref.; idem, *Commentary on John* 32.15f.; idem, *Commentary on Matthew* series 33.

D. van den Eynde, *Les Normes de l'enseignement chrétien dans la littérature patristique des trois premiers siècles* (Gembloux: Duculot, 1933); A.C. Outler, "Origen and the *Regulae Fidei*," *ChHist* 8 (1939):212–221, repr. in *SCent* 4 (1984):133–141; C.H. Dodd, *The Apostolic Preaching and Its Development* (New York: Harper, 1944); L.W. Countryman, "Tertullian and the Regula Fidei," *SCent* 2 (1982):208–277; W.R. Farmer, "Galatians and the Second-Century Development of the *Regula Fidei*," *SCent* 4 (1984):143–170.

RUTH. Ancestress of David; book in Bible. One of the five scrolls in the collection of the Writings (Hagiographa) in the Hebrew Bible, the Book of Ruth is in some lists counted with Judges but otherwise always follows it. Josephus summarizes the content of the book (*Antiquities* 5.9.1–4 [318–337]). The book is first listed in Christian lists by Melito of Sardis (Eusebius, *H.E.* 4.26.13f.).

The Moabite widow Ruth left her people to go with her mother-in-law Naomi, married Boaz, and became the ancestress of David; the book is set in the period of the judges. Ruth is included in the Gospel of Matthew's genealogical list of ancestors of Christ (Matt. 1:5). She is later mentioned by several Christian writers (J. Allenbach et al., *Biblia Patristica*, 4 vols. and Supplement [Paris: Editions du Centre National de la Recherche Scientifique, 1975–1987]). [J.P.L.]

Bibliography

Theodoret, *Quaestiones in Octateuchum*, PG 80.517–528.

A.E. Cundall and L. Morris, *Judges and Ruth* (Downers Grove: Inter-Varsity, 1968); E.F. Campbell, *Ruth* (Garden City: Doubleday, 1975).

S

SABA (439–532). Eastern monastic founder. A native of Cappadocia, Saba entered the monastic life there but later (457) migrated to Jerusalem. After living as a solitary for some time, he founded in 478 the important laura of Mar Saba. (John of Damascus would later be one of its monks.) He established a number of other lauras, monasteries, and hospices throughout Judea. Ordained reluctantly to the priesthood in 490, he was made archimandrite of all hermits in Palestine (492). His influence on later monasticism was substantial. He was a firm defender of orthodoxy against both the teachings of Origen and those of the Monophysites. A typicon, or liturgical manual, that appears under his name is of later date. Feast day December 5.   [M.P.McH.]

Bibliography
Cyril of Scythopolis, *Vita Sabae*.

SABBATH. Religious observance of the seventh day as a day of rest. Early Christianity depended upon Judaism for its understanding of the Sabbath. The earliest commands to keep the Sabbath occur after Israel's deliverance from Egyptian bondage (Exod. 16:23–30). These commands were based on God's hallowing of the seventh day in creation, remembrance of deliverance from bondage, and humanitarian values allowing all equally to enjoy rest from toil and joy in celebration (Gen. 2:1–4; Exod. 20:10–12; Deut. 5:14–15). The seventh-year sabbatical and the fiftieth-year jubilee are additional dimensions of God's Sabbath gift to Israel (Lev. 25; Deut. 15).

The Gospels present Jesus often in conflict with the Pharisees' legalistic view of Sabbath laws; Jesus acted to fulfill the liberating purposes of the Sabbath (Mark 2:23–3:6; Luke 13:10–18; John 5; 9). Although the New Testament writings show that Christian believers continued to go to the synagogue on the Sabbath, Paul says that believers should not pass judgment on one another regarding differences over Sabbath observances (Col. 2:16f.). The Epistle to the Hebrews (8:5) regards the Sabbath as a shadow of its fulfillment, Jesus Christ. Luke presents Jesus' mission as fulfilling the liberating sabbatical and jubilean aspects of the Sabbath (Isa. 61:1–4; Luke 4:16–21).

Most Christians believe that Lord's day observances fulfill or replace Sabbath day observances, although Seventh Day Adventists and other Sabbatarian groups argue that God instituted the Sabbath at creation for all time and all people (Gen. 2:2–3; Isa. 66:22–23). This position holds that no human person or group has authority to change God's divine and eternal command. The Sabbath was replaced by Sunday as a result of three apostate influences in the second century: anti-Judaism, arising from the church's separation from the synagogue; the influence of sun cults in the Roman empire, which led the church into making Sunday the holy day; and the church of Rome's growing authority shown in changing the day.

The predominant Christian position, however, holds that Lord's day (Sunday) celebrations already began to replace Sabbath observances during New Testament times. Just as the Sabbath celebrated Israel's deliverance from Egyptian bondage, so the Lord's day (Sunday) celebrated the Christian community's deliverance from captivity to sin, Satan, and worldly passions, made possible by the resurrection on the first day of the week. On this first day, Christians gathered to celebrate the eucharist, commemorating Jesus' death, God's resurrection victory, and the promised final triumph.

In the early second century, Ignatius says that Christians "who walked in ancient customs came to a new hope, no longer living for [keeping] the Sabbath [*mēketi sabbatizontes*]" (*Magn.* 9.1–3). Ignatius lauded the Christians who ceased to keep the Sabbath (cf. *Barn.* 15). Some Jewish Christians, in contrast, while meeting for the eucharist on Sunday, also observed the Sabbath rest (Eusebius, *H.E.* 3.27.5). With the Christianizing of the empire in the fourth century came laws regulating Sunday activities. Constantine enacted a law on March 3, 321, requiring rest from work, but on July 3 he passed a second law permitting fulfillment of vows and release of slaves on Sunday. Legalizing a day for rest had also practical appeal; it gave protected time for Christians to nurture the spirit.

Both Clement of Alexandria (*Str.* 6.16) and Origen (*Hom. Num.* 23) identified the true meaning of the Lord's day in its inner spiritual character, the drawing of the soul to contemplate the divine. Although Eusebius maintained that Sunday was indeed the Christian Sabbath (*Ps.* 91), thus mandating abstinence from work,

many of the fourth-century fathers, such as Athanasius, Ambrose, and Ambrosiaster, did not link the Sabbath and the Lord's day in this way. They instead saw the Sabbath more legalistically and the Christian Lord's day as a spiritual celebration. Representing this view, Augustine set the direction for later thought. He did not simply transfer Sabbath restrictions against work onto the Lord's day. Rather, as he put it, it would be better for the Jews if they spent the whole day digging than the whole day dancing (*Serm.* 9.3). But indeed the true meaning of the Lord's day and the Sabbath lies in their eschatological significance: both point to their fulfillment in the age to come, God's eighth day of eternal bliss.

Christian liturgical observances on the Sabbath, from the fourth century, appear to be extensions of the Sunday celebration (Socrates, *H.E.* 5.22). *See also* Sunday. [W.M.S.]

Bibliography

A. Heschel, *The Sabbath: Its Meaning for Modern Man* (New York: Farrar, Straus, and Young, 1952); W. Rordorf, *Sunday: The History of the Day of Rest and Worship in the Earliest Centuries of the Christian Church* (Philadelphia: Westminster, 1968); P.K. Jewett, *The Lord's Day: A Theological Guide to the Christian Day of Worship* (Grand Rapids: Eerdmans, 1971); S. Bacchiocchi, *From Sabbath to Sunday: A Historical Investigation of the Rise of Sunday Observance in Early Christianity* (Rome: Pontificia Universitas Gregoriana, 1977); R.T. Beckwith and W. Stott, *This Is the Day: The Biblical Doctrine of the Christian Sunday in Its Jewish and Early Church Setting* (London: Marshall, Morgan and Scott, 1978); D.A. Carson, ed., *From Sabbath to Lord's Day: A Biblical, Historical, and Theological Investigation* (Grand Rapids: Zondervan, 1982); W.M. Swartley, *Slavery, Sabbath, War and Women: Case Issues in Biblical Interpretation* (Scottdale: Herald, 1983), Ch. 2.

SABELLIUS (third century). Figure involved in Christological debates. Sabellius's name is associated with a view that the Son was a different mode of the Father rather than a different person ("Modalist Monarchianism"). The position protected the monarchy of God by refusing any reality to the Son's individual divine existence. A doctrine held in Rome by Noetus and Praxeas, it has led some to see Sabellius as belonging to a Roman circle, but

Greek writers often refer to him as a Libyan or one who came from the Pentapolis. We know far more about the view, known in the West as Patripassianism ("Father sufferers"), than we do about the man. No works from him survive. *See also* Modalism; Monarchianism.   [F.W.N.]

Bibliography

Hippolytus, *Refutation of All Heresies* 9.7; Novatian, *On the Trinity* 12; 18; 21–22; Eusebius, *Church History* 7.6, 26; Basil, *Letter* 210; Athanasius, *On the Opinion of Dionysius* 26; idem, *Discourses Against the Arians* 3.23.4; Epiphanius, *Panarion* 62.

SABINA (second century). Roman who established a place of Christian worship in her home. According to a later legend, Sabina was converted by a slave girl and followed her in martyrdom under the emperor Hadrian (117–138). The Church of Sta. Sabina *(titulus S. Sabinae)* on the Aventine Hill is one of the "title" churches of Rome, so named from the Latin *titulus* ("name-plate"), those churches originally bearing the name of the family or patron in whose house the church met in the days before toleration. Rooms of a second-century house exist under the Church of Sta. Sabina.

The present building was erected in the fifth century and has remained almost intact as the finest example in Rome of an ancient Christian basilica. It houses two ancient art treasures. The mosaic inscription over the entrance on the inside describes the building of the basilica; on each side of the inscription is a matron, the one on the left representing the church of the circumcision and the one on the right representing the church of the Gentiles. Even more outstanding is the set of cypress doors carved with scenes from the Old and New Testaments. The survival of wood carving of such antiquity (ca. 430) is rare, and the intricate work is superb. Among the scenes is one of the earliest depictions in Christian art of the crucifixion. Feast day August 29.   [E.F.]

Bibliography

R. Delbrück, "Notes on the Wooden Doors of S. Sabina," *Art Bulletin* 34 (1952):139–145; F. Darsy,

Church of Sta. Sabina (fifth century) on the Aventine, Rome, Italy.

Recherches archéologiques à Sainte-Sabine sur l'Aventin (Rome: Pontificio Istituto di Archeologia Cristiana, 1968); R. Krautheimer et al., *Corpus Basilicarum Christianarum Romae* (Rome: Pontificio Istituto di Archeologia Cristiana, 1976), Vol. 4, pp. 69–94.

SACRAMENTARY. Book containing the prayers used by the celebrant at Mass over the course of the year, together with diverse prayers used in other liturgical activities. Sacramentaries are particularly associated with the western rites, which had prayers that varied from one mass to the next. Although there are references to sacramentaries compiled in Gaul and Africa during the fifth century, the sacramentary recensions that became most widespread had their origins in Rome during the sixth or seventh century.

In the fifth century, each stational church of Rome had its own *libellus missarum*, presenting the orations (prayers) for the solemnities and for the feast of the saint associated with that church. The Leonine Sacramentary, preserved in a Verona manuscript from the early seventh century, is in fact neither a sacramentary nor the work of Leo I, but rather a sixth-century collection of *libelli*. The orations, grouped into individual masses or into series, are presented in books that correspond to the twelve months of the year.

The Gelasian and Gregorian Sacramentaries constitute the two major sacramentary traditions that coexisted in Rome during the seventh and eighth centuries and were the basis for the later development of the sacramentary and missal. They served as the sacramentaries used respectively by priests in the churches of Rome and by the pope. Although the Gelasian represents a Roman mass tradition, it was possibly compiled in Ravenna, and the sole copy that has come down to us is a Frankish manuscript from ca. 750, including some Gallican elements (Vatican, Reginensis, lat. 316). The Gregorian was probably compiled not by Gregory the Great but shortly after his time, and orations that may have been written by Gregory are found in it along with material from sixth-century sources common

to the Gelasian. The Gregorian tradition had undergone further developments by the time of the earliest extant manuscripts, in the ninth century.

The Gelasian contains masses for the feasts and seasons of the entire liturgical year (beginning with Christmas vigil) in one book, masses for feasts of the saints in a second book, and ordinary Sunday masses, the invariable canon of the mass, and votive or occasional masses in a third book. The Gregorian, on the other hand, has a single series for the liturgical year, with the masses for the saints placed among the solemnities and seasons of the year. An appendix would have been required for the Sundays and for many of the votive masses. The number of orations for each mass also differs: the Gregorian normally has a collect, an *oratio super oblata* (an offertory oration, also called a "secret"), and an *oratio ad complendum* (postcommunion). The Gelasian has a more ancient structure for a number of its masses, with up to three collects, a secret, a postcommunion, and an *oratio super populum* (prayer for the people). Another variable mass element, the preface, is found in both books, but only on certain feasts.

In the mid-seventh century, the Gregorian branched into two types: one retained the papal character and developed into the Hadrianum, which was sent to Charlemagne ca. 785; the other, together with the Gelasian, served as a source for the eighth-century Frankish-Gelasian Sacramentary. This in turn was used by Benedict of Aniane in his ninth-century supplement of the Hadrianum.

Non-Roman sacramentaries and *libelli missarum* have come down to us, with various degrees of Roman influence, from the Ambrosian, Old Spanish, Gallican, and Celtic rites. *See also* Liturgy; Mass. [J.B.]

Bibliography

L.C. Mohlberg, ed., *Sacramentarium Veronense* (Rome: Herder, 1956); idem, *Liber Sacramentorum Romanae Aeclesiae Ordinis Anni Circuli* (Rome: Herder, 1960); J. Deshusses, ed., *Le Sacramentaire Grégorien* (Fribourg: Editions Universitaires Fribourg, 1971), Vol 1: *Spicilegium Friburgense* 16.

A. Chavasse, *Le Sacramentaire Gélasien* (Tournai: Desclée, 1958); K. Gamber, *Sakramentartypen* (Beuron: Beuroner Kunstverlag, 1958); H. Ashworth,

"The Liturgical Prayers of St. Gregory the Great," *Traditio* 15 (1959):107–161; K. Gamber, *Codices Liturgici Latini Antiquiores* (Freiburg: Universitätsverlag, 1968), Vol. 1, pp. 292–318; Vol. 2, pp. 325–428; C. Vogel, *Introduction aux sources de l'histoire du culte chrétien au moyen âge* (Spoleto: Centro Italiano di Studi sull' Alto Medioevo, 1975); J. Deshusses, "Les Sacramentaires: état actuel de la recherche," *Archiv für Liturgiewissenschaft* 24 (1982):19–46.

SACRAMENTS. Actions or ceremonies believed to have been instituted by Christ as channels of divine grace. Unlike the Christians of the medieval west, early Christians did not develop a theology of the sacraments. Nonetheless, they were the architects of later Christian sacramental thought and practice, embodying their sacramental thought largely in catechetical instructions on the liturgy of initiation (baptism and the eucharist). Their overriding conviction about the importance of sacrament, and worship generally, is that liturgy provides for the Christian access to Christ as savior.

Biblical Terminology. The term "sacrament" came into English from the Greek *mysterion* through the Latin *sacramentum*, which denotes oath-taking, for instance, the oath that bound the soldier to the emperor and the Roman gods. In its cultural context, however, the term connotes a transaction by which subject and deity bind themselves to each other in a sacred commitment—a sense that left its stamp on western sacramental thinking for the first four centuries, especially in North African writers like Tertullian, Cyprian, and Arnobius, for whom baptism is a commitment that binds the baptized to Christ in loyalty to the point of death, the baptismal creed being the terms of the oath.

The earliest Latin versions of the Bible use *sacramentum* and its plural, *sacramenta*, along with the transliterations *mysterium* and *mysteria* to translate *mysterion* and its plural, *mysteria*, found in the later books of the Greek Bible (Wisd. Sol. 2:22; 6:22; 8:4, 13; Dan. 2:28–29, 47; 4:9). In the New Testament, *mysterion* is primarily a Pauline term (1 Cor. 2:1; 4:1; Col. 1:26f.; 2:2; Eph. 1:9; 3:3, 4, 9; but cf. Mark 4:11) and reflects a Hellenistic Jewish background. For Paul, the *mysterion* is first and foremost God's counsel and will to save humankind through the life, death, and resurrection of his Son, Jesus Christ. Further, because Christ embodies God's plan and will to save, he is equally the *mysterion*. Finally, as the body of Christ (cf. Col.; Eph.), the church is the place where the believer has access to the *mysterion*.

Patristic Terminology. Christian writers of the first two centuries rarely used the term "mystery," and when they did they reflected the meanings common to the Greek-speaking world rather than the Greek Bible. Among the Greeks, it was used largely in the plural and had a double reference. In Greek religion, it designated the ancient cultic rites in which key events in a god's life were ritually enacted, in order to convey to both devotees and candidates for entry into the cult a share in the god's life and accomplishments, that is, salvation (*sōtēria*). Among the philosophers, it referred to the hidden wisdom (*sophia*) accessible only to those who pursue with devotion (*philosophoi*) the mysterious teachings (*mysteria*) that elevate the spirit to union with the divine.

It was in the struggle with Gnostics and with the mystery cults that "mystery" and "mysteries" became Christian terms. Clement of Alexandria, for instance, consistently presents Christ as mystery-cultist and Gnostic. For him and for Alexandrian Christianity generally, Christ is at once the "Teacher of the Mysteries" (*Str.* 4.25.162.3) who leads the initiate to immortality (*Protr.* 12) and the Gnostic who leads the seeker through the lesser mysteries to the greater, and beyond to the revelation of sacred things (*Str.* 4.3.1–4). In developing his thought, however, Clement laid the groundwork for the use of "mysteries" to designate the rites by which the Christian is initiated into the mystery of Christ. About baptism, he writes: "Listen to the Savior: 'I regenerated you, unhappily born to the world of death. I set you free, I healed you, I redeemed you. I will give you life that is unending, eternal, beyond the world. I will show you the face of God, the good Father. . . . I am the teacher of heavenly learning. On your behalf, I fought with death and paid your debt which you owed for your past sins and your unbelief toward God" (*Q.d.s.* 23).

Symbolic Participation. Origen was the first of the fathers to address the theme that became uppermost in early Christian sacramental teaching, that is, how Christians can gain direct access to the mystery, specifically to the salvation wrought through the life, death, and resurrection of Christ. He sees the answer in the dynamics of symbol. In his *Commentary on John*, for instance, Origen says about the three days Christ spent in the tomb that "those who have been taken up into Christ by baptism have been taken up into his death and buried with him, and with him they will rise from the dead on the third day. . . . When, therefore, you receive the mystery of the third day [baptism], the Lord himself will begin to guide you and show you the way of salvation" (*Jo.* 2.30–31). Christ is the mystery, according to Origen, and baptism, together with the eucharist, comprises the "mysteries" through which one participates in Christ, especially in his death, burial, and resurrection. Indeed, Origen is the first of the church fathers to bring Paul's doctrine of symbolic participation in the death and resurrection of Christ (Rom. 6:1–11) to bear on the sacraments.

In the fourth century, an heir of Origen, Cyril of Jerusalem, took the decisive step. In his baptismal instructions, he explains that the recipient of baptism, through the sacramental enactment of Christ's death, burial, and resurrection, participates in the redemption that these events accomplished (*Catech.* 20). In short, the rites of baptism give the baptismal candidate living access to redemption through the symbolic drama, in this case, of baptism. Cyril, however, is quick to distinguish between the historical and liturgical event: "O paradox! . . . Christ was in reality crucified, and truly buried, and actually rose again; and all these things he has freely bestowed upon us, that, sharing in his sufferings by enacting them symbolically [in baptism], we might gain salvation in reality" (*Catech.* 20.5). The key is the par-

ticipatory character of the liturgical symbolism that undergirds baptismal instruction in both east and west.

Culture, however, conditioned perception. Theodore of Mopsuestia, for instance, imbued with Neoplatonism, saw the sacraments as the link between what he called the "two ages." The first age is the visible and everchanging world of time, space, and human life and choice; the second is the invisible and immutable future—paradise regained. The ages are linked invisibly by the risen Christ and visibly by the sacrament (here baptism), which makes present the second age through sign and symbol enacted in the first (*Catech. Hom.* 2–3). The sacraments make present the second age because they participate in its reality, the core of which is resurrection. Already achieved by Christ, resurrection, even though inchoative, is paradise regained for the Christian.

Farther east, in Syriac Christianity, with its deeply Semitic culture, past and present and heaven and earth all intersect in Christ, to whom the sacrament is linked by the Holy Spirit. Everything converges: creation, the exodus, the crossing of the Jordan, Christ's baptism in the Jordan, and the Christian's baptism. The Holy Spirit, who hovered over the primal deep, over the Red Sea, over the Jordan, and as the dove over Christ, is the very Spirit who hovers over the baptismal waters, sanctifying the recipient (Ephraem the Syrian, *Hymns*). Thus, what happens to Christ in the Jordan happens also to the Christian in the baptismal font.

In the west, the emphasis is on "re-presentation" (*anamnēsis*). First used among the fathers in the *Apostolic Tradition* of Hippolytus, this biblical term (1 Cor. 11:23–25; Luke 20:29) is often taken to mean "in memory of" or "commemoration." The underlying sense, however, is that the liturgy of the sacraments renders present the events signified, especially the axial event upon which the entire early liturgy turns: the redeeming death and resurrection of Christ, which are "re-presented" in a later time and different place.

Whether east or west, however, the underlying conviction was about the resurrection of

Christ, which, as the early Christians saw it, shattered the normal boundaries of space and time. For them Christ's resurrection makes him and the saving events of his life accessible in their present through the sacramental liturgy.

Sacramental Efficacy and Pattern. Early Christians were convinced that the sacraments receive their saving power from the Christ who is risen and in glory but who died on the cross. Syrian Christianity developed this theme in a striking way: the sacramental mysteries embody the blood and water that burst forth from Christ's pierced side (John 19:34–35). John Chrysostom writes about the eucharist: "Do you wish to learn from another source as well the strength of this blood? . . . He did not say: 'There came out blood and water,' but first water came forth and then blood, since first comes baptism and then the mysteries [eucharist]. It was the soldier, then, who opened Christ's side and dug through the rampart of the holy temple, but I am the one who has found the treasure and gotten the wealth" (*Catech.* 3.16; cf. Tertullian, *Bapt.* 9; 11; 13; 16; 19).

Directly related to the efficacy of the sacraments is the pattern according to which they accomplish their effects. Later ages would call it the "institution" of the sacraments. For the eucharist, the pattern is the Last Supper; for baptism, it is Christ's own baptism. For both, the power of the sacrament issues from Christ's institution. Tertullian sets the tone for the west when he writes that Christ was fashioning baptism throughout his life, but particularly when he was baptized, walked on water, changed water into wine at Cana, washed the feet of his disciples, and finally "when he receives a wound [and] water bursts forth from his side, as the soldier's spear can tell" (*Bapt.* 9). Years later, Ambrose of Milan attempted more precision when he implied that the sacrament was instituted when Jesus washed the feet of the disciples at the Last Supper (John 13:12–18 — *Sacram.* 3.4–7).

For Origen and the eastern tradition generally, the focus is on Christ's own baptism: what happens at the Jordan happens also in the baptismal font (Origen, *Hom.* 21 and 22 *in Lc.*; Ephraem the Syrian, *Hymns on Virginity* 7; *Hymns on the Church* 36; *Hymns on Faith* 10; Narsai, *Hom. On Epiph.*). Coptic tradition, reminiscent of Origen, calls the baptismal font "Jordan."

Sacrament as Sign. That sacraments came to be regarded as signs that cause what they signify is owing largely to Augustine of Hippo. He held that the word was the quintessential human sign because it actualized what it signified, that is, it rendered present to the mind its referent (*Magn.*). But Christ, as the Word, is the perfect sign, in Augustine's view, because he embodies God. The sacraments are of the same order—perfect word—because they are signs that embody Christ to such an extent that even "if Judas baptizes, it is Christ who baptizes" (*In evang. Ioh.* 6.8; cf. *C. Petil.* 1.9.10). Augustine's younger contemporary Leo the Great put the matter even more strikingly: "What was visible in Christ has passed over into the sacraments of the church" (*Serm.* 74).

Augustine's point is that precisely as signs composed of words and material elements (*In evang. Ioh.* 80.2), the sacraments render accessible a reality (*res*), namely, the saving action of Christ. As a result, there is an enduring quality to a sacrament embedded in the words joined to the material elements (cf. Tertullian, *Bapt.* 1; 3; 7; 12). Against the Donatists, for instance, Augustine argues a position already espoused by Optatus of Milevis (*C. Parm.* 5), that the recipient of a sacrament receives "something" from the sacrament irrespective of the moral character of the minister or of his own dispositions (*Bapt. c. Don.* 1.7, 10–13). The issue at hand was heretical baptism, and Augustine argued for two alternatives: either (1) the sacrament gives the recipient something (a seal or character) in virtue of which the "benefit" of the sacrament revives when the recipient is reconciled to the church, or (2) the power of the sacrament forgives sin at the moment of reception, even though sin may return immediately afterward to engulf the ill-disposed recipient. In so arguing, Augustine established for his successors the distinction between the validity of a properly celebrated sacrament and its fruitfulness: the one depends on the act of Christ embodied in the sign; the other, on the dispositions of the recipient.

The Minister. As Augustine asserted, Christ is the primary sacramental minister. John Chrysostom in the east echoes the point. To be sure, the normal (but far from the only) minister of the sacraments was the bishop. As Chrysostom puts the matter, he is the "visible high priest," but the "unseen great High Priest is Christ" (*Catech.* 11.12). The point is reinforced by the fathers' view of sacramental institution, efficacy, and symbolism discussed above.

Ultimately, however, the primary minister is the Trinity. Commenting on the passive impersonal baptismal formula used in Syrian Christianity ("N. is baptized in the name . . . ."), for instance, both Chrysostom and his friend Theodore of Mopsuestia insist that the sacrament summons Father, Son, and Spirit in their consubstantiality to baptize (John Chrysostom, *Catech.* 2.26; Theodore, *Catech. hom.* 3.16–17). Like Optatus and Augustine, both are convinced that the visible minister is only an instrument in the hands of the Trinity, and, as a result, that his moral character cannot impede God's action. The two Syrians did, however, hold that defective faith in the Trinity could invalidate the action. Chrysostom, for instance, argues against the validity of Arian baptism by asserting that unless the minister professes true (Nicene) Trinitarian faith neither remission of sin nor filial adoption is granted (*Catech.* 2.26). His conviction was widespread in the fourth-century east, although not in the west.

Sacramental Faith. From the outset, faith entered into the very constitution of the sacraments, not precisely the person's subjective believing—that was presupposed; rather, the faith in question was the objective teaching that articulated the convictions of the community—in short, the creed. Considered the scriptures in capsule form, the creed formed the syllabus of instruction for those coming to Christianity, and it was elicited from them as they stood in the baptismal pool. According to the *Apostolic Tradition* of Hippolytus, for instance, the late-second-century Roman baptismal creed constituted the form according to which baptism was administered. The candidate was asked about each of the creedal articles gathered in three questions, namely, whether the candidate believed. At each response the candidate was immersed (20).

At different times, different customs obtained. In fourth-century Syria, the creed was given to the candidates for baptism orally article-by-article at the beginning of Lent and then professed by them just before baptism, when they renounced Satan. In North Africa, the custom was for the candidate to profess the creed twice before the assembled congregation, the first time on the Sunday before (Easter) baptism and the second time during the Easter vigil. However structured, the church's faith entered into the constitution of the sacraments. The inner disposition of the recipient was not thereby down-played. In the case of baptism, in the west, for instance, the candidates customarily underwent a searching examination called "scrutiny" shortly before baptism. Something of an ordeal, its purpose was to ferret out ill-disposition and defective faith. Those who could not pass muster were judged unfit for the sacrament and set aside. Indeed, the principle that guided early Christian catechists was that conduct mirrors conviction and that deeds embody faith. About those baptized but not converted, Gregory of Nyssa warns: "Although it may be a bold thing to say, yet I will say it and will not shrink; in these cases the water is but water, for the gift of the Holy Spirit in no way appears in him who is thus baptismally born" (*Or. catech.* 40).

Early Christian sacraments had in view adults, but infants and children (and the incapacitated) were not thereby excluded. In the *Apostolic Tradition* of Hippolytus, for instance, there stands a rubric that enjoins baptizing children ahead of everyone else (*Trad. ap.* 20). Although Tertullian rejected infant baptism (*Bapt.* 18), Cyprian, bishop of Carthage, urged his people not even to wait the customary eight days after birth to baptize their children (*Ep.* 74). Origen gives the reason: "While the church's baptism is given for the remission of sin, it is the custom of the church that baptism be administered even to infants. Certainly, if there were nothing in infants that required remission . . . the grace of baptism would seem unnecessary" (*Hom. 8.3 in Lev.*). Early Christian sacramental liturgy had primarily the adult in view, but it reached out also to embrace infant and incapacitated. For the faith that entered into the very constitution of the sacraments was the faith of the church. *See also* Anointing; Baptism; Confirmation; Eucharist; Infant Baptism; Marriage; Ordination; Penance.

[T.M.F.]

Bibliography

Clement of Alexandria, *Miscellanies* 4; idem, *Who Is the Rich Man That Is Saved?* 23; Tertullian, *On Baptism*; Hippolytus, *Apostolic Tradition* 20; Origen, *Commentary on John* 2.30–31; idem, *Homiliae in Leviticum* 8.3; Cyprian, *Letter* 74; Cyril of Jerusalem, *Lectures on the Mysteries*; Ephraem the Syrian, *Hymns on the Church* 36; idem, *Hymns on Faith* 10; idem, *Hymns on Virginity* 7; Gregory of Nyssa, *Catechetical Oration* 40; Ambrose, *On the Sacraments*; John Chrysostom, *Baptismal Instructions*; Theodore of Mopsuestia, *Baptismal Homilies*; Augustine, *On Baptism*; idem, *Against Petilian*; idem, *On the Teacher*; idem, *Commentary on Gospel of John*; Optatus of Milevis, *Against the Donatists* 5; Leo the Great, *Sermon* 74; "The Baptismal Rite of the Coptic Church," *Bulletin de la société d'archéologie Copte* 6 (1945):27–80.

J. de Ghellinck, *Pour l'histoire du mot "Sacramentum"* (Paris: Champion, 1924); J.C. Navickas, "The Doctrine of St. Cyprian on the Sacraments" (Diss., Würzburg, 1924); A. Dondeyne, "La Discipline des scrutins dans l'église latin avant Charlemagne," *RHE* 28 (1932):5–33; A. Michel, "Sacréments," DTC (1939), Vol. 14.1, cols. 478–643; G. Dix, *The Shape of the Liturgy* (New York: Seabury, 1945); J. Daniélou, *Liturgy and the Bible* (Notre Dame: U of Notre Dame P, 1956); O. Casel, *The Mystery of Christian Worship* (Westminster: Newman, 1962); E. Schillebeeckx, *Christ the Sacrament of the Encounter with God* (New York: Sheed and Ward, 1963); E.J. Kilmartin, "Patristic Views of Sacramental Sanctification," *Readings in Sacramental Theology*, ed. C.S. Sullivan (Englewood Cliffs: Prentice-Hall, 1964), pp. 144–164; B. Neunheuser, *Baptism and Confirmation* (New York: Herder and Herder, 1964); J.M. Gallagher, *Significando Causant: A Study of Sacramental Efficacy* (Fribourg: University Press, 1965); O. Semmelroth, *Church and Sacrament* (Notre Dame: Fides, 1965); T. Warden, ed., *Sacraments in Scripture: A Symposium* (London: Chapman, 1966); T.M. Finn, *The Liturgy of Baptism in the Baptismal Instructions of St. John Chrysostom* (Washington, D.C.: Catholic U of America P, 1967); idem, "Baptismal Death and Resurrection: A Study in Fourth Century Eastern Baptismal Theology," *Worship* 43 (1969):175–189; F.S.B. Gavin, *The Jewish Antecedents of the Christian Sacraments* (New York: Ktav, 1969); D. Michaélidès, *Sacramentum chez Tertullien* (Paris: Etudes Augustiniennes, 1970); E. Yarnold, *The Awe-Inspiring Rites of Initiation: Baptismal Homilies of the Fourth Century* (Middlegreen: St. Paul, 1971); A. Schmemann, *For the Life of the World: Sacraments and Orthodoxy*, 2nd ed. (Crestwood: St. Vladimir's Seminary P, 1973); L. Weil, *Sacraments and Liturgy: The Outward Signs: A Study in the Liturgical Mentality* (Oxford: Blackwell, 1983); A. Ganoczy, *An Introduction to Catholic Sacramental Theology* (New York: Paulist, 1984), esp. pp. 7–28; S. Brock, *The Luminous Eye: The Spiritual World Vision of St. Ephrem* (Rome: Center for Indian and Inter-Religious Studies, 1985); D.J. Sheerin, *The Eucharist* (Wilmington: Glazier, 1986); E. Kilmartin, *Christian Liturgy* (Kansas City: Sheed and Ward, 1988), Vol. 1: *Theology*; T.M. Finn, *Early Christian Baptism and the Catechumenate* (Wilmington: Glazier, 1989).

SACRIFICE. An offering to deity. Religion in the ancient world meant to offer sacrifice. The offering might be an animal, grain, fruit, oil, honey, incense, or drink. Sacrifices among pagans and Jews may be broadly classified according to purpose as acts of communion, gifts, or sin offerings. The Greek attitude toward sacrifice was "I give to you so that you may give me" (Plato, *Euthyphro*). Voices were raised, however, against this view, as in Euripides's declaration, "God, if indeed he truly is God, has need of nothing" (*Hercules furens* 1345). The philosophers began to express a more disinterested view of sacrifice: the gods are concerned more with the attitude of the heart of the worshiper than with the quantity of the sacrifices (Seneca, *On Benefits* 16.3; cf. Persius, *Satires* 2.69–75), and the good person is more likely to obtain the answer to petitions than the wicked person (Xenophon, *Memorabilia* 1.3.3; Plato, *Laws* 4.716D–E). Some philosophers developed the idea of rational sacrifice (*Corpus Hermeticum* 13.18–19). The Neoplatonist Porphyry in his treatise *On Abstinence* developed a comprehensive theory of different kinds of sacrifice for different levels of divine beings: meditation for the supreme God, spoken praise for the intellectual gods, fruits of the earth for the planetary gods, and animals for the demons.

The philosophical criticism of traditional religion and the idea of spiritual sacrifice influenced the Jewish philosopher Philo (d. before A.D. 50), who, without rejecting the temple sacrifices, said that the best sacrifice is to offer the self (*Special Laws* 1.272). The Jewish prophets and psalmists had earlier insisted on the need for obedience to accompany sacrifice and to regard praise and obedience as themselves a sacrifice (Isa. 1:10–17; Hosea 6:6; Ps. 51:16f.; 141:2). This emphasis on purity of soul and right conduct continued in Judaism (Sirach 34:18–35:11; Prayer of Azariah 15–17 [Dan. 3:38–40]). After the destruction of the temple in A.D. 70, the rabbis found substitutes for the sacrificial ritual in the study of the Law ("The study of the Torah is more beloved of God than burnt offerings"—'*Abot R. Nathan* 4), prayer (which replaced the daily sacrifices—b. Berakoth 26a, b), fasting (b. Berakoth 17a), almsgiving ("We have an atonement equal to the temple, the doing of loving deeds"—'*Abot R. Nathan* 4), and suffering ("The death of the righteous makes atonement"—b. Mo'ed Qatan 281).

Christians made a clear break with the material sacrifices of paganism (viewed as offered to demons and not to God—Origen, *Mart.* 45) and of Judaism (treated as temporary shadows of the perfect sacrifice of Christ—*Barn.* 2.4–10; 7.3; Origen, *Jo.* 1.35, 37, 39, 40), but they continued to employ sacrificial terminology.

New Testament Basis. The principal use of the language of sacrifice in Christianity was in interpretations of the death of Christ (Eph. 5:2; Heb. 9:12–14, 25–28; 10:1–14). His death was understood as an expiation, a covering over or wiping away of sin (Heb. 2:17; 1 John 2:2; 4:10).

Sacrificial language was applied also to various Christian activities. Since Christ's death was an all-sufficient atonement for sin, the sacrifices of Christians were viewed either as a communion with Christ's sacrifice or as a thank offering in response to it. The activities described as a sacrifice were praise and thanksgiving (Heb. 13:15), benevolence (Heb. 13:16), preaching the gospel (Rom. 15:15–21), and financial support for preaching (Phil. 4:18). The high point of the sacrificial language of the New Testament with reference to Christians is Romans 12:1, "to present your bodies a living sacrifice, which is your rational service" (cf. 1 Peter 2:5).

The Sacrifice of Christ. The death of Christ was seen as fulfilling the whole of the sacrificial system of the Old Testament, including its sacrifices of praise and worship, for he offered his pure body in perfect obedience to God (Origen, *Hom.* 2.3 *in Lev.*; Athanasius, *Ar.* 2.7ff.). Nevertheless, it was especially the sacrifices for atonement that were applied to Christ. For Christians, the sacrifice of Christ was God's way of dealing with sin, and this was understood according to the various types of sin offering known in the Greek and Jewish background: as a means of averting punishment (notably in Origen, *Cels.* 1.31; *Comm. in Rom.* 4.11), a propitiation of God (Eusebius, *Dem. evang.* 1.10; 10.8), and an expiation that removes sin (John Chrysostom, *Hom.* 15, 16, and 18 *in Heb.*).

Sacrifice was only one explanation of the atonement to be found in early Christian literature, but it has come to have the greatest influence, especially through its classic reformulation in the Middle Ages by Anselm in his satisfaction theory of Christ's death. The New Testament Epistle to the Hebrews presents Christ as both the high priest and the victim, and Augustine later summed up the thought succinctly, "Himself both the offered and the offering" (*Civ. Dei* 10.20). Nevertheless, the attention focused on Christ as the victim. This sacrificial interpretation of the death of Christ was more characteristic of the Latin fathers. The emphasis on sacrifice was natural, given the nature of religion in the milieu in which Christianity arose. The preference by westerners for this line of thinking may have had something to do with the ritual nature of Roman religion; the legal, transactional tendency of Roman thought; and the emphasis on the humanity as well as the divinity in Latin Christology. Tertullian presented Christ as the victim offered for the sins of all (*Marc.* 3.7; *Jud.* 13–14) and underscored the vicarious nature of his death (*Pud.* 22). Cyprian spoke of Christ carrying the sins of others (*Ep.* 62.13; *Bono pat.* 6). For Hilary of Poitiers, the death of Christ served to satisfy the penalty of sin (*Comm. in Ps.* 54.12f.; 129.9). Ambrose expressly stated that the purpose of the incarnation was redemption: Christ was sent to die in order to redeem the flesh (*Sacram.* 6.56). He underlined the substitutionary character of Christ's death (*In Psalm.* 37.6).

Although Greek theologians, such as Athanasius and the two Gregorys, expressed their soteriology mainly in terms of divinization, the recreation of the perfect humanity through the incarnation and teachings of Christ, they did use sacrificial language. For Athanasius, the death of Christ was a sacrifice offered by God himself to satisfy the demands of his truthfulness and pay the debt to his integrity (*Inc.* 8–10; *Ar.* 2.7–11). Although Gregory of Nyssa is more famous for the ransom theory of the atonement, he could also speak of Christ as priest who propitiates the Father by the sacrifice of himself as the victim (*C. Eun.* 3.4.18–20 [Jaeger]). Gregory of Nazianzus rejected Gregory of Nyssa's view that the death of Christ was a ransom offered to the devil (*Or.* 45.22), but he too used the language of propitiation. By it, he did not mean that God needed the sacrifice; rather, this was God's means of sanctifying human nature. Christ as priest and sacrifice cleanses the world (*Or.* 30.21; 33; 38.16).

The Sacrifices of Christians. The Christians' spiritual sacrifices were seen as imitating and participating in Christ's all-sufficient sacrifice. They were primarily sacrifices of praise and thanksgiving for the salvation brought by the atoning sacrifice of Christ. The sacrifice of martyrdom, which brought one into close identification with the death of Christ, was also given atoning significance. Sacrificial language was early applied to martyrdom: Ignatius likened his death to the pouring out of a libation on the altar while the church formed a chorus to sing a hymn (*Rom.* 2.2; cf. from the New Testament Phil. 2:7 and Rev. 6:9), and Polycarp, when led out to be burned, was described as "a noble ram . . . for an oblation, a whole burnt offering" (*M. Polyc.* 14.1) and in his last prayer asked that he might be received "as a rich and acceptable sacrifice" (*M. Polyc.* 14.2; cf. Eusebius, *H.E.* 5.1.40, 51, 56). Origen described the martyrs as offering themselves in sacrifice, and he expressly says that martyrs mediate forgiveness of sins to those who pray (*Mart.* 30; cf. *Jo.* 6.54.36). Sometimes, other Christian acts, such as repentance, were regarded as propitiatory (John Chrysostom, *Hom.* 20 *in Heb.*; Gregory of Nazianzus, *Or.* 16.12).

Constantine's oration "To the Assembly of the Saints" 12 refers to the eucharist as a bloodless sacrifice of thanksgiving in memory of the martyrs (cf. Cyprian, *Ep.* 39.3), and special interest attaches to the understanding of the eucharist as a sacrifice. As the name suggests, the eucharist was primarily a thank offering (Justin, *Dial.* 116). Sacrificial language in reference to the eucharistic assembly began quite early (*Did.* 14, without specifying what the sacrifice was) and in the earliest writings occurred mainly in relation to Old Testament types (Justin, *Dial.* 41) or to the prophecy of Malachi 1:11 (Irenaeus, *Haer.* 4.18.1). The contrast of Christian worship with the bloody sacrifices of Jews and pagans was also influential on Christian thought (Athenagoras, *Leg.* 13; Eusebius, *L.C.* 16.9, 10). Although Justin identified the sacrifice primarily with the prayers (*Dial.* 117), he also spoke of the bread and cup as the sacrifice (*Dial.* 41). Irenaeus more explicitly spoke of the bread and cup as an oblation of the first fruits of creation (*Haer.* 4.17.5). Origen failed to include the eucharist among the things that bring forgiveness of sin (*Hom.* 2.4 *in Lev.*), but within a few years Cyprian took a big step in that direction by saying that in the eucharist there is offered "the sacrifice of the Lord's passion" (*Ep.* 63.14, 17). Cyprian freely spoke of the bishop as a priest and of his sacrifices on the altar (e.g., *Ep.* 67.3; 73.2). He brought together the ideas of offering the eucharistic elements and of the real presence of Christ in the elements to produce the new thought that the eucharist was an offering of the Lord's passion. This prepared the way for the eucharist to be described in the fourth century as a propitiatory sacrifice (Cyril of Jerusalem, *Catech.* 23.8–10; *Const. app.* 8.2.12).

Following the lead of the New Testament, early writers used the language of sacrifice to describe a wide variety of other Christian acts and virtues. (1) Worship in general is perhaps the idea behind the use of the analogy of the Old Testament cult in *1 Clement* 36; 41.1; 44. (2) Specifically, praise and prayer were viewed as an offering (Justin, *1 Apol* 13; *A. Apoll.* 8; Clement of Alexandria, *Str.* 7.6.31; Origen, *Cels.* 8.13). This is perhaps the act of spiritual sacrifice most frequently mentioned, with the exception of the eucharist. (3) Hymns and songs were closely associated with prayers as sacrifices (Clement of Alexandria, *Str.* 7.7.49; *Orac. Sib.* 8.332–336), and one passage suggested that David's hymns replaced the Mosaic sacrifices (Hippolytus, *Ps.* [PG 10.712B]). (4) Preaching was a priestly ministry (*Did.* 13; 15). (5) As in Jewish teaching, benevolence was presented as an act of sacrifice (Hermas, *Sim.* 5.3.7f.), and the poor were the altar of the church (Polycarp, *Ep.* 4.3; Methodius, *Symp.* 5.6, 8). (6) Purity of heart or mind, in view of the philosophical background, was naturally seen as a spiritual sacrifice (*Odes of Sol.* 20; *Acts of Phileas*, col. 3). (7) Accordingly, a virtuous life was an important expression of spiritual sacrifice (Minucius Felix, *Oct.* 32; Origen, *Hom.* 23.3 *in Num.*). (8) Indeed, the very self was to be a sacrifice (Clement of Alexandria, *Str.* 7.3; Lactantius, *Div. inst.* 6.24). This partial list of activities and qualities to which sacrificial terminology was applied in early Christian literature shows how the language permeated Christian thought but had been thoroughly reapplied from its earlier material aspect. *See also* Almsgiving; Atonement; Eucharist; Liturgy; Martyrdom; Mass; Real Presence. [E.F.]

Bibliography
H.E.W. Turner, *The Patristic Doctrine of Redemption* (London: Mowbray, 1952); J. Watteville, *Le Sacrifice dans les textes eucharistiques des premiers siècles* (Neuchâtel: Delachaux et Niestlé, 1966); W. Rordorf, "Le Sacrifice eucharistique," *ThZ* 25 (1969):335–353; R. J. Daly, *Christian Sacrifice: The Judaeo-Christian Background Before Origen* (Washington, D.C.: Catholic U of America P, 1978); R.P.C. Hanson, *Eucharistic Offering in the Early Church* (Bramcote: Grove, 1979); F. Young, *The Use of Sacrificial Ideas in Greek Christian Writers from the New Testament to John Chrysostom* (Cambridge: Philadelphia Patristic Foundation, 1979); E. Ferguson, "Spiritual Sacrifice in Early Christianity and Its Environment," ANRW (1980), Vol. 2.23.1, pp. 1151–1189; K.W. Stevenson, *Eucharist and Offering* (New York: Pueblo, 1986); E. Ferguson, *Early Christians Speak* (Abilene: ACU, 1987), pp. 119–127.

ST. CATHERINE'S. Monastery on Mt. Sinai. St. Catherine's is rich in Byzantine treasures, no doubt because it is far from the main route through the desert. Besides its collections of icons, the earliest painted in the sixth or seventh century, and a library with manuscripts in many languages—which formerly included the famous biblical codex Sinaiticus and now houses the newly discovered fragments of it and other manuscripts—the church and its decorations are excellently preserved. The place was holy for Jews before it became a Christian monastery (Josephus, *Antiquities* 3.299). In 382, Egeria was shown many holy places (*Itin. Ether.* 1–5). For her, the main monastery commemorated Moses' burning bush (Exod. 3:2), but there were churches on Mt. Sinai (Jebel Musa), where Moses had received the Law, and on nearby Horeb, where Elijah heard a still, small voice (1 Kings 19:8). The memory of St. Catherine of Alexandria (learned virgin and martyr of the early fourth century) was celebrated on Sinai only from ca. 800, when her body was miraculously found nearby.

For the protection of Palestine, the emperor Justinian (527–565) enclosed the monastery with a square fortress. Food was brought in on a rope to an upper entrance, since there was no door at ground level. Justinian built a new church between 548 and 565. Its builders were poor sculptors, to judge by their execution of the column capitals, but the mosaic at the east end is excellent. The flat wall contains angels flying toward a lamb representing Christ, and the apse, surrounded by medallions of prophets and apostles, has as its main subject the transfiguration. This is perhaps the earliest church yet discovered that retains the original woodwork for its ceiling. [J.W.]

St. Catherine's Monastery, Mt. Sinai, Egypt. (Photograph furnished by B.J. Humble.)

Bibliography
H. Skrobucha, *Sinai* (Oxford: Oxford UP, 1966); G.H. Forsyth and K. Weitzmann, *The Monastery of St. Catherine on Mount Sinai: The Church and the Fortress of Justinian* (Ann Arbor: U of Michigan P, 1973); K. Weitzmann, *The Monastery of St. Catherine on Mount Sinai: The Icons* (Princeton: Princeton UP, 1976); J.H. Charlesworth, *The New Discoveries in St. Catherine's Monastery: A Preliminary Report on the Manuscripts* (Cambridge: American Schools of Oriental Research, 1981); P. Mayerson, "Codex Sinaiticus: An Historical Observation," *Biblical Archaeologist* 46 (1983):54–56; G. Galey, *Sinai and the Monastery of St. Catherine* (New York: Columbia UP, 1986).

ST. PAUL'S OUTSIDE THE WALLS, CHURCH OF.

One of the four papal basilicas and a major pilgrimage church in Rome. The existing church is a rebuilding after a disastrous fire in 1823 of the church begun in 385 by the Roman emperors Valentinian II, Theodosius I, and Arcadius and completed under Honorius at the turn of the fifth century. It follows the same basic plan and incorporates significant remains of the original church.

The basilica of the three emperors was built over a shrine to Paul along the Ostian Way about a mile and a quarter outside the Aurelian Walls and about 220 yards from the Tiber River. The shrine, perhaps from the first century, had been enclosed in a small church with an apse at its western end in the time of Constantine. Only the outline of the apse is known from this earlier church.

The basilica was copied after Constantine's Church of St. Peter and rivaled it in size with an overall length of about 423 feet and a width of 213 feet. The apse to the east was some 40 feet deep and 80 feet across. The transept, which housed the shrine of Paul, was nearly as tall as the nave, deeper than that of St. Peter's, but only slightly wider than the main body of the church. The columns of the nave carried arches, and lower arched colonnades separated the double-side aisles. There was a clerestory with large windows above each of the twenty-one intercolumniations. A colonnaded atrium to the west with a narthex or porch at the entrance measured about 220 by 194 feet.

A major restoration and redecoration of the basilica took place under pope Leo the Great in the middle of the fifth century after damage by lightning. *See also* Basilica.

[G.T.A.]

Bibliography
R. Krautheimer, S. Corbett, and A.K. Frazer, *Corpus Basilicarum Christianarum Romae* (Rome: Pon-

tificio Istituto di Archeologia Cristiana, and Institute of Fine Arts, New York University, 1977), Vol. 5, pp. 93–164; R. Krautheimer, *Early Christian and Byzantine Architecture*, 3rd ed. (Harmondsworth: Penguin, 1979), pp. 91–93.

ST. PETER, CHURCH OF. One of the papal basilicas and the most important pilgrimage church in Rome. Located within Vatican City, since the return of the papacy from Avignon it has been the church in which new popes are consecrated. The existing building was erected between 1506 and 1626 on the same site as the original Church of St. Peter, which was begun by Constantine ca. 320 and substantially completed by 329.

Constantine directed the original church to be built at the place revered by Christians since the late second century as the site of the apostle Peter's burial and/or martyrdom (Eusebius, *H.E.* 2.25.5–7). Excavations beneath the existing building have found a shrine to Peter of that date within a pagan cemetery that had been covered by Constantine's basilica, and they confirm that his church, like the present one, was focused on this shrine. The customary basilican plan was modified by the introduction of a great cross hall or transept between the nave and the apse. The shrine had its place in the transept directly in front of the apse and was given a new monumental setting under a baldacchino, or canopy, supported by four spiral columns and surrounded by bronze railings. The altar was probably in front of the shrine near the triumphal arch between the nave and transept. To build the church around the shrine, great quantities of earth had to be moved, and the ancient cemetery had to be desecrated in violation of Roman law and religious custom.

The nave had double side-aisles marked off by double rows of twenty-two columns each, which came from older Roman buildings, tall walls above the inner columns with a clerestory, and a timber roof. The basilica was about 210 feet wide and 390 feet long—larger than any other Constantinian church. The arch of the apse and the triumphal arch were decorated with mosaic inscriptions in the time of Constantine, and in the next century the nave walls were decorated with biblical scenes.

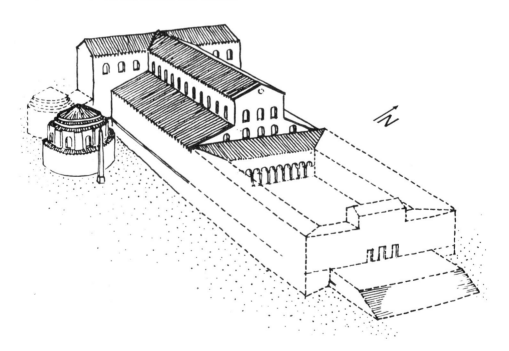

Reconstruction of the fourth-century Church of St. Peter, Vatican City, Italy. (Based on R. Krautheimer, *Early Christian and Byzantine Architecture* [Harmondsworth: Penguin, 1986, fig. 21].)

Because of the location of Peter's shrine on a hill rising to the north and west away from the Tiber River, the entrance was to the east with an arcaded porch or narthex. It formed the western side of an atrium that was as long and wide as the church itself, and not completely enclosed until pope Symmachus's time, at the beginning of the sixth century. In the center of the atrium was a fountain in the form of a second-century bronze pine cone under a canopy with porphyry columns.

The church thus combined the nave of a basilica with a martyrion in the form of the very large transept that gave pilgrims access to the shrine of St. Peter. The church soon became a desired place of burial, in effect a covered cemetery like four other Constantinian churches in Rome, and an imperial mausoleum was built at the south end of the transept ca. 400. The plan was copied in the Church of St. Paul's Outside the Walls in 385 and again in several churches of the Carolingian period and later. The last parts of old St. Peter's were taken down between 1608 and 1618. *See also* Basilica; Martyrion. [G.T.A.]

Bibliography

D.W. O'Connor, *Peter in Rome: The Literary, Liturgical, and Archaeological Evidence* (New York: Columbia UP, 1969); G.T. Armstrong, "Constantine's Churches: Symbol and Structure," *Journal of the Society of Architectural Historians* 33 (1974):5–16; B. Fletcher, *A History of Architecture*, 18th ed., rev. J.C. Palmes (New York: Scribner, 1975), pp. 352–354 (on the old) and pp. 838–845 (on the new St. Peter's); R. Krautheimer, S. Corbett, and A.K. Frazer, *Corpus Basilicarum Christianarum Romae* (Rome: Pontificio Istituto di Archeologia Cristiana, and Institute of Fine Arts: New York University, 1977), Vol. 5, pp. 165–279; R. Krautheimer, *Early Christian and Byzantine Architecture*, 3rd ed. (Harmondsworth: Penguin, 1979), pp. 33–35, 55–62, 66–70, 91–92.

SAINTS. Holy men and women. Originally the whole body of the faithful, later an elite. The saints in Christian tradition are to be understood in their relationship to God and in their social function. In biblical faith, God alone is truly holy (Isa. 1:4; 6:3). The chosen people, sharing in the holiness of God, became a "kingdom of priests and a holy nation" (Exod.

19:6). The essence of this holiness is consecration to the service of God (Lev. 19:2). In the social sphere, the faithful constitute a social group exercising spiritual power. This emphasis often recurs in the New Testament, clearly echoing the Hebrew Bible (1 Peter 2:9; Rev. 20:6). The Gospels consistently present Jesus as exercising power in the social sphere through his teaching and healing works; those possessed by demons acclaimed his holiness and his relationship to God (Mark 1:24; 5:7). Otherwise, only in Acts does this understanding of Jesus become common (Acts 3:14; 4:27, 30).

In the world to come, the disciples will share in Christ's power (Matt. 19:28; Luke 22:30); already, Abraham served as the model of the righteous dead (Luke 16:19–31). For Paul, it is Christ himself who is at the right hand of God and thus able to "intervene on our behalf" (Rom. 8:34; cf. Heb. 7:25; 1 Tim. 2:5). All believers are one body in Christ (Rom. 12:4–8); as members of God's household, all share in his holiness (Eph. 2:19). The living can clearly support one another with prayer (Rom. 15:30–32; Eph. 6:18–19). It was a logical inference that the holy dead, especially those who have borne witness by their death (Rev. 2:26–27; 6:9f.), have similar powers to intervene with God on behalf of human beings, as Judas Maccabee had believed at a time of national crisis (2 Macc. 15:12). At this point, among the "holy faithful" or "saints" only the martyrs who have died for their faith stood out as a special group.

The martyr acts confirm this picture: already, the account of Polycarp's death (ca. 156–157) insists on the theme of "martyrdom." At Lyons, the faithful reserved the title "martyr" for Christ alone but at length conceded it also to those who had died for their faith (Eusebius, *H.E.* 5.2.1–4). While still awaiting torture, they claimed the charismatic power of "free speech against the pagans" (ibid. 5.2.4). Like Stephen, they were considered to bear maternal affection for weaker brethren, helping them with their prayers (ibid. 5.2.5–8); truly, they had earned the titled "blessed" (ibid. 5.2.8). All these elements are essential to the definition of sanctity in the Christian tradition; like Christ himself, the saints were "liminal beings" who had passed over through death to life. They were born again and baptized by blood (ibid. 5.1.11), becoming one with Christ (ibid. 5.1.41–42; cf. *M. Polyc.* 17). Elements of this transformation appear very clearly in the *Passion of Perpetua and Felicitas.* Perpetua was estranged from her father and infant child but drew nearer to a baby brother long dead of cancer (2–8): she became a bride of Christ and the lover of God (18). This reflects a striking redefinition of family. Hostile observers were impressed (17; 19–21) and a soldier received a relic (9; 21). Separation from family, repudiation of the authority of the state, confrontation with death—all this led to a "transvaluation of values." The martyr reentered society personifying Christ in his suffering: the martyr's kinship with Christ gave special powers; the love and memory of witnesses gave rise to the cult in which the "love feast" (agape) and the martyr shrine (*memoria*) played a major part. The tomb of the dead saint was the center of the new social order and a model for living holy men and women.

The early martyrs lived in a settled social order characterized by small groups in which "face to face" conflict was common and intense. During the period ca. 150–350, the locus of power increasingly shifted from the institutions of the towns to exceptional human agents, the friends of God. The church orchestrated this change to a new order. The acts of the martyrs, Eusebius's *Life of Constantine,* Athanasius's *Life of Anthony,* Augustine's *Confessions*—all are evidence for an interest in outstanding individuals, with their orientation to the supernatural and their new source of power. Over against the secular hierarchy appeared a spiritual hierarchy, already exemplified by Cyprian, bishop and martyr (d. 258). The saints who led this hierarchy increasingly followed the model of secular patronage. Paradoxically, the new believer could choose his or her own leader and often chose a saint. The Lives of Anthony and Pachomius document this relationship. The saints distanced themselves from family and village; the temptations of sexuality were clearly associated with family

life. The control of anger and the self-exorcism of the demonic within were stages in social death and the acquisition of a new identity.

In the Roman world, followers tended to see living holy men and dead saints in their tombs as the saintly equivalents of secular patrons, bringing the holy down to the level of everyday life. The writings of Gregory of Tours richly document how the Roman language and practice of patronage (*patrocinium*) was applied to the saints in the Latin west in the century and a half after Martin's death in 397. Appeals to the saints here appear as one form of the traditional Roman appeal to a patron. But closer study of the Martin tradition also reveals what a distance was covered (ca. 400–550) during the evolution of Martin from wandering charismatic to great patron and friend of God—the model of sanctity in the medieval west. In the west, apart from Martin, there were few living holy men; here, the holy was much more closely associated with existing power structures, usually in a tomb shrine under control of the local bishop; control of relics played a significant part in this drama. In the east, an analogous process is evident in the many living saints who served as patrons and mediators for the villages of Syria and Egypt; Symeon Stylites is the great exemplar (Theodoret, *H. rel.,* ca. 393–460). But the Syriac *Life of Symeon* with its insistent emphasis on "taking a stand [for the Lord]" reminds us that the Syriac church had always preferred a different model of sanctity, emphasizing the virginity/chastity of those singleminded "sons and daughters of the covenant"; their heroic virtues were modeled after the warriors who responded to Joshua's call to holy war (Aphraates, *Dem.* 7.18f.). This archaic tradition calls to mind both the prophets and the military metaphor in Paul (Eph. 6:10f.). In any case, the role of the saint as patron is much less emphasized in the Syriac and other eastern traditions.

From the beginning, saints were set apart from ordinary society and consecrated to God, as were the people Israel and indeed the whole church, at least in early times. Certain saints, who testified to their faith by loyalty to the point of death, acquired special powers as friends of God, just as they were decisively separated from their kin and community by the ordeal of death. This model of separation, consecration, and social power was later appropriated by living holy men and women, confessors and ascetics. It reached its most developed form in the shrines of the dead saints, into which were gathered relics, and in *passiones*—the great liturgical dramas that served to make tangible the power of the saint and to reorder society on the model that was to become characteristic for Christendom in east and west. *See also* Martyr, Martyrdom; Relics.   [J.H.Co.]

Bibliography

Martyrdom of Polycarp 17 and *Passion of Perpetua* 2–9, 17–21, tr. H. Musurillo, pp. 3–21, 107–131; *The Acts of the Christian Martyrs* (Oxford: Clarendon, 1972); Pontius, *Life of Cyprian*, tr. M.M. Müller and R.J. Deferrari, FOTC (1952), Vol. 15, pp. 5–23; Eusebius, *Church History* 5.1.11, 41–42; idem, *Life of Constantine*, tr. A.C. McGiffert and E.C. Richardson, NPNF, 2nd ser. (1890), Vol. 1; Athanasius, *Life of Anthony*, tr. R.T. Meyer, ACW (1950), Vol. 10; Aphraates, *Demonstration* 7.18–19; *The Life of St. Pachomius and His Disciples*, ed. A. Veilleux (Kalamazoo: Cistercian, 1980); Theodoret, *A History of the Monks of Syria*, tr. R.M. Price (Kalamazoo: Cistercian, 1985); "The Life of St. Simeon Stylites: A Translation of the Syriac Text," tr. F. Lent, *Journal of the American Oriental Society* 35 (1915–1917):103–198; Augustine, *Confessions*.

H. Delehaye, *Sanctus: Essai sur le culte des saints dans l'antiquité* (Brussels: Société des Bollandistes, 1927); E.W. Kemp, *Canonization and Authority in the Western Church* (London: Oxford UP, 1948); P. Peeters, *Le Tréfonds oriental de l'hagiographie byzantine* (Brussels: Société des Bollandistes, 1950); R. Murray, "The Exhortation to Candidates for Ascetical Vows at Baptism in the Ancient Syrian Church," *NTS* 21 (1974–1975):58–79; P. Brown, "The Rise and Function of the Holy Man in Late Antiquity," *JRS* 61 (1971):80–101; idem, *The Making of Late Antiquity* (Cambridge: Harvard UP, 1978); idem, *The Cult of the Saints: Its Rise and Function in Latin Christianity* (Chicago: U of Chicago P, 1981); J.H. Corbett, "The Saint as Patron in the Work of Gregory of Tours," *JMedHist* 7 (1981):1–13; idem, "Changing Perceptions in Late Antiquity: Martin of Tours," *Toronto Journal of Theology* 3 (1987):236–251; A.G. Elliott, *Roads to Paradise: Reading the Lives of the Early Saints* (Hanover: UP of New England, 1987); D.H. Farmer, ed., *Oxford Dictionary of the Saints*, 2nd ed. (Oxford: Oxford UP, 1987).

SALVATION. What benefits are conferred upon believers, in the view of early Christians? How were those benefits made possible, and how are they communicated to those who are being saved? These questions deal directly with the reasons why people were Christian at all. Salvation can be examined from the point of view of the agent. Here, the questions are "What did God do?" and "How did Jesus's life, death, and resurrection change things for the rest of the world?" Salvation can also be examined from the point of view of the beneficiaries: "What has been changed, so that people's state now is happier than it was before?" "How may people participate in this?" Gospel (Greek *euaggelion*) means "good news"; the meaning of salvation is the explanation of why that news is good.

No single response to these questions does justice to the faith of early Christians, who employed several complementary responses in their effort to express a complex reality.

Earliest Interpretations. Salvation, in earliest Christianity, involved five aspects.

(1) The identification of Jesus as the Messiah who is to come, the embodiment of the Day of the Lord (Matt. 11:3 and parallels; Acts 2:36; 3:20–21). As terrifying as that Day might be, it would be blessed release for the just, those who had completely changed their worldly way of thinking and confessed him as the Christ (from the Greek *christos*, "anointed one"). Those who believed and bravely proclaimed their belief would be vindicated (Matt. 10:32; Rev. 7:13–17), as would all the poor and downtrodden who had never lost their trust in God (*Diogn.* 10).

(2) Deliverance from the threat of death. In the great combat over the human race between God and the forces opposed to him, the decisive battle took place between Jesus and Satan (1 Cor. 15:26; Rom. 6:9–11). Going down into death locked in struggle with the adversary, Jesus emerged victorious and made it possible for his followers in their turn to defeat death by resisting sin to the point of shedding their blood (Heb. 2:14–15; 12:1–4). This he did by sharing with them a new birth, a new life, the life of God, through baptism; death

might rob them of their other old life, but not of this one (John 3:3–7; 6:54; 11:25–26; 2 Cor. 5:1–5; Rev. 20:6; Athanasius, *Inc.* 8–9), and their bodies would rise again (Eusebius, *H.E.* 5.1.62–63).

(3) Atonement (cf. Exod. 32:30), which involved the forgiveness of sins. As a people, the Jews were conscious that they had a special relationship with God, a covenant that bound them to serve the honor of God by worshiping not only in prayers of praise but also in a daily life conformable to the holiness of God (Lev. 19:2). Jesus' preaching, and John the Baptist's before him, made it clear how far short of this full worship people fell (Matt. 3:2; 4:17; cf. Rom. 3:23). Yet Jesus himself, to those who knew and believed in him, was without fault; he died on account of that righteousness (Luke 23:47; Matt. 27:43; cf. Wisd. Sol. 2:12–20), and God raised him up in proof of his acceptability. His unbroken solidarity with sinners, whom he knew and loved and whom he told of God's own tireless love, gave believers confidence that they too were acceptable to God in his company and because of him and that their sins were forgiven (Mark 2:17; John 10:11–15, 27–29; 17:24; Eph. 1:7). To participate in this forgiveness, they had to trust it and to manifest that trust by forgiving others (Luke 6:36; Matt. 6:12; 18:32–35). The scriptural idea of sacrifice and the image of Isaiah's "suffering servant" were woven into this theme (Luke 22:37; Gal. 1:4; Isa. 53).

(4) The conviction that in Jesus one had a personal relationship with God, an indisputable firsthand experience and knowledge of the summit and goal of all human existence (Matt. 11:27; John 14:8–11). This conviction came both from the miracles that Jesus performed and from the authentic wisdom of his teaching, and it was confirmed by encounters with the risen Jesus accompanied by what the early Christians described (following the prophets) as the outpouring of the Spirit of God (John 7:39; Acts 2:4, 17–18, 33). This knowledge of God was enough to make them immortal (Irenaeus, *Haer.* 4.20).

(5) The viewing of Jesus as the person above all others to be imitated. This must have started during his ministry, and even though such imitation proved to have dangerous consequences (Mark 8:34; 10:35–39), it attracted his followers not only because his life attracted them but also because his resurrection demonstrated to them that he was indeed God's idea of a truly just man. This sense of a divine and saving way of life was prominent enough to give rise to an early name for the followers of Jesus (Acts 16:17; 19:9, 23).

These five aspects of salvation all appear in Christian thinking as early as the documents in the New Testament. In different contexts, one or another of these themes may take the lead (for example, Jesus as the anointed one who will judge the world can be presented to a Jewish audience in terms of fulfillment of scriptural expectation, or to a Gentile audience as a sobering threat); but it is not possible to find a first-century Christian context from which any one of these themes is clearly excluded. They constitute the main lines of preaching about salvation in the early church.

Other Contemporary Religious Systems. It would be a mistake to portray this view of salvation as simply a new entrant into a supposed first-century "free market of ideas" on the subject; it was much more a radical shift in how history and the world itself were to be understood, a shift that had good news for the human race among its consequences. Although other systems may not have had good news for people in quite the same way, some of them did use the language of salvation or speak of how human beings could achieve the highest degree of happiness; they can throw light on the early Christian notions described above.

Most important are the ideas current in Judaism, for they are the direct antecedents of Christian beliefs. To know and worship the only true God and to be a part of the people whom God specially loves and rules was such a great privilege that a person could be content with it. Some Jews, like the Essenes, looked forward to a final battle in which God would use the holy ones to overcome evil forever; some, like the Pharisees, expected that the just would be raised from the dead; most believed that in the corporate worship by the whole people of God there was a secure remedy for individual sin. It is clear that in their beliefs about salvation the early Christians' greatest departure from the Jewish understanding lay in the centrality for them of the person of Jesus.

In the Greco-Roman world, there were also notions of salvation, although their similarity to nascent Christian beliefs was less apparent. On a popular level, deliverance from problems with the help of the gods or the assistance of spells was a regular feature of life. Illnesses, economic woes, difficulties in love and friendship, and the malevolent attentions of spirits or cosmic forces could be warded off or cured by recourse to the proper sources of aid. Cities and kingdoms even more than individuals sought and depended on the favor of heavenly powers for their safety and prosperity. Many gods bore the designation of *sōtēr* (Greek, "savior"), and people must have considered that the title was justified.

Of particular relevance to an understanding of early Christian belief in salvation were the so-called mystery religions. "Mystery" referred to the secret ceremonies, especially during the initiation of a new member, by which participants came to belong to a classic story or myth of the gods. These mysteries generally centered not on the classic Greek and Roman deities but on such oriental gods as the Great Mother, Mithras, or Isis and Osiris. One could be initiated into several different mysteries; exclusive claims were rare.

On the borders of Christianity itself, other ideas of salvation attracted many adherents, although only rarely did any one of them predominate in a particular region. Marcion saw Jesus Christ as the messenger of a previously unknown God of mercy and unconditional forgiveness, who came to free human beings from the domination of a "Just God" who had made the world and everything in it and ruled with an iron hand. Essential to this idea of salvation was freedom from punishment and even from matter. Christian Gnostics proclaimed themselves to be sparks of divinity trapped in an inferior and uncomprehending universe, from which Christ, a heavenly, purely spiritual being, came to call them back to unity with their mother, Sophia (Wisdom). Manichaeism, which began in the late third century and exhibited traits of both Marcionite and Gnostic ideas as well as Zoroastrian influence, spoke of one salvation for the elect, who were freed forever from the cycle of reincarnation, and another for their associates, who could hope to rise higher in their next turn on the cycle.

Christian Developments. In the fourth and fifth centuries, there were developments in the Christian understanding of salvation that were of lasting significance. People became more acutely aware of the weakness of human nature and the need for an internal consolidation of the new life, which was offered in baptism. Theologians took two principal tacks in trying to portray how it could be that Jesus had saved people not only from their sins but from the inner instability that continually drew them back into a disordered, unconverted state. The first line of thought, often referred to as "divinization," focused on the way in which Christians could become so assimilated to the Word of God made flesh that he would become their aid, their strength, the source of their every act or desire. This conviction was based on the idea that the Word of God had taken on human nature so that human beings could take on divine nature; what he was by nature, we could become by adoption (Gregory of Nazianzus, *Or.* 29.19; 30.8). The second tack focused on the capacity of Jesus' humanity, once it was united to the Word of God, to progress in love and holiness to the point of perfection, earning for us the possibility of progressing in like fashion (Theodore of Mopsuestia, *Inc.* 7). Some thought that "divinization" endangered the transcendence of God by subjecting the Word of God too closely to the human condition (Theodoret, *Eran.* 3); others suspected that the second line of thought, by insulating the Word from the human experience of Jesus, in effect denied that the divine redeemer had become a real human being (Second Council of Constantinople, *Anathemas* 3–10). Both viewpoints, however, continued to influence Christian thinking.

Two other themes gained prominence in the fourth century. The first is based on the young man's question to Jesus, "What must I do to be saved?" Unlike the call in Acts 2:38, only to repent and be baptized, Jesus' answer (Matt. 19:21) concerns what the practical consequences of accepting the gospel ought to be in people's lives (Athanasius, *V. Anton.* 1–4). This sense that we are saved *in* our lives rather than *from* our lives is basic to the monastic movement, in which, either alone or in communities, men and women dedicated their lives to a permanent and unbroken memory and awareness of God. The second notion is one whose striking expression by Gregory of Nyssa seems so repellent to some that they cannot see its beauty: the image of the humanity of Christ as the bait that drew the adversary, death, to swallow the hook of Christ's divinity, with this result: death's tyranny over the human race is broken, and Satan himself sets out on the way to ultimate salvation (Gregory of Nyssa, *Or. catech.* 20–26). This view, in which even Satan is converted in the end, is the most thoroughly universalist view of salvation in Christianity.

How are these benefits communicated to those who are being saved? Through word (preaching and scripture) and sacrament (especially baptism and the eucharist, which was understood to be capable of changing our mortal flesh into the spiritual being that would be characteristic of the life to come); and through the inner impulse of the Spirit of God and the abiding presence of grace. Augustine and Pelagius, in the fifth century, argued over which was more dangerous: to emphasize God's powerful saving action in Christians and risk denying the importance of individual commitment, or to emphasize the recipient's free acceptance of the gift and risk diminishing the sense of God's freely given love.

Although salvation surely benefited those who received it, the Christians' goal was true knowledge and love of God. The main lines of early Christian tradition fought the self-centered view that such knowledge and love might "bring salvation"; rather, they were themselves all that a Christian could ask or desire (Clement of Alexandria, *Str.* 4.22–23). In this way,

the dominant values of the Jewish view of salvation were preserved in Christianity's. *See also* Atonement; Baptism; Sin. [M.S.]

Bibliography
H.E.W. Turner, *The Patristic Doctrine of Redemption* (London: Mowbray, 1952); G. Aulén, *Christus Victor*, new ed. (New York: Macmillan, 1969); S. Lyonnet and L. Sabourin, *Sin, Redemption, and Sacrifice: A Biblical and Patristic Study* (Rome: Biblical Institute Press, 1970); B. Studer and B. Daley, *Soteriologie: In der Schrift und Patristik* (Freiburg: Herder, 1978); Kelly, pp. 163–188, 375–400; R. MacMullen, *Paganism in the Roman Empire* (New Haven: Yale UP, 1981), pp. 49–130; K. Rudolph, *Gnosis: The Nature and History of Gnosticism* (San Francisco: Harper and Row, 1983), pp. 113–171.

SALVIAN OF MARSEILLES (ca. 400–ca. 480).

Christian writer. Probably born at Cologne, Salvian married Palladia, a pagan whom he converted; they lived for several years in southern Gaul. After the birth of their daughter, they adopted an ascetic life of continence and eventually separated. Salvian entered the monastery at Lérins and later that at Marseilles; he was ordained a priest in 429. His extant writings include letters addressed to several bishops and to his wife's parents, among others. *The Four Books of Timothy to the Church* is a forceful denunciation of avarice and a plea for almsgiving, composed ca. 435–439 under the pseudonym of Timothy. *The Governance of God* is a justification of divine providence written ca. 439–451 under the stress of the barbarian invasions. Salvian's works furnish valuable evidence for contemporary social and political history. CPL 485–487. [M.P.McH.]

Bibliography
Gennadius, *Lives of Illustrious Men* 67.

The Writings of Salvian, the Presbyter, tr. J.F. O'Sullivan, FOTC (1947), Vol. 3; *On the Government of God*, tr. E.M. Sanford (New York: Octagon, 1966).

P.M. Duval, *La Gaule jusqu'au milieu du Ve siècle* (Paris: Picard, 1971), Vol. 1.2, pp. 707–710, no. 304; G.W. Olsen, "Reform After the Pattern of the Primitive Church in the Thought of Salvian of Marseilles," *CHR* 68 (1982):1–12; J.J. O'Donnell, "Salvian and Augustine," *AugStud* 14 (1983):25–34; M.L. Colish, *The Stoic Tradition from Antiquity to the Middle Ages* (Leiden: Brill, 1985), Vol. 2, pp. 109–114.

SAMUEL. Hebrew prophet and name of two biblical books. Samuel, last of the judges and the first of the prophets (Acts 3:24; 13:20), is included in Sirach's notables (46:13-20) and in the New Testament honor roll of faith (Heb. 11:32). Christian writers found various virtues manifested in Samuel. Gnostics used the assigning of Saul to first place among thirty guests (1 Sam. 9:22) to illustrate their Pleroma, as they also did David's hiding in the field (1 Sam. 20:5) (Irenaeus, *Haer.* 1.18.4).

The two books of Samuel are not separated from each other in the Hebrew manuscripts but were divided by the Septuagint and grouped with the books of Kings to give four books of Reigns (or Kingdoms). The Septuagint division was adopted from Latin in the Bomberg Bible (Hebrew) of 1518. Origen (Eusebius, *H.E.* 6.25.2) says they formed one book among the Hebrews. Jerome in his preface to the books of Samuel and Kings implies the same, and the Talmud (b. Baba Bathra 14b) names one book. In early Greek lists, the book is 1–2 *Basileiōn* ("Kingdoms"), most often following the Book of Ruth. In the Latin, the books are *Regum Primus et Secundus*.

As priest (1 Sam. 2:18; 3:1), judge (1 Sam. 7:15), and prophet (1 Sam. 3:20) Samuel was an important transition figure leading to the establishment of the monarchy in Israel. After covering the history of the judges Eli (1 Sam. 1–4) and Samuel (1 Sam. 5–8), the books of Samuel narrate the reigns of Saul (1 Sam. 9–31) and David (2 Sam.). Since Martin Noth, the books of Samuel are often considered a part of "Deuteronomic History" (telling the story from the viewpoint of the Book of Deuteronomy).

[J.P.L.]

Bibliography

Origen, *Homiliae in Regnorum libros* (*GCS* 33 [1925]; 6 [1901]); Ambrose, *De apologia prophetae David* (PL 14.891–960); John Chrysostom, *De Anna sermones* and *De Davide et Saule homiliae* (PG 54.631–708); Basil of Seleucia, *Sermones* (PG 85.182–225); Pseudo-Gregory the Great, *In librum primum Regum expositionum libri sex* (PL 79.17–468).

H.P. Smith, *A Critical and Exegetical Commentary on the Books of Samuel* (New York: Scribners, 1899); H.W. Hertzberg, *I and II Samuel* (Philadelphia: Westminster, 1964); J. Mauchline, *1 and 2 Samuel* (London: Oliphants, 1971); M. Noth, *The Deuteronomistic History* (Sheffield: JSOT 1981); R. Polzin, *Samuel and the Deuteronomist* (San Francisco: Harper, 1989).

S. APOLLINARE IN CLASSE. Basilica near the ancient port of Ravenna dedicated to Ravenna's first bishop, the martyr Apollinaris. The church was financed by Julianus Argentarius and was consecrated by bishop Maximian in 549. The plain interior (182 feet by 99 feet) directs attention to the impressive mosaics of the arch and apse. The dome of the apse depicts a cross with a medallion of Christ at the crossing, the Greek word for "fish" (*ichthus*) above it, and buds at the ends of the cross, indicating the Tree of Life. The figures of Moses and Elijah and three lambs for Peter, James, and John allude to the transfiguration. Apollinaris is shown in the uplifted arms of prayer, flanked by twelve lambs. *See also* Basilica; Mosaics; Ravenna. [E.F.]

Bibliography

M. Mazzotti, *La basilica di Sant' Apollinare in Classe* (Rome: Pontificio Istituto di Archeologia Cristiana, 1954); E. Dinkler, *Das Apsismosaik von S. Apollinare in Classe* (Cologne: Westdeutscher, 1964).

S. APOLLINARE NUOVO. Basilica in Ravenna named for Apollinaris. It was built by Theodoric (493–526) as an Arian church; its present name was given in the ninth century. The inner walls of the clerestory contain three registers of mosaics. The largest band, immediately above the arches, depicts on the south wall a procession of martyrs led by Martin approaching the enthroned Christ and on the north wall a procession of virgins preceded by the three wise men approaching the Madonna with Child. The second zone, between the windows, depicts thirty-two prophets. The highest register has on the south wall thirteen scenes from the ministry of Christ, beginning with the marriage at Cana, and on the north wall thirteen scenes from the passion, beginning with the Last Supper and ending with the unbelief of Thomas. *See also* Basilica; Mosaics; Ravenna. [E.F.]

S. VITALE. Church in Ravenna dedicated to St. Vitalis. After the discovery of the bones of the reputed martyrs Agricola and his slave Vitalis at Bologna in the fourth century, Vitalis was widely venerated in the west. The church of which he is the patron saint in Ravenna was begun by bishop Ecclesius in the second quarter of the sixth century, when the Goths still ruled there. Funds for its construction were supplied by Julianus Argentarius. The church was completed and consecrated by bishop Maximian in 547/8, after control had passed to the Byzantines.

S. Vitale was built on an octagonal plan, with eight heavy piers supporting the drum and dome. The inspiration for the central plan likely came from the east, for Ecclesius had recently returned from a visit to Constantinople, but the construction is Roman. Of special interest are the mosaics of the sanctuary and apse. The great arch contains medallions of the twelve apostles and two martyrs, seven on each side of Christ at the top of the arch. The side walls near the altar depict the four evangelists and sacrificial scenes from the Old Testament— Abel, Melchizedek, and Abraham offering Isaac and receiving the three heavenly visitors. Immediately above the altar is the lamb of God, surrounded by four angels. The side walls of the apse have the famous life-sized mosaics of Justinian (bearing a paten) and his court, including the bishop Maximian, and of Theodora (bearing a chalice) and her court. In the dome of the apse is the heavenly court, with the youthful Christ seated as an emperor on the orb of the universe and flanked by two angels. He extends the crown of martyrdom to Vitalis, who approaches from his right; on his left, Ecclesius presents a model of the church of S. Vitale. *See also* Justinian; Mosaics; Ravenna. [E.F.]

STA. MARIA MAGGIORE. One of the four papal basilicas of Rome. Sta. Maria Maggiore is the largest of Rome's churches dedicated to Mary. The first church was built by bishop Liberius in the fourth century; the existing magnificent church was built under Sixtus III (432–440). Although the floor and ceiling are later, the interior gives a good impression of a fifth-century basilica. The church commemo-

Octagonal Church of S. Vitale, completed 547–548, Ravenna, Italy. (Photograph P. Marzari, S.A.F. Milan.)

rated the Council of Ephesus (431), which declared Mary to be *Theotokos* ("God-bearer" or "mother of God"). Along the flat architrave of the nave, mosaics depict scenes from Old Testament history. Although some argue that they are preserved from the Liberian basilica, most attribute them to the fifth-century reconstruction. Originally, there were twenty-one pairs (one above the other) of pictures on each side of the nave, but several have been damaged. They are in four groups: Abraham, Jacob, Moses, and Joshua. Within each cycle, a chronological order is not observed. These nave mosaics are the oldest narrative cycle in mosaic preserved to the present. The mosaics of the triumphal arch are the finest Christian mosaics in size and quality from Roman times. The lowest zone on each side of the arch depicts Jerusalem and Bethlehem, representing the churches of the Jews and of the Gentiles respectively. The next three zones above on each side depict scenes connected with the infancy of Jesus. At the top of the arch is shown the apocalyptic throne prepared for Jesus, flanked by Peter and Paul and the four figures of the Revelation (Apocalypse), along with the dedi-

catory inscription of Sixtus. *See also* Basilica; Mosaics; Rome; Sixtus III. [E.F.]

Bibliography

C. Cecchelli, *I mosaici della basilica de S. Maria Maggiore* (Turin: ILTE, 1956); H. Karpp, *Die frühchristlichen und mittelalterlichen Mosaiken in Santa Maria Maggiore zu Rom* (Baden-Baden: Grimm, 1966); R. Krautheimer, S. Corbett, and W. Frankl, *Corpus Basilicarum Christianarum Romae* (Rome: Pontificio Istituto di Archeologia Cristiana, 1967), Vol. 3, pp. 1–60; B. Brenk, *Die frühchristlichen Mosaiken in S. Marie Maggiore zu Rom* (Wiesbaden: Steiner, 1975).

SARCOPHAGUS. Lidded stone coffin (from the Greek *sarkophagos*, "flesh eating"). The term became popular only in the eighteenth century. Ancient testimonies for the word exist, but they are few; Juvenal 10.172 is the earliest. Generally, the Romans used the words *capulus* and *arca*. The adjectival form was originally applied to stones. Pliny the Elder (*Natural History* 36.27.131) refers to a *lapis sarcophagus* quarried at Assos that was said to possess the property of devouring cadavers, the teeth excepted, and of petrifying grave goods. Pliny lived (A.D. 23/4–79) at a time when cremation

Sarcophagus (third century) from Sta. Maria Antiqua on the Roman Forum, Italy. (Courtesy P.C. Finney.)

Columnar sarcophagus (last quarter of the fourth century) depicting sacrifice of Isaac, apostle Paul, Christ giving the Law to Peter, and Christ before Pilate. Now in Vatican Grotto, formerly Lateran 174. (Courtesy P.C. Finney.)

was the preferred form of burial, especially among Romans of his class. In any case, his story of *lapis sarcophagus* is curious: sarcophagi were introduced to preserve cadavers, not destroy them.

Although sarcophagi were manufactured all over the Mediterranean in antiquity, Rome (and its affiliates) was the relevant market for most of early Christianity. Roman sarcophagi were normally displayed against a wall—hence, when they were decorated with relief sculpture, it appeared on only three sides, the front and the two ends. The front of the lid was also frequently sculpted in relief. The front of the chest, especially the front center, was the visual focus; the display side of the lid was next in importance; reliefs on the left and right ends of the chest were relatively unimportant; and the back side (though occasionally marked with very low reliefs) played no role at all. Most Roman sarcophagi are in the rectangular-chest form, although we have a small group of sarcophagi executed in the tub (rounded ends), or *lenos*, form, as for example the Sta. Maria Antiqua sarcophagus (illustrated page 829).

The cost of sarcophagi was substantial. The marble, much of it Greek, had to be cloven into blocks at the quarry site. There, it was also roughly hewn and placed on pallets for transport across rough roads to the dock, where it was stowed away in ships' holds for transport

to Ostia (or Marseilles). The fine carving, finishing, and polishing were often performed in Italian workshops (*officinae*). Material, transportation, and labor costs were thus high, probably hundreds of times greater than the cost of a simple *loculus* interment in a Roman catacomb. Catacombs, we presume, were financed in considerable degree out of a communitarian purse, whereas an individual buyer bore the full cost of interment in a sarcophagus—he or she had to pay not only for the monument but also for the mausoleum (sometimes underground, as in the Hypogeum of the Flavians in the Domitilla catacomb) or plot where it was to be housed. Thus, the relief decoration of a sarcophagus was a personal matter, a decision that the buyer reached no doubt in consultation with the workshop foreman.

Romans began to prefer interment in a sarcophagus (instead of cremation and preservation of the ashes in urns often set up in *columbaria*) in the early second century. Roman Christians bought into the market approximately 120 years later, ca. 240–260; by happy coincidence, this period corresponded to the apogee of Roman sarcophagus production overall.

In the period from ca. 260 to ca. 315, Christian products were closely tied to pagan workshops. Gradually, patrons called for explicitly Christian themes (Jonah, Noah, baptism) to be inserted into the stock maritime, bucolic, philosophical, and fluted traditions. The tub sarcophagus, dated ca. 260–270, discovered in the floor of the church of Sta. Maria Antiqua in the Roman Forum, is the masterpiece of the pre-Constantinian period. The orant at center left must have been intended as a portrait of the deceased: the portrait physiognomy was never finished. The same is true for the seated philosopher at center right. At the far left, Jonah rests in the posture of the sleeping Endymion under a gourd vine supported by a frame, and on the far right a diminutive baptizand receives his initiation with the hand of the administrator on his head. All the iconographic images here have precedents in Greco-Roman pagan traditions.

The importance of pagan tradition receded in the period ca. 315–380. Pre-Constantinian Christians bought sarcophagi at pagan workshops and were forced to accommodate their requirements to market forces dominated by pagan buyers; but in the fourth century Christian clients came increasingly to dominate the market. Although Christians may have become principals in one or more of the Roman workshops for sculpture, most Roman workshops remained under pagan ownership. The foreman, however, increasingly was forced to satisfy the requirements of Christian clientele.

Double-register (superimposed registers) sarcophagi entered the market, and the mix of pagan and Christian themes gave way to an exclusively Christian (i.e., biblical) iconography. In the second half of the fourth century, the repertory of subjects drawn from the New Testament was expanded considerably. Columnar sarcophagi (single-register columns relieving *aediculae* niches for sculpture), a genus rooted in a third-century pagan format, were popular among Christian buyers (see illustration, page 830). Triumphalist Christian themes also commenced in this period and reached their apogee at the end of the century under Theodosius. The quality of Christian sarcophagi remained mediocre for two-thirds of the fourth century, but then the quality dramatically rose. The masterpiece of this second period is the well-known Junius Bassus sarcophagus at the Vatican, produced in 359 for the Christian son of a praetorian prefect and consul.

Gradually, over the latter half of the fourth century, the Christian center of sarcophagus production shifted from Rome to Constantinople. From ca. 400, Arles-Marseilles and Ravenna also became important centers of Chris-

Sarcophagus (mid-fifth century) depicting Christ handing scroll to Paul, S. Apollinare in Classe, Ravenna, Italy. (Courtesy P.C. Finney.)

tian sarcophagus manufacture. Ravenna was under the impress of Constantinopolitan tradition; southern Gaul remained Roman in its workshop tradition. Although in Rome the tendency was still to group several themes across the front of the chest, in Ravenna and Constantinople one scene alone came to occupy the entire chest front. Shown on page 831 is the Ravennate *traditio legis* ("giving of the Law" to Paul) sarcophagus (ca. 440–450/60) with corner pilasters. On the front chest register and surrounding the chest is a barrel-vaulted lid marked with three crosses that combine the x and the +. On the chest front, Christ enthroned faces front and, with his right arm outstretched, hands the Law to Paul on his right. Peter, carrying cross and key, advances from the other side. Farther right and left are apostles and martyrs. *See also* Art; Burial; Catacombs; Iconography. [P.C.F.]

Bibliography

C.R. Morey, "The Christian Sarcophagus in Sta. Maria Antiqua," *Supplemental Papers of the American School of Classical Studies, Rome* 1 (1905):148–156; M. Lawrence, "City Gate Sarcophagi," *Art Bulletin* 10 (1927–1928):1–45; G. Wilpert, *I sarcofagi cristiani antichi* (Rome: Pontificio Istituto di Archeologia Cristiana, 1929–1936); M. Lawrence, "Columnar Sarcophagi in the Latin West," *Art Bulletin* 14 (1932–1933):103–185; H.U. von Schönbeck, *Der Mailänder Sarkophag und seine Nachfolge* (Rome: Pontificio Istituto di Archeologia Cristiana, 1935); E. Dinkler, "Die ersten Petrusdarstellungen. . .," *Marburger Jahrbuch für Kunstwissenschaft* 11/12 (1938–1939):1–80; F. Gerke, *Die christlichen Sarkophage der vorkonstantinischen Zeit* (Berlin: de Gruyter, 1940); J. Kollwitz, *Oströmische Plastik der theodosianischen Zeit* (Berlin: de Gruyter, 1941); M. Lawrence, *The Sarcophagi of Ravenna* (New York: College Art Association of America, 1945); F. Benoît, *Sarcophages paléochrétiens d'Arles et de Marseille, Gallia*, Suppl. 5 (Paris: Centre National de la Recherche Scientifique, 1954); T. Klauser, "Studien zur Entstehungsgeschichte der christlichen Kunst I," *JAC* 1 (1958):20ff.; "III," *JAC* 3 (1960):112ff.; "V," *JAC* 5 (1962):113ff.; "VI," *JAC* 6 (1963):71ff.; "VII," *JAC* 7 (1964):67ff.; "VIII/IX," *JAC* 8/9 (1965–1966):126ff.; F.W. Deichmann, G. Bovini, and H. Brandenburg, *Repertorium der christlich-antiken Sarkophage I: Rom und Ostia* (Wiesbaden: Steiner, 1967); E. Sauser, "Das Paschamysterium in den sogenannten frühchristlichen Passionssarkophagen," *Kyriakon: Festschrift Johannes Quasten*, ed. P. Granfield and J.A. Jungmann (Münster: Aschendorff, 1970), Vol. 2, pp. 654–662; J. Kollwitz and H. Dittmers-Herdejürgen, *Die ravennatischen Sarkophage* (Berlin: Mann, 1979); G. Koch and H. Sichtermann, *Römische Sarkophage* (Munich: Beck, 1982).

SARDICA. Modern Sofia, site of a church council summoned in 343 by the emperors Constans and Constantius II at the request of the Roman bishop Julius I. The Council of Sardica was convoked to examine the orthodoxy of Athanasius and other eastern bishops who had been removed from their sees at the Council of Tyre (335) by the followers of Eusebius of Nicomedia, adherents of a moderate Arianism. Most of the eastern bishops refused upon their arrival to particpate, because the westerners accepted Athanasius as a member of the synod. The western bishops, with a few of the easterners, met under the presidency of Hosius of Cordova. The council confirmed the orthodoxy of Athanasius and cleared Marcellus of Ancyra of heresy, while condemning Acacius of Caesarea, Basil of Ancyra, and others as adherents of Arianism. It issued various disciplinary decrees, among them one touching on the Paschal controversy that set the date of Easter for the next fifty years, and another that forbade promotions to a higher church order by omitting an intermediate one. More significantly, the council upheld the right of bishops to appeal to Rome, thus advancing the jurisdictional authority of the papacy in opposition to imperial intervention in ecclesiastical controversies. (Constantius II was active in the east in favoring the Arians.)

The canons of Sardica were joined with those of Nicaea (325) so as to promote the claims of the Roman see and were quoted as Nicene by the Roman bishop Zosimus in a letter to a council in Carthage (418), a procedure that met with the objection of the church of Africa. A letter sent by the bishops at Sardica criticizing Constantius II for interfering in church affairs and asking him to end persecutions against supporters of Nicene orthodoxy is extant among the works of Hilary of Poitiers (CPL 461); the writings of Hosius of Cordova (CPL 537–539) bear on the council in one way or another. CPG IV, 8560–8574.

[M.P.McH.]

Bibliography

H. Hess, *The Canons of the Council of Sardica AD 343: A Landmark in the Early Development of Canon Law* (Oxford: Clarendon, 1958); L.W. Barnard, "The Council of Sardica: Two Questions Reconsidered," *Ancient Bulgaria: Papers Presented to the International Symposium on the Ancient History and Archaeology of Bulgaria, University of Nottingham, 1981*, ed. A.G. Poulter (Nottingham: U of Nottingham, 1983), pp. 215–232; idem, *The Council of Sardica 343 A.D.* (Sofia: Synodal Publishing House, 1983).

SATAN. The devil. The Hebrew noun *Satan*, "adversary," is used in the Old Testament both as a common noun for human adversaries and as a proper noun to refer to a suprahuman personal adversary of Yahweh (Job 1:6–12; 2:1–7; Zech. 3:1–2; 1 Chron. 21:1) who accuses men but with divine permission. The Old Testament contains no explicit account of the origin of Satan, although his creation by God may be inferred from the universality of creation.

The Jewish postbiblical writings considerably elaborated the concept of Satan. The fall of certain angels is connected with Genesis 6:1–4 (*Jubilees* 4.22; *1 Enoch* 6–8); its cause is traced to Michael's unsuccessful attempt to have the angels worship Adam (*Life of Adam and Eve* 12–17). Demons are subject to Mastema or Satan until the messianic age (*Jubilees* 10.8; 23.29; cf. *Assumption of Moses* 10.1), and Satanael is the prince of rebellious angels (*2 Enoch* 18.3; 29.4–5). Satan, or Beliar, tempts human beings through seven spirits, which are the personified lusts of men (*Testament of the Twelve Patriarchs* passim), and spiritual death comes by the envy of the devil (Wisd. Sol. 2:24). According to the rabbinical literature, Sammael, the chief of all Satans, is said to have been created on the sixth day of creation and to be a fallen angel (b. Pesachim 54a). With his threefold office as accuser, seducer, and destroyer, Satan selected the serpent as his instrument, is closely identified with the evil impulse in man, and will be finally destroyed. In the literature from Qumran, two spirits, one of light and the other of darkness, seek opposite effects among humans until the spirit of darkness will be finally destroyed.

New Testament References. The New Testament uses *ho diabolos* ("the slanderer," "false accuser") thirty-seven times, *ho Satan* ("the adversary") thirty-five times, and *Beelzeboul* seven times. In the Synoptic Gospels, Satan is the prince or chief of demons or evil spirits in the kingdom of evil. He tempts Jesus in the wilderness (Mark 1:13 and parallels), is mentioned in the parables of the soils and of the tares (Mark 4:15 and parallels; Matt. 13:38–39 and parallels) and probably in the Lord's prayer (Matt. 6:13), and is said mistakenly to be the one casting out demons (Mark 3:22 and parallels). He "entered into Judas Iscariot" and sought Simon Peter (Luke 22:3, 31) and with his angels will ultimately go into "the eternal fire" (Matt. 25:41). In the Acts of the Apostles, Satan causes Ananias to lie (5:3), and believing Gentiles are turned from Satan's power to God (25:18). In the Pauline letters, "Satan" or "the devil" is mentioned in numerous and varied contexts. Paul also refers to "the tempter" (1 Thess. 3:5), "the god of this world" (2 Cor. 4:4), "Belial" (2 Cor. 6:15), "the prince of the power of the air" and "the spirit that is now at work in the sons of disobedience" (Eph. 2:2), and "the evil one" (Eph. 6:16). The devil "prowls. . .like a roaring lion" (1 Peter 5:8b) and must be resisted (James 4:7b). Jesus by his death destroyed the devil's power of death (Heb. 2:14–15). In 2 Peter 2:4 and Jude 9, one finds the doctrine of the incarceration of fallen angels. The Gospel of John alludes to "the devil" (8:44; 13:2) and "Satan" (13:27), especially in reference to Judas Iscariot, and to "the ruler of this world" (12:31; 14:30; 16:11), and 1 John refers to "the devil" (3:8, 10) and "the evil one" (2:13, 14; 3:12; 5:18–19). In Revelation, "Satan" or "the devil" is mentioned in four of the seven letters to churches (2:9–10, 13, 24; 3:9) and is called "the destroyer" (9:11), "the deceiver of the whole world" (12:9), and "the accuser of our brethren" (12:10). Whereas Genesis 3 does not identify "the serpent" as "Satan," Revelation 12:9 and 20:2 equate the "dragon," "the ancient serpent," "the devil," and "Satan," whose binding, loosing, and final punishment are anticipated (20:2–10).

Postbiblical Christian Literature. Among the apostolic fathers, the teaching about Satan is extended to heretics. Ignatius of Antioch warns of the "snares" and "torments" of the devil (*Trall.* 8; *Rom.* 5; 8). False teachings have a "bad odor" as "inventions of the devil" (*Eph.* 17; cf. *Trall.* 10). The devil invents falsehoods against Christian martyrs (*M. Polyc.*). Christians ought not to fear the devil even though doubt and lust after another man's wife and after luxuries are "the daughter of the devil" (Hermas, *Mand.* 7; 9; 12.2, 6).

Justin Martyr includes the serpent in the Eve–Mary contrast and stresses the devil's role in Jesus' wilderness temptations (*Dial.* 100; 125).

The *Gospel of Nicodemus* dramatizes Satan's role in Hades's unsuccessful resistance to the crucified Jesus, the binding of Satan, and the release of human captives (2.21–24), whereas in the *Gospel of Bartholomew* the devil at first thinks that Jesus is only a prophet (1.16, 18). King Manasseh of Judah, a follower of Beliar or Sammael, was used by Beliar to saw asunder Isaiah the prophet (*Ascens. Is.* 1–5; 11.41–43). According to the Pseudo-Clementines, the serpent is the author and promoter of polytheism (*Recogn.* 2.44–45; 5.17; *Hom.* 10.10–14) and was created by God to enforce the radical choice by humans for or against God (*Recogn.* 9.4; *Hom.* 19.9, 12).

For Irenaeus, the devil is a fallen angel who motivated the murderous Cain (*Dem.* 16–17). He lied in claiming earthly kingdoms (*Haer.* 5.24.1), and he and his house were spoiled and bound by the strong man (Jesus), who in recapitulation abolished death and perfected humans after the image of God (*Haer.* 3.8.2; 3.18.6; 3.23.1; 5.21.2–3; 5.22.3; 5.22.1). The Antichrist will come in the power of the devil (*Haer.* 5.25.1).

According to Clement of Alexandria, the "adversary is not the body. . ., but the devil, and those associated with him" (*Str.* 4.14). The devil is a "thief and robber" (*Str.* 1.17), and Christians are the first to be "wrenched away" from him, for Christ "vanquished the serpent," enslaved death, and set humans free (*Exh.* 9; 11).

Origen conceives of the fall of "preangelic intelligences" as both "ontological diversification" and "moral lapse" (Russell, *Satan,* pp. 126, 130), and the devil's pride-motivated sin as prior to the creation of the material universe (*Princ.* 1.5.5; 1.8.3). Jesus was delivered as ransom to a deceived or tricked devil, whom Jesus overcame via resurrection (*Comm. in Mt.* 13.8–9; 16.8; *Cels.* 7.17; 8.54; *Hom. in Lc.* 6.6). The Christian life is a struggle against the devil's "fiery darts" and "nets," possible only with divine help (*Cant.* 3.8, 13; *Princ.* 3.2.5; *Or.* 22.4), for the devil works to produce signs and wonders (*Cels.* 6.45), and some return to him after having renounced him in their baptism (*Mart.* 17). At the second coming, the devil and the Antichrist will be overcome and condemned to hell (*Princ.* 2.5.2.; *Cels.* 6.25–26). Origen, holding that the devil will be destroyed not as to essence but as to hostility, seems to allow for his ultimate restoration (*Princ.* 3.6.5).

The devil, according to Tertullian, perversely used a woman, Eve, who wrongly persuaded Adam (*Cult. fem.* 1), is responsible for the making of idols (*Idol.* 3), is the originator of impatience (*Pat.* 5) and the instrumental agent for persecution (*Fuga* 2–3), and blinds the hearts of unbelievers (*Marc.* 5.11). He works through Patripassianism to destroy the true doctrine of God (*Prax.* 1), leads Christian wives to participate in pagan rites and revelry (*Ux.* 2.6), and strives against the postpuberty veiling of virgins (*Virg. vel.* 3). The "shows" (circus, theater, wrestling, gladiatorial games) were instituted for the devil's sake (*Spec.* 24).

According to Cyprian, the warfare with the devil is a 6,000-year conflict (*Mart.* pref. 2) and yet a daily struggle (*Mort.* 4). Christians suffer more from the devil than do others (*Mort.* 9), and Catholics more than heretics and schismatics (*Ep.* 60.3; 61.3). Baptism administered by schismatics produces children of the devil (*Unit. eccl.* 11). Confessors "cast down" the devil (*Ep.* 39.3), but the lapsed have served him (*Laps.* 6; 15), and lax treatment of the lapsed is a fallacy derived from him (*Ep.* 43.3). Cosmetics, no less than jealousy and envy, are from the devil (*Habit. virg.* 14; 15; 20; *Zelo et liv.* 3; 4).

For Hippolytus, Jesus suffered that he might "rend the bonds of the devil"; the sign of the cross on the forehead is to be "displayed" against the devil (*Trad. ap.* 4.8; 37.1); and the eschatological Antichrist will be "a son of the devil" (*Antichr.* 19; 57).

Virgins, Methodius wrote, are to imitate the overcoming of the dragon by the church in the wilderness, for the devil is unable to deceive concerning virginity (*Symp.* 8.7, 13; 10.2, 4).

According to Lactantius, God has designed evil, including the adversary, so that men may know goodness and virtue (*Div. inst.* 3.29; 5.7; 6.4; *Epit.* 29), and God has given men wisdom for the discernment of good and evil (*Ira* 13; *Div. inst.* 2.8). Dualistic tendencies are subsumed under God's creation of all (*Div. inst.* 2.9; 6.6), and the devil's final defeat will occur at the end of the millennium (*Div. inst.* 7.26). *See also* Angels; Demons; Hell.   [J.L.G.]

Bibliography

Cyril of Jerusalem, *Catechetical Lectures* Prologue 16; 2.3-5; 4.1, 37; 6.12-13, 35; 15.9, 11, 14-17; 16.15; 19.2-10, tr. E.H. Gifford, NPNF, 2nd ser. (1893), Vol. 7; Gregory of Nazianzus, *Orations* 38.9; 40.10, tr. C.G. Browne, NPNF, 2nd ser. (1893), Vol. 7; Gregory of Nyssa, *Great Catechism* 23-24, tr. W. Moore, NPNF, 2nd ser. (1893), Vol. 5; Ambrose, *On the Christian Faith* 5.19.229; idem, *On Repentance* 1.5, 13-14; idem, *On the Duties of the Clergy* 1.49, tr. H. DeRomestin, NPNF, 2nd ser. (1896), Vol. 10; John Chrysostom, *Homilies on Matthew* 41, tr. S.G. Prevost, NPNF, 1st ser. (1889), Vol. 10; idem, *Three Homilies Concerning the Power of Demons*, tr. T.P. Brandram, NPNF, 1st ser. (1889), Vol. 9; Jerome, *Against Jovinian* 2.1-3; idem, *Against the Pelagians* 1.28, tr. W.H. Fremantle, NPNF, 2nd ser. (1893), Vol. 6; Augustine, *Confessions* 7.5; 10.67; idem, *On Patience* 9, 21; idem, *On the Trinity* 4.13; idem, *Enchiridion* 60; idem, *City of God* 11.13-17; 14.27; 18.51; 19.13; 20.7-8, 11-14; 21.23, NPNF, 1st series (1886–1887), Vols. 1–3.

E. Langton, *Satan, a Portrait: A Study of the Character of Satan Through All the Ages* (London: Skeffington, 1945), pp. 9–65; idem, *Essentials of Demonology: A Study of Jewish and Christian Doctrine; Its Origin and Development* (London: Epworth, 1949); W.L. Hendricks, "The Concept of Satan: A Biblical and Historical Approach and Its Relevance to the Christian Life" (Th.D. diss., Southwestern Baptist Theological Seminary, 1958); H.A. Kelly, *The Devil, Demonology and Witchcraft: The Development of Christian Beliefs in Evil Spirits* (Garden City: Doubleday, 1968; rev. ed., 1974), pp. 11–53; W.E.G. Floyd, *Clement of Alexandria's Treatment of the Problem of Evil* (London: Oxford UP, 1971), esp. Ch. 4; J.B. Russell, *The Devil: Perceptions of Evil from Antiquity to Primitive Christianity* (Ithaca: Cornell UP, 1977), Chs. 5–6; idem, *Satan: The Early Christian Tradition* (Ithaca: Cornell UP, 1981); H.A. Kelly, *The Devil at Baptism: Ritual, Theology, and Drama* (Ithaca: Cornell UP, 1985); N. Forsyth, *The Old Enemy: Satan and the Combat Myth* (Princeton: Princeton UP, 1987).

SATURNINUS (late first century). Gnostic teacher. A native of Antioch, Saturninus (or Satornilus) emerges in patristic heresiologies as an early master of Christian Gnosticism, first trained by the Samaritan Gnostic Menander. Irenaeus (*Haer.* 1.24.1–2) credits Saturninus with an elaborate cosmology, according to which the ineffable God created certain lower powers, including the seven angels who formed the world and humanity. Human beings were endowed with a divine spark of life but could be saved from wretchedness only through the descent of Christ as Gnostic redeemer and vanquisher of the God of the Jews. This doctrine also inspired among Saturninus's disciples a rigorous asceticism that repudiated marriage and sexual procreation.   [P.M.Bl.]

Bibliography

R.M. Grant, *Gnosticism and Early Christianity* (New York: Columbia UP, 1959), pp. 15–17, 100–119.

SCHAFF, PHILLIP (1819–1893). Church historian and Reform theologian. Born in Switzerland, Schaff studied at Tübingen, Halle, and Berlin. He was much influenced by August Neander in his final studies at Berlin. While serving as a Privatdozent there, he received an invitation to join the faculty at the Reformed Seminary in Mercersburg, Pennsylvania. His inaugural address, *The Principles of Protestantism*, in 1844, so clearly defined the debt of the Reformation to the interplay between Protestants and Catholics that he was tried for the heresy of Puseyism. Not convicted, he and his colleague John William Nevin led what has been called the Mercersburg theology, an ecumenical, liturgical, and revived Reformed theology movement. Schaff taught at Mercersburg until 1868, then at Union Theological Seminary in New York from 1870 until his death.

Through his teaching, writing, and organizations his influence in the study of early Christianity has been great. He wrote a *History of the Christian Church* to A.D. 600 (New York: Scribner, 1858). With ten other scholars, he created the *Select Library of Nicene and Post-Nicene Fathers*, which, in two series, eventually amounted to twenty-eight volumes of the fathers in English translation. He organized the American Society of Church History in 1888 and served as the general editor of the *Schaff-Herzog Encyclopedia of Religious Knowledge* (New York: Funk and Wagnalls, 1882–1884). His *Creeds of Christendom* (3 vols.; New York: Harper, 1877) is still a useful compendium.

[F.W.N.]

Bibliography

D. Schaff, *The Life of Phillip Schaff in Part Autobiographical* (New York: Scribner, 1897); J.H. Nichols, *Romanticism in American Theology: Nevin and Schaff at Mercersburg* (Chicago: U of Chicago P, 1961); K. Penzel, "Church History and the Ecumenical Quest: A Study of the German Background and Thought of Phillip Schaff" (Diss., Union Theological Seminary, New York, 1962); H. Bowden, "Science and the Idea of Church History: An American Debate," *ChHist* 36 (1967):308-326; G.H Shriver, *Phillip Schaff: Christian Scholar and Ecumenical Prophet* (Macon: Mercer UP, 1987).

SCHISM. Term deriving from the Greek *schisma* ("division"). Schism gradually came to be distinguished from heresy and was often understood as a division by which Christians seceded from the church to form a separate sect, but not one denying church doctrine. However, divisions of the church have often occurred for theological reasons; in addition, divisions based on disagreement about church discipline inevitably involve a disagreement about theology. For example, the Donatist schism of the early fourth century revolved around the question of whether bishops who had handed over scriptures or church property to the persecuting Roman government could perform sacramental acts that were valid. Although this issue focused on discipline and involved no disagreement about fundamental Christian beliefs, it did imply differing theologies of the church. Consequently, it seems best to define "schism" as any breach of ecclesiastical unity that involves setting up a separate and rival church.

Granted this definition, it is difficult to speak of schism in the church earlier than the third century. Before then, Christianity was developing from diversity toward unity, and the unity of the church was the achievement of the second century rather than the condition of the first. We do, of course, find a great many different churches in the early period. There were Valentinian and other Gnostic churches, as well as Montanist ones. And even if we speak of the Great Church (or "early Catholicism") as the mainline development destined to persist, there was a lack of uniformity that sometimes compromised the unity of the church. For this reason, the Quartodeciman controversy over the date of Easter has sometimes been treated as involving a schism between Rome and Asia Minor.

From the third century on, schism took place in the church for a variety of reasons. At a local level, rivalry among church leaders was a factor. For example, Hippolytus became a rival bishop in Rome in 217 partly because he lost the episcopal election to his rival Callistus. At an ecumenical level, competition between episcopal sees helps explain the schism produced by the Nestorian and the Monophysite controversies. The aftermath of the Decian and Diocletian persecutions (250 and 303) involved the creation of schismatic churches that took a rigorist view of church discipline. The Novatianist church (from 251) and the Donatist church (from 312) persisted for centuries, and Donatism seems to have involved social and economic factors that were at least as important as disciplinary ones. After the Council of Chalcedon (451), Nestorian and Monophysite churches were established for theological reasons. Finally, the schisms that punctuated the separation of Roman Catholicism and Eastern Orthodoxy from 484 on are to be explained not only theologically but also in the light of the social, economic, and political division of the west and the east. A consideration of schism in the early church must take account of these broader historical factors as well as of the more obvious issues of ecclesiastical discipline and Christian belief. *See also* Donatism; Heresy; Monophysites; Montanism; Nestorianism; Novatian; Pasch, Paschal Controversy. [R.A.G.]

Bibliography
A.H.M. Jones, "Were Ancient Heresies National or Social Movements in Disguise?," *JThS* n.s. 10 (1959):280–298; S.L. Greenslade, *Schism in the Early Church*, 2nd ed. (London: SCM, 1964); D. Baker, ed., *Schism, Heresy, and Religious Protest* (Cambridge: Cambridge UP, 1972), pp. 1–63.

SCOTLAND. *See* Great Britain, Iona, Ninian.

SEBASTIAN (d. ca. 303–305). Roman martyr. Sebastian was martyred under Diocletian and buried on the Appian Way near the present Basilica of S. Sebastiano. According to Ambrose (*Expos. Ps. 118* 20.44), he was a native of Milan; nothing else is known of his life. An unreliable account from the fifth century (*Pass. S. Seb.*, CPL 2229), erroneously ascribed to Ambrose, transmits the legend that he was an officer in Diocletian's legions sentenced to be shot with arrows. Left for dead, he recovered with the help of a widow, Irene, and again came before the emperor, who had him beaten to death with clubs. The story probably derives from a monastic foundation established by Sixtus III (432–440) to promote devotion to the saint. Sebastian's iconography is extensive. In earlier portrayals, he appears as an older man holding the martyr's crown. More familiar is his Renaissance depiction as a young man pierced with arrows or holding an arrow. A patron of archers and soldiers, he was invoked in time of plague. Feast day January 20 (west), December 18 (east). [M.P.McH.]

Bibliography
V. Kraehling, *Saint Sébastien dans l'art* (Paris: Alsatia, 1938); B. Pesci, "Il culto di san Sebastiano a Roma nell' antichità e nel medioevo," *Antonianum* 20 (1945):177–200; A. Ferrua, *S. Sebastiano fuori le mura e la sua catacomba* (Rome: Marietti, 1968); R. Krautheimer et al., *Corpus Basilicarum Christianarum Romae* (Vatican City: Pontificio Istituto di Archeologia Cristiana, 1970), Vol. 4, pp. 99–147.

SECUNDUS (third–fourth century). Bishop of Tigisi and metropolitan of Numidia. Together with Donatus, Secundus was a sympathizer with the opponents of bishop Mensurius of Carthage, who had complied with the demands of the imperial authorities in the persecution under Diocletian (304). He presided as primate of Numidia at a council held in Cirta (305–307), where he in turn was accused of having yielded to the authorities to secure his safety. In 311, he presided at a council that resulted in the election of Majorinus to the see of Carthage in opposition to Mensurius's regularly chosen successor, Caecilian. This marked the beginning of the schism known as Donatism.

Among numerous other persons bearing the name Secundus are a Gnostic disciple of Valentinus (second century); a martyr at Amelia in Umbria in the Diocletianic persecution (304); and a monk of Trent (d. 612) who wrote a lost history of the Lombards that was used by Paul the Deacon (ca. 720–ca. 800) in his work on the same topic. [M.P.McH.]

Bibliography
Secundus, bishop of Tigisi: S. Lancel, "Les Débuts du Donatisme: la date du 'Protocole de Cirta' et l'élection épiscopale de Silvanus," *REAug* 24 (1979):217–229.
Secundus, Gnostic: D.J. Good, "Sophia in Valentinianism," *SCent* 4 (1984):193–201, esp. 195–197.
Secundus, martyr: F. Scorza Barcellona, "S. Secondo (*BHL* 7558–7560) tra Amelia e Gubbio," *Augustinianum* 24 (1984):281–292.

SEDULIUS (early fifth century). Christian Latin poet. After devoting his earlier life to secular literature, Sedulius became a priest. His principal work, the *Paschale carmen*, is an account of miracles in both Old and New Testaments. With its blending of biblical, patristic, and classical elements—Virgil was an exemplar—the poem was popular in the Middle Ages. The *Paschale opus*, a recasting of the poem into prose, as well as two hymns to Christ, are also his. CPL 1447–1454. [M.P.McH.]

Bibliography
F.J.E. Raby, *A History of Christian Latin Poetry*, 2nd ed. (Oxford: Clarendon, 1953), pp. 108–110; C. Springer, *Sedulius' Paschale Carmen: The Gospel as Epic in Late Antiquity* (Leiden: Brill, 1988).

SENECA THE YOUNGER (ca. 4 B.C.–A.D. 65). Latin Stoic philosopher and statesman. Lucius Annaeus Seneca was born of an equestrian family in Cordova. His father, L. Annaeus Seneca the Elder, was known for rhetorical writings. An elder brother, who after adoption became L. Junius Gallio, served as proconsul of Achaia under the emperor Claudius (cf. Acts 18:12). A brother Mela was father of the poet Lucan, author of the *Pharsalia*. The young Seneca was brought to Rome for education and for a senatorial career. He became best known for his philosophical treatises and letters, which popularized in Latin a practical Stoicism. His eclecticism allowed a blending of Stoic monism with resurgent Platonism. His ethics reflect the strongly moralistic and ascetical tendencies of Cynicism.

Seneca was marked for death by the emperor Caligula but survived, only to be exiled for a time under Claudius. In A.D. 49, he was recalled to become the tutor to the young Nero. He became wealthy and famous as Nero's court philosopher and adviser until he retired in 62. He was charged in the Pisonian conspiracy of 65 and, in Stoic fashion, committed suicide. Gallio and Lucan also perished in the Neronian purge (Tacitus, *Annals* 14.64).

Seneca's fame and his fate under Nero led to the production of a legendary correspondence with Paul, in which the pagan philosopher offers to put the thought of the apostle into good Latin. The first twelve letters were known to Jerome in 392 (*Vir. ill.* 12); two others were added later. Written in Latin, they derive probably from third-century Italy, part of the apocryphal tradition that grew up around the apostolic legacy. The correspondence is reflected in the later Latin version (Ps.-Linus, *Passio s. Pauli apost.* 1) of the *Martyrdom of Paul*, from the second-century apocryphal *Acts of Paul*. Legend and philosophical affinities had already prompted Tertullian to cite Seneca often and refer to him as "ever *our* Seneca" (*Anim.* 20). Consequently, Augustine (*Ep.* 153.14), following Jerome, thought him a convert. *See also* Nero; Stoicism.   [L.M.W.]

Bibliography
L. Bocciolini Palagi, ed., *Epistolario apocrifo di Seneca e San Paolo* (Florence, Nardini, 1985).

J.B. Lightfoot, "St. Paul and Seneca," *Saint Paul's Epistle to the Philippians* (London: Macmillan, 1913), pp. 270–333; J.N. Sevenster, *Paul and Seneca* (Leiden: Brill, 1961); A. Kurfess, "Correspondence Between Paul and Seneca," NTA, Vol. 2, pp. 133–141; M. Hadas, *The Stoic Philosophy of Seneca* (Garden City: Doubleday, 1968); H.B. Timothy, *The Tenets of Stoicism Assembled and Systematized from the Works of L. Annaeus Seneca* (Amsterdam: Hakkert, 1973); C.D.N. Costa, ed., *Seneca* (London: Routledge and Kegan Paul, 1974); M.T. Griffin, *Seneca: A Philosopher in Politics* (Oxford: Clarendon, 1976).

SEPTIMIUS SEVERUS (145 or 146–211). Roman emperor (193–211). An African of equestrian descent, Septimius Severus became emperor with the support of the legions of the Rhine and the Danube. At the beginning of the reign, he was victorious over rival claimants and, in a campaign against the Parthians, took their capital. Relying heavily upon equestrians for the administration of the empire, he denied the senate an active role in government, and its composition changed through the introduction of new members. Justice was administered fairly, the pay and prestige of the army increased, an extensive building program began, and new colonies were established in Africa and Syria. After campaigning for several years (208–211) in Britain, Septimius died at York. The authenticity of the report in the *Historia Augusta* (*V. Severi* 17.1) that he forbade new conversions to Christianity, like much else in that document, is in dispute. It is certain that local persecutions occurred, as at Alexandria, where Origen's father and a number of his students were executed, and in Africa, where Perpetua and Felicitas were martyred at Carthage (203).   [M.P.McH.]

Bibliography
Eusebius, *Church History* 6.1.1–8.7.

M. Platnauer, *The Life and Reign of the Emperor Lucius Septimius Severus* (Oxford: Oxford UP, 1918); T.D. Barnes, "Legislation Against the Christians," *JRS* 58 (1968):32–50; W.H.C. Frend, "A Severan Persecution? Evidence of the *Historia Augusta*," *Forma Futuri: studi in onore del Cardinale Michele*

Pellegrino (Turin: Bottega d'Erasmo, 1975), pp. 470–480.

SEPTUAGINT (LXX). Most important translation of the Hebrew Bible into Greek. Its origin is explained in the legend contained in the *Letter of Aristeas* (latter half of the second century B.C.), which claims that the translation was made by seventy-two Jewish elders (hence the name "Septuagint," meaning "seventy") at the request of Ptolemy II Philadelphus (283–246 B.C.), who desired a copy for his immense library at Alexandria. Only two facts can be determined from the legend: that the Septuagint is Alexandrian in origin and that the translation of the Pentateuch dates from the third century B.C. The rest of the Septuagint is later, the work of individual translators, although the whole was completed by 132 B.C., as indicated by remarks made in the prologue to Sirach (Ecclesiasticus).

The Septuagint was translated for the use of synagogues in Egypt so that they could have the Bible in the daily language then in use, the *koine* Greek that Alexander the Great had spread across the entire Near East. This language was a vehicle for an active literary development within Hellenistic Judaism. To the books of the canon of the Hebrew Bible were added those of the Apocrypha: 1 and 2 Esdras, Tobit, Judith, Additions to Esther, Wisdom of Solomon, Sirach, Baruch, Letter of Jeremiah, Prayer of Azariah, Song of the Three Young Men, Susanna, Bel and the Dragon, Prayer of Manasseh, and 1 and 2 Maccabees. Many Jews regarded these books as scripture, and they were followed by most Christians for centuries.

The Septuagint is significant for a number of reasons. First, it is an invaluable source of information about Jewish religious thought and piety in the Hellenistic period and is our earliest commentary on the meaning of the Hebrew text. The biblical revelation takes on a new world of thought: Yahweh, for instance, becomes in Greek *kurios* ("Lord"). The additions to the Hebrew canon belong to various categories of literature, from wisdom to history. Even the way in which translators ap-proach their task is illuminating; there is a view of scripture inherent in their work. They translated some books with much greater literalness than others. To cite an extreme example, the translator of Job shortened the book by some 800 lines, eliminating excessive repetition and merely summarizing what was too difficult to translate. Such an approach would have been unthinkable for a book of the Law (i.e., the Pentateuch).

The Septuagint was the Bible of the earliest church. The parting of the church from the synagogue was a bitter one. The Septuagint had been regarded as the inspired Word of God; Christians used such translations as *parthenos* ("virgin") for *'almāh* ("young woman") at Isaiah 7:14, cited by Matthew 1:23 as proof of Jesus' birth as the fulfillment of scripture in argumentation (Justin, *Dial.* 43; 66f.). Further, Christian copyists tended to corrupt the text by introducing Christological data. So it was that the synagogue rejected the Septuagint and turned to other more literal translations, especially that of Aquila. The church spread the Septuagint, together with its own writings contained in the New Testament, throughout the world in its missionary activities. The Greek Bible was translated into Latin, Coptic, Syriac, Ethiopic, Armenian, Georgian, Arabic, and other languages. Even after Jerome translated the Latin Vulgate on the basis of the Hebrew, the Septuagint-based translation of Psalms continued in use, so great was its influence. Until the Protestant Reformation, the canon of the church was the expanded canon of the Septuagint; only then did the Hebrew text of the Old Testament replace the Septuagint.

The Septuagint has traditionally been used to restore the text of the Hebrew Bible where the latter is corrupt. Such a use of the LXX depends on a thorough understanding of the techniques employed by individual translators. The helpfulness of the Septuagint for this purpose thus varies from book to book. Further, its importance for the textual criticism of the Hebrew has diminished since the discovery and publication of the Dead Sea Scrolls, which antedate the Christian era. Still, for some books, like Samuel–Kings, the witness of the Septuagint remains crucial, since it is a witness to a form of Hebrew text that is no longer extant.

The Septuagint has had a complex textual history. From the time of its translation, there were attempts, conscious and unconscious (especially as long as copyists were bilingual in Hebrew and Greek), to bring it into greater agreement with the Hebrew original. Revisions and even new translations were made, connected in particular with the names of Aquila, Symmachus, and Theodotion. The literal version of Aquila was favored in rabbinical circles. The translation of Daniel connected with the name of Theodotion all but eclipsed the Septuagint Daniel, which has survived in only two manuscripts. The translation of Ecclesiastes in manuscripts containing the Septuagint belongs to the Aquila type of translation. Although Theodotion lived in the late second century, the translation associated with his name was known more than a century earlier, causing scholars to see his work as part of an ongoing process of revision. The awareness that almost immediately after its creation the Septuagint text was subject to revision of various kinds, to replacement, and to competition from other translations has been one of the accomplishments of recent research. For example, the Septuagint Jeremiah, with a text much shorter and differently ordered than the traditional Hebrew text, attests the existence of a Hebrew edition of Jeremiah having the same character. Origen's work in the *Hexapla*, which was intended to sort out the conflict between supporters of the Septuagint and adherents of the received Hebrew text by presenting the two texts together in an analytical fashion, inadvertently led to the corruption of much of the LXX manuscript tradition. No field of textual criticism is more complicated than that dealing with the Septuagint.

There are two major modern editions of the Old Testament in Greek. The Cambridge edition reproduces the text of the codex Vaticanus (fourth century) and relates all other witnesses to that manuscript in an apparatus. Edited by A.E. Brooke, N. McLean, and H. St. J. Thackeray, it is unfortunately incomplete and out of print, the last volume having appeared

in 1940. The Göttingen edition of the Septuagint offers an eclectic, critical text, theoretically as close to the original as is possible. Among its editors are A. Rahlfs, J. Ziegler, J.W. Wevers, R. Hanhart, and W. Kappler. Since the Cambridge and Göttingen editions began at opposite ends of the canon, we now have one or the other edition for most of the Old Testament.

The tools that scholars use to establish the original text of the Septuagint are three: Greek manuscripts, quotations from the Septuagint made by the church fathers (e.g., Justin Martyr, Origen, John Chrysostom), and the versions into which the Septuagint was translated (Latin, Coptic, and so on). These various witnesses divide themselves into groups, somewhat like a family tree; understanding their relationships is a major step toward reconstructing the original text.

Septuagint studies today are concerned with establishing and understanding the original text, its history of transmission along with relevant linguistic and theological issues, and the Hellenistic Judaism out of which it grew. The International Organization for Septuagint and Cognate Studies is devoted to the study of the LXX; it publishes an annual *Bulletin*. TLG 0527. *See also* Aquila; Hexapla; Symmachus; Text Criticism; Theodotion.   [C.C.]

Bibliography

Justin, *Dialogue with Trypho* 71; Pseudo-Justin, *Hortatory Address to the Greeks* 13; Irenaeus, *Against Heresies* 3.21.2f.

H.B. Swete, *An Introduction to the Old Testament in Greek*, rev. R.R. Ottley (Cambridge: Cambridge UP, 1902); J.W. Wevers, "Septuagint," *The Interpreter's Dictionary of the Bible*, ed. G.A. Buttrick (Nashville: Abingdon, 1962), Vol. 4, pp. 273–278; S. Jellicoe, *The Septuagint and Modern Study* (Oxford: Clarendon, 1968); S.P. Brock, C.T. Fritsch, and S. Jellicoe, eds., *A Classified Bibliography of the Septuagint* (Leiden: Brill, 1973); E. Tov and R.A. Kraft, "Septuagint," *Interpreter's Dictionary of the Bible, Supplementary Volume*, ed. K. Crim (Nashville: Abingdon, 1976), pp. 807–815; E. Tov, *The Text-Critical Use of the Septuagint in Biblical Research* (Jerusalem: Simor, 1981); A. Pietersma and C. Cox, eds., *De Septuaginta: Studies in Honour of John William Wevers on His Sixty-fifth Birthday* (Toronto: Benben, 1984); N. Fernández Marcos, *La Septuaginta en la Investigacion Contemporanea* (Madrid: Instituto Arias Montano, 1985).

SERAPION OF THMUIS (d. after 362). Superior of a group of monks and later bishop of Thmuis in the Nile Delta from 339 until his death. Serapion was a friend of Anthony, who confided in him his visions and bequeathed to him one of his two sheepskin cloaks, and of Athanasius, who wrote important letters to him, including four on the Holy Spirit. Serapion himself wrote a learned treatise, *Contra Manichaeos*, exposing the Manichaeans' dualistic errors. A collection of thirty prayers attributed to him is an important witness to the Egyptian liturgy in the fourth century. Feast day March 21. CPG II, 2485–2495. [E.F.]

Bibliography

Athanasius, *Life of Anthony* 82; 91; idem, *Festal Letter* 12; idem, *Letter* 54; *Letters Concerning the Holy Spirit*, tr. with int. and notes by C.R.B. Shapland (New York: Philosophical Library, 1951); Jerome, *Lives of Illustrious Men* 99; Sozomen, *Church History* 4.9.

R.P. Casey, *Serapion of Thmuis Against the Manichees* (Cambridge: Harvard UP, 1931); F.E. Brightman, "The Sacramentary of Serapion of Thmuis," *JThS* 1(1900):88–113, 247–277.

J. Wordsworth, *Bishop Serapion's Prayer-book* (London: SPCK, 1923); G.A. Hamman, *Early Christian Prayers* (Chicago: Regnery, 1961).

G. Dix, *The Shape of the Liturgy* (Westminster: Dacre, 1945), pp. 162–172.

SETHIANS. Gnostics who identified themselves as the spiritual descendants of Seth, the third son of Adam and Eve. The Sethians flourished in the Mediterranean area (perhaps Egypt or Palestine, according to Epiphanius) from the early second to at least the fourth century.

Although their teachings show considerable variation, Sethian mythology has a number of distinctive characteristics. The heavenly realm includes a divine triad: the Father, often named the Invisible Spirit; the Mother, named Barbelo; and the Son, often associated with Autogenes. The Primal Human Being, Adam, is connected with this triad. Beneath the heavenly realm exists an inferior demiurge, Yaldabaoth, who is often associated with the disparaged creator God of Genesis. It is he who creates the world in an attempt to dominate the heavenly realm by imprisoning spiritual substance in flesh. Although originally ignorant of the heavenly world's existence, Yaldabaoth becomes angry when his arrogance in declaring himself to be the sole and highest god is punished by the appearance of the heavenly Adam. The creation of humankind is a direct result of Yaldabaoth's envy: he tries to create a being in Adam's image that he can dominate. Salvation is required because in the process of creation, spiritual substance from the heavenly realm is imprisoned in the created world, an evil act that brings tremendous suffering upon the imprisoned souls who desire to escape from creation and return to the heavenly realm.

Seth is the true spiritual representative of his father, Adam; hence, Sethians understand themselves to be descendants of Seth ("the Seed of Seth") and as such possess spiritual substance. Since both Adam and Seth can have a heavenly and an earthly aspect, they function as saviors. The Sethians divide human history into four periods: the age of Adam, the age of Seth, the age of the original Sethians, and the present time. The final resting place for Adam, Seth, and the Seed of Seth is located above the realm of the demiurge with the four aeons and "illuminators" of Autogenes, named Harmozel, Oroiael, Daveithe, and Eleleth.

Due to the confusion of the patristic accounts about the existence, location, and beliefs of Sethians, as well as the variety and complexity of the primary texts themselves, considerable debate has ensued about whether a Sethian group in fact ever existed. The general coherence of Sethian mythology and the appearance of references to ritual practice, such as baptism and ritual of ascent, seem to indicate, however, that behind these texts there was a definable group or sect, not just a number of creative individuals.

From the Nag Hammadi documents, the following texts have been identified as Sethian: *The Apocryphon of John, The Hypostasis of the Archons, The Gospel of the Egyptians, The Apocalypse of Adam, The Three Steles of Seth, Zostrianos, Melchizedek, The Thought of Norea, Marsanes, Allogenes,* and *The Trimorphic Protennoia.* Also included in the list of

Sethian works is *The Untitled Treatise* from the codex Brucianus. *See also* Gnosticism; Nag Hammadi. [K.L.K.]

Bibliography
Irenaeus, *Against Heresies* 1.29; Pseudo-Tertullian, *Against All Heresies* 2; Hippolytus, *Refutation of All Heresies* 5.19–22; Epiphanius, *Panarion* 39; 40; Philastrius, *Haereses* 3.

W. Foerster and R.McL. Wilson, eds., *Gnosis: A Selection of Gnostic Texts* (Oxford: Clarendon, 1972), Vol. 1, pp. 293–305; B. Layton, *The Gnostic Scriptures* (Garden City: Doubleday, 1987); J.M. Robinson and R. Smith, eds., *The Nag Hammadi Library in English*, 3rd ed. (San Francisco: Harper and Row, 1988).

H.M. Schenke, "Das sethianische System nach Nag-Hammadi-Handschriften," *Studia Coptica*, ed. P. Nagel (Berlin: Akademie-Verlag, 1974), pp. 163–173; B. Layton, ed., *The Rediscovery of Gnosticism: Proceedings of the International Conference on Gnosticism at Yale, New Haven, Connecticut, March 28–31, 1978* (Leiden: Brill, 1981), Vol. 2: *Sethian Gnosticism*; K. Rudolph, *Gnosis: The Nature and History of Gnosticism* (San Francisco: Harper and Row, 1983); J.D. Turner, "Sethian Gnosticism: A Literary History," *Nag Hammadi, Gnosticism, and Early Christianity*, ed. C.W. Hedrick and R. Hodgson, Jr. (Peabody: Hendrickson, 1986), pp. 55–86.

SEVERIAN OF GABALA (d. after 408).

Bishop and exegete. Bishop of Gabala in Syria and a skillful preacher, Severian was an opponent of John Chrysostom and took a leading role in the Synod of the Oak (403), convened to depose Chrysostom. A prolific writer, Severian left more than fifty homilies, including six on the Hexaemeron (days of creation) theme, as well as a commentary on the epistles of Paul, portions of which are preserved in catenae. His sermons are widely diffused, appearing mostly in Greek, but some in Armenian, Syriac, and other languages; many have survived under the names of John Chrysostom and others. CPG II, 4185–4295. [M.P.McH.]

Bibliography
John Chrysostom, *Homilia de recipiendo Severiano*; Socrates, *Church History* 6.11, 16, 17; Sozomen, *Church History* 8.10, 19, 22; Gennadius, *Lives of Illustrious Men* 21.

Un traité inédit de christologie de Sévérien de Gabala In Centurionem et Contra Manichaeos et Apollinaristas, exploitation par Sévère d'Antioche

(519) et le synode du Lateran (649), ed. M. Aubineau (Geneva: Cramer, 1983).

SEVERINUS (d. 482). Missionary and monk.

Severinus, an eastern monk, entered the province of Noricum about the time of Attila's death (453) and spent some thirty years evangelizing in the region around the rivers Danube and Inn. He founded monasteries and engaged in extensive charitable works at a time when the province was crumbling under the barbarian invasions. Six years after his death, his body was removed to the abbey of Lucullanum, presided over by his disciple Eugippius, who wrote his biography (ca. 511). [M.P.McH.]

Bibliography
Eugippius, *The Life of Saint Severin*, FOTC (1965), Vol. 55.

SEVERUS OF ANTIOCH (ca. 465–538).

Monophysite bishop. Although Severus insisted on the dominant divine nature of Christ, he had a place for Jesus' humanity and attacked Julian of Halicarnassus and the Aphthartodocetae, who taught that Jesus' body was always incorruptible. Educated at Alexandria and Berytus, he was also a monk. At Constantinople, he received imperial backing for Monophysite monks, becoming bishop of Antioch when Flavian was deposed in 512. In 518, he himself was deposed because of his Monophysite beliefs on the accession of the orthodox emperor Justin, went to Egypt, and was formally excommunicated by a Constantinopolitan synod in 528. A number of his homilies and letters survive in Syriac. CPG III, 7022-7080. *See also* Monophysites. [F.W.N.]

Bibliography
PO (1907), Vols. 2.1 and 3, ed. M.A. Kugener, collects sources for his life.

J. Lebon, *Le Monophysisme sévérien* (Louvain: van Linthout, 1909); W.H.C. Frend, *The Rise of the Monophysite Movement* (Cambridge: Cambridge UP, 1972), pp. 201–295; A. Grillmeier, *Christ in Christian Tradition* (Atlanta: John Knox, 1987), Vol. 2, pp. 269–284.

SEXTUS, SENTENCES OF. Philosophical

(Neopythagorean) collection of maxims revised

by a Christian (ca. 200). Originally in Greek, the *Sentences of Sextus* is best known in the Latin translation by Rufinus, who incorrectly ascribed the work to Sixtus (Xystus) II, bishop of Rome (d. 258). It comprises 451 ethical and religious aphorisms. The *Sentences of Sextus* advocates moderation and temperance in all things and apparently aims to show that Christianity helps people to live the philosophical life, that is, a life of practical, moral wisdom. The work was popular. In addition to Greek and Latin versions, there were translations into Syriac, Armenian, and Coptic (now known from the Nag Hammadi library, Codex XII, 15–16, 17–34). CPG I, 1115. TLG 1666.

[E.F.]

Bibliography

Origen, *Against Celsus* 8.30; idem, *Homilia in Ezechielem* 1.11; Jerome, *In Hieremiam prophetam* 4.41; idem, *Commentarii in Ezechielem* 6; idem, *Letter* 133.3; idem, *Against Jovininian* 1.49; Gennadius, *Lives of Illustrious Men* 17.

H. Chadwick, *The Sentences of Sextus: A Contribution to the History of Early Christian Ethics* (Cambridge: Cambridge UP, 1959); R.A. Edwards and R.A. Wild, eds. and trs., *The Sentences of Sextus* (Chico: Scholars, 1981).

R.L. Wilken, "Wisdom and Philosophy in Early Christianity," *Aspects of Wisdom in Judaism and Early Christianity*, ed. R.L. Wilken (Notre Dame: U of Notre Dame P, 1975), pp. 143–168.

SEXUALITY. Despite the antimarital and antifamilial sentiments attributed to Jesus in the Synoptic Gospels (Matt. 8:21–22; 10:21, 35–37; 19:10–12 and parallels; Luke 8:10–21; 11:27–28), the Gospels' representation of Jesus with no wife or children in evidence, and the strong ascetic preference expressed by Paul (1 Cor. 7), marriage with its attendant sexual activity nonetheless persisted in early Christianity. Given the delay of the eschaton (the return of Christ and end of the world), Christians continued to make use of worldly institutions, hoping to make them, marriage included, more "Christian."

The tension between Christian visions that exalted sexual renunciation and those that assumed Christians would be engaged in sexual intercourse within marriage is noticeable in early Christian literature. Thus, the Pastoral Epistles warn against those who forbid marriage (1 Tim. 4:3) and take for granted that marriage and reproduction are the norm for Christians, whereas the apocryphal acts stress that the gospel carries a message of sexual abstinence (e.g., *A. Paul. et Thecl.* 5–6). To counter some Gnostic and (later) Manichaean teachings that they thought denigrated the body and reproduction, the church fathers tended to accept marriage as a "good," at the same time trying to regulate permissible forms of sexual activity within it.

All the church fathers assume that Christians should not engage in premarital or extramarital sex. Some counseled the early marriage of Christian youths destined for secular life so that the probability of premarital sexual experience would be forestalled (e.g., John Chrysostom, *Inani gloria* 81–82) and were adamant that Christian marriage demanded absolute sexual fidelity from men as well as from women (e.g., 1 Cor. 6:15–20; 7:4; John Chrysostom, *Hom. 5 in 1 Thess.* 2). Within marriage, the fathers advised moderation both in the amount of sexual activity—less being better—and in the concomitant psychological states—"passionlessness" being an ideal for Christian life (e.g., Ignatius, *Polyc.* 5.2; Tertullian, *Anim.* 27; *Marc* 1.29; Clement of Alexandria, *Paed.* 2.10.91; *Str.* 3.5.42–44; 3.7.57; 3.11.71; 3.12.87; Augustine, *Civ. Dei* 14; *Coniug. et concup.* passim). For sexual activity, they frequently revert to the metaphor of a farmer sowing his field, thus revealing the reproductive intent they assume (e.g., Clement of Alexandria, *Paed.* 2.10.83, 92–93; Augustine, *Civ. Dei* 14.23). Most church fathers thought that even within the confines of marriage sexual intercourse ideally should be undertaken only for the sake of reproduction (Justin, *1 Apol.* 29; Athenagoras, *Leg.* 33; Clement of Alexandria, *Paed.* 2.10.91, 95–96; *Str.* 3.7.58; 3.12.79; Augustine, *Coniug. et concup.* 1.5.4; 1.16.14; 1.17.15). Yet given the scorn of some church fathers that Christians should wish for heirs—Christians who supposedly "take no thought for the morrow" and who themselves expect immortality—even a modest desire for children might fall suspect (Tertullian, *Cast.* 12; Jerome, *Jov.* 1.47; *Ep.* 54.4.2). Contraception, abortion, and child exposure are viewed as three related phenomena and are all condemned (e.g., *Did.* 2.2; *Barn.* 19; Athenagoras, *Leg.* 29; 35; Justin *1 Apol.* 27; 29; Tertullian, *Apol.* 9; Clement of Alexandria, *Paed.* 2.10.96; Jerome, *Ep.* 22.13; Augustine, *Coniug. et concup.* 1.17.15; Basil, *Ep.* 188.2; *Const. app.* 7.3; John Chrysostom, *Hom.* 24 *in Rom.*).

Two gauges of the antisexual tendency of early Christian theology are the campaign against second marriage and the growing acceptance of belief in the perpetual virginity of Mary. Second marriage is treated largely as a matter of moral weakness, appropriate only for those lacking sexual self-control (Justin, *1 Apol.* 15; Athenagoras, *Leg.* 33; Tertullian, *Ux.* 1.7; *Cast.* 5–6; 9; 12; *Monog.*; Jerome, *Ep.* 54.4.2; 79.10.4; John Chrysostom, *Non iter. coniug.* 1). The theory of Mary's perpetual virginity, stimulated by the second-century *Protevangelium of James*, served to bolster the ascetic movement of the fourth century (e.g., Jerome, *Helv.*; Ambrose, *Instit. virg.* 17.111; *Ep.* 42.5–6). Ascetic ideals also probably varied from region to region: some scholars think that in Syria baptism may not have been permitted to married Christians in the first centuries of Christianity's existence.

In the fourth century, thousands of Christians flocked to the desert and the wilderness, impelled by asceticism's message of "becoming perfect" through the renunciation of worldly ties, including sexuality. Ascetic theorists like Evagrius of Pontus and John Cassian analyzed how lust attacks celibates and developed techniques to help younger monks conquer such solitary manifestations of sexual desire as the demonic production of erotic visions and dreams and nocturnal emissions. Their teaching undergirded monastic practice for centuries to come.

Although a few Christian writers, such as Jovinian, feared that the exaltation of sexual renunciation denigrated marriage and reproduction, which were created and blessed by God, the mainline western church edged toward an uneasy compromise, one that was promulgated by Augustine and that became standard theological teaching for centuries thereafter. Although virginity was superior to marriage, Augustine affirmed, marriage should be considered a "good" not only for the "sacramental bond" it conferred but also because it issued in reproduction and provided a control for lust. Ideally, if original sin had not intervened, married couples from the time of Adam and Eve would have engaged in the sexual act in order to reproduce, but their sexual organs would have been under the perfect control of the will, and they would not have been stimulated by the "concupiscence of the flesh." Sin having entered human life with raging concupiscence following as its consequence, sexual activity is permitted to married couples even if they are impelled more by lust than by desire for children—if, and only if, no contraceptive measures are taken. Such sexual acts, although not ideal, were deemed within the range of forgiveness (Augustine, *Civ. Dei* 14; *C. Faust* 15.7; 22.84; *Coniug. et concup.* 1.16.14; 1.17.15; 2.35.20; *C. Iul.* 2.15.7; 2.16.7; 2.30.26; 4.12.2; 6.59.19). Through this teaching, Augustine countered the Manichaean promotion of contraception and abhorrence of reproduction. Although many eastern Christians and some westerners, such as Julian of Eclanum, were hesitant to link their sexual teaching to Augustine's concept of original sin, transmitted through the reproductive act, all of them nonetheless counseled chaste moderation within the sexual lives of Christian couples.

Homosexual activity, especially pederasty, was strongly condemned by early Christian writers. They were perhaps motivated in part by their rejection of pagan sexual practices, as well as by their eagerness to limit all sexual activity to the marriage couch (e.g., Justin, *1 Apol.* 27; Athenagoras, *Leg.* 34; John Chrysostom, *Oppugn.* 3). They stressed that homosexual activities were "contrary to nature" (e.g., Clement of Alexandria, *Paed.* 2.10.87)—just as was any form of heterosexual intercourse that could not result in conception (Augustine, *Bon. coniug.* 11.12). And, unlike Old Testament authors, Christian writers explicitly condemned female homosexual practices as well as male (e.g., Tertullian, *Pall.* 4; Clement of Alexandria, *Paed.* 3.3; John Chrysostom, *Hom.* 4 *in Rom.*). It is unclear whether the patristic writers' abhorrence of overturning customary gender roles and activities, as revealed in their diatribes against effeminate men and aggressive women, are linked to a fear of homosexual behavior. There is little in the writings of the church fathers that could bolster a modern argument for "sexual liberation." *See also* Asceticism; Body; Homosexuality; Virgins.   [E.A.C.]

Bibliography

D.S. Bailey, *Sexual Relation in Christian Thought* (New York: Harper, 1959); H. Crouzel, *Mariage et divorce, célibat et caractère sacerdotaux dans l'église ancienne* (Turin: Bottega d'Erasmo, 1982); B.J. Brooten, "Patristic Interpretations of Romans 1:26," *SP* 18 (1985):287–291; J. Noonan, *Contraception: A History of Its Treatment by the Catholic Theologians and Canonists* (Cambridge: Harvard UP, 1986), esp. pp. 1–170; E.A. Clark, *Ascetic Piety and Women's Faith: Essays on Late Ancient Christianity* (Lewiston: Mellen, 1986); idem, "'Adam's Only Companion': Augustine and the Early Christian Debate on Marriage," *Recherches augustiniennes* 21 (1986):139–162; V. Burrus, *Chastity as Autonomy: Women in the Stories of the Apocryphal Acts* (Lewiston: Mellen, 1987); C. Munier, *Ehe und Ehelosigkeit in der alten kirche* (Berne: Lang, 1987); P. Brown, *The Body and Society: Men, Women, and Sexual Renunciation in Early Christianity* (New York: Columbia UP, 1988); A. Rousselle, *Porneia: On Desire and the Body in Antiquity* (London: Blackwell, 1988).

SHENOUTE OF ATRIPE (d. ca. 450).

Abbot of the White Monastery in Upper Egypt (388–ca. 450). The community grew to about 4,000 and supported a large farming population that was repeatedly threatened by invasions. Shenoute required written oaths and allowed mature monks to live as hermits. He opposed Nestorius at Ephesus in 431, but his strength was not theological. Feast day July 1 (Coptic).   [F.W.N.]

Bibliography

Besa: The Life of Shenoute, tr. D.N. Bell (Kalamazoo: Cistercian, 1983).

J. Leipoldt and W.E. Crum, eds., CSCO (1906–1951), Vols. 41, 42, and 73 (Coptic); 96, 108, and 129 (trans.).

J. Leipoldt, *Schenute von Atripe und die Entstehung des national ägyptischen Christentums* (Leipzig: Hinrichs, 1903).

SHEPHERD, GOOD.

Gods, kings, and other political and military leaders were commonly viewed as shepherds in the ancient Near East. The Old Testament often portrays Yahweh as a shepherd and Israel as his flock. The Gospel writers apply this metaphor to Jesus. At John 10:11,14, in an extended allegory, he is the good shepherd; at Hebrews 13:20, he is the great shepherd. In Clement of Alexandria's famous "Hymn to Christ the Savior," he is the holy shepherd (*Paed.* 3.101.3, line 30). In Luke 15:3–7, the parable of the lost sheep (cf. Ezek. 34:12, 16; Ps. 119:176), the shepherd, having found his lost sheep, lays the animal on his shoulders and carries it home, where he rejoices with his neighbors at his good fortune.

Primarily on the basis of this latter pericope, but taken in consort with the rest of New Testament and early patristic tradition, which associates Jesus with shepherding, art historians have long identified the pictorial image of a shepherd carrying a sheep as Jesus the good shepherd. Writing in Carthage in 210 or 211, Tertullian is the first to make the identification explicit. In *On Modesty* 7.1–4 and 10.12, he says that the *physici*, his Catholic Christian opponents, depict on their breakable eucharistic cups the image of Jesus as a shepherd carrying a sheep on his shoulders. The image is ubiquitous in early Christian art: it appears in third- and fourth-century catacomb paintings and on the lunette over the Dura-Europos baptismal font, in relief sculpture, and in freestanding statuary, such as the fourth-century example in Baltimore illustrated on page 846, and in a host of examples in the minor arts. There can be no doubt that this image was a compelling one to early Christians and that they used it almost instinctively in funerary and liturgical contexts from an early date. Because the image is attested in many pre-Christian contexts (as Hermes-criophoros, or ram-bearer, for example), its association with Jesus has been questioned (e.g., by Klauser). The Dura-Europos shepherd-

Shepherd carrying a lamb, early Christian (early fourth century) marble statuette of Roman provenance. (Walters Art Gallery, Baltimore, Maryland.)

criophoros, however, was almost certainly intended to evoke the memory of Jesus. *See also* Abercius; Art; Chalice; Dura-Europos; Orant. [P.C.F.]

Bibliography
T. Klauser, "Studien zur Entstehungsgeschichte der christlichen Kunst I–IX," *JAC* 1 (1958)–10 (1967); W. Schumacher, *Hirt und Guter Hirt, Römische Quartalschrift Suppl.* 34 (Freiburg: Herder, 1977); N. Himmelmann, *Über Hirtengenre in der antiken Kunst* (Opladen: Westdeutscher Verlag, 1980); W. Wischmeyer, "Die Aberkiosinschrift als Grabepigramm," *JAC* 23 (1980):22–47; B. Ramsey, "A Note on the Disappearance of the Good Shepherd from Early Christian Art," *HThR* 76 (1983):375–378.

SIBYLLINE ORACLES. Jewish and Christian imitations of pagan prophetic books. Magistrates in Rome kept an official collection of the prophecies of the inspired women known as Sibyls, but many unofficial sayings were in circulation. The present collection of the *Sibylline Oracles*, written in Greek hexameters, was edited in the fifth–sixth century in fifteen books (9, 10, and 15 are now missing). Books 3–5 are Jewish (second century B.C. to second century A.D.); the others are Christian or revised by Christians (dated second century to fourth century for the most part). The collection is notable for its words of judgment against pagan Rome. The apologists used the *Sibylline Oracles* extensively as pagan testimonies to Christian teachings. CPG I, 1352. TLG 1551. [E.F.]

Bibliography
Athenagoras, *Plea* 30; Theophilus, *To Autolycus* 2.3, 36; Clement of Alexandria, *Exhortation* 6; 8; idem, *Miscellanies* 3.3; Origen, *Against Celsus* 7.53; Lactantius, *Divine Institutes* 1.6, 15; 2.12; 4.6; 7.18–20; Constantine, *Address to the Assembly of the Saints* 18–19; 21; Augustine, *City of God* 18.23.

A.-M. Kurfess, *Sibyllinische Weissagungen* (Munich: Heimeran, 1951).

J.J. Collins, "Sibylline Oracles," *The Old Testament Pseudepigrapha*, ed. J.H. Charlesworth (Garden City: Doubleday, 1983), Vol. 1, pp. 318–472.

B. Thompson, "Patristic Use of the Sibyllin Oracles," *Review of Religion* 16 (1952):115–136.

SIDONIUS APOLLINARIS (ca. 430–ca. 487). Political figure, writer, orator, and bishop of Clermont. A member of a Gallo-Roman aristocratic family and a friend of Claudianus Mamertus, Sidonius married (ca. 450) Papianilla, daughter of the future Roman emperor Avitus, and entered on a public career. He addressed a panegyric (456) to his father-in-law, and others subsequently to the emperors Majorian (458) and Anthemius (468); for the last, he was appointed prefect of Rome. Elected bishop of Clermont ca. 472, he was exiled upon the occupation of the city by the Goths in 475 but was soon reinstated. He left twenty-four poems, modeled on such classical writers as Virgil and Claudius Claudianus, as well as 147 letters reminiscent of Pliny the Younger. The letters are an important source for the history and life of southern Gaul. CPL 986–987a.

[M.P.McH.]

Bibliography

Gennadius, *Lives of Illustrious Men* 92a (92); *Sidonius, Poems and Letters*, tr. W.B. Anderson, LCL, Vol. 1 (1936) and Vol. 2 (1965).

N.K. Chadwick, *Poetry and Letters in Early Christian Gaul* (London: Bowes and Bowes, 1955), pp. 296–327; R.P.C. Hanson, "The Church in Fifth-Century Gaul: Evidence from Sidonius Apollinaris," *JEH* 21 (1970):1–10.

SIGN OF THE CROSS. Tracing a cross on the forehead with thumb or index finger of the right hand. This custom is early; eventually, it was incorporated into the liturgy. A similar drawing of the cross on the breast is attested later, in the late fourth century. The earliest evidence for the signing of the lips appears to come only after the patristic period, in the eighth century. The sign of the cross traced with the thumb and one or two fingers on forehead, breast, and shoulders was used outside the liturgy by the fifth century. It is made in modern times by directing the right hand with all fingers extended from forehead to breast to shoulders—from the left shoulder to the right in the west, from the right to the left in the east.

The *Acts of Peter* (latter half of second century) has Peter describe Theon's baptism: "washed and signed with thy holy sign." The reverence in which the cross was held in the second century is clear from the *Paschal Homily* by the so-called Anonymous Quartodeciman: "This is my nourishment when I am hungry, my covering when I am stripped, my safeguard when I fear God, my support when I falter, my prize when I enter combat, and my trophy when I triumph." From the time of Tertullian, patristic writers testify to the use of the sign of the cross to sanctify actions in daily life. Tertullian observes (*Coron.* 3.4): "At every step forward, at every entrance and exit, when we put on our clothes and shoes, when we bathe, when we sit at table, when we light the lamps, on couch, on seat, in all the ordinary actions of life, we trace upon the forehead

the sign of the cross." Elsewhere (*Resurr.* 8), he gives the reason: "The flesh is signed that the soul may be fortified." Cyprian warns that on the last day only those can escape who have been reborn and signed with the sign of Christ (*Demet.* 22). The *Apostolic Tradition* of Hippolytus (215–220) talks of the bishop ending the anointing with oil: "Sealing him on the forehead, he shall give him the kiss [of peace]." The *Canons of Hippolytus*, which depends on the *Apostolic Tradition*, says: "Sign your forehead with the sign of the cross to overcome Satan and to give glory to God." Lactantius (*Div. inst.* 4.27) says that just as Christ put all demons to flight by a word when he was alive, so now his followers by the name of their master and the sign of his passion exclude those same defiled spirits from men. Prudentius (*Cathem.* 6.130–136) counsels that at bedtime the believer should sign on the breast and forehead the cross of the redemption.

The *Apostolic Constitutions* 8.12 prescribes that the celebrant of the eucharist "at the beginning makes the sign of the cross on his forehead with his hand." Leo the Great (*Serm.* 61) says: "The cross is the fount of all blessings, the source of all graces, and through it the believers receive strength for weakness, glory for shame, and life for death." And Augustine (*In evang. Ioh.* 118) says: "Unless that sign be applied, whether it be to the foreheads of believers, or to the very water out of which they are regenerated, or to the oil with which they receive the anointing chrism, or to the sacrifice that nourishes them, none of them is properly administered."

John Chrysostom is probably the most eloquent witness of all (*Jud. et Gent.* 9.8): "Everyone is constantly making the sign of the cross on the noblest part of his body. Each day people carry around the sign formed on their foreheads as if it were a trophy on a column. We see this sign shining forth on the sacred table, at ordinations, and along with the body of Christ at the sacred mysteries. Anyone could see a whole chorus of these signs of the cross in houses, in the marketplaces, . . . on the hills, at sea, on ships, on beds, garments, weapons, in bridal chambers, on golden vases, on gems, wall paintings. . . . All vie in searching out this wondrous gift and this ineffable grace." *See also* Cross. [T.H.]

Bibliography

E. Beresford-Cooke, *The Sign of the Cross in the Western Liturgies* (London: Longmans, Green, 1907); B. Leoni, *La croce e il segno* (Verona: SAT, 1968); G.Q. Reijners, *The Terminology of the Holy Cross in the Early Christian Literature as Based upon Old Testament Typology* (Nijmegen: Dekker & Van de Vegt, 1965); E. Dinkler, *Signum Crucis* (Tübingen: Mohr, 1967), pp. 1–76.

SIMON MAGUS (first century). Religious leader. First attested in Acts 8:9–24 as a popular charlatan in Samaria won over to Christianity, only to bargain for a share in the apostles' spiritual powers, Simon Magus ("the Magician") was magnified in early Christian tradition as the original mastermind behind Christian Gnosticism and the virtual founder of all heresy (cf. Irenaeus, *Haer.* 1.23.2; Eusebius, *H.E.* 2.13.1ff.). The Acts account notes that Simon had drawn a loyal following who hailed him as "that power of God which is called Great" (8:10); and by the middle of the second century Justin Martyr reported that Simon had engendered a cult in Rome and was still touted as the "first god" by Samaritans and other nationals (*1 Apol.* 26.1–3).

Actually, Simon was probably one among many messianic pretenders of first-century Palestine, hailed as a gifted Gnostic by later "Simonians," who developed their speculative doctrines accordingly. Justin Martyr and Irenaeus (*Haer.* 1.23.2–4) testify that Simon was believed to have been escorted by a Phoenician prostitute, Helen, who, in the Simonian myth, represented his primary "Thought" (*ennoia*). Helen was creator of the lower world but had herself become entrapped there and transmigrated into a harlot's body, being rescued only through the descent of the redeemer Simon. The mature speculations of Simonian gnosis were embodied in a *Great Exposition* (*Apophasis megalē*), mistakenly attributed to Simon himself by Hippolytus (*Haer.* 6.9–18). Later Christian pseudepigraphy immortalized Simon Magus as the archenemy of the primitive Christian mission who was continuously debated and thwarted by the apostle Peter (cf. *Acts of Peter*; Ps.-Clement, *Recogn.* 2.1–3.49; *Hom.* 2; 3; 7; 16–19). [P.M.Bl.]

Bibliography

L. Cerfaux, "La Gnose simonienne," *RecSR* 15 (1925):489–511, and 16 (1926):5–20, 265–285, 481–503; S.V. McCasland, "Simon Magus," *Interpreter's Dictionary of the Bible* (Nashville: Abingdon, 1962), Vol. 4, pp. 358–360; H. Jonas, *The Gnostic Religion*, 2nd ed. (Boston: Beacon, 1963), pp. 103–111; K. Beyschlag, *Simon Magus und die christliche Gnosis* (Tübingen: Mohr, 1974); K. Rudolph, *Gnosis: The Nature and History of Gnosticism* (San Francisco: Harper and Row, 1983), pp. 294–298.

SIMPLICIUS. Bishop of Rome (468–483). Simplicius's pontificate was marked by the fall of the Roman empire in the west and the rule of Odoacer, an Arian, over Italy. Attempts to intervene in the east in defense of orthodoxy as proclaimed at the Council of Chalcedon (451) against the growing influence of the Monophysites met with little success. Simplicius exercised firm disciplinary control over the bishops of Italy and appointed the bishop of Seville as his vicar in Spain. He established new churches in Rome and encouraged church building in his native Tivoli as well. Some twenty of his letters are extant. Feast day March 10. CPL 1664, cf. 1605. [M.P.McH.]

Bibliography

Liber Pontificalis 49 (Duchesne 1.249–251).

SIN. Turning away from God and the consequent moral disorder of the self in will, disposition, and action. Early Christian usage of the Greek and Latin words usually translated "sin" (*hamartia* and *peccatum* respectively) provides only a partial guide to the understanding of sin in the early church. In fact, Christianity developed a complex variety of terms and concepts to designate and interpret the ways in which human beings go astray. At the most general level, sin was construed as moral evil understood in its specifically religious significance. It is moral evil because in one form or another it represents a violation of the requirements of morality on the part of agents who can rightly be held responsible for what they do (i.e., whose capacity for moral action is not constrained or impaired in some way that exempts them from responsibility); and it acquires its specifically religious significance in that it is reckoned above all to be rooted in and to follow from an underlying departure from God. Thus, in a particularly vivid passage, Tertullian claimed that idolatry involves every other form of moral fault (e.g., murder: idolaters kill themselves; fraud: idolaters defraud God of God's due) and intimated, conversely, that all moral evils are forms of idolatry (*Idol.* 1).

Nature of Sin. Early Christianity never elaborated a formal and normative doctrine of sin in the sense in which, during the fourth and fifth centuries, it gave creedal definition to its Trinitarian and Christological doctrines; and theologians rarely treated sin as a separate topic in its own right: there were, for example, no early Christian treatises *De peccato*, "On Sin." Rather, discussions of sin were most often interwoven with other themes, especially, perhaps, the Christian life as the disciplined effort to vanquish sin and conform oneself to God. Nevertheless, these discussions do display common features and address certain dominant questions: how is it that human beings are vulnerable to sin? how does sin exercise its hold over human beings? how can that hold be broken? It is first important, however, to sketch the broad scheme within which the early Christian view of sin took shape.

Virtually from the beginning, Christianity was marked by the sense that there is an opposition between two ways of life, one oriented to "this world" and the other to God. This sense was expressed in (although certainly not limited to) what has come to be called the "two ways" tradition. Drawing on both Jewish and Hellenistic antecedents, the "two ways" notion sets in stark contrast the way of darkness or death and the way of light or life, each delineated in terms of qualities of human character as well as types of behavior and each presided over by its corresponding angel. Literary versions of the tradition were incorporated in several Christian writings of the second century (*Did.* 1.1–6.2; *Barn.* 18–21; cf. Hermas, *Mand.*, with the repeated refrain that those who follow the commands will "live to God"); and the basic antithesis was most vividly and fully elaborated in Augustine of Hippo's famous vision of the two cities, the heavenly formed by love of God even to contempt of self and the earthly by love of self even to contempt of God (*Civ. Dei* 14.28; and, generally, 11–22).

Given this antithesis, it is not surprising that Christianity should have presented itself as a religion of repentance, a final opportunity provided by a gracious and patient God to turn from death to life before the moment of judgment arrives (*1 Clem.* 7.4–8.5; Ignatius, *Smyrn.* 9.1; *2 Clem.* 8.1–4; 16.1–3; Justin, *1 Apol.* 28; Tertullian, *Paenit.* 2). Nor is it surprising that Christian baptism should have been understood to mark the critical point of transition from the one to the other, requiring a repudiation of the Satan who had, so to speak, regulated one's former life and an affirmation of the God to whom one's life was now to be directed (cf. the baptismal liturgy in Hippolytus, *Trad. ap.* 21). Similarly, the Christian life, after baptism, was construed as an ongoing struggle to uproot one's previous orientation to "this world," together with the value commitments on which it rested and the behavior patterns in which it resulted, and to realize a new orientation to God with its new value commitments and new behavior patterns (Hermas, *Mand.* and *Sim.*, with the repeated exhortation not to be "double-minded," that is, not to straddle the two orientations but to achieve the new one). The difficulty of achieving and sustaining such a complex shift in orientation was widely recognized; and, especially among the monks and the monastic theologians of the fourth and later centuries, there emerged a sophisticated "psychology" of the redirecting of the self, deeply aware of the fragility of human efforts to maintain a new orientation and acutely sensitive to the often subtle ways in which the old might retain or reassert its hold upon the self (Evagrius, *Cap. pract.*; John Cassian, *Coll.*).

The basic pattern, then, was a scheme of antithesis between two forms of life, marked out in qualities of character and types of behavior, and of transition, through repentance, from the one to the other, with the shift in one respect concentrated at the moment of baptism and in another extended through the drawn-out struggle of the Christian life. Within this scheme, the early Christian understanding of sin served both as an account of the form of life opposed to God and as a reckoning of the continuing hold of that form of life on the Christian even after repentance and baptism. This understanding, it should be noted, was multidimensional, ranging in its coverage from individual misdeeds through connected patterns of behavior to the deepest dispositions of the self and their underlying value commitments. Thus, the "way of darkness" (*Barn.* 20) includes not only kinds of wrongdoing, such as adultery, robbery, fraud, and magic, but also such dispositional qualities as arrogance, pride, hypocrisy, and malice; and it is rooted most basically in a lack of the knowledge and fear of God, that is, of any controlling respect for the divine. It can therefore be depicted as a fundamental inversion of values in which persons become persecutors of the good and pursuers of the evil. Similarly, Augustine portrayed his two cities, the earthly and the heavenly, as living respectively according to the human (*secundum hominem*) or according to the divine (*secundum Deum*) standard (*Civ. Dei* 14.4); according to two different patterns of value and orientations of will (14.6–7), and not merely as acting in two different ways. Thus, although the emphasis could vary from one discussion to another, early Christianity never construed sin as simply a matter of acts alone, of mere misdeeds; it recognized that sin was a far more complex human phenomenon than that. Sin is not only the religiously based moral failure to do what one ought to do; it is also, and more importantly, the religiously based moral failure to be what one is supposed to be.

Basis of Sin. How is it that human beings are vulnerable to sin? How does it happen that they actually fall into sin? Human vulnerability to sin rests first of all on the status of humans as created beings. Just because humans came into existence from nothing, rather than existing from all eternity, they are—like all created beings—subject to a kind of ontological instability; that is, they are capable of change, including moral change, and thus of sin (Athanasius, *Gent.* 4; *Inc.* 3–5; Gregory of Nyssa, *Or. catech.* 6; 21; Augustine, *Civ. Dei* 14.11, 13). Early Christianity also recognized that sin and evil have a more than human force, that they are not simply or straightforwardly under human control. This power could be represented by speaking of the demons, as when Tertullian, echoing a widespread Christian theme, ascribed idolatry to the malice of the demons who deceive human beings into taking them as gods (*Idol.* 1; cf. Justin, *1 Apol.* 5; Minucius Felix, *Oct.* 26) or especially in accounts of Satan's role in humanity's first fall into evil (Gregory of Nyssa, *Or. catech.* 5–6; Augustine, *Gen. ad litt.* 11.2–30; *Civ. Dei* 14.11–13). It could also be represented by speaking—as did Augustine, in what was a significant break with the previous tradition—of the impairment of the human will and the vitiation of human nature, after Adam's sin, with the result that human beings, on their own, are no longer capable of willing and doing the good (*Nat. et grat.* and the anti-Pelagian writings in general).

Despite these themes, however, early Christianity insisted that sin is not inflicted or imposed on human beings apart from or contrary to their own inclinations. At stake here was the specifically moral character of sin: if persons cannot avoid sinning, they cannot be held (morally) responsible for sin. Thus, early Christianity rejected the fatalistic and deterministic currents in Roman culture, arguing that moral assessment—praise for virtue, blame for vice—makes sense only if persons are free to will either the good or the evil (Justin, *1 Apol.* 43; Origen, *Princ.* 3.1; *Cels.* 4.3; Augustine, *Soliloq.* 1.1.4); and what was to become the dominant form of Christianity resisted Gnostic and Manichaean views that persons are good or evil, saved or lost, either by nature or through the interplay of external cosmic forces (Irenaeus, *Haer.* 4.37, 39; Augustine, *Duab. anim.*; *C. Fort.*). Where there is no free will, Augustine declared (*C. Fort.* 20), there is no sin, because there is no *moral* action at all.

Thus, if human beings are vulnerable to sin due to the instability of created existence, they nevertheless actually sin of their own accord; and, in particular, it was precisely through the exercise of free will that humanity first fell from its initial state of created goodness (Athanasius, *Gent.* 4; *Inc.* 3–5; Gregory of Nyssa, *Or. catech.* 5; Augustine, *Civ. Dei* 14.11), bringing death upon itself, rendering itself liable to demonic assault, and subjecting itself to sin's power. The more-than-human force of sin, then, is itself the result rather than the cause of sin; and sin remains a specifically moral fault.

To interpret the hold that sin takes on persons, early Christianity turned to the internal realm of the psyche. Sin was construed as a disordering of the self in which the passions—desire, joy, fear, grief, anger, etc.—which belong to the lower or irrational part of the soul and function in relation to the immediate objects and actions of the material and social order, come to dominate the self as a whole and in particular the higher or rational part of the soul (Gregory of Nyssa, *Beat.* 2; 3; 5). In this case, the person's mental and emotive life is directed not toward God as the supreme good, but toward the lesser goods and the false ambitions of the temporal realm. This misdirection of the self has several characteristics. It involves a cognitive failure, as persons now conceive God in terms drawn from sense experience rather than in terms appropriate to the divine (Gregory of Nazianzus, *Or.* 28.12–13; Augustine, *Trin.* 1.1) and lose their capacity to discern what is truly good (Gregory of Nyssa, *Beat.* 5; Athanasius, *Gent.* 3–5). There is a rending of the social fabric, as persons turn from God, the common good of all, and seek instead their private good (Augustine, *Lib. arb.* 2.19.53; *Gen. ad litt.* 11.15.19), inevitably in competition with and at the expense of others (Augustine on Romulus and Remus in *Civ. Dei* 15.5); and above all there is pride, the assertion of independence from God and the exaltation of the self that are the root of all sin, as persons take up life for themselves (*secundum se*) rather than for God (Gregory of Nyssa, *Beat.* 1; Augustine, *Gen. ad litt.* 11.15.19–20; *Civ. Dei* 14.13). Thus, sin's disordering of the self is reflected in and reinforced by a false inversion of the true order of value, the lower goods of self and temporal prosperity being treated as if they were of highest worth and being preferred to God, who is in fact the true supreme good for human beings.

This disordering of the self was understood to be habitual and to exercise all the force of habit, controlling the range of the imagination and keeping the will in check (Gregory of Nyssa, *Virg.* 9; Augustine, *Conf.* 8.5.10–12; 8.6.19–11.27). Its hold on the self, however, could be variously estimated. On the one hand, it was possible to picture human nature as basically unimpaired and sin as a kind of rust or stain dulling its otherwise bright surface (Gregory of Nyssa, *Beat.* 6; Pelagius, *Ep. ad Demetr.* 2; 4; 8). In this case, although the self was subject to the tyranny of the passions (Gregory of Nyssa, *Beat.* 3) and had exchanged the free exercise of will for the slavery of sin (Gregory of Nyssa, *Or. dom.* 5), it retained the freedom of the will and thus the capacity to will the good (Gregory of Nyssa, *Beat.* 5; Pelagius, *Ep. ad Demetr.* 3–4). On the other hand, Augustine portrayed human nature as vitiated by sin (*Nat. et grat.*, an extended argument against Pelagius) and sin as so deeply rooted that it becomes a kind of "second nature" to the self (*Lib. arb.* 3.19.54). In Augustine's view, then, habit takes on the force of necessity (*C. Fort.* 22; *Conf.* 8.5.10); and although the will remains free, it no longer suffices on its own to will or to do the good (*Lib. arb.* 2.20.54; *Nat. et grat.* 23.25; *Corrept.* 11.31). Since it is exercised *by* the disordered self, it holds no cure *for* the disordered self.

Overcoming of Sin. On either view, however, the breaking of sin's grip on human beings was understood to be a complex matter involving a variety of elements. Christ's incarnation, life, death, and resurrection were central. The human presence of the divine Word made God accessible, so to speak, within the temporal sphere to which humans had reduced their imagination and their patterns of thought; and thus it initiated a reversal of the cognitive failure involved in sin (Athanasius, *Inc.* 11–19). It vanquished Satan and the demons, robbing them of power and thus putting human beings in a position to unmask their deceptions and repel their assaults (Gregory of Nyssa, *Or. catech.* 18; 22–24; Athanasius, *Inc.* 27; *V. Anton.* 21–43). It defeated death and thus held out the promise of an ultimate ontic stability in which human beings would no longer be vulnerable to sin or subject to mortality (Athanasius, *Inc.* 6–10; Gregory of Nyssa, *Or. catech.* 8). Not least, as the expression of the humility of God (Gregory of Nyssa, *Or. catech.* 14–15), it provided the divine antidote to human pride (Gregory of Nyssa, *Beat.* 1; Augustine, *Conf.* 7.20.26–7.21.27; *En. 2 in Ps.* 18.25; and note that humility could be reckoned the foundation of all virtue: John Cassian, *Coll.* 9.3); and, in general, the pattern of Christ's human life was understood to stand in direct antithesis to the disordered life of the disordered self (Augustine, *En. in Ps.* 72.16) as both its condemnation and its cure.

At the same time, of course, the breaking of sin's grip had also to be realized in a redirection of the self through which the lower element—the passions—would again be properly subordinated to the higher, rational element of the soul and the person properly oriented to God as the supreme good. Thus, the Christian life was understood as an ongoing struggle to vanquish the passions or at least to hold them decisively in check under rational control (Gregory of Nyssa, *Beat.* 2; Evagrius, *Cap. pract.* 6–33). It was in this context that there first emerged lists of what would eventually be formalized as the "seven deadly sins." The Greek monastic theologian Evagrius of Pontus (*Cap. pract.* 6–14) spelled out eight basic thoughts which he also characterized as passions (since entertaining these thoughts arouses the passions) or as demons (since the passions are the avenues of demonic access to and influence on the self). These eight—gluttony, impurity (or lust), avarice, sadness, anger, *acedia* (religious tedium), vainglory, and pride—represent, in ascending order, the lingering and ever more subtle forms of the old orientation's hold on the self as it seeks to mold itself to God; and they are matched, in Evagrius's scheme, by a corresponding set of religious disciplines de-

signed to extinguish the passions and bring them under control (*Cap. pract.* 15–39). John Cassian, who had come under Evagrius's influence in Egypt, conveyed the list to the Latin west; he devoted a full book of his *Institutes*, a guide for monks living the communal life, to each of the eight vices, describing its characteristic effects and indicating appropriate remedies (*Inst.* 5–12). Late in the sixth century, Gregory the Great reduced the list from eight to seven—combining vainglory and pride in pride, combining sadness and *acedia* in sadness (subsequently called accidie), adding the sin of envy—and partially reversed its order, thus producing what has since been the standard listing of the "seven deadly sins": pride, envy, anger, sadness (accidie), avarice, gluttony, and lust (*Mor. in Job* 31.45).

The aim of the struggle against the passions was to attain a state of *apatheia*, or passionlessness, in which human beings, no longer bound to the immediacies of the material order or driven by the false ambitions of an unreconstructed society, would again come to know the divine, to discern the true good, and to love God—that is, in which their mental and affective life would again be rightly ordered to God (Gregory of Nyssa, *Beat.* 6; Evagrius, *Cap. pract.* 63–89). The great difficulty of effecting such a transformation was universally emphasized (Gregory of Nyssa, *Beat.* 1; 2), as was the constant danger of taking pride in one's religious success and thus slipping back into the very pattern of sin one was trying to escape (Evagrius, *Cap. pract.* 13; 14; Augustine, *Nat. et grat.* 32.36); but the underlying integrity of human nature and the enduring freedom of the human will were understood to provide the resources through which, in the light of God's action in Christ and with the assistance of God's grace (Origen, *Princ.* 3.1.19), human beings could bring such a transformation about (Gregory of Nyssa, *Beat.* 6).

Here again, however, Augustine—as in his views on the vitiation of human nature and on the impairment of the human will—took a significantly different tack. Under the influence of his study of Paul and again in his bitter controversy with Pelagius and the Pelagians, he became convinced that human beings cannot control the direction of their love: they cannot make themselves love what they do not love (*Quaest. Simpl.* 1.2.21). Thus, it is only through the interior action of divine grace that a person comes to acknowledge and to delight in the good and to love God. Apart from that grace, free will avails only to sin (*Spir. et litt.* 3–5). In this regard, Augustine set the direction that would subsequently be followed, more or less consistently, in western Christianity, shifting the emphasis from sin as overcome through the discipline of the Christian, and especially of the monastic, life to sin as overcome only by the interior working of divine grace, through which alone the reorientation of the self takes place. In stressing the sheer strength of sin's psychic hold, however, Augustine also came dangerously close to evacuating it of its specifically moral character. After the fall and apart from grace, persons cannot help but will sinfully. Only because he insisted that all humans were somehow participants in the first and freely chosen sin of Adam (*Civ. Dei* 13.14; *C. Pelag.* 4.4.7), and thus shared the responsibility for bringing upon themselves the condition of being unable to will the good, did Augustine retain the critical notion that sin is an act of will for which its agents can rightly be held morally responsible. The tension between sin's strength and sin's moral character is one of the marks of the Augustinian legacy in the theological and intellectual traditions of western culture. *See also* Ethics; Original Sin. [W.S.B.]

Bibliography

Epistle of Barnabas 18–21; *Didache* 1–6; Hermas, *Mandates*; Tertullian, *On Penitence*; Origen, *On First Principles* 3.1–2; Athanasius, *On the Incarnation*; Gregory of Nyssa, *Catechetical Oration*; idem, *Beatitudes*; Evagrius of Pontus, *Praktikos*; Pelagius, *Letter to Demetrias*; Augustine, *Against Fortunatus the Manichaean*; idem, *Confessions* 1; 8; idem, *Literal Meaning of Genesis* 11; idem, *City of God* 11–22; idem, *Spirit and the Letter*; idem, *On Nature and Grace*; John Cassian, *Conferences* 1; 10; 11; idem, *Institutes*.

K. Heussi, *Der Ursprung des Mönchtums* (Tübingen: Mohr, 1936); G. Bardy, "Apatheia," *Dictionnaire de spiritualité* (Paris: Beauchesne, 1937), Vol. 1, pp. 727–746; M.W. Bloomfield, "The Origin of the Concept of the Seven Cardinal Sins," *HThR* 34 (1941):121–128; A. Vögtle, "Affekt," RLAC (1950), Vol. 1, pp. 160–173; M.W. Bloomfield, *The Seven Deadly Sins: An Introduction to the History of a Religious Concept with Special Reference to Medieval English Literature* (East Lansing: Michigan State UP, 1952); J. Gaith, *La Conception de la liberté chez Grégoire de Nysse* (Paris: Vrin, 1953); P. Delhaye et al., *Théologie du péché*, 2 vols. (Tournai: Desclée, 1960–1961); L. Bouyer, *The Spirituality of the New Testament and the Fathers*, (New York: Desclée, 1963); G. Quell, G. Bertram, G. Stählin, and W. Grundmann, "Hamartanō, Hamartēma, Hamartia," *Theological Dictionary of the New Testament* (Grand Rapids: Eerdmans, 1964), Vol. 1, pp. 267–316; W. Jaeger, *Two Rediscovered Works of Ancient Christian Literature: Gregory of Nyssa and Macarius* (Leiden: Brill, 1965), pp. 70–114; R. Kraft, *Barnabas and the Didache* (New York: Nelson, 1965); C. Vogel, *Le Pécheur et la pénitence dans l'église ancienne* (Paris: Cerf, 1966); O. Chadwick, *John Cassian*, 2nd ed. (Cambridge: Cambridge UP, 1968); R. Evans, *Pelagius: Inquiries and Reappraisals* (New York: Seabury, 1968); J. Pelikan, *The Emergence of the Catholic Tradition (100–600)* (Chicago: U of Chicago P, 1971), pp. 278–331; M. Alflatt, "The Development of the Idea of Involuntary Sin in St. Augustine," *REAug* 20 (1974):113–134; idem, "The Responsibility for Involuntary Sin in Saint Augustine," *Recherches augustiniennes* 10 (1975):171–186; A. Vanneste, "Nature et grâce dans la théologie de saint Augustin," *Recherches augustiniennes* 10 (1975):143–169; J.P. Burns, ed., *Theological Anthropology* (Philadelphia: Fortress, 1981); W. Babcock, "Augustine's Interpretation of Romans (A.D. 394–396)," *AugStud* 10 (1979):55–74; idem, "Augustine on Sin and Moral Agency," *Journal of Religious Ethics* 16 (1988):28–55.

SINGING. *See* Music.

SIRICIUS. Bishop of Rome (384–399). Siricius was a supporter of his predecessor, Damasus I, and a presbyter before his election as bishop. Seven of his letters have been preserved. The letter to bishop Himerius of Tarragona in Spain (385) is the first genuine work included in the later collections of papal decretals. It upholds the authority of the Roman see and is the first papal document insisting on celibacy for priests and deacons. A synod under Siricius excommunicated Jovinian for teaching that virginity is not superior in sanctity to marriage. He communicated to the African churches nine canons on the clergy and ordination. Feast day November 26. CPL 1637. [E.F.]

Bibliography

E. Diehl, *Inscriptiones latinae christianae veteres* (Berlin: Weidmann, 1961), nos. 971–972; Ambrose, *Letter* 42; Innocent, *Epistulae* 1.13; 6; *Liber Pontificalis* 40 (Duchesne 1.216-217).

E.G. Weltin, *The Ancient Popes* (Westminster: Newman, 1964), pp. 238–251; C. Pietri, *Roma Christiana* (Rome: Ecole Française de Rome, 1976), pp. 468–474; D. Callam, "Clerical Continence in the Fourth Century," *ThS* 41 (1980):3–50.

SIXTUS I. Bishop of Rome (ca. 117–ca. 127). Sixtus I held office for some ten years in the reign of the emperor Hadrian; nothing else is known with certainty of his life. Feast day April 6. [M.P.McH.]

Bibliography

Eusebius, *Church History* 4.4, 5; 5.6, 24; *Liber Pontificalis* 8 (Duchesne 1.128).

SIXTUS II. Bishop of Rome (257–258). While upholding the validity of baptism administered by heretics, Sixtus II effected a reconciliation with Cyprian of Carthage, who had broken with Sixtus's predecessor Stephen I over the issue. Martyred under Valerian, he was greatly venerated. Feast day August 6. [M.P.McH.]

Bibliography

Eusebius, *Church History* 7.5–7, 9, 27; Cyprian, *Letter* 80; *Liber Pontificalis* 25 (Duchesne 1.155–156).

SIXTUS III. Bishop of Rome (432–440). An opponent of Pelagianism, although he had once been sympathetic to it, Sixtus III refused the reinstatement of Julian of Eclanum (439). Sixtus maintained the claim of the Roman see to jurisdiction over Illyricum, and supervised the rebuilding of the basilica of Sta. Maria Maggiore as well as other construction projects at Rome. Several of his letters are extant. Feast day March 28. CPL 1623, 1624, 1655. *See also* Sta. Maria Maggiore. [M.P.McH.]

Bibliography

Augustine, *Letters* 191; 194; *Liber Pontificalis* 46 (Duchesne 1.232–237).

R. Krautheimer, "The Architecture of Sixtus III," *De artibus opuscula XL: Essays in Honor of Erwin Panofsky*, ed. M. Meiss (Zurich: Buehler Buchdruck, 1960, and New York: New York UP, 1961), pp. 291–302; repr. in R. Krautheimer, *Studies in Early Christian, Medieval, and Renaissance Art* (New York: New York UP, and London: U of London P, 1969), pp. 181–196.

SLAVERY. Aristotle developed the theory that some persons were servile by their very nature. The accepted justification for slavery in the Hellenistic and Roman periods was rather that advanced by the adherents of Stoicism. They held that all were equal and considered slavery to be merely an accident of fortune; as such, it was not a cause of complaint nor was it a matter of great importance. Yet the Stoics consistently urged the compassionate and humane treatment of slaves, and the Stoic philosopher Seneca the Younger argued forcefully on their behalf in a letter (*Moral Epistles* 47) that would figure in the debates of the Renaissance humanists on the subject.

There was a tendency, starting in the late Roman republic and continuing in the empire, to restrict the absolute rights of the master over the slave. A number of pagan jurists, such as Florentinus (second century; *Digest* 1.5.4.1) and Ulpian (third century; *Digest* 50.17.32), recognized the incompatibility of slavery with natural law.

The economy of ancient Israel was not nearly as dependent on slave labor as was the Greco-Roman. Most slaves were engaged in domestic service or small farming, although some war captives served in the Jerusalem temple (Num. 31:25–47; Josh. 9:22–27; Ezra 8:20). Hebrew slaves who had sold themselves because of debt were to be freed after six years (Exod. 21:2–11; Deut. 15:12–18), a provision not always observed (Jer. 34:14–18); foreigners could be permanently enslaved (Lev. 25:44–46).

For Paul and the church of the New Testament, slavery was, as it was for the Stoics, an external (1 Cor. 7:20–24) and not relevant in the spiritual realm, where there was neither slave nor free in Christ (1 Cor. 12:13; Gal. 3:28; Col. 3:11). Christian slaves were to remain obedient to their masters (Eph. 6:5–8;

Col. 3:22–25; 1 Tim. 6:1–2; Titus 2:9–10; 1 Peter 2:18–25), who in turn were to behave toward them with fairness and respect (Eph. 6:9; Col. 4:1). The classic statement on the matter appears in Paul's Epistle to Philemon. The apostle returned the fugitive slave Onesimus, whom he had converted, to his master, but pled that Onesimus be received as a brother rather than a slave (Philem. 15–16).

In the early church, masters and slaves, who participated in the same assembly, might be called on to endure a common martyrdom. Early Christian writings follow the Pauline teaching in calling for respect on the part of masters and obedience from slaves (*Did.* 4.10–11; Ignatius, *Polyc.* 4.3; *Barn.* 19.7).

John Chrysostom, while urging liberal manumission and echoing Paul's thought that slaves are to be treated as brothers in Christ (*Hom.* 1–3 *in Philm.*), considered slavery as arising from sin. Other church fathers likewise located its origin in sin, among them Augustine, who viewed it as a punishment inflicted for the transgression of Adam (*Civ. Dei* 19.15–16). Yet he vigorously protested against the actions of slavetraders who were kidnapping young children and others, and used church funds to ransom them (*Ep.* 10* Divjak).

Generally, the church encouraged the freeing of slaves. But the practice of manumission by Christian communities in their churches (*manumissio in ecclesia*), authorized by Constantine (316, 323), was in no sense obligatory and probably not widespread in use. At times, individual clerics were slaveowners. Slaves could not receive ordination or enter the monastic life so as to avoid their secular obligations, nor could they do so without the consent of their masters. Yet fugitive slaves were at times received into monasteries, and the rule was abrogated in favor of monasticism by Justinian I, who provided (*Code* 1.3.37[38]) that three years' stay in a monastery gave the monk free status so long as he remained therein.

The persistence of slavery can be demonstrated from Bede's account (*H.E.* 2.1) of Gregory the Great's encounter with English slaves for sale in Rome. The institution only gradually withered away in Europe, being replaced by serfdom.

Slavery was pervasive in ancient civilization. Early Christianity, by its teachings and actions, sought on balance to mitigate the abuses and inhumanity of the system, but it would be left mostly to later ages to realize fully the incompatibility of slavery with human rights and dignity and to seek its abolition. *See also* Social Thought.   [M.P.McH.]

Bibliography

W.W. Buckland, *The Roman Law of Slavery* (Cambridge: Cambridge UP, 1908); L.D. Agate, "Slavery (Christian)," *Encyclopedia of Religion and Ethics,* ed. J. Hastings (Edinburgh: T. and T. Clark, 1920), Vol. 11, pp. 602–612 (valuable esp. for its citation of passages); W.L. Westermann, *The Slave Systems of Greek and Roman Antiquity* (Philadelphia: American Philosophical Society, 1955), esp. pp. 149–159; G. de Ste. Croix, "Early Christian Attitudes to Property and Slavery," *Church, Society, and Politics,* ed. D. Baker (Oxford: Blackwell, 1975), pp. 1–38, esp. pp. 15–24; J. Vogt, *Ancient Slavery and the Ideal of Man* (Cambridge: Harvard UP, 1975); M.I. Finley, *Ancient Slavery and Modern Ideology* (New York: Viking, 1980); G. de Ste. Croix, *The Class Struggle in the Ancient Greek World: From the Archaic Age to the Arab Conquests* (Ithaca: Cornell UP, 1981), esp. pp. 418–425; T. Wiedemann, *Greek and Roman Slavery* (Baltimore: Johns Hopkins UP, 1981); J. Vogt et al., *Bibliographie zur antiken Sklaverei,* rev. ed., 2 vols. (Bochum: Studienverlag Dr. N. Brockmeyer, 1983); H. Chadwick, "New Letters of St. Augustine," *JThS* 34 (1983):425–452, esp. pp. 432–434; A.C.J. Phillips, "The Laws of Slavery: Exodus 21:2–11," *Journal for the Study of the Old Testament* 30 (1984):51–66; G. Corcoran, *Saint Augustine on Slavery* (Rome: Institutum Patristicum "Augustinianum," 1985); H. Schulz-Falkenthal et al., *Sklaverei in der griechisch-römischen Antike: Eine Bibliographie wissenschaftlicher Literatur vom ausgehenden 15. Jahrhundert bis zur Mitte des 19. Jahrhunderts* (Halle [Saale]: Universitäts- und Landesbibliothek Sachsen-Anhalt, 1985); R. MacMullen, "Late Roman Slavery," *Historia* 36 (1987):359-382; Y. Garlan, *Slavery in Ancient Greece* (Ithaca: Cornell UP, 1988).

SOCIAL THOUGHT. The social thought of the early church fathers was a dynamic and creative interpretation of the Old Testament message of justice and the New Testament insistence on love of neighbor, influenced by the ethic of Platonism and Stoicism. This Christian teaching, articulated mainly in homilies and scripture commentaries reflecting the social and historical conditions of the age, never became an integrated system or a comprehensive philosophy. Christians, during their first three centuries as members of an illicit and often persecuted religion, exercised their social consciousness by way of charity and almsgiving, mainly among their coreligionists. With its emancipation under Constantine in 313, Christianity extrapolated the concept of charity into a social consciousness gradually encompassing the whole human race.

From the earliest documents—the *Didache*, the *Epistle to Diognetus*, and *1 Clement*—Christian teaching stressed the basic equality of all human beings; private ownership of material goods modified by the conviction that earthly possessions were to be administered by the rich for the benefit of the poor; the necessity of a social structure and a political organization for the pursuit of humankind's temporal ends; the obligation of Christians as citizens to respect the public authority; hospitality; and the sacredness of work over the evil of idleness.

Under the guidance of the bishops, deacons distributed the gifts gathered at the eucharistic liturgy to widows and orphans, captives and prisoners at forced labor for the faith, the sick, the shipwrecked, and the impoverished. Great care was exercised in the burial of the dead. Early Christians dealt with the evil of slavery following Paul's assertion, "There is neither Jew nor Greek, slave nor free . . ." (Gal. 3:28). Convert slaves were welcomed as brothers and sisters; ecclesial offices were open to them—as was martyrdom (e.g., Blandina and Felicitas). Masters were threatened with ecclesial penalties for mistreating slaves, and efforts were made to buy their freedom. Nevertheless, with few exceptions (Gregory of Nyssa for one—*Hom. 4 in Eccl.*), no condemnations of this grave evil were forthcoming.

Although persecuted by the Roman state, most early Christians recognized their obligations as citizens stemming from Christ's admonition to "Render to Caesar . . ." (Matt. 22:21). The *Epistle to Diognetus* insisted that Christians "play their full role as citizens" (5.5). Although Hippolytus saw the reign of Satan be-

hind the Roman imperium, Clement of Alexandria affirmed the obligation to pay taxes and respect the civil authority (*Paed.* 2.14.1). Origen upheld the binding of the law except for idolatry and participation in the cult of the emperor (*Comm. in Rom.* 9.39). And even Tertullian, for all his opposition to the Roman state, agreed that its authority was from God (*Apol.* 30).

The leaders of the church made no direct effort to reform the unjust social and economic structure of their society, but bishops from Cyprian and Ambrose to Basil of Caesarea and John Chrysostom made a considerable effort to defend the rights of the poor and exploited. They proclaimed the ownership of material possessions as a stewardship, insisting that the creation of worldly goods by God is for all of humankind. Thus, "those who have, must share with their neighbor" (Cyprian, *Op. et eleem.* 25). According to Ambrose, "God ordered all things to be produced so that there should be food for all" (*Off. minis.* 1.32); he advised the rich: "You are not making a gift to the poor. You are handing them what is theirs" (*Nabuth.* 12.53). Both Basil and John Chrysostom excoriated the rich who in time of famine refused to open their granaries to feed the starving, to clothe the naked, and to rescue the widow and the orphan. Almost without exception, the church leaders denounced usury as unjust exploitation. They insisted on the sacred character of work and stressed the Christian virtue of hospitality (although the *Didache* cautions that the itinerant who desires to stay should be given work but not be fed if he refuses to ply his trade).

Gradually, the great Christian centers saw the establishment of hospitals, orphanages, shelters for the poor and travelers, granaries for the distribution of food, and asylums for the persecuted. They were administered by deacons, dedicated monks, nuns, and laity.

Despite their inability to confront the grave injustice of slavery, the early fathers provided the Christian community with an attitude toward earthly possessions and secular affairs based on the excoriation of injustice by the ancient Hebrew prophets and Christ's New

Testament injunction, "You shall love your neighbor as yourself." Their social teaching is the basis for the current Judeo-Christian involvement in the struggle for social justice in our world. *See also* Almsgiving; Church and State; Slavery; War; Widows. [F.X.M.]

Bibliography

R. Sierra Bravo, *Doctrina social y económica de los padres de la iglesia* (Madrid: Compañía Bibliográfica Española, 1967); J.G. Gager, *Kingdom and Community: The Social World of Early Christianity* (Englewood Cliffs: Prentice-Hall, 1975); P.C. Phan, *Social Thought* (Wilmington: Glazier, 1985); F.X. Murphy, *The Early Christian Way of Life* (Wilmington: Glazier, 1986).

SOCIETIES. The Association Internationale d'Etudes Patristiques/International Association for Patristic Studies (AIEP/IAPS) was founded in 1965 at a colloquium in Paris. Incorporated in France, it seeks to promote the study of Christian antiquity by acting as a link among patristic scholars of all nations. It publishes a *Bulletin d'information et de liaison* (1:1968; 2:1970; 3:1971; 4:1973; 5:1980; and annually thereafter), which is valuable for its reports of work planned or in progress both on the part of individuals and in series, and an *Annuaire*, or directory of members. The Association has provided subventions to scholars from eastern Europe for the purchase of books and attendance at the Oxford patristic conferences.

The North American Patristic Society (NAPS), founded in 1970 in New York in conjunction with a meeting of the American Philological Association, consists primarily of scholars from the United States and Canada. It originally met with various scholarly organizations but now holds its own annual conference for the presentation of papers and discussion. Its semiannual publication *Patristics* began (1972) as a newsletter. Although continuing to carry reports of the Society's activities and other announcements, it is particularly useful for its book reviews, which currently constitute the greater part of each issue. The Society has recently (1986) undertaken publication of the Patristic Monograph Series formerly issued by the Philadelphia Patristic Foundation.

The Canadian Society of Patristic Studies/Association Canadienne des Etudes Patristiques was begun by Canadians attending the Seventh International Conference on Patristic Studies at Oxford in 1975 and held its first meeting in 1977. It meets annually for the presentation of papers as part of the Learned Societies Conference sponsored by the Canadian Federation for the Humanities. It is represented both in the Federation and in the Canadian Corporation for Studies in Religion, which issues a monograph series. The Society distributes a short bulletin to keep members informed of its activities.

There are many regional and local groups engaged in patristic studies and the investigation of Christian origins. Their status tends to be informal, and they are subject to change and development. From one such group, the Seminar on the Development of Early Catholic Christianity, meeting in the Southwest, there arose the impetus for the founding of the quarterly publication, *The Second Century: A Journal of Early Christian Studies* (*SCent*, from 1981). [M.P.McH.]

Bibliography

M.P. McHugh, "The North American Patristic Society: Retrospect and Prospect," *Classical Folia* 25 (1971):5–8; (no author listed), "Research Groups in North America Studying Early Christianity," *SCent* 1 (1981):55–58.

SOCRATES (469–399 B.C.). Athenian philosopher, teacher of Plato. Knowledge of the life and teachings of Socrates rests almost exclusively on the firsthand portraits of him in Aristophanes's *Clouds*; Xenophon's *Apology*, *Symposium*, and *Memorabilia*; and Plato's dialogues. Each of these portraits is animated and skewed by the purposes of the author: to lampoon and criticize in the case of Aristophanes; to vindicate the nobility and virtue of Socrates's character in the case of Xenophon; and in the case of Plato to dramatize, explore, and expound philosophy and philosophical inquiry. Socrates himself wrote nothing.

Socrates is said to have taken up his father's trade of stonemason; more certain is that in his middle years he took an interest in natural philosophy and eventually abandoned his trade in his pursuit of philosophy, becoming impoverished in his later years. At the age of seventy, he was brought to trial on the charges of introducing his own gods, refusing to recognize those sanctioned by the state, and of corrupting the youth of Athens. His spirited defense of himself and his philosophical activities, reported in Plato's *Apology*, proved ineffective. He was convicted and sentenced to death by drinking hemlock.

Socrates's first studies of the natural world left him dissatisfied, for they did not address the question of the good life. He turned to human affairs and inquired after ethical knowledge. His mode of inquiry was distinctive. He cross-examined those who claimed to know what was best for an individual or the city. The examination usually proceeded by Socrates professing ignorance and drawing forth claims and explanations from the respondent. The claims were examined for content and for consistency in application. A definition of general ethical terms was sought, then applied to various cases. An interlocutor's claims to ethical knowledge were usually wrecked, as a result of Socrates's refutation (*elenchus*), resulting in a perplexing impasse (*aporia*): no clear definition was applicable in all cases. The conclusion was an exhortation to further inquiry.

Socrates himself held several principles, among them that virtue (*aretē*) is knowledge, specifically, knowledge of good and evil, that no one does wrong voluntarily (wrongdoing follows from ignorance), and that what is good is beneficial. The notion behind these is that a person's actions express his or her knowledge of the world and self. Wrongdoing shows a failure to grasp what is really beneficial for one's true self, a mistake Socrates thought no one would really want to make. Inquiry and refutation purged the respondent of a false conceit of knowledge, revealing ignorance. The frequent protestations of ignorance on the part of Socrates were taken as ironic, even as insincere, by those subject to his effective refutations. Still, the principles he held give no direct answer to the question, What is the good life?

More positive was his tenet that one's primary concern is care of one's soul (*psuchē*).

For Socrates, the soul was the seat of knowledge and so the locus and true nature of the ethical agent; the body was an instrument of the soul. Proper care of the soul was guided by the Delphic injunction, "Know thyself" and carried out by Socratic inquiry, purging the soul of false notions and pursuing ethical knowledge. Although he seems to have inclined to view the soul as immortal, he did not expound this belief, and, as with his theological views, his attitude was a modest piety toward the traditional beliefs. Such matters lay outside his concern with the good life for humans. In Plato's dialogues, he often alludes to a single, impersonal, and ultimate divinity.

Socrates's importance in philosophy is neatly summed up by Aristotle, who points to his practice of collecting several relevant cases with a view to finding the common feature and his demand for definition of general terms. More profound was his assumption of and pursuit of scientific knowledge in ethics. His greater importance in the tradition is as the exemplary philosopher, firmly committed to the pursuit of right and truth and yet modest in any claim to final knowledge of such matters. Justin Martyr took up the image of Socrates in Plato's *Apology*, the pious man's rational defense of professed beliefs in the face of death, and sets it as an anticipation of Christian apologetics and martyrdom (*1 Apol.* 5; *2 Apol.* 10). *See also* Philosophy; Plato.   [C.Co.]

Bibliography

Xenophon, *Memorabilia, Symposium, Apology*, tr. E.C. Marchant and O.J. Todd, LCL (1923); Plato, *Collected Dialogues*, ed. E. Hamilton and D. Cairns (Princeton: Bollingen, 1963).

A.E. Taylor, *Socrates* (Boston: Beacon, 1951); A.H. Chroust, *Socrates, Man and Myth* (Notre Dame: Notre Dame UP, 1957); G. Vlastos, ed., *The Philosophy of Socrates* (Garden City: Anchor, 1971); D. Jackson, "Socrates and Christianity," *CF* 31 (1977):189–206; G. Santas, *Socrates* (London: Routledge and Kegan Paul, 1979); I. Opelt, "Das Bild des Socrates in der christlichen Literatur," *JAC* 10 (1983):192–207.

SOCRATES SCHOLASTICUS (ca. 380–450).

Church historian. Socrates spent his entire life in Constantinople. His profession was law; he held no church office. Between 438 and 443, he wrote his *Church History*, which covered the period from 306 to 439 and continued the work of Eusebius. Modern historians regard Socrates highly for both his citation of sources and his good judgment in assessing materials. His work is one of the most important sources for the period he covers.

Socrates did not write from an objective viewpoint. Well read and interested in theology, he portrayed Origen as a figure of lasting importance. Socrates was a Platonist and supported those who shared that philosophy, but he also knew various schools of logic, including the Aristotelian. He brought a sense of sophistic dialectic to his description of the Arian movement. One unexpected aspect of his work is the sympathetic treatment of the Novatianists.

Socrates also was a humanist, a lover of Hellenic culture. He respected pagan oracles and looked for the *kairos*, the key event, in a given historical development. He felt history was the recording of the disturbance of cosmic peace and closed his work with the prayer that the future would bring nothing for historians to write about. CPG III, 6028.   [F.W.N.]

Bibliography
PG 67.28–872.
A.C. Zenos, tr., NPNF, 2nd ser. (1890), Vol. 2.
F. Geppert, *Die Quellen des Kirchenhistorikers Socrates Scholasticus* (Leipzig: Dieterichsche Verlag, 1898; repr. Aalen: Scientia-Verlag, 1972); P. Périchon, "Pour une édition nouvelle de l'historien Socrate: les manuscrits et les versions," *RecSR* 53 (1965):112–120; M. Mazza, "Sulla teoria dello storiografia cristiana: osservazione sui proemi degli storici ecclesiastici," *La storiografia ecclesiastica della tarda antichità* (Messina: Centro di Studi Umaniste, 1980), pp. 335–389; G.F. Chesnut, *The First Christian Histories: Eusebius, Socrates, Sozomen, Theodoret and Evagrius*, 2nd ed. (Macon: Mercer UP, 1986).

SOLOMON (tenth century B.C.). King of Israel (ca. 970–ca. 930 B.C.). A son of David by Bathsheba, Solomon gained the throne through the efforts of his mother and the prophet Nathan. For several years, he ruled jointly with his father, then rapidly consolidated his own power by removing his opponents. He engaged in an ambitious building program, including construction of the temple of Jerusalem, and developed a considerable foreign commerce. He married a number of foreign wives in political alliances, for which he was severely criticized. The kingdom was split shortly after his death by the secession of the ten northern tribes (1 Kings 1–11; 2 Chron. 1–9). Matthew (1:6–7) recorded Solomon in the genealogy of Jesus, who referred to his glory and wisdom (Matt. 6:29; 12:42).

References to Solomon were frequent in the church fathers, who attributed to him the books of Proverbs, Ecclesiastes, the Song of Solomon (Song of Songs, or Canticles), and Wisdom of Solomon. He was proverbial for his wisdom (e.g., Gregory of Nazianzus, *Or.* 43.73). Because of this, and as David's descendant, the builder of the temple, and a king who ruled in peace, he was taken to prefigure Christ (e.g., Gregory of Nyssa, *Hom.* 1 and 7 *in Cant.*; Augustine, *In Psalm.* 126.1). Christ's claim to be greater than Solomon (Matt. 12:42) was linked with God's promise to the latter "that none like you shall arise after you" (1 Kings 3:12) as evidence for Christ's divinity (Ambrosiaster, *Quaes. V. et N. Test.* 91.12). The church was bride of the true Solomon or peacemaker, Christ (Ambrose, *Isaac* 5.45), while the king's famous judgment in the case of the child whose identity was in dispute between two mothers (1 Kings 3:16–28) was said to have been effected through the Holy Spirit (Ambrose, *Sp. Sanct.* 2.6.36–38; cf. 3.22.169). The story of Solomon furnished rich themes for Christian art, and pseudepigraphical works appeared under his name. *See also* Odes of Solomon; Song of Solomon; Testament of Solomon.   [M.P.McH.]

SONG OF SOLOMON. Biblical book. The Song of Solomon (or Song of Songs, or Canticles) is the first of the five Megilloth (rolls) in the Writings (Hagiographa) of the Hebrew Bible. It is read at Passover. The book consists of love songs by a king, his beloved, and their friends. Although some of the poems may be early, some could be as late as the Hellenistic period. The rabbis interpreted the book allegorically as depicting the love of God for Israel

(b. Abodah Zarah 29a). Christians followed this approach, substituting the love of Christ for the church. However, the most influential interpretation in patristic times took the bride as the individual human soul. With this interpretation, the book became important for spirituality and the development of mysticism. [E.F.]

Bibliography

Origen, *Commentary and Homilies on the Song of Songs*, tr. R. P. Lawson, ACW (1957), Vol. 26; Gregory of Nyssa, *Commentary on the Song of Songs*, tr. C. McCambley (Brookline: Hellenic CP, 1988); Ambrose, *Isaac, or the Soul*, tr. M.P. McHugh, FOTC (1972), Vol. 65, pp. 659–665; Theodoret, *Explanatio in Canticum Canticorum*, PG 81.27–214; Procopius of Gaza, *In Cantica Canticorum*, PG 87(2).1545–1780.

H.H. Rowley, "The Interpretation of the Song of Songs," *JThS* 38 (1937):337–363; R. Gordis, *The Song of Songs* (New York: Jewish Theological Seminary, 1954); M.H. Pope, *Song of Solomon* (Garden City: Doubleday, 1977).

SOPHIA. Greek noun from the adjective, *sophos*, "wise," signifying unusual knowledge and ability, a mastery of practical and theoretical skills combining to form the ideal picture of the wise man. Commenting on 1 Corinthians 1:21 ("Since in God's wisdom the world did not come to know him through wisdom"), Theodoret of Cyrus wrote (*Interp. 1 Cor.*; PG 82.236): "The text means the two wisdoms of God, or rather the three. The first wisdom is that given to man, in virtue of which we are endowed with reason, by which we discern what we must do, and discover the arts and sciences, and get to know God. The second is concerned with the contemplation of created things, the heavens, the sky, etc. And the third is that which is shown through our Savior, which is called folly by those who do not accept it."

In the Old Testament, the fear of the Lord is the beginning of wisdom (Ps. 111:10). Divine wisdom is manifested in creation (Wisd. Sol. 10–19). It is already personified in Proverbs 8 and Wisdom 7:22. In the New Testament, Christ is the wisdom of God (1 Cor. 1:24). "The Greeks look for 'wisdom' but we preach Christ crucified" (1 Cor. 1:22–23). Paul's preaching had none of the persuasive power of "wise" argumentation; "what we utter is God's wisdom, a hidden wisdom" (1 Cor. 2:4, 7).

Clement of Alexandria wrote that philosophy is the study of *sophia*, and *sophia* is the knowledge of things divine and human, and of their causes. Wisdom is therefore the queen of philosophy, as philosophy is of preparatory culture (*Str.* 5.13; 6.18; 7.2). In Hellenistic Judaism, and especially in Philo, *sophia* enables humans to free themselves from everything worldly and material, and wisdom is at once the way, the guide, and the goal of life.

Justin Martyr cited Proverbs 8:21–36 as a testimony to the preexistence of God the Son: before all creatures, God begot a Beginning, a certain rational power from himself, who is called glory of the Lord by the Holy Spirit, at one time Son, at another Wisdom (*Dial.* 61). In the *Shepherd* of Hermas, the God of powers is said by his own wisdom and providence to have created his own church (*Vis.* 1.3.4).

Wisdom is an agent in creation. Origen taught that all things came into being according to wisdom and according to the models of the system that are present in God's thoughts. Having created wisdom ensouled, so to speak, he confided to her the task to give to beings and to matter, from the types that were in her, the model, the form, and perhaps even the essences of things (*Jo.* 1.19.133).

In the church fathers, wisdom is mainly a synonym for the Logos, but already in Theophilus of Antioch (*Autol.* 2.10) and Irenaeus (*Haer.* 4.7.4) it is equated with the Third Person of the Trinity, the Holy Spirit. In Gregory of Nazianzus (*Or.* 30.20), among the names for God the Son is Wisdom, "as being the knowledge of matters divine and human." But the Holy Spirit likewise is (quoting Isa. 11:2–3) "spirit of wisdom, understanding, counsel, might, knowledge, true religion, and the fear of God" (*Or.* 31.29). The continued designation of Christ as Wisdom is seen in the dedication in Constantinople in the sixth century of the Church of Hagia Sophia (Holy Wisdom) to Christ.

Sophia was prominent in Gnostic speculations. In the Valentinian system Sophia is a divine emanation, the last of the aeons, dissolute, smitten with a passion to search into the nature of the Father's greatness, fallen but redeemed by the Christ born of Mary, and reunited with her consort. The myth is found in the Coptic Gnostic codex Berolinensis 8502, especially the *Apocryphon of John* and the *Sophia of Jesus Christ.* It is rejected by Irenaeus (*Haer.* 1.2.2f.; 2.18) and Hippolytus (*Haer.* 6.30–31). *See also* Gnosticism. [T.H.]

Bibliography

Irenaeus, *Against Heresies* 1.1.2; 1.2.2; 1.29–30; Theophilus, *To Autolycus* 2.10; Clement of Alexandria, *Miscellanies* 5.13; 6.18; 7.2: Hippolytus, *Refutation of All Heresies* 6.30–31; Origen, *Commentary on John* 1; 19; 133; Gregory of Nazianzus, *Orations* 30.20; 31.29.

SOPHRONIUS (seventh century). Bishop of Jerusalem (634–639). Sophronius and his good friend John Moschus entered the ascetic life probably in the late 570s. They spent twenty-five years mostly in Palestinian monasteries but took at least one trip to visit Egyptian centers. Because of Persian invasions, they fled to Alexandria in 605 and worked the following years in various Egyptian monasteries. By 616, the Persian advance caused them to flee to Rome. Back in Jerusalem (from 619), Sophronius lived to see its fall to the Muslims (637). In 633, Sophronius resisted the reunion based on the teaching that there is one will (Monothelitism) in Christ that was supported by Cyrus of Alexandria and emperor Heraclius. Although his confession of faith does not mention two wills in Christ, his collection of sayings from the fathers opposes Monothelitism. A prolific writer, his style is prolix. Feast day March 11. CPG III, 7635–7681. [F.W.N.]

Bibliography

G. Cosmas, *De oeconomia incarnationis secundum S. Sophronium Hierosolymitanum* (Rome: Dissertatione ad lauream assequendam, 1940); C. von Schönbron, *Sophrone de Jerusalem: vie monastique et confession dogmatique* (Paris: Beauchesne, 1972); W.H.C. Frend, *The Rise of the Monophysite Movement* (Cambridge: Cambridge UP, 1972), pp. 348–351; H. Chadwick, "John Moschus and His Friend Sophronius the Sophist," *JThS* n.s. 25 (1974):41–74; A. Cameron, "The Epigrams of Sophronius," *CQ* 33 (1983):284–292; J. Duffy, "Observations on Sophronius' *Miracles of Cyrus and John*," *JThS* n.s. 35 (1984):71–90.

SOTER. Bishop of Rome (ca. 166–ca. 174). Little is known of Soter and his episcopate, which occurred in the reign of Marcus Aurelius (161–180). Soter was perhaps from Campania. He evidently sent a letter to Corinth along with a contribution for the church there; portions of a reply by his contemporary Dionysius of Corinth are extant (Eusebius, *H.E.* 4.23.9–11). He may have been involved in the Paschal controversy; at least, Easter appears to have been first celebrated at Rome as an annual feast in his time. Evidence for his supposed martyrdom is lacking. Feast day April 22. [M.P.McH.]

Bibliography

Eusebius, *Church History* 4.19; 4.22.3; 4.23.9–11; 4.30.3; 5.1; 5.6.4; 5.24.14–17; *Liber Pontificalis* 13 (Duchesne 1.135).

P. Nautin, *Lettres et écrivains chrétiens des iie et iiie siècles* (Paris: Cerf, 1961); M. Richard, "La Question pascale au iie siècle," *L'Orient syrien* 6 (1961):179–212.

SOTERIOLOGY. *See* Atonement; Salvation.

SOUL. The Greek word *psuchē* (Latin *anima*), often simply transliterated into English as "psyche," has more traditionally been translated as "soul." In Homeric Greek, it referred normally to the life-principle associated with breath (cf. the Hebrew *nephesh*), which departs the body at death "across the teeth's barrier" (*Iliad* 9.409) and leads an isolated, insubstantial, and unconscious existence in Hades. Not until the end of the sixth century B.C. do we find—in Orphic and Pythagorean circles, where the belief that a person might be rewarded or punished after death was central—that *psuchē* is used to denote the essential human "self": not only the life-principle, and thus the principle of growth and motion, but also the seat of feeling, thought, and decision. This understanding assumed a distinction between soul and body (and sometimes more: it is in Orphic sources that we first find the body described as the soul's "tomb"). It is presupposed in Socrates's belief that one's principal and primary concern ought to be not body or possessions but the soul, "that it may be the best possible" (Plato, *Apology* 30B).

Philosophical Background. For Plato, soul as the self-moving principle of motion and change is a centerpiece not merely of his anthropology but also of his cosmology. The soul *par excellence* is the eternal, because incorruptible, soul of the cosmos that directly governs the motion of the heavens. The human soul is in fact tripartite. Its two lower, and mortal, parts are the seats of desire and of assertive action; its superior part, the rational (*to logistikon*), shares with the world-soul the attributes of incorruptibility and of affinity with the unchanging realm of the Forms ("being"), although it represents a strain of soul inferior to that of the world-soul. It thus preexists its union with any particular earthly body and survives the dissolution of that union.

Plato's account of the soul, however, did not prevail in most of later philosophy. Aristotle envisaged the soul as the "form of a natural body having life potentially within it" (*On the Soul* 412a20f.)—that is, as the formal principle in any living organism. Hence, he denied the capacity of the individual soul to exist independently and, perforce, its survival of the organism's death. He also repudiated Plato's division of the soul into parts and preferred to speak of its "powers" or faculties (*dunameis*): "the nutritive, the appetitive, the sensory, the locomotive, and the power of thinking," as one list has it (ibid. 414a.30f.). The classical Stoics differed from both Plato and Aristotle. The individual human soul, as they saw it, was that particular portion of the all-pervading cosmic soul which conferred intelligent life on an individual human body. They conceived it, moreover, as corporeal: as constituted of "fiery spirit," a stuff so fine and ethereal as to be capable of totally interpenetrating another body, thus conferring on it life and self-motion, sensation and the power of rational judgment. This last power they lodged in the soul's "commanding faculty" (*to hēgemonikon*), the rough equivalent of Plato's rational soul, although not, in Plato's sense, a "part" of the soul. Like Aristotle, but for different reasons, the Stoics tended to deny the incorruptibility of the individual

soul and hence its ability to survive the death of the human organism.

There was, therefore, in the world of Christianity, a traditional set of philosophical agenda regarding soul and its nature. These agenda included not only the question of soul's "immortality" but the issues of its origin or derivation, its corporeal or incorporeal character, and its unity. Platonists continued to speak of the soul as having "parts" and to envisage the rational soul or "intellect" (*nous*) as distinct from its nonrational, merely animal counterpart.

New Testament. The literature of primitive Christianity, however, shows little awareness of these questions and uses the term *psuchē* for the most part in a popular and nontechnical way. Thus, *psuchē* can mean simply a person's "life" or, after the fashion of the Hebrew scriptures, an individual person, as at Acts 2:41 ("three thousand souls") or Luke 1:46 (where "my soul" means simply "I"). It also denotes the person as the subject both of such interior dispositions as love, sorrow, or disturbance, and of God's salvation. Soul as the person's proper, intrinsic life and self can be contrasted with external goods (Luke 12:23) and even with the body (Matt. 12:28; cf. 1 Peter 2:11), but it is only in 1 Corinthians 15:44–46, where Paul, whose references to *psuchē* are otherwise sparse and nontechnical, is concerned with problems about the exegesis of Genesis 2:7, that the New Testament betrays even a slight acquaintance with the technical or learned uses of "soul" that had already become common in Hellenistic Judaism.

Second Century. By the middle of the second century, however, Christians were beginning to address the philosophical agenda regarding soul. Justin Martyr, for example, observes the inconsistency between the Platonist doctrine of the eternity and incorruptibility of the soul and the Christian belief that the individual soul is "generated" (*genētos*), that is, has a beginning in God's act of creation. If the soul survives death, he suggests, that is only because God wills it to do so and not because of its intrinsic nature (*Dial.* 4–5). Irenaeus of Lyons agrees with Justin on this score. He describes the human person as a composite of soul and body and envisages the soul, in a fashion essentially Stoic, as a material or quasi-material reality that has a shape corresponding to that of its body (*Haer.* 2.19, 29, 33–34). He equates the Platonist *nous* ("intellect" or "rational soul") with the Stoic "commanding faculty" but follows the Stoics again in seeing this precisely as a phase or faculty of soul and not as a "part" that is separable from a nonrational, animal soul. On this ground, he denies the Valentinian tripartition of humanity into spirit (or *nous*), soul, and body. Confronted with 1 Thessalonians 5:23, where Paul uses the formula "spirit and soul and body," he insists in effect that "spirit" there means not the Platonist intellect or rational soul, but rather the divine Spirit conferred in baptism (*Haer.* 5.6, 9). The soul, then, is a unity, the principle of life, of intelligence, and hence of freedom of choice in the human person. Irenaeus's account of the human soul agrees in all essentials with that given slightly later by Tertullian in his learned treatise *On the Soul*—the earliest systematic and argumentative treatment of the subject by a Christian author. One may suspect that Irenaeus, although he does not discuss the issue, would have concurred in Tertullian's judgment that the individual soul, with the body, is derived from the father's semen (*ex traduce*).

Origen. A different perspective emerged in Alexandrian Christian circles. Origen outlines the standard set of problems about the soul in his commentary on Song of Solomon 1:8 as well as in the preface to his treatise *On First Principles.* He takes it as a given of the church's catechesis that the soul is a "substance," possessed by nature of life, intelligence, and freedom of choice. He disagrees, however, with Irenaeus and Tertullian on two significant points. First, he insists that the soul is in its own nature incorporeal. Second, he argues, on the basis of the two narratives of Adam's creation (Gen. 1:26f.; 2:6f.), that the world that God originally created was a spiritual world consisting entirely of "rational beings" (*logikoi*) and that the soul that we know as united to an earthly body is just such a rational being, but subsisting in the fallen and diminished state

brought about by a primordial sin. Thus, the individual soul preexists its embodiment as a human being and cannot, in Origen's view, be derived *ex traduce.* Hence, too, it is the soul, "the inner person," and not, as Irenaeus had thought, the body, that is the seat of that which "corresponds to the image" (*kat' eikona*) of God. In all this, Origen doubtless exhibits the influence of the Platonism of his time, an influence that emerges also in his tendency to regard the soul, rather than the union of soul and body, as the real human person. He departs from Platonism, however, in declining to acknowledge separate referents for "intellect" and "soul"; for him, these terms tend to refer to different and successive states of the rational creature and not (as with Clement of Alexandria before him) to distinct parts of the life-principle.

Speaking very broadly, one can say that the basic premises of Origen's position triumphed in the Christian thought of the fourth and fifth centuries. The idea that the soul is corporeal tends to disappear, at least from learned theology, and soul as the locus of intelligence and freedom is universally regarded as the seat of the human person's affinity and capacity for God: that is, as that in virtue of which it images God at the level of the creature. Similarly, the soul is generally acknowledged to be immortal in the sense that it survives the dissolution of the human organism, although not in the sense that it is eternal and uncreated, as Platonists continued to teach; and the unity of the soul is by and large maintained (Apollinaris of Laodicea is one exception to this statement). The point on which Origen's teaching was generally repudiated was his thesis concerning the preexistence of the soul, with its concomitant tendency to identify the soul alone as the real person. Thus, even Gregory of Nyssa (*Hom. opif.* 18–29) denies the doctrine of preexistence, asserts that soul and body come into existence together, and teaches that soul, as an immaterial reality, is operative even in the father's semen.

Augustine. In the west, Augustine of Hippo, despite his early addiction to Neoplatonism, subscribed to this broad consensus. The human person is a union of soul and body, and soul itself is a unity: spirit or "mind" (*animus*) is the ultimate principle of animal life and of growth as well as the seat of the divine image. On the question of the origin of the soul, however, Augustine suffered profound doubts. In his mature years, he dismissed the idea of the soul's preexistence. He also repudiated Tertullian's notion of the corporeality of the soul but was nevertheless drawn, by his views on the transmission of Adam's original sin, to a form of the theory that soul, even though immaterial, is conveyed *ex traduce*. At the same time, though, he wondered whether the doctrine that all souls ultimately spring from one (i.e., Adam's) is consonant with human individuality. Hence, he was equally drawn to the theory that each individual soul is directly created by God—whether at the time of its union with body, or (so to speak) ahead of time, at the moment of creation itself. There is no evidence that he ever resolved these issues in his own mind, although it was the creationist hypothesis that eventually became the standard teaching of the church. *See also* Immortality; Spirit; Traducianism.   [R.A.N.]

Bibliography

Epistle to Diognetus 6; Tertullian, *On the Soul*; idem, *On the Testimony of the Soul*; Origen, *Dialogue with Heraclides*; Gregory of Nyssa, *On the Soul and Resurrection*; Nemesius of Emesa, *On the Nature of Man* 2–3; 15–22; Ambrose, *Isaac, or the Soul*; Augustine, *On the Immortality of the Soul*; idem, *On the Soul and Its Origin*; idem, *On the Greatness of the Soul*.

J.H. Waszink, *Tertulliani De anima* (Amsterdam: North-Holland, 1947); H. Karpp, *Probleme altchristlicher Anthropologie* (Gütersloh: Bertelsmann, 1950); R. Norris, *Manhood and Christ* (Oxford: Oxford UP, 1963); A.H. Armstrong and R.A. Markus, *Christian Faith and Greek Philosophy* (New York: Sheed and Ward, 1964), pp. 43–58; R.J. O'Connell, *The Origin of the Soul in St. Augustine's Later Works* (New York: Fordham UP, 1987.)

SOZOMEN (fifth century). Church historian. Evidently born in Bethelia near Gaza in Palestine, Sozomen arrived at Constantinople sometime after 425. The dedication of his history to Theodosius II mentions an event in the emperor's life that dates to the summer of 443.

Sozomen's history, which covers the years 325–425, follows the pattern of Eusebius but gives evidence of the literary activities of the capital more clearly than does the work of Socrates Scholasticus. The lost ending of Sozomen's history may have been deleted by government censors, for he offered the work to the emperor for editing. Although he draws on Socrates's history, he does look independently at some problems and on occasion supplies information from fresh sources. His unacknowledged dependence on Socrates, however, and his failure to cite or quote his sources have made him less attractive to modern historians, despite his rather good literary style.

Sozomen did not become a cleric; often he is critical of bishops who abused their office. He has little interest in and understanding of philosophical or theological issues, yet his coverage of the development of Arianism is essential to its story. He also reports the expansion of Christianity among Armenians, Goths, and Saracens and shows particular concern for liturgy, monasticism, and the life of hermits. CPG III, 6030.   [F.W.N.]

Bibliography

PG 67.844–1630; *Sozomène: Histoire ecclésiastique*, ed. A.J. Festigière et al., SC (1983), Vol. 306. C.D. Hartranft, tr., NPNF, 2nd ser. (1890), Vol. 2. G. Schoo, *Die Quellen des kirchenhistorikers Sozomenus* (Berlin: Trowitzsch, 1911; repr. Aalen: Scientia-Verlag, 1973); M. Mazza, "Sulla teoria della storiografia cristiana: osservazione sui proemi degli storici ecclesiastici," *La storiografia ecclesiastica della tarda antichità* (Messina: Centro di Studi Umaniste, 1980), pp. 335–380; G.F. Chesnut, *The First Christian Histories: Eusebius, Socrates, Sozomen, Theodoret and Evagrius*, 2nd ed. (Macon: Mercer UP, 1986).

SPAIN. Iberian peninsula, first named *Hispania* by the Romans and by A.D. 600 called *Spania* by the peninsula's most punctilious Latinist, Isidore of Seville. The Roman conquest of the Iberian and Celtic inhabitants began in the late third century B.C.; it was declared complete by Augustus in 19 B.C. Organized in two proconsular provinces as early as 197 B.C., Roman Spain was finally divided into five provinces by Theodosius I (379–395). The capitals of these provinces—Tarragona for Hispania

Tarraconensis, Cartagena for Hispania Carthaginensis, Seville for Hispania Baetica, Merida for Lusitania, and Braga for Gallaecia—became metropolitan sees in the subsequent ecclesiastical organization of Christian Spain.

The Roman peace was not decisively broken until 409, when the Vandals, Alans, and Suevi crossed the Pyrenees. The most influential of the Germanic invaders were to be the Visigoths, who entered Spain in 418 at Roman invitation, returned in 456 under the same auspices, then asserted their autonomy and by 477 (under king Euric) once more united the peninsula politically. In 552, Justinian launched a reconquest of Spain for the empire but succeeded in holding only coastal Carthaginensis; Roman garrisons were withdrawn in 624. The Visigothic monarchy lasted until the Arabs overthrew it in 711. Most Visigothic kings strove to maintain the Roman civil and ecclesiastical structures. The major obstacle to this policy was Visigothic heterodoxy: the Goths had been adherents of Arianism since their conversion by Ulfilas (ca. 311–ca. 383). Religious unity was achieved by the conversion of king Reccared (586–601) to the Catholicism of the Hispano-Roman majority. He proclaimed his orthodoxy at the third of the councils of Toledo—by then the royal capital—in 589; almost all ruling-class Arians and apparently the mass of the Gothic people accepted his invitation to conform.

Christian legend attributed the evangelization of Spain to Paul (*1 Clem.* 5.7; *Mur. Frg.*). The mythic mission of Santiago (either James the Great, James the Less, or a conflation of the two) is not attested until after the Muslim conquest. Most of the traditional martyrs, such as Vincent of Saragossa and Eulalia of Barcelona or Merida (or both), are shadowy, formulaic figures.

The first major document of the Spanish church, the acts of the Council of Elvira (ca. 306), predates the Constantinian peace: the canons indicate a strain of moral rigorism along with concern about pollution from participation in pagan civic ritual. Hosius, bishop of Cordova, served as Constantine's primary religious adviser during much of his reign. Monas-

ticism, at once ascetic and erudite, arrived from North Africa; the double monastery of monks and nuns centered on a founding family later became a regional peculiarity.

Spanish patristic thought is distinguished by its historical, exegetical, and rhetorical strains. Prudentius (348–after 405), a patriotic, aristocratic poet, vividly related the sufferings of the martyrs and celebrated the seasons of the liturgical year. Orosius, who fled Spain in 414, admired Augustine's *City of God* and composed a lengthy, pessimistic account of Roman and recent history. Idatius composed a spare, apocalyptic chronicle of the barbarian invasions and general calamity between 409 and the reign of Euric. His contemporary Apringius of Beja composed an influential commentary on the book of Revelation, a favorite text of Spanish exegetes for centuries to come.

The greatest Spanish patristic author was the encyclopedic Isidore of Seville (ca. 560–636). Isidore succeeded his elder brother, Leander, as metropolitan bishop of Seville (ca. 600) and exercised great influence over political and cultural life until his death. Striving to preserve the legacy of Christian antiquity, he became one of the key sources of medieval thought. *See also* Elvira; Goths; Hosius of Cordova; Isidore of Seville; Leander; Priscillian; Prudentius; Toledo, Councils of.

[J.duQ.A.]

Bibliography

E.S. Bouchier, *Spain Under the Roman Empire* (Oxford: Blackwell, 1914); Z. García Villada, *Historia ecclesiástica de España* (Madrid: Compañía Iberoamericana de Publicaciones, 1929–1936), Vols. 1, 2; A.K. Ziegler, *Church and State in Visigothic Spain* (Washington, D.C.: Catholic U of America P, 1930); S.J. McKenna, *Paganism and Pagan Survivals in Spain up to the Fall of the Visigothic Kingdom* (Washington, D.C.: Catholic U of America P, 1938); E.A. Thompson, "The Conversion of the Visigoths to Catholicism," *Nottingham Medieval Studies* 4 (1960):4–35; A.C. Vega, "La venida de San Pablo a España y los Varones Apos.ólicos," *Boletín de la Real Academia de Historia* 94 (1964):7–78; J. Fontaine, "Conversion et culture chez les visigoths d'Espagne," *Settimane di Studio* 14 (Spoleto: Centro Italiano di Studi Sull' Alto Medioevo, 1967), pp. 86–147; E.A. Thompson, *The Goths in Spain* (Oxford: Clarendon, 1969); M. Avilés Fernández et al., eds., *Nueva historia de España* (Madrid: EDAF, 1973–1978), Vols. 1: *Prehistoria*; 2: *Primeras colonizaciones*; 3: *Cartago y Roma*; 4: *La España visigoda*; J. Bermejo Barrera, *Mitología y mitos de la Hispania prerromana* (Madrid: Akal, 1982); J.E. Salisbury, *Iberian Popular Religion, 600 B.C. to 700 A.D.: Celts, Romans, and Visigoths* (Lewiston: Mellen, 1985); M. Sotomayor, "Leyenda y realidad en los orígenes del cristianismo hispano," *Proyección* 36 (1989): 179–198.

SPIRIT. The term "spirit" (Greek *pneuma*) had a wide, diverse, and yet multifariously interrelated set of meanings in the Hellenistic-Roman and late-antique worlds. In various authors and at various times, it entered into the languages of medicine, of philosophical anthropology and cosmology, and of theology narrowly conceived. Its range of connotation was, moreover, only rendered the more complex by the fact that the Greek translators of the Jewish scriptures chose it as their principal equivalent for the Hebrew *ruach*. In the patristic period, starting with the opening of the second century, the whole range of the term's traditional usage was, in one way or another, reflected; but there were nevertheless three doctrinally central ways in which it was habitually used, though of these only one eventually gave rise to explicit, self-conscious reflection and debate.

Spirit as Divine. In the first place, *pneuma* and its derivatives were used to denote the divine and, in general, what belongs to the divine realm. It is this sense of the word that surfaces when, for example, Ignatius of Antioch (*Eph.* 7.2; *Phil.* 7.1) and the author of *2 Clement* (9.5) speak of Christ as being both "flesh" (i.e., creature, humanity) and "spirit" (i.e., divinity). Tertullian follows the same usage when, quoting John 4:24 (cf. Rom. 7:14; Wisd. Sol. 7:22; Isa. 31:3), he avers that "God is spirit" and goes on to express the deity of the divine Word by the statement: "The Word is made of spirit, and spirit is, as it were, the body of the Word" (*Prax.* 7–8). Hence, the divine "substance" in Christ, to be distinguished from his "flesh" or humanity, is spirit (*Prax.* 27). It was probably not peculiar to Tertullian that he held, in accordance with Stoic teaching, that the spirit that is God's substance is corporeal: "spirit . . . is body of its own sort" (*Prax.* 7).

Origen knew people who took John 4:24 in that sense and was at pains to contradict them. In his view, the Gospel calls God spirit "to distinguish him from bodies"; the spiritual is that which is "intellectual" (*Princ.* 1.1.2f.) and hence immaterial. Origen's view on this score prevailed.

Human Spirit. In the second place, *pneuma* had, as in the biblical tradition, an anthropological use. Paul had distinguished, or had accepted a distinction between, "pneumatic" and "psychic" persons (1 Cor. 2:13–15). But he had also spoken of "the spirit of a human being," which was different from "the Spirit of God" and which he described as "within" the person (1 Cor. 2:11); and he appeared further to characterize the human person as constituted of "spirit and soul and body" (1 Thess. 5:23). At around the same time, the Jewish exegete Philo of Alexandria associated this human "spirit" with the "intellect" (*nous*) of Hellenic philosophical tradition, as Paul himself may have done (cf. Rom. 7:22–23): that is, with the rational, governing soul that, Philo insisted, was the element in the human constitution that was made "after the image" of God (cf. *Making of the World* 135; *Allegorical Laws* 3.161; *Who Is the Heir* 55–56). Thus, the human being was said to be composed of "earthy substance and divine spirit," the latter in its turn being distinct from the animal life-principle or nonrational soul. The interpretation of this "trichotomous" scheme, which was itself related to a long tradition of the interpretation of Genesis 2:7, constituted a serious problem for early Christian exegetes. In Valentinian circles, human "spirit" was taken to refer to the true and innermost self, exiled from the divine world and destined to be reintegrated into it: one such source compares spirit to the marrow, soul to the bone, and body to the flesh. Irenaeus of Lyons, however, took Paul in another sense. As he saw it, "spirit" in 1 Thessalonians 5:23 refers to the divine Spirit, the gift of which in baptism completes and perfects the human person constituted of body and soul (*Haer.* 5.6). For the most part, however, the equation of (human) spirit with rational soul or intellect prevailed, although this equation did not of itself entail the Platonizing thesis that "spirit" denotes a third, separable "part" of the human constitution. It was, for example, this tradition, somewhat reconsidered, that enabled Apollinaris of Laodicea in his Christological ruminations to equate the Pauline "spirit and soul and body" with intellect, soul, and body. Something like the Irenaean position, however, was maintained by teachers in the tradition of the Antiochene school, who tended to take references to *pneuma* in human beings as denoting neither a part of the human constitution, nor a faculty of the soul, nor even the divine Spirit itself, but the *charisma* that the latter's presence bestows on a human person.

Holy Spirit in Early Church. Finally, *pneuma* was employed to refer to "the Holy Spirit," the "Spirit of God" or "Spirit of Christ." From the letters of Paul onward, it is clear that the active presence of God's Spirit, bestowed by and through Christ, was a primary mark of Christian existence, because it was seen as a sign of the dawning of the time of redemption. Closely associated with baptism and initiation into the life of the church (1 Cor. 6:11; 1 Peter 1:2), the Spirit made people children of God in Christ (Gal. 4:6) and endowed them with the gifts of prophecy, service, and, above all perhaps, knowledge. The Spirit empowered public confession of Christ and witness to him. In the view of Ignatius of Antioch, himself a Spirit-borne prophet and martyr, the Holy Spirit is the "rope" that lifts people into their places as "stones in the Father's temple" (*Eph.* 9.1: cf. 1 Cor. 3:16f.; Eph. 2:18–22). It is not surprising, then, that the Spirit figured in summary accounts of baptism and its meaning (Matt. 28:19) or that in the second century it became one of the subjects of the confession of faith made at baptism and one of the topics under which catechesis was organized in the "Rule of Faith" (and of course in later declaratory creeds). As Origen observed, "Saving baptism is not complete except when performed with the authority of the whole most excellent Trinity . . .; and . . . the name of the Holy Spirit must be joined to that of the unbegotten God the Father and his only begotten Son" (*Princ.* 1.3.2).

In the second and third centuries, the Spirit was not an explicit focus of doctrinal debate save indirectly, in the controversy occasioned by Montanist prophesyings, with their claim to contain new and binding revelation. The mainstream of Christian thinking, as represented by Irenaeus, saw the revelatory work of the Spirit in the inspiration of the Jewish scriptures; in the inspiration of the apostles and their immediate followers, to whom authorship of the Christian scriptures was attributed; and in the inspiration of the church and its teachers, charged as both were with the faithful transmission of the apostolic gospel and the interpretation of the scriptures. The Spirit was in the first instance the teacher and illuminator of the church and of the individual believer; "for all knowledge of the Father, when the Son reveals him, is made known to us through the Holy Spirit" (Origen, *Princ.* 1.3.4). At the same time, it was the Spirit who endowed the church's members with gifts of prophecy, healing, and government; and who, indeed, in baptism, became the "seed . . . of a divine race [*genus*]," dwelling in the bodies of believers and sanctifying them against the time of the resurrection (Novatian, *Trin.* 29). The Holy Spirit was the present source of the new life in Christ, associated primarily with the work of the redemption whose sphere was the church.

Holy Spirit in Theological Reflection. The Holy Spirit became the subject of doctrinal controversy in the course of the long debate over the teachings of Arius and his successors. At the Council of Nicaea (325), the sole matter considered was the question whether, as Arius maintained, the Logos/Son was a creature. The question of the Spirit surfaced, however, in the debate between Marcellus of Ancyra and Eusebius of Caesarea, the latter of whom maintained that the Spirit is a creature of the Son. During his third exile (358–361), Athanasius wrote a series of letters addressed to Serapion of Thmuis in refutation of certain teachers in Egypt. These "Tropici," although they confessed the deity of the Son, maintained that the Spirit was an angel and a creature. Athanasius's reply is based on the principle that all of God's activity "is . . . originated and actuated through the Word in the Spirit" (*Ep. Serap.* 1.31). The work of the Spirit is thus one "moment" in the work of God the Trinity. Athanasius drives this point home by repeated allusion to baptism, in which, as he points out, the Trinity's salvific action derives from the Father and is accomplished "through the Son in the Spirit." Athanasius reiterated this stand in the synodical letter *To the Antiochenes* (362), which in effect called for confession of the deity of the Spirit as a necessary supplement to the Nicene faith. In this, he was supported by his younger Alexandrian contemporary Didymus the Blind, and his work was continued in Asia Minor, partly against a conservative group referred to as Pneumatomachians (and later as "Macedonians") by Basil of Caesarea. The latter, in his treatises *Against Eunomius* and *On the Holy Spirit,* argued from the unity of the salvific work of the Spirit with that of Father and Son to their unity of being. His position was ultimately summed up in the phrase of the Niceno-Constantinopolitan Creed that affirms that the Spirit is "worshiped and glorified together with the Father and the Son."

In the writings of Augustine of Hippo, who was not directly engaged in the debate with Arianism, the Holy Spirit appears as the divine power that, working inwardly, "sheds abroad the love of God in our hearts" (Rom. 5:5). The Spirit, for Augustine, reorients human desire upon God and so enables the saving knowledge of God in Christ. It represents at once the transformative self-sharing on God's part that Augustine understands by the word "grace" and at the same time the power in which human persons share themselves with one another in love (*caritas*). The Spirit, then, is that which joins humanity to God and human beings to one another in the unity of the church: two themes that Augustine developed polemically in his debates with the Pelagians and the Donatists respectively. In his treatise *On the Trinity*, Augustine accordingly envisages the "person" or hypostasis of the Spirit as constituted by the love or fellowship that Father and Son bestow on one another and in which they are joined, so that it can truly be said that Spirit proceeds "from the Father and

the Son" (*ex Patre Filioque*). This formula, the mark of an Augustinian and "western" Trinitarianism, came eventually to be incorporated in the Latin version of Niceno-Constantinopolitan Creed, where its presence stimulated a centuries-old debate between the Greek and Latin churches. *See also* Holy Spirit; Soul.

[R.A.N.]

Bibliography

A.M. Festugière, "La Trichotomie de I Thess., V, 23, et la philosophie grecque," *RecSR* 20 (1930):385–415; G.L. Prestige, *God in Patristic Thought,* 2nd ed. (London: SPCK, 1952); G. Verbeke, *L'Evolution de la doctrine du pneuma, du Stoïcisme à s. Augustin* (Paris and Louvain: Desclée de Brouwer, 1945); D. Dockrill and R.G. Tanner, eds., *Spirit* (Auckland: U of Auckland P, 1985).

STEPHEN (early first century). Leader of the Hellenists in the first church at Jerusalem and the first Christian martyr. Stephen was one of the Seven, chosen to administer relief to the widows (Acts 6:1–6). His miracles and preaching led to his being brought before the Sanhedrin. His speech recorded in Acts 7, utilizing Jewish history in order to relativize the temple and point to Jesus as the true prophet predicted by Moses, led to his stoning. Some lines of Stephen's theology have been traced in the Epistle to the Hebrews, *Barnabas*, the Pseudo-Clementines, and the Christian apologists. Stephen and the Seven were recalled in the ordination prayers for deacons as exemplars of this ministry. Feast day December 26 (west), December 27 (east). [E.F.]

Bibliography

Gregory of Nyssa, *In sanctum Stephanum Protomartyrem* 1 and 2, PG 46.701–736; Asterius of Amasea, *Homilia* 12, *Laudatio sancti protomartyris Stephani,* G. Anderson and E.J. Goodspeed, *Ancient Sermons for Modern Times* (New York: Pilgrim, 1904); Basil of Seleucia, *Sermo* 41, PG 85.461–473.

M. Simon, *St. Stephen and the Hellenists in the Primitive Church* (New York: Longmans, Green, 1958); M. Scharlemann, *Stephen: A Singular Saint* (Rome: Pontifical Biblical Institute, 1968).

STEPHEN I. Bishop of Rome (254–257). Stephen's short tenure was marked by disputes with Cyprian of Carthage, who, together with other African bishops, opposed Stephen's reinstatement of two Spanish bishops charged with yielding under persecution. Cyprian also wanted the deposition of Marcian of Arles, charged with involvement in the schism of Novatian. Further controversy arose over the question of baptism administered by heretics, which was considered invalid by Cyprian and most of the African church. Stephen did not receive Cyprian's envoys, sent to Rome with African conciliar decrees in support of his stand, while he himself was denounced by Firmilian, bishop of Caesarea in Cappadocia. The dispute virtually came to an end with the death of Stephen (probably not as a martyr). His successor, Sixtus II, effected a reconciliation, and Africa adopted the Roman position within a few decades. Stephen was probably the first Roman bishop to make an explicit claim to primacy over the church on the basis of Christ's words to Peter (Matt. 16:18–19).   [M.P.McH.]

Bibliography

Cyprian, *Letters* 67–75; Eusebius, *Church History* 7.2–5; *Liber Pontificalis* 24 (Duchesne 1.154).

E. Dekkers, "Symbolo Baptizare," *Fides Sacramenti Sacramentum Fidei, Studies in Honour of Pieter Smulders*, ed. H.J. auf der Maur et al. (Assen: Van Gorcum, 1981), pp. 107–112; S.G. Hall, "Stephen of Rome and the One Baptism," *SP* 17.2 (1982):796–798.

STEPHEN GOBARUS (sixth century). Monophysite theologian. An adherent of the tritheism of John Philoponus, Stephen wrote in Egypt or Syria; only fragments of his works are extant. CPG III, 7300.   [M.P.McH.]

STOICISM. Greek philosophical school. Stoicism was founded by Zeno (333/2–262 B.C.) in the early part of the third century B.C. It is named after the *Stoa Poikilē* ("Painted Colonnade"), a public hall in Athens where Zeno and his followers taught. The history of Stoicism is usually divided into three periods.

Early Stoa. Zeno arrived in Athens from Cyprus in 312/1 B.C. He first acquainted himself with the philosophy of the Cynic Crates of Thebes and thereafter studied under Polemo, the head of the Academy. As Zeno developed his ideas, his growing fame drew many people to listen to him at the Stoa. He was succeeded by Cleanthes of Assos (331–232 B.C.) and he by Chrysippus of Soli (ca. 280–ca. 204 B.C.), who elaborated and modified the Stoic system and defended it against the attacks of the Academy. Alongside Zeno, Chrysippus was the greatest figure of the ancient Stoa, and his philosophy became identified with Stoic orthodoxy.

Middle Stoa. The two great leaders of the Middle Stoa were Panaetius of Rhodes (185/80–ca. 100 B.C.) and Posidonius of Apamea (ca. 135–ca. 50 B.C.). After studying in the Stoic school in Athens, Panaetius went, ca. 146 B.C., to Rome, where he introduced Stoicism to leading Romans. In 129 B.C., Panaetius returned to Athens to take over the leadership of the Stoic school. Posidonius, after studying under the aged Panaetius, settled in Rhodes. He mastered both natural science and philosophy and undertook extensive travels throughout the Mediterranean.

Roman Stoa. Seneca (ca. 4 B.C.–A.D. 65) was the earliest representative of the Roman Stoa. Other representatives were Musonius Rufus (A.D. 30–101), who revived the severe ethics of the ancient Stoics, and Epictetus (ca. 50–130), a former slave. Marcus Aurelius (121–180) was emperor of Rome from 161 to 180 and one of the last great Stoics. Stoicism was gradually replaced by other philosophies and religions. One of its main rivals was Christianity.

Teaching. It is difficult to distinguish the views of the first Stoics; a composite picture of their teachings must suffice (although not all Stoics agreed on all points). They divided philosophy into three branches: physics, ethics, and logic. Their system was pantheistic, positing that the divine reality could be found in everything; they declared that all substances were corporeal, including even the deity and emotions. According to them, the world is made up of four elements: fire, air, water, earth. God, the creative fire, generates air, which generates water, which generates earth. In the conflagration phase of the cycle, the universe is consumed by the divine fire: the earth becomes water, water becomes air, and air becomes fire. At a preordained time, the cycle will be repeated; the universe is an endless succession of creation and destruction. Since the world is perfect, all these innumerable successions of worlds are identical. The *logos* (reason) ordains the whole universe; there is no place for chance in the Stoic system. Since everything in the universe is mutually connected, what happens in one part of the universe has an effect on what happens in another part. There is also a correspondence between human affairs and events in the universe (a belief used in defense of divination).

The Stoic ethics defined virtue as the end or goal of life. A virtuous person is one who lives in accordance with nature or the *logos*. All people are interrelated, since they have the same origin, destiny, and *logos*; slavery and social inequality were thus inconsistent with the law of nature and the Stoic system. The Stoics regarded it as their duty to participate in civic affairs and they placed much value on friendship. They believed that evil stemmed from vice, and that in turn from the passions. One should attempt to achieve a state of *apatheia*, in which one is free from negative passions, and replace them with good passions (*eupatheia*).

The Stoics divided all things into three categories: the good (defined as virtue), the bad (defined as vice), and the *adiaphora* (which are indifferent as far as virtue is concerned—such as wealth or poverty, health, or sickness). Among the *adiaphora*, some things were preferred to others.

The Stoics were empiricists and believed that knowledge was derived from perceptions. At birth, the soul is like a clean sheet of paper. It derives its contents from objects. The impression that is then deposited in the mind is called a representation, or *phantasia*. This *phantasia* is evaluated, and when it is considered to be correct it becomes a *phantasia kataleptikē* (a comprehensive presentation held with certainty). Since the Stoics believed that the soul was rational, they paid much attention to logic and hypothetical syllogisms.

Influence. Many early Christians were either converts from paganism or had a classical upbringing. Since Stoicism was an integral part of classical culture, one can assume that it played an important role in the formation of early Christian thinking. Some fathers of the church (such as Justin Martyr and Clement of Alexandria) conceded that there were true elements in pagan philosophies; others condemned them outright (Tatian, Hippolytus). Still others drew subjects or principles from Stoicism and used them in defense of Christine doctrine (Tertullian, Lactantius). It is difficult to determine the extent of either the Stoic influence on Christian thought or the possible influence of Christianity on the Roman Stoa. Modern scholars may draw attention to the parallels between Stoicism and Christianity, mainly in the area of ethics, or else emphasize the radical differences. Although some theologians derived their terminology from Stoicism, they placed these terms in an entirely different worldview and thus gave them a completely different significance. *See also* Philosophy; Seneca.

[H.F.S.]

Bibliography

Hippolytus, *Refutation of All Heresies* 1.18; Tertullian, *On the Soul* 5; Lactantius, *Divine Institutes* 1.5, 12, 17; 3.18; 7.3; idem, *On the Wrath of God* 5.

R. Stob, "Stoicism and Christianity," *Classical Journal* 30 (1934–1935):217–224; M. Spanneut, *Le Stoïcisme des pères de l'église de Clément de Rome à Clément d'Alexandrie* (Paris: Seuil, 1957); R.M. Wenley, *Stoicism and Its Influence* (New York: Cooper Square, 1963); J.M. Rist, *Stoic Philosophy* (Cambridge: Cambridge UP, 1969); F.H. Sandbach, *The Stoics* (London: Chatto and Windus, 1975); J.M. Rist, *The Stoics* (Berkeley: U of California P, 1978); M.L. Colish, *The Stoic Tradition from Antiquity to the Early Middle Ages*, 2 vols. (Leiden: Brill, 1985).

SUBDEACON. Assistant to the deacon. The first mention of the subdeacon is in the *Apostolic Tradition* of Hippolytus, which provided for the bishop to name a subdeacon to "serve the deacon" (14; cf. Laodicea, *can.* 20). Since some churches limited the number of deacons to seven, the office of subdeacon was created to assume some of the subordinate duties of deacons. Thus, Cornelius reported that there were seven deacons and seven subdeacons in the church at Rome (Eusebius, *H.E.* 6.43.11). The *Apostolic Constitutions* 8.21 provided for ordination of subdeacons by laying on of hands, contrary to other sources (Basil, *Ep. Canon.* 217.51; Fourth Council of Carthage, *can.* 5). *See also* Deacon. [E.F.]

Bibliography

J.G. Davies, "Deacons, Deaconesses and the Minor Orders in the Patristic Period," *JEH* 14 (1963):6–7, 14–15; J.M. Barnett, *The Diaconate: A Full and Equal Order* (New York: Seabury, 1981), p. 83.

SUBSTANCE. One of the English terms (others being, e.g., "essence" or "nature") used to render the Greek *ousia*; derived from the latter's normal Latin equivalent, *substantia*. The Greek term itself is an abstract noun formed from the participle of the verb "to be" (*einai*) and has much the same richness and ambiguity of meaning as the modern English word "reality." In classical Attic, *ousia* often meant that which is proper to someone or something, that is, broadly speaking, it connoted "property"—either in the sense of goods and possessions or in the sense of an attribute or character, but always with the suggestion of permanence and solidity.

Plato introduced the term into the vocabulary of philosophy, although he gave it no precise definition and used it to mean, variously, "what something is," "that which is," and "state of being [something]." In all of these senses, however, "substance" (or "being") connoted for Plato that which is at once intelligible and unchanging in its intelligibility: it was the reality that the mind sought in its search for the abiding substance of things. Hence, it became in his thought a general characterization of the realm of Forms or Ideas, which is substance or being *par excellence*, to be contrasted with the phenomenal realm of becoming (*to gignomenon*). Aristotle, rejecting Plato's transcendent realm of Forms, originally identified *ousia* (in the sense of "that which is") as the concrete individual that is referred to by the subject-term in a proposition, or (in the sense of "what something is")

as the species or genus to which such an individual belongs. Thus, on this account Socrates is a substance in the first sense, and humanity is a substance in the second. He later revised this view somewhat: substance is understood less as the subject (of predication or change) than as the essence or actualization of something. The later Stoic school, on the other hand, tended to identify substance as the original or basic material stuff of the ordered, evolving cosmos—a view that in some authors made it out to be a passive, qualityless subject or substratum of change.

The wide variability in the meaning of "substance" persisted into the Christian era. The word *ousia* occurs in the sense of "existence" or "reality," for example; or as denoting "that which is" in the sense of the cosmos or created order as a totality. Equally common is the (Stoic) sense of "stuff," or the school-Platonist sense in which the term refers to the immaterial realm of intelligible or intelligent beings as opposed to the material realm perceived by sense—presumably because the former is permanent and more real. There is reminiscence of Aristotle's usage in the distinction between substance and accident or quality (where substance means something taken in its abiding self-identity) and in the partly analogous distinction between substance and activity or operation (*energeia*). There is no indication that authors of this period attempted to be consistent in their use of *ousia*.

Prior to the Council of Nicaea (325), there was no agreement about the use of the word *ousia* in relation to God, perhaps because in some of its ordinary senses it seemed inappropriate for such use. Although Justin Martyr could identify God as "that which [preeminently] is" (*to on*), Origen, who belonged to the Platonist tradition that saw the ultimate Deity as "beyond *ousia*" (i.e., beyond intelligible form, and hence intellectual grasp: cf. Plato, *Republic* 509B), seemed to doubt, at least on occasion, whether such a classification of God is possible. He could, nevertheless, in at least one place speak of the "unity of nature and substance" that obtains between Father and Son, even while elsewhere he insisted that they are distinct in substance (i.e., in this case, as individual subjects). Tertullian, on the other hand, employed the Latin *substantia* to mean not only "something solidly real" (*Prax.* 7), but also that which something is made of, as constituting the thing and giving it its permanent character (cf. *Anim.* 32). Hence, in the treatise *Against Praxeas* 9.2 he can allege, in a thoroughly Stoic fashion, that the substance of God is the special sort of "body" called "spirit" (cf. John 4:24); and on this view, the Son is envisaged as a "derivative" (*derivatio*) or "portion" of God's substance and as being "of one substance" with God.

The dogmatic confession of the Council of Nicaea employed *ousia* twice (Theodoret, *H.E.* 1.11). First, it asserted against Arius and his supporters that the Son is "from [or "out of"] the substance of the Father." This phrase seems intended primarily to deny that the Son is "out of nothing" (i.e., a creature). In its setting in the creedal text, it asserts in effect that the relation of Father and Son is more like a relation of generation than it is like a relation of positing or creating: it is not merely that the Father accounts for the Son, but that the Son derives from *what the Father is* qua *God*, and in that sense from his substance. Second, the council denies, in one of its anathemas, that the Son is "of [or "from"] a different hypostasis or substance." This phrase, in which "hypostasis" and "substance" are used as synonyms, is ambiguous. It may mean that the Son is not differently composed, or a different sort of thing from the Father. On the other hand, it can mean, as it did for some contemporaries of the council, that the Son does not originate from some reality or "stuff" distinct from the Father.

Clarity—or relative clarity—in the specifically theological use of *ousia* was achieved only in the Trinitarian teaching of the Cappadocian fathers during the last third of the fourth century. This clarification was achieved through their effort to explain how, if Father, Son, and Spirit are distinct from one another as hypostases (existent objective realities), they could at the same time be "consubstantial" (*homoousioi*, "the same as to substance"), as the Nicene formula had asserted. Their solution, as it gradually emerged, was to suggest that hypostasis is related to substance as the particular is to "the common" (*to koinon:* i.e., the specific nature). "Substance," then, denotes the divine "nature" (*phusis*), which is fully and identically present as each of the three hypostases because it becomes Son through "begetting," and Spirit through "procession," from the Father. *Ousia*, then, in this narrow theological context, was to refer as such not to existence, or to an ontological status, or to the immaterial realm of intelligible existence, or to the subject of predication or change, but to "what something is." In other contexts, the other uses of *ousia* of course persisted. *See also* Hypostasis; Spirit. [R.A.N.]

Bibliography

G.L. Prestige, *God in Patristic Thought*, 2nd ed. (London: SPCK, 1952), pp. 190–196, 265–281; J. Moignt, *Théologie trinitaire de Tertullien*, 3 vols. (Paris: Aubier, 1966); C. Stead, *Divine Substance* (Oxford: Clarendon, 1977).

SUETONIUS, GAIUS TRANQUILLUS (ca. 70–ca. 140). Roman biographer. A scholar and friend of Pliny the Younger, Suetonius served as secretary to the emperor Hadrian but was dismissed (122), perhaps as a result of court intrigue. His *Lives of Illustrious Men* survives mostly in fragments, although the lives of Terence, Horace, Virgil, and Lucan are preserved. Jerome used the work for chronology; later, it would influence Einhard's *Life of Charlemagne*. The *Lives of the Caesars* (composed beginning ca. 120), containing biographies of the twelve emperors from Julius Caesar through Domitian, is a source for the history of the early empire. The life of *Claudius* 25.4 has an early, although confused, reference to Christianity—the emperor is reported to have expelled the Jews from Rome because of disturbances arising from the instigation of "Chrestus" (i.e., Christ).

[M.P.McH.]

Bibliography

Pliny the Younger, *Letters* 1.18,24; 3.8; 5.10; 9.34; 10.94.

Suetonius, 2 vols., tr. J.C. Rolfe, LCL (1914); *Lives of the Twelve Caesars*, tr. R. Graves (Harmondsworth: Penguin, 1957).

G.B. Townend, "Suetonius and His Influence," *Latin Biography*, ed. T.A. Dorey (London: Routledge and Kegan Paul, 1967), pp. 79–111; R. Syme, "The Travels of Suetonius Tranquillus," *Hermes* 109 (1981):105–117; A. Wallace-Hadrill, *Suetonius: The Scholar and His Caesars* (New Haven: Yale UP, 1984); R.C. Lounsbury, *The Acts of Suetonius: An Introduction* (New York: Lang, 1987).

SULPICIUS SEVERUS (ca. 360–ca. 420). Christian biographer and historian. After studies at Bordeaux, Sulpicius entered on a legal career but took up the ascetic life upon his wife's early death (ca. 394). His friendship with Paulinus of Nola was longstanding. He was a disciple of Martin of Tours. His *Life of Saint Martin* (ca. 396), given its emphasis on the miraculous and its affinities with the historical novel, yet remains by far the principal source for the saint's life. Through its employment in a poem by Paulinus of Périgueux (CPL 1474) and a life by Venantius Fortunatus (CPL 1037) it became an exemplar for medieval hagiography. It is supplemented by three *Letters* concerning Martin's death and defending him against detractors, along with *Dialogues* (ca. 400) comparing the miracles of Martin with those of the monks of the Egyptian desert. The *Chronicles* (after 404), a sacred history from creation up to A.D. 400 is valuable for its treatment of Priscillian. CPL 474–480. *See also* Martin of Tours. [M.P.McH.]

Bibliography

Paulinus of Nola, *Letters* 1; 5; 11; 17; 22–24; 27–32; Gennadius, *Lives of Illustrious Men* 19.

Sulpice Sévère, Vie de saint Martin, 3 vols., ed. J. Fontaine, SC (1967, 1968, 1969), Vols. 133, 134, 135.

Sulpicius Severus: Writings, tr. B.M. Peebles, FOTC (1949), Vol. 7.

P.M. Duval, *La Gaule jusqu'au milieu du Ve siècle* (Paris: Picard, 1971), Vol. 1.2, pp. 656–662, no. 275; C. Stancliffe, *Saint Martin and His Hagiographer: History and Miracle in Sulpicius Severus* (Oxford: Clarendon, 1983); F. Ghizzoni, *Sulpicio Severo* (Rome: Bulzoni, 1983).

SUNDAY. The first day of the week, the Lord's day. The "day of the sun" (Justin, *1 Apol.* 67) was the pagan name for the second day in the planetary week, which name continues in the Germanic languages of northern Europe. Its equivalent in the Jewish calendar was the day called "the first day of the week" (the first day between the Sabbaths—1 Cor. 16:2). Christians sometimes spoke of the day as the eighth day (*Barn.* 15.8f.; Justin, *Dial.* 41.4; Asterius, *Hom.* 20 *in Ps.* 11.1) in contrast to the Jewish seventh day, because the number eight had associations with immortality and the world to come (*Ep. apos.* 18; Clement of Alexandria, *Exc. Thdot.* 63.1; *Str.* 6.14, 16). The common Christian designation was "the Lord's day" (Rev. 1:10; *A. Jo.* 106), the name that continues in Greek and the romance languages of southern Europe. That Christians coined a new name for Sunday shows that the day was especially important to them.

Various efforts have been made to find a pre-Christian origin for the Christian observance of Sunday: (1) the pagan day of the sun (although there was a day named for the sun, a day that assumed special importance in the cult of Mithras, there remains no evidence of a Sunday celebration in paganism); (2) an anti-Judaic reaction by Gentile Christians in the second century, aided by the pagan solar theology (this hypothesis has difficulties with the New Testament evidence and the consistent evidence of later sources); (3) Jewish sectarian influences represented by the solar calendar followed at Qumran (speculative, for a specific link is lacking); (4) the Jewish Sabbath extended into the first day by Christians meeting on the Sabbath and then "breaking bread" together in the evening (natural enough, but the first evidence points to a Sunday evening rather than a Sabbath evening meeting by Christians). Despite these theories, the Christian Sunday observance can best be explained from motives within Christianity itself.

Sunday, or the first day of the week, was significant for Christians as the day of the week on which Jesus arose from the dead (Mark 16:2ff. and parallels; Ignatius, *Magn.* 9; Clement of Alexandria, *Str.* 7.12.76). Sometimes, other associations were noted, as the beginning of creation (Justin, *1 Apol.* 67), the symbol of the new world (*Barn.* 15.8), or the spiritual fulfillment of circumcision on the eighth day (Justin, *Dial.* 41), but in all of these instances there was also the association with the resurrection. The same is implicit in the connection of the ascension of Jesus with the Lord's day (*Barn.* 15.8f.; *Ev. Petr.* 13.56). Some expected the return of Christ on Sunday (Justin, *Dial.* 100; Melito, *Bapt.* 4; Origen, *Hom.* 9.10 in *Lev.*). Because of this association with the resurrection, Christian sources associate the first day of the week with joy (*Barn.* 15.8f.; Tertullian, *Nat.* 1.13). Psalm 118:24 was applied to Sunday (Clement of Alexandria, *Str.* 6.16; Cyprian, *Dom. or.* 35). Fasting was forbidden on Sunday, and prayer was said standing in representation of the resurrection instead of kneeling (Tertullian, *Cor.* 3; *Or.* 23).

Christians had their regular meeting, particularly to partake of the eucharist, on the first day of the week. The likely origin of this practice was the meeting of Jesus with his disciples on the day of the resurrection and the following Sunday, as noted in John 20:1, 19, 26. The Greek adjective "the Lord's" (*kuriakos*) occurs in the New Testament for the Lord's day (Rev. 1:10) and the Lord's supper (1 Cor. 11:20) and had its principal usage in Christianity in reference to Sunday. Acts 20:7–11 describes a meeting on the evening of the first day of the week, but whether this was Saturday night or Sunday night is uncertain, because it is disputed whether the method of time reckoning was Jewish (Saturday night) or Greek or Roman (Sunday night). Thereafter, Christian sources give uniform testimony to meetings on Sunday (*Did.* 14; Justin, *1 Apol.* 67; Bardesanes, *On Fate*). At some early point, it became common for Christians to have their meeting in the morning (Pliny the Younger, *Ep.* 10.96; Tertullian, *Cor.* 3)—perhaps to make explicit the connection with the resurrection—with the agape in the evening (Tertullian, *Apol.* 39).

Apart from Acts 2:46, which is ambiguous, there is no evidence in the early Christian literature for a daily Lord's supper, or indeed for its observance on any day other than Sunday. The eucharist came to be observed at other special occasions, for instance on the anniversary of the deaths of martyrs, and in the fourth century some churches took the eucharist on Saturday as well as Sunday (Socrates, *H.E.* 5.22; 6.8). The Paschal observance from early times began on the Saturday and continued into Sunday. Vigils were held at other times than Sunday, and there were daily meetings for prayer and Bible study, but these extra occasions did not take away from the central importance of the weekly Sunday assembly in the life of the church.

The Lord's day was consistently distinguished from the Sabbath as a different day (Ignatius, *Magn.* 9; *A. Paul.* 7; *Ev. Petr.* 9.34f.; 12.50f.; Tertullian, *Jejunio* 15), and it was explicitly stated that Christians did not observe the Sabbath (Justin, *Dial.* 10; *A. Petr.* 1.1; Tertullian, *Adv. Judaeos* 2.10; 4.1). Some Jewish Christians observed both the Sabbath and the Lord's day (Eusebius, *H.E.* 3.27.5). This practice shows the different nature of the two days: the Sabbath was a day of rest, and Sunday was a day of assembly. Although the Sabbath had come to be the day of meeting at the synagogue, its essential nature as prescribed by Old Testament law was a day of rest (Exod. 20:8–11). The two days commemorated two different acts of deliverance and salvation—the Exodus of the Jews from Egypt (Deut. 5:15) and the resurrection of Jesus Christ, which brought deliverance from death (Rom. 4:25; 1 Cor. 15:12–57).

When Constantine made it a legal holiday in 321, Sunday began to take on some of the characteristics of a day of rest (rest enjoined in Elvira, *can.* 6; Laodicea, *can.* 29), and some Christians began to apply the Sabbath commandment of the Decalogue to Sunday (Eusebius, *Ps.* 91; John Chrysostom, *Hom.* 10.7 in *Gen.*). The Christian interest in abstinence from work on Sunday, however, was for the purpose of encouraging participation in the services of the church on this day. *See also* Sabbath. [E.F.]

Bibliography

F.H. Colson, *The Week* (Cambridge: Cambridge UP, 1926); P. Cotton, *From Sabbath to Sunday* (Bethlehem: Times Publ. Co., 1933); C. Callewaert, "La Synaxe eucharistique à Jérusalem, berceau du dimanche," *Ephemerides Theologicae* (Louvain) 15 (1938):34–74; F.A. Regan, *Dies Dominica and Dies*

Solis: The Beginnings of the Lord's Day in Christian Antiquity (Washington, D.C.: Catholic U of America P, 1961); W. Rordorf, *Sunday: The History of the Day of Rest and Worship in the Earliest Centuries of the Christian Church* (Philadelphia: Westminster, 1968); idem, *Sabbat und Sonntag in der alten Kirche* (Zurich: Theologischer Verlag, 1972); S. Bacchiocchi, *From Sabbath to Sunday: A Historical Investigation of the Rise of Sunday Observance in Early Christianity* (Rome: Pontifical Gregorian UP, 1977); R.T. Beckwith and W. Stott, *This Is the Day: The Biblical Doctrine of the Christian Sunday in Its Jewish and Early Church History Setting* (Greenwood: Attic, 1978); E. Ferguson, "Sabbath: Saturday or Sunday? A Review Article," *Restoration Quarterly* 23 (1980):172–181; D.A. Carson, ed., *From Sabbath to Lord's Day: A Biblical, Historical and Theological Investigation* (Grand Rapids: Zondervan, 1982); E. Ferguson, *Early Christians Speak* (Abilene: ACU, 1987), pp. 67–79.

SURSUM CORDA. "Lift up your hearts," part of the widely used introductory dialogue preceding the eucharistic prayer in early liturgies. According to the earliest text, the bishop spoke these words and the people responded, "We have them with the Lord" (Hippolytus, *Trad. ap.* 4). The eucharistic prayer was said with the congregation standing, arms outstretched (Justin, *1 Apol.* 67; *Didas.* 12; Tertullian, *Apol.* 30.4; *Spect.* 25). It may be that the exhortation *sursum corda* was the signal for the congregation to rise, if it had been seated, or to lift arms for the prayer. If so, the physical posture was also a call for lifting the attention to heaven (Cyprian, *Dom. or.* 31). [E.F.]

Bibliography
F.J. Dölger, *Sol Salutis* (Münster: Aschendorff, 1925), pp. 228–244; C.A. Bouman, "Variants in the Introduction to the Eucharistic Prayer," *VChr* 4 (1950):94–115; J.A. Jungmann, *The Mass of the Roman Rite* (New York: Benziger, 1955), Vol. 2, pp. 110–115; E. Ferguson, "The Liturgical Function of the 'Sursum Corda,'" *SP* 12 (1975):360–363.

SYLVESTER I. Bishop of Rome (314–335). Little is known of Sylvester's life. During his pontificate, Constantine the Great summoned councils at Arles (314) and Nicaea (325); the emperor gave the Lateran basilica to Sylvester. Legends concerning him were influential in medieval civilization: notably the Donation of Constantine, a gift of lands and authority to the papacy purportedly addressed to Sylvester, an eighth-century forgery. [M.P.McH.]

Bibliography
Liber Pontificalis 34 (Duchesne 1.170–201).

SYMEON STYLITES (ca. 390–459). First pillar saint. Symeon in 423 took up residence in northern Syria not far from Antioch of Syria, where he spent the rest of his life living on a column. The monastery at the modern Qalʿat Sim ʿān, although in ruins, is quite impressive. According to Symeon's biographies, he was responsible for many conversions of whole pagan peoples and influenced policies of Roman emperors. Theodosius II gave up his idea of giving synagogues back to Jews in Antioch when Symeon protested. Leo I requested his opinion on Christological controversies in Egypt; Symeon supported the Chalcedonians.

Daniel (d. ca. 493), Symeon's most famous pupil, took up residence on a pillar near Constantinople. A rather remarkable monastic complex just west of Antioch of Syria grew up around Symeon the Younger (d. ca. 596), named after this Symeon. Feast day January 5 (west), September 1 (east). CPG III, 6640–6650. [F.W.N.]

Bibliography
Theodoret, *History of the Monks of Syria* 26; Evagrius, *Church History* 1.13; Theodore Lector, *Historia ecclesiastica* 1.12; 2.42; *Simeon Stylites: The Biographies*, tr. R. Doran (Kalamazoo: Cistercian, 1988).
A.J. Festugière, *Antioche païenne et chrétienne* (Paris: Boccard, 1959), pp. 388–401; S.A. Harvey, "The Sense of a Stylite: Perspectives on Simeon the Elder," *VChr* 42 (1988):376–394.

SYMMACHUS. Bishop of Rome (498–514). Much of Symmachus's pontificate was troubled by the schism of Laurentius, elected pope in opposition to him by a pro-Byzantine party of the Roman clergy. Symmachus rejected the *Henoticon* of the emperor Zeno, expelled the supporters of Manichaeism from Rome, upheld the primacy of the church of Arles and its bishop Caesarius in the dispute with Avitus of Vienne, extensively renovated the Church of

St. Peter, and ordered the singing of the *Gloria in excelsis* on Sundays. Letters dealing with several of these matters are extant. Feast day July 19. CPL 1678–1682.   [M.P.McH.]

Bibliography

Liber Pontificalis 53 (Duchesne 1.260–268).

On the Laurentian schism: P.A.B. Llewellyn, "The Roman Church During the Laurentian Schism: Priests and Senators," *ChHist* 45 (1976):417–427; J. Moorhead, "The Laurentian Schism: East and West in the Roman Church," *ChHist* 47 (1978):125–136; S.T. Stevens, "The Circle of Bishop Fulgentius," *Traditio* 38 (1982):327–341.

SYMMACHUS (late second century). Translator of Old Testament. Eusebius states that Symmachus was an Ebionite (*H.E.* 6.17). He is important for his idiomatic Greek translation of the Old Testament. Unlike Aquila, whose translation he seems to have known, Symmachus sought to convey the sense of the Hebrew in Greek that had literary style. Origen placed Symmachus's translation in the fourth column of the *Hexapla*. Only fragments of his work are extant. *See also* Hexapla; Septuagint.   [C.C.]

SYMMACHUS, QUINTUS AURELIUS (ca. 340–ca. 402). Roman orator and civil official. A leading orator of his time, and a friend of Ausonius, Symmachus completed his administrative career with service as prefect of Rome (384), in which capacity he recommended Augustine for a post as teacher of rhetoric in Milan. Despite his support of the usurper Maximus (388), he attained the consulship (391). His extant writings include ten books of letters—among them several letters to Ambrose (3.30–37)—and fragments of a number of orations. His best-known work is his third *relatio* (report) to the emperor Valentinian II (384), written in support of the restoration of the altar and statue of Victory, which had been removed from the Roman senate house by Gratian (382); it may well have been composed in concert with Praetextatus, the praetorian prefect. The effort was thwarted by Ambrose; some two decades later, Prudentius would recall the controversy in his *Contra Symmachum*. CPL 160, *epist.* 17a.   [M.P.McH.]

Bibliography

Ambrose, *Letters* 17; 18; 57; Augustine, *Confessions* 5.13.23.

J.F. Matthews, "The Letters of Symmachus," *Latin Literature of the Fourth Century*, ed. J.W. Binns (London and Boston: Routledge and Kegan Paul, 1974), pp. 58–99; J.J. O'Donnell, "The Demise of Paganism," *Traditio* 35 (1979):45–88, esp. 69–80; F. Paschoud, "Le Rôle du providentialisme dans le conflit de 384 sur l'autel de la Victoire," *MH* 40 (1983):197–206.

SYNAXIS. Assembly of the faithful for worship. Ecclesiastical writers employed the Greek word *synaxis* in various ways. It most often referred to the group gathered for worship (John Chrysostom, *Hom.* 29 *in Act.*), or to the worship service itself, sometimes specifying the entire service that included the eucharist (John Chrysostom, *Bapt. chr.* 1), or the act of celebrating the eucharist (Theodoret, *Ep.* 160), or the eucharist itself (Cyril of Alexandria, *Jo.* 12.1). It could also mean the time when worship was held, such as after a vigil (Athanasius, *Fug.* 24) or on a particular day of the week (Epiphanius, *Exp. fid.* 22). Particularly in reference to the monastic life, it designated the prayers, the eucharist, or the office (*Apophth. Patr.*, PG 65.220).

Synaxis could also be used to indicate worship services that were based on the Psalter and distinguish them from those that were centered on catechetical orations (Cyril of Jerusalem, *Catech.* 14.24). Egeria's travel diary describes a *synaxis* with Psalms and antiphon, a lesson from the Old Testament or the New Testament, an Alleluia, and a Gospel reading. *See also* Liturgy.   [F.W.N.]

SYNESIUS OF CYRENE (ca. 370–ca. 414). Bishop of Ptolemais in North Africa from 410. During his early years, Synesius studied at Alexandria under the Neoplatonist philosopher Hypatia, represented Cyrenaica at Constantinople in obtaining tax relief, married a Christian, and defended his city against a Berber invasion. It is doubtful that he had been baptized when out of gratitude for his service to the state he was elected bishop. He accepted only on the condition that he could keep his wife and some of his philosophical beliefs. Most of his writings are philosophical rather than Christian and are of value primarily for studying contemporary life. CPG III, 5630–5640. TLG 2006.   [J.A.B.]

Bibliography
PG 66.1021–1756.

A. Fitzgerald, tr., *The Letters of Synesius of Cyrene* (London: Oxford UP, 1926), and *The Essays and Hymns of Synesius of Cyrene*, 2 vols. (London: Oxford UP, 1930).

A.J. Bregman, *Synesius of Cyrene, Philosopher-Bishop* (Berkeley: U of California P, 1982); S. Vollenweider, *Neuplatonische und christliche Theologie bei Synesios von Kyrene* (Göttingen: Vandenhoeck & Ruprecht, 1985).

SYRIA, SYRIAC. Northern Mesopotamia, the country that stretches between the Euphrates and the Tigris rivers, and adjoining regions; dialect of the Aramaic family of the Semitic languages that was spoken in that vast territory. The cities of Edessa (Urhay, modern Urfa in southeastern Turkey), Nisibis, and Mosul mark the principal cultural centers of the Syriac-speaking peoples, from west to east across the territory. Syriac was spoken there as the mother tongue of most of the people from shortly before the time of Christ until the thirteenth century, when Arabic became the dominant language.

Christianity spread quickly in the Syriac-speaking world, beginning in the first century A.D. According to the indigenous traditions, enshrined in the fifth-century *Doctrina Addai*, the gospel was first preached in Edessa by the disciple Addai at the behest of the apostle Thomas. Early Christian writings in Syriac, with their roots in the second century, are the *Odes of Solomon* and the *Acts of Thomas*, with the strong possibility that other early works now available only in the Greek or Coptic, such as the *Pseudo-Clementines* and the *Gospel of Thomas*, were composed originally in Syriac. Among the earliest members of the Syriac-speaking Christian communities whose names we know are Bardesanes (Bar Dayṣān) (d. ca. 222) and Mani (d. 276), two men whose ideas eventually came to be considered heretical but whose teachings lived on long after their authors. Other early groups were Jewish Christian in origin, such as the Elkesaites and the "Baptist" (Mandaean) communities of southern Iraq. Early Christian ascetics, the Encratites, also found a welcome in the Syriac-speaking communities, among whom there first appeared the distinctly Syrian communities of the "Sons and Daughters of the Covenant," celibate, single people who devoted themselves to various forms of communal ministry in the local churches. Their distinctive forms of asceticism exercised an influence beyond the confines of the Syriac-speaking territories and even as far as Egypt, where the Syriac word for a "Single" (*iḥîdāyâ*) in the Lord's service may have prompted Greek-speaking Christians there to begin using the term *monachos* to describe a celibate ascetic.

The period encompassing the fourth through the sixth centuries was the era of the greatest and most significant productivity for Syriac writers. During this time, the language came to flourish in its classical form, in two distinct idioms with their own typical orthography and scribal usages, called western (Jacobite, *serṭo*) and eastern (Nestorian) respectively, together with a common bookhand (Estrangelo). After the Council of Chalcedon (451), and especially after the first decades of the sixth century, Syriac-speaking Christians throughout their territories came to be organized into three religious denominations, owing allegiance to three separate hierarchies, all in some way claiming the legitimacy of the patriarchate of Antioch: the Jacobites, the Nestorians, and the Melkites. Today, these communities are called the Syrian Orthodox Church, the Church of the East, and the Antiochian Orthodox Church respectively, all with a number of further divisions and allegiances as a result of the vicissitudes of the intervening centuries. The denominations reflect, in the order of the list just given, their members' adherence to the first three ecumenical councils, the first two ecumenical councils, or to the first six ecumenical councils, as the Greek Orthodox Church counts them.

Among the most important early Christian documents in Syriac are the translations of the Bible that appeared in the classical period. The Peshitta, as the most common Syriac version of the scriptures is called, is a valuable witness to the textual traditions behind both the Masoretic Text of the Hebrew Bible and the *Textus Receptus* of the Greek New Testament. For Gospel research, the Syriac witness to the text of the *Diatessaron* attributed to Tatian is indispensable.

The most significant writers in the Syriac tradition, whose works had an influence in the church at large, are Aphraates (fl. 336–345), Ephraem the Syrian (d. 373), Narsai (d. ca. 503), Jacob of Sarug (d. 521), Philoxenus of Mabbūg (d. 523), Babai the Great (d. 628), Jacob of Edessa (d. 708), and Isaac of Nineveh (d. ca. 700). Many of them cultivated the distinctive style of rhythmic prose that Syriac preachers prized, as well as the metrical hymns and homilies for which such writers as Ephraem the Syrian ("the Harp of the Holy Spirit") and Jacob of Sarug ("the Flute of the Holy Spirit") were later remembered. Ephraem in particular was a noted poet and composer of hymns whose works and favorite themes exerted an influence not only on other Syriac writers but on such an original Greek hymnographer as Romanos Melodos.

The historical chronicles of Syriac writers are particularly interesting because they often record details of late Roman and early Byzantine history not found in Greek or Latin narratives. Particularly significant are the Chronicle of Pseudo-Dionysius of Tel-Maḥrē, the Ecclesiastical History of John of Ephesus, the Chronicle of Joshua the Stylite, the Chronicle to the Year 1234, the Chronicle of Michael the Syrian, and the Chronography of Bar Hebraeus. All of these works, and others, preserve memories of life in the oriental churches that do not otherwise appear in the documentary sources for the history of the early church. The same may be said for collections of ecclesiastical canons preserved in Syriac, as the text of the *Synodicon Orientale* makes clear. This compilation preserves documents from the period of the beginnings of independent church life in Persia, during the first part of the fifth century,

as well as later documentary evidence regarding the governance of the Christian communities beyond the borders of the Roman empire to the east.

By the first half of the seventh century, Syriac-speaking Christians had spread the faith as far east as China, according to the testimony of a bilingually inscribed monument erected in Siganfu in 781, which proclaimed in Syriac and in Chinese the presence of Christians in the area since ca. 635. Even earlier, Syriac-speaking Christians had brought the gospel to India, where their descendants are today called "Thomas Christians," because of the story that the apostle Thomas was the first to preach Christianity in India. They are collectively the largest group of Christians now in the world with a Syriac heritage, although they are divided into a number of denominations and ecclesial allegiances.

In the first half of the seventh century, Islam spread rapidly in the Syriac-speaking Christian communities, and it is clear that in many important ways it was through the mediating role of these communities that, along with a knowledge of Greek logic, rhetoric, and science, a good deal of Christian mysticism and even theological influence passed to the Arabs. Nevertheless, within the Syriac-speaking communities many ancient liturgical texts were continually copied and recopied, with the result that they have provided modern liturgical historians with some of their most useful data for the reconstruction of the earliest Christian liturgies.

A number of important early Christian works originally written in Greek have been preserved only in Syriac, for example, Cathedral Homilies of Severus of Antioch, assorted works of Evagrius of Pontus, and the Life of Peter the Iberian by John Rufus. As for works composed originally in Syriac that have exerted a great influence in the Greek- and Latin-speaking worlds, one may mention in addition to the writings of Ephraem, which inspired many imitators in the west, the Ascetical Homilies of Isaac of Nineveh. *See also* Antioch; Edessa; Monophysitism; Nestorianism; Nisibis; Persia; Peshitta.   [S.H.G.]

Bibliography

W. Wright, *A Short History of Syriac Literature* (London: Black, 1894); R. Duval, *La Littérature syriaque*, 3rd ed. (Paris: Lecoffre, 1907); A. Baumstark, *Geschichte der syrischen Literatur* (Bonn: Marcus & Weber, 1922); C. Moss, *Catalogue of Syriac Printed Books and Related Literature in the British Museum* (London: British Museum, 1962); I. Ortiz de Urbina, *Patrologia Syriaca*, 2nd ed. (Rome: Pontificium Institutum Orientalium Studiorum, 1965); S.P. Brock, "Syriac Studies 1960–1970: A Classified Bibliography," *ParOr* 4 (1973):393–465; B.M. Metzger, *The Early Versions of the New Testament* (Oxford: Clarendon, 1977), pp. 3–98; S.P. Brock, "Syriac Studies 1971–1980: A Classified Bibliography," *ParOr* 10 (1981–1982):291–412; W.S. McCullough, *A Short History of Syriac Christianity to the Rise of Islam* (Chico: Scholars, 1982); S.P. Brock, "Syriac Studies 1981–1985: A Classified Bibliography," *ParOr* 14 (1987):289–360; S.P. Brock and S.A. Harvey, *Holy Women of the Syrian Orient* (Berkeley: U of California P, 1987).

T

TACITUS, CORNELIUS (ca. A.D. 56–after 113). Roman historian. Tacitus's career is known from references in his writings and correspondence from Pliny the Younger. He served in various administrative positions, becoming praetor (A.D. 88), consul (97), and proconsul of Asia under Trajan (ca. 112–113). His extant works are the *Agricola* (98), a biography of his father-in-law; *Germania* (98), a description of the manners and customs of the early peoples of Germany; *Dialogus de oratoribus* (perhaps ca. 102, although some scholars place it considerably earlier), on reasons for the decline of oratory; the *Histories* (date uncertain), covering the years 69–96, of which only the account of the years 69–70 is preserved; and the *Annals* (date uncertain), covering 14–68, most of which survives. His description of the suffering of the Christians under Nero as scapegoats for the great fire of A.D. 64 at Rome (*Annals* 15.44) includes a very early Roman reference to the crucifixion of Christ under Pontius Pilate in the reign of Tiberius. The martyrdoms of Peter and Paul would have occurred in this or a later Neronian persecution.

[M.P.McH.]

Bibliography
Pliny the Younger, *Letters* 1.6, 20; 2.1, 11; 4.13, 15; 6.9, 16, 20; 7.20, 33; 8.7; 9.10, 14, 23.

Tacitus, 5 vols., LCL (1914–1937: Vol. 1 rev. 1970); *The Agricola and the Germania*, tr. H. Mattingly, rev. S.A. Handford (Harmondsworth: Penguin, 1975); *The Histories*, tr. K. Wellesley (Harmondsworth: Penguin, 1972, 1975); *The Annals of Imperial Rome*, tr. M. Grant (Harmondsworth: Penguin, 1973, 1975).

R. Syme, *Tacitus*, 2 vols. (Oxford: Clarendon, 1958); H.W. Benario, "Recent Work on Tacitus," *CW* 58 (1964–1965):69–83; 63 (1969–1970): 253–267; 71 (1977–1978):1–32; 80 (1986–1987): 73–147 (bibliographical surveys covering 1954–1983).

TALL BROTHERS. Monks of Egypt in the late fourth–early fifth century. The desert monks Dioscorus (a bishop), Ammonius, Eusebius, and Euthymius, known as the Tall Brothers because of their height, were excommunicated by Theophilus of Alexandria in 401 as adherents of Origen, but also for reasons of ecclesiastical politics. They were received at Constantinople by John Chrysostom, who tried to bring about a reconciliation of the dispute; the incident was one of the events that led to the Synod of the Oak in 403. *See also* Ammonius; Oak, Synod of. [M.P.McH.]

Bibliography
Socrates, *Church History* 6.7, 9, 16; Sozomen, *Church History* 6.30; 8.12, 13, 17.

TATIAN (second century). Greek apologist, creator of the *Diatessaron*. Born into a pagan family in east Syria, Tatian was educated as a rhetorician, but he seems to have read widely in philosophy, both in compendia and in individual authors. His travels took him west to major Mediterranean cities, including Antioch. At Rome, he met Justin Martyr and may have become a Christian there (Eusebius, *H.E.* 4.16, 29). Later, he made his way back to Mesopotamia, where he founded a school. His influence was particularly strong in Syria, Cilicia, and Pisidia.

His *Diatessaron*, a harmony of four (or five) Gospels, may have been created for lessons in his school. It became the normal text of many Syriac-speaking churches well into the fifth century, when it was replaced by the four Gospels. The work is lost, but a Greek fragment found at Dura-Europos has strengthened the case for its being written in Greek, although it may have been composed in Syriac.

Tatian also wrote *On Morals* and *On Perfection According to the Savior*, and he perhaps planned a piece on *Those Who Have Propounded Ideas About God*. His Encratite beliefs, opposing marriage and the eating of meat, were related to Gnostic doctrines (Eusebius, *H.E.* 4.29; Epiphanius, *Haer.* 1.3). His *Oration to the Greeks* is interesting rhetorically as an example of Asiatic style. CPG I, 1104–1106. TLG 1766.   [F.W.N.]

Bibliography

Irenaeus, *Against Heresies* 1.28; 3.23.8; Clement of Alexandria, *Miscellanies* 3.12.81–82; *Selections from Prophetic Scriptures* 36; Origen, *On Prayer* 24.5; idem, *Against Celsus* 1.16; Eusebius, *Church History* 4.16.7; 4.29; 5.13.8.

H.W. Hogg, tr. "The Diatessaron of Tatian," ANF (1896), Vol. 10, pp. 35–138; M. Whittaker, ed. and tr., *Tatian: Oratio ad Graecos and Fragments* (Oxford: Clarendon, 1982).

G.F. Hawthorne, "Tatian and His Discourse to the Greeks," *HThR* 57 (1964):161–188; W.L. Petersen, "New Evidence for the Question of the Original Language of the Diatessaron," *Studien zum Text und zur Ethik des Neuen Testaments: Festschrift . . . Heinrich Greeven*, ed. W. Schrage (Berlin: de Gruyter, 1986), pp. 325–343.

TE DEUM. Latin hymn ("To You, O God," we offer praise). The *Te Deum* offers the praise of all creation to God the Father and to Christ the Savior. Although it has been attributed to Ambrose or Augustine since the ninth century, modern scholarship has suggested that Niceta of Remesiana was the author. The rhythmic prose is unusual for Latin hymns of the fourth century and later. The content combines biblical formulas with imperial acclamations. The *Te Deum* may have originated in the Paschal vigil service, perhaps as a translation from Greek. It found a daily use in the office of Matins in monastic circles and has remained popular in many modern musical settings. *See also* Hymns; Niceta of Remesiana.
                                    [E.F.]

Bibliography

Caesarius of Arles, *Regula ad monachos* 21.

A.E. Burn, *The Hymn Te Deum and Its Author* (London: Faith, 1926); E. Kähler, *Studien zum Te Deum und zur Geschichte des 24 Psalmes in der alten Kirche* (Göttingen: Vandenhoeck & Ruprecht, 1958).

TEACHER. In Greco-Roman society, teachers ranged from those who instructed children to philosophers and professors of rhetoric. Teaching among the Jews was the responsibility of wise men, scribes, rabbis, and the synagogue *chazan* (servant). One of the common titles of address to Jesus was "Teacher" (Matt. 8:19; 12:38; 22:16; "Rabbi" in John 1:39; cf. 20:16). In the early church, teaching was performed by apostles, prophets, bishops, and presbyters; but there was also a separate order of teachers. Teachers were among the Spirit-inspired ministers, listed after apostles and prophets (1 Cor. 12:28; cf. Acts 13:1) and closely associated with pastors (Eph. 4:11; cf. 1 Tim. 5:17), but were also persons with ordinary gifts (Rom. 12:7; James 3:1; Heb. 5:12). Teaching took place in the assembly (1 Cor. 14:26; cf. 1 Tim. 4:13) as well as in smaller groups. It is usually assumed that teachers were concerned mainly with instruction in morals and drawing out the implications of the revelation, but the texts do not give much guidance about the content of the instruction given by teachers. The principle was laid down that teachers should be supported by those whom they taught (Gal. 6:6).

The *Didache* 11; 13; 15 refers to traveling teachers, but such itinerant ministers soon had their function absorbed in the located ministries. Teachers appear in Hermas in lists of functionaries, associated with but distinct from apostles and bishops (*Vis.* 3.5.1; 9.15.4; 9.25). The author of *2 Clement* may have been a teacher, and the author of *Barnabas* refers to himself in such a way as to make it likely that he was a teacher (1.8; 4.9; 9.9). Private schools were conducted by Justin Martyr (*Acts of Justin* 3–4), Tatian (Irenaeus, *Haer.* 1.28), and Pantaenus (Eusebius, *H.E.* 5.10). The great Gnostic leaders, such as Valentinus (Irenaeus, *Haer.* 1.11), were independent teachers.

The church at Alexandria from early days had teachers in addition to the clergy (Clement of Alexandria, *Str.* 1.1.11; for the villages of Egypt, cf. Dionysius of Alexandria in Eusebius, *H.E.* 7.24.7). The most famous of these teachers was Origen, who while still a youth was called by bishop Demetrius to give up his private teaching and take charge of the instruction of catechumens (Eusebius, *H.E.* 6.3.1–3, 8). Origen was one of the last great voices in the early church on behalf of the rights of the teacher, the one learned in the word of God, over against the organized hierarchy of the church (*Jo.* 1.3–4; *Hom.* 2.1 *in Num.*; *Hom.* 1.4 *in Lev.*).

Teachers as a separate category are found principally in the role of catechists preparing converts for baptism (Hippolytus, *Trad. ap.* 16; 18; 19). This activity was under the direction of the bishop, and increasingly the activities of the ordained ministers left no room for the unordained teachers. *See also* Bishop; Catechesis, Cathumenate; Evangelist; Presbyter; Prophet, Prophecy.　　　　　　　　[E.F.]

Bibliography

C.V. Harris, "Origen's Interpretation of the Teacher's Function in the Early Christian Hierarchy and Community" (Ph.D. diss., Duke University, 1952); U. Neymeyer, *Die christlichen Lehrer in 2. Jahrhundert* (Leiden: Brill, 1988).

TERTULLIAN (fl. 200). North African Christian writer and apologist. The traditional account of Tertullian's life has relied heavily upon Jerome (*Vir. ill.* 53) and Eusebius of Caesarea (*H.E.* 2.2): born in Africa ca. 160, the son of a centurion, he became a jurisconsult at Rome, then was converted in middle age, was made a presbyter of the church, but finally lapsed into Montanism and died at a very great age. However, neither Eusebius nor Jerome is in this matter a dependable witness, and what can be known with certainty about Tertullian's life must be gathered from his own writings; unfortunately, their highly rhetorical character often makes inference insecure. We cannot determine the date of his birth or death, and we are able to date confidently only some of his writings between the years 196/7 and 212. His apparently extensive education suggests that he came from a family of some means and perhaps social standing: one of his relatives was a man of letters (*Praesc.* 39.4). He himself wrote in both Latin and Greek and was highly skilled in rhetoric, and his writings reveal a wide if not always deep knowledge of literature, philosophy, and medicine. In general, his intellectual formation appears to reflect the modalities of the Second Sophistic (a rhetorical movement dominant from the second to fourth centuries). From two treatises *To His Wife*, it is natural to infer that he was married, although it is possible that the addressee is a rhetorical fiction. That he was a convert from paganism is suggested by his use of the first person plural in several passages: "the kind of persons we ourselves once were—blind, without the light of the Lord" (*Paenit.* 1.1; cf. *Fug.* 6.2; *Apol.* 18.4). From a similar comment (*Cult. fem.* 1.7.2), it is usually assumed that Tertullian spent some time in Rome, but allusions in his writings leave no doubt that he pursued his career as a Christian literary artist in Carthage. Scholarly opinion is sharply divided on the question of his relations with the Jews, but it is not altogether untenable that he had an intimate knowledge of them and was influenced by Judaism. His later writings reveal a growing commitment, beginning possibly ca. 205, to Montanism, but neither the form of Montanism he espoused nor the manner in which he espoused it can be clearly determined. It is quite possible that Tertullian never formally separated from the church of Carthage.

Writings. The manuscript tradition has handed down thirty-one of Tertullian's treatises. References in his own writings, however, as well as the allusions of others, primarily Jerome, indicate that a number of treatises (possibly a dozen) have been lost; three of these were written in Greek for which we have Latin counterparts: *On the Shows*, *On Baptism*, *On the Veiling of Virgins*. It is convenient to divide the extant treatises into three groups: Apologetic; Controversial; and Disciplinary, Moral, and Ascetical.

(1) Apologetic: From a rhetorical point of view, Tertullian's *Apology* (A.D. 197) marks the climax of Christian efforts in the second century to speak to pagans in polished literary forms, for it combines into a tightly knit whole two genres, the "defense" on behalf of Christians and the "exhortation" to the pagans to turn to Christianity. It was preceded by an artistically less satisfactory "exhortation" *To the Nations*. Probably from the same year comes the little literary jewel *On the Witness of the Soul*, based on the forensic image of the court-witness; possibly also the treatise *Against the Jews*, of which, however, only the first eight chapters are regarded as genuine.

(2) Controversial: During the datable middle years of his literary activity (ca. 203–208), Tertullian wrote against Gnosticism a series of treatises that taken together appear to form a deliberate "program" for the defense and exposition of nascent orthodox doctrine. The works include a discussion of Christian belief about scripture, tradition, and reason (*On the Prescription Against Heretics*); God (*Against Hermogenes*); Christ (*On the Flesh of Christ*); the soul (*On the Soul*); and the creation and destination of the body and the final judgment (*On the Resurrection of the Flesh*). These doctrinal discussions culminate in the massive work *Against Marcion* in five books. Somewhat later (ca. 210), now in his clearly Montanist phase, Tertullian addressed to the church his treatise *Against Praxeas*, defining the formula for what became the orthodox doctrine of the Trinity.

(3) Disciplinary, Moral, and Ascetical: A large number of treatises address problems of Christian ethics and ecclesiastical discipline. They are spread over Tertullian's entire literary career and are marked by a gradually increasing rigidity of tone and extravagance of argument. They include two treatises, *On Penitence* and *On Modesty*, long central to discussions on the ancient practice of penance, while a number of others offer vivid images of the life and practices of the early church, and particularly of Christian women in antiquity.

Importance. Tertullian's penchant for the sharply defined formula and for the colorful word pictures of contemporary life has given his writings considerable importance in modern theological discussion, particularly on such issues as the relation between faith and reason and between Christianity and culture; he is germane as well to any reflection on the traditional Christological and Trinitarian formulations. Recent scholarship has stressed the importance of his writings as a witness to the creative impulse in early African Christianity toward the development of language and literary forms in which Christian faith could find appropriate expression in a Latin-speaking culture. Tertullian was the first significant Christian author to write in Latin. Although it is open to question to what extent Christian Latin literature existed before him, there can be no doubt about his own creativity in the use of Latin to convey Christian concepts. Similarly, his experimentation in literary forms, although not always producing the success of the *Apology*, remains an important witness to early efforts to domicile Christian faith in the contemporary culture.

In spite of his later commitment to Montanism, Tertullian enjoyed a measure of popularity in antiquity, the Middle Ages, and the Renaissance. Lactantius read him, and Jerome's admiration is implied in the story he records of Cyprian, who was said to have called Tertullian his "master" (*Vir. ill.* 53). Four major manuscript traditions, the first traceable to the mid-fifth century, transmitted his work through the Middle Ages. Shortly after the invention of the printing press, an edition of the *Apology* appeared (1483). In 1521, Johann Froben of Basel published the first "Collected Works," edited by Beatus Rhenanus. CPL 1–36.

[R.D.S.]

Bibliography

A. Reifferscheid and G. Wissowa, eds., CSEL (1890), Vol. 20; A. Kroymann, ed., CSEL (1939), Vol. 47; H. Hoppe, ed., CSEL (1939), Vol. 69; A. Kroymann, ed., CSEL (1942), Vol. 70; J.W. Ph. Borleffs et al., eds., CCSL (1954), Vols. 1–2; J.H. Waszink and J.C.M. van Winden, eds., *De Idolatria* (Leiden: Brill, 1987).

P. Holmes and S. Thelwell, trs., ANF (1885), Vols. 3–4; R. Arbesmann et al., trs., FOTC (1950), Vol. 10 and (1959), Vol. 40.

T.D. Barnes, *Tertullian: A Historical and Literary Study* (Oxford: Oxford UP, 1971); R.D. Sider, *Ancient Rhetoric and the Art of Tertullian* (Oxford: Oxford UP, 1971); J.C. Fredouille, *Tertullien et le conversion de la culture antique* (Paris: Etudes Augustiniennes, 1972); R. Braun, *Deus Christianorum: recherches sur le vocabulaire doctrinal de Tertullien*, 2nd ed. (Paris: Etudes Augustiniennes, 1977); R.D. Sider, "Approaches to Tertullian: A Study of Recent Scholarship," *SCent* 2 (1982):228–260; G. Hallonsten, *Satisfactio bei Tertullian: Überprüfung einer Forschungstradition* (Malmö: Gleerup, 1984); A. Viviano, *Cristo Salvador y Liberador del hombre: Estudio sobre la soteriologia de Tertulliano* (Pamplona: Universidad de Navarra, 1986).

TESTAMENT OF OUR LORD. Church order based on the *Apostolic Tradition* of Hippolytus and dated variously from the fourth to the sixth century. The Greek original is lost, but the work survives in a Syriac translation made by the Monophysite Jacob of Edessa in the seventh century; it exists also in Ethiopic and Arabic. The *Testament* is cast in the form of a report by the apostles of Jesus' conversation with them after the resurrection. Book 1 begins with an apocalyptic section giving signs preceding the coming of Antichrist and then gives directions for the construction of church buildings. Instructions concerning the ordination and duties of the clergy discuss the bishop, presbyters, deacons, confessors, widows, subdeacons, readers, virgins, and spiritual gifts. Book 2 covers catechumens, baptism, confirmation, eucharist, agape, Pasch, burial, Psalms, and prayer. The compiler had a high doctrine of the Trinity and enthusiastic praise for celibacy. CPG I, 1743. [E.F.]

Bibliography

A. Vööbus, *The Synodicon in the West Syrian Tradition* I, CSCO (1975), Vols. 367, pp. 1–49 (text), and 368, pp. 27–64 (tr.); J. Cooper and A.J. Maclean, *The Testament of Our Lord Translated into English from the Syriac* (Edinburgh: T. & T. Clark, 1902).

J. Wordsworth, "The Testament of Our Lord," *Internationale theologische Zeitschrift* 8 (1900):452–472; R.G. Coquin, "Le Testamentum Domini: problèmes de tradition textuelle," *ParOr* 5 (1974):165–188.

TESTAMENT OF SOLOMON. Pseudepigraphic writing (ca. third century) by a Greek-speaking Christian. The *Testament of Solomon* presents Solomon as a great magician with power over demons who prophesies the coming of Christ. That Solomon's knowledge (1 Kings 4:29–34) included magical powers frequently appears in Jewish sources (e.g., Josephus, *Antiquities* 8.2.5 [44–49]), and Jewish tales lie behind the present *Testament*. The contents have contacts with Jewish haggadic traditions, Gnostic texts from Nag Hammadi, and the magical papyri. The author substitutes Christian magic for pagan magic. The *Testament* is a rich source for popular ideas about demons, angels, and astrology but affirms the authority of Christ over demons. TLG 2679.

[E.F.]

Bibliography

C.C. McCown, ed., *The Testament of Solomon* (Leipzig: Hinrich, 1922).

D.C. Duling, tr., "Testament of Solomon," *The Old Testament Pseudepigrapha*, ed. J. H. Charlesworth (Garden City: Doubleday, 1983), Vol. 1, pp. 935–987.

TESTAMENT OF THE FORTY MARTYRS OF SEBASTE. The fourth-century story, minimal details of which are given by Sozomen, of forty soldiers martyred under the emperor Licinius (308–324) in Sebaste, Armenia. These martyrs were eulogized by Basil the Great, Gregory of Nyssa, and Ephraem the Syrian. The historicity of their martyrdom and the *Testament* is much debated. TLG 2015. [D.M.S.]

Bibliography

Sozomen, *Church History* 9.2; Basil of Caesarea, *In quadraginta martyres Sebastenses* (PG 31.508–525); Gregory of Nyssa, *Encomium in xl martyres* I and II (PG 46.749–788).

Musurillo, pp. xlix–1, 354–361.

TEXT CRITICISM. Science that attempts to establish the original text and later transmission of ancient documents. The need for such work on the Greek Old Testament (LXX) and the New Testament results from factors prevailing in the early church. Most of the copying errors that made their way into the stream of history were created during the first 300 years of Christianity. However, the sacred character of these documents resulted in the preservation of an abundance of evidence: ancient copies of the Greek text itself, copies of early translations (e.g., Latin, Syriac, Coptic), and biblical citations in the early church fathers. The following discussion will concentrate on the contributions of patristic literature to the discipline of textual criticism.

Patristic citations, when carefully reconstructed and evaluated, offer datable evidence from a specific geographical location, but the difficulty lies in gathering and evaluating the data. The gathering of citations has recently been aided by two major projects: *Biblia Patristica: index des citations et allusions bibliques dans la littérature patristique* (Paris: Centre National de la Recherche Scientifique, 1975–), which indexes all patristic biblical citations, including every imaginable allusion, and *The New Testament in the Greek Fathers* (Atlanta: Scholars, 1987–), a series that seeks to present the New Testament text of the Greek fathers, with a full evaluation of the evidence's usefulness for text criticism. It is evaluating the data that presents the most problems. One cannot always be sure whether an author was copying from his Bible directly or was citing from memory. Furthermore, the citation habits of authors are diverse: some quotations are precise; others are close but reflect a lack of concern for exactness (cf. Paul's citations of the Old Testament); still others are notoriously loose. In addition, the writings of the fathers have themselves gone through a long process of transmission, so that one cannot always be sure that our extant copies represent exactly what a given father wrote or whether copyists modified the biblical citations to conform to later texts with which they were more familiar.

Nonetheless, there remains a large body of valuable evidence. A citation can be evaluated as to its degree of certainty. It can be considered absolutely certain, for example, when in the subsequent discussion the author makes a point of the very words of the biblical text; or when he refers to an alternative reading to the one in his text; or when in a homily or controversial treatise the author repeatedly cites the text in the same way. A relative degree of certainty can also be sustained where scholarship has clearly established a father's overall text and habits of citation.

An example of how patristic evidence is of great value in determining the original New Testament text on any given point of variation is John Chrysostom's reading of John 7:1 as "For he did not *have authority* to go about in Judea," instead of "He did not *wish* to." This evidence, along with the evidence of one Old Syriac version and the Latin versions, as well as Codex W from Egypt, places the reading in every corner of the ancient world at a very early date. It is probably the original text at this point: the reading that best explains how the other(s) came about is to be preferred as the original.

Once the patristic material has been carefully worked through, enough certain evidence remains to help put some pieces into place, at least for the history of the New Testament text. During the second century, the citing of the New Testament tended to be more relaxed, since the documents, even though authoritative, were not yet considered sacred scripture. Thus, Clement of Rome, who tended to cite the Old Testament rather exactly, used the New Testament materials much more loosely. This phenomenon is in part responsible for a large number of the variant readings that exist in the textual tradition. By the time of Irenaeus, Tertullian, and Origen, the situation had changed. Origen, in particular, cited his New Testament generally with great precision and is a significant witness for the text as it circulated in Alexandria in the first half of the third century, and later in Caesarea, where he moved in 230. Even among some later writers with the loosest habits in citation, such as Epiphanius of Salamis, who cites some texts in as many as seven different forms and seldom if ever cites precisely, one can still determine the general character of the New Testament they used.

What we learn from this evidence is that two distinct forms of the New Testament existed in the east and west. The last authors in the west to write in Greek, Hippolytus of Rome and Irenaeus, used Greek texts that looked very much like those that lay behind the earliest Latin versions on which Tertullian, and all subsequent writers in Latin, were clearly dependent. A different picture emerged in Egypt, where the basic text, such as that found in Origen and the earliest Greek manuscripts from this area, seems to be a good preservation of the original texts themselves. When Origen moved to Caesarea, however, he began to use a New Testament that differed considerably from that in Alexandria. A similar, somewhat mixed text can also be found in other early writers from this area, such as Eusebius, Epiphanius, and Basil. At a still later date, John Chrysostom in Antioch and then in Constantinople was using a text much like that of Basil but one that had been modified considerably, so that it was about seventy-five percent along the way to the text that would eventually dominate in the Greek church and that lay behind the King James Version of the New Testament. *See also* Hexapla; Manuscripts; Papyri; Septuagint.   [G.D.F.]

Bibliography

B.M. Metzger, "The Practice of Textual Criticism Among the Church Fathers," *New Testament Studies: Philological, Versional, and Patristic* (Leiden: Brill, 1950), Ch. 12; idem, *The Text of the New Testament*, 2nd ed. (New York: Oxford UP, 1968); G.D. Fee, "The Text of John in Origen and Cyril of Alexandria: A Contribution to Methodology in the Recovery and Analysis of Patristic Citations," *Biblica* 52 (1971):357–394; B.M. Metzger, "Patristic Evidence and the Textual Criticism of the New Testament," *NTS* 18 (1971–1972):379–400; G.D. Fee, "The Text of John in *The Jerusalem Bible*: A Critique of the Use of Patristic Citations in the New Testament Textual Criticism," *JBL* 90 (1971):163–173; K. and B. Aland, *The Text of the New Testament: An Introduction to the Critical Editions and to the Theory and Practice of Modern Textual Criticism* (Grand Rapids: Eerdmans, 1987).

THECLA (first century?). Virgin and martyr. Thecla is described in the apocryphal *Acts of Paul* as a convert and then companion of Paul who, after baptizing herself, cutting her hair, and dressing like a man, was commissioned by Paul to teach the word of God. The Thecla story was popular and circulated independently as the *Acts of Paul and Thecla* (and under other titles), known in Greek, Latin, Syriac, Slavic, and Arabic versions. The example of Thecla was cited, as by the *Acts of Paul*, in support of women's leadership role in the church (including teaching and baptizing), as indicated by Tertullian's polemic (*Bapt.* 17).

The cult of Thecla became widespread, holding special attraction for women. She was frequently referred to and discussed in the literature of the church as a virgin of great virtue and importance. Many women were named after her. A chapel was built in her honor at Seleucia of Isauria in southern Asia Minor, the place of her death. The pilgrim Egeria describes a fourth-century visit to the chapel, noting that the "Acts of Holy Thecla" were read in their entirety in the service (*Itin. Aeth.* 22–23). Emperor Zeno enlarged this chapel in the fifth century. In the sixth century, Justinian built a church in Constantinople in her honor. Many inscriptions and sculptures also honor Thecla. Feast day September 23 (west), September 24 (east). *See also* Acts of Paul.   [D.M.S.]

Bibliography

Methodius, *Symposium* 11; Gregory of Nyssa, *Homily* 14 *on the Song of Songs*; idem, *Life of Macrina* 2; Gregory of Nazianzus, *Oration Against Julian* 1.69; Ambrose, *Letter* 63; idem, *Concerning Virgins* 2.3; John Chrysostom, *Homily* 25 *on the Acts of the Apostles* 4; Pseudo-Chrysostom, *De s. Thecla martyre*; Pseudo-Basil of Seleucia, *De vita et miraculis s. Theclae*; Epiphanius, *Panarion* 47.1–2; Jerome, *Letter* 22.41; Sulpicius Severus, *Dialogues* 2.13.5; *Acts of Xanthippe and Polyxena* 36.

NTA, Vol. 2, pp. 322–390.

G. Dagron, *Vie et miracles de sainte Thécle* (Brussels: Société des Bollandistes, 1978); J. Wilkinson, *Egeria's Travels to the Holy Land* (Jerusalem: Ariel; Warminster: Aris and Phillips, 1981), pp. 288–292; D.R. MacDonald, *The Legend and the Apostle: The Battle for Paul in Story and Canon* (Philadelphia: Westminster, 1983).

THEMISTIUS (ca. 317–388). Pagan rhetorician and statesman. Themistius taught rhetoric in Constantinople, became a member of the city's senate, and was prefect of the city (383–384). His official speeches set forth the political ideology of monarchy, and the emperor Julian wrote to him a letter setting forth his program for the restoration of paganism. Themistius's explanatory paraphrases of Aristotle are important in the history of the interpretation of Aristotle. Although a pagan, he had the respect of Christians, many of whom studied under him.   [E.F.]

Bibliography

Julian, *Letter to Themistius*; Gregory of Nazianzus, *Epistulae* 24; 38.

THEMISTIUS (sixth century). Deacon at Alexandria. A Monophysite, Themistius nonetheless advocated Christ's ignorance of some things on the basis of Mark 13:32 and John 11:34 and became a founder of the sect of Agnoetae. Only fragments of his writings survive. Eulogius of Alexandria attacked his views; he was anathematized by Sophronius of Jerusalem and Gregory the Great. CPG III, 7285–7292.   [E.F.]

Bibliography

Leontius of Byzantium, *De sectis* 10.3; John of Damascus, *Haereses* 85; Photius, *Library* 23; 108; 230.

THEODORA (ca. 500–548). Eastern empress (527–548), wife of Justinian I. An actress, Theodora married Justinian several years before their accession to the throne as co-rulers in 527. Throughout the joint reign, she had the full confidence of her husband, and it was through her firm exercise of political skills that Justinian and she were able to withstand the Nika rebellion in 532. She aimed at moral reform and, along with her husband, promoted the foundation of hospitals. She supported the revival of Byzantine art; her portrait appears in the mosaics in the Church of S. Vitale in Ravenna.

Upon the death of the Roman bishop Agapetus I in Constantinople (536), Theodora supported Vigilius for the Roman see as one who would be sympathetic, she thought, to her religious purposes. When Byzantine forces captured Rome from the Goths in 537, Justinian's general Belisarius forced the election of Vigilius despite the fact that Silverius had been elevated to the see in the meantime. Silverius was sent into exile, then promised a fair hearing by Justinian, and finally sent into a second, fatal exile through the agency of Belisarius and Vigilius.

The empress consistently favored the Monophysites and, in an unsuccessful bid to reconcile them to the imperial church, influenced Justinian to issue his condemnation of the Three Chapters (544) to the detriment of the decrees of the Council of Chalcedon. (The complex affair of Vigilius and the Three Chapters produced a schism in the west that would continue for many years.)

Jacob Baradaeus lived for some time under Theodora's protection in Constantinople; after his consecration as bishop (ca. 542), he devoted himself to missionary efforts that led to the foundation of the Monophysite church of Syria, the Jacobites. With the empress's support, Julian, a Monophysite priest, made the first attempt to convert the inhabitants of Nubia (542–543).

The account of Theodora's career reported in the *Secret History* of Procopius of Caesarea (sixth century) must be used with great caution, since it is in large measure biased against both the empress and Justinian. *See also* Justinian; Monophysites; Three Chapters; Vigilius.   [M.P.McH.]

Bibliography

H. de Lancker, *Théodora, impératrice d'Orient* (Paris: Hachette, 1968); R. Browning, *Justinian and Theodora* (New York: Praeger, 1971; 2nd ed., London and New York: Thames and Hudson, 1987); C. Diehl, *Theodora, Empress of Byzantium* (New York: Ungar, 1972); A.C. Bridge, *Theodora: Portrait in a Byzantine Landscape* (London: Cassell, 1978); J.A.S. Evans, "The Nika Rebellion and the Empress Theodora," *Byzantion* 54 (1984):380–382.

THEODORE OF MOPSUESTIA (ca. 350–428). Bishop and theologian. Like John Chrysostom, Theodore was a pupil of the pagan rhetor Libanius and of Diodore of Tarsus.

It seems likely that he was the Theodore whom Chrysostom urged to return to monasticism from a worldly career and a projected marriage. Little else is known of Theodore's life save that he was bishop of Mopsuestia in Asia Minor from 392 until his death in 428. Like Diodore, Theodore was a vigorous supporter of the new Nicene orthodoxy of the Council of Constantinople (381) and was a foe of both the Arians and the Apollinarians. Also like Diodore, he was regarded by Cyril of Alexandria as a Nestorian before Nestorius. Theodore was condemned by the Second Council of Constantinople in 553, when Justinian sought to appease the Monophysites by condemning Nestorianizing views.

Theodore's theological views are known to us largely through fragments of his dogmatic writings in Greek, a Syriac translation of his *Controversy with the Macedonians*, and his catechetical homilies, discovered in Syriac translation in 1932. His Christology strongly distinguishes Christ's natures. The divine Word is the subject of Christ's divine activities. The "assumed Man" is the subject of Christ's human activities, including his miracles and his special knowledge. The major problem of Theodore's Christology is to explain how these two subjects make up a single Christ. He says that they are one and the same in *prosōpon* (person). Theodore's most careful exposition of the unity of Christ's person makes use of the analogy of grace and repudiates the Apollinarian (and Alexandrian) use of the analogy of the body-soul relation. He says that the Word of God indwelt the assumed man "by good pleasure [grace] as in a Son." He seeks to distinguish this gracious indwelling from what can be found in the prophets, the righteous, and the wise.

Only a small part of Theodore's exegetical writings is preserved. His youthful commentary on Psalms has been partially reconstructed, some of it only in Latin translation. His commentary on the minor prophets is preserved in Greek, and that on the minor epistles of Paul has been found in a Latin translation. A Syriac translation of his commentary on John was published in 1940. Fragments from his other commentaries have been found and collected.

Enough remains to give us a reasonably clear idea of Theodore's approach to scripture. His concern is with a careful exposition of the text at the narrative level (*historia*). Most striking is Theodore's preoccupation with giving the Old Testament autonomy. Trinitarian references are excluded in principle from the Old Testament, and predictive prophecy is severely reduced. David in the Psalms prophesied the whole of Israel's future, but only four Psalms (2; 8; 45; 110) are predictions of Christ. None of the prophets predicts Christ save for Malachi, who revived David's messianic prophecy on the eve of the incarnation. On the other hand, much of the Old Testament has not only a narrative meaning but also a spiritual meaning (*theoria*) that is typological. Without abolishing the narrative meaning for its own time, the interpreter can often also see a typological hint that intimates what may be found clearly in Christ. CPG II, 3827–3873.   [R.A.G.]

Bibliography

H.B. Swete, *Theodori episcopi Mopsuesteni in epistulas B. Pauli commentarii*, 2 vols. (Cambridge: Cambridge UP, 1880–1882); K. Staab, *Pauluskommentare aus der griechischen Kirche* (Münster: Aschendorff, 1933), pp. 113–172; R. Devreesse, *Le Commentaire de Théodore de Mopsueste sur les Psaumes* (Vatican City: Biblioteca Apostolica Vaticana, 1939).

A. Mingana, *Woodbrooke Studies* (Cambridge: Cambridge UP, 1932, 1933), Vol. 5 ("The Commentary of Theodore of Mopsuestia on the Nicene Creed"), Vol. 6 ("The Commentary of Theodore of Mopsuestia on the Lord's Prayer and on the Sacraments of Baptism and the Eucharist").

R. Devreesse, *Essai sur Théodore de Mopsueste* (Vatican City: Biblioteca Apostolica Vaticana, 1948); F.A. Sullivan, *The Christology of Theodore of Mopsuestia* (Rome: Pontifical Gregorian UP, 1956); R.A. Greer, *Theodore of Mopsuestia, Exegete and Theologian* (London: Faith, 1961); R.A. Norris, *Manhood and Christ: A Study in the Christology of Theodore of Mopsuestia* (Oxford: Clarendon, 1963); A. Vööbus, "Regarding the Theological Anthropology of Theodore of Mopsuestia," *ChHist* 33 (1964):115–124; R.P. Vaggione, "Some Neglected Fragments of Theodore of Mopsuestia's 'Contra Eunomium,'" *JThS* n.s. 30 (1980):403–470; D.Z. Zaharopoulos, *Theodore of Mopsuestia on the Bible* (New York: Paulist, 1989).

THEODORET OF CYRUS (393–460 [or 457/8 or 466]). Bishop and theologian. Born of devout Christian parents at Antioch, Theodoret was educated in monastic schools and appointed bishop of Cyrus in 423. He was scholarly and retiring by nature but led an active episcopal life, becoming deeply involved in both secular affairs and theological controversies. According to his letters, he guided the erection of bridges and public buildings in his diocese and strove vigorously, and successfully, to uproot pagan and Arian elements that survived there. Often described as an unoriginal and derivative theologian, he was nevertheless dominant in his primary area of theological influence, Christology. In the controversy between Nestorius and Cyril of Alexandria, he emerged as a leading figure, defending the two-nature Christology, which was typical of theologians from Antioch and which Nestorius pushed to extreme limits. He was the principal spokesperson for this view in the deliberations that surrounded the Council of Ephesus in 431. Although he composed major documents for the Nestorian party at this time, he was reluctant to join John of Antioch and other episcopal colleagues who used those same documents to make peace with Cyril and his adherents in the years following the council. His *Eranistes*, written in 447, was a thinly veiled attack on Cyril's Christology, which Theodoret viewed as Apollinarian and intrinsically Monophysite; such views and activity brought him into conflict with Cyril's successor Dioscorus, and led, first, to his being confined to his diocese as a troublemaker, and then, in 449, to his deposition and exile by the "Robber Council" of Ephesus. During this disastrous period, his letters expressed the anger and unhappiness he felt because of a judgment, considered by him unjust, that forced him to live in the very monastic tranquility that he had often professed to desire. In his frustration, he even sent to Dioscorus a statement of faith in which he denies teaching two Sons and accepts the use of *Theotokos* for the mother of Jesus. With the accession of Marcian to the imperial throne in 450, Theodoret's fortunes changed; he was restored to his position and to an active role in the church by the Council of Chalcedon in 451, after proving his orthodoxy through the repudiation, seemingly under compulsion, of

Nestorius and his teachings. In 553, his writings against Cyril of Alexandria and the Council of Ephesus were anathematized as part of the Three Chapters condemned by the Council of Constantinople under the influence of the emperor Justinian.

Many writings attributed to him, especially those against Cyril and the Council of Ephesus, have perished. Those that survive include commentaries on numerous books of the Old Testament and on Paul's letters; *A History of the Monks of Syria*, which relates the lives of holy monks (including three women); a *Church History* from 323 to 428; a *Haereticarum fabularum compendium*, which also provides information on his contemporaries Nestorius and Eutyches; doctrinal discourses, as *De providentia*; an apologetical treatise against paganism, *Graecarum affectionum curatio*; a Christological dialogue, *Eranistes* (see above); a few homilies; some 200 letters; and several brief works, mostly on Christology, some of which are spurious. CPG III, 6200-6288. TLG 4089. *See also* Christ, Christology; Cyril of Alexandria; Nestorius; Three Chapters. [G.H.E.]

Bibliography

PG 80–84; *Correspondance*, ed. Y. Azéma, SC (1955, 1964, 1965), Vols. 40, 98, 111; *Thérapeutique des maladies helléniques*, ed. P. Canivet, SC (1958), Vol. 57, 2 parts; *Historie des moines de Syrie*, ed. P. Canivet and A. Leroy-Molinghen, SC (1977, 1979), Vols. 234, 257; *Eranistes. Critical Text and Prolegomena*, ed. G.H. Ettlinger (Oxford: Clarendon, 1975); *Commentaire sur Isaïe*, ed. J.-N. Guinot, SC (1980, 1982), Vols. 276, 295; *Kirchengeschichte*, ed. F. Scheidweiler, GCS (1954), Vol. 44(19).

B. Jackson, tr., NPNF, 2nd ser. (1892), Vol. 3; R.M. Price, tr., *Theodoret of Cyrrhus: A History of the Monks of Syria* (Kalamazoo: Cistercian, 1986); T. Halton, tr., *On Divine Providence*, ACW (1989), Vol. 49.

M. Richard, "L'activité littéraire de Théodoret avant le Concile d'Ephèse," *Revue des Sciences Philosophiques et Théologiques* 24 (1935):83–106; idem, "Notes sur l'évolution doctrinal de Théodoret," *Revue des Sciences Philosophiques et Théologiques* 25 (1936):459–481; E. Honigmann, "Theodoret of Cyrrhus and Basil of Seleucia: The Time of Their Death," *Patristic Studies*, Studi e Testi 173 (Vatican City: Biblioteca Apostolica Vaticana, 1953), pp. 174–184; R.V. Sellers, *The Council of Chalcedon: A Historical and Doctrinal Survey* (London: SPCK,

1953); idem, *Two Ancient Christologies* (London: SPCK, 1954); G. Koch, *Strukturen und Geschichte des Heils in der Theologie des Theodoret von Kyros* (Frankfurt: Knecht, 1974); P. Canivet, *Le Monachisme syrien selon Théodoret de Cyr* (Paris: Beauchesne, 1977); Y. Azéma, "La Date de la mort de Théodoret de Cyr," *Pallas* 31 (1984):137–155 and 192–193; G.F. Chesnut, *The First Christian Histories: Eusebius, Socrates, Sozomen, Theodoret and Evagrius*, 2nd ed. (Macon: Mercer UP, 1986).

THEODORIC (ca. 455–526). Ruler of the Arian Ostrogothic kingdom in Italy (493–526). The reign of Theodoric saw the first significant attempt to fuse an invading Germanic people with the indigenous Roman population. The critical factor in the social process was religion, and the religious context was Christian—Arian Goths and Catholic Rome and Italy.

Theodoric was exposed to Mediterranean culture and polity very early, spending nine years in the imperial court at Constantinople as a guarantee of favorable conduct by his father, ruler of the Ostrogoths in the Roman province of Pannonia. In 475, Theodoric, born of a father who adhered to Arianism and a Catholic mother, succeeded to the tribal leadership. The emperor Zeno was relieved to have Theodoric and his Goths move west to Italy, where the Germanic Odoacer, having deposed the imperial claimant Romulus Augustulus in 476, was the *de facto* ruler. Personally disposing of his rival, Theodoric emerged in 493 as the sole ruler of Italy.

From his court at Ravenna, Theodoric implemented a policy of social and religious toleration that lasted for two decades. He won the respect of contemporary Catholics because he recognized the autonomy of the church. The crucial religious issue of this era was schism, between Constantinople and Rome (the Acacian) and within the Roman church (the Laurentian), both intimately related. Theodoric supported the canonical claim of pope Symmachus against Laurentius and the successful efforts of pope Hormisdas to end the Acacian schism. The resolution of this complex ecclesiastical-imperial-papal dispute unfortunately led to a sad conclusion to Theodoric's reign, when toleration and cooperation were replaced by suspicion, bitterness, and executions. Theodoric had aggressively sought to Romanize his Goths

Mausoleum of Theodoric, king of the Ostrogoths (493–526), in Ravenna, Italy.

and to reinvigorate Rome and its institutions and cultural tradition. This policy involved the wide use of Roman administrators and close cooperation with the Roman senatorial aristocracy. Cassiodorus is the preeminent example of the Arian Gothic ruler's use of Catholic Roman administrators. Boethius, whom Theodoric had executed, is, however, the tragic demonstration of a social policy that ultimately failed because of the congruence of Byzantine political aims (the desire of Justinian I to reconquer the western half of the empire) and Catholic loyalists who sought deliverance from a heretical ruler. *See also* Boethius; Cassiodorus; Goths; Ravenna. [H.R.]

Bibliography

Cassiodorus, *Variae*, ed. T. Mommsen in MGH, *Auctores Antiquissimi* (1894), Vol. 12.

T. Hodgkin, *The Letters of Cassiodorus* (London: Frowde, 1886).

T. Hodgkin, *Italy and Her Invaders* (Oxford: Clarendon, 1885), Vol. 3: *The Ostrogothic Invasion, 476–535*, while dated, is useful for detailed exposition of political and ecclesiastical events; W. Ensslin, *Theoderich der Grosse*, 2nd ed. (Munich: Bruckmann, 1959); P. Llewellyn, *Rome in the Dark Ages* (New York: Praeger, 1970), esp. pp. 21–51; J. Richards, *Popes and the Papacy in the Early Middle Ages, 476–752* (Boston and London: Routledge and Kegan Paul, 1979), esp. "Part II, The Papacy and the Ostrogoths"; E.A. Thompson, *Romans and Barbarians: The Decline of the Western Empire* (Madison: U of Wisconsin P, 1982); T.A.S. Burns, *A History of the Ostrogoths* (Bloomington: Indiana UP, 1984), pp. 56–107; H. Wolfram, *History of the Goths* (Berkeley: U of California P, 1988), esp. Ch. 5.

THEODOSIUS I (346/7–395). Last emperor of the undivided Roman empire (379–395) and father of Arcadius, Honorius, and Galla Placidia. Of Spanish origin, the son of a *magister equitum* of the same name, Theodosius followed a military career but retired to his family estates in 375. Summoned by the emperor Gratian to a command against the barbarians in Illyricum after the Battle of Adrianople, he was proclaimed Augustus on January 19, 379. Theodosius managed to pacify the barbarians through military action and a treaty of 382, which allowed the Visigoths to settle within the empire under their own chiefs and to fight under their command as *foederati*, a policy that ultimately led to the dissolution of the empire in the west. After Gratian's death in 383, Theodosius ruled over the whole of the empire. In 384, he recognized the usurper Maximus, but in 388 he yielded to the plea of Valentinian II, marched westward, and defeated Maximus. He remained in Italy for three years, leaving the east under the nominal rule of his son Arcadius. In 391, he returned to Constantinople but in 394 again marched west to deal with Eugenius, who was supported by pagans opposed to the religious policies of the emperor. Supported by large numbers of federate barbarians, Theodosius was victorious at the Battle of the Frigidus on September 6. He died at Milan early the next year.

Theodosius was a staunch supporter of orthodoxy after nearly half a century of Arian emperors. In 380, shortly after his elevation, he issued an edict that declared the faith taught by the bishop of Rome to be correct, and in 381 he ordered all churches to be surrendered to the adherents of Nicaea. He summoned the first Council of Constantinople, which met in May 381 and produced a definition of faith that condemned Arianism and issued a canon that placed the bishop of Constantinople second in honor to the bishop of Rome. Theodosius at first took only mild measures against paganism, but many temples were destroyed or (often violently) converted into churches— such as the Sarapeum in Alexandria. Beginning in 391, probably under the influence of Ambrose, Theodosius issued a series of harsh laws prohibiting public or private sacrifice. These laws were a severe blow to paganism, but they did not put an end to its cults. In 390, Theodosius punished the citizens of Thessalonica for their murder of a barbarian *magister militum*, for which he was compelled by Ambrose to do penance, one of the first instances in which imperial power bowed to the moral authority of the church. [T.E.G.]

Bibliography

Ambrose, *Letter* 51, tr. H. DeRomestin, NPNF, 2nd ser. (1896), Vol. 10; idem, *Funeral Oration on Emperor Theodosius*, tr. R.J. Deferrari, FOTC (1953), Vol. 22; Pacatus, *Panegyric to the Emperor Theodosius*, tr. C.E.V. Nixon (Liverpool: Liverpool UP, 1987); Aurelius Victor, *Epitome* 48; Socrates, *Church History* 5.2–6.1; Sozomen, *Church History* 7.2–29.

W. Ensslin, *Die Religionspolitik des Kaisers Theodosios des Grosse* (Munich: Beck, 1953); N.Q. King, *The Emperor Theodosius and the Establishment of Christianity* (Philadelphia: Westminster, and London: SCM, 1961).

THEODOSIUS II (401–450). Eastern Roman emperor (408–450), son of Arcadius, brother of Pulcheria. Proclaimed Augustus on January 10, 402, Theodosius became ruler of the east upon the death of his father in 408. Theodosius was young when he came to the throne, and throughout his reign he was dominated by more powerful personalities: the prefect Anthemius, his sister Pulcheria, his wife Athenais, and the chamberlain Chrysaphius. Such a milieu presented considerable opportunity for intrigue among the political, religious, and personal factions at court. Nevertheless, important events transpired during his reign: construction of the Theodosian walls of Constantinople (begun in 413); continued struggle against paganism (e.g., the murder of Hypatia in 415 and further restrictive legislation); probable formation of a school in Constantinople (425); codification of law (*Codex Theodosianus*, 438); the ecumenical Council of Ephesus in 431 and the "Robber Council" of 449. The struggle over developing Christology dominated the religious scene and the power of the patriarchs of Constantinople continued to grow, despite the opposition of successive bishops of Alexandria. Theodosius's orthodoxy has often been questioned: he supported Nestorius until well after the latter's condemnation in 431; he then reluctantly agreed to the prohibition of Nestorianism. The controversy between Eutyches and Flavian led to the "Robber Council" of 449, whose decisions Theodosius initially supported; by the end of his life, however, influenced by Pulcheria, he seems to have had second thoughts. Personally, Theodosius was of a scholarly temperament; he had a large collection of theological books and was interested in science. According to Socrates (*H.E.* 7.22), he was of gentle and kindly nature and was reluctant to inflict capital punishment.

[T.E.G.]

Bibliography
Socrates, *Church History* 6.23–7.48; Sozomen, *Church History* 9.1; Isidore of Pelusium, *Epistulae* 1.35, 311.
J.B. Bury, *A History of the Later Roman Empire* (London and New York: Macmillan, 1889), Vol. 1, pp. 212–235; A. Güldenpenning, *Geschichte des östromischen Reiches unter den Kaisern Arcadius und Theodosius II* (Halle: Niemeyer, 1889); C. Luibhéid, "Theodosius II and Heresy," *JEH* 16 (1965):13–38.

THEODOTION (late second century). Translator of the Old Testament into Greek. According to Irenaeus, Theodotion was a Jewish proselyte from Ephesus (*Haer.* 3.21.1). He probably only revised an existing translation, since the type of translation associated with his name (typified, for example, by transliteration) is in evidence more than a century earlier. Theodotionic Daniel was so popular that it eclipsed the Septuagint version. Origen placed Theodotion's work in the sixth column of the *Hexapla* and used it extensively to fill in what was lacking where the Septuagint is shorter than the Hebrew. *See also* Hexapla; Septuagint. [C.C.]

THEODOTUS (second century). Eastern Valentinian Gnostic. Theodotus is known only from fragments, the *Excerpts from Theodotus*, preserved at the end of Clement of Alexandria's *Miscellanies*. Here, Theodotus and other anonymous Gnostics advocate common Valentinian doctrines, such as the *plērōma*, the Ogdoad, and the ranking of persons into three classes. They further describe baptism, eucharist, and anointing as means to bring freedom from the power of evil. CPG I, 1139. [R.R.]

Bibliography
R.P. Casey, *The Excerpta ex Theodoto of Clement of Alexandria* (London: Christophers, 1934); F. Sagnard, *Clément d'Alexandrie: Extraits de Théodote*, SC (1948), Vol. 23.

THEODOTUS THE BANKER (second century). Figure in the Roman church. A supporter of Theodotus the Leatherworker, Theodotus the

Banker belonged to a group that evidently claimed Jesus was a mere man and that Zephyrinus, bishop of Rome ca. 199, in his Christology had destroyed the true tradition of the church. The group is described and attacked in a work referred to by Eusebius (*H.E.* 5.28). Theodotus the Banker and Asclepiades are said to have created expurgated copies of New Testament books that conformed to the "old tradition," but they themselves could not agree on the proper contents.   [F.W.N.]

Bibliography
Hippolytus, *Refutation of All Heresies* 7.24; 10.20; Pseudo-Tertullian, *Against All Heresies* 24; Eusebius, *Church History* 5.28; Epiphanius, *Panarion* 54f.

THEODOTUS THE LEATHERWORKER

(second century). A native of Byzantium, Theodotus taught a form of Adoptionism at Rome. According to Hippolytus, Theodotus claimed that "Christ" descended upon the human Jesus at his baptism as a reward for his virtue. Epiphanius recorded that Theodotus relied on Isaiah 53:3, Jeremiah 17:9, and John 8:40 to form his theology. He is traditionally associated with other teachers of Adoptionism in second-century Rome, including Theodotus the Banker. He was condemned by Victor I of Rome. [R.L.]

Bibliography
Hippolytus, *Refutation of All Heresies* 7.35; 10.23; Eusebius, *Church History* 5.28; Epiphanius, *Panarion* 54.

THEOGNOSTUS

(d. 282). Head of the catechetical school of Alexandria (ca. 265–282) after Dionysius and before Pierius. Theognostus closely followed the thought of Origen, and his *Hypotyposeis* follows the latter's *On First Principles*. Although he spoke of the Son as a creature, he affirmed that he derived from the essence (*ousia*) of the Father. CPG I, 1626, 1628.   [E.F.]

Bibliography
Athanasius, *Letter 4 to Serapion* 11; idem, *Defense of the Nicene Definition* 25; Gregory of Nyssa, *Against Eunomius* 4.6 (3.2.121; GNO II, p. 92); Photius, *Library* 106.

L.B. Radford, *Three Teachers of Alexandria: Theognostus, Pierius, Peter* (Cambridge: Cambridge UP, 1908), pp. 1–43.

THEOPASCHITE FORMULA.

Affirmation that "one of the Trinity suffered in the flesh." The Theopaschite ("God suffered") Formula was advanced by the archimandrite John Maxentius and a group of Scythian monks active at Constantinople (ca. 519). Orthodox in itself, it was susceptible of an interpretation favorable to the Monophysites. Hormisdas, the Roman bishop, although not condemning the formula, refused his approval; it was received by the African bishops under Fulgentius of Ruspe. The emperor Justinian, concerned to gain the adherence of the moderate Monophysites, favored it; and at his request it was accepted by the Roman bishop John II in 533, a decision confirmed by his successor, Agapetus I, in 536.   [M.P.McH.]

Bibliography
J.A. McGuckin, "The 'Theopaschite Confession' (Text and Historical Context): A Study in the Cyrilline Re-interpretation of Chalcedon," *JEH* 35 (1984):239–255.

THEOPHILUS OF ALEXANDRIA (d. 412).

Bishop of Alexandria (385–412). Theophilus preceded his nephew Cyril as bishop. Energetic, decisive, even vindictive, he carried out a series of attacks against his enemies. During his early years in office, he concentrated on pagans and pagan shrines. In 391, he was actively involved in the destruction of the Sarapeum and its library. Later, he turned toward uprooting Origenism through a strong confrontation with the Tall Brothers. His running battle with the see of Constantinople and thus with John Chrysostom was also a part of this struggle. Theophilus seldom lost a chance to enhance the status of his own see. CPG II, 2580–2684; cf. CPL 484, 585, 620. TLG 4115. Feast day October 15 (Coptic), October 17 (Syrian).

           [F.W.N.]

Bibliography
PG. 65.229–268, 401–404; PL 22.758–769, 773-790, 792–812, 813–828.

A. Favale, *Teofilo d'Alessandria, 345–c. 412; scritti, vita e dottrina* (Turin: Società Editrice Internazionale, 1958).

THEOPHILUS OF ANTIOCH (second century). Bishop and apologist. Born near the Euphrates and converted as an adult, Theophilus wrote three books *To Autolycus* (ca. 180) that attack pagan idolatry and emperor worship, contrast the pagan descriptions of their gods with sayings from Old Testament prophets, and compare Christian morality with the immorality of paganism. The work is a defense of the meaning and importance of the name "Christian," a detailed allegorical interpretation of the creation accounts of Genesis, and a sketch of world chronology provided to demonstrate the historical priority of Moses and the prophets to Greek philosophers. The apology shows that Theophilus had a command of rhetoric and a knowledge of Greek philosophy that went beyond cursory handbook reference. He also quotes the *Sibylline Oracles* as authorities on monotheism and seems to be versed in contemporary Jewish apologetics, the arguments of which he employs.

Other works were lost. Eusebius (*H.E.* 4.24) mentions two treatises by name, *Against the Heresy of Hermogenes* and *Against Marcion*, as well as some catechetical writings. Jerome (*Vir. ill.* 25) speaks of those catechetical pieces and *Commentaries on the Gospel* and *On the Proverbs of Solomon*. Elsewhere, Jerome (*Ep.* 121.6.15) notes that Theophilus composed a Gospel harmony. In *To Autolycus*, Theophilus refers to *The History*, which appears to have been a history of humankind.

Theophilus is the first to use the word *trias* (triad) for God, his Word, and his Wisdom. He also distinguishes the Word immanent in God and the Word uttered by God. CPG I, 1107–1109. TLG 1725.   [F.W.N.]

Bibliography
Eusebius, *Church History* 4.20, 24; Jerome, *Lives of Illustrious Men* 25.

R.M. Grant, ed., *Theophilus of Antioch: Ad Autolycum* (Oxford: Oxford UP, 1970).

J. Bentivegna, "A Christianity Without Christ by Theophilus of Antioch," *SP* 13 (1975):107–130.

THEOTOKOS. "God-bearer" (from the Greek *theos*, "God," and *tikto*, "to bear," "bring forth"), a title of Mary, mother of Jesus, often expressed in English by "Mother of God." The ancient church held Mary as the *Theotokos* in a position of the highest honor, but always in a Christological context.

The term *Theotokos* appeared early in the history of the church. Papyrologists trace it in the papyrus known as *Sub tuum* found in Alexandria and dated to the third century. Hippolytus or Origen may have coined the term. Apparently, Alexander, bishop of Alexandria, used the term officially for the first time, and later it appeared frequently in the fathers, among them Athanasius, Cyril of Jerusalem, Basil of Caesarea, Gregory of Nazianzus, and Gregory of Nyssa. The term became controversial when it was rejected by Nestorius. Cyril of Alexandria championed its use, and it was accepted by the Council of Ephesus (431) under his presidency and by the Council of Chalcedon (451).

Theotokos became one of the most common titles of the Virgin Mary in the Greek church, frequently used simply as a proper name. Its original usage was a means of affirming the full deity of the incarnate Son of God from his conception in the womb of Mary. Its use in popular piety enhanced the veneration of Mary. The theological position of the church regarding the Virgin Mary is summarized by John of Damascus (eighth century): "Hence, it is rightly and truly that we call holy Mary the Mother of God, for this name expresses the entire mystery of the incarnation . . . . In this, the Mother of God, in a manner surpassing the cause of nature, made it possible for the Fashioner to be fashioned, and for the God and Creator of the universe to become man and deify human nature" (*F.O.* 12). *See also* Christ, Christology; Mary; Papyri.   [G.S.B.]

Bibliography
J. Karmiris, *A Synopsis of the Dogmatic Theology of the Orthodox Catholic Church* (Scranton: Christian Orthodox Edition, 1973); G.A. Maloney, "Mary and the Church as Seen by the Early Fathers," *Diakonia* 9 (1974):6–19; M. O'Carroll, *Theotokos: A Theological Encyclopedia of the Blessed Virgin Mary* (Wilmington: Glazier, 1982); N.D. Patrinacos, *A Dictionary of Greek Orthodoxy* (New York: Greek Orthodox Archdiocese of North and South America, 1984), s.v.; G.S. Bebis, "The Virgin Mary in the Eastern Traditions," *New Catholic World* 229 (November–December 1986):258–263.

THERAPEUTAE. Jewish sect related to the Essenes. The Therapeutae (Greek, "healers" or "worshipers") are known only from the description in Philo's treatise *The Contemplative Life*. They lived in a kind of monastic community near Lake Mareotis south of Alexandria in Egypt. From Philo's account of their conduct, assemblies, and meals, Eusebius thought they were Christians. The practices that he selects from Philo were these: the Therapeutae abandoned their property and went to live in deserted areas, spent all day in the study of scripture and in fasting, composed psalms, and observed chastity so that the male and female members lived separately (*H.E.* 2.16–17). Eusebius compared their practices specifically with the Paschal vigils and hymn singing of Christians. Although Eusebius is wrong in the identification, his reference is important for what it indicates about Christian observances and the continuity between early Christianity and sectarian Judaism. *See also* Philo.   [E.F.]

Bibliography

F.C. Conybeare, *Philo: About the Contemplative Life* (Oxford: Clarendon, 1895).

G. Vermes, "Essenes-Therapeutai-Qumran," *Durham University Journal* 52 (1960):99–117; idem, "Essenes and Therapeutae," *Revue de Qumran* 3 (1961–1962):219–240.

THESSALONICA, THESSALONIANS. City in northern Greece (modern Saloniki) to which the apostle Paul wrote two letters. Acclaimed by the poet Antipater as the "Mother of Macedonia," Thessalonica stands at the head of the Thermaic Gulf as a natural crossroads of the Balkans. It affords access to central and eastern Europe from the Aegean and to points east and west along important routes connecting Europe with Asia. Cassander, son of Alexander the Great's regent in Macedonia, founded the city in 315 B.C. by the unification of twenty-six towns and villages and named it after Thessaloniki, his wife and a stepsister of Alexander. In 168 B.C., the Romans defeated the last of the Macedonian monarchs, Perseus, and, after suppressing an uprising twenty years later, created the province of Macedonia with Thessalonica as its capital.

Interior of the first church (fourth century) dedicated to St. Demetrius (martyred 303), beneath the present basilica of Hagios Demetrios in Thessalonica, Greece.

The apostle Paul's missionary work at Thessalonica was undertaken probably in A.D. 49 (Acts 17:1–13). In 1 Thessalonians, the earliest of Paul's extant letters, the apostle praised the church of the Thessalonians for the good example it had manifested throughout Greece and the world (1:7–8). Paul related that his desire to return to the city had been thwarted by "Satan" (2:18) and so he wrote to exhort the church to remain steadfast in the face of continuing pressure. He also responded to the question of what happens to church members who had died before Christ's coming. The apostle affirmed that at the Lord's descent from heaven "the dead in Christ will rise first" (4:16), then those alive will be "caught up together with them in the clouds to meet the Lord" (4:17). The letter ends with a polemical observation on the suddenness with which the "day of the Lord" will come (5:1–11) directed against a position proclaiming "peace and security," a possible allusion to promotion of the Roman imperial program of *pax et securitas* ("peace and security"). Many scholars view 1 Thessalonians 2:13–16, in which "the Jews" are characterized as killing Jesus and the prophets and are singled out for divine wrath, as a later non-Pauline interpolation.

On stylistic, form-critical, and theological grounds, some consider 2 Thessalonians as a later forgery intended to "correct" the expectation of the imminent end-time promoted in 1 Thessalonians. Other scholars accept the letter's authenticity and have attempted to recreate a situation at Thessalonica that might have occasioned such an apparent revision of Paul's eschatological views, such as a radical millenarian tendency that had developed subsequent to Paul's visit and that the apostle attempted through correspondence to diffuse. Although scholarly consensus has tipped in favor of inauthenticity, those who promote theories of forgery have yet to develop a generally acceptable occasion for the forgery and a rationale for the forger's explicit use of the apostle's signature and the claim that such was his practice in all of his letters (2 Thess. 3:17).

Although little else is known about Christians at the city during the first and second centuries A.D., there is evidence of dramatic changes in Thessalonica's civic religions. An earlier civic cult of "the gods" was superseded by a cult of the Cabirus as the city's patron deity and its principal divine protector. A cult of the divine Fulvus (Marcus Aurelius's son, who died at the age of four in 165) flourished for over a century at Thessalonica. There also are indications of devotion to "the highest god" (*theos hypsistos*) and to the mother goddess Cybele, as well as continued attention to Dionysus. The cult of the Egyptian gods maintained its popularity and attracted adherents from every quarter of the socioeconomic spectrum. It must have proved a formidable competitor to early Christianity at the city.

In the third century, Gothic invasions threatened Macedonia's political and economic security. Twice, Thessalonica was besieged (252 and 269) but managed to escape destruction. Toward the end of the century, persecution of Christians intensified under the reign of Diocletian and his three co-rulers. One of these was Galerius, who for some time maintained at Thessalonica an imperial residence, much of which has been excavated. A triumphal arch and rotunda (intended but not used as a mausoleum) were also constructed by Galerius at the city. Parts of the structures have survived to the present.

One of the victims of Galerius's vigorous anti-Christian policies was Demetrius, who, according to legend, was assassinated on imperial orders ca. 303. Demetrius was to become the object of a large and enduring cult and emerged as Thessalonica's patron saint and protector. In 313, Galerius was party to an imperial rescript rescinding the persecution of Christians and ensuring their right to assemble and to build churches. Probably soon thereafter, a small martyrion was built near the legendary site of Demetrius's death at a bath complex.

An unnamed bishop of Thessalonica was present at the Council of Nicaea (325), as was his successor, Alexander. At the Council of Tyre (335), bishop Alexander promoted the cause of Athanasius in opposition to Arian views supported by the imperial court. During this period, Thessalonica was under the ecclesiastical jurisdiction of the bishop of Rome, and Alexander's position at Tyre is the first clear evidence of what was to be a fairly consistent policy of Thessalonica's ecclesiastical alignment with Rome and Alexandria over against the empire's new capital, Constantinople. By 342, bishop Aetius had emerged as successor to the see of Thessalonica (342–355) and attended the Council of Sardica (343). Bishop Herenius, who succeeded Aetius, at the Council of Milan (355) reversed the Thessalonian see's policy of support for Athanasius. Herenius's successor, Acholius (374–384), reverted to the previous policy in alignment with Rome.

In 379, under the emperor Theodosius I, Constantinople was given political authority over Thessalonica. Although the city remained under the ecclesiastical jurisdiction of Rome, bishop Damasus I of Rome (366–384) moved to strengthen his position by making Acholius of Thessalonica his vicar apostolic. It was under Acholius's influence that Theodosius, after an illness at the city, converted to Christianity and issued the famous Edict of Thessalonica on February 28, 380. The edict stipulated that "Catholic Christianity" as represented by Damasus of Rome and Peter II of Alexandria was to be the only religion legally tolerated in the empire. Theodosius's order of the massacre of 7,000 Thessalonians for an insurrection caused Ambrose of Milan to place him under discipline.

During the fifth and sixth centuries, Thessalonian Christians maintained their attachment to Rome and embarked on an ambitious program of construction, converting a number of Galerian monuments to ecclesiastical use in addition to building new churches. Already in the late fourth century, the rotunda erected as Galerius's mausoleum had been transformed into a church dedicated to St. George. By the sixth century, splendid mosaics depicting martyr saints adorned the interior. At least some portions of Galerius's palace also were adapted for church use. In the largest apse of an octagonal structure at the palace—perhaps an imperial throneroom—Christian brickwork was inserted. The composition depicts a cross sur-rounded by a circle of rayed bricks with a branch on either side and may represent the emperor Constantine's vision of a cross on the sun accompanied by the injunction "by this, conquer."

By the fifth century, the martyrion of St. Demetrius had gained a reputation for the miraculous qualities of its water. One of the shrine's beneficiaries was a prefect of Illyricum, Leontius (412–413), whose paralysis reputedly had been cured by a visit to the site. Through Leontius's benefactions, an enormous new basilica was built over the martyrion and dedicated to the saint.

Early and enthusiastic devotion to Mary was manifested at Thessalonica in the fifth-century construction of a Church of the Holy Virgin *Acheiropoietos* ("made without hands"). According to legend, an icon of the Virgin "not made by human hands" descended directly from heaven to the site and stimulated construction of the church. Visible to the present day are mosaic decorations between the columns of the nave in the church reflecting marked continuity with late-imperial artistic conventions and motifs. Also dating from the fifth or sixth century is the mosaic decoration of the chapel of Hosios David. A restored mosaic in one of the chapel's apses presents a young, unbearded Christ *Pantocrator* ("ruler of all") standing in the disk of the sun against a rainbow and surrounded by cherubim wings and symbols of the four evangelists (see illustration, page 198).

Despite attempts to bring Thessalonica under the jurisdiction of the patriarchate of Constantinople, the city often persisted in displaying loyalty to the pope. Observance of an imperial order issued by Theodosius II in 421 asserting Constantinople's authority over the bishops of easterrn Illyricum was, at most, superficial. Jurisdiction over Illyrian Christianity reverted to the pope during the reign of Anastasius (491–518). In 535, the emperor Justinian divided Illyricum into two ecclesiastical dioceses, and authority over Thessalonian Christianity was returned to Constantinople. The correspondence of pope Gregory I the Great (590–604) suggests that by the beginning of the seventh century papal authority had been reasserted over the region. Not until the mid-ninth century, after the Iconoclast period, did Roman authority in the area wane.

[H.L.H.]

Bibliography

John Chrysostom, *Homilies on Thessalonians*, ed. J.A. Broadus, NPNF, 1st ser. (1889), Vol. 13; Theodoret, *Interpretatio in epistulas Pauli*, PG 82.627–674; Ambrosiaster, *Commentarius in epistulas Paulinas*, PL 17; Pelagius, *Expositio in I et II Thessalonicenses*, TS 9.3 (1926):417–450.

C. Edson, *Inscriptiones graecae Epiri, Macedoniae, Thraciae, Scythiae, Pars II Inscriptiones Macedoniae, Fasciculus I Inscriptiones Thessalonicae et viciniae* (Berlin: de Gruyter, 1972); E. Tsigaridas and K. Louverdou-Tsigarida, *Catalogue of Christian Inscriptions at the Museum of Thessaloniki* [in Greek] (Thessalonica: Institute for Balkan Studies, 1979); I. Touratsoglou, *Die Münzstätte von Thessaloniki in der römischen Kaiserzeit. Antike Münzen und geschnittene Steine XII* (Berlin: de Gruyter, 1988).

O. Tafrali, *Thessalonique des origines au XIVe siècle* (Paris: Guenther, 1919); B. Rigaux, *Saint Paul: Les Epitres aux Thessaloniciens* (Paris: Gabalda; Gembloux: Duculot, 1956); D. Kanatsoulis, *History of Macedonia* [in Greek] (Thessalonica: Institute for Balkan Studies, 1964); W. Elliger, *Paulus in Griechenland: Philippi, Thessaloniki, Athen, Korinth* (Stuttgart: Katholisches Bibelwerk, 1978); R. Collins, *Studies on the First Letter to the Thessalonians* (Louvain: Louvain UP, 1984); K.P. Donfried, "The Cults of Thessalonica and the Thessalonian Correspondence," *NTS* 31 (1985):333–356; C. Mavropoulou-Tsioumi, ed., *Thessaloniki and Its Monuments* (Thessalonica: Ephorate of Byzantine Antiquities, 1985); R. Jewett, *The Thessalonian Correspondence* (Philadelphia: Fortress, 1986); A.J. Malherbe, *Paul and the Thessalonians* (Philadelphia: Fortress, 1987).

THOMAS. One of the twelve apostles (Matt. 10:3; Mark 3:18; Luke 6:15; Acts 1:13). The name Thomas is a Graecized form of the Aramaic name Tomâ. We learn from John 11:16; 20:24; and 21:2 that Thomas was also called Didymus, a translation of Tomâ meaning "twin." The Hebrew form of the name, Teôm (Song of Solomon 7:4), corresponds almost exactly to the English colloquial abbreviation Tom.

Nearly all we know about Thomas comes from John's Gospel, in which he plays a fairly prominent role. In John 11:16, after the death

of Lazarus when Jesus determined to go to Judea in spite of threats against his life, Thomas called on his fellow disciples to go and die with Jesus. In John 14:5, after Jesus had told his disciples that they knew the way to where he was going, Thomas asked how they could know the way, since they did not know where he was going. In John 21:2, he is included among the seven who participated in the extraordinary catch of fish and to whom Jesus appeared on the shore of the Sea of Tiberias. All of these are significant statements, but it is for the event in John 20:24–29 that Thomas was best remembered. Thomas had not been present on the evening of the first day of the week when Christ appeared and bestowed the Holy Spirit on the disciples (John 20:19–23). When told of the event, he refused to believe unless he saw the nail wounds in the Lord's hands, placed his finger in the wounds, and inserted his hand in his side. When Jesus appeared again a week later and invited Thomas to do just that, he confessed Jesus as his Lord and his God. With that, Thomas, who was called "the Twin" in New Testament times, became, somewhat unjustly, the doubting Thomas of future generations.

Early Christian writings beyond the New Testament era often referred to Thomas as the apostle who doubted. Jesus' last statement in John 20:19–29, which calls blessed those who have not seen and have believed, was especially influential in the homiletic tradition of the early church. This tradition can be summed up in a statement that Gregory the Great made in a homily on John 20:19–29: "Thomas's lack of faith did more for our faith than did the faith of the disciples who believed" (*Hom. 26 in Evang.*; PL 76.1201).

Most of the early traditions focused on Thomas's mission as an apostle. Thomas was particularly prominent in Syriac Christianity and those regions that received Christianity from Syria. According to Eusebius of Caesarea, he brought the gospel to Parthia (*H.E.* 3.1); Jerome (*Vita Apost.* 5) and Rufinus of Aquileia (*H.E.* 2.4) say Persia. Gregory of Nazianzus held that he preached the gospel in India and was martyred there (*Or.* 25), a position also found in the *Acts of Thomas* 1. John Chrysostom referred to his burial place at Edessa (*Hom. in Heb.* 26).

Two significant apocryphal works concerned Thomas, the *Gospel of Thomas* and the *Acts of Thomas*. Until recently, the *Gospel of Thomas* was known only from references to it in early Christian writings and from a single quotation in Hippolytus (*Haer.* 5.7.20). Its full text in Coptic is now known from the Gnostic library found in Egypt near Nag Hammadi around 1945. The *Gospel of Thomas*, a collection of sayings, prophecies, and parables of Jesus, is to be distinguished from a later infancy gospel of the same name. It was composed in Greek sometime before 200 and later translated into Coptic. Many of the sayings have parallels in the Synoptic Gospels. It provides an early witness outside of the canonical writings of the New Testament to the teachings of Jesus and shows how the sayings of Jesus were transmitted in Encratite and Gnostic circles. The *Gospel of Thomas* was eventually accepted by the Manichaeans.

The *Acts of Thomas*, a Syriac work from the early third century, introduces Thomas as Judas Thomas, that is, Judas the Twin. It constitutes the oldest witness to the tradition that Thomas visited and evangelized India. The *Acts of Thomas* is divided into thirteen distinct acts, which are followed by the "Martyrdom of the holy and esteemed apostle Thomas." The eleventh act introduces Thomas's twin, the other Didymus, as an identical twin who is the Lord Jesus himself. What appears to be an older part of the work presupposed a mission to northwest India, which received Christianity from Parthia. However, most of the *Acts* assume a mission in south India, which received Christianity from Persia ca. 200; Persia in turn had received it from Edessa. Early traditions associate Thomas with all three, Parthia, Persia, and Edessa. The *Acts of Thomas* represents the Gnostic Christianity of Syria in the region of Edessa. Like the *Gospel of Thomas*, the *Acts* were later accepted in Manichaeism. Feast day July 3 (Roman Catholic and Syrian), October 6 (Greek Orthodox), December 21 (Anglican). TLG 1375, 2038. *See also* Acts of Thomas; Gospel of Thomas (Infancy); Gospel of Thomas (Sayings). [E.LaV.]

Bibliography

B. Gärtner, *The Theology of the Gospel According to Thomas* (New York: Harper, 1961); A.F.J. Klijn, *The Acts of Thomas* (Leiden: Brill, 1962); NTA, Vol. 1, pp. 278–307, 388–401; Vol. 2, pp. 425–531; R. Brown, *The Gospel According to John* (Garden City: Doubleday, 1970), Vols. 29A, 29B; A. Guillaumont et al., *The Gospel According to Thomas*, 2nd ed. (Leiden: Brill, 1976).

THREE CHAPTERS. Emperor Justinian's edict on Christology (543–544) condemning the person and writings of Theodore of Mopsuestia, the works of Theodoret of Cyrus against Cyril of Alexandria, and a letter of Ibas of Edessa to Maris (all advocates of the Antiochene Christology that spawned Nestorianism). The term "Three Chapters" has often been transferred from the anathemas themselves to the persons and writings condemned. Justinian's reasons for issuing the edict were certainly political and probably religious as well. By a frontal attack on Nestorius's supporters and friends, he hoped to win to his many causes the allegiance of the Monophysite Christians, who adhered to the one divine nature of Christ. The Monophysites were strong in both Egypt and Syria and well represented in Palestine and Asia Minor; they were thus necessary to his plans for rebuilding the empire. Those Christians distrusted the decisions made by the Council of Chalcedon (451) because it had received Theodoret and Ibas as in good standing and could be interpreted as allowing a Christology that sharply distinguished the divine and human natures in Christ. During a conference held in Justinian's palace in 533, Monophysites questioned that acceptance of Theodoret and Ibas. A bishop at the court, Theodore Ascidas, suggested that Justinian publish a decree on those questions.

By condemning Theodore, but only specific works of Theodoret and Ibas, a subtle distinction was being made. First, the full rejection of the root of Nestorianism should satisfy Monophysite misgivings about a possible Nestorian interpretation of Chalcedon. By condemning only certain writings of Theodoret and Ibas, and thus highlighting their recantation of support for Nestorius and their disavowal of their attacks on Cyril at Chalcedon, that council would be given higher standing in Monophysite circles.

In the east, this attempt might have worked; masses of people followed Cyril and distrusted Chalcedon because it seemed to permit Nestorian interpretation. But the effort was doomed to failure. The west, through Leo's exposition of Christology in his *Tome*, accepted a position of Christ *in* two natures, not *out of* two natures. Pope Vigilius rejected the *Three Chapters* and was called to Constantinople to explain himself. In a document called the *Iudicatum*, sent in 548 to Menas, bishop of Constantinople, Vigilius accepted the specific condemnation of the three in Justinian's edict and offered a defense of the Chalcedonian formula from the vantage point of Leo's *Tome*. That provoked so much opposition that Vigilius withdrew the *Iudicatum* and waited to see what the consensus would be at the coming council at Constantinople (553).

As with Zeno's *Henoticon*, the attempt at rapprochement was a failure. The west stood too close to an Antiochene interpretation of Christology to accept fully any large concessions to Monophysites. More important, the *Three Chapters* represented a sad method in theological/political decisions: a figure who had died "orthodox" was exhumed and condemned as a person. The intellectual life and biblical interpretation of the eastern churches have had great difficulty recovering from the condemnation of both Theodore and Origen at the Fifth Ecumenical Council (Constantinople, 553). *See also* Monophysitism; Nestorianism.   [F.W.N.]

Bibliography
C.J. Hefele, *A History of the Councils of the Church* (Edinburgh: T. and T. Clark, 1895), Vol. 4, pp. 229–365; J.W. Barker, *Justinian and the Later Roman Empire* (Madison: U of Wisconsin P, 1966), pp. 108–111; W.H.C. Frend, *The Rise of The Monophysite Movement* (Cambridge: Cambridge UP, 1972), pp. 274–282.

TIBERIUS (42 B.C.–A.D. 37). Roman emperor (A.D. 14–37). Tiberius was the son of Tiberius Claudius Nero and Livia Drusilla. His mother divorced her husband (38 B.C.) to marry Octavian, the future emperor Augustus. Tiberius was himself compelled to divorce his wife, Vipsania (12 B.C.), to enter into an unhappy union with Augustus's daughter, the widowed Julia. His military career (20 B.C.–A.D. 12) was remarkably successful. He lived for several years in Rhodes (6 B.C.–A.D. 2), perhaps in dismay over the imperial succession, since Augustus hoped to be followed by his grandsons. His stepfather adopted him and recognized him as successor (A.D. 4) only after the death of the two grandsons.

As emperor, Tiberius professed his adherence to Augustus's policies. His goal was to ensure peace along the borders and within the empire. He largely succeeded in this aim, apart from several local disturbances. He enforced strict economy, allowing few building projects, donations, or public games, so that he was able to leave considerable wealth to the state at his death. For himself, he refused divine honors.

His rule was marred by an increasing incidence of trials for treason owing to the influence of Sejanus, the prefect of the guard and his principal adviser (23–31). During this period, the emperor took up residence at Capri (26); he never returned to Rome, but conducted public business thereafter by correspondence with the senate. Upon the execution of Sejanus on dubious charges of conspiracy (31), the prosecutions were continued by enemies of the prefect who sought revenge.

During Tiberius's reign, John the Baptist initiated his preaching (29; cf. Luke 3:1); Jesus conducted his public ministry, was crucified (Tacitus, *Annals* 15.44), and was resurrected; Stephen suffered martyrdom, and Paul was converted. Tiberius is the Caesar to whom reference is made in the Gospels (except for Luke 2:1), and it was doubtless a coin with his name and portrait that was shown to Christ when he was questioned about the lawfulness of paying taxes to Caesar (Matt. 22:15–22; Mark 12:13–17; Luke 20:20–26).

Tertullian (*Apol.* 5) reports a legend that Tiberius, informed by Pontius Pilate of Christ's miracles, unjust death, and resurrection, wished to include him in the Roman pantheon but was refused by the senate. This apocryphal story is repeated by Eusebius of Caesarea (*H.E.* 2.2) and Orosius (*Hist.* 7.4). [M.P.McH.]

Bibliography

Velleius Paterculus, *History of Rome* 2.94–131; Tacitus, *Annals* 1–6; Suetonius, *Life of Tiberius*; Dio Cassius, *Roman History* 57–58.

F.B. Marsh, *The Reign of Tiberius* (London: Oxford UP, Milford, 1931); M.P. Charlesworth, "Tiberius," *The Cambridge Ancient History,* ed. S.A. Cook et al. (Cambridge: Cambridge UP, 1934), Vol. 10, pp. 607–652, 960–969 (bibliography); R.S. Rogers, *Studies in the Reign of Tiberius* (Baltimore: Johns Hopkins, 1943), esp. pp. 1–88; G. Marañón, *Tiberius: A Study in Resentment* (London: Hollis and Carter, 1956); R. Seager, *Tiberius* (Berkeley: U of California P, 1972); B.M. Levick, *Tiberius the Politician* (London: Thames and Hudson, 1976); J. Ober, "Tiberius and the Political Testament of Augustus," *Historia* 31 (1982):306–328; G.W. Houston, "Tiberius on Capri," *Greece and Rome* 32 (1985):178–196.

TILLEMONT, LOUIS SEBASTIEN LE NAIN DE (1637–1698).

Historian. Tillemont was a notable figure in an era that saw major advances in the study of church history. After the era of Reformation confrontation in historical writing—e.g., the Magdeburg *Centuries* and Baronius's *Ecclesiastical Annals*—the second half of the seventeenth century witnessed a more reasoned and moderate approach. French Catholic scholars led by the Maurists were in the vanguard of an extraordinary effort that made possible a dispassionate study of the origins of Christianity. Tillemont was associated with this circle of scholars, which also included Mabillon and Montfaucon.

Tillemont was educated at the Jansenist center of Port Royal near Paris but was not associated with the bitter Jansenist controversies. Leisurely trained, he did not become a priest until age thirty-nine. While still at Port Royal, he committed himself to his life's work, thanks to the influence of Baronius's *Annals.* His goal of collecting all the sources for the history of the early church led to his two major works, which complement each other and demonstrate Tillemont's awareness of the importance of the secular environment for the history of the church. When the royal censor objected to some parts of the initial volume of his *magnum opus, Mémoirs pour servir à l'histoire ecclésiastique des six premiers siècles,* Tillemont turned to secular history, which did not require approval by the censor, and in 1690 there appeared the first volume of his *Histoire des empereurs . . . durant les six premiers siècles de l'église.* With a new and less captious royal censor in office, the first volume of the *Mémoirs* appeared in 1693. Only the first four volumes of each of these works appeared before Tillemont's death; his close personal secretary saw the remainder of the volumes into print.

Together, the *Mémoirs* and *Histoire* comprise twenty-two volumes and are an extraordinary compendium of information related to the historical development of the church to 513. Tillemont's historical labors in assembling critically evaluated source material both prepared the way for and anticipated Edward Gibbon's seemingly radical approach to the history of the church in the Roman empire.

[H.R.]

Bibliography

L.S. Tillemont, *Mémoires pour servir à l'histoire ecclésiastique des six premiers siècles,* 16 vols. (Paris, 1693–1712); rev. ed. with Tillemont's corrections and additional notes by Jacques le Mineur (Paris, 1701–1714); Eng. tr. of Vol. 1–2 (down to A.D. 177) by Thomas Deacon, *Ecclesiastical Memoirs of the First Six Centuries . . .* (London, 1733–1735), and Vol. 6, *The History of the Arians and of the Council of Nice* (1721); idem, *Histoire des empereurs . . . durant les six premiers siècles de l'église . . .,* 6 vols. (Paris, 1693–1739); idem, *Vie de saint Louis, roi de France,* 6 vols. (Paris, 1847–1851); idem, *La vie de ste. Geneviève* (Paris, 1823).

B. Neveu, *Un Historien a l'école de Port-Royal: Sébastien Le Nain de Tillemont, 1637–1698* (The Hague: Nijhoff, 1966); M.R.P. McGuire, "Louis Sébastien de Tillemont," *CHR* 52 (1966):186–200.

TIMOTHY (first century).

Companion of the apostle Paul and addressee of two New Testament epistles. Timothy, a native of Lystra in Asia Minor whose mother was a Jew and whose father was a pagan (Acts 16:1–3; 2 Tim. 1:5), was converted by Paul on his first journey to the region (1 Tim. 1:2) and joined Paul on the second journey. He was with Paul during the apostle's house arrest in Rome (Col. 1:1; Philem. 1). After his release, Paul took Timothy east with him and left the young man at Ephesus.

Most scholars since the nineteenth century have regarded the two New Testament epistles to Timothy as pseudo-Pauline. In this view, the conception of the gospel as tradition and the sense of apostleship as accepted authority represent a second or even third generation beyond Paul, even though the epistles do not speak of apostolic succession. The vocabulary and style of the Pastoral Epistles—Titus, 1 and 2 Timothy—are different from those of the major Pauline letters. The situations they describe do not fit easily into what is known of Paul's life from the genuine letters and the Book of Acts. The polemic against heretics, too, has a different tone and style, and in fact may fit best as a response to Marcion. In his letters, Paul responds directly to opponents; here, the author teaches right and wrong doctrine.

More conservative scholars, however, note that tradition and apostolicity are concerns in 1 Corinthians and Galatians. The difference in vocabulary could result from the different situations Paul faced, or even represent a change of approach. The polemical shift could be due to the personal character of the letters, addressed to one leader rather than to a congregation. These scholars believe that Paul may have made these shifts himself.

In either case, 1 and 2 Timothy represent important changes in the early Christian community in the direction of the Great Church of the second and third centuries.

According to later tradition, Timothy was first bishop of Ephesus (Eusebius, *H.E.* 3.4.5.; *Const. app.* 7.46). *Biblia Patristica* finds references to the epistles in Ignatius of Antioch, Polycarp, Hermas, Justin Martyr, Clement of Alexandria, Irenaeus, and Tertullian. Feast day January 26 (west), January 22 (east). [F.W.N.]

Bibliography

Biblia Patristica, ed. J. Allenbach et al. (Paris: Centre National de la Recherche Scientifique, 1975), pp. 510–517; John Chrysostom, *Homilies on Timothy*, tr. C. Marriot, NPNF, 1st ser. (1889), Vol. 13, pp. 401–518; Theodoret, *Interpretatio Epistolae I et II ad Timotheum*, PG 82.787–858; Pelagius, *Expositio in I et II Timotheum*, ed. A. Souter, TS 9.2 (1926):474–524; Ambrosiaster, *Commentarius in Epistulas I et II ad Timotheum*, PL 17.

J.N.D. Kelly, *A Commentary on the Pastoral Epistles: I Timothy, II Timothy, Titus* (London: Black, 1963); M. Dibelius and H. Conzelmann, *The Pastoral Epistles: A Commentary* (Philadelphia: Fortress, 1972); L. Keck, "On the Ethos of Early Christians," *Journal of the American Academy of Religion* 42 (1974):435–452.

TIMOTHY AELURUS (d. 477). Monophysite patriarch of Alexandria (457–460, 475–477), called "The Cat" from his small stature. Although a leader of the Monophysite opposition to Chalcedon (451), he agreed with Cyril and Severus later against Eutyches that the body of Christ was of the same substance as other human bodies. CPG III, 5475–5489.   [E.F.]

TIMOTHY OF JERUSALEM (sixth century?). Homilist. The manuscript tradition assigns to Timothy two homilies on the presentation of Jesus in the temple; four others on biblical topics are attributed to him. His *Oratio in Symeonem*, a presentation homily on Simeon's blessing, has figured in the discussion of the assumption of Mary. CPG III, 7405–7410.

[M.P.McH.]

Bibliography

B. Capelle, "Les Homélies liturgiques du prétendu Timothée de Jérusalem," *Ephemerides Liturgicae* 63 (1949):5–26.

TITUS. Companion of apostle Paul and addressee of a New Testament epistle. Titus was most probably converted by Paul to Christianity from paganism (Titus 1:4), and he remained uncircumcised (Gal. 2:1, 3). It is clear from Galatians 2, although it is not mentioned in Acts 15:1, 2, that he was included among those who accompanied Paul and Barnabas on their journey to Jerusalem on the occasion of the apostles' council.

Titus was sent to Corinth by Paul, probably on two, possibly three, occasions to deliver Paul's letters to the church there, to make arrangements for a collection for the poor brethren of Jerusalem, and to help in restoring church order after the failure of both Paul and Timo-

Church of St. Titus (sixth century?) at Gortys, the metropolitan see of Crete, showing the narthex, the nave, and at the back the triple apse.

thy to do so. His success, described in Paul's second letter to the Corinthians, indicates that he must have been a strong leader as well as a dedicated and zealous missionary (2 Cor. 2:13; 7:6, 13, 14; 8:6, 16, 23; 12:18). It is not surprising that he was subsequently involved in missions to several places, including Crete and Dalmatia. The letter of Paul to Titus, which was sent to Crete probably after Paul's release from his first imprisonment in Rome, includes a request that he should join the apostle in Nicopolis (3:12). Since Paul's second letter to Timothy mentions Titus as having gone to Dalmatia (4:10), we may assume that the above request was met. According to tradition, Titus returned from Dalmatia to Crete, where he served the church until his death. His relics, kept at Gortyna, were brought to the Church of St. Mark in Venice after the invasion of the Arabs in 823, but were returned to the Church of St. Titus in Herakleion in May 1966.

Paul's letter to Titus is understood to have been written after the first letter to Timothy during the interval between Paul's two Roman imprisonments (ca. A.D. 67). Its similarities to 1 Timothy have led several scholars to accept its authenticity, at least in a fragmentary sense. Titus did not leave any writings. The Latin text of a so-called *Epistle of Titus* (published by D. De Bruyne in *RBén* 37 [1925]:47–72), which attacks the custom of having *virgines subintroductae* (spiritual marriage) and defends chastity, is of Priscillianist origin (sixth century). Finally, a Greek apocryphal text *Acta Titi*, which seems to be related to the apocryphal *Acts of Paul* and possibly to the *Apocalypse of Paul*, supplies interesting, although often disputable, information. Feast day January 26 (west), August 15 (east). *See also* Epistle of Titus.   [G.D.D.]

Bibliography

John Chrysostom, *Homilies on Titus*, tr. C. Marriot, NPNF, 1st ser. (1889), Vol. 13, pp. 519–543; Theodoret, *Interpretatio Epistolae ad Titum*, PG 82.857–869; Pelagius, *Expositio in Titum*, ed. A. Souter, TS 9.2 (1926):525–535; Ambrosiaster, *Commentarius in Titum*, PL 17; Jerome, *Commentarii in Titum*, PL 26.

M.R. James, "The Acts of Titus and the Acts of Paul," *JThS* 6 (1905): 549–556; *AB* 79 (1961):241–256.

J.N.D. Kelly, *A Commentary on the Pastoral Epistles: I Timothy, II Timothy, Titus* (London: Black, 1963); M. Dibelius and H. Conzelmann, *The Pastoral Epistles: A Commentary* (Philadelphia: Fortress, 1972).

TITUS (A.D. 39–81). Roman emperor (79–81). Titus joined his father, Vespasian, in putting down the Jewish rebellion against Roman rule (66–70). After Vespasian became emperor in 69, Titus concluded the siege of Jerusalem the following year with the destruction of the city and its temple. His reign, like that of his father, was free of persecutions of the church.

[M.P.McH.]

Bibliography

Eusebius, *Church History* 3.5–7, 13.

B.W. Jones, *The Emperor Titus* (New York: St. Martin, 1984).

TITUS OF BOSTRA (d. 371). Bishop of Bostra (362–371). Both learned and eloquent, Titus wrote four books against the Manichaeans. Julian the Apostate intervened in disputes between Christians and pagans at Bostra, warned Titus he would hold him and the clergy responsible if problems continued, and finally called on the Christians to renounce Titus. His efforts failed. CPG II, 3575–3581. [F.W.N.]

Bibliography

Jerome, *Lives of Illustrious Men* 102; idem, *Letter* 70 (84); Socrates, *Church History* 3.25; Sozomen, *Church History* 3.14; 5.15.

TOLEDO, COUNCILS OF. The sixteen councils of the Spanish church meeting at Toledo under royal supervision between 589 and 702 constitute a distinctive institution of the Visigothic union of the church and state. They were summoned by the monarch; their acts were subscribed (signed) by royal officials as well as bishops, abbots, and other higher clergymen in attendance; and several served as occasions for secular assemblies and legislative actions. The primary evidence for these councils are their *acta*, consisting of the addresses (*allocutiones*) and legislative proposals (*tomi*) of kings, statements of orthodox doctrine, and subscription lists, as well as the laws (*canones*) voted by the attending clergy (after 675, perhaps by lay officers as well).

These councils derived from ecclesiastical councils of local or regional competence, such as the Council of Elvira (ca. 306), as well as the ecumenical councils convoked and enforced by Roman emperors beginning with Constantine, such as Nicaea (325). They may also have been influenced by earlier assemblies of the Gothic people under royal leadership, although this is a much disputed question. In several regards, the councils of Toledo suggest the main lines along which the *Cortes* and other medieval parliaments would later develop.

The first council held at Toledo (ca. 397) was a minor assembly attended mostly by local clergy and presided over by the city's bishop. The Second Council of Toledo (527) was little more. King Reccared transformed the Third Council (589) into a new institution by summoning Catholic and Arian clergy from the entire kingdom and making the council's central business the public conversion of the Goths. The first appearance of the addition of the *Filioque* clause to the Nicene Creed occurs in texts of this council. The Fourth Council (633), summoned by king Sisenand but dominated by Isidore of Seville, was equally national in scope. Except for one final canon on royal election, its lengthy reform program was ecclesiastical in character. The Fifth, Sixth, and Seventh Councils, summoned by kings Khintila (in 636 and 638) and Khindaswinth (in 646), were less ambitious undertakings.

The Eighth Council, convoked with pomp and high rhetoric by king Recceswinth in 653, became the model for subsequent Toledan councils. Its twelve canons dealt with a wide range of issues; it served further as the occasion for promulgating the omnicompetent code of Visigothic law prepared by a royal commission. Recceswinth also summoned the Ninth and Tenth Councils (655 and 656); the former dealt only with the affairs of Toledo's ecclesiastical province. King Wamba's Eleventh Council (675) was comparably limited.

The Twelfth Council of Toledo (681), presided over by king Erwig and by bishop Julian of Toledo as primate of Spain, strongly asserted its national jurisdiction. The next five Toledan councils (Thirteenth through Seventeenth) were likewise shaped by Julian's sense of that institution's function. Sixty bishops attended the Fifteenth Council in 688, more than came to any Toledan council but the Third; they voted no canons but reproved the papacy for failing to comprehend the refinements of Julian's Christology. In retrospect, these six Toledan councils seem obsessed with the effort to legitimize the series of coups d'état perpetrated by rival dynasties and with punitive legislation against the Jews. The Sixteenth and Seventeenth Councils (693 and 694, summoned, as was the Fifteenth, by Erwig's successor, Egica) were especially severe in the latter regard. The acts of the Eighteenth and last Council of Toledo (702) were lost in the general collapse of the Visigothic state after 711.

[J.duQ.A.]

Bibliography

J. Vives et al., eds., *Concilios Visigóticos e Hispano-Romanos* (Barcelona: Consejo Superior de Investigaciones Científicas, Instituto Enrique Flóres, 1963); E.A. Thompson, *The Goths in Spain* (Oxford: Clarendon, 1969); P.D. King, *Law and Society in the Visigothic Kingdom* (Cambridge: Cambridge UP, 1972); J. duQ. Adams, "The Eighth Council of Toledo (653): Precursor of Medieval Parliaments?," *Religion, Culture, and Society in the Early Middle Ages*, ed. T.F. Noble and J.J. Contreni (Kalamazoo: Medieval Institute, 1987), pp. 41–54.

TRADITION. Authoritative teaching transmitted in the church. In the New Testament, the word "tradition" (*paradosis*) usually refers to a body of teaching, a collection of precepts, or a set of customs or usages to which a given group adheres. There is reference in the Gospel narratives, for instance, to the "tradition of the elders," in this case having to do with Jewish dietary laws. Some of the religious leaders, it is recorded (Mark 7:1–13; Matt. 15:1–9), complained that Jesus' disciples were not washing their hands before eating, thus failing to observe the regulations in respect to ritual cleanliness (cf. Luke 11:37–38). Jesus, however, citing Isaiah 29:13, replied that the "commandments of God" take precedence over merely human traditions (Mark 7:8–9; Matt. 15:3) and that the word of God is vitiated by too scrupulous attention to ritualistic concerns.

A less ambiguous use of "tradition," and certainly a more positive one, is found in the letters of Paul. Here, "tradition" refers specifically to what Paul taught, preached, or wrote. He commended the Corinthians for maintaining the "traditions even as I have delivered them to you" (1 Cor. 11:2) and urged the Thessalonians to "stand firm and hold to the traditions you were taught by me" (1 Thess. 2:15), and even warned them to "keep away" from those who did not live "in accord with the traditions you received from us" (3:6). For Paul, "tradition" clearly refers to his teaching concerning Christian doctrine, such as the resurrection; ethical precepts, such as faith, hope, and love; and liturgical usage, such as the institution of the eucharist. Tradition, however, is not merely to be adhered to faithfully, it is also to be "handed on" or "handed over," as the verb form (*paradidōmi*) suggests. The essence of the Christian tradition, as Paul understood it, is found in 1 Corinthians 15:3–4: "For I delivered (*paredōka*) as of first importance what I also received, that Christ died for our sins in accordance with the scriptures, that he was buried, that he was raised on the third day in accordance with the scriptures. . . ." This passage suggests, if nothing else, that that which was "handed over" (delivered) was not something new; it had its authoritative basis in scripture and, for Paul, in Christ himself (1 Cor. 15:7).

The verb form of "tradition" has other meanings as well, among them to "give up" and thus, in some cases, to "betray." There were those customs that were "delivered" by Moses (Acts 6:14); the followers of Jesus could expect to be brought to trial and "delivered up" (Mark 13:11; Matt. 10:19); Jesus died on the cross, that is, he "gave up his spirit" (John 19:30); and it was Judas who was Jesus' "betrayer" (Matt. 26:46). In subsequent generations, when Christians were persecuted, a person who "handed over" the Christian scriptures or sacred vessels to the imperial authorities so as to avoid arrest was referred to as a *traditor*, a word having a common root with *traditio* ("tradition"). For the New Testament, however, the predominant meaning of "tradition" lies within the oft-quoted exhortation from Jude 3 that Christians "contend for the faith which was once for all delivered [*paradotheisē*] to the saints" (cf. 1 Tim. 6:20). To this extent, tradition may properly be equated with the content—doctrinal, ethical, and liturgical—of the Christian faith. That "content" was not fixed; tradition took on increasingly diverse meanings and was brought into play to serve a variety of purposes in the subapostolic and later periods, particularly as the New Testament itself came to be regarded by many as the primary but not exclusive depository of the Christian tradition.

Second and Third Centuries. In the subapostolic period, tradition was a concept to which little attention was paid. The books of the New Testament were still in the process of being gathered into what was to become the canon. Considerable impetus to this process was given by Marcion's out-of-hand rejection of Hebrew scriptures, which he believed depicted a despotic and vindictive creator God in no way to be equated with the God and Father of Jesus Christ. Accordingly, he produced a severely expurgated version of Luke's Gospel and a radically edited collection of Paul's letters, with the intent of portraying a God who sent Jesus to save human beings from the creator God, or demiurge. Yet Marcion's views were themselves rejected, because the early church had already appropriated the Jewish Bible as its book and therefore as an authoritative source for Christian tradition. This appropriation can be seen as early as Clement of Rome, who, toward the end of the first century, exhorted the congregation at Corinth to eschew futile and vain concerns and to embrace the "glorious and honorable rule of our tradition" (*1 Clem.* 7.2). The wider context in which this phrase occurs indicates that Clement was anxious that the Corinthians emulate a posture of piety and penitence, a posture demonstrated primarily by the "blood of Christ," but also by such worthies as Noah, Abraham, Jonah, and Enoch. There is no reference here to tradition as based upon or as encompassing apostolic

teaching. An unwary reader of Eusebius of Caesarea's *Church History* might conclude that Ignatius of Antioch did appeal to apostolic faith, since Eusebius quotes him as urging others to "hold fast to the tradition of the apostles" (3.36.4), but nowhere in Ignatius's letters does such a phrase occur. In Polycarp's *Letter to the Philippians*, however, there is found for the first time an appeal to that tradition which has the New Testament as its source: "Let us give up the vanity of the crowd and false teaching, and let us return to the word which was delivered [*paradothenta*] from the beginning" (7.2). Here, the context indicates that Polycarp's concern is to insist, against the false teaching of the Gnostics, that Jesus Christ "came in the flesh" and that anyone who denies this is the Antichrist. This passage also intimates that tradition would become more precisely defined as it was employed in conscious opposition to competing views and that it would therefore be increasingly articulated in reference to the New Testament as well as to the Old. Apart from this, there are numerous patristic allusions to liturgical and other traditions, such as Justin Martyr's description of eucharistic practice as based upon the "memoirs of the apostles" that have been "delivered" to us (*1 Apol.* 66). And later, Tertullian could speak of specific customs that were enjoined or forbidden by virtue of unwritten traditions, that is, without specific scriptural warrant (*Coron.* 4; *Jejun.* 10). Best known, perhaps, is the manual of church order written by Hippolytus, the *Apostolic Tradition*, in which he boldly asserts that his subject is "our most important theme," namely "the Tradition, our teacher" (*Trad. ap.* 1).

It was, however, specifically in respect to the correct interpretation of scripture and to the orthodox ("Catholic") articulation of the Christian faith, that the role of tradition became a major concern on the early church's agenda. There were adherents of Gnosticism, for instance, such as Valentinus and Basilides, who were boldly promoting their own cosmological/theological systems and who, with equal boldness, were quoting scripture to authenticate their views. Irenaeus of Lyons in his massive *Refutation and Overthrow of Gnosis*

Falsely So Called challenged these Gnostic "heretics." They may claim to use scripture, he said, but in fact they misuse it. The reason for this is that they do not possess the "key" to proper scriptural interpretation; they "falsify the oracles of God and prove themselves evil interpreters of the good word of revelation" (*Haer.* 1. *praef.* 1). They have, he went on to say, no awareness of the basic underlying structure and interconnectedness of scripture. It is as if the Bible were, for them, composed of an infinite number of precious gems that they put together at random, the result being that they produce an ugly mosaic portraying a "fox" or a "dog." Christians, on the other hand, knowing how these gems are to be placed in relation to each other and to the overall purpose of the design, produce a beautiful mosaic that depicts a "king," Jesus Christ (1.8.1.).

The "key" to scriptural interpretation for Irenaeus was what he called the "canon of truth" (*Haer.* 3.2.1), often referred to in its Latin form as the *regula fidei* or *regula veritatis*, a tradition that is to be found only in the church. His intent, however, was not only to refute the Gnostics' "tissue of falsehoods" but, more importantly, to assert that the Christian faith as encapsulated in the canon of truth is the same throughout the whole church and is held by all Christians everywhere. Grounded in scripture, bequeathed to the apostles who delivered it to subsequent generations of bishops and presbyters, and articulated (perhaps) in baptismal formulas, tradition is the hallmark of the authenticity and unchangeableness of Christian preaching and teaching (1.10.1–2). To whatever land one travels, this teaching and preaching will be the same, a proof that the universality of the faith is identical with the unity of the faith: "The tradition of the apostles, made clear in all the world, can be clearly seen by those who wish to behold the truth" (3.3.1). "Apostolic succession," for Irenaeus, means not the succession of bishops but the unwavering succession of Christian teaching—the tradition—as delivered from apostle to bishop and from bishop to bishop. In this succession, "the apostolic tradition in the church and the preaching of the truth have come down to us" (3.3.3; cf. 4.26.2; 4.33.8). The truth is therefore to be found only in those churches professing the apostolic doctrine. An example of this doctrine is the quasi-creedal confession of God the Father as creator of heaven and earth; of Jesus Christ, who came in the flesh for our salvation; of the virginal conception, passion, death, and resurrection of Jesus; and of the Holy Spirit, who through the prophets declared this godly dispensation (1.10.1). Heresies, since they are not rooted in the tradition, are little else than inventions and groundless, unscriptural speculations. (A similar argument was to be used by Tertullian, *Praesc.* 19–22.)

Even if there were no written documents, that is, scripture, available, wrote Irenaeus in a moment of enthusiasm, untutored "barbarians" would need nothing more than the apostolic tradition to detect heresy (3.42). Yet Irenaeus in no way denigrates the importance of scripture. Tradition is the quintessential apostolic teaching both arising out of scripture and in turn used to interpret scripture, or, to put it another way, the church could interpret the Bible by means of the tradition and the tradition by means of the Bible. Scripture and tradition were related dialectically. It is not a question of whether scripture *or* tradition has the primacy; nor is it even a question of scripture *and* tradition; rather, it is more properly a question of *scriptural tradition*.

Was not Irenaeus's assertion as to the oneness and universality of tradition unrealistic? Could there not be variations within a tradition or among a number of traditions as well as variations among principles of scriptural interpretation? And what of those traditions, written or oral, that developed apart from any specific reference to scripture? In the writings of Origen, these and similar questions come to the fore. Although Origen realized that there were not only differences among contemporary Christians on a given subject but also differences with earlier generations, he claimed that the "teaching of the church, handed down in unbroken succession from the apostles, is still preserved and continues to exist in the churches up to this present day" (*Princ.* 1. *praef.* 2).

However, he added a caveat: some of the apostolic doctrines, that is, those found in scripture, are clear and unambiguous, but others are not patient of immediate comprehension inasmuch as they are statements for which no "how?" or "why?" is supplied. Such statements, Origen believed, were invitations to "lovers of wisdom" who wished to exercise their speculative gifts. Divergences of interpretation were therefore bound to arise, especially since not all people were gifted by the Holy Spirit with the "word of wisdom and knowledge." "Who," asked Origen, "on reading the revelations made to John, could not fail to be amazed at the deep obscurity of the unspeakable mysteries contained therein?" (4.2.3). Since not everyone is capable of comprehending such mysteries, Origen suggested a hierarchy of those who would interpret scripture: some will understand its "flesh" (the obvious, literal meaning); others, who have made some progress in the faith, will understand its "soul" (the deeper meaning); those who are "perfect" will discern its true "spirit" (4.2.4). (Here, Origen reflected the views of his Alexandrian predecessor Clement; cf. *Str.* 7.16.104.) Apart from the intellectual elitism implicit in such a statement, Origen was the first to delineate a distinction between the growing tradition that is to be believed by all and the growing types of interpretation of that tradition that allow for doctrinal pluralism. Origen's own highly allegorical and often wildly speculative approach to scripture was in fact a palpable example of the potential for the Christian tradition to take a variety of forms and to move in several directions, some of them based consciously on scripture and some of them articulated and developed apart from any scriptural warrant. There was in subsequent generations, however, an almost universal unwillingness to admit this phenomenon, since for the vast majority of Christians truth was perceived to be one, and if one, therefore unchanging and unchangeable.

Classical Period. The fourth and fifth centuries of the Christian era may be thought of as a period of creed-making. Many of these creeds were rejected as heterodox, while some of them achieved orthodox status. Competing views and heightened doctrinal controversies lay behind this phenomenon. Theological sparring—often more than sparring—led to anathemas and excommunications, with opposing parties all claiming to base their views on scripture. Textual missiles were hurled with seeming abandon. The authorities, ecclesial as well as imperial, used the formation of creeds to stem the tide of doctrinal disarray. To this extent, creeds, at least those assessed as "orthodox," came to be equated with the church's tradition. The creed of Nicaea (325), for instance, was initially promulgated as a statement intended to exclude Arius and his followers; it concludes with the unrelenting assertion that those who adopt Arianism "the holy, Catholic, and apostolic church anathematizes." As creedal tradition, therefore, the Nicene Symbol became, as it were, a defender of the faith. More than this, such creedal pronouncements were no longer viewed only as confessions of faith; rather, they became tests of orthodoxy. An individual's profession ("I believe") became the vehicle for episcopal authority ("We believe").

Athanasius, the primary contender for Nicene orthodoxy, could and did use arguments against the Arians similar to those used by Irenaeus against the Gnostics. The Arians' distortion of the Christian faith, he said, grew out of their inability to apprehend the "scope" (*skopos*) of scripture. For Athanasius, the Old and New Testaments, the teaching of the apostles, and the "tradition of the fathers" (*Ep. Adelph.* 6) were all summed up in the creed of Nicaea (*Decr.* 2) as a unified, internally cohesive, and eternally relevant statement of Christian truth—even though he had to go to exegetical extremes to show how the Son could be of one essence (*homoousios*) with the Father and how such a doctrine could be based in scripture.

The same kind of creed/tradition was composed a century later, in response to a host of doctrinal adversaries, at the Council of Chalcedon (451). The document framed by the participants defined Jesus as one person, "acknowledged in two natures, unconfusedly, unchangeably, indivisibly, inseparably," a statement believed to be strictly in line with Christian tradition and therefore in no way novel. The definition, the council said, was "even as from the beginning the prophets have taught, and as the Lord Jesus Christ himself has taught us, and as the Symbol of the Fathers has handed down [paradedōke] to us." That at best was an unhistorical, if not patently audacious claim. Yet it was a serious claim. The expansion and development of the creedal tradition was believed to be in the best interest of those who sought to protect the purity of the "faith that was once for all delivered to the saints." Unquestionably, however, as the writings of this period clearly show, innovation could not be avoided, even if novelty and heresy were seen by most as equivalent if not synonymous. In spite of the desire for doctrinal antiquity, unity, and universality, innovations of the most radical kind did take place. Tradition therefore served a twofold purpose: publicly, it guarded ancient truth; privately, it disguised innovation as ancient truth. Which is to say, tradition itself was from the beginning a fluid and elusive thing, sometimes rooted in scripture, sometimes going beyond scripture, and always open to new directions.

To combat the innovative nature of doctrinal heresies, Vincent of Lérins wrote that the authority of Catholic tradition rested in its being that which has been believed "everywhere, always, and by all" (*Comm.* 2). The early church surely held this as an ideal to be pursued diligently as it sought to be faithful to Christian tradition. Yet the history and development of Christian doctrine, in the early church and beyond, just as surely suggests a more realistic view: that the essence of Christian faith is not static but is always just beyond our grasp and therefore never patient of timeless definition. *See also* Apostolic Succession; Creeds; Rule of Faith.   [D.F.W.]

Bibliography
G.L. Prestige, *Fathers and Heretics* (London: SPCK, 1940), esp. Ch. 1; J. Moffatt, *The Thrill of Tradition* (New York: Macmillan, 1944); R.P.C. Hanson, *Origen's Doctrine of Tradition* (London: SPCK, 1954); F.W. Dillistone, ed., *Scripture and Tradition* (Greenwich: Seabury, and London: Lutterworth, 1955); O. Cullman, "The Tradition," *The Early Church* (Philadelphia: Westminster, 1956), pp. 59–99; R.P.C. Hanson, *Tradition in the Early Church* (London: SCM, 1962); G. Florovsky, "The Function of Tradition in the Ancient Church," *GOTR* 9 (1963):181–200; K.E. Skydsgaard and L. Vischer, eds., *Schrift und Tradition* (Zurich: EVZ, 1963); Y.M.-J. Congar, *Tradition and Traditions* (New York: Macmillan, 1966); J.P. Mackey, *Tradition and Change in the Church* (Dayton: Pflaum, 1968); H. von Campenhausen, *Tradition and Life in the Church* (London: Collins, 1968); J.F. Kelly, ed., *Perspectives on Scripture and Tradition* (Notre Dame: Fides, 1976); M.F. Wiles, "The Patristic Appeal to Tradition," *Explorations in Theology 4* (London: SCM, 1979); W. Rordorf and A. Schneider, *L'Evolution du concept de tradition dans l'église ancienne* (Berne: Lang, 1982).

TRADUCIANISM. Theory that individual human souls originate by derivation from the souls of the generating parents, in a way similar to the generation of individual bodies. The proponents of traducianism explain that God does indeed create individual souls but that the souls of parents provide a subject or matter for the divine activity, just as the bodies of the parents provide the matter for the creation of the body of their offspring. Thus, this process of creation is different from the original making from nothing, in which the divine activity presupposed no prior subject.

Although less popular than the theory that souls are created individually from nothing at the time of their infusion into a newly conceived body, the traducianist hypothesis was preferred to theories that asserted that individual souls preexist in an immaterial condition and are subsequently joined to bodies by their own choice or God's decree.

Two different forms of the traducianist theory were considered by early Christian thinkers. Tertullian (fl. 200) was the primary proponent of a materialist form of traducianism. He built the theory on an interpretation of Genesis 1:27 and 2:7. God formed humanity from a coarse matter, body, and a finer matter, soul. Each part obeys the divine command to multiply by secreting its seed. The two seeds are emitted simultaneously in copulation and grow together into a new human being (*Anim.* 27). Tertullian's views on the materiality of the soul were not widely shared, and his theory of human generation attracted little support.

The more widely considered traducianist theory was developed by Augustine of Hippo (354–430) in an attempt to understand the sin and death of all humanity in Adam, which are asserted in 1 Corinthians 15:22 and Romans 5:12. Augustine rejected Tertullian's materialism and proposed the hypothesis that God creates the soul of the offspring by working on a spiritual substrate drawn from the souls of the generating parents. Such a theory of the origin of the human soul could, he argued, explain the inheritance of the guilt and punishment of original sin and provide a mechanism for the transmission of its consequences, particularly mortality and concupiscence. Augustine provided extended discussions of this theory in *The Literal Meaning of Genesis* 10, in two letters (166 and 190), and in *On the Nature and Origin of the Soul*. Ultimately, he was willing to endorse neither the traducianist nor the alternative creationist theory of the origin of the soul. He judged that scripture simply did not provide an answer to the question.

The traducianist theory was subsequently condemned by pope Anastasius II (d. 498). In his defense of the theory of original sin, however, Fulgentius of Ruspe (ca. 462–ca. 527) argued that the traducianist theory could not be shown to be contrary to scripture. At the end of the sixth century, Gregory I the Great (ca. 540–604) pronounced the question unresolved. *See also* Anthropology; Original Sin; Soul.   [J.P.B.]

Bibliography

Tertullian, *On the Soul*, ed. J.H. Waszink, CCSL (1954), Vol. 2, pp. 779–869; tr. P. Holmes, ANF (1887), Vol. 3, pp. 181–235; Augustine, *The Literal Meaning of Genesis*, ed. J. Zycha, CSEL (1894), Vol. 28; tr. J.H. Taylor, ACW (1982), Vol. 41; idem, *Letters* 166 and 190, ed. A. Goldbacher, CSEL (1895–1923), Vols. 34, 44, 57, 58; tr. W. Parsons, FOTC (1951–1956), Vols. 12, 18, 20, 30, 32; idem, *On the Nature and Origin of the Soul*, ed. C. Urba and J. Zycha, CSEL (1913), Vol. 60; tr. P. Holmes, NPNF, 1st ser. (1887), Vol. 5, pp. 310–371.

A. Michel, "Traducianisme," DTC, Vol. 15, cols. 1350–1365; M.C. Preus, *Eloquence and Ignorance in Augustine's "On the Nature and Origin of the Soul"* (Atlanta: Scholars, 1985).

TRAJAN (53–117). Roman emperor (98–117). After a successful military career and service as consul (91), Trajan was adopted by the emperor Nerva (97), whom he succeeded. Extensive building and rebuilding of roads, bridges, and other public works took place in his reign, and a system of state loans (*alimenta*) to landowners, the interest on which was used for the maintenance of poor children in Italy, was put in place. He was popular with the army and brought the empire to its maximum extent by military campaigns and annexations. His final few years were marked by a revolt of the diaspora Jews and costly campaigns in the east. His rescript to Pliny the Younger (*Ep.* 10.97) in response to the latter's inquiry (10.96) set imperial policy toward Christians for some time to come: they were not to be hunted out; those proved guilty were to be punished; those who denied that they were Christians were to be pardoned upon worshiping the gods; anonymous accusations were not to be received in any case. A legend that Gregory the Great obtained the release of Trajan's soul from hell through prayer, once he became aware of the emperor's concern for justice, enjoyed widespread popularity in the Middle Ages. *See also* Persecution; Roman Empire.   [M.P.McH.]

Bibliography

Dio Cassius, *Roman History* 68; Pliny the Younger, *Panegyric on Trajan*; idem, *Letters*, Book 10; Eusebius, *Church History* 3.32, 33, 36.

G. Whatley, "The Uses of Hagiography: The Legend of Pope Gregory and the Emperor Trajan in the Middle Ages," *Viator* 15 (1984):25–63.

TRINITY. Christian doctrine of God as three in one. The doctrine of the Trinity is one of the most distinctive and fundamental tenets of the Christian faith. It declares that God is trinity, that the one indivisible Godhead exists and is known in three eternally distinct "persons"—Father, Son, and Spirit. It was during the patristic centuries that the church's Trinitarian faith assumed the shape it has largely retained throughout its history. Athanasius and the Cappadocians in the fourth century, and later Augustine, played a formative role. The

Nicene and "Athanasian" Creeds embody the determinations of the fathers on the Trinity.

Primitive Christianity, like Judaism, was distinguished from paganism by its unqualified monotheism (1 Cor. 8:4–6; cf. Acts 17:24–29; Gal. 3:20). What distinguished it within, and later from, Judaism was its conviction that Jesus was the Christ, the unique Son of God (Matt. 16:16; Rom. 1:2–4; Heb. 1:1–3). Moreover, the Spirit sent to give new birth to the church was in a special sense the Spirit of God or the Spirit of Christ (John 7:39; Rom. 8:9, 14). In various ways, the early Christians confessed both Christ and the Spirit to be "Lord," and spoke of them and their work in terms proper to God himself—albeit less explicitly of the Spirit (cf. John 14–16; 2 Cor. 3:17–18) than of the Son (cf. John 1:1, 18; 8:58; 20:28; Mark 2:7; Col. 2:9; Titus 2:13; Heb. 1:8, 10). The correlation of these new data of the Christian revelation with faith in one God had already begun in the New Testament, in semiformal confessional statements, both twofold (Father and Son: 1 Cor. 8:6; 1 Tim. 2:5–6; 2 Tim. 4:1; Gal. 1:3; 2 John 3; 1 Thess. 3:11) and threefold (Eph. 4:4–6; 1 Cor. 12:4–6; 1 Peter 1:2; with the clearest ones the most obviously liturgical—Matt. 28:19; 2 Cor. 13:14).

Apostolic Fathers. The earliest Christian writings outside the New Testament, the works of the apostolic fathers, likewise contain dyadic and triadic formulas side by side but show little interest in attempting more systematic explanations. A tendency to greater explicitness is nevertheless evident. For Ignatius, Christ is "God incarnate," "our God," "God made manifest in human form" (*Eph.* 7.2; 18.2; 19.3); and *2 Clement*, the oldest extant sermon outside the New Testament, teaches Christians to "think of Jesus as of God" (1.1). Although the three are juxtaposed almost instinctively by Clement of Rome (*1 Clem.* 46.6), the *Shepherd* of Hermas seems to identify the Spirit with the preincarnate Son or the divine in Christ (*Sim.* 5.6.4–7; 9.1.1). Christian faith readily worshiped and prayed to Christ as God and as a consequence was too easily tempted to compromise his humanity (cf. Docetism).

Greek Apologists. The Greek apologists, who flourished ca. 150–200, were the pioneers of a more articulated account of the relation between God and his Word or Son. To refute objections that, for example, creation and incarnation were incompatible with divine transcendence and immutability, they pressed into service, no doubt partly prompted by John 1, the concept of the Logos (Greek, "word" or "reason"), familiar to Hellenistic philosophical theology, especially in Philo, where it tended to merge with the figure of God's Wisdom (cf. Prov. 8:22–31). In these contexts, the Logos was viewed as a power intermediate between God and the world, and a rational principle of order in creation and providence, enabling human beings by reason to apprehend God. This cosmological framework of thought, invaluable apologetically as it was, cast Christian theology in a mold that it found difficult to break.

In summary, the apologists portrayed the Logos as eternally preexisting with or in the Father as his wisdom or mind and as emitted or generated as his Word or Son for creation and revelation. Neither change nor separation from God was entailed in the transition from immanent (*endiathetos*, according to the Stoic distinction, used explicitly by Theophilus, *Autol.* 2.10, 22) Logos to uttered (*prophorikos*) Logos. The being of the Logos was placed firmly in the Godhead; the Son, "being Logos and first-begotten of God, is also God" (Justin, *1 Apol.* 63.15). Although to Justin the Logos was numerically distinct from the Father ("another who is, and is called, God and Lord," *Dial.* 56.4), his personal character remained obscure ("God, being eternally rational [*logikos*], from the beginning had his Logos in himself," Athenagoras, *Leg.* 10), at least prior to his extrapolation as the agent of God's dealings with the world, for not until then, according to the apologists, was he "generated" as Son. The whole presentation was colored by notions of divine rationality.

Theophilus was the first Christian writer to use the Greek word *trias* in this context. His "triad" was God, his Word, and his Wisdom (*Autol.* 2.15). The apologists generally identified Word and Wisdom and not infrequently confused Word and Spirit (e.g., Justin, *1 Apol.* 33.6). Although Christian theology now for the first time talked explicitly about "three" divine beings (cf. Justin, *1 Apol.* 13.3; 60.6–7), the apologists' stress fell on a plurality within the Godhead that was manifested in sequence, as a human being puts forth his mind and spirit in his outward activity (cf. Athenagoras, *Leg.* 10). This approach has come to be called "economic," because of the successive manifestations of the triad in the course of the "economy" (Greek *oikonomia*), the ordered unfolding of God's dealings with the world and humankind in creation, revelation, incarnation, and judgment.

Irenaeus. Irenaeus's teaching falls within a similar pattern, although it is far more biblical in flavor, for example in its interest in the interrelations among Father, Son, and Spirit in the economy. Irenaeus gives greater prominence to the Spirit, whom he identifies with God's Wisdom, and his language (but not the basic structure of his thinking) even suggests the Son's generation from the Father from eternity, and not merely prior to creation. He depicts God's Word and Spirit as becoming his "hands" for the work of the economy—an image indicative both of his biblical temper and of the limitations of his thought. He scarcely broaches the question of the eternal relationships among Father, Son, and Spirit or conceives of them as divine "persons."

Monarchianism. Reactionary defenders of the divine unity found a ready hearing ca. 200, chiefly in the west and especially at Rome. These Monarchians (Greek *monarchia*, "single source/principle") feared that the theology of the Logos and the economy implied two (or three) Gods. They all denied distinct being to God's Word and Spirit—the "Modalist Monarchians," such as Noetus and the mysterious Praxeas, by treating "Father," "Son," and "Spirit" as mere names for the single Godhead's changing modes or roles; the "Dynamic" or "Adoptionist Monarchians" by envisaging Christ as an ordinary man indwelt or inspired by divine power. They all appeared to safeguard not only God's oneness but even Christ's divinity, in a theology that had an immediate resonance with popular piety. Sabellius presented a subtler form of Monarchianism, with

some suggestion of successiveness in the three manifestations of the one God.

Economic Trinity. Early in the third century, Hippolytus of Rome (*Noet.*) and Tertullian (*Prax.*) rebutted Monarchianism by means of a refined economic Trinitarianism. Both still placed the Son's generation prior to his work of creation but sharpened the distinct individuality of the Logos immanent eternally in the Godhead. Tertullian, the creative pioneer of Christian Latin, significantly advanced understanding by his more technical analysis and more precise terminology. He was the first to use the word *trinitas* (*Prax.* 3). The Godhead was a single *substantia*, shared by the Son and the Spirit. The three *personae* were three not in their basic quality or power but in "grade" or "sequence" (*gradus*), "aspect" (*forma*), and "manifestation" (*species*). The Spirit issues from the Father through the Son, being "third from the Father and the Son, just as the fruit derived from the shoot is third from the root" (*Prax.* 8). Although the economic perspective is inescapable (he spoke of the economy "distributing the unity into Trinity," *Prax.* 2), Tertullian clarified both the oneness of the divine "substance," of which the three were embodiments, and their distinctness in almost personal terms. He provided the basic configuration of the Latin west's approach to this doctrine, but in terminology confusing or even scandalous to the east. *Substantia*, fixed upon by Tertullian for the single divine being, had its precise Greek equivalent in *hypostasis*, which easterners would soon be insistently applying to the three!

Novatian and Origen. By the mid-third century, an obvious weakness of economic theology was overcome. Novatian of Rome, author of the first treatise *On the Trinity*, insisted that, since the Father is always Father, he must always have had a Son, although he still affirmed his being "in the Father" before he was "with the Father" (16; 31). In the east, Origen's account of the Son's "eternal generation" unambiguously established the Word's eternal distinctness as that of a Son in relation to his Father. Against Monarchianism, he emphasized that Father, Son, and Spirit are three eternally distinct *hypostaseis*. *Hypostasis* became in time the Greek counterpart to the Latin *persona*, but to Origen it meant a concretely existent being. The divinity of Son and Spirit is not in doubt, for it derives from the Father (through the Son, in the Spirit's case), who is alone *autotheos*, God in the absolute sense, "(the) God" (*ho theos*) rather than merely "God" (*theos*; *Comm. in Jo.* 2.2–3). The hierarchical structure of Platonism's vision of reality left Origen's Trinity a graded one, with the Son ("a secondary God," *Cels.* 5.39) sharply subordinated to the Father, and the Spirit to the Son. The Father's operation extends to the whole cosmos, the Son's only to rational beings, the Spirit's only to the sanctified. So the three shared in a community of divine being, but at three levels, as it were. Origen's teaching had immense influence in the east. Its different strands are not easily harmonized, but the accent fell on the plurality of distinct *hypostaseis* united in a subordinationist schema in which derivation implied inferiority.

The Dionysii. The diverging tendencies of eastern and western triadic theology were starkly revealed ca. 260 in an exchange between Dionysius of Alexandria and Dionysius of Rome. The former's insistence on three distinct *hypostaseis* in refuting Sabellian Monarchianism sounded suspiciously like tritheism to his Roman namesake. The correspondence showed that, apart from some confusion of terminology (Rome was much happier with *homoousios* than was Alexandria—Origen had probably not used it), the Latins approached the Trinity from the oneness and the Greeks from the threeness. To western churchmen, the east imperilled the divine unity; to easterners, the west smacked of Sabellianism.

Arian Controversy. The teaching of Arius, an Alexandrian presbyter, sparked ca. 318 a long controversy in the east that issued in a creedally defined doctrine of the Trinity before the end of the century. Citing John 17:3, he propounded a monotheism of the Father, who alone was truly God. The Word was a perfect creature (according to Col. 1:15 and Prov. 8:22, the latter an influential passage in early Christian thought in this area, which in the Septua-

gint more obviously implied creation than generation). As created, the Word had a beginning of existence, albeit "before times," for he was the agent of the rest of creation including time. Although by courtesy he could be called Son of God or God, he did not share God's being or any of his perfections.

Arius won support beyond Alexandria, from Eusebius of Caesarea, for example, whose views represented a radical Origenism; however, the Council of Nicaea (325) convincingly condemned Arius's teaching. The Council's creed anathematized a set of Arian maxims and affirmed that the Son was "begotten, not made," "true God from [out of] true God," begotten "from the substance [*ousia*] of the Father" and "of one substance with [*homoousios*] the Father." The sequel revealed how contentious these last two statements could be. *Ousia* could mean "a being" (like *hypostasis*) or "the being" (i.e., nature, essence) of a thing. Churchmen like Eusebius feared that *homoousios* implied a materialistic division of the Godhead between Father and Son, while others suspected Sabellianism, contrary to the Origenist distinction of *hypostaseis*. *Homoousios* had not had a happy history in the east, having been used by Gnostics and heretics (possibly Paul of Samosata) more than by anyone else.

The meaning of *homoousios* in the creed has long been debated. To most present at Nicaea, it probably bore a generic sense ("homogeneous"), asserting that the Son was as divine as the Father was. This left unclear how the two were one God. The ensuing debate showed that, if ditheism or the splitting of the Godhead were to be guarded against, it was necessary to affirm not only that Father and Son were equally divine but that they each fully possessed the single (numerically one) being of Godhead. A few at Nicaea may have read *homoousios* in this stronger sense (parallel to Tertullian's "one *substantia*"), but the council did not itself address the issue of the divine unity.

An anti-Nicene reaction soon set in, fueled by the extremism of a few of the creed's keenest champions, notably Marcellus of Ancyra, whose teaching bore too much resemblance to Sabellianism. His notion of the divine monad diversifying into a triad and, at the end, being reabsorbed into the monad (he cited 1 Cor. 15:24) eventually led to the inclusion of "whose kingdom shall have no end" in the later version of the Nicene Creed. The theology of Marcellus confirmed fears aroused by *homoousios*, which suffered also from being extrabiblical.

Athanasius. The great Athanasius, bishop of Alexandria 328–373, indefatigably resisted any refinement of Arianism. Not only was it polytheistic and incompatible with baptism in the threefold name, but it struck at the heart of Christian confidence that in Christ the divine Son reunited humanity with God. Athanasius's own Trinitarian teaching marked an enormous step forward in its depth and comprehensiveness. One statement sums it up: "If the Son as offspring is other than the Father, he is identical with him as God" (*Ar.* 3.4). He did not depend heavily on technical vocabulary. (Only later did he regularly use *homoousios*, and he had no fixed term for "person.") He made full use of the eternal generation of the Son (the Father is "always generative," *Ar.* 3.66), showing that the Son fully shared the Father's divine substance and was completely like him. Because the divine nature was indivisible, the Godhead of Father and Son is a single entity. They are like light and its shining—distinguishable but the same one substance.

Athanasius maintained his position against a variety of counterpresentations, of which some were not far removed from the faith of Nicaea, but none tolerated *homoousios*. Yet from the mid-350s a bridge-building movement began. Basil of Ancyra led a group that rejected identity of *ousia* (and hence *homoousios*) but affirmed that Father and Son were of like *ousia*—*homoiousios*. Hilary of Poitiers, almost the only significant western contributor to these fourth-century debates, saw the potential of this interpretation and argued that each of the two positions not only allowed for but required the other as a corrective complement.

Athanasius also welcomed the *homoiousios* development, and held a synod at Alexandria (362) that clarified the confusingly indiscriminate use of *ousia* and *hypostasis* (seen in the creed of Nicaea itself). "Those who had been blamed for saying there were three *hypostaseis* agreed with the others, while those who had spoken of one *ousia* also confessed the doctrine of the former" (Athanasius, *Tom.* 6).

Another achievement of Athanasius was to bring the Holy Spirit into the center of reflection and to insist on his full divinity. (Although the Arians generally regarded the Spirit as created through the Son, Nicaea said nothing on the subject. No treatise on the person of the Spirit seems to have been written before 350.) Athanasius's *Letters to Serapion* (ca. 360) refuted the views of some Egyptians who accepted *homoousios* of the Son but regarded the Spirit as created out of nothing. He argued his case from the Bible's close association of the Spirit with the Father and Son, especially in creation, the inspiration of the prophets, the incarnation, and the imparting of the life of God to humankind. As earlier concerning the Son, so now concerning the Spirit, Athanasius is emphatic that only the divine can bestow divine life. "By the participation of the Spirit, we are knit into the Godhead" (*Ar.* 3.24).

Cappadocians. Yet even Athanasius declined to call the Spirit "God." A similar hesitation is evident in those Cappadocian theologians who were chiefly responsible for the rehabilitation of Nicaea in the Nicene Creed, which, according to a tradition accepted by most scholars, was approved by the Council of Constantinople in 381 (and hence is also known as the Niceno-Constantinopolitan Creed). Its most obvious difference from the creed of 325 is its much fuller statement about the Spirit: "The Lord and Life-giver, who proceeds from the Father, who with the Father and the Son is jointly worshiped and jointly glorified, who spoke through the prophets."

This restrained wording reflected the thinking of the Cappadocians, who were very conscious of the development of the doctrine of the Spirit, both in themselves and in salvation history as a whole. Basil's *On the Holy Spirit* (375) appealed to the church's threefold baptismal formula and doxology and the Spirit's intimate connection in scripture with the being and activities of the Father and Son. To Gregory of Nazianzus, such evidence warranted calling the Spirit "God" and *homoousios* (*Or.* 31.10). But scripture provided no obvious category for relating the Spirit to the Father or Son, comparable with "generation" for the Son. Gregory picked up "procession" from John 15:26; Gregory of Nyssa laid the basis for the standard eastern view that the Spirit "proceeds" (a term whose meaning was no less ineffable than "generation") *from* the Father *through* the Son. Thus, the distinctiveness of Son and Spirit was grounded in their modes of origin.

The Cappadocian theology undergirding the Nicene Creed, which reiterates Nicaea's keynote confession that the Son is "*homoousios* with the Father," reconciled Athanasius's teaching with the traditional insistence on the distinctness of the three. The key formula was "one *ousia* in three *hypostaseis*"—agreement having at last been reached on the differentiation of these two terms. The Cappadocians' numerous discussions (backed by the writings of Didymus the Blind of Alexandria, Amphilochius of Iconium, Evagrius of Pontus, and others) acknowledged that, although revelation required us to express the internal relations between the persons in such terms as "begottenness" and "procession," we could not penetrate to the realities they denoted. The Cappadocians' emphasis lay on the individuality of the three *hypostaseis*, which they compared to three particulars of a universal, like three human beings. This analogy was easily misconstrued (even when its Platonic inspiration was remembered) and exposed them to accusations of tritheism. Yet ultimately they believed that deity was an indivisible reality, of which the *hypostaseis* were eternally and simultaneously existing modes of being or forms of objective presentation. The divine unity was also highlighted by their exposition of the mutual interpenetration or co-inherence of the three (later to be called *perichoresis*) and the inseparability of their works.

Augustine. Before Augustine, few western theologians had much to contribute on the Trinity. Augustine derived some inspiration from the complex, heavily Neoplatonic writings of Marius Victorinus (e.g., on the soul as an analogy of the Trinity, and on the Spirit as the bond between Father and Son). Victorinus portrayed the relation between the persons in dynamic or mobile terms, like "an immanent dialectal process" (J.N.D. Kelly) in the Godhead, with a strong stress on their mutual indwelling or circuminsession.

Augustine's teaching, set forth supremely in *On the Trinity*, a work as much of contemplation as of speculative dogmatics, is suggestive and profound. The divine unity and the equality of the three are to the fore. None is greater or lesser than either of the others in respect of divinity, and each is identical with the divine *essentia* (which he preferred to "substance," to exclude any Aristotelian implication that in God substance is distinguishable from attributes). The three co-inhere with each other, and their operation is inseparable, by virtue of a single, indivisible will and action. He disliked the term *personae*, because it implied separate individuals. In one of his most original insights, he identified their distinctiveness precisely with their relations with one another—the Father's begetting, the Son's begottenness, and the Spirit's proceeding being the mutual love or communion between the two. The Spirit was therefore identically related to both Father and Son, and proceeded from the Father "and the Son" (Latin *Filioque*), not "through the Son," as the eastern church had come to believe. The insertion of the *Filioque* into the Latin version of the Nicene Creed, probably first made late in the sixth century, proved a major bone of contention between east and west.

Augustine thus focused attention more heavily than his predecessors on the immanent interrelationships within the eternal Trinity. His most distinctive contribution was probably to fasten on the human being, and particularly the soul, as the best analogy of the Trinity (cf. Gen. 1:26, "Let *us* make man in *our* image"). Of the several possibilities he considered, the most satisfying was that of the mind as remembering, knowing, and loving God. He was aware of the limitations of all analogies but typically preferred one that grounded theological discernment in spirituality and worship.

The "Athanasian" Creed (*Quicunque vult*), compiled in southern Gaul ca. 500, is deeply indebted to Augustine in its Trinitarian section, which sums up patristic understanding in the west. "The Godhead of the Father, the Son, and the Holy Spirit is one, their glory is equal, their majesty co-eternal. . . . In this Trinity, there is nothing before or after, nothing greater or less, but all three persons are co-eternal with each other and co-equal." In the end, the western tradition views the Trinity on a triangular model, the eastern on a linear model. The difference is significantly encapsulated in their divergent accounts of the procession of the Spirit.

Conclusion. Neither human analysis nor human language was equal to the demands of Trinitarian theology, as the fathers were only too aware. They were provoked to reflect on the limitations of words, not least those of technical definition. They came to realize that the father-son analogy did not require that the Father preexisted the Son, that is, that its application was not unrestricted. Early Trinitarianism was also an area in which the axiom *lex orandi lex credendi* (literally, "the law of praying [determines] the law of believing") was most evidently operative. From the outset, Father, Son, and Spirit were named together in baptism and in benediction. Christians at worship regularly expressed what theologians struggled to articulate satisfactorily. Believers "lived" tensions and antinomies that reasoned faith found hard to resolve. *See also* God; Homoousios; Hypostasis; Logos; Monarchianism; Nicaea, Council of; Substance.   [D.F.Wr.]

Bibliography

J. Lebreton, *Histoire du dogme de la Trinité des origines au concile de Nicée*, 2 vols. (Paris: Beauchesne, Vol. 1, 1927; Vol. 2, 1928), Engl. tr. of Vol. 1 (London: Burns, Oates, 1939); A.E.J. Rawlinson, ed., *Essays on the Trinity and the Incarnation* (London: Longmans, Green, 1928); G. Kretschmar, *Studien zur frühchristlichen Trinitätstheologie* (Tübingen: Mohr, 1956); G.L. Prestige, *God in Patristic Thought*, 2nd ed. (London: SPCK, 1952); H.A. Wolfson, *The Philosophy of the Church Fathers*, Vol. 1, 2nd ed. (Cambridge: Harvard UP, 1964); A.W. Wainwright, *The Trinity in the New Testament*, 2nd ed. (London: SPCK, 1969); J. Pelikan, *The Emergence of the Catholic Tradition (100-600)* (Chicago: U of Chicago P, 1971); J.N.D. Kelly, *Early Christian Creeds*, 3rd ed. (London: Longmans, 1972); B. Lonergan, *The Way to Nicaea* (London: Darton, Longman and Todd, 1976); C. Stead, *Divine Substance* (Oxford: Oxford UP, 1977); Kelly, pp. 83–137, 223–279; B. Studer, *Gott und unser Erlösung im Glauben der Alten Kirche* (Düsseldorf: Patmos, 1985); M. O'Carroll, *Trinitas: A Theological Encyclopedia of the Holy Trinity* (Wilmington: Glazier, 1986); R.P.C. Hanson, *The Search for the Christian Doctrine of God: The Arian Controversy 318-381* (Edinburgh: T. & T. Clark, 1988); T.F. Torrance, *The Trinitarian Faith: The Evangelical Theology of the Ancient Catholic Church* (Edinburgh: T. and T. Clark, 1988).

TRISAGION. A doxology. Literally, from the Greek, "thrice holy," the Trisagion appears in the form "O holy God, O holy mighty One, O holy immortal One, have mercy on us." The threefold repetition of "holy" goes back to Isaiah 6:3, where it expresses the superlative (cf. Jer. 7:4; 22:29; Ezek. 21:32). Use of the Trisagion in the liturgy in the east dates from the mid-fifth century. It appeared in the Gallican rite as the *Aius*, sung in both Greek and Latin, and from there was introduced in the eleventh century into the Roman liturgy of Good Friday, to be sung as one refrain during the veneration of the cross. It must be distinguished from the *Sanctus*, the threefold "holy" that concludes the Preface and introduces the Canon of the Mass. *See also* Doxology.

[M.P.McH.]

Bibliography

J. Quasten, "Oriental Influence in the Gallican Liturgy," *Traditio* 1 (1943):55–78; J. Mateos, "La Célébration de la parole dans la liturgie byzantine," *Orientalia Christiana Analecta* 191 (1971):91–126.

TYCONIUS (fl. 370–390). Lay theologian and biblical commentator of the Donatist church of Roman Africa. Against the views of his fellow Donatists, Tyconius argued that the church was not a perfect society restricted to the African Donatists. The nature of the church was "bipartite," that is, composed of both good and bad members. Tyconius's insistence upon the universality of the church earned him the censure of his bishop, Parmenian, in 378 but ensured a respectful hearing from the Catholics, notably from his younger contemporary Augustine after his return to Africa in 388.

Tyconius is best remembered for two works, the *Book of Rules*, the first manual of scriptural interpretation in the Latin west, and for his commentary on the Book of Revelation. The *Book of Rules* elaborates a theory about seven "mystical rules" found throughout scripture, and focuses attention upon the interpretation of scriptural promises or threats directed at certain peoples or nations. Tyconius argues that, whether these prophecies address a remote past or the "last days," they are fulfilled "spiritually" in the church. Likewise, in his commentary on Revelation, Tyconius opposes the literal interpretation of such passages as the thousand-year reign in Jerusalem (Rev. 20:1–5). The "first resurrection" is already experienced "spiritually" in the church. The influence of Tyconius's commentary, now known only in fragments, can be traced from the fifth to the eleventh century. The *Book of Rules* has survived intact, but its fame has been eclipsed by the summary and commentary on Tyconius's "seven rules" that Augustine included in the third book of *On Christian Doctrine*. CPL 709–710. [P.B.]

Bibliography

PL 18.15–66; F.C. Burkitt, *The Rules of Tyconius* (Cambridge: Cambridge UP, 1894); F. LoBue and G.C. Willis, *The Turin Fragments: Commentary on Revelation* (Cambridge: Cambridge UP, 1963).

D.L. Anderson, *The Book of Rules of Tyconius: An Introduction and Translation with Commentary* (Ph.D. diss., Southern Baptist Theological Seminary [Louisville], 1974; Ann Arbor: University Microfilms, 1980); K. Froelich, *Biblical Interpretation in the Early Church* (Philadelphia: Fortress, 1984); W.S. Babcock, *Tyconius: The Book of Rules* (Atlanta: Scholars, 1989).

T. Hahn, *Tyconius-Studien: Ein Beitrag zur Kirchen und Dogmengeschichte des 4. Jahrhunderts* (Leipzig: Dietrich, 1900); A. Pincherle, "Da Ticonio a Sant' Agostino," *Ricerche religiose* 1 (1925):443–466; W.H.C. Frend, *The Donatist Church: A Movement of Protest in Roman North Africa* (Oxford: Clarendon, 1952); K. Steinhausen, *The Apocalypse Commentary of Tyconius: A History of Its Reception and Influence* (Berne: Lang, 1987); P. Bright, *The Book of Rules of Tyconius: Its Purpose and Inner Logic* (U of Notre Dame P, 1988).

U

ULFILAS (ca. 311–ca. 383). Bishop among the Goths and Bible translator. Descended from a Christian family of Cappadocia that had been captured by the Goths, Ulfilas (or Wulfila) was fluent in Greek and Latin as well as in Gothic. He was consecrated bishop (ca. 341) by Eusebius of Nicomedia, an adherent of Arianism who was then occupying the see of Constantinople. (Ulfilas was not the first bishop of the Goths, for a bishop Theodore of the Goths took part in the Council of Nicaea in 325.) After working in the area along the lower Danube for several years (ca. 341–348), to escape persecution he settled his followers in Moesia within the Roman empire, in response to the invitation of the emperor Constantius II. The creed he preached was Arian. Thus, Arianism spread from the Goths to the other Germanic tribes and then reentered the empire when those peoples later invaded the west and established their kingdoms there. He died at Constantinople, where he was attending a synod.

Ulfilas composed a profession of faith that was reproduced in the *Epistula de fide, vita, et obitu Ulfilae* of his student Auxentius, the Arian bishop of Durostorum; that letter was itself preserved through its inclusion in the work of another Arian bishop directed against Ambrose (383; CPL 689, 692). Ulfilas's most significant work, undertaken either alone or with the help of collaborators, was his translation of the Bible into Gothic, for which purpose he may have devised the Gothic alphabet. He is reported to have omitted the books of Kings (because of their martial nature); of his New Testament, much of the four Gospels and letters of Paul survives, but only fragments of Ezra and Nehemiah remain from the Hebrew scriptures. Other writings by Ulfilas are lost. *See also* Goths. [M.P.McH.]

Bibliography

Philostorgius, *Church History* 2.5; Socrates, *Church History* 2.41; 4.33–34; Sozomen, *Church History* 4.24; 6.37; Theodoret, *Church History* 4.33.

G.W.S. Friedrichsen, *The Gothic Version of the Gospels: A Study of Its Style and Textual History* (London: Oxford UP, 1926); idem, *The Gothic Version of the Epistles: A Study of Its Style and Textual History* (London: Oxford UP, 1939); E.A. Thompson, *The Visigoths in the Time of Ulfila* (Oxford: Clarendon, 1966); M.J. Hunter, "The Gothic Bible," *The Cambridge History of the Bible*, ed. G.W.H. Lampe (Cambridge: Cambridge UP, 1969), Vol. 2, pp. 338–362; M. Simonetti, "L'arianesimo di Ulfila," *RomBarb* 1 (1976):297–323; H. Schäferdiek, "Wulfila: vom Bischof von Gotien zum Gotenbischof," *ZKG* 90 (1979):253–292.

V

VALENS (fl. 357–371). Bishop of Mursa in Pannonia. Valens and his fellow Balkan bishop Ursacius of Singidunum (Belgrade) led the cause of Arianism and the religious policy of emperor Constantius II. The Roman provinces of Illyricum and Pannonia were the center of Arianism in the western half of the empire. Valens achieved the episcopacy early in life and strongly, if inconsistently, supported Constantius's anti-Nicene and anti-Athanasian efforts in the west, following the death of Constantine's other son and ruler in the west, the pro-Nicene Constans.

At various synods in the 350s and 360s, especially that of Sirmium in 357, which drafted the earliest Latin statement on Arianism extant today, Valens and Ursacius asserted in varying degrees the Arian position. The boldness of the "Blasphemy of Sirmium," as Hilary of Poitiers (*Syn.* 10) characterized it, aroused the western church to confront the challenge to Nicene orthodoxy. CPL 450, 451, 455, 682–684. *See also* Arianism. [H.R.]

Bibliography

M. Meslin, *Les Ariens d'Occident* (Paris: Seuill, 1967), pp. 335–430.

VALENS (ca. 328–378). Roman emperor (364–378). Valens was made emperor of the east by his elder brother, Valentinian I, who took for himself the rule of the west. Valens's campaign against the Visigoths (367–369) was unsuccessful. Later, he assented to their request to enter the empire across the Danube in Moesia in order to escape the pressure of the Huns. Ill-treatment by the Romans caused them to revolt; Valens died fighting them in the Roman disaster at Adrianople. The last emperor to adhere to Arianism, he ordered (365) the exile of the orthodox bishops previously expelled by Constantius II but restored by Julian; but he failed to remove Basil of Caesarea and was compelled to restore Athanasius to Alexandria. There is strong evidence that he recalled the Nicene exiles in the last year of his rule. CPL 1574. [M.P.McH.]

Bibliography

Ammianus Marcellinus, *History* 26.4–31.14; Basil, *Letters* 242–243; Gregory of Nazianzus, *On His Father* 37; idem, *On Saint Basil the Great* 30–33; 44–45; Gregory of Nyssa, *Against Eunomius* 1.12; Socrates, *Church History* 4.1–3, 5–6, 8–9, 13–22, 24, 32–38; Sozomen, *Church History* 6.6–18, 21, 35–37, 39–40; Theodoret, *Church History* 2.6; 4.5, 7, 11–19, 28–33; 5.1, 20.

J.A. Arvites, "The Military Campaigns of Adrianople," *HT* 31.4 (1981):30–35; R. Snee, "Valens' Recall of the Nicene Exiles and Anti-Arian Propaganda," *GRBS* 26 (1985):395–419; R. van Dam, "Emperor, Bishops, and Friends in Late Antique Cappadocia," *JThS* n.s. 37 (1986):53–76; P. Heather, "The Crossing of the Danube and the Gothic Conversion," *GRBS* 27 (1986):289–318.

VALENTINIAN I (321–375). Roman emperor (364–375). A career military officer, Valentinian came to the throne as successor to Jovian. Shortly after his accession, he designated Valens, his younger brother, as eastern emperor. He succeeded in defending the northern frontiers of the empire against unremitting barbarian incursions on the Rhine and Danube. His religious policy was one of broad toleration. He was orthodox in faith but did not forbid pagan worship; he confirmed the elections to the see of Milan of both Auxentius, an adherent of Arianism, and later of the Catholic Ambrose. Forced to intervene (366) in a disputed election to the see of Rome because of severe disturbances in the city, he supported Damasus I against Ursinus, the rival claimant; in 371, he intervened to clear Damasus of charges of sexual immorality. A number of laws directed against abuse of the clerical state were issued in his reign. CPL 1574.   [M.P.McH.]

Bibliography

Ammianus Marcellinus, *History* 26.1–30.9; Ambrose, *On the Death of Valentinian (II)* 20; 55; idem, *Letters* 17.16; 21.2–5; Socrates, *Church History* 4.1–2, 30–31; Sozomen, *Church History* 6.6–7, 21, 36; Theodoret, *Church History* 3.12; 4.5–8; Symmachus, *Laudatio in Valentinianum Seniorem Augustum prior*, ed. F. Del Chicca (Rome: Herder, 1984).

R. Soraci, *L'imperatore Valentiniano I* (Catania: Edigraf, 1971).

VALENTINIAN II (371–392). Roman emperor (375–392). The son of Valentinian I, Valentinian II was accepted while still a young child as joint ruler, with his half-brother, Gratian, of Italy, Africa, and Illyricum. After Gratian was killed by the usurper Maximus (383), Valentinian was allowed a limited authority for a few years but was eventually driven from Italy (387). He was restored a year later by the eastern emperor, Theodosius I, who left the general Arbogast as his protector. He died at the age of twenty, either by suicide or more likely by murder at Arbogast's instigation. Throughout his career, Valentinian II was much involved with Ambrose, who undertook two missions to Maximus (383, 384) on his behalf in order to avert an invasion of Italy. Ambrose successfully opposed the *relatio* of the Symmachus seeking the restoration of the altar and statue of Victory at Rome (386) and withstood the efforts of Valentinian's mother, Justina, to gain a basilica in Milan for the adherents of Arianism (385–386). Ambrose arranged for Valentinian's burial and delivered the funeral oration. CPL 1572–1575, 1624.   *See also* Ambrose.   [M.P.McH.]

Bibliography

Ammianus Marcellinus, *History* 30.10; Ambrose, *Letters* 17; 18; 20; 21; 24; 53; 57.2–3, 5; idem, *Sermon Against Auxentius on the Giving Up of the Basilicas*; idem, *Joseph* 6.30–7.38; idem, *On the Death of Valentinian (II)*; Socrates, *Church History* 4.10; 31; 5.11–12, 14, 25; Sozomen, *Church History* 6.36; 7.13–14, 22; Theodoret, *Church History* 5.13–15, 24.

VALENTINIAN III (419–455). Roman emperor (425–455). Valentinian III was the son of Constantius III and Galla Placidia. His mother (d. 450) was the effective ruler for many years; later, his general Aetius held considerable power. Africa and Britain were lost during his reign, and there were serious uprisings in Spain and Gaul, although Aetius was able to check Attila in battle (451). Valentinian murdered Aetius (454) but was himself killed in the next year by members of the slain general's retinue. In his reign, the law code of Theodosius II (the Theodosian Code) was promulgated in the west as well as the east (438). His religious policy was much influenced by Leo the Great. Most notably, when Hilary of Arles attempted to depose a bishop (444), Leo deprived Hilary of jurisdiction and gained from Valentinian a decree recognizing Roman primacy over the western church. CPL 1656, *epist.* 8, 11, 55, 73, 100, 110.   [M.P.McH.]

Bibliography

Socrates, *Church History* 7.24,46; Sozomen, *Church History* 9.16.

C.D. Gordon, *The Age of Attila: Fifth Century Byzantium and the Barbarians* (Ann Arbor: U of Michigan P, 1960).

VALENTINUS (fl. 120–160). Christian teacher whose doctrines the church fathers condemned as Gnostic heresy. Born in Egypt and educated in Alexandria, Valentinus arrived in Rome sometime between 136 and 140. He is said to have left for Cyprus in 160; details of his death are unknown. According to Tertullian (*Val.* 4) and Eusebius (*H.E.* 4.11.1), he may have left Rome due to conflict within the Christian church there.

Valentinus was noted even by his most virulent detractors for his brilliance and eloquence. He produced a wide variety of writings—letters, sermons, a psalm, and a tractate *On the Three Natures*—of which only fragments remain. Many scholars, however, believe that the *Gospel of Truth* from Nag Hammadi may be attributed to Valentinus. If so, the text is of inestimable importance, since it is extremely difficult to distinguish his teachings from those of his students and followers based on the fragments and descriptions from the church fathers, especially Clement of Alexandria, Irenaeus, Tertullian, Hippolytus, and Epiphanius.

The works of Valentinus show an interest in speculative theology and biblical interpretation that is tied to deep spiritual sensibilities. His speculative thinking clearly shows a knowledge of Christian, Gnostic, and Platonic materials.

According to Valentinus, the divine world of the *plērōma* ("fullness") consists of a primordial male-female duality, "Ineffable" and "Silence." From these, a second duality is emitted, and from them a quartet. These form the first Ogdoad; eleven pairs of male-female aeons (or powers) follow from them, forming the completion (thirty aeons) of the *plērōma*. The last and therefore youngest of these is Sophia. Being the farthest from the primordial duality, she is said to be "lacking" and becomes filled with desire or revolt. From this emotion or "error" arises the whole of the created world, including its creator, the Demiurge (identified with the God of Genesis). In an attempt to separate her desire from the darkness outside the *plērōma*, portions of spirit and soul become encased in flesh. This gives rise in some Valentinian systems to the division of humanity into three classes: spiritual, psychic (soul), and choic (material). To save the imprisoned spirit, the heavenly Christ sends down the savior Jesus to teach the lost souls about their true nature and destiny so that at death they may ascend once again to their true home above. The *Gospel of Truth* is a magnificent and eloquent monument to the profundity of Valentinus's understanding of the human desire to escape the bonds of ignorance and attain mystical, saving knowledge of God.

The influence of Valentinus as a teacher is shown by the number and importance of his followers, among them Florinus, Heracleon, Marcus, Ptolemy, and Theodotus. Valentinian Christianity flourished from the second to the fourth centuries, and its exclusion from the church played a decisive role in the development of Christian orthodoxy. *See also* Gnosticism.   [K.L.K.]

Bibliography

Irenaeus, *Against Heresy* 1.1–8, 11–21; Clement of Alexandria, *Miscellanies* 2.36.2–4; 2.114.3–6; 3.59.3; 4.89.1–4.90.1; 6.52.3–4; Hippolytus, *Refutation of All Heresies* 6.16–50, esp. 6.37.7–8; 6.42.2; Tertullian, *Against the Valentinians*; idem, *Prescription Against Heretics* 30; Pseudo-Tertullian, *Against All Heresies* 12–14; Eusebius, *Church History* 4.10–11; Marcellus of Ancyra, *On the Holy Church* 9; Epiphanius, *Panarion* 31.

W. Foerster and R.McL. Wilson, *Gnosis: A Selection of Gnostic Texts* (Oxford: Clarendon, 1972), Vol. 1, pp. 239–243; B. Layton, *The Gnostic Scriptures* (Garden City: Doubleday, 1987), pp. 215–264.

W. Foerster, *Von Valentin zu Heracleon: Untersuchungen über die Quellen und die Entwicklung der valentinianischen Gnosis* (Giessen: Töpelmann, 1928); H. Leisegang, "Valentinus 1) Valentinianer," *Paulys Real-Encyclopädie der classischen Altertumswissenschaft* (Stuttgart: Metzler, 1943), Series 2, Vol. 7.2, cols. 2261–2273; H. Jonas, *The Gnostic Religion: The Message of the Alien God and the Beginnings of Christianity*, 2nd ed. (Boston: Beacon, 1963); B. Layton, ed., *The Rediscovery of Gnosticism: Proceedings of the International Conference* on *Gnosticism at Yale, New Haven, Connecticut, March 28–31, 1978* (Leiden: Brill, 1980), Vol 1: *The School of Valentinus*; K. Rudolph, *Gnosis: The Nature and History of Gnosticism* (San Francisco: Harper and Row, 1983).

VALERIAN (ca. 200–ca. 260). Roman emperor (253–260). Valerian reputedly was born to an aristocratic family; he appears to have been a prominent senator by 238. In 253, he was commanding an army in the Alpine province of Raetia when a revolt by Marcus Aemilius Aemilianus, governor of Moesia on the lower Danube, prompted the assassination of the incumbent emperor, Trebonianus Gallus. The army of Raetia hailed Valerian as emperor. Valerian's hold on the office was secured when Aemilianus was himself murdered by his own soldiers.

Intermittent civil war, repeated incursions along the northern frontier by nomadic tribes and in the east by the Sassanian Persian monarchy, and a major outbreak of plague had combined to debilitate the Roman empire. To deal with these circumstances—and setting a notable precedent—Valerian proclaimed his son, Gallienus, co-emperor to govern independently the western half of the empire, but he was otherwise less innovative.

Valerian attempted to placate the traditional Roman state gods by persecutions of the Christian church, thereby to ensure success in military operations on the eastern frontier. In 257 and 258, he issued edicts that outlawed the Christian clergy, effectively banned Christian assembly, and aimed at purging Christians from the upper classes. Thus, there was satisfaction in the church when Valerian was captured alive and carried off as a trophy in 260 by the Persian king, Sapor I. *See also* Persecution.   [G.J.J.]

Bibliography

P.J. Healy, *The Valerian Persecution* (Boston: Houghton-Mifflin, 1905); M. Christol, "Les Règnes de Valérien et de Gallien (253–268): travaux d'ensemble, questions chronologiques," ANRW (1975), Vol. 2.2, pp. 803–827; P. Keresztes, "Two Edicts of the Emperor Valerian," *VChr* 29 (1975):81–95; C.J. Haas, "Imperial Religious Policy and Valerian's Persecution of the Church, A.D. 257–260," *ChHist* 52 (1983):133–144.

VANDALS. Group of "East Germans." The Vandals are believed to have had their distant origin in Scandinavia. First-century Roman writers, such as Tacitus and Pliny the Elder, refer to the *Vandilii* as a major Germanic group. By the second century, the Vandals were divided into the Silings, who occupied Silesia, and the Asdings on the upper Tisza (or Theiss) River. Their later distinctive cloisonné jewelry had its origins in the art of the southern Russian steppes. During the third and fourth centuries, the Vandals frequently raided the Roman empire. In 401, Asding Vandals and other barbarians took part in Radagaisus's invasion of Noricum and Raetia on the upper Danube but were driven back by the Roman general Stilicho.

On December 31, 406, a horde of Asding and Siling Vandals, accompanied by Alans, Burgundians, and Suevi, crossed the frozen and unprotected Rhine near Mainz and invaded Gaul. After sacking Mainz, Trier, Rheims, Amiens, and other cities, they slowly moved south. In 409, they traversed the undefended passes of the Pyrenees into Spain. After a few years of devastation, the Silings under Fredbal settled in Baetica in the south, the Asdings under Gunderic and the Suevi in Gallaecia occupied the northwest, and the Alans took Lusitania (Portugal). Around 416, the Asdings and Alans were recognized as Roman "allies," but the Silings and Alans were overwhelmingly defeated by the Visigoths. The Alan remnants then joined the Asdings, whose kings henceforward were known as "Kings of the Vandals and Alans." After a war with the Suevi, the Vandals moved south and settled in Baetica.

In 428, Gunderic was succeeded by his brother Gaiseric, one of the most able Germanic kings of the period. In the next year, Gaiseric led his estimated 80,000 Vandals and Alans across to Africa. According to one account, he had been invited across by the disaffected Roman count Boniface. In 431, an eastern relief army was defeated, and in 435 a treaty recognized Vandal possession of the poor western provinces of Africa. The Vandal advance, however, soon resumed, and in 439 Carthage itself was captured. A new treaty in 442 reversed the division of territory and confirmed the Vandals as the rulers of Carthage and the rich surrounding area. Roman efforts to recover North Africa in 460 and 468 met with failure.

The loss of North Africa was a disaster for the western empire. Not only did it put much of the grain supply of Italy into enemy hands, it also gave the Vandals the opportunity to take to piracy. Vandal raiders fell upon the coasts of Italy, Spain, and even Greece and in general disrupted Mediterranean trade. In 455, Gaiseric went so far as to land at Ostia, the port of Rome. Bishop Leo the Great was said to have met him and prevented an out-and-out sack, but the Vandals nevertheless looted and plundered for fourteen days. They carried back to Carthage not only the spoils taken by Titus from Jerusalem in A.D. 70 but also the empress Eudoxia herself and her daughters Eudocia and Placidia. The last of these then was wed to Gaiseric's son Huneric.

Unlike the Germanic settlers in Europe, such as the Visigoths, Franks, and Ostrogoths, the Vandals in Africa made little effort to conciliate the local Roman population. Their reputation for harshness was in part a result of their adherence to Arianism. They undertook a persecution of the Catholic population, expropriating Catholic churches and property, exiling bishops, and forbidding priests to administer the sacraments. Under Gaiseric's successor, Huneric (477–484), forcible conversions were attempted, and Catholics were removed from office. Some 4,966 Catholic clerics were said to have been exiled to the south. In 484, Catholicism was declared a heresy at a council at Carthage, and other Catholic bishops were deported to Corsica. Still more bishops later were exiled to Sardinia.

The Vandals also seem simply to have confiscated the property of the landed Roman aristocracy and distributed it in tax-free allotments to the Vandal warriors. Some landowners were even enslaved. As a result, many Romans fled to Italy and the east. The Vandals retained the Roman administration, in simplified form. Such policies, however, seem to have been implemented primarily in the immediate neighborhood of Carthage, the

Vandal capital, and Hippo. More outlying areas were only loosely controlled. The failure of the Vandals to maintain the Roman defensive system in North Africa resulted in increased raiding by desert and hill peoples, such as the Mauri (Moors).

Unlike other Germanic peoples, such as the Franks, Gaiseric was successful in establishing a strong centralized government. He broke the power of the old warrior aristocracy, replacing it with men dependent upon himself. He also established the policy whereby there was but a single heir to the throne, the king's eldest son. By so doing, he avoided the fragmentation of the kingdom that was to afflict the Franks.

Subsequent Vandal kings included Gunthamund (484–496) and Thrasamund (496–523). Both were increasingly troubled by Moorish raids. Catholic churches remained closed, and ordination of new bishops was forbidden. Hilderic (523–531), the son of Huneric and the Roman princess Placidia, had lived in Constantinople and adopted the Catholic religion. He allowed the Catholics to reopen their churches and recalled their bishops. As a result, he was imprisoned and dethroned by his cousin Gelimer (531–534), the last Vandal king. This turn of events gave the eastern Roman emperor Justinian (527–565) the pretext for an invasion of Africa. In 533, his general Belisarius landed in Africa, and in two battles Gelimer was totally defeated. Not only the Vandal kingdom but all traces of the Vandal culture disappeared from North Africa. Of all the Germans who occupied the Roman empire, the Vandals probably had the least lasting impact. *See also* Carthage.   [R.W.M.]

Bibliography
Anthologia latina; Ferrandus, *Vita Fulgentii*; Procopius, *On the Vandal War*; Victor of Vita, *Historia persecutionis Africanae provinciae*.

E.F. Gautier, *Genséric: roi des Vandales* (Paris: Payot, 1935); L. Schmidt, *Geschichte der Wandalen*, 2nd ed. (Munich: Beck, 1942); C. Courtois, *Les Vandales et l'Afrique* (Paris: Arts et Métiers Graphiques, 1955).

VENANTIUS FORTUNATUS (ca. 535–ca. 610). Latin poet, hagiographer, and bishop.

Born near Venice, Fortunatus studied at Ravenna before proceeding to Gaul (566). After visiting the shrine of Martin of Tours, he settled at Poitiers. He eventually became a priest in Poitiers and was associated with a convent founded by Radegunde, a princess of Thuringia and former queen of the Franks, although he continued to travel extensively in Gaul. He was elected bishop of Poitiers toward the end of the sixth century. Fortunatus's collected works exhibit a great diversity. They include (besides a few prose pieces) elegies, epigrams, and panegyrics, as well as hymns, the best known of which, the *Pange lingua* and the *Vexilla regis*, he composed on the occasion of the presentation of a relic of the true cross to Radegunde's convent (ca. 569). Other poems include a lament on the extinction of the royal house of Thuringia and a life of Martin of Tours based on the account of Sulpicius Severus. Several prose lives of saints, among them Hilary of Poitiers and Radegunde, are also his. CPL 1033–1052. [M.P.McH.]

Bibliography

F.J.E. Raby, *A History of Christian Latin Poetry*, 2nd ed. (Oxford: Clarendon, 1953), pp. 86–95; B. Brennan, "The Career of Venantius Fortunatus," *Traditio* 41 (1985):49–78.

VERECUNDUS (d. 552).

Bishop of Junca in North Africa and exegete. An opponent of the *Three Chapters*, Verecundus wrote a commentary on nine Old Testament canticles as well as a penitential hymn; a collection of excerpts from the Council of Chalcedon (451) may also be his. CPL 869–871. [M.P.McH.]

Bibliography

Verecundus Iuncensis, Opera, ed. R. Demeulenaere, CCSL (1976), Vol. 93; *Verecundi Iuncensis carmen de paenitentia*, ed. M.G. Bianco (Naples: D'Auria, 1984).

J.L. Kugel, "Is There but One Song?," *Biblica* 63 (1982):329–350.

VERONICA.

Woman with the issue of blood healed by Jesus (Matt. 9:20–22), according to the *Acts of Pilate* 7. The developed form of Veronica's legend (fourteenth century) states that Jesus on his way to the cross wiped his face on her head cloth, leaving the imprint of his features marked on it. Feast day July 12.

[E.F.]

Bibliography

M.R. James, *The Apocryphal New Testament* (Oxford: Clarendon, 1953), pp. 102, 157–159.

VESPASIAN (A.D. 9–79).

Roman emperor (69–79). Vespasian was proclaimed emperor by the eastern Roman legions while he was engaged in putting down the Jewish rebellion (66–70); the campaign was concluded by his elder son, Titus, with the destruction of Jerusalem (70). Christianity was free of persecutions under his rule, although both Vespasian and his younger son, Domitian, are reported by Hegesippus to have searched out supposed descendants of the royal family of David, relatives of Christ, as a possible political threat (Eusebius, *H.E.* 3.12, 19–20). [M.P.McH.]

Bibliography

Tertullian, *Apology* 5.7; Eusebius, *Church History* 2.23.18; 3.5.1; 3.8.10f., 3.12; 3.17; 3.19–20; 5.5.7.

VICTOR I.

Bishop of Rome (ca. 189–ca. 198). Victor's effort to gain uniformity in the celebration of Easter on Sunday, as against the practice of keeping the feast on the fourteenth day of the Jewish month Nisan, met with general acceptance. Polycrates of Ephesus and a number of other Asiatic bishops stood in opposition. Irenaeus of Lyons was one of several who protested Victor's threatened excommunication of them. Victor's implicit assertion of Roman authority would become important in subsequent debate over papal supremacy. He excommunicated Theodotus the Leatherworker for promoting Adoptionism. Victor was the author, according to Jerome, of works on the Paschal controversy as well as of other writings, but none is extant. Feast day July 28. *See also* Pasch, Paschal Controversy.

[M.P.McH.]

Bibliography

Eusebius, *Church History* 5.22.1–24.18, 28.6–9; Jerome, *Lives of Illustrious Men* 34; cf. 35; *Liber Pontificalis* 15 (Duchense 1.137–138).

VICTOR OF VITA (late fifth century). North African church historian. A priest of Carthage, Victor became bishop, probably of Vita. His *Historia persecutionis Africanae provinciae*, an account of the persecution of the African Catholic church by the Arian Vandals under their kings Gaiseric (428–477) and Huneric (477–484), is a valuable if partisan historical source. Of interest to theologians is the profession of faith contained therein drawn up by Eugenius, bishop of Carthage (484). CPL 798–799. [M.P.McH.]

VICTORINUS, CAIUS MARIUS (d. after 363). Rhetorician and theologian. An African, Victorinus taught rhetoric at Rome (from ca. 350) under Constantius II. His conversion to Christianity took place in old age (ca. 355); he gave up his teaching post under the emperor Julian (362). His writings before his conversion include grammatical works, commentaries on Cicero, and translations of parts of Aristotle, Porphyry, and probably Plotinus; an *Ars grammatica* and a treatise on Cicero's *De inventione* are extant. His Christian writings include the earliest Latin commentaries on Pauline epistles (Galatians, Ephesians, and Philippians), as well as four books *Against Arius*, a short work *On the Necessity of Accepting the Homoousion*, and letters and hymns. He presented the doctrine of the Trinity in Neoplatonic terms, with dependence on Porphyry. Augustine was influenced by Victorinus's conversion. CPL 94–100, 680–681, 1543–1544a. [M.P.McH.]

Bibliography
Jerome, *Lives of Illustrious Men* 101; Augustine, *Confessions* 8.2.3–5.

Marius Victorinus: traités théologiques sur la Trinité, ed. P. Henry and P. Hadot, SC (1960), Vols. 68, 69; *Marii Victorini Opera: I, Opera Theologica*, ed. P. Henry and P. Hadot, CSEL (1971), Vol. 83.1; II, *Opera Exegetica*, ed. F. Gori, CSEL (1986), Vol. 83.2; *Marii Victorini Afri Commentarii in Epistulas Pauli . . . Opera Theologica*, 2 vols., ed. A. Locher (Leipzig: Teubner, 1972, 1976).

Marius Victorinus, Theological Treatises on the Trinity, tr. M.T. Clark, FOTC (1981), Vol. 69; see review by S. Gersh, *VChr* 38 (1984):302–303, for bibliographical orientation.

A. Souter, *The Earliest Latin Commentaries on the Epistles of St. Paul* (Oxford: Clarendon, 1927), pp. 8–38; T.P. Halton and R.D. Sider, "A Decade of Patristic Scholarship 1970–1979," *CW* 76 (1982–1983):347–348 (bibliography).

VICTORINUS OF PETTAU (d. ca. 304). Bishop and exegete. Victorinus, bishop of Pettau in Pannonia, suffered martyrdom, probably under Diocletian. He was the earliest known exegete to write in Latin. Relying on Greek authors, Origen especially, he treated numerous biblical passages, but only a commentary on the Book of Revelation and a fragment of a work on the creation of the world survive. He may also have translated into Latin from the Greek *Against All Heresies*, mistakenly attributed to Tertullian and perhaps written by the Roman bishop Zephyrinus. His works were condemned by the *Decretum Gelasianum* (late fifth–early sixth century) because of their tendency to millenarianism, the belief in a future thousand-year reign of Christ and the saints. Feast day November 2. CPL 79–83 (see also 34). [M.P.McH.]

Bibliography
Jerome, *Lives of Illustrious Men* 74; idem, *Letters* 58.10; 70.5.

VICTORIUS, CLAUDIUS MARIUS (d. between 425 and 450). Christian Latin poet and rhetorician. A teacher of rhetoric at Marseilles, Victorius composed (ca. 420 or thereafter) the *Alethia* (the title is Latinized from the Greek word for "truth"). The poem as it now exists consists of some 2,000 hexameter verses in an opening prayer and three books; a fourth book may also have been lost. The work is a paraphrase of material from Genesis, from creation through the destruction of Sodom (Gen. 1–19), and was intended for the instruction of youth. The poem shows a wide knowledge of authors both classical and Christian, but its role in subsequent literary history has been slight. CPL 1455. [M.P.McH.]

Bibliography
Gennadius, *Lives of Illustrious Men* 60.

Claudius Marius Victorius, Alethia, ed. P. Hovingh, CCSL (1960), Vol. 128.

O. Ferrari, *Un poeta cristiano del quinto secolo: Claudio Mario Vittore* (Pavia: Mattei, Speroni, 1912); E.S. Duckett, *Latin Writers of the Fifth Century* (New York: Holt, 1930), pp. 57–64; P.M. Duval, *La Gaule jusqu'au milieu du Ve siècle* (Paris: Picard, 1971), Vol. 1.2, pp. 702–704, no. 300; D.J. Nodes, "The Seventh Day of Creation in *Alethia* of Claudius Marius Victor," *VChr* 42 (1988):59–74.

VIGILANTIUS (late fourth–early fifth century). Presbyter in southwestern Gaul. Vigilantius was the target of one of Jerome's most virulent polemics, *Against Vigilantius*, in 406. The immediate issues concerned Vigilantius's attack on ascetic practices, but Jerome's alienation stemmed from their confrontation in 395, when Vigilantius visited Jerome's monastery in Bethlehem. Vigilantius's assertion that Jerome was guilty of Origenism and his objection to financial support for the Bethlehem community were the prelude to Jerome's polemic of 406, when he received an account of Vigilantius's views, known to us only through Jerome's treatise.

Vigilantius challenged the growing cult of martyrs and their relics. He rejected the value of prayers to martyrs and questioned miracles attributed to their shrines. He also questioned the value of the monastic life and virginity. These values had long been championed by Jerome, as his prolific writings demonstrate. Vigilantius disappeared from the Gallo-Roman church; the final historical reference (late fifth century) placed him in Barcelona (Gennadius, *Sect. eccl.* 35). *See also* Jerome. [H.R.]

Bibliography
Jerome, *Letters* 61; 109; idem, *Against Vigilantius*, tr. W.H. Fremantle, NPNF, 2nd ser. (1892), Vol. 6, pp. 131–133, 212–214, 417–423.

J.N.D. Kelly, *Jerome: His Life, Writings, and Controversies* (London: Duckworth, and New York: Harper and Row, 1975), pp. 286–290.

VIGILIUS. Bishop of Rome (537–555). Vigilius was a Roman deacon chosen by Boniface II as his successor, a designation withdrawn in the face of protest (532). He served as *apocrisarius* (representative) to Constantinople (535–536), where he entered into an accord with the empress Theodora; he may have agreed to reinstate several Monophysites to church office and to set aside the decrees of the Council of Chalcedon (451). He had some involvement in the deposition of his predecessor in the Roman see, Silverius. His role in the controversy over the Three Chapters was complex. On Justinian's order, he was taken to Constantinople (545–546), where he assented to the emperor's demand that he condemn them, although he did not repudiate Chalcedon. Shortly thereafter, he withdrew his condemnation because of strong objections in the west, the issue to await decision in a general council. When the council finally met at Constantinople (553), he refused to attend on the ground of insufficient western representation, but he offered a compromise, which was rejected. The council condemned the Three Chapters, a decision to which he yielded under considerable duress six months later. Allowed to return to his see, he died on the homeward journey. He was vigorous in dealing with western affairs. CPL 1612, 1616, 1625, 1694–1697. *See also* Three Chapters. [M.P.McH.]

Bibliography
Liber Pontificalis 61 (Duchesne 1.296–302).

VIGILS. Numerous distinct forms of worship at night in early Christian liturgy. The liturgical observances before Easter morning, before other solemnities, and before saints' feasts were vigils having separate structural components and origins. The canonical hour of Matins in the Divine Office was also designated as a vigil. Earlier types of vigils were private and communal night observances outside the liturgy: monastic daily prayer, gatherings at saints' tombs, nocturnal preparations for Sunday Mass, and wakes.

Opposing views concerning the relative antiquity of the various types of liturgical and aliturgical vigils make it difficult to determine whether one type evolved from another, and any attempt to schematize the basic types is complicated by the diverging practices in the rites of the east and west. It is known, however, that some vigils consisted primarily of scriptural readings (Easter and Ember days); some consisted primarily of psalmody (monastic prayer and Matins) or included the full recitation of the Psalter (Ambrosian saints' vigils); some consisted of a repetitive unit of psalmody, readings, and prayer; and some included a vigil Mass, celebrated in addition to the Mass of the feast day that followed.

Only certain types of vigils were all-night observances. The Office vigils occupied a part of the night, and other types, which included the vigil Mass, were celebrated in the evening preceding the feast or even earlier. Later in the Middle Ages, the vigil Office and Mass could occupy the entire day before a major feast.

[J.B.]

Bibliography

Niceta, *Vigils of the Saints*, tr. G. Walsh, FOTC (1949), Vol. 7, pp. 55–64; Basil, *Letter* 207, tr. B. Jackson, NPNF, 2nd ser. (1895),Vol. 8, pp. 246–248; *Pilgrimage of Egeria*, 9, 24–25, tr. G. Gingras, ACW (1970), Vol. 38.

O. Heiming, "Die altmailändische Heiligenvigil," *Heilige Überlieferung*, ed. O. Casel (Münster: Aschendorff, 1938), pp. 174–192; A. Baumstark and O. Heiming, *Nocturna Laus* (Münster: Aschendorff, 1957; repr. 1967); J. Mateos, "La Vigile cathédrale chez Egérie," *Orientalia Christiana Periodica* 27 (1961):281–312; J.A. Jungmann, *Pastoral Liturgy* (New York: Herder, 1962), esp. pp. 105–122; A. Van der Mensbrugghe, "Fausses pistes de recherche sur les origines des Vigiles et des Matines," *Überlieferungsgeschichtliche Untersuchungen*, TU (1981), Vol. 125, pp. 553–572; R. Taft, *The Liturgy of the Hours in East and West* (Collegeville: Liturgical, 1986), esp. pp. 165–190.

VINCENT OF LERINS (d. before 450). Monk and writer. Among the many influential writers associated with the monastic center of Lérins, Vincent stands out as one of the most significant. The sparse biographical details come from *Lives of Illustrious Men*, by Gennadius, who ascribes to Vincent the composition of a "very powerful dissertation" against heresies and notes that the author used the pen-name of "Peregrinus," that is, one who had sought solitude in a monastery (*Vir. ill.* 64). This "dissertation" alone merits the recognition of Vincent as one of the architects of the Catholic doctrine of tradition that emerged out of the crucible of the patristic era. His *Commonitorium* ("Aid to Memory") had considerable in-

Vincent of Lérins, sixteenth-century wood sculpture in St. Honorat monastery, Lérins, France.

fluence, which was multiplied through numerous translations, beginning in the Reformation, when Christendom again entered into a profound and prolonged discussion regarding the nature of the authentic Christian tradition. In addition to his great apology, Vincent's writings probably include some *Objections* to Augustinianism (included in Prosper of Aquitaine's works) that formed part of the vigorous dialogue concerning Semipelagianism in the church of southern Gaul, particularly in regard to predestination and the nature of divine grace. In addition, Vincent may well be the author of some *Excerpts*, related to Augustine's teachings on the Trinity and incarnation, with which he fully agreed.

In Chapter 2 of the *Commonitorium*, there appears Vincent's famed canon for defining the true Catholic faith: "what has been believed everywhere, always, and by all." He provided a threefold formula as a defense against heretical teaching: the scriptures, the church universal as their reliable interpreter, and the complementary authority of a general council. Feast day May 24. CPL 510–511.   [H.R.]

Bibliography

Gennadius, *Lives of Illustrious Men* 64.

The Commonitorium of Vincent of Lérins, ed. B.S. Moxon (Cambridge: Cambridge UP, 1915); ed. R. Demeulenaere, CCSL (1985), Vol 64.

A Commonitory, tr. C.A. Heurtley, NPNF, 2nd ser. (1894), Vol. 11, pp. 123–159; tr. R.E. Morris, FOTC (1949), Vol. 7, pp. 257–342; tr. G.E. MacCracken, LCC (1957), Vol. 9, pp. 23–89.

E.S. Duckett, *Latin Writers of the Fifth Century* (New York: Archon, 1969, repr. of 1930 ed.); N.K. Chadwick, *Poetry and Letters in Early Christian Gaul* (London: Bowes and Bowes, 1955); J. Pelikan, *The Christian Tradition: A History of the Development of Doctrine* (Chicago: U of Chicago P, 1971), Vol. 1: *The Emergence of the Catholic Tradition (100–600)*, pp. 333-339 (for the "Vincentian Canon").

VIRGINS. Those voluntarily consecrated to sexual abstinence. Virginity did not appear as a central theme in the history of Israel until the apocalyptic period (200 B.C.), when certain sects arose that prized this attribute, including the Essenes and Therapeutae. Philo (ca. 20 B.C.–A.D. 50) defends the celibacy of the (male) Essenes on the grounds that it preserves the fellowship of their community (*Apology for the Jews*). Another sect comprising male and female virgins, the Therapeutae of Egypt, is depicted as practicing virginity for the sake of contemplation (Philo, *Contemplative Life*). Eusebius (*H.E.* 2.17) and Jerome (*Vir. ill.* 8) thought that the Therapeutae were early Christians.

Regulations for the practice and continuance of virginity in pagan religion abound among peoples of antiquity. The cultic requirement for the governance of virginity is based on the twin considerations of avoidance of the ritual pollution resulting from sexual intercourse (Hesiod, *Works and Days* 733f.) and furtherance of union with the divinity (Herodotus 1.182). In later times, the Pythagoreans distinguished between the ritual pollution resulting from illicit intercourse and matrimony, which was not subject to such interdiction (Diogenes Laertius 8.43). Priests who maintained lifelong chastity are rewarded in the underworld (Virgil, *Aeneid* 6.661).

Early Church Practice. Irrespective of the possible influence of their environment, the second-century apologists attest that Christians of both sexes practiced voluntary continence as a form of asceticism (Justin, *1 Apol.* 15; Athenagoras, *Leg.* 32; Tatian, *Orat.* 32f.). Galen, the pagan philosopher and physician, confirms this ascendancy of Christians over pagan eroticism. Origen compares the Christian virgins, who are preserved in their righteous integrity by God, with pagan virgins, whose claims of virginity are not unmixed with drugs, bribe-taking, or other forms of constraint (*Cels.* 7.48). Athanasius mentions virgins as one proof of the power of Christ and the truth of Christianity (*Inc.* 48.2; 51.1; *Const. app.* 33).

Although living in their own homes until well into the fourth century, the continent were honored in the liturgy and by the community—so much so that pride was considered an "occupational hazard" (Ignatius, *Polyc.* 5.2). The two Pseudo-Clementine letters addressed to virgins reveal that virginity was a common lifestyle in third-century Syria and that male ascetics functioned as itinerant evangelists (*Ep. virg.* 2.4.2; 5.11; 7.3). The first letter also contains a protest against virgins of both sexes living together under one roof (*Ep. virg.* 1.10–13). The Council of Nicaea (325) forbids the not-infrequent arrangement of a "spiritual marriage" between two ascetics (*can.* 3). The third and fourth centuries in Egypt marked the beginning of the monastic movement; the ascetics, first male and later female, ceased living in the cities and withdrew to the desert. Soon, mo-

Part of the procession of twenty-two virgins from the mosaic decoration (557–572) of the north wall of S. Apollinare Nuovo, Ravenna, Italy. (Photograph Editore Dante, Ravenna.)

nasticism spread all over the ancient world, and the monastery became the permanent institutional home of the Christian virgin, including the *ordo* of virgins (i.e., female ascetics), who remained in the church under the supervision of the bishop (but not ordained—Hippolytus, *Trad. ap.* 13). Similarly, celibacy became the approved state for the clergy (Elvira, *can.* 33).

Patristic Commentary. Paul, interpreting Christ's counsels of renunciation, taught that virginity is the ideal, but not obligatory, state for a Christian of either sex (1 Cor. 7:8f.). Cyprian was apparently the first to state explicitly that virginity is a superior way of life to marriage (*Hab. virg.* 23; *Mortal.* 26). A homily erroneously attributed to John Chrysostom awards virginity a crown, marriage moderate praise, and fornication punishment and torment (*Hom. in Ps.* 50.8). The first to write a full-length literary defense of virginity was Methodius of Olympus (ca. 300), whose dialogue *The Banquet of the Ten Virgins* is

modeled upon Plato's *Symposium*. Gregory of Nyssa, John Chrysostom, Jerome, Augustine, and Ambrose wrote treatises on the subject of virginity. All taught that the Christian virgin should be detached from the world and concerned with spiritual matters and that true virginity resides in the soul rather than the body. The virginity of the Trinity and of the angels, virginity as revealed by the dispensation of Christ, and the superiority of the virgin over the married person are the topics of Gregory of Nazianzus's poem *In laudem virginitatis*, which constitutes a convenient summary of the patristic understanding of the Christian ethic of virginity. *See also* Marriage; Mary; Sexuality; Widows; Women. [M.A.S.]

Bibliography

Pseudo-Clement, *Two Epistles Concerning Virginity*, ANF (1886), Vol. 8; Methodius, *The Banquet, or On Virginity*, ACW (1958), Vol. 27; Basil of Ancyra, *De vera virginitate*, PG 30.669–810; Gregory of Nazianzus, *In laudem virginitatis*, PG 37.521–573; Gregory of Nyssa, *De virginitate*, SC (1966), Vol. 119; NPNF, 2nd ser. (1893), Vol. 5;

John Chrysostom, *On Virginity; Against Remarriage*, tr. S.R. Shore (New York: Mellen, 1984); Ambrose, *Concerning Virgins*, NPNF, 2nd ser. (1896), Vol. 10; idem, *On Virginity*, tr. D. Callam (Kalamazoo: Cistercian, 1989); Augustine, *Of Holy Virginity*, FOTC (1955), Vol. 27.

M.R. Nugent, *Portrait of the Consecrated Woman in Greek Christian Literature of the First Four Centuries* (Washington, D.C.: Catholic U of America P, 1941); H. von Campenhausen, "Early Christian Asceticism," *Tradition and Life in the Church* (Philadelphia: Fortress, 1968), pp. 90–122; E.A. Clark, *Jerome, Chrysostom and Friends: Essays and Translations* (New York: Mellen, 1979); J.A. McNamara, *A New Song: Celibate Women in the First Three Christian Centuries* (New York: Institute for Research in History, 1983); U. Bianchi, ed., *La Tradizione dell' Enkrateia. Motivazioni Ontologiche* (Rome: Dell' Ateneo, 1985); C. Munier, *Ehe und Ehelosigkeit in der Alten Kirche* (Berne: Lang, 1987); A. Rouselle, *On Desire and the Body in Antiquity* (Oxford: Blackwell, 1988); P. Brown, *The Body and Society: Men, Women, and Sexual Renunciation in Early Christianity* (New York: Columbia UP, 1988).

VISION OF PAUL. Apocalyptic work (also known as the *Apocalypse of Paul*, but not the work in the Nag Hammadi library) describing a journey of Paul through heaven, where he saw many of the righteous from the Old Testament, and through hell, where he saw the punishments of various types of sinners. Although drawing on earlier sources, the *Vision of Paul* took its basic shape in the late fourth or early fifth century and was modified in many versions during the Middle Ages. It is notable for the description of the separation of soul and body at death, the matching of punishments to sins, the granting of a respite from punishment on Sunday, and the insistence on using the Psalms of David at the eucharist. *See also* Apocalyptic Literature; Heaven; Hell. [E.F.]

Bibliography
NTA, Vol. 2, pp. 755–798; R.P. Casey, "The Apocalypse of Paul," *JThS* 34 (1933):1–32; T. Silverstein, "The Date of the 'Apocalypse of Paul,'" *Medieval Studies* 24 (1962):335–348; E. Ferguson, "Psalm-Singing at the Eucharist: A Liturgical Controversy in the Fourth Century," *Austin Seminary Bulletin* 98 (1983):52–77 (has information on English translations of different versions).

VISIONS. See Mysticism.

VULGATE. Bible of the Latin church from the early Middle Ages until the Second Vatican Council. The Vulgate is essentially the work of one man, Eusebius Hieronymus, or Jerome (ca. 347–419/20). Jerome was working as a secretary to pope Damasus I when the latter suggested (382) that the Old Latin version of the Gospels in use by the church was in need of correction. Damasus did not have in mind a completely new translation but merely a revision of the Latin by means of the Greek. The scholar Jerome also corrected the Old Latin Psalter at this time; he could accomplish no more before the death of Damasus ended his Roman patronage. Jerome next settled in Bethlehem (386) in a monastery founded by his spiritual disciple the Roman matron Paula. For the next twenty years, he produced biblical translations, not as a systematic project commissioned by the church but in response to the demands of his patrons and friends.

In the library at Caesarea, Jerome had access to the *Hexapla* of Origen. This parallel collection of Greek translations of the Hebrew Bible contained a critical text of the Septuagint (LXX) in Column 5. At this point, he became convinced of the futility of working from any other text than this, the Bible of the Christian east and the source of the Old Latin version. In what might be termed the second phase of Jerome's methodological evolution, he translated from Origen's LXX the books of Job, 1–2 Chronicles, Proverbs, Ecclesiastes, and the Song of Solomon. He also provided prefaces that discuss his methods and answer those critics who objected to his new translations of the Bible. At this time, he also translated the LXX Psalms, a work that would eventually be known as the Gallican Psalter and become enshrined in the Roman liturgy and breviary. Jerome claimed he had translated the entire Old Testament from the LXX (*Apol. c. Ruf.* 2.24; 3.25), but it is quite certain that he abandoned this project when he could no longer deny the superiority of the Hebrew original.

To prepare himself for translating the Hebrew Bible, Jerome engaged a learned Jew named Baranina; he had in fact been employing Hebrew tutors for twenty years and would continue to do so for the rest of his life. Yet it must not be concluded that Jerome had any ecumenical inclinations; he was simply weary of losing arguments to Jews who could show that his claims were based on faulty Christian translations (*Pref. Isa.*, PL 28.774). Now, he would battle them on their own ground. Jerome's translation of the Hebrew began in 389 and continued through 405. The first book finished was his third version of the Psalms. For practice in Hebrew, he next tackled the relatively straightforward historical books of Samuel and Kings. By 392, he had completed his work on the Prophets and Job, followed by Ezra–Nehemiah (394), 1–2 Chronicles (396), and the three Solomonic books—Proverbs, Ecclesiastes, and the Song of Solomon (398). Work began on the Pentateuch by the turn of the fifth century but was hampered by a long controversy with Rufinus of Aquileia over Origenism, which consumed much of the time and energy of this combative scholar. By 405, Jerome had completed Joshua, Judges, and Ruth/Esther, thus ending his serious translation work on the Bible. Until his death in 420, however, he continued to write commentaries on virtually every biblical book. Because he devoted himself to the Hebrew Bible, Jerome also restricted his work after 390 to the Hebrew canon (only books written in Hebrew). The complete Christian Bible (Vulgate), which eventually included Jerome's Hebrew translations, also contains deuterocanonical books written in Greek, which he never touched (Wisdom, Sirach, Baruch, 1–2 Maccabees). And although Jerome claims (*Vir. ill.* 135; *Ep.* 71.5) that he revised the entire New Testament, there is substantial scholarly opinion that the books other than the Gospels show no trace of Jerome's style.

Jerome's extensive classical education enabled him to write a fine Latin style, but he willingly foreswore elegance for faithfulness to the simple Hebrew syntax (*Ep.* 49.4). Although he valued accuracy, he knew that a good translator must render ideas and not just words. His impetuous nature at times led him on a capricious search for stylistic novelty. More damaging still is Jerome's tendency to slap-dash haste;

he himself admits that he spent only eight days on the Solomonic books. Nevertheless, Peebles (p. 441) credits the popularity and perdurance of the Vulgate version solely to Jerome's learning and scholarship; Kelly writes that Jerome "raised the Vulgar Latinity of Christians to the heights of great literature" (p. 163).

Because Jerome's translations were done from private initiative, it is not surprising that they were not quickly accepted throughout the church. There was understandable reluctance by the faithful to abandon the Old Latin they virtually knew by heart. Augustine worried that ignoring the Septuagint would cut the Latin church off more severely from the Greeks, who considered that translation divinely inspired. He also told Jerome of a riot that occurred at Oea (Tripoli) when the bishop tried to introduce the new text of Jonah at Mass (*Ep.* 71.5). Nevertheless, Jerome staunchly defended his work against all critics, especially his archrival Rufinus (*Apol. c. Ruf.* 2.24–35). In the fifth century, the main proponents of the new translations were the followers of Pelagius in Italy and several bishops in Gaul. By the end of the sixth century, however, such weighty writers as Gregory the Great and Isidore of Seville regularly quoted Jerome's version. Isidore explicitly recommended it for the liturgy (*Etym.* 6.4.5). By the eighth century, the great Carolingian Bibles all incorporated the new version. In 1546, the Council of Trent called the Vulgate the "authentic" text to be used in the Roman church but admitted that the text needed a thorough correction. Although a papal commission attempted to carry out that mandate with the Clementine Vulgate of 1592, this work was recognized to be less than adequate. In 1933, pope Pius XI erected the Abbey of S. Girolamo in Rome, where a team of monk-scholars have worked diligently ever since at the critical edition of the Vulgate Bible. *See also* Jerome; Old Latin Versions. [T.G.K.]

Bibliography

J. Wordsworth, H.J. White, and H.F.D. Sparks, *Novum Testamentum . . . latine* (Oxford: Clarendon, 1889–1954); F.A. Gasquet et al., *Biblia Sacra iuxta latinam vulgatam versionem*, 16 vols. (Rome: Vatican, 1926–); R. Weber, ed., *Biblia Sacra*, 2 vols. (Stuttgart: Wurttembergische Bibelanstalt, 1969; 2nd ed. 1975); *Novum Vulgata Bibliorum Sacrorum Editio* (Vatican City: Libreria Editrice Vaticana, 1979; 2nd ed. 1986).

H. Quentin, "Mémoire sur l'établissement du texte de la Vulgate, I. Octateuch," *Collectanea Biblica Latina*, VI (Rome: Pustet, 1922); J. Gribomont, "L'Eglise et les versions bibliques," *Maison-Dieu* 62 (1960):41–68; B.R. Peebles, "Vulgate," NCE (1967), Vol. 2, pp. 439–457; H.F.D. Sparks, "Jerome as Biblical Scholar," *The Cambridge History of the Bible*, Vol. 2, ed. G.W.H. Lampe (Cambridge: Cambridge UP, 1970), pp. 510–540; J.N.D. Kelly, *Jerome: His Life, Writings, and Controversies* (London: Duckworth, and New York: Harper and Row, 1975), pp. 141–168.

WALES. *See* David of Wales; Great Britain.

WALKER, WILLISTON (1860–1922). Church historian. Walker was born in Portland, Maine; graduated from Amherst College in 1883 and Hartford Theological Seminary in 1886; received his doctorate from the University of Leipzig in 1888. Returning to the United States, he taught for one year at Bryn Mawr College, then for twelve years at Hartford Theological Seminary. In 1901, he succeeded George Park Fisher as Titus Street Professor of Ecclesiastical History at Yale, a position he held until his death.

A member of the Congregational Church, Walker was instrumental in its reorganization in 1913. He showed great interest both in unity among Christians and in missions to those who were not Christian. The bulk of his scholarly writing dealt with the Congregational heritage in New England.

Nearly three generations of American students of church history, however, began their study through his text *A History of the Christian Church*, a thorough and concise introduction to the subject. First published by Scribner in 1918, it has gone through four editions.

[F.W.N.]

Bibliography
W. Walker, R.A. Norris, D.W. Lotz, and R.T. Handy, *A History of the Christian Church*, 4th ed. (New York: Scribner, 1985).

WAR. The early church received from the Jewish scriptures a specific understanding of warfare: God is the divine warrior who fights for Israel; the human role is to trust in Yahweh's defense and victory (Exod. 14:14; Isa. 7:9; 30:1–5, 15–18; Ps. 33:10–21). The battles that receive lengthy narrative space are those in which the victory is won by divine miracle: the defeat of the Egyptians (Exod. 14–15 with prelude in 5–13), the crashing of Jericho's walls (Josh. 6), the blinding of the army of Syria through Elisha's word (1 Kings 6), Jehoshaphat's victory over the Ammonites (2 Chron. 20). The prophets often criticized Israel for relying on military alliances and weapons (Hos. 5:11–12; 8:9–10; Isa. 31:1–3); in judgment, God fought against Israel (Isa. 3; 10:5–19; 13; Jer. 21:3–6). The imagery of Zion, occurring often in the Psalms and Isaiah, extolled God's power to defend the people, called for complete trust in Yahweh, and repudiated human pride in and boasting of one's own defense and powers (Ps. 20; 44:1–8; 46; 48; 124; Isa. 2:1–11; 28). Within this context, the Old Testament describes many bloody wars. The so-called Deuteronomic history (Josh.–Kings) accents God's command for *ḥerem*, a holy sacrifice of all war booty to Yahweh (Deut. 20 contains rules for warfare). Israel's failure in this action is used to explain her idolatries, worshiping pagan gods and goddesses; this led to her exile.

New Testament. New Testament emphases show both continuity and discontinuity with the Old Testament. The themes of continuity include the call to complete trust in God, exemplified by Jesus' own life and teaching; God's continuing fight against evil in the ministry of Jesus—note especially the exorcisms (Matt. 12:28ff. and parallels); and God's defeat of evil through Jesus' death and resurrection. In this conquest the principalities and powers were disarmed and are ultimately to be defeated (1 Cor. 2:6–8; Col. 2:15; 1 Cor. 15:24–27). Among the points of discontinuity: covenant promises, peoplehood, and Zion-temple imagery are universalized so that neither God nor God's enemies are identified with a particular nation or race of people; evil has an invisible spiritual depth (Satan and demons) that impartially manifests itself in people and structures and must be fought with spiritual weapons; and Jesus commands his followers to love human enemies (Matt. 5:43–44; Rom. 12:19–21). The early church saw itself as one new humanity in which previously hostile groups, Jews and Gentiles, could live together in one body of peace (Eph. 2:12–23).

Additional New Testament teachings, rooted also in the Old Testament, contributed further to the Christian ethical response to war: (1) nonretaliation, i.e., do not repay evil for evil (Matt. 5:39–41; Rom. 12:17, 19–21; 1 Peter 3:9; 1 Thess. 5:15); (2) overcome evil with good (Rom. 12:21); and (3) Christ's kingdom is not of this world; therefore his servants do not fight (John 18:36).

At the same time, Jesus fought against evil, especially the hypocrisy of the Pharisees, and took prophetic action against temple abuses (Mark 11:13–17). These conflicts, however, stand clearly in the biblical prophetic tradition and were not comparable to participation in

war. Nevertheless, there are cases of crucial textual silence: John the Baptist did not ask the soldiers to quit army duty (Luke 3:14); Jesus commended a soldier's faith (Luke 7:5–17) and did not request him to quit his vocation. Also, a Roman army official, Cornelius, was the first Gentile admitted to the church, and the text makes no critical comment on his army position (Acts 10–11). Some consider these silences as approval of these roles; others hold them to be insignificant, since these texts, at least the last two, accent other themes.

In the Pauline writings, the death and resurrection of Jesus defeat the "principalities and the powers." This phrase comprises both spiritual (angelic and demonic) and human, historical dimensions; the spiritual dimension works in and through political leaders and structures—as it does in all of life. This double dimension of the powers is found most clearly in 1 Corinthians 2:6–8 and Ephesians 6:10–18; it is present in other texts as well (Eph. 1:19–23, 3:9–10; 1 Peter 3:22; 1 Cor. 5:24–27; and likely Rom. 13:1–2). In Luke, the gospel promises true peace (*eirēnē*) on earth (2:14, used fourteen times in the Gospel); in Ephesians, Christ is our peace, making one new humanity that replaces former hostile divisions among peoples (Eph. 2:11–23). This peace of Jesus Christ was not only personal peace with God or peace in personal relationships but peace between peoples alienated from each other for the very reasons wars are fought. This peace of Jesus Christ was a new distinct alternative to the peace of the empire.

Although Christians were often persecuted by political rulers (Mark 13:9–13; Acts 8:1; Rev. 6:9; 12:11), they believed it to be their God-willed duty to be subject to the powers, for they are instituted by God. Both divine and demonic powers work through the political rulers, demonstrated by the divergent images of rulers in Romans 13 and Revelation 13. Revelation depicts the early church in a time of persecution. The victory of Christ as a lamb (Rev. 5) dominates the book and becomes the model that inspires Christians to endure suffering, and thus conquer and overcome by their faithfulness to the way of the lamb.

Second and Third Centuries. The early church continued a dual view of the state. We have no evidence of Christians in the army prior to A.D. 170. When the pagan philosopher Celsus asserted that Christians were not bearing their duty to the empire but only reaping the benefits, the apologetic defense was threefold: they were duty-bound to follow the way of Jesus Christ, for the "law of Christ" means "beating swords into plowshares," refusal of military warfare, and doing good to, even loving, the enemy (Justin, *1 Apol.* 39; Irenaeus, *Haer.* 4.34.4; Tertullian, *Iud.* 3; Origen, *Cels.* 5.33; 3.7–8; Hippolytus, *Trad. ap.* 17a; 19); they could not participate in the nation's idolatry especially manifest in the army, since army service required a sacred oath to the emperor and at times emperor worship (Tertullian, *Idol.* 19; *Coron.* 1; 11; Hippolytus, *Trad. ap.* 17b, 19); and their warfare was on a more significant level, namely, praying against the demons that inspire fighting and war (Tertullian, *Apol.* 32; Origen, *Cels.* 8.68–75; Athanasius, *Inc.* 52.4–6). Thus, the Christians replied by arguing that they were the true defenders of the peace of the empire; they worshiped the true God, who gave earthly kings their power. Christians also prayed for the armies to maintain peace as instruments of God's sovereignty (Tertullian, *Apol.* 30.4).

Between 175 and the Edict of Toleration (311), Christians in unknown numbers were enrolled in the army. During the same time, some Christians refused army service on the basis of refusal to kill and became martyrs for the faith (e.g., Maximilian in 295 [Musurillo, pp. 244–249]). Others left the army upon conversion (e.g., Martin of Tours in 339). In some cases, Christians continued in the army but when asked to take the oath or do sacrifice to the emperor refused and were then martyred (e.g., Marinus, 260 [Eusebius, *H.E.* 7.15]; Marcellus, 298 [Musurillo, pp. 250–259]; Dasius, 303 [Musurillo, pp. 272–279; Julius the Veteran, 303 [Musurillo, pp. 260–265]). A certain tension emerged during this period between the teachings of the church, which spoke against Christian participation in war, and the prac-

tice of a significant number of members who entered the army. Toward the end of this period, a greater number of Christians were in the army; willing to suffer death, an unknown number refused to continue because of some point of religious dissent, often emperor worship. Their defense would state "it is not fitting that a Christian . . . should fight for the armies of this world" (Marcellus in Musurillo, p. 253). Early in Diocletian's reign (284–305), Christians were frequently expelled from the army or martyred, a prelude to Diocletian's later fierce persecution of Christians.

Fourth and Fifth Centuries. With the dramatic change from Diocletian's persecution to Constantine's acceptance of Christianity, the relation between church and empire changed. To unify the church and consolidate the empire, Constantine called and presided over the Council of Nicaea in 325; in 336, he was baptized. Eusebius of Caesarea in his later writings regarded the empire's victories against the pagans as expressive of divine blessing and developed a theological apologetic for the empire's success. In this changing social situation of the church, in the late fourth century Ambrose and Augustine (*C. Faust* 22.69–76) formulated the concept of the just war. Because of the church's earlier teaching against Christians serving in the army, Augustine formulated criteria to justify going to war (*jus ad bellum*) and gave some, but less, attention to just means of war (*jus in bellum*). In 439, a new law permitted *only* Christians to serve in the army! The formerly persecuted minority church had now become the cohesive cement of the empire.

Augustine's formulation of the just-war policy sought to apply Jesus' teaching on love for God and neighbor to the sociopolitical and economic realm in which Christians now carried responsibility to maintain order and peace. The just-war criteria thus included limitation of violence, assurance of victory, and certainty that the good to be achieved will outweigh the harm done. Lacking in this formulation are the earlier distinctive teachings of Jesus: love for the enemy, nonretaliation, and refusal of the sword because Christ's kingdom is not of a worldly nature.

Summary. Through all this period, military imagery was used in order to describe the Christian's spiritual warfare against evil (Eph. 6:10–18 and 2 Cor. 10:3–5 provided the model). Always, the Christian church is called to resist evil, to use spiritual resources in Christ to defeat demonic power, and to proclaim Christ's victory over all principalities and powers. The first six centuries of early Christian history leave a complex legacy for the church's enduring call to know how to love God, neighbor, and enemy in the context of the nations' wars. *See also* Church and State; Ethics; Martyr, Martyrdom; Persecution; Social Thought.

[W.M.S.]

Bibliography

A. von Harnack, *Militia Christi: The Christian Religion and the Military in the First Three Centuries* (Philadelphia: Fortress, 1981; orig. German ed., 1905); C.J. Cadoux, *The Early Christian Attitude to War* (London: Headley, 1919; New York: Seabury, 1982); J.-M. Hornus, *It Is Not Lawful For Me to Fight: Early Christian Attitudes Toward War, Violence, and the State* (Scottdale: Herald, 1980; orig. French ed., 1960); R.H. Bainton, *Christian Attitudes Toward War and Peace: A Historical Survey and Critical Re-evaluation* (Nashville: Abingdon, 1960), pp. 66–84; J. Fontaine, "Christians and Military Service in the Early Church," *Concilium* 7 (1965):107–119; H.F. von Campenhausen, "Christians and Military Service in the Early Church," *Tradition and Life in the Church: Essays and Lectures in Church History* (Philadelphia: Fortress, 1968), pp. 160–170; K. Aland, "Das Verhältnis von Kirche und staat in der Frühzeit," P. Keresztes, "The Imperial Government and the Christian Church I" and "II," W. Shäfke, "Frühchristlicher Widerstand," J. Helgeland, "Christians and the Roman Army from Marcus Aurelius to Constantine," L.J. Swift, "War and the Christian Conscience," ANRW (1979), Vol. II.23.1, pp. 60–246, 247–315, 375–386, 460–723, 724–834, 835–868; M.C. Lind, *Yahweh Is a Warrior* (Scottdale: Herald, 1980); T.D. Barnes, *Constantine and Eusebius* (Cambridge: Harvard UP, 1981); W.M. Swartley, *Slavery, Sabbath, War and Women: Case Issues in Biblical Interpretation* (Scottdale: Herald, 1983), Ch. 3; idem, "Politics and Peace (*Eirēnē*) in Luke's Gospel," in *Political Issues in Luke–Acts,* ed. R.J. Cassidy and P.J. Scharper (New York: Orbis, 1983), pp. 18–37; L.J. Swift, *The Early Fathers on War and Military Service* (Wilmington: Glazier, 1983); W. Klassen, *Love of Enemies* (Philadelphia: Fortress, 1984); D.M. Scholer, "Early Christian Attitudes to War and Military Service: A Selective Bibliography," *TSF Bulletin* 8.1 (1984):23–24; R. McSorley, *New Testament Basis of Peacemaking* (Scottdale: Herald, 1985); J. Helgeland, R.J. Daly, and J.P. Burns, *Christians and the Military: The Early Christian Experience* (Philadelphia: Fortress, 1985); W.L. Elster, "The New Law of Christ and Early Pacifism," and J. Friesen, "War and Peace in the Patristic Age" in *Essays on War and Peace: The Bible and Early Church,* ed. W.M. Swartley (Elkhart: Institute of Mennonite Studies, 1986), pp. 108–129; 130–154; J.T. Johnson, *The Quest for Peace: Three Moral Traditions in Western Cultural History* (Princeton: Princeton UP, 1987); E. Ferguson, *Early Christians Speak* (Abilene: ACU, 1987), pp. 219–228; B.C. Ollenburger, *Zion the City of the Great King* (Sheffield: Sheffield Academic Press, 1987); K. Wengst, *Pax Romana and the Peace of Jesus Christ* (Philadelphia: Fortress, 1987); E. Pucciarelli, *I cristiani e il servizio militare* (Florence: Nardini, 1987).

WIDOWS. Widowhood in antiquity was a difficult condition to bear, and pagan public opinion attributed to widowhood both shame and dishonor. The misfortunes that the widow had to suffer are enumerated in John Chrysostom's account of his widowed mother, Anthusa (*Sac.* 1.5). If the unfortunate widow was wealthy, she became a target for human predators. The plight of the poor widow was worse; in fact, poverty and hunger were associated with the "true widow" (John Chrysostom, *Hom. in 1 Tim.* 15.2; *Sac.* 3.12).

The literature of the early church, starting with the apostles and apostolic fathers, inculcates the twin duty of supporting widows and orphans (James 1:27; Hermas, *Mand.* 8.10; *Sim.* 1.8; 5.3; Ignatius, *Polyc.* 4; Polycarp, *Ep.* 4; *1 Clem.* 8; *Const. app.* 4.2). A prayer of Basil of Caesarea includes the petition: "defend the widows; protect the orphans" (J. Goar, *Euchologion* [Venice, 1730], p. 146). This concern derives from the ethical injunctions of the Old Testament (Exod. 22:22; Deut. 10:18). The special title given to widows—"God's altar"—is revelatory of the early Christian concept of sacrifice. Historians suggest that the church made an important contribution to the amelioration of poverty in antiquity by supporting widows. According to its bishop Cornelius (253), the Roman church supported 1,500 widows and poor persons (Eusebius, *H.E.* 6.43). John Chrysostom (end of fourth century) estimated the number of widows and virgins supported by the church of Antioch at 3,000 (*Hom.* 66.3 *in Mt.*). *Chērotropheia*, or homes for poor widows, were erected in the fourth and fifth centuries.

Whereas necessity, that is, having no other means of support (1 Tim. 5:5), was the only requirement for a widow to receive sustenance from the church, there also came into being at an early date an order of widows (1 Tim. 5:9–11). Thus, widows were formally enrolled and constituted within the community as a distinct group whose organization was attributed to the apostle Peter (Ps.-Clement, *Recogn.* 6.15; *Hom.* 11.35). Origen states that the order of widows achieved the dignity of ecclesiastical rank (*Jo.* 32.7). In any event, whether supported by the church or by private means, its members had to meet certain requirements: "Let a widow be put on the list only if she is not less than sixty years old, having been the wife of one man, having a reputation for good works; and if she has brought up children, if she has shown hospitality to strangers, if she has washed the saints' feet, if she has assisted those in distress, and if she has devoted herself to every good work" (1 Tim. 5:9–10). These requirements seem to have been strictly enforced until the fourth century, when the order of widows declined and was replaced by that of deaconesses. Duties of the order of widows included nursing the sick, almsgiving, and evangelizing pagan women (Clement of Alexandria, *Str.* 3; *Const. app.* 3.5).

The *Lex Julia* (18 B.C.) and *Lex Papia Poppaea* (A.D. 9) of the emperor Augustus imposed on Roman citizens the obligation to marry and, in the case of widowhood, to remarry, under penalty of serious disabilities. The first Christian emperor, Constantine, eased these statutory requirements as a consequence of the Christian devotion to the principle of celibacy—a devotion based upon the moral qualities demanded, moral qualities perhaps greater than those required by the office of bishop, according to John Chrysostom. Ignoring the teaching that younger widows should remarry to avoid temptation (1 Tim. 5:14), the church fathers applied Paul's admonition not

to remarry (1 Cor. 7:39–40) to widows of all ages and social stations, as a rule not condemning remarriage after widowhood but considering it a less perfect way. After virginity, widowhood was considered the state most worthy of a Christian. It was meritorious for a widow not only to abstain from a second marriage but to take a vow of continence and wear special dress. By reversing the prevailing negative estimation of widowhood, the fathers felt that they were promoting Christian values: the "grace of widowhood" is a plant unique to Christian agriculture (Ambrose), and even the pagans were beginning to admire it (Libanius). John Chrysostom's homily *Vidua eligatur* recounts this profound social transformation and deems it permanent. *See also* Deaconess; Virgins; Women. [M.A.S.]

Bibliography

Tertullian, *To His Wife*, tr. W.P. LeSaint, ACW (1951), Vol. 13; *Apostolic Constitutions* 3, SC (1986), Vol. 329; John Chrysostom, *Letter to a Young Widow*, ed. G.H. Ettlinger, SC (1968), Vol. 138; tr. W.R.W. Stephens, NPNF, 1st ser. (1889), Vol. 9; Ambrose, *On Widows*, tr. H. deRomestin, NPNF (1896), Vol. 10; Jerome, *Letters* 46; 79; tr. W.H. Fremantle, NPNF, 2nd ser. (1893), Vol. 6; Augustine, *On the Good of Widowhood*, tr. M.C. Eagan, FOTC (1952), Vol. 16.

C.H. Turner, "Ministries of Women in the Primitive Church: Widow, Deaconess and Virgin in the First Four Christian Centuries," *Catholic and Apostolic*, ed. H.N. Bate (London: Mowbray, 1931), pp. 316–351; J. Mayer, *Monumenta de viduis, diaconissis, virginibusque tractantia* (Bonn: Hanstein, 1938); G. Stählin, "Das Bild der Witwe," *JAC* 17 (1974):5–20; J. Daniélou, *The Ministry of Women in the Early Church* (Leighton Buzzard: Faith, 1974), pp. 13–22; C. Osiek, "The Widow as Altar: The Rise and Fall of a Symbol," *SCent* 3 (1983):159–169; B.B. Thurston, *The Widows—A Women's Ministry in the Early Church* (Minneapolis: Fortress, 1989).

WINE. The Greek (*oinos*) and Latin (*vinum*) words for wine, although they could be used for the juice of the grape however preserved or for the fermented juice of other fruits, primarily meant fermented grape juice. The ordinary table beverage of the Mediterranean world was a mixture of wine and water. The proportions varied according to the period and purpose. Popular combinations involved two to three parts of water and one part of wine. Plutarch mentions that three parts of water to one of wine was suitable for "grave magistrates sitting in the council-hall," two parts to one left a person "neither fully sober nor . . . altogether witless," and three parts to two caused "a man to sleep peaceably and forget all cares" (*Table Talk* 3.9 [657B–C]; cf. Athenaeus, *Learned Banquet* 10, 426B–427C, 430D–431F). Half and half or unmixed wine in quantity brought on drunkenness or collapse (Athenaeus 2, 36B). The Jews adopted the Greek and Roman practice of mixing water and wine (2 Macc. 15:39), and rabbinic literature speaks of the ratios of two or three parts of water to one of wine (b. Pesach. 108b; b. Shabb. 77a). The mixed cup was part of the Passover meal (m. Pesach. 10.2, 4, 7) and was expected by the Dead Sea Scrolls (1QSa 2.18) to be part of the eschatological meal. The medicinal use of wine (Luke 10:34) was well known (Pliny the Elder, *Natural History* 23.23.43; 23.25.50f.), and it was recognized that wine had a purifying effect on water (1 Tim. 5:23).

Jesus' miracle of turning water into wine at Cana (John 2:1ff.) was early given a eucharistic interpretation (Irenaeus, *Haer.* 3.11.5), and the most frequent reference to wine in Christianity is at the eucharist. Jesus at the Last Supper identified one of the cups employed at the Passover with his blood, which consecrated the new covenant (Mark 14:24; 1 Cor. 11:25). The "one cup" was an important symbol of "unity with his blood" (Ignatius, *Philad.* 4), even as the vine was a symbol of the church (John 15:1ff.) and had been of Israel (Isa. 5:1ff.). Cyril of Jerusalem was one of the first to teach the doctrine of the conversion of the wine into the blood of Christ (*Catech.* 19.7; 23.7). The wine at the eucharist was the mixture of water and wine that was the ordinary table drink (Justin, *1 Apol.* 65; 67). Cyprian gave a theological significance to the mixture, interpreting the water as the people and the wine as the blood of Christ mingled together so that "the people is made one with Christ" (*Ep.* 63.13). Certain groups used water without wine in the eucharist: Ebionites (Irenaeus, *Haer.* 5.1.3), Encratites (Hippolytus, *Haer.* 8.13), and Mar-

cionites (Epiphanius, *Haer.* 42.3.2). The mainstream of the church insisted that wine must be included (Clement of Alexandria, *Str.* 1.19.96).

Total abstinence from wine was a sign of asceticism, and this abstinence could be practiced for orthodox reasons (Eusebius, *H.E.* 5.3). Ambrose preferred the use of water but allowed the sparing use of wine (*Ep.* 63.27). The prevalent teaching of the church fathers was to warn against drunkenness and counsel moderation. Clement of Alexandria says that wine is not for young people and that as much water as possible should be mixed with it (*Paed.* 2.2).

Since "unmixed" meant "undiluted," "unmixed wine" became a metaphor for unmitigated punishment (Rev. 14:10; cf. Origen, *Hom.* 12.2 *in Jer.*). More often, wine had more positive metaphorical uses: divine teachings (Origen, *Jo.* frg. 74), Holy Spirit (Hippolytus, *Ben. Jac.* 18), or the grace of the Holy Spirit (Origen, *Princ.* 1.3.7). *See also* Bread; Chalice; Eucharist.　　　　[E.F.]

Bibliography

Clement of Alexandria, *Instructor* 2.2; Basil, *Homilia 14 In ebriosos*; John Chrysostom, *Concerning the Statues Homily* 1; idem, *Ecloga de ingluvie et ebrietate*, *Hom.* 12; Simeon Metaphrastes, *Sermo* 16 *De ingluvie et ebrietate*; Ambrose, *De helia et jejunio* 12; 14; 16; Jerome, *Against Jovinian* 1–2; *Letters* 52; 54; 69; 22; 107; 108; Augustine, *Against Faustus* 20; 22; 30; 32; idem, *De moribus ecclesiae* 1.15; 19; 21; 33; 31.

I.W. Raymond, *The Teaching of the Early Church on the Use of Wine and Strong Drink* (New York: Columbia UP, 1927); C. Seltman, *Wine in the Ancient World* (London: Routledge and Kegan Paul, 1957); H.W. Allen, *A History of Wine* (New York: Horizon, 1962); W. Rordorf, "La Vigne et le vin dans la tradition juive et chrétienne," *Université de Neuchâtel Annales* (1969–1970):131–146; E. Ferguson, "Wine as a Table-Drink in the Ancient World," *Restoration Quarterly* 13 (1970):141–153.

WOMEN. Considerable caution must be exercised in interpreting the roles and status of women in early Christian history. The sources are scanty, and their authors are males who often wrote prescriptively. The interpretation now generally accepted is as follows: after an initial stage of relatively public activity by women—characteristic of enthusiastic new sects throughout the ages—their roles were increasingly regulated and curtailed. The restrictions appear to relate both to the increasing formalization and hierarchization of the ministry and to "mainstream" Catholicism's wish to distinguish itself from heretical or schismatic groups that sometimes allowed women wider roles. Two areas in which women's presence was nonetheless strong were martyrdom and asceticism.

Jesus' relatively open treatment of women has often been noticed; less frequently observed is that the Gospels represent him as accompanied by female as well as male followers (Mark 15:40–41; Matt. 27:55; Luke 8:2–3). The Lucan version represents these women as financial supporters of Jesus and "the twelve." The Gospels' evidence on women, however, is sometimes contradicted or ignored by (or perhaps remained unknown to) other New Testament authors. For example, the Gospels' reports that women were the first witnesses to the empty tomb and the resurrection (Mark 16:1–13; Matt. 28:1–10; Luke 24:1–11; John 20:1–18) are omitted in Paul's version of the resurrection appearances (1 Cor. 15:3–8).

The earliest New Testament documents, the letters of Paul, preserve interesting evidence about women, although it is difficult to generalize from the situations of a few possibly unrepresentative communities. Paul depicts women as active in the mission and work of the early Christian movement: nine of the twenty-eight persons he specifically greets in Romans 16 are women. Women were among the owners of houses in which early Christians met, and their roles as patrons may well have entailed responsibilities as church leaders (Acts 12:12; Rom. 16:3–5; 1 Cor. 16:19; Col. 4:15; Philem. 2). There were also missionary couples, such as Prisca/Priscilla and Aquila (Rom. 16:3–5; Acts 18:1–3, 18, 24–28) and Junia and Andronicus (called "apostles" in Rom. 16:7; cf. 1 Cor. 9:5). The exact status of Phoebe, called by Paul a *diakonos* ("deacon" or "servant") of the church at Cenchreae and a *prostatis* ("patroness" or "supporter") "of many and of myself as well" (Rom. 16:1–2), has been much debated. On the basis of 1 Corinthians 11:5, we gather that women prayed and prophesied along with men in worship. The author of Acts, as well as Paul, notes the important role women played in early Christianity, but he tends to view them as providers of hospitality, not as missionaries or leaders in their own right (e.g., Lydia in Acts 16:15).

Later New Testament books, especially the Pastoral Epistles, reveal Christianity's growing conservatism toward women. By the second century, Christian writers presented the new religion to potential converts as one encouraging domestic order. Women were counseled to remain in their traditional roles of wife and mother; for the first time in Christianity, a theological justification was given that explains why women should not be permitted to teach or to have authority over men (1 Tim. 2:12–15). The Pastoral Epistles report that older women were allowed to enroll as "widows"; the group must have been popular, for 1 Timothy 5:3–16 seeks to raise the eligibility requirements. In literature from the late second century onward, however, the widows are a recognized group. They are commended for their prayers and pious deeds, but they are not admitted to clerical rank.

Likewise unclear is how early the word *diakonos* designated clerical office. Were, for example, the *ministrae* that Pliny the Younger mentions in his letter to Trajan (ca. 112) "deaconesses"? By the late third and early fourth centuries, especially in eastern Christendom, the office of deaconess was widely recognized. Although the Council of Nicaea (325) counts deaconesses among the laity, other texts (e.g., *can.* 15 of the Council of Chalcedon, 451) speak of their ordination, and *Apostolic Constitutions* 8.20 gives the prayer to be recited during the ordination service. Deaconesses visited sick women, assisted with the postbaptismal anointing of women, instructed women, and accompanied them on visits to clergymen. Yet they were forbidden to baptize (*Const. app.* 3.9), and in the western church we have no early record of deaconesses being ordained.

Thus, with the increasing formalization of the sacraments and hierarchization of church office, women's earlier public roles in the church were restricted and regulated. Whether the shift from a private to a public worship space influenced this restriction is a question that has recently provoked discussion. Also debated is whether such literature as the *Acts of Paul and Thecla* should be read as a rejection of contemporary (second-century) restrictions on women or simply as entertainment literature.

Catholic Christianity's wish to distinguish itself from sects that it deemed either schismatic or heretical provided another reason for church authorities to limit women's roles, since some of these sects permitted higher positions of leadership to women. Two women prophetesses, Priscilla and Maximilla, were hailed by Montanists as among their founders and were said to enjoy direct revelations of the Holy Spirit (Hippolytus, *Haer.* 8.12; Eusebius, *H.E.* 5.16). Montanist women may also have baptized and celebrated the eucharist (Cyprian, *Ep.* 75[74].10; Epiphanius, *Haer.* 49.2). And some Gnostic groups, according to the church fathers, allowed women to serve as priests and to baptize (Hippolytus, *Haer.* 6.35; Irenaeus, *Haer.* 1.13.1–2; Epiphanius, *Haer.* 42.4; Tertullian, *Praescr.* 41). Catholic women were thus told not to seek such offices.

Women in two categories, however, were extravagantly praised by Catholic churchmen: martyrs and ascetics, deemed to be the equals of men and often praised as "manly." For example, five of the twelve Scillitan martyrs (A.D. 180) were women. The famous martyrs of Lyons and Vienne (A.D. 177) counted the slave girl Blandina and her mistress among them (Eusebius, *H.E.* 5.1.3–2.8). A most famous pair of female martyrs in third-century North Africa were Perpetua and Felicitas; some of their account (*Pass. Perp.*) was written by Perpetua herself.

Asceticism was a second avenue that involved rejection of customary societal values. According to patristic authors, asceticism provided a new arena for Christian combat once martyrdom was no longer an option, given the offical Christianization of the Roman empire in the fourth century. To be sure, asceticism

had been praised by some Christian authors since the earliest decades of Christianity (e.g., 1 Cor. 7) and in some areas of the Mediterranean world, such as Syria, was thought to be the most genuine form of the Christian religion; the fourth century, however, saw the flowering of the ascetic movement. Several women ascetics celebrated in Christian literature founded monasteries: Mary, sister of Pachomius; Melania the Elder; Paula; Macrina, sister of Gregory of Nyssa and Basil of Caesarea; Olympias; Melania the Younger; Caesaria, sister of Caesarius of Arles. Often, their monastic leadership went hand in hand with patronage, for some of them paid for the monasteries they founded. (The elite character of women's monastic leadership can thus be extended backward from the early Middle Ages to the patristic era.) Monastic life offered such women an alternative to marrriage, which was still often arranged for girls of the elite classes: a life of religious devotion, scholarly reading, travel in the form of pilgrimage, and the possibility for close friendships with male ecclesiastical and monastic leaders. Thus, a few facets of early Christian life gave women the chance for special honor. For other women, Christianity offered little by way of progress: its disapproval of divorce from even abusive husbands, and often of second marriage under any circumstances, its prohibition of contraception and abortion, and its encouragement of wifely submission regulated women's lives even more than did secular custom and Roman law. *See also* Deaconess; Eve; Mary; Virgins; Widows.

[E.A.C.]

Bibliography

R. Ruether, "Misogynism and Virginal Feminism in the Fathers of the Church," *Religion and Sexism: Images of Woman in the Jewish and Christian Tradition*, ed. R.R. Ruether (New York: Simon and Schuster, 1974); R. Gryson, *The Ministry of Women in the Early Church* (Collegeville: Liturgical, 1980); P. Wilson-Kastner et al., *A Lost Tradition: Women Writers of the Early Church* (Washington, D.C.: UP of America, 1981); E.A.Clark, *Women in the Early Church* (Wilmington: Glazier, 1983); E. Schüssler-Fiorenza, *In Memory of Her: A Feminist Theological Reconstruction of Christian Origins* (New York: Crossroad, 1983); B.J. Brooten, "Early Christian Women and Their Cultural Context: Issues of

Method in Historical Reconstruction," *Feminist Perspectives on Biblical Scholarship*, ed. A.Y. Collins (Chico: Scholars, 1985); E.A. Clark, *Ascetic Piety and Women's Faith: Essays on Late Ancient Christianity* (Lewiston: Mellen, 1986); S.F. Brock and S.A. Harvey, *Holy Women of the Syrian Orient* (Berkeley: U of California P, 1987); V. Burrus, *Chastity as Autonomy: Women in the Stories of the Apocryphal Acts* (Lewiston: Mellen, 1987); R.S. Kraemer, *Maenads, Martyrs, Matrons, Monastics: A Sourcebook on Women's Religions in the Greco-Roman World* (Minneapolis: Fortress, 1988).

WORSHIP. *See* Eucharist; Liturgy; Office, Divine.

Z

ZENO (d. 491). Eastern Roman emperor (474–475, 476–491). Zeno was an Isaurian who placed his troops at the disposal of the emperor Leo I at a time when the empire was suffering pressure from the Goths. He married Leo's daughter, and shortly after the death of his father-in-law became joint ruler with his own son, Leo II, a young child who died within a year. For a time, he was driven from the capital by a revolt instigated by Basiliscus, brother of Leo I's widow, but he returned and resumed power (476). He sent Theodoric and the Goths into Italy (488) to replace Odoacer, thus relieving the eastern empire of any Gothic threat or burden. On the counsel of Acacius, the patriarch of Constantinople, he published the *Henoticon* (482), a document intended to effect a reconciliation with the Monophysites. It failed of its purpose and led to the Acacian schism (482–519). CPG III, 5999. *See also* Acacius of Constantinople; Henoticon. [M.P.McH.]

Bibliography
Excerpts of Valesius 9.39–44; 11.56.

ZENO OF VERONA (d. ca. 380). Bishop and preacher. Perhaps a North African by birth, Zeno, bishop of Verona (ca. 362–ca. 380), showed pastoral care for the liturgical and sacramental life of his congregation, insisted on almsgiving and concern for the poor, and resisted Arianism and paganism in his diocese. He left some ninety sermons, many in draft form, which show the influence of Tertullian, Cyprian, Lactantius, Hilary of Poitiers, and, among the classical authors, Virgil and Apuleius. The sermons frequently discuss baptism and the Paschal mystery; moral and doctrinal themes also appear. In art, Zeno is represented with a fish, perhaps as a baptismal symbol. Feast day April 12. CPL 208–209. [M.P.McH.]

Bibliography
T.P. Halton and R.D. Sider, "A Decade of Patristic Scholarship 1970–1979," *CW* 76 (1982–1983):380 (bibliography); V. Boccardi, "L'esegesi di Zenone di Verona," *Augustinianum* 23 (1983):453–485; C. Truzzi, *Zeno, Gaudenzio e Cromazio, Testi e contenuti della predicazione christiana per le chiese di Verona e Aquileia (360–410 ca.)* (Brescia: Paideia, 1985).

ZEPHYRINUS. Bishop of Rome (ca. 198–217). Zephyrinus probably stood against Montanism, but with his chief assistant, Callistus, may have supported Monarchianism. The Monarchians apparently denied a separate personality to

Christ and were opposed by both Tertullian and Hippolytus. Zephyrinus was also accused of Patripassianism and laxity of discipline in allowing adulterers back to communion. Feast day August 26. [F.W.N.]

Bibliography

Hippolytus, *Refutation of All Heresies* 10.1–2, 6–7; Eusebius, *Church History* 5.28; 6.21; *Liber Pontificalis* 16 (Duchesne 1.139–140).

Frend, pp. 340–345.

ZOSIMUS. Bishop of Rome (417–418). Zosimus's brief pontificate was troubled by controversy. His attempt to establish the jurisdiction of Arles over Gaul met with considerable resistance and was abandoned by his successor, Boniface I. He accepted the professions of faith of Pelagius, by letter, and Celestius, in person. They were, however, banished by order of the emperor Honorius, and after the African bishops reiterated the previous condemnation issued by his predecessor, Innocent I, Zosimus issued his *Epistula tractoria* in final condemnation of Pelagianism, an action that led to the schism of Julian of Eclanum. Sixteen of Zosimus's letters are extant. CPL 1644–1647. [M.P.McH.]

Bibliography

Liber Pontificalis 43 (Duchesne 1.225–226).

Index

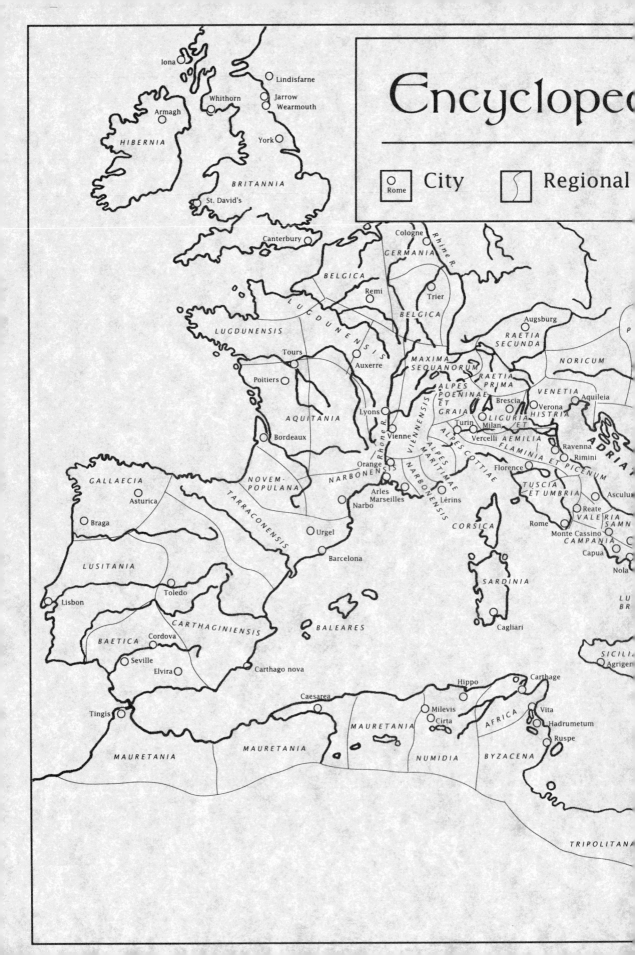

Encyclope...

City ○ Rome **Regional**

Iona
Lindisfarne
Whithorn
Jarrow
Wearmouth
Armagh
York
HIBERNIA
BRITANNIA
St. David's
Canterbury

Cologne
Rhine R.
GERMANIA
BELGICA
Remi
Trier
BELGICA
Augsburg
RAETIA SECUNDA
LUGDUNENSIS
LUGDUNENSIS
NORICUM
Tours
Auxerre
MAXIMA SEQUANORUM
RAETIA PRIMA
Poitiers
ALPES POENINAE ET GRAIA
Brescia
VENETIA
Aquileia
Verona
HISTRIA
AQUITANIA
Lyons
LIGURIA ET
Turin
Milan
Bordeaux
Vienne
Vercelli
AEMILIA
FLAMINIA ET PICENUM
Ravenna
Rimini
VIENNENSIS
Orange
ADRIA...
GALLAECIA
NOVEM-POPULANA
NARBONEN...
Florence
ALPES COTTIAE
TUSCIA ET UMBRIA
Asculum
Asturica
TARRACONENSIS
Arles
Marseilles
Lérins
ALPES MARITIMAE
NARBONENSIS
Reate
VALERIA
SAMN...
Braga
Narbo
Rome
CORSICA
Monte Cassino
CAMPANIA
Urgel
Capua
LUSITANIA
Barcelona
Nola
Toledo
SARDINIA
Lisbon
CARTHAGINIENSIS
BALEARES
LU...
BR...
Cagliari
BAETICA
Cordova
Seville
Elvira
Carthago nova
SICILI...
Agrigen...
Caesarea
Hippo
Carthage
Milevis
Vita
Tingis
Cirta
AFRICA
Hadrumetum
MAURETANIA
Ruspe
MAURETANIA
NUMIDIA
BYZACENA
MAURETANIA
TRIPOLITANA